TOURO COLLEGE LIBRARY
Kings Hwy

WITHDRAWN

THE HANDBOOK OF LIFE-SPAN DEVELOPMENT:

COGNITION, BIOLOGY, AND METHODS

VOLUME 1

THE HANDBOOK OF LIFE-SPAN DEVELOPMENT:

COGNITION, BIOLOGY, AND METHODS

VOLUME 1

Volume Editor

WILLIS F. OVERTON
TEMPLE UNIVERSITY

Editor-in-Chief

RICHARD M. LERNER
TUFTS UNIVERSITY

TOURO COLLEGE LIBRARY
Kings Hwy

WILEY

John Wiley & Sons, Inc.

KH

This book is printed on acid-free paper. ∞

Copyright © 2010 by John Wiley & Sons, Inc. All rights reserved.

Published by John Wiley & Sons, Inc., Hoboken, New Jersey.
Published simultaneously in Canada.

No part of this publication may be reproduced, stored in a retrieval system, or transmitted in any form or by any means, electronic, mechanical, photocopying, recording, scanning, or otherwise, except as permitted under Section 107 or 108 of the 1976 United States Copyright Act, without either the prior written permission of the Publisher, or authorization through payment of the appropriate per-copy fee to the Copyright Clearance Center, Inc., 222 Rosewood Drive, Danvers, MA 01923, (978) 750-8400, fax (978) 646-8600, or on the web at www.copyright.com. Requests to the Publisher for permission should be addressed to the Permissions Department, John Wiley & Sons, Inc., 111 River Street, Hoboken, NJ 07030, (201) 748-6011, fax (201) 748-6008.

Limit of Liability/Disclaimer of Warranty: While the publisher and author have used their best efforts in preparing this book, they make no representations or warranties with respect to the accuracy or completeness of the contents of this book and specifically disclaim any implied warranties of merchantability or fitness for a particular purpose. No warranty may be created or extended by sales representatives or written sales materials. The advice and strategies contained herein may not be suitable for your situation. You should consult with a professional where appropriate. Neither the publisher nor author shall be liable for any loss of profit or any other commercial damages, including but not limited to special, incidental, consequential, or other damages.

This publication is designed to provide accurate and authoritative information in regard to the subject matter covered. It is sold with the understanding that the publisher is not engaged in rendering professional services. If legal, accounting, medical, psychological or any other expert assistance is required, the services of a competent professional person should be sought.

Designations used by companies to distinguish their products are often claimed as trademarks. In all instances where John Wiley & Sons, Inc. is aware of a claim, the product names appear in initial capital or all capital letters. Readers, however, should contact the appropriate companies for more complete information regarding trademarks and registration.

For general information on our other products and services please contact our Customer Care Department within the U.S. at (800) 762-2974, outside the United States at (317) 572-3993 or fax (317) 572-4002.

Wiley also publishes its books in a variety of electronic formats. Some content that appears in print may not be available in electronic books. For more information about Wiley products, visit our website at www.wiley.com.

Library of Congress Cataloging-in-Publication Data:
  The handbook of life-span development / editor-in-chief, Richard M. Lerner.
    p. cm.
  Includes author and subject indexes.
  ISBN 978-0-470-39011-5 (v. 1 : cloth); ISBN 978-0-470-39012-2 (v. 2 : cloth); ISBN 978-0-470-39013-9 (set : cloth); 978-0-470-63433-2 (ebk); 978-0-470-63434-9 (ebk); 978-0-470-63435-6 (ebk)
  1. Developmental psychology. 2. Maturation (Psychology) 3. Aging–Psychological aspects. I. Lerner, Richard M.
  BF713.H3648 2010
  155–dc22   2009049300

Printed in the United States of America

10 9 8 7 6 5 4 3 2 1

1/13/11

Contents

VOLUME 1: Cognition, Biology, and Methods

Preface

Until the early 1960s, the field of human development was dominated by either descriptions of the behavioral or psychological phenomena presumptively unfolding as a consequence of genetically controlled timetables of maturational change (e.g., see the chapters by Hess and by McClearn in the third edition of the *Handbook of Child Psychology*; Mussen, 1970) or by descriptions of the behaviors presumptively elicited in response to stimulation encountered over the course of early life experiences (e.g., see the chapters by Stevenson or by White in the same edition of the *Handbook*). Framed within a Cartesian dualism that split nature from nurture (Overton, 2006), developmental science focused in the main on the generic human being (Emmerich, 1968) and on the earliest years of life or, at most, the years surrounding the stages of pubertal change. These periods were regarded as the portions of ontogeny in which the fundamental processes of human development emerged and functioned to shape the subsequent course of human life (Brim & Kagan, 1980).

Today, the study of development has evolved from a field embedded within the domain of developmental psychology to an area of scholarship labeled *developmental science* (Bornstein & Lamb, 2005, 2010; Magnusson & Stattin, 1998, 2006). Substantively, developmental science is a field that conceptualizes the entire span of human life as potentially involving developmental change. The possibility of developmental change across life exists because the basic process of development is seen as involving mutually influential relations between an active organism and a changing, multilevel ecology, a relation represented as individual ↔ context relations (Lerner, 2006). These relations provide the fundamental impetus to systematic and successive changes across the life span (Brandtstädter, 1998; Overton, 1973, 2003; Lerner, 2006).

Thus, the contemporary study of human development involves placing postmodern, relational models at the cutting edge of theoretical and empirical interest (Overton, 2006).

These models consider all levels of organization—from the inner biological through the physical ecological, cultural, and historical—as involved in mutually influential relationships across the breadth of the entire life course (Bronfenbrenner & Morris, 2006; Riegel, 1975, 1976). Variations in time and place constitute vital sources of systematic changes across ontogeny—even into the 10th and 11th decades of life—and, as such, human life is variegated and characterized by intraindividual change and interindividual differences (Baltes, Lindenberger, & Staudinger, 2006; Elder, Modell, & Parke, 1993). Accordingly, because ontogenetic change is embodied in its relation to time and place (Overton, 2006), contemporary developmental science regards the temporality represented by historical changes as imbued in all levels of organization, as coacting integratively, and as providing a potential for this systematic change—for plasticity—across the life span.

In short, as a consequence of the relational coactions of changes at levels of organization ranging from the biological and the psychological and behavioral to the sociocultural, designed and natural physical ecological, and through the historical (see Gottlieb, 1997; Overton, 2006), processes of development are viewed in contemporary developmental science through a theoretical and empirical lens that extends the study of change across the human ontogenetic span and, as well, through generational and historical time (Elder, 1998; Elder et al., 1993). The variations in the actions of individuals on their contexts and contexts on individuals integratively propel and texture the course of life (Baltes, Freund, & Li, 2005; Brandtstädter, 2006; Freund & Baltes, 2000 Freund, Li, & Baltes, 1999). As a result, the breadth of the life span and all levels of organization within the ecology of human development must be considered to fully describe, explain, and optimize the course of intraindividual change and of interindividual differences in such change (Baltes et al., 2006; Baltes, Reese, & Nesselroade, 1977).

There exist both historical (Baltes, 1979,1983; Cairns & Cairns, 2006), philosophical, and theoretical (Lerner, 1984; Overton, 1973, 1975, 2006) accounts of the nature and bases of the evolution of developmental science. These accounts document that the field changed from one dominated by psychological, environmental, or biological reductionist, split, and age-period-restricted conceptions of human development processes to become a field focused on relational, systems, and life-span developmental models. As Edwin G. Boring (1950, p. ix) noted, Hermann Ebbinghaus once remarked that "psychology has a long past, but only a short history." In many ways, the same statement may be made about the evolution of the life-span view of human development.

A BRIEF HISTORY OF THE LIFE-SPAN DEVELOPMENTAL PERSPECTIVE

The life-span ideas that we today summarize as "the" life-span perspective began to emerge in the United States in the mid-1960s and early 1970s. However, the conception that was forwarded was neither a newly created perspective of human development nor the only extant conception of life-span development present at the time (or even now). To a great extent, the history of the emergence and refinement of this life-span perspective arose through the discussions at, and the subsequent edited volumes derived from, a series of conferences held in the late 1960s and early to mid-1970s at the University of West Virginia in Morgantown. The conferences were held under the aegis of the Department of Psychology, which was chaired by K. Warner Schaie. As Baltes (1979, 1983) and Cairns and Cairns (2006) explained, the roots of the approach that began to crystallize in Morgantown can be traced to 19th-century scholarship in the United States and to philosophical ideas forwarded about 200 years earlier in Europe. In turn, although there was a different concentration of empirical attention paid to successive portions of human ontogeny (with most attention paid to infancy and childhood and comparatively less work devoted to studying people as they aged into the adolescent and adult periods), many U.S. developmental psychologists might argue that the study of human life within the social and behavioral sciences has always included a focus on behavior across the breadth of ontogeny. Despite the fact that the label *life-span developmental psychology* was not used, there was, at least since G. Stanley Hall's work on senescence (1922), attention paid in some way to periods of life beyond childhood and adolescence.

Nevertheless, despite any claims made that developmental science has been concerned for at least 90 years with development across life, the structure and function of academic work would contradict such assertions. Indeed, it was not until the 1970s and early 1980s, when the term *life-span developmental psychology* became popular in developmental psychology (e.g., Baltes & Schaie, 1973; Goulet & Baltes, 1970; Nesselroade & Reese, 1973), that many departments began offering life-span development courses.

Moreover, most people involved in teaching these courses were trained in infancy, childhood, or, in a few cases, adolescence. They taught what they knew most and, as such, courses were mostly modestly revised child development courses with a few lectures at the end of the course devoted to "adult development and aging." The textbooks that were written for use in these courses—in the main by colleagues also not involved in the study of developmental change across the breadth of human ontogeny—reinforced the approach taken by classroom instructors. Texts were in fact slightly revised child development books with a couple of chapters (and in some cases only one chapter) added about adult development and aging; at the time, the late adult years were still not seen as a part of the process of development. In short, authors wrote these books, and publishers structured them, to meet the "needs" of the instructors, which were to present mostly infancy and childhood, perhaps a chapter on adolescence (puberty, the identity crisis, and problem behaviors were in large part the focus of such chapters) and, finally, "adulthood and aging."

When the work of the key scholars studying the latter portion of the life span, for instance, developmental scientists such as Paul B. Baltes, James Birren, John R. Nesselroade, or K. Warner Schaie, among others, were cited, this scholarship was reduced to the fact that these scholars had promoted the idea of studying development across the life span. Therefore, because the existence of such life-span work required some treatment in the textbook, the author of the textbook would commence to present such topics as the life tasks of adulthood (as discussed, for instance, by Robert Havighurst, 1951), some ideas about intellectual decline with aging, and "death and dying." What was wrong with such approaches to life-span human development?

THE VIEW FROM THE HILLS

These early textbooks in life-span development missed the points being made by the scholars who were gathering in Morgantown, West Virginia, and who were shaping quite a different approach to the study of development across the life span. The work of Baltes, Schaie, Nesselroade, and other major contributors (e.g., scholars such as Nancy Datan, Lawrence Goulet, Willis Overton, Hayne Reese, and Klaus Riegel) to the foundation of the approach to life-span development that has evolved to frame developmental science had, at best, been misinterpreted and, at worst (and in fact most of the time), trivialized. What, then, were the ideas being developed by the scholars meeting in Morgantown? Answering this question is central to the present work: The ideas that began to be developed in the West Virginia hills provide the foundation of the scholarship represented in this *Handbook*. Indeed, one cannot overestimate the impact on developmental science theory and methodology of the books that were derived from the West Virginia conferences (Baltes & Schaie, 1973; Datan & Reese, 1977; Goulet & Baltes, 1970; Nesselroade & Reese, 1973) and from a subsequent series of "annual" advances volumes, *Life-Span Development and Behavior*, first edited by Paul Baltes (1978); then by Baltes and Orville G. Brim, Jr. (1979, 1980, 1982, 1983, 1984); by Baltes, David L. Featherman, and Richard M. Lerner (1986, 1988a, 1988b,1990); and by Featherman, Lerner, and Marion Perlmutter (1992, 1994). These works pushed the study of human development beyond the split and reductionist conceptual boundaries to which the field had accommodated (Overton, 2006).

As Baltes (1987; Baltes et al., 2006) explained, the life-span view of human development was associated with the integration of a set of ideas, each of which could be found as "stand-alone" concepts within the developmental literature; however, when taken as an integrated or, in fact, a fused, or relational, whole, these ideas changed the conceptual landscape of the field. As such, the set of concepts introduced in the late 1960s and early 1970s at the University of West Virginia life-span development conferences embodied an approach to the study of the human life span that stood in sharp contrast to the simplistic, additive approach to development found in the early textbooks and associated courses in life-span development. Although these "West Virginian" ideas have of course evolved across the ensuing decades and were refined and extended by the their originators and by those who were influenced or trained by them, the fundamental character of these ideas remains the same and constitutes at least a sea change, if not a true paradigm shift, in the nature of thinking about human development.

First, development was seen as a process, one that began at conception and continued through the end of life. For example, developmental processes were conceptualized as involving systematic and successive changes in the organization of relations within and across the levels of organization comprising the ecology of human development (e.g., Bronfenbrenner, 1979; Bronfenbrenner & Morris, 2006; Lerner, 2002, 2006; Overton, 1973, 1978, 2006; Overton & Reese, 1981; Reese & Overton, 1970). There were both qualitatively and quantitatively continuous and discontinuous facets of this process. Accordingly, mutidirectionality of development (increases, decreases, curvilinearity, smooth or abrupt change, etc.) were all possible forms for a developmental process, and the shape or form of a developmental trajectory for an individual or group was a matter of theory-predicated empirical inquiry (Wohlwill, 1973).

In addition, because variation in the form of developmental trajectories may occur for different people (e.g., people who vary with regard to age, sex, race, birth cohort, etc.), living in different settings, or in different historical eras, developmental process may take a different form at different points in ontogeny, generational time, or history across individuals or groups. Thus, diversity—with regard to within-person changes but also to differences between people in within-person change—rose to the level of substantive significance (as opposed to error variance) within the life-span view. For instance, as explained by Bornstein (1995), in regard to his "specificity principle" of infant development "specific experiences at specific times exert specific effects over specific aspects of infant growth in specific ways" (p. 21). In turn, a similar idea was advanced by Freund, Nikitin, and Ritter (2009), albeit one focused at the other end of the life span. Underscoring the importance of viewing the developmental process across the breadth of ontogeny, Freund et al. noted that a person's development during a historical period of extended life expectancy is likely to have important implications for development during young and middle adulthood.

Accordingly, although it would make sense from a life-span developmental perspective to study individuals and groups within (as well as across) ontogenetic "age periods," an age period–specific focus should not be adopted because of the mistaken belief that the developmental process that occurs in childhood or adolescence is somehow a different developmental process than the one that occurs in adulthood and late adulthood. Rather, the life-span developmental scientist has the task of describing and explaining and, as noted again later in this preface, optimizing the form of such change across life. He or she must detail the ways in which changes within one period are derived from changes at earlier periods and affect changes at subsequent periods.

As well, explanations of continuities and discontinuities across life, and of the form (the shape) of the developmental trajectory and of its rate of change, involve a very different theoretical frame than the ones that had been dominant in other approaches to the study of development (i.e., the split and reductionist approaches of past eras). As explained by Overton, both in his prior work (e.g., 1973, 2006) and in the chapter that introduces Volume 1 of the present *Handbook*, a relational metamodel frames the contemporary, cutting-edge study of human development within and across all portions of ontogeny. The use of this relational perspective emerged through the influence of Overton and other developmental scientists (e.g., Sameroff, 1975), including those studying infancy (e.g., Bornstein, 1995; Lamb, 1977; Lewis, 1972; Lewis & Rosenblum, 1974; Thelen & Smith, 1998), as well as through the contributions of comparative scientists (e.g., Gottlieb, 1997; Greenberg & Tobach, 1984; Kuo, 1976; Schneirla, 1957) and biologists (e.g., Novikoff, 1945a, 1945b; von Bertalanffy, 1933, 1968). This scholarship resulted in the elaboration of several variants of a developmental systems theoretical model of development (e.g., Ford & Lerner, 1992; Lerner, 2002); more recently, by explicitly incorporating a relational perspective, these models have been termed *relational developmental systems* models of development (Lerner, 2006; Lerner & Overton, 2008).

Because it may seem counterintuitive that the scholarship of developmental scientists studying infancy was integral in the foundation of the life-span approach to human development, it is useful to illustrate briefly the contributions of such work to the life-span approach. The scholarship of Michael Lewis (e.g., 1972; Lewis & Lee-Painter, 1974) built on the insights of Bell (1968), about the potential presence in correlational data about socialization, of evidence for the bidirectional influences between parents and children. Lewis and his colleagues launched a program of research that provided a new, relational model of infant–parent interaction. In *The Effect of the Infant on Its Caregiver* (Lewis & Rosenblum, 1974), a volume that represents a watershed event in the history of the study of human development through the use of person↔context relational models, Lewis and colleagues argued that "Not only is the infant or child influenced by its social, political, economic and biological world, but in fact the child itself influences its world in turn" (Lewis & Rosenblum, 1974, p. xv) and maintained that "only through interaction can we study, without distortion, human behavior (Lewis & Lee-Painter, 1974, p. 21). Envisioning the relational, developmental systems models that would come to the fore

in the study of human development a quarter century later, Lewis noted that a

> relational position not only requires that we deal with elements in interaction but also requires that we not consider the static quality of these interactions. Rather, it is necessary to study their flow with time…. Exactly how this might be done is not at all clear. It may be necessary to consider a more metaphysical model, a circle in which there are neither elements nor beginnings/ends. (Lewis & Lee-Painter, 1974, pp. 46–47).

Lewis's scholarship fostered an intellectual climate among other infancy researchers that resulted in a reconceptualization of phenomena of infant development within the sorts of relational, individual ↔ context relational models he forwarded. I noted earlier in this preface the contributions of Marc Bornstein (1995) in this regard. Here, too, however, we should point out another, foundational instance of the contributions of infancy researchers to the life-span perspective, found in the work of Michael Lamb. For instance, Lamb and his colleagues (e.g., Lamb, 1977; Lamb, Thompson, Gardner, & Charnov, 1985; Thompson & Lamb, 1986) approached the study of infant attachment within the context of the assumptions that (a) children influence their "socializers" and are not simply the receptive foci of socializing forces, (b) early social and emotional/personality development occurs in the context of a complex family system rather than only in the context of the mother–infant dyad, and (c) social and psychological development are not confined to infancy or childhood but involve a process that continues from birth to death (Lamb, 1978, p. 137; cf. Riley, 1979).

Within this conceptual framework, Lamb and his colleagues found that prior interpretations of infant attachment, which included "an emphasis on the formative significance of early experiences, a focus on unidirectional influences on the child, a tendency to view development within a narrow ecological context, and a search for universal processes of developmental change" (Thompson & Lamb, 1986, p. 1), were less powerful in accounting for the findings of attachment research than an interpretation associated with person↔context relational models. Accordingly, in a review of attachment research conducted through the mid-1980s, Lamb and colleagues concluded that "reciprocal organism–environment influences, developmental plasticity, individual patterns of developmental change and broader contextual influences on development can better help to integrate and interpret the attachment literature, and may also provide new directions for study" (Thompson & Lamb, 1986, p. 1).

Lamb's work challenged the field of infancy to move the study of the early years of life beyond the use of narrow, split, or reductionist conceptions of the exclusive influences of heredity or early experiences or of simplistic views of proximal dyadic relationships acting in isolation from the fuller and richer ecology of human development. He provided instead a relational vision for the understanding of infancy as part of the entire life span, of the life-span development of the other people in the infant's world, and of the complex set of infant ↔ social context relations as reciprocal exchanges in and with a multilevel and dynamic context (e.g., see Lamb, 1977; Lamb et al., 1985).

In short, as exemplified by the work embedding the study of infancy within a life-span approach to human development, the theoretical approaches that emerged in the 1970s from the impetus given developmental science by the scholars gathering in the hills of West Virginia constituted an integrative approach to variables across the levels of organization within the relational developmental system. As such, these models rejected as counterfactual the split conceptions, theories, and metatheories that partitioned the sources of development into nature and nurture. Rejected as well were "compromise" views that, although admitting that both of these purportedly separate sources of influence were involved in development, used problematic (i.e., additive) conceptions of interaction (conceptualized much as are interaction terms in an analysis of variance or in other instantiations of the general linear model; see Gottlieb, Wahlsten, & Lickliter, 2006). Instead, the theoretical models promoted by the scholars contributing to the foundation and evolution of the life-span perspective stressed that the basic process of human development involves developmental regulations—that is, individual ↔ context relations that link all levels of the ecology of human development within a thoroughly integrated, or "fused" (Tobach & Greenberg, 1984), dynamic, relational system.

For instance, these levels of the ecology involve ecological systems within the person (i.e., biosocial influences) or most proximal to him or her (what Bronfenbrenner [1979] termed the *microsystem*), extend to the set of contexts within which the individual interacts (the *mesosystem*; Bronfenbrenner, 1979) and to the systems in the ecology within which components of the mesosystem (e.g., parents) interact (e.g., the workplace) that may not directly involve the person but nevertheless may have an impact on him or her. In addition, the ecology includes the *macrosystem*—the broadest level of the ecology; the macrosystem influences all other systems and includes social policies, major intuitions of society (such as education, health care, and the economy),

the designed and natural physical ecology, and, ultimately, history. As noted, this latter level of organization within the relational, integrated developmental system provides a temporal component for all other facets of the developmental system and creates the potential for systematic change, for plasticity, in individual ↔ context relations.

One recent instantiation of such relational, developmental systems thinking in regard to the dynamics of the person's exchanges with his or her ecology involves the work of Freund and colleagues in regard to the nature of the goals that individuals pursue within their changing context (e.g., Freund, 2007; Nikitin & Freund, 2008). Freund argues that the interplay of different levels of organization is important not only at the levels of person, family, and society (or other nested levels) but also for understanding the role of specific constructs—in this case, goals—for development. Extending action-theoretical concepts that have tended to view goals as primarily personal constructs, Freund explained that goals are located at multiple levels of the developmental system and that mutually influential relations among these levels need to be assessed to understand fully the nature and role of goals in human development. These levels involve social norms and expectations that inform about age-related opportunity structures and goal-relevant resources; personal beliefs about the appropriate timing and sequencing of goals; personal goals that are influenced by social norms, personal beliefs, the individual's learning history, and external (e.g., social and physical environment) and internal (e.g., talent) resources; and nonconscious goals and motives that might be particularly influential in times of transition or in times of routine.

CONCLUSIONS

A relational developmental systems model of human development constitutes the approach to studying the life span that evolved from the ideas developed among the scholars gathering in the formative conferences at the University of West Virginia (Baltes & Schaie, 1973; Datan & Reese, 1977; Goulet & Baltes, 1970; Nesselroade & Reese, 1973). It is this dynamic, relational perspective that constitutes a radical departure from approaches that study nature, or nurture, or additive, linear (or even curvilinear) combinations (even if cast as "interactions") between the two. Because of the emphasis on the dynamics of relations between the multiple levels of organization involved in the individual and the multiple levels of organization that are part of the ecology of human development, we need to adopt an ontogenetically all-encompassing—a fully life-span—approach to studying relational developmental processes. Such a conceptual frame is required if we are to understand the import of individual ↔ context relations for fostering specific changes, for a specific individual or group, living in a specific context, at a specific point in history (Bornstein, 1995). Clearly, such scholarship requires a multidisciplinary integrative (truly interdisciplinary) approach to the study of human development. Indeed, this need for collaboration across disciplines is in large part why developmental psychology has been transformed into developmental science (Lerner, 2006).

In addition, the concepts of developmental regulation and plasticity integral to a developmental systems framing of the study of development across the life span have another quite important implication for the conduct of developmental science. These concepts in combination afford optimism about the possibility of finding or instantiating individual ↔ context relations that may increase the probability of positive developmental change. Indeed, the life-span approach to developmental science suggests that applications of relational, theory-predicated research findings (in the form of policies or programs) may promote more positive courses of development across life. Efforts to optimize the course of human life through the application of relationally framed developmental science provide, then, an opportunity to test developmental systems ideas about the impact of changes in individual ↔ context relations. As well, such applied efforts constitute a way for developmental scientists to contribute to the improvement of human life among diverse people and their settings. Ultimately, then, such applications of developmental science may contribute to the enhancement of social justice (Lerner & Overton, 2008).

THE GOALS OF THIS *HANDBOOK*

The innovative ideas associated with a developmental systems–framed approach to the study of life-span development is coupled with an admittedly ambitious agenda of basic and applied developmental science devoted to studying and optimizing processes of individual ↔ context relations across the life span. Nevertheless, despite the methodological complexities of adopting this relational approach to developmental science, the past 40 years have provided depth and breadth of empirical evidence in support of the usefulness of these ideas in framing methodologically rigorous and substantively significant developmental science.

As such, one might think that numerous scholarly references exist for scholars to draw on to understand the state-of-the art of the study of life-span development. However, such resources have not existed before the present *Handbook*. Because of this absence, there was no single reference work that developmental scientists or their students could consult to find a thorough, integrative presentation of the breadth of scholarship documenting the use of the relational, developmental systems ideas that frame the life-span study of human development. There was no single high-level reference that provided discussions of the usefulness of relational concepts in integrating and extending the range of substantive areas involved in studying development across the life span.

Instead, to date, the key reference works available to developmental scientists and their students about the nature and scope of life-span change processes have been—paradoxically—age-segmented resources (e.g., Damon & Lerner, 2006; Lerner & Steinberg, 2009). In short, despite the important and rich theoretical and substantive work that is framed by perspectives on human development that encompass the life span, there has been no single reference work that presents the top-tier developmental science work pertinent to such processes.

The goal of this *Handbook* is to provide such a scholarly resource. It is the first-ever reference work to present—through the top-tier scholars in developmental science—the accumulated knowledge about the description, explanation, and implications for optimizing applications (i.e., applications that have the potential to maximize the chances for positive human development) of development across the life span. My fellow editors and I have the aspiration that this *Handbook* will constitute a watershed event in the development of life-span developmental scholarship. With the publication of this *Handbook*, we believe a compelling scholarly alternative will exist to counter both split depictions of developmental processes (e.g., studying childhood and adulthood as if they were composed of distinct, completely discontinuous processes) and split explanations of the changes that occur across the life span.

We hope that this first edition of the *Handbook* will serve as a touchstone for current and future researchers and instructors. As such, future editions of the *Handbook* may provide an even richer depiction of the course of development across the breadth of the life span than is possible in this edition. Given that developmental science has had for so long an age-specific focus, several topics discussed across the two volumes of this *Handbook* remain underexplored, perhaps particularly with respect to the later adult years. When the literature was not available to discuss a particular topic in depth with regard to a portion of the life span, the authors point to this situation and suggest ways to expand the topic more fully across the life span. We believe that their ideas for future scholarship are persuasive—indeed, compelling. As such, our ultimate hope is that future editions of the *Handbook* will reflect the continued theoretical, methodological, and empirical refinement of the concepts about development that began to coalesce in the hills of West Virginia more than four decades ago.

ACKNOWLEDGMENTS

There are numerous people to whom the editors of this *Handbook* owe enormous thanks for their contributions. Clearly, we are deeply grateful to the colleagues who contributed to this work, both for their superb scholarly contributions and for their commitment to working collaboratively to produce this *Handbook*. We also appreciate greatly the unflagging support of our superb editor at John Wiley & Sons, Patricia Rossi. Her commitment to the vision of this *Handbook* and her support for the quality of contribution we sought to make to developmental science were essential, indeed invaluable, assets throughout our work. We are also grateful to Leslie Dickinson and Jarrett M. Lerner, successive Managing Editors at the Institute for Applied Research at Tufts University, for their superb editorial work. Their commitment to quality and productivity, and their resiliency in the face of the tribulations of manuscript production, are greatly admired and deeply appreciated. I am also grateful to the National 4-H Council, the Philip Morris Smoking Prevention Department, the John Templeton Foundation, the Thrive Foundation for Youth, and the National Science Foundation for supporting my work during the development of this project.

Finally, my co-editors and I dedicate this *Handbook* to Paul B. Baltes, one of the pillars of 20th century developmental science and, across the last third of the 20th century, the key intellectual and professional force involved in establishing and enabling the flourishing of theory and research about life-span development. His intellect, leadership, generosity, kindness, and wisdom are warmly remembered and sorely missed.

Richard M. Lerner
Medford, MA
October 1, 2009

REFERENCES

Baltes, P. B. (Ed.). (1978). *Life-span development and behavior* (Vol. 1). New York: Academic Press.

Baltes, P. B. (1979). On the potential and limits of child development: Life-span developmental perspectives. *Newsletter of the Society of Research in Child Development,* 1–4.

Baltes, P. B. (1983). Life-span developmental psychology: Observations on history and theory revisited. In R. M. Lerner (Ed.), *Developmental psychology: Historical and philosophical perspectives* (pp. 79–111). Hillsdale, NJ: Erlbaum.

Baltes, P. B. (1987). Theoretical propositions of life-span developmental psychology: On the dynamics between growth and decline. *Developmental Psychology, 23,* 611–626.

Baltes, P. B., & Brim, O. G. (Eds.). (1979). *Life-span development and behavior* (Vol. 2). New York: Academic Press.

Baltes, P. B., & Brim, O. G. (Eds.). (1980). *Life-span development and behavior* (Vol. 3). New York: Academic Press.

Baltes, P. B., & Brim, O. G. (Eds.). (1982). *Life-span development and behavior* (Vol. 4). New York: Academic Press.

Baltes, P. B., & Brim, O. G. (Eds.). (1983). *Life-span development and behavior* (Vol. 5). New York: Academic Press.

Baltes, P. B., & Brim, O. G. (Eds.). (1984). *Life-span development and behavior* (Vol. 6). New York: Academic Press.

Baltes, P. B., Featherman, D. L., & Lerner, R. M. (Eds.). (1986). *Life-span development and behavior* (Vol. 7). Hillsdale, NJ: Erlbaum.

Baltes, P. B., Featherman, D. L., & Lerner, R. M. (Eds.). (1988a). *Life-span development and behavior* (Vol. 8). Hillsdale, NJ: Erlbaum.

Baltes, P. B., Featherman, D. L., & Lerner, R. M. (Eds.). (1988b). *Life-span development and behavior* (Vol. 9). Hillsdale, NJ: Erlbaum.

Baltes, P. B., Featherman, D. L., & Lerner, R. M. (Eds.). (1990). *Life-span development and behavior* (Vol. 10). Hillsdale, NJ: Erlbaum.

Baltes, P. B., Freund, A.M., & Li, S.-C. (2005). The psychological science of human aging. In M. Johnson, V. L. Bengston, P. G. Coleman, & T. B. L. Kirkwood (Eds.), *The Cambridge handbook of age and ageing* (pp. 47–71). Cambridge, England: Cambridge University Press.

Baltes, P. B., Lindenberger, U., & Staudinger, U. M. (2006). Lifespan theory in developmental psychology. In R. M. Lerner (Ed.) *Handbook of child psychology: Vol. 1. Theoretical models of human development* (6th ed., pp. 569–664). Editors-in-chief: W. Damon & R. M. Lerner. Hoboken, NJ: John Wiley & Sons.

Baltes, P. B., Reese, H. W., & Nesselroade, J. R. (1977). *Life-span developmental psychology: Introduction to research methods.* Monterey, CA: Brooks/Cole.

Baltes, P. B., & Schaie, K. W. (Eds.). (1973). *Life-span developmental psychology: Personality and socialization.* New York: Academic Press.

Bell, R. Q. (1968). A reinterpretation of the direction of effects in studies of socialization. *Psychological Review, 75,* 81–95.

Boring, E. G. (1950). *A history of experimental psychology* (2nd ed.). New York: Appleton-Century-Crofts.

Bornstein, M. H. (1995). Parenting infants. In M. H. Bornstein (Ed.), *Handbook of Parenting* (Vol. 1, pp. 3–39). Mahwah, NJ: Erlbaum.

Bornstein, M. H., & Lamb, M. E. (Eds.). (2005). Developmental *science: An advanced textbook* (5th ed.). Mahwah, NJ: Erlbaum.

Bornstein, M. H., & Lamb, M. E. (Eds.). (2010). *Developmental science: An advanced textbook* (6th ed.). New York: Psychology Press/Taylor & Francis.

Brandtstädter, J. (1998). Action perspectives on human development. In R. M. Lerner (Ed.), *Handbook of child psychology: Vol. 1. Theoretical models of human development* (5th ed., pp. 807–863). Editor in chief: W. Damon. New York: John Wiley & Sons.

Brandtstädter, J. (2006). Action perspectives on human development. In R. M. Lerner (Ed.), *Handbook of child psychology: Vol. 1. Theoretical models of human development* (6th ed., pp. 516–568). Editors-in-chief: W. Damon & R. M. Lerner. Hoboken, NJ: John Wiley & Sons.

Brim, O. G., & Kagan, J. (Eds.). (1980). *Constancy and change in human development.* Cambridge, MA: Harvard University Press.

Bronfenbrenner, U. (1979). *The ecology of human development.* Cambridge, MA: Harvard University Press.

Bronfenbrenner, U., & Morris, P. A. (2006). The bioecological model of human development. In R. M. Lerner (Ed.), *Handbook of child psychology: Vol. 1. Theoretical models of human development* (6th ed., pp. 793–828). Editor in chief: W. Damon. Hoboken, NJ: John Wiley & Sons.

Cairns, R. B., & Cairns, B. D. (2006). The making of developmental psychology. In R. M. Lerner (Ed.), *Handbook of child psychology: Vol. 1. Theoretical models of human development* (6th ed., pp. 89–165). Editors-in-chief: W. Damon & R. M. Lerner. Hoboken, NJ: John Wiley & Sons.

Damon, W., & Lerner, R. M. (Editors-in-Chief). (2006). *Handbook of child psychology* (6th ed.). Hoboken, NJ: John Wiley & Sons.

Datan, N., & Reese, H. W. (Eds.). (1977). *Life-span developmental psychology: Dialectical perspectives on experimental research.* New York: Academic Press.

Elder, G. H., Jr. (1998). The life course and human development. In R. M. Lerner (Ed.), *Handbook of child psychology: Vol. 1. Theoretical models of human development* (5th ed., pp. 939–991). Editor in chief: W. Damon. New York: John Wiley & Sons.

Elder, G. H., Modell, J., & Parke, R. D. (Eds.). (1993). *Children in time and place: Developmental and historical insights.* New York: Cambridge University Press.

Emmerich, W. (1968). Personality development and concepts of structure. *Child Development, 39,* 671–690.

Featherman, D. L., Lerner, R. M., & Perlmutter, M. (Eds.). (1992). *Life-span development and behavior* (Vol. 11). Hillsdale, NJ: Erlbaum.

Featherman, D. L., Lerner, R. M., & Perlmutter, M. (Eds.). (1994). *Life-span development and behavior* (Vol. 12). Hillsdale, NJ: Erlbaum.

Ford, D. H., & Lerner, R. M. (1992). *Developmental systems theory: An integrative approach.* Newbury Park, CA: Sage.

Freund, A. M. (2007). Differentiating and integrating levels of goal representation: A life-span perspective. In B. R. Little, K. Salmela-Aro, J. E. Nurmi, & S. D. Phillips (Eds.), *Personal project pursuit: Goals, action and human flourishing* (pp. 247–270). Mahwah, NJ: Erlbaum.

Freund, A. M., & Baltes, P. B. (2000). The orchestration of selection, optimization, and compensation: An action-theoretical conceptualization of a theory of developmental regulation. In W. J. Perrig & A. Grob (Eds.), *Control of human behaviour, mental processes and consciousness* (pp. 35–58). Mahwah, NJ: Erlbaum.

Freund, A. M., Li, K. Z. H., & Baltes, P. B. (1999). The role of selection, optimization, and compensation in successful aging. In J. Brandtstädter & R. M. Lerner (Eds.), *Action and development: Origins and functions of intentional self-development* (pp. 401–434). Thousand Oaks: Sage.

Freund, A. M., Nikitin, J., & Ritter, J. O. (2009). Psychological consequences of longevity: The increasing importance of self-regulation in old age. *Human Development, 52,* 1– 37.

Gottlieb, G. (1997). *Synthesizing nature–nurture: Prenatal roots of instinctive behavior.* Mahwah, NJ: Erlbaum.

Gottlieb, G., Wahlsten, D., & Lickliter, R. (2006). The significance of biology for human development: A developmental psychobiological systems view. In R. M. Lerner & W. Damon (Eds.), *Handbook of child psychology: Vol. 1. Theoretical models of human development* (6th ed., pp. 210–257). Hoboken, NJ: John Wiley & Sons.

Goulet, L. R., & Baltes, P. B. (Eds.). (1970). *Life-span developmental psychology: Research and theory.* New York: Academic Press.

Greenberg, G., & Tobach, E. (Eds.) *Behavioral evolution and integrative levels.* Hillsdale, NJ: Erlbaum.

Hall, G. S. (1922). *Senescence: The last half of life.* New York: Appleton.

Havighurst, R. J. (1951). *Developmental tasks and education.* New York: Longmans.

Hess, E. H. (1970). Ethology and developmental psychology. In P. H. Mussen (Ed.), *Carmichael's manual of child psychology* (3rd ed., pp. 1–38). New York: John Wiley & Sons.

Kuo, Z.-Y. (1976). *The dynamics of behavior development: An epigenetic view.* New York: Plenum.

Lamb, M. E. (1977). A reexamination of the infant social world. *Human Development, 20,* 65–85.

Lamb, M. E., Thompson, R. A., Gardner, W. P., & Charnov, E. L. (1985). *Infant–mother attachment.* Hillsdale, NJ: Erlbaum.

Lerner, R. M. (1984). *On the nature of human plasticity.* New York: Cambridge University Press.

Lerner, R. M. (2002). *Concepts and theories of human development* (3rd ed.). Mahwah, NJ: Erlbaum.

Lerner, R. M. (2006). Developmental science, developmental systems, and contemporary theories of human development. In R. M. Lerner (Ed.), *Handbook of child psychology: Vol. 1. Theoretical models of human development* (6th ed., pp. 1–17). Editors-in-chief: W. Damon & R. M. Lerner. Hoboken, NJ: John Wiley & Sons.

Lerner, R. M., & Overton, W. F. (2008). Exemplifying the integrations of the relational developmental system: Synthesizing theory, research, and application to promote positive development and social justice. *Journal of Adolescent Research, 23,* 245–255.

Lerner, R. M., & Steinberg, L. (Eds.). (2009). *Handbook of adolescent psychology* (3rd ed.). Hoboken, NJ: John Wiley & Sons.

Lewis, M. (1972). State as an infant–environment interaction: An analysis of mother infant behavior as a function of sex. *Merrill-Palmer Quarterly, 18,* 95–121.

Lewis, M., & Lee-Painter, S. (1974). An interactional approach to the mother–infant dyad. In M. Lewis & L. A. Rosenblum (Eds.), *The effect of the infant on its caregivers* (pp. 21–48). New York: John Wiley & Sons.

Lewis, M., & Rosenblum, L. A. (Eds.). (1974). *The effect of the infant on its caregivers.* New York: John Wiley & Sons.

Magnusson, D., & Stattin, H. (1998). Person–context interaction theories. In R. M. Lerner (Ed.), *Handbook of child psychology: Vol. 1. Theoretical models of human development* (5th ed., pp. 685–759). Editor in chief: W. Damon. New York: John Wiley & Sons.

Magnusson, D., & Stattin, H. (2006). The person in context: A holistic–interactionistic approach. In R. M. Lerner & W. Damon (Eds.), *Handbook of child psychology: Vol. 1. Theoretical models of human development* (6th ed., pp. 400–464). Hoboken, NJ: John Wiley & Sons.

McClearn, G. R. (1970). Genetic influences on behavior and development. In P. H. Mussen (Ed.), *Carmichael's manual of child psychology* (3rd ed., pp. 39–76). New York: John Wiley & Sons.

Mussen, P. H. (Ed.). (1970). *Carmichael's manual of child psychology* (3rd ed.). New York: John Wiley & Sons.

Nesselroade, J. R., & Reese, H. W. (Eds.). (1973). *Life-span developmental psychology: Methodological issues.* New York: Academic Press.

Nikitin, J., & Freund, A. M. (2008). Hoping to be liked or wishing not to be rejected: Conflict and congruence of social approach and avoidance motivation. *Applied Psychology: An International Review, 57,* 90–111.

Novikoff, A. B. (1945a). The concept of integrative levels and biology. *Science, 101,* 209–215.

Novikoff, A. B. (1945b). Continuity and discontinuity in evolution. *Science, 101,* 405–406.

Overton, W. F. (1973). On the assumptive base of the nature–nurture controversy: Additive versus interactive conceptions. *Human Development, 16,* 74–89.

Overton, W. F. (1975). General systems, structure and development. In K. Riegel & G. Rosenwald (Eds.), *Structure and transformation: Developmental aspects* (pp. 61–81). New York: Wiley Interscience.

Overton, W. F. (1978). Klaus Riegel: Theoretical contribution to concepts of stability and change. *Human Development, 21,* 360–363.

Overton, W. F. (2003). Development across the life span: Philosophy, concepts, theory. In R. M. Lerner, M. A. Easterbrooks, & J. Mistry (Eds.), *Handbook of psychology: Vol. 6. Developmental psychology* (pp. 13–42). Editor in chief: B. Weiner. Hoboken, NJ: John Wiley & Sons.

Overton, W. F. (2006). Developmental psychology: Philosophy, concepts, methodology. In R. M. Lerner (Ed.). *Handbook of Child Psychology: Vol. 1. Theoretical models of human development.* Volume 1 of (6th ed.) (pp. 18–88). Editors-in-chief: W. Damon & R. M. Lerner. Hoboken, NJ: John Wiley & Sons.

Overton, W., & Reese, H. (1981). Conceptual prerequisites for an understanding of stability–change and continuity–discontinuity. *International Journal of Behavioral Development, 4,* 99–123.

Reese, H. W., & Overton, W. F. (1970). Models of development and theories of development. In L. R. Goulet & P. B. Baltes (Eds.), *Life-span developmental psychology: Research and theory* (pp. 115–145). New York: Academic.

Riegel, K. F. (1975) Toward a dialectical theory of human development. *Human Development, 18,* 50–64.

Riegel, K. F. (1976). The dialectics of human development. *American Psychologist, 31,* 689–700.

Riley, M. W. (Ed.). (1979). *Aging from birth to death.* Washington, DC: American Association for the Advancement of Science.

Sameroff, A. (1975). Transactional models in early social relations. *Human Development, 18,* 65–79.

Schneirla, T. C. (1957). The concept of development in comparative psychology. In D. B. Harris (Ed.), *The concept of development: An issue in the study of human behavior* (pp. 78–108). Minneapolis: University of Minnesota Press.

Stevenson, H. W. (1970). Learning in children. In P. H. Mussen (Ed.), *Carmichael's manual of child psychology* (3rd ed., pp. 849–938). New York: John Wiley & Sons.

Thelen, E., & Smith, L. B. (1998). Dynamic systems theories. In R. M. Lerner (Ed.), *Handbook of child psychology: Vol. 1. Theoretical models of human development* (5th ed., pp. 563–633). Editor in chief: W. Damon. New York: John Wiley & Sons.

Thompson, R. A., & Lamb, M. E. (1986). Infant–mother attachment: New directions for theory and research. In P. B. Baltes, D. L. Featherman, & R. M. Lerner (Eds.), *Life-span development and behavior* (Vol. 7, pp. 1–41). Hillsdale, NJ: Erlbaum.

Tobach, E., & Greenberg, G. (1984). The significance of T. C. Schneirla's contribution to the concept of levels of integration. In G. Greenberg & E. Tobach (Eds.), *Behavioral evolution and integrative levels* (pp. 1–8). Hillsdale, NJ: Erlbaum.

von Bertalanffy, L. (1933). *Modern theories of development.* London: Oxford University Press.

von Bertalanffy, L. (1968). *General systems theory.* New York: Braziller.

White, S. H. (1970). The learning theory tradition and child psychology. In P. H. Mussen (Ed.), *Carmichael's manual of child psychology* (3rd ed., pp. 657–701). New York: John Wiley & Sons.

Wohlwill, J. F. (1973). *The study of behavioral development.* New York: Academic Press.

Contributors

Ellen Bialystok
York University
Toronto, Ontario, Canada

Susan A. J. Birch
University of British Columbia
Vancouver, British Columbia, Canada

Clancy Blair
New York University
New York, New York

Matthew J. Bundick
Stanford University
Palo Alto, California

Jeremy I. M. Carpendale
Simon Fraser University
Burnaby, British Columbia, Canada

Michael J. Chandler
University of British Columbia
Vancouver, British Columbia, Canada

Fergus I. M. Craik
Rotman Research Institute
Toronto, Ontario, Canada

William Damon
Stanford University
Palo Alto, California

Andreas Demetriou
University of Cyprus
Cyprus, Greece

Kurt W. Fischer
Harvard University
Cambridge, Massachussetts

Susan Goldin-Meadow
University of Chicago
Chicago, Illinois

Gary Greenberg
Wichita State University
Wichita, Kansas

Jana M. Iverson
University of Pittsburgh
Pittsburgh, Pennsylvania

Sophie Jacques
Dalhousie University
Halifax, Nova Scotia, Canada

Linda Jarvin
Tufts University
Medford, Massachusetts

Tzur M. Karelitz
Education Development Center, Inc
Newton, Massachussetts

Pamela Ebstyne King
Fuller Theological Seminary
Pasedena, California

Wendy S. C. Lee
University of Minnesota
Minneapolis, Minnesota

Richard M. Lerner
Tufts University
Medford, Massachusetts

Charlie Lewis
Lancaster University
Lancaster, United Kingdom

Michael Lewis
University of Medicine and Dentistry of New Jersey
Piscataway, New Jersey

Leah L. Light
Pitzer College
Claremont, California

Stella F. Lourenco
Emory University
Atlanta, Georgia

Brian MacWhinney
Carnegie Mellon University
Pittsburgh, Pennsylvania

Stuart Marcovitch
University of North Carolina at Greensboro
Greensboro, North Carolina

Michael F. Mascolo
Merrimack College
North Andover, Massachusetts

John J. McArdle
University of Southern California
Los Angeles, California

Megan M. McClelland
Oregon State University
Corvallis, Oregon

Emily E. Messersmith
University of North Carolina at Chapel Hill
Chapel Hill, North Carolina

Peter C. M. Molenaar
The Pennsylvania State University
University Park, Pennsylvania

Antigoni Mouyi
Pedagogical Institute of Cyprus
Cyprus, Greece

Ulrich Müller
University of Victoria
Victoria, British Columbia

John R. Nesselroade
University of Virginia
Charlottesville, Virginia

Peter A. Ornstein
University of North Carolina at Chapel Hill
Chapel Hill, North Carolina

Willis F. Overton
Temple University
Philadelphia, Pennsylvania

Ty Partridge
Wayne State University
Detroit, Michigan

Claire Cameron Ponitz
University of Virginia
Charlottesville, Virginia

Timothy P. Racine
Simon Fraser University
Burnaby, British Columbia

Robert B. Ricco
California State University at San Bernardino
San Bernardino, California

Sebastiano Santostefano
Private Practice
Boston, Massachusetts

George Spanoudis
University of Cyprus
Cyprus, Greece

Robert J. Sternberg
Tufts University
Medford, Massachusetts

Shauna Tominey
Oregon State University
Corvallis, Oregon

Elliot Turiel
University of California
Berkeley, Berkeley, California

Marina Vasilyeva
Boston College
Boston, Massachusetts

David S. Yeager
Stanford University
Palo Alto, California

Philip David Zelazo
University of Minnesota
Minneapolis, Minnesota

CHAPTER 1

Life-Span Development
Concepts and Issues

WILLIS F. OVERTON

LIFE-SPAN DEVELOPMENT: CONCEPTS AND ISSUES

A *Handbook of Life-Span Development* would seem to merit some serious discussion of the meaning of life-span development. *Life-span development* is a phrase that has been a prominent feature of developmental psychology and developmental science since the early 1970s, but few attempts have been made to conceptually clarify its core meaning(s). One could, of course, take the classic empiricist approach and argue that the work of conceptual clarification is quite meaningless—perhaps producing more heat than light—and the phrase is sufficiently defined operationally by the chapters that the reader encounters in the two volumes of this handbook, together with all other volumes of text that in the past have included the phrase *life-span development*. The advantage of this radically empirical and radically pragmatic approach—life-span development is what life-span developmental researchers do—is that it allows us to glide over possible fissures and tensions that might be present in the study of development across the life span, thus offering the broadest of possible umbrellas under which research fortuitously might flourish. On the other hand, such an approach seems somewhat akin to

I express my appreciation to all of the authors in this volume for their tireless work and creative efforts and for their putting up with my obsessions as an editor, but most of all for teaching me so much about life-span development. I send a special note of appreciation to those who entered into a conversation with me about the shape and breadth of life-span development, and those who helped through editorial suggestions and feedback on this introductory chapter, including Ellen Bialystok, Fergus Craik, Jeremy Carpendale, Rich Lerner, Leah Light, Ulrich Müller, John Nesselroade, K Warner Schaie, and Hayne Reese. I must also single out two people for an additional acknowledgment: first, to Rich Lerner, for his constant and unwavering friendship and support over many years, for inviting me to edit this volume, and for his help in numerous ways throughout the process; and second, to Hayne Reese, for his friendship and support over even more years, as well as for being the person who introduced me to life-span development by inviting me to write a paper with him for the very first Life-Span Development Conference at West Virginia University in 1969. That paper—our first of many dialectical collaborations—later became a chapter in the first volume of the life-span development series: Reese, H. W., & Overton, W. F. (1970). Models of development and theories of development. In L. R. Goulet & P. B. Baltes (Eds.), *Life-span developmental psychology: Research and theory* (pp. 115–145). New York: Academic Press. How different my life would have been had we never met.

dropping a group of people into a dark forest and telling them to walk out. If they did enough walking, they might succeed, but they also might forever walk in circles. Some kind of additional directions would be helpful.

This chapter focuses on conceptual clarifications—providing some direction—designed to avoid confusion and facilitate progress toward the goal of enhancing our knowledge and understanding of "life-span development." It is recognized that the directions suggested here may have to be supplemented by finer details, and also that there may be other successful paths. However, the chapter is partially designed to undercut philosopher Ludwig Wittgenstein's acerbic remark when he maintained that "in psychology there are empirical methods and conceptual confusions" (1958, p. xiv), and partially it is designed in acknowledgment of Robert Hogan's comment that "all the empiricism in the world can't salvage a bad idea" (2001, p. 27); but most broadly, it is designed in the hopes of producing more light than heat and providing at least some suggestions for pathways in moving forward in the field of *life-span development.*

The second section of the chapter, The Concept of Development, explores various meanings of the general concept of "development." These meanings have, at times, been taken as competing alternatives, and here a proposal is made that formulates a more inclusive integrative understanding of the area that defines the core of life-span development. Because formulating an integrative understanding requires the application of some principles of integration, the following section, Relational Metatheory, presents "relationism" as a broad-principled method designed to achieve this goal. As a set of principles, relationism is also used to explore other concepts that are central to a life-span approach to development. It will become obvious early in the chapter that "system" plays a central role in the definition and exploration of development. The third section of the chapter, Relational Developmental Systems, discusses "system" and system approaches to the study of development. In this section, various system concepts, such as "closed and open systems," "complex systems," "adaptive systems," and especially "relational developmental systems," are examined. In turn, the notion of relational developmental systems operates as the grounding for the fourth and final substantive section of the chapter, Age, Life-Span Development, and Aging, which focuses on the "life-span" nature of life-span development. In this section, considerations of "adult development," "age," "aging," "time," "description," and "processes" establish the context for a relational (see Relational Metatheory),

developmental (see Concept of Development), systems (see Relational Developmental Systems) proposal that integrates life-span development, adult development, and aging within a single-process, dual-trajectory understanding of *life-span development.*

In entering this conceptual arena of inquiry, a few introductory words are needed concerning a distinction that will be central to the exploration of life-span development. This is the distinction between metatheory, theory, and methods. In the heydays of neopositivism, or radical empiricism, theory and method lost their status as two distinguishable but interdependent spheres of science, and in radical empiricism's insistence on monistic materialist solutions, theory became squeezed down into method. A consequence, which has lasted even into the present, is that "theory" came often to designate merely the empirical interrelations among the various antecedent variables associated with outcome or dependent variables. So, for example, when asked about a theory or model of aggression, one could, and often still can, point to a structural equation diagram and show—with lines, arrows, and circles—the correlations and weightings among associated variables and aggression outcomes. Today in a postpositivist scientific world, these concepts of theory and method again need to be differentiated: theory constitutes the distinguishable means of conceptual exploration in any designated area of enquiry; methods are the distinguishable means of observational exploration of that area; and they are differentiated and relationally joined spheres that are necessary coactors in scientific enquiry. To paraphrase Immanuel Kant, theories without methods are empty speculations; methods without theories are meaningless data. This brings us to the notion of "metatheory."

With the emergence of postpositivist science developed in the works of Steven Toulmin (1953), N. R. Hanson (1958), Thomas Kuhn (1962), Imre Lakatos (1978), and Larry Laudan (1977), among others, it became clear that any viable scientific research program entails a set of core assumptions that frame and contextualize both theory and methods. These core, often implicit, assumptions have come to be called *metatheoretical,* and their primary function is to provide a rich source of concepts out of which theories and methods emerge. Metatheories transcend (i.e., "meta") theories and methods in the sense that they define the context in which theoretical concepts and specific methods are constructed. A *metatheory* is a set of interlocking rules, principles, or stories (narrative) that *both describes and prescribes* what is acceptable and unacceptable as theoretical concepts and as methodological procedures. For example, one metatheory may prescribe that no "mental" concepts (e.g., "mind") may enter theory, and that all change must be understood as strictly additive (i.e., no emergence, no gaps, strict continuity), and hence will be measured by additive statistical techniques. This is a description of some features of early behaviorism. Another metatheory may prescribe that mind is an essential feature of the system under consideration, that the system operates holistically, that novel features emerge, and that nonadditive statistical techniques are a welcome feature of any methodological toolbox. This is a description of some metatheoretical features of what is termed a "relational developmental systems approach," which is described in detail later in the chapter. Metatheoretical assumptions also serve as guidelines that help to avoid conceptual confusions. Take, for example, the word *stage.* In a metatheory that allows discontinuity of change and emergence, "stage" will be a theoretical concept referring to a particular level of organization of the system; in a metatheory that allows only continuity, if "stage" is used at all—it will be a simple descriptive summary statement of a group of behaviors (e.g., the stage of adolescence), but never as a theoretical concept.

Together with metatheory, theory, and method, it needs to be kept in mind that concepts can and do operate at different levels of discourse (see Figure 1.1). Theories and methods refer directly to the empirical world, whereas metatheories refer to the theories and methods themselves. The most concrete and circumscribed level of discourse is the *observational level.* This is one's current commonsense level of conceptualizing the nature of objects and events in the world. For example, one does not need a professional degree to describe a child as "warm" "loving," "distant," "angry," "bright," or even "attached," "aggressive," or "depressed." This observational, commonsense, or folk level of analysis has a sense of immediacy and concreteness, but when reflected on, it is often unclear, muddy, and ambiguous. It is the reflection on folk understanding that moves the level of discourse to a *reflective level,* which is the beginning of theoretical discourse. Here, reflection is about organizing, refining, and reformulating observational understandings in a broader, more coherent, and more abstract field. At the *theoretical reflective level,* concepts are *about* the observational level, and these range from informal hunches and hypotheses to highly refined theories about the nature of things, including human behavior and change. Relatively refined theories may themselves be narrow or broad. For example, some theories of memory are relatively narrow, whereas Demetriou and

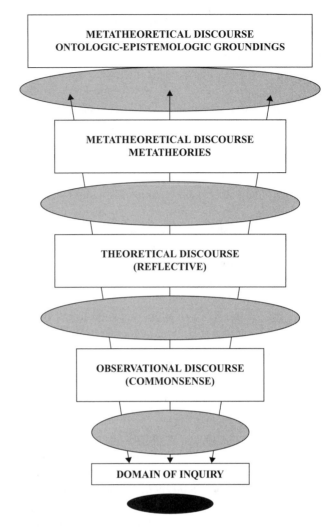

Figure 1.1　Levels of discourse.

colleagues (Chapter 10 of this volume) present a theory of the architecture of mind that is very broad. Similarly, the theories of Piaget, Vygotsky, Erikson, and Werner are grand theories—theories designed to explain a broad sweep of the development of psychological functioning— whereas Bowlby's theory more narrowly focuses on attachment and its development.

The metatheoretical level itself operates above, and functions as a grounding for, the theoretical level. At the metatheoretical level, reflective thought is about basic concepts that, as mentioned earlier, form the contextual frame for the theoretical and observational levels. And here, to make matters a bit more complicated, it is further possible to discriminate levels of metatheory. Thus, arguably, theories such as "relational developmental systems," "dynamical systems," "embodiment," "action," and even "information processing," and "behaviorism" actually constitute metatheories that frame specific theories. These metatheories are each grounded in a coherent sets of broader metatheoretical principles. And these, in turn, are grounded at the final apex of the levels of discourse; in those coherent sets of universal ontological and epistemological propositions termed *worldviews,* including at least the classic "mechanistic," "contextualist," "organicist," and a more recent set, representing the synthesis of contextualism and organicism, termed "relationism."

If all of this abstract talk of levels of discourse and metatheories seems too abstract for pragmatic minds, it should be remembered that most of the fundamental issues in psychology originated in abstract concepts, and it is at that level, and only at that level, that they can begin to be resolved. Of course, one can throw away all abstract maps and yielding to the pragmatic urge, just start walking in the forest; but again, although that may get us out of the woods, it may also just keep us wandering in circles.

THE CONCEPT OF DEVELOPMENT

With metatheories, theories, methods, and levels of discourse as background, we can embark on an exploration of *life-span development.* At first blush it would seem that the "life-span" portion is simple enough: life-span development is the study of the development of living organisms from conception to the end of life. This is a satisfactory initial working definition of life span, but later discussions (especially in the final section of the chapter, Age, Life-Span Development, and Aging) point to some rather thorny conceptual and practical issues presented by such a definition of life span. But from this starting point we can say that the field of life-span development entails the scientific study of *systematic intraindividual changes*—from conception to the end of life—of an organism's behavior, and of the systems and processes underlying those changes and that behavior. The field encompasses the study of several categories of change such as ontogenesis (development of the individual across the life span), embryogenesis (development of the embryo), orthogenesis (normal development), pathogenesis (development of psychopathology), and microgenesis (development on a very small time scale such as development of a single percept). But the field is also comparative and thus includes the study of phylogenesis and evolution (development of the species), as well as historical and cultural development. Human ontogenesis/orthogenesis is the most familiar focus of attention of life-span development,

and within this series a number of age-related areas of study exist—infancy, toddlerhood, childhood, adolescence, early adult, mature adult, and late adulthood. Both within and across areas, life-span developmental scientists explore biological, cognitive, emotional, social, motivational, and personality dimensions of individual development. The field also maintains a strong research focus on contextual ecological systems that impact on development including the family, home, neighborhoods, schools, and peers, and on interindividual differences.

Organization, Sequence, Direction, Epigenesis, and Relative Permanence

Individual change constitutes the fundamental defining feature of development, but it is important to immediately emphasize that not all change is necessarily developmental change. Developmental change entails five necessary defining features: (1) *organization of processes* (also termed *structure* and *system*), (2) *order* and *sequence*, (3) *direction*, (4) *epigenesis* and *emergence,* and (5) *relative permanence* and *irreversibility.* These features frame two broad forms of change that traditionally have been considered developmental, but have also at times been considered competing alternative definitions of developmental change—transformational change and variational change.

Understanding the place of transformational and variational change in development requires a type-token distinction, which is also a distinction between structure and content. Perception, thinking, memory, language, affect, motivation, and consciousness are *universal* psychological processes *(types),* characteristic of the human species as a whole. Any given percept, concept, thought, word, memory, emotion, and motive represents a *particular expression* of a universal process *(tokens).* Although each form of change is entailed by any behavioral act, transformational change primarily concerns the acquisition, maintenance, retention, or decline of universal processes or operations (types), whereas variational change primarily concerns the acquisition, maintenance, retention, or decline of particular expressions (tokens) and individual differences in expressions.

Transformational Change

Organization

Transformational change is change in the form, organization, or structure of a system. In the case of ontogenesis, the system is the living organism, whereas subsystems consist

of cognitive, affective, and motivational (i.e., psychological) processes together with their biological correlates. Embryological changes constitute some of the clearest and most concrete examples of transformational or morphological change (Edelman, 1992; Gottlieb, 1992). Through processes of differentiation and reintegration, movement occurs from the single-celled zygote to the highly organized functioning systems of the 9-month fetus. Some cognitive and social-emotional phenomena of human ontogenesis have also been conceptualized as reflecting transformational change. For example, sensorimotor action undergoes a sequence of transformations to become symbolic thought, and further transformations lead to a reflective symbolic thought exhibiting novel logical characteristics (see Mascolo & Fischer in Chapter 6 of this volume for an extended discussion of several transformational cognitive levels, and Müller & Racine, Chapter 11 of this volume, for an extended discussion of transformation of the representational system). Memory may reflect transformational changes moving from recognition memory to recall memory. The sense of self and identity (Chandler, Lalonde, Sokol, & Hallett, 2003; Damon & Hart, 1988) has been portrayed by some as moving through a sequence of transformations. Emotions have been understood as differentiations from an initial relatively global affective matrix (Lewis, 1993; Sroufe, 1979). Physical changes, such as changes in locomotion, have also been conceptualized as transformational changes (Thelen & Ulrich, 1991). Transformational change has several closely interrelated defining features, and these give further specification to the concept of developmental change.

System

Transformational change implies an object that is changed. In the epoch when reductionist neopositivism and behaviorism constituted the standard psychological metatheory—when psychology identified itself as a *discipline that took substance rather than process as its ontological* base (Bickhard, 2008)—the object changed was simply observable behavior. At the core of neopositivism and behaviorism—and even more recently in what is later described as "strict" contextualism (see Relational Developmental Systems section later in this chapter)—observed behavior and its associations with biological and environmental variables form the bedrock and exclusive context of inquiry. As a consequence, within these metatheoretical frames, it is possible to identify developmental change with a behavioral change that is split off from (i.e., not relationally connected to) any organization of processes. As psychology

moves to a more postpositivist and relational stance—becoming a *process rather than a substance discipline*—it is the living, active, open, self-organizing, and self-regulating system of processes that constitutes the object changed. As an inherently and spontaneously active system, the system acts, and its acts, have the following characteristics: (1) They express the underlying organization of the system (i.e., any act is *expressive*), (2) They function as the means for communicating with the sociocultural world, while changing that and the physical world (i.e., any act is *communicative/instrumental*), and (3) They constitute the basic change mechanism that, through co-action with the world, results in system's transformation. As discussed in detail later in this chapter (see Relational Developmental Systems), it is the active psychological system that organizes and regulates itself through complex and multidirectional relational coactions with its biological, sociocultural, and physical environments (see Greenberg & Partridge, Chapter 5 of this volume, for an extended discussion of a psychology that is biopsychosocial in character). In summary, it is the *relational developmental system* itself that is the object of transformational change.

Order and Sequence

The overt or observable acts of a developmental system exhibit variations (e.g., there are many ways to reach for and grasp a cup), and these variations produce sequences. These behavioral sequences are *contingent* (i.e., under changed conditions can be different). However, change in the form or organization of the system itself exhibits a *necessary order* and *universal sequence* (e.g., the development of "grasping"). Any living system is an adaptive system, and any adaptive system, if it is to live and thrive, necessarily moves from lesser to greater levels of complexity. The transformations from zygote to embryo to fetus, for example, are not contingent; they are universal, and could not be otherwise. Similarly, the transformation of a system characterized by sensorimotor functioning to a system characterized by complex reflective thought represents a necessary and universal ordered sequence.

Directionality

Any notion of order implies a *direction* to the change. That is, any ordered system implies an *orientation toward a goal* or end state. The notion of a goal orientation *(telos)* has often befuddled and even frightened those developmental scientists who continue to grasp on to the anachronism called *neopositivism*. To talk of a telos seems to raise the worry of admitting a discredited teleology into the science. This fear is based on competing metatheoretical assumptions and conceptual confusions. One conceptual confusion concerns subjective versus objective teleology. Subjective teleology involves *subjectively held* "purposes," "aims," or "goals" (e.g., "I intend to become a better person") and is irrelevant to the definition of transformational developmental change. Objective teleology, in contrast, involves the construction of principles or rules designed to explain—in the sense of making intelligible—phenomena under investigation (e.g., "the development of X moves from lack of differentiation to more equilibrated levels of differentiation and hierarchic integration"). The rule so constructed conceptually "finds" or "discovers" or "identifies" the sequential order and the end state. Any position that seriously accepts the idea of transformational change necessarily accepts both goal directedness and the fact that the specific goal articulated is a theoretical concept—not a slice of physical nature—designed to illuminate the nature of the transformational change under study.

It is simply a conceptual confusion to argue that adequate descriptions are more important than the positing of end points (e.g., Sugarman, 1987), or similarly to suggest a movement away from end points and toward "a more neutral, person-time-and-situation-geared conception of development" (Demetriou & Raftopoulos, 2004, p. 91). There is no "neutral" standpoint, and no description could possibly occur without a positing of end points. The question here is what one would possibly describe if one did not understand development as tending toward some specified end? If one wishes to describe/explain the course of acquiring language, then adult language is, of necessity, the end point toward which development moves. No "description" of the language of the child would be possible without this ideal end point. In a similar fashion, if one wishes to describe/explain the transformational development of reasoning, or thought, or problem solving, or personality, or anything, a conceptual end point must serve as the ideal ultimate model.

A related feature of this confusion over the positing of developmental end point arises from the mistaken notion that positing a goal or end point necessarily leads to an "adultomorphic perspective [that] forces one to view earlier behaviors and functions as immature versions of adult functions" (Marcovitch & Lewkowicz, 2004, p. 113). Central to this argument is its faulty assumption that all developmental change, including transformational change, is additive (linear, strict continuity) and, conversely, the failure to recognize a feature further discussed later in this chapter (see Relational Developmental Systems) that, in open self-organizing systems, nonlinearity (nonadditivity; discontinuity) is frequently the rule. For example, Piaget's interest in examining the development of reasoning process from a self-organizing systems perspective resulted in his identifying deductive propositional reasoning as the end point of inquiry; whether this was a good idea or a poor idea is irrelevant to the current argument. What is relevant is that Piaget described several quite different forms of reasoning (e.g., preoperational and concrete operational) that function as discontinuous precursors to this adult form, and these early forms are not simply immature versions of the adult function. Rather, they are qualitatively distinct forms of reasoning.

A final conceptual confusion is the notion—abroad for many years—that focusing on sequences and positing end points introduces rigidity and denies the *plasticity* of development. This notion is quickly debunked by recognizing that the concept of *equifinality* (i.e., that there are multiple means to the same end) is a core concept in any open, self-organizing systems perspective. Although each level of organization of the system is a part of the normative sequence moving toward a normative end, there are multiple means or action paths to each system level.

From a strictly metatheoretical, especially an epistemological metatheoretical perspective, the centrality of transformational change—including the relational developmental system, order, sequence, and directional characteristics—is meaningful only to the extent that our understanding of developmental science and scientific method in general have advanced beyond the neopositivism of what has been traditionally termed *Newtonian mechanical explanation* (Overton, 1991). In that conceptual system, scientific explanation, and hence science, was ultimately reduced to the search for individual and additive observable forces that were taken as the *causes,* and hence the explanation of development. In a relational postpositivist scientific world, the identification of dynamic *pattern*—both momentarily as a "self-organizing system" and temporally as the organized, sequential directional "relational developmental system"—is logically prior to a detailed analysis of the resources this system uses to grow. From a relational developmental systems perspective—given the system's open, active, transforming, self-organizing, and self-regulating character—neither individual nor combined forces cause development. The developmental system defines the resources and their participation in system change. To consider "genes," "neurons," "brain changes," "cultural objects," "parents," "peers," or "neighborhoods" to be sets of additive causes that drive development is to miss the point that these are all resources that the developmental system uses to grow. It is the relational developmental system itself that is the cause of development, and this system enacts this development by engaging in a multitude of complex relational actions with these resources. Classically, these actions have been termed *interactions,* but that term is totally inadequate to describing the relational interpenetrations of coacting parts that operate as the developmental system. In order to capture both the merging (or "fusion"; Greenberg & Tobach, 1984) of parts into a single identity, while maintaining their individual identity as differentiations, this chapter uses the terms *interpenetration* (merging) and *coaction* (differentiation; Gottlieb, Wahlsten, & Lickliter, 2006) in place of *interaction,* except in those cases that refer to the simple additive combination of elements. *Interpenetration* and *coaction* are also used in place of *bidirectional interaction* found in other chapters in this volume. However, it should be noted that when other authors use the term *bidirectional interaction,* they reference the same activity termed *interpenetration* and *coaction* in this chapter.

Although a developmental telos is another necessary feature of transformational change, there is an open and empirical question as to what universal telos most adequately captures the broad course of life-span development. Is it "differentiation and integration" (see Mascolo & Fischer, Chapter 6 of this volume, and Müller & Racine, Chapter 11 of this volume, for extended discussions of the place of "differentiation" as the telos of life-span development)? Or might it be some form of the concept "adaptation" (see Bundick & colleagues, Chapter 24 of this volume, for an extended discussion of "adaptation" as the telos of life-span development)? Or some notion of "balance" (see Bialystok & Craik, Chapter 7 of this volume, and Sternberg, Chapter 23 of this volume, for extended discussions of "balance" as the telos of life-span development)? Or could it be some notion of an "attractor" as discussed within systems approaches to the understanding of changes in "open" systems (Overton, 1975)? Or perhaps some integration of all of these concepts? As discussed further later in this chapter (see Relational Developmental Systems), any telos is an interpretation designed to bring conceptual order into system change, and posited end points can vary as a function of a specific area of inquiry. Because this question of the nature of an adequate developmental telos for life-span development becomes critical when considering "life span" itself, an exploration of this issue is postponed until later in this chapter (see Age, Life-Span Development, and Aging).

Epigenesis and Emergence

The concept of epigenesis was originally introduced in biology as a counterweight to the idea of "preformation" in the explanation of the appearance of increasingly organized complexity from a relatively undifferentiated egg to a highly differentiated organism. Although epigenesis has a long history with several twists and turns (see Lickliter & Honeycutt, in press), today, conceptualized as "probabilistic epigenesis" (Gottlieb, 1992), it designates a *holistic* approach to understanding developmental complexity (transformational change). Probabilistic epigenesis is the principle that the role played by any part of a relational developmental system—gene, cell, organ, organism, physical environment, culture—is a function of all of the interpenetrating and coacting parts of the system. It is through complex relational bidirectional and multidirectional reciprocal interpenetrating actions among the coacting parts that the system moves to levels of increasingly organized complexity. Thus, epigenesis identifies the system as being completely *contextualized* and *situated.* The contextualization of the system is important because it points to the necessity of exploring contextual variables as a part of the overall developmental research enterprise (Bronfenbrenner & Morris, 2006).

Epigenesis also points to a closely related feature of transformational developmental change: *emergence.* Transformational change results in the *emergence of system novelty.* As forms change, they become increasingly complex. This increased complexity is a complexity of pattern rather than a linear additive complexity of elements (see Relational Developmental Systems later in this chapter). The butterfly emerges from the caterpillar through the differentiation and reintegration of organization, the frog from the tadpole, the plant from the seed, the organism from the zygote. In an identical fashion, higher order psychological structures emerge from lower order structures; also in an identical fashion, new patterns of organization exhibit novel characteristics that cannot be reduced to (i.e., completely explained by) or predicted from earlier forms. The novel properties are termed *systemic,* indicating that they are properties of the whole system and not properties of any individual part. This emergence of novelty is commonly referred to as *qualitative* change in the sense that it is change that cannot be represented as purely additive. Similarly, reference to "discontinuity" in development is simply the recognition of emergent novelty and qualitative change of a system (Overton & Reese, 1981). Concepts of "stages" and "levels" of development are theoretical concepts, which within a relational developmental systems perspective reference transformational change together with the associated emergent novelty, qualitative change, and discontinuity. Each of the classic grand developmental figures of the 20th century—Piaget (1967), Vygotsky (1978), Werner (1948), and Erikson (1968)—acknowledged the centrality of nonlinearity and emergence: Piaget and Werner via their ideas of development proceeding through phases of differentiation and reintegration; Erikson through his epigenetic principle of development; Vygotsky in his argument that development is not "the gradual accumulation of separate changes…[but] a complex dialectical process characterized by…qualitative transformations of one form into another [with an] intertwining of external and internal factors" (1978, p. 73).

Systemic emergence is not limited to homogeneous stages such as those offered by the grand theories. Mascolo and Fischer (Chapter 6 of this volume; see also Fischer & Bidell, 2006), for example, in discussing "skill theory" describe development as an "emergent developmental web":

> The developmental web represents development in terms of a series of partially distinct pathways that, depending on developmental circumstances, move in different diverging or converging directions. Higher order psychological structures emerge from the integration or coordination of lower-level structures that develop along partially distinct trajectories. The splitting and converging of developmental trajectories is not something that can be specified or predicted a priori. (p. 163)

In this volume, several other chapters also reference emergence, explicitly or implicitly, as central to their life-span developmental research programs. Demetriou, Mouyi, and Spanoudis (Chapter 10 of this volume) in reviewing the development of mental processing claim that a language of thought—general inferences patterns—and metarepresentational processes are not present at birth but are the "emergent product of guided and reflected-upon domain-specific functioning." (p. 331)

Greenberg and Partridge (Chapter 5 of this volume), following Schneirla (1957), argue that mind is best understood as an emergent systemic feature of organizational transformation:

> Although our view of mind is sympathetic to that of Sperry's, in that we are certainly physical monists and agree that what we call mind is an emergent property, our view extends that of Sperry's to what could be deemed relational emergent

monism. Sperry's emergent monism view of mind is still fundamentally reductionistic, arguing that mind is essentially the dynamic macrostate of underlying neurological activity. Although this dynamic macrostate is emergent in the sense that its properties are not fully predictable from the individual states of the underlying neurologic matrix, it is still a state that is subordinate to neurology.

> By accepting the pragmatic definition of mind as an integration of cognitive, emotional, and organism ← → context relational behaviors within the developmental system, you place the concept of mind and its subsidiary constructs within the operational realm of psychology.…Thus, we see mind as an emergent function of the dynamic transactions over the entire course of development of the individual organism and its ecological context. (p. 129)

MacWhinney (Chapter 14 of this volume) places emergentism at the center of his analysis of language development:

> Emergentist thinking is basic to the natural sciences. However, it applies equally well to the social, neural, and behavioral sciences (Lerner, 2006; Overton, 2006). The application of emergentism to the study of language and language development over the last two decades has proven to be particularly rewarding. In this chapter, we will explore how emergentist theory helps us understand the growth of language across the life span. (p. 470)

Lewis's (Chapter 18 of this volume) presentation of the development of self and consciousness argues for the centrality of transformational emergence in this process:

> For the adult human, both spheres of consciousness are functional. The implicit sphere of the self is composed of the core processes of the body or implicit consciousness; the other sphere is the idea of me, explicit consciousness that represents an emergent transformation of the core processes.…From a developmental perspective, the core processes of self are present at birth, and the mental state of the idea of me emerges as a developmental transformation in the first two years of the child's life. (p. 651)

In a similar context, Santostefano's (Chapter 22 of this volume) exploration of the development of several forms of self as they relate to developmental psychopathology has at its core the following idea:

> New forms of cognition, emotion, and behavior emerge through this process of self-organization…[and] cause and effect is a relational bidirectional, circular process.

...Lower order features provide the foundation from which higher order features emerge. But these higher order features, in turn, exert a top-down influence. (p. 798)

Carpendale and Lewis's (Chapter 17 of this volume) theory of the development of social cognition also explicitly recognizes emergent novelty in their discussion of the transformational gap that operates between neurological and psychological functioning. Finally, Müller and Racine (Chapter 11 of this volume) consider symbolic representations as they have been conceptualized in the classic developmental theories:

Essential for Piaget, Vygotsky, and Werner was the idea that earlier symbolic representations emerge out of pragmatic, communicative activities. For Werner, symbols results from a shift of function: "A novel emerging function becomes actualized at first through the use of means articulated and structured in the service of...[developmentally] earlier ends" (Werner & Kaplan, 1963, p. 66). (p. 379)

Relative Permanence and Irreversibility

A final feature of transformational change of a system is that it is not circular, transitory, or willy-nilly reversible. Transformational change—system change—is relatively permanent, relatively irreversible. This eliminates sleep, digestion, going to the movies, and any behaviors that are readily extinguishable from the list of transformational changes. Although this attribute is generally a straightforward feature of transformational change, it raises an issue with respect to life-span development. If it were found empirically that there were declines in middle or late adulthood in behaviors associated with transformational systems (e.g., if the form of thinking deteriorated or regressed to an earlier form), would this change be considered something other than development? Would it be necessary to introduce two radically different processes into our life-span understanding such as "development" on the one hand and "aging" on the other? Not necessarily. The modifier "relatively" partially addresses this issue. And it might be possible to conceptualize the late adult years as having their own order, sequence, epigenesis (if not emergence), and permanence. However, these issues are better saved for the Age, Life-Span Development, and Aging section of this chapter.

Variational Change

Variational change refers to the degree or extent that a change varies from a standard, norm, or average. Nesselroade and

Molenaar (chapter 2 of this volume) describe three kinds of comparisons that constitute the most elemental character of variation: (1) comparisons among kinds of entities (e.g., qualitative differences), (2) comparisons of an entity with itself over different occasions (intraindividual differences), and (3) comparisons among entities of the same kind (interindividual differences). The first of these refers to the outcome of transformational change; the second, intraindividual variation, is the focus of this section. The third comparison, interindividual differences, is related to the concept of development only to the extent that the focus is on change of these differences, and these changes themselves ultimately devolve back into intraindividual variation. The contingent reaching and grasping patterns of the infant's behavior, the toddler's improvements in walking precision, the growth of vocabulary, and receiving grades on an exam are all examples of variational intraindividual change. From an instrumental point of view, intraindividual variational change is about a skill or ability (token) emerging (but not emergent) and becoming more precise and more accurate. Intraindividual variations are generally represented as linear, as additive in nature. As a consequence, this change is generally understood as *quantitative* and *continuous*.

At any given level of form (i.e., any level of a relational developmental system), there are variants that constitute intraindividual variational changes. If thinking is understood as undergoing transformational change, then at any given transformational level, variational changes are found in variants of thought (e.g., analytic styles and synthetic styles). If emotions are presented as undergoing transformational change, then at any transformational level, variational change is reflected, for example, in differences in the degree of emotionality (more or less anxious, empathic, altruistic, and so on). If identity is thought of as undergoing transformational change, then at any transformational level, there is variational change in the type of identity assumed (e.g., individualistic or communal). If the structure of memory undergoes transformational change, there is variational change in memory capacity, speed of processing, memory style, and memory content.

Transformational change has been identified with domain general normative structural issues such as changes that are *typical* of phyla, species, and individuals. In ontogenesis, for example, normative changes in cognitive, affective, and motivational systems have been the central issue of concern. The focus here is sequences of universal forms whose movement defines a path or trajectory. Intraindividual variational change has been identified with domain-specific content and skill issues. In this case, interest focuses on local changes that suggest a particularity, and a to-and-fro movement or a contingent directionality. Concepts of contingent rather than necessary organization, and contingent rather than necessary change, and concepts of reversibility, continuity, and cyclicity are associated with intraindividual variational change. An example that is central to a number of chapters in this volume is that of intelligence, where fluid intelligence ("for the most part, has been defined by reasoning," Blair, Chapter 8 of this volume) or the similar "control processes" (Bialystok & Craik, Chapter 7 of this volume) are associated with transformational features, whereas crystallized intelligence (knowledge and specific skills) (Blair) or "representations" (Bialystok & Craik), together with processing speed (Blair), are associated with variational features of change.

Transformational and variational changes have also been associated with different mechanisms of change. Transformational change has been associated with the embodied action-in-the-world characteristic of open complex self-organizing and self-regulating systems. Variational change has been associated with information-processing mechanisms related to the encoding, storage, and retrieval of information.

We are here faced with a logical difficulty. As noted earlier, developmental change entails five necessary defining features. However, as it turns out, each feature is associated with transformational change, and none are associated with variational change. Yet, it was also stated earlier that development entails both transformational and variational change. How can this be resolved? Mascolo and Fischer (Chapter 6 of this volume) suggest that the resolution is to identify transformational change as developmental change, and variational as historical change. The difficulty with this solution lies in its exclusivity. The study of change with respect to the individual's acquisition of specific concepts and skills (i.e., variational or historical change), as well as processing mechanisms entailed by those skills, has traditionally been housed within the broad study of development. It would seem prudent to explore whether there might be some principled way this variational component and the transformational component might be integrated into an inclusive framework. That is, it would seem prudent to find a way in which a *de facto* situation—the current field of life-span development includes scientists who study each type of change—can be justified in a coherent, principled fashion.

Transformation and Variation: A Relational Integration

From a metatheoretical perspective, there are two alternative resolutions to the transformational-variational dichotomy: a split resolution and a relational resolution. The split resolution denies the reality of or marginalizes one type of change, thus claiming the other constitutes the really real development. The relational resolution—to be expanded later in the Relational Metatheory section—maintains that the apparent dualism, like any dualism, can better be understood as two interconnected features of the same whole. From the relational perspective, transformation and variation are not alternatives competing for the mantle of "development"; they constitute a whole reflecting two coequal and indissociable complementary process. This solution claims a reality in which the processes assume differentiated functional roles, but each process in itself explains and is explained by the other. Put simply, open, active, holistic systems produce variations, and variations transform the system (Overton & Ennis, 2006a). As discussed later, any living system is open, complex, self-organizing, and self-regulating. Complex open systems by their very nature are inherently and spontaneously active; they produce acts consistent with the structure of the system (flies produce fly acts; pigeons, pigeon acts; and humans, human acts). *Acts are embodied actions-in-the-world, and they succeed or fail to various degrees in attaining their intended goals.* Partial success feeds back to the system, which uses the feedback as a resource in changing (transforming) the system. The transformed system, in turn, produces further variants of the act. Thus, all development entails cyclical movements between transformation and variation that result in increasing complexity of the system and increasingly refined variants (Overton, 2006; Gestsdóttir & Lerner, 2008). As Demetriou, Mouyi, and Spanoudis (Chapter 10 of this volume) state:

> The relations between the general and the specialized processes are complex and bidirectional. On the one hand, general processes set the limits for the construction, operation, and development of the domain-specific systems. On the other hand, specialized processes provide the frame and raw material for the functioning of general processes. (pp. 322)

The relational solution clarifies the *de facto* situation that much of life-span scientific study currently takes place at one or the other pole of the whole, and it encourages an integrated vision for future study. On the other hand, the relational solution discourages any notion of a systems approach and an information processing approach or a social learning approach as necessarily being competing alternatives. They become competing alternatives only when they become split and one or the other claims the totality.

In this life-span volume, the analyses and reviews by Carpendale and C. Lewis on social understanding (Chapter 17 of this volume), M. Lewis on consciousness (Chapter 18 of this volume), and Müller and Racine on concepts and representations (Chapter 11 of this volume) are examples of inquiry primarily embedded within the transformational pole, stressing the self-organizing system and its mechanisms. On the other hand, the analyses and reviews by Goldin-Meadow and Iverson on gesture (Chapter 21 of this volume), Vasilyeva and Lourenco on spatial development (Chapter 20 of this volume), and Ornstein and Light on memory development (Chapter 9 of this volume) exemplify a primary focus on the variational pole. As a microlevel example of the variational, consider Ornstein and Light's analysis. Research programs that focus on transformations of knowing and thought, moving from the concrete sensorimotor to the abstract reflective, often conceptualize these transforms as *levels*, including levels termed *the metacognitive* and *the metamemorial*. Ornstein and Light's work, in contrast, centers its analysis on information-processing mechanisms; as a consequence, metacognition and metamemory appear within this analysis not as transformational levels, but as one set of factors that among others impact on the encoding, storage, and retrieval of information.

Although less common, some research programs explicitly incorporate both poles of the developmental whole. Despite their seeming acceptance of a development-history dichotomy, Mascolo and Fischer (Chapter 6 of this volume) offer a well-articulated example of an integrated program in their discussion of the development of psychological structures as these are related to behavioral skills: "Psychological structures consist of dynamic integrations [transformational changes] of motive-relevant meaning, feeling, and motor action as they emerge within particular behavioral domains and contexts [variational changes]." (p. 150) Also, Demetriou, Mouyi, and Spanoudis' (Chapter 10 of this volume) presentation of a theory of mental processing considers the developing architecture of the mind as entailing both levels of mental structures (transformational change) and a level of processing capacity (variational changes). And similarly, Ricco (Chapter 12 of this volume) describes a dual processing theory of reasoning development proposed by Overton and colleagues (Overton &

Dick, 2007). In this theory, a distinction is drawn between a domain general transformational system termed the *competence system*, and a domain specific variational system termed the *procedural system*. The competence system is characterized by the acquisition of the universal logical features of reasoning, while the procedural system is characterized by highly contextualized on line processing mechanisms.

RELATIONAL METATHEORY

In the course of discussing the concept of development, the term *relational* has frequently appeared. It has appeared as a metatheory at the level of a worldview. It has been featured as a methodology as in "a relational postpositivist scientific world." It has been argued to be an integrative solution to the need for an inclusive and integrated understanding of development. "Relational" has served to qualify the phrases and terms *bidirectional interpenetration, multidirectional interpenetration,* and *differentiation.* It has also been used to point to a specific type of "developmental system." Similar usages are found in a number of the chapters in this volume. Given these multiple usages, and because later discussions—especially of the role of systems and the place of age/aging in life-span development—will involve relationism in a central fashion, this section elaborates on the meaning of this concept.

Relationism—a relational metatheory—represents a principled synthesis of what Stephen Pepper (1942) referred to as the contextualist and the organismic worldviews (Overton, 2007a; Overton & Ennis, 2006a, b). As a synthesis, relationism is composed of a coherent set of ontological and a coherent set of epistemological principles. The ontology of relationism entails a reality based on *process* rather than substance (Bickhard, 2008). This ontology has classically been defined as an ontology of *Becoming* (Allport, 1955; Overton, 1991). It includes process, activity, change, and necessary organization as defining categories. Becoming contrasts with categories of substance, stability, fixity, and contingent organization found in other worldview-level metatheories. M. Lewis (Chapter 18 of this volume) in his exploration of consciousness and Müller and Racine (Chapter 11 of this volume) in their analysis of representations and concepts discuss a number of implications that arise from taking an active versus a passive organism approach to the study of life-span development. The active organism concept is a direct consequence of the ontology of Becoming found in relationism, whereas the passive (or reactive) organism concept reflects the ontology of stasis and uniformity (Overton, 1976), found in the atomistic, reductionistic worldview called *mechanistic*.

The ontologies of active versus passive organism, as M. Lewis (Chapter 18 of this volume) and Müller and Racine (Chapter 11 of this volume) demonstrate, have critical implications for both theory and methods in the study of life-span development. *In fact, the notion of a self-organizing, self-regulating system is incomprehensible unless it is embedded in a Becoming ontology.* Nevertheless, despite this importance, this section is more directly concerned with the epistemological principles of relationism. The epistemology of relationism is, first and foremost, a *relatively inclusive* epistemology, involving both knower and known as equal and indissociable complementary processes in the construction, acquisition, and growth of knowledge. It is "relatively" inclusive, because "inclusion" itself—much like Hegel's master–slave dialectic—can be grasped only in relation to its complement "exclusion." Thus, just as "freedom" must be identified in the context of "constraint," "inclusion" must be identified in the context of "exclusion."

Relational epistemology specifically *excludes* Cartesian dualistic ways of knowing, because Cartesian epistemology trades on absolute exclusivity; it is a "nothing-but" epistemology that was founded on atomism. Here, in the last analysis, nothing counts but "atoms" in their additive combination, whether the atoms are genes, or neurons, or responses, or pieces of the sociocultural world. Cartesian dualism claims to cut nature at its joint, dividing any whole into pure forms that constitute absolutely decomposable pieces (i.e., it "splits" the whole and converts it into an aggregate of elements) resulting in a dichotomy. This "divide-and-conquer" strategy is not simply analysis, but analysis in which the whole is treated as epiphenomenal. For example, subject is split from object, mind from body. Having forced the dichotomy, Cartesian thought makes these epistemological claims: (1) The natural (material, physical, objective) constitutes the ultimate foundational real, the ultimate "atoms" on which all else is built; (2) one of the pieces of the whole is more real than the other; and (3) therefore, the less real must be explained (i.e., reduced) to the more real. As one example among many possible examples of fundamental split dichotomies (Table 1.1), consider the splitting of subject from object, mind from body. After the split, a decision is required as to which constitutes the foundational real that will do the explaining and which constitutes the apparent real that will be explained. If the ontological position is that the physical constitutes

Table 1.1   Fundamental Relational Categories

Subject	Object
Form	Matter
Stability	Change
Transformation	Variation
Universal	Particular
Transcendent	Immanent
Analysis	Synthesis
Unity	Diversity
Interpretation	Observation
Certainty	Doubt
Absolute	Relative
Expressive	Instrumental
Variation	Transformation
Intrapsychic	Interpersonal
Reason	Emotion
Biology	Culture
Person	Biology
Culture	Person
Nature	Nurture

the foundational real—as in all neopositivist and many behavioristic approaches—thinking, reasoning, perception, motivation, affect, and so forth must necessarily be explained by the atoms of biology (genes, neurons), and the sociocultural and physical environments. Because splitting is pervasive in Cartesian epistemology, these "atoms" are themselves treated as split pieces, and attempts to explain specifically how they might come to constitute the whole are necessarily additive. Any behavior or process thus becomes the additive "interaction" of genetic, neurological, and environmental pieces. "Interaction" is here placed in scare quotes to emphasize that this is not an interaction of relational interpenetration, coaction, or reciprocal bidirectionality or multidirectionality, but an interaction in which the pieces maintain their split-off identity.

The epistemology of relationism heals splits and resolves dualisms—false dichotomies—that in a postpositivist era are recognized as retardants to scientific progress. And, importantly, relationism does this healing in a coherent, principled manner. Efforts at moving beyond Cartesian dichotomies are not new, but since the 19th century's rejection of Hegel's metaphysical system, few systematic efforts at doing this healing in a principled fashion have been attempted. Calls for relational thinking are also not new. Holism was a central characteristic of William James's work, and Putnam (1995) describes how James's commitment led to the "obvious *if implicit* rejection of many familiar dualisms: fact, value, and theory are all seen by James as interpenetrating and interdependent" (p. 7, emphasis added). James (1975) addresses virtually all the traditional dichotomies of split-off traditions, and he, together with Dewey (1925), argue for a relational interpenetrating understanding of universal-particular, inner-outer, subject-object, theory-practice, monism-pluralism, and unity-diversity. However, neither James nor Dewey articulated an *explicit set of principles* designed to support this argument.

In recent times, the scientific significance of thinking relationally has been discussed from the vantage point of several disciplines including physics (Smolin, 1997: "Twentieth century physics represents a partial triumph of this relational view over the older Newtonian conception of nature" [p. 19]); anthropology (Ingold, 2000: "How can one hope to grasp the continuity of the life process through a mode of thought that can only countenance the organic world already shattered into a myriad of fragments?... What we need, instead, is a quite different way of thinking about organisms and their environments. I call this 'relational thinking'" [p. 295]); biology (Robert, 2004: "To understand the relationship between genotype and phenotype, we must transcend the dichotomy between them in two ways: we must grasp the phenotype of the gene and we must recognize that the relevant developmental space does not begin nor does it end with the genome-in-context. It begins, instead, with the genetically *co*-defined primary, initially unicellular, organism" [p. 66]); and science studies (Latour, 2004: "Their [the sciences] work consists precisely in inventing through the intermediary of instruments and the artifice of the laboratory, the *displacement of point of view*....They make it possible to shift viewpoint constantly by means of experiments, instruments, models, and theories....Such is their particular form of relativism—that is, *relationism*" [emphasis added] [p. 137]). However, again, despite the many calls for a relational approach to science, there has been little in the way of articulating a coherent set of metatheoretical principles that may then serve as a guide for how one actually might do relational thinking.

Relationism then is a metatheoretical space representing a synthesis of contextualism and organicism where foundations are groundings, not bedrocks of certainty, and analysis is about creating categories, not about cutting nature at its joints. In place of a rejected atomism, holism becomes the overarching first epistemological principle. Building from the base of holism, relational metatheory moves to specific principles that define the relations among

parts and the relations of parts to wholes. In other words, relational metatheory articulates principles of analysis and synthesis necessary for any scientific inquiry. These principles are: (1) the Identity of Opposites, (2) the Opposites of Identity, and (3) the Synthesis of Wholes.

Holism

Holism is the principle that the identities of objects and events derive from the relational context in which they are embedded. Wholes define parts and parts define wholes. The classic example is the relation of components of a sentence. Patterns of letters form words, and particular organizations of words form sentences. Clearly, the meaning of the sentence depends on its individual words (parts define whole). At the same time, the meaning of the words is often defined by the meaning of the sentence (wholes define parts). Consider the word meanings in the following sentences: (1) The *party leaders* were *split* on the *platform*; (2) The *disc jockey* discovered a *black rock star*; and (3) The *pitcher* was *driven home* on a *sacrifice fly*. The meaning of the sentence is obviously determined by the meaning of the words, but the meaning of each word is determined by context of the sentence it is in. Parts determine wholes; wholes determine their parts (Gilbert & Sarkar, 2000).

Holistically, the whole is not an aggregate of discrete elements but an organized system of parts, each part being defined by its relations to other parts and to the whole. Complexity in this context, as further discussed in the next section, is *organized complexity* (Luhmann, 1995; von Bertalanffy, 1968a, b), in that the whole is not decomposable into elements arranged in additive linear sequences of cause/effect relations (Overton & Reese, 1973). In the context of holism, principles of splitting, foundationalism, and atomism are rejected as meaningless approaches to analysis, and "fundamental" antimonies are similarly rejected as false dichotomies. In an effort to avoid "standard" (i.e., neopositivistic) misunderstandings here, it must be strongly emphasized that *nondecomposability does not mean that analysis itself is rejected*. It means that *analysis of parts must occur in the context of the parts' functioning in the whole*. The context-free specifications of any object, event, or process—whether it be a gene, cell, neuron, the architecture of mind or culture—is illegitimate within a holistic system.

Although holism is central to relationism, the acceptance of holism does not in itself offer a detailed program for resolving the many dualisms that have framed an understanding of life-span development and other fields of scientific inquiry. A complete relational program requires principles according to which the individual identity of each concept of a formerly dichotomous pair is maintained while simultaneously it is affirmed that each concept constitutes, and is constituted by, the other. A program is needed in which, for example, both nature and nurture maintain their individual identity while it is simultaneously understood that the fact that a behavior is a product of biology does not imply that it is not equally a product of culture, and the fact that a behavior is a product of culture does not imply that is not equally a product of biology. This understanding is accomplished by considering identity and differences as two *moments of analysis*. The first moment is based on the principle of the identity of opposites; the second moment is based on the principle of the opposites of identity.

The Identity of Opposites

The principle of the identity of opposites establishes the *identity among parts* of a whole by casting them not as exclusive contradictions as in the split epistemology but as differentiated polarities (i.e., coequals) of a unified (i.e., indissociable), inclusive matrix—as a relation. As differentiations, each pole is defined recursively; each pole defines and is defined by its opposite. In this identity moment of analysis, the law of contradiction is suspended and each category contains and, in fact, *is* its opposite. Further— and centrally—as a differentiation, this moment pertains to character, origin, and outcomes. The character of any contemporary behavior, for example, is 100% nature because it is 100% nurture; 100% biology because it is 100% culture. There is no origin to this behavior that was some other percentage—regardless of whether we climb back into the womb, back into the cell, back into the genome, or back into the DNA—nor can there be a later behavior that will be a different percentage. Similarly, any action is both expressive and communicative/instrumental, and any developmental change is both transformational and variational.

There are a number of ways to articulate this principle, but a particularly clear illustration is found in considering the famous ink sketch by M. C. Escher titled "Drawing Hands." As shown in Figure 1.2, a left and a right hand assume a relational posture according to which each is simultaneously drawing and being drawn by the other. In this matrix, each hand is identical—thus coequal and indissociable—with the other in the sense of each drawing and each being drawn. This is a moment of analysis in which the law of contradiction (i.e., Not the case that A = not A) is relaxed and identity (i.e., A = not A) reigns.

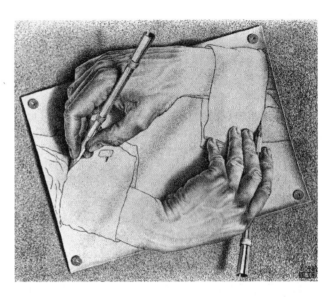

Figure 1.2   M.C. Escher's "Drawing Hands" © 2009 The M.C. Escher Company-Holland. All rights reserved. www.mcescher.com.

In this identity moment of analysis, pure forms collapse and categories flow into each other. Here each category contains and is its opposite. As a consequence, there is a broad inclusivity established among categories. If we think of "inclusion" and "exclusion" as different moments that occur when we observe a reversible figure (e.g., a Necker cube or the vase-women illusion), then in this identity moment we observe only inclusion. In the next (opposite) moment of analysis, the figures reverse, and there we will again see exclusivity as the hands appear as opposites and complementarities.

Within this identity moment of analysis, it is a useful exercise to write on each hand one of the bipolar terms of a traditionally split dualisms (e.g., biology and culture) and to explore the resulting effect. This exercise is more than merely an illustration of a familiar bidirectionality of cause and effects. The exercise makes tangible the central feature of the relational metatheory; seemingly dichotomous ideas that are often thought of as competing alternatives can, in fact, enter into inquiry as coequal and indissociable. It also concretizes the meaning of any truly nonadditive reciprocal determination (Overton & Reese, 1973) and any "circular causality" in a way that simple bidirectionality cannot.

If inquiry concerning, for example, person, culture, and behavior is undertaken according to the principle of identity of opposites, various constraints are imposed, as constraints are imposed by any metatheory. An important example of such a constraint is that behavior, traits, styles, and so forth cannot be thought of as being decomposable into the independent and additive pure forms of biology and culture. Thus, the notion occasionally put forth by some sociocultural or social constructivist approaches, that society and culture occupy a privileged position in developmental explanation, is simply a conceptual confusion in the context of relational metatheory.

If the principle of the identity of opposites introduces constraints, it also opens possibilities. One of these is the recognition that, to paraphrase Searle (1992), the fact that a behavior implicates activity of the biological system does not imply that it does not implicate activity of the cultural system, and the fact that the behavior implicates activity of the cultural system does not imply that it does not implicate activity of the biological system. In other words, the identity of opposites establishes the metatheoretical rationale for the theoretical position that biology and culture (like culture and person, biology and person, etc.) operate in a truly *interpenetrating* manner. Of course, the identity of opposites also justifies the claim that development is not the transformational change of system or the variational change of behavior, but the transformational/system-variational/behavioral change of the organism.

The justification for the claim that a law of logic (e.g., the law of contradiction) can reasonably both be applied and relaxed depending on the context of inquiry requires a recognition that the laws of logic themselves are not immutable and not immune to background ideas. In some metatheoretical background traditions, the laws of logic are understood as immutable realities given either by a world cut off from the human mind or by a prewired mind cut off from the world. However, in the background tradition currently under discussion, the traditional laws of logic are themselves ideas that have been constructed through the reciprocal action of human minds and world. The laws of logic are simply pictures that have been drawn or stories that have been told. They may be good pictures or good stories in the sense of bringing a certain quality of order into our lives, but nevertheless, they are still pictures or stories, and it is possible that other pictures will serve us even better in some circumstances. Wittgenstein (1953/1958), whose later works focused on the importance of background or what we are calling "metatheoretical ideas," made this point quite clearly when he discussed another law of logic—the law of the excluded middle—as being one possible "picture" of the world among many possible pictures.

The law of the excluded middle says here: It must either look like this, or like that. So it really…says nothing at all, but gives us a picture…And this picture *seems* to determine what we have to do and how—but it does not do so.…Here saying "There is no third possibility"…expresses our inability to turn our eyes away from this picture: a picture which looks as if it must already contain both the problem and its solution, while all the time we *feel* that it is not so. (paragraph 352)

The Opposites of Identity

Although the identity of opposites sets constraints and opens possibilities, it does not in itself set a positive agenda for empirical inquiry. The limitation of the identity moment of analysis is that, in establishing a flow of categories of one into the other, a stable base for inquiry that was provided by bedrock "atoms" of the split metatheory is eliminated. Here no relativity entered the picture; all was absolute. Reestablishing a *stable base*—not an absolute fixity, nor an absolute relativity, but a relative relativity (Latour, 1993)—within relational metatheory requires moving to a second moment of analysis. This is the oppositional moment, where the figure reverses and the moment becomes dominated by a relational exclusivity. Thus, in this opposite moment of analysis, it becomes clear that despite the earlier identity, Escher's sketch does illustrate both a *right* hand and a *left* hand. In this moment, the law of contradiction (i.e., Not the case that A = not A) is reasserted and categories again exclude each other. As a consequence of this exclusion, parts exhibit *unique* identities that differentiate each from the other. These unique differential qualities are stable within any holistic system and, thus, may form relatively stable platforms for empirical inquiry. The platforms created according to the principle of the opposites of identity become *standpoints, points-of-view, or lines-of-sight,* in recognition that they do not reflect absolute foundations (Latour, 1993). They may also be considered under the common rubric *levels of analysis,* when these are not understood as bedrock foundations. Again considering Escher's sketch, when left hand as left hand and right as right are each the focus of attention, it then becomes quite clear that, were they large enough, one could stand on either hand and examine the structures and functions of that hand, as well as its relation to the other hand (i.e., the *coactions* of parts). Thus, to return to the nature-nurture example, although explicitly recognizing that any behavior is 100% biology and 100% culture, alternative points-of-view permit the scientist to analyze the behavior from a *biological* or from a *cultural standpoint.* Biology and culture no longer constitute competing alternative explanations; rather, they are two points-of-view on an object of inquiry that has been created by and will be fully understood only through multiple viewpoints. More generally, the unity that constitutes human identity and human development becomes discovered only in the diversity of multiple interrelated lines-of-sight.

The Synthesis of Wholes

Engaging fundamental bipolar concepts as relatively stable standpoints opens the way, and takes an important first step, toward establishing a broad stable base for empirical inquiry within a relational metatheory. However, this solution is incomplete as it omits a key relational component, the relation of parts to the whole. The oppositional quality of the bipolar pairs reminds us that their contradictory nature still remains, and still requires a resolution. Furthermore, the resolution of this tension cannot be found in the split approach of reduction to a bedrock absolute reality. Rather, the relational approach to a resolution is to move away from the extremes to the center and above the conflict, and to there discover a novel system that will coordinate the two conflicting systems. This is the principle of the synthesis of wholes, and this synthesis itself will constitute another standpoint.

At this point, the Escher sketch fails as a graphic representation. Although "Drawing Hands" illustrates the identities and the opposites, and although it shows a middle space between the two, it does not describe a coordination of the two. In fact, the synthesis for this sketch is an unseen hand that has drawn the drawing hands and is being drawn by these hands. The synthesis of interest for the general metatheory would be a system that is a coordination of the most universal bipolarity one can imagine. Undoubtedly, there are several candidates for this level of generality, but the polarity

between matter or nature, on the one hand, and society, on the other, is sufficient for present purposes (Latour, 1993).

Matter and society represent systems that stand in an identity of opposites. To say that an object is a social or cultural object in no way denies that it is matter; to say that an object is matter in no way denies that it is social or cultural. And further, the object can be analyzed from either a social-cultural or a physical standpoint. The question for synthesis becomes the question of what system will coordinate these two systems. Arguably, the answer is that it is *life* or living systems that coordinate matter and society. Because our specific focus of inquiry is the psychological, we can reframe this matter–society polarity back into a nature–nurture polarity of *biology* and *culture*. In the context of psychology, then, as an illustration, write "biology" on one and "culture" on the other Escher hand, and consider what system coordinates these systems. It is life, the human organism, the *person* (Figure 1.3a). A person—as a self-organizing, self-regulating system of cognitive, emotional, and motivational processes, and the actions this system expresses—represents a novel level or stage of structure and functioning that emerges from, and constitutes a coordination of, biology and culture (see Magnusson & Stattin, 1998 for an analysis of a methodological focus on the person).

At the synthesis, then, a standpoint coordinates and resolves the tension between the other two components of the relation. This provides a particularly broad and stable base for launching empirical inquiry. A *person standpoint* opens the way for the empirical investigation of universal dimensions of psychological structure–function relations (e.g., processes of perception, thought, emotions, values), the particular variations associated with these wholes, their individual differences, and their development across

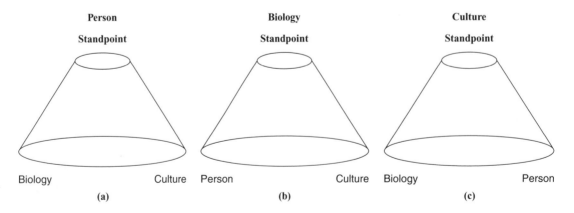

Figure 1.3 Three research program standpoints representing the relational synthesis of wholes: person, biology, and culture.

the life span. Because universal and particular are themselves relational concepts, no question can arise here about whether the focus on universal processes excludes the particular; it clearly does not as we already know from the earlier discussion of polarities. The fact that a process is viewed from a universal standpoint in no way suggests that it is not situated and contextualized.

It is important to recognize that one standpoint of synthesis is relative to other synthesis standpoints. Life and Society are coordinated by Matter; thus, within psychological inquiry, biology represents a standpoint as the synthesis of person and culture (see Figure 1.3b). The implication of this is that a relational biological approach to psychological processes investigates the biological conditions and settings of psychological structure–function relations and the behaviors they express. This exploration is quite different from split foundationalist approaches to biological inquiry that assume an atomistic and reductionistic stance toward the object of study. Neurobiologist Antonio Damasio's (1994, 1999) work on the brain–body basis of a psychological self and emotions is an excellent illustration of this biological relational standpoint. In the context of his biological standpoint, Damasio (1994) emphasizes:

> A task that faces neuroscientists today is to consider the neurobiology supporting adaptive supraregulations [e.g., the psychological subjective experience of self]…I am not attempting to reduce social phenomena to biological phenomena, but rather to discuss the powerful connection between them….Realizing that there are biological mechanisms behind the most sublime human behavior does not imply a simplistic reduction to the nuts and bolts of neurobiology. (pp. 124–125)

A similar illustration comes from the Nobel laureate neurobiologist Gerald Edelman's (1992; 2006) work on the brain–body base of consciousness:

> I hope to show that the kind of reductionism that doomed the thinkers of the Enlightenment is confuted by evidence that has emerged both from modern neuroscience and from modern physics….To reduce a theory of an individual's behavior to a theory of molecular interactions is simply silly, a point made clear when one considers how many different levels of physical, biological, and social interactions must be put into place before higher order consciousness emerges. (Edelman, 1992, p. 166)

A third synthesis standpoint recognizes that Life and Matter are coordinated by Society, and again granting that the psychological inquiry is about psychological processes,

culture or sociocultural represents a standpoint as the synthesis of person and biology (see Figure 1.3c). Thus, a relational cultural approach to psychological processes explores the cultural conditions and settings of psychological structure–function relations. From this cultural standpoint, the focus is on cultural differences in the context of psychological functions as complementary to the person standpoint's focus on psychological functions in the context of cultural differences.

This standpoint is illustrated by "cultural psychology," or "developmentally oriented cultural psychology." However, not all cultural psychologies emerge from relational metatheory. When, for example, a cultural psychology makes the social constructivist assertion that social discourse is "prior to and constitutive of the world" (Miller, 1996, p. 99), it becomes clear that this form of cultural psychology has been framed by split foundationalist background ideas. Similarly, when sociocultural claims are made about the "primacy of social forces," or claims arise suggesting that "mediational means" (i.e., instrumental-communicative acts) constitute the necessary focus of psychological interest (e.g., see Wertsch, 1991), the shadow of split foundationalist metatheoretical principles is clearly in evidence.

Valsiner (1998) gives one illustration a relational, developmentally oriented cultural standpoint in his examination of the "social nature of human psychology." Focusing on the "social nature" of the person, Valsiner stresses the importance of avoiding the temptation of trying to reduce person processes to social processes. To this end, he explicitly distinguishes between the dualisms of split foundationalist metatheory and "dualities" of the relational stance he advocates. Another recent relational cultural perspectives is found in the work of Mistry and Wu (2010), whose sociocultural perspective views culture and individual psychological functioning as mutually constitutive and "individual development is situated and constituted through participation in ongoing, dynamic communities of practice…notions [which] are consistent with the relational metatheory position that culture and person operate in a 'truly interpenetrating manner'" (p. 8). Carpendale and Lewis (Chapter 17 of this volume) further illustrate the relational posture of person and sociocultural points of view in the development of social knowledge (see also Mueller & Carpendale, 2004).

When the three primary points of synthesis—biology, person, and socioculture—are cast as a unity of interpenetrating/coacting parts, there emerges what Greenberg and Partridge describe (Chapter 5 of this volume) as a "biopsychosocial" approach to psychology and life-span development. In this tripartite relational systems approach to life-span human development, each part interpenetrates and "coconstructs" the other or "coevolves" with the other. Development begins from a relatively undifferentiated biosocial action matrix, and through coconstructive (epigenetic) interpenetrating coactions, the biological, the cultural, and the psychological or person part systems emerge, differentiate, and continue their interpenetrating coconstruction, moving through levels of complexity toward developmental ends (Figure 1.4). A critical feature of this synthesis is that once the psychological part system emerges, like any synthesis, it participates as an equal indissociable partner in the total interpenetrating, coconstructive, coevolution, coaction process. Only in a split-off reductionistic context is it possible to envision a "coconstructive biocultural" approach with its clear implication that the psychological system is explained by, driven by, and reducible to the "coevolution" of two pure forms termed the *biological system* and the *cultural system* (Baltes, Lindenberger, & Staudinger, 2006).

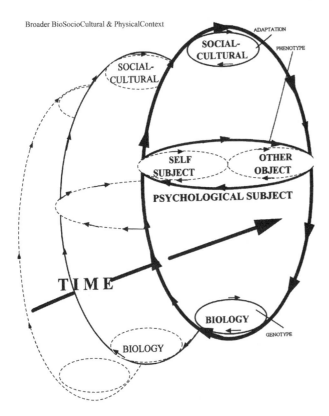

Figure 1.4 Relational emergence and development of the biopsychosocial organism. Within a biosociocultural world, through action mechanisms (*arrows*), a relatively undifferentiated biopsychosocial organism emerges. Through reciprocal interpenetrating coactions, biological, person, and cultural subsystems emerge, and move toward greater articulation, differentiation, and integration.

As a final note concerning syntheses and the view from the center, it needs to be recognized that a relational metatheory is not limited to three syntheses. For example, *discourse* or *semiotics* may also be taken as a synthesis of *person* and *culture* (Latour, 1993). In this case, biology and person are conflated, and the biological/person and culture represents the opposites of identity that are coordinated by discourse.

As a set of epistemological principles, relationism frames a general scientific research methodology or "research programme" (Lakatos, 1978; Overton, 1984) that moves beyond the reductionistic atomism of the positivist era; a methodology in which synthesis and analysis, together with reason and observation, operate in an interpenetrating reciprocal fashion; a methodology that promotes a truly multidisciplinary, multimethod approach to inquiry in which each individual approach is valued not as a potentially privileged vantage point, but as a necessary line of sight on the whole. This methodology facilitates the conceptual integration of theoretical concepts previously considered as competing alternatives as, for example, the integration of transformational and variational change into an inclusive concept of development. From the perspective of this methodology, "relational" becomes an appropriate qualifier for "bidirectional interpenetration" and "multidirectional interpenetration," in clarifying a form of "interaction" that begins and ends in an integrated, interpenetrating coaction of parts, not an aggregate of additive pieces. It serves as a similar qualifier for "differentiation" in emphasizing that differentiations necessarily occur in the context of the integrated parts of the whole.

Relationism also serves as a principled justification for an argument made by several authors in this volume: It is scientifically counterproductive to ignore the integrated whole when analyzing part process, and conversely counterproductive to ignore part processes when exploring the whole. Thus, Turiel (Chapter 16 of this volume) with respect to moral development; McClelland, Ponitz, Messersmith, and Tominey (Chapter 15 of this volume), in regard to self-regulation; Mascolo and Fischer (Chapter 6 of this volume), concerning thinking, feeling, and acting; M. Lewis (Chapter 18 of this volume) examining consciousness; and Santostefano (Chapter 22 of this volume) considering psychopathology, all argue that treating cognition and emotion as if they were split-off, decomposable processes leads to a scientific dead end. In a similar fashion, Carpendale and Lewis (Chapter 17 of this volume) argue against the splitting of social processes and cognitive process in the understanding of "social cognition." And Karelitz,

Jarvin, and Sternberg (Chapter 23 of this volume) discuss the importance to many theories of wisdom—including Sternberg's own theory—of explicitly recognizing and articulating the inherent integration of cognitive and affective development.

Central to the issues of this chapter is the fact that relationism has also served as the metatheoretical frame for the construction for some, but not all, of a family of theoretical approaches termed *relational developmental systems* and a subset of this family termed *dynamical systems*. The following section focuses on the nature of relational developmental systems (Lerner, 2006; Lerner & Overton, 2008; Overton, 2006), keeping in mind the aim of exploring conceptual distinctions in an effort to avoid or ameliorate conceptual confusions, and the aim of clarifying the nature of life-span development.

RELATIONAL DEVELOPMENTAL SYSTEMS

In the exploration of the nature of developmental change it was stated that the object that undergoes developmental change is the *relational developmental system*. In considering the nature of this it should first be noted that "system" represents a *subpersonal* level of explanation (Dennett, 1987; Dick & Overton, 2010; Russell, 1996), which stands in a complementary relation to the *person* level. The person level is constituted by genuine psychological concepts (e.g., thoughts, feelings, desires, wishes) that have intentional qualities, are open to interpretation, and are available to consciousness (Shanon, 1993); in other words, they have psychological meaning. The subpersonal level is constituted by various action systems that are described by concepts such as "scheme," "operation," "ego," "self," or "attachment behavioral system." In fact, consistent with several chapters in this volume, "mind" may be defined as an emergent system that subsumes cognition, emotion, and motivation as relational subsystems.

How then is the relational developmental system to be characterized? What are its identifying features? From the earlier discussion, we know that the system is inherently and spontaneously active, and inherently and spontaneously changing. Activity and change are not the products of other forces; as a consequence, when discussing psychological development, neither biological factors, nor cultural factors, nor any simple additive "interactions" of the two, can be considered to be mechanisms of development. And we know from the earlier discussion that a relational

developmental system is one that does not privilege any individual part (the biological, the psychological, the sociocultural). A more detailed specification will further elaborate on these and other system features mentioned earlier, especially as they relate to life-span development.

A system can be defined in various ways. For example, it can be defined as "any collection of phenomena, components, variables" (van Geert, 2003, p. 655). However, this and other "collection" or aggregate-like definitions are inconsistent with holism and, consequently, inconsistent with relationism. A more adequate relational definition of system is "a whole which functions as a whole by virtue of the interdependence of its parts" (Overton, 1975). Thus, a system is by its nature organized and organized holistically. Historically, a general method with the goals of classifying holistic systems in terms of how the parts are organized and establishing *typical patterns* of behavior for different types of holistic systems was called *general systems theory*. The acknowledged father of general systems theory, Ludwig von Bertalanffy, more than 40 years ago pointed to the fact that "general systems"—itself a metatheory—was being interpreted by some within the framework of a "mechanistic" worldview and by some within the framework of an "organismic" worldview (Overton, 1975; von Bertalanffy, 1968a, b). The impact of this often unrecognized conflation was to obscure the specific nature and methods of general systems theory and to obscure the explanatory structure of the approach. Von Bertalanffy—who evidently knew nothing of Steven Pepper's (1942) systematization of "mechanism" and "organicism" as contradictory worldviews—characterized the mechanistic formulation in terms of its principles of the primacy of ontological stasis, atomistic reductionism, and additive and linear organization. He characterized his own organismic perspective in terms of the principles of ontological activity and change, holism, and nonadditive, nonlinear organization. Over the years, the organismic version of the general systems approach was refined and modified (Luhmann, 1995) to include a synthesis with a "contextualist" worldview, and today's direct descendents are termed *developmental* or *dynamic* systems approaches.

Against this historical backdrop, Witherington (2007) has analyzed recent interpretations of "systems" and has demonstrated how again today "systems" is receiving alternative worldview interpretations that fall along similar divergent ontological and epistemological lines as those found in von Bertalanffy's time. Although the mechanistic formulation has moved somewhat to the background—being explicitly identified as taking a "mechanistic approach" is not currently fashionable—Witherington points out that among current research programs that carry the "systems" label, some operate within the framework of a split-off "strict contextualist" worldview and some within the framework of an integrated "organismic-contextualist" (relational) worldview (Overton, 2007a). Thelen and Smith's (1994, 2006; Smith, 2005) approach is representative of the strict contextualist interpretation, whereas Mascolo and Fischer (Chapter 6 of this volume); Ford and Lerner (1992), Lerner (2006), van Geert (2003; van Geert & Steenbeck, 2005), and Gottlieb, Wahlsten, and Lickliter (2006), among others, represent a relational approach. The main point of differentiation is that *strict contextualists privilege here-and-now explanations* of development, whereas *relationists accept both local contexts and higher order forms (patterns of organization) as explanatory* (van Geert & Steenbeck, 2005). As Witherington says, these differences "affect how each camp views the process of self-organization, the principle of circular [relational bidirectional] causality and the very nature of explanation in developmental science" (p. 127). Stated slightly differently, the relational approach takes the developmental system *qua* developmental system seriously and does not view it as merely the outcome of behavioral variation, whereas the strict contextualist sees variation as the determining cause of system structures.

An understanding of the nature of relational developmental systems requires that a distinction be made between closed and open systems, and between near and far from equilibrium states. All systems operate according to the Second Law of Thermodynamics; all systems exhibit a directionality, moving toward a maximum state of disorder (randomness, death), which is the definition of thermodynamic "equilibrium." The quantitative measure of randomness is termed *entropy*. Thus, systems exhibit an "arrow of time" (Overton, 1994) or irreversible directionality of change moving toward maximum entropy (i.e., a direction from order to disorder). However, before reaching this state, also termed a *target* or *fixed-point attractor* by systems theorists (e.g., van Geert & Steenbeck, 2005), a system evolves to a "steady" or "stable" state.

A system may exchange energy, matter, and information with its environment. A *closed system* is defined as one that *exchanges only energy with its surroundings*. Closed systems have relatively rigid boundaries; they are nonflexible, impermeable. A watch is a standard example of a closed system. Such systems operate in ways similar to a thermostat; other than changing the temperature, little environmental input is needed to maintain effective operation, and causality is one way. Closed systems

"near equilibrium" reach the steady state mentioned earlier, and this state is the area where energy dissipation reaches a minimum. This state is also called *homeostasis* (Waddington, 1971). At this steady state, the system is stable and completely analyzable (reducible) into individual components and functional relations between components (i.e., "interactions"). The relation between parts of such a system is one of simple complexity in the sense that these "interactions" between components may be treated as trivial or decomposable. Thus, such a system may be considered uniform, stable, and linear (summative)—the fundamental categories of the machine. This view of a system is exactly the background model used in psychology and other fields to justify both the denial of irreversible directional increases in structure or organization across various evolutionary series and treating biological organisms as steady state input-output computational devices. This was, for example, exactly the model that Fodor (1980) used in his dismissal of the Piagetian perspective that stronger (more complex, more organized) logical systems emerge from weaker logical systems. It is also the model that Levins and Lewontin (1985) criticized when they noted that "modern evolutionary thought denies history by assuming equilibrium" (p. 23). Closed systems near equilibrium do entail an Arrow of Time. However, this end point can be ignored for most practical purposes when considering large-scale thermodynamic (or psychological) issues.

Living systems, as well as other physical systems, according to any plausible interpretation, are not closed: "When we examine a biological cell or a city…not only are these systems open, but also they exist only because they are open" (Prigogine & Stengers, 1984, p. 127). And *open systems*—defined through their *active exchange of matter, energy, and information* with their surroundings—*build and maintain complex order* or organization by exporting entropy into their surroundings. An open system takes inputs from the environment, transforms them, and releases the transformations as outputs. At the same time in this coaction of system and environment, there are reciprocal effects on the system itself (change of organization) and on the environment (transformed environment). That is, the organization becomes part and parcel of the environment (biological and cultural with respect to living systems) in which it is situated just as the environment becomes part and parcel of the system. To borrow from Piaget, open systems are assimilation/accommodation wholes that resist the twin assumptions of trivial "interactions" and additivity of parts. They are dialectical, active, and holistic, and they define some of the basic features of relational developmental systems.

Open systems resist stable-state machine interpretations. They also attain a steady state, but it is a dynamic state where the rate of input of energy, matter, and information is equal to the rate of energy dissipation of energy and output of material and information. This state is called *homeorrhesis,* meaning that what is stabilized in an active system is not a particular value (homeostasis) but, instead, is "a particular course of change in time" (Waddington, 1971, p. 36). Finally, open systems *maintain* their state of homeorrhesis through "self-regulatory" mechanisms (i.e., processes of maintaining structure and order without explicit instructions or guidance from outside forces; (see McClelland, Ponitz, Messersmith, & Tominey, Chapter 15 of this volume, for an extended discussion of self-regulation).

Although steady state open systems define some of the basic features of relational developmental systems, they do not in themselves introduce a novel directionality to change. In fact, early work in the field of general systems was criticized because it was relatively silent on the issue of directionality; it addressed no developmental direction and was generally content with examining the holistic features of open systems (Overton, 1975). A directionality or arrow of time of *increasing complexity* emerges when *open systems* are driven or exist—as is the case of organisms and of the biosphere as a whole—*far from equilibrium.*

Work on the movement of open systems from lesser to greater levels of complexity was pioneered in the field of thermodynamics by the chemist Ilya Prigogine and his colleagues (Glansdorff & Prigogine, 1971; Nicolis & Prigogine, 1977, 1989; Prigogine & Stengers, 1984). When open systems are far from equilibrium, relatively stationary states become unstable through a fluctuation (i.e., variations or variability) that is "first localized in a small part of the system and then spreads and leads to a new macroscopic state" (Prigogine & Stengers, p. 178). With respect to human development, this means that small behavioral variation occurs in the context of the current organization of the system, and these variations ultimately lead, through positive and negative feedback mechanisms, to a new more complex level of organization. The centrality of variability here is the reason that all relational systems perspectives take intraindividual variability seriously rather than casting it off as error, as is done in classic nonsystems or closed system approaches. As the complex system becomes unstable, a "crisis point" or "bifurcation point" arises and abrupt changes, called *phase transitions,* occur,

resulting in the system *evolving into a novel more complex state* that may have properties different from those of the original. The new states, which, *in principle,* are not predictable from the original states, exhibit increased degrees of organization. That is, at a certain point, differentiation and reorganization (transformation) takes place, and this change yields a more complex organization, as well as emergent systemic properties. For example, at birth, the human organism is a complex sensorimotor system, and through variational actions-in-the-world, and their positive and negative feedback loops, this system becomes transformed into a more complex reflective symbolic system, where conscious reflection and symbols constitute emergent properties.

Prigogine termed these states *dissipative structures* and the complex holistic processes that lead to the formation of these states *self-organization.* Self-organization occurs only in complex systems, and it is "a *process of creating structure* [emphasis added] and order without explicit instructions or guidance from outside" (van Geert, 2003, p. 654). Thus, the system is self-organizing in the sense that it operates according to its own principles and not according to the dictates of external forces. It is important to emphasize that self-organization most empathetically does not mean that the system is split off or isolated from its environment. As stated earlier, it exchanges energy and matter with the environment, and it increases in complexity by acting in that environment; it is part and parcel of its environment as its environment is part and parcel of it. When viewed from the psychological standpoint, "environment" refers to both the person's biological and external environments. The psychological system self-organizes and self-regulates using its biological and cultural/physical contexts as resources, not as driving forces.

Although the randomness of the arrow of thermodynamic equilibrium will prevail in the long run—importantly here for a life-span approach, living organisms do eventually decline and die—on the way, the arrow of irreversible nonequilibrium thermodynamics "allows for the possibility of spontaneous self-organisation leading to structures ranging from planets and galaxies to cells and organisms" (Coveney & Highfield, 1990, p. 168).

A close relation exists between self-organization and the chaos called *dynamical chaos* or *deterministic chaos.* These terms are used to define irreversible, nonlinear systems that are incredibly sensitive to initial conditions. Deterministic chaos differentiates this kind of paradoxically predictable randomness, which is internally generated by a system, from the uncontrolled effects of "stochastic" fluctuations caused by the environment. When an irreversible process (e.g., chemical clock reaction) is pushed far from equilibrium, the evolution that occurs can be represented as a series of alternative choices or, as mentioned earlier, moves to new states. As a system fluctuates and reaches new bifurcation points or phase transitions, choices available to the system multiply in ways that lead to unpredictable dynamic behavior. Although this behavior appears random, it is, in fact, minutely organized. Furthermore, the evolution of a system can still be understood in terms of a target, goal, end point, or *attractor*. In this case, however, it is not a fixed-point attractor of thermodynamic equilibrium, but what is called a *strange attractor*. More broadly, attractors are end states or goals or recurrent patterns that ultimately stabilize and become increasingly predictable (Thelen & Smith, 1994). Van Geert (2003) points out that attractors can take a number of forms. As examples, there is the simple *point* attractor where the system develops toward a stable state (e.g., "the adult speaker's stable level of linguistic skill [p. 658]" or a given overall developmental level such as Piaget's "concrete operational" or "formal operational" states). There are also *cyclical* attractors where, as the name implies, states of the system run through cycles as, for example, in neo-Piagetian stage theory, "which assumes that every stage is characterized by a repetitive cycle of substages" [Case, 1990] (p. 658). In fact, all developmental acquisitions can be described as attractor patterns that emerge across time.

As structure is to function, the organization of the living system is to the activity called *adaptation*. Open systems far from equilibrium have been termed *adaptive*. Adaptation here refers how the system responds to changing environments—"perturbations" in systems language (see Santostefano, Chapter 22 of this volume)—so as to increase its probability of survival or to maintain its far from equilibrium state, not in the sense of "adjusting" to an environment. Adaptive systems are defined in contrast with "determined" systems. In determined systems (see Jones, 2003), the relation between inputs and outputs are exactly and reproducibly connected. For example, an automobile is a determined system. Whenever the driver presses the accelerator or turns the steering wheel, both driver and passenger expect the auto to speed up or turn. All components of the auto must be fully determined to achieve this collective response. And determined systems are linear—small inputs resulting in small outputs; large inputs in large outputs—thus, outputs are predictable. In adaptive systems, the parts follow simple rules, whereas the behavior of the whole system is not determined. A flock of birds is a simple

adaptive system. There is no bird-in-chief. Each bird follows simple rules such as "avoid obstacles," "align flight to match neighbors," and "fly an average distance from the neighbors." Each bird has a choice of response within the rules; thus, individual behavior is not highly determined. However, given these simple rules, highly complex and adaptive flock behavior emerges (Jones, 2003).

This short introduction to adaptive open systems far from equilibrium reveals that they exhibit a relational complementarity of structure and function—an integration of transformation and variation. They are epigenetic. The system grows through relational multidirectional interpenetrations/coactions of parts including "circular causality" (i.e., the relational bidirectional interpenetration of interlevel—top down and bottom up—causality); they are ordered, sequenced, directional, and irreversible. In summary, they are *relational developmental systems.*

It again needs to be pointed out that relational developmental systems are subpersonal level constructs, and they constitute both formal and dynamic pattern explanations of personal-level meanings and changes of meanings (cognitive, emotional, motivational meanings). As an example, consider a favorite among dynamic systems investigators: "Theory-of-Mind." Leaving aside the general controversial issues surrounding this concept (see Chandler & Birch, Chapter 19 of this volume; Carpendale & Lewis, Chapter 17 of this volume), theory-of-mind is an inference made about a changed pattern of meanings concerning social understandings of self in relation other people. (i.e., the change from "I know that others have the *same* thoughts, beliefs, wishes, desires as me," to "I know that others have thoughts, beliefs, wishes, desires that are *different* from mine"). Notice that this inference is made at the person level, which entails, as stated earlier, genuine psychological concepts (e.g., thoughts, feelings, desires, wishes). That is, there is a change in the way the child thinks. If we look at this same change in pattern at a subpersonal level (i.e., the level of "system"), this change pattern *qua* pattern is the relational developmental system. The ontogenesis of theory-of-mind considered as a system operates according to the principles of open systems far from equilibrium in moving from a lower to a higher level of complexity. Furthermore, when the system activity—termed a *generator* in system language—is translated to a behavioral level, it is called *embodied action* (van Geert & Steenbeck, 2005). In the final analysis, *the microscopic mechanism of all psychological development is the organism's embodied action-in-the-world* (Overton, 2007b; Overton, Mueller, & Newman, 2007). However, to be clear, embodied action is not simply physical movements and states; action entails intentionality, and intentionality is a feature of all acts from the most sensorimotor to the most reflective or metarepresentational. Thus, to claim that embodied action is the mechanism of development in no way contradicts, for example, Demetriou, Mouyi, and Spanoudis's argument (Chapter 10 of this volume) that metarepresentation is a significant mechanism of development. Similarly, when MacWhinney claims that "language depends on a set of domain-general mechanisms that ground language on the shape of the human body, brain, and society" (Chapter 14 of this volume, p. 472), he is arguing the relational developmental systems position that action of the embodied system ultimately constitutes the mechanism of development.

This introduction to relational developmental systems opens the way to now focus more directly on the life-span meaning of life-span development.

AGE, LIFE-SPAN DEVELOPMENT, AND AGING

One may wonder whether this lengthy abstract discussion might successfully have been avoided by simply defining development as changes in behavior that occur with age, or age-related changes in behavior. Some, especially those functioning within a strict contextualist behavioral orientation, do, in fact, follow this path, arguing that both "development" and the concept "aging" are merely descriptive, and reduce to "age-related change" in behavior. In the context of this choice, the behavioral change group goes on to conceptualize biological factors, cultural factors, and additive combinations of biological and cultural factors as "mechanisms" of behavioral change, or factors that "influence" or "shape" change. On the other hand we have already seen that from a relational developmental systems perspective, although cultural and biological factors are important resources of the system, the general mechanism of development is the developmental system itself, whereas the microscopic mechanism is embodied action-in-the-world; there is no shaping or influencing by split-off forces.

Furthermore, "age-related change" has other problems associated with its use. "Age-related change" is a phrase that is embedded in method; it is not a substantive term. Although it is a convenient empirical marker, when the phrase spreads from the results section to the introductory and discussion sections of a research study, one can be reasonably confident that the project lacks *conceptual*

substance. Age has no unique features that differentiate it from time; age is simply one index of time, and there is nothing unique or novel about units of age-time (i.e., years, months, weeks, minutes). Should it be said that development is about changes that occur in time, as some have (e.g., Elman, 2003), or that time is a "theoretical primitive"? Time can hardly be a theoretical anything, as time, in and of itself, does nothing and implies nothing. As Wohlwill (1970, 1973) pointed out, time certainly cannot be an independent variable; it is merely a dimension along which processes operate. All change, even changes discussed earlier in this chapter that are entirely transitory and entirely reversible, occurs "in" time. Thus, if "changes in time" were accepted as definitional, this statement would collapse into the proposition that development is about any and all change. Such a position could be adopted only within the most radical neopositivist and strict split-off contextualist framework. Outside this framework, "development" has always been a far richer and more substantive concept.

When it comes to considering "life-span development," or "adult development," or "aging," the situation becomes more complex and difficult. This complexity involves not only issues of metatheory and theory. As made clear by McArdle (Chapter 3 of this volume), there are specific and complex methodological and data analytic challenges that must be addressed when we extend our developmental perspective across the life span, especially through the use of the long-term, longitudinal research. In addition, however, the sociology of developmental science adds to the difficulty of considering life-span development, adult development, or aging. There are professional groups, journals, and funding agencies that are dedicated to the study of "development," including "life-span development" and "adult development." There are professional groups, journals, and funding agencies dedicated to the study of "aging." And there are some groups and journals that lay claim to the combination of "life-span development and aging" as their field of inquiry. In an effort to discover whether there might be a consensus with respect to the difference/similarity of life-span development and aging, while editing this volume and writing this chapter, I consulted with a number of senior research scientists whose work spans both areas. The outcome of this nonscientific survey was the fairly uniform agreement that the distinction is quite unclear. Reading the history of the American Psychological Association (APA), Division 20—currently named the "Division of Adult Development and Aging" (Birren & Stine-Morrow, 1996)—one finds that as originally established in 1947, the division was called the "Division on Maturity and Old Age." Its current title did not appear until 1970. In 1975, a Division 20 committee report asked whether a proposed curriculum should "focus on the subject of aging, of life-span development, or both?" (Birren & Stine-Morrow, 1996, p. 6). However, there was no discussion about what "either" or "both" might mean. And when the APA began its publication of the journal *Psychology and Aging,* the first editorial of this new journal declared that it was to be dedicated to "dealing with adult development and aging." (Lawton & Kausler, 1986, p. 3). Clearly from early on there has been some sort of implicitly felt difference between life-span development and aging, but this difference has remained vague at best.

One of my consultants, Fergus Craik, pointed out that, "whereas 'adult development' is a rather positive term, suggesting improvement, clearly 'aging' is negative, suggesting decline and decay" (personal communication, September, 2009). Craik suggests retaining both terms for exactly this reason, but placing both under the umbrella of "life-span development." Craik further argues that both "adult development" and "aging" constitute process rather than neutral descriptive terms; thus, under this proposal, there are two separate processes, a developmental process and an aging process. This approach seems to be a solution that has some positive features and one with which many are comfortable. However, a significant problem for others is that the proposal tends to marginalize "life-span development," as this term becomes simply a descriptive umbrella phrase that subsumes several seemingly disconnected process terms including "infant development," "child development," "adolescent development," "adult development," and "aging."

An alternative to the type of solution Craik proposes begins by representing "life-span development" itself as a process, not a simple descriptive umbrella term. Life-span development is about the relational developmental system, and the relational developmental system is an active self-organizing process that functions across the life span. However, and this is the key to this alternative proposal, although the life-span developmental process necessarily entails trajectory, there is nothing associated with the concept that requires that the trajectory remain an absolute constant from conception to the end of life. It is entirely consistent with the concept of a single life-span developmental process that life begins on one broad trajectory and at some point or during some epoch, moves on to another broad trajectory. Despite the change in direction, features associated with the process, including sequence, order, directionality,

epigenesis, and irreversibility, are all retained. When the broad trajectory changes during the life course, the emergence of structural novelty is ultimately replaced by its relational twin—the devolution or dedifferentiation of the system. Nevertheless, development continues as a process across the life span from conception to the end of life. A related feature of this "single process" proposal is that, within the life-span process, the epochs of infancy, childhood, adolescence, adulthood, and late adulthood constitute the purely descriptive parsing of time. In the adult and late adult epoch, adult development and aging become two sides of the same coin. As the trajectory changes, a primary interest in the stability of the system, and resources that the system uses to maintain itself, avoid devolution, and generate new adaptive goals, would tend to be described as the study of "adult development." On the other hand, a primary interest in issues related to decline would tend to be described as the study of "aging." And, of course, there would often be mixed interests, which would constitute "adult development and aging."

Consider this proposal in the context of relational developmental systems concepts. Structure and function constitute a relational bipolarity: Systems are active and activity implies system. We know that adaptive (function) open systems (structure) far from equilibrium both build and maintain complexity (structure); early development is about both building and maintaining system complexity. From some time in the middle years of life, the building of increased system complexity necessarily slows and moves into a dynamical "phase space" of maximum complexity. As an open system, however, the system continues to maintain complexity by exporting entropy into its surroundings. That is, in human terms, the adaptive intraindividual behavioral variations, which across several epochs serve to build complexity, increasingly come to serve the function of maintaining complexity. Adaptive strategies can result in maintaining the structure of the developmental system. However, the fixed point attractor of thermodynamic equilibrium necessarily comes into play and ultimately describes a trajectory of systems devolution completing its developmental course at the end of life. Exactly when this attractor comes into play is an empirical issue, undoubtedly related to developmental resources and undoubtedly exhibiting large individual differences. For some, devolution could begin quite early, whereas in another, it might not emerge until shortly before the end of life.

Thus, the relational developmental system has two *telos*: one an inclined plane leading to maximum complexity and efficiency, and the other a declined plane leading to a final equilibrium. The availability of both biological and cultural resources constitutes a central issue with respect to building and maintaining a psychological system's complexity, and they remain a central issue in the devolution of this competence. It bears repeating, however, that neither biological resources, nor cultural resources, nor any additive "interactions" of these resources drive development. The motor of the developmental system is the system itself, and the microscopic mechanism of this is the organism's embodied action-in-the-world regardless of trajectory.

This integrative single-process dual-directionality approach to life-span development is consistent with concepts presented in this volume and elsewhere. "Fluid intelligence" (Blair, see Chapter 8 of this volume), "control processes" (Bialystok & Craik, see Chapter 7 of this volume), and "fluid mechanics" (Baltes et al., 2006) represent behavioral manifestations of the transformational pole of the developmental system. In early development, these systems become increasingly complex, and in late adult development, devolution ultimately occurs (Bialystok & Craik). "Crystallized intelligence" (Blair), "representations" (Bialystok & Craik), and "crystallized pragmatics" (Baltes et al., 2006) are behavioral manifestations of the variational or information-processing pole of the developmental system. Processes at this pole become increasingly effective and efficient, and generally maintain this status across early and late developmental epochs, although some decline may occur in the ability to access and manipulate representations (Bialystok & Craik, see Chapter 7 of this volume). It is the skills and procedures developed in relation to this pole that serve as resources for system maintenance, as well as for novel adaptive goals in late adulthood. Taken together, according to Bialystok and Craik, the two-part processes of control and representation maintain an adaptive dynamic *balance* across course of life:

> Thus, although there may be a tendency for control to dominate in middle life and representations to dominate in both early and later life, all cognitive performance throughout the life span rests on the *interaction* between these two sets of factors, although the balance may tilt from one to the other for various reasons. (p. 218)

Mascolo and Fischer (Chapter 6 of this volume) focus, as do Müller and Racine (see Chapter 11 of this volume), on the inclined plane of increasing organizational complexity, and within this context, they emphasize the importance of environmental supports in the expression and maintenance of this competence. Although they argue that because there is a decline with advancing age, there is no development in this epoch, this part of their general approach loses its force in the single-process dual-trajectory life-span development proposal. That is, their argument is premised on the notion that there is no structural or system "progression" involved in adult and late adult development. Within the integrated process proposal, however, there is, in fact, progression toward those very features that Mascolo and Fischer claim as necessary criteria for developmental change, that is, an *"optimal outcome, end point* or *form"* (Mascolo & Fischer, Chapter 6 this volume). It is only from a human subjective experiential perspective that thermodynamic equilibrium or the complete devolution of the system is not "optimal"; but regardless, it is certainly an outcome, an end point, and a form.

The single-process dual-directionality approach is also consistent with positions that focus on the positive features of early development and late adult development (for a discussion of "thriving," see Bundick, Yeager, King, & Damon, Chapter 24 of this volume; for positive features of late adult development, see the discussion of "cognitive reserve" and "compensation" by Bialystok & Craik, Chapter 7 of this volume). In early development, for example, Lerner and colleagues' (2005) "5 Cs" (confidence, competence, character, compassion, connection) model of positive youth development focuses on skills that enhance early development as it moves toward greater complexity.

Although the developmental trajectory of all individuals during the late adult years is necessarily toward the ultimate end of life, *successful late adult development* (also called *successful aging* in the literature) refers to individuals whose cognitive and emotional spheres of life, as well as their social goals and satisfactions, operate well above the average. To account for both the enhancements of successful late adult development and the losses, the Balteses and their colleagues (Baltes & Baltes, 1990; Baltes & Freund, 2003; Baltes et al., 2006) posited a Selection, Optimization, and Compensation (SOC) model, where *selection* entails choosing and committing to goals, *optimization* refers to acquiring and refining the means needed to accomplish these goals, and *compensation* refers to maintaining a given level of functioning via the discovery of alternative means when existing means are lost. Returning to the co-relative enhancement of early development, Gestsdottir and Lerner (2007) refer to the SOC model as it applies to adolescence as "intentional self-regulation" (p. 508). And in Chapter 15, McClelland,

Ponitz, Messersmith, and Tominey elaborate on this feature of system self-regulation as it applies across life-span development:

> …self-regulation is involved when an adolescent selects a college and/or career path, and it underscores how adaptively an adult navigates life transitions such as becoming a parent, planning for a child going to college, being a productive citizen, retiring, and optimizing health and development in late adulthood. Self-regulation also enables us to manage the mental and physical challenges that become increasingly prevalent as we age and confront difficult events, such as a partner or spouse dying. Thus, throughout the life span, self-regulation is a critical factor in our ability to manage our emotions, cognitions, and behavior. (p. 510)

A corollary of this proposed integrative single-process dual-directionality of life-span development is the fact that "aging" is considered a descriptive, not a process term. Although processes take place during aging, there is no "aging process" or "process of aging." As discussed earlier, age itself reduces to time, and although processes operate within time, time itself cannot be a process. It appears that when the phrase *aging process* is used, it most frequently entails making an implicit appeal to a split-off biological process. Here again, however, it is important to guard against importing a context-free biology, however implicitly, as a mechanism that drives the system. To repeat, biological processes and their development constitute a resource of the life-span relational developmental system, not a mechanism of its early or late development. The fact that this resource declines during the later years of life is important, in the same way that the decline of cultural resources is important, but this loss does not constitute a mechanism. "Aging" is a descriptive term that refers to the late adult years; it is not an explanation of what occurs in those years. There is, for example, no such thing as "aging-induced decline." On the other hand, "late adult development" as a part of the life-span process of development is a process term, and as such it has broad explanatory powers.

As a final issue with respect both to the concept of life-span development and the single-process dual-trajectory proposal to the relation between life-span development and aging, it is worth noting that the concept "maturation" sometimes enters life-span discussions in a manner similar to that of "aging." "Maturity" itself is simply a surrogate term for end point, goal, or attractor. One may reach biological maturity, cognitive maturity, or emotional maturity, and we may speak of the mature perceptual system, language system, self system, adults, and so on. Occasionally, one also finds mentioned the "maturation" of these systems. In this case, the term either functions as an extremely vague and uninformative substitute for "development," and is best avoided, or functions as surrogate for "biologically determined," and is best avoided. Used in either of these latter two fashions, the term is as empty as its twin "growth."

"Maturation" does become more problematic when it is introduced in life-span human developmental discussions to reference a context-free biological process, as in, for example, a statement such as "cognitive mechanics reflect the influence of maturational processes, whereas cognitive pragmatics reveal the power of culture." Splitting-off biological processes as context-free causal agents and encapsulating these processes as a vaguely defined "maturational process" add nothing to advancing an understanding of cognitive, affective, social, or motivational life-span development.

CONCLUDING REMARKS

This chapter represents a conceptual exploration of what it means to say that we are life-span developmental scientists who study life-span development. As it turns out, the meaning of this proposition is relative to the metatheoretical grounding on which it rests. Split metatheoretical groundings characteristic of the era of neopositivist or radical empiricist methodology, as well as contemporary "strict" contextualism, cut the very nature of development into sets of dualistic competing alternatives. Within this grounding, variational change is pitted against transformational change, continuity of change is pitted against discontinuous change, nature is pitted against nurture, structure against function, constructivist perspectives against information-processing perspectives. On the other hand, relational metatheory, emerging as a viable scientific grounding in the postpositivist era, functions as the context for an integrative perspective on development and developmental issues. Relationism, as a synthesis of the worldviews contextualism and organicism, conceptualizes development as a holistic, active system in which variational and transformational change, continuity and novelty, biology and culture, structure and function, constructivism and information processing operate as integrative, interpenetrating/coactive components. Within split approaches, external forces—environmental or biological—drive psychological development. Within a relational developmental systems approach, the active system's actions-in-the-world constitutes the overriding mechanism of development, whereas biology and culture constitute system resources. Split perspectives faced with life-span issues of growth and decline resolve these issues—true to their metatheoretical directives—by assuming competing alternative processes: one "developmental," one "aging." Relational developmental systems resolve the same issues through an integrative single-process dual-trajectory understanding of a single overarching process called *development.* Thus, in the final analysis, what life-span developmental scientists, in fact, do is study *development* from conception to the end of life.

REFERENCES

Allport, G. (1955). *Becoming.* New Haven, CT: Yale University Press.

Baltes, P. B., & Baltes, M. M. (1990). Psychological perspectives on successful aging: The model of selective optimization with compensation. In P. B. Baltes & M. M. Baltes (Eds.), *Successful aging: Perspectives from the behavioral sciences* (pp. 1–34). New York: Cambridge University Press.

Baltes, P. B., & Freund, A. M. (2003). Human strengths as the orchestration of wisdom and selective optimization with compensation (SOC). In L. G. Aspinwall & U. M. Staudinger (Eds.), *A psychology of human strengths: Fundamental questions and future directions for a positive psychology* (pp. 23–35). Washington, DC: APA Books.

Baltes, P. B., Lindenberger, U., & Staudinger, U. M. (2006). Lifespan theory in developmental psychology. In W. Damon & R. M. Lerner (Series Eds.) & R. M. Lerner (Vol. Ed.), *Theoretical models of human development: Vol. 1, Handbook of child psychology* (6th ed., pp. 569–664). Hoboken, NJ: John Wiley & Sons.

Bickhard, M. H. (2008). Are you social? The ontological and developmental emergence of the person. In U. Mueller, J. I. M. Carpendale, N. Budwig, & B. Sokol (Eds.), *Social life and social knowledge: Toward a process account of development* (pp. 17–42). New York: Taylor & Francis Group.

Birren, B., & Stine-Morrow, L. (1996). The development of division 20. In S. K. Whitborne (Ed.), *Division 20: Past and future perspectives.* Washington, DC: American Psychological Association.

Bronfenbrenner U., & Morris P. A. (2006). The bioecological model of human development. In R. M. Lerner (Ed.) *Theoretical models of human development.* Volume 1 of *The Handbook of child psychology* (pp. 793–828). (6th ed.), Editor-in-Chief: William Damon; Richard M. Lerner. Hoboken, NJ: John Wiley & Sons.

Case, R. (1990). Neo-Piagetian theories of child development. In R. Sternberg & C. Berg (Eds.), *Intellectual development* (pp. 161–196). New York: Cambridge University Press.

Chandler, M. J., Lalonde, C. E., Sokol, B. W., & Hallett, D. (2003). Personal persistence, identity development, and suicide. *Monographs of the Society for Research in Child Development, 68,* (2 Serial No. 272. Whole Issue).

Coveney, P., & Highfield, R. (1990). *The arrow of time.* New York: Fawcett Columbia.

Damasio, A. (1994). *Descartes' error: Emotion, reason, and the human brain.* New York: Avon.

Damasio, A. (1999). *The feeling of what happens: Body and emotion in the making of consciousness.* New York: Harcourt Brace.

Damon, W., & Hart, D. (1988). *Self-understanding in childhood and adolescence.* New York: Cambridge University Press.

Demetriou, A., & Raftopoulos, A. (2004). The shape and direction of development: Teleologically but erratically lifted up or timely harmonious? *Journal of Cognition and Development, 5,* 89–95.

Dennett, D. (1987). *The intentional stance.* Cambridge, MA: The MIT Press.

Dewey, J. (1925). *Experience and nature.* La Salle, IL: Open Court Press.

Dick, A. S., & Overton, W. F. (2010). Executive function: Description and explanation. In B. Sokol, U. Müller, J. I. M. Carpendale, A. R. Young, & G. Iarocci (Eds.), *Self- and social-regulation: Exploring the relations between social interaction, social cognition, and the development of executive functions* (pp. 7–34). New York: Oxford University Press.

Edelman, G. M. (1992). *Bright air, brilliant fire: On the matter of the mind.* New York: Basic Books.

Edelman, G. M. (2006). *Second nature: Brain science and knowledge.* New Haven: Yale University Press.

Elman, J. (2003). Development: It's about time. *Developmental Science, 6,* 430–433.

Erikson, E. H. (1968). *Identity youth and crisis.* New York: Norton.

Fischer, K. W., & Bidell, T. R. (2006). Dynamic development of action, thought, and emotion. In W. Damon & R. M. Lerner (Eds.), *Theoretical models of human development: Vol. 1, Handbook of child psychology* (6th ed., pp. 313–399). Hoboken, NJ: John Wiley & Sons.

Fodor, J. (1980). Fixation of belief and concept acquisition. In M. Piatteli-Palmarini (Ed.), *Language and learning: The debate between Jean Piaget and Noam Chomsky* (pp. 143–149). Cambridge, MA: Harvard University Press.

Ford, D. H., & Lerner, R. M. (1992). *Developmental systems theory: An integrative approach.* Newbury Park, CA: Sage.

Gestsdóttir, S., & Lerner, R. M. (2007). Intentional self-regulation and positive youth development in early adolescence: Findings from the 4-H Study of Positive Youth Development. *Developmental Psychology, 43*(2), 508–521.

Gestsdóttir, G., & Lerner, R. M. (2008). Positive development in adolescence: The development and role of intentional self regulation. *Human Development, 51,* 202–224.

Gilbert, S. F., & Sarkar S. (2000). Embracing complexity: Organicism for the 21st century. *Developmental Dynamics, 219,* 1–9.

Glansdorff, P., & Prigogine, I. (1971). *Thermodynamic theory of structure.* New York: John Wiley & Sons.

Gottlieb, G. (1992). *Individual development and evolution: The genesis of novel behavior.* New York: Oxford University Press.

Gottlieb, G., Wahlsten, D., & Lickliter, R. (2006). The significance of biology for human development: A developmental psychobiological systems view. In W. Damon & R. M. Lerner (Series Ed.) & R. M. Lerner (Vol. Ed.), *Handbook of child psychology: Vol. 1, Theoretical models of human development* (6th ed., pp. 210–257). Hoboken, NJ: John Wiley & Sons.

Greenberg, G., & Tobach, E. (Eds.). (1984). *Behavioral evolution and integrative levels.* Hillsdale, NJ: Erlbaum.

Hanson, N. R. (1958). *Patterns of discovery.* London: Cambridge University Press.

Hogan, R. (2001). Wittgenstein was right. *Psychological Inquiry, 12,* 27.

Ingold, T. (2000) Evolving skills. In H. Rose & S. Rose (Eds.), *Alas, poor Darwin: Arguments against evolutionary psychology* (pp. 273–297). New York: Harmony Books.

James, W. (1975). *Pragmatism and the meaning of truth*. Cambridge, MA: Harvard University Press.

Jones, W. (2003). Complex adaptive systems. In G. Burgess & H. Burgess (Eds.), *Beyond intractability*. Boulder, CO: Conflict Research Consortium, University of Colorado. Retrieved from http://www.beyondintractability.org/essay/complex_adaptive_systems/ November 2009,

Kuhn, T. S. (1962). *The structure of scientific revolutions*. Chicago: University of Chicago Press.

Lakatos, I. (1978). *The methodology of scientific research programmes: Philosophical papers* (Vol. 1). New York: Cambridge University Press.

Latour, B. (1993). *We have never been modern*. Cambridge, MA: Harvard University Press.

Latour, B. (2004). *Politics of nature*. Cambridge, MA: Harvard University Press.

Laudan, L. (1977). *Progress and its problems: Towards a theory of scientific growth*. Berkeley, CA: University of California Press.

Lawton, M. P., & Kausler, D. H. (1986). Editorial. *Journal of Psychology and Aging*, 1, 3.

Lerner, R. M. (2006). Developmental science, developmental systems, and contemporary theories of human development. In W. Damon & R. M. Lerner (Series Eds.) & R. M. Lerner (Vol. Ed.), *Handbook of child psychology: Vol. 1, Theoretical models of human development* (6th ed., pp. 1–17). Hoboken, NJ: John Wiley & Sons.

Lerner, R. M., Lerner, J. V., Almerigi, J., Theokas, C., Phelps, E., Gestsdóttir, S., Naudeau, S., Jelicic, H., Alberts, A. E., Ma, L., Smith, L. M., Bobek, D. L., Richman-Raphael, D., Simpson, I., Christiansen, E. D., & von Eye, A. (2005). Positive youth development, participation in community youth development programs, and community contributions of fifth-grade adolescents: Findings from the first wave of the 4-H Study of Positive Youth Development. *Journal of Early Adolescence, 25*(1), 17–71.

Lerner, R. M., & Overton, W. F. (2008). Exemplifying the integrations of the relational developmental system: Synthesizing theory, research, and application to promote positive development and social justice. *Journal of Adolescent Research, 23*, 245–255.

Levins, R., & Lewontin, R. C. (1985). *The dialectical biologist*. Cambridge, MA: Harvard University Press.

Lewis, M. (1993). The emergence of human emotions. In M. Lewis & J. Haviland (Eds.), *Handbook of emotions* (pp. 223–235). New York: Guilford.

Lickliter, R., & Honeycutt, H. (in press). Rethinking epigenesis and evolution in light of developmental science. In M. Blumberg, J. Freeman, & S. Robinson (Eds.), *Oxford handbook of developmental behavioral neuroscience* (pp. 30-47). New York: Oxford University Press.

Luhmann, N. (1995). *Social systems*. Stanford, CA: Stanford University Press.

Magnusson, D., & Stattin, H. (1998). Person-context interaction theories. In W. Damon (Series Ed.) & R. M. Lerner (Ed.), *Theoretical models of human development: Vol. 1, Handbook of child psychology* (5th ed., pp. 685–760). New York: John Wiley & Sons.

Marcovitch, S., & Lewkowicz, D. J. (2004). U-Shaped functions: Artifact or hallmark of development? *Journal of Cognition and Development, 5*, 113–118.

Miller, J. G. (1996). Theoretical issues in cultural psychology. In J. W. Berry, Y. H. Poortinga, & J. Pandey (Eds.), *Handbook of cross-cultural psychology: Theory and method* (pp. 85–128). Boston: Allyn & Bacon.

Mistry, J., & Wu, J. (2010). Navigating cultural worlds and negotiating identities: A conceptual model. *Human Development, 53*, 1–21.

Mueller, U., & Carpendale, J. I. M. (2004). From joint activity to joint attention: A relational approach to social development in infancy. In J. I. M. Carpendale & U. Mueller (Eds.), Social interaction and the development of knowledge (pp. 215–238). Mahwah, NJ: Erlbaum.

Nicolis, G., & Prigogine, I. (1977). *Self-organization in nonequilibrium systems*. New York: John Wiley & Sons.

Nicolis, G., & Prigogine, I. (1989). *Exploring complexity*. New York: Freeman.

Overton, W. F. (1975). General systems, structure and development. In K. Riegel & G. Rosenwald (Eds.), *Structure and transformation: Developmental aspects* (pp. 61–81). New York: Wiley InterScience.

Overton, W. F. (1976). The active organism in structuralism. *Human Development, 19*, 71–86.

Overton, W. F. (1984). World views and their influence on psychological theory and research: Kuhn—Lakatos—Laudan. In H. W. Reese (Ed.), *Advances in child development and behavior* (Vol. 18, pp. 191–2226). New York: Academic.

Overton, W. F. (1991). Historical and contemporary perspectives on developmental theory and research strategies. In R. Downs, L. Liben, & D. Palermo (Eds.), *Visions of aesthetics, the environment, and development: The legacy of Joachim Wohlwill* (pp. 263–311). Hillsdale, NJ: Erlbaum.

Overton, W. F. (1994). The arrow of time and cycles of time: Concepts of change, cognition, and embodiment. *Psychological Inquiry, 5*, 215–237.

Overton, W. F. (2006). Developmental psychology: Philosophy, concepts, methodology. In W. Damon & R. M. Lerner (Series Ed.) & R. M. Lerner (Vol. Ed.), *Theoretical models of human development: Vol. 1, Handbook of child psychology* (6th ed., pp. 18–88). Hoboken, NJ: John Wiley & Sons.

Overton, W. F. (2007a). A coherent metatheory for dynamic systems: Relational organicism-contextualism. *Human Development, 50*, 154–159.

Overton, W. F. (2007b). Embodiment from a relational perspective. In W. F. Overton, U. Mueller, & J. L. Newman (Eds.), *Developmental perspective on embodiment and consciousness* (pp. 1–18). Hillsdale, NJ: Erbaum.

Overton, W. F., & Dick, A. S. (2007). A competence-procedural and developmental approach to logical reasoning. In Maxwell. J. Roberts (Ed.), *Integrating the mind* (pp. 332–366). Hove, UK: Psychology Press.

Overton, W. F., & Ennis, M. (2006a). Cognitive-developmental and behavior-analytic theories: Evolving into complementarity. *Human Development, 49*, 143–172.

Overton, W. F., & Ennis, M. (2006b). Relationism, ontology, and other concerns. *Human Development, 49*, 180–183.

Overton, W. F., Mueller, U., & Newman, J. L. (Eds.). (2007). *Developmental perspective on embodiment and consciousness*. Hillsdale, NJ: Erlbaum.

Overton, W. F., & Reese, H. W. (1973). Models of development: Methodological implications. In J. R. Nesselroade & H. W. Reese (Eds.), *Life-span developmental psychology: Methodological issues* (pp. 65–86). New York: Academic.

Overton, W. F., & Reese, H. W. (1981). Conceptual prerequisites for an understanding of stability-change and continuity-discontinuity. *International Journal of Behavioral Development, 4*, 99–123.

Pepper, S. (1942). *World hypotheses*. Los Angeles: University of California Press.

Piaget, J. (1967). *Six psychological studies*. New York: Random House.

Prigogine, I., & Stengers, I. (1984). *Order out of chaos: Man's new dialogue with nature*. New York: Bantam.

Putnam, H. (1995). *Pragmatism*. Cambridge, MA: Blackwell.

Robert, J. S. (2004). *Embryology, epigenesis, and evolution: Taking development seriously.* Cambridge: Cambridge University Press.

Russell, J. (1996). *Agency: Its role in mental development.* Hillsdale, NJ: Erlbaum.

Schneirla, T. C. (1957). The concept of development in comparative psychology. In D. B. Harris (Ed.), *The concept of development* (pp. 78–108). Minneapolis, MN: University of Minnesota Press.

Shanon, B. (1993). *The representational and the presentational: An essay on cognition and the study of mind.* New York: Harvester Wheatsheaf.

Smith, L. B. (2005). Cognition as a dynamic system: Principles from embodiment. *Developmental Review, 25,* 278–298.

Smolin, L. (1997). *The life of the cosmos.* New York: Oxford University Press.

Sroufe, L. A. (1979). Socialemotional development. In J. Osofsky (Ed.), *Handbook of infant development* (pp. 462–516). New York: John Wiley & Sons.

Sugarman, S. (1987). The priority of description in developmental psychology. *International Journal of Behavioral Development, 10,* 391–414.

Thelen, E., & Smith, L. B. (1994). *A dynamic systems approach to the development of cognition and action.* Cambridge, MA: MIT Press.

Thelen, E., & Smith, L. B. (2006). Dynamic systems theories. In W. Damon & R. M. Lerner (Series Ed.) & R. M. Lerner (Vol. Ed.), *Theoretical models of human development: Vol. 1, Handbook of child psychology* (6th ed., pp. 258–312). Hoboken, NJ: John Wiley & Sons.

Thelen, E., & Ulrich, B. D. (1991). Hidden skills. *Monographs of the Society for Research in Child Development, 56* (1, Serial No. 223, Whole Issue).

Toulmin, S. (1953). *The philosophy of science.* New York: Harper & Row.

Valsiner, J. (1998). *The guided mind: A sociogenetic approach to personality.* Cambridge, MA: Harvard University Press.

van Geert, P. (2003). Dynamic systems approaches and modeling of developmental processes. In J. Valsiner & K. J. Connolly (Eds.), *Handbook of developmental psychology* (pp. 640–672). London: Sage.

van Geert, P., & Steenbeck, H. (2005). Explaining after by before: Basic aspects of a dynamic systems approach to the study of development. *Developmental Review, 25,* 408–442.

von Bertalanffy, L. (1968a). *General system theory.* New York: George Braziller, Inc.

von Bertalanffy, L. (1968b). *Organismic psychology and systems theory.* Barre, MA: Barre Publishing Company.

Vygotsky, L. S. (1978). *Mind in society: The development of higher psychological processes.* Cambridge, MA: Harvard University Press.

Waddington, C. H. (1971). *Biology, purpose and ethics.* Worcester, MA: Clark University Press with Barre Publishers.

Werner, H. (1948). *Comparative psychology of mental development.* New York: International Universities Press. (Originally published 1940).

Werner, H., & Kaplan, B. (1963). *Symbol formation.* New York: John Wiley & Sons. Wertsch, J. V. (1991). *Voices of the mind: A sociocultural approach to mediated action.* Cambridge, MA: Harvard University Press.

Witherington, D. C. (2007). The dynamic systems approach as metatheory for developmental psychology. *Human Development, 50,* 127–153.

Wittgenstein, L. (1958/1953). *Philosophical investigations* (G. E. M. Anscombe, Trans.) (3rd ed.). Englewood Cliffs, NJ: Prentice Hall.

Wohlwill, J. F. (1970). The age variable in psychological research. *Psychological Review, 77,* 49–64.

Wohlwill, J. F. (1973). *The study of behavioral development.* New York: Academic.

CHAPTER 2

Emphasizing Intraindividual Variability in the Study of Development Over the Life Span
Concepts and Issues

JOHN R. NESSELROADE and PETER C. M. MOLENAAR

Age cannot wither her, nor custom stale her infinite variety.

— William Shakespeare, *Antony and Cleopatra*

Animate objects, including behavioral scientists, respond to variation. There is an old adage to the effect that "we don't know who discovered water, but we're pretty sure it was not a fish." This piscine allusion harbors the fundamental notion of variation, or actually, in this case, the lack of variation. The fish that only experiences water as its surrounding milieu must remain "unaware" of it because constancy does not register on its senses. If variation is not present, the organism may actively produce it. For instance, the microsaccades of the human eye create variation on the retina of an image that would otherwise be still. We remain vertical by continuously beginning

to fall, and subtly and exquisitely correcting for it. The successful sculptor may be the one who is able to introduce "movement" into an otherwise immobile representation of nature. The basic sentiment is captured in such utterances as "variety is the spice of life." In this chapter, we focus directly on variation, especially a particular kind—that manifested by an individual over time, conditions, and situations—intraindividual variation.

Study of intraindividual variation began early in the history of psychological research (Wundt, 1897). Classical discussions of intraindividual variation include those by Cattell (1966a), Fiske and Rice (1955), Flugel (1928),

This work was supported by R21 Grant AG034284-01 from the National Institute on Aging, National Institutes of Health (USA), and National Science Foundation Grant 0852417. We are grateful to Jerry Clore for helpful comments on an earlier version of this chapter, and to Bill Overton for his patient and insightful overseeing of its development through a series of revisions.

Horn (1972), Thouless (1936), and Woodrow (1932). More recent, quite illuminating portrayals of the nature of intraindividual variability include those by Hultsch and MacDonald (2003), Hultsch, Strauss, Hunter, and MacDonald (2008), Moskowitz and Hershberger (2002), and Overton (2006). Diverse applications of intraindividual variability concepts are found in personality (e.g., Cattell, 1973; Mischel, Shoda, & Mendoza-Denton, 2002), cognition (e.g., Hertzog, Dixon, & Hultsch, 1992; Hultsch et al., 2008; Salthouse, Nesselroade, & Berish, 2006; Sliwinski, Smyth, Hofer, & Stawski, 2006), health-related behaviors (e.g., Ghisletta, Nesselroade, Featherman, & Rowe, 2002), religious beliefs (Kim, Nesselroade, & McCullough, 2009), and many other areas.

Taken seriously, we believe that a sincere appreciation for variation within the individual over time or situation, or both, has powerful, far-reaching implications for how one studies most behavioral phenomena, including developmental ones (e.g., see Baltes, Reese, & Nesselroade, 1977; Lerner, Schwartz, & Phelps, 2009; Magnusson, 2000; Molenaar, 2004; Nesselroade, 1988, 1991; Overton, 2006; Wohlwill, 1973). We have some sense that these implications have not been understood and allowed to play out to the extent warranted by their significance, and as a result, the study of developmental phenomena has not prospered as much as it might otherwise have. In addition to the exceedingly broad influences of overarching models and worldviews (e.g., Overton & Reese, 1973; Reese & Overton, 1970), sincere concern of developmentalists with intraindividual variability also influences fundamentally how the study of development proceeds. Attention to intraindividual variability leads to favoring some kinds of research designs over others, how and what one measures, and the data analyses one performs. Even more fundamentally, intraindividual variability concerns help to delimit the very way one formulates his or her research questions and the manner in which one conceptualizes and deals with fundamental scientific matters such as prediction and generalizability. These latter concerns, in turn, rightfully have strong "trickle-down" effects on the design, measurement, and modeling efforts of students of development.

It is our belief that over the past several decades discrepancies between professed substantive concerns and preferred methods have had unintended negative consequences for the study of behavioral change processes, including developmental ones. This chapter aims to take a close look at the matter with the goal of being constructive regarding several methodological issues that bear directly on the study of human development over the life span.

Although it may not always seem so as we lay out our views, some of which will appear to be in conflict with contemporary developmental research efforts, we are intent on trying to strengthen the developmental research enterprise, especially as we view it from a life-span perspective, a perspective that, as delineated by Baltes (1987) and his colleagues (Baltes, Lindenberger, & Staudinger, 1997; see also Baltes et al., 1977), leans heavily on methodological variety and innovation.

CHARACTER OF VARIATION

Differences are the most elemental character of variation, and they are defined on three fundamental kinds of comparisons (e.g., Nesselroade, 2002): (1) comparisons among kinds of entities (e.g., qualitative differences); (2) comparisons among entities of the same kind (interindividual differences); and (3) comparisons of an entity with itself over different occasions (intraindividual differences). This characterization is not so dissimilar from the definition of variation used by Molenaar (2004): "The degree to which something differs, for example, from a former state or value, from others of the same type, or from a standard" (pp. 204–205). Variation that represents differing from a standard is at base akin to variation attributed to interindividual differences. If the standard remains constant, the ways individuals differ from the standard are the ways they differ from each other. In any case, taken together, these definitions cover well the phenomena of our concern in writing this chapter.

Clearly, the operation of "differencing," in one form or another, is at the heart of the variation concept. Even the psychologist's arguably most common index of variation, the standard deviation, can be calculated by first taking every possible difference of each pairing of scores in a distribution, although far more efficient ways are typically invoked, such as taking the square root of the average squared deviation about the mean.

Whichever working definition one uses, the study of behavior has a long history of emphasizing differences among individuals (variation), whether they are differences created by Mother Nature or by experimental manipulation (e.g., see Cattell, 1966a; Cronbach, 1957, 1975). Study of the former, differential psychology, involves primarily comparisons among entities of the same kind (interindividual differences) and, to some extent, comparisons among kinds of entities (e.g., qualitative differences). In contrast, the production and study of the latter, experimental psychology, rests on treatment manipulations and comparisons among entities of the same kind that have been treated differently or on comparisons of the same entities before and after treatments.

Somewhat ironically, given the rightful emphasis on variability, a basic, if generally stated goal of science is to ascertain what attributes of entities remain invariant under which transformations (Keyser, 1956)—a question of generality. Put simply, out of the variability that we study, we strive to find invariant relations. The goal is to establish invariance, but the road to that goal is paved with variability. Like the watery milieu of the aforementioned fish, without variability, not much surrounding us is of interest to either the layperson or the developmental scientist. As we were writing this chapter, a brief piece by Barlow and Nock (2009) was published in which they quote Sidman (1960) to the effect that generality and variability are antithetical concepts. At one level, we agree. However, Sidman was referring to unaccounted for variability—the kind that weakens relations. Here, we focus on the very process of accounting for variability through the articulation of general relations.

Students of behavior and development should understand that the underlying theme of this chapter is that the most meaningful and informative differences to examine are those at the level of the individual, as the individual behaves over time. This perspective leads to the conclusion that one's primary focus should be on intraindividual variation. More specifically, we argue that a primary scientific research focus should be on identifying similarities in patterns of intraindividual variation defined over multiple variables simultaneously. Furthermore, we suggest that the sought-after similarities may not be found to reside at the manifest variable level, but rather at the more abstract, latent variable level (see later for further discussion). Given these considerations, we train our major emphasis in the remainder of this chapter on the third kind of difference mentioned earlier—comparisons within the same entity over different occasions, conditions, or situations—as the basis on which to build more general lawful relations concerning development over the life span.

INTRAINDIVIDUAL VARIATION AND THE STUDY OF CHANGE PROCESSES

A major objective of developmental research is to study processes of change. Development includes many processes occurring simultaneously. Whether that time frame is limited to some early portion of life or encompasses the entire human life span has been a key distinction between more traditional views of development (e.g., infancy, child development, adolescence) and the life-span development perspective (e.g., Goulet & Baltes, 1970), which, in large measure, is oriented toward long-term processes that span decades (e.g., Baltes, 1987; Baltes et al., 1997).

The history of behavioral science is rich with discussion and debate concerning the measurement of change (e.g., see Cronbach & Furby, 1970; Harris, 1963), and the measurement of change would seem to be a *sine qua non* for the rigorous study of development. Despite the best efforts of large numbers of sophisticated methodologists, many of the basic questions about change measurement remain unresolved (see also McArdle, Chapter 3 of this volume). A general reaction of methodologists to this dilemma, if such it be, over the past three decades or so has been to move beyond two occasions of measurement and change scores to many occasions of measurement (e.g., see Rogosa, 1988; Wohlwill, 1973) and some version of growth curve modeling (see McArdle, Grimm, Hamagami, & Bowles, 2009; and McArdle & Nesselroade, 2003, for reviews). In general, we believe this change of emphasis from two occasion differences to multi-occasion change functions has been constructive and can be seen as the opening of a renewed effort to focus on process. Indeed, we subscribe enthusiastically to the value of going beyond basic notions of change to focus on more highly structured temporal organizations, which is what we believe researchers are trying to convey with the use of the term *process* and the application of a variety of approaches, including "person-centered" ones and various systems theoretic ideas and models such as the damped linear oscillator (Boker & Nesselroade, 2002) that has been used to model bereavement and adjustment to widowhood (e.g., Bisconti & Bergeman, 2007). A difference score based on two occasions of measurement cannot begin to convey the same richness of content as does a more or less invariant sequence of events that constitutes a process. For example, studying the inexorable losses of physical and cognitive resources, and the continuing adaptations one makes to them described in the Selection, Optimization, Compensation (SOC) model (Baltes & Baltes, 1990; see also Carstensen, 1993) contrasts sharply with merely taking the difference in one's cognitive performance scores over a similar period. However, as we proceed, we advocate for even more intensive measurement schemes than the typical growth curve and some other longitudinal modeling efforts to emphasize time-series designs. Such designs enable researchers to obtain the kinds of data that allow them to capitalize on the power of methods and procedures that we believe offer increased promise for better understanding of development. If the reader's "inner ear" is beginning to detect rumblings that can be construed as leading to an emphasis on the general themes of relational developmental systems theory (e.g., Ford, 1987; Ford & Lerner, 1992; Lerner & Overton, 2008, Overton, 2006), we do not discourage that line of speculation.

The study of processes is rightly a basic activity of the developmentalist, but as has been suggested elsewhere (Browne & Nesselroade, 2005; Nesselroade & Molenaar, 2003), from a methodological perspective, developmentalists can hardly be satisfied with the way processes are being conceptualized and modeled. Capturing the nature of process in a quantitatively rigorous way is not easy, and yet doing so is necessary for building a scientifically valuable knowledge base concerning developmental phenomena—their description and their explanation. Subsequently, we focus on this topic in some detail.

Here, however, we first want to examine more closely the role of intraindividual variability in this most important arena to the developmentalist—the study of process. To get started, we again use a working definition of the concept of process (Nesselroade & Molenaar, 2003) provided by the Oxford English Dictionary (1989): "A continuous and regular action or succession of actions, taking place or carried on in a definite manner, and leading to the accomplishment of some result." What this definition lacks in quantitative rigor is compensated for with its stark implication for the need to measure changes over time—a clear signal to study intraindividual variation. We attempt to flesh out the definition more extensively and precisely in the following text.

In the context of developmental research and the analysis of variability, a dichotomy that has surfaced in the late 20th century under a variety of labels pits *persons* against *variables,* For example, the terms *person-centered* versus *variable-centered* are preferred by some life-span developmentalists (Bergman, Magnusson, & El-Kouri, 2003; Magnusson, 1997, 2003) who have contributed extensively to both the methodology and the substance of developmental research. Although good reasons exist for wanting to clarify differences in orientation and procedures via the use of dichotomies, it is also the case that students of human behavior do not study persons without using variables, and they do not study variables without using persons. One need only hark back to what Cattell called the "data box" or basic data relations matrix

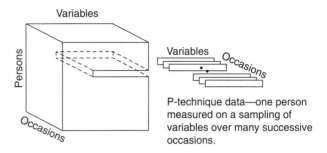

Figure 2.1   A version of Cattell's data box emphasizing the nature of data involved in P-technique factor analysis. One individual is measured on a sampling of variables over a sampling of successive occasions, resulting in a multivariate time series.

(Cattell, 1966a) to be reminded that empirical data inevitably involve at least one person, at least one variable, and at least one occasion of measurement. Figure 2.1 depicts a version of the data box emphasizing that any datum is simultaneously defined as an intersection of person, variable, and occasion coordinates. Usually, several elements of at least one of this triad are involved in defining a set of data.

The data box in Figure 2.1 is more than an anchoring heuristic for contemplating the nature of data acquired in empirical research, especially with regard to the study of process and change. The various covariation techniques can be derived from it (Cattell, 1952), out of which one can begin to fashion a systematic approach to the study of processes. The version of the data box shown in Figure 2.1 emphasizes what we believe to be a fundamentally important locus of intraindividual variability—multiple variables measured over multiple occasions of measurement on one individual—and a covariation procedure called *P-technique,* which will play a highly visible role in our discussion because of the features of the empirical data on which it rests. The (factor) analysis of P-technique data is described in more detail at appropriate places in the text. It suffices here to emphasize that P-technique analysis involves exploiting data arising from the intensive measurement of the single case, both over many successive occasions of measurement and with the use of many measurement variables. This data configuration sets the stage for modeling intraindividual variability at both the manifest and latent variable levels, with the individual as the primary unit on which the analysis is focused. As explained in the next section, coupled with the appropriate measurement methods, design conditions, and analysis techniques, some of which are rather novel and innovative, we believe such data are the key ingredients for a powerful approach to the study of developmental processes.

THREE KEY EMPHASES IN STUDYING DEVELOPMENTAL PROCESSES THROUGH INTRAINDIVIDUAL VARIABILITY

Efforts to further the study of processes via capitalizing on the riches of intraindividual variation by means of relatively recent methodological developments have led us both jointly (Nesselroade & Molenaar, 2003) and separately (e.g., Browne & Nesselroade, 2005; Molenaar, 2004; Nesselroade, 2005) to examine more critically the way behavioral research in general is conducted, but always with due concern for the particularly demanding challenges of studying developmental change. As our thinking has evolved on these matters, we have come to believe that the study of behavior should rely on a strong focus on intraindividual variability, and that three key emphases can be identified for capitalizing on intraindividual variability that are critical to further strengthening the study of development as a life-span phenomenon. We see these emphases, each of which has a long history in our science, to be instrumental in defining an approach that amounts to something distinctly different from the experimental and differential traditions that Cronbach (1957, 1975) discussed. Moreover, for the study of developmental phenomena, these emphases are especially critical because they provide a direct approach to the modeling of process. The three emphases are as follows:

1. *Recognize the individual as the appropriate unit of analysis in behavioral research, including the study of development.* Obviously, a focus on the individual requires adopting some kind of repeated measurements regimen to obtain variance to study, which necessarily involves some version of a time-series design (e.g., univariate or multivariate time series, panel studies). But time-series designs do seem, after all, to produce the kind of data appropriate for students of development and other kinds of changes—a lot of information regarding the individual over substantial time spans. Clearly, these notions are, in many respects, compatible with the general approach of relational developmental systems theory.

2. *Define patterns of intraindividual variation on multiple variables, thus allowing one to rely on the methods and techniques of multivariate analysis, including powerful multivariate measurement models that emphasize and target for closer scrutiny unmeasured, latent variables* (e.g., see Cattell, 1966b). Baltes and Nesselroade (1973) and Nesselroade and Ford (1987) laid out a rationale for the use of multivariate measurement in developmental research (see later). Such a multivariate perspective is compatible with a more holistic view of the organism promoted by other developmental scientists (e.g., see Baltes et al., 1997; Bergman et al., 2003; Magnusson, 2000; Overton, 2006) and offers considerable flexibility in building promising, technically sound measurement schemes. We believe that the capacity to model relations at the latent variable level is a virtue of multivariate measurement, the value of which is difficult to overestimate because it affords the use of some of the most powerful measurement innovations that behavioral/ social scientists have developed to date.

3. *Identify similarities and differences among persons in patterns of intraindividual variation.* Somewhat in contrast with the prevalent emphasis on interindividual differences one sees in most correlational research, it is our contention that with an emphasis on establishing lawful relations, one is actually more intent on identifying and studying the similarities than the differences among persons. Therefore, individuals are neither conceived of as interchangeable elements nor as randomly equivalent entities, but rather as distinct entities among whom one seeks to replicate lawful relations. Considerably more will be said about this later because the locus of such similarities may be found only at more abstract latent levels rather than in the interrelations of the manifest variables.

In addition to serving as an important corollary of emphasizing the individual as the unit of analysis, emphasizing interindividual similarities rather than interindividual differences dictates a quite different approach to data aggregation than most behavioral scientists practice (e.g., see Molenaar, 2004; Nesselroade & Molenaar, 1999; Ram, Carstensen, & Nesselroade, 2009; Zevon & Tellegen, 1982). Rather than blindly aggregating information across multiple individuals as the initial step in data analysis, as is done in computing the usual "descriptive statistics" (e.g., means, variances, and covariances) of traditional individual differences research, one takes an informed approach to aggregation that features using as much knowledge about the individual as possible.

Our emphasis on identifying similarities in multivariate patterning of variables also leads us to argue for some alternate conceptions of measurement (Nesselroade, Gerstorf, Hardy, & Ram, 2007; Nesselroade, Ram, Gerstorf, & Hardy, 2009), as is discussed more fully later in this chapter.

These three key features—individuals as the units of analysis, modeling with latent variables, and emphasizing similarities rather than differences across persons—help define an approach to scientific psychology that we believe has important implications for the conduct of behavioral research in general and developmental science in particular. Moreover, each of the three features is rooted deeply in the history of our discipline (Nesselroade, in press), and in concert, they define an approach that appears to be distinct from the two disciplines of scientific psychology that Cronbach (1957, 1975) discussed. In those highly influential articles, Cronbach (1957, 1975) identified two disciplines of scientific psychology: experimental psychology and differential (correlational) psychology. The latter is often referred to as the study of individual differences. There is no doubt that, in many respects, this distinction has served psychology well. We believe signs exist that a third discipline incorporating features from both the experimental and differential disciplines but with different emphases and methods can be identified. It was characterized by Molenaar (2004) as *idiographic science*. As noted earlier, idiographic science emphasizes the individual as the primary unit of analysis, but individuals are not viewed as randomly equivalent replicates of one another; nor is the emphasis on synthesizing the behaving individual from the differences among the ways individuals behave. Rather, the individual is the focus of analysis, and identifying similarities of behavior patterns across individuals is a key goal of applying empirical inquiry to the study of lawful relations. This third discipline of scientific psychology is driven by substantive interests and methodological developments that extend primarily the analytical tools of differential psychology, including latent variable modeling.

We recognize that much empirical research in the operant conditioning/learning paradigm was conducted on very small samples and involved careful attention to intraindividual variability in performance. In some ways, the recognition of the importance of the topography of a response versus its specific features agrees with the notion of idiosyncratic aspects of observable behavior that we discuss in detail later in considering measurement issues. Where we diverge remarkably from an operant perspective is on the use of multivariate measurement

schemes to model interesting phenomena at the latent variable level.

THE INDIVIDUAL AS THE UNIT OF ANALYSIS

Emphasizing the individual as the unit of analysis is by no means new to behavioral research, and the arguments supporting it have appeared in quite diverse contexts. Indeed, over the years, many writers have promoted the individual as the proper unit of analysis for studying behavior. Allport (1937) argued elegantly for it. Carlson (1971) asked: Where is the person in personality research? Gottlieb (2003) called for more emphasis on the individual in behavior genetics studies. Lamiell (1981, 1988) proposed an idiothetic approach to blend the strengths of individual-level– and group-based analyses. In developmental research, Magnusson (2000, 2003) pleaded for more emphasis on the individual. Molenaar (2004) argued rigorously for such an emphasis generally in behavioral science. Zevon and Tellegen (1982) illustrated how one could use the intensive study of the individual in the service of reaching conclusions of greater generality by focusing first on the structuring of the individual's behavior (through intraindividual variability) and then looking for common patterns across these individual structures at a more abstract level (e.g., see Friedman & Santucci, 2003). Clearly, a critical feature of empirical research in any discipline concerns not only how the basic unit of analysis is defined but how it is used.

As indicated later in this chapter, emphasizing the individual as the unit of analysis is not the same as arguing for single-case studies, although they tend to be somewhat related in the perspective of many researchers. Two of the key corollary matters in this regard are replication and generalizability, which will receive explicit attention toward the end of this chapter.

Molenaar (2004) described how a sample of scientists nominated the revolutionary idea of Brownian motion as the single most important scientific breakthrough of the 20th century. Molenaar went on to point out that a central feature of Brownian motion—that it applies to the random, time-dependent behavior of a single particle—has been substantially ignored by behavioral scientists even though the latter rely heavily, for example, on various statistics resting on probability models. Parenthetically, it seems that probability models are sometimes convenient and sometimes not. In any case, behavioral scientists tend *not* to focus on the time-dependent behavior of a single individual—our counterpart to a single particle. Obviously, there are exceptions (e.g., operant learning paradigms, psychotherapeutic process analysis), but by and large, our research designs do not capitalize on the individual *qua* individual, but rather on the individual as either one of many interchangeable parts or one of many randomly equivalent parts.

In spite of the fact that psychologists generally tend not to embrace an N = 1 time-series perspective and its emphasis on variation within individuals, it is our belief that the appropriate unit of analysis for the study of behavior is the individual (and his or her intraindividual variability), and that the principal domain for building generalizations regarding behavior is *across* individuals. Following Molenaar (2004) and in line with the Brownian motion concept, we conceive of each person as a system of interacting dynamic processes, the unfolding of which produces an individual life trajectory in a high-dimensional psychological space (Figure 2.2).

Focusing in this way on N = 1 research designs empha–sizes the time-dependent variation within a single individual and invites the dedicated, intensive study of intraindividual variation, before a second, equally important step—aggregating information across individuals. This is discussed in further detail later because there are other important aspects of generalization to which we should attend, including variables and occasions of measurement, as implied by Figure 2.1.

As noted earlier, identifying the individual as the primary unit of analysis carries with it the necessary corollary of performing a sufficiency of repeated measurements if one is to have variation to analyze. This, of course, tends to "fly in the face" of the traditional individual differences

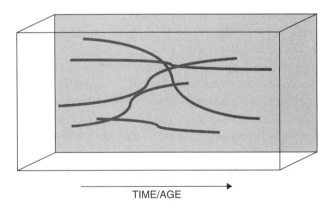

Figure 2.2 Schematic of a set of life trajectories in a high-dimensional space.

orientation that has carried many of us through the bulk of our careers—obtaining the variation needed for further analysis over people instead of over occasions of measurement. As alluded to earlier, within the study of behavior, however, intensive examination of the individual traces back to various sources, including the old distinction between idiographic and nomothetic approaches to the study of behavior; this distinction has helped shape behavioral research over the past century in important ways. Idiographic concerns emphasize the uniqueness of the individual, whereas nomothetic concerns emphasize generality in behavioral lawfulness (e.g., Allport, 1937; Barlow & Nock, 2009; Friedman & Santucci, 2003; Lamiell, 1981, 1988; Molenaar, 2004; Rosenzweig, 1958, 1986; van Kampen, 2000; Zevon & Tellegen, 1982).

Of the many writers who have called for greater emphasis on the individual as the unit of analysis for studying behavior, Cattell (1963b; see also Cattell, Cattell, & Rhymer, 1947) not only described and promoted P-technique factor analysis (applying the factor model to multivariate time series) as a way of identifying individual traits, but in the process exemplified the use of multivariate measurement models to represent underlying constructs at the individual level; we attend closely to this application in the next section.

Molenaar (2004) greatly strengthened the case for elevating the individual to prime status as the unit of analysis for behavioral science through the use of the ergodicity theorems of classical mechanics. In the context of Molenaar's discussion, ergodicity is a characteristic of multidimensional systems evolving through time such that an individual trajectory over time yields the same information as a cross section of trajectories at one point in time and vice versa. The pertinence of this concept has to do with the extent to which one can synthesize one individual's longitudinal trajectory from an instantaneous snapshot of many individuals' trajectories. Molenaar's arguments, which are summarized here, conclude that by their very nature, developmental phenomena, although intraindividual, are nonergodic behavioral systems, in large measure because they are not stationary processes, but rather manifest time-related trends. This conclusion carries the striking implication that the traditional study of individual differences—one of two disciplines of scientific psychology mentioned earlier—is certainly not optimal and most likely unable to provide a sound basis for synthesizing intraindividual processes. Molenaar states, "Only under very strict conditions—which are hardly obtained in real psychological processes—can a generalization be made from a structure of interindividual variation to the analogous structure of intraindividual variation" (p. 201).

Thus, Molenaar rested his arguments on the contrast of what we have been calling *intraindividual* and *interindividual variation,* and focused his attention primarily on covariation matrices of the observations—a common concern for those who quantitatively model behavior and behavior change. These covariation matrices of concern include the usual information regarding the extent to which measured variables rise and fall together over occasions of measurement, but also the extent to which the measured variables rise and fall together when the variables are lagged on each other (and themselves) by different amounts. For example, if x and y are out of phase, they may not covary at all if one does not correct for the phase differences. But if x at time 1 is paired with y at time 3, x at time 2 paired with y at time 4, x at time 3 paired with y at time 5, and so on, x and y might be found to covary substantially. Under these circumstances, lagging y on x by two occasions of measurement reveals a relation between x and y that has a strong temporal component. For example, ingesting food and feeling satiated for having done so are not contemporaneous events. A relation clearly exists between the two, but feelings of satiation lag food ingestion by perhaps 30 minutes. Developmental researchers have long understood the basic ideas concerning how early events may be predictors, if not causes, of later events (e.g., see Kagan, 1994, 2007). For example, differences in heart-rate variability in infants predict much later personality characteristics (e.g., Fox & Porges, 1985).

In a similar way, when a variable is lagged on itself (autocorrelation), the magnitude of the relation tends to vary with the amount of lag. The dependence of autocorrelation on lag is valuable information in time-related modeling of individual-level data (Newell & Molenaar, in press).

Molenaar defined the *phase space* as the multivariate domain whose dimensions were the measured variables of interest. Addition of another dimension—time—to the phase space yielded the behavior space. The values of a person's variables at a given time, t, define a point in the phase space. The values of all the variables for that same person at successive repeated measurements define a trajectory (life history) in the behavior space, and the complete set of such trajectories represents the life spans of a population of persons (see Figure 2.2). To define a *random process,* Molenaar considered the trajectory of a specific person in the behavior space up to some arbitrary time point, t, through which time point all the relevant

information for that person is available. Predicting the value of the trajectory at $t + 1$ will, in general, not be exact; thus, the trajectory is considered to be the result of a random process—a process characterized by some amount of uncertainty. If the amount of uncertainty approaches zero, which happens seldom, if ever, with human behavior, the process becomes deterministic. Illustrating the act of predicting in this way, within the individual over time (e.g., from t to $t + 1$), foreshadows a discussion presented later in this chapter concerning the roles of prediction and selection within the general intraindividual variability approach considered here.

Molenaar concluded his line of argument by indicating that the projection of a random trajectory along the time axis of the multidimensional behavior space yields a multivariate time series. He then used the time series literature to argue that such a process is ergodic (affords generalization from a structure of interindividual variation to the analogous structure of intraindividual variation) only if its first-order moment function (mean vector) and second-order moment function (lagged covariance matrices) are invariant in time. Such conditions scarcely seem to characterize developmental processes. Indeed, developmentalists are generally indifferent to phenomena that do not show growth or decline as the individual ages.

Finally, Molenaar (2004) demonstrated that longitudinal factor models based on interindividual differences, even though the participants may have been measured multiple times, do not meet the stringent assumptions necessary to conclude that the processes described by interindividual variation accurately characterize those described by intraindividual variation. The rather striking conclusion, as noted earlier, is that with regard to development, one cannot synthesize intraindividual processes from interindividual differences. Harking back to Figure 2.2, one can get a sense of the ergodicity argument by imagining comparing a cross section of all the trajectories at one point in time with one of the individual trajectories over all the time points. Would these be likely to yield the same picture? Most likely they would not in the case of developmental phenomena (e.g., cognitive development) because a developmental process that involves incremental gains (or losses) over long periods is not a stationary phenomenon. Somewhat in contrast, variation in emotion/affect seems a more likely candidate to behave according to ergodic principles in the sense that emotions do wax and wane repeatedly over time. It is not completely out of the question that the individual, over his or her lifetime, might experience the gamut of emotions that one might find in a cross section of the population at one point in time. Thus, over the course of an individual's lifetime, the array of affective behavior might well approximate the array of affective behavior of many individuals at a given point in time and vice versa. In any case, the contrast between the more or less unidirectional changes in cognitive measurements and more or less reversible changes in emotion measurements, while representing two very different kinds of intraindividual variability, helps to convey the nature of the ergodicity argument.

In summary, behavior is what individuals do. Therefore, the articulation of lawful relations regarding behavior should involve the individual as the main unit of analysis. Classical experimental psychology involves the manipulation of variables at the individual level but does not allow for systematic differences among individuals unless they receive different manipulations. Classical differential psychology capitalizes on differences among individuals but does not necessarily reconstitute a meaningful individual from those differences. We are arguing for maintaining the individual as the unit of analysis but for seeking similarities in patterns of individuals' behavior, thereby describing a functioning individual of some generality rather than trying to synthesize an individual from the ways people differ from one another.

In terms of variation, we are primarily seeking similarities in intraindividual variability. Baltes, Reese, and Nesselroade (1977) defined developmental research as seeking interindividual differences (and similarities) in patterns of intraindividual change. This view rather closely parallels traditional differential psychology but with an initial emphasis on individual-level measurement to identify intraindividual change patterns. In their discussion of rationales for conducting longitudinal research, Baltes and Nesselroade (1979) saw interindividual differences and similarities in patterns of intraindividual variability and change as a key means by which to identify developmental influences.

Of course, it is understood that if one does not find similarities in intraindividual variability patterns, then one still has to deal with interindividual differences in those patterns. However, given interindividual differences, we do not believe the appropriate next step is to blindly aggregate those differences by, for example, averaging them, as was done often before the seminal work of Tucker (1958, 1966; see also Rao, 1958) in analyzing data from learning studies. Tucker's proposal is now recognized as one of the key lead-ins to what is currently known as *growth curve modeling* (e.g., see Meredith & Tisak, 1990; and McArdle,

Chapter 3 of this volume). Tucker (1966) proposed the decomposition of learning performance (repeated measurements over many trials on a learning task) in such a way that distinctly different trajectories could be identified. Up to that time, most learning data were simply averaged over participants to provide a relatively smooth curve that was used to describe the learning process. Tucker's proposal, which applies more widely than merely to learning data, recognized the possibility that individual trajectories were not necessarily well described by an average curve. Rather, he proposed methods for identifying different subgroup trajectories, as well as multiple functions underlying the observed performance. Cronbach (1975) hailed Tucker's influential proposal as an example of rapprochement between the classical experimental and differential approaches to the study of behavior because it yielded both general curves applicable to multiple participants and individualized weights by which those general curves could be combined to produce a close approximation to the unique performance of each of the individual participants.

Rather than ignoring *among* persons differences by, for example, summarizing with an average curve, it may be possible to fashion patterns that do manifest similarities across persons, if the comparisons involve other levels of abstraction. For example, the more *abstract* process of exhibiting a stress reaction may accurately describe what happens to many individuals placed in a public speaking context even though the actual symptoms displayed (e.g., sweaty palms, shallow respiration, accelerated heart rate) during that stress reaction may well differ substantially from one individual to the next. Two very different child-rearing styles, one featuring physical coercion and the other abusive verbal attempts at control, both reflect domineering behavior on the part of the parent over the child. Similarly, one child may manifest resistance to such coercion by "acting out," whereas another displays passive-aggressive behavior. Obviously, admission of such a variety of manifestations under common labels is required if theories are to have generality, but it places a strong burden on our ability to measure behavioral constructs at the individual level very well, a topic to which we now turn.

MULTIVARIATE MEASUREMENT SCHEMES

Lobbying as energetically as we have for recognizing the individual as the unit of analysis in developmental research carries with it the responsibility to examine the implications for measurement. It is rather clear that the general orientation we are propounding impinges heavily on the area of measurement. Measurement is always a thorny issue in behavioral research and it is no less so when studying development, especially if one takes seriously the individual as the unit of analysis with its corollary repeated measurements. There are two broad concerns we want to examine here. The first concern has to do with general psychometric practice; the second has to do with recognizing idiosyncrasy, and whether and how a multivariate perspective on measurement can accommodate it. This, in turn, has implications for how one models processes; we elaborate on this topic in the next section.

Many of the current debate topics in measurement theory hinge on such matters as how true scores are defined, the nature of measurement error, and the quantification of item difficulty level. We propose to enter the discussion of measurement a level or so above these concerns that, for example, pit definitions from item response theory against those of classical test theory. These are interesting, important matters ultimately in need of resolution, but their resolution is not critical for our discussion and further scrutiny at that level would distract us from our principal concerns for this chapter. Valuable examinations of these issues can be found, for example, in works by Embretson (1996) and Schmidt and Embretson (2003).

Bearing more directly on this discussion—from the joint perspective of emphasizing the individual as the unit of analysis and viewing the study of development as not fitting well with the individual differences orientation because of the ergodicity principles—Molenaar (2004) raised fundamental concerns regarding traditional approaches to psychological measurement when he argued "that test theory, yielding the formal and technical underpinning of psychological test construction (Lord & Novick, 1968), gives rise to serious questions regarding its applicability to individual assessment" (p. 203). For example, true scores and errors of measurement in classical test theory are individual-level concepts linked to intraindividual variability, but in practice, they are typically estimated from data that involves many people measured once rather than one person measured many times. Such substitution of interindividual variation for intraindividual variability is not uncommon in the quantitative modeling lore of psychology. For example, descriptions of various scaling methods (e.g., Torgerson, 1958) illustrate how the judgments of many participants are substituted for the behavior of one participant rendering many judgments.

One of our guiding premises here is that focusing on the individual as the appropriate unit of analysis and looking for similarities in intraindividual change patterns is inadequate if undertaken solely at the level of manifest variables. Although we do not go so far as to "declare a pox" on standardized measurement, we depart from the traditional measurement orientation to recognize that the sought-after similarities among individuals simply may not be found at the manifest variable level, but rather should be sought at the latent variable level. This means, for example, that somewhat different emphases must be applied to issues of measurement and matters of analysis. For this, we turn to a more general discussion of multivariate measurement schemes.

Because of their prominent role in modeling with latent variables, multivariate measurement schemes have held an important place in the psychometric literature for several decades. From early work in the human abilities area by such pioneers as Burt, Spearman, Thomson, and Thurstone through large programs of research on personality traits by investigators such as Cattell, Eysenck, and Guilford, multivariate, factor analytic approaches to studying interrelations among arrays of variables have made important contributions to the study of behavior. Since the 1970s, multivariate measurement schemes have reached a fairly dominant position in psychometrics through the evolving sophistication of measurement models within a structural equations modeling framework. Research on the so-called big 5 personality factors well illustrate the progression (e.g., see Costa, 1992; Goldberg, 1990; McCrae & Costa, 1999), as does work on human abilities and cognition (see McArdle, Chapter 3 of this volume; Tucker-Drob, 2009).

As mentioned earlier, Baltes and Nesselroade (1973) articulated three primary aspects of a rationale for why measurement schemes should be multivariate in nature in studying developmental processes. Subsequently, Nesselroade and Ford (1987) elaborated the rationale to emphasize its pertinence to dynamical systems representations. The elements of the combined rationale are: (1) any dependent variable (or consequent) is potentially a function of multiple determinants; (2) any determinant or antecedent has potentially multiple consequents; (3) any determinant or antecedent may also be considered a consequent of other determinants or antecedents, and any consequent may also be considered a determinant or antecedent of some other consequents; and (4) the study of multiple antecedent-consequent relations provides a useful model for the organization of complex systems.

With the encouragement and contributions of a large cadre of methodologically sophisticated behavioral scientists, the variety and power of multivariate modeling procedures increased enormously during the latter half of the 20th century (e.g., see Cudeck & MacCallum, 2007; Little, Bouvaird, & Card, 2007). Probably one of the most influential aspects has been the improvements in the ways to measure latent variables coupled with the ability to evaluate how well this is being done, much of it tracing back to the seminal work of Jöreskog (1969). Confirmatory factor analysis and structural equation modeling have come of age during this period and, both because of its intuitive appeal and its technical advantages such as the innate correction for attenuation of relations because of measurement error, the measurement model has virtually become a "fixture" for representing latent variables or constructs in a wide variety of modeling efforts.

P-technique factor analysis and its newer derivatives such as dynamic factor analysis (Browne & Nesselroade, 2005; Molenaar, 1985; Nesselroade, McArdle, Aggen, & Meyers, 2002), state-space modeling (e.g., Molenaar, Sinclair, Rovine, Ram, & Corneal, 2009), and other time-series analysis approaches (see, e.g., Chow, Ferrer, & Hsieh, 2010; Hamaker, Dolan, & Molenaar, 2005; Newell & Molenaar, in press), which also feature multivariate measurement but are much more oriented toward the study of process at the individual level, have an important role to play in this context (Boker, 2002; Nesselroade, 2007). Early on, Cattell and Williams (1953) anticipated a multivariate, person-oriented approach by acknowledging a trend toward measuring many variables simultaneously on one animal instead of a few variables measured on many animals, whereas decrying the fact that this "holistic" functional understanding had not availed itself of P-technique as a statistical device for discovering the functional unities. Cattell and Williams went on to warn that being able to generalize to people broadly would require "the accumulation of quite a number of P-technique studies" (p. 142).

Somewhat in cadence with these arguments we have made regarding the importance of the individual as the unit of analysis and the centrality of latent variable modeling, Nesselroade et al. (2007) described and empirically illustrated an approach to multivariate measurement that, although initially resting on P-technique, and therefore oriented toward the individual level, was designed to strengthen the individual orientation by filtering out idiosyncratic features of measurement—features that can interfere with the measurement process but are basically irrelevant to the constructs being measured. We describe this later in more detail, but first, some additional background on idiosyncrasy will help to set the stage for our description.

In one of the debriefing sessions following up a P-technique study of mother/daughter dyads (Mitteness & Nesselroade, 1987), it was learned that whereas one member of the dyad in responding to the self-report item ANXIOUS had anxious and jittery in mind, the other member of the dyad thought of it as eagerness. Thus, the same objective stimulus was eliciting markedly different response patterns from the participants. Although the folly of aggregating responses of such different quality to what is objectively the same stimulus material is quite obvious, traditional approaches to measurement do not appropriately take into account such differences.

The intention of Nesselroade et al. (2007) was to present a method for measuring abstract qualities (constructs) such as depression, life satisfaction, morale, wisdom, and expertise in ways that are appropriately different for different individuals or age groups while holding constant the meaning of those abstract qualities being assessed. The rationale for Nesselroade et al.'s (2007) proposal is that at its heart, good theory rests on constructs and their interrelations. But without appropriate measurement operations to give the constructs empirical representation either directly through observable indicators of the construct or through other constructs, empirical deductions cannot be tested and hypotheses are not falsifiable. Nesselroade et al. (2007) sought alternative measurement operations that permitted the maintenance of rigorous mathematical concepts of invariance whereas accommodating idiosyncratic features of individuals and of subgroups that differ by variables such as age. A way to meet these conditions with mathematical rigor was discussed, and the procedures were illustrated with extant data. Subsequently, Nesselroade and Estabrook (2009) extended the general line of argument to the case of subgroups and presented an examination of how the factorial nature of the items of the Center for Epidemiologic Studies-Depression Depression Scale (CES-D; Radloff, 1977) varied with age.

How was this alternative measurement goal accomplished? From a multivariate measurement perspective, in psychology, the measurement model of structural equation modeling and a conception of measurement invariance relying heavily on the common factor model have become mainstays in the effort to build and empirically test models involving latent variables. The various elements of the common factor model—loading patterns, factor covariance matrices, unique parts covariance matrices, and intercepts—are central in distinguishing among weak, strong, and strict invariance (Meredith, 1993; Millsap & Meredith, 2007). Traditional measurement invariance in structural modeling work in psychology relies heavily on the relations between factors and manifest variables (relations described by the factor loadings). Invariance of factor loadings, although sometimes difficult to achieve in practice, has in many ways been the gold standard for the traditional evaluation of measurement models.

When one focuses on intraindividual variability and the individual as the primary unit of analysis, of necessity the specter of idiosyncrasy looms into the picture. Indeed, idiosyncrasy is a natural, substantial phenomenon when the unit of analysis is the person, but under standard measurement invariance notions, there is virtually no place for it in the manifest and latent variables or in their relations. Ignoring it does not make it go away; rather, it continues to hover and attenuate relations among variables. Trying to corner it into a "catchall" error term is not satisfying if one truly believes in the appropriateness of individual-level analysis. In the conventional notions of measurement invariance, there is virtually no useful place for idiosyncrasy in the manifest and latent variables or in their relations when the unit of analysis is the person.

How pervasive is the notion of idiosyncrasy? Many concepts for which we attempt to provide empirical representation imply some idiosyncrasy (e.g., expertise, intelligence, and creativity). Expertise, for instance, can be equally great in some sense in two individuals, but it may be manifested in entirely different domains. Can expertise be measured in a standardized format? Must it be measured in a standardized format? The medical concept of a syndrome, which presumes a common core of meaning across individuals, whereas allowing for different but overlapping subsets of indicators of that core from one individual to another, allows for idiosyncrasy in the pattern of manifest variables that pertain, but our traditional notions of rigorous, standardized measurement do not. Individual specificity of psychophysiological response patterns (Friedman & Santucci, 2003; Stemmler, 1992) represents another arena in which idiosyncrasy is present in the observable manifestations of behavior patterns and must somehow be accommodated in the measurement operations if lawful relations between context and behavior are to have generality.

Thus, the objective of Nesselroade et al. (2007) was to allow measurement operations to accommodate idiosyncrasy and still provide representation for the *same* construct across individuals. An individually oriented modeling procedure (P-technique factor analysis) was used to provide

a measurement approach that accommodated idiosyncrasy but continued to impose rigorous mathematical concepts of invariance. The standard measurement invariance approach was replaced with one in which invariance was imposed at a higher level of abstraction—in the relations (correlations) among the factors. Nesselroade et al. (2007) retained the traditional concept of factorial invariance but in a somewhat different way, by allowing the P-technique factor loading patterns, which are the relations between manifest variables and unmeasured or latent variables, to reflect some idiosyncrasy for the different individuals who were being studied. At the same time, out of respect for the traditional scientific values on eventually building nomothetic relations and the role that factorial invariance has played in trying to establish them, a necessary condition of invariance was imposed. In this case, however, the invariance constraints were imposed on the factor intercorrelation matrices *across* the multiple individuals under consideration. This condition, in turn, yields second-order factors (factors based on the intercorrelations of the first-order factors) that manifested the traditional factor loading pattern invariance.

This *higher order invariance* approach is somewhat analogous to the use of the syndrome concept in medicine that was mentioned earlier. Many observable indicators are associated with a given syndrome, but not all individuals so afflicted will manifest all of the symptoms. For instance, suppose there are nine symptoms known to be part of syndrome A. Each of three persons could manifest six of the nine symptoms, but any pair of individuals might have only three of the symptoms in common. Still, all three individuals would be characterized as manifesting syndrome A. This thinking is not unrelated to that underlying the measurement of developmental risk as a predictor of later adjustment by counting the number of risk factors for each person, regardless of their precise nature, and using the count as the measurement (e.g., see Sameroff, Peck, & Eccles, 2004).

Nesselroade et al. (2007) allowed the factor loadings to differ somewhat from person to person even though the driving argument involved measuring the same underlying constructs. But the interrelations among the latent variables (the factor intercorrelations) characterized by the individually tailored loading patterns were rigidly constrained to be the same from individual to individual. This was the "idiographic filter" aspect of the approach. The idea was that the constructs were the "same" constructs for different individuals and would share some common structural features, albeit each construct could manifest itself somewhat differently in the observable behaviors of different persons.

The essential idiographic filter ideas are portrayed in Figures 2.3 and 2.4. Figure 2.3 illustrates the general idea of the idiographic filter—to separate the idiographic space from the nomothetic relations space by means of the idiographic filter. The idiographic filter consists of the first-order factors and their loadings on the manifest variables. These loadings are allowed to reflect idiosyncrasy in the relations between the latent and manifest variables without necessarily indicating why these idiosyncratic relations obtain.

In Figure 2.4, three spaces are identified. A measurement space is identified for each of two individuals, but it could just as well include many individuals. The measurement space contains a set of manifest variables (a through f) that are made distinct for each individual because they may not be the "same" variables for each person, even though they have the "same" name. Spanning the measurement space for multiple individuals is the idiographic filter space, which includes the first-order factors (latent variables) and the factor loadings, which describe the manifest variables in the measurement space as linear combinations of the

primary factors. This is the site of traditional factorial invariance of factor loading patterns, which if it holds across individuals, affords an interpretation that the manifest variables are "measuring the same thing" in different individuals. In Figure 2.4, the loading patterns for individuals i and j are different to indicate that the manifest variables are not the same measures from individual to individual; hence the need for the idiographic filter. The third space is labeled nomothetic relations because, as the figure portrays, the higher order factors (F_I and F_{II}), which derive from the interrelations among the first-order factors, are the same for different individuals. This is the case because the relations (e.g., factor intercorrelations) of the primary factors (in the idiographic filter space) are identical for different individuals, thus defining identical higher order factors.

More concretely, we have elsewhere (Nesselroade et al., 2007) illustrated the basic idea with the concepts of *Area* and *Volume* in geometric objects playing the role of higher order constructs. Both cylinders and boxes, for example, have volumes equal to their cross-sectional area times their length. But the cross-sectional area of a cylinder (a circle) is π times the square of the radius, and the cross-sectional area of a box (a rectangle) is length times width. A rectangle does not have a radius and a circle does not have a length, so the measures (manifest variables) defining the area are different in the two cases, but no one doubts that the concept *Area* is the same. Similarly, *Volume* in both cases is cross-sectional *Area* times the length of the three-dimensional object (cylinder or box). Thus, the relation between *Area* and *Volume* is the same for the cylinder and the box, but the two concepts rest on different measures (radius and length vs. width, height, and length). The basic idea, we would argue, is not unfamiliar to developmental psychologists. Designers of longitudinal research, for example, have long had to deal with devising age-appropriate measurement instruments to study continuity and change over longer spans of time.

Procedurally, fitting this idiographic filter model involves conducting multiple P-technique analyses simultaneously, constraining the factor intercorrelations to be equal across individuals but allowing, within the conditions of identifiability, the factor loading patterns to reflect some idiosyncrasy, and then testing the fit of this model to the multiple P-technique data. If the model fits the data, one can interpret the outcome as having identified an invariant second-order factor solution while "filtering" out the idiosyncratic aspects of measurement at the first-order factor level.

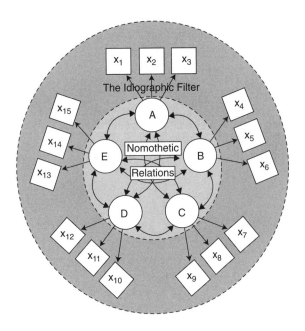

Figure 2.3 Schematic portrayal of the measurement space, the idiographic filter space, and the nomothetic relations space. *Circles* represent latent variables (factor); *boxes* represent manifest variables; *straight arrows* represent factor loading; *curved double arrows* represent factor intercorrelation.

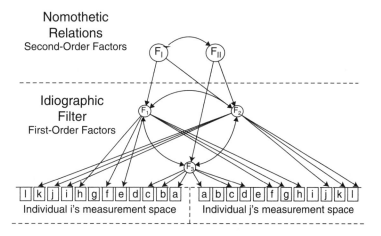

Figure 2.4 Kinds of models tested in evaluating the idiographic filter's fit to data. Two hypothetical individuals (i and j) are measured on 12 variables (a through l) representing three first-order factors (F_1, F_2, and F_3), the loadings of which are idiosyncratically patterned. The factor intercorrelations are invariant between individuals, thus defining invariant factor loading patterns for the second-order factors (F_I and F_{II}). (Note that the figure is meant to be illustrative. One would not define two second-order factors on the intercorrelations of only three first-order factors.) *Circles* represent latent variables (factor); *boxes* represent manifest variables; *straight arrows* represent factor loading; *curved double arrows* represent factor intercorrelations.

Higher order measurement invariance is highly pertinent to the study of development because each of us has a unique history of experience, learning, conditioning, language usage, and so forth that, in part, contributes idiosyncrasy to our behavior patterns ranging over the gamut from self-reporting in a testing room to neurological activity in a magnetic resonance imaging (MRI) chamber. Nesselroade et al. (2007) argued that it is desirable to separate idiosyncratic aspects of the linkages between latent and manifest variables from the core meaning of constructs. But the question is *how* to filter out the irrelevant aspects of behavior. The example given earlier with ANXIOUS as a self-report stimulus item illustrates how differences in the use of what purports to be a common language can introduce interindividual variation that is not just irrelevant, but actually damaging, into one's data. One promising answer was to use some form of P-technique to capture intraindividual variability. However, it was also clear that it would need to be linked to the simultaneous use of multiple P-technique cases to capitalize on the strengths of the approach. Obviously, this *filtering effort represents an attempt to eliminate some interindividual differences en route to emphasizing similarities among individuals.*

Something akin to what we are calling *idiographic filtering* is found in a wide variety of contexts ranging from other approaches to measurement (e.g., Sameroff, Peck, & Eccles, 2004), to developmental concepts such as vicariance (e.g., Lautrey & de Ribaupierre, 2004), to the modeling of electroencephalograph/magnetoencephalography and functional MRI time series. In the latter, for example, multivariate time series are collected for a sample of N subjects. In the first phase, each subject is analyzed individually. In neural source modeling of electroencephalograph/magnetoencephalography time series, for instance, often an individual (idiographic) head model for each subject is determined by means of an MRI scan and then used in the source model fits. In functional MRI studies, the scans of individual subjects can be compared only after "warping" them unto a common atlas; this is a rather drastic idiographic filtering step based on diffeomorphic transformations of the scans.

We acknowledge that the idiographic filter proposal represents a daring (some would say foolhardy) assault on the principles and traditional notions of standardized measurement. For a diversity of viewpoints on this proposal, refer to the critical commentaries appearing with Nesselroade et al.'s (2007, 2009) articles. The commentaries on the higher order invariance article are both substantive and technical in nature. More important for this chapter are the technical commentaries. In brief, there are two primary arguments against the idiographic filter proposal. The first has to do with the matter of identification, which is explained later. The second argument, which is related to the first, has to do with relying on the interrelations of first-order factors as a sufficient basis for construct identification.

The essential issue is that because the higher order invariance measurement approach relaxes the strict invariance of factor loading patterns, there is the possibility that unless sufficient constraints are placed on the loadings, one can always find a solution that will appear to yield higher order invariance regardless of the fit (in the abstract sense) to the data. In other words, one is not entitled to take a completely laissez-faire approach to representing the relations between constructs and manifest variables. Currently, we are in the process of working out the specific identification conditions to be imposed to be able to provide a rigorous test of the hypothesis that one has a reasonable fit to one's data using the higher order invariance approach (Molenaar & Nesselroade, 2010; Zhang, Browne, & Nesselroade, 2009). Being able to reject or falsify the hypothesis of higher order invariance is key if the idiographic filter is to be a valuable measurement tool.

Some commentators who were critical of the idiographic filter conception were opposed to the notion that invariant factor intercorrelations could be relied on to identify constructs as the same from one individual to another. Working out the conditions for identification of the measurement models will, in large measure, help take care of this second concern regarding higher order invariance. Our aim is not to ignore completely any information regarding the nature of the constructs that is provided by the manifest variables, but rather to augment the condition of invariant construct interrelations with what useful information the manifest variables can supply. It is important to recognize, however, that we do not rely solely on the manifest variables to define the constructs as is the case with the traditional measurement invariance approach. Instead, the idiographic filter allows for the manifest variables to exhibit some idiosyncratic features and set these aside rather than allow them to dilute or obscure important relations.

Relying more on the interrelations among constructs, as we do with the higher order invariance approach, stands in marked contrast to the traditional measurement invariance notions. It is our belief, however, that this alternative is timely, especially when one is emphasizing the individual as the primary unit of analysis. From a traditional perspective, when one's emphasis is on modeling interindividual variation, it is easy to avoid asking the difficult question, namely, Do the differences among people represent common phenomena, that is, variation that can be analyzed meaningfully between individuals? Our contention is that some of the ways individuals differ from each other, for instance, when they are responding to stimulus material in a measurement context, are idiosyncratic rather than common, and aggregating across them interferes with the relations one is trying to establish.

A version of our concern with idiosyncrasy seems to be reflected in currently popular modeling procedures that aim to deal with so-called heterogeneity. However, they tend to emphasize "fixes" at the level of modeling, rather than at the level of measurement. For example, many solutions to the problem of "heterogeneity," including mixture modeling, spline regression, latent class analysis, and so forth, tacitly reinforce the idea that all people do not fit the same mold and segregate them into subgroups of like individuals. We question the value of this line of approach in the sense that we all abhor the idea of a science of individuals, so we have to ask just how much better is a science that explicitly involves many different subgroups?

Although the possible gains in the measurement of constructs are considerable, the higher order invariance model obviously must involve strong constraints, and the appropriateness of imposing them can (and should) be evaluated as a hypothesis. As noted earlier, minimum conditions for identification are currently being worked out for such statistical tests to be practical (Molenaar, 2009; Molenaar & Nesselroade, 2010; Zhang, Browne, & Nesselroade, 2009). However, to the extent that this hypothesis is supported by the data, it means that the structure of the factors at the second-order level (factors derived from the factor intercorrelations) is invariant across individuals in the traditional sense. Thus, one can indeed have an invariant measurement framework at a more general level by filtering out idiosyncratic aspects at another level. This speaks directly to our aim of looking for similarities among individuals, but at the measurement level. This is discussed more generally in the following text.

An important distinction must be made here and, to broaden the scope of our discussion, it can be illustrated with subgroup, rather than individual comparisons. What is considered to be irrelevant for one investigator's research question may be the focus of another's. More concretely, suppose one is studying age differences in depression in younger and older adults, and measures depression with a self-report instrument such as the CES-D (Radloff, 1977). Younger and older adults represent different cohorts, different educational systems, perhaps different socioeconomic levels, and so on—differences that may result in the content of some of the items being interpreted differently by participants. This, in turn, may cause the responses not to be comparable, jeopardizing any age comparisons. Such differences are irrelevant to making age comparisons on depression (as a construct), and it would be appropriate to eliminate them, if possible, from the calculations. Another investigator, however, might be interested in the nature of age differences in the semantic meaning of such items and the differences would be highly pertinent. In the first case, the differences jeopardize the comparisons; in the second case, they are the focus of the comparisons.

Let us consider some of the implications of the idiographic filter for the measurement of constructs; later, we examine the approach in the broader context of modeling processes, for we believe that imposing such measurement operations "steers" the researcher's interpretation of data in the right direction for further examination of similarities in more explanatory relations among constructs. The approach is multivariate; it does, in fact, focus on the individual as the unit of analysis, and its primary objective in getting rid of the irrelevant idiosyncratic features of behavior is to create a basis for the identification of similarities across individuals. So, for example, the "same" constructs can be identified from one person to another or one subgroup to another even though the linkages between those constructs and the empirical world are somewhat idiosyncratic. In disciplines other than developmental science, syndromes in medicine and response specificity in the psychophysiological literature exemplify this notion. Thus, even at the measurement level, one can emphasize the two primary aspects discussed earlier, namely, the individual as the unit of analysis and seeking similarities as opposed to differences among individuals.

In summary, we have explored the use of multivariate measurement schemes and the idiographic filter primarily by means of P-technique as an approach to structuring intraindividual variability in what we believe are more powerful and general ways than those currently in use. In so doing, we have deliberately emphasized latent variables rather more than manifest variables as the key to identifying invariant relations. The next section goes beyond the matter of measurement of more or less static attributes to focus on the study of relations involving the concept of process.

SIMILARITIES IN INTRAINDIVIDUAL VARIABILITY PATTERNS

It is our contention that people are neither interchangeable parts nor randomly equivalent entities. Still, we believe that a primary goal of science is the enunciation of nomothetic relations that reflect generality across individuals. Reconciling these perspectives of nomothetic and idiographic orientations has been the focus of considerable effort for much of the documented history of behavioral science (Barlow & Nock, 2009; Lamiell, 1998; Zevon & Tellegen, 1982). In this chapter, we are interested in more general patterns of intraindividual variability organized over time—process—and the general tack we are taking is to use the basic idiographic filter idea as described earlier in a measurement context as a key component of a basis for identifying similarities (and differences) among individual patterns of intraindividual variability. This section explores how this can be accomplished.

An important piece of both the historical lore and current practice regarding individual level analysis and modeling is P-technique factor analysis, to which we have alluded several times. Applications of P-technique exemplify both the individual as the unit of analysis and the use of multivariate measurement schemes because it involves repeated measurements of one individual with a battery of measures over many successive occasions as was depicted in Figure 2.1.

P-technique factor analysis has played a pivotal role in the quantitative study of intraindividual variability (for reviews of the substantive literature, see Jones & Nesselroade, 1990; Luborsky & Mintz, 1972). Cattell et al. (1947; see also Cattell, 1963a) promoted P-technique as an integral way to get at individual-level traits of personality. For example, P-technique was instrumental in the articulation of the state (as opposed to trait) anxiety concept (Cattell & Scheier, 1961), which subsequently led to the development of various measurement instruments such as the Spielberger State Trait Anxiety Inventory (STAI; Spielberger, Gorsuch, & Lushene, 1969).

The developmental trajectory for P-technique was by no means a smooth one, despite the great interest in factor analytic procedures in general in the mid-20th century. Fifteen years after the first P-technique article was published (Cattell et al., 1947), Anderson (1963) essentially dismissed it as an inappropriate procedure (see also Holtzman, 1963). At the same time, however, Bereiter (1963, p. 15) was calling P-technique "the logical technique for studying the interdependencies of measures." Despite the controversies, P-technique has continued to be instrumental in a variety of substantive research contexts including the analysis of psychophysiological recordings (e.g., Friedman & Santucci, 2003), studying short-term affective variability at the individual level (Lebo & Nesselroade, 1978; Nesselroade & Ford, 1985; Zevon & Tellegen,

1982), and introducing alternative conceptions of construct measurement (Nesselroade et al., 2007). Subsequent important elaborations of the basic P-technique idea (Browne & Nesselroade, 2005; Molenaar, 1985) led to the dynamic factor model and various state-space modeling approaches (e.g., Browne & Zhang, 2007; Chow et al., 2010; Molenaar et al., 2009) that promise to enhance substantially our ability to study developmental processes because they offer mathematically rigorous ways to model relational systems at the individual level (Newell & Molenaar, in press). Thus, although epitaphs for P-technique have been written a few times, to paraphrase Mark Twain, "the reports of its death have been greatly exaggerated." The basic P-technique model still retains merit in both its own right and as a relatively efficient way to establish the basic dimensionality of a multivariate time series (Molenaar & Nesselroade, 2009)—something one may want to determine before undertaking more complex analyses.

Measurement and modeling procedures in psychology are rather firmly built on the premise that much of what is common—the stuff of lawful relations—resides at the observable or manifest level rather than at the abstract level. This view, which reflects the epistemologic stance taken by early and mid-20th-century neopositivists and behaviorists that concepts must be reducible to observables, is exemplified by the concept of factorial invariance and the strong role it has played in measurement and modeling, as most discussions will attest. However, the use of the idiographic filter represents a deliberate attempt to "alter the playing field" somewhat in the sense of emphasizing the latent variables as the level of abstraction for which invariance was sought.

Given our concern with merging the individual level of analysis and modeling with a focus on ascertaining similarities, it seems timely to explore approaches other than the traditional group-based, interindividual differences designs that emphasize invariant relations between latent and manifest variables. Instead, we focus on invariant relations found at a more abstract level, for example, among latent variables. Consider an example that comes from the structural literature of physics of separating a system's idiosyncratic features from its general features. Eddington (1956) described the behavior of an atom that had one electron that, at a given time, circled the nucleus in one of nine orbits. The electron could perform nine possible behaviors. It could jump to any of the other eight orbits or it could remain in the orbit in which it was currently. Eddington went on to illustrate how the jumping operations exemplified the closure property of a mathematical group

because the result of combining any two operations in succession was equal to executing one of the other operations. For example, jumping two orbits and then three orbits had the same effect as jumping five orbits. Eddington then erased the atom from the equations to dramatize the idea that the structure of interest was in the interrelations of the jumping operations rather than in the behavior of the electron itself. Eddington went on to argue that this was not trivial because, as he put it, another well-known "jumper," the knight on a chessboard, also had a repertoire of nine possible moves. It could jump to any of eight squares or it could remain in its current location. However, a knight on a chessboard can get to a square in two successive jumps that it could not reach in one jump, thereby negating the closure property characterizing the atom's jump operations. This example illustrates looking for similarities (and differences) in systems at the abstract rather than the manifest variable level because the two systems are so disparate in virtually every aspect except the jumping operations.

But consider still another "jumper": the baseball. During a baseball game, at any given inning there are nine gloved players on the field. The baseball "jumps" from one glove to another, much like the electron in the Eddington example. The baseball can "jump" to any of the other eight gloves or it can remain in the one in which it is currently. Moreover, like the electron, the baseball could get in one "jump" where it can get in two successive "jumps." For example, in the service of putting out a runner who is about to score, the ball may "jump" from the left fielder's glove to the third baseman's glove to the catcher's glove, or it may "jump" directly from the left fielder's glove to the catcher's glove. Perhaps this stretches the metaphor a bit, but it is for the sake of making a key point: Two very different systems—the atom in Eddington's case and the baseball in ours—that have virtually no resemblance in their physical forms (manifest variables) or in their behavioral repertoires (manifest variables) do share a common abstract structure in their behavior.

The example involving the atom, the knight, and the baseball illustrates a key feature for the study of development over the life span. Indeed, the example reflects a general disavowal of neopositivism by emphasizing the "reality" of the abstract interrelations rather than the manifest ones. Overton (2006) discusses in more detail the nature of this philosophical position and its pertinence to the study of development.

The "idiographic filter" within a measurement context strongly reflects these sentiments. In the context of studying development as a life-span phenomenon, we believe that the ideas are reflected in one of our major goals stated earlier—the search for generality in patterns of behavior across time/age. Clearly, this search does not have to be constrained to the relations among manifest variables; nor, we argue, should the search be so constrained. Had the atom, the knight, and the baseball been thrown together, some measurements taken, and then a mean and standard deviation calculated, the two statistics would have been utter nonsense—descriptions of a jumping nonentity. But by focusing on properties residing at a more abstract level, similarities could be identified between the baseball and the atom that were, however, not shared by the knight. Indeed, the aggregation of information, which is at the heart of such important issues as generalizability, should be so informed by these abstract relations rather than blindly conducted at the level of manifest variables (e.g., see Molenaar, 2004).

Referring back to the analyses of imaging time series involving "warping" images to a common reference scheme, in the second phase of such studies, selected aspects of the models or warped scans obtained in P-technique, like analyses of the time series data for each individual subject are entered in analysis of variance analyses. The results of these analyses can be generalized to the population from which the sample was drawn. This exemplifies one traditional, yet effective way to address the matter of generalizability in analyses of intraindividual variation.

It is the case that we do not yet have a great variety of innovative tools on which to base the search for similarities in intraindividual variability patterns, but as noted earlier, important steps have been taken with the extensions of P-technique factor analysis such as dynamic factor analysis and state-space models. As we have argued elsewhere (Molenaar & Nesselroade, 2010; Nesselroade & Molenaar, 2003), these methods offer a promising, rigorous approach to the concept of process. Processes involve sequential organizations of events that are related within a larger scheme. However, all events occurring simultaneously are not necessarily part of the same process, and multiple processes can simultaneously influence the same variables, thus complicating the task of the developmentalist trying to detail the nature of developmental change. Nesselroade and Molenaar illustrated the ideas with the example of children simultaneously growing physically, learning to read and write, and so forth, at the same time they were being "socialized" through influences at home, school, and other environments. The child's sense of self, for instance, is simultaneously impacted by all

these processes (physical growth, cognitive development, socialization), some of which are individual and some institutional. To go beyond a mere static description of what is going on by plotting the child's sense of self-trajectory over age, you can remarkably enrich the picture by incorporating dynamics into it. How this can be done is easily illustrated. Suppose that the rate of change (velocity) in the developing child's sense of self is inversely proportional to the child's current sense of self, implying that the child with a strong sense of self is changing less rapidly than a child with a weak sense of self—both are approaching some equilibrium value by the same general rule, but the rate of change differs for the two.

How to model the kind of system just described? As we have been arguing, a focus on modeling process at this stage of life-span developmental psychology's evolution needs to rest on both a multivariate orientation to measurement and analysis, and an idiographic emphasis in pursuing nomothetic relations. Models that look promising for this purpose represent significant elaborations of the basic P-technique approach, such as dynamic factor models, as well as state-space models and dynamical systems models, among others. Furthermore, we believe that the dynamical models can be made even more valuable for the study of process by implementing two innovations. The first is to create versions of the modeling procedures that can cope with nonstationary time-series data (e.g., see Molenaar et al., 2009). The second is to extend the idiographic filter notion to the modeling of process. Molenaar and Nesselroade (2010) discuss how this can be accomplished in a rigorous way.

Somewhat analogous to the way other constructs are conceptualized, processes are latent entities that are "realized" in the empirical world via a set of manifest or indicator variables. In the spirit of the "multivariate orientation" (Baltes & Nesselroade, 1973; Cattell, 1966b; Nesselroade & Ford, 1987) and discussed earlier in a measurement context, we believe that dynamic factor models, state-space models, and so forth can play for processes a role similar to that played by P-technique for latent variables as in the idiographic filter described earlier. In this vein, the dynamic factor models, for example, represent a kind of invariant "wire frame" for the "same" process that can be realized differently at the manifest variable level for different individuals. For example, socialization is generally conceptualized as a process, but the specific socializing behaviors of parents and socialized outcomes displayed by their offspring are not necessarily the same from one family unit to another. Therefore, developing a general understanding of how the process of socialization unfolds cannot be tied to a particular set of manifest variables. Rather, in analogy to the "jumping operations" of the atom and the baseball, a set of abstract principles must be determined if a claim to "understanding the process of socialization" is to be validly made. This is the general direction in which we believe the study of developmental processes can profitably head. It features a dynamic orientation and assumes that there are common, underlying processes, whereas allowing the actual physical manifestations (indicators or manifest variables) to differ from individual to individual. This is the underlying idea of the idiographic filter applied to the notion of process. For futher discussion of the issues and procedures see the article by Molenaar and Nesselroade (2010).

SOME FINAL METHODOLOGICAL ISSUES

The somewhat unique perspective that we have been discussing may have seemingly foreclosed on a couple of general concerns that have been of major interest to behavioral scientists for decades. One of these is the matter of prediction, which we may seem to have placed in some jeopardy by our indifference to the traditional differential psychology orientation. The other is the matter of generalizability, the traditional notion of which we may seem to have threatened with our strong focus on the individual case. We want to consider each of these in more detail because we think their roles are different in the intraindividual variability approach we have been discussing. We hasten to add, however, that far from being diminished in our intraindividual variability scheme, we believe that their importance may actually be enhanced.

Prediction and Selection

Prediction and the traditional differential psychology approach go together nicely because prediction typically rests on differential inputs pointing to differential outcomes. One measures differences among the attributes of individuals and, to the extent that these differences remain stable, they can be used at a later point to predict other differences such as those in performance. However, from an intraindividual variability perspective, prediction takes a somewhat different form. As we have been pointing out in this chapter, we are intent on focusing more on the similarities among individuals than on their differences. But the similarities among individuals do not lend themselves to differential predictions regarding future behavior.

Have we backed ourselves into a difficult corner? We don't think so. From a perspective emphasizing intraindividual variability, concern is on predicting what an individual will do in the future based on his or her past behavior rather than on what one individual will do relative to another. This is a further illustration of how a focus on intraindividual variability leads us into a somewhat different kind of issue than those on which the traditional nomothetic perspective rests. *Predicting* whether a given individual, X, can accomplish feat Y can be based on X's past performance. Given that X is predicted to succeed at Y, whether X should actually be the person *selected* out of a larger pool of those capable to do Y is *not* an individual question. Rather, it is a different kind of question; perhaps one requiring knowledge of how X *differs* from others. This forced discrimination between prediction and selection obviously calls for richer information on the individual than might otherwise be the case, but obtaining such information is quite in line with the fundamental thrust of our arguments.

Generalizability

Generalizability is another key concern of behavioral researchers, and emphasizing the individual case usually invites a vigorous critique centered on the lack of it. Campbell and Stanley (1963) defined generalizability or external validity in terms of the range of other variables, groups, treatments, and so on, for which a given finding held. One of the obstacles to be overcome from an intraindividual variability perspective is that research designs involving a time-series orientation often involve small numbers of cases, even single cases sometimes, and thus are probably among the most heavily criticized for their lack of generalizability. Yet, a dominant recommendation that we have been discussing is basing the search for similarities across individuals on patterns of intraindividual variability generated by such designs. It seems to us that the search for similarities in patterns of intraindividual variability over individuals is very much in the spirit of generalizability from our idiographic perspective. Moreover, as Molenaar (2004) has argued, technology for the kinds of designs we are describing will surely make them feasible for much larger numbers of cases in the near future. As the numbers of cases on which such research can be conducted increases, concerns regarding generalizability of findings will decrease accordingly.

Aggregation of information is closely bound to the matter of generalizability, which in traditional interindividual differences designs is often considered accomplished if one simply uses large, representative samples of participants. We cannot underscore strongly enough, however, that simply gathering information on large samples of participants and averaging over them as the way to develop general conclusions is a false hope for developmental science. The most likely outcome of basing averages on larger and larger samples is weaker and weaker relations among important variables. We should remember, and take seriously, the old adage regarding learning less and less about more and more until one knows nothing about everything.

As Molenaar (2004) indicated, there is much more to be concerned about in large aggregations than sheer numbers of participants. Heterogeneity of within-person structures in large numbers of participants may be obscured, and standard kinds of analyses such as factor analysis of cross sections of the participants can fail to detect that is the case. Plausible modeling outcomes can be obtained under such conditions, and no indications arise to warn the data analyst that the apparently meaningful results are, in fact, meaningless. A thorough examination of intraindividual variability is necessary to detect such circumstances. That is a primary reason why our approach to aggregation (and generalizability) is more one of accretion based on informed judgments regarding the appropriateness of combining cases rather than blithely aggregating and finding some kind of average.

DEVELOPMENTAL RESEARCH ISSUES AND QUESTIONS

Closing a methodological chapter with a discussion of research issues and questions may seem a little like putting the horse after the cart. But in this case, we believe that it is first imperative to state a number of points regarding methodology if the comments we wanted to make regarding research issues and questions are to be construed the way we intend. This final section examines the matter of research issues and questions in light of our emphases on individuals and intraindividual variability, latent variable modeling via multivariate measurement models, and looking at similarities rather than differences.

Browne and Nesselroade (2005) distinguished between studying changes from a stasis/equilibrium versus studying change from a process/change perspective. The stasis/equilibrium perspective dominated psychology, even developmental psychology (e.g., see Overton, 2006), the biological sciences (Levins & Lewontin, 1985), and the

physical sciences (Holling, 1973), well into the 20th century. One need only attend to the psychometric literature on the measurement of change up through the 1960s and beyond (e.g., see Cronbach & Furby, 1970) to understand the profound grip an ontological commitment to a world that is ultimately static and fixed has had on the nature of the research enterprise. A strong parallel exists here with the distinctions raised by Baltes (1973) in discussing the significance of bringing a "developmental perspective" to bear on research problems, and not just developmental research problems—any research problems. This distinction implies that not only are the measurement, design, and modeling efforts at stake but also the very phrasing of the research questions. In the presentation of some individual-level modeling techniques, Browne and Nesselroade (2005) illustrated the point simply with the contrast between asking, "Which of these intelligence tests shows the highest test-retest correlation?" versus "How much more does Anxiety fluctuate than Guilt?" Underlying the first question is the belief that intelligence is a highly stable attribute, and departures of the test-retest correlation from 1.00 are mainly indicative of unreliability of measurement. Underlying the second question is the belief that emotions naturally fluctuate. Given that, it is of interest to see how they fluctuate. In one view, stability and equilibrium are tacitly assumed; in the other view, change is a given.

It bears repeating (see Browne & Nesselroade, 2005) that one can measure and analyze intraindividual variation from a purely static perspective, if that is one's goal. For example, in a sample of older adults, Eizenman, Nesselroade, Featherman, and Rowe (1997) found that those who showed greater week-to-week fluctuation in their reported control (internality) beliefs were at greater risk for mortality than those who showed small amounts of week-to-week fluctuation, regardless of mean level around which the fluctuations occurred. Here the predictor was the magnitude of within-person fluctuations (intraindividual variability). In this case, however, the analytical thrust was the traditional one of predicting between-person differences from between-person differences. Although the between-person differences had to do with within-person variability, the emphasis was on stable features (amount of intraindividual variability) of the within-person changes.

Psychological research has not had the rich history with the study of intraindividual variability via time series modeling that it has enjoyed with other kinds of variability that is typically modeled via various forms of regression analysis. It is not easy to collect sufficient numbers of repeated measurements on N = 1 to provide reliable parameter estimates. Multiplying the number of such intensively measured cases further increases the difficulties of collecting such data. Moreover, outspoken concerns regarding generalizability have been detrimental in this regard. We believe the concerns over generalizability have been overstated, because of a narrow interpretation of the important features of generalizability. With a few exceptions (e.g., psychophysiology; see also Glass, Willson, & Gottman, 1972; Gottman, McFall, & Barnett, 1969; Larsen, 1987), psychologists have tended to frame their research questions, and collect and analyze their data from other perspectives. If the study of development is to embrace what we believe is a much needed, more process-oriented, intraindividual variability perspective, this will have to change.

Finally, we believe that a commitment to the intraindividual variability emphasis promoted in this chapter is highly consistent with, and perhaps even foundational to, a life-span perspective in the study of development. We close with three points for why we believe this to be the case. The three ideas underlying these points are by now familiar to the reader.

First, focusing on the individual as the proper unit of analysis sets the stage for an examination of developmental processes, first and foremost, as an individual phenomenon. Of course, individuals develop in contexts, typically contexts that include other people who are also undergoing changes. But as Baltes, Reese, and Nesselroade (1977) stated several decades ago, the fundamental task of life-span developmental researchers involves identifying intraindividual change patterns first, and then interindividual differences and similarities in those intraindividual change patterns. Specifying intraindividual change patterns precisely requires making a sufficiency of repeated measurements of the individual—one of the central ideas running throughout this chapter.

Second, to be of value to the elaboration of a knowledge base, theories of development need to have the level of generality that can be achieved only when key elements include latent variables and their interrelations. We would argue that our most useful current level of sophistication in "tying down" latent variables both in terms of their manifest representations and their interrelations resides in the so-called measurement models of structural equation modeling. The measurement model approach, in turn, is highly dependent on multivariate measurement schemes of one kind or another. As discussed several times in this chapter, multivariate measurement models provide the kinds of data that we think are appropriate and necessary for exploiting

intraindividual variability conceptions and data. By carefully evaluating the proper role of concepts such as invariance, proposals such as the idiographic filter are meant to help us further capitalize on the inherent strengths of a multivariate measurement orientation.

Third, we have vigorously promoted the identification of similarities and differences among persons in patterns of intraindividual variation as a key aspect of the capitalization on intraindividual variability phenomena to understand behavior. Tools such as the idiographic filter used at the measurement level can help to eliminate irrelevant differences whereas emphasizing similarities. Clearly, this fits well with the life-span objective of identifying interindividual differences and similarities in intraindividual change patterns. Obviously, some interindividual differences can be central to our understanding of developmental mechanisms, but others ought to be minimized or even ignored. Being able to make the difficult call regarding which is which is a task with which the idiographic filter should be able to help.

Do other general approaches to building a scientific knowledge base also mesh with the objectives of elaborating the life-span approach to the study of development? Of course they do. The two disciplines of scientific psychology that Cronbach (1957, 1975) described so well involve methods that have served the study of development substantially for a century or more. However, from the perspective of extracting the most from a growing body of life-span development research and the further elaboration of a knowledge base, the surface has barely been scratched. We want more and we believe that a clearer focus on the individual and the exploitation of intraindividual variability approaches through more sophisticated measurement and modeling techniques opens some promising avenues to new advances.

REFERENCES

Allport, G. W. (1937). *Personality: A psychological interpretation.* New York: Holt, Rinehart, and Winston.

Anderson, T. W. (1963). The use of factor analysis in the statistical analysis of multiple time series. *Psychometrika, 28,* 1–24.

Baltes, P. B. (1973). Prototypical paradigms and questions in life-span research on development and aging. *The Gerontologist, 13,* 458–467.

Baltes, P. B. (1987). Theoretical propositions of life-span developmental psychology: On the dynamics between growth and decline. *Developmental Psychology, 23*(5), 611–626.

Baltes, P. B., & Baltes, M. M. (1990). Psychological perspectives on successful aging: The model of selective optimization with compensation. In P. B. Baltes & M. M. Baltes (Eds.), *Successful aging: Perspectives from the behavioral sciences* (pp. 1–34). New York: Cambridge University Press.

Baltes, P. B., Lindenberger, U., & Staudinger, U. M. (1997). Life-span theory in developmental psychology. In W. Damon (Series Ed.) & R. M. Lerner (Vol. Ed.), *Theoretical models of human development: Vol. 1, Handbook of child psychology* (5th ed.). New York: John Wiley & Sons.

Baltes, P. B., & Nesselroade, J. R. (1973). The developmental analysis of individual differences on multiple measures. In J. R. Nesselroade & H. W. Reese (Eds.), *Life-span developmental psychology: Methodological issues* (pp. 219–249). New York: Academic.

Baltes, P. B., & Nesselroade, J. R. (1979). History and rationale of longitudinal research. In J. R. Nesselroade & P. B. Baltes (Eds.), *Longitudinal research in the study of behavior and development* (pp. 1–39). New York: Academic.

Baltes, P. B., Reese, H. W., & Nesselroade, J. R. (1977). *Life-span developmental psychology: Introduction to research methods.* Monterrey, CA: Brooks/Cole.

Barlow, D. H., & Nock, M. K. (2009). Why can't we be more idiographic in our research? *Perspectives on Psychological Science, 4,* 19–21.

Bereiter, C. (1963). Some persisting dilemmas in the measurement of change. In C. W. Harris (Ed.), *Problems in measuring change.* Madison, WI: University of Wisconsin Press.

Bergman, L. R., Magnusson, D., & El-Kouri, B. M. (2003). Studying individual development in an interindividual context. Mahwah, NJ: Erlbaum.

Bisconti, T. L., & Bergeman, C. S. (2007). Understanding the adjustment to widowhood: Using dynamical systems to assess and predict trajectories of well-being. In A. D. Ong & M. Dulman (Eds.), Oxford handbook of methods in positive psychology (pp. 395–408). New York: Oxford University Press.

Boker, S. M. (2002). Consequences of continuity: The hunt for intrinsic properties within parameters of dynamics in psychological processes. *Multivariate Behavioral Research, 37,* 405–422.

Boker, S. M., & Nesselroade, J. R. (2002). A method for modeling the intrinsic dynamics of intraindividual variability: Recovering the parameters of simulated oscillators in multi-wave data. *Multivariate Behavioral Research, 37,* 127–160.

Browne, M. W., & Nesselroade, J. R. (2005). Representing psychological processes with dynamic factor models: Some promising uses and extensions of ARMA time series models. In A. Maydeu-Olivares & J. J. McArdle (Eds.), *Psychometrics: A festschrift to Roderick P. McDonald* (pp. 415–452). Mahwah, NJ: Erlbaum.

Browne, M. W., & Zhang, G. (2007). Developments in the factor analysis of individual time series. In R. Cudeck & R. C. MacCallum (Eds.), *100 years of factor analysis: Historical developments and future directions* (pp. 265–291). Mahwah, NJ: Erlbaum.

Campbell, D. T., & Stanley, J. C. (1963). Experimental and quasi-experimental designs for research on teaching. In N. L. Gage (Ed.), *Handbook of research on teaching.* Chicago: Rand McNally.

Carlson, R. (1971). Where is the person in personality research? *Psychological Bulletin, 75,* 203–219.

Carstensen, L. (1993). Motivation for social contact across the life span: A theory of socioemotional selectivity. In J. E. Jacobs (Ed.), *Nebraska symposium on motivation* (pp. 209–254). Lincoln, NE: University of Nebraska Press.

Cattell, R. B. (1952). The three basic factor–analytic research designs—their interrelations and derivatives. *Psychological Bulletin, 49,* 499–520.

Cattell, R. B. (1963a). The interaction of hereditary and environmental influences. *British Journal of Statistical Psychology, 16,* 191–210.

Cattell, R. B. (1963b). The structuring of change by P-technique and incremental R-technique. In C. W. Harris (Ed.), *Problems in measuring change* (pp. 167–198). Madison, WI: University of Wisconsin Press.

Cattell, R. B. (1966a). The data box: Its ordering of total resources in terms of possible relational systems. In R. B. Cattell (Ed.), *Handbook of multivariate experimental psychology* (pp. 67–128). Chicago, IL: Rand McNally.

Cattell, R. B. (1966b). Guest editorial: Multivariate behavioral research and the integrative challenge. *Multivariate Behavioral Research, 1,* 4–23.

Cattell, R. B. (1973). *Mood and personality.* San Francisco: Jossey-Bass.

Cattell, R. B., Cattell, A. K. S., & Rhymer, R. M. (1947). P-technique demonstrated in determining psychophysical source traits in a normal individual. *Psychometrika, 12,* 267–288.

Cattell, R. B., & Scheier, I. H. (1961). *The meaning and measurement of neuroticism and anxiety.* New York: Ronald.

Cattell, R. B., & Williams, H. F. (1953). P-technique: A new statistical device for analysing functional unities in the intact organism. *British Journal of Preventive and Social Medicine, 7,* 141–153.

Chow, S.-Y., Ferrer, E., & Hsieh, F. (Eds.). (2010). *Statistical methods for modeling human dynamics: An interdisciplinary dialogue.* New York: Routledge.

Costa, P. T., Jr. (1992). Trait psychology comes of age. In T. B. Sonderegger (Ed.), *Nebraska symposium on motivation* (pp. 169–204). Lincoln, NE: University of Nebraska Press.

Cronbach, L. J. (1957). The two disciplines of scientific psychology. *American Psychologist, 12,* 71–84.

Cronbach, L. J. (1975). Beyond the two disciplines of scientific psychology. *American Psychologist, 30*(2), 116–127.

Cronbach, L. J., & Furby, L. (1970). How should we measure "change"—or should we? *Psychological Bulletin, 74*(1), 68–80.

Cudeck, R., & MacCallum, R. C. (Eds.). (2007). *100 years of factor analysis.* Mahwah, NJ: Erlbaum.

Eddington, A. S. (1956). The theory of groups. In J. R. Newman (Ed.), *The world of mathematics* (Vol. 3, pp. 1558–1573). New York: Simon and Schuster.

Eizenman, D. R., Nesselroade, J. R., Featherman, D. L., & Rowe, J. W. (1997). Intra-individual variability in perceived control in an elderly sample: The MacArthur Successful Aging Studies. *Psychology and Aging, 12,* 489–502.

Embretson, S. E. (1996). The new rules of measurement. *Educational Assessment, 8,* 341–349.

Fiske, D. W., & Rice, L. (1955). Intra-individual response variability. *Psychological Bulletin, 52,* 217–250.

Flugel, J. C. (1928). Practice, fatigue, and oscillation. *British Journal of Psychology, Monograph Supplement, 4,* 1–92.

Ford, D. H. (1987). *Humans as self-constructing living systems.* Hillsdale, NJ: Erlbaum.

Ford, D. H., & Lerner, R. M. (1992). *Developmental systems theory: An integrative approach.* Newbury Park, CA: Sage.

Fox, N. A., & Porges, S. W. (1985). The relationship between neonatal heart period patterns and developmental outcome. *Child Development, 56,* 28–37.

Friedman, B. J., & Santucci, A. K. (2003). Idiodynamic profiles of cardiovascular activity: A P–technique approach. *Integrative Physiological & Behavioral Science, 38*(4), 295–315.

Ghisletta, P., Nesselroade, J. R., Featherman, D. L., & Rowe, J. W. (2002). The structure, validity, and predictive power of weekly intraindividual variability in health and activity measures. *Swiss Journal of Psychology, 61,* 73–83.

Glass, G. V., Willson, V. L., & Gottman, J. M. (1972). *Design and analysis of time-series experiments (Laboratory of Educational Research Report).* Boulder, CO: University of Colorado.

Goldberg, L. R. (1990). An alternative "Description of Personality": The big–five factor structure. *Journal of Personality and Social Psychology, 59,* 1216–1229.

Gottlieb, G. (2003). On making behavior genetics truly developmental. *Human Development, 46,* 337–355.

Gottman, J. M., McFall, R. M., & Barnett, J. T. (1969). Design and analysis of research using time series. *Psychological Bulletin, 72*(4), 299–306.

Goulet, L. R., & Baltes, P. B. (Eds.). (1970). *Life-span developmental psychology: Research and theory.* New York: Academic.

Hamaker, E. L., Dolan, C. V., & Molenaar, P. C. M. (2005). Statistical modeling of the individual: Rational and application of multivariate stationary time series analysis. *Multivariate Behavioral Research, 40,* 207–233.

Harris, C. W. (Ed.). (1963). *Problems in measuring change.* Madison, WI: University of Wisconsin Press.

Hertzog, C., Dixon, R. A., & Hultsch, D. F. (1992). Intraindividual change in text recall of the elderly. *Brain and Language, 42,* 248–269.

Holling, C. S. (1973). Resilience and stability of ecological systems. *Annual Review of Ecology and Systematics, 4,* 1–23.

Holtzman, W. H. (1963). Statistical models for the study of change in the single case. In C. W. Harris (Ed.), *Problems in measuring change* (pp. 199–211). Madison, WI: University of Wisconsin Press.

Horn, J. L. (1972). State, trait, and change dimensions of intelligence. *British Journal of Educational Psychology, 42,* 159–185.

Hultsch, D. F., & MacDonald, S. W. (2003). Intraindividual variability in performance as a theoretical window onto cognitive aging. In R. A. Dixon, L.-G. Nilsson, & L. Beckman (Eds.), *New frontiers in cognitive aging.* New York: Oxford University Press.

Hultsch, D. F., Strauss, E., Hunter, M. A., & MacDonald, S. W. S. (2008). Intraindividual variability, cognition, and aging. In F. I. M. Craik & T. A. Salthouse (Eds.), *The handbook of aging and cognition* (pp. 491–556). New York: Psychology Press.

Jones, C. J., & Nesselroade, J. R. (1990). Multivariate, replicated, single-subject designs and P-technique factor analysis: A selective review of the literature. *Experimental Aging Research, 16,* 171–183.

Jöreskog, K. G. (1969). A general approach to confirmatory maximum likelihood factor analysis. *Psychometrika, 34,* 183–202.

Kagan, J. (1994). *Galen's prophecy.* New York: Basic Books.

Kagan, J. (2007). A trio of concerns. *Perspectives on Psychological Science, 2,* 361–376.

Keyser, C. J. (1956). The group concept. In J. R. Newman (Ed.), *The world of mathematics* (Vol. 3, pp. 1538–1557). New York: Simon and Schuster.

Kim, J., Nesselroade, J. R., & McCullough, M. E. (2009). Dynamic factor analysis of worldviews/religious beliefs and well-being among older adults. *Journal of Adult Development, 16,* 87–100.

Lamiell, J. T. (1981). Toward an idiothetic psychology of personality. *American Psychologist, 36,* 276–289.

Lamiell, J. T. (1988, August). Once more into the breach: Why individual differences research cannot advance personality theory. Paper presented at the Annual Meeting of the American Psychological Association, Atlanta, GA.

Lamiell, J. T. (1998). "Nomothetic" and "idiographic": Contrasting Windelband's understanding with contemporary usage. *Theory and Psychology, 8*(1), 23–38.

Larsen, R. J. (1987). The stability of mood variability: A spectral analytic approach to daily mood assessments. *Journal of Personality and Social Psychology, 52,* 1195–1204.

Lautrey, J., & De Ribaupierre, A. (2004). Psychology of human intelligence in France and French-speaking Switzerland. In R. J. Sternberg (Ed.), *International handbook of intelligence* (pp. 104–134). Cambridge: Cambridge University Press.

Lebo, M. A., & Nesselroade, J. R. (1978). Intraindividual differences dimensions of mood change during pregnancy identified in five P-technique factor analyses. *Journal of Research in Personality, 12,* 205–224.

Lerner, R. M., & Overton, W. F. (2008). Exemplifying the integrations of the relational developmental system: Synthesizing theory, research, and application to promote positive development and social justice. *Journal of Adolescent Research, 23,* 245–255.

Lerner, R. M., Schwartz, S. J., & Phelps, E. (2009). Problematics of time and timing in the longitudinal study of human development: Theoretical and methodological issues. *Human Development, 52,* 44–68.

Levins, R., & Lewontin, R. (1985). *The dialectical biologist.* Cambridge: Harvard University Press.

Little, T. D., Bouvaird, J. A., & Card, N. A. (Eds.). (2007). *Modeling contextual effects in longitudinal studies.* Mahwah, NJ: Erlbaum.

Luborsky, L., & Mintz, J. (1972). The contribution of P-technique to personality, psychotherapy, and psychosomatic research. In R. M. Dreger (Ed.), *Multivariate personality research: Contributions to the understanding of personality in honor of Raymond B. Cattell* (pp. 387–410). Baton Rouge, LA: Claitor's Publishing Division.

Magnusson, D. (1997). The logic and implications of a person approach. In R. B. Cairns, L. R. Bergman, & J. Kagan (Eds.), *The individual as a focus in developmental research.* New York: Sage.

Magnusson, D. (2000). The individual as the organizing principle in psychological inquiry: A holistic approach. In L. R. Bergman, R. B. Cairns, L. G. Nilsson, & L. Nystedt (Eds.), *Developmental science and the holistic approach* (pp. 33–47). Mahwah, NJ: Erlbaum.

Magnusson, D. (2003). The person approach: Concepts, measurement models, and research strategy. In *New directions for child and adolescent development* (pp. 3–23). New York: Wiley Periodicals, Inc.

McArdle, J. J., Grimm, K. J., Hamagami, F., & Bowles, R. P. (2009). Modeling life-span growth curves of cognition using longitudinal data with multiple samples and changing scales of measurement. *Psychological Methods, 14,* 126–149.

McArdle, J. J., & Nesselroade, J. R. (2003). Growth curve analysis in developmental research. In J. Schinka & W. Velicer (Eds.), *Comprehensive handbook of psychology: Vol. 2, Research methods in psychology.* New York: Pergamon.

McCrae, R. R., & Costa, Jr., P. T. (1999). A five-factor theory of personality. In L. A. Pervin & O. P. John (Eds.), *Handbook of personality* (2nd ed.). New York: Guilford.

Meredith, W. (1993). Measurement invariance, factor analysis and factor invariance. *Psychometrika, 58,* 525–543.

Meredith, W., & Tisak, J. (1990). Latent curve analysis. *Psychometrika, 55,* 107–122.

Millsap, R. E., & Meredith, W. (2007). Factorial invariance: Historical perspectives and new problems. In R. Cudeck & R. C. MacCallum (Eds.), *100 years of factor analysis* (pp. 131–152). Mahwah, NJ: Erlbaum.

Mischel, W., Shoda, Y., & Mendoza-Denton, R. (2002). Situation-behavior profiles as a locus of consistency in personality. *Current Directions in Psychological Science, 11,* 50–54.

Mitteness, L. S., & Nesselroade, J. R. (1987). Attachment in adulthood: Longitudinal investigation of mother-daughter affective interdependencies by P-technique factor analysis. *The Southern Psychologist, 3,* 37–44.

Molenaar, P. C. M. (1985). A dynamic factor model for the analysis of multivariate time series. *Psychometrika, 50*(2), 181–202.

Molenaar, P. C. M. (2004). A manifesto on psychology as idiographic science: Bringing the person back into scientific psychology —

this time forever. *Measurement: Interdisciplinary Research and Perspectives, 2,* 201–218.

Molenaar, P. C. M. (2009). Commentary on Nesselroade et al. Idiographic filters. *Measurement: Interdisciplinary Research and Perspectives, 7,* 13–15.

Molenaar, P. C. M., & Nesselroade, J. R. (2009). The recoverability of p-technique factor analysis. *Multivariate Behavioral Research, 44,* 130–141.

Molenaar, P. C. M., & Nesselroade, J. R. (2010). "Modeling process with the idiographic filter." Unpublished manuscript, Department of Psychology, University of Virginia.

Molenaar, P. C. M., Sinclair, K. O., Rovine, M. J., Ram, N., & Corneal, S. E. (2009). Analyzing developmental processes on an individual level using nonstationary time series modeling. *Developmental Psychology, 45,* 260–271.

Moskowitz, D. S., & Hershberger, S. L. (Eds.). (2002). *Modeling intraindividual variability with repeated measures data.* Mahwah, NJ: Erlbaum.

Nesselroade, J. R. (1988). Some implications of the trait–state distinction for the study of development across the life span: The case of personality research. In P. B. Baltes, D. L. Featherman, & R. M. Lerner (Eds.), *Life-span development and behavior* (Vol. 8, pp. 163–189). Hillsdale, NJ: Erlbaum.

Nesselroade, J. R. (1991). The warp and woof of the developmental fabric. In R. Downs, L. Liben, & D. Palermo (Eds.), *Visions of development, the environment, and aesthetics: The legacy of Joachim F. Wohlwill* (pp. 213–240). Hillsdale, NJ: Erlbaum.

Nesselroade, J. R. (2002). Elaborating the different in differential psychology. *Multivariate Behavioral Research, 37*(4), 543–561.

Nesselroade, J. R. (2005). Quantitative modeling in adult development and aging: Reflections and projections. In C. S. Bergeman & S. M. Boker (Eds.), *Quantitative methods in aging research* (pp. 1–17). Mahwah, NJ: Erlbaum.

Nesselroade, J. R. (2007). Factoring at the individual level: Some matters for the second century of factor analysis. In R. Cudeck & R. MacCallum (Eds.), *100 years of factor analysis* (pp. 249–264). Mahwah, NJ: Erlbaum.

Nesselroade, J. R. (in press). On an emerging third discipline of scientific psychology. In K. M. Newell & P. C. M. Molenaar (Eds.), *Individual pathways of change and development.* Washington, DC: American Psychological Association.

Nesselroade, J. R., & Estabrook, C. R. (2009). Factor invariance, measurement, and studying development over the lifespan. In H. Bosworth & C. K. Hertzog (Eds.), *Aging and cognition: Research methodologies and empirical advances* (pp. 39–53). Washington, DC: American Psychological Association.

Nesselroade, J. R., & Ford, D. H. (1985). P-technique comes of age: Multivariate, replicated, single-subject designs for research on older adults. *Research on Aging, 7,* 46–80.

Nesselroade, J. R., & Ford, D. H. (1987). Methodological considerations in modeling living systems. In M. E. Ford & D. H. Ford (Eds.), Humans as self-constructing living systems: Putting the framework to work (pp. 47–79). Hillsdale, NJ: Erlbaum.

Nesselroade, J. R., Gerstorf, D., Hardy, S. A., & Ram, N. (2007). Idiographic filters for psychological constructs. *Measurement: Interdisciplinary Research and Perspectives, 5,* 217–235.

Nesselroade, J. R., McArdle, J. J., Aggen, S. H., & Meyers, J. M. (2002). Alternative dynamic factor models for multivariate time-series analyses. In D. M. Moskowitz & S. L. Hershberger (Eds.), *Modeling intraindividual variability with repeated measures data: Advances and techniques* (pp. 235–265). Mahwah, NJ: Erlbaum.

Nesselroade, J. R., & Molenaar, P. (2003). Quantitative models for developmental processes. In J. Valsiner & K. Connolly (Eds.), *Handbook of developmental psychology* (pp. 622–639). London: Sage.

Nesselroade, J. R., & Molenaar, P. C. M. (1999). Pooling lagged covariance structures based on short, multivariate time-series for dynamic factor analysis. In R. H. Hoyle (Ed.), *Statistical strategies for small sample research* (pp. 224–250). Newbury Park, CA: Sage.

Nesselroade, J. R., Ram, N., Gerstorf, D., & Hardy, S. A. (2009). Rejoinder to commentaries on Nesselroade, Gerstorf, Hardy, and Ram. *Measurement: Interdisciplinary Research and Perspectives, 7,* 17–26.

Newell, K. M., & Molenaar, P. C. M. (Eds.). (in press). *Individual pathways of change and development.* Washington, DC: American Psychological Association.

Overton, W. F. (2006). Developmental psychology: Philosophy, concepts, methodology. In W. Damon (Series Ed.) & R. M. Lerner (Vol. Ed.), *Theoretical models of human development: Vol. 1, Handbook of child psychology* (6th ed., pp. 18–88). Hoboken, NJ: John Wiley & Sons.

Overton, W. F., & Reese, H. W. (1973). Models of development: Methodological implications. In J. R. Nesselroade & H. W. Reese (Eds.), *Life-span developmental psychology: Methodological issues* (pp. 65–86). New York: Academic.

The Oxford English Dictionary. 2nd ed. 1989. OED Online. Oxford University Press. http://dictionary.oed.com/cgi/entry/501891487.

Radloff, L. S. (1977). The CES-D scale: A self-report depression scale for research in the general population. *Applied Psychological Measurement, 1,* 385–401.

Ram, N., Carstensen, L. L., & Nesselroade, J. R. (2009). "Age differences in the structure of emotional experience across the adult lifespan: Articulating individual-level theory via individual-level method." Unpublished manuscript, Department of Human Development and Family Studies, The Pennsylvania State University.

Rao, C. R. (1958). Some statistical methods for the comparison of growth curves. *Biometrics, 14,* 1–17.

Reese, H. W., & Overton, W. F. (1970). Models of development and theories of development. In L. R. Goulet & P. B. Baltes (Eds.), *Life-span developmental psychology: Research and theory* (pp. 116–145). New York: Academic.

Rogosa, D. (1988). Myths about longitudinal research. In K. W. Schaie, R. T. Campbell, W. Meredith, & S. C. Rawlings (Eds.), *Methodological issues in aging research* (pp. 171–209). New York: Springer.

Rosenzweig, S. (1958). The place of the individual and of idiodynamics in psychology: A dialogue. *Journal of Individual Psychology, 14,* 3–20.

Rosenzweig, S. (1986). Idiodynamics vis-a-vis psychology. *American Psychologist, 41,* 241–245.

Salthouse, T. A., Nesselroade, J. R., & Berish, D. E. (2006). Short-term variability and the calibration of change. *Journal of Gerontology: Psychological Sciences, 61,* 144–151.

Sameroff, A. J., Peck, S. C., & Eccles, J. L. (2004). Changing ecological determinants of conduct problems from early adolescence to early adulthood. *Development and Psychopathology, 16,* 873–896.

Schmidt, K. M., & Embretson, S. E. (2003). Item response theory and measuring abilities. In I. B. Weiner (Series Ed.) & J. Schinka & W. F. Velicer (Eds.), *Research methods in psychology: Vol. 2, Handbook of Psychology.* Hoboken, NJ: John Wiley & Sons.

Sidman, M. (1960). *Tactics of scientific research: Evaluating experimental data in psychology.* New York: Basic Books.

Sliwinski, M. J., Smyth, J. M., Hofer, S. M., & Stawski, R. S. (2006). Intraindividual coupling of daily stress and cognition. *Psychology and Aging, 21,* 545–557.

Spielberger, C. D., Gorsuch, R. L., & Lushene, R. (1969). *The State-Trait Anxiety Inventory (STAI) test manual, form x.* Palo Alto, CA: Consulting Psychologists Press.

Stemmler, G. (1992). *Differential psychophysiology: Persons in situations.* Berlin: Springer-Verlag.

Thouless, R. H. (1936). Test unreliability and function fluctuation. *British Journal of Psychology, 26,* 325–343.

Torgerson, W. J. (1958). *Theory and methods of scaling.* New York: John Wiley & Sons.

Tucker, L. R. (1958). Determination of parameters of a functional relation by factor analysis. *Psychometrika, 23,* 19–23.

Tucker, L. R. (1966). Learning theory and multivariate experiment: Illustration by determination of generalized learning curves. In R. B. Cattell (Ed.), *Handbook of multivariate experimental psychology* (pp. 476–501). Chicago: Rand McNally.

Tucker-Drob, E. M. (2009). Differentiation of cognitive abilities across the life span. *Developmental Psychology, 45,* 1097–1118.

van Kampen, V. (2000). Idiographic complexity and the common personality dimensions of insensitivity, extraversion, neuroticism, and orderliness. *European Journal of Personality, 14,* 217–243.

Wohlwill, J. F. (1973). *The study of behavioral development.* New York: Academic.

Woodrow, H. (1932). Quotidian variability. *Psychological Review, 39,* 245–256.

Wundt, W. (1897). *Outlines of psychology* (C. H. Judd, Trans.). Leipzig: Wilhelm Engleman.

Zevon, M., & Tellegen, A. (1982). The structure of mood change: Idiographic/nomothetic analysis. *Journal of Personality and Social Psychology, 43,* 111–122.

Zhang, Z., Browne, M. W., & Nesselroade, J. R. (2009). Factor invariance and mapping constructs to idiographic patterns of observables. Unpublished manuscript, Department of Psychology, University of Notre Dame.

CHAPTER 3

What Life-Span Data Do We Really Need?

JOHN J. MCARDLE

This chapter reviews various methodological innovations in life-span research that have come as a direct result of advances in dealing with incomplete data using structural equation models (SEMs). The broad methodological topics include statistical power, multivariate scale and item measurement, and longitudinal and dynamic measurements.

Some of the newest presentations on longitudinal data analysis based on latent curve analysis seem to promote these techniques as entirely new methodology. In fact, the classical analysis of variance (ANOVA) designs (e.g., Fisher, 1925, 1940) set the stage for the majority of contemporary analyses. Another important contribution to this area

This work was supported by the National Institute on Aging (grant AG-7137–20). This chapter is dedicated to the memory of R. Q. Bell (University of Virginia), who became my friend and mentor during the 1990s. I thank my colleagues John R. Nesselroade (University of Virginia), Kevin J. Grimm (University of California at Davis), and John J. Prindle (University of Southern California), as well as the editor, Willis Overton, for their important contributions to earlier versions of this work.

was the classic set of articles that R. Q. Bell (1953, 1954) wrote on accelerated longitudinal data and convergence analysis. New computer programs for latent curve/mixed-effects modeling have allowed these interesting concepts to be more fully realized, and this has been extended to deal with multivariate dynamic models as well. Although it does not seem clear to many contemporary researchers, the current work is far less revolutionary than the past work. The main methodological point made in this chapter is that "less can be more" in terms of data collection and data analyses, but we need to be aware of "how many" and "which ones" when we eliminate some of our data. Some historical highlights are merged with my own research to illustrate that several contemporary design features can be seen as practical solutions to otherwise prohibitively costly life-span research.

THE NEED FOR APPROXIMATIONS IN LIFE-SPAN RESEARCH

Life-Span Approximations

The human life span is fairly long, at least compared with other mammals and insects (Finch, 2007). So what do we want to know about humans during this time period? Some of us want to know about specific things that happen to some people and not to other people—especially the bad and good things. Others of us want to know about why these things happen at all—mainly to avoid the bad and accumulate the good. A variety of compelling questions such as these are often asked in specific contexts by psychological researchers who want answers soon (i.e., "Actually right now!"). Others are willing to wait a bit longer (i.e., "Before I die would be nice."), but hardly anyone wants to wait until after they are dead and gone for reasonable answers. Sadly, most of the things we would like to know about the full life span we probably cannot live long enough to find out. So we approximate the answers, and how well we do these approximations forms our own life story.

It is not surprising that all kinds of approximations surround us (see McKibben, 1992). When we take pictures of our children at various ages and line them up on a wall, we end up with a sort of chronology of their life up to some point. It is only when we talk about these pictures that we realize these are discrete snapshots and largely incomplete descriptions of the children. This chronology seems to improve in accuracy if we have taken more and more pic-

tures, but we realize this is never as much depth as would be a continuous stream, or a movie, of their life—being there makes all the difference. Movies of children's lives do provide more depth at a particular time, but movies do not show everything of importance largely because we focus on specific individual events (e.g., birthday parties or graduations). Of course, it does not seem humanly possible to have a movie of an entire life, although people have considered it (see *Seven Up!* directed by P. Almond, 1964; *The Truman Show,* directed by Peter Weir, 1998, with Jim Carrey; *The Final Cut,* written and directed by Omar Naim, 2004, with Robin Williams). And yet, our discrete approximations can be surprisingly useful. When we compare these chronological snapshots across several different children, the individual differences can be striking, and it is clear no child within the family has developed in exactly the same way. When looking at pictures in other people's houses, it is also clear that members of my family are more similar than members of other families. So, as children will themselves often ask, where is the limit to this family chronology? That is, how many snapshots or movies are actually needed?

Although the title of this chapter is intentionally provocative, this chapter is not flippant. Instead, it is intended to be a serious consideration about what we have already learned about the life-span approximations we can use and still tell a reasonable life-span story. This chapter focuses on which aspects of these life-span approximations are most crucial, and by recognizing what we do not need to do, hopefully we will learn more about what we actually need to do.

The Analysis of Variance Approach to Incomplete Design Structures

As with most topics in methodology, the newest approaches are not radically new at all. In early work on this topic, R. A. Fisher (1925, 1940; see Box, 1980) developed several key suggestions for researchers. In the first part of this work, a model based on the "ANOVA of a two-way layout" was used to separate conditional means of main effects (i.e., A and B) from the potential of an interaction (A by B). These statistical developments have been widely used by psychological researchers even in cases where the design factors are not explicitly controlled by the experimenter (see Shadish, Cook, & Campbell, 2002). However, of most importance here are advanced designs discussed at considerable length in the classical ANOVA literature—the so-called Split Plots, the Latin Square, the Fractional Factorial, or the Randomized Blocks designs.

In each of these well-known design features, the main effects or specific interactions were considered of paramount importance, so less emphasis is placed on having a fully crossed set of independent factors. These statistical models require less data to be collected, but under strictly prespecified design conditions, and the analytic models based on less degrees of freedom (i.e., no interaction is assumed; see Maxwell & Delany, 1990). Without going into too much detail on this algebra, it is fair to say that these designs represent clear-cut cases where the information in the independent manipulated factors is spread out to cover a wider range of treatments using the same number of participants (or possibly plants!).

One important variation on this ANOVA formulation that was subsequently developed in clinical psychology was the Solomon four-group design (Solomon, 1949; see Figure 3.3a). It was clear that pretest and post-test measurement led to a powerful way to examine treatment effects, but the practical problem raised was that the act of measuring might, in fact, create difference in outcomes, either by learning something from the testing or by creating (and then expressing) expectations about the treatment efficacy. Thus, the act of pretesting created a potential bias and added to potential confounds of results (i.e., those not treated might get better by testing alone). To answer these practical questions using a structured design, researchers first randomly assigned individuals to treatment groups, and then randomly assigned individuals to be measured (or not) on the pretest variable. Individuals were either trained or not, and all individuals participated in the post-test measurement. This creative four-group design allowed for less ambiguous estimation of potential treatment effects separated from potential testing effects (see What People Do We Really Need? section later in this chapter).

Researchers have found many creative ways to analyze average trends in longitudinal data using ANOVA. When the observations are repeated measurements on the same individuals, research in the behavioral sciences has relied on advanced versions of the linear growth models (e.g., Bock, 1975). There is no doubt that these classical methods provide powerful and accurate tests. However, the introduction of individual differences in change analyses has led to a great deal of statistical controversy in model fitting. For example, there are many published data analyses where the *observed difference scores* or *rates of change scores* are used as outcomes in data analyses (e.g., Allison, 1990). These change score calculations are relatively simple and theoretically meaningful. However, the potential confounds because of the accumulation of random errors has been a key concern in previous studies using observed change scores or rate of change scores (e.g., Burr & Nesselroade, 1990; Rogosa & Willett, 1983).

Cross-Sectional and Longitudinal Designs in Life-Span Research

In life-span research, we, out of necessity, often live with simple observational experimental designs that do not require continuous measurement over a whole life span. In essence, we try to *accelerate* the production of answers to our questions. Of course, we still want to build in some empirical checks against making the wrong claims, so we try to keep in mind that the purpose of any experimental design is *to minimize variation that we are not interested in and to maximize variation in what we are interested in* (Thurstone, 1937). We require that the same picture taken from different angles yields the same story—we require *convergence* of information (see next section).

It seems that the simplest way we can do this is to take a cross-sectional approach to measurement—measure people right now but include people of various ages. To claim that the *differences* between ages is a good surrogate for the *changes* within people over age, we typically make the assumption that the younger ones will turn into the older ones, or that the older ones were, at some prior time, just like the younger ones. These cross sections allow us to characterize the *differences* between the younger and older persons as if these were the expected *changes*. This is the most common experimental design in life-span research, and many researchers have pointed out how this is obviously flawed (e.g., Nesselroade & Baltes, 1979; Wohlwill, 1973). Although cross-sectional design is a rather rapid way to understand changes, the cost of the design comes when our measurements are susceptible to what are widely known as "cohort" effect—in simple terms, the younger ones now are *not* exactly like the younger ones then, and the younger ones may *not* be traveling on the same path as the older ones. Cross sections do accelerate or speed up information acquisition, but they do not provide a test of convergence; that is, they do not look at the same people from different angles (different ages).

As a result, we move toward the other extreme—the longitudinal method. Here we know we can measure the same people, on the same instruments, and under the same conditions (i.e., measure convergence); thus, we can evaluate the changes directly. The term *growth curve analysis* is a common research technique in developmental investigations. In a general sense, this term denotes the processes of describing, testing hypotheses, and making scientific inferences about the growth and change patterns in a wide range of time-related phenomena. Growth curve data have unique features: (1) the same entities are repeatedly observed, (2) the same procedures of measurement and scaling of observations are used, and (3) the timing of the observations is known. These features lead to unusual opportunities for developmental data analysis.

This longitudinal talk all sounds perfectly reasonable, even special, and as a result, longitudinal data analysis enjoys a great deal of practical face validity (see McArdle, 2009). But what do we do if the people do not want to participate in this testing again? Or what if we cannot locate the same people to again ask the same questions? Or what if they die before we can measure them again? Or what if the first experience has altered their behavior (i.e., they are better at taking the test)? Or what if the conditions of measurement have changed? Or what if not enough time has gone by for the people to change very much? These are all real threats to the validity of the longitudinal change information.

Nevertheless, we are often stuck somewhere between the simplest measurement procedure, the cross-sectional design, and the most complex measurement design, the longitudinal time-series approach. Many others have grappled with these questions before, and often people defend results from cross-sectional differences or longitudinal changes. More well- reasoned answers almost always come in the form of some mixture of the cross-sectional and longitudinal methods. In gerontology, this general strategy is termed a *cohort-sequential design* (Schaie, 1965; but see Cattell, 1970). In sociology, this data collection is often termed a *longitudinal panel* (Frees, 2004). In econometrics, this data collection is often termed a *cross-sectional time-series design* (Hsiao, 2003). In other scientific areas, there are likely to be other terms for this same data collection design.

Contributions of R. Q. Bell on Accelerated Data and Convergence Analysis

Many of the newest presentations on longitudinal data analysis are based on the concept of a *trajectory over time,* and many new presentations seem to promote the available techniques as entirely new methodology. For example, methodological summaries in the 2000s of the *Annual Review of Psychology* includes articles by Raudenbush (2001), Collins (2006), MacKinnon, Fairchild, and Fritz (2007), and McArdle (2009), which are all based on

this trajectory concept. However, a few classical studies actually set the stage for the great majority of contemporary trajectory analyses. One of these was the classic set of articles written by R. Q. Bell (1953, 1954). Of course, new computer programs for latent curve/mixed-effects modeling have allowed these classical concepts to be realized, but the current work is far less revolutionary than the past work. To illustrate these issues, this section uses contemporary techniques to fit the longitudinal concepts of growth from the classic study of Bell (1954).

In this context, some of Bell's (1953, 1954)[1] early conjectures were both interesting and provocative—one of these important conjectures is depicted in the theoretical growth curves of Figure 3.1. In the early 1950s, Bell was working at the National Institute of Mental Health (NIMH) developmental laboratories studying various ways to examine changes in physical and mental health. The problems of inferences about changes from cross-sectional differences were already well known, so the longitudinal data collection approach was gaining momentum. However, Bell, although supporting longitudinal data collection, also critiqued the potential problems of longitudinal retesting, including both selection effects and practice effects. As a resolution of these problems, he suggested a combination of longitudinal and cross-sectional data; a data collection he termed *accelerated longitudinal* data. The plots of Figure 3.1a show a hypothetical "true curve" over ages 6 to 14 (white triangles) for both a 13-year longitudinal collection of data (white circles) and a 3-year set of cross-sectional and longitudinal sequences (black circles).

In this first article, he suggested this complex accelerated longitudinal data collection design would be a nearly optimal way to understand growth and change processes both within and between individuals. In a second article, Bell (1954) showed that these statistical procedures could be evaluated by eliminating or "masking" existing data from a more time-consuming longitudinal collection. Indeed, masking existing data is one common form of "sensitivity" analysis in statistics (e.g., Daniels & Hogan, 2008). To ensure uniformity of the outcomes, Bell suggested a test of "convergence" of the cross-sectional and longitudinal data, created by joining the shorter spans of data from people together who appeared most similar at the end points. What Bell did was to form long longitudinal segments of data on the same attribute by joining shorter

---

[1] Among many interesting paradoxes, Bell's (1953) original article was actually written the year after it was published (for details, see McArdle, 2002).

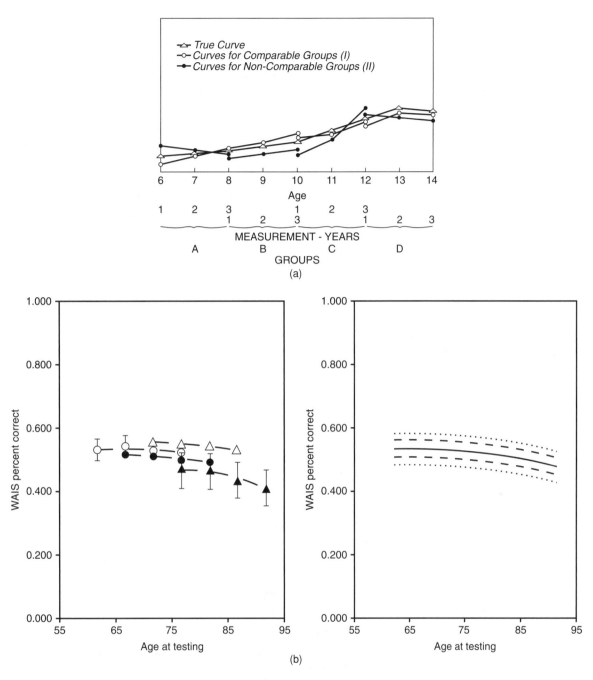

Figure 3.1 Accelerated data and convergence analysis (from Bell, 1953, 1954). (a) The "accelerated longitudinal data collection." *Triangles* represent true curve; *white circles* represent curves for comparable groups; *black circles* represent curves for noncomparable groups. (b) Bell's "convergence analysis" applied to cohort-sequential data. WAIS, Wechsler Adult Intelligence Scale.
(From McArdle, J. J., & Anderson, E. (1990). Latent variable growth models for research on aging. In J. E. Birren & K. W. Schaie (Eds.), *The handbook of the psychology of aging* (pp. 21–43). New York: Plenum Press, by permission.)

segments of longitudinal data from different persons who appeared to be maximally similar at the same age of measurement. He then demonstrated that the key model predictions were basically the same even though the data collection was much shorter—that is, the same parameters

from a repeated-measures ANOVA. Thus, Bell was both an advocate of accelerated 3-year sequences and a critic of other longitudinal measurement biases.

This general convergence approach was later revived for use with life-span data (McArdle & Anderson,

1990; McArdle & Bell, 2000; McArdle et al., 2002; Miziaki & Raudenbush, 2000). For example, McArdle and Anderson (1990) examined Wechsler Adult Intelligence Scale (WAIS) data from the Duke Longitudinal Study, where a small sample of individuals (N = 87) were initially tested on the WAIS at ages of about 60, 64, 68, and 72. The means of these groups at these ages appears in Figure 3.1b. These individuals were all measured again on the WAIS at about 3 years later at ages 63, 67, 71 and 75, and the lines in Figure 3.1b are used to connect the means at this second age. In previous work, these kinds of cohort-sequential data had been analyzed using both repeated-measures *t* test of the differences over time (within age group) and a more comprehensive between-within ANOVA model with group differences between ages (Botwinick & Seigler, 1980). However, McArdle and Anderson (1990) did something different in their analyses. They first plotted four different group trajectories over age and then asked whether a single functional growth curve over age could be used to account for these data (see the right side of Figure 3.1b). This is a contemporary form of a convergence question—for this single model to fit these four-group data, the patterns of change across individuals must yield the same ability level at the same age no matter what cohort they were in or what occasion of measurement they were tested (as in the model of Figure 3.1b). As McArdle and Anderson (1990) pointed out, this data collection design was powerful enough to reject this simplistic age-convergence idea. However, a combined four-group latent growth model fit these data well, and more complex alternatives were not needed (as presented). The general point made was that these individuals, who were in different cohorts and measured at different time points, provided cognitive data that could be viewed as simply specific samples of an age-based process (i.e., loss of cognition in older ages). McArdle and Bell (2000) and McArdle et al., (2002) extended this convergence sampling analysis with real data (see later), and Miziaki and Raudenbush (2000) provided an in-depth look at the test statistics required.

The Utility of an Experiment and Structural Equation Modeling Solutions

This chapter examines experimental designs from several perspectives, including measurements of people, scales, items, repetitions, occasion, and dynamics. But regardless of perspective, a simple principle can always be applied to evaluate the optimality of any data collection design. This principle is:

$$\text{Utility (experiment)} = \text{Information (experiment)}/ \text{Costs (experiment)} \quad (1)$$

where the Utility of an Experiment (or data collection) is defined by the Information it creates divided by the Costs it takes to carry it out. This concept of Information is intentionally vague so it can be defined in many ways (i.e., scientific insights, increased popularity, publications of results). Likewise, Costs may be defined in many ways as well (i.e., money, participant time, experimenter time). But by keeping this simple principle in mind, we can better judge the virtues of different types of data collections, and this, hopefully, will lead to the most reasonable design for our purposes.

Suppose the choice we make is a rather advanced model of analysis for our data—analyses of the dynamic relations of latent trajectories for well-measured common factors (following McArdle, 2009). Of course, to gain some direction, we may divide this more comprehensive model into smaller parts. But even with this division into smaller units, we are still required to answer some basic questions: How many people should we try to measure? How many measures should we use? How long should we measure them for? Of course, the answers to these questions depend a lot on both what we want to know (i.e., power) and the real cost of doing the data collection (e.g., money, time). The issues surrounding information versus costs (see Allison, Faith, Paultre, & Pi-Sunyer, 1997; Maxwell, 2004) is viewed here as the fundamental question of the limits of acceleration and the costs of convergence. Of course, there are many highly technical presentations on optimal experimental designs (e.g., Pukelsheim, 1993; Singer, 1995), but our goal is decidedly less formal: We simply summarize these highly technical questions and ask, "What life-span data do we really need?"

Structural Equation Modeling Solutions

When we ask questions such as "What do we really need?" we are essentially conducting a cost-benefit analysis as a thought experiment (see Equation 1), where any measurement on any person takes time and money for both the investigator and the participant. This chapter highlights how new *SEMs* can be used to deal with convergence of incomplete data (McArdle, 1994). By combining SEM with deleting, degrading, or *masking data* we have already collected (from Bell, 1954), we can consider what would have happened if we had collected only a specific selection of data in a particular way. My own view is that it behooves us to minimize, or at least trim down, the time and money it takes to obtain the life-span information (McArdle, 1994; cf., Maxwell, 2004).

In general, in the next few sections of this chapter, the masking approach used by Bell is expanded to highlight key design issues. Specifically, we want to know what information (i.e., results) would have been obtained if less data (i.e., less cost) had been collected from the very start. Many of the research articles discussed here contain detailed tables of information, and although I refer to this information, these details are not presented again here. As it turns out, this masking of data is not considered a foolproof approach; it is likely that participants will behave somewhat differently if they are asked to provide less data, or if they are not measured over longer periods, or if they are offered less money overall. But it is a good start at a better understanding of what could have been done to improve the approach. If we can ask for less data, the participants may not experience testing fatigue, may volunteer at higher rates, and there may be less impact of practice. On the other hand, the design originally chosen may be focused on answering specific questions with great precision, and these questions may turn out to be less important than originally thought. These are all questions of practical concern to any investigator, but some useful guidelines may be provided by this SEM approach.

This is not the first time that similar points about *planned missing data* have been made, especially if we consider the ANOVA designs and Bell's conjectures as versions of a more general theme (e.g., see Horn & McArdle, 1980). However, the SEM logic of dealing with incomplete data is again presented here to demonstrate just how broad and useful such a design concept can be in multivariate, longitudinal, and measurement research. In the remainder of this chapter, I more fully defend and clarify what can be inferred from life-span research based on these kinds of design statements, and I will show how the design concept has already been used.

INCOMPLETE DATA AND THE STRUCTURAL EQUATION MODEL APPROACH

Modeling Incomplete Data

It is now clear that many contemporary methods for dealing with approximations can be based on fitting observed raw-score longitudinal data—typically estimates from a theoretical model—using either likelihood-based techniques (Little & Rubin, 2002; McArdle, 1994; see later) or using some form of imputation (Gellman & Meng, 2004). Recent statistical research has focused on this incomplete data problem and has demonstrated how the previous statements about complete-case analysis are not typically true (Enders, 2001; Little & Rubin, 1987). In fact, well-meaning complete-case analyses are likely to yield unintentionally biased results.

Lord (1955) provided one of the first examples of this kind where one test *(x)* was administered to N = 1,200 people, whereas two other tests (y_1 and y_2) were each administered to only a split half of the whole group. The resulting data and analysis are reprinted in Cudeck (2000), who shows that the assumption of a single-factor model for all three tests (x, y_1, y_2) made it possible to identify a unique *maximum likelihood estimation* (MLE) of the correlation among the two variables that were never measured on the same persons (y_1 and y_2). In contemporary terms, the common score *(x)* served as an "anchor" for the correlation of the other two scores, and this simple design is one version of what is termed a *nonequivalent anchor test* (McArdle, Grimm, Hamagami, Bowles, & Meredith, 2009; von Davier, Holland, & Thayer, 2004).

This same principle can be used when individuals drop out of a longitudinal study. A typical indicator of attrition bias caused by dropouts is expressed as the mean differences at time 1 between groups that *(a)* participate at both occasions and *(b)* those that are not available at the second occasion. When we find mean differences between these groups, we have selection bias, and the question becomes, what inferences are now possible? One of the more popular features of SEM is the ability to deal directly with common problems of incomplete data. Following the well-developed lead of many statisticians (Cudeck, du Toit, & Sorbom, 2001; Hsiao, 2003; Little & Rubin, 2002), we can write any change model in terms of a sum of misfits (L_g) for multiple groups, where groups are defined as persons with the identical pattern of complete data. In this context, the SEM approach is relatively easy to understand (Enders, 2001; McArdle & Bell, 2000). In one important sense, the new SEM approach can be thought of as *dealing with all the available data,* and this can be described using path diagrams.

Structural Equation Modeling of Incomplete Data

Figure 3.2a shows an autoregressive model for data where two groups of persons have been measured on two occasions, *Y*[1] and *Y*[2] (drawn as squares), and separated by

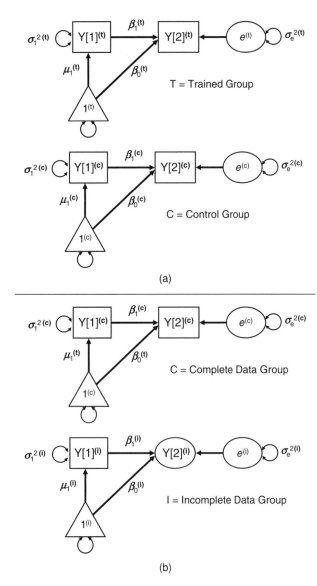

Figure 3.2 Path diagrams of multigroup structural equation models (SEMs). (a) Simplified multigroup autoregression model with group differences. (b) Simplified multigroup autoregression model with incomplete data differences.

an unspecified interval of time. The typical model of autoregression predicts observed time 2 scores from observed time 1 scores by estimating a set of regression parameters (β_0, β_1) under the assumption of unobserved and independent residuals—latent variable e (drawn as a circle). To mimic the design of a randomized experiment, we can draw this model for two independent groups of persons labeled Group T (for Trained) and Group C (for Control Subjects). In a typical analysis of experimental data, we would compare the parameters of this kind of model using a standard two-group SEM with invariance constraints, and hopefully find some differences caused by training in

the expected direction (see McArdle, 2007; McArdle & Prindle, 2008).

Figure 3.2b illustrates how it is possible to deal with incomplete data using an additional latent variable. We draw the same kind of multigroup autoregression model, but here the groups are separated by the pattern of available data—Group C (Complete on $Y[1]$ and $Y[2]$) are separated from Group I (Complete on $Y[1]$ but incomplete on $Y[2]$). This, of course, mimics the common problem of having attrition in longitudinal studies. But rather than analyzing only the data from the first group, we fit a model where that the second score ($Y[2]$) is treated as a latent variable (drawn as a circle) in the second (incomplete) group. To fit this model, we typically restrict all the parameters to be invariant over both groups. This kind of latent variable has little formal status, but it mainly act as a "placeholder" in the required matrix expressions. Horn and McArdle (1980) and McArdle (1980) termed these latent variables as *nodes* and used this device extensively to deal with age by time by cohort equations. In a subsequent and independent development, Rindskopf (1984) used the term *phantom variable* to express the same concept.

Statistical Terminology and Formulations

The SEM approach may benefit from classical terminology used in incomplete data statistical analysis (e.g., Little & Rubin, 2002). Here, the misfit of this model is a test of equality of groups only on the time 1 data, and this allows us to evaluate the *missing completely at random* (MCAR) assumptions. By requiring the invariance of the parameters over both groups, assume all data at the first time are from one population. However, because we will never know if the parameters at time 2 are the same over the two groups, we simply use the standard *missing at random* (MAR) assumptions. When we have a selection effect that is not related to the observed scores, we use the term *nonignorable missingness* (NIM). Of course, we do not solve all problems of incomplete data by simply using statistical terminology based on a clearer set of assumptions. But what this terminology does do is help us understand and classify the severity of the likely problems.

In a more general sense, we can describe the key equations used for many variables and many groups of persons ($g = 1$ to G) with the identical *pattern of incomplete data* (defined in a filter matrix F_g; for details, see McArdle & Hamagami, 1992). We assume the persons in these groups have data vectors (Y_g), and we assume some population model (as in Figure 3.2) is based on expected means (μ)

and covariances (Σ). We then can deal with incomplete data by assuming that this population model is the same for all persons no matter what pattern of data is available. This implies any model can be fit and compared with the observations by simply selecting (filtering) the relevant expectations (i.e., $\mu_g = F_g \, \mu$ and $\Sigma_g = F_g \, \Sigma \, F_g{}'$). These definitions allow us to write the *MLE* function as a model written as:

$$L^2 \text{ (model)} = \sum\nolimits_{g=1 \text{ to } G} \{ n_g \cdot L^2{}_g \}, \text{ where}$$
$$L^2{}_g = K_g + (Y_g - \mu_g)' \, \Sigma_g{}^{-1} \, (Y_g - \mu_g) \qquad (2)$$

where Y = scores of persons with a common pattern of data, K = a constant, $(Y - \mu)$ is the difference between the observed data and expected means, and Σ^{-1} = the inverse of the submatrix of observed variables within the group. The technical reader will note that the squared mean difference divided by a covariance matrix is a typical form in statistics (as Hoteling's T^2 or Mahalanobis distance, etc.; see Anderson, 1958). However, this simplified form of the model tells us a particularly interesting story. This formulation implies that the overall misfit function (L^2) and the estimated parameters (used to form μ and Σ) are based *solely on the available observed scores in each group*.

Novel Opportunities

These incomplete data SEM techniques are often used when the data could not be obtained, because of refusals, attrition, or even lack of money. If we want to make an inference about all people as if they were from the same population of interest, we start by assuming invariance of all parameters over all groups. In general, this multigroup SEM approach uses all available data on any measured variable, so it is a reasonable starting point for all further change analysis. The inclusion of all the cases, both complete and incomplete, allows us to examine the impact of attrition and possibly to correct for these biases. MAR results represent a convenient starting point, but other techniques are available for dealing with incomplete data.

Although we expect nonrandom attrition, our goal is to include all the longitudinal and cross-sectional data to provide the best estimate of the parameters of change as if everyone had continued to participate (McArdle & Anderson, 1990; McArdle & Bell, 2000; McArdle & Hamagami, 1991; McArdle, Prescott, Hamagami, & Horn, 1998). In computational terms, the available information

for any participant on any data point (i.e., any variable at any occasion) is used to build up MLEs that optimize the model parameters with respect to any available data. We can assess the goodness of fit of each model using classical statistical principles about the model likelihood (L^2) and change in fit (χ^2).

In most models to follow, we use the MAR assumption to deal with incomplete longitudinal records, and we must consider the implications of these assumptions. That is, we should try to measure the reasons why people do not participate, because nonrandom selection can create additional biases (e.g., McArdle, Small, Backman, & Fratiglioni, 2005; McArdle & Bell, 2000; Raudenbush, 2001). We are able to analyze all the data collected using these and other incomplete-data techniques (e.g., MI).

Now what may seem like minor variations of these unintentionally incomplete data SEMMAR methods can be used to improve the intentional designs of our new studies. As stated in McArdle (1994):

> Many researchers worry a great deal about incomplete data while other researchers seem not to worry at all. Such responses may indicate more about the people than the problems. With this in mind I want to say that I like incomplete data and think there should be more of it. I do not intend to be facetious, but I do wish to make a key point: *Structural equation models do not require all variables to be measured on all individuals under all conditions.* (p. 409)

The numerical examples to follow emphasize some relatively new work on this SEM approach, and this is now commonly available in much of the existing software (e.g., SAS MIXED, NLMIXED, Mplus, Mx). Although we discuss technical and substantive features of contemporary model fitting and the inferences that follow, this presentation is not intended to be overly technical. The general basis of computer software for these analyses is described, but we expect the results from different programs will be the same, and only the model to be fitted makes a real difference (for demonstration, see Ferrer, Hamagami, & McArdle, 2004). However, the key feature to note about this approach is that by using SEM, we can easily change the way we can think about the design of experiments in life-span research. Rather than simply ask, "What data can we collect?" we can ask, "What data do we really need to collect?" We will try to show how this simple conjecture poses new challenges for developmental researchers and also how aspects of these new tasks can be informed by prior research.

WHAT PEOPLE DO WE REALLY NEED?

Statistical Power and the Selection of Persons

Statistics is often defined as the sampling of people. Thus, the initial sampling of individuals is a primary concern to most researchers. The typical question asked here is, "How many can we get?" Less concern seems to be placed on the need for a *representative sampling of people*. There are now a lot of useful articles on statistical power (Allison et al., 1997; Maxwell, 2004; Maxwell, Kelley, & Rausch, 2008). Of course, the power of the *chi-square (χ^2) statistic* is well known (since 1920) for contingency table analysis. But statistical power was not a highlight of most SEM studies until the mid-1980s, and certainly did not include issues about incomplete data (see Cudeck, 2000).

Important articles by Saris and Satorra (1985, 1993) altered the way people considered power in the SEM context. The ideas used here are similar to standard SEM tests but are most useful for planning a study. In this article they suggested we generally use four specific steps:

Step 1: Create a population model Σ_0 from a prespecified path structure A_0.

Step 2: Create an alternative and more restricted population Σ_1 by eliminating terms to have a reduced path model (A_1).

Step 3: Fit the restricted model (A_1) to the initial population Σ_0 (with an SEM program).

Step 4: Using the noncentral distribution of the L^2, we can examine the power curve for many different samples sizes (n) as a test(s) of the significance of the parameters.

The resulting noncentrality index (based on $\chi^2/N - 1$) is an index of the statistical distance between population model (Σ_0) and alternative model (Σ_1). Following this simple logic, the comparison of two likelihoods has become a popular way to examine potential power ($1 - \beta$), and the basic requirement is that we have at least one model (A_0) and one alternative (A_1) based on slightly different parameters (i.e., in one model, a parameter $\beta_j = 0.5$, and in the other, the same parameter $\beta_j = 0.0$). Using this approach, we can model complex impacts by having different numbers of people measured in different ways under different models (see Fan, 2003; MacCallum, Browne, & Sugawara, 1996; Muthén & Curran, 1997; Muthén & Muthén, 2002; Raudenbush & Liu, 2000).

Random Experiments with Pretest/Post-Test Data

A basic example of pretest and post-test data can be found in the training experiment (done by Kvaschev) is reported by Stankov and Chen (1988). In this study, N = 204 high-schools students were semirandomly assigned to one of two groups: *(T)* participant in after-school training or *(C)* no-participation control. The training was focused on engagement with intellectually challenging tasks conducted by Kvaschev himself. The pretesting was done on a large set of intellectual ability measures at the beginning of the ninth grade (at about age 14), and post-testing was on the same measures at the end of the 12th grade (at about age 18). The available data for a measure of Reasoning ability *(Gf)* are plotted for on all persons in both groups as the trajectory plots in Figure 3.3a. Here the data for each individual are plotted so the pretest and the post-test are connected by a straight line. Of course, we are fairly certain that the changes do not occur in a straight line for anyone, and this is a clear limit of two-occasion data (Wohlwill, 1973). These trajectory plots represent $D = 408$ points of data (N = 204 × 2).

The initial models fitted to these data included a two-group repeated-measures ANOVA, and this was followed by an analysis of covariance (ANCOVA) model (see Stankov & Chen, 1988). For the purposes of the analysis described here, the only model used is a two-group latent difference model (from McArdle & Nesselroade, 1994). This model can be most easily seen in the first two groups of Figure 3.3b, where the $Y[1]$ and $Y[2]$ parameter expectations are formed from fixed parameters (= 1) and an unobserved or latent change score (*d* here). More details on the construction of a latent change score model, and the alternative autoregression model, can be found in McArdle (2009).

These data were used in a series of SEM analyses by McArdle and Aggen (1998). In a first model, we found that the numerical result of forcing invariance of all model parameters over both groups yields an $L^2 = 65$ with $df = 5$ (i.e., 5 parameters held the same over groups). This misfit is considered significant at the $\alpha = 0.05$ test level, so we conclude there is a significant difference between groups. In a second model, we allowed the mean of the change score to vary over groups (differences of 9.4 and 15.5) the misfit is reduced to $L^2 = 4$ with $df = 4$, and this is not significant. For our purposes, the most important index is the difference between the two models is a $\chi^2 = 61$ on $df = 1$, and this has very high power ($1 - \beta > 0.95$). From these numerical results, we conclude that the only significant

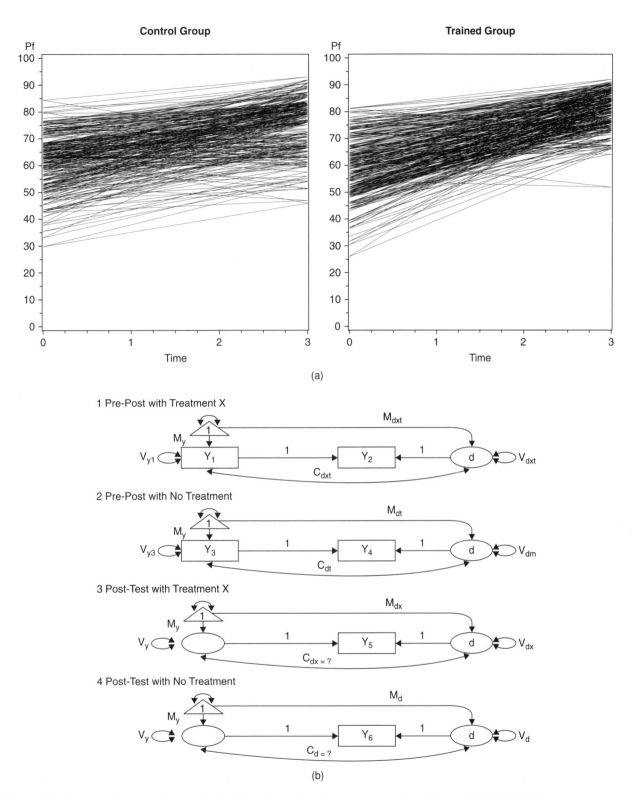

Figure 3.3   Pretest and post-test longitudinal training data and multigroup structural equation model (SEM). (a) Two-group complete case data from Kvashchev's pretest and post-test training experiment. (b) Solomon four-group analysis of variance design as a multigroup SEM with latent changes.

(From McArdle, J. J., & Aggen, S. (1998). *Structural equation models with randomized and non-randomized experiments*. Unpublished manuscript, Department of Psychology, University of Virginia, by permission.)

difference between groups comes from the means of the changes, and this mimics the typical repeated-measures *t* test. This kind of effect size would be significant (assuming $\alpha = 0.05$, $1 - \beta > 0.80$) using the Satorra–Saris approach if we had used only about n = 50 persons in each group (N = 100 with $D = 200$).

To inform future experiments, we might like to know "What would be the results if some people had not been tested at time 1?" To examine this issue, we used the same training design as in the previous change model, but now we create two additional groups by masking some of the available data—we assumed about half the persons in each group had not been measured on $Y[1]$ by design, and this creates two additional groups now included as groups 3 and 4 of Figure 3.3b. This Solomon four-group design is drawn as a multigroup SEM path model in Figure 3.3a. This is methodologically interesting because we know that the change score cannot be calculated directly using the last two groups (i.e., because they have only one score). In this case, we randomly masked half of the data at time 1 and fitted a four-group SEM with invariance constraints between and within groups (as in Figure 3.3b). After fitting the model again, now including four groups and two additional latent variables, we obtained lower power but similar results. This effect size would be significant if we had measured only n = 45 persons in each of 4 groups (N = 180, $D = 270$). This means that the lack of measurement of some participants at time 1 in this experiment would have only a small effect on this overall result.

Nonrandom Experiments with Pretest/ Post-Test Data

We also considered the potential problems of nonrandom dropout. When these data were obtained, no indicator of any dropout was present. However, for the purposes of future work, we might like to know "What would be the results if some people had dropped out by time 2?" Missing data seem quite likely for participants in this age range (ages 14–18). To examine this potential event, we randomly masked a subset of the data at time 2 for the participants and fit a four-group model similar to Figure 3.3b, but now with the last two groups having latent variables at time 2. This four-group attrition design is similar and can be drawn as a multigroup SEM path model where the four groups are separated vertically and the circles are used for $Y[2]$ variables. We slightly obtained lower power but similar results, so it appears that the lack of measurement of some participants at time 1 would have only a small effect

on this overall result. This effect size would be significant if we had only used n = 45 persons in each of 4 groups (N = 180, $D = 270$). Once again, the change score is not possible to calculate directly using the last two groups because they have only one score at $Y[2]$. The result of random assignment missing data again lowers the power of the test.

Finally, we assumed that any dropout would be selective; we split the data for both groups at the median, resulting in an upper half and a lower half, and then we split this again into training groups. By treating this as a four-group model with all data available, we obtain the same parameter values as before, but we now create a misfit ($L^2 = 325$ on $df = 10$), and this suggests the data are not MCAR equivalent over the four groups. However, the differences between C and T groups are retained, and the test of invariance of two groups of C with two groups of T is even worse ($L^2 = 390$ on $df = 15$, so $\chi^2 = 65$ on $df = 5$). If we selectively use only the data from the two groups representing the selected upper half of the data, the difference because of training is only $\chi^2 = 37$ on $df = 5$. Even worse, if we selectively use only data from the upper half of the score distribution, much like assuming these are the only ones with complete data, the difference because of training is only $\chi^2 = 19$ on $df = 5$. If this had occurred, these differences would not be significant until we had about n = 300 persons in each of 2 groups (N = 300, $D = 600$).

One way to avoid the problem of requiring more cases because of nonrandom selection (see earlier) is to use some mixture of the available data. For example, if we use both lower scoring groups plus just the upper group at the first time, the misfit of invariance is large ($L^2 = 318$ on $df = 4$), and the test of invariance over C and T is almost as high ($L^2 = 360$ on $df = 9$, so $\chi^2 = 42$ on $df = 5$). Alternatively, by using the upper groups at two times and the lower group at one occasion, we find the misfit of invariance is large ($L^2 = 318$ on $df = 4$), and the test of invariance over C and T is not as high ($L^2 = 342$ on $df = 9$, so $\chi^2 = 24$ on $df = 5$).

It may be useful to consider even more complex selection models for these data, because selective attrition may work in many ways. But two lessons can be found in this masking of data. First, the statistical power of the simple test of mean changes is more than doubled when the same person is measured twice—in fact, it is almost tripled! This mimics the well-known results of repeated-measures *t* test, where the size of the correlation over measures increases the power of the test (e.g., Bock, 1975). For studies of this size, the Solomon four-group design could be used without a big loss of power for these hypotheses. Second, the evidence provided by the incomplete data analyses suggests that the inclusion of partial attrition information (i.e., data from time 1 for people who have no data at time 2) will move us back in the direction of the unbiased answer (i.e., matching the result of the full data). Any correction for bias of the $Y[2]$ parameters cannot come from the missing data, so it must come from the differences between groups at $Y[1]$. Unfortunately, the explicit form of selection of persons to attrition groups is a critical missing piece in this statistical puzzle.

WHAT SCALES DO WE REALLY NEED?

The Common Factor Model of Scales

Psychometrics is often defined as the sampling of measures or scales, although this history is often overlooked (see McDonald, 1999). Most of these multivariate measurement models are not formed from specific items but are based on specific scales. In such cases, the common factor model of scale measurement (McDonald, 1985; McArdle, 2007) is a useful starting point.

Models for different scales can be seen to have a common basis when we write

$$Y_n = \lambda_0 + \lambda_1 c_n + u_n \tag{3}$$

where the Y is a vector of measurements (of size M), based on a smaller set of common factor scores c (of size $K < M$), and a set of unique factor scores (K). The factor loadings for the intercept (λ_0) and slope (λ_1) will have a dimensionality defined by the number of factors. The question that is raised is exactly how many measures M do we need to accurately indicate K common factors.

Experiments with Incomplete Measurements

The benefits and limitations of the SEM approach for multivariate experiments with incomplete data have been discussed by many others (e.g., McDonald, 1985). In McArdle (1994), the basic common factor model was expanded to a latent variable path model and examined from the perspective of incomplete data. Four different kinds of incomplete data were created by masking the original data to investigate the loss of accuracy or potential biases caused by having less complete multivariate data: (1) latent variables, (2) omitted variables, (3) randomly missing data, and (4) nonrandomly missing data. Power-based cost-benefit

analyses for experimental design and planning were also presented. These incomplete data approaches were closely related to models used in classical experimental design, interbattery measurement analysis, longitudinal analysis, and behavioral genetic analyses. Indeed, these SEMs for old experimental design problems indicated new opportunities for future multivariate research.

This experiment started with complete case data from eight scales on the *Wechsler Adult Intelligence Scale—Revised* (WAIS-R; N = 1,680; see Wechsler, 1955, 1981). These raw data ($D = 1,690 \times 4 = 13,520$ scale scores) were examined using a latent variable model with one or two common factors, and included age and education as extension variables for the common factors. Strong evidence initially was found using these population data that favored a two-factor (*Gf/Gc*) structure compared with a one-factor *(G)* structure ($\chi^2 = 1833$, $df = 5$). The omitted variable analyses was considered to be a set of *short forms*—exactly half the measures were masked ($M = 4$), but each selection of measures yielded a different answer to the basic question. In some cases, if four measures were chosen representing one construct, the test of one versus two factors was moot (i.e., it was always one factor, but a different one each time). In other cases, where the measures crossed the constructs (with two indicators each), some differentiation was possible, but the biggest differences between one and two factors were reduced severely. In general, it was considered easy to use the same set of scales, and the testing time would have been cut in half, but it was still difficult to choose among the short forms.

Results Based on Incomplete Measurements

The issue of results based on incomplete measurements was partly resolved by using a more complex selection design of Figure 3.4a. In the top part of this figure, we give a schematic form of the data selection: Each column here defines one of eight groups of participants, selected at random, and administered $m = 4$ (of $M = 8$) specific tests. The squares represent scales to be measured, and the circles represent scales that are not to be measured. Each column (group) has the same number of scales (4 of 8) and each scale is measured in the same number of groups (4 of 8). This was termed a *fractional block* selection of measures to recognize its ANOVA origin. The multigroup SEM analysis is presented here as if there were one group, mainly because it assumes complete invariance across all model parameters, but the locations where the scales may or may not be measured was drawn as a "circle inside a square."

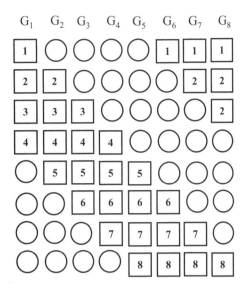

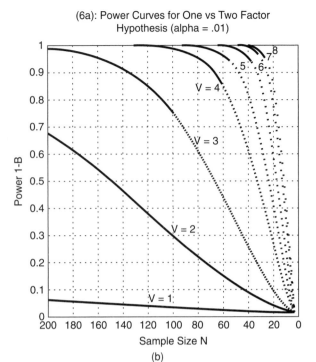

(6a): Power Curves for One vs Two Factor Hypothesis (alpha = .01)

(b)

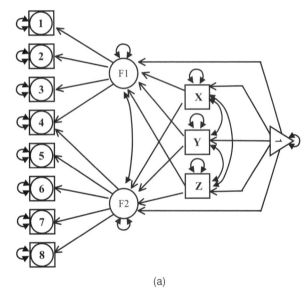

(a)

Figure 3.4 Alternative incomplete data measurement models. (a) A "fractional block" data design with the structural equation model multigroup model solution. (b) Likelihood-based power curves for subject and variables with fractional block incomplete data.

(From McArdle, J. J. (1994). Structural factor analysis experiments with incomplete data. *Multivariate Behavioral Research, 29*(4), 409–454, by permission.)

The general results from applying this kind of multigroup SEM to masked data were presented in detail, and the general result is lower but reasonable power ($\chi^2 = 544$, $df = 5$), which was considered reasonable because of the lack of half the data ($d = 6,720$ scores).

This same procedure was reapplied to the fractional factorial sampling of measures for different numbers of scales per person. The available power common factors are presented for each of these sampling conditions in Figure 3.4b. In this figure, the x-axis is the theoretical number of participants per group (N = 1–200), and the y-axis is the resulting statistical power of the χ^2 test for 1 versus 2 common factors. Each curve in the diagram is for a specific number of measures, $m = 1$ to 8, and we can see the lowest power is found for having only $m = 1$ or 2 measures; but as

soon as we reach $m = 3$ or 4 measures, we are moving up the power chart rapidly. For example, 80% power would be achieved with only $m = 4$ scales and about n = 50 in each of the 8 groups ($N = 400$, $D = 1,600$ scores). The same level of power could be obtained for $m = 3$, but this would require about n = 110 per group (n = 880, $d = 2,640$ scores). On the other hand, the advances in power for having more people on more scales ($m > 4$) seem relatively small, especially for the increased cost of testing.

Additional Results with Incomplete Measurements

Although Figure 3.4 shows most of the key ideas, a few other observations are useful. First, it was clear that a design of measurement that included some key variables (i.e., one per common factor) and randomly selected the other three indicators—a *reference variable design*—could easily be seen as the optimal design (i.e., highest power for the amount of observed data). The main problem with this design is that the best indicator needs to be known in advance of the data, so some prior results are essential.

Second, these designs were also studied under conditions of nonrandom selection to groups. One case examined was where the best scores for a person defined the group of measures used (i.e., the lowest four scores for the person were masked). This complex selection led to complex results, and it seems that this form of self-selection will not lead to a fair test of the common factor structure. Indeed, any nonrandom self-selection to group needs careful consideration, and more results are presented in McArdle (1994).

WHAT ITEMS DO WE REALLY NEED?

The Rasch Model of Item Measurement

If we examine these issues as the sampling of items, several historical treatments become clear (see Rasch, 1960; McDonald, 1999). First, two practical problems of using multiple measurements with an adult population are well known: unwanted "cognitive fatigue" and "practice effects" (see McArdle, et al., 2002; Ferrer et al., 2005). Thus, tests based on a small number of items are essential, and this begins with simply counting the items in a scale of measurement. In one extremely basic form of measurement, we assume that some attribute or construct *(c)* score exists for each individual (n = 1 to N), and a set of items (i = 1 to I) with different levels of difficulty (δ_i) can be found. We may assume the person responses to these items follow the simple expression

$$\pi_{in} = f\{c_n - \delta_i\} \tag{4a}$$

where π_{in} = the probability of the person *n* responding correctly to item *i* is some undefined function *(f)* of the score on the person's score on the underlying construct (c_n) compared with the difficulty of the item (δ_i). This simple idea that the probability of a correct response (π) is simply and directly related to the distance of the individuals' construct

score compared with the item difficulty is a fundamental form of the models in *item response theory* (IRT; see Rasch, 1960). In practice, the function *(f)* is typically a logarithmic or probit function, there may be a constant and multiplier in the fitted equation, and more complex models can be created for more complex responses (see Baker & Kim, 2004; Wilson, 2005).

Also important here is the notion of a *standard error of measurement (sem)*, and this is typically defined for binary items as

$$sem\{c_n\} = 1 / \left(\sum_{i=1\,to\,I} (\pi_{in} \cdot 1 - \pi_{in}) \right)^{1/2} \tag{4b}$$

where the accuracy with which a person is measured is both a function of the specific items selected *(i)* and their relevant probability for the specific individual. If many items are measured at many levels of difficulty, then the resulting *sem* will be very small.

It is no surprise that the number of items used in a scale can be used to estimate the overall internal consistency reliability of the scale—the Spearman and Brown prophecy formula is an index of the loss of reliability with less than a full set of items (as reported by Guilford, 1956, p. 453; McArdle & Woodcock, 1997). Furthermore, if we have a test with 10 items (*I* = 10), but we eliminate half the items to create a test with only 5 items (*i* = 5), we will inevitably reduce the accuracy of the individual score (i.e., its *sem*). But if the simple model of measurement (5) is assumed to be correct, then the number of individual items (I_n) required to measure any construct on any specific person can actually be eliminated in a more efficient fashion.

There has been a great deal of work on incomplete data problems at the level of items. Linking, equating, and calibrating refer to a series of statistical methods for comparing scores from tests (scales, measures, etc.) that do not contain the same exact set of measurements but presume to measure the same underlying construct. Most of the recent work on this topic is summarized in Dorans, Pommerich, and Holland (2007), and a good readable overview of linking scores is provided by Dorans (2007). Here he examines the general assumptions of different data collection designs and gives explicit definitions of equating, calibrating, and linking. Dorans (2007) also provides a compelling example of the importance of adequate linking using multiple health outcome instruments and how an individual's health may be misunderstood if alternative tests presumed to measure the same construct fail to do so.

The general theme of individualized adaptive testing has followed from this logic (see Embretson & Reise, 2000; Wainer, 2000). These adaptive tests are "abbreviated" but not "shortened" forms of classic tests based on some form of IRT. In a fully adaptive strategy, we administer a first set of items somewhere in the middle of the scale; then as soon as a person gets one right and one wrong, we can create an *MLE* of the estimated c_I score for that person and select the next item so it is as close to that difficulty level δ_i as possible. We can then stop at i items (or when *sem* < 1; for further details, see Baker & Kim, 2004). In theory, the newly estimated ability is based on far less than the full set of complete items (e.g., $i_n = \frac{1}{5}*I$), without major loss of reliability, adequate accuracy, and without the need to repeat any item in a second testing (i.e., no item-specific practice).

A Recent Experiment in Adaptive Testing

An experiment in cognitive adaptive testing has recently been under study by me and several colleagues. In one such collaborative study (see McArdle, Fisher, & Kadlec, 2007; Cog USA), we tried to measure Fluid Reasoning (*Gf*) using the Woodcock-Johnson (WJ-III) Number Series test in a variety of different ways, including the creation of a six-item adaptive scale. This was initiated with the normative data on the Woodcock-Johnson scales (WJ-R, WJ-III) for Number Series. In our most recent data collection and analysis, we have used the full $I = 47$ item published version of the Number Series task and evaluated its adaptive capacity with N > 1,400 adults. We have done this by evaluating the loss of reliability and validity compared with more complete data. We started with the full dataset of $I = 47$ completed items and assigned each person a total score. We then wrote an algorithm that would look at only $i = 6$ specific items in a specific adaptive order—that is, we started at a first item; if this was correct, we looked at a harder item, the next was chosen (by *MLE*), and so on. At the end of this procedure, each person was assigned a score based only on the unmasked $i_n = 6$ items (i.e., not the same 6 for each person).

The broad goal of this procedure was to assign the same score to each person for either $I = 47$ or $i = 6$, and the result is presented graphically in Figure 3.5a. Although it is difficult to see it here, the means of the total scores are nearly identical (517 vs. 516), but the standard deviations of the original scores are much smaller (26 vs. 37).

This increased spread is evident at almost every level of the scores in Figure 3.5a. However, the Pearson correlation among the two scores is $r = 0.87$, suggesting a strong positive relation of the relative rank ordering of persons on the scale. We note that this is not a perfect correlation, so some unnecessary noise is apparent in the new scores. But although the new scores are decidedly less accurate at the individual level, this needs to be compared with the benefits of faster administration (i.e., time used on 6 items instead of 47!). Incidentally, this strategy could have been used on the WAIS scales described earlier, but we did not have the item-level data.

Considering Alternative Adaptive Strategies

In further analyses, it also seemed useful to see what our subjects' new scores "would have been" if they had taken even less items using different forms of adaptive strategies:

1. *Fixed items:* Pick a set of i items that represent an equal spread across the scale. This mimics a "short form."
2. *Random items:* Pick a set of i items that are randomly selected across the scale.
3. *Half-adaptive items:* Pick a set of i_n items that are based on prior responses. If the prior response is correct, the next item is "halfway up" the scale. If incorrect, the next item is "halfway down" the difficulty scale. Stop at i items or when *sem* < 1.
4. *Fully adaptive items:* Pick a set of i_n items using MLE as described earlier (see Baker & Kim, 2004).

The results presented in the histograms of Figure 3.5b show the Pearson correlations of the $I = 47$ item scale score with scores that have been estimated using from $i = 3$ to 7 items under each of the four adaption schemes. It seems the random selected items is the least like using all $I = 47$ items, and this approaches $r > 0.7$ only when we have $i > 7$. The used of a fixed set of items is not as close to the full score until we use $i = 6$ or 7 items. However, the half-adaptive and fully adaptive strategies have reasonably high correlations after only $i_n > 3$ items are used. Of course, such results will vary with the content and the construct, but it is fairly evident here that $I = 47$ items is needed only if we want to make precise statements about each individual. If not, only $i_n = 6$ adaptive items are really needed for group-level accuracy using this scale.

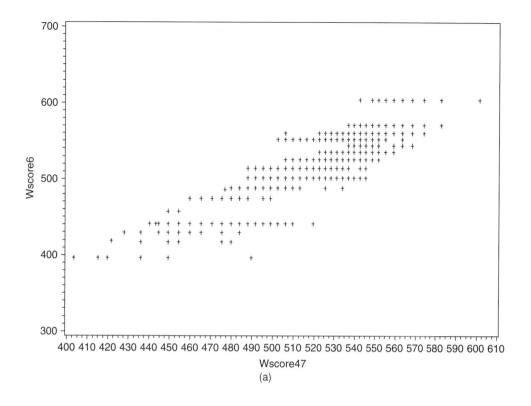

(a)

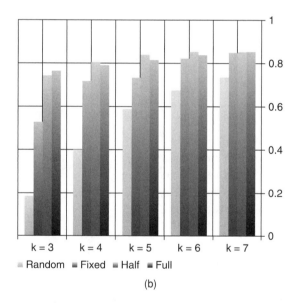

(b)

Figure 3.5 Incomplete item-level data based on adaptive test strategies. (a) Plot of full test scores ($I = 47$) versus adaptive test scores ($I = 6$) on N > 1,400 adults. (b) Comparative histograms where fewer items ($I = 3$–7) used in different adaptive strategies are correlated (y-axis) with full score ($I = 47$).

(From McArdle et al. 2009; unpublished, by permission.)

WHAT OCCASIONS DO WE REALLY NEED?

Longitudinal Data Analysis Models

Longitudinal data analysis can be highlighted by the sampling of occasions (e.g., McArdle & Bell, 2000; Nesselroade & Baltes, 1979; Singer, 1995). Formal models for the analysis of these complex longitudinal data have been developed in many different substantive domains. Early work on these problems led to the polynomial growth models by Fisher (as reported by Box, 1980) and Wishart (1938), where an individual regression coefficient was used to describe a growth characteristic of the person (see Rogosa & Willett, 1983). An interesting approach to different times between retests was proposed by Thorndike (1941). The contemporary basis of latent growth curve analyses can also be found in the recent developments of *multilevel models* or *mixed-effects models* or *latent curve models (LCMs)*. In further work by Browne and du Toit (1991), classical nonlinear models were added as part of this same framework (see Cudeck & Harring, 2007). It is now clear that there is no single optimal way to analyze these kinds of mixed longitudinal and cross-sectional data collections.

Most of these models are now presented using a common factor basis and written in this fashion. At the individual level, all individual observations (Y_n) at any occasion (t) are fitted to a functional form of

$$Y[t]_n = g0_n + g1_n A[t] + u[t]_n \qquad (5)$$

where the basis function $A[t]$ is a function of age at testing, and latent variables $g0$ = the intercept, and $g1$ = the slope. In this approach, the choice of the basis defines a scale for the timing of the changes, and we can scale it (i.e., $A[t] = \{(Age[t] - 60)/10\}$) so the intercept is estimated near the center of the observed data ($Age[t] = 60$), and a one-unit change in the resulting slope represents *latent score change per decade*. We should note that once a linear model of this type is estimated, approximations to scores at other ages can be calculated directly implied by the coefficients and can be calculated by classical Bayesian methods (see McArdle et al., 2005).

Experiments with Latent Curves Models

After the general expression for the LCM was promoted (e.g., McArdle, 1986, 1988; McArdle & Epstein, 1987; Meredith & Tisak, 1990), it became interesting to examine

the limits of what could be done with fewer occasions of measurement. As discussed earlier, McArdle and Anderson (1990) used this LCM to fit incomplete longitudinal data that naturally arise from an age-cohort data collection design, but it was not clear whether any of these results were actually correct or would generalize to other problems.

To explore some of these questions, McArdle and Hamagami (1991, 1992) examined several results using a masking data strategy. As a population dataset, N = 100 vectors were simulated based on a simple five-time-point model with an $A[t] = [0, 1, 2, 2, 1]$ basis function. This essentially led to a set of trajectories that over the five occasions rose gradually (0, 1, 2), flattened out (2, 2), and then declined (2, 1). The variance of the levels and slopes was allowed, as was some unique within-time residual, so the outcome looked like real data (i.e., as in McArdle & Anderson, 1990). The available SEM programs at the time (i.e., LISREL, Mx) were used to fit the LCM, and the results were nearly perfect. The power to test any hypothesis was based on N = 100 with D = 500, and this power was surprisingly large for typical alternative hypotheses—that is, Was the curve simply linear? Was the model an autoregressive structure? This work initially demonstrated that the SEM worked when the correct model was fitted to the data.

But of focal interest here is what was done next to examine the convergence SEM. The same data were masked in four different ways, conforming to the plots of Figure 3.6a. In the first case (dataset A), a dataset was created by randomly selecting only two occasions of measurement for each of the N = 100 people. This masked dataset was designed to mimic the typical two-time panel study where four groups of people born in different decades were measured 10 years apart, but only twice, $Y[t]$ and $Y[t + 10]$. So n = 25 were assumed to have observations only at $Y[1]$ and $Y[2]$, n = 25 had observations only at $Y[2]$ and $Y[3]$, n = 25 had observations only at $Y[3]$ and $Y[4]$, and n = 25 had observations only at $Y[4]$ and $Y[5]$. Overall, the number of data points was much smaller (d = 200), and no one was measured three times. Although the typical analysis of these longitudinal data would be to fit a two-time-point model with initial age as a covariate, the model fitted was the original LCM (from earlier), this time with patterns of incomplete data—that is, the convergence SEM. This required a four-group LCM with an abundance of nodes, invariance of all LCM parameters, and this SEM appears as the first four groups of Figure 3.6b. The most remarkable result was that this SEM yielded nearly identical results as the full data model (d = 500), and it retained most of the power to test the more basic alternatives.

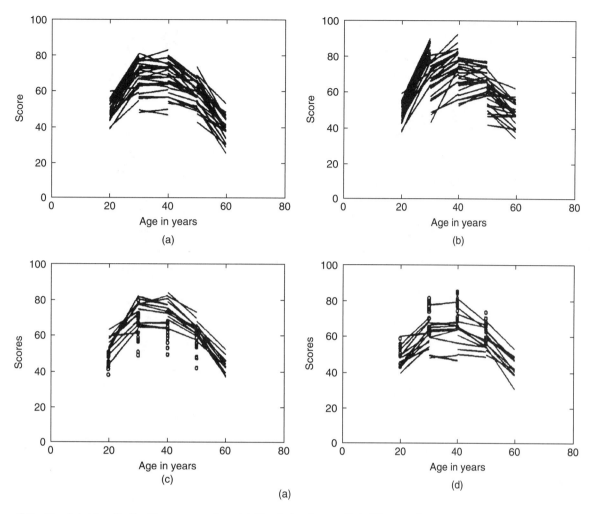

Figure 3.6 Simulated longitudinal latent curve data. (a) Simulating four realistic life-span datasets based on two occasions. (b) Path diagram of eight-group latent curve structural equation model used in fitting.

(From McArdle, J. J., & Hamagami, E. (1992). Modeling incomplete longitudinal and cross-sectional data using latent growth structural models. *Experimental Aging Research, 18*(3), 145–166, by permission.)

Indeed, this simple demonstration of masking is completely consistent with Bell's principle of accelerated data collection and techniques of convergence analysis. This demonstration also showed how LCM based on only 10 years of data could be used to correctly estimate what would have happened over 50 years of data collection, thus giving some backing to the cohort-sequential design. This approach also provided a formal statistical test of convergence, using the standard SEM likelihood ratio indices, and this was essentially a statistical basis for the distance measures originally used by Bell (1954). The observed data from optimally matching people were not actually joined together using SEM (as in Figure 3.1b), and this matching technique was not needed. Instead, the SEM expectations were formed using the principle of a common LCM, and the statistical test of

change in fit because of adding convergence constraints was used to indicate that such individual-level matches were possible. If the misfit was relatively high, then we must conclude that no simple convergence was possible with this LCM. Of course, many additional assumptions were made in the data masking, such as random selection to groups, and this is a continuing concern for this convergence-SEM approach.

Nonrandom Experiments with Latent Curve Models

The next part of this work is probably of most relevance to the key concerns about cohort sequential designs (see McArdle & Hamagami, 1991, 1992). The three other sets of data of Figure 3.6a were created in slightly unusual

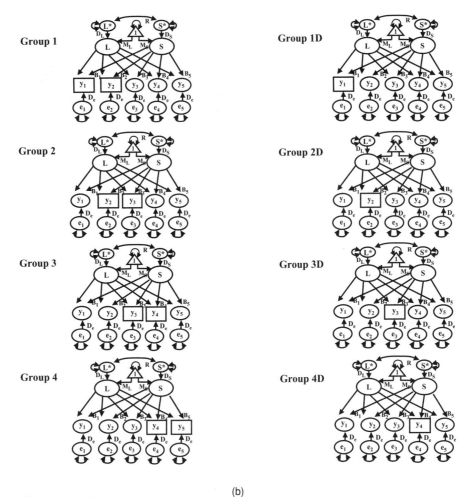

(b)

Figure 3.6 (*Continued*)

ways. In the next dataset (B), we examined retest effects, and in the last two datasets (C, D), we examined the impacts of selective attrition at the second occasion.

In simulated data (dataset B in Figure 3.6a), we started with the previously selected data (dataset A) and added a "practice" effect. This was construed as a positive shift (with mean and variance) for persons taking the same test for a second occasion. Because people did not all take the second test at the second age, this positive shift because of prior exposure (i.e., practice) was not created to be at the same age for each person, but it was independent of other model features (i.e., level and slope). But now, when the previous model four-group LCM was fitted, the results were not at all the same: The parameters were incorrect and the power of the alternative tests was lowered. Obviously, the original LCM was no longer appropriate for these data (i.e., the misfit was large), and we needed to add a practice component as a latent variable common to all second occasions to correctly recover the population model. In general, this alerted us to the potentially serious

problems of ignoring retest effects in longitudinal data (see Ferrer et al., 2007; McArdle & Woodcock, 1997).

In the third dataset (dataset C in Figure 3.6a), we selectively dropped about half the scores with a higher probability for those who had lower latent level scores. Of course, this was possible to do only because we had created the latent scores! The resulting sample of data still had N = 100, but now with much less observed data ($d =$ 150). This was intended to mimic dropout for those who scored the lowest at time 1. To fit this model, we used the full eight-group model of Figure 3.6b, where four groups have two occasions of observed data (and three incomplete occasions) and four other groups have only one occasion of observed data (and four incomplete occasions). When fitted using only the first four groups, the parameters are biased upward, but when all the available data of eight groups are fitted, the parameters are essentially correct. This demonstrates the MAR correction for selection, and this is similar to what happened in the pretest/post-test example presented earlier. That is, because a variable (time

1 scores) that was related to the selection (probabilistically) was included in the analysis, the correct population result was obtained even in the presence of nonrandom selection.

In a final analysis, we went one step further. In the fourth dataset (see Figure 3.6a, dataset D), the same kind of attrition data was created, but here the attrition was based on the latent slope scores: There was a higher probability of dropping out for persons with a higher slope. Because a higher slope implied the person changed a lot, this dataset mimicked what we termed a "High School Reunion" selection—that is, people who change are less likely to return. Because the resulting data layout was the same at the previous eight-group model (see Figure 3.6b), we used the same SEM program. However, the results were not at all the same: The LCM parameters were largely incorrect, and the power to reject alternative models was low. In retrospect, the problem with this data-model combination is fairly obvious: Any indication of the slope must come from at least two points of data, and here we had observed only one. This is not a case of MAR selection, but this is an example of NIM selection. Problems of inference can be created by this type of selection because, without at least three points in time on the critical variables, we will not be able to know what selection has happened or what correction would be most appropriate.

We have learned at least two more principles from these simple experiments in masking simulated data. First, under the typical assumptions of constant age selection, the incomplete data SEM works perfectly. Second, if the assumptions are violated, either by retest or slope selection, the multigroup SEM will fail. The problem in the selection of the occasions in real data is that we are unlikely to know which selection problem is actually operating. This leads us to consider more complex designs and more complex model fitting strategies. For example, McArdle and Bell (2000) advocated using *age-as-the-basis* for changes instead of *time-as-the-basis*. This novel approach created large amounts of seemingly incomplete data, but these data were not due to person self-selection, so the MCAR or MAR assumptions may be reasonable. This data analysis design also provides a way to separate changes in the construct from practice-retest effects, and this is now a common theme in longitudinal data analysis of many functions (e.g., Ferrer et al., 2007).

Practical Planning in National Growth and Change Study

We actually implemented the prior design ideas at the planning stages of a longitudinal study termed the *National Growth and Change Study* (NGCS). At the start, the NGCS was an experimental measurement study. We collected new data from N = ~300 participants of various ages (18–95 years) to improve on the internal validity of the common factors of the WAIS, but we also added many Rasch-based scales from the Woodcock-Johnson (WJ) tests (see Woodcock, 1990). The overall NGCS measurement design used here included some of the 11 subscales of the WAIS, as well as some of the 22 measures from the WJ-R subscales. But to cut down on time, yet have the full factorial description, the data collection was conducted so that no person was measured on more than 20 variables at any one occasion (i.e., following a reference variable selection model; McArdle, 1994).

Our analysis of NGCS data used MLE and MAR applied to the scales (the same programs in McArdle, 1994), and was based on an eight-factor model proposed by Woodcock (1990). A target rotation using Browne's (2001) approach (termed CEFA) resulted in the solution, which showed a remarkable agreement between the eight-factor WJ-R model and smaller number of WAIS factors. A few WAIS variables exhibited only one large loading on one factor (e.g., VO on *Gc*, DSS on *Gs*, MS on *Gsr*, and AR on *Gq*). Other key variables of the WAIS did not exhibit simplicity of any form (e.g., BD, PC). These factor analytic results strongly suggest that six of the eight main cognitive factors of *Gf-Gc* theory are complexly measured in the WAIS; that is, no pure *Gf* or *Ga* (as reported in Browne, 2001). In the most recent extension of this measurement analysis, we used raw data from three groups: (1) the NGCS data (N = 294) with both the WAIS-R and WJ-R, (2) the national norming sample of the WAIS-R (N = 1,880), and (3) the national norming sample of the WJ-R (N = 2,700). The results of this analysis show a remarkable simplicity of factor loadings for the WJ-R and a remarkable complexity of factor loadings for the WAIS-R. These results clarify some limitations in the prior isolated factor analyses of the WAIS and show the need for a joint battery factor analysis with reference groups is an improved way to achieve this degree of factorial description.

Probably the most innovative aspect of the current research was our intentional sampling of occasions of measurement where we could more clearly separate age changes from retest effects. In McArdle and Woodcock (1997), we presented the formal basis of what we called a *time-lag* design. In this data collection design, people were first measured at an initial age (ages = 5–95 years), and then a second time at a random distance in time ($\Delta t = 1$ month to 5 years). Of critical importance is that we controlled the interval of time between tests, and we made

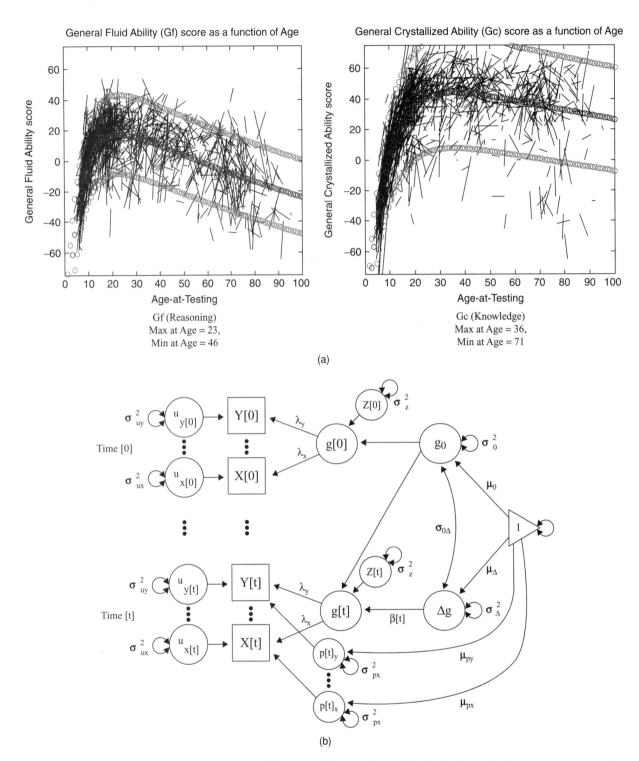

Figure 3.7   Longitudinal time-lag data from National Growth and Change Study. (a) Multilevel longitudinal age trajectories of two broad cognitive abilities (plus model expected means and 95% confidence intervals). For general Fluid ability *(Gf)* scores, maximum occurs at age 23 and minimum at age 46; for general Crystallized ability *(Gc)* scores, maximum occurs at age 36 and minimum at age 71. (b) A path model of the multivariate multilevel growth model used to evaluate common factors (fitted using SAS NLMIXED, Mplus, or Mx).

(From McArdle, J. J., Ferrer-Caja, E., Hamagami, F., & Woodcock, R. W. (2002). Comparative longitudinal multilevel structural analyses of the growth and decline of multiple intellectual abilities over the life-span. *Developmental Psychology, 38*(1), 115–142, by permission.)

sure this was largely uncorrelated with the initial ages. Using this logic, we were able to collect a sample of N = 1,074 participants from the WJ-R norming files already measured on the WJ-R scales, and we remeasured people over a variable length time lag (0–5 years between tests). Figure 3.7a is a plot of the WJ-R growth curve data for the Crystallized Knowledge *(Gc)* scale and the Fluid Reasoning scale.

Our subsequent analyses utilize the full NGCS data collections and incomplete data time-lag analysis. McArdle and Woodcock (1997) focused on the short-term time-sequence effects of the tests in the NGCS data. These unique time-lag data were analyzed using a novel SEM, and the new WJ-R factors had these results: (1) substantial growth components, (2) some simple retest components, and (3) little or no trait change in this short period. Most of the reliable components could be traced to true score effects, and the long-term change effects were relatively small in most variables. The cognitive factors displayed some practice effects but little trait changes. The only substantial trait-change component was seen in Visualization *(Gv)*, and this parallels a result previously described by Horn (1972). In contrast with these Cognitive factors, the Achievement clusters and the *Gc* factor all displayed substantial trait changes and small practice effects.

When it became clear that we could estimate practice effects separately from growth and decline, we went one step further. In a second NGCS article using these data, we examined the life-span growth curves of children and adults using standard and nonstandard multilevel models (McArdle, Ferrer-Caja, Hamagami, & Woodcock., 2002; see Figure 3.7a). These data included N > 1,100 persons who were given 16 WJ-R subtests at intervals ranging from 6 months to 5 years. Notice that no person is actually measured at exactly the same ages or time lag. Standard multilevel models with connected segments (splines) provided a reasonable fit to these data. In addition, a nonlinear multilevel model of "two competing forces" used in information-processing research achieved excellent fit. This model has the functional form of

$$Y[t]_n = g0_n + g1_n A[t] + g2_n P[t] + u[t]_n \qquad (6)$$

where the basis function $A[t]$ was the sum of and exponential gain $(+\pi^a)$ and an exponential loss $(-\pi^b)$, and the additional loading $P[t] = 0$ or 1, so the additional latent variable $g2 =$ the practice slope. The parameters of this complex model were identified by the time-lag collection.

We found most cognitive ability changes in the WJ-R in the adult age range can be described as linearly decreasing with age; but in some cases, a first growth segment (18–40) was characterized by no changes, and a second growth segment (41–95) showed substantial average decreases. *Gc* exhibit the smallest decline, and *Gf* and *Gs* have largest rates of decline (as listed in Figure 3.7a). The addition of demographic or psychosocial factors improved the fit, and all WJ-R scores have the following characteristics: (1) appear to be substantially improved with years of education, especially after high school graduation; (2) are considerably lower for members of minority groups than for whites; (3) do not exhibit sex differences; (4) have no noteworthy differences in the trend components for demographic groupings; (5) have positive relations with good mental health; and (6) physical health and social networks have only small effects.

The central core of these convergence analyses are based on a multivariate model (see Figure 3.7b) that allowed us to mimic Equation 6 and separate practice-retest in components in a variable from changes over time in a common construct (i.e., *G*). Although the SEM with incomplete ages worked fine for some functions (coded in NLMIXED or Mplus), the models of common factors for higher level components was rejected for these cognitive longitudinal data. It seems as if a common factor labeled *G* is not a useful developmental construct (see McArdle, 2007).

WHAT DYNAMICS DO WE REALLY NEED?

Latent Change Score Models

The prior problems have led us to the much larger issue of what constructs influence the others over time, and in what sequence, to test specific adult development hypotheses. These multivariate dynamic concepts are indicative of a complex system of relations, but this can be simplified in terms of a set of leading and lagging indicators as presented in Figure 3.8a. Here we have four constructs and five alternative systems. In the first four cases (see Figure 3.8a, parts a–d), only one of the constructs is an important leading indicator of the changes in the others. In the fifth alternative (see Figure 3.8a, part e), a single "higher order" factor common to all four "lower order" constructs influences all the changes over time. These alternatives lead to different model expectations both within and over time (see McArdle, 2007), so these can be examined using standard confirmatory SEM techniques.

To begin to get a grasp on this dynamic problem, let us first consider that all of the prior SEMs can be seen to have a common basis if we write the expressions as an accumulated function of the changes:

$$Y[t]_n = g0_n + \left\{ \sum_{j=1 \text{ to } t} (\Delta y[j]_n) \right\} + e[t]_n,$$

$$\text{where } \Delta y[t]_n = f\{\alpha, \beta, y[t - \Delta t]\} \tag{7a}$$

In this expression, the change scores ($\Delta y[t]$) are considered to be unobserved, and the accumulation of all prior changes (the summation) provides a description of the current status. These kinds of simple linear expressions can be used to fit latent curves of high complexity (see Hamagami & McArdle, 2007), and they can be used with common factors as well (as in McArdle, 2001).

These simple linear change models also lead directly to a bivariate dynamic model of changes among more than

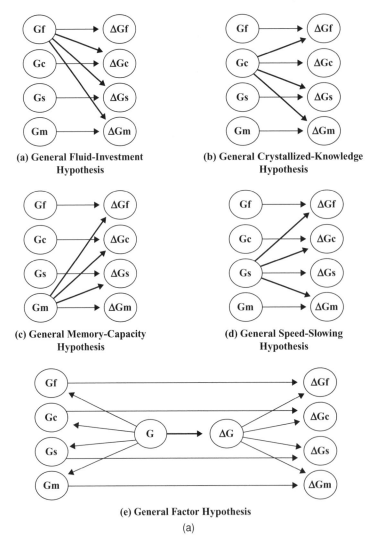

(a) General Fluid-Investment Hypothesis

(b) General Crystallized-Knowledge Hypothesis

(c) General Memory-Capacity Hypothesis

(d) General Speed-Slowing Hypothesis

(e) General Factor Hypothesis

(a)

Figure 3.8 Simulation of life-span dynamic systems. (a) Alternative model of bivariate latent variable dynamic impacts among cognitive factors over multiple time points. (b) Six (of 12) sets of observed longitudinal data (N = 100, *T* = 20) simulation from an explicit dynamic process.

(a: From McArdle, J. J., Hamagami, F., Meredith, W., & Bradway, K. P. (2000). Modeling the dynamic hypotheses of Gf-Gc theory using longitudinal life-span data. *Learning and Individual Differences, 12,* 53–79, by permission; b: From Hamagami, F., & McArdle, J.J. (2000). Advanced studies of individual differences linear dynamic models for longitudinal data analysis. In G. Marcoulides & R. Schumacker (Eds.), *New developments and techniques in structural equations modeling* (pp. 203–246). Mahwah, NJ: Erlbaum, by permission.)

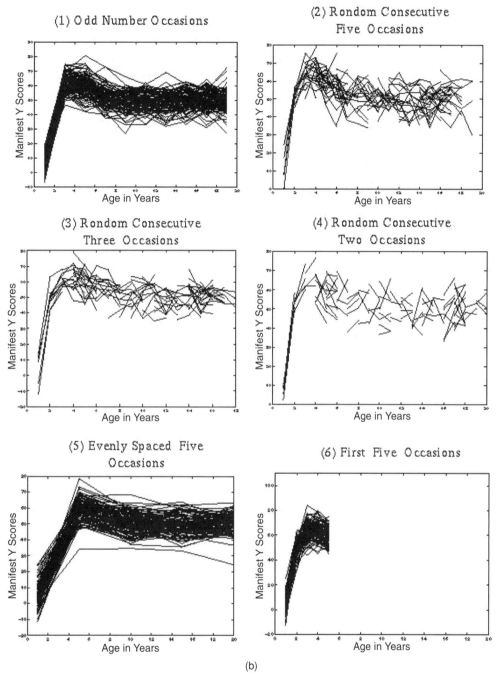

(b)

Figure 3.8 *(Continued)*

one variable. If we consider two variables measured over multiple occasions, $Y[t]$ and $X[t]$, we can write

$$\Delta y[t]_n = \alpha_y + \beta_y \, y[t-1]_n + \gamma_y \, x[t-1]_n + z[t]_n \text{ and}$$

$$\Delta x[t]_n = \alpha_x + \beta_x \, x[t-1]_n + \gamma_x \, y[t-1]_n + w[t]_n \qquad (7b)$$

so the latent changes in one variable ($\Delta y[t]$ or $\Delta x[t]$) can be a function of the past accumulation in that latent scores

($y[t-1]$ or $x[t-1]$), as well as prior influences in the other score. This need not be the case, and some of the key parameters of the changes can be forced to zero. This kind of linear dynamic restrictions can be fully represented and fitted using standard SEM logic, and some alternative models are presented in Figure 3.8a. This is fairly important, because it implies we can include incomplete time points and incomplete groups in the same way as done earlier here. In theory, this model also deals with many of the most persistent problems of lead-lag sequences in observation longitudinal data.

In practice, this model has been used in many substantive applications (for review, see McArdle, 2009). For example, the bivariate dual-change model has only been available only since 2000, but many researchers have already applied this dynamic SEM to their substantive problems. In our own applications, we used dynamic SEM to investigate the lead-lag relations in: (1) Wechsler Intelligence Scales for Children (WISC) intelligence scales in children (McArdle, 2001), (2) WAIS intelligence factors changing over adulthood (McArdle et al., 2001), (3) antisocial behaviors and Reading Achievement in the National Longitudinal Survey of Work Experience of Youth (NLSY) cohort (McArdle & Hamagami, 2001), (4) cognitive dynamics in longitudinal twin data (McArdle & Hamagami, 2003), (5) experimental impacts of cognitive training (McArdle, 2007; McArdle & Prindle, 2008), and (6) brain changes in lateral ventricle size (LVS) and the Wechsler Memory Scale (WMS; McArdle et al., 2004). Research led by others has examined different lead-lag relations using similar bivariate latent change score models, including: (1) personality disorders and changes (Hamagami, McArdle, & Cohen, 2000), (2) perceptual speed and knowledge changes in older ages (Ghisletta & Lindenberger, 2003, 2005), (3) specific cognitive abilities and achievement using the WJ-R (Ferrer & McArdle, 2004); (4) social participation and perceptual speed in late adult development (Lövdén, Ghisletta, & Lindenberger, 2005), (5) physical activity and cognitive declines (Ghisletta, Bickel, & Lövdén, 2006), (6) reading and cognition over all ages (Ferrer et al., 2007), and (7) forgiveness and psychological adjustment (Orth, Berking, Walker, Meier, & Znoj, 2008). What is not clear yet is the potential limitations of this kind of dynamic SEM, in terms of variable reliabilities, and the number of persons, occasions, and time lags.

Exploring the Limits of Structural Equation Model–Based Dynamic Systems

In Hamagami and McArdle (2000), we used Monte Carlo simulation analyses to investigate how the structural change scores equations for two variables behave when a variety of incompleteness of data was imposed by masking. A SEM approach to dynamical system modeling was utilized to accomplish the analyses. And this method was contrasted with the traditional regression model with a change score as a dependent variable. The research here uses the principles of masking data and incorporates ideas of bivariate linear difference equation dynamics, structural equation modeling,

and concept of individual differences about observed data. These analyses were considered necessary to determine whether the proposed models (Equations 7a and 7b) are tenable to reconstruct a predetermined dynamical system.

To be more specific, we first generated data for $N = 100$ individuals measured over $T = 20$ occasions (so $D = 2,000$) using a dynamic models where X controlled Y— more formally, where $x[t - 1] \rightarrow \Delta y[t]$ but $y[t - 1] \rightarrow \Delta x [t]$. This overall model was examined with various levels of within time variance (noise σu^2), but this SEM fit the data well at all levels. We also fit incorrect alternatives, and we had high power to detect the correct model of sequential influence in almost all cases, as long as the latent variance was at least 30% of the total variance.

Next, we masked the data in 12 different ways, and 6 of these are presented in the plots of Figure 3.8b. In the first case (see Figure 3.8b, panel 1), we masked either the odd or even occasions of data (so $N = 100$, $T = 10$, and $D = 1,000$), and we refit the model without any problems at all. In the second case (see Figure 3.8b, panel 2), we selected only $T = 5$ occasions (masking 15 data points), and we chose these at random for each person. The statistical behavior of this model was also nearly perfect. In time sampling (see Figure 3.8b, panel 3), we lowered this to $t = 3$ random time points per person (17 time points masked), and this still led to a very strong accuracy and power. Time sampling (see Figure 3.8b, panel 4) used only $t = 2$ time points per person, and although certainly not as accurate as the model fitted to the previous samplings, this still led to acceptable results for the sequential inferences. Time sampling (see Figure 3.8b, panel 5) used only $t = 5$ points, but these were fixed values but spread out for everyone. This was not as accurate as the prior random selections, but it was acceptable because it was spread out so far over the time span. In sampling (see Figure 3.8b, panel 6), we used only the first $t = 5$ time points and, as Figure 3.8b seems to show, it is difficult to approximate latent dynamic influences until they have had time to work their way into observations. From this first set of six samplings, we learned that the use of random selections could be a reasonable way to approach such a dynamic problem. Of course, we did not try to simulate retest effect parameters, because these would have distorted every parameter. So in some sense, models of practice-retest need to be considered seriously.

Six other data sampling models were considered in this research, and most of these led to ways to get the wrong answers, but they will not be considered further here. In general, the latent change score dynamic models do enable us to recover dynamic parameters, including interindividual variability of initial conditions and of constant slopes. These dynamic models seem to be fairly robust in recovering a predetermined population parameter set, but the way that occasions are sampled form the bigger picture can make a big difference in the resulting accuracy and power. These analyses of missing data patterns showed that proposed dynamic models were fitted to recover features of dynamic systems even if data structures were seriously masked. In contrast, we demonstrated that the traditional regression model failed to recover dynamic parameters if missing data patterns were imposed in simulation data structure. In this presentation, we also provided cautionary notes about expecting too much from latent variable dynamic modeling. Not surprisingly, we must measure the constructs of interest or we will never be able to estimate their impacts.

DYNAMIC EXAMPLES FROM THE BERKELEY–BRADWAY STUDY

Combining Longitudinal Datasets

In our applied research, we developed and used a variety of these SEM concepts with real longitudinal data, and many

of these applications used the WAIS cognitive scales. The basic ideas of the SEMs for multiple variable growth curve analysis were given in earlier publications (e.g., McArdle, 1986, 1988, 1989; McArdle & Epstein, 1987; McArdle & Anderson, 1990; McArdle, Hamagami, Elias, & Robbins, 1991). We were especially interested in the application of a "factor of curves" (after McArdle, 1988) model to growth components of these life-span data. In McArdle and Nesselroade (1994), we demonstrated why the invariance of a longitudinal factor model is formally identical to the invariance of a factor of change and initial level scores. Our results show that the common factors of WAIS measurement, complex as they may be, are consistent over the adult life span. Perhaps the most important lesson that we have learned is that datasets are not better because they are simple; complex data arrays can be analyzed, and these may give sturdier results; and data sets used in one analysis may encompass more than one actual study (see McArdle et al., 2009). In our prior work, existing data from several longitudinal studies have been combined to provide more breath and depth of measurement across the whole life span, and one kind of example is provided in Figure 3.9.

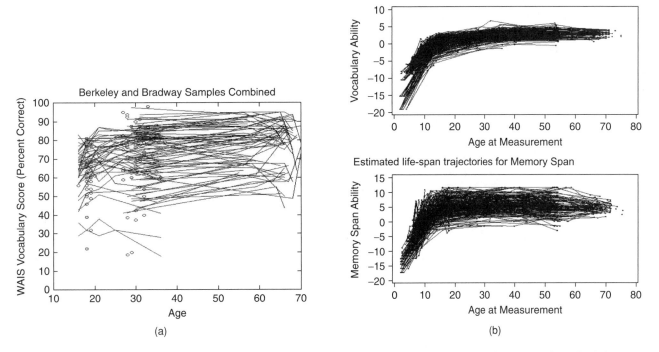

(a)   (b)

Figure 3.9   Accelerate longitudinal data from combinations of the Berkeley and Bradway study samples. (a) Bradway–Berkeley combination allows coverage over the adult life span. WAIS, Wechsler Adult Intelligence Scale. (b) Longitudinal life-span trajectories from estimated ability scores for each person.

(a: From McArdle, Hamagami, et al., 2001, *Learning and Individual Differences*, by permission; b: from McArdle, J. J., Grimm, K., Hamagami, F., Bowles, R., & Meredith, W. (2009). A multiple-group longitudinal item response model of vocabulary abilities over the life-span. *Psychological Methods, 14*(2), 126–149, by permission.)

McArdle, Hamagami, Meredith, and Bradway's (2000) study attempted to describe the dynamics of late cognitive development, with specific hypotheses defined by the alternative dynamics of Figure 3.8a, using a combination of longitudinal WAIS data from two different but complementary studies. This analysis used WAIS data from the *Bradway–McArdle Longitudinal* (BML) study. These N = 111 individuals in this study were first measured in 1932 as children aged 2 to 5 years as part of the standardization sample of the Stanford–Binet test. They were measured again about 10 years later by Katherine P. Bradway as part of her doctoral dissertation (Bradway & Thompson, 1962). These same persons were measured again by Bradway as adults at average ages of 30 and 42 (Kangas & Bradway, 1971). About half (N = 55) of these persons were measured again by McArdle in 1984 at ages 55 to 57 years and in 1993 to 1997 at ages ranging from 64 to 72 years. All recent testing on the WAIS was completed in the subjects' homes (mainly in the San Francisco Bay Area), and the recent wave of subject recruitment included n = 51 (46%) retested, n = 21 (19%) not located, n = 20 (18%) deceased, n = 12 (10%) refused testing, and n = 7 (6%) with incomplete tests.

The second data collection used was WAIS data from the *Berkeley Growth Study* (BGS) participants (e.g., McArdle et al., 2009). The BGS was initiated by Nancy Bayley with N = 61 healthy infants born between 1928 and 1929. This was initially in a study designed to trace normal intellectual, motor, and physical development through the first year, but it continued with a wide variety of measurements taken each year until the children were 16 years old. Bayley first administered the Wechsler–Bellevue (WB) scales at 16, 18, 21, and 26 years of age, and then administered the WAIS at age 36. A second adult follow-up was conducted at age 50 and another at 60, and the WAIS or WAIS-R was administered at each age. At these latter ages, spouses of the original subjects were measured as well, and this provided more longitudinal information (N = 76 persons total).

Figure 3.9a shows the full data collection when we combined the WAIS scores of the BGS (n = 76) data and the Bradway longitudinal data (n = 111). Figure 3.9a includes a plot for the WAIS Vocabulary scores where the multiple scores measured for a specific person (n) on that specific variable *(y)* at a particular age *(t)* are connected by a line. This combination of early adult data from Berkeley with later adult data from Bradway allows this collection to be considered over the whole life span. This combination of longitudinal data for the Bradway and Berkeley samples

still has several selective limitations. Among these, the participants are all from one birth cohort (~1928) in the same geographical area (San Francisco), are all of one ethnicity (white), all come from volunteer families with above-average socioeconomic status, and as a group score above average on most cognitive tasks. However, even given these selection limitations, the selected data from the Bradway–Berkeley combination do permit an inference about growth over a relatively long life span. This collection of individual growth curves plotted over the adult life span is the focus of all analyses to follow.

Latent Change Score Analysis of Combined Data

In a first set of analyses, we use linear dynamic models in a formal evaluation of the growth and declines of abilities through latent growth and linear dynamic models. Our first results indicate separate trends over age for different intellectual abilities including broad knowledge, spatial reasoning, perceptual speed, and immediate memory. In a second set of analyses, we extend these multivariate dynamic SEMs to explore the age-based leading and lagging indicators as previously defined in Figure 3.8a. These SEM created misfit indices for each hypothesis, and these point to a relatively complex system of relations, with memory losses as an important leading indicator. For example, the dynamic equations suggested

$$\Delta Gf[t]_n = -0.05 - \mathbf{0.29}\ Gf[t-1]_n + 0.03\ Gc[t-1]_n$$
$$+ 0.09\ Gm[t-1]_n + \mathbf{0.30}\ Gs[t] \qquad (8a)$$

and

$$\Delta Gc[t]_n = 0.02 - \mathbf{0.27}\ Gc[t-1]_n - 0.04\ Gf[t-1]_n$$
$$+ \mathbf{0.30}\ Gm[t-1]_n + 0.02\ Gs[t] \qquad (8b)$$

This implies the age-related changes in Fluid ability (Equation 8a) are impacted by itself and only by the Speed construct at earlier ages. In contrast, the age-related changes in Crystallized abilities (Equation 8b) are impacted by itself and by the Memory construct at the earlier ages. The way these dynamic models make explicit forecasts of different ages require much more detail (see McArdle et al., 2000, p. 67).

In a third set of analyses, we use confirmatory techniques to test specific late adult development hypotheses. These results indicate support for both the "general memory loss" hypothesis and the "general slowing" hypothesis, and provide some support the "investment theory" at the adult level. Once again, this suggests a single *G* factor does not describe the complexity of late adult cognitive development. In a related set of articles, we went a bit further and used a latent "growth-mixture" approach to estimate latent groupings in the Verbal (and Non-Verbal) dynamic scores of these longitudinal data (see McArdle & Hamagami, 2004; McArdle & Nesselroade, 2003), but we did not find strong evidence for latent classes. These results, when taken as a whole, synthesize prior WAIS studies and provide methods for further research on the dynamics of the growth and decline of intellectual abilities across the adult life span (also see McArdle & Hamagami, 2005, 2007).

Additional Longitudinal Possibilities

We examined additional methodological possibilities using these longitudinal life-span data in a slightly different way (McArdle et al., 2002). Here we reconstructed different scales in these data in terms of common item level Rasch models, so the constructs of Verbal Ability and Memory Ability were measured in common units over time. Over this time course, nine different Vocabulary tests, including the Stanford–Binet (L & LM), WISC, WAIS (WB, WB-II, WAIS, WAIS-R), and WJ-R tests had been administered to these individuals at several different occasions. When considered as one large test, we have N > 2,500 individual vocabulary tests with 230 items measured. These data were used in a Rasch-based item analysis, and the results suggested there was enough item overlap for a good fitting model and the calibration of a single dimension of Vocabulary. This led to a person-item map showing the distribution of each person-test on the ordered set of items and allowed us to calculate a new Vocabulary Ability in a common metric (i.e., no matter what test was used).

By putting together these different scales into a common metric, we could use these linked scores in subsequent growth curve analysis. This scaling into Rasch units allowed us to interpret the intellectual changes over the life span in terms of individual differences in the following factors: (1) growth rates, (2) asymptotes (or final size achieved), and (3) distances from the asymptotes (or age shifts). These results show a strong relation between childhood changes and later adulthood levels, very little adulthood changes for any factor between ages 30 and 50, and some decrements in nonverbal abilities starting between ages 55 and 62. Although many segments of these growth curves are "incomplete," it is possible to use all measurement data and obtain maximum likelihood estimates and

tests for expected exponential curves. These new growth analyses suggest that the growth of Vocabulary ability does not decline even in the seventh decade of life, and there are only small differences because of Gender, Educational Level, and Military Service. We have also examined these issues in every analysis where we combined different datasets. For example, power analyses were done based on combining the Berkeley and Bradway samples, and the results (using $\alpha = 0.05$, $\eta^2 = 0.30$) showed a clear increase in the power of the test statistics used to compare alternative growth models (also see Grimm & McArdle, 2007).

WHAT LIFE-SPAN DATA DO WE REALLY NEED?

The main objective of this chapter has been to review evidence that shows, after we have collected some data, how we are in the position to figure out how much information we really need. This sounds like a bit of an odd way to make an experimental design plan, and this is correct. Also, the plan may shift when some people are actually measured. But planning with existing data turns out to be an essential and powerful idea!

What People Do We Really Need?

The people we typically need are a sample of individuals who are representative of the population of interest. This requires some sense of the population of inference, and this is often not so easy. One could say we want a sample of individuals who are representative of the entire U.S. population (e.g., McArdle et al., 2007). But even here we have to ask "when?" because this population is in constant flux. If we propose to study the full life span, we must recognize that some life spans are shorter or longer than others, and a truly representative sample is considerably more difficult to create. If we want to make a projection to a population, we need to be very specific. We did not formally deal with this fundamental problem of sample representativeness, but it is crucial.

We did deal with this sample size problem. If this primary condition of representative is met, then we need as large a sample as needed to have precision in our estimates and power to test alternative hypotheses. We found that any solution to this problem implies we have some alternative hypotheses, and we need to make sure we have at least two key alternatives to guide the sample size selection. Of course, if this proves too difficult, we can simply avoid these questions and analyze some data on hand or some data that are easy to obtain. But these alternatives are not desirable. If we end up with a sample of individuals who are not representative, we may need to down-weight the data so the "effective" sample will be much smaller with less power (Stapleton, 2002). If we end up with a representative sample that is small, we may not have enough power to test the hypothesis of key interest.

What Scales Do We Really Need?

The scales we need are basically surrogates for the key constructs we wish to examine. The scales we need are the ones that uniquely identify the constructs of interest. We need to have enough of these scales to identify the key constructs over time, but the scales do not need to remain the same over all occasions. Because there may be many relevant constructs, we may need many scales of measurement. The minimal identification conditions suggest we need to measure at least three indicators per factor (McArdle, 2007), but the masking experiments suggest that not all three are needed for every individual (McArdle, 1994). If these scales are sensitive to retest or practice effects, they should simply not be repeated (see McArdle & Hamagami, 1992; McArdle & Woodcock, 1997).

There are many different ways to introduce variation in the scales of measurement, including fractional factorial and reference variable designs. Sound measurement plans may be related to broader characteristics of the constructs, such as some key hypotheses about how these constructs are related to one another. Any plan of reduced measures should be tested out on existing data before being put into practice.

What Items Do We Really Need?

We want to have an accurate measure of the person on any key construct, so we need items that are most appropriate for the individuals to be studied. We probably do not need to measure individuals on many items that are either too hard or too easy for that person, because these will simply be answered with probability 0 or 1. Instead, we want to focus our items near the expected construct score for each person, so the expected probability is closer to $p_n = 0.5$, because this will give the best precision (i.e., smallest *sem*).

We have examined what happens to our estimate of the latent score when only some of the information is available on any person. What we find is what probably has been

known for a long time: If we can focus our items so that they are closer to the individual's latent score, then we can obtain as much accuracy as possible with the fewest items. This also means we will take less time with each person, and this could have important effects on validity of measurement and the probability of a repeated testing.

What Occasions Do We Really Need?

It is clear that the optimal time to measure change is right before and right after it happens (see Albert, Blacker, Moss, Tanzi, & McArdle, 2007). Unfortunately, this timing is not typically known in advance of the data collections, and it is likely not to be the same for everyone. If not known, the use of random selections may be a better way to deal with the pushes and pulls, the ups and downs, of dynamic effects. This is consistent with an informative theoretical starting point. The "Nyquist–Shannon sampling theorem" (see Grenander, 1959) suggests that if we want to avoid biases in picking up signals, termed *aliasing,* in understanding a discrete signal processing system, aliasing can be avoided if the frequency of sampling is greater than the bandwidth. In practice, this means we should consider measurements at half the sampling frequency of the changes—that is, if the change occurs over 2 years, we should measure every 1 year. This is used in oversampling of signals of music on a CD, but six times is typical in these cases. Although our longitudinal models have little to do with the typical information theory models, this approach to oversampling seems to be useful in a number of practical contexts (see Wohlwill, 1973).

This incomplete measure SEM approach advocated here is now commonly used as a practical solution for dealing with the attrition problem in longitudinal research—that is, when some of the participants do not return for a repeated testing. It is less widely known that these same SEM techniques can be used in situations where the psychometric *measures are not exactly repeated over time.* This is a common problem in life-span developmental research where the measure for a construct is necessarily chosen to be "age appropriate" or where a new "test form" has been introduced. In recent work, we assumed: (1) some generic measurement or factorial model, (2) metric factorial invariance over time, (3) the noncommensurate variables are treated as incomplete data (latent), and (4) these variables are *MAR.* We can now highlight the alternative model derived from IRT that has similar assumptions but proved to be far more practical when dealing with the item level data (McArdle et al., 2009).

What Dynamics Do We Really Need?

The simulation results described earlier suggest that the most important data are found where the dynamic changes occur. This is such an obvious statement that it hardly needs to be made. But this is not often the way life-span studies are conducted. Instead, a fixed number of people are administered a fixed number of items on a fixed number of scales at a fixed number of occasions, at fixed intervals of time. This seems largely because any other time-sampling design would require some advanced knowledge of the phenomena, some prior beliefs about the dynamic system.

The dynamic research presented here has demonstrated the use of dynamic models with sets of combined longitudinal data. The overlapping Bradway–Berkeley longitudinal data used here provided individual information about changes in multiple cognitive abilities from early childhood to later adulthood. These models allow us to test hypotheses about the following topics: (1) the rise (or fall) of a construct toward (or away from) an equilibrium age (at an asymptote or peak), and (2) the deflection of this equilibrium age by influences of levels on other constructs. Although these linear SEMs for dynamic analysis are relatively new, they deal directly with the challenges created by multivariate longitudinal life-span data.

As life-span studies accumulate, mature as they are, these methodological results suggest it is foolish to use a fixed approach when a more random selection of occasions is likely to yield more precise information. There seems to be very few problems with the model fitting with incomplete data, except that our assumptions about the missing data may be incorrect and not possible to check. But this means that, in the new era of incomplete data modeling, the possibilities of spreading variation about key features of most concern makes it necessary to try.

What Life Span Do We Really Need?

As stated earlier, the title of this chapter is provocative but not flippant. One key suggestion being made here is to consider the possibility of intentionally collecting less data but basing all of the key data collections on fitting specific model-based hypotheses. Some people have referred to this general logic as "planned incompleteness," but such terminology was not used in the early ANOVA designs based on optimizing specific effects, and I doubt if it is very helpful now because we always have planned incompleteness. What can be very helpful is the methodological approach that Bell (1954) suggested: Mask some

of the data you already have and see if it makes any difference to the results. This is, of course, related to any "sensitivity" analysis and to incomplete data theories (e.g., Wainer, 1989). Using such a strategy, combined with the expressions presented here, it is possible to determine the statistical power of alternative hypotheses even in the most complex cohort-sequential design. This approach also has many other real-life analogies, such as the family pictures and movies described earlier.

From a life-span perspective, it is both practical and important not to measure some of the people some of the time. It is mainly important to measure: (1) as many people as possible who are representatives of the population of interest; (2) on a small set of scales that best represent the key factors of interest; (3) on a small set of items (stimuli) that best represent their underlying scores (responses) to a full scales; (4) at key moments in time, especially when they are changing the most; and (5) on key factors that clearly influence the dynamics of the changes. Although we cannot be certain we know the answer to these questions in advance of the data collection, we should still ask these questions using whatever data are available. The creative use of available data can be used to guide the optimal experimental design.

Of course, it is difficult to know with any certainty that any SEM answer is absolutely correct! So, in most cases, we would rather have all the data, including all the latent scores! But this is not different than making identification assumptions in ANOVA designs (i.e., no interactions), and some practical problems may require some of the models described in this chapter (e.g., practice, fatigue, attrition). There are now a variety of alternative statistical techniques that can be used (e.g., SEM, multiple imputation) for any complex analysis, so there is no longer any excuse for gathering more data than are needed for these purposes. This assertion that a plan to collect less data may actually lead to improved research results does not seem to be the collective wisdom in most of the behavioral sciences. But at the very least, if we are planning to collect lots of longitudinal data, we should take a step back and ask "why?" And we should no longer blame the data analysis requirements on what turns out to be the data analysis limitations of the investigators.

REFERENCES

Albert, M., Blacker, D., Moss, M. B., Tanzi, R., & McArdle, J. J. (2007). Longitudinal change in cognitive performance among individuals with mild cognitive impairment. *Neuropsychology, 21*(2), 158–169.

Allison, D. B., Allison, R. L., Faith, M. S., Paultre, F., & Pi-Sunyer, F. X. (1997). Power and money: Designing statistically powerful studies while minimizing financial costs. *Psychological Methods, 2*(1), 20–33.

Allison, P. D. (1990). Change scores as dependent variables in regression analysis. In C.C. Clogg (Ed.), *Sociological methodology 1990* (pp. 93–114). San Francisco, CA: Jossey-Bass.

Anderson, T. W. (1958). *An introduction to multivariate statistical analysis.* New York: John Wiley & Sons.

Baker, F. B., & Kim, S.-H. (2004). *Item Response Theory parameter estimation techniques* (2nd ed.). New York: Marcel Dekker.

Bell, R. Q. (1953). Convergence: An accelerated longitudinal approach. *Child Development, 24*(2), 145–152.

Bell, R. Q. (1954). An experimental test of the accelerated longitudinal approach. *Child Development, 25,* 281–286.

Bock, R. D. (1975). *Multivariate statistical methods in behavioral research.* New York: McGraw-Hill.

Botwinick, J., & Seigler, I. (1980). Intellectual ability comparisons among the elderly: Simultaneous cross-sectional and longitudinal comparisons. *Developmental Psychology, 16*(1), 49–53.

Box, J. F. (1980). R. A. Fisher and the Design of Experiments, 1922–1926. *The American Statistician, 34*(1), 1–7.

Browne, M. (2001). An overview of analytic rotation in exploratory factor analysis. *Multivariate Behavioral Research, 36* (1), 111–150.

Browne, M., & du Toit, S. H. C. (1991). Models for learning data. In L. Collins & J. L. Horn, (Eds.), *Best methods for the analysis of change* (pp. 47–68). Washington, DC: APA Press.

Burr, J. A., & Nesselroade, J. R. (1990). Change measurement. In A. Von Eye & M. Rovine (Eds.), *Statistical methods in longitudinal research.* New York: Academic.

Cattell, R. B. (1970). Separating endogenous, exogenous, ecogenic, and epogenic component curves in developmental data. *Developmental Psychology, 3*(2), 151–162.

Collins, L. M. (2006). Analysis of longitudinal data: The integration of theoretical model, temporal design, and statistical model. *Annual Review of Psychology, 57,* 505–528.

Cudeck, R. (2000). An estimate of the covariance between two variables which are not jointly observed. *Psychometrika, 65*(4), 539–546.

Cudeck, R., du Toit, S., & Sorbom, D. (Eds.). (2001). *Structural equation modeling: Present and future.* Lincolnwood, IL: Scientific Software International.

Cudeck, R., & Harring, J. R. (2007). Analysis of nonlinear patterns of change with random coefficient models. *Annual Review of Psychology, 58,* 615–637.

Daniels, M. J., & Hogan, J. W. (2008). *Missing data in longitudinal studies: Strategies for Bayesian modeling and sensitivity analysis.* New York: Chapman & Hall.

Dorans, N. J. (2007). Linking scores from multiple health outcome instruments. *Quality of Life Research, 16,* 85–94.

Dorans, N. J., Pommerich, M., & Holland, P. W. (2007). *Linking and aligning scores and scales.* New York: Springer.

Embretson, S. E., & Reise, S. P. (2000). *Item Response Theory for psychologists.* Mahwah, NJ: Erlbaum.

Enders, C. K. (2001). A primer on maximum likelihood algorithms for use with missing data. *Structural Equation Modeling, 8,* 128–141.

Fan, X. (2003). Power of latent growth modeling for detecting group differences in linear growth trajectory parameters. *Structural Equation Modeling, 10*(3), 380–400.

Ferrer, E., Hamagami, F., & McArdle, J. J. (2004). Modeling latent growth curves with incomplete data using different types of structural equation modeling and multilevel software. *Structural Equation Modeling, 11*(3), 452–483.

Ferrer, E., & McArdle, J. J. (2004). An experimental analysis of dynamic hypotheses about cognitive abilities and achievement from childhood to early adulthood. *Developmental Psychology, 40,* 935–952.

Ferrer, E., McArdle, J. J., Shaywitz, B. A., Holahan, J. M., Marchione, K., & Shaywitz, S. E. (2007). Longitudinal models of developmental dynamics between reading and cognition from childhood to adolescence. *Developmental Psychology, 43,* 1460–1473.

Ferrer, E., Salthouse, T. A., McArdle, J. J., Stewart, W. F., & Schwartz, B. (2005). Multivariate modeling of age and retest effects in longitudinal studies of cognitive abilities. *Psychology and Aging, 20*(3), 412–442.

Finch, C. E. (2007). *The biology of human longevity: Inflammation, nutrition, and aging in the evolution of lifespans.* New York: Academic.

Fisher, R. A. (1925). *Statistical methods for field workers.* London: Oliver and Boyd.

Fisher, R. A. (1940). An examination of the different possible solutions of a problem in incomplete blocks. *Annals of Eugenics, 10,* 52–75.

Frees, E. W. (2004). *Longitudinal and panel data: Analysis and applications in the social sciences.* New York: Cambridge Press.

Gelman, A., & Meng, X.-L. (2004). *Applied Bayesian modeling and causal inference from incomplete-data perspectives.* Hoboken, NJ: John Wiley & Sons.

Ghisletta, P., Bickel, J.-F., & Lövdén, M. (2006). Does activity engagement protect against cognitive decline in old age? Methodological and analytical considerations. *Journal of Gerontology B Psy Sciences, 61,* 253–261.

Ghisletta, P., & Lindenberger, U. (2003). Age-based structural dynamics between perceptual speed and knowledge in the Berlin Aging Study: Direct evidence for ability dedifferentiation in old age. *Psychology and Aging, 18*(4), 696–713.

Ghisletta, P., & Lindenberger, U. (2005). Exploring the structural dynamics of the link between sensory and cognitive functioning in old age: Longitudinal evidence from the Berlin Aging Study. *Intelligence, 33,* 555–587.

Grenander, U. (1959). Probability and statistics: The Harald Cramér volume. New York: John Wiley & Sons.

Grimm, K. J., & McArdle, J. J. (2007). A dynamic structural analysis of the potential impacts of major context shifts on lifespan cognitive development. In T. D. Little, J. A. Bovaird, & N. A. Card (Eds.), *Modeling contextual effects in longitudinal studies* (pp. 363–386). Mahwah, NJ: Erlbaum.

Guilford, J. P. (1956). Fundamental statistics in psychology and education. New York: McGraw-Hill.

Hamagami, F., & McArdle, J. J. (2000). Advanced studies of individual differences linear dynamic models for longitudinal data analysis. In G. Marcoulides & R. Schumacker (Eds.), *New developments and techniques in structural equations modeling* (pp. 203–246). Mahwah, NJ: Erlbaum.

Hamagami, F., & McArdle, J. J. (2007). Dynamic extensions of latent difference score models. In S. M. Boker et al. (Eds.), *Quantitative methods in contemporary psychology* (pp. 47–85). Mahwah, NJ: Erlbaum.

Hamagami, F., McArdle, J. J., & Cohen, P. (2000). Bivariate dynamic systems analyses based on a latent difference score approach for personality disorder ratings. In V. J. Molfese & D. L. Molfese (Eds.), *Temperament and personality development across the life span.* Mahwah, NJ: Erlbaum.

Horn, J. L. (1972). State, trait, and change dimensions of intelligence. *The British Journal of Mathematical and Statistical Psychology, 42*(2), 159–185.

Horn, J. L., & McArdle, J. J. (1980). Perspectives on mathematical and statistical model building (MASMOB) in research on aging.

In L. Poon (Ed.), *Aging in the 1980s: Psychological issues* (pp. 503–541). Washington, DC: American Psychological Association.

Hsiao, C. (2003). *Analysis of panel data* (2nd ed.). New York: Cambridge Press.

Little, R. J. A., & Rubin, D. J. (2002). *Statistical analysis with missing data* (2nd ed.). New York: John Wiley & Sons.

Lord, F. M. (1955). Estimation of parameters from incomplete data. *Journal of the American Statistical Association, 50,* 870–876.

Lövdén, M., Ghisletta, P., & Lindenberger, U. (2005). Social participation attenuates decline in perceptual speed in old and very old age. *Psychology and Aging, 20,* 423–434.

MacCallum, R. C., Browne, M. B., & Sugawara, H. M. (1996). Power analysis and determination of sample size for covariance structure modeling. *Psychological Methods, 1*(2), 130–149.

MacKinnon, D. P., Fairchild, A. J., & Fritz, M. S. (2007). Mediation analysis. *Annual Review of Psychology, 58,* 593–614.

Maxwell, S. E. (2004). The persistence of underpowered studies in psychological research: Causes, consequences, and remedies. *Psychological Methods, 9*(2), 147–163.

Maxwell, S. E., & Delaney, H. D. (1990). *Designing experiments and analyzing data: A model comparison perspective.* Belmont, CA: Wadsworth.

Maxwell, S. E., Kelley, K., & Rausch, J. R. (2008). Sample size planning for statistical power and accuracy in parameter estimation. *Annual Review of Psychology, 59,* 537–563.

McArdle, J. J. (1980). Causal modeling applied to psychonomic systems simulation. *Behavior Research Methods & Instrumentation, 12,* 193–209.

McArdle, J. J. (1986). Latent variable growth within behavior genetic models. *Behavior Genetics, 16*(1), 163–200.

McArdle, J. J. (1988). Dynamic but structural equation modeling of repeated measures data. In J. R. Nesselroade & R. B. Cattell (Eds.), *The handbook of multivariate experimental psychology* (Vol. 2, pp. 561–614). New York: Plenum.

McArdle, J. J. (1989). Structural modeling experiments using multiple growth functions. In P. Ackerman, R. Kanfer, & R. Cudeck (Eds.), *Learning and individual differences: Abilities, motivation, and methodology* (pp. 71–117). Hillsdale, NJ: Erlbaum.

McArdle, J. J. (1994). Structural factor analysis experiments with incomplete data. *Multivariate Behavioral Research, 29*(4), 409–454.

McArdle, J. J. (2000). Obituary for Richard Q. Bell (1919–2001). *American Psychologist, 57*(6), 791.

McArdle, J. J. (2001). A latent difference score approach to longitudinal dynamic structural analysis. In R. Cudeck, S. du Toit, & D. Sorbom (Eds.). *Structural Equation Modeling: Present and future* (pp. 342–380). Lincolnwood, IL: Scientific Software International.

McArdle, J. J. (2007). Five steps in the structural factor analysis of longitudinal data. In R. Cudeck & R. MacCallum (Eds.), *Factor analysis at 100 years* (pp. 99–130). Mahwah, NJ: Erlbaum.

McArdle, J. J. (2009). Latent variable modeling of longitudinal data. *Annual Review of Psychology, 60,* 20.1–20.29.

McArdle, J. J., & Aggen, S. (1998). *Structural equation models with randomized and non-randomized experiments.* Unpublished manuscript, Department of Psychology, University of Virginia.

McArdle, J. J., & Anderson, E. (1990). Latent variable growth models for research on aging. In J. E. Birren & K. W. Schaie (Eds.), *The handbook of the psychology of aging* (pp. 21–43). New York: Plenum.

McArdle, J. J., & Bell, R. Q. (2000). An introduction to latent growth curve models for developmental data analysis. In T. D. Little, K. U. Schnabel, & J. Baumert (Eds.), *Modeling longitudinal and multiple-group data: Practical issues, applied approaches, and scientific examples* (pp. 69–107). Mahwah, NJ: Erlbaum.

McArdle, J. J., & Epstein, D. B. (1987). Latent growth curves within developmental structural equation models. *Child Development, 58*(1), 110–133.

McArdle, J. J., Ferrer-Caja, E., Hamagami, F., & Woodcock, R. W. (2002). Comparative longitudinal multilevel structural analyses of the growth and decline of multiple intellectual abilities over the life-span. *Developmental Psychology, 38*(1), 115–142.

McArdle, J. J., Fisher, G. G., & Kadlec, K. M. (2007). Latent variable analysis of age trends in tests of cognitive ability in the health and retirement survey, 1992–2004. *Psychology and Aging, 22*(3), 525–545.

McArdle, J. J., Grimm, K., Hamagami, F., Bowles, R., & Meredith, W. (2002, October). A dynamic structural equation analysis of vocabulary abilities over the life-span. Presented at the Annual meeting of the Society of Multivariate Experimental Psychologists, Charlottesville, VA.

McArdle, J. J., Grimm, K., Hamagami, F., Bowles, R., & Meredith, W. (2009). A multiple-group longitudinal item response model of vocabulary abilities over the life-span. *Psychological Methods, 14*(2), 126–149.

McArdle, J. J., & Hamagami, E. (1991). Modeling incomplete longitudinal and cross-sectional data using latent growth structural models. In L. Collins & J. L. Horn (Eds.), *Best methods for the analysis of change* (pp. 276–304). Washington, DC: APA Press.

McArdle, J. J., & Hamagami, E. (1992). Modeling incomplete longitudinal and cross-sectional data using latent growth structural models. *Experimental Aging Research, 18*(3), 145–166.

McArdle, J. J., & Hamagami, F. (2001). Linear dynamic analyses of incomplete longitudinal data. In L. Collins & A. Sayer (Eds.), *Methods for the analysis of change* (pp. 137–176). Washington, DC: APA Press.

McArdle, J. J., & Hamagami, F. (2003). Structural equation models for evaluating dynamic concepts within longitudinal twin analyses. *Behavior Genetics, 33*(2), 137–159.

McArdle, J. J. & Hamagami, F. (2004). Methods for dynamic change hypotheses In K. van Montfort, J. Oud, & A. Satorra. (Ed.) *Recent developments in structural equation models* (pp. 295–336). London: Kluwer.

McArdle, J. J., Hamagami, F., Elias, M. F., & Robbins, M. (1991). Structural modeling of mixed longitudinal and cross-sectional data. *Experimental Aging Research, 17*(1), 29–52.

McArdle, J. J., Hamagami, F., Jones, K., Jolesz, F., Kikinis, R., Spiro, A., et al. (2004). Structural modeling of dynamic changes in memory and brain structure using longitudinal data from the normative aging study. *Journal of Gerontology Series B: Psychological Sciences, 59B*(6), P294–P304.

McArdle, J. J., Hamagami, F., Meredith, W., & Bradway, K. P. (2000). Modeling the dynamic hypotheses of Gf-Gc theory using longitudinal life-span data. *Learning and individual differences, 12,* 53–79.

McArdle, J. J., & Nesselroade, J. (1994). Structuring data to study development and change. In S. H. Cohen & H. W. Reese (Eds.), *Life-span developmental psychology: Methodological innovations* (pp. 223–267). Hillsdale, NJ: Erlbaum.

McArdle, J. J., & Nesselroade, J. R. (2003). Growth curve analyses in contemporary psychological research. In J. Schinka & W. Velicer (Eds.), *Comprehensive handbook of psychology: Vol. 2, Research methods in psychology* (pp. 447–480). New York: Pergamon.

McArdle, J. J., Prescott, C. A., Hamagami, F., & Horn, J. L. (1998) A contemporary method for developmental-genetic analyses of age changes in intellectual abilities. *Developmental Neuropsychology, 14*(1), 69–114.

McArdle, J. J., & Prindle, J. J. (2008). A latent change score analysis of a randomized clinical trial in reasoning training. *Psychology and Aging, 23*(4), 702–719.

McArdle, J. J., Small, B. J., Backman, L., & Fratiglioni, L. (2005). Longitudinal models of growth and survival applied to the early detection of Alzheimer's disease. *Journal of Geriatric Psychiatry and Neurology, 18*(4), 234–241.

McArdle, J. J., & Woodcock, J. R. (1997). Expanding test-rest designs to include developmental time-lag components. *Psychological Methods, 2*(4), 403–435.

McDonald, R. P. (1985). *Factor analysis and related methods.* Hillsdale, NJ: Erlbaum.

McDonald, R. P. (1999) *Test theory: A unified treatment.* Mahwah, NJ: Erlbaum.

McKibben, B. (1992). *The age of missing information.* New York: Random House.

Meredith, W., & Tisak, J. (1990). Latent curve analysis. *Psychometrika, 55,* 107–122.

Miyazaki, Y., Raudenbush, S. W. (2000). Tests for linkage of multiple cohorts in an accelerated longitudinal design. *Psychological Methods, 5,* 24–63.

Muthén, B. O., & Curran, P. (1997). General longitudinal modeling of individual differences in experimental designs: A latent variable framework for analysis and power estimation. *Psychological Methods, 2,* 371–402.

Muthén, L. K., & Muthén, B. O. (2002). How to use a Monte Carlo study to decide on sample size and determine power. *Structural Equation Modeling, 4,* 599–620.

Nesselroade, J. R., & Baltes, P. B. (Eds.). (1979). *Longitudinal research in the study of behavior and development.* New York: Academic.

Orth, U., Berking, M., Walker, N., Meier, L. L., & Znoj, H. (2008). Forgiveness and psychological adjustment following interpersonal transgressions: A longitudinal analysis. *Journal of Research in Personality, 42,* 365–385.

Pukelsheim, F. (1993). *Optimal design of experiments.* New York: John Wiley & Sons.

Rasch, G. (1960). *Probabilistic models for some intelligence and attainment tests.* Chicago: University of Chicago Press.

Raudenbush, S. W. (2001). Comparing personal trajectories and drawing causal inferences from longitudinal data. *Annual Review of Psychology, 52,* 501–525.

Raudenbush, S. W., & Liu, X. (2000) Statistical power and optimal design for multisite randomized trials. *Psychological Methods, 5*(2), 199–213.

Rindskopf, D. (1984). Using phantom and imaginary latent variables to parameterize constraints in linear structural models. *Psychometrika, 49*(1), 37–47.

Rogosa, D., & Willett, J. (1983). Demonstrating the reliability of the difference score in the measurement of change. *Journal of Educational Measurement, 20*(4), 335–343.

Saris, W. E., & Satorra, A. (1985). Power of the likelihood ratio test in covariance structure analysis. *Psychometrika, 50,* 1, 83–89.

Saris, W. E., & Satorra, A. (1993). Power evaluations in structural equation models. In K. Bollen & S. Long (Eds.), *Testing structural equation models* (pp. 181–204). Beverly Hills, CA: Sage.

Schaie, K. W. (1965). A general model for the study of developmental problems. *Psychological Bulletin, 64*(2), 92–107.

Shadish, W., Cook, T. D., & Campbell, D. T. (2002). *Experimental and quasi-experimental design for generalized causal inference.* Boston: Houghton Mifflin.

Singer, H. (1995). Analytical score function for irregularly sampled continuous time stochastic processes with control variables and missing values. *Econometric Theory, 11*(4), 721–735.

Solomon, R. L. (1949). An extension of the control group design. *Psychological Bulletin, 46,* 137–150.

Stankov, L., & Chen, K. (1988). Can we boost fluid and crystallised intelligence? A structural modelling approach. *Australian Journal of Psychology, 40*(4), 363–376.

Stapleton, L. M. (2002). The incorporation of sample weights into structural equation modeling. *Structural Equation Modeling, 9*(4), 475–502.

Thorndike, R. L. (1941). The effect of the interval between test and retest on the constancy of the IQ. *Journal of Educational Psychology,* 1–7.

Thurstone, L. L. (1937). Psychology as a quantitative rational science. *Science, 85*(2201), 227–232.

von Davier, A. A., Holland, P. W., & Thayer, D. T. (2004). *The kernel method of equating.* New York: Springer.

Wainer, H. (1989). Eelworms, bullet holes, and Geraldine Ferraro: Some problems with statistical adjustment and some solutions. *Journal of Educational and Behavioral Statistics, 14*(2), 121–140.

Wainer, H. (Ed.). (2000). Computerized Adaptive Testing: A primer (2nd ed). Mahwah, NJ: Erlbaum.

Wechsler, D. (1955). *Manual for the Wechsler Adult Intelligence Scale.* New York: The Psychological Corporation.

Wechsler, D. (1981). *Manual for the Wechsler Adult Intelligence Scale-Revised.* New York: The Psychological Corporation.

Wilson, M. (2005). *Constructing measures: An item response approach.* Mahwah, NJ: Erlbaum.

Wishart, J. (1938). Growth rate determinations in nutrition studies with the bacon pig, and their analyses. *Biometrika, 30,* 16–28.

Wohlwill, J. F. (1973). *The study of behavioral development.* Oxford: Academic.

Woodcock, R. W. (1990). Theoretical foundations of the WJ-R measures of cognitive ability. *Journal of Psychoeducational Assessment, 8*(3), 231–258.

CHAPTER 4

Brain Development
An Overview

PHILIP DAVID ZELAZO and WENDY S. C. LEE

This chapter first reviews research on the structural development of the brain across the life span, addressing changes in white matter, gray matter, sex differences in brain development, relations between brain structure and behavior, and the influence of experience on brain development. A final section, intended to illustrate changes in brain function across the life span, focuses on prefrontal cortical function, associated with executive function, or the conscious control of thought, action, and emotion. This review demonstrates that brain development is a lifelong phenomenon characterized by considerable regional specificity and also by a series of overlapping, dynamic processes that yield both progressive events, such as increases in white matter, and regressive events, such as decreases in gray matter. A good deal is now known about the structural development of the brain, but links to function are only starting to be understood. Evidence suggests, however, that specific neural changes are linked to the attainment of specific cognitive capabilities, and that both may be influenced by experience, consistent with the view that the human brain, like other biological systems, develops through a complex series of reciprocal interactions.

BRAIN STRUCTURE

The mere fact that the human brain develops across the life span is obvious even from gross measures, such as brain weight (e.g., Dekaban & Sadowsky, 1978). At birth, the brain typically weighs about 370 g, about a fourth to a third of the weight of the adult brain, which is roughly 1,400 to 1,500 g, or 3 lbs. Overall brain weight increases rapidly during early childhood, tripling by age 3 years, and then increases more slowly, gradually reaching a plateau by about 10 years of age. Brain weight then begins to decrease by about the fifth decade of life, reaching a level after 86 years that is about 11% less than that of young adults. In general, this inverted-U–shaped developmental pattern fits with what we know about the rapid rise and gradual fall of our cognitive functions (e.g., Craik & Bialystok, 2006). This broad outline, however, obscures a much more complex set of dynamic processes and omits important changes that occur before birth.

In fact, a great deal of brain development occurs before birth, and research has now traced this prenatal development in detail, from the formation of the neural plate at about 20 days after conception through a series of processes that include neuronal proliferation, neuronal migration, synaptogenesis, and myelination, among other processes (see Table 4.1 for a brief summary; for a detailed review, see Stiles, 2008). The pace of this development is remarkable. During the second trimester of pregnancy, for example, as many as 250,000 new neurons are formed every minute in the fetal brain. Indeed, by 5 months gestational age, the fetal brain already has nearly as many neurons as the typical adult brain—one hundred billion neurons, an astronomical number that is more than 15 times the Earth's current population. Despite this early start and remarkably rapid pace, however, brain development is a protracted process that continues into adulthood, with major changes taking place after increases in brain weight have slowed. Moreover, brain development involves both progressive events, such as synaptogenesis, and regressive events, such as synaptic pruning, and many of these events occur both before and after birth.

Historically, research on brain development in human beings has either relied on limited postmortem samples (e.g., Molliver, Kostović, & Van der Loos, 1973) or used relatively indirect measures such as head circumference (Epstein, 1986) or scalp electrical activity (e.g., Bell & Fox, 1992). Although these approaches have been valuable, revealing, for example, that synaptic density is higher in childhood than it is in adulthood (e.g., Huttenlocher, 1979), recent technologic advances have allowed unprecedented opportunities to observe detailed developmental changes in the living brain. Techniques such as near-infrared spectroscopy,

Table 4.1 Summary of Selected Processes in Human Brain Development

Processes	Description	Time Frame
Gastrulation	Differentiation of embryonic (epiblast) cells into 3 cell lines (primary germ layers) forming the trilaminar disc. Cells from the ectodermal germ layer will become neurons (via a process called neural induction).	14–18 days g.a.
Primary Neurulation	Creation of the neural plate and neural tube.	18–28 days g.a. Closure of rostral end of neural tube at 24 days g.a.
Neuronal Proliferation (Neurogenesis)	The creation of neurons (through cell division) from neural progenitor cells.	Onset at 52 days g.a., peak rate at 70–140 days g.a. May continue across the lifespan, at least in some areas (e.g. hippocampus).
Neuronal Migration	Movement of neurons from proliferation zones to final locations in the brain, including the 6 cortical layers.	Primarily between 52–140 days g.a.
Neuritogenesis	Growth of neuronal processes (axons and dendrites with dendritic spines).	Axonal growth starts as early as 52 days g.a., and dendritic arborization, which begins around 100 days g.a., continues postnatally, especially during the first 2 years.
Synaptogenesis	Formation of synapses between the axon of one neuron and (usually) a dendritic spine of another, allowing for communication via electrochemical signals. Average number of synapses per neuron may be as high as 80,000 (in prefrontal cortex).	Starts prenatally, as soon as axons and dendrites come into contact (around 160 days g.a.); occurs rapidly during the first postnatal years; continues across the lifespan. During the second postnatal year, about 40,000 new synapses are being formed every second, and during early childhood the total number of synapses is about a quadrillion (10^{15}).
Dendritic Pruning and Synaptic Elimination	Experience-dependent removal of excess synaptic contacts.	Starts postnatally and continues until late adolescence for some brain regions.
Myelination	Wrapping of axons in myelin (formed from oligodendrocytes).	Starts prenatally (end of 2nd trimester) for some cortical regions and continues well into adulthood, at least for some regions.
Gyrification	The folding of the surface of the brain, creating gryi and sulci.	Begins around 126 days g.a., increases through the preschool period, resulting in higher-than-adult levels of gyrification. Decrease in gyrification during the school age years.

Note: "g.a." = gestational age.

structural magnetic resonance imaging (MRI), functional magnetic resonance imaging (fMRI), and diffusion tensor imaging (DTI) have provided a much clearer picture of the structural and functional changes that occur over the course of childhood and adolescence, and during adulthood (see Table 4.2 for a brief description of these and other commonly used methods in brain research).

PATTERNS OF CHANGE

A great deal of variability exists within brain structures, even among healthy, typically developing individuals (e.g., Sowell et al., 2002). There are, however, some relatively consistent patterns of structural and functional change in the brain that are seen over the course of development. These are

Table 4.2   Methods and Techniques Used in Brain Imaging and the Measurement of Brain Electrical Activity

Method	Description
Electroencephalogram (EEG)	EEGs record the background electrical activity of the brain generated by the firing of neurons, and are well suited for measuring state processes over a short period of time. The recordings are obtained by placing electrodes on the scalp. The procedure is noninvasive and relatively inexpensive, but has poor spatial resolution, although this is improving with increasing numbers of electrodes used (e.g., over 200 electrodes can be used via cap or net).
Event-Related Potential (ERP)	ERPs are EEGs that are time-locked to a discrete event (stimulus or response). Because potentials are difficult to discriminate from the background activity, the event is repeated many times and the brain activity is averaged. ERPs provide temporal resolution on the scale of milliseconds. An ERP consists of several positive (P) and negative (N) waves referenced to the time (msec) it occurs after the event (e.g., P_{300}). Because a verbal or motor response from the participants is not necessary, ERPs can be used in infant research. One challenge that remains is the loss of data due to artifacts from muscle and eye movements.
Positron Emission Tomography (PET)	PET scans can produce two- or three-dimensional images of functional processes in the brain. Subjects ingest glucose with a radioisotope of carbon, nitrogen, oxygen, or fluorine. Brain areas that are particularly active during a task will have greater glucose uptake, be more radioactive, and emit more positrons during decay. A detector analyzes the emissions and reconstructs their origin to localize brain activity. Because the brain is always active, baseline activity must be measured and subtracted from the activity during the task of interest. Unfortunately, there is limited spatial resolution with fairly large voxels (cubic centimeters) and limited temporal resolution on the scale of minutes. PET scans are expensive, and although the radioisotopes are not usually harmful and have a very short life (only minutes), ethnical constraints limit the use of PET scans with children.
Magnetic Resonance Imaging (MRI)	For MRI scans, participants are placed in a scanner with a very powerful magnetic field that causes the hydrogen atoms in the body or brain to align in the direction of the field. When radio waves are beamed at the atoms, the atoms emit radio wave signals that characterize the density of atoms present and their chemical environment. This allows for the construction of a more accurate and dense image that shows the composition of the tissue structure. Cross-sectional "slices" of brain images at various orientations can be used to construct three-dimensional images of the brain. MRI scans are non-invasive, do not involve radioisotopes or x-rays, and can be performed in a short period of time.
Functional MRI (fMRI)	fMRI scans reveal functional processes within the brain. When certain regions of the brain are more active during a task, there is increased blood flow and increased oxygen. Changes in the relative concentrations of oxygenated hemoglobin to deoxygenated hemoglobin attenuate MRI signals, which provide a link to neural activity (e.g., BOLD signals; Blood-Oxygen-Level-Dependent). These changes are tracked moment to moment, and by taking consecutive slices of the brain in different orientations, the areas of greatest activation can be reconstructed. Activation patterns during a task and baseline are compared to allow researchers to determine task-related activity. The spatial resolution allows accurate mapping on the order of several millimeters. While having greater spatial resolution than PET, fMRI also has poor temporal resolution.
Magnetoencephalogram (MEG)	MEG is another non-invasive procedure, but unlike fMRI and PET which both measure brain metabolism, MEG measures brain function directly. The magnetic fields created by neural activity in the brain are detected by super-conducting detectors and amplifiers (SQUIDs), and the spatial distribution of these fields is used to localize the sources of brain activity. This can be superimposed on anatomical images such as those from MRI to reveal both structure and function. MEG has both high temporal resolution and high spatial resolution on the order of milliseconds and millimeters, respectively. However, the signal is very small and can easily be overwhelmed by signals in the environment, and thus, specialized shields are required to eliminate interference. Because the procedure is entirely non-invasive without exposure to radioisotopes, x-rays, or even magnetic fields, it can be used safely with children and infants.

(Continued)

Table 4.2 *Continued*

Method	Description
Near Infrared Spectroscopy (NIRS)	NIRS is a spectroscopic method that uses the near infrared (NIR) range of the electromagnetic spectrum to measure brain function. The transmission and absorption of NIR light in human body tissues provides information about changes in hemoglobin concentrations. When an area of the brain is activated, localized blood volumes change quickly (on the order of seconds). By continuously monitoring blood hemoglobin levels in specific regions and locations, activity can be determined using optical absorption coefficients. NIRS is a non-invasive assessment of brain function because NIR light can pass safely through skin, bones, and other tissues, especially in infants. Fiber-optic bundles or optodes are placed on opposite sides of the head or close together at acute angles. Light enters the head through one optode and a fraction of the photons are captured by the other optode. Multiple light emitters and detectors can be used. While NIRS is non-invasive and can be used with infants, it can only scan cortical tissues, unlike fMRI, which can measure activation throughout the brain. The terms optical topography (OT; which usually refers to three-dimensional NIRS) and Near Infrared Imaging (NIRI) are sometimes used interchangeably with NIRS, although there are distinctions.
Diffusion Tensor Imaging (DTI)	DTI is an MRI-based technique that is used to visualize the anisotropy of white matter tracts, providing information about location, orientation, and degree of myelination. Axons in parallel bundles and their myelin sheaths facilitate the diffusion of water along their main direction (anisotropic diffusion). DTI images this property by applying a series of magnetic field variations in the MRI magnet (diffusion gradients) that allows the calculation of a tensor for each voxel that produces a three-dimensional shape of the diffusion pattern. With DTI, tractography can be performed within the white matter to track a fiber along its whole length with estimation of its orientation and strength. Such methods can be particularly useful in the study of aging pathology and the degeneration of white matter.

summarized later, with occasional reference to Figure 4.1, which depicts some of the broad structural categories in question, including the frontal, temporal, parietal, and occipital (visual) lobes; prefrontal cortex; the language areas of the frontal (Broca's area) and temporal (Wernicke's area) cortices; gray versus white matter; and the corpus callosum. Locations within the brain are often described in terms of two perpendicular axes, one ranging from rostral (anterior) to caudal (posterior), and the other ranging from dorsal (superior) to ventral (inferior). The following sections address changes in white matter, gray matter, sex differences in brain development, relations between brain structure and behavior, and the influence of experience on brain development. A final section, intended to illustrate changes in brain function across the life span, focuses on a topic of considerable recent interest: prefrontal cortical function. Prefrontal cortical function is associated with executive function, or the conscious control of thought, action, and emotion. Executive function develops across the life span, with important improvements occurring during the preschool years (between about 2 and 5 years of age) and adolescence, and substantial declines associated with the late adult years.

White Matter

Myelination, the process whereby neuronal axons are wrapped in a white, fatty substance (myelin) formed from the cell membranes of glia (oligodendrocytes), insulates

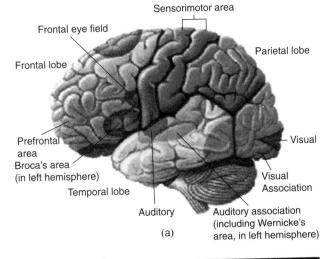

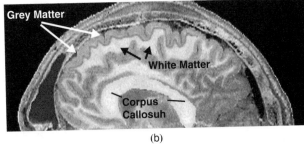

Figure 4.1 (a) Lateral view of the brain showing the four lobes of the cerebral cortex, as well as selected functional areas. (b) Sagittal section of the brain showing gray and white matter, including the corpus callosum. Rostral is left and caudal is right in these images.

axons and facilitates the conduction of electrical impulses—increasing conduction speed by about 100%. This process of white matter development starts before birth (at the end of the second trimester) for some brain regions and after birth for others, and both histologic analyses (e.g., Yakovlev & Lecours, 1967) and more recent neuroimaging methods (segmentation methods and DTI) suggest that myelination continues at a slow and steady pace into adulthood, when it appears to taper off and eventually decline (e.g., Klingberg, Vaidya, Gabrieli, Moseley, & Hedehus, 1999; Pfefferbaum, Mathalon, Sullivan, Rawles, Zipursky, & Lim, 1994; see Figure 4.2).

In general, myelination starts and finishes first for inferior versus superior regions (e.g., brainstem and cerebellum before cortex), for posterior versus anterior regions (e.g.,

occipital cortex before frontal cortex), and for central regions versus polar regions (e.g., regions around the central sulcus before the cortical poles). The occipital poles myelinate before the frontal poles, which, in turn, myelinate before the temporal poles (Sampaio & Truwit, 2001).

Research has also investigated the myelination of particular fiber tracts. Paus, Zijdenbos, Worsley, Collins, Blumenthal, Giedd, et al. (1999) found increases in white matter density (image intensity) between 4 and 17 years in the internal capsule bilaterally (a key corticospinal pathway) and the arcuate fasciculus on the left (connecting Broca's and Wernicke's areas). The corpus callosum, which connects the left and right hemispheres, shows peak growth rates between 3 and 6 years in the anterior regions that connect the two frontal lobes (Thompson, Giedd, Woods, MacDonald, Evans, & Toga, 2000), followed in later childhood by more rapid growth in more posterior regions (i.e., there is a rostral-to-caudal wave of growth in corpus callosum). Evidence also has been reported that corticolimbic pathways may show marked changes around puberty (Benes, Turtle, Khan, & Farol, 1994).

Studies examining changes in white matter during late adulthood have produced mixed findings that may partially be explained by the use of different methodologies and different ages and populations. Another difficulty in the measurement of white matter volume in late adulthood is that, although there may be real decreases in myelin during late adult development (Ansari & Loch, 1975), this may be offset to some degree by the expansion of capillary networks and perivascular spaces (Meier-Ruge, Ulrich, Brühlmann, & Meier, 1992), leading to the appearance of limited or no white matter volume loss. In any case, some studies have failed to find significant decreases in white matter with age, at least in some cerebral regions (e.g., Guttmann et al., 1998; Jernigan, Archibald, Berhow, Sowell, Foster, & Hesselink, 1991; Jernigan, Press, & Hesselink, 1990; Raz, Gunning, Head, Dupuis, McQuain, Briggs, et al., 1997), but there are reasons to believe that late adult development is indeed associated with white matter loss. Although Jernigan and colleagues (1990, 1997) did not find evidence of white matter loss, for example, they did observe greater signal hyperintensities in the white matter of their subjects aged 30 to 79 years. White matter hyperintensities are believed to reflect small, irregularly distributed lesions in white matter, and although poorly understood, these lesions are generally viewed as pathological and may be related to hypertension, transient cerebral ischemia, and cerebrovascular disease (Park, Polk, Mikels, Taylor, & Marshuetz, 2001). Moreover, in a later study,

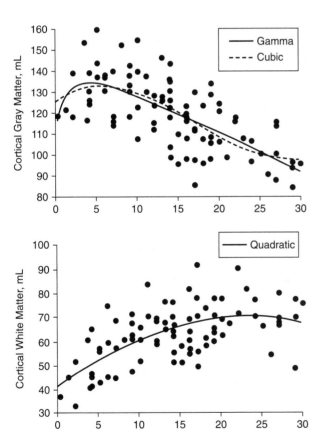

Figure 4.2 Quantitative magnetic resonance imaging estimates of cortical volume of gray (top) and white matter (bottom) as a function of age.

(Reprinted from Pfefferbaum, A., Mathalon, D. H., Sullivan, E. V., Rawles, J. M., Zipursky, R. B., & Lim, K. O. (1994). A quantitative magnetic resonance imaging study of changes in brain morphology from infancy to late adulthood. *Archives of Neurology, 51*, 874–887, by permission.)

Jernigan, Archibald, Fennema-Notestine, Gamst, Stout, Bonner, and Hesselink (2001) expanded the age range of their earlier investigation to include participants as old as 99 years; they found that between 30 and 90 years, the loss of cerebral white matter was estimated at 26%. White matter loss occurred later than gray matter loss in the cerebral cortex and the cerebellum, but the total volume loss was ultimately greater for white matter. This suggests that white matter may show a more precipitous decline in the very late adult years.

Gray Matter

Neuroimaging research (e.g., Gogtay et al., 2004; Jernigan & Tallal, 1990; O'Donnell, Noseworthy, Levine, Brandt, & Dennis, 2005; Pfefferbaum et al., 1994; Reiss, Abrams, Singer, Ross, & Denckla, 1996) suggests that, in contrast with the generally monotonic (and negatively accelerating) growth of white matter during childhood, adolescence, and early adulthood, gray matter, which is composed of neurons with dendritic and synaptic processes, as well as glia and vasculature, shows more complex patterns that vary not only quantitatively but qualitatively by region. One prominent pattern seen in many cortical regions (especially dorsal regions) is that of increases in infancy and early childhood, followed by gradual decreases that start in late childhood and continue into adulthood, reaching a plateau (see Figure 4.2). In broad terms, this pattern confirms the trend seen by Huttenlocher (e.g., 1979, 1990) in his histologic studies of synaptic density. Huttenlocher noted that synaptic density in layer III of the middle frontal gyrus reaches a peak at about 1 year of age that is considerably greater than the adult level, remains high until at least age 7 years, and then declines by about 40% until about age 16, when the adult level is finally attained. A similar pattern was found in occipital cortex, but the inverted-U–shaped process was accelerated, with a peak reached at about 5 months of age (Huttenlocher & Dabholkar, 1997).

Cross-sectional and longitudinal MRI studies have found evidence for an inverted-U–shaped pattern of changes in gray matter in several regions. For example, Sowell et al.'s (1999) cross-sectional MRI study found marked reductions in gray matter density in frontal and parietal cortices between childhood (between 7 and 10 years of age) and adolescence (between 12 and 16 years of age), with the largest decreases occurring in parietal cortex. Subsequent work comparing the adolescents in that sample with a group of young adults (17–30 years of age) found that the most prominent reductions occurred in frontal cortex

(Sowell et al., 2003). Together, these findings suggest that, on average, parietal cortex may reach maturity earlier than frontal cortex.

Giedd and colleagues' (1999) longitudinal MRI study demonstrated that increases in gray matter volume may continue much later than had previously been believed. In this study, 145 participants between the ages of 4.2 and 21.6 years were scanned between 1 and 5 times, with approximately 2 years between scans. Results for most cortical regions revealed increases in gray matter volume followed by postadolescent decreases, with peak volumes occurring at different times for different regions (and earlier for girls than for boys). For frontal cortex, peak volume occurred at 12.1 years for boys and 11 years for girls; for parietal cortex, it occurred at 11.8 years for boys and 10.2 years for girls; for temporal cortex, it occurred at 16.5 years for boys and 16.7 years for girls. In contrast with this pattern, however, gray matter volume continued to increase over the age range studied (4–22 years) for occipital cortex, suggesting that changes in gray matter volume as measured by MRI do not necessarily correspond to changes in synaptic density (cf. Huttenlocher & Dabholkar, 1997).

Age-related increases in gray matter in some regions have also been observed by Sowell and colleagues (2004), who measured cortical thickness (in millimeters) in a longitudinal study of 45 children between the ages of 5 and 11 years scanned twice (about 2 years apart). Gray matter thickness at the time of the first scan (between 5 and 9 years of age) ranged from 1.5 mm in occipital cortex to 5.5 mm in the dorsomedial prefrontal cortex. From time 1 to time 2, gray matter thinning, together with increases in brain size (radial expansion from the center of the brain), was seen in right frontal and bilateral parietooccipital areas, but gray matter thickening was seen in the left inferior frontal and bilateral temporal lobes (i.e., including Broca's and Wernicke's areas), with changes occurring at rates between −0.3 and +0.3 mm/year. Two-year changes in dorsal parietal and dorsal frontal cortices (i.e., thinning) were correlated with changes in performance (raw scores) on the vocabulary subtest of the WISC-R, pointing to the possible functional role of these structural changes (see Relations between Structural Changes and Behavior section later in this chapter).

Gogtay and colleagues (2004) measured regional cortical density (a measure related to both cortical volume and cortical thickness) in 13 individuals between 4 and 21 years of age, who were scanned every 2 years for 8 to 10 years. This study reported different trajectories of decline across the cortical surface. In general, gray matter decline started in sensorimotor regions (primary motor cortex, primary visual cortex, and primary sensory areas of parietal cortex) and then extended rostrally to prefrontal cortex. Dorsolateral prefrontal cortex and the superior temporal cortex were the last regions to show substantial decline (see Figure 4.3). The findings are generally consistent with a hierarchical view of cortical development that follows the phylogenetic sequence: lower-order somatosensory and visual cortices develop first (i.e., reach adult levels of gray matter density), followed by higher order association areas that integrate information from the lower order areas.

A more recent longitudinal study by Shaw et al. (2008) revealed more complex patterns of change that were related to cytoarchitectonic complexity (i.e., the complexity of the cellular architecture of different brain regions, ranging from the homotypical six-layered regions of cortex to more primitive allocortical regions). In particular, Shaw et al. examined data from 375 typically developing individuals and found a relatively complex cubic pattern of increase followed by decrease followed by stabilization in the regions with the largest number of cortical layers (i.e., six-layered cortex): the frontal pole, lateral frontal cortex, lateral temporal cortex, parietal cortex, and occipital isocortex. The simpler, transitional regions of the insula and anterior cingulate cortex showed a simpler quadratic trend of increase followed by decrease. Finally, the allocortical piriform cortex (important for olfaction) showed the simplest, linear pattern of thinning. Examples of these trajectories are shown in Figure 4.4.

Reductions in gray matter volume have been attributed to synaptic pruning, which may occur as a function of learning and experience (Casey, Giedd, & Thomas, 2000; Durston, Hulshoff Pol, Casey, Giedd, Buitelaar, & Van Engeland, 2001; Giedd et al., 1999). Indeed, by first overproducing synapses and then eliminating those that do not prove useful, brain development may be operating according to Darwinian principles of environmental selection. Childhood and early adolescence may, therefore, be periods of relative plasticity, where the brain is prepared for a great deal of learning from the environment (discussed

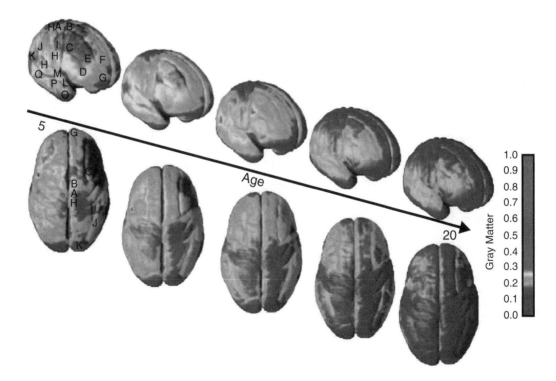

Figure 4.3   Right lateral and dorsal views of age-related changes (decreases) in gray matter volume on the cortical surface. Varying shades represent units of gray matter volume.

(Reprinted from Gogtay, N., Giedd, J. N., Lusk, L., Hayashi, K. M., Greenstein, D., Vaituzis, A. C., et al. (2004). Dynamic mapping of human cortical development during childhood through early adulthood. *Proceedings of the National Academy of Sciences, 101*, 8174–8179, by permission.)

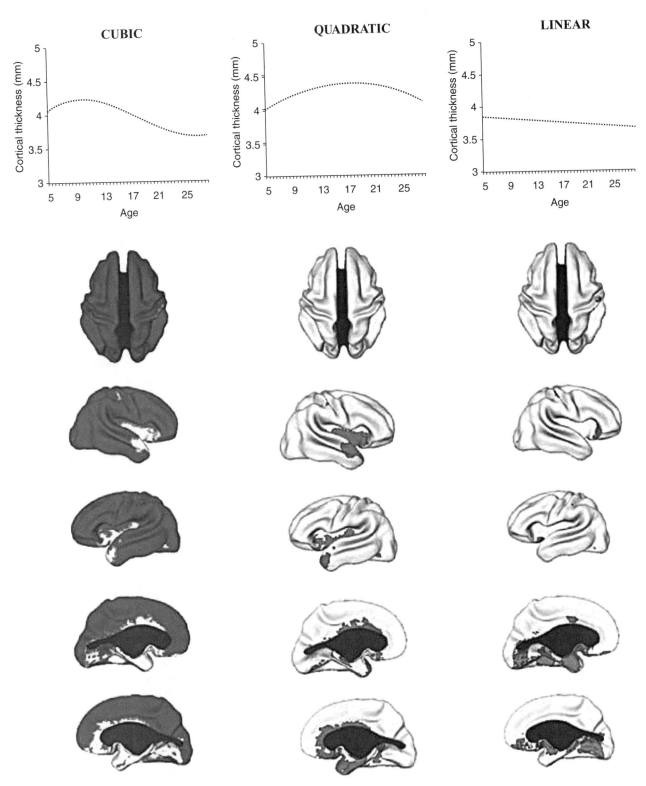

Figure 4.4 Regional variation in the complexity of developmental trajectories in cortical thickness, ranging from cubic (red) to quadratic (green) to linear (blue) for the regions shown in five different views: dorsal, right lateral, left lateral, right medial, and left medial. (Reprinted from Shaw, P., Kabani, N. J., Lerch, J. P., Eckstrand, K., Lenroot, R., Gogtay, N., et al. (2008). Neurodevelopmental trajectories of the human cerebral cortex. *Journal of Neuroscience, 28*, 3586–3594, by permission.)

further later). One caveat that should be noted, however, is that it is currently difficult to distinguish on the basis of MRI data between decreases in gray matter and increases in white matter, so to some (unknown) extent, what appears to be gray matter reduction may reflect the continued myelination of axons and dendrites (e.g., Gogtay et al., 2004; Paus, 2005).

Relatively few studies have examined gray matter across the life span, but there is good evidence for decreases in gray matter volume during later adulthood, especially in dorsal and lateral regions of the cortex (Bartzokis, Beckson, Lu, Nuechterlein, Edwards, & Mintz, 2001; Raz et al., 1997). For example, in one MRI study examining 465 healthy adults ranging from 17 to 79 years of age (Good, Johnsrude, Ashburner, Henson, Friston, & Frackowiak, 2001), researchers found accelerated gray matter loss bilaterally in the insula, superior parietal gyri, central sulci, and the cingulate sulci. Little change was observed in the amygdala, hippocampus, and entorhinal cortex, although other studies have found accelerated declines in the hippocampus (e.g., Jernigan et al., 2001; Kemper, 2000). Sowell et al. (2003) found that gray matter density reaches its lowest points in the lateral parietal cortex between 40 and 50 years, and in the lateral frontal cortex between 50 and 60 years. In the posterior temporal and inferior parietal regions, however, there was a different pattern, with a gradual increase until around 30 years, followed by a gradual decrease, and then by a steeper decrease occurring after about age 50 years. There are also increases in ventricular volume (e.g., Resnick et al., 2000), and as noted earlier, decreases in white matter volume (Bartzokis et al., 2001; Courchesne et al., 2001; Pfefferbaum et al., 1994). The Baltimore Longitudinal Study of Aging (Resnick, Pham, Kraut, Zonderman, & Davatzikos, 2003), provides a rare longitudinal look at brain development during the late adult years. Researchers followed older adults over 4 years, performing MRI scans at baseline, 2 years later, and 4 years later. They found a decrease of an average of 5.4 cm^3/year for total brain matter, 2.4 cm^3/year for gray matter, and 3.1 cm^3/year for white matter. There was also an increase of 1.4 cm^3/year in ventricle size.

Although observed decreases in gray matter earlier in life may reflect continued myelination of axons, decreases in gray matter later in life are more likely to reflect degenerative processes, including neuronal shrinkage in frontal and temporal cortices (Terry, De Teresa, & Hansen, 1987) and reduction in the length of myelinated axons (Marner, Nyengaard, Tang, & Pakkenberg, 2003). Structural changes associated with late adult development

at the neuronal level include the formation of neurofibrillary tangles, which are created when fibers in the axons become twisted together forming abnormal filaments, as well as the formation of neuritic or senile plaques, extracellular deposits of amyloid protein associated with damaged or dying neural structures (Morrison & Hof, 1997; Scheibel, 1996). Although a part of normal late adult development, large concentrations of neurofibrillary tangles and plaques can be indicative of Alzheimer disease. It was previously thought that widespread neuronal loss was also a part of normative late adult development, but with the advent of more accurate stereological procedures for counting neurons as opposed to measuring neuronal density, evidence suggests that neuronal decrease occurring during normal late adult development may be limited (Gómez-Isla et al., 1997; Morrison & Hof, 1997; Pakkenberg & Gundersen, 1997).

Sex Differences in Brain Development

Males, on average, have larger brains than females by about 10%, and this difference appears as early as 5 years of age (Reiss et al., 1996). Some studies have also reported a greater number of neurons across the cortex in the male brain (e.g., Pakkenberg & Gundersen, 1997), although this is inconsistent with some other reports, suggesting perhaps that differences in neuronal numbers may vary by region or cortical layer (Witelson, Glezer, & Kigar, 1995). Beyond global differences, a number of regional variations in structure by sex have been documented. One MRI report (Goldstein et al., 2001) studied 48 adults between the ages of 25 and 51 years, matching male and female subjects on characteristics such as socioeconomic status, education, ethnicity, and handedness. Results revealed that female subjects had greater cortical volume relative to the cerebrum, particularly in the frontal and medial paralimbic cortices, and male subjects had greater volume in the frontomedial cortex, amygdala, and hypothalamus. One possible explanation for sexual dimorphisms in the brain is the influence of sex hormones on brain development. The majority of evidence comes from research with nonhuman animals, but the regions with the greatest sex differences in Goldstein and colleagues' study correspond to homologous regions in nonhuman animals shown to have high levels of sex steroid receptors during critical developmental periods. This finding suggests indirectly that sex hormones may play a role in human brain sexual dimorphisms (see Collaer & Hines, 1995, for discussion of sex differences and the role of gonadal hormones).

Areas of particular interest with respect to sexual divergences include the amygdala, hypothalamus, hippocampus, and corpus callosum. The amygdala has been found to be larger in female than males adjusted for total brain size (Goldstein et al., 2001), and sex differences may exist in how the amygdala covaries in size with other brain structures (Mechelli, Friston, Frackowiak, & Price, 2005). Functional differences have also been reported, such as different patterns of lateralization of amygdala involvement in memory for emotional stimuli. Cahill, Uncapher, Kilpatrick, Alkire, and Turner (2004) found that activity in the right amygdala while viewing emotionally arousing images was more related to subsequent memory in females, whereas activity in the left amygdala was more related to subsequent memory in males.

Within the hypothalamus, one area of interest has been the sexually dimorphic nucleus in the preoptic area, which was reported to be larger in males (Swaab & Hofman, 1988). Postmortem examination of brains with a wide age range revealed that sexually dimorphic nucleus cell numbers began to differ for boys and girls around the ages of 2 to 4 years, primarily because of cell decreases in girls. The developmental pattern observed following early childhood was one of relative stability, followed by a decrease in cell numbers in males at age 50, and another period of decrease in females around age 60, with peak sex differences around the ages of 30 and after 80 years.

The hippocampus, which is important for learning and memory, has been found to be larger in female than males relative to total brain size (e.g., Goldstein et al., 2001). Interestingly, animal models have shown that the female hippocampus suffers more damage from chronic stress than does the male hippocampus (McEwen, 2000), which could have relevance in the study and treatment of disorders such as post-traumatic stress disorder and depression that disproportionately affect women.

Finally, because the corpus callosum is the main fiber tract that connects the left and right hemispheres, some researchers have suggested that it may underlie some of the sex differences seen in cognitive function (e.g., language and visuospatial ability), as well as in lateralization (e.g., language lateralization and handedness; Collaer & Hines, 1995). Although evidence has been conflicting since De Lacoste-Utamsing and Holloway (1982) reported females having a wider and more bulbous splenium (the posterior portion of the corpus callosum; see Collaer & Hines, 1995), studies with larger sample sizes and similar methodology to the original study suggest that small differences do exist (e.g., Allen, Richey, Chai, & Gorski,

1991; Clarke, Kraftsik, Van der Loos, & Innocenti, 1989). Moreover, individuals with reversed lateralization for language (i.e., with right hemisphere dominance for language) had a larger corpus callosum (O'Kusky et al., 1988), and females who showed reduced lateralization had larger spleniums (Hines, Chiu, McAdams, Bentler, & Lipcamon, 1992).

Differences in rates of sexual development may also play a significant role in sex differences. Waber (1977) examined spatial and verbal abilities in boys and girls classified as early or late maturing, with reference to puberty. Late-maturing children performed better than early-maturing children of the same sex on spatial measures, suggesting that because boys mature later than girls, their advantage in spatial performance may be related to their maturation rate.

The influence of rate of development more generally has also been implicated in male selective vulnerability to central nervous system insults (Gualtieri & Hicks, 1985) and to male vulnerability to cerebral injury during the perinatal period (Raz et al., 1995). Raz and colleagues found that, in a group of children who had suffered from perinatal intracranial hemorrhage, girls showed greater cognitive recovery with higher scores on standard intelligence tests, with no sex differences found in a comparison group. The authors hypothesized that a more developed system at the time of insult is less susceptible to injury because critical developmental processes have already taken place.

Sex differences have also been observed in the rate of development of different regions. For example, orbitofrontal cortex seems to develop more rapidly in male than in females (e.g., Overman, Bachevalier, Schumann, & Ryan, 1996), and work with nonhuman primates suggests that the rate of development of this region is under gonadal hormonal control (Clark & Goldman-Rakic, 1989). More generally, De Bellis et al. (2001) studied 118 individuals between the ages of 6 and 17 years, and found that the general patterns of developmental increases in white matter volume and decreases in gray matter volume are more pronounced for boys than they are for girls. That is, boys show faster rates of white matter increase, as well as faster rates of gray matter decrease. Figure 4.5 shows these patterns, adjusted for cerebral volume. In adults, the ratios of gray to white matter in different brain regions have been found to differ for males and females (Allen, Damasio, Grabowski, Bruss, & Zhang, 2003).

Sex differences in the brain have also been observed in adult and late adult development. In their cross-sectional sample of participants spanning the ages of 17 to 79 years,

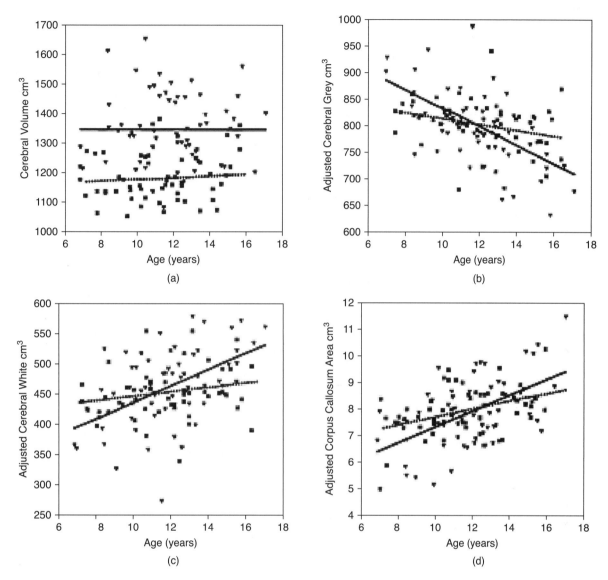

Figure 4.5 Scatterplots of (a) cerebral volume, (b) cerebral volume–adjusted cerebral gray matter volume, (c) cerebral volume–adjusted cerebral white matter volume, and (d) cerebral volume–adjusted cerebral corpus callosum volume. *Solid lines* show linear trends for males; *dotted lines* show linear trends for females.

(Reprinted from De Bellis, M. D., Keshavan, M.S., Beers, S. R., Hall, J., Frustaci, K., Masalehdan, A., et al. (2001). Sex differences in brain maturation during childhood and adolescence. *Cerebral Cortex, 11*, 552–557, by permission.)

Good et al. (2001) reported a steeper linear decline of global gray matter for male individuals, although no sex differences were observed in white matter loss. Other researchers have demonstrated region-specific differences in age-related changes that varied by sex. Using volumetric MRI, Murphy et al. (1996) compared young adults (20–35 years of age) with older adults (60–85 years of age) and found greater volume loss in the hippocampus and the parietal lobes in female subjects, and greater loss in the frontal and temporal lobes in male subjects. Similarly, Raz et al.

(1997) reported steeper decreases in volume in the inferior temporal cortex in male subjects. Examining subregions of the cortical lobes, Xu, Kobayashi, Yamaguchi, Iijima, Okada, and Yamashita (2000) found more age-related atrophy in the posterior right frontal lobe, the middle part of the right temporal lobe, the left basal ganglia, the parietal lobe, and the cerebellum in males. Despite the evidence for sex differences in the brain during late adult development, however, it is not yet clear whether they are related to hormonal differences, rate of development, and/or life

TOURO COLLEGE LIBRARY

history (e.g., smoking, alcohol consumption, education, family), although it seems likely that they reflect complex, reciprocal interactions among many aspects of the developing system.

Relations between Structural Changes and Behavior

A growing body of evidence suggests that individual differences in key aspects of brain structure (e.g., gray and white matter volume) are related to individual differences in behavior. As noted earlier, in their longitudinal study of 5- to 11-year-olds, Sowell et al. (2004) found positive correlations between the amount of gray matter thinning in left frontal and parietal regions, and changes in children's vocabulary scores. The authors suggested that these changes may correspond to individual differences in general intellectual function, as indexed by IQ tests, rather than language per se. Indeed, Amat, Bansal, Whiteman, Haggerty, Royal, and Peterson (2008) found that full-scale IQ scores in adults were negatively correlated with hippocampal volume (especially the anterior hippocampus). In a sample of 85 participants between 5 and 17 years, however, Reiss et al. (1996) found that IQ was positively, not negatively, correlated with gray matter volume in the prefrontal cortex.

Another study may shed some light on this inconsistency by revealing the complex, dynamic, age-related association between IQ and gray matter. Shaw et al. (2006) examined gray matter thickness in relation to IQ in 307 typically developing individuals (from 3.8–29 years) who were classified as average IQ (83–100), high IQ (109–120), or superior IQ (121–149). The superior IQ group initially had thinner cortices and showed peak thickness later (11.2 vs. 8.5 years for high and 5.6 years for average), followed by a steeper decline after the peak. The differences among IQ groups were especially pronounced in the superior frontal gyri extending into medial prefrontal cortex. The pattern for the high IQ group appeared intermediate between the patterns for the other two groups, and it is as if IQ was associated with a developmental pattern that may reflect a protracted period of cortical plasticity in prefrontal cortex. In any event, however, the relation between IQ and gray matter volume varies as a function of age, and IQ may be more meaningfully related to the developmental trajectory of gray matter volume than to gray matter volume at any particular point in development.

In a study observing more focused anatomic differences, Casey, Trainor, Giedd, et al. (1997) examined the relation

between the anterior cingulate region and controlled attentional processes in children 5 to 16 years of age. Children were given a visual discrimination task that involved determining which of three presented stimuli were different from the other two, either in shape or color. In the controlled processes condition, the key dimension changed between trials, and in the automatic processes condition, the dimension remained the same within a block. The size of the right anterior cingulate region was positively correlated with age and IQ, and also with response time and accuracy during the controlled condition, even when adjusting for age and IQ. The authors hypothesized that the correlation between the anterior cingulate volume and better attentional processes may reflect greater myelination of important projections from the posterior parietal and dorsolateral prefrontal cortex, consistent with the faster reaction times with age. Alternatively or additionally, it may reflect growth of dendritic connections and supporting glial cells.

Differences in white matter have also been related to behavioral differences more directly. Nagy, Westerberg, and Klingberg (2004) examined 23 children between the ages of 8 and 18 years, and compared reading and working memory performance with white matter as assessed by DTI. Working memory was positively related to white matter in the anterior corpus callosum and in two regions of the left frontal lobe, including a region linking the frontal and parietal cortices—two areas of cortex shown to be important for working memory (e.g., Klingberg, Forssberg, & Westerberg, 2002). In contrast, reading was related to white matter in the left temporal lobe in that study.

Liston et al.'s (2005) study used DTI to measure white matter in relation to children's (7–14 years) versus young adults' (18–31 years) performance on a go/no-go task, a paradigm often used to measure inhibitory or cognitive control. In the go/no-go task, participants were required to respond by pressing a button when they saw one type of stimulus ("go" stimuli), presented on the majority of trials, and withhold or inhibit responding when they saw a different, less frequent stimulus (the "no-go" stimulus). Results revealed evidence of age-related increases in myelination in tracts connecting right ventral prefrontal cortex to the striatum, and these increases were correlated with improvement in performance (decreases in reaction time).

White and gray matter have also been related to cognitive function later in life. Van Petten, Plante, Davidson, Kuo, Bajuscak, and Glisky (2004) found memory and executive function decline to be associated with increased white matter hyperintensities in older adults 65 to 85 years of age. Consistent with these findings, in a meta-analysis of 23 studies, Gunning-Dixon and Raz (2000) found that white matter hyperintensities were generally associated with attenuated performance on tasks measuring cognitive functioning, including processing speed, recall memory, and executive function in older adults; however, no significant relations were found between white matter hyperintensities and estimates of IQ or fine motor skill.

Van Petten and colleagues (2004) also reported associations between memory performance and gray matter volume in the middle frontal gyrus and regions of temporal neocortex. In this case, the association was negative, with greater memory performance related to decreased volume. Other researchers have also found negative correlations between cognitive performance and gray matter volume, including lower hippocampal volume associated with better immediate and delayed verbal recall (Köhler et al., 1998), and smaller prefrontal cortex gray matter volume associated with better working memory (Salat, Kaye, & Janowsky, 2002). Van Petten and colleagues suggest that when subjects are primarily healthy older adults, the relation between memory and volume may be negative, consistent with that seen in younger adults (e.g., Chantôme et al., 1999; Foster et al., 1999). In cases where there is pathology or true age-related decline, then we may expect to see positive correlations (e.g., Barber, McKeith, Ballard, Gholkar, & O'Brien, 2001; Mungas et al., 2002; Petersen et al., 2000). In a meta-analytic review, Van Petten (2004) found that the volume-memory correlation became more positive with age, and that strikingly, there was great variability in the correlations found in older adults, ranging from negative to positive (see Van Petten, 2004, for further discussion).

Experience and the Brain

The epigenetic importance of early experience in aspects of cognitive, social, perceptual, and physical development has been well observed at the behavioral level. This is often manifested as sensitive or critical periods that occur early in development and involve rapid and efficient learning (e.g., of language); learning typically is more difficult after the specified period and involves lower levels of attainment. It has been proposed that the neural mechanism implicated in this early sensitivity to experience is the decline in synaptic density after birth and in early childhood, as noted earlier (Greenough, Black, & Wallace, 1987). According to Greenough and colleagues, there are two mechanisms through which experience shapes the developing brain. *Experience-expectant* processes are involved in storing environmental information that is expected to

be present in the species-typical environment (e.g., motion, edge contrasts). There is an intrinsic overgeneration of synaptic connections early in life, and as the system is provided with experiential input, a subset of the synapses are strengthened and maintained, whereas others are lost. Thus, lack of the expected experiences or abnormal experiences will result in non-normative neural patterns. In contrast, *experience-dependent* processes are those involved in storing information specific to the individual (e.g., the location of food or shelter) that can vary by timing and character. Because these inputs cannot be anticipated, they likely involve the formation of new synaptic connections as each learning occasion arises, as opposed to the selection of preexisting connections (and thus they are less restricted by timing of experience).

Much of the evidence supporting the importance of early experiences for brain development comes from sensory deprivation studies with animals that involve the experimental manipulation of early perceptual experience (see Greenough et al., 1987). This includes total pattern deprivation, monocular deprivation, and selective deprivation (e.g., specific contours, movement) that are associated with impaired visual processing in various tasks. Neurophysiological changes can include decreased sensitivity of visual cortical neurons to visual characteristics that were missing in the rearing environment (e.g., horizontal line orientation, movement), as well as decreases in dendrites, spines on dendrites, and synaptic connections in the visual cortex. A commonly cited example is the role of deprivation in the development of stereoscopic depth perception (LeVay, Wiesel, & Hubel, 1980). In the adult, each eye has connections terminating in layer IV of the visual cortex, creating alternating bands or ocular dominance columns (innervated either by the left or right eye, respectively). In infancy, however, the axons from both eyes have overlapping terminal fields and no clear bands exist, consistent with the notion of an early surplus of synapses. With binocular visual experience, certain axons from each eye regress, leaving the sharply defined bands. If one eye is deprived of sight, as experimentally manipulated in the classic research with monkeys, the terminals of the deprived eye regress more than normal, and the intact eye retains a larger portion of the terminal field, resulting in alternating narrow and wide bands. Behaviorally, this disrupts the normal development of stereoscopic vision. Even if the deprived eye is later provided with normal input, there may or may not be recovery depending on whether the number of synapses is nearing adult values and the critical period is coming to a close.

Demonstration of experience-dependent processes in brain development come from studies that examine young rats raised in different laboratory environments (see Greenough et al., 1987). Generally when rats are housed in more enriched or complex environments, such as those including other rats, stimulating objects, and the opportunity to explore and play, they perform better at complex tasks (e.g., mazes). Associated neurological changes can include a heavier and thicker cortex in certain regions, a greater number of dendrites per neuron, and greater frequency of postsynaptic spines.

In human beings, one of the most striking examples of sensitivity to experiential timing is the learning of language, as seen in the challenges associated with acquiring a second language. For example, the native language we learn appears to be associated with brain changes to the point that we only hear certain phonetic contrasts, and this can impede second language learning (Kuhl, 2004). In Japanese, [r] and [l] are part of the same phonemic category, and Japanese speakers have trouble discriminating between the two sounds. In English, these phonetic units form separate phonemes, and native speakers easily discriminate between these two categories (Kuhl, 2004). Infants, however, have the potential to learn any language, and at 6 months of age (and possibly as young as 5 weeks), they can discriminate not only contrasts in their own native language, but also those in other languages (Werker & Desjardins, 1995). By about 12 months of age, however, this ability is lost and infants perform similar to adults. This may reflect neural commitment as a result of first language experience, akin to the selection of synapses involved in experience-expectant processes (Kuhl, 2004).

These changes have also been shown at the neural level of activity. The mismatch negativity (MMN) is an event-related potential (ERP) component elicited by changes in repeated sound patterns, and it can be observed in the left hemisphere for native-language sounds. Cheour et al. (1998) demonstrated the presence of the MMN in infants, and between the ages of 6 and 12 months, the MMN amplitude increased for native phonemes and decreased for non-native phonemes. Interestingly, more recent research suggests this decline in phonetic discrimination can be reversed or stalled with just 12 short sessions of second-language exposure at 9 months (Kuhl, Tsao, & Liu, 2003). This has also been demonstrated by changes in MMN in 3- to 6-year-olds after 2 months of second-language exposure at preschool (Cheour, Shestakova, Alku, Ceponiene, & Näätänen, 2002). Other evidence of the impact of language-related training on neural function comes from Temple and colleagues (2003), who examined the effects of 8 weeks of training on auditory processing and oral language in 8- to 12-year-old children with dyslexia. Pretraining and post-training fMRI scans showed increased activity in left temporoparietal cortex, which was also correlated with improvements in oral language, as well as increased activity in the left inferior frontal gyrus. These patterns of activation were closer to those seen in control children. Greater activation was also found in the right-hemisphere frontal and temporal regions, and the anterior cingulate gyrus.

The development of expertise in childhood and adulthood has also been related to structural and functional differences in the brain. A famous study by Maguire et al. (2000) examined the hippocampi of taxi drivers in London. Taxi drivers, who have to pass a rigorous test demonstrating their knowledge of London streets, were found to have larger posterior hippocampi (and smaller anterior hippocampi) than age-matched control subjects. Moreover, the number of years that they had been driving a cab was positively related to the volume of their posterior hippocampi and negatively related to the volume of their anterior hippocampi. This finding demonstrates that relying heavily on spatial memory (and engaging regularly in navigation) is relevant to the reshaping of relevant regions of cortex—and not necessarily increases in volume.

Similar findings have been obtained for white matter and for measures of brain function. For example, Bengtsson, Nagy, Skare, Forsman, Forssberg, and Ullén (2005) found positive relations between the number of hours spent practicing the piano (especially as a child) and white matter (measured via DTI), with different regions being implicated at different ages. An early study by Elbert, Pantev, Wienbruch, Rockstroh, and Taub (1995) used magnetoencephalography (MEG) to measure cortical representations of fingers in violin players and found larger representation in sensorimotor cortex of the digits of the left (fingering) hand (but not the thumb), as would be expected if experience were implicated in these changes.

Indeed, experimental studies support a causal interpretation of these correlations. Extensive work with nonhuman animals has demonstrated environmental effects on both behavioral and brain development (for reviews, see Huttenlocher, 2002; Stiles, 2008). In human beings, the experimental evidence is more limited but encouraging. For example, Olesen, Westerberg, and Klingberg (2003) conducted two studies with adults (a total of eight participants) and used fMRI to measure brain activity before and after 5 weeks of working memory training. Results showed increases after training in activity in frontal and parietal areas, and decreases in activity in cingulate cortex.

Neurological effects of training have also been demonstrated in young children. For example, Rueda, Rothbart, McCandliss, Saccomanno, and Posner (2005) improved 4- and 6-year-olds' performance on a computerized attention task within five training sessions using computerized games. Children in the training condition showed improvement on an attention task and a measure of general intelligence, as well as differences in ERPs recorded during the attention task. Children in the training conditions showed more adult-like patterns in an ERP component (the N2) located over frontoparietal and prefrontal areas.

Although late adult development is associated with various patterns of decline, as outlined earlier, certain activities and experiences are associated with positive brain effects and may be implicated in the prevention of cognitive and neurological deterioration. The construct of *behavioral brain reserve* or *cognitive reserve* refers to the potential protection against dementia and cognitive decline that is associated with cumulative complex mental activity across the life span. Valenzuela and Sachdev (2006a) reviewed 22 longitudinal cohort studies of dementia incidence, looking at the effect of education, occupation, and leisure or mental activities. Results showed that higher brain reserve (i.e., cumulative complex mental activity) was related to lower rates of dementia; in particular, increased mental activity in late life was an independent predictor of lower incidence of dementia. In a related analysis of 18 studies, Valenzuela and Sachdev (2006b) found that higher behavioral brain reserve was related to decreased longitudinal cognitive decline, suggesting that the link between brain reserve and dementia is likely due to different cognitive trajectories.

Recently, researchers have examined bilingualism as a possible contributor to cognitive reserve, because bilingualism has been associated with better attention and cognitive control in both children (Bialystok, 2001) and older adults (Bialystok, Craik, & Ryan, 2006). Bialystok, Craik, and Freedman (2007) conducted analyses on records from patients at a memory clinic who had been diagnosed with dementia, 51% of whom were bilingual, and found that bilingual individuals showed symptoms of dementia 4 years later than monolingual individuals.

Cognitive activity may not be the only source of brain reserve, and new research has shown that physical activity may also be implicated in the prevention of age-related brain decline. In a meta-analysis of 18 intervention studies (Colcombe & Kramer, 2003), researchers found robust positive effects of fitness training on cognition, particularly executive control processes, in healthy but sedentary adults. These effects can be demonstrated at the neural level. Colcombe et al. (2006) observed 59 healthy older adults, aged 60 to 79 years, who were enrolled in a 6-month randomized, clinical trial. Half of the participants were assigned to an aerobic training group, and the other half were assigned to a toning and stretching group. MRI scans before and after training revealed increased brain volume in both gray and white matter for the aerobic group but not for the control group. These increases were found primarily in the prefrontal and temporal cortices, which typically show age-related decline.

Clearly, the environment and experience play a significant role in shaping brain structure and function, from prenatal stages to old age, consistent with an epigenetic view. Early experiences are important for guiding basic normative development (e.g., sensory, language), and through childhood and adulthood, learning continues to impact the developing brain. In the later stages of life, how individuals interact with the world mentally and physically can also have an important impact on the cognitive and neurological health of the brain.

DEVELOPMENT OF PREFRONTAL CORTEX

A great deal of research on functional changes in brain activity across the life span has focused on the prefrontal cortex, a region associated with late-developing, higher order cognitive functions, including executive function (see Jacques & Marcovitch, Chapter 13 of this volume)— the conscious control of thought, action, and emotion. Developmental research on executive function has revealed that executive function first emerges early in development, probably around the end of the first year of life; it develops across a wide range of ages, with important changes occurring between about 2 and 5 years of age, and during adolescence; and its development appears to follow an inverted-U–shaped curve when considered across the life span. For example, life-span studies of the ability to switch rapidly between rules and/or responses suggest that the development of switching follows a U-shaped curve, with reductions in switch cost throughout childhood and adolescence, and subsequent increases in older adults (Cepeda, Kramer, & Gonzalez de Sather, 2001; Crone, Bunge, Van der Molen, & Ridderinkhof, 2006; Reimers & Maylor, 2005; Zelazo, Craik, & Booth,

2004). Cepeda et al. (2001), for example, observed task-switching performance over the life span (ages 7–82 years). In a series of trials, participants were shown either one or three numerical ones or threes (i.e., 1, 111, 3, or 333) and were required to classify these stimuli differently depending on a cue (i.e., they were required to indicate either which numeral was displayed or how many numerals were displayed). A U-shaped function was obtained for switch costs—the increase in reaction time on switch trials compared with nonswitch trials. Switch costs (above and beyond perceptual speed, working memory, and nonswitch reaction time) decreased from childhood into young adulthood and stayed fairly constant until about 60 years of age, after which they increased. Cepeda et al. (2001) also found evidence that life-span changes in switch costs could be attributed primarily to changes in the time needed to prepare for a new task, as opposed to changes in the decay rate of a previous task (i.e., task set inertia; Allport, Styles & Hsieh, 1994). Other well-known "signs" of decline during late adult development, such as increased forgetting and unwanted intrusions in one's speech, may be attributable, to some extent, to impaired executive function associated with the deterioration of the functioning of prefrontal cortex. Indeed, there is some reason to believe that the functions that are the "last in" during childhood and adolescence may the "first out" during late adult development.

Regions of Prefrontal Cortex

As shown in Figure 4.1, the prefrontal cortex is the region of the frontal cortex anterior to the premotor cortex and the supplementary motor area—a region that in human beings comprises between a quarter and a third of the cortex (Fuster, 1989). In fact, however, the prefrontal cortex is a heterogeneous region, with several distinct subregions, including the orbitofrontal cortex, anterior cingulate cortex, and ventrolateral, dorsolateral, and rostrolateral prefrontal cortices (Figure 4.6). These regions show cytoarchitectonic differences, different patterns of connectivity with other brain regions, different patterns of cognitive impairment associated with lesions, and different developmental profiles (see Zelazo, Carlson, & Kesek, 2008, for review).

Traditionally, conceptualizations of executive function have focused on its relatively "cool," cognitive aspects, often associated with lateral prefrontal cortex and elicited by relatively abstract, decontextualized problems. Recently, however, there has been growing interest in the

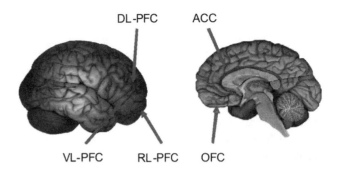

Figure 4.6 The human brain, showing various regions of prefrontal cortex on the lateral surface (left) and the medial surface (right). ACC, anterior cingulate cortex; DL-PFC, dorsolateral prefrontal cortex; OFC, orbitofrontal cortex; RL-PFC, rostrolateral prefrontal cortex; VL-PFC, ventrolateral prefrontal cortex.

development of relatively "hot" aspects of executive function, more associated with the orbitofrontal cortex and seen in situations that are emotionally and motivationally significant because they involve meaningful rewards or punishers (e.g., Happaney, Zelazo, & Stuss, 2004; Zelazo & Müller, 2002). This characterization of hot executive function is consistent with recent proposals regarding the function of the orbitofrontal cortex. For example, on the basis of evidence that the orbitofrontal cortex is required for successful performance on simple tests of object reversal and extinction in lesioned monkeys and patients with orbitofrontal cortex damage, Rolls (e.g., Rolls, Hornak, Wade, & McGrath, 1994) suggests that the orbitofrontal cortex is required for the flexible representation of the reinforcement value of stimuli.

Damasio (1994) also proposed that the orbitofrontal cortex is important in the processing of learned associations between affective reactions (somatic markers) and certain scenarios. Somatic markers are affectively induced physiological states evoked by rewards or punishments that can signal the potential outcome and guide behavior in complex decision-making tasks where outcomes are uncertain. Damasio, Bechara, and colleagues (e.g., Bechara, Damasio, & Damasio, 2000; Bechara, Damasio, Damasio, & Anderson, 1994) developed a gambling task that involves choosing cards from four decks, two of which are advantageous over time, with low wins but even lower losses, and two of which are disadvantageous over time, with high wins but even higher losses. Healthy subjects usually learn to avoid the bad decks and produce anticipatory skin conductance responses before selecting from bad decks. However, patients with ventromedial damage that encompasses the orbitofrontal region continue to select from disadvantageous decks and fail to produce anticipatory responses.

Changes in Prefrontal Cortical Function

Recent fMRI evidence suggests a few general changes in patterns of neural recruitment within and involving prefrontal cortex. Specifically, several researchers have noted a shift from more diffuse to more focal activation within prefrontal cortex (e.g., Bunge, Dudukovic, Thomason, Vaidya, & Gabrieli, 2002; Casey, Trainor, Orendi, et al., 1997). This increasing focalization, which is associated with behavioral improvements, suggests more specialized and efficient processing with development. That is, older children and children who perform better on measures of executive function show more focal patterns of neural activation (i.e., more activation in areas related to executive function performance, less activation in unrelated areas). For example, in a combined longitudinal and cross-sectional design, Durston et al. (2006) scanned children while they performed a target detection task. Older children (11 years) recruited a more limited range of brain regions than younger children (9 years), and this shift was accompanied by an improvement in performance. For example, there was a decrease in activation in dorsolateral prefrontal cortex and increases in activation in right ventrolateral prefrontal cortex. An earlier example comes from Casey, Trainor, Orendi, et al. (1997), who administered a go/no-go task to 9 children (aged 7–12 years) and 9 young adults (aged 21–24 years). Although there was considerable overlap between the prefrontal regions showing activation in the two age groups, the volume of prefrontal cortex that was activated was greater in children than adults, and this was particularly true for the dorsal and lateral prefrontal cortex. Only activations in the ventral and medial prefrontal cortex correlated with performance.

Another general trend in neural development is increasing reliance on more anterior regions of cortex (i.e., frontalization). Rubia et al. (2000) had adolescents and young adults perform a stop signal task and a motor synchronization task, and found a general pattern of increased frontal activation with age. For example, in the motor synchronization task, the better performance demonstrated by adults was accompanied by increased activity in a fronto-striato-parietal network. Rubia et al. (2006) administered three measures of inhibitory control: a go/no-go task, where participants responded only to left and right pointing arrows

on a screen by pressing the corresponding keys, and not to an up arrow; a Simon task, where the left arrow would sometimes appear on the right side of the screen and vice versa (incongruent trials); and a Switch task, where a four square grid was presented with a circle appearing in one of the squares on each trial, together with a cue indicating whether the participant should decide if the circle was in the left or right side of the grid, or the top or bottom half of the grid. Results showed that during these tasks, adults were more likely to recruit prefrontal cortex, anterior cingulate cortex, and the striatum when compared with children and adolescents. Frontalization has also been seen using EEG. Lamm, Zelazo, and Lewis (2006) used high-density EEG to measure ERPs as children and adolescents performed a go/no-go task, and collected a number of behavioral measures of executive function. The N2 component of the ERP, an index of cognitive control, was source localized to the cingulate cortex and to the ventrolateral prefrontal cortex. However, the source of the N2 in those children who performed well on the executive function tasks was more anterior than that of children who performed poorly. This suggests that children rely more heavily on more anterior regions of prefrontal cortex as performance on independent measures of executive function increases.

A third developmental trend may be a shift from greater reliance on left-hemisphere regions to greater reliance on right hemisphere regions. In adults, many regions of right prefrontal cortex and related areas play a prominent role in executive function (e.g., Garavan, Ross, & Stein, 1999). Right lateralization is not always seen in studies of younger participants, however. Bunge et al. (2002), for example, examined correlates of performance during a flanker task, a commonly used task to measure attention and inhibitory control. Participants had to identify the left/right direction of a central arrow while ignoring the direction of arrows "flanking" the central arrow (e.g., ← ← → ← ←). It was found that successful performance was correlated with activation in the inferior frontal gyrus in both children and adults, but this activation was lateralized to the right hemisphere in adults and to the left hemisphere in children.

A Model of Prefrontal Cortical Function

Bunge and Zelazo (2006) reviewed research on the development and neural correlates of executive function and hypothesized that the pattern of developmental changes seen in childhood reflects the different rates of development of specific regions within prefrontal cortex. In particular, the use of relatively complex rules to control one's thought, action, and emotion is acquired late in development because it involves the hierarchical coordination of regions of prefrontal cortex—a hierarchical coordination that parallels the hierarchical structure of children's rule systems and develops in a bottom-up fashion, with higher levels in the hierarchy operating on the products of lower levels (cf. Badre & D'Esposito, 2007; Botvinick, 2008; Christoff & Gabrieli, 2000; Goldberg & Bilder, 1987; Koechlin, Ody, & Kouneiher, 2003). Indeed, as noted earlier, there is evidence that within prefrontal cortex, dorsolateral prefrontal cortex may be the last to develop (e.g., Gogtay et al., 2004). Moreover, measures of cortical thickness suggest that the dorsolateral prefrontal cortex and the rostrolateral

prefrontal cortex exhibit similar, slow rates of structural change (O'Donnell et al., 2005).

Figure 4.7 illustrates the way in which regions of prefrontal cortex may correspond to rule use at different levels of complexity. The function of prefrontal cortex is proposed to be hierarchical in a way that corresponds to the hierarchical complexity of the rule use underlying executive function. As individuals engage in reflective processing and formulate more complex rule systems, they recruit an increasingly complex hierarchical network of prefrontal regions. This can also be viewed as a shift from hotter to cooler aspects of executive function.

Zelazo and Cunningham (2007; Cunningham & Zelazo, 2007) incorporated this hypothesis into their

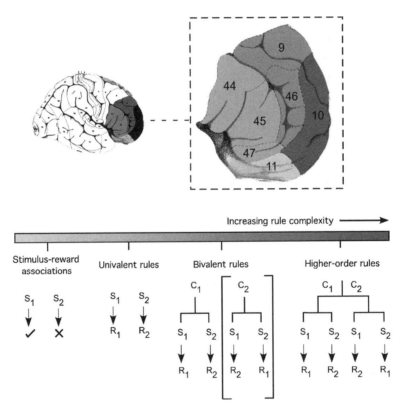

Figure 4.7   Hierarchical model of rule representation in prefrontal cortex (PFC). A lateral view of the human brain is depicted at the top, with regions of PFC identified by the Brodmann areas (BA) that comprise them: orbitofrontal cortex (BA 11), ventrolateral PFC (BA 44, 45, 47), dorsolateral PFC (BA 9, 46), and rostrolateral PFC (BA 10). The PFC regions are shown in various shades of gray, indicating which types of rules they represent. Rule structures are depicted below, with darker shades of gray indicating increasing levels of rule complexity. The formulation and maintenance in working memory of more complex rules depends on the reprocessing of information, which, in turn, depends on the recruitment of additional regions of PFC into an increasingly complex hierarchy of PFC activation. *Check mark* indicates reward; *X* indicates nonreward; *brackets* indicate a bivalent rule that is currently being ignored. C, context, or task set; R, response; S, stimulus.

(Reprinted from Bunge, S., & Zelazo, P. D. (2006). A brain-based account of the development of rule use in childhood. *Current Directions in Psychological Science, 15,* 118–121, by permission.)

Iterative Reprocessing model, which addresses the role of prefrontal cortex in evaluation and hot executive function. According to their model, the thalamus and amygdala generate quick emotional response tendencies that are then fed into orbitofrontal cortex. Orbitofrontal cortex then generates simple approach-avoidance (stimulus-reward) rules and is also involved in learning to reverse these rules. If these relatively unreflective processes fail to provide an adequate response to the situation, anterior cingulate cortex, thought to act as a performance monitor, signals the need for further, higher level processing in lateral prefrontal cortex. Different regions of lateral prefrontal cortex are involved in reprocessing information and representing rules at different levels of complexity—from sets of conditional rules (ventrolateral prefrontal cortex and dorsolateral prefrontal cortex) to explicit consideration of task sets (rostrolateral prefrontal cortex), as proposed by Bunge and Zelazo (2006). In the following text, a few selected pieces of research on the neural correlates of executive function development are reviewed with reference to this model.

Anterior Cingulate Cortex Function

A crucial element of executive function is the ability to recognize when actions do not have the intended effect, which may signal the need for more elaborate processing dependent on lateral prefrontal cortex, and anterior cingulate cortex is a key component of this system (e.g., Ridderinkhof, Ullsperger, Crone, & Nieuwenhuis, 2004; Zelazo & Cunningham, 2007).

Typically, younger children make more errors on tasks that require executive function than do adults, and they may be less aware of them. One way to assess performance monitoring is using ERPs. The error-related negativity (ERN) is a negative-going ERP component, probably originating in anterior cingulate cortex, which is associated with the realization that an error has been committed (Segalowitz & Davies, 2004). Segalowitz, Davies, Santesso, Gavin, and Schmidt (2004) measured the ERN in participants from age 10 to 25 as they completed the Eriksen flanker task. This task requires participants to identify the letter in the center of a string of either congruent (e.g., SSSSS) or incongruent flankers (e.g., SSHSS). The results suggest that the development of anterior cingulate cortex follows a protracted course, which may be related to puberty. In general, ERN amplitude increased with age, but there was also a U-shaped dip in the amplitude of the ERN that was maximal for boys at age 13 years and maximal for girls

at age 10 years, consistent with what one would expect if this dip were related to puberty.

A number of other studies have also found similar increases in ERN amplitude in older adolescents (Hogan, Vargha-Khadem, Kirkham, & Baldeweg, 2005; Ladouceur, Dahl, & Carter, 2004). The observed changes in the ERN correspond to improved task performance, including fewer errors and quicker response times, suggesting that the ability to perform online error monitoring is, indeed, an important element in the development of executive function.

At older ages, relations between ERN amplitude and performance are less clear. A growing number of studies have shown that healthy older adults produce smaller ERNs compared with their younger counterparts (e.g., Falkenstein, Hoormann, & Hohnsbein, 2001; Mathalon, Bennett, Askari, Gray, Rosenbloom, & Ford, 2003; Nieuwenhuis et al., 2002). However, these reductions in ERN amplitude are often only marginally related to behavioral differences in performance. The ERN is specifically associated with errors that are slips (when the correct response is known but not supplied) rather than mistakes (when the correct response is unknown; Dehaene, Posner, & Tucker, 1994). Because age differences are typically greatest when the ratio of mistakes to slips is large (Hester, Fassbender, & Garavan, 2004), diminished ERNs in older adults may reflect a greater proportion of mistakes (Mathalon et al., 2003). Consistent with this view, patients with Alzheimer disease show further reductions in ERN amplitude compared with healthy adults, which may be related to greater mistakes caused by disease-related knowledge loss (Mathalon et al., 2003). Also, when errors are reported primarily as slips, greater activation in anterior cingulate cortex has been found in older adults in their 30s and 40s compared with those in their early to mid-20s (Hester et al., 2004). Others have proposed that a decline in dopaminergic reinforcement learning signals may underlie reduced ERN amplitudes and age-related changes in error processing (see Nieuwenhuis et al., 2002).

Lateral Prefrontal Cortex Function

The activation of anterior cingulate cortex, signaling that the simple approach-avoidance tendencies generated by orbitofrontal cortex have not resolved the present situation, may lead to more elaborate processing in lateral areas of prefrontal cortex, including the formulation of increasingly complex rules for controlling behavior. Both ventrolateral and dorsolateral prefrontal cortex have been consistently implicated in the retrieval, maintenance, and use of more complex sets of conditional rules in both lesion and fMRI studies (Bunge, 2004). For example, using fMRI, Crone, Wendelken, Donohue, van Leijenhorst, and Bunge (2006) found that both ventrolateral and dorsolateral prefrontal cortex are active during the maintenance of sets of conditional rules, and that they are sensitive to rule complexity, showing more activation for bivalent rules than for univalent rules. Bunge, Kahn, Wallis, Miller, and Wagner (2003) observed that these two regions are also more active for more abstract conditional rules ("match" or "nonmatch" rules, whereby different actions are required depending on whether two objects match or not) than for specific stimulus–response associations.

A study with preschool aged children examined the neural correlates of performance on the Dimensional Change Card Sort (DCCS), a measure of flexible rule use that can be used with young children (e.g., Zelazo, Müller, Frye, & Marcovitch, 2003). In the DCCS, children are shown two target cards (e.g., a blue rabbit and a red boat) and asked to sort a series of bivalent test cards (e.g., red rabbits and blue boats) first according to one dimension (e.g., color) and then according to the other (e.g., shape). Most 3-year-olds perseverate during the postswitch phase, continuing to sort test cards by the first dimension (e.g., Dick, Overton, & Kovacs, 2005; Kirkham, Cruess, & Diamond, 2003; Zelazo et al., 2003). In a study comparing 3- and 5-year-olds,

Moriguchi and Hiraki (2009) used near-infrared spectroscopy to measure concentration of oxygenated hemoglobin in ventrolateral prefrontal cortex during performance on this task. During both preswitch and postswitch phases, after presentation of test cards, 5- and 3-year-olds who switched flexibly on the task showed an increase in oxygenated hemoglobin bilaterally, whereas 3-year-olds who failed the task did not (see Figure 4.8).

The hypothesis that lateral prefrontal cortex plays a key role in following bivalent rules—using one pair of rules while ignoring a competing alternative—is consistent with its well-documented role in working memory, the ability to maintain and manipulate information to control responding. That is, working memory involves working on some information (e.g., trial-unique information) while ignoring other information (e.g., information from previous trials). Working memory has been linked to functioning of ventrolateral and dorsolateral prefrontal cortex and superior parietal cortex using a number of different neuropsychological methods, including fMRI and lesion studies (Braver, Cohen, Nystrom, Jonides, Smith, & Noll, 1997; Diamond & Goldman-Rakic, 1989; Kane & Engle, 2002; Smith & Jonides, 1999). In an early study, Casey et al. (1995) had children complete a working memory task in an fMRI scanner. Participants between 9 and 11 years completed a task that required them to respond to a target letter only if an identical letter had been presented two trials previously. Neural activation was observed in dorsolateral

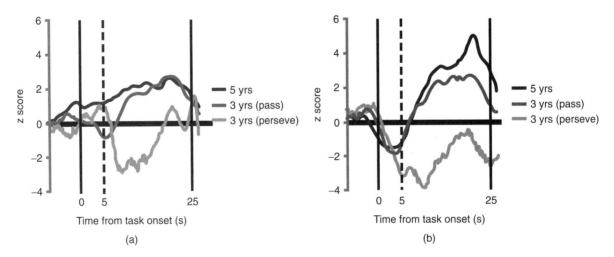

Figure 4.8 Near-infrared spectroscopy (NIRS) standard scores of concentration of oxygenated hemoglobin (oxy-Hb) in ventrolateral prefrontal cortex during performance on this task, for 3- and 5-year-olds who pass versus perseverate (perseve) Dimensional Change Card Sort (DCCS). (a) Preswitch phase. (b) Postswitch phase.

(Reprinted from Moriguchi, Y., & Hiraki, K. (2009). Neural origin of cognitive shifting in young children. *Proceedings of the National Academy of Sciences, 106,* 6017–6021, by permission.)

prefrontal cortex and anterior cingulate cortex, which mirrors the pattern of activation observed in adults who performed an identical task of working memory (Cohen et al., 1997). More recently, Crone et al. (2006) compared children (8–12 years), adolescents (13–17 years), and young adults (18–25 years) during performance on a measure of working memory that allowed for separate assessments of maintenance and maintenance with manipulation. Across participants, activation in right dorsolateral prefrontal cortex and the bilateral superior parietal cortex was associated with better performance on manipulation trials, but only adolescents and adults showed significant activation in these regions that was greater for manipulation than for maintenance.

As noted earlier, relations between functional brain activity and cognitive performance is generally less clear in older adults, and this is also true of lateral prefrontal cortex. Although there are age-related structural declines and volume loss in prefrontal cortex that have been associated with decreased cognitive performance (e.g., Raz, 2000), linking neural activation patterns to cognitive function has been difficult, with various patterns of increases and decreases documented in older adults. Imaging evidence has been reported that older adults tend to show less specificity and differentiation in their brain recruitment during cognitive tasks—that the number of sites recruited increases with age ("dedifferentiation"; see Park et al., 2001, for discussion)—but also that the recruited areas may be different from those seen in young adults.

In Reuter-Lorenz et al.'s (2000) positron emission tomographic study, for example, older adults showed bilateral activation of dorsolateral prefrontal cortex for both verbal and spatial working memory tasks, whereas young adults showed a more lateralized pattern (predominantly left-lateralized for verbal and right-lateralized for spatial). McIntosh et al. (1999) demonstrated unique recruitment of areas in dorsolateral prefrontal cortex by older adults compared with young adults, as well as unique activation in mediotemporal areas when performing a visual discrimination working memory task. Activation in these areas was related to task performance in older adults, whereas no such relation was seen in young adults.

Such differences in activation patterns have also been documented in tasks that require inhibition and task switching. Jonides et al. (2000) presented older adults with a verbal working memory task that required remembering a target set of four letters for 3 seconds, then responding to a probe letter and deciding whether it was in the set. Response conflict was created by presenting familiar test items that were used in previous sets but not in the current set. Older adults showed more behavioral interference from these items than young adults and did not demonstrate the activation in lateral prefrontal cortex that was seen in young adults. Smith et al. (2001) tested young and older adults in a dual-task paradigm that required performing a memory task while verifying simple equations. The results for older adults were poorer than for young adults, and older adults also recruited regions of lateral prefrontal cortex, including dorsolateral prefrontal cortex, that were not seen in young adults.

As Park et al. (2001) suggested, it is difficult to determine whether these differences in activation patterns reflect compensatory mechanisms for maintaining cognitive function or whether they are pathological indices of poor cognitive performance. Some of these differences may also simply reflect neural reorganization that is not associated with performance changes.

CONCLUSION

New technologies have allowed scientists unprecedented opportunities to observe the developing (including the late adult) brain in vivo, and although more work is needed to understand the limitations of the views afforded by different techniques, as well as how these views interrelate, our understanding of brain development has increased enormously in recent years. As this brief review reveals, brain development is a lifelong phenomenon characterized by considerable regional specificity, and also by a series of overlapping, dynamic processes that yield both progressive events, such as increases in white matter, and regressive events, such as decreases in gray matter. Regressive events are prominent in childhood and early adolescence, but also in the late adult years. A good deal is now known about the structural development of the brain, but links to function (both neural function and behavior), especially in young children, are still only starting to be understood. Evidence suggests, however, that specific neural changes are linked to the attainment or loss of specific cognitive capabilities, and that both may be modified by experience.

One region of the brain that undergoes especially noteworthy changes across the life span—during childhood, adolescence, and normal late adult development—is prefrontal cortex, which appears to play a key role in the conscious reprocessing of information that underlies monitoring, working memory, and executive function. Prefrontal cortex is a large, heterogeneous region of hierarchically arranged subregions, and there is emerging evidence that changes in the structural and functional integration of these subregions are associated with changes in cognitive complexity and the cognitive control of thought, action, and emotion.

REFERENCES

Allen, J. S., Damasio, H., Grabowski, T. J., Bruss, J., & Zhang, W. (2003). Sexual dimorphism and asymmetries in the gray-white composition of the human cerebrum. *Neuroimage, 18,* 880–894.

Allen, L. S., Richey, M. F., Chai, Y. M., & Gorski, R. A. (1991). Sex differences in the corpus callosum of the living human being. *Journal of Neuroscience, 11,* 933–942.

Allport, D. A., Styles, E. A., & Hsieh, S. (1994). Shifting intentional set: Exploring the dynamic control of tasks. In C. Umiltà & M. Moscovitch (Eds.), *Attention and performance XV* (pp. 421–452). Cambridge, MA: MIT Press.

Amat, J. A., Bansal, R., Whiteman, R., Haggerty, R., Royal, J., & Peterson, B. S. (2008). Correlates of intellectual ability with morphology of the hippocampus and amygdala in healthy adults. *Brain and Cognition, 66,* 105–114.

Ansari, K., & Loch, J. (1975). Decreased myelin basic protein content of the aged human brain. *Neurology, 25,* 1045–1050.

Badre, D., & D'Esposito, M. (2007). Functional magnetic resonance imaging evidence for a hierarchical organization of the prefrontal cortex. *Journal of Cognitive Neuroscience, 19,* 2082–2099.

Barber, R., McKeith, I. G., Ballard, C., Gholkar, A., & O'Brien, J. T. (2001). A comparison of medial and lateral temporal lobe atrophy in dementia with Lewy bodies and Alzheimer's disease: Magnetic resonance imaging volumetric study. *Dementia and Geriatric Cognitive Disorders, 12,* 198–205.

Bartzokis, G., Beckson, M., Lu, P. H., Nuechterlein, K. H., Edwards, N., & Mintz, J. (2001). Age-related changes in frontal and temporal lobe volumes in men: A magnetic resonance imaging study. *Archives of General Psychiatry, 58,* 461–465.

Bechara, A., Damasio, H., & Damasio, A. R. (2000). Emotion, decision making and the orbitofrontal cortex. *Cerebral Cortex, 10,* 295–307.

Bechara, A., Damasio, A. R., Damasio, H., & Anderson, S. W. (1994). Insensitivity to future consequences following damage to human prefrontal cortex. *Cognition, 50,* 7–15.

Bell, M. A., & Fox, N. A. (1992). The relations between frontal brain electrical activity and cognitive development during infancy. *Child Development, 63,* 1142–1163.

Benes, F. M., Turtle, M., Khan, Y., & Farol, P. (1994). Myelination of a key relay zone in the hippocampal formation occurs in the human brain during childhood, adolescence, and adulthood. *Archives of General Psychiatry, 51,* 477–484.

Bengtsson, S. L., Nagy, Z., Skare, S., Forsman, L., Forssberg, H., & Ullén, F. (2005). Extensive piano practicing has regionally specific effects on white matter development. *Nature Neuroscience, 8,* 1148–1150.

Bialystok, E. (2001). *Bilingualism in development: Language, literacy, and cognition.* New York: Cambridge University Press.

Bialystok, E., Craik, F. I. M., & Freedman, M. (2007). Bilingualism as a protection against onset of symptoms of dementia. *Neuropsychologia, 45,* 459–464.

Bialystok, E., Craik, F. I. M., & Ryan, J. (2006). Executive control in a modified anti-saccade task: Effects of aging and bilingualism. *Journal of Experimental Psychology: Learning, Memory, and Cognition, 32,* 1341–1354.

Botvinick, M. M. (2008). Hierarchical models of behavior and prefrontal function. *Trends in Cognitive Sciences, 12,* 201–208.

Braver, T. S., Cohen, J. D., Nystrom, L. E., Jonides J., Smith E. E., & Noll D. C. (1997). A parametric study of prefrontal cortex involvement in human working memory. *Neuroimage, 5,* 49–62.

Bunge, S. A. (2004). How we use rules to select actions: A review of evidence from cognitive neuroscience. *Cognitive, Affective, and Behavioral Neuroscience, 4,* 564–579.

Bunge, S. A., Dudukovic, N. M., Thomason, M. E., Vaidya, C. J., & Gabrieli, J. D. E. (2002). Development of frontal lobe contributions to cognitive control in children: Evidence from fMRI. *Neuron, 33,* 301–311.

Bunge, S. A., Kahn, I., Wallis, J. D., Miller, E. K., & Wagner, A. D. (2003). Neural circuits subserving the retrieval and maintenance of abstract rules. *Journal of Neurophysiology, 90,* 3419–3428.

Bunge, S., & Zelazo, P. D. (2006). A brain-based account of the development of rule use in childhood. *Current Directions in Psychological Science, 15,* 118–121.

Cahill, L., Uncapher, M., Kilpatrick, L., Alkire, M. T., & Turner, J. (2004). Sex-related hemispheric lateralization of amygdala function in emotionally influenced memory: An fMRI investigation. *Learning and Memory, 11,* 261–266.

Casey, B. J., Cohen, J. D., Jezzard, P., Turner, R., Noll, D. C., Trainor, R. J., et al. (1995). Activation of prefrontal cortex in children during a nonspatial working memory task with functional MRI. *Neuroimage, 2,* 221–229.

Casey, B. J., Giedd, J. N., & Thomas, K. M. (2000). Structural and functional brain development and its relation to cognitive development. *Biological Psychology, 54,* 241–257.

Casey, B. J., Trainor, R. J., Giedd, J., Vauss, Y., Hamburger, S., Kozuch, P., et al. (1997). The role of the anterior cingulate in automatic and controlled processes: A developmental neuroanatomical study. *Developmental Psychobiology, 30,* 61–69.

Casey, B. J., Trainor, R. J., Orendi, J. L., Schubert, A. B., Nystrom, L. E., Giedd, J. N., et al. (1997). A developmental functional MRI study of prefrontal activation during performance of a go-no-go task. *Journal of Cognitive Neuroscience, 9,* 835–847.

Cepeda, N. J., Kramer, A. F., & Gonzalez de Sather, J. C. M. (2001). Changes in executive control across the life span: Examination of task-switching performance. *Developmental Psychology, 37,* 715–730.

Chantôme, M., Perruchet, P., Hasboun, D., Dormont, D., Sahel, M., Sourour, N., et al. (1999). Is there a negative correlation between explicit memory and hippocampal volume? *Neuroimage, 10,* 589–595.

Cheour, M., Ceponiene, R., Lehtokoski, A., Luuk, A., Allik, J., Alho, K., et al. (1998). Development of language-specific phoneme representations in the infant brain. *Nature Neuroscience, 1,* 351–353.

Cheour, M., Shestakova, A., Alku, P., Ceponiene, R., & Näätänen, R. (2002). Mismatch negativity shows that 3- to- 6-year-old children can learn to discriminate non-native speech sounds within two months. *Neuroscience Letters, 325,* 187–190.

Christoff, K., & Gabrieli, J. D. E. (2000). The frontopolar cortex and human cognition: Evidence for a rostrocaudal hierarchical organization within the human prefrontal cortex. *Psychobiology, 28,* 168–186.

Clark, A. S., & Goldman-Rakic, P. S. (1989). Gonadal hormones influence the emergence of cortical function in nonhuman primates. *Behavioral Neuroscience, 103,* 1287–1295.

Clarke, S., Kraftsik, R., Van der Loos, H., & Innocenti, G. M. (1989). Forms and measures of adult and developing human corpus callosum: Is there sexual dimorphism? *Journal of Comparative Neurology, 280,* 213–220.

Cohen, J. D., Perlstein, W. M., Braver, T. S., Nystrom, L. E., Noll, D. C., Jonides, J., et al. (1997). Temporal dynamics of brain activation during a working memory task. *Nature, 386,* 604–608.

Colcombe, S. J., Erickson, K. I., Scalf, P. E., Kim, J. S., Prakash, R., McAuley, E., et al. (2006). Aerobic exercise training increases brain volume in aging humans. *Journals of Gerontology Series A: Biological Sciences and Medical Sciences, 61,* 1166–1170.

Colcombe, S., & Kramer, A. F. (2003). Fitness effects on the cognitive function of older adults: A meta-analytic study. *Psychological Science, 14,* 125–130.

Collaer, M. L., & Hines, M. (1995). Human behavioral sex differences: A role for gonadal hormones during early development? *Psychological Bulletin, 188,* 55–107.

Courchesne, E., Chisum, H. J., Townsend, J., Cowles, A., Covington, J., Egaas, B., et al. (2001). Normal brain development and aging: Quantitative analysis at in vivo MR imaging in healthy volunteers. *Radiology, 216,* 672–682.

Craik, F. I. M., & Bialystok, E. (2006). Cognition through the lifespan: Mechanism of change. *Trends in Cognitive Sciences, 10,* 131–138.

Crone, E. A., Bunge, S. A., Van der Molen, M. W., & Ridderinkhof, K. R. (2006). Switching between tasks and responses: A developmental study. *Developmental Science, 9,* 278–287.

Crone, E. A., Wendelken, C., Donohue, S., van Leijenhorst, L., & Bunge, S. A. (2006). Neurocognitive development of the ability to manipulate information in working memory. *Proceedings of the National Academy of Sciences, 103,* 9315–9320.

Cunningham, W. A., & Zelazo, P. D. (2007). Attitudes and evaluation: A social cognitive neuroscience perspective. *Trends in Cognitive Sciences, 11,* 97–104.

Damasio, A. (1994). *Descartes' error: Emotion, reason, and the human brain.* New York: Putnam.

De Bellis, M. D., Keshavan, M. S., Beers, S. R., Hall, J., Frustaci, K., Masalehdan, A., et al. (2001). Sex differences in brain maturation during childhood and adolescence. *Cerebral Cortex, 11,* 552–557.

Dehaene, S., Posner, M. I., & Tucker, D. M. (1994). Localization of a neural system for error detection and compensation. *Psychological Science, 5,* 303–305.

Dekaban, A. S., & Sadowsky, D. (1978). Changes in brain weights during the span of human life: Relation of brain weights to body heights and body weights. *Annals of Neurology, 4,* 345–356.

De Lacoste-Utamsing, M. C., & Holloway, R. L. (1982). Sexual dimorphism in the human corpus callosum. *Science, 216,* 1431–1432.

Diamond, A., & Goldman-Rakic, P. S. (1989). Comparison of human infants and rhesus monkeys on Piaget's AB task: Evidence for dependence on dorsolateral prefrontal cortex. *Experimental Brain Research, 74,* 24–40.

Dick, A. S., Overton, W. F., & Kovacs, S. L. (2005). The development of symbolic coordination: Representation of imagined objects, executive function, and theory of mind. *Journal of Cognition and Development, 6,* 133–161.

Durston, S., Davidson, M. C., Tottenham, N., Galvan, A., Spicer, J., Fossella, J. A., et al. (2006). A shift from diffuse to focal cortical activity with development. *Developmental Science, 9,* 1–20.

Durston, S., Hulshoff Pol, H. E., Casey, B. J., Giedd, J. N., Buitelaar, J. K., & Van Engeland, H. (2001). Anatomical MRI of the developing human brain: What have we learned? *Journal of the American Academy of Child and Adolescent Psychiatry, 40,* 1012–1020.

Elbert, T., Pantev, C., Wienbruch, C., Rockstroh, B., & Taub, E. (1995). Increased cortical representation of the fingers of the left hand in string players. *Science, 270,* 305–307.

Epstein, H. T. (1986). Stages in human brain development. *Brain Research, 395,* 114–119.

Falkenstein, M., Hoormann, J., & Hohnsbein, J. (2001). Changes of error-related ERPs with age. *Experimental Brain Research, 138,* 258–262.

Foster, J. K., Meikle, A., Goodson, G., Mayes, A. R., Howeard, M., Sünram, S. I., et al. (1999). The hippocampus and delayed recall, bigger is not necessarily better? *Memory, 7,* 715–732.

Fuster, J. M. (1989). *The prefrontal cortex: Anatomy, physiology, and neuropsychology of the frontal lobe.* New York: Raven.

Garavan, H., Ross, T. J., & Stein, E. A. (1999). Right hemispheric dominance of inhibitory control: An event-related functional MRI study. *Proceedings of the National Academy of Sciences, 96,* 8301–8306.

Giedd, J. N., Blumenthal, J., Jeffries, N. O., Castellanos, F. X., Liu, H., Zijdenbos, A., et al. (1999). Brain development during childhood and adolescence: A longitudinal MRI study. *Nature Neuroscience, 2,* 861–863.

Gogtay, N., Giedd, J. N., Lusk, L., Hayashi, K. M., Greenstein, D., Vaituzis, A. C., et al. (2004). Dynamic mapping of human cortical development during childhood through early adulthood. *Proceedings of the National Academy of Sciences, 101,* 8174–8179.

Goldberg, E., & Bilder, R. M. (1987). The frontal lobes and hierarchical organization of cognitive control. In E. Perecman (Ed.), *The frontal lobes revisited* (pp. 159–187). New York: The IRBN Press.

Goldstein, J. M., Seidman, L. J., Horton, N. J., Makris, N., Kennedy, D. N., Caviness, V. S., et al. (2001). Normal sexual dimorphism of the adult human brain assessed by in vivo magnetic resonance imaging. *Cerebral Cortex, 11,* 490–497.

Gómez-Isla, T., Hollister, R., West, H., Mui, S., Growdon, M. D., Petersen, R. C., et al. (1997). Neuronal loss correlates with but exceeds neurofibrillary tangles in Alzheimer's disease. *Annals of Neurology, 41,* 17–24.

Good, C. D., Johnsrude, I., Ashburner, J., Henson, R. N. A., Friston, K. J., & Frackowiak, R. S. J. (2001). Cerebral asymmetry and the effects of sex and handedness on brain structure: A voxel-based morphometric analysis of 465 normal adult human brains. *Neuroimage, 14,* 685–700.

Greenough, W. T., Black, J. E., & Wallace, C. S. (1987). Experience and brain development. *Child Development, 58,* 539–559.

Gualtieri, T., & Hicks, R. (1985). An immunoreactive theory of selective male affliction. *The Behavioral and Brain Sciences, 8,* 427–441.

Gunning-Dixon, F. M., & Raz, N. (2000). The cognitive correlates of white matter abnormalities in normal aging: A quantitative review. *Neuropsychology, 14,* 224–232.

Guttmann, C. R., Jolesz, F. A., Kikinis, R., Killiany, R. J., Moss, M. B., Sandor, T., et al. (1998). White matter changes with normal aging. *Neurology, 50,* 972–978.

Happaney, K., Zelazo, P. D., & Stuss, D. T. (2004). Development of orbitofrontal function: Current themes and future directions. *Brain and Cognition, 55,* 1–10.

Hester, R., Fassbender, C., & Garavan, H. (2004). Individual differences in error processing: A review and reanalysis of three event-related fMRI studies using the go/no-go task. *Cerebral Cortex, 14,* 986–994.

Hines, M., Chiu, L., McAdams, L. A., Bentler, P. M., & Lipcamon, J. (1992). Cognition and the corpus callosum: Verbal fluency, visuospatial ability and language lateralization related to midsagittal surface areas of callosal subregions. *Behavioral Neuroscience, 106,* 3–14.

Hogan, A. M., Vargha-Khadem, F., Kirkham, F. J., & Baldeweg, T. (2005). Maturation of action monitoring from adolescence to adulthood: An ERP study. *Developmental Science, 8,* 525–534.

Huttenlocher, P. R. (1979). Synaptic density in human frontal cortex: Developmental changes and effects of aging. *Brain Research, 163,* 195–205.

Huttenlocher, P. R. (1990). Morphometric study of human cerebral cortex development. *Neuropsychologia, 28,* 517–527.

Huttenlocher, P. R. (2002). Neural plasticity: The effects of environment on the development of the cerebral cortex. Cambridge, MA: Harvard University Press.

Huttenlocher, P. R., & Dabholkar, A. S. (1997). Regional differences in synaptogenesis in human cerebral cortex. *Journal of Comparative Neurology, 387,* 167–178.

Jernigan, T. L., Archibald, S. L., Berhow, M. T., Sowell, E. R., Foster, D. S., & Hesselink, J. R. (1991). Cerebral structure on MRI, Part I: Localization of age-related changes. *Biological Psychiatry, 29,* 55–67.

Jernigan, T. L., Archibald, S. L., Fennema-Notestine, C., Gamst, A. C., Stout, J. C., Bonner, J., et al. (2001). Effects of age on tissues and regions of the cerebrum and cerebellum. *Neurobiology of Aging, 22,* 581–594.

Jernigan, T. L., Press, G. A., & Hesselink, J. R. (1990). Methods for measuring brain morphologic features on magnetic resonance images: Validation and normal aging. *Archives of Neurology, 47,* 27–32.

Jernigan, T. L., & Tallal, P. (1990). Late childhood changes in brain morphology observable with MRI. *Developmental Medicine and Child Neurology, 32,* 379–385.

Jonides, J., Marshuetz, C., Smith, E. E., Reuter-Lorenz, P. A., Koeppe, R. A., & Hartley, A. (2000). Age differences in behavior and PET activation reveal differences in interference resolution in verbal working memory. *Journal of Cognitive Neuroscience, 12,* 188–196.

Kane, M. J., & Engle, R. W. (2002). The role of prefrontal cortex in working-memory capacity, executive attention, and general fluid intelligence: An individual-differences perspective. *Psychonomic Bulletin & Review, 9,* 637–671.

Kemper, T. (2000). Neuroanatomical and neuropathological changes during ageing and dementia. In M. Albert & E. Knoepfel (Eds.), *Clinical neurology of aging* (pp. 3–67). New York: Oxford University Press.

Kirkham, N. Z., Cruess, L. M., & Diamond, A. (2003). Helping children apply their knowledge to their behavior on a dimension-switching task. *Developmental Science, 6,* 449–467.

Klingberg, T., Forssberg, H., & Westerberg, H. (2002). Increased brain activity in frontal and parietal cortex underlies the development of visuospatial working memory capacity during childhood. *Journal of Cognitive Neuroscience, 14,* 1–10.

Klingberg, T., Vaidya, C. J., Gabrieli, J. D. E., Moseley, M. E., & Hedehus, M. (1999). Myelination and organization of the frontal white matter in children: A diffusion tensor MRI study. *Neuroreport, 10,* 2817–2821.

Koechlin, E., Ody, C., & Kouneiher, F. (2003). The architecture of cognitive control in the human prefrontal cortex. *Science, 302,* 1181–1185.

Köhler, S., Black, S. E., Sinden, M., Szekely, C., Kidron, D., Parker, J. L., et al. (1998). Memory impairments associated with hippocampal versus parahippocampal-gyrus atrophy: An MR volumetry study in Alzheimer's disease. *Neuropsychologia, 36,* 901–914.

Kuhl, P. K. (2004). Early language acquisition: Cracking the speech code. *Nature Reviews Neuroscience, 5,* 831–843.

Kuhl, P. K., Taso, F. M., & Liu, H. M. (2003). Foreign-language experience in infancy: Effects on short-term exposure and social interaction on phonetic learning. *Proceedings of the National Academy of Sciences, 100,* 9096–9101.

Ladouceur, C. D., Dahl, R. E., & Carter, C. S. (2004). ERP correlates of action monitoring in adolescence. *Annals New York Academy of Science, 1021,* 329–336.

Lamm, C., Zelazo, P. D., & Lewis, M. D. (2006). Neural correlates of cognitive control in childhood and adolescence: Disentangling the contributions of age and executive function. *Neuropsychologia, 44,* 2139–2148.

LeVay, S., Wiesel, T. N., & Hubel, D. H. (1980). The development of ocular dominance columns in normal and visually deprived monkeys. *Journal of Comparative Neurology, 191,* 1–51.

Liston, C., Watts, R., Tottenham, N., Davidson, M. C., Niogi, S., Ulug, A. M., et al. (2005). Frontostriatal microstructures modulates efficient recruitment of cognitive control. *Cerebral Cortex, 16,* 553–560.

Maguire, E. A., Gadian, D. G., Johnsrude, I. S., Good, C. D., Ashburner, J., Frackowiak, R. S. J., et al. (2000). Navigation-related structural change in the hippocampi of taxi drivers. *Proceedings of the National Academy of Sciences, 97,* 4398–4403.

Marner, L., Nyengaard, J. R., Tang, Y., & Pakkenberg, B. (2003). Marked loss of myelinated nerve fibers in the human brain with age. *Journal of Comparative Neurology, 462,* 144–152.

Mathalon, D. H., Bennett, A., Askari, N., Gray, E. M., Rosenbloom, M. J., & Ford, J. M. (2003). Response-monitoring dysfunction in aging and Alzheimer's disease: An event-related potential study. *Neurobiology of Aging, 24,* 675–685.

McEwen, B. S. (2000). The neurobiology of stress: From serendipity to clinical relevance. *Brain Research, 886,* 172–189.

McIntosh, A. R., Sekuler, A. B., Penpeci, C., Rajah, M. N., Grady, C. L., Sekuler, R., et al. (1999). Recruitment of unique neural systems to support visual memory in normal aging. *Current Biology, 9,* 1275–1278.

Mechelli, A., Friston, K. J., Frackowiak, R. S., & Price, C. J. (2005). Structural covariance in the human cortex. *Journal of Neuroscience, 25,* 8303–8310.

Meier-Ruge, W., Ulrich, J., Brühlmann, M., & Meier, E. (1992). Age-related white matter-atrophy in the human brain. *Annals of the New York Academy of Sciences, 673,* 260–269.

Molliver, M. E., Kostović, I., & Van der Loos, H. (1973). The development of synapses in cerebral cortex of the human fetus. *Brain Research, 50,* 403–407.

Moriguchi, Y., & Hiraki, K. (2009). Neural origin of cognitive shifting in young children. *Proceedings of the National Academy of Sciences, 106,* 6017–6021.

Morrison, J. H., & Hof, P. R. (1997). Life and death of neurons in the aging brain. *Science, 278,* 412–419.

Mungas, D., Reed, B. R., Jagust, W. J., DeCarli, C., Mack, W. J., & Kramer, J. H., et al. (2002). Volumetric MRI predicts rate of cognitive decline related to AD and cerebrovascular disease. *Neurology, 59,* 867–873.

Murphy, D. G., DeCarli, C., McIntosh, A. R., Daly, E., Mentis, M. J., Pietrini, P., et al. (1996). Sex differences in human brain morphometry and metabolism: An in vivo quantitative magnetic resonance imaging and positron emission tomography study on the effect of aging. *Archives of General Psychiatry, 53,* 585–594.

Nagy, Z., Westerberg, H., & Klingberg, T. (2004). Maturation of white matter is associated with the development of cognitive functions during childhood. *Journal of Cognitive Neuroscience, 16,* 1227–1233.

Nieuwenhuis, S., Ridderinkhof, K. R., Talsma, D., Coles, M. G., Holroyd, C. B., Kok, A., et al. (2002). A computational account of altered error processing in older age: Dopamine and the error-related negativity. *Cognitive, Affective, and Behavioral Neuroscience, 2,* 19–36.

O'Donnell, S., Noseworthy, M., Levine, B., Brandt, M., & Dennis, M. (2005). Cortical thickness of the frontopolar area in typically developing children and adolescents. *Neuroimage, 24,* 948–954.

O'Kusky, J., Strauss, E., Kosaka, B., Wada, J., Li, D., Druhan, M., et al. (1988). The corpus callosum is larger with right-hemisphere cerebral speech dominance. *Annals of Neurology, 24,* 379–383.

Olesen, P. J., Westerberg, H., & Klingberg, T. (2003). Increased prefrontal and parietal activity after training of working memory. *Nature Neuroscience, 7,* 75–79.

Overman, W. H., Bachevalier, J., Schumann, E., & Ryan, P. (1996). Cognitive gender differences in very young children parallel biologically based cognitive gender differences in monkeys. *Behavioral Neuroscience, 110,* 673–684.

Pakkenberg, B., & Gundersen, H. J. G. (1997). Neocortical neuron number in humans: Effect of sex and age. *Journal of Comparative Neurology, 384,* 312–320.

Park, D. C., Polk, T. A., Mikels, J. A., Taylor, S. F., & Marshuetz, C. (2001). Cerebral aging: Integration of brain and behavioral models of cognitive function. *Dialogues in Clinical Neuroscience, 3,* 151–165.

Paus, T. (2005). Mapping brain maturation and cognitive development during adolescence. *Trends in Cognitive Sciences, 9,* 60–68.

Paus, T., Zijdenbos, A., Worsley, K., Collins, D. L., Blumenthal, J., Giedd, J. N., et al. (1999). Structural maturation of neural pathways in children and adolescents: In vivo study. *Science, 283,* 1908–1911.

Petersen, R. C., Jack, C. R., Xu, Y. C., Waring, S. C., O'Brien, P. C., Smith, G. E., et al. (2000). Memory and MRI-based hippocampal volumes in aging and AD. *Neurology, 54,* 581–587.

Pfefferbaum, A., Mathalon, D. H., Sullivan, E. V., Rawles, J. M., Zipursky, R. B., & Lim, K. O. (1994). A quantitative magnetic resonance imaging study of changes in brain morphology from infancy to late adulthood. *Archives of Neurology, 51,* 874–887.

Raz, N. (2000). Aging of the brain and its impact on cognitive performance: Integration of structural and functional findings. In F. I. M. Craik & T. A. Salthouse (Eds.), *The handbook of aging and cognition* (2nd ed., pp. 1–290). Mahwah, NJ: Erlbaum.

Raz, N., Gunning, F. M., Head, D., Dupuis, J. H., McQuain, J., Briggs, S. D., et al. (1997). Selective ageing of the human cerebral cortex observed in vivo: Differential vulnerability of the prefrontal gray matter. *Cerebral Cortex, 7,* 268–282.

Raz, S., Lauterbach, M. D., Hopkins, T. L., Glogowski, B. K., Porter, C. L., Riggs, W. W., et al. (1995). A female advantage in cognitive recovery from early cerebral insult. *Developmental Psychology, 31,* 958–966.

Reimers, S., & Maylor, E. A. (2005). Task switching across the lifespan: Effects of age on general and specific switch costs. *Developmental Psychology, 41,* 661–671.

Reiss, A. L., Abrams, M. T., Singer, H. S., Ross, J. L., & Denckla, M. B. (1996). Brain development, gender, and IQ in children: A volumetric imaging study. *Brain, 119,* 1763–1774.

Resnick, S., Goldszal, A., Davatzikos, C., Golski, S., Kraut, M., Metter, E., et al. (2000). One-year age changes in MRI brain volumes in older adults. *Cerebral Cortex, 10,* 464–472.

Resnick, S., Pham, D. L., Kraut, M. A., Zonderman, A. B., & Davatzikos, C. (2003). Longitudinal magnetic resonance imaging studies of older adults: A shrinking brain. *Journal of Neuroscience, 23,* 3295–3301.

Reuter-Lorenz, P. A., Jonides, J., Smith, E. E., Hartley, A., Miller, A., Marshuetz, C., et al. (2000). Age differences in the frontal lateralization of verbal and spatial working memory revealed by PET. *Journal of Cognitive Neuroscience, 12,* 174–187.

Ridderinkhof, K. R., Ullsperger, M., Crone, E. A., & Nieuwenhuis, S. (2004). The role of the medial frontal cortex in cognitive control. *Science, 306,* 443–447.

Rolls, E. T., Hornak, J., Wade, D., & McGrath, J. (1994). Emotion related learning in patients with social and emotional changes associated with frontal lobe damage. *Journal of Neurology, Neurosurgery & Psychiatry, 57,* 1518–1524.

Rubia, K., Overmeyer, S., Taylor, E., Brammer, M., Williams, S. C. R., Simmons, A., et al. (2000). Functional frontalisation with age: Mapping neurodevelopmental trajectories with fMRI. *Neuroscience and Biobehavioral Reviews, 24,* 13–19.

Rubia, K., Smith, A. B., Woolley, J., Nosarti, C., Heyman, I., Taylor, E., et al. (2006). Progressive increase of frontostriatal brain activation from childhood to adulthood during event-related tasks of cognitive control. *Human Brain Mapping, 27,* 973–993.

Rueda, M. R., Rothbart, M. K., McCandliss, B. D., Saccomanno, L., & Posner, M. I. (2005). Training, maturation, and genetic influences on the development of executive attention. *Proceedings of the National Academy of Sciences, 102,* 14931–14936.

Salat, D. H., Kaye, J. A., & Janowsky, J. S. (2002). Greater orbital prefrontal volume selectively predicts worse working memory performance in older adults. *Cerebral Cortex, 12,* 494–505.

Sampaio, R. C., & Truwit, C. L. (2001). Myelination in the developing brain. In C. A. Nelson & M. Luciana (Eds.), *Handbook of developmental cognitive neuroscience* (pp. 35–44). Cambridge, MA: MIT Press.

Scheibel, A. B. (1996). Structural and functional changes in the aging brain. In J. E. Birren & K. W. Schaie (Eds.), *Handbook of the psychology of aging* (4th ed., pp. 105–128). San Diego, CA: Academic.

Segalowitz, S. J., & Davies, P. L. (2004). Charting the maturation of the frontal lobe: An electrophysiological strategy. *Brain and Cognition, 55,* 116–133.

Segalowitz, S. J., Davies, P. L., Santesso, D., Gavin, W. J., & Schmidt, L. A. (2004). The development of the error negativity in children and adolescents. In M. Ullsperger & M. Falkenstein (Eds.), *Errors, conflicts, and the brain: Current opinions on performance monitoring* (pp. 177–184). Leipzig, Germany: Max Planck Institute for Cognition and Neuroscience.

Shaw, P., Greenstein, D., Lerch, J., Clasen, L., Lenroot, R., Gogtay, N., et al. (2006). Intellectual ability and cortical development in children and adolescents. *Nature, 440,* 676–679.

Shaw, P., Kabani, N. J., Lerch, J. P., Eckstrand, K., Lenroot, R., Gogtay, N., et al. (2008). Neurodevelopmental trajectories of the human cerebral cortex. *Journal of Neuroscience, 28,* 3586–3594.

Smith, E. E., Geva, A., Jonides, J., Miller, A., Reuter-Lorenz, P., & Koeppe, R. A. (2001). The neural basis of task switching in working memory: Effects of performance and aging. *Proceedings of the National Academy of Sciences, 98,* 2095–2100.

Smith, E. E., & Jonides, J. (1999). Storage and executive processes in the frontal lobe. *Science, 283,* 1657–1661.

Sowell, E. R., Peterson, B. S., Thompson, P. M., Welcome, S. E., Henkenius, A. L., & Toga, A. W. (2003). Mapping cortical change across the human life span. *Nature Neuroscience, 6,* 309–315.

Sowell, E. R., Thompson, P. M., Holmes, C. J., Batth, R., Jernigan, T. L., & Toga, A. W. (1999). Localizing age-related changes in brain structure between childhood and adolescence using statistical parametric mapping. *Neuroimage, 9,* 587–597.

Sowell, E. R., Thompson, P. M., Leonard, C. M., Welcome, S. E., Kan, E., & Toga, A. W. (2004). Longitudinal mapping of cortical thickness and brain growth in normal children. *Journal of Neuroscience, 24,* 8223–8231.

Sowell, E. R., Thompson, P. M., Rex, D., Kornsand, D., Tessner, K. D., Jernigan, T. L., et al. (2002). Mapping sulcal pattern asymmetry and local cortical surface gray matter distribution in vivo: Maturation in perisylvian cortices. *Cerebral Cortex, 12,* 17–26.

Stiles, J. (2008). *The fundamentals of brain development: Integrating nature and nurture.* Cambridge, MA: Harvard University Press.

Swaab, D. F., & Hofman, M. A. (1988). Sexual differentiation of the human hypothalamus: Ontogeny of the sexually dimorphic nucleus of the preoptic area. *Developmental Brain Research, 44,* 314–318.

Temple, E., Deutsch, G. K., Poldrack, R. A., Miller, S. L., Tallal, P., Merzenich, M. M., et al. (2003). Neural deficits in children with dyslexia ameliorated by behavioral remediation: Evidence from functional MRI. *Proceedings of the National Academy of Sciences, 100,* 2860–2865.

Terry, R. D., De Teresa, R., & Hansen, L. A. (1987). Neocortical cell counts in normal adult aging. *Annals of Neurology, 21,* 530–539.

Thompson, P. M., Giedd, J. N., Woods, R. P., MacDonald, D., Evans, A. C., & Toga, A. W. (2000). Growth patterns in the developing brain detected by using continuum mechanical tensor maps. *Nature, 404,* 190–193.

Valenzuela, M. J., & Sachdev, P. (2006a). Brain reserve and dementia: A systematic review. *Psychological Medicine, 36,* 441–454.

Valenzuela, M. J., & Sachdev, P. (2006b). Brain reserve and cognitive decline: A non-parametric systematic review. *Psychological Medicine, 36,* 1065–1073.

Van Petten, C. (2004). Relationship between hippocampal volume and memory ability in healthy individuals across the lifespan: Review and meta-analysis. *Neuropsychologia, 42,* 1394–1413.

Van Petten, C., Plante, E., Davidson, P. S. R., Kuo, T. Y., Bajuscak, L., & Glisky, E. L. (2004). Memory and executive function in older adults: Relationships with temporal and prefrontal gray matter volumes and white matter hyperintensities. *Neuropsychologia, 42,* 1313–1335.

Waber, D. P. (1977). Sex differences in mental abilities, hemispheric lateralization, and rate of physical growth in adolescence. *Developmental Psychology, 13,* 29–38.

Werker, J. F., & Desjardins, R. N. (1995). Listening to speech in the 1st year of life: Experiential influences on phoneme perception. *Current Directions in Psychological Science, 4,* 76–81.

Witelson, S. F., Glezer, I. I., & Kigar, D. L. (1995). Women have greater density of neurons in posterior temporal cortex. *Journal of Neuroscience, 15,* 3418–3428.

Xu, J., Kobayashi, S., Yamaguchi, S., Iijima, K., Okada, K., & Yamashita, K. (2000). Gender effects on age-related changes in brain structure. *American Journal of Neuroradiology, 21,* 112–118.

Yakovlev, P. I., & Lecours, A. R. (1967). The myelogenetic cycles of regional maturation of the brain. In A. Minkowski (Ed.), *Regional development of the brain in early life* (pp. 3–70). Oxford: Blackwell.

Zelazo, P. D., Carlson, S. M., & Kesek, A. (2008). Development of executive function in childhood. In C. A. Nelson & M. Luciana (Eds.), *Handbook of developmental cognitive neuroscience* (2nd ed., pp. 553–574). Cambridge, MA: MIT Press.

Zelazo, P. D., Craik, F. I. M., & Booth, L. (2004). Executive function across the lifespan. *Acta Psychologica, 115,* 167–183.

Zelazo, P. D., & Cunningham, W. (2007). Executive function: Mechanisms underlying emotion regulation. In J. Gross (Ed.), *Handbook of emotion regulation* (pp. 135–158). New York: Guilford.

Zelazo, P. D., & Müller, U. (2002). Executive functions in typical and atypical development. In U. Goswami (Ed.), *Handbook of childhood cognitive development* (pp. 445–469). Oxford: Blackwell.

Zelazo, P. D., Müller, U., Frye, D., & Marcovitch, S. (2003). The development of executive function in early childhood. *Monographs of the Society for Research on Child Development, 68,* vii–137.

CHAPTER 5

Biology, Evolution, and Psychological Development

GARY GREENBERG and TY PARTRIDGE

WHAT IS PSYCHOLOGY?

Taking a cue from *Alice in Wonderland*, we always believe it is best to start at the beginning. Thus, we start this discussion of the relation of biology to psychology with an understanding of the nature of the science of psychology. Succinctly, *Psychology is the biopsychosocial science of animal behavior.* Animal behavior is included to avoid references to other uses of the term, such as the physicist's description of the behavior of particles. Furthermore, the implication here is that only animals behave in the psychological sense; in addition, we believe that behavior requires a nervous system, again restricting psychological behavior to animals. The idea that plants can behave in the psychological sense rears its head every so often and is quickly dismissed: "The past three years have witnessed the birth and propagation of a provocative idea in the plant sciences. Its proponents have suggested that higher plants have nerves, synapses, the equivalent of a brain localized somewhere in the roots, and an intelligence" (Alpi et al., 2007, p. 135; see also Dudley & File,

2007). This same sentiment can be extended to recent developments in the realm of artificial intelligence and naturalistic theologies such as the Gaia hypothesis (Lovelock, 1979). The adaptive behavior of complex systems and neural network computing systems are qualitatively different than psychology.

Implied by the perspective that psychology is the biopsychosocial science of behavior is the assumption that behavior is influenced by biological, psychological, and social factors, among others. In this context, it is critical to understand the significance of the important organizing principle of integrative levels: "a view of the universe as a family of hierarchies in which natural phenomena exist in levels of increasing organization and complexity" (Aronson, 1984, p. 66). This is a refutation of atomistic/reductionistic principles and an affirmation of holism—that wholes cannot be reduced to their parts; that "more is different" (Anderson, 1972; Kauffman, 2007; Overton, 2006). Indeed, "hierarchy is a central phenomenon of life. Yet it does not feature as such in traditional biological theory" (Vrba & Eldredge, 1984, p. 146). Psychology is one of a growing number of areas of study falling under the metasciences of holism and complexity.

Psychology, then, is a more complex science than is biology, and sociology more so than is psychology (Cole, 1983; Feibleman, 1954). Although a student may struggle more through her physics class, psychology can be seen to be more complex than is physics, which not only can describe its phenomena with equations but can identify the variables on both sides of those equations. Psychology, of course, has not yet identified all variables pertinent to understanding behavioral origins. Nevertheless, psychology is a science sufficiently mature to stand on its own as unique, and not as a subset of biology (Greenberg, Partridge, Mosack, & Lambdin, 2006; Kantor, 1959; Schneirla, 1949), the discipline from which it emerged. A similar situation existed with regard to biology in the early 1900s when Woodger (1929) argued that biology needed an explanatory model distinct from physics and chemistry. This was a mere 120 years after the "founding" of biology as the "science of life" by Lamarck (Keller, 2002). Similarly, psychology is presented as a unique science, separate and distinct from biology, with its own unique principles, searching for its own unique laws. Notably, this has been recognized by scientists other than psychologists. The physicist P. W. Anderson, for example, has said: "At each stage [i.e., level of organization] entirely new laws, concepts, and generalizations are necessary. Psychology is not applied biology, nor is biology applied chemistry" (1972, p. 393). The ecologist Vincent Bauchau (2006) points out that just as there are principles in biology that do not belong to physics, so there are principles in the other sciences, from chemistry to psychology, that cannot be reduced and that do not belong to sciences lower in the hierarchy. Natural selection, for example, a "universal law of biology," cannot be reduced to physics. Of course, the idea of a hierarchy of the sciences is not new. That the sciences themselves can be divided into areas of study based on qualitative changes in complexity of organization, with physics and chemistry addressing the lower levels of complexity, and biology, psychology, and sociology addressing higher levels of complexity, is an idea that seemingly was originated by Auguste Comte in the late 1800s (see Boorstein, 1998, p. 223) and was later developed by others such as Novikoff (1945) and Feibleman (1954). The study of learning, of cognition, of personality development, and of species-typical behaviors are subject areas that the psychologist can address from the orientation proposed here—from the perspective of psychology and not from biology. The theme of this chapter, therefore, is that although psychology cannot be reduced to biology, biology remains a necessary perspective for a complete understanding of events at the level of psychology.

Although psychology is generally viewed from a natural science perspective (i.e., behavior is as natural a phenomenon as rolling balls down inclined planes was to Galileo), the discipline has few genuine "laws." Arguably, this is due both to the relative immaturity of the field and to its involvement with misguided intellectual efforts. Scientific progress in psychology has been retarded by frequently being lost and enamored in its own blind alleys of alchemy, phrenology, and atomistic reductionism. Hence, it is worthwhile to heed the admonition of Lerner (2004a) when he suggests, "We are at a point in the science of human development where we must move on to the more arduous task of understanding the integration of biological and contextual influences in terms of the developmental system of which they are a dynamic part" (p. 20).

Psychology, then, is the unique science of behavior, although greatly influenced by principles of the other sciences. For example, as Medawar (1974) frames it:

> Every statement which is true in physics is true also in chemistry and biology and ecology and sociology. Likewise, any statement that is true in biology and "belongs" to biology is true in sociology. Thus a characteristically physical proposition like $E = mc^2$ is true also in all the sciences. More usually, however, a physical or chemical statement such as "the atomic weight of potassium is 39" is simply not interesting in a subject like sociology and does not bear at all upon its distinctive problems. (p. 62)

This same idea was more recently posed by Gilbert and Sarkar (2000), who stated that when examining cells, the spin of a quark is simply not relevant. In addition, "If one asks why peacocks have long tail[s], it will not help to inquire about the physico-chemistry of feathers" (Bauchau, 2006, p. 37). However, the atomic weight of potassium would be relevant to studies in physiological psychology, especially when examining neuronal functioning, just as are principles of physics when studying animal locomotion (Vogel, 1998). Thus, although psychology strives to develop its own unique principles and laws, these will of necessity be compatible and consistent with those of all of the other sciences. For the most part, the properties of the physical world, organized at lower levels of complexity than at least biology, function as background constants for the study of psychology. So, although it is important that the atomic weight of potassium is 39, insofar as this molecular structure affords potassium a role in the action potential of neurons, for pragmatic purposes there is no point in discussing them as psychological variables, because they do not vary. In contrast, the specific organization and function of the endocrine system across mammalian species does vary, and thus should be considered when defining the psychological capacities or potentials for a given species or individual (see Nesselroade & Molenaar, Chapter 2 of this volume for an extended discussion of the role of variation in psychology).

Presenting psychology as a unique science is, of course, not a new approach. As early the 1920s, J. R. Kantor (1924, 1926) was making this case and arguing that, although biology is important for psychological events, psychology was not a biological science but was, rather, a psychological science. T. C. Schneirla (1949) later joined in discussing psychology in this way. Contemporary relational developmental systems psychologists have more recently also embraced this understanding of psychology (e.g., Lerner & Overton, 2008).

A RELATIONAL DEVELOPMENTAL SYSTEMS APPROACH

Dynamic systems "theory" (Lewin, 1992; Michel & Moore, 1995) or what in developmental psychology has been termed *relational developmental systems* (Lerner & Overton, 2008) is an organizing metatheory that recognizes the importance of *relations* between events. From this perspective, organisms are not simply collections of organs and other parts; rather, they operate holistically, their parts are interdependent, regulating each other. The importance of this distinction cannot be overstated. Indeed, the modus operandi of psychology is the study of dynamic relations between the multiple elements comprising psychological systems. The philosophical shift in psychological science away from a reductionistic and static orientation aimed at understanding the structural elements of behavior (i.e., psychological causes must be physically located in either a biological, psychological, or sociological entity) toward a dynamic, holistic, and relational orientation extends from metatheory through the articulation of methodologies to the conceptualization of all psychological constructs (Overton, 2006). This was recognized early on by the Nobel Laureate Charles Sherrington (1906/1947, 1951/1964). Furthermore, organisms are not separate from or independent of their environments but are *fused* with them. The environment, thus, is seen to be part of the organismic "whole." This important way of looking at organisms has a long history in modern psychology (von Bertalanffy, 1933; Kantor, 1959;

Lerner, 1998; Overton, 1975). Our discussion of the relation of biology to behavior is framed in this perspective.

Approaching psychology as a biopsychosocial science resolves the ancient nature–nurture controversy by recognizing that organisms are simultaneously biological and psychological/social beings, and that each of these perspectives plays necessary roles in the origin and maintenance of behaviors. Ingold (2000) put it this way: "We do not progress, in the course of our lives, from a stage of biological incompletion as 'mere' organisms, to one of social completion as fully fledged persons. We are fully and indissolubly organism and person from beginning to end" (p. 285). As Donald Hebb (1953) once remarked, behavior is 100% biology (nature) and 100% psychology (nurture). In a more contemporary formulation of this same idea, Overton (2006) remarked, "The character of any contemporary behavior…is 100% nature because it is 100% nature" (p. 33). Accordingly, following Seay and Gottfried (1978), behavior is understood to be a result of the dynamic interplay of five sets of factors:

1. *Phylogenetic set*—refers to the organism's evolutionary status, that is, what it is as a species. This is embodied in Kuo's (1967) "principle of behavioral potentials," which suggests that each species is endowed with the potential to behave in species-typical ways (Haraway & Maples, 1998). Of course, there is no guarantee that those potentials will be actualized. Thus, as Montagu (1952/1962) points out, "The wonderful thing about a baby…is its promise" (p. 17), suggesting that we are born *Homo sapiens,* but we have to *become* human beings. Another way of saying this is that human nature (or that of any species) is not a direct product of biology, but rather a set of characteristics acquired during the course of growth and development.

2. *Ontogenetic set*—refers to the developmental history of the organism, from the moment of its conception to its death. Included here is biological maturation, the process of bringing the various tissues, organs, and other parts of the organism to full functional development. The probabilistic nature of this ontogeny is underscored. Nothing in development—embryologic or behavioral—is guaranteed by genes; nothing is preformed or preordained (Gottlieb, 1992; Nieuwkoop, Johnen, & Albers, 1985). It is crucial to note that the developmental stage of the organism profoundly impacts its behavior and the way in which it reacts to stimuli.

3. *Experiential set*—the multitude of experiences an organism accrues throughout its life course does much to direct its future development (Lerner & Ross-Bushnagel, 1985). Here, following Schenirla's (1972/1957) definition of experience as "all stimulative effects upon the organism through its life history…" (p. 269), it also refers to all actions initiated by the organism (Overton, 2006). Thus, experience is both what happens to the organism and what it does. Kantor (1959) referred to this experiential history as the "reactional biography." The reactional biography begins at conception and continues to be built up until the organism's death. Every stimulus and each act affects the organism and changes it, though some stimulation and some acts have much more profound and obvious effects than others. Learning, for example, is an important process in behavioral change, but it is nothing more than a special set of experiences.

4. *Cultural set*—refers to the organism's function in environments. The organism-environment forms a functional whole, and consequently, environments are necessary features of the organism's biological and behavioral development. This is most obvious in humans, who have developed contextual cultural systems (e.g., religion, dietary practices, social institutions) that impact in multiple ways on behavioral development. But all living organisms, though perhaps at less complex levels, function within environments of their own making. Different species may inhabit different environments, eat different foods, and so forth. This important point was stressed by the ethologist Jacob von Uexküll (1957), who termed the behavioral environment of an animal its *Umwelt,* its sensory-perceptual world (see also Michel, in press). Chimpanzees, for example, display different behavioral adaptations related to their unique environments (Matsuzawa, 1998). Two communities separated by only 10 km display markedly different behaviors. These differences include nest building, ant dipping, use of leaves for water drinking, food choices, and many others. These differences are less complex cultural traditions than are found in more complex species.

5. *Individual set*—refers to the uniqueness of each individual organism and how that uniqueness relates to its development. One animal may be more or less sensitive to sounds, or may have a developmental abnormality that limits its interactions with its world,

or may be larger or smaller than its conspecifics, and so forth. This set of factors recognizes the contribution of the individual's unique genotype and how that, in dynamic interaction with contextual influences, may render it a different behaving creature than all others.

These five organizational sets provide the ontological structure of psychology. The common theme that runs through all of these organizational sets is that temporal processes and relational constructs are the central conceptual features of each set. The challenge for the study of psychology is to account for these dynamic relational processes that occur at multiple spatial and temporal streams, becoming manifest in the nexus of the individual organism.

BIOLOGICAL FACTORS IN BEHAVIORAL DEVELOPMENT: EVOLUTION AND GENETICS

We turn now to a discussion of the several aspects of biology that play a role in the genesis of behavior and development. It should again be emphasized at the outset of this discussion that the position taken here is that biology plays an important, but not foundational, role in behavior and development. The impact of biology in psychological phenomena is relatively recent, it being the case that "Biology as a unified science did not exist until well into the 20th century" (Smith, 2008, p. x).

Evolution

Evolution is an appropriate starting point for an enquiry into the relation of biology and psychology because, in a sense, everything in life can be said to begin here. Science speaks of cosmic evolution, the universe originating with the Big Bang (Singh, 2005), though, of course, the principles and mechanisms of cosmic evolution are different from those of biological evolution (Darwin, 1859). One corollary of cosmic evolution is that given enough time, hydrogen and helium become living organisms (and eventually sentient beings)—it is at this point that biological evolution and natural selection emerge and become possible (Weber, 2007). Biological evolution can be described as change in the characteristics of populations of organisms over time. The concept applies only to groups (species) and not to individuals; individuals develop over time but do not themselves evolve. Evolutionary changes are inherited, biologically and culturally, in the sense of being passed down across generations. Of course, as Reid (2007) has pointed out, the path to sentience is not inevitable, merely a result of emergent evolution:

> Thus, mind, as a manifestation of those novel internal relations, becomes a likely outcome at the higher levels. But it is not predetermined by the early generative conditions. And it certainly does not reside hylozoically in the Big Bang nor in the simplicities of solid-state physics… An expanding universe has the potential to develop carbon etc. Carbon etc. have the potential to originate life, Life has the potential to complexify through reproduction…and it is as a *result* of biological evolution that energy flow increases in the biosphere. (pp. 428–429)

It is instructive to begin our discussion of evolution with a quotation from Ernst Mayr, one of the 20th century's leading evolutionary biologists:

> The most consequential change in man's view of the world, of living nature and of himself came with the introduction over a period of some 100 years beginning only in the 18th century, of the idea of change itself, of change over long periods of time: in a word, of evolution. Man's world view today is dominated by the knowledge that the universe, the stars, the earth and all living things have evolved through a long history that was not foreordained or programmed, a history of continual, gradual change shaped by more or less directional processes consistent with the laws of physics. (1979, p. 47)

The modern theory of evolution dates from a joint presentation on behalf of Charles Darwin and Alfred Wallace to the Linnean Society of London in 1856. Of course, Darwin and not Wallace is remembered as the founder of modern evolution ideas because of the weight of the evidence he collected and presented in his 1859 discourse, *The Origin of Species*. One of the basic ideas of evolution, that present forms of plant and animal life have changed over vast periods to become as they now are, is at least as old as the Greek philosopher Anaximander, who believed that all life began in the sea and gradually evolved to take advantage of land and ocean environments (Futuyma, 1998). What was missing in older ideas of evolution was a mechanism or guiding principle by which evolution would be given order and direction. That principle was supplied by the idea of natural selection and later by the ideas of genetics.

It is well known that Darwin formed his idea of natural selection after a mapping expedition over much of the world with the British Navy in the late 1830s. He noted the wide variety of animals and how their variations were related to their unique environments. His observations lay dormant, incubating several years while he experimented with breeding and cross-breeding animals and plants. The key idea of Darwin's theory, which distinguished it from earlier evolution ideas, was that of natural selection. All species and all individuals must survive a natural selection. Here was a principle to give guidance and direction to the process of evolution. Evolution must flow always in the direction of functional effectiveness, in the direction of survivability.

Darwin had formed the basic ideas of his theory of evolution by the end of the 1830s, but came forth to publish those ideas only when Wallace independently conceived his own similar ideas in the mid-1850s. Following the joint publication with Wallace in 1856, Darwin made use of his 20-year head start in working with his own theory of evolution. In 1859 he published his basic book on the subject. *The Origin of Species* became an international sensation, and the theory of evolution soon became known as "Darwin's Theory." It has become one of the most influential ideas in the history of thought. Mayr (1979) has said that the synthetic theory of evolution is "*the* organizing principle of biology" (p. 47, emphasis added). Dobzhansky (1973), another important contributor to the development of modern evolutionary theory, titled an article, "Nothing in Biology Makes Sense Except in the Light of Evolution." Indeed, our understanding of life, the world we stand upon, and the universe which surrounds us is an evolutionary understanding.

As with all major scientific theories, Darwinism is an exemplar of simplicity. It can be summarized in three fundamental principles: (1) Species produce many more eggs and offspring than can survive and reproduce themselves; (2) sexual reproduction permits a wide variety of genetically different offspring to be produced by each breeding pair, male and female; (3) from among this variability, nature selects individuals whose characteristics result in survival and breeding capability. Note that these principles hold for all organisms, animals as well as plants. Because species evolution results from differing rates of survival and reproduction among various types, the relative frequencies of the types change over time. In this sense, then, evolution can be seen to be a sorting process (Griffiths et al., 2005).

Darwin knew that characteristics that permit the organisms possessing them to survive were likely to be passed on through the successful reproduction of those organisms. He knew nothing, however, about the mechanism of such inheritance. Our current understanding of genetics, which began with the work of the monk Gregor Mendel, provides this mechanism. The canonical theory of evolution, referred to as "The Modern Synthesis," combines Darwin's ideas of natural selection and Mendel's ideas of genetics (e.g., Mayr & Provine, 1980).

Theories in science are of necessity dynamic. All the facts are never fully collected; that is why science is characterized as a self-correcting discipline. New discoveries and new facts rarely result in the discarding of a strong theory; rather, the course taken is to tweak the theory to accommodate the new findings. So it is with Darwinism. Although Darwin provided the fundamental law of his theory, that of Natural Selection, Saunders and Ho (1976, 1981) suggested that an increase in complexity over geologic time (i.e., with evolution) can be understood as a second law of Darwinism. We have discussed complexity theory and its corresponding idea of emergence fully in other publications (Greenberg, Partridge, & Ablah, 2007; Partridge & Greenberg, in press). It is sufficient here to state that increases in complexity and the epigenetic emergence of novelty are the rule in evolution. This should come as no surprise, for as many, including Stephen J. Gould (1997b; see also Krasny, 1997), Maynard Smith (1970), Sean Carroll (2001), and others, have pointed out, when you begin with a single cell, with simplicity, there is only one direction to go in and that is up toward greater complexity. Maynard Smith (1970) explains, "It is in some sense true that evolution has led from the simple to the complex: prokaryotes precede eukaryotes, single-celled precede many-celled organisms, taxes and kineses precede complex instinctive or learnt acts...And if the first organisms were simple, evolutionary change could only be in the direction of complexity" (p. 271).

It is in this context that the important evolutionary concept of anagenesis becomes significant. Anagenesis is a concept that implies evolutionary progress (Aronson, 1984; Greenberg, 1995; Overton, 1975; Yarczower, 1984): "The cardinal defining features of behavioral and psychological anagenesis [are] increases in ontogenetic plasticity and improvements in behavioral versatility, the latter through enhanced perceptual, cognitive, learning, social, and/or motor skills" (Gottlieb, 1984, p. 454). The progress referred to here is evolutionary change. Although "progress" is often a highly charged and controversial idea in evolutionary thinking, misunderstandings are avoided by adopting Stephen Jay Gould's (1988) argument that "we can preserve the deep (and essential) theme of direction in history, while abandoning the intractable notion of progress" (p. 321). The fossil record presents virtually undeniable evidence that organismic complexity has increased

with time. Stated differently, with few exceptions, more recently evolved forms are more complex in their behavior than are earlier evolved forms. As evolution has continued, it has preserved many simple forms, perhaps unchanged over millennia, but the new forms produced have tended strongly in the direction of increasing complexity. Chaisson (2001) has thoroughly discussed the idea of complexity in nature. With respect to the application of complexity to development in psychology, the following statement by Arthur (1993) is telling: "The writer Peter Matthiessen once said, 'The secret of well-being is simplicity.' True. Yet the secret of evolution is the continual emergence of complexity. Simplicity brings a spareness, a grit; it cuts the fat. Yet complexity makes organisms like us possible in the first place" (p. 144).

The issue here is not only controversial, it is contentious, with debate frequently occurring from ideologic perspectives (Lewin, 1992). However, in the context of the argument presented in this chapter, Bonner's (1988) position is persuasive:

> There is an interesting blind spot among biologists. While we readily admit that the first organisms were bacteria-like and that the most complex organism of all is our kind, it is considered bad form to take this as any kind of progression... It is quite permissible for the paleontologist to refer to strata as upper and lower, for they are literally above and below each other...But these fossil organisms in the lower strata will, in general, be more primitive in structure as well as belong to a fauna and flora of earlier times, so in this sense "lower" and "higher" are quite acceptable terms...But one is flirting with sin if one says a worm is a lower animal and a vertebrate a higher animal, even though their fossil origins will be found in lower and higher strata. (pp. 5–6)

Reid (2007) offers a simpler way of saying the same thing: "To say that human is higher does not disparage the worm, but implies that perfection-of-adaptation-to-environment is a totally inadequate assessment" (pp. 432–433). Bonner's (1988) book is an exposition on the evolution of biological complexity, a phenomenon he likens to a "law" of evolution. That this trend toward complexity in evolution is so pervasive and agreed on has led some to identify it as "The Arrow-of-Complexity hypothesis" (Miconi, 2008).

The idea of evolutionary progress has been troublesome to scientists since Darwin's time (Nitecki, 1988). The problem lies in finding a reasonable and objective basis on which to judge one species as representing an improvement, or an advance, over another. Progressive change may be identified as a sustained or continuing change in any particular direction. Maier and Schneirla (1935/1964) found it useful to equate evolutionary progress with increases in behavioral complexity and plasticity as one ascends through a hierarchy of behavioral levels of organization. Associated with that hierarchy are increases in nervous system complexity, organization, and integrative functions (Bonner, 1988; Jerison, 1994). The idea of complexity is no longer the poorly defined construct it once was. By wide agreement (e.g., Carroll, 2001), complexity in biological systems can be assessed by the number of different components—cell types, structures, even gene number—possessed by organisms. As pointed out earlier, Saunders and Ho (1976, 1981) have gone so far as to identify a positive relation between progressive complexity and evolutionary advancement as a second law of evolution, together with natural selection. Increasing complexity is closely related to improved organization and increased plasticity of behavior, which accompany evolutionary elaboration of the nervous system. Indeed, as Chaisson (2001) has pointed out, "Whatever measure of complexity is used, it is hard to avoid the notion that 'things'—whether galactic clouds, slimy invertebrates, luxury automobiles, or the whole universe itself—have generally become more complicated throughout the course of history" (p. 7).

A cornerstone of Darwinian theory is that evolutionary change is slow and gradual, taking millions of years. The absence of a corresponding fossil record is one source of challenge to this idea. However, Eldredge and Gould (1972) provided an explanation for these gaps in the fossil record and at the same time demonstrated the dynamism of Darwinian theory—that it can be tweaked. Their idea is referred to as *punctuated equilibrium*. The proposal, now widely accepted as another modification of Darwinian theory (Gould & Eldredge, 1993), is that species remain unchanged for long periods (i.e., in equilibrium), and that these long periods of no change are punctuated by episodes of relatively rapid (e.g., in geologic time, tens or hundreds of thousands of years) change. Thus, there is no gradual fossil record to be discovered. This is saltatory, rather than gradual, evolution and is an example of how the principle of emergence plays a role in our contemporary understanding of evolution (Reid, 2007). (See MacWhinney, Chapter 14 of this volume, for an extended discussion of emergence in human language development.)

We entered the 21st century on the heels of two expensive and popular scientific efforts, the Decade of the Brain (http://www.loc.gov/loc/brain) and the Human Genome Project (http://www.ornl.gov/sci/techresources/Human_Genome/home.shtml). Both purported to put to rest the search for the origins of behavior. The former endeavor sought to put the entire burden of behavior on the brain, the latter on the human genome. Both, of course, celebrated the nature side of the nature–nurture equation and, importantly, both failed to "take development seriously" (Robert, 2004). This has changed with the most recent modification of Darwinism in its rerecognition of the significance of development in the evolutionary process. This takes the form of a newly developed area of study, evolutionary developmental biology or evo-devo. In the 20th century, the study of embryology and genetics took different paths, the two failing to acknowledge the importance of each for the other. This "was a conceptual block that continued to be an issue among biologists until the1980s and 1990s, when the application of molecular genetics to development promised to bring the two fields [i.e., genetics and embryology] back together in the new disciplinary synthesis of 'evo-devo'" (Allen, 2007, p. 151).

Evo-devo entails, among other things, a new understanding of genetic functioning and the role of development in this functioning. And with the introduction of evo-devo, there has been a reemergence of the centrality of concept of epigenesis (i.e., increasing system complexity and the *emergence* of irreducible *novel* systems properties and competencies occurring through biological-environmental interactions). The novelty of this newly emerging discipline has been summarized as follows by Jason Robert (2004), a philosopher (of biology) who has argued forcefully for the return of development in the understanding of modern approaches to biology in general and evolution in particular:

> Despite differences in approach, evo-devoists tend to hold to a core of theoretical presuppositions, including: (a) the hierarchical nature of development and evolution; (b) the need to focus on developmental processes—interactions—between genotype and developing phenotype; and (c) the belief that analysing developmental processes and mechanisms, and their evolution, improves our understanding of both evolution and development. Studying development in evolutionary context, and evolution in developmental context, increases the explanatory scope of both sciences. (p. 97)

Before the Human Genome Project, it was believed that the human genome contained about 100,000 genes. We now know that number to be a somewhat more modest figure of

20,000 to 30,000, no more really than the common house mouse. It is also known that the genomes of *Homo sapiens* and our closest relative, the chimpanzee, are some 98.7% identical. The question thus arises, if the genomes of so disparate animals are so similar, what accounts for the vast differences in the phenotypes between these organisms?

The answer lies not in the genes themselves but in the arrangement of these genes on chromosomes. To be more precise, "It is not so much mutational events and new genes that are the origin of complex novel structures, but rather developmental reorganization and the cooptation of established regulatory pathways into new developmental functions" (Miller, 2007). As Evelyn Fox Keller (2002) describes, the spatial position of genes plays a major role in their expression; context, then, is key, and positional information and the central dogma (which is discussed later in this chapter) are now understood to be "the two theoretical cornerstones of molecular developmental biology (the other being the central dogma)" (p. 180). Genes, then—and this is a major point of the evo-devo movement—do not exist in a vacuum; rather, they function in a cell with many components and other genes, the myriad contents of which interact and play a role in the turning on and off of different genes. It is safe to agree with the philosopher of biology, Michael Ruse (2006), that the development of evo-devo has opened the way to some of the most interesting discoveries in molecular biology, not the least of which are the "amazing homologies between humans and fruitflies for starters" (p. 36). It is of interest to note that some of these ideas have been known for a long time, though they did not make their way into the popular literature until more recently. For example, as early as 1972, Hull wrote: "As it turns out, the same gene frequently functions differently, depending on its position on the chromosome, a phenomenon known as the position effect" (p. 498). It is now recognized that this, and other cellular environmental influences and developmental processes, have profound effects on genetic expression. Some genes are not even found in the embryo (e.g., those for B- and T-cell antigen receptors) but are constructed during development (Gilbert & Sarkar, 2000).

Problems of Evolutionary Psychology

The perspective of atomistic reductionism has been the cornerstone of the relatively new field of Evolutionary Psychology, which presents a genocentric explanation of human behavior. The basic argument here has been that the genome has been fixed since the days of our hunter-gatherer ancestors, and all behavior is accounted for by random genetic variation and natural selection. The alternative to this perspective is the holistic relational position that, although evolution, like genes, represents partial processes in the nature and development of behavior, there is ample evidence that evolution has continued across history, and factors are at work beyond variation and selection.

This alternative position has been expressed by Lickliter and Honeycutt (2003), among others (e.g., Blumberg, 2005; Kaplan & Rogers, 2003), in their critique of atomistic reductionistic application of evolution to psychology and development. Although evolutionary psychology posits a universal human nature, Ingold (2000) discusses the crucial role of culture in making us all different, identical twins included! Here the first important point to be made is that many evolutionary forces have been at work since the appearance of our species in the Pleistocene. It is an error to suggest that our behavior as *Homo sapiens* is the result of our adaptation to Pleistocene events, as evolutionary psychologists not only imply but explicitly state (e.g., Buss, 1999, 2005; Pinker, 2002). For evolutionary psychologists, adaptation to Pleistocene events is perhaps the fundamental principle involved in behavioral evolution. However, as Buller (2005) stresses, "There is ongoing evolution in human psychological adaptations, so it is mistaken to believe that our minds are adapted to our Pleistocene past" (p. 13). Indeed, as Ingold (2000) points out, nothing has been transmitted to us by our Pleistocene ancestors, "For the growth of practical knowledge in the life history of a person is a result not of information transmission but of guided rediscovery" (p. 288).

Rejection of the atomistic reductionistic approach also entails a rejection of the adaptationist agenda of evolutionary psychology. As many have pointed out, including such notable evolution scientists as Gould (1997a), even Darwin suggested that mechanisms other than adaptation are at work in evolution. It is a mistake and a misunderstanding of Darwinism to suppose that there is anything approaching the consensus claimed by evolutionary psychologists. Rather, pluralism of mechanisms is the rule in the still developing paradigm of evolution. For example, we now understand evolution to involve punctuated equilibrium, genetic drift, mutation, and other processes, as well as natural selection. In fact, evolution does not always involve changes in the genome. It is now recognized that not all genes of the human genome get expressed. Evolution can occur if different portions of the genome are expressed, the result perhaps of environmental impact. This would result in new phenotypes (see Honeycutt, 2006).

Some have also argued that "evolutionary psychology has recently gone too far in its epistemological agenda, as it attempts to uncover the brain 'mechanisms' that constitute 'human nature'" (Panskepp & Panskepp, 2000, p. 108). The holistic relational alternative to this notion of innate and universal human nature is found in Montagu's position that we are born *Homo sapiens,* but we become human beings. This too was the point of Kuo (1967), who raised the issue of whether a cat was a rat killer or a rat lover, and *empirically* answered the question in this way: Kittens raised with rats out of sight of cats which kill and eat rats, never kill rats themselves, even when hungry. Never having seen a rat killed or eaten, it is simply not a food object for them. Animal nature is a result not of biology alone, but of developmental history. Behavior, thus, even human behavior, is enormously plastic (Lerner, 1984). Herein lies the significance of relational developmental systems theory for psychology and especially for developmental psychology.

Another related serious difficulty with contemporary evolutionary psychology is its genocentric arguments from animal to human behavior. Of course, it is almost universally accepted now in psychology that there is continuity in behavioral processes from animals to humans. This is reflected in current research in cognition, studies of the origins of language, the fundamental workings of learning, and so forth. Animal models can be extremely useful in this regard, in the search for the evolutionary origins of much of human behavior. Strains of mice and the fruit fly, for example, have been the workhorses of behavior geneticists for 50 years or more. But such models have their limitations; the social climate, empowered by the enormous success of the Human Genome Project, one of the most costly scientific endeavors in history, has fostered an almost frenzied search for the "gay gene" and the "schizophrenia gene." Nevertheless, "There is so far only one known example of male to male matings being switched on by one gene. This is the fruit fly…[However] one would be hard pressed to call a fruit fly homosexual" (Kaplan & Rogers, 2003 p. 223). Lewontin's (1997, p. 29) comment is germane in this context:

The concentration on the genes implicated in cancer is only a special case of a general genomania that surfaces in the form of weekly announcements in *The New York Times* of the location of yet another gene for another disease. The revealing rhetoric of this publicity is always the same; only the blanks need to be filled in: "It was announced today by scientists at [Harvard, Vanderbilt, Stanford] Medical School that a gene responsible for [some, many, a common form of] [schizophrenia, Alzheimer's, arteriosclerosis, prostate cancer] has been located and its DNA sequence determined. This exciting research, say scientists, is the first step in what may eventually turn out to be a possible cure for this disease."

Unfortunately, there is rarely a follow-up announcement that the findings were in error or have failed to be replicated! One of the best recent discussions of this issue is found in Joseph (in press). A good example concerns the ongoing search for the gene(s) for depression. There have been many reports of finding them, but a new meta-analysis of 14 studies before 2008 revealed *no* evidence of a relation between genes and the risk for depression (Risch et al., 2009). Of course, genetics is involved in depression, this report indicates, but as a fusion with experience. The behavioral sciences in general and evolutionary psychology in particular have tended to ignore or perhaps are not even aware of contemporary empirical findings in molecular biology, evolutionary biology, and genetics, a point emphasized by others (e.g., Gottlieb 2004; Kaplan & Rogers, 2003; Lickliter & Honeycutt, 2003). As Lewontin (1997) has remarked, "Even individual scientists are ignorant about most of the body of scientific knowledge" (p. 28). Thus, it is now known that genes are not directly responsible for phenotypic expression, but rather, the environmental context of development plays a crucial role in this process; that genes not only work from the inside out, but that behavior, too, can influence the expression of genes (referred to as "downward causation" by Campbell, 1990); that not all genes of a genome get expressed; that natural selection is but one of several mechanisms responsible for evolutionary change; and that the path from genes to physical or behavioral traits is enormously complex and indirect. It is now recognized that social behavior itself can turn genes on and off (Robinson, Fernald, & Clayton, 2008). Thus, foraging by honeybees occurs as a result of the effect of colony pheromones that alter the expression of hundreds of genes in the bee brain. In the swordfish, some genes are turned on as the female swordfish interacts with some male swordfish and off when the interaction is with other female swordfish. Genomes remain active throughout life to many environmental stimuli including those from the social context. Some of these social signals have epigenetic effects that are inheritable, but not through changes in the DNA sequence—transgenerational inheritance via epigenetic pathways (Harper, in press). That social behavior has been shown to affect brain genetics, which affects neuronal activity, provides a bidirectional pathway from altered brains to altered behavior. This work calls to mind the discussion of social effects on brain disorders, labeled sociogeneic brain damage (Montagu, 1972). Social deprivation, economics, and malnutrition all have dramatic effects on brain development. Indeed, we have known for some time that social conditions have a profound effect not only on brain development, but on physical development in general, a phenomenon labeled *psychosocial dwarfism* (Reinhart & Drash, 1969). It is also the case that drug addictions may be related to drug-induced changes in gene expression in key brain reward areas (Renthal & Nestler, 2008). Work of this nature suggests that we still have a great deal to learn about the nature and role of the gene in the overall developmental system.

Another idea at the center of the evolutionary psychology program is that the human mind is constructed of innate, domain-specific cognitive modules, evolutionary adaptive holdovers from the Pleistocene (Pinker, 2002). (See discussions by Buller [2005], Kaplan and Rogers [2003], and Uttal [2001] on mental modules.) Mental modules constitute a rather vague concept, and information is seldom provided concerning their specific nature or numbers (though some have speculated that the number might be in the "hundreds or thousands" [Toobey & Cosmides, 1995, p. xiii]). As Panskepp and Panskepp (2000) argue, we too "believe that some currently fashionable versions of evolutionary psychology are treading rather close to neurologically implausible views of the human mind... there is no [convincing] evidence in support of highly resolved genetically dictated adaptations that produce socioemotional cognitive strategies within the circuitry of the human neocortex" (p. 111).

Other critical features of the biological sciences are misunderstood or ignored, or both, by evolutionary psychologists. A common response by evolutionary psychologists to such criticism has been that it is they who are misunderstood, and that they do not suggest that behavior is genetically determined or innate. However, and unfortunately, these responses amount to little more than lip service, as reference to a recently established web site illustrates (University of Sheffield, n.d.). This is the web site of a group known as *The AHRB Project on Innateness and the Structure of the Mind,* the members of which are a veritable Who's Who of the evolutionary psychology elite. In their own words, from their web site: "The project brought together top scholars in a broad range of disciplines—including animal psychology, anthropology, cognitive psychology, developmental psychology, economics, linguistics and psycholinguistics, neuroscience,

and philosophy—to investigate the current status and most promising future directions of nativist research."

Evolution and Behavior

An organism's status as a species endows it with the potentials to behave in ways unique to that species. This idea is captured by Kuo's (1967) "principle of behavioral potentials," which asserts that each species is endowed with the potential to behave in species-typical ways. The same idea is the basic assumption of contemporary work on "embodiment" (see Overton, Mueller, & Newman, 2007), embodiment being the claim that perception, thinking, feelings, and desires are contextualized by our being *active agents* with this particular kind of body. A concrete illustration of these concepts is found in the song "Can't Help Lovin' Dat Man" from the musical *Show Boat:* "Fish gotta swim, birds gotta fly." Of course, there is no guarantee that potentials are actualized. This is why the notable evolutionary biologist Paul Ehrlich suggested that we are better off thinking of human (or species) natures in the plural, rather than a single nature (Ehrlich, 2000).

As species evolve, their behavioral potentials change. In fact, there is a close tie between behavior and evolution. Surprisingly, the relation goes not from evolution to behavior, but from behavior to evolution. In an important and real sense, it is what an organism does that allows it to survive and pass on its genes to future generations. Said another way, it is the phenotype, in this case, the animal's behavior, and not the genotype that drives evolution. The Nobel biologist Waddington (1969) stated:

> Now natural selection obviously acts on the phenotype. If for instance, natural selection demands that a horse can run fast enough to escape from a predatory wolf, what matters is not what genes the horse has got, but how fast it can run. It is irrelevant whether it can run fast because it has been trained by a good race horse trainer, or because it has got a nice lot of genes. (p. 360)

Ernest Mayr (1985) pointed out that, in addition to being adaptive, behavior serves as a pacemaker in evolution, "by leading organisms into new niches or environments which exert a new set of selection pressures and thus may lead to major evolutionary changes" (pp. 59–60). As an example, consider the following: For almost 50 years, Japanese primatologists (Nishida, 1986) have been studying the social behavior and emergent traditions of Japanese macaque monkeys. Provisioned with novel foods—potatoes and rice—the monkeys soon began to toss handfuls of rice gathered from the sandy beach into the water, where the rice would float and the sand would sink. The monkeys thus discovered a way to wash sand from their food. These practices spread throughout the colony and are now part of the animals' normal behavioral repertoire. The practice is handed down from generation to generation—a primitive form of cultural transmission, though alternative explanations of this behavior have been proposed (Heyes, 1998). Once they began spending more time near and in the water, young macaques began playing in it. This play led to the development of new behavioral skills, such as swimming. The animals also incorporated new foods into their diets, fish, for example, and may now be capable of swimming to distant islands. Behavior such as this would subject them to new ecologic pressures and potentially affect the course of their evolution—a form of "Darwin's finches" scenario. This is an example of how behavior may drive evolution. Of course, as organisms change over time and new species evolve, the new biologies of these species endow them with new behavioral potentials. In this way, we see that evolution affects behavior as well.

Genetics—The Mechanism of Evolution?

When Darwin first put forth his theory of evolution by natural selection, he knew that traits were passed on from one generation to the next, but he knew nothing of how that was accomplished. It was only in the early part of this century that a group of biologists, including Ernst Mayr, Theodosius Dobzhansky, and George Gaylord Simpson, incorporated the Mendelian system of genetics into evolutionary theory. The result produced what is now referred to as the Modern Synthesis, or the Synthetic Theory of Evolution, or "neo-Darwinism," a synthesis of natural selection and genetics (Futuyma, 1998).

Evolution is now understood to involve the formation of new species by changes in the gene pool that characterizes a parent species (Mayr, 1970). These changes arise in several ways, most dramatically when a natural barrier arises and separates groups of animals. The flow of genes between them is halted and each species, or isolated gene pool, now becomes subject to different ecological pressures. Because the flow of genes is the result of reproduction, the successful attracting of mates becomes a crucial event in evolution. This is accomplished by behavioral means—bird song, courtship displays, flash rates by fireflies. Again, we see the important links between behavior and evolution.

What is a gene? "It is almost common knowledge among biologists and philosophers of biology…that the classical molecular gene concept is not sufficient any

longer in the face of the complex interactive processes being reported by molecular biology" (Neumann-Held, 2001, p. 69). Neumann-Held and others (e.g., Keller, 2000, 2002; Moss, 2003) also point out that since the end of the 20th century, the very notion of just what a gene is has changed. It is no longer sufficient to speak of "the" gene; the term has come to mean different things to different people. The term *gene* is now understood to be shorthand for several different kinds of units. It may be that "gene" is not so much an identifiable *thing* as it is a *process* involved in binding DNA to other factors that act together in polypeptide production. At its inception, and indeed until only very recently, the gene, seemingly so concrete and definitive a structure, was nothing more than a hypothetical construct in a statistical equation (Burian, 1985; Keller 2002). Even with the discovery of the unique and highly functional structure of deoxyribonucleic acid (DNA) by Watson and Crick (1953), little more empirical light was shown on the subject than simply having a molecule with the kinds of properties through which the hypothetical gene might work.

However, it is now understood that there is no explanation in attributing a trait, behavioral or structural, to genetics in light of what converging current research from several disciplines indicates (Moss, 2003). Many behavioral scientists, behavior geneticists, and evolutionary psychologists seem to be unaware of these recent developments in our understanding of genetics, as Gottlieb (1998, 2004) and others (e.g., Lickliter & Honeycutt, 2003) have pointed out. It turns out that there is no information in the genome to be triggered or nurtured by the environment, though this is the current consensus in the behavioral and much of the biological sciences. This has been consistently and reliably demonstrated empirically in data from a large number of studies, which give us a new picture of the role of genes in development in general. "For instance, genes are not informational in the way supposed, nor do they initiate or direct ontogeny, there is no such thing as a genetic programme, and there is no straightforward 'unfolding' relation from genotype to phenotype" (Robert, 2004, p. 39). This type of information is only recently making its way into the popular press (e.g., Angier, 2008), where it is likely to have a greater impact in educating the public than do scientific publications. Our own students, for example, reluctantly accept what we have to say about such things but readily believe in what they read in *Time* magazine or hear on the nightly news!

It is now known that genes do little more than code for the many different proteins that go into making up living things; the proteins are themselves incorporated into the ever-changing molecular and cellular structure and physiology that is an individual organism. One way of looking at an organism is as a chemical soup. The biologist Garrett Hardin (1956) said that humans and other animals are not so much *things* as they are *places* where very interesting things are occurring. From this view, the DNA part of this chemical soup sees that certain chemical reactions take place at certain times. Genes participate in turning reactions on or off; they function as catalysts. Similarly, they really operate by participating in the timing of important chemical events. When the default schedule is followed, certain interactions inevitably occur. "There is no need for genes to encode and control those interactions directly. Instead, they follow from the laws of physics, geometry, topology—laws of great generality" (Elman et al., 1996, pp. 41–42).

In this context, it is useful to recall the distinction between the genotype and the phenotype. The genotype is the actual genetic code, the genetic blueprint that influences every cell of our bodies. Because all cells trace their beginnings to a single daughter cell, the genotypes of each cell must be identical. The result of how those genes express themselves is the phenotype, but there is no direct relation here. It is not the case that the genotype codes for the phenotype. Although all cells have the same genotype, some become bone cells, some blood cells, some skin cells. Human beings possess some 256 different types of cells. These different cells arise as a result of epigenetic forces acting on the genes to cause them to express themselves in different ways (e.g., "Cellular differentiation is a classic example where epigenetic phenomena have a critical role" [Renthal & Nestler, 2008, p. 341]). Genes express themselves in the context of a field of internal and external forces that impinge on them (Stoltenberg & Hirsch, 1998). It is known that, in addition to a cell's own internal chemistry, genes can be switched on and off by signals from other cells and from other aspects of the environment (Geard & Wiles, 2005), including positional information referred to earlier in this chapter. "The path linking genes or molecules to the expression of behavior is long and complex…There are innumerable ways genes can influence development, physiology and the nervous system to affect behavior. Further, the genome has a dynamic relation with behavior, and each influences the other through complex regulatory mechanisms" (Barron & Robinson, 2008, p. 257). The relation between genetics and behavioral phenotypes is extremely indirect. Thus, two strains of inbred mice, C57BL10J and A/J, differ substantially in their aggressive behaviors, not a result of their inheriting

aggressive or nonaggressive genes, but rather the result of their sensitivity to stimulation, a biological factor that is, indeed, an inherited trait, much as myopia is in human beings (Greenberg, 1972). The title of a review of T. C. Schneirla's writings reflected this: "A Long Way from Genes to Behavior…" (Jaynes, 1973).

Molecular biology has learned a great deal about the functioning of genes in the past few decades, exploding a number of ideas we now see to be myths. These include the notion that single genes affect single traits—eye color, for example. Although some single gene/single traits are known to exist, the common mode is for genes to act in concert with others. What a gene does, then, is very much influenced by which other genes are being turned on or off at any particular time during development. In other words, genes do their work together with other genes, rather than individually. The developmental process, therefore, is not a predetermined one, but rather a probabilistic one. Put another way, "Since it has become evident that genes interact with their environment at all levels, including the molecular, there is virtually no interesting aspect of development that is strictly 'genetic,' at least in the sense that it is exclusively a product of information contained within the genes" (Elman et al., 1996, p. 21).

These ideas are in conflict with what came to be known as the central dogma of molecular biology (Crick, 1970), which states that genetic information flows in one direction only—from inside to out, from the genotype to the phenotype. Many have convincingly shown this to be false, most significantly for psychologists such as Gilbert Gottlieb, whose entire body of work showed empirically that structure–function relations were bidirectional (e.g., 2004). Gottlieb (2001) has suggested that few psychologists, and, in fact, many biologists, are simply unaware of recent developments in molecular biology that render no longer valid the standard program of genetics as an unfolding of a set genetic code: "While this fact is not well known in the social and behavioral sciences, it is surprising to find that it is also not widely appreciated in biology proper…[!]" (p. 47). He was not alone in this assessment, as even a molecular biologist has noted (Strohman, 1997). Within this assumptive framework, gene theory derived its key principles (Gottlieb, 2006):

1. Genes must be discrete causal agents "located" in the germ cells. This principle is derived entirely from the Newtonian assumptions of linear, singular, additive, and deterministic causes. Indeed, it was completely assumed as an a priori "given." The only empirical

observations related to this principle were the basic, observable aspects of sexual reproduction.

2. Genes behaved statistically "as if" they contained independent and unique causal information, which additively combine to form the adult organism, although there were no formal tests of this assumption. The logic was: If our atomistic and additive conceptualization is true, then the statistical properties of the organism would follow certain parameters. The statistical properties follow these parameters; therefore, our conceptualization of the gene is true. Philosophers of science refer to this logical fallacy as "affirming the consequent."

3. Because traits are predictable from the statistical estimations of Mendel and then later Fisher, both of whom did not include terms representing either development or environmental variation, it was further asserted that the causal information contained in genes was effectively isolated and independent of external influence (either biological or ecological).

BIOLOGICAL FACTORS IN BEHAVIORAL DEVELOPMENT: THE BRAIN AND NERVOUS SYSTEM

We begin our discussion of the role of the brain and nervous system in behavior with a quote from an introductory physiological psychology textbook (Plotnik & Mollenauer, 1978). Although the book was published in 1978, this statement reflects the still prevalent neurologic reductionistic materialism of contemporary psychology. Indeed, it reflects an important goal of the recently completed Decade of the Brain, an international research effort geared to resolving much of our still poor understanding of the functioning of the brain.

> If your brain were removed and another put into your skull, who would you be? Your friends would recognize your face but you would not recognize your friends or know their names. You would not know where you lived or who your parents were. You would not joke like or think like or dream like the original you. You would be a different you since the original you was stored in the brain that was removed. With a new brain you would have a different mind and personality even though your original body remained. (Plotnik & Mollenauer, 1978, p. 10)

This is incredibly fanciful stuff, especially for a textbook! Of course, it is entirely speculative because

such a procedure has never been performed even with the simplest of organisms. It does, however, reflect the still widely accepted idea that you are your brain, in the same sense that genetic reductionism holds that you are your genome. In more contemporary terms, this is often referred to as the "brain in a vat" theory.

Of course, just as we are more than the sum our genes (Kaye, 1992), we are much more than merely our brains and nervous systems. Again, the notion of embodiment is central here. The Noble laureate Sir Charles Sherrington put it this way, "A healthy man is a set of organs of interlocking action regulating each other, the whole making a self-regulating system" (1951, p. 163). The human being is a highly complex organism, actually a self-organizing and self-regulating system of interrelated and interdependent parts, all of which regulate each other, no one system more crucial to one's survival than all of the others. An organism cannot survive, or behave, without its heart or liver or lungs, and so forth, or without its nervous system. Although the nervous system links all of the other systems together, it is inaccurate to say that it is more important than any of the other systems, because the very life of the organism depends on the interdependent functioning of *all* of its biological systems as they function in the world. Although it has become habitual to say that the brain does various things such as think and remember, the fact is that it is the *person* who does these things, not his or her brain (Bennett & Hacker, 2003).

Unfortunately, the history of science is riddled with master-organ scenarios. In ancient Egypt, the heart ruled; the early Chinese looked to the liver, heart, lungs, and kidneys in trying to understand the emotions, until, as Critchley (1969) has pointed out, the history of neurology shows that the cerebralists gradually attained increasing acceptance. An excellent recent history of neuroscience (Zimmer, 2004) demonstrates:

> More than any other individual, Thomas Willis ushered in the Neurocentric Age...In redefining the brain, Willis redefined the soul as well. It was banished from the liver and the heart, restricted now to the brain and nerves...Willis's doctrines of the brain and the soul became part of the bedrock of Western thought, and they still lurk beneath many of our beliefs about ourselves today. (p. 240)

At the heart of this reductionistic thinking is a particular form of the materialist position adopted with respect to behavior and its development, reflecting the still dominant influence of mind–body dualism. Behavior, in this view, must be some *thing* and must be in some *place,* and that place is routinely identified as the brain. This line of thought stems from the reductionistic belief "that physiology is somehow nearer to reality than psychology" (Bannister, 1968, p. 231). This appears to be as true today as it was when Bannister made that statement. Thus, Weisberg, Keil, Goodstein, Rawson, and Gray (2008) found the current popular perception of neuroscience to be as follows:

> The presence of neuroscience information may be seen as a strong marker of a good explanation, regardless of the actual status of that information within the explanation. That is, something about seeing neuroscience information may encourage people to believe they have received a scientific explanation when they have not. People may therefore uncritically accept any explanation containing neuroscience information, even in cases when the neuroscience information is irrelevant to the logic of the explanation. (p. 470)

In their words, neurologic explanations are "alluring." Although the results of their investigation indicated that "experts" were not lulled into accepting false neurologic explanations, there is little reason to believe that psychology as a whole is less susceptible to this illusion than is the lay public. Our discussion of brain imaging (see later) is directed at this point.

Brain and Mind

Since adopting the model of experimental science around 1879, psychology has been identified as a dualistic enterprise, that is, the study of behavior *and* of the mind. Although the discipline has had little difficulty in defining what is meant by behavior (i.e., what organisms *do*), we have yet to achieve anything near consensus about what is meant by mind, or even whether such a thing or process exists. Although ideas of the mind can be traced back to the beginnings of philosophy, there is little dispute that the modern concept of the mind (i.e., mind/body dualism) can be attributed to Descartes (Leahy, 2000; Overton, 2006). Descartes believed mind and body to be truly different substances, as expressed in this statement: "There is no physiology of the mind any more than there is a psychology of the nervous system" (cited in Reise, 1958, p. 122). Of course, with Descartes, the brain had by then become the seat of the mind/soul (Pronko, 1988), although as early as Hippocrates, four centuries before Christ, the brain had been identified as the organ of the mind (Penfield, 1958b). We are in full agreement with Richard Rorty's assessment that the "mind-body problem is an historical artifact created by Descartes—and it should be dissolved rather than positively solved" (cited by Niiniluoto, 1994, p. 40). Indeed, the mind–brain relation was thoroughly discussed by Uttal (2005), who concluded this to be a virtually unsolvable problem when cast in a dualistic, nonrelational manner.

It can be argued that the mind was not a phenomenon that was discovered as the result of patient and arduous empirical work, but rather an invention, first by the Greeks and for modern psychology, by Descartes, to avoid the Catholic Church's power of thumbscrew, and later by others, such as Freud, as a way of legitimizing some extremely creative, imaginative, and most likely wrong ideas (e.g., Bailey, 1965; Thornton, 1984). Indeed, in pointing out that we still have no satisfactory definition of the mind, Uttal agrees that today's mind was yesterday's *soul*:

> In previous times the word soul served the role that mind does now…I use soul here with the understanding that its theological overtones are to be ignored and that soul is, for all practical purposes, synonymous with what modern science now calls mind. (p. 50)

Skinner's (1977) understanding is pertinent here:

> The Greeks invented the mind to explain how the real world could be known. For them, to know meant to be acquainted with, to be intimate with. The term cognition itself is related to coitus, as in the biblical sense in which a man is said to know a woman. Having no adequate physics of light and sound nor any chemistry of taste and odor, the Greeks could not understand how a world outside the body, possibly some distance away, could be known. There must be internal copies. Hence cognitive surrogates of the real world…The mental apparatus studied by cognitive psychology is simply a rather crude version of contingencies of reinforcement and their effects. (pp. 5, 9)

It is appropriate for us to recognize the brilliant work of neuroscientists such as Broca, Frisch and Hitzig, Flourens, Gall, Spurzheim, and others in elucidating important aspects of brain functioning. "But with what consequences to psychology? The upshot of all this research was to saddle the materialistic brain with the functions of the immaterial mind. Thus was the brain made successor to the less scientifically palatable mind. And that's the way it has been ever since: soul → mind → brain" (Pronko, 1988, p. 189). However, as suggested earlier, we are in agreement with Kantor (1959) and Schneirla (1949) in believing that psychology is mature enough to be a uniquely psychological science with its own principles that are distinct from biological ones (Greenberg, Partridge, Mosack, & Lambdin, 2006; Pronko, 1980).

We certainly do not move forward with the same hubris of some reductionistic cognitive scientists who can putatively explain how the mind works (e.g., Pinker, 1999). These attempts generally turn out to be more descriptive statements about the manifestations of cognitive and emotional behaviors as opposed to explanatory statements. Rather, we have formed our perspective on the mind by drawing on a long history of multidisciplinary data and a relational developmental systems orientation. In many ways, our view of mind is consistent with the pragmatic views of early American functionalists. From a definitional perspective, we see merit in Schneirla's (e.g., 1949, 1957) understanding of mind and mental events as simply an overarching term referring to the integration across several developmental levels of sensory, perceptual, emotional, and cognitive behaviors of an organism. This definitional perspective has important ontologic consequences, prominent among which is the conception of mind as a term summarizing the set of cognitive, emotional, and individual $\leftarrow \rightarrow$ context relational variables fused within developmental systems. Of course, then, the mind can thus be understood as a collection of psychological variables with no lesser nor greater explanatory attribute than any other psychological variable. The Noble laureate Gerald Edelman (Edeleman & Tononi, 2000) referred to memory, one important aspect of the mind and mental events, in the following way:

> Whatever its form, memory itself is a system property. It cannot be equated exclusively with circuitry, with synaptic changes, with biochemistry, with value constraints, or with behavioral dynamics. Instead, it is the dynamic result of the interactions of *all* these factors acting together, serving to select an output that repeats a performance or an act. (p. 99)

Mentalism—split apart from the relational developmental system—can be seen as a crutch that gets in the way of our undertaking the arduous tasks necessary to unmask it. No psychologist has made this point more succinctly than Schneirla (1949), by pointing out that: "'Mind,' ostensibly a term for a generalized functional entity, a very impressive term, actually is only an introductory expression for all of man's intellectual capacities and attainments considered as a system" (p. 225). We take some solace in the conception of the mind as an extended phenomenon, not confined to the head, but as part of a person-context system (e.g., Marshall, 2009).

In seeing the mind this way as opposed to some secretion or product of the brain, several philosophical conundrums are addressed. Foremost is the problem regarding the on-

tological nature of the Universe—can there be explanatory entities that are fundamentally distinct from the material universe? Cognitive scientist Roger Sperry outlined the traditional philosophical positions with regard to this question: physical monism, mental monism, and dualism. In discussing these positions in the context of cognitive psychology and neuroscience, Sperry (1991, 1993) argued for an intermediary position, that of emergent monism. This, too, is the position of Bunge (1980). The assumption is that physical monism is the only scientifically defensible philosophical position to take, but that the cognitive and emotional behaviors that we refer to as mind are emergent properties of organism/environment dynamism. It is this viewpoint that underscores the contemporary hardware (neuroscience)/software (mind) metaphor. Although our view of mind is sympathetic to that of Sperry's, in that we are certainly physical monists and agree that what we call mind is an emergent property, our view extends that of Sperry's to what could be deemed relational emergent monism. Sperry's emergent monism view of mind is still fundamentally reductionistic, arguing that mind is essentially the dynamic macrostate of underlying neurological activity. Although this dynamic macrostate is emergent in the sense that its properties are not fully predictable from the individual states of the underlying neurologic matrix, it is still a state that is subordinate to neurology.

By accepting the pragmatic definition of mind as an integration of cognitive, emotional, and organism $\leftarrow \rightarrow$ context relational behaviors within the developmental system, you place the concept of mind and its subsidiary constructs within the operational realm of psychology, which, as we have presented in this chapter, is an independent science with explanatory principles that are uniquely psychological and neither subordinate nor superordinate to other phenomenological levels of analysis. Thus, we see mind as an emergent function of the dynamic transactions over the entire course of development of the individual organism and its ecological context. In a seminal essay, Freeman (2001) outlines what he refers to as three centuries of category errors in trying to relate neurology to cognition and other aspects of the mind. At the heart of his argument is the fact that cognitive neuroscience and its philosophical and scientific predecessors have failed to recognize the importance of both development and context as shapers of mind rather than simply being sources of information. In summary, we see mind as an emergent function of the dynamic transactions over the entire course of development of the individual organism and its ecological context rather than as some vague, obscure, and ill-defined secretion of the brain.

Contemporary Neuroscience and Its Problems

What the Brain Does Not Do

The statement that the human brain is the most complex structure in the known universe and that it defies full understanding is a familiar one. Though admitting there remain a myriad of questions about the brain despite the enormous successes of The Decade of the Brain, the assessment itself seems overzealous. As Bullock (1965/1970) stated:

> The gulf between our present level of physiological understanding and the explanation of behavior as we see it in higher forms is wider than the gulf between atomic physics and astronomy and is indeed the widest gap between disciplines in science. (p. 451)

Despite having made that comment in the 1960s, we are no closer to understanding the brain–behavior relation as underscored by Uttal's (2005) explorations of why the mind–brain problem will never be resolved. Indeed, the workings of the brain itself are still poorly understood—even the simplest of brains still defy the most basic understanding (Koch & Laurent, 1999). Professionals, as well as the lay public, are led to believe that our studies of the brain, although not complete, are extensive. However, 45% of contemporary brain studies involve only three species: the mouse, the rat, and the human (Manger et al., 2008). Much of what we know about brain functioning is the result of comparative studies. Examples include giant axons in the squid, dendritic spines in the central nervous system in chickens, conditioned reflexes in dogs, receptive fields in limulus, and nerve growth factor in the chicken. It is safe to say that the relative lack of such comparative studies today limits our full understanding of the brain and its evolution.

Nevertheless, psychology is today characterized by many as a reductionistic biological or brain science. In arguing that morphology is a phrenologic tool for assessing behavior, Gallup, Frederick, and Pipitone (2008) state, "Behavior is first and foremost a biological phenomenon" (p. 302). Similarly, Uttal understands psychology as a field that "can be completely explained in the language and data of neurophysiology—in principle if not in fact" (2005, p. 155). The most mainstream of psychology journals, *The American Psychologist,* often includes articles that promote the reductionist biological nature of behavior. For example, Heinrichs (1993) claims, "Schizophrenia is a kind of brain disease that should be approached as a problem in neuroscience. There are no

viable alternatives" (p. 221). Even one of the editors of a major behaviorist journal, the *Journal of the Experimental Analysis of Behavior,* has argued that psychology is a biological science: "Behavior is a biological property of organisms—what else could it be?" (J. Maar, personal communication, June 7, 2006). And, of course, the general public is led to believe this as well:

> In the 1950s, the common view was that humans begin as nearly blank slates and that behavior is learned through stimulus and response. Over the ages, thinkers have argued that humans are divided between passion and reason, or between the angelic and the demonic. But now the prevailing view is that brain patterns were established during the millenniums when humans were hunters and gatherers, and we live with the consequences. Now, it is generally believed, our behavior is powerfully influenced by genes and hormones. Our temperaments are shaped by whether we happened to be born with the right mix of chemicals. (Brooks, 2006, p. 14)

The alternative view is summed up nicely by Bennett and Hacker (2003):

> Such assertions as these—namely, that human beings are machines, or that the behaviour of a human being is no more than the behaviour of their nerve cells, or that decisions are taken in and (apparently) by the brain—are not science but metaphysics…Could neuroscience explain why birthdays are celebrated, why *Tosca* is worth going to, and why a husband might think it appropriate to get tickets to the opera for his wife's birthday treat? (pp. 356, 364)

The Executive Director for Science of the American Psychological Association has summed up an important reason for current biological reductionism: "[Today's] newest age of reductionism is being fueled by the federal funding agencies, the Congress, and by the general public. Everyone seems to think that focusing on ever finer grains of sand will hasten cures for the worst of human afflictions and produce enormous leaps forward in our understanding of the human condition" (Breckler, 2006, p. 23).

One of us has argued against psychology's reliance on the brain as *the* organ of behavior (e.g., Greenberg, 1983). Indeed, although we do not deny the necessity of the brain for behavior (or any life process for that matter), we cannot dismiss the ignored and neglected writings of John Lorber, who in the 1970s accidentally came upon several young adults, normal in all respects, with virtually no brains at all, a result of early childhood hydrocephalus (Lewin, 1980; Lorber, 1983)! The most that critics of these reports can say is that is simply not possible, but no empirical evidence is ever offered to refute Lorber's reports. Critical comments typically suggest that the full brain is there only in compacted form. On the other hand, a University of Michigan doctoral dissertation (Berker, 1985) concluded:

> Despite a marked reduction in neuroanatomical economy both hydrocephalics and hemispherectomy patients have demonstrated development of above average and even superior intellectual capacities. For example, one hydro-cephalic (RW) with over 95% of the cranium filled with CSF [cerebrospinal fluid] now has an honors degree in math, superior verbal (VIQ=140) and bright normal performance IQ (PIQ=112) and now has been success-fully employed as an accountant. Smith and Sugar (1975) reported a case of left hemispherectomy with similar superior development of verbal, and above average devel-opment of non-verbal abilities who has a college degree and has been successfully employed as an executive. Thus our findings of early onset hydrocephalus and studies of patients with hemispherectomy for infantile hemiplegia illustrate the remarkable capacity and versatility of the young brain for functional reorganizations despite marked reductions in cerebral economy.

That these findings have been ignored by the neuro-science community is no surprise to Lewontin (1997): "Repeatable observations that do not fit into an existing frame have a way of disappearing from view" (p. 30).

But as asserted earlier, from the holistic developmental systems approach, it is the *whole* organism that behaves. This is the point of Noë's (2008) statement:

> We should reject the idea that the mind is something inside of us that is basically matter of just a calculating machine. There are different reasons to reject this. But one is, simply put: there is nothing inside us that thinks and feels and is conscious. Consciousness is not something that happens in us. It is something we do.

Having just completed two major research efforts, the Decade of the Brain and the Human Genome Project, one goal of which was to elucidate the neural and genetic underpinnings of behavior, it may be understandable why biology, why brains and genes, is seen to control behav-ior, and why psychology is understood to be a biological science in the reductionist sense of the term. No one would deny the significance of the biological in our understand-ing of behavior; however, evolution, genetics, hormones, and neurophysiology are not, even together, *foundational* or bedrock explanations of behavior and development.

They are all necessary, although not necessary and suffi-cient, participating factors in the development of behavior. The Decade of the Brain and the Human Genome Project purported to put to rest the search for the bedrock origins of behavior. The former endeavor sought to place the entire burden of behavior on the brain, the latter on the human genome. Each effort yielded much significant and im-portant information about the brain and the genome, but their impact on our understanding of neural and genetic influences on behavior were minimal (Lewontin, 2000; Strohman, 1997). Although each effort arose from and attempted to endorse the nature side of the nature–nurture equation, "The Decade of the Brain has led to a realization that a comprehensive understanding of the brain cannot be achieved by a focus on neural mechanisms alone, and advances in molecular biology have made it clear that genetic expressions are not entirely encapsulated, that heri-table does not mean predetermined" (Cacioppo, Bernston, Sheridan, & McClintock, 2000).

In support of a perspective that approaches behavioral understanding holistically and relationally, we may con-sider evidence from several areas, evidence both present and absent.

Lateralization and the Split Brain. It is widely accepted that the brain and its functions are lateralized, and that this lateralization is the result of developmental dynamics (Rogers, in press). For example, chickens de-velop in their eggs with one side of their heads against the shell exposed to light stimulation. Rogers' research has elegantly shown this prehatching experience to affect brain lateralization in these animals. A similar situation may exist in primates. Michel (1981) and Michel and Goodwin (1979) argued that the position of the fetus in the uterus, the orientation of its head after birth, and left-right hand preference are all associated.

However, Sperry's (1982; see also Gazzaniga, 1967, 1983) idea that the two hemispheres are specialized for different cognitive functions remains in dispute. The most significant argument against this is the empirically based discussion by Efron (1990), which is summarized as follows:

> The degree to which studies of split-brain patients have, in fact, confirmed the existence of right-hemisphere speech is a matter of debate: Gazzaniga (1983) has claimed, "Indeed, it could well be argued that the cognitive skills of a normal disconnected right-hemisphere without language are vastly inferior to the cognitive skills of a chimpanzee" (p. 536).

Myers (1984), in a detailed review of the data on 21 of Gazzaniga's split-brain patients, asserts that Gazzaniga has seriously misinterpreted the facts. As you might expect, in his rebuttal Gazzaniga (1984) defends his own interpretation. I mention this dispute to alert the reader that many of the conclusions drawn from the study of split-brain patients, and not merely those pertaining to right-hemisphere linguistic competence, are not as convincing as you might have been led to believe. (p. 40)

Efron discusses the misinterpretations of their own data by researchers in this field and points out the many design flaws in their experiments. His conclusions are buttressed by his own research, which draws fundamentally different conclusions about hemispheric specialization.

A more telling criticism is that of Myers (1984), cited earlier by Efron. Myers reveals that there are a surprisingly small number of "split-brain" patients to begin with, and more significantly, most of them have only partially split hemispheres. We have seen dogma developed based on a small N in psychology before. Today's psychology textbooks still cite Penfield's "findings" that memories "stored" in the brain can be released by the application of a mild current to the cortex (e.g., Penfield, 1958a; Penfield & Perot, 1963). Some of his patients reported vivid memories during brain stimulation, and this led him to conclude that memories are highly stable and the brain contains a complete record of our past experiences. Rarely, if ever, mentioned are the facts that, of his 520 temporal cortex–stimulated patients, only 40 (7.7%) reported such memories (Loftus & Loftus, 1980). It is a very weak science, indeed, based on 7% of events. Could it be that the auditory sensations produced brain stimulation function as a kind of auditory projective test in which the patient interprets auditory buzzing as memories? This is the suggestion of Pronko (1973). About memory, we prefer Skinner's (1974) understanding, that memories are not stored and later retrieved as from some filing cabinet, but are rather *re*membered, stimulated by substitute stimuli.

Finally, it was recognized early that split-brain findings have been characterized as follows: (1) by their capriciousness, (2) by replication failures, (3) by widespread individual performance differences between experimental subjects on similar tasks, (4) by the lack of consistency within the same individuals on experimental tasks, and (5) by the then and continued absence of a global theory accounting for such phenomena (Friedman & Polson, 1981). Pronko (1973) points out that split-brain subjects only show split-brain phenomena in the special settings of laboratory conditions. In real life, such subjects

are intellectually and cognitively "normal." In the end, one has to wonder about the meaning and validity of these split-brain reports.

Localization of Function.   The findings of Frisch and Hitzig in the 1870s gave substantial credence to the notion that the brain is partitioned into areas that control various bodily and mental functions (Uttal, 2001). Every textbook shows and describes which brain areas and structures control which psychological processes (e.g., Kalat, 2009). However, the picture of this has changed in 150 years. Even those who still adhere to some form of localization admit it holds only for the basest of functions—reflexes, sensory inputs—and not for higher cognitive processes (Linden, 2007). Valenstein (1973) stated:

The impression exists that if electrodes are placed in a specific part of the brain, a particular behavior can be reliably evoked. Those who have participated in this research know that this is definitely not the case. (p. 87)

He describes research, especially involving hypothalamic stimulation, showing that evoked behavior differs depending on the presence of different objects in the environment. For example, stimulating the ventromedial hypothalamus is supposed to elicit eating, excessive eating in some cases; and it does in the presence of food, but it evokes drinking in the presence of water and gnawing in the presence of objects to gnaw on (Valenstein, Cox, & Kakolewski, 1970). Interestingly, as early as 1808, Cuvier was "an early opponent of the cerebral localization of mental phenomena" (Reise, 1958, p. 129). Reise points out that a similar view was expressed at the 1861 meeting of the Paris Society of Anthropology by Gratiolet, in almost identical terms. How prescient these men would turn out to be.

Sex/Gender Differences.   The terms *sex* and *gender* are not so easily defined. One seemingly refers to biology (sex), the other to culture (gender) (Rogers, 1999). Nevertheless, there are certainly differences, behavioral *and* biological, between male and female individuals. However, as Rogers explains, these differences are not directly explained by genetic (or other biological) foundations, but rather by a fusion of nature and nurture effects. Readers of this handbook are undoubtedly aware of the fact that this area of study has been, and remains, controversial. As Rogers points out, "No other area of biology is more influenced by social attitudes than the study of differences between human groups" (p. 6). This is, of course, as true for psychology and development as it is for biology, as a recent discussion in the journal *Nature* of the genetics of intelligence makes clear (Ceci & Williams, 2009; Rose, 2009). Rogers's own research (1999, in press) confirms brain differences between the sexes, though she has identified experiential reasons for those differences. Others, she points out, carelessly ignore conducting research to determine the reasons for such differences.

Rogers's arguments are buttressed by those of Anne Fausto-Sterling (1985). Of course, male and female individuals show differences—in relatively trivial ways such as hair length and body shape. But the search for "root causes" of behavioral differences has been fruitless. She argues instead for "a more complex analysis in which an individual's capacities emerge from a web of interactions between the biological being and the social environment" (p. 8).

Neural Imaging. The development of neural imaging techniques, such as CAT (computer-assisted X-ray tomography) scans, PET (positron emission tomography) scans, MRIs (magnetic resonance images), NMR (nuclear magnetic resonance) scans, and others, were heralded as ushering in a new age of understanding brain function (Uttal, 2001). Indeed, for years it was difficult for psychology articles involving brain activity to be published in prestigious journals such as *Science* without accompanying them with brains scans. However, as Uttal indicates, such scans are not the same as looking at photographs of one's honeymoon in Tuscany. They must be interpreted; the devices producing the scans must be calibrated, and that is subject to human error and individuality. In short, he tells us that brain scans leave much to be desired. And woe to the resulting scan if the person being scanned moves his or her head! This is exactly the argument that Roskies (2007) presented: fMRIs are not photographs at all. They allow us to visualize magnetic properties of water in the brain. That such scans light up when parts of the brain are active "is an illusion" (p. 863). The many inferences that have to be made in reading or interpreting brain scans leaves a great deal of room for making errors (Dobbs, 2005).

Uttal is not alone in his cautions about the meanings of brain scans. Although not critical of the scientific validity of the vast amount of neuroimaging reports in recent years, Page (2006) nevertheless points out that that does not "constitute good cognitive science" (p. 428). He indicates that, for the most part, imaging research is geared to address "where" questions and not "how" questions. That is, that a part of the brain lights up in a scan indicates where in the brain some function is being processed.

However, in his review, Page questions "whether the engagement of two different regions, even regions well separated in the brain, *necessarily* implies two different functions" (p. 431). Whether scans might be identifying epiphenomena is a legitimate question to raise. Page raises an important criticism, not only of neuroimaging research but of research in general, that touches on the sociology of science. Scanning devices are expensive, and the expense could color one's judgments and interpretations of findings to justify the outlay of huge sums of money for equipment. Indeed, scans do not necessarily even indicate brain activity. Sirotin and Das (2009) report findings that blood flow changes in the brain are not always linked to changes in neuronal activity.

A more serious criticism of neuroimaging is raised by Vul, Harris, Winkielman, and Pashler (2009). They analyzed the results of 54 articles reporting imaging and found the statistical analyses to be seriously faulty, especially with respect to the overstating of correlations between scanning results and brain functions. They state that in half of the reports they examined "correlation coefficients mean almost nothing, because they are systematically inflated by the biased analysis" (p. 281). Finally, as we discussed above, scanning images are "alluring." We tend to be persuaded by things we can see, that is, scanned brain images, regardless of what those images might mean. As McCabe and Castel (2007) point out, images appeal to our intuitive understanding that the brain is doing something important!

It is quite clear that when the record is closely examined, many facts about neuroscience are not facts at all. This is, of course, not peculiar to neuroscience, or to psychology, but perhaps to science in general. Pertinent examples for this discussion include the often erroneously reported facts about Broca and his role in uncovering the locus of speech defects (Thomas, 2007; Willems & Hagoort, 2009), and the incorrectly reported story of Phineas Gage, which occupies a special place in the history and our understanding of the brain and behavior (Macmillan, 2008). We have provided only a small sample of other similar "facts."

What the Brain Does *Do*

The Brain and Cognition. "The anatomical and functional architecture of the brain is neither established genetically nor fixed at birth. Instead, the system has extraordinary plasticity; its formation reacts in response to the structure and influence of its environment…Brain and culture are co-producing partners" (Baltes, Reuter-Lorenz, & Rösler, 2006, p. 20). This, of course, is consistent with our relational, holistic, epigenetic, developmental system perspective regarding not only behavior but anatomy, and for this chapter, especially the brain. As Benno (1990) makes abundantly clear, the development of the brain is itself regulated by a complex set of epigenetic processes.

Coltheart (2006) said, "Rather a lot of people believe that you can't learn anything about cognition by studying the brain" (p. 330). In his discussion, Coltheart described several research projects that failed to provide support for one or another cognitive theory based on neuroimaging data collected. He concludes that the techniques have taught us nothing about the mind. He also cited several authors who support the idea of the fruitlessness of such work. Fodor (1999), for example, is cited suggesting that such work seeks merely to collect data showing that certain brain areas light up during certain tasks—that is, experimental data are taken *ipso facto* as a scientific contribution. Coltheart also pointed out that, although a great number of imaging articles are published today, few are critical of the technique and of its use in studying cognition. Three recent exceptions are publications by Page (2006), Uttal (2005), and Vul, Harris, Winkielman, and Pashler (2009).

However, as in an earlier discussion of this topic (Greenberg, Partridge, Weiss, & Haraway, 1998), we focus on a single crucial question: How is it that one species among millions developed the ability to use language (Deacon, 1997)? Was it due to increased brain size and functional brain organization? An important relation exists between brain development, complexity, and language, but this does not appear to be the whole story. There is disagreement regarding the anatomy and the structure-function relations of brain areas and behaviors. Griffiths and Warren (2002), for example, discuss this with respect to the *planum temporale,* a structure implicated in speech. The brains of chimpanzees contain this structure (Gannon, Holloway, Broadfield, & Braun, 1998), but they are incapable of speech. Therefore, although it is tempting to draw broad conclusions and make judgments about the brain, behavior, and development, it appears that little about the brain is so simple. Consistent with our understanding that the brain is an integrating organ system, in their analysis of the *planum temporale,* Griffiths and Warren make the case that it is a "computational 'hub' that directs further processing in other cortical regions" (p. 348). Of course, modern brain scans show that many brain areas are active in any function, cognitive or otherwise (Uttal, 2001; Vul, Harris, Winkielman, & Pashler, 2009).

Cultural complexity has also been thought to be an important influence in the appearance of language. For example, human children fail to develop language in the extreme absence of adult role models and interaction (Lieberman, 1998). And many nonhuman primates and other mammals do live in quite complex social communities without developing language. Yet, if we conceive of language, culture, and brain complexity holistically and relationally as parts of a large, complex developmental system, small incremental changes in all three may be seen eventually to reach a critical level of both capacity and interconnectivity, leading to a cascade of large-scale increases across all of the system components. Thus, brain complexity, language, and cultural complexity all begin to drive each other to exponential increases. Large-scale and sudden changes often lead to (novel) qualitative changes in system behavior (Bak, 1996). Such changes are analogous to the concept of phase transitions in physics—what we have referred to as emergent properties (Greenberg, Partridge, & Ablah, 2007; Partridge & Greenberg, in press). Thus, the shift from protolanguage skills of chimpanzees, which on close examination differ dramatically from "true language," to language used by humans would be an emergent "phase-transition." The development of language by bonobos (Savage-Rumbaugh, Shanker, & Taylor, 1998) is preceded by their immersion in a complex and unrelenting social setting (see MacWhinney, Chapter 14 of this volume, for an extended discussion of language development across the life span).

Tobach and Schneirla's (1968) formulation of behavioral levels (applied to the full range of behaviors in Greenberg & Haraway, 2002) correlates highly with nervous system evolution and complexity. There is little disagreement regarding the evolutionary trend toward more complex nervous systems and larger brains (e.g., Rose, 1989). Related to this are two fruitful ideas, seen by some as competing but by us as complementary. The first is that evolution provided larger brains and with that, increased amounts of neocortex, or association cortex. Indeed, among the primates there is

> ...a profound enhancement of the neocortex in relation to the rest of the brain as one moves from the most primitive primate forms, the prosimians, to the New and Old World monkeys in turn, and to the lesser apes, great apes, and humans. The brain becomes more complex in its dendritic interlacings, its convolutions, and its gyrii. The cortex becomes disproportionately large relative to the rest of the brain. (Rumbaugh & Pate, 1984, p. 571)

These developments provide greater computational or information-processing power by these brains.

The second fruitful idea is that the crucial dimension for the appearance of higher cognitive processes in these larger brained species is not mere volume of neocortex, but the ratio of log brain mass (especially neocortex) to log body mass, referred to as the "encephalization quotient," or EQ (Jerison, 1973). Scaling features such as brain size and body size against each other is known as *allometry* (Thiessen & Villarreal, 1998). As Rumbaugh and Pate (1984) and others have pointed out, this latter allometric trend does not become clear until the variance has been smoothed by using a logarithmic transformation on brain mass and body mass. The encephalization quotient provides an objective measure, "a true dimension based upon objectively measured structural attributes" (Plotkin, 1983, p. 128). Olson (1976) has shown that progressive encephalization, in particular an increased amount of cerebral cortex, represents a greater capacity to process information. Killackey (1990) presented an argument that agrees with this line of thought, showing that neocortical expansion and improved information processing follow along phylogenetic lines. The ratio of neocortical mass to total brain mass (the neocortical ratio), which is a refinement of the encephalization quotient, is correlated to yet a higher degree with cognitive processes. The increased neocortex relative to total brain mass results are what Deacon (1997) refers to as *net computing power*. Accordingly, the neocortical ratio is thought to be a proxy measure for the ratio of neurons available and neurons needed for basal functions such as sensorimotor regulation, autonomic responses, and metabolic demand.

The brains of primitive vertebrates consist of three swellings: forebrain, midbrain, and hindbrain. All evolutionary advance has preserved this arrangement, simply increasing the size of these swellings. Advanced vertebrate brains are thus larger, though the same pattern of hindbrain, midbrain, and forebrain is preserved. Larger brains mean more neurons, and this, in turn, means more pathways, circuits, and tracks in the nervous system (Deacon, 1990). More of these processes resulted in greater and more refined differentiation, permitting greater integration of neural functioning. As the nervous system increased in size, its information-processing capacities differentiated and increased as well. Improved information processing was recognized early by Pantin (1951) to be a crucial indicator of evolutionary advance. According to Michel and Moore (1995), "The essence of neuronal function is to integrate input from one group of cells and to transmit the resulting activity to yet other cells. The pattern of connections that a neuron maintains with other cells defines, to a very great extent, the nature of its functioning" (p. 260). Of course, this was the point of Sherrington's important book, *Integrative Action of the Nervous System* (1906). The increase in neural integration that accompanied increased brain size allowed for greater behavioral plasticity and diversity. Thus, we expect, and find, increased behavioral plasticity and complexity as we ascend the behavioral levels, across a corresponding increase in brain size (Jerison, 1994). Other evolutionary trends are those of increasing body size and of numbers of specialized cell types. Increases in size and complexity require increases in brain size to permit the coordination of more cell and muscle types. Some now understand the brain as a relational, bidirectional processing system that functions between inputs and outputs (Marshall, 2009). This conception underscores the plasticity of the nervous system. Contemporary thinking about complexity and cognition is summed up nicely by Goodwin (2009): "When an organism has a nervous system of sufficient complexity, subjective experience and feelings can arise. This implies that something totally new and qualitatively different can emerge from the interaction of 'dead,' unfeeling components such as cell membranes, molecules, and electrical currents" (p. 3).

This perspective is also applicable to the difficult concept of "consciousness," such that we would hypothesize that critical levels of neuronal connectivity and activity lead to qualitative shifts from "unintelligent" functions to "intelligent" functions. Although not discussed here, this has been dealt with from a hierarchical organizational point of view by both Bickerton (1995) and Edelman (1992; Tononi & Edelman, 1998). Our own earlier treatment of this topic showed how other human cognitive processes, particularly the broad category of "culture," can be understood from this relational, holistic, developmental systems perspective (Greenberg, Partridge, Weiss, & Haraway, 1998).

Of course, although we have presented psychology not as a biological but as a developmental, psychological science, we underscore the significance of biology, and of brain, for psychological development. In the end, however, we are forced to agree with Hardcastle and Stewart (2002), who ask, "What do all the brain data we have amassed tell us about how the brain works? Precious little so far" (p. S80).

BIOLOGY AND DEVELOPMENT

A common question, whether implicitly or explicitly posed, in theoretical articles regarding biology, evolution, and development, asks what the role of biology is in shaping development. Such questions take the form of hypotheses regarding the relation between a given allele and trajectories of behavioral outcomes such as adolescent smoking (Malaiyandi, Sellers, & Tyndale, 2005) or the heritability of attachment (Finkle, Wille, & Matheny, 1998), or the findings of functional MRI studies correlating age-related declines in spatial abilities with changes in regional neural metabolism during a spatial memory task (Moffat, Kennedy, Rodrigue, & Raz, 2007). In the case of evolution, if the research questions posed are even reasonably empirically testable, they tend to be framed in the form of the constraints that evolution places on behavioral development (Buss, 2005). Alternatively, evolutionary perspectives simply articulate putative adaptive explanations for developmental phenomena (Buss, 2005). In all of these situations, there is an underlying assertion that development is subsidiary to evolutionary trajectories and biological factors. In other words, ontogeny is a function of phylogeny and behavioral development is shaped by the organism's biology. From this perspective, biology is the fundamental and guiding force that drives individual differences in developmental trajectories of behavior.

However, a relational, holistic position takes a dramatically different perspective on the relations between biology, evolution, and psychological development. From this perspective, development is an active system of processes superordinate to biology and evolution. Thus, it is not that the gene or evolution explains development, but that the developmental system explains the functioning of both the gene and evolution. From this perspective, it is the developmental system that integrates biological functions into coordinated patterns that support behavior. It is the process of development that shapes biological organization and provides a temporal context for biology-behavior-ecology interrelations. So the question really becomes, how does development shape biology and the relation of genes and neurons with behavioral outcomes in a given environmental context?

In endorsing this relational, holistic position, we believe that the focus of study in psychology should be on the pattern of interrelations between biological structure, psychological states, and ecological contexts. A clear characterization of development, be it biological or behavioral, is that organisms are initially composed of relatively undifferentiated biological and behavioral features that, over time, become increasingly differentiated and reintegrated into a coherent biological and behavioral system. It is the probabilistic epigenetic and self-organizing principles of development within a dynamic ecological

context that shape the process of differentiation and integration that characterize a given individual's genetic, neurologic, and behavioral attributes, rather than the other way around.

As early as 1929, Woodger made an important distinction between the study of development in the form of embryogenesis and the study of genetics. The study of development has as its focus the patterns of biological and behavioral differentiation within a single organism over time. This notion of development is echoed in the recent work of Nesselroade and colleagues (e.g., Molenaar, 2007; Nesselroade & Molenaar, 2006; Chapter 2 of this volume) emphasizing the importance of methods for the study of intraindividual variability. The study of genetics, in contrast, has as its focus the pattern of differences in attributes between organisms at a given point in time. In relating the two sciences, Woodger (1929) stated that even at the turn of the 20th century, the source of individual differences in patterns of differentiation were sought both in the nucleus and the cytoplasm of the germ cells, yet these attempts were unsuccessful. But despite the consistent lack of empirical support for the genesis of developmental differentiation in the physical attributes of the germ cells, it is an assumption that has yet to yield. However, what has consistently been demonstrated empirically from experimental embryology at the turn of the 20th century to contemporary molecular genetic studies is that the physical attributes of the cell, including protein formation and structure, are a direct result of developmental transactions of the biological aspects of an organism and the environmental context of that organism. As Woodger (1929) put it:

> The cells of a given developing embryo are internally related to one another in the sense that the rate and plane of division, at least, of a given cell, depend upon its relations to the neighbouring cells, and hence on its position in the whole....At a certain period of development the cells of an embryo undergo intracellular elaboration depending partly on their mutual relations, and partly on their intrinsic properties so that the latter may be the same in all cells, [and] which of them are realized in a given cell will depend upon its relations to the whole, which will of course differ from place to place. (p. 384)

And so it would seem that nearly 90 years of empirical findings suggest that, rather than searching for the source of intraindividual differentiation in interindividual differences, we should perhaps be looking for the source of interindividual differences in the patterns of intraindividual differentiation.

Role of the Gene in Development

At least since the broad acceptance of the modern synthesis in biology, the gene construct has served as the central biological organizing feature assumed to guide biological and behavioral development. Indeed, it was tacitly assumed by behavior geneticists that once the human genome was sequenced, behavioral science would be able to incorporate genetic profiles into a general linear model calculus and be able to predict with a reasonable amount of statistical precision the general trajectory of behavioral development, especially those that had been demonstrated to be highly heritable, and thus largely under genetic control. This assumption was based on the premise that packets of nucleotides contained developmental information guiding biological development. Behavioral geneticists, being primarily interested in genetically guided neurologic development, could then argue for genotypic control of the behavioral phenotype via the neurologic endophenotype. The sequencing of the human genome (Venter et al., 2001) has not yielded the scientific fruit for behavioral science that many leading behavioral geneticists envisioned, as we discussed earlier. Rather, there has been a realization among cell biologists that genes do not carry biological or developmental information, and that they have the capacity to differentially respond to environmental and developmental signals originating at multiple levels of biosocial organization. As a result, there has been a resurgence of interest in epigenesis as a developmental process and of epigenetics as a mechanism through which genes and contexts transact through development.

Although the concept of epigenesis originated in biology, with respect to behavioral development, the usefulness of *probabilistic* epigenesis was recognized and promoted throughout the 20th century by psychologists such as Zing-Yang Kuo (1967), Gilbert Gottlieb (1992), Susan Oyama (2000), and T. C. Schneirla (Aronson, Tobach, Rosenblatt, & Lehrman, 1972), though Schneirla never specifically used the term *epigenesis* in his writing. Probabilistic epigenesis has gained support from an exciting set of developments in contemporary science subsumed under the rubric of "dynamic systems theory and relational developmental systems theory," in which complex developmental processes are understood as composed of interrelations among many active system components of the whole developmental system. The implication of this position is that in a dynamic and changing environment, rather than genes specifying a particular developmental outcome, be it structural or behavioral, *every outcome is an emergent result of the transaction between genes and their cellular, organismic, ecologic, and temporal contexts.* This view of epigenesis is epitomized by recent discoveries in biology that even identical genomes in extremely similar environments do not always follow the same developmental pathways. Ko and colleagues (Ko, Yomo, & Urabe, 1994), studying enzyme activity in bacteria, found that despite identical genomes and extremely uniform culture conditions, individual cells developed different levels of enzyme activity and grew into colonies of different size. Ko's studies showed that cell state in bacteria is determined not only by genotype and environment. Rather, "Changes of state can occur spontaneously, without any defined internal or external cause. By definition, these changes are epigenetic phenomena: dynamic processes that arise from the complex interplay of all the factors involved in cellular activities, including the genes" (Solé & Goodwin, 2000, p. 63).

In an impressive review of developmental processes shaping biological phenotypes, Rudel and Sommer (2003) have identified ten basic developmental principles that can adequately describe biological development.[1]

What is perhaps most intriguing about these principles is how few of them are genocentric. In fact, nearly all of them involve either epigenetic factors or epistatic genetic regulation. For the purposes of this chapter, we briefly review four of these core principles:

Asymmetric cell division. One of the key factors in establishing the morphologic and functional capacities of differentiated cell lines is the relative spatial position within the developing embryo. Most cellular division produces two homogeneous daughter cells from a single progenitor cell. This results in a cellular symmetry by maintaining an undifferentiated state from mother to daughter cells. However, asymmetric cell division occurs when the differential concentrations of cell fate determinant factors align with the mitotic spindle, producing daughter cells with different exposures to cell fate factors, and thus differentiating the ultimate cell line morphology

---

[1] Rudel and Sommer (2003) outline 10 principles of biological development: Fate Maps, tracing the lineage of a given cell line; Asymmetric Cell Division; Cellular Induction; Developmental Genomics; Cell Competence, referring to the cell's differential responses to biochemical gradients; Genetic Redundancy; Positional Information; Differential Determination; Lateral Inhibition; and Genetic Networks. Rudel and Sommer (2003) claim that with these basic concepts much of the biological development of organisms can be described.

and function. This asymmetric cell division process has been shown to occur both spontaneously and in response to extracellular signaling mechanisms (Knoblich, 2001). Therefore, although both daughter cells contain the same genetic capacity to achieve the same cell fate, differential exposures to cell fate factors elicit differential genetic activity within those identical genomes, which leads ultimately to cellular differentiation.

Cellular induction. Cellular induction is a fundamental cell signaling process whereby biochemical signals are produced through the activity of a given cell or tissue that influences the developmental fate of neighboring cells. Rudel and Sommer (2003) review a study of eye development in two populations of Mexican cavefish *(Astyanax mexicanus).* The epigean type of *A. mexicanus* lives in surface waters and develops a normally functioning eye. The hypogean type, however, dwelling in dark, underground cave waters, develops a nonfunctional occluded eye, a common adaptation in animals living in darkness. Yamamoto and Jeffery (2000) performed a lens transplantation experiment in which they placed the hypogean lens vesicle in an epigean optic cup and also placed an epigean lens vesicle in a hypogean optic cup. Via local cellular induction processes, transplanted epigean type fish developed occluded eyes that did not have an iris, cornea, or anterior chamber. Similarly, the transplanted hypogean fish developed fully functional eyes. Such induction processes have played a vital role in our understanding of the neuropharmacologic responses to chronic nicotine exposure (Joshi & Tyndale, 2006), as well as cancer cell proliferation (Barcellos-Hoff, 2008).

Lateral inhibition. Lateral inhibition is also a cellular signaling process in which the activity of a cell inhibits or restricts the ability of neighboring cells to develop along a similar pathway. This cellular signaling process is critical to cellular differentiation, which is necessary for biological and behavioral development. For example, recent work by Amoyel and colleagues (Amoyel, Cheng, Jiang, & Wilkinson, 2005) found that the cellular signaling molecule Wnt1 expressed by boundary cells in the zebrafish hindbrain is a mechanism through which cellular differentiation occurs in zebrafish hindbrain development.

Positional information. As a result of cellular signaling processes such as cellular induction and lateral inhibition, every cell is exposed, throughout development, to an ever-changing biochemical information field. Based on the specific signaling factors present, the relative gradients of exposure, and the developmental history of the cell in terms of patterns of genetic expression and cell fate, cells follow self-organized developmental sequences as a function of their spatial and temporal location in the developing organism. The role of positional information can be seen in the cellular differentiation of limb formation in arthropods via the differential expression of the *Ultrabithorax (Ubx) Hox* genes. The differential expression patterns arise from epigenetic influences that vary along spatial dimensions (see Rudel & Sommer, 2003).

These developmental processes or mechanisms are just a few exemplars of the developmental principles that Rudel and Sommer (2003) outlined for understanding biological development. We highlight these four processes because they typify the extent to which epigenetic and sequential processes are regulating patterns of genetic expression, and thereby leading to differential cell morphology, cell function, and cellular organization. This is in stark contrast with the genocentric reductionistic viewpoint of the central dogma of genetics and behavioral genetics in which the gene is the regulator of development. Indeed, what we view here at the most basic biological level is that genes require differential exposure to epigenetic factors to function at all, and a given extragenetic factor will yield differential cell fates depending on the genetic background in terms of sequencing history of the cellular DNA. In other words, in biological development, it is quite clear that genetic and extragenetic processes coregulate each other and become organized through development rather than being the organizers of development. If this complex transactional developmental process serves as the organizing feature of basic cell morphology and embryogenesis, it seems a far reach, indeed, to speculate on the regulating role of genes for a complex social phenomena such as social network membership (Fowler, Dawes, & Christakis, 2009).

Development in Complex Adaptive Systems

As stated earlier, the science of molecular genetics is still in its empirical infancy. Before the turn of the century or so, the functioning of specific genes had to be largely inferred from indirect observations. The ability to work with specific genes has revealed an astounding complexity and requires a paradigmatic realignment of the reductionistic conceptualization of "the gene as blueprint or instruction set." Rather, what we are learning, as highlighted in the earlier discussion, is that genes serve as relatively passive biochemical production mechanisms. More developmental information is stored in the gene than there is in the metal stamping machine in an auto factory—they simply produce parts. This is not to negate their importance in biological and behavioral development. It is simply to recognize that they are but a single element in a vast developmental complex operating on multiple spatial and temporal scales. Furthermore, this biobehavioral complex becomes organized and displays a consistent morphologic and behavioral regularity through the developmental sequencing of multiple internal and local coregulating transactions among genes, cells, tissues, organs, organ systems, organisms, and their environmental and historical ecologies. This is much the same realization that the Chinese comparative psychologist Z. Y. Kuo (1970) articulated: "Every response is determined not only by the stimuli or stimulating objects, but by the total environmental context, the status of anatomic structures and their functional capacities, the physiological (biochemical and biophysical) conditions, and the developmental history up to that stage" (p. 189).

Despite the hubris that often accompanied the Human Genome Project, The Decade of the Brain, and other heralds of reductionistic biocentric social science, we are seeing that at the genetic, proteinomic, neurological, cognitive, and social levels of analysis, these phenomena typify all of the fundamental attributes of a complex adaptive system (CAS) (see Holland, 1995). The atomistic decompositional quest for the genetic or neurological basis of behavior has ironically taught us that we can understand biological and behavioral phenomena only by treating the biopsychosocial system holistically as an integrated whole. CAS models provide a uniquely suited methodology for this task. Over the past couple decades of work on CASs, one lawlike finding has been that the organization and behavior of the system is a function of its developmental transactions, and as such, it is the act of developing that shapes the fate of the system and influences the behavior of the elements rather than the elements guiding the developmental process. This is a profound, if topsy-turvy, lesson for those of us working at the interface of biology and behavior.

Psychology Is a Developmental Science

Contemporary developmental science has successfully provided a dialectical synthesis of earlier organismic and mechanistic theories (Overton & Reese, 1973) by positing that behavioral development is a function of an active or-

ganism interacting with an active sociohistorical ecology. This family of theories includes perspectives such as relational developmental systems theory (Lerner, 2006; Lerner & Overton, 2008; Overton, 2006), the life-span approach (Lerner, 2002), the person-oriented approach (Mangnusson, 1995), transactional models (Sameroff, 1975), and the bioecologic developmental systems model (Bronfenbrenner & Morris, 2006). The success of these theoretical formulations is indicated by the radical change in the scope and content of developmental psychology.

Concurrent with advances in developmental science, science in general has been revolutionized by developments in the study of nonlinear dynamic systems, as discussed earlier. Under the general rubric of nonlinear dynamics are several subfields: chaos theory, the study of complex behavior resulting from simple and deterministic processes; fractal geometry, the study of geometrical forms invariant across scale; and complex systems theory, the study of stable, organized behavior resulting from complex and stochastic processes. It is the latter that seems to hold the most relevance for current formulations of developmental science.

Relational developmental systems theory has built steadily on the ideas of such early biological and behavioral theorists as Kantor (1924, 1926), Kuo (1967), Morgan (1923), Needham (1929), Novikoff (1945), Schneirla (Aronson et al., 1972), and Woodger (1929). These early foundations provided a fertile source from which developmental systems theorists such as Bronfenbrenner (Bronfenbrenner & Morris, 2006), Cairns (Cairns, Elder, & Costello, 1996), Lerner (Ford & Lerner, 1992), Overton (2006), Oyama (1985), and many others have successfully drawn. A new vigor has been infused into this longstanding developmental framework through the incorporation of analytic and conceptual tools from the recent study of CASs. Until the 2000s, relational developmental systems models were often restricted to metaphorical statements. However, advances in complex systems science have allowed for more specific and grounded assertions about how complex behavioral systems develop over time. This has the potential to profoundly impact developmental science.

The ideas of the scientists (behavioral and biological) and philosophers we cited earlier have coalesced since about the late 1980s in a form germane to psychology under the rubric of "developmental systems theory" or "relational developmental systems theory." Despite the terminology, this is not a specific theory, nor is there universal agreement among these diverse sources (Keller, 2005; Griffiths & Gray, 2005).

It is possible, however, to identify at least seven interrelated themes among them (Robert, Hall, & Olson, 2001):

1. *Developmental contextualism:* organisms are fused with their environments, all features of which affect the developmental course of their behavior, as well as their biologies (Lerner, 1998). The idea of a genetic program becomes unnecessary. Indeed, from this perspective, the claims of geneticists and behavior geneticists can be seen as "grandiose" (Nelkin, 1993).

2. *Nonpreformationism:* the role of probabilistic epigenesis in the course of development. The "rules" governing the developmental process are not locally encoded in some external control process but rather are derived from the recursive mutual interactions of all the system variables as an organized whole. Thus, it is the process of development itself that drives the course that development takes.

3. *Causal co-interactionism:* developmental causes interact in complex, nonadditive, ways.

4. *Causal dispersion:* the many causes of development are diffuse and fluid. Genes and brains, then, are participating and not causative factors in development.

5. *Expanded pool of interactants:* genes themselves are influenced by other genes and all the constituents of the cell, among numerous other factors.

6. *Extended inheritance:* inheritance is not the sole purview of genetics. Phylogenetic change can also be induced by environmental causes, as discussed by Honeycutt (2006).

7. *Evolutionary developmental systems:* transmission across generations is not simply of traits but of developmental systems themselves. A complete understanding of evolution requires an understanding of development (evo-devo) and vice versa (devo-evo) (Robert, 2004).

Psychology, like biology during the early 20th century (see Woodger, 1929), has matured into an independent natural science and is poised at the threshold of a paradigmatic shift. On the one hand, there are those suggesting that our understanding of human behavior ultimately lies in the gene or the neuron and, as a consequence, can be fully accounted for by panselectionist evolutionary biology. In strong contrast, we argue that psychology as a discipline must be understood as a developmental science in which ontogeny itself serves to weave together biology and ecology into coherent behavioral trajectories across the life span of the organism. This paradigmatic transition requires a fundamental shift in the metatheoretic principles guiding psychological theory and the corresponding methodologies away from a conception of static, independent, and additive relations among biological, psychological, and social variables to an orientation that is dynamic, self-referential, and interdependent. In this chapter, we have provided a synopsis of just such a metatheoretical overview and associated methodologies. Furthermore, although explanations of behavior from a population genetic, braincentric, or evolutionary perspective seem reasonable on the surface, when the full weight of empirical data is examined, these views are left wanting. We have attempted to show the fundamental limits of each of these perspectives and how, by adopting a developmental systems perspectives, a more complete and coherent account of behavior can be given.

Neuroscience. Many of the ideas we have presented have been incorporated into contemporary neuroscience. Notable among these are the organism-environment system theory that Jarvilehto (1998) proposed and Freeman's (1991, 1992) work on brain dynamics. The organism-environment system theory asserts that the distinction between organism and environment is artificial, and that one cannot understand the neurophysiological functioning of organisms independent of their ecological context. Similarly, the organism's ecology can only be meaningfully understood in relation to its neurophysiology. This idea is consistent with the integrative systems view articulated in our approach to comparative psychology (Greenberg, Partridge, Weiss, & Pisula, 2004).

Freeman has been one of the pioneers of applying systems notions to the study of brain functioning. In the examples of his work cited above, he implicitly utilizes many of the principles of organization and integrative levels that we have proposed here in understanding how we get complex brain dynamics from neuronal functioning. These ideas have led to a new understanding of how unintelligent agents such as neurons can, through aggregate behavior, lead to intelligent functions (see also Dean, 2000, and Holland, 1995). Some of these ideas and formulations form the very foundations of contemporary neuroscience (Pribram, 1993, 1996). Uttal's (2001) critique of the localizationist hypothesis also incorporates a dynamic systems approach to neural functioning. Thus, rather than consisting of numerous independent cognitive modules, the brain is conceptualized as a dynamic set of circuits functioning as a unit.

Perception and motor development. The study of perceptual and motor development has also been imbued with many of the ideas we have proposed. The leading advances in this area of study focus on the origins of coherent patterns of motion through a dynamic coupling of independent functional units (Goldfield, 1995; Kugler & Turvey, 1987; Smith & Thelen, 2003; Thelen, 1989, 1990, 2004). Many of the ideas such as emergence, integration of activity on multiple temporal and spatial scales, and self-organization are fundamental to our understanding of human perception and action. Interestingly, Gibson's (1966) "ecological approach" to perception is again in vogue.

Developmental science. Since the late 1980s, there has been a burgeoning of theoretical developments across a diverse set of disciplines, including developmental psychology, sociology, developmental epidemiology, psychobiology, and embryology, that have a common conceptual foundation—and in many cases, methodological approach—with the comparative psychology we have outlined here. Although these theoretical formulations differ in specifics, they share a core set of common assumptions. These interdisciplinary advances can be referred to as an "emergent convergence and isomorphism" (Cairns et al., 1996, p. ix). Indeed, theoretical frameworks such as relational developmental systems (Lerner, 2006; Lerner & Overton, 2008; Overton, 2006), bioecologic systems (Bronfenbrenner & Morris, 2006), life span (Baltes, Reuter-Lorenz, & Rösler, 2006), person centered (Magnusson, 1995), transactional (Sameroff, 1975), and developmental psychopathology (Cicchetti & Cohen, 1995) have such a degree of commonality that Cairns (Cairns et al., 1996) has proposed incorporating them under the umbrella concept of Developmental Science.

One of the leading proponents of this perspective is Richard M. Lerner, who has made significant contributions at basic theoretical levels (e.g., see references throughout this chapter) and at the policy-level (e.g., Lerner, 2004b) applications of this perspective. The empirical research that Lerner and colleagues have conducted has focused primarily on the natural contextual shifts found in adolescence (e.g., Talwar, Nitz, & Lerner, 1990). For instance, the transition from junior high to high school connotes a significant shift in the contextual demands placed on an adolescent. By studying the interaction of these contextual shifts with variables such as temperament, it can be shown empirically how these mutual influences not only shape each other, but how they conjointly influence other behavioral outcomes.

Many scientists are already examining social behavior from a developmental contextual perspective. Building on the youth development work of Weiss and her colleagues, Lerner described a Development-In-Context Evaluation (DICE) model for program design and evaluation as a framework for interventions addressing social problems (Ostrom, Lerner, & Freel, 1995). The DICE model explicitly incorporates program designs and policies, as well as evaluation into the nested ecology of behavioral development. Indeed, not only are children and adolescents influenced by program design, implementation, and evaluation activities, they also directly influence those activities in a reciprocal manner. In addition, multiple levels of a developmental system are assessed qualitatively and quantitatively at multiple levels of analysis.

Personality and social psychologist Albert Bandura (1977) proposed his belief that dynamically interactive, person-context developmental models must become incorporated into the theory and research of personality and social psychology. Bandura explains that need for reliance on reciprocal effects in a triadic system of reciprocity among the person or organism, behavior or action, and the environmental or contextual influences. Although Bandura recognizes that current methods that investigate what he calls initial effects, or effects that do not rely on interactional assessment, are important to our understanding of development, he argues that, to understand psychological functioning, our methods must include reciprocal and initial effects. Bandura also believes that, in a reciprocal system, change and context must take a primary focus if the field is to advance.

James Garbarino (1992) explains individual development as a process that occurs in the context of several different levels of influence. Like Lerner and Bandura, Garbarino stresses the importance of being aware of the changing contexts that individuals develop in, the changes over time in the individual's relations to those contexts, and how individuals and contexts continually shape one another. The work of Lerner, Bandura, and Garbarino represents a trend evident across a variety of different researchers who examine individual and social systems problems away from simple cause-and-effect and reductionist models toward an approach to development that incorporates a developmental contextual perspective.

CONCLUSIONS

We have tried to show that, although we envision psychology not as a biological science but as a unique science of its own, the principles of all aspects of biology are pertinent for a full understanding of psychology and especially for the development of behavior. This is reflected in how we define psychology: the biopsychosocial science of behavior. Our discussion attempted to show that biological factors are necessary *participating* but not causative factors in behavior development. Along the way, we took the opportunity to dispel some myths and misunderstandings about the relations of biological factors to behavior: the "true" role of genes; the question of whether there really are minds, and if so, whether they are products of the brain; the value of the overused procedures of brain scans; and the perniciousness of evolutionary psychology, a misguided application of the principles of evolution as they apply to behavioral origins. We concluded our discussion with a treatment of the general topic of development, as it applies in biology in general and in psychology in particular. We earlier made the case that development is crucial to psychology, and that the science can be understood to be a developmental science (Greenberg, Partridge, Mosack, & Lamdin, 2006).

REFERENCES

Allen, G. E. (2007). A century of evo-devo: The dialectics of analysis and synthesis in twentieth-century life science. In M. D. Laubichler & J. Maienschein (Eds.), *From embryology to evo-devo: A history of developmental evolution* (pp. 123–167). Cambridge, MA: MIT Press.

Alpi, A., Amrhein, N., Bertl, A., Blatt, A., Blumwald, E., Cervone, F., et al. (2007). Plant neurobiology: No brain, no gain. *Trends in Plant Science, 12,* 135–136.

Amoyel, M., Cheng, Y., Jiang, Y., & Wilkinson, D. G. (2005). Wnt1 regulates neurogenesis and mediates lateral inhibition of boundary cell specification in the zebrafish hindbrain development. *Development, 132,* 775–785.

Anderson, P. W. (1972). More is different. *Science, 177,* 393–396.

Angier, N. (2008, November 11). Scientists and philosophers find that "gene" has a multitude of meanings. *The New York Times,* p. D2.

Aronson, L. R. (1984). Levels of integration and organization: A re-evaluation of the evolutionary scale. In G. Greenberg & E. Tobach (Eds.), *Evolution of behavior and integrative levels* (pp. 57–81). Hillsdale, NJ: Erlbaum.

Aronson, L. R., Tobach, E., Rosenblatt, J. R., & Lehrman, D. H. (Eds.). (1972). *Selected writings of T. C. Schneirla.* San Francisco: Freeman.

Arthur, W. B. (1993). Why do things become more complex? *Scientific American, 268*(5), 144.

Bailey, P. (1965). *Sigmund the unserene: A tragedy in three acts.* Springfield, IL: Thomas.

Bak, P. (1996). *How nature works: The science of self-organized criticality.* New York: Springer-Verlag.

Baltes, P. B., Reuter-Lorenz, P. A., & Rösler, F. (2006). Prologue: Biocultural co-constructivism as a theoretical metascript. In P. B. Baltes, P. A. Reuter-Lorenz, & F. Rösler (Eds.), *Lifespan development and the brain: The perspective of biocultural co-constructivism.* (pp. 3–39). Cambridge: Cambridge University Press.

Bandura, A. (1977). Self-efficacy: Toward a unifying theory of behavioral change. *Psychological Review, 84,* 191–215.

Bannister, D. (1968). The myth of physiological psychology. *Bulletin of the British Psychological Society, 21,* 229–231.

Barcellos-Hoff, M. H. (2008). Cancer as an emergent phenomenon in systems radiation biology. *Radiation and Environmental Biophysics, 47,* 33–37.

Barron, A. B., & Robinson, G. E. (2008). The utility of behavioral models and modules in molecular analyses of social behavior. *Genes, Brain and Behavior, 7,* 257–265.

Bauchau, V. (2006). Emergence and reductionism: From the game of life to the science of life. In B. Feltz, M. Crommerlinck, & P. Goujon (Eds.), *Self-organization and emergence in life sciences* (pp. 29–40). Dordrecht, The Netherlands: Springer.

Bennett, M. R., & Hacker, P. M. S. (2003). *Philosophical foundations of neuroscience.* Malden, MA: Blackwell.

Benno, R. H. (1990). Development of the nervous system: Genetics, epigenetics, and phylogenetics. In M. E. Hahn, J. K. Hewitt, N. D. Henderson, & R. H. Benno (Eds.), *Developmental behavior genetics: Neural, biometrical, and evolutionary approaches* (pp. 113–143). New York: Oxford University Press.

Berker, E. A. (1985). *Principles of brain function in neuropsychological development of hydrocephalics.* Unpublished doctoral dissertation, University of Michigan, Ann Arbor.

Bertalanffy, L. von. (1933). *Modern theories of development.* London: Oxford University Press.

Bickerton, D. (1995). *Language and human behavior.* Seattle, WA: University of Washington Press.

Blumberg, M. (2005). *Basic instinct: The genesis of behavior.* New York: Thunders Mouth Press.

Bonner, J. T. (1988). *The evolution of complexity.* Princeton, NJ: Princeton University Press.

Boorstein, D. J. (1998). *The seekers.* New York: Vintage.

Breckler, S. J. (2006). The newest age of reductionism. *Monitor on Psychology, 27*(8), 23.

Bronfenbrenner, U., & Morris, P. A. (2006). The bioecological model of human development. In W. Damon (Series Ed.) & R. M. Lerner (Vol. Ed.), *Theoretical models of human development: Vol. 1, Handbook of child psychology* (6th ed., pp. 793–828). Hoboken, NJ: John Wiley & Sons.

Brooks, D. (2006, September 17). Is chemistry destiny? *The New York Times,* Section 4, p. 14.

Buller, D. J. (2005). *Adapting minds: Evolutionary psychology and the quest for human nature.* Cambridge, MA: MIT Press.

Bullock, T. H. (1965/1970). Physiological bases of behavior. In J. A. Moore (Ed.), *Ideas in evolution and behavior.* Garden City, NY: Natural History Press.

Bunge, M. (1980). *The mind-body problem.* Oxford: Pergamon.

Burian, R. M. (1985). On conceptual change in biology: The case of the gene. In D. J. Depew & B. H. Weber (Eds.), *Evolution at a crossroads: The new biology and the new philosophy of science* (pp. 21–42). Cambridge, MA: MIT Press.

Buss, D. M. (1999). *Evolutionary psychology: The new science of the mind.* Boston: Allyn & Bacon.

Buss, D. M. (Ed.). (2005). *The handbook of evolutionary psychology.* Hoboken, NJ: John Wiley & Sons.

Cacioppo, J. T., Bernston, G. G., Sheridan, J. F., & McClintock, B. (2000). Multiple integrative analyses of human behavior: Social neuroscience and the nature of social and biological approaches. *Psychological Bulletin, 126,* 829–843.

Cairns, R. B., Elder, G. H., & Costello, E. J. (1996). *Developmental science.* New York: Cambridge University Press.

Campbell, D. T. (1990). Levels of organization, downward causation, and the selection-theory approach to evolutionary epistemology. In G. Greenberg & E. Tobach (Eds.), *Theories of the evolution of knowing* (pp. 1–17). Hillsdale, NJ: Erlbaum.

Carroll, S. B. (2001). Chance and necessity: The evolution of morphological complexity and diversity. *Nature, 409,* 1102–1109.

Ceci, S., & Williams, W. M. (2009). Darwin 200. Should scientists study race and IQ? Yes: The scientific truth must be pursued. *Nature, 457*(7231), 788–789.

Chaisson, E. J. (2001). *Cosmic evolution: The rise of complexity in nature.* Cambridge, MA: Harvard University Press.

Cicchetti, D., & Cohen, D. J. (1995). *Developmental psychopathology.* New York: John Wiley & Sons.

Cole, S. (1983). The hierarchy of the sciences? *American Journal of Sociology, 89,* 111–139.

Coltheart, M. (2006). What has functional neuroimaging told us about the mind (so far)? *Cortex, 42,* 323–331.

Crick, F. (1970). Central dogma of molecular biology. *Nature, 227,* 561–563.

Critchley, M. (1969). Disorders of higher nervous activity: Introductory remarks. In P. J. Vinken & G. W. Bruyn (Eds.), *Handbook of clinical neurology* (Vol. 3). New York: John Wiley & Sons.

Darwin, C. (1859). *The origin of species.* London: John Murray.

Deacon, T. W. (1990). Rethinking mammalian Brain Evolution. *American Zoologist, 30,* 229–705.

Deacon, T. W. (1997), *The symbolic species: The co-evolution of language and the brain.* New York: Norton.

Dean, A. (2000). *Complex life: Nonmodernity and the emergence of cognition and culture.* Aldershot, United Kingdom: Ashgate.

Dobbs, D. (2005). Fact or phrenology? *Scientific American Mind, 16*(1), 24–31.

Dobzhansky, T. (1973). Nothing in biology makes sense except in the light of evolution. *American Biology Teacher, 35,* 125-129.

Dudley, S. A., & File, A. L. (2007). Kin recognition in an annual plant. *Biology Letters, 3,* 435–438.

Edelman, G. M. (1992). *Bright air, brilliant fire: On the matter of mind.* New York: Basic Books.

Edelman, G. M., & Tononi, G. (2000). *A universe of consciousness: How matter becomes imagination.* New York: Basic Books.

Efron, R. (1990). *The decline and fall of hemispheric specialization.* Hillsdale, NJ: Erlbaum.

Ehrlich, P. (2000). Human natures: Genes, cultures, and the human prospect. Washington, DC: Island Press.

Eldredge, N., & Gould, S. J. (1972). Punctuated equilibria: An alternative to phyletic gradualism. In T. J. M. Schopf (Ed.), *Models in paleobiology* (pp. 82–115). San Francisco, CA: Freeman.

Elman, J. L., Bates, E. A., Johnson, M. H., Karmiloff-Smith, A., Parisi, D., & Plunkett, K. (1996). *Rethinking innateness: A connectionist perspective on development.* Cambridge, MA: MIT Press.

Fausto-Sterling, A. (1985). Myths of gender: Biological theories about women and men. New York: Basic Books.

Feibleman, J. K. (1954). Theory of integrative levels. *British Journal for the Philosophy of Science, 5,* 59–66.

Finkel, D., Wille, D. E., & Matheny A. P. (1998). Preliminary results from a twin study of infant-caregiver attachment. *Behavior Genetics, 28*(1), 1–8.

Fodor, J. (1999, September 30). Let your brain alone. *London Review of Books,* p. 21.

Ford, D. H., & Lerner, R. M. (1992). *Developmental systems theory: An integrative approach.* Newbury Park, CA: Sage.

Fowler, J. H., Dawes, C. T., & Christakis, N. A. (2009). Model of genetic variation in human social networks. *Proceedings of the National Academy of Science, 106*(6), 1720–1724.

Freeman, W. J. (1991). The physiology of perception. *Scientific American, 264*(2), 78–85.

Freeman, W. J. (1992). Tutorial in neurobiology: From single neurons to brain chaos. *International Journal of Bifurcation and Chaos, 2,* 451–482.

Freeman, W. J. (2001). Three centuries of category errors in studies of the neural basis of consciousness and intentionality. In W. Sulis & I. Trofimova (Eds.), *Nonlinear dynamics in the life and social sciences* (pp. 275–285). Amsterdam: IOS Press.

Friedman, A., & Polson, M. C. (1981). Hemispheres as independent resource systems: Limited-capacity processing and cerebral specialization. *Journal of Experimental Psychology: Human Perception and Performance, 7,* 1031–1058.

Futuyma, D. J. (1998). *Evolutionary biology* (3rd ed.). Sunderland, MA: Sinauer Associates Inc.

Gallup, G. G., Frederick, M. J., & Pipitone, R. N. (2008). Morphology and behavior: Phrenology revisited. *Review of General Psychology, 12,* 297–304.

Gannon, P. J., Holloway, R. L., Broadfield, D. C., & Braun, A. R. (1998). Asymmetry of chimpanzee planum temporale: Humanlike brain pattern of Wernicke's language area homolog. *Science, 279,* 222–226.

Garbarino, J. (1992). *Children and families in the social environment.* New York: Aldine.

Gazzaniga, M. S. (1967). The split-brain in man. *Scientific American, 217,* 24–29.

Gazzaniga, M. S. (1983). Right hemisphere language following brain bisection: A 20-year perspective. *American Psychologist, 38,* 525–537.

Gazzaniga, M. S. (1984). Right hemisphere language: Remaining problems. *American Psychologist, 39,* 1494–1496.

Geard, N., & Wiles, J. (2005). A gene network model for developing cell lineages. *Artificial Life, 11*(1–2), 249–268.

Gibson, J. J. (1966). *The ecological approach to visual perception.* Mahwah, NJ: Erlbaum.

Gilbert, S. F., & Sarkar, S. (2000). Embracing complexity: Organiscism for the 21st century. *Developmental Dynamics, 219,* 1–9.

Goldfield, E. C. (1995). *Emergent forms: Origins and early development of human action and perception.* New York: Oxford University Press.

Goodwin, B. (2009). Pan-sentience. In J. Brockman (Ed.), *What have you changed your mind about? Today's leading minds rethink everything* (pp. 2–4). New York: Harper.

Gottlieb, G. (1984). Evolutionary trends and evolutionary origins: Relevance to theory in comparative psychology. *Psychological Review, 91,* 448–456.

Gottlieb, G. (1992). *Individual development and evolution: The genesis of novel behavior.* New York: Oxford University Press.

Gottlieb, G. (1998). Normally occurring environmental and behavioral influences on gene activity: From central dogma to probabilistic epigenesis. *Psychological Review, 105,* 792–802.

Gottlieb, G. (2001). A developmental psychobiological systems view: Early formulation and current status. In S. Oyama, P. E. Griffiths, & R. D. Gray (Eds.), *Cycles of contingency: Developmental systems and evolution* (pp. 41–54). Cambridge, MA: MIT Press.

Gottlieb, G. (2004). Normally occurring environmental and behavioral influences on gene activity: From central dogma to probabilistic epigenesis. In C. G. Coll, E. L. Bearer, & R. M. Lerner (Eds.), *Nature* and *nurture: The complex interplay of genetic and environmental influences on human behavior and development* (pp. 85–106). Mahwah, NJ: Erlbaum.

Gottlieb, G. (2006). Developmental neurobehavioral genetics: Development as explanation. In B. C. Jones & P. N. Mormede (Eds.), *Neurobehavioral genetics: Methods and applications* (2nd ed., pp. 17–27). Boca Raton, FL: CRC Press.

Gould, S. J. (1988). On replacing the idea of progress with an operational definition of directionality. In. M. H. Nitecki (Ed.), *Evolutionary progress* (pp. 319–338). Chicago: University of Chicago Press.

Gould, S. J. (1997a). Darwinian fundamentalism. *New York Review of Books, 44*(10), 34–37.

Gould, S. J. (1997b). *Full house: The spread of excellence from Plato to Darwin.* New York: Three Rivers Press.

Gould, S. J., & Eldredge, N. (1993). Punctuated equilibrium comes of age. *Nature, 366,* 223–227.

Greenberg, G. (1972). The effects of ambient temperature and population density on aggression in two strains of mice, *Mus musculis. Behaviour, 42,* 119–131.

Greenberg, G. (1983). Psychology without the brain. *Psychological Record, 33,* 49–58.

Greenberg, G. (1995). Anagenetic theory in comparative psychology. *International Journal of Comparative Psychology, 8,* 31–41.

Greenberg, G., & Haraway, M. H. (2002). *Principles of comparative psychology.* Boston, MA: Allyn & Bacon.

Greenberg, G., Partridge, T., & Ablah, E. (2007). The significance of the concept of emergence for comparative psychology. In D. Washburn (Ed.), *Primate perspectives on behavior and cognition* (pp. 81–98). Washington, DC: American Psychological Association.

Greenberg, G., Partridge, T., Mosack, V., & Lambin, C. (2006). Psychology is a developmental science. *International Journal of Comparative Psychology, 19,* 185–205.

Greenberg, G., Partridge, T., Weiss, E., & Haraway, M. M. (1998). Integrative levels, the brain, and the emergence of complex behavior. *Review of General Psychology, 3,* 168–187.

Greenberg, G., Partridge, T., Weiss, E., & Pisula, W. (2004). Comparative psychology: A new perspective for the 21st century. Up the spiral staircase. *Developmental Psychobiology, 44,* 1–15.

Griffiths, A. J. F., Wessler, S. R., Lewontin, R. C., Gelbart, W. M., Suzuli, D. T., & Miller, J. H. (2005). *Introduction to genetic analysis* (8th ed.). New York: Freeman.

Griffiths, P. E., & Gray, R. D. (2005). Discussion: Three ways to misunderstand developmental systems theory. *Biology and Philosophy, 20,* 417–425.

Griffiths, T. D., & Warren, J. D. (2002). The planum temporale as a computational hub. *Trends in Neuroscience, 25,* 348–353.

Haraway, M. H., & Maples, E. (1998). Species-typical behavior. In G. Greenberg & M. H. Haraway (Eds.). *Comparative psychology: A handbook.* New York: Garland.

Hardcastle, V. G., & Stewart, C. M. (2002). What do brain data really show? *Philosophy of Science, 69,* S72–S82.

Hardin, G. (1956). Meaninglessness of the word protoplasm. *Scientific Monthly, 82*(3), 112–120.

Harper, L. V. (in press). Trans-generational epigenetic inheritance. In K. Hood, C. Halpern, G. Greenberg, & R. Lerner (Eds.), *Handbook of developmental science, behavior and genetics.* Malden, MA: Blackwell.

Hebb, D. O. (1953). Heredity and environment in mammalian behavior. *British Journal of Animal Behaviour, 1,* 43–47.

Heinrichs, R. W. (1993). Schizophrenia and the brain. *American Psychologist, 48,* 221–233.

Heyes, C. M. (1998). Theory of mind in nonhuman primates. *Behavioral and Brain Sciences, 21,* 101–148.

Holland, J. H. (1995). *Hidden order: How adaptation builds complexity.* Reading, MA: Addison-Wesley.

Honeycutt, H. (2006). Studying evolution in action: Foundations for a transgenerational comparative psychology. *International Journal of Comparative Psychology, 19,* 170–184.

Hull, D. (1972). Reduction in genetics—biology or philosophy? *Philosophy of Science, 39,* 491–499.

Ingold, T. (2000). Evolving skills. In H. Rose & S. Rose (Eds.), *Alas poor Darwin: Arguments against evolutionary psychology* (pp. 273–297). New York: Harmony Books.

Jarvilehto, T. (1998). The theory of theorganism-environment system: I. Description of the theory. *Integrative Psychological and Behavioral Science, 33*(4), 321–334.

Jaynes, J. (1973). A long way from genes to behavior and molecules to man. [Review of *Selected writings of T. C. Schneirla*]. *Contemporary Psychology, 18,* 611–613.

Jerison, H. (1973). *Evolution of the brain and intelligence.* New York: Academic.

Jerison, H. J. (1994). Evolution of the brain. In D. W. Zaidel (Ed.), *Neuropsychology. Handbook of perception and cognition* (2nd ed., pp. 53–82). San Diego: Academic.

Joseph, J. (in press). Genetic research in psychiatry and psychology: A critical overview. In K. E. Hood, C. T. Halpern, G. Greenberg, & R. M. Lerner (Eds.), *Handbook of developmental science, behavior, and genetics.* Malden, MA: Blackwell.

Joshi, M., & Tyndale, R. F. (2006). Regional and cellular distribution of CYP2E1 in monkey brain and its induction by chronic nicotine. *Neuropharmacology, 50,* 568–575.

Kalat, J. W. (2009). *Biological psychology* (10th ed.). Belmont, CA: Wadsworth.

Kantor, J. R. (1924). *Principles of psychology* (Vol. 1). Bloomington, IN: Principia Press.

Kantor, J. R. (1926). *Principles of psychology* (Vol. 2). Bloomington, IN: Principia Press.

Kantor, J. R. (1959). *Interbehavioral psychology* (2nd ed.). Chicago: Principia Press.

Kaplan, G., & Rogers, L. J. (2003). *Gene worship: Moving beyond the nature/nurture debate over genes, brain, and gender.* New York: Other Press.

Kauffman, S. (2007). Beyond reductionism: Reinventing the sacred. *Zygon, 42,* 903–914.

Kaye, H. L. (1992, Spring). Are we the sum of our genes? *Wilson Quarterly, 16,* 77–84.

Keller, E. F. (2000). *The century of the gene.* Cambridge, MA: Harvard University Press.

Keller, E. F. (2002). *Making sense of life: Explaining biological development with models, metaphors, and machines.* Cambridge, MA: Harvard University Press.

Keller, E. F. (2005). DDS: Dynamics of developmental systems. *Biology and Philosophy, 20,* 409–416.

Killackey, H. P. (1990). Neocortical expansion: An attempt toward relating phylogeny and ontogeny. *Journal of Cognitive Neuroscience, 2,* 1–17.

Knoblich, J. A. (2001). Asymmetric cell division during animal development. *Nature Reviews Molecular Cell Biology, 2,* 11–20.

Ko, E. P., Yomo, T., & Urabe, I. (1994). Dynamic clustering of bacterial populations. *Physica D. 75*(1–3), 81–88.

Koch, C., & Laurent, G. (1999). Complexity and the nervous system. *Science, 284,* 96–98.

Krasny, M. (1997). Stephen Jay Gould. *Mother Jones, 22*(1), 60–63.

Kugler, P. N., & Turvey, M. T. (1987). *Information, natural law and the self-assembly of rhythmic movement.* Mahwah, NJ: Erlbaum.

Kuo, Z. Y. (1967). *The dynamics of behavior development.* New York: Random House.

Kuo, Z. Y. (1970). The need for coordinated efforts in developmental studies. In L. R. Aronson, E. Tobach, D. S. Lehrman, & J. S. Rosenblatt (Eds.), *Development and evolution of behavior: Essays in memory of T. C. Schneirla* (pp. 182–193). San Francisco, CA: Freeman.

Leahey, T. H. (2000). *A history of psychology: Main currents in psychological thought.* Upper Saddle River, NJ: Prentice Hall.

Lerner, R. M. (1984). *On the nature of human plasticity.* Cambridge: Cambridge University Press.

Lerner, R. M. (1998). Developmental contextualism. In G. Greenberg & M. M. Haraway (Eds.), *Comparative psychology: A handbook* (pp. 88–97). New York: Garland.

Lerner, R. M. (2002). *Concepts and theories of development* (3rd ed.). Mahwah, NJ: Erlbaum.

Lerner, R. M. (2004a). Genes and the promotion of positive human development: Hereditarian versus developmental systems perspectives. In C. G. Coll, E. L. Bearer, & R. M. Lerner (Eds.), *Nature and nurture: The complex interplay of genetic and environmental influences on human behavior and development* (pp. 1–33). Mahwah, NJ: Erlbaum.

Lerner, R. M. (2004b). *Liberty: Thriving and civic engagement among America's youth.* Thousand Oaks, CA: Sage.

Lerner, R. M. (2006). Developmental science, developmental systems, and contemporary theories of human development. In W. Damon (Series Ed.) & R. M. Lerner (Vol. Ed.), *Theoretical models of human development: Vol. 1, Handbook of child psychology* (pp. 1–17, 6th ed.). Hoboken, NJ: John Wiley & Sons.

Lerner, R. M., & Busch-Rossnagle, N. A. (Eds.). (1981). *Individuals as producers of their development: A life-span perspective.* New York: Academic.

Lerner, R. M., & Overton, W. F. (2008). Exemplifying the integrations of the relational developmental system: Synthesizing theory, research, and application to promote positive development and social justice. *Journal of Adolescent Research, 23,* 245–255.

Lewin, R. (1980). Is your brain really necessary? *Science, 210,* 1232–1234.

Lewin, R. (1992). *Complexity: Life at the edge of chaos.* New York: Macmillan.

Lewontin, R. (1997). Billions and billions of demons. *New York Review of Books, 44*(1), 28–32.

Lewontin, R. (2000). It ain't necessarily so: The dream of the Human Genome and other illusions. *New York Review of Books.*

Lickliter, R., & Honeycutt, H. (2003). Developmental dynamics: Toward a biologically plausible evolutionary psychology. *Psychological Bulletin, 129,* 819–835.

Lieberman, P. (1998). *Eve spoke.* New York: Norton.

Linden, D. J. (2007). *The accidental mind.* Cambridge, MA: Harvard University Press.

Loftus, E. F., & Loftus, G. R. (1980). On the permanence of stored information in the brain. *American Psychologist, 35,* 409–420.

Lorber, J. (1983). Is your brain rally necessary? In D. Voth (Ed.), *Hydrocephalus im frühen Kindesalter: Fortschritte der Grundlagenforschung, Diagnostik und Therapie* (pp. 2–14). Stuttgart, Germany: Ferdinand Enke Verlag.

Lovelock, J. E. (1979). *Gaia, a new look at life on earth.* New York: Oxford University Press.

Macmillan, M. (2008). Phineas Gage: Unravelling [sic] the myth. *The Psychologist, 21*(9), 828–831.

Magnusson, D. (1995). Individual development: A holistic integrated model. In P. Moen, G. H. Elder, & K. Luscher (Eds.), *Examining lives in context: Perspectives on the ecology of human development* (pp. 19–60). Washington, DC: American Psychological Association.

Maier, N. R. F., & Schneirla, T. C. (1964). *Principles of animal psychology (Enlarged edition).* New York: Dover. (Original work published 1935)

Malaiyandi, V., Sellers, E. M., & Tyndale, R. F. (2005). Implications of CYP2A6 genetic variation for smoking behaviors and nicotine dependence. *Perspectives in Clinical Pharmacology, 77,* 145–158.

Manger, P. R., Cort, J., Ebrahim, N., Goodman, A., Henning, J., Karolia, M., et al. (2008). Is 21st century neuroscience too focussed on the rat/mouse model of brain function and dysfunction? *Frontiers in Neuroanatomy, 2,* 1–7.

Marshall, P. J. (2009). Relating psychology and neuroscience. *Perspectives on Psychological Science, 4,* 113–125.

Matsuzawa, T. (1998). Chimpanzee behavior: A comparative cognitive perspective. In G. Greenberg & M. M. Haraway (Eds.). *Comparative psychology: A handbook* (pp. 360-375). New York: Garland.

Maynard Smith, J. (1970). Time in the evolutionary process. *Studium Generale, 23,* 266–272.

Mayr, E. (1970). *Populations, species, and evolution.* Cambridge, MA: Harvard University Press.

Mayr, E. (1979). Evolution. *Scientific American, 239*(3), 46–55.

Mayr, E. (1985). How biology differs from the physical sciences. In D. J. Depew & B. H. Weber (Eds.), *Evolution at a crossroads: The new biology and the new philosophy of science* (pp. 44–63). Cambridge, MA: MIT Press.

Mayr, E., & Provine, W. B. (1980). *The evolutionary synthesis: Perspectives on the unification of biology.* Cambridge, MA: Harvard University Press.

McCabe D. P., & Castel, A. D. (2007). Seeing is believing: The effect of brain images on judgements of scientific reasoning. *Cognition, 107,* 343–352.

Medawar, P. (1974). A geometric model of reduction and emergence. In F. C. Ayala & T. Dobzhansky (Eds.), *Studies in the philosophy of biology* (pp. 57–63). Los Angeles: University of California Press.

Michel, G. F. (1981). Right handedness: A consequence of infant supine head orientation preference? *Science, 212,* 685–687.

Michel, G. F. (in press). The meaning of the concept of experience in behavioral development. In K. E. Hood, C. T. Halpern, G. Greenberg, & R. M. Lerner (Eds.), *Handbook of developmental science, behavior, and genetics.* Malden, MA: Blackwell.

Michel, G. F., & Goodwin, R. (1979). Intrauterine birth position predicts newborn supine head position preference. *Infant Behavior and Development, 2,* 29–38.

Michel, G. F., & Moore, C. L. (1995). *Developmental psychobiology.* Cambridge, MA: MIT Press.

Miconi, T. (2008). Evolution and complexity: The double-edged sword. *Artificial Life, 14,* 325–344.

Miller, G. (2007). Six memos for evo-devo. In M. D. Laubichler & J. Maienschein (Eds.), *From embryology to evo-devo: A history of developmental evolution* (pp. 499–524). Cambridge, MA: MIT Press.

Moffat, S. D., Kennedy K. M., Rodrigue, K. M., & Raz, N. (2007). Extrahippocampal contributions to age differences in human spatial navigation. *Cerebral Cortex, 17*(6), 1274–1282.

Molenaar, P. C. M. (2007). Psychological methodology will change profoundly due to the necessity to focus on intra-individual variation. *Integrative Psychological and Behavioral Science, 41*(1), 1932–4502.

Montagu, A. (1962). Our changing conception of human nature. In *The humanization of man* (pp. 15–34). New York: Grove Press. (Reprinted from Impact [UNESCO], 1952, 3, 219–232)

Montagu, M. (1972). Sociogenic brain damage. *American Anthropologist, 74,* 1045–1061.

Morgan, C. L. (1923). *Emergent evolution: The Gifford lectures.* London: Williams and Norgate.

Moss, L. (2003). *What genes can't do.* Cambridge, MA: MIT Press.

Myers, J. J. (1984). Right hemisphere language: Science or fiction? *American Psychologist, 39,* 315–320.

Needham, J. (1929). *The skceptical biologist.* London: Chatto.

Nelkin, D. (1993). The social power of genetic information. In D. Kevles and L. Hood (Eds.), *The code of codes: Scientific and social issues in the human genome project* (pp. 177–190). Cambridge, MA: Harvard University Press.

Nesselroade, J. R. (2006). Quantitative modeling in adult development and aging: Reflections and projections. In C. S. Bergman & S. M. Boker (Eds.), *Methodological issues in aging* (pp. 1–18). Mahwah, NJ: Routledge.

Neumann-Held, E. M. (2001). Let's talk about genes: The process molecular gene concept and its context. In S. Oyama, P. E. Griffiths, & R. D. Gray (Eds.), *Cycles of contingency: Developmental systems and evolution* (pp. 69–84). Cambridge, MA: MIT Press.

Nieuwkoop, P. D., Johnen, A. G., & Albers, B. (1985). *The epigenetic nature of early chordate development: Inductive interaction and competence.* Cambridge, England: Cambridge University Press.

Niiniluoto, I. (1994). Scientific realism and the problem of consciousness. In A. Revonsuo & M. Kamppinen (Eds.), *Consciousness in philosophy and cognitive neuroscience* (pp. 33–34). Hillsdale, NJ: Erlbaum.

Nishida, T. (1986). Learning and cultural transmission in nonhuman primates. *Folia Primatologica, 12,* 273–283.

Nitecki, M. H. (1988). *Evolutionary progress.* Chicago: University of Chicago Press.

Noë, A. (2008). The problem of consciousness: A talk with Alva Noë. *Edge: The third culture.* Retrieved December 26, 2008, from http://www.edge.org/3rd_culture/noe08/noe08_index.html#rc.

Novikoff, A. (1945). The concept of integrative levels and biology. *Science, 101,* 209–215.

Olson, E. C. (1976). Rates of evolution of the nervous system and behavior. In R. B. Masterton, W. Hodos, & H. Jerison (Eds.), *Evolution, brain and behavior: Persistent problems* (pp. 47–77). Hillsdale, NJ: Erlbaum.

Ostrom, C. W., Lerner, R. M., & Freel, M. A. (1995). Building the capacity of youth and families through university-community collaboration. *Journal of Adolescent Research, 10,* 427–448.

Overton, W. F. (1975). General systems, structure and development. In K. Riegel & G. Rosenwald (Eds.), *Structure and transformation: Developmental aspects* (pp. 61–81). New York: Wiley Interscience

Overton, W. F. (2006). Developmental psychology: Philosophy, concepts, methodology. In W. Damon (Seried Ed.) & R. M. Lerner (Vol. Ed.), *Theoretical models of human development: Vol. 1, Handbook of child psychology* (6th ed., pp. 18–88). Hoboken, NJ: John Wiley & Sons.

Overton, W. F., Mueller, U., & Newman, J. L. (Eds.). (2007). *Developmental perspective on embodiment and consciousness.* Hillsdale, NJ: Erlbaum.

Overton, W. F., & Reese, H. W. (1973). Models of development: Methodological implications. In J. R. Nesselroade & H. W. Reese (Eds.), *Life-span developmental psychology: Methodological issues* (pp. 65–86). New York: Academic.

Oyama, S. (1985). *The ontogeny of information: Developmental systems and evolution.* Cambridge: Cambridge University Press.

Oyama, S. (2000). *Evolution's eye: A systems view of the biology-culture divide.* Durham, NC: Duke University Press.

Page, M. P. A. (2006). What can't functional neuroimaging tell the cognitive psychologist? *Cortex, 42,* 428–443.

Panskepp, J., & Panskepp, J. B. (2000). The seven sins of evolutionary psychology. *Evolution and Cognition, 6,* 108–131.

Pantin, C. F. A. (1951). Organic design. *The Advancement of Science, 30,* 138-150.

Partridge, T., & Greenberg, G. (in press). Contemporary ideas in physics and biology in Gottlieb's psychology. In K. Hood, C. Halpern, G. Greenberg, & R. Lerner (Eds.), *Handbook of developmental science, behavior and genetics.* Malden, MA: Blackwell.

Penfield, W. (1958a). Some mechanisms of consciousness discovered during electrical stimulation of the brain. *Proceedings of the National Academy of Sciences, 44*(2), 51–66.

Penfield, W. (1958b). Hippocratic preamble: The brain and intelligence. In F. N. L. Poynter (Ed.), *The brain and ins functions: An Anglo-American symposium* (pp. 1–4). Oxford: Blackwell Scientific Publications.

Penfield, W., & Perot, P. (1963). The brain's record of auditory and visual experience: A final summary and discussion. *Brain, 86,* 595–697.

Pinker, S. (1999). *How the mind works.* New York: W. W. Norton.

Pinker, S. (2002). *The blank slate: The modern denial of human nature.* New York: Penguin.

Plotkin, H. C. (1983). The functions of learning and cross-species comparisons. In G. C. L. Davey (Ed.). *Animal models of human behavior* (pp.117–134). New York: John Wiley & Sons.

Plotnik, R., & Mollenauer, S. (1978). *Brain and behavior.* San Francisco: Canfield Press.

Pribram, K. (Ed.). (1993). *Rethinking neural networks: Quantum fields and biological data.* Mahwah, NJ: Erlbaum.

Pribram, K. (Ed.). (1996). *Learning as self-organization.* Mahwah, NJ: Erlbaum.

Pronko, N. H. (1973). *Panorama of psychology* (2nd ed.). Monterey, CA: Brooks/Cole.

Pronko, N. H. (1980). *Psychology from the standpoint of an interbehaviorist.* Belmont, CA: Wadsworth.

Pronko, N. H. (1988). "Soul": The transformation of "soul" to "mind" and "mind" to "brain." In N. H. Pronko (Ed.), *From AI to Zeitgeist: A philosophical guide for the skeptical psychologist* (pp. 188–189). New York: Greenwood Press.

Reid, R. G. B. (2007). *Biological emergences: Evolution by natural experiment.* Cambridge, MA: MIT Press.

Reinhart, J. B., & Drash, A. L. (1969). Psychosocial dwarfism: Environmentally induced recovery. *Psychosomatic Medicine, 31,* 165–172.

Reise, W. (1958). Descartes' ideas of brain function. In F. N. L. Poynter (Ed.), *The brain and ins functions: An Anglo-American symposium* (pp. 115–134). Oxford: Blackwell Scientific Publications.

Renthal, W., & Nestler, E. J. (2008). Epigenetic mechanisms is drug addiction. *Trends in Molecular Medicine, 14,* 341–350.

Risch, N., Herrell, R., Lehner, T., Liang, K-Y., Eaves, L., Hoh, J., et al. (2009). Interaction between the serotonin transporter gene (5-HTTLPR), stressful life events, and risk of depression: A meta-analysis. *Journal of the American Medical Association, 301*(23), 2462–2470.

Robert, J. S. (2004). *Embryology, epigenesis, and evolution: Taking development seriously.* Cambridge: Cambridge University Press.

Robert, J. S., Hall, B. K., & Olson, W. M. (2001). Bridging the gap between developmental systems theory and evolutionary developmental biology. *BioEssays, 23,* 954–962.

Robinson, G. E., Fernald, R. D., & Clayton, D. F. (2008). Genes and social behavior. *Science, 322,* 896–900.

Rogers, L. (1999). *Sexing the brain.* London: Weidenfeld & Nicolson.

Rogers, L. J. (in press). Interactive contributions of genes, hormones and early experience to behavioural development discussed in a social and ecological context. In K. E. Hood, C. T. Halpern, G. Greenberg, & R. M. Lerner (Eds.), *Handbook of developmental science, behavior and genetics: Honoring the work of Gilbert Gottlieb.* Malden, MA: Wiley-Blackwell.

Rose, S. (1989). *The conscious brain* (Rev. ed.). New York: Paragon House.

Rose, S. (2009). Darwin 200: Should scientists study race and IQ? No: Science and society do not benefit. *Nature, 457*(7231), 786–789.

Roskies, A. L. (2007). Are neuroimages like photographs of the brain? *Philosophy of Science, 74,* 860–872.

Rudel, D., & Sommer, R. J. (2003). The evolution of developmental mechanisms. *Developmental Biology, 264,* 15–37.

Rumbaugh, D. M., & Pate, J. L. (1984). The evolution of cognition in primates: A comparative perspective. In H. L. Roitblatt, T. G. Bever & H. S. Terrace (Eds.), *Animal cognition* (pp. 569-587). Hillsdale, NJ: Erlbaum

Ruse, M. (2006). Forty years a philosopher of biology: Why evo-devo makes me still excited about my subject. *Biological Theory, 1,* 35–37.

Sameroff, A. (1975). Transactional models in early social relations. *Human Development, 18*(1–2), 65–79.

Saunders, P. T., & Ho, M. W. (1976). On the increase in complexity in evolution. *Journal of Theoretical Biology, 63,* 375–384.

Saunders, P. T., & Ho, M. W. (1981). On the increase in complexity in evolution. II. The relativity of complexity and the principle of minimum increase. *Journal of Theoretical Biology, 90,* 515–530.

Savage-Rumbaugh, S., Shanker, S. G., & Taylor, T. J. (1998). *Apes, language, and the human mind.* New York: Oxford University Press.

Schneirla, T. C. (1949). Levels in the psychological capacities of animals. In R. W. Sellars, V. J. McGill, & M. Farber (Eds.), *Philosophy for the future* (pp. 243–286). New York: Macmillan.

Schneirla, T. C. (1957). The concept of development in comparative psychology. In D. B. Harris (Ed.), *The concept of development: An issue in the study of human behavior* (pp. 78–108). Minneapolis: University of Minnesota Press.

Schneirla, T. C. (1972). The concept of development in comparative psychology. In L. R. Aronson, E. Tobach, J. S. Rosenblatt, & D. S. Lehrman, (Eds.). (1972). *Selected writings of T. C. Schneirla* (pp. 259–294). San Francisco: Freeman. (Reprinted from *The concept of development,* pp. 78-108, D. B. Harris, Ed., 1957, Minneapolis: University of Minnesota Press)

Seay, B., & Gottfried, N. (1978). *The development of behavior: A synthesis of developmental and comparative psychology.* Boston: Houghton Mifflin.

Sherrington, C. (1951/1964). *Man on his nature* (Rev. ed.). New York: Mentor.

Sherrington, C. S. (1906/1947). *The integrative action of the nervous system* (2nd ed.). New Haven, CT: Yale University Press.

Singh, S. (2005). *Big bang.* New York: Harper.

Sirotin, Y. B., & Das, A. (2009). Anticipatory haemodynamic signals in sensory cortex not predicted by local neuronal activity. *Nature, 457,* 475–480.

Skinner, B. F. (1974). *About behaviorism.* New York: Knopf.

Skinner, B. F. (1977). Why I am not a cognitive psychologist. *Behaviorism, 5,* 1–10.

Smith, A., & Sugar, O. (1975). Development of above normal language and intelligence 21 years after left hemispherectomy. *Neurology, 25,* 813.

Smith, E. (2008). Before Darwin: How the earth went from lifeless to life. *The Scientist, 22*(6), 32.

Smith, L. B., & Thelen, E. (2003). Development as a dynamic system. *Trends in Cognitive Science, 7,* 343–348.

Solé, R., & Goodwin, B. (2000). *Signs of life: How complexity pervades biology.* New York: Basic Books.

Sperry, R. W. (1982). Some effects of disconnecting the cerebral hemispheres. *Science, 217,* 1223–1226.

Sperry, R. W. (1991). In defense of mentalism and emergent interaction. *Journal of Mind and Behavior, 12,* 221–245.

Sperry, R. W. (1993). The impact and promise of the cognitive revolution. *American Psychologist, 48,* 878–885.

Stoltenberg, S. F., & Hirsch, J. (1998). Behavior-genetic analysis. In G. Greenberg & M. M. Haraway (Eds.), *Comparative psychology: A handbook* (pp. 226–235). New York: Garland.

Strohman, R. C. (1997). The coming Kuhnian revolution in biology. *Nature Biotechnology, 15,* 194–200.

Talwar, R., Nitz, K., & Lerner, R. M. (1990). Relations among early adolescent temperament, parent and peer demands, and adjustment: A test of the goodness of fit model. *Journal of Adolescence, 13*(3), 279–298.

Thelen, E. (1989). Self-organization in developmental processes: Can systems approaches work? In M. R. Gunnar & E. Thelen (Eds.), *Systems and development: The Minnesota symposium in child psychology, 22,* 77–117.

Thelen, E. (1990). Coupling perception and action in development of skill: A dynamic approach. In H. Bloch & B. Bertanthal (Eds.), *Sensory motor organizations and development in infancy and early childhood* (pp. 39–56). Dordrecht, The Netherlands: Kluwer.

Thelen, E. (2004). Motor development as a foundation and future of developmental psychology. In W. W. Hartup & R. K. Silbereisen (Eds.), *Growing points in developmental science* (pp. 1–23). New York: Psychology Press.

Thiessen, D., & Villarriel, R. (1998). Allometry and comparative psychology: Technique and theory. In G. Greenberg & M. M. Haraway (Eds.), *Comparative psychology: A handbook* (pp. 51–65). New York: Garland.

Thomas, R. (2007). Recurring errors among recent history of psychology textbooks. *American Journal of Psychology, 120,* 477–495.

Thornton, E. M. (1984). *The Freudian fallacy: An alternative view of Freudian theory.* Garden City, NY: Doubleday.

Tobach, E., & Schneirla, T. C. (1968). The biopsychology of social behavior of animals. In R. E. Cook & S. Levin (Eds.), *The biological basis of pediatric practice* (pp. 68–82). New York: McGraw-Hill.

Tononi, G., & Edelman, G. M. (1998). Consciousness and complexity. *Science, 282,* 1846–1851.

Toobey, J., & Cosmides, L. (1995). Forward. In S. Baron-Cohen (Ed.), *Mind-blindness: An essay on autism and theory of mind* (pp. xi–xviii). Cambridge, MA: MIT Press.

University of Sheffield. (n.d.). The AHRC *Innateness and the Structure of the Mind* Project. Retrieved from http://www.philosophy.dept.shef.ac.uk/AHRB-Project. Accessed January 2, 2010.

Uttal, W. R. (2001). *The new phrenology: The limits of localizing cognitive processes in the brain.* Cambridge, MA: MIT Press.

Uttal, W. R. (2005). *Neural theories of mind: Why the mind-brain problem may never be solved.* Mahwah, NJ: Erlbaum.

Valenstein, E. S. (1973). *Brain control.* Hoboken, NJ: John Wiley & Sons.

Valenstein, E. S., Cox, V. C., & Kakolewski, J. W. (1970). Reexamination of the role of the hypothalamus in motivation. *Psychological Review, 77,* 16–31.

Venter, J. C., Adams, M. D., Myers, E. W., Li, P. W., Mural, R. J., Sutton, G. G., et al. (2001). The sequence of the human genome. *Science, 291*(5507), 1304–1351.

Vogel, S. (1998). Locomotor behavior and physical reality. In G. Greenberg & M. M. Haraway (Eds.), *Comparative psychology: A handbook* (pp. 713–719). New York: Garland.

von Uexküll, J. (1957). A stroll through the world of animals and men. In C. H. Schiller (Ed.), *Instinctive behavior* (pp. 5–80). New York: International Universities Press.

Vrba, E. S., & Eldredge, N. (1984). Individuals, hierarchies and processes: Towards a more complete evolutionary theory. *Paleobiology, 10,* 146–171.

Vul, E., Harris, C., Winkielman, P., & Pashler, H. (2009). Puzzlingly high correlations in fMRI studies of emotion, personality, and social cognition. *Perspectives on Psychological Science, 4,* 274–290.

Waddington, C. H. 1969. "The Theory of Evolution Today." In A. Koestler and S. Smythies (eds.), *Beyond Reductionism* (pp. 357–374). London: Hutchinson.

Watson, J. D., & Crick, F. H. C. (1953). A structure for deoxyribose nucleic acid. *Nature, 171,* 737–738.

Weber, B. H. (2007). Emergence of life. *Zygon, 42,* 837–856.

Weisberg, D. S., Keil, F. C., Goodstein, J., Rawson, E., & Gray, J. R. (2208). The allure of neuroscience explanations. *Journal of Cognitive Neuroscience, 20,* 470–477.

Willems, R. E., & Hagoort, P. (2009). Broca's region: Battles are not won by ignoring half of the facts. *Trends in Cognitive Neuroscience, 13*(3), 101.

Woodger, J. H. (1929). *Biological principles: A critical study.* London: Routledge and Kegan Paul.

Yamamoto, Y., & Jeffery, W. R. (2000). Central role for the lens in cave fish eye degeneration. *Science, 289,* 631–633.

Yarczower, M. (1984). Behavior and evolutionary progress: Anagenesis, grades, and evolutionary scales. In G. Greenberg & E. Tobach (Eds.), *Behavioral evolution and integrative levels: The T. C. Schneirla Conference Series* (Vol. 1, pp. 105–120). Hillsdale, NJ: Erlbaum.

Zimmer, C. (2004). *Soul made flesh: The discovery of the brain—and how it changed the world.* New York: Free Press.

CHAPTER 6

The Dynamic Development of Thinking, Feeling, and Acting over the Life Span

MICHAEL F. MASCOLO and KURT W. FISCHER

These are exciting times for life-span developmental psychology. In the last several decades, advances in theory and research have produced profound changes in the ways in which we understand human action and development. These changes involve a reversal of many long-held assumptions about the nature of psychological functioning. The most salient of these changes involve refutations of the legacy of strong dualities that have long constrained progress in the study of human behavior and development. These include strong distinctions such as mind/body, emotion/reason, biology/psyche, organism/environment, inner/ outer, behavior/mental process, individual/culture, and similar dualities (Overton, 2006). The most exciting developments have come from the recognition that the components and contexts of human activity cannot be understood independent of each other. Instead, human development occurs in *medias res*—in the middle of everything. When taken seriously, the implications of this idea are vast. Instead of operating as separate modules, thought and emotion, experience and action, biology and agency, person and environment, and other ostensibly opposing processes are highly dependent on each other. This chapter elaborates a model

We acknowledge our tremendous gratitude to Dr. McCullough and the Lady Cloaked in Fog for their generosity and courage in making videotapes of their work available for analysis.

of human development that takes seriously the idea that the structures and processes of human action operate as dynamic processes that take diverse forms and trajectories as they develop in *medias res.*

A recurring theme that has emerged in developmental theory and research over the past several decades is the profound lack of independence of the systems that make up human action, as well as the systems and contexts within which human action is embedded (Gangestad & Simpson, 2007; Gottlieb, Wahlsten, & Lickliter, 2006; Lerner & Overton, 2008). Instead of postulating sequences of internal cognitive processes without reference to brain, body, and social context, psychologists have examined the *embodied* nature of thought and action (Gallagher, 2005; Gibbs, 2006; Overton, Mueller, & Newman, 2007; Thompson, 2007). Thought has its origins in actions that occur within the medium of the body and that operate within physical and social contexts (Johnson, 1987; Noë, 2004). Instead of studying cognition and emotion as separate and distinct psychological modules, psychologists, philosophers, and neuroscientists currently maintain that emotion plays a necessary role in the organization of all human action (Freeman, 2000; Mascolo, Fischer, & Li 2003; see also McClelland, Ponitz, & Tominey, Chapter 15 of this volume, and Santostefano, Chapter 22 of this volume). Instead of viewing individual persons as entities that can function independent of physical and social contexts, current theory and research support the idea that person and context operate as distinct parts of an interlocking system (Clark, 1997; Fischer & Bidell, 2006; Gottlieb & Lickliter, 2007; Overton, 2006).

This emergence of these approaches has important implications in the ways in which we address central questions about human development. First, consider the foundational question: *What is it that develops in psychological development?* Emerging perspectives proceed with an appreciation of how seemingly different psychological functions codevelop and influence each other over time. For example, Campos and his colleagues (Campos et al., 2000; Lejeune et al., 2006; Uchiyama et al., 2008) have shown that early locomotor experience, and not simply visual experience, plays a key role in the development of visual proprioception (i.e., the perception of self-motion in response to visual motion cues). Eight-month-olds with experience walking or creeping exhibited higher rates of postural adjustment and emotionality to the induction of motion parallax than did prelocomotor infants. The developmental literature includes many examples of similar effects. These findings underscore the coparticipation of multiple organismic systems in the development of any given psychological structure. Calling into question the practice of analyzing discrete psychological processes, these findings suggest a need to analyze development in terms of increasingly integrative couplings among ostensibly distinct psychological processes (Ayoub & Fischer, 2006; Overton, 2007; Sneed, Hamagami, McArdle, Cohen, & Chen, 2007; Witherington, 2007).

How do psychological structures undergo developmental change? Human development is dynamic; it does not occur according to fixed plans, whether those plans are regarded as genetic, psychological, or cultural in origin (Fogel, Lyra, & Valsiner, 1998; Thelen & Smith, 2006; van Geert, 1994). To understand the processes by which development occurs, we can no longer focus on individual forces, or even multiple forces acting independently; instead, it is necessary to analyze how biology, action, and context interact within a *relational developmental system* (Gottlieb & Lickliter, 2007; Lerner, 2006; Lerner & Overton, 2008; Overton, 2006; Oyama, 2000). For example, Gottlieb (2008; Gottlieb et al., 2006) has shown numerous examples of the ways in which anatomical and behavioral structures in different species take different forms depending on local rearing conditions. For example, the capacity to respond selectively to maternal calls in mallard ducks is dependent on having been exposed to the duck's own or to another duck's vocalizations in utero; sex determination in varieties of reptiles is influenced by incubation temperature; genetically identical parasitic wasps that gestate in different animal hosts develop different anatomical structures. Thus, if development occurs *in medias res,* it follows that it is not possible to predict the shapes of development simply from knowing initial conditions. To identify the shapes of development, one must examine developmental trajectories as they emerge for particular configurations of psychological processes under particular developmental conditions (Gottlieb & Lickliter, 2007; Lewontin, 2000).

In what follows, we begin first by offering a model of the integrative nature of human action and experience. Articulation of such a basic framework is necessary if we are to understand the integrative nature of "what develops" in human development. We define integrative *psychological structures* as a basic unit of conceptual and empirical analysis. Psychological structures consist of dynamic integrations of motive-relevant meaning, feeling, and motor action as they emerge within particular behavioral domains and contexts. We then examine how a theory of skill development (Fischer, 1980; Fischer & Bidell, 2006; Mascolo & Fischer, 2005) can illuminate the ways in which psychological structures develop over the life span. Skill theory (Fischer, 1980) provides conceptual and empirical tools for identifying the shifting structure of any given system of acting, thinking, and feeling as they take shape within particular psychological domains and social contexts. We then track developmental changes in psychological structures within specific psychological domains. We focus first on age-related and developmental changes in representations of *what makes life meaningful* over the course of adulthood. The question of what makes life meaningful is an integrative one. As a result, its analysis can help illuminate the integrative nature of individual development over the life span. Our discussion then shifts from the analysis of macrodevelopmental changes over long periods to more focused analyses on the microdevelopment of integrative psychological structures in moment-by-moment face-to-face interactions *between* people. In so doing, we extend our analysis of the development of psychological structures in *individual* actors to a discussion of methods for assessing the dynamic structure of *joint* action between individuals over time (Basseches & Mascolo, 2010; Fogel, Garvey, Hsu, & West-Stromming, 2006; see also Nesselroade & Molenaar, Chapter 2 of this volume, and McArdle, Chapter 3 of this volume, for extended discussions of life-span methods). The port of entry for this discussion is the analysis of developmental changes in representational and emotional aspects of psychological structures that occur over the course of psychotherapy in adulthood. We conclude this chapter with a discussion of challenges elaborating integrative models of life-span development.

FOUNDATIONS OF AN INTEGRATIVE THEORY OF DYNAMIC DEVELOPMENT

Psychological structures are motive-relevant *integrations* of meaning, affect, and experience that have their origins in *action*. The concepts of *action* and *activity*—common to the seminal developmental theories erected by Baldwin, Dewey, Piaget, Vygotsky, and others—bring together the various processes that we call *psychological* into a single unit. Although the term *action* is often used as a synonym for "overt behavior" or movement, the concept of action *transcends* the distinction between inner experience and outer movement. The concept of action implies some capacity for *agency* or *control;* an action is a type of *doing* (Burke, 1966; Taylor, 1970). Analysis of even the simplest actions reveals properties that incorporate but extend well beyond mere movement. Actions are intentional processes (in the sense that they are "directed toward" or are "about" something; Searle, 1969; Zahavi, 2005), goal directed (Miller, Galanter,

& Pribram, 1960), and mediated by meaning (Wertsch, 1998; Vygotsky, 1978). However, the meanings that mediate action are not simply "cognitive" or "intellectual" affairs. Instead, emotion and bodily experience play central roles in the organization of the varied components action (Brown, 1994; Damasio, 1994; Freeman, 2000). Figure 6.1 is a schematic diagram of the integrative structure of action. We illustrate the integral nature of action through analysis of the everyday act of drinking a cup of coffee.

First, actions are intentional processes in the sense that they are either performed *on* something, directed *toward* something, or are *about* something, real or imagined (Merleau-Ponty, 1945; Searle, 1969; Vedeler, 1994). Actions and their objects are represented at points a and b in Figure 6.1. In the case of drinking a cup of coffee, coordinated actions of reaching, grasping, and drinking are performed *on* the coffee. The coffee is the *object* of the person's act of drinking. The relation between action and object is an intimate one; actions and their objects *mutually constitute each other,* whether those actions are sensorimotor acts of *drinking a cup of coffee* or social activity such an *engaging in a conversation* over coffee. For example, when grasping a mug, one must extend one's arm and accommodate one's hand and fingers around the mug's contours. In this way, the physical structure of the mug constrains the structure the act of grasping (Bateson, 1972; Gibson, 1979; Rosey, Golomer, & Keller, 2008). Simultaneously, the act of grasping the mug is organized by the goals and meaning that the mug has for the person—specifically, the idea that the mug operates as a vehicle for bringing the coffee to the mouth. Thus, action is always *action-on-objects;* a change in object necessitates a change in actions performed on the object and vice versa.

Second, and perhaps more important, psychological activity is mediated by *meaning* and *experience;* meaning and experience are aspects or forms of action (Overton, 2006). More than any other feature, it is *meaning,* broadly defined, that makes any given process a *psychological* one. A psychological process is a process that is mediated by the meaning that events have for an experiencing organism. The 5-week-old's smile on recognizing her mother, the 20-year-old's anticipation of the kick that will come from her next sip of coffee, and the 40-year-old's fear that spending too much time cultivating a career will interfere with his relationship are mediated not by events per se but by the *meaning* events have for persons. The role of meaning in mediating action is represented at point c of Figure 6.1. It is important to understand that meaning does not *precede* action; psychological acts are mediated by meaning.

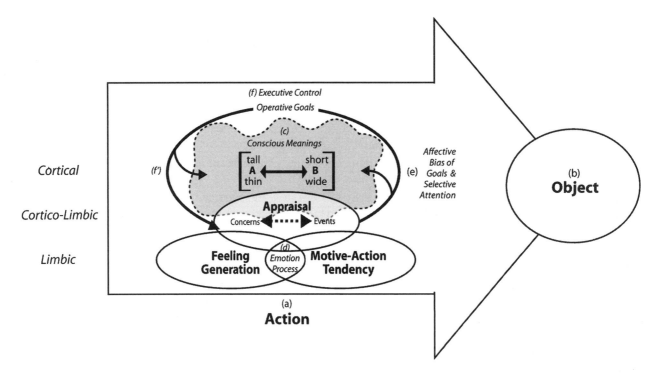

Figure 6.1   Architecture of human action. Psychological processes are understood as forms or components of meaning-mediated action *(a)*. Psychological acts exhibit intentionality (aboutness), in the sense that they are directed toward some object *(b)*, real or imagined. Psychological activity is mediated by meaning *(c)*. The structure of meaning in consciousness emerges from multiple sources. Nonconscious affect-generating processes *(d)* function to select and amplify conscious activity and attention *(e)*. Simultaneously, in any given context, higher order executive processes *(f)* exert downward and conscious control over the construction of meaning *(f′)* and the regulation of affect *(f′)*. In this way, any psychological act involves the integration of cognitive, conative, and affective processes at multiple levels of functioning.

Third, acting is a form of *doing*. The concept of action implies some degree of *agency* on the part of the person performing the action; persons exert some degree of control over representational, experiential, and motor processes. The capacity to exert control implies that action is goal directed or otherwise motivated. Agency and goal directedness are represented in Figure 6.1 by the arrow depicted at point d. Research clearly indicates a capacity of primitive forms of goal directedness from birth onward (de Casper & Carstens, 1980; Sullivan & Lewis, 2003). Thus, to exert control over the act of grasping a coffee mug implies the presence of a goal—namely, to bring the coffee to the mouth. The coordinated acts of reaching, grasping, lifting, and sipping are all subordinated to this particular goal, which itself may be subordinated to a still higher order goal (e.g., having a conversation over coffee). In this way, actions function as hierarchically nested control structures (Mascolo, Fischer, & Neimeyer, 1999).

The Role of Emotion in Human Action

Although psychological acts function as control structures, they are not simply cognitive processes. Any action necessarily involves an integration of cognitive, conative, and emotional processes. Current theory and research underscore the idea that emotion plays a central role in selecting, amplifying, and organizing attention, consciousness, thinking, and action (Freeman, 2000; Keltner & Gross, 1999; Lewis, 1996; Tomkins, 1984). In addition to these intrapersonal functions, emotion also serves social, moral, and cultural functions (Keltner & Haidt, 1999; Mascolo & Fischer, 2007; Tangney, Stuewig, & Mashek, 2007). It follows that affective processes must operate as part of the basic architecture of human action.

It is helpful to think of emotional states with reference to three broad classes of components (Mascolo, Fischer, & Li, 2003). Emotions are composed of motive-relevant *appraisals* (Lazarus, 1991; Scherer, 2004), a core bodily experience or *phenomenal tone* (Bermond, 2008; Scherer, 2004), and characteristic *motor expressions and motive-action tendencies* (Frijda, 1987). Appraisals refer to embodied assessments of the relation between perceived events and a person's motives, goals, and concerns (Frijda, 1986; Scherer, 2004). Different emotional states reflect variations in the ways in which individuals appraise events relative to their motives and desires (Ellsworth & Scherer, 2003). Positive emotions accompany motive-consistent appraisals; negative emotion arises when events clash with goals, motives, and concerns. Although appraisals are often conceptualized as "cognitive" processes, they are always *motive relevant;* they are assessments of how events relate to what one desires, wants, expects, and so forth. Appraisals reflect changes in the *fate of one's motives* (Roseman, 1984). Thus, although appraisals *involve* cognitive processes, the cognitive aspects of appraisal function in the service of a person's motives. As a result, appraisal processes that operate in emotion are fast-acting, nonconscious, and nondeliberate (Barrett, Ochsner, & Gross, 2007). With development, event appraisals become increasingly mediated by higher order meanings (Mascolo, Fischer, & Li, 2003; Sroufe, 1996).

Feeling tone refers to the phenomenal experience of an emotional state. Most laypersons report that different experiences of emotions have different characteristic feeling tones. Although it is often difficult for people to describe their felt states, when they do, they often resort to telling stories about the circumstances under which feelings arose (Sarbin, 1989), describing the events that precipitate them (e.g., "It felt as if I were punched in the stomach"), or invoking metaphor (Davitz, 1969; Kovecses, 2000; Santostefano, Chapter 22 of this volume). For example, the experience of anger is often described in terms of "heat" ("I felt hot") and "pressure" ("I felt like I was going to explode"). *Motive-action tendencies* consist of voluntary, involuntary, and communicative actions that function in the service of the appraisals involved in the emotional experience. Different classes of motive-action tendencies reflect what a person typically *wants to do* and what a person has a tendency to *actually do* within the emotional experience in question. These include both voluntary and involuntary actions. Motive-action tendencies are *functional.* They operate in the service of the motives implicated in the appraisals that participate in an emotional state. For any given category of emotion, action tendencies encompass characteristic patterns of facial, vocal, postural, and instrumental activity.

The tripartite structure of appraisal-affect-action processes is represented in Figure 6.1 in terms of the interlocking circles within the broad arrow signifying action. No single or fixed sequence is in the construction of any particular emotional experience. Appraisal, affect, and motor action *regulate each other* in real time; each is always operative in continuously modulating each other's functioning over time (Lewis, 1996; Mascolo & Harkins, 1998; Scherer, 2004). In any given context, appraisal processes—most of which proceed without conscious awareness—continuously generate, modify, and modulate the production of affect and action; different affective patterns are generated by different types of appraisal activity. At the same time, however, affect *amplifies, organizes,* and *selects* these same appraisals *for conscious attention* (Brown, 1994; Phelps, Ling, & Carrasco, 2006; Tomkins, 1984). At any given point in time, motive-relevant appraisal systems are active in monitoring event-related information from thousands of different sources (e.g., different classes of visual, auditory, vestibular, tactile, bodily inputs) at a variety of different levels of meaning (i.e., homeostatic regulation, bodily feedback, higher order meanings). Only a small minority of these appraisal processes result in conscious awareness.

For example, most drivers have had the experience of "automatic driving"—operating a car for long periods without being aware of one's driving. During such an episode, if a child were to run into the road, the child's presence would immediately be drawn to conscious awareness. "Without thinking," the driver would maneuver the car to avoid hitting the child. This common example illustrates the typically *nonconscious* ongoing appraisal processes; at any given moment, appraisal processes monitor the status of *full range* of a person's goals, motives, and concerns. Change in the relation between events and a person's important motives and concerns result in affective changes: The person may experience bodily changes that are described with terms like *fear, terror,* or *horror.* Most important for this discussion, *affective changes thereupon select, organize, and amplify one's motive-relevant appraisal for conscious awareness whereas simultaneously activating broad classes of adaptive action.* In this case, *before* the driver in the example provided is able to respond to the situation in terms of higher order deliberative activity, the emotional state of fear amplifies and selects the appraisal *"a child is in danger"* for conscious awareness whereas simultaneously activating action tendencies that function to *remove the danger* to the child. In this way, *affect plays a central role in the selection and organization motive-relevant appraisals for conscious awareness, attention, and action. Affect operates as an actual part of any given action structure.*

Completing an Integrative Conception of Action

The emotion process is depicted in Figure 6.1 in terms of the three interlocking ellipses identified at point d. At any given moment, appraisal processes monitor relations between perceived events and a person's goals, motives, and concerns. An individual's goals, motives, and concerns undergo profound developmental change over the course of life. By the time an individual reaches adulthood, a person's motivational system is constituted by a broad range of goals, motives, and concerns. Appraisal processes are continuously operative in monitoring the flow of events with reference to a person's motive hierarchies. The emotional selection and organization of goal-directed consciousness is represented in Figure 6.1 in terms of the arrow indicated at point e. Conscious control over meaning, experience, and motor action is depicted in terms of the activity of higher order executive functions depicted at points f and f′. It is through the operation of executive processes that individuals exert coordinative control over meaning, experience, and motor movement. Conscious control over action occurs as one is able to bring structures of meaning, experience, and movement into correspondence with those goals, motives, and concerns that have been organized in consciousness through the generation of affect (point e in Figure 6.1) (Scherer, 2004). Of course, the capacity for higher order cortical control does not emerge *ex nihilo;* it is organized by lower-level processes (including affect) that function outside of awareness. Thus, human action functions as a complex, integrated, and dynamic process.

Neurobiological Grounding of an Integrated Model of Action

Although they are still in their infancy, the fields of cognitive (Gazzaniga, Ivry, & Mangun, 2008), affective (Davidson, 2000; Panksepp, 1998), and social (Cacioppo, Visser, & Picket, 2006; Harmon-Jones & Winkielman, 2007) neuroscience have produced research that provides the psychobiological grounding supporting the basic process model of human action depicted in Figure 6.1. The neurobiological grounding of a model of action would identify interconnected systems of brain structures and processes that mediate the production of meaning and experience in action. Neuroscience has evolved well beyond the point attempting to localize complex psychological processes within single brain areas (Cacioppo, Visser, & Picket, 2006). According to Panskepp (1998), "There are no unambiguous 'centers' or loci for discrete emotion in the brain that do not massively interdigitate with other functions, even though certain key circuits are essential for certain emotions to be elaborated" (p. 147). Similarly, particular brain areas have multiple functions. For example, many areas that mediate particular modes of cognitive processes have also been implicated in emotional and motor functioning (Cozolino, 2006; Davidson, 2000; Phelps, 2005). As such, the biological substrata that mediate psychological activity are best understood as products of the activation of neural systems that are distributed throughout the brain (Thompson, 2007).

A first step to elaborating a model of the social brain can be informed by MacLean's (1990) conception of the *triune brain.* MacLean (1990) represents the anatomy of the brain in terms of three phylogenetic layers that have their origins different phases of evolution. These systems include the reptilian (i.e., inner core), paleomammalian (i.e., limbic system), and neomammalian (i.e., cortex) brain systems. These systems are sometimes loosely understood as three nested brains, each higher level brain wrapped around each lower level brain. The reptilian brain, the evolutionary oldest system shared by snakes and reptiles, consists of the inner core of the brain (e.g., thalamus and basal ganglia). The reptilian brain plays a role in regulating hunger, thirst, bodily homeostasis, fight/flight responses, and similar processes. The paleomammalian brain, shared by dogs, cats, and rats, corresponds to the structures of the "limbic system," a system of structures that are thought to play a leading role in mediating emotion. The neomammalian brain consists of the cortex, shared by primates and great apes, which is most developed in humans. The cortex mediates the higher order functions of planning, deliberation, complex thought, executive functioning, conscious inhibition of action, among others. The concept of the "triune brain" is almost certainly an oversimplification, but it is a helpful heuristic in understanding the gross functions of different brain areas. Although structures in the entire brain are relevant to production of emotion, the structures of the limbic system play a dominant role in mediating the production of emotion and motor behavior.

As indicated in Figure 6.1, executive functions and the production of higher order symbolic representations are largely mediated by activity in the frontal and prefrontal cortex of the brain (Cozolino, 2006). Pathways that mediated motive-relevant appraisal processes are nested throughout cortical and corticolimbic areas of the brain. In any given context, sensory information is filtered through the sensory thalamus. From this point, processing moves in two different directions (Berridge, 2003; LaBar & LeDoux, 2003).

A fast-acting pathway links directly to the amygdala, which is involved in assessing the emotional salience of motive-relevant events. A slower moving path directs processing toward the prefrontal cortex, which plays an important role in higher order meaning analysis and in mediating links between salient goals and possible actions. The fast-acting pathway is most important for immediate adaptive action. The amygdala plays an important role in assessing the emotional significance of events (e.g., the biological equivalent of "good for me/bad for me"). The amygdala has rich interconnections with the hippocampus, which plays a central role in the representation and consolidation of episodic memory structures. In emotion, the hippocampus appears to function to connect representations of particular environmental contexts with the emotional salience of those events. Once activated, the amygdala modulates the arousal and attention functions of the prefrontal cortex. In this way, the fast-acting emotional processing performed by the amygdala plays a role in directing attention toward the source of a stressful event. This process organizes and facilitates conscious processing of emotionally salient aspects of a person's environs (Cacioppo, Visser, & Picket, 2006; LaBar & LeDoux, 2003; Phelps, 2005).

At the same time, the amygdala activates the hypothalamus, which is involved in mediating a suite of affective and behavioral processes. The hypothalamus functions as the apex of the hypothalamus-pituitary-adrenal axis, which is instrumental in the release of stress hormones, including cortisol. During times of stress, the hypothalamus stimulates the pituitary gland (located below the hypothalamus) to secrete ACTH (adrenocorticotropic hormone). ACTH activates the adrenal cortex, which secretes stress hormones, including cortisol, which functions to increase blood pressure and glucose metabolism needed to support an individual's adaptive reaction to stress. Similarly, during stress, the hypothalamus also plays a role in activating the sympathetic nervous system. Furthermore, through connections that pass through the central gray, the amygdala activates particular classes of emotional motor behavior, including the fight-or-flight response (LaBar & LeDoux, 2003). Recent research, however, suggests limitations in the traditional characterization that fight-or-flight responses function as foundational fear responses. Research suggests that low levels of amygdala activation are associated with freezing behavior, whereas higher levels of activation are associated with the fight-or-flight response. Freezing under relatively lower levels of danger may allow the organism to more fully assess the situation to weigh different options for responding to the situation (Cozolino, 2006).

The picture that emerges from current affective and social neuroscience is one that depicts affective processes as broadly distributed throughout multiple levels of neural organization (Pessoa, 2008; Winkielman & Cacioppo, 2006). Lower level limbic and corticolimbic systems mediate fast-acting, nonconscious affective processing of motive-relevant events (LaBar & LeDoux, 2003). Cortical functions are implicated in more deliberate, higher order acts that involve executive control (Zelazo & Cunningham, 2007). In any given context, conscious awareness is organized by the nonconscious activation of affect-producing neural pathways (Mitchell & Phillips, 2007). Higher order executive functions, mediated by the frontal cortex, exert downward control over thought, feeling, and muscle action (Lewis, 2005). The interaction between cognition and affect is mediated by systems of massively interconnected corticolimbic pathways (Phelps, 2005; Winkielman & Cacioppo). With development, through such interconnected circuitry, emotional reactions come to be mediated by increasingly higher order meanings and event appraisals, whereas implicitly activated affective processes continue to organize higher order thought and action (Lewis & Todd, 2007). Thus, contemporary neuroscience supports the view that psychological structures are simultaneously affective and cognitive events. They arise through the dynamic coupling of cognitive and affective processes as they adjust to each other in contexts that have implications for the fate of one's motives.

DYNAMIC DEVELOPMENT OF INTEGRATIVE PSYCHOLOGICAL STRUCTURES

Psychological structures consist of dynamically integrated configurations of meaning, experience, and affect that operate within particular domains and social contexts (Fischer & Bidell, 2008; Mascolo, 2008). To speak of the development of psychological structures is not the same as speaking of the development of a person. There are no general or "all-purpose" psychological structures. Although they undergo massive development over the life span, psychological structures consist of localized skills that are tied to particular situational demands, psychological domains, and social contexts (Fischer, Bullock, Rotenberg, & Raya, 1993). Knowing that a 40-year-old can operate at high levels of functioning while leading a meeting at work does not allow one to predict that same person's level of performance when conducting an emotional family meeting at home. Developmental trajectories can be predicted reliably only within specific tasks, task domains, and contexts.

As defined in dynamic skill theory (Fischer, 1980; Fischer & Bidell, 2006; Mascolo & Fischer, 2005), within particular domains and contexts, psychological structures develop over the life span through 13 levels that begin shortly after birth and continue to undergo transformation until an individual reaches about 25 to 30 years of age. As indicated in Figure 6.2, the process of development occurs through a reiterative series of two nested growth cycles (Fischer, 2008). The first consists of a longer term growth cycle involving the progression of skills through a series of *broad-based* developmental *tiers*. A tier consists of a particular mode or quality of action or thought. There are five broad tiers of development: *reflexes* refer to preadapted action components (e.g., sucking on an object placed in the mouth); *sensorimotor actions* refer to smoothly controlled actions on objects (e.g., reaching for a bottle); *representations* consist of symbolic meanings about concrete aspects of objects (e.g., "Mommy likes candy."); *abstractions* consist of higher order representations about intangible and generalized aspects of objects and events (e.g., "Conservation refers to the concept that the quantity of something remains the same despite a change in its appearance."); and *abstract principles* are high-level, abstract conceptions that tie together multiple abstract systems. Abstract principles are rare in development, and occur in people with high levels of education, experience, and/or specialization in a given field.

The second shorter term growth cycle recurs within each longer term cycle. Within each of broad tier of development, skills develop through a series of four *levels*. These levels of individual skill development include *single sets, mappings, systems,* and *systems of systems*. Within the short-term growth cycle, higher levels within a tier arise as persons are able to coordinate one or more lower level skill components. Figure 6.3 describes the short-term growth cycle in terms of a series of mapping relations involved in forming a cube. Mappings involve the coordination of two or more single sets; they are represented in Figure 6.3 in terms of a single line connecting two points. Systems arise from the coordination of two or more mappings; they are represented in terms of the mapping of two lines onto each other to form a square. Finally, a system of systems emerges as two systems are mapped onto each other. This is represented in Figure 6.3 in terms of the mapping of two two-dimensional squares onto each other to form a three-dimensional cube. The coordination of two systems into a system of systems is the equivalent of the first level of a tier of skill development. This is indicated in Figure 6.3

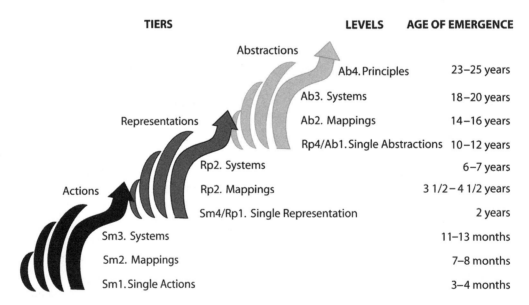

Figure 6.2   Developmental cycles of tiers and levels of skills. Development proceeds through 10 levels of skills grouped into 3 tiers between 3 months of age and adulthood. The ages of emergence are for optimal levels (the most complex skill a person can perform within a social context) and are based on research with middle-class American and European children. They may differ across social groups. There is some evidence for an additional tier of preadapted action components corresponding to the first few months of life (see Fischer, 1980; Fischer & Hogan, 1989).

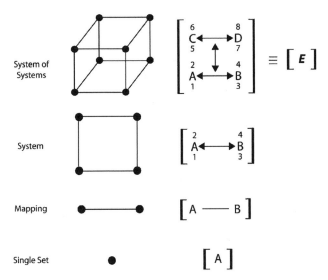

Figure 6.3 Levels of skill development within tiers. Within any given tier, skills develop through four levels. The first level consists of single sets, such as single sensorimotor acts, representations, or abstractions. Mappings emerge with the capacity to coordinate two single sets into a single seamless skill; an individual is able to map one single set onto another. A system arises with the capacity to intercoordinate to mapping level skills into a single organized structure. Finally, a system of systems is constructed through the intercoordination of two systems level structures. In skill theory, a system of systems at one tier is the equivalent of a single set of the next broad tier of development. For example, a system of representation systems arises through the intercoordination of at least two representational systems level skills and is the equivalent of a single abstraction—the first level of the next tier of development.

by the statement of equivalence between the skill structure representing a system of systems (Level 5) and the skill structure identifying the first level of the next broad tier in terms of a single higher order set (Level 5/1).

Within any given tier of development, a single set refers to a single organized reflex, action, representation, or abstraction. For example, within the representational tier, which begins to emerge around 18 to 24 months of age, a toddler can coordinate multiple systems of action into a single symbolic representation. At this level, a child can begin to make one thing stand for another. For example, in contexts that support the construction of such actions, a child can use a doll or a block to stand for a person in pretend play. Alternatively, she can begin to represent the meaning of words (sound sequences) that refer to absent objects. At its most basic level, a single representation corresponds to the meaning of a single, concrete, declarative sentence (e.g., "Mommy is mad," "Do it myself!" or "The milk spilled.").

Mappings refer to coordinations between two or more single sets. A mapping arises when an individual constructs a skill by putting together two lower level single sets. Within the representational tier, in contexts that support a child's attempts to do so, a 3½- to 4-year-old child can begin to map one single representation onto another single representation to form a *representational mapping.* Using a representational mapping, a child can represent the concrete relation between two basic ideas. The preschooler can represent relations between two or more ideas in terms of a variety of possible concrete relations, including cause/effect, part/whole, big/little, reciprocity, contiguity, temporality, and so forth. For example, a 4-year-old child can construct a representation of herself in terms of concrete social comparisons (e.g., "I can run into the water [beach] *just like* all the big girls do!"). At this level, a child can compare the height of two glasses of water and understand that the level in a tall beaker is *higher than* the level of a short beaker. Alternatively, he can understand that a coffee mug is *wider than* a water glass. Representational mappings are indicated as follows.

Systems arise when an individual is able to bring together two lower-level mappings into a single, seamless skill. A system thus consists of the mapping of at least two mappings. Within the representational tier of development, beginning around 6 to 7 years of age, with contextual support, a child is able to bring together at least two lower level skills at the level of representational mappings into a single integrated *representational system.* For example, in a traditional conservation task, a 4- or 5-year-old, using representational mappings, can compare the amount of water contained in a tall, thin glass with the amount of water poured from an identical glass into a short and wide glass. Using representational mappings, the younger child is able to compare relative height of the level of water contained in the two glasses (e.g., "the water in the tall glass is higher than the water in the short glass"). Alternatively, the child can compare the width of the two glasses (e.g., "the tall glass is thinner than the short glass"). However, it is not until the child is able to represent both of these mapping relations simultaneously that she can solve the traditional water conservation task. Thus, beginning around 6 to 7 years of age, with the capacity to construct representational systems, a child can coordinate these two lower level mapping relations to understand that when water is poured from a tall, thin glass to a short and wide one, *changes in height from tall to short are made up for by changes in width from narrow to wide.*

Using representational systems, a child is able to represent a variety of such concrete, systematic relations. For example, a child can construct an understanding that "Joey is better than I am in music, but I am better than Joey in soccer," or "Mom will be mad when she sees the note from my teacher, so I better put it under my mattress so that she can't find it," or "I like playing with Sarah because we can play with dolls, but it's also not fun because she can be so bossy."

Within any given tier of development, the final level produced within the short-term growth cycle consists of systems of systems. A *system of systems* arises through the process of coordinating two or more systems level skills into a single integrated skill. The production of a system of systems serves a dual function. Within a given tier of development, a system of systems constitutes the *final level of the short-term growth cycle;* simultaneously, a system of systems is the equivalent of the *first level of the next broad tier of development.* For example, in the representational tier of development, a *system of representational systems* is the equivalent of the *first level* of the next broad tier of development—abstractions. Beginning around 10 or 11 years of age, in contexts that support their construction, a preadolescent can begin to represent the relation between two concrete representational systems conceptions in terms of a single, intangible, generalized abstract concept. For example, using representational systems, children can construct skills for understanding conservation in a variety of different concrete domains—conservation of number, mass, volume, and so forth. However, constructing a *generalized* concept of conservation requires abstracting what is common or typical across concrete instances of conservation. Using *single abstractions,* under favorable conditions, a preteen can represent what is common to concrete examples of conservation of volume and conservation of mass in terms of an abstraction, such as "Conservation is the idea that the quantity of something remains the same despite a change in its appearance."

Such a conception represents the meaning of conservation in a general and intangible way, free of any specific concrete content. However, facility with the use of abstractions requires the capacity to apply abstract ideas to particular concrete content. Given the appropriate degree of experience and support, the capacity to construct single abstract sets provides the foundation for the development of different generalized concepts within different domains of psychological activity, whether they be conceptions related to morality (e.g., "justice," "mercy"), identity (e.g., "I want to be *popular*"), scientific concepts (e.g., *energy, variable*), or politics (e.g., *democracy, nation*).

Particular skills continue to develop through four levels as the short-term growth cycle reiterates through the abstract tier. Building on multiple single abstract sets, beginning around 14 to 15 years of age, given appropriate contextual support, teens begin to coordinate two single abstract sets into an *abstract mapping.* At the level of abstract mappings, individuals can represent the relations between at least two abstractions. For example, an American teenager can represent the relation between two different conceptions of self, such as "I'm relaxed with friends that I know well, but I'm nervous when I'm around the popular kids." Alternatively, a teen who is studying physics can construct a higher order understanding of the relation between *mass* and *energy.*

Abstractions and abstract mappings are not confined to the midteen years. In older individuals, abstract mapping can be used to organize conceptions of identity-related issues that accompany one's social position. For example, a 40-year-old can use an abstract mapping to represent relations between goals related to career and family.

Further, higher order abstractions and abstract mappings are not decontextualized modes of thought that are available only to the highly learned; abstract mappings have real-world consequences and are used by people in a variety of different domains of life. For example, an accomplished cook or chef understands abstract conceptions of how ingredients can be adjusted to make just the right type of muffins. The structure of the chef's thinking may be represented as follows:

Beginning at around 17 to 19 years of age, under conditions that support their development, young adults are able to coordinate two or more abstract mappings into an *abstract system.* At this level, an individual can represent relations between abstract relations. Abstract systems operate at a high-level functioning and signify advanced development within particular psychological domains. At this level, an individual can construct an abstract and integrated conception of the relation between two differentiated aspects of one abstract idea and two similarly differentiated aspects of a second abstract idea. For example, at the level of abstract systems, a 20-year-old college student can construct a sophisticated abstract plan to map out her desired career in law. To *become a lawyer in a prestigious firm,* the student plans to *specialize in college* so that she can attend a good law school. However, knowing that schooling alone is insufficient, the student plans to *delay starting a family* to devote herself full time to her ambitions, which involve *forming networks of connections* to people in the legal field. This abstract system can be represented as follows.

Abstract systems are highly developed psychological structures. They involve the systematic integration of multiple abstractions, each of which is founded on and incorporates a rich network of concrete meanings. As highly developed as these structures are, the highest level of psychological structures begins to emerge in adulthood beginning at around 23 to 24 years of age in the form of single abstract principles. *Single principles* arise in highly educated and/or experienced individuals with their capacity to coordinate two abstract systems level conceptions into a system of abstract systems. Single principles constitute the final broad tier of development and are the product of the final iteration of the short-term growth cycle that occurs in the abstract tier. We elaborate further on abstract principles later in the chapter.

Central Role of Context in the Construction of Psychological Structures

Psychological structures are the products of individual adaptation to particular social and environmental demands. As a result, psychological structures are not static properties of single individuals, but instead are *dynamic* products of persons-in-context. A change in situational demand,

psychological domain, or social context necessitates a change in the structure and content of skilled action. The act of running 100 yards as quickly as possible will depend on whether one is running on the beach, uphill at a high elevation, or on a rubberized track using spiked running shoes. Contexts differ in the extent to which they support an individual's attempt to produce skilled activity (Mascolo, 2005; Morrow & Rogers, 2008; Rosey et al., 2008). Contexts that involve *high support* provide assistance that supports an individual's actions (e.g., modeling desired behavior; providing cues, prompts, or questions that prompt key components to help structure children's actions). Contexts that involve *low support* provide no such assistance. Level of contextual support contributes directly to the level of performance a person is able to sustain in deploying a given skill. A person's *optimal level* refers to the highest level of performance one is capable of achieving, usually in contexts offering high support. A person's *functional level* consists of their everyday level of functioning in low support contexts. In general, a person's optimal level of performance under conditions of high support is several steps higher than his functional level in low support contexts (Fischer, Bullock, Rotenberg, & Raya, 1993; Fischer & Pipp, 1984). Figure 6.4 depicts developmental

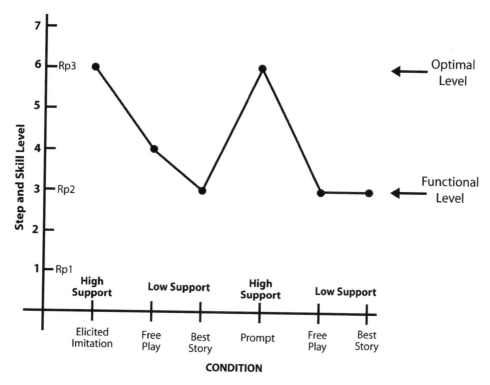

Figure 6.4 The developmental range. Variation in optimal and functional level of skill in a story-telling task as a function of social context.

variation in a child's story telling in a variety of high and low support conditions. In the context of elicited imitation, a child is asked to imitate a complex story modeled by an adult. In elicited imitation, the child's story functions at a level that is several steps higher than when he or she tells stories in free play, or is asked to tell his or her best story—both conditions of low support. Minutes later, when an adult prompts the child by stating the key components of the story, the child again functions at optimal level. Then after a few more minutes, low support conditions result in reduction of the child's performance to functional level again. These fluctuations in skill level occur in the same child on the same task across varying conditions of contextual support separated by mere minutes.

The importance of environmental support in organizing the structure of skilled activity is not limited to children. Environmental support increases the level of performance in skilled activity across the life span (Bialystok & Craik, Chapter 7 of this volume, Luo & Craik, 2008; Park & Shaw, 1993). More important, environmental support becomes increasingly important in structuring the production of everyday and skilled activity in older individuals (Sharps, Martin, Nunes, Neff, & Woo, 2004). A particularly compelling example comes from assessing the capacity of pilots to understand air traffic control communications over the course of adulthood (Morrow et al., 2003). Pilots in younger, middle-aged, and late adult years listened to air traffic communications describing the route of a plane through airspace. Level of environmental support was manipulated by either allowing or not allowing participants to take notes during the communication. The variable of interest was the capacity of the participants to repeat back the message. Without the benefit of notes, the capacity to repeat back air traffic control communications declined with advancing age. However, the decrement in performance was eliminated when pilots were allowed to take notes. We interpret these data as indicating that environmental support is not simply an adjunct to task performance; it is part of the process of skilled activity itself. Furthermore, these data suggest that during late adulthood, environmental support plays an increasingly important role in structuring meaningful skilled activity for many tasks.

Contexts that involve high and low support differ from contexts that involve *scaffolded* support (Gauvain, 2002; Mascolo, 2005; Wood, Bruner, & Ross, 1976). In contexts that involve high or low support, the individual alone is responsible for coordinating the components of a given skill. For example, an adult may model a complex story for a child who then produces the story without further assistance; a pilot repeats back the air traffic control message just provided to her. In contrast, in scaffolded contexts, a more accomplished other assists the person by performing part of the task or by otherwise structuring a person's actions during the course of skill deployment. Within scaffolded interactions, an individual is able to participate at levels that *surpass* her optimal level (Fischer, Yan, & Stewart, 2003; Mascolo, 2005). When a mentor assists a graduate student in composing a master's thesis, the student is able to produce a thesis at a higher level of quality than he could have accomplished without such assistance. Skill development occurs as individuals differentiate and coordinate higher order skills and meanings from their *participation* in joint activity with others (Mascolo, Pollack, & Fischer, 1997; Rogoff, 1993). By pulling a learner's performance beyond that which she can sustain alone, scaffolding awakens and directs the process of development.

The process of scaffolding occurs throughout the life span (Yan & Fischer, 2002, 2007). In adulthood, scaffolding occurs in contexts ranging from mentor–mentee relationships (Dennen, 2004), learning novel skills (Murray & McPherson, 2006), and novel learning in organizational contexts (Hoare, 2005; Kristensen, 2004), psychotherapy, and coaching (Basseches & Mascolo, 2010). Emotional scaffolding and support is an important aspect of the types of supportive social interactions that occur between caregivers and persons with dementia (Cavanaugh, Dunn, Mowery, & Feller, 1989; Rabins, 1998). As is well known, the primary deficits in individuals with Alzheimer's disease involve difficulties in memory and thought. Human factors researchers have shown that there are many ways to design the physical and social environments to support the memory functions of persons living with Alzheimer's disease (Charness & Holley, 2001; Cohen & Day, 1993). These include populating a person's environs with redundant cuing, such as familiar objects, photographs, or even auditory and olfactory cues such as familiar music or cooking smells. Schafer (1985) suggested that caregivers adopt the strategy of adapting the physical and social environment to the familiar behaviors of the Alzheimer's patient rather than attempt to foster novel skills, especially at later phases of the disease (Charness & Holley).

Emergent Webs of Development

Traditional models of development generally conceptualize development in terms of a series of homogeneous stages, whether those stages are taken to reflect different levels of cognition (Piaget, 1983), identity formation (Erikson,

1963), or personality (Freud, 1917/1965). Although there are a variety of important transitions and milestones in ontogenesis (e.g., primary and secondary intersubjectivity in infancy, social referencing, the semiotic function, puberty), decades of research suggest that development is not characterized by changes in singular, broad-based, homogeneous competencies. Instead, within particular social contexts, psychological structures develop within particular psychological domains (Fischer & Bidell, 2006; Mascolo, 2008; Turiel, 1989, and Chapter 16 of this volume). For example, Piaget designed a series of logical tasks (e.g., conservation, seriation, transitivity, class inclusion) to reflect the onset of concrete operational thinking—the capacity to manipulate representations in a logically consistent and systematic way. Although all such tasks were thought to reflect a single broad system of psychological competence, there are dramatic differences in the ages at which individual children are able to succeed at these different tasks (Gelman & Baillargeon, 1983). Children can solve some conservation tasks years before they are able to solve class inclusion tasks. There is even variability in the age at which children perform different versions of the conservation task (e.g., number, mass, or volume).

Table 6.1 depicts trajectories in the development of skills in three basic domains: mathematical skills, narrative understanding, and artistic skill. The trajectories depicted in Table 6.1 illustrate the principle of systematic development within domains: Although skills develop through the same abstract sequence of structural transformations across different conceptual domains, skills in different conceptual domains develop along their own trajectories. Even if one controls for social context, is not possible to predict the level of skill development that a person will exhibit in one target domain from knowing a person's level of performance on any single task or set of tasks in another target domain. The age of emergence of skills at similar levels of structural complexity show only weak correlations between conceptual domains. Such findings underscore the idea that "what develops" in psychological development is not the "person-as-a whole," but instead increasingly integrated local skills within particular contexts and domains.

Much research conducted in the latter part of the 20th century tended to treat psychological domains as if they were rigidly bounded areas of activity. Developmental psychologists have been able to track stable developmental orderings within the areas of moral understanding (Kohlberg, 1981), understanding of social conventions (Turiel, 1989, and Chapter 16 of this volume), social perspective taking (Selman, 1980), mathematical thinking (Saxe, 1982), and

so forth. However, just as meaning-mediated actions are dynamic rather than fixed, *so are the psychological domains and contexts with which psychological structures operate* (Ayoub & Fischer, 2006; Mascolo, 2008b). The trajectories depicted in Table 6.1 identify transformations in skills within rather bounded domains of psychological activity. Although many contexts call for skills within such encapsulated domains (e.g., academic study), the domains and contexts in which we operate in everyday life are not so neatly structured. Over the course of a day, the skills that we use to meet the demands of any given context require the integration of meaning, knowledge, and feeling from a wide variety of diverse areas. The domains and social contexts in which we function are not static structures existing in a predefined reality. Instead, they reflect *emergent systems of meaning and practice that arise within particular social and cultural contexts, motivated by social and economic need, and—especially in current times—mediated by increasingly novel technologies.*

For example, consider the task of teaching a course in psychology. What set of tasks, meanings, skills, and skill domains do we use when we teach such a course? The most obvious consists of the knowledge and skills that constitute the specific discipline or psychological area that we are teaching. On a superficial level, it might seem that *teaching psychology* constitutes a clear and distinct domain of activity. However, the act of teaching requires the coordination of skills in a myriad of domains that extend beyond the formal discipline of psychology. It requires the capacity to speak to a particular audience of students, to assess their level of engagement, to design and assess the outcomes of various teaching and learning activities, to provide feedback on papers and in discussion, to calculate grades, to manage disputes and emergent problems, to fight with the Dean for resources, and so forth. There are few pure domains of action. Any particular pedagogic act involves the coordination of skills and meanings from multiple partially overlapping spheres of activity.

Coordinating across these different spheres of activity, over time, one might feel that one has identified a stable, if emergent, skill set to define the domain of "teaching psychology." However, at the time of this writing, many skills used to teach psychology a mere 10 years ago would appear to require dramatic revision (Espiritu, 2007). The age of the Internet has ushered in novel technologies that both support innovation and produce new challenges (Davis & Fill, 2007). Online and hybrid courses have proliferated (Hahs-Vaughn, Zygouris-Coe, & Fiedler, 2007; Quilter & Weber, 2004). The skills that one requires to teach an effective

Table 6.1   Developmental Transformations in Hierarchical Complexity in Three Domains

Number	Narrative	Drawing (Arts)
Abstract Principles (25 years +) **Manipulations of Higher-Order Mathematical Structures and Objects.** Relations among abstract structures of mathematical operations (e.g., detecting structural isomorphisms between groups of mathematical operations in disparate areas).	**Principled Integration of Literary Forms and Genres.** Principled articulation and integration of relations among multiple literary genres, methods, styles, etc. into a stable and consolidated style or narrative system that organizes a given narrative.	**Principled Consolidation of Style.** Visual expression organized in terms of systematic principles that organize multiple dimensions of visual, expressive, methodological, conventional forms, and content.
Abstract Systems (18–21 years +) **Higher-Order Mathematical Relations.** Capacity to manipulate abstract relations involving change over time (e.g., calculus as an integration of algebra, geometry, and arithmetic); capacity to solve two simultaneous abstract relations; abstract algebraic proofs.	**Narratives Structured by Integrative Relations.** Complex or interweaving narratives organized by relations among multiple qualities of characters and events; integrative use of higher-order literary devices (e.g., anachrony, embedded narrative, higher-order tropes).	**Higher-Order Visual-Conceptual Integrations.** Manipulation of multiple visual, conventional, and/or methodological means to represent intangible, emotional, or abstract content. Modification of convention to express abstract, emotional, and other visual content.
Abstract Mappings (14–15 years+) **Transformation of Algebraic Relationships.** Capacity to coordinate the relation between two abstract variables (e.g., $f = m * a;\ a^2 + b^2 = c^2$)	**Dialectic Relations among Stable Characters.** Complex narratives involving characters with inner states and continuity over time. Conflicts derive from relations among characters or events.	**Visual-Conceptual Integration.** Intentional use of variation in form, content, or technique in the service of conceptual goal (use of distortion, color variations to represent emotional themes); abstract themes.
Single Abstractions (10–11 years) **Simple Algebraic Representations.** Incipient representation of single abstract variables representing quantity (e.g., $2x = 4$)	**Conflict-Driven Multi-Lined Narrative.** Complex stories involving characters with mental states, motives, organized plots, and subplots driven by conflicts and attempts to resolve conflicts.	**Three Dimensional Scenes.** Draws scenes with fore-, middle-, and background in continuous space; realistic details; use of visual metaphor (drawing a teacher as a "witch").
Representational Systems (6–7 years) **Mental Number Line.** Understanding relations between numbers on a "mental" number line; capacity for addition and subtraction. By 8–9 years, multiplication and division.	**Intentional Story Lines.** Temporal-causal plot lines involving characters with mental states and motives (e.g., "We went to the zoo, but then I got hungry so we took the train to go buy some yummy hot dogs…"	**Mental Reference Line.** Child can draw identifiable persons and objects placed within a particular location or scene (e.g., person and a house; flower under the sun), often with lines indicating ground or sky.
Representational Mappings (3½ to 4 years) **Mental Counting Line.** Representation of relations between numbers; comparison of more vs. less.	**Causal-Temporal Action Sequences.** Child relates multiple actions/events in time or cause-effect relation (e.g., "We went to the zoo and then we got a hot dog").	**Identifiable Objects and Figures.** Able to draw barely articulated figure or object (e.g., person), often hovering over bottom of page.
Single Representations (18–24 months) **Counting Actions.** Begins to count objects, slowly developing one-to-one correspondence, sequencing, and idea that last number counted represents total items.	**Global Descriptions and Shift of Focus.** Simple descriptions of individual events (e.g., "We went to the zoo") without links to other elements. Adults move narrative forward (shift focus) using questions.	**Scribbles and Post-Hoc Labeling.** Scribbling and primate figures; child labels figure after rather than before completion.

online course are dramatically different from those that undergird face-to-face classes (Palloff & Pratt, 1999). Some learning goals are facilitated in an online format; others are made more difficult (Tutty & Klein, 2008). Viewed in this way, the seemingly stable domain of teaching psychology becomes exposed as a dynamic and emergent one. In this way, skill domains are dynamic and emergent processes that mutually constitute each other over time.

Traditional accounts have portrayed development in terms of a linear series of steps (Erikson, 1963; Freud, 1917/1965; Piaget, 1983) much like a ladder or staircase. However, in light of all of the above, rather than viewing development as if it were a ladder, staircase, or set of distinct silos, it is more helpful to view development in terms of an *emergent developmental web* (Fischer & Bidell, 2006; Fischer et al., 2003). Figure 6.5 depicts a model of the developmental web. The developmental web represents development in terms of a series of partially distinct pathways that, depending on developmental circumstances, move in different diverging or converging directions. Higher-order psychological structures emerge from the integration or coordination of lower-level structures that develop along partially distinct trajectories. The splitting and converging of developmental trajectories is not something that can be specified or predicted *a priori*. As described earlier, skill theory provides a universal yardstick for gauging the developmental trajectories of particular skills. However, the specific skill structures, pathways, and timing that emerge in ontogenesis cannot be predicted beforehand (Fogel, & Lyra, & Valsiner, 1997). Development takes different paths depending on local developmental conditions (Gottlieb & Lickliter, 2007; Thelen & Smith, 2006). In this way, development emerges as a process of "laying down a path in walking" (Thompson, 2007, p. 166).

The developmental web differs from a developmental ladder in at least six fundamental ways (Fischer et al., 2003):

1. The web highlights *local variation of activity within global order;* the developmental ladder tends to marginalize variation by regarding it as an indication of error or individual differences.

2. The web can be used to represent developmental order and variability of *individuals or groups* because it

represents a series of steps along a universal dimension; the ladder tends to focus attention of the performance of groups.

3. Use of the web presumes that an individual can function at multiple levels at any given point in time; the ladder metaphor assumes that a skill operates on only a single step or rung at any given time.

4. The web distinctions multiple tasks, domains, social contexts, and their relation; the ladder represents tasks and domains along a single unidirectional dimension.

5. The developmental web is defined in terms of a complex network of connections among developmental strands and trajectories; the ladder has no provisions for representing interconnections among diverse developmental strands.

6. The web represents the multidirectional nature of development, including forward progression and backward transitions; the ladder metaphor assumes a single unidirectional progression in developmental levels over time.

The developmental web can be used to represent development in different ways. The strands that compose the web can reflect the development of different domains of psychological structures *within individuals;* alternatively, the trajectories can represent alternative pathways taken by different *individuals* or *groups* of individuals. Within the developmental web, an individual cannot be said to operate at a single level of development, even for particular skills. As indicated throughout, the developmental level of a persons' skills vary both as a function of domain and of social context. Across domains, a pilot may function at very high levels in the domain of receiving and using air traffic control communications or performing mathematical calculations. However, it is possible that this same pilot may function at dramatically lower levels of development in the domain of taking care of an infant child, tending bar, or fixing a lawn mower. Equally important, within individuals, a person's skill level varies as a function of social context. As indicated in Figure 6.4, the level of performance that a child is able to achieve when telling a story varies according to whether the child is operating in the context of low, high, or scaffolded support. In light of such data, it is not appropriate to say that an individual functions at a single developmental level—*even for a particular skill.* Instead, it is more appropriate to say that an individual's skills function at a *range of levels* depending on context, domain, time of day, emotional state, and other variables.

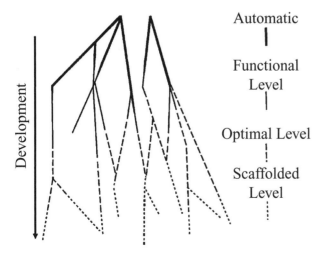

Figure 6.5   The developmental web.

The *developmental range* is illustrated in Figure 6.5. As indicated, along any given strand of development, there are four basic regions corresponding to different levels of stability in the construction and consolidation of any given skill. Automatized skills have been over-learned in such a way that their deployment requires little or no conscious attention, effort, conscious control, or processing resources (Hassin, Uleman, & Bargh, 2005). They are represented in terms of the bold lines depicted lower-level processes along any given strand of the developmental web. For example, many of the tasks involved in driving a car are automatized in such a way that it is not only possible to perform a variety of tasks while driving, drivers often cover long stretches of road without having been consciously aware of their driving actions (Mascolo et al., 1999). In some cases, automatized skills are deployed involuntarily in such a way that once begun, they cannot be inhibited. Reading is an example of such an automated task. The profound robustness of the Stroop color word task attests to the involuntary nature of the fast-acting process of reading color names over the slower process of naming the colors in which color names are printed (Brown, Joneleit, Robinson, & Brown, 2002). Skills that operate at a person's functional, optimal, and scaffolded levels are indicated in Figure 6.5 in terms of nonbolded, heavily dotted lines, and lightly dotted lines, respectively.

To illustrate, imagine the process of learning to drive an automobile with a manual transmission. When a novice teenager or adult embarks upon the process of learning to drive, she brings with her a series of highly automatized skills that can be deployed without effort and often without awareness. These tend to include overlearned sensorimotor skills such as turning a wheel, depressing a pedal, or pushing a stick shift. After several weeks of instruction, the novice's functional level might include the capacity to drive around a large, empty parking lot. The novice's functional level—the level of skill in the absence of contextual support—would include a series of representational and motor skills, including the capacity to shift gears, maneuver the clutch, and depress the accelerator at the same time; to steer the car to make broad, slow, and perhaps jerky turns around corners. This same individual would be able to function at a higher level in the context of high levels of contextual support. For example, if, before starting her practice, her instructor reminded her to "stop at the stop sign between Parking Lot A and B," the student would be more likely to avoid her habitual error of failing to attend to the stop sign. Finally, this same student would be able to function at a still higher level in the context of scaffolded support. For example, the instructor may offer continuous verbal feedback to scaffold the novice's attempt to perform a three-point turn. Over time, as the driver achieves more coordination, the instructor would gradually relax the scaffolding provided. Conditions of high support, coconstruction with others, and scaffolding are at least as important in the construction and consolidation of novel skills in adults as they are in children.

The developmental web can also be used to represent individual differences in trajectories of development between different groups. Drawing on a large literature on temperament–caregiver interaction, Mascolo and Fischer (2007) described six pathways in the development of emotion-based personality dispositions in adolescence and adulthood. These paths are depicted in Figure 6.6. Each pathway is defined with reference to relations between a child's temperamental dispositions and social experience over time. *Normative* pathways (a, b, and c) result in the capacity for self-regulation and competent social relations. Children who exhibit generalized positive affect and the capacity for high levels of effortful control (Eisenberg, Hofer, Vaughan, 2007; Rothbart, 2007), and who are cared for by sensitive and authoritative parents, are more likely to develop through the Positive-Normative pathway (a). The Negative-Normative path (b) involves children with dispositions toward negative affect (i.e., irritability, frustration), but with a high capacity for attentional focus. Despite their affective dispositions, given their capacity for self-regulation, they can learn to regulate their emotion when given consistently firm but nonhostile parental discipline. The Inhibited/Normative path (c) occurs in children who exhibit "fearful" (Kochanska, Forman, Aksan, & Dunbar, 2005) or "inhibited" (Kagan & Snidman, 2004) emotional biases. Because such children are disposed to attend to parental prohibitions, gentle discipline is often sufficient to promote rule induction.

The model also specifies three non-normative developmental pathways. Children who are temperamentally disposed to *negative affect* and *poor self-regulation* are at risk for developing externalizing and antisocial behavior in adolescence and adulthood (Eisenberg et al., 2007; Loeber & Stouthamer-Loeber, 1998; Tremblay, 2000) or behavior reflecting a *shame-anger dynamic* (Ferguson, Eyre, & Ashbaker, 2000; Scheff & Retzinger, 1991). Given their relative inability to regulate aggression, such children are more likely to engender harsh or extreme discipline, thus

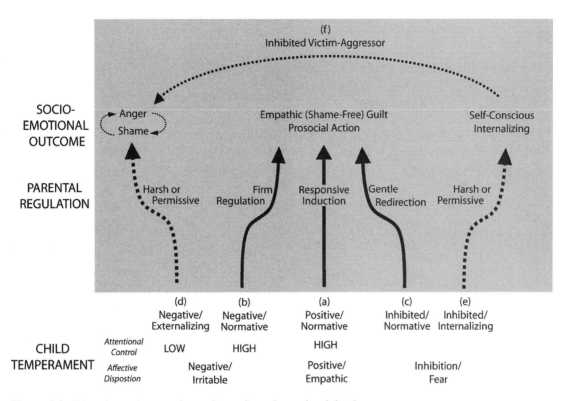

Figure 6.6 Diverging and converging pathways in socioemotional development.

promoting both shameful affect and angry aggression. Children who are disposed temperamentally toward "fearful/inhibited" affect and who are the recipients of harsh or affectively insensitive discipline are disposed to develop tendencies toward internalizing emotion-regulation strategies and self-conscious social interaction (Pathway e, Inhibited-Internalizing). Recent research also shows that, in some circumstances (e.g., when children are humiliated or raised in violent homes), temperamentally inhibited children may also develop toward the externalizing pathway and become highly aggressive (Pathway f, Victim-Aggressor; Watson, Fischer, & Andreas, 2004; Smith, 2004).

Dynamics of Developmental Trajectories

Psychological structures are capable of undergoing developmental change throughout the entire life span. However, psychological skills show different trajectories over time depending on the nature of the skill and the circumstances under which those skills emerge and are assessed. Research from a variety of sources converges to indicate that, within particular domains and contexts, developmental changes in

an individual's functional and optimal levels of skill show different growth curves over time. Within any given domain of functioning, a person's functional level consists of the level of performance that one spontaneously exhibits in everyday tasks without the benefit of high support or scaffolding. Optimal-level performance occurs in the context of high contextual support (e.g., well-defined and familiar tasks, practice, priming of memory for task components) and occurs far less frequently than functional level performance. Within a given domain of activity, a person's spontaneous, everyday functional level performance is generally several levels lower than his optimal-level performance. Figure 6.7 shows a characteristic growth curve tracking changes in optimal and functional developmental level from preadolescence through early adulthood. As indicated in Figure 6.7, over time, functional level performance tends to be characterized by slow, gradual, and continuous growth, whereas optimal levels exhibit stagelike spurts and plateaus. Over time, growth curves for functional and optimal-level performance diverge with age (Fischer, Kenny, & Pipp, 1990; Kitchener, King, & DeLuca, 2006).

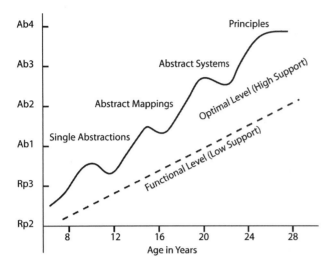

Figure 6.7 Development of optimal and functional levels of skill over the life span.

Role of Brain Development in the Emergence of Optimal-Level Performance

This divergence arises because changes in functional and optimal-level performance depend on different growth processes and developmental conditions. What is the source of the developmental spurts and plateaus that characterize growth curves in tracking optimal-level performance within particular domains of activity? The emergence of optimal-level performance is supported by three basic sets of processes: (1) biological changes, including measurable discontinuities in brain growth, synaptic density, head size, and shifts in activity in different brain regions; (2) the activity of the individual actor, who, in the creation of any given psychological structure, must actively and effortfully perform acts of coordination that "put together" components of any emerging skill to meet task demands; and (3) high levels of contextual support, as indicated earlier. A series of findings supports the proposition that developmental changes in the brain play a central role in supporting the emergence of new levels of optimal-level performance within particular domains of activity. Evidence for this assertion comes in the form of similarities between trajectories of brain growth and development and growth curves tracking the emergence of optimal-level psychological skills. Research on the development of cortical (electroencephalogram [EEG]) activity, synaptic density, and head growth provides evidence for discontinuities in brain growth for at least 9 of the 10 levels of skill development listed in Figure 6.2. Little research exists to test hypothesized brain–behavior relations for the 10th level.

In infancy, discontinuities in EEG power arise at approximately 3 to 4, 6 to 8, 11 to 13 months, and 2 years (Hagne, Persson, Magnusson, & Petersén, 1973). For example, in a study of relative power for occipital EEG in Japanese infants, Mizuno et al. (1970) found spurts at approximately 4, 8, and 12 months. These ages are similar to those found for psychological development in infancy. Bell and Fox (1992) assessed the relations between growth functions for EEG activity and the development of object search, vocal imitation, and crawling skills in infancy. They found that, for many individual infants between 8 and 12 months of age, connections between specific cortical regions involving planning, vision, and control of movement exhibited a surge while the infants were mastering crawling. The surge disappeared after they had become skilled crawlers. During childhood and adolescence, clusters of discontinuities arise at approximately 2, 4, 7, 11, 15, and 20 years (Somsen, van't Klooster, van der Molen, van Leeuwen, & Licht, 1997; Thatcher, 1994). A classic Swedish study assessing changes in relative EEG power with age produced evidence of spurts at approximately 2, 4, 8, 12, 15, and 19 years (Hudspeth & Pribram, 1992; Matousek & Petersén, 1973).

Additional converging evidence comes from studies on the development of EEG coherence (Thatcher, 1994). EEG coherence is a measure of the correlation between wave patterns from different cortical regions. High EEG coherence indicates that two regions have similar EEG wave patterns. Similarity in EEG wave patterns suggests that the cortical regions in question are interconnected and communicating with each other. In his study of the development of EEG coherence, Thatcher described evidence documenting discontinuities in EEG coherence at age regions associated with transformations in optimal-level skill performance. With development, coherence for any pair of EEG sites typically oscillates up and down. These oscillations show growth cycles that move through cortical regions in a regular pattern. The oscillations demonstrate discontinuities that relate to shifts in levels of psychological skills. That is, shifts in optimal level of psychological skill occur around the time that oscillation patterns show abrupt shift to a different period. These occur at approximately 4, 6, and 10 years. These patterns of brain growth suggest correspondence between phases of brain growth and transformations in optimal-level psychological performance.

Still further, the cycles of coherence that Thatcher (1994) reported suggest not only a series of discontinuities in brain growth and development, but also a growth cycle indicating different patterns of connectivity among cortical regions for each level (Fischer & Bidell, 2006; Fischer & Rose, 1994). Surges and drops in connectivity are measured by change in EEG coherence cycle through brain regions in systematic and repetitive patterns. The growth cycle moves in a systematic pattern around the cortex, showing a full cycle of interconnectivity for each level of psychological skill. The connections typically begin in the frontal cortex and involve long-distance connections between frontal and occipital regions for both hemispheres. The growth cycle then moves systematically around the cortex, extending through the right hemisphere and then through the left. For the right hemisphere, growth patterns first establish global, long-distance connections and then contract to establish more local ones. In contrast, in the left hemisphere, growth begins by establishing more local connections before it moves toward the consolidation of more distant ones. Growth moves systematically through different cortical areas until it consolidates networks throughout the cortex.

Within the representational and abstract tiers of development, transformation from one level of skill to another (e.g., from single sets to mappings) seems to be supported by the production of new systems of neural networks that link different brain regions. Matousek and Petersén (1973) examined changes in EEG activity for each of four cortical brain regions (viz., frontal, occipital/parietal, temporal, and central) in children and adolescents. Their results suggested that, for the representational (2–10 years of age) and abstract tiers (10–20 years), transitions to different levels within a developmental tier are marked by cyclic changes in brain activity in different cortical regions. Within this cycle, a new tier emerges with a maximal spurt in the *frontal cortex;* the first level is marked by a maximal spurt in the *occipitoparietal region;* one in the *temporal region* marks the second level; and one in the *central region* marks the third. Another maximal surge in the *frontal region* marks the onset of the next broad tier of development. These changes illustrate the systematic relations between movement through skill levels and cyclic changes in brain activity.

Meaning of Development over the Life Span

Under high support conditions, adults begin to gain the capacity to construct skills at the level of single abstract principles—the highest level of skill functioning—beginning around 23 to 25 years of age. Does this mean that optimal-level development ceases at age 25? That no meaningful developmental changes occur after age 25? When does development stop and decline begin? Although these questions appear on the surface to be reasonable ones, they have meaning only under the presupposition of certain conceptions of development—for example, that development consists of an age-related sequence of broad stages of psychological functioning. If this were so, it might make sense to say that individuals enter a final period of development at a particular point in time. However, as argued throughout this chapter, development is dynamic and does not proceed in a linear fashion. Many types of changes occur over the life span. Not all of these changes can be properly regarded as *developmental* changes. For example, the mere fact that some events (e.g., the onset of Alzheimer disease) occur at later periods of life does not mean that the transition to those events mark periods of *development.* It is necessary to differentiate the concept of *development* from a series of related and overlapping concepts, such as *change, growth, age-related change, history,* and the *life course* to understand the nature of development over the course of the life span. Having done so, it will become possible to identify how developmental change occurs within the context of various other types of changes that occur over the life span.

The concept of development is used in different ways by different theorists. To say that a structure or process is undergoing development certainly implies that it is undergoing some sort of *change.* However, the mere fact that something is changing does not imply that it is undergoing development (Overton, 2006). *Change* simply implies reference to any type of alteration over time; for example, one can alter the position of one's hand in space, ice can melt into water, and hair grows over time. Although each of these events reflects a type of change, none is an example of development. Having longer hair, for example, does not mark a developed state compared with having shorter hair. Thus, although *development* involves change, it cannot be reduced to change alone. Similarly, in psychology, the concept of development is sometimes used to refer to *age-related changes.* From this view, developmental changes consist of transitions in psychological functioning that arise systematically at different ages across the life span. From this view, the task of the life-span psychologist is to track transitions in psychological processes from one period to the next. The main problem with this conception of development, of course, is that not all ordered or age-related changes can be regarded as developmental changes. Researchers who study late adult development routinely report examples of the *decline* in psychological capacities with advancing age. Although such declines may be *age related,* the mere use of the term *decline* suggests a movement *away* from some high point of psychological functioning, however defined.

The concept of development differs from the concepts of change and age-related change in its implication of *progression.* To say that a psychological process is undergoing development implies change toward a *higher level of functioning,* however defined. In this way, developmental changes must be judged, either implicitly or explicitly, with reference to some conception of the *optimal outcome, end point,* or *form* of the psychological process in question. Furthermore, to say that in development involves movement to a higher *level* of functioning implies some type of change in the structure or hierarchical organization of the developing function. Thus, to say that the capacity to construct narratives undergoes development requires some conception, however tacit, of what would constitute fully developed acts of narrative construction. It is this latter point that differentiates the concept of development from the concept of *growth.* At base, the concept of growth implies a difference in quantity or amount; to say that a flower, a coral reef, or a salary grows is to speak of an increase in quantity. Thus, yet again, although developmental process often involves growth, development implies more than growth. Development implies some type change in the *structure* of the entity as it moves in directions defined by some conception of the optimal outcome(s) or form(s) of the entity in question.

The 10 levels of skill depicted in Figure 6.2 provide a yardstick for tracking *developmental* change defined in terms of *structural transformation* in patterns of thinking, feeling, and acting within particular domains and context. From this view, to speak of the development of psychological skills is to speak of transformations in the *structure* of action from less differentiated lower level actions to increasingly differentiated and hierarchically integrated *forms* of acting, thinking, and feeling. In this sense, the developmental progression postulated by dynamic skill theory reflects a more precise articulation of Werner & Kaplan, (1962/1984) *orthogenetic principle of development.* The orthogenetic principle states that when development occurs, it moves from more global and undifferentiated states to increasingly differentiated, integrated, and hierarchically integrated states. The levels and tiers specified by skill theory reflect increasingly levels of differentiation and hierarchical integration of skill components.

When addressing the issue of the nature of psychological change over the life span, it is important to differentiate the overlapping concepts of development, on the one hand,

and history and the life course, on the other. An analysis of an individual's *life history* often proceeds a *causal-temporal accounting* (narrative) of the sequence of events that make up an individual's life. A satisfying account of a person's life course provides an explanation of how a person's life, character, or psychological attributes came to be the way that they are or were. The narrative accounting of lives overlaps considerably with developmental analyses (Elder & Shanahan, 2006; Roy & McAdams, 2006); both are concerned with identifying the processes and pathways through which psychological processes and outcomes take shape over time. However, identifying the pathways through which psychological events move is not the same as tracking *developmental changes* in those events. A narrative accounting of such a person's life course can illuminate the processes and pathways through which an individual experiences shifts in jobs, careers, relationships, attachments, beliefs, health, and other conditions en route to, say, a state of contented retirement. However, such analyses are silent when it comes to the question of *developmental level.* Over any given period, the developmental level of a person's psychological structures and processes in particular contexts and domains may rise, fall, remain the same, or show any number of movements toward or away from any given developmental outcome. Thus, although historical and narrative analyses document *what happens over time,* developmental analyses document how psychological structures and processes *undergo transformation in the direction of higher order structures.* The distinction between *what happens over time* and *movement toward a higher level* is revealed in the use of terms to refer to the developmental status of events as they change over time. It is only with reference to some conception of a developmental end point that we can properly speak of *progression or advance, regression or decline, backward transitions, deviations, lateral change,* and so forth (Fischer & Granott, 1995; Mascolo, Li, Finke, & Fischer, 2002). Thus, although developmental changes take place within historical time, historical changes are not necessarily developmental changes.

The distinction between change-over-time (historical changes) and developmental changes can be illuminated through an analysis of microdevelopment of skilled action over time (see Siegler, 2006; Yan & Fischer, 2007). Granott (1993, 2002) reported the results of a study in which groups of adults worked together to perform a task of joint problem solving. Adults observed the behavior of a Lego robot, called a "wuggle," which was programmed to respond to changes in light, shadow, sound, and touch. Their task was to figure out and explain how and why the wuggle operated. In analyzing videotaped interactions among pairs of participants, Granott (1993) classified the complexity of each partner's actions and explanations of the wuggle's movements. An analysis of changes in the skill complexity of one dyad (Ann and Donald) is provided in Figure 6.8. Over the course of 27 minutes and 148 interchanges, Ann and Donald worked together to explain how the wuggle operated. Although both Ann and Donald were intelligent adults capable of functioning with high levels of skill, as they began to collaborate, the complexity of their actions fell to levels that were comparable with actions at the *sensorimotor tier* of development. The dyad's actions were characterized by particular *descriptions* (representations) of particular *observations of the concrete movements* (akin to sensorimotor actions) of the wuggle. Given their hybrid nature, Granott referred to these sensorimotor-like skills as *actions*. A *single action* (Sm1) might include a description of the act of *seeing the wuggle move* or *hearing a sound* made by the wuggle. An *action mapping* (Sm2) might include noticing that *hearing a loud sound* goes with *seeing the wuggle change movement*. *Action systems* (Sm3) involved combinations of several movements or sounds into a single observation. Finally, *single representations* (Sm4/Rp1) result from coordinating several action systems. Abstracting across observations of how the wuggle moved in response sound, the dyad constructed a representation that "The wuggle reacts to sound."

A series of important findings resulted from Granott's (1993) study. First, as indicated earlier, even though Ann and Donald were capable of operating at extremely high levels of abstract functioning, when they began to work on the novel problem of figuring out how the unfamiliar Lego robot operated, the dyad's level of functioning fell to very low levels. Granott referred to such shifts to lower levels of functioning as *backward transitions*. Backward transitions or regressions seem to arise when people are trying to construct novel skills in unfamiliar domains, when they attempt to simplify a task by breaking it down into parts, or when it is otherwise possible to construct some parts of a larger task before moving on to construct other such parts. In an extremely novel domain of action (like Ann and Donald's), an individual's level of performance can fall to very low levels—even to sensorimotor actions. Constructing skills for a new and unfamiliar task required the dyad to "begin at the beginning." As indicated in Figure 6.8, over the course of the first 60 interchanges, the dyad moved gradually through the action tier and into the representational tier.

At interchange 65, however, the dyad experienced an unexpected event. A wire fell out of the wuggle. In their attempt to repair the wuggle, the dyad placed the wire in the wrong hole. As a result, the wuggle began to behave differently. As the dyad resumed their joint problem solving, their novel and still unstable skills for representing the movement of the wuggle failed. The dyad experienced a

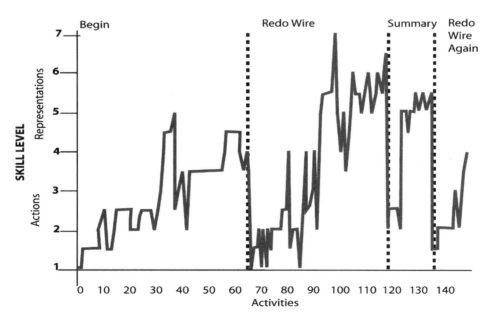

Figure 6.8 The microdevelopment of joint representations: Ann and Donald.

second backward transition; the level of their explanations returned again to the first level of the action tier of development. The dyad had to "start over again" and make new observations of the wuggle's novel behavior. Over the next several minutes, the dyad rebuilt their understanding of the wuggle's behavior, moving through the action and representational tiers, and finally onto construct abstract tier of development. The dyad experienced additional backward transitions as they continued to be asked to perform novel tasks related to the wuggle's behavior.

The changes in skill complexity depicted in Figure 6.8 show the importance of differentiating historical *changes in what occurs over time* from *developmental progressions*. As indicated in Figure 6.8, historically, the level of complexity of Ann and Donald's skilled performance fluctuated over time. The growth curve is nonlinear and characterized by both increases and decreases in complexity, developmental progressions, and backward transitions. Some of the backward transitions occurred as the dyad moved from one aspect of the task to another; others occurred as the dyad focused on a single task component (e.g., representing the wuggle before and then after the changing of the wire). The upward and downward fluctuations are not simply random; instead, they function in the service of the dyad's attempt to construct higher order skills. In this way, forward and backward transitions reflect important and perhaps even universal aspects of the *process* of development—the construction of higher order skills by coordination of lower level components.

As individuals reach the years of late adult development, they experience decline in a wide variety of psychological functions, including processing speed, memory functioning (especially under conditions of low support), capacity to inhibit thought and action, and so forth. However, decline in some psychological functions and domains does not imply decline in all areas (see Bialystok & Craik, Chapter 7 of this volume, and Blair, Chapter 8 of this volume for extended discussions of declines and advances during late adult development). For example, although speed of processing may undergo gradual decline in late adult development, individuals often embark on new developmental projects during their retirement years. Despite decline in particular memory functions, adults in the late mature years show advances in reflective thinking and the capacity for "wisdom" (see Karelitz, Jarvin & Sternberg, Chapter 23 of this volume). Furthermore, among older adults, novel developmental pathways emerge as adaptive reactions to the decline in other areas. Thus, when we adopt psychological structures as the unit of developmental

analysis, it becomes easier to see how development occurs throughout the life span through the process of adapting to novel demands and challenges.

DEVELOPMENTAL CHANGES IN LIFE GOALS OVER THE ADULT YEARS

How do overarching life goals undergo developmental change over adulthood? In contrast with traditional developmental (Erikson, 1963; Freud, 1917/1965; Piaget, 1983) and life-phase approaches (Gould, 1980; Levinson, 1978), development does not occur in a linear series of homogeneous stages throughout the life span (Clark & Caffarella, 1999; Fischer & Bidell, 2006; Valsiner, 1998). Different cultures parse the life course in different ways for different people. For example, unlike in Western societies, in traditional India, during the last phase of life, many Brahmin men leave the family in search of spiritual fulfillment (Mascolo, Rapisardi, & Misra, 2004). Even within the same culture, the nature, form, and timing of life transitions varies across groups. As cultures change, the developmental tasks associated with different life phases also shift. With economic and demographic changes, for example, many retired individuals in the United States have faced the challenge of returning to work. Many adults who have encountered economic difficulty have found it necessary to return to their parents' homes for some period of time. In contrast, in the economically burgeoning India, the tradition of extended families is unraveling (Sharma, 2003). Thus, no single normative trajectory of change or development exists across the life span.

Over the course of life, a person's processes are psychologically channelized by those tasks and developmental goals that are most adaptive, salient, or meaningful at a particular phase of life. In keeping with the distinction between historical and developmental change described earlier, some of these changes will be historical changes—shifts from one culturally embedded life theme to another—whereas others will be developmental changes. Although no single trajectory exists in the emergence of life goals, to the extent that life goals undergo genuine development, they will move in the direction of increased differentiation and hierarchic integration. Over time, context-specific skills and meanings will become increasingly intercoordinated to form more generalized and encompassing higher order structures. For example, lower level structures (e.g., *making a cup of coffee; talking about the weather*) can increasingly come under the regulative control of higher order goal structures (e.g., *being a good host to one's guests*). Over time, higher level psychological structures can function as higher order goals (e.g., *be a good host*) that drive social action in particular social contexts (e.g., *making coffee for one's guests*). In this way, the task of tracking changes in central life goals is tantamount to charting changes in core self-defining meanings that individuals use to organize and regulate self and social activity.

Figure 6.9 identifies the results of a cross-sectional study in which 409 English-speaking individuals from the United States and United Kingdom responded to an online questionnaire. Participants were asked to enter written responses to the question, "What do you experience as the most important thing in your life right now?" to explain why the event in question was important to them and to provide a concrete example. Responses were classified into a series of core life goals, including education (i.e., attending school or college), family (i.e., relationships to parents, children, siblings), love relationships (i.e., relationships to spouse, boyfriends, girlfriends), career, friends, health (i.e., concern about maintaining health), and reflection (i.e., reflections about the life course, one's legacy, spiritual connections beyond the self). Figure 6.9 identifies the percentage of respondents indicating core life goals for each of five age groups. The top panel of Figure 6.9 identifies the most frequent themes indicated within each different age group. Goals and themes related to *family* were the most frequently indicated theme for *all* age groups (the proportion of participants nominating family themes is identified on the secondary *y*-axis using an expanded scale). Nonetheless, the importance of family increased gradually over the first three cohorts, reaching a peak among 36- to 45-year-olds—around the time when parents are busy raising children.

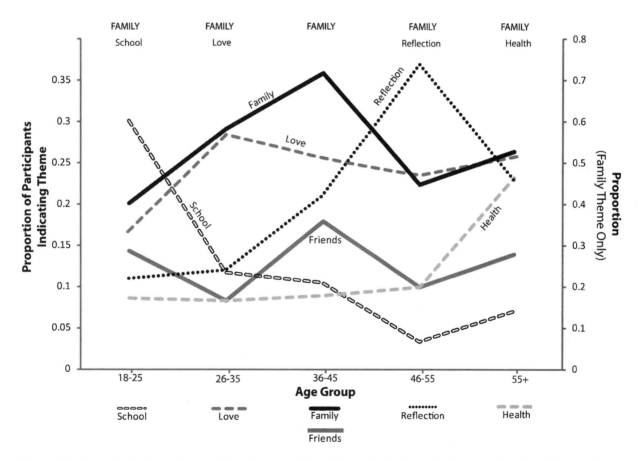

Figure 6.9   Age-related changes in core life goals over adulthood. Age-related changes in the proportion of participants who identified family, school, love relationships, health, and reflection/generative as their most important goals over the course of the life span. Although family was by far the most frequently nominated category for all age groups, with increasing age, salient core life goals shifted from school (18–25 years), to love relationships (26–35 years), family (36–45 years), reflection-generativity (46–55 years), and health (55+ years).

Beyond these overarching investments in family, over the five cohorts, the most salient life goals included *school* for 18- to 25-year-olds, *love relationships* for 26- to 35-year-olds, *family* for 36- to 45-year-olds, *reflection* for 46- to 55-year-olds and *health, love relationships,* and *reflection* for individuals 56 years and older. These dominant concerns are sensible for individuals in Western culture. Late adolescence and early adulthood is the time that most individuals attend high school and college. As indicated in Figure 6.9, education-related goals drop off precipitously after age 25. Earlier to early-mid adulthood is a time when individuals typically seek partners for love relationships. As indicated in Figure 6.9, after reaching a peak between ages 26 and 35, the percentage of individuals nominating love-related goals declines somewhat but remains relatively stable over the final three age cohorts. The percentage of individuals who nominate reflection-related goals increases precipitously in the 46 to 55 age group, around the time when many individuals report so-called midlife crises (Lachman, 2004). At this point, many individuals become concerned about their generativity, their life work, and connecting to social or spiritual realms outside of the self. Health concerns are nominated by relatively small proportions of people in each cohort with the exception of the 56+ cohort. Although friendship-related goals (not indicated in Figure 6.9) were higher among 18- to 25-year-olds, they were rarely elevated to the status of most important concerns for any age group. Surprisingly, career-related goals (not indicated in Figure 6.9) never emerged as a singly dominant motive for any cohort. It is possible that career goals were subordinated to family goals in the lives of participants in this study.

Figure 6.9 tracks age-related shifts in life goals across five different cohorts. However, without assessing the level of complexity of shifting life goals over time or cohort, such changes cannot be regarded as genuine developmental changes. A subsample of 200 individuals was selected for further analysis to assess developmental changes in the *structural complexity* of life goals. Participants in this subsample completed an extended version of the task described earlier; they described, justified, and provided examples of the *first, second,* and *third* most important things in their lives. They were also asked to describe principles that would explain how the life goals that they had described were related to each other. We refer to the representations of each participant's life goals as a *core goal structure.* The level of complexity of each participant's core goal structure was identified in terms of the developmental levels indicated in Figure 6.2. In this online

questionnaire, because there was no opportunity for an investigator to ask follow-up questions that would probe the depth of a person's goal structure, participants are best regarded as operating at their *functional* rather than optimal or scaffolded levels of performance. Consistent with this assertion, the level of complexity of core goal structures increased gradually with each age cohort, taking the shape of the *functional* rather than the *optimal* level curve depicted in Figure 6.7.

Figure 6.10 provides examples of core goal structures at give different levels of complexity. The bottom panel portrays an 18- to 25-year-old man's core goal structure for whom school, work, and relationships constitute important goals. For this individual, school, work, and relationships are all organized around the generalized value of *taking responsibility,* which functions at the level of single abstractions (Level 10/Ab1). The second panel from the bottom depicts the protocol of a 26- to 35-year-old woman. This woman identified family, personal goals, and securing financial assets as fundamental goals. Operating at the level of abstract mappings (Level 11/Ab2), this individual represents her life goals in terms of a paradoxical relation between two primary concerns: although *family* comes before *personal goals* (i.e., becoming a nurse) and *making money,* one nonetheless needs money and personal fulfillment to make one's family happy. The third panel from the bottom displays the protocol of a 40-year-old man who is at a point of transition in his life. The man's protocol functions at the level of abstract systems (Level 12/Ab3). The respondent's goal structure is organized in terms of multiple integrated comparisons between his current station in life and his future sense of who he wants to be. Specifically, this individual wishes to *complete his current position* before moving on to *a career and lifestyle that will bring him happiness;* simultaneously, the respondent maintains the importance of being *flexible and adjusting his sense of who he wants to be* as he confronts the *stabilities and changes involved in getting older.*

The top panel of Figure 6.10 depicts a rare example of a core goal structure that operates at the level of abstract principles (Level 13: Ab4/Pr1). Abstract principles are the highest level of functioning postulated by dynamic skill theory (Bidell & Fischer, 2006; Mascolo & Fischer, 2003). The protocol is that of a 55+-year-old woman with a graduate-level education (master's degree). This individual's protocol is characterized by a high degree of integration over a series of highly differentiated values, goals, and meanings. The principle of *living a spiritual life,* represented in terms of the metaphor of *a fortunate*

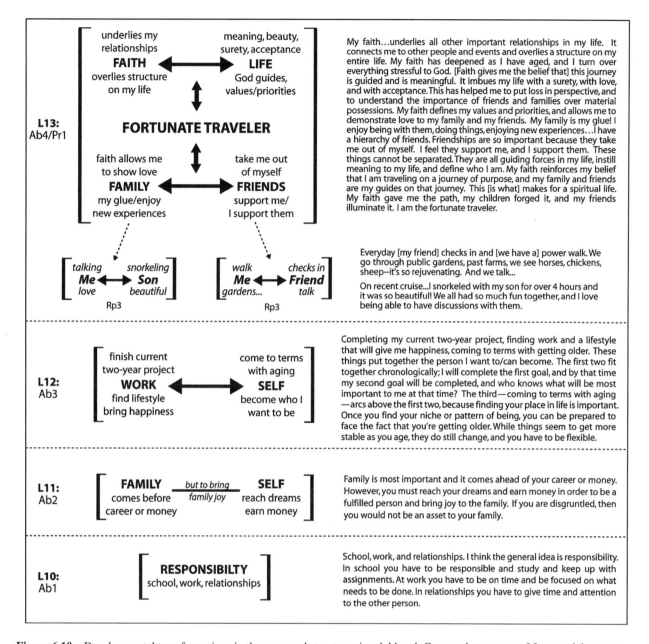

Figure 6.10   Developmental transformations in the core goal structures in adulthood. Core goal structures of four participants at four levels of development. The bottom through top panels depict protocols from an 18- to 25-year-old (single abstractions, L10/Ab1); 26- to 35-year-old (abstract mapping, L11/Ab2); 36- to 45-year-old (abstract systems, L12/Ab3), and 55+-year-old (single principles, L13/Ab4/Pr1). The top panel depicts how higher order principles regulate lower level goal structures.

traveler, structures the various components of her life goal representation. For this individual, *faith in God* provides a structure that *overlays her entire life*. Her faith gives her a sense of *surety, acceptance, and love*; it helps her to *define values and priorities*, *deal with loss,* and perceive *beauty and meaning* in her everyday experiences in the world. This last point is reflected in her relationships with other people, namely, her family and friends. Given the certainty, acceptance, and capacity to love that stems from her faith, the respondent is able to *give and receive support* to a *hierarchy of friends,* to *enjoy* the time she spends with her children, and to *appreciate her son with loving acceptance of his serious disabilities.* In her protocol, this respondent described a series of concrete examples of the ways in which she is able to put her core goals into *praxis*. Two such examples (i.e., enjoying spending time on a cruise with her sons; enjoying power walks with a close friend) are provided in Figure 6.10 in the form of skill diagrams depicting activities at the level of representational systems (Level 9/Rp3). The respondent's descriptions of these concrete activities flow easily from the abstract idealizations that she describes. This is an important feature of her core goal structure. Within any given level of functioning, core goal representations operate as *hierarchically organized control structures;* lower level actions and meanings function in the service of higher order meanings, values, and goals. There is a high level of integration and coherence between the abstractions that make up the respondent's core goal representation and the concrete examples provided to illustrate them. This degree of coherence suggests a high capacity to regulate concrete behavior in terms of abstract ideals—that is, to put abstract principles into practice. With advancing development, individuals are increasingly able to put higher order enduring beliefs into concrete practice (McNamee, 1977). Thus, higher order abstractions need not function as "mere conceptualizations." Like the lower level actions and concrete meanings from which they ultimately arise, higher order abstract concepts function as control structures. With development, individuals are increasingly able to draw on high-level abstractions to exert regulative control over their everyday actions.

Changes in Emotional Aspects of Psychological Structures over the Adult Years

Core goal structures are not simply *conceptual* structures; they are *embodied* structures that are built from the constructive integration of lower level actions and concrete meanings over long periods. Affective changes over the life span have been studied in a variety of ways. Although research on affective changes over the life span has produced many conflicting results (Consedine & Magai, 2006), findings suggest some general conclusions. At the most basic level, researchers have examined age-related changes in the experience of and negative emotional experiences over the life span. Trajectories in the frequency of positive and negative affect over the life span take different shapes as a function of sex, personality dispositions, socioeconomic status, and other variables (Gruenewald, Mroczek, Ryff, & Singer, 2008; Mroczek & Kolarz, 1998). Over the life span, reports of positive emotions are dramatically higher than reports of negative emotions (Carstensen & Mikels, 2005). Between the ages of 20 and 75, in Western samples, there appears to be a modest increase in the frequency with which people report positive emotion and a gradual

decrease in the frequency with which people negative affect (Mroczek, 2001). With respect to negative emotion, Schieman (1999) has suggested that older individuals are less likely to find themselves in situations that produce experiences of anger and related emotions; other studies suggest that decrements in anger among older individuals are mediated by differential use of emotion coping strategies (Blanchard-Fields & Coats, 2008; Charles & Carstensen, 2008). In their review of research on emotional expressivity, Consedine and Magai (2006) have suggested that, contrary to conventional wisdom, research suggests that emotional expressivity remains robust and may even increase with age. A variety of studies have examined age-related changes in complexity of emotional experience with age. Malatesta and Izard (1984) have demonstrated that in comparison with younger women, older women exhibited more complex blends of emotion-related facial activity when recounting memories of emotional experiences, suggesting an increase in the complexity of emotional expression in older individuals.

Although much research addressing age-related changes in emotional experience has examined quantitative differences in emotion over time (Consedine & Magai, 2006), some researchers have examined how emotion undergoes qualitative transformation throughout childhood (Mascolo & Griffin, 1998; Sroufe, 1996), adulthood, and late adulthood (Labouvie-Vief, 2003; Strayer, 2002). Labouvie-Vief and her colleagues (Labouvie-Vief & Diehl, 2000; Labouvie-Vief, Diehl, Jain, & Zhang, 2007) have examined development changes in what they call *affective optimization* and *affective complexity* over the life span. Affective optimization consists of an emotional regulation strategy involving the maximization of positive affect and the minimization of negative emotion in connection to emotionally challenging circumstances. Affective complexity consists of the capacity to differentiate, experience, and coordinate multiple emotions at the same time. Labouvie-Vief and her colleagues have shown different trajectories in the development of affective optimization and affective complexity across the life span. Affective complexity increases over time, peaking at about middle age, and begins to decline from about age 60 onward. In contrast, affective optimization shows gradual increases over the adult years, leveling off but not declining after about age 80 (Labouvie-Vief & Diehl, 2000; Labouvie-Vief et al., 2007). These findings corroborate a suite of findings that suggest that there are both quantitative and qualitative changes in emotional life over the life span. With development, individuals become able to construct (1) complex combinations of emotional states

(Malatesta & Izard, 1984; Ready, Carvalho, & Weinberger, 2008), (2) higher order experiences of emotion (e.g., pride, resentment, patriotism, contentment; Mascolo & Fischer, 1995; Zinck & Newen, 2008), and (3) complex and nuanced emotional regulation strategies (Diehl, Coyle, & Labou- vie-Vief, 1996; Freund, 2007; Riediger & Freund, 2006). For example, when confronted with stressful life events, younger individuals are more likely to exhibit "primary" coping reactions (i.e., attempts to directly solve the prob- lem); in contrast, older individuals are more likely to adopt "secondary" coping strategies (i.e., managing emotion and accepting events over which they have little control; Diehl, Coyle, & Labovie-Vief, 1996; Riediger & Freund, 2006).

Thus, as integrative and embodied processes, psycho- logical structures do not simply have cognitive or repre- sentational content; they are also organized in terms of significant *emotional* content. Table 6.2 identifies four dominant emotional themes contained in the core goal structures in participants in the study described earlier: *happiness, love, emotional support,* and *emotional coping.* Three levels of emotional complexity were defined for each emotional theme as indicated in Table 6.2. Figure 6.11 dis- plays the proportion of participants in each age cohort who made reference to each form and level of emotional con- tent in their core goal structures. As indicated in each panel

of Figure 6.11, the frequency with which participants made reference to higher order forms of emotion increased with age for each of the four emotional themes. The top left panel displays age-related and developmental changes in reports of *happy themes*. Reference to simple happy states (Level 1) peaked between ages 26 and 35 but were fre- quent in all age groups. Enduring feelings of contentment and fulfillment (Level 2) emerged between ages 26 and 45, and showed a mild decline after age 46. At this time, participants began to make reference to more highly devel- oped modes of happiness such as taking joy in moment- by-moment experiencing, actively choosing to be happy, and finding joy in connecting to the world (Level 3). The top right panel displays changes in *love-related themes.* Again, the most frequently cited theme involves simple statements of love for various objects (people, family, activities, etc.). The proportion of participants who make reference to object love (Level 1), mutual/enduring love (Level 2), and love as an active process (Level 3) gradually increases with age. Mutual/enduring love begins to emerge between 26 and 35 years of age, whereas love as an active process begins to emerge after age 45.

References to *emotional support* and *caring for oth- ers* showed dramatic differences over time. An extremely common theme in the protocols of 18- to 25-year-olds

Table 6.2 Levels of Emotional Complexity

	Happiness	Love	Emotional Support	Emotional Coping
1	• **General Reference to Happiness** • **Having Fun** Relaxation; pleasure • **Other/Job/Activity Makes Me Happy**	• **Self Loves Other(s)** Partner; children; family; God, work; activity, thing; pet • **Self Feels Loved by Other(s)**	• **Others Support Self** Family, parents, partner, children, etc. • **Taking Care of Specific Persons** • **Putting Specific Others Before Self**	• **Depend on Others in Crisis** Family, parents, partner • **Give Up/Don't Know How to Respond to Stress**
2	• **Happy About Life Trajectory or Station** • **Sense of Fulfillment** Contentment, security satisfaction	• **Mutuality of Love** Affection, respect, caring • **Love within Enduring Relationship** • **Appreciation of Deep Attributes of Other**	• **Take Care of Specific Classes of People** Children at school; clients	• **Event-Related Coping** Optimism, perseverance, directly confronting problem • **Distraction/Discharge** Avoiding object of stress; stress-relieving activities
3	• **Happiness as Process** Mindful experiencing; flow; choosing happiness moment-by-moment • **Deep Peace** • **Happiness as Connection to World** Exchange or connection with that beyond self	• **Love as Activity or Way of Relating to Others and World** • **Love as a Process of Valu- ing, Experiencing Connec- tion to World**	• **Care for Embedded Processes, Entities or Events** Humanity; planet; ecosystem; social activism (with reference to concrete action)	• **Balance of Acceptance and Assertion** Accepting what cannot be changed; mindful appreciation; balancing controllable with non-controllable; Putting stress in perspective; nonattachment

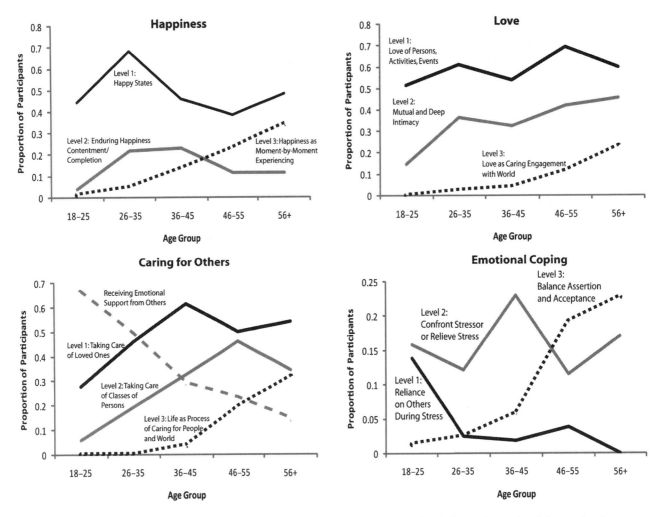

Figure 6.11 Age-related and developmental changes in emotional themes over adulthood. For each emotional theme, the changes depicted reflect transformations in the form or quality of emotional dispositions rather than simply changes in the extent to which particular emotional themes were represented in participant protocols.

involved feelings of being supported by others, particularly parents. Over and over again, the youngest cohort made reference to the ways in which family was "there" for them and supported them through their primary activities. The frequency with which participants made reference to feelings of emotional support declined gradually with increasing age. In contrast, references to caring for others increased with age. References to taking care of specific loved ones (Level 1) emerged among 18- to 25-year-olds and peaked between age 36 and 45. Caring for specific *classes* of people (e.g., teachers caring for students; professionals caring for clients; Level 2) began to emerge among the 26- to 35-year-old cohort and peaked between 46 and 55 years of age. Finally, references to caring for both individuals and broad classes of people as a duty or way of life (Level 3) began to emerge with the 46- to

55-year-old cohort, and increased in individuals over 55 years of age. The lower right quadrant of Figure 6.11 displays changes in styles of *emotional coping* as represented in the core goal structures of participants. Descriptions of emotional coping involved reference to ways of addressing situations that were described as explicitly stressful or challenging. As indicated in Figure 6.11, descriptions of nonadaptive coping strategies (i.e., giving up; not knowing how to manage stress) and dependency on others during stress (Level 1) declined with age, and was evident only among 18- to 25-year-olds. References to proactive emotional coping strategies (Level 2) were evident in all age cohorts. Reference to a *balance between acceptance and assertion* as an emotional coping strategy began to emerge only later in life, beginning with the 46- to 55-year-old cohort and increasing thereafter.

Overall, these data suggest, in development, core goals structures undergo both emotional and representational transformation. With age, individuals increasingly made reference to a range of higher order emotional experiences (i.e., cognitive-affective differentiation; emotional complexity) and to modes of regulating emotion in ways that reflect a balance between acceptance and agency in the world (i.e., affective optimization; the coordination of primary and secondary emotion regulation strategies). Indeed, among very highly developed goal structures, it is sometimes difficult to differentiate representational, affective, and regulatory aspects of a person's reflections; any given statement involves a highly integrative melding of meaning, affect, and social understanding. Such higher order integrations reflect a sense of "feeling whole within the self" and "feeling connected to the world" that some view as representative of healthy adult development (Sinnott & Berlanstein, 2006).

ADULT DEVELOPMENT THROUGH SOCIAL RELATIONSHIPS

Earlier in the chapter, we argued for the need to identify an integrative unit of psychological analysis. We suggested that the concept of *situated meaning-mediated action* can function as such a unit. As indicated in Figure 6.1, the concept of action brings together a series of essential psychological processes, including agency, meaning, experience, affect, motor movement, and so forth. From this view, thinking, experiencing, and movement are understood either as aspects of ongoing action or as forms of contextualized action. Throughout this chapter, we have emphasized the importance of social context as part of the process of structuring human action. In this section, we extend the model of individual action developed earlier to elaborate a more comprehensive model of the person-environment system (Magnusson & Stattin, 2006). Having done so, we then extend the conceptual and empirical tools described thus far for the analysis of individual action and development to elaborate a system for assessing the dynamic structure of joint activity. In so doing, we describe tools for analyzing how individual psychological structures develop within the context of meaning-mediated interactions with others. We illustrate these principles through an analysis of the microdevelopment (Granott, Fischer, & Parziale, 2002; Siegler, 2006) of meaning and emotion over the course of single sessions of psychotherapy.

Extending a Model of Integrative Action: The Coactive Person-Environment System

Figure 6.12 incorporates and builds on Figure 6.1. Like Figure 6.1, the model begins with a representation of individual action (A) on physical and psychological objects (B). The components of individual action are represented

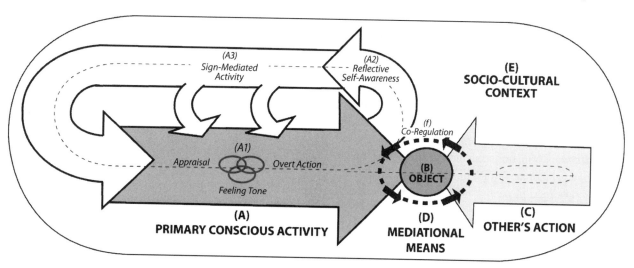

Figure 6.12 The social context of development: the person-environment system. The person-environment system is composed of five categories of interlocking processes. The *gray arrow (A)* represents a person's primary conscious activity. The *gray circle* toward which the base arrow points represents the objects *(B)* of intentional action. The intentional object of action can be either real or representational, and consists of the focus of a person's attentional activity. Many instances of human action involve *(C)* another person or persons. In face-to-face interaction, individuals coregulate each other's actions both verbally and nonverbally. Higher order coregulation occurs using some form of meditational means *(D),* the most significant of which is language. All interaction occurs within a particular social-cultural-historical context *(E)* consisting of socially shared meanings, practices, and artifacts.

in Figure 6.12 at point A1. Figure 6.12 extends Figure 6.1 though its depiction of the fundamentally embedded nature of individual action within sociocultural context (E). In so doing, Figure 6.12 augments Figure 6.1 by representing three additional propositions:

1. In social interaction, social partners (A, C) coregulate (f) each other's actions, thoughts, and feeling.
2. Face-to-face coregulation is mediated by the use of cultural tools, most notable among them being language and other symbol systems, broadly defined (Wertsch, 1998; Vygotsky, 1978).
3. Higher order experiences of *self* are coconstructed in discursive interactions with others; in any given discursive context, self-awareness emerges as primary conscious activity (A)—which normally is focused on external objects (B)—loops back and takes itself as its own object of awareness (A2, A3).

Once constructed, higher order representations of self function as goal structures that individuals use to regulate thinking, feeling, and action in particular social contexts.

The coactive systems view goes beyond the everyday idea that the social environment "has an effect" on individuals. The main point of the coactive person-environment system is that the components of the person-environment system *do not function independently of one another.* This statement calls for a shift in the ways in which we often think about the analysis of causality in psychology. The various components of the person-environment system are not "factors" or "forces" that exert individual or collective "effects" on an individual (Rogoff, 1990). Because control over action is *distributed* among components of the person-environment system, at any given moment, even subtle shifts in relations among system components can lead to significant transformation in an individual's action. In what follows, we elaborate further on the ways in which Figure 6.12 elaborates a coactive model of social interaction.

Social Interaction Is Coregulated

The coregulation of action in face-to-face social exchanges is indicated at point f in Figure 6.12. The concept of coregulation can be illuminated through an analysis of human communication systems. The process of communication is often represented mechanistically in terms of individual senders forwarding discrete and bounded messages back and forth to each other. Such a process is characteristic of discrete state communication systems (Fogel, 1993;

Semin, 2007; Trevarthen, 1998). From this view, a discrete message originates within a single individual, and is encoded and then sent through a fixed communicational channel (e.g., as in telegraph, mail, or e-mail). After the individual sends the message, it remains fixed and cannot be changed throughout the process of transmission. After the correspondent receives the message, she must decode it. Only *after* she has decoded the message can she switch roles from receiver to sender, and continue the exchange. This form of communication is typical of those that involve the use of letters sent through the mail, e-mail, telegraph, and related mechanical exchanges of information.

Face-to-face communication, however, does not proceed in this way. Face-to-face exchange provides an example of a continuous process communication system (Fogel, 1993, 2006; Mascolo & Margolis, 2005). In ordinary interaction, interlocutors are simultaneously active as both senders and receivers. As one person speaks, the other person provides *continuous feedback* in the form of verbal and nonverbal indicators (e.g., nodding of the head, changing facial expression, direction of gaze, and even the time allowed to elapse before speaking). As a result, the "message" is not fixed and is free to change in the very process of communication. In social interaction, meanings are jointly constructed as social partners coregulate each other's actions, thoughts, and feelings. In this sense, *coregulation* refers to the process by which social partners simultaneously and continuously adjust their ongoing actions, thoughts, and feelings to each other (Fogel, 1993; Mascolo & Fischer, 1998). It follows that, within coregulation, the actions of the other are part of the process of the self's actions and vice versa.

Current research suggests that infant-caregiver dyads are able to establish rudimentary forms of intersubjectivity soon after infants are born. Intersubjectivity can be defined in terms of the capacity for shared or coordinated action or experience within episodes of joint action (Matusov, 1996; Rommetveit, 1979; Trevarthen, 1993). Support for this proposition comes from many sources. Melzoff and Moore (1999) have described evidence that neonates are capable of matching facial actions modeled by others. By two months of age, infants and their caregivers engage in emotionally charged turn-taking involving sequences of smiling, cooing, and related coordinated acts (Trevarthen, 1993, 1998; Trevarthen & Hubley, 1978). Through these richly coregulated interchanges, infant and caregiver not only coordinate their facial and vocal actions, *they also coordinate the emotional experiences that arise within the facial and vocal dance that occurs between them* (Gallagher & Hutto, 2008). The idea that infants enter the world capable of achieving primitive forms of intersubjective activity is bolstered by the recent discovery of "mirror neurons" (Gallese, Eagle, & Migone, 2007; Rizzolatti, 2005). "Mirror neurons" consist of neurons, initially discovered in the prefrontal lobes of monkeys, which become activated both when observing behavior in others and when executing the same action by the self. The existence of mirror neurons suggests that a common neurologic system underlies both the observation and production of certain classes of motor behavior. Such common pathways provide a foundation for understanding how infants are capable of entering into socioemotional interactions from the start of life. Although individual persons are separate and distinct organisms, the mirror neuron system (or systems like it) provides a means for experiencing correspondences, however primitive at first, between experience of others and experiences within the self (Meltzoff, 2002; Meltzoff & Brooks, 2007).

These findings suggest an *inversion* of traditional conceptions of the relation between social and cognitive development. Whereas traditional approaches maintain that intersubjectivity is a *derivative product* of cognitive development, recent research suggests that psychological development *builds on* a primordial intersubjectivity with others (see Bråten, 2007; Carpendale & Lewis, Chapter 17 of this volume, Overgaard, 2006; Ter Hark, 1990). Thus, whether we are talking about infants (Fogel, Garvey, Hsu, & West-Stromming, 2006; Trevarthen & Aiken, 2000) or adults (Beebe, Knoblauch, Rustin, Sorter, Jacobs, & Pally, 2005), development is founded on the capacity for intersubjectivity with others.

Higher Order Social Interaction and Development Is Mediated by the Use of Language and Symbol Systems

Higher order operations are produced and maintained through the use of semiotic systems (Rommetveit, 1985; Wertsch, 1998). We use the term *semiotic function* to refer broadly to any form of representation, where representation refers to the capacity to make one thing stand for or refer to something else. In so doing, following a long tradition, we draw a distinction between *signs* and *symbols.* Sign systems are particularly important in mediating social interaction and higher order psychological processes that have their origins in sociocultural activity. Signs and symbols can be differentiated along a continuum. On one end of the continuum, *signs* (e.g., words, mathematical or musical notation) function as: (1) *generative* systems that represent (2) *arbitrary* and (3) *shared* meanings. In contrast, on the other end of the continuum, *symbols* (e.g., images, pictures, objects that are used to stand for other meanings) are: (1) *nongenerative,* (2) less arbitrary in the sense that they tend to *resemble* their referents in some way, and (3) represent *personal* rather than shared meanings. In what follows, we focus primarily on articulating the special properties of sign systems that make them such useful vehicles of social interaction and enculturation.

First, signs are *generative* in the sense that given a finite number of components and rules of combination (e.g., phonemes, letters), persons can generate an infinite number of meanings. For example, using the rules for combining the 26 letters of the English alphabet, one can construct an infinite number of possible meanings. Second, signs are *arbitrary* in the sense that the concepts and meanings to which they refer can be constructed in alternative ways based on purpose, history, and context. Words are not used simply to refer to physical or concrete objects in the world. Instead, they represent systems of *meanings.* The meanings to which words and expressions refer are arbitrary in the sense that they *could be otherwise* depending on the ways in which they are used (Mascolo, 2008; Wittgenstein, 1953) to make social distinctions that serve *human* purposes. For example, the meaning of the term *mother* does not come from its correspondence a particular entity in the world, fixed or otherwise. The concept of mother has evolved over time to incorporate meanings that would be foreign to speakers of earlier generations (e.g., adoptive mother, stepmother, surrogate mother). The third feature of signs is that they represent *shared* rather than personal meanings. Unlike pictures or images, words represent meanings that are shared within a linguistic community. Thus, it is through the use of language that we are able to construct and reconstruct novel meanings that mediate thinking, feeling, and action.

In light of these special properties, language organizes human action at multiple levels. At the level of *culture,* language functions as a dynamic repository of shared and contested meanings that have evolved as means of solving personal and collective problems; at the level of *social interaction,* in light of its capacity to represent shared meanings, language plays a central (but not exclusive) role in mediating the coconstruction and exchange of meaning between people. Given its generative properties and capacity to represent arbitrary meanings, language makes it possible to construct an infinite number of social meanings by drawing on a finite number of meaning components. Language thus functions as the quintessential medium for communicating, transforming, and cocreating *novel* meanings in social interaction. Once novel meanings are created in social action, language provides the vehicle through which such meanings can be disseminated throughout a linguistic community. Cultural change occurs as novel meanings, practices, and artifacts are disseminated, accepted, and transformed by members of a given linguistic community.

At the level of *individual action,* language is used for purposes that extend beyond communicative functions. From their participation in joint activity with others, individuals internalize, appropriate, and use language and other semiotic vehicles to *think* with (Wertsch, 1998), to *regulate* their feeling and action (Diaz & Berk, 1992; Vygotsky, 1978), and to direct their *participation* in (Rogoff, 1993, 2002) sociocultural activities. It is largely through the use of language that individuals are able to profit from social interaction in the acquisition of higher order skills and meanings that have their origins in cultural rather than individual history (e.g., mathematics; use of the Internet; the formation of personal and professional relationships; identity construction within cultural contexts). The use of language to mediate action in individual actors is not, however, a static process. Sign-mediated meanings do not simply "pass through" individuals as if persons were merely conduits of cultural activity. On the contrary, individuals actively transform cultural meanings in the process of coconstructing and using them. Thus, although the individual minds are shaped by the cultural meanings conveyed in ordinary language, individuals are able to transform those meanings and externalize them in an attempt to advance their own personal and communal objectives.

Discursive Construction of Self and the Regulation of Action

The third main issue highlighted in Figure 6.12 involves clarification of the concept and role of self in individual and joint action. We follow a long tradition of regarding self as a type of *experience* (Mead, 1934; Sarbin, 1952; Zahavi, 2005). In so doing, we differentiate between primary and secondary modes of self-experience. The primary experience of self consists of a type of prereflective background experience that accompanies primary or core conscious activity on objects (Damasio, 1999; Mascolo, 2004; Zahavi). Primary conscious activity is a form of prereflective awareness directed toward external objects in the world. In primary conscious activity, because one's full attention is focused on the object of one's activity, it is common for people to get "lost in the experience" (Csikszentmihalyi, 1991); a person is primarily aware of the external object rather than of his own experience. However, despite the primary focus on the "external" in primary consciousness (e.g., what our interlocutor is saying, the movie we are watching, the passage in the book we are reading), it is nonetheless sensible to speak of an implicit or prereflective experience of self (Damasio, 1999; Emde, 1983; Zahavi, 2005). Looming in the background is an implicit and prereflective awareness of our body in space, emotional feeling tone, and a sense of the agency of acting. It is likely even very young infants experience a subjective sense of self in this way (Damasio, 1999; Emde, 1983;). Primary experience of self is indicated at point A1 in Figure 6.12.

The secondary form of self-experience is a reflective and most often mediated experience of *self-consciousness.* Self-consciousness occurs as an act of self-reflection and is indicated at point A2 in Figure 6.12. Self-consciousness occurs as primary conscious activity loops reflexively back onto itself and *takes itself as its own object* (Mascolo & Fischer, 1998; Mead, 1934). If follows that there are multiple levels and forms of conscious experience, of which we have differentiated only two broad categories. As a higher order process, secondary self-awareness begins to emerge in the middle of the second year of life with the onset of the semiotic function. It is at this time that children begin to use both signs and symbols to construct explicit representations of self. Throughout development, in everyday interactions, one's interlocutors use language to draw a person's attention to aspects of her own functioning. Imagine a supervisor who instructs her new employee: "When you interact with customers, you represent not only yourself, but also the ABC Corporation. Be sure to greet your customers with a pleasant telephone voice." The supervisor has not only called the employee's attention to himself, but also, through the vehicle of language, offered a sociomoral category in relation to which the employee is asked to define himself. Over time, higher order representations of self are constructed as individuals appropriate the language of their social community to identify experiential states, to regulate their actions, and to form social identities. The use of language to mediate the higher order construction of self is indicated in Figure 6.12 at points A2 and A3.

With development, the secondary, higher order construction of representations of self is of vital importance to understanding the regulation of action. With development, representations of self come to operate as high-level goals or reference standards that direct and drive social action (Baumeister, 1998; Carver & Scheier, 2002; Mascolo & Fischer, 1998). Tangney has suggested that valued representations of self function as a kind of moral guide to action (Tangney, 2002). Kagan (1996) has suggested that the quest to create and conform to personally valued images of self operates as the most important motivational force in human action. With higher order development, the desire to live up to valued conceptions of a worthy self can usurp even basic motives (e.g., hunger, thirst, safety). Dunning (2007) has reviewed research suggesting that much consumer behavior arises in an attempt to bolster views of the self as capable, valued, or moral. To the extent that the desire to experience the self in terms of valued sociomoral standards operates as a central human motive, representation of self plays an important role in the development and construction of psychological structures within any given social context.

Tracking Individual Development within Joint Action: Relational Action Analysis

If the patterns of acting, thinking, and feeling produced in face-to-face therapeutic interactions are coregulated, it is not possible to understand the developmental course of psychological structures by focusing only on individual actors. Instead, it becomes necessary to develop methods to analyze the ways in which meanings arise and are distributed with the broader person-environment system. Such a goal requires a shift in the unit of psychological analysis from the individual to the *joint activity* (Rogoff, 1990) or *social ensemble* (Granott, 1998, 2005). Mascolo (Basseches & Mascolo, 2010; Mascolo & Margolis, 2004) has developed a method for analyzing the *structure of joint action,* meaning, and feeling in development. One can analyze the structure of joint action using a procedure called the *relational action analysis*. The basic principles for performing a relational activity analysis are simple. For any given unit of social interaction, a researcher performs the following steps: (1) identifies the structure of action, thinking, and feeling produced by each social partner; (2) identifies the form of coregulated social interaction that occurs *between* social partners; and (3) tracks changes in the structure of the resulting jointly constructed actionover time. It is possible using these procedures to identify and chart changes in the *structure of joint action* and how novel forms of individual thinking, feeling, and acting arise as a product of joint action as it unfolds over time.

The process of analyzing the structure of joint action proceeds by identifying *relational action structures.* Relational activity structures are represented visually using *relational action diagrams.* To illustrate, consider the difference between *individual skill structures* and *relational action structures.* Diagram I of Figure 6.13 displays an individual skill diagram that depicts the structure skill components for manipulating a handheld jack-in-the-box. To manipulate a jack-in-the-box, a child must coordinate skill components at the level of compounded sensorimotor systems. She must be able to *hold the box* while *holding, looking at,* and *turning* the crank *up and down* long enough *to see the jack pop.* Although this skill is within the skill sets of most children older than 2 years, it is beyond the capacity for most 15-month-olds. When provided with a handheld jack-in-the box, a 15-month-old might be able to hold the box but could not simultaneously turn the crank. Having successfully grasped the box, a 15-month-old will often have to let go of the box as he attempts to turn the crank. However, if a caregiver holds the box for the child, an infant can begin to turn the crank up and down. In the context of joint action, the child exerts control over part of the task while the adult supports the child by performing the remainder of the task. The structure of this joint activity can be represented using a relational activity diagram.

The structure of the joint manipulation of the jack-in-the-box is depicted in Diagram II of Figure 6.13. As indicated in Diagram II, a relational action diagram is composed of several basic components. The left and right side of the diagram depict the specific *structure of the meaning or action* produced by each social partner in a given episode of social interaction. In this case, the structure on the left depicts an infant's capacity to skills at the level of sensorimotor system (SM3) to coordinate acts of looking at the caregiver's modeled action and using looking to guide turning the crank. The structure on the right represents the caregiver's act of holding the box and modeling the act of turning the crank. The symbol located in between each partner's meaning structure identifies the specific form of coactive scaffolding that occurs between the two social partners. Table 6.3 describes different forms and levels of coactive scaffolding and the symbols used to represent them within relational action diagrams. In this example, the caregiver provides multiple forms scaffolding by breaking down and performing part of the task (holding the box). However, the highest level of scaffolding involves modeling the act of turning the crank (Scaffolding Level 8). In so doing, as indicated in Figure 6.13, the mother *MODELS* the act while the child *IMITATES.*

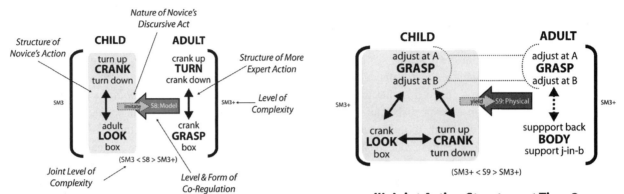

Figure 6.13 Individual and relational activity diagrams. Top panel shows a task analysis for the skill of manipulating a handheld jack-in-the-box. The task analysis indicates the structure of what an individual must do and know to manipulate the toy independently. The lower panels depict relational activity diagrams that show how control over elements of the jack-in-the-box task are distributed between a 15-month-old child and his mother. Relational activity structures identify: (1) the structure and level of complexity of each individual's actions, (2) the form of coregulated activity occurring between persons, (3) and the level of joint complexity exhibited by the dyad itself.

In development, the production of novel meanings and experiences cannot be attributed to the actions of individual persons. Individual actors are often not capable of producing or sustaining emergent forms of action, thought, or feeling in the absence of social partners. As a representation of joint activity, the relational action diagram depicts the dynamic structure and control over action as it is distributed throughout the dyad (Salomon, 1993). The action that emerges in social action is a dynamic product of the ensemble itself. By representing the ways in which the actions of social partners are constituted in relation to each other, a relational activity diagram provides a visual snapshot of how novel structures have their origins in coregulated social interaction. Tracking relational action structures over time produces a visual representation of changes in the structure of joint action, and the processes by individual and joint meanings are created.

Individual Coordination within Joint Action

What is the role of individual actors within the moment-by-moment coconstruction of meaning in joint action? Within social interaction, individual development occurs within as

individuals appropriate meanings and novel experiences from their participation in joint action with others (Rogoff, 1990, 1993). However, what do individual actors *do* when they appropriate meaning from their interactions with others (Mascolo, Pollack, & Fischer, 1997)? For example, the process by which an infant imitates an action modeled by a caregiver (e.g., turning the crank on a jack-in-the-box) does not follow as a simple reproduction or internalization of the adult's action. To imitate a modeled action, the imitator must actively coordinate components of action and meaning in ways that approximate the modeled action. To do so, individual actors must draw on and extend their existing skill repertoires to produce novel action; furthermore, individuals must incorporate novel meanings and actions arising in joint action into their existing meaning and skill repertoires. It follows that individuals *transform* the meanings and actions that they acquire in the very act of appropriating them. How is this accomplished?

Fischer (1980; Fischer & Pipp, 1984) has proposed a series of transformation rules that describe how individual actors create higher order structures through the coordination of lower level skills and meanings. These transformation rules also describe change processes that occur at

Table 6.3   Levels and Forms of Coactive Scaffolding

FORM AND LEVEL OF SCAFFOLDED SUPPORT	SYMBOL Less Expert More Expert
Sc1. Cue/Prompt (CUE, PROMPT). A cues or prompts existing skill in B. B deploys full skilled action without further support. *Example. A: "Hello, Bob..." B: "and?" C: "Oh yeah, I shake hands."*	Sc1: Cue
Sc2. Encouragement/Acknowledgment/Affirm (ENC, ACK, AFF). A reassures or encourages B's ongoing efforts to perform task, or acknowledges B's statement so to motivate continued action. *Example. You can do it; it's just like the last time.*	Sc2: Ack/Enc
Sc3. Restatement (RS). A restates B's utterance to clarify or consolidate B's meaning. *B: "It's too hard!" A: "You don't think you can do it..."*	Sc3: Ack/Enc
Sc4. Distancing (QUES, EXP, PROBE). A creates cognitive demand that motivates novel constructive action to meet demand (open-ended questions; probes; expansions; requests for evaluation, inference, etc.). *Example. "What would happen if you told her that?"*	**?** Sc4: Distance
Sc5: Emotional Holding (SUPP). A empathically communicates willingness to share the burden of managing intense feelings that result from B's attending to painful experience. *Example. B: "I'm really embarrassed to tell you this." A: "Don't worry, I'm here for you."*	As5: Hold
Sc6. Interpretation (INT). A offers explicit explanation or way to understand the meaning of a given issue or event. *A: "I think she did that because she felt insecure."*	I6: Interpret
Sc7. Direction (DIR). A actively directs B's actions or instructs B on how to perform action or represent an event.	E7: Direction
Sc8. Guided Enactment (MODEL, RP). (a) A models (most often with direction) an activity that B imitates concurrently; (b) A and B engage in role play. *Examples. (1) A models how to "shake hands" for a child; (2) A: "I'll be your mother and you be you. Say how you feel."*	E8: Model
Sc9. Physical Guidance (PHYS). A uses *physical* direction or other types of physical support to directly modulate or organize B's actions or experiences (e.g., hand-over-hand guidance; touching to regulate calming; providing physical pressure to foster sensory-integration; biofeedback, etc).	E9: Physical Guidance

the level of individual action. The term *coordination* is the general process of bringing into correspondence two or more previously unrelated meanings or actions. There are multiple forms of coordination. Several forms of coordination result in movement within a given developmental level of skill. *Differentiation* refers to the process of articulating a new meaning or action component in contradistinction to a previous or existing one. For example, an infant notices that moving the crank of a jack-in-the-box one way turns it up, whereas moving it a different way turns it down; in comparing two paintings, an adult is able to discriminate the realism characteristic in the work of the young Picasso from the abstraction in the work of Picasso later in his life.

Shift of focus occurs when an individual changes the focus of his or her attention from one part of a task to another without fully connecting to two parts. For example, having succeeded in grasping and lifting a jack-in-the-box, as a child shifts his limited attention to turning the crank, he may release the box. Shift-of-focus functions as an early form of juxtaposing skill components that are beyond an individual's capacity for full coordination. *Compounding* occurs when an individual brings into juxtaposition two or more skill components within the same developmental level of functioning. The process of building novel skill structures within joint action is illustrated in the bottom right of Figure 6.13. This figure depicts the structure of joint activity between the same infant and caregiver whose actions are represented in Diagram III of Figure 6.13. The joint action structure represented in the bottom right occurred only minutes after the one displayed in the bottom left panel. There are two major differences in these joint action structures. First, in the latter structure, the caregiver provides a high level of scaffolding in the following forms: (1) hand-over-hand guidance in assisting the child's attempt to hold the jack-in-the-box while simultaneously turning the crank, and (2) the resulting increase in the child's skill level. In the latter structure, using skills at the level of sensorimotor systems (SM3), given the caregiver's scaffolding, the child has begun to use compounding to coordinate novel skill components (i.e., holding the box) with existing skills (i.e., visually guided turning of the crank). Compounding differs from *intercoordination,* which involves coordinating two or more skills at a lower developmental level to form a skill at a higher level or tier. *Intercoordination* is the only change process that moves a skill from a lower level to a higher developmental level. Intercoordination occurs, for example, when an infant is able to coordinate two previously independent sensorimotor *mapping* skills (e.g., looking at a crank to grasp it; turning the crank up and then turning the crank down) into a single and stable sensorimotor *system* for manipulating a jack-in-the-box (e.g., using looking to guide the coordinated acts of grasping and turning the crank up and down).

Tracking Adult Development through Social Relationships: The Microdevelopment of Self and Emotion over the Course of Psychotherapy

To illustrate the ways in which a relational action analysis can be used to track microdevelopmental processes as they occur in moment-to-moment social exchanges, we provide an analysis of transformations in emotionally charged representations of self and other over the course of psychotherapy (Basseches & Mascolo, 2010; Mascolo, 2008a; Mascolo, Craig-Bray, & Neimeyer, 1997). The case involves a single session of short-term "anxiety-regulating" dynamic psychotherapy (McCullough, Kuhn, Andrews, Kaplan, Wolf, & Hurley, 2003; McCullough & Magill, 2009) between a therapist and the *Lady Cloaked in Fog* (McCullough, 1999)—a 44-year-old unmarried, depressed woman who exhibited difficulty experiencing feelings of closeness. The *Lady* had experienced intractable depression all of her adult life and had been in some form of therapy for the previous 24 years. Of the 64 sessions that constituted the early phases of the *Lady's* treatment, we

focus on changes that occurred in the pivotal 15th session. During this session, dramatic transformations occurred in the structure and content of the client's emotionally structured representation of self in relation to her therapist. At the beginning of the session, the dyad was able to identify a core emotional theme related to the client's relationships with others, namely, "I matter onstage (when I'm at work, doing things for others) but not off stage (not at work; home alone)." By the end of the session, the client was able to represent the therapist in terms of the metaphor of a "harbor light." The client was able to represent herself as the captain of a ship at sea and the therapist as a harbor light—a beacon of care shining on shore regardless of whether the client was with her. When it was stormy or foggy, the client could "perk my head up" and see the harbor light beaming on shore. She could then decide whether to go toward the beacon of care, or just know it was there. This metaphor, built over the course of the session, provided the foundation for further development that occurred throughout the remainder of the client's therapy.

Figure 6.14 tracks the development of the representational and emotional aspects of client's psychological structures over the course of the pivotal session. The bottom curve displays changes in the complexity of the client's meaning structures over the course of the session. The top curve shows changes in the development of structural complexity of the client's skill. The complexity of the client's meaning structures began at the high level of abstract mappings (Level, 11, Ab2) and fluctuated between representational systems (Level 9/Rp3) and abstract mappings until the final episode in which the client coordinated the harbor light insight at the level of abstract systems (Level 11/Ab2). Whereas this curve charts changes in the level of hierarchical complexity of the client's representational activity, there are many configurations of meaning that can be formed at any given level of complexity. A second index of developmental change included the number of thematic components contained in the harbor light insight that were coordinated by the client on any given conversational turn. Changes in the coordination of thematic components reveal how the content of the harbor light insight developed over time. This curve clearly shows the ways in which the harbor light insight has built up gradually over time. Forward progression of certain aspects of the harbor light insight was followed by a series of backward transitions as the dyad encountered novel emotional and representational conflicts to address. Although multiple configurations of meaning components developed over the course of the session, an abrupt change occurred at conversational turn

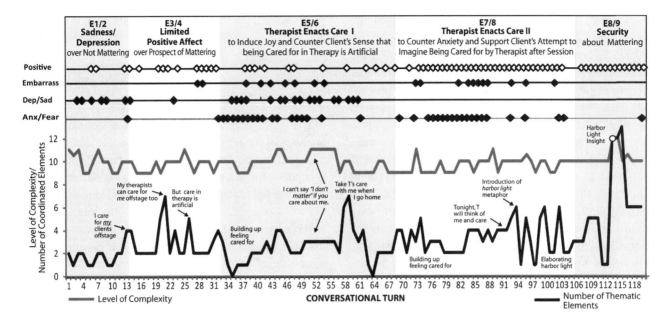

Figure 6.14 Codevelopment of representational and emotional activity over the course of a therapy session. The *curves* represent changes in the complexity of the client's representation of her sense of mattering to her therapist over the course of the session. *Gray curve* reflects changes in the hierarchical complexity of the client's utterances over the course of the session; *black curve* identifies changes in the number of meaning components that would eventually be coordinated into the "harbor light insight" at the end of the session.

114 when the various sets of components were coordinated into a single highly integrated insight. In what follows, we examine structural changes in the client's construction of the harbor light insight.

The experience of emotion plays a central role in organizing the developmental course of meaning in development (Fischer, Shaver, & Carnochan, 1990; Mascolo, Fischer, & Li, 2003). This is especially the case in psychotherapy (Basseches & Mascolo, 2010; Greenberg, Rice, & Elliot, 1993; Mascolo, Mancuso, & Dukewich, 2005; Toomey & Ecker, 2007). The top of Figure 6.14 depicts changes in expressed emotion over the course of the harbor light session. Four categories of emotion are identified: positive affect (i.e., smile, laughter, excited voice, statements expressing positive emotion), embarrassment/shame (i.e., smiling and gaze aversion; laughter inconsistent with events), depression/sadness (i.e., crying; tears; thin, constricted voice, as to cry; tremor; low/guttural voice; downturned lips; sitting heavily in the chair; long pauses/staring into space), and anxiety/fear (i.e., tightening of muscles or posture; increase in bodily movement; increase in pace of speech and/or decrease in clarity of speech; gaze aversion; verbal expressions). As indicated in Figure 6.14, the client's emotions evolved in five phases, each characterized by a different pattern of expressed emotion.

Over the course of the session, the therapist adopted the therapeutic strategy of repeatedly inducing emotional meanings and experiences that were incompatible with the emotional meanings and experiences expressed by the client (see McCollough & Magill, 2009; Ecker & Toomey, 2008). In the first phase, the client's emotions were organized primarily around sadness/depression as she articulated her sense of not mattering to others "off stage." During the second phase, the client expressed occasions of positive affect; she contemplated the prospect that she *might* matter to others (her present and previous therapist) when the client was "off stage" and not at work. Progress in imagining feeling cared for by the client's therapists was interrupted by the client's statement, accompanied by deep sadness, that feelings of care expressed by a therapist are "artificial." The therapist responded to the client by enacting deep feelings of care for the client (i.e., "Do I seem artificial to you?"). The therapist's expressed emotion had the effect of inducing both *positive affect* and *embarrassment* over feeling cared for by the therapist. Throughout the session, the therapist adopted the strategy of responding to the client's negative emotion with expressions of care intended to induce joyful experiences of feeling cared about by the therapist. This occurred repeatedly in both the third and fourth emotional phases of the session. In the third phase, the therapist's expression of care functioned to challenge the client's *anxiety* and *sadness* about the artificiality about the therapist's care. By the fourth phase, as the client was able to accept the therapist's expression of care as genuine, the client's expressions of sadness dissipated completely. At this point, the therapist raised the possibility that the client could draw on the therapist's feelings of care outside of the therapy session (i.e., "I wonder if you can take me with you, and take these feelings with you."). This produced deep anxiety (but not sadness) in the client, which the therapist again addressed by explicitly enacting feelings of care to the client. At the end of the fourth phase, the therapist guided the client through the extremely painful emotional task of imagining how the therapist would feel about the client that night when she was home at dinner. Throughout the process, the client relied on the therapist's overtly supportive expressions of care to manage her deep feelings of anxiety, fear, and embarrassment through the process: "This ability to look at you is a real, real barometer for me [to answer that question]." With such support, the client was able to imagine that she would matter to her therapist that evening after the session. Soon thereafter, the client invoked the metaphor of the therapist as a "harbor light" who beamed care to the client whether the therapist was present or absent. During the last phase, in her elaboration of the "harbor light insight," the client expressed considerable positive emotion, presumably reflecting feelings of security and closeness to the therapist.

These observed changes have several notable implications. First, the microdevelopmental changes that occurred over this session were not simply representational or cognitive ones; meaningful emotional transformation occurred over the course of the session. However, emotional transformation is not simply reflected in the superficial transition from predominantly negative to positive affect over the course of the session. Instead, it is manifested in the transformation of core emotional theme that organizes the client's relationship to her therapist. The shift from *not mattering "off stage"* to *"mattering to the therapist off stage"* reflects a transformation in the client's socioemotional orientation toward others. Second, the emotional changes observed over the course of the client's session were not simply adjuncts to the representational changes that occurred en route to the harbor light insight. On the contrary, the representational changes observed throughout the session *were organized by and made possible by* the emotional changes that occurred within the context of coregulated interaction between the client and therapist. In this way, emotion is not only necessary for the formation of novel

psychological structures in development; emotion is part of the process that defines a dynamic psychological structure.

Discursive Construction of Individual Meaning within Joint Action

Figure 6.15 provides the results of relational activity analyses of the four moments in the coconstruction of the client's "harbor light insight"—the client's emotionally grounded representation that the therapist can function as a "harbor light" whose beacon of care shines for the client whether the client is "onshore" or "offshore." The bottom right panel of Figure 6.15 contains an individual skill diagram that depicts the structure of the client's "harbor light insight," which functions at the high level of abstract systems (Ab3). The relational activity analyses depicted in the first three panels illuminate the processes by which the structural changes in the client's evolving representation emerged as a product of specific forms of coregulated activity that occurred between the therapist and client. The top left panel provides a representation of the starting point of the session, in which the following dialogue occurred:

C: Essentially me, my vote matters, but *I don't matter…* the things I can do, and, um, changes I can make and, uh, stuff I do to make the world a better place.

T: But there is a part of you that doesn't [feel you matter]. It's important because your actions are you, too. But something you were saying, the core of you, the feeling of like of you, your feelings don't matter…

C: Yeah, I guess that's it. It's like I, it's like when I'm at work, I matter, and when I go home, am by myself, I don't matter. It sort of on or off…Onstage or off stage.

Even in these few conversational turns, the client's representation of her sense of mattering undergoes change. In C1, at the level of abstract mappings, the client articulates the main conflict between mattering and not mattering that undergirds the entire session. In responding to the client, the therapist abstracted across the examples that the client provided of "mattering" to create the interpretation: "Your actions matter." The client then abstracted across her own and her therapist's statements to produce a more consolidated representation of her conflict in terms of mattering "onstage" but not mattering "off stage." The movements that produced this higher order representation of the conflict are represented in Figure 6.15.

The top right panel of Figure 6.15 illustrates a simple, yet important exchange involving the induction of emotion

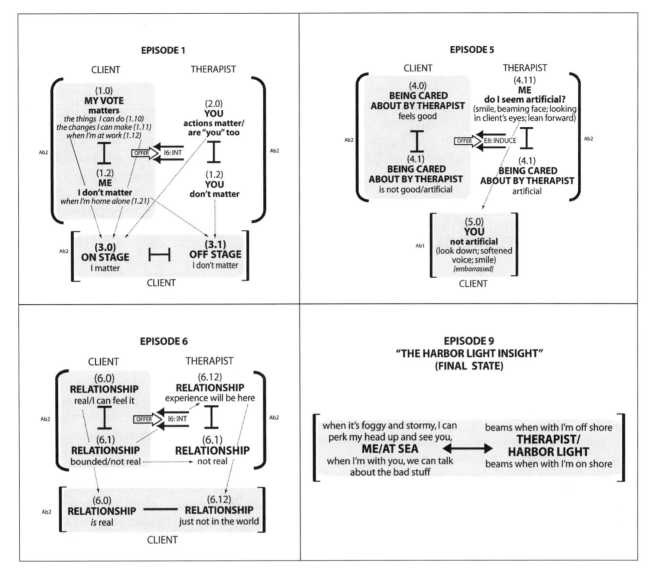

Figure 6.15   Four moments in the development of a client's representation of self and other. Figure depicts a series of relational activity diagrams and individual skill diagrams that chart developmental changes in a client's representation of self and other over the course of a psychotherapy session. Relational activity diagrams are enclosed in *rounded brackets;* individual skill diagrams are enclosed in *square brackets.* The first three quadrants identify the origins of a significant change in the client's psychological structure (individual structures) as products of specific coregulated exchanges between client and therapist (relational structures). The last panel shows the structure of the client's representation of self and other that emerged from the session.

in the client. Throughout the session, the therapist used the strategy of inducing emotional experiences that were incompatible with the client's expressed emotions and meanings. Specifically, the therapist enacted feelings of "caring for" the client as a counter to the client's sense that the client did not matter to others. In Episode 5, the client had just expressed anxiety (see earlier for criteria) about her sense that being cared for by a therapist is "artificial." In response, the therapist, with a beaming face, asked, "Do I seem artificial to you?" This simple interchange induced

embarrassment in the client, which signaled some degree of acceptance of the therapist's expressed feelings and provided a context for further development.

The bottom left panel of Figure 6.15 provides a simple example of how subtle interchanges that occur between social partners can produce profound transformations in emotionally charged representations in individual partners. In this case, building on her initial acceptance of the therapist's expressions of care, the client continues to struggle with the idea that expressions of care in therapy are "artificial and bounded" and thus "not real." This is represented in the left portion of the relational activity diagram. In response, the therapist states, "That's right, our experience will be here." In this utterance, the therapist differentiated two meanings that until this point were undifferentiated in the client, namely, the distinction that a relationship that is "bounded" ("our experience will be here") can produce "real" feelings of care. The client is able to use this distinction to restructure the conflict that she articulated just moments before.

DEVELOPMENTAL THEORY AND RESEARCH: THINK GLOBALLY, ACT LOCALLY

In his call for a developmental behavioral genetics, Gottlieb (2003) wrote:

> The population view of behavioral genetics is not developmental. It is based on the erroneous assumption that a quantitative analysis of the genetic and environmental contributions to individual differences sheds light on the developmental process of individuals. Any light shed on individuals development from a population view of behavioral genetics would be of a very general, nonspecific nature...Two reasons: (1) The finding of variance between individuals cannot be validly applied to an explanation of variation within individuals...(2) Because an understanding of the changes in individual development over the lifespan cannot be ascribed to singular causes (e.g., hereditary factors) operating in isolation: Understanding the development of individuals requires a relational concept of causality. (p. 338)

Human psychological functioning and its development are dynamic. To the extent that psychological functioning consists of a type of *activity*, it must operate as a *process* that occurs *over time*. To study a *process*, it is necessary to examine how the components of the process change over time in relation to each other within particular contexts. Traditionally, however, instead of thinking of psychological functioning in terms of systems of contextualized processes, theorists and researchers have understood human action in terms of a series of abstract and more-or-less static entities or structures. Examples of static units include the concepts such as *trait, general stages of operative competence, genetic plans, memories* as *stored representations,* and so forth. Such units are static because they are assumed to reflect more or less fixed or stable attributes of individuals. To gain evidence for the existence of such static attributes, it is necessary to *abstract across* and *ignore* the dynamic *variation* that occurs across the multiple situations or contexts in which indicators of a presumed variable are observed.

The new developmental science is a dynamic one. Within this new and exciting paradigm, the *development* of psychological functioning can be seen in terms of the *dynamic emergence of increasingly differentiated and integrated structures of meaning-mediated activity over time within particular physical and social contexts.* Although human psychological functioning is composed of multiple component processes, no single component process is primary in the constitution of action; any psychological act necessarily involves some integration of all such processes. As dynamic *processes* rather than static entities, it is necessary to study *integrative human action* in particular behavioral *domains* as it assumes successively different *forms over time* within particular contexts. As Gottlieb (2003) suggested, to capture the nature of the process of development, one must go beyond the partitioning of variance within populations to the study of trajectories of growth and development in *individual* actors over time (Fogel et al., 2003; Piaget, 1953; Van Geert, 1994; see Nesselroade & Molenaar, Chapter 2 of this volume, for an extended discussion of methods for assessing intraindividual variation). In so doing, it is necessary to draw on methods, many of which have been illustrated in this chapter, to analyze the moment-to-moment process by which discursive organism-environment interchanges create novel integrations of thinking, feeling, and action over time. Toward this end, because they lend themselves to finely textured analysis of the moment-by-moment emergence of novel behavior, the study of *microdevelopment* will prove to be an invaluable analytic tool (Flynn & Siegler, 2007; Granott, Fischer, & Parziale, 2002). In the coming decades, although the study of development *in medias res* will require psychological theorizing of a *global* and *integrative* nature, empirical progress will be found in the application of theory and method to analyze the developmental course of human action in *local* domains and contexts over the life span.

REFERENCES

Ayoub, C. C., & Fischer, K. W. (2006). Developmental pathways and intersections among domains of development. In K. McCartney & D. Phillips (Eds.), *Handbook of early child development* (pp. 62–82). Oxford: Blackwell.

Barrett, L. F., Ochsner, K. N., & Gross, J. J. (2007). On the automaticity of emotion. In J. Bargh (Ed.), *Social psychology and the unconscious: The automaticity of higher mental processes* (pp. 173–218). New York: Psychology Press.

Basseches, M., & Mascolo, M. F. (2010). *Psychotherapy as a developmental process.* New York: Routledge.

Bateson, G. (1972). *Steps to an ecology of mind.* New York: Aronson.

Baumeister, R. (1998). The self. In *The handbook of social psychology* (Vols. 1 and 2, 4th ed., pp. 680–740). New York: McGraw-Hill.

Beebe, B., Knoblauch, S., Rustin, J., Sorter, D., Jacobs, T., & Pally, R. (2005). *Forms of intersubjectivity in infant research and adult treatment.* New York: Other Press.

Bell, M., & Fox, N. (1992). The relations between frontal brain electrical activity and cognitive development during infancy. *Child Development, 63*(5), 1142–1163.

Bermond, B. (2008). The emotional feeling as a combination of two qualia: A neurophilosophical-based emotion theory. *Cognition & Emotion, 22,* 897–930.

Berridge, K. C. (2003). Comparing the emotional brain of humans and other animals. In R. J. Davidson, H. H. Goldsmith, & K. Scherer (Eds.), *Handbook of affective sciences* (pp. 25–51). Oxford: Oxford University Press.

Blanchard-Fields, F., & Coats, A. (2008). The experience of anger and sadness in everyday problems impacts age differences in emotion regulation. *Developmental Psychology, 44,* 1547–1556.

Bråten, S. (Ed.). (2007). *On being moved: From mirror neurons to empathy.* Philadelphia: John Benjamins.

Brown, T. (1994). Affective dimensions of meaning. In W. Overton & D. Palermo (Eds.), *The nature and ontogenesis of meaning.* Hillsdale, NJ: Erlbaum.

Brown, T. L., Joneleit, K., Robinson, C. S., & Brown, C. R. (2002). Automaticity in reading and the Stroop task: Testing the limits of involuntary word processing. *American Journal of Psychology, 4,* 515–543.

Burke, K. (1966). *Language as symbolic action.* Los Angeles: University of California Press.

Cacioppo, J. T., Visser, P. S., & Picket, C. L. (Eds.). (2006). *Social neuroscience: People thinking about thinking people.* Cambridge, MA: MIT Press.

Campos, J. J., Anderson, D. I., Barbu-Roth, M. A., Hubbard, E. M., Hertenstein, M. J., & Witherington, D. (2000). Travel broadens the mind. *Infancy, 1,* 149–219.

Carstensen, L., & Mikels, J. (2005). At the intersection of emotion and cognition: Aging and the positivity effect. *Current Directions in Psychological Science, 14,* 117–121.

Carver, C. S., & Scheier, M. F. (2002). Control processes and self-organization as complementary principles underlying behavior. *Personality and Social Psychology Review, 6,* 304–315.

Cavanaugh, J., Dunn, N., Mowery, D., & Feller, C. (1989). Problem-solving strategies in dementia patient-caregiver dyads. *The Gerontologist, 29,* 156–158.

Charles, S., & Carstensen, L. (2008). Unpleasant situations elicit different emotional responses in younger and older adults. *Psychology and Aging, 23,* 495–504.

Charness, N., & Holley, P. (2001). Human factors and environmental support in Alzheimer's disease. *Aging & Mental Health, 5,* 65–73.

Clark, A. (1997). *Being there.* Cambridge, MA: MIT Press.

Clark, M., & Caffarella, R. (1999). Theorizing adult development. *New Directions for Adult & Continuing Education, 84,* 1–8.

Cohen, U., & Day, K. (1993). *Contemporary environments for people with dementia.* Baltimore: Johns Hopkins Press.

Consedine, N., & Magai, C. (2006). Emotional development in adulthood: A developmental functionalist review and critique.

Handbook of adult development and learning (pp. 123–148). New York: Oxford University Press.

Cozolino, L. (2006). *The neuroscience of human relationships: Attachment and the developing social brain.* New York: Norton.

Csikszentmihalyi, M. (1991). *Flow: The psychology of optimal experience.* New York: Harper & Row.

Damasio, A. (1994). *Descartes' error: Emotion, reason, and the human brain.* New York: Putnam.

Damasio, A. (1999). *The feeling of what happens: Body and emotion in the making of consciousness.* New York: Harcourt Brace.

Davidson, R. J. (2000). Cognitive neuroscience needs affective neuroscience (and vice versa). *Brain & Cognition, 42,* 89–92.

Davis, H., & Fill, K. (2007). Embedding blended learning in a university's teaching culture: Experiences and reflections. *British Journal of Educational Technology, 398,* 817–828.

Davitz, J. R. (1969). *The language of emotion.* New York: Academic.

de Casper, A., & Carstens, A. (1980). Contingencies of stimulation: Effects on learning and emotion in neonates. *Infant Behavior and Development, 4,* 19–36.

Dennen, V. (2004). Cognitive apprenticeship in educational practice: Research on scaffolding, modeling, mentoring, and coaching as instructional strategies. In *Handbook of research on educational communications and technology* (2nd ed., pp. 813–828). Mahwah, NJ: Erlbaum.

Diaz, R. M., & Berk, L. E. (1992). *Private speech. From social interaction to self-regulation.* Hillsdale, NJ: Erlbaum.

Diehl, M., Coyle, N., & Labouvie-Vief, G. (1996). Age and sex differences in strategies of coping and defense across the life span. *Psychology and Aging, 11,* 127–139.

Dunning, D. (2007). Self-image motives and consumer behavior: How sacrosanct self-beliefs sway preferences in the market place. *Journal of Consumer Psychology, 17*(4), 237–249.

Ecker, B., & Toomey, B. (2008). Depotentiation of symptom-producing implicit memory in coherence therapy. *Journal of Constructivist Psychology, 21,* 87–150.

Eisenberg, N., Hofer, C., & Vaughan, J. (2007). Effortful control and its socioemotional consequences. *Handbook of emotion regulation* (pp. 287–306). New York: Guilford

Elder, G., & Shanahan, M. (2006). The life course and human development. In *Handbook of child psychology: Vol. 1, Theoretical models of human development* (6th ed., pp. 665–715). Hoboken, NJ: John Wiley & Sons.

Ellsworth, P., & Scherer, K. (2003). Appraisal processes in emotion. *Handbook of affective sciences* (pp. 572–595). New York: Oxford University Press.

Emde, R. N. (1983). The prerepresentational self and its affective core. *Psychoanalytic Study of the Child, 38,* 165–192.

Erikson, E. H. (1963). *Childhood and society.* New York: Norton.

Espiritu, L. (2007). E-teaching skills. *Communication and cognition: An Interdisciplinary Quarterly Journal, 40,* 119–126.

Ferguson, T. J., Eyre, H. L., & Ashbaker, M. (2000). Unwanted identities: A key variable in shame-anger links and gender differences in shame. *Sex Roles, 42,* 133–157.

Fischer, K. W. (1980). A theory of cognitive development: The control and construction of hierarchies of skills. *Psychological Review, 87,* 477–531.

Fischer, K. W. (2008). Dynamic cycles of cognitive and brain development: Measuring growth in mind, brain, and education. In A. M. Battro, K. W. Fischer, & P. Léna (Eds.), *The educated brain* (pp. 127–150). Cambridge: Cambridge University Press.

Fischer, K. W., & Bidell, T. R. (2006). Dynamic development of action, thought, and emotion. In W. Damon & R. M. Lerner (Eds.),

Theoretical models of human development: Vol. 1, Handbook of child psychology (6th ed., pp. 313–399). Hoboken, NJ: John Wiley & Sons.

Fischer, K. W., Bullock, D. H., Rotenberg, E. J., & Raya, P. (1993). The dynamics of competence: How context contributes directly to skill. In R. Wozniak & K. W. Fischer (Eds.), *Development in context: Acting and thinking in specific environments* (pp. 93–117). Hillsdale, NJ: Erlbaum.

Fischer, K., & Granott, N. (1995). Beyond one-dimensional change: Parallel, concurrent, socially distributed processes in learning and development. *Human Development, 38*(6), 302–314.

Fischer, K. W., and Hogan, A. E. (1989) The big picture for infant development: Levels and variations. In J. J. Lockman & N. L. Hazen (Eds.). *Action in social context: Perspectives on early development* (pp. 275–305) New York: Plenum.

Fischer, K. W., Kenny, S. L., & Pipp, S. L. (1990). How cognitive processes and environmental conditions organize discontinuities in the development of abstractions, In C. N. Alexander, E. J. Langer, & R. M. Oetzel (Eds.), *Higher stages of development* (pp. 162–187). New York: Oxford University Press.

Fischer, K. W., & Pipp, S. L. (1984). Processes of cognitive development: Optimal level and skill acquisition. In R. J. Sternberg (Ed.), *Mechanisms of cognitive development* (pp. 45–80). San Francisco, CA: Freeman.

Fischer, K., & Rose, S. (1994). Dynamic development of coordination of components in brain and behavior: A framework for theory and research. *Human behavior and the developing brain* (pp. 3–66). New York: Guilford.

Fischer, K. W., Shaver, P., & Carnochan, P. (1990). How emotions develop and how they organize development. *Cognition and Emotion, 4,* 81–127.

Fischer, K. W., Yan, Z., & Stewart, J. (2003). Adult cognitive development: Dynamics in the developmental web. In J. Valsiner & K. Connolly (Eds.), *Handbook of developmental psychology* (pp. 491–516). Thousand Oaks, CA: Sage.

Flynn, E., & Siegler, R. (2007). Measuring change: Current trends and future directions in microgenetic research. *Infant and Child Development, 16,* 135–149.

Fogel, A. (1993). *Developing through relationships.* Chicago: University of Chicago Press.

Fogel, A. (2006). Dynamic systems research on interindividual communication: The transformation of meaning-making. *The Journal of Developmental Processes, 1,* 7–30.

Fogel, A., Garvey, A., Hsu, H-C., & West-Stromming, D. (2006). *Change processes in relationships: A relational-historical approach.* New York: Cambridge University Press.

Fogel, A., Lyra, M. C. D. P., & Valsiner, J. (Eds.). (1997). *Dynamics and indeterminism in developmental and social processes.* Mahwah, NJ: Erlbaum.

Freeman, W. (2000). Emotion is essential to all intentional behaviours. In M. D. Lewis & I. Granic (Eds.), *Emotion, development, and self-organization* (pp. 209–235). New York: Cambridge University Press.

Freud, S. (1917/1965). *New introductory lectures on psychoanalysis.* New York: Norton.

Freund, A. (2007). Differentiating and integrating levels of goal representation: A life-span perspective. *Personal project pursuit: Goals, action, and human flourishing* (pp. 247–270). Mahwah, NJ: Erlbaum.

Frijda, N. H. (1986). *The emotions.* Cambridge: Cambridge University Press.

Frijda, N. H. (1987). Emotion, emotion structure, and action tendency. *Cognition and Emotion, 1,* 115–143.

Gallagher, S. (2005). *How the body shapes the mind.* Oxford: Oxford University Press.

Gallagher, S., & Hutto, D. D. (2008). Understanding others through primary interaction and narrative practice. In J. Zlatev, T. Racine, C. Sinha, & E. Itkonen (Eds.), *The shared mind: Perspectives on intersubjectivity.* Amsterdam: John Benjamins.

Gallese, V., Eagle, M. N., & Migone, P. (2007). Intentional attunement: Mirror neurons and the neural underpinnings of interpersonal relations. *Journal of the American Psychoanalytic Association, 55,* 131–176.

Gangestad, S., & Simpson, J. (2007). *The evolution of mind: Fundamental questions and controversies.* New York: Guilford.

Gazzaniga, M. S., Ivry, R. B., & Mangun, G. R. (Eds.). 2008. *Cognitive neuroscience: The biology of the mind* (3rd ed.). New York: Norton.

Gelman, R., & Baillargeon, R. (1983). A review of some Piagetian concepts. In J. H. Flavell & E. Markman (Eds.), *Handbook of child psychology: Vol. 3, Cognitive development.* New York: John Wiley & Sons.

Gibbs, R. (2006). *Embodiment and cognitive science.* New York: Cambridge University.

Gibson, J. J. (1979). *The ecological approach to visual perception.* Boston: Houghton Mifflin.

Gottlieb, G. (2003). On making behavioral genetics truly developmental. *Human Development, 46,* 337–355.

Gottlieb, G., & Lickliter, R. (2007). Probabilistic epigenesis. *Developmental Science, 10,* 1–11.

Gottlieb, G., Wahlsten, D., & Lickliter, R. (2006). The significance of biology for human development: A developmental psychobiological systems perspective. In W. Damon & R. M. Lerner (Series Eds.) & R. M. Lerner (Vol. Ed.), *Handbook of child psychology: Vol. 1, Theoretical models of human development* (6th ed., pp. 210–257). Hoboken, NJ: John Wiley & Sons.

Gould, R. L. (1980). Transformational tasks in adulthood. In S. I. Greenspan & G. H. Pollock (Eds.), *The course of life: Psychoanalytic contributions toward understanding personality development* (Vol. 3). Washington, DC: National Institute of Mental Health.

Granott, N. (1993). Patterns of interaction in the co-construction of knowledge: Separate minds, Joint effort, and Weird creatures. In R. Wozniak & K. W. Fischer (Eds.), *Development in context: Acting and thinking in specific environments* (pp. 183–207). Hillsdale, NJ: Erlbaum.

Granott, N. (1998). Unit of analysis in transit: From the individual's knowledge to the ensemble process. *Mind, Culture, and Activity: An International Journal, 5*(1), 42–66.

Granott, N. (2002). How microdevelopment creates macrodevelopment: Reiterated sequences, backward transitions, and the zone of current development zone. In N. Granott & J. Parziale (Eds.), *Microdevelopment: Transition processes in development and learning* (pp. 213–242). New York: Cambridge University Press.

Granott, N., Fischer, K. W., & Parziale, J. (2002). Bridging to the unknown: A fundamental mechanism in learning and problem-solving. In N. Granott & J. Parziale (Eds.), *Microdevelopment.* Cambridge: Cambridge University Press.

Greenberg, L. S., Rice, L. N., & Elliot, R. (1993). *Facilitating emotional change: The moment by moment process.* New York: Guilford.

Gruenewald, T., Mroczek, D., Ryff, C., & Singer, B. (2008). Diverse pathways to positive and negative affect in adulthood and later life: An integrative approach using recursive partitioning. *Developmental Psychology, 44,* 330–343.

Hagne, I., Persson, J., Magnusson, R., & Petersén, I. (1973). Spectral analysis via fast Fourier transform of waking EEG in normal infants. In P. Kellaway & I. Petersén (Eds.), *Automation of clinical electroencephalography* (pp. 103–143). New York: Raven.

Hahs-Vaughn, D., Zygouris-Coe, V., & Fiedler, R. (2007). A hybrid evaluation model for evaluating online professional development. *Technology, Pedagogy & Education, 16,* 5–20.

Harmon-Jones, E., & Winkielman, P. (Eds.). (2007). *Social neuroscience: Integrating biological and psychological explanations of social behavior.* New York: Guilford.

Hassin, R., Uleman, J., & Bargh, J. (Eds.). (2005). *The new unconscious.* New York: Oxford University Press.

Hoare, C. (2006). Work as the catalyst of reciprocal adult development and learning: Identity and personality. *Handbook of adult development and learning* (pp. 344–380). New York: Oxford University Press.

Hudspeth, W. J., & Pribram, K. H. (1992). Psychophysiological indices of cerebral maturation. *International Journal of Psychophysiology, 12,* 19–29.

Johnson, M. (1987). *The body in the mind: The bodily basis of meaning, imagination, and reason.* Chicago: University of Chicago Press.

Kagan, J. (1996). Three pleasing ideas. *American Psychologist, 51,* 901–908.

Kagan, J., & Snidman, N. (2004). *The long shadow of temperament.* Cambridge, MA: Belknap Press/Harvard University Press.

Keltner, D., & Gross, J. J. (1999). Functional accounts of emotions. *Cognition and Emotion, 13,* 467–480.

Keltner, D., & Haidt, J. (1999). The social functions of emotions at four levels of analysis. *Cognition and Emotion, 13,* 505–522.

Kitchener, K., King, P., & DeLuca, S. (2006). Development of reflective judgment in adulthood. *Handbook of adult development and learning* (pp. 73–98). New York: Oxford University Press.

Kochanska, G., Forman, D., Aksan, N., & Dunbar, S. (2005). Pathways to conscience: Early mother-child mutually responsive orientation and children's moral emotion, conduct, and cognition. *Journal of Child Psychology and Psychiatry, 46,* 19–34.

Kohlberg, L. (1981). *Essays on moral development, Vol. I: The philosophy of moral development.* San Francisco, CA: Harper & Row.

Kovecses, Z. (2000). *Metaphor and emotion.* New York: Oxford University Press.

Kristensen, T. (2004). The physical context of creativity. *Creativity and Innovation Management, 13,* 89–96.

LaBar, K. S., & LeDoux, J. E. (2003). Emotional learning circuits in animals and humans. In R. J. Davidson, K. Scherer, & H. H. Goldsmith (Eds.), *Handbook of affective sciences* (pp. 52–65). New York: Oxford University Press.

Labouvie-Vief, G. (2003). Dynamic integration: Affect, cognition, and the self in adulthood. *Current Directions in Psychological Science, 12,* 201–206.

Labouvie-Vief, G., & Diehl, M. (2000). Cognitive complexity and cognitive-affective integration: Related or separate domains of adult development? *Psychology and Aging, 15,* 490–504.

Labouvie-Vief, G., Diehl, M., Jain, E., & Zhang, F. (2007). Six-year change in affect optimization and affect complexity across the adult life span: A further examination. *Psychology and Aging, 22,* 738–751.

Lachman, M. (2004). Development in midlife. *Annual Review of Psychology, 55,* 305–331.

Lazarus, R. S. (1991). *Emotion and adaptation.* New York: Oxford University Press.

Lejeune, L., Anderson, D., Campos, J., Witherington, D., Uchiyama, I., & Barbu-Roth, M. (2006). Responsiveness to terrestrial optic flow in infancy: Does locomotor experience play a role? *Human Movement Science, 25,* 4–17.

Lerner, R. M. (2006). Developmental science, developmental systems, and contemporary theories of human development. In W. Damon & R. M. Lerner (Series Eds.) & R. M. Lerner (Vol. Ed.), *Handbook of child psychology: Vol. 1, Theoretical models of human development* (6th ed., pp. 1–17). Hoboken, NJ: John Wiley & Sons.

Lerner, R. M., & Overton, W. F. (2008). Exemplifying the integrations of the relational developmental system: Synthesizing theory, research, and application to promote positive development and social justice. *Journal of Adolescent Research, 23,* 245–255.

Lewis, M. D. (1996). Self-organising cognitive appraisals. *Cognition and Emotion, 10,* 1–25.

Lewis, M. D. (2005). Bridging emotion theory and neurobiology through dynamic systems modeling. *Behavioral and Brain Sciences, 28,* 169–245.

Lewis, M., & Todd, R. (2007). The self-regulating brain: Cortical-subcortical feedback and the development of intelligent action. *Cognitive Development, 22,* 406–430.

Lewontin, R. C. (2000). *The triple helix: Gene, organism and environment.* Cambridge, MA: Harvard University Press.

Loeber, R., & Stouthamer-Loeber, M. (1998). The development of juvenile aggression and violence: Some common misconceptions and controversies. *American Psychologist, 53,* 242–259.

Luo, L., & Craik, F. I. (2008). Aging and memory: A cognitive approach. *Canadian Journal of Psychiatry, 53,* 346–353.

MacLean, P. D. (1993). Perspectives on cingulate cortex in the limbic system. In B. A. Vogt & M. Gabriel (Eds.), *Neurobiology of cingulate cortex and limbic thalamus: A comprehensive handbook* (pp. 1–15). Boston: Brikhauser.

Magnusson, D., & Stattin, H. (2006). The person in the environment: Towards a general model for scientific inquiry. In W. Damon & R. M. Lerner (Series Eds.) & R. M. Lerner (Vol. Ed.), *Handbook of child psychology: Vol. 1, Theoretical models of human development* (6th ed., pp. 400–464). Hoboken, NJ: John Wiley & Sons.

Malatesta, C., & Izard, C. (1984). Facial expression of emotion in young, middle-aged, and older adults. In C. Malatesta & C. E. Iard (Eds.), *Emotion in adult development.* Beverly Hills, CA: Sage.

Mascolo, M. F. (2004). The coactive construction of selves in cultures. In W. Damon (Series Ed.) & M. F. Mascolo & J. Li (Vol. Eds.), *Culture and self: Beyond dichotomization: New directions in child and adolescent development series* (pp. 79–90). San Francisco, CA: Jossey-Bass.

Mascolo, M. F. (2005). Change processes in development: The concept of coactive scaffolding. *New Ideas in Psychology, 23,* 185–196.

Mascolo, M. F. (2008a). Wittgenstein and the discursive analysis of emotion. *New Ideas in Psychology, 27,* 258–274.

Mascolo, M. F. (2008b). The concept of domain in developmental models of hierarchical complexity. *World Futures: The Journal of General Evolution. 64*(5–7), 330–347.

Mascolo, M. F., Craig-Bray, L., & Neimeyer, R. (1997). The construction of meaning and action in development and psychotherapy: An epigenetic systems approach. In G. Neimeyer & R. Neimeyer (Eds.), *Advances in personal construct psychology* (Vol. 4, pp. 3–38). Greenwich, CT: JAI Press.

Mascolo, M. F., & Fischer, K. W. (2005). Constructivist theories. In B. Hopkins, R. G. Barre, G. F. Michel, & P. Rochat (Eds.), *Cambridge encyclopedia of child development.* Cambridge: Cambridge University Press.

Mascolo, M. F., & Fischer, K. W. (2007). The co-development of self-awareness and self-evaluative emotions across the toddler years. In C. A. Brownell & C. B. Kopp (Eds.), *Transitions in early socioemotional development: The toddler years.* New York: Guilford.

Mascolo, M. J., Fischer, K. W., & Li, J. (2003). Dynamic development of component systems of emotions: Pride, shame, and guilt in China and the United States. In R. J. Davidson, K. Scherer, & H. H.

Goldsmith (Eds.), *Handbook of affective science.* Oxford: Oxford University Press.

Mascolo, M., & Fischer, K. (1998). The development of self through the coordination of component systems. *Self-awareness: Its nature and development* (pp. 332–384). New York: Guilford.

Mascolo, M., & Fischer, K. (1995). Developmental transformations in appraisals for pride, shame, and guilt. *Self-conscious emotions: The psychology of shame, guilt, embarrassment, and pride* (pp. 64-113). New York: Guilford.

Mascolo, M. F., Fischer, K. W., & Neimeyer, R. (1999). The dynamic co-development of intentionality, self and social relations. In J. Brandstadter & R. M. Lerner (Eds.), *Action and development: Origins and functions of intentional self-development* (pp. 133–166). Thousand Oaks, CA: Sage.

Mascolo, M., & Harkins, D. (1998). Toward a component systems approach to emotional development. *What develops in emotional development?* (pp. 189–217). New York: Plenum.

Mascolo, M., Li, J., Fink, R., & Fischer, K. (2002). Pathways to excellence: Value presuppositions and the development of academic and affective skills in educational contexts. *The pursuit of excellence through education* (pp. 113–146). Mahwah, NJ: Erlbaum.

Mascolo, M. F., & Mancuso, J. C., & Dukewich, T. (2005). Trajectories in the development of anger in development: Appraisal, action and regulation. In J. Cummins (Ed.), *Working with anger: A practical perspective.* Hoboken, NJ: John Wiley & Sons.

Mascolo, M. F., & Margolis, D. (2005). Social meanings as mediators of the development of adolescent experience and action: A coactive systems approach. *European Journal of Developmental Psychology, 1,* 289–302.

Mascolo, M., Misra, G., & Rapisardi, C. (2004). Individual and relational conceptions of self in India and the United States. *Culture and developing selves: Beyond dichotomization* (pp. 9–26). San Francisco, CA: Jossey-Bass.

Mascolo, M. F., Pollack, R., & Fischer, K. W. (1997). Keeping the constructor in constructivism: An epigenetic systems approach. *Journal of Constructivist Psychology, 10,* 25–29.

Matousek, M., & Petersén, I. (1973). Frequency analysis of the EEG in normal children and adolescents. In P. Kellaway & I. Petersén (Eds.), *Automation of clinical electroencephalography* (pp. 75–102). New York: Raven.

Matusov, E. (1996). Intersubjectivity without agreement. *Mind, culture and activity, 3,* 25–45.

McCullough, L. (1999). Short term psychodynamic therapy as a form of desensitization: Treating affective phobias. *In session: Psychotherapy in practice, 4,* 35-53.

McCullough, L., Kuhn, N., Andrews, S., Kaplan, A., Wolf, J., & Hurley, C. (2003). *Treating affect phobia: A manual for short-term dynamic psychotherapy.* New York: Guilford.

McCullough, L., & Magill, M. (2009). Affect-focused short-term dynamic therapy. *Handbook of evidence-based psychodynamic psychotherapy: Bridging the gap between science and practice* (pp. 249–277). Totowa, NJ: Humana.

McNamee, S. (1977). Moral behavior, moral development and motivation. *Journal of Moral Education, 7,* 27–31.

Mead, G. H. (1934). *Mind, self and society from the standpoint of a social behaviorist.* Chicago: University of Chicago Press.

Meltzoff, A. N. (2002). Elements of a developmental theory of imitation. In A. N. Meltzoff & W. Prinz (Eds.), *The imitative mind: Development, evolution, and brain bases* (pp. 19–41). Cambridge: Cambridge University Press.

Meltzoff, A. N., & Brooks, R. (2007). Intersubjectivity before language: Three windows on preverbal sharing. In S. Bråten (Ed.), *On being moved: From mirror neurons to empathy* (pp. 149–174). Philadelphia: John Benjamins.

Meltzoff, A. N., & Moore, M. K. (1999). Persons and representation: Why infant imitation is important for theories of human development. In J. B. G. Nadel (Ed.), *Imitation in infancy: Cambridge studies in cognitive perceptual development* (pp. 9–35). New York: Cambridge University Press.

Merleau-Ponty, M. (1945). *The phenomenology of perception* (C. Smith, Trans.). London: Routledge and Kegan Paul.

Miller, G. A., Galanter, E., & Pribram, K. H. (1960). *Plans and the structure of behavior.* New York: Henry Holt.

Mitchell, R., & Phillips, L. (2007). The psychological, neurochemical and functional neuroanaticalal mediators of the effects of positive and negative mood on executive functions. *Neuropsychologia, 45,* 617–629.

Mizuno, T., Yamauchi, N., Watanabe, A., Komatsushiro, M., Takagi, T., Linuma, K., et al. (1970). Maturation of patterns of EEG: Basic waves of healthy infants under 12 months of age. *Tohoku Journal of Experimental Medicine, 102,* 91–98.

Morrow, D., Ridolfo, H., Menard, W., Sanborn, A., Stine-Morrow, E., Magnor, C., et al. (2003). Environmental support promotes expertise-based mitigation of age differences on pilot communication tasks. *Psychology and Aging, 18,* 268–284.

Morrow, D., & Rogers, W. (2008). Environmental support: An integrative framework. *Human Factors, 50,* 589–613.

Mroczek, D. (2001). Age and emotion in adulthood. *Current Directions in Psychological Science, 10,* 87–90.

Mroczek, D., & Kolarz, C. (1998). The effect of age on positive and negative affect: A developmental perspective on happiness. *Journal of Personality and Social Psychology, 75,* 1333–1349.

Murray, D., & McPherson, P. (2006). Scaffolding instruction for reading the web. *Language Teaching Research, 10,* 131–156.

Noë, A. (2004). *Action in perception.* Cambridge, MA: MIT Press.

Overgaard, S. (2006). The problem of other minds: Wittgenstein's phenomenological perspective. *Phenomenology and the Cognitive Sciences, 5,* 53–73.

Overton, W. F. (2006). Developmental psychology: Philosophy, concepts, methodology. In W. Damon & R. M. Lerner (Series Ed.) & R. M. Lerner (Vol. Ed.), *Handbook of child psychology: Vol. 1, Theoretical models of human development* (6th ed., pp. 18–88). Hoboken, NJ: John Wiley & Sons.

Overton, W. F. (2007). A coherent metatheory for dynamic systems: Relational organicism-contextualism. *Human Development, 50,* 154–159.

Overton, W. F., Mueller, U., & Newman, J. (Eds.). (2007). *Developmental perspectives on embodiment and consciousness.* Mahwah, NJ: Erlbaum.

Oyama, S. (2000). *Evolution's eye: A systems view of the biology-culture divide.* Durham, NC: Duke University Press.

Palloff, R., & Pratt, K. (1999). *Building learning communities in cyberspace: Effective strategies for the online classroom.* San Francisco, CA: Jossey-Bass.

Panksepp, J. (1998). *Affective neuroscience: The foundations of human and animal emotions.* New York: Oxford University Press.

Park, D. C., & Shaw, R. J. (1992). Effect of environmental support on implicit and explicit memory in younger and older adults. *Psychology and Aging, 7,* 632–642.

Pessoa, L. (2008). On the relationship between emotion and cognition. *Nature Reviews Neuroscience, 9,* 148–158.

Phelps, E. (2005). *The interaction of emotion and cognition: The relation between the human amygdala and cognitive awareness. The new unconscious* (pp. 61–76). New York: Oxford University Press.

Phelps, E., Ling, S., & Carrasco, M. (2006). Emotion facilitates perception and potentiates the perceptual benefits of attention. *Psychological Science, 17,* 292–299.

Piaget, J. (1953). *The origins of intelligence in children.* London: Routledge and Kegan Paul.

Piaget, J. (1983). Piaget's theory. In W. Kessen (Ed.), *Handbook of child psychology* (Vol. 1). New York: John Wiley & Sons.

Quilter, S., & Weber, R. (2004). Quality assurance for online teaching in higher education: Considering and identifying best practice for e-Learning. *International Journal on E-Learning, 3,* 64–73.

Rabins, P. (1998). The caregiver's role in Alzheimer's disease. *Dementia and Geriatric Cognitive Disorders, 9,* 25–28.

Ready, R., Carvalho, J., & Weinberger, M. (2008). Emotional complexity in younger, midlife, and older adults. *Psychology and Aging, 23*(4), 928–933.

Riediger, M., & Freund, A. (2006). Focusing and restricting: Two aspects of motivational selectivity in adulthood. *Psychology and Aging, 21,* 173–185.

Rizzolatti, G. (2005). The mirror neuron system and imitation. In S. Hurley & N. Chater (Eds.), *Perspectives on imitation: From neuroscience to social science* (Vol. 1, pp. 55–76). Cambridge, MA: MIT Press.

Rogoff, B. (1990). *Apprenticeship in thinking: Cognitive development in social context.* New York: Oxford University Press.

Rogoff, B. (1993). Children's guided participation and participatory appropriation in sociocultural activity. In R. H. Wozniak & K. W. Fischer (Eds.), *Development in context* (pp. 121–153). Hillsdale, NJ: LEA.

Rommetveit, R. (1979). On the architecture of intersubjectivity. In R. Rommetveit & R. M. Blaker (Eds.), *Studies of language, thought and verbal communication.* New York: Academic.

Rommetveit, R. (1985). Language acquisition as increasing linguistic restructuring of experience and symbolic behavior control. In J. V. Wertsch (Ed.), *Culture, communication and cognition* (pp. 57–68). Cambridge: Cambridge University Press.

Roseman, I. J. (1984). Cognitive determinants of emotions: A structural theory. In P. Shaver (Ed.), *Review of personality and social psychology* (Vol. 5, pp. 11–36). Beverly Hills, CA: Sage.

Rosey, F., Golomer, E., & Keller, J. (2008). Precocity of fine motor control and task context: Hitting a ball while stepping. *Journal of Motor Behavior, 40,* 347–357.

Rothbart, M. (2007). Temperament, development, and personality. *Current Directions in Psychological Science, 16,* 207–212.

Roy, K., & McAdams, D. (2006). Second chances as transformative stories in human development: An introduction. *Research in Human Development, 3,* 77–80.

Salomon, G. (1993). (Ed.). *Distributed cognitions. Psychological and educational considerations.* Cambridge: Cambridge University Press.

Sarbin, T. (1989). Emotion as situated action. In L. Cirillo, B. Kaplan, & S. Wapner (Eds.), *The role of emotion in ideal human development* (pp. 77–99). Hillsdale, NJ: Erlbaum.

Sarbin, T. R. (1952). A preface to a psychological analysis of the self. *Psychological Review, 59,* 11–22.

Saxe, G. B. (1982). Developing forms of arithmetic operations among the Oksapmin of Papua New Guinea. *Developmental Psychology, 18,* 583–594.

Schafer, S. (1985). Modifying the environment. *Geriatric Nursing, 3,* 157–159.

Scheff, T., & Retzinger, S. (1991). *Emotions and violence.* Lexington, MA.

Scherer, K. R. (2004). Feelings integrate the central representation of appraisal-driven response organization in emotion. In A. S. R. Manstead, N. H. Frijda, & A. H. Fischer (Eds.), *Feelings and emotions* (pp. 136–157). Cambridge: Cambridge University Press.

Schieman, S. (1999). Age, physical impairment, and symptoms of anxiety: A test of mediating and moderating factors. *International Journal of Aging and Human Development, 49,* 43–59.

Searle, J. R. (1969). *Intentionality.* Cambridge: Cambridge University Press.

Selman, R. L. (1980). *The growth of interpersonal understanding.* New York: Academic.

Semin, G. (2007). Grounding communication: Synchrony. In *Social psychology: Handbook of basic principles* (2nd ed., pp. 630–649). New York: Guilford.

Sharma, D. (2003). *Childhood, family, and sociocultural change in India: Reinterpreting the inner world.* New York: Oxford University Press.

Sharps, M. J., Martin, S. S., Nunes, M. A., Neff, A., & Woo, E. (2004). Relational and imageric recall in young and older adults under conditions of high task demand. *Current Psychology, 22,* 379–393.

Siegler, R. S. (2006). Microgenetic analyses of learning. In D. Kuhn & R. S. Siegler (Vol. Eds.), *Handbook of child psychology* (6th ed., pp. 464–510). Hoboken, NJ: John Wiley & Sons.

Sinnott, J., & Berlanstein, D. (2006). The importance of feeling whole: Learning to "feel connected," community, and adult development. *Handbook of adult development and learning* (pp. 381–406). New York: Oxford University Press.

Smith, L. B. (2004). Cognition as a dynamic system: Principles from embodiment. *Developmental Review, 25,* 278–298.

Sneed, J., Hamagami, F., McArdle, J., Cohen, P., & Chen, H. (2007). The dynamic interdependence of developmental domains across emerging adulthood. *Journal of Youth and Adolescence, 36,* 351–362.

Somsen, R. J. M., van't Klooster, B. J., van der Molen, M. W., van Leeuwen, H. M. P., & Licht, R. (1997). Growth spurts in brain maturation during middle childhood as indexed by EEG power spectra. *Biological Psychology, 44,* 187–209.

Sroufe, L. A. (1996). *Emotional development.* Chicago: University of Chicago Press.

Strayer, J. (2002). The dynamics of emotions and life cycle identity. *Identity, 2,* 47–79.

Sullivan, M. W., & Lewis, M. (2003). Contextual determinants of anger and other negative expressions in young infants. *Developmental Psychology, 39,* 693–705.

Tangney, J. P. (2002). Self-conscious emotions: The self as a moral guide. In A. Tesser & D. A. Stapel (Eds.), *Self and motivation: Emerging psychological perspectives* (pp. 97–117). Washington, DC: American Psychological Association.

Tangney, J. P., Stuewig, J., & Mashek, D. J. (2007). Moral emotions and moral behavior. *Annual Review of Psychology, 58,* 345–372.

Taylor, R. (1970). Simple action and volition. In M. Brand & W. K. Frankena (Eds.), *The nature of human action.* Glenville, IL: Scott, Foresman.

Ter Hark, M. (1990). *Beyond the inner and the outer: Wittgenstein's philosophy of psychology.* Dordrecht, the Netherlands: Kluwer.

Thatcher, R. W. (1994). Cyclic cortical reorganization: Origins of human cognitive development. In G. Dawson & K. W. Fischer (Eds.), *Human behavior and the developing brain* (pp. 232–266). New York: Guilford.

Thelen, E., & Smith, L. B. (2006). Dynamic systems theories. In W. Damon & R. M. Lerner (Series Eds.) & R. M. Lerner (Vol. Ed.), *Handbook of child psychology: Vol. 1, Theoretical models of human development* (6th ed., pp. 258–312). Hoboken, NJ: John Wiley & Sons.

Thompson, E. (2007). *Mind in life.* Cambridge, MA: Harvard University Press.

Tomkins, S. S. (1984). Affect theory. In K. R. Scherer & P. Ekman (Eds.), *Approaches to emotion* (pp. 163–195). Hillsdale, NJ: Erlbaum.

Toomey, B., & Ecker, B. (2007). Of neurons and knowings: Constructivism, coherence psychology and their neurodynamic substrates. *Journal of Constructivist Psychology, 20,* 201–245.

Tremblay, R. E. (2000). The development of aggressive behaviour during childhood: What have we learned in the past century? *International Journal of Behavioral Development, 24,* 129–141.

Trevarthen, C. (1993). The self born in intersubjectivity: The psychology of an infant communicating. In U. Neisser (Ed.), *The perceived self: ecological and interpersonal sources of self-knowledge* (pp. 121–173). New York: Cambridge University Press.

Trevarthen, C. (1998). The concept and foundations of infant intersubjectivity. In S. Braten (Ed.), *Intersubjective communication and emotion in early ontogeny* (pp. 15–46). Cambridge: Cambridge University Press.

Trevarthen, C., & Aitken, K. J. (2000). Infant intersubjectivity: Research, theory, and clinical applications. *Journal of Child Psychology and Psychiatry and Allied Disciplines, 42,* 3–48.

Trevarthen, C., & Hubley, P. (1978). Secondary intersubjectivity: Confidence, confiding and acts of meaning in the first year. In A. Lock (Ed.), *Action, gesture and symbol: The emergence of language* (pp. 183–229). London: Academic.

Turiel, E. (1989). Domain-specific social judgments and domain ambiguities. *Merrill-Palmer Quarterly, 35,* 89–114.

Tutty, J., & Klein, J. (2008). Computer-mediated instruction: A comparison of online and face-to-face collaboration. *Educational Technology Research & Development, 56,* 101–124.

Uchiyama, I., Anderson, D., Campos, J., Witherington, D., Frankel, C., Lejeune, L., et al. (2008). Locomotor experience affects self and emotion. *Developmental Psychology, 44,* 1225–1231.

Valsiner, J. (1998). *The guided mind: A sociogenetic approach to personality.* Cambridge, MA: Harvard University Press.

Van Geert, P. (1994). *Dynamic systems of development: Change between complexity and chaos.* London: Harvester Wheatsheaf.

Vedeler, D. (1994) Infant intentionality as object directeness: Toward a method of observation. *Scandinavian Journal of Psychology, 35,* 343–366.

Vygotsky, L. (1978). *Mind in society.* Cambridge, MA: Harvard University Press.

Watson, M. W., Fischer, K. W., & Andreas, J. B. (2004). Pathways to aggression in children and adolescents. *Harvard Educational Review, 74,* 404–430.

Werner, H., & Kaplan, B. (1962/1984). *Symbol formation.* Hillsdale, NJ: Erlbaum.

Wertsch, J. V. (1998). *Mind as action.* Cambridge: Harvard University Press.

Winkielman, P., & Cacioppo, J. (2006). A social neuroscience perspective on affective influences on social cognition and behavior. *Affect in social thinking and behavior* (pp. 41–63). New York: Psychology Press.

Witherington, D. C. (2007). The dynamic systems approach as metatheory for developmental psychology. *Human Development, 50,* 127–153.

Wittgenstein, L. (1953). *Philosophical investigations* (G. E. M. Anscombe, Trans.). Oxford: Blackwell.

Wood, D., Bruner, J., & Ross, G. (1976). The role of tutoring in problem-solving. *Journal of Child Psychology and Psychiatry, 17,* 89–100.

Yan, Z., & Fischer, K. (2002). Always under construction. *Human Development, 45,* 141–160.

Yan, Z., & Fischer, K. W. (2007). Pattern emergence and pattern transition in microdevelopmental variation: Evidence of complex dynamics of developmental processes. *Journal of Developmental Processes, 2,* 39–62.

Zahavi, D. (2005). *Subjectivity and selfhood.* Cambridge, MA. MIT Press.

Zelazo, P., & Cunningham, W. (2007). Executive function: Mechanisms underlying emotion regulation. *Handbook of emotion regulation* (pp. 135–158). New York: Guilford.

Zinck, A., & Newen, A. (2008). Classifying emotion: A developmental account. *Synthese: An International Journal for Epistemology, Methodology and Philosophy of Science, 161,* 1–25.

CHAPTER 7

Structure and Process in Life-Span Cognitive Development

ELLEN BIALYSTOK and FERGUS I. M. CRAIK

There are two great truths in studies of cognitive change: developmental research shows that older children perform better than younger children on virtually every measure that can be administered, and cognitive research on late adulthood shows that older adults perform more poorly than younger adults on almost an equally large range of tests. A single-factor model in which cognitive ability rises and falls in a smoothly defined parabolic trajectory is consistent with both experimental observation and intuitive experience: whatever mechanism improves performance throughout childhood begins to fail in late adulthood. However, at least two factors make it difficult to verify such an account empirically. The first is that researchers working on each trajectory of this overall curve have little contact with each other; they base their research on different models, different methodologies, and to some extent, different questions, making the discovery of a common cause difficult or impossible. The second is that the explanation is naively simple and suggests no mechanism for either direction of change.

Figure 7.1 (Craik & Bialystok, 2006a) illustrates three basic approaches to the understanding of life-span changes in cognitive performance. Figure 7.1a shows a single-factor model, based on the idea that one set of variables underlies cognitive growth in childhood, and that the same variables decline in efficiency during the late adult years. The second model, shown in Figure 7.1b, takes account of the observation that, whereas cognitive growth in childhood is associated with an increase in both knowledge and efficiency of control processes operating on that knowledge

Preparation of this chapter was supported by the Canadian Institutes of Health Research (grant MOP57842 to E.B. and F.I.M.C.) and the National Institutes of Health (grant R01HD052523 to E.B.). We thank Lynn Ossher for her help in preparing the manuscript.

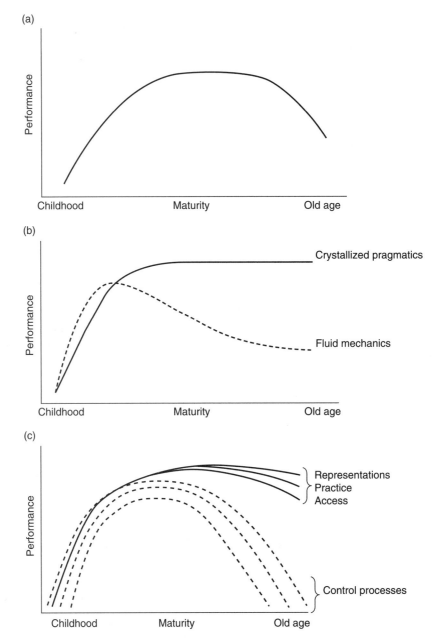

Figure 7.1 Three speculative models of cognitive change across the life span. (a) A single "mirror-image" view; performance increases in childhood, is maintained in middle age, and declines in late adulthood. (b) The different life-span trajectories of crystallized intelligence (crystallized pragmatics) and fluid intelligence (fluid mechanics); the former is well maintained in late adulthood, whereas the latter declines. (c) A more realistic version of (b) in that representations are generally well maintained in late adulthood, but some knowledge is either lost (especially with lack of practice) or becomes inaccessible. Control processes develop at different ages and also decline differentially, depending, in part, on the brain areas involved.

base, cognitive decline in older adults is associated with a marked decline in efficiency of control processes but with relative preservation of vocabulary and other types of general world knowledge (Craik & Bialystok, 2006a; Salthouse, 1991, 2003). In the terminology of Li and Baltes (2006), these two factors are labeled "fluid mechanics" and "crystallized pragmatics," respectively. The argument that we develop in this chapter refers to the same basic constructs as "control processes" and "representations," respectively. The notion again is that control processes first increase and then decrease in efficiency across the life span—likely because of concomitant changes in the efficiency of frontal lobe processes—whereas cognitive representations, once established, are relatively stable across early development and late adult development. The model in Figure 7.1c portrays a more realistic version of the model in Figure 7.1b in that it allows for some decline in the ability to access and manipulate acquired knowledge—as a function of practice and recency of access, for example—and also for the growth and decline of control processes to differentiate as a function of such factors as the material, type of processing, and specific brain areas involved. In the following sections, we elaborate the arguments for and against each of the three models.

EVALUATING MODELS OF CHANGE

Single-Factor Explanations of Early and Late Development

There has historically been little interaction between researchers of early and late development, even when the interest is in the same types of cognitive processes. The majority of studies of early development stop at adolescence, and the majority of late adult development studies focus on cognitive abilities for individuals in their 60s and later years. Ironically, the baseline for both types of studies is the performance of young adults, typically college students in their 20s; although in one case, these individuals represent an end point, and in the other, a starting point. Such divergent research programs, therefore, are unlikely to converge on a single mechanism differing only in direction to explain the changes inherent in each.

This cultural isolation between the two subareas of life-span cognitive change is particularly difficult to understand when the few studies that do cover all ages report substantial similarities between the cognitive mechanisms responsible for these changes in children and adults. For example, Salthouse and Davis (2006) analyzed the structural organization of cognition in 3,400 individuals ranging in age from 5 to 93 years old, and reported a qualitatively similar organizational structure of cognitive variables between children (5–17 years), students (18–22 years), and adults (23–93 years). The investigators concluded that "at least with respect to these aspects of cognition, age differences across the life span appear to be more quantitative than qualitative" (p. 52).

One reason for the division between researchers in child development and late adult development may be the different evolutionary histories of the two areas. Infant and child cognitive development research emerged from observational studies of children's intellectual growth, often recorded as diaries by scientist–parents, and from studies of educational abilities and attainments. Research on cognition during the adult and late adult years, in contrast, grew out of psychometric studies of abilities and the methods of experimental cognitive psychology.

Exceptions exist that override these segregated cultures and apply a more coherent framework to describing cognitive change across the life span. Beginning with the problem of late adult cognitive development and working backward toward child development, Baltes and his colleagues (e.g., Baltes, 1987; Baltes, Reese, & Lipsitt, 1980; Li, 2002; Lindenberger, 2001) have been instrumental in advocating a comprehensive developmental framework for understanding cognition across the life span; although as we describe later, their solution is not for the single factor or mechanism indicated in Figure 7.1a. In contrast, however, Salthouse's (1991, 1998) approach both stresses the importance of a full life-span view of development and endorses a single-factor explanation for the changes on both sides of the trajectory. In an extensive research program, Salthouse has demonstrated the fundamental role played by speed of processing in cognitive performance, and how that speed first quickens throughout childhood and then slows in the late adult years, providing a possible mechanism for cognitive change that can be plotted monotonically across the life span.

Fewer theories of child development have been applied comprehensively to processes associated with late adult development, but some cases exist. For example, there were some early attempts to extend Piaget's stage theory to adult and late adult development (Hooper, Fitzgerald, & Papalia, 1971). In an influential chapter, Riegel (1977) described the "dialectics of development"—the growth-related interactions between individuals and their inner biology on the one hand, and their outer sociological conditions on the other. This dialectical approach, which is currently represented by the relational developmental systems approach (Lerner, 2006; Lerner & Overton, 2008; Overton, 2006) is rooted in the study of adult development but is applicable to childhood and adolescence as well.

Even if the methodological issues of incorporating participants of all ages into the same experimental designs could be solved and undertaken as a standard research procedure, there remains the conceptual problem of imagining what the mechanism for a single-factor model would look like. Behaviorally, the only suggestion has been Salthouse's proposal for speed of processing. Equally, however, it would be necessary to demonstrate that neurological changes in the brain across the life span could also support a smooth transition in cognitive function that would be reflected in the rise and fall of ability across the life span.

Little evidence in brain development and decline has been documented, however, to support a symmetrical account of child and older adult development. There are approximately 100 billion neurons in the human brain, and these are all present at birth. This number remains relatively constant, at least until young adulthood, but the number of synapses changes dramatically—from roughly 2,500 per cortical neuron at birth to 15,000 at age 2 to 3 years (Goswami, 2002). This explosive growth of connectivity is seen as an increase in synaptic density in the cerebral cortex (gray matter). It produces an overabundance of connections that are then pruned by experience— essentially, a strengthening of connections that are used and an elimination of connections that are not used. The balance between progressive synapse formation and increasing dendritic arborization on the one hand, and synaptic pruning on the other hand, produces an inverted-U–shaped rise and fall of gray matter that peaks at different ages for different brain regions (Casey, Tottenham, Liston, & Durston, 2005; Gogtay et al., 2004). These peaks occur at approximately 11 years for the parietal lobes, 11½ years for the frontal lobes, and 16½ years for the temporal lobes (Giedd et al., 1999).

In contrast with the growth and decline of gray matter during childhood, white matter (representing increasing myelinization and neuronal conductivity) increases linearly with age throughout childhood and young adulthood (Giedd et al., 1999), although again following a different timetable for different brain regions (Konner, 1991; Taylor, 2006). In the late adult years, there is a decline in white matter, attributable to the gradual process of demyelinization (Raz, 2000). The combined effects of synaptic growth, synaptic pruning, and increasing myelinization results in high levels of plasticity and learning ability in infants and young children; these abilities level off in middle life and then decline at older ages. The apparent outcome of these processes is growth and decline of function across the life span, but importantly, the changes in the brain responsible for the level and type of cognitive function available at different stages of the life span are different and are based on different neuronal structures.

The neuronal explanation for adult cognition and decline is actually more complex than the processes described earlier. Ultimately, neuronal models are linked to genetic and other biological systems that are associated with all development. Furthermore, although genetics is central to understanding, the notion that specific genes can be linked to identifiable behavioral outcomes has been replaced by more complex models that are based on networks of genes, and interactions between genetic and environmental influences (see Greenberg & Partridge, Chapter 5 of this volume, for an extended discussion of the role of genes in development). Plomin (1995) points to two aspects of these complex views: First, disorders, such as Alzheimer disease and mental retardation, are the outcome of a number of constituent disorders each with its own genetic background; and second, multiple linkages combine to produce specific outcomes, making all genetic expression more probabilistic than certain. These examples from atypical development signal the untenability of assuming that simple models can explain typical development.

Genetic predispositions not only interact with each other, but they also interact with the environment, a concept known as "epigenetics" or "norm of reaction" (Gottlieb, 2003). The range of probabilistic outcomes that is established by genetic networks is influenced by features in the environment and by the interactions that the individual carries out in those environments. In child development, the most dramatic example of this process is the variability in outcome of intelligence as measured by IQ test results. The variability is found by placing an individual with a given genetic range into environments that are more or less supportive of the development of intelligence as measured in this way. Importantly, the extent of influence of the environment is not constant but interacts with the genetic base as well, with more supportive environments exerting greater influence on intelligence than more impoverished ones. In a dramatic study based on 319 pairs of monozygotic and dizygotic twins, Turkheimer, Halye, Waldron, D'Onofrio, and Gottesman (2003) calculated the contribution of genotype and environmental influence on full-scale IQ, and showed a shift in the proportion toward an increasing role for genotype in children in families that were higher in socioeconomic status. Thus, more enriched environments better enabled genotypic expression than did less enriched environments. The authors are appropriately cautious in their interpretation of how socioeconomic status functions in these interactions but emphasize the unequivocal result that genetic factors alone do not determine cognitive development.

In late adult development, the mitigating effect of environmental influence on the biological predisposition for cognitive decline is largely dealt with under the heading of cognitive reserve (Stern, 2002). A large body of evidence shows that engagement in intellectual, social, and physical activities leads to a reduction in the rate of cognitive decline. Thus, higher levels of cognitive functioning in older age are associated with higher occupational status, continuing involvement in education, stimulating leisure activities, and physical fitness (see Kramer, Bherer, Colcombe, Dong, & Greenough, 2004; Valenzuela & Sachdev, 2006 for reviews). The most dramatic outcome of cognitive reserve is that these stimulating mental activities can delay the onset of dementia, although whether such activities slow the rate of cognitive decline or simply raise the level of performance for the same rate of decline is still a matter of debate. One large-scale meta-analysis by Valenzuela and Sachdev found evidence for the former position, whereas a second large-scale review by Salthouse (2006) showed strong evidence for the latter conclusion. Further analyses are clearly needed, but one possibility is that the pattern of outcomes may differ between normal late adult development and development complicated by the presence of dementia.

Another way of considering the impact of the environment on cognitive performance is through the notion of compensation, the idea that both neural and behavioral systems change their functional organization to cope better with age-related declines. At the level of brain organization, there is growing agreement about the changes that take place, but also some interesting debates on how best to characterize these changes. The evidence suggests that some functions represented unilaterally in the brains of young adults are bilaterally represented in the brains of older adults. Grady, McIntosh, Horwitz, and Maisog (1995) and Cabeza (2002) have shown that retrieval from episodic memory is typically associated with activity in the right dorsal prefrontal cortex (PFC) in young adults (the HERA model suggested by Tulving, Kapur, Craik, Moscovitch, & Houle, 1994), but episodic retrieval in older adults is associated with *bilateral* activity in the frontal lobes. Cabeza (2002; Dennis & Cabeza, 2008) has termed this shift from unilateral to bilateral representations the *HAROLD* model (Hemispheric Asymmetry Reduction in Older Adults). Although the shift to bilaterality is well recognized, whether the shift is compensatory remains an open question. The main alternative is that representations differentiate in the growing brain, going from general bilateral representations to more specific representations that are typically unilateral

(Durston et al., 2006). As the brain ages, the process of differentiation reverses to one of dedifferentiation, and cognitive systems change from precisely focused representations in younger adults to fuzzier, less well-focused representations in older adults. There is a satisfying symmetry to this approach and one that is compatible with a neurological analogue for a single-factor mechanism: In contrast with the dedifferentiation found in older adults, representations in the developing child progressively undergo differentiation. This process of differentiation happens in terms of both cognitive structures (e.g., "doggy" used to name all animals, to "doggy" for dogs alone, to "terrier," "poodle" etc., for specific breeds of dog) and brain representations where there is a developmental shift from diffuse to focal, lateralized representations (Casey, Giedd, & Thomas, 2000). Efforts to support these models, however, have yielded inconsistent results (Dennis & Cabeza, 2008; Raz, 2000; Rubin, 1999; Stuss et al., 2002).

In principle, it is always prudent to follow the rule of Occam and refrain from postulating more devices than necessary. Logically, therefore, this strategy endorses the preference for a single developmental process that grows and wanes over the decades. It is also appealing to think that there is a consistent explanation for the rapid cognitive changes that are visible at both ends of the life span and the relative stability that characterizes the middle years. But the simple model also needs to provide a reasonable account of the data, and for methodological, conceptual, and biological reasons, it seems that a single-factor account that places child development and late adult development at opposite sides of a mirror will not work.

Two-Factor Frameworks for Cognitive Development

Little evidence has been reported to support an explanation based on the assumption that child and late adult development reflect a single common process that reverses its effect across the life span. The appeal of that approach rested on the apparent continuity with which these cognitive changes are observed, but the appearance of continuous change does not necessarily indicate a single continuous factor. Instead, continuous change can be an emergent property of at least two processes, each of which has its own role in cognitive functioning and its own life-span trajectory, but that are typically highly correlated with each other. In this case, continuous change reflects these individual correlated progressions. Two-factor models of intelligence have been around for some time; for example, theorists have distinguished "fluid" from "crystallized" intelligence (Horn, 1989; see also Blair, Chapter 8 of this volume), and Baltes and his coworkers have drawn the distinction between fluid mechanics (genetic inheritance, maturation, and decline of neurological processes) and crystallized pragmatics (reflecting the person's interactions in his or her sociocultural environment). Both of these pairs of descriptions generally map onto the distinction we are making between cognitive control and representations of schematic knowledge.

A two-factor account of this type was used to propose that the apparently smooth development in children's language abilities from oral conversational competence, to simple metalinguistic awareness, and finally to literacy concealed two developmental processes that interact to produce each of these achievements (Bialystok, 1991). The observable evidence is that language acquisition follows a smooth and continuous progression: children first demonstrate linguistic ability through oral production; during the preschool years there is an increasing interest and ability to participate in various word games and manipulate word properties such as sounds; and finally, literacy is achieved normally under the formal structure of schooling, incorporating all of a child's linguistic knowledge accumulated to that point. This progression was traditionally attributed to the forward movement of "language acquisition," a vague process that enhanced children's linguistic resources, enabling them to perform increasingly complex tasks and demonstrate steadily improving verbal ability. The problem, however, is that, although all children experience the major milestones in the same order, there are differences in the variability among children at different points, especially regarding metalinguistic development. In particular, the linguistic development of bilingual children through these primary stages is nonsynchronous with the linguistic development of comparable monolingual children.

The idea that Bialystok (1991) proposed is that each of the main domains of linguistic development—oral, metalinguistic, and literate—is supported by the development of two underlying processes. The two processes were called *analysis of representational structure* (analysis) and *control of attention* (control), and were considered to be theoretically orthogonal but practically highly correlated because of their common reliance on maturation and experience for development, factors that are constant for any individual child. In general, the progressive domains of linguistic expertise—oral, metalinguistic, and literate— require increasing competence in each of these underlying

processes. The correlation, in conjunction with the gradually increasing demands across these domains, makes it appear as though there is only one evolving mechanism underlying these developmental progressions.

Analysis is the process through which representations of knowledge are modified to become more explicit, more structured, and therefore more accessible to intentional access and manipulation. Children increasingly appear to know not only unrelated facts but also the relations among various concepts and ideas. Other theorists have described this development in different terms; for example, Karmiloff-Smith (1992) pointed to representational redescription as the fundamental cognitive change for children, and Zelazo and Frye (1997) described cognitive complexity as the mechanism for cognitive development. Both of these perspectives describe a process similar to the role that analysis of representational structures plays in building up mental representations in that children's cognitive development is attributed to qualitative modifications in the child's representation of knowledge that enable increasingly complex performance. In both cases, however, the explanation for cognitive development in childhood rests exclusively on this single process. Nonetheless, these structural and organizational changes in knowledge representation through childhood are clearly among the most fundamental aspects of cognitive development.

Control refers to the level of attention recruited during cognitive processing, with different levels of control required for different types of tasks, or for different stages of development or expertise. This is the process that allows the child to direct attention to specific aspects of either a stimulus field or a mental representation as problems are solved in real time. The need for control is most apparent when a problem contains conflict or ambiguity. In these cases, two or more mental representations may be constructed, each of which bears some relation to the problem, and the correct solution requires attending to only one of these possible representations whereas inhibiting or resisting attention to the other. A classic Stroop task presents exactly this conflict: representations for both ink color and color name are activated, and control is required to attend only to the representation that conforms to the task instructions. Higher levels of control are associated with processing that is more intentional, and models of late adult cognitive development often use the decline of such control as the primary explanation for those changes (e.g., Braver & West, 2008; Daniels, Toth, & Jacoby, 2006; Jacoby, 1991). Thus, unlike models of child and adolescent cognitive development that tend to focus on changes in the representational structure of performance, models of late cognitive development tend to focus on changes in the level of available control.

The separability of these processes becomes apparent in research with bilingual children. It seems that, although both analysis and control develop through experience, the experiences supporting the development of each are different. Therefore, changes in children's experiences could disrupt the correlation and the apparently linear progression would disappear. In general, in this research, analysis was responsive to increasing language proficiency, literacy instruction, and so on, experiences common to a wide range of children. Control, however, was responsive to bilingualism, so children learning two languages progressed more rapidly in this underlying skill.

This distinction makes it possible to understand how bilingualism affects children's progression through the general trajectory of oral, metalinguistic, and literate uses of language. In tasks that were based primarily on linguistic knowledge, or determined by the representational structure of linguistic knowledge, monolingual and bilingual children performed equivalently. However, in tasks that were similar but included the need for control of attention to resolve competition from competing information, bilingual children outperformed monolingual children who were otherwise comparable. Thus, tasks that have relatively higher demands for analysis than for control were solved similarly by all children, but tasks that have relatively higher demands for control than for analysis were solved better by bilingual children. These processes that are jointly responsible for language acquisition in the broad sense do not develop at similar rates in children with different language experiences.

This dissociation was first demonstrated in a task in which children were asked to make judgments about the grammaticality of simple sentences, the most commonly used metalinguistic task. Typically, the task is considered to assess knowledge of grammatical structure, and it has been used successfully with young children (de Villiers & de Villiers, 1972, 1974). In several studies, monolingual and bilingual children between the ages of 6 and 9 years were trained extensively to respond only to the grammaticality of simple sentences, irrespective of their meaning. Children in both groups were equally able to determine when the sentence contained a grammatical error *(Apples growed on trees)*, but when the sentences were manipulated so that they were grammatically correct but contained a semantic anomaly *(Apples grow on noses)*, bilingual children performed significantly better than monolingual children in focusing attention on the structure and responding correctly that the sentence is acceptable under the stated rules (Bialystok, 1986,

1988; Bialystok & Majumder, 1998; Cromdal, 1999). For both types of sentences, the task was to judge only the grammaticality, so the differential performance of children in the two groups indicates that different processes are involved in each case. Specifically, bilingual children were better than monolingual children at resisting interference from misleading meanings. This suggests that bilingual children are better able to control attentional processes. A similar pattern of results has recently been found for adults using similar sentence types in an event-related potential study (Moreno, Wodniecka, Bialystok, & Alain, submitted 2009). This grammaticality judgment paradigm illustrates a case in which two relevant processes, knowledge of grammar (analysis) and selective attention to grammar in the context of interference (control), are both involved in a simple task. Children's ability to solve the task increases with age in an apparently smooth progression, but examining children for whom the two processes have different developmental trajectories reveals the more complex structure of the abilities underlying the task.

These studies of children's metalinguistic development led to a framework for considering cognitive development in terms of two processing types, one describing changes in the representational structure of a domain of knowledge and the other describing changes in the attentional control resources available to children (Bialystok, 2001). These two processes have several important differences that are relevant for development. First, representational development is largely specific to a domain of knowledge or experience, and the evolution of more articulated and more accessible representational structures proceeds individually for each domain of expertise. In contrast, the development of control is largely tied to the resource-limited systems of executive functions, and these processes apply broadly across domains. Second, each of these processes develops in response to a set of common factors concerned with maturation and experience, but each additionally develops in response to a unique set of factors. A growing body of research has identified bilingualism as an experience that promotes the development of attentional control in childhood across all domains, including nonverbal ones, although it does not affect levels of representational knowledge. Therefore, monolingual and bilingual children perform comparably in nonverbal tasks that require explicit representations of knowledge, but bilingual children outperform monolingual children in conditions that are similar but have increased demands for control through the inclusion of distracting or interfering information (see review in Bialystok, 2001). Thus, both processes are central to development, but they cannot be seen independently until they are dissociated through their differential response to experience.

The component processes of analysis and control were proposed to solve a specific problem in explaining language development in monolingual and bilingual children. Thus, they were extracted from the evidence for children's performance on particular problems and then generalized to predict performance first to other problems in the same domain and eventually to performance in completely different domains, namely, nonverbal cognitive performance. Although various refinements in the definition and conception of these processes were necessary as the breadth of application increased, the essential idea behind them has remained relatively constant. Thus, it appears that there is an essence to each of these processes that is broader than language, and potentially broader than development. A similar conceptualization has been proposed to explain the decline of cognition in the late adult years (Craik & Bialystok, 2006b), again a process that appears to be continuous but may instead reflect two processes that decline on different trajectories. Henceforth, we refer to these processes as representation and control.

Representation and Control in Life-Span Development

The two-factor model shown in Figure 7.1b is substantially more satisfactory than the one-factor model (Figure 7.1a), but it is probably unrealistic to postulate two monolithic constructs, each of which follows only one trajectory across the life span. Instead, it seems more likely that different representational systems develop and decline at different ages, depending on such factors as complexity, interest, schooling, and use. Similarly, whereas control may be a domain-general construct, it again seems more likely that the manifestations of control will depend on the representational system in which control is exercised; control is greater when the system in question is a highly practiced and "expert" one for the particular person observed. This last point makes it likely that representations and control are two broad factors that determine cognitive performance across the life span, but they are essentially interactive rather than being truly orthogonal (Craik & Bialystok, 2006a).

One example of how representations and control interact comes from a consideration of the role of context in governing behavior. In simple animals, the external environment *provides* control, in that the animal is hard-wired to react differentially and adaptively (within limits) to different environmental contingencies. As the evolutionary scale is ascended, animals internalize aspects of the environment as mental representations that can then be controlled to some extent independently of external changes. This differential reliance on representation and control, and their independence from the external environment can also be seen developmentally. As described later in this chapter, babies are relatively dependent on reinstatement of learning contexts to exhibit learned habits (Rovee-Collier & Hayne, 2000). As the child develops toward adulthood, control can then select aspects of the external world to be represented internally, and these internal representations can then be selected and held in working memory (WM) to act as an "internal context" to guide further selection and processing (Braver et al., 2001). Finally, as control weakens in older adults, individuals again become progressively more dependent on the external context for guidance and support (Craik, 1983, 1986).

There are two further complications of the two-factor model. First, representations are not arranged democratically but rather are organized in a hierarchical manner, with abstract context-free representations occupying higher positions than representations of specific details and episodic events. Young children develop the higher level concepts first (as described later) and gradually fill in detailed knowledge. Second, older adults presumably still retain representations at various levels, but there is a progressive difficulty in accessing the more specific representational levels (e.g., names and episodic memory details; Craik, 2002). Again, therefore, it appears that there is a commonality between the processing outcomes of early childhood and late adulthood, but little evidence to indicate a common mechanism and good reason to expect quite different explanations in each case. These complications of the two-factor model are illustrated in the following sections on language and memory as they change over the life span.

LANGUAGE REPRESENTATION AND PROCESS ACROSS THE LIFE SPAN

The processes of representation and control are similar to the components of crystallized pragmatics and fluid mechanics that Paul Baltes and his colleagues proposed in their model developed to explain cognitive change across the life span (Baltes, 1987; Li & Baltes, 2006). As we have seen, however, they also resemble the processes of analysis and control that were proposed in a much narrower context

to model language development in early childhood. Therefore, the first test of a two-factor model for cognitive change would be to assess the fit with changes in language ability across the life span.

Theories of Language Acquisition

The acquisition of language is one of the more dramatic developments in childhood (see MacWhinney, Chapter 14 of this volume, for an extended discussion of the life-span development of language). In a breathtakingly short time, infants progress from babbling (about 6 months old), to single words (about 1 year old), with word combinations before 2 years old, and complex syntax and rich vocabulary by the time they start school. Their use of language by about the age of 5 years observes rules of grammar and indicates mastery of several thousand words spoken with native-like pronunciation, following the constraints of pragmatic usage. During the late adult years, speech becomes marked by difficulties in word retrieval and a noticeably simplified grammar, both for production and comprehension. Thus, the changes that characterize linguistic performance at both ends of the life span are vast. They are also roughly similar: children learn words, and older adults forget them; children increase grammatical complexity, and older adults reduce it. As we have seen, however, the temptation to examine these phenomena as instances of symmetric development and decline gains little support from the evidence.

Theories of language acquisition can be positioned along a dimension that varies in the extent to which this process is driven primarily by preadapted biological biases in the system to learn language or by experiences that lead the child to language through meaningful interactions. Theories that rely more strongly on biological biases to ensure learning are domain specific in that these biases apply only to language; the linguistic representations that emerge from this development will inevitably be unique to language, and possibly idiosyncratic in form and structure. The syntax of natural languages is an example of a representational system that is considered to be a unique construction constrained by linguistic universals, as in the account that Pinker (1994) proposed. Theories that rely more strongly on experience and interaction appeal to all-purpose cognitive and social processes to guide language acquisition; the linguistic representations that develop in response to these experiences will be continuous with other representational forms and largely integrated with them, as in the account that Tomasello (2003) proposed.

On these views, there is little in the representation of language that is distinct from other representational systems, even though much of it is unique. Along this dimension that describes the process of language acquisition in vastly different ways, the salient problem to be solved is how the child establishes the underlying knowledge system that defines the forms and structures of language.

The decline of linguistic ability during the late adult years is similarly different under these two perspectives, appealing either to the decline of language-specific mechanisms that require more salient input and longer processing times, or to the decline of general cognitive mechanisms that define the overall changing cognitive profile that occurs with age (see Demetriou, Mouyi, & Spanoudis, Chapter 10 of this volume, for an extended discussion of the life-span development of general cognitive mechanisms). For example, a language-specific explanation of decline, such as that by Caplan and Waters (1999), points to the decline in components of WM that are involved only in language processing, whereas the explanation offered by Wingfield (1996) based on the effect of cognitive slowing leads to a more domain-general account of decline that connects changes in language ability with other cognitive systems. Again, however, the central problem addressed by these different explanatory mechanisms is an account of how access to linguistic knowledge and the productive use of linguistic knowledge changes with later development. Unlike the problem in explaining children's acquisition of representational structures that form the core of linguistic knowledge, the problem in the late adult years is to understand changes in the control systems that interact with that knowledge.

The difference in emphasis on the identification of the linguistic problem converges on a differential focus at each end of the life span in considering representational structure (children) or control processes (older adults) as the primary locus of change. When child and adult/late adult development are examined independently, the isolation of only one of these components can be interpreted as providing a sufficient account of changes in language behavior, and complementary changes in the less salient component are often neglected. However, a complete account of language change across the life span will need to integrate the role of both representation and control at all points in the life span. Moreover, the bias for attention on one or the other of these components has also led to a bias for accepting theories that are more biological and domain specific (children) or more experiential and domain general (older adults) as the more useful perspective. Again, however, a complete account will ultimately require a synthesis that addresses the contribution of both biology and experience. With a more fully elaborated account, the mechanisms of change responsible for linguistic ability throughout the life span will be clearer. These ideas will be illustrated by considering explanations for changes in vocabulary and syntax across the life span.

Vocabulary Learning and Semantic Knowledge

Vocabulary acquisition proceeds at a stunning rate through childhood. Bates, Dale, and Thal (1995) report that, by 16 months of age, children could reliably understand a mean of 191 words and produce a mean of 64 words; by 30 months, the mean number of words in productive vocabulary was 534. This period of rapid vocabulary growth during the second year of life has been called the "vocabulary burst" (Bloom, 1973; Dromi, 1987; Nelson, 1973), and researchers have calculated different rates for this achievement, ranging from about 5 words (Anglin, 1993) to 10 words per day (Clark, 1995) through the school years. Other researchers describe word acquisition in terms of an accelerated rate of learning with no identifiable burst (Bloom, 2002; Elman et al., 1996), but the outcome is the same for the present purposes.

Biology-based accounts of this development rely on mechanisms that guide children to understand how labels heard in the speech around them are the names for specific objects, a process called "fast-mapping" (Carey, 1978; Markson & Bloom, 1997). The mechanisms enabling this one-trial learning of new words are posited as biological constraints and include taxonomic constraints, mutual exclusivity, and whole-object constraint (Clark, 1993; Markman, 1989). However, the same outcome can be achieved without biases that are dedicated to the language system. For example, Smith, Jones, and Landau (1996) propose that simple attention processes automatically focus on the correct level of description for a new word and guarantee the correct representation, a point that Bloom (2000) takes as evidence for the importance of domain-general cognitive constraints in language acquisition. Similarly, Golinkoff and Hirsh-Pasek (2006) attribute word learning to a fortunate confluence of children's attentional biases and developing cognitive systems in interaction with adults who guide the process of word learning.

In these accounts of vocabulary development, the focus is on explaining the rapid and efficient acquisition of a complex system of symbols to denote the full range of meanings that humans intend to express. The problem,

therefore, is to explain how representations are built, but the solution invokes various degrees and types of control to establish that representational system. The solutions differ in whether the responsible mechanisms are specific to language or part of a set of general cognitive processes, but they share the feature of addressing the single most crucial issue in vocabulary development: How do children figure out how words refer and solve the mapping problem between words and their meanings? In none of these proposals are the cognitive and executive monitoring systems (e.g., WM) that are involved in vocabulary acquisition either complex or central to the story.

Evidence on the fate of vocabulary knowledge in the late adult years is more mixed. There is consensus that vocabulary continues to increase throughout middle age and holds up well but eventually begins to decline in late adulthood (Hultsch, Hertzog, Dixon, & Small, 1998; Schaie, 1996). However, these deficits in vocabulary knowledge are not reported until individuals reach about 70 (Au et al., 1995), 80 (Alwin & McCammon, 2001), or even 90 years of age (Singer, Verhaeghen, Ghisletta, Lindenberger, & Baltes, 2003), an achievement that attests to the durability of the representations. Therefore, the eventual decline of vocabulary in the late adult years cannot be attributed to the same factors responsible for the increase of vocabulary in childhood when children are establishing representational structures that connect symbols to concepts.

The main diagnostic experience of vocabulary failures in the late adult years is the problem of word retrieval (Burke, MacKay, Worthley, & Wade, 1991; Cohen & Faulkner, 1986; Mortensen, Meyer, & Humphreys, 2006). Inherent in this description is an assumption about its locus: Word retrieval implies that the knowledge is present but inaccessible, and the responsibility for accessibility is control. Not surprisingly, therefore, most explanations of the word retrieval problem center on failures in aspects of control, including reductions in processing speed, WM, and inhibitory control (Braver & West, 2008; Salthouse, 1996; Wingfield & Stine-Morrow, 2000; Zacks, Hasher, & Li, 2000).

In contrast with these control-based views, Burke and her colleagues propose an explanation for vocabulary failure in the late adult years that is rooted in the representational system called the "transmission deficit hypothesis" (Burke & Laver, 1990; Burke et al., 1991). The essence of the model is that the connections between concepts and lexical details, especially phonologic and orthographic information, are strengthened by use but weakened by processes associated with late adult development. These weak connections are characteristics of the representation, as opposed to characteristics of control, but are experienced as general processing deficits. Put another way, late adult development is associated with deterioration in the connectivity of the representational structure, making word retrieval problematic. Deterioration of connective links between word representations and their orthography also occur, resulting in an increase in spelling errors in older adults (Burke & Shafto, 2004; MacKay & Abrams, 1998). Aspects of the system that are based on single connections, such as the links between a word and its phonology, are vulnerable to decay and result in word retrieval failures; however, aspects of the system that are connected through built-in redundancy, such as lexical-semantic links, are more robust, preserving semantic processing for older adults. Thus, age-related changes in representational structures account for changes in lexical processing in the late adult years. This view is contrary to those claiming that knowledge representations are insensitive to processes associated with late adult development (e.g., Baltes, Staudinger, & Lindenberger, 1999). An intermediate position might be that they are *relatively* insensitive to the effects of processes associated with late adult development.

To summarize, both representation and control are involved in the acquisition of vocabulary for children and the failure to access vocabulary in the late adult years. What is different is the balance between them and the mechanism required by each. For children, the primary challenge for representation is to solve the mapping problem between concepts and symbols so that a representational structure can be created and developed; for adults, the primary challenge for representation is to maintain the connections between ideas and the specific lexical details because those links weaken in late adult development. The control restrictions on vocabulary acquisition and decline are defined by the processing resources required for access to specific items. These resources may be insufficient for young children, thus limiting the extent of new vocabulary acquisition, and diminished for older adults, thus reducing access to vocabulary that has been previously represented but is now weakly activated or confusable with competing terms. As a result, both young children and older adults may rely on more general terms to express specific concepts: "dog" instead of "collie." For children, the reason is that the representational system may not have been elaborated to include all the relevant distinctions between the subcategories of the concept, and the attentional processes may not have been sufficiently focused to identify the relevant distinguishing feature between subcategories. In some real sense, therefore, all dogs are the same for

children. For older adults, the reason is that the less frequently used specific vocabulary is less strongly integrated into the representation of the semantic network, and the control processes for accessing intended lexical items default to the more general level of the hierarchy where fewer attentional distinctions are required. Thus, both representation and control define the richness and accessibility of vocabulary knowledge throughout the life span.

Syntax and Grammatical Processing

The second major index of language ability in both child development and late adult development is mastery of the complex syntax that defines natural language. At about 2 years old, children begin to produce two-word utterances, and syntactic complexity emerges as the utterance length, generally measured as mean length of utterance (MLU) increases (Brown, 1973). Traditional explanations for this increase in grammatical competence appeal to children's improvements in processing capacity and cognitive resources, either in terms of domain-general mechanisms for processing complex information or language-specific information for discovering the rules of language. The majority of the explanations have traditionally fallen into the latter category (e.g., Meisel, 1995), but more recently a shift toward cognitive accounts comprises the majority of the research (e.g., Tomasello, 2003).

The domain-specific language accounts of syntactic development begin with the assumption that the brain is strongly biased for language learning through its innate structure (Pinker, 1994). The developing processing capacity allows children to uncover grammatical rules and to produce increasingly complex linguistic utterances that conform to them (de Villiers & de Villiers, 1992). An empirical demonstration that combines this approach with an account of general processing resources has been supplied by Valian and her colleagues, who have shown that the restrictions on the grammaticality and completeness of children's utterances are determined more by processing limitations than by knowledge failures. For example, children find it easier to imitate complex sentences that have predictable objects that serve to reduce the processing load (Valian, Prasada, & Scarpa, 2006), and are more likely to drop subjects from their utterances as a function of sentence length, indicating performance deficits, and not grammatical complexity, indicating competence deficits (Valian, Hoeffner, & Aubry, 1996). Children are capable of reproducing complex syntax if the sentence falls within their resource capacity.

This processing-based view of syntactic development fits well with evidence from children's developing cognitive resources and the appearance of increasingly complex grammatical forms in their speech. However, it is also possible to consider the acquisition of grammar in terms of the representation system and not the control system. Bates and colleagues (Bates & Goodman, 1999; Elman et al., 1996) have noted that children begin to combine words and demonstrate grammatical constraints at the point at which their vocabulary exceeds a base level of 50 words, and the development of both vocabulary and syntax from that point are entirely intertwined; they argue, in fact, that they are aspects of the same development. For example, in a longitudinal study of children between 10 and 28 months old, the correlations between measures of grammar and measures of vocabulary were just as high as measures within one of those domains, and generally greater than +0.75. The explanation is that grammar emerges as a natural organizational property of representations of words and the need to use those words in a linear speech channel for communication. Thus, increasing grammatical complexity is a reflection of the growth of representations of the lexicon.

Changes in grammatical competence become apparent again in late adulthood, although basic syntactic processes appear to be unaffected by processes associated with late adult development (Kemper, Herman, & Nartowitz, 2003). Part of this may reflect the ability of adults to recruit representations of context and meaning as a support for more detailed linguistic structures. In several studies, the facilitating effect of context on the ability to interpret complex language has been shown to be greater for older adults than younger individuals (Schneider, Daneman, & Murphy, 2005), suggesting the reliance on larger representational structures for language processing in older adults.

In contrast with intact comprehension, there is a characteristic simplification of speech production in late adulthood (Cooper, 1990; Kemper, Kynette, Rash, Sprott, & O'Brien, 1989; Shewan & Henderson, 1988). Kemper, Thompson, and Marquis (2001) quantified this age-related simplification by computing values for Developmental Level (D-Level) and Propositional Density (P-Density) indexing syntactic and propositional complexity, respectively, and showed declines for both in late adulthood. Kemper (2006) attributes this decline to WM limitations (Kemper et al., 1989), reductions in processing speed (Wingfield, 1996), and reduced inhibitory control (Hasher & Zacks, 1988). Van der Linden et al.'s (1999) large-scale study confirmed a model in which age-related differences in language comprehension and verbal memory were mediated

through changes in WM, indirectly incorporating reduced processing speed and decreased resistance to interference. Similarly, Burke and Shafto (2008) offer six explanations for age-related change in syntactic complexity—resource deficits, general slowing, inhibition deficits, transmission deficits, declining WM, and sensory/perceptual deficits—all of which are based on reductions in control processes that occur during the late adult years.

As in the explanation for child and adolescent development, the issue of whether the relevant processes are specific to language or part of general cognitive systems applies to adult and later adult development as well. In contrast with the views described earlier in which general resource reduction is responsible, some theorists identify processing declines in systems that are specific to language processing. Caplan and Waters (1999), for example, consider that linguistic processing is conducted by dedicated systems involved only in the processing of language, and the reduction in syntactic complexity in late adulthood is attributable to the changes in the WM components of these language-specific processors. Again, the scope of the processes as being general cognitive or language-specific functions is different from the thematic argument that it is reduction in such control systems that is responsible for declining complexity in syntactic structure for older adults.

It is apparent in this brief review that no account of language acquisition and decline is possible without considering the contributions of both representation and control. In this sense, the development and decline of language-processing abilities are, indeed, symmetric, rising and falling for reasons rooted in the same ultimate mechanisms. However, it is equally apparent that the changes in linguistic abilities that characterize each end of the life span are dramatically different from each other. Our view is that these differences reflect two aspects of the functioning of representation and control systems. The first is that the bias for each of these systems is different at the two ends of the life span, with greater emphasis on representation in childhood and on control in older adulthood. The second is that the precise responsibility of each of these systems is different, with representation changing from establishing concepts to maintaining them, and control changing from directing attention to language-relevant events in the environment to monitoring attention and WM for online processing.

These differences in the responsibilities for representation and control come from different linguistic challenges in childhood and in late adulthood. Language acquisition is defined by the development of the linguistic system and the accumulation of language-specific knowledge about the forms and functions of language. Language decline is defined by a decrease in the cognitive systems that support language, not necessarily in the language systems themselves. For these reasons, children's challenges are not with control but with representation, the most important being the need to establish conceptual structures that can relate abstract symbolic forms and structures to meanings. The depth of this problem has led many researchers to invoke a large degree of biological preparedness as a means of overcoming the formidable problem of creating such representational structures from nothing. In contrast, the challenges of older adulthood come from the diminishing resources that are available to carry out the comprehension and production of a system as complex as language.

Language Ability across the Life Span

The case of language makes clear the joint involvement of representation and control across the life span. As the balance between them shifts and demands of mastering a linguistic system grow, different aspects of these processes are highlighted. Even taking the same evidence, for example, reduced vocabulary in childhood and late adulthood, the explanation for children's deficit is predominantly lack of knowledge or representation of words, but for adult deficits, it is lack of access to words. Development and decline are different to be sure, but their progress and dynamic rests on the same small set of processes that define all human cognition.

PROCESS CHANGES IN MEMORY AND EXECUTIVE CONTROL

An understanding of the development, maintenance, and deterioration of the processes involved in the regulation of mental functions is central to the study of cognitive changes over the life span. Despite this pivotal role of the executive functions, the nature of cognitive control is still poorly understood. Is there a single domain-general controller, or does each content area have its own mechanisms for selection, inhibition, goal setting, and conflict resolution? Are the representational and control systems independent or interdependent? What is the role of the external environment in guiding behavior, and does that role change as a function of early and later development? Similar questions can be raised about the role of schematized past learning in controlling choices and actions.

The question of whether there is one general controller or a family of task-specific controllers is a matter of current debate. On the one hand, Luria (1973) proposed that the PFC performed a set of general regulatory functions (manifested as inhibition, activation, planning, conflict resolution, etc.) that acted on posterior areas of the brain devoted to representations and associations. On the other hand, more recent work in neuropsychology and neuroanatomy has made it progressively clearer that the frontal lobes do not act in a holistic manner but are composed of regions that have specific functions (Petrides & Pandya, 1999; Stuss et al., 2002). The finding that various tasks claiming to measure executive functions typically correlate poorly with each other also seems at odds with the idea of one controller (see Daniels et al., 2006, for a review). The interesting notion that executive control is not a thing in itself but is rather an emergent property from the interactions among various representational systems (Barnard, 1985) also suggests that such interactions would result in characteristics specific to the particular systems involved. However, two recent proponents of the unity view concede that only certain areas of the PFC are concerned with executive control (specifically, dorsal and ventral lateral regions), but claim that these areas have a *general* regulatory function. Thompson-Schill, Bedny, and Goldberg (2005) make a case for the left ventrolateral PFC acting to regulate various functions in WM and language, and Duncan and colleagues (2000; Duncan & Miller, 2002) have presented compelling data showing that a variety of executive function tasks activate similar areas of the lateral PFC and dorsal anterior cingulate. Duncan and Miller (2002) make the further suggestion that "to some extent at least, the same frontal neurons may be configured to aid in solution of many different cognitive challenges" (p. 281). That is, the same PFC areas may be involved in the control of different tasks but using different network configurations. Thompson-Schill and colleagues (e.g., Thompson-Schill et al., 2005) take the view that specificity of function is achieved as a result of connectivity between the same frontal regions and different domain-specific posterior regions.

It is important to understand the relation between the PFC and other brain areas when examining life-span changes in executive functions because it is universally agreed that the frontal lobes are the primary locus of control. It is also well established that the frontal lobes are the last areas of the brain to develop fully (Casey et al., 2005; Diamond, 2002) and among the first to decline (Raz, 2000; Raz et al., 2005). These latter conclusions suggest a degree of symmetry between early development and development in the late adult years, but whereas early cortical development involves much sculpting of networks through *selective* loss of dendritic connectivity, the losses accompanying late adult development are less selective and, therefore, less adaptive.

At the cognitive/behavioral level, the functions of executive control processes are largely agreed on. Their essential task is to overcome the "default mode" of automatic habitual perceptual-motor tendencies (Mesulam, 2002) in situations where an alternative response would be beneficial. The possession of efficient control processes thus enables the person (or animal) to break free from rigid, stereotyped behaviors, and exhibit flexibility, adaptability, choice, and planning. Studies of control processes have focused on a variety of supposed components of executive functions, for example, inhibition, conflict resolution, decision making, selection, concentration, and resistance to interference. It is often essential to hold information in mind temporarily, to manipulate or transform that information mentally, and to integrate pieces of information from a variety of sources. These functions are performed by WM, which thus combines the short-term storage of incoming or recently retrieved information with controlled operations performed on or with that information (see Diamond, 2006, for a useful discussion of the relations between WM and executive functions).

Cognitive theorists agree on these components of executive functioning but stress different aspects when defining the fundamental roots of mental control. Current candidates include processing speed (Salthouse, 1996), attentional resources (Craik & Byrd, 1982), inhibition (Hasher & Zacks, 1988; Hasher, Zacks, & May, 1999), the ability to reflect consciously on integrated higher order rules (Zelazo, 2004), and recollection (Daniels et al., 2006; Jacoby, 1991; Jennings & Jacoby, 1997; see also Jacques & Marcovitch, Chapter 13 of this volume, for an extended discussion of the development of executive function). All of these constructs are well described and analyzed, and life-span changes in all of them are well documented, but it is reasonable to conclude that no one aspect is *the* crucial root cause of cognitive success and failure, and that all of them play some part in the overall regulation of behavior and thought.

Cognitive Control and the External Environment

The behavior of lower animals is largely controlled by the external environment, in that appropriate responses to salient stimuli are biologically wired into the organism. One major accomplishment of evolution is to relocate control within the animal as a mental construct or ability, thereby giving behavior more independence and flexibility. Nonetheless, the external environment continues to play some part in control even for humans, and its importance is greater at the two ends of the life span than in later childhood and adulthood (Piaget, 1959). An obvious difference between young children and older adults is that the latter have acquired rich stores of schematic knowledge, with the result that environmental influences are filtered through these systems of habitual responses. As an example, an older person's actions and reactions become attuned and finally become overdependent on domestic surroundings, so when the person moves into sheltered housing there is often a period of disorientation and confusion before new habit systems are learned. Craik (1983, 1986) has discussed the related notion of environmental support as the mechanism by which the late adult relies on local contexts to guide behavior because of the declining efficiency of executive functions (self-initiated activities). The behavior of some severely impaired frontal patients is occasionally *over* determined by the current context in interaction with learned schemas, so that patients will automatically eat when food is presented or attempt to sew if sewing materials are presented. These are the "utilization behaviors" described by Lhermitte (1986). Infants lack such schematic knowledge, so environmental control may be seen in more direct reflex behaviors such as sucking and rooting reflexes. In summary, the external environment acts on the young child and older adult to support appropriate behaviors; the older child is progressively freed from this influence as the frontal lobes develop, but the reliance on environmental support reemerges in the older adult, although with the difference that the influence is now mediated and modified by schematic habits.

One corollary of life-span changes in environmental dependence is the changing vulnerability to interference and distraction from external stimuli. As a speculation, if young children and older adults are more dependent on the external environment to support appropriate behaviors, they may also be prone to the misleading effects of external stimuli when such stimuli are *not* in accord with optimal thoughts or actions. This idea was suggested by Dempster (1992), who argued that the ability to resist interference is a major function of the frontal lobes and, therefore, waxes and wanes over the life span. In what might be considered an extension of Dempster's view, Enns and Trick (2006) propose that the key feature of attention is *selection*, and that selective attention may be classified in terms of two dimensions: automatic-controlled and exogenous-endogenous.

Enns and Trick use the terms *exogenous* and *endogenous* to refer to the contrast between external stimuli whose selection is not learned, and selection in terms of learned expectations and goals. Their framework generates a 2 × 2 classification in which automatic-exogenous selection is labeled *reflex*, automatic-endogenous selection is labeled *habit*, controlled-exogenous selection is termed *exploration*, and controlled-endogenous selection is termed *deliberation*. Like Dempster, Enns and Trick attribute life-span changes in their automatic-controlled dimension to the growth and decline of frontal lobe processes. Their exogenous-endogenous dimension, however, depends on degree of relevant learning. The Enns and Trick framework thus suggests that automatic-exogenous behaviors, that is, reflex, will show the least amounts of life-span developmental change and controlled-endogenous behaviors, that is, deliberation, will show the greatest degree of change but also the greatest degree of variability (Enns & Trick, 2006).

Consistent with the view we are developing here, the Enns and Trick framework stresses the interactions between raw control as mediated by the frontal lobes and representations in the sense of learned schemas. Indeed, learned representations can act *as* mechanisms of control, for example, in situations where the person is set to expect a specific stimulus configuration on the basis of past experience. Typically, however, accumulated past experiences push the person to respond in the habitual manner associated with current circumstances. In many cases, this default mode may be the best option, but a major function of executive processes is to monitor the situation and either proceed with the habitual response or substitute a more appropriate one. In fact, most methods that have been used to assess the development, integrity, and deterioration of executive control processes have measured the effectiveness of control in overcoming the prepotent influences of both environmental and schematic pressures. The Stroop task fits this description, as does the ability to overcome the tendency to move the eyes toward a visual object appearing suddenly in peripheral vision and instead move the eyes *away* from the object in the antisaccade task. The automatic-exogenous (reflex) tendency to look toward a visual target is so strong that the ability to perform antisaccadic eye movements does not develop until the child is 6 or 7 years old (Diamond, 2006).

Procedural Learning and Implicit Memory

For Piaget (1959), the world of the infant is confined to the "here and now." Piaget's observation was that infants lack the means to symbolically represent information from the outside world until they are 18 to 24 months old, restricting conscious experience to the relatively immediate present. Therefore, although an infant's behavior is responsive to perceived events, infants do not necessarily *recollect* those events in the sense of consciously reexperiencing them. The difference here between memories that can experience events that potentially alter future behavior and memories that are confined to the relative present is the form in which these events have been represented (see Müller & Racine, Chapter 11 of this volume, for an extended discussion of the development of representations). The structure of the infant's memory cannot yet support the control processes necessary for fully conscious recollection.

A significant problem facing researchers of memory and learning in preverbal infants and very young children is how to assess those abilities. Rovee-Collier and colleagues devised an ingenious solution (reviewed by Rovee-Collier & Hayne, 2000). They had infants age 2 to 6 months lie in their cribs with one foot tied by a ribbon to an attractive mobile suspended above the crib. Initially, spontaneous foot-kicks moved the mobile, thereby reinforcing further kicking movements. Learning was revealed 24 hours later when the infant kicked in the presence of the original mobile, even though it no longer moved. This learning was specific to the original mobile, as kicking did not occur in response to a different mobile. A study by Timmons (1994) demonstrated how this "hyperspecificity" of learning is modified later by conditioning 6-month-old infants to move a mobile by kicking and to activate a music box by performing an arm movement. These learned responses were apparently forgotten after 3 weeks, but when the child was reminded of the learning by again allowing the music box to be activated by an arm movement, foot-kicks to the mobile were also emitted. In other words, the representation of the action to activate the mobile and the music box were somehow associated, presumably through the common training context, allowing a form of generalization to take place. Rovee-Collier and Hayne give further examples of how with age, infants' responses can increasingly generalize to novel task cues. The supportive effects of context are, therefore, quite specific at first but can be overridden by training in multiple contexts. By 8 months old, infants learn to generalize, decreasing the dependency on exact context reinstatement to support retrieval of the learned response.

Another method used to study infant learning is novelty preference, sometimes in a paired-comparison setting. The infant is familiarized with one stimulus and then exposed to the choice of that stimulus or a novel stimulus; the infant demonstrates learning by attending more to the novel stimulus. This phenomenon reflects a mechanism for learning new patterns and objects—the starting point for a system of representations. When the same pattern is exposed on repeated occasions, it becomes habituated, no longer attracting attention but presumably gaining in familiarity. As children mature, they can deal with more complex patterns and retain them for longer periods; at the age of 5 months, children will select a novel black and white pattern after 2 days but will select a novel facial photograph after 2 weeks (Fagan, 1973). It seems likely that the advantage to faces reflects some relatively innate ability that has obvious biological value.

These examples of early learning, although impressive, are unlikely to involve memory in the sense of recollecting anything about the original event but are more akin to demonstrations of procedural memory or priming in adults (Mandler, 1998). As Tulving (1983) has also pointed out, some forms of memory and learning appear to be more fundamental and primitive, occurring in lower animals and also occurring early in ontogeny (see Ornstein & Light, Chapter 9 of this volume, for an extended discussion of memory development). Does this mean that they are also the last to survive in the late adult's brain?

In general, the answer is yes; most studies show that older adults are essentially unimpaired on implicit or procedural tasks of memory and learning. In the serial reaction time task, for example, participants must press the key corresponding to one of several lights in a display. Over a long, continuous series of stimuli and responses, some conditions contain a repeated sequence of 8 to 12 stimuli, whereas other series are random. Learning is exhibited by faster responding to the repeated series, and older participants show as much learning as young adults in this task, although they are less able to explicitly report knowledge of the repetitions (Howard & Howard, 1989). A similar age-related dissociation between implicit and explicit memory occurs in the word-stem completion paradigm. In this task, participants first study a long list of words, often under conditions of incidental learning in which they simply make decisions about each studied word. In the test phase, the first three letters of studied and unstudied words (e.g., PAR_, LEA_) are presented, either with the instruction to use the word stem as a cue to recall studied words (explicit memory) or with the instruction to complete the stem with "the first word that comes to mind." In this second condition, implicit learning is shown to the extent that stems of studied words are completed correctly more often

than stems of comparable unstudied control words. The typical result is that older adults show a deficit relative to young participants in the explicit condition but none in the implicit condition (La Voie & Light, 1994; Light & Singh, 1987).

Although age constancy in priming and related tasks is generally a good thing, the likelihood that older adults have intact implicit but impaired explicit memory means that the older person's experience of past events tends to be dominated by feelings of familiarity rather than by recollection of specific detail. For this reason, feelings of familiarity may be misconstrued as genuine memories or known facts. Dywan and Jacoby (1990) presented a list of fictitious names to older and younger adults, and later gave them a test in which names of famous people were mixed with the previously presented fictitious names. Older adults were more likely to misattribute the familiarity of fictitious names to fame in the real world. Similarly, Jennings and Jacoby (1997) found that older adults were more likely to confuse repetitions of words on a test list with words previously presented in a study list. Thus, the early development and late retention of implicit modes of learning and memory is clearly advantageous in general, yet has its costs in terms of vulnerability to error.

The finding that young children and older adults perform well on tasks of procedural or implicit memory and learning does *not* mean that their learning is as good as that of young adults. Encoding processes are likely to be less deep and elaborate in children and older adults, sufficient to support a feeling of familiarity and to bias certain responses, but insufficient to support conscious recollection that the word or other event has been perceived recently. This explanation accounts for life-span differences in terms of the quality of the representation underlying the memory or learning. An alternative account is that children and older adults utilize their developed representations (of perceptual-motor sequences or words at a later stage in children) but do not possess the control processes that would enable retrieval of the stored event plus its context in a way that yields the experience of recollection.

Semantic Memory

Tulving (1983) has suggested that memory systems evolved phylogenetically in the order procedural, semantic, and finally episodic, and that the same order is seen ontogenetically, placing semantic memory as one of the most significant developments of early childhood. The growth of semantic memory, or general knowledge of the world, is obviously one of the major achievements of development. Explaining the mechanisms that signal its emergence from the prior procedural memory in terms of a single linear development, however, is untenable in the same way that the apparent linear progression from oral to metalinguistic to literate competence with language could not be attributed to a single factor.

Semantic memory is a complex system of representations that, like episodic memory, are declarative in the sense that the stored pieces of information may be contemplated consciously, considered individually, and communicated to others. Our contention is that semantic memory is one major area of asymmetry between young children and older adults. That is, knowledge of facts, numbers, and details all increase markedly during child development but remain relatively stable in older adults (Light, 1992; Nilsson, 2003). What *does* change in the course of late adult development is the ability to access information quickly—or even at all. A difficulty in retrieving names is universally reported by adults older than 60 years. Thus, lifelong changes in the ability to access specific facts, or details of a representational structure, are parallel to the lifelong changes described earlier for retrieving specific lexical items. Young children and older adults both find this to be more difficult than young adults do, but the reason in each case is different.

Children and older adults undoubtedly differ in their ability to add new information to their knowledge store; younger children rapidly acquire both vocabulary and grammar, as described earlier, but even the acquisition of interesting new facts is less efficient in older than in younger adults (McIntyre & Craik, 1987). As Keil (2006) pointed out, there are adaptive reasons why certain core functions should be preserved in early childhood, whereas there are no such evolutionary pressures on retention of these abilities in late adulthood. Both the acquisition of new information and the ability to access that information rapidly and effectively appear to favor children over older adults.

One factor that may preferentially favor older adults is the benefit associated with expertise. It is well established that new learning is facilitated when it is congruent with existing schematic knowledge (Bransford, Franks, Morris, & Stein, 1979). It seems reasonable to suppose that older adults possess more schematic knowledge and will, therefore, outperform children if the new material is relevant to their current knowledge base. However, if a child is an expert in some domain of knowledge, that child will show a correspondingly good ability to learn and remember

new material in that domain. In an influential study, Chi (1978) showed that chess-playing 10-year-olds were better at remembering chess positions than non–chess-playing adults, although the adults were better at remembering digit strings. Bäckman, Small, Wahlin, and Larsson (2000) point out an interesting parallel between fluid and crystallized intelligence on the one hand, and the learning of completely new versus schema-relevant information on the other hand. Just as fluid intelligence declines with age, so does the ability to learn new information; in contrast, crystallized intelligence holds up well with age, just as does the ability to learn using preexisting knowledge structures.

One final point of comparison for semantic memory across the life span is the access to different levels of specificity of stored information. Brainerd and Reyna (1990) have proposed "fuzzy trace theory," in which acquired information is represented both in a literal verbatim form and in terms of gist or conceptual meaning. The verbatim form is dominant in early childhood but gradually gives way to the encoding and retrieval of gist. The consequence is that young children tend to recall events in terms of their surface form, but older children interpret incoming information to a greater degree and, therefore, show a greater tendency to recall the meaning of events. Efficient memory performance in older children and young adults reflects both types of representation—gist and inference, as well as perceptual and contextual detail. As adults age, specific detail becomes less accessible, and recall of both factual and episodic material reflects abstracted generalities (Craik, 2002; Dixon, Hultsch, Simon, & von Eye, 1984). This developmental sequence, moving from verbatim to gist, to conceptual plus specific, to abstract/general, reflects the interplay of representation and control processes at different ages. Young children represent incoming events largely in terms of surface form; as conceptual representations develop, events are interpreted in those terms, and control processes allow access to both general and specific levels of detail. In older adults, representational systems remain intact, but control processes are less effective, affording easy access to generalities but not to specifics.

Episodic and Strategic Memory

The developmental course for the recollection of autobiographical events is clear, but explanations for that pattern vary substantially. By the end of the first year of life, infants can reproduce a sequence of actions after some time has elapsed. Bauer (2002) points out that such deferred imitations reflect declarative memory in that a complex sequence can be recalled and expressed. Recall becomes increasingly reliable during the second year, and by 3 to 4 years old, the child's personal memories are primarily expressed in verbal terms (Bauer, 2002). However, for these forms of declarative memory to indicate control of episodic memory as formulated by Tulving (1983), they would need to include "mental time travel" (Tulving, 1993), that is, the ability to relive the experience through recollection of details of the original event. This seems unlikely for such declarative recall as deferred imitation or remembering where a toy is hidden. Thus, Tulving (1983) suggests that episodic memory does not develop until the age of 4 years (see also Perner & Ruffman, 1995).

Episodic memory ability continues to increase until the teenage years and then levels off by the age of 25 to 30 years (Ornstein, Haden, & Elischberger, 2006; Schneider, 2002), when it begins a steady decline through adulthood (Nilsson, 2003; Park et al., 2002). Again, however, this surface symmetry likely conceals important differences between children of 10 to 12 years old and older adults of 70 to 80 years. First, good episodic memory performance reflects good encoding in terms of the person's organized schematic knowledge base, especially expert knowledge in such specialized domains as chess, physics, music or sport (Chi, 1978; Schneider & Bjorklund, 1998). This is the basis for the levels-of-processing effect that Craik and Lockhart (1972) and Craik and Tulving (1975) discussed. As described earlier, schematic knowledge develops over childhood but remains relatively intact in the course of late adult development, so the decline of episodic memory in older adults must have another major cause. Two other linked factors are the use of strategies and the efficiency of executive control processes. Viewing material passively results in poor memory performance, so between the ages of 5 and 10 years, children learn to use such strategies as rehearsal and organization (see Harnishfeger & Bjorklund, 1990, for review). Children younger than this neither use strategies nor profit from them when they are taught, a situation labeled *mediation deficiency*. Older children can and do use strategies but often do not produce them spontaneously, a situation labeled *production deficiency* (Schneider & Pressley, 1997). The probable reason for this latter deficiency is that strategy use is effortful and costly in terms of attentional resources (Guttentag, 1984), and exactly this pattern of production deficiency has also been reported for older adults (e.g., Craik & Byrd, 1982; Naveh-Benjamin, Craik, Guez, & Kreuger, 2005).

Knowledge of strategies and their use is part of metamemory, a type of knowledge that increases in the course of child development. Metamemory knowledge is effective; Schneider and Pressley (1989) found a correlation of +0.41 between levels of metamemory and levels of memory performance in a large sample of children and young adults. In the later adult years, metamemory knowledge remains largely intact, but knowledge of such memory strategies does not guarantee they will be used (Hertzog & Hultsch, 2000); therefore, in general, the correlation between metamemory and memory performance becomes less reliable with age (Cavanaugh & Poon, 1989; Dunlosky, Kubat-Silman, & Hertzog, 2003). Nonetheless, Valentijn et al. (2006) reported a study with older adults demonstrating a relation between metamemory and memory performance that was stronger 6 years after the initial testing.

Older adults exhibit production deficiencies much as children do, and probably for the same reason, namely, strategies are laborious, time-consuming, and effortful to use. In one classic study, Kliegl, Smith, and Baltes (1990) taught older adults to use the method of loci based on Berlin landmarks, increasing their recall substantially over the course of extensive training. The problem, however, is that this strategic skill did not generalize to other memory situations in real life. In summary, strategy use develops in children aged 10 and older, and falls off in older adults because of the associated processing resource costs. Case (1985) commented that, in younger children, the use of strategies leaves little capacity for processing the material. The trick is to integrate new material into existing schematic knowledge and to practice this skill until it becomes at least somewhat automatic and effortless (see Demetrio, Mouyi, & Spanoudis, Chapter 10 of this volume, for an extended discussion of the development of mental processing).

Memory performance typically benefits from the reinstatement of the original learning context at the time of retrieval, a benefit labeled "environmental support" in the adult development literature (Craik, 1983, 1986). Craik has shown that memory tasks such as free recall and time-based prospective memory lack such support and, therefore, require self-initiated activities by the person trying to remember, and that such mental activities are especially difficult for older adults. The consequence is that age-related memory decrements are typically largest in tasks that require the greatest amount of self-initiation and least in tasks, such as recognition memory, where the environment helps to cue the appropriate retrieval processes (Craik & McDowd, 1987). Interestingly, although older adults benefit substantially from reinstatement of the original encoding context at the time of recollection, they are considerably worse than young adults when asked to *recall* the original context (Schloerscheidt, Craik, & Kreuger, 2007; Spencer & Raz, 1994; but see also Siedlecki, Salthouse, & Berish, 2005, for evidence suggesting equivalent age-related declines in memory for context and content).

Children's memory retrieval is also helped by reminders of aspects of the original situation. In a useful discussion of these effects, Ornstein, Haden and Elischberger (2006) describe how a mother's questions and prompts act as a scaffolding to support her child's narrative recall. Apart from the obvious effect of providing retrieval cues, this type of mother–child interaction can help the child's *understanding* of the situation, thereby providing a framework that acts to facilitate retrieval. Ornstein and colleagues go on to suggest that schooling in older children provides similar benefits to aid strategy development. That is, just as the young child's memory development is facilitated by "parent talk," so older children's further development is facilitated by "teacher talk," which provides semantic structure via hints, suggestions, and formal requirements.

Addressing another important aspect of memory retrieval, Jacoby and his colleagues (e.g., Jennings & Jacoby, 1993, 1997) have pointed out that recognition memory comprises two components—familiarity and conscious recollection—that can be dissociated in various ways, as described later in the section on cognitive control. Although the feeling of familiarity of a studied item, person, or event is not very affected by the aging process, the ability to recollect the original encoding context decreases substantially over the course of late adult development (Jennings & Jacoby, 1993, 1997). The age-related decrease in recollection has obvious similarities to the age-related difficulty in retrieving context (referred to as "source amnesia" in more severe cases). This difficulty of recollection may also partly reflect an age-related inefficiency in binding or associating two events at the time of learning (Chalfonte & Johnson, 1996; Naveh-Benjamin, 2000).

Memory and the Involvement of Control

The three aspects of memory we have discussed—procedural, semantic, and episodic—each shows a different trajectory across the life span. In general, procedural and implicit learning remain relatively constant across the life span, semantic memory increases rapidly in childhood and then remains relatively intact, and episodic memory displays the symmetrical inverted-U–shaped pattern of increasing in childhood and declining in the late adult years. These patterns can be explained by considering the reliance of each of these types of memory on representational

and control processes: Semantic memory is largely based on knowledge representations that increase in development and then remain intact, whereas episodic memory depends much more on control and is most reliable for young adults for whom control processes are at their peak efficiency, as discussed in the next section. However, interactions between representation and control affect all three types of memory, changing their pattern of development and decline. For example, both younger children and older adults profit from environmental or schematic support to bolster memory performance. Although context reinstatement is especially helpful to children and older adults, both groups also show some impairment in binding or associative memory (Chalfonte & Johnson, 1996; Cowan, Naveh-Benjamin, Kilb, & Saults, 2006; Naveh-Benjamin, 2000). Finally, more detailed descriptions that isolate the relevant aspects of representation and control are required to understand memory performance across the life span, as Jacoby has demonstrated through his process-dissociation technique that distinguishes between familiarity and recollection. The success with which individuals can demonstrate control and flexibility of memory depends on the availability of representation and control processes at that developmental stage of life.

The process dissociation (PD) procedure that Jacoby and his colleagues (Daniels et al., 2006; Jacoby, 1991; Jennings & Jacoby, 1997) developed provides a means of separating the controlled and automatic aspects of responses in a memory task. The method yields estimates of recollection (R) reflecting cognitive control, and a second measure that has been variously termed "automatic," "unconscious," "familiarity," and "accessibility bias," reflecting the pull exerted by recent learning or deeply ingrained habits. Jennings and Jacoby (1997) showed that R estimates decline from young to late adulthood in a memory paradigm, whereas automatic estimates do not change with age. In a similar demonstration, Zelazo, Craik, and Booth (2004) found that R estimates in a word-stem completion task rose from a group of children aged 8 to 10 years to young adults (22 years on average) and then fell to a group of older adults (71 years on average), but that estimates of automatic influences in the task showed no life-span differences.

Jacoby has also applied his PD analysis to young children. In the classic Piagetian "A-not-B task," infants up to 12 months old will continue to search for a desired object in the place that it has been successfully found on previous trials in spite of watching as it was rehidden in a different location. This behavior has been attributed to an inability on the part of younger infants to maintain the correct information in WM long enough to carry out the appropriate action (Diamond, 2006), but Jacoby argues that location information from previous trials is well learned and thus creates an accessibility bias that influences the direction of the current choice (Daniels et al., 2006). In this way, the initial trials create a temporary habit that must be overruled by an efficiently functioning cognitive control mechanism to avoid the error and perform correctly in the recollection (R) condition.

Jacoby, Debner, and Hay (2001) have used this method to evaluate age-related differences in recollection and accessibility bias at the older end of the age scale. They asked older and younger adults to learn related word pairs with two possible associated words (e.g., knee-BONE or knee-BEND). In a series of training trials, one response (e.g., BONE) was presented 75% of the time and the other (BEND) was presented 25% of the time. After biasing this learned habit, participants were given short lists of the word pairs to be studied for a following cued-recall test. In this retrieval test, first words were presented with a word fragment cue for the second word (e.g., knee-B_N_) that could cue either response. The pairs presented in the to-be-remembered list were either congruent or incongruent with the previously biased (75%) response; Jacoby and colleagues argue that successful recall of congruent responses could be caused by either recollection or habit, but correct recall of incongruent responses demonstrates that recollection overruled the accessibility bias created by the training phase. After applying the PD formulas (see Jacoby, 1991; Daniels et al., 2006), the authors found that conscious control decreased in older adults, reflected in lower R values, but left accessibility bias unchanged. In contrast, training in the 75% condition increased accessibility bias relative to a 50% control condition but left R unchanged. Jacoby and his colleagues concluded that this result points to an age-related deficit in recollection, rather than to an age-related failure of inhibition, being the reason for older adults' increased vulnerability to interference (e.g., Hasher et al., 1999). That is, older adults do not differ from younger adults in their reliance on accessibility bias when recollection fails; the difference in performance between the age groups is attributable more to failures of recollection in the older adults caused by less efficient control.

The PD perspective illustrates how behavior can be governed both by control (R) and by learned representations (accessibility bias) acting either in concert or in opposition. The illustrations provided by Jacoby and colleagues have focused on situations in which accessibility bias is manipulated by varying *new* habit learning, and in these cases, age-related differences are slight as they are for priming and other cases of automatic learning such as the generation effect (Mitchell, Hunt, & Schmitt, 1986; Rabinowitz, 1989) and the self-performed task paradigm (Rönnlund, Nyberg, Bäckman, & Nilsson, 2003). It might be expected, however, that in situations where accessibility bias is provided by long-standing real-life habits, older adults would show larger effects of accessibility bias than younger adults. As the effectiveness of control processes declines with age in adulthood, behavior is progressively more influenced by accumulated habits rather than by the contingencies of the current situation.

Finally, the effect of experience on the development of control may systematically benefit some groups for whom control is better maintained on memory tasks that assess R. Recent studies have shown that tasks that rely on high levels of control to resolve conflict or avoid distraction are solved better by bilingual than monolingual individuals, and that these differences persist into older age (Bialystok, Craik, Klein, & Viswanathan, 2004; Bialystok, Craik, & Ryan, 2006; Costa, Hernandez, & Sebastián-Gallés, 2008). Just as bilingual children performed sentence judgment tasks better than monolingual children when the sentence included a conflict between form and meaning (e.g., Bialystok, 1986), so, too, bilingual adults outperform comparable monolingual adults on tasks such as the Stroop color naming on the conflict conditions but do not differ in control conditions for color naming or word reading (Bialystok, Craik, & Luk, 2008). Wodniecka, Craik, Bialystok, and Luo (in press) tested the hypothesis that this control advantage may extend to recollection in a memory paradigm. Younger and older monolinguals and bilinguals completed a memory task that led to estimates of familiarity and recollection. No differences were found among any of the participants for estimates of familiarity, but bilingual subjects obtained higher estimates for R than monolingual subjects. Such dissociations by groups that differ in experience offer a method for isolating the role of the individual components of representation and control in complex behavior.

Working Memory

Since its proposal by Baddeley and Hitch (1974), the construct of WM has played an increasingly important role in theories of cognitive performance. These authors have focused largely on the short-term storage aspects of WM, but others have explored the role of WM in governing ongoing behavior. Over the life span, the data are clear on the general point that WM abilities increase throughout early development (Diamond, 2006; Hitch, 2006) and decrease with age in adulthood (Gick, Craik, & Morris, 1988). Performance on WM tasks may begin to decline as early as the 30s, although initial declines may be slight (Park & Payer, 2006). As with other complex cognitive constructs, the exact nature of WM appears to depend on the task being performed. For example, span tasks for relatively meaningless material (e.g., digit or letter span) largely reflect control processes of the central executive and speed of processing (Case, Kurland, & Goldberg, 1982; Hitch, Towse, & Hutton, 2001), although speed of processing is unlikely to be the whole story (Diamond, 2006). However, when the WM task involves meaning, as with sentence span or reading span (where participants judge the truth or falsity of short statements and then attempt to remember the final words in each statement), long-term memory representational systems are clearly involved. In these latter cases, developmental changes depend on the development and organization of the relevant representational system. In other words, such tasks involve representations at least as much as they involve control. Commenting on individual differences in WM, Hitch (2006) suggests that "domain-specific variance might be explained by assuming that complex span tasks involve a general resource interacting with domain-specific knowledge representations" (p. 120). Ericsson and Kintsch (1995) made a similar point to account for why WM capacity in adults is larger for domains in which the participants have expertise. These ideas and the data behind them make it quite unlikely that WM is a single, fixed system. It seems more likely that the term applies to a family of related functions whose exact characteristics will depend on the representational systems involved.

Diamond (2006) and Kane and Engle (2003) have stressed the importance of the control functions of WM. One such function is goal maintenance, the ability to keep key aspects of the task in mind across a time delay or during performance of the task itself. This ability is tied to the maturity and integrity of frontal lobe functioning (Duncan, Emslie, Williams, Johnson, & Freer, 1996) and, therefore, improves during childhood (Diamond, 2006) and declines in later adulthood (Phillips, MacLeod, & Kliegel, 2005). Craik (1983, 1986) described self-initiated activities as a group of processes brought online in memory retrieval situations when the information provided by the task and context is insufficient to support recollection. In these cases, such as free recall, the participant must actively generate information related to the context of learning or to the items themselves. Described in this way, self-initiated activities involve "going beyond the information given" in Bruner's (1957) useful phrase, and are clearly similar to the control processes of conscious recollection (R) described by Jacoby and others. Craik's point was that such self-initiated activities appear to decline with age in adulthood. Recent work by Engle and Kane (2004) has also stressed the executive role of WM and the important part played by the ability to generate relevant information from long-term memory.

Two further sets of studies relevant to cognitive control, WM, and older adult development are described here briefly. First, Braver and his colleagues (Braver, Cohen, & Barch, 2002; Braver et al., 2001) have developed an ingenious paradigm to study control successes and failures in a WM context. Participants view a long sequence of letters presented as a series of successive cue-probe pairs, and the task is simply to respond rapidly to each letter X, but only if the X probe is preceded by the cue letter A. Such AX events occur on 70% of trials; the remaining 30% are composed of BX, AY, and BY pairs, none of which should receive a response. Braver argues that failure to maintain the context cue B in WM will result in a false alarm to the succeeding X in BX trials, producing a "context-failure error"; in contrast, false alarms to Y in AY trials represent "context-induced errors." If older adults are less able to maintain context information in WM to control ongoing behavior, then they should make more BX errors but *fewer* AY errors than young adults, and this was the pattern observed (Braver et al., 2001, 2002). As Braver and West (2008) described, these age-related results have been tied both to frontal lobe functions and the efficiency of dopamine regulation in older adults.

The second set of studies concerns the idea that WM in older adults is compromised by a failure to delete irrelevant information from this mental workspace (Hasher & Zacks, 1988; Hasher et al., 1999; Zacks & Hasher, 1994). These authors follow Cowan (1988) in suggesting that conscious awareness is restricted to some highly activated subset of representations (the focus of attention), and that it is this active fragment that controls thought and action. To maximize efficiency and, therefore, control, Hasher and colleagues suggest that inhibition serves three functions in WM: access, deletion, and restraint. First, inhibition controls *access* to WM by monitoring and screening out irrelevant sources of activation from the environment and from intruding mental processes; failure to do so will result in interference and loss of concentration. Second, inhibition acts to *delete* or suppress information in WM that is no longer relevant to the current goal; if the goal shifts (commencing a new task, for example), this function is crucial to maintain mental flexibility. Third, inhibition has a *restraining* function by dampening down habitual or prepotent stimulus–response tendencies, again in the service of keeping thought and action focused on the task at hand. Hasher and colleagues illustrate these notions in cognitive adult development research by showing that older adults have less effective inhibitory functions, with a consequent reduction in the efficiency of WM as a control mechanism.

Task Switching and Mental Flexibility

Mental flexibility, defined as the ability to switch attention among two or more sources of information or to switch between alternative stimulus–response mappings with changes in task demands, is another central component of cognitive control. This ability has been explored in studies of task switching in which participants respond to stimuli on the basis of two different rules; for example, respond to a display of colored shapes by making a judgment based on either the color or the shape. Zelazo et al. (2004) carried out such an experiment on three groups: children aged 8 to 9 years, young adults aged 19 to 26 years, and older adults aged 65 to 74 years. Each trial presented a visual stimulus that was one of four shapes in one of four colors, and participants classified the stimulus by color if it was presented with the letter X and by shape if it was presented with the letter Y. Eighty percent of the trials required color responses to bias that classification. The primary dependent measure was the proportion of perseverative errors—a response that would have been correct according to the other rule. This proportion declined from 10% in children to 4% in young adults, and then rose again to 10% in older adults. Flexible control was, therefore, symmetrically poor in children and older adults, relative to younger adults (see also Jacques & Marcovitch, Chapter 13 of this volume).

Cepeda, Kramer, and Gonzalez de Sather (2001) reported a task-switching study in which displays of three digits (e.g., 1 1 1 or 3 3 3) were preceded by the question, "How many?" or "What digit?" The requirement for cognitive control varies with the display: The display 3 3 3 yields the same response ("3") regardless of the question, so it requires little control; whereas the display 111 leads to different responses for each of the questions ("3" and "1," respectively), so it requires greater control. The authors measured speed of response in participants ranging in age from 7 to 82 years and found a U-shaped function, with higher switch costs for children and older adults.

Switch costs were defined as the extra time needed to switch between tasks relative to a repeated-task baseline. All participants benefited from practice, with children and older adults showing the greatest benefits. Task set inertia was assessed by varying the time between one response and the cue for the next display. On this measure, older adults benefited more than younger adults as this interval was lengthened, showing that older adults take longer to disengage from the current task set. Interestingly, children benefited less than older adults as the response–cue interval was lengthened, but both groups benefited from longer preparation times—the interval between the cue and the relevant display. The study thus demonstrated both symmetries (equivalent decrements in active preparation times in children and older adults relative to young adults) and asymmetries (children were less able than older adults to disengage from a previous task set) across the life span in the ability to manage attention to two tasks.

Several studies have now shown that specific switch costs show comparatively slight life-span changes, whereas general switch costs decline from children to young adults and then increase in older adults. Specific switch cost is the difference in response speed between successive trials requiring a switch to the other rule and successive trials requiring the same rule; general switch cost or mixing cost is the difference in response speed between trials in a mixed block containing two interspersed rules and single blocks containing only one rule. Thus, perhaps unexpectedly, children and older adults can easily switch between rules on successive trials, but their responses are slowed in mixed blocks, even on nonswitch trials, where the *possibility* of a switch is present. This pattern was shown in a large-scale Internet study of more than 5,000 participants ranging in age from 10 to 66 years (Reimers & Maylor, 2005). Their results showed that general switch costs declined from children aged 10 to 11 years to adolescents aged 16 to 17 years; thereafter, costs increased monotonically to a group aged 61 to 66 years. That is, performance peaked at age 17! However, specific switch costs showed no age-related trend across the age range 10 to 60 years, although the 61 to 66 year group showed slight amounts of slowing. The changes in general switch costs may be attributed to the developmental rise and fall of WM abilities; the necessity to bear two rules in mind slows performance in children and in older adults.

Another method used to assess inhibitory control is the stop-signal procedure (Williams, Ponesse, Schachar, Logan, & Tannock, 1999). In this task, participants perform a long series of visual two-choice reaction-time (RT) trials; but if a tone sounds, they must inhibit their response on that trial. Williams and colleagues measured both the RTs to perform go-trials successfully and the shortest time between the visual go-stimulus and the auditory stop-signal for which participants could inhibit their responses on 50% of occasions. Both go-stimulus and stop-signal RTs showed life-span developmental trends (measured on participants ranging in age from 6–81 years), but the trends were very different. Whereas go-signal RTs declined from 675 ms in early childhood to an average of 362 ms in young adulthood and then rose to 538 ms in participants aged 60 to 81 years, stop-signal RTs declined from 274 ms in early childhood to approximately 200 ms in late adolescence, but then rose only 30 ms, to 230 ms, in the older adult group. In this case, inhibition is equivalent to a simple (one-choice) RT, however, as opposed to the two-choice go-signal; therefore, the conclusion that response execution shows a more symmetrical life-span trend than does inhibitory control should be tempered by difference in the degree of choice involved.

These examples from memory and cognitive performance point to at least two processes that change over the life span and produce somewhat different trajectories from childhood to late adulthood. Different types of memory project differently across the life span, and different aspects of cognitive performance, such as task switching, reveal significant breaks in the alleged symmetry of cognitive change across the life span.

LIFE-SPAN CHANGES IN REPRESENTATION AND COGNITIVE CONTROL

Our proposal for a comprehensive explanation of cognitive change is that processes concerned with representation, control, and their interaction evolve across the life span and determine cognitive ability. *Representations* are the set of crystallized schemas that are the basis for memory, learned procedures, and knowledge of the world; *control* is the set of fluid operations that enable intentional processing and adaptive cognitive performance. These systems are interactive: Representations of the world are not constructed randomly but are selected on the basis of needs and desires. In turn, these representations influence the further selection of schema-relevant information from the outside world, thereby demonstrating control. In this way, control processes determine the construction of representations, and these representations later play a part in

further controlled processing. We assume that representational knowledge increases markedly during childhood and continues to accumulate at a slower pace throughout adulthood, but remains relatively stable in the late adult years. This is the pattern depicted for crystallized intelligence or crystallized pragmatics in Figure 7.1. In contrast, cognitive control increases in power, speed, and complexity from infancy to young adulthood, and declines thereafter, as shown for fluid intelligence or fluid mechanics.

Evidence for this conceptualization can be seen in our discussion of the life-span changes in the specific content areas of language ability and cognitive skills. Across the various tasks described earlier, cognitive control over behavior improves from infancy to young adulthood and then declines throughout the adult years. This inverted-U–shaped function parallels the growth and decline of efficient frontal lobe functioning. It is generally agreed that specific areas of the PFC interact with parietal and other brain areas to mediate control processes, but the exact manner in which these neural networks function to regulate behavior is still quite poorly understood. Different theorists have emphasized different aspects of controlled behavior and their developmental changes; for example, Salthouse (1996) has focused on speed and slowing, Hasher and Zacks (1988) emphasize inhibition, Craik and Byrd (1982) stress processing resources, and Jacoby and colleagues (Daniels et al., 2006) have emphasized conscious control. These interpretations are not necessarily mutually exclusive, and Dennis and Cabeza (2008) explore the relations between them and how they relate to current ideas about brain structure and function. Thus, it seems likely that *all* of these factors play some role in the mechanisms of cognitive control across the life span, rather than one being correct and the others wrong.

Mechanisms of Change: Context, Representation, and Control

Early child development is dominated by the acquisition of knowledge of various types—sensorimotor, procedural, declarative, and episodic—and thus by the growth and organization of representations. In contrast, the decline of cognitive functioning in the late adult years is more dominated by changes in control functions operating on the knowledge base. However, the context in which behavior occurs is crucially important at both ends of the life course. The external environment is obviously the source of new information at all stages of life, and in that sense the context establishes, shapes, and confirms the knowledge incorporated in the representational systems. This function of context is particularly important during childhood, but the external context also has an important role in older age. Young children (like simple animals perhaps) are heavily influenced by the current environment in their feelings, thoughts, and behavior, but as they mature and accumulate internal representations, such thoughts and behaviors are progressively more dominated by these internal schemas. In this way, the developing child is able to act independently of the pressures of "here and now," and more in response to longer term plans and goals. In older adulthood, the support of the environment is again needed to compensate for the increasing difficulty in accessing representational knowledge. Thus, environmental support again becomes progressively more necessary at older ages, both to complement self-initiated behaviors that are difficult to manage, and to guide thoughts and actions appropriately (Craik, 1983).

Our main point is that cognitive change across the life span can be understood largely in terms of the growth and decline of representational structures and control systems, the interactions between them, and their joint interactions with the environmental context. It is clear that "context" in this sense must include social and cultural aspects of the environment (Baltes, Reuter-Lorenz, & Rösler, 2006; Vygotsky, 1978), although a thorough analysis of their profound effects on cognition is beyond the scope of this chapter. The framework provided by this interactional scheme further suggests a number of general questions.

One issue that we have already discussed in the sections examining the two specific domains of language and cognition is whether the *balance* between representation and control in their effect on performance remains constant or changes through different periods of life. Our answer is to endorse the latter option, namely, that these relations change continually through life as a function of both biology and experience. In general, representations play a dominant role when they are first established in early childhood and then become more crystallized (Cattell, 1971; Horn, 1982). These representational systems are well developed in adults, and the use of this represented knowledge is guided by effective control systems. In the late adult years, representations are again dominant but for a different reason; on the assumption that representational systems include schematic habit patterns, as well as structures that represent abstract knowledge, the declining power of control systems leaves behavior influenced predominantly by previously established habits, which may no longer guide behavior adaptively. Thus, although there

may be a tendency for control to dominate in middle life and representations to dominate in both early and later life, all cognitive performance throughout the life span rests on the *interaction* between these two sets of factors, although the balance may tilt from one to the other for various reasons.

Describing the relative balance between representation and control in terms of life-span stages, however, misses the important influence of task-specific influences on these interactions. Even within a single cognitive domain, there are changes in the involvement of representation and control, and the ways in which they interact across the life span. For example, vocabulary development and decline are largely a reflection of representational change, but syntactic development and decline are more dependent on cognitive control; semantic memory is primarily based on representational structure, but episodic memory requires more control; WM depends substantially on established representational schemas, but task switching involves high levels of cognitive control. No single formula associates each of these two central processes with any specific higher cognitive function.

Finally, this approach can be used to understand the development of expertise and the transfer of training to new skills. In the interactive view, in which performance depends on both specific representational knowledge and control procedures to utilize that knowledge in performance, expertise can be described in terms of the relevant networks that incorporate these components through experience and practice. Thus, as Salthouse and Mitchell (1990) have shown, architects have expertise that enables them to perform better than nonarchitects on visuospatial tasks. For any expertise, the extent to which transfer facilitates performance on other tasks will depend on the extent to which the representation and control structures overlap in the networks underlying performance in the two tasks. Thus, expertise based on a narrowly defined set of abilities, for example, video-game players, will have less potential to generalize to other tasks than those for whom the expertise is broadly based, such as musicians. This conception may have application to remediation and rehabilitation in which individuals may be taught to take advantage of skills developed in one domain to facilitate performance in another.

From this perspective, we can then return to the initial question regarding the extent to which development in the mature and late adult years can be regarded as child and adolescent development in reverse. Superficially, this seems to be an attractive idea, given that cognitive abilities obviously increase throughout childhood and generally wane from middle age on, although with markedly different trajectories depending on the relative involvement of such factors as fluid versus crystallized abilities, automatic versus controlled processes, and the like (Craik & Bialystok, 2006a; Park et al., 2002; Salthouse, 1991). However, on the basis of the evidence reviewed here, we reject this possibility on the grounds that even though overall performance first rises and then falls, the *components* of cognitive performance vary at different stages in life. That is, intellectual abilities in young children are relatively poor largely because they have not yet built up adequate knowledge structures, whereas cognitive inefficiencies in older adults stem principally from failures of control. This analysis suggests that equivalent overall performance between 12-year-olds and 80-year-olds is the result of substantially different component processes.

Another question concerns changes in the neural underpinnings of cognitive performance across the life span. Although research in the area of cognitive neuroscience is still at an early stage, there may be some hints about this question to be gleaned from a consideration of brain changes related to early and late development. For example, planning and control are functions generally considered to depend on frontal lobe processes.

Our suggestion is that the role of representations, control, and their interactions in cognitive performance depends on the potential for change afforded by neural structures and brain organization at a particular stage of life. Specifically, the execution of a successful cognitive action at a given moment depends on the interactions among these components, resulting in a fluent act that is not readily decomposed into its components. Instead, it exists as a gestalt at a higher level, much as a winning shot in tennis depends on past knowledge of how to prepare for a particular stroke, current knowledge of the opponent's likely moves, the speed of the ball, the surface, and the racquet, all interacting to create the final fluent action. It is in this sense that it is somewhat artificial to decompose mental processes into their constituent representational, control, and contextual components. Nonetheless, our analysis requires that we do just that. Performance described at the level of the gestalt conceals important differences in the underlying neural and cognitive structures that support those performances. Although overall performance may, indeed, be adequately described by a model such as Figure 7.1a and be consistent with the conclusion that early and late development rerun the same story in different directions, that account is not compatible with any notion of the mechanism of change

and with the important developmental dissociations found for the component abilities of representation and control.

In the cognitive domains we have discussed, change across the life span takes different forms, sometimes appearing to follow a symmetrical pattern of rising and falling ability, sometimes best characterized as childhood development of a skill that is well maintained through late adulthood, and sometimes requiring a more complex description based on interactions between systems of knowledge and control. Our contention is that what unites these trajectories through the diverse domains is their reliance on the same basic cognitive mechanisms that themselves have a predictable evolution through the life span and a unique relation to neural organization and development.

Processes involved in establishing representational structure and organization develop rapidly through childhood, consolidating knowledge structures and schemas that become available to guide further acquisition of knowledge and to participate in the control of behavior. This latter function becomes especially important with mature adult and late adult development, when the processes that comprise cognitive control begin to wane. In addition, these representational processes appear to be largely specific to different domains of thought, allowing for the development of expertise in certain areas in which attention, memory, and learning are enhanced by virtue of more elaborate schemas for that domain. More highly developed representational structures are also associated with more focal activation in the cortex, as neural connectivity becomes more specialized. This *increasing* localization of skill in the developing brain may be related to the finding that late adult development is associated with greater bilateral activity, in other words, *decreasing* localization, although the reasons for these changes at the two ends of the life span are likely quite different.

Processes involved in cognitive control are associated with the PFC, an area of the brain that develops late and declines early, limiting the availability of these processes at the end points of life. In addition, control processes demand high levels of resources for attention and capacity, limiting the extent to which they can operate on a specific task at any time in the life span. Thus, the development and decline of cognitive control is constrained both neurologically and cognitively, shaping the type of mental activity that can be engaged at each stage of life.

Cognitive control includes a variety of skills and abilities, such as processing speed, inhibition, and WM, and the relation among them is a matter of debate, as described in the previous section. Whatever that relation is ultimately determined to be, however, all of the proposed components follow this common path of rising in childhood and waning in the late adult years, and all are associated to some degree with the growth and decline of the PFC. Therefore, it is reasonable to assume that even under a model attributing the greatest independence to each component, there is some common core underlying their function. It is likely, in fact, that no one of these control components overrides the others for its centrality to cognitive processing. In his classic *Textbook of Psychology* (1972), Hebb pointed to the dual roles of sensory stimulation in guiding behavior, one being a nonspecific arousal function and the other being a behavioral steering or cue function. Similarly, it may be that cognitive functions require both sufficient processing resources and adequate cognitive control to be effective. Processing speed may be a *consequence* of these resource and control factors rather than being causative. In turn, all these factors reflect the integrity of brain mechanisms and functions, and how they change across the life span.

The cognitive changes that occur across the life span are vast, and we do not suggest that a simple framework based on only two underlying processing mechanisms can account for those changes in all their complexity. However, we do believe that these two mechanisms allow us to understand both what is similar and what is different about the significant changes that occur over the life span. The observation that early and late development appear to share certain features needs to be explained in a way that allows the mechanisms underlying those shared descriptions to be quite different from each other—adults do not lose the ability to process complex syntactic structures for the same reason that children acquire that ability—but the explanations nonetheless need to be compatible. It would be extraordinary to think that the *types* of mechanisms responsible for cognitive development and decline were completely different in the young child and the older adult. Our purpose is to discover the continuity of these processes by attempting to examine the details of children's development and older adults' decline in specific areas of cognitive performance. We hope that this approach will reveal a clearer understanding of how thinking evolves and how the brain supports those developments.

REFERENCES

Alwin, D. F., & McCammon, R. J. (2001). Aging, cohorts, and verbal ability. *Journal of Social Sciences, 56B,* S151–S161.

Anglin, J. M. (1993). Vocabulary development: A morphological analysis. *Monographs for the Society for Research in Child Development, 58*(10, Serial No. 238).

Au, R., Joung, P., Nicholas, M., Kass, R., Obler, L. K., & Albert, M. L. (1995). Naming ability across the lifespan. *Aging and Cognition, 2,* 300–311.

Bäckman, L., Small, B. J., Wahlin, Å., & Larsson, M. (2000). Cognitive functioning in very old age. In F. I. M. Craik & T. A. Salthouse (Eds.), *The handbook of aging and cognition* (2nd ed., pp. 499–558). Mahwah, NJ: Erlbaum.

Baddeley, A. D., & Hitch, G. (1974). Working memory. In G. H. Bower (Ed.), *The psychology of learning and motivation: Advances in research and theory* (Vol. 8, pp. 47–89). New York: Academic.

Baltes, P. B. (1987). Theoretical propositions of life-span developmental psychology: On the dynamics between growth and decline. *Developmental Psychology, 23,* 611–626.

Baltes, P. B., Reese, H. W., & Lipsitt, L. P. (1980). Life-span developmental psychology. *Annual Review of Psychology, 31,* 65–110.

Baltes, P. B., Reuter-Lorenz, P. A., & Rösler, F. (Eds.). (2006). *Lifespan development and the brain: The perspective of biocultural co-constructivism.* New York: Cambridge University Press.

Baltes, P. B., Staudinger, U. M., & Lindenberger, U. (1999). Lifespan psychology: Theory and application to intellectual functioning. *Annual Review of Psychology, 50,* 471–507.

Barnard, P. J. (1985). Interacting cognitive subsystems: A psycholinguistic approach to short term memory. In A. Ellis (Ed.), *Progress in the psychology of language* (Vol. 2, pp. 197–258). London: Erlbaum.

Bates, E., Dale, P. S., & Thal, D. J. (1995). Individual differences and their implications for theories of language development. In P. Fletcher & B. MacWhinney (Eds.), *Handbook of child language* (pp. 96–151). Oxford: Basil Blackwell.

Bates, E., & Goodman, J. C. (1999). On the emergence of grammar from the lexicon. In B. MacWhinney (Ed.), *The emergence of language* (pp. 29–70). Mahwah, NJ: Erlbaum.

Bauer, P. J. (2002). Early memory development. In U. Goswami (Ed.), *Blackwell handbook of childhood cognitive development* (pp. 127–146). Malden, MA: Blackwell.

Bialystok, E. (1986). Factors in the growth of linguistic awareness. *Child Development, 57,* 498–510.

Bialystok, E. (1988). Levels of bilingualism and levels of linguistic awareness. *Developmental Psychology, 24,* 560–567.

Bialystok, E. (1991). Metalinguistic dimensions of bilingual language proficiency. In E. Bialystok (Ed.), *Language processing in bilingual children* (pp. 113–140). London: Cambridge University Press.

Bialystok, E. (2001). *Bilingualism in development: Language, literacy, and cognition.* New York: Cambridge University Press.

Bialystok, E., Craik, F. I. M., Klein, R., & Viswanathan, M. (2004). Bilingualism, aging, and cognitive control: Evidence from the Simon task. *Psychology and Aging, 19,* 290–303.

Bialystok, E., Craik, F. I. M., & Luk, G. (2008). Cognitive control and lexical access in young and older bilinguals. *Journal of Experimental Psychology: Learning, Memory, and Cognition, 34,* 859–873.

Bialystok, E., Craik, F. I. M., & Ryan, J. (2006). Executive control in a modified anti-saccade task: Effects of aging and bilingualism. *Journal of Experimental Psychology: Learning, Memory, and Cognition, 32,* 1341–1354.

Bialystok, E., & Majumder, S. (1998). The relationship between bilingualism and the development of cognitive processes in problem-solving. *Applied Psycholinguistics, 19,* 69–85.

Bloom, L. (1973). *One word at a time.* The Hague: Mouton.

Bloom, P. (2000). *How children learn the meaning of words.* Cambridge, MA: MIT Press.

Bloom, P. (2002). Mindreading, communication, and the learning of names for things. *Mind and Language, 17,* 37–54.

Brainerd, C. J., & Reyna, V. F. (1990). Gist is the grist: Fuzzy-trace theory and the new intuitionism. *Developmental Review, 10,* 3–47.

Bransford, J. D., Franks, J. J., Morris, C. D., & Stein, B. S. (1979). Some general constraints on learning and memory research. In L. S. Cermak & F. I. M. Craik (Eds.), *Levels of processing in human memory* (pp. 331–354). Hillsdale, NJ: Erlbaum.

Braver, T. S., Barch, D. M., Keys, B. A., Carter, C. S., Cohen, J. D., & Kaye, J. A., et al. (2001). Context processing in older adults: Evidence for a theory relating cognitive control to neurobiology in healthy aging. *Journal of Experimental Psychology: General, 130,* 746–763.

Braver, T. S., Cohen, J. D., & Barch, D. M. (2002). The role of prefrontal cortex in normal and disordered cognitive control: A cognitive neuroscience perspective. In D. T. Stuss & R. T. Knight (Eds.), *Principles of frontal lobe function* (pp. 428–447). New York: Oxford University Press.

Braver, T. S., & West, R. (2008). Working memory, executive control, and aging. In F. I. M. Craik & T. A. Salthouse (Eds.), *The handbook of aging and cognition* (3rd ed., pp. 311–372). New York: Psychology Press.

Brown, R. (1973). *A first language: The early stages.* Cambridge, MA: Harvard University Press.

Bruner, J. S. (1957). On perceptual readiness. *Psychological Review, 64,* 123–152.

Burke, D. M., & Laver, G. D. (1990). Aging and word retrieval: Selective age deficits in language. In E. A. Lovelace (Ed.), *Aging and cognition: Mental processes, self-awareness, and interventions* (pp. 281–300). New York: Elsevier-North Holland.

Burke, D. M., MacKay, D. G., Worthley, J. S., & Wade, E. (1991). On the tip of the tongue: What causes word finding failures in young and older adults? *Journal of Memory and Language, 30,* 542–579.

Burke, D. M., & Shafto, M. A. (2004). Aging and language production. *Current Directions in Psychological Science, 13,* 21–24.

Burke, D. M., & Shafto, M. A. (2008). Language and aging. In F. I. M. Craik & T. A. Salthouse (Eds.), *The handbook of aging and cognition* (3rd ed., pp. 373–443). New York: Psychology Press.

Cabeza, R. (2002). Hemispheric asymmetry reduction in older adults: The HAROLD model. *Psychology and Aging, 17,* 85–100.

Caplan, D., & Waters, G. (1999). Verbal working memory and sentence comprehension. *Behavioral and Brain Sciences, 22,* 114–126.

Carey, S. (1978). The child as word learner. In M. Halle, J. Bresnan, & G. A. Miller (Eds.), *Linguistic theory and psychological reality* (pp. 264–293). Cambridge, MA: MIT Press.

Case, R. (1985). *Intellectual development: Birth to adulthood.* New York: Academic.

Case, R., Kurland, D. M., & Goldberg, J. (1982). Operational efficiency and the growth of short-term memory span. *Journal of Experimental Child Psychology, 33,* 386–404.

Casey, B. J., Giedd, J. N., & Thomas, K. M. (2000). Structural and functional brain development and its relation to cognitive development. *Biological Psychology, 54,* 241–257.

Casey, B. J., Tottenham, N., Liston, C., & Durston, S. (2005). Imaging the developing brain: What have we learned about cognitive development? *Trends in Cognitive Sciences, 9,* 104–110.

Cattell, R. B. (1971). *Abilities: Their structure, growth, and action.* Oxford: Houghton Mifflin.

Cavanaugh, J. C., & Poon, L.W. (1989). Memorial predictors of memory performance in young and older adults. *Psychology and Aging, 4,* 363–368.

Cepeda, N. J., Kramer, A. F., & Gonzalez de Sather, J. C. M. (2001). Changes in executive control across the life span: Examination of task-switching performance. *Developmental Psychology, 37,* 715–730.

Chalfonte, B. L., & Johnson, M. K. (1996). Feature memory and binding in young and older adults. *Memory & Cognition, 24,* 403–416.

Chi, M. T. H. (1978). Knowledge structure and memory development. In R. S. Siegler (Ed.), *Children's thinking: What develops?* (pp. 73–96). Hillsdale, NJ: Erlbaum.

Clark, E. V. (1993). *The lexicon in acquisition.* Cambridge: Cambridge University Press.

Clark, E. V. (1995). Later lexical development and word formation. In P. Fletcher & B. MacWhinney (Eds.), *The handbook of child language* (pp. 393–412). Oxford: Blackwells.

Cohen, G., & Faulkner, D. (1986). Memory for proper names: Age differences in retrieval. *British Journal of Developmental Psychology, 4,* 187–197.

Cooper, P. V. (1990). Discourse production and normal aging: Performance on oral picture tasks. *Journal of Gerontology: Psychological Sciences, 45,* P210–P214.

Costa, A., Hernandez, M., & Sebastián-Gallés, N. (2008). Bilingualism aids conflict resolution: Evidence from the ANT task. *Cognition, 106,* 59–86.

Cowan, N. (1988). Evolving conceptions of memory storage, selective attention, and their mutual constraints within the human information-processing system. *Psychological Bulletin, 104,* 163–191.

Cowan, N., Naveh-Benjamin, M., Kilb, A., & Saults, J. S. (2006). Life-span development of visual working memory: When is feature binding difficult? *Developmental Psychology, 42,* 1089–1102.

Craik, F. I. M. (1983). On the transfer of information from temporary to permanent memory. *Philosophical Transactions of the Royal Society of London, Series B, 302,* 341–359.

Craik, F. I. M. (1986). Selective changes in encoding as a function of reduced processing capacity. In F. Klix, S. Hoffman, & E. Van der Meer (Eds.), *Cognitive research in psychology* (pp. 152–161). Berlin: Deutscher Verlag der Wissenschaften.

Craik, F. I. M. (2002). Human memory and aging. In L. Bäckman & C. von Hofsten (Eds.), *Psychology at the turn of the millennium: Vol. 1, Cognitive, biological, and health perspectives* (pp. 261–280). Hove, United Kingdom: Psychology Press/Taylor & Francis (UK).

Craik, F. I. M., & Bialystok, E. (2006a). Cognition through the lifespan: Mechanisms of change. *Trends in Cognitive Sciences, 10,* 131–138.

Craik, F. I. M., & Bialystok, E. (2006b). On structure and process in lifespan cognitive development. In E. Bialystok & F. I. M. Craik (Eds.), *Lifespan cognition: Mechanisms of change* (pp. 3–14). New York: Oxford University Press.

Craik, F. I. M., & Byrd, M. (1982). Aging and cognitive deficits: The role of attentional resources. In F. I. M. Craik & S. E. Trehub (Eds.), *Aging and cognitive processes* (pp. 191–211). New York: Plenum.

Craik, F. I. M., & Lockhart, R. S. (1972). Levels of processing: A framework for memory research. *Journal of Verbal Learning and Verbal Behavior, 11,* 671–684.

Craik, F. I. M., & McDowd, J. M. (1987). Age differences in recall and recognition. *Journal of Experimental Psychology: Learning, Memory, and Cognition, 13,* 474–479.

Craik, F. I. M., & Tulving, E. (1975). Depth of processing and the retention of words in episodic memory. *Journal of Experimental Psychology: General, 104,* 268–294.

Cromdal, J. (1999). Childhood bilingualism and metalinguistic skills: Analysis & control in young Swedish-English bilinguals. *Applied Psycholinguistics, 20,* 1–20.

Daniels, K., Toth, J., & Jacoby, L. (2006). The aging of executive functions. In E. Bialystok & F. I. M. Craik (Eds.), *Lifespan cognition: Mechanisms of change* (pp. 96–111). New York: Oxford University Press.

Dempster, F. N. (1992). The rise and fall of the inhibitory mechanism: Toward a unified theory of cognitive development and aging. *Developmental Review, 12,* 45–75.

Dennis, N. A., & Cabeza, R. (2008). Neuroimaging of healthy cognitive aging. In F. I. M. Craik & T. A. Salthouse (Eds.), *The handbook of aging and cognition* (3rd ed., pp. 1–54). New York: Psychology Press.

de Villiers, J. G., & de Villiers, P. A. (1972). Early judgments of semantic and syntactic acceptability by children. *Journal of Psycholinguistic Research, 1,* 299–310.

de Villiers, J. G., & de Villiers, P. A. (1974). Competence and performance in child language: Are children really competent to judge? *Journal of Child Language, 1,* 11–22.

de Villiers, P. A., & de Villiers, J. G. (1992). Language development. In M. H. Bornstein & M. E. Lamb (Eds.), *Developmental psychology: An advanced textbook* (pp. 337–418). Hillsdale, NJ: Erlbaum.

Diamond, A. (2002). Normal development of prefrontal cortex from birth to young adulthood: Cognitive functions, anatomy, and biochemistry. In D. T. Stuss & R. T. Knight (Eds.), *Principles of frontal lobe function* (pp. 466–503). New York: Oxford University Press.

Diamond, A. (2006). The early development of executive functions. In E. Bialystok & F. I. M. Craik (Eds.), *Lifespan cognition: Mechanisms of change* (pp. 70–95). New York: Oxford University Press.

Dixon, R. A., Hultsch, D. F., Simon, E. W., & von Eye, A. (1984). Verbal ability and text structure effects on adult age differences in text recall. *Journal of Verbal Learning & Verbal Behavior, 23,* 569–578.

Dromi, E. (1987). *Early lexical development.* Cambridge: Cambridge University Press.

Duncan, J., Emslie, H. Y., Williams, P., Johnson, R., & Freer, C. (1996). Intelligence and the frontal lobe: The organization of goal-directed behavior. *Cognitive Psychology, 30,* 257–303.

Duncan, J., & Miller, E. K. (2002). Cognitive focus through adaptive neural coding in the primate prefrontal cortex. In D. T. Stuss & R. T. Knight (Eds.), *Principles of frontal lobe function* (pp. 278–291). New York: Oxford University Press.

Duncan, J., Seitz, R. J., Kolodny, J., Bor, D., Hertzog, H., & Ahmed, A., et al. (2000). A neural basis for general intelligence. *Science, 289,* 457–460.

Dunlosky, J., Kubat-Silman, A. K., & Hertzog, C. (2003). Effects of aging on the magnitude and accuracy of quality-of-encoding judgments. *American Journal of Psychology, 116,* 431–454.

Durston, S., Davidson, M. C., Tottenham, N., Galvan, A., Spicer, J., Fossella, J. A., et al. (2006). A shift from diffuse to focal cortical activity with development. *Developmental Science, 9,* 1–20.

Dywan, J., & Jacoby, L. (1990). Effects of aging on source monitoring: Differences in susceptibility to false fame. *Psychology and Aging, 5,* 379–387.

Elman, J. L., Bates, E. A., Johnson, M. H., Karmiloff-Smith, A., Parisi, D., & Plunkett, K. (1996). *Rethinking innateness: A connectionist perspective on development.* Cambridge, MA: MIT Press.

Engle, R. W., & Kane, M. J. (2004). Executive attention, working memory capacity, and a two-factor theory of cognitive control.

The psychology of learning and motivation (Vol. 44, pp. 145–199). Oxford: Academic.

Enns, J. T., & Trick, L. M. (2006). Four modes of selection. In E. Bialystok & F. I. M. Craik (Eds.), *Lifespan cognition: Mechanisms of change* (pp. 43–56). New York: Oxford University Press.

Ericsson, K. A., & Kintsch, W. (1995). Long-term working memory. *Psychological Review, 102,* 211–245.

Fagan, J. F. (1973). Infants' delayed recognition memory and forgetting. *Journal of Experimental Child Psychology, 16,* 424–450.

Gick, M. L., Craik, F. I. M., & Morris, R. G. (1988). Task complexity and age differences in working memory. *Memory & Cognition, 16,* 353–361.

Giedd, J. N., Blumenthal, J., Jeffries, N. O., Castellanos, F. X., Liu, H., & Zijdenbos, A., et al. (1999). Brain development during childhood and adolescence: A longitudinal MRI study. *Nature Neuroscience, 2,* 861–863.

Gogtay, N., Giedd, J. N., Lusk, L., Hayashi, K. M., Greenstein, D., & Vaituzis, A. C., et al. (2004). Dynamic mapping of human cortical development during childhood through early adulthood. *Proceedings of the National Academy of Sciences of the United States of America, 101,* 8174–8179.

Golinkoff, R. M., & Hirsh-Pasek, K. (2006). The emergentist coalition model of word learning in children has implications for language in aging. In E. Bialystok & F. I. M. Craik (Eds.), *Lifespan cognition: Mechanisms of change* (pp. 207–222). New York: Oxford University Press.

Goswami, U. (Ed.). (2002). *Blackwell handbook of childhood cognitive development.* Malden, MA: Blackwell.

Gottlieb, G. (2003). On making behavioral genetics truly developmental. *Human Development, 46,* 337–355.

Grady, C. L., McIntosh, A. R., Horwitz, B., & Maisog, J. M. (1995). Age-related reductions in human recognition memory due to impaired encoding. *Science, 269,* 218–221.

Guttentag, R. E. (1984). The mental effort requirement of cumulative rehearsal: A developmental study. *Journal of Experimental Child Psychology, 37,* 92–106.

Harnishfeger, K. K., & Bjorklund, D. F. (1990). Children's strategies: A brief history. In D. F. Bjorklund (Ed.), *Children's strategies: Contemporary views of cognitive development* (pp. 1–22). Hillsdale, NJ: Erlbaum.

Hasher, L., & Zacks, R. T. (1988). Working memory, comprehension, and aging: A review and a new view. In G. H. Bower (Ed.), *The psychology of learning and motivation* (Vol. 22, pp. 193–226). New York: Academic.

Hasher, L., Zacks, R. T., & May, C. P. (1999). Inhibitory control, circadian arousal, and age. In D. Gopher & A. Koriat (Eds.), *Attention and performance XVII: Cognitive regulation of performance: Interaction of theory and application* (pp. 653–675). Cambridge, MA: MIT Press.

Hebb, D. O. (1972). *Textbook of psychology* (3rd ed.). Philadelphia: Saunders.

Hertzog, C., & Hultsch, D. F. (2000). Metacognition in adulthood and old age. In F. I. M. Craik & T. A. Salthouse (Eds.), *The handbook of aging and cognition* (2nd ed., pp. 417–466). Mahwah, NJ: Erlbaum.

Hitch, G. J. (2006). Working memory in children: A cognitive approach. In E. Bialystok & F. I. M. Craik (Eds.), *Lifespan cognition: Mechanisms of change* (pp. 112–127). New York: Oxford University Press.

Hitch, G. J., Towse, J. N., & Hutton, U. (2001). What limits children's working memory span? Theoretical accounts and applications for scholastic development. *Journal of Experimental Psychology: General, 130,* 184–198.

Hooper, F. H., Fitzgerald, J., & Papalia, D. (1971). Piagetian theory and the aging process: Extensions and speculations. *Aging & Human Development, 2,* 3–20.

Horn, J. L. (1982). The theory of fluid and crystallized intelligence in relation to concepts of cognitive psychology and aging in adulthood. In F. I. M. Craik & S. Trehub (Eds.), *Aging and cognitive processes* (pp. 237–278). New York: Plenum.

Horn, J. L. (1989). Models of intelligence. In R. L. Linn (Ed.), *Intelligence: Measurement, theory, and public policy* (pp. 29–73). Urbana, IL: University of Illinois Press.

Howard, D. V., & Howard, J. H. (1989). Age differences in learning serial patterns: Direct versus indirect measures. *Psychology and Aging, 4,* 357–364.

Hultsch, D. F., Herzog, C., Dixon, R. A., & Small, B. J. (1998). *Memory change in the aged.* New York: Cambridge University Press.

Jacoby, L. L. (1991). A process dissociation framework: Separating automatic from intentional uses of memory. *Journal of Memory and Language, 30,* 513–541.

Jacoby, L. L., Debner, J. A., & Hay, J. F. (2001). Proactive interference, accessibility bias, and process dissociations: Valid subject reports of memory. *Journal of Experimental Psychology: Learning, Memory, and Cognition, 27,* 686–700.

Jennings, J. M., & Jacoby, L. L. (1993). Automatic versus intentional uses of memory: Aging, attention, and control. *Psychology and Aging, 8,* 283–293.

Jennings, J. M., & Jacoby, L. L. (1997). An opposition procedure for detecting age-related deficits in recollection: Telling effects of repetition. *Psychology and Aging, 12,* 352–361.

Kane, M. J., & Engle, R. W. (2003). Working-memory capacity and the control of attention: The contributions of goal neglect, response competition, and task set to Stroop interference. *Journal of Experimental Psychology: General, 132,* 47–70.

Karmiloff-Smith, A. (1992). *Beyond modularity: A developmental perspective on cognitive science.* Cambridge, MA: MIT Press.

Keil, F. (2006). Patterns of knowledge growth and decline. In E. Bialystok & F. I. M. Craik (Eds.), *Lifespan cognition: Mechanisms of change* (pp. 264–273). New York: Oxford University Press.

Kemper, S. (2006). Language in adulthood. In E. Bialystok & F. I. M. Craik (Eds.), *Lifespan cognition: Mechanisms of change* (pp. 223–238). New York: Oxford University Press.

Kemper, S., Herman, R. E., & Nartowitz, J. (2003). The costs of doing two things at once for young and older adults: Talking while walking, finger tapping, and ignoring speech or noise. *Psychology and Aging, 18,* 181–192.

Kemper, S., Kynette, D., Rash, S., Sprott, R., & O'Brien, K. (1989). Life-span changes to adults' language: Effects of memory and genre. *Applied Psycholinguistics, 10,* 49–66.

Kemper, S., Thompson, M., & Marquis, J. (2001). Longitudinal change in language production: Effects of aging and dementia on grammatical complexity and propositional density. *Psychology and Aging, 16,* 600–614.

Kliegl, R., Smith, J., & Baltes, P. B. (1990). On the locus and process of magnification of age differences during mnemonic training. *Developmental Psychology, 26,* 894–904.

Konner, M. (1991). Universals of behavioral development in relation to brain myelination. In K. R. Gibson & A. C. Petersen (Ed.), *Brain maturation and cognitive development* (pp. 181–223). New York: Aldine de Gruyter.

Kramer, A. F., Bherer, L., Colcombe, S. J., Dong, W., & Greenough, W. T. (2004). Environmental influences on cognitive and brain plasticity during aging. *Journals of Gerontology: Series A: Biological Sciences and Medical Sciences, 59,* 940–957.

La Voie, D., & Light, L. L. (1994). Adult age differences in repetition priming: A meta-analysis. *Psychology and Aging, 9,* 539–553.

Lerner, R. M. (2006). Developmental science, developmental systems, and contemporary theories of human development. In W. Damon & R. M. Lerner (Series Eds.) & R. M. Lerner (Vol. Ed.), *Handbook of child psychology: Vol. 1, Theoretical models of human development* (6th ed., pp. 1–17). Hoboken, NJ: John Wiley & Sons.

Lerner, R. M., & Overton, W. F. (2008). Exemplifying the integrations of the relational developmental system: Synthesizing theory, research, and application to promote positive development and social justice. *Journal of Adolescent Research, 23,* 245–255.

Lhermitte, F. (1986). Human autonomy and the frontal lobes. Part II: Patient behavior in complex and social situations—the "environmental dependency" syndrome. *Annals of Neurology, 19,* 335–343.

Li, S.-C. (2002). Connecting the many levels and facets of cognitive aging. *Current Directions in Psychological Science, 11,* 38–43.

Li, S.-C., & Baltes, P. B. (2006). Cognitive developmental research from lifespan perspectives: The challenge of integration. In E. Bialystok & F. I. M. Craik (Eds.), *Lifespan cognition: Mechanisms of change* (pp. 344–363). New York: Oxford University Press.

Light, L. L. (1992). The organization of memory in old age. In F. I. M. Craik & T. A. Salthouse (Eds.), *The handbook of aging and cognition* (pp. 111–165). Hillsdale, NJ: Erlbaum.

Light, L. L., & Singh, A. (1987). Implicit and explicit memory in young and older adults. *Journal of Experimental Psychology: Learning, Memory, and Cognition, 13,* 531–541.

Lindenberger, U. (2001). Lifespan theories of cognitive development. In N. J. Smelser & P. B. Baltes (Eds.), *International encyclopedia of the social & behavioral Science* (1st ed., pp. 8848–8854). Oxford: Elsevier.

Luria, A. R. (1973). *The working brain: An introduction to neuropsychology.* New York: Basic Books.

MacKay, D. G., & Abrams, L. (1998). Age-linked declines in retrieving orthographic knowledge: Empirical, practical, and theoretical implications. *Psychology and Aging, 13,* 647–662.

Mandler, J. M. (1998). Representation. In W. Damon (Ed.), *Handbook of child psychology: Vol. 2, Cognition, perception, and language* (pp. 255–308). Hoboken, NJ: John Wiley & Sons.

Markman, E. M. (1989). *Categorization and naming in children: Problems of induction.* Cambridge, MA: MIT Press.

Markson, L., & Bloom, P. (1997). Evidence against a dedicated system for word learning in children. *Nature, 385,* 813–815.

McIntyre, J. S., & Craik, F. I. M. (1987). Age differences in memory for item and source information. *Canadian Journal of Psychology, 41,* 175–192.

Meisel, J. M. (1995). Parameters in acquisition. In P. Fletcher & B. MacWhinney (Eds.), *The handbook of child language* (pp. 10–35). Oxford: Blackwell.

Mesulam, M. (2002). The human frontal lobes: Transcending the default mode through contingent encoding. In D. T. Stuss & R. T. Knight (Eds.), *Principles of frontal lobe function.* (pp. 8–30). New York: Oxford University Press.

Mitchell, D. B., Hunt, R. R., & Schmitt, F. A. (1986). The generation effect and reality monitoring: Evidence from dementia and normal aging. *Journal of Gerontology, 41,* 79–84.

Moreno, S., Wodniecka, Z., Bialystok, E., & Alain, C. (2009). *Conflict resolution in sentence processing by bilinguals.* Manuscript submitted for publication.

Mortensen, L., Meyer, A. S., & Humphreys, G. W. (2006). Age-related slowing of object naming: A review. *Language and Cognitive Processes, 21,* 238–290.

Naveh-Benjamin, M. (2000). Adult age differences in memory performance: Tests of an associative deficit hypothesis. *Journal of Experimental Psychology: Learning, Memory, and Cognition, 26,* 1170–1187.

Naveh-Benjamin, M., Craik, F. I. M., Guez, J., & Kreuger, S. (2005). Divided attention in younger and older adults: Effects of strategy and relatedness on memory performance and secondary task costs. *Journal of Experimental Psychology: Learning, Memory, and Cognition, 31,* 520–537.

Nelson, K. (1973). Structure and strategy in learning to talk. *Monographs of the Society for Research in Child Development, 38*(1 and 2), Serial No. 149.

Nilsson, L. (2003). Memory function in normal aging. *Acta Neurologicala Scandinavica, 107,* 7–13.

Ornstein, P. A., Haden, C. A., & Elischberger, H. B. (2006). Children's memory development: Remembering the past and preparing for the future. In E. Bialystok & F. I. M. Craik (Eds.), *Lifespan cognition: Mechanisms of change* (pp. 143–161). New York: Oxford University Press.

Overton, W. F. (2006). Developmental psychology: Philosophy, concepts, methodology. In W. Damon & Richard M. Lerner (Series Eds.) & R. M. Lerner (Vol. Ed.), *Theoretical models of human development: Vol. 1, Handbook of child psychology* (6th ed., pp. 18–88). Hoboken, NJ: John Wiley & Sons.

Park, D. C., Lautenschlager, G., Hedden, T., Davidson, N. S., Smith, A. D., & Smith, P. K. (2002). Models of visuospatial and verbal memory across the adult life span. *Psychology and Aging, 17,* 299–320.

Park, D. C., & Payer, D. (2006). Working memory across the adult lifespan. In E. Bialystok & F. I. M. Craik (Eds.), *Lifespan cognition: Mechanisms of change* (pp. 128–142). New York: Oxford University Press.

Perner, J., & Ruffman, T. (1995). Episodic memory and autonoetic consciousness: Developmental evidence and a theory of childhood amnesia. *Journal of Experimental Child Psychology. Special Issue: Early Memory, 59,* 516–548.

Petrides, M., & Pandya, D. N. (1999). Dorsolateral prefrontal cortex: Comparative cytoarchitectonic analysis in the human and the macaque brain and corticocortical connection patterns. *European Journal of Neuroscience, 11,* 1011–1036.

Phillips, L. H., MacLeod, M., & Kliegel, M. (2005). Adult aging and cognitive planning. In G. Ward & R. Morris (Eds.), *The cognitive psychology of planning* (pp. 111–134). Hove, United Kingdom: Psychology Press.

Piaget, J. (1959). *The language and thought of the child* (3rd ed.). London: Routledge & Kegan Paul.

Pinker, S. (1994). *The language instinct.* New York: William Morrow.

Plomin, R. (1995). Molecular genetics and psychology. *Current Directions in Psychological Science, 4,* 114–117.

Rabinowitz, J. C. (1989). Judgments of origin and generation effects: Comparisons between young and elderly adults. *Psychology and Aging, 4,* 259–268.

Raz, N. (2000). Aging of the brain and its impact on cognitive performance: Integration of structural and functional findings. In F. I. M. Craik & T. A. Salthouse (Eds.), *The handbook of aging and cognition* (2nd ed., pp. 1–90). Mahwah, NJ: Erlbaum.

Raz, N., Lindenberger, U., Rodrigue, K. M., Kennedy, K. M., Head, D., Williamson, A., et al. (2005). Regional brain changes in aging healthy adults: General trends, individual differences and modifiers. *Cerebral Cortex, 15,* 1679–1689.

Reimers, S., & Maylor, E. A. (2005). Task switching across the life span: Effects of age on general and specific switch costs. *Developmental Psychology, 41,* 661–671.

Riegel, K. F. (1977). History of psychological gerontology. In J. E. Birren & K. W. Schaie (Eds.), *Handbook of the psychology of aging* (1st ed., pp. 70–102). New York: Van Nostrand Reinhold.

Rönnlund, M., Nyberg, L., Bäckman, L., & Nilsson, L. (2003). Recall of subject-performed tasks, verbal tasks, and cognitive activities across the adult life span: Parallel age-related deficits. *Aging, Neuropsychology, and Cognition, 10,* 182–201.

Rovee-Collier, C., & Hayne, H. (2000). Memory in infancy and early childhood. In E. Tulving & F. I. M. Craik (Eds.), *The Oxford handbook of memory* (pp. 267–282). New York: Oxford University Press.

Rubin, D. C. (1999). Frontal-striatal circuits in cognitive aging: Evidence for caudate involvement. *Aging, Neuropsychology, and Cognition, 6,* 241–259.

Salthouse, T. A. (1991). *Theoretical perspectives on cognitive aging.* Hillsdale, NJ: Erlbaum.

Salthouse, T. A. (1996). The processing-speed theory of adult age differences in cognition. *Psychological Review, 103,* 403–428.

Salthouse, T. A. (1998). Independence of age-related influences on cognitive abilities across the life span. *Developmental Psychology, 34,* 851–864.

Salthouse, T. A. (2003). Interrelations of aging, knowledge, and cognitive performance. In U. Staudinger & U. Lindenberger (Eds.), *Understanding human development: Dialogues with lifespan psychology* (pp. 265–287). Dordrecht, the Netherlands: Kluwer.

Salthouse, T. A. (2006). Mental exercise and mental aging: Evaluating the validity of the "use it or lose it" hypothesis. *Perspectives on Psychological Science, 1,* 68–87.

Salthouse, T. A., & Davis, H. P. (2006). Organization of cognitive abilities and neuropsychological variables across the lifespan. *Developmental Review, 26,* 31–54.

Salthouse, T. A., & Mitchell, D. R. D. (1990). Effects of age and naturally occurring experience on spatial visualization performance. *Developmental Psychology, 26,* 845–854.

Schaie, K. W. (1996). *Intellectual development in adulthood: The Seattle longitudinal study.* New York: Cambridge University Press.

Schloerscheidt, A. M., Craik, F. I. M., & Kreuger, S. (2007). *The influence of aging and context change on the recognition of pictures and words.* Manuscript submitted for publication.

Schneider, B. A., Daneman, M., & Murphy, D. R. (2005). Speech comprehension difficulties in older adults: Cognitive slowing or age-related changes in hearing? *Psychology and Aging, 20,* 261–271.

Schneider, W. (2002). Memory development in childhood. In U. Goswami (Ed.), *Blackwell handbook of childhood cognitive development* (pp. 236–256). Malden, MA: Blackwell.

Schneider, W., & Bjorklund, D. F. (1998). Memory. In W. Damon (Ed.), *Handbook of child psychology: Vol. 2, Cognition, perception, and language* (pp. 467–521). New York: John Wiley & Sons.

Schneider, W., & Pressley, M. (1989). *Memory development between 2 and 20.* New York: Springer-Verlag.

Schneider, W., & Pressley, M. (1997). *Memory development between two and twenty* (2nd ed.). Mahwah, NJ: Erlbaum.

Shewan, C. M., & Henderson, V. L. (1988). Analysis of spontaneous language in the older normal population. *Journal of Communication Disorders, 21,* 139–154.

Siedlecki, K. L., Salthouse, T. A., & Berish, D. E. (2005). Is there anything special about the aging of source memory? *Psychology and Aging, 20,* 19–32.

Singer, T., Verhaeghen, P., Ghisletta, P., Lindenberger, U., & Baltes, P. B. (2003). The fate of cognition in very old age: Six-year longitudinal findings in the Berlin aging study. *Psychology and Aging, 18,* 318–331.

Smith, L. B., Jones, S. S., & Landau, B. (1996). Naming in young children: A dumb attentional mechanism? *Cognition, 60,* 143–171.

Spencer, W. D., & Raz, N. (1994). Memory for facts, source, and context: Can frontal lobe dysfunction explain age-related differences? *Psychology and Aging, 9,* 149–159.

Stern, Y. (2002). What is cognitive reserve? Theory and research application of the reserve concept. *Journal of the International Neuropsychological Society, 8,* 448–460.

Stuss, D. T., Alexander, M. P., Floden, D., Binns, M. A., Levine, B., & McIntosh, A. R., et al. (2002). Fractionation and localization of distinct frontal lobe processes: Evidence from focal lesions in humans. In D. T. Stuss & R. T. Knight (Eds.), *Principles of frontal lobe function* (pp. 392–407). New York: Oxford University Press.

Taylor, M. (2006). Neural bases of cognitive development. In E. Bialystok & F. I. M. Craik (Eds.), *Lifespan cognition: Mechanisms of change* (pp. 27–42). New York: Oxford University Press.

Thompson-Schill, S. L., Bedny, M., & Goldberg, R. F. (2005). The frontal lobes and the regulation of mental activity. *Current Opinion in Neurobiology, 15,* 219–224.

Timmons, C. R. (1994). Associative links between discrete memories in early infancy. *Infant Behavior & Development, 17,* 431–445.

Tomasello, M. (2003). *Constructing a language: A useage-based theory of language acquisition.* Cambridge, MA: Harvard University Press.

Tulving, E. (1983). *Elements of episodic memory.* New York: Oxford University Press.

Tulving, E. (1993). What is episodic memory? *Current Directions in Psychological Science, 2,* 67–70.

Tulving, E., Kapur, S., Craik, F. I. M., Moscovitch, M., & Houle, S. (1994). Hemispheric encoding/retrieval asymmetry in episodic memory: Positron emission tomography findings. *Proceedings of the National Academy of Sciences, 91,* 2016–2020.

Turkheimer, E., Halye, A., Waldron, M., D'Onofrio, B., & Gottesman, I. I. (2003). Socioeconomic status modifies the heritability of IQ in young children. *Psychological Science, 14,* 623–628.

Valentijn, S. A. M., Hill, R. D., Van Hooren, S. A. H., Bosma, H., Van Boxtel, M. P. J., Jolles, J., et al. (2006). Memory self-efficacy predicts memory performance: Results from a 6-year follow-up study. *Psychology and Aging, 21,* 165–172.

Valenzuela, M. J., & Sachdev, P. (2006). Brain reserve and dementia: A systematic review. *Psychological Medicine, 36,* 441–454.

Valian, V., Hoeffner, J., & Aubry, S. (1996). Young children's imitation of sentence subjects: Evidence of processing limitations. *Developmental Psychology, 32,* 153–164.

Valian, V., Prasada, S., & Scarpa, J. (2006). Direct object predictability: Effects on young children's imitation of sentences. *Journal of Child Language, 33,* 247–269.

Van der Linden, M., Hupet, M., Feyereisen, P., Schelstraete, M-A., Bestgen, Y., Bruyer, R., et al. (1999). Cognitive mediators of age-related differences in language comprehension and verbal memory performance. *Aging, Neuropsychology, and Cognition, 6,* 32–55.

Vygotsky, L. S. (1978). *Mind in society: The development of higher psychological processes.* Cambridge, MA: Harvard University Press.

Williams, B. R., Ponesse, J. S., Schachar, R. J., Logan, G. D., & Tannock, R. (1999). Development of inhibitory control across the life span. *Developmental Psychology, 35,* 205–213.

Wingfield, A. (1996). Cognitive factors in auditory performance: Context, speed of processing, and constraints of memory. *Journal of the American Academy of Audiology, 7,* 175–182.

Wingfield, A., & Stine-Morrow, E. A. L. (2000). Language and speech. In F. I. M. Craik & T. A. Salthouse (Eds.), *The handbook of aging and cognition* (2nd ed., pp. 359–416). Mahwah, NJ: Erlbaum.

Wodniecka, Z., Craik, F. I. M., Bialystok, E., & Luo, L. (in press). Does bilingualism help memory? Impact of bilingualism and aging on recollection and familiarity. *International Journal of Bilingual Education and Bilingualism.*

Zacks, R. T., & Hasher, L. (1994). Directed ignoring: Inhibitory regulation of working memory. In D. Dagenbach & T. H. Carr (Eds.), *Inhibitory processes in attention, memory, and language* (pp. 241–264). New York: Academic.

Zacks, R. T., Hasher, L., & Li, K. Z. H. (2000). Human memory. In T. A. Salthouse & F. I. M. Craik (Eds.), *Handbook of aging and cognition* (2nd ed., pp. 293–357). Mahwah, NJ: Erlbaum.

Zelazo, P. D. (2004). The development of conscious control in childhood. *Trends in Cognitive Sciences, 8,* 12–17.

Zelazo, P. D., Craik, F. I. M., & Booth, L. (2004). Executive function across the life span. *Acta Psychologica, 115,* 167–183.

Zelazo, P. D., & Frye, D. (1997). Cognitive complexity and control: A theory of the development of deliberate reasoning and intentional action. In M. Stamenov (Ed.), *Language structure, discourse, and the access to consciousness* (pp. 113–153). Amsterdam: John Benjamins.

CHAPTER 8

Fluid Cognitive Abilities and General Intelligence

A Life-Span Neuroscience Perspective

CLANCY BLAIR

This chapter examines the development of intelligence from the perspectives of life-span developmental psychology and developmental neuroscience. It contrasts the developmental approach to the study of intelligence with the psychometric approach and addresses a broad distinction in both approaches between fluid and crystallized aspects of mental ability. A variety of evidence is reviewed suggesting that this distinction is central to understanding intelligence both behaviorally and at the neurobiological level. Although the psychometric tradition continues to emphasize a single general factor in the study of intelligence, analyses of longitudinal data in the developmental approach indicate distinct trajectories for fluid and crystallized aspects of intelligence, and present no evidence of a single underlying factor that can explain change over time in various domains of intelligence. As well, in the neuroimaging literature, studies attempting to identify the neural basis for intelligence using various brain imaging methodologies demonstrate that distinct brain areas are associated

with fluid and crystallized abilities, and as yet have been unable to identify a single unitary neural substrate for general intelligence. In conclusion, available evidence from the developmental and neuroimaging literatures points to the role of experience in shaping the behavioral and biological expression of intelligence in both its fluid and crystallized forms.

FLUID COGNITIVE ABILITIES AND GENERAL INTELLIGENCE

The study of mental ability has been a central theme in psychology since the founding of the discipline. In many ways, the interests and concerns of inquiry into mental abilities provided a platform on which some of the defining questions and research methods of the emerging science of psychology were built at the turn of the 20th century. For both practical and basic science reasons, interest in the definition and measurement of mental abilities was strong at this time. Practical in that with the advent of industrialization came an increase in the formal schooling of young children and concerns about the ability of children to succeed in elementary education. Basic in that advances in measurement and theory led to questions concerning the extent to which parameters could be established for specific physical, physiological, and psychological characteristics that could be used to explain individual differences in mental abilities. These basic and practical concerns, and the empirical approaches they generated remain strong today.

The practical and basic science interests in the study of mental abilities converged in two approaches to the study of intelligence. The first, the psychometric approach, refers to a method of measurement and analysis that is primarily concerned with the structure of intelligence and with differences among individuals in intelligence. The second, the developmental approach, refers to a theory-driven experimental approach that focuses on the mechanisms and processes by which intelligence changes across the life span. Rather than focusing solely on differences among individuals, however, this approach is concerned with how intelligence varies with chronological age or culture, as well as with how intelligence changes within persons across the life span (see Nesselroade & Molenaar, Chapter 2 of this volume, for an extended discussion of methodological features of the psychometric and developmental approaches). Although the psychometric and developmental approaches are distinct, and at times opposed in their conclusions about central issues in intelligence, they are similar in that each indicates fluid intelligence—the ability to reason about novel information—to be a central, if not the central, aspect of mental ability. Why this is and how fluid intelligence is central to intelligence in both approaches reflects the specific methodological and analytical techniques that each uses to study intelligence.

PSYCHOMETRIC APPROACH

In the psychometric approach to the study of intelligence, a large number of measures of cognitive ability are administered to representative samples of individuals, and statistical relations among the various measures are investigated using the technique of factor analysis. The goal of this area of research is to determine the extent to which distinct aspects of cognitive ability can be identified and also to determine the extent to which the distinct aspects, or factors, are united by one common underlying general factor. Over the

past 100 or more years, literally hundreds of factor analytic studies of human mental ability have been conducted, and in a comprehensive reanalysis and review of these studies by John Carroll (1993), a generally accepted structure of intelligence was confirmed. This structure merged the central factor theory of Spearman (1904), which identifies specific cognitive abilities that are united under a single general factor, with the two-factor theory of fluid and crystallized intelligence of Cattell and Horn (1967), which identifies broad fluid and crystallized categorizations of specific abilities without a general factor.

Referred to as the Cattell-Horn-Carroll (CHC) model of intelligence (McGrew, Flanagan, Keith, & Vanderwood, 1997), the CHC model, shown in Figure 8.1, identifies 64 first stratum or specific abilities that are subsumed under approximately 9 second stratum or broadband factors that are themselves subsumed under a third stratum by g, or the general factor of intelligence. In addition to gF, fluid reasoning ability, and gC, crystallized knowledge, these broad second stratum abilities include gS, speed of processing, gV, visual processing, gA, auditory processing, and gLR, long-term storage and retrieval, as well as several other potential broadband factors. The assumption is that the broadband factors in combination define the range of cognitive skills involved in any mental endeavor, from solving a problem in mathematics, to writing an essay, to composing a symphony, to solving a crossword puzzle.

An important point about the study of intelligence within the psychometric tradition is that the number and types of factors extracted from any factor analysis of test performance is dependent on the types of measured abilities that go into it. By and large, the types of mental abilities that have been measured in a great number of factor analytic studies have to do with what might be considered academic types of abilities (e.g., remembering facts, discriminating quantities and symbols, and solving problems). The type of information presented with the measures is at times purposefully arcane and distinct from everyday types of experiences so as to presumably reduce bias in the constructs being measured. These aspects of intelligence testing within the psychometric tradition have given rise to some pointed criticisms of the assumptions on which well established and widely used measures of intelligence are based, and has resulted in alternative conceptualizations and measures of intelligence (e.g., Gardner, Lewkowicz, Rose, & Karmel, 1986; Sternberg, 1991).

Although the set of broad factors retrieved from factor analyses of mental test batteries have been reliably replicated many times and are presumably of more or less

Stratum III

Stratum II

Stratum I

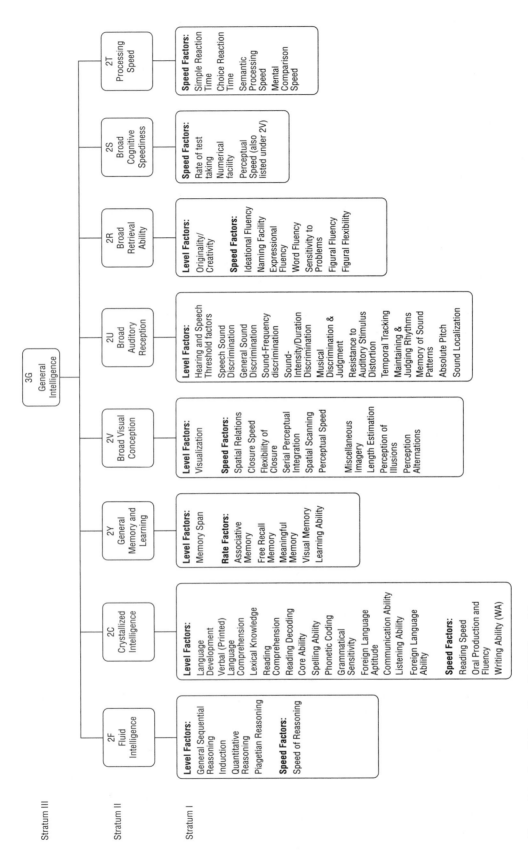

Figure 8.1 Cattell-Horn-Carroll (CHC) model.

equal importance to overall mental ability, gF is of strong interest in that time and again it has been shown to be highly similar, if not identical, to general intelligence, both scientifically and popularly defined. This can be seen in the following, in which gF in the CHC model is defined as:

[The] deliberate and controlled mental operations to solve novel problems that cannot be performed automatically. Mental operations often include drawing inferences, concept formation, classification, generating and testing hypotheses, identifying relations, comprehending implications, problem solving, extrapolating, and transforming information. Inductive and deductive reasoning are generally considered the hallmark indicators of gF. (McGrew, 2009, p. 5)

Encapsulated in this definition is the idea that fluid intelligence describes the ability to reason, to manipulate and organize information in ways that promote the application of that information to a specific end, as in solving a problem, planning a sequence of actions, or extracting higher order rules and making inferences from diverse bodies of information. Of further importance is the deliberate and controlled nature of fluid cognitive tasks; that they are effortful, as opposed to automatic, and that they are applied within a task-specific context and toward a specific goal. In this, fluid intelligence describes what is considered to be the essence of intelligence; the domain general ability to think carefully and clearly about things, the eduction of relations and correlates, to use Spearman's phrase, or more simply, in Carroll's words, "Reasoning abilities are traditionally considered to be at or near the core of what is ordinarily meant by intelligence" (Carroll, 1993, p. 196).

Types of Reasoning Ability

Within the CHC model of intelligence, gF, for the most part, has been defined by reasoning and defined by tasks that are grouped into ability domains labeled as sequential deductive reasoning, inductive reasoning, quantitative reasoning, and Piagetian reasoning. *Sequential deductive reasoning* refers to the ability to begin with a stated set of rules or premises and to arrive through a series of steps at a logically derived conclusion. Tasks that assess sequential reasoning include syllogisms and picture arrangement, among others. In contrast with sequential reasoning in which rules are stated, *inductive reasoning* refers to the ability to infer, or educe common characteristics or rules that determine relations among a set of stimulus materials. Tasks that assess inductive reasoning include pattern completion, matrices completion, and similarities tests. *Quantitative reasoning* combines elements of both sequential and inductive reasoning but is distinct in terms of its content, referring to the ability to reason both deductively and inductively about mathematical concepts. Tasks that assess quantitative reasoning ability include number series and necessary arithmetic operations tasks. And presumably distinct from sequential, inductive, and quantitative types of reasoning, *Piagetian reasoning* refers to the ability to complete conservation, seriation, and classification types of tasks that are the primary indicators of mental development of children described by Piagetian theory. However, as these tasks are present in fewer data sets, the clear demarcation of Piagetian reasoning from other types of reasoning is sometimes questioned.

Distinguishing reliably among the indicators of different reasoning components (e.g., quantitative vs. inductive) of fluid intelligence is difficult and of necessity somewhat arbitrary. This reflects the fact that reasoning factors identified through factor analysis are a function of the types of tasks that have been included in intelligence batteries. That is, there may be other types of reasoning that could be contributing to gF, but there are not enough batteries that include this type of reasoning for it to be reliably identified using factor analysis of multiple data sets. Furthermore, an important point with all reasoning tasks, known and unknown concerns the extent to which they are independent of other aspects of mental ability, such as crystallized intelligence and processing speed. To the extent to which variance associated with knowledge or speed rather than reasoning ability is assessed, the tasks will fail to primarily assess reasoning ability.

At root, however, the defining common feature of fluid reasoning tasks is that they require the individual to organize information, whether novel or familiar, and to identify patterns or rules for grouping or classifying information. As such, the archetypal and most widely used measure of fluid intelligence is the Raven Progressive Matrices (RPM) test. As shown in a hypothetical Raven test item in Figure 8.2, the object of this task is to determine the pattern of relations among the figural elements and to determine which item from the multiple choices presented best completes the pattern. As the complexity of the items increases, the task requires the individual to hold an increasing number of relations among the problem elements in mind and to avoid distracting choices that complete the pattern in terms of one or two relations, but that are incorrect and must be inhibited.

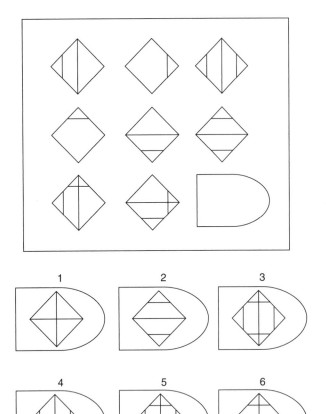

Figure 8.2 Hypothetical Raven Progressive Matrices test item.

In the organization of information, completion of patterns, and identification of relations among problem elements in measures such as RPM, gF is presumed to be closely dependent on specific cognitive control abilities that are to a greater or lesser extent present in all types of reasoning tasks and that include the set of information-processing abilities described under constructs such as working memory (Baddeley, 1986), working memory capacity (Kane & Engle, 2002), or executive functions (EFs; Diamond, 2002; Jacques & Marcovitch, Chapter 13 of this volume; Zelazo & Müller, 2002). EFs describe information-processing abilities that allow for actively maintaining and processing task-relevant information in working memory, for flexibly sustaining and shifting attention between distinct but related aspects of a given task, and for inhibiting extraneous information and automatic responding associated with prepotent stimuli (Diamond; Zelazo et al., 2003). In this tripartite division into working memory, inhibitory control, and attention shifting or flexibility, EFs have been related to multiple aspects of

developing social and cognitive competence in children (Blair & Razza, 2007; Carlson & Moses, 2001; Hughes & Ensor, 2007), to declines in fluid intelligence in research on late adult cognitive development (Schretlen et al., 2000; West, 1996), and have been identified as highly salient, if not central, aspects of cognitive deficits in a number of developmental disorders and psychopathologies in children (Pennington & Ozonoff, 1996; Zelazo & Müller, 2002) and adults (Hedden & Gabrieli, 2004; see Jacques & Marcovitch, Chapter 13 of this volume, for an extended discussion of the life-span development of EF).

Executive Functions, Fluid Reasoning Ability, and General Intelligence

Furthermore, as abilities central to reasoning, and conceptually very close to the definition of general intelligence, it is perhaps not surprising that in a number of psychometric studies, the relation of latent ability factors for EFs, working memory capacity, in particular, to the gF factor is very high (Ackerman, Beier, & Boyle, 2005; Kane, Hambrick, & Conway, 2005; Süß, Oberauer, Wittmann, Wilhelm, & Schulze, 2002), and the relation of gF to g at times approaches unity (Embretson, 1995; Gustafsson, 1984; Kyllonen & Christal, 1990). This similarity of gF to g is represented in the structure of intelligence as presented in a multidimensional scaling analysis of the relation of various intelligence tests to the general factor (Marshalek, Lohman, & Snow, 1983). In that analysis, RPM emerged at the center of a "complexity continuum," meaning that it had the highest loading on the general factor of intelligence and was surrounded by reasoning tasks of similar complexity to RPM, with successively less complex and more knowledge based, and therefore lower g content, tasks radiating outward.

The close associations of EFs with gF and gF with g has led to a number of attempts to determine whether individual differences in EF abilities, particularly, working memory (Kyllonen & Christal, 1990) and inhibitory control (Dempster, 1992), may, in fact, account for individual differences in general intelligence. Working memory refers to the ability to hold information in mind and to operate on it or integrate it with other information; that is, to hold it in the focus of attention. As such, information in working memory is in a state that is vulnerable to interference; therefore, the ability to inhibit shifting the focus of attention to prepotent or distracting information or responses is a key component of working memory ability (Kane & Engle, 2002; see also Bialystok & Craik, Chapter 7 of this volume, and Demetriou, Mouyi, & Spanoudis, Chapter 10 of this volume, for extended discussions of working memory development).

The association between EFs and intelligence has been investigated in a variety of ways and has produced the general conclusions that the ability to hold information in mind and resist interference from competing or prepotent information or responding is a central aspect of mental ability that is highly related to general intelligence, but that speed of processing, as an independent aspect of mental ability, may be as important, if not more so, for explaining the relation of EF to gF and to g (Kail & Salthouse, 1994; Salthouse & Pink, 2008). This is particularly so when considering the development of fluid intelligence and the extent to which age-related increases (Fry & Hale, 1996) and decreases (Salthouse, 1996) in mental ability may be attributable to changes in speed of processing as much or more so than to change in the EF of working memory capacity. An important point in this research, however, concerns the extent to which measures of speed and working memory can be convincingly differentiated and demonstrated to be relatively "process pure" measures of their respective constructs. To the extent that studies have been able to demonstrate this distinction in measurement, findings indicate in young adults that working memory capacity, not speed, is the primary correlate of gF (Conway, Cowan, Bunting, Therriault, & Minkoff, 2002).

Although working memory capacity would appear to be a primary determinant of gF, and perhaps by extension the g factor itself, somewhat ironically, gF and EF have been shown in clinical and developmental research to be distinct from the general factor, as well as from other aspects of intelligence (Blair, 2006). The finding that gF is so highly similar to g in the psychometric literature but so clearly distinct from it in others, including clinical neuropsychology and developmental disabilities, as well as the literature on the secular rise in intelligence over the 20th century, referred to as the "Flynn effect," has been a central point in the study of intelligence (Blair, 2006; Colom, Rebollo, Palacios, Juan-Espinosa, & Kyllonen, 2004) and also of the neurobiology of intelligence (Jung & Haier, 2007; Kane & Engle, 2002). Although perhaps viewed as anomalies within the psychometric tradition, the associations and disassociations of gF with g fundamentally serve to highlight generative and insightful research reviewed in the following sections about the development of intelligence and the neural basis for intelligence.

DEVELOPMENTAL APPROACH

Without question, the psychometric tradition has provided a foundational and enduring definition of the structure of intelligence and produced highly reliable and valid measures of various aspects of intelligence. Despite this precision and emphasis on structure, however, two primary issues for the psychometric approach are an absence of a theoretical basis for the structure and an absence of a consideration of its development. The psychometric approach defines the structure of intelligence empirically without specifying any prior reason or explanation for this structure. As such, the approach is largely atheoretical, leading to some uncertainty as to what general intelligence is exactly (Jensen, 1998). As well, the psychometric approach treats development and change in the underlying cognitive abilities that define the structure of intelligence as extraneous variance. That is, the approach is adevelopmental, meaning that the structure of intelligence has been demonstrated to be generally the same from childhood through later adulthood. Although the tasks increase in complexity with age, they measure the same underlying constructs and accurately assess individual differences among representative samples at different ages. This characteristic of the measurement of intelligence is reflected in the impressive stability in intelligence from childhood through adulthood (Deary, Whalley, Lemmon, Crawford, & Starr, 2000) and in the excellent psychometric properties that many intelligence measures demonstrate.

Two-Factor Theory

Although stability and precision in intelligence measured psychometrically are the case, and in combination represent a defining scientific accomplishment for psychology, the absence of theory and of development to explain stability and precision, and to account for growth despite stability (or what is more accurately considered as continuity), obscures much that is meaningful about intelligence. Here, a developmental perspective (see Overton, 2006) provides a theoretically meaningful approach, and like the psychometric tradition, one in which fluid intelligence is central to understanding the structure of intelligence and its development. This is seen in the two-factor Gf-Gc theory of intelligence of Cattell and Horn (Cattell, 1971; Horn & Cattell, 1967; Horn & Noll, 1997). In the Cattell-Horn theory, distinct fluid (Gf) and crystallized (Gc) factors are needed to adequately represent the structure of human mental abilities, and in the Gf-Gc model the general intelligence factor is notably absent. (Here, the abbreviations Gf and Gc are used to represent the constructs in the two-factory theory, in which g is absent, and gF and gC are used to represent the constructs in the CHC model of intelligence in which g is present.) As Cattell and Horn noted, the two factor Gf-Gc theory goes beyond the methodology of the psychometric approach as the sole criterion for determining the structure of intelligence to address issues in intelligence research raised by developmental and neurobiological research on mental abilities. "The theory of fluid and crystallized intelligence does not rest only on factor-analytic researches of the structure itself…It draws further support from…five or six additional directions of evidence—developmental, physiological, etc." (Cattell, 1971, p. 97).

In brief, Gf-Gc theory, as with a similar two-factor theory from Baltes, Staudinger, and Lindenberger (1999), which refers to a distinction between the pragmatics (Gc) and mechanics (Gf) of intelligence, is premised on longitudinal data describing what can be considered the classic adult and late adult developmental pattern of intelligence, in which both Gf and Gc exhibit a steep increase in early childhood with an earlier asymptote and steeper decline with increasing age for Gf, as opposed to a later asymptote and general stability in Gc throughout adulthood. Furthermore, this age-related pattern of change in Gf and Gc is presumed to reflect a distinction in the two realms of intelligence in the relative dependence of each on biology (Gf) and culture (Gc), and a presumed developmental relation between them, referred to as the *investment hypothesis*. In the investment hypothesis, abilities grouped together as Gf and presumed to be primarily dependent on physiological parameters and the integrity of the central nervous system will pave the way for the acquisition of learned and acculturated abilities and information, such as vocabulary, grouped together as Gc.

Furthermore, to address the idea that certain aspects of mental ability are presumed to be primarily determined by biology and decline more rapidly with age and that others are primarily determined by acculturation and preserved with age, Baltes et al. (1999) proposed a developmental hypothesis referred to as *selective optimization with compensation*. In selective optimization with compensation, individual-level competence in a particular pragmatic domain is determined by the extent to which the individual can narrow the scope of activities within that domain and rely on social and cultural supports to maintain ability even as functioning in biologically based mechanistic abilities declines (Baltes, Lindenberger, & Staudinger, 2006).

Theorizing about relations between Gf and Gc, or between pragmatics and mechanics, also led to a further hypothesis referred to as the *differentiation-dedifferentiation hypothesis*. The differentiation-dedifferentiation hypothesis addresses the idea present in the two-factor theory that Gf, or mechanics, will form the basis for the early development of intelligence. As individuals develop and encounter increasingly diverse opportunities and environments, however, variation in Gc, or pragmatics, would be increasingly distinct from Gf/mechanics, resulting in differentiation of the two broad aspects of mental ability. With advancing age, however, and the more rapid decline of Gf, variation in Gc is once again more closely linked to Gf (see Bialystok & Craik, Chapter 7 of this volume).

Developmental Data

From the point of view of development and the identification of sources of variation in mental ability, the investment hypothesis and the differentiation-dedifferentiation hypothesis represent coherent theory-based models of intelligence development. It is important to note, however, that both fluid and crystallized aspects of intelligence are rooted in neurobiology, and affected by experience and acculturation in a bidirectional fashion as suggested by relational developmental systems theory discussed later (Lerner, 2006; Lerner & Overton, 2008; Overton, 2006). It may be, however, that the neurobiological systems and processes of experience and acculturation that underlie each are distinct. Furthermore, examinations of longitudinal data have demonstrated that the general trends of the classic Gf-Gc adult and late adult development pattern are more descriptive than determined, with considerable interindividual and intraindividual variation in patterns of change (McArdle, Ferrer-Caja, Hamagami, & Woodcock, 2002) and, notably, variation between historical cohorts (Schaie, 1994).

Empirical examinations of both the investment hypothesis and the differentiation-dedifferentiation hypothesis provide mixed results (Li et al., 2004; Tucker-Drob & Salthouse, 2008). In one of the more interesting longitudinal examinations of developmental relations among diverse mental abilities, McArdle and colleagues (McArdle et al., 2002) demonstrated that trajectories for each of the various second stratum abilities of the CHC model are distinct. In an analysis of the test-retest sample of the Woodcock-Johnson Psychoeducational Battery–Revised [WJ-R], a mental test battery grounded in the CHC model, including the WJ-R Tests of Cognitive Abilities and the WJ-R Tests of Achievement, these authors found that individual broad second stratum abilities were characterized by very rapid increase in childhood followed by decline, with each distinguished by a unique asymptote and by differing rates of change across childhood and adulthood. Of particular interest in the developmental analysis was the absence of any evidence in support of the hypothesis that a single general factor underlies development in each of the domains. Change in the second stratum domains could not be explained by any one underlying determinant such as a general intelligence factor.

In addition, when examining interrelations among the broad second stratum abilities over development in childhood, and also their relation to academic achievement, Ferrer and McArdle (2004) observed subtest-specific relations. Important for the Gf-Gc investment hypothesis, there was no direct evidence of a relation between Gf and Gc; Gf was, however, a strong predictor of quantitative ability and academic knowledge latent factors derived from the subtests of the WJ-R Tests of Achievement. As well, relations of Gf with academic ability were reciprocal, indicating that, although Gf fostered growth in academic ability, academic ability also fostered growth in Gf. In contrast, Gc had only weak relations with knowledge factors, a finding that was confirmed in a second sample examining longitudinal relations of intelligence, as assessed by the Wechsler Intelligence Scales for Children (WISC), to reading achievement assessed by the WJ-R in children between first and twelfth grade. In this analysis, Ferrer and collaborators identified relations between intelligence and the development of reading ability that were stronger for the performance scales of the WISC, which are more closely tied to Gf, than for the verbal scales, which are more closely tied to Gc (Ferrer et al., 2007).

Developmental Theory

Evidence in favor of the role of fluid cognitive abilities in the development of academic ability, including reading as well as quantitative knowledge studied longitudinally, is consistent with the general framework of Gf-Gc theory and provides additional support for what is an enduring emphasis on fluid reasoning abilities in the study of cognitive development extending back to Jean Piaget and beyond (Piaget, 1952). The relation of fluid intelligence to Piagetian theory is, of course, seen in the psychometric tradition by the presence of a Piagetian reasoning ability domain in the factor structure of gF. In the Piagetian tradition, however, the development of the ability to reason about relations among problem elements, whether objects

or hypothetical constructs, is the chief characteristic and central aspect of cognitive development in childhood.

Although Piaget's intellectual legacy is far reaching, the specific tasks that he devised to examine the emergence of reasoning abilities in young children became the focus of interest of many psychologists working in child development. This interest and attention led to numerous research programs designed to examine the development of reasoning abilities using now classic conservation, seriation, classification, and transitive inference tasks with young children. However, although the interest in Piagetian reasoning tasks has been strong, the relevance of Piagetian reasoning to the development of intelligence specifically has received only limited attention. This is somewhat ironic in that the relation of Piagetian theory to the study of intelligence, as defined in the psychometric tradition, was noted early on by J. McVicker Hunt (1961) in his book *Intelligence and Experience.* In his book, Hunt examined the evidence for a fixed and predetermined intelligence, rejected it, and outlined a developmental approach in which the ability to reason and to problem solve is central to the development of intelligence. In doing so, Hunt examined a variety of sources of information, eventually turning to Piaget in Chapter 5, which he opens as follows:

> A conception of intelligence as problem-solving capacity based on a hierarchical organization of symbolic representations and information-processing strategies deriving to a considerable degree from past experience, has been emerging from several sources. These sources include observations of human behavior in solving problems, the programming of electronic computers, and neuropsychology. It is interesting, therefore, to find such a conception coming also from Piaget's observations of the development of intelligence in children. The various lines of evidence appear to be coalescing to flow in one direction, a direction that makes interaction between the environment and the organism continuous. Piaget's observations of the homely interactions of the child with his everyday environment demonstrate empirically the formation of a vertical hierarchy of operations for the processing of information to guide action. His observations begin to show what these concepts of a vertical hierarchy of information-processing operations and a continuous interaction between the organism and the environment mean empirically in human development, where they most need to be understood. (p. 109)

More recently, examinations of the cognitive processes involved in Piagetian and other types of reasoning tasks, and the neurobiology that underlie aspects of these reasoning processes have confirmed the role of fluid cognitive abilities, of EFs in Piagetian reasoning (Houdé & Tzourio-Mazoyer, 2003). In several experiments, Houdé and collaborators have demonstrated that the EF of inhibitory control, the ability to inhibit the interference or distraction of previously acquired information and associations, is central to the successful completion of Piagetian reasoning tasks (Daurignac, Houdé, & Jouvent, 2006; Schirlin & Houdé, 2007). Specifically, in number and weight conservation tasks, in which length and number of objects or weight and number of objects are congruent or incongruent, negative priming effects of incongruent on congruent trials were observed. Similar negative priming effects were observed in the judgment of the veracity of syllogistic reasoning conclusions in which belief biases are incongruent with conclusions (e.g., All elephants eat hay, all hay eaters are light, all elephants are light.) followed by syllogisms in which belief biases are consistent with conclusions (e.g., All men are mortal, Socrates is a man, Socrates is mortal.) (Moutier, Plagne-Cayeux, Melot, & Houde, 2006; see also Ricco, Chapter 12 of this volume). These studies support the idea that the ability to override or inhibit well-learned associations concerning relations among elements in the natural world is an important contributor to the development of reasoning ability.

A further implication of this research is that experience on reasoning tasks may be an important aspect of pedagogy, particularly in mathematics education, that contributes to the development of fluid intelligence, as well as to academic achievement (Blair, Knipe, & Gamson, 2008). This possibility is consistent with Ferrer and McArdle's (2004) finding in which Gf and academic knowledge latent factors were reciprocally related. In the domain of mathematics education, the acquisition of crystallized knowledge, including knowledge of numbers, algorithms, and other knowledge-based aspects of mathematics are important contributors to achievement. Simultaneously, however, an important goal of mathematics education is to develop the ability to reason about relations among numbers, to use algorithms flexibly, and to understand the transitive relations among processes. In many instances, these reasoning processes require learners to inhibit previously learned information and strategies in favor of new ones, such as inhibiting large real number values in favor of small ones when learning fractions, or acquiring a flexible understanding of zero when acquiring an understanding of place value (Blair et al., 2008). In each of these examples, previously acquired associations must be inhibited while information is maintained in working memory and attention flexibly shifted between problem elements and task goals. The

recognition of the role of EFs in mathematics education is evident in the content of mathematics textbooks for young children (Blair, Gamson, Thorne, & Baker, 2005), and their role in the process through which knowledge and ability are generated is central to neo-Piagetian approaches to relations among action and cognitive development in education (Fischer & Bidell, 2006; see also Mascolo & Fischer, Chapter 6 of this volume).

Further evidence of a bidirectional development relation between fluid cognition and academic ability is evident in training studies in young children. In several experiments using randomized designs and learning set methods, preschool and kindergarten children receiving almost daily experience over several months with Piagetian reasoning problems have demonstrated increases in reasoning ability, as well as on standardized measures of achievement and intelligence (Pasnak, Madden, Malabonga, & Holt, 1996; Pasnak, McCutcheon, Holt, & Campbell, 1991). In these studies, Pasnak and collaborators have shown that the provision of gamelike experiences that teach young children to reason about class inclusion, seriation, and transitivity problems result in gains in reasoning abilities, and in some instances, these gains generalize to academic abilities, particularly numeracy and particularly for children experiencing learning difficulty in preschool and kindergarten. Through repeated experience with Piagetian reasoning activities in 15-minute sessions, several days per week over several months, children in experimental conditions have demonstrated sustained gains in cognitive development.

Despite the foregoing research demonstrating the role of fluid reasoning ability in cognitive development and the development of intelligence, the study of the development of reasoning in young children has seen limited research activity (Goswami, 1991), and longitudinal research on the development of fluid intelligence specifically in children has been essentially nonexistent. As noted by A. F. Fry & Hale (2000), "Despite the well known age-related improvement (in fluid intelligence)…there is no empirical literature that examines the development of fluid intelligence, per se" (p. 9). Although interest in age-related changes in specific information-processing abilities, namely, working memory, short-term memory, and speed of processing as a basis for individual differences in fluid intelligence, both early and late in the life span, has been strong (Fry & Hale, 1996; Park & Reuter-Lorenz, 2009; Rabbitt, 1993; Salthouse, 1996), in many ways, the study of fluid intelligence has labored in the shadow of the study of general intelligence. Given the close similarity of gF to g in the psychometric literature, this is perhaps understandable; however, given the large dissociations between gF and other aspects of mental ability in clinical research and in the study of secular trends in intelligence test performance (reviewed in Blair, 2006), it is clear that it is important to study fluid reasoning ability as an independent construct. To this end, research on the neurobiology of fluid intelligence has done much to reveal the multiple ways in which biology and experience bidirectionally interact to influence its development. As reviewed in the following sections, this research has demonstrated the ways in which fluid intelligence is important for, but also dependent on, the self-regulation of behavior, particularly aspects of self-regulation associated with emotional reactivity and stress response systems. In the study of self-regulation, gF and its component processes can be considered, to some extent, as distinct from the psychometric structure of intelligence, helping to focus attention on fluid intelligence as a unique and specific aspect of human behavior and development.

NEUROBIOLOGICAL MODEL

As with research on brain–behavior relations generally, hypotheses about fluid intelligence in cognitive development both early and late in the life span and in research on self-regulation, including emotional and physiological aspects of self-regulation, have been derived, in many instances, from the study of brain injury. Generally speaking, the observation of specific cognitive and behavioral deficits associated with injury or dysfunction in specific brain areas has provided the basis for theorizing about typical age-related changes in mental ability and influences on them. Furthermore, with the advent of brain imaging technologies and continuing advances in animal models that allow for linking brain areas and circuitry with behavior and cognitive abilities, knowledge of the neural basis for fluid intelligence has advanced considerably.

In research on intelligence, one of the most interesting findings of clinical neuropsychology has been a discrepancy between fluid intelligence and crystallized intelligence in the instance of damage to prefrontal cortex (PFC). For many years it has been known that damage to frontal cortex in adults does not drastically impair performance on intelligence measures that primarily assess crystallized abilities (Hebb, 1939, 1942). More recently, however, it has been shown that, although patients with damage to PFC exhibit crystallized intelligence in the normal range, levels of performance on measures of fluid intelligence

such as the RPM and the Cattell Culture Fair Test of Gf are in the range of mental retardation (MR; Duncan, Burgess, & Emslie, 1995; Waltz et al., 1999). As well, the identification of social and emotional problems, and problems with the self-regulation of behavior associated with damage to PFC, extending as far back as the celebrated case of Phineas Gage in 1848 (Damasio, Grabowski, Frank, Galaburda, & Damasio, 1994), provide an indication that frontal cortex, which is composed of many distinct regions, is associated with the regulation of behavior and with the moral sense, and that cognitive and emotional aspects of behavior are integrated in PFC.

As defined earlier, fluid intelligence includes reasoning abilities associated with deduction and induction, and with reasoning in specific domains such as quantitative reasoning and reasoning on Piagetian tasks. As well, it has been shown in a number of computational modeling and behavioral studies that reasoning skills and performance on measures of fluid intelligence such as the Raven and Cattell tests are dependent on working memory and related EFs (Carpenter, Just, & Shell, 1990) and on speed of processing (Fry & Hale, 1996; Salthouse, 1996). As such, fluid intelligence, as with EF, has been closely associated with a network of brain structures and neural circuitry based in PFC. Furthermore, fluid intelligence has to a limited extent (primarily through its association with working memory) been linked to specific neurotransmitters and neuromodulators, and variants of genes that are relevant to brain structure and function of PFC and related neural circuitry (Arnsten, 2000; Ramos & Arnsten, 2007; Tunbridge, Harrison, & Weinberger, 2006).

Life-Span Development and Relational Developmental Systems Theory

Before describing aspects of the neural and chemical architecture of brain areas important for fluid intelligence, it is important to consider the relation of neurobiology to experience. What has been absent to a considerable extent from research on the neural basis of intelligence is much explicit consideration of the ways in which biology and experience are related in development. Here, life-span developmental theory is needed to address the ways in which biology and experience are coactive contributors to development through the process defined as *probabilistic epigenesis* (Gottlieb, 1983; Gottlieb & Halpern, 2002). Probabilistic epigenesis is a central tenet of developmental psychobiology, as well as being a central feature of relational developmental system theory (Lerner, 2006; Lerner

& Overton, 2008; Overton, 2006). Probabilistic epigenesis refers to a developmental analysis that seeks to explain how influences on behavior at multiple levels combine over time to shape development (Gottlieb, 1998). Specifically, bidirectional and coactive relations are acknowledged among levels of analysis ranging from the genetic, to the neural, to the behavioral, to the physical, social, and cultural. A key aspect of the relational developmental systems model is a questioning of the assumption that relations between levels of influence or between structure and function in the development of any organ or organism are unidirectional, and to explore possible bidirectionalities between structures and functions. With respect to brain development, it has long been known that experience influences brain structure, and that brain structure plays an important role in brain function and behavior. Yet most, if not all, of the research on brain structure and function in development frequently makes only passing reference to experience when interpreting findings and relating brain structure and brain activity to behavior. Furthermore, as noted earlier, the study of intelligence has placed great emphasis on defining the structure of intelligence with little or no attention to the idea that the structure of intelligence might be determined as much by its function as its function is determined by its structure. Therefore, in the review of the literature on fluid intelligence that follows, the role of experience on bidirectionality of influences is emphasized.

Neural Basis for Fluid Intelligence

Fluid intelligence and associated information-processing abilities, such as working memory, inhibitory control, and attentional flexibility, are dependent on neural circuitry that is associated primarily with PFC. This circuitry extends throughout neocortex, particularly parietal cortex (Jung & Haier, 2007), but the central and primary point of interest is PFC (Duncan, 2001; Duncan & Owen, 2000). The association between PFC neural circuitry and cognitive abilities important for fluid intelligence has been established in a number of ways. One is through functional neuroimaging, including functional magnetic resonance (fMRI) and positron emission tomography (PET), of brain activity during the performance of measures of fluid intelligence, and on tasks such as working memory and related EFs. Neuroimaging studies have indicated that when completing measures of fluid intelligence, as well as working memory tasks, a network of regions in PFC is reliably activated. These regions include at a minimum the

mid-dorsal lateral frontal cortex and midventrolateral areas of PFC bilaterally, bilateral dorsal anterior cingulate cortex (ACC), and bilateral posterior parietal cortex (PPC), including inferior and superior parietal lobules and the intraparietal sulcus. A number of studies have differentiated frontal regions by identifying their relation to specific aspects of EF, such as storage and processing aspects of working memory (MacDonald, Cohen, Stenger, & Carter, 2000) or differentiation of attentional flexibility and inhibitory control systems (Sylvester et al., 2003; Wager, Jonides, Smith, & Nichols, 2005). The integration of these regions in specific fluid reasoning tasks such as RPM, however, indicates that PFC serves as the neural basis for this aspect of intelligence.

Associations of frontal cortex with executive cognitive abilities that are important for fluid intelligence form the basis for theories of frontal cortex function that emphasize the adaptive nature of neural activity in this part of the brain, and that prioritize its role in general intelligence (Duncan & Owen, 2000; Miller & Cohen, 2001). Simply put, if this brain area is highly flexible and adaptive, exerting control in response to various sources and types of information, coordinating brain systems with more specialized jobs in the execution of diverse tasks that underlie conscious, purposeful goal-directed behavior, then for all intents and purposes, PFC must be the seat of general intelligence. Given the near identity between gF and g in the psychometric literature, it has not been too difficult to make the case for the idea that the neural basis for intelligence is located in PFC, and as such, that a major scientific goal been reached in the study of brain and behavior (Duncan et al., 2000). This is seen most clearly in studies that have shown increased activation in frontal regions in response to increasing demands on reasoning processes. For example in studies by Duncan et al. (2000) and Prabhakaran, Smith, Desmond, Glover, and Gabrieli (1997), as an individual's progress from 0 relations—that is, no reasoning demand at all—to tasks that require reasoning about 1 or 2 more relations among problem elements, or from tasks with few reasoning demands and, therefore, low loading on the general factor of intelligence to tasks with high g loadings, PFC and related regions (Brodmann areas [BA]; see Figure 8.3) are activated, including lateral and medial frontal regions (BA 6, 8, 45, 46), parietal regions (BA 7, 40), and occipital regions (BA 18, 19).

The association of fluid intelligence with PFC and of PFC with EFs is consistent with anatomic study of the brain (Barbas, 2000; Barbas & Zikopoulos, 2007) and with theories of PFC function that attempt to describe the myriad

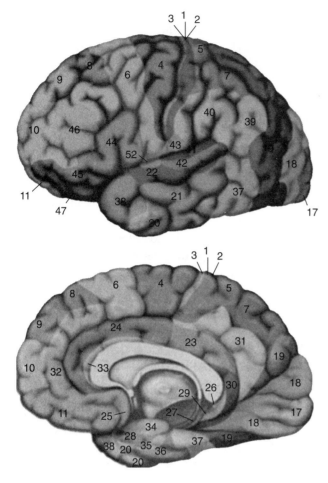

Figure 8.3   Broadmann areas of the brain.

either are weakly established relative to other existing ones or are rapidly changing" (p. 168). In its top-down biasing role, PFC function is critical and most sorely missed in situations in which information and goal states are novel, and bottom-up, automatized responding must be overridden to avoid a disadvantageous outcome.

To fulfill its top-down biasing function, PFC is understood to rely on intrinsic connections among its distinct subregions: dorsolateral PFC for maintaining information in readily accessible form (MacDonald et al., 2000), ventromedial and orbital PFC for registering reward and goal state (Rolls & Grabenhorst, 2008), inferofrontal PFC for overriding automatized stimulus-response mappings (Aron, 2007), as well as extrinsic connections with parietal cortex, anterior cingulate, and visual, motor, and limbic areas for appropriately shifting and maintaining attention (Wager et al., 2005), registering conflict or error (Botvinick, Cohen, & Carter, 2004), regulating visceral arousal (Critchley, 2005), and inhibiting and enacting responses as needed. The extent to which diverse regions, and intrinsic and extrinsic connections among them are associated with distinct aspects of cognitive control and reasoning ability versus the extent to which they function as an integrated adaptive whole has been a major focus of research on PFC and EFs in both behavioral and neuroscience research (Duncan, 2001). Also, a foundational but difficult-to-address concern is the source of control and the way in which control occurs (i.e., the homuncular problem; see Zelazo, Chapter 4 of this volume, for an extended discussion of life-span cognitive and neural development).

Although research addressing questions about unity and diversity in cognitive control functions and their underlying circuitry is extensive, for the purposes of this chapter, research on fluid intelligence suggests that the reasoning requirements of fluid intelligence measures such as the Raven Progressive Matrices test are dependent on the specific network of PFC and related regions. For example, in drawing on interrelated control processes, one region of PFC that has received specific attention in the study of reasoning and decision making is the most anterior region of PFC, the frontopolar complex, referred to as rostral or polar PFC (BA 10) (Bunge, Burrows, & Wagner, 2004; Crone et al., 2009; Koechlin & Summerfield, 2007). Functional neuroimaging studies indicate that polar PFC is active in tasks that make high demands on the integration of information and require subgoal processing during maintenance of the primary goal (Koechlin, Basso, Pietrini, Panzer, & Grafman, 1999). The limited capacity of polar PFC to engage in subgoal processing, however, suggests that its

ways in which the brain processes information. Consistent with a two-factor theory of intelligence, Miller and Cohen (2001) propose an integrative theory in which the essential function of PFC is to maintain a relevant goal state and to exert top-down influence to bias other systems, including motor, vision, long-term memory, and emotion-relevant systems to meet that goal state. In this way, information processing in PFC is differentiated from bottom-up, automatized, and efficient information processing associated with previously acquired knowledge and highly learned routines, also known as crystallized intelligence and acquired aspects of visual, auditory, somatosensory processing as in automatic stimulus and response mappings, and also in visceral, motoric, or emotional responding to specific stimuli. In coordinating and resolving conflicting information in the planning and execution of intentional actions, however, the role of PFC is apparent. As Miller and Cohen note, "The PFC is critical in situations when the mappings between sensory inputs, thoughts, and actions primary function is to maintain overall problem focus and engagement rather than to function as the seat of complex reasoning (Koechlin, Ody, & Kounelher, 2003).

Individual Differences

Neural Efficiency

Having identified overlap between EFs and fluid intelligence both behaviorally and in brain regions and neural circuitry of PFC, a natural question arises concerning the extent to which individual differences in these regions and circuitry are associated with individual differences in intelligence: If these brain areas are important for fluid intelligence, as the structural and functional neuroimaging literatures indicate, then are they larger in individuals with higher intelligence, are they more active?

In an initial attempt to address this question of individual differences in fluid intelligence, Gray, Chabris, and Braver (2003) used fMRI with adults between 18 and 37 years of age as they completed a "verbal" (as opposed to visuospatial) n-back working memory task. In the n-back, participants are required to view individual letters presented sequentially and to indicate when one of the letters is the same as the letter presented on the previous 1, 2, or 3 presentations. That is, in the 1-back condition, the participant indicates whether a letter is the same as that presented on the immediately preceding presentation; on the 2-back, the same as that on the presentation before last; on the 3-back, the same as that presented two presentations before last, and so on. In this way, the task requires the participant to continually update the contents of short-term memory, and to do so while updating and maintaining the target and correctly enacting or withholding a response to each sequentially presented letter. Furthermore, the difficulty of the task can be increased on 2- and 3-back trial blocks by inserting lures, that is, letters in the 2- or 4-back position that match the target in a 3-back trial. Examining regions of the brain that were active in response to the difficult lure trial items in the 3-back condition, Gray et al. (2003) found that activity in specific frontal (BA 9, 10, 44, 45, 46), parietal (BA 40, 31), temporal (BA 22, 39), anterior cingulate (BA 24), and cerebellar regions was positively correlated with participants' scores on the Raven Progressive Matrices test, with the size of the relation ranging from about 0.40 to about 0.60, depending on brain region in a sample of 48 young adults.

The interesting result of Gray et al.'s (2003) study was that relations among gF and brain activity were present only for the difficult working memory items, the lure trials. Although gF was correlated with accuracy on the nonlure ($r = 0.29$) and the lure ($r = 0.36$) trials, no relations between gF and brain activity on nonlure trials were observed. This result is noteworthy in that the emphasis in definitions of fluid intelligence and EFs is on the ability to coordinate information in the face of interference, such as that caused by the presence of the lures, and to maintain information and act on it appropriately while processing additional information or performing subgoals, such as continuously updating the contents of short-term memory and updating the target.

When relating gF to the brain regions identified in response to the difficult lure trial items on the n-back task in Gray et al.'s (2003) study, however, it is also necessary to consider relations between levels of brain activity and task difficulty. Although the relation between activity and difficulty appears to be linear (i.e., as difficulty increases, so does activity), it is not. Functional imaging studies examining relations between activity in PFC across the range of difficulty levels in working memory tasks indicate that individuals with lower working memory capacity exhibit higher levels of PFC activation at lower levels of task difficulty relative to individuals with higher working memory capacity (Callicott et al., 1999; Perfetti et al., 2009; Rympa & Prabhakaran, 2009; Rympa, Prabhakaran, Desmond, Glover, & Gabrieli, 1999). This relation reflects the capacity constraint of working memory in which activation in PFC is low in task conditions with little or no working memory demand and increases linearly with task difficulty up to a threshold beyond which activation decreases thereafter. This inverted U relation between difficulty and activation has been demonstrated at the group level in individuals of generally similar working memory ability as they complete working memory tasks at increasing levels of difficulty (Callicott et al., 1999) and between groups of individuals with greater or lesser working memory capacity (Tan et al., 2007).

The inverted U relation between working memory capacity and functional activity in PFC suggests that individuals with higher working memory capacity and higher gF are more efficient problem solvers than are individuals with lower working memory capacity and lower gF, and that this efficiency can be seen at the neural level. Consistent with the *neural efficiency hypothesis*, one of the earliest imaging studies to examine relations between brain activity and fluid intelligence using PET demonstrated lower rather than higher glucose metabolic rate (GMR) in high relative to low gF individuals as they completed the Raven Progressive Matrices test (Haier, Siegel, Nuechterlein, Hazlett,

Wu, Paek, et al., 1988). This finding was then extended and replicated in a study demonstrating that the effect could be reversed by matching task difficulty to gF ability level. Here individuals with higher ability solving more difficult problems exhibited increased GMR relative to individuals of lower ability levels solving difficult problems (Larson, Haier, LaCasse, & Hazen, 1995).

The findings of functional studies demonstrating an inverted U relation between working memory capacity and activity in PFC, and between GMR and fluid intelligence are consistent with Gray et al.'s (2003) findings relating PFC activity to performance on difficult working memory items and also with a similar functional study designed to examine the neural correlates of superior fluid intelligence in a sample of adolescents, all of whom were 17 years of age (Lee et al., 2006). Here, as with prior studies of the neural basis for fluid intelligence, activation in frontal and parietal regions was greater for complex relative to simple trials on a visuospatial reasoning task modeled on the RPM. When examining correlations between individual gF ability and activation, however, regions most strongly associated with gF were located in PPC bilaterally rather than PFC. Functional activations in right PFC and ACC were associated to some extent with individual ability, but the largest relations were observed in PPC. These findings suggest that even on ostensibly more difficult problems, higher ability individuals are able to solve RPM-type reasoning problems more efficiently through visuospatial attention systems of the PPC rather than more effortful working memory processes associated with PFC.

Such an association between increased parietal relative to prefrontal activation in the neural efficiency hypothesis is also supported by the findings of a functional imaging study that examined brain activity in response to RPM-type problems in high gF relative to low gF individuals (Perfetti et al., 2009). Participants (n = 18) completed simple RPM problems that required reasoning about only one figural relation among problem elements to activation in response to problems requiring reasoning about multiple relations (both activations were observed relative to a control condition in which participants completed a matching task requiring no reasoning). Consistent with the neural efficiency hypothesis, high gF individuals exhibited lower prefrontal activation relative to low gF individuals in response to the low reasoning demand figural problems and increasing activation in response to the more complex relational reasoning problems. The opposite pattern was observed among the low gF individuals who exhibited

reduced prefrontal activation in the complex reasoning relative to the simple reasoning problems.

Similar support for the efficiency interpretation is also found in a functional imaging study examining activity in response to the digit-symbol substitution subtest of the Wechsler battery (Rympa et al., 2006). This task, which is timed and ostensibly a speed of processing task, also requires the ability to hold in mind relations between digits and arbitrary symbols for successful completion. The interesting result, in a sample of 12 young adults, was that faster performers exhibited greater parietal activation and less dorsal lateral PFC activation relative to slower performers. In addition, connectivity analysis indicated that slower performers exhibited increases in prefrontal activation in advance of parietal activation, suggesting increased prefrontal coordination and control of posterior information-processing activity in individuals who completed the task more slowly.

Neuromodulators and Gene Variants

Individual differences in the neural efficiency of brain systems that underlie fluid intelligence have also been related to differences in levels of neuromodulators present in PFC neural circuitry and in variants of genes that code for receptors for these neuromodulators. The demonstration of the inverted U relation between fluid intelligence and brain activity in functional imaging studies is consistent with research in animal models demonstrating an inverted U relation between levels of neuromodulators, such as the catecholamines dopamine and norepinephrine, and neural activity in the PFC. Although the animal models do not address individual differences, they are highly instructive as to how gene variants and aspects of experience may affect performance on measures of fluid intelligence and EFs.

Using a variety of manipulations to alter catecholamine levels, studies have shown that synaptic activity in neurons of the PFC is a function of levels of dopamine and norepinephrine (Arnsten, 2000; Goldman-Rakic, Muly, & Williams, 2000). Using single-unit physiology to record from individual neurons in PFC in nonhuman primates and rodents, performance on working memory types of tasks, primarily those imposing a delay period over which information must remain active, have shown that the activity of neurons in PFC is dependent on catecholamine levels in an inverted U relation. When levels of the catecholamines dopamine and norepinephrine are very low, synaptic long-term potentiation (LTP) is minimal, but with catecholamine increase up to a given threshold, LTP increases. At levels beyond this threshold, LTP decreases. In the instance of norepinephrine (NE), Arnsten and collaborators have shown that this relation is a function of neural receptors in PFC. Moderate increases in NE result in increased occupation of a specific type of neural receptor, alpha-2A adrenoceptors, which have a high affinity for NE and are predominantly located in PFC (Ramos & Arnsten, 2007). At increases beyond a moderate level, however, alpha-2A receptors become saturated, LTP in PFC decreases, and adrenoceptors with a lower affinity for NE become active. These lower affinity receptors are predominantly located in subcortical and posterior brain regions associated with reflexive and reactive responses to stimulation. In this way, levels of NE act to influence the neural response to stimulation, promoting neural activity in PFC associated with reflective and reasoned responses to stimulation at moderate levels, whereas at high levels, NE reduces neural activity in PFC and increases neural activity in posterior brain areas associated with reactive and automatized responses to stimulation (Arnsten & Li, 2005).

The inverted U quadratic relation between catecholamine levels and LTP in PFC is also evident for another neuromodulator, the glucocorticoid hormone cortisol (corticosterone in rodents). Of the two types of corticosteroid receptors in the brain, glucocorticoid (GR) and mineralocorticoid (MR), GRs bind (take up) cortisol with less affinity than do MRs and, therefore, remain largely unoccupied at low levels of arousal. However, with increasing arousal and moderate cortisol increase, GR occupation increases, supporting synaptic LTP. Increases in cortisol with arousal beyond a moderate level, indicating increasingly high GR occupation, however, are associated with synaptic long-term depression rather than LTP (de Kloet, Oitzl, & Joëls, 1999; Erickson, Drevets, & Schulkin, 2003).

As an aspect of experiential influences on fluid intelligence, catecholamine and glucocorticoid levels are important in that they are controlled to a large extent by the body's physiological response to stress. Catecholamine levels are controlled by the activity of the sympathetic-adrenal-medullary system, an aspect of central and peripheral nervous system physiology that reacts quickly in response to stress. Cortisol is under the control of the hypothalamic-pituitary-adrenal axis stress response system, the slower acting component of the stress response that prepares the individual to deal with stress over an extended period (McEwen, 2000). Individual differences in the sensitivity of these systems to stress and in the experience of stress across the life span are likely to be important influences on the development of fluid intelligence (Blair, 2006).

Genetic background is another individual differences factor that affects catecholamine and glucocorticoid levels, and thereby neural activity in PFC. In keeping with relations between PFC-related neural activity and levels of catecholamines and glucocorticoids, a number of studies have demonstrated relations among variants of genes that code for processes that determine levels of these neuromodulators and activity in PFC neural circuitry in response to EF tasks. Occasionally, these studies also demonstrate relations among genetic background, brain activity, and task performance, but relations to observed performance are not consistently observed. This has been evident in a particularly well-studied single-nucleotide polymorphism, the *catechol-o-methyl-transferase (COMT)* gene. In *COMT,* a relatively common substitution of valine (val) to methionine (met) determines the activity of the gene in inactivating (catabolizing) dopamine in PFC. Accordingly, individuals with the val allele of this polymorphism exhibit more rapid dopamine inactivation and lower levels of performance on working memory tasks, whereas those with the met version of the allele inactivate dopamine more slowly and exhibit higher levels of performance on working memory tasks. Individuals with the met/met genotype tend to display high levels of performance on tests of working memory, whereas individuals with the val/val genotype tend to perform worse. Individuals who are heterozygous display performance intermediate to those who are homozygous (Egan et al., 2001; Weinberger et al., 2001). In a particularly illuminating functional imaging study, however, Tan et al. (2007) found that individuals homozygous for valine and who also possessed a polymorphism of a glutamate receptor, metabotropic glutamate receptor 3 (GRM3), also associated with inefficient PFC activity in working memory tasks, and exhibited increased levels of PFC activation and decreased levels of coupling between PFC and PPC, indicative of less efficient processing of information at the neural level in response to a working memory task (Tan et al., 2007). Importantly, however, levels of performance on the task, the n-back, in this small sample study did not vary between the groups. That is, both groups completed the task successfully but with differing levels of neural efficiency.

Although gene variants have been related to brain activity in response to a number of working memory and EF tasks, consistent with the role in PFC of the neuromodulators with which they are associated, these gene variants remarkably appear to be unrelated to performance on intelligence tests, including measures of fluid intelligence. Although this is perhaps unexpected, given the close association between working memory and fluid intelligence, attempts to link genetic polymorphisms such as COMT to neural activity have been far more successful and consistent than have attempts to link these polymorphisms to task performance (Tunbridge et al., 2006). When attempting to link neurobiology to task performance, it is necessary to consider another principle of relational developmental systems, *equifinality*—that is, there are multiple ways in which an individual might solve a complex problem. Given the inverted U relation linking catecholamine and glucocorticoid levels to synaptic LTP in PFC, the relation of genetic background (val or met COMT polymorphism, for instance) to neural activity in PFC will depend on the background state of PFC, individual arousal levels, and susceptibility to arousal. Accordingly, whereas met carriers tend to exhibit increased neural efficiency and higher levels of performance, val carriers under certain conditions exhibit increased efficiency and performance (Mattay et al., 2003), or in at least one instance (Bishop, Fossella, Croucher, & Duncan, 2008), reduced efficiency but higher performance. Furthermore, in the study of Bishop et al. (2008), which indicated reduced neural efficiency but higher working memory performance, examination of the relation of COMT to gF found no association between val-met genotype and performance on the Cattell Culture Fair Test in a sample of 145 adults.

Search for Neuro-g

Evidence linking fluid cognitive abilities with activity in PFC neural circuitry, with neuromodulators, and gene variants for these neuromodulators, as well as with task difficulty, indicates, as expected, that intelligence test performance reflects a complex mix of biology and experience. This evidence indicates not only that both biology (including genetic background and brain structure and function) and experience (including strategy knowledge and use, and levels of arousal and engagement, and by extension beliefs about the self) are important for intelligence test performance, but that they are likely to be bidirectionally interactive and mutually influential.

Relations among genetic background, arousal, and neural activity in relation to intelligence test performance suggest limits on or caveats to the attempt to identify individual differences in intelligence in the structure of the brain—to identify a "neuro-g." Although the neural basis for the types of cognitive abilities that support fluid intelligence is well established, it is increasingly clear that individual differences in these abilities are not consistently related to individual differences in brain structure and function, and that the relation of neurobiology to intelligence is complex. At a minimum, it appears that to understand the relation of neurobiology to intelligence, it is necessary to take into account the role of experience as an influence on brain development and brain activity, and also on the relation of genetic background and neuromodulator function to brain activity. The brain is, of course, a highly complex but plastic organ and one that demonstrates considerable developmental change in response to both short and long-term experience (Liston et al., 2006). At most, it would appear that knowledge of the structure and function of the brain, while providing the foundation for fluid intelligence, can provide only limited information about individual differences in intelligence; that it is a foundation or platform that individuals use in various ways that are as dependent on experience as much as on biology to arrive at a given level of ability.

In the attempt to identify a neural basis for intelligence, a number of studies have correlated the findings of functional and structural neuroimaging studies with individual differences in ability. Using a variety of intelligence measures and ways of measuring intelligence (e.g., full-scale IQ vs. a g factor), these studies have identified a number of associations throughout the brain. These associations, however, have tended to vary across studies and across various operationalizations of intelligence (Colom et al., 2009). Perhaps the most thorough and comprehensive examination of the relation of neuroimaging findings to intelligence has been in the research of Richard Haier and his collaborators Rex Jung and Roberto Colom. Both in a number of experiments designed to address important issues in the measurement of brain and intelligence, and in a comprehensive review of the literature, Haier and collaborators have extensively examined the relation of brain structure and function to intelligence test performance using measures of g derived from factor analytic (correlated vectors) methods, as well as observed full-scale, crystallized, and fluid measures of intelligence. As with the functional imaging findings described earlier, in a review of 37 structural and functional neuroimaging studies of "intelligence and reasoning tests," Jung and Haier (2007, p. 138) identified frontal (BA 6, 9, 10, 32, 45, 46, 47) and parietal (BA 7, 39, 40) cortex, as well as specific temporal (BA 21, 37) and occipital (BA 18, 19), as central to the neural basis for intelligence in a parietofrontal integration theory of intelligence, or P-FIT, that attempts to elucidate *"the critical interaction between association cortices within parietal and frontal brain regions that, when effectively linked by white matter structures (i.e., arcuate fasciculus, superior longitudinal fasciculus), underpins individual differences in reasoning competence in humans, and perhaps in other mammalian species, as well."*

Importantly, Jung and Haier included in their review studies examining relations between intelligence and brain structure, as well as brain function. The association between brain size and general intelligence is moderate but well established (McDaniel, 2005). Relations are present for both total gray and white matter volume, for volume in specific regions such as frontal cortex with median correlations of about 0.30 (Chiang et al., 2009; Hulshoff Pol et al., 2006), and present in children and adults (van Leeuwen et al., 2009). Accordingly, a number of regions were identified that, similar to Miller and Cohen's integrative theory, would seem to emphasize the role of PFC in the coordination of numerous brain systems important for processing information at various levels of complexity. Although consistency in the functional and structural neuroimaging literatures in support of the P-FIT model is considerable, the authors, as well as several commentators on the theory, also noted the considerable heterogeneity in the findings of the various studies included in the review. Many brain regions were implicated by a small percentage of the studies reviewed, whereas relatively few were identified by more than 50% of the studies examined (Colom, 2007). Overall, there is perhaps as much heterogeneity as homogeneity in the findings of studies examining the functional and structural basis of intelligence. Possible sources of variation across studies could, of course, be attributable to extraneous influences, such as variation in sample size, or to substantive reasons such as variation in the way in which intelligence was measured in various studies. To address these concerns, the authors have conducted subsequent experiments with larger samples and with observed and factor analytically derived measures of intelligence, and have provided general support for the P-FIT (Colom, Jung, & Haier, 2006; Haier et al., 2009). Importantly, however, direct comparison of neuroanatomical correlates of a general factor derived from two distinct intelligence test batteries revealed little overlap in brain areas in which structural variation was associated with performance (Haier et al., 2009). The implication that the identification of the structural correlates of g is dependent on the test battery with which g is measured suggests inherent limits on the identification of a neuroanatomic structure of g in the brain (Haier et al., 2009).

An additional indication of limits to relations between structural variation in the brain and intelligence is provided by twin studies examining the heritability of brain structure, both gray and white matter, and intelligence. Although the samples included in these studies are small (n < 25), brain imaging with adults who vary in degree of relatedness (monozygotic [MZ], dizygotic [DZ], unrelated individuals) has demonstrated that regional structural variation in the brain is, not surprisingly, highly heritable (Chiang et al., 2009; Hulshoff Pol et al., 2006; Thompson et al., 2001; Toga & Thompson, 2005; van Leeuwen et al., 2009). Gray matter in frontal, parietal, and occipital cortex in MZ twins is, as with most aspects of morphology in these individuals, essentially identical (within-pair correlation in excess of 0.95). In DZ twins, however, a very high but somewhat lesser degree of similarity is observed in gray matter in parietooccipital cortex and areas of frontal cortex associated with language. Surprisingly, however, similarity in gray matter in frontal cortex areas associated with fluid intelligence is less substantial in DZ twins. Even more so than in gray matter, white matter similarity between MZ twins is very high, whereas many regions are uncorrelated in DZ twins (Chiang et al.). Furthermore, although neuroimaging studies have established the very high heritability of brain structure, as with the literature on brain structure and intelligence reviewed earlier, correlations between brain structure and measures of intelligence in these studies are in the moderate range.

Further indication of the challenges of identifying an integrated brain structure and function model of general intelligence, whether measured by the general factor or full-scale IQ, is seen in the finding in a large neuroimaging study. Here, gC was demonstrated to be more closely related to brain structure, whereas gF was more closely related to brain function (Choi et al., 2008). In this large neuroimaging sample (225 participants between 18 and 23 years of age), gC was positively associated with gray matter thickness in numerous regions of left temporal cortex and negatively associated with gray matter thickness in left superior parietal cortex. In contrast with the predominantly left hemisphere relation between gC and brain structure, gF was associated structurally with frontal cortex, presumably bilaterally, but was more closely associated with functional activity in parietal cortex bilaterally. Although gC and gF had very different correlates in this study, the authors were able to derive parameter estimates from both the structural and functional data, and use these parameters in an independent sample to predict more than half of the variance in IQ. The impressive result of this study, which essentially differentiated gF and gC at the neural level, is that in the prediction of intelligence from the neuroimaging data, both the structural and functional data made unique and substantial contributions.

Additional indication of the complexity of identifying a specific neural substrate for fluid intelligence is seen in the lack of a consistent pattern of activation in brain regions in functional neuroimaging of diverse reasoning tasks. Across various types of reasoning tasks, ranging from deductive reasoning to inductive reasoning, to visuospatial reasoning such as the Raven Progressive Matrices test, to various types of syllogisms, including tasks such as Wechsler Similarities, little commonality among regional activations has been noted (Goel, 2007; Kroger, Nystrom, Cohen, & Johnson-Laird, 2008). In a review of the functional neuroimaging literature on deductive reasoning tasks, Goel (2007) noted that the data indicate a fractionated rather than unitary relation between brain activity and reasoning ability. Variation in brain activity in different types of tasks can be understood to reflect systems for reasoning with different types of information, such as certain versus uncertain information, familiar versus unfamiliar information, and information that does or does not involve conflict and belief bias. Furthermore, in a direct comparison of deductive reasoning and mathematical reasoning, limited overlap was observed among participants as they completed hard versions of each type of task relative to easy versions. As Kroger et al. noted:

> Several general roles for prefrontal cortex and for widespread networks have been proposed to serve flexible information processing, including working memory and executive function (Baddeley, 2000), biasing control networks (Miller & Cohen, 2001), and supervisory control (Shallice, 1988). It would not be surprising to find that deduction depends on many of the same circuits. What is surprising, rather, is that consistent patterns of recruitment of these networks across different neuroimaging studies of deduction have not occurred. (p. 86)

Further, in reviewing the literature from neuroimaging studies of diverse reasoning tasks, Kroger et al. noted, "Our objective is not to build a consistent model from the findings of these studies, but rather to show that doing so is impossible" (p. 87).

Developmental Imaging Studies

Structural Imaging

Structural imaging of the developing brain both cross sectionally and longitudinally has confirmed that brain anatomy changes over time and further suggests that attempts to link brain structure to intelligence must take into account the dynamic nature of brain development and the myriad ways in which individuals solve diverse problems. Structurally, early histological research demonstrated that brain growth is characterized by synaptic proliferation followed by pruning, and that the time course of proliferation and pruning varies from region to region (Huttenlocher, 1979). This pattern of differential gray matter change in the brain by region has been confirmed in longitudinal structural imaging studies (Toga, Thompson, & Sowell, 2006). In samples, followed over several years and imaged at regular intervals, a pattern of progressive gray matter decrease and white matter increase has been demonstrated throughout the brain. One study (Gogtay et al., 2004) that followed 13 children between the ages 4 and 21 over 10 years with structural MRI taken every 2 years indicated progressive gray matter change across the cortex. A pattern was identified in which gray matter loss initially occurs in dorsal parietal and sensorimotor regions between 4 and 8 years of age, and then progresses laterally and caudally into temporal regions and anteriorly into prefrontal areas. This pattern is one in which gray matter in brain regions associated with basic sensory functions reaches mature levels relatively early, followed by regions associated with language and visuospatial cognition around puberty, followed still later by areas associated with fluid intelligence in late adolescence and early adulthood (Gogtay et al., 2004).

Although gray matter loss follows a general posterior-to-anterior progression, moving from brain areas associated with basic information-processing abilities to those associated with higher order information-processing abilities, change is not linear. As shown by several longitudinal imaging studies, gray matter increases to asymptote followed by linear decline, and this pattern of nonlinearity holds across the life span, with higher order association areas showing a cubic trend of increase followed by decrease and leveling, whereas phylogenetically older sensory regions such as limbic areas exhibit early peak and linear decline. Transitional regions, such as cingulate cortex, exhibit a quadratic curve of increase followed by decrease to mature levels (Toga et al., 2006). In later adulthood, variability in patterns of gray matter decrease is also observed. Frontal regions tend to show linear decrease to asymptote in mid to late adulthood, whereas temporal regions demonstrate stability in adulthood followed by late decrease (Sowell et al., 2003). In the study of cognitive development in late adulthood, for example, use of an accelerated longitudinal design in which individuals between 20 and 77 years old underwent structural MRI at 5-year intervals suggested progressive gray matter loss in frontal, striatal, hippocampal, and cerebellar regions but relative stability in gray matter in occipital, temporal, parietal, and entorhinal cortex (Raz et al., 2005). In contrast, a large cross-sectional study examining 6 datasets with 883 participants ranging in age from early to late adulthood indicated generally widespread thinning across the cortex and consistency across the samples in age-related thinning in frontal cortex. Age-related change in other regions, however, was more variable (Fjell et al., 2009). It is important to note in all longitudinal studies examining age-related change in gray matter, particularly those with a wide age span to examine change across adulthood, the data are from sequential cohorts followed longitudinally over short periods; therefore, they include individuals of different historical cohorts and cannot correct for potential cohort differences in total or region-specific brain volume.

As with gray matter, the study of white matter change with age indicates differential rates of change. Unlike gray matter, however, this change is best represented by a linear increase in all brain regions in the early part of the life span followed by linear or quadratic decrease in later adulthood. Similar to gray matter changes, most reliable relations with age have been observed in fiber tracts associated with frontal cortex (Head et al., 2004; Pfefferbaum, Adalsteinsson, & Sullivan, 2005).

Studies that examine relations of gray and white matter development to measures of intelligence and fluid cognitive abilities have indicated expected region-specific relations between brain development and aspects of cognition. For example, in a short-term longitudinal study in children, change in verbal ability as assessed by Wechsler and WJ-R subtests was associated with greater gray matter thinning (i.e., an inverse association with cortical thickness) in left-hemisphere language areas (Sowell et al., 2003). This change in the relation between cortical thickness and cognitive ability is consistent with the idea that increases in cognitive ability are associated with the progressive pruning and refinement of cortical networks in the brain. The interpretation is consistent with the finding of a general relation between cortical thickness and intelligence as measured by the full-scale IQ estimate from the Wechsler batteries in children between the ages of 7 and 19 (Shaw et al., 2006). In this study, however, higher intelligence was associated with a pattern of gray matter increase in the middle childhood years followed by decrease in adolescence, suggesting a dynamic relation between change in cortical thickness in childhood and intelligence. Furthermore, these relations

are distinct from Choi et al.'s (2008) findings described earlier in a same age sample at approximately 21 years, in which left temporal lobe gray matter thickness was positively associated with gC. In the study of white matter, similar region-specific relations have been noted between white matter increase in fiber tracts connecting frontal and parietal areas, and intelligence as measured by Wechsler full-scale IQ (Schmithorst, Wilke, Dardzinski, & Holland, 2005).

In studies of cognitive development in late adulthood, the relation between gray matter change and cognition would seem to be essentially reversed from that of early development. Gradual cortical thinning in frontal and other cortical regions with age is associated with improvements in fluid cognitive abilities early in the life span. In later life, however, the opposite is sometimes observed. In cognitive developmental research in late adulthood, volumetric decreases in later adulthood have been associated with declining performance on measures of specific cognitive abilities including EF. The relation of gray and white matter change to cognition, however, varies across studies of late adult cognitive development, and this is particularly true for measures of fluid intelligence (Park & Reuter-Lorenz, 2009; Raz & Rodrigue, 2006). For example, Rabbitt and colleagues (2006, 2007) found that gray matter decrease and white matter degradation are robustly associated with measures of speed of processing but not with measures of fluid intelligence.

Functional Imaging

A number of functional imaging studies with children, nearly all using MRI, have examined the development of EFs, particularly working memory, primarily in cross-sectional designs, although few have examined brain activity in response to measures of fluid intelligence. Generally, these studies have tended to indicate that younger age is associated with more diffuse activation in a greater extent of cortex in regions identified in functional imaging studies with adults. These studies suggest the progressive refinement of cortical pathways in childhood and adolescence leading to increasingly efficient and mature activation patterns in adulthood (Bunge & Wright, 2007).

To the extent that various studies have accounted for task difficulty and task accuracy, the developmental functional imaging literature is consistent with a neural efficiency hypothesis. That is, these studies suggest that when task difficulty is equated, children will exhibit activation of a greater extent of cortical regions involved, and that this will be particularly true for frontal regions associated with fluid cognitive abilities. At low levels of task difficulty, when performance between children and adults is equated, children will tend to exhibit larger and more diffuse activation in frontal cortex (e.g., Durston et al., 2002). As task difficulty increases, however, and performance becomes correlated with age, older individuals will tend to demonstrate greater activity in frontal and parietal, if not cingulate, and striatal regions associated with fluid cognitive abilities (Crone et al., 2009; Kwon, Reiss, & Menon, 2002).

In contrast with numerous functional imaging studies of working memory in the child developmental imaging literature, only one study has directly examined developmental change (cross sectionally) in children in functional activity in response to relational reasoning problems of the type presented by the Raven Progressive Matrices test (Crone et al., 2009). Here the authors focused on regions of interest in brain areas associated with working memory ability, including dorsolateral PFC, polar PFC, and superior and inferior parietal regions. Results indicated that children compared with adults tended to exhibit lower levels of activity in dorsolateral PFC and in parietal regions in response to the requirement to reason about one and two relations among problem elements relative to problems that required no relational reasoning. In polar PFC, however, children exhibited high levels of activity early in the time course of activation in response to two-relation problems, on which they were less accurate than were adults, but unlike adults did not sustain the activity. As well, and also unlike patterns of activation in adults, children exhibited increased activation in polar PFC late in problem solving in response to one-relation problems, on which they were as accurate as adults. These results indicate the absence of adult-like activation patterns in response to reasoning problems in children and suggest that in regions in which younger and older problem solvers overlap, younger problem solvers activate brain areas differently than do adults.

A somewhat different result was obtained in a cross-sectional developmental imaging study using a simpler type of relational reasoning task than that associated with the Raven Progressive Matrices test, but that is frequently present in mathematical textbooks for children in kindergarten through third grade (Eslinger et al., 2009). This study also identified age-related differences in activation patterns. Unlike the group analysis in regions of interest on Raven-type problems described earlier, however, this study examined linear relations between activation and age throughout the brain in a sample of children age

8 to 19 years. As expected, results indicated that older children primarily activated posterior regions, primarily in superior parietal cortex bilaterally when solving problems that required simple pattern completion determined by the shape and/or the color of the object arrays compared with a task involving no reasoning. Relative to younger children, older children exhibited less frontal activation in response to these tasks, suggesting that they were able to solve the simple reasoning problems using primarily visuospatial processing of relations among task elements. In contrast, younger participants exhibited primarily frontal activation, as well as activation in the striatum and anterior cingulate. This pattern of activation suggests that younger children were solving the reasoning problems through more deliberative information processing associated with the coordination of information maintenance and inhibitory control processes associated with activity in PFC-cingulate-striatal neural circuitry. The cingulate, particularly its anterior region, is a transitional one between PFC and subcortical structures, and is important for the detection of error and for the detection of conflicting information. As well, the striatum, composed of the caudate and putamen, is important for the acquisition, coordination, and activation of routines, such as in motor processes but also in cognitive processes.

Results similar to those obtained by Eslinger et al. (2009) in response to relational reasoning were obtained in a child sample, also 8 to 19 years of age, in response to simple addition and subtraction problems (Rivera, Reiss, Eckert, & Menon, 2005). Accuracy rates of older and younger children on the mathematics problems were identical, whereas reaction time was inversely related to age. As with simple relational reasoning, younger participants demonstrated greater activation in frontal, cingulate, and striatal regions, and also in mediotemporal lobe including the hippocampus, whereas older participants demonstrated greater activation in posterior regions, namely, parietal and occipitotemporal cortex associated with rapid information processing and fact retrieval. Given that quantitative reasoning constitutes a component of gF, the consistency of these results with those for simple relational reasoning in Eslinger et al. suggests the maturation of frontal-cingulate-striatal networks associated with reasoning in childhood leading to more rapid reasoning processes occurring in posterior systems associated with visuospatial attention and knowledge of relations among problem elements. Furthermore, the brain regions observed in simple relational reasoning and in simple calculation in child samples

(Eslinger et al., 2009; Rivera et al., 2005) are similar to those observed in a sample of 18- to 24-year-olds completing a transitive inference reasoning task in which participants learned relations among 11 novel figures and then were asked to make judgments about these relations in ordered pairs (e.g., if A > B and B > C, then A > C). Relative to a control condition in which participants either passively viewed the objects or made judgments concerning the height of the objects, participants activated frontal, parietal, anterior cingulate, and striatal regions (Acuna, Eliassen, Donoghue, & Sanes, 2002).

The similarity in activation in response to ostensibly different types of reasoning tasks in child samples is in contrast with the variation among regions activated in response to diverse reasoning tasks noted by Kroger et al. (2008) and by Goel (2007). This may suggest greater overlap in brain regions activated by reasoning tasks in childhood than in adulthood. Additional imaging studies of various types of reasoning tasks with similar age ranges and careful attention to task difficulty, task accuracy, and reaction time are needed, however, to further establish the development of the neural basis of fluid reasoning in both children and adults. Functional neuroimaging of fluid reasoning in older adults, also primarily using fMRI, has indicated a relation between brain activation and neural efficiency not unlike that seen in the child development imaging literature. Studies that examine fluid cognitive abilities in older versus younger adults, primarily in working memory types of tasks, indicate that older adults tend to activate a larger extent of cortex, and that this increased activation appears to be a compensatory response to the increased processing demand that older individuals experience in response to these types of problems (Cabeza et al., 2004; Park & Reuter-Lorenz, 2009; Persson et al., 2006). Here, unlike the child imaging literature as yet, the neuroimaging literature that examines reasoning tasks in older versus younger adults indicates a potentially central role for the hippocampus in neural systems that underlie the ability to reason among multiple relations within a given problem and to make transitive inferences of the type if A > B and B > C, then A > C. In research on typical late adult development, as well as in the study of neurodegenerative disease, the hippocampus is indicated in the rapid coding of spatial and temporal contiguity among problem elements that underlies reasoning ability. As an aspect of impaired performance on reasoning tasks in schizophrenia or Alzheimer disease, for example, reduced hippocampal activations and compensatory increases in frontal activity have been observed

(reviewed in Park & Reuter-Lorenz, 2009; Ryan, Moses, & Villate, 2009).

THE NEUROBIOLOGICAL MODEL AND DEVELOPMENT

The literature reviewed earlier examining the structural and functional neural basis for intelligence provides a clear indication that diverse brain regions are active in response to the information-processing demands of intelligence tests, and that fluid cognitive ability, neurobiologically speaking, is primarily based in neural circuitry of PFC. This literature on the neural basis of fluid intelligence also suggests differences among individuals in the efficiency of PFC circuitry related to fluid intelligence and indicates that greater neural efficiency is associated with higher level of ability. Determining why some individuals are more efficient than others, however, is a complex problem. Variation in genes that code for neural receptors and for levels of neural modulators account to some extent for efficiency. To date, however, this variation has been more relevant to neural activity in PFC circuitry than to cognitive performance itself. Also, levels of emotion and stress arousal are relevant to the role of neuromodulators that influence activity in PFC networks important for fluid intelligence. As such, it would seem a logical conclusion that efficiency is the product of numerous short- and long-term influences, including genetic background, but also an individual's developmental history, including experience with cognitive tasks.

Against the backdrop of a number of variable intersecting contributors to performance on measures of fluid intelligence, it is perhaps surprising that fluid ability is so remarkably stable from one instance to the next, at least in terms of rank order stability. Of course, within-person (intraindividual) variability is considerable, but this variability is not well studied and is usually considered as nuisance or error variance, rather than as the source of meaningful information that it is (Molenaar, 2001; Ram, Rabbitt, Stollery, & Nesselroade, 2005; see Nesselroade & Molenaar, Chapter 2 of this volume, for a discussion of issues related to development and intraindividual variation). However, when viewed across groups of individuals, stability, or more accurately continuity, in intelligence test performance is the rule rather than the exception. Here a distinction between stability and continuity is important as stability implies stasis, an underlying mechanism or process that functions in the same way across time and contexts. Continuity, however, recognizes change with development and implies a predominant dependence of later behavior on earlier behaviors and events. That is, continuity focuses on the ways in which behavior at any time point is a product of prior development (Gottlieb, 1983). As such, with an eye toward continuity in fluid intelligence, it is valuable to consider continuity in the development of the neurobiology underlying fluid intelligence and to consider influences on it across the life span.

Infancy

In research on the development of intelligence in infancy, it is well established that the best predictors of intelligence in later life are measures of information-processing ability, namely visual habituation and dishabituation behavior, also referred to as *visual recognition memory* (Rose, Feldman, & Jankowski, 2004). In the programs of research of several different investigators, a robust finding is that habituation efficiency is moderately correlated with later intelligence (Bornstein et al., 2006; Colombo, 2001; McCall & Carriger, 1993). Findings across several studies indicate relations from habituation efficiency measured at anywhere from 4 to 12 months of age and later IQ measured using standardized intelligence tests from age 4 through adulthood. In most, if not all, instances, later intelligence in these studies has been measured with Wechsler or Stanford-Binet full-scale IQ. Results from a meta-analysis of studies of the relation habituation efficiency in infancy to IQ in later childhood (studies ranged for outcome at age 2 through 11 years) indicated an overall correlation of 0.37 (Kavsek, 2004). Similarly, a study with longitudinal follow-up into young adulthood found a correlation between habituation efficiency measured between 6 and 12 months of age and adult IQ measured at age 21 of 0.34, with the magnitude of the correlation increasing to 0.59 when correcting for unreliability in the measures (Fagan, Holland, & Wheeler, 2007).

Although reasons for the strength of the relation between infant attention and later intelligence are not entirely clear, it is evident that the neural basis for infant habituation-dishabituation of attention is rooted in early developing altering and orienting reflexes (Colombo, 2001; Posner & Petersen, 1990) that precede the development of executive attention ability important for the development of EF and fluid intelligence. As such, habituation-dishabituation in infancy likely serves as an early indicator of the efficiency of PFC networks, particularly PFC connectivity with the striatum and limbic system that underlie fluid reasoning ability. In adults, activation in PFC and hippocampus has been detected in response to unattended novel events using fMRI (Yamaguchi, Hale, D'Esposito, & Knight, 2004), and developmental

imaging studies have shown that PFC-striatal connectivity is a central feature of developing reasoning ability (Eslinger et al., 2009; Rivera et al., 2005). Overall, habituation of attention in infancy would appear to reflect neuronal efficiency in PFC networks that underlie intelligence. An early developing attention system that facilitates the detection of similarity versus difference is important for survival, and as such, the integrity of this neural system is perhaps a good indicator of the integrity of brain systems generally.

Given that habituation-dishabituation in infancy would likely represent an indicator of the development of PFC systems important for fluid intelligence, it is interesting to note that PFC has a protracted developmental course extending into early adulthood and thought perhaps to be relatively quiet in infancy. The few studies that have specifically examined PFC activity in infancy in response to the detection of novelty and in habituation-dishabituation, however, have clearly demonstrated that PFC is involved in these abilities. At least three studies have demonstrated PFC activity in response to novelty in infants within the first year of life. At 3 month olds, detection of novel syllables, a robust phenomenon in language development, was associated with event-related potentials associated with left PFC (Dehaene-Lambertz & Dehaene, 1994). Similarly, two studies using near-infrared spectroscopy, an optical imaging technology that uses infrared light to measure levels of oxygen in hemoglobin, have demonstrated blood oxygenation increases in PFC in response to novelty in infants. In the first of these, increased oxyhemoglobin was detected in PFC in 7- to 12-month-old infants as they acquired an early indicator of the Piagetian reasoning ability referred to as object permanence as demonstrated in the AnotB task (Baird et al., 2002). The second directly examined habituation-dishabituation in 3-month-old infants and demonstrated increased deoxyhemoglobin in response to habituation trials in temporal cortex and most frontal regions, and increasing oxyhemoglobin only in PFC and only in response to dishabituation trials (Nakano, Watanabe, Homae, & Taga, 2009). Given that PFC development is protracted and undergoes extensive development in later childhood and adolescence, these studies suggest that early experience with novelty detection and habituation-dishabituation may play an important role in the experience-dependent maturation of PFC neural circuitry.

Early Childhood

The attention systems that provide the basis for habituation and dishabituation in infancy are joined in early childhood by a third system that provides for the regulation of attention, referred to as *executive attention,* an important aspect of EF and fluid intelligence (Posner & Rothbart, 2000; Rueda, Rothbart, McCandliss, Saccomanno, & Posner, 2005). The executive attention system, as opposed to orienting and alerting responses, is associated with the detection of conflict or error, and as such is assessed by tasks that require the focusing of attention in a goal-directed context and resistance to distracting stimuli that interfere with attention focus and goal completion. To this end, executive attention is reliably assessed by a type task known as a flanker task in which the direction of a central stimulus, usually an arrow, is either congruent or incongruent with the flanking arrows that are to the left and right of the central arrow. Functional MRI studies with flanker tasks indicate that they reliably activate the ACC (Fan, Hof, Guise, Fossella, & Posner, 2007), a central component of PFC networks associated with fluid intelligence and a transitional region between striatal, limbic, and brainstem structures associated with alerting, orienting, emotional and stress reactivity, and areas of PFC associated with EF. As such, the executive attention system is thought to signal the need for top-down control and to either engage regions of PFC associated with EF or to increase autonomic and neuroendocrine levels needed for a full-blown response to stress that acts to inhibit PFC activity (Arnsten & Li, 2005). Although no studies have specifically examined relations between executive attention and fluid intelligence, it is noteworthy that one study that attempted to increase executive attention in 4- to 6-year-old children through a computer-based training program demonstrated an effect of the training in a randomized design in 6-year-olds on the matrix completion subtest of the Kaufman Brief Intelligence Test (Rueda et al., 2005). These findings suggest that the development of the executive attention system, like habituation-dishabituation in infancy, is an important precursor of the development of fluid intelligence.

Childhood and Adolescence

In childhood and adolescence, PFC networks important for fluid intelligence continue to develop as evidenced by gray matter loss and white matter increase. This change in PFC is associated with increases in fluid reasoning ability and in performance on progressively complex EF tasks (Conklin, Luciana, Hooper, & Yarger, 2007; Luciana, Conklin, Hooper, & Yarger, 2005). This rapid increase in ability during a time of ongoing brain growth and physical development, accompanied by heightened self-awareness and

social interaction, has focused attention on adolescence as time of profound change. During adolescence, biological, social, and psychological aspects of development come together in ways that lead not only to improvements in cognitive and social-emotional competence, but also, somewhat paradoxically, to increased morbidity and mortality, and to increased risk for psychopathology (Cicchetti & Rogosch, 2002; Santostefano, Chapter 22 of this volume). Of particular interest in the study of the brain in adolescent populations is development in areas of the brain that are important for processing social information (Blakemore, 2008). These areas include orbital frontomedial and ventromedial areas of PFC that are responsible for registering the reward value of stimuli and for modulating relations between limbic and brainstem regions, important for catecholamine and glucocorticoid levels, and PFC areas associated with EFs. As these areas undergo neuronal pruning and dendritic reorganization during adolescence, this corticolimbic connectivity is altered (Spear, 2000). The changing relation between bottom-up emotion-motivational signaling and top-down executive control of behavior in adolescence is thought to underlie increased risk taking in adolescence, increased experience of and susceptibility to stress, and the occasional disconnect between reason and emotion, generally speaking. In terms of fluid intelligence, the developmental changes of adolescence indicate an overall progressive increase in reasoning ability, as in the onset of formal operations in Piagetian theory. The neurobiology of PFC connectivity, however, suggests that within-person variability in performance and possible divergence of measured fluid intelligence from decision making, academic achievement, and other aspects of behavior may be caused by a changing balance and ongoing experiential reshaping of relations between emotion and cognition.

Adulthood and Late Adult Development

Although the literature on cognitive changes with age and the neurobiology underlying various changes with age is vast and was touched on earlier, study of the ways in which PFC networks and reasoning ability may be affected by the events of adulthood and late adulthood are less well studied. Although the adult years are characterized by continuity in cognitive and social-emotional functioning, the effects of job stress, of family conflict, and of other life events on reasoning ability are perhaps profound. As noted earlier, the study of stress response systems have demonstrated that working memory ability is increased at moderate elevations but reduced at high elevations of glucocorticoids (Lupien, Gillin, & Hauger, 1999) and catecholamines (Arnsten & Li, 2005). As such, it is likely that stressful experience will influence the development of fluid intelligence throughout adulthood, and that fluid intelligence and stressful experience will be reciprocally related, with the ability to manage stress both affecting and being affected by fluid intelligence. However, only a few studies have examined the relation of stress to working memory, and none has examined fluid intelligence specifically in relation to stress. In a study that involved exposure to a laboratory stressor in 40 young adults randomly assigned to a stress (the Trier test) or to a control condition, reduced working memory ability, both accuracy and reaction time, was observed in the stress group (Schoofs, Preuss, & Wolf, 2008). Similarly, an examination of daily stress in a repeated-measures design with younger and older adults demonstrated stress effects on within-person variability in reaction time (but not accuracy) on the 2-back condition of n-back and n-count working memory tasks (Sliwinski, Smyth, Hofer, & Stawski, 2006). The indication that both young and older individuals reporting higher levels of daily stress were more variable in their performance of the tasks across six sessions over approximately 2 weeks suggests the importance of looking within as well as between persons to examine expected relations between stress and reasoning ability in adults and children.

THE NEUROBIOLOGICAL MODEL IN CONTEXT

Poverty

Relations between psychosocial stress and the functioning of PFC neural circuitry important for EFs and fluid reasoning suggest the importance of examining contexts that may promote or impede the development of intelligence. The environment of childhood poverty is of strong interest given the indication that it is one that is stressful for children (Evans, 2004), and can result in family environments that increase stress and influence the development of stress response systems (Repetti, Taylor, & Seeman, 2002). Although, as noted earlier, the development of fluid intelligence in children is not well studied, fluid intelligence as measured by a version of the Raven Progressive Matrices test in a sample of kindergarten children from low-income homes has been shown to be closely related, as expected, to EF ability. Furthermore, EF in this study

was shown to account for a relation between fluid intelligence and academic ability (Blair & Razza, 2007). Also, in keeping with the role of stress response systems in circuitry of the PFC, individual differences in EF in this sample were also associated with flexible reactivity in the glucocorticoid hormone cortisol in response to mild stress; and both EF and cortisol were related to teachers' ratings of children's ability to regulate behavior in the classroom (Blair, Granger, & Razza, 2005). The indication in this research is that for children in poverty, stress associated with conditions of the home or neighborhood may lead to chronic elevations in stress response systems, a condition referred to as *allostasis* (Evans, 2004; McEwen, 2000), and thereby to increased basal levels of stress response systems and to problems with fluid reasoning, self-regulation, and academic achievement. Although a chronically increased stress response may be adaptive in low-resource and unpredictable contexts, because of its potentiation of reactive and automatized responses to stimulation, it is injurious to physical health and to the development of reflective and self-regulatory aspects of cognition and behavior associated with the development of PFC (Blair, Willoughby, Mills-Koonce, & FLP Investigators, 2009; Holmes & Wellman, 2009; Meaney, 2001). Children who by benefit of positive early experiences and perhaps also genetic background are characterized by lower resting or baseline levels of glucocorticoids and catecholamines (taking into account a diurnal pattern of decrease across the day in cortisol) will exhibit an increase in these neurochemicals in response to stress when needed, and greater levels of EF ability and self-regulation. In contrast, children presumably from higher stress homes, characterized by higher allostatic load, present greater baseline levels of cortisol and exhibit a decrease rather than an increase in cortisol in response to mild stress, lower levels of EF, and experience greater difficulty with self-regulation. These distinct patterns of stress response suggest important influences of early experience on the development of PFC connectivity, with implications for self-regulation and fluid intelligence, and ultimately progress in school (Blair, in press). Given that animal models in both rodents and nonhuman primates indicate the importance of early rearing experience for the development of the stress response, and for cognitive and self-regulation ability (Liu, Liao, & Wolgemuth, 2000; Meaney, 2001; Parker, Buckmaster, Justus, Schatzberg, & Lyons, 2005), findings suggest that stress and self-regulation development are important aspects of early intervention and educational daycare programs designed to promote intelligence and school achievement. Findings also suggest the importance of a focus on self-regulation and the embedding of academic learning in self-regulation–promoting activities in early and elementary education curricula (Bodrova & Leong, 2007; Diamond, Barnett, Thomas, & Munro, 2007).

Intellectual Disability

Relations between psychosocial stress and the functioning of PFC circuitry important for fluid intelligence are also relevant to the study of intellectual disability. Relative to typically developing individuals, persons with intellectual disability, primarily idiopathic mental retardation (MR), exhibit delay in a wide variety of cognitive processes and functions that result in IQ scores of 70 or less. Persons with MR exhibit delays in memory, speed of processing, inspection time, perceptual acuity, and a number of domains, including fluid intelligence. Fluid intelligence, however, is not well studied in persons with MR, and the limited research that is available suggests that it is a unique aspect of mental ability in these persons (Blair & Patrick, 2006). For example, measures of working memory or measures that make substantial demand on fluid cognitive processes tend to be unrelated to measured IQ in individuals with MR (because of the high emphasis on crystallized abilities in most measures) but are uniquely associated with aspects of academic ability, such as literacy acquisition (Conners, Atwell, Rosenquist, & Sligh, 2001; Numminen et al., 2000). Furthermore, although individuals with idiopathic MR exhibit levels of ability and sequences of development similar to individuals of equivalent mental age (MA) across essentially all aspects of mental ability (Zigler & Bennett-Gates, 1999), this is not necessarily the case for working memory and presumably fluid intelligence. For example, comparison of adults with MR to children with equivalent fluid intelligence as measured by the Raven Progressive Test identified reduced WM ability in individuals with MR relative to the MA control subjects on tasks containing nonsemantic information. On a measure of working memory that involved semantic information, digit-span backward, however, performance of individuals with MR and MA control subjects was equivalent. These results may indicate a qualitative difference in the working memory of individuals with MR. Specifically, performance of individuals with MR on working memory tasks may be more dependent on crystallized knowledge, on familiarity with task content, than is the case in typically developing individuals. Also, given the role of arousal and stress in the neurobiological

model of fluid intelligence and EF, individuals with MR would perhaps be expected to perform less well on working memory tasks involving unfamiliar stimuli because unfamiliarity might lead to a high or low level of physiological or emotional arousal and to reduced performance. Although much more research is needed on fluid intelligence and EF in persons with MR, the available data are consistent with the motivational approach to MR (Zigler, 1969) and to the characterization of MR as a disorder of self-regulation and of mental disability (Whitman, Hantula, & Spence, 1990). These approaches suggest that a focus on personality and temperament characteristics, and efforts to assist the development of self-regulation in individuals with MR could yield meaningful benefits to fluid intelligence, and to aspects of daily living and self-regulation associated with fluid intelligence.

Historical Context

A third area to which research on the neurobiology of fluid intelligence is relevant is historical context and the phenomenon of rising mean IQ (Flynn, 1984). Data from successive normative samples of major intelligence test batteries indicate a linear increase in mean levels of performance over the past 100 years, particularly on measures of fluid intelligence. Although increases in mean levels of performance on measures of crystallized intelligence have been documented, the gains are small in comparison with those on measures of fluid abilities. As Flynn (2009) estimated and as shown in Figure 8.4, between 1947 and 2002, mean increases on the Vocabulary, Information, and Arithmetic subtests of the WISC, the verbal or crystallized subtests, were slight, at roughly 2 to 4 points. In contrast, gains for Picture Completion, Block Design, Coding, and Similarities, the performance subtests, were nothing short of massive, being orders of magnitude larger than those for crystallized intelligence, ranging from 11 to 24 points, or an approximate 1.0 to 1.65 standard deviation increase. In addition, in further confirmation of the extent to which performance on measures of fluid reasoning ability in the population has been increasing, gains on the Raven Matrices outpace even those for Similarities. Population increases on the Raven have been so great that performance of a 65-year-old individual in 1942 that would result in a 90th percentile ranking relative to same-age individuals, would place that person in roughly the 25th percentile relative to same-age individuals in 1992 and in the 5th percentile, the range of profound MR, relative to 25-year-olds completing the test in 1992.

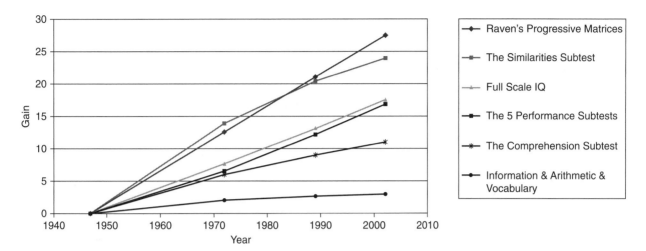

Figure 8.4 Generational change in IQ (Flynn effect). *Diamonds* represent Raven Progressive Matrices test; *small squares* represent the Similarities subtest; *triangles* represent the full-scale IQ; *large squares* represent the five Performance subtests; *asterisks* represent the Comprehension subtest; *circles* represent Information, Arithmetic, and Vocabulary.

In and of themselves, the increases in mean level of IQ across the 20th century are astounding and pose problems for intelligence research begging for solution. Of course, the findings cannot indicate that the mean level of intellectual ability in prior generations was in the range of MR. This was clearly not the case. Nor do the gains indicate that the world is increasingly populated with geniuses. The gains do indicate, however, that human beings as a whole have been getting better and better at specific mental abilities that are important for performance on measures of fluid intelligence. One of the most fascinating and puzzling aspects of population changes in intelligence test performance is that the gains have been largest on the measures, namely, the Raven Progressive Matrices test, that are known to be the "purest" measures of general fluid intelligence. However, in attempting to solve problems posed by an increasing mean IQ, it is worth noting that the gains are actually one instance of a larger set of phenomena indicating a clear distinction between fluid and crystallized aspects of mental ability (Blair, 2006). As with the dissociation between fluid and crystallized abilities seen in the instance of damage to PFC in clinical neuropsychology, and in the instance of numerous developmental disorders and psychopathologies ranging from attention deficit/hyperactivity disorder (ADHD) to schizophrenia, increasing mean intelligence appears to be a clear indication of change in aspects of mental ability that are closely tied to gF and the function of PFC, albeit at the population rather than the individual level. As such, it would seem that the rapid population-level change in the neural function or efficiency of PFC

circuitry has occurred, and that the mechanism is likely experiential. Through changes in education, visual media, and/or other aspects of experience with more or less uniform population-level exposure, human beings have been getting better and better at fluid reasoning types of tasks but not noticeably better at information or memorization types of abilities. In this, increasing mean IQ would appear to be highly consistent with the wealth of evidence indicating the brain and cognitive abilities are plastic and open to the effects of experience, particularly in the phylogenetically recent PFC, which appears to have evolved to promote adaptability and responsiveness to the environment. As well, the phenomenon of increasing mean fluid IQ, as with findings in clinical neuropsychology and developmental disability, help to focus interest on fluid intelligence as a unique and distinctive aspect of mental ability. However, just what gains over time in this aspect of mental ability mean for the world population are difficult to determine.

CONCLUSION

This chapter reviewed research on fluid intelligence as studied in the psychometric and developmental literatures, and in the growing literature on the neurobiology of intelligence. Overall, this review has emphasized the distinction between gF and gC, and also the association of gF with coordinated PFC brain systems active in the completion of goal-directed activities. The association of gF with effortful top-down control and gC with fast and automatic aspects of mental ability is a distinction that has been supported in both behavioral and neuroscientific research on intelligence. Attempts to understand the developmental relation between these broad aspects of intelligence, in Gf-Gc theory, and in the theory of pragmatics and mechanics, have focused on ways in which gF in its top-down role is expected to be a primary mechanism of development. In these theories, gF is primarily a function of biology and changes as a function of biological growth and decline, and gC is primarily a function of biology plus acculturation, with culture providing increasing and selective support for specific crystallized abilities.

Although these theories are insightful and have received some empirical support, what has been lacking in nearly all theories of intelligence development is some consideration of intelligence from the relational developmental systems perspective of probabilistic epigenesis. As a relational theory, probabilistic epigenesis addresses the idea that biological and behavioral aspects of the developing person are intertwined and coactive influences on development. The approach suggests that biology and experience can be understood only in relation to one another, as opposed to individually, in which one broad influence unconditionally precedes and causes change in the other. The hallmark of the probabilistic epigenetic approach as a relational theory is that multiple biological and experiential contributors to development combine and organize in a dynamic and nonlinear fashion, meaning that the combination of biological and environmental influences is not additive or conventionally interactive but catalytic, producing systemic change and reorganization of relations among neural, physiological, behavioral, psychological, and sociocultural influences on the individual.

In the relation between biology and experience, however, it is behavior itself that is understood to be the primary mechanism through which development occurs. That is, behavior is the initial expression of numerous biological and environmental influences that then feeds back on and thereby directs development in these influences. This cyclic feedback loop relating behavior to biological and environmental systems avoids problems inherent in theories in which development is largely determined by either biology or environment.

Application of the probabilistic epigenetic relational model to the development of fluid intelligence is relatively straightforward in light of the literature reviewed in this chapter. In infancy, initial neural systems that underlie attention and habituation-dishabituation behavior respond to the environment and are strengthened in specific ways. In appropriately stimulating and supportive environments, meaning that opportunities for stimulation are appropriately paced to avoid excessive overstimulation or understimulation, attentional ability increases and leads to the emergence of the ability to actively regulate behavior through attention. In turn, this active regulation then leads to the regulation of physiological arousal and stress response systems that are conducive to higher forms of self-regulation, including EFs that promote gF, as well as aspects of behavior that promote positive social interactions with caregivers, siblings, and peers. In contrast, in less supportive and more unpredictable environments, processes of attention development would not necessarily be supported in ways that lead to the regulation of behavior. This would then likely lead to more reactive forms of self-regulation, to physiological and behavioral reactivity to stimulation, and ultimately to a less rapid pace for the development of higher order forms of cognition and gF.

As an important component of intelligence development and ultimately of school readiness and early school success, behavior conducive to the development of higher order self-regulation and gF might lead at school age to a developing sense of self as one who is good at and enjoys school. Conversely, children with poor attention ability and more reactive forms of regulation might derive little positive feedback from formal schooling and develop negative attitudes and self-perceptions. In addition, these influences on the developing sense of self would likely lead to peer group affiliations and to socialization processes that either value or devalue fluid intelligence abilities, leading to a further feedback-driven process in which behavioral tendencies either conducive to or detrimental to fluid intelligence are reinforced. These experiences and self-perceptions would be expected to feedback on and further strengthen the development of PFC networks in ways that serve to maintain continuity in development and trajectories toward high or low gF ability. As trajectories for development become established, behavior would become increasingly difficult to change, ultimately resulting in school and socialization experiences that influence lifelong patterns and consequences of those patterns, such as in school completion, pursuit of higher education, career and employment opportunities, and choices that ultimately and perhaps profoundly reinforce behaviors and the functioning of neural systems that support gF.

Although plausible developmental scenarios can be described that could lead to considerable continuity in development, even to the appearance of a highly determined, essentially inevitable process, change is clearly possible through the life span in the probabilistic epigenetic model. It may be, however, that behavior, as the leading edge of the epigenetic process, may become increasingly difficult to change with development. If behavior change can be sustained, however, it is likely to lead to effects on biology and on experience that can alter developmental trajectories. This would seem to be apparent in the evidence of training regimens for working memory and EFs that through behavior alter neural networks important for attention control and for gF that should have consequences later in behavior, cognitive ability, and life outcomes (Jaeggi, Buschkuehl, Jonides, & Perrig, 2008; Olesen, Westerberg, & Klingberg, 2004). Experience with working memory and attention-focusing activities in early and later adulthood is associated with delayed cognitive decline and higher level of well-being (Park & Reuter-Lorenz, 2009). Programs of research demonstrating these associations provide support for the probabilistic epigenetic model of development. Although much research is needed to further the application of the probabilistic epigenetic model to the development of fluid intelligence, it is clear that the elements needed for this application are in place. It is also clear from the literature reviewed in this chapter that an overarching implication of recent findings on the neurobiology of intelligence is that attempts to understand the biology of intelligence are incomplete without a close examination of behavior and experience.

REFERENCES

Ackerman, P. L., Beier, M. E., & Boyle, M. O. (2005). Working memory and intelligence: The same or different constructs? *Psychological Bulletin, 131*(1), 30–60.

Acuna, B. D., Eliassen, J. C., Donoghue, J. P., & Sanes, J. N. (2002). Frontal and parietal lobe activation during transitive inference in humans. *Cerebral Cortex, 12*(12), 1312–1321.

Arnsten, A. F., & Li, B. M. (2005). Neurobiology of executive functions: Catecholamine influences on prefrontal cortical functions. *Biological Psychiatry, 57*(11), 1377–1384.

Arnsten, A. F. T. (2000). Through the looking glass: Differential noradenergic modulation of prefrontal cortical function. *Neural Plasticity, 7*, 133–146.

Aron, A. R. (2007). The neural basis of inhibition in cognitive control. *The Neuroscientist: A Review Journal Bringing Neurobiology, Neurology and Psychiatry, 13*(3), 214–228.

Baddeley, A. (1986). *Working memory*. New York: Clarendon Press/ Oxford University Press.

Baird, A. A., Kagan, J., Gaudette, T., Walz, K. A., Hershlag, N., & Boas, D. A. (2002). Frontal lobe activation during object permanence: Data from near-infrared spectroscopy. *NeuroImage, 16*(4), 1120–1125.

Baltes, P. B., Lindenberger, U., & Staudinger, U. M. (2006). Life span theory in developmental psychology. In W. Damon & R. M. Lerner

(Series Eds.) & R. M. Lerner (Ed.) *Theoretical models of human development: Vol. 1, Handbook of child psychology* (pp. 569–664, 6th ed.). Hoboken, NJ: John Wiley & Sons.

Baltes, P. B., Staudinger, U. M., & Lindenberger, U. (1999). Lifespan psychology: Theory and application to intellectual functioning. *Annual Review of Psychology, 50,* 471–507.

Barbas, H. (2000). Complementary roles of prefrontal cortical regions in cognition, memory, and emotion in primates. *Advances in Neurology, 84,* 87–110.

Barbas, H., & Zikopoulos, B. (2007). The prefrontal cortex and flexible behavior. *The Neuroscientist, 13,* 532–545.

Bishop, S. J., Fossella, J., Croucher, C. J., & Duncan, J. (2008). COMT val158met genotype affects recruitment of neural mechanisms supporting fluid intelligence. *Cerebral Cortex, 18*(9), 2132–2140.

Blair, C. (2006). How similar are fluid cognition and general intelligence? A developmental neuroscience perspective on fluid cognition as an aspect of human cognitive ability. *Behavioral and Brain Sciences, 29*(2), 109–160.

Blair, C. (in press). Stress and the development of self-regulation in context. *Child Development Perspectives.*

Blair, C., Gamson, D., Thorne, S., & Baker, D. (2005). Rising mean IQ: Cognitive demand of mathematics education for young children, population exposure to formal schooling, and the neurobiology of the prefrontal cortex. *Intelligence, 33*(1), 93–106.

Blair, C., Granger, D., & Razza, R. P. (2005). Cortisol reactivity is positively related to executive function in preschool children attending head start. *Child Development, 76*(3), 554–567.

Blair, C., Knipe, H., & Gamson, D. (2008). Is there a role for executive functions in the development of mathematics ability? *Mind, Brain, and Education, 2*(2), 80–89.

Blair, C., & Patrick, M. (2006). Fluid cognitive abilities neglected aspects of cognition in research on mental retardation. In L. Glidden (Ed.), *International review of research in mental retardation* (pp. 131–158). San Diego: Academic.

Blair, C., & Razza, R. P. (2007). Relating effortful control, executive function, and false belief understanding to emerging math and literacy ability in kindergarten. *Child Development, 78*(2), 647–663.

Blair, C., Willoughby, M., Mills-Koonce, R., & FLP Investigators. (2009). The measurement of executive function at age 3: Early prediction from child and family characteristics in a population-based, longitudinal sample. The Biennial Meeting of the Society for Research in Child Development, Denver, CO.

Blakemore, S. (2008). The social brain in adolescence. *Nature Reviews Neuroscience, 9*(4), 267–277.

Bodrova, E., & Leong, D. J. (2007). Play and early literacy: A Vygotskian approach. In K. A. Roskos & J. F. Christie (Eds.), *Play and literacy in early childhood: Research from multiple perspectives* (2nd ed., pp. 185–200). Mahwah, NJ: Erlbaum.

Bornstein, M. H., Hahn, C. S., Bell, C., Haynes, O. M., Slater, A., Golding, J., et al. (2006). Stability in cognition across early childhood. A developmental cascade. *Psychological Science, 17*(2), 151–158.

Botvinick, M. M., Cohen, J. D., & Carter, C. S. (2004). Conflict monitoring and anterior cingulate cortex: An update. *Trends in Cognitive Sciences, 8*(12), 539–546.

Bunge, S. A., Burrows, B., & Wagner, A. D. (2004). Prefrontal and hippocampal contributions to visual associative recognition: Interactions between cognitive control and episodic retrieval. *Brain and Cognition, 56*(2), 141–152.

Bunge, S. A., & Wright, S. B. (2007). Neurodevelopmental changes in working memory and cognitive control. *Current Opinion in Neurobiology, 17*(2), 243–250.

Cabeza, R., Daselaar, S. M., Dolcos, F., E. Prince, S., Budde, M., & Nyberg, L. (2004). Task-independent and task-specific age effects on brain activity during working memory, visual attention and episodic retrieval. *Cerebral Cortex, 14*(4), 364–375.

Callicott, J. H., Mattay, V. S., Bertolino, A., Finn, K., Coppola, R., Frank, J. A., et al. (1999). Physiological characteristics of capacity constraints in working memory as revealed by functional MRI. *Cerebral Cortex, 9*(1), 20–26.

Carlson, S. M., & Moses, L. J. (2001). Individual differences in inhibitory control and children's theory of mind. *Child Development, 72*(4), 1032–1053.

Carpenter, P. A., Just, M. A., & Shell, P. (1990). What one intelligence test measures: A theoretical account of the processing in the Raven Progressive Matrices test. *Psychological Review, 97*(3), 404–431.

Carroll, J. B. (1993). *Human cognitive abilities: A survey of factor-analytic studies.* New York: Cambridge University Press.

Cattell, R. B. (1971). *Abilities: Their structure, growth, and action.* Oxford: Houghton Mifflin.

Chiang, M. C., Barysheva, M., Shattuck, D. W., Lee, A. D., Madsen, S. K., Avedissian, C., et al. (2009). Genetics of brain fiber architecture and intellectual performance. *Journal of Neuroscience, 29*(7), 2212–2224.

Choi, Y. Y., Shamosh, N. A., Cho, S. H., DeYoung, C. G., Lee, M. J., Lee, J. M., et al. (2008). Multiple bases of human intelligence revealed by cortical thickness and neural activation. *Journal of Neuroscience, 28*(41), 10323–10329.

Cicchetti, D., & Rogosch, F. A. (2002). A developmental psychopathology perspective on adolescence. *Journal of Consulting and Clinical Psychology, 70*(1), 6–20.

Colom, R. (2007). Intelligence? What intelligence? *Behavioural and Brain Sciences, 24,* 867–878.

Colom, R., Haier, R. J., Head, K., Álvarez-Linera, J., Quiroga, M. Á., Shih, P. C., et al. (2009). Gray matter correlates of fluid, crystallized, and spatial intelligence: Testing the P-FIT model. *Intelligence, 37*(2), 124–135.

Colom, R., Jung, R. E., & Haier, R. J. (2006). Distributed brain sites for the g-factor of intelligence. *NeuroImage, 31*(3), 1359–1365.

Colom, R., Rebollo, I., Palacios, A., Juan-Espinosa, M., & Kyllonen, P. C. (2004). Working memory is (almost) perfectly predicted by g. *Intelligence, 32,* 277–296.

Colombo, J. (2001). The development of visual attention in infancy. *Annual Review of Psychology, 52,* 337–367.

Conklin, H. M., Luciana, M., Hooper, C. J., & Yarger, R. S. (2007). Working memory performance in typically developing children and adolescents: Behavioral evidence of protracted frontal lobe development. *Developmental Neuropsychology, 31*(1), 103–128.

Conners, F. A., Atwell, J. A., Rosenquist, C. J., & Sligh, A. C. (2001). Abilities underlying decoding differences in children with intellectual disability. *Journal of Intellectual Disability Research, 45*(4), 292–299.

Conway, A. R. A., Cowan, N., Bunting, M. F., Therriault, D. J., & Minkoff, S. R. B. (2002). A latent variable analysis of working memory capacity, short-term memory capacity, processing speed, and general fluid intelligence. *Intelligence, 30*(2), 163–183.

Critchley, H. D. (2005). Neural mechanisms of autonomic, affective, and cognitive integration. *Journal of Comparative Neurology, 493*(1), 154–166.

Crone, E. A., Wendelken, C., van Leijenhorst, L., Honomichl, R. D., Christoff, K., & Bunge, S. A. (2009). Neurocognitive development of relational reasoning. *Developmental Science, 12*(1), 55–66.

Damasio, H., Grabowski, T., Frank, R., Galaburda, A. M., & Damasio, A. R. (1994). The return of Phineas Gage: Clues about the brain from the skull of a famous patient. *Science (New York, N.Y.), 264*(5162), 1102–1105.

Daurignac, E., Houdé, O., & Jouvent, R. (2006). Negative priming in a numerical Piaget-like task as evidenced by ERP. *Journal of Cognitive Neuroscience, 18*(5), 730–736.

Deary, I. J., Whalley, L. J., Lemmon, H., Crawford, J. R., & Starr, J. M. (2000). The stability of individual differences in mental ability from childhood to old age: Follow-up of the 1932 Scottish mental survey. *Intelligence, 28*(1), 49–55.

Dehaene-Lambertz, G., & Dehaene, S. (1994). Speed and cerebral correlates of syllable detection in infants. *Nature, 370,* 292–295.

de Kloet, E. R., Oitzl, M. S., & Joëls, M. (1999). Stress and cognition: Are corticosteroids good or bad guys? *Trends in Neurosciences, 22*(10), 422–426.

Dempster, F. N. (1992). The rise and fall of the inhibitory mechanism: Toward a unified theory of cognitive development and aging. *Developmental Review, 12*(1), 45–75.

Diamond, A. (2002). Normal development of prefrontal cortex from birth to young adulthood: Cognitive functions, anatomy, and biochemistry. In D. Stuss & R. Knight (Eds.), *Principles of frontal lobe function* (pp. 466–503). New York: Oxford.

Diamond, A., Barnett, W. S., Thomas, J., & Munro, S. (2007). Preschool program improves cognitive control. *Science (New York, N.Y.), 318*(5855), 1387–1388.

Duncan, J. (2001). An adaptive coding model of neural function in prefrontal cortex. *Nature Reviews Neuroscience, 2*(11), 820–829.

Duncan, J., Burgess, P., & Emslie, H. (1995). Fluid intelligence after frontal lobe lesions. *Neuropsychologia, 33*(3), 261–268.

Duncan, J., & Owen, A. M. (2000). Common regions of the human frontal lobe recruited by diverse cognitive demands. *Trends in Neurosciences, 23*(10), 475–483.

Duncan, J., Seitz, R. J., Kolodny, J., Bor, D., Herzog, H., Ahmed, A., et al. (2000). A neural basis for general intelligence. *Science, 289,* 457–460.

Durston, S., Thomas, K. M., Yang, Y., Ulug, A. M., Zimmerman, R. D., & Casey, B. J. (2002). A neural basis for the development of inhibitory control. *Developmental Science, 5*(4), F9–F16.

Egan, M. F., Goldberg, T. E., Kolachana, B. S., Callicott, J. H., Mazzanti, C. M., Straub, R. E., et al. (2001). Effect of COMT Val108/158 met genotype on frontal lobe function and risk for schizophrenia. *Proceedings of the National Academy of Sciences of the United States of America, 98*(12), 6917–6922.

Embretson, S. E. (1995). The role of working memory capacity and general control processes in intelligence. *Intelligence, 20*(2), 169–189.

Erickson, K., Drevets, W., & Schulkin, J. (2003). Glucocorticoid regulation of diverse cognitive functions in normal and pathological emotional states. *Neuroscience & Biobehavioral Reviews, 27*(3), 233–246.

Eslinger, P. J., Blair, C., Wang, J., Lipovsky, B., Realmuto, J., Baker, D., et al. (2009). Developmental shifts in fMRI activations during visuospatial relational reasoning. *Brain and Cognition, 69*(1), 1–10.

Evans, G. W. (2004). The environment of childhood poverty. *American Psychologist, 59*(2), 77–92.

Fagan, J. F., Holland, C. R., & Wheeler, K. (2007). The prediction, from infancy, of adult IQ and achievement. *Intelligence, 35*(3), 225–231.

Fan, J., Hof, P. R., Guise, K. G., Fossella, J. A., & Posner, M. I. (2007). The functional integration of the anterior cingulate cortex during conflict processing. *Cerebral Cortex, 18*(4), 796–804.

Ferrer, E., & McArdle, J. J. (2004). An experimental analysis of dynamic hypotheses about cognitive abilities and achievement from childhood to early adulthood. *Developmental Psychology, 40*(6), 935–952.

Ferrer, E., McArdle, J. J., Shaywitz, B. A., Holahan, J. M., Marchione, K., & Shaywitz, S. E. (2007). Longitudinal models of developmental dynamics between reading and cognition from childhood to adolescence. *Developmental Psychology, 43*(6), 1460–1473.

Fischer, K. W., & Bidell, T. R. (2006). Dynamic development of action, thought, and emotion. In R. M. Lerner & W. Damon (Eds.), *Handbook of child psychology: Vol. 1, Theoretical models of human development* (6th ed.). Hoboken, NJ: John Wiley & Sons.

Fjell, A. M., Westlye, L. T., Amlien, I., Espeseth, T., Reinvang, I., Raz, N., et al. (2009). High consistency of regional cortical thinning in aging across multiple samples. *Cerebral Cortex, 19*(9), 2001–2012.

Flynn, J. R. (1984). The mean IQ of Americans: Massive gains 1932 to 1978. *Psychological Bulletin, 95*(1), 29–51.

Flynn, J. R. (2009). *What is intelligence? Beyond the Flynn effect*. New York: Cambridge University Press.

Fry, A. F., & Hale, S. (1996). Processing speed, working memory, and fluid intelligence: Evidence for a developmental cascade. *Psychological Science, 7*(4), 237–241.

Fry, A. F., & Hale, S. (2000). Relationships among processing speed, working memory, and fluid intelligence in children. *Biological Psychology, 54*(1–3), 1–34.

Gardner, J. M., Lewkowicz, D. J., Rose, S. A., & Karmel, B. Z. (1986). Effects of visual and auditory stimulation on subsequent visual preferences in neonates. *International Journal of Behavioral Development, 9*(2), 251–263.

Goel, V. (2007). Anatomy of deductive reasoning. *Trends in Cognitive Sciences, 11*(10), 435–441.

Gogtay, N., Giedd, J. N., Lusk, L., Hayashi, K. M., Greenstein, D., Vaituzis, A. C., et al. (2004). Dynamic mapping of human cortical development during childhood through early adulthood. *Proceedings of the National Academy of Sciences of the United States of America, 101*(21), 8174–8179.

Goldman-Rakic, P. S., Muly, E. C., 3rd, & Williams, G. V. (2000). D(1) receptors in prefrontal cells and circuits. *Brain Research. Brain Research Reviews, 31*(2–3), 295–301.

Goswami, U. (1991). Analogical reasoning: What develops? A review of research and theory. *Child Development, 62*(1), 1–22.

Gottlieb, G. (1983). The psychobiological approach to developmental issues. In P. M. Mussen (Ed.), *Handbook of child psychology* (4th ed., p. 1). New York: John Wiley & Sons.

Gottlieb, G. (1998). Normally occurring environmental and behavioral influences on gene activity: From central dogma to probabilistic epigenesis. *Psychological Review, 105*(4), 792–802.

Gottlieb, G., & Halpern, C. T. (2002). A relational view of causality in normal and abnormal development. *Development and Psychopathology. Special Issue: Multiple Levels of Analysis, 14*(3), 421–435.

Gray, J. R., Chabris, C. F., & Braver, T. S. (2003). Neural mechanisms of general fluid intelligence. *Nature Neuroscience, 6*(3), 316–322.

Gustafsson, J. (1984). A unifying model for the structure of intellectual abilities. *Intelligence, 8*(3), 179–203.

Haier, R. J., Colom, R., Schroeder, D. H., Condon, C. A., Tang, C., Eaves, E., et al. (2009). Gray matter and intelligence factors: Is there a neuro-g? *Intelligence, 37*(2), 136–144.

Haier, R. J., Siegel, B. V., Nuechterlein, K. H., Hazlett, E., Wu, J. C., Paek, J., et al. (1988). Cortical glucose metabolic rate correlates of abstract reasoning and attention studied with positron emission tomography. *Intelligence, 12,* 199–217.

Head, D., Buckner, R. L., Shimony, J. S., Williams, L. E., Akbudak, E., Conturo, T. E., et al. (2004). Differential vulnerability of anterior white matter in nondemented aging with minimal acceleration in dementia of the Alzheimer type: Evidence from diffusion tensor imaging. *Cerebral Cortex, 14*(4), 410–423.

Hebb, D. O. (1939). Personality changes after operations on the frontal lobes: A clinical study of 32 cases. *Psychological Bulletin, 36*(9), 796–797.

Hebb, D. O. (1942). Psychosurgery: Intelligence, emotion and social behavior following prefrontal lobotomy for mental disorders. *Psychological Bulletin, 39*(6), 417–419.

Hedden, T., & Gabrieli, J. D. E. (2004). Insights into the ageing mind: A view from cognitive neuroscience. *Nature Reviews Neuroscience, 5*(2), 87–96.

Holmes, A., & Wellman, C. L. (2009). Stress-induced prefrontal reorganization and executive dysfunction in rodents. *Neuroscience and Biobehavioral Reviews, 33*(6), 773–783.

Horn, J. L., & Cattell, R. B. (1967). Age differences in fluid and crystallized intelligence. *Acta Psychologica, 26,* 107–129.

Horn, J. L., & Noll, J. (1997). Human cognitive capabilities: Gf-gc theory. In D. P. Flanagan, J. L. Genshaft, & P. L. Harrison (Eds.), *Contemporary intellectual assessment: Theories, tests, and issues* (pp. 53–91). New York: Guilford.

Houdé, O., & Tzourio-Mazoyer, N. (2003). Neural foundations of logical and mathematical cognition. *Nature Reviews Neuroscience, 4*(6), 507–514.

Hughes, C., & Ensor, R. (2007). Executive function and theory of mind: Predictive relations from ages 2 to 4. *Developmental Psychology, 43*(6), 1447–1459.

Hulshoff Pol, H. E., Schnack, H. G., Posthuma, D., Mandl, R. C., Baare, W. F., van Oel, C., et al. (2006). Genetic contributions to human brain morphology and intelligence. *Journal of Neuroscience, 26*(40), 10235–10242.

Hunt, J. M. (1961). *Intelligence and experience*. Oxford: Ronald.

Huttenlocher, P. R. (1979). Synaptic density in human frontal cortex—developmental changes and effects of aging. *Brain Research, 163*(2), 195–205.

Jaeggi, S., Buschkuehl, M., Jonides, J., & Perrig, W. (2008). Improving fluid intelligence with training on working memory. *Proceedings of the National Academy of Sciences of the United States of America, 105,* 6829–6833.

Jensen, A. R. (1998). *The g factor: The science of mental ability*. Westport, CT: Praeger Publishers/Greenwood Publishing Group.

Jung, R. E., & Haier, R. J. (2007). The parieto-frontal integration theory (P-FIT) of intelligence: Converging neuroimaging evidence. *The Behavioral and Brain Sciences, 30*(2), 135–154; discussion 154–187.

Kail, R., & Salthouse, T. A. (1994). Processing speed as a mental capacity. *Acta Psychologica. Special Issue: Life Span Changes in Human Performance, 86*(2–3), 199–225.

Kane, M. J., & Engle, R. W. (2002). The role of prefrontal cortex in working-memory capacity, executive attention, and general fluid intelligence: An individual-differences perspective. *Psychonomic Bulletin & Review, 9*(4), 637–671.

Kane, M. J., Hambrick, D. Z., & Conway, A. R. A. (2005). Working memory capacity and fluid intelligence are strongly related constructs: Comment on Ackerman, Beier, and Boyle (2005). *Psychological Bulletin, 131*(1), 66–71.

Kavsek, M. (2004). Predicting later IQ from infant visual habituation and dishabituation: A meta-analysis. *Journal of Applied Developmental Psychology, 25*(3), 369–393.

Koechlin, E., Basso, G., Pietrini, P., Panzer, S., & Grafman, J. (1999). The role of the anterior prefrontal cortex in human cognition. *Nature, 399*(6732), 148–151.

Koechlin, E., Ody, C., & Kounelher, F. (2003). The architecture of cognitive control in the human prefrontal cortex. *Science, 302*(5648), 1181–1185.

Koechlin, E., & Summerfield, C. (2007). An information theoretical approach to prefrontal executive function. *Trends in Cognitive Sciences, 11*(6), 229–235.

Kroger, J. K., Nystrom, L. E., Cohen, J. D., & Johnson-Laird, P. N. (2008). Distinct neural substrates for deductive and mathematical processing. *Brain Research, 1243,* 86–103.

Kwon, H., Reiss, A. L., & Menon, V. (2002). Neural basis of protracted developmental changes in visuo-spatial working memory. *Proceedings of the National Academy of Sciences of the United States of America, 99*(20), 13336–13341.

Kyllonen, P. C., & Christal, R. E. (1990). Reasoning ability is (little more than) working-memory capacity? *Intelligence, 14*(4), 389–433.

Larson, G., Haier, R. J., LaCasse, L., & Hazen, K. (1995). Evaluation of a "mental effort" hypothesis for correlations between cortical metabolism and intelligence. *Intelligence, 21,* 267–278.

Lee, K. H., Choi, Y. Y., Gray, J. R., Cho, S. H., Chae, J. H., Lee, S., et al. (2006). Neural correlates of superior intelligence: Stronger recruitment of posterior parietal cortex. *NeuroImage, 29*(2), 578–586.

Lerner, R. M. (2006). Developmental science, developmental systems, and contemporary theories of human development. In W. Damon & R. M. Lerner (Series Eds.) & R. M. Lerner (Ed.) *Theoretical models of human development:* Vol. 1, *Handbook of child psychology* (6th ed., pp. 1–17). Hoboken, NJ: John Wiley & Sons.

Lerner, R. M., & Overton, W.F. (2008). Exemplifying the integrations of the relational developmental system: Synthesizing theory, research, and application to promote positive development and social justice. *Journal of Adolescent Research, 23,* 245–255.

Li, S. C., Lindenberger, U., Hommel, B., Aschersleben, G., Prinz, W., & Baltes, P. B. (2004). Transformations in the couplings among intellectual abilities and constituent cognitive processes across the life span. *Psychological Science, 15*(3), 155–163.

Liston, C., Watts, R., Tottenham, N., Davidson, M. C., Niogi, S., Ulug, A. M., et al. (2006). Frontostriatal microstructure modulates efficient recruitment of cognitive control. *Cerebral Cortex 16*(4), 553–560.

Liu, D., Liao, C., & Wolgemuth, D. J. (2000). A role for cyclin A1 in the activation of MPF and G2–M transition during meiosis of male germ cells in mice. *Developmental Biology, 224*(2), 388–400.

Luciana, M., Conklin, H. M., Hooper, C. J., & Yarger, R. S. (2005). The development of nonverbal working memory and executive control processes in adolescents. *Child Development, 76*(3), 697–712.

Lupien, S. J., Gillin, C. J., & Hauger, R. L. (1999). Working memory is more sensitive than declarative memory to the acute effects of corticosteroids: A dose-response study in humans. *Behavioral Neuroscience, 113*(3), 420–430.

MacDonald, A. W., 3rd, Cohen, J. D., Stenger, V. A., & Carter, C. S. (2000). Dissociating the role of the dorsolateral prefrontal and anterior cingulate cortex in cognitive control. *Science (New York, N.Y.), 288*(5472), 1835–1838.

Marshalek, B., Lohman, D. F., & Snow, R. E. (1983). The complexity continuum in the radex and hierarchical models of intelligence. *Intelligence, 7*(2), 107–127.

Mattay, V. S., Goldberg, T. E., Fera, F., Hariri, A. R., Tessitore, A., Egan, M. F., et al. (2003). Catechol O-methyltransferase val158-met genotype and individual variation in the brain response to amphetamine. *Proceedings of the National Academy of Sciences of the United States of America, 100*(10), 6186–6191.

McArdle, J. J., Ferrer-Caja, E., Hamagami, F., & Woodcock, R. W. (2002). Comparative longitudinal structural analyses of the growth and decline of multiple intellectual abilities over the life span. *Developmental Psychology, 38*(1), 115–142.

McCall, R. B., & Carriger, M. S. (1993). A meta-analysis of infant habituation and recognition memory performance as predictors of later IQ. *Child Development, 64*(1), 57–79.

McDaniel, M. A. (2005). Big-brained people are smarter: A meta-analysis of the relationship between in vivo brain volume and intelligence. *Intelligence, 33*(4), 337–346.

McEwen, B. S. (2000). The neurobiology of stress: From serendipity to clinical relevance. *Brain Research, 886,* 172–189.

McGrew, K. S. (2009). CHC theory and the human cognitive abilities project: Standing on the shoulders of the giants of psychometric intelligence research. *Intelligence, 37*(1), 1–10.

McGrew, K. S., Flanagan, D. P., Keith, T. Z., & Vanderwood, M. L. (1997). Beyond g: The impact of gf-gc specific cognitive abilities research on the future use and interpretation of intelligence tests in the schools. *School Psychology Review, 26,* 189–210.

Meaney, M. J. (2001). Maternal care, gene expression, and the transmission of individual differences in stress reactivity across generations. *Annual Review of Neuroscience, 24*(1), 1161.

Miller, E. K., & Cohen, J. D. (2001). An integrative theory of prefrontal cortex function. *Annual Review of Neuroscience, 24,* 167–202.

Molenaar, P. C. M. (2001). Systems modeling. In Neil J. Smelser & Paul B. Baltes (Eds.), *International encyclopedia of the social & behavioral sciences* (pp. 15423–15428). Oxford: Pergamon.

Moutier, S., Plagne-Cayeux, S., Melot, A. M., & Houde, O. (2006). Syllogistic reasoning and belief-bias inhibition in school children: Evidence from a negative priming paradigm. *Developmental Science, 9*(2), 166–172.

Nakano, T., Watanabe, H., Homae, F., & Taga, G. (2009). Prefrontal cortical involvement in young infants' analysis of novelty. *Cerebral Cortex, 19*(2), 455–463.

Numminen, H., Service, E., Ahonen, T., Korhonen, T., Tolvanen, A., Patja, K., et al. (2000). Working memory structure and intellectual disability. *Journal of Intellectual Disability Research, 44*(5), 579–590.

Oleson, P., Westerberg, H., & Klingberg, T. (2004). Increased prefrontal and parietal activity after training of working memory. *Nature Neuroscience, 7,* 75–79.

Overton, W. F. (2006). Developmental psychology: Philosophy, concepts, methodology. In W. Damon & R. M. Lerner (Series Eds.) & R. M. Lerner (Ed.), *Theoretical models of human development: Vol. 1, Handbook of child psychology* (6th ed., pp. 18–88). Hoboken, NJ: John Wiley & Sons.

Park, D. C., & Reuter-Lorenz, P. (2009). The adaptive brain: Aging and neurocognitive scaffolding. *Annual Review of Psychology, 60,* 173–196.

Parker, K. J., Buckmaster, C. L., Justus, K. R., Schatzberg, A. F., & Lyons, D. M. (2005). Mild early life stress enhances prefrontal-dependent response inhibition in monkeys. *Biological Psychiatry, 57*(8), 848–855.

Pasnak, R., Madden, S. E., Malabonga, V. A., & Holt, R. (1996). Persistence of gains from instruction in classification, seriation, and conservation. *Journal of Educational Research, 90*(2), 87–92.

Pasnak, R., McCutcheon, L., Holt, R. W., & Campbell, J. W. (1991). Cognitive and achievement gains for kindergartners instructed in Piagetian operations. *Journal of Educational Research, 85*(1), 5–13.

Pennington, B. F., & Ozonoff, S. (1996). Executive functions and developmental psychopathology. *Journal of Child Psychology and Psychiatry, and Allied Disciplines, 37*(1), 51–87.

Perfetti, B., Saggino, A., Ferretti, A., Caulo, M., Romani, G. L., & Onofrj, M. (2009). Differential patterns of cortical activation as a function of fluid reasoning complexity. *Human Brain Mapping, 30*(2), 497–510.

Persson, J., Nyberg, L., Lind, J., Larsson, A., Nilsson, L. G., Ingvar, M., et al. (2006). Structure-function correlates of cognitive decline in aging. *Cerebral Cortex, 16*(7), 907–915.

Pfefferbaum, A., Adalsteinsson, E., & Sullivan, E. V. (2005). Frontal circuitry degradation marks healthy adult aging: Evidence from diffusion tensor imaging. *NeuroImage, 26*(3), 891–899.

Piaget, J. (1952). *The origins of intelligence in children.* Oxford: International Universities Press.

Posner, M. I., & Petersen, S. E. (1990). The attention system of the human brain. *Annual Review of Neuroscience, 13,* 25–42.

Posner, M. I., & Rothbart, M. K. (2000). Developing mechanisms of self-regulation. *Development and Psychopathology, 12*(03), 427–441.

Prabhakaran, V., Smith, J. A., Desmond, J. E., Glover, G. H., & Gabrieli, J. D. (1997). Neural substrates of fluid reasoning: An fMRI study of neocortical activation during performance of the Raven Progressive Matrices test. *Cognitive Psychology, 33*(1), 43–63.

Rabbitt, P. (1993). Does it all go together when it goes? The nineteenth Bartlett memorial lecture. *Quarterly Journal of Experimental Psychology, 46*(3), 385–434.

Rabbitt, P., Scott, M., Lunn, M., Thacker, N., Lowe, C., Pendleton, N., et al. (2007). White matter lesions account for all age-related declines in speed but not in intelligence. *Neuropsychology, 21*(3), 363–370.

Rabbitt, P., Scott, M., Thacker, N., Lowe, C., Jackson, A., Horan, M., et al. (2006). Losses in gross brain volume and cerebral blood flow account for age-related differences in speed but not in fluid intelligence. *Neuropsychology, 20*(5), 549–557.

Ram, N., Rabbitt, P., Stollery, B., & Nesselroade, J. R. (2005). Cognitive performance inconsistency: Intraindividual change and variability. *Psychology and Aging, 20*(4), 623–633.

Ramos, B. P., & Arnsten, A. F. T. (2007). Adrenergic pharmacology and cognition: Focus on the prefrontal cortex. *Pharmacology & Therapeutics, 113*(3), 523–536.

Raz, N., Lindenberger, U., Rodrigue, K. M., Kennedy, K. M., Head, D., Williamson, A., et al. (2005). Regional brain changes in aging healthy adults: General trends, individual differences and modifiers. *Cerebral Cortex, 15*(11), 1676–1689.

Raz, N., & Rodrigue, K. M. (2006). Differential aging of the brain: Patterns, cognitive correlates and modifiers. *Neuroscience and Biobehavioral Reviews, 30*(6), 730–748.

Repetti, R. L., Taylor, S. E., & Seeman, T. E. (2002). Risky families: Family social environments and the mental and physical health of offspring. *Psychological Bulletin, 128*(2), 330–366.

Rivera, S. M., Reiss, A. L., Eckert, M. A., & Menon, V. (2005). Developmental changes in mental arithmetic: Evidence for increased functional specialization in the left inferior parietal cortex. *Cerebral Cortex, 15*(11), 1779–1790.

Rolls, E. T., & Grabenhorst, F. (2008). The orbitofrontal cortex and beyond: From affect to decision-making. *Progress in Neurobiology, 86*(3), 216–244.

Rose, S. A., Feldman, J. F., & Jankowski, J. J. (2004). Infant visual recognition memory. *Developmental Review, 24*(1), 74–100.

Rueda, M. R., Rothbart, M. K., McCandliss, B. D., Saccomanno, L., & Posner, M. I. (2005). Training, maturation, and genetic influences on the development of executive attention. *Proceedings of the National Academy of Sciences of the United States of America, 102*(41), 14931–14936.

Ryan, J. D., Moses, S. N., & Villate, C. (2009). Impaired relational organization of propositions, but intact transitive inference, in aging: Implications for understanding underlying neural integrity. *Neuropsychologia, 47*(2), 338–353.

Rypma, B., Berger, J. S., Prabhakaran, V., Bly, B. M., Kimberg, D. Y., Biswal, B. B., et al. (2006). Neural correlates of cognitive efficiency. *NeuroImage, 33*(3), 969–979.

Rypma, B., & Prabhakaran, V. (2009). When less is more and when more is more: The mediating roles of capacity and speed in brain-behavior efficiency. *Intelligence, 37*(2), 207–222.

Rypma, B., Prabhakaran, V., Desmond, J. E., Glover, G. H., & Gabrieli, J. D. (1999). Load-dependent roles of frontal brain regions in the maintenance of working memory. *NeuroImage, 9*(2), 216–226.

Salthouse, T. A. (1996). The processing-speed theory of adult age differences in cognition. *Psychological Review, 103*(3), 403–428.

Salthouse, T. A., & Pink, J. E. (2008). Why is working memory related to fluid intelligence? *Psychonomic Bulletin & Review, 15*(2), 364–371.

Schaie, K. W. (1994). The course of adult intellectual development. *American Psychologist, 49,* 304–313.

Schirlin, O., & Houdé, O. (2007). Negative priming effect after inhibition of weight/number interference in a Piaget-like task. *Cognitive Development, 22*(1), 124–129.

Schmithorst, V. J., Wilke, M., Dardzinski, B. J., & Holland, S. K. (2005). Cognitive functions correlate with white matter architecture in a normal pediatric population: A diffusion tensor MRI study. *Human Brain Mapping, 26*(2), 139–147.

Schoofs, D., Preuss, D., & Wolf, O. T. (2008). Psychosocial stress induces working memory impairments in an n-back paradigm. *Psychoneuroendocrinology, 33*(5), 643–653.

Schretlen, D., Pearlson, G. D., Anthony, J. C., Aylward, E. H., Augustine, A. M., Davis, A., et al. (2000). Elucidating the contributions of processing speed, executive ability, and frontal lobe volume to normal age-related differences in fluid intelligence. *Journal of the International Neuropsychological Society, 6*(1), 52–61.

Shaw, P., Greenstein, D., Lerch, J., Clasen, L., Lenroot, R., Gogtay, N., et al. (2006). Intellectual ability and cortical development in children and adolescents. *Nature, 440*(7084), 676–679.

Sliwinski, M. J., Smyth, J. M., Hofer, S. M., & Stawski, R. S. (2006). Intraindividual coupling of daily stress and cognition. *Psychology and Aging, 21*(3), 545–557.

Sowell, E. R., Peterson, B. S., Thompson, P. M., Welcome, S. E., Henkenius, A. L., & Toga, A. W. (2003). Mapping cortical change across the human life span. *Nature Neuroscience, 6*(3), 309–315.

Spear, L. P. (2000). The adolescent brain and age-related behavioral manifestations. *Neuroscience & Biobehavioral Reviews, 24*(4), 417–463.

Spearman, C. (1904). "General intelligence," objectively determined and measured. *American Journal of Psychology, 15*(2), 201–293.

Sternberg, R. J. (1991). Death, taxes, and bad intelligence tests. *Intelligence, 15*(3), 257–269.

Süß, H., Oberauer, K., Wittmann, W. W., Wilhelm, O., & Schulze, R. (2002). Working-memory capacity explains reasoning ability—and a little bit more. *Intelligence, 30*(3), 261–288.

Sylvester, C., Wagner, T. D., Lacey, S. C., Hernandez, L., Nichols, T. E., Smith, E. E., et al. (2003). Switching attention and resolving interference: FMRI measures of executive functions. *Neuropsychologia. Special Issue: Functional Neuroimaging of Memory, 41*(3), 357–370.

Tan, H. Y., Chen, Q., Sust, S., Buckholtz, J. W., Meyers, J. D., Egan, M. F., et al. (2007). Epistasis between catechol-O-methyltransferase and type II metabotropic glutamate receptor 3 genes on working memory brain function. *Proceedings of the National Academy of Sciences of the United States of America, 104*(30), 12536–12541.

Thompson, P. M., Cannon, T. D., Narr, K. L., van Erp, T., Poutanen, V. P., Huttunen, M., et al. (2001). Genetic influences on brain structure. *Nature Neuroscience, 4*(12), 1253–1258.

Toga, A. W., & Thompson, P. M. (2005). Genetics of brain structure and intelligence. *Annual Review of Neuroscience, 28,* 1–23.

Toga, A. W., Thompson, P. M., & Sowell, E. R. (2006). Mapping brain maturation. *Trends in Neurosciences, 29*(3), 148–159.

Tucker-Drob, E. M., & Salthouse, T. A. (2008). Adult age trends in the relations among cognitive abilities. *Psychology and Aging, 23*(2), 453–460.

Tunbridge, E. M., Harrison, P. J., & Weinberger, D. R. (2006). Catechol-o-methyltransferase, cognition, and psychosis: ValÂ¹-sup-5-sup-8Met and beyond. *Biological Psychiatry, 60*(2), 141–151.

van Leeuwen, M., Peper, J. S., van den Berg, S. M., Brouwer, R. M., Hulshoff Pol, H. E., Kahn, R. S., et al. (2009). A genetic analysis of brain volumes and IQ in children. *Intelligence, 37*(2), 181–191.

Wager, T. D., Jonides, J., Smith, E. E., & Nichols, T. E. (2005). Toward a taxonomy of attention shifting: Individual differences in fMRI during multiple shift types. *Cognitive, Affective & Behavioral Neuroscience, 5*(2), 127–143.

Waltz, J. A., Knowlton, B. J., Holyoak, K. J., Boone, K. B., Mishkin, F. S., de Menezes Santos, M., et al. (1999). A system for relational reasoning in human prefrontal cortex. *Psychological Science, 10*(2), 119–125.

Weinberger, D. R., Egan, M. F., Bertolino, A., Callicott, J. H., Mattay, V. S., Lipska, B. K., et al. (2001). Prefrontal neurons and the genetics of schizophrenia. *Biological Psychiatry, 50*(11), 825–844.

West, R. L. (1996). An application of prefrontal cortex function theory to cognitive aging. *Psychological Bulletin, 120*(2), 272–292.

Whitman, T. L., Hantula, D. A., & Spence, B. H. (1990). Current issues in behavior modification with mentally retarded persons. In J. L. Matson (Ed.), *Handbook of behavior modification with the mentally retarded* (2nd ed., pp. 9–50). New York: Plenum.

Yamaguchi, S., Hale, L. A., D'Esposito, M., & Knight, R. T. (2004). Rapid prefrontal-hippocampal habituation to novel events. *Journal of Neuroscience, 24*(23), 5356–5363.

Zelazo, P. D., & Müller, U. (2002). The balance beam in the balance: Reflections on rules, relational complexity and developmental processes. *Journal of Experimental Child Psychology, 81*(4), 458–465.

Zelazo, P. D., Muller, U., Frye, D., Marcovitch, S., Argitis, G., Boseovski, J., et al. (2003). The development of executive function in early childhood. *Monographs of the Society for Research in Child Development, 68*(3), vii–137.

Zigler, E. (1969). Developmental versus difference theories of mental retardation and the problem of motivation. *American Journal on Mental Deficiency, 73,* 536–556.

Zigler, E., & Bennett-Gates, D. (Eds.). (1999). *Personality development in individuals with mental retardation.* Cambridge, England: Cambridge University Press.

CHAPTER 9

Memory Development across the Life Span

PETER A. ORNSTEIN and LEAH L. LIGHT

This chapter provides an integrated account of age-related changes in memory skills across the life span, focusing on both the growth of memory in childhood and its decline in later adulthood. Our aim is to characterize the changing abilities of children and adults, and when possible, to discuss factors that may serve to moderate or mediate these changes across the life span. We recognize that the rich bodies of work on memory in the early cognitive development and late adult cognitive development literatures have been summarized separately in recent reviews (e.g., Hess,

2005; McDaniel, Einstein, & Jacoby, 2008; Ornstein, Haden, & San Souci, 2008). We also acknowledge that there have been attempts to have "child people" talk with "older adult people," as in the pair of chapters by Ornstein, Haden, and Elischberger (2006) and Zacks and Hasher (2006) in a recent volume edited by Bialystok and Craik (2006). However, by and large, there has been little "cross-talk" between these two communities of researchers. To some extent, the separate treatments of research on developmental changes in memory in children and adulthood is quite understandable, given differences across these research areas in fundamental questions of interest, interpretive frameworks, and tasks, as well as the lack of a standard metric for evaluating performance of children and adults on the same scale.

These differences notwithstanding, there may, in fact, be more commonality among "child people" and "older adult people" in their approaches to memory and its development than is at first apparent. Consider, for example, that researchers in both areas accept key classification systems for thinking about long-term memory. To illustrate, researchers who study children's memory and those who examine late adult cognitive development both accept the utility of differentiating between explicit and implicit forms of memory, with explicit or declarative memory being tapped by tasks that require the deliberate retrieval of information in memory, and implicit memory being assessed in tasks that do not call for deliberate recollection but nonetheless reflect the influence of prior experience (Graf & Schacter, 1985). In a similar fashion, both early child cognitive development and late adult cognitive development researchers are comfortable with distinguishing between episodic and semantic memory as subdivisions of memory, with episodic memory referring to our memory for specific events in the contexts in which they were experienced, and semantic memory referring to our general knowledge about the world, including especially our understanding of the meanings of words and concepts (Tulving, 1985). Further, both groups of researchers are comfortable in discussing development in terms of key changes with age in the encoding, consolidation, storage, retrieval, and reporting of information, and often in attributing causal linkages between changes in these processes and changes in a small set of underlying mechanisms, such as speed of processing (Demetriou, Mouyi, & Spanoudis, Chapter 10 of this volume; Kail, 1991; Salthouse, 1996), working memory (Bopp & Verhaeghen, 2005; Cowan & Alloway, 2009), executive function (Jacques & Markovitch, Chapter 13 of this volume; Braver & West, 2008; Zelazo, Muller, Frye, & Marcovitch, 2003), or inhibition (Bjorklund & Harnishfeger, 1990; Hasher & Zacks, 1988).

Given these points of agreement in terms of underlying principles, it seems worthwhile to attempt to put the two separate literatures together to construct a picture of the development of memory across the life span. The verb *to construct* is chosen deliberately, as our integration of the literatures reflects a highly constructive process that is necessitated by the paucity of studies of memory that are truly life span in their orientation. Most researchers in the

area of young children's memory have focused on a fairly narrow age range (e.g., infancy, the preschool years, or the elementary school years), and only rarely is the performance of young children contrasted with that of adolescents or young adults. In contrast, developmentalists who study the late adult development of memory typically make use of extreme age group designs (e.g., contrasting individuals in their 20s with those in their 60s or 70s, the modal contrast seen in studies of adult development that we review here), or sample participants systematically to cover the decades from 20 to 80, or even beyond. We recognize, of course, that a few research groups have included children and adults of varying ages in the same studies (e.g., Shing, Werkle-Bergner, Li, & Lindenberger, 2008; Zelazo, Craik, & Booth, 2004), but even these projects do not include individuals from across the entire life span. Admittedly, for many reasons, it would be difficult to do so, especially given the absence of a common set of tasks that could be used on both neonates and individuals in their 90s.

From our perspective, longitudinal and microgenetic methods are needed to make clear statements about developmental change within individuals (e.g., McArdle, Chapter 3 of this volume; Nesselroade & Molenaar, Chapter 2 of this volume; Ornstein & Haden, 2001; Schaie, 1996), and studies that make use of these designs to chart the development of memory are relatively few in number. With regard to children, the Munich LOGIC study, launched by Franz Weinert and Wolfgang Schneider, is an exception, as participants were followed from the preschool years until their early 20s (Schneider & Bullock, 2009; Weinert & Schneider, 1999). There are a fair number of longitudinal studies of memory across a substantial portion of the adult life span (see Piccinin & Hofer, 2008, for examples). Nonetheless, many conclusions about the course of memory found in the child development and late adult development literatures represent inferences from cross-sectional studies, which, when taken together, suggest a pattern of growth in episodic memory from childhood to early adulthood, with a systematic downward trend thereafter. Establishing the precise trajectories of developmental change, however, is heavily dependent on whether cross-sectional or longitudinal methods are used. For instance, in cross-sectional studies, it is generally in the 20s and 30s that peak memory performance is seen with declines beginning in the 20s and perhaps accelerating after 50 (Salthouse, 2009; Verhaeghen & Salthouse, 1997), but estimates from longitudinal studies across portions of the life span place the peak later and the course of decline less precipitous (Ronnlund, Nyberg, Backman, & Nilsson, 2005). Cross-sectional methods may also present a picture of relatively smooth trajectories over time, but individuals may show fairly abrupt qualitative changes over short periods (Kron-Sperl, Schneider, & Hasselhorn, 2008) that when averaged appear more gradual.

In this review, we focus on the age-related changes that are observed over the life span in explicit memory, as opposed to implicit memory, which exhibits relative stability across a wide age range, although there may be some variability as a function of the nature of the tasks used in particular studies (Light, Prull, LaVoie, & Healy, 2000; Lloyd & Newcombe, 2009). Moreover, within the domain of explicit memory, we concentrate on episodic memory, although we cover aspects of semantic memory under the rubric of *knowledge* and its impact on remembering. Furthermore, we emphasize deliberate memory, although we will make occasional reference to incidental memory (including autobiographical memory) for events that were experienced without an overt memory goal. Given the research methods represented in the child and late adult cognitive development literatures, most of the findings that we report will be drawn from cross-sectional studies, although when available we will include data from microgenetic and longitudinal studies.

To set the stage for our consideration of deliberate episodic memory, we begin with brief discussions of the nonverbal memory of infants as it is reflected in behavioral tasks, coupled with preschoolers' memories for past experiences as they are observed in the context of parent–child conversations, although we readily admit that the precise linkages between these competencies and the later deliberate skills of children have yet to be established. Then we turn to the discussion of deliberate memory skills across the life span, emphasizing the deployment of strategies for remembering. We discuss the growth of children's intentionality—that is, their understanding that something specific typically needs to be initiated if one is to remember a set of material—and examine changes with age in the effectiveness of children's strategic efforts. Context will play a considerable role in the developmental story, as seemingly slight variations in aspects of the task will make children and older adults seem more or less strategic. We will also devote a considerable amount of attention to theory-based treatments of the recollection- and familiarity-driven processes that are assumed to underlie the mnemonic skills of both children and adults. In addition, to the extent to which they can be discerned, we discuss factors that contribute to memory performance and development.

SETTING THE STAGE FOR THE DEVELOPMENT OF DELIBERATE MEMORY

Although our focus is on deliberate memory, it is important to recognize the foundational mnemonic skills that are already in place as children begin to learn how to remember. In this regard, it is clear that preschoolers, toddlers, and even infants can demonstrate substantial skill in remembering events that were most likely encoded without the operation of memory goals. To illustrate, we consider briefly the abilities of infants and toddlers that have been revealed in a variety of tasks that do not require the use of language, and we discuss preschoolers' developing facility in talking about past events with their parents and other adults.

Behavioral Indicators of Early Memory

It all begins in the womb! Indeed, newborn infants' memory for aspects of a story read to them in the last weeks of their mothers' pregnancies has been revealed by their differential sucking patterns in the context of an operant conditioning paradigm. In a procedure in which contrasting rates of sucking (either fast or slow) can provide opportunities for newborns to hear either the story passage that they had previously heard or a novel control passage, these infants, only hours old, showed clear preferences for the passage that they had heard in utero (DeCasper & Fifer, 1980; DeCasper & Spence, 1986). In addition, researchers using a wide variety of behavioral measures—including visual preference and habituation (e.g., Bahrick & Pickens, 1995; Rose, Gottfried, Melloy-Carminar, & Bridger, 1982), conjugate reinforcement (e.g., Rovee-Collier & Cuevas, 2008), and elicited and delayed reinforcement (e.g., Bauer, Wenner, Dropik, & Wewerka, 2000; Meltzoff, 1985)—have pieced together an impressive picture of what infants can remember over various delays, as well as age-related changes in these skills.

Although additional work is necessary to understand how these different indicators converge to characterize children's skill at any one point in development (Ornstein et al., 2008), it is clear that a high-functioning memory system is in place before language is available for the encoding and reporting of information. It is also clear that memory performance is affected by reminding, context, prior knowledge, repeated experience, active participation, and enabling relations in ways similar to that observed with older children (see Bauer, 2007). These similarities notwithstanding, it must be admitted that little is known about the ways in which children's nonverbal memory performance leads to (or predicts) subsequent performance on tasks that require verbal reports. Nonetheless, one might expect linkages between the imitation-based techniques and subsequent verbally based measures because, as Bauer (2006, 2007) has argued convincingly, these imitation-based techniques seem to capture the essence of explicit memory: rapid learning, forgetting over time, preservation of memory over contexts (for a contrasting perspective, see Rovee-Collier & Cuevas, 2008). Admittedly, the imitation tasks do not involve verbal reports, and thus it is impossible to know whether the infants whose performance is assessed experience a sense of conscious recollection. However, an additional finding is relevant to the argument: Adult humans with amnesia that impairs their performance on explicit memory tasks also exhibit deficits on elicited imitation tasks (McDonough, Mandler, McKee, & Squire, 1995).

Of course, children's memory abilities change markedly once they are able to use language to express what they remember about previously experienced events. These changes have been observed in a wide range of situations, some of which involve assessing children's memory in the context of mother–child conversations about jointly experienced events, whereas others explore memory for specified events. We turn now to a discussion of memory as expressed in conversations about the past and then to a treatment of children's memory for salient "target" events.

Adult–Child Conversations

Studies of naturally occurring conversation indicate that children begin to verbally reference the past between 18 and 24 months of age (e.g., Hudson, 1990; Nelson, 1986). Their skills for reporting experienced events develop rapidly between 2 and 4 years of age, and they soon become able to provide coherent, well-organized accounts of routine, everyday activities (e.g., Nelson, 1986) and can also generate information about novel, one-time past experiences. Indeed, by 29 to 35 months of age, in response to only general "open-ended" prompts (e.g., "Tell me about Disneyland."), children are able to recall in somewhat coherent form events that they experienced only once or twice, such as a visit to a zoo or a museum, that occurred more than 6 months in the past (Fivush, Gray, & Fromhoff, 1987). These abilities notwithstanding, it is also clear that children's early reports of their past experiences are limited both in content and structure (see Fivush, Haden, & Reese, 2006). For example, when parents and children first begin conversing about past events, the discussions are usually initiated and heavily scaffolded by an adult. Indeed, a central focus of research on parent–child reminiscing has been directed to an examination of this scaffolding and has revealed marked differences in the "reminiscing styles" that parents use to structure conversations about the past with their young children (see Fivush et al., 2006, for a review).

In contrast to *low-elaborative mothers, high-elaborative mothers* frequently ask questions and continually add new information that serves to cue memory, even when their children do not provide much in the way of spontaneous recall (e.g., McCabe & Peterson, 1991; Reese, Haden, & Fivush, 1993). Importantly, the evidence indicates that the nature of mothers' talks with their children about past experiences has both an immediate and a long-term impact on children's remembering. Indeed, longitudinal data reveal that differences in maternal style are associated with later differences in children's independent abilities to generate information about past events. To illustrate, Reese et al. showed that mothers' elaborations during early conversations with their 40-month-olds were associated positively with children's independent contributions of memory information in conversations at 58 and 70 months of age. Also, other research (e.g., Hudson, 1993; McCabe & Peterson, 1991) demonstrates that the more elaborative mothers of 2-year-olds were, the better their children's independent skills for remembering events with an examiner as much as a year and a half later.

These findings concerning linkages between mothers' reminiscing styles and children's memory skills have been widely replicated (e.g., Farrant & Reese, 2000; Leichtman, Pillemer, Wang, Koreishi, & Han, 2000; Peterson, Jesso, & McCabe, 1999) and extended with training studies that demonstrate causal linkages between mothers' conversational styles and children's later independent memory skills (e.g., Peterson, 1999; Reese & Newcombe, 2007). The evidence seems clear that social-communicative interactions between parents and children provide several opportunities: (1) to focus children's attention on salient aspects of an event, (2) to search memory for information concerning the experience, (3) to understand what is involved in communicating about the past, and (4) to use narrative conventions to express what they remember. Moreover, it is important to emphasize that, just as adult–child conversations about the past can influence the recovery and reporting of information, verbal interactions that occur as salient events unfold may also have positive mnemonic consequences. Parents and other adults may be able to provide information during an ongoing event that facilitates children's comprehension and subsequent remembering. Indeed, a growing body of evidence supports the idea that language-based interactions during ongoing events can serve to focus children's attention on various aspects of the situation that are particularly salient, and in the process influence encoding and the establishment of a representation (e.g., Boland, Haden, & Ornstein, 2003; McGuigan & Salmon, 2004; Ornstein, Haden, & Hedrick, 2004).

Memory for Salient Activities

In part as a result of conversational interactions, children make rapid gains in their understanding of the goals of communicating about the past and their abilities to report on the details of salient events that they have experienced. A substantial amount is now known about the mnemonic skills of children between 2½ and 8 years of age. In a range of studies, children have been exposed to specially constructed "stimulus" events, such as a staged "visiting the pirate" activity (e.g., Murachver, Pipe, Gordon, & Owens, 1996) or a pretend zoo (e.g., McGuigan & Salmon, 2004), whereas in others, they experienced naturally occurring (mostly medical) events such as routine pediatric checkups, and other less familiar and more stressful procedures (e.g., Goodman, Quas, Batterman-Faunce, Riddlesberger, & Kuhn, 1997; Merritt, Ornstein, & Spicker, 1994; Peterson & Bell, 1996).

This corpus of work indicates young children's prowess in remembering the details of salient experiences. For example, Baker-Ward, Gordon, Ornstein, Larus, and Clubb (1993) explored 3-, 5-, and 7-year-olds' retention of the details of a routine visit to the pediatrician and observed that the children recalled 83% of the component features of the physical examination. Nonetheless, Baker-Ward et al. (1993) reported substantial age differences in various aspects of the children's memory performance, and their findings are consistent with the results of numerous other studies. To illustrate, with increases in age, it is clear that children demonstrate higher levels of overall recall of medical and other salient experiences, provide more information in response to open-ended questions, and thus are less dependent on the use of yes/no questions to elicit remembering (e.g., see Baker-Ward et al., 1993; Ornstein, Baker-Ward, Gordon, & Merritt, 1997). In addition, older children evidence less forgetting over time (e.g., Brainerd,

Reyna, Howe, & Kingma, 1990) and may be less susceptible to suggestive questions than younger children (Ceci & Bruck, 1995; Ornstein et al., 1997). Moreover, the available evidence also indicates that with age and increased experience in talking about the past, children's reports become more richly detailed and complex, and less dependent on information being provided by adult conversational partners (e.g., Haden, Haine, & Fivush, 1997).

To what extent do these developing skills in reporting the details of salient experiences set the stage for children's performances in tasks that require deliberate remembering? Currently, there are only hints in the literature of possible linkages between a child's event and deliberate memory performance. For example, Haden, Ornstein, Eckerman, and Didow (2001) observed young children as they took part in three specially constructed "adventures" with their mothers: at 30 months, a camping trip; at 36 months, a bird-watching adventure; and at 42 months, the opening of an ice-cream shop. Although they focused on associations between aspects of mother–child conversations as the events unfolded and the preschoolers' memories for the details of these experiences, Haden et al. (2001) also reported moderate correlations between the children's memories of the activities at all three assessment points and their performance on a deliberate memory task that was introduced at 42 months. Admittedly, the necessary longitudinal data are not yet available to support the claim, but we suspect that skills in talking about the past and in deploying mnemonic strategies may lie at different points on a developmental continuum. As we see it, just as early expressions of nonverbal memory give way to later uses of language to make reference to past experiences, it seems likely that growing sophistication in talking about the past may precede later competencies in deliberate planning for future assessments of remembering.

A PERSPECTIVE ON DELIBERATE MEMORY

In sharp contrast to the research on the social origins of memory for personally-experienced events, much of the research on episodic memory involves the examination of the deliberate deployment of strategies for remembering by individuals in laboratory settings. Moreover, although event memory is largely incidental, the use of strategies for remembering involves intentional behavior that is initiated in order to prepare for a future assessment of memory.

Orienting Assumptions

As we see it, contemporary work on deliberate memory reflects the merging of two separate cognitive traditions, the information-processing approach (e.g., Atkinson & Shiffrin, 1968) and the organizational tradition (e.g., Bousfield, 1953; Tulving, 1962), which itself reflects the application of Gestalt concepts to problems of remembering (Katona, 1940). Reflecting these perspectives, research on strategies for remembering represents a staple feature of the child and older adult research literatures, and is based on the assumption that selection and application of a task-appropriate mnemonic strategy will facilitate remembering. Moreover, there is a further assumption that developmental changes in deliberate memory can be accounted for, at least in part, by the age-related differences in the likelihood of selecting an appropriate strategy and in the subsequent efficacy of the use of this technique. Strategies are seen as influencing all aspects of information processing, from the encoding and the establishment of a representation in memory through memory search, retrieval, and reporting. Indeed, remembering has been viewed by many as a type of cognitive problem, with the selection of an appropriate strategy taken to be the solution to a memory problem (Brown & DeLoache, 1978).

Our treatment of mnemonic skills across the life span is informed by an awareness of linkages between age-related changes in remembering and corresponding changes in other domains such as knowledge, on the one hand, and factors that can limit performance, such as attentional capacity, processing speed, and executive function, on the other hand. The distinction between these two clusters of abilities is partially captured by such dichotomies as crystallized versus fluid abilities (Blair, Chapter 8 of this volume; Horn, 1968, 1970), cognitive pragmatics versus cognitive mechanics (Baltes, Lindenberger, & Staudinger, 1998), and representations versus control processes (Bialystok & Craik, Chapter 7 of this volume). In contrast to many other domains of cognition, *knowledge* (crystallized intelligence, cognitive pragmatics, representations) is believed to grow across the life span, at least into the 60s, with acquisition influenced primarily by cultural factors such as education, as well as by choices made by individuals that depend on their interests. Growth is seen in both general world knowledge, often indexed by measures of semantic memory such as vocabulary (Bowles & Salthouse, 2008; Ronnlund et al., 2005; Schaie, 1996; Verhaeghen, 2003; Waxman & Lidz, 2006), and in more domain-specific knowledge in the humanities, civics, social sciences, and some natural sciences (P. L. Ackerman, 2008; Vosniadou, 1992).

In contrast to crystallized abilities, fluid abilities or cognitive mechanics or control processes (including memory, reasoning, and perceptual speed) are thought to be driven primarily by biological factors and to follow a life-span trajectory of increase followed by decrease. To illustrate, Li and colleagues (2004) administered a battery of tasks that tapped both fluid and crystallized abilities to people between 6 and 89 years of age. For processing speed and fluid abilities, peaks were seen in the mid-20s, with declines visible by the mid-30s. Crystallized intelligence, in contrast, showed a peak in the 40s, with stability observed until a decline began after age 70. These age gradients describe a lead-lag pattern with fluid abilities rising earlier and showing earlier peaks than crystallized abilities. Li et al. (2004) also observed stronger correlations between crystallized and fluid abilities in childhood and later adulthood than during the middle years, in keeping with a set of assumptions about the interrelations between biological and cultural and experiential factors in development. That is, they make the following arguments: (1) during maturation, growth in crystallized abilities depends on the availability of fluid abilities; (2) once maturation occurs, further growth in knowledge depends on experience; and (3) in late adult development, the further growth expression of knowledge is limited by reduced fluid abilities. In addition, there is abundant evidence that top-down processes dependent on knowledge and expectations play an important role in comprehension and memory in late adulthood (for reviews, see Stine-Morrow, Miller, & Hertzog, 2006, Thornton & Light, 2006; Zacks, Hasher, & Li, 2000).

In our treatment of deliberate memory, we build on these ideas. We make frequent reference to the *changing knowledge system,* focusing on the positive effects of prior knowledge on individuals' changing abilities to use memory strategies that draw on that knowledge, as well as on ways in which knowledge activation can lead to errors in remembering (Brainerd & Reyna, 2005; Brewer & Nakamura, 1984; Ornstein et al., 1998). We also consider the ways in which attentional resources and knowledge contribute to the deployment of effective strategies, emphasizing the degree to which certain techniques may be too effortful for young children (Bjorklund & Harnishfeger, 1987; Case, 1985; Guttentag, 1984; Ornstein, Baker-Ward, & Naus, 1988). These relations can be quite complex. Knowledge, working memory, and speed are known to predict episodic memory in adulthood (e.g., P. L. Ackerman, 2008; Hultsch, Hertzog, Dixon, & Small, 1998; Johnson,

2003). However, the extent to which these predictors interact or make independent contributions to performance is not fully understood. For instance, vocabulary can be a stronger mediator of performance in cued recall in older than in younger samples (Hedden, Lautenschlager, & Park, 2005), arguing that, under some conditions, knowledge can partially compensate for declines in other aspects of processing, possibly by facilitating generation of mediators (Dunlosky & Hertzog, 1998; Dunlosky, Hertzog, & Powell-Moman, 2005). On the other hand, working memory and domain knowledge can be independent predictors of acquisition of new domain-specific knowledge (Hambrick & Engle, 2002).

Additional examples are to be found in the expertise literature. For example, studies that focus on the development of expertise in specific domain (e.g., chess, soccer) have demonstrated repeatedly that the highly organized and accessible knowledge of experts enables them to encode and remember domain-relevant information more effectively than novices, so much so that child experts outperform older novices in memory for materials drawn from their areas of expertise (e.g., Chi, 1978; Schneider, Korkel, & Weinert, 1989). Of course, when both younger and older children have equivalent expertise in a given domain, the typical age-related improvement in remembering is observed (Schneider et al., 1989). Moreover, expertise enhances learning of new domain-specific information, but it does not protect against age-related declines in acquisition in domains as heterogeneous as baseball (Hambrick & Engle, 2002), chess (Charness, 1981), music (Meinz, 2000), Go (Masunaga & Horn, 2001), or aviation (e.g., Morrow, Leirer, & Altieri, 1992; Morrow, Menard, Stine-Morrow, Teller, & Bryant, 2001; but see Morrow, Leirer, Altieri, & Fitzsimmons, 1994).

The importance of both knowledge and limited capacity as mediators of growth and decline cannot be underestimated. Knowledge and capacity are not, however, the whole story. In our review, we go beyond the distinction between two kinds of abilities, inasmuch as we are concerned with the contexts in which remembering is carried out and the extent to which the expression of memories is dependent on the goals of the individual.

Conceptual Issues: Identification of Deficiencies in Strategy Use

Despite their acceptance of a common set of assumptions, researchers in children's cognitive development and late adult cognitive development have focused on somewhat different sets of developmental questions. A good deal of the early research on episodic memory conducted by child developmentalists focused on issues concerning when children understand that they must do "something" to attempt to remember, as well as on changes with age in the nature of that "something" and its effectiveness in mediating recall. Moreover, given that dramatic gains in the use of strategies such as rehearsal (Ornstein & Naus, 1978), organization (Lange, 1978), and elaboration (Rohwer, 1973) are observed over the course of the elementary and junior high school years, one focus of researchers who study adults is on the strategic repertoires of this population and the conditions under which these techniques continue to be maintained (as opposed to abandoned) and deployed successfully with increasing age (Hertzog & Dunlosky, 2004).

This discussion of deliberate memory in children and older adults revolves to a considerable extent around the degree to which individuals produce relevant strategies, and if so, whether, in fact, these "mediators" seem to "work." It therefore behooves us to be clear at the outset about the ways in which strategizing can go awry in the context of remembering. Within the literature on children's memory, issues concerning the production and effectiveness of mnemonic techniques were first articulated by Flavell (e.g., 1970) and his colleagues. In framing the questions, Flavell was influenced by mediational approaches to the study of children's learning (e.g., Kendler & Kendler, 1962; Reese, 1962) in which the central issues concerned children's use (or lack thereof) of words as mediators of performance in various discrimination learning and concept utilization tasks. Drawing a parallel between the use of verbal mediators in these tasks and the deployment of memory strategies such as rehearsal, Flavell, Beach, and Chinsky (1966; see also Flavell, 1970) discussed two general types of potential "deficiencies" in performance: a *production deficiency* in which a mediator (strategy) is not spontaneously generated by the child, and thus cannot affect performance, and a *mediation deficiency* in which the relevant mediator (i.e., strategy) is produced by the child or can be prompted but does not mediate performance (i.e., affect remembering).

As Flavell (1970) and many others have demonstrated (e.g., Brown & DeLoache, 1978), mediation deficiencies in young children's memory strategies (e.g., active rehearsal, organized sorting) are quite rare, with most difficulties being described as production deficiencies; that is, initial failures to generate spontaneously relevant task-appropriate strategies, coupled with strategy production that "works" in response to prompts or training. However, as developed later in this chapter, even though young children's performance can be facilitated under some conditions, they do not typically derive as much benefit from the use of a given strategy as do older children. In this regard, in his initial treatment of mediation and production deficiencies, Flavell (1970) pointed out that "there can be a whole gamut of intermediaries between a smooth and flawless execution of some mediational response and no attempt to execute it at all" (p. 199). Indeed, in his discussion of the transition from nonuse to effective use of particular mnemonic techniques, Flavell (1970) indicated that "production inefficiency may be a fairly frequent developmental precursor to efficient production" (p. 201).

Miller (1990; Miller & Seier, 1994; see also Bjorklund & Coyle, 1995; Bjorklund, Miller, Coyle, & Slawinski, 1997) identified a third type of deficiency, *utilization deficiency*, in which a young child may generate spontaneously a strategy in response to a request for remembering, but the strategy either does not "work" or it does but is not as effective as when generated by an older individual. Although many developmental researchers have embraced the concept of the utilization deficiency, Waters (2000) in an insightful critique raised a number of questions about its usefulness as a construct, beginning with problems that arise with its overly broad definition, one that includes the concept of the mediation deficiency (the strategy does not "work"), as well as the notion of strategy inefficiency (it "works," but the benefits are limited). Concerning the first of these issues, she contrasted the findings of Flavell (1970) that mediation deficiencies are rather rare with the claims of Miller and her colleagues (e.g., Bjorklund et al., 1997; Miller & Seier, 1994) that they are routinely observed before a period of strategy inefficiency. In doing so, Waters (2000) indicated that the diagnosis of a mediation deficiency requires evidence that the very same strategy is being used by subjects of different ages, with only older children deriving a benefit from its application. She then indicated that such evidence is rarely available, as it is often possible for children to appear as though they are using the same technique, when, in fact, close analysis may reveal the presence of are-related differences in the strategy being applied. These issues, as well as others (e.g., a lack of attention to alternative hypotheses), led Waters (2000, p. 1007) to the position that the "jury is still out" on questions concerning the frequency of early mediation deficiency. She also argued that it would be most worthwhile to focus research efforts on the range of production inefficiencies that Flavell (1970) suggested.

Although the mediation, production, and utilization deficiency constructs were introduced in the child development literature, they have come to be used frequently to characterize the performance of older adults as well (Dunlosky et al., 2005; Kausler, 1970, 1994), albeit with occasional differences in the ways in which the terms are used in the two literatures. The greatest discrepancy seems to be in the use of the term *mediation deficiency*. Whereas Flavell (1970) and others have talked about this deficiency in terms of a produced strategy (mediator) not working, Dunlosky et al. (2005, p. 389) present it as a situation in which an individual does not "generate mediators even when support is available." Moreover, Dunlosky et al.'s (2005) use of the term *utilization deficiency* is not as broad as that used by Miller, Bjorklund, and their colleagues, and seems to focus only on the strategy inefficiency component: "When a mediator is produced, it affects memory but does so less effectively" (p. 389). In addition, Dunlosky et al. (2005) introduce two additional deficiencies that focus on the use of mediators when remembering is assessed, especially within the context of associative learning tasks. Under these conditions, a response must be provided to a stimulus word, and if mediators were generated at encoding to link the stimulus and response terms, they can, in principle, be used during test. As Dunlosky et al. (2005) indicate, a *retrieval deficiency* refers to problems at test with gaining access to an original mediator, whereas a *decoding deficiency* refers to difficulties with decoding the retrieved mediator, and hence in getting it to cue the appropriate response. Although these deficiencies have not been treated at length in the child developmental literature, Pressley and his colleagues (e.g., Pressley & Levin, 1980; Pressley & MacFayden, 1983) have examined conditions under which children may fail to retrieve and use at test a mediator that had been established at the time of encoding.

From our perspective, the use of strategic deficiency constructs has played an important role in focusing attention on processes central to performance on deliberate memory tasks. They have also helped to identify the nature of the difficulties faced by young children and older adults, in comparison with older children and younger adults. However, we do not believe that the deficiency constructs afford sufficient insight into what individuals are actually doing when they attempt to deal with sets of to-be-remembered materials (see Ornstein et al., 1988; Waters, 2000). As we see it, an understanding of development requires as an initial step a characterization of the strategic efforts of individuals of different ages, and not just statements concerning the production (or lack thereof) of strategies under certain conditions. For these reasons, as well as the conceptual problems discussed earlier, we focus on actual behaviors to the extent to which this is possible. Although we make occasional references to one or another deficiency to tie a particular finding to the literature, we believe that it is more productive to focus on actual behaviors, including various subcomponents of mature strategies, so as to discern to the extent possible just what individuals of different ages do when asked to remember.

LEARNING TO BE STRATEGIC

Over the course of the preschool, elementary school, and middle school years, children become increasingly skilled in the deployment of deliberate strategies for remembering information. Even school-aged children who are rather sophisticated in terms of reporting the details of salient events that they have experienced are nonetheless rather limited in their use of techniques that require study-like behaviors. We trace the development of these types of deliberate mnemonic techniques, focusing especially on rehearsal and organization, although other strategies (e.g., verbal and visual elaboration) are mentioned. The literature on strategy use by children and adults is voluminous, and additional details can be found in a number of reviews (e.g., Bjorklund, Dukes, & Brown, 2009; Burke & Light, 1981; Hertzog & Dunlosky, 2004; Schneider & Bjorklund, 1998). As we see it, many subcomponent processes are involved in the use of memory strategies, but perhaps the most fundamental is metacognitive in nature, namely, an understanding that one needs to behave intentionally to prepare for a future assessment of memory (Folds, Footo, Guttentag, & Ornstein, 1990; Ornstein et al., 1988; Wellman, 1988). We thus begin our treatment of strategies with a discussion of this form of intentionality, returning later to a discussion of other aspects of metacognition.

Early Strategies and the Development of Intentionality

The roots of children's understanding that "something" must be done in the service of the goal of remembering can be seen in the preschool years in the behaviors that children direct to objects that are to be remembered (e.g., Baker-Ward, Ornstein, & Holden, 1984; DeLoache, Cassidy, & Brown, 1985; Wellman, 1988). To illustrate, consider a study by DeLoache et al. (1985) in which

preschoolers watched familiar stuffed toys such as Snoopy and Big Bird being hidden (e.g., behind a chair, under a pillow), and were told to remember the locations so that the toys could be retrieved later. Under these conditions, even 18-month-olds directed a variety of strategy-like behaviors (e.g., naming, pointing, and "peeking") toward the objects or hiding places, and even though the deployment of these behaviors was not related unambiguously to success in remembering, their use suggests that the young children have a rudimentary understanding of the need to do "something" in response to a memory demand. Furthermore, these displays of mnemonic regulation seem to emerge in an "unplanned" fashion as part of ongoing pleasurable activities (e.g., hide-and-seek) in settings that are highly salient. As such, these behaviors might be more aptly characterized as *protostrategies* that may, or may not, be linked to later expressions of mnemonic skill (see Wellman's [1988] discussion of the concept of intentionality).

Older preschoolers certainly have a firmer understanding of the need to do "something" to prepare for memory assessment, but their strategic efforts may be no more effective than those of the 18-month-olds studied by DeLoache et al. (1985). Consider, for example, Baker-Ward et al.'s (1984) experiment in which 4-, 5-, and 6-year-olds were directed to interact with a set of objects and toys for a 2-minute activity period, and were placed in one of three conditions: Target Remember, Target Play, and Free Play. The children in the Target Remember condition were told that they could play with all of the objects, but that they should try especially to remember a subset of the items (i.e., the target objects). In contrast, the participants in the Target Play group were given instructions that did not mention remembering but rather stressed playing with a subset of the target objects, whereas those in the Free Play condition were given general play instructions.

Observation of the children's behavior during the activity period indicate clearly that even 4-year-olds who were told to remember behaved differently from those in the Free Play condition. More specifically, Baker-Ward et al. (1984) observed that spontaneous labeling or naming of the objects occurred almost exclusively among the 4-, 5-, and 6-year-olds in the Target Remember condition, that is, those participants who were instructed to remember a subset of the objects, who also played less than those in the Free Play and Target Play conditions. It was also the case that the children who received instructions to remember engaged in more visual inspection and evidenced more "unfilled time" than did their peers in the play conditions. Unfilled time was coded when a child was not paying direct attention to the items, but nonetheless did not seem to be off-task; informally, it seemed to involve reflection and self-testing. These findings indicate that the instructions to remember engendered a "studious" approach to the task among the 4-, 5-, and 6-year-olds alike, but it is important to note that only among the 6-year-olds were the strategic behaviors associated with higher levels of recall.

Two aspects of their findings seemed noteworthy to Baker-Ward et al. (1984). First, the observation that even 4-year-olds respond to the challenge of a memory goal with clear, deliberate, study-like behaviors is interesting, but it stands in contrast to the findings (presented later) that strategies that can be applied when remembering sets of words undergo a prolonged period of development during the elementary school years (Schneider & Pressley, 1997). Indeed, within the context of these more complex verbally based tasks, even 8- and 9-year-olds can seem unfocused in their strategic efforts (Bjorklund, Ornstein, & Haig, 1977). Second, the fact that the strategic efforts of the younger children do not facilitate remembering, whereas similar behaviors of the 6-year-olds are associated with enhanced recall, raises a number of challenges for understanding the linkage between strategic production and subsequent remembering. For example, why should similar strategic activities differ in their mnemonic effectiveness? Clearly, many factors may be necessary for strategies to be effective in supporting recall.

Although Baker-Ward et al.'s (1984) findings can and have been interpreted in terms of utilization deficiencies (e.g., Miller & Seier, 1994), as discussed earlier in our treatment of these deficiencies, the differential effects of younger and older children's strategic effects may be resolved to some extent with more precise coding of the techniques that are deployed. For example, even though the observable behaviors (e.g., naming, visual inspection) of Baker-Ward et al.'s 4-, 5-, and 6-year-olds were similar, they may have been the external manifestation of quite different underlying strategies. As such, the similarity across ages in strategic efforts may be illusory, with, for example, the children of different ages combining the observable behaviors into qualitatively different strategies. This possibility is consistent with Baker-Ward et al.'s observation that the younger children seemed to combine verbal naming or labeling and manipulation, whereas the older children put naming together with visual examination. It would thus be worthwhile to develop higher order coding schemes to capture adequately these age-related changes in the coordination of different mnemonic behaviors. Efforts of this kind may well contribute to more precise definitions of

effective mnemonic techniques, but it is also possible that these fine-grained analyses will still leave open questions about the conditions under which the application of strategies may and may not impact remembering. Moreover, as discussed later, other factors—for example, age-related changes in underlying knowledge (Bjorklund, 1985), speed of processing (Kail, 1991), and the effort requirements of strategy usage (Case, 1985; Guttentag, 1984)—may affect whether a given strategy influences remembering.

This brief treatment of young children's strategies that do not "work" highlights the fact that *intentionality* is only one component of strategic behavior and that two others, *consistency* and *effectiveness*, must be considered. This is especially the case when it is recognized that it is not until the middle school years that children evidence mastery of a broad set of mnemonic techniques. In terms of consistency, skilled strategy users have command over a wide repertoire of strategies (e.g., rehearsal, organization, elaboration) and can apply them in a skillful manner across a wide range of situations that call for remembering (Brown, Bransford, Ferrara, & Campione, 1983; Ornstein et al., 1988; Pressley, Borkowski, & Schneider, 1989). In contrast, novice strategy users have limited sets of techniques at their disposal, and their application of any given procedure is often characterized by *context specificity*. Indeed, the evidence suggests that children may initially evidence strategic "sophistication" only in some highly salient and supportive settings, but not in others (Ornstein et al., 1988). Similarly, as already demonstrated, young children's initial strategic efforts may not facilitate remembering, and it is with age and experience that strategies come to be increasingly effective (Bjorklund et al., 2009; Ornstein et al., 1988; Wellman, 1988).

Encoding Strategies during the Elementary and Middle School Years

To illustrate this passive-to-active progression, we focus here on studies of children's use of two seemingly simple classes of strategies, rehearsal and organization, as observed in tasks designed to "externalize" these techniques. Consider first the performance of 9- and 14-year-olds who are given a list of words to be remembered and asked to rehearse aloud as each item is presented. In this type of "overt rehearsal" task (Rundus, 1971), 9-year-olds tend to rehearse each to-be-remembered item alone as it is displayed, whereas older children (and young adults) rehearse each one with several previously presented stimuli (Ornstein & Naus, 1978; Ornstein, Naus, & Liberty, 1975).

To illustrate, if the first three items on a to-be-remembered list are *table, car,* and *flower,* a typical third grader would rehearse *table, table, table,* when the first word is shown; *car, car, car,* when *car* is presented; and *flower, flower, flower,* when the third word is shown. In contrast, the average 14-year-old is likely to rehearse *table, table, table,* when *table* is presented; *table, car, table, car,* when *car* is presented; and *table, car, flower,* when *flower* is displayed. These children thus differ considerably in the extent to which rehearsal is limited (or passive) versus more cumulative (or active), and these differences in rehearsal style are related to substantial differences in recall. Indeed, with increases in age, not only does rehearsal become more active, with several different items being intermixed, but recall improves dramatically, especially that of the early list items. As such, children's increasingly active rehearsal styles are associated with enhanced recall of the primacy portion of the serial position curve (Ornstein et al., 1975), and it is the "activity" of rehearsal as opposed to its sheer frequency that is responsible for improved performance (see also Craik & Watkins, 1973).

Paralleling these changes in rehearsal style are comparable differences in the deployment of organizational techniques, both those demonstrated at recall output (e.g., category clustering; see Bousfield, 1953) and those shown in sorting patterns at input (Mandler, 1967). In tasks that involve the remembering of categorically related items, the subjects' organizational efforts may be reflected in the extent to which recall output is clustered or structured according to the categories that comprise the list, whereas in sort-recall tasks, organization may be seen in the degree to which the sorting patterns that are produced before recall are semantically constrained. Although both types of organization are of interest, clustering in recall provides only an indirect index of subjects' mnemonic efforts because grouping according to categories at output could reflect deliberate encoding according to the categories when the materials were presented, the deliberate use of categories when recall is prompted, or both. For this reason, we emphasize the organizational patterns that are reflected in sorting before recall, although we begin our treatment of organization with a brief discussion of clustering. We do so because the clustering literature provides us with a vehicle for introducing one issue that must be considered in any treatment of the development of mnemonic strategies, namely, the role played by the developing knowledge base in permanent memory.

When presented with a set of taxonomically organized materials (e.g., a list of 16 items composed of 4 instances of each of 4 categories: *clothing, vehicles, furniture, things to eat*), clustering at output in terms of the categories increases with age over the elementary school years (e.g., Cole, Frankel, & Sharp, 1971). Nonetheless, in addition to the uncertainty whether the observed organization reflects activities at input, output, or both, there has been some controversy concerning the age at which clustering can be unambiguously observed in children's recall protocols. Lange (1973, 1978), for example, argued that clustering as a deliberate strategy may not be observed until the later elementary school years. Indeed, he suggested (see also Bjorklund, 1985, 1987) that demonstrations of clustering among younger children may reflect the selection of to-be-remembered materials in which the members of the categories may be linked by strong interitem associations, in addition to category membership. Thus, from this point of view, early clustering may reflect the automatic activation of associations, and the age-related progression that Cole et al. (1971) observed may be a by-product of an increasingly articulated knowledge system.

This perspective on children's category clustering underscores a set of important issues concerning the linkage between the developing knowledge base and children's increasing mnemonic skill. Although claims can be made about direct effects of knowledge on memory (e.g., Bjorklund, 1985; Lange, 1978), there seems to be a consensus concerning the importance of both knowledge and strategies (e.g., Muir-Broaddus & Bjorklund, 1990; Ornstein et al., 1988; Schneider & Pressley, 1997). It thus becomes possible to pose questions concerning the extent to which the deployment of a deliberate mnemonic strategy is supported by associative activation in the knowledge base. Moreover, these questions become important for a developmental analysis of remembering because it is likely that children's early deliberate efforts are first observed in highly supportive settings. Just as early behavioral strategies are seen with the salient toys and objects that DeLoache et al. (1985) and Baker-Ward et al. (1984) employed, so children's verbal strategies may first be observed with highly associated items.

We turn now to a treatment of age-related changes in children's organizational efforts when they are given an opportunity to group or sort materials before recall (Mandler, 1967). For example, when presented with relatively unrelated or low-associated items and told to *"form groups that will help you remember,"* third and fourth graders will rarely sort on the basis of semantic relations, but rather tend to form fragmented groupings that are not consistent from trial to trial (Bjorklund et al., 1977; Liberty

& Ornstein, 1973). In contrast, older children (sixth grade and above) and young adults routinely form semantically constrained groups; that is, they sort on the basis of meaning, even though the instructions only make reference to a memory goal and do not prompt semantic grouping. These older children seem to have the metacognitive understanding that sorting on the basis of meaning will facilitate recall, readily translating a remembering instruction into one that involves a search for a meaning-based organization (Ornstein, Trabasso, & Johnson-Laird, 1974). Moreover, consistent with the rehearsal literature, these age differences in the extent to which sorting is driven by the semantic organization of the materials are associated with corresponding differences in recall. However, it should be emphasized that younger children's failure to use a meaning-based grouping strategy does not imply that they lack understanding of the semantic linkages among the items, as they can readily sort even low-associated items on the basis of meaning when instructed to do so (Bjorklund et al., 1977; Corsale & Ornstein, 1980). Indeed, a number of studies suggest that young children are aware of semantic relations, at least to some extent, both when the items are taxonomically related (Nelson, 1974) and when the organizational structure is less salient (Bjorklund et al., 1977; Liberty & Ornstein, 1973; Worden, 1975).

These findings suggest that the apparent failure of young children to organize in recall does not stem from a lack of knowledge of organizational structures, but rather from a failure to apply this knowledge strategically. Evidence in support of this view can be seen in Corsale and Ornstein's (1980) study in which third and seventh graders were given a set of low-associated words in the context of a sort-recall task. The instructions were varied such that some children were asked to sort the items so that the groups formed would help them remember ("recall" instructions), some children were asked to sort items so that the pictures classified together "go together in some way" ("meaning" instructions), and some were given a combination of recall and meaning instructions. Consistent with expectations, these different sets of instructions resulted in quite different sorting and recall patterns for the younger children, but not for the older children. Consistent with previous findings, the third graders who were given recall instructions sorted in a basically random fashion, whereas those who were given meaning instructions grouped in a semantically constrained fashion. Those third graders who were given both sets of instructions sorted like their peers in the meaning group, indicating that it is not a recall instruction per se that is responsible for the young children's

failure to use an organizational strategy spontaneously. At the seventh-grade level, all children in all instructional conditions sorted in a meaningful fashion, confirming previous work and demonstrating again that these children clearly knew that semantically constrained sorting would facilitate recall. Interestingly, the sorts of the third graders in the "meaning" condition were equivalent to those in the seventh graders.

In terms of recall, it should be noted that there were no differences in the seventh-graders' recall as a function of instructions. Importantly, the third graders who had been given the meaning or the meaning-plus-recall instructions performed essentially at the level of the seventh graders, even though the children in the meaning group did not expect a recall trial. In contrast, those third graders given the recall instructions, who were supposedly preparing for recall, performed at a considerably lower level. Thus, it should be noted that the incidental recall of children who had been led to engage in task-appropriate activities (i.e., semantic sorting) was greater than the intentional recall of their peers whose preparation led them to engage in activities that were inappropriate in terms of recall.

These findings are consistent with the thinking of Russian psychologists (e.g., Smirnov, 1973) who have pointed out that young children may be able to engage in memory-related activities when they are a means to another goal (e.g., comprehension), but not necessarily when they are goals in and of themselves. Nonetheless, these researchers emphasize that if a child does engage in the appropriate behavior (even when it is not seen as a memory strategy), recall should follow. This perspective is also consistent with Jenkins's (1974) demonstrations of variations in incidental recall as a function of the level of semantic analysis called for in an orienting task.

Context Specificity in Children's Strategy Use and Development

A salient feature of young children's deliberate use of memory strategies is the context specificity that characterizes many aspects of their performance (Ornstein & Myers, 1996). In brief, estimates of children's cognitive skills can vary dramatically as a function of certain features of the context, as can be vividly illustrated by Corsale and Ornstein's (1980) finding that third graders' sorting (and subsequent recall) varied markedly as a function of whether they were instructed to form groups that would help them remember or to sort on the basis of meaning. The success of Corsale and Ornstein's instructional manipulation is consistent with the results of numerous studies that demonstrate direct links between strategy use and recall. For example, in addition to the facilitation that is observed in sort-recall tasks when young children are instructed to sort on the basis of meaning (Bjorklund et al., 1977; Corsale & Ornstein, 1980), performance can be enhanced by yoking them to the sorting patterns of older children (Bjorklund et al., 1977; Liberty & Ornstein, 1973), or even just by providing experience with highly organized materials (Best & Ornstein, 1986). In addition, instructing younger children to rehearse more actively leads to improved recall, whereas asking older children to rehearse in a passive manner interferes with remembering (e.g., Naus, Ornstein, & Aivano, 1977; Ornstein, Naus, & Stone, 1977).

These demonstrations of context specificity in the use of rehearsal and organizational techniques provide information concerning the operation of several key factors that may underlie strategy production. Although Corsale and Ornstein (1980) found that age differences on a sort-recall task could be eliminated when younger children were led to group the to-be-remembered materials on the basis of meaning, recall differences typically remain following instructions in multi-item active rehearsal (Naus et al., 1977; Ornstein et al., 1977). However, by making it easier for young children to perform the active rehearsal strategy—by combining instructions with a reduction in the information-processing demands of the task—dramatic improvements in strategy use and recall can be obtained (Ornstein, Medlin, Stone, & Naus, 1985). These findings suggest that the use of an active rehearsal technique may require more attentional effort for younger than older children; indeed, Guttentag (1984), working with a dual-task paradigm in which rehearsal is carried out in conjunction with a secondary tapping task, provided support for this interpretation. Further, using the dual-task procedure, Bjorklund and Harnishfeger (1987) found that a trained clustering in free recall requires more effort for younger than for older children, and Kee and Davies (1990) reported similar findings in the context of a trained elaboration strategy. Finally, increases in working memory capacity are associated with enhanced benefits of strategy use—as assessed in terms of recall—by both children (Woody-Dorning & Miller, 2001) and adults (Gaultney, Kipp, & Kirk, 2005).

Not only do contextual factors influence the success of instructional manipulations, they can also affect the likelihood that young children will engage spontaneously in activities that are judged to be strategic, as well as the "sophistication" of their efforts. For example, by permitting third graders visual access to all previously presented items (thereby reducing the attentional demands of active rehearsal), some typically passive rehearsers were observed to engage spontaneously in a more complex, active rehearsal strategy (Guttentag, Ornstein, & Siemens, 1987). Importantly, it was these "transitional" children—that is, those who rehearsed actively under the scaffolded conditions of visual access to the materials, while they rehearsed passively under the typical mode of presentation—who moved the next year to active rehearsal under both presentation conditions, in contrast to the children who consistently rehearsed in a passive fashion. In addition, variations in children's knowledge and understanding of the materials to be remembered can have a profound impact on the strategies that they use when confronted with a memory goal (Ornstein & Naus, 1985). Age-related changes in both the contents of the knowledge base and the ease of access to stored information may influence significantly just what can be done strategically with the to-be-remembered materials. In fact, as suggested earlier in the discussion of clustering, it is possible that a child will appear to be "strategic" when trying to remember some types of materials (e.g., those with strong interitem associations) and nonstrategic with others, most likely leading to the first expressions of deliberate memorization with highly meaningful materials (Ornstein & Naus, 1985; Ornstein et al., 1988; cf., Lange, 1978; Bjorklund, 1985). Furthermore, it is likely that the increasing growth and organization of the knowledge system may facilitate information retrieval, and thus bring about a reduction in the effort required to execute various subcomponents of memory strategies (Ornstein et al., 1988).

Use of Multiple Encoding Strategies

The passive-to-active transition in children's mnemonic efforts has focused thus far on changes in the sophistication—and effectiveness—of individual memory techniques such as organization or rehearsal. Nonetheless, it is often the case that when faced with a task involving remembering, children make use of more than one strategy at a time, and with increases in age, there are corresponding increments in the number of such techniques that are deployed (e.g., see Coyle & Bjorklund, 1997; Cox, Ornstein, Naus, Maxfield, & Zimler, 1989; Lehmann & Hasselhorn, 2007). For example, Coyle and Bjorklund (1997) examined children's simultaneous use of up to four strategies—sorting, rehearsing, category naming, and clustering in recall—in the context of a sort-recall task with categorized items. Children at all age levels from second through the fourth grades made use of more than one technique at a time, with the older children making greater use of multiple techniques and evidencing corresponding gains in remembering. It should be pointed out that an impetus for some of this research can be found in Siegler's (1996) strategy choice model, reflecting the notion that at any point in time, children may have a repertoire of techniques under their control that may be more or less effective, depending on the task. As children get older, however, their use of less effective strategies decreases, as they choose to implement more efficient techniques (see, e.g., Coyle & Bjorklund, 1997).

Retrieval Strategies

The strategies discussed thus far are techniques that aid in the encoding of information and the establishment of memory representations. But it is one thing for material to be represented in memory and another for it to be retrieved in an efficient manner when needed. In this regard, children have much to learn about the use of deliberate techniques for cueing and searching memory, and with increases in age, they become more effective in the implementation of these strategies (B. P. Ackerman, 1985; Kobasigawa, 1977; Schneider & Pressley, 1997). In contrast to the voluminous literature on encoding strategies, relatively little work has been conducted on children's developing repertoire of retrieval skills. Nonetheless, it is clear that with age and experience, children acquire skills in reinstating spontaneously the encoding context and utilizing cues independently. Evidence concerning these accomplishments is presented here, and then we mention briefly other age-related changes in retrieval.

A considerable amount of work in the adult literature indicates that recall is facilitated to the extent to which aspects of the context prevailing when material was encoded are reinstated at the time of test (Light & Carter-Sobell, 1970; Tulving & Thompson, 1971). Research by B. P. Ackerman (e.g., 1985, 1986) indicates a developmental progression in children's abilities to reestablish the encoding context when recall is requested. Consider, for example, a study in which children study sets of three categorized words (e.g., *horse–pig–cow*), with the task being that of remembering the third word in each set. Later, when recall was tested, the children could be cued with one or two cues (*horse* and/or *pig*) for each target word *(cow),* or with a related word that had not been presented at the time of encoding (e.g., *goat).* The findings indicated clearly that the recall of second graders was facilitated when they were

provided with the full encoding context (i.e., both cues), but not when they were given only a single cue, whereas older fourth graders and adults could benefit from the partial cues, presumably because they were able to spontaneously reconstruct the full context, and thus to prompt their recall effectively. The young children clearly had much information available in memory, but they could not access this material without the reminders provided by the complete context reinstatement.

An important study by Kobasigawa (1974) illustrates comparable age-related differences in children's use of external cues to facilitate the recall of categorized sets of pictures. First, third, and sixth graders were asked to remember lists of 24 items that were composed of three exemplars (e.g., *monkey, camel, bear*) of each of eight categories (e.g., zoo animals). The materials were presented together with eight pictures that represented the list categories (e.g., a picture of a zoo with three empty cages), and the children classified the to-be-remembered items according to these pictures, thus ensuring that they were encoded in terms of the categories. After study, the children were assigned to one of three different assessment conditions. Children in a Free Recall condition were told to remember as many of the items as they could, in any order. In contrast, those in an Available Cue condition were given the eight pictorial cue cards and told that they could use these cues to facilitate remembering, but no instructions were provided concerning the order in which the items should be recalled. Moreover, children in the Directive Cue condition were given the eight cue cards, one at a time, told that three items had been paired with each picture, and then instructed to recall as many items as they could for the first picture, then the second picture, and so on. The findings indicated that the recall performance of the children in the Free Recall condition increased directly with age, and that age differences were eliminated for the children in the Directive Cue condition; indeed, the combination of cues and instructions to recall according to the categories facilitated the performance of all participants, with the younger children benefitting more than the sixth graders. In contrast, the presence of the pictorial prompts in the Available Cue condition facilitated the performance of the sixth graders, but not that of the two younger groups. These findings demonstrate not only that the first and third graders stored as much information as the older children, but also that they had difficulty in spontaneously using the external pictorial cues to gain access to the material.

Other investigators provide evidence that is consistent with Kobasigawa's (1974) finding of age-related improvement in the independent use of retrieval cues (e.g., Scribner & Cole, 1972), as well as corresponding developmental changes in the generation of task-appropriate search strategies (e.g., Kenniston & Flavell, 1979). In each of these cases and others (e.g., Mistry & Lange, 1985), younger children profit from specific prompts to make use of the strategies, and they do so more than older children, presumably because they do not generate systematic retrieval plans, either as they study the to-be-remembered material or as they attempt to remember. Taken as a whole, these findings have implications for the debate concerning mediation and utilization deficiencies (see earlier discussion). It is possible that the reason that younger children's spontaneously produced encoding strategies may not always appear to "work" (or work completely) has nothing to do with the effectiveness of these techniques in establishing representations in memory; indeed, it may be the case that, under some conditions, the appropriate representations have been established, but that the younger children may not be able to gain access to them, and thus retrieve the stored information.

MEMORY STRATEGIES IN THE ADULT YEARS

Our account of children's memory as they move through the elementary school years and into adolescence has focused on their increasing facility in the use of a wide range of mnemonic techniques. Given the extent to which children's growing facility in the use of encoding and retrieval strategies is linked to their increasing abilities to remember, it seems important to ask about the ways in which age-related declines in strategy use and effectiveness may contribute to corresponding declines in deliberate memory in adulthood. However, it should be noted that researchers in late adult cognitive development have not focused their efforts on identifying transition points in strategy usage, largely because of an emphasis on extreme group designs in the literature. As a result, we do not know whether there is a clear progression away from the proficient use of strategies that mirrors the developmental pattern seen in childhood.

A considerable amount of research has been devoted to looking for possible production deficiencies over the life span. For example, in their early review of the deliberate memory skills of younger and older adults, Burke and Light (1981) posed two contrasting hypotheses concerning production deficiencies in older adulthood: the *depth-of-processing* and the *search deficit* hypotheses. According

to the depth-of-processing hypothesis, the source of older adults' memory impairment might stem from a failure to encode the meaning of new information as thoroughly as do young adults, whereas the search deficit hypothesis could reflect older adults' failure to either formulate good retrieval plans as new information is being studied or to use such plans when they later search memory. These two hypotheses share the assumption that there are no qualitative changes in the nature of memory functioning across the adult years, and thus memory impairment in late adulthood is simply the product of failure to engage in strategies that improve memory. Moreover, the search deficit hypothesis predicts that age differences should be most apparent when memory search demands are heavy, as in free recall, and least apparent when search demands are reduced, as in recognition.

Burke and Light's (1981) characterization of production deficiencies is similar in many respects to Craik's influential view that age-related differences in memory arise from the failure of older adults to engage in self-initiated processing at storage and retrieval, and that their memory problems can be repaired by appropriate environmental support at both encoding and retrieval (Craik, 1977, 1983, 1986; Craik & Jennings, 1992). Moreover, a related position concerning deficiencies in the production of encoding and retrieval strategies can be seen in the "disuse" or "use it or lose it" hypothesis (e.g., Salthouse, 1991, 2006). From this perspective, young adults are routinely positioned in educational and workforce settings that foster the goals of acquiring new information, and hence make more demands on memory than do the environments of older adults. With less pressure to acquire new information and fewer memory demands placed on them, older adults would have less need to practice the kinds of mnemonic techniques that they used previously in their younger years, and thus would be less likely to use these strategies spontaneously when they might, in fact, be beneficial.

Hypotheses about various types of production deficiencies have been examined extensively. As discussed later, however, it seems unlikely that age-related declines in memory can be fully accounted for by the failure to spontaneously produce a variety of strategies. It certainly is the case that older adults often evidence reduced strategy use in comparison with younger adults, and that their performance can often be improved by prompting them to make use of mnemonic techniques. However, such manipulations are by no means always sufficient to eliminate age differences in performance, and sometimes exacerbate them.

Deployment of Task-Appropriate Strategies and Their Effectiveness in Young and Older Adults

Let us consider first older adults' use of strategies in free recall tasks in which techniques such as category clustering (Bousfield, 1953) can be observed in the order in which items are recalled. Several reviews of this literature (Burke & Light, 1981; Kausler, 1994; Light, 1991) have concluded that when older adults were asked to recall sets of taxonomically structured materials, the observed levels of category clustering were sometimes substantially below those of younger adults. Further, when category structure is made manifest both at study (e.g., by displaying all members of a category together) and at test (by providing the names of the categories), older adults' clustering increases, along with their recall, but not invariably to the levels of young adults (e.g., Hultsch & Craig, 1976; Smith, 1974). From analyses of free and cued recall of taxonomically organized lists, it appears that this result rests on both poorer spontaneous retrieval of categories and poorer memory for items within categories. Hultsch (1975) found that providing category names at test eliminated an age difference in retrieval of categories (as indexed by recall of at least one member of a category) seen in free recall, but that the age difference in words per category found in free recall persisted under cued recall. This latter finding could stem from age differences in organization of taxonomic structure in semantic memory, but this seems unlikely because category norms for young and older adults generally show fairly strong agreement (Howard, 1980; Yoon et al., 2004). Thus, as was observed with young children (cf. Corsale & Ornstein, 1980), older adults' deficiencies in producing meaning-based strategies for remembering may stem from their failure to make use of what they already know (i.e., their semantic knowledge) in the service of a memory goal. As such, providing them with scaffolding in the form of prompts or instructions can often facilitate their use of these techniques.

Recent studies using multitrial recall have cast additional light on these matters. Wingfield, Lindfield, and Kahana (1998) investigated the course of acquisition of lists of words that contain members of taxonomic categories and also examined the temporal structure of recall when perfect performance was achieved. Young adults reached 100% recall more quickly than older adults, but even on trials before reaching this criterion, the output of both groups showed virtually perfect category clustering and almost no intrusion errors despite the fact that there were age differences in recall on these precriterion trials.

When no category cues were present at study or recall, older adults were less likely to generate all categories on the first trial of acquisition, which is consistent with Hultsch's (1975) observations. Moreover, examination of the time between initiation of successive words when recall was perfect showed that the time to begin recall from a given category increased with its position in recall, with this increment being much greater for older than younger adults and no age difference in within-category retrieval times. Age differences in intercategory transitions were abolished, however, when the names of the categories were displayed throughout study and recall. Wingfield et al. note that pre-existing semantic relations within categories support bursts of responding within categories, and age differences in semantic organization and access to semantic information are negligible (e.g., Light, 1992). However, there are no such pre-existing semantic relations to support transitions between categories. Instead, the temporal context of items must be encoded so that the presence of particular categories on a list can be determined. In their view, age-related reductions in temporal context learning lead to poorer binding of temporal and semantic information, as well as more difficult retrieval of category information at test.

Rather than trying to classify these results as production or utilization deficiencies, we simply note here that consideration of more microlevel processes conveys more information about the nature of the relations between organization and recall across the adult years. The fruitfulness of this approach can be seen in its extension to free and serial recall of uncategorized word lists (Golomb, Peelle, Addis, Kahana, & Wingfield, 2008). In separate sessions, young and older adults were given either free or serial recall instructions. Young adults had higher recall under both instructional conditions than older adults, with age-related differences greater for serial recall than free recall, consistent with older adults having particular difficulty with order information. Indeed, the age by task interaction disappeared when all items recalled, regardless of order, were counted as correct. Further examination of the basis for the proximity of items produced in recall showed that both actual contiguity in the study list and semantic interrelations among items affected recall order. However, young adults had reduced dependence on semantic similarity in serial recall relative to free recall, but older adults did not show this shift in the basis for ordering, possibly because of reduced accuracy in temporal encoding of list items, coupled with preserved semantic knowledge. Another possibility is that older adults have greater difficulty in flexibly adjusting strategies to task demands. The latter account is made somewhat less plausible by the fact that, whereas young and older adults produced final list items early in free recall (a common finding), they gave initial list items early in serial recall, thereby demonstrating sensitivity to serial recall instructions. Detailed examination of the properties of recall protocols thus helps us localize the nature of age differences in list recall in a way that goes beyond simply categorizing the results in terms of particular production or utilization deficiencies.

Similar conclusions are derived from an examination of the performance of older and younger adults on tasks involving the learning of lists of paired associates, as opposed to free recall. On these tasks, strategies take the form of verbal or imaginal mediators that link the members of each stimulus–response pair. Although the generation and use of mediators in paired-associate learning is not available to inspection—as is the use of a clustering strategy in free recall—people can be questioned directly about the techniques they use to link the members of each to-be-remembered pair. These reports of both older and younger adults can then be examined and related to recall success, and when this has been done, older participants sometimes evidence deficits in the spontaneous production of effective mediators, deficits that are associated with reduced memory performance, but this pattern is by no means universal.

To illustrate, consider Naveh-Benjamin, Keshet Brav, and Levy's (2007) study in which younger (21–28 years old) and older (65–83 years old) participants were asked to study and remember a list of word pairs. Memory was assessed on an associative recognition test that required discrimination of previously studied pairs from rearranged lures that were composed of words that also had been studied, but with other partners. After the test, they were given open-ended questions about how they had encoded the pairs. In response to these questions, the mediators reported by younger adults 92% of the time involved generating sentences and forming interactive mental images, techniques that are known to improve remembering, whereas the older adults indicated that they never used these strategies. In contrast, the older adults reported using rehearsal—a relatively inefficient strategy in the context of this task—67% of the time, whereas the younger adults stated that they never used this procedure.

These results are consistent with earlier findings in the literature indicating that when queried after being tested, older adults report using linking imagery in paired-associate learning less often than do young adults (e.g., Hulicka & Grossman, 1967). However, Naveh-Benjamin et al. (2007) also found that there were substantial effects of telling participants that research demonstrated that linking the two words in a pair with a sentence facilitated remembering and encouraging them to use this strategy at encoding, or at both encoding and retrieval. Indeed, this information facilitated remembering, and 100% of older adults (and about 90% of young adults) reported using sentence creation. In general, memory performance was consistent with the amount of guidance people received in their strategy instructions, such that better memory was found when the utility of sentence generation was emphasized at encoding, and even better memory was found when participants were also exhorted to use strategies at test. Older adults benefited more than young ones from instructions to the extent that age differences in associative recognition were nonsignificant for the most constraining instructional condition.

In contrast with Naveh-Benjamin et al.'s (2007) questioning their participants about the use of strategies after testing memory for all of the pairs, Dunlosky and Hertzog (1998) probed their subjects after each to-be-remembered pair had been studied. They combined the use of this technique with the presentation of information about a set of strategies—sentence generation, interactive imagery, and rote repetition—that are commonly used in paired associate learning. In two experiments, Dunlosky and Hertzog (1998) asked younger and older adults to learn lists of conceptually related or unrelated pairs, and after each individual pair was studied to indicate which strategy, if any, they had used. Under these conditions of strategy assessment, both younger and older adults reported more effective (sentence generation, interactive imagery) than ineffective techniques, and age differences in strategy production were minimal. However, the near-equivalence of older and younger adults' strategy production notwithstanding, there were still differences in remembering. Dunlosky and Hertzog (1998) also instructed some participants to use interactive imagery as a strategy for learning the pairs, a technique that has been thought to pose difficulty for older adults (e.g., see Dror & Kosslyn, 1994), whereas others were told to make use of whatever strategy worked best for them. They found that both age groups were able to follow these instructions, with reports of imagery increasing and reports of sentence formation and repetition decreasing, although it was nonetheless easier to make use of imagery as a strategy when learning related as opposed to unrelated word pairs. Nonetheless, Dunlosky and Hertzog (1998) also found that despite the deployment of similar strategies, age differences in memory remained. In addition, with unrelated word pairs, the gain in cued recall when strategies were reported was less for older than for younger adults.

The results of other studies also indicate clearly that when given explicit instructions to use either imagery or sentence generation to link words during study, young and older adults may be similar in mediator production at study (e.g., Cohn, Emrich, & Moscovitch, 2008), or older adults may actually show greater evidence of mediator production than young adults (Dunlosky et al., 2005). Moreover, Dunlosky et al. (2005) found similar distributions of types of strategies across age and negligible evidence that mediators differed in length, number of content words, or syntactic organization (see also Marshall et al., 1978; Nebes & Andrews-Kulis, 1976). Thus, there is little support for age differences among adults in the quality of mediators.

As indicated earlier, older adults can produce appropriate mediators when prompted, but age differences in remembering often remain. These findings, however, do not necessarily conflict with other evidence that strategy utilization can produce comparable benefits across adulthood. To examine this issue, Dunlosky et al. (2005) compared cued recall of paired associates when mediators had or had not been produced during study, and found that younger and older adults demonstrated substantial and equivalent benefits from mediator production. Naveh-Benjamin, Craik, Guez, and Kreuger (2005) also found equivalent benefits in cued recall when young and older adults were instructed to relate the two words in a pair by using sentences or interactive imagery. Given these findings of equivalent benefits being derived from the use of similar strategies but with age differences nonetheless remaining, it seems likely that other nonstrategic factors must contribute to the superior performance of younger in contrast with older adults.

Luo, Hendriks, and Craik (2007) proposed an interesting hypothesis to account for the heterogeneity of outcomes of studies that manipulate encoding conditions. Using the same experimental procedure in a series of experiments, they varied the nature of the encoding manipulation, comparing performance when words were presented alone or with pictures, when words were presented or generated from definitions and fragments (e.g., *riding animal*: *H_RS_*), and when words were presented alone or with a sound characteristically associated with them (e.g., the sound of a door closing). With the first manipulation, older adults benefited more than young adults. With the second, the gain in performance from generation was constant across age, and with the third, the younger group got a bigger boost than the older one. Luo et al. suggest that the pattern of benefits from various manipulations depends on whether older adults are less likely to spontaneously engage in the processes that are induced by the manipulation (such as imaging), and whether the benefits to be accrued by these processes tax the limited resources of older adults more than those of young adults (as in forming associations between words and sounds). This intriguing hypothesis merits systematic investigation and extension to a wider range of memory paradigms involving the use of strategies.

Thus far, in our treatment of the memory skills of adults, we have focused for the most part on encoding strategies; we turn now to a discussion of potential age differences in strategy use at retrieval. To illustrate, Dunlosky et al. (2005) obtained reports, both at study and after attempted recall, of mediators that subjects used to link word pairs. Interestingly, older adults evidenced poorer memory for the mediators than did younger adults, and also had reduced recall of the correct responses when mediators were remembered correctly, thus demonstrating both retrieval and decoding deficiencies. Cohn et al. (2008) also had young and older participants generate sentence mediators for word pairs at study, and used an associative recognition procedure to assess memory for the word pairs. After giving a recognition judgment, subjects were asked to recall the sentences they had produced at study for intact pairs and to recall the study pairs for rearranged lures. When sentence recall was covaried, age differences in hits were eliminated, consistent with the idea of a retrieval deficiency. Moreover, when pair recall was covaried, age differences in false alarms were no longer significant, implicating reduced retrieval of the originally studied pair as a mechanism responsible for poorer correct rejection in older adults, a point to which we return later in this chapter.

In summary, when subjective reports are used to make inferences regarding strategy production in paired associate learning, older adults may lag behind younger adults in spontaneous strategy production, just as they do in free recall. However, the data indicate clearly that older adults can generate task-appropriate strategies when asked to do so or when given even minimal information concerning strategies (Dunlosky & Hertzog, 1998, 2001; Dunlosky et al., 2005). Thus, paralleling findings in the child development literature, contextual factors are important in terms of whether older adults appear to be deficient in the production of strategies. Nonetheless, the use of apparently similar mnemonic techniques by both younger and older adults does not always translate into equivalent performance on memory tasks. In addition, the findings are consistent with retrieval deficiencies among older adults. In closing this treatment of strategies, we do want to sound a cautionary note. The evidence suggests minimal differences between younger and older adults when they are queried about strategies they use in everyday life while going about their ordinary routines (Dixon & Hultsch, 1983; Lane & Zelinski, 2003; Perlmutter, 1978). In contrast, as demonstrated earlier, when strategy use is assessed in laboratory-based situations, the context is critical, with more support being required for older adults to seem to be "strategic," a constellation of findings reminiscent of those seen in the literature on children's use of strategies.

Strategy Training in Adulthood

Our review has suggested that, in laboratory studies of memory, older adults need relatively little encouragement to use effective encoding strategies. As we have seen, simply telling people that research has shown certain approaches to be beneficial can increase reports of strategy use, with concomitant memory improvement but without elimination of age differences in memory. Although these findings indicate clearly that older adults are able to use strategies that they might not ordinarily engage in spontaneously, these "one-shot" instructional manipulations given in laboratory settings are, for the most part, inadequate to overcome long-standing habits of inefficient strategy use. On this view, more extended training may be required to effect substantial change, and to reduce and possibly eliminate adult age differences in memory. This helps to explain why a sizable cottage industry is devoted to investigating the effects of programs to train and maintain memory skills in healthy older adults (for reviews, see Hertzog, Kramer, Wilson, & Lindenberger, 2009; Salthouse, 2006).

The evidence from these programs indicates that there is considerable plasticity in late adult development, with both younger and older adults benefiting from training, but that age differences in performance are not eliminated. Older adults, including those aged 75 to 101, show improvements immediately after training, but their gains are smaller than those of young adults, even with extensive practice or adaptive training (Baltes & Kliegl, 1992; Kliegl, Smith, & Baltes, 1989; Singer, Lindenberger, & Baltes, 2003). Moreover, older adults may show less improvement with strategy training than do children (Brehmer, Li, Muller, von Oertzen, & Lindenberger, 2007; Shing et al., 2008).

One intervention of considerable interest focuses on consciously controlled recollection. Jennings, Webster, Kleykamp, and Dagenbach (2005) implemented an adaptive training procedure in which older participants gained skill in discriminating not only between old and new items on a recognition test, but also between new and repeated lure items. Recollection training in which participants engaged in a continuous recognition task was successful in increasing the lag between repetitions over which participants could identify repeated items. Moreover, the extent to which participants benefit from this recollection training appears to depend on how they distribute their time on encoding and retrieval (Bissig & Lustig, 2007). People who devoted a greater proportion of their time to studying words showed greater improvements over time than did those who focused more on retrieval. Good performers also reported more self-initiated encoding strategies, such as creating narrative structures or relating words to personal experiences, whereas poor performers reported either poorly specified strategies or rote repetition. Thus, the effectiveness of recollection training seems to have its locus in the encouragement of self-initiated strategic processing at study. Lustig and Flegal (2008) suggested that improved training results in the establishment of representations that permit participants to use more highly specified retrieval criteria that, in turn, increase the likelihood of correct recognition. This, therefore, is an example of the difficulty of sorting out the locus of effects of manipulations that improve performance in older adults (storage vs. retrieval), an issue to which we return later.

Flexibility and Selectivity of Strategies in Adulthood

There is overwhelming evidence for an age-related decline in working-memory capacity (e.g., Bopp & Verhaeghen, 2005; Park, Lautenschlager, Hedden, Davidson, Smith, & Smith, 2002; Park, Smith, Lautenschlager, Earles, Frieske, Zwahr, & Gaines, 1996) that can mediate age-related declines in episodic memory. Both encoding and retrieval operations that require memory search appear to be more demanding of working memory or attentional capacity in older adults than in younger adults (e.g., Anderson, Craik, & Naveh-Benjamin, 1998; Naveh-Benjamin et al., 2005). There is also evidence that memorizing may be selectively underemphasized by older adults because their maintenance of everyday functions requires more attention than in younger adults (Li, Lindenberger, Freund, & Baltes, 2001).

Surprisingly, dividing attention does not produce a greater reduction in associative recognition than in item recognition in either young or older adults; nor are attentional costs on secondary tasks greater for associative recognition tasks relative to item recognition tasks in either age group (Kilb & Naveh-Benjamin, 2007). Finding null effects of divided attention on costs for item and associative recognition is, at least on the surface, inconsistent with the idea that declines in available resources are responsible for associative deficits in late adulthood, which predicts a larger cost for binding two words than for encoding single items, a difference that should be exacerbated during late adult development. However, Kilb and Naveh-Benjamin gave intentional learning rather than strategy instructions in their study. When strategy instructions are given, the results are more in line with expectations. To illustrate, Naveh-Benjamin et al. (2005) examined the costs of dividing attention at encoding or retrieval in young and older adults given either standard intentional learning instructions or instructions to use imagery or sentence mediation to learn word pairs. Costs on the continuous tracking secondary task were greater during both encoding and retrieval for strategy instructions than for standard learning instructions, documenting the greater attentional demands of this condition. Moreover, a fine-grained analysis examined costs at points in the encoding and retrieval periods where particular processes were thought to be occurring. The pattern of costs was the same for young and older adults across both encoding and retrieval periods under standard instructions, but these costs were disproportionally greater for older adults during times when mediator formation and retrieval would be expected to take place. It is also noteworthy that dividing attention at encoding lowered recall to the same extent for young and older adults, but dividing attention at retrieval only impacted negatively the recall of older adults, suggesting that strategic retrieval operations are particularly effortful for older adults.

The effortful nature of strategy use during encoding and retrieval may lead older adults to steer clear of mnemonic strategies known to be highly effective in the laboratory and to prefer approaches that are seen as less demanding. On this view, age differences in memory arise in part from constraints imposed by limited attentional capacity that, in turn, lead to choices of particular modes of operation with respect to encoding and retrieval. We first describe some studies that illustrate this point and then consider findings that show that older adults encode more information than they make use of when tested for

memory. We believe that results from studies bearing on such hypotheses favor the idea that what appear to be age decrements in performance can arise from age differences in preferences for modes of information storage and/or utilization.

Differences in Preference for Retrieval Strategies in Adulthood

Consider first an experiment by Reder, Wible, and Martin (1986) in which young and older adults read stories and took one of two types of tests: either a recognition test that required direct retrieval of actually studied statements, or a plausibility judgment test that required only a judgment that the test item was consistent with the story. The test for a given story occurred either immediately after it was read or after all stories had been read. The pattern of the latency and accuracy data suggests that young adults engaged in direct retrieval on recognition tests when memory was expected to be reliable (i.e., on immediate tests), switching to reliance on plausibility when memory was less good (i.e., on delayed tests). Older adults, in contrast, seem to engage in plausibility judgments even when asked to carry out a recognition task, regardless of test delay.

Reder et al.'s (1986) results, suggesting older adults' preference for a plausibility strategy, could reflect gist-based (Brainerd & Reyna, 2005) or situation model encoding biases (Radvansky & Dijkstra, 2007; Stine-Morrow et al., 2006) in older adults, so that specific information cannot be recollected as readily for close matches of probes to information in memory, or it could reflect a form of retrieval aversion, even in recognition, in which the alternative plausibility strategy cannot lead to success. According to Reder (1982), direct retrieval requires access to a single matching trace in memory, whereas plausibility judgments can be accomplished by locating any one of a number of similar traces. A related argument has been put forth by Jacoby, Shimizu, Velanova, and Rhodes (2005), who conceptualize familiarity as a less constrained form of memory access than recollection, which involves elaboration of the recognition probe to recapitulate study processing. On their hypothesis, familiarity, rather than recollection, is the preferred basis for recognition decision in older adults, who sometimes may simply not bother to invoke recollection processes at all.

Further evidence that older adults may prefer not to use direct retrieval strategies comes from a look-up task that resembles the digit-symbol task. A pair of nouns is presented and participants must decide whether the two words go together. A key that indicates the correct pairings is presented together with the test pair. If the pairing is learned during the course of the task, the participant can retrieve the answer directly, bypassing inspection (i.e., scanning) of the key. Thus, two strategies both lead to success—direct retrieval and scanning. The question of interest concerns the extent to which older and younger adults differ in their strategy choices. As would be expected, the proportion of direct retrievals in the look-up task increases with repetitions, but it does so more slowly in older than in younger adults. Critically, this finding is obtained even when it can be shown that older adults have committed the pairs to memory, and thus could use direct retrieval (Rogers & Gilbert, 1997; Rogers, Hertzog, & Fisk, 2000), suggesting that older adults are averse to using direct retrieval. Older adults do respond to manipulations that increase the utility or salience of direct retrieval (Touron & Hertzog, 2004; Touron, Swaim, & Hertzog, 2007) but nonetheless report use of direct retrieval under such conditions less frequently than do younger adults, although monetary incentives to increase use of retrieval can largely eliminate the age difference.

There is related evidence from other sources that older adults do not use all of the information that they have at hand in some deliberate memory tasks. For instance, older adults do not differ from young adults in recognition when the criterion for accepting test items includes not only actually studied material but also similar material—that is, under what constitutes less constrained retrieval instructions (Chung & Light, 2009; Cohn et al., 2008; Koutstaal, 2006). Here we note that this result cannot be interpreted as support for the view that older adults store less contextual information, because both young and older adults have higher recognition when the test item is physically identical to the studied item than when it is physically different (i.e., a different picture of an umbrella, a noun studied in singular form but tested in plural form, intact versus rearranged pairs in associative recognition). A related finding of age equivalence in performance is observed when study context is reinstated at test, for instance, when words are presented and tested in the same auditory or visual modality (e.g., Light, LaVoie, Valencia-Laver, Albertson Owens, & Mead, 1992). Such findings indicate that perceptual information is available in memory that is not always utilized by older adults, consistent with there being a strategic component in their approach to memory tasks that differs from that of young adults.

RECOLLECTION AND FAMILIARITY

Thus far, our discussion of the role of strategic processes in the growth and decline of memory has been concerned almost exclusively with memories that are faithful to people's actual experiences, and we have made little reference to representations or processes that engender spurious, but not infrequently compelling, subjective experiences of episodes that never occurred. However, the discrimination of true from false memories is a topic central to most contemporary dual-process models of memory (see Diana, Reder, Arndt, & Park, 2006; Malmberg, 2008; Yonelinas, 2002, for reviews). These models posit two processes—*recollection* and *familiarity*—that underlie both recall and recognition. In most dual-process models, recollection is taken to involve remembering particular aspects of a prior episode, such as perceptual details, spatial or temporal information, the source of information, or thoughts and feelings that accompanied the event; these assumptions reflect a shared perspective with the source monitoring framework (Johnson, Hashtroudi, & Lindsay, 1993). Familiarity, in contrast, usually refers to experiences of prior events that may arise from activated semantic representations (as in the activation monitoring framework of Roediger & McDermott, 2000); these experiences, however, lack the phenomenology associated with recollection. Dual-process models differ in various ways, but typically characterize recollection as deliberate, attention demanding, and slow in rise time, whereas familiarity is thought to be a relatively automatic process that is recruited more rapidly. Moreover, recollection is usually considered to be the preferred basis for responding in recognition tasks, at least in young adults, unless speeded responding is required or other aspects of the task encourage familiarity-based responding (e.g., Diana et al., 2006; Reder, 1988).

Some of the work in this area has been quantitative, generating model-based estimates of the contributions of recollection and familiarity processes to remembering, but much of it depends on qualitative comparisons of people of different ages for evidence of the roles of different mental operations in performance. With respect to the development of memory, the main questions have been the nature of changes from childhood to late adulthood (if any) in the relative contribution of recollection and familiarity to remembering, and the extent to which such changes can account for changes in true and false memory across the life span. We begin by examining efforts to obtain quantitative estimates of these processes and then take up more qualitative research.

Recollection and Familiarity Processes in Children—Quantitative Estimates

Several techniques have been used to derive quantitative estimates of recollection and familiarity. These methods include the process dissociation technique (Jacoby, 1991), the remember/know procedure (Gardiner, 1988; Tulving, 1985), the conjoint recognition paradigm (Brainerd, Reyna, & Mojardin, 1999), and the receiver operating characteristic (ROC) fitting approach (Yonelinas, 1994). These techniques were originally developed for use with adult populations, so their extension to research with children as young as 4 or 5 has required considerable design ingenuity. Even with modifications, they are used with some caveats about whether they presume too much about children's abilities to understand complex instructions about their subjective experiences (Brainerd, Holliday, & Reyna, 2004; Ghetti & Angelini, 2008).

In the process dissociation procedure, estimates of recollection are obtained by contrasting performance on inclusion tasks in which both recollection and familiarity contribute to accurate performance, and exclusion tasks where successful performance requires using recollection to oppose familiarity. Anooshian (1999) used the process dissociation procedure to derive estimates of recollection and familiarity in young children (mean age, 4.5 years) and college students (mean age, 22.4 years). In the first phase of the study, participants viewed a film in which a narrator told a story while pictures that illustrated the story were presented. In the second phase, they saw pictures that were marked with a dot in the top-left corner and were told that these were pictures from the first story that the film maker was saving for a second story film. In the third phase, they were given a forced-choice recognition task. With this procedure, the inclusion test involved pictures from the first and second phases paired with similar lure pictures. In contrast, for the exclusion test, the participants were told to choose pictures for a new story film (i.e., only pictures that had originally been presented with dots), because only these were eligible for a new film. Estimates of recollection increased with age, but estimates of familiarity were age invariant.

In the *remember/know* task, participants are asked to decide not only whether or not test items had been studied previously, but also to evaluate the conscious experiences that led to each decision. A *remember* response is given when elements of the original study episode are recollected, whereas a *know* response is made when study-phase contextual details cannot be retrieved, but the test

item feels sufficiently familiar to warrant an *old* judgment. This procedure measures phenomenological states rather than processes that mediate these states, but the proportions of *remember* and *know* responses are nonetheless sometimes treated as relatively pure measures of recollection and familiarity (Yonelinas & Jacoby, 1995). Billingsley, Smith, and McAndrews (2002) used the *remember/know* judgment technique with samples of children from 8 to 10, 11 to 13, 14 to 16, and 17 to 19 years of age in both recall and recognition tasks. *Remember* reports increased with age in both tasks. The probability of *know* judgments in recall did not vary with age. In recognition, there was a decrease in raw *know* judgments across age for studied items, but no age effect for *know* judgments that were corrected for baseline *know* responses to lure items; thus, the decline in know responses appears to be due to generally poorer discrimination between studied and unstudied materials in the younger children.

The conjoint recognition paradigm is based on Brainerd and Reyna's fuzzy-trace theory (e.g., Brainerd & Reyna, 1995, 2005; Reyna & Brainerd, 1995). In fuzzy-trace theory, exposure to a stimulus event simultaneously gives rise to independent verbatim (i.e., surface) and gist (i.e., semantic) representations (e.g., Reyna & Kiernan, 1994). Children, as well as adults, make use of their prior knowledge to interpret incoming information and, in the process, to extract the underlying gist. Memory of actually experienced events may be based on either recollection (retrieval of verbatim traces) or familiarity (retrieval of gist traces), or both. Two additional cognitive operations, *phantom recollection* and *recollection rejection,* are hypothesized to be involved in the production and prevention of false memory reports. As Brainerd and Reyna claim, phantom recollection builds on gist traces to produce vivid and highly confident false reports, whereas recollection rejection is a type of editing operation that makes use of verbatim traces to suppress false memories (cf. Rotello, Macmillan, & Van Tassel's [2000] discussion of *recall to reject*).

In the typical conjoint recognition experiment, participants study material that has obvious semantic structure (e.g., a list of semantically related words, a story). The recognition test materials include studied words (e.g., *bed, rest, awake*), semantically related new items (e.g., *sleep*), and semantically unrelated new items. Participants receive one of three types of test—verbatim, gist, and verbatim plus gist—in which they are asked to respond positively only to studied test items, only to test items that are semantically related to studied items, or to both studied and related test items (cf. the plausibility judgment condition of Reder et al., 1986), respectively. A mathematical model is then used to obtain estimates of various parameters for recollection and familiarity from the acceptance rates in the three test conditions, as well as estimates of recollection rejection and phantom recollection for lures related to targets.

In one of Brainerd et al.'s (2004) applications of this technique with Deese–Roediger–McDermott (DRM) materials (see Roediger & McDermott, 1995), second-, sixth-, and ninth-grade children were tested on recognition for words from lists in which the items were semantically related, and in fact, all converged on a common target associate such as *sleep*. Estimates of recollection for studied words increased dramatically from the second to the ninth grade, regardless of whether these were recollection of the targets themselves or retrieval of targets from semantically related lures. Phantom recollection also increased across grade level for semantically related lures that attracted many false alarms. Estimates of familiarity did not show a consistent age-related pattern.

In the ROC technique, participants make confidence-rated recognition judgments. A plot is then made of the cumulative proportion of hits (old judgments correctly given to studied items) as a function of the cumulative proportion of false alarms (the proportion of old judgments incorrectly given to new items) at various levels of confidence. Theoretical models of the recognition process are fit to the ROC curves, and estimates of recollection and familiarity are derived. Ghetti and Angelini (2008) used the dual-process signal detection model to examine recollection and familiarity in children from childhood to late adolescence. In one experiment, children aged 6, 8, 10, 14, and 18 years received a recognition test for drawings. In addition to an *old* or *new* recognition response, the participants were asked to make a judgment of their confidence using a 3-point confidence rating board, with a picture of a child with a confident facial expression at one end and a child with a doubtful facial expression at the other end. At study, the drawings were in either red or green, and children either named the color of the drawing (shallow processing) or made a semantic judgment (deep processing) for each drawing, with different judgments for red and green drawings. A significant increase with age was observed for recollection, but only in the deep encoding condition. Interestingly, familiarity estimates were lower for 6-year-olds than for other groups, though, oddly, estimates were lower for 18-year-olds than for 14-year-olds. For items judged old, children indicated whether the drawing had been seen originally in red or in green. Recollection

was a better predictor of memory for context (color) in both studies than was familiarity, supporting the notion that contextual information processing and recollection are related abilities.

To summarize the results from paradigms for estimating recollection and familiarity in childhood, we see reliable increments with increasing age in childhood for recollection, a not altogether consistent pattern for familiarity estimates, and evidence that increases in phantom recollection depend on the balance of gist and verbatim information available in particular paradigms. In general, growth in recollection appears to outpace any change in familiarity, but as seen in the Brainerd et al. (2004) studies, under some conditions, increases in reliance on gist may be substantial.

Recollection and Familiarity Processes in Young and Older Adults—Quantitative Estimates

Quantitative estimates of the contributions of recollection and familiarity to memory in young and older adults have been obtained from the process dissociation procedure, from the *remember/know* procedure, and from fitting ROCs to confidence judgment data from recognition memory experiments. Estimates from the process dissociation procedure usually show age differences in recollection and age constancy in familiarity, although the latter finding is not universal (Davidson & Glisky, 2002; Jennings & Jacoby, 1997; Luo et al., 2007; Salthouse, Toth, Hancock, & Woodard, 1997; Schmitter-Edgecombe, 1999; for reviews, see Light et al., 2000; Prull, Crandell Dawes, McLeish Martin, Rosenberg, & Light, 2006; Yonelinas, 2002). In the only life-span study that we know of that used process dissociation to get estimates of recollection and familiarity, Zelazo et al. (2004) found an inverted-U–shaped function, with 8- to 9-year-olds having lower estimates of recollection than 19- to 27-year-olds, and 65- to 74-year-olds not differing from the children; estimates of familiarity were invariant with age.

In the *remember/know* task, older adults generally have reduced *remember* judgments and may also have somewhat greater rates of *know* judgments (e.g., Parkin & Walter, 1992; Perfect, Williams, & Anderton-Brown, 1995). However, when Light et al. (2000) applied a correction that assumes independence of familiarity and recollection to data from several published studies, they found that both estimates tended to be smaller for older adults (see also Prull et al., 2006). Thus, the *remember/ know* paradigm appears to yield somewhat inconsistent outcomes with respect to familiarity. This conclusion is perhaps not altogether surprising. *Know* judgments, like *remember* judgments, assign items to the category of recently studied material. At some level, then, both may tap recollection, although *know* judgments represent less detailed information about acquisition. By this account, *know* judgments would not yield pure estimates of familiarity in the absence of recollection and would consequently not necessarily show stability across age.

Two investigations have reported fits of Yonelinas's (1994, 1997) high threshold model to ROCs for item recognition (Howard, Bessette-Symons, Zhang, & Hoyer, 2006; Prull et al., 2006). Both found higher estimates of recollection, but Howard et al. observed a trend toward higher familiarity values in older adults, and Prull et al. found smaller values of familiarity in this group. Healy, Light, and Chung (2005) obtained estimates of recollection and familiarity from ROCs for confidence-rated associative recognition tests from several different dual-process models. In models that included recollection, two recollection parameters were estimated: one indexed the extent to which recognition of a previously studied pair is based on recollection that the two words were studied together (recall-to-accept), and the other indexed the extent to which rearranged foils are rejected by recollecting that one of the words in the pair was studied with another item (recall-to-reject or recollection rejection). For all models examined, recollection parameters were lower for older than for younger adults, with this being especially evident for recall-to-reject. Age effects for familiarity estimates were inconsistent and were highly model dependent. The lack of totally consistent results from different procedures for deriving quantitative estimates of familiarity in young and older adults is puzzling. However, the conclusion that estimates of recollection are lower in later adulthood stands on very firm ground.

Recollection and Familiarity Processes in Children—More about False Memory

Brainerd and Reyna (2005; Brainerd, Reyna, & Ceci, 2008) have developed an extensive theory-based research program directed at questions about the origins and phenomenology of false memories, both those that are spontaneously produced and those that can be viewed as implanted by suggestive modes of questioning. Building on fuzzy trace theory's core assumptions of the parallel formation of gist and verbatim traces, and of dissociations in the retrieval of these traces, Brainerd and Reyna

have been able to predict and observe a number of effects, including surprising increases in children's production of false memories, forcing modification of claims (see Brainerd et al., 2008) of age-related decreases in suggestibility in childhood. Based on fuzzy-trace theory, together with the additional assumption that children's knowledge base becomes increasingly rich and interconnected in later childhood (e.g., Bjorklund, 1987), they predict (and they and others find) that false memory increases across childhood for materials that make it easy to form semantic connections among targets. These include DRM lists (Roediger & McDermott, 1995) in which list words all converge on a common target associate, lists of pictures that are highly similar (e.g., multiple instances of the categories *cats, bears,* or *birds*), and lists that contain words that share category membership (e.g., Brainerd et al., 2004; Brainerd, Reyna, & Forrest, 2002; Howe, 2006; Sloutsky & Fisher, 2004).

An impressive body of work now supports predictions from fuzzy-trace theory about factors that change the pattern of increasing false memory for semantically related materials in childhood (see Brainerd & Reyna, 2005, and Brainerd et al., 2008, for more complete reviews, including work on paradigms relevant to eye-witness testimony). We touch here on a few findings that have parallels in the strategy development literature or have been of particular interest in investigations with older adults. First, consistent with a theory in which extraction of semantic gist plays a core role, lists of *phonologically* related words do not produce a pattern of false memory increasing with age in childhood (Brainerd & Reyna, 2007; Dewhurst & Robinson, 2004; Holliday & Weekes, 2006). Second, manipulations designed to draw attention to list structure by providing category names for taxonomically related lists, telling children what the thematic gist of each list will be, or telling them that the words within a list will all be related, appear to have their strongest effects on false memory in later childhood or early adolescence, presumably because very young children do not have the requisite level of semantic knowledge (or do not make use of that knowledge) and late adolescents already spontaneously extract gist (e.g., Brainerd et al., 2004; Lampinen, Leding, Reed, & Odegard, 2006; but see Holliday, Reyna, & Brainerd, 2008; Howe, 2006; and Howe, Wimmer, Gagnon, & Plumpton, 2009, for somewhat contrary views). Third, manipulations that reduce the saliency of the global gist of lists eliminate the increase in the DRM illusion with age in childhood (e.g., Lampinen et al., 2006; Odegard, Holliday, Brainerd, & Reyna, 2008).

An interesting question is whether repetition of items within a list has beneficial or harmful effects on recollection rejection and phantom recollection when study materials are used that foster false memory. In young adults, repeating DRM lists leads to fewer false alarms for related words, i.e., less false memory (Benjamin, 2001; Kensinger & Schacter, 1999; Skinner & Fernandes, 2009), and repeating lists of paired associates leads to increasing hit rates accompanied by flat false alarm rates for rearranged pairs in associative recognition, i.e., stable false memory (Kelley & Wixted, 2001; Light, Patterson, Chung, & Healy, 2004), a finding to which we will return. Fuzzy-trace theory predicts that repetition of lists should strengthen both verbatim and gist traces, but that the effect for verbatim traces should be greater because gist extraction is largely complete with a single presentation. This prediction was borne out in a study of children aged 7 to 15 years (Holliday et al., 2008); though false recall of critical lures increased with age, repeating DRM lists three times rather than just once before testing decreased false recall of critical lures for all ages equally, presumably because repetition differentially strengthens verbatim traces, increasing the likelihood of successful recollection rejection. Similar findings of the effects of repetition have been obtained in recognition—to wit, repetition produces a decrease in false alarms to critical lures that is greater in older than in younger children (Brainerd, Reyna, & Kneer, 1995).

In addition to the recollection rejection mechanism of fuzzy-trace theory, the rejection of nonpresented but similar lures on a recognition test can be based on more metacognitive strategies. To illustrate, Schacter, Israel, and Racine (1999) found that both young and older adults had fewer familiarity-based false alarms on a word recognition test after they studied pictures than after they studied words. Schacter et al. reasoned that after studying pictures, which contain distinctive visual information, people expect to be able to recollect the pictorial information when tested with words, enabling them to reject test words for which visual information is not retrieved. Unlike the recall-to-reject process, which involves the retrieval of information inconsistent with test lures, the distinctiveness heuristic involves rejection of related word lures based on an *expectation* that they would be remembered if they had been presented as pictures. Howe (2006) also found that under conditions in which words alone produced an age increase in false memory, these effects were nullified by using pictures, with older children showing reductions in false memory for pictures, suggesting the utility of distinctiveness for young children. In other paradigms,

young adults are also able to reject highly salient distractors by the use of memorability-based strategies, both in list learning contexts (i.e., members of categories with fewer instances presented are more salient) and in situations in which false autobiographical events (e.g., "going to the Grand Canyon") are suggested to them, but children younger than 9 years of age are not able to do so (e.g., Ghetti, 2003; Ghetti & Castelli, 2006). These results indicate that a complete explanation of children's false memory will need to include memorability-based strategies such as distinctiveness and salience heuristics.

Research is also needed to evaluate the claims of fuzzy-trace theory against an alternative account offered by Howe (e.g., Howe, 2005, 2008; Howe, Wimmer, & Blease, 2008). According to Howe, the fuzzy-trace theory notion that growth in false memory is due to increased ability to extract global gist (common meaning) from separate items is hard to tie down conceptually and runs counter to findings that even children as young as 7 years encode semantic relations, though they may not use semantic information during retrieval. On Howe's (2008) associative-activation theory, it is not a separate gist extraction mechanism that is responsible for growth in false memory, but rather it is "changes in representational (e.g., associative) structures (knowledge base) that alter the speed and automaticity with which children access, activate, and use associations" (p. 769). Many of the same false memory phenomena can be explained by associative-activation theory and fuzzy-trace theory. Clearly, as Brainerd et al. (2008) and Ghetti (2008) both noted, there is a need for research designed to produce empirical evidence that directly links independent measures of children's gist or meaning extraction to the occurrence and magnitude of false memory.

In addition, the relations among growth of recollection, increased accuracy in source memory (Cycowicz, Friedman, & Duff, 2003; Foley & Johnson, 1985; Sluzenski, Newcombe, & Kovacs, 2006), metacognitive strategies, and patterns of false memory in children remain to be fully worked out. For instance, increases in accuracy of source memory across age in children would lead to the expectation that false memory should also decrease across childhood, and this is what activation-monitoring theories predict; but as we have seen, this is not what is found. Moreover, it is not known whether gist extraction and other associative processes are automatic or strategic, and how changes in these might be related to other automatic and attentional processes in semantic memory (e.g., semantic priming, see Plaut & Booth, 2000). Finally, we note that not all varieties of false memory show age-related increases in childhood. False alarms to rearranged lures in associative recognition show a U-shaped function in which there is a decline from childhood to adulthood and an increase in late adulthood (Shing et al., 2008). Such false alarms are thought to arise from a failure of recollection to counter the familiarity of individual items in rearranged lures, but the familiarity here is based on recent exposure to list words and not to gist-based familiarity. Clarifying the relations between episodic familiarity and gist-based familiarity, and the effects of these on different forms of false memory across the life span is a topic for further research.

Recollection and Familiarity Processes in Young and Older Adults—Qualitative Studies

Several lines of research have produced convergent evidence that age-related deficits in recall and recognition in adulthood stem from reduced efficiency in recollection, with relative preservation of familiarity-based mechanisms (for reviews, see Hoyer & Verhaeghen, 2006; Light et al., 2000; Yonelinas, 2002). Older adults have poorer memory for contextual information, even when item recognition is held constant (e.g., see Old & Naveh-Benjamin, 2008, and Spencer & Raz, 1995, for meta-analytic reviews; see Siedlecki, Salthouse, & Berish, 2005, for a different perspective). Moreover, adult age differences appear to be particularly marked when specific aspects of the initial study episode must be discriminated (whether a word was studied with a drawing or with a photograph), even when performance is matched across age on a task that requires use of more general information (whether a word was studied alone or with any image; Luo & Craik, 2009). Associative recognition also shows a decline with age, even when item recognition is held constant (e.g., Healy et al., 2005; Light et al., 2004; Naveh-Benjamin, 2000; see Old & Naveh-Benjamin, 2008, for a meta-analytic review).

Findings from other paradigms also provide converging evidence that late adult development is accompanied by impaired recollection and relatively spared familiarity. After studying lists of items associated semantically or phonologically with target concepts or words (i.e., DRM lists), older adults may have higher false alarm rates in recognition, as well as higher intrusion rates in recall for the nonpresented targets than do young adults (e.g., Balota et al., 1999; Gallo & Roediger, 2003; Koutstaal & Schacter, 1997; Norman & Schacter, 1997; Tun, Wingfield, Rosen, & Blanchard, 1998; but see Salthouse

& Siedlecki, 2007). Although we know of no life-span studies of the DRM effects or meta-analyses that combine the findings from literature on children and adults of various ages, our review suggests that there is an increase in false memory from childhood through late adulthood, a finding compatible with the growth of semantic and general world knowledge through the adult years. The observation of increased levels of phonological false alarms in older adults, however, runs counter to findings of children's constant or decreasing false memory for lists of phonologically related words and is not compatible with theories that predict growth only in associative false memories.

Jacoby (1999) reported an ironic effect of repetition in recognition memory in young and older adults. After seeing a list in which words appeared one, two, or three times, and then hearing a second list of words, participants took a recognition test on which they were asked to respond *old* only to previously heard words. For young adults, false alarms to previously seen words declined as a function of repetition, but the opposite was true for older adults, implicating an age-related deficit in the use of recollection to oppose enhanced familiarity produced by item repetition. Young adults show effects of repetition in associative recognition resembling those of older adults when required to respond before a deadline short enough to prevent recruitment of recollective processes (Light et al., 2004). Similar effects of repetition and deadline have been found for the DRM memory illusion task (Benjamin, 2001; Kensinger & Schacter, 1999; see also Watson, McDermott, & Balota, 2004) and the plurality discrimination task (Light, Chung, Pendergrass, & Van Ocker, 2006). In associative recognition, the effects of repetition appear to be attributable to greater strengthening of items than of associations in older adults, whereas the effects of strengthening are more similar for items and associations in young adults (Buchler, Faunce, Light, Reder, & Gottfredson, 2009; Overman & Becker, 2009).

There is evidence, albeit mixed, that older adults can invoke recollection to reject familiar test lures under some circumstances. This evidence comes from studies using manipulations that are designed to focus attention toward or away from the structure of the lists or the requirements of the test task (e.g., Koutstaal, Reddy, Jackson, Prince, Cendan, & Schacter, 2003; Thomas & Sommers, 2005), and from studies in which warnings about the nature of the lures in DRM tasks are given before study (McCabe & Smith, 2002; Watson et al., 2004). Older adults have also shown reduced false memory when required to make specific source decisions during recognition. This result was also obtained when people were asked to make *old and identical* versus *new and related* versus *new and unrelated* judgments, rather than simple *old/new* judgments, for categorically related lures (Koutstaal, Schacter, Galluccio, & Stofer, 1999). Similar findings have been seen for false fame and misleading information paradigms (Multhaup, 1995; Multhaup, De Leonardis, & Johnson, 1999; Roediger & Geraci, 2007).

In the paradigms discussed earlier, successful performance requires that familiarity be opposed by recollection. As we have discussed, older adults usually have difficulty in doing this (Cohn et al., 2008; Dunlosky et al., 2005), but they can do so if conditions are favorable. For instance, one way to arrive at the correct decision that a rearranged pair was not previously studied on an associative recognition test is to retrieve the original pair mate, that is, to use recall-to-reject. Patterson, Light, Von Ocker, and Olfman (2009) found that it was easier for both young and older adults to reject rearranged lures (e.g., *chair jealousy*) that consist of words studied in semantically related pairs (*chair table* and *envy jealousy*) than to reject rearranged lures (e.g., *zero technique*) that were seen originally in semantically unrelated pairs (*zero sad, dog technique*). Presumably, the existence of pre-experimental associations makes it easier to recover the original study pairs from the test probe in the former than in the latter situation. Under some circumstances, older adults may also use distinctive information about aspects of studied items to reject related lures on recognition tests (Dodson & Schacter, 2002; Gallo, Cotel, Moore, & Schacter, 2007; Schacter et al., 1999).

In addition to experimental variables that affect mean performance on false memory tasks, there are also individual difference variables that play a role. Not all older adults are more susceptible to false memory effects than are young adults. In particular, several studies have reported that only older adults who score low on neuropsychological measures thought to tap frontal lobe function (e.g., Wisconsin Card Sorting Task, verb fluency, digits backward) have higher rates of false alarms on DRM lists (Butler, McDaniel, Dornburg, Price, & Roediger, 2004), in the misinformation paradigm (Roediger & Geraci, 2007), in tests requiring discrimination of perceptually similar stimuli (Henkel, Johnson, & DeLeonardis, 1998; Koutstaal, 2006), and in the exclusion condition of the process dissociation procedure (Davidson & Glisky, 2002). Neuropsychological measures of frontal lobe function are also known to predict source memory in older adults (Glisky & Kong, 2008; Glisky, Polster, & Routhieaux, 1995; Glisky, Rubin, & Davidson, 2001). By inference, then, a plausible source of difficulty in older adults' discrimination among similar items in false memory studies is impaired source memory, a notion that comports well with the activation-monitoring framework and with dual-process models of memory in general.

There are nonetheless some caveats that must be made with reference to the frontal lobe deficit model. Tests thought to tap medial-temporal lobe function also predict source memory in some studies (see Glisky & Kong, 2008, for a review), so the dissociation between frontal and medial-temporal lobe measures as predictors of source memory is not always clean. Moreover, Chan and McDermott (2007) found independent contributions of age and frontal lobe measures to performance on the DRM task, so that the story is more complex than portrayed by a simple frontal lobe deficit model. Furthermore, to the extent that recollection is dependent on retrieval of contextual or source information, one would predict that measures of frontal lobe function would be good predictors of estimates of recollection from the process-dissociation procedure, the *remember/know* task, and ROC fitting methods. This literature is, however, rather inconsistent across studies, and even when recollection is estimated by different techniques in the same individuals, patterns of correlations may not replicate across estimates (see Prull et al., 2006, for an example and for a review). Moreover, the frontal lobes are not the only brain structures involved in memory that are impacted in late adulthood, as can be seen, for example, in reports of linkages between various aspects of memory and brain volume measures for areas such as the hippocampus and entorhinal cortex (e.g., Yonelinas et al., 2007; see also Dennis & Cabeza, 2008).

Are Recollection Deficits in Older Adults Really Encoding Deficits?

The focus of dual-process models is on retrieval. However, it is highly unlikely that late adulthood deficits can be localized uniquely to retrieval processes. Naveh-Benjamin and his colleagues (e.g., Naveh-Benjamin, 2000; Naveh-Benjamin, Hussain, Guez, & Bar-On, 2003) have formulated an associative deficit hypothesis. According to their view, problems underlying age-related deficits in recall and recognition, including associative recognition, are due to difficulties in forming associations between items or between items and their contexts, pointing to an encoding locus for effects that we have been discussing in terms of retrieval. Li and her colleagues have provided evidence from simulations that less distinctive encoding of associations can account for a number of findings (Li, Naveh-Benjamin, & Lindenberger, 2005). For instance, Shing et al. (2008) suggest that less distinct encoding in older adults makes it more difficult to differentiate between studied pairs and rearranged lures in associative recognition. Moreover, on their account, suboptimal neuromodulation can lead to more highly activated, though less specific, representations, producing a pattern of increased false alarming with high confidence in late adulthood (Dodson, Bawa, & Krueger, 2007; Shing et al., 2008; Shing, Werkle-Bergner, Li, & Lindenberger, 2009).

FACTORS THAT CONTRIBUTE TO AGE-RELATED CHANGES IN PERFORMANCE

How can we understand the developmental changes in strategy deployment and effectiveness that have been outlined in our selective review of the literature? As already indicated, prior knowledge about the materials being remembered and the effort requirements of strategy utilization are linked clearly to both age-related changes in the deployment of mnemonic techniques and the patterns of context specificity that characterize the literature. We now turn to a brief treatment of several factors that may influence the differential use of strategies across the life span and serve as mediators of the observed age-related progression: (1) the metamnemonic understanding of children and adults, (2) the impact of context of remembering and the goals that are operative, and (3) the broader developmental context in which skills may be acquired and maintained.

Metamemory

What children and adults know about the operation of memory is likely to be quite important for the deployment of various techniques, as well as for developmental changes in the use of these strategies. In this section, we consider children's growing metamnemonic understanding and focus on the extent to which growth in this knowledge about remembering is associated with subsequent increases in strategy deployment. We also consider aspects of adults' metacognition, including the role of common stereotypes concerning cognitive loss during late adult development, and the extent to which these beliefs are linked to declines in strategy effectiveness.

Metamemory in Children

To illustrate the importance of children's understanding of the operation of memory, consider Corsale and Ornstein's (1980) demonstration (see earlier) that seventh but not fourth graders seemed to know what to do in the context of a sort-recall task when told to form groups that would help them remember. These seventh graders readily translated the remember-based instructions into sort-on-the-basis-of-meaning instructions, whereas the younger children did not, even though they had the basic semantic knowledge needed to form effective groups. What was missing was their understanding that this semantic knowledge could be used effectively when confronted with a memory goal. In short, the children who Corsale and Ornstein studied differed in terms of their metamemory, or their understanding of the operation of the memory system and the demands of various tasks that require remembering (Cavanaugh & Perlmutter, 1982; Flavell & Wellman, 1977; Schneider, 1985).

Metamemory as a construct and a field of investigation was introduced by Flavell (1971), who launched serious study of the topic in an early study in which first, third, and fifth graders were asked a series of questions about memory (Kreutzer, Leonard, & Flavell, 1975). The results indicated clearly that young children know relatively little about the conditions under which they remembered things or the types of materials that would be easy or difficult to remember. Flavell and Wellman (1977) then systematized the early study of metamemory by creating a taxonomy that distinguished between "sensitivity" and "variables," with the former dealing with knowledge that memory activity (e.g., the deployment of a strategy) is necessary in some settings, and the latter concerning understanding of person, task, and strategy factors that influence remembering. These distinctions between sensitivity and variables correspond to what has come to be called *procedural metacognitive knowledge* and *declarative metacognitive knowledge.*

Much research has focused on children's growing metacognitive knowledge, declarative ("knowing that" and "knowing why") and procedural ("knowing how"). Research on declarative metamemory has followed the lead of Kreutzer et al. (1975) in using interview studies (e.g., Schneider, Borkowski, Kurtz, & Kerwin, 1986; Yussen & Bird, 1979), although the use of nonverbal judgment tasks has also added to our understanding of children's developing knowledge concerning the types of strategies that may facilitate remembering (e.g., Justice, 1985, 1986).

Research on procedural metamemory has also proceeded apace, with explorations of developmental changes in self-monitoring (e.g., Borkowski, Milstead, & Hale, 1988). Particular attention has been given to the changing accuracy of children's Ease-of-Learning judgments (e.g., Pressley, Levin, Ghatala, & Ahmad, 1987; Schneider, Visé, Lockl, & Nelson, 2000; Visé & Schneider, 2000), Judgments of Learning (e.g., Koriat & Shitzer-Reichert, 2002; Schneider et al., 2000), and Feeling-of-Knowing judgments (DeLoache & Brown, 1984; Lockl & Schneider, 2002).

Procedural Metamemory

In terms of procedural metamemory, the available evidence suggests that even young children possess some rudimentary self-monitoring skills, and that these skills increase substantially across childhood and adolescence (Schneider, 2009). To illustrate, in contrast to the accurate Ease-of-Learning Judgments of children in the early elementary school years, those of kindergarten-aged children reveal a tendency to overestimate how well they will do at remembering information (e.g., Visé & Schneider, 2000). Interestingly, the errors of these young children do not necessarily reflect a total lack of understanding, but to some extent stem from both wishful thinking and beliefs that effort will result in enhanced performance (Schneider, 1998). In contrast to explorations of Ease-of-Learning judgments, there have been relatively few studies of children's Judgments of Learning after to-be-remembered material has been presented and studied. As expected, these investigations reveal age-related trends in the ability to monitor the progress of one's learning, but even so, young children evidence rudimentary monitoring skills, particularly when judgments are made after a delay interval (Schneider et al., 2000). Furthermore, children's Feeling-of-Knowing judgments also improve across childhood and adolescence, but as is the case with their Judgments of Learning, young children are more likely to overestimate their future ability to remember information than are older children and adults (Schneider & Lockl, 2008).

Linkages between Metamemory and Strategy Use

These developmental trends in children's abilities to monitor their performance are interesting, but important questions remain concerning the linkages among these skills and the use of control processes for remembering. For example, in contrast to evidence that young adults allocate study time on the basis of their metacognitive monitoring (e.g., Metcalfe, 2002; Nelson & Narens, 1990), relatively little is known about the about the ways in which children's

monitoring influences their behavior. To be sure, children aged 10 and older are able to devote more time to studying "hard" as opposed to "easy" items, and this ability to efficiently allocate study time increases with age (e.g., Lockl & Schneider, 2004). However, in these studies, the age-related trend was observed in study behavior and not in metacognition per se, as there were few differences in the ability to differentiate between "hard" and "easy" items. As such, what seems to be developing here is not so much metacognitive understanding but rather its application to strategies that involve self-regulation.

Much of the research on the development of metamemory has been motivated by an assumption that children's knowledge about memory influences their selection of specific strategies in tasks that require remembering (e.g., Brown, 1978). Indeed, to a considerable degree, Flavell (1971) was interested in metamemory as a partial determinant of production deficiencies in children's strategy usage. Given these assumptions about linkages between children's metamemory and strategy use, it is somewhat surprising that the correlational evidence has been quite mixed (Schneider, 1985; Schneider & Pressley, 1997). That is, these metamemory-strategy associations increase somewhat with age (e.g., Joyner & Kurtz-Costes, 1997) and vary as a function of methods of measurement (Best & Ornstein, 1986) and children's motivation (Schneider & Lockl, 2002), but they also tend to be relatively modest (e.g., Cavanaugh & Perlmutter, 1982).

Additional problems, moreover, have been noted in cases in which children are able to verbalize knowledge of a specific mnemonic technique but then fail to make use of it (Sodian, Schneider, & Perlmutter, 1986), and also in situations in which children use what might be viewed as a deliberate strategy but are unable to demonstrate any corresponding metamnemonic awareness (Bjorklund & Zeman, 1982). These difficulties notwithstanding, Schneider and Pressley (1997) reported a meta-analysis of 60 investigations in which they obtained a correlation of 0.41 between metamemory and strategy use. Nonetheless, interpretation of this finding is difficult because these correlations may reflect bidirectional linkages, with metamnemonic understanding influencing strategic behavior on the one hand, and strategic efforts leading to increases in understanding on the other (Borkowski, Carr, Rellinger, & Pressley, 1990; Kuhn, 1999; Schneider & Pressley, 1997).

Despite the mixed results of these correlational investigations, evidence consistent with the fundamental assumption of a linkage between children's metamnemonic understanding and their use of strategies for remembering comes from a series of short-term training studies (see Cox, Ornstein, & Valsiner, 1991). As discussed earlier, children can be instructed in the use of mnemonic techniques, with improvements in remembering being noted. However, the effectiveness of the instructional manipulation, particularly in terms of the extent to which transfer is observed in different contexts, varies markedly as a function of the degree to which strategy information is supplemented by the provision of metacognitive information (e.g., Paris, Newman, & McVey, 1982; Pressley, Ross, Levin, & Ghatala, 1984; Ringel & Springer, 1980). Indeed, as Cox et al. (1991) point out, the most effective instructional protocols were those in which the provision of metacognitively relevant information—about the value and effectiveness of the strategies being taught—was made a central feature of the instructional regimen.

These findings of the importance of metacognitive information for effective strategy maintenance and transfer prompt a number of basic developmental questions. The correlational studies summarized earlier for the most part have been focused on the issue of whether there are concurrent associations at any point in developmental time between children's metamnemonic understanding and their use of strategies. Notwithstanding the importance of concurrent linkages between metamemory and strategy deployment, perhaps a more significant developmental question concerns the extent to which children's metamnemonic understanding at any time (time t) is linked with more effective strategy use at a later time (time $t + 1$). The instructional literature, with its emphasis on transfer, focuses attention on this critical question. In this regard, it is important to note that in their microgenetic study, Schlagmüller and Schneider (2002) reported that children who acquired an organizational strategy over the course of the project showed increases in declarative metamemory well ahead of actually showing the strategy.

Metamemory and the Late Adult Development of Memory

Extending our treatment of children's growing metamnemonic understanding, we now consider three aspects of metamemory that have been examined in some depth across the adult life span: memory self-efficacy, stereotype threat, and monitoring and updating. The first and second of these topics have been relatively unexplored in children other than in at-risk populations but have been of considerable interest in the cognitive late adult development arena because of their potential to provide explanations of age differences in adult memory. In particular, it

has been hypothesized that older adults' culturally based beliefs about memory in late adult development and their concerns about perceived changes in their own mnemonic skills contribute to age-related declines in memory performance. Given this orientation, we first consider possible linkages between memory self-efficacy and stereotype threat and memory changes in later adulthood, and then address issues related to memory monitoring and updating.

Memory Self-Efficacy

Adults of all ages in Western cultures believe that there are negative consequences for memory during the late adult years. Moreover, older adults are more likely than young adults to believe that their memory is poor, that it has gotten (and will continue to get) worse over time, and that they have less control over their memory than they did when they were younger (Dixon & Hultsch, 1983; Gilewski, Zelinski, & Schaie, 1990; Lachman, Bandura, Weaver, & Elliott, 1995; for a review, see Lane & Zelinski, 2003). If older adults believe their ability to remember is poor, either because they have observed changes in their own performance over time or because they have internalized cultural stereotypes about cognition in late adulthood, they may set lower memory goals for themselves and reduce their efforts to remember (Berry, 1989; West, Welch, & Thorn, 2001). They then remember less, experience further feelings of reduced memory self-efficacy, try less hard to remember, and so on.

There is evidence for this set of propositions from both cross-sectional and longitudinal research. For instance, Lachman and Andreoletti (2006) found that a domain-specific measure of cognitive control beliefs was correlated with recall of a categorized word list in middle-aged and older adults, but not in young adults. Further, the association between control beliefs and recall was mediated by category clustering of words at recall, pinpointing the locus of the effect in greater use of strategies by those with higher control beliefs. Similar findings of the mediation of age-memory relations by self-referent beliefs about cognition have been reported by Jopp and Hertzog (2007) for paired-associate recall. Hertzog, McGuire, and Lineweaver (1998) found that people who claim to use strategies in a free recall task reported higher levels of control over their present memory performance. The negative relation between age and free recall, however, remained substantial after removing the effects of memory control beliefs and strategy use, and there was no direct relation between memory control and recall.

In longitudinal studies, the relation between memory self-efficacy and performance has been variable (see Lane & Zelinski, 2003, and McDonald-Misczak, Hertzog, & Hultsch, 1995, for discussions of these issues). Moreover, even when self-assessments of memory and performance both decline across measurement occasions, there are competing explanations for the covariation other than the influence of self-efficacy on memory. Changes in the assessment of memory could simply track performance changes, or changes in self-assessment could reflect implicit theories of memory change, whereas performance changes reflect actual memory decline.

Supplementing these studies of linkages between self-efficacy are experiments in which efforts have been made to change people's beliefs about their memory ability, with the hope of observing corresponding changes in memory performance. If negative expectations drive performance downward, increasing confidence in memory should improve recall, presumably by encouraging appropriate strategy use. To illustrate, Lachman, Weaver, Bandura, Elliot, and Lewkowicz (1992) assigned older adults to one of a number of training conditions that differed in the extent to which the focus was on cognitive restructuring or memory skills training. They found that participants' beliefs about memory ability and control were influenced by cognitive restructuring, and that people exposed to memory skills training were more likely than others to indicate that they were using new strategies. However, all groups showed equivalent performance increases from pretest to post-test, such that neither changes in memory self-efficacy nor reports of increased strategy use translated into differential gains in remembering.

Stereotype Threat

Steele (1997) has argued that negative stereotypes about a group may harm performance of group members when they perceive that their actions could confirm those stereotypes. Stereotype threat is hypothesized to have its effects by producing distraction, increasing anxiety, or lowering motivation, and to most affect individuals who identify strongly with the stereotyped domain. Several lines of research have now investigated these claims with respect to late adult development, accruing varying degrees of support.

One line of work compares young and older adults in cultures that have more or less negative stereotypes of late adult development. For example, Levy and Langer (1994) examined memory in younger and older samples of Chinese, deaf Americans, and hearing Americans, and found that the first two groups have more positive stereotypes of late adult development than the third. They also observed that there was no effect of culture on memory in young adults, but clear evidence that the older Chinese outperformed the two older American groups. Moreover, the age difference was not significant in the Chinese samples. Although this study provides support for the stereotype threat hypothesis, other reports have not fully replicated these results (e.g., Yoon, Hasher, Feinberg, Rahhal, & Winocur, 2000).

Another tack is to vary the instructions of the task so that memory per se is made more or less salient, under the assumption that stereotype threat is minimized when older adults do not expect a memory assessment. To illustrate, Rahhal, Hasher, and Colcombe (2001) tested younger and older adults under conditions that either explicitly mentioned a subsequent test of memory or de-emphasized memory. When a forthcoming memory assessment was not mentioned, the memory performance of younger and older adults was equivalent, whereas age differences were observed in the condition that emphasized remembering. A similar result was reported by Desrichard and Kopetz (2005), who found, in addition, that memory self-efficacy mediated age differences in planning a route for an imaginary shopping trip.

Other studies have involved manipulations in which positive or negative stereotypes of late adult development have been primed—sometimes with quite overt priming techniques, and other times with subliminal procedures—so as to examine the impact of priming on age differences in memory (e.g., Hess, Auman, Colcombe, & Rahhal, 2003; Hess, Hinson, & Statham, 2004; Levy & Leifheit-Limson, 2009). In general, these studies have shown that the priming of negative stereotypes results in degraded memory performance among older adults, with little effect being observed with young adults, consistent with the idea that only groups for whom poor memory is the stereotype should be influenced by priming. Positive priming has been observed as well, but not universally (e.g., see Hess et al., 2003). Support for the idea that stereotype threat has its strongest impact on individuals who identify with the threatened domain (here memory) has also been obtained (Hess et al., 2003; but see Hess et al., 2004, for a different outcome). There is also evidence that stereotype priming effects are mediated by strategy use inasmuch as older adults who invest greater value in their memory abilities show reduced clustering when given negative primes (Hess et al., 2003).

Memory Monitoring and Updating

Although it might be expected that lower self-efficacy for memory or reduced processing resources would reduce older adults' accuracy in estimating how much they will remember (prediction) or have remembered (postdiction), how they might allocate attention to strategies that could improve performance, and how much they modify their encoding and retrieval strategies based on recent experience (updating), the evidence on these points is inconsistent. For example, older adults seem to be as good as younger adults in accessing feelings of knowing (e.g., Butterfield, Nelson, & Peck, 1988; Marquie & Huet, 2000). Moreover, younger and older adults differ little in their ability to predict how much they will be able to remember, either when asked on an item-by-item basis as items are studied (or shortly thereafter), or in postdicting the correctness of responses after they have been made (e.g., Devolder, Brigham, & Pressley, 1990; Rabinowitz, Ackerman, Craik, & Hinchley, 1982; see Hertzog and Dunlosky, 2004, for a review). In addition, older adults, like younger adults, may use cues from the task they are performing—such as item relatedness (Hertzog, Kidder, Dunlosky, & Powell-Moman, 2002; Robinson, Hertzog, & Dunlosky, 2006) or text coherence (Dunlosky, Baker, Hertzog, & Rawson, 2006)—to inform their Judgments of Learning.

These studies suggest that monitoring is relatively spared in late adulthood, but there is also evidence to the contrary. For instance, when adults are asked to indicate whether memories for particular items are based on the retrieval of specific details of the experiences under which they were studied (*remember* judgments) or whether the test items "just feel familiar," Judgments of Learning correlate more strongly with memory for items given *remember* responses than for items judged to be *familiar,* but the difference between the remember and familiar response correlations is smaller for older than for younger adults (Daniels, Toth, & Hertzog, 2009). This result is compatible with the idea that the mapping of subjective experiences of remembering onto actual memories is less accurate in older than in younger adults. As another example, individuals across adulthood may be equally good at predicting recall in paired-associate learning, but older adults appear to be less adept than younger ones in using this knowledge to allocate more study time to less well-learned pairs on subsequent trials (Dunlosky & Connor, 1997). In addition, updating processes also become less proficient with increasing age in adulthood. After exposure to encoding strategies or retrieval cues that vary in

effectiveness, older adults are less likely to modify their predictions about the relative effectiveness of strategies or their assessments of the relative utilities of these strategies, or both (e.g., Bieman-Copland & Charness, 1994; Brigham & Pressley, 1988; Matvey, Dunlosky, Shaw, Parks, & Hertzog, 2002).

Older adults also lag behind younger adults in strategically regulating the accuracy of their memory reports and are less likely to shift to a more conservative output criterion when the payoff matrix leads to greater negative consequences for incorrect reports (e.g., Kelley & Sahakian, 2003; Rhodes & Kelley, 2005; Pansky, Goldsmith, Koriat, & Pearlman-Avnion, 2009). Moreover, they are more prone than younger adults to making false recollection errors (i.e., giving *remember* judgments to unstudied but highly related lures) when recalling lists of words (Skinner & Fernandes, 2009) and in associative recognition (Van Ocker, Light, Olfman, & Rivera, 2009), and to giving higher confidence ratings in incorrect answers in various other tasks (e. g., Dodson et al., 2007; Shing et al., 2008). These are all clear signs of failures in monitoring.

Context Effects and Goals

As discussed earlier in our treatment of children's use of strategies, variations in the to-be-remembered materials, the instructions, the effort demands of the task, and so forth, can influence dramatically children's performance and hence the "diagnoses" that we make of their abilities. The performance of young children thus reflects a considerable degree of context specificity (Ornstein & Myers, 1996). We turn now to a broader treatment of context, focusing on the settings in which researchers make assessments of the mnemonic skills of the individuals who take part in their studies. As such, we discuss the extent to which the laboratory setting per se, in contrast to "everyday" contexts, makes a difference in the performance of children and older adults. We also focus on potential differences between the (memory) goals of researchers and those of the children and adults they study.

To begin, consider that, in laboratory studies of memory, researchers set the goals for participants, or at least attempt to do so. The chief of these goals is typically to reproduce verbatim what has been presented for study. In everyday life, however, memory goals are likely to be multifarious, and what is remembered will, at least to some extent, be conditioned by the short- and long-term goals of the individual (Conway & Pleydell-Pearce, 2000). Cohen (1998) has identified three categories of memory functions: (1) knowledge-based—construction of general knowledge from particular experiences and problem solving; (2) interpersonal—namely, social interaction, self-disclosure in the service of establishing and maintaining intimacy, and empathy; and (3) intrapersonal—mood regulation and self-concept formation. Moreover, the contents of memories reported in social settings depend on the perspective and goals of the narrator and the intended audience (Pasupathi, 2001). For instance, college students' narratives contained fewer sensory details and more references to affect when instructed to retell a story to be entertaining than when asked to focus on accuracy (Dudukovic, Marsh, & Tversky, 2004).

What is the relevance of this for late adult development? In an influential chapter, Hasher and Zacks (1988) noted that researchers may have ignored the extent to which older adults give increased importance to personal values and experience in determining what is reported, and may be more intent on telling a good story than on reproducing exact details of their experiences. Thus, the goals of older persons and those of memory researchers may be at odds in the typical laboratory setting in which memory abilities are assessed (see Istomina, 1975, for a similar view with regard to children's memory). For instance, there is evidence that young and older adults differ in pragmatic aspects of discourse, placing greater value on meaningful interpretation of past events rather than concise factual descriptions. Older adults perform less well than younger adults when asked to recall literal propositional content of narratives, but when asked to interpret stories they have read, they generate more elaborated, integrative, symbolically rich responses than do younger adults (Adams, Smith, Nyquist, & Perlmutter, 1997). Adams, Smith, Pasupathi, and Vitolo (2002) also found that older adults reported less information from a story than younger adults when the listener was an experimenter, but not when the listener was a child who might be presumed to need more specifics. Interestingly, Best and Ornstein (1986) found a similar result in that third graders evidenced more metacognitive knowledge when they had to provide instructions to first graders in how to carry out a memory task than when assessed in a standard metamemory interview with an adult experimenter. In this context, it is interesting that discourse produced by older adults is rated at least as highly (and sometimes more highly) than that of young adults for story quality, interest, clarity, and informativeness (James, Burke, Austin, & Hulme, 1999; Kemper, Rash, Kynette, & Norman, 1990; Pratt & Robins, 1991).

A consideration of shifts in the goals of older adults from acquiring new information to focusing on social and emotional aspects of their lives may also help to explain the results of a series of studies by Hashtroudi, Johnson and their colleagues. To illustrate, Hashtroudi, Johnson, and Chrosniak (1990) found that when describing perceived (enacted) and imagined scenarios such as packing a picnic basket or visiting a seminar room, older adults reported more thoughts and feelings and evaluative statements, and fewer perceptual and spatial details than younger adults. These findings seem in keeping with a shift with age in interpretive focus to personal value systems and feelings. To explore this idea, Hashtroudi, Johnson, Vnek, and Ferguson (1994) had younger and older adults engage in an interactive simulated situation—a short play—and then talk about and rehearse the factual or affective aspects of the play, or talk about the play in whatever ways they preferred. Older adults' source memory was impaired in the affective and control conditions, relative to younger adults, but an emphasis on facts reduced age differences in source memory. Notably, the affective focus reduced recall for both age groups and increased the likelihood that older adults would inject nonpresented elaborative information (thoughts, feelings, evaluations, incorrect details) into their reports. Overall, then, the evidence suggests that interpretive focus may vary with age and influence the balance of verbatim and elaborative information generated by younger and older adults.

These results are consistent with the predictions of socioemotional selectivity theory proposed by Carstensen and her colleagues (e.g., Carstensen, Isaacowitz, & Charles, 1999; Carstensen & Mikels, 2005; Carstensen, Mikels, & Mather, 2006). On their view, with increasing age (or in any context in which people perceive that the time left in life is relatively short) there is a shift in goals from acquiring novel information to emotion regulation. Because selective cognitive processing is a component of effective emotion regulation, older adults are likely to devote their attention and memory capacity to positive information that will enhance their current mood (Carstensen et al., 2006). Indeed, the use of memory to support emotional regulation goals in older adults is limited by declines in cognitive control processes. For instance, older adults who do well on tasks that involve cognitive control (e.g., executive function, working memory) have greater positivity effects (i.e., higher proportions of their recall that are positive than negative), whereas those with lower cognitive control scores and younger adults in general have greater negativity effects (Mather & Knight, 2005). Moreover, with divided attention at encoding, older adults' positivity effect is abolished (Knight et al., 2007; Mather & Knight, 2005).

Before leaving this topic, we should note that findings with respect to positivity and negativity effects have not been altogether consistent across emotional memory studies—or, indeed, within studies (e.g., Carstensen & Turk-Charles, 1994; Charles, Mather, & Carstensen, 2003; see Murphy & Isaacowitz, 2008, for a meta-analysis). Moreover, there is some controversy as to whether age differences in positivity and negativity effects are due to differences in ability to discriminate between different types of old and new information (sensitivity) or to differences in bias to respond *old* to test materials with particular emotional valences (e.g., Kapucu, Rotello, Ready, & Seidl, 2008; Thapar & Rouder, 2009). Thus, our understanding of the extent and nature of differences in the emotional contents of memory in adults of different ages is incomplete.

Developmental Context

Although the bulk of evidence presented in this chapter suggests that the deployment of deliberate strategies for remembering facilitates the storage and retrieval of information, relatively little is known about the contextual factors that are associated with the emergence of these mnemonic techniques. Yet these skills typically develop in the context of social settings, such as school, in which remembering is both expected and valued (Cole, 1992; Rogoff & Mistry, 1990; Wagner, 1981). As such, it seems likely that aspects of the elementary school classroom may serve to mediate developmental changes in children's skills for remembering. Moreover, if exposure to the demands of formal schooling is associated with the emergence and refinement of skills for remembering, it is possible that continued exposure to school-like environments would serve to maintain memory skills across the life span. Indeed, the use-it-or-lose-it hypothesis (Salthouse, 2006) predicts that people who continue to be engaged in intellectually demanding professional activities, or who are experts in various domains, should continue to have memory demands in those domains and, therefore, should show little or no decline in memory, at least for domain-relevant materials. A related perspective is reflected in the view that continued participation in intellectually stimulating activities should help to maintain or enhance cognitive function in normal late adult development (Havighurst, Neugarten, & Tobin, 1968; Rowe & Kahn, 1997).

Schooling

A number of lines of evidence lead to the inference that formal schooling may contribute to the development of children's increasing skill in the use of memory strategies. Consider first comparative-cultural investigations in which researchers contrasted the performance of children matched in chronological age but who differed in terms of whether they had or had not participated in Western-style schooling. In studies conducted in Liberia (e.g., Scribner & Cole, 1978), Mexico (e.g., Rogoff, 1981), and Morocco (e.g., Wagner, 1978), children who attended school demonstrated superiority in the types of mnemonic skills that have typically been studied by Western psychologists and anthropologists. Rogoff, for example, reported that non-schooled children generally do not make use of organizational techniques for remembering unrelated items, and that school seemed necessary for the acquisition of these skills. These findings suggest that something in the formal school context is most likely related to the emergence of skills that are important for success on tasks that involve deliberate memorization.

To explore these issues, Ornstein, Grammer, and Coffman (2010) have carried out a series of studies to characterize memory-relevant behaviors that teachers use that may support children's deliberate memory skills. Some of their findings are consistent with Moely, Hart, Leal, Santulli, Rao, Johnson, and Hamilton's (1992) report that it is rare to find explicit instruction in mnemonic techniques by teachers throughout the elementary school grades.

However, even though mnemonic strategies are not generally taught in an explicit fashion, Coffman, Ornstein, McCall, and Curran (2008) have observed that first-grade teachers employed a considerable amount of "memory talk" in the course of their whole-class instruction. For example, even though the teachers rarely informed their students that remembering was an expressed goal, they nonetheless often required the active use of memory in the context of teaching language arts and mathematics. Indeed, they found that memory seems to permeate the classroom environment, with teachers frequently making direct or indirect requests of their students to recall information from memory. In addition, Coffman et al. observed that teachers also made strategy suggestions and posed metacognitive questions.

Coffman et al. (2008) also noticed that there was considerable variability across teachers in the extent to which they made use of this type of "memory talk" in the course of their instruction, and this variability enabled the measurement of the teachers' *mnemonic style* and the identification of two distinct groups of teachers that were high and low in their orientation. Moreover, children in first-grade classes taught by the *high mnemonic* teachers evidenced a greater facility in the use of strategies for remembering than did children in the classes of *low mnemonic* teachers. It is also the case that substantial long-term effects of mnemonic style can be seen in later years when the children are taught by other teachers. For example, teachers' mnemonic style in the first grade is linked to the children's organized sorting patterns and study skills on more difficult tasks (sorting: Bjorklund et al., 1977; studying: Brown & Smiley, 1977) administered in the fourth grade (Ornstein, Haden, & Coffman, in press). These findings that aspects of the language used by teachers may be relevant for the emergence and refinement of mnemonic skills is consistent with the research discussed earlier that suggests that "parent talk" about events can impact preschoolers' developing abilities to talk about events that they have experienced in the past (e.g., Boland et al., 2003; Reese et al., 1993).

Disuse, Expertise, and Engagement

Returning to the presumed protective effects of expertise, as we have discussed earlier, a considerable amount of research has been carried out in which young and older adults who are experts in selected areas are compared on a variety of memory tasks. As we have also stressed, prior knowledge in specific areas can influence all aspects of the processing of information drawn from those domains, from the encoding and storage through subsequent retrieval. The facilitative effects of knowledge are certainly consistent with the view that expertise should have a protective effect on memory performance across the life span, but the typical finding is that when younger and older experts in specific areas are compared, substantial differences in performance remain (see Salthouse, 1991, 2006, for reviews). Indeed, even within academic settings in which demands on memory might be expected to be prominent in the daily lives of academics throughout their careers, age differences in memory tasks are generally observed (Shimamura, Berry, Mangels, Rusting, & Jurica, 1995).

We should also point out that these studies of expertise among young and older adults may not be altogether relevant for a consideration of the types of mnemonic strategies emphasized in this chapter. Little work has been carried out on the role of domain-specific expertise in promoting the maintenance of verbally based strategies such

as organization and rehearsal, but there is one study in which researchers focused on the method of loci, a classical mnemonic technique that requires the use of visual imagery. In this investigation, Lindenberger, Kliegl, and Baltes (1992) contrasted the performance of young and older graphic designers, reasoning that the field of graphic design places a great deal of emphasis on visual skills, and thus that age differences in performance would be eliminated on a task involving the method of loci; the data were inconsistent with the use-it-or-lose-it hypothesis, as the younger experts outperformed their older counterparts.

We turn now to work on the possible role of active engagement in intellectually stimulating everyday activities in reducing memory declines found in the late adult years. The intriguing nature of this idea notwithstanding, the evidence for it is decidedly mixed. For instance, Salthouse, Berish, and Miles (2002) examined the relation between cognitive stimulation and cognitive performance in a sample of 204 individuals ranging from 20 to 91 years of age. The activity index included activities that ranged in cognitive demand from teaching or attending class, working on crossword puzzles, and handling finances down to gardening, doing housework, and watching television, whereas the memory composite included story recall, list recall, and paired-associate recall. There was no evidence that the strength of the age-memory association was mediated or moderated by activity level, as would be predicted by the use-it-or-lose-it hypothesis. A similar failure of age to moderate the linkage between age and cognition, including memory, has been reported by Jopp and Hertzog (2007). These authors, however, presented evidence that engaging in an active lifestyle may nonetheless benefit cognition in late adulthood by increasing overall performance even in the absence of moderation effects. There have also been suggestive findings that the risk for cognitive decline or dementia is reduced for people who engage in cognitive activities (for a review that systematically assesses rival hypotheses about the nature of this association, see Hertzog et al., 2009).

Evaluating the contribution of active lifestyles to the preservation of memory in older adults is complicated by the fact that determining the directionality of effects is not always straightforward. That is, rather than intellectually stimulating mental life supporting memory performance, it is possible that older adults who engage in intellectually stimulating activities have better preserved cognitive abilities, including memory (e.g., see Bosma et al., 2002; Hultsch, Hertzog, Small, & Dixon, 1999; Schooler & Mulatu, 2001; Schooler, Mulatu, & Oates, 1999). It seems quite plausible that there could be a reciprocal relation between engaged lifestyle and cognition. Of course, the way to establish causal linkages between lifestyle variables and cognition is through interventions in which an experimental group receives enrichment in the form of intellectually stimulating activities, whereas a control group does not. Research in this area is potentially promising, but at this point in time, the extant data do not permit us to draw firm conclusions about the generality of effects or the type and intensity of activities that are necessary for the promotion of better memory in older adults (e.g., see Carlson et al., 2008; Smith et al., 2009).

Overview

In our treatment of factors that may influence strategy development, we have emphasized linkages between metamnemonic understanding and memory performance, and the importance of considering the assessment context and the goals that are operative in our diagnoses of the memory skills of children and adults. Although much remains to be learned about these topics, the basic questions are being asked by researchers. In contrast, we have devoted less attention to explorations of the developmental context in which memory skills are acquired and maintained. To some extent, this is because not a great deal of research has been devoted to these issues, and some of that which has been conducted does not speak directly to questions of strategy development. For example, although we now have suggestive evidence concerning the importance of the elementary school classroom for the emergence of verbally based strategies for remembering, additional research— both observational and experimental—is clearly needed. Moreover, the extant research on expertise and lifestyle as factors that may serve to maintain strategies in adulthood does strongly support a view of the importance of these key aspects of the context. Clearly, additional research needs to be carried out on those settings across the life span that serve to maintain the strategies that are acquired in childhood and adolescence.

CONCLUSIONS

The research summarized here indicates that much has been learned in recent years about the development of memory across the life span, but also that there are many gaps in our understanding. We have focused our efforts on the deliberate memory skills in children and older adults

largely because developmentalists working with these age groups have devoted a great deal of attention to the development of memory strategies. We were motivated to attempt this integration, in part, because both cognitive developmentalists and cognitive psychologists interested in memory in older adults differentiate between explicit and implicit forms of remembering, and emphasize the key roles of capacity and underlying knowledge in their accounts of memory. However, in doing so, we are conscious of the limitations of our efforts at integration.

By constructing an overview of deliberate memory skills in children and older adults, we recognize that we have not been able to discuss other important features of memory, including the development of autobiographical memory, semantic memory, and implicit memory. Nor have we been able to provide coverage of developmental changes in the neurobiological systems that subserve memory or of pathological changes in these systems that lead to Alzheimer's disease and other dementias of late adulthood. Moreover, as indicated at the outset, we also recognize that we have had to *construct* an integrated overview, at times literally forcing studies together that represent work carried out in different research traditions. In doing so, we are conscious of the limitations of the largely cross-sectional literatures that provide much of the foundation for our integration. In general, the age groups represented in the different studies do not "line up" adequately to provide a truly life-span account, though cross-sectional studies do not in any case make claims about development within individuals.

These limitations notwithstanding, our hope is that this chapter will encourage further collaborations between students of cognition in child and adult development that, in turn, will lead to integrated investigations of memory across the life span. By capitalizing on the insights of these two research traditions, we hope that such collaborations will spark research that increases our understanding of the skills of children and adults of different ages, and of the factors that contribute to the developmental trends that are observed.

REFERENCES

Ackerman, B. P. (1985). Constraints on retrieval search for episodic information in children and adults. *Journal of Experimental Child Psychology, 40,* 152–180.

Ackerman, B. P. (1986). Differences in the associative constraint on retrieval search from a context cue for children and adults. *Journal of Experimental Child Psychology, 42,* 315–344.

Ackerman, P. L. (2008). Knowledge and cognitive aging. In F. I. M. Craik & T. A. Salthouse (Eds.), *The handbook of aging and cognition* (3rd ed., pp. 445–489). New York: Psychology Press.

Adams, C., Smith, M. C., Nyquist, L., & Perlmutter, M. (1997). Adult age-group differences in recall for the literal and interpretive meanings of narrative text. *Journal of Gerontology: Psychological Sciences, 52B,* 187–195.

Adams, C., Smith, M. C., Pasupathi, M., & Vitolo, L. (2002). Social context effects on story recall in older and younger women: Does the listener make a difference? *Journal of Gerontology: Psychological Sciences, 57B,* P28–P40.

Anderson, N. D., Craik, F. I. M., & Naveh-Benjamin, M. (1998). The attentional demands of encoding and retrieval in younger and older adults: Evidence from divided attention costs. *Psychology and Aging, 13,* 405–423.

Anooshian, L. J. (1999). Understanding age differences in memory: Disentangling conscious and unconscious processes. *International Journal of Behavioral Development, 23,* 1–18.

Atkinson, R. C., & Shiffrin, R. M. (1968). Human memory: A proposed system and its control processes. In K. W. Spence & J. T. Spence (Eds.), *The psychology of learning and motivation* (Vol. 2, pp. 89-195). New York: Academic.

Bahrick, L. E., & Pickens, J. N. (1995). Infant memory for object motion across a period of three months: Implications for a four-phase attention function. *Journal of Experimental Child Psychology, 59,* 343–371.

Baker-Ward, L., Gordon, B. N., Ornstein, P. A., Larus, D. M., & Clubb, P. A. (1993). Young children's long-term retention of a pediatric examination. *Child Development, 64,* 1519–1533.

Baker-Ward, L., Ornstein, P. A., & Holden, D. J. (1984). The expression of memorization in early childhood. *Journal of Experimental Child Psychology, 37,* 555–575.

Balota, D. A., Cortese, M. J., Duchek, J. M., Adams, D., Roediger III, H. L., McDermott, K. B., et al. (1999). Veridical and false memories in healthy older adults and in dementia of the Alzheimer's type. *Cognitive Neuropsychology, 16,* 361–384.

Baltes, P. B., & Kliegl, R. (1992). Further testing of limits of cognitive plasticity: Negative age differences in a mnemonic skill are robust. *Developmental Psychology, 28,* 121–125.

Baltes, P. B., Lindenberger, U., & Staudinger, U. M. (1998). Life-span theory in developmental psychology. In W. Damon & R. M. Lerner (Eds.), *Handbook of child psychology: Vol. 1, Theoretical models of human development* (5th ed., pp. 1029–1143). New York: John Wiley & Sons.

Bauer, P. J. (2006). Event memory. In D. Kuhn, R. S. Siegler, W. Damon, & R. M. Lerner (Eds.), *Handbook of child psychology: Vol. 2, Cognition, perception, and language* (6th ed., pp. 373–425). Hoboken, NJ: John Wiley & Sons.

Bauer, P. J. (2007). *Remembering the times of our lives: Memory in infancy and beyond.* Mahwah, NJ: Erlbaum.

Bauer, P. J., Wenner, J. A., Dropik, P. L., & Wewerka, S. S. (2000). Parameters of remembering and forgetting in the transition from infancy to early childhood. *Monographs of the Society for Research in Child Development, 65* (4, Serial No. 263).

Benjamin, A. S. (2001). On the dual effects of repetition on false recognition. *Journal of Experimental Psychology: Learning, Memory, and Cognition, 27,* 941–947.

Berry, J. M. (1989). Cognitive efficacy across the life span: Introduction to the special series. *Developmental Psychology, 25,* 683–686.

Best, D. L., & Ornstein, P. A. (1986). Children's generation and communication of mnemonic organizational strategies. *Developmental Psychology, 22,* 845–853.

Bialystok, E., & Craik, F. I. M. (Eds.). (2006). *Lifespan cognition: Mechanisms of change.* New York: Oxford University Press.

Bieman-Copland, S., & Charness, N. (1994). Memory knowledge and memory monitoring in adulthood. *Psychology and Aging, 9,* 287–302.

Billingsley, R. L., Smith, M. L., & McAndrews, M. P. (2002). Developmental patterns in priming and familiarity in explicit recognition. *Journal of Experimental Child Psychology, 82,* 251–277.

Bissig, D., & Lustig, C. (2007). Who benefits from psychological training? *Psychological Science, 18,* 720–726.

Bjorklund, D. F. (1985). The role of conceptual knowledge in the development of organization in children's memory. In C. J. Brainerd & M. Pressley (Eds.), *Basic processes in memory development: Progress in cognitive development research* (pp. 103–142). New York: Springer-Verlag.

Bjorklund, D. F. (1987). How age changes in knowledge base contribute to development of children's memory: An interpretive review. *Developmental Review, 7,* 93–130.

Bjorklund, D. F., & Coyle, T. R. (1995). Utilization deficiencies in the development of memory strategies. In F. E. Weinert & W. Schneider (Eds.), *Memory performance and competencies: Issues of growth and development* (pp. 161–180). Mahwah, NJ: Erlbaum.

Bjorklund, D. F., Dukes, C., & Brown, R. D. (2009). The development of memory strategies. In M. Courage & N. Cowan (Eds.), *The development of memory in infancy and childhood* (pp. 145–175). Hove East Sussex, United Kingdom: Psychology Press.

Bjorklund, D. F., & Harnishfeger, K. K. (1987). Developmental differences in the mental effort requirements for the use of an organizational strategy in free recall. *Journal of Experimental Child Psychology, 44,* 109–125.

Bjorklund, D. F., & Harnishfeger, K. K. (1990). The resources construct in cognitive development: Diverse sources of evidence and a theory of inefficient inhibition. *Developmental Review, 10,* 48–71.

Bjorklund, D. F., Miller, P. H., Coyle, T. R., & Slawinski, J. L. (1997). Instructing children to use memory strategies: Evidence of utilization deficiencies in memory training studies. *Developmental Review, 17,* 411–441.

Bjorklund, D. F., Ornstein, P. A., & Haig, J. R. (1977). Developmental differences in organization and recall: Training in the use of organizational techniques. *Developmental Psychology, 13,* 175–183.

Bjorklund, D. F., & Zeman, B. R. (1982). Children's organization and metamemory awareness in the recall of familiar information. *Child Development, 53,* 799–810.

Boland, A. M., Haden, C. A., & Ornstein, P. A. (2003). Boosting children's memory by training mothers in the use of an elaborative conversational style as an event unfolds. *Journal of Cognition and Development, 4,* 39–65.

Bopp, K. L., & Verhaeghen, P. (2005). Aging and verbal memory span: A meta-analysis. *Journal of Gerontology: Psychological Sciences, 60,* 223–233.

Borkowski, J. G., Carr, M., Rellinger, E., & Pressley, M. (1990). Self-regulated cognition: Interdependence of metacognition, attributions, and self-esteem. In B. F. Jones & L. Idol (Eds.), *Dimensions of thinking and cognitive instruction* (pp. 53–92). Hillsdale, NJ: Erlbaum.

Borkowski, J. G., Milstead, M., & Hale, C. (1988). Components of children's metamemory: Implications for strategy generalization. In F. E. Weinert & M. Perlmutter (Eds.), *Memory development: Universal changes and individual differences* (pp. 73–100). Hillsdale, NJ: Erlbaum.

Bosma, H., van Boxtel, M. P., Ponds, R. W., Jelicic, M., Houx, P., Metsemakers, J., et al. (2002). Engaged lifestyle and cognitive function in middle and old-aged, non-demented persons: A reciprocal association? *Zeitschrift für Gerontologie und Geriatrie, 35,* 575–581.

Bousfield, W. A. (1953). The occurrence of clustering in the recall of randomly arranged associates. *Journal of General Psychology, 49,* 229–240.

Bowles, R. P., & Salthouse, T. A. (2008). Vocabulary test format and differential relations to age. *Psychology and Aging, 23,* 366–377.

Brainerd, C. J., Holliday, R. E., & Reyna, V. F. (2004). Behavioral measurement of remembering phenomenologies: So simple a child can do it. *Child Development, 75,* 505–522.

Brainerd, C., & Reyna, V. F. (1995). Fuzzy-Trace Theory: An interim synthesis. *Learning and Individual Differences, 7,* 1–75.

Brainerd, C. J., & Reyna, V. F. (2005). *The science of false memory.* New York: Oxford University Press.

Brainerd, C. J., & Reyna, V. F. (2007). Explaining developmental reversals in false memory. *Psychological Science, 18,* 442–448.

Brainerd, C. J., Reyna, V. F., & Ceci, S. J. (2008). Developmental reversals in false memory: A review of data and theory. *Psychological Bulletin, 134,* 343–382.

Brainerd, C. J., Reyna, V. F., & Forrest, T. J. (2002). Are young children susceptible to the false-memory illusion? *Child Development, 73,* 1363–1377.

Brainerd, C. J., Reyna, V. F., Howe, M. L., & Kingma, J. (1990). The development of forgetting and reminiscence. *Monographs of the Society for Research in Child Development, 55*(3–4), 1–109.

Brainerd, C. J., Reyna, V. F., & Kneer, R. (1995). False-recognition reversal: When similarity is distinctive. *Journal of Memory and Language, 34,* 157–185.

Brainerd, C. J., Reyna, V. F., & Mojardin, A. H. (1999). Conjoint recognition. *Psychological Review, 106,* 160–170.

Braver, T. S., & West, R. (2008). Working memory, executive control, and aging. In F. I. M. Craik & T. A. Salthouse (Eds.), *The handbook of aging and cognition* (3rd ed., pp. 311–372). New York: Psychology Press.

Brehmer, Y., Li, S.-C., Muller, V., von Oertzen, T., & Lindenberger, U. (2007). Memory plasticity across the life span: Uncovering children's latent potential. *Developmental Psychology, 43,* 465–478.

Brewer, W. F., & Nakamura, G. V. (1984). The nature and functions of schemas. In R. S. Wyer & T. K. Srull (Eds.), *Handbook of social cognition* (Vol. 1, pp. 119–160). Hillsdale, NJ: Erlbaum.

Brigham, M. C., & Pressley, M. (1988). Cognitive monitoring and strategy choice in younger and older adults. *Psychology and Aging, 3,* 249–257.

Brown, A., Bransford, J., Ferrara, R., & Campione, J. (1983). Learning, remembering, and understanding. In P. H. Mussen, J. H. Flavell, & E. M. Markman (Eds.), *Handbook of child psychology: Vol. 3, Cognitive development* (4th ed., pp. 77–166). New York: John Wiley & Sons.

Brown, A. L. (1978). Knowing when, where, and how to remember: A problem of metacognition. In R. Glaser (Ed.), *Advances in instructional psychology* (Vol. 1, pp. 77–165). Hillsdale, NJ: Erlbaum.

Brown, A., & DeLoache, J. S. (1978). Skills, plans, and self-regulation. In R. Siegler (Ed.), *Children's thinking: What develops?* (pp. 3–35). Hillsdale, NJ: Erlbaum.

Brown, A. L., & Smiley, S. S. (1977). The importance of structural units of prose passages: A problem in metacognitive development. *Child Development, 48,* 1–8.

Buchler, N. G., Faunce, P., Light, L. L., Reder, L. M., & Gottfredson, N. (2009). *Associative memory deficits in old age: Dissociating the dual-process contributions of recognition and familiarity.* Manuscript in preparation.

Burke, D. M., & Light, L. L. (1981). Memory and aging: The role of retrieval processes. *Psychological Bulletin, 90,* 513–546.

Butler, K. M., McDaniel, M., Dornburg, C. C., Price, A. L., & Roediger III, H. L. (2004). Age differences in veridical and false recall are not inevitable: The role of frontal lobe functioning. *Psychonomic Bulletin & Review, 11,* 921–925.

Butterfield, E. C., Nelson, T. O., & Peck, V. (1988). Developmental aspects of the feeling of knowing. *Developmental Psychology, 24,* 654–663.

Carlson, N. E., Moore, M. M., Dame, A., Howieson, D., Silbert, L. C., Quinn, J. F., et al. (2008). Trajectories of brain loss in aging and the development of cognitive impairment. *Neurology, 70,* 828–833.

Carstensen, L. L., Isaacowitz, D. M., & Charles, S. T. (1999). Taking time seriously: A theory of socioemotional selectivity. *American Psychologist, 54,* 165–181.

Carstensen, L. L., & Mikels, J. A. (2005). At the intersection of emotion and cognition: Aging and the positivity effect. *Current Directions in Psychological Science, 14,* 117–121.

Carstensen, L. L., Mikels, J. A., & Mather, M. (2006). Aging and the intersection of cognition, motivation, and emotion. In J. E. Birren & K. W. Schaie (Eds.), *Handbook of the psychology of aging* (6th ed., pp. 343–362). Amsterdam: Elsevier.

Carstensen, L. L., & Turk-Charles, S. (1994). The salience of emotion across the adult life span. *Psychology and Aging, 9,* 259–264.

Case, R. (1985). *Intellectual development: Birth to adulthood.* New York: Academic.

Cavanaugh, J. C., & Perlmutter, M. (1982). Metamemory: A critical examination. *Child Development, 53,* 11–28.

Ceci, S. J., & Bruck, M. (1995). *Jeopardy in the courtroom: A scientific analysis of children's testimony.* Washington, DC: American Psychological Association.

Chan, J. C. K., & McDermott, K. B. (2007). The effects of frontal lobe functioning and age on veridical and false recall. *Psychonomic Bulletin & Review, 14,* 606–611.

Charles, S. T., Mather, M., & Carstensen, L. L. (2003). Aging and emotional memory: The forgettable nature of negative images for older adults. *Journal of Experimental Psychology: General, 132,* 310–324.

Charness, N. (1981). Search in chess: Age and skill differences. *Journal of Experimental Psychology: Human Perception and Performance, 7,* 467–476.

Chi, M. T. H. (1978). Knowledge structures and memory development. In R. Siegler (Ed.), *Children's thinking: What develops?* (pp. 73–96). Hillsdale, NJ: Erlbaum.

Chung, C., & Light, L. L. (2009). Effects of age and study repetition on plurality discrimination. *Aging, Neuropsychology, and Cognition, 16,* 446–460.

Coffman, J. L., Ornstein, P. A., McCall, L. E., & Curran, P. J. (2008). Linking teachers' memory-relevant language and the development of children's memory skills. *Developmental Psychobiology, 44,* 1640–1654.

Cohen, G. (1998). The effects of aging on autobiographical memory. In C. P. Thompson, D. J. Herrmann, D. Bruce Darryl, J. D. Read, D. G. Payne, & M. P. Toglia (Eds.), *Autobiographical memory: Theoretical and applied perspectives* (pp. 105–123). Mahwah, NJ: Erlbaum.

Cohn, M., Emrich, S. M., & Moscovitch, M. (2008). Age-related deficits in associative memory: The influence of impaired strategic retrieval. *Psychology and Aging, 23,* 93–103.

Cole, M. (1992). Cognitive development and formal schooling: The evidence from cross-cultural research. In L. C. Moll (Ed.), *Vygotsky and education: Instructional implications and applications of sociohistorical psychology* (pp. 89–110). New York: Cambridge University Press.

Cole, M., Frankel, F., & Sharp, D. (1971). Development of free recall learning in children. *Developmental Psychology, 4,* 109–123.

Conway, M. A., & Pleydell-Pearce, C. W. (2000). The construction of autobiographical memories in the self-memory system. *Psychological Review, 107,* 261–288.

Corsale, K., & Ornstein, P. A. (1980). Developmental changes in children's use of semantic information in recall. *Journal of Experimental Child Psychology, 30,* 231–245.

Cowan, N., & Alloway, T. (2009). Development of working memory in childhood. In M. L. Courage & N. Cowan (Eds.), *The development of memory in infancy and childhood* (pp. 303–342). Hove, East Sussex, United Kingdom: Psychology Press.

Cox, B. D., Ornstein, P. A., Naus, M. J., Maxfield, D., & Zimler, J. (1989). Children's concurrent use of rehearsal and organizational strategies. *Developmental Psychology, 25,* 619–627.

Cox, B. D., Ornstein, P. A., & Valsiner, J. (1991). The role of internalization in the transfer of mnemonic strategies. In L. Oppenheimer & J. Valsiner (Eds.), *The origins of action: Interdisciplinary and international perspectives* (pp. 101–131). New York: Springer-Verlag.

Coyle, T. R., & Bjorklund, D. F. (1997). Age differences in, and consequences of, multiple- and variable-strategy use on a multitrial sort-recall task. *Developmental Psychology, 33,* 372–380.

Craik, F. I. M. (1977). Age differences in human memory. In J. E. Birren & W. Schaie (Eds.), *Handbook of the psychology of aging* (pp. 384–420). New York: Van Nostrand Reinhold.

Craik, F. I. M. (1983). On the transfer of information from temporary to permanent memory. *Philosophical Transactions of the Royal Society, Series B302,* 341–359.

Craik, F. I. M. (1986). A functional account of age differences in memory. In F. Klix & H. Hagpendorf (Eds.), *Human memory and cognitive capabilities, mechanisms, and performances* (pp. 409–422). Amsterdam: Elsevier.

Craik, F. I. M., & Jennings, J. M. (1992). Human memory. In F. I. M. Craik & T. A. Salthouse (Eds.), *The handbook of aging and cognition* (pp. 51–110). Hillsdale, NJ: Erlbaum.

Craik, F. I. M., & Watkins, M. J. (1973). The role of rehearsal in short-term memory. *Journal of Verbal Learning and Verbal Behavior, 12,* 599–607.

Cycowicz, Y. M., Friedman, D., & Duff, M. (2003). Pictures and their colors: What do children remember? *Journal of Cognitive Neuroscience, 15,* 759–768.

Daniels, K. A., Toth, J. P., & Hertzog, C. (2009). Aging and recollection in the accuracy of judgments of learning. *Psychology and Aging, 24,* 494–500.

Davidson, P. S. R., & Glisky, E. L. (2002). Neuropsychological correlates of recollection and familiarity in normal aging. *Cognitive, Affective, & Behavioral Neuroscience, 2,* 174–186.

DeCasper, A. J., & Fifer, W. P. (1980). Of human bonding: Newborns prefer their mothers' voices. *Science, 208,* 1174–1176.

DeCasper, A. J., & Spence, M. J. (1986). Prenatal maternal speech influences newborns' perception of speech sounds. *Infant Behavior and Development, 9,* 133–150.

DeLoache, J., & Brown, A. (1984). Where do I go next? Intelligent searching by very young children. *Developmental Psychology, 20,* 37–44.

DeLoache, J. S., Cassidy, D. J., & Brown, A. L. (1985). Precursors of mnemonic strategies in very young children's memory. *Child Development, 56,* 125–137.

Dennis, N. A., & Cabeza, R. (2008). Neuroimaging of healthy cognitive aging. In F. I. M. Craik & T. A. Salthouse (Eds.), *The handbook of aging and cognition* (3rd ed., pp. 1–54). Mahwah, NJ: Erlbaum.

Desrichard, O., & Kopetz, C. (2005). A threat in the elder: The impact of task-instructions, self-efficacy and performance expectations on

memory performance in the elderly. *European Journal of Social Psychology, 35,* 537–552.

Devolder, P. A., Brigham, M. C., & Pressley, M. (1990). Memory performance awareness in younger and older adults. *Psychology and Aging, 5,* 291–303.

Dewhurst, S. A., & Robinson, C. A. (2004). False memories in children: Evidence for a shift from phonological to semantic associations. *Psychological Science, 15,* 782–786.

Diana, R., Reder, L. M., Arndt, J., & Park, H. (2006). Models of recognition: A review of arguments in favor of a dual-process account. *Psychonomic Bulletin & Review, 13,* 1–21.

Dixon, R. A., & Hultsch, D. F. (1983). Structure and development of metamemory in adulthood. *Journal of Gerontology, 38,* 682–688.

Dodson, C. S., Bawa, S., & Krueger, L. E. (2007). Aging, metamemory, and high-confidence errors: A misrecollection account. *Psychology and Aging, 22,* 122–123.

Dodson, C. S., & Schacter, D. L. (2002). Aging and strategic retrieval processes: Reducing false memories with a distinctiveness heuristic. *Psychology and Aging, 17,* 405–415.

Dror, I. E., & Kosslyn, S. M. (1994). Mental imagery and aging. *Psychology and Aging, 9,* 90–102.

Dudukovic, N. M., Marsh, E. J., & Tversky, B. (2004). Telling a story or telling it straight: The effects of entertaining versus accurate retellings on memory. *Applied Cognitive Psychology, 18,* 125–143.

Dunlosky, J., Baker, J. M. C., Hertzog, C., & Rawson, K. A. (2006). Does aging influence people's metacomprehension? Effects of processing ease on judgments of text learning. *Psychology and Aging, 21,* 390–400.

Dunlosky, J., & Connor, L. T. (1997). Age differences in the allocation of study time account for age differences in memory performance. *Memory & Cognition, 25,* 691–700.

Dunlosky, J., & Hertzog, C. (1998). Aging and deficits in associative memory: What is the role of strategy production? *Psychology and Aging, 13,* 597–607.

Dunlosky, J., & Hertzog, C. (2001). Measuring strategy production during associative learning: The relative utility of concurrent versus retrospective reports. *Memory & Cognition, 29,* 247–253.

Dunlosky, J., Hertzog, C., & Powell-Moman, A. (2005). The contribution of mediator-based deficiencies to age differences in associative learning. *Developmental Psychology, 41,* 389–400.

Farrant, K., & Reese, E. (2000). Maternal style and children's participation in reminiscing: Stepping stones in autobiographical memory development. *Journal of Cognition and Development, 1,* 193–225.

Fivush, R., Gray, J. T., & Fromhoff, F. A. (1987). Two year olds talk about the past. *Cognitive Development, 2,* 393–410.

Fivush, R., Haden, C. A., & Reese, E. (2006). Elaborating on elaborations: Role of maternal reminiscing style in cognitive and socioemotional development. *Child Development, 77,* 1568–1588.

Flavell, J. H. (1970). Developmental studies of mediated memory. In H. W. Reese & L. P. Lipsitt (Eds.), *Advances in child development and behavior* (Vol. 5, pp. 181–211). New York: Academic.

Flavell, J. H. (1971). Stage-related properties of cognitive development. *Cognitive Psychology, 2,* 421–453.

Flavell, J. H., Beach, D. R., & Chinsky, J. M. (1966). Spontaneous verbal rehearsal in a memory task as a function of age. *Child Development, 37,* 283–299.

Flavell, J. H., & Wellman, H. M. (1977). Metamemory. In R. V. Kail & J. W. Hagen (Eds.), *Perspectives on the development of memory and cognition* (pp. 3–33). Hillsdale, NJ: Erlbaum.

Folds, T. H., Footo, M., Guttentag, R. E., & Ornstein, P. A. (1990). When children mean to remember: Issues of context specificity, strategy effectiveness, and intentionality in the development of memory. In D. F. Bjorklund (Ed.), *Children's strategies: Contemporary views of cognitive development* (pp. 67–91). Hillsdale, NJ: Erlbaum.

Foley, M. A., & Johnson, M. K. (1985). Confusions between memories for performed and imagined actions: A developmental comparison. *Child Development, 56,* 1145–1155.

Gallo, D. A., Cotel, S. C., Moore, C. D., & Schacter, D. L. (2007). Aging can spare recollection-based retrieval monitoring: The importance of event distinctiveness. *Psychology and Aging, 22,* 209–213.

Gallo, D. A., & Roediger III, H. L. (2003). The effects of associations and aging on illusory recollection. *Memory & Cognition, 31,* 1036–1044.

Gardiner, J. M. (1988). Functional aspects of recollective experience. *Memory & Cognition, 16,* 309–313.

Gaultney, J. F., Kipp, K., & Kirk, G. (2005). Utilization deficiency and working memory capacity in adult memory performance: Not just for children anymore. *Cognitive Development, 20,* 205–213.

Ghetti, S. (2003). Memory for nonoccurrences: The role of metacognition. *Journal of Memory and Language, 48,* 722–739.

Ghetti, S. (2008). Processes underlying developmental reversals in false-memory formation: Comment on Brainerd, Reyna, and Ceci (2008). *Psychological Bulletin, 134,* 764–767.

Ghetti, S., & Angelini, L. (2008). The development of recollection and familiarity in childhood and adolescence: Evidence from the dual-process signal detection model. *Child Development, 79,* 339–358.

Ghetti, S., & Castelli, P. (2006). Developmental differences in false-event rejection: Effects of memorability-based warnings. *Memory, 16,* 762–776.

Gilewski, M. J., Zelinski, E. M., & Schaie, K. W. (1990). The Memory Functioning Questionnaire for assessment of memory complaints in adulthood and old age. *Psychology and Aging, 5,* 482–490.

Glisky, E. L., & Kong, L. L. (2008). Do young and older adults rely on different processes in source memory tasks: A neuropsychological study. *Journal of Experimental Psychology: Learning, Memory, and Cognition, 34,* 809–822.

Glisky, E. L., Polster, M. R., & Routhieaux, B. C. (1995). Double dissociation between item and source memory. *Neuropsychology, 9,* 229–235.

Glisky, E. L., Rubin, S. R., & Davidson, P.S.R. (2001). Source memory in older adults: An encoding or retrieval problem? *Journal of Experimental Psychology: Learning, Memory, and Cognition, 27,* 1131–1146.

Golomb, J. D., Peelle, J. E., Addis, K. M., Kahana, M. J., & Wingfield, A. (2008). Effects of adult aging on utilization of temporal and semantic associations during free and serial recall. *Memory & Cognition, 36,* 947–956.

Goodman, G. S., Quas, J. A., Batterman-Faunce, J. M., Riddlesberger, M. M., & Kuhn, J. (1997). Children's reactions to and memory for a stressful event: Influences of age, anatomical dolls, knowledge and parental attachment. *Applied Developmental Science, 1,* 54–74.

Graf, P., & Schacter, D. L. (1985). Implicit and explicit memory for new associations in normal and amnesic subjects. *Journal of Experimental Psychology: Learning, Memory, and Cognition, 11,* 501–518.

Guttentag, R. E. (1984). The mental effort requirements of cumulated rehearsal: A developmental study. *Journal of Experimental Child Psychology, 37,* 92–106.

Guttentag, R. E., Ornstein, P. A., & Siemens, L. (1987). Children's spontaneous rehearsal: Transitions in strategy acquisition. *Cognitive Development, 2,* 307–326.

Haden, C. A., Haine, R. A., & Fivush, R. (1997). Developing narrative structure in parent-child reminiscing across the preschool years. *Developmental Psychology, 33,* 295–307.

Haden, C. A., Ornstein, P. A., Eckerman, C. O., & Didow, S. M. (2001). Mother-child conversational interactions as events unfold: Linkages to subsequent remembering. *Child Development, 72,* 1016–1031.

Hambrick, D. Z., & Engle, R. W. (2002). Effects of domain knowledge, working memory capacity, and age on cognitive performance: An investigation of the knowledge-is-power hypothesis. *Cognitive Psychology, 44,* 339–387.

Hasher, L., & Zacks, R. T. (1988). Working memory, comprehension, and aging: A review and a new view. In G. H. Bower (Ed.), *The psychology of learning and motivation: Advances in research and theory* (Vol. 22, pp. 193–225). New York: Academic.

Hashtroudi, S., Johnson, M. K., & Chrosniak, L. D. (1990). Aging and qualitative characteristics of memories for perceived and imagined complex events. *Psychology and Aging, 5,* 119–126.

Hashtroudi, S., Johnson, M. K., Vnek, N., & Ferguson, S. A. (1994). Aging and the effects of affective and factual focus on source monitoring and recall. *Psychology and Aging, 9,* 160–170.

Havighurst, R., Neugarten, B., & Tobin, S. (1968). Disengagement and patterns of aging. In B. Neugarten (Ed.), *Middle age and aging* (pp. 161–172). Chicago, IL: University of Chicago Press.

Healy, M. R., Light, L. L., & Chung, C. (2005). Dual-process models of associative recognition in young and older adults: Evidence from receiver operating characteristics. *Journal of Experimental Psychology: Learning, Memory, and Cognition, 31,* 768–788.

Hedden, T., Lautenschlager, G., & Park, D. C. (2005). Contributions of processing ability and knowledge to verbal memory tasks across the adult life-span. *Quarterly Journal of Experimental Psychology, 58A,* 169–190.

Henkel, L. A., Johnson, M. K., & De Leonardis, D. M. (1998). Aging and source monitoring: Cognitive processes and neuropsychological correlates. *Journal of Experimental Psychology: General, 127,* 251–268.

Hertzog, C., & Dunlosky, J. (2004). Aging, metacognition, and cognitive control. In B. H. Ross (Ed.), *The psychology of learning and motivation: Advances in research and theory* (Vol. 45, pp. 215–251). San Diego, CA: Elsevier.

Hertzog, C., Kidder, D. P., Dunlosky, J., & Powell-Moman, A. (2002). Aging and monitoring associative learning: Is monitoring accuracy spared or impaired? *Psychology and Aging, 17,* 209–225.

Hertzog, C., Kramer, A. F., Wilson, R. S., & Lindenberger, U. (2009). Enrichment effects on adult cognitive development: Can the functional capacity of older adults be preserved and enhanced? *Psychological Science in the Public Interest, 9,* 1–65.

Hertzog, C., McGuire, C. L., & Lineweaver, T. T. (1998). Aging, attributions, perceived control, and strategy use in a free recall task. *Aging, Neuropsychology, and Cognition, 5,* 85–106.

Hess, T., Auman, C., Colcombe, S., & Rahhal, T. (2003). The impact of stereotype threat on age differences in memory performance. *Journals of Gerontology: Psychological Sciences, 58B,* P3–P11.

Hess, T. M. (2005). Memory and aging in context. *Psychological Bulletin, 131,* 383–406.

Hess, T. M., Hinson, J. T., & Statham, J. A. (2004). Explicit and implicit stereotype activation effects on memory: Do age and awareness moderate the impact of priming. *Psychology and Aging, 19,* 495–505.

Holliday, R. E., Reyna, V. F., & Brainerd, C. J. (2008). Recall of details never experienced: Effects of age, repetition, and semantic cues. *Cognitive Development, 23,* 67–78.

Holliday, R. E., & Weekes, B. S. (2006). Dissociated developmental trajectories for semantic and phonological false memories. *Memory, 14,* 624–636.

Horn, J. L. (1968). Organization of abilities and the development of intelligence. *Psychological Review, 75,* 242–259.

Horn, J. L. (1970). Organization of data on life-span development of human abilities. In L. R. Goulet & P. B. Baltes (Eds.), *Life-span developmental psychology: Research and theory* (pp. 423–466). New York: Academic.

Howard, D. V. (1980). Category norms: A comparison of the Battig and Montague (1969) norms with the responses of adults between the ages of 20 and 80. *Journal of Gerontology, 35,* 225–231.

Howard, M. W., Bessette-Symons, B., Zhang, Y., & Hoyer, W. J. (2006). Aging selectively impairs recollection in recognition memory for pictures: Evidence from modeling and receiver operating characteristic curves. *Psychology and Aging, 21,* 96–106.

Howe, M. L. (2005). Children (but not adults) can inhibit false memories. *Psychological Science, 16,* 927–931.

Howe, M. L. (2006). Developmentally invariant dissociations in children's true and false memories: Not all relatedness is created equal. *Child Development, 77,* 1112–1123.

Howe, M. L. (2008). What is false memory development the development of? Comment on Brainerd, Reyna, and Ceci (2008). *Psychological Bulletin, 134,* 768–772.

Howe, M. L., Wimmer, M. C., & Blease, K. (2009). The role of associative strength in children's false memory illusions. *Memory, 17,* 8–16.

Howe, M. L., Wimmer, M. C., Gagnon, N., & Plumpton, S. (2009). An associative-activation theory of children's and adults' memory illusions. *Journal of Memory and Language, 60,* 229–251.

Hoyer, W. J., & Verhaeghen, P. (2006). Memory and aging. In J. E. Birren & K. W. Schaie (Eds.), *Handbook of the psychology of aging* (6th ed., pp. 209–232). Amsterdam: Elsevier.

Hudson, J. A. (1990). The emergence of autobiographical memory in the mother-child conversation. In R. Fivush & J. A. Hudson (Eds.), *Knowing and remembering in young children* (pp. 166–196). New York: Cambridge University Press.

Hudson, J. A. (1993). Reminiscing with mothers and others: Autobiographical memory in young two-year-olds. *Journal of Narrative and Life History, 3,* 1–32.

Hulicka, I. M., & Grossman, J. L. (1967). Age group comparisons for the use of mediators in paired-associate learning. *Journal of Gerontology, 22,* 46–51.

Hultsch, D. F. (1975). Adult age differences in retrieval: Trace-dependent and cue-dependent forgetting. *Developmental Psychology, 11,* 197–201.

Hultsch, D. F., & Craig, E. R. (1976). Adult age differences in the inhibition of recall as a function of retrieval cues. *Developmental Psychology, 12,* 83–84.

Hultsch, D. F., Hertzog, C., Dixon, R. A., & Small, B. J. (1998). *Memory change in the aged.* Cambridge: Cambridge University Press.

Hultsch, D., Hertzog, C., Small, B., & Dixon, R. (1999). Use it or lose it: Engaged lifestyle as a buffer of cognitive decline in aging? *Psychology and Aging, 14,* 245–263.

Istomina, Z. M. (1975). The development of voluntary memory in preschool-age children. *Soviet Psychoology, 13,* 5–64. (Originally published 1948.)

Jacoby, L. L. (1991). A process dissociation framework: Separating automatic from intentional uses of memory. *Journal of Memory and Language, 30,* 513–541.

Jacoby, L. L. (1999). Ironic effects of repetition: Measuring age-related differences in memory. *Journal of Experimental Psychology: Learning, Memory, and Cognition, 25,* 3–22.

Jacoby, L. L., Shimizu, Y., Velanova, K., & Rhodes, M. G. (2005). Age differences in depth of retrieval: Memory for foils. *Journal of Memory and Language, 52,* 493–504.

James, L. E., Burke, D. M., Austin, A., & Hulme. E. (1998). Production and perception of "verbosity" in younger and older adults. *Psychology and Aging, 13,* 355–367.

Jenkins, J. J. (1974). Remember that old theory of memory? Well, forget it. *American Psychologist, 29,* 785–795.

Jennings, J. M., & Jacoby, L. L. (1997). An opposition procedure for detecting age-related deficits in recollection: Telling effects of repetition. *Psychology and Aging, 12,* 352–361.

Jennings, J. M., Webster, L. M., Kleykamp, B. A., & Dagenbach, D. (2005). Recollection training and transfer effects in older adults: Successful use of a repetition-lag procedure. *Aging, Neuropsychology, and Cognition, 12,* 278–298.

Johnson, M. K., Hashtroudi, S., & Lindsay, D. S. (1993). Source monitoring. *Psychological Bulletin, 114,* 3–28.

Johnson, R. E. (2003). Aging and the remembering of text. *Developmental Review, 23,* 261–346.

Jopp, D., & Hertzog, C. (2007). Activities, self-referent memory beliefs, and cognitive performance: Evidence for direct and mediated relations. *Psychology and Aging, 22,* 811–825.

Joyner, M. H., & Kurtz-Costes, B. (1997). Metamemory development. In N. Cowan (Ed.), *The development of memory in childhood* (pp. 275–300). East Sussex, United Kingdom: Psychology Press.

Justice, E. M. (1985.) Categorization as a preferred memory strategy: Developmental changes during elementary school. *Developmental Psychology, 21,* 1105–1110.

Justice, E. M. (1986). Developmental changes in judgments of relative strategy effectiveness. *British Journal of Developmental Psychology, 4,* 75–81.

Kail, R. (1991). Developmental change in speed of processing during childhood and adolescence. *Psychological Bulletin, 109,* 490–501.

Kapucu, A., Rotello, C. M., Ready, R. E., & Seidl, K. M. (2008). Response bias in "remembering" emotional stimuli: A new perspective on age differences. *Journal of Experimental Psychology: Learning, Memory, and Cognition, 34,* 703–711.

Katona, G. (1940). *Organizing and memorizing.* New York: Columbia University Press.

Kausler, D. H. (1970). Retention-forgetting as a nomological network for developmental research. In L. R. Goulet & P. B. Baltes (Eds.), *Life-span developmental psychology: Research and* theory (pp. 305–353). New York: Academic.

Kausler, D. H. (1994). *Learning and memory in normal aging.* San Diego, CA: Academic.

Kee, D. W., & Davies, L. (1990). Mental effort and elaboration: Effects of accessibility and instruction. *Journal of Experimental Child Psychology, 49,* 264–274.

Kelley, C. M., & Sahakyan, L. (2003). Memory, monitoring, and control in the attainment of memory accuracy. *Journal of Memory and Language, 48,* 704–721.

Kelley, R., & Wixted, J. T. (2001). On the nature of associative information in recognition memory. *Journal of Experimental Psychology: Learning, Memory, and Cognition, 27,* 701–722.

Kemper, S., Rash, S., Kynette, D., & Norman, S. (1990). Telling stories: The structure of adults' narratives. *European Journal of Cognitive Psychology, 2,* 205–228.

Kendler, H. H., & Kendler, T. S. (1962). Vertical and horizontal processes in problem solving. *Psychological Review, 69,* 1–16.

Kenniston, A. H., & Flavell, J. H. (1979). A developmental study of intelligent retrieval. *Child Development, 50,* 1144–1152.

Kensinger, E. A., & Schacter, D. L. (1999) When true memories suppress false memories: Effects of ageing. *Cognitive Neuropsychology, 16,* 399–415.

Kilb, A., & Naveh-Benjamin, M. (2007). Paying attention to binding: Further studies assessing the role of reduced attentional resources in the associative deficit of older adults. *Memory & Cognition, 35,* 1162–1174.

Kliegl, E., Smith, J., & Baltes, P. B. (1989). On the locus and process of magnification of age differences during mnemonic training. *Developmental Psychology, 26,* 894–904.

Knight, M., Seymour, T. L., Gaunt, J. T., Baker, C., Nesmith, K., & Mather, M. (2007). Aging and goal-directed emotional attention: Distraction reverses emotional biases. *Emotion, 7,* 705–714.

Kobasigawa, A. (1974). Utilization of retrieval cues by children in recall. *Child Development, 45,* 127–134.

Kobasigawa, A. (1977). Retrieval strategies in the development of memory. In R. V. Kail & J. W. Hagen (Eds.), *Perspective on the development of memory and cognition* (pp. 177–201). Hillsdale, NJ: Erlbaum.

Koriat, A., & Shitzer-Reichert, R. (2002). Metacognitive judgments and their accuracy. *Metacognition: Process, function and use* (pp. 1–17). Dordrecht, The Netherlands: Kluwer.

Koutstaal, W. (2006). Flexible remembering. *Psychonomic Bulletin & Review, 13,* 84–91.

Koutstaal, W., Reddy, C., Jackson, E. M., Prince, S., Cendan, D. L., & Schacter, D. L. (2003). False recognition of abstract versus common objects in older and younger adults: Testing the semantic categorization account. *Journal of Experimental Psychology: Learning, Memory, and Cognition, 29,* 499–510.

Koutstaal, W., & Schacter, D. L. (1997). Gist-based false recognition of pictures in older and younger adults. *Journal of Memory and Language, 37,* 555–583.

Koutstaal, W., Schacter, D. L., Galluccio, L., & Stofer, K. A. (1999). Reducing gist-based false recognition in older adults: Encoding and retrieval manipulations. *Psychology and Aging, 14,* 220–237.

Kreutzer, M. A., Leonard, C., & Flavell, J. H. (1975). An interview study of children's knowledge about memory. *Monographs of the Society for Research in Child Development, 40*(1, Serial No. 159).

Kron-Sperl, V., Schneider, W., & Hasselhorn, M. (2008). The development and effectiveness of memory strategies in kindergarten and elementary school: Findings from the Wurzburg and Gottingen longitudinal memory studies. *Cognitive Development, 23,* 79–104.

Kuhn, D. (1999). Metacognitive development. In L. Balter & C. S. Tamis-LeMonda (Eds.), *Child psychology: A handbook of contemporary issues* (pp. 259–286). Philadelphia: Psychology Press.

Lachman, M., Bandura, M., Weaver, S., & Elliott, E. (1995). Assessing memory control beliefs: The Memory Controllability Inventory. *Aging and Cognition, 2,* 67–84.

Lachman, M. E., & Andreoletti, C. (2006). Strategy use mediates the relationship between control beliefs and memory performance for middle-aged and older adults. *Journal of Gerontology: Psychological Sciences, 61B,* P88–P94.

Lachman, M. E., Weaver, S. L., Bandura, M., Elliott, E., & Lewkowicz, C. J. (1992). Improving memory and control beliefs through cognitive restructuring and self-generated strategies. *Journal of Gerontology: Psychological Sciences, 47,* P293–P299.

Lampinen, J. M., Leding, J. K., Reed, K. B., & Odegard, T. N. (2006). Global gist extraction in children and adults. *Memory, 14,* 952–964.

Lane, C. J., & Zelinski, E. M. (2003). Longitudinal hierarchical linear models of the Memory Functioning Questionnaire. *Psychology and Aging, 18,* 38–53.

Lange, G. (1973). The development of conceptual and rote recall among school age children. *Journal of Experimental Child Psychology, 15,* 394–406.

Lange, G. (1978). Organization-related processes in children's recall. In P. A. Ornstein (Ed.), *Memory development in children* (pp. 101–128). Hillsdale, NJ: Erlbaum.

Lehmann, M., & Hasselhorn, M. (2007). Variable memory strategy use in children's adoptive intratask learning behavior: Developmental changes and working memory influences in free recall. *Child Development, 78,* 1068–1082.

Leichtman, M. D., Pillemer, D. B., Wang, Q., Koreishi, A., & Han, J. G. (2000). When Baby Maisy came to school: Mothers' interview style and preschoolers event memory. *Cognitive Development, 15,* 99–114.

Levy, B., & Langer, E. (1994). Aging free from negative stereotypes: Successful memory in China and among the American deaf. *Journal of Personality and Social Psychology, 66,* 989–997.

Levy, B. R., & Leifheit-Limson, E. (2009). The stereotype-matching effect: Greater influence on functioning when age stereotypes correspond to outcomes. *Psychology and Aging, 24,* 230–233.

Li, K. Z. H., Lindenberger, U., Freund, A. M., & Baltes, P. B. (2001). Walking while memorizing: Age-related differences in compensatory behavior. *Psychological Science, 12,* 230–237.

Li, S.-C., Lindenberger, U., Hommel, B., Aschersleben, G., Prinz, W., & Baltes, P. B. (2004). Transformations in the couplings among intellectual abilities and constituent cognitive processes across the life span. *Psychological Science, 15,* 155–163.

Li, S-C., Naveh-Benjamin, M., & Lindenberger, U. (2005). Aging neuromodulation impairs associative binding. *Psychological Science, 16,* 445–450.

Liberty, C., & Ornstein, P. A. (1973). Age differences in organization and recall: The effects of training in categorization. *Journal of Experimental Child Psychology, 15,* 169–186.

Light, L.L., & Carter-Sobell, L. (1970). Effects of changed semantic context on recognition memory. *Journal of Verbal Learning and Verbal Behavior, 9,* 1–11.

Light, L. L. (1991). Memory and aging: Four hypotheses in search of data. *Annual Review of Psychology, 42,* 333–376.

Light, L. L. (1992). The organization of memory in old age. In F. I. M. Craik & T. Salthouse (Eds.), *Handbook of aging and cognition* (pp. 111–165). Hillsdale, NJ: Erlbaum.

Light, L. L., Chung, C., Pendergrass, R., & Van Ocker, J. C. (2006). Effects of repetition and response deadline on item recognition in young and older adults. *Memory & Cognition, 34,* 335–343.

Light, L. L., LaVoie, D., Valencia-Laver, D., Albertson Owens, S. A., & Mead, G. (1992). Direct and indirect measures of memory for modality in young and older adults. *Journal of Experimental Psychology: Learning, Memory, and Cognition, 18,* 1284–1297.

Light, L. L., Patterson, M. M., Chung, C., & Healy, M. R. (2004). Effects of repetition and response deadline on associative recognition in young and older adults. *Memory & Cognition, 32,* 1182–1183.

Light, L. L., Prull, M. W., LaVoie, D. J., & Healy, M. R. (2000). Dual-process theories of memory in old age. In T. J. Perfect & E. A. Maylor (Eds.), *Models of cognitive aging* (pp. 238–300). New York: Oxford University Press.

Lindenberger, U., Kliegl, R., & Baltes, P. B. (1992). Professional expertise does not eliminate age differences in imagery-based memory performance during adulthood. *Psychology and Aging, 7,* 585–593.

Lloyd, M., & Newcombe, N. (2009). Implicit memory in childhood: Reassessing developmental invariance. In M. L. Courage & N. Cowan (Eds.), *The development of memory in infancy and childhood* (pp. 93–113). New York: Psychology Press.

Lockl, K., & Schneider, W. (2002). Developmental trends in children's feeling-of-knowing judgments. *International Journal of Behavioral Development, 26,* 327–333.

Lockl, K., & Schneider, W. (2004). The effects of incentives and instructions on children's allocation of study time. *European Journal of Developmental Psychology, 1,* 53–169.

Luo, L., & Craik, F.I.M. (2009). Age differences in recollection: Specificity effects at retrieval. *Journal of Memory and Language, 60,* 421–436.

Luo, L., Hendriks, T., & Craik, F. I. M. (2007). Age differences in recollection: Three patterns of enhanced encoding. *Psychology and Aging, 22,* 269–280.

Lustig, C., & Flegal, K. E. (2008). Targeting latent function: Encouraging effective encoding for successful memory training and transfer. *Psychology and Aging, 23,* 754–764.

Malmberg, K. J. (2008). Recognition memory: A review of the critical findings and an integrated theory for relating them. *Cognitive Psychology, 57,* 335–384.

Mandler, G. (1967). Organization and memory. In K. W. Spence & J. T. Spence (Eds.), *The psychology of learning and motivation: Advances in research and theory* pp. 327–372. New York: Academic.

Marquie, J. C., & Huet, N. (2000). Age differences in feeling-of-knowing and confidence judgments as a function of knowledge domain. *Psychology and Aging, 15,* 451–461.

Marshall, P. H., Elias, J. W., Webber, S. M., Gist, B. A., Winn, F. J., & King, P. (1978). Age differences in verbal mediation: A structural and functional analysis. *Experimental Aging Research, 4,* 175–193.

Masunaga, H., & Horn, J. (2001). Characterizing mature human intelligence: Expertise development. *Learning and Individual Differences, 12,* 5–33.

Mather, M., & Knight, M. (2005). Goal-directed memory: The role of cognitive control in older adults' emotional memory. *Psychology and Aging, 20,* 554–570.

Matvey, G., Dunlosky, J., Shaw, R., Parks, C., & Hertzog, C. (2002). Age-related equivalence and deficit in knowledge updating of cue effectiveness. *Psychology and Aging, 17,* 589–597.

McCabe, A., & Peterson, C. (1991). Getting the story: A longitudinal study of parental styles in eliciting narratives and developing narrative skill. In A. McCabe & C. Peterson (Eds.), *Developing narrative structure* (pp. 217–253). Hillsdale, NJ: Erlbaum.

McCabe, D. P., & Smith, A. D. (2002). The effect of warnings on false memories in young and older adults. *Memory & Cognition, 30,* 1065–1077.

McDaniel, M. A., Einstein, G. O., & Jacoby, L. L. (2008). New considerations in aging and memory: The glass may be half full. In F. I. M. Craik & T. A. Salthouse (Eds.), *The handbook of aging and cognition* (3rd ed., pp. 251–310). New York: Psychology Press.

McDonald-Misczak, L., Hertzog, C., & Hultsch, D. F. (1995). Stability and accuracy of metamemory in adulthood and aging: A longitudinal analysis. *Psychology and Aging, 10,* 553–564.

McDonough, L., Mandler, J. M., McKee, R. D., & Squire, L. R. (1995). The deferred imitation task as a nonverbal measure of declarative memory. *Proceedings of the National Academy of Sciences, 92,* 7580–7584.

McGuigan, F., & Salmon, K. (2004). The time to talk: The influence of the timing of adult-child talk on children's event memory. *Child Development, 75,* 669–686.

Meinz, E. J. (2000). Experience-based attenuation of age-related differences in music cognition tasks. *Psychology and Aging, 15,* 297–312.

Meltzoff, A. N. (1985). Immediate and deferred imitation in fourteen and twenty-four-month-old infants. *Child Development,* 56, 62–72.

Merritt, K. A., Ornstein, P. A., & Spicker, B. (1994). Children's memory for a salient medical procedure: Implications for testimony. *Pediatrics, 94,* 17–23.

Metcalfe, J. (2002). Is study time allocated selectively to a region of proximal learning? *Journal of Experimental Psychology: General, 131,* 349–363.

Miller, P. H. (1990). The development of strategies of selective attention. In D. F. Bjorklund (Ed.), *Children's strategies: Contemporary views of cognitive development* (pp. 157–184). Hillsdale, NJ: Erlbaum.

Miller, P. H., & Seier, W. L. (1994). Strategy utilization deficiencies in children: When, where, and why. In H. W. Reese (Ed.), *Advances in child development and behavior* (Vol. 25, pp. 107–156). New York: Academic.

Mistry, J. J., & Lange, G. W. (1985). Children's organization and recall of information in scripted narratives. *Child Development, 56,* 953–961.

Moely, B. E., Hart, S. S., Leal, L., Santulli, K. A., Rao, N., Johnson, T., & Hamilton, L.B. (1992). The teacher's role in facilitating memory and study strategy development in the elementary school classroom. *Child Development, 63,* 653–672.

Morrow, D. G., Leirer, V. O., & Altieri, P. A. (1992). Aging, expertise, and narrative processing. *Psychology and Aging, 7,* 376–388.

Morrow, D. G., Leirer, V. O., Altieri, P., & Fitzsimmons, C. (1994). When expertise reduces age differences in performance. *Psychology and Aging, 9,* 134–148.

Morrow, D. G., Menard, W. E., Stine-Morrow, E. A. L., Teller, T., & Bryant, D. (2001). The influence of task factors and expertise on age differences in pilot communication. *Psychology and Aging, 16,* 31–46.

Muir-Broaddus, J. E., & Bjorklund, D. F. (1990). Developmental and individual differences in children's memory strategies: The role of knowledge. In W. Schneider & F. E. Weinert (Eds.), *Aptitudes, strategies and knowledge in cognitive performance* (pp. 99–116). New York: Springer-Verlag.

Multhaup, K. S. (1995). Aging, source, and decision criteria: When false fame errors do and do not occur. *Psychology and Aging, 10,* 492–497.

Multhaup, K. S., De Leonardis, D. M., & Johnson, M. K. (1999). Source memory and eyewitness suggestibility in older adults. *Journal of General Psychology, 126,* 74–84.

Murachver, T., Pipe, M. E., Gordon, R., & Owens, J. L. (1996). Do, show, and tell: Children's event memories acquired through direct experience, observation, and stories. *Child Development, 67,* 3029–3044.

Murphy, N. A., & Isaacowitz, D. M. (2008). Preferences for emotional information in older and younger adults: A meta-analysis of memory and attention tasks. *Psychology and Aging, 23,* 263–286.

Naus, M. J., Ornstein, P. A., & Aivano, S. (1977). Developmental changes in memory: The effects of processing time and rehearsal instructions. *Journal of Experimental Child Psychology, 23,* 237–251.

Naveh-Benjamin, M. (2000). Adult age differences in memory performance: Tests of an associative deficit hypothesis. *Journal of Experimental Psychology: Learning, Memory, and Cognition, 26,* 1170–1187.

Naveh-Benjamin, M., Craik, F. I. M., Guez, J., & Kreuger, S. (2005). Divided attention in younger and older adults: Effects of strategy and relatedness on memory performance and secondary task costs. *Journal of Experimental Psychology: Learning, Memory, and Cognition, 31,* 520–537.

Naveh-Benjamin, M., Hussain, Z., Guez, J., & Bar-On, M. (2003). Adult age differences in episodic memory: Further support for an associative deficit hypothesis. *Journal of Experimental Psychology: Learning, Memory, and Cognition, 29,* 826–837.

Naveh-Benjamin, M., Keshet Brav, T., & Levy, O. (2007). The associative memory deficit of older adults: The role of strategy utilization. *Psychology and Aging, 22,* 202–208.

Nebes, R. D., & Andrews-Kulis, M. E. (1976). The effect of age on the speed of sentence formation and incidental learning. *Experimental Aging Research, 2,* 315–331.

Nelson, K. (1974). Variation in children's concepts by age and category. *Child Development, 45,* 557–584.

Nelson, K. (1986). *Event knowledge: Structure and function in development.* Hillsdale, NJ: Erlbaum.

Nelson, T. O., & Narens, L. (1990). Metamemory: A theoretical framework and new findings. In G. H. Bower (Ed.), *The psychology of learning and motivation: Advances in research and theory* (Vol. 26, pp. 125–173). New York: Academic.

Norman, K. A., & Schacter, D. L. (1997). False recognition in younger and older adults: Exploring the characteristics of illusory memories. *Memory & Cognition, 25,* 838–848.

Odegard, T. N., Holliday, R. E., Brainerd, C. J., & Reyna, V. F. (2008). Attention to global gist processing eliminates age effects in false memories. *Journal of Experimental Child Psychology, 99,* 96–113.

Old, S., & Naveh-Benjamin, M. (2008). Differential effects of age on item and associative measures of memory: A meta-analysis. *Psychology and Aging, 23,* 104–118.

Ornstein, P., Grammer, J., & Coffman, J. (2010). Teachers' "mnemonic style" and the development of skilled memory. In H. S. Waters & W. Schneider (Eds.), *Metacognition, strategy use, and instruction* (pp. 23–53). New York: Guilford.

Ornstein, P. A., Baker-Ward, L., Gordon, B. N., & Merritt, K. A. (1997). Children's memory for medical experiences: Implications for testimony. *Applied Cognitive Psychology, 11,* S87–S104.

Ornstein, P. A., Baker-Ward, L., & Naus, M. J. (1988). The development of mnemonic skill. In F. E. Weinert & M. Perlmutter (Eds.), *Memory development: Universal changes and individual differences* (pp. 31–49). Hillsdale, NJ: Erlbaum.

Ornstein, P. A., & Haden, C. A. (2001). Memory development or the development of memory? *Current Directions in Psychological Science, 10,* 202–205.

Ornstein, P. A., Haden, C. A., & Coffman, J. L. (in press). Learning to remember: Mothers and teachers talking with children. In N. L. Stein & S. Raudenbush (Eds.), *Developmental science goes to school.* New York: Taylor & Francis.

Ornstein, P. A., Haden, C. A., & Elischberger, H. B. (2006). Children's memory development: Remembering the past and preparing for the future. In E. Bialystok & F. I. M. Craik (Eds.), *Lifespan cognition: Mechanisms of change* (pp. 143–161). New York: Oxford University Press.

Ornstein, P. A., Haden, C. A., & Hedrick, A. M. (2004). Learning to remember: Social-communicative exchanges and the development of children's memory skills. *Developmental Review, 24,* 374–395.

Ornstein, P. A., Haden, C. A., & San Souci, P. P. (2008). The development of skilled remembering in children. In J. H. E. Byrne & H. Roediger III (Vol. Eds.), *Learning and memory: A comprehensive reference: Vol. 4, Cognitive psychology of memory* (pp. 715–744). Oxford: Elsevier.

Ornstein, P. A., Medlin, R. G., Stone, B. P., & Naus, M. J. (1985). Retrieving for rehearsal: An analysis of active rehearsal in children's memory. *Developmental Psychology, 21,* 633–641.

Ornstein, P., Merritt, K., Baker-Ward, L., Furtado, E., Gordon, B., & Principe, G. (1998). Children's knowledge, expectation, and long-term retention. *Applied Cognitive Psychology, 12,* 387–405.

Ornstein, P. A., & Myers, J. T. (1996). Contextual influences on children's remembering. In K. Pezdek & W. P. Banks (Eds.), *The recovered memory/false memory debate* (pp. 211–223). San Diego, CA: Academic.

Ornstein, P. A., & Naus, M. J. (1978). Rehearsal processes in children's memory. In P. A. Ornstein (Ed.), *Memory development in children* (pp. 69–99). Hillsdale, NJ: Erlbaum.

Ornstein, P. A., & Naus, M. J. (1985). Effects of the knowledge base on children's memory strategies. In H. W. Reese (Ed.), *Advances in child development and behavior* (Vol. 19, pp. 113–148). New York: Academic.

Ornstein, P. A., Naus, M. J., & Liberty, C. (1975). Rehearsal and organizational processes in children's memory. *Child Development, 46,* 818–830.

Ornstein, P. A., Naus, M. J., & Stone, B. P. (1977). Rehearsal training and developmental differences in memory. *Developmental Psychology, 13,* 15–24.

Ornstein, P. A., Trabasso, T., & Johnson-Laird, P. N. (1974). To organize is to remember: The effects of instructions to organize and to recall. *Journal of Experimental Psychology, 103,* 1014–1018.

Overman, A. A., & Becker, J. T. (2009). The associative deficit in older adult memory: Recognition of pairs is not improved by repetition. *Psychology and Aging, 24,* 501–506.

Pansky, A., Goldsmith, M., Koriat, A., & Pearlman-Avnion, S. (2009). Memory accuracy in old age: Cognitive, metacognitive, and neurocognitive determinants. *European Journal of Cognitive Psychology, 21,* 303–329.

Paris, S. G., Newman, R. S., & McVey, K. A. (1982). Learning the functional significance of mnemonic actions: A microgenetic study of strategy acquisition. *Journal of Experimental Child Psychology, 34,* 490–509.

Park, D. C., Lautenschlager, G., Hedden, T., Davidson, N. S., Smith, A. D., & Smith, P. K. (2002). Models of visuospatial and verbal memory across the adult life span. *Psychology and Aging, 17,* 299–320.

Park, D. C., Smith, A. D., Lautenschlager, G., Earles, J. L., Frieske, D., Zwahr, M., et al. (1996). Mediators of long-term memory performance across the life span. *Psychology and Aging, 11,* 621–637.

Parkin, A. J., & Walter, B. M. (1992). Recollective experience, normal aging, and frontal dysfunction. *Psychology and Aging, 7,* 290–298.

Pasupathi, M. (2001). The social construction of the personal past and its implications for adult development. *Psychological Bulletin, 127,* 651–672.

Patterson, M. M., Light, L. L., Van Ocker, J. C., & Olfman, D. (2009). Discriminating semantic from episodic relatedness in young and older adults. *Aging, Neuropsychology, and Cognition, 16,* 535–562.

Perfect, T. J., Williams, R. B., & Anderton-Brown, C. (1995). Age differences in reported recollective experience are due to encoding effects, not response bias. *Memory, 3,* 169–186.

Perlmutter, M. (1978). What is memory aging the aging of? *Developmental Psychology, 14,* 330–345.

Peterson, C. (1999). Children's memory for medical emergencies: Two years later. *Developmental Psychology, 35,* 1493–1506.

Peterson, C., & Bell, M. (1996). Children's memory for traumatic injury. *Child Development, 67,* 3045–3070.

Peterson, C., Jesso, B., & McCabe, A. (1999). Encouraging narratives in preschoolers: An intervention study. *Journal of Child Language, 26,* 49–67.

Piccinin, A. M., & Hofer, S. M. (2008). Integrative analysis of longitudinal studies on aging: Collaborative research networks, meta-analysis, and optimizing future studies. In S. M Hofer & D. F. Alwin (Eds.), *Handbook of cognitive aging: Interdisciplinary perspectives* (pp. 446–476). Thousand Oaks, CA: Sage.

Plaut, D. C., & Booth, J. R. (2000). Individual and developmental differences in semantic priming: Empirical and computational support for a single-mechanism account of lexical processing. *Psychological Review, 107,* 786–823.

Pratt, M. W., & Robins, S. L. (1991). That's the way it was: Age differences in the structure and quality of older adults' personal narratives. *Discourse Processes, 14,* 73–85.

Pressley, M., Borkowski, J. G., & Schneider, W. (1989). Good information processing: What it is and how education can promote it. *International Journal of Educational Research, 13,* 857–897.

Pressley, M., & Levin, J. R. (1980). The development of mental imagery retrieval. *Child Development, 51,* 558–560.

Pressley, M., Levin, J. R., Ghatala, E. S., & Ahmad, M. (1987). Test monitoring in young grade school children. *Journal of Experimental Child Psychology, 43,* 96–111.

Pressley, M., & MacFayden, J. (1983). The development of mnemonic mediator usage at testing. *Child Development, 54,* 474–479.

Pressley, M., Ross, K. A., Levin, J. R., & Ghatala, E. S. (1984). The role of strategy utility knowledge in children's decision making. *Journal of Experimental Child Psychology, 38,* 491–504.

Prull, M. W., Crandell Dawes, L. L., McLeish Martin III, M. A., Rosenberg, H. F., & Light, L. L. (2006). Recollection and familiarity in recognition memory: Adult age differences and neuropsychological test correlates. *Psychology and Aging, 21,* 107–118.

Rabinowitz, J. C., Ackerman, B. P., Craik, F. I. M., & Hinchley, J. L. (1982). Aging and metamemory: The roles of relatedness and imagery. *Journal of Gerontology, 37,* 688–695.

Radvansky, G. A., & Dijkstra, K. (2007). Aging and situation model processing. *Psychonomic Bulletin & Review, 14,* 1027–1042.

Rahhal, T. A., Hasher, L., & Colcombe, S. J. (2001). Instructional manipulations and age differences in memory: Now you see them, now you don't. *Psychology and Aging, 16,* 697–706.

Reder, L. M. (1982). Plausibility judgments versus fact retrieval: Alternative strategies for sentence verification. *Psychological Review, 89,* 250–280.

Reder, L. M. (1988). Strategic control of retrieval strategies. In G. H. Bower (Ed.), *The psychology of learning and motivation: Advances in research and theory* (Vol. 22, pp. 227–259). San Diego, CA: Academic.

Reder, L. M., Wible, C., & Martin, J. (1986). Differential memory changes with age: Exact retrieval versus plausible inference. *Journal of Experimental Psychology: Learning, Memory, and Cognition, 12,* 72–81.

Reese, E., Haden, C. A., & Fivush, R. (1993). Mother-child conversations about the past: Relationships of style and memory over time. *Cognitive Development, 8,* 403–430.

Reese, E., & Newcombe, R. (2007). Elaborative reminiscing enhances children's autobiographical memory and narrative. *Child Development, 78,* 1153–1170.

Reese, H. W. (1962). Verbal mediation as a function of age level. *Psychological Bulletin, 59,* 502–509.

Reyna, V. F., & Brainerd, C. J. (1995). Fuzzy-trace theory: An interim synthesis. *Learning and Individual Differences, 7,* 1–75.

Reyna, V. F., & Kiernan, B. (1994). The development of gist versus verbatim memory in sentence recognition: Effects of lexical familiarity, semantic content, encoding instructions, and retention internal. *Developmental Psychology, 30,* 178–191.

Rhodes, M. G., & Kelley, C. M. (2005). Executive processes, memory accuracy, and memory monitoring: An aging and individual difference analysis. *Journal of Memory and Language, 52,* 578–594.

Ringel, B. A., & Springer, C. J. (1980). On knowing how well one is remembering: The persistence of strategy use during transfer. *Journal of Experimental Child Psychology, 29,* 322–333.

Robinson, A. E., Hertzog, C., & Dunlosky, J. (2006). Aging, encoding fluency, and metacognitive monitoring. *Aging, Neuropsychology, and Cognition, 13,* 458–478.

Roediger III, H. L., & Geraci, L. (2007). Aging and the misinformation effect: A neuropsychological study. *Journal of Experimental Psychology: Learning, Memory, and Cognition, 33,* 321–334.

Roediger III, H. L., & McDermott, K. B. (1995). Creating false memories: Remembering words not presented on lists. *Journal of Experimental Psychology: Learning, Memory, and Cognition, 21,* 803–814.

Roediger III, H. L., & McDermot, K. B. (2000). Tricks of memory. *Current Directions in Psychological Science, 9,* 123–127.

Rogers, W., & Gilbert, D. (1997). Do performance strategies mediate age-related differences in associative learning? *Psychology and Aging, 12,* 620–633.

Rogers, W. A., Hertzog, C., & Fisk, A. D. (2000). An individual differences analysis of ability and strategy influences: Age-related differences in associative learning. *Journal of Experimental Psychology: Learning, Memory, and Cognition, 26,* 359–394.

Rogoff, B. (1981). Schooling and the development of cognitive skills. In H. C. Triandis & A. Heron (Eds.), *Handbook of cross-cultural psychology* (Vol. 4, pp. 233–294). Boston: Allyn and Bacon.

Rogoff, B., & Mistry, J. (1990). The social and functional context of children's remembering. In R. Fivush & J. A. Hudson (Eds.), *Knowing and remembering in young children* (pp. 197–222). New York: Cambridge University Press.

Rohwer, W. D. (1973). Elaboration and learning in childhood and adolescence. In H. W. Reese (Ed.), *Advances in child development and behavior* (Vol. 8, pp. 1–57). New York: Academic.

Ronnlund, M., Nyberg, L., Backman, L., & Nilsson, L.-G. (2005). Stability, growth, and decline in adult life span development of declarative memory: Cross-sectional and longitudinal data from a population-based study. *Psychology and Aging, 20,* 3–18.

Rose, S. A., Gottfried, A. W., Melloy-Carminar, P., & Bridger, W. H. (1982). Familiarity and novelty preferences in infant recognition memory: Implications for information processing. *Developmental Psychology, 18,* 704–713.

Rotello, C. M., Macmillan, N. A., & Van Tassel, G. (2000). Recall-to-reject in recognition: Evidence from ROC curves. *Journal of Memory and Language, 43,* 67–88.

Rovee-Collier, C., & Cuevas, K. (2008). Multiple memory systems are unnecessary to account for infant memory development: An ecological model. *Developmental Psychology, 45,* 160–174.

Rowe, J. W., & Kahn, R. L (1997). Successful aging. *The Gerontologist, 37,* 433–440.

Rundus, D. (1971). Analysis of rehearsal processes in free recall. *Journal of Experimental Psychology, 89,* 63–77.

Salthouse, T. A. (1991). *Theoretical perspectives on cognitive aging.* Hillsdale, NJ: Erlbaum.

Salthouse, T. A. (1996).The processing-speed theory of adult age differences in cognition. *Psychological Review, 103,* 403–428.

Salthouse, T. A. (2006). Mental exercise and mental aging: Evaluating the validity of the "use it or lose it" hypothesis. *Perspectives on Psychological Science, 1,* 68–87.

Salthouse, T. A. (2009). When does age-related cognitive decline begin? *Neurobiology of Aging, 30,* 507–514.

Salthouse, T., Berish, D., & Miles, J. (2002). The role of cognitive stimulation on the relations between age and cognitive functioning. *Psychology and Aging, 17,* 548–557.

Salthouse, T. A., & Siedlecki, K. L. (2007). An individual difference analysis of false recognition. *American Journal of Psychology, 120,* 429–458.

Salthouse, T. A., Toth, J. P., Hancock, H. E., & Woodard, J. L. (1997). Controlled and automatic forms of memory and attention: Process purity and the uniqueness of age-related influences. *Journal of Gerontology: Psychological Sciences, 52B,* P216–P228.

Schacter, D. L., Israel, L., & Racine, C. (1999). Suppressing false recognition in younger and older adults: The distinctiveness heuristic. *Journal of Memory and Language, 40,* 1–24.

Schaie, K. W. (1996). *Intellectual development in adulthood: The Seattle Longitudinal Study.* New York: Cambridge University Press.

Schlagmüller, M., & Schneider, W. (2002). The development of organizational strategies in children: Evidence from a microgenetic longitudinal study. *Journal of Experimental Child Psychology, 81,* 298–319.

Schmitter-Edgecombe, M. (1999). Effects of divided attention and time course on automatic and controlled components of memory in older adults. *Psychology and Aging, 14,* 331–345.

Schneider, W. (1985). Developmental trends in the metamemory-memory behavior relationship: An integrated review. In D. L. Forrest-Pressley, G. E. Mackinnon, & T. G. Waller (Eds.), *Cognition, metacognition, and human performance: Vol. 1, Theoretical perspectives* (pp. 57–109). New York: Academic.

Schneider, W. (2009). Metacognition and memory development in childhood and adolescence. In H. S. Waters & W. Schneider (Eds.), *Metacognition, strategy use, and instruction* (pp. 54–81). New York: Guilford.

Schneider, W., & Bjorklund, D. F. (1998). Memory. In W. Damon, D. Kuhn, & R. S. Siegler (Eds.), *Handbook of child psychology: Cognition, perception, and language* (Vol. 2, pp. 467–521). New York: John Wiley & Sons.

Schneider, W., Borkowski, J. G., Kurtz, B. E., & Kerwin, K. (1986). Metamemory and motivation: A comparison of strategy use and performance in German and American children. *Journal of Cross-Cultural Psychology, 17,* 315–336.

Schneider, W., & Bullock, M. (Eds.) (2009). *Human development from early childhood to early adulthood: Findings from a 20 year longitudinal study.* New York: Psychology Press.

Schneider, W., Korkel, J., & Weinert, F. E. (1989). Domain-specific knowledge and memory performance: A comparison of high- and low-aptitude children. *Journal of Educational Psychology, 81,* 306–312.

Schneider, W., & Lockl, K. (2002). The development of metacognitive knowledge in children and adolescents. In T. J. Perfect & B. L. Schwartz (Eds.), *Applied metacognition* (pp. 224–257). Cambridge: Cambridge University Press.

Schneider, W., & Lockl, K. (2008). Procedural metacognition in children: Evidence for developmental trends. In J. Dunlosky & R. A. Bjork (Eds.), *A handbook of metamemory and memory* (pp. 391–410). New York: Psychology Press.

Schneider, W., & Pressley, M. (1997). *Memory development between 2 and 20.* New York: Springer-Verlag.

Schneider, W., Visé, M., Lockl, K., & Nelson, T. O. (2000). Developmental trends in children's memory monitoring: Evidence from a judgment-of-learning (JOL) task. *Cognitive Development, 15,* 115–134.

Schooler, C., & Mulatu, M. (2001). The reciprocal effects of leisure time activities and intellectual functioning in older people: A longitudinal analysis. *Psychology and Aging, 16,* 466–482.

Schooler, C., Mulatu, M. S., Oates, G. (1999). The continuing effects of substantively complex work on the intellectual functioning of older workers. *Psychology and Aging, 14,* 483–506.

Scribner, S., & Cole, M. (1972). Effects of constrained recall training on children's performance in a verbal memory task. *Child Development, 43,* 845–857.

Scribner, S., & Cole, M. (1978). Literacy without schooling: Testing for intellectual effects. *Harvard Educational Review, 48,* 448–461.

Shimamura, A., Berry, J., Mangels, J., Rusting, C., & Jurica, P. J. (1995). Memory and cognitive abilities in university professors: Evidence for successful aging. *Psychological Science, 6,* 271–277.

Shing, Y. L., Werkle-Bergner, M., Li, S.-C., & Lindenberger, U. (2008). Associative and strategic components of episodic memory: A life-span dissociation. *Journal of Experimental Psychology: General, 137,* 495–513.

Shing, Y. L., Werkle-Bergner, M., Li, S-C., & Lindenberger, U. (2009). Committing memory errors with high confidence: Older adults do but children don't. *Memory, 17,* 169–179.

Siedlecki, K. L., Salthouse, T. A., & Berish, D. E. (2005). Is there anything special about the aging of source memory? *Psychology and Aging, 20,* 19–32.

Siegler, R. S. (1996). *Emerging minds: The process of change in children's thinking.* New York: Oxford University Press.

Singer, T., Lindenberger, U., & Baltes, P. B. (2003). Plasticity of memory for new learning in very old age: A story of major loss? *Psychology and Aging, 18,* 306–317.

Skinner, E. I., & Fernandes, M. A. (2009). Illusory recollection in older adults and younger adults under divided attention. *Psychology and Aging, 24,* 211–216.

Sloutsky, V. M., & Fisher, A. V. (2004). When development and learning decrease memory: Evidence against category-based induction in children. *Psychology Science, 15,* 553–558.

Sluzenski, J., Newcombe, N. S., & Kovacs, S. L. (2006). Binding, relational memory, and recall of naturalistic events: A developmental perspective. *Journal of Experimental Psychology: Learning, Memory, and Cognition, 32,* 89–100.

Smirnov, A. A. (1973). *Problems of the psychology of memory.* New York: Plenum.

Smith, A. D. (1974). Response interference with organized recall in the aged. *Developmental Psychology, 10,* 867–880.

Smith, G. E., Housen, P., Yaffe, K., Ruff, R., Kennison, R. F., Mahncke, H. W., et al. (2009). A cognitive training program based on principles of brain plasticity: Results from the Improvement in Memory with Plasticity-Based Adaptive Cognitive Training (IMPACT) study. *Journal of the American Geriatric Society, 57,* 594–603.

Sodian, B., Schneider, W., & Perlmutter, M. (1986). Recall, clustering, and metamemory in young children. *Journal of Experimental Child Psychology, 41,* 395–410.

Spencer, W. D., & Raz, N. (1995). Differential effects of aging on memory for content and context: A meta-analysis. *Psychology and Aging, 10,* 527–539.

Steele, C. M. (1997). A threat in the air: How stereotypes shape intellectual identity and performance. *American Psychologist, 52,* 613–629.

Stine-Morrow, E. A. L., Miller, L. M. S., & Hertzog, C. (2006). Aging and self-regulated language processing. *Psychological Bulletin, 132,* 582–606.

Thapar, A., & Rouder, J. N. (2009). Aging and recognition memory for emotional words: A bias account. *Psychonomic Bulletin & Review, 16,* 699–704.

Thomas, A. K., & Sommers, M. S. (2005). Attention to item-specific processing eliminates age effects in false memories. *Journal of Memory and Language, 52,* 71–86.

Thornton, R., & Light, L. L. (2006). Language comprehension and production in normal aging. In J. E. Birren & K. W. Schaie (Eds.), *Handbook of the psychology of aging* (6th ed., pp. 261–287). Amsterdam: Elsevier.

Touron, D. R., & Hertzog, C. (2004). Strategy shift affordance and strategy choice in young and older adults. *Memory & Cognition, 32,* 298–310.

Touron, D. R., Swaim, E. T., & Hertzog, C. (2007). Moderation of older adults' retrieval reluctance through task instructions and monetary incentives. *Journal of Gerontology: Psychological Sciences, 62B,* P149–P155.

Tulving, E. (1962). Subjective organization in free recall of unrelated words. *Psychological Review, 69,* 344–354.

Tulving, E. (1985). Memory and consciousness. *Canadian Psychology, 26,* 1–12.

Tulving, E., & Thompson, D. M. (1971). Retrieval processes in recognition memory: Effects of associative context. *Journal of Experimental Psychology, 87,* 116–124.

Tun, P. A., Wingfield, A., Rosen, M. J., & Blanchard, L. (1998). Response latencies for false memories: Gist-based processes in normal aging. *Psychology and Aging, 13,* 230–241.

Van Ocker, J. C., Light, L. L., Olfman, D., & Rivera, J. (2009). *Effects of repetition and test type on age differences in associative recognition.* Manuscript submitted for publication.

Verhaeghen, P. (2003). Aging and vocabulary score: A meta-analysis. *Psychology and Aging, 18,* 322–339.

Verhaeghen, P., & Salthouse, T. A. (1997). Meta-analyses of age-cognition relations in adulthood: Estimates of linear and nonlinear age effects and structural models. *Psychological Bulletin, 122,* 231–249.

Visé, M., & Schneider, W. (2000). Determinanten der Leistungsvorhersage bei Kindergarten- und Grundschulkindern: Zur Bedeutung metakognitiver und motivationaler Einflußfaktoren. *Zeitschrift für Entwicklungspsychologie und Pädagogische Psychologie, 32,* 51–58.

Vosniadou, S. (1992). Knowledge acquisition and conceptual change. *Applied Psychology: An International Review, 41,* 347–357.

Wagner, D. A. (1978). Memories of Morocco: The influence of age, schooling, and environment on memory. *Cognitive Psychology,* pp. 1–28.

Wagner, D. A. (1981). Culture and memory development. In H. Triandis & A. Heron (Eds.), *Handbook of cross-cultural psychology* (Vol. 4, pp. 187–232). Boston: Allyn & Bacon.

Waters, H. S. (2000). Memory strategy development: Do we need yet another deficiency? *Child Development, 71,* 1004–1012.

Watson, J. M., McDermott, K. B., & Balota, D. A. (2004). Attempting to avoid false memories in the Deese/Roediger-McDermott paradigm: Assessing the combined influence of practice and warnings in young and older adults. *Memory & Cognition, 32,* 135–141.

Waxman, S., & Lidz, J. (2006). Early word learning. In D. Kuhn & R. Siegler (Eds.), *Handbook of child psychology: Vol. 2, Cognition, perception, and language* (6th ed., pp. 299–335). Hoboken, NJ: John Wiley & Sons.

Weinert, F. E., & Schneider, W. (Eds.). (1999). *Individual development from 3 to 12.* Cambridge, MA: Cambridge University Press.

Wellman, H. (1988). The early development of memory strategy. In F. E. Weinert & M. Perlmutter (Eds.), *Memory development: Universal changes and individual differences* (pp. 3–29). Hillsdale, NJ: Erlbaum.

West, R. L., Welch, D. C., & Thorn, R. M. (2001). The effects of goal-setting and feedback on memory performance and beliefs among older and younger adults. *Psychology and Aging, 16,* 240–250.

Wingfield, A., Lindfield, K. C., & Kahana, M. J. (1998). Adult age differences in temporal characteristics of category free recall. *Psychology and Aging, 13,* 256–266.

Woody-Dorning, J., & Miller, P. H. (2001). Children's individual differences in capacity: Effects on strategy production and utilization. *British Journal of Developmental Psychology, 19,* 543–557.

Worden, P. E. (1975). Effects of sorting on subsequent recall of unrelated items: A developmental study. *Child Development, 46,* 687–695.

Yonelinas, A. P. (1994). Receiver-operating characteristics in recognition memory: Evidence for a dual-process model. *Journal of Experimental Psychology: Learning, Memory, and Cognition, 20,* 1341–1354.

Yonelinas, A. P. (1997). Recognition memory ROCs for item and associative information: The contribution of recollection and familiarity. *Memory & Cognition, 25,* 747–763.

Yonelinas, A. P. (2002). The nature of recollection and familiarity: A review of 30 years of research. *Journal of Memory and Language, 46,* 441–517.

Yonelinas, A. P., & Jacoby, L. L. (1995). The relation between remembering and knowing as bases for recognition: Effects of size congruency. *Journal of Memory and Language, 34,* 622–643.

Yonelinas, A. P., Widaman, K., Mungas, D., Reed, B., Weiner, M. W., & Chui, H. C. (2007). Memory in the aging brain: Doubly dissociating the contribution of the hippocampus and entorhinal cortex. *Hippocampus, 17,* 1134–1140.

Yoon, C., Feinberg, F., Hu, P., Hedden, T., Jing, Q., Park, D. C., et al. (2004). Category norms as a function of culture and age: Comparisons of item responses to 105 categories by American and Chinese adults. *Psychology and Aging, 19,* 379–393.

Yoon, C., Hasher, L., Feinberg, F., Rahhal, R. A., & Winocur, G. (2000). Cross-cultural differences in memory: The role of culture-based stereotypes about memory. *Psychology and Aging, 15,* 694–704.

Yussen, S. R., & Bird, J. E. (1979). The development of metacognitive awareness in memory, communication, and attention. *Journal of Experimental Child Psychology, 28,* 300–313.

Zacks, R. T., & Hasher, L. (2006). Aging and long-term memory: Deficits are not inevitable. In E. Bialystok & F. I. M. Craik (Eds.), *Lifespan cognition: Mechanisms of change* (pp. 162–177). New York: Oxford University Press.

Zacks, R. T., Hasher, L., Li, K. Z. H. (2000). Human memory. In F. I. M. Craik & T. A. Salthouse (Eds.), *The handbook of aging and cognition* (2nd ed., pp. 293–357). Mahwah, NJ: Erlbaum.

Zelazo, P. D., Craik, F. I. M., & Booth, L. (2004). Executive function across the life span. *Acta Psychologica, 115,* 167–183.

Zelazo, P. D., Müller, U., Frye, D., & Marcovitch, S. (2003). The development of executive function in early childhood. *Monographs of the Society for Research in Child Development, 68* (3, Serial No. 274).

CHAPTER 10

The Development of Mental Processing

ANDREAS DEMETRIOU, ANTIGONI MOUYI, and GEORGE SPANOUDIS

This chapter reviews theory and research concerned with the development of mental processing. Mental processing can be defined in terms of three dimensions: content, processes and mechanisms, and potentials or capacity. The content refers to mental representations. That is, it refers to functional mental entities that can stand for entities in the world. Mental representations may be anything that carries information about the world. Therefore, mental images, words, numbers, bodily sensations, or any combination of them, are mental representations that can feed mental processing for the sake of understanding or problem solving (see Müller & Racine, Chapter 11 of this volume, for an extended discussion of the development of representation). External symbols, such as pictures, written language, mathematical symbolism, or any other kind of symbolism stand for, activate, or generate mental representations. Processes refer to mental actions that can be applied on representations to transform, connect, combine, or integrate them for the sake of understand-ing and problem solving. Reasoning of all kinds, such as analogical, inductive, and deductive reasoning, forms a universe of mental processes that bind mental representations together to derive or generate meaning from them, or to go beyond them by drawing inferences about meaning that exists in the relations between representations rather than in the representations themselves. In addition, there are representation-specific or domain-specific processes that operate on representations, such as mental rotation for mental images, grammar and syntax for words, arithmetic operations for numbers, and so forth. Potentials or capacity refer to the volume of representations and processes that can be handled at a particular moment. The higher they are, the more complex the realities that can be represented and processed.

Mental processing develops. Content, processes, and capacity change with development. With development, new representations or processing skills, patterns, or mecha-nisms are acquired or formed as a result of experience or learning. With development, representations and processes may be transformed, differentiated, integrated with each other, abolished, abandoned, or fade away. Language, quantitative relations, and visuospatial representation are examples of domains where all kinds of changes mentioned earlier may be observed. Finally, potentials or capacity expand systematically from birth to middle age and then decline. Obviously, the development of mental processing is dynamic. Change in each of the dimensions may cause changes in the other dimensions. For instance, acquisition of new representations may cause changes in processes, and changes in processes may cause the transformation or better handling of representations. Moreover, change in mental capacity enhances the amount of representations and processes that can be handled, and changes in processing strategies may result in more efficient use of capacity.

This chapter first summarizes theories and research that focused on different aspects of mental processing and its development. Then it focuses on our research that aimed to integrate models into a comprehensive theory. Finally, this chapter summarizes research on the organization and development of the brain with the aim to show that the theory proposed here about the mind is compatible with what is known about the brain.

MODELS FOR MENTAL PROCESSING

For almost a century, scientific study of the human mind was conducted from the perspective of three distinct epistemological traditions: the experimental, the differential, and the developmental. The experimental tradition focused primarily on the more dynamic aspects of mental functioning to explain how information from the environment is recorded, processed, represented, and stored for the purpose of understanding and problem solving. Thus, this tradition has been successful in developing models of the flow and manipulation of information in the mind. The differential or psychometric tradition aimed primarily to measure and to explain individual differences in mental abilities. This tradition has been successful in two respects. First, psychometric research uncovered a number of stable dimensions of ability and cognitive functioning that can be used to compare individuals. Second, this research produced valid and reliable tests that can be used to measure each individual's relative standing on each of the dimensions. Finally, the developmental tradition focused primarily on the development of mental functions to specify both their

state and form at different phases of life, and the causes and mechanisms underlying their transformation with growth. Thus, this tradition modeled the stages and the dynamics of the development of mental functions.

Despite large conceptual and methodological differences, the three traditions converge in their assessment of the most important constructs in the architecture of the mind. At the same time, they diverge considerably in terms of the relative importance of the various constructs in the functioning and development of the mind and their dynamic interrelations. This chapter specifies the status, development, and interrelations of cognitive functions and processes that have been the focus of these three traditions. Specifically, these are speed of processing, controlled attention and inhibitory processes, short-term and working memory, and reasoning and problem solving. We first describe each tradition separately; then we provide an integrative model and summarize supportive research.

Experimental Tradition

In the experimental tradition, information-processing models have dominated research and theorizing since the early 1950s. According to these models, humans usually operate under conditions of uncertainty caused by conflicting or incongruent information relative to a specific goal. Thus, to meet their goals, humans must be able to focus attention and process goal-relevant information efficiently, filtering out goal-irrelevant information. In effect, speed of processing, controlled attention, and working memory are considered to be important variables in understanding, learning, and problem solving.

Speed of processing basically refers to the maximum speed at which a given mental act may be efficiently executed. Usually in tests of speed of processing, the individual is asked to recognize a simple stimulus as quickly as possible, such as naming a letter, reading single words in one's native language, or identifying a certain stimulus (e.g., a geometrical figure). Under these conditions, speed of processing indicates the time needed by the system to record and give meaning to information. Traditionally, the faster an individual can recognize a stimulus, the more efficient his information processing is considered (McLeod, 1991; Posner & Raicle, 1997).

Controlled attention refers to processes that enable the thinker to stay focused on the information of interest while filtering out interfering and goal-irrelevant information (McLeod, 1991; Neil, Valdes, & Terry, 1995). In laboratory situations, the Stroop phenomenon is the paradigmatic example of the conditions that require efficient handling of conflicting information. In the classic version of the task, participants are presented with cards that involve color words printed either in black ink or in an ink color that is different from the color denoted by the word itself (for example, the word *red* is printed in blue ink). The participants may be examined under several conditions. Of primary interest is the condition of having to *read* the color words that are printed in black ink and the condition of having to *name* the ink color of words where meaning and ink color differ. Under these conditions, word reading is much faster (43.30s) than naming the ink color (110.3s). The time difference between these two conditions has been ascribed to the interference of the dominant aspect of the stimulus (i.e., the tendency to read a word) with the processing of the weaker but goal-relevant aspect (i.e., the naming of ink color). Thus, this difference is taken as a measure of inhibition, which is the basic component of controlled attention (McLeod, 1991; Stroop, 1935).

Working memory refers to the processes enabling a person to hold information in an active state while integrating it with other information until the current problem is solved. A common measure of working memory is the maximum amount of information and mental acts that the mind can efficiently activate simultaneously. The common assumption is that understanding, learning, and problem solving are positively related to working memory capacity because enhanced working memory increases the connections and associations that can be built either between the units of the newly encountered information or between this information and information already stored in long-term memory. Baddeley's (1990, 2000) model, which has received extensive empirical and theoretical scrutiny since it was first published, is widely regarded as a good approximation of the architecture of working memory. According to this multicomponent model (Baddeley, 1990, 2000; Baddeley & Hitch, 1974), working memory consists of a central executive that is an attention-controlling system that coordinates and processes the information of the other components of the model, two unimodal storage systems, namely, the phonological loop and the visuospatial sketchpad, which manipulate and store acoustic information and visual images, respectively, and a multimodal limited capacity system capable of integrating information into unitary episodic representations, the episodic buffer. The central executive is an attentional control system that is responsible for monitoring and coordinating the operation of the two slave systems, namely the phonological loop and the visuospatial sketchpad for strategy selection, and coordinating the

information in working memory with information in long-term memory. The phonological loop involves a short-term phonological buffer and a subvocal rehearsal loop. The first stores verbal information as encountered. Information in this buffer decays rapidly. The second counteracts this decay by refreshing memory traces through rehearsal. The faster the rehearsal is, the more the information that can be held in the phonological loop. The visuospatial sketchpad is responsible for the retention and manipulation of visual or spatial information. The two slave systems draw on partially different resources. As a result, each is amenable to interference from system-specific information that does not affect the other system. That is, the phonological loop is affected by interference from verbal but not visuospatial information; the visuospatial sketchpad is affected by visuospatial but not verbal information (Shah & Miyake, 1996). However, these systems are interrelated, and information from one can be translated into the code of the other through rehearsal guided by the central executive.

The episodic buffer is assumed to be "a limited-capacity temporary storage system that is capable of intergrading information from a variety of sources" (Baddeley, 2000, p. 421) into unitary multidimensional representations using a multimodal code. It integrates information from the other working memory components and the long-term memory into more complex structures, namely, scenes or episodes. It serves as a mediator between subsystems with different codes. The limited capacity of the attentional system, namely, the central executive, affects the integration and maintenance of information within the episodic buffer. The process of retrieving and binding information from multiple sources and modalities is primarily based on conscious awareness. Baddeley's model allows for both specificity and generality in cognitive functioning. Specificity is defined in terms of the modality in which information is received (i.e., acoustic vs. visual) and the ensuing symbol systems, which are developed to handle information presented in these modalities (i.e., language vs. mental imagery). Generality is defined in terms of the episodic buffer and the central executive. The very existence of the episodic buffer ensures the communication and production of integrated mental products, and the operating capacity of the central executive sets the general constraints under which the two slave systems can function.

Differential Tradition

All of these constructs attracted the interest of researchers in the differential tradition. Specifically, in this tradition, agreement is growing that intelligence is a three-level hierarchical system. This hierarchy involves general intelligence, or *g*, at the third level; a set of broad abilities, such as spatial, verbal, and mathematical reasoning at the second level; and a variety of narrow abilities within each of the second-level broad abilities at the first level.

The three-stratum theory advanced by Carroll (1993), which is based on a thorough reanalysis of a large number of factorial studies, is the prototypical model of this architecture. According to Carroll, the first stratum includes very narrow task- or medium-specific abilities, such as reasoning in different contexts, speed of processing in different contexts, different types of memory and perception, and so forth. The second stratum contains factors that organize the specialized processes of the first stratum. That is, the second stratum includes factors that represent the constructs discussed earlier (i.e., speed, control, and working memory), very broad constructs such fluid and crystallized intelligence (see Blair, Chapter 8 of this volume, for an extended discussion of intelligence, including fluid and crystallized intelligence across the life span), and also domain-specific abilities such as visual and auditory perception. The third stratum is *g* itself. Carroll posits that *g* involves complex higher-order reasoning and cognitive processes, such as induction and quantitative reasoning. Thus, Carroll's conception of *g* is similar to Spearman's classic theory (1904), which identifies *g* with general inferential processes. This general architecture is generally accepted by differential psychologists as the most accurate representation of the organization of human intelligence (Gustafsson & Undheim, 1996; Jensen, 1998).

It must be stressed, however, that Carroll's conception of *g* as inferential processes has been strongly disputed (Jensen, 1998). According to Jensen (1998), *g* is a biological rather than a psychological or behavioral construct, which reflects the ability of the brain itself to process information. Thus, according to Jensen (1998, 2006) measures of this ability must be as simple and content-free as possible to reflect the quality of information registering, transmission, and processing in the nervous system.

Numerous studies have investigated how these factors interrelate across the different levels or strata attempting to specify the relation among all three dimensions of information processing (i.e., speed of processing, controlled attention, and working memory) and psychometric *g*. It must be noted that correlations between psychometric *g* and various measures of speed of processing vary enormously (between −0.2 and −0.8) because the degree of correlation depends on the complexity of the speed of processing task.

That is, the more complex and/or semantically laden the task is in terms of decisions required before responding, the higher the correlation (see Bors, McLeod, & Forrin, 1993). Thus, several studies have suggested that general control processes rather than sheer speed are responsible for this relation (Embretson, 1995). Others have argued that the crucial variable in this relation is controlled attention capacity, which is part of working memory. In fact, Kyllonen went so far as to argue that *g is* working memory (Kyllonen, 1996). Concurring with this claim, Conway, Cowan, Bunting, Therriault, and Minkoff (2002) presented evidence suggesting that working memory but not speed of processing was related to *g*. In agreement with these findings, Miller and Vernon (1992) showed that working memory predicts *g* better than speed of processing. However, these authors also noted that working memory mediates the relation between speed of processing and *g*, because it is itself based on processing efficiency. This possibility justifies one to argue that the contribution of working memory may be overestimated, compared with measures of processing efficiency, because working memory depends on processing efficiency. Thus, working memory and processing efficiency must be clearly dissociated if their relative contribution to thought is to be specified.

Developmental Tradition

Piaget himself was indifferent to research in the differential and the experimental tradition. However, a number of scholars attempted to draw concepts and methods from these traditions to clarify the development of problem solving and thinking. There have been two lines of research in this direction, both of which have generated valuable findings and hypotheses. The first focused on the role of speed of processing and inhibition on the development of thinking and problem solving. The second, followed mostly by the so-called neo-Piagetian theorists (see Demetriou, 1998a, 1998b), that is, Case (1985, 1992), Demetriou (1998a; Demetriou, Christou, Spanoudis, & Platsidou, 2002; Demetriou, Efklides, & Platsidou, 1993), Pascual-Leone (1970, 1988), and Halford (1993, 2002), focused on the role of working memory. These two lines of research are discussed in the following section.

Role of Speed of Processing and Inhibition in Cognitive Development

Abundant evidence has been reported that speed of processing increases systematically with age. Kail (1991, 2000) showed that reaction times for a wide range of tasks, including motor, perceptual, and cognitive tasks (such as mental addition, mental rotation, and memory search), decrease exponentially with age, leveling off at about the age of 17 to 18 years. That is, Kail found that the change in speed of processing is constrained by a common factor, which operates across all types of tasks. This suggests the operation of a common underlying mechanism, which may be correlated to age-related change in the rate of neural communication or other parameters related to the representation and processing of information in the brain. Kail (2000) suggested that changes in speed of processing result in more efficient use of working memory, which, in turn, enhances reasoning and thinking.

Kail and Salthouse (Kail, 2000, 2007; Kail & Salthouse, 1994; Salthouse, 1996, 2000) extended this model to account for cognitive changes during late adult development. Specifically, they argued that impairment in cognitive performance, which occurs after middle age (Baltes, 1991; Schaie, Willis, Jay, & Chipuer, 1989), is caused by a slowing in speed of processing that begins at about the age of 40 years and continues systematically until death. Salthouse (1996) ascribed this effect of cognitive slowing to two mechanisms: the limited time mechanism and the simultaneity mechanism. According to the first mechanism, when processing speed is slower than the demand of a given task, performance is degraded because there is competition between the currently executed operations and the operations of the immediate past. That is, "the time to perform later operations is greatly restricted when large proportions of the available time are occupied by the execution of early operations" (Salthouse, 1996, p. 404), resulting in a processing that always lags behind current needs. According to the second mechanism, "products of early processing may be lost by the time that later processing is completed. To the extent this is the case, relevant information may no longer be available when it is needed" (Salthouse, 1996, p. 405). Thus, the operation of higher level mental functions, such as working memory or reasoning, may be impaired because of lack of critical information.

Inhibition may be perceived as the gatekeeper of information processing. It refers to active suppression processes that protect processing from the interference of irrelevant information, remove task-irrelevant information from the field or space of processing, and block mental or overt actions that may divert processing from the current goal (Bjorklund & Harnishfeger, 1995; Dempster, 1991, 1992, 1993; Harnishfeger, 1995). Empirical research has shown that inhibition changes systematically with age, following a pattern similar to that observed in the development of speed of processing. That is, it improves from early childhood to late adolescence, remains stable until middle age, and declines thereafter. This pattern was observed in the context of various task conditions, including the Stroop phenomenon (Comalli, Wapner, & Werner 1962; Demetriou, Efklides, & Platsidou, 1993; Harnishfeger, 1995; see also McLeod, 1991) and working memory tests. In the case of working memory, children become more able, with development, to retain storage-relevant information and ignore distracting information. In the later years, the tendency to distribute attention over both relevant and distracting information surges again, impairing working memory performance.

Obviously, the information-processing efficiency of a system that operates under limited resources is a dynamic condition that must be defined in reference to both speed of processing and inhibition. These two aspects of processing efficiency may be causally related. That is, on the one hand, improvement in speed of processing may result in an improvement in the ability to work on and finish a task before distractors can interfere, thereby resulting in improved inhibition. On the other hand, improvement in inhibition may conserve resources that are used for the sake of the current goal, thereby reducing the time needed to work on the task. To our knowledge, information referred to answer this question is not yet available.

Role of Working Memory

In the developmental tradition, neo-Piagetian theorists attempted to explain cognitive growth along Piaget's stages by invoking processing capacity as the causal factor of stage transitions. Although several researchers in the early 1960s envisaged this possibility (McLaughlin, 1963), Pascual-Leone (1970; Pascual-Leone & Goodman, 1979) was the first to propose a model of cognitive development in which he systematically attempted to integrate the fundamental assumptions of information-processing theory with the fundamental assumptions of Piagetian theory. Specifically, he argued that human thought is organized as a two-level system. The first and more basic level involves a number of constructs and functions, which define the volume of information that the individual can represent and process at a given time, and also the style and preferred ways of processing. In other words, the constructs involved at this level define the potentials or the capabilities of the individual for what information can be processed, how much of it can be processed, and how processing will be done. The second level involves both the mental operations that the thinker can execute and the concepts or knowledge that she has about the world. Pascual-Leone accepts that this level involves the structures of thought described by Piaget. Therefore, in Pascual-Leone's theory, the first of the two levels of mental architecture is derived from information-processing theory and the second originated from Piaget's theory. Pascual-Leone invokes the first level to explain the functioning and the development of the second level.

Mental attention is the fundamental construct of the causal level. It involves three constituents: the M-operator, which reflects the mental energy available at a given moment; the I-operator, which reflects central inhibition processes that enable the person to stay focused on a goal; and the currently dominant set of executive schemes, which specify the current goal. Working memory involves, in addition to all of these operators, the various content schemes that need to be held in memory when working on tasks. Mental power, or *Mp*, is the measured manifestation of working memory as defined earlier (Pascual-Leone & Baillargeon, 1994). Thus, *Mp* refers to the maximum number of independent information units or mental schemes that the person can hold simultaneously in mind at a given moment; it is quantitatively defined by Equation 1a:

$$Mp = e + k \text{ (1a)}$$

where *e* stands for the mental energy required to hold the current goal (or executive) active, and *k* stands for the number of independent schemes that can be represented and operated on. According to Pascual-Leone (Pascual-Leone & Baillargeon, 1994), *e* grows during the period of sensorimotor development until it stabilizes at the age of 2 to 3 years; *k* is equal to 1 scheme or unit of information at the age of 3, and it increases by 1 unit every second year until reaching its maximum of 7 units at the age of 15.

Pascual-Leone attempted, very systematically, to show that the increase in *Mp is the cause* of the transition from one Piagetian stage or substage to the next (Johnson, Pascual-Leone, & Agostino, 2001; Pascual-Leone & Baillargeon, 1994; Pascual-Leone & Morra, 1991). Thus, he maintains that the classic Piagetian tasks that can be solved at the stage of preoperational, intuitive, early concrete, late concrete, transitional from concrete to formal, early formal, and late formal thought require an *Mp* of 1, 2, 3, 4, 5, 6, and 7 mental schemes, respectively. Having an amount of mental power lesser than what is required by a task makes the solution of this task impossible. Thus, each increase in the capacity of *Mp* opens the way for the construction of concepts and skills up to the new level of capacity. Although a considerable number of empirical studies confirmed the expected relation between *Mp* devel-

opment and stage attainment by children and adolescents (de Ribaupierre & Pascual-Leone, 1984; Pascual-Leone & Goodman, 1979), both the analysis of tasks in terms of their *Mp* demands and the presumed direction of causality from *Mp* to stage attainment were under debate (Flavell, Miller, & Miller, 2001).

We note here that Pascual-Leone and his colleagues (Johnson, Im-Bolter, & Pascual-Leone, 2003; Pascual-Leone, 1988; Rocadin, Pascual-Leone, Rich, & Dennis, 2007) studied the role and the development of other aspects of mental attention supposedly involved in *Mp*, such as the role and the development of speed of processing and of inhibitory processes. In relation to speed, they present some evidence showing that the development of *Mp* and reaction time in a motor task follow the same developmental pattern. This finding was taken to suggest that they both reflect the same underlying construct of mental attention (Pascual-Leone, 1988). In relation to inhibitory processes, it is suggested that effortful inhibition is closely related to *Mp* as opposed to automatic inhibition, although, as it is noted, inhibition is multidimensional in nature, and its application may be affected by task demands (Johnson et al., 2003). Moreover, changes in inhibitory control are related to changes in working memory (Rocadin et al., 2007).

Several studies (Kemps, De Rammelaere, & Desmet, 2000; Morra, 2000; de Ribaupierre & Bailleux, 1994, 1995) have compared Pascual-Leone's model with the model of Baddeley (Baddeley & Hitch, 1974; Baddeley, 1990, 2000). The general conclusion is that the two models are complementary. These studies suggest that Pascual-Leone's theory can accommodate the evidence related to the development of the central aspects of working memory because the pattern of age differences found approximates the developmental pattern proposed by this theory. It is also concluded that Baddeley's model is better able to accommodate the evidence referring to the architecture of working memory and the phenomena related to this architecture. That is, Baddeley's model can accommodate the differentiation between phonological and visual memory, and also the effect of processes used to facilitate the retention of information, such as rehearsal.

Robbie Case (1985, 1992) advanced an alternative model of capacity development. This model is similar to Pascual-Leone's model in some respects and different in others. Specifically, the mental architecture in Case's theory is the same as in Pascual-Leone's theory. That is, it involves two levels, one defined in terms of processing capacity and another defined in terms of mental structures.

Moreover, causality in the relation between the two levels runs in the same direction as in Pascual-Leone's theory. That is, the development of processing capacity drives the development of mental structures.

However, there are some crucial differences between the two models. First, Case (1985) rejected the idea that changes in processing capacity can be described as a progression along a single line of development as Pascual-Leone suggested. Instead, Case maintained that processing capacity development recycles over a succession of four main stages, each one characterized by its own executive control structures. Executive control structures are systems of goal-directed representations and strategies rather than operational systems organized according to the laws of some kind of logic. In Case's (1985) words:

> An executive control structure is an internal mental blueprint, which represents a subject's habitual way of construing a particular problem situation, together with his or her habitual procedure for dealing with it. All executive control structures are supposed to contain (1) a representation of the *problem situation*, (2) a representation of their most common *objectives* in such a situation, and (3) a representation of the *strategy* needed to go from the problem situation to the objectives in as efficient manner as possible. (pp. 68–69)

Case maintained that there are four types of executive control structures: sensorimotor (e.g., seeing or grasping; 1–18 months), interrelational (e.g., words or mental images; 18 months to 5 years), dimensional (e.g., numbers; 5–11 years), and vectorial (ratios or numbers; 11–19 years).

Second, Case (1985, 1992) maintained that development within each of these four main stages evolves along the same sequence of four levels: (1) operational consolidation, (2) unifocal coordination, (3) bifocal coordination, and (4) elaborated coordination. As implied by their names, structures of increasing complexity can be understood or assembled at each of the four levels. Successive stages are not unrelated, however. According to Case, the final level of a given stage is at the same time as the first level of the following stage. Thus, when the structures of a given stage reach a given level of complexity (which corresponds to the level of elaborated coordination), a new mental unit is created and the cycle starts up from the beginning.

Case (1992) used the term *total processing space* (TPS) to refer to processing capacity. Like Pascual-Leone, he defined TPS as the sum of operating space (OS) and short-term storage space (STSS). Equation 1b is a formal expression of Case's model:

$$TPS = OS + STSS \quad (1b)$$

The OS refers to the operations that need to be performed by the thinker to attain the goal. At each of the four major stages of development, the OS is occupied by sensorimotor, relational, dimensional, and vectorial operations, respectively. The STSS refers to the maximum number of mental schemes that the thinker can focus on at a single centration of attention. An example is when one has to count how many elements are involved in several groups of objects and at the end recall all values found. In this example, the operation of counting occupies the OS component of TPS, and the values found as a result of counting occupy the STSS.

Unlike Pascual-Leone, Case (1992) maintained that TPS does not change with development. Only the relations between OS and STSS change. That is, Case asserted that, with development, the quantity of mental resources required by OS decreases because of increasing processing efficiency. The space left free because of these changes is used by the STSS. Thus, STSS increases as processing efficiency increases. Case maintained that the capacity of STSS is 1, 2, 3, and 4 schemes, at the levels of operational consolidation, unifocal coordination, bifocal coordination, and elaborated coordination, respectively.

In a series of experiments, Case (1992) tried to show that increases in STSS are, indeed, related to increases in operational efficiency. In these experiments, operational efficiency was defined as the speed of execution of the required operation. For instance, children were asked to count the elements of different sets of objects as fast as possible to measure operational efficiency in the dimensional stage. In this experiment, the children were also tested for their STSS of the sets involved. It was found that the faster the children executed the counting operation, the more items they were able to store in STSS. Baddeley and Hitch (2000) noted, however, that in this experiment, Case (1992) did not directly observe the resource demands of processing, but rather inferred them from changes in processing speed. Thus, an alternative to the assumption that increased processing efficiency frees resources that can then be used to retain more information might be that faster processing enables one to process more items per time unit, thereby increasing span. Obviously, this interpretation is fully consistent with the limited time mechanism that Salthouse (1996) proposed and directly connects the functioning of working memory to processing speed.

Halford (1993; Halford, Wilson, & Phillips, 1998) raised a number of objections regarding Case's definition of processing capacity and its role in cognitive growth. First, Halford rejected Case's position that TPS does not increase with age, because there is evidence to suggest that total capacity does increase with age (Halford, 1993). Second, he also objected to Case's fundamental assumption that development in problem solving is due to the increase in STSS, because there is evidence gathered in the context of Baddeley's model (1990; see also Halford, Maybery, O'Hare, & Grant, 1994) that suggests that STSS is not the workspace of thinking. According to this evidence, a person can keep one type of information in storage and still be able to work on a problem of a different type. This is taken to imply that it is the central executive that is involved in current problem solving and neither of the two storage systems (i.e., the phonological loop and the visuospatial sketchpad). Halford (1993) believes that the two storage systems are only used to store information that will be used at steps subsequent to the current one in a given problem-solving attempt.

The third main objection refers to Case's analysis of the complexity of problems. The reader is reminded that, according to Case, the complexity of a problem is a function of the number of goals or subgoals that must be represented as subservient to the attainment of the main goal. The more they are, the larger the STSS needed to represent them. Halford (1993, 2002; Halford & Andrews, 2004) argued that Case's definition of complexity and ensuing processing load in terms of processing steps or subroutine hierarchies is flawed for two reasons. First, subroutine hierarchies are not intrinsically constrained; that is, there is nothing inherent in them, which ensures that everybody will always analyze the goal stack of the problem in the same way. Thus, there is no way to standardize problem difficulty, making it impossible to ascribe problems unequivocally to a specific developmental level. Second, Case's assumption that more steps or subgoals make a problem more difficult is contradicted by a rather common assumption in cognitive psychology that breaking a problem into more steps makes it simpler or easier to solve.

Halford (2002; Halford & Andrews, 2004) proposed an alternative way to analyze the processing demands of problems that is supposed to explain the most crucial component of problem solving: understanding what the problem is about, as the construction of a representation of the problem that is meaningful to the person and that fully captures all the crucial relations involved. According to Halford, this understanding is built through *structure mapping.* Structure mapping is analogical reasoning that thinkers use to give meaning to problems by translating the givens of a problem into a representation or mental model that they already have and that allows them to understand the problem. The structure mappings that can be constructed depend on the relational complexity of structures they involve. The relational complexity of structures depends on the number of entities or the number of dimensions that are involved in the structure. The processing load of a task corresponds to the number of dimensions, which must be simultaneously represented if their relations are to be understood. For example, to understand any comparison between two entities (e.g., "larger than," "better than"), one must be able to represent two entities and one relation between them. To understand a transitive relation, one must be able to represent at least three entities and two relations (e.g., $A > B$; $C < B$); otherwise, it would not be possible to mentally arrange the entities in the right order that would reveal the relations between all entities involved.

Halford (2002; Halford & Andrews, 2004) identified four levels of dimensionality. The first is the level of unary relations or element mappings. Mappings at this level are effected on the basis of a single attribute. For instance, the mental image of a cat, or the word *cat,* is a valid representation of the animal cat because it is similar to it. The second level is the level of binary relations or relational mappings. At this level, two-dimensional concepts of the type "larger than" can be constructed. Thus, two elements connected by a given relation can be considered at this level. The next level is the level of system mappings, which requires that three elements or two relations be considered simultaneously. At this level, ternary relations or binary operations can be represented. The example of transitivity, which can be understood at this level, has already been explained earlier. The ability to solve simple arithmetic problems, where one term is missing, such as "3 + ? = 8" or "4 ? 2 = 8," also depends on system mappings, because all three known factors given must be considered simultaneously if the missing element or operation is to be specified. At the final level, multisystem mappings can be constructed. At this level, quaternary relations or relations between binary operations can be constructed. For example, problems with two unknowns (e.g., 2 ? 2 ? 4 = 4) or problems of proportionality can be solved. That is, at this level, four dimensions can be considered at once. The four levels correspond to Piaget's sensorimotor, intuitive, concrete, and formal stages, or Case's sensorimotor, interrelational, dimensional, and vectorial stages, respectively, and are thought to be attainable at the age of 1, 3, 5, and 10 years, respectively.

To conclude, Halford's theory is intended as a "hard capacity theory," in that it supposedly explains the mechanism underlying the transition across the main cycles of cognitive development. In other words, it might be assumed that processing capacity as conceived by Halford, which is equivalent to Baddeley's central executive, determines what can be represented in Case's OS. Case's theory, with its emphasis on the role of STSS and the analysis of processing steps, can explain progression across the sublevels involved within each of the main cycles. Halford (1993; Halford, Wilson, & Phillips, 1998) maintained that the first kind of developmental progression depends more on biological maturation than experience because it draws on the capacity of the brain to represent information. The second kind of progression depends more on experience because it depends on conceptual chunking and segmentation, which can be learned.

A COMPREHENSIVE MODEL OF THE MENTAL ARCHITECTURE AND DEVELOPMENT

We propose that the mind is a three-level architecture; two of the levels comprising general-purpose mechanisms and processes, namely, the *Processing Potentials* and the *Hypercognitive System*, and one comprising specialized capacity systems, namely, the *Specialized Systems of Thought*. The levels are functionally distinguished from each other. Each one of them is itself a complex network of processes and systems involving multiple dimensions and tiers of organization that may be uncovered if appropriately examined. The most basic of these levels involves general processes and functions, such as speed and control of processing and working memory capacity, that define the processing potentials available at a given time. The other two levels are *knowing* levels, in that they involve systems and functions underlying understanding both the surrounding environment and the self and problem solving. The first of these two *knowing* levels is primarily directed to the environment. It involves systems of cognitive functions and abilities specializing in the representation and processing of the different aspects of the physical and the social environment, such as information, relations, and problems. The other *knowing* level, namely, the *hypercognitive system*, is directed to the self. That is, it involves processes underlying self-monitoring,

self-representation, and self-regulation. In other words, this level comprises processes underlying awareness and consciousness, intentionality, and self-control. Understanding, learning, or performing any task, at a particular point in time, is a mixture of the processes involved in all three levels.

The relations between the three levels are synergic in that the condition of the processes in each constrains the operation of the processes in the other levels, and changes in any of the levels can open the way for changes in the other levels. That is, the processes comprising the level of processing potentials constrain the condition and functioning of the systems included in the other two levels. The executive and control processes in the hypercognitive system channel how efficiently processing potentials may be used, and the condition of the specialized systems of thought are the interface through which both processing potentials and executive processes are expressed (Demetriou et al., 2002). Figure 10.1 shows an illustration of this model. The following section first outlines this architecture and presents supporting empirical evidence. Then, the discussion focuses on the development of and the dynamic interrelations between the various constructs.

Processing Potentials

In this model, processing potentials are specified in terms of three dimensions: speed of processing, control of processing, and representational capacity. *Speed of processing* refers to the maximum speed at which a given mental act may be efficiently executed. *Control of processing* is considered as part of a broader mental ability, namely, executive control, which refers to inhibiting attention to irrelevant stimuli, to inhibiting prepotent or premature responses, to concentrating on goal-relevant information, to shifting focus to other information, if this is required, and to maintaining information and the appropriate rules in working memory so that a strategic plan of action can be made (Zelazo, 2004). *Representational capacity* is defined as the maximum amount of information and mental acts that the mind can efficiently activate at a given moment. Working memory is regarded as the functional manifestation of representational capacity. It is a hypothetical construct that comprises mental processes that keep a limited amount of information in an especially retrievable form, long enough for it to be used in ongoing mental tasks (Cowan, Morey, Chen, & Bunting, 2007). It is generally accepted that working memory involves central executive processes that are common across domains and modality-specific storage

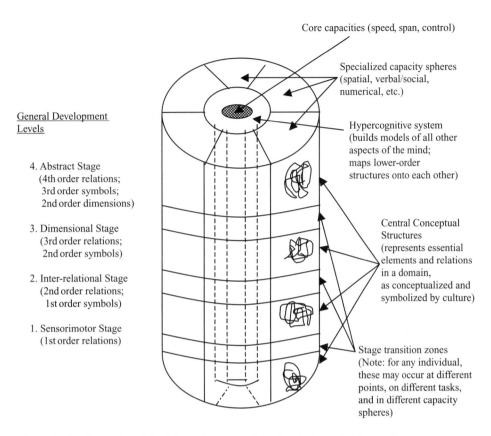

Figure 10.1   General model of the architecture of the developing mind integrating concepts from the theories of Demetriou and Case.

(Based on Figure 13 in Demetriou, A., Efklides, A., & Platsidou, M. (1993). The architecture and dynamics of developing mind: Experiential structuralism as a frame for unifying cognitive developmental theories. *Monographs of the Society for Research in Child Development, 58* [Serial Number 234].)

processes specializing in the representation of different types of information.

Specialized Domains of Thought

Specialized processes refer to mental operations and problem-solving skills that are suitable for handling (i.e., comparing, combining, transforming) different types of information, relations, and problems. We propose that to qualify for the status of a domain of thought, a block of mental operations must satisfy the following criteria. First, it must serve an identifiable *special function or purpose* vis-à-vis the organism's adaptational needs. Second, it must be responsible for the representation and processing of a particular *type of objects and relations* between environmental entities and environmental relations. Third, it must involve *specialized operations and processes* that are appropriate for the representation and processing of the type

of relations that are characteristic of each system's domain of application. Fourth, it must be *biased to a particular symbol system* that is better appropriate than other symbol systems to represent the type of relations concerned and facilitate the execution of the operations concerned. Because of these differences, the development of each system may proceed through partially different types of developmental sequences and at different rates of progression (Demetriou, 1998b; Demetriou, Efklides, & Platsidou, 1993; Demetriou & Raftopoulos, 1999; Kargopoulos & Demetriou, 1998).

The domains may be organized in three levels, each of which comprises different types of components. Specifically, each domain involves: (1) core processes; (2) mental operations, processing skills, and rules and principles integrating their functioning and use; and (3) knowledge and beliefs. Core processes are special kinds of mental processes within each system. That is, they are fundamental processes that ground each of the domains into its respective environmental realm. Therefore, these processes are obviously the result of our evolution as a species, and they somehow characterize the cognitive functioning of other species as well (Rumbaugh & Washburn, 2003). During development, core processes are the first manifestations of the systems, and they are predominantly action and perception bound. A minimum set of conditions needs to be present in the input information, to activate the core processes to provide an interpretation of the input. In other words, core processes act as inferential traps within each of the systems that respond to informational structures with core-specific interpretations that have adaptive value and "meaning" for the organism. Core elements form the background for the development of operating rules and knowledge to be described next.

The operations, rules, and processing skills are systems of mental (or, frequently, physical) actions that are used to intentionally deal with information and relations in each of the domains. At the initial phases of development, operations, skills, rules, and knowledge arise as a result of the bidirectional interactions between domain-specific core processes, the informational structures of the environment, and the functioning of the hypercognitive system as this is manifested via the executive, the self-monitoring, and the self-regulation processes.

The systems of operations and processes within each domain emerge as a process of differentiation and expansion of the core processes when these do not suffice to meet the understanding and problem-solving needs of the moment. In other words, the initial inferential traps are gradually transformed into inferential ability that is increasingly self-guided and reflected on to produce inferential patterns of thought.

Finally, each system involves knowledge of the domain with which it is affiliated. This is knowledge accumulating over the years as a result of the bidirectional interactions between a particular system and its respective domain. The acquisition of new knowledge and the formation of new representations may, under certain circumstances (such as the condition of the processing efficiency parameters and the mental capacity of the system), cause changes in processes in such ways that the system can better and more efficiently deal with more aspects of the respective domain of reality, and changes in processes may cause the transformation or better handling of representations that already exist in the system. Conceptual and belief systems pertaining to the physical, biological, psychological, and social worlds are found at this level of the organization of the various systems. Table 10.1 presents the three levels of organization of each specialized system of thought, as these will be analytically presented later.

Table 10.1   The Three Levels of Organization of Each Specialized System of Thought

Domain	Core Processes	Mental Operations	Knowledge and Beliefs
Categorical	Perception according to perceptual similarity; inductive inferences based on similarity-difference relations	Specification of the semantic and logical relations between properties, classification; transformation of properties into mental objects; construction of conceptual systems	Conceptions and misconceptions about the world
Quantitative	Subitization; counting, pointing, bringing in, removing, sharing	Monitoring, reconstruction, execution, and control of quantitative transformations, the four arithmetic operations	Factual knowledge about the quantitative aspects of the world, algebraic, and statistical inference rules
Spatial	Perception of size, depth, and orientation; formation of mental images	Mental rotation, image integration, image reconstruction, location and direction tracking and reckoning	Stored mental images, mental maps, and scripts about objects, locations, scenes, or layouts maintained in the mind
Causal	Perception of overt and covert causal relations	Trial and error; combinatorial operations; hypothesis formation; systematic experimentation (isolation of variables); model construction	Knowledge, attributions, and understanding of the reasons underlying physical and social events and the dynamic aspects of the world
Social	Recognition of conspecifics, recognition of emotionally laden facial expressions	Deciphering the mental and emotional states and intentions of others; organization of actions accordingly; imitation; decentering and taking the other's perspective	System of social attributions about other persons, their culture, and their society
Verbal	Use of the grammatical and syntactical structures of language	Identifying truth in information; abstraction of information in goal-relevant ways; differentiation of the contextual from the formal elements; elimination of biases from inferential processes; securing validity of inference	Knowledge about grammar, syntax, and logical reasoning; metalogical knowledge about nature and justifiability of logical inferences; metacognitive awareness, knowledge, and control of inferential processes

Our research has uncovered six domains of thought, namely, the categorical, quantitative, spatial, causal, social, and verbal thought, that satisfy the criteria summarized earlier (Demetriou, 1998a, 1998b, 2000; Demetriou & Bakracevic, 2009; Demetriou & Efklides, 1985, 1988, 1989; Demetriou, Efklides, Papadaki, Papantoniou, & Economou, 1993; Demetriou, Efklides, & Platsidou, 1993; Demetriou & Kazi, 2001; Demetriou, Pachaury, Metallidou, & Kazi, 1996; Demetriou, Platsidou, Efklides, Metallidou, & Shayer, 1991; Kargopoulos & Demetriou, 1998; Shayer, Demetriou, & Pervez, 1988). Clearly, the domains of quantitative, spatial, and verbal thought satisfy all four criteria discussed earlier. That is, each has a special function, deals with a special type of relation in the environment, involves characteristic operations and rules that can be easily discerned from those of the other domains, and is biased to a different symbol system (mathematical notation, mental images, and language, respectively). The other three domains (i.e., categorical, causal, and social reasoning) clearly satisfy the first three criteria (i.e., function, type of relations, and mental operations) but not the fourth one (i.e., there is no symbol system distinctly associated with each of them).

According to many studies, all six domains do come out as distinct factors in factor analysis (Case, Demetriou, Platsidou, & Kazi, 2001; Demetriou & Kyriakides, 2006; Demetriou, Kyriakides, & Avraamidou, 2003). It is interesting that using Case's (1992) analysis of central conceptual structures reveals that each of these domains involves its own semantic networks for the representation of domain-specific information, and that each of these domains activates relevant actions and operations from the part of the reasoner. It must be noted that a cognitive analysis of these systems from the point of view of their logical composition suggests that each operates according to its own logical principles (Kargopoulos & Demetriou, 1998). These logical and semantic differences between the domains suggest that they are cognitive entities, distinct from each other, in addition to being dimensions of systematic individual differences, as suggested by their factorial autonomy. Therefore, it is clear that the psychometric methods of classic and modern confirmatory factor analysis that capture dimensions of individual differences converge with the cognitive methods of logical and semantic analysis that capture the formal and mental composition of cognitive domains.

Categorical Reasoning

Categorical reasoning specializes in the handling of relations of similarity and difference between objects. The primary function of categorical reasoning is to reduce unnecessary complexity by building broad conceptual classes about the world that would facilitate future encounters on the basis of features of the objects already encountered. An example of the core elements involved in this system is processes related to categorical perception according to elements of perceptual similarity such as shape and color. Inductive inferences based on perceptual similarity can be drawn from the very first days of life, if not at birth. In fact, infants are able to recognize and register similarities and differences among various stimuli (see Butterworth, 1998). Thus, the core processes in this domain are the seeds of inductive inference. At the second level of organization, this domain involves operations and rules enabling the person to systematically represent attributes between objects, and process their similarities and differences by activating classification skills and strategies to allow for their inclusion in or exclusion from a category or a class. The third level of organization in this system accommodates our conceptions and misconceptions about the world, such as the concepts that we have about physical phenomena and living beings in general.

Quantitative Reasoning

Quantitative transformations happen on various features of the world at many levels. Things aggregate or separate so that they increase, decrease, split, or multiply in space or time for many different reasons. Subitization is one of the main core processes in this system. It refers to the ability of humans, as well as many other animals (Dehaene, 1997), to specify the number of elements in small sets (smaller than three or four elements) by simply looking at them. At the second level of organization, quantitative reasoning involves operations that enable the thinker to deal with the various quantitative transformations in ways that changes in reality can be internalized and transformations can be monitored, reconstructed or executed, and controlled by the thinker. Prominent among these operations are counting, pointing, bringing in, and removing and sharing, and their internalized mental counterparts, that is, the four arithmetic operations. The third level of the organization of this system involves all kinds of factual knowledge about the quantitative aspects of the world, algebraic and statistical inference rules.

Spatial Reasoning

Spatial reasoning enables thinking about objects and episodes as such, and orientation and movement in space. Thus, spatial reasoning enables the thinker to visualize spatial patterns and spatial relations between objects and mentally manipulate them (see Vasilyeva and Lourenco, Chapter 20 of this volume, for an extended discussion of spatial reasoning). Therefore, in this domain, spatial relations within objects (the composition and structure of objects) and between objects (relative distances, directions, and orientations) become important because they are crucial in the representation of the objects themselves, their location in space, and the space that surrounds them, as such. Formation of mental images and mental processes, such as perception of size, depth, and orientation of objects, are examples of this system's core processes. Operations, such as mental rotation or direction tracking and reckoning, allow the thinker to represent mental images and operate on them from the perspective needed so as to be able to recognize and locate them, and efficiently move between them, toward them, or away from them. The thinker can acquire, code, store, recall, and decode information about the relative locations and attributes of objects or phenomena in their everyday spatial environment. Stored mental images, mental maps, and scripts about objects, locations, scenes, or layouts maintained in the mind belong to the third level of the organization of this system (Kosslyn, 1980). This information can be of crucial importance when the reasoner plans space-related activities or selects routes over previously traveled areas.

Causal Reasoning

Causal reasoning refers to the ability to identify causal relations between objects or events. When the thinker assumes that one or more events may cause some other events, it becomes possible first to establish if there, indeed, is a causal relation and then act accordingly to manipulate this relation to reinforce, weaken, or even remove it for the sake of changing the sequence of events in the preferred direction. Perception of fundamental causal relations, such as when there is a direct transfer of energy from one object to another (e.g., we push something to move it), is an example of the core processes involved in this system. At the second level of organization, causal reasoning involves operations that enable the thinker to manipulate and represent causal relations. Prominent among these is trial-and-error manipulations that aim to uncover the causal role of objects. Isolation of variables (or systematic experimentation) is a more elaborate process used to systematically manipulate dynamic causal relations. Knowledge related to the "why" and "how" of things pertains to the third level of the organization of this system. Our understanding of the reasons underlying physical and social events, as well as their procedural aspects, comes from the functioning of

the operations mentioned earlier and constitutes our ready-made attributions about the dynamic aspects of the world (Demetriou, Efklides, & Platsidou, 1993; Demetriou, Efklides et al., 1993).

Social Reasoning

Social reasoning focuses on how people think about and make sense of themselves, others, and the world of social affairs by understanding the social relationships and interactions. These range from the dynamics concerned with ongoing interpersonal interactions and relationships between individuals to general rules and principles governing the relationships between individuals and social or cultural institutions. In this latter case, one may refer to the moral principles and conventions that regulate what is permissible in a given society at particular historical times or the rules governing the political organization of society. Core processes in this system involve the recognition of conspecifics (i.e., recognition of the members of the same species), such as the infant's preference for the human face as contrasted with other objects, or the recognition of particular emotionally laden facial expressions, such as a smile or growl, which are adaptively important for the individual. At the second level of organization, there are operations and processes that enable the individual to decipher the mental and emotional states and the intentions of others, and organize his or her actions toward others accordingly. Imitation, actual or mental, decentering, and taking the other's perspective are examples of operations explicitly involved in understanding and handling social interactions. The role of such operations in internalizing knowledge or information and shaping conceptual structures is important. Accumulated experience shapes and fosters these structures that act as the basis for mental representations, and they serve as a frame of reference for interpreting, storing, processing, and using information and experiences. These mental representations and the well-differentiated and integrated cognitive structures that are developed over the course of time belong to the third level of organization of this system. At this level, the knowledge and beliefs that constitute the person's system of social attributions about other persons, their culture, and their society enable the thinker to select, process, and use social information in a relatively efficient, automatic fashion. The likelihood that at this level the individual might use incoming social information in a biased way and in a manner conforming to existing conceptual structures is increasing or decreasing as a function of the person's ability to control the tendency of automatically categorizing and socially stereotyping in terms of a conceptual structure that represents a particular group of people.

Verbal Reasoning

Verbal reasoning refers to the ability to listen (or read) critically and to identify relevant information about facts, opinions, and inferences that can be used to facilitate interaction between persons, guide action, and organize inference across different domains and occasions. As a facilitator of interpersonal interactions, verbal reasoning enables persons to share information, cooperate, and check for consistency in the information provided, and thus avoid deception, if present (Cosmides & Tooby, 1994). As a guide of action, it enables persons to specify the results of their possible actions from the beginning, and thus choose between alternative courses of action according to the goals selected. As an inference organizer, it enhances mental economy and efficiency by generating mental tools that can be readily called on in the future. Core processes in this system underlie the ability to use the grammatical and syntactical structures of language (e.g., "*if* this *then* that," "*either* this *or* that") to infer the relations between the events or situations mentioned in a sequence of sentences (Braine, 1990; Demetriou, 1998b). At the second level of organization, operations and processes in this domain are primarily directed to identifying the truth in relations as these are presented in verbal statements and securing the validity of the extracted inference. These processes enable the person to judge the accuracy of the information received, decipher deception, eliminate the likelihood that conclusions are biased by personal knowledge and beliefs, and so forth. Two types of skills are used to attain these aims. First, grammatical and syntactical skills enable the individual to interpret and relate the components in verbal statements so that information may be abstracted in goal-relevant, meaningful, and coherent ways. Second, there are skills that enable one to differentiate the contextual from the formal elements in a series of statements and operate on the latter. The content and, therefore, the meaning of the verbal information are strongly related to the reasoning procedure where their role in each type of reasoning is clearly differentiated. In deduction, knowledge and belief biases may intrude in the process and distort the effect of the logical form of the argument on the extraction of the outcome. In induction, the content of the premises defines the outcome because it activates the retrieval of knowledge stored in long-term memory (see Ricco, Chapter 12 of this volume, for an extended discussion of deductive reasoning). These processes enable one to construct and express the basic logical relations of negation, conjunction, disjunction, and implication (Efklides, Demetriou, & Metallidou, 1994). When available, these relations can be invoked for the sake of dealing with problems in any of the other domains. With development and experience, it becomes easier to intentionally call on these relations for the sake of the functioning of different domains. Explicit knowledge about grammar and syntax, and explicit knowledge about logical reasoning belong to the third level of the organization of this system. Metalogical knowledge about the nature and justifiability of logical inferences, and metacognitive awareness, knowledge, and control of one's inferential processes belong to the third level of the organization of verbal reasoning as well (Moshman, 2004).

The Hypercognitive System

Problem-solving creatures, other than humans, can draw inferences, and they possess many domain-specific abilities, such as orientation in space, object recognition, quantification, and so forth (Rumbaugh & Washburn, 2003). Even modern robots possess these abilities (Pfeifer & Scheier, 1999). However, possession of these abilities is not sufficient to credit these creatures with a mind. For this to be possible, a cognitive system must be able to reflect on its own reasoning and to use the product of this reflection to organize complex reasoning processes. In other words, the system must be capable of *self*-mapping: record its own cognitive experiences and keep maps of them that can be used in the future, if the need arises (Demetriou, 2000; Demetriou & Efklides, 1989; Demetriou, Efklides, & Platsidou, 1993; Demetriou & Kazi, 2001, 2006; Demetriou, Kyriakides, & Avraamidou, 2003). This metacognitive ability to think about thinking and to explicitly control the organization of one's reasoning processes is what accounts for a major part of the individual differences between reasoners of the same age, as well as for the age-related differences between children and adults (Moshman, 2004).

We postulate that creatures capable of self-mapping possess a second-order level of *knowing*. This is the *hypercognitive system*. It may be noted here that the adverb *hyper* in Greek means "higher than" or "on top of" or "going beyond," and when added to the word *cognitive*, it indicates the supervising and coordinating functions of the hypercognitive system. Thus, this term is preferable to the term *metacognition*, which is commonly used in the literature, because the adverb *meta* it often taken to mean "after" or "later." The input to this system is information coming from the other levels of the mind (sensations, feelings, and conceptions caused by mental activity). This information is organized into the maps or models of mental functions to be described later. These are used to coordinate and control the functioning of the domain-specific systems and the processing potentials available. Thus, the hypercognitive system is defined by the self-awareness and self-regulation knowledge and strategies, and is conceived as the interface between (a) mind and reality, and (b) any of the various systems and processes of the mind. The hypercognitive system involves two central functions, namely, the *working hypercognition* and the *long-term hypercognition.*

Working hypercognition revolves around a strong directive-executive function that is responsible for setting and pursuing mental and behavioral goals until they are attained. This function involves five basic components: (1) a directive function oriented to setting the mind's current goals; (2) a planning function that proactively constructs a road map of the steps to be made toward the attainment of the goal; (3) a comparator or monitoring function that regularly effects comparisons between the present state of the system and the goal; (4) a negative feedback control function that registers discrepancies between the present state and the goal, and suggests corrective actions; and (5) an evaluation function that enables the system to evaluate each step's processing demands vis-à-vis the available skills and strategies of the system so as to make decisions about the value of continuing or terminating the endeavor and evaluate the final outcome achieved. These processes operate recursively in such a way that goals and subgoals may be renewed according to the online evaluation of the system's distance from its ultimate objective. These regulatory functions operate under the current structural constraints of the system that define the system's current maximum potentials (Demetriou, 2000; Demetriou & Efklides, 1989; Demetriou & Kazi, 2001).

Consciousness is an integral part of the hypercognitive system. The very process of setting mental goals, planning their attainment, monitoring action vis-à-vis both the goals and the plans, and regulating real or mental action requires a system that can remember and review and, therefore, know itself. Therefore, conscious awareness and all ensuing functions, such as a self-concept (i.e., awareness of one's own mental characteristics, functions, and mental states) and a theory of mind (i.e., awareness of others' mental functions and states) are part of the very construction of the system. In fact, long-term hypercognition comprises the models and representations concerning past cognitive experiences that result from the functioning of working hypercognition. These models involve descriptions about the general structural and dynamic characteristics of the

mind, and prescriptions and rules about the efficient use of the functions—for instance, that excessive information requires organization if it is to be retained in memory, or that rehearsal is needed if one is to learn quickly and permanently. Research on theory of mind (e.g., Fabricius & Schwanenflugel, 1994; Flavell, Green, & Flavell, 1986; Schneider, Lockl, & Fernadez, 2005; Wellman, 1990; Zelazo & Müller, 2002) and on implicit theories of intelligence (Grigorenko et al., 2001; Sternberg, Conway, Ketron, & Bernstein, 1981) sheds light on this aspect of long-term hypercognition. Moreover, research on self-evaluation and self-representation with regard to intellectual functioning is related to the evaluative and regulatory aspects of hypercognition (Demetriou & Bakracevic, 2009; Demetriou & Kazi, 2001, 2006; Harter, 1999; Nicholls, 1990). Finally, we have shown that the hypercognitive system mediates the relations between cognitive processes and personality, enabling the individuals to have an integrated cognitive-affective view of themselves that is accessible to consciousness (Demetriou, Kyriakides, & Avraamidou, 2003).

Long-term hypercognition involves the control and executive functions ascribed by Baddeley's model to the central executive and the episodic buffer of working memory, or by experimental researchers to functions underlying control of processing, inhibition, and selective attention. All these processes usually refer to using the hypothetical constructs of selective attention, working memory, inhibition, and sustained attention or alertness, and are part of the generic construct of executive functions (Polderman et al., 2007). Ascription of these functions to the hypercognitive system rather than to working memory or control of processing conveys our assumption that self-awareness and control emanate from a higher-order system that specializes in the surveillance and regulation of cognitive functions oriented to the environment. This system may have evolved from primary inhibition and control mechanisms associated with perception and automated action sequences (Demetriou, 2000; Demetriou & Bakracevic, 2009; Demetriou & Kazi, 2001, 2006; Gibson, 1966; Zelazo, 2004; Zelazo et al., 2003).

Davidson, Amso, Anderson, and Diamond (2006) place much value on the functions of working memory, inhibition, and cognitive flexibility, and they postulate that mature cognition is characterized by the specific abilities that refer to these functions. As children enter adolescence and early adulthood, they become increasingly more able to control their thoughts and actions (Huizinga, Dolan, & van der Molen, 2006). Specifically, their ability to select input from the environment that is relevant to their goals and suppress distracting or conflicting information, to hold that information in mind and to process it according to the demands of the task at hand, to inhibit inappropriate or premature reactions, and to maintain alertness during the problem-solving procedure is increasingly developed (Diamond, 1990; Zelazo, 2004; Zelazo et al., 2003).

Relations between the Levels of Mind

Three-Level Architecture

Several studies on the three-level architecture of the mind, which includes processing potentials as such, the specialized domains, and the hypercognitive system, have been conducted (see Demetriou, 2003, 2006; Demetriou & Kazi, 2001, 2006). One of them is summarized here (Demetriou & Kazi, 2006). This study addressed all three dimensions of processing potentials—that is, speed and control of processing and representational capacity (phonological, visual, and executive working memory), three domains of reasoning (verbal, quantitative, and spatial reasoning), and self-awareness about the domains of reasoning mentioned earlier in a group of 11- to 15-year-old adolescents. The model that captures the relations between the levels of the mind is shown in Figure 10.2.

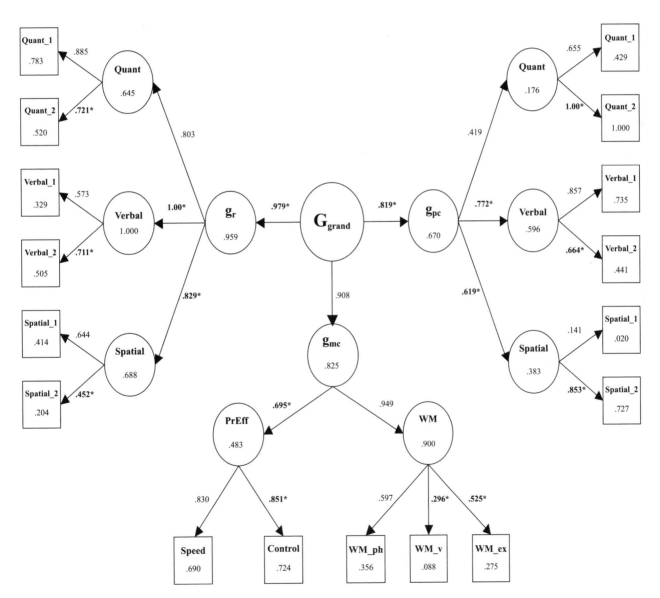

Figure 10.2 Confirmatory factor analysis for processing efficiency and capacity, and self-representation of the cognitive processes. *Boldface* denotes free parameters; *asterisks* denote significant coefficients.

It can be seen that this model includes a first-order factor standing for processing efficiency and another first-order factor standing for working memory. These two factors are related to a second-order factor that stands for general mental capacity. Also, there are three first-order factors standing for performance on quantitative, verbal, and visuospatial reasoning. These three factors relate to another second-order factor that stands for general reasoning. Finally, there are three first-order factors that stand for self-representation in each of the three reasoning domains. The three factors relate to another second-order factor that stands for general perceived competence. Obviously, these three second-order factors stand for the three main levels of the mental architecture proposed in our theory. These three second-order factors were regressed on a third-order factor, the Ggrand. Attention is drawn to the relations between the three second-order factors and the Ggrand factor. They are all very strong (all coefficients greater than 0.82), clearly suggesting that processing efficiency and representational capacity, inferential and problem-solving processes, and self-awareness about them are all complementary and strong components of *g*. All in all, this study clearly shows that all three types of processes are equally strong constituents of the human mind.

Dynamic Relations between Processes and Systems

The relations between the general and the specialized processes are complex and bidirectional. On the one hand, general processes set the limits for the construction, operation, and development of the domain-specific systems. On the other hand, specialized processes provide the frame and raw material for the functioning of general processes. Thus, individual differences in the functioning of general processes reflect, to a large extent, differences in the specialized processes.

The models of the effects of general processes on specialized processes adopt a bottom-up approach. That is, they assume that general-purpose processes constrain the condition of complex, and thus more specialized, processes, though there is no consensus yet on the exact nature of this relation and on the role of the various general-purpose processes in the functioning and development of specialized processes. For some scholars, speed of processing is the most important factor both for individual differences (Deary, 2000; Jensen, 1998) and intellectual development (Kail, 1991; Kail & Salthouse, 1994; Salthouse, 1996). For other scholars, attentional and executive control processes are more important factors in explaining individual

differences and intellectual development (Bjorklund & Harnishfeger, 1995; Dempster, 1991, 1992; Engle, 2002; Harnishfeger, 1995; Schweizer, Moosbrugger, & Goldhammer, 2005; Stankov & Roberts, 1997; Zelazo, Qu, & Müller, 2005; see also Jacques & Marcovitch, Chapter 13 of this volume). Finally, for other scholars, working memory is the crucial causal factor underlying individual differences in intelligence (Cowan et al., 2007; Hale & Fry, 2000; Kyllonen & Christal, 1990; Oberauer, Süß, Schulze, Wilhelm, & Wittmann, 2000) and intellectual development (Case, 1985, 1992; Halford, 1993; Halford & Andrews, 2004; Pascual-Leone, 1970, 1988; Rocadin et al., 2007).

Obviously, the integrative theory to come will have to specify accurately the role of each of these processes. A series of studies in our laboratory has tried to meet this challenge. The main methodological consideration guiding the design of these studies lies in the construction of the tasks. Specifically, tasks are constructed so as to differ systematically in their composition, from very simple to very complex, in such a way that tasks at each next level of complexity involve all of the processes of the previous level together with the processes that are specific to this particular level. Performance on such an array of tasks must conform to a simplex model, in terms of modern structural equation modeling. That is, a model where performance on the tasks of each level, *L*, is regressed on performance on the tasks of the lower level, *L—1*, must fit the data very well because of the common components running through the sequence in the cascade fashion explicated earlier.

In one of these studies (Demetriou, Mouyi, & Spanoudis, 2008), we designed tasks addressed to the following processes: speed of processing (SP), perceptual discrimination (PD), perceptual control (PC), conceptual control (CC), working memory (WM), information integration (InfI), and deductive and inductive reasoning (Reason). The first four processes address various aspects of processing efficiency by speeded performance tasks, and the last three address representational and inferential processes. The tasks addressed to these processes are assumed to include the components as specified in Equations 2a to 2f:

$$PD = SP + \textit{perceptual discrimination processes} \quad (2a)$$

$$PC = SP + PD + \textit{control of interference from perceptual attributes} \quad (2b)$$

CC = SP + PD + PC + *control of interference from*
conceptual attributes to knowledge in long-term
memory   (2c)

WM = SP + PD + PC + CC + *storage and retrieval*
processes   (2d)

InfI = SP + PD + PC + CC + WM + *planning and*
integration processes   (2e)

Reason = SP + PD + PC + CC + WM + InfI +
inferential processes   (2f)

Speed of processing tasks studied the ability to locate the position of a stimulus as fast as possible. Perceptual discrimination tasks addressed the ability to specify which of two objects drawn to clearly differ in size (e.g., a leaf and a tree) is the bigger one. Therefore, it is assumed that perceptual discrimination reflects sheer speed of processing together with the processes required to discriminate between two simple stimuli and identify the target one. In the perceptual control tasks, participants were presented stimuli where one strong perceptual attribute interfered with a weaker but relevant attribute that was to be responded as well. For instance, participants were presented a big number digit (e.g., 7) composed of small 4s. Their task was to recognize the small component digit as fast as possible. Thus, it is assumed that perceptual control reflects the processes involved in perceptual discrimination and also the processes required for the control of the interference of the strong but irrelevant dimension of the stimulus condition in the identification of the weaker but relevant dimension. In conceptual control tasks, participants were presented with a pair of objects or animals where their actual size relations were reversed, such as an ant bigger than a bear, and they were asked to choose which is bigger in reality. Therefore, conceptual knowledge (bears are bigger than ants) would have to dominate over the perceptual setup of the stimuli. Conceptual control is assumed to reflect all of the processes included in perceptual control and also the processes required to control interference from conceptual attributes to knowledge in long-term memory. Working memory tasks addressed both simple storage and executive processes using spatial, numerical and verbal information. Working memory is assumed to involve all of the processes above and also the processes required to store and recall information. In the information integration tasks, participants were presented

with a stimulus in the top-right corner of the screen (e.g., a word) and they were asked to specify whether its components (i.e., syllables), which were scrambled on the rest of the screen together with other stimuli, were all present. Information integration is assumed to involve all of the processes above and also the processes required to execute an action plan for the identification and integration of information as specified by the task requirements. Finally, reasoning tasks addressed various types of deductive and inductive reasoning in spatial, mathematical, and verbal relations. It is assumed that reasoning involves all of the processes above and also the inferential processes required to go beyond the information given to draw the relevant logically sound conclusions. These tasks were administered to 140 children about equally drawn from the 6 primary school grades, that is, children from 6.5 to 11.5 years of age.

To test the model capturing the structural relations between the various processes specified earlier, we evaluated a series of structural equation models. Two of these models are presented in Figure 10.3. These models are built on the assumption, specified by Equations 2a through 2f, that processes are hierarchically organized so that the processes at each subsequent higher level in the hierarchy are largely based on the processes of the previous levels together with processes specific to this level. In this case, the various processes were represented by the seven first-order factors. Specifically, speed of processing, perceptual discrimination, perceptual control, conceptual control, working memory, information integration, and reasoning were identified by relating each of the corresponding sets of measures to a separate factor. These factors were regressed on each other in the cascade fashion shown in Figure 10.3. The fit of this model was excellent (see fit indices in Figure 10.3). It can be seen that all structural relations were significant and high. Therefore, it is clear that cognitive processes are hierarchically organized so that effects are carried over from one level of organization to the other where new processes are constructed in level-specific fashion.

One might object that the relations captured by this model are spurious relations emanating from the operation of a powerful common factor that pulls the strings of the interaction between the various processes. One such factor is age, which represents the general maturational and experiential state, and the developmental direction of the organism. To test how age as such affects the relations between the various constructs, we reran the model above after partialing out the effect of age. Technically, this was effected by regressing each of the

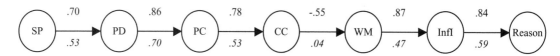

Figure 10.3 Simplex model of the structural relations between the factors. Coefficients in italics come from fitting the model after partialing out the effect of age. All coefficients are significant but the correlation between conceptual control (CC) and working memory (WM) when the effect of age is partialed out. Fit indices of the model before [$\chi^2(143) = 166.741$; $p = 0.085$; CFI = 0.974; RMSEA = 0.045] and after partialing out the effect of age [$\chi^2(143) = 156.621$; $p = 0.206$; CFI = 0.987; RMSEA = 0.034], respectively. SP, speed of processing; PD, perceptual discrimination; PC, perceptual control; CC, conceptual control; WM, working memory; InfI, information integration; Reason, deductive and inductive.

observed variables involved in the model on age, in addition to the factors they are related to as specified earlier. The fit of this model was also excellent (see indices in Figure 10.3).

Naturally, the relations between factors did become weaker, suggesting that the force of development does bind the factors together, to some extent. However, most of the relations remained significant and generally high, suggesting that the cascade hierarchical structure of cognitive processes is part of their construction. Special attention, however, is drawn to the fact that this manipulation resulted in the annihilation of the relation between conceptual control and working memory. This finding reflects a division between the level of processing potentials and the representational level of the mind that is bridged by development. In other words, through development, the possibilities afforded by processing potentials are transformed into actual representational and inferential capabilities.

A second study confirmed and extended the findings of the study summarized earlier (Demetriou et al., 2002). This study included 120 children and adolescents from 8 to 14 years of age who were tested longitudinally for 3 consecutive years so that by the end of the study their age ranged from 10 to 16 years. The tasks used in this study overlapped with those used in the study summarized earlier only to some extent. Specifically, we used the perceptual discrimination and perceptual control tasks to examine processing efficiency. For memory, we used both tasks addressed to short-term storage and executive control in working memory. For reasoning, there were tasks addressed to three domains: deductive and inductive reasoning as in the earlier study, and also quantitative (a series of numerical analogies and arithmetic operations tasks) and spatial reasoning (a series of mental rotation and coordination of perspectives tasks). A series of cascade models similar to the model presented earlier (see Figure 10.3) was applied on this study as well. The

general pattern of relations built into the model is shown in Figure 10.4.

In Figure 10.4a, each level was regressed on the previous level but the last three reasoning factors, which were all regressed on the executive working memory factor. In this case, however, we included in the model performance on perceptual discrimination and perceptual control of the first testing wave, performance on the short-term and executive working memory of the second testing wave, and performance on the three reasoning domains of the third testing wave. This model is a robust test of the structural relations between processes because each of the three main types of processes (processing efficiency, working memory, and reasoning) is measured at different points in time. That is, prediction here acquires its true meaning because we predict reasoning at time 3 from the condition of working memory at time 2, and we predict the condition of working memory at time 2 from the condition of processing efficiency at time 1. All relations are strong and similar to the relations found by the first study. Moreover, partialing out the effect of age resulted in a mild reduction of the strength of the relations in all cases but in the case of the relation between perceptual control and short-term memory, where the reduction was very large (from −0.62 to −0.28).

Figure 10.4b presents a slightly different version of the model explicated earlier. Specifically, the reasoning factor (of the second testing wave) was taken as a separate tier in this model. It can be seen that this factor was regressed on the executive memory factor (of the second testing wave), and the other two reasoning domains (of the third testing wave), that is, the domains of mathematical and spatial thought were regressed on this reasoning factor. Obviously, this manipulation conveys the assumption that the thought processes involved in spatial and mathematical thought build on and go beyond the deductive and inductive inferential processes. In other words, inferential processes are taken to be basic processes that are used for the construction of the domain-specific strategies, skills, and processes involved in the various domains. This model was found to hold well and, in fact, to be statistically more powerful than the model presented earlier (see the fit indices in Figure 10.4).

The convergence between the two studies summarized earlier suggests the following conclusions. First, the separation between the level of processing potentials and the environment-oriented representational level is clear in both studies. Second, it is also clear that the first level functions as a developmental factor for the latter. This is suggested by the fact that partialing out the effect of age drastically diminishes the relation between processing efficiency and working memory, which suggests that these levels are connected by the developmental factors associated with age. Thus, changes in the dimensions of processing efficiency, that is, speed and control of processing, make changes in the various representational functions, such as information storage, integration, and inference, possible. Attention is drawn to the fact that working memory seems to belong to the representational level of the mind's organization rather than the level of processing potentials. Attention is also drawn to the relations of the executive working memory factor with the three reasoning

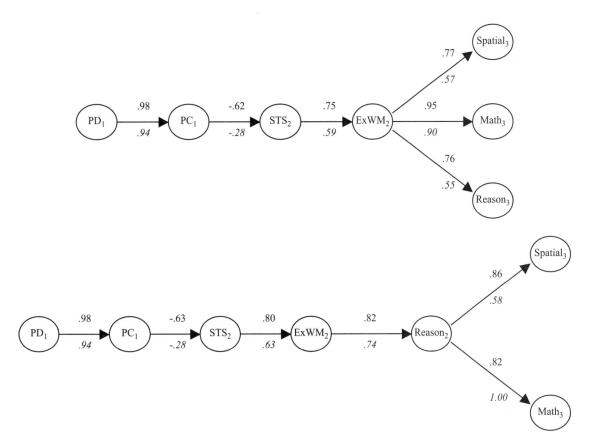

Figure 10.4 Simplex model of the structural relations of the longitudinal study. (a) Perceptual discrimination (PD) and perceptual control (PC) were taken from the first testing wave; short-term storage (STS) and executive working memory (ExWM) from the second testing wave; and spatial, mathematical, and propositional reasoning from the third testing wave. (b) PD and PC were taken from the first testing wave; STS, ExWM, and propositional reasoning from the second testing wave; and spatial and mathematical reasoning from the third testing wave. Coefficients above the *arrows* show relations before partialing age out, and coefficients below the *arrows* (in italics) show relations after partialing age out. All coefficients are significant. Fit indices of the models before [a: $\chi^2(163) = 192.381$; $p = 0.067$; CFI = 0.961; RMSEA = 0.040; b: $\chi^2(163) = 188.112$; $p = 0.087$; CFI = 0.967; RMSEA = 0.037] and after partialing age out [a: *$\chi^2(163) = 189.200$; $p = 0.078$; CFI = 0.971; RMSEA = 0.038;* b: *$\chi^2(163) = 187.536$; $p = 0.083$; CFI = 0.971; RMSEA = 0.038*].

domains. It can be seen that these relations vary, reflecting differences between domains in the transformation of processing potentials and representational capacity into domain-specific skills, operations, and processes. Finally, it also seems to be the case that inferential processes as such form an extra tier in the architecture of the mind that intervenes between general executive processes and domain-specific computational and operational processes, strategies, and skills.

General Developmental Patterns

All of the processes mentioned earlier develop systematically with age. The structural models summarized suggest that there are strong developmental relations between the various processes, such that changes at any level of organization of the mind open the way for changes in other levels. Specifically, the simplex cascade models suggest that changes in speed of processing open the way for changes in the various forms of control of processing. These, in turn, open the way for the enhancement of working memory capacity, which subsequently opens the way for development in inferential processes as such. Eventually, all of these changes result in the development of the various specialized domains through the reorganization of domain-specific skills, strategies, and knowledge, and the

acquisition of new ones. Other studies, to be summarized later, show that there is top-down escalation of change as well (Demetriou et al., 2002). The following section summarizes the basic developmental trends in each of the main levels of the mind.

Processing Efficiency and Working Memory

Our research (Demetriou et al., 2008) shows that reaction times decrease with age in all of the processing efficiency functions described earlier (Figure 10.5). Although absolute values vary depending on the complexity of the process concerned, the pattern of change is exponential. Kail (1991) conducted a meta-analysis of 72 studies on speeded performance to provide additional evidence on the relation between the mean response times in groups of different ages. Kail showed that the mean reaction time of young children and adolescents is equal to the mean reaction time of the young adults, which is the age with the smallest reaction time recorded, multiplied with a slowing coefficient. The value of the slowing coefficient became smaller with age, in a nonlinear fashion: It changed substantially in early and middle childhood, and more slowly thereafter. Overall, processing efficiency remains stable from early adulthood to the mid-50s, when it starts to decline systematically (Salthouse, 2004; Schaie, 1995).

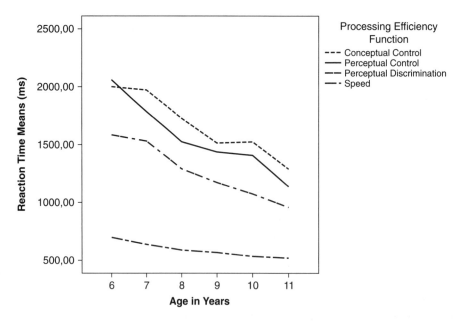

Figure 10.5 Processing efficiency as a function of age and process. *Dotted line* represents conceptual control; *solid line* represents perceptual control; *short dashed and dotted line* represents perceptual discrimination; *long dashed and dotted line* represents speed.

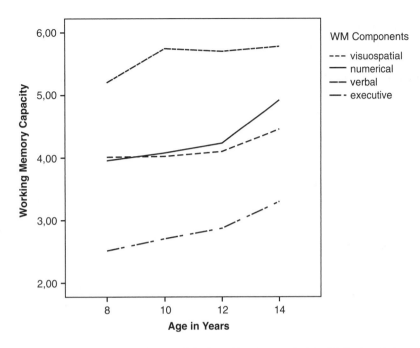

Figure 10.6 Short-term visuospatial *(dotted line)*, numerical *(solid line)*, verbal *(dashed line)*, and executive working memory *(dashed and dotted line)* as a function of age in a sample of Chinese children.

Working memory is a hypothetical construct that comprises mental processes that keep a limited amount of information in an especially retrievable form, long enough for it to be used in ongoing mental tasks (Cowan et al., 2007). A consistent understanding of the function of working memory should successfully address both of its components, namely, the storage component and the attention component (Conway et al., 2002), by studying its function in maintaining memory representations in the face of concurrent processing and under the plausible distractions and attention shifts (Ackerman, Beier, & Boyle, 2005; Engle, Tuholski, Laughlin, & Conway, 1999; Miyake & Shah, 1999). There are many ways to measure the capacity of working memory. This explains why scholars differ in their specification of the capacity of working memory at different periods of life.

According to our studies, all components of working memory (i.e., executive processes, numerical, phonological and visuospatial storage) increase with age (Demetriou, Efklides, & Platsidou, 1993; Demetriou et al., 2002, Demetriou et al., 2008). In fact, the development of the components of working memory seems to follow the same pattern of change and can be described by a logistic curve that is very similar to the exponential curve that describes the change of processing efficiency (Demetriou et al.,

2005). This pattern of change of the components of working memory is illustrated in Figure 10.6.

It can be seen that there is an inverse trade-off between the central executive and the storage buffers, so that the higher the involvement of executive processes, the less the manifested capacity of the modality-specific buffers. This is so because the executive operations themselves consume part of the available processing resources. However, with age, executive operations and information are chunked into integrated units. As a result, with development, the person can store increasingly more complex units of information. For instance, primary school children can remember single numbers, whereas adolescents can store the products of operations applied on numbers. This pattern is in agreement with Case's (1985) claim that the development of OS is inversely related to the development of STSS. In line with the findings on processing efficiency, the various aspects of working memory remain stable from early adulthood to the 50s, and they start to decline thereafter (Salthouse, 2004; Schaie, 1995).

To account for this evidence, we proposed the functional shift model (Demetriou, Efklides, & Platsidou, 1993). This model presumes that when the mental units of a given level reach a maximum degree of complexity, the mind tends to reorganize these units at a higher level of representation or integration to make them more manageable. Having created a new mental unit, the mind prefers to work with this rather than the previous units because of its functional advantages. An example in the verbal domain would be the shift from words to sentences and in the quantitative domain from natural numbers to algebraic representations of numerical relations. The model suggests that working memory cannot be completely disentangled from its content. By definition, then, working memory is representational in nature. This explains why in the earlier models working memory is tied to the representational rather than the efficiency level of the mind.

Development of the Specialized Domains

The specialized domains are developing through the life span in terms of both general trends and the modal characteristics of each domain. In the age span from birth to middle adolescence, the changes are faster in all of the domains. This developmental profile of each specialized domain in the period between 3 and 15 years of age is outlined in Table 10.2. Inspection of Table 10.2 suggests that with development, each of the domains moves from fewer

and reality-referenced to more and reciprocally referenced representations.

As a result, concepts in each of the domains become increasingly defined in reference to rules and principles bridging more local concepts and creating new, broader concepts that are subject to change should such a need occur. Moreover, understanding and problem solving in each of the domains evolve from global and less integrated to differentiated, but better integrated, mental operations (Werner, 1948). As a result, planning and operation from alternatives become increasingly part of the person's modus operandi, as well as the increasing ability to efficiently monitor the problem-solving process. This offers flexibility in cognitive functioning and problem solving across the whole spectrum of specialized domains. Finally, as shown in the next section, increasing reflection on cognitive and problem-solving processes, self-guidance, and self-awareness become part of the system.

Hypercognition

Hypercognition develops along a number of different fronts (see Table 10.2), including the various functions of

Table 10.2 Modal Characteristics of the Specialized Domains with Development

Age	Class	Number	Cause	Space	Verbal	Hyper
3 to 4	Proto-categories	Proto-quantitative schemes	Proto-causal schemes	Global images	Primary reasoning	Differentiation between modalities (perception vs. knowing)
5 to 6	Single criterion classes	Coordination of proto-quantitative schemes	Coordination of proto-causal schemes	Single spatial dimensions or operations	Permission rules	Understanding the stream of consciousness and inner speech
7 to 8	Logical multiplication	Number concepts and quantitative dimensions	Experience-based proto-theories	"Fluent" mental imagery	Explicit inference	Grasp of the constructive nature of thought
9 to 10	Logical multiplication on unfamiliar context	Construction of simple math relations	Testable theories in action	Representation of complex realities	Logical necessity	Differentiation between cognitive functions (memory vs. attention)
11 to 12	Flexible logical multiplication	Proportional reasoning Coordination of symbolic structures	Suppositions, isolation of variables	Imagination of the nonreal	Logical validity of propositions	Differentiation between clearly different domains (space vs. math)
13 to 14	Strategic classification including relevant-irrelevant information	Algebraic reasoning based on mutually specified symbol systems	Hypothesis driven experimentation	Originality in mental images	Grasp of formal relations	Awareness of specialized mental operations within a domain
15 to 16	Multilevel classes Networks of classification criteria	Generalized concept of variable	Integrated theory building	Personal imaginal worlds, aesthetic criteria	Reasoning on reasoning	Integrated cognitive theory

working hypercognition, such as the directive-executive function and self-evaluation, and the various dimensions of long-term hypercognition, such as the theory of mind, implicit theories of cognition and intelligence, and the self-concept. Space considerations do not allow a complete discussion of the development of these functions. Discussion here focuses on the development of awareness of cognitive processes because they are instrumental in the functioning and development of the other levels of the mind.

We (Demetriou & Kazi, 2006) conducted a study to examine how, if at all, 3- to 7-year-old children are aware of the cognitive processes involved in tasks addressed to three domains of reasoning (i.e., spatial, quantitative, and categorical reasoning). We found that the judgments of similarity between processes activated by tasks addressed to these domains moved, with age, from the perceptual characteristics of the tasks to the mental operations involved. Specifically, pairs of cards, each of which showed a child trying to solve a task, were presented to participants who were asked to evaluate if the two tasks were similar to each other and to justify their answers. In some pairs, these model children were required to use the same processes, applied either on the same or on different objects. For example, two of the pairs addressed classification, two addressed counting, and two addressed visuospatial reasoning. Finally, there were pairs where the two children were required to use different mental processes, such as counting, classification, or model figure reproduction. The judgments of similarity between processes in these self-awareness tasks moved, with age, from the perceptual characteristics of the tasks to the mental operations involved. Specifically, from the age of 3 to 5 years, the majority of children based their judgments on perceptual similarity across all nine task pairs. More than half of 6-year-old children and more than the two-thirds of the 7-year-old children were able to recognize that the three task pairs involving tasks that belong to a different domain require different mental processes. However, it was only at the age of 7 years that the majority of children were able to recognize the mental process required by similar process tasks where the objects of application of the process differed. This pattern suggests that the development of self-awareness about mental processes develops with the development of reasoning processes as such (Demetriou & Kazi, 2006).

In another study (Demetriou & Kazi, 2006), aiming at identifying patterns in the relation of self-concept on reasoning performance and reasoning performance in the age span of 11- to 17-year-old adolescents, tasks addressed to four specialized domains, namely, quantitative reasoning, causal reasoning, social reasoning, and drawing, were administered. In addition to solving the various tasks addressed to each of these domains, participants were asked to evaluate their performance on the tasks by answering to a general self-representation inventory probing their general self-concept related to each of the domains. Table 10.3 shows the structural relations between the factors standing for reasoning, self-evaluation, and self-representation.

Table 10.3 Structural Relations between Reasoning, Self-Evaluation, and Self-Representation as a Function of Age

Age	Self-Evaluation—Reasoning	Self-Representation—Reasoning	Self-Representation—Self-Evaluation
11	.18	.00	.08
12	.33*	.06	.12
13	.78*	.01	−.10
14	.80*	.34*	−.30*
15	.97*	.54*	−.80*

It can be seen that the relation of self-evaluation and reasoning is very low and nonsignificant at the age of 11 years, and then Lt increases steadily and systematically until approaching unity at the age of 15 to 16 years ($r = 0.97$). Interestingly, the relation of self-representation and reasoning does follow the same trend but with a considerable age lag: It is very low until the age of 13, it increases to moderate and significant at the age of 14 ($r = 0.34$), and to high ($r = 0.54$) at the age of 15 to 16 years. In a similar fashion, the relation of self-representation and self-evaluation is very low until the age of 13 years, it increases to moderate and significant at the age of 14 ($r = -0.30$), and to very high at the age of 15 to 16 years ($r = -0.80$). The negative relation implies that with increasing accuracy in self-evaluations, adolescents become more conservative and strict in their self-representation.

These findings suggest that self-awareness and self-evaluation of cognitive processes develop in a recycling fashion, which involves three major age cycles: 3 to 7, 8 to 12, and 13 to 18 years. Within each phase of development, self-evaluation and self-awareness concerning the relevant mental operations are very low and inaccurate at the beginning, and they tend to increase and to become more accurate with development until the end of the phase. Entering the next phase resets both of them to an initial low level, from where they gradually take off again with the development of the new phase-specific problem-solving operations and skills. This pattern of change indicates that the thinker needs time and experience to acquire knowledge and sensitivity to the condition of the operations and processes of the new phase. It also indicates, as shown in the study summarized in Figure 10.2, that increasing self-awareness of cognitive processes becomes part of the very functioning of the processes concerned. As shown later, this intertwining of cognitive functioning with awareness about it, which makes metarepresentation or, in other words, the explicit representation of cognitive processes possible, is, in fact, a very robust mechanism of cognitive development.

Development of the Specialized Domains and Hypercognition in Adulthood

A recent study (Demetriou & Bakracevic, 2009) examined the development of spatial, propositional, and social reasoning, as well as awareness and accuracy of self-evaluation about problem solving in these domains from adolescence (13–15 years) through young (23–25 years) and early adulthood (33–35 years) to mature adulthood (43–45 years). This study showed that changes with age vary greatly across abilities, most likely reflecting the differential importance and role of different types of processes or abilities in different phases of life. Specifically, in agreement with the developmental patterns summarized earlier, the study showed that a basic level of spatial and propositional reasoning is established from early adolescence, and this level is generally maintained through the 20s, the 30s, and the 40s. It is noted, however, that there is a slight decline in propositional reasoning starting from the mid-30s. This pattern is consistent with the findings of longitudinal studies reviewed earlier (Reynolds et al., 2005; Schaie, 1995). The development of social reasoning lags behind spatial and propositional reasoning by many years as it is only in the mid-30s that a satisfactory level of performance is attained. Self-evaluations improved in all three domains of thought despite the fact that clear performance improvement occurred only in social reasoning, indicating that, with age, self-evaluation becomes generally more accurate and self-confident, increasingly reflecting actual task performance.

These results suggest that intellectual development gradually shifts from the dominance of systems that are oriented to the processing of the environment and are power hungry in terms of computational resources (such as spatial and propositional reasoning) to systems that require

social support, and self-understanding and management. This shift in the orientation of thought was associated with an improvement in the accuracy of self-evaluation, indicating that in the years from early adolescence to middle age, persons become more aware of their cognitive experiences and the products of their cognitive activity. Thus, the transition to mature adulthood makes persons intellectually stronger and self-aware of their strengths, even if they start to feel that processing in some domains that require sheer mental manipulations, such as propositional reasoning, becomes effortful and demanding.

This pattern of changes in actual cognitive attainment and self-evaluation indicates that cognitive development in adulthood is much more complicated than it is suggested by previous research. In fact, it raises questions about the validity of the gain-loss model that has been dominant in the life-span study of cognitive development (e.g., Baltes, Dittmann-Kohli, & Dixon, 1984). Specifically, this study suggests that positive changes in social reasoning and self-awareness cannot come from a compensatory reaction to losses in fluid abilities (represented here by spatial and propositional reasoning), because no significant losses were observed in these abilities and, if any, they have not been registered by the self-monitoring and self-representation system. Thus, this study suggests that the transition from young to mature adulthood is associated with a functional shift of the mind from dealing with environment-oriented relations to dealing with person-oriented relations, involving either other persons or the self.

This shift renders thinking both flexible and principled. The social life of the adult requires flexibility so that one can consider and negotiate, if necessary, the multiple perspectives that are usually associated with different individuals, groups, or institutions one normally encounters. The handling of this very reality is conducive for a principled approach to problems and situations, because the consideration of alternative perspectives, solutions, or approaches necessitates unifying or reference principles or frames that can be used to compare and contrast the alternatives. Thus, relational and dialectical thinking emerges from the flexibility that is associated with the multiplicity of perspectives that the social environment forces onto the adult, rather than from a compensatory reaction to the loss of inferential and computational power. Principled thinking emerges from the need to give coherence to understanding and meaning making. The powers of reasoning and logical analysis already attained in the years of adolescence and early adulthood are, of course, used in the sake of both the conception of alternatives and their orchestration or evaluation. Under this interpretation of development from adolescence to maturity, the attainments of thought in adolescence and early adulthood are integrated into the attainments of maturity. Thus, sheer inferential powers and skills can be used as such for the analysis of problems posed by the physical environment and for specification of the alternatives necessitated by social and personal problems that require a relational and dialectical approach.

Under this model, critical, relational, and dialectical thought (Basseches, 1984; Kitchener & King, 1981; Labouvie-Vief, 1994; Overton, 2006; Riegel, 1973) refer to the orientation of the thinking of the mature adult. Systematic and metasystematic thought refer to the integrative and constructive capabilities of this thinking, because they enable the thinker to bring variables and components together into systems, to compare the systems across contexts and domains, and reflect on them (Commons & Richards, 2002; Commons, Richards, & Kuhn, 1982). Both the orientation and the constructive capabilities may be applied on the physical (Kuhn, 2000), as well as the social and the moral world (Kohlberg, 1984; Turiel, Chapter 16 of this volume). In fact, problems of increasing complexity require both an increasing relational thought to cover all of the aspects or facets involved and an increasing abstractness to conceive or construct general principles that would govern all aspects or facets involved. Thus, it is perfectly reasonable that recent research suggests that there may be a common system of hierarchical complexity where different lines of development may be reduced (Dawson & Gabrielian, 2003; Dawson & Wilson, 2003). In conclusion, this study suggests that different models of development that captured different aspects of it all appear to be alternative perspectives on the same complex developmental process.

Metarepresentation as a Mechanism of Cognitive Development

Metarepresentation is a significant mechanism of developmental change. It is a hypercognitive process that looks for, codifies, and typifies similarities between mental experiences to enhance understanding and problem-solving efficiency. So defined, metarepresentation is the constructive aspect of working hypercognition that integrates the contents of the episodic buffer, in Baddeley's (1990) terms, or the screen of conscience, in James's terms (1890), thereby generating new mental schemes and operations. In a sense, metarepresentation is inductive inference applied to mental experiences, representations, or operations, rather than to

environmental stimuli and information as such. The distillation of this transformation process is the metarepresentations. Metarepresentations act as criteria that are activated any time the thinker needs to find a solution to a problem, monitor its implementation, and evaluate its outcome in terms of its validity. We explicate this process here in reference to the development of logical reasoning itself.

According to many theorists, reasoning reflects a universal language of thought that comprises a limited set of ready-made inference patterns. Both psychometric and developmental theorists would feel perfectly happy with the assumption of a universal language of thought. For psychometric theorists, it maps onto their construct of fluid intelligence as a system of general reasoning processes, such as Spearman's (1904) eduction of relations and correlates. For developmental theorists, it maps onto operative intelligence (Piaget, 1970), executive control structures (Case, 1985), skill structures (Fischer, 1980), or structure mappings (Halford, 1993).

We maintain that these general inference patterns do not exist at the beginning. Instead, they are constructed by mapping domain-specific inference patterns onto each other through the process of metarepresentation. Accommodating these general inference patterns, or the so-called metarepresentations, is affected by a general language of thought that, like the process of metarepresentation, is an emergent product of guided and reflected-on domain-specific functioning. The general language of thought is gradually constructed when the patterns of thought are compared across domains and reduced to schemes that can be intentionally activated across domains. A good criterion of the power and the effectiveness of this general language of thought is logical necessity. That is, taking the conclusion of an inferential scheme as logically necessary implies that this scheme has been lifted from a context-bound processing frame to an advanced rule-bound organizer of relations, which does not allow any exceptions or knowledge and belief-based biases to intrude in the inferential process. Therefore, this general language of thought is a construction that gradually expands and stabilizes through the bidirectional interaction between domain-specific processing and executive, self-awareness, and self-regulation processes of the hypercognitive system. It should be recognized that the development of this general logical language is confined by the potential of the processing system. We elaborate on that later when we present recent experimental data on the relation of the logical reasoning developmental process with the processing efficiency and the representational parameters.

Natural language has a privileged relation with this emergent universal language of thought because it is the main symbol system that can be used to express and manipulate its constructions. Thus, natural language and the emergent language of thought are gradually intertwined, and increasingly used to guide and facilitate inference and processing within each of the domains. Structural modeling shows that the relations between propositional reasoning as such and the other domains of thought become stronger with age. However, these relations always deviate considerably from unity, suggesting that there are other processes in these domains in addition to propositional reasoning (Demetriou, 2006). Thus, there is a dynamic bidirectional interaction such that the functioning of domains feeds in the development of general inferential processes and these, once in place, guide and facilitate the functioning of the domains.

In conclusion, according to this theory, metarepresentation is the mechanism that drives the development of reasoning from stimulus-driven and content-bounded inference to explicit logical reasoning and ability to reflect on the process and its outcomes. Metarepresentation reminds one of Piaget's (1977/2001) "reflective abstraction" and Karmiloff-Smith's (1992) "representational redescription." Like reflective abstraction, it abstracts general patterns from different mental functions or activities. Like representational redescription, it reorganizes them at a higher, more efficient representational level. However, its primary constituent is self-awareness. Although its accuracy and degree of involvement varies from age to age because it is subject to development itself, self-awareness is always part of the abstraction and reconstruction processes that generate new concepts and schemes out of old ones. Our studies about self-evaluation and self-awareness summarized earlier suggest that moving across developmental phases is a product of increasing binding between actual cognitive processing and awareness about it. Moreover, there is accruing evidence that self-awareness and executive control are part of the learning process, and that the efficiency of learning process changes during development because of changes in both of them (Kuhn & Pease, 2006). These processes ensure that future use of the new construct is under the intentional control of the thinker and not just under the control of external stimuli.

Reasoning Development, Processing Efficiency, and Representational Capacity

In a recent study, Mouyi (2008) attempted to specify the relations between inductive and deductive reasoning development, and the development of processing efficiency and representational capacity. Children from 7 to 12 years of age were examined by a large array of tasks addressed to inductive and deductive reasoning, and also a large array of tasks addressed to speed and control of processing and various aspects of working memory, such as short-term storage and executive control (see Ricco, Chapter 12 of this volume, for an extensive discussion on the development of reasoning in general and on the study of the development of reasoning in late adulthood and its relation to processing speed, storage and maintenance components of working memory, and the executive control component of working memory). Rasch scaling of performance on the reasoning items revealed three levels for each type of reasoning. These levels are summarized next.

At the first level of inductive reasoning, inference based on concrete observations can be drawn. That is, children can identify patterns and formulate generalizations on the basis of a single dimension or relation. However, at this level, the child's experiences and specific knowledge may bias inference drawing against generalizations suggested by patterns. These biases suggest that control processes are not powerful enough to sustain the inferential processes against privileged knowledge and experiences. At the second level, inductive reasoning can handle *hidden* or *implied* relations that require from the thinker to combine information present to the senses with knowledge stored in long-term memory. Mapping out the implied relation requires that nonrelevant information in the premises or in long-term memory are inhibited. Moreover, inductive inferences based on the syntactical components of verbal premises can be drawn. Negative premises may be manipulated at this level. Thus, it is suggested that control processes at this level are powerful enough to direct the inferential process on target and protect representational capacity from overloading with irrelevant information. Finally, at the third level, inductive reasoning is based on theoretical supposition. That is, possibilities can be specified in advance, and information in the premises is analyzed in reference to them. As a result, multiple parameters and relations can be simultaneously considered and manipulated. Generalizations can therefore be extracted from the relations and elevated to mental models.

In so far as the deductive reasoning is concerned, the three levels are defined in terms of the four types of logical arguments: modus ponens, modus tollens, affirming the consequent, and denying the antecedent (see also Ricco, Chapter 12 of this volume). Specifically, at the first level of deductive reasoning, modus ponens inferences can be handled, simple at the beginning (involving only affirmative premises) and more complex later on (negations may be involved). Negation calls for the activation of the control processes ensuring that alternatives in meaning emanating from the negation are taken into consideration. Constructing, or retrieving from memory, the complement of a negation calls on further cognitive resources allocation. At the second level, deductive reasoning can deal with modus tollens inferences. In comparison with modus ponens, modus tollens requires a model construction process that takes the modus ponens argument as a basis and then constructs alternative models that are compared with each other. Toward

the end of this level, the *denial of the antecedent* and the *affirmation of the consequent* fallacies can be processed. Specifically, arguments with binary propositions can be solved. These higher reasoning functions are a big step forward because they enable the thinker to go beyond the obvious. Overall, reasoning at this level involves more steps and more operations. This poses higher needs to both representational capacity and control processes. Finally, at the third level of deductive reasoning, all fallacies can be solved. Fallacies place high demands on the system. Many alternatives must be retrieved from memory and be processed. Moreover, the very nature of the outcome of processing is

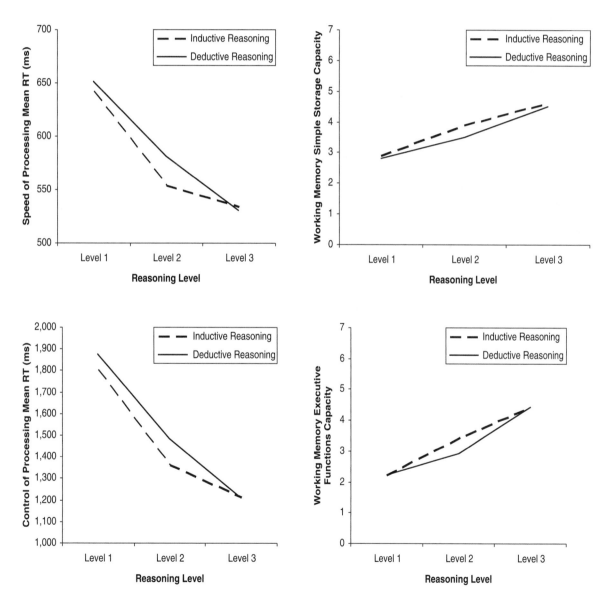

Figure 10.7 Cognitive processes as a function of reasoning developmental level. *Dotted lines* represent inductive reasoning; *solid lines* represent deductive reasoning.

peculiar because the conclusion is that no conclusion can be reached. Therefore, the reasoner at this level must accept that not all arguments are determinate, and thus uncertainty may be part of the reasoning process itself.

To specify the processing and representational profile of individuals at each of the three levels in the development of inductive and deductive reasoning, mean reaction time in speed and control of processing tasks, and mean capacity for short-term storage and executive function of working memory were estimated. The relations between processing efficiency, working memory, and reasoning level are illustrated in Figure 10.7. It can be seen that clear developmental trends are in all dimensions. Reaction time to speed and control of processing tasks decreases and working memory capacity increases systematically across all three levels in both types of reasoning. Specifically, it can be seen that, at the first level, reaction times to speed and control of processing tasks are approximately 650 and 1,800 ms, respectively; at the third level, these values decline to approximately 530 and 1,200 ms, respectively. The values for short-term and executive working memory at the first level are about 3 and 2 units, respectively, and they increase to about 4.5 units for both. Therefore, it is clear that ascension across these levels of reasoning development is associated with developments in processing efficiency and representational capacity.

In line with these findings, we have shown (Demetriou et al., 2002; see Figure 10.8) by means of dynamic sys-

tems modeling that the development of reasoning is slower when it is assumed to draw only on itself than when it receives influences from any one of the processes involved in processing potentials (e.g., speed of processing or working memory). Moreover, development is considerably faster when it receives influences from both of these processes (i.e., speed of processing and working memory) than when it receives effects from one or none of them). It is also highly interesting that the contribution of each of these two potentiation factors to the growth of reasoning is different in its initiation and termination, because of their differences in growth rate. When both effects are present, the development of reasoning takes off and levels off considerably earlier than when it is influenced from any of these two effects.

In line with our assumption that development is synergic, we have shown that top-down effects are also present (Figure 10.9). That is, the development of reasoning does influence the development of processing efficiency. We have shown that the development of processing efficiency and working memory is faster when they receive effects from reasoning than when they are supposed to capitalize only on their own capacity for development. Specifically, the curves of development for these two constructs are steeper, reflecting faster progression toward their end state, when effects from reasoning are assumed as compared with the curves reflecting the development of each of them alone. This means that changes in reasoning function as a

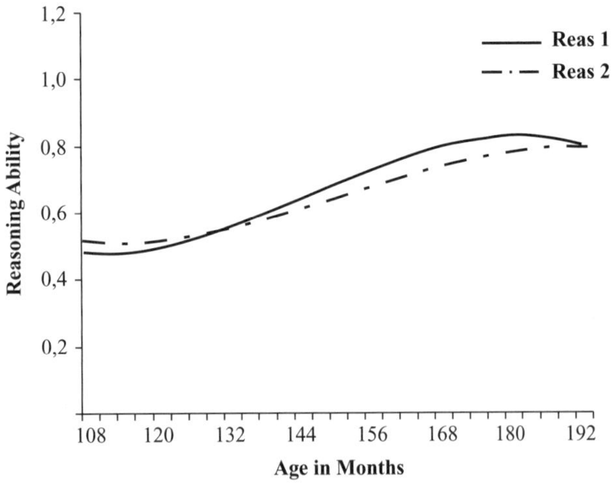

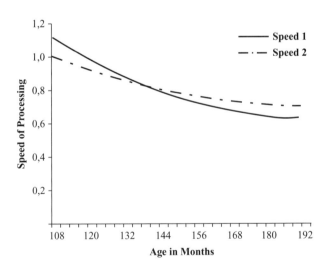

Figure 10.8 Cumulative effects of processing efficiency and working memory on reasoning ability. *Solid line* denotes reasoning ability when influences from processing efficiency and working memory are assumed. *Dashed line* denotes reasoning ability when no influences from processing efficiency and working memory are assumed.

Figure 10.9 Effect of reasoning ability on the development of speed of processing. Speed 1: Speed of processing when influence from reasoning ability is assumed (*solid line*). Speed 2: Speed of processing when no influence from reasoning ability is assumed (*dashed line*).

mediator for the improvement of memory and processing efficiency.

MAPPING THE DEVELOPING MIND—DEVELOPING BRAIN RELATIONS

Questions to Be Answered

The human mind and the human brain are the two sides of the same coin. The human brain is the underlying biological mechanism of the human mind. In other words, the mind in all of its expressions emerges from the structure and functioning of the brain. Research in cognitive neuroscience in both its empirical (Kandel, Schwartz, & Jessell, 1995) and its computational (O'Reilly & Munakata, 2000) branches blossomed in recent years (see also Gazzaniga, Ivry, & Mangun, 2008, for an excellent synthesis). The guiding question of this research is simple: What are the neuronal underpinnings of the various functions and processes modeled by theories of intelligence and intellectual development? This section reviews research on the brain that reveals the neuronal analogue of the architecture proposed in this chapter.

However, a note of caution is in order here, because simple questions do not always have simple answers. Specifically, we must bear in mind that psychological and brain functions reside on different levels of analysis and involve different "research objects" (Overton, 2006). The objects of psychological research include: (1) observable responses (ranging from reaction times to various types of stimuli to solutions to various types of problems), and (2) subjective experiences and related reports. The objects of neuroscience research include biological entities, such as the nature, volume, and organization of neuronal matter itself, and the responses and correlates of neuronal matter. This last type of objects is extremely variable and includes: (1) blood supply and glucose consumption of different brain areas; (2) the electrochemical activity of neuronal networks; (3) the pattern of chemical responses related to the communication between neurons through the release and use of neurotransmitters; and (4) at a more basic level, the various types of protein synthesis that, under the direction of genes, express the responses of the brain to ongoing cognitive needs raised by the environment. We still do not know how to map the different levels of analysis onto each other. In fact, the lack of a commonly accepted language for describing each of these levels renders their mapping onto each other difficult.

With this caution in mind, we can outline the questions that neuroscience must answer, from the perspective of our theory:

1. Is the architecture of mind specified by our theory reflected in the various levels of the organization and functioning of the brain? Specifically, are the various structures posited by our model also present at the various levels of the organization and functioning of the brain? For example, are the various environment-oriented systems of thought represented by different regions or networks in the brain?

2. What entities and conditions in the brain stand for the general processes and mechanisms specified by our model? That is, are actual structural analogues in the brain associated with general inferential processes related to fluid intelligence and general self-representation? Is there any structural analogue for whatever is common between all kinds of cognitive activity?

3. How are different networks differentiated subjectively so that intentional decisions can be made in advance about their activation? What other regions are involved when processing surfaces to consciousness? Does awareness emerge from particular structures or networks, or does it result from particular coactivation patterns that may involve alternative networks?

4. Brain itself changes ontogenetically for reasons genetically controlled (such as increases in neuronal volume, myelination, and neuronal pruning within particular time windows). These changes are, to a large extent, although not completely, independent from the environment. How are these changes related to the changes of the various cognitive processes described here?

Obviously, the grand neurocognitive developmental theory of intelligence to come would have to answer the questions above, thereby integrating brain with functional and subjective maps of mental functions into a common landscape. The following sections review recent research and theorizing in cognitive and developmental neuroscience to show that the structural and functional organization of the brain can, indeed, be mapped on the general levels and tiers of mind described by the present model. Overall, this research shows that the brain, like the mind, involves structures and processes that serve general cognitive processes, and structures and functions dedicated to more specialized cognitive processes.

Brain–Mind Maps

Domain-Specific Networks

It is already well documented that different brain networks serve different cognitive domains. In fact, the evidence suggests that each of the cognitive domains mapped here is served by a number of overlapping or interacting neural networks (see Galaburta, Kosslyn, & Christen, 2002). The clearest differentiation in neuronal infrastructure supporting the functioning of different cognitive processes is between verbal and visuospatial information. In recent years, there has been a clear substantiation of this differentiation in regard to the short-term storage of verbal and visuospatial storage of information. That is, neuroimaging shows that verbal storage is served by two distinct circuits, one specializing in verbal rehearsal as such (i.e., a left-lateralized premotor-parietal network) and another one subserving nonarticulatory maintenance of phonological information (i.e., a bilateral anterior-prefrontal/inferior parietal network). In contrast, visuospatial storage relies on only one bilateral brain system (i.e., the posterior parts of the superior frontal sulcus and the entire interparietal sulcus). Some brain regions are activated during processing of both the verbal and the visuospatial tasks, which is in line with the assumption that a central episodic buffer (Baddeley & Hitch, 2000; Repovš & Baddeley, 2006) may exist (i.e., right middle frontal gyrus and the presupplementary motor area [SMA], as well as bilaterally in the deep frontal opercular cortex and the cortex along anterior and middle parts of the intraparietal sulcus).

Quantitative information is processed in the inferior parietal cortex, particularly its posterior convolution called the "angular gyrus" (BA 39; Dehaene, 1997). Understanding of causal relations between objects is processed in the medial and dorsal part of the superior frontal cortex, whereas perception of causality is served by visual cortices, such as V5 (Fonlupt, 2003). Crucial aspects of social understanding are related to the activation of the medial prefrontal cortex, the superior temporal sulcus, and the temporal poles bilaterally. Processing of categorical information is closely related to language understanding, and is thus associated with the entire superior temporal gyrus, which analyzes the "object" properties of auditory signals (Galaburda et al., 2002).

With respect to verbal reasoning, there is evidence that different types of reasoning are served by different neural networks. According to Osherson et al. (1998), inductive and deductive reasoning are served by different but partially overlapping neural networks (frontal gyrus and the right insular cortex for inductive reasoning and associative visual areas, the right superior parietal lobule and thalamus, and the right anterior cingulate for deductive reasoning). Even the same type of reasoning, such as deductive reasoning, activates different networks depending on the information to be integrated (Goel, 2007; Goel, Buchel, Frith, & Dolan, 2000; Goel & Dolan, 2000, 2001). Specifically, content-based propositions activate temporal (BA 21, 22) and frontal regions (BA 44, 8, 9). Formal propositions activate occipital (BA 18, 19), left parietal (BA 40), bilateral dorsal frontal (BA 6), left frontal (BA 44, 8, 10), and right frontal (BA 46) regions, suggesting the construction of visual mental models of the relations implied by the formal propositions.

Networks Underlying General Inferential Processes

In their review of a large number of neuroimaging and lesion studies, Jung and Haier (2007) attempted to synthesize this evidence into an integrated model associating brain functioning with the aim to pinpoint the networks underlying fluid or general intelligence, which they called the "parietofrontal integration theory" (P-FIT) of general intelligence. According to this theory, information is first registered and processed in regions of the cortex that specialize to deal with different types of sensory information, such as the visual (BA 18, 19) and the auditory cortex (BA 22), mentioned earlier. From there, information is then fed forward to several regions in the parietal cortex (BA 7, 39, 40) for symbolism, abstraction, and elaboration. Then there is an interaction of these regions with frontal regions (BA 6, 9, 10, 45–47) for the conception and hypothesis testing of alternative solutions to the problem at hand. Finally, the anterior cingulate (BA 32) is engaged to constrain response selection and inhibit alternative responses. If interference is caused by the fact that the same neural networks are activated by different blocks of information (Gruber & von Cramon, 2003; Klingberg, 1998), the anterior cingulate may be conceived as a conductor orchestrating when different players must come into play. Individual differences in the volume, quality, efficiency, and connectivity of these neuronal ensembles, and the underlying white matter are associated with individual differences in general IQ.

Mapping the P-FIT onto our model suggests some interesting isomorphisms related to the first two of the questions posed earlier. Overall, there are indeed brain structures related to the mind structures uncovered by our research. Specifically, the sensory areas involved in the P-FIT model, as well as other information-specific networks, may be more related to the domain-specific processes represented by first-order factors in this model, such as verbal, spatial, or quantitative reasoning. The parietal areas of the P-FIT model may be related to the information integration, meaning making, and inferential processes applied on domain-specific information and emerging as second-order factors in structural models. The frontal areas of the P-FIT model may be related to working memory, attention, and executive control, as reflected by the working memory and control factors of this model. Finally, the anterior cingulate of the P-FIT model may be related to intentional planning, inhibition, and conscious selection of responses included in the hypercognitive system of this model.

Networks Underlying Awareness and Consciousness

The discussion about consciousness and awareness requires special attention. There is no consensus as to the brain bases of consciousness and self-awareness. According to some scholars, these distinctive functions of the human mind do not reside in a particular locus of the brain. Specifically, according to Edelman and Tononi (2000) and Lamme (2006), evidence shows that awareness emerges from brain functioning as such rather than from any particular brain region dedicated to it. Specifically, it is assumed that awareness emerges from two characteristics of the brain functioning: recurrent activation of the same network and coordinated activation of complementary networks. That is, the person becomes aware of stimuli and processes whose processing is recycled over the same neuronal networks so that they are coordinated or tuned to each other, thereby producing an experience of functioning, so to speak.

Crick and Koch (2005) have questioned this interpretation of consciousness. These scholars have argued that consciousness emerges from the functioning of a particular brain structure that is connected to all sensory and motor regions of the cortex and the amygdala, which is related to emotion. This small structure, the claustrum, is located below the cortex. According to Crick and Koch (2005), it functions as the spot of attention as it receives input from all areas activated at a particular moment and it binds them together.

The reader is reminded that it was argued earlier that consciousness emerges from directive executive functions because these functions are recursive. That is, as they are repeated, observed, and recorded, they engender awareness about them that becomes increasingly explicit. In a sense, then, mind maps of cognitive functions, which reflect self-awareness about cognitive functions, may be considered as subjective representations of maps of recurrent brain activity underlying cognitive functioning of different kinds that gradually become explicitly represented. Our studies on self-evaluation and self-representation show that explicit representation of cognitive processes is a slow process that grows side by side with the development of the cognitive processes themselves, slightly lacking behind them and recycling with them. An important task for future research is to provide crucial evidence about these models of the neuronal bases of consciousness. What is the neuronal mechanism underlying the emergence of awareness? Does it emerge from the increasing coordination of different distributed networks in the brain, as suggested by Edelman's model, or from the functioning of a particular brain nucleus, as suggested by Crick and Koch's model, or from both—that is, a combination of these two models—that a single structure such as the claustrum orchestrates the coordination of different networks?

The structural equation and development models presented in this chapter lean toward the third option. That is, the presence of domain-specific factors at both the performance and the self-representation levels of the model may be taken to correspond to the networks that carry the different types of processing and their registration in awareness and self-representation as such. The presence of level-specific factors (such as the general reasoning and the general self-representation factors) may be taken to correspond to general patterns of neuronal activity that run through each of these levels, that is, patterns related to processing as such (e.g., general associative and inferential mechanisms) and patterns related to self-monitoring and self-awareness as such (i.e., general self-observation processes), respectively. Finally, the presence of a grand factor binding the general performance and self-representation factors may reflect the operation of a common central neuronal structure binding everything together and pulling the strings of different systems at different levels.

Factors Related to Speed of Processing

In the models presented earlier, speed of processing was found to be a powerful factor of intellectual functioning and development. Evidence suggests that this factor stands for general qualities of the brain networks involved, or even the brain as a whole, rather than for a particular region or network. These qualities may be the sheer neuronal volume, myelination, and connectivity between and within regions. Efficiency of operation and response to environmental demands by building the required neural networks may also be important parameters of this general quality.

Garlick (2002) proposed that the underlying neural correlate of general intelligence might be the plasticity of the nervous system to respond appropriately to stimulation and build the required networks that may be spatially differentiated and distributed for different kinds of tasks. For instance, evidence indicates that more intelligent individuals use less brain volume and, therefore, less energy to process a task than do individuals of average intelligence (Jausovec & Jausovec, 2004). Thus, higher speed may reflect plasticity and flexibility in the construction and use of the networks needed to deal with cognitive tasks (Neubauer, Grabner, Freuddenthaler, Beckman, & Guthke, 2004).

Brain–Mind Development

How is cognitive development related to the developmental changes in the organization and functioning of the brain? Case (1992) suggested that increases in the myelination of neuronal axons, which protect the transmission of electrical signaling along the axons from leakage, are related to changes in general processing efficiency. This, in turn, enhances the capacity of working memory, thereby facilitating transition across the stages of cognitive development. Thatcher (1992) maintained that changes within stages of cognitive development are associated with improvements in neuronal networking within brain regions, whereas transitions across stages are associated with improvements in networking between brain regions. These findings are consistent with connectionist modeling of cognitive development, suggesting that limited changes are associated with strengthening the connections between the existing networks subserving a particular behavior or skill. Major changes leading to higher levels of cognitive development (e.g., increasingly abstract cognitive structures in different domains) are associated with the gradual construction of intervening higher level hidden units (new neural networks) that encode and compact the functioning of lower level information-specific networks already in existence (Shultz, 2003).

In fact, the development from core processes to mental operations within each of the domains mentioned earlier (see Table 10.1) and from these to general reasoning patterns, as suggested in the section about metarepresentation, is a good example of levels of intellectual development that may require the construction of superimposed levels of neuronal networks, if they are to come into existence. For instance, the neuronal networks for core processes, such as subitization and counting acts, within the quantitative domain, may be projected and integrated into a higher

level neuronal network underlying the mental number line. Subsequently, this network, together with another network within another domain, such as the categoric, associated with mental representations of class relations, may be integrated, at a higher level, into a network underlying the grasp of transitive relations. This is so because in both cases, mental representations are transitively connected. That is, numbers along the number line are ordered so that $1 < 2 < 3 \ldots < n$; classes in class hierarchies are similarly ordered, such as sparrows $<$ birds $<$ animals $\ldots <$ living beings, and so on.

A study of the relations between intelligence and cortical development suggests that the brain expression of intelligence is dynamic. Specifically, this study (Shaw et al., 2006) showed that the trajectory of change in the thickness of the cerebral cortex rather than thickness itself is most closely related to the level of intelligence. That is, more intelligent children demonstrate a very plastic cortex, particularly in the frontal regions, with an initial accelerated and prolonged phase of cortical increase followed by an equally vigorous cortical thinning in early adolescence. Moreover, other research suggests that developmental changes in patterns of brain activity appear to involve a shift from diffuse to more focal activation, which probably represents a fine-tuning of relevant neural systems with experience. That is, these changes reflect an increasing efficiency in the selection of the right networks and the deactivation of the less relevant or proper ones (Durston & Casey, 2006). Moreover, Bunge and Zelazo (2006) show that there is a correspondence in the developmental levels of mastering rules of increasing complexity in executive tasks and the maturation of different regions in the prefrontal cortex (orbitofrontal first, followed by ventrolateral, and then by the dorsolateral prefrontal cortex). These patterns of brain development explain both increasing speed and control efficiency. That is, blocks of neurons that are not used are pruned, yielding faster, more focused, and efficient processing. In turn, these changes make possible the increasing intertwining of networks as directed by experience, thereby increasing the person's storage, integration, and reasoning capabilities.

The isomorphisms between the cognitive model presented here and the neuronal model emerging from neuroscience research is encouraging and justifies further research. Overall, it is clear that cognitive structures are associated with different brain structures, and different levels of cognitive organization are associated with different levels in the organization of the brain. Moreover, changes in structures, their functioning, and their connectivity are clearly associated with both intellectual growth and differentiation. However, this research has many unanswered questions and problems to solve. For example, there is no cognitive structure whose corresponding brain structures are fully known. Moreover, we still do not know what is truly general and what is truly specific in both the brain and the mind. Specifically, how much of each of the general processes of the mind, such as speed, control, or representational capacity, is associated with various general brain qualities (i.e., sheer total brain volume, overall physical state of neurons and neurotransmitters, connectivity), and how much is accounted by the fact that particular brain regions (such as the anterior cingulate) are always engaged in cognitive processing? Also, we still do not know how each of the various networks carry on its own job, how the networks interact with each other, and how they are integrated into a final solution behaviorally and subjectively. And, of course, we know little about how the various types of change in the brain (e.g., myelination, electrical activity, volume, dispersion, activity of neurotransmitters, connectivity) interact with cognitive developmental changes. Therefore, the grand neurocognitive developmental theory of intelligence that would integrate brain with functional and subjective maps of mental functions into a common landscape is still far ahead of us.

CONCLUSIONS

This chapter aimed to integrate evidence and concepts from cognitive, differential, and developmental models of the human mind into an overarching theory. This theory aspires to be able at one and the same time to describe and explain the architecture of the mind, its development, and individual differences in regard to both architecture and development. In concern to the architecture of the mind, our findings support our assumption that both general and specialized capabilities and processes do exist. These are organized hierarchically so that more simple or general processes are embedded in more complex and specialized processes. This architecture, which is the culmination of more than a century of psychometric research (Carroll, 1993; Gustafsson & Undheim, 1996; Jensen, 1998), is largely consistent with findings in both the cognitive and the developmental tradition (Case et al., 2001; Demetriou et al., 2002). A large part of what is defined as psychometric *g* (i.e., the factors that are responsible for the positive correlations between all mental tests) includes mechanisms that have been of primary interest in research

and theory in cognitive psychology, such as underlying processing efficiency, processing capacity, and directive-executive control. These very mechanisms seem able to explain, to a considerable extent, the person's state of understanding and problem solving at successive age periods, which is the object of developmental psychology and individual differences in regard to it.

In the proposed overarching model, intelligence is a function of a person's mental efficiency, flexibility, capability, and insightfulness, in regard to both other individuals and a general developmental hierarchy. That is, excelling in understanding, learning, reasoning, and problem solving, in comparison with other individuals of the same age or in comparison with one's own performance in younger ages, is, to a considerable extent, a function of differences or increases in these processes. In psychometric terms, this is tantamount to saying that differences in the processes associated with *g* cause differences in general inferential and reasoning mechanisms. In developmental terms, this is tantamount to saying that changes in the processes underlying *g* result in the qualitative transformation of the general structures of thought underlying understanding and reasoning at successive ages so that more complex and less familiar problems can be solved, and more abstract concepts can be constructed. It may be noted here that a general factor of intelligence was recently found to be able to explain differences in intellectual achievements between different primates (Deaner, van Schaik, & Johnson, 2006; Lee, 2006). These findings suggest that there has been a directional selection for general cognitive ability in the lineage leading to *Homo sapiens*.

Regarding change, the three traditions also seem to meld into this overarching model. On the one hand, transition mechanisms underlying progress across developmental levels, as these are specified by developmental theory, are useful for differential theory because they highlight why and how change in mental age occurs. On the other hand, mechanisms of change underlying the automation of performance, as these are specified in cognitive theory or in models of learning, highlight how newly acquired developmental structures in a given phase may get established and consolidated, thereby preparing the way for the transition to the next developmental phase. In effect, both kinds of these mechanisms may explain underlying cognitive differences between persons of different IQs.

The differentiation of development across domains is an integral part of the organization and functioning of the human mind. This is so because in each of the domains there are constraints coming directly from the particularities in the mental operations, the representations, and the skills that characterize each of the domains. Performance within and across persons may vary even if general processes are kept constant, because the dynamics of functioning and development differ across domains, and the mastering of these dynamics depends on both special domain-specific disposition and domain-specific experience. Domain-specific disposition is a multiplier of general potentials. If domain-specific disposition falls short of general potentials in a given domain, attainment in this domain will obviously prove to fall below the level of general potentials. For instance, visuospatial ability will fall below general potentials in the blind, even if general potentials are very high. If domain-specific disposition is high, such as a special proclivity in visualization, visuospatial ability will exceed the level expected on the basis of the condition of general potentials. Domain-specific experience is needed to give the chance to the developing person to customize, so to speak, the general possibilities and processes to particularities and constraints of each of the domains. Obviously, practice to the extreme in a domain will elevate this domain to the upper limit of general potentials. Overall, the particular combination of general potentials, domain-specific disposition, and domain-specific experience determines the momentum, stability, and direction of development in the individual. Moreover, shifts in life needs and experiences that are associated with different phases of life are also reflected in the general patterns of changes in the different abilities. It is reminded that our study of development from adolescence to mature adulthood (Demetriou & Bakracevic, 2009) showed that from early adulthood, development shifts from the environment-oriented domains to the domain of social understanding and self-awareness. Obviously, the complexities of the social life in adulthood necessitate the development of understanding and managing others, and self-understanding, self-evaluation, and self-management.

It is hoped that this chapter suggests clearly that neither Gardner-like theories (e.g., Gardner, 1983), which postulate the existence of autonomous multiple intelligences, nor Jensen-like theories (e.g., Jensen, 1998), which stress the primacy of general processes, do justice to the complexity of the human mind. The human mind involves both general and specialized abilities, each of which functions as a dimension of intraindividual and interindividual differences during both online functioning and developmental time. That is, general processes are everywhere, but they can never be seen alone, and specialized domains are the interfaces through which the mind interweaves with the different realms of the world, but specialized processes involve general processes as part of their construction, and they need them for their functioning and development. Relational developmental systems (Lerner, 2006; Lerner and Overton, 2008; Overton, 2006) provide the melting pot where general and specialized processes become integrated and refined into world-relevant systems of understanding and action.

Finally, it is highly interesting that modern research on the organization and functioning of the brain lends support to this architecture. The evidence summarized earlier suggests that some general aspects of the brain, such as myelination, plasticity, and neuronal connectivity, are related to some dimensions of general intelligence, such as speed of processing and learning efficiency. Moreover, there are brain regions, located mainly in the frontal and parietal cortices, that subserve functions that are central to all cognitive processing, such as control and working memory. Also, there are many neural networks that specialize in the representation of different types of information such as spatial, causal, quantitative, social, and categorical. In fact, it is highly interesting that new mental schemes emerge from the interaction and integration of existing schemes in a way that is reminiscent of the fact that consciousness may emerge from the dialogue between overlapping neuronal networks and/or through the coordinating operation of neuronal structures orchestrating this dialogue. Obviously, future research on the developing mind–developing brain relations is one of the most exciting fields of research in its promises to shed light on some of the most central aspects of human life and existence. That is, how immaterial experiences gradually sculpt the gray and white matter of the brain, making it able to get in tune with the physical, social, and cultural environment, and how the organization, functioning, and change of the brain make the construction of experience, understanding, and consciousness possible.

REFERENCES

Ackerman, P. L., Beier, M. E., & Boyle, M. O. (2005). Working memory and intelligence: The same or different constructs? *Psychological Bulletin, 1,* 30–60.

Baddeley, A. D. (1990). *Human memory: Theory and practice.* Hillsdale, NJ: Erlbaum.

Baddeley, A. D. (2000). The episodic buffer: A new component of working memory? *Trends in Cognitive Sciences, 4,* 417–423.

Baddeley, A. D., & Hitch, G. J. (1974). Working memory. In G. A. Bower (Ed.), *The psychology of learning and motivation* (pp. 47–89). San Diego: Academic Press.

Baddeley, A. D., & Hitch, G. H. (2000). Development of working memory: Should the Pascual-Leone and the Baddeley and Hitch models be merged? *Journal of Experimental and Child Psychology, 77,* 128–137.

Baltes, P. B. (1991). The many faces of human aging: Toward a psychological culture of old age. *Psychological Medicine, 21,* 837–854.

Baltes, P. B., Dittmann-Kohli, F., & Dixon, R. A. (1984). New perspectives on the development of intelligence in adulthood: Toward a dual-process conception and a model of selective optimization with compensation. In P. B. Baltes & O. G. Brim (Eds.), *Life-span development and behavior* (Vol. 6, pp. 33–76). San Diego: Academic Press.

Basseches, M. (1984). Dialectical thinking as a metasystematic form of cognitive organization. In M. L. Commons, F. A. Richards, & C. Armon (Eds.), *Beyond formal operations: Late adolescent and adult cognitive development* (pp. 216–238). New York: Praeger.

Bjorklund, D. F., & Harnishfeger, K. K. (1995). The evolution of inhibition mechanisms and their role in human cognition and behavior. In F. N. Dempster & C. J. Brainerd (Eds.), *Interference and inhibition in cognition* (pp. 141–173). New York: Academic Press.

Bors, D. A., McLeod, M. C., & Forrin, B. (1993). Eliminating the IQ-RT correlation by eliminating an experimental confound. *Intelligence, 17,* 475–500.

Braine, M. D. S. (1990). The "natural logic" approach to reasoning. In W. F. Overton (Ed.), *Reasoning, necessity, and logic: Developmental perspectives* (pp. 133–157). Hillsdale, NJ: Erlbaum.

Bunge, S., A., & Zelazo, D. P. (2006). A brain-based account of the development of rule use in childhood. *Current Directions in Psychological Science, 15,* 118–121.

Butterworth, G. (1998). Perceptual and motor development. In A. Demetriou, W. Doise, & C. F. M. van Lieashout (Eds.), *Life-span developmental psychology* (pp. 101–136). Chichester, United Kingdom: John Wiley & Sons.

Carroll, J. B. (1993). *Human cognitive abilities: A survey of factor-analytic studies.* New York: Cambridge University Press.

Case, R. (1985). *Intellectual development. Birth to adulthood.* New York: Academic Press

Case, R. (1992). *The mind's staircase: Exploring the conceptual underpinnings of children's thought and knowledge.* Hillsdale, NJ: Erlbaum.

Case, R., Demetriou, A., Platsidou, M., & Kazi, S. (2001). Integrating concepts and tests of intelligence from the differential and the developmental traditions. *Intelligence, 29,* 307–336.

Comalli, P. E., Jr., Wapner, S., & Werner, H. (1962). Interference effects of Stroop color-word test in childhood, adulthood, and aging. *Journal of Genetic Psychology, 100,* 47–53.

Commons, M. L., & Richards, F. A. (2002). Organizing components into combinations: How stage transition works. *Journal of Adult Development, 3,* 159–177.

Commons, M. L., Richards, F. A., & Kuhn, D. (1982). Systematic and metasystematic reasoning: A case for levels of reasoning beyond Piaget's stages of formal operations. *Child Development, 53,* 1058–1069.

Conway, A. R. A., Cowan, N., Bunting, M. F., Therriault, D. J., & Minkoff, S. R. B. (2002). A latent variable analysis of working memory capacity, short-term memory capacity, processing speed, and general fluid intelligence. *Intelligence, 30,* 163–183.

Cosmides, L., & Tooby, J. (1994). Beyond intuition and instinct blindness: Toward an evolutionarily rigorous cognitive science. *Cognition, 50,* 41–77.

Cowan, N., Morey, C. C., Chen, Z., & Bunting M. F. (2007). What do estimates of working memory capacity tell us? In N. Osaka, R. Logie, and M. D'Esposito (Eds.), *The cognitive neuroscience of working memory.* Oxford: Oxford University Press.

Crick, F. C., & Koch, C. (2005). What is the function of the claustrum? *Philosophical Transactions of the Royal Society: Brain and Biological Sciences, 30,* 1271–1279.

Davidson, M. C., Amso, D., Anderson, L. C., & Diamond, A. (2006). Development of cognitive control and executive functions from 4 to 13 years: Evidence from manipulations of memory, inhibition and task switching. *Neuropsychologia, 44,* 2037–2078.

Dawson, T. L., & Gabrielian, S. (2003). Developing conceptions of authority and contract across the lifespan: Two perspectives, *Developmental Review, 23,* 162–218.

Dawson, T. L., & Wilson, M. (2003). Domain-general and domain-specific developmental assessments: Do they measure the same thing? *Cognitive Development, 18,* 61–78.

Deaner, R. O., van Schaik, C. P., & Johnson, V. (2006). Do some taxa have better domain-general cognition than others? A metaanalysis of nonhuman primate studies. *Evolutionary Psychology, 4,* 149–196.

Deary, I. J. (2000). *Looking down on human intelligence.* Oxford: Oxford University Press.

Dehaene, S. (1997). *The number sense: How the mind creates mathematics.* New York: Oxford University Press.

Demetriou, A. (1998a). Nooplasis: 10 + 1 Postulates about the formation of mind. *Learning and Instruction: The Journal of the European Association for Research on Learning and Instruction, 8,* 271–287.

Demetriou, A. (1998b). Cognitive development. In A. Demetriou, W. Doise, & K. F. M. van Lieshout (Eds.), *Life-span developmental psychology* (pp. 179–269). London: John Wiley & Sons.

Demetriou, A. (2000). Organization and development of self-understanding and self-regulation: Toward a general theory. In M. Boekaerts, P. R. Pintrich, & M. Zeidner (Eds.), *Handbook of self-regulation* (pp. 209–251). San Diego: Academic Press.

Demetriou, A. (2003). Self-formations: Toward a life-span model of the developing mind and self. *Journal of Adult Development, 17,* 151–171.

Demetriou, A. (2006, July). *Mind, personality, and emotions: Deciphering their relations.* Keynote address presented at the 13th Conference of the European Association of Personality, Athens, Greece.

Demetriou, A., & Bakracevic, K. (2009). Cognitive development from adolescence to middle age: From environment-oriented reasoning to social understanding and self-awareness. *Learning and Individual Differences, 19,* 181–194.

Demetriou, A., Christou, C., Spanoudis, G., & Platsidou, M. (2002). The development of mental processing: Efficiency, working memory, and thinking. *Monographs of the Society of Research in Child Development, 67* (Serial Number 268).

Demetriou, A., & Efklides, A. (1985). Structure and sequence of formal and postformal thought: General patterns and individual differences. *Child Development, 56,* 1062–1091.

Demetriou, A., & Efklides, A. (1988). Experiential structuralism and neo-Piagetian theories: Toward an integrated model. In A. Demetriou (Ed.), *The neo-Piagetian theories of cognitive development: Toward an integration* (pp. 173–222). Amsterdam: North-Holland.

Demetriou A., & Efklides, A. (1989). The person's conception of the structures of developing intellect: Early adolescence to middle age. *Genetic, Social, and General Psychology Monographs, 115,* 371–423.

Demetriou, A., Efklides, E., Papadaki, M., Papantoniou, A., & Economou, A. (1993). The structure and development of causal-experimental thought. *Developmental Psychology, 29,* 480–497.

Demetriou, A., Efklides, A., & Platsidou, M. (1993). The architecture and dynamics of developing mind: Experiential structuralism as a frame for unifying cognitive developmental theories. *Monographs of the Society for Research in Child Development, 58* (Serial Number 234).

Demetriou, A., & Kazi, S. (2001). *Unity and modularity in the mind and the self: Studies on the relationships between self-awareness, personality, and intellectual development from childhood to adolescence.* London: Routledge.

Demetriou, A., & Kazi, S. (2006). Self-awareness in g (with processing efficiency and reasoning). *Intelligence, 34,* 297–317.

Demetriou, A., & Kyriakides, L. (2006). A Rasch-measurement model analysis of cognitive developmental sequences: Validating a comprehensive theory of cognitive development. *British Journal of Educational Psychology, 76,* 209–242.

Demetriou, A., Kyriakides, L., & Avraamidou, C. (2003). The missing link in the relations between intelligence and personality. *Journal of Research in Personality, 37,* 547–581.

Demetriou, A., Mouyi, A., & Spanoudis, G. (2008). Modeling the structure and development of g. *Intelligence, 5,* 437–454.

Demetriou, A., Pachaury, A., Metallidou, Y., & Kazi, S. (1996). Universal and specificities in the structure and development of quantitative-relational thought: A cross-cultural study in Greece and India. *International Journal of Behavioral Development, 19,* 255–290.

Demetriou, A., Platsidou, M., Efklides A., Metallidou, Y., & Shayer, M. (1991). Structure and sequence of the quantitative-relational abilities and processing potential from childhood and adolescence. *Learning and Instruction: The Journal of the European Association for Research on Learning and Instruction, 1,* 19–44.

Demetriou, A., & Raftopoulos, A. (1999). Modeling the developing mind: From structure to change. *Developmental Review, 19,* 319–368.

Demetriou, A., Zhang, X. K., Spanoudis, G., Christou, C., Kyriakides, L., & Platsidou, M. (2005). The architecture and development of mental processing: Greek, Chinese or Universal? *Intelligence, 33,* 109–141.

Dempster, F. N. (1991). Inhibitory processes: A neglected dimension of intelligence. *Intelligence, 15,* 157–173.

Dempster, F. N. (1992). The rise and fall of the inhibitory mechanism: Toward a unified theory of cognitive development and aging. *Developmental Review, 12,* 45–75.

Dempster, F. N. (1993). Resistance to interference: Developmental changes in a basic processing mechanism. In M. L. Howe & R. Pasnak (Eds.), *Emerging themes in cognitive development: Vol. 1, Foundations* (pp. 3–27). New York: Springer.

de Ribaupierre, A., & Bailleux, C. (1994). Developmental change in a spatial task of attentional capacity: An essay toward an integration of two working memory models. *International Journal of Behavioral Development, 17,* 5–35.

de Ribaupierre, A., & Bailleux, C. (1995). Development of attentional capacity in childhood: A longitudinal study. In F. E. Weinert & W. Schneider (Eds.), *Memory performance and competencies: Issues in growth and development* (pp. 45–70). Hillsdale, NJ: Erlbaum.

de Ribaupierre, A., & Pascual-Leone, J. (1984). Pour une intégration des methods en psychologie: Approaches expérimentale, psycho-génétique et différentielle. *L'Année Psychologique, 84,* 227–250.

Diamond, A. (1990). The development and neural bases of memory functions as indexed by the AB and delayed response tasks in

human infants and infant monkeys. In A. Diamond (Ed.), *The development and neural bases of higher cognitive functions. Annals of the New York Academy of Sciences: 608* (pp. 239–266). New York: New York Academy of Sciences.

Durston, S., & Casey, B. J. (2006). What have we learned about cognitive development from neuroimaging? *Neuropsychologia, 44,* 2149–2157.

Edelman, G. M., & Tononi, G. A. (2000). *Universe of consciousness.* New York: Basic Books.

Efklides, A., Demetriou, A., & Metallidou, A. (1994). The structure and development of propositional reasoning ability. In A. Demetriou and A. Efklides (Eds.), *Mind, intelligence, and reasoning: Structure and development* (pp. 151–172). Amsterdam: Elsevier.

Embretson, S. E. (1995). The role of working capacity and general processes in intelligence, *Intelligence, 20,* 169–189.

Engle, R. W. (2002). Working memory capacity as executive attention. *Current Directions in Psychological Science, 11,* 19–23.

Engle, R. W., Tuholski, S. W., Laughlin, J. E., & Conway, A. R. A. (1999). Working memory, short-term memory, and general fluid intelligence: A latent-variable approach. *Journal of Experimental Psychology: General, 128,* 309–331.

Fabricius, W. V., & Schwanenflugel, P. J. (1994). The older child's theory of mind. In A. Demetriou & A. Efklides (Eds.), *Intelligence, mind, and reasoning: Structure and development* (pp. 111–132). Amsterdam: North-Holland.

Fischer, K. W. (1980). A theory of cognitive development: The control and construction of hierarchies of skills. *Psychological Review, 87,* 477–531.

Flavell, J. H., Green, F. L., & Flavell, E. R. (1986). Development of knowledge about the appearance-reality distinction. *Monographs of the Society for Research in Child Development, 51* (Serial Number 212).

Flavell, J. H., Miller, P. H., & Miller, S. A. (2001). *Cognitive development* (4th ed.). Englewood Cliffs, NJ: Prentice Hall.

Fonlupt, P. (2003). Perception and judgement of physical causality involve different brain structures. *Cognitive Brain Research, 17,* 248–254.

Galaburta, A. M., Kosslyn, S. M., & Christen, Y. (2002). *The languages of the brain.* Cambridge, MA: Harvard University Press.

Gardner, H. (1983). *Frames of mind. The theory of multiple intelligences.* New York: Basic Books.

Garlick, D. (2002). Understanding the nature of the general factor of intelligence: The role of individual differences in neural plasticity as an explanatory mechanism. *Psychological Review, 109,* 116–136.

Gazzaniga, M. S., Ivry, R. B., & Mangun, G. R. (2008). *Cognitive neuroscience: The biology of the mind.* New York: W. W. Norton & Company.

Gibson, J. J. (1966). *The senses considered as perceptual systems.* London: Allen & Unwin.

Goel, V. (2007). The anatomy of deductive reasoning. *Trends in Cognitive Sciences, 11,* 435–441.

Goel, V., Buchel, C., Frith, C., & Dolan, R. J. (2000). Dissociation of mechanisms underlying syllogistic reasoning. *NeuroImage, 12,* 504–514.

Goel, V., & Dolan, R. J. (2000). Anatomical segregation of component processes in an inductive inference task. *Journal of Cognitive Neuroscience, 12,* 1–10.

Goel, V., & Dolan, R. J. (2001). Functional neuroanatomy of three-term relational reasoning. *Neuropsychologia, 39,* 901–909.

Grigorenko, E. L., Geissler, P. W., Prince, R., Okatcha, F., Nokes, C., Kenny, D. A., et al. (2001). The organization of Luo conceptions of intelligence: A study of implicit theories in a Kenyan village. *International Journal of Behavioral Development, 25,* 367–378.

Gruber, O., & von Cramon, D. Y. (2003). The functional neuroanatomy of human working memory revisited—Evidence from 3T-fMRI studies using classical domain-specific interference tasks. *NeuroImage, 19,* 797–809.

Gustafsson, J. E., & Undheim, J. O. (1996). Individual differences in cognitive functions. In D. C. Berliner & R. C. Calfee (Eds.), *Handbook of educational psychology* (pp. 186–242). New York: Macmillan.

Hale, S., & Fry, A. F. (2000). Relationships among processing speed, working memory, and fluid intelligence in children. *Biological Psychology, 54,* 1–34.

Halford, G. S. (1993). *Children's understanding: The development of mental models.* Hillsdale, NJ: Erlbaum.

Halford, G. S. (2002). Information-processing models of cognitive development. In U. Gowsami (Ed.), *Handbook of child cognitive development* (pp. 556–574). Oxford: Blackwell.

Halford, G. S., & Andrews, G. (2004). The development of deductive reasoning: How important is complexity? *Thinking & Reasoning, 10,* 123–145.

Halford, G. S., Maybery, M. T., O'Hare, A. W., & Grant, P. (1994). The development of memory and processing capacity. *Child Development, 65,* 1330–1348.

Halford, G. S., Wilson, W. H., & Phillips, S. (1998). Processing capacity defined by relational complexity: Implications for comparative, developmental, and cognitive psychology. *Behavioral and Brain Sciences, 21,* 803–864.

Harnishfeger, K. K. (1995). The development of cognitive inhibition: Theories, definitions, and research evidence. In F. N. Dempster & C. J. Brainerd (Eds.), *Interference and inhibition in cognition* (pp. 175–204). New York: Academic Press.

Harter, S. (1999). *The construction of the self.* New York: Guilford Press.

Huizinga, M., Dolan, C. V., & van der Molen, M. W. (2006). Age-related change in executive function: Developmental trends and a latent variable analysis. *Neuropsychologia, 44,* 2017–2036.

James, W. (1890). *The principles of psychology* (Vol. 1). New York: Hold.

Jausovec, N., & Jasovec, K. (2004). Differences in induced brain activity during performance of learning and working memory tasks related to intelligence. *Brain and Cognition, 54,* 65–74.

Jensen, A. R. (1998). *The G factor: The science of mental ability.* New York: Praeger.

Jensen, A. R. (2006). *Clocking the mind: Mental chronometry and individual differences.* Amsterdam: Elsevier.

Johnson, J., Im-Bolter, N., & Pascual-Leone, J. (2003). Development of mental attention in gifted and mainstream children: The role of mental capacity, inhibition, and speed of processing. *Child development, 74,* 1594–1614.

Johnson, J., Pascual-Leone, J., & Agostino, A. (2001). *Solving multiplication word problems: The role of mental attention.* Presented at the meeting of the Society for Research in Child Development, Minneapolis, MN.

Jung R. E., & Haier, R. J. (2007). The Parieto-Frontal Integration Theory (P-FIT) of intelligence: Converging neuroimaging evidence. *Behavioral and Brain Sciences, 30,* 135–154.

Kail, R. (1991). Developmental functions for speed of processing during childhood and adolescence. *Psychological Bulletin, 109,* 490–501.

Kail, R. (2000). Speed of information processing: Developmental change and links to intelligence. *Journal of School Psychology, 38,* 51–61.

Kail, R. (2007). Longitudinal evidence that increases in processing speed and working memory enhance children's reasoning. *Psychological Science, 4,* 312–313.

Kail, R., & Salthouse, T. A. (1994). Processing speed as a mental capacity. *Acta Psychologica, 86,* 199–225.

Kandel, E. R., Schwartz, J. H., & Jessell, T. M. (1995). *Essentials of neural science and behavior.* New York: Appleton & Lange.

Kargopoulos, P., & Demetriou, A. (1998). What, why, and whence logic? A response to the commentators. *New Ideas in Psychology, 16,* 125–139.

Karmiloff-Smith, A. (1992). *Beyond modularity: A developmental perspective on cognitive science.* Cambridge, MA: MIT Press.

Kemps, E., De Rammelaere, S., & Desmet, T. (2000). The development of working memory: Exploring the complementarily of two models. *Journals of Experimental Child Psychology, 77,* 89–109.

Kitchener, K. S., & King, P. M. (1981). Reflective judgment: Concepts of justification and their relationship with age and education. *Journal of Applied Developmental Psychology, 2,* 89–116.

Klingberg, T. (1998). Concurrent performance of two working memory tasks: Potential mechanisms of interference. *Cerebral Cortex, 8,* 593–601.

Kohlberg, L. (1984). *Essays in moral development: Vol. 2, The psychology of moral development.* New York: Harper & Row.

Kosslyn, S. M. (1980). *Image and mind.* Cambridge, MA: Harvard University Press.

Kuhn, D. (2000). Metacognitive development. *Current Directions in Psychological Science, 9,* 178–181.

Kuhn, D., & Pease, M. (2006). Do children and adults learn differently? *Journal of Cognition and Development, 7,* 279–293.

Kyllonen, P. C. (1996). Is working memory capacity Spearman's g? In I. Dennis & P. Tapsfield (Eds.), *Human abilities: Their nature and measurement* (pp. 49–75). Mahwah, NJ: Erlbaum.

Kyllonen, P., & Christal, R. E. (1990). Reasoning ability is (little more than) working-memory capacity? *Intelligence, 14,* 389–433.

Labouvie-Vief, G. (1994). *Psyche and Eros: Mind and gender in the life course.* New York: Cambridge University Press.

Lamme, V. A. F. (2006). Towards a true neural stance on consciousness. *Trends in Cognitive Sciences, 10,* 494–501.

Lee, J. J. (2006). A g beyond Homo sapiens: Some hints and suggestions. *Intelligence, 35,* 253–265.

Lerner, R. M. (2006). Developmental science, developmental systems, and contemporary theories of human development. In W. Damon & R. M. Lerner (Series Eds.) & R. M. Lerner (Vol. Ed.), *Handbook of child psychology: Vol. 1, Theoretical models of human development* (6th ed., pp. 1–17). Hoboken, NJ: John Wiley & Sons.

Lerner, R. M., & Overton, W. F. (2008). Exemplifying the integrations of the relational developmental system: Synthesizing theory, research and application to promote positive development and social justice. *Journal of Adolescent Research, 23,* 245–255.

McLaughlin, G. H. (1963). Psycho-logic: A possible alternative to Piaget's formulation. *British Journal of Educational Psychology, 33,* 61–67.

McLeod, C. M. (1991). Half a century of research on the Stroop effect: An integrative review. *Psychological Bulletin, 109,* 163–203.

Miller, L. T., & Vernon, P. A. (1992). The general factor in short-term memory, intelligence, and reaction time. *Intelligence, 16,* 5–29.

Miyake, A., & Shah, P. (1999). *Models of working memory: Mechanisms of active maintenance and executive control.* Cambridge: Cambridge University Press.

Morra, S. (2000). A new model of verbal short-term memory. *Journal of Experimental Child Psychology, 75,* 191–227.

Moshman, D. (2004). From inference to reasoning: The construction of rationality. *Thinking & Reasoning, 10,* 221–239.

Mouyi, A. (2008). *Developmental dynamics binding processing efficiency, working memory, and reasoning: A longitudinal study.*

Unpublished doctoral dissertation, University of Cyprus, Nicosia, Cyprus.

Neil, W. T., Valdes, L. A., & Terry, K. M. (1995). Selective attention and inhibitory control of cognition. In F. N. Dempster & C. J. Brainerd (Eds.), *Interference and inhibition in cognition* (pp. 207–263). New York: Academic Press.

Neubauer, A. C., Grabner, R. H., Freuddenthaler, H. H., Beckman, J. F., & Guthke, J. (2004). Intelligence and individual differences in becoming neurally efficient. *Acta Psychologica, 116*, 55–74.

Nicholls, J. G. (1990). What is ability and why are we mindful of it? A developmental perspective. In R. J. Sternberg & J. Kolligian, Jr. (Eds.), *Competence considered* (pp. 11–40). New Haven, CT: Yale University Press.

Oberauer, K., Süß, H.-M., Schulze, R., Wilhelm, O., & Wittmann, W. W. (2000). Working memory capacity. Facets of a cognitive ability construct. *Personality and Individual Differences, 29*, 1017–1045.

O'Reilly, R. C., & Munakata, Y. (2000). *Computational explorations in cognitive neuroscience: Understanding the mind by simulating the brain.* Cambridge, MA: MIT Press.

Osherson, D., Perani, D., Cappa, S., Schnur, T., Grassi, F., & Fazio, F. (1998). Distinct brain loci in deductive versus probabilistic reasoning. *Neuropsychologia, 36*, 369–376.

Overton, W. F. (2006). Developmental psychology: Philosophy, concepts, methodology. In W. Damon & R. M. Lerner (Series Ed.) & R. M. Lerner (Vol. Ed.), *Theoretical models of human development: Vol. 1, Handbook of child psychology* (6th ed., pp. 18–88). Hoboken, NJ: John Wiley & Sons.

Pascual-Leone, J. (1970). A mathematical model for the transition rule in Piaget's developmental stages. *Acta Psychologica, 32*, 301–345.

Pascual-Leone, J. (1988). Organismic processes for neo-Piagetian theories: A dialectical causal account of cognitive development. In A. Demetriou (Ed.), *The neo-Piagetian theories of cognitive development: Toward an integration* (pp. 25–64). Amsterdam: North-Holland.

Pascual-Leone, J., & Baillargeon, R. (1994). Developmental measurement of mental attention. *International Journal of Behavioral Development, 17*, 161–200.

Pascual-Leone, J., & Goodman, D. R. (1979). Intelligence and experience: A neo-Piagetian approach. *Instructional Science, 8*, 301–367.

Pascual-Leone, J., & Morra, S. (1991). Horizontality of water level: A neo-Piagetian developmental review. *Advances in Child Development and Behavior, 23*, 231–275.

Pfeifer, R., & Scheier, C. (1999). *Understanding intelligence.* Cambridge, MA: MIT Press.

Piaget, J. (1970). Piaget's theory. In P. H. Mussen, (Ed.), *Carmichael's handbook of child development* (pp. 703–732). New York: John Wiley & Sons.

Piaget, J. (2001). *Studies in reflecting abstraction* (R. L. Campbell, Trans.). London: Psychology Press. (Original work published 1977)

Polderman, T. J. C., Posthuma, D., De Sonneville, L. M. J., Stins, J. F., Verhulst, F. C., & Boomsma, D. I. (2007). Genetic analyses of the stability of executive functioning during childhood. *Biological Psychology, 76*, 11–20.

Posner, M. I., & Raicle, M. E. (1997). *Images of mind.* New York: Scientific American Library.

Repovš, G., & Baddeley, A. (2006). The multi-component model of working memory: Explorations in experimental cognitive psychology. *Neuroscience, 139*, 5–21.

Reynolds, C. A., Finkel, D., McArdle, J. J., Gatz, M., Berg, S., & Pedersen, N. L. (2005). Quantitative genetic analysis of latent growth curve models of cognitive abilities in adulthood. *Developmental Psychology, 41*, 3–16.

Riegel, K. F. (1973). Dialectic operations: The final period of cognitive development. *Human Development, 16*, 346–370.

Rocadin, C., Pascual-Leone, J., Rich, J. B., & Dennis, M. (2007). Developmental relations between working memory and inhibitory control. *Journal of the International Neuropsychological Society, 13*, 59–67.

Rumbauch, D. M., & Washburn, D. A. (2003). *Intelligence of apes and other rational beings.* New Haven, CT: Yale University Press.

Salthouse, T. A. (1996). The processing-speed theory of adult age differences in cognition. *Psychological Review, 103*, 403–428.

Salthouse, T. A. (2000). Aging and measures of processing speed. *Biological Psychology, 54*, 35–54.

Salthouse, T. A. (2004). What and when of cognitive aging. *Current Directions in Psychological Science, 13*, 140–144.

Schaie, K. W. (1995). *Intellectual development in adulthood: The Seattle Longitudinal Study.* New York: Cambridge University Press.

Schaie, K. W., Willis, S. L., Jay, G., & Chipuer, H. (1989). Structural invariance of cognitive abilities across the adult life span: A cross-sectional study. *Developmental Psychology, 25*, 652–662.

Schneider, W., Lockl, K., & Fernandez, O. (2005). Interrelationships among theory of mind, executive control, language development, and working memory in young children: A longitudinal analysis. In W. Schneider, R. Schumann-Hengsteler, & B. Sodian (Eds.), *Young children's cognitive development* (pp. 259–284). Hillsdale, NJ: Erlbaum.

Schweizer, K., Moosbrugger, H., & Goldhammer, F. (2005). The structure of the relationship between attention and intelligence. *Intelligence, 33*, 589–611.

Shah, P., & Miyake, A. (1996). The separability of working memory resources for spatial thinking and language processing: An individual differences approach. *Journal of Experimental Psychology: General, 125*, 4–27.

Shaw, P., Greenstein, D., Lerch, J., Clasen, L., Lenroot, R., Gogtay, A., et al. (2006). Intellectual ability and cortical development in children and adolescents. *Nature, 440*, 676–679.

Shayer, M., Demetriou, A., & Pervez, M. (1988). The structure and scaling of concrete operational thought: Three studies in four countries. *Genetic, Social, and General Psychology Monographs, 114*, 307–376.

Shultz, T. R. (2003). *Computational developmental psychology.* Cambridge, MA: MIT Press.

Spearman, C. (1904). "General intelligence" objectively determined and measured. *American Journal of Psychology, 15*, 201–293.

Stankov, L., & Roberts, R. (1997). Mental speed is not the 'basic' process of intelligence. *Personality and Individual Differences, 22*, 69–84.

Sternberg, R. J., Conway, B. E., Ketron, J. L., & Bernstein, M. (1981). People's conceptions of intelligence. *Journal of Personality and Social Psychology, 41*, 37–55.

Stroop, J. R. (1935). Studies of interference in serial verbal reactions. *Journal of Experimental Psychology, 18*, 643–662.

Thatcher, R. W. (1992). Cyclic cortical reorganization during early childhood. *Brain and Cognition, 20*, 24–50.

Wellman, H. M. (1990). *The child's theory of mind.* Cambridge, MA: MIT Press.

Werner, H. (1948). *Comparative psychology of mental development.* New York: International Universities Press. (Originally published 1940)

Zelazo, P. D. (2004). The development of conscious control in childhood. *Trends in Cognitive Sciences, 8,* 12–17.

Zelazo, P. D., & Müller, U. (2002). Executive function in typical and atypical development. In U. Gowsami (Ed.), *Handbook of child cognitive development* (pp. 445–469). Oxford: Blackwell.

Zelazo, P. D., Müller, U., Frye, D., Marcovitch, S., Argitis, G., Boseovski, J., et al. (2003). The development of executive function in early childhood. *Monographs of the Society for Research in Child Development, 68* (Serial No. 3).

Zelazo, P. D., Qu, L., & Müller, U. (2005). Hot and cool aspects of executive function: Relations with early development. In W. Schneider, R. Schumann, R. Hengsteler, & B. Sodian (Eds.), *Young children's cognitive development: Interrelationships among executive functioning, working memory, verbal ability, and theory of mind.* Mahwah, NJ: Erlbaum.

CHAPTER 11

The Development of Representation and Concepts

ULRICH MÜLLER and TIMOTHY P. RACINE

Reviewing the development of representation and concepts is a difficult task because the terms representation and concept are notoriously ambiguous. Almost two decades ago, Russell (1992) remarked that the word representation "is as dangerously versatile as 'consciousness,' a Humpty-Dumpty word" (p. 500). Since then, the situation has not much improved: "[T]here is nothing remotely like a consensus on the nature of mental representation. Quite the contrary, the current state of affairs is perhaps best described as one of disarray and uncertainty" (Ramsey, 2007, p. xi). When we turn to the term *concept*, we encounter the same kind of problem: "Despite numerous attempts to pin down what we mean when we speak of concepts, the notion continues to defy a single, agreed-upon, applicable-to-all instances definition" (Flavell, Miller, & Miller, 2002, p. 108). Compounding this already complicated situation is the fact that different uses of the terms representation and concept reflect opposing approaches to the study of the mind (Margolis & Laurence, 2006).

Given this state of affairs, in the next section, we discuss multiple uses of the term *representation* before we examine the development of representation in various content areas. Later in this chapter, we examine various theories of concepts and then review conceptual development across the life span.

REPRESENTATION

Historically "representation" has had four distinct meanings as used in philosophy and psychology (Scheerer, 1990a, 1990b, 1993), and these meanings partially overlap with the everyday use of the word *representation* (Oxford English Dictionary, 2009). Although one might worry about the relation between these more technical uses of *representation* and the everyday concept itself and express some concern about how the former can be cashed out in the latter, we will set these issues aside and focus on how

Preparation of this chapter was supported by the Human Early Learning Partnership (to U.M.) and the Social Sciences and Humanities Research Council of Canada (to T.P.R.). We thank Bill Overton for comments on previous drafts.

the term is actually used. First, *representation* refers to any type of meaningful mental content (i.e., content characterized by aboutness) regardless of its function. However, unlike the other three other uses of representation, this need not denote a standing-in-for relation. This meaning can be traced back to Descartes' theory of ideas, although Descartes himself left open whether representations are mental objects or mental acts (Judge, 1985; Kemmerling, 2004; Scheerer, 1993). Whereas perceptual content is included in the first meaning of representation, this is not the case for the second meaning. Rather, the second meaning of representation contrasts direct, "presentational" (perceptual) content or functions and mediated, re-presentational content and functions. *Re-presentational content* refers to content that was formerly directly given by perception but is now stood-in-for and reproduced by acts of thought. For example, Gillett (1988) defines representation in this second sense: "To have a representation of some item is to be able to take account of that item in behaviour even when current circumstances do not *present* it to the organism's sensory systems" (italics in original; p. 261). This second meaning of representation can be traced back to the philosophers Tetens and Hegel, and the distinction between presentational and re-presentational acts plays an important role in phenomenology (Marbach, 1993).

Third, *representation* has been referred to as an image or replica of a thing. Representation in this sense can mean either internal or external representation (e.g., paintings, maps; see Liben, 2008). To be considered a representation, the replica need not resemble the thing it represents. In fact, in mathematics, a representation consists of a mapping of elements from one structure onto elements of another structure such that the structure of the represented system is preserved in the structure of the representing system. Finally, the fourth meaning of representation involves the sense of a person standing in for or looking after the interests of another person or group of persons.

These several meanings appear in the various fields of psychology in which the term *representation* is used. For example, representation is used to refer to neurophysiologic functioning (Elman et al., 1997; Metzinger & Gallese, 2003a), perceptual content (e.g., Marr, 1980), higher cognitive functions (Zelazo, Carter, Reznick, & Frye, 1997), language (Bühler, 1934/1990), mental images (Mandler, 2004), external representation (Liben, 2008), and collective representation (Nicolopoulou & Weintraub, 1998). In some of these fields, it is strongly contested whether the use of the term *representation* is

appropriate (Gibson, 1979; Glock, 2003; Metzinger & Gallese, 2003b; Prinz, 2003). Regardless of whether there are good reasons to discuss all of these as instances of representation, it seems unlikely that such a notion could be defined by necessary and sufficient conditions. Here, Wittgenstein's (1958) notion of family resemblance among members of a category seems more appropriate, and problems would arise when the different uses of terms are confused for one another.

From our brief delineation of representation, it would seem that an important distinction could be made between uses of the term that imply a standing-in-for relation and those that do not. Thus, Scheerer's first use of representation as meaningful mental content may be too general to be helpful here. For psychologists who are almost always concerned with meaningful mental content, a distinction between presentational, perceptual, direct, and re-presentational, mediated content seems essential. Both denote a reference to an object, but in the first instance, the reference is direct, and in the second instance, the reference is mediated by some entity. To limit the scope and, hence, the length of this chapter, we primarily restricted the review of representational development to the second instance, the notion of representation as re-presentation. This is a reasonable restriction as re-presentation has been the meaning adopted by both classical (Baldwin, 1906; Piaget, 1945/1962; Werner & Kaplan, 1963) and contemporary (DeLoache, 2004; Mandler, 2004; Perner, 1991) theories of human development. It also is consistent with the ordinary, everyday use of the term.

Our working definition of representation differs from those provided by Bialystok and Craik (Chapter 7 of this volume) and Demetriou and colleagues (Chapter 10 of this volume). In these chapters (see also Burke, 2006), *representation* is used in the sense of a mapping, and equated with information and stored knowledge. In this chapter, representation involves the intentional use of a stand-in that refers to something other than itself. Thus, we distinguish between information, stored knowledge, and representation, and use a narrower definition of representation in the context of which information and stored knowledge do not constitute representation. For example, we can identify informational correspondences between brain states and states in the world, but these correspondences do constitute meaningful representations for the person himself or herself. In a way, this chapter stresses the human agency involved in the constitution of representations and deals with representation at a personal level of analysis, whereas other chapters in this volume provide a more detailed summary of representation at a subpersonal level of analysis (for the subpersonal-personal distinction in philosophy, see e.g., Dennett, 1969; in psychology, see e.g., Overton, 2006; Russell, 1996).

Historically, there have been two conflicting traditions to the study of mind in general and representation in particular: the passive mind and the active mind (Judge, 1985; Overton, 1976). These traditions only partially overlap with the distinction between empiricism and rationalism. Classical philosophers who adhere to the view that the mind is passive include empiricist philosophers such as Locke and Hobbes, and at least partly, the rationalist philosopher Descartes (Judge, 1985; Overton, 2006). According to this view, the external world becomes represented in the mind through mechanistic cause-and-effect relations, that is, minds "causally register the impingements of the world and thereby carry causally produced representations of it" (Gillett, 1992, p. 1). Here, mental contents are simply the effects of stimuli external to the mind. From this point of view, the human mind, then, is analogous to a camera passively receiving impressions that mirror the separately identifiable entities, or pieces of reality, thought to exist in the external world (Bickhard, 1993; Lakoff, 1987; Rorty, 1979; Taylor, 1995). Any notion of human agency, or activity, in constructing representations is omitted. The meaning of a representation is presumed to be encapsulated in its content. In turn, the mind is more or less a container for such content, which becomes an object of thought by hovering in front of the "mind's eye" for inspection (Judge, 1985).

By contrast, the tradition of understanding mind as an active system, which includes philosophers such as Aristotle, Aquinas, Leibniz, Kant, Hegel, Brentano, Husserl, Merleau-Ponty, and partly Descartes, stresses the importance of the activity of the person in constructing representations (Judge, 1985; Overton, 2006). Because the activity of mind is directed toward things and includes a content, it is construed as intentional (Brentano, 1874/1995, p. 88). In fact, the notion of intentionality highlights that both the activity of the person and the content constituted by this activity are inextricably interwoven. From this point of view, mental content cannot be separated from the activity that supplies the forms or structures by which the content is organized and understood.

A good deal of contemporary psychological thinking about representations is strongly shaped by what is termed the *representational theory of mind* (RTM; see Heil, 2004). Cash (2009) describes the core assumptions of RTM as follows:

People's mental states and processes (their knowledge, beliefs, perceptions, intentions, musings, plans, imaginings and so on) can be about things or have content because of representational structures in the brain and their contents. These representations contain information about things; information that is computationally processed to produce actions sensitive to the information represented. Such contentful representations are caused by perceptual activity, and they are part of processes that cause actions. Their causal connections with people's perceptions, judgments, utterances and other actions help us determine exactly which mechanisms in the brain are representational, the information such representations contain, and their causal (or computational) relationships with other representations. (p. 134)

Because RTM assumes that mental representation receives its meaning from the events that reliably trigger them (e.g., Fodor, 1987), and thus explains reference and intentionality of representations causally, RTM is metatheoretically committed to the passive mind tradition. This conceptualization of the mind, which has dominated in much of current thinking about representation in life-span development (Müller, & Overton, 1998a, 1998b; Müller, Sokol, & Overton, 1998), stands in fundamental conflict with classical developmental theories of representation.

In brief, within classical theories, "re-presentation"[1] is defined as a three-term relation that entails: (1) the item represented; (2) the representative item (i.e., the item doing the representing); and (3) the agent or individual who constructs the representation (Judge, 1985). This notion is made explicit in the pragmatist philosopher Peirce's (1931–1935/1966) definition of representation:

Represent: to stand for, that is, to be in such relation to another that for certain purposes it is treated by some mind as if it were that other. Thus, a spokesman, deputy, attorney, agent, vicar, diagram, symptom, counter, description, concept, premise, testimony, all represent something else, in their several ways, to minds who consider them in that way. (p. 155)

The implication of this working definition of representation is that to make something present that is not immediately given involves the ability to use representative items such as symbols and signs. Symbols and signs serve

---

[1] In the following text, we use, for the sake of simplicity, the term *representation* to refer to "re-presentation."

a proxy function (Bühler, 1933/1982, 1934/1990; Werner & Kaplan, 1963). Bühler illustrates the proxy function in terms of an actor, say Sir Lawrence Olivier, who is playing Shakespeare's Hamlet. On the one hand, the actor is Hamlet, but on the other hand, he is actually not Hamlet. As Bühler (1933/1982) observes, "There is a curious duality in the words, 'He is something and yet he is not that'" (p. 95). This curious duality is due to the fact that the perceptual accidents of the actor (Olivier) do not inhere in the substance they normally belong to (Olivier), but rather in the substance of another object (Hamlet; see Bühler 1934/1990, p. 49). In a similar fashion, in a painting, the canvas lends its accidents (spots of color) to the imagined or imaginary thing it represents, and in symbolic or pretend play, the substitute object (e.g., block) lends its attributes to the imagined thing it stands in for. According to a contemporary definition, which succinctly brings out these complex relations, a symbol is "something that someone intends to represent something other than itself" (DeLoache, 2004, p. 66).

Contemporary research on the development of representation in infancy has been heavily influenced by the work of Jean Piaget, which is briefly outlined later, then followed by a review of contemporary research on representational development. We then summarize theories and empirical research on different areas of representational development, including pretend play, symbolic gestures, and the development of the use and comprehension of external representations (models, pictures; for reviews of the life-span development of representation as it concerns language and memory and maps [as external spatial representations], see McWhinney, Chapter 14 of this volume; Bialystok & Craik, Chapter 7 of this volume; Vasilyeva & Lourenço, Chapter 20 of this volume). Extant research in these areas has largely focused on infancy and the early childhood. As a result, information about representational development across the entire life span in these areas is sparse.

Piaget's Theory of the Emergence of Representation

It is critical to understand that Piaget's theory incorporates two developmentally distinct definitions of "representation." The first, and developmentally primary, definition makes reference to *nonsymbolic meanings* (similar to the first sense of representation as any type of meaningful content, see earlier). For example, Piaget (1936/1952) refers to this understanding of representation when he discusses "the capacity to confer upon things a meaning before the action which this meaning permits... The act of looking under a shawl for a shoe in order to strike it with a piece of wood (Obs. 129) is the prototype of this behavior pattern" (p. 242). Representation in this sense can be traced back to the very beginning of mental life (Piaget, 1936/1952, p. 38). As this citation demonstrates, critics who argue that Piaget conceived of the infant as a simple stimulus-response machine fail to realize his emphasis here is on representation in the sense of nonsymbolic, but actual, meaning (and as actively constructed in applying schemes to the world).

The second, and developmentally more advanced, definition makes reference to *symbolic meanings*. Here, *representation* (re-presentation in the second sense of representation as discussed earlier) entails the capacity to use symbols and signs to evoke an absent object. Symbolic representational thought is a structuring activity that synthesizes concepts or schemes and symbolic representational items (Piaget, 1945/1962, p. 67). Symbolic representational thought requires signifiers (i.e., representative items that convey meaning) and signifieds (i.e., the meaning carried by the signifier) that are *differentiated* from their referents. A system of such signifiers is termed the *semiotic function* (Piaget & Inhelder, 1966/1969, p. 51), which subsumes both symbols and signs. Following the tradition of de Saussure (1916/1986, pp. 67–69), Piaget (Piaget & Inhelder, 1966/1969, p. 56) defined symbols such as mental images as motivated signifiers (i.e., they present some resemblance to the things signified), and signs, such as words, as arbitrary and conventional signifiers. The developmental emergence of the semiotic function opens the possibility of thinking—itself involving the manipulation of symbols and signs—about absent objects, as well as past, future, and even fictitious events.

For Piaget, signifiers and signified are not limited to symbolic representational intelligence but are already present at the sensorimotor level, because meaning is always constituted by signifiers and signified (Piaget, 1936/1952, pp. 189–190). However, in contrast with the signifiers at the symbolic–representational level, signifiers at the sensorimotor level are not differentiated from what they refer to (Piaget, 1936/1952, p. 191). Piaget (1936/1952, p. 191) used the generic term *indications* to refer to undifferentiated signifiers. Signifieds at this level are sensorimotor schemes that confer meaning on the elements they interacted with (Piaget, 1936/1952, p. 189). An indication is an "objective aspect of external reality" (Piaget, 1936/1952, p. 193), "a perceptible fact which announces the presence of an object or the imminence of an event (the door which opens and announces a person)" (Piaget, 1936/1952, pp. 191–192).

Symbolic representations emerge in the second year of life in the form of mental images. The emergence of mental images is captured in an observation of Piaget's daughter Lucienne (Piaget, 1936/1952, Obs. 180). When Lucienne was 16 months old, Piaget gave her a box, the opening of which was too narrow to remove a chain it contained. Piaget observed that Lucienne opened and closed her mouth, and then widened the opening of the box to pull out the chain. Piaget interpreted the opening and closing of the mouth as a differentiated signifier that signified the motor operations required for the successful solution of the problem. Piaget (1936/1952, p. 248) was adamant that symbolic representations are only "tools of nascent thought" supporting the dynamic process of invention.

Symbolic representation can also be observed in other areas such as deferred imitation (i.e., the imitation of absent models using mental images as signifiers), pretend play, and object permanence. Specifically, infants solve object permanence tasks in which objects are invisibly displaced. For example, when Piaget hid a small pencil in his hand, moved his hand successively to hiding places A, B, and C, and left the pencil under C, his daughter Jacqueline, at the age of 19 months, was able to retrieve the pencil. According to Piaget (1937/1954, pp. 83–86), the retrieval of invisibly displaced objects presupposes the emergence of symbolic representation.

Contemporary Research on Early Infant Representation

A significant proportion of the study of representational development emerged from various critiques of Piaget's account of the development of representation. The major critique argued that Piaget's methods of assessing representation (i.e., his reliance on sensorimotor actions such as manual search) systematically underestimated infants' representational competencies. In place of tasks involving motor actions, some investigators adopted tasks using "looking behavior" in their studies of representational development. A commonly used method in this line of research is termed the violation of expectation (VOE) paradigm (see Bremner, 2001). In the VOE paradigm, infants are familiarized with an event sequence (e.g., a screen rotating back and forth through an arc of 180 degrees; see Baillargeon, 1987). Following habituation to this event, infants are pre-

sented with test events that either do or do not violate the physical principle under study (e.g., the screen either stops at the box or appears to pass through it). Investigators have assumed that if infants look longer at the impossible than at the possible event, they have formed a representation of the box and understand the physical principle under study. Using the VOE paradigm, researchers have found that 3- to 4-month-old infants already look longer at "impossible" than at "possible" events (see Baillargeon, 2004a; Bremner, 2001). These findings have been interpreted by some as evidence that "young infants are able to represent the existence and the location of hidden objects and to reason about these objects in sophisticated, adult-like ways" (Baillargeon, 1993, p. 294).

This rich interpretation of an infant's looking time behavior has not gone unchallenged (e.g., Cohen & Cashon, 2006; Haith & Benson, 1998; Kagan, 2008; Rakison, 2007). It has been argued that possible and impossible events in the VOE paradigm are confounded with other factors, which, in turn, may explain the looking time differences (e.g., Bogartz, Shinskey, & Speaker, 1997; Cashon & Cohen, 2000; Rivera, Wakeley, & Langer, 1999; Schöner & Thelen, 2006). A counterargument is that confounds may explain some findings but cannot account for numerous demonstrations of representational competence in infants (Baillargeon, 2002, 2004a, 2004b; Bremner, 2001). However, a recent dynamic systems model claims to account for all the findings gathered with the VOE paradigm on the basis of action-perception cycles (Schöner & Thelen, 2006). Furthermore, it has been argued that because the VOE paradigm assesses only whether infants perceptually discriminate between two different events, it is generally compatible with a perceptual interpretation and does not warrant the ascription of advanced cognitive processes to infants (Cohen & Cashon, 2006; Haith & Benson, 1998; Kagan, 2008; Müller & Overton, 1998a; Rakison, 2007; Schöner & Thelen, 2006; but see Baillargeon, 2004a, 2004b). A further problem for the rich interpretation of looking time data is that it fails to explain why infants' precocious knowledge is not revealed in their actions (e.g., in the A-not-B task) even several months after they have acquired the necessary motor skills (Bremner, 2001; Müller & Overton, 1998a).

What we add for consideration in this debate is that Baillargeon is equivocating in her use of representation. She has introduced a technical notion of the concept wherein *representation* means looking longer at an impossible rather than a possible event. However, this is not how this term normally is used, and in fact we use it in our chapter in its ordinary sense of indicating a standing-in-for relation. In its everyday sense, the grounds for attributing such a concept to a pre-linguistic, or for that matter non-linguistic, agent have to be that they actually do something that demonstrates such a standing-in-for relation. However, no such thing has been done, and in fact *could* be done, using the VOE paradigm. Of course, scientists are free to introduce technical concepts to guide their empirical and theoretical work, but when these technical concepts are not distinguished from ordinary ones, confusion is the inevitable result. In Baillargeon's case, the damage done is that her theoretical claims only follow if the everyday use of the term is in play. That is, VOE needs to show a "simpler" form of re-presentation. What it has shown is representation in the empiricist sense of a perceptual representation. This is simply how an empiricist describes VOE; it is in this sense an alternate description and not an explanation of representational development.

As these considerations suggest, contemporary uses of the term *representation* are often rooted in an epistemological framework entirely at odds with Piaget's epistemological framework. More specifically, a good deal of contemporary research, including Baillargeon's, is based on a causal RTM, which itself is rooted in the empiricist passive mind tradition (Goldberg, 1991; McDonough, 1989). As discussed earlier, RTM explains meaning and behavior according to internal representations that mediate between input and output. These representations are causally produced by input (i.e., perceptual information) and, in turn, effect some output (i.e., bodily movements). For example, in Baillargeon's (2004a, 2004b, 2008) account of physical reasoning, representations of events are triggered by some input and run through some computations performed by the physical reasoning system, which then produces an output (i.e., increased attention to the physically impossible event). Baillargeon (2004b) explicitly states that reasoning in her theory is performed by some device: "It seems very unlikely that infants possess explicit beliefs about anything. What they do possess is an abstract computational system, a physical reasoning system that monitors physical events and flags those that do not unfold as expected for further scrutiny" (p. 422). In causal representational theories such as Baillargeon's, representations seem to become entities that take on a life of their own and the "person as agent becomes superfluous" (Judge, 1985, p. 51).

This necessarily brief discussion indicates the fundamental differences in the way in which contemporary neonativist theories (exemplified by Baillargeon's theory)

and Piaget differently conceptualize the working of the mind (for a more detailed treatment, see Müller & Overton, 1998a, 1998b; Müller et al., 1998). Basically, in the tradition of empiricist causal representational theories, Baillargeon's theory conceptualizes the mind as passive and relations between infants and the world as extrinsic, whereas Piaget's theory conceptualizes the mind as active and the relation between infant and world as intrinsic.

A second critique of Piaget's account of representation emerged over the issue of deferred imitation (Mandler, 2004). Following Piaget, research on deferred imitation used tasks that were modeled on Piaget's own observations. For example, Meltzoff (1988) examined immediate (study 1) and deferred (study 2) imitation in 9-month-olds. In each study, Meltzoff used one imitation group and three control groups. The infants in the imitation group viewed a model applying three simple actions to toys that were novel to them. For example, they observed a model shaking a plastic egg that made a rattling noise. Infants in the baseline control group did not observe modeled actions. The baseline control group was introduced to establish the probability that infants would produce the target actions spontaneously. In the adult-touching control group, the model approached and touched each toy but did not model the target actions. In the adult-manipulation control group, the model manipulated the toy and produced the same consequences (e.g., noise) as in the imitation group but did not produce the target actions. The latter two groups were introduced to control for the possibility that infants would produce the target action either because they were aroused by the adult approaching the toys, or because they heard the consequences of the model's manipulations. Meltzoff (1988) found that infants in the imitation group reproduced significantly more target actions than the three control groups combined, both when the toys were handed to the infants immediately after the modeling period (study 1) and when the infants were given the objects 24 hours later (study 2). Meltzoff (1988, 1990) interpreted these findings as demonstrating that deferred imitation is already present in 9-month-old infants, a claim that is inconsistent with Piaget's theory, according to which deferred imitation, and thus symbolic representation, does not emerge until the second year of life.

The deferred imitation research points to a problem involving the operational criteria that Piaget used to diagnose the presence of representation. It is not clear why success on deferred imitation tasks should require symbolic representation: Once a target action is understood, it can be enacted whenever the proper cues (target object, place, presence of the model) are present. It is not necessary to assume that deferred imitation requires that infants form a mental image or are conscious of having perceived the imitated action in the past. Understanding the target action leads to a modification of the action scheme, and memory of the past exists in nothing but the preservation of the modified scheme. Following this line of argument, deferred imitation (at least in infants) can be explained without invoking symbolic representation: Infants assimilate the target action through observational learning and reproduce it after a 24-hour delay because they recognized the toy and model, and assimilate them to the scheme that had been activated earlier. This interpretation receives empirical support from the findings that immediate and deferred imitation performances of assimilable actions do not substantially differ (Abravanel, 1991; Mandler & McDonough, 1995), and that changing some features of the context and of the target object leads to a significant decrease of imitative performance (Barnat, Klein, & Meltzoff, 1996). Furthermore, deferred imitation is acquired considerably (i.e., about 6 months) earlier than other symbolic representational abilities such as pretend play (Nielsen & Dissanayake, 2004), which is also consistent with the suggestion that it is based on less complex, nonsymbolic processes.

Development of Pretend Play

Because Piaget's description of the development of pretend play still constitutes the main reference point for most of recent research on pretend play, we briefly summarize his work on this topic. According to Piaget (1945/1962), pretend play is a vehicle that reflects and promotes symbolic representational development. Specifically, in pretend play, the child uses one action or object as a signifier to stand in for something else (e.g., use a banana as if it were a telephone). Pretend play emerges from sensorimotor rituals that are applied out of context:

> The child is using schemas which are familiar, and for the most part already ritualized…but (1) instead of using them in the presence of the objects to which they are usually applied, he assimilates to them new objects unrelated to them from the point of view of effective adaptation; (2) these new objects, instead of resulting merely in an extension of the schema (as is the case in the generalisation proper to intelligence), are used with no other purpose than that of allowing the subject to mime or evoke the schemas in question. (Piaget, 1945/1962, p. 97)

Piaget observed the first instances of pretend play in the second year of life. For example, when she was 1 year and 3 months old, Piaget's daughter Jacqueline used a cloth as if it were a pillow and pretended to sleep (Piaget, 1945/1962, Obs. 64). The fact that Jacqueline was laughing was taken by Piaget as an indicator that her actions were not meant seriously. Piaget (1945/1962, p. 101) did not regard this action as properly symbolic because the action was both signifier and signified. However, because the action remained unfinished and was done only for fun, there was a differentiation between signifier (the movements actually made) and signified (the whole movements if the action were completed seriously). In more advanced pretend play, additional objects are assimilated to the play actions. Take, for example, Jacqueline's action of using the tail of her rubber donkey as if it were a pillow (Piaget, 1945/1962, Obs. 64). Here, the donkey's tail and the actions performed on it serve as a signifier, and the signified is constituted by the action as it would normally unfold and the object to which this action would be applied if the action were performed seriously (Piaget, 1945/1962, p. 101).

Initially, children use pretend actions that are derived from their own ritualized actions. In the second half of the second year of life, children generalize their pretend actions to others (e.g., pretending that a toy dog is crying; see Piaget, 1945/1962, Obs. 75), and they use actions they have borrowed from others, but they apply these actions to new objects (Piaget, 1945/1962, Obs. 76a, 76b). The projection of pretend actions to others and the projection of imitative actions to objects represent a further differentiation between signifier and signified because in the first case, children's actions symbolize somebody else's actions, and in the second case, children's actions imitate another person's actions using substitute objects (e.g., pretending to talk on the phone, using a leaf as a receiver; Piaget, 1945/1962, Obs. 76a). The further development of pretend play at the end of the second year of life is marked by a more explicit use of substitute objects and by the identification of the child's own body with that of others and with things. Whereas substitute objects were implicitly used in the projection of imitative actions onto new objects, the identification of one object with another object now is explicitly used as the central motive setting up the play. To illustrate, when Jacqueline was 22 months old, "she put a shell on the edge of a big box and made it slide down saying: 'Cat on the wall'" (Piaget, 1945/1962, Obs. 77). In the third year of life, children start to combine various schemes to create more elaborate pretend scenarios (Piaget, 1945/1962, Obs. 81) that frequently serve an affective function (Piaget, 1945/1962, Obs. 84, 85, 86). Piaget (1945/1962, Obs. 87a, 87b) observed that around the age of 4 years, children made deductive-like inferences in the context of their pretend play, anticipating which consequences would ensue if certain actions were taken. Finally, Piaget (1945/1962, pp. 135–139) noted that the pretend play of 4- to 7-year-olds is distinguished from that of younger children by three features: (1) It is more orderly, (2) it strives toward an exact imitation of reality, and (3) it frequently involves social pretend play in the context of which children gradually learn to take complementary roles. After the age of 7, pretend play declines and is replaced by games with rules and symbolic constructions (e.g., external models of landscapes, maps; Piaget, 1945/1962, Obs. 92; but see Göncü & Perone, 2005).

Consistent with Piaget's description, subsequent research has identified four trends in the development of pretend play. First, pretend play becomes increasingly decentered as children move from using only the self as agent to using a doll or substitute object as active agents (e.g., pretending that the doll herself pours tea into the cup; Fenson & Ramsay, 1980; Watson & Jackowitz, 1984). Second, substitute objects used in pretend play become increasingly less perceptually and functionally similar to the objects they signify (Bigham & Bourchier-Sutton, 2007; Jackowitz & Watson, 1980; Musatti & Mayer, 1987; Ungerer, Zelazo, Kearsley, & O'Leary, 1981). Third, children integrate actions into more complex hierarchical action sequences (Fenson & Ramsey, 1980). Fourth, complex sociodramatic play emerges around the age of 3 years, but it may appear earlier when children's pretense is scaffolded by a more proficient social partner (Howes & Matheson, 1992).

Building on Piaget's work, and incorporating findings from cross-sectional and longitudinal studies, McCune (1995, 2010; McCune-Nicolich, 1981) developed a detailed account of the development of pretend play in terms of five levels. Essential to this developmental sequence are successive differentiation and integration processes that lead to the increasing distancing between signifier and signified (see also Werner & Kaplan, 1963; Vygotsky, 1978). At the presymbolic level (level 1; typically attained at 8–11 months of age), infants use familiar everyday objects in well-practiced sensorimotor actions, but these actions are enacted outside their regular context. For example, a child of this age encountering an empty cup may pick the cup up and bring it to her lips. These actions are usually quite brief and are enacted with a serious expression. It is likely that the object reminded the child of its typical use, leading to an enactment of the action meaning this object usually affords. At the next level (autosymbolic play, 11–13 months

of age), the infant performs self-pretend actions that are accompanied by smiles and looks to the observer that seem to indicate a sense of playfulness. Infants elaborate on the actions used at the presymbolic level by adding sound effects (e.g., simulating the sounds made when liquid is really consumed). This elaboration suggests that, at this level, the real and pretend acts do not completely overlap because the simulated sound effects, for example, stand in for aspects of the real act. At level 3, symbolic play becomes decentered (12–13 months of age), and children perform pretend actions on other people and objects (e.g., pretending to give mother or doll a drink from an empty cup). Other-directed pretense involves a different physical movement of the body than autosymbolic play, and for that reason reflects a further distancing between signifier and signified. At level 4 (13–18 months of age), infants start to combine several different pretend actions. For example, a single pretend scheme such grooming may be successively applied to different recipients (doll, mother, teddy bear, etc.), or different thematically related schemes may be applied to the same recipient (e.g., putting a dress and shoes on a doll, putting a toy purse over her arms). Finally, hierarchical pretend play emerges between 18 and 24 months of age as children's behavior shows signs of advance planning. Advance planning is displayed in prior designation of the meaning of a substitute object (e.g., saying, "This is a car" in reference to a block) by performing preparatory actions indicating a plan, or by search for objects needed to accomplish the play activity. At this level, children are capable of guiding their symbolic activity by a dynamic schema, rather than being dependent on enactment with objects to support the meaning. The representational intention can now arise without external perceptual support, with internal plans (dynamic schematizing) guiding the action.

In contrast with the classical theories that conceptualize pretend play as being fueled by the gradual differentiation between signifier and signified, contemporary theories of pretend play are founded on the assumptions of the RTM (Friedman & Leslie, 2007; Leslie, 1987; Lillard, 2002). There are currently two main RTM theories of pretend play, both of which are based on a causal (external, disembodied) understanding of the relation between mind and behavior. On the one hand, Leslie (1987, 1994; Friedman & Leslie, 2007) and Fodor (1992) have argued that children as young as 2 years of age apply the same concept of pretense as do adults. According to Leslie (1987, 1994), pretense makes use of a specialized innate cognitive architecture that decouples a pretense representation (e.g., "This is a telephone" when holding a banana) from primary representations about the real world. The decoupling mechanisms copy the primary representation into a metarepresentational context that quarantines it off its normal semantics by giving a quotation of it. For example, when a child pretends that a banana is a telephone, the specialized cognitive architecture would produce the metarepresentation, MOTHER PRETENDS (of) THIS BANANA (that) "IT IS A TELEPHONE" (Friedman & Leslie, 2007, p. 108). The quotation marks indicate that the expression contained in them is decoupled from its normal semantics (i.e., truth conditions). In this manner, the decoupling mechanism transforms the previously transparent expression into an opaque expression (Leslie, 1987).

According to Leslie (1987), metarepresentation is necessary for understanding and production of pretense, because otherwise the child would have a primary representation (*this is a banana*) and a pretend representation (*this is a telephone*) that both refer to the same situation. This poses the threat of representational abuse because both representations contradict each other semantically (Leslie, 1987). Metarepresentation, thus, is necessary to prevent the child's representational system from becoming totally undermined: "If children did not quarantine pretense representations then every instance of pretense would be an instance of confusion and ultimately pretending would alter the meaning (for example, the truth conditions) of representations in arbitrary ways" (Friedman & Leslie, 2007, p. 108).

However, ter Hark (2006) argued that Leslie's theory misconstrues pretend play and fails to properly account for its central features. In Leslie's theory, the postulated decoupling mechanism protects the primary representation from contamination by making a copy of the primary representation, the normal semantics of which is suspended. But as ter Hark (2006) points out, Leslie's use of the term *copy* here trades on an ambiguity:

> On the one hand he refers to the analogy with editing a copy of a word-processing file which implies that the copy and the original are identical in content but physically separated. But then the copy, contrary to what Leslie intends, should have the very same semantic properties as the original. On the other hand decoupling is said to effect a mental copy, a representation of a primary representation but without the semantic properties of the latter. Conceived this way it cannot have the same meaning as the primary representation. Such an account of pretense makes it impossible to explain that the child, if asked what it meant by "pain" when pitying its doll, will not refer to its doll but to

the primary use of this concept. Yet it is precisely in virtue of this dependency relation with the primary use that the child is inclined to treat its doll with care and to find the word "pain" appropriate here. (p. 312)

As a result, so ter Hark (2006, p. 312) concludes, Leslie's explanation of the concept of pretence in terms of metarepresentations "undermines the conditions of sense."

The competing account to Leslie's metarepresentational theory of pretend play is what has been called the "behaving-as-if" theory of children's early pretend play (e.g., Jarrold, Carruthers, Smith, & Boucher, 1994; Lillard, 1994; Nichols & Stich, 2000; Perner, Baker, & Hutton, 1994). Proponents of the "behaving-as-if" theory claim that young children do not yet understand that pretense is based on mental states that knowingly construe a situation in a counterfactual way. Rather, young children have a concept of "pretending-that-p" as "behaving in a way that would be appropriate if p (the counterfactual situation) were the case" (Nichols & Stich, 2000, p. 139). As a result, young children overextend the concept of pretense and apply it to a wider set of cases than do adults. Young children mistakenly include instances of a person behaving-as-if x but does not know x into the class of pretense actions (Lillard, 1993, 1996; Lillard, Zeljo, Curenton, & Kaugars, 2000; Perner et al., 1994). For example, Lillard (1993) introduced 4- to 5-year-old children to a troll named Moe who hopped around like a rabbit but lacked any knowledge about rabbits. Then children were asked whether Moe was pretending to be a rabbit. Over several trials, most 4-year-olds and even many 5-year-olds consistently (and incorrectly) claimed that Moe was pretending to be a rabbit. On the basis of these findings, Lillard (1993) concluded that 4- to 5-year-old children are not in the command of the concept of pretense because they fail to understand that pretense involves the enactment of a knowingly construed counterfactual situation.

The behaving-as-if theory has also claimed that young children include the instance of a person who behaves-as-if unintentionally into the class of pretense actions. For example, Lillard (1998) presented children with the (by now familiar) troll Moe and told them that he hopped like a rabbit, but that he did not want to, or did not try to, hop like a rabbit. When asked whether Moe was pretending to be a rabbit, the majority of 4-year-olds consistently claimed that Moe was pretending to be a rabbit. However, when a reason was provided for why Moe hopped like a rabbit even if he did not want to (e.g., he was walking on a hot pavement and did not want to burn his feet), fewer children believed that Moe was pretending to be a rabbit (Richert & Lillard, 2002). Furthermore, Ganea, Lillard, and Turkheimer (2004) found that, under certain facilitating conditions (e.g., intention of the protagonist is made salient), even 3- and 4-year-old children display a more mentalistic understanding of pretense. Taken together, these results suggest that the children in the Lillard's (1998) original study might have ignored the premise that Moe did not want to hop like a rabbit (Rakoczy, Tomasello, & Striano, 2004; see German & Leslie, 2001, for an extended critique of Lillard's study).

The behaving-as-if perspective has been criticized for a number of theoretical reasons (Friedman & Leslie, 2007; ter Hark, 2006). Friedman and Leslie (2007) argue that the behaving-as-if perspective does not account for how children can possibly understand the pretend actions of others. Ter Hark (2006) criticizes Lillard for illegitimately equating the knowledge required for the possession of the concept of pretend with having a theory of mental representations, the way they are produced, and how they issue in behavior.

Consequently, both Leslie's metarepresentational theory and the behaving-as-if perspective suffer from theoretical problems: Whereas Leslie's theory ascribes too much knowledge and fails to explain the phenomenon of pretend play, the behaving-as-if perspective ascribes too little knowledge. An intermediary position (still from within the RTM framework) is taken by Rakoczy and colleagues (2004). In a series of experiments, Rakoczy and colleagues showed children a person either pretending or trying to do something (in both cases, the person did not actually perform the act to a final result). Thus, children saw the same act presented in one of two different forms. In the first form, the demonstrator was trying (unsuccessfully) to write with a pen. In the second form, the demonstrator was pretending to do something, for example, to write with a pen. Both models were superficially alike: The demonstrator made writing movements with the pen on a sheet of paper, but no marks were made on the paper. The first model was marked by signs of surprise and frustration as trying to write; the second model was marked by signs of fun and playfulness as pretending to write. The child was then given the object. Importantly, the object could be made to work on closer inspection; for example, the pen could be made to really write. The findings were that 3-year-olds, and to some degree 2-year-olds, performed the real action themselves (or tried to really perform it) after the trying model, whereas after the pretense model, they only pretended. Following Rakoczy and colleagues (2004), these findings require an

interpretation richer than that offered by behaving-as-if theories but not as rich as that offered by Leslie's (1994) metarepresentational claim. Specifically, the findings are not consistent with the claim of the behaving-as-if theory that young children do not understand pretense as intentionally acting as-if. Rather, these findings suggest that by 2 to 3 years of age, children understand that someone is acting intentionally according to a counterfactual proposition. At the same time, the findings leave open whether young children fail to distinguish between pretending and other forms of behaving-as-if in their cognitive aspects (e.g., that pretending differs from believing in being defined by the suspension of commitment to truth).

For the reader familiar with the history of psychology, the current controversy about the status and interpretation of pretend play may evoke a déjà vu experience. A similar argument over the status of pretend play raged between William Stern (1914/1930) and Karl Bühler (1918). In a seminal article, the philosopher Ernst Cassirer (1932/1985) pointed out that the conceptualizations by both Bühler and Stern were based on an adultocentric and mentalistic analysis of children pretend play. In a similar vein, it could be argued that contemporary RTM theories of pretend play misconstrue the phenomenon. Instead of viewing pretend play as being based on some special inner mechanism, it may be more appropriate to view it, paraphrasing an expression by ter Hark (2006), as the transferred use of action meaning. The development of the transferred use of action meaning is not an one-time event, but a gradual process of differentiation between signifier and signified, along which different levels of pretend play can be distinguished; not surprisingly, these different levels are not addressed in RTM theories. Furthermore, the transferred use is learned in a social context: The actions used in pretense are often adapted from others, and thus socially shared (Rakoczy, Tomasello, & Striano, 2005), and adults provide a variety of manner cues (e.g., exaggerated motions, smiling) that signal for children that their actions should not be taken literally (Lillard, 2006; Lillard et al., 2007; Nishida & Lillard, 2007). To again paraphrase ter Hark (2006, p. 310), representational abuse arises as a problem only because of the failure to realize that socially shared meaning of action is necessary for a child to be able to pretend-play and make-believe.

Symbolic Representation in the Gestural Medium

In their classic work, *Symbol Formation*, Werner and Kaplan (1963) suggested that gestures constitute one medium in which symbolic representation emerges. Symbolic "motor-gestural depiction" as they (Werner & Kaplan, 1963, p. 84) termed it, is based on nonsymbolic, affective and pragmatically oriented motor action that does "not 'refer' to or represent the affective content but rather includes this content in the reactive pattern" (Werner & Kaplan, 1963, p. 85). Gestural depiction requires the differentiation of the gesture (signifier) from the contents it depicts (signified). Initially, the perceived event and the immediate reaction constitute a global, undifferentiated unit, as evident in "coaction," in which the infants' motor actions resonate with the motor actions of others (Werner & Kaplan, 1963, p. 87). The emergence of intentional motor imitation leads to a differentiation between perceived event and action, and paves the way for the distancing between the gesture and its content, "both in regard to the degree of similarity between the material of the depictive element and of the depicted content and in regard to the temporal-spatial relations between the depictive and the depicted moments" (Werner & Kaplan, 1963, p. 88). At the end of the second year of life, children start to use bodily movements to imitate nonkinetic properties of things such as their form. For example, they may imitate the form of an orange by inflating their cheeks (Werner & Kaplan, 1963, p. 89). According to Werner and Kaplan (1963), the formation of descriptive gestures indicates that the "child has begun to translate realistic events into a medium with its own expressive features: the imitative expressions have developed into truly *pictorial* or *iconic* representations" (p. 89).

More recently, Acredolo and Goodwyn (1985, 1988; for a review, see Acredolo, Goodwyn, Horobin, & Emmons, 1999) systematically examined the emergence of nonverbal gestures (or what they called "baby signs") that 1- to 2-year-old children use to symbolically represent objects (e.g., sniffing gesture for "flower"), requests (e.g., up-and-down movement of the hands to ask for the opportunity to play the piano), and attributes (e.g., hand gesture for "big"). To qualify as a symbolic gesture, these gestures, among others, had to be produced repeatedly in reference to conceptually similar objects or events and had to be used in a context-flexible way (i.e., had to be applied to different exemplars of the concept; Acredolo et al., 1999). A good example of the flexible use of gestures is provided by a 15-month-old girl who rubbed her index fingers together to represent a spider in reference to real spiders, toy spiders, and pictures of spiders (Acredolo & Goodwyn, 1985). Symbolic gestures were acquired either in the context of highly structured interactive routines or through the imitation of actions of the depicted object (e.g., waving hands for "butterfly") outside

of social routines (Acredolo & Goodwyn, 1988). Acredolo and Goodwyn (1988) found that symbolic gestures are quite common among 1- to 2-year-olds (85% of all infants used symbolic gestures). Furthermore, the number of symbolic gestures was significantly correlated with vocabulary development (Acredolo & Goodwyn, 1988), and the training of symbolic gestures in infancy resulted in an increased rate of expressive and receptive vocabulary development at 2 and 3 years, compared with a nonintervention control group (Goodwyn, Acredolo, & Brown, 2000). Symbolic gestures might promote verbal language development because they elicit verbal responses and elaboration from the caregiver, and increase the amount of language to which the infant is exposed. With the growth of verbal language, the spontaneous production of symbolic gestures declines (Iverson, Capirci, & Caselli, 1994; Stefanini, Bello, Caselli, Iverson, & Volterra, 2009). However, gesture continues to play an important role in communication, as well as in cognitive and emotional development (Goldin-Meadow & Wagner, 2005).

Features of symbolic gestures such as their movement pattern and shape often resemble what they depict. Thus, the early emergence of symbolic gestures might be taken as support for Piaget's (1945/1962; Piaget & Inhelder, 1966/1969) and Werner and Kaplan's (1963) position that iconic signifiers (i.e., signifiers that are related to their referent by some sort of resemblance) emerge before and are a prerequisite for the acquisition of signs such as words, which are arbitrarily related to their referents. A number of findings, however, are inconsistent with this position. First, symbolic gestures develop simultaneously with words (Acredolo & Goodwyn, 1988). Second, research on hearing infants and infants learning sign language from native signing parents shows that iconic gestures are not acquired before arbitrary gestures (Morford, Singleton, & Goldin-Meadow, 1995; Namy, 2008; Namy, Campbell, & Tomasello, 2004; Namy & Waxman, 1998; Orlansky & Bonvillian, 1984). Third, the advantage of iconic gestures over arbitrary gestures in facilitating the selection of the appropriate referent is absent in 18-month-olds, emerges in the third year of life, and disappears when children are 4 years old (Namy et al., 2004).

Namy (2008; Namy et al., 2004) provides the following explanation of this developmental pattern. First, 18-month-olds might not understand iconicity at all because the understanding of correspondences between features of the symbolic medium and the referent may be beyond the reach of 18-month-olds. Evidence for this proposal comes from a study by Namy (2008) that showed that children younger than 26 months failed to reliably select the target when a novel gesture was used to indicate an object with which the children were not familiar. Furthermore, Tomasello, Striano, and Rochat (1999) examined the emergence of 18-, 26-, and 35-month-old children's use of single objects and gestures as symbolic representations in an interactive gamelike context in which the experimenter asked the children to slide one of four objects down a chute. The experimenter indicated the target object in the following ways: (1) by holding a toy replica of the target object (e.g., shoe) up in front of the child; (2) by performing a conventional gesture (e.g., acting as if putting on a shoe); (3) by acting on an object symbolically to transform it into another object (e.g., rolling up a piece of paper and throwing it the air, thus pretending the piece of paper to be a ball); and (4) by acting on an object symbolically to transform it into another object and holding up a real ball (with the rolled-up paper serving as the target object); thus, the real object in this condition was not a replica of the target object but exemplified what the target object had previously been used to symbolically indicate. Eighteen-month-olds performed above chance only in the conventional gesture condition; 26-month-olds performed above chance in the conventional and symbolic gesture conditions, but children at this age did not perform above chance when they had to treat the replica as a symbol. Thirty-five-month-olds performed above chance in all four conditions. Namy and colleagues (2004, p. 39) argue that, taken together, these findings cast doubt on whether the symbolic gestures that Acredolo and Goodwyn (1998) documented are truly symbolic and not an "artifact of the type of gestures that parents tend to employ in everyday interactions with their infants." That is, children may simply imitate what they receive in their input and not understand the iconicity of these gestures at all (Tomasello et al., 1999). However, as Acredolo and Goodwyn (1988) showed, not all symbolic gestures can be traced back to a social communicative context, and early symbolic gestures are characterized by some context flexibility. Instead of renouncing the symbolic status of these gestures, it may be more fruitful to conceptualize them at one end of a continuum that is characterized by different degrees of differentiation between signifier and signified.

Namy and colleagues (2004) attribute the finding that by 26 months, children are less likely to map arbitrary gestures than iconic gestures and words to object categories (Namy & Waxman, 1998) to their increasing reliance on verbal language. The reliance on verbal language may bootstrap the detection of similarities, and thus the

construction of iconic symbols, or, alternatively, may reflect the newly gained understanding of the conventions that govern symbolic representation in general, which, in turn, would have ramifications for children's understanding of iconic symbols. As a result of understanding conventions, and perhaps coupled with a more sophisticated understanding of other persons' communicative intent, 4-year-olds perform equally well on arbitrary and iconic gestures.

However, it is not clear whether Namy's (2008; Namy et al., 2004) studies tell us much about the development of iconic gestures. As noted by Namy (2008, fn):

> Strictly speaking, "iconic" refers specifically to representation of visual form (such as the whiskers of a cat or the shape of a ball) whereas the term "indexic" refers to symbols resembling an action associated with the referent (see e.g., Peirce, 1932). I use the term here in a broader sense to refer to the resemblance between a symbol and its referent more generally, encompassing both iconic and index elements.

For Peirce (1955), however, indices and icons are characterized by different relations between signifier and referent. An index refers to an object by virtue of some physical relation (e.g., relation of contiguity as between the pointing finger and the object pointed at; a causal relation as between smoke and fire). An icon refers to an object by virtue of some sort of resemblance between features of the signifier and the referent. The novel gestures used in Namy's (2008) study had not much to do with icons. Furthermore, for Werner and Kaplan (1963), iconicity means that the gestures (and early words as well) imitate some internal expressive feature of the actions or objects. In Eco's (1977) typology, such gestures would perhaps best be classified as a type of ostensive sign (i.e., an iconic sign that refers to the referent by virtue of displaying a part of the referent; Eco [1977, p. 64] provides the example of referring to a gun by stretching the index finger, putting up the thumb, and closing the other fingers). Clearly, future research on the development of symbolic gestures should be based on a thorough semiotic analysis of the relations between signifier and signified.

Another area in which the development of symbolic gestures has been studied is pantomime. In a seminal study, Overton and Jackson (1973) asked 3- to 8-year-old children to pretend to execute different action sequences (e.g., to brush their teeth). Younger children used a body part to model the action (e.g., used a finger to substitute for a toothbrush), whereas older children pretended to hold an imaginary toothbrush (e.g., used a hand as if *correctly* holding and operating a toothbrush; Overton & Jackson, 1973; see also Boyatzis & Watson, 1993; Dick, Overton, & Kovacs, 2005). Although it has been argued that the progression from using a body part to model the action to using an imaginary object to model the action is completed by age 5 (Boyatzis & Watson, 1993), recent evidence suggest that this development is more protracted and continues beyond the preschool years (Dick et al., 2005). O'Reilly (1995; but see Bigham & Bourchier-Sutton, 2007) found that the frequency of using a body part in 3-year-olds' production was mirrored by their failure to label pantomime with imaginary objects correctly, suggesting that their performance reflects difficulties with the conceptualization of symbolic gestures and is not just due to motor problems. In addition, children produced more imaginary object substitutions when they were required to simply hold the object instead of performing a dynamic action with it, and when the pantomime was self-directed instead of other-directed (Dick et al., 2005). Holding the object may simplify the action representation (Dick et al., 2005) or remove the pragmatic context from the action (Werner & Kaplan, 1963). Taken together, these findings provide support for Werner and Kaplan's (1963) idea that representational development is characterized by a process of distancing in which the representation and object represented are initially similar (body part as object) but become increasingly dissimilar (symbolic object) with development.

Later in life, healthy adults have been found to rarely use a body part to model an action (O'Reilly, 1995); however, adults with neurologic conditions such as limb apraxia tend to substitute body parts for imagined objects in action sequences on trials subsequent to having been reinstructed (Raymer et al., 1997). Findings with respect to pantomime and late adult development are not entirely consistent. Ska and Nespoulous's (1987) study found that 60- to 82-year-olds produced significantly more body-part-as-object substitutions than younger cohorts; however, in their study, educational level was confounded with age, which hampers the interpretation of the age-related effects. When educational level was controlled, older adults (mean age, 65 years) made significantly more body-part-as-object substitutions than young adults (mean age, 23 years; Peigneux & van der Linden, 1999). However, older adults were likely to correct this error in a second trial after reinstruction. There was no difference between cohorts in the number of body-part-as-object substitutions that persisted after reinstruction, indicating that in normal late adult development, these substitutions do not reflect difficulties with the conceptualization of symbolic gestures as such but with the inhibition of prepotent emblem gestures (Peigneux & van der Linden, 1999).

Developmental Trends in Children's Drawings

The ability to create pictorial or plastic representations in a two- or three-dimensional medium that can stand for a real or an imagined object or event seems to be a uniquely human ability (Golomb, 1992, 2007; Tanaka, Tomonaga, & Matsuzawa, 2003, but see Savage-Rumbaugh, Fields, & Taglialatela, 2001, pp. 290–291). The development of representational drawing is a complex process that involves the development of fine motor skills, visuospatial abilities, memory, verbal abilities, working memory, the understanding of intention, and the acquisition of cultural conventional forms (Golomb, 2007; Morra, 2005; Toomela, 2002).

The development of drawing has been approached from different perspectives, which have focused on different questions. The so-called classic approach to the development of drawing, perhaps best exemplified by Piaget and Inhelder's work (Piaget & Inhelder, 1948/1956; Piaget & Inhelder, 1966/1969), uses children's drawings as an indicator of their cognitive development. Though not without its problems, as recognized by Piaget and Inhelder (1948/1956, p. 46) themselves, this approach has led to the use of drawings as a measure of intelligence in children (Goodenough, 1926), cognitive functioning in older adults (Ericsson, Winblad, & Nilsson, 2001), and as a screening device for pathology in older adults (Jungwirth et al., 2009). This approach to the development of drawing has been criticized for lacking awareness "that art is a unique symbolic domain that needs to be investigated in its own terms before one can establish similarities to other symbolic domains" (Golomb, 1992, pp. 1–2). Based on Rudolf Arnheim's (1954/1974) seminal work, Golomb (1992, 2007) has argued that children's drawings are grounded in a graphic logic with its own syntax and semantics that deserves to be studied in its own right.

Further controversy exists over the criterion against which to measure artistic development (Golomb, 2007; Matthews, 2010). According to one view, as proponents of which Golomb (2007) mentions Piaget and Neo-Piagetians (Case, 1992), the development of drawing culminates in realism, that is, exact replications of the objects as if recorded from a projective retinal image (Matthews, 2010). If realism is accepted as the ultimate measure of artistic development, then deviation from realism is understood as a mark of deficiency:

> From this perspective, the typical childhood drawings with their unrealistic proportions, transparencies, overlapping forms, and omission and misplacement of parts are seen as seriously flawed. Altogether, the absence of such three-dimensional pictorial cues as foreshortening, size diminution with distance, and lack of perspective are taken as indices of an early, primitive mental orientation. (Golomb, 2007, p. 32)

Following this view, graphic deficiencies gradually are overcome by the development of increasingly complex concepts of geometry, space, and measurement that make possible a more accurate graphic copy of reality and result in more realistic drawings. According to Golomb (2007), this description of development reflects the (ill-conceived) idea that the "accurate imitation of an object or scene is considered to be at the heart of pictorial representation and its development" (p. 32).

Instead, Golomb (2007, p. 33) endorses Arnheim's view that drawing aims at the *"invention of forms that are structurally or dynamically equivalent to the object"* (italics in original), and not at an exact replication of the object. Children are faced with the constraints of the medium to produce these equivalences. Through experience they learn to understand the medium and its possibilities, and master increasingly complex forms to produce equivalences. "Thus, *inexperience, not childhood,* according to Arnheim, is the true starting point for representational development in the arts, and experience with the two-dimensional medium becomes a major force leading to the differentiation of forms and their composition" (Golomb, 2007, p. 33, italics in original).

It is not entirely clear, however, whether Golomb (1992, 2007), in her description of the realistic approach, does not set up a straw man. Piaget (Piaget & Inhelder, 1948/1956) certainly did not believe that spatial concepts are simple copies of reality, and he also had no particular sympathy for realism. Rather, for Piaget (1970/1983), knowledge originates and is based on action and transformation. Furthermore, there is a difference between describing a developmental sequence and placing value judgments on this sequence (Chapman, 1988; Kesselring, 2009). In any case, Golomb's points that children's drawings testify to their creativity and that the medium plays an important role in drawing are certainly well taken.

The study of the development of drawing tackles a variety of different topics; the complexity of this research cannot be covered in this review (for overviews,

see Milbrath, & Trautner, 2008; Willats, 2005). We focus on two specific areas, the development of human figure drawing and the development of shape drawing, as these areas have received a large amount of attention. The developments in these two areas will provide us with the opportunity to show that some general principles apply to the development of drawing. We also briefly address the development of expressiveness in drawing. Finally, we discuss the processes and factors involved in the development of drawing.

Scribbling and the Emergence of Representational Drawing

Representational drawing emerges from motor activity that, in the process of exploring the properties of papers and pens, leaves behind dots and lines. These early artistic productions have been described as scribbles (Kellogg, 1969; Matthews, 2010). In its initial phases, scribbling is not guided by planning or visual attention, and children simply rejoice in the motor activity that provides them with functional pleasure (Bühler, 1918; Piaget & Inhelder, 1966/1969). In the second year of life, motor movements (e.g., vertical and horizontal arcs; see Matthews, 2010) are systematically varied, and children explore the effects of these movements on a piece of paper and pay increasingly more attention to the products and forms that result from their drawing activity. There is some controversy over whether 2-year-olds' scribbles are symbolic (Golomb, 1992; Matthews, 1984). If the differentiation between graphic symbol and referent is taken as a criterion for the emergence of symbols (Werner & Kaplan, 1963), then these scribbles are not symbolic because children's movements, their vocal utterances, and the actions of the drawing instrument are all combined to simulate the referent (Golomb, 1992). At this stage, the drawing is a representation in action, and the drawing activity is closely tied to the child's embodied expression. For example, the developmental psychologist Martha Muchow observed that a 3-year-old, after having been presented with several straight-line figures and then asked to copy a circle, inflated his cheeks and then drew an inordinately big, puffed-out circle (cited in Werner & Kaplan, 1963, p. 90). To provide another example, 2-year-olds may make "hopping" movements with their hand when asked to draw a rabbit (Winner, 1986). The motor action sustains the meaning of the graphic symbol, and once the motor action is finished, the graphic symbol loses its meaning (Golomb, 1992).

In a study by Adi-Japha, Levin, and Solomon (1998), 2- to 3-year-old children either provided no answer to the question what their scribbles meant, or they provided an answer that had no representational meaning (Adi-Japha et al., 1998). Even though these children did not attribute a representational meaning to the whole scribble, they attributed such meaning to individual line segments of the scribble. In particular, angular curves were much more likely to elicit representational responses than smooth curves. However, the scribbles were not yet fully representational because independent observers could not recognize them, nor did the majority of children when presented with the same line segments several weeks after production give them the same meaning (Adi-Japha et al., 1998). Angular curves are likely to draw more attention than smooth curves because, among others, they involve the intentional change of direction. Being relatively closed, angular curves may also be more likely to suggest the contour of an object and, thus, would be more likely to elicit the attribution of representational meaning (Freeman, 1980). Initially, these representational meanings were rarely expressed in advance of the drawing. Rather, these meanings emerged after the drawing had been completed, and were prompted by the process of social interaction that revolved around the drawing (Adi-Japha et al., 1998) and by children's recognition that their marks resembled a recognizable shape (Golomb, 1992; Piaget & Inhelder, 1966/1969). For example, Winner (1986) reported the case of a 2-year-old who made some random marks on a paper and then, realizing the similarity between his scribbles and noodles, named his drawing, "Chicken Pie and Noodles."

The intention to represent a particular object subsequently becomes planned and occurs in advance of the drawing activities by the age of 3 to 4 years (Freeman, 1993; Gardner, 1980; Vygotsky, 1978). According to Bühler (1934/1990, p. 62), the onset of preplanned drawing marks the transition from functional pleasure to creative joy. Creative joy entails the tendency or need to construct more perfect forms ("Formwille"), as well as struggle with resistance encountered in perfecting forms. The developmental transition from functional pleasure to creative joy takes place when children begin to regard the product of their activity as a work, reflected in the sense of ownership and pride they display for their representational drawings, whereas their interest in scribbles was only transient (Golomb, 1992). At the same time, the product of children's activity becomes increasingly independent of the drawing movements by means of which it is accomplished.

Human Figure Drawing

The human figure has received considerable attention in the study of the development of children's drawing be-

cause it is the favorite referent in their drawing (Cox, 1993; Golomb, 1992; Milbrath, 1998; Silk & Thomas, 1986). The most basic human figure drawing consists of a large oval with roundish facial features on its inside (Golomb, 1992). Next, children add vertical lines representing legs to the oval, creating what has been termed the *tadpole figure* (Cox, 1993; Golomb, 1992). Thereafter, this figure tends to be restructured by first lengthening the vertical extensions, creating an *open trunk figure,* which is followed by drawing a separate unit for the torso to which often arms are attached as straight lines at right angles. Five- and 6-year-olds introduce further detail to the drawing by adding, among other features, clothing and hair, and in middle childhood, the body formation becomes more realistic, and later on, proportions of body features are drawn more accurately (Cox, 1993). Children also start to draw the human figure using one continuous outline instead of composing the human figure of separately drawn parts (Goodnow, 1977). For preschoolers, the human figure serves as a template for drawing animal figures, as illustrated by the finding that 3- to 6-year-old children included human features in their drawings of animals (e.g., vertical orientation of animals; Silk & Thomas, 1986).

Once the major forms have been differentiated, children also start to pay attention to the orientation of figures (Cox, 1993). The figure is mostly drawn in a canonical view, with no overlap in parts of the body, facing the viewer rather than in profile, and static rather than in action (Cox, Koyasu, Hiranuma, & Perara, 2001). If children are provided with specific instructions regarding the orientation of the figure, they will alter the canonical view. For example, when instructed to draw a person running, preschoolers widened the angle of the legs; 6- to 10-year-olds bent the legs, and some 9- and 10-year-olds also bent the torso (Goodnow, 1978; Smith, 1993). When asked to draw a person running to the right, there was a significant increase between the ages of 7 and 11 years in the use of a profile view, the depiction of arms and legs asymmetrical in relation to the torso, and occlusion (Cox et al., 2001). However, few older children used foreshortening (i.e., proportionately contracted some parts of the figure to create the illusion of depth) when asked to draw a figure running toward them (Cox et al., 2001).

According to Luquet (1913, 1927) and Piaget (Piaget & Inhelder, 1966/1969), representational drawing is characterized by the transition from intellectual realism to visual realism. Preschool children essentially draw an object as they know it, not how they see it. For example, when children draw a human figure in profile, they will draw the person with two eyes because they know a person has two eyes (Golomb, 1992; Piaget & Inhelder, 1966/1969). Another characteristic of intellectual realism is that children's drawing of human figures is not limited to what is visible, but they will draw the body's insides (e.g., a baby inside the mother's womb; see Golomb, 1992; Piaget and Inhelder [1966/1969] termed this phenomenon "transparency") and fail to occlude the parts that remain hidden from the viewer. By 8 to 9 years of age, children make the transition to visual realism. Their drawings are now limited to what they see from a particular perspective, and the objects in their drawings are arranged according to an overarching plan that is guided by a spatial coordinate system (Lange-Küttner, 2009; Piaget & Inhelder, 1966/1969). The idea that children make a transition from intellectual realism to visual realism is supported by findings that children often depict generic features of the model that are occluded, whereas they omit nongeneric features (e.g., decorative detail) that are visible (Barrett & Light, 1976; Ford & Rees, 2008; Freeman & Janikoun, 1972).

The interpretation of intellectual realism errors, however, has been controversial. According to Golomb (1992), these intellectual realism errors do not indicate children's confusion but reflect their "limited skills to cope with the vexing task of translating the three-dimensional object to the flat two-dimensional surface of the paper" (p. 67). Following Golomb, one would expect that children's production of drawings lags behind their comprehension, and that they select as the best drawing from an array of drawings one that is at a higher level than they are capable of producing. Pertinent findings are not entirely consistent (e.g., Hart & Goldin-Meadow, 1984; Taylor & Bacharach, 1981). This inconsistency is likely due to the ambiguous instruction to select the "best" drawing, which can be interpreted cognitively or affectively (i.e., "Which one do you like best?"). When this ambiguity is removed, 2- to 14-year-old children preferred and considered to be more advanced a human figure drawing from a higher level than shown in their own production (Jolley, Knox, & Foster, 2000). These findings suggest that drawings are not simple "printouts" of children's conception of a particular topic. Rather, it is possible that children use different conceptual models for production and comprehension of pictures. Production makes cognitive and graphic demands that are more complex than those made by comprehension. To complete a representational drawing, children need to hold in mind the conceptual and perceptual components of a chosen topic, sequentially translate these components into graphic schemes on a two-dimensional surface, constantly

monitor this translation process, and plan ahead to properly allocate space on the two-dimensional surface (Freeman, 1980). As a result of these difficulties involved in production, children may use a graphic form that is within their graphic abilities and that satisfactorily represents the topic (Arnheim, 1954/1974; Golomb, 1992).

The level of detail included in human figure drawings remains unchanged over adulthood (Ericsson et al., 2001). After the age of 60 years, however, there is a slight decline in the body details, head-to-body ratio, and centeredness of human figure drawings. Number of body details, height, and centeredness also discriminate between individuals with pathological aging and controls (Ericsson, Hillerås, Holmén, & Winblad, 1996; Ericsson et al., 1991, 2001; Wang, Ericsson, Winblad, & Fratiglioni, 1998). However, it is unclear whether human figure drawing predicts pathology in older adults beyond other measures of cognition (Jungwirth et al., 2009).

Drawing of a Cube

In addition to the human figure, the development of the drawing of geometrical shapes such as a cube has received considerable attention (Cox, 1986; Cox & Perara, 1998; Nicholls & Kennedy, 1992; Piaget & Inhelder, 1948/1956; Toomela, 1999). The main goal of this line of research is to determine the extent to which children can successfully convey the three-dimensionality of the cube and draw what they see from a particular viewpoint. In this research, children are typically presented with a cube such that three faces of the cube are visible and asked to draw it, with the cube remaining in sight (Cox & Perara, 1998; Nicholls & Kennedy, 1992). Toomela (1999; see also Cox & Perara, 1998) found that the development of drawing a cube follows an orderly sequence, along which four different broader stages can be distinguished. Up to 2.5 years of age, children drew only scribbles. At the second stage, which Toomela (1999) termed *Single Units,* children started to draw a single square that stood for the whole cube. At the third stage, which emerged around 4 years of age and was termed *Differentiated Figures*, children decomposed the single unit into subparts; they also depicted some of the qualities of the different faces of a cube in a visually realistic manner, but they were not able to represent in a visually realistic manner the relations between the faces and the edges of a cube as a whole (Toomela, 1999). Finally, at the fourth stage (*Integrated Wholes*), which emerged at about 8 years of age, children integrated the formerly differentiated units and created visually realistic drawings of cubes. For example, they represented a cube by a square with foreshortened obliques to indicate depth (Cox & Perara, 1998; Toomela, 1999).

Expression in Drawings

Like other symbols, drawings have an expressive function. The different elements of the drawing do not only represent literally but also metaphorically moods and ideas (Parsons, 1987). Using a selection task that required 4- to 11-year-olds to complete line drawings on a mood consistent basis, Jolley and Thomas (1995) found that preschool children already were able to complete the happy mood scene. However, it was not until 11 years of age that children were able to complete the sad scene. Furthermore, when participants were asked to justify their selections, only adults provided mood-based justifications. A further study (Jolley, Zhi, & Thomas, 1998) showed that Chinese children completed the sad scene and provided mood-based justifications for their selections at an earlier age than British children. One reason for this cross-cultural difference may be that Chinese children were more attentive to detail, because of the fact that Chinese art education places more weight on monitoring fine detail (Jolley et al., 1998).

Controversy exists over whether the emergence of realism would negatively affect the quality of children's expressive drawings (Jolley, Fenn, & Jones, 2004). In a study that assessed both how children used the subject matter (e.g., a countryside scene on a summer's day) and formal properties (e.g., bright colors) to express mood, Jolley and colleagues (2004) found that developmental increases in the use of subject matter themes preceded the use of formal properties to express mood. Furthermore, scores on an expressive drawing task were weakly (small positively) correlated with visual realism scores, indicating that there is some overlap between expressive drawing and visual realism. Jolley and colleagues (2004) concluded that visual realism does not negatively affect expressive drawing.

Development of Drawing: Processes and Factors

Golomb (1992, 2007) proposes that drawing develops according to an intrinsic logic, characterized by differentiation and restructuring of forms. However, the specific way in which forms are differentiated and restructured is influenced by the nature of the medium, the tools used in the production of a drawing, and the sociocultural context. The process of differentiation does not have to proceed along a single pathway to one ideal end point (see Mascolo & Fischer, Chapter 6 of this volume, for an extended discussion of differentiation and developmental trajectories). Rather, multiple ways of solving the problem of how to create equivalences are possible that can lead to different end points. Differentiation of forms can be seen in the human figure drawing and cube drawing, which starts with undifferentiated global patterns (Golomb, 1992, 2007; Werner, 1948, pp. 118–124) that become increasingly enriched by adding further detail to make finer distinctions (e.g., facial features in human figure drawing, additional faces in cube drawing). Restructuration refers to the integration of differentiated forms into a new synthesized whole (e.g., the open-trunk figure restricts circular form to the head; different faces of a cube are spatially coordinated).

The differentiation and restructuration/integration process in the development of drawing is impacted by numerous factors. The role of cognitive factors in drawing has received considerable attention. Piaget (Piaget & Inhelder, 1948/1956, 1966/1969) attributed progress in drawing to the development of children's conceptions of space, in particular the emergence of a concept of projective geometry. Even though there is empirical support for Piaget's theory (e.g., Lange-Küttner, 2009), for the most part, it has been strongly criticized (Golomb, 1992; Willats, 2005). In particular, research has shown that drawing is not constrained by the development of spatial cognition to the extent as might be expected on the basis of Piaget's theory; rather, the conditions under which children are asked to produce drawings affect whether children include elements of projective geometry (Golomb, 1992; but see Vinter & Marot, 2007).

Neo-Piagetian theory has used the concept of working memory capacity and the ability to construct more complex relations between elements to explain drawing development in general (Case, 1992). Neo-Piagetian theory has also focused on specific aspects of drawing development such as drawing flexibility and explained these in terms of an increase of attentional resources (Morra, 2005), or in terms of the representational redescription of drawing procedures at a higher level of consciousness (Karmiloff-Smith, 1990; Spensley & Taylor, 1999).

Language also impacts the development of drawing. Toomela (2002) has shown that, in addition to motor abilities, perceptual skills, and visuospatial skills, language (vocabulary for objects, object properties, and spatial relations between objects) is strongly associated with drawing skills. Toomela (2002) suggested that different aspects of language might fulfill different functions in drawing. Object names and names for object properties may be important for the selection of particular aspects of the object to be represented in the drawing. Consequently, the development of vocabulary results in a differentiation of shapes in representational drawing. In support of this suggestion, empirical studies have revealed that children's verbal descriptions of human figures resemble the structure of their drawing (Golomb, 1992; Harris, 1963). However, the naming of body parts is only a necessary but not a sufficient condition for the drawing of differentiated human figures because Cox (1993) has shown that naming each part of the body to a tadpole drawer does not change the tadpole structure of the human figure. According to Toomela (2002), the second function of language in the development of drawing consists in the support it provides for planning activities. Self-directed speech guides children's planning of how to place objects onto the two-dimensional surface.

Finally, two studies by Callaghan (1999) highlight the role of social factors in the development of drawing. In the first study, children played a social-communicative game with an experimenter in which they had to draw pictures to indicate to an experimenter which objects to put down a tunnel. Whereas the social-communicative game was associated with 3- and 4-year-old children's production of more detailed drawings, this was not the case for 2-year-olds. The second study revealed that providing 3- and 4-year-old children with feedback that their drawings did not effectively communicate their referents was related to improvements in their drawings. In addition, Callaghan and Rankin (2002) demonstrated that providing 28-month-olds with extensive training that highlighted the relation between drawing and referent led to significant improvement in their representational drawing skills at 42 months.

Furthermore, the finding that there are cultural differences in different aspects of drawing attests to the impact of social factors in the development of drawing. For example, there is evidence that the way children draw the human figure is not universal but varies from culture to culture (Cox, 1998; Golomb, 1992). These cross-cultural differences likely result from a number of factors such as copying the drawings of other children or adults (Cox, 1998), art education in school, and copying graphic images in the popular media (Wilson, 1997).

Comprehension of Drawings, Pictures, and Models

A picture can be displayed in different media (e.g., photograph, video, drawing). To understand and interact with

pictures properly, children need to develop what has been called "pictorial competence" (DeLoache, Pierroutsakos, & Uttal, 2003):

> Full pictorial competence involves both perceptual abilities and conceptual knowledge. In perceiving and interpreting a picture, a viewer not only sees the representation—the picture surface—but also "sees through" it to its referent. At the same time, the viewer must understand and keep in mind the nature of the relation between representation and referent. Finally, pictorial competence also includes pragmatic knowledge about how pictures are produced and used. (p. 115)

Two kinds of knowledge are acquired in the course of developing pictorial competence: (1) the knowledge that pictures are merely representations of something other than themselves—*representational knowledge*; and (2) the knowledge that pictures are cultural artifacts, and thus intentionally created through human action—*intentional knowledge*.

Representational Knowledge and Pictures

From a young age, infants are able to recognize objects and people depicted in pictures, and to discriminate depicted objects from actual objects (e.g., DeLoache, Strauss, & Maynard, 1979; Rose, 1977). Even though infants discriminate pictures from real objects, they do not seem to understand these differences. For example, Perner (1991) reported that his 16-month-old son attempted to put on a picture of a shoe. In a systematic study of the early understanding of pictures, DeLoache, Pierroutsakos, Uttal, Rosengren, and Gottlieb (1998) presented infants with pictures of objects and systematically examined their behaviors. They found that 9-month-old infants initially manually investigated the pictured objects (colored photographs of single objects such as common plastic toys). They even grasped at the pictures as if trying to pick up the depicted objects from the page. Subsequent studies showed that manual exploration of pictured objects was not due to an infant's inability to discriminate between two- and three-dimensional stimuli (DeLoache et al., 1998). Further studies (Troseth, Pierroutsakos, & DeLoache, 2004) suggested that infants expected the depicted objects to have some of the same qualities (e.g., texture, solidity) as the real objects. In addition, infants' behaviors toward the depictions were impacted by the extent to which the depicted objects resembled their real-world counterparts (Pierroutsakos & DeLoache, 2003). In 9-month-olds, manual investigation varied as a function of the degree of realism in the pictures. Furthermore, 9-month-olds also manually investigated video images and tried to pluck depicted objects off the video screen (Pierroutsakos & Troseth, 2003). Their emotional reactions to live events and video images of these events were also similar, but emotional reactions to live presentations were somewhat stronger (Diener, Pierroutsakos, Troseth, & Roberts, 2008).

According to Troseth et al. (2004), although infants perceive the two-dimensionality of the depicted objects, they do not conceptually understand the meaning of two-dimensionality. Infants' manual explorations of pictures and video images reflect their attempts at coming to understand them better, and thanks to repeated explorations, infants eventually learn the significance of two-dimensionality through these experiences. As children in the second year of life come to understand pictures better, their need to manually explore them decreases and is replaced by communicative behaviors (e.g., pointing at pictures, vocalizing; DeLoache et al., 1998; Pierroutsakos & Troseth, 2003). "Through experience, infants learn that what is depicted is not a real object—it is not manipulable or eatable. They learn to point to and label objects as their parents do" (Troseth et al., 2004, p. 16).

By about 18 months, infants appear to appreciate that pictures are symbols and refer to a real entity in the world. Preissler and Carey (2004) showed that 18- and 24-month-olds always chose the real object when shown a picture of an object and its actual counterpart after they had learned a new word in the presence of a picture. For example, if these young children saw a line drawing of a whisk and heard it named ("This is a whisk."), they later extended the name to real-world whisks, not to other drawings (Preissler & Carey, 2004), suggesting that they did not learn a simple association between the name and the picture. Similar findings emerged from a study by Preissler and Bloom (2007, Experiment 1), who examined whether when presented with a simplified task, 2-year-olds can flexibly understand pictures both as representations and as objects in their own right. Preissler and Bloom tested 2-year-olds on four items: an unfamiliar object, a line drawing of that object, a second unfamiliar object, and a line drawing of this second object. In one condition, the experimenter pointed to one of the drawings, described it with a novel word, and asked the child to generalize the word (e.g., "This is a wug. Can you show me another one?"). In another condition, the experimenter asked the same question without using a new label (e.g., "Look at this. Can you show me another one?"). For adults, common nouns refer to kinds of objects (see Bloom, 2000), and so the "wug" question should be taken as applying not to the picture but to what the picture

depicts, and hence should be extended to the corresponding object. In contrast, the "look at this" question should more likely be taken as simply referring to the picture itself, and therefore is more likely to be extended to the other picture. Consistent with these hypotheses, Preissler and Bloom found that when asked to show another "wug," children chose the corresponding object 90% of the time; however, when no word was provided, children chose the corresponding object only 30% of the time.

It is not clear, however, to what extent this early understanding of pictures includes a comprehension of pictures. Sigel (1978) sharply distinguished between recognition and comprehension of pictures. Whereas recognition refers to the identification or labeling of a picture, "to comprehend a picture is to *extract meaning* from the picture, to relate it as a *representation* of a referential object or event either in the knowledgeable past or as projected in the future" (Sigel, 1978, p. 95, italics in original). Indeed, research suggests that younger children frequently do not fully appreciate the representational status of pictures. Beilin and Pearlman (1991; see also Robinson, Nye, & Thomas, 1994; Thomas, Jolley, Robinson, & Champion, 1999; Thomas, Nye, & Robinson, 1994) found that 3-year-olds often fail to distinguish between the properties of the photographs and the properties of the objects depicted in those photographs. Specifically, in about 40% of their responses, 3-year-olds attributed a property of the real object to the picture (e.g., they said that a picture of an ice-cream cone would feel cold if they touched it). By contrast, in only about 15% of their responses did 5-year-olds make this iconic realism error. After being challenged (e.g., children were asked to touch the picture of the ice-cream cone), only about 37% of the iconic realism errors originally elicited in response to physical property questions remained.

Preschool children also appear to have a broader and more inclusive conception of what might count as a picture than do older children (Thomas, Nye, Rowley, & Robinson, 2001). When presented with a variety of items (e.g., realistic drawings, abstract drawings, repetitive patterns such as rows of Os and Xs, nonsense words, and a drinking mug with an image on it), 3- to 4-year-olds categorized all drawings as pictures, even repetitive patterns and numbers. However, they were less likely than 6- to 10-year-olds to accept a mug with an image on it as a picture. Nine- to 10-year-olds were likely to reject abstract drawings as pictures, probably because they used visual realism as a criterion for judging whether something was a drawing. In judging whether something is a picture, preschoolers thus relied on the substrate (paper) as a criterion, whereas older children disregarded substrate status and used subject matter as a criterion (see Thomas et al., 2001).

The comprehension of spatial variables such as viewing distance, viewing angle, and viewing azimuth that together define the vantage point from which a picture is taken undergoes protracted development from early childhood to adulthood (Liben, 2003). For example, when presented with a pair of pictures that were taken of the same objects (e.g., tulips) but from different viewing angles, 3-year-olds did not notice any difference between photographs. Five-year-olds noticed a difference in the pictures and attributed this to the referent rather than the viewing angle. One 5-year-old commented: "The tulips are up and the tulips are down... First, in the spring they were closed and then in the summer they came out again" (Liben, 2003, p. 15). Seven-year-olds were more likely to attribute the differences between photographs to viewing angle, and adults performed almost at ceiling in this task. Similar developmental trends were observed for viewing distance and viewing azimuth (Liben, 2003).

Liben (2003) suggested that five factors play a role in children's understanding of external representations such as drawings and photographs. First, exposure to different kinds of external representations, particularly when these depict the same referent, promotes attention to the representational medium itself. Second, by exposing children to alternative representations of the same referent in the same medium, children learn to differentiate between the properties of the representational medium and the properties of objects depicted in that medium. Third, socially mediated experiences direct children's attention to the surface features of the external representation. This suggestion is supported by the research of Callaghan (1999; Callaghan & Rankin, 2002), who showed that the comprehension of drawings is facilitated through incorporation into a communicative context and through training that highlights the relation between drawings and their referents. Fourth, experience in creating external representations and learning about graphic techniques would promote the understanding of external representations. Finally, Liben (2003) proposes that exposure to ego-deictic representations (i.e., pictures that refer back to themselves such as Escher's "Drawing Hands," thereby highlighting their representational status) enhances the comprehension of representations. Future research is necessary to more systematically evaluate whether and how different factors promote the understanding of drawings and photographs.

Intentional Knowledge and Pictures

Intentionality is crucial for the understanding of symbols because something (e.g., a gesture, a mark on a piece of paper) is a symbol, representing something other than itself, only by virtue of being intended this way (DeLoache, 2004). Before explicitly considering children's understanding of intentions in pictures or symbols in general, it is worth pausing to return again to researchers' epistemological commitments. These issues will come up again when considering conceptual development, because representation and conceptual development are tightly intertwined *and* here we are discussing the grounds for the attribution of the understanding of a concept ("intention") to children. The most important thing to understand is that the grounds for the attribution of a concept to an agent are logically distinct from the factors that are causally responsible for an agent behaving in such a manner as to satisfy such grounds (Racine & Müller, 2009; Susswein & Racine, 2008). Thus, if a child behaves in such a way as to demonstrate an understanding of another's intentions, this does not entail that the child has done the *additional* act of representing the agents' intentions to do so. This would be to confuse the RTM theoretical redescription of these actions with the grounds for attribution.

This section discusses several studies of children's understanding of artists' intentions to assess children's understanding of representation in pictures. A child attributes intentions to an artist by virtue of what the latter does. The understanding is tied up with, internally related to, the situation in which it takes place (Racine, 2004; Racine & Carpendale, 2007). This is one sense in which researchers sometimes speak of intentions as embodied, as opposed to disembodied, in that the intentions are tied up with some pattern of action rather than having some private a priori causal status (Racine & Carpendale, 2008). Now, of course, mental processes can and do cause things to happen; for example, you might now intend to take a break from reading this chapter and go for a walk instead. But this is to confuse two completely different things—one about grounds for attribution, the other about particular capacities. Therefore, according to RTM, to understand the intention is to understand the mental state that created it. Setting this aside, another problem in RTM is that this deliberative, reflective sort of awareness that we sometimes have about our projects is taken to be the paradigm case. But this collapses levels of competence. A child who can think about and sequence intentions in the way seemingly presumed by RTM has a different degree of competence than a child who demonstrates such an understanding through practical action. And in neither case is this what we mean by, that is, what constitutes, an intention. With this caveat in mind, we now turn to the empirical studies.

Preissler and Bloom (2008) investigated whether 2-year-olds are sensitive to the intent of an artist (as reflected in direction of gaze) when understanding what a drawing depicts and extending a name for that drawing. They found that when 2-year-olds are asked to interpret the name of a drawing, they choose the object that the speaker was looking at when the drawing was created (Experiment 1), and they did this to a greater extent than when the speaker was looking at the object but not creating a drawing (Experiment 2). This suggests that 2-year-olds attend to intention when interpreting the name of a picture. Given the preceding discussion, it should be clear that we mean the child is showing an understanding of intention in their actions, not that they are literally attending to some discrete internal state in the experimenter. Perhaps no researcher would explicitly suggest that the latter is the case, but it is less clear that such a disembodied view is not being assumed.

When asked what an ambiguous drawing represents, 3- to 4-year-olds rely on the creator's stated intention in determining the representational meaning of the drawing. For example, Bloom and Markson (1998) asked 3- and 4-year-old children to draw four pictures: a balloon, a lollipop, themselves, and the experimenter. The drawings of the different objects looked very similar as these children still had rather limited artistic skills. When later asked to name the drawings they had produced, the children considered the representational intent in naming the picture and overwrote perceptual similarity. For example, they named their drawing of a lollipop a "lollipop" even when it was similar to a balloon and corrected the experimenter when she described their drawing of a lollipop as a balloon. Similarly, 3-year-olds treat a picture differently depending on whether it was produced accidentally or intentionally (Gelman & Bloom, 2000; Gelman & Ebeling, 1998). When children were made to believe that a picture was intentionally created, they named it according to what it looked like; by contrast, when they were made to believe that the picture was created accidentally, they did not.

However, when conflicting cues are presented, young children are less likely to use the creator's stated intention in determining the representational meaning of the picture. For example, Richert and Lillard (2002, Experiments 2 and 3) pitted the appearance of an object (e.g., the experimenter pointed out that the picture looked like a lollipop) against the creator's stated intention (the creator, a troll named Luna, who came from a land where there were no lollipops, intended to draw a balloon). They found that 3- and 4-year-olds did not use the creator's stated intention to determine what the picture represented. Even

older children have problems overwriting iconic similarity when it conflicts with the stated intention of the creator of a drawing. In Myers and Liben's (2008) study, children observed how actors added colored dots to a map; the actors displayed either a symbolic or an aesthetic intention. In the first study, most 5- to 6-year-olds understood the actors' intentions, but when asked which graphic would help find hidden objects, most selected the incorrect (aesthetic) one whose dot color matched the referent color. On a similar task in the second study, 5- and 6-year-olds systematically selected the incorrect graphic, most 9- and 10-year-olds selected the correct graphic, and 7- and 8-year-olds showed mixed performance. When referent color matched neither symbolic nor aesthetic dot colors, children performed better overall, but only the oldest children universally selected the correct graphic and justified choices by referring to the creator's intent. Thus, with a more challenging situation (when a creator intentionally creates a symbol that is not iconically matched to the referent), even older children encounter difficulties with using the stated intention to interpret the referent of the picture. The understanding of the creator's intention and general conventions also plays a role in children's understanding of spatial maps, because some features of graphic symbols are iconic, but others are arbitrary (see Liben, 2008, for a review).

Model Room Task

A widely used paradigm for studying the development of external representation in young children is the Model Room task (DeLoache, 2002). In this task, 2- to 3-year-old children are provided with information about the location of a hidden toy via an external symbolic representation—a scale model, a picture, a video, or a map. For example, in the scale model task, children observe an experimenter hide a miniature toy at a location in a realistic scale model of a room, and they are told that a larger version of the object is hidden in the corresponding place in the room itself. Research on the model room task has revealed dramatic developmental changes in very young children's ability to use the information provided by models, with excellent performance by 3.0-year-olds in the standard model task but very poor performance by 2.5-year-olds (DeLoache, 1987; DeLoache, Kolstad & Anderson, 1991; Dow & Pick, 1992; Kuhlmeier, 2005; O'Sullivan, Mitchell, & Daehler, 2001). Both age groups are able to remember and find the hiding place of the toy in the model, but only the older children are able to retrieve the model in the room itself.

DeLoache (1987, 2002) suggested that successful performance in the model room task involves *representational insight*, that is, the appreciation of the symbolic or representational relation between the two spaces. According to this proposal, sensitivity to the higher order "stands for" relation between model and room supports older children's successful performance in the standard model task. Representational insight, in turn, requires *dual representation*— that is, being able to think about the model both as an object and at the same time as a representation of something other than itself. That is, one must mentally represent the concrete object itself and its abstract relation to what it stands for. One has to perceive the symbol and interpret its relation to its referent. The need for dual representation constitutes a challenge for young children, who have difficulty considering both the symbolic object and its referent, and focus more on the concrete object itself rather than its relation to what it represents.

Several lines of evidence support the dual representation hypothesis. First, manipulation of the salience of the model as an object in its own right impacts performance. When the salience of the model as an object was decreased by placing it behind a window, even 30-month-olds succeeded in the model task (DeLoache, 2000). By contrast, when the physical salience of the model was increased by having children play with the model for several minutes before the retrieval task, the performance of 3-year-olds decreased (DeLoache, 2000). Thus, interaction with the model interferes with the appreciation of its symbolic representational status. Second, younger children solve the task when the requirement to construct a dual representation is entirely removed. DeLoache, Miller, and Rosengren (1997) made children believe that a "shrinking machine" could transform a large-sized tent into a small-scale model. The children first observed a large toy being hidden in the tent, left the tent while the shrinking machine was operated, and then were asked to retrieve the toy in the scale model. Already 30-month-olds successfully retrieved the toy, suggesting that the ability to construct a dual representation is critical in the standard scale model task. Third, media such as video and photographic images that are not as physically salient as a scale model facilitate performance on the model room task (DeLoache & Burns, 1994; Troseth & DeLoache, 1998). Moreover, when 2-year-old children who performed relatively poorly in the video task, even if they watch on a monitor as the experimenter models finding the toy in the room, were led to believe that they were looking through a window at a person hiding a toy in the room next door (they were actually watching the event on video), they could find the toy (Troseth & DeLoache). Thus, 2-year-olds can learn from an event when they directly observe it or think they are directly observing it, but not when they knowingly view the same event via a symbolic medium.

DeLoache and colleagues' research established that the more salient or appealing the physical aspects of a symbolic object appear, the more difficult it is for young children to achieve dual representation. Focusing too much on the symbolic object underlies their difficulty using scale models, which are very salient and attractive as objects. Emphasizing the physical model itself makes it more difficult for children to use it symbolically, whereas diminishing its physical salience makes it easier. Similarly, children younger than 2 years can interpret symbolic gestures more easily than replica objects, which are interesting in and of themselves, and hence pose more of a challenge for dual representation (Johnson, Younger, & Cuellar, 2005; Tomasello et al., 1999; Younger & Johnson, 2006).

DeLoache's proposal that success at the model room task requires representational insight has been challenged. For example, Perner (1991), Lillard (1993), and Blades and Cooke (1994) suggest that it is not necessary to posit awareness of the higher level model–room relation to explain success in the retrieval task. Instead, they argue that 3-year-olds could solve the problem simply by noticing lower level correspondences between objects (e.g., a miniature chair in model room with larger chair in real room) in the two spaces. Troseth, Pickard, and DeLoache (2007) examined whether detection of low-level object correspondences is sufficient for success in the model room task by having children either simply match objects between model and real room or use the correspondences to find objects hidden in the room. They found that children in the matching group accurately detected the corresponding individual objects in the two spaces but, nevertheless, were unsuccessful at using those object correspondences as a basis for performing the symbolic retrieval in the room. In fact, the performance of these children on the search task was comparable with that of a comparison group who had not experienced the matching task first. This study thus suggests that 2.5-year-olds are capable of identifying the lower level object correspondences involved in the model task, but the very same children fail to rely on those object correspondences to solve the standard retrieval task—even when tested immediately afterward. By showing that success in the model task involves something more than detecting correspondences between objects, the results provide support for the representational insight account: To solve the retrieval task, children must detect the representational relation between model and room. Thus, although establishing the lower level object matches between model and room is necessary, it is not sufficient for successful symbolic retrieval.

CONCEPTS

Life-span developmental psychologists would doubtlessly agree that concepts organize experience (Gelman & Kalish, 2006) and "are the glue that holds our mental world together" (Murphy, 2002, p. 1). Already Kant (1787/1933, B76) stated, "Thoughts without content are empty, intuitions without concepts are blind. It is, therefore, just as necessary to make our concepts sensible [i.e., to add the object to them in intuition] as to make our intuitions understandable [i.e., to bring them under concepts].

However, as for representation, a problem is that various understandings of "concept" emerge from conflicting metatheoretical positions and result in alternative meanings (Bolton, 1977; Gelman & Kalish, 2006). In the empiricist tradition, concepts are formed rather passively through inductive abstraction ("drawing away") of similarities among otherwise dissimilar physical stimuli. Importantly, the abstraction itself is not the product of actions on the part of the person, but a label given to the generalization of associations based on contiguity, reinforcement, and similarity among physical features. In this view, a concept is a generalized representation of physical features observed across our many particular perceptions. In the rationalist tradition, concepts are rules or hypotheses—produced through the mind's activity—designed to bring order and organization into the world of perception and thought. For example, the concept "chair" may be deployed across a wide range of objects that share no physical features. However, sitting on a fragile box that breaks may modify the concept to exclude nonweight-bearing objects. In the course of development, concepts become organized to form conceptual systems, and in this sense it can be said that people construct their view of the world.

In a discussion of the concept of intentional action, Machery (2008) has noted an additional difficulty:

> To put it simply, the controversy can be resolved only if there is a principled distinction between what constitutes our competence with a given concept and what results merely from the multitude of factors that affect our use of this concept at a given time on a given occasion. Unfortunately, the literature on concepts has not converged and does not seem to be converging on such a principled distinction. (pp. 172–173)

Although Machery is primarily referring to the philosophical literature, the failure to distinguish definitional from causal issues contributes to some of the confusion in the psychological literature concerning conceptual development. The problem is that, as previously discussed when considering the grounds for attributing to a child an understanding of an artists' intention, the grounds for the attribution of a concept to an agent are distinct from what is responsible for an agent to be behaving in such a manner as to satisfy such grounds. Thus, to attribute an understanding of a concept to an agent is not to say anything about how or why the agent is able to act in such manner. However, if one holds, for example, an RTM view of conceptual development, one automatically credits the infant with particular causal powers that are not warranted by the evidence.

Understood in this manner, theories, and metatheories like RTM embody conceptual frameworks that need to be judged on their own logical merits. Some of the most important work in philosophy is explicitly laying out, comparing, and defending such positions from one another. Unfortunately, psychologists rarely explicitly do such exacting conceptual work but are still content to frame their interpretations in terms of RTM or other overarching metatheories without at all justifying the use of their frameworks. This would be fine if there was some neat division of labor between philosophy and psychology such that the former handled conceptual definitional issues and psychology investigated the fruits of such labor. But this is not the case and rests on a naïve view of science. Even more troubling is that a trend in both the philosophy of mind and the developmental psychology of children's understanding of concepts of mind seems to be an informal rapprochement between proponents of theory-theory in both disciplines where developmentalists use the philosophy as justification for their empirical programs and philosophers use these empirical programs as support for the very views that they were propagating in the first instance.

Setting aside the issue of the relation between conceptual, theoretical and empirical work (for a fuller treatment, see Machado & Silva, 2007; Overton, 2006), as we discussed previously in considering children's understanding of drawing, an added problem is that this again collapses levels of competence. That is, the infant who can discriminate x from y demonstrates a different degree of competence than does an agent who can actively sort x from y in an array or one who can answer questions concerning x and y. Thus, researchers must not only be careful not to confuse definitional and causal issues but to also carefully distinguish levels of competence. In any case, given that the goal of this chapter is mainly to characterize rather than diagnose the state of the field, we will not develop these cautionary remarks further in this context.

In contemporary life-span developmental theories, proponents of both empiricist and rationalist traditions can be found, but for the most part, contemporary theories of conceptual development are eclectic, borrowing elements from both traditions (Gelman & Kalish, 2006). We briefly summarize six important approaches to conceptual development: (1) the classical view; (2) the ecological view; (3) the perceptual symbol system view; (4) the associative-learning and similarity-based view; (5) the naïve theory view; and (6) the Piagetian view (see Barsalou, 2008; Medin, Lynch, & Solomon, 2000; Murphy, 2002).

The first approach is the *classical view* of concepts (e.g., Bruner, Goodnow, & Austin, 1956), which is largely only of historical interest because of several major theoretical and empirical problems (see Murphy, 2002). The classical view conceives of concepts as being mentally represented as definitions. Concepts are defined by features that are necessary and jointly sufficient. Furthermore, the classical view does not make any distinction between category members. Anything that meets the category definition is just as good a category member as anything else. Wittgenstein (1958) already questioned the assumption of the classical view that important concepts could be defined. Instead of necessary and sufficient features, Wittgenstein thought that concepts are characterized by family resemblance. Empirically, the demonstration of typicality effects (i.e., graded membership, the idea that some category members are considered better exemplars than others; Rosch, 1975) essentially made the classical view obsolete (see Murphy, 2002).

The *ecological view* that Rosch (1975) introduced argues that every category is represented by a summary representation that is a description of the category as a whole (i.e., a prototype). The summary representation is described in terms of a family resemblance: Some of the features that are usually found in category members are more important than others. Therefore, there is graded membership among category members. For example, it is important for dogs to bark, but not so important that they are brown, even though many dogs are. Thus, the feature, "can bark," would be highly weighted in the representation, whereas the feature, "is brown," would not be. Gabora, Rosch and Aerts (2008) have recently provided a mathematical formalization of this approach that is inspired by concepts in use in quantum physics. Gabora

and her colleagues (2008) note that the problems plaguing the classical view also seem to apply to contemporary views such as Barsalou's (2008), which is summarized as follows:

> [T]o define a concept in terms of weighted averages for certain features presupposes that it is possible to state objectively what the relevant features *are*. Unless a context is specified, there is no basis for supposing that one feature is more relevant than another; otherwise one might just as well reason that because Ann could sit in either Chair A, Chair B, or Chair C, Ann can be defined as some sort of average of a human sitting in each of these three chairs. Clearly, Ann is more than this, much as BEAUTY is more than an average taken across certain features of salient instances of BEAUTY. This sort of problem also plagues a related approach to concepts in which they are viewed as *perceptual symbol systems*, that is, simulators of sets of similar perceptually based memories. (Gabora et al., 2008, pp. 91–92)

The *perceptual symbol systems* approach that Barsalou (1999, 2008) defended is one form of a grounded cognition approach to concepts (e.g., see also Gallese & Lakoff, 2008). This class of approaches focuses on roles of the body and modality-specific processing in cognition. Barsalou rejects the standard view of amodal concepts and replaces it with a modality-sensitive model that relies on processes of simulation in the utilization of these amodal concepts. He emphasizes introspection because he argues that there is an overreliance on sensorimotor coupling in many grounded theories:

> During perception, states of perceptual systems become stored in memory (e.g., for vision and audition). Similar stimuli perceived later trigger these memories, simulating the perceptual states they contain. As these simulations become active they produce perceptual inferences that go beyond perceived stimuli in useful ways. (Barsalou, 2008, p. 624)

Despite his emphasis on internal processing, Barsalou's (2008) model is part of the passive empiricist mind tradition and seems largely a terminological respecification with "simulation of concept of x" for "concept of x": "simulations of internal states could provide much of the conceptual content central to abstract concepts" (p. 634). Simulation as a basis for conceptual development also has a storied and largely unsuccessful history.

In the empiricist tradition, contemporary approaches to conceptual development emphasize *general associative learning* mechanisms (Rakison & Lupyan, 2008) that operate on the basis of featural similarity (Sloutksy, Kloos, & Fisher, 2007a, 2007b). For example, according to Similarity-Induction-Naming-Categorization theory (Sloutsky & Fisher, 2004; Sloutsky et al., 2007a, 2007b) categorization as well as the extension of category membership to new exemplars is initially based on overall similarity of the objects that are being compared. Thus, early in development, concept learning does not depend on top-down conceptual knowledge but is "grounded in powerful learning mechanisms, such as statistical and attentional learning" (Sloutsky et al., 2007a, p. 180). A general problem of empiricist approaches is that associative and similarity-based learning appears to require the possession of the very concept that is supposed to be learned (for a thorough discussion, see Cassirer, 1923, 1953).

A central feature of *naïve theory* approaches (Gelman & Kalish, 2006; Wellman & Gelman, 1992) is the assumption that concepts are embedded in commonsense theories. This network of theoretical beliefs provides the basis for categorization and inferential processes, which, in turn, promotes further conceptual development. Similar to paradigm shifts in the history of science (Kuhn, 1962), conceptual change involves a radical reorganization of the cognitive framework (Gelman & Kalish, 2006). Naïve theory approaches often stipulate *natural kinds* and *essentialism* (Kalish, 2002; Gelman, 2004). *Natural kinds* is the realist assumption that certain groupings of particulars truly exist in the world independently of humans (i.e., the boundaries of these categories are fixed by nature and are only discovered [not constructed] by humans [see Overton, 2006]). Just as an individual tiger has a reality beyond our perception of it, so too does the category of tigers. Natural kinds contrast with artificial or nominal kinds. *Nominal kinds* are arbitrary or conventional collections that have no basis outside the mind.

A goal of research in this framework is to explore when in development children begin to form natural kinds concepts, and different theories have been formulated to explain the development of these concepts. According to Keil (1989), children initially form concepts by keeping track of co-occurrences of the features of entities, and only later on, when they have acquired more detailed knowledge about different content domains as well as a better grasp of causality, do they attempt to find explanations of the groupings they have formed. An alternative perspective is that children initially assume that all concepts are natural kinds concepts, and only with development do they come

to differentiate between natural and nominal kinds concepts (Gelman & Kalish, 2006).

The concept of natural kinds, however, is deeply problematic. Philosophers (Dupré, 2004; Hacking, 2007) and psychologists (Danziger, 1997, pp. 181–193) have argued that until now criteria for delineating natural kinds have not yet clearly been outlined. Furthermore, classifications are flexible and change depending on the goals of the classification. Along with the goal of the classification, the definition of what is essential changes as well. As a result, Hacking (2007) concludes:

> Philosophical research programmes connected with natural kinds have brought many logical truths to light. They have fallen on hard times. They have split into sects, to the extent that paradigm natural kinds for one set are not natural kinds at all for another. The doctrine of natural kinds is in such disarray that it does tend to humptyism. Advocates will refer to the class of classifications they most admire, as the class of natural kinds. The class is often of great interest. Yet the chief reason for calling it the class of natural kinds is that that sounds good. It confers a rhetorical pedigree on the class. When natural kinds become redefined as some special-interest class, one is tempted to invoke Imre Lakatos's phrase, and speak of a degenerating research programme.[2] (p. 206)

Essentialism is the view that categories have underlying (i.e. not directly observable) and unchanging characteristics or properties that a member of the category must possess in order to belong to that category (Gelman, 2003, 2004, 2009). The underlying essence gives an object its context-independent identity. As a consequence, the essentialist position subscribes to realism: "categories are real in several senses: they are discovered (versus invented), they are natural (versus artificial), they predict other properties, and they point to natural discontinuities in the world" (Gelman & Kalish, 2006, p. 708). The rich causal structure of the essence guides children's conceptual development. It is not necessary that children possess specialized knowledge to be guided by essences in conceptual development because they may possess an essence placeholder without knowing what the essence is (Medin, 1989; but see Newman & Keil, 2008). Gelman and Kalish (2006, p. 708) illustrate the placeholder notion using the example

---

[2] Even Locke, who is frequently referred to as endorsing the notions of natural kind and essentialism (Gelman & Kalish, 2006) actually criticized both notions (see Crane, 2003).

of a child who "might believe that girls have some inner, nonobvious quality that distinguishes them from boys and is responsible for the many observable differences in appearance and behavior between boys and girls, before ever learning about chromosomes and human physiology." It is important to note that proponents of essentialism claim that the study of essentialism in children and adults makes no claims about the "objective reality" of the world; rather, it concerns people's implicit beliefs about the world (Gelman, 2003, 2004, 2009).

The naïve theory view is currently dominant in conceptual development, but it should be noted that the realist flavor of this approach is tantamount to the endorsement of a passive mind perspective of the RTM. As a consequence, concepts are largely treated as objects and are equated with mental representations (Margolis & Laurence, 2006; Murphy, 2002). As a result, in many contemporary theories of conceptual development, the mind remains passive, and concepts become reified and take on a life of their own. For example, the notions of natural kinds and essentialism (Gelman & Kalish, 2006; Medin et al., 2000) suggest that these concepts are based on the structure intrinsic to concepts as if concepts were independent of their use and the goals of the person using them. But if Wittgenstein is right about family resemblance, of what could such an intrinsic structure consist? This view also contrasts with the active mind perspective illustrated in Continental philosophy (e.g., Cassirer, 1923/1953; Merleau-Ponty, 1945/1962). For example, stressing the constitutive activity of the person, Kant (1787/1933, B130) argued:

> [W]e cannot represent to ourselves anything as combined in the object without having previously combined it ourselves, and that of all representations combination is the only one which cannot be given through objects, but is an act of the subject's self-activity, can only be carried out by the subject itself.

Finally, the *Piagetian approach* to concepts unites features of the different approaches to conceptual development. Piaget distinguished between practical concepts on the sensorimotor level (action schemes) that supply the meaning for children's activities, and prototypes and more complex definitional concepts on the representational level. Importantly, Piagetian concepts do not have an intrinsic structure, but concepts are grounded in and used by the active child in interacting with the world. Piaget's approach shares with the grounded cognition perspective the belief that concepts are ultimately rooted in embod-

ied activity and are elaborated through modality-specific coordination (e.g., visual and motor systems; Mounoud, Duscherer, Moy, & Perraudin, 2007). In contrast with the grounded cognition approach, Piaget, however, based schemes in sensorimotor embodiment and not in neurophysiological embodiment (see Overton, Müller, & Newman, 2008). With the prototype theory, Piaget's approach shares the idea that concepts are always accompanied by an individualized feature that is constituted by imagery (Piaget & Inhelder, 1966/1969). In fact, Piaget (1945/1962) thought that during early childhood, concepts are prototypes. With the naïve theory view, Piaget's view of concepts shares the assumption that concepts are holistic and inferential, and cannot be reduced to simple processes of association (this much follows from the function of assimilation). However, as a constructivist, Piaget naturally would have rejected the realist underpinnings of naïve theory. Finally, with the classical view of concepts, Piaget shares the idea that at a certain level of development, children become indeed capable of operating with concepts in a way that they identify necessary and sufficient features, and in an amodal manner.

This latter view is probably responsible for the fact that Piaget's theory of conceptual development is classified as a classical view and sometimes considered obsolete (Murphy, 2002). However, this classification overlooks that for Piaget, concepts are used in acts of judgment, and that children (and adults) may become or are capable of identifying necessary and sufficient features in a restricted reference class (e.g., when presented with picture cards depicting seven eagles and five sparrows) when they have acquired the thought operations involved in such definitions. Piaget never meant to argue that concepts are represented somewhere in the brain as definitions; this would be at odds with his active view of the mind. For Piaget, concepts were not simply mental representations. Rather, with respect to representational thought, Piaget (1945/1962, pp. 67–68) distinguished between representative items (signifiers such as symbols or signs) and a system of concepts and schemes. The concepts are used to structure the representative items and thereby impress them with meaning; the items are the concrete, sensible matter necessary for thought to express itself. In this sense, Piaget's view of concepts is rather Kantian.

In the next section, we review conceptual development in infancy. We then focus on selective topics of conceptual development in childhood and late adulthood. Specifically, we summarize research on thematic and taxonomic relations, category induction, and the hierarchic organization of the development of taxonomies and the hierarchic organization of concepts.

Conceptual Development in Infancy

Concepts are believed to underlie the ability to categorize, that is, to respond similarly to members from the same categories and differently to members from a different category. This section first describes different methodologies that have been used to infer categorization in infants. Next, we discuss recent trends in infant categorization. Finally, we tackle the thorny issue of how to interpret the findings generated on infant categorization.

A modified version of the familiarization novelty preference paradigm is widely used to access infants' preference for looking at novel stimuli. In the familiarization/preference novelty paradigm, infants are presented with identical stimuli of one category over several trials and then are presented a stimulus pair consisting of the familiar stimulus and a novel stimulus. Longer looking time to the novel stimulus indicates discrimination between the novel and the familiar stimulus (Quinn, 2007).

Effective use of the familiarization/novelty preference paradigm to study categorization in infants requires additional procedures and control conditions (Quinn, 2007). First, different stimuli from the same category are presented during a series of familiarization trials. Second, after familiarization, the novel category preference test is administered and infants are presented with two novel stimuli: one from the familiar category, and the other from a new category. If infants look longer at the novel instance from the novel category than at the novel instance from the familiar category, it can be inferred that they treated as equivalent the instances of the familiar category and discriminated them against the novel instance from the novel category (Quinn, 2007). The possibility that the preference for the novel category instance occurred because of an a priori preference must be excluded to make sure that infants formed a category. A control group of infants is administered only the preference test exemplars and not the familiarization exemplars to establish that category formation has taken place. In this way, infants' spontaneous preferences for those category exemplars can be obtained that were presented on the preference test trials of the category formation study. A second control condition is necessary to determine whether infants discriminated between members of the familiar category. For this purpose, infants in a separate control group are first familiarized with one exemplar from the familiar category and

subsequently presented with a preference test pairing the familiar exemplar and a novel exemplar from the same category.

In addition to the familiarization/novelty preference procedure, three further paradigms are frequently used to assess categorization in infants. The first is called the "sequential touching paradigm," and it has been used with older infants and toddlers in the age range of 12 to 30 months (Quinn, 2007). In the sequential touching paradigm, infants are presented with several exemplars from two or more categories that are arranged randomly in front of them (Mareschal & Tan, 2007). Usually, the exemplars are small, three-dimensional, realistic-scale models of prototypical real-world objects. Categorization is inferred if the infant touches exemplars from one category in sequence before touching members of the other category (for more complex ways of assessing categorization in sequential touching, see Mareschal & Tan, 2007).

Another procedure for assessing infant categorization is the generalized imitation paradigm (McDonough & Mandler, 1998; Quinn, 2007). In this paradigm, an infant is presented with stimuli similar to those used in the sequential touching studies. In the generalized imitation procedure, the experimenter picks up a particular object and models an action appropriate for that object (e.g., a cat drinking from a bowl). Infants are considered to categorize the objects if they generalize the action to other members of the same category (e.g., animals), but not to members of contrast categories (e.g., vehicles).

Finally, the free classification method has been used with somewhat older infants (Langer, 1980, 1986; Sugarman, 1982). In this paradigm, infants are presented with several objects that belong to different categories, and the experimenter records whether infants sort objects into groups. Sometimes, the experimenter may model sorting behavior (Gopnik & Meltzoff, 1987).

Using the familiarization/novelty preference, it has been shown that already 3- to 4-month-old infants can form categories for a variety of different stimuli such as animals, artifacts, and people (Murphy, 2002; Quinn, 2002, 2007). Infants also seem to be able to discriminate between categories at different levels of inclusiveness because they can make distinctions at the superordinate (e.g., animals) and more specific level (e.g., cat vs. Siamese cat; see Quinn, 2002, 2004). According to Quinn (2002; see also Rakison & Lupyan, 2008), infants at this age use perceptual surface features (e.g., faces, fur, tail) to discriminate between categories. Quinn (1999, 2002; Quinn & Eimas, 1996, 1997) suggests that the development of categorization consists of the differentiation of global categories to include increasingly more fine-grained detail.

An alternative framework for thinking about categories in infancy has been suggested by Mandler (1998, 2004). Mandler claims that early in infancy, categories are formed on the basis of static perceptual attributes. Perceptual attributes, however, are limited and remain on the surface of things because they do not define the true meaning or nature of something (what kind of thing it is). In the second half of the first year of life, true categories are formed on the basis of image schemas, which, in turn, are produced by a process of perceptual analysis. Perceptual analysis generates global categories (e.g., animals) but not basic level categories (e.g., trucks, cars). Mandler (2004) presents a number of empirical findings in support of this interpretation. For example, in a series of studies, Mandler and McDonough (1993) explored the concept of animacy and found that 7-month-old infants looked longer at objects from the global category of *inanimate objects* (e.g., a toy vehicle) after they had been habituated to different objects from another global category (e.g., toy rabbits). At the same time, infants did not dishabituate to a fish (i.e., toy fish) after they had been habituated to several dogs (i.e., toy dogs); that is, they failed to discriminate on the basic level. A similar distinction between animate and inanimate objects was found when the conceptual development of older infants was assessed using the sequential touching and the generalized imitation paradigms (Mandler, Bauer, & McDonough, 1991; Mandler & McDonough, 1996).

Mandler's dual-process model of early categorization has been severely criticized for theoretical and empirical reasons (e.g., Müller & Overton, 1998a, 1998b; Murphy, 2002; Quinn, 2002). For example, Behl-Chadha (1996) found that already 3- and 4-month-olds can make discriminations on the global level. This finding calls into question the claim that global categories are conceptually based because it is unlikely that infants this young could have relied on conceptual knowledge in making their discriminations. Furthermore, it is likely that even in older infants, the discrimination between global categories is based on (more complex) perceptual features (Murphy, 2002, p. 297).

The familiarization/novelty preference, sequential touching, and generalized imitation paradigms are limited in terms of the inferences that can be drawn about infants' competencies. Specifically, these paradigms do not permit the conclusion that infants relate different objects from one category to another because infants in these studies merely successively visually explore and touch only one object at a time. When infants successively identify objects that share a salient property, their behavior does not imply that they compare and relate objects from the same category to each other. Their behavior implies only that they discriminate between those objects having a specific property and those objects not having that property. "Recognizing individual items as x does not amount to an awareness that several things exist that are the *same*. Identifying x is not the same as explicitly equating x with some x1. These are concepts of different logical types" (Sugarman, 1982, p. 86). Recognizing individual items as x on the basis of some property does not imply that infants grasp the relation existing between their categorizations. Each action might exist independently of the other, and the stimuli be unrelated to each other.

In general, the findings just described are consistent with Piaget's characterization of sensorimotor intelligence. Infants begin psychological life with sensorimotor schemes, including perceptual schemes, which are deployed in the pursuit of practical goals. A scheme is an organized set of expectations, which, by assimilating environmental objects, endows these objects with meaning (Overton, 1994). In a way, each scheme can be said to entail an informal rule that determines its range of application. By integrating different objects into the same scheme, these objects are experienced and treated as equivalent. Practical, sensorimotor concepts thus allow the identification of objects on the basis of intensive properties by assimilating these objects to habitual schemes (Inhelder & Piaget, 1959/1969, p. 13; Sugarman, 1983). Piaget termed this type of identification *schematic membership relation* (Inhelder & Piaget, 1959/1969, p. 9) and suggested that it is present from early infancy on (Piaget, 1936/1952).

The free classification paradigm allows somewhat richer inferences about infants' competencies. Studies using this procedure have revealed that by 12 months, infants start to put two or more objects that are alike into a spatially separated group. Sugarman (1983) termed this the *single iterative phase:* individual elements are related to one another on the basis their functional properties or visual similarity. Children compare objects on one dimension and realize that an object (x) is like *a* or not like *a*. During the second year of life, children begin increasingly to compose two groups of objects simultaneously, which provides them with the opportunity to construct relations between both groups. Furthermore, infants start to flexibly shift between different relations. For example, infants become capable of composing two groups of objects by manipulating objects from both groups (Gopnik & Meltzoff, 1987, 1992; Langer, 1986; Ricciuti, 1965; Sugarman, 1982, 1983). However, infants rarely switch from one group to the other group while constructing these groups (Langer, 1986; Sugarman, 1983). Rather, they first group all the objects belonging to one category and then the objects belonging to the second category, a behavior that implies that at any one point of time, only one property is used to evaluate objects in terms of their similarities and differences. Successive grouping of objects into two different groups involves a flexible shift from one similarity relation to another similarity relation. This cognitive organization that manifests in this kind of classificatory behavior may be described as follows: an object (x) is like a or not like a—shift to another dimension b—an object (x) is like b or not like b (Sugarman, 1983). The same level of flexibility is also evidenced by an 18-month-old's ability to switch between categorizing at the basic (e.g., trucks, airplanes) and global (e.g., vehicles) level in the sequential touching paradigm (Mareschal & Tan, 2007).

At the end of their second and in their third year of life, children recursively shift between groups when they construct two groups (Sugarman, 1983). Their advanced sorting behavior suggests that they have judged an object as not belonging to one class but still consider it as a possible member of another group: what is not like a may be like b (Sugarman, 1983). The iterations that were previously executed successively become coordinated, and guided by a higher order scheme that integrates relations between relations, children order objects according to two schemes at once (Langer, 1986). Children now simultaneously use two properties to compare objects in terms of their similarities and differences, although these comparisons are still made on a step-by-step basis, that is, inductively (Sugarman, 1983).

Conceptual Development in Childhood and Beyond

A common assumption of classical theories of concept development is that younger children's concepts are perceptually based (e.g., Werner, 1948). Support for this claim comes from the use of the free classification paradigm with preschool children. For example, Inhelder and Piaget (1959/1969, pp. 17–46) presented children with a number of objects that differed, for example, in terms of shape (triangles, squares, circles) and color (red, blue, green), and asked children to collect together the objects that were alike. On the basis of the way children grouped the objects, Inhelder and Piaget distinguished between different types of graphic and nongraphic levels in the development of

classification. For example, a graphic collection consisted in the sorting of objects on the basis of thematic relations (i.e., objects were involved in the same kind of event [putting woman and a car together with the explanation that the woman would drive the car]). Nongraphic collections were based on similarity relations (e.g., blue objects were placed in one group, red objects in a different group). Inhelder and Piaget (1959/1969) argued that children at these levels (i.e., between 3 and 6 years old) cannot construct a stable classification that is independent of space; rather, the perceptual features of the spatial layout determine the extension of a collection. This failure was manifest in the failure to understand class inclusion (to be discussed later).

Subsequent research has shown that preschool children are not limited to constructing thematic relations. Rather, when 3-year-olds were given the instruction, "Can you find me another one?" (instead of "Put things together that go together."), they were likely to group together objects belonging to the same semantic category (i.e., they sorted by taxonomic relations; Waxman & Namy, 1997). Markman and Hutchinson (1984) showed that giving the target an object name (e.g., "dax") increased the number of taxonomic responses. The likelihood of giving taxonomic or thematic responses also appears to depend on experience and object category (Bonthoux & Kalenine, 2007).

Recent work on category induction also suggests that 4-year-olds do not necessarily perform category membership on a perceptual basis. In a category induction task, children are shown two picture cards (e.g., a tropical fish and a dolphin) and are told new information about the object displayed on each picture card (e.g., the tropical fish can breathe under water, the dolphin breathes above the water). After each pair had been presented, the experimenter shows a third picture that closely resembles one member of the original pair but receives the same label as the other member (e.g., a shark, which is perceptually similar to the dolphin, receives the label "fish"). The child's task then is to infer whether the shark breathes like a fish or like a dolphin. Thus, in the category induction task, the common label and category membership are pitted against perceptual similarity. Using the category induction task, Gelman and Markman (1986) found that 4-year-olds generalized properties on the basis of category membership and common label, and not on the basis of perceptual appearance, suggesting that children's concepts are not simply collections of perceptual features (see Gelman & Kalish, 2006, for a review of this line of research). Gelman (2004) interprets these findings as supporting the theory of psychological essentialism, because in category induction, children infer properties that are not visible, internal features (e.g., breathing, having bones), and they draw inferences even when category membership competes with perceptual similarity.

However, Sloutsky and colleagues (Fisher & Sloutsky, 2005; Sloutsky & Fisher, 2004; Sloutsky, Kloos, & Fisher, 2007a; 2007b) have challenged this rich interpretation of category induction. In a series of experiments, they demonstrated that preschool children generalize category membership not on the basis of category knowledge but on the basis of similarities. Because labels are considered by preschoolers as being a part of objects, they contribute to overall similarity (Sloutsky & Fisher, 2004). Induction based on category knowledge emerges gradually from early childhood to adulthood (Fisher & Sloutsky, 2005). As Sloutsky and colleagues (2007b) point out, a major problem of the conceptual knowledge (naïve theory) approach is that "although the knowledge-based approach account argues that conceptual knowledge is important, it offers little detail as to what conceptual knowledge is, where it comes from, under which conditions it is employed, and how it mediates associative mechanisms" (p. 557). We would add that the failure to provide a more detailed analysis of the cognitive activities involved in category induction (and theory formation) results from the realist basis of the naïve theory approach.

Few studies have examined classification behavior across the life span. In older adults, taxonomic categorization seems to be less available than in younger adults. When the free classification paradigm is used, older adults are less likely than younger people to group objects by taxonomic relations (Annett, 1959; Cicirelli, 1976; Kogan, 1974). Similarly, the results of Denney and Lennon's (1972) developmental study showed that whereas middle-aged persons (ranging in age from 25–55 years) tended to use taxonomic relations to exhaustively group geometric stimuli, older adults (ranging in age from 65–95 years) used thematic relations to arrange these stimuli. In a matching-to-sample task, Smiley and Brown (1979) observed a majority of thematic choices in older adults but a majority of taxonomic choices in young adults. Thus, studies that compared the categorization skills of older adults with those of young adults reflect a decrease in the use of taxonomic relations after 60 years of age (in addition to an increase in the use of thematic relations in these experiments).

However, Lin and Murphy (2001; see also Denney, 1974) showed that thematic categorization was frequent in young adults. To explain their results, Lin and Murphy hypothesized that the relative salience of taxonomic and thematic relations affects category construction. In two further experiments, they induced different response preferences by emphasizing either thematic or taxonomic relations. Results showed that performing a similarity comparison task or a difference judgment task before category construction was related to enhanced taxonomic categorization, a finding that supports Lin and Murphy's hypothesis that the relative salience between taxonomic and thematic relations affects the way categories are formed and used.

Pennequin and colleagues (2006) examined whether the relative salience of thematic and taxonomic relations depends on the associative strength between stimuli, and whether differences in associative strength may account for the increase of thematic relations in older adults. They compared the relative effects of associative strength on taxonomic and thematic choices of young adults and older adults, controlling for associative strength on an individual level. Participants performed a picture matching task. In each trial, the target was shown first, followed by two comparison pictures associated to the target. The two comparison pictures were either two thematically or two thematically related associates (homogenous conditions), or one thematically and one taxonomically related associate (heterogeneous condition). In each condition, one comparison picture was a strong associate, the other a weak associate. The results revealed that the pattern of categorical choices was similar for young and older adults. Both groups displayed the same effect of associative strength and type of relation. In the homogeneous conditions (two thematic or two taxonomic associates), the strong associate was always selected. However, in the heterogeneous condition, strong thematic associates were dominant over weak taxonomic associates, but strong taxonomic associates were not dominant over weak thematic associates. This finding contradicts the idea that the ability to perceive and use taxonomic relations declines in late adulthood (Annett, 1959; Cicirelli, 1976; Denney & Lennon, 1972). Rather, it suggests that the predominance of taxonomic choices in young adults and their decrease in older adults, which have frequently been observed, reflect an experimental bias in the choice of stimulus material. When associative strength is equated at the individual level, age effects disappear.

Pennequin and colleagues (2006) interpret these findings in terms of Baltes's (1987) distinction between three broad systems of developmental influences: age-graded influences, history-graded influences, and non-normative influences.[3] Age-graded influences are defined as biological and environmental factors that have a strong relation to chronological age and exert a similar influence across individuals. History-graded influences involve those biological and environmental determinants that are associated with historical time. Two types of history-graded influences on aging are the availability of pharmaceutical drugs and educational opportunities. Non-normative influences refer to unique life experiences that are not tied to either age-graded or historical influences and differ from individual to individual. According to Baltes, the relative role of these three types of influence varies throughout life. Non-normative influences increase throughout life, and in late adulthood, they constitute the most important factor in cognitive performance. As a consequence, adult development can be viewed as an individuation and a personalization process that is partially under the person's control. It is likely that in the context of this personalization process, autobiographical (i.e., non-normative) experiences influence the perception of commonalities and differences between stimuli, and thus modify the associative strength between stimuli, which, in turn, affects categorical choices in classification tasks.

Adult concepts form a hierarchy such that general concepts such as animal are superordinate and include lower level or subordinate concepts such as dogs and cats. The hierarchical relation between concepts was extensively investigated by Inhelder and Piaget (1959/1969). Inhelder and Piaget referred to the hierarchical relation between concepts as class inclusion. Classes are defined in terms of two important features, their intension and their extension (Inhelder & Piaget, 1959/1969, pp. 7–8). The *intension of a class* is the set of properties that are common to the members of the class and that differentiate them from other classes. The *extension of a class* is the set of members or individuals comprising that class. For Piaget, the development of the hierarchical organization between concepts involves the coordination of extension (i.e., part–whole relation) with the intension (i.e., similarity and difference of properties).

One criterion for the coordination of intension and extension is the understanding of class inclusion. A typical class inclusion task asks children to compare the number of objects in the including or superordinate class with the number of objects in the most numerous of its subclasses (Inhelder & Piaget, 1959/1969, pp. 100–118). For example, given 12 daisies and 4 roses, children are asked, "Are there more daisies or more flowers?" A correct answer requires that children conserve the including class (B) while making the quantitative comparison between it and the included class (A).

In Piaget's theory, class inclusion is explained as the result of the coordination or grouping of operations having the form $A + A' = B$. This formula represents the operation of putting together individual objects (daisies [A] and roses [A']) into two subclasses, and the operation of combining the subclasses into a superordinate class (flowers [B]). The plus sign indicates the reversibility of the operations in the sense that each term of the equation can be derived from the other two: (1) B from the composition of A and A', (2) A' from B ignoring A, and (3) A from B ignoring A' (Chapman & McBride, 1992). Inhelder and Piaget (1959/1969) considered the mastery of class inclusion as a criterion for concrete operational thought and observed that it emerged usually around the age of 7 years.

Inhelder and Piaget's (1959/1969) work on class inclusion has been criticized for numerous reasons. A major methodologic criticism is that the standard class inclusion question (e.g., "Are there more birds or eagles?") is ambiguously worded: It lacks the normal linguistic marker for part–whole comparisons (Campbell, 1991; Hodkin, 1981; Shipley, 1979). In everyday language, we usually attach linguistic modifiers to labels to specify the reference to a particular class (e.g., *only* the eagles, or *all* the birds). Because of the lack of linguistic modifiers, the standard class inclusion may be confusing or may be understood as a request for a subclass comparison. There are several ways in which the ambiguity can be removed to countermand the subclass-subclass comparison, including: (1) provision of linguistic markers for the subordinate class ("only") and superordinate class ("all"), (2) perceptual or linguistic marking of the superordinate class, and (3) asking for a subclass-subclass comparison before the standard class inclusion question (see Chapman & McBride, 1992; McGarrigle, Grieve, & Hughes, 1978; Shipley, 1979). Using these modified procedures, researchers have found the children solve the class inclusion task somewhat earlier (5–6 instead of 7 years of age; see Winer, 1980).

However, it has been argued that superordinate class cuing effects do not facilitate genuine class inclusion reasoning but reflect nonlogical figurative and intuitive processes that increase the rate of guessing (Dean, Chabaud, & Bridges,

---

[3] These influences should not be considered as unidirectional causes; rather, the effects of these influences depend on how the multilayered, self-organizing organism deals with them.

1981; Hodkin, 1987; Winer, 1980). Using an elegant design that controlled for guessing, Chapman and McBride (1992) provided evidence that perceptual and linguistic marking of the superordinate class facilitated inclusion reasoning.

Another methodologic criticism of the standard class inclusion task is that it makes requirements for the ascription of a hierarchical organization of concepts that are too strict (see Murphy, 2002, for a discussion). As an alternative to the standard class inclusion task, Markman (1989) proposed to assess the hierarchical organization of concepts using the principles of transitivity and asymmetry. Transitivity exploits the property of hierarchical classification systems that classes at a lower level of the system are included in classes at a higher level (e.g., if it is known that members of the class of dogs are included in the class of mammals, and if it is known that members of the class of mammals are included in the class of animals, then it necessarily follows that members of the class of dogs are included in the class of animals). The vertical relations between classes are asymmetric in that, even though all members of the class of dogs are included in the class of mammals, the reverse is not true (i.e., not all members of the class of mammals are included in the class of dogs). Because transitivity and asymmetry are the principles that define the vertical relation between classes, Markman (1989) suggested that a more appropriate and direct test of the understanding of class inclusion should be based on the evaluation of children's comprehension of transitivity and asymmetry.

In a systematic assessment of 5- to 9-year-olds' understanding of the principles of transitivity and asymmetry, as well of class inclusion, Denault and Ricard (2006) found that knowledge of the transitivity of inclusion relations increased significantly between 5 and 7 years of age. In contrast, the understanding of asymmetry was acquired more slowly, and was not complete even by 9 years of age. Whereas the ability to make qualitative inferences that involved the transitivity principle preceded the ability to make quantitative class inclusion inferences, the ability to make qualitative inferences involving the comprehension of the asymmetry principle was as difficult as the ability to make quantified class inclusion inferences. Halford, Andrews, and Jensen (2002) compared preschoolers' performance on category induction, the asymmetry principle, and class inclusion. Preschool children performed significantly better on category induction tasks than on tasks that assess the asymmetry principle. Although not directly compared with category induction

and the comprehension of the asymmetry principle, the standard class inclusion task appeared to be more difficult than the former tasks. Halford and colleagues (2002) argued that category induction tasks are easier than tasks that assess hierarchical classification (comprehension of the asymmetry principle and standard class inclusion) because the former involves only a comparison between categories at the same level of the hierarchy (binary relation), whereas the latter involve a comparison between classes at different levels of the hierarchy (ternary relations).

Overall, these findings on the development of hierarchical relations between concepts suggest that the knowledge of categorical hierarchies in children is not an all-or-nothing acquisition but a continuum in which different levels of understanding emerge at different moments in the course of development. The findings are largely consistent with Blewitt's (1994) three-level model, although this model likely needs to be further differentiated. At level 1 of Blewitt's model, children (at 2–3 years of age) are able to form categories at different levels of generality and to include the same object (e.g., Fido) into two categories (in the dog category, as well as in the animal category). At level 2, children are able to make qualitative inferences (inductive and deductive) about novel objects. When told that a "dax" is a dog, they can infer that a dax is an animal. At this level, children realize that different categories are related, and their inferences reflect this newly gained understanding. Finally, at level 3, children are able to make quantitative inferences about the relative size of sets of objects that are vertically connected in the same hierarchy. At this level, children succeed at Inhelder and Piaget's (1959/1969) standard class-inclusion task.

Performance on the class inclusion task appears to decline in older adults (Denney & Cornelius, 1975), particularly in elderly men (Sinnott, 1975). Consistent with these findings, Fontaine and Pennequin (2000) more recently demonstrated that older adults performed more poorly on class inclusion tasks than children and adolescents. However, children and older adults had difficulties in different aspects of the class inclusion task: Whereas children had problems representing the subclass as a class on its own and, at the same time, as being a part of the superordinate class, older adults had problems with the selection of relevant information to make the appropriate inferences (see also Howe & Rabinowitz, 1996). These findings suggest that older adults recruit different resources in class inclusion reasoning than do children.

CONCLUSION

We conclude the review of representational and conceptual development by raising three issues that we believe are central to the development in both areas. The first issue concerns the process of distancing, the second the role of social interaction in promoting representational and conceptual development, and the third the process of differentiation and integration.

Distancing

The process of distancing between signifier or symbol and referent surfaced in several places in discussions of the development of symbolic representation. The development of pretend play, drawing, symbolic gestures, and the understanding of pictures and scale models each involve the creation of an increasing differentiation between the representational medium and the thing or event represented in the representational medium.

In fact, the process of distancing between subject and object may be essential to the emergence of symbolic representation (Werner & Kaplan, 1963). For example, the ability to use words as symbols requires some sort of removal from immediate stimulation: "To be able to talk about things is to be potentially aware of them outside of any particular transaction with them; it is to be potentially aware of them not just in their behavioral relevance to some activity we are now engaged in, but also in a 'disengaged' way" (Taylor, 1971, p. 404).

Animals may lack this distancing capacity. Their behaviors appear, to different degrees, to be tied to their environment and cannot be divided into a series of independent actions to be somehow separately considered or reflected on. Objects in an organism's perceptual field are at this level, which Werner (1948) has called *things-of-action*. They are limited to an instrumental meaning relative to the one or many behavior patterns activated (von Uexküll, 1926, 1934/1957). In von Uexküll's (1909) words, "The stimuli of the environment constitute a rigid barrier which surrounds the animal like the walls of a house, closing it off from the entire world outside..." (p. 212, our translation). Overcoming this barrier involves loosening, or even cutting altogether, the direct tie between the stimulus and the consequent action (von Herder, 1772/1967; Werner, 1948). When this tie between a given situation and the organism's actions is severed, the organism's opportunities for different actions afford it a larger degree of freedom, allowing it to become aware of things in a disengaged way and to look at its field of action as a reflective observer, rather than an engrossed participant. This notion is nicely captured in the following remarks by Gehlen (1988):

> The things in our world thus have the essentially human character of *acquired neutrality*. This is not the indifference toward anything that does not appeal directly to instincts, as is the case in the environments of the higher animals. In contrast, the things around us are thoroughly known and "worked through," but remain "undecided" for the most part, available for interaction at any time. This is how man masters the overwhelming barrage of impressions, this is how he obtains relief: He actively "checkmates" *the forcefulness of the world's impressions, making the world potentially available at any time.* (pp. 162–163, emphasis in original)

In contemporary theories, distancing is either conceived as an agent-independent mechanism (in the sense of a computer function, see Leslie, 1987), or it is simply stipulated without being explained (Perner, 1991). The concept of psychological distancing has received more attention as an important aspect of development in many classical theories of development, most notably those of Piaget, Vygotsky, and Werner. In Piaget's theory, distancing (or what he calls "decentration") is closely tied to the idea that any form of knowledge results from the bidirectional reciprocal interactions of the child (subject) and the world (object), and that at the beginning of development, subject and object are relatively undifferentiated. For him, intelligence originates and perpetuates itself, as he claims, "neither with knowledge of the self nor of things as such but with knowledge of their interaction, and it is by orienting itself simultaneously toward the two poles of that interaction that intelligence organizes the world by organizing itself" (Piaget, 1937/1954, pp. 354–355). In the course of their bidirectional interactions with the world, children develop more complex coordinations between action schemes and representational schemes. More complex coordinations constitute higher order control structures that lead to the progressive distancing between child and world, and result in increasingly successful ways of regulating interactions with the world. In Piaget's theory, distancing then results from a gradual process of differentiation and integration of, first, action schemes, and later, conceptual schemes.

Whereas Piaget emphasized the importance of the coordinatory or operative aspect of intelligence in psychological distancing, Vygotsky emphasized the role of signs, or more specifically, speech (i.e., the figurative aspect of intelligence; see Amin & Valsiner, 2004). For Vygotsky, psychological distance is achieved through semiotic mediation (i.e., language) and play. Functionally, both facilitate the "emancipation from situational constraints" that derives from its "demands on the child to act against immediate impulse" (Vygotsky, 1978, p. 99). Speech and play transform the child's relation to the world by creating a representational "space" that is psychologically removed from the immediate perceptual field:

> The child is much more easily able to ignore the vector that focuses attention on the goal itself, and to execute a number of complex preliminary acts, using for this purpose a comparatively long chain of auxiliary instrumental methods. The child proves able to include independently, in the process of solution of the task, objects which lie neither within the near nor the peripheral visual field. By creating through words a certain intention, the child achieves a much broader range of activity, applying as tools not only those objects that lie near at hand, but searching for and preparing such articles as can be useful in the solution of its task and planning its future actions. (Vygotsky & Luria, 1994, p. 110)

In play, the relation between perception and activity loses its determining force: "In play thought is separated from objects and action arises from ideas rather than from things: a piece of wood begins to be a doll and a stick becomes a horse" (Vygotsky, 1978, p. 97). At the same time, speech and play transform the child's relation to himself or herself and his or her own behavior with the same consequence: "With the aid of speech the child for the first time proves able to the mastering of its own behaviour, relating to itself as to another being, regarding itself as an object. Speech helps the child to master this object through the preliminary organization and planning of its own acts of behaviour" (Vygotsky & Luria, 1994, p. 111). Following Vygotsky, then, speech plays an important part in the process of distancing.

Contemporary research supports the idea that language in general facilitates the development of symbolic representational abilities. As reviewed earlier, there is empirical evidence for the role of language in the development of drawing (Toomela, 2002). Language supports the use of substitute objects in pretend play (Ungerer et al., 1981) and the planning of more complex pretend play scenarios

(McCune, 2010). Metacommunicative language helps children assign and coordinate several roles in social pretend play (Giffin, 1984). The understanding of drawings, pictures, and replica objects may be mediated by language (Callaghan, 2000; Younger & Johnson, 2006). Language also has been shown to play an important role in conceptual development (Gelman, 2009; Gelman & Kalish, 2006; Kemler Nelson, O'Neil, & Asher, 2008; Smith 2003). However, for the most part, these findings did not directly test Vygotsky's claim that self-directed speech (not language ability more generally) promotes the process of distancing. The more direct testing of Vygotsky's claim, therefore, remains a task for future research.

Werner (1948; Werner & Kaplan, 1963) conceived of distancing as a gradual process between four poles: between addressor and addressee, addressor and vehicle, addressor and referent (or subject and object), and symbol and referent. In the course of the distancing between symbolic vehicle and referential object, the vehicle becomes desubstantialized and loses its thing-like status (i.e., it becomes transparent). At the same time, the properties of the vehicle become increasingly dissimilar from those of the referent (e.g., in substitute play), which results in the denaturalization of the vehicle. A symbolic expression becomes denaturalized and loses its close tie to a specific referent when it is applied to qualitatively different situations rather than to just one event. Concomitantly, the symbol is gradually decontextualized; that is, the child creates an increasing distance in time and increasing differentiation of context of execution from the context of original presentation.

Essential for Piaget, Vygotsky, and Werner was the idea that earlier symbolic representations emerge out of pragmatic, communicative activities. For Werner, symbols results from a shift of function: "A novel emerging function becomes actualized at first through the use of means articulated and structured in the service of genetically earlier ends" (Werner & Kaplan, 1963, p. 66). That is, a newly emerging function appropriates existing behavioral structures and only gradually transforms them. Even though the same gradual process of distancing is present in the different domains of representational development, it may be heavily influenced by domain-specific constraints. For example, language and pretend play appear to emerge before children demonstrate representational drawing or understand scale models. Werner (1948) attributed this "horizontal decalage" to the fact that "language permits a far greater use of syncretic representation (i.e., representation embedded in concrete motor-affective activity) than does drawing" (pp. 250–251). Alternatively (or in addition), different representational media may differ in terms of transparency. For example, the use of a scale model requires children to identify certain relations between the model and the real room to successfully retrieve the object in the real room. In this sense, the extent to which children need to focus on the material features of the representational medium might influence the emergence and trajectory of symbolic development.

Empirical research on developmental relations between different symbolic domains is sparse. One exception is Callaghan and Rankin's (2002) study that showed that the production of drawing was significantly correlated with scaffolded pretend play and language skills, suggesting that these three domains of symbolic development are systematically related to each other. Clearly, the developmental relations between different symbolic representational media need to be studied in more detail.

The role of distancing in conceptual development has received relatively little attention. Piaget (1936/1952) alludes to this distancing process in the context of sensorimotor development. By being applied to varied objects, embodied sensorimotor concepts (or what Piaget termed *schemes*) lose their close ties to particular stimuli and become more flexible, which is a prerequisite for their coordination with other schemes. Werner (1948) believed that conceptual thought processes develop as they become increasingly detached from affective and sensorimotor functions. Vygotsky (1934/1986) advanced the idea that mediation through language and other cultural tools such as writing leads to a distancing of conceptual thought from the immediate here-and-now. Unfortunately, the specific mechanisms by means of which distancing is accomplished in the symbolic-representational domain and the conceptual domain, and how these mechanisms are related to each other has not received much attention in contemporary research.

Social Interaction

Developmental theories of representational and conceptual development differ in the emphasis they place on social interaction and the larger sociocultural context. Braswell (2006) distinguishes *individualistic and sociocultural models*. Individualistic models adopt an information-processing or RTM approach, and account for symbolic and conceptual development in terms of internal mechanisms and endogenous constraints with social and cultural factors playing a minor role at best. For example, according to Braswell (2006), with respect to pretend play, the

theory of Leslie (1987) provides an example of a highly individualistic model of pretense. Leaving open whether this characterization of Leslie's theory is entirely correct (see Friedman & Leslie, 2007), individualistic models are certainly insufficient to explain representational and conceptual development because there is ample evidence for the important role of social interaction in these domains (see Braswell, 2006). Let us provide some examples from different domains. Children and adults participate in collaborative drawing activities in the context of which adults scaffold children's activities (Boyatzis, 2000; Yamagata, 1997). Children's drawing skills and their understanding of drawing improves if it is embedded in a social-communicative context (Callaghan, 1999; Callaghan & Rankin, 2002). Likewise, pretend play is more advanced when scaffolded by an older peer or an adult (Bornstein, 2006). Infants' pretend play with mothers is more complex, diverse, and sustained than is their solitary pretend play (Bornstein, Haynes, O'Reilly, & Painter, 1996; Haight & Miller, 1992), and children often pick up new pretend actions by imitating those of others (Rakoczy, Tomasello, & Striano, 2005). Moreover, researchers are now beginning (again) to pay more attention to the way in which the input children receive affects their conceptual development (Gelman, 2009).

The importance of social interaction (and cultural context, see Braswell, 2006) in development of representation and concepts would seem to support the sociocultural model. The sociocultural model replaces the focus on the individual child as a unit of analysis with the focus on the activities in which the child takes part (Braswell, 2006; Gauvain, 2001; Göncü, 1999; Göncü, Jain, & Tuermer, 2006; Rogoff, 1998). Cognition and behavior are viewed as being embedded within a specific sociocultural context that is defined by particular values, customs, tools, and practices. Development occurs as a function of participating in the particular cultural context (Rogoff, 1990, 1998, 2003).

However, it is not clear whether sociocultural approaches, isolated from a comprehensive theory of the developing person as a unit of analysis, can supply a sufficient explanation of the sequential nature of representational and conceptual development. Both symbolic-representational and conceptual development have their own logic that follows from the fact that human beings are multilayered self-organizing systems (Piaget, 1975/1985). Sociocultural approaches themselves are ambiguous as to the role of the person in development (Lawrence & Valsiner, 1993). Either sociocultural approaches rely on a transmission model of enculturation in which the developing person is viewed as passive and simply copies conventions and practices, or they rely on an active transformation model in which the developing person actively reconstructs and appropriates the cultural forms and practices for himself or herself. The former model falls squarely into the category of the passive mind, whereas the latter subscribes to the view of the active mind and necessitates a theory that focuses on the developing person in relation and interaction with his or her world.

In either case, future research is necessary to elaborate in further theoretical and empirical detail how social interaction and social practices impact the logic of representational and conceptual development (Chapman, 1988; see Carpendale & Lewis, Chapter 17 of this volume, for a relational approach that avoids an individualistic–sociocultural split perspective on mind in general). One avenue of approach could be to focus on the process of distancing and elucidate the types of interactions that promote or impede it. For example, Sigel (2002; Sigel, Stinson, & Kim, 1993) has outlined a model of distancing that emphasizes the manner in which parents construct a linguistic environment that activates the synthesis and organization of representational schemes. In particular, Sigel focuses on the discursive practices of parents, which he views as a primary source of intellectual stimulation (Sigel et al., 1993). For example, parents create psychological distance for children by drawing their attention to aspects of a problem they had not considered before. In Sigel's model, these "distancing strategies function to create temporal and/or spatial, and/or psychological distance between self and object" (Sigel et al., 1993, p. 214) by placing a "cognitive demand on the child to separate the self mentally from the ongoing present" (Sigel, Stinson, & Flaugher, 1991, p. 126). According to Sigel's distancing model, individual differences in children's symbolic-representational and conceptual development should be related to individual distancing strategies used by parents (Sigel et al., 1991). Sigel's distancing model has yet to be systematically applied to symbolic representational and conceptual development (but see Giesbrecht, Müller, & Miller, 2010).

Differentiation and Integration

Current research on representational and conceptual development is all too often mired in the futile controversy of when an ability first emerges. However, as Werner (1948) pointed out, this is not a very productive question:

> It is more or less futile to inquire into the absolute genetic [in the sense of developmental] origin of any mental activity. It would seem to be more constructive to analyze mental development in terms of genetically related, analogous processes. We must not frame the question to ask: "At what age level does concept formation first come into existence?" Rather, we must ask: "What are the different function patterns underlying the concept formation which appears at different age levels? (p. 215)

The controversy over category induction (Fisher & Sloutsky, 2005; Sloutsky & Fisher, 2004) showed that the more detailed analysis of the processes that are involved in a specific performance is tantamount to achieving an accurate picture of the developmental trajectory. In a similar vein, older adults appear to use different cognitive processes in class inclusion reasoning than younger adults; failure to be attentive to these processes can lead to a premature identification of aging with decline.

Werner (1957; see also Piaget, 1975/1985) believed that development proceeds from an initial state of relative lack of differentiation to a state of increasing differentiation and integration. With respect to symbolic representational development, we have indicated that development can be productively conceptualized as a differentiation-integration process that leads to increasingly more complex forms—a view that is consistent with relational developmental systems approaches to development (Lerner, 2006; Lerner & Overton, 2008; Overton, 2006). It is, however, an open question to what extent late adult development is characterized as a dedifferentiation process. There is little life-span research on symbolic-representational development, and research on conceptual development has not indicated clear-cut patterns of dedifferentiation. At the same time, there is some indication that older adults engage different resources in classification and class inclusion. Clearly, this area needs to receive more empirical attention.

Contemporary researchers (e.g., Flavell et al., 2002; Gelman & Kalish, 2006; Murphy, 2002) often arrive at the conclusion that there are no qualitative changes in conceptual development (even though research on early sorting and hierarchical classification indicate otherwise; see Halford et al., 2002; Langer, 1986; Sugarman, 1983). Partly, as we have indicated, this view derives from the epistemologic perspective pervasive in contemporary research. Adopting the RTM framework, contemporary researchers treat representations and concepts as if they had a life of their own and fail to analyze, or even outright ignore, the cognitive processes that constitute representations and concepts. As a consequence, the question as to how a particular use of concepts is cognitively instantiated does not even come into view. Against this backdrop, Werner's call that we must analyze the different function pattern underlying the concept formation at different age levels is as timely as ever.

REFERENCES

Abravanel, E. (1991). Does immediate imitation influence long-term memory for observed actions? *Journal of Experimental Child Psychology, 51,* 235–244.

Acredolo, L., & Goodwyn, S. (1985). Symbolic gesturing in language development: A case study. *Human Development, 28,* 40–49.

Acredolo, L., & Goodwyn, S. (1988). Symbolic gesturing in normal infants. *Child Development, 59,* 450–466.

Acredolo, L. P., Goodwyn, S. W., Horobin, K. D., & Emmons, Y. D. (1999). The signs and sounds of early language development. In I. L. Balter & C. S. Tamis-LeMonda (Eds.), *Child psychology: A handbook of contemporary issues* (pp. 116–139). Philadelphia: Psychology Press.

Adi-Japha, E., Levin, I., & Solomon, S. (1998). Emergence of representation in drawing: The relation between kinematic and referential aspects. *Cognitive Development, 13,* 25–51.

Amin, T. G., & Valsiner, J. (2004). Coordinating operative and figurative knowledge: Piaget, Vygotsky, and beyond. In J. I. M. Carpendale & U. Müller (Eds.), *Social interaction and the development of knowledge* (pp. 87–109). Mahwah, NJ: Erlbaum.

Annett, M. (1959). The classification of instances of four common class concepts by children and adults. *British Journal of Educational Psychology, 29,* 223–236.

Arnheim, R. (1974). *Art and visual perception.* Berkeley, CA: University of California Press. (Original work published 1954)

Baillargeon, R. (1987). Object permanence in 3½- and 4½-month-old infants. *Developmental Psychology, 23,* 655–664.

Baillargeon, R. (1993). The object concept revisited: New directions in the investigation of infants' physical knowledge. In C. Granrud (Ed.), *Visual perception and cognition in infancy* (pp. 265–315). Hillsdale, NJ: Erlbaum.

Baillargeon, R. (2002). The acquisition of physical knowledge in infancy: A summary in eight lessons. In U. Goswami (Ed.), *Handbook of childhood cognitive development* (pp. 47–83). Oxford: Blackwell.

Baillargeon, R. (2004a). Infants' reasoning about hidden objects: Evidence for event-general and event-specific expectation. *Developmental Science, 7,* 391–414.

Baillargeon, R. (2004b). Can 12 large clowns fit in a Mini Cooper? Or when are beliefs and reasoning explicit and conscious? *Developmental Science, 7,* 422–424.

Baillargeon, R., (2008). Innate ideas revisited: For a principle of persistence in infants' physical reasoning. *Perspectives on Psychological Science, 3,* 2–12.

Baldwin, J. M. (1906). *Thought and things: Vol. 1, Functional logic.* New York: Macmillan.

Baltes, P. B. (1987). Theoretical propositions of life-span developmental psychology: On the dynamics between growth and decline. *Developmental Psychology, 23,* 611–626.

Barnat, S. B., Klein, P. J., & Meltzoff, A. N. (1996). Deferred imitation across changes in context and object: Memory and generalization

in 14-month-old infants. *Infant Behavior and Development, 19,* 241–251.

Barrett, M. D., & Light, P. H. (1976). Symbolism and intellectual realism in children's drawings. *British Journal of Educational Psychology, 46,* 198–202.

Barsalou, L. W. (1999). Perceptual symbol systems. *Behavioral and Brain Sciences, 22,* 577–660.

Barsalou, L. W. (2008). Grounded cognition. *Annual Review of Psychology, 59,* 617–645.

Behl-Chadha, G. (1996). Basic-level and superordinate-like categorical representations in early infancy. *Cognition, 60,* 105–141.

Beilin, H., & Pearlman, E. G. (1991). Children's iconic realism: Object versus property realism. In H. W. Reese (Ed.), *Advances in child development and behavior* (Vol. 23, pp. 73–111). New York: Academic Press.

Bickhard, M. H. (1993). Representational content in humans and machines. *Journal of Experimental & Theoretical Artificial Intelligence, 5,* 285–333.

Bigham, S., & Bourchier-Sutton, A. (2007). The decontextualization of form and function in the development of pretence. *British Journal of Developmental Psychology, 25,* 335–351.

Blades, M., & Cooke, Z. (1994). Young children's ability to understand a model as a spatial representation. *Journal of Genetic Psychology, 155,* 201–218.

Blewitt, P. (1994). Understanding categorical hierarchies: The earliest levels of skill. *Child Development, 65,* 1279–1298.

Bloom, P. (2000). *How children learn the meaning of words.* Cambridge, MA: MIT Press.

Bloom, P., & Markson, L. (1998). Intention and analogy in children's naming of pictorial representations. *Psychological Science, 9,* 200–204.

Bogartz, R. S., Shinskey, J. L., & Speaker, C. J. (1997). Interpreting infant looking: The event set × event set design. *Developmental Psychology, 33,* 408–422.

Bolton, N. (1977). *Concept formation.* Oxford: Pergamon Press.

Bonthoux, F., & Kalenine, S. (2007). Preschoolers' superordinate taxonomic categorization as a function of individual processing of visual vs. contextual/functional information and object domain. *Cognition, Brain, & Behavior, 11,* 713–731.

Bornstein, M. H. (2006). On the significance of social relationships in the development of children's earliest symbolic play: An ecological perspective. In A. Göncü & S. Gaskins (Eds.), *Play and development: evolutionary, sociocultural, and functional perspectives* (pp. 101–129). Mahwah, NJ: Erlbaum.

Bornstein, M. H., Haynes, O. M., O'Reilly, A. W., & Painter, K. M. (1996). Solitary and collaborative pretense play in early childhood: Sources of individual variation in the development of representational competence. *Child Development, 67,* 2910–2929.

Boyatzis, C. J. (2000). The artistic evolution of mommy: A longitudinal case study of symbolic and social processes. In C. J. Boyatzis & M. W. Watson (Eds.), *Symbolic and social constraints on the development of children's artistic style* (pp. 5–29). San Francisco: Jossey-Bass.

Boyatzis, C. J., & Watson, M. W. (1993). Preschool children's symbolic representation of objects through gestures. *Child Development, 64,* 729–735.

Braswell, G. S. (2006). Sociocultural contexts for the early development of semiotic production. *Psychological Bulletin, 132,* 877–894.

Bremner, G. (2001). Cognitive development: Knowledge of the physical world. In G. Bremner & A. Fogel (Eds.), *Blackwell handbook of infant development* (pp. 98–138). Oxford: Blackwell.

Brentano, F. (1995). *Psychology from an empirical standpoint*. London: Kegan. (Original work published in 1874)

Bruner, J. S., Goodnow, J. J., & Austin, G. A. (Eds.). (1956). *A study of thinking*. New York: John Wiley & Sons.

Bühler, K. (1918). *Die geistige Entwicklung des Kindes* [The mental development of the child]. Jena, Germany: Verlag Gustav Fischer.

Bühler, K. (1982). The axiomatization of the language sciences. In R. E. Innis (Ed.), *Karl Bühler: Semiotic foundations of language theory* (pp. 91–164). New York: Plenum Press. (Original work published in 1933)

Bühler, K. (1990). *Theory of language: The representational function of language*. Amsterdam: Benjamins. (Original work published in 1934)

Burke, D. M. (2006). Representation and aging. In E. Bialystok & F. I. M. Craik (Eds.), *Lifespan cognition: Mechanisms of change* (pp. 193–206). New York: Oxford University Press.

Callaghan, T. C. (1999). Early understanding and production of graphic symbols. *Child Development, 70*, 1314–1324.

Callaghan, T. C. (2000). Factors affecting children's graphic symbol use in the third year: Language, similarity, and iconicity. *Cognitive Development, 15*, 185–214.

Callaghan, T. C., & Rankin, M. P. (2002). Emergence of graphic symbol functioning and the question of domain-specificity: A longitudinal study. *Child Development, 73*, 259–276.

Campbell, R. L. (1991). Does class inclusion have mathematical prerequisites? *Cognitive Development, 6,*169–194.

Case, R. (1992). Neo-Piagetian theories of child development. In R. J. Sternberg (Ed.), *Intellectual development* (pp. 161–196). New York: Cambridge University Press.

Cash, M. (2009). Normativity is the mother of intention: Wittgenstein, normative practices and neurological representations. *New Ideas in Psychology, 27*, 133–147.

Cashon, C. H., & Cohen, L. B. (2000). Eight-month-old infants' perceptions of possible and impossible events. *Infancy, 1*, 429–446.

Cassirer, E. (1953). *Substance and function*. New York: Dover. (Original work published 1923)

Cassirer, E. (1985). Die Sprache und der Aufbau der Gegenstandswelt [Language and the construction of the objective world]. In E. W. Orth & J. M. Krois (Eds.), *Ernst Cassirer: Symbol, Technik, Sprache. Aufsätze aus den Jahren 1927–1933* (pp. 121–160). Hamburg: Felix Meiner Verlag. (Original work published in 1932)

Chapman, M. (1988). Contextuality and directionality of cognitive development. *Human Development, 31*, 92–106.

Chapman, M., & McBride, M. L. (1992). Beyond competence and performance: Children's class inclusion strategies, superordinate class cues, and verbal justifications. *Developmental Psychology, 28*, 319–327.

Cicirelli, V. G. (1976). Categorization behavior in aging subjects. *Journal of Gerontology, 31*, 676–680.

Cohen, L. B., & Cashon, K. H. (2006). Infant cognition. In W. Damon & R. Lerner (Series Eds.), D. Kuhn & R. Siegler (Vol. Eds.), *Handbook of child psychology: Vol. 2, Cognition, perception, and language* (6th ed., pp. 214–251). Hoboken, NJ: John Wiley & Sons.

Cox, M. (1993). *Children's drawings of the human figure*. Hove, United Kingdom: Erlbaum.

Cox, M. V. (1986). Cubes are difficult things to draw. *British Journal of Developmental Psychology, 4*, 341–345.

Cox, M. V. (1998). Drawings of people by Australian Aboriginal children: Intermixing of cultural styles. *Journal of Art and Design Education, 17*, 71–79.

Cox, M. V., Koyasu, M., Hiranuma, H., & Perara, J. (2001). Children's human figure drawings in the UK and Japan: The effects of age, sex, and culture. *British Journal of Developmental Psychology, 19*, 275–292.

Cox, M. V., & Perara, J. (1998). Children's observational drawings: A nine-point scale for scoring drawings of a cube. *Educational Psychology, 18*, 309–317.

Crane, J. K. (2003). Locke's theory of classification. *British Journal for the History of Philosophy, 11*, 249–259.

Danziger, K. (1997). *Naming the mind: How psychology found its language*. London: Sage.

Dean, A. L., Chabaud, S., & Bridges, E. (1981). Classes, collections, and distinctive features: Alternative strategies for solving inclusion problems. *Cognitive Psychology, 13*, 84–112.

DeLoache, J. S. (1987). Rapid change in the symbolic functioning in very young children. *Science, 238*, 1556–1557.

DeLoache, J. S. (2000). Dual representation and young children's use of scale models. *Child Development, 71*, 329–338.

DeLoache, J. S. (2002). Early development of the understanding and use of symbolic artifacts. In U. Goswami (Ed.), *Handbook of childhood cognitive development* (pp. 206–226). Oxford: Blackwell.

DeLoache, J. S. (2004). Becoming symbol-minded. *Trends in Cognitive Sciences, 8*, 67–70.

DeLoache, J. S., & Burns, N. M. (1994). Early understanding of the representational function of pictures. *Cognition, 52*, 83–110.

DeLoache, J. S., Kolstad, D. V., & Anderson, K. N. (1991). Physical similarity and young children's understanding of scale models. *Child Development, 62*, 111–126.

DeLoache, J. S., Miller, K. F., & Rosengren, K. S. (1997). The credible shrinking room: Very young children's performance with symbolic and nonsymbolic relations. *Psychological Science, 8*, 308–313.

DeLoache, J. S., Pierroutsakos, S. L., & Uttal, D. H. (2003). The origins of pictorial competence. *Current Directions in Psychological Science, 12*, 114–118.

DeLoache, J. S., Pierroutsakos, S. L., Uttal, D. H., Rosengren, K. S., & Gottlieb, A. (1998). Grasping the nature of pictures. *Psychological Science, 9*, 205–210.

DeLoache, J. S., Strauss, M. S., & Maynard, J. (1979). Picture perception in infancy. *Infant Behavior and Development, 2*, 77–89.

Deneault, J., & Ricard, M. (2006). The assessment of children's understanding of inclusion relations: Transitivity, asymmetry, and quantification. *Journal of Cognition and Development, 7*, 551–570.

Dennett, D. (1969). *Content and consciousness*. London: Routledge.

Denney, N. D. (1974). Classification criteria in middle and old age. *Developmental Psychology, 10*, 901–906.

Denney, N. W., & Cornelius, S. W. (1975). Class inclusion and multiple classification in middle and old age. *Developmental Psychology, 11*, 521–522.

Denney, N. W., & Lennon, M. L. (1972). Classification: A comparison of middle and old age. *Developmental Psychology, 7*, 210–213.

de Saussure, F. (1986). *Course in general linguistics*. La Salle, IL: Open Court Classics. (Original work published in 1916)

Dick, A. S., Overton, W. F., & Kovacs, S. L. (2005). The development of symbolic coordination: Representation of imagined objects, executive function, and theory of mind. *Journal of Cognition and Development, 6*, 133–161.

Diener, M., Pierroutsakos, S. L., Troseth, G. L., & Roberts, A. (2008). Video versus reality: Infants' attention and affective responses to video and live presentations. *Media Psychology, 11*, 418–441.

Dow, G. A., & Pick, H. L. (1992). Young children's use of models and photographs as spatial representations. *Cognitive Development, 7*, 351–363.

Dupré, J. (2004). Human kinds and biological kinds: Some similarities and differences. *Philosophy of Science, 71*, 892–900.

Eco, U. (1977). *Zeichen*. Frankfurt: Suhrkamp.

Elman, J. L., Bates, E. A., Johnson, M. H., Karmiloff-Smith, A., Parisi, D., & Plunkett, K. (1997). Rethinking innateness: A connectionist perspective on development. Cambridge, MA: MIT Press.

Ericsson, K., Forsell, L., Amberla, K., Holmén, K., Viitanen, M., & Winblad, B. (1991). Graphic skills used as an instrument for detecting higher cortical dysfunctions in old age. *Human Movement Science, 10,* 335–349.

Ericsson, K., Hilleräs, P., Holmén, K., & Winblad, B. (1996). Human Figure Drawings (HFD) in the screening of cognitive impairment in old age. *Journal of Medical Screening, 3,* 105–109.

Ericsson, K., Winblad, B., & Nilsson, L.-G. (2001). Human-figure drawing and memory Functioning across the adult life span. *Archives of Gerontology and Geriatrics, 32,* 151–167.

Fenson, L., & Ramsey, D. S. (1980). Decentration and integration of the child's play in the second year. *Child Development, 51,* 171–178.

Fisher, A. V., & Sloutsky, V. M. (2005). When induction meets memory: Evidence for gradual transition from similarity to category-based induction. *Child Development, 76,* 583–597.

Flavell, J. H., Miller, P. H., & Miller, S. A. (2002). *Cognitive development* (4th ed.). Upper Saddle River, NJ: Prentice Hall.

Fodor, J. A. (1987). *Psychosemantics: The problem of meaning in the philosophy of mind.* Cambridge, MA: MIT Press.

Fodor, J. A. (1992). A theory of the child's theory of mind. *Cognition, 44,* 283–296.

Fontaine, R., & Pennequin, V. (2000). Effect of aging on inferential reasoning about class inclusion. *Current Psychology of Cognition, 19,* 453–482.

Ford, R. M., & Rees, E. L. (2008). Representational drawing and the transition from intellectual to visual realism in children with autism. *British Journal of Developmental Psychology, 26,* 197–219.

Freeman, N. H. (1980). *Strategies of representation in young children: Analysis of spatial skills and drawing process.* London: Academic Press.

Freeman, N. H. (1993). Drawing: Public instrument of representation. In C. Pratt & A. F. Garton (Eds.), *Systems of representation in children: Development and use* (pp. 113–132). Chichester, United Kingdom: John Wiley & Sons.

Freeman, N. H., & Janikoun, R. (1972). Intellectual realism in children's drawings of a familiar object with distinctive features. *Child Development, 43,* 1116–1121.

Friedman, O., & Leslie, A. M. (2007). The conceptual underpinnings of pretense: Pretending is not 'behaving-as-if'. *Cognition, 105,* 103–124.

Gabora, L., Rosch, E., & Aerts, D. (2008). Toward an ecological theory of concepts. *Ecological Psychology, 20,* 84–116.

Gallese, V., & Lakoff, G. (2008). The brain's concepts: The role of the sensory-motor system in conceptual knowledge. *Cognitive Neuropsychology, 22,* 455–479.

Ganea, P. A., Lillard, A. S., & Turkheimer, E. (2004). Preschoolers' understanding of the role of mental states in action and pretense. *Journal of Cognition and Development, 5,* 213–238.

Gardner, H. (1980). *Artful scribbles: The significance of children's drawings.* New York: Basic Books.

Gauvain, M. (2001). *The social context of cognitive development.* New York: Guilford Press.

Gehlen, A. (1988). *Man, his nature and place in the world.* New York: Columbia University Press. (Original work published 1940)

Gelman, S. A. (2003). *The essential child: Origins of essentialism in everyday thought.* New York: Oxford University Press.

Gelman, S. A. (2004). Psychological essentialism in children. *Trends in Cognitive Sciences, 8,* 404–409.

Gelman, S. A. (2009). Learning from others: Children's construction of concepts. *Annual Review of Psychology, 60,* 115–140.

Gelman, S. A., & Bloom, P. (2000). Young children are sensitive to how an object was created when deciding what to name it. *Cognition, 76,* 91–103.

Gelman, S. A., & Ebeling, K. S. (1998). Shape and representational status in children's early naming. *Cognition, 66,* B35–B47.

Gelman, S. A., & Kalish, C. W. (2006). Conceptual development. In W. Damon (Series Ed.) & D. Kuhn & R. Siegler (Vol. Eds.), *Handbook of child psychology: Vol. 2, Cognition, perception, and language* (5th ed., pp. 687–733). Hoboken, NJ: John Wiley & Sons.

Gelman, S. A., & Markman, E. M. (1986). Categories and induction in young children. *Cognition, 23,* 183–209.

German, T. P., & Leslie, A. M. (2001). Children's inferences from 'knowing' to 'pretending' and 'believing'. *British Journal of Developmental Psychology, 19,* 59–83.

Gibson, J. J. (1979). *The ecological approach to perception.* Hillsdale, NJ: Erlbaum.

Giesbrecht, G. F., Müller, U., & Miller, M. R. (2010). Psychological distancing in the development of executive function and emotion regulation. In B. F. Sokol, U. Müller, J. I. M. Carpendale, A. R. Young, & G. Iarocci (Eds.), *Self- and social-regulation: Social interaction and the development of social understanding and executive function* (pp. 337–357). Oxford: Oxford University Press.

Giffin, H. (1984). The coordination of meaning in the creation of a shared make believe reality. In I. Bretherton (Ed.), *Symbolic play: The development of social understanding* (pp. 73–100). New York: Academic Press.

Gillett, G. (1988). Representation and cognitive science. *Inquiry, 32,* 261–276.

Gillett, G. (1992). *Representation, meaning, and thought.* Oxford: Clarendon.

Glock, H.-J. (2003). Neural representationalism. *Facta Philosophica, 5,* 105–129.

Goldberg, B. (1991). Mechanism and meaning. In J. Hyman (Ed.), *Investigating psychology* (pp. 48–66). London: Routledge.

Goldin-Meadow, S., & Wagner, S. M. (2005). How our hands help is learn. *Trends in Cognitive Sciences, 9,* 234–241.

Golomb, C. (1992). *The child's creation of a pictorial world.* Berkeley, CA: University of California Press.

Golomb, C. (2007). Representational conceptions in two- and three-dimensional media: A developmental perspective *Psychology of Aesthetics, Creativity, and the Arts, 1,* 32–39.

Göncü, A. (1999). Children's and researchers' engagement in the world. In A. Göncü (Ed.), *Children's engagement in the world: Sociocultural perspectives* (pp. 3–22). New York: Cambridge University Press.

Göncü, A., Jain, J., & Tuermer, U. (2006). Children's play as cultural interpretation. In A. Göncü & S. Gaskins (Eds.), *Play and development: Evolutionary, sociocultural, and functional perspectives* (pp. 155–178). Mahwah, NJ: Erlbaum.

Göncü, A., & Perone, A. (2005). Pretend play as a life-span activity. *Topoi, 24,* 137–147.

Goodenough, F. L. (1926). *The measurement of intelligence by drawings.* New York: World Book Company.

Goodnow, J. (1977). *Children's drawings.* Cambridge, MA: Harvard University Press.

Goodnow, J. J. (1978). Visible thinking: Cognitive aspects of change in drawings. *Child Development, 49,* 637–741.

Goodwyn, S. W., Acredolo, L. P., & Brown, C. A. (2000). Impact of symbolic gesturing on early language development. *Journal of Nonverbal Behavior, 24,* 81–103.

Gopnik, A., & Meltzoff, A. N. (1987). The development of categorization in the second year and its relation to other cognitive and linguistic developments. *Child Development, 58,* 1523–1531.

Gopnik, A., & Meltzoff, A. N. (1992). Categorization and naming: Basic-level sorting in eighteen-month-olds and its relation to language. *Child Development, 63,* 1091–1103.

Hacking, I. (2007). Natural kinds: Rosy dawn, scholastic twilight. *Royal Institute of Philosophy Supplement, 82,* 203–239.

Haight, W. L., & Miller, P. J. (1992). The development of everyday pretend play: A longitudinal study of mothers' participation. *Merrill-Palmer Quarterly, 38,* 331–349.

Haith, M. M., & Benson, J. B. (1998). Infant cognition. In W. Damon (Series Ed.) & D. Kuhn & R. Siegler (Vol. Eds.), *Handbook of child psychology: Vol. 2, Cognition, perception, and language* (5th ed., pp. 199–254). New York: John Wiley & Sons.

Halford, G. S., Andrews, G., & Jensen, I. (2002). Integration of category induction and hierarchical classification: One paradigm at two levels of complexity. *Journal of Cognition and Development, 3,* 143–177.

Harris, D. B. (1963). *Children's drawings as measures of intellectual maturity. A revision and extension of the Goodenough Draw-a-Man test.* New York: Harcourt, Brace & World.

Hart, L. M., & Goldin-Meadow, S. (1984). The child as nonegocentric art critic. *Child Development, 55,* 2122–2129.

Heil, J. (2004). *Philosophy of mind: A contemporary introduction* (2nd ed.). New York: Routledge.

Hodkin, B. (1981). Language effects in the assessment of class-inclusion ability. *Child Development, 52,* 470–478.

Hodkin, B. (1987). Performance model analysis in class inclusion: An illustration with two language conditions. *Developmental Psychology, 23,* 683–689.

Howe, M. L., & Rabinowitz, F. M. (1996). Reasoning from memory: A lifespan inquiry into the necessity of remembering when reasoning about class inclusion. *Journal of Experimental Child Psychology, 61,* 1–42.

Howes, C., & Matheson, C. (1992). Sequences in the development of competent play with peers: Social and social pretend play. *Developmental Psychology, 28,* 961–974.

Inhelder, B., & Piaget, J. (1969). *The early growth of logic in the child.* New York: Norton. (Original work published 1959)

Iverson, J. M., Capirci, O., & Caselli, M. C. (1994). From communication to language in two modalities. *Cognitive Development, 9,* 23–43.

Jackowitz, E. R., & Watson, M. W. (1980). Development of object transformation in early pretend play. *Developmental Psychology, 16,* 543–549.

Jarrold, C., Carruthers, P., Smith, P. K., & Boucher, J. (1994). Pretend play: Is it metarepresentational? *Mind & Language, 9,* 445–468.

Johnson, K. E., Younger, B. A., & Cuellar, R. E. (2005). Toddlers' understanding of iconic models: Cross-task comparison of selection and preferential looking responses. *Infancy, 8,* 189–200.

Jolley, R. P., Fenn, K., & Jones, L. (2004). The development of children's expressive drawing. *British Journal of Developmental Psychology 22,* 545–567.

Jolley, R. P., Knox, E. L., & Foster, S. G. (2000). The relationship between children's production and comprehension of realism in drawing. *British Journal of Developmental Psychology, 18,* 557–582.

Jolley, R. P., & Thomas, G. V. (1995). Children's sensitivity to metaphorical expression of mood in line drawings. *British Journal of Developmental Psychology, 13,* 335–346.

Jolley, R. P., Zhi, Z., & Thomas, G. V. (1998). The development of understanding moods metaphorically expressed in pictures: A cross-cultural comparison. *Journal of Cross-Cultural Psychology, 29,* 358–376.

Judge, B. (1985). *Thinking about things: A philosophical study of representation.* Edinburgh: Scottish Academic Press.

Jungwirth, S., Zehetmayer, S., Bauer, P., Weissgram, S., Tragl, K.-H., & Fischer, P. (2009). Screening for Alzheimer's dementia at age 78 with short psychometric instruments. *International Psychogeriatrics, 21,* 548–559.

Kagan, J. (2008). In defense of qualitative changes in development. *Child Development, 79,* 1606–1624.

Kalish, C. W. (2002). Gold, jade, and emeruby: The value of naturalness for theories of concepts and categories. *Journal of Theoretical and Philosophical Psychology, 22,* 45–66.

Kant, I. (1933). *Critique of pure reason* (2nd ed.). London: Macmillan. (Original work published in 1787)

Karmiloff-Smith, A. (1990). Constraints on representational change: Evidence from children's drawing. *Cognition, 34,* 57–83.

Keil, F. (1989). *Concepts, kinds, and cognitive development.* Cambridge, MA: MIT Press.

Kellogg, R. (1969) *Analyzing children's art.* Palo Alto, CA: Mayfield Publishing.

Kemler Nelson, D. G., O'Neil, K. A., & Asher, Y. M. (2008). A mutually facilitative relationship between learning names and learning concepts in preschool children: The case of artifacts. *Journal of Cognition and Development, 9,* 171–193.

Kemmerling, A. (2004). As it were pictures: On the two-faced nature of Cartesian ideas. In R. Schumacher (Ed.), *Mental representation and reality: Philosophical theories of perception from Descartes to today* (pp. 43–68). Berlin: Walter de Gruyter.

Kesselring, T. (2009). The mind's staircase revisited. In U. Müller, J. I. M. Carpendale, & L. Smith (Eds.), *The Cambridge companion to Piaget* (pp. 372–399). New York: Cambridge University Press.

Kogan, N. (1974). Categorizing and conceptualizing styles in younger and older adults. *Human Development, 17,* 218–230.

Kuhlmeier, V. (2005). Symbolic insight and inhibitory control: Two problems facing young children on symbolic retrieval tasks. *Journal of Cognition and Development, 6,* 365–380.

Kuhn, T. S. (1962). *The structure of scientific revolutions.* Chicago, IL: University of Chicago Press.

Lakoff, G. (1987). *Women, fire, and dangerous things.* Chicago: University of Chicago Press.

Lange-Küttner, C. (2009). Habitual size and projective size: The logic of spatial systems in children's drawings. *Developmental Psychology, 45,* 913–927.

Langer, J. (1980). *The origins of logic: Six to twelve months.* New York: Academic Press.

Langer, J. (1986). *The origins of logic: One to two years.* New York: Academic Press.

Lawrence, J. A., & Valsiner, J. (1993). Conceptual roots of internalization: From transmission to transformation. *Human Development, 36,* 150–167.

Lerner, R. M. (2006). Developmental science, developmental systems, and contemporary theories of human development. In W. Damon & R. M. Lerner (Series Eds.) & R. M. Lerner (Vol. Ed.), *Handbook of child psychology: Vol. 1, Theoretical models of human development* (6th ed., pp. 1–17). Hoboken, NJ: John Wiley & Sons.

Lerner, R. M., & Overton, W. F. (2008). Exemplifying the integrations of the relational developmental system: Synthesizing theory, research and application to promote positive development and social justice. *Journal of Adolescent Research, 23,* 245–255.

Leslie, A. M. (1987). Pretense and representation: The origins of "theory of mind." *Psychological Review, 94,* 412–426.

Leslie, A. M. (1994). Pretending and believing: Issues in the theory of ToMM. *Cognition, 50,* 211–238.

Liben, L. S. (2003). Beyond point and shoot: Children's developing understanding of photographs as spatial and expressive representations. *Advances in Child Development and Behaviour, 31,* 1–42.

Liben, L. (2008). Embodiment and children's understanding of the real and represented world. In W. F. Overton, U. Müller, & J. Newman (Eds.), *Developmental perspectives on embodiment and consciousness* (pp. 191–224). New York: Taylor & Francis.

Lillard, A. S. (1993). Pretend play skills and the child's theory of mind. *Child Development, 64,* 348–371.

Lillard, A. (1994). Making of pretense. In C. Lewis & P. Mitchell (Eds.), *Children's early understanding of mind: Origins and development* (pp. 211–234). Hove, United Kingdom: Erlbaum.

Lillard, A. S. (1996). Body or mind: Children's categorizing of pretense. *Child Development, 67,* 1717–1734.

Lillard, A. S. (1998). Wanting to be it: Children's understanding of intentions underlying pretense. *Child Development, 69,* 981–993.

Lillard, A. (2002). Pretend play and cognitive development. In U. Goswami (Ed.), *Handbook of childhood cognitive development* (pp. 188–205). Oxford: Blackwell.

Lillard, A. (2006). Guided participation: How mothers structure and children understand pretend play. In A. Göncü & S. Gaskins (Eds.), *Play and development: Evolutionary, sociocultural, and functional perspectives* (pp. 131–153). Mahwah, NJ: Erlbaum.

Lillard, A., Nishida, T., Massaro, D., Vaish, A., Ma, L., & McRoberts, G. (2007). Signs of pretense across age and scenario. *Infancy, 11,* 1–30.

Lillard, A. S., Zeljo, A., Curenton, S., & Kaugars, A. (2000). Children's understanding of the animacy constraint on pretense. *Merrill-Palmer Quarterly, 46,* 21–44.

Lin, E. L., & Murphy, G. L. (2001). Thematic relations in adults' concepts. *Journal of Experimental Psychology: General, 130,* 3–28.

Luquet, G. (1913). *Les dessins d'un enfant.* Paris: Alcan.

Luquet, G. (1927). Le realisme intellectuel dans l'art primitif. 1. Figuration de l'invisible. *Journal de Psychologie, 24,* 765–797.

Machado, A., & Silva, F. J. (2007). Toward a richer view of the scientific method. *American Psychologist, 7,* 671–681.

Machery, E. (2008). The folk concept of intentional action: Philosophical and experimental issues. *Mind & Language, 23,* 165–189.

Mandler, J. M. (1998). Representation. In W. Damon (Series Ed.) & D. Kuhn & R. Siegler (Vol. Eds.), *Handbook of child psychology: Vol. 2, Cognition, perception, and language* (5th ed., pp. 255–308). New York: John Wiley & Sons.

Mandler, J. M. (2004). *The foundations of mind.* New York: Oxford University Press.

Mandler, J. M., Bauer, P. J., & McDonough, L. (1991). Separating the sheep from the goats: Differentiating global categories. *Cognitive Psychology, 23,* 263–298.

Mandler, J. M., & McDonough, L. (1993). Concept formation in infancy. *Cognitive Development, 8,* 291–318.

Mandler, J., & McDonough, L. (1995). Long-term recall of event sequences in infancy. *Journal of Experimental Child Psychology, 59,* 457–476.

Mandler, J., & McDonough, L. (1996). Drinking and driving don't mix: Inductive generalization in infancy. *Cognition, 59,* 307–335.

Marbach, E. (1993). *Mental representation and consciousness. Towards a phenomenological theory of representation and reference.* Dordrecht, the Netherlands: Kluwer Academic.

Mareschal, D., & Tan, S. H. (2007). Flexible and context-dependent categorization by eighteen-month-olds. *Child Development, 78,* 19–37.

Margolis, E., & Laurence, S. (2006). *Concepts.* Retrieved May 29, 2009, from http://www.plato.stanford.edu/entries/concepts/.

Markman, E. M. (1989). *Categorization and naming in children. Problems of induction.* Cambridge, MA: MIT Press.

Markman, E. M., & Hutchinson, J. E. (1984). Children's sensitivity to constraints on word meaning: Taxonomic versus thematic relations. *Cognitive Psychology, 16,* 1–27.

Marr, D. (1980). *Vision: A computational investigation into the human representation and processing of visual information.* San Francisco, CA: W. H. Freeman.

Matthews, J. (1984). Children's drawings: Are young children really scribbling? *Early Child Development and Care, 18,* 1–9.

Matthews, J. (2010). Scribble: The origin of expression, representation and symbolisation. In B. Wagoner (Ed.), *Symbolic transformations: The mind in movement through culture and society* (pp. 209–231). London: Routledge.

McCune, L. (1995). A normative study of representational play at the transition to language. *Developmental Psychology, 31,* 198–206.

McCune, L. (2010). Developing symbolic activities. In B. Wagoner (Ed.), *Symbolic transformations: The mind in movement through culture and society* (pp. 193–208). London: Routledge.

McCune-Nicolich, L. (1981). Toward symbolic functioning: Structure of early use of early pretend games and potential parallels with language. *Child Development, 52,* 785–797.

McDonough, L., & Mandler, J. M. (1998). Inductive generalization in 9- and 11-month-olds. *Developmental Science, 1,* 227–232.

McDonough, R. (1989). Towards a non-mechanistic theory of meaning. *Mind, 98,* 1–21.

McGarrigle, J., Grieve, R., & Hughes, M. (1978). Interpreting inclusion: A contribution to the study of the child's cognitive and linguistic development. *Journal of Experimental Child Psychology, 26,* 528–550.

Medin, D. L. (1989). Concepts and conceptual structure. *American Psychologist, 44,* 1469–1481.

Medin, D. L., Lynch, E. B., & Solomon, K. O. (2000). Are there kinds of concepts? *Annual Review of Psychology, 51,* 121–147.

Meltzoff, A. N. (1988). Infant imitation and memory: Nine-month-olds in immediate and deferred tests. *Child Development, 59,* 217–225.

Meltzoff, A. N. (1990). Towards a developmental cognitive science: The implications of crossmodal matching and imitation for the development of representation and memory in infancy. *Annals of the New York Academy of Sciences, 608,* 1–37.

Merleau-Ponty, M. (1962). *Phenomenology of perception.* New York: Humanities Press. (Original work published 1945)

Metzinger, T., & Gallese, V. (2003a). The emergence of a shared action ontology: Building blocks for a theory. *Consciousness and Cognition, 12,* 549–571.

Metzinger, T., & Gallese, V. (2003b). Of course they do. *Consciousness and Cognition, 12,* 574–576.

Milbrath, C. (1998). *Patterns of artistic development in children: A comparative study of talent.* New York, NY: Cambridge University Press.

Milbrath, C., & Trautner, H. M. (Eds.). (2008). *Children's understanding and production of pictures, drawings, and art: Theoretical and empirical approaches.* Ashland, OH: Hogrefe & Huber Publishers.

Morford, J. P., Singleton, J. L., & Goldin-Meadow, S. (1995). The genesis of language: How much time is needed to generate arbitrary symbols in a sign system? In K. Emmorey & J. Reilley (Eds.), *Language, gesture, and space* (pp. 313–332). Hillsdale, NJ: Erlbaum.

Morra, S. (2005). Cognitive aspects of change in drawings: A neo-Piagetian theoretical account. *British Journal of Developmental Psychology, 23,* 317–341.

Mounoud, P., Duscherer, K., Moy, G., & Perraudin, S. (2007). The influence of action perception on object recognition: A developmental study. *Developmental Science, 10,* 836–852.

Müller, U., & Overton, W. F. (1998a). How to grow a baby: A reevaluation of image-schema and Piagetian action approaches to representation. *Human Development, 41,* 171–211.

Müller, U., & Overton, W. F. (1998b). Action theory of mind and representational theory of mind: Is dialogue possible? *Human Development, 41,* 127–133.

Müller, U., & Sokol, B., & Overton, W. F. (1998). Reframing a constructivist model of the development of mental representation: The role of higher-order operations. *Developmental Review, 18,* 155–201.

Murphy, G. L. (2002). *The big book of concepts.* Cambridge, MA: MIT Press.

Musatti, T., & Mayer, S. (1987). Object substitution: Its nature and function in early Pretend play. *Human Development, 30,* 225–235.

Myers, L. J., & Liben, L. S. (2008). The role of intentionality and iconicity in children's developing comprehension and production of cartographic symbols. *Child Development, 79,* 668–684.

Namy, L. L. (2008). Recognition of iconicity doesn't come for free. *Developmental Science, 11,* 841–846.

Namy, L. L., Campbell, A. L., & Tomasello. M. (2004). The changing role of iconicity in non-verbal symbol learning: A U-shaped trajectory in the acquisition of arbitrary gestures. *Journal of Cognition and Development, 5,* 37–57.

Namy, L. L., & Waxman, S. R. (1998). Words and gestures: infants' interpretations of different forms of symbolic reference. *Child Development, 69,* 295–308.

Newman, G. E., & Keil, F. C. (2008). Where is the essence? Developmental shifts in children's beliefs about internal features. *Child Development, 79,* 1344–1356.

Nicholls, A. L., & Kennedy, J. M. (1992). Drawing development: From similarity of features to direction. *Child Development, 63,* 227–241.

Nichols, S., & Stich, S. (2000). A cognitive theory of pretense. *Cognition, 74,* 115–147.

Nicolopoulou, A., & Weintraub, J. (1998). Individual and collective representations in social context: A modest contribution to resuming the interrupted project of a sociocultural developmental psychology. *Human Development, 41,* 215–235.

Nielsen, M., & Dissanayake, C. (2004). Pretend play, mirror self-recognition and imitation: A longitudinal investigation through the second year. *Infant Behavior & Development, 27,* 342–365.

Nishida, T. K., & Lillard, A. S. (2007). The informative value of emotional expressions: 'Social referencing' in mother-child pretense. *Developmental Science, 10,* 205–212.

O'Connell, B., & Bretherton, I. (1984). Toddler's play, alone and with mother: The role of maternal guidance. In I. Bretherton (Ed.), *Symbolic play: The development of social understanding* (pp. 337–368). New York: Academic Press.

O'Reilly, A. W. (1995). Using representations: Comprehension and production of actions with imagined objects. *Child Development, 66,* 999–1010.

Orlansky, M. D., & Bonvillian, J. D. (1984). The role of iconicity in early sign language acquisition. *Journal of Speech and Hearing Disorders, 49,* 287–292.

O'Sullivan, L. P., Mitchell, L. L., & Daehler, M. W. (2001). Representation and perseveration: Influences on young children's representational insight. *Journal of Cognition and Development, 2,* 339–365.

Overton, W. F. (1976). The active organism in structuralism. *Human Development, 19,* 71–86.

Overton, W. F. (1994). Contexts of meaning: The computational and the embodied mind. In W. F. Overton & D. S. Palermo (Eds.), *The nature and ontogenesis of meaning* (pp. 1–18). Hillsdale, NJ: Erlbaum.

Overton, W. F. (2006). Developmental psychology: Philosophy, concepts, methodology. In W. Damon & R. M. Lerner (Series Ed.) & R. M. Lerner (Vol. Ed.), *Handbook of child psychology* (Vol. 1, 6th ed., pp. 18–88). Hoboken, NJ: John Wiley & Sons.

Overton, W. F., & Jackson, J. P. (1973). The representation of imagined objects in action sequences: A developmental study. *Child Development, 44,* 309–314.

Overton, W. F., Müller, U., & Newman, J. L. (Eds.). (2008). *Developmental perspective on embodiment and consciousness.* Hillsdale, NJ: Erlbaum.

Oxford English Dictionary. (2009). *Representation.* Retrieved March 22, 2009, from http:/www.oed.com/.

Parsons, M. J. (1987). *How we understand art: A cognitive developmental account of aesthetic experience.* Cambridge: Cambridge University Press.

Peigneux, P., & van der Linden, M. (1999). Influence of aging and educational level on the prevalence of the body-part-as-objects in normal subjects. *Journal of Clinical and Experimental Neuropsychology, 21,* 547–552.

Peirce, C. S. (1955). *Philosophical writings of Peirce.* New York: Dover.

Peirce, C. S. (1966). Elements of logic. In C. Hartshorne & P. Weiss (Eds.), *Collected papers* (Vol. 2). Cambridge, MA: Harvard University Press. (Original work written 1931–1935)

Pennequin, V., Fontaine, R., Bonthoux, F., Scheuner, N., & Blaye, A. (2006). Categorization deficit in old age: Reality or artefact? *Journal of Adult Development, 13,* 1–9.

Perner, J. (1991). *Understanding the representational mind.* Cambridge, MA: Bradford Books, MIT Press.

Perner, J., Baker, S., & Hutton, D. (1994). Prelief: The conceptual origins of belief and pretence. In C. Lewis & P. Mitchell (Eds.), *Children's early understanding of mind: Origins and development* (pp. 261–286). Hove, United Kingdom: Erlbaum.

Piaget, J. (1952). *The origins of intelligence in children.* New York: International Universities Press. (Original work published 1936)

Piaget, J. (1954). *The construction of reality in the child.* New York: Basic Books. (Original work published 1937)

Piaget, J. (1962). *Play, dreams and imitation in childhood.* New York: W. W. Norton & Co. (Original work published 1945)

Piaget, J. (1983). Piaget's theory. In P. Mussen (Ed.), *Handbook of child psychology* (4th ed., pp. 103–128). New York: John Wiley & Sons. (Original work published in 1970)

Piaget, J. (1985). *The equilibration of cognitive structures: The central problem of intellectual development.* Chicago: University of Chicago Press. (Original work published in 1975)

Piaget, J., & Inhelder, B. (1956). *The child's conception of space.* London: Routledge and Kegan Paul. (Original work published 1948)

Piaget, J., & Inhelder, B. (1969). *The psychology of the child.* New York: Basic Books. (Original work published 1966)

Pierroutsakos, S. L., & DeLoache, J. S. (2003). Infants' manual exploration of pictorial objects varying in realism. *Infancy, 4,* 141–156.

Pierroutsakos, S. L., & Troseth, G. L. (2003). Video verité: Infants' manual investigation of objects on video. *Infant Behavior & Development, 26,* 183–199.

Preissler, M. A., & Bloom, P. (2007). Two-year-olds appreciate the dual nature of pictures. *Psychological Science, 18,* 1–2.

Preissler, M. A., & Bloom, P. (2008). Two-year-olds use artist intention to understand drawings. *Cognition, 106,* 512–518.

Preissler, M. A., & Carey, S. (2004). Do both pictures and words function as symbols for 18- and 24-month-old children? *Journal of Cognition and Development, 5,* 185–212.

Prinz, W. (2003). Neurons don't represent. *Consciousness and Cognition, 12,* 572–573.

Quinn, P. C. (1999). Development of recognition and categorization of objects and their spatial relations in young infants. In I. L. Balter & C. S. Tamis-LeMonda (Eds.), *Child psychology: A handbook of contemporary issues* (pp. 85–115). Philadelphia: Psychology Press.

Quinn, P. C. (2002). Early categorization: A new synthesis. In U. Goswami (Ed.), *Handbook of childhood cognitive development* (pp. 84–101). Oxford: Blackwell.

Quinn, P. C. (2004). Development of subordinate-level categorization in 3- to 7-month-old infants. *Child Development, 75,* 886–899.

Quinn, P. C. (2007). Infant categorization. In A. Slater & M. Lewis (Eds.), *Introduction to infant development* (pp. 119–136). Oxford: Oxford University Press.

Quinn, P. C., & Eimas, P. D. (1996). Perceptual cues that permit categorical differentiation of animal species by infants. *Journal of Experimental Child Psychology, 63,* 189–211.

Quinn, P. C., & Eimas, P. D. (1997). A reexamination of the perceptual-to-conceptual shift in mental representations. *Review of General Psychology, 69,* 151–174.

Racine, T. P. (2004). Wittgenstein's internalistic logic and children's theories of mind. In J. I. M. Carpendale & U. Müller (Eds.), *Social interaction and the development of knowledge* (pp. 257–276). Mahwah, NJ: Erlbaum.

Racine, T. P., & Carpendale, J. I. M. (2007). The role of shared practice in joint attention. *British Journal of Developmental Psychology, 25,* 3–25.

Racine, T. P., & Carpendale, J. I. M. (2008). The embodiment of mental states. In W. F. Overton, U. Müller, & J. Newman (Eds.), *Body in mind, mind in body: Developmental perspectives on embodiment and consciousness* (pp. 159–190). Mahwah, NJ: Erlbaum.

Racine, T. P., & Müller, U. (2009). The contemporary relevance of Wittgenstein: Reflections and directions. *New Ideas in Psychology, 27,* 107–117.

Rakison, D. H. (2007). Is consciousness in its infancy in infancy? *Journal of Consciousness Studies, 14,* 66–89.

Rakison, D. H., & Lupyan, G. (2008). Developing object concepts in infancy: An associative learning perspective. *Monographs of the Society for Research in Child Development, 73,* 1–110.

Rakoczy, H., Tomasello, M., & Striano, T. (2004). Young children know that trying is not pretending: A test of the "behaving-as-if" construal of children's understanding of pretense. *Developmental Psychology, 40,* 388–399.

Rakoczy, H., Tomasello, M., & Striano, T. (2005). On tools and toys: How children learn to act on and pretend with 'virgin objects'. *Developmental Science, 8,* 57–73.

Ramsey, W. R. (2007). *Representation reconsidered.* New York: Cambridge University Press.

Raymer, A. M., Maher, L. M., Foundas, A. L., Heilman, K. M., & Gonzalez Rothi, L. J. (1997). The significance of body part as tool errors in limb apraxia. *Brain & Cognition, 34,* 287–292.

Ricciuti, H. (1965). Object grouping and selective ordering behavior in infants 12 to 24 months old. *Merrill-Palmer Quarterly, 11,* 129–148.

Richert, R. A., & Lillard, A. S. (2002). Children's understanding of the knowledge prerequisites of drawing and pretending. *Developmental Psychology, 38,* 1004–1015.

Rivera, S. M., Wakeley, A., & Langer, J. (1999). The drawbridge phenomenon: Representational reasoning or perceptual preference? *Developmental Psychology, 35,* 427–435.

Robinson, E. J., Nye, R., & Thomas, G. V. (1994). Children's conceptions of the relationship between pictures and their referents. *Cognitive Development, 9,* 165–191.

Rogoff, B. (1990). *Apprenticeship in thinking: Cognitive development in social context.* Oxford: Oxford University Press.

Rogoff, B. (1998). Cognition and a collaborative process. In D. Kuhn & R. S. Siegler (Eds.), *Handbook of child psychology: Vol. 2, Cognition, perception and language* (5th ed., pp. 679–744). New York: John Wiley & Sons.

Rogoff, B. (2003). *The cultural nature of human development.* Oxford: Oxford University Press.

Rorty, R. (1979). *Philosophy and the mirror of nature.* Princeton, NJ: Princeton University Press.

Rosch, E. (1975). Cognitive representations of semantic categories. *Journal of Experimental Psychology: General, 104,* 192–233.

Russell, J. (1992). The theory theory: So good they named it twice. *Cognitive Development, 7,* 485–519.

Russell, J. (1996). *Agency: Its role in mental development.* Bristol, PA: Taylor and Francis.

Savage-Rumbaugh, S., Fields, W. M., & Taglialatela, J. P. (2001). Language, speech, tools, and writing: A cultural imperative. *Journal of Consciousness Studies, 8,* 273–292.

Scheerer, E. (1990a). *Mental representation: Its history and present status. I. 'Repraesentatio' from Cicero to Suarez.* Zentrum für interdisplinäre Forschung, Bielefeld: Mind and Brain, Report 27.

Scheerer, E. (1990b). *Mental representation: Its history and present status. II A. Descartes, his followers and his opponents.* Zentrum für interdisplinäre Forschung, Bielefeld: Mind and Brain, Report 43.

Scheerer, E. (1993). Mentale Repräsentation in interdisziplinärer Perspektive [Mental representation in interdisciplinary perspective]. *Zeitschrift für Psychologie, 201,* 136–166.

Schöner, G., & Thelen, E. (2006). Using dynamic field theory to rethink infant habituation. *Psychological Review, 113,* 273–299.

Shipley, E. F. (1979). The class inclusion task: Question form and distributive comparisons. *Journal of Psycholinguistic Research, 8,* 301–331.

Sigel, I. E. (1978). The development of pictorial comprehension. In B. S. Randhawa & W. E. Coffman (Eds.), *Visual learning, thinking, ands communication* (pp. 93–111). New York: Academic Press.

Sigel, I. E. (2002). The psychological distancing model: A study of the socialization of cognition. *Culture and Psychology, 8,* 189–214.

Sigel, I. E., Stinson, E. T., & Flaugher, J. (1991). Socialization of representational competence in the family: The distancing paradigm. In L. Okagaki & R. J. Sternberg (Eds.), *Directors of development: Influences on the development of children's thinking* (pp. 121–144). Hillsdale, NJ: Erlbaum.

Sigel, I. E., Stinson, E. T., & Kim, M. (1993). Socialization of cognition: The distancing model. In R. Wozniak & K. W. Fischer (Eds.), *Development in context: Acting and thinking in specific environments* (pp. 211–224). Hillsdale, NJ: Erlbaum.

Silk, A. M. J., & Thomas, G. V. (1986). Development and differentiation in human figure drawing. *British Journal of Developmental Psychology, 77,* 399–410.

Sinnott, J. D. (1975). Everyday thinking and Piagetian operativity in adults. *Human Development, 18,* 430–443.

Ska, B., & Nespoulous, J.-L. (1987). Pantomimes and aging. *Journal of Clinical and Experimental Neuropsychology, 9,* 754–766.

Sloutsky, V. M., & Fisher, A. V. (2004). When development and learning decrease memory. *Psychological Science, 15,* 553–558.

Sloutsky, V. M., Kloos, H., & Fisher, A. V. (2007a). When looks are everything: Appearance similarity versus kind information in early induction. *Psychological Science, 18,* 179–185.

Sloutsky, V. M., Kloos, H., & Fisher, A. V. (2007b). What's beyond looks? Reply to Gelman and Waxman. *Psychological Science, 18,* 556–557.

Smiley, S. S., & Brown, A. L. (1979). Conceptual preference for thematic or taxonomic relations: A nonmonotonic age trend from preschool to old age. *Journal of Experimental Child Psychology, 28,* 249–257.

Smith, L. B. (2003). Learning to recognize objects. *Psychological Science, 14,* 244–250.

Smith, P. M. (1993). Young children's depiction of contrast in human figure drawing: Standing and walking. *Educational Psychology, 13,* 107–118.

Spensley, F., & Taylor, J. (1999). The development of cognitive flexibility: Evidence from children's drawings. *Human Development, 42,* 300–324.

Stefanini, S., Bello, A., Caselli, M. C., Iverson, J. M., & Volterra, V. (2009). Co-speech in a naming task: Developmental data. *Language and Cognitive Processes, 24,* 168–189.

Stern, W. (1930). *Psychology of early childhood.* New York: Henry Holt. (Original work published in 1914)

Sugarman, S. (1982). Transitions in early representational intelligence: Changes over time in children's production of simple block structures. In G. E. Forman (Ed.), *Action and thought* (pp. 65–93). New York: Academic Press.

Sugarman, S. (1983). *Children's early thought.* Cambridge: Cambridge University Press.

Susswein, N., & Racine, T. P. (2008). Sharing mental states: Causal and definitional issues in intersubjectivity. In J. Zlatev, T. P. Racine, C. Sinha, & E. Itkonen (Eds.), *The shared mind: Perspectives on intersubjectivity* (pp. 141–162). Amsterdam: Benjamins.

Tanaka, M., Tomonaga, M., & Matsuzawa, T. (2003). Finger drawing by infant chimpanzees *(Pan troglodytes). Animal Cognition, 6,* 245–251.

Taylor, C. (1971). What is involved in a genetic psychology? In T. Mischel (Ed.), *Cognitive development and epistemology* (pp. 393–416). New York: Academic Press.

Taylor, C. (1995). *Philosophical arguments.* Cambridge, MA: Harvard University Press.

Taylor, M., & Bacharach, V. R. (1981). The development of drawing rules: Metaknowledge about drawing influences performance on nondrawing tasks. *Child Development, 52,* 372–375.

ter Hark, M. (2006). Wittgenstein, pretend play and the transferred use of language. *Journal for the Theory of Social Behaviour, 36,* 299–318.

Thomas, G. V., Jolley, R. P., Robinson, E. J., & Champion, H. (1999). Realist errors in children's responses to pictures and words as representations. *Journal of Experimental Child Psychology, 74,* 1–20.

Thomas, G. V., Nye, R., & Robinson, E. J. (1994). How children view pictures: Children's responses to pictures as things in themselves and as representations of something else. *Cognitive Development, 9,* 141–164.

Thomas, G. V., Nye, R., Rowley, M., & Robinson, E. J. (2001). What is a picture? Children's conceptions of pictures. *British Journal of Developmental Psychology, 19,* 475–491.

Tomasello, M., Striano, T., & Rochat, P. (1999). Do young children use objects as symbols? *British Journal of Developmental Psychology, 17,* 563–584.

Toomela, A. (1999). Drawing development: Stages in the representation of a cube and a cylinder. *Child Development, 70,* 1141–1150.

Toomela, A. (2002). Drawing as a verbally mediated activity: A study of relationships between verbal, motor, and visuospatial skills and drawing in children. *International Journal of Behavioral Development, 26,* 234–247.

Troseth, G. L., & DeLoache, J. S. (1998). The medium can obscure the message: Young children's understanding of video. *Child Development, 69,* 950–965.

Troseth, G. L., Pickard, M. E. B., & DeLoache, J. S. (2007). Young children's use of scale models: Testing an alternative to representational insight. *Developmental Science, 10,* 763–769.

Troseth, G. L., Pierroutsakos, S. L., & DeLoache, J. S. (2004). From the innocent to the intelligent eye: The early development of pictorial competence. *Advances in Child Development and Behaviour, 32,* 1–35.

Ungerer, J. A., Zelazo, P. R., Kearsley, R. B., & O'Leary, K. (1981). Developmental changes in the representation of objects in symbolic play from 18 to 34 months of age. *Child Development, 52,* 186–195.

Vinter, A., & Marot, V. (2007). The development of context sensitivity in children's graphic copying strategies. *Developmental Psychology, 43,* 94–110.

von Uexküll, J. (1909). *Umwelt und Innenwelt der Tiere* (The external and internal world of animals). Berlin: Julius Springer Verlag.

von Uexküll, J. (1926). *Theoretical biology.* London: Kegan Paul, Trench, Trubner.

von Uexküll, J. (1957). A stroll through the worlds of animals and men. A picture book of invisible worlds. In C. H. Schiller (Ed.), *Instinctive behavior. The development of a modern concept* (pp. 5–80). New York: International Universities Press. (Original work published 1934)

von Herder, J. G. (1967). Essay on the origin of language. In J. H. Moran (Ed.), *On the origin of language.* New York: F. Ungar. (Original work published 1772)

Vygotsky, L. S. (1978). *Mind in society.* Cambridge, MA: Harvard University Press.

Vygotsky, L. S. (1986). *Thought and language.* Cambridge, MA: MIT Press. (Original work published 1934)

Vygotsky, L. S., & Luria, A. (1994). Tool and symbol in child development. In R. van der Veer & J. Valsiner (Eds.), *The Vygotsky reader* (pp. 99–174). Oxford: Blackwell.

Wang, H.-X., Ericsson, K., Winblad, B., & Fratiglioni, L. (1998). The Human Figure Drawing test as a screen for dementia in the elderly: A community-based study. *Archives of Gerontology and Geriatrics 27,* 25–34.

Watson, M. W., & Jackowitz, E. R. (1984). Agents and recipients in the development of early object play. *Child Development, 55,* 1091–1097.

Waxman, S. R., & Namy, L. L. (1997). Challenging the notion of a thematic preference in young children. *Developmental Psychology, 33,* 555–567.

Wellman, H. M., & Gelman, S. A. (1992). Cognitive development: Foundational theories of core domains. *Annual Review of Psychology, 43,* 337–375.

Werner, H. (1948). *Comparative psychology of mental development.* New York: International Universities Press.

Werner, H. (1957). The concept of development from a comparative and organismic point of view. In D. B. Harris (Ed.), *The concept of development: An issue in the study of human behavior* (pp. 125–148). Minneapolis, MN: University of Minnesota Press.

Werner, H., & Kaplan, B. (1963). *Symbol formation.* New York: John Wiley & Sons.

Willats, J. (2005). *Making sense of children's drawings.* Mahwah, NJ: Erlbaum.

Wilson, B. (1997). Types of child art and alternative accounts: Interpreting the interpreters. *Human Development, 40,* 155–168.

Winer, G. A. (1980). Class-inclusion reasoning in children: A review of the empirical literature. *Child Development, 51,* 309–328.

Winner, E. (1986). Where pelicans kiss seals. *Psychology Today, 20,* 25–35.

Wittgenstein, L. (1958). *Logical investigations.* New York: Macmillan.

Yamagata, K. (1997). Representational activity during mother–child interaction: The scribbling stage of drawing. *British Journal of Developmental Psychology, 15,* 355–366.

Younger, B. A., & Johnson, K. E. (2006). Infants' developing appreciation of similarities between model objects and their real-world referents. *Child Development, 77,* 1680–1697.

Zelazo, P. D., Carter, A., Reznick, J. S., & Frye, D. (1997). Early development of executive function: A problem-solving framework. *Review of General Psychology, 1,* 198–226.

CHAPTER 12

Development of Deductive Reasoning across the Life Span

ROBERT B. RICCO

Even a cursory review of the deductive reasoning literature reveals some striking inconsistencies both within the developmental findings, and between those findings and the results of adult research (Evans, 2002; Klaczynski, Schuneman, & Daniel, 2004; Markovits & Barrouillet, 2004). Research with children has often been interpreted as indicating substantial innate deductive reasoning competence (Braine & O'Brien, 1998a; Cheng & Holyoak, 1985), but also significant development from childhood to adolescence (Moshman, 2004; Overton & Dick, 2007). The adult literature, by contrast, has generated considerable evidence of young adults failing to reason logically, even under reasonably favorable conditions (Evans, 2002; Markovits, 2004). Resolving these inconsistencies represents a major challenge for any theory of deductive reasoning. This chapter offers both a summary of the developmental findings concerning deductive reasoning and a consideration of the existing developmental theories with regard to their capacity to explain both the findings and the inconsistencies.

This chapter begins with a discussion of the nature of deductive reasoning and a brief description of some key

methods used in empirical research on deduction. The discussion then moves to a critique of the major developmental theories of deductive reasoning and a review of the findings generated by research associated with the theories. These theories are primarily concerned with providing an account of deduction through early adulthood and have surprisingly little to say about late adult development. For this reason, the unexpectedly limited and somewhat atheoretical late adult development literature on deductive reasoning is presented separately in a final section of the chapter.

NATURE AND SCOPE OF
DEDUCTIVE REASONING

Reasoning consists of a goal-directed, inferential process in which a conclusion is drawn on the basis of one or more premises taken as true or acceptable, at least provisionally (Moshman, 2004; Overton, 1990). There are many types of inference and, therefore, of reasoning. However, most inference types entail the general category of inductive inference and are thus secondary to the basic distinction between deduction and induction.

Deductive inference is unique in several, interrelated respects. Most importantly, it is the only form of inference that can support judgments of necessity (Overton, 1990; Piaget, 1986, 1987; Ricco, 1990, 1993). In both formal and lay accounts of deduction, the truth of the premises is taken to provide an absolute guarantee for the truth of the conclusion, the latter being logically necessary given the former (Haack, 1978, pp. 13–15). This is because in a valid deduction, the conclusion is implicit within the premises. It is the form of a deductive inference, therefore, and not its content, that preserves the certainty of the premises in the conclusion. Two important consequences of this are that deduction cannot yield new information and deduction is monotonic (Adler, 2008). That is, the addition of new premises to a valid deductive argument cannot render the argument invalid. One last property of deductive inference worth noting here is that deduction proceeds from the general to the specific, thereby providing a basis for the application of general rules or categories to particular instances (Overton, 1990). This property is not unique to deduction, but the grounding of deduction in logical necessity provides a unique and powerful warrant for this process of instantiation (Piaget & Garcia, 1989; Ricco, 1993).

The several forms of inductive inference (e.g., probabilistic, presumptive, plausible, etc.) stand in sharp contrast with deduction as just described. Inductive inference cannot guarantee the truth of the conclusion and is non-monotonic. Although the truth of the premises may make the conclusion highly likely in inductive inference, there is always the potential for new information to render the conclusion false (Reiter, 1987). In addition, inductive inference yields genuinely (nontrivially) new information and often proceeds from the specific to the general (Kahane, 1973, pp. 248–250).

Some recent discussions of deductive reasoning have argued that human beings generally do not engage in this kind of thinking, except under very explicit instructions to do so (Evans, 2002, 2007, p. 10; Evans & Thompson, 2004). At the same time, it is claimed that the mental competencies and processes involved in performance on deductive reasoning problems do not differ in principle from those used in other kinds of reasoning and in problem-solving in general (Evans, 2002; Kuhn & Franklin, 2006; Markovits & Barrouillet, 2002). In these views, in other words, the unique properties of deductive inference described earlier are of limited use or relevance to ordinary cognition and

are, at best, characteristic of a highly specialized, acquired mode of thinking favored by logicians. Inductive inference, in contrast, is viewed as far more central to ordinary cognition, and its properties are considered better analogs to the properties of thought itself (Oaksford, Chater, & Hahn, 2008; Reiter, 1987). A full discussion of this controversy lies beyond the scope of this chapter, though the theories of deductive reasoning that proceed from this view are discussed and considered later in this chapter.

One factor, however, contributing to the recent tendency to trivialize deductive inference has been the surprisingly narrow range of methods used by cognitive psychologists in the study of deduction. This has led many to equate deductive reasoning, narrowly, with specific patterns of responding on a small set of problems and tasks. Ironically, this current methodological limitation contrasts sharply with the now unfashionable approach taken by Inhelder and Piaget (1958, 1964), who used a wide range of methods in their pioneering research into deductive processes, underscoring their basic assumption that deductive inference is an essential property of mind and not an arbitrary or specialized skill.

In contrast with the previously noted discussions, this chapter favors the position that deductive reasoning involves unique psychological processes (Braine, 1978; Inhelder & Piaget, 1958; Moshman, 2004; Overton, 1990) and is central to higher order cognition, providing a core competence underlying the various formalisms of which mature human thought is capable, including scientific thinking, hypothetical thinking, and critical thought (Grice, 1989; Overton & Dick, 2007; Piaget, 1986; Rips, 1994). In particular, the complete independence of form and content in deductive inference makes it uniquely suited to supporting the decontextualization of thought, that is, the freeing of thinking from the influence of merely local necessities, allowing an appreciation of necessary relations extending across series of inferences (Markovits, 2004).

Before discussing theory and research on the development of deductive reasoning, it would be helpful to elaborate further on the properties of deductive inference and to describe the principle measures that have been used in empirical research on deduction. Cognitive and developmental psychologists have focused largely on two forms of deductive reasoning, considering them to be representative—syllogistic reasoning and conditional reasoning. Syllogistic reasoning involves the construction or evaluation of arguments about relations between statements featuring quantified terms (*Some* A, *All* B, etc.), and consisting of two premises and a conclusion such that the premises share a common term and the conclusion shares a unique term with each of the premises.

Table 12.1 contains examples of deductively valid and invalid syllogisms. In the former, the truth of the premises guarantees the truth of the conclusion. Common experimental manipulations in syllogism studies involve varying the complexity of the syllogism and the relation between believability of content and validity of form (Markovits & Nantel, 1989; Morley, Evans, & Handley, 2004). Complexity can be varied in several ways having to do with the specific quantifiers used and the arrangement of the terms in the argument. Table 12.1 presents a simple manipulation of whether the order of terms in the conclusion

matches the order of these terms in the premises. More complex syllogisms are presumed to require additional inferences, processing steps, or mental models, or more sophisticated deductive reasoning strategies (Braine & O'Brien, 1998a; Halford & Andrews, 2004; Markovits & Barrouillet, 2002). Believability of the argument's content and validity of the argument's form can be made to be consistent or inconsistent, as presented in Table 12.1. Conflicts between validity and believability are of particular interest in research on deductive reasoning because they pit logic against belief.

Conditional reasoning concerns arguments that contain a conditional statement ("If…then…") as the major premise and a statement indicating whether the antecedent or consequent of the conditional applies in a given case as the minor premise. The four possible forms of conditional argument are described in the following list. Note that two of the forms are determinate or valid; that is, the conclusion is necessary given the premises. These are formally referred to as modus ponens (MP) and modus tollens (MT). The other two forms are indeterminate or invalid; that is, they allow for no certain conclusion. These are affirming the consequent (AC) and denying the antecedent (DA).

TABLE 12.1 Manipulations of the Logic-Belief Relation and the Ordering of Terms in Syllogistic Reasoning

Consistency and Inconsistency in the Relation of Logic and Belief

Valid—Unbelievable	Invalid—Believable
All animals with four legs are dangerous.	All things that have a motor need oil.
Poodles are not dangerous.	Automobiles need oil.
Thus, poodles do not have four legs.	*Thus, automobiles have motors.*
Valid—Believable	Invalid—Unbelievable
No deep-sea divers are smokers.	No millionaires are hard workers.
Some smokers are good swimmers.	Some hard workers are rich people.
Thus, some good swimmers are not deep-sea divers.	*Thus, some millionaires are not rich people.*

Manipulating the Order of Terms in the Conclusion Relative to the Premises

Preferred Order

Some healthy people are unhappy.	Some A are B.
No unhappy people are astronauts.	No B are C.
Thus, some healthy people are not astronauts.	*Thus, some A are not C.*

Nonpreferred Order

Some nutritional things are inexpensive.	Some A are B.
No inexpensive things are vitamins.	No B are C.
Thus, some vitamins are not nutritional.	*Thus, some C are not A.*

Adapted from Markovits, H., & Nantel, G. (1989). The belief-bias effect in the production and evaluation of logical conclusions. *Memory and Cognition, 17*(1), 11–17; and Morley, N. J., Evans, J. S., & Handley, S. J. (2004). Belief bias and figural bias in syllogistic reasoning. *Quarterly Journal of Experimental Psychology, 57A*(4), 666–692, by permission.

Modus Ponens (MP)

If it is raining, then the street is wet.	If p, then q.
It is raining.	p.
Therefore, the street is wet.	*Therefore, q.*

Modus Tollens (MT)

If it is raining, then the street is wet.	If p, then q.
The street is not wet.	−q.
Therefore, it is not raining.	*Therefore, −p.*

Affirming the Consequent (AC)

If it is raining, then the street is wet.	If p, then q.
The street is wet.	q.
Therefore, it is raining.	*Therefore, p. (Invalid)*

Denying the Antecedent (DA)

If it is raining, then the street is wet.	If p, then q.
It is not raining.	−p.
Therefore, the street is not wet.	*Therefore, −q. (Invalid)*

Unquestionably, the key manipulation in research on conditional reasoning concerns the content of the problem.

Conditionals can vary in whether their content is familiar or unfamiliar (Griggs & Cox, 1982), concrete (relatively meaningful) or abstract (relatively meaningless; Markovits, Doyon, & Simoneau, 2002), fantastic or realistic (Dias & Harris, 1990), and relevant, featuring a meaningful connection between antecedent and consequent, or nonrelevant, featuring an arbitrary relation (Ward & Overton, 1990). Two particularly pivotal content manipulations concern the availability of counterexamples to the two indeterminate argument forms (AC and DA) and the availability of disabling conditions regarding the conditional rule itself (Markovits, 2000, 2004; Markovits & Barrouillet, 2002). Table 12.2 presents some examples of these manipulations. The ease with which alternative antecedents (cases of –p) can be paired with the consequent (q) is directly related to the likelihood with which the individual will recognize that AC and DA do not allow for a definitive conclusion (Barrouillet, Markovits, & Quinn, 2002; Daniel & Klaczynski, 2006). Similarly, ease of access to conditions under which the conditional rule does not hold is related to the

likelihood that MP and MT will be rejected (Klaczynski et al., 2004; Vadeboncoeur & Markovits, 1999).

Although explicit examples of syllogistic reasoning occurring naturally in conversation may be limited, the four conditional argument forms are ubiquitous across ordinary language usage, though their validity or invalidity may or may not be appreciated by the reasoner.

At a metalogical level, MP is the general form of *any* valid deductive argument (LeBlanc & Wisdom, 1976, pp. 282, 292). We can represent this as "If P1, P2, P3, etc., then C; P1, P2, P3, etc. Therefore, C." The conditional argument forms are frequently used in hypothetical thinking and decision making, among various other types of reasoning (Evans, 2007). MT is the basic form of any falsification strategy, including that generally associated with scientific inquiry, whereas AC is the form of a confirmation strategy. The argument forms are also important embodiments of the logical constructs of necessity and sufficiency as they pertain to conditions (O'Brien, Costa, & Overton, 1986). The antecedent of a conditional statement is merely a sufficient condition for the consequent, and the consequent is a necessary condition for the antecedent.

Contemporary methods used in the study of deductive reasoning generally involve *evaluation tasks* where the reasoner must determine whether a given argument or inference is valid, and *inference tasks* where the reasoner must arrive at the appropriate conclusion to draw from a set of premises or must infer some other missing element to a valid argument. With each of these approaches, a crucial instructional manipulation concerns whether the researcher attempts to induce a deductive set in the participant (Evans, 2002; Markovits & Barrouillet, 2002). Instructions that seek to elicit a logical approach to the problem typically require the participant to assume that the premises are true and to draw the conclusion strictly on the basis of the information contained in the argument.

One important paradigm that does not fit neatly into the evaluation/inference dichotomy is the Wason (1983) selection task. In this task, the subject is presented with a rule or hypothesis in the form of a conditional statement for example, "If it is raining, then the street is wet." The participant is shown four cards. One side of each card indicates whether it is raining, whereas the other side indicates whether the street is wet. Thus, the four cards instantiate all four possible combinations of truth values for the antecedent and consequent of the conditional. The task requires that the participant select the card or cards that would have to be turned over to determine whether the rule is being

TABLE 12.2 Variation across Conditionals in the Availability of Alternative Antecedents and Disablers

Conditional	Alternative	Disabler
Many Alternatives and Many Disablers		
If the brake is depressed, then the car slows down.	Uphill.	Brake broken.
If Jenny turns on the air conditioner, then she feels cool.	Took off clothes.	Air conditioner broken.
Many Alternatives and Few Disablers		
If Mary jumps into the pool, then she gets wet.	Rains.	Pool empty.
If water is poured on the campfire, then the fire goes out.	Died out.	Too little water.
Few Alternatives and Many Disablers		
If the ignition key is turned, then the car starts.	Hot wired.	Engine broken.
If the trigger is pulled, then the gun fires.	Faulty design.	No bullets.
Few Alternatives and Few Disablers		
If Larry grasps the glass with his bare hands, then his fingerprints are on it.	Still on from earlier grasp.	Hands not greasy.
If water is heated to 100° C, then it boils.	Already hot.	Not pure water.

(*Note:* Examples of alternative antecedents and disablers represent the most common responses on a generation task from data by De Neys, Schaeken, & D'Ydewalle [2005].)

broken. The correct response is to select the card indicating that "it is raining" (p) and the card indicating that "the street is not wet" (–q). This is the so-called falsification solution because this combination of cards is necessary and sufficient to test the rule.

A number of additional measures of deductive reasoning are not discussed in this introduction, including problem-solving paradigms (Arenberg, 1974; Byrnes & Beilin, 1991) and psychometric measures (Salthouse, 2005a), and there are other content manipulations of interest, including the basic distinction between indicative and deontic content (Cheng & Holyoak, 1985; Noveck & O'Brien, 1996). These variations will be discussed as they come up in the literature review.

DEVELOPMENTAL THEORIES OF DEDUCTIVE REASONING

Mental Logics

The *mental logic* group of theories of deductive reasoning (Braine & O'Brien, 1998a; Inhelder & Piaget, 1958; Overton, 1990; Piaget & Garcia, 1991; Rips, 1994) maintains that the rules that govern operations within classic or standard symbolic logic—either propositional (sentential) logic or first-order predicate logic—are an idealization of the rules that underlie mature human thought (Overton & Dick, 2007). Thus, classical symbolic logic bears a non-arbitrary relation to the psychological processes involved in deductive reasoning. For this reason, symbolic logic, in its essentials, can be profitably employed as a model of the logical competence underlying at least some aspects of formal thought. Mental logic theories do not maintain, however, that any particular rule of symbolic logic constitutes a mental representation in real-time processing on deductive reasoning problems (Overton, 1990, 1991, 2003). The competence model—the mental logic—makes no claims regarding the specific representations or procedures that might engage this competence on any given occasion of reasoning.

It is also recognized by mental logic theorists that verisimilitude to psychological processes was never more than a tacit, implicit motive for the development of classical symbolic logic (Kneale & Kneale, 1962, pp. 406–407). The development of logic is first and foremost an explicit attempt to identify valid forms of argument and to distinguish these from invalid forms (Haack, 1978; p. 5). Consistent with this agenda, there has been an interest in

ensuring that certain metalogical properties hold in standard logic and in developing proof procedures to determine this (O'Brien, 2004; Rips, 1994). In particular, it is important that any statement that is derivable from a set of premises is also entailed by that set (soundness), and that any statement that is entailed by the set is derivable from the set (completeness) (LeBlanc & Wisdom, 1976, pp. 282, 292). This enterprise has certain consequences for standard logic that are not necessarily relevant to the use of the logic as a competence model of deductive reasoning. For this reason, some elements of classic logic are considered largely arbitrary or even counterproductive to the general project of modeling human deductive reasoning (Ricco, 1990, 1993). Certainly the notorious property of standard propositional logic wherein a contradiction or inconsistency entails any statement whatsoever does not, it is hoped, reflect our basic intuitions about the nature of inference. It also seems more profitable to represent the mental logic as a natural deduction system featuring inference rules (Braine, 1978; Piaget & Garcia, 1991), rather than as an axiomatic system.

On occasion, extensions of classical logic such as modal logic and epistemic logic have been used as competence models to directly represent constructs such as necessity and possibility (Pieraut-LeBonniec, 1990). In addition, certain so-called deviant logics, which retain most aspects of the classic systems but reject or modify others, are sometimes proposed as better candidates for a logical competence model of human reasoning. Piaget and Garcia (1991), for example, proposed a revision of the formal operational logic as an entailment or relevance logic (Anderson & Belnap, 1975) to capture the importance of meaningful implications and relevance to human reasoning. In summary, it is important to recognize that proposed mental logics are not, and need not be, isomorphic to any particular formal logic (O'Brien, 1998a; Overton, 1990).

There are three major mental logic accounts of the development of deductive reasoning: Inhelder and Piaget's (1958) combinatorial logic (and its revision as a logic of meanings by Piaget and Garcia [1991]), Overton's (1990) competence-procedural theory, and the natural deduction system of Braine and O'Brien (1998a, 1998b). Overton's theory, which is formulated within the theoretical context of a relational developmental systems perspective (Overton, 2006; Lerner & Overton, 2008), generally adopts Piaget's mental logics as competence models and achieves a kind of rapprochement between mental logic theories and alternative accounts of deductive reasoning. As such, Piaget's theory is discussed in the context of Overton's

Neo-Piagetian account. Another important mental logic theory is that of Rips (1994). However, Rip's theory is largely nondevelopmental and, as such, is not a focus of discussion in this chapter.

Overton's Competence-Procedural Theory

The competence-procedural theory of Overton and colleagues (e.g., Byrnes & Overton, 1986, 1988; Chapell & Overton, 2002; Foltz, Overton, & Ricco, 1995; Müller, Overton, & Reene, 2001; Müller, Sokol, & Overton, 1999; O'Brien & Overton, 1980, 1982; Overton & Dick, 2007; Overton, Ward, Noveck, Black, & O'Brien, 1987; Pollack, Overton, Rosenfeld, & Rosenfeld, 1995; Takahashi & Overton, 1996; Ward & Overton, 1990) holds strongly to the fundamental distinction between the competence to reason logically and the individual's actual performance on a particular task and occasion, the latter being subject to a wide range of influences, any of which could support or hinder the underlying competence. This distinction is essential because the two systems serve different functions or goals. The competence system is concerned with understanding or knowing, whereas the procedural system makes success possible on particular problems (Overton, 1990; Overton & Dick, 2007). Performance or procedural factors cannot substitute for competence, and the latter cannot be reduced to some set of procedures. The competence system for formal reasoning in Overton's account is assumed to consist of a mental logic that resembles standard propositional logic. In particular, the combinatorial logic (INRC group) of Inhelder and Piaget (1958) along with its revision as an entailment logic or logic of meanings (Piaget & Garcia, 1991, pp. 141–158) have been proposed by the Overton group as reasonable candidates for the competence model (Overton, 1990; Ricco, 1993).

One potential advantage of the Piagetian propositional logic as a competence model is that it can be derived from a more fundamental logic of classes and relations, and as such, it comprises part of a theoretically viable account of the emergence of deductive reasoning from earlier, more limited, logical competencies. In fact, Piaget's logical competence model is unique in this regard. The derivation of Piaget's propositional logic involves, in part, an expansion of the scope of negation in the class and relational logics (Byrnes, 1988; Byrnes & Overton, 1988; Müller et al., 1999; Piaget, 2001), and the emergence of formal deductive competence from an earlier, concrete competence can be represented as a process of increasing flexibility in the use of partial or local negations leading to the differentiation and coordination of two forms of negation—one bounded and the other unbounded (Byrnes, 1988; Piaget, 1980, pp. 297–299; Piaget & Garcia, 1991, p. 164). This theoretical claim has been supported empirically. Müller et al. (1999) provide evidence that the a priori ordering of logic problems in terms of their complexity with regard to the role of negation corresponds to a developmental progression.

An account of the development of deductive reasoning that stresses its origins in class reasoning is central to the competence-procedural theory and can explain a number of developmental effects concerning deductive reasoning. For that reason, it is worth more detailed discussion. We can consider *implication,* or the conditional, in terms of class relations (Byrnes, 1988; Müller et al., 1999). Given the implication "if p, then q" (e.g., "If something is a rose, then it is a flower."), we may refer to the extension of the antecedent as the set P (roses) and the extension of the consequent as the set Q (flowers). The implication asserts that P is nested within Q (roses are a type of flower). When the antecedent p is negated, there are two possible states of affairs that might obtain. These are [–p and q] (something that is not a rose, but is a flower) and [–p and –q] (something that is neither a rose nor a flower). In terms of the extensions, then, the negation of the antecedent p can denote an affirmation of a set P′, which is the complement of P with respect to Q (all flowers that are not roses), *or* an affirmation of the set Q′, which is the complement of Q (all things that are not flowers). Negation has two different senses here: one relatively more constrained, bounded, or narrower in scope (the set P′); and the other relatively unconstrained or unbounded (the set Q′).

Class logics, such as the groupings that Piaget proposes as competence models of reasoning in middle childhood (Inhelder & Piaget, 1964), can represent bounded or partial negations. The negation of a class A (e.g., roses) within a hierarchical classificatory system is partial because it is equivalent to the affirmation of the complementary class (A′; other flowers) under the nearest superordinate (B; flowers). Partial negations are signifying negations because they affirm and delimit (Piaget & Garcia, 1991). Full, unbounded, or nonsignifying negation (e.g., all nonflowers) cannot be directly represented within the groupings, though it can be approximated by expanding the reference frame for negation beyond the immediate superordinate (e.g., by abstracting from the class of flowers to the class of plants) (Müller et al., 1999). In the competence-procedural account, experience with class relations yields increasing flexibility with regard to several operations including the decomposition of classes into alternative sets of subclasses

$B = A_1 + A_1'$, $B = A_2 + A_2'$, etc.; The class of flowers consists of all roses and all flowers that are not roses OR all tulips and all flowers that are not tulips, etc.), the inclusion of primary classes (A_1; e.g., roses) in the complement of other primary classes (A_2'; e.g., flowers that are not tulips), comparison of the extensions of alternative secondary classes (A_1' vs. A_2'; nonrose flowers vs. nontulip flowers), and the addition and subtraction of classes at different levels of a hierarchy. This flexibility tends toward an understanding of relatively unbounded negation and eventually to its coordination with bounded negation (Piaget, 2001).

Before the differentiation and coordination of bounded and unbounded negation, the child is likely to conflate the two possibilities for the denial of the antecedent in conditional argument, namely, [–p and q] and [–p and –q]. Such a conflation amounts to an interpretation of the conditional as a biconditional (p if and only if q). This conflation is, indeed, significantly more common in childhood than in adolescence (Byrnes, 1988; Overton, 1990; Overton et al., 1987). The account of the emergence of conditional reasoning from class reasoning also predicts that this conflation should go hand in hand with a fundamental difficulty in generating alternative antecedents for the consequent q. That is, not only should children be more likely than adolescents to interpret conditionals as biconditionals, they should also be less likely to generate alternatives to p that could obtain along with q. Again, this prediction is substantially supported in the literature (Daniel & Klaczynski, 2006; Janveau-Brennan & Markovits, 1999; Markovits & Barrouillet, 2002). For the competence-procedural account, then, the primary restriction on the range of possibilities that the child can generate in reasoning about conditional arguments is a logical one—difficulty in appreciating that the truth of the conditional is consistent with situations where the consequent obtains despite the absence of the antecedent.

Reasoning for both Piaget and Overton is intentional, goal-directed, and involves some manner of organization or coordination across inferences. Any given inferential act by the child assumes and implicates various other inferences that are part of the competence, though not manifest in performance on this occasion (Markovits, 2004; Müller et al., 2001; Piaget, 1986). Any attempt to analyze inferences in isolation represents a reduction of competence to procedure. Claims of *reductionism*, therefore, are central to critiques by competence-procedural theorists of evidence of early deductive reasoning competence from within domain-specific theories, mental model theories,

and other accounts (Overton, 1990, 2006; Overton & Dick, 2007). Research based in these theoretical perspectives is discussed later, but one set of findings frequently referenced as evidence of early competence concerns the use of fantasy settings or instructional sets to dissuade empirical, nonlogical approaches to deduction problems. These studies are purported to provide evidence of deductive reasoning in preschool or the early school years (Dias and Harris, 1988, 1990; Hawkins, Pea, Glick, & Scribner, 1984; Kuhn, 1977; Leevers & Harris, 1999). Early success across these studies, however, is generally limited to a few isolated inference forms such as MP or valid syllogisms. Similar levels of success with indeterminate argument forms (e.g., AC or DA) is only occasionally found (Markovits, Schleifer, & Fortier, 1989; Markovits et al., 1996). From the competence perspective, therefore, such evidence of early reasoning is necessarily suspect insofar as it is limited to success with a particular type of inference in the absence of success on other, logically related inferences.

In addition, evidence of early-onset deductive inferences that are relatively automatic and nonintentional in nature is also suspect from the perspective of competence-procedural theory. Inferences resembling deductions are common in language comprehension processes, for example, and are embedded in domain-specific or modular forms of cognition (Braine, 1978; Braine & O'Brien, 1998a). As such, even young children show evidence of such inferences. As part of domain-specific processing, however, these inferences are not subject to reflection, and young children generally fail to demonstrate an understanding of their deductive nature (Moshman, 1990, 2004; Moshman & Franks, 1986).

Initial research from within the competence-procedural perspective suggested that formal deductive reasoning was not available before twelfth grade (O'Brien & Overton, 1980, 1982; Overton, Byrnes, & O'Brien, 1985). However, this was based, in large part, on a demanding conditional inference task requiring participants to determine whether a given minor premise and conclusion of a conditional argument were sufficient to fill in the missing antecedent of the major premise (conditional rule). This task format appears to require additional processing steps when compared with the selection task or with conditional reasoning tasks that merely require participants to infer or evaluate conclusions to conditional arguments. A similarly late age of acquisition for deductive competence has been obtained using the selection task when low-socioeconomic status (SES) samples were used (Chapell & Overton, 2002).

More recent findings by Overton's research group suggest an earlier emergence of deductive competence. There is some indication that an understanding of logical uncertainty, that is, indeterminacy, in the context of formal implication and an ability to appreciate relations of equivalence and nonequivalence among propositional forms may be emerging as early as fifth grade (Byrnes & Overton, 1986, 1988). However, the most consistent pattern evident in Overton's findings, particularly on versions of the selection task, is that formal reasoning competence is lacking in fourth through sixth grades, coming online in eighth/ninth grade, and readily available in tenth to twelfth grades (Chapell & Overton, 1998; Foltz et al., 1995; Overton et al., 1987; Ward & Overton, 1990). This pattern is not limited to cross-sectional comparisons. It has been corroborated with longitudinal research as well (Müller et al., 2001).

The preceding developmental pattern is also indirectly supported by findings regarding training effects and the role of moderator variables. Interventions such as contradictory training, meant to discourage invited inferences on indeterminate problems, are beneficial, but only for ages at which prior research suggests the competence is typically present (Overton et al., 1985). At the same time, older adolescents are less likely than younger ones to need cues and assistance, presumably because the competence is more intact (Müller et al., 2001). Moderator variables, such as SES and instructional set, have more relevance at ages where deductive competence is typically emerging or present. Thus, success on the selection task is more suppressed in low SES samples for tenth and twelfth graders than it is for sixth graders (Chapell & Overton, 2002). Explicit instructions to maintain a deductive set by assuming the truth of the premises, accepting only logically necessary conclusions, or working merely with the information contained in the problem, improves performance on conditional reasoning problems for adolescents (e.g., 13 and 16 years of age) but generally not, or less so, for preadolescents (e.g., 10 years) (Daniel & Klaczynski, 2006).

The competence-procedural account provides plausible explanations for a variety of *content* effects. Importantly, most of these explanations are a priori rather than post hoc. Familiar content, meaningful content, and increased relevance of antecedent to consequent facilitate performance on deductive reasoning problems, but only subsequent to the availability of the logical competence (Müller et al., 2001; Overton et al., 1987; Ward & Overton, 1990), and the greatest degree of variability in performance across content is found during periods of competence consolidation (Overton et al., 1987). Abstract content is problematic

at all ages, but improvement is clearly evident from eighth through twelfth grades (Overton et al., 1987; see also Markovits & Vachon, 1990). Findings of this sort make it difficult to argue that success on deductive reasoning tasks is strictly a function of domain-specific processes (Cheng & Holyoak, 1985). Familiarity, relevance, and other aspects of content that would be expected to maximize the efficiency of processing in working memory support the application of an *existing* logical competence. Those same processes, however, are ineffective in the absence of that competence.

The pitting of one content effect against another has also provided support for a competence account. Specifically, the perceived relevance of consequent to antecedent is a better predictor of conditional reasoning performance than mere familiarity of content, and a meaningful connection between antecedent and consequent enhances performance even in the absence of familiarity (Ward, Byrnes, & Overton, 1990). This finding is consistent with the competence-procedural account because it suggests that domain-specific processes responsible for familiarity effects are not sufficient for success on conditional reasoning problems and are secondary in importance to organizational processes in working memory. This result is to be expected from within a competence-procedural account because real-time organizations such as a semantic connection between antecedent and consequent provide optimal conditions for the application of a logical competence (Ricco, 1990; Ward et al., 1990; Ward & Overton, 1990). This is because the latter is, itself, organizational in nature. By contrast, although familiarity should generally support access to a logical competence, it could also elicit local or domain-specific inferences of a nondeductive nature (Cummins, 1996; Harris & Nunez, 1996).

The competence-procedural theory is also able to account for the emergence, in middle childhood, of various concrete precursors to formal deductive competence. These include an appreciation of *logical indeterminacy* and the *logic of falsification* within concrete, problem-solving settings (Byrnes & Overton, 1986; Ricco, 1997). A logical competence based in class reasoning should be sufficient for success in this regard. Representing the set of viable alternatives on an indeterminate problem in terms of an equivalence class would provide a basis for regarding them as equally viable despite the presence of various arbitrary features that might otherwise be used by the child to attach a greater likelihood to one alternative rather than another (Byrnes & Beilin, 1991). Consideration of alternatives from within the logical construct of an equivalence class would also promote an appreciation of the epistemic legitimacy of uncertainty, that is, an appreciation that uncertainty is a necessary and irreducible state within logical relations. Consistent with this claim, children do not show clear evidence of an appreciation of the irreducibility of uncertainty on indeterminate problems before 8 or 9 years (Byrnes & Overton, 1986; Horobin & Acredolo, 1989; Ricco, McCollum, & Wang, 1997)—the age at which success on class reasoning problems is initially found—and possibly not until 11 or 12 years (Acredolo & Horobin, 1987; Scholnick & Wing, 1988). Evidence of earlier success on indeterminate problems (Fabricius, Sophian, & Wellman, 1987; Rai & Mitchell, 2006; Sodian & Wimmer, 1987; Sodian, Zaitchik, & Carey, 1991; Sommerville, Hadkinson, & Greenberg, 1979; Wollman, Eylon, & Lawson, 1979) is not accompanied by evidence that indeterminacy can be maintained in the face of task-based and internally based cues to close prematurely on problem solutions.

Similar results obtain in regard to a concrete understanding of falsification. Appreciating that a falsification strategy is the only basis for solving proof construction problems in the minimal number of moves is absent before 8 or 9 years of age (Ricco, 1997), and the capacity to *generate* conclusive tests of concrete hypotheses including a *search* for disconfirming or falsifying evidence is rarely found earlier than 8 years (Chen & Daehler, 1989; Chen & Klahr, 1999).

Overton (2006) has presented a broad relational metatheory designed to overcome many of the classic dualisms in psychology and, thus, form the basis for a rapprochement among seemingly competing theories (e.g., see Overton & Ennis, 2006). The competence-procedural theory of deductive reasoning illustrates this relational approach and affords a promising basis for rapprochement among the theories discussed in this chapter. From the standpoint of a competence account, theories of deductive reasoning that do not include a logical competence model (mental logic) are essentially procedural theories that, to varying degrees, accomplish one or both of the following. First, all of these theories serve to work out important components of the real-time processing involved in deductive reasoning (Cosmides & Tooby, 1992, 1994; Cummins, 1996; Girotto, Light, & Colbourn, 1988; Markovits & Barrouillet, 2002) and, in this capacity, are complementary to, and potentially compatible with, competence theories. Second, some of these theories include aspects of logical competence in a procedural form. As long as the reductionism is strictly avoided, research grounded in these theories could be interpreted as identifying important indicators,

manifestations, or direct consequences of an emergent logical competence. The prime example here is research into the development of conceptual knowledge about logic (metalogical knowledge) in the metacognitive theories of Kuhn (Kuhn & Franklin, 2006) and Moshman (1990, 2004).

Braine and O'Brien's Natural Deduction System

Another key mental logic theory that differs in several respects from the theories of Overton and Piaget features, as its competence model, a natural deduction system, the core of which consists of a set of basic inference schemas adapted from those proposed by Gentzen (1964) for standard propositional logic. These schemas license the elimination or introduction of logical operators into an expression. They provide the basis for substituting some proposition for one or more other propositions. For example, given that "there is a D or a T" and "there is not a D," a schema for the elimination of disjunction allows the inference to "there is a T" (Braine & O'Brien, 1998a, p. 80). MP can be construed as a rule for the elimination of the conditional, and it represents another basic inference schema in the logic. Complementing the basic schemas is a direct reasoning routine containing procedures for applying the schemas in lines of reasoning (Braine, 1990). For example, one such procedure ensures that any propositions derived by applying the basic schemas will be added to the premise set for all future derivations. These procedures are minimally effortful, and both the basic schemas and the direct reasoning routine are claimed to be significantly innate or automatized at an early point in development (Markovits, 2004). The system operates on propositional structures that comprise a syntax or logic of thought (Braine & O'Brien, 1998b; O'Brien, 2004).

Like other mental logic theories, the natural deduction system of Braine and O'Brien differs in many ways from standard symbolic logic. In fact, it is not a logic per se, but a set of independent schemas and procedures (Braine & O'Brien, 1998a, 1998b; Markovits, 2004; Overton & Dick, 2007). There is no notion of the structure d'ensemble so central to the competence-procedural account. Furthermore, some of the schemas have no equivalent in formal logic because they are based in observations of how logical connectives naturally function in thinking and in language (Braine & O'Brien, 1998b). The basic schemas purportedly provide definitions of the natural meanings of logical connectives. Another major departure from both formal logic and other mental logic theories is that the notion of validity is downplayed and is not considered to be a salient consideration in human reasoning (O'Brien, 1998b).

The inference schemas selected by Braine and O'Brien as basic or primary components of their natural deduction system are arrived at empirically; they are supposedly among the most common of inferences involved in discourse comprehension and in the integration of information across time (Braine, 1990). The basic inference schemas and direct reasoning routines are supplemented by a set of complex schemas or indirect reasoning strategies that are not innate or universal, and that are particularly dependent on formal tuition and related experiences (Braine & O'Brien, 1998a; O'Brien, 2004). Thus, the theory presents a kind of dualism with respect to logical thinking. The basic or primary schemas are used automatically when the appropriate propositions are encountered. Given its automaticity, it would be inappropriate to consider this process to involve the "drawing" of a "conclusion" from some set of "premises," because this latter characterization implies conscious, deliberate, effortful thinking. By contrast, the complex or secondary inference schemas are used only under special conditions and are strategic, deliberative, and intentional. The complex schemas include MT and the reductio ad absurdum. The latter is a suppositional argument strategy that involves demonstrating the falsehood of a proposition by showing that a contradiction follows from its supposition. For example, to prove that my daughter must have cleaned up her room, I might suppose that she did not clean it. If I can show that, in such a case, her mom would be unhappy, whereas, in fact, her mom is happy, then I can conclude that my daughter cleaned her room (Leblanc & Wisdom, 1976, p. 83). Interestingly, other suppositional procedures are treated by Braine and O'Brien as basic schemas. They are not regarded as complex, secondary schemas. These include conditional supposition that authorizes the assertion of the conditional (if p, then q) if the consequent q can be derived with the aid of the antecedent p (O'Brien, 2004).

There is also an *interpretive* component of the theory that is essentially an account of the language comprehension processes that provide input to the reasoning programs, with specific focus on pragmatic factors that might influence comprehension (Braine, 1990; O'Brien, 1998a). Interpretive processes, therefore, become the origin and basis for any "extralogical" processes involved in reasoning. The interpretive component operates, at times, as a theory of performance because it is sometimes invoked to account for occasions of departure from the straightforward application of the schemas and reasoning programs of the logical competence model.

Language comprehension processes play a critical role in determining the specific propositions, connectives (e.g., "or" "and"), and inference forms that become input for the mental logic. An initial level of interpretation assesses the goal of the problem and initiates one of two stances accordingly: natural or analytic (Braine, 1990; Markovits, 2004). The natural stance allows for the use of existing real-world knowledge to supplement the literal or propositional content of language expressions, whereas the analytic stance mandates limiting oneself to the strict content of the premises and reasoning on the basis of that information along with the syntactic properties of the argument. Instructions that convey a deductive set would invoke the analytic stance (Daniel & Klaczynski, 2006; Evans, 2002). Subsequent levels of interpretation involve a search for conversational implicatures (Adler, 2008) in accordance with the cooperative principle—the basic notion that the speaker is attempting to be truthful, relevant, and clear. Interpretive processes also consider the appropriateness of invited inferences. For example, although the logical disjunctive "either p or q" permits both p and q, it invites the inference "only one or the other." Also, the conditional "if p, then q" invites the inference "if not p, then not q" (Braine, 1990). The theory does not always make clear predictions on the basis of the interpretive component; for example, should tendencies to interpret conditionals ('If… then') as biconditionals (i.e., 'if and only if') increase or decrease across childhood. On the one hand, we might expect that cumulative experience would yield increasing knowledge of situations where it is important to avoid such an invited inference, whereas on the other hand, age should be accompanied by an increasing ability to appreciate the subtle linguistic and situational cues legitimating such inferences.

The mental logic of Braine and O'Brien finds substantial support in several respects. There is little dispute at this point that problems tapping into the basic inference schemas of the theory are generally easier or more effortlessly engaged than problems that tap into the secondary or complex schemas. In addition, findings support predictions about the order in which the schemas might be invoked in real-time processing, and problems requiring combinations of schemas are perceived to be more difficult than problems requiring individual schemas (O'Brien, 1998b, 2004). A potential strength of the theory is its interpretive component based in the pragmatics of ordinary language usage. If further developed, this aspect of the theory could deliver on Grice's (1989) project of defending the role of a mental logic in ordinary cognition by complementing it with a pragmatic logic of conversation (Grice, 1975).

At the same time, some of the theory's successes point to its limitations as a theory of deductive reasoning competence. The bulk of the theory's utility has been in explaining relatively automatic and isolated inferences such as might be involved in language comprehension. Several other theories of deductive reasoning dispute whether inferences of this kind constitute reasoning per se (Kuhn & Franklin, 2006; Moshman, 2004; Overton, 1990). Another concern is that the quasi-empirical process used to select inference schemas for the natural deduction system leads to some degree of arbitrariness. For example, why are certain suppositional schemas considered to be basic or primary inferences, whereas other forms of supposition are treated as complex, secondary, or indirect inferences? Finally, it should be noted that various findings indicate that reasoners can self-report, with considerable specificity, regarding the basic inference schemas they are employing on problems (O'Brien, 1998b). This seems to contradict claims that the basic schemas are relatively automatic and distinct from the secondary schemas.

Domain-Specific Accounts

Some models of deductive reasoning have attempted to explain age-related differences in performance on conditional and syllogism tasks in terms of domain-specific factors. Early attempts to reduce deductive reasoning to a purely content-driven process predicted that the availability of relevant experiences and knowledge in long-term memory within the same domain as the reasoning problem would promote success (Griggs & Cox, 1982; Reich & Ruth, 1982). However, familiarity of content, degree of expertise within a content domain, and even the availability of experiences representing counterexamples to an argument do not always, or simply, facilitate performance or allow prediction of age-related effects (Cheng & Holyoak, 1985; Manktelow & Evans, 1979).

More successful approaches within the domain-specific paradigm have proposed that deductive reasoning reduces to the application of pragmatic or deontic schemas rather than domain-general inference rules (Cheng & Holyoak, 1985; Girotto, Blaye, & Farioli, 1989). These schemas include permission and obligation rules. The *permission* schema interprets a conditional statement as asserting that a specified action can only be performed if a certain precondition is met. Thus, rather than asserting a specific relation between the truth-status of the antecedent and the

consequent, the conditional statement, "If a person is driving a motor vehicle, then the person must be over 16," could be interpreted as indicating, simply, a condition under which someone is or is not permitted to undertake an action. The *obligation* schema interprets a conditional as asserting that a specific action must be undertaken when a certain condition holds. Conditionals that lend themselves to such interpretations typically use modal terms representing necessity (must) or possibility (may, can). Pragmatic schemas have been alleged, by some, to have an innate basis because of their importance to interpersonal success across a range of typical interactions within human societies (Cummins, 1996). On the other hand, the schemas may be largely acquired through experience in social exchange and related settings (Cheng & Holyoak, 1985).

It has been shown in some research that children and adults are better at finding cases of individual violators (cheaters) of pragmatic rules than they are at finding cases that falsify indicative rules or that represent counterexamples to arguments (Cosmides & Tooby, 1992, 1994; Cummins, 1996; Girotto, Light, & Colbourn, 1988). Even preschool children can successfully apply a violation detection strategy on deontic content when they are still using confirmation strategies on indicative content (Cummins, 1996; Harris & Nunez, 1996). This allows for precocious performance on deductive reasoning problems when these can be presented as pragmatic or deontic problems. The salience of pragmatic schemas to children is apparent from findings that early competence is evident with relatively abstract permission rules. Thus, even when the pragmatic rule is unfamiliar to the child (Girotto, Gilly, Blaye, & Light, 1989; Girotto et al., 1988, 1989), we see success in 9- or 10-year-olds as long as a rationale for the relation in the rule can be constructed by the child.

Results such as the ones just discussed make it clear that pragmatic schemas, in some form, are available to children and adults alike. They do not demonstrate, however, that logical competence is irrelevant to reasoning with deontic content conditionals, and they do not show that pragmatic schemas are invoked, routinely, in reasoning about indicative conditionals. In addition, results for the obligation schema are generally not as consistent as those for the permission schema (Noveck & O'Brien, 1996), making it dubious that the construct of pragmatic schemas is any broader in scope than that of permission rules per se. Also, the superior performance for pragmatic or deontic content found by Cheng and Holyoak (1985) in their original studies does not always obtain (Klaczynski et al., 2004), and, in a recent replication, was attributed to factors other than the rule content per se. These factors included task features such as the role-playing set, the explicit marking of negation, and the type of inference required (i.e., reasoning *from* the conditional as contrasted with reasoning *to* the conditional; Noveck & O'Brien, 1996). The results of training studies also suggest limitations in schema theory as a general account of deductive reasoning. In particular, training transfer from permission content to arbitrary content is not as effective as transfer from causal content to arbitrary content or from arbitrary to causal. This suggests that domain-general rules or operations are accessed by training on arbitrary or causal conditionals but not on permission conditionals. The latter content does not appear to elicit or access domain-general rules as readily (Klaczynski, 1993).

Markovits's Developmental Revision of Mental Models Theory

Markovits and colleagues (e.g., Barrouillet, Markovits, & Quinn, 2002; Janveau-Brennan & Markovits, 1999; Markovits, 2000, 2004; Markovits & Barrouillet, 2002; Markovits, Fleury, Quinn, & Venet, 1998; Markovits et al., 1989; Venet & Markovits, 2001) have extended *mental models theory* into a genuinely developmental account of deductive reasoning whereas modifying some aspects of the parent theory. Markovits's theory seeks to improve on the predictive accuracy of mental logic theories by developing a sophisticated account of the encoding processes involved in conditional reasoning. Two important claims of Markovits's account are, first, that deductive reasoning involves the same basic mental processes and competencies at all ages or levels of development, and second, that deductive processes do not draw on any set of mental rules akin to those of formal logic.

Mental models theory maintains that the cognitive representations with which lay deductive reasoning proceeds are semantic, rather than syntactic (Johnson-Laird, 2008). In this view, the cognitive processes used by children and adults when engaged in deductive reasoning are not related to the rules of formal logic. Syntax is presumably involved only at the linguistic level where the grammatical structure of premises must be interpreted. A mental model is a real-time representation of possible states of affairs denoted by the premises of an argument (Markovits, 2004). Tokens represent these possible states of affairs. Using Markovits' notation (Markovits & Barrouillet, 2002), the major premise (if p, then q) in a conditional argument would be represented as follows where "—" stands for the relation denoted by "if…then."

$$p — q$$

Consider our earlier example of a conditional: "If it is raining (p), then the street is wet (q)." The p term represents one possible object or event (it is raining) from among many (e.g., it is a clear day, the street is being cleaned, someone is washing their car, etc.). The q term, in Markovits's account, represents a simple dichotomy consisting of the possibility that q is affirmed (the street is wet) and the possibility that q is denied (the street is dry). This representation then opens onto a conceptual space consisting of three distinct classes of objects or events (Markovits, 2004; Markovits & Barrouillet, 2002). One class consists of possibilities that are *complementary* to the conditional. These are cases where something other than p is combined with the denial of q (e.g., it is a clear day and the street is dry). A second class comprises *alternatives* to the antecedent. These are cases involving objects or events that are different from p and where q is affirmed (e.g., the street is being cleaned and the street is wet). In other words, these are alternative ways in which q is realized. The third class comprising this conceptual space consists of *disablers* of the conditional in the major premise. Disablers represent conditions (e.g., the street is covered with a tarp) that, when paired with p, render the conditional false. Disablers qualify the applicability of the conditional and must be suppressed or bracketed for the rule to hold.

Once a minor premise is added to the problem, any of these three classes may or may not be activated, and the degree of activation can vary depending on a host of factors (Markovits, Doyon, & Simoneau, 2002; Markovits & Vachon, 1990; Simoneau & Markovits, 2003). The familiarity or novelty of the problem content, the availability of alternative antecedents or of disabling conditions, the degree of relatedness of antecedent and consequent, and constraints pertaining to speed of processing, amount of information to be retrieved, and the capacity of short-term store in working memory (see Demetriou, Mouyi, & Spanoudis, Chapter 10 of this volume) can all determine whether, and to what degree, a given class of object/event is activated (Markovits & Barrouillet, 2002). The resulting pattern of activation, in turn, determines the mental models that will be generated. Additional considerations enter at this point—primarily, the number of models that can be accommodated by working memory and the availability of inhibitory processes that can block specific models in compliance with the demands of the task (Markovits, 2004).

If the sole class activated in the conceptual space consists of cases where something other than p is combined with the denial of q (e.g., it is a clear day and the street is dry), then the mental models generated will consist merely of the affirmation of the major premise (p — q) and the complementary of the conditional.

$$p — q$$
$$a — not\text{-}q$$

Here, "a" represents something (e.g., it is a clear day) other than p. Where these mental models prevail, it is likely that the child will demonstrate the classic biconditional pattern of responding to the conditional arguments. In contrast, if the class of alternatives to p (call any of these "b") should be activated, providing alternative ways in which q can be realized (e.g., the street is being cleaned, someone is washing their car), then an important model is generated allowing for an appreciation that AC and DA are uncertain.

$$p — q$$
$$b — q$$

This is because pairings of the consequent with alternative antecedents alerts the individual to the indeterminacy of these argument forms. If disabling conditions (d) (e.g., the street is covered with a tarp) are activated, then at least the following two models will be represented, making it likely that the child will indicate that MP is uncertain.

$$p — q$$
$$p.d — not\text{-}q$$

A critical characteristic of mental models is that not all possibilities are initially represented because there is an overriding concern to minimize cognitive load. Additional states or models (e.g., those other than p — q) can be fleshed out according to the properties of the logical connectives involved. However, in Markovits's account, any additional models result from the activation pattern in the conceptual space. The fleshing-out process is thus an *automatic* one in Markovits's theory (Markovits, 2004; Markovits & Barrouillet, 2002). This represents a key distinction between the developmental theory and the parent theory. The Johnson-Laird (2008) formulation of mental models theory, which has been widely applied in the adult literature on deductive reasoning, involves active searches for counterexamples, that is, cases where the premises are true and the conclusion false.

By accounting for a myriad of content and context effects on an a priori basis, Markovits's adaptation of mental models theory provides a plausible way to reconcile findings of early success in deductive reasoning with evidence of substantial non-normative responding among adolescents and adults. Some highlights in this regard are discussed here, but for a thorough treatment, see Markovits and Barrouillet (2002).

Like the natural deduction theory of Brain and O'Brien, Markovits's theory readily explains the fact that MP is the inference form associated with the most success among young children, as well as findings that MT is more difficult at these ages. From a mental models perspective, the representation of MP requires only a single mental model (p — q; e.g., it is raining and the street is wet), whereas MT requires two models (p — q and a — not-q; e.g., it is raining and the street is wet AND it is a clear day and the street is dry) and places greater demands on young children's limited working memory capacity. At the same time, the theory predicts the counterintuitive finding that MP inferences decline or show greater variability across contexts as children get older, particularly under instructional sets that do not make explicit a need to work exclusively with the information provided in the premises (Janveau-Brennan & Markovits, 1999; Markovits et al., 1998). This trend would be expected if the expansion of various knowledge bases with age increases both the likelihood that disablers will be activated and the variety of factors that can trigger disabling conditions. Indeed, we generally do not find sensitivity to disabling conditions or a tendency to withhold acceptance of MP before second or third grade (Janveau-Brennan & Markovits, 1999).

Another set of findings readily addressed by the theory concerns the relatively precocious performance of children on conditionals expressing class relations. Class-based conditionals (e.g., "If something is a rose, then it is a flower") lead to earlier success than causal conditionals ("If it is raining, then the street is wet"), and there is evidence that 7- to 8-year-olds produce uncertainty responses (Markovits et al., 1996) to the indeterminate argument forms when class relations are involved. By contrast, Janveau-Brennan and Markovits (1999) found only limited success on AC for causal conditionals in second or third grade. In addition, success on DA was delayed until fifth or sixth grade on causal conditionals, and certainty responses were still more common than uncertainty responses for those grades. Also, content factors that affect availability of alternative antecedents influence responding on *class-based* conditionals for young children. That is, success on the indeterminate argument forms is a function of the ease with which children can think of alternative antecedents on conditionals such as "If something is a rose, then it is a flower." By contrast, the availability of alternative antecedents is more likely to affect responding on *causal* conditionals for adolescents and adults (Markovits, 2000; Markovits et al., 1998; Quinn & Markovits, 1998). The greater difficulty of causal conditionals compared with class-based conditionals and the earlier evidence of success with the latter can be explained within a mental models account by the fact that class-based conditionals map more directly onto semantic and conceptual relations in long-term memory. Interestingly, competence-procedural theory also predicts some precocity on class-based conditionals because of their amenability to representation within the class-based logic that precedes the propositional logic of formal deductive competence.

Perhaps mental models theory's most significant strength is its capacity to make specific predictions about the ages and conditions for which success might be expected on the indeterminate forms (AC and DA) of conditional argument. According to the theory, early success on the indeterminate forms would be expected when problem content and child knowledge are such that alternative antecedents are readily activated, minimizing early limitations in retrieval processes and processing capacity. At the same time, success rates should be low, even among adolescents, when problem content does not favor retrieval of alternatives. In support of this prediction, the likelihood of responding with uncertainty to AC and DA is associated with the number of alternative antecedents children and adolescents produce (Janveau-Brennan & Markovits, 1999; Markovits, 2000), and the age of success on the indeterminate forms depends on the ease with which alternative antecedents can be generated (Markovits et al., 1996).

The theory also sheds light on findings that there are more uncertainty responses to AC and DA when there is a weak relation or association between antecedent and consequent (Quinn & Markovits, 1998). Evidently, such conditionals readily activate alternative antecedents for which the consequent also holds. This effect lessens across the adolescent years, suggesting that older adolescents are better at generating alternative antecedents under conditions of minimal support, that is, where there is less information in long-term memory or less real-world content that might yield concrete alternatives (Barrouillet, Markovits, & Quinn, 2002; Markovits et al., 1998). Although the weakening of this effect with age is

also consistent with competence-procedural theory, the preferred explanation from within mental models theory is that older children, fifth and sixth grade, have more flexible retrieval of information relevant to the problem than second and third graders (Markovits et al., 1998). Mental models theory has also provided evidence for the increasing role of inhibitory mechanisms with age in the suppression of disabling conditions and other products of automatic retrieval processes when deductive instructional sets call for such suppression. Inhibitory processes have been particularly associated with arguments that feature a logic-belief incongruity (Handley, Capon, Beveridge, Dennis, & Evans, 2004).

It is clear from the available evidence that situating performance on deductive reasoning tasks within a sophisticated account of the development of encoding processes, retrieval processes, and inhibitory mechanisms makes possible accurate predictions of the extent to which alternative, specifically indeterminate models will be generated leading to responses of uncertainty on the various argument forms. Overall, Markovits's model is able to account for a wide range of findings from both the developmental and adult literatures on conditional reasoning. At the same time, the theory seems best suited to explaining deductive reasoning with nonabstract, meaningful content problems. This is because concrete content allows, in principle, for activation of information in long-term memory and, therefore, construction of the three sets of potential models. Genuinely abstract content, that is, content whose semantic interpretation is wholly arbitrary ("If rems are full, then braks are soft," "If there is a vowel on one side, then there is an odd number on the other.") is problematic for the theory because it provides no obvious basis for the activation of information in long-term memory. Consequently, we might expect that for abstract content, the tripartite conceptual space and the set of mental models derived from this space would be impoverished to the point that they would support only the biconditional interpretation. Yet, clearly, some individuals, including adolescents, can reason successfully with more abstract content. Furthermore, success on abstract content increases across the adolescent years (Markovits & Vachon, 1990).

Markovits suggests that success on abstract problems might result from some manner of structure mapping based in analogies between the abstract relation in the conditional and similar relations manifest in schematic structures in long-term memory (Markovits & Barrouillet, 2002). It is difficult to see, however, what the nature of such analogies might be. Nonetheless, Venet and Markovits (2001) have shown that abstract reasoning is more readily facilitated by realistic contexts than by fantasy contexts, as might be expected if the analog explanation is correct. It is also suggested in recent accounts of the theory that metacognitive processes might lead to self-reflection with regard to reasoning processes, resulting in a more formal representation of the inferential process or a redescription of tokens from concrete to abstract, together with some manner of monitoring and conscious control over the fleshing out process. Each of these developments could support reasoning with abstract content. However, the addition of these explanatory principles to the theory seems somewhat ad hoc and has the potential to fundamentally alter the nature of the theory. As Markovits himself notes (Markovits & Barrouillet, 2002), the distinction between more automatic activation based in semantic networks in long-term memory, as favored by his theory, and a deliberate process of search, such as might be important with abstract content, is similar to the distinction between heuristic and analytical processing within a dual-process model of cognition (Evans, 2002). Recent findings indeed suggest that the fleshing out of mental models is more effortful and less automatic than Markovits's theory has typically claimed. DeNeys, Schaeken, and d'Ydewalle (2005) demonstrate that retrieval of counterexamples on indeterminate conditional arguments is impeded when participants must perform a second task that places demands on attentional resources, thus implicating an executive component of working memory. Clearly, then, an interesting area of revision for the theory concerns possible modifications in response to findings regarding abstract content.

However, from a competence-procedural perspective, the difficulty in accounting for results with abstract content is symptomatic of a deeper problem with the mental models approach. That problem is the absence of a competence model. By exclusively focusing on real-time psychological processes and their development, whether domain general (improvements in retrieval, increases in working memory capacity and efficiency) or domain specific (expansion of a knowledge base), the theory provides the best currently available account of the conditions under which an existent logical competence might be manifest on a deductive reasoning task. However, it provides little basis for explaining the development of that logical competence per se. The retrieval of alternative antecedents or of disabling conditions from long-term memory can prevent premature closure on a problem, but does it, in itself, amount to an understanding of logical indeterminacy or logical necessity?

Another concern arising from the absence of a competence component to mental models theory is why we do not see more early success than we do. Arguably, if logical competence were present in young children or if it were immaterial to success, as the theory claims, we would expect more consistent evidence of early success across a broader set of inferences. Certainly there are studies that indicate some success with formal implication in young children, but it remains the case that these are relatively few and are more likely to reflect success with determinate inferences and valid argument forms such as MP than with indeterminate inferences or invalid forms.

Metacognitive Theories

Metacognition is central to the developmental accounts of deductive reasoning offered by Kuhn (Kuhn & Franklin, 2006) and Moshman (2004). Both theorists place significant emphasis on the basic notion of thought becoming an object for itself. Metacognitive theories of deductive reasoning share with Piaget, and with the competence-procedural account, the claim that the most powerful forms of reflexive thinking are largely an achievement of adolescence.

Kuhn's account of development across several areas of higher order cognition, including deductive reasoning (Kuhn & Franklin, 2006), scientific thinking (Kuhn, 2002), and argumentation (Kuhn, 1991), places particular emphasis on the progressive overcoming of belief-bias effects and other aspects of motivated reasoning. The *belief-bias effect* within a deductive reasoning paradigm refers to a tendency to accept or reject the conclusion of an argument on the basis of the believability of the premises and/or conclusion, rather than the logical form of the argument. Vulnerability to belief-bias can be assessed by setting up a conflict between logic and belief, as previously noted (see Table 12.1). This can be accomplished by way of arguments that have an invalid form, but true premises or a true conclusion, or both. Alternatively, one could employ arguments with a valid form, but false premises or a false conclusion, or both. Belief bias is evident when the former argument is judged to be valid and the latter invalid. When task instructions stress the importance of a logical or formal evaluation of the argument, susceptibility to belief bias tends to decrease across later childhood and adolescence (Markovits & Vachon, 1989), though it is substantially present even in adults (George, 1997). This trend is similar to what we find for hypothesis-testing studies under conditions where the individual is not neutral with respect to the hypothesis being assessed. Where there are expectations about the fate of the hypothesis, as would be the case where the individual's own beliefs or naïve theories are at stake, we see fundamental problems during the middle childhood years in conceptualizing evidence as separate from theory or belief and in appreciating the falsifiable nature of the latter, and we tend to see relatively fewer problems in adolescence and/or adulthood (Kuhn, 2002; Kuhn & Franklin, 2006). This developmental progression in the coordination of belief and evidence appears to be largely contemporary with the similar progression in the separation of form and content (i.e., overcoming belief bias) on deductive reasoning tasks.

Kuhn maintains that metacognition and executive functions are implicated in the ability to overcome belief bias in at least two respects. First, children and adolescents become less susceptible to belief bias as they develop knowledge of the formal properties of deductive inference (Kuhn & Franklin, 2006). This is a kind of *metalogical knowledge.* Moshman (2004; see following discussion) provides a detailed account of what the development of knowledge about logic might involve. The second relevant aspect of metacognitive development concerns an increasing awareness of, and control over, beliefs (Kuhn, 2001, 2002; Kuhn, Katz, & Dean, 2004). As with Markovits's mental models account, inhibitory capabilities are seen as key here (Handley et al., 2004). Where real-world knowledge and the rules of reasoning are in conflict on logic problems, that knowledge, which otherwise represents an aid and support to the application of inferences rules, becomes a hindrance and must be suppressed (Daniel & Klaczynski, 2006; Kuhn & Franklin, 2006). Overriding heuristic responses based in real-world knowledge, and avoiding premature closure, make it possible to consider alternatives and to recognize indeterminacy or invalidity despite believable content.

Adapting Kuhn's general account of knowing to this discussion of deductive reasoning, we can identify other metalevel elements of cognition that are both subject to development and potentially relevant to performance on deductive reasoning problems. The competence to apply reasoning strategies, including deductive strategies such as falsification, is dependent on an appreciation of what the use of these strategies achieves for the individual—why they are important and when they should be used. This is a kind of *procedural metacognitive* knowledge (Kuhn, 2001; Kuhn & Franklin, 2006; Kuhn, Katz, & Dean, 2004). The *disposition* to apply a competence is important in Kuhn's account as well. Need for cognition, resistance to closure,

or flexibility and openness of thinking are cognitive styles that would provide favorable conditions for separating belief from evidence and inhibiting more heuristic forms of processing (Evans, 2002; Stanovich & West, 1997). In Kuhn's account, disposition can also reflect both intellectual values and level of epistemological understanding or awareness, where the latter concerns an appreciation of the nature of knowing and knowledge (Kuhn, 2001; Kuhn & Park, 2005). Concerning intellectual values, deductive strategies are more likely to be invoked by individuals when the goal of arriving at veridical judgments and maximizing knowledge is given priority over the protection of existing beliefs and personal theories (Klaczynski & Robinson, 2000). Likewise, a personal epistemology in which knowing is understood to be a relatively transparent process that yields facts and opinions, rather than a theory-laden process yielding testable and falsifiable claims (Overton, 2003), is likely to favor inductive reasoning strategies over deductive strategies (Klaczynski, 2000).

Moshman's theory of the development of deductive reasoning also places great emphasis on metacognition (Moshman, 1990, 1998, 2004). In his view, reasoning involves explicit conceptual knowledge regarding inference (metalogical knowledge) and metacognitive awareness of, and control over, inference. Moshman identifies two aspects of metalogic that correspond to the distinction between procedural and declarative metaknowledge. The first aspect concerns metalogical *strategies* for the derivation of conclusions from premises and for the coordination of inferences. These strategies can include reductio ad absurdum, systematic generation of possible states of affairs consistent with the premises, and a search for counterexamples. The second, more declarative, aspect of metalogic consists of metalogical *understanding* and includes a recognition that inference is a basis for knowledge, an understanding of key distinctions among types of inference, an appreciation that conclusions must be consistent with all possible states of affairs represented by the premises, and an understanding of logical indeterminacy, inconsistency, and necessity.

The development of reasoning and rationality is viewed by Moshman as a process of reflection on implicit metalogical knowledge. This is essentially the developmental mechanism common to Piaget's notion of reflective abstraction (Piaget, 2001) and Karmiloff-Smith's (1986) representational redescription. Development involves a self-reflective process by which elements implicit in intellectual acts are rendered explicit and, as such, come under conscious, intentional control, thereby becoming applicable across a wider set of circumstances. This is an internal process, though it is supported by specific types of social interaction (Moshman, 1998, 2004). It does not involve a process of transmission from external authorities to the child.

Preschool and early-school-aged children are able to make a variety of deductive inferences that comply with logical norms, but in Moshman's view, these inferences do not represent reasoning because they are not consciously or purposefully constrained by particular inferential norms. Conclusions as the outcomes of inferential acts are not conclusions per se for the young child but simply facts, in principle indistinguishable from observational facts. Moshman, however, considers some knowledge of inference and of inferential form and norms to be implicit in children's thinking at this stage. During the middle childhood years, these implicit elements become explicit. According to Moshman's account, we should see a developing awareness of inference as a source of knowledge across the elementary school years. This includes an appreciation of premises and conclusion as distinct components of inference, and an increasing understanding of the premise-conclusion relation and of inference as a process that derives the conclusion specifically from the premises. However, still implicit during much of middle childhood is an appreciation of the different syntactic forms for premises (e.g., disjunction, conjunction, implication) and an understanding of key differences among types of inference, and between determinate (valid) and indeterminate (invalid) arguments. Explicit awareness of inferential validity as a function of argument form and independent of the truth and falsehood of the premises is alleged to emerge in adolescence, and this appreciation of logical truth as distinct from empirical truth enables success in reasoning with contrary-to-fact arguments. When the adolescent appreciates that empirical evidence is irrelevant and superfluous in the face of logical truth or falsehood, she should also recognize that only logical truths will hold in all times and places.

Findings regarding child and adolescent metalogical knowledge provide a pattern of purely intuitive or implicit understandings of logical concepts preceding more explicit understandings. This pattern generally conforms to Moshman's predictions. There is also evidence of implicit understanding of more advanced concepts existing alongside explicit command of less advanced constructs. Some relevant findings are discussed here (see Moshman, 2004, for a more thorough treatment). Consistent with Moshman's expectations, there is evidence by 6 years of age of certain implicit metalogical knowledge. Children are sensitive to

logical inconsistencies within individual propositions and across statements in a simple story (Ruffman, 1999; Nesdale, Tunmer, & Clover, 1985; Tunmer, Nesdale, & Pratt, 1983). Young children also treat logically determinate statements differently than contingent statements. Six-year-olds consider a logically false proposition (e.g., "Peter is eating an apple, and not only that, Peter is not eating an apple.") to make less sense than empirical inconsistencies in the form of a nonsensical fact ("Peter is eating a television, and not only that, Peter is not eating an apple.") and a difference of opinion between two people (according to one person, "Peter is eating an apple," whereas according to another person, "Peter is not eating an apple.") (Ruffman, 1999; Russell, 1982).

It is evident, however, that these early successes are based on largely implicit knowledge. This is clear from two findings. First, there appears to be a developmental lag between children's success in distinguishing logical *falsehoods* from contingent statements and their success in distinguishing logical *truths* from contingent statements. Even 8- and 9-year-olds have difficulty distinguishing between necessarily *true* statements or tautologies (e.g., "The walking man is on his feet.") and contingent statements ("The walking man is on his own.") on learned discrimination tasks, though they benefit from training (Nicholls & Thorkildsen, 1988; Russell, 1982). Second, children in the early elementary school years do not appear to understand the basis for the distinctions they are able to make between logically determinate propositions and merely contingent propositions. When presented with various logical truths or tautologies ("Either the counter in my hand is not white or it is white.") and logical inconsistencies or contradictions ("The counter in my hand is blue and it is not blue."), and required to judge whether the statement is true or false on a priori grounds, only 20% to 36% of third graders (Cummins, 1978) or 23% to 56% of second graders (Osherson & Markman, 1975) were successful across the individual items, and these percentages decline dramatically when adequate justifications are required (0–17% of third graders). Even sixth graders have difficulty judging the truth status of logically determinate statements. Only 27% to 42% of sixth graders were successful in their response and 11% to 42% were successful if justification is required (Cummins, 1978). Similarly, Morris and Sloutsky (2001) found that third graders did not appear to understand that the truth of contingent statements could not be determined before data gathering, whereas the truth of tautologies and contradictions could be known a priori.

There is additional evidence of implicit metalogical knowledge becoming available in the early school years with subsequent, explicit forms emerging later. Children as young as 7 years appear to realize that logical truths meet two of three key conditions: first, they are true everywhere, and second, they will never change. However, this appears to be a largely implicit grasp of logical necessity because children of this age typically do not appreciate the additional condition that logical truths cannot be imagined to be different (Miller, 1986; Miller, Custer, & Nassau, 2000). Even most third graders and a sizable number of fifth graders are willing to draw a picture that would portray the contradiction of class inclusion or a necessary proposition. In addition, 7-year-olds do not recognize how nonlogical truths (social conventions, physical laws, arbitrary facts) differ from logical truths in terms of these three conditions (Miller et al., 2000). An appreciation, for example, that logical necessities hold everywhere whereas physical laws need not may not be present even by 10 years of age (Komatsu & Galotti, 1986).

As predicted by Moshman's account, explicit appreciation of validity as a property of argument form appears to be a relatively late achievement and is uncommon in the elementary school years. Moshman and Franks (1986) presented children and adolescents with several argument types including transitivity, class instantiation, disjunction, conjunction, and reverse conjunction. Each of these arguments is considered by Braine (1978) to be a basic inference scheme available to young children. The arguments also varied systematically in terms of the truth of the premises and conclusion and the validity of the argument's form. In general, fourth graders did not sort the arguments on the basis of validity, did not provide explanations for their sorts that referred to the notion of validity, and did not succeed in identifying arguments as valid or invalid even after feedback was provided following individual trials and explanations, and examples of valid and invalid arguments were presented. There was also a strong tendency for this age group to interpret "most logical" as "most empirically correct or sensible." A substantial minority of seventh graders, by contrast, was able to sort arguments in terms of validity and to provide adequate explanations, and most seventh graders could correctly identify arguments as valid or invalid after an explanation of the construct with examples. Training by way of explanation and feedback was successful in elevating the performance levels of seventh graders to that of college students. In follow-ups to Moshman and Frank's work (Morris, 2000), additional training techniques have proved

somewhat more successful with third and fourth graders. In particular, cuing the child to attend to the structural relations inherent in the arguments and the use of fantasy content to cue the child to monitor (and presumably suppress) the introduction of personal knowledge about the premises led to sortings and explanations based in validity for 35% of fourth and fifth graders.

Other research also points to the general inability of children in the elementary years to provide justifications for their responses on logic problems that adequately capture the notion of validity (Markovits et al., 1989). This is also reflected in findings that justifications for uncertain responses develop from reference to specific alternatives (e.g., "It might be a street cleaner making the street wet.") to mention of general justifications ("It might be something else."), and then to abstract or formal considerations (mentioning logical terms like necessity, possibility, etc.; Venet & Markovits, 2001). Consistent with these results, significant differences have been found between early and middle adolescents in understanding the role of mathematical proofs in establishing logical necessity and in appreciating that proofs do not require or benefit from empirical verification (Morris & Sloutsky, 1998).

Unlike mental models theory or the domain-specific accounts, the theories of Kuhn and Moshman appear to include aspects of logical competence, but to represent these in procedural form. Logical competence becomes, in effect, conceptual knowledge about logic and about logical strategies, together with adherence to intellectual values and personal epistemologies that entail a conscious conformity to logical norms in approaching certain problems. In this way, the theories attempt to avoid any notion of a mental logic. The claim here is that explicit conceptual knowledge about logical necessity and validity can obtain in the absence of an inherently logical-mathematical organization to thought itself. From within the metacognitive perspective, mature thinking is not inherently logical, but it can avail itself of different rule systems, including that of symbolic logic, to accomplish specific goals. These theories also posit the development of metacognitive functioning as contributing in key ways to the controlled and strategic use of deductive inference.

Comparison and Conclusions Regarding the Theories

At this point in time, and despite considerable focus on deduction in developmental research, the available empirical evidence does not allow any decisive test of the competing theories of deductive reasoning because the majority of these findings are consistent with more than one theory. The one exception here may be the domain-specific account. This account indeed seems unlikely to carry the day at this point because evidence of content effects and of pragmatic schemas do not argue against mental logic, mental models, or metacognitive theories of deductive reasoning. In the absence of decisive tests that might rule out particular theories, it may be profitable to seek some means of reconciling competing claims (Overton, 2006; Overton & Ennis, 2006). In this regard, the rapprochement afforded by competence-procedural theory offers a promising basis for resolving differences and preserving the obvious strengths of each theory.

The competence-procedural theory is able to explain, on an a priori basis, the various age-related effects that have been found for deductive reasoning, together with a host of findings regarding key moderators of these age-related effects, including such factors as training, content, and SES. The theory is also able to reconcile the striking inconsistencies typically present when the adult and developmental literatures on deductive reasoning are compared. Evidence of early success on deductive reasoning problems is explained within the competence-procedural account in two ways. Some of this evidence appears to identify concrete precursors to formal deductive competence (Acredolo & Horobin, 1987; Byrnes & Beilin, 1991; Byrnes & Overton, 1986; Klahr & Chen, 2003; Muller et al., 1999; Ricco, 1997). These precursors are predicted by the theory on the basis of class and relational reasoning competencies present in middle childhood. Other evidence of early success consists of relatively isolated, localized inferences in the absence of explicit understanding (Dias & Harris, 1988, 1990; Hawkins et al., 1984; Leevers & Harris, 1999) and, consequently, does not meet reasonable criteria of deductive competence (Markovits et al., 1989, 1996). The theory explains apparent evidence of adult incompetence as occasions where procedural obstacles to the accessing and implementation of a logical competence are present (see Overton, 1990, and Overton & Dick, 2007, for discussions).

The specific nature of the rapprochement offered by the competence-procedural account is to interpret the findings from research conducted within competing theories as providing important elaborations of the procedural component of the theory while, at the same time, rejecting interpretations that blur distinctions between competence and performance or that reduce aspects of competence to procedural factors. The role of encoding, retrieval, executive,

and pragmatic-interpretive processes in age, task, and content effects in deductive reasoning have been significantly clarified by research within domain-specific, mental models, and metacognitive theories.

The competence-procedural account also recognizes the findings of Kuhn and Moshman regarding metalogical development and some aspects of broader metacognitive development as confirming the logical competence model of the theory and as identifying key indicators, manifestations, and consequences of an emergent logical competence. The course of development for conceptual knowledge about logic (Komatsu & Galotti, 1986; Markovits, 1989; Miller, 1986; Miller et al., 2000; Morris, 2000; Morris & Sloutsky, 2001; Moshman & Franks, 1986), documented in the earlier review of research, is entirely consistent with the emergence of a class-based mental logic supporting concrete precursors to deductive competence followed by the emergence of a propositional mental logic supporting a mature formal competence. In addition, at least some aspects of metacognitive or executive functioning that have been linked to success on deductive reasoning problems by Kuhn, Moshman, and others could be seen as a manifestation or consequence of an emergent logical competence. Parallels, both empirical and theoretical, exist between the formal operational model of Inhelder and Piaget and certain metacognitive or executive functions (Emick & Welsh, 2005), such as planning, cognitive flexibility, and cognitive monitoring.

An important obstacle to the proposed rapprochement concerns fundamental differences in views of the scope and importance of deductive reasoning, with competence-performance theory giving a privileged and foundational status to deductive processes in mature thought (Overton, 1990; Piaget, 1986; Ricco, 1993; Rips, 2001), and alternative theories viewing deduction as of less significance (Evans, 2002; Kuhn & Franklin, 2006; Moshman, 2004) and as a competence made possible by other, more significant, aspects of cognitive development (Markovits & Barrouillet, 2002). In support of the rapprochement, it could be argued that the core claim of competence-procedural theory that thought is inherently logico-mathematical does not preclude the development of a variety of inductive or nonmonotonic forms of reasoning. In addition, the claim is reasonably consistent with a view that analysis in terms of logical relations is not the default mode of responding even on most deductive reasoning problems, and that logical analysis represents an override of more heuristic responding as the default (Daniel & Klaczynski, 2006; Evans, 2002; Klaczynski, 2000; Klaczynski & Robinson, 2000). In this interpretation of the core claim to competence-procedural theory, the gap between the theory and the metacognitive approach of Kuhn and Moshman would seem to be narrowed, and the theory is also compatible with dual-processing accounts of cognition. There is no reason, in principle, why the analytic system in a dual-process theory cannot include a logical competence model. Some dual-process theorists have acknowledged the importance of an "appreciation of the logic of necessity and indeterminacy" (Daniel & Klaczynski, 2006, p. 351) to success on deductive reasoning tasks. What the competence-procedural account *does* require, however, is evidence of the increasing availability of a deductive competence with age—evidence that seems readily available—and evidence that the development of deductive thinking plays at least some role in the progressive decontextualization of thought and in the emergence of more formal kinds of thinking such as hypothetical, scientific, and argumentative thinking (Ricco, 2007). For the most part, research programs that might generate the latter kind of evidence have yet to be conducted.

In contrast with competence-procedural theory, the other leading mental logic theory of the development of deductive reasoning does not appear to offer the same basis for rapprochement. The natural deduction system of Braine and O'Brien has a somewhat ambiguous status as a mental logic theory. Although the theory is clear in its claim that human thought is inherently logical, and the mental rules or schemas invoked by the theory are unambiguously logical, the rules bear a merely arbitrary relation to one another and do not comprise a logic per se. As a result, the theory blurs the lines between a competence model and a performance or procedural model. Specifically, there does not seem to be any distinction, *in principle*, among a logical rule (inference scheme), a procedural rule from the direct reasoning routine, and a pragmatic inference or conversational implicature from the interpretive component of the model. As such, the theory is basically procedural.

This state of affairs contrasts sharply with the logical competence models that Piaget and Overton proposed. For each of these theorists, the claim that thinking is inherently logical is a claim that cognitive structures are systems of logical implications or entailments obtaining among a set of cognitive transformations (Piaget, 1986). Each transformation entails the possibility of certain other transformations to which it is necessarily related. Thus, the relations that obtain among the transformations are *never* arbitrary. For example, in grouping I, the logical addition of classes in a hierarchy, the generation of a class B by the additive combination of its subclasses (A + A′ = B) is logically equivalent to the combination of two other transformations

decomposing B into its subclasses, (B − A′ = A) + (B − A = A′). It is this logical equivalence that supports the logical implication defining the crucial grouping property of reversibility (Inhelder & Piaget, 1964, pp. 288–289).

With development, structures become more integrated and recursive, where the latter refers to a structure's capacity to define a given transformation in terms of other transformations. Consider the four transformations comprising Inhelder and Piaget's (1958, p. 134) model of formal deductive reasoning—the INRC group (identity, negation, reciprocity, and correlativity). These transformations apply to propositions in the logic, altering the truth values of atomic components and/or changing the logical operator:

$$I(p \lor q) = (p \lor q), N(p \lor q) = (-p \,\&\, -q), R(p \lor q)$$
$$= (-p \lor -q); C(p \lor q) = (p \,\&\, q)$$

The key property of the INRC group is that each transformation is definable in terms of each of the other transformations (e.g., N = RC, R = NC, etc.). Thus, there is a greater recursiveness to the INRC group than there is to the groupings (Byrnes, 1988; Ricco, 1990). In the additive combination of classes, relations of logical equivalence among transformations are confined to immediate vertical relations within the hierarchical structure of the logic. The INRC group, however, is not so restricted.

The use of largely isolated rules in the absence of any greater organization in the mental logic theory of Braine and O'Brien carries a cost in regard to explaining the development of logical thinking. The explanatory value of logical-mathematical organizations to any theory of cognitive development is their inherent capacity to model the development of judgments of necessity. A given logico-mathematical structure is an index of the scope and complexity of the necessary relations the child can construct on the basis of that structure (Piaget, 1986, 1987). The extent of the role of necessity in the child's organization of experience will be a direct function of the necessary relations (logical implications) comprising the particular structures available to the child at a given phase of development (Ricco, 1990). This explains why valid judgments of necessity are both present at all levels of development, and become more complex and general with development. With the progressive integration and recursiveness of cognitive structures, their logical implications become more numerous and richer (Piaget, 1986, 1987, p. 139). Corresponding to this structural development, the child's judgments of necessity develop from stimulus- or data-bound and local in scope to deductive and universal (Piaget, 1986). The logical implications within structures become manifest in necessary relations among meanings constructed by the child. Thus, the full recursiveness that defines the INRC group corresponds to the construction of multiple and simultaneous necessary relations by the child, allowing more general and complex judgments of necessity than are afforded by groupings.

By way of its impressive explanatory scope, and on the basis of its markedly different set of assumptions, Markovits's mental models theory is an obvious alternative to the rapprochement offered by competence-procedural theory. The mental models account predicts a wide range of developmental and adult findings on conditional and syllogistic reasoning problems. In general, it successfully links the relative likelihood of success on the various forms of conditional argument to specific task features controlling the availability of alternative antecedents and disablers, and to viable developmental claims concerning cognitive procedures such as retrieval, encoding, cognitive inhibition, and representation. This linkage of task properties and aspects of information processing enables a comprehensive account of patterns of responding in early childhood that have suggested early competence, and patterns of responding in adulthood that have suggested a lack of competence. At the same time, mental models theory is a strictly procedural account of performance on deductive reasoning problems. Procedural elements function to maximize success in performance (Overton, 1990, 1991; Overton & Dick, 2007). As such, it is not surprising that a detailed procedural theory is effective in predicting patterns of success and failure. Missing, however, is an account of the development of the understanding or competence underlying at least the more consistent manifestations of success. By middle adolescence, an appreciation of specifically logical constructs such as inference, indeterminacy, necessity, sufficiency, and validity appears to be relatively normative, as findings reviewed in discussing Moshman's theory indicate. Developmental mental models theory does not directly address the nature and development of this competence. In addition, as noted previously, the theory is primarily an account of reasoning with meaningful content and is less convincing as an account of reasoning with nonmeaningful content.

LATE ADULT DEVELOPMENT AND DEDUCTIVE REASONING

The late adult development literature contains dramatically fewer studies of deductive reasoning than the child and adolescent literatures. There is some research, primarily from the 1970s, with original or modified versions of standard Piagetian tasks (class reasoning, transitivity, formal operations; Blackburn, 1984; Clayton & Overton, 1976; Denney & Cornelius, 1975; Fontaine & Pennequin, 2000; Muhs, Hooper, & Papalia-Finlay, 1979–1980; Sinnott, 1975; Sinnott & Guttmann, 1978; Tomlinson-Keasey, 1972) and a small number of studies using conditional reasoning or syllogistic reasoning problems, or both (Cohen, 1981; Fisk & Sharp, 2002; Gilinski & Judd, 1994; McKinnon & Moscovitch, 2007; Morgan, 1956; Nehrke, 1972; Overton, Yaure, & Ward, 1986; Pollack, Overton, Rosenfeld, & Rosenfeld, 1995; Takahashi & Overton, 1996). A somewhat larger body of late adult development literature concerns problem-solving tasks that, to varying degrees, resemble proof construction problems (Foltz, Overton, & Ricco, 1995; Piaget, 1987; Ricco, 1997) and, to that extent, would appear to involve relatively concrete forms of deductive competence (e.g., Arenberg, 1974; Denney & Palmer, 1981; Denney & Wright, 1976; Haught, Hill, Nardi, & Walls, 2000; Kesler, Denney, & Whitely, 1976; Sanders & Sanders, 1978; Wetherick, 1964; Young, 1971). Finally, there are studies conducted on relatively large adult samples that use reasoning measures originating in, or deriving from, psychometric tests. Some of these measures would appear to be assessing deductive reasoning (see Salthouse, 2005a, in particular, for a review of relevant studies conducted in his laboratory). However, because such psychometric measures have no obvious basis in any theory of reasoning, identifying the specific type or types of reasoning being assessed is far from straightforward.

This discussion begins with a review of research assessing both deductive and inductive reasoning using *psychometric measures*. Consideration of this body of research allows us to compare the developmental course for deduction with the course of the other major category of reasoning addressed in late adult development research, and to identify mediators and intervention-based moderators of the general development-reasoning relation in adult development. These mediators are prime candidates for explaining age-related effects in deductive reasoning per se. Next, a review of the adult development problem-solving literature, including Piagetian measures and proof construction paradigms, is presented. This literature is useful in identifying possible age-related effects regarding relatively concrete forms of deduction. It is less well suited to explaining the basis for these age-related effects. Following this section, the review turns to studies employing standard syllogistic and conditional reasoning measures familiar from the child/adolescent literature and from the nondevelopmental, adult reasoning literature. These are relatively uncontroversial measures of formal deductive reasoning. Most of this literature goes beyond description of age-related effects per se and allows us to address the key question of whether age-related differences in performance on reasoning problems are best construed as reflective of competence changes or changes in procedural components of adult cognition. This latter discussion will be further informed by the results of the earlier discussion of mediators of the relation between age and reasoning in the adult years.

As noted at the outset of this chapter, the major theories of the development of deductive reasoning typically do not make clear claims about late adult development. The one exception here is competence-procedural theory. Nonetheless, some basic, albeit crude, predictions can be made from the theories considered earlier. Mental logic theories, including the competence-procedural account, would seem to predict that late adult development should not compromise the basic competence to reason deductively. From this standpoint, we would expect to find substantial logical competence in late adulthood once the effects of decline in various procedural factors are controlled. By contrast, Markovits's mental models account and the metacognitive theories of Moshman and Kuhn view the ability to reason deductively as fundamentally dependent on a set of factors that are known to show decline in the later years of life. These would include self-initiated retrieval processes and various executive functions such as cognitive inhibition. Because there is no competence-procedure distinction in these theories, decline in procedural factors should be tantamount to decline in deductive capability itself. On the other hand, the metacognitive theories also stress the importance of metalogical knowledge, for which there is no evidence of decline in adulthood. Thus, we might predict significant late adult age effects from within Markovits's theory, but less so for the metacognitive theories.

Psychometric Measures of Deductive and Inductive Reasoning

A number of studies have been conducted on the fate of various cognitive abilities across the adult years that include psychometric assessments of reasoning taken from standard cognitive test batteries (see Blair, Chapter 8 of this volume, for discussion of the psychometric approach to the study of adult cognitive development). The nature of this research is such that it is particularly difficult to determine whether deductive reasoning per se is involved. There are

several reasons for this. First, psychometric measures are generally not based on any theory of reasoning and are clearly measuring multiple reasoning processes. Second, the primary focus of these studies has been to identify cognitive processing and resource components that might explain age-related effects in a fluid reasoning ability (gF) (Horn & Cattell, 1967; see also Blair, Chapter 8 of this volume), without particular concern for distinguishing among types of reasoning. Nonetheless, some of the psychometric measures used in the study of late adult development, as well as certain derivative measures, would appear to assess deductive reasoning. Although these tasks do not present verbal arguments featuring premise-conclusion relations that must be evaluated in terms of validity, they generally involve information that could be readily represented in propositional form, and their solution requires an appreciation of necessary relations among such propositions. Examples of such measures include the *logical steps* and *mystery codes* subtests of the Kaufman Adult Intelligence Test (KAIT; Kaufman & Kaufman, 1993), and the *analysis-synthesis* subtest of the Woodcock-Johnson III Tests of Cognitive Abilities (WJ-III; Woodcock, McGrew, & Mather, 2001). All three measures load heavily on fluid intelligence.

The logical steps measure is verbal in nature but loads minimally on crystallized intelligence. The following sample item is representative of the measure: "Here is a staircase with seven steps. Bob is always one step above Ann. Bob is on step 6. What step is Ann on?" The mystery codes subtest of the KAIT pairs each of several pictorial stimuli with an identifying code. By analyzing the codes, the participant must deduce the correct code for an uncoded stimulus. This measure is speeded. The analysis-synthesis subtest of the Woodcock-Johnson III similarly involves the analysis of symbolic formulations to determine the missing elements in a puzzle. In addition to these measures, Salthouse and colleagues (e.g., Salthouse, 1992, 2001a, 2001b) have used two reasoning measures in their research that are derived from psychometric assessments and that appear to assess deductive reasoning. These are *analytical reasoning* and *integrative reasoning*. The former measure requires participants to construct all possible models (e.g., possible arrangements of individuals around a table) that are consistent with a series of premises (relative positions of individuals seated at the table). This involves a key element in several accounts of deductive reasoning—an exhaustive construction of possibilities consistent with a set of constraints. The integrative reasoning measure presents participants with information about relations among several variables (e.g., "F and G do the same. E does the opposite of F."). The participant is then asked a question about an additional relation not included in the premises (e.g., "If E increases, will G increase.").

In a recent review, Salthouse (2005a) presents an analysis of cross-sectional data on adult intellectual development consisting of large norming samples (ranging from 1,300–2,500 subjects) for the KAIT, Wechsler Adult Intelligence Scale (WAIS) III, and WJ-III, and a series of laboratory studies by Salthouse and colleagues featuring from 980 to 1,976 participants for each individual measure. Although the analysis does not address deductive reasoning per se, the findings provide useful information on the fate of deduction in the adult years.

Participants were administered the above deductive reasoning measures, together with several measures of inductive reasoning (matrix reasoning, concept formation, and series completion). On each of the inductive reasoning tasks, participants must generate (induce) a rule from a series of instances of the rule and must then use the rule to identify a new instance from a set of possibilities. Induction is the most frequently assessed form of reasoning in late adult development research, where it typically serves as an assessment of fluid intelligence.

The cross-sectional comparisons for both the norming samples and the laboratory studies show linear to mildly curvilinear age functions for all of the reasoning measures. *No clear difference is evident between the functions for deductive and inductive reasoning.* In general, performance of 70-year-olds is about one standard deviation (SD) less than that of the typical adult in their 20s. Thus, the relation between psychometric measures of deductive or inductive reasoning and age appears to be substantial in cross-sectional studies. Accounting for sample size, Verhaegen and Salthouse (1997) characterize the weighted correlation of reasoning with age to be moderate across 38 studies and to be at least as strong as that evident for various memory variables.

Available findings for longitudinal studies of reasoning using psychometric measures are, to a significant extent, at odds with the above cross-sectional comparisons. Unfortunately, longitudinal research does not use the above measures of deductive reasoning and tends to focus on inductive reasoning. Nonetheless, given the similar age functions for deductive and inductive reasoning described earlier, these findings are relevant to claims about the fate of deductive reasoning. Schaie's (1994) review of research stemming from the Seattle Longitudinal Study presents a more optimistic assessment of the fate of complex cognitive abilities

in middle and late adulthood than strictly cross-sectional research generally has. This review found sizable cohort effects for the primary mental abilities of verbal meaning, spatial orientation, and inductive reasoning, calling into question the accuracy of cross-sectional data as an estimate of age functions for these variables. In fact, the review reveals very different age functions for the same cognitive variables in cross-sectional studies as compared with longitudinal studies.

Cross-sectional comparisons within the Seattle data set suggest that most of the mental abilities are in decline by the early 40s, with inductive reasoning showing a consistent decline from the mid-20s onward, and demonstrating a greater overall decline than most of the other abilities. This is consistent with the Salthouse (2005a) analysis. Although declines are evident in the longitudinal comparisons, they tend to be preceded by gains and to begin later than in the cross-sectional data. This is particularly the case for inductive reasoning, which does not decline until the mid-50s, and shows only moderate change until the mid-70s. In addition, longitudinal comparisons indicate that the decline for inductive reasoning is more moderate than for most of the other abilities. Inductive reasoning shows a decline of only 0.5 SD from 25 to 88 years. It is also noteworthy that the difference between cross-sectional and longitudinal findings for inductive reasoning is most apparent when multiple indices are used to measure this ability, allowing for the analysis of latent variables. Recent considerations of cohort effects in inductive reasoning support the findings of Schaie (1994). Using inductive reasoning measures requiring the discovery of a rule, Zelinski and Kennison (2007) found significant cohort effects that did not eliminate the age-related effects but did account for substantial variability in the development–reasoning relation. The older adults were performing at a level equivalent to adults 15 years younger from the prior generation.

Attempts to train older adults on strategies for approaching psychometric assessments of inductive reasoning have been successful (Boron, Turiano, Willis, & Schaie, 2007; Willis & Schaie, 1986a, 1986b, 1988), though the effectiveness of the training is sometimes a function of age and level of education (Saczynski, Willis, & Schaie, 2002). In one study (Saczynski et al., 2002), older adults (64 years of age and older) were trained on a series completion problem. The training involved saying the series aloud, and marking any repeating sequences and skipped elements in a sequence. On subsequent inductive problems, the trained group spontaneously used the strategies and showed gains in inductive reasoning as a result. More intensive interventions have yielded gains that endure well beyond the training sessions. Willis and Schaie (1986a, 1986b, 1988) provided participants from the Seattle Longitudinal Study with five 1-hour sessions of strategy training for inductive reasoning or spatial orientation problems. The trained participants demonstrated gains on the average of 0.5 SD and performed significantly better than control subjects. Greater gains were evident for inductive reasoning than for spatial orientation. The intervention groups continued to perform better than control groups 7 years later and also demonstrated additional gains after a booster session.

Training on inductive reasoning has also been found to produce gains that go beyond performance on post-training reasoning measures. Benefits have been noted with respect to self-reported degree of difficulty in completing cognitively demanding tasks in participants' everyday activities. Such transfer to everyday activities was not found for training in speed of processing or memory (Willis et al., 2006). Recent findings from the National Institutes of Health Socio-Environmental Studies Section longitudinal research program (Caplan & Schooler, 2008; Schooler, 2007) also provide evidence that reasoning abilities are readily supported in the later years. Performance by the elderly on a composite measure of intellectual functioning that includes an argument construction exercise is positively related to the degree of cognitive demand of participants' everyday environments including paid work, leisure activities, and housework. The argument construction measure reflected the extent to which participants could generate both pro and con arguments in regard to an issue. This form of reasoning has been identified as a sophisticated achievement of the adolescent years (Kuhn & Franklin, 2006).

Indirect evidence supports claims that declines in reasoning are not inevitable. Reasoning measures show increasing heterogeneity with normal adult and late adult development, whereas other cognitive abilities such as visuoconstructive abilities and general knowledge measures show more stability across the adult years in terms of their dispersion within age groups (Ardila, 2007). Presumably, this indicates that reasoning is an ability where there is significant variability in the age function across middle and later adulthood. Some individuals show considerably less decline than others, and this suggests important individual difference factors that might account for the variability. There is also evidence that age and biological markers (e.g., sensory, pulmonary, or cardiovascular functioning) are somewhat independent predictors of reasoning performance in older adults suggesting that biological components of normal adult development are not responsible for the age-related decline in reasoning during late adulthood. Rather, individual-specific biological and experiential factors, together with sociocultural factors, are implicated (MacDonald, Dixon, Cohen, & Hazlitt, 2004).

The available findings on psychometric assessments of reasoning in the adult years are useful to the extent that we can generalize from the results for inductive reasoning, for which we have a great deal of psychometric data, to deduction, for which we have little data. The case for generalization stems from the similarity in age functions for inductive and deductive measures in cross-sectional research. The varieties of inductive reasoning assessed in the literature reviewed earlier show substantial decline across the middle and later adult years in cross-sectional research. At the same time, there is significant evidence of cohort effects and only modest declines even in the later years when longitudinal research is considered. In addition, intervention studies regarding inductive reasoning have generally been successful with the elderly.

Mediators of the Development–Reasoning Relation

Several information-processing variables have been proposed as possible mediators of the development–reasoning relation across the adult years. These include domain-general and domain-specific processing speed, storage and maintenance components of working memory, and the executive control component of working memory (see Demetriou and colleagues, Chapter 10 of this volume), together with other executive functions. Most, if not all, of these variables are, in part, fluid mechanics, and it is their decline that may underlie decline in other cognitive functions, such as reasoning (Craik & Bialystok, 2006; Bialystok & Craik, Chapter 7 of this volume). The executive functions that appear to be particularly susceptible to the neurologic changes taking place in late adult development include inhibition and task management (Park & Payer, 2006). Resistance to interference from task-irrelevant information has been found to decline with age (Kramer & Kray, 2006; Zacks, Hasher, & Li, 2000), as has the inhibition of experimentally induced prepotent responses (Verhaeghen & DeMeersman, 1998a, 1998b). Aspects of task management that show evidence of decline include dividing attention between tasks (Zacks et al., 2000), set shifting, the spontaneous use of cognitive strategies (De Luca et al., 2003; Verhaeghen, Steitz, Sliwinski, & Cerella, 2003), and cognitive monitoring (Hertzog & Hultsch, 2000). For the most part, these effects appear to be relatively modest in middle adulthood (Treitz, Heyder, & Daum, 2007) but become significant after the age of 60 (see Bialystok & Craik, Chapter 7 of this volume, for an extended discussion of normative change in control functions during adulthood).

The role of mediator variables in the developmental course of reasoning processes in the later years has been explored by way of statistical controls and experimental manipulation of candidate variables. Verhaeghen and Salthouse (1997) conducted an extensive meta-analysis of findings regarding relations between age and cognitive abilities across the adult years. The analysis covered 91 studies and included the primary abilities of working memory, processing speed, spatial ability, episodic memory, and reasoning. The latter consisted primarily of inductive, analogical, and spatial reasoning as represented by several measures including matrices, series completion, analogies, and figural relations. The meta-analysis indicated that processing speed and the central executive component of working memory—that is, the manipulation, and not merely the maintenance, of information—mediated the association of age and cognitive variables including reasoning, spatial ability, and episodic memory. Nearly 80% of age-related variance in reasoning scores was associated with processing speed alone, and 40% of the variance was associated with the working memory measures (Verhaeghen & Salthouse, 1997). Salthouse (2005a) also reports that controlling for working memory measures reduces age-related variance in integrative reasoning (deduction) and inductive reasoning from 43% to 88% depending on the study.

Other evidence for working memory as a mediator of age-related effects in reasoning comes from the findings of a 16-year longitudinal study in which declines of inductive reasoning were positively related to declines in recall but not recognition, arguing for the relevance of more effortful memory processes (Zelinski & Stewart, 1998). There is evidence that more static and basic aspects of working memory, such as maintenance and storage capacity, might be involved as well. Salthouse presents evidence that the availability of premise information on reasoning problems seems more compromised in older adults than the integration of information across relevant premises (Salthouse, 1992; Salthouse, Legg, Palmon, & Mitchell, 1990; Salthouse, Mitchell, Skovronek, & Babcock, 1989), thus implicating maintenance functions of working memory. In addition, Mutter, Haggbloom, Plumlee, and Schirmer (2006) found age-related decrements in inductive reasoning in discrimination learning problems and also found that creating conditions that reduced working memory capacity in young adults by having them simultaneously perform a digit-span task together with the discrimination learning task resulted in performance levels comparable with those of older adults.

Although a mediator role for speed of processing and several aspects of working memory seems well established, findings are inconsistent concerning specific executive functions. Salthouse and colleagues found that the functions of task switching (Salthouse, 2001b; Salthouse, Fristoe, McGuthry, & Hambrick, 1998), division of attention (Salthouse, Fristoe, Lineweaver, & Coon, 1995), and inhibition (Salthouse & Meinz, 1995) do not clearly meet the criteria of a mediator. In particular, they are not sufficiently independent of reasoning and other higher order cognitive abilities (Salthouse, 2005b). When mediator effects for executive functions are present in the Salthouse research program, as in the case of time sharing, they appear to be small and less than perceptual speed (Salthouse & Miles, 2002). These findings of a fundamental lack of independence between executive function measures and reasoning measures is related to our earlier discussion of metacognitive theories of deductive reasoning and the generally unresearched issue of whether metacognitive factors implicated in the development of reasoning are genuinely independent of logical competence per se.

Despite the findings of Salthouse and colleagues, executive functions remain viable candidates for mediators of the development–reasoning relation in adulthood, as discussed later in considering more experimental research. Darowski, Helder, Zacks, Hasher, and Hambrick (2008) found a partial mediator role for distraction control (inhibiting the processing of distracting information) in age-related deficits in both working memory and matrix reasoning, though the mediational role was stronger for working memory than for reasoning. We return to this discussion later in this section.

Problem-Solving Studies

Problem-solving paradigms for the study of deductive reasoning in the late adult years provide data regarding more concrete manifestations of deduction, as was the case for the use of these paradigms in child development research. A small body of research within a traditional Piagetian approach is reviewed first. In addition, several paradigms have been used that resemble proof construction problems, a type of task of particular interest to Piaget in the later years of his research program.

Piagetian Measures of Logical Thinking

Standard or modified Piagetian measures of logical thinking have been used with older adults in research primarily from the 1970s. The findings are mixed and seem to vary by task. Age-related effects are consistently found for versions of the class inclusion problem including a version with familiar or everyday materials (Denney & Cornelius, 1975; Fontaine & Pennequin, 2000; Muhs et al., 1979–1980; Sinnott, 1975), though the effects of education are sometimes stronger than age-related effects (Muhs et al., 1979–1980). The basis for the age-related effects is far from clear. In one informative study involving children and older adults, the child participants had difficulty with the simultaneous status of elements as members of a superordinate class and a subclass, an aspect of the problem directly implicating logical competence. The older adults, however, had difficulty with selectively attending to key information in the problem, a deficit that is arguably more procedural than competence based (Fontaine & Pennequin).

Results for formal operational measures are less clear-cut than the class reasoning findings. Sinnot (1975) found age-related effects on combinatorial reasoning and proportional reasoning problems for both formal content and familiar content versions. The familiar content versions were easier than the formal content versions for all age groups, but especially for late adulthood. Muhs et al. (1979–1980) found age-related effects for combinatorial reasoning, and Clayton and Overton (1976) found age-related effects for combinatorial reasoning and the pendulum problem, with each of two older groups doing more poorly than the young group. However, neither study found any age-related effect for transitive reasoning. Other research, by contrast, has failed to find age-related differences across the adult years on formal operational measures. Using a large sample, Sinnott and Guttmann (1978) found that 54% of adults older than 60 years passed the familiar materials version of the proportional reasoning problem. Tomlinson-Keasey (1972) found comparable percentages of young and middle-aged adults (mean age, 54 years) reaching the formal operational level using Piaget's criteria (67% and 54%, respectively). The older and younger groups also benefited from training as evident from performance on a near-transfer, but not a far-transfer, task. Blackburn (1984) found no age-related effects for formal operational measures including recipe, chemicals, and flexibility-of-a-rod problems, together with analogies and number relations. The older adults in his study were generally at the formal operational level. However, this was a highly motivated and educationally elite group of individuals attending college. In summary, the Piagetian literature does not present a clear picture with regard to age-related effects, but the latter appear more often than not in the existing research. Curiously, age-related effects

have been more consistent with class reasoning measures than with formal operational measures.

Proof Construction Problems

Three closely related paradigms are used in the adult problem-solving literature that, in most cases, involve a kind of proof construction (Piaget, 1987). To this extent, these paradigms are measures of deductive reasoning, albeit at a relatively more concrete level than propositional reasoning tasks. The paradigms referred to are logical analysis problems (e.g., Kesler et al., 1976; Wetherick, 1964; Young, 1971), concept acquisition or concept learning studies (e.g., Arenberg, 1974; Haught et al., 2000), and 20 questions problems (e.g., Denney, Pearce, & Palmer, 1982; Hartley & Anderson, 1983; Heidrich & Denney, 1994). The deductive nature of these problems is evident from several of their properties. First, some combinatorial reasoning process is required to generate a finite set of possible solutions or possible hypotheses to test. Second, each of the participant's responses potentially provides information that, when combined across responses, leads to the solution. In particular, the moves eliminate possible solutions from a finite solution set. Third, the solution to the problem is logically necessary given specific information learned from the participant's responses. Fourth, some measure of move efficiency, that is, the informative value of the move with regard to eliminating possible solutions, is used in the scoring. Fifth, the problem involves a constraint of reaching solution in as few moves as possible—an instruction that might be expected to induce a deductive set in the participant. As a result of this constraint, a falsification strategy is essential to success on the problem.

Similar to producing a logical proof, the task of each paradigm requires participants to produce moves that are individually necessary and jointly sufficient to reach solution. Not all the studies employing these paradigms meet each of these five criteria, and this seems to be closely related to the outcomes of the studies. For example, in some studies, it is not clear that the participant is instructed to reach solution in the minimal number of moves. These studies, therefore, are less likely to induce a deductive set in the participant or to otherwise access a deductive competence. Interestingly, studies that meet the above criteria are less likely to find age-related effects than those that do not.

The *logical analysis* paradigm makes use of some variant of a task developed by John (1957) and referred to as a Logical Analysis Device. Although multiple versions of this device have been used, they each require the participant to identify which of several possible sequences of switches or button presses is logically necessary and sufficient to turn on a target light. The participant must select switches or switch combinations and note the outcomes of those selections to arrive at the correct solution. In the *concept attainment* paradigm (see Bruner, Goodnow, & Austin, 1956, for the introduction of this problem into the developmental literature), participants seek to identify a rule indicating a specific combination of attributes along several dimensions; for example, what specific foods in a three-course meal have been poisoned. Participants choose a particular combination (e.g., salad for the first course, pot roast for the second, and apple pie for the third) and indicate whether they believe it follows the rule or breaks the rule. They are then told whether they are correct about this particular combination. In the *20 questions* paradigm, participants are presented with an array of cards, each of which depicts an object or item belonging to multiple categories. One of these cards is designated as the solution and the participant must determine it by asking "yes" or "no" questions.

The *logical analysis* paradigm has produced mixed findings regarding age-related effects. The different outcomes produced by this paradigm appear to be a function, in part, of the degree of difficulty of the problem. Using close variants of the original task, cross-sectional (Jerome, 1962; Young, 1966) and longitudinal (Arenberg, 1974) studies report poorer performance in older adults relative to younger adults. The longitudinal comparison finds significant age-related decrements only in adults 70 years and older, whereas the cross-sectional studies find evidence of age-related effects by the 60s. Attempts to reduce the short-term memory and selective attention demands of the problem, and efforts to provide training in a set of heuristics for reaching solution had only limited effectiveness for the older adults (Young, 1966). Other studies, however, using a simpler one-attribute logical rule (i.e., a single button or switch, rather than a combination, represents the solution) report either no age-related differences (Kesler et al., 1976; Wetherick, 1964) or age-related effects for men but not women (Young, 1971). Most importantly, age-related differences favoring younger over older participants are least in evidence when the procedure for the task meets all five of the earlier proof construction criteria, including the minimal move constraint (Kesler et al., 1976; Wetherick, 1964; Young, 1971).

The results for *concept attainment* problems also seem to depend on crucial aspects of the procedure, including

the extent to which it involves proof construction. Many versions of concept attainment tasks clearly do not qualify as proof construction problems. For example, several studies involve experimenter control over stimulus presentation; that is, the experimenter dictates the attribute combinations to test. Consequently, participants are not instructed to solve in the minimal number of moves. Also, scoring in these versions of the task generally does not consist of a measure of the relative informativeness, hence efficiency, of moves (e.g., number of trials to solution, cumulative value of moves in eliminating possible solutions; but see West, Odom, & Aschkenasy, 1978). Instead, scoring involves the number of problems correctly solved or the number of errors of a certain type. Under this format, cross-sectional studies report age-related effects (Arenberg, 1968; Brinley, Jovich, & McLaughlin, 1974; Hartley, 1981; Hess & Slaughter, 1986; Offenbach, 1974; West et al.; Wetherick, 1966) even with basic, one-concept problems, and in one study (Brinley et al., 1974), age-related differences were present before age 50. By contrast, on those concept attainment studies that have the participant select moves, that is, choose hypotheses to test, and that assess informativeness or efficiency of moves, the available results present a different picture. Two studies report age-related differences in time to solution, but not in number of trails to solution (Haught et al., 2000) or in number of errors (Haught et al.; Wiersma & Klausmeier, 1965), even when considering groups 65 to 80 years of age (Haught et al.). A third, longitudinal study (Arenberg, 1974) meeting the proof construction criteria finds age-related differences across middle and older adulthood. However, the age-related effects are small until the eighth or ninth decade of life. Thus, the results for this paradigm, as with the logical analysis problems, suggest little, if any, age-related differences on versions of the task that seem most likely to involve deductive reasoning.

Even where age-related effects are present on concept attainment problems, they do not seem to involve competence deficits. West et al. (1978) found that on problems of *high* perceptual salience for the participant, older adults performed at levels comparable with those achieved by the young adults on problems of *low* perceptual salience, suggesting that a basic competence for concept attainment was available to the older participants. In Wetherick's (1966) study, there were more errors of a given type by the older participants but no age-related difference in the overall number of all types of errors. In the Brinley et al. (1974) study referred to earlier, the two older age groups found low organization problems, where two relations needed to be processed, much harder than high organization problems. Thus, older adults can approximate the performance of young adults when the level of complexity is adjusted. Most significantly, training procedures that seek to induce effective hypothesis-testing strategies through the use of strategy hints, memory cues, verbal feedback, and cumulative experience with problems at different levels of complexity have been successful in significantly improving the performance of older adults (e.g., 65–83 years; Sanders, Sterns, Smith, & Sanders, 1975; Sanders, Sanders, Mayes, & Sielski, 1976). In addition, training effects have been found up to one year later and to transfer to problems of greater complexity than those used in training (Sanders & Sanders, 1978).

On *20 questions* problems, some studies (Denney & Palmer, 1981; Kesler et al., 1976) have found that education is more strongly related to performance than is age, and that age-related effects are absent once education is taken into account, suggesting that some age-related effects, when present, may actually be cohort effects. The majority of studies, however, find that even when significant education effects are present (e.g., Denney & Palmer; Denney & Denney, 1973), age-related effects contribute significantly and uniquely to variance in performance measures, such as the number of constraint-seeking questions, the number of questions to solution, and the average amount of information gain from the participant's questions (Denney et al., 1982; Hartley & Anderson, 1983; Heidrich & Denney, 1994; Hybertson, Perdue, & Hybertson, 1982). Once again, however, training studies with older adults has generally been successful. Interventions involving either modeling constraint-seeking questions or explicitly verbalizing the rule underlying this strategy significantly improved the performance of adults 60 to 90 years of age (Denney & Denney, 1974; Denney, Wells Jones, & Krigel, 1979), suggesting that the competence to use a falsification strategy and to reason deductively on this problem is present even quite late in life (Denney & Wright, 1976). The use of practice has also been found to lead to improvement (Hybertson et al., 1982). Motivational interventions, in contrast, have not been effective (Denney, 1980a). Further indication that older adults have the competence to use the falsification strategy of constraint seeking is evident in findings that older adults are actually more likely to spontaneously use the strategy on problems that are designed to be easier (e.g., playing cards) or harder than on the standard format (Denney, 1980b), though this result was not replicated by Hartley and Anderson (1983).

To summarize the research using proof construction paradigms, it is evident that for two of the three paradigms, age-related effects are generally absent when the studies adhere, strictly, to the criteria of a proof construction. These are conditions under which the paradigm is most likely to be assessing deductive reasoning, albeit it in relatively concrete forms. In addition, success by older adults is fairly readily trained and is significantly more likely when task complexity is reduced while preserving the logical demands of the task.

Formal Deductive Reasoning—Syllogism and Conditional Reasoning Studies

Adult developmental research using syllogistic or conditional reasoning tasks is limited, but the cumulative findings are informative with regard to possible bases for any age-related effects that have been found. This characterization, however, applies more to the later studies in this category. The early research is particularly difficult to interpret. In two initial cross-sectional studies of *syllogistic* reasoning across the adult years, Morgan (1956) and Nehrke (1972) used formally diverse sets of syllogisms and found evidence of age-related deficits as early as 30 to 39 years in the ability to distinguish between valid and invalid argument forms. However, education moderated these effects in strikingly different ways across the two studies. Morgan found age-related effects for participants with bachelor's degrees, but not participants with master's degrees. Nehrke, in contrast, found that the age-related decline was delayed until midlife, and was preceded by age-graded increases in performance, for those participants whose education did not go beyond high school.

The earliest research on *conditional* reasoning across the adult years also reports age-related effects that are difficult to interpret. Cohen (1981) found evidence of poorer performance among older adults (65–79 years) when compared with young adults (19–29 years) on conditional reasoning problems requiring participants to evaluate the validity of the argument. However, a response option of "perhaps" was included and was interpreted by Cohen as an indication that the participant was responding on an empirical (incorrect), rather than a logical, basis. As subsequent research has indicated, the more appropriate interpretation of this response is that the participant considers the problem to be logically indeterminate. Also, it is not clear how the individual problems may have varied in terms of their content or complexity. At least some of the examples supplied by Cohen make relatively high demands on language processing by using negation, multiple comparatives, and extraneous language (Light, Zelinski, & Moore, 1982).

An important limitation of these three early studies is that, while identifying possible age functions for deductive reasoning, they leave open the question of whether the apparent declines concern logical competence per se or, alternatively, age-related changes in various performance factors that might mask the presence of logical thinking. Several, more contemporary studies (Fisk & Sharp, 2002; Gilinski & Judd, 1994; McKinnon & Moscovitch, 2007; Overton et al., 1986; Pollack et al., 1995; Takahashi & Overton, 1996) include design elements that address the competence-performance distinction. Two of these studies use syllogistic arguments, whereas the other four studies concern conditional reasoning.

Gilinski and Judd (1994) had adults from 19 to 96 years of age either evaluate or construct conclusions to a series of syllogistic arguments that varied systematically in their complexity and the relation between logic (validity) and belief. In general, the findings indicated an apparent decline in syllogistic reasoning with development beginning in midlife. This negative relation between syllogistic reasoning and age was partially mediated by performance on measures of vocabulary and working memory, construed as the capacity to process and simultaneously retain information. Some of the age-related effects in reasoning, however, were independent of these performance factors. In particular, older adults were more likely than younger adults to make errors on syllogisms requiring the construction of multiple mental models. In addition, older adults were more vulnerable than younger adults to belief-bias effects. That is, age-related effects were stronger for syllogisms where logic and belief were in conflict. Syllogisms with believable conclusions but an invalid form were especially problematic for older adults. When no logic-belief conflict was present, performance was largely unrelated to age (Gilinski & Judd). Individual differences in susceptibility to belief-bias effects have been linked to effectiveness of inhibitory processes in children and adults (Handley et al., 2004).

In a study designed to directly address the findings of Gilinski and Judd (1994), Fisk and Sharp (2002) obtained somewhat different results using strictly abstract syllogisms. A negative relation between reasoning performance and age was present, but it was fully mediated by an age-related decline in processing speed. By contrast, measures assessing the apprehension span of the phonologic and visuospatial short-term stores, as well as the efficiency

of the central executive component of working memory, were only partial mediators and did not account for enough age-related variance to eliminate the age-related effect for syllogism performance. Thus, both Gilinski and Judd and Fisk and Sharp identify significant mediators of age-related effects in syllogistic reasoning performance. Taken together, these sets of findings suggest that aspects of working memory may play an important, if limited, mediational role with regard to late adult development in deductive reasoning. However, the findings also raise the possibility that the status of working memory measures as mediators in age-related declines in reasoning may, in turn, be the result of declines in processing speed. The findings also identify key forms of problem complexity (e.g., number of mental models, belief-logic conflicts) that might be intricately linked to age-related declines.

Three additional studies (Light et al., 1982; McKinnon & Moscovitch, 2007; Viskontas, Holyoak, & Knowlton, 2005) have specifically explored the role of working memory in age-related differences in adult performance on deductive reasoning tasks. McKinnon and Moscovitch (2007) presented younger and older adults with one of two versions of the selection task. In a standard version, featuring both descriptive and abstract content, task instructions framed the problem as one of needing to verify or determine the truth status of the rule. In a deontic version, participants were presented with rules describing a social contract or a precaution. In this condition, instructions framed the problems in terms of needing to detect cheaters or individuals not adopting the precaution. Older adults made more errors than younger adults, but only in one of two experiments. For both age groups, the deontic problems were easier than the standard problems, but this was more the case for the younger adults. Requiring the young adults to perform a second, simultaneous task that tapped working memory resources (n-back task) eliminated the difference between standard and deontic content, thus producing results that more closely paralleled those for the older adults. This would seem to implicate working memory in the age-related effects (McKinnon & Moscovitch, 2007).

Light et al. (1982) and Viskontas et al. (2005) looked at working memory as a mediator of age-related effects in deductive reasoning by manipulating the level of complexity on transitive inference problems involving unfamiliar or novel content. Complexity was operationalized in terms of the number of relations that needed to be processed or integrated simultaneously (see Halford & Andrews, 2004) and was manipulated by varying the terms (e.g., A, B, C) in the premises, the order of the terms in a premise (AB vs. BA), and the ordering of the premises. Thus, the presentation order consisting of AB, BC, CD requires only a single relation to be processed at one time because neighboring premises consistently share adjacent terms and can be integrated into a single representation. This order, therefore, is most conducive to the sequence of transitive inferences necessary for solution. By contrast, the order **AB**, BC, **DA** requires that two relations (in bold) be processed simultaneously because the last two premises share no terms. The order **AB, CD, DA** requires the simultaneous processing of three relations because the first two premises share no term and cannot be integrated without the last premise.

Light et al. (1982) found that older adults (50–86 years of age across three experiments) performed comparable with younger adults (17–36 years of age) under task conditions that presumably did not tax working memory resources. No age-related effects were found when the premises were available for viewing at the time of inference or when the order of premise presentation (AB, BC, CD) required the processing of a single relation. On the other hand, making the premises unavailable at the time of inference, or using presentation orders that require processing multiple relations (BC, AB, CD), degraded the performance of the older adults more so than the younger adults. Viskontas et al. (2005) found that older adults (66–81 years) took more time and made more errors than young adults (18–26 years) on problems with two or more relations. Middle-aged adults (41–55 years) were comparable with younger adults on two-relation problems, but not on three- or four-relation problems. When only a single relation was involved, older adults had longer response times than younger adults but did not differ in accuracy (Viskontas et al., 2005). Notably, the role of real-world knowledge and the role of the phonologic and visuospatial storage systems of working memory were held constant across difficulty levels in the latter study. This would suggest that executive components of working memory, rather than storage or maintenance components, are implicated in the age-by-complexity interaction. This is consistent with findings from the manipulation of relational complexity on inductive reasoning and analogical reasoning problems. Similar degradation of performance in older adults with increased complexity was found for these types of reasoning, and difficulty in ignoring irrelevant information increased for these adults with increasing complexity. In addition, computer modeling that manipulated attentional and inhibitory processes in working memory produced results that were similar to the age-related effects obtained

in these studies (Viskontas, Morrison, Holyoak, Hummel, & Knowlton, 2004; Viskontas et al., 2005).

The results reviewed in this section so far, though lacking in consistency to some degree, suggest that age-related effects in deductive reasoning are mediated by several factors. The most convincing case for mediation seems to be in regard to processing speed, more executive components of working memory, and inhibitory processes, though there is some evidence for more static aspects of working memory capacity as mediators as well. When problems making fewer demands in these respects are employed, age-related effects are small or absent. These studies also provide a useful measure of problem complexity in terms of the number of relations or models to be processed simultaneously.

Findings consistent with those just discussed are reported across three studies by Overton and colleagues (Overton et al., 1986; Pollack et al., 1995; Takahashi & Overton, 1996) using the selection task to assess conditional reasoning in older adults. These studies manipulated problem content and the presence or absence of a metacognitive strategy designed to access logical competence, particularly in older adults. In general, older adults performed more poorly than younger adults on problems with affect-laden content (Pollack et al.; Takahashi & Overton) and problems with content directly relevant to the experience of older individuals (Overton et al., 1986). The latter problems appear to have elicited some degree of emotional arousal in the older participants. No age-related differences were found for affect-neutral content problems and for problems that were not any more relevant to the elderly than to younger adults. In addition, the affect-laden problems were more difficult than the affect-neutral problems for the older adults, but not for the younger adults (Pollack et al.).

The most parsimonious account of Overton's findings would be that deductive reasoning does not decline significantly across the adult years, and that when older participants are reasoning with emotionally arousing content, they are at a disadvantage relative to younger adults. Existing research is mixed, though generally supportive, with respect to this latter claim. Several findings indicate that late adult development is, indeed, associated with problems in the inhibition of emotional arousal (Hasher & Zacks, 1989), and with poorer integration of emotion and cognition (Coats & Blanchard-Fields, 2008). Compared with younger adults, older adults appear to devote more resources to regulating their emotions in coping with interpersonal or everyday problems, and the elderly give relatively higher priority to achieving emotion regulation goals in interpersonal settings (Coats & Blanchard-Fields). In selecting emotion regulation strategies, older adults opt more frequently than younger adults for relatively passive regulation strategies such as withdrawal from the situation, avoidance, suppressing feelings, or self-distraction (Blanchard-Fields, 2007; Blanchard-Fields, Jahnke, & Camp, 1995; Coats & Blanchard-Fields). Late adult age effects in emotion regulation have been observed in decision-making settings as well. Denburg, Reckner, Bechara, and Tranel (2006) have found that older adults with impaired decision making do not demonstrate the anticipatory skin conductance responses that younger adults do on a gambling decision-making problem. Although the autonomic nervous system responses of the young consistently discriminate between impending choices that are advantageous or disadvantageous to the individual, the responses of the elderly appear to be abnormal somatic responses that may not be adaptive.

Two of the Overton studies provided younger and older adults with a relatively simple metacognitive strategy involving a recitation procedure (Pollack et al., 1995; Takahashi & Overton, 1996). Participants in the strategy condition were instructed to pose the question, "Will this card help me decide if the rule is being broken," before considering each alternative card on the selection task. Results indicated that on neutral content problems, older adults who were instructed to use the metacognitive strategy produced more deductive solutions than older adults who were not provided with the strategy. For younger adults, however, the strategy did not facilitate performance. On affect-laden problems, the results were mixed. The strategy facilitated performance in the older adults in one study (Pollack et al.) but not in the other (Takahashi & Overton). Thus, a relatively simple strategy was effective in orienting the older adults to key task information, although this relatively minimal intervention may not be sufficient to offset the effects of emotional arousal.

Summary and Conclusions of Late Adult Development Research

This review of research on the fate of deductive reasoning in the adult and late adult years has considered two key questions. First, are there significant age-related declines in performance on deductive reasoning measures? Second, what is the basis for any age-related effects that are identified? Do they reflect a decline in deductive reasoning competence per se, or alternatively, are they the result of declines in various procedural factors that are instrumental to success in applying a deductive competence? An additional concern is to consider the available theories of the development of deductive reasoning in light of our answers to these questions.

Findings of age-related effects with regard to inductive and deductive reasoning are not difficult to come by. A closer examination of the literature, however, as presented earlier, suggests that, in many cases, the size or even the presence of the effect is misleading. From the empirical finding that deductive reasoning and inductive reasoning show similar age functions in adulthood (Salthouse, 2005a), we attempted to generalize from the substantial research on psychometric measures of induction to the less researched case of deductive reasoning. Despite substantial age differences in cross-sectional research on inductive reasoning within the psychometric approach (Salthouse, 1992, 2001b, 2005a; Salthouse et al., 1989), longitudinal comparisons suggest only moderate decline from the mid-50s to the mid-70s (Schaie, 1994). Evidence of cohort effects (Zelinski & Kennison, 2007) and consistent success in training interventions (Boron et al., 2007; Willis & Schaie, 1986a, 1986b, 1988) support this conclusion. To the extent that conclusions based on psychometric measures of inductive reasoning can be generalized to deductive processes, the psychometric literature suggests that age-related decline in deductive reasoning performance in adulthood is generally moderate, even into the later years.

Results from the substantial problem-solving literature on relatively concrete forms of deductive reasoning, though mixed, do not present clear age-related effects. Once again, there is evidence that decline in deductive reasoning is not inevitable. To the extent that problem-solving paradigms conform to the criteria of proof construction (e.g., Arenberg, 1974; Haught et al., 2000; Kesler et al., 1976; Wetherick, 1964; Wiersma & Klausmeier, 1965; Young, 1971) and, as such, are most clearly assessing deductive reasoning strategies, we are less likely to find differences in performance between younger and older adults. The one possible exception to this concerned 20 questions tasks. Regarding the latter, however, there is ample evidence of success in attempts to train effective approaches to the task (Denney & Denney, 1974; Denney et al., 1979; Hybertson et al., 1982). In addition, performance on lower complexity versions of problems is less likely to show age-related differences.

The key literature regarding the question of age-related effects in deductive reasoning is clearly the relatively small set of studies of syllogistic and conditional reasoning.

These studies are particularly informative because they are the least controversial measures of deduction, and because they vary important potential mediators of the adult development–reasoning relation. Age-related effects in performance are found across most of these studies. However, a consistent finding is that age-related effects are absent or substantially reduced when relatively minimal training is provided (Overton et al., 1986; Pollack et al., 1995; Takahashi & Overton, 1996) or when various mediators of the development–reasoning relation are controlled (Fisk & Sharp, 2002; Gilinski & Judd, 1994; Light et al., 1982; McKinnon & Moscovitch, 2007; Overton et al., 1986; Pollack et al.; Takahashi & Overton, 1996; Viskontas et al., 2005). These mediators include working memory demands, and demands on inhibitory processes and emotion regulation.

Taken as a whole, the body of findings presented in this section provides reasonable support for a claim that the logical competence implicated in deductive reasoning is relatively enduring across the later years. Declines in performance on deductive reasoning tasks are generally mediated by declines in procedural factors that are important to success on these problems. A fairly consistent pattern emerges implicating more executive components of working memory, such as attention regulation, together with other executive functions, particularly inhibitory and regulatory processes (Light et al., 1982; McKinnon & Moscovitch, 2007; Pollack et al., 1995; Takahashi & Overton, 1996; Viskontas et al., 2004, 2005). Speed of processing has also been found to mediate the adult development–reasoning relation in studies that assessed it (Fisk & Sharp, 2002; Verhaeghen & Salthouse, 1997). By contrast, more inert resources within working memory, such as storage capacity and maintenance, do not appear to be implicated to the same extent in age-related effects in deductive reasoning, though they seem to have greater significance as mediators of age-related effects in inductive reasoning (Salthouse, 1992; Salthouse et al., 1989, 1990).

It was noted at the outset of this section that the major developmental theories of deductive reasoning are weighted heavily toward explaining changes across childhood and adolescence, and give dramatically less consideration to late adult development and deductive reasoning. Only competence-procedural theory has undertaken a systematic research program regarding deductive reasoning and late adult development. Insofar as predictions can be derived from the theories, the findings from late adult development research would seem to support the mental logic account in general and competence-procedural theory in

particular. This assessment is based on the earlier conclusion that deductive reasoning competence is largely intact in the later years of life. Mental logic accounts argue that deductive inference is a fundamental characteristic of mature human thought. As inherent to thinking, deductive processes should be relatively immune to the age effects during late adult development (Pollack et al., 1995; Takahashi & Overton, 1996). By contrast, a variety of procedural factors important to accessing and implementing this competence might be expected to be relatively more at risk for the compromising effects found in late adulthood. Similarly, the emphasis, within metacognitive theories, on conceptual knowledge of logic as an important basis for deductive reasoning is consistent with expectations of an intact deductive competence because there is little evidence of age-related decline in declarative aspects of metacognition (Hertzog & Hultsch, 2000). Because mental models theory is wholly dependent on procedural factors in its account of success on deductive reasoning problems, this theory seems most consistent with a decline in deductive reasoning capability with late adult development and is less well-supported by the available adult development findings.

Research on the fate of deductive processes across the adult years is sorely lacking. The conclusions drawn in this review are tentative given the relative absence of systematic research into this question. This chapter concludes with a call for a renewal of interest in the fate of deductive reasoning in the middle and later years of life, and for efforts at extending existing developmental theories to include comprehensive accounts of the basis for age-related effects in reasoning across the adult years.

FUTURE DIRECTIONS

The review of developmental research on deductive reasoning presented in this chapter provides a basis for several brief recommendations regarding future empirical work in this area. There has been a notable decline in studies of deductive reasoning in recent years, and this is particularly the case with regard to developmental studies. On the one hand, this is a positive indication that researchers are increasingly aware of, and interested in, nonmonotonic forms of reasoning. As has been noted in several recent discussions, an *exclusive* focus on deductive processes, deductive instructional sets, and the norms of classic symbolic logic is counterproductive and misplaced (Evans, 2002; Markovits, 2004; Moshman, 2004). The lesser emphasis on deduction in current research also reflects the currently influential view that deductive processes play only a minor role in cognition. Despite the current ascendancy of this view, it is important to recognize that the matter is far from resolved. The precise role and scope of deductive processes in mature cognition is unknown, and claims that it is substantial or insignificant continue to function mostly as higher order assumptions rather than as tested or testable aspects of theory (Overton, 2006). Research is clearly needed in this regard.

One approach that might be taken is to attempt to identify the extent to which deductive processes are implicated in specific thinking skills and on particular problems assessing these skills. In addition to standard skill areas such as decision making and scientific thinking, argumentation (Kuhn, 1991; Kuhn & Franklin, 2006; Ricco, 2002, 2007, 2008) represents a recent and promising area of study in which we might assess the relevance of deductive processes to critical, skeptical, or analytic modes of thinking. Although generally an informal and nonmonotonic process for subjecting disputed claims to rational doubt (van Eemeren & Grootendorst, 1988), everyday argumentation may also involve deductive processes (Ricco, 2007). For example, when cooperative and credulous processing in discourse breaks down and a communicant cannot arrive at an adequate interpretation of an utterance, critical or skeptical processing and a more argumentative discourse ensue (Stenning & van Lambalgen, 2008). Crucial to such a conversational repair process could be the explication of assumptions underlying claims, and the use of a more closed and monotonic form of reasoning in which an attempt is made to derive claims strictly from the assumptions, bracketing supplementary information.

Moving from the question of whether deductive processes play a significant role in cognition to the topic addressed by this review, it seems clear that despite substantial data, fundamental questions remain about the development of deductive reasoning. The existing evidence does not dramatically favor one developmental theory over another, and there are obvious inconsistencies within the developmental findings concerning when and whether deductive competence is available. It is the primary recommendation of this review that the rapprochement afforded by competence-procedural theory be seriously considered as an impetus for future research. One potential area for empirical work from within such a theoretical perspective would be to systematically consider the implications of a formal deductive competence for various executive or metacognitive functions. The frameworks of Kuhn and Moshman provide

interesting theoretical resources for such an inquiry. Such a research program would seek to determine which aspects of epistemic awareness/understanding and of executive control are intrinsic to logical competence itself, and which are either manifestations or direct consequences of that competence or moderators of that competence. The findings of Salthouse (2005b) and colleagues regarding the substantial extent of shared variance between reasoning measures and executive measures in adult development are relevant to such a project as well.

The discussion of late adult development research with which this chapter concluded makes it particularly clear that serious study of deductive processes beyond early adulthood has been occasional and unsustained. The bulk of the findings reviewed are more than a decade old and speak merely to the general question of whether age-related effects in deductive reasoning are normative during the adult years. There is substantially less research that can contribute to our understanding of the basis for late adult development. Do age-related effects reflect declines or other manners of change in reasoning processes per se, or are they indicative, merely, of changes in procedural factors instrumental to the access and implementation of reasoning competence? If the latter, then what specific factors are involved? With the exception of research conducted within competence-procedural theory, the existing research is also largely atheoretical, which reflects the lack of a life-span perspective in current theories of deductive reasoning.

Particularly useful would be experimental studies that can verify the tentative conclusions drawn here concerning the specific aspects of working memory and executive control that function as mediators of the development-reasoning relation in late adulthood. Such studies should include both direct measures of working memory or executive processing and indirect assessments involving a manipulation of problem complexity on the deductive reasoning task. Based on the above review, one promising way in which to use problem complexity as an indirect measure of working memory resources would be to define it in terms of the number of simultaneous relations or mental models that must be processed in working on a problem (Gilinski & Judd, 1994; Light et al., 1982; Viskontas et al., 2005).

Another pertinent issue for future adult and late adult development research is raised by findings from one of the few sustained research programs on deductive processes and late adult development. Research from within the Overton laboratory suggests that older adults may be relatively more susceptible than younger adults to content effects on reasoning tasks. Some more contemporary findings are consistent with this claim as well and additional research into this question is clearly merited. Recent research on motivated reasoning provides evidence that older and middle-aged adults have a greater tendency than young adults to adopt an uncritical stance, using primarily heuristic processing, when encountering evidence consistent with their preexisting beliefs (Klaczynski & Robinson, 2000). Thus, older individuals appear to be more likely to engage in motivated reasoning. Klaczynski and Robinson suggest several possible reasons for this. In particular, they focus on the possibility that late adult development may impact lower order mechanisms such as selective attention and cognitive inhibition, which could lead to greater interference of personal belief with more critical reasoning processes or may compromise metacognitive awareness. Both of these outcomes would lead to a greater susceptibility to content effects (see Bialystok & Craik, Chapter 7 of this volume, for a similar argument with regard to a greater dependence on context in the late adult years). It is also possible that the beliefs of older individuals have become more integrated into the self such that they have assumed the epistemological status of truths and, as such, are largely unassailable. At the same time, the greater reliance on content knowledge by older, relative to younger, adults may serve an adaptive function by compensating for general processing deficits (Masunaga & Horn, 2000, 2001; Salthouse, 2005a).

In conclusion, the development of deductive reasoning remains a viable and fresh area of study with many questions still unresolved. Even the role and scope of deductive reasoning in human cognition remains an open and empirical question that must be addressed in new phases of research. Future work on the development of deductive processes would do well to recognize points of compatibility among the extant theories. This review has suggested what the nature of these compatibilities might be.

REFERENCES

Acredolo, C., & Horobin, K. (1987). Development of relational reasoning and avoidance of premature closure. *Developmental Psychology, 23*(1), 13–21.

Adler, J. E. (2008). Philosophical foundations. In J. E. Adler & L. J. Rips (Eds.), *Reasoning: Studies of human inference and its foundations*. Cambridge, MA: Cambridge University Press.

Anderson, A. D., & Belnap, N. D. (1975). *Entailment: The logic of relevance and necessity* (Vol. 1). Princeton, NJ: Princeton University Press.

Ardila, A. (2007). Normal aging increases cognitive heterogeneity: Analysis of dispersion in WAIS III scores across age. *Archives of Clinical Neuropsychology, 22,* 1003–1011.

Arenberg, D. (1968). Concept problem solving in young and old adults. *Journal of Gerontology, 23,* 279–282.

Arenberg, D. (1974). A longitudinal study of problem-solving in adults. *Journal of Gerontology, 29*(6), 650–658.

Barrouillet, P., Markovits, H., & Quinn, S. (2002). Developmental and content effects in reasoning with causal conditionals. *Journal of Experimental Child Psychology, 81*(3), 235–248.

Blackburn, J. A. (1984). The influence of personality, curriculum, and memory correlates on formal reasoning in young adults and elderly persons. *Journal of Gerontology, 39*(2), 207–209.

Blanchard-Fields, F. (2007). Everyday problem-solving and emotion. *Current Directions in Psychological Science, 16*(1), 26–31.

Blanchard-Fields, F., Jahnke, H. C., & Camp, C. (1995). Age differences in problem-solving style: The role of emotional salience. *Psychology and Aging, 10*(2), 173–180.

Boron J. B., Turiano, N. A., Willis, S. L., & Schaie, K. W. (2007). Effects of cognitive training on change in accuracy in inductive reasoning ability. *Journals of Gerontology: Psychological Sciences and Social Sciences, 62B*(3), P179–P186.

Braine, M. D. S. (1978). On the relation between the natural logic of reasoning and standard logic. *Psychological Review, 85*(1), 1–21.

Braine, M. D. S. (1990). The "natural logic" approach to reasoning. In W. F. Overton (Ed.), *Reasoning, necessity, and logic: Developmental perspectives*. Hillsdale, NJ: Erlbaum.

Braine, M. D. S., & O'Brien, D. P. (1998a). The theory of mental-propositional logic: Description and illustration. In M. D. S. Braine & D. P. O'Brien (Eds.), *Mental logic*. Mahwah, NJ: Erlbaum.

Braine, M. D. S., & O'Brien, D. P. (1998b). How to investigate mental logic and the syntax of thought. In M. D. S. Braine & D. P. O'Brien (Eds.), *Mental logic*. Mahwah, NJ: Erlbaum.

Brinley, J. F., Jovick, T. J., & McLaughlin, L. M. (1974). Age, reasoning, and memory in adults. *Journal of Gerontology, 29*(2), 182–189.

Bruner, J. S., Goodnow, J. J., & Austin, G. A. (1956). *A study of thinking*. New York: John Wiley & Sons.

Byrnes, J. P. (1988). Formal operations: A systematic reformulation. *Developmental Review, 8*(1), 66–87.

Byrnes, J. P., & Beilin, H. (1991). The cognitive basis of uncertainty. *Human Development, 34*(4), 189–203.

Byrnes, J. P., & Overton, W. F. (1986). Reasoning about certainty and uncertainty in concrete, causal, and propositional contexts. *Developmental Psychology, 22*(6), 793–799.

Byrnes, J. P., & Overton, W. F. (1988). Reasoning about logical connectives. A developmental analysis. *Journal of Experimental Child Psychology, 46*(2), 194–218.

Caplan, L. J., & Schooler, C. (2008). Household work complexity, intellectual functioning, and self-esteem in men and women. *Journal of Marriage and Family, 68*(4), 883–900.

Chapell, M. S., & Overton, W. F. (1998). Development of logical reasoning in the context of parental style and test anxiety. *Merrill Palmer Quarterly, 44*(2), 141–156.

Chapell, M. S., & Overton, W. F. (2002). Development of logical reasoning and the school performance of African American adolescents in relation to socioeconomic status, ethnic identity, and self-esteem. *Journal of Black Psychology, 28*(4), 295–317.

Chen, Z., & Daehler, M. W. (1989). Positive and negative transfer in analogical problem-solving by 6-year-olds. *Cognitive Development, 4*(4), 327–344.

Chen, Z., & Klahr, D. (1999). All other things being equal: Acquisition and transfer of the control of variables strategy. *Child Development, 70,* 1098–1120.

Cheng, P. W., & Holyoak, K. (1985). Pragmatic reasoning schemas. *Cognitive Psychology, 17*(4), 391–416.

Clayton, V., & Overton, W. F. (1976). Concrete and formal operational thought processes in young adulthood and old age. *International Journal of Aging and Human Development, 7*(3), 237–245.

Coats, A. H., & Blanchard-Fields, F. (2008). Emotion regulation in interpersonal problems: The role of cognitive-emotional complexity, emotion regulation goals, and expressivity. *Psychology and Aging, 23*(1), 39–51.

Cohen, G. (1981). Inferential reasoning in old age. *Cognition, 9,* 59–72.

Cosmides, L., & Tooby, J. (1992). Cognitive adaptations for social exchange. In J. Barkow, L. Cosmides, & J. Tooby (Eds.), *The adapted mind: Evolutionary psychology and the generation of culture.* New York: Oxford University Press.

Cosmides, L., & Tooby, J. (1994). Beyond intuition and instinct blindness: Toward an evolutionarily rigorous cognitive science. *Cognition, 50*(1–3), 41–77.

Craik, F. I. M., & Bialystok, E. (2006). Cognition through the life span: Mechanisms of change. *Trends in Cognitive Science, 10*(3), 131–138.

Cummins, D. D. (1996). Evidence of deontic reasoning in 3- and 4-year-old children. *Memory and Cognition, 24*(6), 823–829.

Cummins, J. (1978). Language and children's ability to evaluate contradictions and tautologies: A critique of Osherson and Markman's findings. *Child Development, 49,* 895–897.

Daniel, D. B., & Klaczynski, P. A. (2006). Developmental and individual differences in conditional reasoning: Effects of logic instructions and alternative antecedents. *Child Development, 77*(2), 339–354.

Darowski, E. S., Helder, E., Zacks, R. T., Hasher, L., & Hambrick, D. Z. (2008). Age-related differences in cognition: The role of distraction control. *Neuropsychology, 22*(5), 638–644.

De Luca, C. R., Wood, S. J., Anderson, V., Buchanan, J., Proffitt, T. M., Mahony, K., & Pantelis, C. (2003). Normative data from the Cantab. I: Development of executive function across the life span. *Journal of Experimental and Clinical Neuropsychology, 25*(2), 242–254.

Denburg, N. L., Reckner, E. C., Bechara, A., & Tranel, D. (2006). Psychophysiological anticipation of positive outcomes promotes advantageous decision-making in normal older persons. *International Journal of Psychophysiology, 61*(1), 19–25.

DeNeys, W., Schaecken, W., & d'Ydewalle, G. (2005). Working memory and counterexample retrieval for causal conditionals. *Thinking and Reasoning, 11*(2), 123–150.

Denney, D. R., & Denney, N. W. (1973). The use of classification for problem solving: A comparison of middle and old age. *Developmental Psychology, 9*(2), 275–278.

Denney, N. W. (1980a). The effect of the manipulation of peripheral, noncognitive variables on the problem-solving performance of the elderly. *Human Development, 23*(4), 268–277.

Denney, N. W. (1980b). Task demands and problem solving strategies in middle-aged and older adults. *Journal of Gerontology, 35,* 559–564.

Denney, N. W., & Cornelius, S. (1975). Class inclusion and multiple classification in middle age and old age. *Developmental Psychology, 11*(4), 521–522.

Denney, N. W., & Denney, D. R. (1974). Modeling effects on the questioning strategies of the elderly. *Developmental Psychology, 10*(3), 458.

Denney, N. W., & Palmer, A. M. (1981). Adult age differences in traditional and practical problem-solving measures. *Journal of Gerontology, 36,* 323.

Denney, N. W., Pearce, K. A., & Palmer, A. M. (1982). A developmental study of adults' performance on practical and traditional problem-solving tasks. *Experimental Aging Research, 8*(2), 115–118.

Denney, N. W., Wells Jones, F., & Krigel, S. H. (1979). Modifying the questioning strategies of young children and elderly adults with strategy-modeling techniques. *Human Development, 22*(1), 23–36.

Denney, N. W., & Wright, J. C. (1976). Cognitive changes during the adult years: Implications for developmental theory and research. In H. W. Reese (Ed.), *Advances in child development and behavior.* New York: Academic Press.

Dias, M., & Harris, P. L. (1988). The effect of make-believe play on deductive reasoning. *British Journal of Developmental Psychology, 6*(3), 207–221.

Dias, M., & Harris, P. L. (1990). The influence of the imagination on reasoning in young children. *British Journal of Developmental Psychology, 8*(4), 305–318.

Emick, J., & Welsh, M. (2005). Association between formal operational thought and executive function as measured by the Tower of Hanoi-Revised. *Learning and Individual Differences, 15,* 177–188.

Evans, J. S. (2002). Logic and human reasoning: An assessment of the deduction paradigm. *Psychological Bulletin, 128*(6), 978–996.

Evans, J. S. (2007). *Hypothetical thinking: Dual processes in reasoning and judgment.* Hove, United Kingdom: Psychology Press.

Evans, J. S., & Thompson, V. A. (2004). Informal reasoning: Theory and method. *Canadian Journal of Experimental Psychology, 58*(2), 69–74.

Fabricius, W. V., Sophian, C., & Wellman, H. M. (1987). Young children's sensitivity to logical necessity in their inferential search behavior. *Child Development, 58,* 409–423.

Fisk, J. E., & Sharp, C. (2002). Syllogistic reasoning and cognitive ageing. *Quarterly Journal of Experimental Psychology, 55A*(4), 1273–1293.

Foltz, C., Overton, W. F., & Ricco, R. B. (1995). Proof construction: Adolescent development from inductive to deductive problem-solving strategies. *Journal of Experimental Child Psychology, 59*(2), 179–195.

Fontaine, R., & Pennequin, V. (2000). Effect of aging on inferential reasoning about class inclusion. *Cahiers de Psychologie Cognitive, 19*(4), 453–482.

Gentzen, G. (1964). Investigations into logical deduction. *American Philosophical Quarterly, 1,* 288–306. (Original work published 1935)

George, C. (1997). Reasoning from uncertain premises. *Thinking and Reasoning, 3*(3), 161–189.

Gilinski, A. S., & Judd, B. B. (1994). Working memory and bias in reasoning across the life span. *Psychology and Aging, 9*(3), 356–371.

Girotto, V., Blaye, A., & Farioli, F. (1989). A reason to reason: Pragmatic basis of children's search for counterexamples. *Cahiers de Psychologie Cognitive/Current Psychology of Cognition, 9*(3), 297–321.

Girotto, V., Gilly, M., Blaye, A., & Light, P. (1989). Children's performance on the selection task: Plausibility and familiarity. *British Journal of Psychology, 80*(1), 79–95.

Girotto, V., Light, P., & Colbourn, C. J. (1988). Pragmatic schemes and conditional reasoning in children. *Quarterly Journal of Experimental Psychology: Human Experimental Psychology, 40A*(3), 469–482.

Grice, H. D. (1975). Logic and conversation. In P. Cole & J. L. Morgan (Eds.), *Syntax and semantics 3: Speech acts.* New York: Academic Press.

Grice, H. P. (1989). *Studies in the way of words.* Cambridge, MA: Harvard University Press.

Griggs, R. A., & Cox, J. R. (1982). The elusive thematic-materials effect in Wason's selection task. *British Journal of Psychology, 73*(3), 407–420.

Haack, S. (1978). *Philosophy of logics*. Cambridge: Cambridge University Press.

Halford, G. S., & Andrews, G. (2004). The development of deductive reasoning: How important is complexity? *Thinking and Reasoning, 10*(2), 123–145.

Handley, S. J., Capon, A., Beveridge, M., Dennis, I., & Evans, J. S. (2004). Working memory, inhibitory control, and the development of children's reasoning. *Thinking and Reasoning, 10*(2), 175–195.

Harris, P. L., & Nunez, M. (1996). Understanding of permission rules by preschool children. *Child Development, 67*, 1572–1591.

Hartley, A. A. (1981). Adult age differences in deductive reasoning processes. *Journal of Gerontology, 36*(6), 700–706.

Hartley, A. A., & Anderson, J. W. (1983). Task complexity and problem-solving performance in younger and older adults. *Journal of Gerontology, 38*(1), 72–77.

Hasher, L., & Zacks, R. T. (1989). Working memory, comprehension, and aging: A review and a new view. In G. H. Bower (Ed.), *The psychology of learning and motivation: Advances in research and theory* (Vol. 22). San Diego, CA: Academic Press.

Haught, P. A., Hill, L. A., Nardi, A. H., & Walls, R. T. (2000). Perceived ability and level of education as predictors of traditional and practical adult problem solving. *Experimental Aging Research, 26*(1), 89–101.

Hawkins, J., Pea, R. D., Glick, J., & Scribner, S. (1984). "Merds that laugh don't like mushrooms": Evidence for deductive reasoning by preschoolers. *Developmental Psychology, 20*(4), 584–594.

Heidrich, S. M., & Denney, N. W. (1994). Does social problem solving differ from other types of problem solving during the adult years. *Experimental Aging Research, 20*(2), 105–126.

Hertzog, C., & Hultsch, D. (2000). Metacognition in adulthood and old age. In F. I. M. Craik & T. A. Salthouse (Eds.), *The handbook of aging and cognition* (2nd ed.). Mahwah, NJ: LEA.

Hess, T. M., & Slaughter, S. J. (1986). Aging effects on prototype extraction and concept identification. *Journal of Gerontology, 41*(2), 214–221.

Horn, J. L., & Cattell, R. B. (1967). Age differences in fluid and crystallized intelligence. *Acta Psychologica, 26*, 107–129.

Horobin, K., & Acredolo, C. (1989). The impact of probability judgments on reasoning about multiple possibilities. *Child Development, 60*, 183–200.

Hybertson, D., Perdue, J., & Hybertson, D. (1982). Age differences in information acquisition strategies. *Experimental Aging Research, 8*(2), 109–113.

Inhelder, B., & Piaget, J. (1958). *The growth of logical thinking from childhood to adolescence*. New York: Basic Books.

Inhelder, B., & Piaget, J. (1964). *The early growth of logic in the child*. New York: W. W. Norton & Co.

Janveau-Brennan, G., & Markovits, H. (1999). The development of reasoning with causal conditionals. *Developmental Psychology, 35*(4), 904–911.

Jerome, E. A. (1962). Decay of heuristic processes in the aged. In C. Tibbitts & W. Donahue (Eds.), *Social and psychological aspects of aging*. New York: Columbia University Press.

John, E. R. (1957). Contributions to the study of the problem-solving process. *Psychological Monographs, 71*, 1–39.

Johnson-Laird, P. N. (2008). Mental models and deductive reasoning. In J. E. Adler & L. J. Rips (Eds.), *Reasoning: Studies of human inference and its foundations*. Cambridge, MA: Cambridge University Press.

Kahane, H. (1973). *Logic and philosophy*. Belmont, CA: Wadsworth.

Karmiloff-Smith, A. (1986). From meta-processes to conscious access: Evidence from children's metalinguistic and repair data. *Cognition, 23*(2), 95–147.

Kaufman, A. S., & Kaufman, N. L. (1993). *Kaufman Adolescent and Adult Intelligence Test (KAIT)*. Circle Pines, MN: American Guidance Service.

Kesler, M. S., Denney, N. W., & Whitely, S. E. (1976). Factors influencing problem-solving in middle-aged and elderly adults. *Human Development, 19*(5), 310–320.

Klaczynski, P. A. (1993). Reasoning schema effects on adolescent rule acquisition and transfer. *Journal of Educational Psychology, 85*(4), 679–692.

Klaczynski, P. A. (2000). Motivated scientific reasoning biases, epistemological beliefs, and theory polarization: A two process approach to adolescent cognition. *Child Development, 71*(5), 1347–1366.

Klaczynski, P. A., & Robinson, B. (2000). Personal theories, intellectual abilities, and epistemological beliefs: Adult age differences in everyday reasoning biases. *Psychology and Aging, 15*(3), 400–416.

Klaczynski, P. A., Schuneman, M. J., & Daniel, D. (2004). Theories of conditional reasoning: A developmental examination of competing hypotheses. *Developmental Psychology, 40*(4), 559–571.

Klahr, D., & Chen, Z. (2003). Overcoming the positive-capture strategy in young children's learning about indeterminacy. *Child Development, 74*(5), 1275–1296.

Kneale, W., & Kneale, M. (1962). *The development of logic*. Oxford: Oxford University Press.

Komatsu, L. K., & Galotti, K. M. (1986). Children's reasoning about social, physical, and logical regularities: A look at two worlds. *Child Development, 57*, 413–420.

Kramer, A. F., & Kray, J. (2006). Aging and attention. In E. Bialystok & F. I. M. Craik (Eds.), *Life span cognition: Mechanisms of change* (pp. 57–69). Oxford: Oxford University Press.

Kuhn, D. (1977). Conditional reasoning in children. *Developmental Psychology, 13*(4), 342–353.

Kuhn, D. (1991). *The skills of argument*. New York: Cambridge University Press.

Kuhn, D. (2001). How do people know? *Psychological Science, 12*(1), 1–8.

Kuhn, D. (2002). What is scientific thinking and how does it develop? In U. Goswami (Ed.), *Handbook of childhood cognitive development* (pp. 371–393). Oxford: Blackwell.

Kuhn, D., & Franklin, S. (2006). The second decade: What develops (and how). In W. Damon & R. M. Lerner (Series Eds.) & D. Kuhn & R. S. Siegler (Vol. Eds.), *Handbook of child psychology: Vol. 2, Cognition, perception, and language*. Hoboken, NJ: John Wiley & Sons.

Kuhn, D., Katz, J. B., & Dean, D. Jr. (2004). Developing reason. *Thinking and Reasoning, 10*(2), 197–219.

Kuhn, D., & Park, S. (2005). Epistemological understanding and the development of intellectual values. *International Journal of Educational Research, 43*, 111–124.

LeBlanc, H., & Wisdom, W. A. (1976). *Deductive logic*. Boston: Allyn and Bacon.

Leevers, H. J., & Harris, P. L. (1999). Persisting effects of instruction on young children's syllogistic reasoning with incongruent and abstract premises. *Thinking and Reasoning, 5*(2), 145–173.

Lerner, R. M., & Overton, W. F. (2008). Exemplifying the integrations of the relational developmental system: Synthesizing theory, research, and application to promote positive development and social justice. *Journal of Adolescent Research, 23*, 245–255.

Light, L. L., Zelinski, E. M., & Moore, M. (1982). Adult age differences in reasoning from new information. *Journal of Experimental Psychology: Learning, Memory, and Cognition, 8*(5), 435–447.

MacDonald, S. W. S., Dixon, R. A., Cohen, A., & Hazlitt, J. E. (2004). Biological age and 12-year cognitive change in older adults: Findings from the Victoria Longitudinal Study. *Gerontology, 50*(2), 64–81.

Manktelow, K. I., & Evans, J. S. (1979). Facilitation of reasoning by realism: Effect or non-effect? *British Journal of Psychology, 70*(4), 477–488.

Markovits, H. (2000). A mental model analysis of young children's conditional reasoning with meaningful premises. *Thinking and Reasoning, 6*(4), 335–347.

Markovits, H. (2004). The development of deductive reasoning. In J. P. Leighton & R. J. Sternberg (Eds.), *The nature of reasoning*. Cambridge: Cambridge University Press.

Markovits, H., & Barrouillet, P. (2002). The development of conditional reasoning: A mental model account. *Developmental Review, 22*(1), 5–36.

Markovits, H., & Barrouillet, P. (2004). Introduction: Why is understanding the development of reasoning important? *Thinking and Reasoning, 10*(2), 113–121.

Markovits, H., Doyon, C., & Simoneau, M. (2002). Individual differences in working memory and conditional reasoning with concrete and abstract content. *Thinking and Reasoning, 8*(2), 97–107.

Markovits, H., Fleury, M., Quinn, S., & Venet, M. (1998). The development of conditional reasoning and the structure of semantic memory. *Child Development, 69*(3), 742–755.

Markovits, H., & Nantel, G. (1989). The belief-bias effect in the production and evaluation of logical conclusions. *Memory and Cognition, 17*(1), 11–17.

Markovits, H., Schleifer, M., & Fortier, L. (1989). Development of elementary deductive reasoning in young children. *Developmental Psychology, 25*(5), 787–793.

Markovits, H., & Vachon, R. (1989). Reasoning with contrary-to-fact propositions. *Journal of Child Experimental Psychology, 47(3)*, 398–412.

Markovits, H., & Vachon, R. (1990). Conditional reasoning, representation, and level of abstraction. *Developmental Psychology, 26*(6), 942–957.

Markovits, H., Venet, M., Janveau-Brennan, G., Malfait, N., Pion, N., & Vadeboncoeur, I. (1996). Reasoning in young children: Fantasy and information retrieval. *Child Development, 67*, 2857–2872.

Masunaga, H., & Horn, J. (2000). Characterizing mature human intelligence: Expertise development. *Learning and Individual Differences, 12*(1), 5–33.

Masunaga, H., & Horn, J. (2001). Expertise and age-related changes in components of intelligence. *Psychology and Aging, 16*(2), 293–311.

McKinnon, M. C., & Moscovitch, M. (2007). Domain-general contributions to social reasoning: Theory of mind and deontic reasoning explored. *Cognition, 102*(2), 179–218.

Miller, S. A. (1986). Certainty and necessity in the understanding of Piagetian concepts. *Developmental Psychology, 22*(1), 3–18.

Miller, S. A., Custer, W. L., & Nassau, G. (2000). Children's understanding of the necessity of logically necessary truths. *Cognitive Development, 15*(3), 383–403.

Morgan, A. B. (1956). Differences in logical reasoning associated with age and higher education. *Psychological Reports, 2*, 235–240.

Morley, N. J., Evans, J. S., & Handley, S. J. (2004). Belief bias and figural bias in syllogistic reasoning. *Quarterly Journal of Experimental Psychology, 57A*(4), 666–692.

Morris, A. K. (2000). Development of logical reasoning: Children's ability to verbally explain the nature of the distinction between logical and nonlogical forms of argument. *Developmental Psychology, 36*(6), 741–758.

Morris, A. K., & Sloutsky, V. M. (1998). Understanding of logical necessity: Developmental antecedents and cognitive consequences. *Child Development, 69*(3), 721–741.

Morris, B. J., & Sloutsky, V. (2001). Children's solutions of logical versus empirical problems: What's missing and what develops? *Cognitive Development, 16*(4), 907–928.

Moshman, D. (1990). The development of metalogical understanding. In W. F. Overton (Ed.), *Reasoning, necessity, and logic: Developmental perspectives*. Hillsdale, NJ: Erlbaum.

Moshman, D. (1998). Cognitive development beyond childhood. In W. Damon (Ed.), *Handbook of child psychology: Vol. 2, Cognition, perception, and language* (pp. 947–978). New York: John Wiley & Sons.

Moshman, D. (2004). From inference to reasoning: The construction of rationality. *Thinking and Reasoning, 10*(2), 221–241.

Moshman, D., & Franks, B. A. (1986). Development of the concept of inferential validity. *Child Development, 57*, 153–165.

Muhs, P. J., Hooper, F. H., & Papalia-Finlay, D. (1979–1980). Cross-sectional analysis of cognitive functioning across the life-span. *International Journal of Aging and Human Development, 10*(4), 311–333.

Müller, U., Overton, W. F., & Reene, K. (2001). Development of conditional reasoning: A longitudinal study. *Journal of Cognition and Development, 2*(1), 27–49.

Müller, U., Sokol, B., & Overton, W. F. (1999). Developmental sequences in class reasoning and propositional reasoning. *Journal of Experimental Child Psychology, 74*(2), 69–106.

Mutter, S. A., Haggbloom, S. J., Plumlee, L. F., & Schirmer, A. R. (2006). Aging, working memory, and discrimination learning. *Quarterly Journal of Experimental Psychology, 59*(9), 1556–1566.

Nehrke, M. F. (1972). Age, sex, and educational differences in syllogistic reasoning. *Journal of Gerontology, 27*(4), 466–470.

Nesdale, A. R., Tunmer, W. E., & Clover, J. (1985). Factors influencing young children's awareness of logical inconsistencies. *Journal of Experimental Child Psychology, 36*(1), 97–108.

Noveck, I. A., & O'Brien, D. P. (1996). To what extent do pragmatic reasoning schemas affect performance on Wason's selection task? *Quarterly Journal of Experimental Psychology, 49A*(2), 463–489.

Nicholls, J. G., & Thorkildsen, T. A. (1988). Children's distinctions among matters of intellectual convention, logic, fact, and personal preference. *Child Development, 59*, 939–949.

Oaksford, M., Chater, N., & Hahn, U. (2008). Human reasoning and argumentation: The probabilistic approach. In J. E. Adler & L. J. Rips (Eds.), *Reasoning: Studies of human inference and its foundations*. Cambridge: Cambridge University Press.

O'Brien, D. P. (1998a). Introduction: Some background to the mental-logic theory and to the book. In M. D. S. Braine & D. P. O'Brien (Eds.), *Mental logic*. Mahwah, NJ: Erlbaum.

O'Brien, D. P. (1998b). Mental logic and irrationality: We can put a man on the moon, so why can't we solve those logical reasoning problems? In M. D. S. Braine & D. P. O'Brien (Eds.), *Mental logic*. Mahwah, NJ: Erlbaum.

O'Brien, D. P. (2004). Mental-logic theory: What it proposes, and reason to take this proposal seriously. In J. P. Leighton & R. J. Sternberg (Eds.), *The nature of reasoning*. Cambridge: Cambridge University Press.

O'Brien, D. P., Costa, G., & Overton, W. F. (1986). Evaluation of causal and conditional hypotheses. *Quarterly Journal of Experimental Psychology, 38A*(3), 493–512.

O'Brien, D. P., & Overton, W. F. (1980). Conditional reasoning following contradictory evidence: A developmental analysis. *Journal of Experimental Child Psychology, 30*(1), 44–60.

O'Brien, D. P., & Overton, W. F. (1982). Conditional reasoning and the competence performance issue: A developmental analysis of a training task. *Journal of Experimental Child Psychology, 34*(2), 274–290.

Offenbach, S. I. (1974). A developmental study of hypothesis testing and cue selection strategies. *Developmental Psychology, 10*(4), 284–290.

Osherson, D. N., & Markman, E. (1975). Language and the ability to evaluate contradictions and tautologies. *Cognition, 3*(3), 213–226.

Overton, W. F. (1990). Competence and procedures: Constraints on the development of logical reasoning. In W. F. Overton (Ed.), *Reasoning, necessity, and logic: Developmental perspectives* (pp. 1–32). Hillsdale, NJ: Erlbaum.

Overton, W. F. (1991). Competence, procedures, and hardware: Conceptual and empirical considerations. In M. Chandler & M. Chapman (Eds.), *Criteria for competence: Controversy in the conceptualization and assessment of children's ability.* Hillside, NJ: Erlbaum.

Overton, W. F. (2003). Development across the life span: Philosophy, concepts, theory. In R. M. Lerner, M. A. Easterbrooks, & J. Mistry (Eds.), *Comprehensive handbook of psychology: Developmental psychology* (Vol. 6). Hoboken, NJ: John Wiley & Sons.

Overton, W. F. (2006). Developmental psychology: Philosophy, concepts, and methodology. In R. M. Lerner & W. Damon (Eds.), *Handbook of child psychology: Vol. 1, Theoretical models of human development* (6th ed., pp. 18–88). Hoboken, NJ: John Wiley & Sons.

Overton, W. F., Byrnes, J. P., & O'Brien, D. P. (1985). Developmental and individual differences in conditional reasoning: The role of contradiction training and cognitive style. *Developmental Psychology, 21*(4), 692–701.

Overton, W. F., & Dick, A. S. (2007). A competence-procedural and developmental approach to logical reasoning. In M. J. Roberts (Ed.), *Integrating the mind: Domain general versus domain specific processes in higher cognition.* New York: Psychology Press.

Overton, W. F., & Ennis, M. D. (2006). Cognitive-developmental and behavior-analytic theories: Evolving into complementarity. *Human Development, 49,* 143–172.

Overton, W. F., Ward, S. L., Noveck, I. A., Black, J., & O'Brien, D. P. (1987). Form and content in the development of deductive reasoning. *Developmental Psychology, 23*(1), 22–30.

Overton, W. F., Yaure, R., & Ward, S. L. (1986). *Deductive reasoning in young and elderly adults.* Paper presented at the Southeastern Conference of Human Development, Nashville, TN.

Park, D. C., & Payer, D. (2006). Working memory across the adult life span. In E. Bialystok & F. I. M. Craik (Eds.), *Life span cognition: Mechanisms of change.* Oxford: Oxford University Press.

Piaget, J. (1980). *Experiments in contradiction.* Chicago: University of Chicago Press. (Original work published 1974)

Piaget, J. (1986). Essay on necessity. *Human Development, 29,* 301–314.

Piaget, J. (1987). *Possibility and necessity: Vol. 2, The role of necessity in cognitive development.* Minneapolis, MN: University of Minnesota Press.

Piaget, J. (2001). *Studies in reflecting abstraction* (R. L. Campbell, Ed., Trans.). New York: Psychology Press.

Piaget, J., & Garcia, R. (1989). *Psychogenesis and the history of science.* New York: Columbia University Press.

Piaget, J., & Garcia, R. (1991). *Toward a logic of meanings* (P. M. Davidson & J. Easley, Eds.). Hillsdale, NJ: Erlbaum. (Original work published 1983)

Pieraut-LeBonniec, G. (1990). The logic of meaning and meaningful implication. In W. F. Overton (Ed.), *Reasoning, necessity, and logic: Developmental perspectives.* Hillsdale, NJ: Erlbaum.

Pollack, R. D., Overton, W. F., Rosenfeld, A., & Rosenfeld, R. (1995). Formal reasoning and later adulthood: Role of semantic content and metacognitive strategy. *Journal of Adult Development, 2,* 1–14.

Quinn, S., & Markovits, H. (1998). Conditional reasoning, causality, and the structure of semantic memory: Strength of association as a predictive factor for content effects. *Cognition, 68,* 93–101.

Rai, R., & Mitchell, P. (2006). Children's ability to impute inferentially based knowledge. *Child Development, 77*(4), 1081–1093.

Reich, S. S., & Ruth, P. (1982). Wason's selection task: Verifications, falsifications, and matching. *British Journal of Psychology, 73*(2), 395–405.

Reiter, R. (1987). Nonmonotonic reasoning. *Annual Review of Computer Science, 2,* 147–186.

Ricco, R. B. (1990). Necessity and the logic of entailment. In W. F. Overton (Ed.), *Reasoning, necessity, and logic: Developmental perspectives.* Hillsdale, NJ: Erlbaum.

Ricco, R. B. (1993). Revising the logic of operations as a relevance logic: From hypothesis testing to explanation. *Human Development, 36*(3), 301–314.

Ricco, R. B. (1997). The development of proof construction in middle childhood. *Journal of Experimental Child Psychology, 66*(3), 279–310.

Ricco, R. B. (2002). Analyzing the roles of challenge and defense in argumentation. *Argumentation and Advocacy: Journal of the American Forensic Association, 39*(1), 1–22.

Ricco, R. B. (2007). Individual differences in the analysis of informal reasoning fallacies. *Contemporary Educational Psychology, 32,* 459–484.

Ricco, R. B. (2008). The influence of argument structure on judgments of argument strength, function, and adequacy. *Quarterly Journal of Experimental Psychology, 61*(4), 641–664.

Ricco, R. B., McCollum, D., & Wang, J. (1997). Children's judgments of certainty and uncertainty on a problem where the possible solutions differ in likelihood. *Journal of Genetic Psychology, 158*(4), 401–410.

Rips, L. J. (1994). *The psychology of proof: Deductive reasoning in human thinking.* Cambridge, MA: MIT Press.

Rips, L. J. (2001). Two kinds of reasoning. *Psychological Science, 12*(2), 129–134.

Ruffman, T. (1999). Children's understanding of logical inconsistency. *Child Development, 70*(4), 872–886.

Russell, J. (1982). The child's appreciation of the necessary truth and the necessary falseness of propositions. *British Journal of Psychology, 73*(2), 253–266.

Saczynski, J. S., Willis, S. L., & Schaie, K. W. (2002). Strategy use in reasoning training with older adults. *Aging, Neuropsychology, and Cognition, 9*(1), 48–60.

Salthouse, T. A. (1992). Working-memory mediation of adult age differences in integrative reasoning. *Memory and Cognition, 20*(4), 413–423.

Salthouse, T. A. (2001a). Structural models of the relations between age and measures of cognitive functioning. *Intelligence, 29*(2), 93–115.

Salthouse, T. A. (2001b). Attempted decomposition of age-related influences on two tests of reasoning. *Psychology and Aging, 16*(2), 251–262.

Salthouse, T. A. (2005a). Effects of aging on reasoning. In K. J. Holyoak & R. G. Morrison (Eds.), *The Cambridge handbook of thinking and reasoning* (pp. 589–605). Cambridge: Cambridge University Press.

Salthouse, T. A. (2005b). Relations between cognitive abilities and measures of executive functioning. *Neuropsychology, 19*(4), 532–545.

Salthouse, T. A., Fristoe, N. M., Lineweaver, T. T., & Coon, V. E. (1995). Aging of attention: Does the ability to divide decline? *Memory and Cognition, 23*(1), 59–71.

Salthouse, T. A., Fristoe, N. M., McGuthry, K., & Hambrick, D. Z. (1998). Relation of task switching to age, speed, and fluid intelligence. *Psychology and Aging, 13*(3), 445–461.

Salthouse, T. A., Legg, S. E., Palmon, R., & Mitchell, D. R. D. (1990). Memory factors in age-related differences in simple reasoning. *Psychology and Aging, 5*(1), 9–15.

Salthouse, T. A., & Meinz, E. J. (1995). Aging, inhibition, working memory, and speed. *Journals of Gerontology: Psychological Sciences and Social Sciences, 50*(B), P297–P306.

Salthouse, T. A., & Miles, J. D. (2002). Aging and time-sharing aspects of executive control. *Memory and Cognition, 30*(4), 572–582.

Salthouse, T. A., Mitchell, D. R. D., Skovronek, E., & Babcock, R. L. (1989). Effects of adult age and working memory on reasoning and spatial abilities. *Journal of Experimental Psychology: Learning, Memory, and Cognition, 15*(3), 507–516.

Sanders, R. E., & Sanders, J. A. (1978). Long-term durability and transfer of enhanced conceptual performance in the elderly. *Journal of Gerontology, 33,* 408–412.

Sanders, R. E., Sanders, J. A., Mayes, G. J., & Sielski, K. A. (1976). Enhancement of conjunctive concept attainment in older adults. *Developmental Psychology, 12*(5), 485–486.

Sanders, R. E., Sterns, H. L., Smith, M., & Sanders, R. E. (1975). Modification of concept identification performance in older adults. *Developmental Psychology, 11*(6), 824–829.

Schaie, K. W. (1994). The course of adult intellectual development. *American Psychologist, 49*(4), 304–313.

Scholnick, E. K., & Wing, C. S. (1988). Knowing when you don't know: Developmental and situational considerations. *Developmental Psychology, 24*(2), 190–196.

Schooler, C. (2007). Use it—and keep it, longer, probably: A reply to Salthouse (2006). *Perspectives on Psychological Science, 2*(1), 24–29.

Simoneau, M., & Markovits, H. (2003). Reasoning with premises that are not empirically true: Evidence for the role of inhibition and retrieval. *Developmental Psychology, 39*(6), 964–975.

Sinnott, J. D. (1975). Everyday thinking and Piagetian operativity in adults. *Human Development, 18*(6), 430–443.

Sinnott, J. D., & Guttmann, D. (1978). Piagetian logical abilities and older adults' abilities to solve everyday problems. *Human Development, 21*(5–6), 327–333.

Sodian, B., & Wimmer, H. (1987). Children's understanding of inference as a source of knowledge. *Child Development, 58,* 424–433.

Sodian, B., Zaitchik, D., & Carey, S. (1991). Young children's differentiation of hypothetical beliefs from evidence. *Child Development, 62,* 753–766.

Sommerville, S. C., Hadkinson, B. A., & Greenberg, C. (1979). Two levels of inferential behavior in young children. *Child Development, 50,* 119–131.

Stanovich, K., & West, R. (1997). Reasoning independently of prior belief and individual differences in actively open-minded thinking. *Journal of Educational Psychology, 89*(2), 342–357.

Stenning, K., & van Lambalgen, M. (2008). Interpretation, representation, and deductive reasoning. In J. E. Adler & L. J. Rips (Eds.), *Reasoning: Studies of human inference and its foundations.* Cambridge, MA: Cambridge University Press.

Takahashi, M., & Overton, W. F. (1996). Formal reasoning in Japanese older adults: The role of metacognitive strategy, task content, and social factors. *Journal of Adult Development, 3*(2), 81–91.

Tomlinson-Keasey, C. (1972). Formal operations in females from eleven to fifty-six years of age. *Developmental Psychology, 6*(2), 364.

Treitz, F. H., Heyder, K., & Daum, I. (2007). Differential course of executive control changes during normal aging. *Aging, Neuropsychology, and Cognition, 14,* 370–393.

Tunmer, W. E., Nesdale, A. R., & Pratt, C. (1983). The development of young children's awareness of logical inconsistencies. *Journal of Experimental Child Psychology, 36*(1), 97–108.

Vadeboncoeur, I., & Markovits, H. (1999). The effect of instructions and information retrieval on accepting the premises in a conditional reasoning task. *Thinking and Reasoning, 5*(2), 97–113.

Van Eemeren, F. H., & Grootendorst, R. (1988). Rationale for a pragma-dialectical perspective. *Argumentation, 2,* 271–291.

Venet, M., & Markovits, H. (2001). Understanding uncertainty with abstract conditional premises. *Merrill-Palmer Quarterly, 47*(1), 74–99.

Verhaeghen, P., & DeMeersman, L. (1998a). Aging and the negative priming effect: A meta-analysis. *Psychology and Aging, 13*(3), 435–444

Verhaeghen, P., & DeMeersman, L. (1998b). Aging and the Stroop effect: A meta-analysis. *Psychology and Aging, 13*(1), 120–126.

Verhaeghen, P., & Salthouse, T. A. (1997). Meta-analyses of age-cognition relations in adulthood: Estimates of linear and non-linear age effects and structural models. *Psychological Bulletin, 122*(3), 231–249.

Verhaeghen, P., Steitz, D. W., Sliwinski, M. J., & Cerella, J. (2003). Aging and dual-task performance: A meta-analysis. *Psychology and Aging, 18*(3), 443–460.

Viskontas, I. V., Holyoak, K. J., & Knowlton, B. J. (2005). Relational integration in older adults. *Thinking and Reasoning, 11*(4), 390–410.

Viskontas, I. V., Morrison, R. G., Holyoak, K. J., Hummel, J. E., & Knowlton, B. J. (2004). Relational integration, inhibition, and analogical reasoning in older adults. *Psychology and Aging, 19*(4), 581–591.

Ward, S. L., Byrnes, J. P., & Overton, W. F. (1990). Organization of knowledge and conditional reasoning. *Journal of Educational Psychology, 82*(4), 832–837.

Ward, S. L., & Overton, W. F. (1990). Semantic familiarity, relevance, and the development of deductive reasoning. *Developmental Psychology, 26*(3), 488–493.

Wason, P. C. (1983). Realism and rationality in the selection task. In J. S. Evans (Ed.), *Thinking and reasoning: Psychological approaches.* London: Routledge & Kegan Paul.

West, R. L., Odom, R. D., & Aschkenasy, J. R. (1978). Perceptual sensitivity and conceptual coordination in children and younger and older adults. *Human Development, 21*(5–6), 334–345.

Wetherick, N. E. (1964). A comparison of the problem-solving ability of young, middle-aged, and old subjects. *Gerontologia, 9*(3), 164–178.

Wetherick, N. E. (1966). The inferential basis of concept attainment. *British Journal of Psychology, 57*(1 and 2), 61–69.

Wiersma, W., & Klausmeier, H. J. (1965). The effect of age upon speed of concept attainment. *Journal of Gerontology, 20,* 398–400.

Willis, S. L., & Schaie, K. W. (1986a). Practical intelligence in later adulthood. In R. J. Sternberg & R. K. Wagner (Eds.), *Practical intelligence: Origins of competence in the everyday world.* New York: Cambridge University Press.

Willis, S. L., & Schaie, K. W. (1986b). Training the elderly on the ability factors of spatial orientation and inductive reasoning. *Psychology and Aging, 1*(3), 239–247.

Willis, S. L., & Schaie, K. W. (1988). Gender differences in spatial ability in old age: Longitudinal and intervention findings. *Sex Roles, 18*(3–4), 189–203.

Willis, S. L., Tennstedt, S. L., Marsiske, M., Ball, K., Elias, J., Mann Koepke, K., et al. (2006). Long term effects of cognitive training on everyday functional outcomes in older adults. *Journal of the American Medical Association, 296*(23), 2805–2814.

Wollman, W., Eylon, B., & Lawson, A. E. (1979). Acceptance of lack of closure: Is it an index of advanced reasoning. *Child Development, 50,* 656–665.

Woodcock, R. W., McGrew, K. S., & Mather, N. (2001). *Woodcock Johnson III Tests of Cognitive Abilities.* Itasca, IL: Riverside.

Young, M. L. (1966). Problem-solving performance in two age groups. *Journal of Gerontology, 21,* 505–509.

Young, M. L. (1971). Age and sex differences in problem-solving. *Journal of Gerontology, 26,* 330–336.

Zacks, R. T., Hasher, L., & Li, K. Z. H. (2000). Human memory (pp. 293–358). In F. I. M. Craik & T. A. Salthouse (Eds.), *The handbook of aging and cognition* (2nd ed.). Mahwah, NJ: LEA.

Zelinski, E. M., & Kennison, R. F. (2007). Not your parents' test scores: Cohort reduces psychometric aging effects. *Psychology and Aging, 22*(3), 546–557.

Zelinski, E. M., & Stewart, S. T. (1998). Individual differences in 16-year memory changes. *Psychology and Aging, 13*(4), 622–630.

CHAPTER 13

Development of Executive Function across the Life Span

SOPHIE JACQUES and STUART MARCOVITCH

Humans have the power to think and do the unexpected. They can generate novel ideas and resist engaging in behaviors strongly elicited by the immediate environment. Broadly defined, *executive function* (EF) abilities are higher cognitive processes necessary for the voluntary control of thought and action. The capacity for cognitive and response control develops slowly across childhood, reaches a peak in early adulthood, and declines in late adulthood. The development of EF abilities is recognized as crucial for daily functioning of individuals in both social and nonsocial realms. EF abilities have been linked to prefrontal cortex development, and injury to this region of the brain not only leads to impairments in EF, but also to devastating loss of function for individuals across a wide range of domains. Viewed in this light, sophisticated EF abilities arguably make humans who they are and make them capable of doing what they do.

No consensus has been reached regarding the specific abilities that are thought to be subsumed under the umbrella term of EF. Moreover, whereas some researchers argue for the unitary nature of a single EF process, others argue for the inclusion of multiple, diverse EF abilities. Although researchers disagree about the inclusion of particular EF processes, most agree that EF skills involve only *higher* level cognitive processes necessary for engaging in complex novel behaviors for which immediate solutions are not obvious and for which flexibility is required in how one might think or act. In this respect, researchers explicitly (e.g., Zelazo, Carter, Reznick, & Frye, 1997) or implicitly (Miller & Cohen, 2001) adopt a problem-solving framework for delineating EF abilities: Thoughts and behaviors that require EF must be intentional, goal directed, and relatively novel. Despite the fact that lower cognitive abilities such as speed of processing (e.g., Case, Kurland, & Goldberg, 1982; Salthouse, 2005; see Hitch, 2006; Park & Payer, 2006, for reviews) and attention (e.g., Jones, Rothbart, & Posner, 2003) have been shown to relate to EF abilities, these abilities are rarely considered EF processes per se (but see Posner & Rothbart, 2007, who view executive attention as an executive control process). This is an important point because difficulties on tasks purported to measure EF abilities may result from either one or multiple EF impairments, or from impairments with simpler lower cognitive processes (cf. Stuss, Shallice, Alexander, & Picton, 1995). In contrast, successful performance on EF tasks necessarily means that all underlying EF processes (and all lower cognitive ones too) must be intact. We reiterate this caution about interpreting EF task difficulties throughout the chapter.

Several abilities have been proposed to constitute EF, including planning, verbal fluency, sequencing, error detection and error correction, self-monitoring, attentional control, and conditional learning. However, many researchers agree that working memory, response control/ inhibition, and set shifting (also known as cognitive flexibility) constitute core EF abilities (Miyake et al., 2000), and that other EF abilities are sometimes considered to be by-products of these core abilities (cf. Diamond, 2006b). For example, planning presumably requires the ability to maintain task-relevant information and the goal in mind (working memory), the ability to consider multiple solutions, including correct ones that temporarily detract from the final goal (cognitive flexibility), and the ability to resist the temptation to respond too hastily or prematurely toward the final goal (response control). As another example, Allain and colleagues (2007) reported that older adults are impaired in their ability to produce temporally coherent sequences, and that their ability to produce such sequences correlates with EF measures on which older adults also do more poorly than younger adults. The authors argued that this link is not surprising, as reproducing temporally coherent sequences depends on being able to keep in mind an internally generated script (working memory), switch back and forth between the script and individual elements (set shifting), and update the script (working memory).

Although specific definitions of working memory, cognitive flexibility, and response control differ somewhat, there is considerable agreement on some of the essential properties of these processes. In brief, working memory generally refers to the temporary maintenance and manipulation of information held online while performing cognitive tasks (Baddeley, 1986, 2003; Hitch, 2006; see also Demetriou, Mouyi, & Spanoudis, Chapter 10 of this volume; Bialystok & Craik, Chapter 7 of this volume; and Ornstein & Light, Chapter 9 of this volume). In turn, cognitive flexibility or set shifting is required when individuals must consider multiple *conflicting* perspectives

(or mental sets) on a single object or event (Jacques & Zelazo, 2005b). To be correct on a problem that requires flexibility, individuals must either switch successively between two equivalent perspectives or approach the problem from a less obvious and more difficult perspective, while ignoring a stronger perspective. Problems that require response control—or response inhibition, more specifically—typically require one to overcome the overwhelming tendency to respond in a particular way either because the correct response goes against one's habitual response tendencies or because a particular conflicting response is more strongly suggested by the immediate environment (Verbruggen & Logan, 2008). For example, consider the *object retrieval task* (Diamond, 1990), which requires that infants reach around a transparent barrier (e.g., glass window) to obtain a toy rather than reach directly for it. The object retrieval task is typically viewed as a response control task because to succeed, infants must resist their learned tendency to reach directly for the toy and instead perform a novel, less obvious, and less direct action (i.e., reach around the barrier) to retrieve the desirable object.

This chapter begins with a brief and general overview of major developmental changes that have been documented across the life span in the three core aspects of EF. Following this review of empirical findings, we review theoretical models that have been proposed to account for EF at various points across the life span including early development, normal adulthood, and late adult development. We follow this review of theoretical models by discussing what an idealized integrated developmental model of EF might look like. In doing so, we identify defining characteristics that each process (i.e., working memory, cognitive flexibility, and response inhibition) is likely to possess on the basis of characteristics that have already been identified in different existing models. We then review additional findings documented across the life span in light of this integrated model. We conclude by identifying outstanding issues in the study of EF that any theory of EF will need to address.

DEVELOPMENTAL CHANGES IN EXECUTIVE FUNCTION ACROSS THE LIFE SPAN

Much of the early research into EF processes arose within the neuropsychology literature (e.g., Luria, 1959b; Milner, 1963, 1964) and expanded into the study of psychopathologies such as autism, attention deficit/hyperactivity disorder (ADHD) and conduct disorder in childhood (see Pennington & Ozonoff, 1996, for a review), and schizophrenia in adulthood (Pickup, 2008). Early neuropsychological research equated EF impairments with "frontal lobe impairments" (Stuss et al., 1995) and a "frontal deficit" hypothesis about cognitive declines in late adult development also was proposed (e.g., West, 1996). It is now clear, however, that although frontal function is related to EF, this is not an identity relation. Patients with lesions elsewhere can also demonstrate EF impairments, and not all patients with frontal lobe lesions have EF impairments (see Dick & Overton, 2010; Miyake et al., 2000, for discussions). In recent years, there has been an upsurge of research attempting to map EF processes to specific neurological structural and functional systems (see Zelazo & Lee, Chapter 4 of this volume). Despite the importance of neurophysiological data to our overall understanding of EF, however, we limit our review to psychological and behavioral data on the typical development of EF across the life span.

Research on the development of working memory, cognitive flexibility, and response control is fairly intertwined across much of the life span *within* specific age groups. However, this is not the case across age groups as research on these processes has advanced fairly independently because of the use of different tasks at different ages (see Bialystok & Craik, Chapter 7 of this volume). The high interrelation between cognitive flexibility and response control, in particular, may have arisen, in part, from the fact that the distinction between them can often be blurred (e.g., Botvinick, Braver, Barch, Carter, & Cohen, 2001; Garon, Bryson, & Smith, 2008). On the one hand, *cognitive flexibility* is required when individuals must generate and adopt a weaker internal perspective or mental set when it conflicts with another stronger internal perspective or mental set. On the other hand, *response control* is required when the competition is between strong prepotent motor responses elicited either by the presence of strong external cues or by habitual responding (or both) that must be overcome and replaced with a weaker and more novel internally generated response. In other words, difficulties with response control occur at the level of the response itself, whereas difficulties with cognitive flexibility occur at the level of the underlying representation. However, it is unclear whether a particular novel response can be generated in the absence of an underlying associated internal mental set/perspective. For that reason, if an underlying representation is evoked, then any task that requires response control may require cognitive flexibility, although the opposite may not necessarily hold: Cognitive flexibility

may be required on some tasks that do not require motor response control.

Moreover, difficulties at either the representation or response level will often lead to the same overt mistaken— and typically, perseverative—response, making it difficult to identify the source of the problem. The only real means of identifying the problem's source is by determining whether individuals who commit an error are aware of their mistake *at the time that they commit it*. If they are aware of their error, then the error likely resulted from an action slip or response control failure. However, if individuals do not recognize an error that they or someone else makes, then they likely err on the basis of an incorrect mental representation or perspective of the problem (cf. Jacques, Zelazo, Kirkham, & Semcesen, 1999).

To compound the issue further, tasks used to assess specific EF processes, including working memory, are particularly challenging because they tend to be complex, requiring several cognitive processes, making it impossible to identify the exact source of any difficulty on these tasks (e.g., Daniels, Toth, & Jacoby, 2006; Delis, Squire, Bihrle, & Massman, 1992; Jacques & Zelazo, 2001; Levine, Stuss, & Milberg, 1995; Miyake et al., 2000; Pennington & Ozonoff, 1996; Stuss & Alexander, 2000; Wiebe, Espy, & Charak, 2008). In fact, most complex EF tasks have working memory, set shifting, and response control requirements, although relative requirements for each vary substantially from task to task. In the *go/no-go task*, for example, participants must press a key in response to one stimulus (go responses) and withhold responding to another stimulus (no-go responses). Researchers have argued about whether performance on no-go trials reflects response inhibition or conflict-monitoring difficulties (e.g., Botvinick et al., 2001).

In another task, the *Wisconsin Card Sort Test* (Berg, 1948; Grant & Berg, 1948), participants are shown four target cards consisting of different geometric shapes (i.e., triangles, circles, stars, and crosses) that also differ in terms of color (red, green, yellow, or blue) and number (1, 2, 3, or 4). They are then presented with test cards that they are required to match with one of the target cards, which can be challenging as the test cards can match multiple target cards on different dimensions. Participants are told on every trial only whether they matched correctly. Once they have sorted by one dimension correctly for 10 consecutive trials, the experimenter surreptitiously changes the dimension, and participants must then switch their response set and attempt to discover the new correct dimension. Participants continue to sort until they complete six categories or until they sort all test cards. Although construed primarily as a measure of set-shifting abilities, the Wisconsin Card Sort Test also has working memory and response control requirements (Dunbar & Sussman, 1995; Milner, 1963; Ozonoff & Strayer, 1997). That is, participants must not only keep the relevant category in mind and update that information when the category changes (i.e., working memory), but they must also resist the temptation to sort cards as they did for previous categories (response control). In addition, successful performance requires other non-EF cognitive processing skills (e.g., learning from feedback). Difficulties on any EF or non-EF abilities will lead to difficulties on this task, making it impossible to identify the source of difficulty.

Similarly, the *A-not-B search task*—an EF measure used with infants—has been construed by different researchers as a measure of working memory (Munakata, 1998), response control (Ahmed & Ruffman, 1998), or both (Diamond, Cruttenden, & Neiderman, 1994; Marcovitch & Zelazo, 2009). In addition, infants may fail to search for a toy at the second hiding location because they are stuck on a representation of the toy's initial hiding location instead of their response to that location, which could reflect set-shifting difficulties (cf. Daniels et al., 2006). The root cause of poor performance on this task is difficult to determine on the basis of performance on the standard version of the task. However, many clever manipulations have been introduced that have allowed researchers to disentangle the relative contributions of specific cognitive processes to performance on this task (see Harris, 1987; Marcovitch & Zelazo, 2009, for reviews).

Despite limitations in our ability to differentiate between EF processes on most EF tasks, a great deal is known about the development of EF across the life span. The following sections review common tasks used to assess EF processes at different points in development and general age-related changes documented from the use of these tasks.

Executive Function Development in Infancy

Assessing cognitive development, in particular, EF, in infants is inherently challenging because of limitations in symbolic processing (including language) and restrictions in response execution. Despite these shortcomings, we know a surprising amount about EF in the first 2 years of life. Nonetheless, as discussed in the previous section, EF tasks typically confound various components, and most require a combination of response inhibition, working memory, and set shifting to complete successfully. Tasks developed to assess EF processes in infancy are no exception. In fact, the inability to separate EF components in tasks targeted at infants may be partly responsible for considering EF as a unitary structure, particularly in the first 6 years of life (Wiebe et al., 2008).

Search tasks that require infants to search for objects hidden in one of multiple locations are important paradigms for studying EF in infancy. One of the simplest—the *delayed response* (or *delayed reaction*) task—involves an object that is conspicuously hidden in one location. After a delay, infants are allowed to search for it (Hunter, 1913, 1917). Typically, the task is repeated for a number of trials at different locations following a predetermined order. Success on this task correlates with activation of the dorsolateral prefrontal cortex (see Fuster, 1980; Goldman-Rakic, 1987; Jacobsen, 1936), and the task is often considered to be a measure of working memory (Reznick, Morrow, Goldman, & Snyder, 2004). Diamond and Doar (1989), for example, found improvements on this task between 6 and 12 months of age, with older children capable of tolerating longer delays than younger children (roughly 2.1 seconds per month). Errors on the delayed response task are typically perseverative in nature in that infants have a bias to search at previously searched locations (Diamond & Doar; Smith, Thelen, Titzer, & McLin, 1999).

A common variant of the delayed response task inspired by Piaget (1954)—and less commonly known, by Luria (1959a)—is the A-not-B task mentioned earlier. In this task, an object is hidden repeatedly at one location (A) for a number of trials and then switched to another location (B). Infants often commit the *A-not-B error*, which consists of perseverative responses at location A on B trials. Two separate meta-analyses (Marcovitch & Zelazo, 1999; Wellman, Cross, & Bartsch, 1986) have confirmed the robustness of this phenomenon and identified a number of variables that are associated with the likelihood that A-not-B errors will occur, including age (Sophian & Wellman, 1983), delay (Gratch, Appel, Evans, LeCompte, & Wright, 1974), distance between hiding locations (Horobin & Acredolo, 1986), number of hiding locations (Cummings & Bjork, 1983; Diamond et al., 1994), and number of A trials (Marcovitch, Zelazo, & Schmuckler, 2002).

Remarkably, researchers have demonstrated that hiding the object from view is not required to elicit the A-not-B error, indicating the relative importance of motor habits to performance on this task (Clearfield, Diedrich, Smith, & Thelen, 2006; Clearfield, Dineva, Smith, Diedrich, & Thelen, 2009; Smith et al., 1999; but see Munakata, 1997, for an alternative interpretation). For example, using a version of the A-not-B task in which the object remained visible, Clearfield et al. (2006) assessed perseverative responding in infants who were not yet able to search for *hidden* objects. They showed that perseverative reaching was most likely at 8 months of age but surprisingly less likely to occur at younger ages. They explained this counterintuitive finding by proposing that infants first must establish stable reaching patterns before they can develop potent motor habits.

Consistent with the importance of reaching dynamics, several studies have revealed that infants who only see the object hidden at A outperform infants who reach for the object at A (Ahmed & Ruffman, 1998; Hofstadter & Reznick, 1996; see Munakata, McClelland, Johnson, & Siegler, 1997, for an explanation using a graded representations account). However, using a repeated-measures design with a different coding scheme, Bell and Adams (1999) demonstrated comparable performance on reaching and looking versions of the A-not-B task at 8 months of age (see also Matthews, Ellis, & Nelson, 1996), suggesting that difficulties on the A-not-B extend beyond simple motor response perseveration. Although better performance seems possible with looking-time paradigms than with reaching paradigms, Bell and Adams' results provide evidence that looking-time paradigms can still reliably be used as an assessment of the A-not-B error, making this version particularly useful for neurophysiological studies (Bell, 2001).

Recently, a new and potentially very informative variant of the A-not-B task has been developed for use with infants capable of walking. Using a *locomotor A-not-B task* with 13-month-old infants, Berger (2004) found that all infants in a baseline condition could walk down one flat path and then walk down a different flat path. In contrast, when infants had to walk down paths that involved descending staircases instead of flat paths, 25% of infants went back to the original A staircase on B trials instead of descending the new B staircase. This marked difference in behavior is most likely attributed to additional cognitive demands required for infants of this age to descend staircases as opposed to traversing on flat ground, suggesting that limiting available cognitive resources increases perseverative responding.

Another popular paradigm used to assess EF in infancy, the *delayed nonmatching/matching to sample task,* also capitalizes on delayed responding. In this paradigm, participants are shown an object and then required to choose between it and a novel object after a brief delay. Participants are either rewarded for selecting the previously seen (delayed matching) or the novel (delayed nonmatching)

object. Overman (1990) tested infants on both tasks and found: (1) infants learn the delayed nonmatching version significantly faster than the delayed matching one, and (2) performance on both versions improves with age.

Both the delayed matching and nonmatching to sample versions of the task make EF demands because they require working memory and response inhibition; the previously seen object must be kept in mind and infants must inhibit selecting a particular type of object (either the familiar or novel one). However, Diamond, Churchland, Cruess, and Kirkham (1999) argued that young infants' (under 21 months) difficulty with this task lies in their inability to understand the relation between the stimulus and reward. Specifically, in the standard task (as used by Overman, 1990), a reward is hidden under the correct object. However, Diamond et al. (1999) showed that infants as young as 9 months of age demonstrate remarkable improvement when the reward is physically attached to the object or when verbal praise is used instead of a tangible reward. On the basis of these findings, Diamond (2006a) argued that infants' difficulty with the standard version of the task results from a difficulty with grasping the conceptual connection between the physically unconnected stimulus and reward, and not necessarily with the particular working memory or response control demands of the task.

Another important EF task used with infants that requires them to inhibit a prepotent response is the object retrieval task popularized by Diamond (1990) and mentioned previously. In this task, a desirable object is visible through a transparent box with one opening on one of the sides. To obtain the object, infants must inhibit their tendency to reach directly for the object and instead detour around to the open side. On the basis of a longitudinal study, Diamond reported that 6.5- to 7-month-olds unsuccessfully attempt to retrieve the toy through the closed side facing them. In contrast, 7.5- to 8-month-olds try to change their body position or the box position so that the open side is in line with their reach. The first clear evidence that infants can reach for an opening not directly in their line of sight occurs between 8.5 and 9 months, although infants still need to look through the opening at some point, often resulting in awkward reaches. Between 9.5 and 10.5 months, infants can retrieve a toy without needing to look through the opening.

Executive Function Development in Preschoolers

A panoply of tasks have been developed to assess various aspects of EF in preschoolers (e.g., Carlson, 2005), although we review only a handful here because developmental changes across many of these tasks, especially tasks assessing cognitive flexibility, tend to be similar. In particular, major age-related changes in EF have been noted to occur between 3 and 5 years of age across an impressive array of tasks assessing various EF abilities (for more extensive reviews, see Diamond, 2006b; Garon et al., 2008; Jacques & Zelazo, 2005b; Zelazo et al., 1997; Zelazo & Jacques, 1997).

For example, the *Dimensional Change Card Sort* was developed to assess children's abilities to sort the same cards successively using two incompatible sets of rules (Frye, Zelazo, & Palfai, 1995; Zelazo, 2006; Zelazo, Müller, Frye, & Marcovitch, 2003). In the standard version of this task, preschoolers are presented with test cards that vary on two dimensions (e.g., color and shape) and are asked to sort the cards according to one dimension and then the other. Children are presented with two sorting trays, each depicting a target card that matches each test card on exactly one dimension. For example, if test cards consist of red trucks and blue flowers, then target cards consist of a red flower and a blue truck. Three-year-olds have no difficulties sorting test cards by a first dimension (either color or shape), whatever that dimension happens to be. However, most 3-year-olds fail the *postswitch phase* of the standard version of this task by perseverating and continuing to sort by the preswitch dimension, whereas the majority of 4-year-olds and most 5-year-olds sort the cards correctly by both sets of rules.

Several other tasks developed to assess cognitive flexibility at this age share the same underlying task structure such that children must respond in one way on the basis of one mental set/perspective and then respond in a different, conflicting way on the basis of a different mental set/perspective. In *deductive* versions of such tasks, including the Dimension Change Card Sort (Frye et al., 1995), the *synonym judgment task* (Doherty & Perner, 1998), and the *physical causality task* (Frye, Zelazo, Brooks, & Samuels, 1996), the experimenter tells children explicitly how to respond according to each mental set, whereas in *inductive* versions, including the *discrimination-shift learning paradigm* (Kendler & Kendler, 1961), the *double categorization task* (Blaye & Jacques, 2009), the *false belief task* (Wimmer & Perner, 1983), the *Flexible Item Selection Task* (Jacques & Zelazo, 2001), the *matrix classification task* (Inhelder & Piaget, 1959/1964), and the *novel word inference task* (Deák, 2000), children must infer how to solve at least one aspect of the task (see Jacques & Zelazo, 2005b, for more discussion on the distinction between deductive and inductive tasks).

For example, in the Flexible Item Selection Task (Jacques & Zelazo, 2001), children are shown three items on each trial (e.g., a small red boat, a small blue boat, and a large blue boat). Two of the items match on a specific dimension (e.g., size) and two items match on another dimension (e.g., color). A third dimension is constant across the three items (e.g., shape). Thus, on all trials, one of the items, the *pivot* item (the small blue boat) matches one of the other items on one dimension and the remaining item on the alternate dimension. Children are asked to select a pair of matching items, and then immediately switch and select a different pair that matches on another dimension. Consequently, to succeed, they must be flexible in how they represent the pivot item so that they can select it twice, according to two different dimensions. Unlike the Dimensional Change Card Sort, the Flexible Item Selection Task is an inductive task because children are not told the matching dimensions; they must determine these for themselves. Research with the Flexible Item Selection Task has shown that the majority of 3-year-olds perform worse than both 4- and 5-year-olds on their first selection, suggesting that the inductive nature of the task is especially difficult for them. In contrast, 4-year-olds do well on their first selection but perform worse than 5-year-olds on their second selection, indicating that they have specific difficulties with the switching aspect of the task.

As another example, although initially designed to assess children's understanding of the subjective nature of mental states, *false-belief tasks* are believed to have strong EF requirements and correlate strongly with performance on traditional EF tasks (e.g., Carlson & Moses, 2001; Carlson, Moses, & Hix, 1998; Frye et al., 1995; Hughes, 1998; Hughes & Russell, 1993; Ozonoff, Pennington, & Rogers, 1991; Zelazo, Jacques, Burack, & Frye, 2002; see Perner & Lang, 1999, for a review). Specifically, in false-belief tasks, children are asked to predict the behavior of a protagonist who holds a mistaken belief about the whereabouts of an object or the contents of a container when they themselves know the real location of the object or contents of the container. Hence, to succeed, children must reason from the erroneous perspective of the protagonist and refrain from responding on the basis of their own reality-informed perspective, thereby requiring cognitive flexibility. Research with the false-belief task has shown age-related changes between 3 and 5 years of age in children's ability to predict the behavior of the protagonist correctly (see Carpendale & Lewis, Chapter 17 of this volume; Chandler & Birch, Chapter 19 of this volume; Wellman, Cross, & Watson, 2001, for reviews).

In short, performance on many measures believed to assess cognitive flexibility suggest that 3- and 4-year-olds often experience difficulty, even though 4-year-olds do better on some tasks (especially deductive tasks) than 3-year-olds. Inductive tasks are often solved later than deductive ones, perhaps as a result of the added difficulty of having to infer what to do (see Jacques & Zelazo, 2005b, for a review). However, deductive and inductive tasks also tend to differ in terms of the amount of relevant information that is explicitly *labeled.* Specifically, in the course of telling children what to do, researchers generally label all relevant information in deductive tasks. In contrast, because children are not told explicitly what to do on inductive measures, whether relevant information gets labeled in inductive measures is more variable. As discussed later in this chapter, labeling has a significant impact on performance on measures of cognitive flexibility.

Two types of response control tasks are used with preschoolers, including tasks that assess children's ability to delay their behavior (referred to by Garon et al., 2008, as simple response inhibition tasks) and tasks that require children to inhibit a dominant response while generating a novel response that goes against their existing response tendency. The latter of these tasks used within the preschool period are similar in structure to deductive versions of cognitive flexibility measures, although instead of requiring that children switch between two mental sets that they are taught during the task itself, children are asked to solve a problem that requires them to respond to stimuli in a manner that goes against their preexisting, pre-experimental response tendencies (e.g., the *Interference Control Task*, Müller, Zelazo, Hood, Leone, & Rohrer, 2004; the go/no-go task, Luria, 1959a, 1961; *Bear/Dragon Task*, Reed, Pien, & Rothbart, 1984; *Day-night Stroop-like Test*, Gerstadt, Hong, & Diamond, 1994; Passler, Isaac, & Hynd, 1985; *Detour-Reaching Box*, Hughes & Russell, 1993; *Luria Hand Game*, Hughes, 1996, 1998; *Luria Tapping Game Test*, Diamond & Taylor, 1996; *Deceptive Pointing Task*, Carlson et al., 1998; *Simple Simon Task*, Jones et al., 2003; Reed et al., 1984). For example, in the Day-night Stroop-like task (Gerstadt et al., 1994), children are asked to say "Day" when presented with a picture of a moon and "Night" when presented with a picture of a sun. To succeed, then, children must inhibit their preexisting tendency to respond in a semantically congruent fashion to each stimulus (e.g., to say "Day" in response to the picture of the sun).

Some debate exists as to whether these response inhibition tasks, referred to by some researchers as conflict inhibition tasks (Carlson & Moses, 2001) or complex response inhibition tasks (Garon et al., 2008), really differ from tasks assessing cognitive flexibility (see Jacques & Zelazo, 2005b), or what Garon et al. refer to as response–set-shifting tasks. In particular, preschoolers' performance on both types of tasks correlates well and follows a similar developmental path (e.g., Carlson & Moses, 2001; Carlson et al., 1998; Frye et al., 1995; see Perner & Lang, 1999; Zelazo & Jacques, 1997, for reviews). In addition, as discussed previously, difficulties on these purported response inhibition tasks could easily result from difficulties with switching between two relevant underlying mental sets (i.e., switching from a preexisting mental set to one introduced within the experiment) rather than between overt response sets. Conversely, poor performance on cognitive flexibility tasks could be caused by difficulties with response switching instead of switching between mental sets (but see Jacques et al., 1999, for evidence against such an account of difficulties on the Dimensional Change Card Sort).

Developmental changes on delay tasks, which require children to delay or modulate a prepotent response, follow a different developmental path (Carlson & Moses, 2001; Carlson, Moses, & Breton, 2002; Kochanska, Murray, Jacques, Koenig, & Vandegeest, 1996; Reed et al., 1984; Vaughn, Kopp, & Krakow, 1984). There are two general kinds of delay tasks: simple delay tasks and choice delay tasks. In simple delay task, children must resist the temptation to respond before they are allowed, or they must slow down or modulate a motor activity. In choice delay tasks, such as the *delay of gratification task* (Mischel, Shoda, & Rodriguez, 1989), children are given a choice between responding immediately for a smaller reward or delaying their response to get a larger reward. On simple delay tasks, by 4 years of age, children are capable of holding a candy on their tongue without eating it, or resisting peeking at an experimenter who noisily wraps a gift (Kochanska et al., 1996). On choice delay tasks, same-aged children can also choose to wait for a larger prize instead of receiving a smaller prize immediately (Mischel et al., 1989; Thompson, Barresi, & Moore, 1997). In fact, even 3-year-olds can choose to delay responding for a larger reward for a third person even though they do not do so for themselves at this age (Prencipe & Zelazo, 2005).

As described previously, working memory in infants and young children is often assessed using delayed response tasks (Reznick et al., 2004). For preschoolers, however, different tasks are used to assess working memory. In particular, researchers differentiate working memory tasks into two groups: simple and complex tasks (see Hitch, 2006, for a review). *Simple working memory tasks*, also referred to as *short-term memory tasks*, require only holding information in mind over a delay, whereas *complex working memory tasks* require holding temporary information in mind and manipulating or updating it in some way. Complex working memory tasks in particular are associated with EF, especially beyond the infancy period. As an example of a simple working memory task, Alp (1994) devised an imitation sorting task for use with children in the transition from infancy through the early preschool years. He assessed 12- to 36-month-olds on a task in which children had to imitate an experimenter sorting objects into different containers. The highest number of objects that children sorted correctly was taken as an index of their working memory size. Alp found linear increases in working memory during this period, with age accounting for 55% of the variance in working memory.

Complex working memory tasks also have been devised to assess preschool children's abilities to hold information in mind while processing it in some way. For example, on the basis of Petrides and Milner's (1982) self-ordered pointing task designed for use with adults, Hughes (1998) used a working memory task in which children were required to update their still-to-be-remembered list on each trial. Hughes showed children a spin-the-pots task in which they retrieved rewards that were hidden under eight different pots. Only one reward was hidden under each pot, and between trials, the pots were scrambled and spun. Moreover, on each trial, children were reminded to choose a pot that they had not yet selected. Thus, to succeed, children needed to update their list of searched and still-to-be searched locations, and as a result, they had to process information in addition to remembering it. Hughes found that the majority of 3-year-olds succeeded on this task.

Executive Function Development in School-Aged Children, Adolescents, and Young Adults

A radical change occurs in the assessment of EF during the school-age period. Performance on EF tasks used with preschool children tends to be scored in terms of accuracy because children are generally correct or incorrect (and often perseverative) on individual trials. With school-aged children, however, it is more common to use age-appropriate versions of adult tasks in which the correct answer is expected and EF efficiency is instead inferred from slowed response times indicating increased difficulty (although accuracy is sometimes used with school-aged

children and beyond; e.g., see work by Zelazo, Craik, & Booth, 2004). For this reason, this section reviews performance of school-aged children and adolescents in relation to performance of young adults, who tend to show peak reaction time performance on these EF tasks. In general, performance on EF tasks tends to improve with age for children and adolescents relative to young adults, but then declines again in older adults (see next section). Moreover, like preschoolers (but unlike infants), EF tasks used within these age ranges are often purported to assess specific EF abilities, including cognitive flexibility or set shifting (sometimes referred to as task switching; Allport, Styles, & Hsieh, 1994; Monsell, 2003), response inhibition, and working memory (sometimes referred to as information updating and monitoring; Miyake et al., 2000).

Set shifting has been assessed effectively with school-aged children and adults using card sorting tasks, like the Wisconsin Card Sorting Test (Berg, 1948; Grant & Berg, 1948) described earlier, and task-switching paradigms (Monsell, 2003). In task-switching paradigms, participants are required to switch between two simple tasks, such as adding and subtracting numbers (e.g., Baddeley, Chincotta, & Adlam, 2001). Participants are generally slower immediately after a switch, known as the switch cost (Monsell, 2003). Studies using the Wisconsin Card Sorting Test and other set-shifting tasks (Cepeda, Kramer, & Gonzalez de Sather, 2001; Chelune & Baer, 1986; Crone, Bunge, van der Molen, & Ridderinkhof, 2006; Levin et al., 1991; Passler et al., 1985; Welsh, Pennington, & Groisser, 1991) have found that younger children have difficulty with set shifting but improve throughout the school years. In general, age-related increases have been identified from school-aged children to young adults, although specific ages at which tasks show the most increase and at which performance plateaus vary substantially between tasks.

A number of response inhibition tasks have been used with school-aged children and adults, including most commonly, the *Stroop test* and analogous *spatial Simon task*, the *antisaccade task*, the *flanker task*, modified *Simon Says* paradigms, as well as the go/no-go task and the related *stop-signal paradigm*. In the classic Stroop test (Bub, Masson, & Lalonde, 2006; Comalli, Wapner, & Werner, 1962; Stroop, 1935; see MacLeod, 1991, for a review), participants are presented with a list of color words (e.g., "red," "blue," "green") printed in nonmatching ink colors (e.g., blue, green, red, respectively). They are asked to inhibit reading the word and instead name the color of the ink as fast as possible. Similarly, in the Simon task (Lu & Proctor, 1995; Simon, 1990), participants must respond using one of two keys (one key on the left and one key on the right) on the basis of the direction to which an arrow is pointing (left or right), while ignoring the irrelevant position on the screen in which the arrow appears. In one version used with preschoolers (Gerardi-Caulton, 2000) and school-aged children (Davidson, Amso, Anderson, & Diamond, 2006), children are instructed instead to press the left button in response to one animal and the right button in response to another animal. Crucial incongruent trials occur when stimuli appear spatially over the incorrect response key and participants must inhibit their tendency to respond with that key. In Simon Says tasks (LaVoie, Anderson, Fraze, & Johnson, 1981; Strommen, 1973), children are told simple commands ("Touch your nose!"). They are to obey these commands, but only if these are prefaced by the words "Simon says." As a result, on some trials when "Simon says" is not stated explicitly, children must inhibit direct requests to respond to a command to which they would normally respond. Antisaccade tasks require participants to look away from a target as soon as it appears, thereby requiring inhibition of the tendency to look toward an appearing object (Munoz, Broughton, Goldring, & Armstrong, 1998). Flanker tasks (Eriksen & Schultz, 1979) are computerized tasks in which participants are shown a central stimulus on a screen about which they must make a judgment (e.g., decide whether an arrow is pointing left or right). The central stimulus is flanked by or surrounded by other stimuli that are either all congruent or incongruent with it (e.g., same or opposite pointing arrows, respectively). Any difference in reaction time for trials with congruent and incongruent trials is taken as evidence of inhibition difficulties. Finally, in the go/no-go task (e.g., Lamm, Zelazo, & Lewis, 2006; Luria, 1959a), and one of its variants, the stop-signal paradigm (Schachar & Logan, 1990; Schachar, Tannock, & Logan, 1993; van den Wildenberg & van der Molen, 2004; Williams, Ponesse, Schachar, Logan, & Tannock, 1999), participants are required to respond on most trials except under specific circumstances (e.g., a specific stimulus is presented), at which point they must inhibit their responses despite having built up a strong tendency to respond. Like measures of set shifting, performance on all of these tasks varies during the elementary school years (and in some cases, during the preschool and adolescent years as well), but generally improves with age.

Although many complex working memory span tasks exist for use with school-aged children and beyond, such as operational, reading, counting, and visual pattern span tasks, they share similar underlying methodologies even though they differ in terms of the information retained and the specific processing operations required (see Bialystok & Craik, Chapter 7 of this volume; Hitch, 2006, for a review). Specifically, in complex memory span tasks, participants are required to perform a secondary processing task (e.g., solving math equations) while keeping temporary information associated with the primary task (e.g., the answers to the equations) active in working memory. Complex working memory span is the maximum amount of information participants remember while still effectively performing the processing task (Towse & Hitch, 2007). Case et al. (1982), for example, used a counting span task in which 6- to 12-year-old children counted objects while remembering the total number on each card. They found that age-related differences in counting span was associated with age-related changes in counting efficiency.

Executive Function Development in Older Adults

After reaching peak levels during the young adult years, both performance on cognitive tasks generally, and EF tasks specifically, decline during the late adult years (Mayr & Kliegl, 1993; Touron & Hertzog, 2004; Verhaegen, Kliegl, & Mayr, 1997). These declines have been associated with changes in the prefrontal cortex, specifically the dorsolateral region (Phillips & Della Sala, 1999), resulting in a loss of efficiency in inhibition processes (Albert & Kaplan, 1980; Dempster, 1992, 1993, 1995; Hasher & Zacks, 1988, see Daniels et al., 2006; Phillips & Della Sala, 1999; West, 1996, for reviews). Indeed, there is a greater reduction in the volume of frontal cortex relative to other neural regions in older adults (Haug & Eggers, 1991), and typical neurological changes are associated with increases in perseverative behavior and distractibility.

Lowered EF performance in older adults can be seen across a wide range of contexts including performance on EF tasks themselves, such as the *Wisconsin Card Sorting Task* (Axelrod & Henry, 1992; Daigneault, Braun, & Whitaker, 1992; Libon et al., 1994), problem-solving tasks (Della Sala & Logie, 1998; Shallice & Burgess, 1991), letter fluency (Whelihan & Lesher, 1985), *Tower of London* (Allamanno, Della Sala, Laiacona, Pasetti, & Spinnler, 1987), garden-path sentences (Hartman & Hasher, 1991), visual self-ordered retrieval task (Daigneault & Braun, 1993), temporal-order judgments (Allain et al., 2007; Moscovitch & Winocur, 1995), context processing (i.e., the AX-CPT task; Rush, Barch, & Braver, 2006), and directed forgetting (Zacks, Radvansky, & Hasher, 1996). An example of this age-related decline is evident in prospective memory tasks. In one such task, participants are given instructions to do something in the future either after a certain delay (time based) or when exposed to a cue (event based). Successful performance requires the ability to switch flexibly between attending to the current task and monitoring the appropriateness of engaging in the prospective task, and inhibiting the current task when executing the prospective task. Older adults are less accurate in time-based tasks relative to younger adults (McDaniel & Einstein, 1992; but see Patten & Meit, 1993), and show deficits in event-based tasks with increased complexity (e.g., needing to remember four cues instead of one; Einstein, Holland, McDaniel, & Guynn, 1992) and atypical cues (Mäntylä, 1994).

Life-span studies using set-shifting tasks also have revealed inverted-U–shaped developmental changes with improvements from the school age to the younger adult period and then subsequent declines in the late adult developmental period (Cepeda et al., 2001; Kray, Eber, & Lindenberger, 2004; Mayr, 2001; Reimers & Maylor, 2005; Zelazo et al., 2004). For example, Zelazo et al. (2004) used a modified version of the *Dimensional Change Card Sort* with school-aged children, young adults, and older adults. In this version, participants had to "sort" computerized cards according to either shape or color of the stimuli, but alternate between sorting dimensions from trial to trial depending on the presence or absence of a border surrounding the stimuli. Zelazo et al. found that both school-aged children and older adults between 65 and 75 years of age found the task more challenging than younger adults.

Response inhibition difficulties are also evident on the *Stroop task,* with slower color naming compared with baseline for older adults (Boone, Miller, Lesser, Hill, & D'Elia, 1990; Cohn, Dustman, & Bradford, 1984; Comalli et al., 1962; Daigneault et al., 1992; Houx, Jolles, & Vreeling, 1993), although these deficits are minimal in highly educated adults (Houx et al., 1993) or when color and word information are separated spatially (Hartley, 1993). Paradoxically, decreases in response inhibition can sometimes lead to task improvements. For example, older adults do not exhibit negative priming, the tendency to suppress previously unnecessary material, because of reductions in response inhibition (Hasher, Stoltzfus, Zacks, & Rypma, 1991). Finally, whereas simple working memory performance tends to stay relatively stable with advancing age, complex working memory performance decreases, beginning as early as the 20s, although there is some debate as to whether verbal and visuospatial working memory decline at the same rates (see Park & Payer, 2006, for a review).

THEORETICAL MODELS OF EXECUTIVE FUNCTION

Several models of EF have been proposed to account for the development of EF at various points of the life span. Existing models of EF generally fall under two broad types: On the one hand, *representational models* focus on the kind of representations individuals can hold and the ensuing executive control made possible by these representational abilities (e.g., Figure 13.1); on the other hand, *componential models* see EF as consisting of a group of more-or-less correlated, yet separable cognitive processes that work together to produce executive control (e.g., Figure 13.2). As mentioned previously, there is also a more common distinction made in the literature between unified and diverse models of EF, and although this distinction overlaps somewhat with the representational/componential distinction that we make here, they are not identical. Proponents of unified models (loosely related to representational models) claim that there is a single unified EF process that underlies cognitive and response control, whereas diverse models (related to componential models) suggest that there are multiple dissociable EF processes. Although diverse and componential models are essentially the same, there are unified models that are not representational; for example, models that invoke a single construct (e.g., a general purpose inhibitory mechanism) to account for EF processes assume a single unified process, but such models need not be representational.

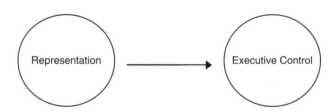

Figure 13.1 Representational models stipulate that *how* information is represented influences executive control.

Representational Models

Childhood Representational Models

One of the earliest developmental models of cognitive and behavioral control was proposed by Vygotsky (1929) in the 1920s, and later tested empirically and expanded on by his colleague Luria—although at that time, these abilities had not been grouped under the modern EF umbrella term. In his sociocultural theory of cognitive development,

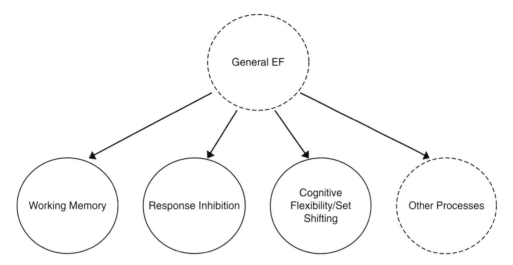

Figure 13.2 Componential models. Most componential models tend to include working memory, response inhibition, and cognitive flexibility/set shifting. Some models include a more general executive function (EF) process, other specific processes, or both (*dashed circles*).

Vygotsky theorized that socially transmitted cultural tools, particularly language, allow for qualitative changes in the structure of human cognition making the voluntary control of behavior possible (Luria, 1969, 1976; Vygotsky, 1978, 1934/1986). In particular, he stated that the "specifically human capacity for language enables children to provide for auxiliary tool in the solution of difficult tasks, to overcome impulsive action, to plan a solution to a problem prior to its execution, and to master their own behavior" (Vygotsky, 1978, p. 28). From our modern perspective, then, Vygotsky viewed the development of EF as rooted in the development of language.

A central tenet of Vygotsky's theory was his belief that cognitive change first manifests itself in social exchanges (interpersonal) and only later becomes internalized by the individual (intrapersonal; Luria, 1961; Vygotsky, 1978). A second fundamental principle in Vygotsky's theory concerned the determining role of speech in the organization of higher psychological processes (Vygotsky, 1978). He proposed that speech and thought first develop independently only to become tightly intertwined in the course of development (Vygotsky, 1929, 1978). Initially, speech serves only a communicative purpose, but later acquires other functions such as semantic, syntactic, and for our purposes, directive functions (Luria, 1957, 1969, 1976). Vygotsky claimed that the emergent directive function of speech allows children to organize and plan their behavior, essentially rendering them capable of voluntary, purposeful behavior (Vygotsky, 1978, 1934/1986). Vygotsky's untimely death prevented him from conducting much of the

experimental research required to test his theory. However, his colleagues—Luria, in particular—conducted empirical studies that tested various aspects of Vygotsky's claims. The results of these experiments allowed Luria to refine and elaborate on Vygotsky's initial theory (e.g., Luria, 1957, 1959a, 1961, 1969).

A key finding in Luria's experimental work was the progressive developmental changes he identified in children's ability to govern their behavior via external and then internal speech or verbal directives (e.g., Luria, 1959a, 1961). More specifically, Luria not only found evidence that infants and preschoolers are able to obey increasingly complex verbal commands with development, but that children younger than 3 years find it more difficult to *inhibit* responses according to verbal instructions than to initiate them (see later in this chapter for experimental details). He further argued that without speech, stimulus-response mappings are extremely inflexible and can be changed only gradually (Luria, 1957). Thus, on both Luria and Vygotsky's account, the advent of language increasingly allows children greater cognitive and response control as they develop. The medium of language provides the vehicle for representing information in the form of self- or other-generated verbal directives that allow children to control their thoughts and behaviors, and developmental changes in control result from developmental changes in language abilities.

A second, more recent representational model of the early development of EF has been elaborated by Zelazo and his colleagues. They take a functional approach to the study of EF, defining the construct by what it accomplishes (Zelazo et al., 1997; Zelazo et al., 2003). From this perspective, Zelazo et al. (1997) presented a problem-solving approach to the study of EF that involves the subfunctions of problem representation, planning, execution, and evaluation; EF impairments can manifest themselves at any of these stages. From Zelazo and colleagues' perspective, increases in representational skills, which most likely are linked to maturation of the prefrontal cortex, account for developmental changes in EF. Three separate, but related, models have been proposed to describe the development of EF at different levels of analyses: levels of consciousness model, hierarchical competing systems model, and cognitive complexity and control theory.

According to the levels of consciousness model (Zelazo, 2004), an intentional representation is formed when an object becomes the content of consciousness. In the simplest case, the object is an external stimulus that triggers a description from semantic memory. This basic process is referred to as minimal consciousness and is thought to be active early in life, perhaps even innate. Reflection occurs when a representation itself becomes the content of consciousness. This allows for memory to be decoupled from experience. The memory can now serve as a goal even in the absence of the original object. Furthermore, reflection is a recursive process such that a level of reflection can then become the object of a representation, resulting in a second-order reflection, and so on. The representational capability of a system is related directly to the highest degree of reflection that is possible.

Focusing on the importance of the development of the representational system, the hierarchical competing systems model (Marcovitch & Zelazo, 2006, 2009) posits that the ability to reflect is a primary determinant of executive control (see Mascolo & Fischer, Chapter 6 of this volume, for an extended discussion of the development of levels of reflection). According to the hierarchical competing systems model, behavior is jointly determined by a habit system that biases responding toward previously rewarded behaviors and a representational system that has the potential to override the habit system via reflection. Thus, EF errors occur in the absence of reflection, which is common in the face of complex or distracting stimuli. One important corollary of the hierarchical competing systems model is the role of task experience, which paradoxically increases the likelihood of repeating previously successful behaviors via the habit system, as well as the likelihood of reflection via the representational system. Consequently, U-shaped relations are observed between EF performance and the amount of experience with the task. Errors are rarely made with little task experience because of a weak habit system or with large amounts of task experience (see Esposito, 1975, for a review of overtraining effects on the discrimination-shift learning paradigm) because reflection becomes likely. Rather, errors are most likely to occur when there is a moderate amount of experience such that the habit system is relatively strong but reflection is not elicited (Marcovitch & Zelazo, 2000, 2006).

High levels of reflection also allow for increases in representational flexibility. According to the cognitive complexity and control theory (CCC, Zelazo & Frye, 1998; CCC-r, Zelazo et al., 2003), behaviors are the products of mentally represented "if-then" rules. Furthermore, age-related advances in levels of reflection are responsible for age-related changes in the level of complexity of the rule structures that children can represent and follow. Specifically, 2.5-year-old children can follow one rule (Zelazo & Reznick, 1991; Zelazo, Reznick, & Piñon, 1995), 3-year-old children can follow a pair of compatible rules, and 5-year-old children can switch between two pairs of incompatible rules (Frye et al., 1995).

Munakata and colleagues also propose a representational model for EF; however, they take the perspective that the strength of representations is critical to solving EF tasks (Cepeda & Munakata, 2007; Morton & Munakata, 2002; Munakata, 2001). By postulating that representations are graded in nature (i.e., some are stronger than others), Munakata (2001) offers a parsimonious explanation for dissociations in behavior, which are common in the EF literature. For example, behavioral dissociations, such as the finding that 8- to 12-month-old infants who search incorrectly for an object are surprised when they observe someone else search incorrectly (Ahmed & Ruffman, 1998), are often explained by proposing separable knowledge systems (e.g., coordination of a means-end routine vs. object permanence) that are assessed using different methods (e.g., reaching vs. looking). According to Munakata (2001), however, dissociations can be explained by the fact that different methods of assessment require different strengths in representations. For example, because their representations of hidden objects are graded, younger infants are more successful at demonstrating their representation of a hidden object on tasks that only require responses that depend on weaker representations, such as looking, than on those that require responses that depend on stronger representations, such as reaching.

The active/latent account put forth by Munakata and colleagues (Cepeda & Munakata, 2007; Morton & Munakata, 2002; Munakata, 1998) emphasizes the importance of representational strength in EF. Active traces, subserved by the prefrontal cortex, involve the maintenance of a representation over a delay. In contrast, latent traces subserved by the posterior cortex contain previously relevant information and arise from repeatedly processing stimuli. Like others, Munakata and colleagues argue that prefrontal active representations code more conceptual, abstract representations, whereas posterior latent representations code stimulus-specific representations. Behavior is determined by the relative strengths of active and latent traces, and failures in EF occur when active traces are not strong enough to compete with latent traces. More important, as the strength of active traces increases with development of the prefrontal cortex, so does the ability to maintain the relevant representation, increasing the capacity for flexible behavior.

Adulthood Representational Models

Miller and Cohen (2001) put forth an important representational model of the role of prefrontal cortex in executive control. They proposed that the prefrontal cortex represents goals and the means to achieve them, thereby allowing for executive control in the face of distraction. Inflexible, automatic behaviors that are stereotyped reactions to specific stimuli are associated with other areas of the brain. According to Miller and Cohen, the prefrontal cortex comes into play when top-down processing is involved and internal representations must be used to select task-relevant, but weakly established or novel behaviors, in the face of competition from task-irrelevant, but stronger, more established responses. Miller and Cohen assumed that processing in the brain is competitive. Consequently, whenever multiple responses are possible and a weak task-relevant response is appropriate but needs to compete with stronger task-inappropriate responses, the prefrontal cortex biases or guides neural activity along specific pathways that lead to the appropriate response. The specific function of the prefrontal cortex is to generate and maintain representations of mean-ends relations. In short, they considered the prefrontal cortex as "active memory in the service of control" (Miller & Cohen, 2001, p. 173) that can sustain active representations over time to guide behavior even in the face of distraction. Moreover, based on Petrides's (1985) research suggesting that patients with frontal damage lose the ability to learn conditional associations, Miller and Cohen suggested that the prefrontal cortex represents contingencies between general abstract rules and responses rather than contingencies between particular cues and responses.

Miller and Cohen (2001) proposed a number of other minimal requirements for top-down control by the prefrontal cortex to be possible. For example, they suggested that representations subserved by the prefrontal cortex must be multimodal and integrative. The prefrontal cortex also must access and integrate internal and external information. Indeed, Miller and Cohen concluded that given its interconnectivity with other brain regions, the prefrontal cortex is not only particularly well suited at representing diverse sources and kinds of information, but it is also well suited for returning feedback to these other brain regions, allowing for learning to take place.

Late Adulthood Representational Models

Both documented changes in prefrontal cortex and decreased performance on EF tasks with advancing age have led some to propose the *frontal-lobe hypothesis* of late adult cognitive development (e.g., West, 1996). This hypothesis has been criticized, however, for its lack of specificity and because some have demonstrated that age-related variation on EF tasks disappears when lower cognitive processing abilities have been controlled (see Daniels et al., 2006, for a review). Recently, more specific models of late adult cognitive development involving EF have emerged. For example, Craik and Bialystok (2006; see also Bialystok & Craik, Chapter 7 of this volume) propose a representational model of cognition and executive control applicable across the life span. In their account, both representational and control processes contribute in an interactive way to the development of EF. Craik and Bialystok argue that representational processes influence cognition in terms of their content: Knowledge schemas are built from interactions with the environment. Control processes are the processes that operate on existing representations. However, both representational and control processes mutually influence each other; specific kinds of representations are limited by the control processes available to individuals to generate them, whereas control processes are influenced by existing knowledge structures. In their words, "control processes determine the construction of representations, and these representations later play a part in further controlled processing" (Craik & Bialystok, 2006, p. 132).

Changes to the representational system show the largest increase during childhood, growing less rapidly during adulthood and remaining relatively stable through late adulthood. Like other accounts of cognitive development (e.g., Gibson, 1969; Inhelder & Piaget, 1959/1964; Smith, 1984, 1989; Vygotsky, 1934/1986; Werner, 1948; Zelazo & Frye, 1997), Craik and Bialystok (2006) proposed that children's representational knowledge structures become increasingly hierarchical with age with the construction of more generalized representations. Thus, as children's representational abilities increase, their representations become more conceptual and less context dependent. In older adults, however, context once again becomes increasingly important for them to access more specific and detailed stored representations, although their more generalized conceptual representations remain relatively intact.

In contrast, internal control processes necessary for overriding prepotent, externally determined responses increase during childhood and early adulthood but decline thereafter. Control processes are intentional and conscious, and likely to be associated with working memory. Because of distinct developmental trajectories of representational and control processes, Craik and Bialystok (2006) argued that each influence EF at different points in development, with representational difficulties contributing more to EF processes in early childhood and control difficulties contributing more in late adulthood. Both processes, however, have at least some impact on EF abilities, but for different reasons. For instance, in children, knowledge-related difficulties that contribute to EF difficulties often arise from incomplete acquisition of relevant information, whereas in late adulthood, knowledge-related difficulties that contribute to EF difficulties often can stem from difficulties with accessing stored relevant information.

Componential Models

Several componential models of EF have been proposed across the life span. Although they differ in many respects, these models have in common that they stipulate a group of more or less correlated but distinct EF abilities. Some of these models have been developed based on findings that EF measures are typically only moderately correlated, suggesting that different yet related EF processes are implicated (e.g., Carlson, Mandell, & Williams, 2004; Carlson & Moses, 2001), whereas others have been proposed as a result of empirical investigations using exploratory or confirmatory factor analyses (e.g., Hughes, 1998; Lehto, Juujärvi, Kooistra, & Pulkkinen, 2003; Miyake et al., 2000; Welsh et al., 1991; see Garon et al., 2008, for a review). Results from such studies have yielded sets of correlated factors suggesting that a number of distinguishable EF abilities exist. Moreover, some models (but not all)

stipulate an overarching common underlying mechanism that relates the separate EF abilities. We present some examples of componential models proposed to account for EF at different points in the life span.

Childhood Componential Models

Diamond (2006b) proposed that there are only three EF processes—namely, inhibition, working memory, and cognitive flexibility—and argued that these processes become better coordinated with development because of maturation of the dorsolateral and ventrolateral prefrontal cortex. According to Diamond (2006b), the dramatic growth of the prefrontal cortex between 7.5 and 12 months of age leads to radical improvements in a variety of infant-appropriate EF tasks (e.g., delayed response task, A-not-B task, object retrieval task). In the second year of life, there is marked improvement in the ability to process physically and conceptually unconnected things (e.g., delayed nonmatching to sample task), which she associated with the growth of the inferior frontal junction. In older children, there is a strong relation between faster processing and EF ability, which Diamond linked to system-wide improvements to neural circuitry (increased myelinization) or to the fact that stronger prefrontal cortex provides better signals for diverse neural regions.

Borrowing from the adult framework that Miyake et al. (2000; described in the next section of this chapter) proposed, Garon et al. (2008) recently presented a new componential model of the development of EF during the preschool years. They suggested that EF consists of a set of common and separable EF components that are organized hierarchically. They proposed that EF processes exist to resolve conflict (cf. Diamond, 2006b; Munakata, 2001) between (1) different representations, (2) representations and prepotent responses, or (3) incompatible response sets. Drawing from Posner and Rothbart's (2007) work on attention, Garon et al. suggested that attention is the common underlying mechanism that influences all three core EF components (working memory, response control, and set shifting). Developments in attentional abilities are believed to underlie developments in EF across the preschool years. For example, early improvements in EF and goal-directed behavior in infancy are thought to occur as a result of an increased ability to focus attention on task-relevant information while ignoring task-irrelevant information. Based on Posner and Rothbart's theory, Garon et al. suggested that developmental changes in selective attention result from changes in two complementary attentional systems, an orienting system that emerges in infancy and allows children to orient to and shift attention between different external stimuli, and an anterior attention system that emerges later in the preschool years and allows children to select and enhance attention on the basis of internal representations. Changes in the preschool years are believed to result from an increase in the control of the anterior attentional system over the orienting one, which, in turn, allows children to stay in a state of focused attention for a longer amount of time (sustained attention) and flexibly shift the focus of their attention as a function of task goals. Infants first learn to shift attention between external stimuli, and later learn to shift attention between internal representations and external stimuli. Furthermore, in early development, focusing and shifting aspects of attentional processes are not fully integrated and actually compete with each other (Jones et al., 2003). However, with development, these two attentional processes become integrated, allowing for advances in EF.

Garon et al. (2008) delineated specific developmental changes for each of the three core EF abilities during the infancy and preschool periods. Young infants show improvements in simple working memory tasks in their first year of life, whereas they do not succeed on complex tasks until their second year. Garon et al. also differentiated between simple and complex response inhibition tasks in that they proposed that simple response inhibition tasks require only withholding or delaying a single prepotent or automatic response. In contrast, complex response inhibition tasks require responding according to a rule held in mind while inhibiting a prepotent response. Finally, they differentiated between simple and complex set-shifting tasks, referring to simpler ones as response-shifting tasks and to more complex ones as attention-shifting tasks. On the one hand, response-shifting tasks require forming an arbitrary stimulus–response set and then shifting to another arbitrary stimulus–response set. On the other hand, attention-shifting tasks also require learning one stimulus–response set and shifting to another, but these mappings involve two different aspects of the same stimuli. Moreover, attention-shifting tasks also require response shifting because some degree of response remapping must necessarily be involved for successful performance.

Adulthood Componential Models

Garon and colleagues (2008) constructed their developmental componential model of EF abilities in preschoolers drawing extensively from Miyake et al.'s (2000) findings regarding the unity and diversity of EF. Miyake et al. used confirmatory factor analysis and structural equation modeling to determine whether EFs can be fractionated into separate distinct functions in adults. They assessed young adults on several relatively simple but diverse tasks purported to assess the "updating function" of working memory, response inhibition, and set shifting. Using confirmatory factor analysis in which they assigned specific tasks to their purported functions, Miyake et al. tested four kinds of models: a single-factor model, separate models with two factors, a model with three independent factors, and a model with three factors that were allowed to correlate. The latter of these models best fit the data.

In addition, they assessed participants on more complex tasks (e.g., Wisconsin Card Sort Test, *Tower of Hanoi, Random Number Generation Task*) that have been used extensively in the literature and assumed to test specific EF abilities. The authors found that some of the tasks tended to load on specific EF processes. For example, the Wisconsin Card Sort Test loaded on the set-shifting factor, whereas the Tower of Hanoi and some of the response variables from the Random Number Generation Task loaded on the inhibition factor. Other response variables from the random number task loaded on the updating factor. Interestingly, dual-task performance—performing two independent tasks simultaneously—did not load on any EF factors, despite the assumption that dual-task performance might require set shifting given that participants need to shift continuously between two tasks. This finding suggests that EF-related set-shifting requirements are not involved when participants must coordinate and engage in two unrelated tasks simultaneously. Set shifting may be implicated only when individuals must switch between two incompatible representations of the same task; that is, when they must consider the same stimuli from different perspectives.

On the basis of their findings, Miyake et al. (2000) concluded that there is sufficient evidence of both unity and diversity of EF processes; that is, each of the EF components (updating, set shifting, and inhibition) appear to be separable, yet they are all interrelated, suggesting that although they share some degree of commonality, they likely do not reflect the same underlying mechanism. Miyake et al. speculated about potential ways in which these processes might relate with each other, but they did not commit themselves to one particular proposal. Moreover, their results suggest that even though individual differences in performance on complex tasks used to assess EF, such as the Wisconsin Card Sort Test, could result for any number of reasons, performance on these complex tasks at least loaded on relevant EF processes for young adults. Thus, at least for typical young adults, individual differences in performance on these complex EF tasks likely result from efficiency of specific EF processes. This interpretation, however, should not be generalized to other age groups or to clinical groups, because difficulties in any of these groups on these same tasks could arise for other reasons given the number of processes that need to be intact for successful performance on these tasks.

Other Models

Other models of EF that do not fall neatly into the representational versus componential model distinction exist. Many of these models, although they differ substantially, actually integrate aspects of both representational and componential models. We briefly highlight some of these models.

Childhood Other Models

Early developmental models of EF tended to emphasize a unitary inhibitory mechanism (e.g., Dempster, 1992; Harnishfeger & Bjorklund, 1993). For example, Dempster (1992) argued that improvements in inhibitory processes during cognitive development, and conversely, impairments in these same processes in late adult cognitive development, can be traced back to the growth and decline of inhibitory processes necessary to resist interference. Likewise, Harnishfeger and Bjorklund (1993; Bjorklund & Harnishfeger, 1990) proposed that inhibitory processes become more efficient over childhood in an "outward-in" direction, with inhibitory control initially arising in response to adult directions, then arising from children's own overt behavior (i.e., self-directed speech), and finally through covert self-direction. Consequently, the developing ability to keep inappropriate information out of working memory leads to vast improvements in cognitive development.

In contrast, Barkley (2001) took a functional view of EF, suggesting that executive acts serve to modify one's own behavior in the future. Specifically, EFs are considered to be classes of self-directed actions used to promote self-regulation; thus, all EFs require response inhibition. Furthermore, EFs have developed across the evolutionary time course; they began as overt behaviors but have become covert as humans have become more adept at self-regulation and have found it increasingly necessary to protect self-directed thoughts from social imitators. Barkley argued that EFs follow the same developmental progression in childhood, developing from overt to covert, although one cannot engage in overt and covert forms of EFs simultaneously.

From this perspective, Barkley (2001) proposed four EFs that form a stage-wise hierarchy such that an earlier EF is needed for a later EF: (1) nonverbal working memory (sensing to the self), (2) verbal working memory (speech to the self), (3) self-regulation of affect/motivational/arousal (emotion/motivation to the self), and (4) reconstitution (play to the self). Nonverbal working memory has both retrospective and prospective functions, and thus becomes the mental module for anticipating the future from the experienced past. It relies heavily on the privatization of visual and auditory events, and these representations form the basis of eventual symbolization. Finally, resensing one's past experiences presumably forms the basis of autonoetic awareness. Verbal working memory is characterized by the privatization of speech that allows for self-description, reflection, self-instruction, self-questioning, and problem solving. Self-regulation of affect/motivation/arousal arises from the existence of the first two EFs. Mentally represented events have associated somatic markers that are paired initially with publically observable behaviors (e.g., laughing out loud). This EF serves to privatize affect and arousal, resulting in covert forms of the paired behaviors, and thus becomes the basis for intrinsic motivation that initiates behavior. Reconstitution, in turn, is the internalization of play, which can be thought of as mental simulations of events. This allows for the internal generation and execution of novel actions without real-world consequences, and is essential for planning and problem solving.

Adulthood Other Models

Engle and Kane (2004; Kane & Engle, 2002) have recognized the importance of working memory capacity in predicting a wide array of psychological functions. From their perspective, individual differences in working memory capacity, typically measured using complex span tasks in the face of demanding secondary tasks, do not reflect storage limitations per se, but rather the executive control needed to maintain information in an active state. Compared with individuals with high working memory capacity ("high spans"), those with low working memory capacity ("low spans") have difficulty maintaining goals in active memory and resolving response competition. Unlike some models of EF that postulate that working memory is a subcomponent of EF, Engle and Kane take a different approach in postulating that executive control is a subfeature of working memory (Engle & Kane; Engle, Kane, & Tuholski, 1999; Kane, Conway, Hambrick, & Engle, 2007; see also Baddeley, 1986; Case, 1992, 1995; Gordon & Olson, 1998;

Olson, 1993; O'Reilly, Braver, & Cohen, 1999; Pascual-Leone, 1970; and Roberts & Pennington, 1996, for other models that give working memory a pivotal role in EF or cognition more generally). In Kane et al.'s (2007) model, short-term memory consists of long-term memory traces that are activated above threshold. Maintaining these traces in an active state requires grouping/chunking, coding, and/or rehearsal strategies, which may be within or outside of consciousness. For example, maintaining the rules of a Stroop task (i.e., name the color of the font but do not read the word) may be easy and relatively automatic for high-span adults, but challenging and resource demanding for low-span children. The central executive is best described by endogenously controlled attention and is responsible for regulating the skills needed to keep memory traces active, retrieve information from outside of conscious focus, and block goal-irrelevant representations or inappropriate responses elicited by the environment. The extent of executive control engagement is determined by the degree of conflict presented in the context, and further modulated by familiarity and practice with particular skills.

Late Adulthood Other Models

Models of EF in older adults typically account for age-related decreases in cognitive abilities, including increased susceptibility to proactive and retroactive interference. Salthouse (1996) postulated that declines in processing speed accounts for a domain-general decrement in cognitive performance in late adult populations. He further proposed that the relation between speed and cognition in older adults arises from limited time because of cognitive processes that are executed too slowly and from deficits in high-level processing because of a reduction in the amount of available information. Verhaeghen et al. (1997) also argued that the ability to coordinate complex components into a reliable sequence is a process that is separable from processing speed (see also Chalfonte & Johnson, 1996; Craik & Byrd, 1982).

Hasher and Zacks (1988) further implicate inhibitory processing failures in working memory as a major determinant in the reduced cognitive functioning of older adults. In their view, deficiencies in inhibition are responsible for hindering the retrieval of critical information, usually because inappropriate information (e.g., previously correct information, distracting stimuli, current concerns of the subject) is not inhibited effectively and persists in working memory for a prolonged period. One consequence of weakened inhibition is that older adults have more difficulty giving up previously held inferences in light of new

information. Furthermore, as the coordination of complex components requires keeping representations encapsulated, inhibition failures make this difficult, leading to "cross talk" among simultaneously active representations. Notably, well-educated older adults with high verbal memory are often protected from the considerable age-related decline in cognitive functioning, suggesting that experience and efficient strategy implementation on cognitive tasks are important in mitigating age-related decline (Hasher & Zacks).

Braver and West (2008) speak directly to the role of EF in cognitive decline (but see Salthouse, Atkinson, & Berish, 2003, for an alternative view) in their goal-maintenance account of late adult cognitive development, suggesting that active maintenance of the goal is a primary indicator of success on cognitive tasks (Kane & Engle, 2003; Marcovitch, Boseovski, & Knapp, 2007). They further postulate that successful goal maintenance requires inhibition of inappropriate goals. Support for this hypothesis comes from a number of sources, including research on prospective memory (i.e., remembering to do something in the future). For example, Smith and Bayen (2006) reported that older adults have more difficulty with prospective memory tasks. One path to efficient prospective memory is through active goal maintenance, which may be difficult for older adults who have trouble maintaining intentions across delays as short as 5 seconds (Einstein, McDaniel, Manzi, Cochran, & Baker, 2000; McDaniel, Einstein, Stout, & Morgan, 2003). Similarly, Braver, Gray, and Burgess (2007) have argued for a distinction between proactive and reactive cognitive control. Simply put, proactive control occurs in anticipation of an event, whereas reactive control is stimulus driven. According to this model, older adults show reductions in their usage of proactive control.

AN INTEGRATED DEVELOPMENTAL MODEL OF EXECUTIVE FUNCTION

We argue that a developmental model encompassing key features from the described existing models provides the best account for EF across the life span. This model includes both componential and representational features. In brief, like Engle and Kane (2004) and others (e.g., Case, 1992, 1995; Gordon & Olson, 1998; Olson, 1993; Pascual-Leone, 1970), we propose that variability in working memory best accounts for variability in EF. In other words, the development of working memory abilities are most likely instrumental in the emergence of the two forms of executive control processes (viz. cognitive and response control). Specifically, in this model, working memory is understood as the representational vehicle that permits relevant information to be kept in mind, information that is critical for one to be able to exert control over one's thoughts and behaviors, permitting cognitive flexibility on the one hand and response control on the other. In this respect, this is a representational model. However, the model is also componential because it distinguishes between the three core EF processes (working memory, cognitive flexibility, and response control). Whereas many componential models often (implicitly, at least) describe working memory as its own independent EF process (e.g., Diamond, 2006b; Garon et al., 2008; Miyake et al., 2000), we, like Engle and Kane (2004), view working memory as a contributor to the other two processes. Figure 13.3 depicts the proposed links between the three core EF processes. Thus, this model is representational in its assertion that how information is represented affects executive control. However, unlike some representational models (e.g., Bialystok & Craik, Chapter 7 of this volume; Craik & Bialystok, 2006; Miller & Cohen, 2001), two forms of executive control (viz. cognitive vs. response control) are differentiated.

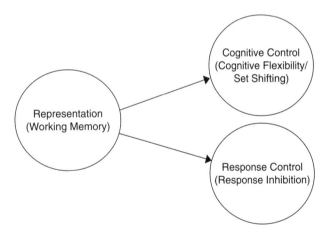

Figure 13.3 An integrated model suggesting a causal link between specific representational capabilities and specific forms of control.

This section describes key characteristics of working memory representations that allow one to exert control over one's own thoughts and behavior. These characteristics are not new; in fact, they are drawn directly from existing theories described in the previous sections—although no existing theory proposes *all* of these characteristics into a single model. For example, Miller and Cohen (2001)

emphasize goal representation and representations that are resistant to distractions, but they do not consider development, which we view as essential in any theory of EF. As another example, Zelazo et al. (2003) place great emphasis on the influence of representational changes across development on EF processes at different ages, but they do not fully incorporate the concept of working memory processes within their conceptualization of EF (see also Zelazo et al., 1997).

Working memory has received considerable attention in recent decades, particularly as a result of the seminal work by Baddeley and Hitch (1974; see Baddeley, 1986, 2003; and Hitch, 2006, for reviews). Baddeley (1986) defined working memory as "a system for the temporary holding and manipulation of information during the performance of a range of cognitive tasks such as comprehension, learning and reasoning" (pp. 33–34). He argued that any model of working memory must distinguish and incorporate at least two components: On the one hand, working memory requires a storage component so that information can be maintained online; on the other hand, it must include a processing component that can manipulate this stored information. Specifically, Baddeley (1986) proposed a working memory model that includes two storage subsystems, namely, an articulatory loop and a visuospatial scratch pad, which differ in terms of the type of information that each is able to hold (i.e., linguistic vs. visuospatial information, respectively), and a supervisory controlling subsystem, referred to as the central executive, which processes information stored in the two storage subsystems.

This initial notion of working memory has evolved and several other models have emerged (see Miyake & Shah, 1999; and Demetriou, Mouyi, & Spanoudis, Chapter 10 of this volume, for reviews of major theoretical approaches). Researchers generally agree about the existence of two types of working memory tasks (e.g., Garon et al., 2008; Hitch, 2006); tasks that place only storage demands on working memory are generally considered simple working memory tasks or short-term memory tasks, whereas those that require participants to store and process information simultaneously are labeled complex working memory tasks. Existing research on the development of working memory across the life span has also tended to focus on developmental changes in working memory *capacity* and *function*. Although capacity and function are important, the particular contents of working memory are also critical for effective executive control (cf. Bialystok & Craik, this volume; Craik & Bialystok, 2006; Zelazo et al., 2003).

Drawing from existing theories, the integrated model proposes that there are several features of working memory that may be essential for successful EF (see Table 13.1). The first of these features is the maintenance of *task goals* (cf. Engle & Kane, 2004; Miller & Cohen, 2001). Second, early working memory representations, especially goal representations, must be *resistant to interference* from task-irrelevant stimulation (cf. Garon et al., 2008; Hasher & Zacks, 1988; Marcovitch et al., 2007; Miller & Cohen). A failure to represent the goal during problem solving in the face of distractions would lead to EF failures. Moreover, *early working memory* representations are likely to be constructed using bottom-up processes from perceptual-motor information (as opposed to internally generated ones) but maintained internally in the form of *sensorimotor representations*. From the perspective of this integrated model, early EF abilities are also likely to develop on the basis of improvements in an infant's basic ability to *maintain information*. As a result, these early working memory abilities can be tapped by simple working memory tasks because maintaining information in working memory suffices for early executive control (cf. Garon et al.).

Table 13.1   Proposed Characteristics of Working Memory Representations

1. Early Executive Control Depends on Storage of Representational Content

    a. Goal representation—actively maintains goal in mind

    b. Representations resistant to distraction

    c. Sensorimotor-derived representations

2. Advanced Executive Control Depends on Storage and Processing of Representational Content (monitoring, manipulating, and/or updating)

    d. Verbally mediated, language-based representations

    e. Internally generated, abstract conceptual representations

Although maintaining representations in working memory is critical at all levels of EF, processing the representational content held in mind by monitoring, manipulating, or updating it becomes increasingly important for the emergence of advanced executive control. With new EF processing requirements come novel constraints on the specific form and content of working memory representations. Specifically, based on early research by Luria (1959a, 1961) and Vygotsky (1929), it is hypothesized that advanced executive control requires complex working memory representations that are *linguistic* in nature. Further, the *abstract and conceptual* (i.e., symbolic as distinct from sensorimotor) nature of these representations provides the base for new levels of executive control to emerge during

the preschool years (cf. Blaye & Jacques, 2009; Carlson & Beck, 2009; Jacques & Zelazo, 2005a; Jacques et al., 2010; Kharitonova, Chien, Colunga, & Munakata, 2009; Luria, 1959a; Zelazo & Frye, 1997). Abstract linguistic representations are necessarily *internally generated* using top-down processing rather than generated from available sensorimotor information. Thus, approaching a task relying on (verbal) representations that are also internally generated allows children greater control over their behavior than relying on externally derived representations. That is, because abstract representations are further separated from perceptual experience, they are more robust and easier to manipulate (cf. Carlson & Beck, 2009; Carlson, Davis, & Leach, 2005; Jacques & Zelazo, 2005a).

EMPIRICAL EVIDENCE FOR REPRESENTATIONAL DEVELOPMENT IN WORKING MEMORY AND EXECUTIVE CONTROL PROCESSES

This section reviews research that provides support for the claim that developmental changes in the representational features of working memory are associated with the development of cognitive flexibility and response control; the review is limited to EF research that has identified links between these processes. In particular, it discusses research across the life span that is relevant to the model features of working memory described in the previous section. Much of the research reported in this section involves child research because less research has been documented with younger and older adults on the specific features identified in this model. When possible, however, this section reviews relevant adult research.

Early Working Memory Representations

With respect to development, the complexity of information held in working memory likely depends on the actual or functional limits of working memory capacity. Thus, the structure and the content of working memory are vital developmental considerations. As a result, the number and complexity of representations that one is able to hold in mind both increase with development. In fact, the complexity of the representations that one is capable of holding in mind may be limited, in part, by the number of items that one can represent (e.g., Case, 1992, 1995; Case et al., 1982; Pascual-Leone, 1970). For example, representing a specific relation between two objects requires not only representing this relation but representing each object as well, thus requiring a minimum of three units of information held in working memory (cf. Guttentag & Lange, 1994; Halford, Wilson, & Phillips, 1998). Thus, if only two units of working memory capacity are available, only two objects could be represented at any one time, leaving no functional space available for representing a relation between them.

For instance, as described earlier, Diamond (Diamond et al., 1999; see Diamond, 2006a, for a review) reported that infants do better at a much earlier age on EF tasks, such as the object retrieval task or the delayed nonmatching-to-sample task, if objects are physically connected to each other than if objects are spatially distinct. Diamond (2006a) argued that the physical connectedness between objects helps infants see their conceptual connectedness earlier, allowing them to deduce abstract rules about their relations. Instead, perhaps infants do better earlier when objects are physically connected because objects and their relation can be represented in working memory using fewer units of information than if they are separated, thereby alleviating constraints on working memory representations that might make it difficult for infants to use these representations to govern their behavior.

Hence, because of limitations in functional working memory capacity, infants are likely to succeed first on EF tasks that require little functional working memory space. The simplest EF tasks are ones in which infants need only represent a goal over a delay in the face of distraction.

Goal Representation and Goal Neglect

Goal representation is a necessary feature of problem solving and, thus, a defining feature of EF tasks. Goal representation may be defined as the ability to maintain the goal in mind and act in a manner consistent with achieving this goal despite distractions. There is clear evidence that children can accomplish this by 2.5 years of age.

For example, Bullock and Lütkenhaus (1988) directly examined goal representation by exploring whether 15- to 35-month-old children could maintain an externally defined goal in mind and act on the basis of that goal. In a block-building task, children were shown how to build a figure (e.g., a house) with three blocks (i.e., the standard). They were then asked to reproduce the same figure as the experimenter. Children were given replicas of the three blocks used by the experimenter in addition to a fourth, irrelevant block to determine whether they could focus on producing the specific goal (i.e., the house) and stop once the goal had been reached despite the presence of a

distracting object designed to lead them to focus on the activity of block building itself instead of the goal. This study found that the majority of the youngest toddlers did not act in an appropriate goal-oriented manner. That is, younger children showed no evidence of using the standard in their manipulation of the task materials and instead manipulated the materials in unsystematic ways (e.g., banging blocks together). Although 26-month-olds were more outcome oriented in that they tried to reproduce figures on the basis of the standard, they were driven by the task materials, building the figure incorrectly and or failing to stop when required. Reproductions of the standard were most consistent for 32-month-olds. Although it is not clear why the younger children failed to reproduce the figure (e.g., they may have failed to understand the task or been particularly susceptible to the presence of a distracting block), it is clear that by 32 months, children can hold a goal in mind and act on the basis of that goal despite distractions. Of particular relevance, in following up this work, Silverman and Ippolito (1997) found that goal-directedness is associated with inhibitory control abilities as assessed using simple delay tasks. These findings are consistent with the idea that goal representation is an important feature of executive control.

There are many reasons why children and adults may fail to solve a particular problem as a result of goal-representation difficulties. On the one hand, they may hold the wrong goal in mind or no particular goal at all, perhaps as a result of not understanding task instructions. For example, Kaler and Kopp (1990) demonstrated that language comprehension limitations are related to young children's ability to control their behavior. The authors found that infants who failed to comply with requests generally did not comprehend nouns or verbs used in these requests when comprehension for these words was assessed independently. Thus, a simple failure to represent the correct goal in mind may account for some EF difficulties. This point is similar to one raised several times in this chapter: Poor performance on EF tasks can occur for several reasons and, therefore, can be difficult to interpret.

On the other hand, there may be situations in which children and adults demonstrate that they can represent the correct goal, but for one reason or another, fail to use this representation when attempting to solve the problem. This failure to behave appropriately in relation to a particular goal despite demonstrating knowledge of the appropriate actions, when this failure is attributable to an inability to maintain the goal in active memory, is referred to as *goal neglect* (Daniels et al., 2006; Duncan, Emslie, Willams, Johnson, &

Freer, 1996; Kane & Engle, 2003; Marcovitch et al., 2007). For example, *failure to maintain set* errors on the Wisconsin Card Sorting Test, errors that occur after a number of correct responses to a particular category, likely reflect goal-neglect errors because participants fail to respond according to the current sorting category despite having demonstrated on previous trials that they can sort by that category.

Other examples of goal neglect are common in the developmental literature, although not reported as such. For instance, despite looking at the correct location, infants around 1 year of age still perseverate on the A-not-B task when required to reach for the hidden object manually (Hofstadter & Reznick, 1996). Similar dissociations between looking and reaching have been noted at 2 years of age on more complex versions of the A-not-B task (Zelazo, Reznick, & Spinazzola, 1998). Moreover, infants who fail the A-not-B task act surprised when they see the object at the wrong location (Ahmed & Ruffman, 1998). Together, these findings indicate that, although young children can fail the A-not-B task (or one of its variants), they still demonstrate some understanding of where the object should be. By 3 years of age, children also exhibit knowledge dissociations on the Dimensional Change Card Sort, in that they are able to point to the correct target despite sorting cards perseveratively (Zelazo, Frye, & Rapus, 1996), and on false-belief tasks, in that they look at the correct location despite reporting the wrong location (Clements & Perner, 1994). Although indirect, all of these dissociations suggest that failures on EF tasks might result from goal neglect because children show some evidence that they know what to do but fail to use that knowledge when attempting to solve these tasks.

More recently, several studies have investigated goal neglect directly in children and adults. For example, based on a goal-neglect task developed by Duncan et al.'s (1996) adult task, Towse, Lewis, and Knowles (2007) presented 4-year-old children with pairs of food stimuli. On some trials, a cue was presented (e.g., an arrow) that prompted children to attend to and name items on a particular side of a computer screen for a number of trials (e.g., a right-pointing arrow indicated naming items on the right-hand side, whereas a left-pointing arrow indicated naming items on the left-hand side). After a series of trials, another type of cue was then presented (e.g., a colored box), which either required that children attend to the same side or shift attention to the other side (e.g., a red box indicated naming items on the left-hand side, whereas a blue box indicated naming items on the right-hand side). Despite demonstrating knowledge of the appropriate cue-direction contingencies, children often persisted in naming items on

the same side even after a new cue prompted them to shift attention to the other side. Towse et al. (2007) argued that this failure to shift attention provides evidence of goal neglect because children failed to update their goal based on the appearance of the cue and incorrectly relied on the old goal. In a very real sense, proficiency in task switching appears to require the ability to remain alert to cues that require a change in goal representations.

Recent research by Marcovitch and colleagues (2007) suggests that active and sustained representation of the goal is important for successful performance on EF tasks, and that conditions that reduce children's tendency to maintain the goal actively in mind may make them prone to err on EF tasks. In Marcovitch et al.'s goal-neglect version of the Dimensional Change Card Sort, devised on the basis of a modified Stroop task used with adults (Kane & Engle, 2003), 4- and 5-year-old children were given two types of test stimuli: standard conflict test cards, which matched each target on a different dimension, and redundant test cards, which were identical to the targets and, therefore, matched one of them on both dimensions. It is necessary to attend to the rules provided to sort conflict cards correctly because successful performance is underdetermined by the stimuli. This is not the case for sorting redundant cards, however, because sorting by either dimension would lead to a correct response. Thus, for redundant cards, active and sustained representation of the goal itself (e.g., "sort by color") is not necessary for successful performance. Marcovitch et al. found that in a mostly redundant condition in which 80% of the cards were redundant and 20% were conflict, 4- and 5-year-old children made relatively large numbers of perseverative errors in the postswitch phase compared with children in a mostly conflict condition in which 80% of the cards were conflict. These findings suggest that despite knowing what to do as demonstrated by their ability to sort correctly in the postswitch of the mostly conflict condition, 4- and 5-year-olds can perseverate on this task if they are placed in a context in which they are less inclined to maintain the goal in mind. Of particular interest, recent work has tied success on this goal-neglect version of the Dimensional Change Card Sort with individual differences in working memory capacity in 4- to 6-year-olds (Marcovitch, Boseovski, Knapp, & Kane, in press), consistent with the idea that working memory development, goal representation, and executive control abilities are related.

Representations Resistant to Distractions

It was proposed earlier that success on simple executive control tasks requires maintaining a goal representation in mind in the face of possible distraction (cf. Garon et al., 2008). However, few studies have directly examined the specific effects of the presence of distractions on EF performance. In one early study, Luria (1959a) examined the role of perceptual and motor distractions in relation to infants' ability to control behaviors that they could control in the absence of distractions. For instance, Luria found that, although 12- to 14-month-olds were able to obey simple directives (e.g., "Give me the horse."), they failed to do so when these same directives conflicted with their prepotent response tendencies. Specifically, when infants were presented with a toy fish and a toy horse, and were asked to give the experimenter one of the two toys (e.g., "Give me the horse."), they succeeded on several successive trials. However, when then asked to switch and give the alternate toy, they perseverated and handed the experimenter the original toy. Fourteen- to 16-month-olds had difficulty obeying similar directives when these conflicted with their current ongoing motor responses. For example, if told to put a ring on a stick while in the process of removing another ring, they failed to suppress the ongoing action (Luria, 1959a). Similarly, their ability to obey directives was easily disrupted by the presence of perceptually salient stimuli. For instance, when asked to retrieve a toy placed farther away from their body than another toy, infants tended to grasp the more proximal and, presumably, perceptually more salient toy. It was not until the age of 16 to 18 months that infants succeeded in guiding their behavior according to directives, without being susceptible to either perceptual or motor conflicts. These findings support the contention that distractions play a role in failures to maintain goal representations in this age range, and that in part what develops in the late infancy period is the ability to maintain representations while resisting distractions.

Representations Constructed from Sensorimotor Information

Luria's (1959a) work also provides evidence supporting the idea that early success on EF tasks is related to sensorimotor rather than abstract representations. Luria found that infants between the ages of 18 and 24 months were unable to follow verbal directives if these directives required searching for hidden (as opposed to visible) objects (e.g., "The coin is under the cup. Find the coin!"). Admittedly, poor performance on Luria's verbal search task could result from a simple lack of understanding of the directives. However, this latter interpretation is unlikely to suffice because Luria also found on a verbal analogue to the A-not-B search task that 20- to 24-month-olds could find a hidden object on the basis of verbal directives alone at a first location, but if the coin was hidden at a second location, they searched perseveratively at the previous hiding location. The finding that 2-year-olds could search at the first location on the basis of verbal directives alone suggests that they understood instructions. Their failure to search correctly at the second location, however, suggests that they failed to use verbal information to overcome their conflicting motor responses.

As discussed earlier, results from numerous studies clearly indicate that by 2 years of age, infants succeed on the conventional version of the A-not-B task. That is, they have no difficulty searching for hidden objects at different locations if provided with perceptual information from which they can generate their goal representation (i.e., directly observing the object being hidden). These findings suggest that they fail this verbal analogue of A-not-B task because they have to *infer* the object's location from verbal information alone (see also Sophian & Wellman, 1983). These findings support the notion that in the first 2 years, young children can exert control over their behavior using sensorimotor working memory representations before they can exert the same sort of control using abstract verbal representations. Obviously, the supportive evidence for this interpretation is still weak: Luria's results need to be replicated and extended to other paradigms. However, Luria's work is at least consistent with the idea that infants and young children initially succeed on simple EF tasks that require sensorimotor representations.

Advanced Working Memory Representations

Whereas sensorimotor working memory representations may suffice for success on early EF tasks, abstract, symbolic, linguistic representations are necessary prerequisites for the emergence of advanced EF abilities in the late preschool period (cf. Blaye & Jacques, 2009; Carlson & Beck, 2009; Jacques & Zelazo, 2005b; Jacques et al., 2010; Kharitonova et al., 2009; Luria, 1959a, 1961; Vygotsky, 1934/1986; Zelazo & Frye, 1997). Young children do not recode visual input into verbal representations in working memory spontaneously until the end of the preschool years. For example, unlike older children and adults, preschoolers are less likely to show phonological effects that are typically associated with verbal recoding on nonverbal working memory tasks (Gathercole, Pickering, Ambridge, & Wearing, 2004;

see Gathercole, 1998; Hitch, 2006, for reviews). By 6 years of age, however, children and adults do recode visuospatial information verbally in working memory, even when it is a detriment to do so. For example, adults who are prevented from verbally recoding ambiguous figures are better at identifying both images contained in the ambiguous figures (Brandimonte & Gerbino, 1993).

Although children in the 3- to 6-year-old range may not spontaneously recode visuospatial information verbally, if prompted to do by the introduction of labels, they demonstrate performance patterns typically associated with older children on cognitive tasks, including EF tasks (e.g., Jacques et al., 2010; Kendler & Kendler, 1961; Luria, 1959a). Thus, children between 3 and 6 years of age acquire the basic competence necessary for visual-verbal recoding, even though this competence may not always be apparent in their overt performance. The next section reviews research that demonstrates that language and labeling manipulations are closely associated with enhanced performance on measures of both cognitive flexibility and response control.

Verbally Mediated, Language-Based Representations

Whereas infants and young children gain control over their behavior through sensorimotor-derived representations, language and verbal mediation come to play an increasingly important role in advanced EF abilities as children develop (Luria, 1959a; Vygotsky, 1978; Zelazo, 1999). Deák (2003) and Jacques and Zelazo (2005b) have reviewed research that explores this topic and have presented evidence that language manipulations conducted with labels impact performance on many measures of cognitive flexibility and response control, including the Dimensional Change Card Sort, the Flexible Item Selection Task, and the go/no-go task. More important, the impact of labels appears to change between 3 and 4 years of age. Luria (1959a) attributed the change in the quality of label effects in this age range to the manner in which children use labels. He argued that younger 3-year-olds use *impulsive* aspects of labels to influence their behavior. That is, they use labels as some sort of auditory cue to act. Older preschoolers, in contrast, begin to use *semantics,* or the meaning of specific labels, to guide their behavior. That is, whereas young 3-year-olds can accompany motor responses on a go/no-go task with overt verbal responses (e.g., "press") that require them to act (i.e., pressing a ball), they cannot use overt verbal responses to inhibit their motor action (e.g., "don't

press"). In the former case, the physical aspect of the verbal response (i.e., producing a verbal response) is congruent with the manual response required (i.e., producing a motor response). However, in the latter case, the physical aspect of the verbal response (i.e., producing a verbal response) is incongruent with the manual response (i.e., inhibiting a motor response), thereby creating a conflict between the impulsive (excitatory in this case) and semantic (inhibitory in this case) aspects of the verbal response. It is not until children are 4-years-old that they appear to use the actual meaning of the verbal responses to guide their motor responding (Luria, 1959a; see Jacques & Zelazo, 2005b, for an extended discussion).

Early research in the learning literature provided some correlational and experimental support for a link between language development and the development of flexible thinking in preschool children (e.g., Bruner & Kenney, 1966; Kendler & Kendler, 1961; Kuenne, 1946). For example, Kuenne found that preschool children who could articulate exactly how they solved transposition problems using appropriate relational terms such as "smaller" versus "bigger" succeeded on complex transposition problems, whereas children who could not verbalize their solutions solved only simpler transposition problems—problems that even nonhuman species can solve. Transposition problems require cognitive flexibility because children must select stimuli on the basis of their simultaneous relation with at least two other items. In a similar vein, Kendler and Kendler and others (see Esposito, 1975, for a review) found that introducing relevant labels experimentally allowed preschoolers to succeed on discrimination-shift learning paradigms, which also require cognitive flexibility (see Jacques & Zelazo, 2005b, for further discussion).

More recently, a body of research has emerged indicating that language abilities predict theory-of-mind development concurrently and longitudinally (see Astington & Baird, 2005; Milligan, Astington, & Dack, 2007). Although investigators disagree as to how language might be implicated in theory of mind development, one possibility is that language abilities influence the cognitive flexibility requirements of some theory-of-mind tasks, such as the false-belief task, rather than (or in addition to) affecting mental-state understanding per se (see Jacques & Zelazo, 2005a).

Several experimental studies have been conducted that manipulate labels with the Dimensional Change Card Sort (Kirkham, Cruess, & Diamond, 2003; McKay & Jacques, 2009; Müller, Zelazo, Lurye, & Liebermann, 2008; Towse, Redbond, Houston-Price, & Cook, 2000; Yerys & Munakata, 2006), but the results of these experiments have been mixed. For example, Kirkham et al. (2003) found that most 3-year-olds who were asked to label test cards by the relevant dimension in both the preswitch and the postswitch phases succeeded on the postswitch phase. However, in several studies, Müller et al. (2008) failed to replicate these findings. Like Kirkham et al. (2003), Towse et al. (2000) also found that children who managed to label correctly in the postswitch phase also tended to sort correctly, however, unlike Kirkham et al. (2003), Towse and colleagues (2000) found that children who labeled correctly represented only a minority of 3-year-olds. The majority of 3-year-olds did not label appropriately when asked about the postswitch dimension.

Jacques and Zelazo (2005b) suggested that labeling manipulations may be unreliable with deductive tasks (i.e., tasks in which children are explicitly told what to do) because the experimenter already provides labels for the relevant information when giving task instructions to children. As a result, labeling manipulations on deductive tasks often involve having a group of children who are exposed to their own and the experimenter's labels, and another group of children who are exposed only to the experimenter's labels (e.g., Kirkham et al., 2003). The comparison between conditions is not about the presence or absence of labels, but rather about being exposed to two kinds of labels versus one. In other words, in deductive tasks, it is difficult to include a group of children who are not exposed to relevant labels at all (but see McKay & Jacques, 2009; Yerys & Munakata, 2003). Consequently, any conclusions drawn from such studies are unclear because potential differences could result from additive effects of receiving a second label or from interactive effects of receiving two different kinds of labels.

As described earlier, the amount of explicitly labeled relevant information by the experimenter varies more in inductive tasks (i.e., tasks in which children must infer what they need to do). In studies in which labeling effects have been reported with inductive tasks, the experimenter (or children) sometimes labeled relevant aspects of the stimuli and sometimes did not. Although the influence of labels on the Dimensional Change Card Sort has been inconsistent, labeling manipulations using inductive measures of cognitive flexibility have been reported more consistently (e.g., the Flexible Item Selection Task, Jacques et al., 2010; the Flexible Induction of Meaning task, Deák, 2000; the discrimination-shift learning paradigm, Kendler & Kendler, 1961; a spatial relational mapping task, Loewenstein & Gentner, 2005).

For example, Jacques et al. (2010) investigated whether attribute (e.g., "red") and dimensional (e.g., "color") labels

are associated with developmental changes in cognitive flexibility. In three studies using the Flexible Item Selection Task, they found that when 4-year-olds were asked to label (or the experimenter labeled) relevant dimensions on their first selection, their performance significantly improved on their second selection. In contrast, 3- and 5-year-olds did not improve in the label condition, likely as a result of floor and ceiling effects, respectively.

The finding that labels on the first selection related to better performance on the second selection is particularly remarkable because it suggests that labels on this task did not affect performance because of simple attention-directing properties. That is, several authors have argued that labeling effects on different tasks occur only because they direct children's attention toward important information about stimuli, helping them both to notice relevant information and to disregard irrelevant information (cf. Gibson, 1969; House, 1989; Kirkham et al., 2003; Murray & Lee, 1977). On this account, labels only have general, attention-directing properties, without promoting changes in children's representation or understanding of the task at hand, or in the cognitive processes that they use to solve the task. If labels acted only by directing children's attention to the relevant dimension on the Flexible Item Selection Task, then it is unlikely that labeling on *Selection 1* could influence *Selection 2* performance. In fact, if only attention-directing properties of labels were operating, then labeling on Selection 1 should have directed children's attention to the relevant dimension on Selection 1, making it even more difficult for them to identify the second dimension.

Instead, Jacques et al. (2010) suggested that labels help children access underlying conceptual knowledge about the stimuli rather than approaching the task at a perceptual level. In support of this interpretation, they found that 5-year-olds were more likely to label stimuli spontaneously than were 3- or 4-year-olds. Even though 4-year-olds were no more likely to label items spontaneously than 3-year-olds, 4-year-olds (but not 3-year-olds) were as likely as 5-year-olds to identify attributes correctly when asked to identify them (e.g., "What color are these pictures?"). In other words, despite not labeling spontaneously, 4-year-olds had well-organized dimensional knowledge. When explicitly provided with or asked to provide relevant labels, 4-year-olds performed better on Selection 2. Jacques et al. suggested that cognitive flexibility is a consequence of having and using underlying conceptual representations of dimensions. Three-year-olds did not benefit from labels because they did not have the underlying conceptual knowledge.

Jacques et al. (2010) proposed that labels help performance on the Flexible Item Selection Task for at least two reasons: labels provide a means of identifying specific dimensions via their members and a means of using the abstract representations themselves. First, because labels convey meaning about specific exemplars, identifying exemplars using distinct labels can help to accentuate the explicit contrastive relations that exist between exemplars of the same dimension (e.g., *red* vs. *blue* items). Second, labels provide useful symbolic tags for representing higher order dimensions (e.g., color), which, by definition, are not grounded in concrete representations (Nelson, 1988). Together, both of these aspects of labels help symbol users to go beyond perceptually given information. Jacques et al.'s approach shares some similarities with Gentner's (2003) structure-mapping approach, which also assigns an important role for abstraction and labeling.

Labeling has also been shown to relate to adults' cognitive flexibility across several tasks, for both younger (e.g., Glucksberg & Weisberg, 1966) and older adults (Kray et al., 2004). For instance, using Duncker's (1945) candle problem—considered a classic measure of cognitive flexibility—Glucksberg and Weisberg (1966) manipulated written labels to determine whether adults could solve the task more rapidly if relevant information was identified explicitly. Adults were presented with a candle, matches, and a box containing tacks. They were asked to affix the candle vertically against a wall, light it, and ensure that wax did not drip on the table or floor. Hence, to succeed, participants had to empty the box and affix it on its side against the wall with a tack before placing the candle on the box and lighting it. Adults often fail to solve the problem because they fail to use the box as a platform for the candle. Their failure to use the box is believed to result from their tendency to fixate on the box's current function (as a container), failing to consider that it could serve another function (as a platform). However, Glucksberg and Weisberg found that adults who were shown a relevant written label for the box found the correct solution more rapidly and demonstrated less *functional fixedness* than adults who were not shown this written label.

Kray and colleagues (2004) recently examined the role of labeling on a task switching paradigm in 9-, 21-, and 65-year-olds. Participants were presented with gray and colored pictures of animals and fruit. For one task, participants had to decide whether a picture was an animal or a fruit. For the other task, participants had to decide whether a picture was gray or colored. The instructional words "OBJECT" or "COLOR" preceded each target picture, informing participants of which task they were expected to do. To assess effects of verbal prompts, a task-compatible, task-incompatible, and task-irrelevant word (e.g., "gray"/"colored," "animal"/"fruit," "sand"/"round," respectively, for the Color task) appeared between the instructional word and the target picture. Participants were asked to read the word before making a decision about the target picture. Two control conditions (one including an intervening motor task and one including no intervening task between the instructional word and the target picture) were also included to assess the overall influence of performing a verbal task on performance. In single-task blocks, participants performed only one or the other task within each block, whereas in mixed-task blocks, they had to switch between tasks.

Kray et al. (2004) found an inverted-U–shaped pattern of developmental change in the cost to participants in selecting between task sets; specifically, young adults outperformed children and older adults. Moreover, only children benefitted from task-relevant verbal prompts relative to task-irrelevant prompts, and only older adults showed interference from task-incompatible prompts relative to task-irrelevant prompts. The finding that children benefitted from labeling task-relevant information is consistent with other studies noted earlier of labeling-related improvements in children. The finding that younger and older adults did not benefit substantially from task-relevant prompts compared with task-irrelevant prompts suggests that they may have spontaneously invoked their own task-relevant prompts. However, the finding that older adults found it difficult to ignore task-incompatible verbal prompts is consistent with the idea that older adults experience more difficulty in keeping distracting information out of working memory (cf. Hasher & Zacks, 1988). The researchers concluded that inner speech plays a central role in developmental changes in EF across the life span, but it may do so in different ways for different age groups.

Several investigations have assessed the relation between labeling and cognitive flexibility in adults by using a dual-task technique in which participants perform a primary task requiring cognitive flexibility and a secondary task that may or may not require verbal processing. The presence of a secondary task is presumed to limit relevant cognitive processes available for the primary task. Thus, if participants selectively do worse on the primary task when required to perform a secondary task that requires verbal processes than when it requires nonverbal processes, then this is taken as evidence that language is important for successful performance on the primary task. Using a dual-task approach, Jacques et al. (2010) gave adults a modified version of the Flexible Item Selection Task while doing a verbal secondary task, a nonverbal secondary task, or no secondary task. They found that participants' performance on their second selections was significantly worse when they simultaneously did a verbal secondary task than in the other two conditions, suggesting that language may be important for flexible thinking in adults. Baddeley et al. (2001; see also Emerson & Miyake, 2003; Goschke, 2000; Miyake, Emerson, Padilla, & Ahn, 2004; Saeki & Saito, 2004a, 2004b) and Dunbar and Sussman (1995) found similar results using task-switching paradigms and the Wisconsin Card Sorting Test.

Labeling also appears to relate to performance on EF tasks that measure response control. For example, as noted previously, Luria (1959a) reported that beginning at around 3 years, children can accompany motor responses on a go/no-go task with overt verbal responses on go trials that require them to act, although they cannot use verbal responses to inhibit their motor actions on no-go trials. However, by 4 years, they can use their own, as well as an experimenter's, verbal responses more selectively (see Luria, 1959a, 1961, for more details). Although much of Luria's work on the relation between verbal labels and the development of response control needs replication under tighter experimental conditions, recent work using the Dimensional Change Card Sort and simpler card sorting tasks have supported his findings on preschoolers' ability to use conditional rules (e.g., Zelazo et al., 1996; see Zelazo & Jacques, 1997).

In addition, using a different paradigm, Müller and colleagues (2004) found that labeling helps 3-year-olds succeed on another response control measure of EF. In their interference-control task, children were shown five different-colored Smarties (a popular British and Canadian candy) placed on large mismatching colored cards and were given five smaller colored cards. To win Smarties, the experimenter pointed to one Smartie and children had to give the experimenter a small colored card that matched the color of the larger card on which the Smartie was placed, while refraining from giving the experimenter the colored card that matched the color of the Smartie itself. Most 3-year-olds failed this version of the task, whereas most 4-year-olds did well. However, 3-year-olds did well when asked to label the color of the larger card before reaching for the small card. Interestingly, 3-year-olds also did well when they were asked to point to the larger card before reaching for the smaller card. These findings suggest that labeling or pointing to the larger card itself reoriented children's attention to the color of the card instead of the color of the Smartie as they were required to do, supporting Luria's (1959a) contention that at age 3, children may be influenced by the impulsive attention-directing aspects of labels.

In summary, as children begin to master language, they use labels as a means of decoupling from the immediate stimulus. This makes possible a wide range of cognitive manipulations, leading to advanced EF abilities including flexible thought and response control. In some instances—and shown empirically with 3- and 4-year-olds—the primary function of language is to orient attention toward the appropriate aspect of a situation, a function that can also be accomplished using other external physical cues like pointing. The impressive power of language's influence on EF, however, arises when it leads to the formation of internally generated, conceptual representations. Research on working memory and on other aspects of EF suggests that children spontaneously begin to use language in this way around age 6. Before then, there is a 2- to 3-year period during which these representations can be elicited from children using labeling manipulations, leading to corresponding gains in their executive control abilities.

Internally Generated, Conceptual Representations

As indicated in the previous section, research suggests that how working memory representations are coded may play an instrumental role in the development of cognitive flexibility and response control seen in preschoolers. In particular, advances in EF have been linked to children's tendency to represent information verbally. According to this integration model, one reason why verbal representations may be particularly helpful for EF is that they are necessarily conceptual and abstract as opposed to sensorimotor, allowing children to approach the task using top-down processes as opposed to bottom-up stimulus-driven processes.

To examine links between conceptual representations and EF directly in preschoolers, Blaye and Jacques (2009) used a modified version of a match-to-sample task used in the categorization literature to examine the development of categorical flexibility, the ability to switch successively between two simultaneously available semantic representations of a given object. In the traditional match-to-sample categorization task, children are presented with a target object (e.g., a dog) and asked to match it to an associate from a set of potential matches. Preschoolers are typically presented with a taxonomic choice (i.e., an object that is the same sort of thing; e.g., another animal) and a thematic choice (i.e., an object that is part of the same event or scheme; e.g., a doghouse). Early research suggested that preschoolers have a thematic preference, and that children come to prefer taxonomic matches only later in development (e.g., Smiley & Brown, 1979). Thematic matches are believed to be easier and preferred throughout the preschool period because they presumably can be made on the basis of learned perceptual associations (D'Entremont & Dunham, 1992; Tversky, 1985). In contrast, taxonomic matches require good underlying conceptual knowledge. As a result, these early findings led to the belief that young children do not have a conceptual understanding of taxonomic relations (Inhelder & Piaget, 1959/1964; Nelson, 1977). Recent research has clearly shown that preschoolers can appreciate both kinds of relations, although different contextual variables (e.g., task instructions or presence of labels) can bias children toward one kind of associate over the other (e.g., Blaye & Bonthoux, 2001; Markman & Hutchinson, 1984; Waxman & Namy, 1997; see Murphy, 2002, for a review).

Although a number of studies have claimed to assess categorical flexibility in infants and preschool children (e.g., Blaye & Bonthoux, 2001; Ellis & Oakes, 2006; Mareschal & Tan, 2007), Blaye and Jacques (2009) argued that existing research has not assessed flexibility directly because the same children have not been asked to categorize a specific set of stimuli into different categories successively and without a delay. Therefore, to assess categorical flexibility directly, Blaye and Jacques adapted the traditional match-to-sample categorization task in two ways. In a Double Categorization task (Experiment 1), children were shown a target picture (e.g., a carrot) and three potential matches: a thematic associate (e.g. a rabbit), a taxonomic associate (e.g., a strawberry), and a nonassociate to the target (e.g., binoculars). They were then asked to make *two* successive matches. In a Simple Categorization task (Experiment 2), children also were shown a target picture and three potential matches. However, on thematic trials, they were shown a thematic associate and two nonassociates, and on taxonomic trials, they were shown a taxonomic associate and two nonassociates. Blaye and Jacques found that on the Double Categorization task, 5-year-olds correctly selected both matches for the target more often than 3- or 4-year-olds, whereas on the Simple Categorization task, 4- and 5-year-olds correctly selected both matches more often than 3-year-olds. The authors concluded that, although performance on the Simple Categorization task demonstrates that both 4- and 5-year-olds have the prerequisite conceptual knowledge of both kinds of associates, only 5-year-olds selected

both associates when these were placed in competition with each other in the Double Categorization task. These findings indicate that advances in conceptual knowledge may precede advances in categorical flexibility. In support of a direct link between conceptual knowledge and flexibility, Blaye and Jacques also found that children who strategically selected one kind of match (either thematic or taxonomic) consistently across trials in the Double Categorization task demonstrated more flexibility than children who showed less consistency across trials in their Selection 1 responses. In other words, children who used a top-down conceptual strategy to select their first matches across trials were more flexible than those who apparently approached the task on a trial-by-trial basis, presumably influenced by the relative strength of particular associates on each particular trial.

On the basis of findings using the Dimensional Change Card Sort, Kharitonova et al. (2009) also came to the conclusion that children who hold more abstract representations of stimuli are also more flexible. In one version of the Dimensional Change Card Sort, they presented 3-year-olds with test cards that only approximated the target cards on both dimensions. For example, if target cards were a blue truck and red flowers, and children had to sort cards by color, they had to sort turquoise, teal, and green cards with the blue target, and orange, yellow, and orange-yellow cards with the red target. Kharitonova et al. found that switchers (i.e., those who switched on the postswitch phase of a standard version of the Dimension Change Card Sort) had more abstract representations of the stimuli in that they were more likely to sort cards that only approximated the targets with the appropriate target. In contrast, perseverators tended to sort these cards randomly.

In a similar vein, Carlson and colleagues (2005), using a measure of response inhibition—the *Less-is-More task*—argued that redirecting attention from salient perceptual features of rewards by using abstract symbols can provide *psychological distance* between rewards and symbol users, and that this distance, in turn, allows symbol users to show more response control (cf. Sigel, 1970). In the Less-is-More task, children are instructed to point to one of two rewards (e.g., either two or five treats) with the understanding that a naughty puppet will take the reward to which they point and they will receive the remaining one. To succeed, then, children need to point to the smaller reward, while resisting the temptation to point to the reward that they really want. In their study, Carlson et al. (2005) placed rewards in boxes and used symbols on top of the boxes to differentiate them. They included four different symbols, each one increasingly more abstract or distant from the salient features of the reward. In the treats condition, the symbols were identical to the treats; in the rocks condition, the symbols were the same number of rocks and were a similar shape to the rewards but did not share an identity relation; in the beads condition, the symbols were dots drawn in a circle representing a discrete, quantitative representation of the reward; and finally, in the animals condition, drawings of a mouse and elephant represented the quantity relation symbolically using the relative size of the real animals to depict small and large, respectively. Carlson et al. (2005) found that children were more likely to point to the lesser reward box in the most distant symbol condition (the animal condition) than in the least distant one (the treats condition), suggesting that the use of psychologically distant or abstract symbols is more effective at helping children control their behavior than the use of perceptually based ones.

Together, Blaye and Jacques (2009) and Kharitonova et al.'s (2009) findings, as well as those by Carlson et al. (2005), strongly suggest that the representations of children who demonstrate more advanced EF are more conceptual and abstract, and less likely to be perceptually driven than those of children who are less advanced. On the flip side, children and adults who use less abstract representations or who are presented with perceptually salient information have more difficulty controlling their thoughts and behavior (Kirkham et al., 2003; Zaitchik, 1991). For example, Zaitchik showed that 3-year-olds have more difficulty on the false-belief task if they are shown the object in its real hiding location than if they are simply told the location of the hidden object. Likewise, Kirkham et al. showed that 4-year-olds are more likely to perseverate on the Dimensional Change Card Sort if they are required to sort cards facing up across both phases. Seeing the specific cards that they sorted by one dimension in the preswitch phase presumably makes it more difficult for them to sort cards by the alternate dimension in the postswitch.

There is also indirect support for the idea that adults who are overly perceptually driven have more difficulty controlling their behavior. Consider *utilization behaviors* sometimes demonstrated by patients with frontal lobe lesions (Lhermitte, 1983, 1986). Patients who exhibit utilization behaviors—especially environmental dependency syndrome—have exaggerated responses to environmental stimuli and difficulty resisting the temptation to engage in specific actions associated with specific objects when these

are presented within their visual field. For example, Lhermitte (1986) reported the case of a female patient, who on being presented with a tongue depressor proceeded to examine the examiner's throat, not because of any previous experience at examining others' throats using tongue depressors (her occupation had consisted of working in the home) or a habit to engage in this particular behavior. Instead, she acted on the basis of what was called for by objects in the immediate environment. It is as though patients with these utilization behaviors cannot overcome the tendency to act on perceptually derived representations of the stimuli by using internally generated representations. The stimuli available in the environment dictate a particular motor response that these patients simply cannot resist doing.

In a rare study that assessed the link between conception and EF in adults, Levine et al. (1995) assessed younger (18–39 years), middle-aged (40–64 years), and older (65–79 years) adults' ability to generate and switch between concepts. They assessed adults on a concept generation task in which participants had to generate six different groupings for six items by separating them into two sets of three items and accurately naming the basis for their groupings. The six items each included an animal word and an abstract figure. The items could be grouped with each other in different ways according to two verbal categories (animal habitat, animal domesticity) and four graphical features (figure shape, figure size, word location, internal properties of the figure). Levine et al. (1995) found that although all age groups attempted the same number of groupings, older adults produced fewer correct groupings, and they erred more often in naming the groups they produced. In addition, older adults were more prone to repeat groupings and names than the younger age groups. However, age group differences were attenuated when the experimenter provided increasingly explicit external cues. For example, all older adults eventually produced the six possible groupings, but many did so only after the experimenter cued them as to how to group items (e.g., "Group the items according to the shape of the figure."). In other words, changing the task from an inductive to a deductive version allowed older adults to identify and switch between all possible groupings. Finally, performance on this task related with measures of cognitive flexibility including the Wisconsin Card Sorting Test and word list generation tasks, suggesting that older adults' difficulties with cognitive flexibility may be related to difficulties in generating appropriate conceptual representations for stimuli.

CONCLUSIONS

Unitary models of EF, unlike diverse models, suggest a single underlying executive process (see Miyake et al., 2000, for further discussion on the distinction between unitary vs. diverse models of EF). However, recent behavioral research suggests that diverse models may be more plausible (Miyake et al., 2000). In this chapter, we proposed that a model that integrates key aspects of existing models into a single model might best account for the development of EF. In particular, the model proposes two major changes in working memory representations that may be important for the development of EF abilities. Specifically, the development of early working memory representations allows infants to gain control over their thoughts and behaviors because they can represent task goals over a delay despite the presence of distractors. These early representations are constructed and supported by sensorimotor representations. In turn, the development of advanced working memory representations allows children and adults to maintain information in mind while processing it simultaneously, permitting them greater executive control abilities. These processing abilities are supported by children's emerging ability to represent information verbally and abstractly (as opposed to perceptually). Although existing empirical research findings are consistent with the features of this model, much research remains to be done to test it directly, especially in older adults, to determine whether this model fits the data better than existing ones. In particular, systematic investigations and comparisons of performance on EF measures across different age groups may help elucidate important information about EF processes themselves and about how these might become linked in development. Moreover, even though neurophysiological findings were beyond the scope of this chapter, these may help to determine the plausibility of specific models of EF. Together, behavioral and neurophysiological data may allow a clearer picture of the nature of interrelations between EF processes throughout the life span to emerge.

REFERENCES

Ahmed, A., & Ruffman, T. (1998). Why do infants make A not B errors in a search task, yet show memory for the location of hidden objects in a nonsearch task? *Developmental Psychology, 34,* 441–453.

Albert, M. S., & Kaplan, E. (1980). Organic implications of neuropsychological deficits in the elderly. In F. Poon (Ed.), *New directions in memory and aging* (pp. 403–432). Hillsdale, NJ: Erlbaum.

Allain, P., Berrut, G., Etcharry-Bouyx, F., Barré, J., Dubas, F., & Le Gall, D. (2007). Executive functions in normal aging: An examination of script sequencing, script sorting, and script monitoring. *Journals of Gerontology: Series B: Psychological Sciences and Social Sciences, 62B,* 187–190.

Allamanno, N., Della Sala, S., Laiacona, M., Pasetti, C., & Spinnler, H. (1987). Problem-solving ability in aging: Normative data on a non-verbal test. *Italian Journal Neurological Sciences, 8,* 111–119.

Allport, A., Styles, E. A., & Hsieh, S. (1994). Shifting intentional set: Exploring the dynamic control of tasks. In C. Umilta & M. Moscovitch (Eds.), *Attention and performance XV: Conscious and nonconscious information processing* (pp. 421–452). Cambridge, MA: MIT Press.

Alp, I. E. (1994). Measuring the size of working memory in very young children: The Imitation Sorting Task. *International Journal of Behavioral Development, 17*(1), 125–141.

Astington, J. W., & Baird, J. A. (Eds.). (2005). *Why language matters for theory of mind.* New York: Oxford University Press.

Axelrod, B. N., & Henry, R. R. (1992). Age-related performance on the Wisconsin Card Sorting, Similarities, and Controlled Oral Word Association Tests. *The Clinical Neuropsychologist, 6,* 16–26.

Baddeley, A. (1986). *Working memory.* Oxford: Oxford University Press.

Baddeley, A. (2003). Working memory: Looking back and looking forward. *Nature Reviews Neuroscience, 4,* 829–839.

Baddeley, A., Chincotta, D., & Adlam, A. (2001). Working memory and the control of action: Evidence for task switching. *Journal of Experimental Psychology: General, 130,* 641–657.

Baddeley, A. D., & Hitch, G. (1974). Working memory. In G. H. Bower (Ed.), *The psychology of learning and motivation: Advances in research and theory* (Vol. 8, pp. 47–89). New York: Academic Press.

Barkley, R. A. (2001). The executive functions and self-regulation: An evolutionary neuropsychological perspective. *Neuropsychology Review, 11,* 1–29.

Bell, M. A. (2001). Brain electrical activity associated with cognitive processing during a looking version of the A-not-B task. *Infancy, 2,* 311–330.

Bell, M. A., & Adams, S. E. (1999). Comparable performance on looking and reaching versions of the A-not-B task at 8 months of age. *Infant Behavior and Development, 22,* 221–235.

Berg, E. A. (1948). A simple objective technique for measuring flexibility in thinking. *The Journal of General Psychology, 39,* 15–22.

Berger, S. E. (2004). Demands on finite cognitive capacity cause infants' perseverative errors. *Infancy, 5*(2), 217–238.

Bjorklund, D. F., & Harnishfeger, K. K. (1990). The resources construct in cognitive development: Diverse sources of evidence and a theory of inefficient inhibition. *Developmental Review, 10,* 48–71.

Blaye, A., & Bonthoux, F. (2001). Thematic and taxonomic relations in preschoolers: The development of flexibility in categorization choices. *British Journal of Developmental Psychology, 19,* 395–412.

Blaye, A., & Jacques, S. (2009). Categorical flexibility in preschoolers: Contributions of conceptual knowledge and executive control. *Developmental Science, 12*(6), 863–873.

Boone, K. B., Miller, B. L., Lesser, I. M., Hill, E., & D'Elia, L. (1990). Performance on frontal lobe tests in healthy, older individuals, *Developmental Neuropsychology, 6,* 215–223.

Botvinick, M. M., Braver, T. S., Barch, D. M., Carter, C. S., & Cohen, J. D. (2001). Conflict monitoring and cognitive control. *Psychological Review, 108,* 624–652.

Brandimonte, M. A., & Gerbino, W. (1993). Mental image reversal and verbal recoding: When ducks become rabbits. *Memory and Cognition, 21,* 23–33.

Braver, T. S., Gray, J. R., & Burgess, G. C. (2007). Explaining the many varieties of working memory variation: Dual mechanisms of cognitive control. In A. R. A. Conway, C. Jarrold, M. J. Kane, A. Miyake, & J. N. Towse (Eds.), *Variation in working memory*. New York: Oxford University Press.

Braver, T. S., & West, R. (2008). Working memory, executive control, and aging. In F. I. M. Craik & A. T. Salthouse (Eds.), *The handbook of aging and cognition* (3rd ed.). New York: Psychology Press.

Bruner, J. S., & Kenny, H. J. (1966). On multiple ordering. In J. S. Bruner, R. R. Olver, & P. M. Greenfield (Eds.), *Studies in cognitive growth* (pp. 154–167). New York: John Wiley and Sons.

Bub, D. N., Masson, M. E. J., & Lalonde, C. E. (2006). Cognitive control in children: Stroop interference and suppression of word reading. *Psychological Science, 17,* 351–357.

Bullock, M., & Lütkenhaus, P. (1988). The development of volitional behavior in the toddler years. *Child Development, 59*(3), 664–674.

Carlson, S. M. (2005). Developmentally sensitive measures of executive function in preschool children. *Developmental Neuropsychology, 28,* 595–616.

Carlson, S. M., & Beck, D. M. (2009). Symbols as tools in the development of executive function. In A. Winsler, C. Fernyhough, & I. Montero (Eds.), *Private speech, executive functioning, and the development of verbal self-regulation* (pp. 163–175). New York: Cambridge University Press.

Carlson, S. M., Davis, A. C., & Leach, J. G. (2005). Less is more: Executive function and symbolic representation in preschool children. *Psychological Science, 16,* 609–616.

Carlson, S. M., Mandell, D. J., & Williams, L. (2004). Executive function and theory of mind: Stability and prediction from ages 2 to 3. *Developmental Psychology, 40,* 1105–1122.

Carlson, S. M., & Moses, L. J. (2001). Individual differences in inhibitory control and children's theory of mind. *Child Development, 72,* 1032–1053.

Carlson, S. M., Moses, L. J., & Breton, C. (2002). How specific is the relation between executive function and theory of mind? Contributions of inhibitory control and working memory. *Infant and Child Development. Special issue: Executive function and its development, 11,* 73–92.

Carlson, S. M., Moses, L. J., & Hix, H. R. (1998). The role of inhibitory processes in young children's difficulties with deception and false belief. *Child Development, 69,* 672–691.

Case, R. (1992). The role of the frontal lobes in the regulation of cognitive development. *Brain & Cognition (Special Issue: The Role of Frontal Lobe Maturation in Cognitive and Social Development), 20,* 51–73.

Case, R. (1995). Capacity-based explanations of working memory growth: A brief history and reevaluation. In F. E. Weinert & W. Schneider (Eds.), *Memory performance and competencies: Issues in growth and development* (pp. 23–44). Mahwah, NJ: Erlbaum.

Case, R., Kurland, M., & Goldberg, J. (1982). Operational efficiency and the growth of short-term memory span. *Journal of Experimental Child Psychology, 33,* 386–404.

Cepeda, N. J., Kramer, A. F., & Gonzalez de Sather, J. C. M. (2001). Changes in executive control across the life-span: Examination of task switching performance. *Developmental Psychology, 37,* 715–730.

Cepeda, N. J., & Munakata, Y. (2007). Why do children perseverate when they seem to know better: Graded working memory, or directed inhibition? *Psychonomic Bulletin and Review, 14,* 1058–1065.

Chalfonte, B. L., & Johnson, M. K. (1996). Feature memory and binding in young and older adults. *Memory & Cognition, 24,* 403–416.

Chelune, G. J., & Baer, R. A. (1986). Developmental norms for the Wisconsin Card Sorting Test. *Journal of Clinical and Experimental Neuropsychology, 8,* 219–228.

Clearfield, M. W., Diedrich, F. J., Smith, L. B., & Thelen, E. (2006). Young infants reach correctly in A-not-B tasks: On the development of stability and perseveration. *Infant Behavior and Development, 29,* 435–444.

Clearfield, M. W., Dineva, E., Smith, L. B., Diedrich, F. J., & Thelen, E. (2009). Cue salience and infant perseverative reaching: tests of the dynamic field theory. *Developmental Science, 12,* 26–40.

Clements, W. A., & Perner, J. (1994). Implicit understanding of belief. *Cognitive Development, 9,* 377–395.

Cohn, N. B., Dustman, R. E., & Bradford, D. C. (1984). Age-related decrements in Stroop Color Test performance. *Journal of Clinical Psychology, 40,* 1244–1250.

Comalli, P. E. J., Wapner, S., & Werner, H. (1962). Interference effects of Stroop color-word test in childhood, adulthood, and aging. *Journal of Genetic Psychology, 100,* 47–53.

Craik, F. I. M., & Bialystok, E. (2006). Cognition through the lifespan: Mechanisms of change. *Trends in Cognitive Sciences, 10,* 131–138.

Craik, F. I. M., & Byrd, M. (1982). Aging and cognitive deficits: The role of attentional resources. In F. I. M. Craik & S. E. Trehub (Eds.), *Aging and cognitive processes* (pp. 191–211). New York: Plenum.

Crone, E. A., Bunge, S. A., van der Molen, M. W., & Ridderinkhof, K. R. (2006). Switching between tasks and responses: A developmental study. *Developmental Science, 9*(3), 278–287.

Cummings, E. M., & Bjork, E. L. (1983). Search behavior on multi-choice hiding tasks: Evidence for an objective conception of space in infancy. *International Journal of Behavioral Development, 6,* 71–87.

D'Entremont, B., & Dunham, P. J. (1992). The noun-category bias phenomenon in 3-year-olds: Taxonomic constraint or translation? *Cognitive Development, 7,* 47–62.

Daigneault, S., & Braun, C. M. (1993). Working memory and the Self-Ordered Pointing Task: Further evidence of early prefrontal decline in normal aging. *Journal of Clinical and Experimental Neuropsychology, 15,* 881–95.

Daigneault, S., Braun, C. M., & Whitaker, H. A. (1992). An empirical test of two opposing theoretical models of prefrontal function. *Brain and Cognition, 19*(1), 48–71.

Daniels, K., Toth, J., & Jacoby, L. (2006). The aging of executive functions. In E. Bialystok & F. I. M. Craik (Eds.), *Lifespan cognition: Mechanisms of change* (pp. 96–111). New York: Oxford University Press.

Davidson, M. C., Amso, D., Anderson, L. C., & Diamond, A. (2006). Development of cognitive control and executive functions from 4 to 13 years: Evidence from manipulations of memory, inhibition, and task switching. *Neuropsychologia, 44,* 2037–2078.

Deák, G. O. (2000). The growth of flexible problem solving: Preschool children use changing verbal cues to infer multiple word meanings. *Journal of Cognition and Development, 1,* 157–191.

Deák, G. O. (2003). The development of cognitive flexibility and language development. In R. V. Kail (Ed.), *Advances in child development and behavior* (Vol. 31, pp. 271–327). Amsterdam: Academic Press.

Delis, D. C., Squire, L. R., Bihrle, A., & Massman, P. (1992). Componential analysis of problem-solving ability: Performance of patients with frontal lobe damage and amnesic patients on a new sorting test. *Neuropsychologia, 30,* 683–697.

Della Sala, S., & Logie, R.H. (1998). Dualism down the drain, thinking in the brain. In R. H. Logie & K. J. Gilhooly (Eds.), *Working memory and thinking* (pp. 45–66). Hove, United Kingdom: Psychology Press.

Dempster, F. N. (1992). The rise and fall of the inhibitory mechanism: Toward a unified theory of cognitive development and aging. *Developmental Review, 12,* 45–75.

Dempster, F. N. (1993). Resistance to interference: Developmental changes in a basic processing mechanism. In M. L. Howe & R. Pasnak (Eds.), *Emerging themes in cognitive development* (Vol. 1, pp. 3–27). New York: Springer-Verlag.

Dempster, F. N. (1995). Interference and inhibition in cognition: An historical perspective. In F. N. Dempster & C. J. Brainerd (Eds.), *Interference and inhibition in cognition* (pp. 3–26). San Diego, CA: Academic Press.

Diamond, A. (1990). Developmental time course in human infants and infant monkeys, and the neural bases, of inhibitory control in reaching. *Annals of the New York Academy of Sciences, 608,* 637–676.

Diamond, A. (2006a). Bootstrapping conceptual deduction using physical connection: Rethinking frontal cortex. *Trends in Cognitive Sciences, 10,* 212–218.

Diamond, A. (2006b). The early development of executive functions. In E. Bialystok & F. I. M. Craik (Eds.), *Lifespan cognition: Mechanisms of change* (pp. 70–95). New York: Oxford University Press.

Diamond, A., Churchland, A., Cruess, L., & Kirkham, N. (1999). Early developments in the ability to understand the relation between stimulus and reward. *Developmental Psychology, 35,* 1507–1517.

Diamond, A., Cruttenden, L., & Neiderman, D. (1994). AB with multiple wells: 1. Why are multiple wells sometimes easier than two wells? 2. Memory or memory + inhibition? *Developmental Psychology, 30,* 192–205.

Diamond, A., & Doar, B. (1989). The performance of human infants on a measure of frontal cortex function, the delayed response task. *Developmental Psychobiology, 22,* 271–294.

Diamond, A., & Taylor, C. (1996). Development of an aspect of executive control: Development of the abilities to remember what I said and to "do as I say, not as I do." *Developmental Psychobiology, 29*(4), 315–334.

Dick, A. S., & Overton, W. F. (2010). Executive function: Description and explanation. In B. W. Sokol, U. Müller, J. I. M. Carpendale, A. R. Young, & G. Iarocci (Eds.), *Self and social regulation: Social interaction and the development of social understanding and executive functions* (pp. 7–34). Oxford: Oxford University Press.

Doherty, M., & Perner, J. (1998). Metalinguistic awareness and theory of mind: Just two words for the same thing? *Cognitive Development, 13,* 279–305.

Dunbar, K., & Sussman, D. (1995). Toward a cognitive account of frontal lobe function: Simulating frontal lobe deficits in normal subjects. *Annals of the New York Academy of Sciences, 769,* 289–304.

Duncan, J., Emslie, H., Williams, P., Johnson, R., & Freer, C. (1996). Intelligence and the frontal lobe: The organization of goal-directed behavior. *Cognitive Psychology, 30,* 257–303.

Duncker, K. (1945). On problem-solving. *Psychological Monographs, 58*(5, Whole No. 270).

Einstein, G. O., Holland, L. J., McDaniel, M. A., & Guynn, M. J. (1992). Age-related deficits in prospective memory: The influence of task complexity. *Psychology and Aging, 7,* 471–478.

Einstein, G. O., McDaniel, M. A., Manzi, M., Cochran, B., & Baker, M. (2000). Prospective memory and aging: Forgetting over short delays. *Psychology and Aging, 15,* 671–683.

Ellis, A. E., & Oakes, L. M. (2006). Infants flexibly use different dimensions to categorize objects. *Developmental Psychology, 42,* 1000–1011.

Emerson, M. J., & Miyake, A. (2003). The role of inner speech in task switching: A dual-task investigation. *Journal of Memory and Language, 48,* 148–168.

Engle, R. W., & Kane, M. J. (2004). Executive attention, working memory capacity, and a two-factor theory of cognitive control. In B. Ross (Ed.), *The psychology of learning and motivation* (pp. 145–199). New York: Academic Press.

Engle, R. W., & Kane, M. J., & Tuholski, S. W. (1999). Individual differences in working memory capacity and what they tell us about controlled attention, general fluid intelligence, and functions of the prefrontal cortex. In A. Miyake & P. Smith (Eds.). Models of working memory: Mechanisms of active maintenance and executive control. Cambridge: Cambridge University Press.

Eriksen, C. W., & Schultz, D. W. (1979). Information processing in visual search: A continuous flow conception and experimental results. *Perception & Psychophysics, 25,* 249–263.

Esposito, N. J. (1975). Review of discrimination shift learning in young children. *Psychological Bulletin, 82,* 432–455.

Frye, D., Zelazo, P. D., & Palfai, T. (1995). Theory of mind and rule-based reasoning. *Cognitive Development, 10,* 483–527.

Frye, D., Zelazo, P. D., Brooks, P. J., & Samuels, M. C. (1996). Inference and action in early causal reasoning. *Developmental Psychology, 32,* 120–131.

Fuster, J. M. (1980). *The prefrontal cortex.* New York: Raven.

Garon, N., Bryson, S. E., & Smith, I. M. (2008). Executive function in preschoolers: A review using an integrative framework. *Psychological Bulletin, 134,* 31–60.

Gathercole, S. E. (1998). The development of memory. *Journal of Child Psychology & Psychiatry & Allied Disciplines, 39,* 3–27.

Gathercole, S. E., Pickering, S. J., Ambridge, B., & Wearing, H. (2004). A structural analysis of working memory from 4 to 15 years of age. *Developmental Psychology, 40,* 177–190.

Gentner, D. (2003). Why we're so smart. In D. Gentner & S. Goldin-Meadow (Eds.), *Language in mind: Advances in the study of language and thought* (pp. 195–235). Cambridge, MA: MIT Press.

Gerardi-Caulton, G. (2000). Sensitivity to spatial conflict and the development of self-regulation in children 24–36 months of age. *Developmental Science, 3,* 397–404.

Gerstadt, C. L., Hong, Y. J., & Diamond, A. (1994). The relationship between cognition and action: Performance of children 3½–7 years old on a Stroop-like day-night test. *Cognition, 53,* 129–153.

Gibson, E. J. (1969). *Principles of perceptual learning and development.* New York: Appleton-Century-Crofts.

Glucksberg, S., & Weisberg, R. W. (1966). Verbal behavior and problem solving: Some effects of labeling in a functional fixedness problem. *Journal of Experimental Psychology, 71,* 659–664.

Goldman-Rakic, P. S. (1987). Circuitry of primate prefrontal cortex and regulation of behavior by representational memory. In F. Plum & V. Mountcastle (Eds.), *Handbook of physiology* (Vol. 5, pp. 373–517). Washington, DC: The American Physiological Society.

Gordon, A. C. L., & Olson, D. (1998). The relation between acquisition of a theory of mind and information processing capacity. *Journal of Experimental Child Psychology, 68,* 70–83.

Goschke, T. (2000). Intentional reconfiguration and involuntary persistence in task set switching. In S. Monsell & J. Driver (Eds.), *Attention and performance XVIII: Control of cognitive processes* (pp. 331–355). Cambridge, MA: MIT Press.

Grant, D. A., & Berg, E. A. (1948). A behavioral analysis of degree of reinforcement and ease of shifting to new responses in a Weigl-type card-sorting problem. *Journal of Experimental Psychology, 38,* 404–411.

Gratch, G., Appel, K. J., Evans, W. F., LeCompte, G. K., & Wright, N. A. (1974). Piaget's stage IV object concept error: Evidence of forgetting or object conception. *Child Development, 45,* 71–77.

Guttentag, R. E., & Lange, G. (1994). Motivational influences on children's strategic remembering. *Learning and Individual Differences, 6,* 309–330.

Halford, G. S., Wilson, W. H., & Phillips, S. (1998). Processing capacity defined by relational complexity: Implications for comparative, developmental, and cognitive psychology. *Behavioral & Brain Sciences, 21,* 803–864.

Harnishfeger, K. K., & Bjorklund, D. F. (1993). The ontogeny of inhibition mechanisms: A renewed approach to cognitive development. In M. L. Howe & R. Pasnak (Eds.), *Emerging themes in cognitive development* (Vol. 1, pp. 28–49). New York: Springer-Verlag.

Harris, P. L. (1987). The development of search. In P. Salapatek & L. B. Cohen (Eds.), *Handbook of infant perception* (Vol. 2). New York: Academic Press.

Hartley, A. A. (1993). Evidence for the selective preservation of spatial selective attention in old age. *Psychology & Aging, 8,* 371–379.

Hartman, M., & Hasher, L. (1991). Aging and suppression: Memory for previously relevant information. *Psychology and Aging, 6,* 587–594.

Hasher, L., Stoltzfus, E. R., Zacks, R. T., & Rypma, B. (1991). Age and inhibition. *Journal of Experimental Psychology: Learning, Memory, and Cognition, 17,* 163–169.

Hasher, L., & Zacks, R. T. (1988). Working memory, comprehension, and aging: A review and a new view. In G. H. Bower (Ed.), *The psychology of learning and motivation* (Vol. 22, pp. 193–225). New York: Academic Press.

Haug, H., & Eggers, R. (1991). Morphometry of the human cortex cerebri and corpus striatum during aging. *Neurobiology of Aging, 12,* 336–338.

Hitch, G. J. (2006). Working memory in children: A cognitive approach. In E. Bialystok & F. I. M. Craik (Eds.), *Lifespan cognition: Mechanisms of change* (pp. 128–142). New York: Oxford University Press.

Hofstadter, M., & Reznick, J. S. (1996). Response modality affects human infant delayed-response performance. *Child Development, 67,* 646–658.

Horobin, K. M., & Acredolo, L. P. (1986). The role of attentiveness, mobility history, and separation of hiding sites on stage IV search behavior. *Journal of Experimental Child Psychology, 41,* 114–127.

House, B. J. (1989). Some current issues in children's selective attention. In H. W. Reese (Ed.), *Advances in child development and behavior* (Vol. 21, pp. 91–119). San Diego: Academic Press.

Houx, P. J., Jolles, J., & Vreeling, F. W. (1993). Stroop interference: Aging effects assessed with the Stroop Color-Word Test. *Experimental Aging Research, 19*(3), 209–224.

Hughes, C. (1996). Control of action and thought: Normal development and dysfunction in autism: A research note. *Journal of Child Psychology and Psychiatry, 37*(2), 229–236.

Hughes, C. (1998). Executive function in preschoolers: Links with theory of mind and verbal ability. *British Journal of Developmental Psychology, 16,* 233–253.

Hughes, C., & Russell, J. (1993). Autistic children's difficulty with mental disengagement from an object: Its implication for theories of autism. *Developmental Psychology, 29,* 498–510.

Hunter, W. S. (1913). The delayed reaction in animals and children. *Behavior Monographs, 2,* 1–86.

Hunter, W. S. (1917). The delayed reaction in a child. *Psychological Review, 24,* 74–87.

Inhelder, B., & Piaget, J. (1964). *The early growth of logic in the child: Classification and seriation* (E. A. Lunzer & D. Papert, Trans.). New York: Harper & Row. (Original work published 1959)

Jacobson, C. F. (1936). Studies of cerebral functions in primates: I. The functions of the frontal association areas in monkeys. *Comparative Psychology Monographs, 13,* 1–30.

Jacques, S., & Zelazo, P. D. (2001). The Flexible Item Selection Task (FIST): A measure of executive function in preschoolers. *Developmental Neuropsychology, 20,* 573–591.

Jacques, S., & Zelazo, P. D. (2005a). Language and the development of cognitive flexibility: Implications for theory of mind. In J. W. Astington & J. A. Baird (Eds.), *Why language matters for theory of mind* (pp. 144–162). Oxford: Oxford University Press.

Jacques, S., & Zelazo, P. D. (2005b). On the possible roots of cognitive flexibility. In B. D. Homer & C. S. Tamis-Lemonda (Eds.), *The development of social understanding and communication* (pp. 53–81). Mahwah, NJ: Erlbaum.

Jacques, S., Zelazo, P. D., Kirkham, N. Z., & Semcesen, T. K. (1999). Rule selection versus rule execution in preschoolers: An error-detection approach. *Developmental Psychology, 35,* 770–780.

Jacques, S., Zelazo, P. D., Lourenco, S. F., Sutherland, A. E., Shiffman, M., & Parker, J. A. (2010). *The roles of labeling and abstraction in the development of cognitive flexibility.* Manuscript under revision.

Jones, L. B., Rothbart, M. K., & Posner, M. I. (2003). Development of executive attention in preschool children. *Developmental Science, 6,* 498–504.

Kaler, S. R., & Kopp, C. B. (1990). Compliance and comprehension in very young toddlers. *Child Development, 61,* 1997–2003.

Kane, M. J., Conway, A. R. A., Hambrick, D. Z., & Engle, R. W. (2007). Variation in working memory capacity as variation in executive attention and control. In A. R. A. Conway, C. Jarrold, M. J. Kane, A. Miyake, & J. N. Towse (Eds.), *Variation in working memory* (pp. 21–48). New York: Oxford University Press.

Kane, M. J., & Engle, R. W. (2002). The role of prefrontal cortex in working-memory capacity, executive attention, and general fluid intelligence: An individual differences perspective. *Psychonomic Bulletin & Review, 9,* 637–671.

Kane, M. J., & Engle, R. W. (2003). Working-memory capacity and the control of attention: The contributions of goal neglect, response competition, and task set to Stroop interference. *Journal of Experimental Psychology: General, 132,* 47–70.

Kendler, H. H., & Kendler, T. S. (1961). Effect of verbalization on reversal shifts in children. *Science, 134,* 1619–1620.

Kharitonova, M., Chien, S., Colunga, E., & Munakata, Y. (2009). More than a matter of getting "unstuck": Flexible thinkers use more abstract representations than perseverators. *Developmental Science, 12,* 662–669.

Kirkham, N. Z., Cruess, L. M., & Diamond, A. (2003). Helping children apply their knowledge to their behavior on a dimension-switching task. *Developmental Science, 6,* 449–467.

Kochanska, G., Murray, K., Jacques, T. Y., Koenig, A. L., & Vandegeest, K. A. (1996). Inhibitory control in young children and its role in emerging internalization. *Child Development, 67,* 490–507.

Kray, J., Eber, J., & Lindenberger, U. (2004). Age differences in executive functioning across the lifespan: The role of verbalization in task preparation. *Acta Psychologica Sinica, 115*(2–3), 143–165.

Kuenne, M. R. (1946). Experimental investigation of the relation of language to transposition behavior in young children. *Journal of Experimental Psychology, 36,* 471–490.

Lamm, C., Zelazo, P. D., & Lewis, M. D. (2006). Neural correlates of cognitive control in childhood and adolescence: Disentangling the contributions of age and executive function. *Neuropsychologia, 44,* 2139–2148.

LaVoie, J. C., Anderson, K., Fraze, B., & Johnson, K. (1981). Modelling, tuition, and sanction effects on self-control at different ages. *Journal of Experimental Child Psychology, 31,* 446–455.

Lehto, J. E., Juujärvi, P., Kooistra, L., & Pulkkinen, L. (2003). Dimensions of executive functioning: Evidence from children. *British Journal of Developmental Psychology, 21,* 59–80.

Levin, H. S., Culhane, K. A., Hartmann, J., Evankovich, K., Mattson, A. J., Harward, H., et al. (1991). Developmental changes in performance on tests of purported frontal lobe functioning. *Developmental Neuropsychology, 7,* 377–395.

Levine, B., Stuss, D. T., & Milberg, W. P. (1995). Concept generation: Validation of a test of executive functioning in a normal aging population. *Journal of Clinical and Experimental Neuropsychology, 17,* 740–758.

Lhermitte, F. (1983). "Utilization behaviour" and its relation to lesions of the frontal lobes. *Brain, 106,* 237–255.

Lhermitte, F. (1986). Human autonomy and the frontal lobes. Part II: Patient behavior in complex and social situations: The environmental dependency syndrome. *Annals of Neurology, 19,* 335–343.

Libon, D. J., Glosser, G., Malamut, B. L., Kaplan, E., Goldberg, E., Swenson, R., et al. (1994). Age, executive functions, and visuospatial functioning in healthy older adults. *Neuropsychology, 8,* 38–43.

Loewenstein, J., & Gentner, D. (2005). Relational language and the development of relational mapping. *Cognitive Psychology, 50,* 315–353.

Lu, C.-H., & Proctor, R. W. (1995). The influence of irrelevant location information on performance: A review of the Simon and spatial Stroop effects. *Psychonomic Bulletin & Review, 2*(2), 174–207.

Luria, A. R. (1957). The role of language in the formation of temporary connections. In B. Simon (Ed.), *Psychology in the Soviet Union* (pp. 115–129). Stanford, CA: Stanford University Press.

Luria, A. R. (1959a). The directive function of speech in development and dissolution. Part I. Development of the directive function of speech in early childhood. *Word, 15,* 341–352.

Luria, A. R. (1959b). The directive function of speech in development and dissolution. Part II. Dissolution of the regulative function of speech in pathological states of the brain. *Word, 15,* 453–464.

Luria, A. R. (1961). *The role of speech in the regulation of normal and abnormal behavior* (J. Tizard, Ed.). New York: Pergamon Press.

Luria, A. R. (1969). Speech development and the formation of mental processes. In M. Cole & I. Maltzman (Eds.), *A handbook of contemporary Soviet psychology* (pp. 121–162). New York: Basic Books.

Luria, A. R. (1976). *Cognitive development: Its cultural and social foundations* (M. Lopez-Morillas & L. Solotaroff, Trans., & M. Cole, Ed.; pp. 3–19). Cambridge, MA: Harvard University Press.

MacLeod, C. M. (1991). Half a century of research on the Stroop effect: An integrative review. *Psychological Bulletin, 109,* 163–203.

Mäntylä, T. (1994). Remembering to remember: Adult age differences in prospective memory. *Journal of Gerontology: Psychological Sciences, 49,* 276–282.

Marcovitch, S., Boseovski, J. J., & Knapp, R. J. (2007). Use it or lose it: Examining preschoolers' difficulty in maintaining and executing a goal. *Developmental Science, 10,* 559–564.

Marcovitch, S., Boseovski, J. J., Knapp, R. J., & Kane, M. J. (in press). Goal neglect and working memory in preschoolers. *Child Development.*

Marcovitch, S., & Zelazo, P. D. (1999). The A-not-B error: Results from a logistic meta-analysis. *Child Development, 70,* 1297–1313.

Marcovitch, S., & Zelazo, P. D. (2000). A generative connectionist model of the development of rule use in children. *Proceedings of the Twenty-second Annual Conference of the Cognitive Science Society* (pp. 334–339). Mahwah, NJ: Erlbaum.

Marcovitch, S., & Zelazo, P. D. (2006). Non-monotonic influence of number of A trials on 2-years-old's perseverative search: A test of the hierarchical competing systems model. *Journal of Cognition and Development, 7,* 477–501.

Marcovitch, S., & Zelazo, P. D. (2009). A hierarchical competing systems model of the emergence and early development of executive function. *Developmental Science, 12*(1), 1–25.

Marcovitch, S., Zelazo, P. D., & Schmuckler, M. A. (2002). The effect of number of A trials on performance on the A-not-B task. *Infancy, 3,* 519–529.

Mareschal, D., & Tan, S. H. (2007). Flexible and context-dependent categorization by eighteen-month-olds. *Child Development, 78,* 19–37.

Markman, E. M., & Hutchinson, J. E. (1984). Children's sensitivity to constraints on word meaning: Taxonomic versus thematic relations. *Cognitive Psychology, 16,* 1–27.

Matthews, A., Ellis, A. E., & Nelson, C. A. (1996). Development of preterm and full-term infant ability on AB, recall memory, transparent barrier detour, and means-end tasks. *Child Development, 67,* 2658–2676.

Mayr, U. (2001). Age differences in the selection of mental sets: The role of inhibition, stimulus ambiguity, and response-set overlap. *Psychology and Aging, 16,* 96–109.

Mayr, U., & Kliegl, R. (1993). Sequential and coordinative complexity: Age-based processing limitations in figural transformations. *Journal of Experimental Psychology: Learning, Memory, and Cognition, 19,* 1297–1320.

McDaniel, M. A., & Einstein, G. O. (1992). Aging and prospective memory: Basic findings and practical applications. In T. E. Scruggs & M. A. Mastropieri (Eds.), *Advances in learning and behavioral disabilities* (Vol. 8, pp. 87–105). Greenwich, CT: JAI Press.

McDaniel, M. A., Einstein, G. O., Stout, A. C., & Morgan, Z. (2003). Aging and maintaining intentions over delays: Do it or lose it. *Psychology and Aging, 8,* 823–835.

McKay, L., & Jacques, S. (2009, June). *Labels or attributes: Preswitch rule learning strategies and their effects on postswitch performance on the DCCS.* Poster presented at the 38th Annual Meeting of the Jean Piaget Society, Park City, Utah.

Miller, E. K., & Cohen, J. D. (2001). An integrative theory of prefrontal cortex function. *Annual Review of Neuroscience, 24,* 167–202.

Milligan, K., Astington, J. W., & Dack, L. A. (2007). Language and theory of mind: Meta-analysis of the relation between language ability and false-belief understanding. *Child Development, 78,* 622–646.

Milner, B. (1963). Effects of different brain lesions on card sorting. *Archives of Neurology, 9,* 100–111.

Milner, B. (1964). Some effects of frontal lobectomy in man. In J. Warren & K. Ackert (Eds.), *The frontal granular cortex and behavior* (pp. 313–334). New York: McGraw-Hill.

Mischel, W., Shoda, Y., & Rodriguez, M. L. (1989). Delay of gratification in children. *Science, 244,* 993–938.

Miyake, A., Emerson, M. J., Padilla, F., & Ahn, J. C. (2004). Inner speech as a retrieval aid for task goals: The effects of cue type and articulatory suppression in the random task cuing paradigm. *Acta Psychologica, 115,* 123–142.

Miyake, A., Friedman, N. P., Emerson, M. J., Witzki, A. H., Howerter, A., & Wager, T. D. (2000). The unity and diversity of executive functions and their contributions to complex "frontal lobe" tasks: A latent variable analysis. *Cognitive Psychology, 41,* 49–100.

Miyake, A., & Shah, P. (Eds.). (1999). *Models of working memory: Mechanisms of active maintenance and executive control.* New York: Cambridge University Press.

Monsell, S. (2003). Task switching. *Trends in Cognitive Sciences, 7,* 134–140.

Morton, J. B., & Munakata, Y. (2002). Active versus latent representations: A neural network model of perseveration, dissociation, and décalage in early childhood. *Developmental Psychobiology, 40,* 255–265.

Moscovitch, M., & Winocur, G. (1995). Frontal lobes, memory, and aging. In J. Grafman, K. J. Holyoak, & F. Boller (Eds.), *Structure and functions of the human prefrontal cortex. Annals of the New York Academy of Sciences* (Vol. 769, pp. 119–150). New York: New York Academy of Sciences.

Müller, U., Zelazo, P. D., Hood, S., Leone, T., & Rohrer, L. (2004). Interference control in a new rule use task: Age-related changes, labeling, and attention. *Child Development, 75,* 1594–1609.

Müller, U., Zelazo, P. D., Lurye, L. E., & Liebermann, D. P. (2008). The effect of labeling on preschool children's performance in the Dimensional Change Card Sort Task. *Cognitive Development, 23,* 395–408.

Munakata, Y. (1997). Perseverative reaching in infancy: The roles of hidden toys and motor history in the AB task. *Infant Behavior and Development, 20,* 405–416.

Munakata, Y. (1998). Infant perseveration and implications for object permanence theories: A PDP model of the AB task. *Developmental Science, 2,* 161–184.

Munakata, Y. (2001). Graded representations in behavioral dissociations. *Trends in Cognitive Sciences, 5*(7), 309–315.

Munakata, Y., McClelland, J. L., Johnson, M. H., & Siegler, R. (1997). Rethinking infant knowledge: Toward an adaptive process account of successes and failures in object permanence tasks. *Psychological Review, 104,* 686–713.

Munoz, D. P., Broughton, J. R., Goldring, J. E., & Armstrong, I. T. (1998). Age-related performance of human subjects on saccadic eye movement tasks. *Experimental Brain Research, 121,* 391–400.

Murphy, G. L. (2002). *The big book of concepts.* Cambridge, MA: MIT Press.

Murray, F. S., & Lee, T. S. (1977). The effects of attention-directing training on recognition memory task performance on three-year-old children. *Journal of Experimental Child Psychology, 23,* 430–441.

Nelson, K. (1977). The syntagmatic-paradigmatic shift revisited: A review of research and theory. *Psychological Bulletin, 84,* 93–116.

Nelson, K. (1988). Where do taxonomic categories come from? *Human Development, 31,* 3–10.

Olson, D. R. (1993). The development of representations: The origins of mental life. *Canadian Psychology, 34,* 293–304.

O'Reilly, R. C., Braver, T. S., & Cohen, J. D. (1999). A biologically-based computational model of working memory. In A. Miyake, & P. Shah (Eds.), *Models of working memory: Mechanisms of active maintenance and executive control* (pp. 375–411). New York: Cambridge University Press.

Overman, W. H. (1990). Performance on traditional matching to sample, non-matching to sample, and object discrimination tasks by 12- to 32-month-old children. In A. Diamond (Ed.), *The development and neural bases of higher cognitive functions, Annals of the New York Academy of Sciences* (Vol. 608, pp. 365–393). New York: New York Academy of Sciences.

Ozonoff, S., Pennington, B. F., & Rogers, S. J. (1991). Executive function deficits in high-functioning autistic individuals: Relationship to theory of mind. *Journal of Child Psychology, Psychiatry and Allied Disciplines, 32,* 1081–1105.

Ozonoff, S., & Strayer, D. L. (1997). Inhibitory function in nonretarded autistic children. *Journal of Autism and Developmental Disorders, 27,* 59–76.

Park, D. C., & Payer, D. (2006). Working memory across the adult lifespan. In E. Bialystok & F. I. M. Craik (Eds.), *Lifespan cognition:*

Mechanisms of change (pp. 128–142). New York: Oxford University Press.

Pascual-Leone, J. (1970). A mathematical model for the transition rule in Piaget's developmental stages. *Acta Psychologica, 32,* 301–345.

Passler, M. A., Isaac, W., & Hynd, G. W. (1985). Neuropsychological development of behavior attributed to frontal lobe functioning in children. *Developmental Neuropsychology, 1*(4), 349–370.

Patten, G. W. R., & Meit, M. (1993). Effect of aging on prospective and incidental memory. *Experimental Aging Research, 19,* 165–176.

Pennington, B. F., & Ozonoff, S. (1996). Executive function and developmental psychopathology. *Journal of Child Psychology and Psychiatry, 37*(1), 51–87.

Perner, J., & Lang, B. (1999). Development of theory of mind and executive control. *Trends in Cognitive Sciences, 3,* 337–444.

Petrides, M. (1985). Deficits on conditional associative-learning asks after frontal- and temporal-lobe lesions in man. *Neuropsychologia, 23,* 601–614.

Petrides, M., & Milner, B. (1982). Deficits on subject-ordered tasks after frontal- and temporal-lobe lesions in man. *Neuropsychologia, 20*(3), 249–262.

Phillips, L., & Della Sala, S. (1999). Aging, intelligence and anatomical segregation in the frontal lobes. *Learning and Individual Difference, 10,* 217–243.

Piaget, J. (1954). *The construction of reality in the child.* New York: Basic Books.

Pickup, G. J. (2008). Relationship between theory of mind and executive function in schizophrenia: A systematic review. *Psychopathology, 41,* 206–213.

Posner, M. I., & Rothbart, M. K. (2007). Research on attention networks as a model for the integration of psychological science. *Annual Review of Psychology, 58,* 1–23.

Prencipe, A., & Zelazo, P. D. (2005). Development of affective decision-making for self and other: Evidence for the integration of first- and third-person perspectives. *Psychological Science, 16,* 501–505.

Reed, M. A., Pien, D. L., & Rothbart, M. K. (1984). Inhibitory self-control in preschool children. *Merrill-Palmer Quarterly, 30,* 131–147.

Reimers, S., & Maylor, E. A. (2005). Task switching across the life span: Effects of age on general and specific switch costs. *Developmental Psychology, 41*(4), 661–671.

Reznick, J. S., Morrow, J. D., Goldman, B. D., & Snyder, J. (2004). The onset of working memory in infants. *Infancy, 6,* 145–154.

Roberts, R. J., & Pennington, B. F. (1996). An interactive framework for examining prefrontal cognitive processes. *Developmental Neuropsychology, 12,* 105–126.

Rush, B. K., Barch, D. M., & Braver, T. S. (2006). Accounting for cognitive aging: Context processing, inhibition or processing speed? *Aging, Neuropsychology, and Cognition, 13,* 588–610.

Saeki, E., & Saito, S. (2004a). Effect of articulatory suppression on task-switching performance: Implications for models of working memory. *Memory, 12,* 257–271.

Saeki, E., & Saito, S. (2004b). The role of the phonological loop in task switching performance: The effect of articulatory suppression in the alternating runs paradigm. *Psychologia: An International Journal of Psychology in the Orient, 47,* 35–43.

Salthouse, T. A. (1996). The processing-speed theory of adult age differences in cognition. *Psychological Review, 103,* 403–428.

Salthouse, T. A. (2005). Relations between cognitive abilities and measures of executive functioning. *Neuropsychology, 19,* 532–545.

Salthouse, T. A., Atkinson, T. M., & Berish, D. E. (2003). Executive functioning as a potential mediator of age-related cognitive decline in normal adults. *Journal of Experimental Psychology: General, 132*(4), 566–594.

Schachar, R. J., & Logan, G. D. (1990). Impulsivity and inhibitory control in normal development and childhood psychopathology. *Developmental Psychology, 26*, 710–720.

Schachar, R. J., Tannock, R., & Logan, G. D. (1993). Inhibitory control, impulsiveness, and attention deficit hyperactivity disorder. *Clinical Psychology Review, 13*, 721–739.

Shallice, T., & Burgess, P. W. (1991). Higher-order cognitive impairments and frontal lobe lesions in man. In H. S. Levin, H. M. Eisenberg, & A. L. Benton (Eds.), *Frontal lobe function and dysfunction* (pp. 125–138). New York: Oxford University Press.

Sigel, I. E. (1970). The distancing hypothesis: A causal hypothesis for the acquisition of representational thought. In M. R. Jones (Ed.), *Miami Symposium on the Prediction of Behavior, 1968: Effects of early experience* (pp. 99–118). Coral Gables, FL: University of Miami Press.

Silverman, I. W., & Ippolito, M. F. (1997). Goal-directedness and its relation to inhibitory control among toddlers. *Infant Behavior & Development, 20*, 271–273.

Simon, J. R. (1990). The effects of an irrelevant directional cue on human information processing. In R. W. Proctor & T. G. Reeve (Eds.), *Stimulus-response compatibility: An integrated perspective* (pp. 31–86). Amsterdam: North-Holland.

Smiley, S. S., & Brown, A. L. (1979). Conceptual preference for thematic or taxonomic relations: A nonmonotonic age trend from preschool to old age. *Journal of Experimental Child Psychology, 28*, 249–257.

Smith, L. B. (1984). Young children's understanding of attributes and dimensions: A comparison of conceptual and linguistic measures. *Child Development, 55*, 363–380.

Smith, L. B. (1989). From global similarities to kinds of similarities: The construction of dimensions in development. In S. Vosniadou & A. Ortony (Eds.), *Similarity and analogical reasoning (*pp. 146–178). Cambridge: Cambridge University Press.

Smith, L. B., Thelen, E., Titzer, R., & McLin, D. (1999). Knowing in the context of acting: The task dynamics of the A-not-B error. *Psychological Review, 106*, 235–260.

Smith, R. E., & Bayen, U. J. (2006). The source of adult age differences in prospective memory: A multinomial modeling approach. *Journal of Experimental Psychology: Learning, Memory, and Cognition, 32*, 623–635.

Sophian, C., & Wellman, H. M. (1983). Selective information use and perseveration in the search behavior of infants and young children. *Journal of Experimental Child Psychology, 35*, 369–390.

Strommen, E. A. (1973). Verbal self-regulation in a children's game: Impulsive errors on "Simon Says." *Child Development, 44*, 849–853.

Stroop, J. R. (1935). Studies of interference in serial verbal reactions. *Journal of Experimental Psychology, 18*, 643–661.

Stuss, D. T., & Alexander, M. P. (2000). Executive function and the frontal lobes: A conceptual view. *Psychological Research, 63*, 289–298.

Stuss, D. T., Shallice, T., Alexander, M. P., & Picton, T. W. (1995). A multidisciplinary approach to anterior attentional functions. *Annals of the New York Academy of Science, 769*, 191–212.

Thompson, C., Barresi, J., & Moore, C. (1997). The development of future-oriented prudence and altruism in preschoolers. *Cognitive Development, 12*, 199–212.

Touron, D. R., & Hertzog, C. (2004). Distinguishing age differences in knowledge, strategy use, and confidence during strategic skill acquisition. *Psychology and Aging, 19*, 452–466.

Towse, J. N., & Hitch, G. J. (2007). Variation in working memory due to normal development. In A. R. A. Conway, C. Jarrold, M. J. Kane, A. Miyake, & J. N. Towse (Eds.), *Variation in working memory* (pp. 109–133). New York: Oxford University Press.

Towse, J. N., Lewis, C., & Knowles, M. (2007). When knowledge is not enough: The phenomenon of goal neglect in preschool children. *Journal of Experimental Child Psychology, 96*(4), 320–332.

Towse, J. N., Redbond, J., Houston-Price, C. M. T., & Cook, S. (2000). Understanding the dimensional change card sort: Perspectives from task success and failure. *Cognitive Development, 15*, 347–365.

Tversky, B. (1985). Development of taxonomic organization of named and pictured categories. *Developmental Psychology, 21*, 1111–1119.

van den Wildenberg, W. P. M., & van der Molen, M. W. (2004). Additive factors analysis of inhibitory processing in the stop-signal paradigm. *Brain and Cognition, 56*(2), 253–66.

Vaughn, B. E., Kopp, C. B., & Krakow, J. B. (1984). The emergence and consolidation of self-control from eighteen to thirty months of age: Normative trends and individual differences. *Child Development, 55*(3), 990–1004.

Verbruggen, F., & Logan, G. D. (2008). Response inhibition in the stop-signal paradigm. *Trends in Cognitive Sciences, 12*, 418–424.

Verhaeghen, P., Kliegl, R., & Mayr, U. (1997). Sequential and coordinative complexity in time-accuracy functions for mental arithmetic. *Psychology and Aging, 12*, 555–564.

Vygotsky, L. S. (1929). The problem of the cultural development of the child. *Journal of Genetic Psychology, 36*, 415–434.

Vygotsky, L. S. (1978). *Mind in society: The development of higher psychological processes* (M. Cole, V. John-Steiner, S. Scribner, & E. Souberman, Eds.). Cambridge, MA: Harvard University Press.

Vygotsky, L. S. (1986). *Thought and language* (A. Kozulin, Ed., Trans.). Cambridge, MA: MIT Press. (Original work published 1934)

Waxman, S. R., & Namy, L. L. (1997). Challenging the notion of a thematic preference in young children. *Developmental Psychology, 33*, 555–567.

Wellman, H. M., Cross, D., & Bartsch, K. (1986). Infant search and object permanence: A meta-analysis of the A-not-B error. *Monographs of the Society for Research in Child Development, 51*(3), Serial No. 214.

Wellman, H. M., Cross, D., & Watson, J. (2001). Meta-analysis of theory-of-mind development: The truth about false belief. *Child Development, 72*, 655–684.

Welsh, M. C., Pennington, B. F., & Groisser, D. B. (1991). A normative-developmental study of executive function: A window on prefrontal function in children. *Developmental Neuropsychology, 7*, 131–149.

Werner, H. (1948). *Comparative psychology of mental development.* New York: Science Editions.

West, R. L. (1996). An application of prefrontal cortex function theory to cognitive aging. *Psychological Bulletin, 120*, 272–292.

Whelihan, W. M., & Lesher, E. L. (1985). Neuropsychological changes in frontal functions with aging. *Developmental Neuropsychology, 1*, 371–380.

Wiebe, S. A., Espy, K. A., & Charak, D. (2008). Using confirmatory factor analysis to understand executive control in preschool children: I. Latent structure. *Developmental Psychology, 44*(2), 575–587.

Williams, B. R., Ponesse, J. S., Schachar, R. J., Logan, G. D., & Tannock, R. (1999). Development of inhibitory control across the life span. *Developmental Psychology, 35*, 205–213.

Wimmer, H., & Perner, J. (1983). Beliefs about beliefs: Representation and constraining function of wrong beliefs in young children's understanding of deception. *Cognition, 13*, 103–128.

Yerys, B. E., & Munakata, Y. (2006). When labels hurt but novelty helps: Children's perseveration and flexibility in a card-sorting task. *Child Development, 77*, 1589–1607.

Zacks, R. T., Radvansky, G. A., & Hasher, L. (1996). Studies of directed forgetting in older adults. *Journal of Experimental Psychology: Learning, Memory, & Cognition, 22*, 143–156.

Zaitchik, D. (1991). Is only seeing really believing? Sources of the true belief in the false belief task. *Cognitive Development, 6*(1), 91–103.

Zelazo, P. D. (1999). Language, levels of consciousness, and the development of intentional action. In P. D. Zelazo, J. W. Astington, & D. R. Olson (Eds.), *Developing theories of intention: Social understanding and self-control* (pp. 95–117). Mahwah, NJ: Erlbaum.

Zelazo, P. D. (2004). The development of conscious control in childhood. *Trends in Cognitive Sciences, 8,* 12–17.

Zelazo, P. D. (2006). The dimensional change card sort (DCCS): A method of assessing executive function in children. *Nature Protocols, 1,* 297–301.

Zelazo, P. D., Carter, A., Reznick, J. S., & Frye, D. (1997). Early development of executive function: A problem-solving framework. *Review of General Psychology, 1,* 198–226.

Zelazo, P. D., Craik, F. I. M., & Booth, L. (2004). Executive function across the life span. *Acta Psychologica, 115,* 167–184.

Zelazo, P. D., & Frye, D. (1997). Cognitive complexity and control: A theory of the development of deliberate reasoning and intentional action. In M. Stamenov (Ed.), *Language structure, discourse, and the access to consciousness* (pp. 113–153). Amsterdam: Benjamins.

Zelazo, P. D., & Frye, D. (1998). II. Cognitive complexity and control: The development of executive function. *Current Directions in Psychological Science, 7,* 121–126.

Zelazo, P. D., Frye, D., & Rapus, T. (1996). An age-related dissociation between knowing rules and using them. *Cognitive Development, 11,* 37–63.

Zelazo, P. D., & Jacques, S. (1997). Children's rule use: Representation, reflection and cognitive control. *Annals of Child Development, 12,* 119–176.

Zelazo, P. D., Jacques, S., Burack, J. A., & Frye, D. (2002). The relation between theory of mind and rule use: Evidence from persons with autism-spectrum disorders. *Infant and Child Development (Special Issue: Executive functions and development), 11,* 171–195.

Zelazo, P. D., Müller, U., Frye, D., & Marcovitch, S. (2003). The development of executive function in early childhood. *Monographs of the Society for Research in Child Development, 68*(3), Serial No. 274.

Zelazo, P. D., & Reznick, J. S. (1991). Age-related asynchrony of knowledge and action. *Child Development, 62,* 719–735.

Zelazo, P. D., Reznick, J. S., & Piñon, D. E. (1995). Response control and the execution of verbal rules. *Developmental Psychology, 31,* 508–517.

Zelazo, P. D., Reznick, J. S., & Spinazzola, J. (1998). Representational flexibility and response control in a multistep multilocation search task. *Developmental Psychology, 34,* 203–214.

CHAPTER 14

Language Development

BRIAN MacWHINNEY

Language provides a remarkably clear window onto the complex workings of the human psyche and the human brain. By studying people's names for animals and foods, we can learn how they think about the biological world. By examining and testing people who have suffered from a brain lesion, we can identify parts of the brain that are important for particular cognitive and emotional functions. By studying infant babbling, we can understand how the brain comes to control the vocal apparatus. By observing how people learn a second language, we can come to understand ways in which the mind and brain change over time and experience. By studying how people describe their solutions to problems, we can track the details of problem solving in activities, such as chess, architecture, medicine, and law. In these and many other ways, we can use language as a window onto the mind and the brain.

Language is also a window onto human society and social relations. Each day, we spend an enormous amount of time engaged in linguistic interactions. Some of this time is spent receiving communications from media such as television, books, or radio. For other blocks of time, we are actively involved in producing conversation. Workers in professions such as law, sales, medicine, education, or public relations spend many of their waking hours using language. When it is time to relax, we do not stop talking. Instead, we seek out friends and go to parties, restaurants, or bars where we can spend still more

time talking. This enormous involvement with spoken language has important consequences for development across the life span.

Because we spend so much time talking, it should come as no surprise that the language we end up acquiring is full of great complexity and detail. On the one hand, much of language is rule-governed. We consistently form plurals in English by adding the suffix "-s" or "-es." We consistently place the adjective before the noun. But underneath this level of consistency is a bubbling sea of idiosyncratic, inconsistent partial patterns. Language is rich in frozen expressions, formulas, exceptions, and irregularities. We use the phrases "how about X" and "what about X" happily enough, but would never dream of using "when about X" or "how under X." We pronounce the "ough" in "plough," "tough," and "slough" in three totally different ways, despite the similar orthography. When we are in Boston, we expect to hear "car" pronounced without the final /r/; when we are in Pittsburgh, we expect to hear "oil" pronounced as "earl." We know that we should not say "good night" to someone until we leave, even if it is late at night, whereas we have no problem using "good morning" and "good evening" as greetings on arrival.

Language is a vast quilt of irregularities, variations, and special cases set against a backdrop of partial regularities (MacWhinney, 1975b; Pinker, 1991). A sure guide to all of these patterns is the modicum that, in language, "all rules leak." Plurals, such as *oxen, sheep,* and *leaves,* break the otherwise well-behaved plural rule. The rule for forming double-object constructions such as *Pat gave John the ball* or *Sarah mailed her Mom the chocolates* seems quite tidy. But then we find that it is impossible to say *Tom delivered the fraternity the pizza* or *He recommended me his book.* This coexistence of regularity with exceptions reflects the fact that language is used for so many purposes across so many complex social situations. When we ask sarcastically, *What is this fly doing in my soup?* we do not expect a literal answer such as "the backstroke" (Kay & Fillmore, 1999). Instead, we are using this unique and rather limited construction to express a very specific type of meaning appropriate in a very narrow context.

Language is a collection of special purpose devices for dealing with a myriad of narrow contexts, complemented by general devices for dealing with broad contexts. We learn how to use language for singing songs, imitating foreign accents, describing mathematical formulas using Greek letters, naming fish, and encoding the hundreds of names of cities, buildings, and streets we encountered on our last trip abroad. In a very basic way, language becomes a faithful record of the entire journey of our lives. When I know that someone knows how to get from Kolozsvár (Cluj) to Kalotaszeg in Romania, I know a great deal about the travels of that person. When I know that someone understands the symptoms of *polycythemia vera* (Frederiksen, Donin, Koschmann, & Myers Kelson, 2004), I know a great deal about the medical training of that person. If they can recite in Sanskrit the first lines of the Bhagavad Gita, I know still more.

Language conveys not just experience and training. It also reveals secrets about our wishes, dreams, fears, and commitments. Applying the methods of Conversation Analysis (Schegloff, 2007), we can study the ways in which pauses and drops in pitch indicate disalignments or misunderstandings between speakers. Words like *just, even,* or *sure* can betray ways in which we question other people's values or refrain from stating our own. In these various ways, the language we acquire across the life span of our development comes to represent the sum of our past experiences and our hopes for the future. Along the way to what we are now, we often pick up pieces of language that we later shed. When I was young, I referred to something interesting as being "a real trip." It has probably been 40 years since I last used that phrase, although I occasionally hear it used still, almost always sardonically.

UNIVERSAL GRAMMAR

As we survey this vast complexity of language, we wonder how children could learn all of this. One answer to this question is that the core shape of language is engraved in our genetics. According to this view, promulgated most famously by Noam Chomsky, language is not learned—it is acquired. This view of language as a Special Gift has led some researchers (Bickerton, 1990) to believe that language arose from a small set of evolutionary events. According to this view, the capacity to learn language is a unique property of the human mind represented neurologically in a separate cognitive module (Chomsky, 1980; Fodor, 1983). Studies of language learning stimulated by this perspective have tended to focus on a small set of syntactic structures that are thought to constitute the core of Universal Grammar (Chomsky, 1965). According to the "principles and parameters" model of language structure (Hyams & Wexler, 1993), the learning of particular languages occurs through the process of parameter setting. During parameter setting, children identify the exact shape of their mother tongue by choosing the proper settings on a small set of binary oppositions. For example, a positive setting on the pronoun omission parameter will select for languages like Italian or Chinese, whereas a negative setting will select for English.

This belief in a core genetic basis for human language is supported by the fact that no other animal species has ever developed a system of communication as rich and complex as human language. Unlike the communication systems of other species, language allows humans to create complete and open-ended descriptions of all manner of objects and activities outside of the here and now. This marked contrast between our species and our nearest primate relatives suggests that, over the 6-million-year course of human evolution, there must have been important genetic changes that allowed humans to develop this particular species-specific ability. Further proof of this genetic basis comes from the fact that children learn their first language "like a duck takes to water," whereas learning of a second language is often slow and incomplete. The claim is that, after some critical period, the species-specific gift for language learning expires, thereby making second language learning difficult or even impossible.

What might be at the core of this uniquely human ability? Hauser, Chomsky, and Fitch (2002) speculated that what makes human language unique is its capacity for recursion. This idea fits in nicely with the emphasis on the centrality of the recursive application of rules that has been at the core of generative grammar since its introduction (Chomsky, 1957). Early on, Miller (1965) showed that structures like relative clauses can be added at will to sentences, making the number of possible sentences in a language uncountably large. Perhaps there is some simple genetic change that occurred in recent human evolutionary history that led to the introduction of this new capacity.

The idea that there might be a gene for recursion seems attractive, because it offers the possibility of linking together facts from linguistics, cultural anthropology, neurology, genetics, and evolution. However, this proposal generates predictions that are problematic. One prediction is that all human language should display recursion. However, many languages make far less use of things like relative or complement clauses than we do in English. Languages of North America, such as Navajo or Mohawk, can break a sentence such as *The boy who shot the arrow dropped the stone*, into components like *That boy, he shot the arrow*, and *That one, he dropped the stone*. In this way, discourse can replace syntactic recursion. In his account of his work with the isolated Pirahã of the Amazon, Everett (2007) explains how these people communicate effectively without relying on recursive syntactic devices at all. In the world of this group of hunter-gatherers, what is important is an accurate description of events, rather than the recursive linkage of events into bigger discourse structures.

The view of language as a species-specific ability linked to a critical period is also problematic. Studies of the neural basis of communication in organisms such as crickets (Wyttenback, May, & Hoy, 1996), quail, and song birds (Marler, 1991) have emphasized the extent to which species-specific communication patterns are stored in highly localized hardwired neurologic structures. However, in many bird species, the consolidation of the song pattern emerges gradually over the first weeks and remains plastic or mutable for several more weeks (Konishi, 1995). When we look at human language learning, we see even more evidence for plasticity and gradual emergence, rather than strong initial canalization. There is little evidence that child language development follows a tight biological timetable of the type that we see in the development of communication systems in other organisms. In fact, children can learn language even when they have been isolated up to the age of 6 (Davis, 1947).

The nativist account of language acquisition emphasizes the idea that language learning is almost trivially easily. In truth, children find language learning not nearly as easy as the nativists suggest. Even with consistent and massive input, children struggle for three full years to acquire the core aspects of articulation in their native language. Children learn language gradually and inductively across a period of many years, rather than abruptly and deductively through the setting of a few simple parameters. No one has ever been able to present evidence for some discrete moment at which a child sets some crucial linguistic parameter (Hyams, 1995; MacWhinney & Bates, 1989). Moreover, it is difficult to use standard experimental methods to prove that children have acquired some of the abstract categories and structures required by Universal Grammar, such as argument chains, empty categories, landing sites, or dominance relations (Gopnik, 1990; van der Lely, 1994).

Language learning is not finished at age three. Rather, the acquisition of new words and constructions continues throughout our lives. In this sense, the view of human language as linked to some core genetic feature fails to tell us what we really want to know about language development across the life span.

EMERGENTISM

For a richer understanding of language development, we can turn to the theory of emergentism, which is a key component of general systems theory (von Bertalanffy, 1968) and its current developmental version—relational developmental systems theory (Lerner, 2006; Lerner & Overton, 2008; Overton, 2006). As an example of an emergent process, consider the forces that determine the length of checkout lines at a supermarket. Over time, you will find that the number of people queued up in each line stays roughly the same. There are rarely six people in one line and two in the next, unless there is a line with special rules. There is no socially articulated rule governing this pattern. Instead, the uniformity of this simple social structure emerges from other basic facts about the goals and behavior of shoppers and supermarket managers. The general principle here is that the emergence of patterns in one domain typically arises from patterns or constraints derived from a separate domain.

Honeybees are certainly no smarter than shoppers. However, working together, bees are able to construct an even more complex structure. When a bee returns to the hive after collecting pollen, she deposits a drop of wax-coated honey. Each of these honey balls has approximately the same globular shape and size. As these balls get packed together, they take on the familiar hexagonal shape that we see in the honeycomb. There is no gene in the bee that codes for hexagonality in the honeycomb, nor any overt communication regarding the shaping of the cells of the honeycomb. Rather, this hexagonal form emerges from the application of packing rules to a collection of honey balls of roughly the same size.

Nature abounds with such examples of emergence. The shapes of crystals emerge from the ways in which atoms can pack into sheets. Crystalline lattice structures (cubic, hexagonal, monoclinic, orthorhombic) emerge as packing solutions based on the relative size of the atoms in ionic compounds. The outlines of beaches emerge from interactions between geology and ocean currents. Consider the shape of Cape Cod near Provincetown, where the northeasterly drift of the Gulf Stream works to push the outline of the cape toward the mainland. Weather patterns like the Jet Stream or El Niño emerge from interactions between the rotation of the Earth, solar radiation, and the shapes of the ocean bodies. Biological patterns emerge in similar ways. For example, the shapes of the spots on a leopard or the stripes on a tiger emerge from the timing of the expression of a pair of competing genes expressing color as they set up standing waves governed by B-Z equilibria across the developing leopard or tiger embryo (Murray, 1988). No single gene directly controls these patterns. Rather, the stripes emerge from the interactions of the genes on the physical surface of the embryo. The shape of the brain is very much the same. For example, Miller, Keller, and Stryker (1989) have shown how the ocular dominance columns that Hubel and Weisel (1963) described emerge from the competition between projections from the two optic areas during synaptogenesis in striate cortex.

In 1794, Huygens demonstrated that two pendulums moving at different periods would couple together to find a single periodicity if they are mounted on a board with springs. During this coupling, one pendulum serves as the strong attractor that entrains the other pendulum to its periodicity. This form of resonant coupling also occurs within language. For example, studies of the mechanics of infant babbling have demonstrated that there is an early period when the child moves the jaw with a consistent rhythm (MacNeilage, 1998). During babbling, the periodicity of this movement then serves to entrain a similar periodicity in the opening and closing of the glottis. The result of this coupling is the emergence of canonical babbling (Vihman, 1996).

The study of interactions between hierarchically structured emergent levels is a familiar theme in sciences, such as biology, astronomy, and physics. Our biological existence is grounded on the operations of thousands of proteins, each with a subtlety different geometry, determined on four emergent levels. The primary structure of a protein is determined by its sequence of amino acids, which is, in turn, a function of the order of base pairs in a codon of DNA. This is the structure that is most tightly linked to evolution and natural selection. The secondary structure of proteins involves coils, fold, and pleats that arise from the formation of hydrogen bonds between CO and NH groups along the polypeptide backbone. Tertiary structure, leading to the folding of single polypeptides, derives from hydrophobic interactions and disulfide bridges that produce bonding between side chains. Quaternary structure emerges from the aggregation of polypeptide subunits, as in the combination of four subunits in hemoglobin. Altogether, "the specific function of a protein is an emergent property that arises from the architecture of the molecule" (Campbell, Reece, & Mitchell, 1999, p. 74).

Emergentist thinking is basic to the natural sciences. However, it applies equally well to the social, neural, and behavioral sciences (Lerner, 2006; Overton, 2006). The application of emergentism to the study of language and language development over the last two decades has proven to be particularly rewarding. In this chapter, we will explore how emergentist theory helps us understand the growth of language across the life span. Two major preliminary issues need to be examined. The first is the way in which language forms emerge in parallel across multiple *time frames*. The second is how language development is facilitated by a variety of core *mechanisms of emergence*.

TIME FRAMES

Lorenz (1958) argued that animal behavior is constrained by processes that operate across four times frames. In the case of human language, we can distinguish seven distinct time frames for emergent processes and structures.

1. *Phylogenetic emergence.* The slowest moving language structures are those that are encoded in the genes. Changes across this time frame are controlled by natural selection (Darwin, 1871). The core engine of emergence is the generation of variation through mutation, followed then by natural selection through both mate choice and differential mortality. Natural selection utilizes the possibilities for reorganization shaped by the DNA and the interactions of polypeptides that it specifies. Emergentist accounts in this area have emphasized

the ways in which language, society, and cognition have undergone coevolution (MacWhinney, 2002) based on the linking of dynamic systems. Changes in linguistic abilities must arise in parallel with advances in cognitive or social abilities to trigger this coevolutionary advantage. Moreover, both effects must interact at the moment of speaking. When this happens in a way that favors reproductive fitness, the mutation will be preserved.

2. *Epigenetic emergence.* The codification of information in the DNA represents a precise meshing between the slow-moving process of evolution and the faster moving process of epigenesis (Waddington, 1957). Embryologists have shown that biological structures emerge from processes of induction between developing tissue structures in the embryo. The shape of these interactions is not hard-coded in the DNA. Instead, the DNA encodes information that can push the process of differentiation in particular directions at crucial epigenetic choice points. The precursors of autism in the embryo can be traced to particular epigenetic effects, as can the formation of stripes in the tiger (Murray, 1988). Epigenetic emergence continues throughout the life span. Later forms of epigenetic emergence include changes such as puberty, menopause, or disorders such as schizophrenia and Huntington chorea. Before birth, epigenetic interactions with the environment are confined to forces that impinge on the uterus and the embryonic fluid. After birth, the environmental interactions can trigger patterns such as diabetes or brain reorganization for language in the deaf (Bellugi, Poizner, & Klima, 1989).

3. *Developmental emergence.* Jean Piaget's genetic psychology (Piaget, 1954) was the first fully articulated emergentist view of development. Impressively complete in its coverage, it failed to specify details regarding mechanisms of development. Current emergentist accounts of development rely on connectionism, embodiment, and dynamic systems theory to provide this missing processing detail (Quinlan, 2003). Emergentist theory has been used to characterize two different, but interrelated, aspects of development. The first is the basic learning process that involves the continual learning of new facts, forms, relations, names, and procedures. Basic models of language learning, such as those that deal with learning of the past tense (MacWhinney & Leinbach, 1991), often focus on this type of development. A second type of development involves the learning of new strategies and frameworks that can alter the overall shape of language and cognition, often through cue focusing (Colunga & Smith, 2000; Regier, 2005). Work linking these two strands together has just begun.

4. *Processing emergence.* The most fast-acting pressures on language form are those that derive from online processing constraints (MacWhinney, 1999b). The basic constraint here is the need to produce language that keeps our listeners' attention and effectively communicates what we want to say. To achieve this, we rely on a variety of well-coordinated mechanisms for attentional focusing, coordination of sentence planning, code switching between languages, and motor control. Many of the pressures we sense in the current moment are themselves driven by long-term processes. For example, a child's failure to understand the meaning of the word *dependability* in a discussion of the reliability of batteries may be the result of problems in understanding previous classroom and computerized lessons on numeric distributions. Similarly, the failure in lexical retrieval that occurs in aphasia is driven by changes to neural tissue subsequent to a stroke. Thus, online processing emergence can reflect the current status of longer term developmental, neuronal, and physiologic processes.

5. *Social emergence.* Many aspects of language are shaped by social mimetics (Mesoudi, Whiten, & Laland, 2006). Our choice of vocabulary, slang, phonetic form, and topics is determined by the nature of the relations we perceive with the people we meet. We can select these options to emphasize solidarity (Brown & Gilman, 1960), impose our power, or seek favors (Brown & Levinson, 1978). The time course of changes in these social commitments is often measured in terms of years or decades, with many remaining constant across the life span.

6. *Interactional emergence.* Apart from our long-term commitments to dialects, languages, and subgroup themes, we also make more short-term commitments to ongoing social interactions. For example, we may engage a real-estate agent to help us purchase a house. Our linguistic interactions with this agent are then shaped by the current status of the buying process. Even after we terminate one set of transactions with this agent, we will maintain an ongoing relation that will then shape our further interactions, days or weeks later (Keenan, MacWhinney, & Mayhew, 1977).

7. *Diachronic emergence.* We can also use emergentist thinking to understand the changes that languages have undergone across the centuries (Bybee & Hopper, 2001). These changes emerge from a further complex interaction of the previous three levels of emergence (evolutionary, developmental, and online).

MECHANISMS OF EMERGENCE

Emergentism agrees with Universal Grammar (UG) on one core issue: human language is uniquely well adapted to human nature. The fact that all people succeed in learning to use language, whereas not all people learn to swim or do calculus, demonstrates how fully language conforms to our human nature. Languages avoid sounds that people cannot produce, words they cannot learn, or sentence patterns they cannot parse. Emergentism differs from UG in that it attributes this match to general versus specific mechanisms. In the UG account, specific genetic mechanisms arose over recent evolutionary history that support this uniquely human ability. In the emergentist account, language depends on a set of domain-general mechanisms that ground language on the shape of the human body, brain, and society. This is the core difference between UG and emergentism.

As noted earlier, much of the complexity of language arises from the shape of society. However, we can also point to a rich array of domain-general mechanisms that serve to support the learning and processing of language. Some of these mechanisms include:

1. *Homeorrhesis:* All neurobiological processes are grounded on the brain's ability to maintain homeorrhesis and homeostasis to provide underlying stability in neural function, despite the fact that cells and protoplasm are continually undergoing change.

2. *Competition:* Like other biological systems, the brain relies on variation and competition (Edelman, 1987) to learn the appropriate matching of responses to stimuli.

3. *Control:* Systems such as the basal ganglia circuit involving the striatum, thalamus, cortex, globus pallidus, and substantia nigra provide multiple loop-back levels (von Bertalanffy, 1968) for attentional control, proceduralization, and error-based learning (Rumelhart & McClelland, 1986).

4. *Topological organization:* The brain depends on a system for connecting areas through topological (tonotopic, somatotopic, retinotopic, etc.) organization that

emerges during embryogenesis. This system links to methods for self-organization in feature maps (Kohonen, 2001) and topological sheets (Elman, 1999; Shrager & Johnson, 1995).

5. *Item basis:* The brain links episodic (McClelland, McNaughton, & O'Reilly, 1995) and procedural systems to support item-based learning (MacWhinney, 1975a; Tomasello, 2000a) of grammatical constructions (Goldberg, 1999).

6. *Statistical learning:* Statistical learning allows both children and adults to learn patterns of sounds, tones, or visual forms (Jusczyk, 1997; Saffran, Aslin, & Newport, 1996), as constituted in sequential groups (Gupta & MacWhinney, 1997; Houghton, 1990).

7. *Redundancy:* The brain supports multiple systems for redundancy to provide plasticity and recovery from injury. For example, the brain can compensate for damage to language areas in the left hemisphere through reorganization to the right hemisphere (Booth et al., 1999; Corina, Vaid, & Bellugi, 1992; MacWhinney, Feldman, Sacco, & Valdes-Perez, 2000).

8. *Learning to learn:* Competition, statistical learning, and control loops can guide learners' attention to cues that have proved useful in learning previous similar forms (Smith, 1999). This then confirms the importance of these cues for further learning.

9. *Analogy:* The interactive and connected nature of neural processing allows problem solvers and learners to structure domains and relations in parallel alignment (Gentner & Markman, 1997).

10. *Resonance:* The consolidation of new learning, particularly in second language learning, can rely on the development of resonance between alternative systems (orthography, phonology, mnemonics) for encoding across multiple languages (MacWhinney, 2005a). For example, when we code-switch from English to Spanish, the initial moments of speaking in Spanish are still under the influence of resonance operating in English (Grosjean & Miller, 1994).

LEVELS OF LANGUAGE

Unlike certain basic systems such as smell or balance, language processing depends on the coordination of activities between many cortical regions. Linguistic theory has traditionally analyzed language across the levels of auditory phonology, articulatory phonology, lexicon, morphology, syntax, and pragmatics. Research in cognitive neurolinguistics (MacWhinney & Li, 2008) provides additional support for this analysis, as summarized in Table 14.1.

TABLE 14.1   The Six Subsystems of Language

Subsystem	Cortical Area	Processes	Theory
Audition	Auditory cortex	Extracting phonemes	Statistical learning
Articulation	Motor cortex	Targets, timing	Resonance, gating
Lexicon	Wernicke's area	Phonology to meaning	DevLex
Syntax	Inferior frontal gyrus	Slots, sequences	Item-based patterns
Mental models	Dorsal cortex	Deixis, perspective	Perspective
Conversation	Social system	Topics, turn taking	Conversation analysis

Before beginning our study of the life-span development of these systems, let us take a quick glance over each of these six components. First, consider the relation between auditory and articulatory learning. Auditory development involves learning how to distinguish the basic sounds of the language and using them to segment the flow of speech into words. This learning involves the receptive or perceptual side of language use. Children's articulatory development, in contrast, involves learning to control the mouth, tongue, and larynx to produce sounds that imitate those produced by adults. This learning involves the productive or expressive use of language. Auditory learning and articulatory learning are the two sides of phonological development. Clearly, we cannot acquire conventional control over articulation until we have learned the target auditory contrasts. Thus, audition logically precedes articulation.

The third dimension of language development is lexical development, or the learning of words. To serve as a means of communication between people, words must have a shared or conventional meaning. Picking out the correct meaning for each new word is a major learning task for the child. But it is not enough for children to just recognize words produced by their parents. To express their own intentions, they have to be able to recall the names for things on their own and convert these forms into actual articulations. Thus, lexical development, like phonological development, includes both receptive and expressive components.

Having acquired a collection of words, children can then put them into combinations. Syntax—the fourth component of language—is the system of rules by which words and phrases are arranged to make meaningful statements. Children need to learn how to use the ordering of words to mark grammatical functions such as subject or direct object.

The fifth linguistic component that a child must learn to master is the system of mental models that relate syntactic patterns to meaningful interpretations. During production, this system takes meanings and prepares them into a form that Slobin (1996) has called "thinking for speaking." During comprehension, this system takes sentences and derives embodied mental models for the meanings underlying these sentences.

The sixth component that the child must acquire encodes the social and pragmatic principles for conversation. This is the system of patterns that determines how we can use language in particular social settings for particular communicative purposes. Because pragmatics refers primarily to the skills needed to maintain conversation and communication, child language researchers find it easiest to refer to pragmatic development as the acquisition of communicative competence and conversational competence (Ochs & Schieffelin, 1983). A major component of communicative competence involves knowing that conversations customarily begin with a greeting, require turn-taking, and concern a shared topic. Children must also learn that they need to adjust the content of their communications to match their listener's interests, knowledge, and language ability.

Auditory Development

William James (1890) described the world of the newborn as a "blooming, buzzing confusion." However, we now know that, at the auditory level at least, the newborn's world is remarkably well structured. The cochlea and auditory nerve provide extensive preprocessing of signals for frequency and intensity. By the time the signal reaches the auditory cortex, it is fairly well structured.

Perceptual Contrasts

Research on the emergence of auditory-processing abilities has identified three major streams of auditory learning and development. The first stream involves the core perceptual features of hearing. In the 1970s, researchers (Eimas, Siqueland, Jusczyk, & Vigorito, 1971) discovered that human infants were specifically adapted at birth to perceive contrasts such as that between /p/ and /b/, as in *pit* and *bit*. However, it soon became apparent that even chinchillas were capable of making this distinction (Kuhl & Miller, 1978). This suggests that much of the basic structure of the infant's auditory world might be attributed to fundamental processes in the mammalian ear and cochlear nucleus, rather than some specifically human adaptation. As infants sharpen their ability to hear the contrasts of their native language, they begin to lose the ability to hear contrasts not represented in their native language (Werker, 1995). If the infant is growing up in a bilingual world, full perceptual flexibility is maintained (Sebastián-Galles & Bosch, 2005). However, if the infant is growing up monolingual, flexibility in processing is gradually traded off for quickness and automaticity (Kilborn, 1989).

Statistical Learning

The second stream of auditory development involves the processing of statistical regularities of spoken language. It is as if the infant has something akin to a tape recorder in the auditory cortex that records input sounds, replays them, and accustoms the ear to their patterns, well before learning the actual meanings of these words. There is now abundant evidence that both infants (Aslin, Saffran, & Newport, 1999; Marcus, 2000) and monkeys (Hauser, Newport, & Aslin, 2001) are able to use sequential statistics to extract background properties of their language involving prosodies (Thiessen & Saffran, 2007), phonotactics (Thiessen, 2007), and possible segments. These stored sequences can help the child solidify preferences for certain voices over others. Thus, a French infant will prefer to listen to French, whereas a Polish infant will prefer to listen to Polish (Jusczyk, 1997). In addition, babies demonstrate a preference for their own mother's voice, as opposed to that of other women. In fact, this learning seems to begin even before birth. DeCasper and Fifer (1980) tape-recorded mothers reading a Dr. Seuss book, and then played back these tapes to newborns before they were 3 days old. Making the playback of the tapes contingent on the sucking of a pacifier, they found that babies sucked harder for recordings from their own mothers than for those from other mothers. Moreover, newborns preferred stories their mothers had read out loud even before they were born over stories that were new (DeCasper, Lecanuet, & Busnel, 1994). Thus, it appears that their prenatal auditory experience shaped their postnatal preference.

One method (Aslin et al., 1999) for studying these early auditory processes relies on the fact that babies tend to habituate to repeated stimuli from the same perceptual class. If the perceptual class of the stimulus suddenly changes, the baby will brighten up and turn to look at the new stimulus. To take advantage of this, experimenters can play back auditory stimuli through speakers placed either to the left or right of the baby. If the experimenter constructs a set of words that share a certain property and then shifts to words that have a different property, the infant may demonstrate awareness of the distinction by turning away from the old stimulus and orienting to the more interesting, new stimulus. For example, if the 6-month-old hears a sequence such as /badigudibagadigu-digagidu/ repeated many times, the parts that are repeated will stand out and affect later listening. In this example, the repeated string is /digudi/. If infants are trained on these strings, they will grow tired of this sound and will come to prefer to listen to new sound strings, rather than one with the old /digudi/ string. This habituation effect is strongest for stressed syllables and syllables immediately following stressed syllables (Jusczyk, 1997).

Words as Cues to Segmentation

The third stream of auditory development involves the storage of sounds as potential candidate words. This type of learning is crucial for the segmentation of speech into meaningful units. By 6 months, children are able to respond to their own name. Using the auditory codes they have developed, they can retain traces of words they have heard, although they may not yet have learned what these words mean. Recent attempts to model the growth of speech segmentation (Batchelder, 2002; Monaghan, Christiansen, & Chater, 2007) have shown that the ability to detect known words within new sequences is a crucial key to language learning. Brent and Siskind (2001) observed that nearly a quarter of the utterances presented to young children involve single words. These forms can be directly and accurately acquired without segmentation. Thus, if the mother points to a dog and says "doggie," the child can directly acquire this as a candidate word form. Then, when the child hears the combination "nice doggie," the familiar form "doggie" can be segmented out from the unfamiliar form "nice." This is what MacWhinney (1978) called the *segmentation of the known from the unknown*. The further task facing the child is then to link the unknown to a specific candidate meaning.

Articulatory Development

Although we have good experimental evidence for a growing auditory awareness in the infant, the first directly observable evidence of language-like behaviors occurs when the child vocalizes. At birth, the child is already capable of four distinct types of cries (Wäsz-Hockert, Lind, Vuoren-koski, Partanen, & Valanne, 1968): the birth cry, the pain cry, the hunger cry, and the pleasure cry. The birth cry occurs only at birth and involves the infant trying to clear out the embryonic fluid that has accumulated in the lungs and trachea. The pain cry can be elicited by pricking the baby with a pin. The hunger cry is a reliable indicator of the infant's need to be fed. The pleasure cry, which is softer and not too frequent at first, seems to be the cry from which later language develops. Moreover, using spectrographic analysis, one can distinguish children with genetic abnormalities such as *cri du chat* or Lesch–Nyan syndrome at this age through their cries (Wäsz-Hockert, Lind, Vuoren-koski, Partanen, & Valanne, 1968).

Fixed Action Patterns

Infant cry patterns can be understood from the framework of the study of animal behavior or ethology (Tinbergen, 1951). In that framework, animals are viewed as capable of producing certain fixed action patterns. For example, bucks have fixed action patterns for locking horns in combat. Birds have fixed action patterns for seed pecking and flying. In humans, fixed action patterns include sucking, crying, eye fixation, and crawling. These various fixed action patterns are typically elicited by what ethologists call *innate releasing mechanisms.* For example, the sight of the nipple of the mother's breast elicits sucking. Mothers respond to an infant's hunger cry by lactating. A pinprick on a baby's foot elicits the pain cry, and parents respond to this cry by picking up and cuddling the child. On this level, we can think of the origins of language as relatively phylogenetically ancient and stable.

During the first 3 months, a baby's vocalizations involve nothing more than cries and vegetative adaptations, such as sucking, chewing, and coughing. However, around 3 months (Lewis, 1936; McCarthy, 1954), at the time of the first social smile, babies begin to make delightful little sounds called "cooing." These sounds have no particular linguistic structure, but their well-integrated intonation makes them sure parent pleasers. During this time, the number and variety of vowel-like sounds the infant produces shows a marked increase. Unlike the vowels of crying, these vowels are produced from pleasure. Irwin (1936) noted that, up to 6 months, the infant's sounds are 90% back consonants like /g/ and /k/ and midvowels like /ɐ/ and /ə/.

Babbling and Cortical Control

At around 6 months of age, there is shift from back to front consonants. This shift may be a result of the shift from the dominance of spinal control of grosser synergisms like swallowing to cortical control of finer movements (Berry & Eisenson, 1956; Tucker, 2002). This shift to cortical control allows the baby to produce structured vocalizations, including a larger diversity of individual vowels and consonants, mostly in the shape of the consonant-vowel (CV) syllables like /ta/ or /pe/. As the frequency of these structured syllable-like vocalizations increases, we begin to say that the infant is babbling. Neural control of early babbling is built on top of patterns of noisy lip-smacking that are present in many primates (MacNeilage, 1998). These CV vocal gestures (Hoyer & Hoyer, 1924) include some form of vocal closure followed by a release with vocalic resonance.

Until the sixth month, deaf infants babble much like hearing children (Oller & Eilers, 1988). However, well before 9 months, deaf infants lose their interest in babbling, diverging more and more from the normal pathway (Mavilya, 1972). This suggests that their earlier babbling is sustained through proprioceptive and somesthetic feedback, as the babies explore the various ways in which they can play with their mouth. After 6 months, babbling relies increasingly on auditory feedback. During this period, the infant tries to produce specific sounds to match up with specific auditory impressions. It is at this point that the deaf child no longer finds babbling entertaining, because it is not linked to auditory feedback. These facts suggest that, from the infant's point of view, babbling is essentially a process of exploring the coordinated use of the mouth, lungs, and larynx.

In the heyday of behaviorism, researchers viewed the development of babbling in terms of reinforcement theory. For example, Mowrer (1960) thought that babbling was driven by the infant's attempt to create sounds like those made by their mothers. In behaviorist terms, this involves secondary goal reinforcement. Other behaviorists thought that parents would differentially reinforce or shape babbling through smiles or other rewards. They thought that these reinforcements would lead a Chinese baby to babble the sounds of Chinese, whereas a Quechua baby would babble the sounds of Quechua. This was the theory of "babbling drift." However, closer observation has indicated that this drift toward the native language does not occur clearly until after 10 months (Boysson-Bardies & Vihman, 1991). After 12 months, we see a strong drift in the direction of the native language as the infant begins to acquire the first words. Opponents of behaviorism (Jakobson, 1968) stressed the universal nature of babbling, suggesting that all children engage in babbling all the sounds of all the world's languages. However, this alternative position also seems to be too strong. Although it is certainly true that some English-learning infants will produce Bantu clicks and Quechua implosives, not all children produce all of these sounds (Cruttenden, 1970).

Although vowels can be acquired directly as whole stable units in production, consonants can be articulated only in combinations with vowels, as pieces of whole syllables. The information regarding the place of articulation for all consonants except fricatives (Cole & Scott, 1974) is concentrated in the formant transitions that occur before and after the steady state of the vowel. In CV syllables like /pa/ or /ko/, each different consonant will be marked by different patterns of transitions before and after different vowels. Thus, in /di/, the second format rises in frequency before the steady state of the vowel, whereas in /du/, the second formant falls before the vowel. Massaro (1975) argued that this blending makes the syllable the natural unit of perception, as well as the likely initial unit of acquisition. By learning syllables as complete packages, the child avoids the problem of finding acoustic invariance for specific phonemes. If the syllable is, in fact, the basic unit of perception, we would expect to find that auditory storage would last at least 200 ms, or about as long as the syllable. In fact, it appears that there is a form of auditory storage that lasts about 250 ms (Massaro, 1975), indicating that it may be adapted to encode and process syllables.

Ongoing practice with whole syllables occurs throughout the babbling period that extends from around 4 months to the end of the first year. In languages like Japanese, which has only 77 syllable types, this learning may allow the child to control some significant part of adult phonology. In English, with more than 7,000 possible syllables, learning of the language through the acquisition of syllables seems to be a less realistic goal.

Infants commonly produce syllables sounding like /ba/ and /di/, but are relatively less likely to produce /bi/, probably because making a /b/ results in a tongue position well suited to following with /a/ but not /i/ (MacNeilage, Davis, Kinney, & Matyear, 2000). Vihman (1996) studied infants and toddlers learning Japanese, French, Swedish, and English. A very small number of syllables accounted for half of those produced in all the groups, and the two most frequent syllables, /da/ and /ba/, were used by all language groups. These patterns suggest that infants use a basic motor template to produce syllables. These same constraints also affect the composition of the first words (Oller, 2000).

Between 6 and 10 months of age, there seems to be a tight linkage between babbling and general motoric arousal. The child will move arms, head, and legs while babbling, as if babbling is just another way of getting exercise while aroused. During the last months of the first year, the structure of babbling becomes clearer, more controlled, and more organized. Some children produce repetitive syllable strings, such as /badibadibadibadigu/; others seem to be playing around with intonation and the features of particular articulations.

Circular Reactions

Piaget's (1952) theory of sensorimotor learning provides an interesting account of many of these developments. Piaget viewed much of early learning as based on circular reactions in which the child learned to coordinate the movements of one process or schema with another. In the case of babbling, the child is coordinating the movements of the mouth with their proprioceptive and auditory effects. In these circular reactions, the child functions as a "little scientist" who is observing and retracing the relations between one schema and another. For example, in the first month, the newborn will assimilate the schema of hand motion to the sucking schema. In babbling, the child assimilates the schema of mouth motions to the perceptual schema of audition, proprioception, and oral somesthesia. There is much to support this view. It seems to be particularly on the mark for those periods of late babbling when the child is experimenting with sounds that are found in other languages. Also, the fact that deaf babies continue to babble normally until about 6 months also tends to support this view.

Phonotactic Processes

The child's first words can be viewed as renditions of adult forms that have gone through a series of simplifications and transformations. Some of these simplifications lead to the dropping of difficult sounds. For example, the word *stone* is produced as *tone*. In other cases, the simplifications involve making one sound similar to those around it. For example, *top* may be produced as *pop* through regressive assimilation. Assimilation is a process that results in the features of one sound being adapted or assimilated to resemble those of another sound. In this case, the labial quality of the final /p/ is assimilated backward to the initial /t/, replacing its dental articulation with a labial articulation. We can refer to these various types of assimilations and simplifications as "phonological processes" (Menn & Stoel-Gammon, 1995; Stampe, 1973). Many of these processes or predispositions seem to be based on something like the principle of "least effort" (Ponori, 1871). A proper theory of least effort has to be grounded on an independent phonetic account of effort expenditure. Ohala (1974, 1981, 1994) has explored many of the components of this theory. However, most child phonologists have not yet made use of phonetically grounded principles, preferring to construct abstract accounts based on Optimality Theory (Kager, 1999).

The child's problems with phonological form are very much focused on production, rather than perception. An illustration of this comes from the anecdote in which a father and his son are watching boats in the harbor. The child says, "Look at the big sip." Echoing his son's pronunciation, the father says, *"Yes, it's quite a big sip."* To this, the child protests, saying, "No, Daddy say 'sip' not 'sip.'" Such anecdotes underscore the extent to which the child's auditory forms for words line up with the adult standard, even if their actual productions are far from perfect.

Detailed observations of the course of phonological development have shown that the development of individual word forms does not follow a simple course toward the correct adult standard. Sometimes there are detours and regressions from the standard. For example, a child may start by producing *step* accurately. Later, under the influence of pressures for simplification of the initial consonant cluster, the child will regress to production of *step* as *tep*. Finally, *step* will reassert itself. This pattern of good performance, followed by poorer performance, and then finally good performance again is known as "U-shaped learning," because a graph of changes in accuracy across time resembles the letter U. The same forces that induce U-shaped learning can also lead to patterns in which a word is systematically pronounced incorrectly, even though the child is capable of the correct pronunciation. For example, Smith (1973) reported that his son systematically produced the word *puddle* as *puggle*. However, he showed that he was able to produce *puddle* as an incorrect attempt at *puzzle*. One possible interpretation of this pattern is that the child produces *puggle* in an attempt to distinguish it from *puddle* as the incorrect pronunciation of *puzzle*. Here, as elsewhere in language development, the child's desire to mark clear linguistic contrasts may occasionally lead to errors.

Word Learning

The emergence of the first word is based on three earlier developments. The first is the infant's growing ability to record the sounds of words. The second is the development of an ability to control vocal productions that occurs in the late stages of babbling. The third is the general growth of the symbolic function, as represented in play, imitation, and object manipulation. Piaget (1954) characterized the infant's cognitive development in terms of the growth of representation or the "object concept." In the first 6 months of life, the child is unable to think about objects that are not physically present. However, a 12-month-old will see a dog's tail sticking out from behind a chair and realize that the rest of the dog is hiding behind the chair. This understanding of how parts relate to wholes supports the child's first major use of the symbolic function. When playing with toys, the 12-month-old will begin to produce sounds such as *vroom* or *bam-bam* that represent properties of these toys and actions. Often, these phonologically consistent forms appear before the first real words. Because they have no clear conventional status, parents may tend to ignore these first symbolic attempts as nothing more than spurious productions or babbling.

Even before producing the first conventional word, the 12-month-old has already acquired an ability to comprehend perhaps a dozen conventional forms. During this period, parents often realize that the prelinguistic infants are beginning to understand what they say. However, it is difficult for parents to provide convincing evidence of this ability. Researchers deal with this problem by bringing infants into the laboratory, placing them into comfortable highchairs, and asking them to look at pictures, using the technique of visually reinforced preferential looking. A word such as *dog* is broadcast across loudspeakers. Pictures of two objects are then displayed. In this case, a dog may be on the screen to the right of the baby and a car may be on the screen to the left. If the child looks at the picture that matches the word, a toy bunny pops up and does an amusing drum roll. This convinces babies that they have chosen correctly and they then continue looking at the named picture on each trial. Some children get fussy after only a few trials, but others last for 10 trials or more at one sitting and provide reliable evidence that they know a few words. Many children demonstrate this level of understanding by the 10th month—2 or 3 months before they have produced their first recognizable word.

Given the fact that the 10-month-old is already able to comprehend several words, why is the first recognizable conventional word not produced until several months later? Undoubtedly, many of the child's first attempts to match an articulation with an auditory target fall on deaf ears. Many are so far away from the correct target that even the most supportive parent cannot divine the relation. Eventually, the child produces a clear articulation that makes sense in context. The parent is amazed and smiles. The child is reinforced and the first word is officially christened. But all is still not smooth sailing. The challenges of word production discussed earlier make early words difficult to recognize. Rather than having to go through sessions of repeated noncomprehension, children may spend a month or two consolidating their conceptual and phonological systems in preparation for an attack on the adult target. However, most children do not go through this silent period. Instead, late babbling tends to coexist with the first words in most cases.

One way of understanding the challenge presented by the first words views the problem from the perspective of the infant. When babbling, the only constraints infants face are those arising from their own playfulness and interest. There are no socially defined constraints on the range of variation of those sounds. Some babies may try to get each sound "just right," but they do this to match their own goals and not ones imposed from outside. When the task shifts to making use of conventional words, the constraints come from unclarity about meaning, variability in the perception of the sound, and the problem of matching the adult articulations. Thus, babbling provides the child with only a small part of the foundation for use of the first words.

It is easy to assume that children have some innate knowledge that tells them that words will always involve some spoken verbal form. However, an innate constraint of this type would severely limit the learning of sign language by deaf children. It would also inhibit gestural learning by hearing children. Rather than obeying some narrow view of the possible shape of a word, children are willing to learn all sorts of meaningful relations between signs and the objects that they represent. For example, Namy and Waxman (1998) found that normal 18-month-olds are happy to learn gestures as object labels. Similarly, Woodward and Hoyne (1999) found that 13-month-olds are happy to respond to the sound produced by an object as if it were its name.

Discovering Meanings

From Plato to Quine, philosophers have considered the task of figuring out word meaning to be a core intellectual challenge. For example, if the child were to allow for the possibility that word meanings might include disjunctive Boolean predicates (Hunt, 1962), then it might be the case that the word grue would have the meaning "green before the year 2000 and blue thereafter." Similarly, it might be the case that the name for any object would refer not to the object itself, but to its various undetached parts. When one

thinks about word learning in this abstract way, it appears to be impossibly hard.

Quine (1960) illustrated the problem by imagining a scenario in which a hunter is out on safari with a native guide. Suddenly, the guide shouts "Gavagai" and the hunter, who does not know the native language, has to quickly infer the meaning of the word. Does it mean "shoot now," or "there's a rhino," or perhaps even "it got away"? If the word refers to the rhino, does it point to the horn, the hooves, the skin, or the whole animal? Worse still, the word could refer to the horn of a rhino if it is before noon and the tail of a jackal after noon. Without some additional cues regarding the likely meaning of the word, how can the poor hunter figure this out?

Fortunately, the toddler has more cues to rely on than the hunter. The first person to recognize the shape of these cues was Augustine, the great Church father, who wrote this in his *Confessions* (1952, original AD 397):

> This I remember; and have since observed how I learned to speak. It was not that my elders taught me words (as, soon after, other learning) in any set method; but I, longing by cries and broken accents and various motions of my limbs to express my thoughts, that so I might have my will, and yet unable to express all I willed or to whom I willed, did myself, by the understanding which Thou, my God, gavest me, practice the sounds in my memory. When they named anything, and as they spoke turned towards it, I saw and remembered that they called what they would point out by the name they uttered. And that they meant this thing, and no other, was plain from the motion of their body, the natural language, as it were, of all nations, expressed by the countenance, glances of the eye, gestures of the limbs, and tones of the voice, indicating the affections of the mind as it pursues, possesses, rejects, or shuns. And thus by constantly hearing words, as they occurred in various sentences, I collected gradually for what they stood; and, having broken in my mouth to these signs, I thereby gave utterance to my will. Thus I exchanged with those about me these current signs of our wills, and so launched deeper into the stormy intercourse of human life, yet depending on parental authority and the beck of elders. (1952, p. 8)

Augustine's reflections are remarkable for several reasons. First, he emphasizes the natural, emergent nature of word learning situated directly in situational contexts. Second, he understood the importance of a preliminary period of auditory learning, followed then by an arduous process of articulatory control. Third, he focused on the learning of words in the direct presence of the referent

(Cartwright & Brent, 1997; Huttenlocher, 1974). Fourth, to further confirm shared attention on a candidate referent, he made use of a variety of gestural and postural cues from his elders.

Recent research has supported and elaborated Augustine's intuitions. The ability to follow eye gaze appears to rely on fundamental developments in the visual system that emerge in the first 4 months of life (Johnson, 1992). These developmental changes involve the linkage of basic phylogenetic abilities to ongoing epigenesis. Similar changes arise in the tracking of postural cues and pointing. By the time the child comes to learn the first words, these cues are generally accessible. Baldwin (1991; Baldwin & Markman, 1989) has shown that children try to acquire names for the objects that adults are attending to. Similarly, Akhtar, Carpenter, and Tomasello (1996) and Tomasello and Akhtar (1995) have emphasized the crucial role of mutual gaze between mother and child in the support of early word learning. Bates, Benigni, Bretherton, Camaioni, and Volterra (1979) showed how 10-month-olds would reliably follow eye gazes, pointing, and gesturing. Gogate, Bahrick, and Watson (2000) showed that, when mothers teach infants a name for a novel toy, they tend to move the toy as they name it, much as Augustine suggested.

One hardly needs to conduct studies to demonstrate the role of gaze, intonation, and pointing, because these cues are so obvious to all of us. However, a second aspect of Augustine's analysis is subtler and less fully appreciated. This is the extent to which children seek to divine the intention of the adult as a way of understanding a word's meaning. They want to make sure that the adult is directly attending to an object, before they decide to learn a new word (Baldwin et al., 1996). If the adult is speaking from behind a screen, children are uncertain about the adult's intentions and fail to learn the new word. Tomasello and Ahktar (1995) illustrated this by teaching 2-year-olds a new verb such as *hoisting*. In some of the trials, the toy character would inadvertently swing away and the experimenter would say "whoops." In those trials, the children would not associate *hoisting* with the failed demonstration. Generalizing from these studies, Tomasello (1999, 2003) and Bloom (2002) have argued that word learning depends primarily on the child's ability to decode the parent's intentions. Further support for this view comes from the fact that autistic children have problems picking up on both gestural and intentional cues, possibly because of the fact that they have incompletely constructed models of the goals and intentions of other people (Baron-Cohen, Baldwin, & Crowson, 1997; Frith & Frith, 1999).

Initial Mapping

Laboratory studies of word learning typically rely on a process of relatively fast initial mapping of a new word to a new meaning. This is the type of quick, but superficial, word learning that occurs when a child encounters a new word for the first time. The initial mapping process involves the association of auditory units to conceptual units (Naigles & Gelman, 1995; Reznick, 1990). For example, the 14-month-old can be brought into the laboratory (Schafer & Plunkett, 1998) and shown a picture of an animal called a "tiv." The child will then demonstrate understanding of the new word by turning to a picture of the new animal, rather than a picture of a dog, when hearing the word "tiv." In these laboratory experiments, children are learning a new concept in parallel with a new word. However, in the real world, children often have developed a clear idea about a concept well before they have learned the word for that concept. The child comes to the task of word learning already possessing a fairly well-structured coding of the basic objects in the immediate environment (Piaget, 1954; Stiles-Davis, Sugarman, & Nass, 1985; Sugarman, 1982). Children treat objects such as dogs, plates, chairs, cars, baby food, water, balls, and shoes as fully structured, separate categories (Mervis, 1984). They also show good awareness of the nature of particular activities such as falling, bathing, eating, kissing, and sleeping. This means that, in reality, conceptual organization often precedes lexical mapping. Thus, word learning is usually not the mapping of a new word to a new meaning, but the mapping of a new word to an old meaning. Moreover, in some cases, the sound of the word may already be a bit familiar and the learning really involves the mapping of an old form to an old meaning. Because natural learning is difficult to control, there have been relatively few studies of this more natural process.

Undergeneralization, Generalization, and Overgeneralization

Because of this specificity, early word uses are often highly *undergeneralized* (Dromi, 1987; Kay & Anglin, 1982). For example, a child may think that *dog* is the name for the family pet or that *car* refers only to vehicles parked at a specific point outside a particular balcony (L. Bloom, 1973). It is sometimes difficult to detect undergeneralization, because it never leads to errors. Instead, it simply leads to a pattern of idiosyncratic limitations on word usage. Early undergeneralizations are gradually corrected as the child hears the words used in a variety of contexts. Each new context is compared with the current meaning. Those features that match are strengthened (MacWhinney, 1989) and those that do not match are weakened. When a feature becomes sufficiently weak, it drops out altogether.

This process of generalization is guided by the same cues that led to initial attention to the word. For example, it could be the case that every time the child hears the word *apple*, some light is on in the room. However, in none of these cases do the adults focus their attention on the light. Thus, the presence or absence of a light is not a central element of the meaning of *apple*. The child may also occasionally hear the word *apple* used even when the object is not present. If, at that time, attention is focused on some other object that was accidentally associated with *apple*, the process of generalization could derail. However, cases of this type are rare. The more common case involves use of *apple* in a context that totally mismatches the earlier uses. In that case, the child simply assumes nothing and ignores the new exemplar (Stager & Werker, 1997).

Gradually, the process of generalization leads to a freeing of the word from irrelevant aspects of the context. Over time, words develop a separation between a "confirmed core" (MacWhinney, 1984, 1989) and a peripheral area of potential generalization. As the confirmed core of the meaning of a word widens and as irrelevant contextual features are pruned out, the word begins to take on a radial or prototype form (Lakoff, 1987; Rosch & Mervis, 1975). In the center of the category, we find the best instances that display the maximum category match. At the periphery of the category, we find instances whose category membership is unclear and which compete with neighboring categories (MacWhinney, 1989).

According to this core-periphery model of lexical structure, overgeneralizations arise from the pressures that force the child to communicate about objects that are not inside any confirmed core. Frequently enough, children's overgeneralizations are corrected when the parent provides the correct name for the object (Brown & Hanlon, 1970). The fact that feedback is so consistently available for word learning increases our willingness to believe that the major determinants of word learning are social feedback, rather than innate constraints or even word learning biases.

This process of initial undergeneralization and gradual generalization is the primary stream of semantic development. However, often children need to go outside this primary stream to find ways of expressing meanings that they do not yet fully control. When they do this, they produce *overgeneralizations*. For example, children may overgeneralize (and alarm their parents) by referring to tigers as *kitties*. Although overgeneralizations are not as frequent as undergeneralizations, they are easier to spot because they always produce errors. Overgeneralization errors arise because they have not yet learned the words they need to express their intentions. It is not that the child actually thinks that the tiger is a kitty. It is just that the child has not yet learned the word *tiger* and would still like to be able to draw the parent's attention to this interesting catlike animal.

The smaller the child's vocabulary, the more impressionistic and global will be the nature of these overgeneralizations. For example, Ament (1899) reported that his son learned the word *duck* when seeing some birds on a lake. Later, he used the word to refer to other ponds and streams, other birds, and coins with birds on them. Bowerman (1978b) reports that her daughter Eve used *moon* to talk about a lemon slice, the moon, the dial of a dishwasher, pieces of toenail on a rug, and a bright street light. But this does not necessarily mean that the child actually thinks that *duck* refers to both lakes and birds or that *moon* refers to both lemon slices and hangnails. Rather, the child is using one of the few words available to describe features of new objects. As the child's vocabulary grows in size, overgeneralization patterns of this type disappear, although more restricted forms of overgeneralization continue throughout childhood.

This model of overgeneralization assumes that the child understands the difference between a *confirmed core* of features for a word and the area of potential further generalization. The confirmed core extends to referents that have been repeatedly named with the relevant word. The area of extension is an area outside this core where no other word directly competes and where extension is at least a possibility.

Flexible Learning

As the child begins to learn new words, the process of learning itself produces new generalizations (Smith, 1999). For example, children soon come to realize that new words almost always refer to whole objects. There is no reason to think that this is some genetically determined, species-specific constraint. Early on, children realize that objects typically function as perceptual wholes. However, a cautious learner will always realize that this assumption can sometimes be wrong. For example, one evening, I was sitting on a Victorian couch in our living room with my son Ross, aged 2.0, when he pointed to the arm of the couch, asking "couch?"

He then pointed at the back and then the legs, again asking if they were also "couch." Each time, I assured him that the part to which he was attending was, indeed, a part of a *couch.* After verifying each component, he seemed satisfied. In retrospect, it is possible that he was asking me to provide names for the subparts of the couch. However, like most parents, I tried to focus his attention on the whole object, rather than the parts. Perhaps, I should have first taught him that all of the parts were pieces of couch and then gone on to provide additional names for the subparts, such as *arm, seat, back*, and *edge*, ending with a reaffirmation of the fact that all of these parts composed a *couch.*

Learning to learn can also induce the child to treat early word meanings in terms of common object functions. For example, Brown (1958) noted that parents typically label objects at the level of their most common function. Thus, parents will refer to *chairs*, but avoid *furniture* or *stool*, because *chair* best captures the level of prototypical usage of a class of objects (Adams & Bullock, 1986). As a result, children also come to realize that the names for artificial objects refer to their functions and not to their shape, texture, or size.

Children are also quick to pick up on a variety of other obvious correlations. They learn that the color of artificial objects such as cars and dresses can vary widely, but that many animals have unique colorings and patterns. They learn that any new word for an object can also refer to a toy characterizing that object or a picture of the object. They learn that people can have multiple names, including titles and nicknames. They learn that actions are mapped onto the human perspective (MacWhinney, 1999a), and that the meanings of adjectives are modulated by the baseline nature of the object modified. Generally speaking, children must adopt a highly flexible, bottom-up approach to the learning of word meanings (Maratsos & Deak, 1995), attending to all available cues, because words themselves are such flexible things.

This flexibility also shows up in the child's handling of cues to object word naming. Because shape is a powerful defining characteristic for so many objects, children learn to attend closely to this attribute. However, children can easily be induced to attend instead to substance, size, or texture, rather than shape. For example, Smith (1999) was able to show how children could be induced, through repeated experiences with substance, to classify new words not in terms of their shape but in terms of their substance.

Children's Agenda

The view of the child as a flexible word learner has to be balanced against the view of the child as having definite personal agenda. Like Augustine, children often see language as a way of expressing their own desires, interests, and opinions. In some extreme cases, children may adopt the position espoused by Humpty Dumpty, when he chastises Alice for failing to take charge over the meanings of words. As Humpty Dumpty puts it, "When I use a word, it means just what I choose it to mean—neither more nor less."

Fortunately, the agenda that children seek to express through early words match up closely with what their parents expect them to express. During the months before the first words, the child may use certain gestures and intonational patterns to express core agenda items such as desire, question, and attention focusing (Halliday, 1975). Later, children seem to seek out words for talking about fingers, hands, balls, animals, bottles, parents, siblings, and food. Much of this early agendum appears to focus initially on the learning of nouns, rather than verbs or other parts of speech. Gentner (1982) argues that this is because it is easier to map a noun to a constant referent. A variant of Gentner's position holds that nouns are learned more readily because it is easier for children to figure out what people are talking about when they use nouns than when they use verbs. Moreover, nouns tend to be used the same categorical and taxonomic ways (Sandhofer, Smith, & Luo, 2000), whereas verbs refer to a wider range of conceptual structures, including wishes, movements, states, transitions, and beliefs.

Input factors play a role as well. Studies of languages other than English show that sometimes children do not produce more nouns than verbs. For example, children learning Korean (Gopnik & Choi, 1995) and Mandarin Chinese (Tardif, 1996) may produce more verbs than nouns under certain conditions of elicitation. Two plausible explanations for this phenomenon have been offered. First, in both Korean and Mandarin, verbs are much more likely to appear at the ends of utterances than in English, where the last word in input sentences tends to be a noun (Nicoladis, 2001). Perceptual studies (Jusczyk, 1997) have shown that it is easier for children to recognize familiar words at the ends of sentences, suggesting that this structural feature of languages influences rates of word learning as well. Second, Korean and Mandarin mothers tend to talk about actions more than do English mothers, who tend to focus on labeling things. Goldfield (1993) showed that American mothers who used more nouns tended to have infants with a higher proportion of nouns in their vocabularies.

Whorf versus Humpty Dumpty

As learning progresses, the child's agendum becomes less important than the shape of the resources provided by the language. For example, languages like Salish or Navajo expect the child to learn verbs instead of nouns. Moreover, the verbs children will learn focus more on position, shape, and containment than do verbs in English. For example, the verb "'ahééníshtiih" in Navajo refers to "carrying around in a circle any long straight object such as a gun." The presence of obligatory grammatical markings in languages for concepts such as tense, aspect, number, gender, and definiteness can orient the child's thinking in certain paths at the expense of others. Whorf (1967) suggested that the forms of language may end up shaping the structure of thought. Such effects are directly opposed to the Humpty Dumpty agenda-based approach to language. Probably the truth involves a dynamic interaction between Whorf and Humpty Dumpty. Important though language-specific effects may be, all children end up being able to express basic ideas equally well, no matter what language they learn.

Learning from Syntactic Contexts

Shared reference is not the only cue toddlers can use to delineate the meanings of words. They can also use the form of utterances to pick out the correct referents for new words. Consider these contexts:

1. Here is a pum. — count noun
2. Here is Pum. — proper noun
3. I am pumming. — intransitive verb
4. I pummed the duck. — transitive (causative) verb
5. I need some pum. — mass noun
6. This is the pum one. — adjective

Each of these sentential contexts provides clear evidence that *pum* is a particular part of speech. Other sentential frames can give an even more precise meaning. If the child hears, "This is not green, it is pum," it is clear that *pum* is a color. If the child hears, "Please don't cover it, just pum it lightly," then the child knows that *pum* is a verb of the same general class as *cover*. The use of cues of this type leads to a fast, but shallow, mapping of new words to new meanings. Learning of this type was first identified in 3-year-olds by Brown (1973) and later in children younger than 2 by Katz, Baker, and Macnamara (1974). Carey (1978) later used the term *fast mapping* to refer to this induction of word meaning from syntactic context. The idea here is that the child can quickly pick up a general idea of the meaning of a new word in this way, although it may take additional time to acquire the

fuller meaning of the word. Fast learning has also been identified in much younger children (Schafer & Plunkett, 1998). However, before age 2, fast mapping depends only on memory for the referent itself and not on induction from syntactic frames.

Words as Invitations to Learning

In a very real sense, words function as invitations for the construction of new categories. The child soon realizes that each new word is a pointer into a whole set of related objects or events that share some discoverable similarity. The more words the child learns, the clearer this effect becomes. New words for animals, like *hedgehog* and *dolphin* invite an exploration of the habits, shapes, colors, and activities of that animal. New words for physical actions, like *gallop* and *knit*, invite an exploration of the ways in which the body can use these motions to act on other objects. Research has shown that the mere presence of a word can induce sharper and more consistent concept formation. For example, Waxman and Kosowski (1990) gave children two stories. In the first story, they used the word *dobutsu* as a label, saying, "There's a being from another planet who wants some dobutsus. I don't know what dobutsus means, but he likes things like a dog, a duck, or a horse. Can you find him something he wants?" In the second story, they provided no label, saying, "This puppet only likes things like dogs, ducks, and horses. Can you find him something he likes?" Children were much more likely to point to another animal when the label *dobutsu* was used than when no label was provided. This effect has also been demonstrated for infants (Waxman & Markow, 1995) and echoed in several further studies, all of which emphasize the role that words play as invitations to categorization and cognition (Gentner, 2005).

Competition and Mutual Exclusivity

Even the most complete set of syntactic cues and the fullest level of shared attention cannot completely preclude the occasional confusion about word meanings. Some of the most difficult conflicts between words involve the use of multiple words for the same object. For example, a child may know the word *hippo* and hear a hippo toy referred to as a *toy*. But this does not lead the child to stop calling the toy a *hippo* and start calling it a *toy*. Some have suggested that children are prevented from making this type of error by the presence of a universal constraint called *mutual exclusivity*. This constraint holds that each object can have only one name. If a child hears a second name for the old object, they can either reject the new name as wrong or else find some distinction that disambiguates the new name from the old. If mutual exclusivity were an important constraint on word meaning, we would expect children to show a strong tendency toward the first solution—rejection. However, few children illustrate such a preference. The fact is that objects almost always have more than one name. For example, a *fork* is also *silverware* and a *dog* is also an *animal*. Linguistic structures expressing a wide variety of taxonomic and metonymic relations represent a fundamental and principled violation of the proposed mutual exclusivity constraint. The most consistent violations occur for bilingual children who learn that everything in their world must, by necessity, have at least two names. Mutual exclusivity is clearly not a basic property of natural language.

One reason why researchers have devoted so much attention to mutual exclusivity stems from the shape of the laboratory situation in which word learning is studied. The child is presented with a series of objects, some old and some new, given a word that is either old or new, and then asked to match up the word with an object. For example, the child may be given a teacup, a glass, and a demitasse. She already knows the words *cup* and *glass*. The experimenter asks her, "Give me the demitasse." She will then correctly infer that *demitasse* refers to the object for which she does not have a well-established name. In this context, it makes sense to use the new name as the label for some new object.

Instead of thinking in terms of mutual exclusivity, the child appears to be thinking in terms of competition between words, with each word vying for a particular semantic niche (Merriman, 1999). At the same time, the child is thinking in terms of the pragmatics of mutual cooperation (Clark, 1987). When two words are in head-on conflict and no additional disambiguating cues are provided, it makes sense for the child to assume that the adult is being reasonable and using the new name for the new object (Golinkoff, Hirsh-Pasek, & Hollich, 1999). The child assumes that the cooperative experimenter knows that the child has words for cups and glasses, so it only makes sense that the new word is for the new object.

In the real world, competition forces the child to move meanings around so that they occupy the correct semantic niche. When the parent calls the toy hippo a *toy*, the child searches for something to disambiguate the two words. For example, the parent may say, "Can you give me another toy?" or even "Please clean up your toys." In each case, *toy* refers not just to the hippo, but also potentially to many other toys. This allows the child to shift perspective and to

understand the word *toy* in the framework of the shifted perspective. Consider the case of a rocking horse. This object may be called *toy, horsey,* or even *chair,* depending on how it is being used at the moment (Clark, 1997). This flexible use of labeling is an important ingredient in language learning. By learning how to shift perspectives, children develop powerful tools for dealing with the competitions between words. In this way, conflicts between meanings create complex structures and cognitive flexibility.

Building Theories

As children learn more and more words, they begin to develop clearer ideas about the ways in which words can refer to objects, properties, and events. The meanings of organized groups of words come to represent many aspects of the cognitive structure of the child's world. Children begin to realize that certain properties of objects are more fundamental and inherent than others. For example, Keil and Batterman (1984) talked to children about a cat that had been given a skunk's tail, nose, and fur. Before the age of 5, children believed that this animal would now actually be a skunk. After age 5, children began to realize that mere addition of these features would not change the fact that the animal was still inherently a cat. In effect, children are beginning to develop belief in a scientific theory that holds that animals cannot change their genetic status through simple transformations. Theories also provide children with conceptual structures they can use to infer the properties of new words. For example, if a child is told that a *dobro* is a fish, then they can also infer that the *dobro* swims and has gills (Gelman, 1998).

Milestones in Vocabulary Growth

Typically, the child demonstrates new language abilities first in comprehension and then only later in production. For example, children comprehend their first words by 9 months or even earlier, but produce the first word only after 12 months. Children are able to comprehend 50 words by about 15 months but do not produce 50 words in their own speech until about 20 months. More generally, children acquire words into their receptive vocabulary more than twice as fast as into their productive vocabulary.

Children tend to produce their first words sometime between 9 and 12 months. One-year-olds have about 5 words in their vocabulary, on average, although individual children may have none or as many as 30; by 2 years, average vocabulary size is more than 150 words, with a range among individual children from as few as 10 to as many as 450 words. Children possess a vocabulary of about 14,000 words by 6 years of age (Templin, 1957); adults have an estimated average of 40,000 words in their working vocabulary at age 40 (McCarthy, 1954). To achieve such a vocabulary, a child must learn to say at least three new words each day from birth.

The growth of children's vocabulary is heavily dependent on specific conversational input. The more input the child receives, the larger the vocabulary (Huttenlocher, Haight, Bryk, Seltzer, & Lyons, 1991). Children from higher socioeconomic status groups tend to have more input and a more advanced vocabulary (Arriaga, Fenson, Cronan, & Pethick, 1998). More educated families provide as much as three times more input than less educated families (Hart & Risley, 1995). Social interaction (quality of attachment, parent responsiveness, involvement, sensitivity, control style) and general intellectual climate (providing enriching toys, reading books, encouraging attention to surroundings) predict developing language competence in children as well (van IJzendoorn, Dijkstra, & Bus, 1995). Children with verbally responsive mothers achieve the vocabulary spurt and combine words into simple sentences sooner than do children with less verbally responsive mothers (Tamis-LeMonda & Bornstein, 2002). These facts have led educators to suspect that basic and pervasive differences in the level of social support for language learning lie at the root of many learning problems in the later school years.

Word Learning in School

Researchers have been focusing on word learning in the first 5 years. This focus on preschoolers tends to ignore the extent to which schooling shapes word meanings. Even for basic concepts such as "cat," schooling can bring about fundamental changes in conceptual structure. For example, Keil (1989) asked children whether a cat that had the fur of a skunk and the shape of a skunk would still be a cat. Preschoolers concluded that the cat would now be a skunk. However, 7-year-olds refused to accept the idea that the change of fur and shape would alter the internal nature of the cat. Schoolchildren will first support their position by just saying that once you are a cat you are always a cat. However, later, they will make reference to scientific constructs such as genetics and DNA to support their view. There is good reason to believe that schooling supports this shift toward essentialism (Astuti, Solomon, & Carey, 2004).

To understand how schooling operates in real time, researchers have begun to rely on detailed analyses of classroom conversations about mathematical and scientific concepts. These analyses are based on transcripts linked to video, which can be viewed directly from http://talkbank. org (using the online browser, the materials discussed in the current example are in ClassBank/JLS). Let us consider one particular instance of a detailed study of lessons by Paul McCabe and Kay McClain in a seventh-grade classroom studying terminology for describing statistical distributions. The students have been interacting for several weeks with a computer interface that allows them to vary treatments and observe outcome effects. In the current lesson, the teacher is discussing a projected graph of battery life for two types of flashlight batteries. Tests of 30 units of the Always Ready batteries showed that 8 lasted longer than 6 hours, although 10 lasted less than 4 hours. Tests of 20 units of the Tough Cells batteries showed that none of them lasted less than 4 hours, although only 3 lasted longer than 6 hours.

The teacher begins the discussion by asking which of the two batteries is more *dependable*. Caesara responds that the Always Ready batteries are more *dependable* because they yielded more "good ones." This interpretation of the concept of *dependability* fails to pay attention to the notion of a minimal performance standard. For example, if you were exploring a cave with a flashlight, you might want to make sure that your battery would not give out in the middle of your 4-hour exploration. If it did, you would call it *undependable*. Understanding this perspective, Blake counters Caesara's position when he notes that, "All of the Tough Cell is above 80." At this point, the teacher asks other students to clarify Caesara's position. Sequoria uses a set of hand gestures to draw a picture of the distribution of batteries in the air and to then point deictically to the segment of the distribution that Caesara is emphasizing. Although Caesara does not overtly withdraw her analysis during this discussion, Blake's provision of a clear account of the meaning of *dependable* and *dependability* helped the class move toward a fuller, statistically grounded understanding of these terms.

In this video interaction, we see a wide range of social forces impinging on the collaborative process of discovering meanings. Forces of gender, age, ethnicity, and group membership are evident in the discussion. The teacher plays a unique role in terms of her ability to recognize students who want to make contributions, revoice their contributions, and question their positions. In this study, Sfard and McClain (2002) tracked learning and reasoning from graphs and charts over several weeks. By examining the growth of interlocked concepts such as "distribution," "effectiveness," and "dependability" over this entire period across various students, we can gain a clearer idea of the process of word learning in the school years.

Increased input during early childhood leads to increases in vocabulary growth and other aspects of language structure. These differences in input quantity and quality continue to widen as children get older, with children from higher socioeconomic status and more educated families receiving more instruction both in the home and in the school in language forms, reading, literature, and composition (Dickinson & Moreton, 1993).

As children move on to higher stages of language development and the acquisition of literacy, they depend increasingly on wider social institutions. They may rely on Sunday school teachers as their source of knowledge about biblical language, prophets, and the geography of the Holy Land. They will rely on science teachers to gain vocabulary and understandings about friction, molecular structures, the circulatory system, and DNA (Keil, 1989). The vocabulary demands placed by such materials can be enormous, with textbooks in biology requiring the learning of as many as 800 technical terms.

Students will rely on peers to introduce them to the language of the streets, verbal dueling, and the use of language for courtship. They will rely on the media for exposure to the verbal expressions of other ethnic groups and religions. When they enter the workplace, they will rely on their coworkers to develop a literate understanding of work procedures, union rules, and methods for furthering their status. By reading to their children, by telling stories, and by engaging in supportive dialogues, parents set the stage for their child's entry into the world of literature and schooling (Snow, 1999). Here, again, the parent and teacher must teach by displaying examples of the execution and generation of a wide variety of detailed literate practices, ranging from learning to write through outlines to taking notes in lectures (Connors & Epstein, 1995).

It is important to recognize that the literate practices used in today's schools are specific adaptations to the requirements of our current educational system. In the past, a great deal of emphasis was placed on the learning of Greek, Latin, and Hebrew. Today, we see a relatively greater emphasis on the acquisition of technical vocabulary, including programming languages. If foreign languages are taught, they are no longer the classics but rather major living languages such as Spanish or Chinese.

Educators and parents often complain about the decrease in young people's abilities to recall culturally significant facts (Hirsch, 1987; Hirsch, Kett, & Trefil, 1988).

However, with the advent of tools for web searching, students have access to an encyclopedia of knowledge far greater than that of their parents. In truth, the very concept of literate practices is undergoing continual transformation as technologic advances in video, telecommunications, and computers allow us to explore new modes of communication (McLuhan & Fiore, 1967). However, to maintain cultural continuity, students will still need to be able to appreciate the structure of a Greek drama, the rules of formal debate, and the allegorical features in the *Divine Comedy*.

Neural Network Models of Word Learning

Ideally, we would like to have precise neurocomputational models that integrate across all of these time frames and cue types. But building such models is a tall task, and no current models can capture all these cues and interactions. However, one framework that allows us to model the core aspects of lexical learning is the self-organizing feature map (SOFM) architecture (Kohonen, 2001), as expressed in the DevLex model of Li, Farkas, and MacWhinney (2004). SOFM networks model initial word learning as patterns of organization in cortical maps. Three local maps are involved in word learning: an auditory map, an articulatory map, and a lexical map (see Figure 14.1). Emergent self-organization on each of these three maps uses the same learning algorithm. Word learning involves the association of elements between these three maps. What makes this mapping process self-organizing is the fact that there is no pre-established pattern for these mappings, and no preordained relation between particular nodes and particular feature patterns.

Evidence regarding the importance of syllables in early child language (Bijeljac, Bertoncini, & Mehler, 1993; Jusczyk, Jusczyk, Kennedy, Schomberg, & Koenig, 1995) suggests that the nodes on the auditory map may best be viewed as corresponding to full syllabic units, rather than separate consonant and vowel phonemes. The demonstration by Saffran et al. (1996) of memory for auditory patterns in 4-month-old infants indicates that children are not only encoding individual syllables but are also remembering sequences of syllables. In effect, prelinguistic children are capable of establishing complete representations of the auditory forms of words. Within the DevLex self-organizing framework, these capabilities can be represented in two ways. The auditory map uses a slot-and-frame feature notation from MacWhinney, Leinbach, Taraban, and McDonald (1989). The articulatory map combines this representation with a sequence-encoding mechanism based on the work of Gupta and MacWhinney (1997). This model treats the

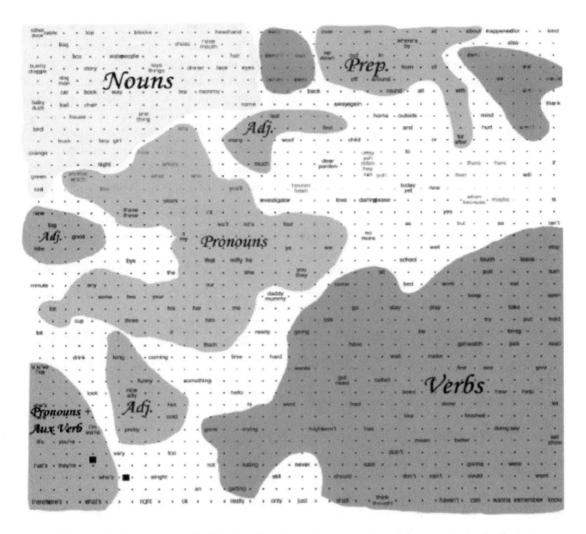

Figure 14.1   Lexical map extracted by DevLex. Organization by parts of speech is suggested by shading patterns. Within each part of speech, words are located next to other semantically similar words.

neural encoding of words as an "avalanche" (Grossberg, 1978) that controls the order of syllables within the word. Each new word is learned as a new avalanche.

The input to the DevLex model includes compressed representations of actual sentences spoken to children as taken from the Child Language Data Exchange System (CHILDES) database (http://www.childes.psy.cmu.edu). This information tells the child about the words with which a new lexical item co-occurs in the input. In addition, for each word, the model receives semantic features extracted from WordNet (Harm, 2002; Miller, Beckwith, Fellbaum, Gross, & Miller, 1990). After some 500 cycles of training on this input, newly learned words organize themselves into groups in the lexical map. As illustrated in Figure 14.1, this organization follows the part of speech organization

described by standard linguistic analyses (Sagae, Davis, Lavie, MacWhinney, & Wintner, 2007). This emergent process allows the SOFM to extract part of speech information implicitly and to encode it in the topology of the lexical map. As discussed later, this topological information is crucial for the linkage of the lexicon to sequential, syntactic processing in the inferior frontal cortex.

The DevLex model focuses on the linkage of the two phonological maps to the lexicon and says nothing about links between the two phonological maps. However, there are now several well-articulated models of the development of these linkages between articulation and audition. These models (Guenther, 2006; Lacerda, 1998; Westermann & Miranda, 2004) use the same SOFM architecture of DevLex but emphasize the ways in which units in auditory space come to be constrained by the possible articulations produced by the child. Lindblom, Diehl, Park, and Salvi (in press) argue that, to work effectively across contexts, this learning has to rely on the fact that the brain is able to compute motor equivalence between targets. This allows the learner to link together a targeted sound with an auditory effect, even when the actual details of the sound production vary radically across contexts. During this learning, the ambient language is providing ongoing input to auditory organization, and this input provides new targets for the process of articulation. In the end, the structures encoded in auditory space become the strongest forces in this coupled system.

In the DevLex self-organizing framework, the learning of a word is viewed as the emergence of an association between a pattern on the auditory map and a pattern on the concept map through Hebbian learning (Hebb, 1949; Kandel & Hawkins, 1992). When the child hears a given auditory form and sees an object at the same time, the co-activation of the neurons that respond to the sound and the neurons that respond to the visual form produces an association across a third pattern of connections that maps auditory forms to conceptual forms. Initially, the pattern of these interconnections is unknown, because the relation between sounds and meanings is arbitrary (de Saussure, 1915/1966). This means that most of the many potential connections between the auditory and conceptual maps will never be used, making it a sparse matrix (Kanerva, 1993). In fact, it is unlikely that all units in the two maps are fully interconnected (Shrager & Johnson, 1995). To support the initial mapping, some researchers (Schmajuk & DiCarlo, 1992; Wittenberg, Sullivan, & Tsien, 2002) have suggested that the hippocampus may provide a means of maintaining the association until additional cortical connections have been established. As a result, a single exposure to a new word is enough to lead to one-trial learning. However, if this initial association is not supported by later repeated exposure to the word in relevant social contexts, the child will no longer remember the word.

Syntax

The transition from the first words to the first sentences is nearly imperceptible. After learning the first words, children begin to produce more and more single-word utterances. As their vocabulary grows, children begin saying words in close approximation (Branigan, 1979). For example, they may say *wanna,* followed by a short pause and then *cookie.* If the intonational contour of *wanna* is not closely integrated with that of *cookie,* adults tend to perceive this as two successive single-word utterances. However, the child may already have in mind a clear syntactic relation between the two words.

As the clarity of the relations between single words strengthens, the temporal gap between the words will decrease. However, the transition from successive single-word utterances to true word combinations requires more than just faster timing. Two other achievements must occur. First, the child has to figure out how to join words together into a single intonational package or breath group. Second, the child also has to figure out which words can be meaningfully combined and in what order.

The level of successive single-word utterances is one that chimpanzees also reach when they learn signed language. Domesticated chimps like Sarah, Washoe, or Kanzi can learn about a hundred conventional signs or tokens. They can then combine these words to produce meaningful communication. However, the combinations that chimpanzees produce never really get beyond the stage of successive single-word utterances. For example, the chimpanzee Washoe, who was raised by the Gardners (Allen & Gardner, 1969), produced strings such as "Open, now, me, now, open, door, please, open, please, me" to express the request to have a door opened. In a sequence like this, the chimp is basically using every item in her lexicon that might apply to the current scene without paying much attention to particular binary combinations of items (Terrace, Petitto, Sanders, & Bever, 1980).

Item-Based Patterns

Eventually, children come to take a more systematic approach to the process of combining words. The description of the growth of this process is the task of the theory of syntactic development. In the early days of psycholinguistic theory, Braine (1963, 1971) explored ways of applying learning theory to the study of syntactic development. The formulation he devised focused on the idea that function words tend to appear in fixed positions vis-à-vis content words. For example, *the* appears before nouns, and the suffix *-ing* appears after verbs. Many of these positional patterns involved combinations of predicates such as *want, more,* or *go* with arguments such as *cookie* or *flower.* Braine found that a small set of semantic combination types could be used to account for nearly all of the sentences in the small corpora that he studied. In some cases, the positional occurrence of the words involved was quite fixed. For example, children always said *my* + X and never X + *my* to express the possession relation. However, in other cases, the order was more variable. Like Harris (1951) or Tesniére (1959), Braine analyzed these constituent structures in terms of slots that could be filled by items of a certain class. Formulating a set of 12 such positional patterns for a small corpus of child utterances, he referred to his account as a "pivot-open" grammar, because it specified the position of pivot words vis-à-vis the open class. However, in the spirit of Chomsky's (1959) critique of Skinner's *Verbal Behavior*, this model was criticized as failing to pay adequate attention to semantic patterning (Bloom, 1971). Later, Braine (1976) revised his account, emphasizing the role of "groping patterns" that established links based not on lexical class, but semantic relations (Schlesinger, 1974, 1975).

Sticking more closely to Braine's original formulations, MacWhinney (1975a) introduced the notion of the item-based pattern (IBP), in contrast with Braine's later concept of groping patterns. Rather than viewing the combination of *more* and *milk* as expressing a pattern such as *recurrence + object*, MacWhinney interpreted the combination as evidence of the IBP *more + X,* where the italicization of the word *more* indicates that it is a particular lexical item and not a general concept. This analysis stresses the extent to which the IBP first emerges as a highly limited construction based on the single lexical item *more*.

In this account, the grammar of the child's first word combinations is extremely concrete. The child learns that each predicate should appear in a constant position with respect to the arguments it requires. For example, in English, the word *more* appears before the noun it modifies and the verb *run* appears after the subject with which it combines. The combination is based on a slot-filler relation. Consider the combination *more milk*, which is generated from the IBP *more + X*. In this combination, *milk* is a filler for the slot that is represented by the X.

MacWhinney (1975a) examined the word order of 11,077 utterances produced by two Hungarian children between the ages of 17 and 29 months. He found that between 85% and 100% of the utterances in these samples could be generated by a set of 42 IBPs. Some examples of these patterns in English translation are*: X + too, no + X, where + X, dirty + X, and see + X.* The IBP model is able to achieve a remarkably close match to the child's output because it postulates an extremely concrete set of abilities that are directly evidenced in the child's output.

MacWhinney made no general claims about a pivot or open class, focusing instead on the idea that the first syntactic patterns involve links between individual lexical items and other words with which they are prone to combine. An example of an IBP is the structure *the + X*. This pattern states that the word *the* occurs before another word with which it is semantically related. In addition to these positional facts, the IBP encodes the shape of the words that can occupy the slot determined by X and the nature of the semantic relation between *the* and *X*. This is to say that an IBP is a predicate-argument relation that encodes:

- the lexical identity of the predicate
- the lexical category of the argument(s)
- the sequential position of the predicate vis-à-vis its argument(s)
- the semantic relation between the predicate and its argument(s)

The predicates of IPBs can specify one, two, or even three arguments. A word such as *want* needs to be completed with two other words to form a complete, meaningful predication. First, there must be a nominal that serves as a direct object, as in *want cookie*. Second, there must be a nominal that serves as the subject, as in *I want cookie*. Because *want* expects these two additional words, we call it a two-argument predicate. Other predicates, such as *under* or *my,* take only one argument, and a few such as *give* take three (*John gave Bill a dollar.*). We can refer to this argument structure as the valency of the predicate (Herbst, 2007), much as atoms have a valency structure in chemistry. Nouns that are derived from verbs, such as *destruction* or *remission* can take optional arguments (*the destruction of the city* or *a decline in the dollar*) to form complex noun phrases. Basic nouns such as *chair* and *goat* do not even have these expectations. However, in English, these require modification with a determiner such as *the* or *this*. Thus, in the phrase *the dog*, there is a covalent relation, because the determiner requires the noun for completion and the noun requires the determiner.

Learning Item-Based Patterns

Children learn IBPs by listening to sentences. For example, if the child's older sister says "my dolly," the child may recognize the word *dolly* from previous experience and then further notice the presence of *my* in front of *dolly*. At this point, the child can compare the phrase *my dolly* with the single word *dolly*, noticing the differences (MacWhinney, 1978). The first difference is the presence of *my* before *dolly*. From this evidence, the child can extract the IBP *my + X*.

In this case, the child is learning the word *my* at the same time as the IBP. Possibly, the older sister may be asserting her control over the doll and wrestling it from the younger sister's possession. Thus, the younger child can pick up not only the meaning of *my* and the IBP, but also the notion of a relation of possession and control between the two words. Thus, it is more accurate to speak of this IBP as combining *my + object possessed,* rather than just *my + X.* By specifying a particular semantic role for the filler, we are emphasizing the fact that the pattern encodes both syntax and semantics.

Initially, this IBP is restricted to the words *my* and *dolly,* and the relation of possession that occurs between them. However, if the older sister then says "and this is my horsey," the child can begin to realize that the open slot for the pattern based on the item *my* refers potentially to any manner of *toy.* Subsequent input will teach the child that any object can fill the slot opened up by the operator *my.* Each IBP goes through this same course of generalization (MacWhinney, 1975a; Tomasello, Akhtar, Dodson, & Rekau, 1997).

Evidence for the Reality of Item-Based Patterns

During the second and third year, children's productions provide extensive evidence for the pervasiveness and productivity of the growing systems of IBPs. One clear form of evidence comes from the application of IBPs to new words. We can also demonstrate the productivity of IBPs by teaching children novel words that serve as slot fillers. For example, we can show a child a picture of a bird-like creature that we call *a wug.* The positioning of the nonce word *wug* after the indefinite article induces the child to treat the word as a common noun. We can show the child two pictures of the strange creature and ask her, "What are these?" By responding with the answer *wugs,* children show productivity of the IBP based on the plural suffix /s/. Also, we can set up a game in which each person names some toys. This will lead the child to produce the combination *my wug,* thereby showing the productivity of the pattern *my + object possessed.* Similarly, a German-speaking child can be taught the nonce name *der Gann* (nominative, masculine, singular) for a toy. The experimenter can then pick up the toy and ask the child what he is holding. By the age of 3, children will correctly produce the accusative form *den Gann* (accusative, masculine, singular).

Although it is easy to convince children to accept new slot fillers, it is far more difficult to teach them to accept new operators. This is because new operators must establish their own new IBPs. As a result, it is difficult to convince children to use novel verbs in a fully produc-

tive fashion. Instead, children tend to be conservative and unsure about how to use verbs productively until about age 5 (Tomasello, 2000b). By then, they start to show productive use of constructions such as the double object, the passive, or the causative (Bowerman, 1988). For example, an experimenter can introduce a new verb such as *griff* in the frame *Tim griffed the ball to Frank,* and the child will productively generalize to *Tim griffed Frank the ball.*

The productivity of IBPs can also be illustrated by errors in word combination. Early child syntax is replete with examples of errors produced by the simple application of IBPs (Brown, Cazden, & Bellugi, 1968; Klima & Bellugi, 1966; Menyuk, 1969). Examples include *where Mama boot, who that, what train, no Rusty hat,* and *that no fish school.* These combinations arise from the application of IBPs such as: *where + object located,* or *no + object denied.* In these patterns, the open slot can hold single nouns, noun phrases, or simple sentences. The fact that slot fillers can themselves be formed from IBPs allows for recursive rule application that we will call *clustering.* How clustering can be implemented on the neuronal level is discussed later in this chapter.

Errors arise because children are omitting articles and auxiliaries, but over time they will learn to add these through additional IBPs. Soon, children learn to use *where's,* rather than *where* for interrogatives, producing correct combinations, such as **where's the wheel?* Some children form an overgeneralized *no + X* negation pattern in which X is not restricted to an object. Errors illustrating this incorrect overextension include: **no do this, *no wipe finger, *no sit there, *no play that, *he no bite you,* and **I no taste them.* Parallel interrogative combination errors include **where go, *what happen, *where put him on a chair, *what happen me,* and **why need them more.* Interrogative errors with missing auxiliaries of the shape **what they are doing* and *where he's going* are extremely common. There are also errors, such as **where the wheel do go* and **what you did eat,* in which the auxiliary is misplaced after the subject. These errors are further evidence for patterns such as *where + S.* Later on, children replace *where + S* with *where + tense.* However, they fail to restrict the *where + tense* pattern to exclude main verbs. Overgeneralization errors attesting to the productivity of this later pattern include: **where goes the wheel, *where could be the shopping place,* or **where's going to be the school?* After the first few months of word combination, there are no reports of errors that go against the basic item-based interrogative patterns. For example, there are no reports of errors such as *he can't do it why* (Labov & Labov, 1978).

The fact that grammatical patterns are often acquired word by word provides further evidence for the operation of IBPs. For example, Kuczaj and Brannick (1979) showed that children are quicker to show placement of the tensed auxiliary after the interrogatives *what* and *where* than after *how long* or *when*. Thus, children will produce *what is he doing?* at the same time they produce **when he coming?* Similarly, Bowerman (1978a) noted that, at 17 months, her daughter Eva used the patterns *want + X* and *more + X* productively. However, these patterns did not generalize to other words like *open, close, bite, no more,* or *all gone*.

One could argue that sentences of the type we have discussed are produced not through word combination, but through analogy. Accounts based on analogy can be used to account for virtually any particular form. However, accounts based on analogy can also predict error types that never occur. For example, Kuczaj and Brannick (1979) noted that questions like *gonna he go?* have never been reported, although children say *he's gonna go, he will go,* and *will he go?* If analogy were operating here, we would expect to find *gonna he go?* on analogy with *will he go?* On the other hand, IBPs account for these data correctly. The auxiliary *will* is combined with *he go* using the IBP *will + action*. This pattern does not generalize to *gonna,* because, by definition, the IBP *will + action* is restricted to the auxiliary *will*. Thus, the learning of IBPs is conservative in a way that correctly predicts nonoccurring overgeneralizations.

Consider another example of how lexical classes help the child avoid overgeneralization. Children may notice that both *big* and *red* pattern together in forms such as *big barn* and *red barn*. This might induce them to produce forms such as *I painted the barn big* on analogy with *I painted the barn red*. A conservative learner would stick close to facts about the verb *paint* and the arguments that it permits. If the child has heard a form like *I painted the barn white,* it would make sense to extend this frame slightly to include the resultative predicate *red*. However, to extend from the word *white* to semantically unrelated words like *happy* or *difficult* would be to go far beyond the attested construction. As a result, this type of category-leaping overgeneralization is extremely infrequent. This type of conservatism is fundamental to the Competition Model's multiple process solution to what is often referred to as the "logical problem of language acquisition" (MacWhinney, 2004, 2005c; Pinker, 1984).

Feature-Based Patterns

Although IBPs can be used to generate nearly all word combinations, there is good evidence that children soon go beyond IBPs to learn more general combinatorial rules. Consider the learning of the pattern that places the adjective before the noun in English. At first, children pick up a few IBPs such as *nice + object, good + object,* and *pretty + object*. They acquire these patterns during the learning of new adjectives from the input. For example, children may hear the form *nice kitty,* from which they create the pattern *nice + X*. At first, the slot filler is limited to the original noun *kitty,* but it is then quickly generalized to all possible objects. When the child then begins to learn the parallel patterns for *good* and *pretty,* the process of slot generalization becomes quicker, as the child begins to realize that words like *nice, good,* and *pretty* that describe characteristics of objects all accept a related object in the following syntactic position. This linking of IBPs then creates a feature-based pattern (FBP) that specifies the combination *modifier + object described* for English. Other early FBPs include *possessor + possession (John's computer)* and *locative + location (behind the tree)*. Once children have learned these more general patterns, they apply immediately to newly learned words.

FBPs can also apply to the positioning of nouns as topics in languages like Hungarian or Chinese. These languages encourage the formation of sentences that place nominal topics in initial position, according to the FBP *topic + comment*. At first, children may pick this up as an IBP. For example, they might hear a Hungarian sentence of the shape *the glass # empty* with the # sign indicating an intonational break between the topic and the comment. They first encode this as a pattern linked to *glass*. However, after hearing a few more parallel patterns for other nouns, they then extract a general FBP, just as they do for the *modifier + object described* pattern for adjectives. Studies such as MacWhinney (1975b) and Lee (1999) have demonstrated that children use these patterns productively by age 2.

Category-Based Patterns

There is a third level of argument generalization, above the levels of the IBP and the FBP. This is the level of the category-based pattern (CBP). Just as feature-based constructions emerge from a process of generalization across IBPs, so these more global CBPs emerge from generalization across feature-based constructions. For example, in English, there are literally dozens of verb groups that share a common placement of the subject before the verb. Together, these constructions give support for a CBP supporting SV (subject-verb) word order in English. The English CBPs of SV and VO work together to produce prototypical SVO (subject-verb-object) order (MacWhinney, Bates, & Kliegl, 1984). Other languages promote different combinations of global patterns. In Hungarian and Chinese, for example, SV, OV, and VO orders operate to express alternative varieties of object definiteness, producing SVO and SOV orders. Italian combines SV and VO patterns with secondary but significant use of VS (Dell'Orletta, Lenci, Montemagni, & Pirrelli, 2005) to produce SVO and VSO orders. Other global patterns control the ordering of topic before comment or the tendency to associate animacy with agency, producing a CBP for AV or AXV.

The sequential processing system is grounded on the individual IBPs that encode all the rich detail of individual constructions. Higher level FBP and CBP constructions emerge when extending patterns to new verbs (Tomasello, 2000b), largely after age 4, and when organizing the whole network of IBPs into a more smoothly functioning whole. However, the data that support IBPs remain available throughout development.

Morphology: Between Lexicon and Syntax

One of the most vexed problems in linguistics and psycholinguistics is the status of morphological processes, such as derivation, inflection, and compounding. Although English is relatively poor in terms of inflectional morphology, it makes full use of compounding and derivational morphology. The problem with morphology is that it seems to have one foot in lexicon and one foot in syntax. Consider a form such as *knives* as the plural of *knife*. In terms of combination, we can view knives as a combination of the stem knife with the plural suffix -s. However, the fact that the stem changes its shape when joining with the suffix is not a fact about combination, but a fact about the sound shape of this lexical item. Morphology differs from syntax in another fundamental way. Earlier, we saw the difficulties involved in viewing syntactic patterns as based on analogy. This is because syntax is produced by combination, not analogy. However, the same is not true for morphology. To the extent that complex words can be stored in posterior cortex as single wholes, they can serve as the analogic bases for new word productions. Thus, *knives* can be produced on analogy with *wives*.

These properties of morphological formations have made them excellent targets for neural network models that can focus on the processes of analogy that operate within the lexicon (MacWhinney & Leinbach, 1991; MacWhinney

et al., 1989; Rumelhart & McClelland, 1987). However, even in morphologically complex languages, such as Turkish or Navajo, morphemes appear in invariable position slots, suggesting that these forms are not produced by the types of free IBPs used for syntax, but rather through analogic processes operating in the lexicon.

Amalgams

Although morphological marking is fixed in sequential terms, it still poses a learning challenge to the child. At first, children seem blissfully unaware of the presence of grammatical markings, treating complex, multimorphemic words as if they were single units. For example, a child might use the word *cookies* even before learning the singular *cookie*. At this point, we can refer to the unanalyzed two-morpheme combination *cookies* as an *amalgam* (MacWhinney, 1978). The child language literature is replete with examples of uses of inflected amalgams before the child has learned the stems. For example, Brown et al. (1968, p. 41) reported use of *can't, won't,* and *don't* at a time when *can, will,* and *do* were absent. Similarly, Leopold (1949, p. 8) reported use of *sandbox* when *sand* was absent. Children also use inflected forms before they have acquired the inflections. Kenyeres (1926) reported that his daughter used the inflected Hungarian word *kenyeret* (bread + accusative) at 16 months, when there was no other evidence for productive use of the accusative *-et*. It makes sense that the word should be learned in this form, because this is how it appears in sentences such as *Do you want some bread?* Moreover, Hungarian children often use *kalapáccsal* (hammer-with) before demonstrating productive use of either the stem *kalapács* (hammer) or the instrumental suffix *-val*. Of course, for the child, the main interest value of a hammer involves its use as an instrument.

Some of the more complex units encoded by amalgams are later produced through syntax. Peters (1977) noted that when her 14-month-old subject could control only 6 to 10 words, he said quite clearly, "Open the door." Similarly, my son Ross produced "No, Mommy, I don't want to go bed" and "I like it; I love it" at a time when the first two-word combinations were just emerging. It is possible that these precocious forms derive from stored full-sentence templates that just happen to work correctly as full units or amalgams in a particular situational context. Although amalgams can produce precocious successes, they can also lead to grammatical errors. For example, if children learn *like it* and *want some* as amalgams, they can produce errors such as *I like it the ball* or *I want some a banana*. Clark

(1977, p. 350) reported the utterance "hat on gone now" in which "hat on" is apparently a unit.

Evidence for the nonproductivity of early affixes or word endings comes from the fact that, when they first appear, affixes are seldom overgeneralized (Ervin, 1964; MacWhinney, 1974, p. 653). Children begin by saying *went* and *saw*, and over-regularizations such as *goed* or *sawed* typically do not occur before correct irregular forms are produced. When errors like *goed* and *sawed* begin to appear, they serve as evidence of the productivity of the past tense suffix, as well as evidence of its earlier nonproductivity. After a few weeks, the child corrects these errors and returns to correct use of *went* and *saw*. This pattern of correct performance with an intermediate period of overgeneralization produces a U-shaped curve that has a different developmental profile for each verb. Children make fewer morphophonological errors on common irregular words than on rare irregular words (MacWhinney, 1975a, 1978). This effect indicates that children rely on rote to produce at least some inflected forms. Frequent forms can be acquired as chunks or amalgams because they are heard so often.

The absence of productivity for a suffix should not be taken as absence of the underlying concept. For example, Brown and Bellugi (1964) found that children would refer to *many shoe* and *two shoe* at a time when there is still no clear evidence for the productivity of the plural suffix. However, the words *many* and *two* by themselves show that the child not only thinks in terms of the concept of plurality but also has succeeded in finding two ways of expressing this concept. At this point, acquisition of the plural is driven not by the child's need to express concepts, but by the need to match the formal structures of the adult language.

Syntactic Processing

The Competition Model (MacWhinney, 1987) characterizes learned grammatical knowledge in terms of the system of IBPs, FBPs, and CBPs. Over time, the child learns to join these various positional patterns into a single network to control both comprehension and production. Although this network is learned, the processing principles that apply the knowledge encoded in this network are not learned. Rather, they are rather fundamental properties of the cognitive system. In this sense, syntax emerges from already existing processes.

The sequential network must communicate with both the lexicon (level 3) and mental models (level 5). In production, the representations of mental models are already active, and the work of syntax is to coordinate lexical activation in a way that will facilitate sequential output. In comprehension, words are recognized by the lexicon and the syntax has the responsibility of fitting these words together into structures that can build up coherent mental models (Gernsbacher, 1990; MacWhinney, 1977). In presenting this analysis of sequential processing, we are bringing emergentist theory to bear on the same question that has been at the center of the theory of Universal Grammar. This is the issue of the role of recursion as a unique feature of human language (Hauser, Chomsky, & Fitch, 2002). However, unlike UG, this account views recursion as an emergent property of other domain-general neural and social processes operating in collaboration, rather than as the result of some totally new structure based on a recent mutation.

The core assumptions of the Competition Model are shared with many other models in current psycholinguistics. The model specifies a series of steps for the competition between constructions during comprehension:

1. Sounds activate competing words as they are heard in speech (Brent, 1999; Marslen-Wilson & Warren, 1994; Monaghan, Christiansen, & Chater, 2007).

2. Each new word activates its own IBPs together with related FBPs (Trueswell & Tanenhaus, 1994; Trueswell, Tanenhaus, & Kello, 1993).

3. IBPs then initiate tightly specified searches for slot fillers (Ford, Bresnan, & Kaplan, 1982; MacDonald, Pearlmutter, & Seidenberg, 1994).

4. Slots may be filled either by single words or by whole phrases. In the latter case, the attachment is made to the head of the phrase (O'Grady, 2005; Taraban & McClelland, 1988).

5. To fill a slot, a word or phrase must receive support from cues for word order, prosody, affixes, or lexical class (MacWhinney, 2005a).

6. If several words compete for a slot, the one with the most cue support wins (Kempe & MacWhinney, 1999).

7. Processing commitments are made when the difference in the activation of two competitors passes over a threshold (Ratcliff, 1978; Ratcliff & Smith, 2004).

These seven design features of the processor work together to achieve fluent production and comprehension in real time. Here, the time frame of the constraints of face-to-face interaction is the critical determinant of the emergent shape of these processes. Consider the German noun phrase *am Haus meiner Mutter* (at my mother's house). The initial preposition *am* is a contraction of *an* "to" and *dem* "the." When producing *am,* the speaker must already know that the following noun will be neuter. If the following noun were feminine, then the form would be *an der,* rather than *am.* It is generally true of German that, when producing articles, adjectives, and even contracted prepositions, one must know the gender of the following noun. For a native speaker, this comes naturally, because the lexicon is organized in terms of gender categories, as suggested by the DevLex model discussed earlier. However, for a second language learner, the gender of a noun is not as obvious, and this means that the second language learner will often produce errors or disfluencies when picking the gender for forms before the noun.

Timing and the just-in-time flow of information are important throughout the processing system. Sometimes the barriers involve anticipation of information that has not yet been determined; sometimes they involve the settling of competitions between attachments. Consider the case of prepositional phrase attachment. Prepositions such as *on* take two arguments; the first argument (arg1) is the object of the preposition, and the second argument (arg2) is the head of the prepositional phrase (i.e., the word or phrase to which the prepositional phrase attaches). We can refer to arg1 as the local head and arg2 as the external head. Consider the sentence *the man positioned the coat on the rack.* Here, the local head of *on* is *rack* and its external head (the head of the whole prepositional phrase) could be either *positioned* or *the coat.* These two alternative attachment sites for the prepositional phrase are in competition with each other.

Competition also governs the interpretation of verbs as either transitive or intransitive. Verbs like *jog* that have both transitive/causative and intransitive readings can be represented by two competing lexical entries. When we hear the phrase *since John always jogs a mile,* we activate the transitive reading. However, if the full sentence then continues as *since John always jogs a mile seems like a short distance,* then the intransitive reading takes over from the transitive one. For detailed examples of the step-by-step operations of this type of processor, consult MacWhinney (1987), MacDonald et al. (1994), or O'Grady (2004).

Neurological Control

The Unified Competition Model (MacWhinney, 2009) links the processes and levels of language we have been discussing to structures in particular brain areas. Understanding the neural basis of language is important for the life-span approach to language development because it allows us to understand many otherwise puzzling aspects of first language learning, second language learning in adulthood, developmental language disorders, and aphasia. The model views the six linguistic levels (audition, articulation, lexicon, syntax, mental models, and conversation) as processed through partially separate neural structures. These structures are not viewed as modules (Fodor, 1983) but as parts of interactive neural circuits (Just & Varma, 2007).

The neural representation for the levels of articulation, audition, and lexicon was discussed in the context of our review of the DevLex model. The three separate maps of the DevLex model represent three of the six core linguistic modules. These modules are each located in separate brain regions, connected by axonal, white matter projections. DexLex trains these connections using Hebbian learning. Input phonology is processed in the auditory cortex of the superior temporal sulcus. Output phonology is controlled by parts of Broca's area, along nearby regions with motor cortex. The core semantic or lexical map is centered in Wernicke's area, although the actual meanings of words are distributed throughout the brain (Mitchell et al., 2008).

Looking first at the control of input phonology, we know that this processing is focused in primary auditory cortex. This area, which spans Brodmann areas BA41 and BA42, lies in the posterior half of the superior temporal gyrus and the transverse temporal gyri or Heschl's gyri. Within this area, there are, in fact, multiple tonotopic maps, each of which appears to represent a different view or processing slant on the whole range of the frequency spectrum. Work with rhesus monkeys has shown that the auditory system involves three levels of auditory processing with 15 different tonotopic maps. This pattern of multiple parallel isotopically organized maps is similar to the pattern of multiple parallel maps found in the motor system. Like many other cortical areas, the auditory cortex is also connected to its own specific thalamic nucleus, the medial geniculate nucleus, from which it receives input.

Syntax gates both lexical production and mental model extraction. The central role played by syntactic gating allows us to understand many features of language development and disorders. The distinction between lexicon and syntax reflects the fundamental linguistic contrast between rote and combination (MacWhinney, 1978; Pinker, 1999). Posterior lexical areas, including Wernicke's area, rely on the detailed coding facilities provided by the ventral neural system (Tucker, 2009). This system relies on the remarkable ability of the hippocampus to store huge quantities of specific episodic experiences through a system of synaptic reentry (Wittenberg, Sullivan, & Tsien, 2002). Anterior sequence-processing areas, including Broca's area, rely on the more action-oriented mechanisms of the dorsal processing system. Ullman (2004) has noted that the dorsal system is also closely allied with thalamic and striatal midbrain systems that work to set up and solidify sequential and procedural processing. Thus, this basic division between rote and combination is honored in a basic way by the brain's division into dorsal and ventral systems.

Although the division of these two processes makes great sense computationally, it leads to a fundamental problem in terms of language coordination. During comprehension, anterior syntactic areas need to listen closely to posterior lexical areas to decide when specific IBPs or FBPs can fire. During comprehension, there are often competing possible interpretations that are controlled by alternative syntactic pathways. Only by maintaining smooth contact with posterior areas can anterior areas make the right choices. During speech production, the problem is even worse. Syntactic areas, taking their cues from mental models, must control or *gate* the firing of lexical items. Multiple lexical items are often ready to fire in parallel (G. Dell, Juliano, & Govindjee, 1993; Stemberger, 1985). However, each word must wait for its appointed moment for entry into the slots opened up by IBPs. When that moment comes, the word fires the articulatory gestures that it commands in motor cortex. The sequence mechanism must gate lexical items in a smooth way that minimizes stuttering, false starts, and pauses. This means that all signals from Broca's to Wernicke's must arrive on time in a coordinated way. Failures in the timing of this gating produce disfluencies in first language learning, second language learning (Yoshimura & MacWhinney, 2007), developmental language disorders, stuttering, and aphasia (Dell, Schwartz, Martin, Saffran, & Gagnon, 1997).

The operations of this processor are not learned; rather, they are grounded on structures in the ventral and dorsal systems that have parallels in all of our primate cousins. There are at least four major anterior-posterior white matter pathways that connect primate areas homologous to those involved in human language (Schmahmann et al., 2007). Although diffusion tensor imaging with humans is in its infancy, it is likely that we will find that the integration of the anterior/dorsal system and the posterior/ventral system has been even more elaborated in recent human evolution. Friederici (in press) and others have begun to trace ways in which these partially separate white matter conduits can gate different levels of information between syntax and lexicon.

These white matter connections must deal with a fundamental issue in neural processing: the binding problem. When an IBP or FBP is activated in inferior frontal gyrus (IFG), it opens up an argument slot that is characterized by a part of speech. This means that this sequential pattern must be connected with lexical cortex in a way that activates potential slot fillers and not other lexical items. The DevLex model is organized to produce exactly this effect, because it manages to organize lexical items in a local topological map in terms of their parts of speech. This means that connections through white matter must terminate in the correct general area of lexical space, and also that the IBPs and FBPs that gate these part of speech areas must be responsive to this information. For a normal child who is learning a first language, this type of connection develops slowly, but consistently and directly. However, if the white matter pathways are damaged in any way, gating will be slow and activation will be erratic. The worst case would be in Wernicke's aphasia where the crucial terminals of these pathways are completely severed. Second language learners must also deal with the fact that they need to rely on the lexical maps and pathways of their first language, and that often these will produce incorrect transfer to L2.

So far, we have not characterized the sequential processor in mechanistic terms. To do this, we need to address two issues. The first is the way in which individual IBPs can operate in real time. The second is how IBPs combine into a coordinated system. On the first issue, there are several models of neural mechanisms for sequence detection and control. One class of models views sequential patterns as avalanches (Grossberg, 1978; McCulloch & Pitts, 1943) that fire in quick sequence without additional feedback control (Houghton, 1990). Simple chains provide a reliable solution to the sequencing problem. However, if the delay between events A and B is either less than or more than the natural timing on the synaptic connections between units A and B, the chain may fail to fire. Sequence detection can rely on additional mediating elements, configured in various ways, to avoid this type of problem (Dominey, Hoen, & Inui, 2006). Pulvermüller (2003) proposes a mechanism that includes bidirectional connections that promote reverberation within the circuit. The fact that forward sequential connections are stronger than backward ones prevents the circuit from firing in the wrong direction. When sequence unit A fires, it primes the control unit C. Unit C then primes sequence unit B, thereby triggering initial reverberation in the whole circuit. At this point, both of the items that have been detected become "visible," which means that they can then pass on information to other processing areas. However, if the unit B fires without first being primed, it fails to trigger the control unit C and activation of unit B is then suppressed. There are many other ways in which the basic sequence detection mechanism could be configured, and it is even possible that nature has utilized several of these alternative ways.

The second problem that must be addressed by a mechanistic model of sequence control for syntax is the problem of how positional patterns are linked. There is, in fact, a very standard computational framework that can serve well to explain this system. This is the finite-state automaton, which is a machine that can produce or recognize sequences as a series of state transitions. In their original formulation, finite-state machines were thought of as systems for transitioning between lexical items. However, as Hausser (1999) has shown, the pathways in this system can also be viewed as transitions between categories, such as parts of speech or grammatical categories. In this sense, an IBP can be viewed as a finite-state machine that maps the transition between a single lexical item and a category. When IBPs are generalized as FBPs, then the resulting categories can form a complete finite-state machine.

However, for this machine to work well in neural terms, there has to be a good way to implement the process of clustering described earlier. Consider a sentence such as *boys with long hair like to ride motorcycles*. Here, the initial cluster is *boys with long hair*. If this cluster can activate a node that treats it as a complex noun, then the whole cluster can fill the subject slot for the verb *ride*. The question is simply how the brain manages to control the activation of clusters as sentences become more and more complex. Gibson (1998), Just and Carpenter (1992), and others have analyzed complex sentences in detail and have concluded that complex syntax places specific burdens on the working memory system. Recent work in cognitive neuroscience has indicated that this system relies primarily on representations in dorsolateral prefrontal cortex (DLPFC; Just & Varma, 2007). But neuroscience has not yet told us exactly how DLPFC manages to perform clustering actions. The basic idea proposed here is that DLPFC interprets individual phrasal chunks in terms of a mental model grounded on embodied cognition. In this process, it assigns action roles to the various phrases in the sentence and uses these to control the process of clustering in the syntactic sequence processing areas. To understand how these roles are assigned, we next turn to the level of processing of mental models.

Mental Models

Recent work in neuroscience has benefitted from four fundamental insights, each relating to the construction of mental models. First, in the 1980s, we learned that the visual system separates processing into an image-oriented ventral stream and an action-oriented dorsal stream. Second, we have learned from imaging work through the last decade that the brain relies on a perception-action cycle to interpret incoming messages. This cycle involves the generation of mental representations for objects in terms of the ways in which we typically act on them (Knoblich, 2008). Much of this cycle is grounded on interactions that include the action-oriented processing of the dorsal stream. Third, we have learned that the brain provides specific mechanisms for mapping the body images of others onto ours. One consequence of this ability is the fact that "mirror" neurons (Rizzolatti, Fadiga, Gallese, & Fogassi, 1996) controlling actions, facial gestures, and postures can fire equally strongly when the actor is the self or the other. As we are now learning, these mirror neurons are components of a general system for social cognition. The larger system also includes mechanisms in the superior temporal cortex for facial processing (Pelphrey, Morris, & McCarthy, 2005) and eye contact (Pelphrey et al., 2003), as well as amygdala and striatal areas for empathy (Meltzoff & Decety, 2003) and projection (Adolphs & Spezio, 2006). Fourth, we have learned that the basal ganglia and hippocampus play a central role in the consolidation of memories, often driven by rewards and error minimization.

Piecing together these results, we can see that one of the additional consequences of the dorsal-ventral dichotomy is a shift of discrete processing of individual elements to the ventral stream and a shift of global model construction to the dorsal stream, with particular additional regulatory control from frontal areas. In recent articles (MacWhinney, 2005d, 2008c), I have suggested that this system provides the neurological basis for a system that constructs dynamic mental models from linguistic input. At the core of this system is the notion of the self as actor. During sentence interpretation, this fictive self is then projected onto the role of sentence subject, and the self reenacts the image underlying the sentence. These images place the self into a set of well-understood roles as agent, experiencer, and source. Even locative and temporal relations can be interpreted from the egocentric frame that begins with a projection of the self onto the object located or the event in time.

Because narrative and dialogue often involve rapid shifts between agents, this system has to be able to use linguistic devices to control perspective shifting. As a result of this core dynamics, we can refer to this system as the Perspective Shift System. This system constitutes the highest level of support for linguistic complexity. Without the mental model construction supported by this system, complex syntax would be useless. This is because the fundamental purpose of virtually all the devices of complex syntax is the marking of perspective shift. This analysis applies across all the major grammatical constructions, including passivization, relativization, clefting, pronominalization, dislocation, existentials, shift reference, split ergativity, serialization, complementation, conjunction, ellipsis, adverbialization, long-distance anaphora, reflexivization, PP-attachment, and participial ambiguity. Each of these structures allows the speaker to combine, maintain, and shift perspectives in communicatively important ways. And these devices allow the listener to trace these movements of the speaker's attention across all of these shifts.

Building Mental Models

The traditional view of mental model construction (Budiu & Anderson, 2004; Kintsch, 1998) focuses on the linking of predicates into a coherent propositional graph. This activity is much like the process of clause combining that we learned in classes in composition. For example, you can combine "the dog chased the bird" and "the bird flew away" to form "the dog chased the bird that flew away." All one needs here is a grammatical device that serves to mark the fact that *the bird* plays a role in both clauses. Language provides a variety of methods or constructions for clause linkage, including conjunction, complementation, relativization, subordination, and adverbialization, as illustrated in these sentences:

If you go down to Shattuck, the bakery is on the corner.

Jim had asked me to bring him a loaf of bread.

Unfortunately, the bread I bought was stale.

Although it was stale, John wanted to pay me.

Shaking my head, I accepted the money.

My refusal of the payment would have made him upset.

These different constructions serve to link together clauses in terms of spatial, temporal, causal, and anaphoric relations. Most of these constructions rely on both lexical and syntactic processes. Typically, there is a linking lexical element, such as a conjunction or relativizer. In some cases, the lexical element is an affix that forms nominalizations or participials. Use of this linking element then triggers additional syntactic processes, such as extraposition, deletion, constituent reordering, agreement, and so on.

Syntactic constructions rely on four key aspects of the current model. First, the lexical items involved must be stored as phonological forms within the posterior systems. These items include both full lexical items and affixes. Second, these lexical forms must be integrated by IFG into positional patterns that control the positioning of the items in the clauses, as well as movement and deletion. Third, these IFG structures must rely on frontal short-term memory (STM) mechanisms that store elements as flexible deictic representations (Ballard, Hayhoe, Pook, & Rao, 1997; Silverstein, 1976). Fourth, these STM items must be pieced together for final mental model construction.

MacWhinney (2008c) argues that mental model construction is driven by a process of perspective taking. Let use consider an example from relative clause processing. Earlier we noted how clause combining through STM joins *the dog chased the bird* and *the bird flew away* to form *the dog chased the bird that flew away.* In this case, the shift moves smoothly from *bird* as the object of chased to *bird* as the subject of *flew away.* However, if the sentence is *the dog chased the bird that the girl loved,* then perspective tracking is more difficult, because a new perspective is introduced after *bird,* and the perspectives of both *the dog* and *the bird* must then be dropped. In this case, there is a greater burden on STM for fragment storage, and hence a higher overall processing load, as reflected by slower latencies and lesser recall accuracy for object relatives. These shifts of perspective are triggered by syntactic patterns linked to lexical devices. To learn these, the child must figure out how to operate on signals from the lexicon or IFG to control the correct shifting in frontal cortex. As the developmental literature amply demonstrates, the learning of this control takes many years (Franks & Connell, 1996). We explore some of these processes in further detail later in this chapter because this is one of the primary loci of the consolidation of linguistic complexity.

Ambiguous sentences illustrate another face of perspective shifting. Consider sentences such as "John saw the Grand Canyon flying to New York." Here, the default syntactic mechanism would favor the local attachment of *flying to New York* to *Grand Canyon.* The competing attachment is to *John.* Of course, the latter perspective is far more plausible. Or consider the processing of "Visiting relatives can be a nuisance." Here, we can either take the perspective of the relatives who become a nuisance to their hosts or the perspective of an unmentioned generalized actor who visits the relatives. In this case, both readings seem plausible. Reflexivity provides another useful example of perspectival processes. Consider these sentences:

a. Jessie stole a photo of herself/her* out of the archives.
b. Jessie stole me a photo of herself/her out of the archives.
c. Jessie stole a silly photo of herself/her out of the archives.

In (a), the reflexive is required because the perspective of Jessie remains active up to the appearance of the anaphor. In (b), on the other hand, the intervening presence of "me" causes a shift of perspective away from Jessie. As a result, when interpretation reaches the anaphor, either the reflexive or the simple pronoun is acceptable. Perspective shift is sensitive not just to other intervening animate perspectives, but also to implicit perspectives triggered by adjectives such as *silly* in (c). This type of phenomena is basic to all levels of mental model construction.

Perspective and Gesture

The frontal-parietal system for perspective shifting is not a recent evolutionary adaptation. Chimpanzees (Tomasello, Call, & Gluckman, 1997), dogs, and other mammals make extensive use of symbolic behaviors in social contexts. However, lacking a lexicon and positional patterns, other animals cannot organize these behaviors into recursive structures. However, Donald (1991) and others have argued that the production of symbolic communication can rely on gestural and vocal devices that may well have been readily accessible to *Homo erectus*. Because gestures can be formed in ways that map iconically to their referents, it is relatively easy to build up communal recognition of a gestural system. As Tucker (2009) argued, such a system would rely primarily on gestures and affordances specific to the action-oriented processes in the dorsal stream. It appears that speakers of sign languages are able to use posterior lexical areas to structure a lexicon of signs, just as they use IFG in the left hemisphere to control the ordering of signs. It is possible that protosign could also have relied on these same neuronal structures for lexical organization. However, looking back 2 million years, it is likely that the depth of support for lexical storage and positional patterning of gesture was still very incomplete. As a result, it is likely that protosign was incompletely lexical and heav-

ily reliant on dorsal processes for direct perspective taking and shifting.

Although sign may not have triggered full linguistic structure, it provided a fertile social bed that supported the development of further articulatory, lexical, and sequence systems. As Darwin (1872) noted, vocal and gestural communication coexisted as parallel streams from the beginning of human evolution. Gesture and prosody were able to keep humans engaged in protoconversations, during which the further elaboration of vocal patterns could refine and complement communication in the gestural-prosodic mode. Of course, humans are not the only primates that engage in conversation. However, as argued in MacWhinney (2008b), the shift in *Homo habilis* to a full upright posture led to two important consequences. One was the freeing of the hands for additional conversational interaction, and the other was the encouragement of full face-to-face interactions linked to full display of the hands and torso. This increasing support for gestural communication brought along with it a supportive social context for the further development of accompanying vocalizations. However, both of these modalities continue to provide important input to conversation in modern humans. Thus, we can best view the transition from a primarily gestural communication to a primarily vocal communication system as gradual, but unbroken, process with no sudden break based on the sudden introduction of an ability to process recursion.

Mental Models and Socialization

Vygotsky (1929), Mead (1934), Bruner (1987), Nelson (2000), and many others have argued that language plays a unique role in the transmission of cultural norms, frames, expectations, roles, and values. According to Vygotsky, the earliest uses of language are primarily social. This interpretation is supported in some detail by analyses from Ninio and Snow (1988) that focus on the heavy use in early vocabulary of forms such as *hi, gimme,* and *Mama*—all with clear social reflexes. Vygotsky argued that, once this initial social configuration is established, language then supports inner speech, a process that uses discourse, grammatical, and narrative forms from the ambient language to guide internal cognitive processing. It is difficult to imagine how this basic story could be wrong. In modern societies, we end up acquiring an enormously complex system of related concepts and frames, based nearly exclusively on verbal and written input. Moreover, this process of acculturation continues across the entire life span. In a very real sense, we can view culture as a roadmap or guidebook for life, and the way in which this guidebook is conveyed to new generations is largely through language and conversation.

These scripts, frames, and plans for social rules and behaviors become encoded as mental models (Fauconnier, 1994), based on the system for perspectival construction described throughout this section. These models are organized in two fundamental ways. One method uses the point of view of the human agent as protagonist. In this method, we use dorsal encoding to remember how to order food at McDonald's by encoding the perspectives of ourselves as clients, as well as those of the clerks who take the orders. These stories are further encoded in terms of the deictic frameworks of space and time supported by the ventral system. In the second method of encoding, we construct views of objects and systems as working mechanisms. This method is important for understanding science (Greeno & MacWhinney, 2006), mathematics (Nuñez & Lakoff, 2000), and mechanical devices. For this encoding, we use a variety of physicalist primitives, or p-prims, together with notions of force dynamics (Talmy, 2000) and basic causation (Hume, 1748).

Conversation

The view of acculturation presented so far suggests that society is encoded only as narratives or mechanics. Although narrative and mechanistic organizations are fundamental to many pieces of social competence, acculturation into conversational patterns also plays a major role in our daily lives. However, unlike narratives and mechanics, the components of conversational competence are stored not as long sequences of actions and causes, but as local networks, much like the systems for encoding IBPs and FBPs. Much of conversational competence can be described in terms of simple rules for turn-taking (Sacks, Schegloff, & Jefferson, 1974), speech act adjacency pairs (Mann & Thompson, 1992), and local cues for the expression of affect (Crystal, 1975). The full system for conversational interaction involves a rich multimedia interplay between gesture, prosody, lexicon, discourse, syntax, gaze, and posture (Kendon, 1982). Perhaps the best way to think of conversation is in terms of the interface between the social and the linguistic world with all the devices of each of these worlds being made available at the time of interaction.

Babies and their parents engage in conversations even before the child has begun to produce words. These conversations may involve shared smiles, gazes, coos, and grunts (Snow, 1977). Parents of young children will speak to them as if they were real conversational participants.

(For examples of this, you can browse the transcripts linked to audio at the CHILDES database: http://www.childes.psy.cmu.edu/data, such as the Brent corpus, or use the online browser at http://www.childes.psy.cmu.edu/browser.) These early dialogues are important for several reasons. First, they demonstrate the extent to which children acquire language not to just solve problems or express themselves, but also to participate fully in conversational interactions. Conversations allow us to engage socially as members of dyads and groups. To the degree that there is a fundamental urge to produce language, it is in large part an urge not to talk, but to converse.

This urge to socialize affects mothers, as well as infants. Papousek and Papousek (1991) showed that mothers use rising pitch contours to engage infant attention and elicit a response, falling contours to soothe their babies, and bell-shaped contours to maintain their attention. In general, these patterns are useful not only for directing attention to new words, but also for involving babies in the "melody" of conversation (Locke, 1995), even before they have learned "the words."

Conversations between mothers and their infants involve a variety of alternating activities. Infants tend to produce positive vocalization when gazing into their parents' eyes (Keller, Poortinga, & Schomerich, 2002). When infants produce negative vocalizations, parents often respond by touching and cuddling them. However, infants will produce more vocalizations when parents vocalize to them, rather than merely responding with touch or gesture (Bloom, Russell, & Wassenberg, 1987). A longitudinal study of naturalistic talk (Snow, Pan, Imbens-Bailey, & Herman, 1996) found a continuing increase in child speech act during 10-minute segments from 4 at 14 months to 7 at 20 months and 11 at 32 months. This ongoing growth of participation in conversations emphasizes the extent to which infants are being mainstreamed into a world of continual conversational turn-taking.

The logic of parent–child conversational turn-taking is not fundamentally different from that used between adults. The basic rule underlying all forms of turn-taking (Sacks, Schegloff, & Jefferson, 1974) is that, at any given moment, one of the participants is said to "have the floor." While that participant holds the floor, the other participants are supposed to pay attention to the conversational contribution. At some point the speaker begins to yield the floor and thereby invites a new conversational contribution. Signals that invite a new contribution include pauses, questions, and drops in intonation. Of course, conversations are not controlled as carefully as the flow of traffic through signal lights.

Often there are collisions between speakers, resulting in overlaps. At other times, there are complete breaks in the interaction. All of these features can be detected in vocal-visual interactions between mothers and children as young as 12 months. What distinguishes parent–child dialogues from adult–adult dialogs is the extent to which the parent uses specific devices to interpret children's ill-formed actions as conversational actions, and the extent to which the parent attempts to maintain and guide the interaction, both verbally and physically.

Toward the end of the first year, children develop increasing ability to control conversations through specific routines. The most well-developed routine is pointing. Children show reliable responding to pointing by about 10 months. They are able to look at their parents' faces, and use their gaze and pointing to locate objects. Soon after this, by about 12 months, children begin to produce their own communicative pointing (Lempers, 1979). In the period between 12 and 15 months of age, just before the first words, children also develop a set of intonational patterns and body postures intended to communicate other detailed meanings (Halliday, 1975).

Parents provide interpretive scaffolding for many of the child's early communicative behaviors (Bruner, 1992). After the child produces a smile, the parent may then respond with a full-fledged verbal interpretation of the meaning implicit in the smile, as in, *Is David having fun?* If the child shakes a spoon, the mother will attempt to interpret this gesture, too, suggesting, *Ready for dinner?* Beginning around 9 months, this sequence of child action and maternal interpretation takes on a choral quality involving alternating, rather than overlapping, contributions (Jasnow & Feldstein, 1986). By combining verbal responses with the child's gestures, mothers are able to produce a scaffold on which children can construct a vision of communicative interactions. The transcripts with videos available from the CHILDES database (http://www.childes.psy.cmu.edu) provide many illustrations of choral sequences of this type.

Snow (1999) argues that early participation in conversational interactions is the primary support for the initial stages of language acquisition. She emphasizes the extent to which early words serve social functions in games and routines, rather than serving merely to request objects. Crucially, language learning depends on the construction of a shared intersubjective understanding of the intentions of the parent. Conversational sequencing is the scaffold on which this understanding develops. However, it is further supported by processes of identification (Rizzolatti et al.,

1996), embodiment (MacWhinney, 2008c), and imitation (Meltzoff, 1995).

Language after Childhood

As noted earlier, certain aspects of language development continue throughout the life span. The clearest example of this is vocabulary development. Although the core vocabulary of a language is largely acquired by the end of childhood, there is continual later development in specialized areas of the lexicon. In some societies (Schieffelin & Ochs, 1987), there are special ceremonial uses of the language that are revealed to young men only after they pass through puberty rites. At this point, they are inducted into men's societies (Levi-Strauss, 1963) that reveal to them traditions that are often linked to special uses of the language. Children and adolescents also come to learn new words and constructions when they acquire specialized skills. In tribal societies, these can involve methods of hunting, names for animals and plants (Berlin & Kay, 1969), or tools for weaving and pottery. In modernized societies, these new concepts may relate to schooling, instruments used in the trades, or new social groups.

Apart from the basic increase in vocabulary, adolescents may acquire a wide range of other semiotic patterns. They may learn segments of the Bible, Torah, Koran, Constitution, or Scout Oath by heart. They may have to study the signs, symbols, and rules for driving, soccer, playing a musical instrument, or skateboarding. Teenagers and young adults often engage in innovative uses of language that introduce new slang, constructions, and phonological patterns (Labov, 1994). In young adulthood, schooling continues in the form of professional development. In areas such as biology, medicine, or chemistry, students may be responsible for learning as many as 10,000 technical terms. These terms are learned in the context of dense semantic networks explaining the role of each term in complex processes (Miller, 1978). In urban societies, we also continue to meet new people, and need to learn their names and many facts about them. In smaller, traditional societies, this type of learning often focuses instead on the learning of the names of ancestors and their life stories.

This continual expansion of language during adulthood depends on the powerful episodic encoding mechanisms of the ventral-temporal stream in the cortex. The ability of this system to store new items is virtually limitless, although some forgetting and interference does occur over time. This system provides much of the basis for the crystalline intelligence (Miller, 1978), which is largely preserved even in old age. Older adults occasionally experience word-finding problems, often revealed through tip-of-the-tongue episodes. The occurrence of effects of this type is in line with findings regarding the fan effect (Reder & Anderson, 1980), which views the growth in declarative memory structures as leading to slowdowns in retrieval and increases in interference.

The continual growth of lexical ability across the life span is not matched by a similar growth in processing ability. Instead, there is evidence for a gradual neural decline beginning in early adulthood (Kemper, 2006) that leads to slow declines in language fluency, speed, coordination, and accuracy. Even in adults who have not suffered from stroke or other neural disabilities, we can see some slowdown of processing in old age. Wear and tear on the vocal cords and loss of muscle tone can affect speech production, further slowing articulation. When evaluating this decline, we need to note that there is little room for improvement during adulthood in the core features of articulation, audition, and syntax, because these abilities are essentially perfected by the end of childhood. For abilities that are already at asymptote, the only possible direction of movement is downward. Although it is true that we do see some downward movement, this movement is relatively minor and seems to be mostly caused by an overall decline in processing speed.

Second Language Acquisition

In predominantly monolingual countries like the United States or Japan, it is easy to forget that the majority of the people in the world are bilingual or multilingual. The ways in which bilingualism can arise are highly diverse. In areas such as Southeast Asia or the Balkans, villages may be fundamentally bilingual, with people from two different language communities living next to each other and interacting on a daily basis. In multilingual countries such as Switzerland, Belgium, and Luxembourg, a child's parents may each speak a different language, and the child will speak one of these languages at home and another with their peers. In regions such as Africa, children may acquire the national language from their life in the capital city, but a local family language when they return to the countryside in vacation times to live with their rural family.

Older learners' abilities to acquire additional languages with full native fluency declines slowly (Hakuta, Bialystok, & Wiley, 2003) across the life span. Some researchers have suggested that there may be a sharp drop in learning success at puberty (Johnson & Newport, 1989). However, more comprehensive studies indicate no sharp drop at this point, but only a slow and gradual decline. A census-based study of hundreds of Chinese and Mexican immigrants to California (Hakuta et al., 2003; Wiley, Bialystok, & Hakuta, 2005) showed that the disadvantage for older learners is equal to the disadvantage arising from the lack of higher education in one's home country. Thus, educated older immigrants learn about as well as less-educated younger immigrants.

Foreign accent is usually revealed in the way in which an adult learner articulates particular sounds. The fact that some adult learners find it difficult to lose their native language accent even after many years in another country has suggested to some that there may be a specific critical period for the learning of articulation. In a study of Italian immigrants to Toronto, Flege, Yeni-Komshian, and Liu (1999) found that, if the immigrant had arrived to Canada after age 6, it was likely that they would have some trace of an Italian accent. However, it is possible that this preservation of native accent was supported, at least in part, from continued interaction with the Italian immigrant community after arrival. If we look at learners who begin second language acquisition after age 20, it is true that the majority maintain some trace of a foreign accent. However, Bongaerts (1999) found that, if these late learners had good phonetic training, they could eventually lose all trace of a foreign accent in their acquired language.

Emergentist accounts for these effects focus on the twin mechanisms of transfer and entrenchment (MacWhinney, 2005b, 2008a). When two languages are acquired in parallel from birth, neither dominates over the other and each is acquired in its own right. When a second language is learned after early childhood, the words of the weaker language are initially parasitic on those of the first (Kroll & Tokowicz, 2005). In terms of the DevLex model (Li, Zhao, & MacWhinney, 2007), this parasitism is expressed by locating the new words in the same lexical space as their translation equivalents. In terms of articulatory form, new words in the second language are initially composed of phonemes from the first languages. With time, these entrenched L1 gestures are restructured for use in L2. Similarly, syntactic patterns from the first language are also used to order sentences in the second language. Over time, as second language forms strengthen, they can compete with the stronger L1 forms and L2 gradually takes on its own independent shape. In this regard, it is particularly important that the learner starts to think and reason in the second language, thereby acquiring new attitudes, thoughts, and linguistic patterns.

SUMMARY

In this chapter, we have seen how language development across the life span emerges from interactions of the brain with input from the social environment. Both first and second languages are learned by step-by-step inductive procedures that focus on gradual, conservative extension of newly acquired words, sounds, and syntactic patterns. After initial acquisition, ongoing competition modifies the shape of individual forms and the overall system across the life span. Beyond its use for communication, language serves to structure thought and wider social relations in patterns that operate at diverse time scales (MacWhinney, 2005e) ranging from the moment, to the minute, the inter-action, the life span, and the evolution of the species.

REFERENCES

Adams, A., & Bullock, D. (1986). Apprenticeship in word use: Social convergence processes in learning categorically related nouns. In S. Kuczaj & M. Barrett (Eds.), *The development of word meaning* (pp. 155–197). New York: Springer.

Adolphs, R., & Spezio, M. (2006). Role of the amygdala in processing visual social stimuli. *Progress in Brain Research, 156,* 363–378.

Akhtar, N., Carpenter, M., & Tomasello, M. (1996). The role of discourse novelty in early word learning. *Child Development, 62,* 635–645.

Allen, R., & Gardner, B. (1969). Teaching sign language to a chimpanzee. *Science, 165,* 664–672.

Ament, W. (1899). *Die Entwicklung von Sprechen und Denken beim Kinder.* Leipzig: Ernst Wunderlich.

Arriaga, R., Fenson, L., Cronan, T., & Pethick, S. (1998). Scores on the MacArthur communicative development inventory of children from low and middle income families. *Applied Psycholinguistics, 19,* 209–223.

Aslin, R. N., Saffran, J. R., & Newport, E. L. (1999). Statistical learning in linguistic and nonlinguistic domains. In B. MacWhinney (Ed.), *The emergence of language* (pp. 359–380). Mahwah, NJ: Erlbaum.

Astuti, R., Solomon, G., & Carey, S. (2004). Constraints on conceptual development: A case study of the acquisition of folkbiological and folksociological knowledge in Madagascar *Monographs of the Society for Research in Child Development,* 1–135.

Augustine, S. (1952). *The confessions* (Vol. 18). Chicago: Encyclopedia Britannica.

Baldwin, D. A. (1991). Infants' contribution to the achievement of joint reference. *Child Development, 62,* 875–890.

Baldwin, D. A., & Markman, E. M. (1989). Establishing word-object relations: A first step. *Child Development, 60,* 381–398.

Baldwin, D. A., Markman, E. M., Bill, B., Desjardins, R. N., Irwin, J. M., & Tidball, G. (1996). Infants' reliance on a social criterion for establishing word-object relations. *Child Development, 67,* 3135–3153.

Ballard, D. H., Hayhoe, M. M., Pook, P. K., & Rao, R. P. (1997). Deictic codes for the embodiment of cognition. *Behavioral and Brain Sciences, 20,* 723–767.

Baron-Cohen, S., Baldwin, D. A., & Crowson, M. (1997). Do children with autism use the speaker's direction of gaze strategy to crack the code of language? *Child Development, 68,* 48–57.

Batchelder, E. (2002). Bootstrapping the lexicon: A computational model of infant speech segmentation. *Cognition, 83,* 167–206.

Bates, E., Benigni, L., Bretherton, I., Camaioni, L., & Volterra, V. (1979). *The emergence of symbols: Cognition and communication in infancy.* New York: Academic Press.

Bellugi, U., Poizner, H., & Klima, E. S. (1989). Language, modality and the brain. *Trends in Neuroscience, 12*(10), 380–388.

Berlin, B., & Kay, P. (1969). *Basic color terms: Their universality and evolution.* Berkeley: University of California Press.

Berry, M., & Eisenson, J. (1956). *Speech disorders: Principles and practices of therapy.* New York: Appleton-Century Crofts.

Bickerton, D. (1990). *Language and species.* Chicago: University of Chicago Press.

Bijeljac-Babic, R., Bertoncini, J., & Mehler, J. (1993). How do four-day-old infants categorize multisyllabic utterances? *Developmental Psychology, 29,* 711–721.

Bloom, K., Russell, A., & Wassenberg, K. (1987). Turntaking affects the quality of infant vocalizations. *Journal of Child Language, 14,* 211–227.

Bloom, L. (1971). Why not pivot grammar? *Journal of Speech and Hearing Disorders, 40,* 40–50.

Bloom, L. (1973). *One word at a time: The use of single word utterances.* The Hague: Mouton.

Bloom, P. (2002). *How children learn the meanings of words (Learning, Development, and Conceptual Change).* Cambridge, MA: MIT Press.

Bongaerts, T. (1999). Ultimate attainment in L2 pronunciation: The case of very advanced late L2 learners. In D. Birdsong (Ed.), *Second language acquisition and the Critical Period Hypothesis.* Mahwah, NJ: Earlbaum.

Booth, J. R., MacWhinney, B., Thulborn, K. R., Sacco, K., Voyvodic, J., & Feldman, H. (1999). Functional organization of activation patterns in children: Whole brain fMRI imaging during three different cognitive tasks. *Progress in Neuropsychopharmocology and Biological Psychiatry, 23,* 669–682.

Bowerman, M. (1978a). Systematizing semantic knowledge: Changes over time in the child's organization of word meaning. *Child Development, 49,* 977–987.

Bowerman, M. (1978b). The acquisition of word meaning: An investigation into some current conflicts. In N. Waterson & C. Snow (Eds.), *The development of communication.* New York: John Wiley & Sons.

Bowerman, M. (1988). The "no negative evidence" problem. In J. Hawkins (Ed.), *Explaining language universals* (pp. 73–104). London: Blackwell.

Boysson-Bardies, B., & Vihman, M. M. (1991). Adaption to language: Evidence from babbling and first words in four languages. *Language, 67,* 297–320.

Braine, M. D. S. (1963). The ontogeny of English structure: The first phase. *Language, 39,* 1–13.

Braine, M. D. S. (1971). On two types of models of the internalization of grammars. In D. I. Slobin (Ed.), The ontogenesis of grammar: A theoretical symposium. New York: Academic Press.

Braine, M. D. S. (1976). Children's first word combinations. *Monographs of the Society for Research in Child Development, 41* (Whole No. 1).

Branigan, G. (1979). Some reasons why successive single word utterances are not. *Journal of Child Language, 6,* 411–421.

Brent, M., & Siskind, J. (2001). The role of exposure to isolated words in early vocabulary development. *Cognition, 61,* 93–125.

Brent, M. R. (1999). An efficient, probabilistically sound algorithm for segmentation and word discovery. *Machine Learning Journal, 34*, 71–106.

Brown, R. (1958). How shall a thing be called? *Psychological Review, 65*, 14–21.

Brown, R. (1973). *A first language: The early stages.* Cambridge, MA: Harvard.

Brown, R., & Bellugi, U. (1964). Three processes in the child's acquisition of syntax. In E. H. Lennenberg (Ed.), *New directions in the study of language.* Cambridge, MA: MIT Press.

Brown, R., Cazden, C., & Bellugi, U. (1968). The child's grammar from I to III. In J. P. Hill (Ed.), *Minnesota symposia on child development*, Minneapolis, MN: University of Minnesota Press.

Brown, R., & Gilman, A. (1960). The pronouns of power and solidarity. In T. A. Sebeok (Ed.), *Style in language.* Cambridge, MA: MIT Press.

Brown, R., & Hanlon, C. (1970). Derivational complexity and order of acquisition in child speech. In J. R. Hayes (Ed.), *Cognition and the development of language* (pp. 11–54). New York: John Wiley & Sons.

Bruner, J. (1987). *Actual minds, possible worlds.* Cambridge, MA: Harvard University Press.

Bruner, J. (1992). *Acts of meaning.* Cambridge, MA: Harvard University Press.

Budiu, R., & Anderson, J. (2004). Interpretation-based processing: A unified theory of semantic sentence comprehension. *Cognitive Science, 28*, 1–44.

Bybee, J., & Hopper, P. (2001). *Frequency and the emergence of linguistic structure.* Amsterdam: Benjamins.

Campbell, N. A., Reece, J. B., & Mitchell, L. G. (1999). *Biology* (5th ed.). Menlo Park, NJ: Addison Wesley.

Carey, S. (1978). The child as word learner. In M. Halle, J. Bresnan, & G. Miller (Eds.), *Linguistic theory and psychological reality* (pp. 264–293). Cambridge, MA: MIT Press.

Cartwright, T. A., & Brent, M. R. (1997). Syntactic categorization in early language acquisition: Formalizing the role of distributional analysis. *Cognition, 61*, 121–170.

Chomsky, N. (1957). *Syntactic structures.* The Hague: Mouton.

Chomsky, N. (1959). Review of Skinner's "Verbal Behavior." *Language, 35*, 26–58.

Chomsky, N. (1965). *Aspects of the theory of syntax.* Cambridge, MA: MIT Press.

Chomsky, N. (1980). *Rules and representations.* New York: Columbia University Press.

Clark, E. (1987). The Principle of Contrast: A constraint on language acquisition. In B. MacWhinney (Ed.), *Mechanisms of language acquisition* (pp. 1–34). Hillsdale, NJ: Erlbaum.

Clark, E. (1997). Conceptual perspective and lexical choice in acquisition. *Cognition, 64*, 1–37.

Clark, R. (1977). What's the use of imitation? *Journal of Child Language, 4*, 341–358.

Cole, R. A., & Scott, B. (1974). Toward a theory of speech perception. *Psychological Review, 81*(4), 358–374.

Colunga, E., & Smith, L. B. (2000). *Committing to an ontology: A connectionist account.* Paper presented at the Cognitive Science Society, Boston.

Connors, L. J., & Epstein, J. L. (1995). Parent and school partnerships. In M. H. Bornstein (Ed.), *Handbook of parenting* (Vol. 4, pp. 437–457). Mahwah, NJ: Erlbaum.

Corina, D. P., Vaid, J., & Bellugi, U. (1992). The linguistic basis of left hemisphere specialization. *Science, 255*(5049), 1258–1260.

Cruttenden, A. (1970). A phonetic study of babbling. *British Journal of Disorders of Communication, 5*, 110–117.

Crystal, D. (1975). *The English tone of voice: Essays in intonation, prosody and paralanguage.* London: Edward Arnold.

Darwin, C. (1871). *The descent of man and selection in relation to sex.* London: John Murray.

Darwin, C. (1872). *The expression of the emotions in man and animals.* London: John Murray.

Davis, K. (1947). Final note on a case of extreme social isolation. *American Journal of Sociology, 52*, 432–437.

de Saussure, F. (1915/1966). *Course in general linguistics.* New York: McGraw-Hill.

DeCasper, A. J., & Fifer, W. P. (1980). Of human bonding: Newborns prefer their mothers' voices. *Science, 208*, 1174–1176.

DeCasper, A. J., Lecanuet, J., & Busnel, M. (1994). Fetal reactions to recurrent mother speech. *Infant Behavior and Development, 17*, 159–164.

Dell, G., Juliano, C., & Govindjee, A. (1993). Structure and content in language production: A theory of frame constraints in phonological speech errors. *Cognitive Science, 17*, 149–195.

Dell, G. S., Schwartz, M. F., Martin, N., Saffran, E., & Gagnon, D. A. (1997). Lexical access in aphasic and non-aphasic speakers. *Psychological Review, 104*, 811–838.

Dell'Orletta, F., Lenci, A., Montemagni, S., & Pirrelli, V. (2005). Climbing the path to grammar: A maximum entropy model of subject/object learning. *Association for Computational Linguistics: PsyComp Models.* ACM, 72–81.

Dickinson, D. K., & Moreton, J. (1991). Predicting specific kindergarten literacy skills from three-year-olds' preschool experiences. *Merrill-Palmer Quarterly, 15*, 249–258.

Dominey, P., Hoen, M., & Inui, T. (2006). A neurolinguistic model of grammatical construction processing. *Journal of Cognitive Neuroscience, 18*, 2088–2177.

Donald, M. (1991). *Origins of the modern mind.* Cambridge, MA: Harvard University Press.

Dromi, E. (1987). *Early lexical development.* New York: Cambridge University Press.

Edelman, G. (1987). *Neural Darwinism: The theory of neuronal group selection.* New York: Basic Books.

Eimas, P. D., Siqueland, E. R., Jusczyk, P., & Vigorito, J. (1971). Speech perception in infants. *Science, 171*, 303–306.

Elman, J. L. (1999). The emergence of language: A conspiracy theory. In B. MacWhinney (Ed.), *The emergence of language* (pp. 1–28). Mahwah, NJ: Erlbaum.

Ervin, S. (1964). Imitation and structural change in children's language. In E. H. Lenneberg (Ed.), *New directions in the study of language.* Cambridge, MA: MIT Press.

Everett, D. (2007). Challenging Chomskyan linguistics: The case of Pirahã. *Human Development, 50*, 297–299.

Fauconnier, G. (1994). *Mental spaces: Aspects of meaning construction in natural language.* Cambridge: Cambridge University Press.

Flege, J. E., Yeni-Komshian, G. H., & Liu, S. (1999). Age constraints on second-language acquisition. *Journal of Memory and Language, 41*, 78–104.

Fodor, J. (1983). *The modularity of mind: An essay on faculty psychology.* Cambridge, MA: MIT Press.

Ford, M., Bresnan, J., & Kaplan, D. (1982). A competence-based theory of syntactic closure. In J. Bresnan & R. Kaplan (Eds.), *The mental representation of grammatical relations.* Cambridge, MA: MIT Press.

Franks, S. L., & Connell, P. J. (1996). Knowledge of binding in normal and SLI children. *Journal of Child Language, 23*, 431–464.

Frederiksen, C., Donin, J., Koschmann, T., & Myers Kelson, A. (2004). *Investigating diagnostic problem solving in medicine through cognitive analysis of clinical discourse.* Paper presented at the Society for Text and Discourse, Chicago.

Friederici, A. (in press). Brain circuits of syntax: From neurotheoretical considerations to empirical tests. In *Biological foundations and origin of syntax*. Cambridge, MA: MIT Press.

Frith, C. D., & Frith, U. (1999). Interacting minds—a biological basis. *Science, 286,* 1692–1695.

Gelman, S. A. (1998). Categories in young children's thinking. *Young Children, 53,* 20–26.

Gentner, D. (1982). Why nouns are learned before verbs: Linguistic relativity versus natural partitioning. In S. Kuczaj (Ed.), *Language development: Language, culture, and cognition* (pp. 301–334). Hillsdale, NJ: Erlbaum.

Gentner, D. (2005). The development of relational category knowledge. In L. Gershkoff-Stowe & D. Rakison (Eds.), *Building object categories in developmental time*. Mahwah, NJ: Erlbaum.

Gentner, D., & Markman, A. (1997). Structure mapping in analogy and similarity. *American Psychologist, 52,* 45–56.

Gernsbacher, M. A. (1990). *Language comprehension as structure building*. Hillsdale, NJ: Erlbaum.

Gibson, E. (1998). Linguistic complexity: Locality of syntactic dependencies. *Cognition, 68,* 1–76.

Gogate, L. J., Bahrick, L. E., & Watson, J. D. (2000). A study of multimodal motherese: The role of temporal synchrony between verbal labels and gestures. *Child Development, 71,* 878–894.

Goldberg, A. E. (1999). The emergence of the semantics of argument structure constructions. In B. MacWhinney (Ed.), *The emergence of language* (pp. 197–213). Mahwah, NJ: Erlbaum.

Goldfield, B. (1993). Noun bias in maternal speech to one-year-olds. *Journal of Child Language, 13,* 455–476.

Golinkoff, R., Hirsh-Pasek, K., & Hollich, G. (1999). Emergent cues for early word learning. In B. MacWhinney (Ed.), *The emergence of language* (pp. 305–330). Mahwah, NJ: Erlbaum.

Gopnik, A., & Choi, S. (1995). Names, relational words, and cognitive development in English and Korean speakers: Nouns are not always learned before verbs. In M. Tomasello & M. Merriman (Eds.), *Beyond names for things* (pp. 63–80). Hillsdale, NJ: Erlbaum.

Gopnik, M. (1990). Feature blindness: A case study. *Language Acquisition, 1,* 139–164.

Greeno, J., & MacWhinney, B. (2006). *Perspective shifting in classroom interactions*. Paper presented at the AERA Meeting, San Francisco, CA.

Grosjean, F., & Miller, J. (1994). Going in and out of languages. *Psychological Science, 5,* 201–206.

Grossberg, S. (1978). A theory of human memory: Self-organization and performance of sensory-motor codes, maps, and plans. *Progress in Theoretical Biology, 5,* 233–374.

Guenther, F. (2006). Cortical interactions underlying the production of speech sounds. *Journal of Communication Disorders, 39,* 350–365.

Gupta, P., & MacWhinney, B. (1997). Vocabulary acquisition and verbal short-term memory: Computational and neural bases. *Brain and Language, 59,* 267–333.

Hakuta, K., Bialystok, E., & Wiley, E. (2003). Critical evidence: A test of the critical period hypothesis for second language acquisition. *Psychological Science, 14,* 31–38.

Halliday, M. (1975). *Learning to mean: explorations in the development of language*. London: Edward Arnold.

Harm, M. (2002). Building large scale distributed semantic feature sets with WordNet. *CNBC Tech Report.* PDP.CNS.02.1 January.

Harris, Z. S. (1951). *Structural linguistics*. Chicago: University of Chicago Press.

Hart, B., & Risley, T. R. (1995). *Meaningful differences in the everyday experience of young American children*. Baltimore: Paul H. Brookes.

Hauser, M., Chomsky, N., & Fitch, T. (2002). The faculty of language: What is it, who has it, and how did it evolve? *Science, 298,* 1569–1579.

Hauser, M., Newport, E., & Aslin, R. (2001). Segmentation of the speech stream in a non-human primate: Statistical learning in cotton-top tamarins. *Cognition, 78,* B53–B64.

Hausser, R. (1999). *Foundations of computational linguistics: Man-machine communication in natural language*. Berlin: Springer.

Hebb, D. (1949). *The organization of behavior.* New York: John Wiley & Sons.

Herbst, T. (2007). Valency complements or valency patterns? In T. Herbst & K. Götz-Votteler (Eds.), *Valency: Theoretical, descriptive and cognitive issues* (pp. 15–35). Berlin: Mouton de Gruyter.

Hirsch, E. D. (1987). *Cultural literacy: What every American needs to know.* Boston: Houghton Mifflin.

Hirsch, E. D., Kett, J. F., & Trefil, J. (1988). *The dictionary of cultural literacy.* Boston: Houghton Mifflin.

Houghton, G. (1990). The problem of serial order: A neural network model of sequence learning and recall. In R. Dale, C. Mellish, & M. Zock (Eds.), *Current research in natural language generation* (pp. 287–319). London: Academic.

Hoyer, A., & Hoyer, G. (1924). über die Lallsprache eines Kindes. *Zeitschrift für angewandte Psychologie, 24,* 363–384.

Hubel, D., & Weisel, T. (1963). Receptive fields of cells in striate cortex of very young, visually inexperienced kittens. *Journal of Neurophysiology, 26,* 994–1002.

Hume, D. (1748). *An inquiry concerning human understanding.* London: Collier & Son (public domain).

Hunt, E. (1962). *Concept learning: An information processing approach.* New York: John Wiley & Sons.

Huttenlocher, J. (1974). The origins of language comprehension. In R. Solso (Ed.), *Theories in cognitive psychology: The Loyola symposium* (pp. 331–388). Potomac, MD: Erlbaum.

Huttenlocher, J., Haight, W., Bryk, A., Seltzer, M., & Lyons, T. (1991). Early vocabulary growth: Relation to language input and gender. *Developmental Psychology, 27*(2), 236–248.

Hyams, N. (1995). Nondiscreteness and variation in child language: Implications for Principle and Parameter models of language development. In Y. Levy (Ed.), *Other children, other languages* (pp. 11–40). Hillsdale, NJ: Erlbaum.

Hyams, N., & Wexler, K. (1993). On the grammatical basis of null subjects in child language. *Linguistic Inquiry, 24*(3), 421–459.

Irwin, O. C. (1936). *Infant speech.* New York: Harcourt, Brace.

Jakobson, R. (1968). *Child language, aphasia and phonological universals.* The Hague: Mouton.

James, W. (1890). *The principles of psychology.* New York: Holt, Rinehart, and Winston.

Jasnow, M., & Feldstein, S. (1986). Adult-like temporal characteristics of mother-infant vocal interactions. *Child Delevopment, 57,* 754–761.

Johnson, J., & Newport, E. (1989). Critical period effects in second language learning: The influence of maturational state on the acquisition of English as a second language. *Cognitive Psychology, 21,* 60–99.

Johnson, M. (1992). Imprinting and the development of face recognition: From chick to man. *Current Directions in Psychological Science, 1,* 52–55.

Jusczyk, P. W. (1997). *The discovery of spoken language.* Cambridge, MA: MIT Press.

Jusczyk, P. W., Jusczyk, A. M., Kennedy, L. J., Schomberg, T., & Koenig, N. (1995). Young infants' retention of information about bisyllabic utterances. *Journal of Experimental Psychology: Human Perception and Performance, 21,* 822–836.

Just, M., & Carpenter, P. (1992). A capacity theory of comprehension: Individual differences in working memory. *Psychological Review, 99*, 122–149.

Just, M., & Varma, S. (2007). The organization of thinking: What functional brain imaging reveals about the neuroarchitecture of complex cognition. *Cognitive, Affective, and Behavioral Neuroscience, 7*, 153–191.

Kager, R. (1999). *Optimality Theory.* New York: Cambridge University Press.

Kandel, E. R., & Hawkins, R. D. (1992). The biological basis of learning and individuality. *Scientific American, 266*, 40–53.

Kanerva, P. (1993). Sparse distributed memory and related models. In M. Hassoun (Ed.), *Associative neural memories: Theory and implementation* (pp. 50–76). New York: Oxford University Press.

Katz, N., Baker, E., & Macnamara, J. (1974). What's in a name? A study of how children learn common and proper names. *Child Development, 45*, 469–473.

Kay, D. A., & Anglin, J. M. (1982). Overextension and underextension in the child's expressive and receptive speech. *Journal of Child Language, 9*, 83–98.

Kay, P., & Fillmore, C. J. (1999). Grammatical constructions and linguistic generalization: The "what's X doing Y?" construction. *Language, 75*, 1–33.

Keenan, J., MacWhinney, B., & Mayhew, D. (1977). Pragmatics in memory: A study in natural conversation. *Journal of Verbal Learning and Verbal Behavior, 16*, 549–560.

Keil, F. C. (1989). *Concepts, kinds, and cognitive development.* Cambridge, MA: MIT Press.

Keil, F. C., & Batterman, N. (1984). A characteristic-to-defining shift in the development of word meaning. *Journal of Verbal Learning and Verbal Behavior, 23*, 221–236.

Keller, H., Poortinga, Y., & Schomerich, A. (2002). *Between culture and biology: Perspectives on ontogenetic development.* New York: Cambridge University Press.

Kempe, V., & MacWhinney, B. (1999). Processing of morphological and semantic cues in Russian and German. *Language and Cognitive Processes, 14*, 129–171.

Kemper, S. (2006). Language in adulthood. In E. Bialystok & F. Craik (Eds.), *Lifespan cognition.* (pp. 223–238). New York: Oxford University Press.

Kendon, A. (1982). The study of gesture: Some observations on its history. *Recherches Sémiotiques/Semiotic Inquiry, 2*(1), 45–62.

Kenyeres, E. (1926). *A gyermek első szavai es a szófajók föllépése.* Budapest: Kisdednevelés.

Kilborn, K. (1989). Sentence processing in a second language: The timing of transfer. *Language and Speech, 32*, 1–23.

Kintsch, W. (1998). *Comprehension: A paradigm for cognition.* New York: Cambridge University Press.

Klima, E., & Bellugi, U. (1966). Syntactic regularities in the speech of children. In J. Lyons & R. J. Wales (Eds.), *Psycholinguistics papers.* Edinburgh: Edinburgh University Press.

Knoblich, G. (2008). Bodily and motor contributions to action perception. In R. Klatzky, B. MacWhinney, & M. Behrmann, (Eds.), *Embodied cognition.* Mahwah, NJ: Erlbaum.

Kohonen, T. (2001). *Self-organizing maps* (3rd ed.). Berlin: Springer.

Konishi, M. (1995). A sensitive period for birdsong learning. In B. Julesz & I. Kovacs (Eds.), *Maturational windows and adult cortical plasticity* (pp. 87–92). New York: Addison-Wesley.

Kroll, J., & Tokowicz, N. (2005). Bilingual lexical processing. In J. F. Kroll & A. M. B. DeGroot (Eds.), *Handbook of Bilingualism: Psycholinguistic approaches.* New York: Oxford University Press.

Kuczaj, S., & Brannick, N. (1979). Children's use of the Wh question modal auxiliary placement rule. *Journal of Experimental Child Psychology, 28*, 43–67.

Kuhl, P. K., & Miller, J. D. (1978). Speech perception by the chinchilla: Identification functions for synthetic VOT stimuli. *Journal of the Acoustical Society of America, 63*, 905–917.

Labov, T., & Labov, W. (1978). The phonetics of cat and mama. *Language, 54*, 316–852.

Labov, W. (1994). *Principles of linguistic change: Vol. 1, Linguistic considerations.* London: Blackwells.

Lacerda, F. (1998). An exemplar-based account of emergent phonetic categories. *Journal of the Acoustical Society of America, 103*, 2980–2981.

Lakoff, G. (1987). *Women, fire, and dangerous things.* Chicago: Chicago University Press.

Lee, T. H. (1999). Finiteness and null arguments in child Cantonese. *Tsinghua Journal of Chinese Studies, 33*, 1–16.

Lempers, J. (1979). Young children's production and comprehension of nonverbal deictic behaviors. *Journal of Genetic Psychology, 135*, 93–102.

Leopold, W. (1949). *Speech development of a bilingual child: A linguist's record: Vol. 3, Grammar and general problems in the first two years.* Evanston, IL: Northwestern University Press.

Lerner, R. (2006). Developmental science, developmental systems, and contemporary theories of human development. In R. Lerner (Ed.), *Handbook of child psychology: Vol. 1, Theoretical models of human development* (6th ed., pp. 1–17). Hoboken, NJ: John Wiley & Sons.

Lerner, R. M., & Overton, W. F. (2008). Exemplifying the integrations of the relational developmental system: Synthesizing theory, research, and application to promote positive development and social justice. *Journal of Adolescent Research, 23*, 245–255.

Levi-Strauss, C. (1963). *Structural anthropology.* New York: Basic Books.

Lewis, M. M. (1936). *Infant speech: A study of the beginnings of language.* New York: Harcourt, Brace and Co.

Li, P., Farkas, I., & MacWhinney, B. (2004). Early lexical development in a self-organizing neural network. *Neural Networks, 17*, 1345–1362.

Li, P., Zhao, X., & MacWhinney, B. (2007). Dynamic self-organization and early lexical development in children. *Cognitive Science, 31*, 581–612.

Lindblom, B., Diehl, R., Park, S.-H., & Salvi, G. (in press). Sound systems are shaped by their users: The recombination of phonetic substance. In N. Clements & R. Ridouane (Eds.), *Where do features come from? The nature and sources of phonological primitives.* Paris: Sorbonne.

Locke, J. (1995). Why do infants begin to talk? Language as an unintended consequence. *Journal of Child Language, 23*, 251–268.

Lorenz, K. Z. (1958). The evolution of behavior. *Scientific American, 199*, 95–104.

MacDonald, M. C., Pearlmutter, N. J., & Seidenberg, M. S. (1994). Lexical nature of syntactic ambiguity resolution. *Psychological Review, 101*(4), 676–703.

MacNeilage, P. (1998). The frame/content theory of evolution of speech production. *Behavioral and Brain Sciences, 21*, 499–546.

MacNeilage, P., Davis, B. L., Kinney, A., & Matyear, C. (2000). The motor core of speech: A comparison of serial organization patterns in infants and languages. *Child Development, 71*, 153–163.

MacWhinney, B. (1974). *How Hungarian children learn to speak.* Berkeley, CA: University of California.

MacWhinney, B. (1975a). Pragmatic patterns in child syntax. *Stanford Papers and Reports on Child Language Development, 10*, 153–165.

MacWhinney, B. (1975b). Rules, rote, and analogy in morphological formations by Hungarian children. *Journal of Child Language, 2,* 65–77.

MacWhinney, B. (1977). Starting points. *Language, 53,* 152–168.

MacWhinney, B. (1978). The acquisition of morphophonology. *Monographs of the Society for Research in Child Development, 43*(Whole no. 1), 1–123.

MacWhinney, B. (1984). Where do categories come from? In C. Sophian (Ed.), *Child categorization* (pp. 407–418). Hillsdale, NJ: Erlbaum.

MacWhinney, B. (1987). The competition model. In B. MacWhinney (Ed.), *Mechanisms of language acquisition* (pp. 249–308). Hillsdale, NJ: Erlbaum.

MacWhinney, B. (1989). Competition and lexical categorization. In R. Corrigan, F. Eckman, & M. Noonan (Eds.), *Linguistic categorization* (pp. 195–242). Philadelphia: Benjamins.

MacWhinney, B. (1999a). The emergence of language from embodiment. In B. MacWhinney (Ed.), *The emergence of language* (pp. 213–256). Mahwah, NJ: Erlbaum.

MacWhinney, B. (Ed.). (1999b). *The emergence of language.* Mahwah, NJ: Erlbaum.

MacWhinney, B. (2002). The gradual evolution of language. In B. Malle & T. Giv—n (Eds.), *The evolution of language* (pp. 233–264). Philadelphia: Benjamins.

MacWhinney, B. (2004). A multiple process solution to the logical problem of language acquisition. *Journal of Child Language, 31,* 883–914.

MacWhinney, B. (2005a). A unified model of language acquisition. In J. F. Kroll & A.M.B. de Groot (Eds.), *Handbook of bilingualism: Psycholinguistic approaches* (pp. 49–67). New York: Oxford University Press.

MacWhinney, B. (2005b). Emergent fossilization. In Z. Han & T. Odlin (Eds.), *Studies of fossilization in second language acquisition* (pp. 134–156). Clevedon, United Kingdom: Multilingual Matters.

MacWhinney, B. (2005c). Item-based constructions and the logical problem. *ACL 2005, 46*–54.

MacWhinney, B. (2005d). The emergence of grammar from perspective. In D. Pecher & R. A. Zwaan (Eds.), *The grounding of cognition: The role of perception and action in memory, language, and thinking* (pp. 198–223). Mahwah, NJ: Erlbaum.

MacWhinney, B. (2005e). The emergence of linguistic form in time. *Connection Science, 191*–211.

MacWhinney, B. (2008a). A unified model. In P. Robinson & N. Ellis (Eds.), *Handbook of cognitive linguistics and second language acquisition.* Mahwah, NJ: Erlbaum.

MacWhinney, B. (2008b). Cognitive precursors to language. In K. Oller & U. Griebel (Eds.), *The evolution of communicative flexibility* (pp. 193–214). Cambridge, MA: MIT Press.

MacWhinney, B. (2008c). How mental models encode embodied linguistic perspectives. In R. Klatzky, B. MacWhinney, & M. Behrmann (Eds.), *Embodiment, ego-space, and action* (pp. 369–410). Mahwah, NJ: Erlbaum.

MacWhinney, B. (2009). The emergence of linguistic complexity. In T. Givon (Ed.), *Linguistic complexity* (pp. 405–432). New York: Benjamins.

MacWhinney, B., & Bates, E. (Eds.). (1989). *The crosslinguistic study of sentence processing.* New York: Cambridge University Press.

MacWhinney, B., Bates, E., & Kliegl, R. (1984). Cue validity and sentence interpretation in English, German, and Italian. *Journal of Verbal Learning and Verbal Behavior, 23,* 127–150.

MacWhinney, B., Feldman, H. M., Sacco, K., & Valdes-Perez, R. (2000). Online measures of basic language skills in children with early focal brain lesions. *Brain and Language, 71,* 400–431.

MacWhinney, B., & Leinbach, J. (1991). Implementations are not conceptualizations: Revising the verb learning model. *Cognition, 29,* 121–157.

MacWhinney, B., Leinbach, J., Taraban, R., & McDonald, J. (1989). Language learning: Cues or rules? *Journal of Memory and Language, 28,* 255–277.

MacWhinney, B., & Li, P. (2008). Neurolinguistic computational models. In B. Stemmer & H. Whitaker (Eds.), *Handbook of the neuroscience of language* (pp. 229–236). Mahwah, NJ: Erlbaum.

Mann, W. C., & Thompson, S. A. (1992). *Discourse description.* Amsterdam: Benjamins.

Maratsos, M., & Deak, G. (1995). Hedgehogs, foxes, and the acquisition of verb meaning. In M. Tomasello & M. Merriman (Eds.), *Beyond names for things* (pp. 377–404). Hillsdale, NJ: Erlbaum.

Marcus, G. (2000). Pabiku and Ga Ti Ga: Two mechanisms infants use to learn about the world. *Current Directions in Psychological Science, 9,* 145–147.

Marler, P. (1991). Song-learning behavior: the interface with neuroethology. *Trends in Neuroscience, 14,* 199–206.

Marslen-Wilson, W., & Warren, P. (1994). Levels of perceptual representation and process in lexical access: Words, phonemes, and features. *Psychological Review, 101,* 653–675.

Massaro, D. (Ed.). (1975). *Understanding language: An introduction-processing analysis of speech perception, reading, and psycholinguistics.* New York: Academic Press.

Mavilya, M. (1972). Spontaneous vocalication and babbling in hearing impaired infants. In G. Fant (Ed.), *International Symposium on Speech Communication Abilities and Profound Deafness.* Washington, DC: Alexander Graham Bell Association for the Deaf, 163–171.

McCarthy, D. (1954). Language development in children. In L. Carmichael (Ed.), *Handbook of child psychology.* New York: John Wiley & Sons.

McClelland, J. L., McNaughton, B. L., & O'Reilly, R. C. (1995). Why there are complementary learning systems in the hippocampus and neocortex: Insights from the successes and failures of connectionist models of learning and memory. *Psychological Review, 102,* 419–457.

McCulloch, W. S., & Pitts, W. H. (1943). A logical calculus of the ideas immanent in nervous activity. *Bulletin of Mathematical Biophysics, 5,* 115–133.

McLuhan, M., & Fiore, Q. (1967). *The medium is the massage.* New York: Bantam Books.

Mead, G. (1934). *Mind, self, and society: From the standpoint of a social behaviorist.* Chicago: Chicago University Press.

Meltzoff, A. N. (1995). Understanding the intentions of others: Re-enactment of intended acts by 18-month-old children. *Developmental Psychology, 31,* 838–850.

Meltzoff, A. N., & Decety, J. (2003). What imitation tells us about social cognition: A rapprochement between developmental psychology and cognitive neuroscience. *Philosophical Transactions of the Royal Society of London B, 358,* 491–500.

Menn, L., & Stoel-Gammon, C. (1995). Phonological development. In P. Fletcher & B. MacWhinney (Eds.), *The handbook of child language* (pp. 335–360). Oxford: Blackwell.

Menyuk, P. (1969). *Sentences children use.* Cambridge, MA: MIT Press.

Merriman, W. (1999). Competition, attention, and young children's lexical processing. In B. MacWhinney (Ed.), *The emergence of language* (pp. 331–358). Mahwah, NJ: Erlbaum.

Mervis, C. (1984). Early lexical development: The contributions of mother and child. In C. Sophian (Ed.), *Origins of cognitive skills* (pp. 339–370). Hillsdale, NJ: Erlbaum.

Mesoudi, A., Whiten, A., & Laland, K. (2006). Towards a unified science of cultural evolution. *Behavioral and Brain Sciences, 29,* 329–383.

Miller, G. (1965). Some preliminaries to psycholinguistics. *American Psychologist, 20,* 15–20.

Miller, G. (1978). Semantic relations among words. In J. B. M. Halle & G. Miller (Eds.), *Linguistic theory and psychological reality* (pp. 60–118). Cambridge, MA: MIT Press.

Miller, G., Beckwith, R., Fellbaum, C., Gross, D., & Miller, K. (1990). Introduction to WordNet: An on-line lexical database. *International Journal of Lexicography, 3.*

Miller, K., Keller, J., & Stryker, M. (1989). Ocular dominance column development: Analysis and simulation. *Science, 245,* 605–615.

Mitchell, T. M., Shinkareva, S. V., Carlson, A., Chang, K.-M., Malave, V. L., Mason, R. A., et al. (2008). Predicting human brain activity associated with the meanings of nouns. *Science, 320,* 1191–1195.

Monaghan, P., Christiansen, M., & Chater, N. (2007). The phonological-distributional coherence hypothesis: Cross-linguistic evidence in language acquisition. *Cognitive Psychology, 55,* 259–305.

Mowrer, O. (1960). *Learning theory and the symbolic processes.* New York: John Wiley & Sons.

Murray, J. D. (1988). How the leopard gets its spots. *Scientific American, 258,* 80–87.

Naigles, L. G., & Gelman, S. A. (1995). Overextensions in comprehension and production revisited: Preferential looking in a study of dog, cat, and cow. *Journal of Child Language, 22,* 19–46.

Namy, L., & Waxman, S. (1998). Words and gestures: Infants' interpretations of different forms of symbolic reference. *Child Development, 69,* 295–308.

Nelson, K. (2000). Emerging theories in the psychology of language and cognition. *Contemporary Psychology, 45,* 159–161.

Nicoladis, E. (2001). Finding first words in the input. In J. Cenoz & F. Genesee (Eds.), *Trends in bilingual acquisition* (pp. 131–148). New York: Benjamins.

Ninio, A., & Snow, C. (1988). Language acquisition through language use: The functional sources of children's early utterances. In Y. Levy, I. Schlesinger, & M. Braine (Eds.), *Categories and processes in language acquisition* (pp. 11–30). Hillsdale, NJ: Erlbaum.

Nuñez, R., & Lakoff, G. (2000). *Where mathematics comes from: How the embodied mind brings mathematics into being.* New York: Basic Books.

Ochs, E., & Schieffelin, B. B. (1983). *Acquiring conversational competence.* London: Routledge & Kegan Paul.

O'Grady, W. (2004). *Syntactic carpentry.* Mahwah, NJ: Erlbaum.

O'Grady, W. (2005). *Syntactic carpentry.* Mahwah, NJ: Erlbaum.

Ohala, J. J. (1974). Phonetic explanation in phonology. In A. Bruck, R. Fox, & M. La Galy (Eds.), *Papers from the parassession on natural phonology* (pp. 251–274). Chicago: Chicago Linguistic Society.

Ohala, J. J. (1981). The listener as a source of sound change. In R. H. C. Masek & M. Miller (Eds.), *Papers from the Parasession on Language and Behavior.* Chicago: Chicago Linguistic Society.

Ohala, J. J. (1994). The frequency codes underlying the symbolic use of voice pitch. In L. Hinton, J. Nichols, & J. Ohala (Eds.), *Sound symbolism* (pp. 325–347). New York: Cambridge University Press.

Oller, D. K. (2000). *The emergence of the speech capacity.* Mahwah, NJ: Erlbaum.

Oller, D. K., & Eilers, R. E. (1988). The role of audition in infant babbling. *Child Development, 59,* 441–449.

Overton, W. (2006). Developmental psychology: Philosophy, concepts, methodology. In R. Lerner (Ed.), *Handbook of child psychology: Vol. 1, Theoretical models of human development* (pp. 18–88). Hoboken, NJ: John Wiley & Sons.

Papousek, M., & Papousek, H. (1991). The meanings of melodies in mothers in tone and stress languages. *Infant Behavior and Development, 14,* 415–440.

Pelphrey, K. A., Mitchell, T. V., McKeown, M. J., Goldstein, J., Allison, T., & McCarthy, G. (2003). Brain activity evoked by the perception of human walking: Controlling for meaningful coherent motion. *Journal of Neuroscience, 23,* 6819–6825.

Pelphrey, K. A., Morris, J. P., & McCarthy, G. (2005). Neural basis of eye gaze processing deficits in autism. *Brain, 128,* 1038–1048.

Peters, A. M. (1977). Language learning strategies: Does the whole equal the sum of the parts? *Language, 53,* 560–573.

Piaget, J. (1952). *The origins of intelligence in children.* New York: International Universities Press.

Piaget, J. (1954). *The construction of reality in the child.* New York: Basic Books.

Pinker, S. (1984). *Language learnability and language development.* Cambridge, MA: Harvard University Press.

Pinker, S. (1991). Rules of language. *Science, 253,* 530–535.

Pinker, S. (1999). *Words and rules: The ingredients of language.* New York: Basic Books.

Ponori, T. E. (1871). A gyermeknyelvról. *Természettudományi Közlöny, 3,* 117–125.

Pulvermüller, F. (2003). *The neuroscience of language.* Cambridge: Cambridge University Press.

Quine, W. V. O. (1960). *Word and object.* Cambridge, MA: MIT Press.

Quinlan, P. T. (2003). *Connectionist models of development: Developmental processes in real and artificial neural networks.* Hove, United Kingdom: Psychology Press.

Ratcliff, R. (1978). A theory of memory retrieval. *Psychological Review, 85,* 59–108.

Ratcliff, R., & Smith, R. L. (2004). A comparison of sequential sampling models for two-choice reaction time. *Psychological Review, 111,* 333–367.

Reder, L. M., & Anderson, J. R. (1980). A partial resolution of the paradox of interference: The role of integrating knowledge. *Cognitive Psychology, 12,* 447–472.

Regier, T. (2005). The emergence of words: Attentional learning in form and meaning. *Cognitive Science, 29,* 819–865.

Reznick, S. (1990). Visual preference as a test of infant word comprehension. *Applied Psycholinguistics, 11,* 145–166.

Rizzolatti, G., Fadiga, L., Gallese, V., & Fogassi, L. (1996). Premotor cortex and the recognition of motor actions. *Cognitive Brain Research, 3,* 131–141.

Rosch, E., & Mervis, C. B. (1975). Family resemblances: Studies in the internal structure of categories. *Cognitive Psychology, 7,* 573–605.

Rumelhart, D. E., & McClelland, J. L. (1986). *Parallel distributed processing.* Cambridge, MA: MIT Press.

Rumelhart, D. E., & McClelland, J. L. (1987). Learning the past tenses of English verbs: Implicit rules or parallel distributed processes? In B. MacWhinney (Ed.), *Mechanisms of language acquisition* (pp. 195–248). Hillsdale, NJ: Lawrence Erlbaum.

Sacks, H., Schegloff, E., & Jefferson, G. (1974). A simplest systematics for the organization of turn-taking for conversation. *Language, 50,* 696–735.

Saffran, J. R., Aslin, R. N., & Newport, E. L. (1996). Statistical learning by 8-month-old infants. *Science, 274,* 1926–1928.

Sagae, K., Davis, E., Lavie, E., MacWhinney, B., & Wintner, S. (2007). High-accuracy annotation and parsing of CHILDES transcripts. In *Proceedings of the 45th Meeting of the Association for Computational Linguistics.* Prague: ACL.

Sandhofer, C., Smith, L., & Luo, J. (2000). Counting nouns and verbs in the input: Differential frequencies, different kinds of learning? *Journal of Child Language, 27,* 561–585.

Schafer, G., & Plunkett, K. (1998). Rapid word learning by 15-month-olds under tightly controlled conditions. *Child Development, 69,* 309–320.

Schegloff, E. (2007). *Sequence organization in interaction: A primer in conversation analysis.* New York: Cambridge University Press.

Schieffelin, B., & Ochs, E. (1987). *Language acquisition across cultures.* New York: Cambridge.

Schlesinger, I. M. (1974). Relational concepts underlying language. In R. L. Schiefelbusch & L. L. Lloyd (Eds.), *Language perspectives–Acquisition, retardation, and intervention.* Baltimore, MD: University Park Press.

Schlesinger, I. M. (1975). Grammatical development—the first steps. In E. H. Lenneberg & E. Lenneberg (Eds.), *Foundations of language development: A multidisciplinary approach* (Vol. 1). New York: Academic Press.

Schmahmann, J., Pandya, D., Wang, R., Dai, G., D'Arceuil, H., de Crespigny, A., et al. (2007). Association fibre pathways of the brain: Parallel observations from diffusion spectrum imaging and autoradiography. *Brain, 130,* 630–653.

Schmajuk, N., & DiCarlo, J. (1992). Stimulus configuration, classical conditioning, and hippocampal function. *Psychological Review, 99,* 268–305.

Sebastián-Galles, N. & Bosch, L. (2005). Phonology and bilingualism. In J. F. Kroll & A. M. B. DeGroot (Eds.), *Handbook of bilingualism: Psycholinguistic approaches.* New York: Oxford University Press.

Sfard, A., & McClain, K. (2002). Special issue: Analyzing tools: Perspective on the role of designed artifacts in mathematics learning. *Journal of the Learning Sciences, 11,* 153–388.

Shrager, J. F., & Johnson, M. H. (1995). Waves of growth in the development of cortical function: A computational model. In B. Julesz & I. Kovacs (Eds.), *Maturational windows and adult cortical plasticity* (pp. 31–44). New York: Addison-Wesley.

Silverstein, M. (1976). Shifters, linguistic categories and cultural description. In K. H. Basso & H. A. Selby (Eds.), *Meaning in anthropology* (pp. 11–55). Albuquerque, NM: University of New Mexico Press.

Slobin, D. I. (1996). From "thought and language" to "thinking for speaking." In J. J. Gumperz & S. Levinson (Eds.), *Rethinking linguistic relativity* (pp. 70–96). Cambridge: Cambridge University Press.

Smith, L. (1999). Children's noun learning: How general processes make specialized learning mechanisms. In B. MacWhinney (Ed.), *The emergence of language* (pp. 277–304). Mahwah, NJ: Erlbaum.

Smith, N. V. (1973). *The acquisition of phonology: A case study.* Cambridge: Cambridge University Press.

Snow, C. E. (1977). The development of conversation between mothers and babies. *Journal of Child Language, 4,* 1–22.

Snow, C. E. (1999). Social perspectives on the emergence of language. In B. MacWhinney (Ed.), *The emergence of language* (pp. 257–276). Mahwah, NJ: Erlbaum.

Snow, C. E., Pan, B., Imbens-Bailey, A., & Herman, J. (1996). Learning how to say what one means: A longitudinal study of children's speech act use. *Social Development, 5,* 56–84.

Stager, C. L., & Werker, J. F. (1997). Infants listen for more phonetic detail in speech perception than in word learning tasks. *Nature, 388,* 381–382.

Stampe, D. (1973). *A dissertation on natural phonology.* Chicago: University of Chicago.

Stemberger, J. (1985). *The lexicon in a model of language production.* New York: Garland.

Stiles-Davis, J., Sugarman, S., & Nass, R. (1985). The development of spatial and class relations in four young children with right-cerebral-hemisphere damage: Evidence for an early spatial constructive deficit. *Brain and Cognition, 4,* 388–412.

Sugarman, S. (1982). Developmental change in early representational intelligence: Evidence from spatial classification strategies and related verbal expressions. *Cognitive Psychology, 14,* 410–449.

Talmy, L. (2000). *Toward a cognitive semantics: Vol. 1, The concept structuring system.* Cambridge, MA: MIT Press.

Tamis-LeMonda, C., & Bornstein, M. H. (2002). Maternal responsiveness and early language acquisition. In R. Kail & J. Reese (Eds.), *Advances in child development and behavior* (Vol. 29, pp. 89–127). San Diego, CA: Academic Press.

Taraban, R., & McClelland, J. L. (1988). Constituent attachment and thematic role assignment in sentence processing: Influences of content-based expectations. *Journal of Memory and Language, 27,* 597–632.

Tardif, T. (1996). Nouns are not always learned before verbs: Evidence from Mandarin speakers' early vocabularies. *Developmental Psychology, 32,* 492–504.

Templin, M. (1957). *Certain language skills in children.* Minneapolis, MN: University of Minnesota Press.

Terrace, H. S., Petitto, L. A., Sanders, R. J., & Bever, T. G. (1980). On the grammatical capacity of apes. In K. Nelson (Ed.), *Children's language* (Vol. 2). New York: Gardner.

Tesniére, L. (1959). *Elements de syntaxe structurale.* Paris: Klincksieck.

Thiessen, E. D. (2007). The effect of distributional information on children's use of phonemic contrasts. *Journal of Memory and Language, 56,* 16–34.

Thiessen, E. D., & Saffran, J. R. (2007). Learning to learn: Acquisition of stress-based strategies for word segmentation. *Language Learning and Development, 3,* 75–102.

Tinbergen, N. (1951). *The study of instinct.* New York: Clarendon Press.

Tomasello, M. (1999). *The cultural origins of human communication.* New York: Cambridge University Press.

Tomasello, M. (2000a). Do young children have adult syntactic competence? *Cognition, 74,* 209–253.

Tomasello, M. (2000b). The item-based nature of children's early syntactic development. *Trends in Cognitive Sciences, 4,* 156–163.

Tomasello, M. (2003). *Constructing a first language: A usage-based theory of language acquisition.* Cambridge: Harvard University Press.

Tomasello, M., & Akhtar, N. (1995). Two-year-olds use pragmatic cues to differentiate reference to objects and actions. *Cognitive Development, 10,* 201–224.

Tomasello, M., Akhtar, N., Dodson, K., & Rekau, L. (1997). Differential productivity in young children's use of nouns and verbs. *Journal of Child Language, 24,* 373–387.

Tomasello, M., Call, J., & Gluckman, A. (1997). Comprehension of novel communicative signs by apes and human children. *Child Development, 68,* 1067–1080.

Truewell, J. C., & Tanenhaus, M. K. (1994). Toward a lexicalist framework for constraint-based syntactic-ambiguity resolution. In J. C. Truewell & M. K. Tanenhaus (Eds.), *Perspectives in sentence processing* (pp. 155–179). Hillsdale, NJ: Erlbaum.

Truewell, J. C., Tanenhaus, M. K., & Kello, C. (1993). Verb-specific constraints in sentence processing: Separating effects of lexical preference from garden-paths. *Journal of Experimental Psychology: Learning, Memory, and Cognition, 19*(3), 528–553.

Tucker, D. (2002). Embodied meaning. In T. Givon & B. Malle (Eds.), *The evolution of language out of pre-language* (pp. 51–82). Amsterdam: Benjamins.

Tucker, D. (2009). Neuronal basis of language. In T. Givon (Ed.), *Linguistic complexity.* New York: Benjamins.

Ullman, M. (2004). Contributions of memory circuits to language: The declarative/procedural model. *Cognition, 92,* 231–270.

van der Lely, H. (1994). Canonical linking rules: Forward vs. reverse linking in normally developing and Specifically Language Impaired children. *Cognition, 51,* 29–72.

van IJzendoorn, M. H., Dijkstra, J., & Bus, A. G. (1995). Attachment, intelligence, and language: A meta-analysis. *Social Development, 4,* 115–128.

Vihman, M. (1996). *Phonological development: The origins of language in the child.* Cambridge, MA: Blackwell.

von Bertalanffy, L. (1968). *General system theory: Foundations, development, applications.* New York: George Braziller.

Vygotsky, L. S. (1929). The problem of the cultural development of the child. *Genetic Psychology, 36,* 415–432.

Waddington, C. H. (1957). *The strategy of the genes.* New York: MacMillan.

Wäsz-Hockert, O., Lind, J., Vuorenkoski, V., Partanen, T., & Valanne, E. (1968). *The infant cry: A spectrographic and auditory analysis* (Vol. 29). Lavenham: Lavenham Press.

Waxman, S., & Kosowski, T. (1990). Nouns mark category relations: Toddlers' and preschoolers' word-learning biases. *Child Development, 61,* 1461–1473.

Waxman, S., & Markow, D. (1995). Words as invitations to form categories: Evidence from 12- to 13-month-old infants. *Cognitive Psychology, 29,* 257–302.

Werker, J. F. (1995). Exploring developmental changes in cross-language speech perception. In L. Gleitman & M. Liberman (Eds.), *An invitation to cognitive science: Language* (Vol. 1, pp. 87–106). Cambridge, MA: MIT Press.

Westermann, G., & Miranda, E. R. (2004). A new model of sensorimotor coupling in the development of speech. *Brain and Language, 89,* 393–400.

Whorf, B. (1967). *Language, thought, and reality.* Cambridge, MA: MIT Press.

Wiley, E., Bialystok, E., & Hakuta, K. (2005). New approaches to using census data to test the Critical-Period Hypothesis for second language acquisition. *Psychological Science, 16,* 341–343.

Wittenberg, G., Sullivan, M., & Tsien, J. (2002). Synaptic reentry reinforcement based network model for long-term memory consolidation. *Hippocampus, 12,* 637–647.

Woodward, A. L., & Hoyne, K. L. (1999). Infants' learning about words and sounds in relation to objects. *Child Development, 70,* 65–77.

Wyttenback, M., May, M., & Hoy, D. (1996). Categorical perception of sound frequency by crickets. *Science, 273,* 1542–1544.

Yoshimura, Y., & MacWhinney, B. (2007). The effect of oral repetition in L2 speech fluency: System for an experimental tool and a language tutor. *SLATE* Conference. New York: ACM.

CHAPTER 15

Self-Regulation

Integration of Cognition and Emotion

MEGAN M. McCLELLAND, CLAIRE CAMERON PONITZ,

EMILY E. MESSERSMITH, and SHAUNA TOMINEY

Self-regulation has emerged as a critical area of interest throughout the life span. Starting at birth, regulatory capacities lay the foundation for the ability to control emotions, cognition, and behavior (Calkins, 2007). For example, 3-month-olds who suck on their fist to soothe themselves are exerting the earliest forms of self-regulation.

Initially, many aspects of regulation are the responsibility of caregivers. When infants cry, their parent calms them through holding and rocking. When an infant is hungry, it is the caregiver's responsibility to provide sustenance. As children develop, regulation moves from external to internal control (Kopp, 1982, 1991). In toddlers, self-regulation enables children to stop from touching a hot burner or from throwing themselves on the floor in a temper tantrum. In young children, self-regulation is a critical component of school readiness and social development (Blair & Razza, 2007; Eisenberg, Smith, Sadovsky, & Spinrad, 2004; M. M. McClelland, Cameron, Connor, et al., 2007), and aspects of self-regulation have been found to uniquely predict academic success throughout childhood, adolescence, and into adulthood (Blair & Razza; Duckworth & Seligman, 2005; M. M. McClelland, Acock, & Morrison, 2006; M. M. McClelland, Morrison, & Holmes, 2000; M. M. McClelland & Piccinin, 2009; Vitaro, Brendgen, Larose, & Trembaly, 2005). Moreover, as individuals enter adulthood, a growing body of evidence suggests that self-regulation plays a role in a variety of arenas, including schooling decisions, employment, choice of occupation, and wages (Heckman, Stixrud, & Urzua, 2006).

Together, these examples illustrate one of the themes woven throughout this chapter: throughout the life span, self-regulation assists individuals with selecting, optimizing, and using compensatory strategies to effectively pursue and refine goals, as well as to manage significant events and transitions in life (Brandtstädter & Lerner, 1999; Gestsdóttir & Lerner, 2007). Self-regulation helps individuals select goals that will be beneficial, optimize those goals, and minimize losses associated with goal accomplishment. In other words, self-regulation encompasses the coping skills we use to manage life events, both minor and major. For example, self-regulation is involved when an adolescent selects a college and/or career path, and it underscores how adaptively an adult navigates life transitions such as becoming a parent, planning for a child going to college, being a productive citizen, retiring, and optimizing health and development in late adulthood. Self-regulation also enables us to manage the mental and physical challenges that become increasingly prevalent as we age and confront difficult events, such as a partner or spouse dying. Thus, throughout the life span, self-regulation is a critical factor in our ability to manage our emotions, cognitions, and behavior. It is from this perspective that we conceptualize this chapter, first beginning with our working definition.

DEFINITIONS OF SELF-REGULATION

In recent years, various definitions have emerged to describe the components comprising self-regulation (Baumeister & Vohs, 2004; Cole, Martin, & Dennis, 2004; Kochanska, Murray, & Harlan, 2000; Rueda, Posner, & Rothbart, 2005; P. D. Zelazo & Müller, 2002). Consensus holds that self-regulation is a multidimensional construct that includes the regulation of emotion, cognition, and behavior. More generally, self-regulation is defined as *a deliberate attempt to modulate, modify, or inhibit actions and reactions toward a more adaptive end* (Barkley, 2004). This broad definition simultaneously solves and belies many theoretical issues related to the study of self-regulation, so we unpack this definition to clarify our meaning. *A deliberate attempt* means altering one's mode of thinking, feeling, or behaving to reach a goal, which one would not obtain by remaining in the current mode (Carver, 2004; Grolnick & Farkas, 2002). *Actions and reactions* pertain to the cognitions, emotional responses, and overt behaviors of a human being. Usually, these responses refer to our own actions (intrinsic regulation or internal control) but can be applied to alter the actions of someone else or change one's environment (extrinsic regulation or external control); for the general purposes of this chapter, self-regulation refers to the intrinsic form (Gross & Thompson, 2007).

Toward a more adaptive end means that altering one's actions results in a more positive outcome than would continuing on the current course (MacCoon, Wallace, & Newman, 2004). Important in contemporary definitions is recognizing that *adaptive* depends on one's perspective, the context, and the time scale (Gross & Thompson, 2007). In other words, *adaptive* might have different (even conflicting) definitions depending on the individual, environment, or society-at-large. Adaptive choices can also be situation specific, such that the same actions might be appropriate in one situation whereas being inappropriate in another. Finally, the term encourages us to ask whether benefits or losses are conferred in the immediate or long-term future. Therefore, *adaptive* is not about a regulatory decision being good versus bad, but instead, it indicates that the eventual outcome of self-regulation depends on other factors. For example, Fernando, who has just retired, may be used to spending his weekends and leisure time relaxing and watching television. Now that Fernando no longer works, he spends most of his time relaxing, but he quickly gets bored, gains weight, and loses touch with his former coworkers. To stay healthy, Fernando realizes he must adopt a new set of strategies, including staying active, exercising, and maintaining relationships with his friends. Though these new behaviors might challenge Fernando's initial expectations about retirement, they will likely improve his potential for sustainable psychological and physical well-being.

We also need to be clear about whether and when self-regulation should be discussed as a term or as an imperfect indicator for a latent construct, representing a complex mechanism that promotes our survival, effective socialization, and healthy development. As a term, *self-regulation* introduces metaphysical wonderings, including "What is the 'self'?" "If there *is* a 'self,' what is it regulating?" and the like (Lewis & Todd, 2007; MacCoon et al., 2004). These are interesting questions but are beyond our present scope. Ultimately, there remains much debate about self-regulation, how to define it, and how to measure it (Pintrich, 2000). Our goals are to describe these diverse perspectives while highlighting commonalities and themes across the life span, in an effort to better understand the latent construct of self-regulation, which we construe broadly as an individual's directed intentionality in making life decisions.

Despite the current definitional muddle, self-regulation is clearly important. In one of two handbooks of self-regulation published recently, Baumeister and Vohs (2004) note that difficulties self-regulating are responsible for many, if not all, of the challenges people face, including school under-achievement, gambling, violence, addiction, crime, and depression. Many of these issues are addressed in Santostefano's (Chapter 22 of this volume) chapter on psychopathology, whereas much (but not all) of the research we cover was conducted in typical populations over the life span.

Throughout this chapter, we highlight transitions in the individual as a particularly relevant context, or metacontext, for understanding self-regulation. Transitions are especially important because they test our adaptive abilities by presenting situations where the way we have been responding may no longer be healthy. For example, we met Fernando above, who, when employed, was accustomed to relaxing in his nonwork hours, but following retirement may need to reassess his behavior. Often, life presents us with situations where maintaining a positive trajectory requires self-regulatory strategies, and we must override our natural or dominant response to execute a set of healthier, though nondominant and potentially even uncomfortable, behaviors. Thus, we view self-regulation as a powerful and necessary strategy for effectively managing and mastering changes in our lives.

EMOTION AND COGNITION IN SELF-REGULATION

As the foregoing discussion indicates, self-regulation has been defined from multiple perspectives and measured in various ways, but some common themes emerge. These include the integration of emotion and cognition in regulatory behavior, and self-regulation as a determinant of how individuals adapt to the world. Notwithstanding these themes, scientists from different perspectives tend to adopt varying methods and terminologies. For example, temperament researchers study a typical style of reaction and regulation to stimuli of varying intensity, valence, and duration. Researchers of executive function may be most interested in brain activation when deliberate choice or planning is required or affective regulation occurs, studying areas of association and disassociation among component skills. Educational researchers often examine feelings, thoughts, and behaviors associated with school success. Though each of these examples highlight different levels of analysis, each include possibilities for integrating what have long been called *cognitive and/or emotional processes*.

We embrace a relational or holistic approach to understanding self-regulation, acknowledging the ultimate futility of the emotion-cognition dichotomy. Distinctions such as this are not without merit, however, if only because they have been so commonly used and are familiar (Overton, 2006). Hence, *emotional regulation* is often used to describe the affective and motivational aspects of self-regulation, whereas *cognitive self-regulation* is often used to describe the "cool" regulatory processes involved in planning, decision making, and problem solving (Bodrova & Leong, 2006; Zelazo & Müller, 2002). In addition, the term *emotion* may indicate an internal process, whose origins and function pertain to signaling information relevant to the individual's *immediate* physical or psychological well-being. In contrast, *cognition* may indicate an internal process whose origin and function pertain to an abstract or future event. One example of this is using mathematics in everyday life. This skill probably originated as an adaptive reaction to a problem with relevance to the *future* survival of the individual or the species. Whether one masters mathematical competence early in life may have ultimate consequences, but in the immediacy of the now, the relevance for well-being is limited. Therefore, cognitions may be considered a reaction to a signal with import for the "future."

It may be most accurate to think of "pure" cognition (as it is typically meant) as the processing of information that occurs under optimal emotional conditions, or in the absence of immediate physical or psychological threat or reward. In other words, there is no situation void of emotional importance. Instead, situations vary in their level, intensity, and immediacy of importance. This is a theme to which we return, but it is helpful for underscoring the ultimate problem with conceptualizing emotion and cognition as separate constructs when trying to understand self-regulation. Cognition and emotion reflect two complementary, synergistic processes within the individual (Lewis & Todd, 2007). Lewis and Todd's work on patterns of neuroactivation during self-regulation tasks showcases this point. They have shown through functional magnetic resonance imaging studies that tasks historically considered to tap "cognition" or "emotion" do not map easily onto distinct areas in the brain (which we could then conveniently label "Cognitive Area" and "Emotion Area"). What Lewis and Todd found more useful in understanding emotion and cognition are three observations. First, certain regulatory tasks differentially activate areas of the brain along the cortical-subcortical continuum, with emotion-laden tasks and stimuli activating subcortical structures (e.g., limbic, hypothalamic, and brainstem), and tasks requiring planning and deliberate manipulation of multiple pieces of information activating cortical structures, such as the prefrontal cortex (PFC). For example, when we see a disturbing image, our amygdala shows more activation, relative to other brain regions. When we are asked to remember whether the digit we have just seen matches the digit we saw two digits ago, our PFC shows more activation, relative to other brain regions.

Second, "regulation," or success on a given task, is best characterized as coordination among areas, not regulation of any single area or process. For example, heightened amygdala activity is followed by PFC activity, which regulates the amygdala. Third, "regulation"—rather than being "emotional" or "cognitive"—may be more accurately said to occur at different levels along the cortical-subcortical continuum. The second and third observations go together. To understand what is happening at the neural level when one is "regulating" means asking which hub (or place on the cortical-subcortical continuum) the other structures are coordinating. In other words, sometimes, our subcortical structures are in charge, whereas at other times, our cortical structures are in charge. The anterior cingulate cortex, relevant in attentional processes, plays a central role in coordinating information from multiple regions and is widely implicated in many different situations where regulation is required.

What does this mean in the context of understanding the development of regulatory competence? We argue that over the life span, and the many transitions and experiences that arise, an individual's ability to self-regulate at the most adaptive level contributes to their optimal functioning. MacCoon and colleagues' have defined self-regulation as the "context-appropriate allocation of attentional capacity to dominant and non-dominant cues" (MacCoon et al., 2004, p. 422). We agree that adaptively regulating means simultaneously coping with emotional signals with immediate importance and aligning cognitive resources to solve problems with future importance. Furthermore, research from different fields indicates that the success of one's attempts to self-regulate is borne out on different levels, both internal (physiological and psychological) and external (social). These points are illustrated in the forthcoming discussion.

ORGANIZATION OF THE CHAPTER: THEORY, DEFINITIONS, MEASUREMENT, AND A LIFE-SPAN VIEW OF SELF-REGULATION

The remainder of this chapter is organized into four main sections. First, we situate self-regulation in a theoretical context and describe the conceptual foundations that have informed its study across multiple sources of influence, settings, and over time. We highlight perspectives that are especially relevant to the study of self-regulation across the life span such as relational developmental systems theories, social cognitive theories, and life-span theories (Lerner, 2006; Lerner & Overton, 2008; Overton, 2006). Our goal in including these theories is to set the stage for a comprehensive understanding of how self-regulation is defined, measured, and characterized across the life span.

Second, we discuss how self-regulation has been defined and operationalized in diverse fields over the life span. In recent years, the study of self-regulation and related constructs have become increasingly popular as efforts to improve child and adult functioning have gained momentum in a variety of areas (e.g., academic success, social competence, career competence, interpersonal relationships). There remains, however, much uncertainty and debate about definitions and underlying constructs comprising this important construct. We review different definitions of self-regulation and discuss how aspects of self-regulation are implicated in constructs, such as temperament and executive function in childhood, and to personality, decision making, and motivation throughout the life course. Finally, within the sphere of self-regulation, we argue for the integration of cognition and emotion, including how these processes are translated into regulated behavior and action.

These conceptual conundrums are inherently linked to methodological challenges. Therefore, we review measurement issues including the *what, where*, and *how* as these questions pertain to measuring self-regulation from a multidimensional perspective. We also discuss recent advances in the assessment of self-regulation, and describe current and future challenges in measuring this construct.

The final section discusses the development of self-regulation over the life span. We describe pathways in developing regulatory competence, with particular emphasis on how self-regulation is important throughout life, but especially during life transitions: from birth to the transition to formal schooling, also known as the 5 to 7 shift (Sameroff & Haith, 1996); from about age 7 to the transition into adolescence; from adolescence to the transition into adulthood, including related adulthood transitions (e.g., career, relationships, children); and finally, how self-regulation functions in the later years, including middle life and older age (e.g., retirement, death of a loved one). We highlight factors that contribute to self-regulation, including internal and external (e.g., environmental) influences that help shape regulatory processes to varying degrees early in development versus later in life. We also examine how these internal and external factors interact over the course of an individual's self-regulatory development. We conclude the chapter with common themes, implications, and future directions for research and intervention.

THEORETICAL FOUNDATIONS IN THE STUDY OF SELF-REGULATION

Self-regulation has been examined from a variety of fields in psychology and education, although an extensive review of all relevant literatures is beyond the scope of this chapter (see Baumeister & Vohs, 2004, and Boekaerts, Pintrich, & Zeidner, 2000, for a complete review of self-regulation models and perspectives). Some recent theoretical perspectives are, however, centrally relevant to understanding self-regulation within a life-span framework in a way that integrates cognition and emotion. These are relational developmental systems theories, social cognitive perspectives, and life-span theories of development. These theories share the feature of viewing development as a *process* that proceeds within a *context* (e.g., a relational developmental system, the person as an active agent in his/her regulation, or across the life span, with time and the landscape of a person's entire life the context). Included in this overview of relevant theoretical perspectives is a discussion of core issues in human development, such as nature versus nurture, continuity versus discontinuity, and stability versus instability. We also focus on how concepts such as equifinality, multifinality, relative plasticity, and the use of compensatory strategies across the life span are central to an individual's ability to regulate thoughts, feelings, and behaviors.

Relational Developmental Systems Perspectives and Self-Regulation

Relational developmental systems theorists describe an individual's development as involving bidirectional and integrated relations between a person and multiple levels of their environment (Lerner, 2006; Lerner & Overton, 2008; Overton, 2006). This process of mutual integration between a person and their context has been termed *developmental regulation* and describes the dynamic interactions between levels of influence from the genetic, proximal level to more distal levels, such as society, culture, and time (Gottlieb, Wahlsten, & Lickliter, 2006; Lerner, 2006; Lerner & Overton, 2008). This perspective also stems from current views of *probabilistic epigenesis*; in other words, how individual development is characterized by an increase in complexity over time based on reciprocal interactions at all levels of analysis (Gottlieb et al., 2006). Perspectives such as dynamic systems theory (Thelen & Smith, 2006), the bioecological model (Bronfenbrenner & Morris, 2006), and the developmental psychobiological systems view (Gottlieb et al., 2006) also reflect this dynamic, interactive conceptualization of human development. Our view of self-regulation is influenced by these perspectives, and for the purposes of this chapter, we focus on the similarities rather than the differences among these theoretical models. We note that these relatively recent theories are more alike to one another than to traditional views of development as static, staged, or separate from the individual's immediate environment (Cairns & Cairns, 2006; Lerner, 2006).

Describing development as a series of relational interactions operating at multiple levels of influence has some advantages over prior views of development. Systems perspectives reject notions of a split between two sides, such as nature versus nurture, continuity versus discontinuity, and stability versus instability (Lerner, 2006; Overton, 2006). Instead, both nature and nurture contribute to an individual's stable, as well as changing, characteristics. For example, evidence supports the notion that self-regulation develops from interactions between individual temperamental characteristics and reciprocal relations between parents and caregivers (Calkins, 2004, 2007; Lengua & Kovacs, 2005). Thus, a child may be good at self-soothing early in life (e.g., sucking on their fist, looking away when he/she is overstimulated), but interactions with parents and caregivers will also shape future regulatory strategies for that child. A number of studies have found that strong levels of effortful control (which underlies self-regulation) serve as a protective factor in children when low parental warmth or negative parenting behaviors are present (Lengua, 2009; M. M. McClelland, Kessenich, & Morrison, 2003). Research has also found that children who are high in negative reactivity are more affected by overall parenting behaviors than children who are less reactive (Belsky, Bakermans-Kranenburg, & van Ijzendoorn, 2007). Thus, reciprocal interactions between individual characteristics and parenting behaviors together influence a child's regulatory behaviors over time.

The development of self-regulation has been described by Kopp (1982, 1991), who suggests that early self-control is characterized by external (other) regulation, which evolves into internalized self-regulation as children develop. From a relational developmental systems perspective, similar interactions can also be found between an individual's self-regulation and contexts, such as child-care settings, formal schooling, culture, and peers, across life transitions and throughout the life span (Baumeister & Vohs, 2004; Calkins, 2007; Lengua, 2002; McCabe, Cunnington, & Brooks-Gunn, 2004). For example, one experiment seeking to improve maternal responsiveness, a parenting behavior linked to strong self-regulation, found evidence for child by experience interactions. In the control group, where mothers did not received sensitivity training, only those infants who were highly reactive developed an insecure attachment. In contrast, the other infants who were less reactive in the control group, and the high- and low-reactive infants in the treatment group, developed secure attachments (Klein Velderman, Bakermans-Kranenburg, Juffer, & van Ijzendoorn, 2006).

In addition to relational interactions between individual characteristics and contexts, self-regulation also shows evidence of stability and instability, and continuity and discontinuity over the life span. Research examining relations between temperament or personality and self-regulation suggests that underlying regulatory characteristics are amenable to change, especially early in life, but they also exhibit stability over time (Rothbart & Bates, 2006). This is especially true as people develop through the life span and developmental pathways are charted (Heckhausen & Schultz, 1999). Moreover, different outcomes emerge depending on child characteristics, as well as aspects of the environment. One longitudinal study followed 15-month-olds who met a stranger in Ainsworth's Strange Situation and then were coded as either socially bold (i.e., approaching, initiating interaction) or socially wary (i.e., cautious, distressed) in the kindergarten classroom. Descriptive analyses showed that bold children spent more time off-task in the classroom, but characteristics of the classroom teacher also contributed to children regulating their behavior. In classrooms where teachers were sensitive and responsive, bold children showed more self-reliance, less off-task behavior, and less anger and aggression than did bold children in classrooms where teachers were less sensitive (Rimm-Kaufman et al., 2002). In general, bold children also interacted more with their teachers. This study demonstrates stability in regulatory behaviors from infancy to early childhood, whereas also showcasing malleability and interactions among child characteristics and other players in the child's life such as kindergarten teachers.

It has also been found that self-regulation and regulatory strategies demonstrate instability over time as pathways are altered and affected by multiple levels of influence and the interactions between these levels (Lerner, 2006; Thelen & Smith, 2006; Werner & Smith, 2001). In other words, according to dynamic systems theories, individual development is characterized by the ability of the system to self-organize to increase efficiency and adaptability (Thelen & Smith, 2006). For example, Thelen and colleagues' research on motor development in young children demonstrates that learning to crawl and walk involves increasingly complex systems of action that help children adapt their skills to more efficiently explore their environment (Thelen & Smith, 2006).

In terms of continuity, patterns of self-regulation appear across different contexts and throughout the life span (Baltes, 1997; Lerner, Freund, De Stefanis, & Habermas, 2001). For example, infants who react strongly to a new stimulus may develop into shy, withdrawn children who must work to enjoy social situations for the rest of their lives (Fox, Henderson, Rubin, Calkins, & Schmidt, 2001; Kagan, 2003). Moreover, throughout the life course, we experience situations that either match or tax our regulatory strategies. Life transitions, in particular, may force individuals to call on existing self-regulatory strategies or develop new ways of coping, or both. Thus, the extent to which an individual can continue to adjust and refine emotional and behavioral regulation skills over time is an important predictor of a person's developmental trajectory (Heckhausen & Schultz, 1999; Skinner, 1999). For example, if Rosario is a relatively easy (e.g., non-reactive) baby with strong regulatory strategies who can adapt well to new situations, she will likely have an easy time adapting her strategies to events and transitions throughout her life. On entering school, Rosario's strong regulatory skills may help her remain calm and use appropriate language to resolve conflicts with peers and ask her teacher for help, rather than becoming overly frustrated in new learning situations in the classroom and giving up. In contrast, Dylan, a difficult, reactive baby with poor regulatory strategies, may be more troubled by life and its many challenges. As Dylan reaches school age, entering kindergarten may be an especially challenging transition. Poor regulatory strategies in infancy may later manifest in difficulty regulating emotions in social interactions with peers and lead to withdrawal or aggressive behavior. In the classroom, rather than asking the teacher for help when frustrated, he may find himself giving up quickly and easily getting off-task.

There is also evidence of discontinuity in self-regulation development over the life span. Early infancy is characterized by almost complete dependence on others, whereas in less than 5 years, most children are able to control their actions, ask for help, express emotion appropriately, initiate action, and work toward their own goals. These qualitative changes in behavior are related to development in areas of the brain that control cognitive processes, namely, the PFC. The PFC undergoes significant maturation in early childhood, including myelination and pruning (see Chapters 8 and 4 in this volume by Blair and Zelazo & Lee, respectively, for a detailed discussion of brain development). In addition, research suggests that site-specific cortex activation co-occurs with particular behavioral responses (Blair, 2002; Shonkoff & Phillips, 2000). For example, deliberate processing of information operates through dorsolateral prefrontal pathways, whereas spontaneous responses to emotionally relevant stimuli operate through ventromedial pathways (Davidson, 2002; Zelazo & Müller, 2002). Together, these processes contribute to a child's regulatory functioning and undergo rapid development between early childhood and adolescence (Diamond, 2002; Rothbart, Posner, & Kieras, 2006).

Taken together, from a relational developmental systems perspective, issues such as nature/nurture, stability/instability, and continuity/discontinuity are relational rather than reflecting an either/or paradigm; furthermore, they help inform the study of self-regulation over the life span. We view the development of self-regulation as including the integration, instead of a conceptual dualism, of these core issues in human development. In addition

to these issues, concepts such as equifinality, multifinality, and relative plasticity are integral to the relational developmental systems perspective. Equifinality refers to aspects of development that demonstrate different starting points or conditions but result in the same outcome or end point. For example, two children, one raised in urban poverty and another in a wealthy suburb, may both become successful college graduates. The outcome could reflect their similar ability to do homework, follow school rules, and initiate prosocial interactions with teachers and peers. For example, one study found that children rated with strong attention abilities by their kindergarten teachers, regardless of their socioeconomic background, were more likely to graduate from high school than kindergartners rated as having attention problems (Vitaro et al., 2005).

In a similar vein, aspects of development can share similar starting points and reach the same outcome via different trajectories or pathways of influence (Gottlieb et al., 2006). Multifinality describes developmental processes that share initial starting points but reach diverse outcomes through differing pathways. For example, two children who are raised in the same family may experience very different pathways: one sibling may become a successful lawyer, whereas the other sibling struggles with substance abuse and is unable to finish college or maintain stable employment. Evidence of multifinality can be seen in a cross-sectional twin study of children aged 4 to 9 years, which suggested that before the school transition, family and early environment played a critical role in participants' observed and rated task persistence. After the transition to school, however, child factors, including genetically related attributes, more strongly predicted task persistence than did family and early environment (Deater-Deckard, Petrill, Thompson, & DeThorne, 2005).

Both equifinality and multifinality are directly relevant to the study of self-regulation over the life span. Early in life, children may differ in their underlying regulatory capacities, but through interaction and experience with multiple levels of their environment (e.g., parents, family members, peers, school, and job contexts), they develop similar abilities to regulate their emotions and behaviors (equifinality). For example, a child who is reactive and who has difficulty regulating herself early in life may have parents who teach her important regulatory strategies to manage her reactivity. This reciprocal interaction can result in the child becoming a well-regulated adult who, although still reactive, is able to draw on successful strategies to regulate thoughts, feelings, and inappropriate behaviors in ways similar to another child who was less reactive and better regulated early in life.

The concept of relative plasticity is also important to our understanding of self-regulation. In general, plasticity refers to the capacity for change. Relative plasticity reflects the notion that our ability to regulate our own development bolsters, but can also constrain, the opportunities for change over the life span (Lerner, 2006). In other words, our potential for change or plasticity is not without limits and may change over the life span. Thus, although we retain the potential for changing our emotional and behavioral regulation throughout our life, our capacity for modifying these skills is not limitless, may differ across various times of our lives, and helps shape our developmental trajectories (Heckhausen & Schultz, 1999; Lerner, 2006). Together, equifinality, multifinality, and relative plasticity are important concepts in the relational developmental systems perspective that can guide our understanding and conceptualization of self-regulation across the life span.

In summary, our conceptualization of self-regulation is well-situated within the assumptions of a relational developmental systems perspective and related theoretical models. According to these perspectives, dynamic interactions at multiple levels of influence describe associations between an individual's underlying self-regulatory characteristics and the environment throughout their lives. In addition, self-regulation directly reflects the core features of the developmental systems perspective through the integration of emotion, cognition, and behavior. For example, the behavioral and emotional aspects of self-regulation include the integration of affective and cognitive processes with motor skills, language, cognition, and social development that depend on the person, context, and time (Calkins, 2004; Kopp, 1982). Overall, we view the development of self-regulation as a dynamic, multilevel, and interactive process over the life span. Moreover, developmental systems perspectives share with social cognitive perspectives the assumption that each person is an active agent in their development of self-regulation whereas acknowledging constraints on the potential for change.

Social Cognitive Perspectives of Self-Regulation

Beyond the view provided by relational developmental systems perspectives for understanding self-regulation, social cognitive perspectives offer additional insight into the role of engagement, self-regulated learning, and motivation in self-regulation. Social cognitive perspectives focus on deliberate or intentional self-regulation, such as when individuals are actively engaged in their own learning and pursuit of goals. Under this perspective, individuals are motivated to achieve their goals and use cognitive strategies to do so. These models focus on how cognitive processes play a role in the behavioral aspects of self-regulation. Albert Bandura (1986), considered the father of social cognitive theory, proposed that the environment, overt behavior, and personal beliefs interact to determine behavior. "Self-efficacy" beliefs are central, based on Bandura's observation that people who believed they would succeed at a task would exert more effort toward the task; this increased effort increased the probability of success, which then fueled the desire to continue to perform the task and sustained regulation.

Research primarily in the realm of educational psychology has focused on how the domains of self-regulated engagement, learning, and motivation (to name a few) are related to school adaptation and success (Pintrich, 2000; Wigfield, Eccles, Schiefele, Roeser, & Davis-Kean, 2006; Zimmerman & Schunk, 2001). According to Zimmerman and Schunk's (2001) social cognitive perspective, regulated behavior can be divided into three parts: *forethought* (or planning of behavior), *performance,* and *self-reflection* (Schunk, Zimmerman, Reynolds, & Miller, 2003; Zimmerman & Schunk, 2001).

Forethought includes planning what needs to be done to complete a task or goal and the motivation needed to achieve the goal. For example, a student (Malia) who has been assigned a collage for an art project must plan how to do the project and motivate herself to get started. Consistent with Bandura's theory, if Malia is interested and engaged in the art activity, she will have an easier time planning and motivating herself to do the collage than classmates who are uninterested or who do not value the activity (Wigfield et al., 2006). *Performance* is often considered the second part of self-regulated behavior and includes the regulatory strategies taking place while doing an activity or task. In other words, how well can Malia pay attention, remember the instructions, and exhibit self-control when constructing the collage for the art activity? Integral to this process is Malia's self-monitoring as she completes the collage. Individuals who successfully monitor their own progress during a task have an easier time staying motivated to finish the task. Thus, if Malia can keep track of what she has done and what she still needs to do, she is more likely to maintain engagement in the activity. Finally, *self-reflection* is the last part of self-regulated behavior in the social cognitive perspective. It refers to the appraisal made by individuals about whether they mastered the task and the attributions made about their success or failure. In our example, if Malia successfully completes the collage, she is more likely to feel a sense of accomplishment and satisfaction and make positive attributions about her performance than if she were unable to finish. Therefore, in addition to retrospective attributions and appraisals, the strategies individuals use to remain motivated and engaged while working on a task are important. Illustrating the transactional, dynamic nature of regulation, these strategies may include self-administered rewards for finishing a task. Thus, to help her persist while working on the collage, Malia decides she can call a friend after she completes the art project.

Overall, social cognitive perspectives provide a useful lens through which to view self-regulatory actions, especially as they relate to learning, engagement, and motivation. These perspectives are, however, somewhat limited, because processes like monitoring, self-reflection, and self-evaluation are sophisticated and require a level of metacognition not usually observed in younger children (Zimmerman, 2000). For example, 5-year-old Mary is able to use strategies to remember something (such as remembering the name of a girl in a story by repeating the name over and over), but she is less able to apply the strategy consistently than would a 7-year-old (Weisner, 1996). In this respect, Mary's thinking is less metacognitive and more "hit and miss." She remembers the name correctly, but applying the same strategy on a future task is more challenging for younger individuals. Thus, social cognitive models of self-regulation become relevant as children develop and are most commonly applied to older children, adolescents, and adults. Notably, however, there is a rapid shift in thinking between the ages of 5 and 7 as metacognitive strategies improve (Sameroff & Haith, 1996). This is illustrated in one study where researchers observed first-grade girls and boys solving math problems three times over the school year and then asked them about the strategies they used to solve the problems (Carr & Jessup, 1997). Metacognitive awareness (measured by the match between observed strategies and children's report of strategies) increased over the course of the year. Girls were more likely to use overt strategies such as manipulatives to solve problems, whereas boys used more memory strategies, which indicate the importance of contextual factors in understanding self-regulation from a social-cognitive perspective. Thus, although social-cognitive perspectives are often used with older children, adolescents, and adults, the basic tenets can also apply to young children.

Life-Span Theories and Self-Regulation

Selective Optimization with Compensation in Self-Regulation

Similar to social cognitive models, the selective optimization with compensation framework (Baltes, 1997; Baltes & Baltes, 1990) is a life-span model of self-regulation and is often applied to older children and adults. This perspective considers how the individual negotiates his or her own life-span development within the context of culture and society. It focuses on three core approaches individuals can use to facilitate adaptation to their cultural and physical environments: *selection, optimization*, and *compensation.*

The first strategy, selection, involves making choices. This process is necessary because of constraints on one's time and other resources (Baltes, 1997; Freund & Baltes, 1998). Because we do not have the time, energy, or wherewithal to pursue every desire, we must set goals and make choices. Selection also may involve defining and revising a hierarchy of goals. Consider, for instance, the conflicting goals that are held by high-school graduates about to enter their first year of college. They likely want to do well in school, but they also probably want to make new friends. When young adults attend college in an atmosphere where students bond during social activities such as drinking alcohol, the relative importance of these academic and social goals results in different behaviors. One study examined entering students at a large university and found that the importance participants placed on their academic goals negatively predicted the frequency with which they planned to drink during the academic year (Rhoades & Maggs, 2006). In contrast, the importance of their social goals positively predicted both the frequency with which they planned to drink and the quantity they planned to drink. These incoming college students weighed their goals and reported acting in accordance to whichever goal they felt was more compelling.

As with other aspects of self-regulation, selection is constrained by one's social environment. Furthermore, according to this perspective, decisions may not always take into account every possible alternative. For example, when Samantha, a young girl, chooses to enroll in dance lessons rather than swimming lessons, she will probably not realize that by choosing to study dance, she is forgoing activities that her parents did not encourage (such as attending a science camp) or activities that were not available locally (such as learning how to surf).

Once individuals have selected goals, the process of optimization can help them achieve their goals (Baltes, 1997;

Freund & Baltes, 1998). When individuals optimize their goals, they devote resources (e.g., time, money, or effort) toward achieving them, or develop toward their peak level of functioning (Wiese, Freund, & Baltes, 2000). Optimization strategies include maintaining one's attention, expending one's energy and time, and practicing and learning skills. Consider Arthur, an overweight man who has decided to begin eating healthier foods and smaller portion sizes to lose weight. For Arthur to be successful, he must remain focused and adhere to his decision when shopping in the grocery store and when planning each meal. He may do so by having his groceries delivered to his house, putting notes on the refrigerator, or taking a class to learn how to cook low-calorie meals.

Finally, compensation is the third strategy described by the Selection, Optimization, Compensation (SOC) model. Like optimization, compensation generally occurs when individuals already have goals and have executed choices. Unlike optimization, compensation focuses on minimizing losses rather than maximizing gains. Compensation involves adapting one's functioning because of incompatible goals, new constraints, or losses (Baltes, 1997; Freund & Baltes, 1998). Examples of compensation include increasing the attention, effort, or time devoted to an activity, and acquiring assistance from others or from external aids (e.g., walking canes, hearing aids). Compensation may be temporary, such as employing a home-care assistant to help with tasks of daily living while recovering from surgery, or permanent, such as modifying one's house to be handicap-accessible after a paralyzing accident.

Typically, the three strategies in the SOC model are studied in combination, reflecting the theoretical notion that they are distinct but complementary facets of self-regulation (Gestsdóttir & Lerner, 2008). Research shows that, collectively, SOC strategies predict adaptive functioning during both daily life and times of stress. For instance, during adolescence, SOC strategies are positively related to positive youth development (such as perceived competence in various domains, self-confidence, caring, and social relationships), and negatively related to depression, engaging in risk behaviors, and delinquency (Gestsdóttir & Lerner, 2007). Moreover, when parents use more SOC strategies with their families, they experience less family-related stress (Young, Baltes, & Pratt, 2007). Furthermore, this effect is more pronounced for parents who experience more strain on their limited resources, for instance, among parents with young children (compared with parents with older children) and parents with few family-friendly policies at work (compared with parents with more flexible jobs). This study suggests that parents who are prone to experiencing the most strain on their time and energy also have the most to gain from using effective self-regulatory strategies (Young et al., 2007).

Each of the SOC concepts has elements of cognition and emotion, as well as illustrating the dynamic nature of self-regulation (Gestsdóttir & Lerner, 2008). For example, a bad experience at the lake last summer may shape Samantha's choice to study dance instead of swimming. The environment itself and the choices presented by Samantha's parents limit the possible path of her learning; perhaps her mother always wanted to be a dancer and secretly believed Samantha would choose dance over swimming. If Samantha turns out to enjoy dance, she may seek out further instruction and become motivated to excel in that area. Or, she may suffer an injury that requires her to stop dancing and then may decide to swim after all.

In addition to highlighting the dynamic nature of self-regulation, the three strategies in the SOC framework share similarities with the forethought, performance, and self-reflection domains found in the social cognitive perspectives where an individual is actively engaged in the pursuit of his or her goals. Thus, although different theoretical perspectives focus on varying aspects of self-regulation and use different terminology, they also share common themes in the study of self-regulation across the life span. One theme that has emerged throughout the foregoing discussion is that of directed intentionality, or the idea that humans are motivated to determine the course of their own development.

Life-Span Theory of Control

Heckhausen and colleagues' (Heckhausen & Schutz, 1995; M. J. Poulin & Heckhausen, 2007) theory of control is drawn from a life-span developmental framework examining how individuals shape their ontogeny. A core assumption of the theory is that humans are motivated to control their environments and themselves. Drawing on the work of Rothbaum, Weisz, and Snyder (1982), Heckhausen and Schulz (1995) suggested that individuals meet their goals through a combination of two processes: *primary control* and *secondary control*. Individuals exert primary control by shaping their environments. For example, a late mature adult whose goal is to live without assistance might choose to move into a single-story home after climbing stairs becomes too difficult to manage on her own. Secondary control occurs when individuals adjust *themselves* to be more aligned with their environments. Consider 13-year-old Tony, who moves to a new town with his family. He finds that the kids in his school dress, talk, and even act a little different than the kids in his old school. To fit in and make new friends, he buys new clothes and starts following the local sports team rather than the teams near his former hometown. In doing so, he modifies his appearance and behaviors to be more congruent with his new environment.

Similar to the SOC notions of selection and compensation as strategies that individuals use to reach their goals, primary and secondary control can be used selectively or as compensation (Heckhausen & Schulz, 1995; Wrosch, Schulz, & Heckhausen, 2004). *Selective primary control* involves investing personal resources (such as effort and time) toward a particular goal, specifically focused on shaping one's environment. Consider Monique and Sean, who have decided to buy their first home. Among other reasons, they have decided to spend time (looking for a home) and money (buying a home) rather than continuing to rent because they want to be able to decorate their home as they wish. Thus, they look for single-family homes rather than townhouses or condos, so that they can plant a garden. They spend many hours online learning what kinds of houses are in their price range and which neighborhoods they find appealing. In buying a home, they invest their own resources to shape part of their environment.

Compensatory primary control, in contrast, draws on one's external resources by obtaining assistance or advice from others. After Monique and Sean decide what features they are looking for in their first home, they hire a real-estate agent to help them look at houses in person and negotiate when making an offer on a house they like. Though Monique and Sean could buy a home without the help of a real-estate agent, they choose to seek such assistance to maximize their ability to buy a house that suits their goals.

Selective secondary control facilitates individuals' continued use of primary control by allowing individuals to focus their effort toward a reasonable number of carefully chosen goals rather than spreading resources across too many different goal pursuits (Heckhausen & Schulz, 1995). For example, Jim is a high-school student who wants to attend Stanford University. He has heard that admissions counselors view participation in extracurricular activities highly, so he wants to excel in several school activities. However, he soon realizes that by participating in too many activities in the same semester, he limits the amount of time and energy that he can devote to each. Instead, Jim uses selective secondary control and chooses to participate in only two activities (e.g., an academic team and track) so that he can focus his efforts toward achieving

a higher level of competence in a fewer number of activities. Selective secondary control can also ameliorate the negative effects of stressful events on goal striving (M. J. Poulin & Heckhausen, 2007).

In contrast, *compensatory secondary control* is utilized when an individual loses primary control or fails at a goal pursuit. It allows the individual to disengage from the goal, focus on alternative goals, or otherwise protect his or her sense of self from threat (M. Poulin, Haase, & Heckhausen, 2005; Wrosch et al., 2004). College track and field athletes whose recent performance is worse than their performance goal tend to revise their goal downward for their next track meet (Williams, Donovan, & Dodge, 2000). In doing so, they exhibit compensatory secondary control and are able to work toward more realistic and achievable goals in the future.

Control theory also provides a lens through which to view transitions across the life span. Many transitions have a "developmental deadline" that marks an ideal (or maximum) age at which a transition may be completed. Such deadlines may be determined primarily by biology (such as childbearing age for women), institutions (such as maximum retirement age), or cultural norms (such as age at marriage or entering a career). When a developmental deadline is distant, individuals may engage in goal pursuit without much urgency. As a developmental deadline draws closer, individuals who have not yet completed a transition begin to use more control strategies and more effort in reaching their goal pursuit. When the deadline is reached and the goal is no longer attainable, the healthy and adaptive individual will disengage from the goal through compensatory secondary control.

One study investigated women of different ages who had not had children (Heckhausen, Wrosch, & Fleeson, 2001). Women who were in their late 20s or early 30s were approaching the social developmental deadline for becoming mothers but had not yet passed it. Women who were in their 40s were approaching or, in some cases, may have passed their biological developmental deadline for becoming mothers. Heckhausen and colleagues (2001) showed that, controlling for their desire to have children, the women in their late 20s or 30s had more goals related to childbearing than the women in their 40s. The older childless women had more self- and health-related goals than the younger childless women. Furthermore, when participants were asked to spontaneously recall sentences that they had read, younger childless women recalled more baby-related sentences than older childless women. Thus, as individuals age, they use self-regulatory strategies to focus on developmentally appropriate goals. Heckhausen's (2000) *action-phase model of developmental regulation* suggests that the amount of effort and the variety of cognitive strategies needed to meet one's goal pursuit immediately before a developmental deadline is extraordinary. Because of the investment, goal pursuit at the verge of a developmental deadline is also more susceptible to disruption.

Taken together, the theoretical frameworks of relational developmental systems perspectives, social cognitive perspectives, and life-span theories provide a strong foundation for understanding underlying issues in self-regulation across the life span. Although these theories present views of self-regulation through different lenses, they share common themes that cut across disciplines and developmental periods. We now turn to how self-regulation has been conceptualized by developmental, personality, cognitive, and educational perspectives.

SELF-REGULATION IN MULTIPLE DISCIPLINES

As we and others have defined it, self-regulation is relevant for the study of how individuals develop and adapt to the world, and the personal, interpersonal, and societal challenges encountered along the way. This diversity of theoretical perspectives and investigators has produced a host of terms that can be subsumed under the umbrella term of *self-regulation.* Common terms related to the study of self-regulation include *effortful control* and *executive attention* (rooted in developmental psychology, particularly in studies of temperament), *ego control/resiliency* (rooted in personality psychology), *executive function* (rooted in clinical and developmental neuropsychology), *decision making* (rooted in cognitive psychology), *engagement* (rooted in educational psychology), and *motivation* (rooted in educational psychology and personality psychology), to name just a few of the most relevant to this discussion. This section discusses these different definitions of self-regulation, before delving into measurement issues, including the *what, where,* and *how* in measuring self-regulation, recent advances in measurement, and current and future challenges in this area.

Developmental Perspectives: Temperament, Effortful Control, and Executive Attention

Consider 4-month-old Theodore, captive in a bouncing seat, who is presented with a colorful, multi-armed mobile. Although his mother is nearby, the mobile is introduced by a bearded, bespectacled stranger wearing a stark white lab coat. Theodore becomes distressed at the appearance of the stranger and the associated unpredictable movement of the mobile; he cries, fusses, and kicks. He looks into his mother's face, orienting his gaze to one side of the mobile and listening to her calming, cooing voice. He calms, and stops crying and kicking. Though occasionally he glances at the mobile, fussing a bit each time, he mainly looks at his mother and remains calm until the mobile is removed.

Temperament has a lot to do with Theodore's reaction to the stranger. Temperament views of self-regulation are based on an assumption of individual, biologically based differences in reactivity and regulation (Rothbart & Bates, 2006). "Biology" implies the study of all biological systems, prenatal indicators, and perceptual predispositions, which have been shown to predict regulatory behavioral tendencies. For example, fetal heart rate and activity levels predict behavior at 36 weeks, with more active fetuses reported by their mothers as being difficult and reactive infants compared with less active fetuses, who as infants are more easy-going (DiPietro, Hodgson, Costigan, & Johnson, 1996).

Temperament research indicates that, although one may be inclined to react either intensely or calmly, one's regulation of that reactivity ultimately predicts levels of functioning. Although Theodore's intense reaction suggests a tendency to react negatively to stimuli, he found an adaptive strategy of looking at his mother instead of at the mobile, thereby successfully regulating this negative reaction. Individual differences also exist in the extent to which we seek out stimuli likely to elicit reactions. Reflecting this view, current research conceptualizes three dimensions of temperament: (1) *negative emotionality* (reactivity to stimuli), (2) *effortful control* (regulation of reactivity), and (3) *extraversion/surgency* (selection of stimuli; Rothbart & Bates, 2006). The effortful control aspect of temperament is most relevant to our study of self-regulation and has been defined as "the ability to suppress a dominant response to perform a subdominant response" (Kochanska & Knaack, 2003, p. 1087).

The three-dimensional structure of temperament and the positive outcomes associated with having stronger effortful control have been supported in a large body of research, as well as cross-culturally (Ahadi, Rothbart, & Ye, 1993; Eisenberg, Liew, & Pidada, 2004; Eisenberg, Smith, et al., 2004; Eisenberg et al., 2003; Kochanska et al., 2000; Rothbart & Bates, 2006; Zhou, Eisenberg, Wang, & Reiser, 2004). Relative to impulsive children, who have trouble inhibiting automatic reactions, those with stronger effortful control have a social advantage, associated with their stronger internalization of rules, greater likelihood of giving a positive response even when faced with disappointment (such as smiling when given a undesirable gift), and lower rates of aggression (Kochanska & Knaack, 2003; Simonds, Kieras, Rueda, & Rothbart, 2007; Zhou et al., 2004). Exercising effortful control means deliberately overriding what we *want* to do, such as grabbing a neighbor's toy, to do what we *should*, such as waiting for a turn with the desired toy or playing with another available toy. In other words, succeeding in social situations often means considering and placing the interests of others above our own. Successfully putting the interests of others before ourselves usually requires effort and deliberation, demonstrated by growing research that connects temperament with social outcomes.

Twin studies attempt to assess genetic background features for aspects of temperament alongside so-called nonshared, experiential sources of influence (Goldsmith, Lemery, Buss, & Campos, 1999; for an alternative perspective on the impact of genetics, see Greenberg & Partridge, Chapter 5 of this volume). Current views of temperament highlight the reciprocal interaction of biological predispositions with experiences and situational factors (i.e., epigenesist; Kochanska & Knaack, 2003; Rothbart, 2007). A good example of this is Ahadi et al.'s (1993) study of cultural differences in temperament. In their investigation of 624 six- and seven-year-olds, American children had higher extraversion/surgency and effortful control scores, whereas Chinese children had higher negative emotionality. This suggests that, although the nature of temperament and presence of factors appear similar in different cultures, the extent and relative strength of those factors may differ. It should be noted that "culture" is not an external, environmental context but also reflects biological predispositions of a population, aggregated over time and history (Pinker, 1994). We focus, however, on the dynamic interactions that occur among multiple levels of influence over a person's life span.

How does effortful control differ from self-regulation? In many ways, self-regulation is influenced by foundational contributions of temperament, of which effortful control is one. Thus, effortful control has origins in temperament, and is a relatively stable style of reaction and regulation. In contrast, self-regulation is commonly framed as situation-specific in samples of all ages (although it is influenced by the bidirectional interactions between aspects of temperament and different levels of the environment throughout the life span). In addition, the underlying cognitive processes that are utilized when effortful control or self-regulation is displayed are also key contributors to this developmental process. For example, *executive attention* has been described as the neural substrate underlying the overt display of effortful control (Rothbart & Posner, 2005), which is related to cognitive or "executive" regulatory processes. We now turn to aspects of personality, which are clearly related to temperament perspectives of self-regulation, but which are usually examined in older children and adults.

Personality Perspectives: Ego Control and Ego Resiliency

In the personality view, individuals' use of strategies to monitor, control, and change their cognitions, emotions, and behaviors tends to follow consistent patterns across multiple contexts and situations. In the traditional view of personality, these patterns—or *traits*—are relatively stable across the life span, though recent research reveals more change among adults than was previously realized (Roberts & Mroczek, 2008). Thus, from this perspective, there is stable between-person variation in the extent to which individuals utilize self-regulation, but individuals can also learn to regulate more or use regulatory strategies less often over time.

In the personality perspective, two aspects of personality functioning are closely related to self-regulation: ego control and ego resiliency (Block & Block, 1980). *Ego control* is an individual's ability to suppress unwanted emotions or thoughts, and to inhibit actions. In contrast, e*go resiliency* refers to an individual's ability to adapt their level of ego control in response to new stimuli or contexts. Although they are occasionally studied as opposing constructs, theoretically, they are orthogonal dimensions. Individuals can range from overcontrolled to undercontrolled, and can also exhibit a high level of resilience to a low level of resilience (which is sometimes referred to as *brittleness*).

Imagine Jerry and Mike, who have both become fathers for the second time. In infancy, each of their first children was relatively calm and easy, but their second children are fussy. Mike, who is undercontrolled and has little resiliency, has a difficult time coping with his infant daughter. He tries to soothe her using the strategies he learned when his first daughter was an infant, but these strategies do not work well. Mike is not the kind of parent who tries new methods of soothing his child; he frequently acts moody around his infant daughter and misplaces his frustration on his wife and other daughter. Jerry, who is more resilient, is able to change his style of interacting with his infant son based on how his son acts; he is sometimes stimulating and playful, and other times quiet and calming. Jerry is also overcontrolled and is thus easily able to suppress lashing out at his wife when he does become frustrated by their infant son. However, because Jerry is overcontrolled, he is hesitant to show affection to his children, even though it is acceptable to do so. In this view, not only can an individual rely too little on self-regulatory strategies, but they can also rely on them too much (Hoyle, 2006). An individual with too much ego control denies himself or herself of desires when it is unnecessary to do so—when the denial will not bring about a greater good. In addition, an overcontrolled individual will persist long after a task has become either obsolete or impossible. In a study of adopted children, those who were undercontrolled exhibited more externalizing problem behaviors than children who were either resilient or overcontrolled, whereas overcontrolled children exhibited more internalizing problem behaviors than children in the other two groups; no children were classified as low in resilience (Juffer, Stams, & van IJzendoorn, 2004). Ego control and ego resiliency are often used to describe personality functioning, and include the degree to which an individual can regulate cognitions, emotions, and behavior. Thus, although terminology differs, ego control and ego resiliency share features with similar constructs that are related to self-regulation in other perspectives, such as executive function and decision making, to which we turn next.

Cognitive Perspectives

Executive Function

Developmental, personality, and cognitive researchers have come together in recent years, contributing insights about how personality and temperament interact with situation-specific functioning in the face of multiple challenges and distracters (Rueda et al., 2005). Whereas personality and temperament perspectives emphasize continuity in regulatory tendencies across situations, cognitive perspectives tend to emphasize the situational aspects and malleability of self-regulation. Cognitive and neuropsychological investigators use specific tasks to elicit variability in self-regulation, and to improve participants' regulatory skills on specific tasks. Researchers emphasize the cognitive processing aspects of self-regulation, most centrally in literature on *executive function*. This construct gained popularity in recent years to describe the ability to plan, organize, and complete tasks (see

Jacques & Marcovitch, Chapter 13 of this volume). The term *executive* indicates our core theme of self-regulation as deliberate and managerial. Executive function is defined as the complexity of cognitive processes involved in conscious control of thought and action (Zelazo & Müller, 2002). The study of executive function originally focused on clinical investigations of the cognitive failures of patients with frontal lobe damage, who tend to be impulsive and lack forethought (Temple, Carney, & Mullarkey, 1996).

With the evolution of the frontal lobe came the ability to perform complex tasks requiring the processing and management of information while executing deliberate responses and overriding automatic tendencies (Zelazo, Carter, Reznick, & Frye, 1997). Rather than mapping onto a single function, executive function includes multiple cognitive skills, although researchers debate about the nature, number, and labels for individual components within the construct, which may change throughout development (Isquith, Crawford, Espy, & Gioia, 2005). Despite this confusion, the component processes usually include a form of *attention,* or the ability to focus on a stimulus, shift attention between relevant stimuli, and sustain attention in the face of distraction (Lyon & Krasnegor, 1996); *working memory*, the ability to manage and process information simultaneously (Demetriou, Christou, Spanoudis, & Platsidou, 2002; Jonides, 1995); and *inhibitory control*, the ability to prevent nonadaptive, automatic responses and initiate adaptive, nonautomatic responses, similar to effortful control (Barkley, 1997; Blair, 2002). Planning, or integrating multiple cognitive skills to create a plan for future action, is also commonly included (Sonuga-Barke, Dalen, Daley, & Remington, 2002; Zelazo et al., 1997). These processes can be considered distinct components of executive function, in that individuals recruit unique areas of the brain to perform attention, working memory, or inhibition tasks (Miyake, Friedman, Emerson, Witzki, & Howerter, 2000). In general, however, regulatory tasks activate multiple areas, as we mentioned in our description of neuroactivation studies (Lewis & Todd, 2007). Specifically, research suggests that after processing emotional stimuli, our brains then engage areas associated with cognitive and attentional tasks (e.g., the anterior cingulate cortex, or ACC) to manage emotional reactions. Hence, recent trends have been to move away from pitting emotion regulation against cognitive regulatory skills (Zelazo et al., 2002) and toward a conceptualization of these two sets of processes as interactive and reciprocally regulating.

The history of studying executive function in clinical populations contributes to its primary appearance in research based in the laboratory and with nontypical adult populations (Singer & Bashir, 1999). Since the late 1990s, however, there has been a growing number of studies of executive function based in ecological contexts, such as classrooms, which consider the development and malleability of executive function (Diamond, Barnett, Thomas, & Munro, 2007). Executive function is still considered a primarily cognitive construct that contributes to self-regulation (Barkley, 1997). In contrast, self-regulation has made broader appearances in multiple literatures, with implications for situational, real-world functioning, such as successful behavior in school (Bronson, 2000).

Behavioral Regulation: Integration of Cognitive Processes

In addition to research examining the components of executive function, a growing body of research has examined how individual cognitive processes are integrated into behavior, especially as they relate to school adjustment (Howse, Calkins, Anastopoulos, Keane, & Shelton, 2003; M. M. McClelland, Cameron, Connor, et al., 2007; M. M. McClelland, Cameron, Wanless, & Murray, 2007; Ponitz et al., 2008). Research in this area has focused on how behavior has different implications than individual cognitive processes, because it is often through overt behavior that self-regulation is seen as successful or maladaptive. Integrating aspects of executive function (including attention, working memory, and inhibitory control) allows children to control their behavior, remember instructions, pay attention, and complete tasks in classroom settings. Moreover, successfully navigating the demands of classroom settings requires the integration of all three skills. Accumulating research suggests that children's behavioral regulation significantly predicts achievement and social outcomes before formal schooling (Blair, 2002; Blair & Razza, 2007; M. M. McClelland, Cameron, Connor, et al., 2007) throughout elementary school (Connor et al., in press; M. M. McClelland et al., 2000, 2006; Pears, Fisher, Heywood, & Bronz, 2007; Rimm-Kaufman, Curby, Grimm, Nathanson, & Brock, 2009), and also predicts high-school graduation and college completion (McClelland, Piccinin, & Stallings, 2010; Vitaro et al., 2005). Behavioral regulation helps children remember and follow teachers' directions and focus on a task without getting distracted. These skills provide a foundation for positive classroom behavior and academic achievement (Alexander, Entwisle, & Dauber, 1993; Ladd, 2003; M. M.

McClelland et al., 2006), and also form the basis for successful decision making throughout life.

Decision Making

Related to aspects of executive function and to self-regulation is another construct from cognitive psychology, *decision making*. There are many approaches to decision-making, including (but not limited to) research on decisions under uncertainty, common biases and heuristics, and models of optimal decision making. Here, we do not discuss all views of decision making, but rather focus on decision making that involves forethought, planning, and evaluation.

Similar to Zimmerman and Schunk's social cognitive perspective (Schunk et al., 2003; Zimmerman & Schunk, 2001), the self-regulation model of decision making (SRMDM; Byrnes, 1998) proposes three consecutive phases: generation (of ideas and possible courses of action), implementation (of one's decision), and evaluation (assessing the outcomes and consequences of one's decision; Miller & Byrnes, 2001b). These three phases are all rooted in self-regulation, and self-regulatory strategies can improve the success of all three phases of decision making. Not all individuals make decisions in an SRMDM framework, and if a person uses self-regulated decision making in some situations, they will not necessarily do so in all situations. Those who engage in this model of decision making are individuals who value the kinds of decisions and goals that this framework facilitates, and who have the self-regulatory skills to implement the three phases. For example, adolescents' value for social goals and self-regulatory decision-making skills predict their social behaviors (Miller & Byrnes, 2001a), and adolescents' value for academic goals and decision-making skills predict academic achievement (Miller & Byrnes, 2001b).

Educational Perspectives

Self-regulation in the context of school adaptation and performance is evident in educational and personality research on engagement (cognitive, emotional, behavioral), which includes the literatures on self-regulated learning and motivation (Boekaerts, 2006; Eccles et al., 1993; Fredricks, Blumenfeld, & Paris, 2004; Pintrich, 2000; Wigfield & Eccles, 2000; Zimmerman, 1989). It is not our intention to focus on self-regulation in academics per se, nor do we wish to highlight education in a particular setting or culture, such as North American classrooms where most research has been conducted. Nevertheless, a discussion of self-regulation as adaptive functioning over the life span requires a mention of schooling for a few reasons. First, challenging life transitions that intersect with schooling trajectories and choices are prevalent (e.g., going to kindergarten; the transition to middle school; the importance of a college degree in industrialized nations; the need for continuing adult education when changing careers). Second, diverse societies see a growing need for their citizenry to attain average levels of education that are higher than in previous generations (Blair, 2002). Third, recent calls for free global education as a basic human right bring self-regulation in school contexts to the fore (National Public Radio, 2008).

Engagement and Self-Regulated Learning

Engagement has been defined as deliberate, active involvement in school and related activities, and includes thoughts about school and willingness to invest cognitive effort in learning (cognitive engagement); attitudes and feelings toward school (emotional engagement); and participation in school and related activities, including completion of homework (behavioral engagement; Fredricks et al., 2004). Essentially, engagement represents self-regulation within a specific setting, toward a discrete outcome—succeeding in academics, for example—with diverse implications for functioning over the life span. Little is currently known about how different types of engagement (cognitive, emotional, and behavioral) relate to one another. In addition, investigators have been most successful connecting behavioral engagement to achievement outcomes. This means that children who actually exhibit the behaviors associated with success in school—going to class, completing homework, showing good classroom behavior, and studying— tend to have higher achievement than children who do not (Greenwood, Horton, & Utley, 2002; Guthrie, Schafer, & Huang, 2001; J. Hughes & Kwok, 2007). Students who are inattentive in school and engage in behaviors that compete with academic engagement achieve at lower levels than children who are able to remain behaviorally engaged (Finn, Pannozzo, & Voelkl, 1995). In many ways, these findings parallel research in developmental psychology documenting links between behavioral regulation and school achievement. Links among emotional and cognitive engagement and achievement are less clear (Patrick, Ryan, & Kaplan, 2007). This could indicate issues of measurement, because behavioral engagement is easier to measure and, therefore, easier to connect to outcomes or issues of mediation; for example, cognitive and emotional engagement may relate to achievement only for children who are also behaviorally engaged.

Motivation

Finally, motivation is inherently related to the study of self-regulation. The realm of motivation is too large for us to comprehensively address in this chapter, but we discuss a few key concepts from the motivational literature that relate to self-regulation. One of the concepts implicated in discussions of both motivation and self-regulation is the idea of goals. *Goals* are desires for the self in the future. Although the concept of a goal does not vary substantially in motivational and self-regulatory perspectives, the two perspectives tend to focus on different goal-related topics. Generally, though, motivation and self-regulation are highly interrelated. As mentioned in the discussion of social cognitive theory, an individual's motivation to reach a goal tends to rely on his or her value for the goal, as well as his or her belief that the goal is achievable (Eccles et al., 1983; Wigfield & Eccles, 2000; Wigfield et al., 2006). The same is true for the use of self-regulatory strategies: Individuals who do not value self-regulation or who do not expect it to lead to desirable outcomes are less likely to use effective strategies.

In addition, by engaging in self-regulation, individuals can increase their motivation for a particular activity. According to control-process theory (Carver, Lawrence, & Scheier, 1996) and self-discrepancy theory (Higgins, 1987), self-change occurs through a self-regulatory process that begins with reflection on oneself. An individual compares his or her current state with his or her ideal state. When one's current and ideal states do not match, the discrepancy between the two motivates the individual to take action (Michie, Hardeman, Fanshawe, Taylor, & Kinmouth, 2008). Discrepancy reduction occurs either by adjusting one's ideal state to be more in line with the current state, or by taking actions to change one's current state to be more ideal. The process is cyclical, such that self-reflection and evaluation continue once change has been implemented; continued discrepancies motivate more change. In contrast with the discrepancy-creating activity of adopting goals, this framework focuses on individuals' reactions to discrepancies that already exist (Bandura, 1991; Bandura & Locke, 2003).

Other motivational perspectives focus on needs. Early research in the motivation literature focused on needs for achievement, power, and affiliation (D. C. McClelland, 1961; D. C. McClelland, Atkinson, Clark, & Lowell, 1953;

Murray, 1938). For example, individuals who have a high need for achievement seek challenges and enjoy receiving feedback regarding their performance, those with a high need for power enjoy having an influence on other people, and those with a high need for affiliation seek to build interpersonal relationships and gain others' approval (Koestner & McClelland, 1990; Koestner, Weinberger, & McClelland, 1991). More recently, a good deal of motivational research has focused on individuals' needs for autonomy, competence, and relatedness. These needs are the focus of self-determination theory, which postulates that when given opportunities to satisfy these three needs, individuals are more likely to be intrinsically motivated (Deci & Ryan, 1985; Ryan & Deci, 2000, 2006). Specifically, contexts that encourage autonomy and competence also encourage self-directed choice and behavior. When an individual is not intrinsically motivated to behave a certain way, being in a context where acting that way allows him or her to feel related to others will encourage him or her to adopt the behavior. Initially, engaging in the behavior will be externally regulated, but over time it can become internally regulated behavior.

Consider Chris, who takes a new job at a company that has very different corporate values than his last company. His old job allowed him to make choices about which projects he would work on, and how and when he accomplished his tasks. His old job also involved working on challenging, but not impossible, tasks, which gave him a sense of competence. Unfortunately, he does not have the same degree of autonomy in his new job, and the tasks he is given are easy and repetitive. Self-determination theory proposes that Chris would exhibit less self-regulation and intrinsic motivation in his new job than in his old job. His job performance may suffer if he starts working at a slower pace and leaving work early.

At the same time, Chris begins dating a new woman, Jenny, whom he likes very much. The only problem is that Chris smokes cigarettes and Jenny strongly dislikes smoking. Jenny externally regulates Chris's smoking by asking him not to smoke around her and by reminding him of the reasons he should quit. Soon, even when Chris is alone, smoking reminds him of Jenny's disapproval. Eventually, Chris internalizes the reasons to quit smoking that Jenny told him, and he quits smoking. Chris's need for relatedness caused him to internalize his inhibition of smoking, and it became a self-regulated behavior. Taken together, motivation is inherently tied to self-regulation and the strategies individuals use to accomplish goals in their lives.

Although different fields have their own names and conceptualizations of self-regulation, we focus on similarities and commonalities in an effort to best understand self-regulation over the life span. One of our goals thus far has been to identify versions of this construct in the various psychological literatures. Self-regulation is a relatively new and vital research area, and as such, it exhibits some of the awkward and frustrating characteristics of an emerging field. Yet, studying this construct is also exciting because we have already seen similar definitional themes emerging from the different fields. The advantage of multiple disciplinary perspectives means a convergence on the importance of being able to control, manage, and direct oneself throughout life.

INTEGRATION OF EMOTION AND COGNITION IN BEHAVIOR

As noted earlier, self-regulation is composed of the integration of emotions and cognitions. Behavioral aspects of regulation demonstrate the importance of overt behavior. In many cases, one's overt behavior, arising from internal regulatory processes, is the strongest predictor of functioning. In other words, whereas emotion and cognition are internal processes, the individual's overt behavior (or actions within a context), represent how these processes interface with the outside world. Behavioral strategies, such as taking oneself out of a dangerous situation, defusing a violent parent with soothing words, or giving oneself a time-out to calm down from anger, help shape the course of our lives. Fields vary considerably in the extent to which they measure the regulation of emotion or cognition directly. Many of the studies we cite, in fact, measure overt behaviors thought to indicate emotion or cognitive regulation; a similar conundrum in measurement has been identified with the study of emotion and is likely inherent in the study of "black box" processes that occur at the neurological or physiological level (Larsen & Fredrickson, 1999). Nonetheless, to simplify things, we use the terms *emotion regulation* and *cognitive regulation*, and clarify their meaning by noting how they were measured.

How we handle our emotions—the *now* signals about our immediate circumstances and well-being—contributes significantly to how we appear to and interact with the outside world. Imagine Brock, a sixth grader who hates doing homework except for science class, which he conscientiously does at his after-school program. One day, his friend Andrew teases him about a girl Brock likes. In anger,

Brock lunges for his friend and begins to chase him around the classroom. His conscience (i.e., regulating system for strong emotions) warns him, "Remember what happened the last time you hit Andrew!" and Brock turns around, sighing, but sitting down to complete his homework.

Brock's ability to avoid attacking his friend, focusing instead on his homework, has a few adaptive advantages. He will avoid punishment by the after-school program director and will also finish his homework. His friend, Andrew, may even decide that, because he cannot get a rise out of Brock, he will not tease him in the future. Other, less adaptive, though often dominant, responses are also possible. Maladaptively regulating means allowing emotional responses to overwhelm one's ability to make planful, thoughtful choices for the future. In an alternate scenario, Brock hits his friend, receives a time-out, becomes too upset to finish his homework, receives detention after school, and is then grounded by his mother. This event may set into motion multiple recurring outbursts and cycles of punishment and, perhaps, escalating violence that ends in Brock's expulsion from school and eventual dropout. Maladaptively regulating may also allow abstract planning to overshadow our emotional lives and the signals that give us information about possibilities for health or happiness. In this case, Brock could decide to stop being Andrew's friend to avoid any future possibility of emotional disruption. He becomes a loner, deeply engrossed in his schoolwork, but depressed and isolated.

Often, we may desire to act inappropriately given the situation, such as when Brock wants to chase his friend in the computer lab. But, as we will show, how we *feel* and how we actually *behave* can be different things. Adaptive self-regulation represents the mastery of emotional responses *and* the coordination of cognitive resources in situations where conditions bring us to the edge of being either better or worse off than we expected. It is this process we seek to understand, providing support for the notion that diverse and interactive processes, including our processing of affectively salient and cognitively salient information, are responsible for our ultimate functioning. Emerging themes argue for a conceptualization of self-regulation that considers the integration of emotion and cognition in contributing to overt behavior.

The bulk of research on the processing of emotion regulation has focused on the early years of development, or on the treatment and prevention of antisocial or problematic outcomes, such as aggression or obsessive-compulsive disorder, in adult populations. We begin our discussion within early childhood (Blair, 2002). Blair (2002) notes that stronger negative emotional reactions, including anger and anxiety, may impede children's ability to regulate their behavior in school settings where they need to deploy attention and persist in their work. In other words, children who are easily angered will have more difficulty concentrating on schoolwork than those who can better regulate their emotional reactions. Thus, variability in emotion regulation as noted by Calkins (2007) is related to, and may challenge or enhance, children's ability to regulate their overt actions. Consistent with this notion is considerable evidence linking children's effective management of their emotions to positive behavioral and academic outcomes (Eisenberg, Smith, et al., 2004; Graziano, Reavis, Keane, & Calkins, 2006; Howse, Calkins, et al., 2003). Children who cannot control their emotions are more likely to act out, behave aggressively, and oppose the perspectives and requests of others (Graziano et al., 2006; C. Hughes, White, Sharpen, & Dunn, 2000; Raver, 2004; Shields et al., 2001).

Some evidence indicates that strong cognitive skills, or the ability to effectively direct attention, may ameliorate the negative effects of poor emotion regulation. In other words, it is the interaction between emotion and one's regulation of that emotion that determines adaptation (Henderson & Fox, 1998; Rothbart & Bates, 2006). One study of toddlers found strong negative emotionality to be associated with greater readiness for school (measured by knowledge related to colors, letters, counting, shapes, and conceptual comparisons), but only when children had strong attention skills (Belsky, Friedman, & Hsieh, 2001). Other research supports the notion that behavioral regulation is the operable determinant of adjustment and academic success. In a study of academic achievement following 122 preschoolers to kindergarten, Howse, Calkins, et al. (2003) found that preschool emotion regulation predicted kindergarten math and literacy achievement by operating through behavioral regulation. Preschoolers who successfully managed their emotions achieved at relatively higher levels in kindergarten compared with peers who had more difficulty regulating emotions, but this was dependent on whether they were able to manage their behavior in the classroom effectively (as rated by their teachers). Children exhibiting poor emotion regulation in preschool, but who demonstrated strong behavioral regulation, also had high achievement. Another recent study found that the relation between teacher ratings of emotional regulation in kindergarten and academic competence in first grade was mediated by first-grade ratings of attention (Trentacosta & Izard, 2007). These findings provide empirical support for a multidimensional, domain-specific, and interactive conceptualization of self-regulation, whereby children with strong emotional responses, who can regulate those responses in their subsequent behavior, fare better compared with individuals with little capacity to regulate their behavior (Eisenberg, Smith, et al., 2004; Rothbart & Bates, 2006).

Studies have recently started to identify the specific mechanisms responsible for whether we successfully translate the need to regulate overt action. For example, there is growing support for attentional allocation as an important organizer and coordinator of multiple responses into adaptive behavioral functioning. One study had 7- to 10-year-olds perform a flanker task, considered an executive attention measure, in two sessions. The task required them to focus on the direction that a target fish was pointing and give a physical response (press a certain button) based on whether the direction of the target fish matched (congruent) or did not match (incongruent) the direction of another group of fish. As part of the same study, children also received a disappointing gift (a wood chip) and their reactions (e.g., smiling, not smiling) were observed; finally, their parents rated their effortful control. Results demonstrated that performance in the executive attention sessions was an important factor. First session performance predicted only both ratings of effortful control, and second session performance predicted only smiling to the undesired gift. Effortful control ratings and smiling were not related to one another (Simonds et al., 2007). Although this study raised additional questions pertaining to training effects (such that by the second session, children's performance no longer related to effortful control ratings), it also demonstrated the central relevance of the ability to manage attention and resist distractors for multiple other situations (laboratory and long-term perceptions of behavior by one's parents). The next challenge involves how to reliably and validly measure self-regulation over the life span. This is not an easy task, in part because the interaction of internal regulatory processes with overt behavior is one area of particular interest. We now turn to different ways researchers have measured self-regulation, which helps shed additional light on similarities, differences, and challenges in studying this vital construct.

MEASUREMENT

Self-regulation is an internal process of coordinating and managing one's responses, the consequences of which are often translated into overt behavior. According to a relational developmental or dynamic systems framework,

self-regulated behavior may create environments or stimuli that lead to new regulatory demands (Mayne & Ramsey, 2001; Sameroff, 1995). For example, if, after some rambunctious play, a child successfully waits for three minutes in a time-out, she may be reintroduced into the play scenario with the condition that she must exercise self-control to avoid another time-out. A child who cannot wait in time-out may not be reintroduced to play, and consequently will be deprived of another chance to practice regulating. The measurement of self-regulation, however, has rarely taken this reciprocal nature of regulation within an environment into account (Gross, 2007). Scientists have more often focused on documenting discrete behaviors and events in response to a single prior event or manipulation. This section starts by describing how researchers have measured self-regulation in terms of the *what, where,* and *how;* we then discuss recent advances in the assessment of self-regulation.

Dimensions of Measurement: What, Where, and How We Measure Self-Regulation

Investigators have commonly used individuals' external behavior as a proxy for internal regulatory processes, either through asking observers (e.g., teacher or parents) to report on children's behavior or observing participants themselves. Low correspondence among regulatory measures, or arguments for one measure and against another, could indicate a number of factors, some of which are avoidable with informed measurement decisions, and others of which are likely inherent to studying this area. For example, until recently, self-regulation research, like emotion research (Larsen & Fredrickson, 1999), has been limited by the fact that many studies rely on teacher or parent ratings or self-reports (especially with older children, adolescents, and adults). As precision and sophistication in the measurement of self-regulation improves, we are successfully addressing many of the methodological issues currently plaguing the field. Thus, we start by describing some currently available methodologies and measures using a dimensional approach. We find this approach addresses the complexity of available measurement options and helps showcase similarities and differences among different methodologies. This is fruitful to the extent that external behavior in a given setting (like the classroom) is the phenomenological level we are interested in measuring and to the extent that we can trust the person doing the reporting. Essentially, different types of measures provide different information (Caspi, 1998). This section finishes by discussing innovations in measures of self-regulation for children, adolescents, and adults.

The What: Measuring Self-Regulation at Different Phenomenological Levels

We use three dimensions to describe how researchers typically measure self-regulation. First is the "what"— What does one intend to measure? This first dimension, which we refer to as the phenomenological level, simply means that we measure regulatory processes varying from the internal (e.g., biology) to the external (e.g., social behavior); sometimes, we measure one process at a time, but it is also possible, and potentially more interesting, to measure the interaction of these processes. For example, in one study, two groups of adults shown disturbing images exhibited different physiological reactions, with the group instructed to hide their emotional reactions having greater sympathetic nervous system activity than the group that was not given instruction regarding emotional reactions (Gross & Levenson, 1993). This study suggested that regulation on one phenomenological level (overt behavior, such as facial expression) impacted regulation on another level (i.e., physiological). The possible health implications of this process are still emerging; a recent study of women with breast cancer found positive associations among the repression of hostility and blood pressure (Giese-Davis, Conrad, Nouriani, & Spiegel, 2008). Findings illustrate that what may be adaptive behavior from one perspective, such as hiding one's anger in front of one's boss, may have negative, nonadaptive consequences in another realm. That is, hiding one's negative emotions and hostility may enhance social relationships but may contribute to increased blood pressure and poor heart health. Together, these studies suggest that it is important to measure self-regulation at a variety of levels and in ways that capture the interaction of internal and external processes. However, research in this area does not often include measures that can tap different levels of regulation. Thus, a remaining challenge in the field is to develop better measures of self-regulation throughout the life span that more accurately gauge varying levels of regulatory processes and can assess the interaction among processes.

The Where: Context in the Measurement of Self-Regulation

The second dimension in our discussion of self-regulation measurement is the "where"—Where is the measurement occurring? This dimension regards *context*, which means the settings where self-regulation is assessed vary from the simple and controlled (e.g., laboratory) to the complex and uncontrolled (e.g., classroom or work settings). "Simple" and "complex" pertain to the presence, number, and variation in unmeasured variables that might impact the data intended to capture the regulatory process. In highly controlled laboratory settings, participants are placed in a space where they can be easily observed, or they are attached to brain monitors. Then they are asked to perform a novel task, such as pressing an arrow that matches the direction a particular fish is pointing on the screen. On the one hand, laboratory settings have their advantages, chief among them being the removal of variables that might interfere with our understanding of how the particular task manipulation affects regulatory success. On the other hand, we do not really know how well these tasks correspond to real-life settings where regulation matters, such as in classrooms or on the job.

The implications of variation in context, although as yet understudied, are significant. Naturalistic contexts are often highly complex but may be of greater practical significance than one's performance on a novel laboratory task. Furthermore, some evidence suggests that individual characteristics (such as sex) predict self-regulation in some contexts, but not in others. For example, a longitudinal study of executive function assessed in the laboratory (including processing speed, disinhibition, and working memory) reported few sex differences, with the single difference indicating boys had an advantage over girls in processing speed (Brocki & Bohlin, 2004). Yet mounting reports reveal that American boys have more difficulty with self-regulation than girls in home and school contexts (Dunn & Hughes, 2001; Fantuzzo, Bulotsky-Sheare, Fusco, & McWayne, 2005; Gilliam, 2005; Vitaro et al., 2005). One study showed that boys' compliant, regulated behavior decreased more than did girls' in conditions of greater classroom chaos (Wachs, Gurkas, & Kontos, 2004). Consistent with the theoretical foundations underpinning self-regulation discussed earlier, these findings indicate that context is an important consideration in the study of self-regulation, and that individual characteristics interact with context.

Another example of the importance of context can be seen when comparing measures of executive function with measures of behavioral regulation in young children. Although there is little research looking at both traditional executive function measures and measures of behavioral regulation, documented correlations have been modest (Blair, 2003; Lan & Morrison, 2008). For example, Blair (2003) found that preschoolers' on-task behaviors (rated by teachers) were not significantly correlated with executive function performance on tasks of inhibitory control. This somewhat surprising noncorrespondence may have to do with contextual differences. Whereas individual aspects of executive function are typically measured in laboratory settings using experimental measures, behavioral regulation is more often observed in naturalistic classroom contexts, where children need to utilize attention, working memory, and inhibitory control to carry out specific tasks, such as taking turns in a game or working on their own to complete a book-making project.

In addition to contextual differences, cognitive scientists often measure aspects of self-regulation using separate tasks of executive function. For example, a common practice has been to assess aspects of attention, inhibitory control, and working memory separately, and then combine the scores on each test into aggregates or an overall behavioral regulation or executive function score (Carlson, 2005; Smith-Donald, Raver, Hayes, & Richardson, 2007). Although this method has its benefits, it is also potentially problematic because separate measures of executive function are often not strongly related to each other (Blair, 2003; Lan & Morrison, 2008). For example, one study reported that measures of attention shifting and inhibitory control were correlated $r = 0.34$ in prekindergarten and $r = 0.41$ in kindergarten (Blair & Razza, 2007). Similarly, a study with preschool children indicated that after controlling for age, the correlation between measures of working memory and attention was $r = 0.34$ (Hongwanishkul, Happaney, Lee, & Zelazo, 2005). Another investigation with elementary students revealed that measures of working memory and inhibitory control were weakly correlated at $r = 0.23$ (Archibald & Kerns, 1999). Creating composite variables based on low intercorrelations may contribute to insensitive measurement and an inability to detect significant effects.

Research indicates that beyond measurement and developmental factors, whether an individual successfully regulates his or her behavior is also sensitive to the particular demands of the context (Bulotsky-Shearer, Fantuzzo, & McDermott, 2008). For example, studies have shown that children's regulatory performance diminishes with both increases in task demands, such as remembering two rules instead of one, and increases in situational demands, such as responsibility for working independently versus working with others (Hala, Hug, & Henderson, 2003; Rimm-Kaufman, La Paro, Downer, & Pianta, 2005; Wilson, Kipp, & Daniels, 2003). Thus, measures that can be delivered in the context in which regulation is important (e.g., the school classroom or work context) might be critical for

a screening tool of regulatory competence to be efficacious in predicting school achievement. Although an individual might score well on an individually administered attention task in a laboratory setting, he or she might not be able to pay attention in a classroom or work situation, which includes many distractions and extraneous activity.

Finally, culture is an important part of context that influences children's self-regulation. Much of the self-regulation research, however, has been conducted in the United States, Canada, or Europe, often with homogenous samples of children. Thus, we do not know whether these results generalize to individuals in other cultures. Research has recently started to address this and documented superior self-regulatory skills in young Asian children compared with children in North America and Europe. In one study, preschoolers in China consistently scored about 6 months ahead of their counterparts in the United States on attention, working memory, and inhibitory control tasks (Sabbagh, Xu, Carlson, Moses, & Lee, 2006). In another study, South Korean 3-year-olds had stronger inhibitory control than British 5-year-olds (Oh & Lewis, 2008). Thus, evidence suggests that the cultural context is important, and that children from several Asian countries outperform children from Western countries on aspects of self-regulation. One possible explanation may have to do with the ideals and behaviors valued by different cultures. For example, interdependence and collectivism are more important than individual interests in many countries located in Asia, Africa, and South and Central America. In contrast, independence and the rights of the individual are highly valued in places like the United States, Canada, and Europe (Markus & Kitayama, 1991). These differences have been linked to how individuals from Asian and American cultures perceive information, and may also be implicated in regulatory differences observed across cultures (Kitayama, Duffy, Kawamura, & Larsen, 2003). The extent to which culture plays a role in self-regulation is a growing area in need of further inquiry. However, the within-culture variation in regulatory competence and life outcomes likely far outweighs the between-culture variation in self-regulation. In other words, all cultures include individuals who make adaptive choices through the life span, as well as individuals who struggle to succeed.

The How: Reported, Observed, and Direct Measurements of Self-Regulation

In addition to the importance of context is the "how" in self-regulation measurement, or how are the data collected? This dimension pertains to how evidence of self-regulation is gathered, from the individual, from observations of the individual, or from third-party reports of the individual's self-regulation (J. Block, 2008). Until fairly recently, participant reports have predominated in the study of self-regulation. Caregiver reports are especially common in the study of children and adolescents, and self-reports are more common with older adolescents and adults. One study asking adolescents about their behaviors related to ADHD found that parent reports of these behaviors were both more numerous and more predictive of significant life outcomes than were children's reports (Fischer, Barkley, Smallish, & Fletcher, 2005). Teachers can be especially reliable reporters of children, and their ratings generally correspond to observed self-regulation and achievement outcomes (Connell & Prinz, 2002; Ladd, Birch, & Buhs, 1999; M. M. McClelland et al., 2000, 2006; Ponitz, McClelland, Matthews, & Morrison, 2009).

Despite their utility, some concerns associated with observer reports of regulatory processes include the possibility of introducing bias, not based on differences in regulation, but in observer perceptions of the subject. For example, one study examining teacher ratings of children's behavior found that up to 33% of the variance was due to rater differences (Mashburn, Hamre, Downer, & Pianta, 2006). Teacher ratings of young children's behavior in the United States, which are often completed by white women, may disadvantage boys and members of minority ethnic groups (Beaman, Wheldall, & Kemp, 2006). Actual differences in self-regulation across sex and culture further cloud this issue (Kochanska, Murray, Jacques, Koenig, & Vandegeest, 1996; Ponitz et al., 2008). During early childhood, one solution is to use multiple measures of self-regulation and not to make important decisions, such as whether a child should go to kindergarten, on the basis of a single instrument (Meisels, 2006).

Another concern with observer report data is that the internal process of self-regulation does not always manifest in immediate behavior. A review of engagement (which we have discussed as a form of self-regulation toward academic and school-related goals) identifies behavioral, cognitive, and emotional engagement but highlights the difficulty of measuring the latter two types of engagement reliably (Fredricks et al., 2004). Cognitive engagement, or the willingness to figure out difficult problems, and emotional engagement, including positive and negative attitudes toward school and learning, are not readily observable, at least as compared with behavior engagement evident in on-task behavior and overt participation in learning activity (Connor, Jakobsons, Crowe, & Meadows, 2009).

Although traditional assessments of self-regulation with young children have often utilized caregiver reports (Howse, Calkins, et al., 2003; M. M. McClelland et al., 2000; Schultz, Izard, Ackerman, & Youngstrom, 2001) or experimental measures (Carlson, 2005), direct measures are becoming more common. Moreover, many direct measures have strong construct validity, which allow for the prediction of social and academic outcomes (Diamond, Kirkham, & Amso, 2002; Gathercole & Pickering, 2000; Hongwanishkul et al., 2005; Kochanska, Coy, & Murray, 2001; Manly et al., 2001; McCabe, Hernandez, Lara, & Brooks-Gunn, 2000; McCabe, Rebello-Britto, Hernandez, & Brooks-Gunn, 2004; Pickering & Gathercole, 2004; Welsh, Pennington, & Groisser, 1991). Nevertheless, existing observational instruments have a number of shortcomings because many are designed for the laboratory or for clinical populations (Pickering & Gathercole, 2004). Thus, developing sensitive, predictive, and longitudinally valid measures of self-regulation that bridge the gap between the laboratory and real world is a current and future challenge.

Research on self-regulated learning in older children, adolescents, and adults has also utilized a number of different types of measures including self-reports, online learning software, structured diary measures, observations, qualitative measures, and microanalytic measures that include open- or closed-ended questions (Boekaerts & Cascallar, 2006; Zimmerman, 2008). One measure of self-regulated learning that is useful with adolescents and college students is the *Motivated Strategies to Learn Questionnaire* (MSLQ; Pintrich, Smith, García, & McKeachie, 1991, 1993), which has shown that students' self-regulated cognitive strategies and behaviors are related to motivational beliefs and achievement, and that educational contexts influence self-regulation (Bandalos, Finney, & Geske, 2003; Brookhart & Durkin, 2003; Dahl, Bals, & Turi, 2005; Pintrich & DeGroot, 1990; Zusho, Pintrich, & Coppola, 2003). However, one challenge for research in this area is that different types of measurement often demonstrate incongruence. For example, in one study, students used an online learning and self-regulation software to improve their study methods and achievement (Winne et al., 2006). Results suggested that students were somewhat overconfident when monitoring their own learning compared with actual tracking by the program (called *traces*), and significant discrepancies were seen when comparing students' monitoring of their use of self-regulation strategies. For example, students overestimated their own use of planning and reviewing by 29% and 26%, respectively, whereas tracking by the program indicated that few strategies were actually utilized by students. These results suggest that self-reports, like parent and teacher reports, may be useful but also share a number of limitations and often may not calibrate with direct measures of self-regulation.

Measuring Self-Regulation Using a Multidimensional Approach

Although the measurement of self-regulation has come a long way, measurement issues still abound in the field and present challenges, especially when self-regulation is viewed within a single dimension. As noted earlier, our conceptualization of self-regulation across the life span stems from a multidimensional, dynamic approach. Furthermore, the three-dimensional approach outlined earlier can be useful when discussing measurement issues in self-regulation. Figure 15.1 displays some examples of measures of self-regulation using the three dimensions of measurement. The axes of Figure 15.1 represent the first two dimensions. On the vertical axis is the phenomenological level, or *what* is measured; on the horizontal axis is the context, or *where* it is measured. The third dimension, or *how* the measurement is collected, is shown with different shades. White boxes indicate information collected directly from the individual; light gray boxes indicate observed behavior; dark gray boxes indicate reports of behavior. For example, biological measures of self-regulation within highly controlled laboratory settings include changes in heart rate and functional magnetic resonance imaging. A biological measure in a naturalistic setting might include taking cheek swabs of preschoolers' cortisol levels, which might then be connected to observed regulatory behavior in that setting. At the level of external, observable phenomena, measures of self-regulation in the laboratory include observable behaviors, such as participants' key presses on a computer task or other overt behavioral responses, such as whether a child gives the experimenter a turn while building a tall tower of blocks. Within highly naturalistic settings, self-regulation can be observed within peer interactions in classrooms or by asking teachers to report on children's social competence.

A final aspect of Figure 15.1 is the box whiskers. These indicate that measurement tools vary in the phenomenological levels they attempt to examine and in the settings in which they are relevant. For example, parent ratings of temperament, while situated at the level of observed behavior, often include questions such as "bright lights bother my child," and "my child responds strongly to particular

food tastes." These questions, although not directly tapping processes at biological levels, are nonetheless suggestive of these processes. We argue that the measures with longer whiskers are those that have successfully spanned multiple phenomenological levels and contexts, because they either implicitly or explicitly attempt to measure self-regulation across multiple dimensions rather than within one dimension.

Advances in Measuring Self-Regulation

In many ways, Figure 15.1 raises more questions than it answers: Do different ends of the continuum represent quantitative or qualitative shifts in self-regulation? What measures are most strongly predictive of other outcomes across settings? What are the ideal phenomenological level, context, and tool for a given research question? A number of measurement advances have been made in recent years to meet the challenges outlined earlier in traditional assessments of self-regulation and to better reflect the conceptualization that self-regulation requires a multilevel and multidimensional approach. For example, to better address the "what" issue or how to best measure different levels of regulatory processes, researchers have worked to develop measures that provide more proximal access to internal regulatory process. A relatively new method, the *Experience Sampling Method* (ESM), shows particular promise for helping us understand the moment-to-moment regulatory decisions made in daily life (Shernoff, Csikszentmihalyi, Schneider, & Shernoff, 2003). With ESM, subjects are given a Palm Pilot, which beeps them at random times during the day and solicits their responses to statements such as "I was concentrating on what I was doing," and "I was distracted from what I was doing" (Kane et al., 2007). New technologies utilizing mobile phones and Web sites such as Twitter also show promise for obtaining immediate information from individuals.

Gathering proximal data reflects a need to open the black box of the cognitive processes underlying self-regulation. Even when we strive to limit bias, participant reports will never provide direct information about the processes contributing to a set of manifest behaviors. Unlike observer reports, which tend to seek information about participants' typical behaviors across a range of naturalistic settings, internal process measures are usually gathered in the laboratory. Significant advances in this area attempt to measure self-regulation internally, including at the physiological and neurological levels. In *event-related potential* studies, the P300 is an electrical marker indicating a failure of

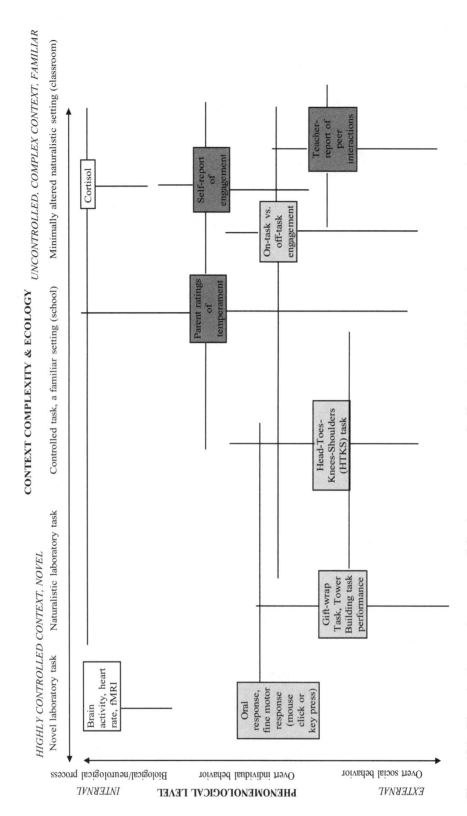

Figure 15.1 Dimensional approach to conceptualizing the measurement of self-regulation. fMRI, functional magnetic resonance imaging. *White boxes* indicate information collected directly from the individual; *light gray boxes* indicate observed behavior; *dark gray boxes* indicate reports of behavior.

self-regulation, of which the subject is cognitively aware. In tasks that require inhibitory control, such as refraining from pressing a key when viewing a stimuli that previously required a fast key press, the P300 is observed when subjects fail the item (by pressing the key).

Another challenge has been to develop measures of self-regulation that take into account the context or "where" self-regulation is best assessed. As one example, we have developed a task called *Head-Toes-Knees-Shoulders* (HTKS) to measure the regulation of overt behavior (Ponitz et al., 2008, Ponitz, McClelland, et al., 2009). The HTKS integrates three aspects of executive function into a short, easy-to-administer game. It involves four paired behavioral rules: "touch your head" and "touch your toes"; "touch your shoulders" and "touch your knees." Children first respond as instructed and then are asked to switch rules by responding in the opposite way (e.g., touch their head when told to touch their toes). The task taps behavioral regulation by requiring children to integrate three skills: (1) paying *attention* to the instructions; (2) using *working memory* to remember and execute new rules while processing the commands; and (3) using *inhibitory control* through inhibiting their natural response to the test command while initiating the correct but unnatural response. These multiple requirements make the HTKS a potentially useful measure of self-regulation. In addition, the ease of administration (a 5- to 10-minute task that can be learned quickly and that demonstrates strong interrater reliability) makes this a practical tool for use in classroom environments. In multiple samples from preschool to elementary school, children who succeed on this task achieve at higher levels academically and receive more positive ratings of behavior from their parents and teachers, compared with children who do less well (Connor et al., in press; Matthews, Ponitz, & Morrison, 2009; M. M. McClelland, Cameron, Connor, et al., 2007; Ponitz et al., 2008).

Research has also worked to examine how culture is an important context when measuring self-regulation. As noted earlier, children from several Asian countries have shown stronger self-regulation compared with children in Western countries (Oh & Lewis, 2008; Sabbagh et al., 2006). However, it has also been common for instruments to be translated into other languages without examining the psychometric properties of the measures in another culture or country (Tsai, McClelland, Pratt, & Squires, 2006; Wanless, McClelland, Acock, Chen, & Chen, in press). Thus, results could be because of culture or of measurement. Recent studies have started to address this by validating measures cross-culturally, although more work is

clearly needed. As one example, the HTKS direct measure of self-regulation and a simpler version called the *Head-to-Toes Task* (HTT) have been found to be reliable and significantly predict early achievement in the United States, Taiwan, South Korea, and China (Lan et al., 2010; Ponitz et al., 2008, 2009; Son et al., 2009; Wanless, McClelland, Acock, et al., in press; Wanless, McClelland, Son, et al., 2010).

As noted earlier, a number of studies have shown that girls have stronger self-regulatory skills compared with boys in childhood and adolescence, but these findings appear unique to North American samples and may not apply in other cultures (Duckworth & Seligman, 2006; Matthews et al., 2009; Ponitz et al., 2008). Recent research has started to examine this in more detail. In one study of Taiwanese preschoolers, girls were rated as having significantly stronger self-regulation than boys on a teacher-rated measure, but no significant sex differences were found when using the HTT direct measure (Wanless, McClelland, Acock, et al., in press). Another study utilized the HTKS and the same teacher-rated measure with preschoolers in the United States, Taiwan, South Korea, and Beijing. In this study, girls were rated more highly on self-regulation by teachers and also exhibited stronger scores on the HTKS direct measure of self-regulation compared with boys. In Taiwan, South Korea, and Beijing, however, no significant sex differences were found on the HTKS, but girls were rated by teachers as having stronger self-regulation (Lan et al., 2010). Thus, examining the same measure cross-culturally can shed light on how factors such as sex influence self-regulation in different cultures and contexts.

Finally, advances in measurement must also address the question of *how* self-regulation is best assessed. It may be most useful to collect data from a variety of sources—parents and teachers, self-report, and direct measures—to best capture self-regulation from a number of levels and dimensions. Traditional self-regulation measures have often relied on other-report (e.g., parent or teacher) or self-report (with older individuals), which each have benefits but also limitations. In addition to these methods, utilizing direct measures of self-regulation in naturalistic settings show particular utility. For example, with younger children, a direct assessment such as the HTKS measure of self-regulation shows promise because it directly taps behavior that closely approximates regulatory demands seen in school settings (Lan et al., 2010; Ponitz, McClelland et al., 2009). For example, inhibitory control required in the HTKS taps processes similar to remembering to raise one's hand before speaking in class. Moreover, a task such as the HTKS, which integrates attention, working memory, and inhibitory control, demonstrates ecological validity because the orchestration of these executive function processes are behavioral demands children encounter in real-world settings such as in classrooms and school settings.

Progress to develop innovative measures that move beyond self-reports commonly used with older children, adolescents, and adults can also be seen especially in the area of self-regulated learning (Zimmerman, 2008). Some of these innovations include software programs such as the gStudy online learning software, which records traces of student activities in the program in addition to self-reports of their self-regulated learning strategies and achievement (Perry & Winne, 2006). Other innovations in measures include think-aloud measures used in hypermedia online learning environments (Azevedo, 2005), combinations of qualitative and quantitative observational and interview measures (Perry, VandeKamp, Mercer, & Nordby, 2002), and microanalytic measures, which include open- and closed-ended questions (Zimmerman, 2008).

Research on older adults has relied more on self-reports but finds that autobiographical methods have important benefits, especially as people age (Hooker & McAdams, 2003). For example, although not often utilized, self-narrative methods such as remembering, reminiscing, and storytelling are important for organizing life stories, which are ways that individuals construct the story of their life and identity (McAdams, 2001). Individuals draw on their life stories and self-narratives as they pursue and refine goals, and navigate transitions throughout adulthood. Moreover, aspects of self-regulation are important for the development of life stories and for maintaining goals in later adulthood. Notably, research suggests that the ability to reminisce about a person's life is linked to their emotion regulation and other cognitive and interpersonal skills (Cappeliez & O'Rourke, 2002; Hooker & McAdams, 2003).

Taken together, research from a number of fields has advanced measures of self-regulation for children, adolescents, and adults. These achievements hold promise for addressing some of the limitations plaguing the field whereas reflecting the dynamic and integrative characteristics of self-regulation. The next section describes how self-regulation develops over the life span. Underlying this discussion is an emphasis on how self-regulation reflects the theoretical perspectives discussed earlier, such as the integration of cognitive, emotional, and behavioral processes that depend on multiple levels of influence, including person, context, and time, and that focus on the individual as an active agent in his or her own development.

DEVELOPMENT OF SELF-REGULATION OVER THE LIFE SPAN

Self-Regulation from Birth to the Transition to School

In infancy, self-regulation first begins to develop within the family context. Embedded in infant–caregiver interactions, early regulation is primarily the responsibility of caregivers. When a newborn cries, a responsive caregiver acts to soothe the infant through feeding, diaper changing, or holding and comforting. The caregiver acts to regulate the infant's needs, and through responsive and repetitive behaviors by the caregiver during the early months and years, children learn to regulate their own emotions and behaviors. Imagine Logan, an infant who is 6 months old. When he cries, his parents react quickly to soothe him by changing his diaper, feeding him, and giving him attention. During his early months, Logan learns that when he cries, his parents always respond quickly; as a result, he stops crying and smiles as soon as they enter the room. He develops a sense of trust and a secure attachment results. Logan begins self-regulating his cries in response to his parents' behaviors; eventually, he stops crying as soon as they enter the room.

A number of biological and environmental factors influence self-regulation starting in infancy. For example, an infant's temperament influences how they express emotions and learn to interpret the emotions and behaviors of others. Moreover, a child's expression of emotions and behaviors elicits different responses from parents. Parents' reactions to their infant's behaviors, as well as subsequent interactions, play a role in shaping the attachment relationship. For example, imagine an infant who is difficult to soothe but who has a responsive and patient caregiver that persists in attempting to calm their child despite prolonged cries. Over time, the infant may spend less time crying as a result of the caregiver's responsiveness. A secure attachment is created between the infant and caregiver where the infant learns that the caregiver will always respond in the same manner. This same infant in a scenario with a depressed caregiver may have a drastically different outcome. When the infant cries, the depressed caregiver attempts to calm the child but quickly grows frustrated and gives up, or even stops responding to the child's cries. The child finds that the caregiver's responses to cries are unpredictable and, as a result, becomes even more difficult to soothe. Together, these early interactions influence the attachment relationship, which is an important predictor of self-regulation (Calkins, 2004).

Differences in children's self-regulation abilities often become apparent in preschool. Early education and care settings represent one of the first environments in which children are exposed to peers and a structured environment in which they are asked to exhibit self-regulation (Phillips, McCartney, & Sussman, 2006). It is also during the preschool years that a number of changes occur that facilitate the development of self-regulation. These changes include a significant increase in vocabulary (Thompson & Lagattuta, 2006) and brain maturation in the PFC, which helps children control, direct, and plan actions (Blair, 2002). Rapid development in the PFC occurs between ages 3 and 6, suggesting that this time is an important period of development for self-regulation.

It is also during the preschool years that a link between aspects of self-regulation and early academic achievement emerges (Blair & Razza, 2007; Duncan et al., 2007; Gathercole & Pickering, 2000; Howse, Lange, Farran, & Boyles, 2003; Kail, 2003; NICHD Early Child Care Research Network, 2003; Trentacosta & Izard, 2007). Self-regulation assessed by measures that integrate inhibitory control, attention, and working memory predicts social and academic success (Bronson, Tivnan, & Seppanen, 1995; Howse, Calkins, et al., 2003; M. M. McClelland et al., 2006; M. M. McClelland, Cameron, Connor, et al., 2007; M. M. McClelland et al., 2000). In one study, prekindergartners who had difficulty regulating their behavior to complete goal-directed activities scored lower on a cognitive achievement measure (Bronson et al., 1995). In another study, self-regulation measured by a direct task significantly predicted emergent literacy, vocabulary, and math skills over the prekindergarten year. Moreover, gains in preschool self-regulation significantly predicted gains in these same academic measures over the school year (M. M. McClelland, Cameron, Connor, et al., 2007). Research has also documented that children with poor self-regulation exhibit more risk factors than their peers, including family problems, lower parental education, and behavioral or emotional problems (Bronson et al., 1995; Howse, Calkins, et al., 2003; M. M. McClelland et al., 2006; M. M. McClelland et al., 2000). Furthermore, research has shown that children with strong self-regulation have better social competence, and that strong behavioral regulation can ameliorate otherwise negative characteristics

or conditions (Connor et al., in press; Eisenberg, Smith, et al., 2004; Fantuzzo, Bulotsky-Sheare, et al., 2005; Lengua, 2002; Lengua, Honorado, & Bush, 2007; Patrick, 1997). For example, negative emotional responses to challenges are linked with poor social competence, except when children have strong attentional skills (Belsky et al., 2001).

Risk Factors and Self-Regulation in Young Children

Risk factors such as socioeconomic status (SES) and ethnic minority status also contribute to children's developing self-regulation. Research has shown that children from sociodemographically disadvantaged backgrounds perform worse than their more advantaged peers on a variety of achievement, language, and school readiness indicators, including self-regulation (Dearing, Berry, & Zaslow, 2006). Low family income and low maternal education also predict decreased levels of attention and self-regulation before school entry and in the early school years (Howse, Lange et al., 2003). Overall, children from minority and disadvantaged backgrounds appear to be at particularly high risk for developing poor self-regulation (Connell & Prinz, 2002; M. M. McClelland et al., 2000). For example, recent research documented that ethnic minority status and poverty predicted lower self-regulation and achievement in young children (Evans & Rosenbaum, 2008), and another study found that multiple risk factors predicted negative adjustment, and that children in elementary school who were low in self-regulation were more vulnerable to multiple risk factors (Lengua, 2002).

Although little research exists on Hispanic children's self-regulation, a recent study suggests that children from disadvantaged Hispanic families enter preschool with significantly lower levels of self-regulation than their classmates (Wanless, McClelland, Tominey, & Acock, 2010). One possible contributor may be a parenting emphasis on compliance, which Hispanic mothers may value more than mothers from other cultural backgrounds (Brooks-Gunn & Markman, 2005; Wasserman, Rauh, Brunelli, & Garcia-Castro, 1990). Furthermore, emphasizing compliance and following parents' rules rather than supporting children's autonomy has been associated with lower levels of behavioral regulation (Kochanska & Knaack, 2003; Stansbury & Zimmermann, 1999; Wachs et al., 2004). Together, this research suggests that children with an accumulation of risk factors, especially those from minority and disadvantaged backgrounds (within the context of the United States), may have more difficulty on tasks requiring that they control, plan, and direct their behavior, which may result in lower self-regulation and academic achievement.

We have also learned much from research on stressful early environments, and how these shape particular patterns of brain activation and behavior (Gunnar, 2006). From a self-regulation perspective, early stressors mean that the bulk of a child's early experiences require immediate and intense reaction. Examples of early stressors associated with poor developmental outcomes include inconsistent or volatile parenting; frequent moves or change in caregivers; intense and frequent violence, abuse, or neglect; or stimulus deprivation (Morales & Guerra, 2006). In other words, stressful situations require young children to spend much of their time managing their emotions, leaving little time for the intellectual exploration and learning that a peaceful, stimuli-rich environment enables. As one example, a recent study found that PFC functioning was lower in low-SES children compared with high-SES children on measures of attention (Kishiyama, Boyce, Jimenez, Perry, & Knight, 2009). Some researchers have observed that neurological pathways, including those used for processing emotion information or cognitive information, are like muscles (Muraven & Baumeister, 2000; Shonkoff & Phillips, 2000). Pathways that are used grow and mature, whereas those that are unused atrophy. A child navigating multiple sustained and severe emotionally charged situations in his early years has little opportunity to develop critical thinking skills, to reflect on his or her learning, or to learn to focus attention on a problem. Thus, as noted earlier, in the United States, children experiencing risk because of SES, family background, or neighborhood violence are more likely to have poorer self-regulation skills than those not experiencing such risks (Esposito, 1999; Fantuzzo, Rouse, et al., 2005; M. M. McClelland et al., 2000; Sameroff & Chandler, 1975).

Some research has focused on examining individual traits that may help children overcome a highly negative early environment (Borman & Overman, 2004; Masten, 2001; Werner & Smith, 2001). However, findings suggest that as environmental and family risks increase, positive outcomes are increasingly less likely (Sameroff, Bartko, Baldwin, Baldwin, & Seifer, 1998). This may be, in part, because negative early environments create a set of emotional, cognitive, and behavioral strategies in children themselves, which may be adaptive for that particular environment but maladaptive in new, mainstream environments such as a classroom. For example, the same response that works with an abusive sibling—hitting back—is not an appropriate response in a preschool setting. Thus, children exposed to accumulated risk over time will have more difficulty developing adaptive self-regulatory strategies. However, viewing self-regulation from a relational developmental systems perspective also acknowledges the importance of plasticity throughout the life span. Thus, although negative risk factors are more likely to cascade over time (Masten et al., 2005), opportunities for change and growth exist throughout the life span (Lerner, 2006; Werner & Smith, 2001). It is especially relevant to consider that development is not static or linear, but reflects interactive processes between individuals and multiple levels of their environment (from biological factors to cultural and societal factors). More research focusing on these developmental pathways and the specific mechanisms involved in charting these paths is clearly needed.

As we describe the growth of self-regulation from infancy through adolescence, it is useful to consider Piaget's stages as a context for this development (E. Fox & Riconscente, 2008; Piaget, 1964/1968). For example, changes in self-regulation between infancy and adolescence parallel the cognitive changes theorized by Piaget as children transition from the sensorimotor period, to preoperational and concrete operational thinking, to formal operations in adolescence (Bronson, 2000). According to Piaget, this process involves intentionality and emotions (E. Fox & Riconscente, 2008; Piaget, 1964/1968). As children move through the Piagetian stages and enter formal operational thinking, they become increasingly able to deliberately control their thoughts and actions, organize, and systematically problem-solve (Gestsdóttir & Lerner, 2008). Thus, children's cognitive development has important implications for their self-regulation as they progress from early childhood to adolescence.

Self-Regulation from the Transition to School to Adolescence

Considerable research demonstrates that self-regulation is important for achievement in kindergarten and throughout elementary school (Howse, Calkins, et al., 2003; M. M. McClelland et al., 2006; M. M. McClelland et al., 2000; Ponitz, Rimm-Kaufman, Grimm, & Curby, 2009). Teachers, however, report significant variability in the self-regulatory skills of children entering kindergarten (Lin, Lawrence, & Gorrell, 2003). Specific aspects of self-regulation (including attention, working memory, and inhibitory control) are essential for children to develop positive behaviors in a classroom context. Students who are unable to pay attention, control their behavior, and complete tasks have difficulty in the classroom (Alexander et al., 1993; Ladd, 2003). In one study, kindergarten self-regulation, as rated by teachers, predicted children's academic achievement over the school year (Howse, Calkins, et al., 2003). Another study found that students' self-regulation in first grade significantly predicted reading comprehension and vocabulary skills growth (Connor et al., in press). Finally, research has documented that kindergarten learning-related skills (including self-regulation and social-emotional competence) predicted literacy and mathematics skills between kindergarten and sixth grade, and growth in literacy and math from kindergarten to second grade (M. M. McClelland et al., 2000, 2006). Children with poor self-regulation skills also had lower performance than their higher-rated peers on reading and mathematics between kindergarten and sixth grade (M. M. McClelland et al., 2006). Together, these results suggest that self-regulation is important for achievement throughout elementary school.

As childhood progresses, self-regulation can be viewed in terms of decision making and motivation. Moreover, as children's cognitive capabilities develop and they move from concrete operations to formal operational thinking, they are able to self-regulate through complex, future-oriented processes such as goal setting, planning, and weighing options in terms of values, expectancies, and possible consequences (E. Fox & Riconscente, 2008; Freund & Baltes, 2002; J. Heckhausen & Schulz, 1995; Wigfield et al., 2006). For example, imagine a middle-school student, Brody. On entering middle school, Brody finds that his teachers require much more homework than his elementary school teachers did. He wants to play soccer in high school, like his brother, and he knows that to develop the skills to do so, he needs to play on the middle-school team. However, his parents require him to maintain a B average to play sports. Brody also enjoys playing the piano but decides that homework and soccer are his top priorities and chooses not to continue private music lessons.

In early and middle childhood, parents play a significant role in shaping the development of self-regulation by providing the environment in which a child grows and develops, including providing opportunities for children to make decisions and practice self-regulation. As students enter adolescence, parental influences become increasingly indirect and adolescents play a more active role in their own decision making and self-regulation. In other words, the nature of the parent–child relationship changes

in adolescence in that the level of control that parents exert over their children tends to decrease. In general, parents spend less time directly monitoring adolescent activities and behaviors, and believe that children can be relied on to follow directives and regulate their own time and behavior (Bulcroft, Carmody, & Bulcroft, 1996). There is evidence, however, that parenting styles continue to have a direct influence on adolescent self-regulation. One study used a combination of observations and adolescent reports to examine the effects of parenting styles in two-parent families on children's school commitment (a construct that includes motivation and self-regulation; Simons & Conger, 2007). Results indicated that adolescents with two authoritative parents had higher school commitment than those whose parents exhibited other parenting style combinations (authoritarian, indulgent, or uninvolved).

Aspects of self-regulation, such as decision making, goal pursuit, and motivation, continue to become increasingly salient as children enter adolescence (Gestsdóttir & Lerner, 2008). In addition, the transition into adolescence is a time when self-regulation may take different forms or involve different processes than self-regulation during childhood transitions. Consistent with the transition to formal operational thinking, not only are adolescents' planning skills still developing, their higher order cognitive processes that are involved in making judgments about important life dilemmas are developing as well. In particular, there are steady age-related gains in knowledge and judgment regarding difficult, ambiguous, real-life scenarios from adolescence to the early 20s, but performance remains level through young adulthood (Pasupathi, Staudinger, & Baltes, 2001). In a review of 94 empirical journal articles focusing on adolescent goal pursuit, though the goals changed slightly as adolescents aged, the most common goals of adolescents related to education, occupation, and social relationships (Massey, Gebhardt, & Garnefski, 2008). The same study found that, with age, adolescents increasingly developed self-regulatory skills pertinent to achieving these goals, including planning abilities and confidence in attaining goals.

Brain development also plays a critical role in self-regulation throughout adolescence. Behavioral studies have shown that the transition to adolescence is characterized by a more fully conscious, self-directed, and self-regulatory mind (Keating, 2004). Moreover, adolescents become increasingly adept at controlling how they process information despite competing demands. Neuroimaging studies in adolescence have shown significant growth in the PFC, the area of the brain related to the development of self-regulation, as well as a significant expansion of the linkages from the PFC to other regions in the brain (Keating, 2004).

Self-Regulation from Adolescence to the Transition to Adulthood

What happens during adolescence and the transition to adulthood to enhance or diminish self-regulation? Again, we turn to transitions as events that, in creating change, also illustrate individual differences in self-regulation (Caspi & Moffitt, 1991; Graber & Brooks-Gunn, 1996). Popular stereotypes of adolescence detail a disordered, hectic time characterized by poor judgment. Indeed, during adolescence, substance use, risk-taking, and delinquent behaviors increase (Bachman et al., 2008; Bryant, Schulenberg, O'Malley, Bachman, & Johnston, 2003; Steinberg, 2008). Accumulating evidence suggests that during adolescence, self-regulation is influenced by physiological changes, which illustrates the dynamic interplay between the body, brain, and behavior. In particular, Steinberg (2008) suggests that an increase in dopaminergic activity in the brain, which occurs during puberty, is associated with (though not necessarily directly causative of) increased risk-taking.

Other models of decision making propose two cognitive processes that individuals use to make decisions (Carver & White, 1994; Epstein, 1994; Gerrard, Gibbons, Houlihan, Stock, & Pomery, 2008). Though the specific nature of these cognitive processes varies by theory, one process is generally considered a conscious, analytic, and rational approach, which is closely associated with self-regulation. This process involves deliberation, planning, and anticipating outcomes and consequences. The other process is a heuristic, intuitive approach, which relies on gut feelings and affect. Consistent with this notion, Piaget viewed self-regulation as including the development of intellect (e.g., intentional behavior), as well as affect (E. Fox & Riconscente, 2008; Piaget, 1964/1968). All individuals use a combination of the dual cognitive processes (analytic vs. heuristic), but some evidence suggests that adolescents are more prone than adults to use a heuristic mode of decision making (Gerrard et al., 2008). Furthermore, adolescents may be especially prone to use the heuristic style of decision making in social situations, when risky activities are most likely to be present. Thus, adolescents' use of heuristic decision making may explain risky adolescent behaviors such as substance use (Leventhal, Keeshan, Baker, & Wetter, 1991; Spijkerman, van den Eijnden, & Engels, 2005) and sexual activity without condoms (van Empelen & Kok, 2006). Life-span differences in the use of the two decision-making styles may also explain why individuals' intentions do not predict adolescent behavior as well as they predict adult behavior (Sheeran & Orbell, 1998).

Over time, adolescents begin to reduce their risky behaviors. This change is thought to be partly related to brain development as synaptic pruning in the PFC (and possibly continued changes in dopaminergic activity) increases individuals' capacity for self-regulation (Steinberg, 2008). Indeed, adolescents who have stronger self-regulatory skills are less prone to endorse and engage in risky behaviors (Crockett, Raffaelli, & Shen, 2006; Magar, Phillips, & Hosie, 2008). As individuals' cognitive capabilities develop, they are more able to self-regulate through complex, future-oriented processes such as goal setting, planning one's actions and investment of resources, and weighing options in terms of values, expectancies, and possible consequences (Freund & Baltes, 2002; J. Heckhausen & Schulz, 1995). This is also reflected in the concept of *intentional self-regulation*, which becomes especially relevant in adolescence (Gestsdóttir & Lerner, 2008). Intentional self-regulation describes the strategies and behaviors that individuals use to accomplish their goals. As individuals move through adolescence, they use intentional self-regulation to select and optimize goals, and compensate for any losses in the pursuit of those goals (Gestsdóttir & Lerner, 2008).

Related to this and similar to Piaget's formal operational thinking, the higher order cognitive processes that are involved in making judgments about important life dilemmas also change during adolescence (E. Fox & Riconscente, 2008). Judgment regarding difficult and ambiguous real-life scenarios increases from early adolescence into the early 20s, before leveling off in young adulthood (Pasupathi et al., 2001). Another likely reason for an increase in individuals' self-regulatory, decision making, and judgment over time is that they have more experience to draw on when evaluating ideas and planning courses of action.

The *transition to adulthood* is a phrase used to describe a period of the life course characterized by many overlapping transitions between the approximate ages of 18 and 30. Key transitions that make up the transition to adulthood in social science literature include moving out of the family home, concluding formal education, entering the workforce full-time (often in a job related to one's aspired career track, rather than in a noncareer-track job), getting married, becoming a parent, and becoming financially independent.[1] Gaining "adult" status does not require the whole sum of these transitions; in general, each of them represents movement away from the relative irresponsibility and dependency of adolescence, and toward the relative responsibility, autonomy, and creation/procreation that marks adulthood.

Furthermore, many of the transitions that comprise the transition to adulthood are temporally flexible and revisable. When young adults who have made a transition find themselves overwhelmed, some may regress as a way of coping with realities that are beyond their capacities. For instance, it is now relatively common in the United States to move away from the family home for an extended amount of time but to move back in with one's parents during the transition to adulthood (Arnett, 2004). As a widespread phenomena, this is not indicative of young adults providing care for an older generation (though that does occur); rather, young adults struggle to become financially independent and find that sharing housing expenses or living rent-free with their parents is one way of coping. Consider the case of Joe, a college graduate with a degree in English. After searching for a job in publishing and having no success, he took a job as a paralegal. After some time in this position, he realized that it would be difficult for him to progress in his desired career field without additional education, and so he quit his full-time job to attend law school. While attending law school, he lived with his parents, but after graduating, he became a lawyer and bought a house of his own. In this case, Joe completed his education twice and entered the full-time workforce twice because he was unsatisfied with his first attempt at navigating these transitions.

As seen with Joe, the transition into adulthood is assisted or hampered by psychological capacities that help determine an individual's decisions and life course. For example, skills such as planfulness, reflective capacity, developmental regulation, and self-efficacy are related to self-regulation, and help individuals pursue goals and make the life decisions inherent in adulthood (Settersten,

2007). Planfulness refers to being aware of available options and taking advantage of them, setting goals, and being flexible if the context or the options change. Developmental regulation includes the ability to use aspects of self-regulation (e.g., inhibitory control) to act in socially appropriate ways. Finally, self-efficacy is related to the ability to self-regulate in young people and adults because it includes individuals' ability to self-evaluate their behavior and manage their actions in future situations. This self-awareness is critical as young adults like Joe begin to navigate a complex array of educational, work, and social situations. As seen throughout this chapter, these capacities overlap with relevant constructs from other perspectives such as Baltes's (1997) SOC model. Aspects of the SOC model can be used to describe how young adults make and pursue goals, and change their plans when faced with failure or obstacles (Settersten, 2007). However, as Lerner and colleagues (2001) have noted, young adults may have difficulty recognizing the need for compensation if they associate compensating with failure.

The transition to adulthood is unique in that it is the first time in the life course that individuals are faced with decreasing probabilities of achieving many major life goals. Although unmet goals occur throughout life, the transition to adulthood is often the first time that life goals can surpass reality, and when this occurs, the mismatch may have substantial long-term social cognitive consequences. Children and adolescents can hypothesize substantial long-term disasters from failing a test or not being invited to a party, but such events do not, by themselves, have a global impact on the quality of the rest of one's life. In contrast, *not* completing one's anticipated level of education or *not* marrying the person to whom one is engaged has more substantial impact on the chances, opportunities, and contexts one will encounter in the future. In addition, such failures to fulfill life plans can result in detriments to physical health (Strauman, Coe, McCrudden, Vieth, & Kwapil, 2008) and well-being (Nurmi & Salmela-Aro, 2002). For instance, after graduation, young adults who have not found employment are more likely than their employed peers to become depressed (Nurmi & Salmela-Aro, 2002). Furthermore, the relation between self-regulation and health is reciprocal, and individuals who are depressed or have other mental disorders perform worse on a task of recalling autobiographical memories (Neshat-Doost, Dalgleish, & Golden, 2008).

Despite increased cognitive self-regulatory capacities, adolescents and young adults may still encounter difficulties when exerting control over themselves and their

---

[1] For the sake of this chapter, we primarily discuss schooling and career-entry transitions in the section on Self-Regulation from Adolescence to the Transition to Adulthood; marital and parenthood transitions are discussed in the section on Self-Regulation in Adulthood and Within-Adulthood Transitions. Although the flexible timing of such transitions makes such distinction rather arbitrary, the American standard is to marry and become a parent slightly after completing school and entering one's career.

environments. At any age, making choices can impair individuals' self-control (Vohs et al., 2008). Because transitions often require making multiple choices, periods of the life course that are full of transitions are likely to be especially stressful, even if those transitions are generally positive. Together, the cognitive and emotional demands on individuals during periods of transition may reduce their capacity to strive to reach additional goals, and the emotional consequences of these "missed opportunities" could be quite negative.

Stressful events also appear to directly reduce individuals' self-regulatory capacity. Poulin and Heckhausen (2007) found that adolescents who had recently experienced a death or divorce in their family had reduced primary control for their educational and career goals. Moreover, this effect was stronger when the developmental deadline of their goals was more immediate (e.g., at the end of their final year of high school) rather than more distant (e.g., early in their final year of high school). Poulin and Heckhausen argue that the intense effort necessary to reach a goal at the brink of its developmental deadline makes immediate goals more susceptible to interference than distant goals. When a goal is more distant, individuals can temporarily reduce their focus on the goal, but recover their focus and effort before the deadline must be met.

Poulin and Heckhausen (2007) also suggest that the process by which stressful life events impact the pursuit of life goals is through the person's beliefs about the world. A stressful event, a series of events, or a long period of being stressed reduces one's perceptions that the world is controllable. Because the world seems less controllable, one's *control means-ends beliefs*, or the belief that a particular goal outcome is controllable, diminish as well. When an individual no longer feels personal control over meeting a goal, then goal-striving efforts are also reduced.

Self-Regulation in Adulthood and Within-Adulthood Transitions

Although adulthood is often less studied by developmentalists, it is as full of transitions and opportunities for self-regulatory changes as other periods of the life course. As adults encounter new transitions and begin to experience more losses, new patterns of adaptation emerge and novel self-regulatory strategies may be used (Freund & Baltes, 2002). For instance, middle-aged adults have more maintenance-focused goal orientations than do younger adults (Ebner, Freund, & Baltes, 2006). In addition, with advancing age, individuals' maintenance and loss-prevention goal orientations are more strongly related to their subjective well-being.

In adulthood, many developmental deadlines become more salient and urgent. Some of these may be socially determined deadlines (Baltes, 1991; Heckhausen, 2000), such as getting married, being promoted, or buying a house. Other developmental deadlines may be more real in their temporal extension, such as childbearing for women. Later in this chapter, we discuss research findings regarding several of these transitions.

Self-regulation strategies appear to influence the quality and satisfaction of intimate relationships. For instance, using selection, optimization, and compensation strategies to achieve one's romantic goals is related to satisfaction with one's partner or relationship, emotional balance in one's relationship, and subjective success in the domain of relationships (Wiese et al., 2000). Persistently using relationship-enhancing strategies (not limited to those in the SOC model) is related to concurrent marital satisfaction (Halford, Lizzio, Wilson, & Occhipinti, 2007). Furthermore, persistence and the use of relationship-enhancing strategies predict subsequent marital satisfaction. However, the relations are weaker over time than concurrently, which suggests that the correlation between self-regulation within a relationship and relationship satisfaction indicates that people are more willing to work for a strong relationship when the relationship already makes them happy. This illustrates the dynamic nature of self-regulation.

Moreover, Bowen's family systems theory suggests that when a spouse has trouble regulating his or her emotions, frustrations within the marriage lead the spouse to seek regulation from a third party (Kerr & Bowen, 1988; Titelman, 2008). These third parties may be romantic interests, but they may also be children, families of origin, or other members of their social network. When both spouses are able to regulate their emotions effectively, they can cope with issues in their relationship without seeking external support.

In the realm of work, during young adulthood, using selection, optimization, and compensation strategies to achieve goals is related to work satisfaction, emotional balance at work, and subjective success in one's occupation (Wiese et al., 2000; Wiese, Freund, & Baltes, 2002). Paralleling findings from childhood and schooling, young adults' progress toward occupational goals is related to greater well-being (Wiese & Freund, 2005). Importantly, making progress toward or meeting one's occupational goals is not by itself related to an increase in well-being.

It is only when a person believes that his or her goals are difficult to achieve that making progress toward achieving them results in greater well-being.

Late Adulthood

As adults enter late adulthood, their use of self-regulatory strategies continues to change. Baltes (1997) suggested that, in childhood, individuals focus on growth and gains, rather than loss, but with age, a stronger emphasis on loss begins to emerge. Though losses and setbacks happen throughout the life course, older adults must increasingly adapt to losses in their social networks, physical health, and cognitive abilities. Therefore, older adults have fewer growth-focused orientations toward their personal goals than do younger adults and middle-aged adults (Ebner et al., 2006). Ebner and colleagues also found that when older adults do have growth-focused orientations toward their goals, such orientations are less strongly related to their subjective well-being than they are among younger adults. Rather than pursuing growth, older adults tend to pursue loss prevention-focused goal orientations. These changes are an appropriate adaptation of self-regulatory strategies in the face of new personal and contextual realities.

One reason for these developmentally appropriate changes is the gradual decline in older adults' cognitive resources. Although crystallized intelligence, or cognitive pragmatics, remains relatively strong and stable throughout adulthood, fluid intelligence, or cognitive mechanics, shows age-related decline throughout middle and late adulthood (Baltes, 1997). In addition, Baltes (1997) argues that cultural supports and resources for individuals' self-regulation strategies become less efficient as individuals' personal (cognitive and physical) resources decline, thereby decreasing the overall resources available to older adults even more. For example, although cultural advantages (e.g., education) can promote greater acquisition of cognitive abilities, they do not protect against these age-related declines (Mayer & Baltes, 1996, cited in Baltes 1997). Goal disengagement processes, though used and valuable throughout the life span, are considered to be even more important during later adulthood, when individuals have fewer opportunities to achieve their goals and fewer resources to engage during goal pursuit (Wrosch et al., 2004).

Although many adults remain active and healthy well into late adulthood, physical declines and illnesses take their toll on this group. For example, older adults have reduced sensorimotor abilities such as balance and speed

(Lindenberger, Marsiske, & Baltes, 2000), and the physical declines associated with late adult development and age-related illness are risk factors for depression (Lenze et al., 2001; Wrosch et al., 2004). Moreover, this relation is reciprocal: Individuals who experience development of health problems are more likely to become depressed than individuals who are otherwise healthy, but depression can also reduce one's ability to cope with illness and to maintain one's level of physical well-being, leading to further health problems.

In addition to physical declines and illness, adults in later life experience changes in brain structure, which may affect their ability to self-regulate. Research suggests that, even in healthy adults, late adult development is accompanied by a decrease in brain volume in the frontal lobe, an area critical for self-regulation (Vinters, 2001). Moreover, brain changes in late adulthood are correlated with declines in working memory and cognitive flexibility (Raz et al., 1997). Additional research has also found age-related declines in explicit memory and executive functions in late adulthood with no other evidence of clinical disease (Albert & Killiany, 2001).

The combination of physical, mental, and cultural declines in older adults' resources results in strains on their self-regulation. This has been demonstrated in dual-task activities in which adults are asked to walk around a narrow track while engaging in a memory task. Recall is lower when individuals walk around difficult tracks than it is when they walk around simple tracks or when they are not walking (Lindenberger et al., 2000). Further, the decrement in physical task performance is larger for older adults than it is for younger adults (Li, Lindenberger, Freund, & Baltes, 2001; Lindenberger et al., 2000).

As adults age, they must regulate many aspects of their lives, including aspects that are not often considered activities requiring self-regulation earlier in life. For example, physical and cognitive declines often lead to the cessation of driving among older adults (Rudman, Friedland, Chipman, & Sciotino, 2006). With advancing age, older adults (age 85 and older) are more likely than young-old adults (age 65–74 years) to report that they would refrain from driving in heavy traffic or in an unfamiliar area (Kostyniuk & Molnar, 2008). Driving is one example of a realm in which older adults often need to cope with a change from independence to dependence—once they are no longer capable of driving, they need to rely on others for transportation. This change can be difficult and frustrating, as many consider driving to be a symbol of personal freedom and mobility, and driving may be a virtual necessity of survival in some suburban and rural communities (Rudman et al., 2006). Coping with the loss of driving can be facilitated with compensation strategies, such as disengaging from driving by focusing on the financial benefits of no longer owning a car.

Finally, another loss that often occurs during older adulthood is bereavement. One recent study described changes in regulation as a response to loss of a partner (Sbarra & Hazan, 2008). In a committed relationship, individuals engage in *coregulation*, which is defined as "the reciprocal maintenance of psychophysiological homeostasis within a relationship" (Sbarra & Hazan, p. 143). When a person loses his or her partner, they must learn to rely more on their own self-regulation to achieve emotional balance. The absence of coregulation sends the remaining partner into "biobehavioral dysregulation," or a state of physical and mental stress. Consider Agatha, who recently lost her husband of many years. At first, she experiences volatile emotions and a sense of insecurity. Over time, she successfully recovers a sense of balance. She does so by packing up her husband's belongings and giving them away, and by not thinking or talking about her husband whenever possible. Her friend Gretchen thinks Agatha's reaction is odd because when Gretchen lost her husband the year before, she felt best when she shared stories about her husband and talked about her emotions. Sbarra and Hazan (2008) suggest that there are many ways to cope with the loss of one's partner. As an illustration of equifinality, for a coping strategy to be adaptive, it must restore the bereaved person's sense of security and mitigate their stress response, returning the individual's homeostasis. Thus, individuals may find different strategies successfully return their sense of balance.

Advancing age brings with it a shorter temporal extension for many life goals. By older adulthood, many developmental deadlines have already passed. Wrosch and colleagues (2004) suggest that older adults who disengage from their goals through compensatory secondary control may experience lower well-being. This is especially true when they are unable to replace their disengaged goals with new goals (Wrosch, Scheier, Miller, Schulz, & Carver, 2003, cited in Wrosch, Schulz, & Heckhausen 2004). Thus, a lifelong runner may experience depression if he stops running races because of arthritis, but would be less likely to experience depression if he replaces running with swimming or another low-impact activity. Challenges associated with disengaging from goals are particularly prevalent during older adulthood.

Fortunately, despite a wide range of resource losses, older adults do not rely solely on compensatory strategies to meet their goals. Rather, many optimizing strategies and other activities can help ward off losses and protect their mental well-being. For instance, most people show a decline in attentional performance and decline in gray matter volume with age (Pagnoni & Cekic, 2007; Sowell et al., 2003). These changes, however, are less present in people who practice Zen meditation, which is a form of cognitive and behavioral (postural) self-regulation (Pagnoni & Cekic, 2007). There are several implications of the life-span control theory for working with older adults who experience health problems (Wrosch et al., 2004). When individuals face health challenges that are, to some degree, controllable, treatment should focus on the individual's ability to exert influence. When health problems are uncontrollable, disengagement and goal replacement or reconstruction may be the best strategies for coping with changes in one's health.

Taken together, the ability to self-regulate begins at birth and continues throughout adulthood, with a variety of factors influencing its development. Although rarely examined across the life span, self-regulation is clearly important and is woven throughout perspectives from a multitude of disciplines. The degree to which individuals successfully learn to manage emotions, cognitions, and behaviors is an important indicator of how well they navigate life domains (e.g., school, peers, family and interpersonal relationships, work) and transitions. Thus, research would benefit from continuing to examine how self-regulation operates at different developmental periods over the life span. We now turn to concluding comments, implications, and future directions in the study of self-regulation.

CONCLUSIONS AND FUTURE DIRECTIONS

Historically, the construct of self-regulation has been studied somewhat in isolation and within a fairly narrow scope. Since the late 1980s, however, there has been an explosion of interest in the area from a number of theoretical perspectives and disciplines. This accumulation of research is particularly exciting because it has moved self-regulation research in important new directions. Along with this growing enthusiasm, however, come an increasing number of definitions of self-regulation and conceptualizations of the various domains underlying this important construct. This complexity makes it particularly challenging when synthesizing research from a number of fields to comprehensively define and describe self-regulation. Perhaps this is also why little research takes a life-span view of self-regulation; the undertaking quickly becomes daunting. For example, when discussing self-regulation in children, much research stems from a developmental or cognitive perspective. In adolescents, educational or personality perspectives have typically been used to investigate self-regulation, and in adults, life-span perspectives such as the SOC model (Baltes, 1997) and the life-span theory of control (J. Heckhausen & Schulz, 1995) are often applied. Finally, most research has been conducted within North American populations, and needs to be expanded into other cultures. Thus, integrating research from a number of fields is especially challenging.

However, given the importance of self-regulation for predicting a multitude of outcomes in individuals, this integration of research is essential to gain a full understanding of how self-regulation is defined, measured, and develops across the life span, and how to intervene with individuals who struggle in this area. Fortunately, as described throughout this chapter, there are many points of agreement among the perspectives examining self-regulation. This concluding section describes some of the common themes that cut across disciplinary fields, and discusses implications and future directions for research and intervention in self-regulation.

Common Themes in Self-Regulation Research

There is little doubt that self-regulation has emerged as an important construct throughout the life span. As noted throughout this chapter, evidence from a variety of disciplines points to the centrality of self-regulation for predicting outcomes such as school readiness, achievement, psychological adjustment, work, career, and interpersonal relationships. This convergence of perspectives has resulted in major advances in the field of self-regulation as research has become increasingly life-span oriented and multidisciplinary. One example of this can be seen in recent work applying life-span theories to self-regulation with children and adolescents, which were first used in research with older adults (Gestsdóttir & Lerner, 2007, 2008; Lerner et al., 2001; Skinner, 1999).

Consistent with this broadening of perspectives is the growing agreement that self-regulation is best viewed as the integration of cognitive, emotional, and behavioral processes. Much of this integrative framework has come from the cognitive and developmental neuropsychology literatures, which have featured recent special issues and books specifically devoted to the integration of cognition

and emotion (Calkins & Bell, in press; Sokol & Müller, 2007). Although more work is clearly needed, this research has greatly increased our understanding of underlying brain and temperamental processes involved in the regulation of thoughts, emotions, and behavior, and adds insight into the mechanism variables involved and how they predict outcomes. Moreover, these results have major implications for strengthening an individual's capacity for effective self-regulation throughout the life span.

As research becomes increasingly multidisciplinary, existing commonalities have become more evident in theoretical frameworks such as developmental systems perspectives, social cognitive, and life-span theories. There is also an increasing emphasis to situate self-regulation within theoretical perspectives that view development as involving mutual interactions between an individual and different levels of influence including person, context, and time experience over the life span. In addition, borrowing from the SOC model (Baltes, 1997), a useful conceptualization is to describe life-span self-regulation in terms of selecting, optimizing, and using compensatory strategies to pursue and refine goals, and manage life events and transitions.

Another common theme woven throughout the theoretical and disciplinary perspectives reviewed here is the notion that each individual is an active agent in his or her self-regulation. This does not negate the importance of the underlying biological and temperamental bases of self-regulation. Instead, we focus on the importance of interactions between these underlying bases and environmental factors, including how process and context influence the capacity for self-regulation. It also reflects the concept of relative plasticity in suggesting that change in an individual's ability to self-regulate is possible throughout the life span, although it is not without limits (Lerner, 2006). Taken together, these themes have clear implications for future research and intervention, which are discussed in this section.

It is also evident that different disciplines measure self-regulation similarly across the life span, and there is growing consensus about the strengths and limitations of existing types of assessment. Although other-report or self-report remain commonly used to assess aspects of self-regulation and have a number of strengths, limitations include possible bias and an inability to tap underlying processes. Direct and observational measures have gained popularity in recent years and have contributed much to research in this area. However, they also have weaknesses; many measures developed for use in clinical or laboratory settings may not adequately tap emotional and behavioral aspects of self-regulation in real-world settings such as school, work, or interpersonal contexts.

Given the importance of precise measurement for studying self-regulation, it is promising to see the advances in measurement in recent years, together with an increasing interest in developing reliable and valid assessments in disciplines such as developmental, cognitive, educational, and personality psychology (Blair, Zelazo, & Greenberg, 2005; Hooker & McAdams, 2003; Ponitz, McClelland et al., 2009; Zimmerman, 2008). It is especially noteworthy that these innovations have occurred in disciplines studying self-regulation throughout the life span, from childhood to adulthood. More work, however, is needed in this area including the development of longitudinally valid and sensitive measures, and research that uses a variety of sources including self-reports, other-reports (e.g., parent, teacher, caregivers), direct assessments, and observational methods.

Related to the issue of measurement is the importance of cultural context and the development of measures that are reliable and valid outside of North America and Western Europe. Although research on measures of self-regulation has been conducted in non-Western countries, especially in the field of developmental psychology and temperament (Ahadi et al., 1993; Lan et al., 2010; Rothbart & Bates, 2006; Son et al., 2009; Wanless, McClelland, Son, et al., 2010), much more remains to be done. In particular, inquiries examining whether cross-cultural differences are because of culture, measurement, or other factors are needed.

Finally, a theme seen throughout this chapter is how individuals' self-regulatory pathways are charted starting early in life. Although self-regulation may be quantitatively and qualitatively different from one developmental period to the next, providing many possible points of intervention, the foundation for these skills is built early in life. Thus, we believe that there are many advantages to using a broad lens to view self-regulation across the life span. Many examples illuminate how research in young children can inform self-regulation research in adulthood and vice versa.

Implications and Future Directions for Research and Intervention

We conclude by noting a number of implications and future directions for research and intervention. First, research can benefit from utilizing theories and perspectives from across the life span to provide the foundation for framing issues in self-regulation. For example, using the SOC model to describe self-regulation in children and adolescents, and relational developmental systems theory to explain aspects of self-regulation in later adulthood is likely to broaden the discussion of important issues. Similarly, incorporating research from a variety of disciplines (e.g., developmental, personality, and educational psychology) can inform individual research perspectives and advance knowledge in important ways.

Second, as noted earlier, many of the common themes present opportunities for intervening with individuals throughout their lives to strengthen aspects of self-regulation. Interventions have recently gained momentum in research with children (Diamond et al., 2007; Pears, Fisher, & Bronz, 2007; Tominey & McClelland, 2010), adolescents, and young adults (Boekaerts, 2006; Perry & Winne, 2006; Winne et al., 2006). Much less work has been done to promote self-regulation in adulthood, although research in other fields such as stress and coping, and health maintenance and improvement have focused on this to some extent (Bode, de Ridder, Kuijer, & Bensing, 2007; Levenson & Aldwin, 2006; Levine et al., 2007; Strauman et al., 2006; Wing et al., 2008). Given the potential for change throughout the life span, and the view that individuals are active agents in their utilization of self-regulation strategies, it seems especially important to design effective interventions that target self-regulation at all developmental periods.

In addition, research should continue to focus on developing reliable, valid, and longitudinally sensitive measures of self-regulation. Although recent research has seen many advances in measurement, more needs to be done to adequately measure these skills. Related to this, research that focuses on how self-regulation operates and is measured cross-culturally would greatly benefit our understanding of this important construct.

Taken together, self-regulation is a critical predictor of developmental outcomes across all stages of the life course. It plays a vital role in an individual's ability to manage emotions, cognitions, and behaviors, and encompasses the coping skills that are essential for managing life transitions. Moreover, self-regulation helps individuals select, optimize, and use compensatory strategies to pursue and refine goals related to major and minor life events. Studying self-regulation from a multidisciplinary and life-span perspective presents challenges but also garners considerable excitement. We look forward to continued momentum and advances that move the field forward in ways that optimize individual development.

REFERENCES

Ahadi, S. A., Rothbart, M. K., & Ye, R. (1993). Children's temperament in the US and China: Similarities and differences. *European Journal of Personality, 7*(5), 359–377.

Albert, M. S., & Killiany, R. J. (2001). Age-related cognitive change and brain-behavior relationships. In J. E. Birren & K. W. Schaie (Eds.), *Handbook of the psychology of aging* (Vol. 5). San Diego, CA: Academic Press.

Alexander, K. L., Entwisle, D. R., & Dauber, S. L. (1993). First-grade classroom behavior: Its short- and long-term consequences for school performance. *Child Development, 64,* 801–814.

Archibald, S. J., & Kerns, K. A. (1999). Identification and description of new tests of executive functioning in children. *Child Neuropsychology, 5*(2), 115–129.

Arnett, J. J. (2004). *Emerging adulthood: The winding road from the late teens through the twenties.* New York: Oxford University Press.

Azevedo, R. (2005). Using hypermedia as a metacognitive tool for enhancing student learning? The role of self-regulated learning. *Educational Psychologist, 40*(4), 199–209.

Bachman, J. G., O'Malley, P. M., Schulenberg, J., Johnston, L. D., Freedman-Doan, P., & Messersmith, E. E. (2008). *The education-drug use connection: How successes and failures in school related to adolescent smoking, drinking, drug use, and delinquency.* New York: Lawrence Erlbaum/Taylor & Francis.

Baltes, P. B. (1991). The many faces of human ageing: Toward a psychological culture of old age. *Psychological Medicine, 21,* 837–854.

Baltes, P. B. (1997). On the incomplete architecture of human ontogeny: Selection, optimization, and compensation as foundation of developmental theory. *American Psychologist, 52,* 366–380.

Baltes, P. B., & Baltes, M. M. (1990). Psychological perspectives on successful aging: The model of selective optimization with compensation. In P. B. Baltes & M. M. Baltes (Eds.), *Successful aging: Perspectives from the behavioral sciences* (pp. 1–34). New York: Cambridge University Press.

Bandalos, D. L., Finney, S. J., & Geske, J. A. (2003). A model of statistics performance based on achievement goal theory. *Journal of Educational Psychology, 95*(3), 604–616.

Bandura, A. (1986). *Social foundations of thought and action: A social cognitive theory.* Englewood Cliffs, NJ: Prentice-Hall.

Bandura, A. (1991). Self-regulation of motivation through anticipatory and self-regulatory mechanisms. In R. A. Dienstbier (Ed.), *Perspectives on motivation: Nebraska Symposium on Motivation* (Vol. 38, pp. 69–164). Lincoln, NE: University of Nebraska Press.

Bandura, A., & Locke, E. A. (2003). Negative self-efficacy and goal effects revisited. *Journal of Applied Psychology, 88*(1), 87–99.

Barkley, R. A. (1997). Behavioral inhibition, sustained attention, and executive functions: Constructing a unifying theory of ADHD. *Psychological Bulletin, 121*(1), 65–94.

Barkley, R. A. (2004). Attention-deficit/hyperactivity disorder and self-regulation: Taking an evolutionary perspective on executive functioning. In R. F. Baumeister & K. D. Vohs (Eds.), *Handbook of self-regulation: Research, theory, and applications* (pp. 301–323). New York: Guilford Press.

Baumeister, R. F., & Vohs, K. D. (2004). *Handbook of self-regulation: Research, theory, and applications.* New York: Guilford.

Beaman, R., Wheldall, K., & Kemp, C. (2006). Differential teacher attention to boys and girls in the classroom. *Educational Review, 58*(3), 339.

Belsky, J., Bakermans-Kranenburg, M. J., & van Ijzendoorn, M. H. (2007). For better and for worse: Differential susceptibility to environmental influences. *Current Directions in Psychological Science, 16,* 300–304.

Belsky, J., Friedman, S. L., & Hsieh, K.-H. (2001). Testing a core emotion-regulation prediction: Does early attentional persistence moderate the effect of infant negative emotionality on later development? *Child Development, 72*(1), 123–133.

Blair, C. (2002). School readiness: Integrating cognition and emotion in a neurobiological conceptualization of children's functioning at school entry. *American Psychologist, 57*(2), 111–127.

Blair, C. (2003). Behavioral inhibition and behavioral activation in young children: Relations with self-regulation and adaptation to preschool in children attending Head Start. *Developmental Psychobiology, 42*(3), 301–311.

Blair, C., & Razza, R. P. (2007). Relating effortful control, executive function, and false belief understanding to emerging math and literacy ability in kindergarten. *Child Development, 78*(2), 647–663.

Blair, C., Zelazo, P. D., & Greenberg, M. T. (2005). The measurement of executive function in early childhood. *Developmental Neuropsychology, 28*(2), 561–571.

Block, J. (2008). *The Q-sort in character appraisal: Encoding subjective impressions of persons quantitatively.* Washington, DC: American Psychological Association.

Block, J. H., & Block, J. (1980). The role of ego-control and ego-resiliency in the organization of behavior. In W. A. Collins (Ed.), *The Minnesota symposia on child psychology* (Vol. 13, pp. 39–101). Hillsdale, NJ: Erlbaum.

Bode, C., de Ridder, D. T. D., Kuijer, R. G., & Bensing, J. M. (2007). Effects of an intervention promoting proactive coping competencies in middle and late adulthood. *Gerontologist, 47*(1), 42–51.

Bodrova, E., & Leong, D. J. (2006). Self-regulation as key to school readiness: How early childhood teachers promote this critical competency. In M. Zaslow & I. Martinez-Beck (Eds.), *Critical issues in early childhood professional development* (pp. 203–224). Baltimore, MD: Paul H. Brookes.

Boekaerts, M. (2006). Self-regulation and effort investment. In K. A. Renninger & I. E. Sigel (Eds.), *Handbook of child psychology: Vol 4, Child psychology in practice* (6th ed., pp. 345–377). Hoboken, NJ: John Wiley & Sons.

Boekaerts, M., & Cascallar, E. (2006). How far have we moved toward the integration of theory and practice in self-regulation? *Educational Psychology Review, 18*(3), 199–210.

Boekaerts, M., Pintrich, P. R., & Zeidner, M. (2000). *Handbook of self-regulation.* San Diego, CA: Academic Press.

Borman, G. D., & Overman, L. T. (2004). Academic resilience in mathematics among poor and minority students. *The Elementary School Journal, 104*(3), 177–195.

Brandtstädter, J., & Lerner, R. M. (Eds.). (1999). *Action and self-development: Theory and research through the life span.* Thousand Oaks, CA: Sage.

Brocki, K. C., & Bohlin, G. (2004). Executive functions in children aged 6 to 13: A dimensional and developmental study. *Developmental Neuropsychology, 26*(2), 571–593.

Bronfenbrenner, U., & Morris, P. A. (2006). The bioecological model of human development. In W. Damon & R. M. Lerner (Series Eds.) & R. M. Lerner (Vol. Ed.), *Handbook on child psychology: Vol. 1, Theoretical models of human development* (6th ed., pp. 793–828). Hoboken, NJ: John Wiley & Sons.

Bronson, M. B. (2000). *Self-regulation in early childhood: Nature and nurture.* New York: Guilford Press.

Bronson, M. B., Tivnan, T., & Seppanen, P. S. (1995). Relations between teacher and classroom activity variables and the classroom behaviors of prekindergarten children in Chapter 1 funded programs. *Journal of Applied Developmental Psychology, 16,* 253–282.

Brookhart, S. M., & Durkin, D. T. (2003). Classroom assessment, student motivation, and achievement in high school social studies classes. *Applied Measurement in Education, 16*(1), 27–54.

Brooks-Gunn, J., & Markman, L. B. (2005). The contribution of parenting to ethnic and racial gaps in school readiness. *The Future of Children, 15*(1), 139–168.

Bryant, A. L., Schulenberg, J., O'Malley, P. M., Bachman, J. G., & Johnston, L. D. (2003). How academic achievement, attitudes, and behaviors relate to the course of substance use during adolescence: A 6-year, multiwave national longitudinal study. *Journal of Research on Adolescence, 13*(3), 361–397.

Bulcroft, R. A., Carmody, D. C., & Bulcroft, K. A. (1996). Patterns of parental independence giving to adolescents: Variations by race, age, and gender of child. *Journal of Marriage & the Family, 58,* 866–883.

Bulotsky-Shearer, R. J., Fantuzzo, J. W., & McDermott, P. A. (2008). An investigation of classroom situational dimensions of emotional and behavioral adjustment and cognitive and social outcomes for Head Start children. *Developmental Psychology, 44*(1), 139–154.

Byrnes, J. P. (1998). *The nature and development of decision-making: A self-regulation model.* Mahweh, NJ: Erlbaum.

Cairns, R. B., & Cairns, B. D. (2006). The making of developmental psychology. In W. Damon & R. M. Lerner (Series Eds.) & R. M. Lerner (Vol. Ed.). *Handbook of child psychology: Vol. 1, Theoretical models of human development* (Vol. 6th, pp. 18–88). Hoboken, NJ: John Wiley & Sons.

Calkins, S. D., & Bell, M. (in press). *The developing human brain: Development at the intersection of emotion and cognition.* Washington, DC: American Psychological Association.

Calkins, S. D. (2004). Early attachment processes and the development of emotional self-regulation. In R. F. Baumeister & K. D. Vohs (Eds.), *Handbook of self-regulation: Research, theory, and applications* (pp. 324–339). New York: Guilford Press.

Calkins, S. D. (2007). The emergence of self-regulation: Biological and behavioral control mechanisms supporting toddler competencies. In C. A. Brownell & C. B. Kopp (Eds.), *Socioemotional development in the toddler years: Transitions and transformations* (pp. 261–284). New York: Guilford.

Cappeliez, P., & O'Rourke, N. (2002). Personality traits and existential concerns as predictors of the functions of remininscience in older adults. *Journal of Gerontology: Psychological Sciences, 57B,* 116–123.

Carlson, S. M. (2005). Developmentally sensitive measures of executive function in preschool children. *Developmental Neuropsychology, 28*(2), 595–616.

Carr, M., & Jessup, D. L. (1997). Gender differences in first-grade mathematics strategy use: Social and metacognitive influences. *Journal of Educational Psychology, 89,* 318–328.

Carver, C. S. (2004). Self-regulation of action and affect. In R. F. Baumeister & K. D. Vohs (Eds.), *Handbook of self-regulation: Research, theory, and applications* (pp. 13–39). New York: Guilford Press.

Carver, C. S., Lawrence, J. W., & Scheier, M. F. (1996). A control-process perspective on the origins of affect. In L. L. Martin & A. Tesser (Eds.), *Striving and feeling: Interactions among goals, affect, and self-regulation* (pp. 11–52). Mahwah, NJ: Erlbaum.

Carver, C. S., & White, T. L. (1994). Behavioral inhibition, behavioral activation, and affective responses to impending reward and punishment: The BIS/BAS scales. *Journal of Personality and Social Psychology, 67,* 319–333.

Caspi, A. (1998). Personality development across the life course. In W. Damon & N. Eisenberg (Eds.), *Handbook of child*

psychology: Vol. 3, Social, emotional, and personality development (5th ed., pp. 311–388). New York: John Wiley & Sons.

Caspi, A., & Moffitt, T. E. (1991). Individual differences are accentuated during periods of social change: The sample case of girls at puberty. *Journal of Personality and Social Psychology, 61,* 157–168.

Cole, P. M., Martin, S. E., & Dennis, T. A. (2004). Emotion regulation as a scientific construct: Methodological challenges and directions for child development research. *Child Development, 75*(2), 317–333.

Connell, C. M., & Prinz, R. J. (2002). The impact of childcare and parent-child interactions on school readiness and social skills development for low-income African American children. *Journal of School Psychology, 40*(2), 177–193.

Connor, C. M., Jakobsons, L. J., Crowe, E. C., & Meadows, J. G. (2009). Instruction, student engagement, and reading skill growth in Reading First classrooms. *Elementary School Journal, 109,* 221–250.

Connor, C. M., Ponitz, C. E. C., Phillips, B., Travis, Q. M., Glasney, S., & Morrison, F. J. (in press). First graders' literacy and self-regulation gains: The effect of individualizing instruction. *Journal of School Psychology.*

Crockett, L. J., Raffaelli, M., & Shen, Y.-L. (2006). Linking self-regulation and risk proneness to risky sexual behavior: Pathways through peer pressure and early substance use. *Journal of Research on Adolescence, 16*(4), 503–525.

Dahl, T. I., Bals, M., & Turi, A. L. (2005). Are students' beliefs about knowledge and learning associated with their reported use of learning strategies? *British Journal of Educational Psychology, 75,* 257–273.

Davidson, R. J. (2002). Anxiety and affective style: Role of prefrontal cortex and amygdala. *Biological Psychiatry, 51*(1), 68–80.

Dearing, E., Berry, D., & Zaslow, M. (2006). Poverty during early childhood. In K. McCartney & D. Phillips (Eds.), *Blackwell handbook of early childhood development* (pp. 399–423). Malden, MA: Blackwell.

Deater-Deckard, K., Petrill, S. A., Thompson, L. A., & DeThorne, L. S. (2005). A cross-sectional behavioral genetic analysis of task persistence in the transition to middle childhood. *Developmental Science, 8*(3), F21–F26.

Deci, E. L., & Ryan, R. M. (1985). *Intrinsic motivation and self-determination in human behavior.* New York: Plenum Press.

Demetriou, A., Christou, C., Spanoudis, G., & Platsidou, M. (2002). The development of mental processing: Efficiency, working memory, and thinking. *Monographs of the Society for Research in Child Development, 67*(1), vii–154.

Diamond, A. (2002). Normal development of prefrontal cortex from birth to young adulthood: Cognitive functions, anatomy, and biochemistry. In D. T. Stuss & R. T. Knight (Eds.), *Principles of frontal lobe function* (pp. 466–503). London: Oxford University Press.

Diamond, A., Barnett, W. S., Thomas, J., & Munro, S. (2007). Preschool program improves cognitive control. *Science, 318*(5855), 1387–1388.

Diamond, A., Kirkham, N., & Amso, D. (2002). Conditions under which young children can hold two rules in mind and inhibit a prepotent response. *Developmental Psychology, 38*(3), 352–362.

DiPietro, J. A., Hodgson, D. M., Costigan, K. A., & Johnson, T. R. B. (1996). Fetal antecedents of infant temperament. *Child Development, 67*(5), 2568–2583.

Duckworth, A. L., & Seligman, M. E. P. (2005). Self-discipline outdoes IQ in predicting academic performance of adolescents. *Psychological Science, 16*(12), 939–944.

Duckworth, A. L., & Seligman, M. E. P. (2006). Self-discipline gives girls the edge: Gender in self-discipline, grades, and achievement test scores. *Journal of Educational Psychology, 98,* 198–208.

Duncan, G. J., Dowsett, C. J., Claessens, A., Magnuson, K., Huston, A. C., Klebanov, P., et al. (2007). School readiness and later achievement. *Developmental Psychology, 43*(6), 1428–1446.

Dunn, J., & Hughes, C. (2001). "I got some swords and you're dead!": Violent fantasy, antisocial behavior, friendship, and moral sensibility in young children. *Child Development: Special Issue, 72*(2), 491–505.

Ebner, N. C., Freund, A. M., & Baltes, P. B. (2006). Developmental changes in personal goal orientation from young to late adulthood: From striving for gains to maintenance and prevention of losses. *Psychology and Aging, 21,* 664–678.

Eccles, J. S., Adler, T. F., Futterman, R., Goff, S. B., Kaczala, C. M., Meece, J. L., et al. (1983). Expectations, values, and academic behaviors. In J. T. Spence (Ed.), *Achievement and achievement motivation* (pp. 75–146). San Francisco, CA: Freeman.

Eccles, J. S., Midgley, C., Wigfield, A., Buchanan, C. M., Reuman, D., Flanagan, C., et al. (1993). Development during adolescence: The impact of stage_environment fit on young adolescents' experiences in schools and in families. *American Psychologist, 48*(2), 90–101.

Eisenberg, N., Liew, J., & Pidada, S. (2004). The longitudinal relations of regulation and emotionality to quality of Indonesian children's socioemotional functioning. *Developmental Psychology, 40,* 805–812.

Eisenberg, N., Smith, C. L., Sadovsky, A., & Spinrad, T. L. (2004). Effortful control: Relations with emotion regulation, adjustment, and socialization in childhood. In R. F. Baumeister & K. D. Vohs (Eds.), *Handbook of self-regulation: Research, theory, and applications* (pp. 259–282). New York: Guilford.

Eisenberg, N., Valiente, C., Fabes, R. A., Smith, C. L., Reiser, M., Shepard, S. A., et al. (2003). The relations of effortful control and ego control to children's resiliency and social functioning. *Developmental Psychology, 39*(4), 761–776.

Epstein, S. (1994). Integration of the cognitive and the psychodynamic unconscious. *American Psychologist, 49,* 709–724.

Esposito, C. (1999). Learning in urban blight: School climate and its effect on the school performance of urban, minority, low-income children. *School Psychology Review: Special Issue: Beginning School Ready to Learn: Parental Involvement and Effective Educational Programs, 28*(3), 365–377.

Evans, G. W., & Rosenbaum, J. (2008). Self-regulation and the income-achievement gap. *Early Childhood Research Quarterly, 23*(4), 504–514.

Fantuzzo, J. W., Bulotsky-Sheare, R., Fusco, R. A., & McWayne, C. (2005). An investigation of preschool classroom behavioral adjustment problems and social-emotional school readiness competencies. *Early Childhood Research Quarterly, 20*(3), 259–275.

Fantuzzo, J. W., Rouse, H. L., McDermott, P. A., Sekino, Y., Childs, S., & Weiss, A. (2005). Early childhood experiences and kindergarten success: A population-based study of a large urban setting. *School Psychology Review, 34*(4), 571–588.

Finn, J. D., Pannozzo, G. M., & Voelkl, K. E. (1995). Disruptive and inattentive-withdrawn behavior and achievement among fourth graders. *The Elementary School Journal, 95*(5), 421–434.

Fischer, M., Barkley, R. A., Smallish, L., & Fletcher, K. (2005). Executive functioning in hyperactive children as young adults: Attention, inhibition, response perseveration, and the impact of comorbidity. *Developmental Neuropsychology, 27*(1), 107–133.

Fox, E., & Riconscente, M. (2008). Metacognition and self-regulation in James, Piaget, and Vygotsky. *Educational Psychology Review, 20*(4), 373–389.

Fox, N. A., Henderson, H. A., Rubin, K. H., Calkins, S. D., & Schmidt, L. A. (2001). Continuity and discontinuity of behavioral inhibition and exuberance: Psychophysiological and behavioral influences across the first four years of life. *Child Development, 72*(1), 1–21.

Fredricks, J. A., Blumenfeld, P. C., & Paris, A. H. (2004). School engagement: Potential of the concept, state of the evidence. *Review of Educational Research, 74*(1), 59–109.

Freund, A. M., & Baltes, P. B. (1998). Selection, optimization, and compensation as strategies of life management: Correlations with subjective indicators of successful aging. *Psychology and Aging, 13,* 531–543.

Freund, A. M., & Baltes, P. B. (2002). Life-management strategies of selection, optimization, and compensation: Measurement by self-report and construct validity. *Journal of Personality and Social Psychology, 82,* 642–662.

Gathercole, S. E., & Pickering, S. J. (2000). Working memory deficits in children with low achievements in the national curriculum at 7 years of age. *British Journal of Educational Psychology, 70,* 177–194.

Gerrard, M., Gibbons, F. X., Houlihan, A. E., Stock, M. L., & Pomery, E. A. (2008). A dual-process approach to health risk decision making: The prototype willingness model. *Developmental Review, 28,* 29–61.

Gestsdóttir, S., & Lerner, R. M. (2007). Intentional self-regulation and positive youth development in early adolescence: Findings from the 4-H study of positive youth development. *Developmental Psychology, 43*(2), 508–521.

Gestsdóttir, S., & Lerner, R. M. (2008). Positive development in adolescence: The development and role of intentional self-regulation. *Human Development, 51,* 202–224.

Giese-Davis, J., Conrad, A., Nouriani, B., & Spiegel, D. (2008). Exploring emotion-regulation and autonomic physiology in metastatic breast cancer patients: Repression, suppression, and restraint of hostility. *Personality and Individual Differences, 44*(1), 226–237.

Gilliam, W. S. (2005). *Prekindergarteners left behind: Expulsion rates in state prekindergarten programs* (No. Policy Brief Series No. 3). New Haven, CT: Yale University Foundation for Child Development.

Goldsmith, H. H., Lemery, K. S., Buss, K. A., & Campos, J. J. (1999). Genetic analyses of focal aspects of infant temperament. *Developmental Psychology, 35*(4), 972–985.

Gottlieb, G., Wahlsten, D., & Lickliter, R. (2006). The significance of biology for human development: A developmental psychobiological systems view. In W. Damon & R. M. Lerner (Series Eds.) & R. M. Lerner (Vol. Ed.), *Handbook of child psychology: Vol. 1, Theoretical models of human development* (6th ed., pp. 210–257). Hoboken, NJ: John Wiley & Sons.

Graber, J. A., & Brooks-Gunn, J. (1996). Transitions and turning points: Navigating the passage from childhood through adolescence. *Developmental Psychology, 32*(4), 768–776.

Graziano, P. A., Reavis, R. D., Keane, S. P., & Calkins, S. D. (2006). The role of emotion regulation in children's early academic success. *Journal of School Psychology, 45*(1), 3–19.

Greenwood, C. R., Horton, B. T., & Utley, C. A. (2002). Academic engagement: Current perspectives on research and practice. *School Psychology Review, 31*(3), 328–349.

Grolnick, W. S., & Farkas, M. (2002). Parenting and the development of children's self-regulation. In M. H. Bornstein (Ed.), *Handbook of parenting: Vol. 5, Practical issues in parenting* (2nd ed., pp. 89–110). Mahwah, NJ: Erlbaum.

Gross, J. J. (2007). *Handbook of emotion regulation.* New York: Guilford.

Gross, J. J., & Levenson, R. W. (1993). Emotional suppression: Physiology, self-report, and expressive behavior. *Journal of Personality and Social Psychology, 64*(6), 970–986.

Gross, J. J., & Thompson, R. A. (2007). Emotion regulation: Conceptual foundations. In J. J. Gross (Ed.), *Handbook of emotion regulation* (pp. 3–24). New York: Guilford.

Gunnar, M. R. (2006). Social regulation of stress in early child development. In K. McCartney & D. Phillips (Eds.), *Blackwell handbook of early childhood development* (pp. 106–125). Malden, MA: Blackwell Publishing.

Guthrie, J. T., Schafer, W. D., & Huang, C.-W. (2001). Benefits of opportunity to read and balanced instruction on the NAEP. *Journal of Educational Research, 94*(3), 145–162.

Hala, S., Hug, S., & Henderson, A. (2003). Executive function and false-belief understanding in preschool children: Two tasks are harder than one. *Journal of Cognition and Development, 4*(3), 275–298.

Halford, W. K., Lizzio, A., Wilson, K. L., & Occhipinti, S. (2007). Does working at your marriage help? Couple relationship self-regulation and satisfaction in the first 4 years of marriage. *Journal of Family Psychology, 21*(2), 185–194.

Heckhausen, J. (2000). Developmental regulation across the life span: An action-phase model of engagement and disengagement with developmental goals. In J. Heckhausen (Ed.), *Motivational psychology of human development: Developing motivation and motivating development* (pp. 213–231). New York: Elsevier Science.

Heckhausen, J., & Schulz, R. (1995). A life-span theory of control. *Psychological Review, 102,* 284–304.

Heckhausen, J., & Schulz, R. (1999). Selectivity in life-span development: Biological and societal canalizations and individuals' developmental goals. In L. J. Brandtstädter & R. M. Lerner (Eds.), *Action and self-development: Theory and research through the life span* (pp. 67–103). Thousand Oaks, CA: Sage.

Heckhausen, J., Wrosch, C., & Fleeson, W. (2001). Developmental regulation before and after a developmental deadline: The sample case of "biological clock" for childbearing. *Psychology and Aging, 16*(3), 100–413.

Heckman, J. J., Stixrud, J., & Urzua, S. (2006). The effects of cognitive and noncognitive abilities on labor market outcomes and social behavior. *Journal of Labor Economics, 24,* 411–482.

Henderson, H. A., & Fox, N. A. (1998). Inhibited and uninhibited children: Challenges in school settings. *School Psychology Review, 27*(4), 492–505.

Higgins, E. T. (1987). Self-discrepancy: A theory relating self and affect. *Psychological Review, 94,* 319–340.

Hongwanishkul, D., Happaney, K. R., Lee, W. S. C., & Zelazo, P. D. (2005). Assessment of hot and cool executive function in young children: Age-related changes and individual differences. *Developmental Neuropsychology, 28*(2), 617–644.

Hooker, K., & McAdams, D. P. (2003). Personality reconsidered: A new agenda for aging research. *Journal of Gerontology: Psychological Sciences, 58B*(6), 296–304.

Howse, R. B., Calkins, S. D., Anastopoulos, A. D., Keane, S. P., & Shelton, T. L. (2003). Regulatory contributors to children's kindergarten achievement. *Early Education and Development, 14*(1), 101–119.

Howse, R. B., Lange, G., Farran, D. C., & Boyles, C. D. (2003). Motivation and self-regulation as predictors of achievement in economically disadvantaged young children. *Journal of Experimental Education, 71,* 151–174.

Hoyle, R. H. (2006). Personality and self-regulation: Trait and information-processing perspectives. *Journal of Personality, 74,* 1507–1525.

Hughes, C., White, A., Sharpen, J., & Dunn, J. (2000). Antisocial, angry, and unsympathetic: "Hard-to-manage" preschoolers' peer problems and possible cognitive influences. *Journal of Child Psychology & Psychiatry & Allied Disciplines, 41*(2), 169–179.

Hughes, J., & Kwok, O. (2007). Influence of student-teacher and parent-teacher relationships on lower achieving readers' engagement and achievement in the primary grades. *Journal of Educational Psychology, 99*(1), 39–51.

Isquith, P. K., Crawford, J. S., Espy, K. A., & Gioia, G. A. (2005). Assessment of executive function in preschool-aged children. *Mental Retardation and Developmental Disabilities Research Reviews, 11*(3), 209–215.

Jonides, J. (1995). Working memory and thinking. In *Thinking: An invitation to cognitive science* (Vol. 3, 2nd ed., pp. 215–265). Cambridge, MA: MIT Press.

Juffer, F., Stams, G.-J. J. M., & van IJzendoorn, M. H. (2004). Adopted children's problem behavior is significantly related to their ego resiliency, ego control, and sociometric status. *Journal of Child Psychology and Psychiatry, 45*(4), 697–706.

Kagan, J. (2003). Biology, context, and developmental inquiry. *Annual Review of Psychology, 54*(1), 1–23.

Kail, R. V. (2003). Information processing and memory. In M. H. Bornstein, L. Davidson, C. L. M. Keyes, & K. A. Moore (Eds.), *Crosscurrents in contemporary psychology.* Mahwah, NJ: Erlbaum.

Kane, M. J., Brown, L. H., McVay, J. C., Silvia, P. J., Myin-Germeys, I., & Kwapil, T. R. (2007). For whom the mind wanders, and when: An experience-sampling study of working memory and executive control in daily life. *Psychological Science, 18*(7), 614–621.

Keating, D. (2004). Cognitive and brain development. In R. M. Lerner & L. Steinberg (Eds.), *Handbook of adolescent psychology* (2nd ed., pp. 45–84). Hoboken, NJ: John Wiley & Sons.

Kerr, M. E., & Bowen, M. (1988). *Family evaluation: An approach based on Bowen Theory.* New York: W. W. Norton.

Kishiyama, M. M., Boyce, W. T., Jimenez, A. M., Perry, L. M., & Knight, R. T. (2009). Socioeconomic disparities affect prefrontal function in children. *Journal of Cognitive Neuroscience, 21*(6), 1106–1115.

Kitayama, S., Duffy, S., Kawamura, T., & Larsen, J. T. (2003). Perceiving an object and its context in different cultures: A cultural look at New Look. *Psychological Science, 14*(3), 201–206.

Klein Velderman, M., Bakermans-Kranenburg, M. J., Juffer, F., & van Ijzendoorn, M. H. (2006). Effects of attachment-based interventions on maternal sensitivity and infant attachment: Differential susceptibility of highly reactive infants. *Journal of Family Psychology, 20*(2), 266–274.

Kochanska, G., Coy, K. C., & Murray, K. T. (2001). The development of self-regulation in the first four years of life. *Child Development, 72*(4), 1091–1111.

Kochanska, G., & Knaack, A. (2003). Effortful control as a personality characteristic of young children: Antecedents, correlates, and consequences. *Journal of Personality, 71,* 1087–1112.

Kochanska, G., Murray, K., Jacques, T. Y., Koenig, A. L., & Vandegeest, K. A. (1996). Inhibitory control in young children and its role in emerging internalization. *Child Development, 67*(2), 490–507.

Kochanska, G., Murray, K. T., & Harlan, E. T. (2000). Effortful control in early childhood: Continuity and change, antecedents, and implications for social development. *Developmental Psychology, 36*(2), 220–232.

Koestner, R., & McClelland, D. C. (1990). Perspectives on competence motivation. In L. Pervin (Ed.), *Handbook of personality theory and research* (pp. 527–548). New York: Guilford.

Koestner, R., Weinberger, J., & McClelland, D. C. (1991). Task-intrinsic and social-extrinsic sources of arousal for motives assessed in fantasy and self-report. *Journal of Personality, 59*(1), 57–82.

Kopp, C. B. (1982). Antecedents of self-regulation: A developmental perspective. *Developmental Psychology, 18*(2), 199–214.

Kopp, C. B. (1991). Young children's progression to self-regulation. In M. Bullock (Ed.), *The development of intentional action: Vol. 22, Cognitive, motivational, and interactive processes* (pp. 38–54). Basel, Switzerland: Karger.

Kostyniuk, L. P., & Molnar, L. J. (2008). Self-regulatory driving practices among older adults: Health, age and sex effects. *Accident Analysis and Prevention, 40,* 1576–1580.

Ladd, G. W. (2003). Probing the adaptive significance of children's behavior and relationships in the school context: A child by environment perspective. In R. V. Kail & H. W. Reese (Eds.), *Advances in child development and behavior* (Vol. 31, pp. 43–103). New York: Academic Press.

Ladd, G. W., Birch, S. H., & Buhs, E. S. (1999). Children's social and scholastic lives in kindergarten: Related spheres of influence? *Child Development, 70*(6), 1373–1400.

Lan, X., & Morrison, F. J. (2008). Inter-correlations among components of behavioral regulation and their relationship with academic outcomes in China. Paper presented at the International Society for the Study of Behavioural Development, Wurzburg, Germany.

Lan, X., Wanless, S. B., McClelland, M. M., Son, S.-H., Ponitz, C. C., Morrison, F. J., et al. (2010). *Gender differences in behavioral regulation in four cultures.* Manuscript in preparation.

Larsen, R. J., & Fredrickson, B. L. (1999). Measurement issues in emotion research. In D. Kahneman & E. Diener (Eds.), *Well-being: The foundations of hedonic psychology* (pp. 40–60). New York: Russell Sage Foundation.

Lengua, L. J. (2002). The contribution of emotionality and self-regulation to the understanding of children's response to multiple risk. *Child Development, 73,* 144–161.

Lengua, L. J. (2009). Effortful control in the context of socioeconomic and psychosocial risk [Electronic Version]. APA Psychological Science Agenda, 23. Retrieved January 20, 2009, from http://www.apa.org/science/psa/jan09-sci-brief.html.

Lengua, L. J., Honorado, E., & Bush, N. R. (2007). Contextual risk and parenting as predictors of effortful control and social competence in preschool children. *Journal of Applied Developmental Psychology, 28,* 40–55.

Lengua, L. J., & Kovacs, E. A. (2005). Bidirectional associations between temperament and parenting and the prediction of adjustment problems in middle childhood. *Journal of Applied Developmental Psychology, 26*(1), 21–38.

Lenze, E. J., Rogers, J. C., Martire, L. M., Mulsant, B. H., Rollman, B. L., Dew, M. A., et al. (2001). The association of late-life depression and anxiety with physical disability: A review of the literature and prospectur for future research. *American Journal of Geriatric Psychiatry, 9,* 113–135.

Lerner, R. M. (2006). Developmental science, developmental systems, and contemporary theories of human development. In W. Damon & R. M. Lerner (Series Eds.) & R. M. Lerner (Vol. Ed.), *Handbook of child psychology: Vol. 1, Theoretical models of human development* (6th ed., pp. 1–17). Hoboken, NJ: John Wiley & Sons.

Lerner, R. M., Freund, A. M., De Stefanis, I., & Habermas, T. (2001). Understanding developmental regulation in adolescence: The use of the Selection, Optimization, and Compensation model. *Human Development, 44,* 29–50.

Lerner, R. M., & Overton, W. F. (2008). Exemplifying theory, research, and application to promote positive development and social justice. *Journal of Adolescent Research, 23*(3), 245–255.

Levenson, M. R., & Aldwin, C. M. (2006). Change in personality processes and health outcomes. In D. Mroczek & T. Little (Eds.), *Handbook of personality change* (pp. 423–444). New York: Guildford.

Leventhal, H., Keeshan, P., Baker, T., & Wetter, D. (1991). Smoking prevention: Towards a process approach. *Addiction, 86*(5), 583–587.

Levine, B., Stuss, D. T., Gordon, W., Binns, M. A., Fahy, L., Mandic, M., et al. (2007). Cognitive rehabilitation in the elderly: Effects of strategic behavior in relation to goal management. *Journal of the International Neuropsychological Society, 13,* 143–152.

Lewis, M. D., & Todd, R. M. (2007). The self-regulating brain: Cortical-subcortical feedback and the development of intelligent action. *Cognitive Development, 22*(4), 406–430.

Li, K. Z. H., Lindenberger, U., Freund, A. M., & Baltes, P. B. (2001). Walking while memorizing: Age-related differences in compensatory behavior. *Psychological Science, 12,* 230–237.

Lin, H.-L., Lawrence, F. R., & Gorrell, J. (2003). Kindergarten teachers' views of children's readiness for school. *Early Childhood Research Quarterly, 18*(2), 225–237.

Lindenberger, U., Marsiske, M., & Baltes, P. B. (2000). Memorizing while walking: Increase in dual-task costs from young adulthood to old age. *Psychology and Aging, 15,* 417–436.

Lyon, G. R., & Krasnegor, N. A. (Eds.). (1996). *Attention, memory, and executive function.* Baltimore, MD: Brookes.

MacCoon, D. G., Wallace, J. F., & Newman, J. P. (2004). Self-regulation: Context-appropriate balanced attention. In R. F. Baumeister & K. D. Vohs (Eds.), *Handbook of self-regulation: Research, theory, and applications* (pp. 422–444). New York: Guilford Press.

Magar, E. C. E., Phillips, L. H., & Hosie, J. A. (2008). Self-regulation and risk-taking. *Personality and Individual Differences, 45,* 153–159.

Manly, T., Anderson, V., Nimmo-Smith, I., Turner, A., Watson, P., & Robertson, I. H. (2001). The differential assessment of children's attention: The Test of Everyday Attention for Children (TEA-Ch), normative sample and ADHD performance. *Journal of Child Psychology and Psychiatry, 42*(8), 1065–1081.

Markus, H. R., & Kitayama, S. (1991). Culture and the self: Implications for cognition, emotion, and motivation. *Psychological Review, 98*(2), 224–253.

Mashburn, A. J., Hamre, B. K., Downer, J. T., & Pianta, R. C. (2006). Teacher and classroom characteristics associated with teachers' ratings of prekindergartners' relationships and behaviors. *Journal of Psychoeducational Assessment, 24*(4), 367–380.

Massey, E. K., Gebhardt, W. A., & Garnefski, N. (2008). Adolescent goal content and pursuit: A review of the literature from the past 16 years. *Developmental Review, 28,* 421–460.

Masten, A. S. (2001). Ordinary magic: Resilience processes in development. *American Psychologist: Special Issue, 56*(3), 227–238.

Masten, A. S., Roisman, G. I., Long, J. D., Burt, K. B., Obradovic, J., Riley, J. R., et al. (2005). Developmental cascades: Linking academic achievement and externalizing and internalizing symptoms over 20 years. *Developmental Psychology, 41*(5), 733–746.

Matthews, J. S., Ponitz, C. C., & Morrison, F. J. (2009). Early Gender Differences in Self-Regulation and Academic Achievement. *Journal of Educational Psychology, 101*(3), 689–704.

Mayer, K. U., & Baltes, P. B. (Eds.). (1996). *Die Berliner Altersstudie* [The Berlin Aging Study]. Berlin: Akademie Verlag.

Mayne, T. J., & Ramsey, J. (2001). The structure of emotions: A nonlinear dynamic systems approach. In T. J. Mayne & G. A. Bonanno (Eds.), *Emotions: Current issues and future directions* (pp. 1–37). New York: Guilford.

McAdams, D. P. (2001). The psychology of life stories. *Review of General Psychology, 5,* 100–122.

McCabe, L. A., Cunnington, M., & Brooks-Gunn, J. (2004). The development of self-regulation in young children: Individual characteristics and environmental contexts. In R. F. Baumeister & K. D. Vohs (Eds.), *Handbook of self-regulation: Research, theory, and applications* (pp. 340–356). New York: Guilford Press.

McCabe, L. A., Hernandez, M., Lara, S. L., & Brooks-Gunn, J. (2000). Assessing preschoolers' self-regulation in homes and classrooms: Lessons from the field. *Behavioral Disorders, 26*(1), 53–69.

McCabe, L. A., Rebello-Britto, P., Hernandez, M., & Brooks-Gunn, J. (2004). Games children play: Observing young children's self-regulation across laboratory, home, and school settings. In R. DelCarmen-Wiggins & A. Carter (Eds.), *Handbook of infant, toddler, and preschool mental health assessment* (pp. 491–521). New York: Oxford University Press.

McClelland, D. C. (1961). *The achieving society.* Princeton, NJ: Van Nostrand.

McClelland, D. C., Atkinson, J. W., Clark, R. A., & Lowell, E. L. (1953). *The achievement motive.* New York: Appleton-Century-Crofts.

McClelland, M. M., Acock, A. C., & Morrison, F. J. (2006). The impact of kindergarten learning-related skills on academic trajectories at the end of elementary school. *Early Childhood Research Quarterly, 21,* 471–490.

McClelland, M. M., Cameron, C. E., Connor, C. M., Farris, C. L., Jewkes, A. M., & Morrison, F. J. (2007). Links between behavioral regulation and preschoolers' literacy, vocabulary and math skills. *Developmental Psychology, 43*(4), 947–959.

McClelland, M. M., Cameron, C. E., Wanless, S. B., & Murray, A. (2007). Executive function, behavioral self-regulation, and social-emotional competence: Links to school readiness. In O. N. Saracho & B. Spodek (Eds.), *Contemporary perspectives on social learning in early childhood education* (pp. 83–107). Charlotte, NC: Information Age.

McClelland, M. M., Kessenich, M., & Morrison, F. J. (2003). Pathways to early literacy: The complex interplay of child, family, and sociocultural factors. In R. V. Kail & H. W. Reese (Eds.), *Advances in child development and behavior* (Vol. 31, pp. 411–447). New York: Academic Press.

McClelland, M. M., Morrison, F. J., & Holmes, D. L. (2000). Children at-risk for early academic problems: The role of learning-related social skills. *Early Childhood Research Quarterly, 15,* 307–329.

McClelland, M. M., Piccinin, A., & Stallings, M. C. (2010). *Relations between preschool attention and sociability and later achievement outcomes.* Manuscript in review.

Meisels, S. J. (2006). *Accountability in early childhood: No easy answers (Occasional Paper No. 6).* Chicago, IL: Herr Research Center for Children & Social Policy, Erikson Institute. Available from http://www.erikson.edu/research.asp?file=publications_topic#assess.

Michie, S., Hardeman, W., Fanshawe, T., Taylor, L., & Kinmouth, A. L. (2008). Investigating theoretical explanations for behaviour change: The case study of ProActive. *Psychology and Health, 23,* 25–39.

Miller, D. C., & Byrnes, J. P. (2001a). Adolescents' decision-making in social situations: A self-regulation perspective. *Journal of Applied Developmental Psychology, 22*(3), 237–256.

Miller, D. C., & Byrnes, J. P. (2001b). To achieve or not to achieve: A self-regulation perspective on adolescents' academic decision-making. *Journal of Educational Psychology, 93*(4), 677–685.

Miyake, A., Friedman, N. P., Emerson, M. J., Witzki, A. H., & Howerter, A. (2000). The unity and diversity of executive functions and their contributions to complex "frontal lobe" tasks: A latent variable analysis. *Cognitive Psychology, 41*(1), 49–100.

Morales, J. R., & Guerra, N. G. (2006). Effects of multiple context and cumulative stress on urban children's adjustment in elementary school. *Child Development, 77*(4), 907–923.

Muraven, M., & Baumeister, R. F. (2000). Self-regulation and depletion of limited resources: Does self-control resemble a muscle? *Psychological Bulletin, 126*(2), 247–259.

Murray, H. A. (1938). *Explorations in personality.* New York: Oxford.

National Public Radio. (2008). Shakira lobbies congress on education for poor [Electronic Version]. Retrieved December 15, 2008 from http://www.npr.org/templates/story/story.php?storyId=89844556.

Neshat-Doost, H. T., Dalgleish, T., & Golden, A.-M. J. (2008). Reduced specificity of emotional autobiographical memories following self-regulation depletion. *Emotion, 8*(5), 731–736.

NICHD Early Child Care Research Network. (2003). Do children's attention processes mediate the link between family predictors and school readiness? *Developmental Psychology, 39,* 581–593.

Nurmi, J.-E., & Salmela-Aro, K. (2002). Goal construction, reconstruction and depressive symptoms in a life-span context: The transition from school to work. *Journal of Personality, 70*(3), 385–420.

Oh, S., & Lewis, C. (2008). Korean preschoolers' advanced inhibitory control and its relation to other executive skills and mental state understanding. *Child Development, 79*(1), 80–99.

Overton, W. F. (2006). Developmental psychology: Philosophy, concepts, methodology. In W. Damon & R. M. Lerner (Series Eds.) & R. M. Lerner (Vol. Ed.), *Handbook of child psychology: Vol. 1. Theoretical models of human development* (6th ed., Vol. 1, pp. 18–88). Hoboken, NJ: John Wiley & Sons.

Pagnoni, G., & Cekic, M. (2007). Age effects on gray matter volume and attentional performance in Zen meditation. *Neurobiology of Aging, 28,* 1623–1627.

Pasupathi, M., Staudinger, U. M., & Baltes, P. B. (2001). Seeds of wisdom: Adolescents' knowledge and judgment about difficult life problems. *Developmental Psychology, 37,* 351–361.

Patrick, H. (1997). Social self-regulation: Exploring the relations between children's social relationships, academic self-regulation, and school performance. *Educational Psychologist, 32*(4), 209–220.

Patrick, H., Ryan, A. M., & Kaplan, A. (2007). Early adolescents' perceptions of the classroom social environment, motivational beliefs, and engagement. *Journal of Educational Psychology, 99*(1), 83–98.

Pears, K. C., Fisher, P. A., & Bronz, K. D. (2007). An intervention to facilitate school readiness in foster children: Preliminary results from the Kids in Transition to School pilot study. *Social Psychology Review, 36,* 665–673.

Pears, K. C., Fisher, P. A., Heywood, C. V., & Bronz, K. D. (2007). Promoting school readiness in foster children. In O. N. Saracho & B. Spodek (Eds.), *Contemporary perspectives on social learning in early childhood education* (pp. 173–198). Charlotte, NC: Information Age.

Perry, N. E., VandeKamp, K. O., Mercer, L. K., & Nordby, C. J. (2002). Investigating teacher–student interactions that foster self-regulated learning. *Educational Psychologist, 37*(1), 5–15.

Perry, N. E., & Winne, P. H. (2006). Learning from learning kits: Study traces of students' self-regulated engagements with computerized content. *Educational Psychology Review, 18*(3), 211–228.

Phillips, D., McCartney, K., & Sussman, A. (2006). Child care and early development. In K. McCartney & D. Phillips (Eds.), *Blackwell handbook of early childhood development* (pp. 471–489). Malden, MA: Blackwell.

Piaget, J. (1968). *Six psychological studies.* New York: Random House (A. Tenzer, Trans.). (Original work published in 1964)

Pickering, S. J., & Gathercole, S. E. (2004). Distinctive working memory profiles in children with special educational needs. *Educational Psychology, 24*(3), 393–408.

Pinker, S. (1994). *The language instinct.* New York: Morrow.

Pintrich, P. R. (2000). Issues in self-regulation theory and research. *Journal of Mind & Behavior, 21*(1), 213–219.

Pintrich, P. R., & DeGroot, E. (1990). Motivational and self-regulated learning components of classroom academic performance. *Journal of Educational Psychology, 82,* 33–40.

Pintrich, P. R., Smith, D. A. F., García, T., & McKeachie, W. J. (1991). *A manual for the use of the Motivated Strategies for Learning Questionnaire (MSLQ).* Ann Arbor, MI: University of Michigan, National Center for Research to Improve Postsecondary Teaching and Learning.

Pintrich, P. R., Smith, D. A. F., García, T., & McKeachie, W. J. (1993). Reliability and predictive validity of the Motivated Strategies for Learning Questionnaire (MSLQ). *Educational and Psychological Measurement, 53,* 801–813.

Ponitz, C. C., McClelland, M. M., Jewkes, A. M., Connor, C. M., Farris, C. L., & Morrison, F. J. (2008). Touch your toes! Developing a direct measure of behavioral regulation in early childhood. *Early Childhood Research Quarterly, 23,* 141–158.

Ponitz, C. C., McClelland, M. M., Matthews, J. M., & Morrison, F. J. (2009). A structured observation of behavioral self-regulation and its contribution to kindergarten outcomes. *Developmental Psychology, 45*(3), 605–619.

Ponitz, C. C., Rimm-Kaufman, S. E., Grimm, K. J., & Curby, T. W. (2009). Kindergarten classroom quality, behavioral engagement, and reading achievement. *School Psychology Review, 38*(1), 102–120.

Poulin, M., Haase, C. M., & Heckhausen, J. (2005). Engagement and disengagement across the life span: An analysis of two-process models of developmental regulation. In G. Werner, K. Rothermund, & D. Wentura (Eds.), *The adaptive self: Personal continuity and intentional self-development* (pp. 117–135). Ashland, OH: Hogrefe & Huber.

Poulin, M. J., & Heckhausen, J. (2007). Stressful events compromise control strivings during a major life transition. *Motivation and Emotion, 31,* 300–311.

Raver, C. C. (2004). Placing emotional self-regulation in sociocultural and socioeconomic contexts. *Child Development, 75*(2), 346–353.

Raz, N., Gunning, F. M., Head, D., Dupuis, J. H., McQuain, J., Briggs, S. D., et al. (1997). Selective aging of the human cerebral cortex observed in vivo: Differential vulnerability of the prefrontal gray matter. *Cerebral Cortex, 7,* 268–282.

Rhoades, B. L., & Maggs, J. L. (2006). Do academic and social goals predict planned alcohol use among college-bound high school graduates? *Journal of Youth and Adolescence, 35*(6), 913–923.

Rimm-Kaufman, S. E., Curby, T. W., Grimm, K. J., Nathanson, L., & Brock, L. L. (2009). The contribution of children's self-regulation and classroom quality to children's adaptive behaviors in the kindergarten classroom. *Developmental Psychology, 45*(4), 958–972.

Rimm-Kaufman, S. E., Early, D. M., Cox, M. J., Saluja, G., Pianta, R. C., Bradley, R. H., et al. (2002). Early behavioral attributes and teachers' sensitivity as predictors of competent behavior in the kindergarten classroom. *Journal of Applied Developmental Psychology, 23*(4), 451–470.

Rimm-Kaufman, S. E., La Paro, K. M., Downer, J. T., & Pianta, R. C. (2005). The contribution of classroom setting and quality of instruction to children's behavior in the kindergarten classroom. *Elementary School Journal, 105*(4), 377–394.

Roberts, B. W., & Mroczek, D. (2008). Personality trait change in adulthood. *Current Directions in Psychological Science, 17,* 31–35.

Rothbart, M. K. (2007). Temperament, development, and personality. *Current Directions in Psychological Science, 16*(4), 207–212.

Rothbart, M. K., & Bates, J. E. (2006). Temperament. In W. Damon & R. M. Lerner (Series Eds.) & N. Eisenberg (Vol. Ed.), *Handbook of child psychology: Vol. 3, Social, emotional, and personality development* (6th ed., pp. 99–166). Hoboken, NJ: John Wiley & Sons.

Rothbart, M. K., & Posner, M. I. (2005). Genes and experience in the development of executive attention and effortful control. *New Directions for Child and Adolescent Development, 109,* 101–108.

Rothbart, M. K., Posner, M. I., & Kieras, J. (2006). Temperament, attention, and the development of self-regulation. In K. McCartney & D. Phillips (Eds.), *Blackwell handbook of early childhood development* (pp. 338–357). Malden, MA: Blackwell.

Rothbaum, F., Weisz, J. R., & Synder, S. S. (1982). Changing the world and changing the self: A two-process model of perceived control. *Journal of Personality and Social Psychology, 42,* 5–37.

Rudman, D. L., Friedland, J., Chipman, M., & Sciotino, P. (2006). Holding on and letting go: The perspectives of pre-seniors and seniors on driving self-regulation in later life. *Canadian Journal on Aging, 25*(1), 65–76.

Rueda, M. R., Posner, M. I., & Rothbart, M. K. (2005). The development of executive attention: Contributions to the emergence of self-regulation. *Developmental Neuropsychology, 28*(2), 573–594.

Ryan, R. M., & Deci, E. L. (2000). Self-determination theory and the facilitation of intrinsic motivation, social development, and well-being. *American Psychologist, 55*(1), 68–78.

Ryan, R. M., & Deci, E. L. (2006). Self-regulation and the problem of human autonomy: Does psychology need choice, self-determination, and will? *Journal of Personality, 74*(6), 1557–1585.

Sabbagh, M. A., Xu, F., Carlson, S. M., Moses, L. J., & Lee, K. (2006). The development of executive functioning and theory of mind: A comparison of Chinese and U.S. preschoolers. *Psychological Science, 17*(1), 74–81.

Sameroff, A. J. (1995). General systems theories and developmental psychopathology. In *Developmental psychopathology: Theory and methods* (Vol. 1, pp. 659–695). New York: John Wiley & Sons.

Sameroff, A. J., Bartko, W. T., Baldwin, A., Baldwin, C., & Seifer, R. (1998). Family and social influences on the development of child competence. In *Families, risk, and competence* (pp. 161–185). Mahwah, NJ: Erlbaum.

Sameroff, A. J., & Chandler, M. J. (1975). Reproductive risk and the continuum of caretaking casualty. In F. D. Horowitz, M. Hetherington, S. Scarr-Salapatek, & G. Siegel (Eds.), *Review of child development research* (Vol. 4, pp. 187–244). Chicago: University of Chicago.

Sameroff, A. J., & Haith, M. M. (Eds.). (1996). *The five to seven year shift: The age of reason and responsibility.* Chicago: University of Chicago Press.

Sbarra, D. A., & Hazan, C. (2008). Coregulation, dysregulation, self-regulation: An integrative analysis and empirical agenda for understanding adult attachment, separation, loss, and recovery. *Personality and Social Psychology Review, 12,* 141–167.

Schultz, D., Izard, C. E., Ackerman, B. P., & Youngstrom, E. A. (2001). Emotion knowledge in economically disadvantaged children: Self-regulatory antecedents and relations to social difficulties and withdrawal. *Development & Psychopathology, 13*(1), 53–67.

Schunk, D. H., Zimmerman, B. J., Reynolds, W. M., & Miller, G. E. (2003). Self-regulation and learning. In *Handbook of psychology: Educational psychology* (Vol. 7, pp. 59–78). Hoboken, NJ: John Wiley & Sons.

Settersten, R. A. (2007). Passages to adulthood: Linking demographic change and human development. *European Journal of Population, 23,* 251–272.

Sheeran, P., & Orbell, S. (1998). Do intentions predict condom use? Meta-analysis and examination of six moderator variables. *British Journal of Social Psychology, 37,* 231–250.

Shernoff, D. J., Csikszentmihalyi, M., Schneider, B., & Shernoff, E. S. (2003). Student engagement in high school classrooms from the perspective of flow theory. *School Psychology Quarterly, 18*(2), 158–176.

Shields, A., Dickstein, S., Seifer, R., Giusti, L., Magee, K. D., & Spritz, B. (2001). Emotional competence and early school adjustment: A study of preschoolers at risk. *Early Education & Development, 12*(1), 73–96.

Shonkoff, J. P., & Phillips, D. A. (2000). *From neurons to neighborhoods: The science of early childhood development.* Washington, DC: National Academy Press.

Simonds, J., Kieras, J. E., Rueda, M. R., & Rothbart, M. K. (2007). Effortful control, executive attention, and emotional regulation in 7–10-year-old children. *Cognitive Development, 22*(4), 474–488.

Simons, L. G., & Conger, R. D. (2007). Linking mother-father differences in parenting to a typology of family parenting styles and adolescent outcomes. *Journal of Family Issues, 28,* 212–241.

Singer, B. D., & Bashir, A. S. (1999). What are executive functions and self-regulation and what do they have to do with language-learning disorders? *Language, Speech, & Hearing Services in Schools, 30*(3), 265–273.

Skinner, E. A. (1999). Action regulation, coping, and development. In J. Brandtstädter & R. M. Lerner (Eds.), *Action and self-development: Theory and research through the life span* (pp. 465–503). Thousand Oaks, CA: Sage.

Smith-Donald, R., Raver, C. C., Hayes, T., & Richardson, B. (2007). Preliminary construct and concurrent validity of the Preschool Self-regulation Assessment (PSRA) for field-based research. *Early Childhood Research Quarterly, 22*(2), 173–187.

Sokol, B. W., & Müller, U. (2007). The development of self-regulation: Toward the integration of cognition and emotion. *Cognitive Development, 22*(4), 401–405.

Son, S.-H., Ponitz, C. C., McClelland, M. M., Lan, X., Wanless, S. B., Morrison, F. J., et al. (in press). *The development of behavioral regulation in four cultures.*

Sonuga-Barke, E. J. S., Dalen, L., Daley, D., & Remington, B. (2002). Are planning, working memory, and inhibition associated with individual differences in preschool ADHD symptoms? *Developmental Neuropsychology, 21*(3), 255–272.

Sowell, E. R., Peterson, B. S., Thompson, P. M., Welcome, S. E., Henkenius, A. L., & Toga, A. W. (2003). Mapping cortical change across the human life span. *Nature Neuroscience, 6,* 309–315.

Spijkerman, R., van den Eijnden, R. J. J. M., & Engels, R. C. M. E. (2005). Self-comparison processes, prototypes, and smoking onset among early adolescents. *Preventive Medicine, 40,* 785–794.

Stansbury, K., & Zimmermann, L. K. (1999). Relations among child language skills, maternal socializations of emotion regulation, and child behavior problems. *Child Psychiatry & Human Development, 30*(2), 121–142.

Steinberg, L. (2008). A social neuroscience perspective on adolescent risk-taking. *Developmental Review, 28,* 78–106.

Strauman, T. J., Coe, C. L., McCrudden, M. C., Vieth, A. Z., & Kwapil, L. (2008). Individual differences in self-regulatory failure and menstrual dysfunction predict upper respiratory infection symptoms and antibody response to flu immunization. *Brain, Behavior, and Immunity, 22*(5), 769–780.

Strauman, T. J., Vieth, A. Z., Merrill, K. A., Kolden, G. G., Woods, T. E., Klein, M. H., et al. (2006). Self-system therapy as an intervention for self-regulatory dysfunction in depression: A randomized comparison with cognitive therapy. *Journal of Consulting and Clinical Psychology, 74*(2), 367–376.

Temple, C. M., Carney, R. A., & Mullarkey, S. (1996). Frontal lobe function and executive skills in children with Turner's syndrome. *Developmental Neuropsychology, 12*(3), 343–363.

Thelen, E., & Smith, L. B. (2006). Dynamic systems theories. In W. Damon & R. M. Lerner (Series Eds.) & R. M. Lerner (Vol. Ed.), *Handbook on child psychology: Vol. 1, Theoretical models of human development* (6th ed., pp. 258–312). Hoboken, NJ: John Wiley & Sons.

Thompson, R. A., & Lagattuta, K. H. (2006). Feeling and understanding: Early emotional development. In *Blackwell handbook of early childhood development* (pp. 317–337). Malden, MA: Blackwell.

Titelman, P. (Ed.). (2008). *Triangles: Bowen family systems theory perspectives.* New York: The Haworth Press/Taylor & Francis.

Tominey, S., & McClelland, M. M. (2010). *Red light, purple light: Initial findings from an intervention to improve self-regulation over the pre-kindergarten year.* Manuscript in review.

Trentacosta, C. J., & Izard, C. E. (2007). Kindergarten children's emotion competence as a predictor of their academic competence in first grade. *Emotion and Academic Competence, 7,* 77–88.

Tsai, H.-L. A., McClelland, M. M., Pratt, C., & Squires, J. (2006). Adaptation of the 36-Month Ages and Stages Questionnaire in Taiwan: Results from a preliminary study. *Journal of Early Intervention, 28*(3), 213–225.

van Empelen, P., & Kok, G. (2006). Condom use in steady and casual sexual relationships: Planning, preparation and willingness to take risks among adolescents. *Psychology and Health, 21,* 165–181.

Vinters, H. V. (2001). Aging and the human nervous system. In J. E. Birren & K. W. Schaie (Eds.), *Handbook of the psychology of aging* (Vol. 5). San Diego, CA: Academic Press.

Vitaro, F., Brendgen, M., Larose, S., & Trembaly, R. E. (2005). Kindergarten disruptive behaviors, protective factors, and educational achievement by early adulthood. *Journal of Educational Psychology, 97*(4), 617–629.

Vohs, K. D., Baumeister, R. F., Schmeichel, B. J., Twenge, J. M., Nelson, N. M., & Tice, D. M. (2008). Making choices impairs subsequent self-control: A limited-resources account of decision making, self-regulation, and active initiative. *Journal of Personality and Social Psychology, 94,* 883–898.

Wachs, T. D., Gurkas, P., & Kontos, S. (2004). Predictors of preschool children's compliance behavior in early childhood classroom settings. *Journal of Applied Developmental Psychology, 25*(4), 439–457.

Wanless, S. B., McClelland, M. M., Acock, A. C., Chen, F., & Chen, J. (in press). Behavioral regulation and early academic achievement in Taiwan. *Early Education and Development.*

Wanless, S. B., McClelland, M. M., Son, S. H., Lan, X., Ponitz, C. C., Morrison, F. J., et al. (2010). Measuring behavioral regulation in four societies. Manuscript in review.

Wanless, S. B., McClelland, M. M., Tominey, S. L., & Acock, A. C. (2010). *The influence of demographic risk factors on children's behavioral regulation in prekindergarten and kindergarten.* Manuscript in review.

Wasserman, G. A., Rauh, V. A., Brunelli, S. A., & Garcia-Castro, M. (1990). Psychosocial attributes and life experiences of disadvantaged minority mothers: Age and ethnic variations. *Child Development, 61*(2), 566–580.

Weisner, T. S. (1996). The 5 to 7 transition as an ecocultural project. In A. J. Sameroff & M. M. Haith (Eds.), *The five to seven year shift: The age of reason and responsibility* (pp. 295–326). Chicago: University of Chicago Press.

Welsh, M. C., Pennington, B. F., & Groisser, D. B. (1991). A normative-developmental study of executive function: A window on prefrontal function in children. *Developmental Neuropsychology, 7*(2), 131–149.

Werner, E. E., & Smith, R. S. (2001). *Journeys from childhood to midlife: Risk, resilience, and recovery.* Ithaca, NY: Cornell University Press.

Wiese, B. S., & Freund, A. M. (2005). Goal progress makes one happy, or does it? Longitudinal findings from the work domain. *Journal of Occupational and Organizational Psychology, 78,* 287–304.

Wiese, B. S., Freund, A. M., & Baltes, P. B. (2000). Selection, optimization, and compensation: An action-related approach to work and partnership. *Journal of Vocational Behavior, 57,* 273–300.

Wiese, B. S., Freund, A. M., & Baltes, P. B. (2002). Subjective career success and emotional well-being: Longitudinal predictive power of selection, optimization, and compensation. *Journal of Vocational Behavior, 60,* 321–335.

Wigfield, A., & Eccles, J. S. (2000). Expectancy-value theory of achievement motivation. *Contemporary Educational Psychology: Special Issue: Motivation and the Educational Process, 25*(1), 68–81.

Wigfield, A., Eccles, J. S., Schiefele, U., Roeser, R. W., & Davis-Kean, P. (2006). Development of achievement motivation. In W. Damon & R. M. Lerner (Eds.) & N. Eisenberg (Vol. Ed.), *Handbook of child psychology: Vol. 3, Social, emotional, and personality development* (6th ed., pp. 933–1002). Hoboken, NJ: John Wiley & Sons Inc.

Williams, K. J., Donovan, J. J., & Dodge, T. L. (2000). Self-regulation of performance: Goal establishment and goal revision processes in athletes. *Human Performance, 13*(2), 159–180.

Wilson, S. P., Kipp, K., & Daniels, J. (2003). Task demands and age-related differences in retrieval and response inhibition. *British Journal of Developmental Psychology, 21*(4), 599–613.

Wing, R. R., Papandonatos, G., Fava, J. L., Gorin, A. A., Phelan, S., McCaffrey, J., et al. (2008). Maintaining large weight losses: The role of behavioral and psychological factors. *Journal of Consulting and Clinical Psychology, 76*(6), 1015–1021.

Winne, P. H., Nesbit, H. C., Kumar, V., Hadwin, A. F., Lajoie, S. P., Azevedo, R., et al. (2006). Supporting self-regulated learning with gStudy software: The learning kit project. *Technology, Instruction, Cognition, and Learning, 3,* 105–113.

Wrosch, C., Scheier, M. F., Miller, G. E., Schulz, R., & Carver, C. S. (2003). Adaptive self-regulation of unattainable goals: Goal disengagement, goal reengagement, and subjective well-being. *Personality and Social Psychology Bulletin, 29,* 1494–1508.

Wrosch, C., Schulz, R., & Heckhausen, J. (2004). Health stresses and depressive symptomatology in the elderly: A control-process approach. *Current Directions in Psychological Science, 13,* 17–20.

Young, L. M., Baltes, B. B., & Pratt, A. K. (2007). Using selection, optimization, and compensation to reduce job/family stressors: Effective when it matters. *Journal of Business and Psychology, 21*(4), 511–539.

Zelazo, P. D., Carter, A., Reznick, J. S., & Frye, D. (1997). Early development of executive function: A problem-solving framework. *Review of General Psychology, 1*(2), 198–226.

Zelazo, P. D., & Müller, U. (2002). Executive function in typical and atypical development. In U. Goswami (Ed.), *Blackwell handbook of childhood cognitive development* (pp. 445–469). Malden, MA: Blackwell.

Zhou, Q., Eisenberg, N., Wang, Y., & Reiser, M. (2004). Chinese children's effortful control and dispositional anger/frustration: Relations to parenting styles and children's social functioning. *Developmental Psychology, 40*(3), 352–366.

Zimmerman, B. J. (1989). Models of self-regulated learning and academic achievement. In B. J. Zimmerman & D. H. Schunk (Eds.), *Self-regulated learning and academic achievement: Theory, research, and practice* (pp. 1–25). New York: Springer-Verlag.

Zimmerman, B. J. (2000). Attaining self-regulation: A social cognitive perspective. In M. Boekaerts, P. R. Pintrich, & M. Ziedner (Ed.), *Handbook of self-regulation* (pp. 13–39). San Diego: Academic Press.

Zimmerman, B. J. (2008). Investigating self-regulation and motivation: Historical background, methodological developments, and future prospects. *American Educational Research Journal, 45*(1), 166–183.

Zimmerman, B. J., & Schunk, D. H. (Eds.). (2001). *Self-regulated learning and academic achievement: Theoretical perspectives* (2nd ed.). Mahwah, NJ: Erlbaum.

Zusho, A., Pintrich, P. R., & Coppola, B. (2003). Skill and will: The role of motivation and cognition in the learning of college chemistry. *International Journal of Science Education, 25*(9), 1081–1094.

CHAPTER 16

The Development of Morality
Reasoning, Emotions, and Resistance

ELLIOT TURIEL

Human behaviors appear to be complex and to entail a great deal of planning and purposefulness. People seem to make decisions about their life goals, including family life; educational pathways; occupational choices; religious commitments; how to participate in society, culture, and politics; how to balance necessities and pleasures in recreational activities; how to coordinate self-fulfillment and contributing to the welfare and well-being of others, to fairness and justice, and to the good of the community and perhaps humanity; whether to pursue peace or war; and how to prepare for late adulthood and ultimately death. People seem to form understandings of the world around them, including through artistic, scientific, and religious endeavors that appear to contain intricate forms of knowledge and thought. People also seem to form understandings of social relationships, cultural practices, and societal organizations, which include efforts toward accommodation and social harmony, as well as conflict, opposition, and moral resistance. The list could go on and on.

IS ALL THIS AN ILLUSION?

According to many psychologists, all this is illusory. Psychologists, and other social scientists, have traditionally viewed most, if not all, of these types of endeavors as only giving the appearance of reasoning, purpose, understandings, choices, and balancing of alternatives. They have looked for the hidden and mysterious as a way of explaining human behavior. Some of the most prominent psychological theories of the first part of the twentieth century were organized around explanations of the hidden or unknown. This was certainly the goal of the psychoanalytic movement led by Freud (1923/1960, 1930/1961). As is well known (or at least used to be well known until recently), Freud attempted to generate a general psychological theory on the premise that the mysteries of psychopathology were different only in degree from psychological processes in those who functioned outside of the realm we would call psychopathological, and that there is a continuum between the pathological and the supposedly "normal." Early in life (during the first 5–7 years), much of significance moves out of consciousness into unconscious processes of a timeless nature about which there is almost insurmountable resistance to bringing the emotions and thoughts into awareness. Pathological and neurotic symptoms are manifestations of that which lies in a dynamic and conflictful unconscious.

An informative example of how seemingly complex systems of thought, knowledge, and emotion ostensibly aimed at explaining the universe at institutional and individual levels actually reflect hidden and mysterious processes can be seen in Freud's explanation of the psychology and sociology of religion in a slim volume entitled *The Future of an Illusion,* first published in 1927. The illusion referred to in the title is religion. Of course, many have maintained that religion has it wrong regarding particular dimensions (e.g., creationism) or general premises, such as the existence of deities or a deity (and religions differ from each other). The use of the term *illusion* was not meant to convey inaccuracies or errors ("An illusion is not the same thing as an error" [Freud, 1927/1961, p. 30]), but that which is motivated by wishes or desires, involves a disregard of reality, and maintains no concern with verification. In the case of religion, the motivations and structure of beliefs are unconsciously conceived as something different from what they actually are psychologically. As one example, religion portrays moral prohibitions, such as the prohibition on killing, as emanating from God, whereas such prohibitions, Freud asserted, actually stem from society and are aimed at protecting individuals from the instinctual aggression they would otherwise inflict on one another. Developmentally, prohibitions are internalized at early ages through superego formation with the resolution of the Oedipal conflict (Freud, 1930/1961). Freud maintained that in the process of becoming "civilized," children must pass through a phase of neurosis caused by the necessity for repression of instinctual demands. Religion, he asserted, represents an analogous form of neurosis caused by repression in prehistoric times: "Religion would thus be the universal obsessional neurosis of humanity; like the obsessional neurosis of children, it arose out of the Oedipus complex, out of the relation of the father" (Freud, 1927/1961, p. 43). The conceit in Freud's position was that he, as a scientist, could see through the illusory, and that psychoanalysis, as a therapeutic method, could further the progress of civilization (with sufficient time) so that science and rationality would triumph over the illusion.

There are other examples of social scientific pronouncements of the ubiquity of illusions in systems of thought and in everyday understandings of psychological functioning. From a sociological perspective, Durkheim (1912/1965) maintained that the sense of sacredness and adherence to rituals in religious life actually represents the attachment and sense of respect for the collectivity—though it is not recognized as such. Durkheim (1925/1961) theorized that morality is manifested in an attachment to society that includes incorporation of societal rules and standards, as well as symbolic values, which can take secular or religious forms. Religion, however, is a disguised manifestation of the attachment to society. The behaviorist movement was also predicated on the proposition that most psychological concepts are illusory and need to be reduced to conditioning or learning theory explanations of behavior to the exclusion of internal processes. Watson (1924) dismissed the idea of consciousness, equating it with the superstitious, nonscientific concept of a soul in religious frameworks. Skinner (1971) explicitly excluded most other common psychological constructs in his contention that the science of human behavior needs to abandon terminology pertaining to inner mental states or mediating states of mind: "Physics did not advance by looking more closely at the jubilance of a falling body, or biology by looking at the nature of vital spirits, and we do not need to try to discover what personalities, states of mind, feelings, traits of character, plans, purposes, intentions, or other perquisites of autonomous man really are to get on with a scientific analysis of behavior" (Skinner, 1971, pp. 12–13).

Skinner was one of the few strict behaviorists who lived to witness the cognitive revolution of the second part of the 20th century and the advent of cognitive science, a movement he lamented and dismissed by drawing an analogy with the opposition of creationism and evolutionary theory: "The role of variation and selection in the behavior of the individual suffers from the same opposition. Cognitive science is the creation science of psychology, as it struggles to maintain the position of a mind or self" (Skinner, 1990, p. 1209).

Skinner would have been somewhat heartened to know that some quarters of psychology have gone in the direction of dramatically downplaying mind, cognition as entailing goal-directed thinking or rationality, and choice or autonomy. In research on neuroscience, there are increasingly frequent assertions that brain processes are causal in determining decisions and actions that are not rational and are predetermined without freedom or choice (e.g., Cushman, Young, & Hauser, 2006; Greene & Haidt, 2002;

Wegner, 2002). Freud would have been somewhat heartened to know that those researchers also assert that decisions and choices are made out of, and before, conscious awareness. Both Freud and Skinner would have gravitated to explanations of morality, among neuroscientists and others, that decisions and actions are due to emotional reactions of a nonrational type stemming from nonconscious brain process or in-built intuitions, or both. In these views, the bases for moral choices are unknown and inexplicable to the actor. Insofar as reasons or explanations are invoked, they are irrelevant to decisions made. The decisions precede the explanations or reasons, which are after-the-fact and ad hoc rationalizations perhaps invoked to convince oneself or others.

IS DEVELOPMENT A CONSEQUENCE OF ONLY ENVIRONMENT OR BIOLOGY (OR ADDITIONS OF THE TWO)?

It is important to recognize that positions on the pervasiveness of hidden or unknown features of human functioning are intricately connected to the general theoretical propositions, including propositions on acquisition or development. In Freud's case, propositions regarding the nature of instinctual forces in early life and their inevitable clash with the requirements of interpersonal relationships and group life (civilization, as he put it) result in a repression of instinctual impulses (with the assumption of a dynamic unconscious into which they can be placed) and the child's incorporation of societal standards that serve to regulate behavior. Therefore, moral development (or superego formation) entails the acquisition of external societal prohibitions handed down to the child in a way people are not consciously aware. In Skinner's case, moral development is also a process of acquiring group values or standards, but through the vehicle of mechanistic processes of conditioning. Behaviors, therefore, are to be explained scientifically as determined by environmental contingencies, which is why we need to do away with explanations based on notions such as states of mind, purposes, intentions, autonomy, freedom, or dignity. In the early part of the 20th century, many also proposed that biological processes in the form of instincts determined behaviors (e.g., McDougall, 1926).

Explanations of moral development, and development more generally, have often oscillated between environmental and biological propositions, which are sometimes connected to debates about moral relativism and universalism. In addition to the environmentalism of behaviorists (Freudian theory is also environmentalist with regard to the content of values and standards acquired), other psychologists and anthropologists at the time were proposing nativistic views of social and moral behavior. In reaction to nativist propositions, several prominent cultural anthropologists (e.g., Ruth Benedict, Frans Boas, and Margaret Mead) argued vociferously against what they perceived as a lack of respect and tolerance for the integrity of different and unique cultural patterns in theories that engaged in comparative analyses from the vantage point of Western cultures and ordered cultures on some scale of adequacy or levels of civilization. In the process, however, a clear environmentalism was assumed by cultural anthropologists in their presumptions about children's development: "The life-history of the individual is first and foremost an accommodation to the patterns and standards traditionally handed down in his community" (Benedict, 1934, pp. 2–3). The corollary of this view of acquisition is moral relativism in the sense that, "Within each culture there comes into being characteristic purposes not necessarily shared by other types of society" (Benedict, p. 46). Social learning and socialization theorists in much of psychology proposed some version of this type of environmentalism in the second half of the 20th century (e.g., Aronfreed, 1968; Bandura & Walters, 1963; Hoffman, 1970; Mischel & Mischel, 1976). By the end of the 20th century and beginning of the 21st century, biological theories of the development of morality reemerged. In current formulations, the biological basis of moral acquisition is emphasized by evolutionary psychologists who propose either that emotionally based brain functions determine moral choices (Greene, Sommerville, Nystrom, Darley, & Cohen, 2001) or that there is a built-in universal moral grammar (Hauser, 2006; Mikhail, 2007).

However, the ever-present oscillations between environmentalism and nativism are not the only alternatives, though sometimes it appears we are stuck in the oscillation. In the past few centuries, many philosophical analyses have been aimed at formulating rationales and frameworks for welfare, beneficence, justice, freedom, equality, and rights (e.g., Dworkin, 1977; Frankena, 1963; Gewirth, 1982; Habermas, 1990; Kant, 1785/1964; Mill, 1863/2001; Nussbaum, 1999; Okin, 1989; Rawls, 1971). In this regard, moral philosophy, which has been concerned with defining morality, has stood apart from both environmental and biological formulations. It could be said that this schism is due to the mechanistic propositions of the environmental and biological theories that are largely formulated in the absence of concern with the epistemological underpinnings of the nature of the moral realm. There are, however, alternative positions to the mechanistically framed environmentalism and nativism; alternatives that, together with avoiding either/or approaches, also avoid approaches that are predicated on mechanistic additivity, aiming at an explanation of the whole by taking some of this (environment) and adding it with some of that (biology). The alternative positions, which are readily integrated with epistemological analyses, at a general level are called *structural-developmental* (Kohlberg, 1969) and *relational developmental systems* approaches to life-span development (Lerner, 2006; Lerner & Overton, 2008; Overton, 2006). Relational developmental systems incorporate an understanding that environment and biology—like cognition and emotion, intrapersonal and interpersonal, self and other, mind and body, and so on—are separable only for analytic purposes: a *relational bidirectionality,* and hence, an understanding that in both causality and interactions each part is composed of and composed by the other; an *epigenetic* model of life-span development, and hence, an understanding that development is sequential, ordered, directional, relatively permanent and emergent; and a *temporal plasticity,* and hence, an understanding that there can be multiple individual trajectories toward the same end. Within this broad relational developmental systems understanding there are specific theories that further articulate the alternatives to split-off environmentalism, split-off nativism, and split-off additive conceptions. These theories are rooted in the works of Baldwin (1906), Piaget (1947), and Werner (1957), each of which conceptualizes development as entailing mental constructions arising from the person's relational bidirectional interactions with the physical and social environment. Across the life span, individuals construct understandings of the physical world and social relationships; in the process, they develop moral judgments that include an integration of reasoning, emotions, and action (Kohlberg, 1963a, 1971).

Autonomy of the Mind and Persons: Taking Thought and Morality Seriously

A major feature of an integrated developmental systems perspective on human functioning and development differs from positions of split-off biological and environmental determinisms by taking seriously the relational interweaving of thought, emotions, and actions. Actions constitute the foundation of thought and the development of thought, and thought, in turn, feeds back on actions (Kohlberg, 1969; Overton, 2006; Piaget, 1932; Turiel, 2003a, 2008a; see also Mascolo & Fischer, Chapter 6 of this volume; Santostefano, Chapter 22 of this volume; McClelland, Ponitz, Messersmith, & Tominey, Chapter 15 of this volume). The formulations of Baldwin (1906), Piaget (1947), and others (e.g., Werner, 1957) take the relational character of mind and the person seriously in that human beings are, indeed, seen as thinking beings, and development is viewed as a function of their relational bidirectional interactions, with complex and multifaceted environments continuing throughout the life span. In these views, thought and emotions are not independent pieces of a puzzle. Thought and emotions are interdependent parts of a whole (Kohlberg, 1969; Piaget, 1981; Turiel, 2006). Emotions are not so powerful and thinking so weak that emotions dominate reasoning. Emotions do not drive thought and behavior, and individuals do not simply act nonrationally or irrationally because of unconscious or unreflective emotional reactions. Emotional appraisals are part of reasoning that involves taking into account the reactions of others and self (Nussbaum, 1999). The emotional reactions of people are a central part of moral judgments, and it is relational reciprocal interactions, together with reflections on one's own judgments and cultural practices or societal arrangements, that are central to the development system (Kohlberg, 1969; Turiel, 2002). Moreover, the primary emotions associated with morality are positive ones, such as sympathy, empathy, and respect; they are not negative or aversive emotions, such as fear, anxiety, disgust, and guilt. The proposition that moral thought and emotions are closely linked to actions is based on the assumptions that individuals are active in thinking about the social environment, that they have mental/emotional propensities to care about the welfare of others and fairness in their relationships, that they scrutinize their world and reflect on their own and others judgments and actions, and that in the process they are not driven solely by emotional or unconscious biological or psychological forces to act without choice. However, an understanding of social and moral decisions and actions must also be connected to situational contexts and account for the variety of different types of social judgments that individuals make, including moral, social, and personal judgments. The embodiment of reasoning in actions (Overton, 2007) involves a coordination of different types of judgments in particular contexts (Turiel, 2003a, 2008b). Consequently, we cannot approach the question of how moral judgments might be related to decisions and actions by assessing moral judgments only, as discussed further later in this chapter.

These propositions imply that morality is a substantive realm of thought and study, and that more is required in the exploration of moral behavior and development than a reliance solely on psychological mechanisms. As a substantive realm of thought, knowledge, and discourse, the psychological study of morality requires epistemological analyses and formulations of conceptual bases that are not reducible to psychological mechanisms. This is consistent with Piaget's (1970) broad call for a genetic epistemology entailing collaboration between scholars from multiple disciplines. Whether it be through face-to-face collaboration among scholars or collaboration based on print and electronic media, the basic point is, as stated by Chomsky (1979): "No discipline can concern itself in a productive way with the acquisition or utilization of a form of knowledge, without being concerned with the *nature* of that system of knowledge" (p. 43).

In contrast with this position expressed by Piaget, Chomsky, and Kohlberg, the sociobiologist E. O. Wilson (1975) famously argued for the opposing stance in the study of morality and biology when he asserted: "Scientists and humanists should consider together the possibility that the time has come for ethics to be removed temporarily from the hands of the philosophers and biologicized" (p. 562). Wilson's proclamation of the need to split off from philosophy was criticized and largely unheeded until the recent reemergence of research on morality by evolutionary psychologists (Hauser, 2006; Krebs & Denton, 2005) and neuroscientists (Greene et al., 2001) emphasizing the biological bases of moral evaluations and decisions (a topic to be discussed further later in this chapter). In developmental psychology, at least, Wilson's pronouncements went unheeded for a time, perhaps because of the influence of researchers of morality like Kohlberg (1971), who was influential not only because of his empirical contributions through his cross-sectional and longitudinal research on a developmental sequence of moral judgments, but also because of his detailed analyses of the shortcomings of psychological research that ignored philosophical-conceptual analyses.

The historical context for Kohlberg's analyses was that much of the research of the time (some based on psychoanalytic theory, more based on behaviorist and social learning theories) merely attended to psychological constructs in attempts to explain the acquisition of vaguely defined values, standards, or behaviors. The research based on psychoanalytic theory focused on instincts, impulses, and conflicts in parent–child relationships as the mechanisms for acquisition. In the behaviorist and social learning accounts, the focus was on reinforcement, imitation, modeling, parental child rearing practices, and the learning of self-control in relation to a set of largely undefined moral outcome variables, such as rules, norms, standards, and restrictions often arbitrarily identified in laboratory or naturalistic settings. For the most part, the moral outcome variables, lacking theoretical formulations related to definitional criteria, were by-products stemming from the requirement that measures be included of moral acquisition to connect to the psychological constructs. Moreover, Kohlberg (1963b, 1964) demonstrated that the moral outcome measures produced inconsistent and inconclusive results regarding the validity of the proposed psychological mechanisms of acquisition. Kohlberg's research, by contrast, attempted to coordinate analyses of the individual's thought and development with analyses (as guided by philosophical inquiry) of the nature of moral systems entailing welfare, equality, justice, and rights (Kohlberg, 1971). If morality is not taken seriously—if there is an absence of concern with the nature of systems of moral knowledge—psychological theory and research are simply guided by intuitions about the moral realm and ad hoc choices of empirical tasks.

Much of the research that Kohlberg reviewed in arriving at the conclusion that the study of morality could not be restricted to the narrow confines of psychological analyses also did not lend support to the propositions that parental child rearing practices, positive and negative reinforcements, and processes of identification and imitation were associated with the moral measures used, such as "strength of conscience" or extent of feelings of guilt, adherence to societal rules or norms, or the acquisition of abilities to resist temptation (Kohlberg, 1963b, 1964). In addition to the problem that such research was not based on sound conceptual frameworks concerning the moral domain, nor sound assessments of moral evaluations, judgments, decisions, or actions, the research operated from the perspective that development is largely adult driven. Within that framework, adults, including adult psychologists, tended to approach childhood as if it is what adults do to children—how they shape and guide them—that largely determines behavior and development. An exception was made for unsocialized children's behaviors, which were understood as the negative consequence of peers or, more recently, forces such as the media, television, and the Internet. Part of the idea of taking morality seriously (i.e., as a realm of autonomous decision making based on substantive understandings) is that humans should be taken seriously.

Studying Morality and Development: Taking Humans Seriously

What I mean by taking humans seriously is that it is necessary to recognize that people are not simply objects buffeted by the force of directives emanating from others (or the force of biology). From the beginning, the developing person acts to give meaning to and to understand the world, and to make sense of social relationships. And with development, they come to evaluate the dictates of others, to distinguish between what they judge to be legitimate and illegitimate demands and directives, and to engage in relational reciprocal interpersonal interactions and communications. In the process of early development, they evaluate social relationships and consequently come to accept and reject parental directives, sometimes leading to conflicts with adults and peers. Children, like adults, also approach social relationships from the viewpoint of moral concerns, including concerns with the welfare of others and fairness. A good deal of research supports this general view of the developing person, the person's social interactions, and the person's social and moral worlds.

Mark Twain, Childhood, and Society

Before exploring this research, however, these ideas can be illustrated in illuminating ways through the writings of one of America's great writers of the 19th century, Mark Twain. Two of his novels are particularly well known, *The Adventures of Tom Sawyer* and *The Adventures of Huckleberry Finn. The Adventures of Tom Sawyer,* published in 1876, largely portrays the escapades of Tom and his friends in their relationships with each other, with parents, siblings, other family members, teachers, and religious authorities. Tom, who lives with his Aunt Polly (his main caretaker), half-brother Sid, and cousin Mary, is always sneaking away at night to seek new adventures, often plays hooky from school, gets into mischief at home and school, engages in hijinks at Sunday school, and occasionally gets lost for days on end. He runs away from home not out of anger with his family, but to undertake irresistible adventures. In Mark Twain's portrayal, the boys are often in conflict with adults and reject many of society's mores because of their desires for fun and to pursue the personal pleasures of life. The boys rarely hurt people (their fights are benign), act unfairly, or deprive

others of their just due. The boys get into a lot of trouble with the parents, teachers, and ministers, but they also are portrayed as having a keen sense of sympathy for people and a strong desire to correct injustices. It is adults who are more often portrayed as engaging in moral affronts, including serious physical violence and in their treatment of slaves.

Perhaps it is Huck Finn, as he is portrayed in the Tom Sawyer volume, who best illustrates Mark Twain's view of the early periods of the life span. Huck made his appearance as the vagabond son of the Town Drunkard, who "was cordially hated and dreaded by all the mothers of the town, because he was idle and lawless, and vulgar and bad—and because all their children admired him so, and delighted in his forbidden society" (*The Adventures of Tom Sawyer,* 1876, p. 61). Tom was under strict orders not to play with Huck, "so he played with him every time he got a chance." In one of the last adventures in *The Adventures of Tom Sawyer,* Huck became a hero by risking his life to save the Widow Douglas from someone out to kill her. Just before that, Tom and Huck had found a fortune during one of their adventures. In her gratitude, the Widow Douglas insisted on taking Huck under her wing:

> Huck Finn's wealth and the fact that he was now under the Widow Douglas's protection introduced him into society—no, dragged him into it, hurled him into it—and his sufferings were almost more than he could bear. The widow's servants kept him clean and neat, combed and brushed, and they bedded him nightly in unsympathetic sheets that had not one little spot or stain which he could press to his heart or know for a friend. He had to eat with knife and fork; he had to use napkin, cup, and plate; he had to learn his book, he had to go to church; he had to talk so properly that speech was become insipid in his mouth; whithersoever he turned, the bars and shackles of civilization shut him in and bound him hand and foot.
>
> He bravely bore his miseries three weeks, and then one day turned up missing. (*The Adventures of Tom Sawyer,* pp. 278–279)

The adults were worried about his well-being and looked everywhere for him. But Tom knew where to find Huck. Huck protested Tom's efforts to bring him home, but Tom first invoked convention: "Well, everybody does that way, Huck." Huck retorted that he was not everybody, and blamed his entire predicament on the found fortune. He offered it all to Tom. But Tom would have none of that because "Tain't fair." Finally, Huck consented to try again with the Widow Douglas mainly because it was the only way he could join Tom and their friends in the "gang of robbers" and participate that night in the initiation rites.

Mark Twain and Childhood Morality

Here Tom displays his sense of fairness, and Huck was concerned with preventing harm and the value of life when he saved the Widow Douglas. Nevertheless, *Tom Sawyer* dealt less with children's moral orientation than with their rejection of customs and conventions, many parental directives, and their pursuit of pleasurable activities. It is in *The Adventures of Huckleberry Finn,* published in 1885, that Mark Twain deals directly with children's moral orientations, including concerns with justice, equality, and the enslavement of people. In this volume, Mark Twain deals with these issues through the portrayal of Huck Finn's actions in helping free the runaway slave, Jim.

Huck Finn's defiance in helping free Jim from slavery, however, was not without ambivalence and intense conflict. Huck's initial judgment was that he should help Jim run away on their raft to a free state. In Mark Twain's portrayal, conflict and inner struggle were generated by feelings and thoughts about what is right to do as given in society's expectations, and about what is right and good for individuals whose dignity and freedom are taken away. The inner struggle comes to a head when Huck Finn becomes torn as to what to do about Jim and as to whether it would be better for Jim to go home or be free. He first thinks that he should not reveal Jim's whereabouts because Jim would be punished and because "It would get all around, … and if I was to ever see anybody from that town again, I'd be ready to get down and lick his boots for shame" (*The Adventures of Huckleberry Finn,* p. 178). However, the mental struggle continued as he thought better of it again, until he thinks about Jim, about all they went through, about their sad and happy times, about their close friendship, and about how Jim cared for him.

Huck Finn's turmoil over his decision means that he understood what the social expectations were, and how they conflicted with the dignity of human beings and with the importance of freedom and equality. The expectations that he would be shamed in front of the townsfolk means that he understood the consequences of moral defiance. These two volumes illustrate three research-based issues about children and adults that I discuss in this chapter. One is that at an early age children form moral judgments, connected to emotions, which they distinguish from understandings of society's customs and conventions, and from what they judge to be legitimate realms of personal choice and jurisdiction. The second is that across the life span, moral and social decisions often involve coordinating or balancing different considerations from the moral, social, and personal domains. The third is that across the life span, individuals engage in social opposition and moral resistance in their everyday lives in that they scrutinize and critique existing social arrangements and cultural practices.

A constant theme in Mark Twain's writing was the divide between society's ways and the desires of individuals. He did this, I believe, with two goals in mind: One goal was to portray injustices at the societal level, and thereby critique society; the second was to illustrate that children are often at odds with the expectations of adults and do not simply accommodate or adjust to societal ways. As an example, Twain's descriptions of Huck's predicament in the home of the Widow Douglas had to do with the myriad conventions and arbitrary restrictions imposed on children by adults who thought such restrictions necessary for civilization. Twain conveyed children's desires for enjoyment, fulfillment, adventures, play, and pleasures in areas that were part of their personal lives. And in Twain's characterization, children's rejection of conventions and their pursuit of the pleasures of life did not interfere with their moral sense, feelings for the welfare of others, or a sense of fairness. Children's moral sense included a rejection of societal practices they see as wrong.

Mark Twain's depiction of childhood is more consistent with the position that children construct judgments through social interactions than depictions of childhood represented in characterizations of moral development as a process of socialization into society's values and norms. He portrayed children as capable of discriminating between the demands of convention and the requirements of justice. Mark Twain also depicted people across the life span as individuals with abilities to scrutinize, critique, and attempt to transform societal arrangements that include inequalities and injustices. Through his writings of the risks that Jim took in becoming a runaway slave, Twain also captured the resistance of those in subordinate positions to unjust institutionalized practices.

Research on Moral, Social, and Personal Judgments: Domains of Reasoning

Of course, this is all presented in fictional form by way of novels. Nevertheless, *Tom Sawyer* and *Huckleberry Finn* provide great insights into moral resistance, and the inner mental workings and social lives of children. Making distinctions among morality, convention, and realms of personal choice, as well as between adult demands and the perspectives of youth, are important not merely because Mark Twain tells us so. It is important because a large number of studies inform us that these distinctions are important for understandings of development, and moral and social decision making. More than 100 studies conducted since the 1970s in several cultures have shown that by a fairly young age, children make distinctions between morality and the social conventions of the family, school, or society. Morality entails concepts about welfare, justice, and rights, and pertains to issues such as inflicting harm, theft, violation of rights, and unequal treatment. Social conventions are tied to social systems and involve concepts of expectations that coordinate social interactions (issues such as modes of dress, forms of address, eating habits). Research also shows that children distinguish the domains of morality and social convention from the personal domain, which pertain to arenas of personal choice and jurisdiction that do not involve impinging on the welfare or rights of others.

Because the research on *domains* has been widely published and a number of comprehensive reviews are available (e.g., Nucci, 2001; Smetana, 2006; Tisak, 1995; Turiel, 1983, 1998, 2002, 2006), I summarize in fairly brief fashion the features of children's thinking in the domains, and then consider how a domain approach is similar to and different from the approaches of Piaget (1932) and Kohlberg (1969) to moral development. This is followed by consideration of moral and social decision making that involves coordination of different domains of judgments and different aspects of moral judgments.

The first fact that the research has demonstrated is that, contrary to assumptions made from mechanistic perspectives, young children do not make moral judgments on the basis of extrinsic factors such as punishment, the power and status of adults, or reverence for authority. Nor are their moral judgments based on personal interests and needs. By 4 to 6 years of age (and perhaps earlier), children make judgments about welfare and in a more rudimentary way about justice and rights. Moral issues of welfare, justice, and rights are not confused with issues of punishment, obedience, power, or the needs and interests of the self. Furthermore, the fact that young children are quite capable of discriminating the various types of rules speaks to the fact that morality is not primarily based on the incorporation of parental or societal rules, standards, or norms. Standards or norms pertaining to moral issues are judged differently from those pertaining to conventions. These distinctions do not solely involve a simple discrimination between categories. A complex configuration is connected to each domain, including what have

been referred to as criterion judgments and justifications. The criterion judgments, which are not age related, refer to whether morality or convention is seen as contingent on rules, dependent on authority dictates, or based on common practice or existing social arrangements.

Many studies show that moral norms are judged to be obligatory and noncontingent on rules, authority, or existing practices and agreements (for reviews, see Smetana, 2006, and Turiel, 1998). Studies also show that children and adolescents do not accept directives from authorities they consider unjustified (Laupa, 1991; Laupa & Turiel, 1986; Tisak, 1986). By contrast, conventional norms are judged to be contingent on rules, authority, and common practice, and are based on social agreements. Justifications—or reasons for evaluations and criterion judgments—also differ by domain and do involve age-related changes. Justifications in the moral domain are based on concepts of welfare, justice, and rights, whereas in the conventional domain they are based on tradition, social agreement, and social coordinations. The domains, which constitute distinct developmental pathways, are associated with the early emergence of emotions such as sympathy, empathy, and respect (Eisenberg & Fabes, 1991; Hoffman, 2000; Piaget, 1932). In saying that the domains constitute distinct developmental pathways, I mean that age-related changes occur within each domain. For instance, the development of thinking about social conventions involves a series of changes connected with conceptions of social systems and the role of conventions in coordinating social interactions within social systems (Turiel, 1983). Levels of development have also been identified for the personal domain (Nucci, 1977, 2001). Although less is known about development in the moral domain, shifts occur from a focus on harm among younger children to concerns with welfare and justice in later childhood (Davidson, Turiel, & Black, 1983; Nucci, 2001; Turiel, 1998).

Recent research (Nucci & Turiel, 2009) has shown that age-related changes in moral judgments are far from straightforward and involve complex patterns related to the application of basic concepts of harm in situational contexts, and that also involve increased capacities to coordinate concepts of welfare and justice with the demands of the situation. It was found that children as young as 6 to 8 years understand the need to avoid harm to persons and promote fairness, but do so with less ambiguity than young adolescents. Young adolescents exhibit an expanded capacity to include facets of the situation so that the application of moral concepts is more ambiguous and less categorical. Older adolescents are better able to apply moral concepts in unambiguous ways without ignoring the features of the situation.

The evidence, therefore, indicates, in keeping with the relational developmental system notion of temporal plasticity, that there are different strands of developmental transformations within individuals in the context of maintaining the domain distinctions across ages. Because we have emphasized that domains are distinguished across ages starting in early childhood, some have misconstrued our position as sympathetic to a nativistic modularity (Glassman & Zann, 1995).

Domain Theory Is Not About Modularity and Not About Nativism

As Piaget (1932) pointed out long ago, findings of the early emergence of moral and social judgments should not be taken to mean that they are innately (i.e., biologically) determined. The context for Piaget's claim was assertions by Antipoff (1928, as cited in Piaget, 1932) that a sense of justice was "innate and instinctive," and that its emergence did not require social experiences. Because Antipoff's research was with children from 3 to 9 years of age, Piaget (1932) noted that by the age of 3 years, children have experienced a good deal of social interaction that could influence their development. Findings with young children do not necessarily speak to the question of innateness.

In fact, research has shown that a variety of young children's social experiences are distinctly associated with the development of judgments in the moral, conventional, and personal domains. In one line of research, observations were made of children's interactions with other children and adults in the context of moral and social conventional transgressions. These studies, conducted with preschoolers (Nucci & Turiel, 1978; Nucci, Turiel, & Encarcion-Gawrych, 1983; Nucci & Weber, 1995) and older children (Nucci & Nucci, 1982a, 1982b; Turiel, 2008a), demonstrate that interactions around moral transgressions are different from interactions taking place when conventional transgressions occur. Interactions around moral transgressions typically do not involve commands or communications about rules and expectations of adults (which do occur for conventional events), but are about feelings and the perspectives of actors, as well as communications about welfare and fairness. Interactions and communications about moral issues revolve around the effects of acts on people, the perspectives of others, the need to avoid harm, and the pain and emotions experienced, whereas with regard to conventional events, they revolve around adherence to rules, commands from those in authority, and an emphasis on social order.

A second line of research examined children's discussions, in narrative form, about events involving harm they had experienced as either perpetrators or victims (Wainryb, Brehl, & Matwin, 2005). The many narratives provided by children and adolescents illustrated that they focus on interactions and exchanges between people, the feelings evoked, and the effects of acts on self and others. This is true even for preschoolers. For example, a preschool boy talking about his experiences as a victim recalled the physical and emotional hurt involved (from Wainryb et al., 2005): "He was a friend…he hit me with his hammer in the middle of the head and it really hurt" (p. 54). A preschool girl recalled that her friend "said she really didn't want to play with me and she um she hit me and um and I felt bad and so I asked her mom…if I could go home and she said yes" (p. 54). At this young age, children also are aware of their acts as a perpetrator. One boy stated, "I said something that really hurt him and he said, 'I don't like that.' And I stopped" (p. 55).

Older children express their reflections about their actions and those of others, as well as the nature of their relationships. One first-grade girl discussed a time she felt slighted by her "best friend" who referred to another child as her best friend: "And I kind of thought to myself that was kind of making me feel bad. So I wonder if I can go over there and tell her that I that that kind of hurt my feelings" (Wainryb et al., 2005, p. 56).

Not surprisingly, adolescents also expressed these types of concerns and reflections on social relationships. One example comes from a tenth-grade girl who talked about the time she evaded a planned evening with one of her best friends to spend time with other friends: "…she figured it out and found out and she felt really bad and was hurt and so it wasn't good. Cause I bet she felt betrayed maybe even she thought I don't care about her but I do um I didn't want to hurt her feelings because she was one of my best friends and so I know sometimes being honest is hard but it would definitely be worth it, but it was hard just because I felt so pressured like it happens a lot I know it happens to a lot to people my age" (Wainryb et al., 2005, p. 59–60).

These examples illustrate that the dynamics of social interactions in childhood and beyond include a large measure of scrutiny of events that are experienced, what people say to each other, concerns with feelings, and concerns with how others will react. Children are not solely responding to adult directives or to adults' attempts to shape them. Children's many everyday social experiences involve participating in and observing events of many types. Children participate in events that involve, as examples, people harming or helping each other, sharing or failing to share, excluding or including others, treating people equally or unequally. Children's lives are full of these types of experiences, about which they are neither unaware nor passive. Their observations and reflections of events are major sources of formation and changes of moral and social judgments.

Contrasts with Adult-Driven Conceptions of Development

Clearly, the findings that young children maintain systems of thought that differ by domains, that they do not make moral judgments on the basis of existing standards, that they do not base moral evaluations on directives by authorities, and that those domains are associated with different types of social experiences are not consistent with theories of internalization and socialization, which attempt to explain development as the shaping of behavior through an external agent (the adult). One such shaping approach—asserting the strong position that development is adult driven—conceptualizes morality as entailing the formation of an internal set of traits (Bennett, 1993, 1995; Bennett & Delattre, 1978; Ryan, 1989; Sommers, 1984; Wynne, 1985). The basic proposition of this theory is that children must be taught in ways that lead them to acquire behaviors that are consistently applied and that come to operate as a set of internal dispositions of personality. The internal dispositions are identified as traits such as honesty, obedience, loyalty, friendship, responsibility, persistence, courage, and faith. Presumably, those who acquire these traits act according to them consistently across situations, and thus appear to possess the self-control to withstand temptations to act in their own self-interest. The "character traits" are defined as nonrational dispositions that involve habits of behavior. These habits must be instilled in children though indoctrination (Bennett & Delattre, 1978; Wynne, 1985), direct instruction, and the transmission of society's traditions through stories and lived examples of good works. Other socialization perspectives, although not necessarily relying on the idea of internal dispositions, nevertheless also portray children as needing to be socialized by external agents (adults), and socialization here means to be trained or shaped in some way that results in compliance with the values, standards, and practices of one's society or culture (e.g., Aronfreed, 1968; Kochanska, 1993; Mischel & Mischel, 1976). This view of children fails to account for the complex types of moral and social judgments they form. Children do not operate according to a set of abstract and fixed dispositions, or by incorporated values and actions.

Contrasts with Differentiation Models of Moral Development

Although Piaget and Kohlberg proposed that the development of moral judgments is a process of construction, the findings on domains do not support their specific characterizations of the sequence of the development of moral judgments and especially their characterizations of young children's morality. In each of their formulations, moral development is characterized as a process of a series of differentiations leading to "autonomous morality" (Piaget) or "postconventional morality" (Kohlberg). Piaget (1932) proposed that, in a developed state, moral judgments are autonomous in that individuals participate in the elaboration of norms in the sense that they construct judgments and have their own understandings of fairness, equality, and the need for cooperation. However, before this type of autonomous morality, children are understood to be heteronomous in that morality is seen as adherence to fixed rules and to infallible adult authorities. The claim is that moral obligation is tied to a one-way or unilateral respect for adults. In heteronomous thinking, when justice is in conflict with authority or custom, children believe authority and custom right, and justice wrong (Piaget, 1932). Piaget proposed that at later ages, children form distinct moral understandings of justice in an autonomous orientation that entails differentiating the moral from the nonmoral. One of the salient confusions resolved with the claim that development moves from heteronomy to autonomy is the differentiation of "what ought to be from what is" (Piaget, 1932, p. 350). Heteronomous thought identifies "what is with what ought to be" (Piaget, 1932, p. 347).

For Piaget, the development of autonomous moral thinking involved a differentiation of justice from adult authority and the force of custom. Although Kohlberg's six-stage sequence of moral judgments differed in its details from the sequence proposed by Piaget, a similar differentiation model was proposed that entailed progressive differentiations of what ought to be from what exists. In this formulation as well, distinct moral understandings do not emerge until the highest stages of thinking. Development is here explained as a process of increasing differentiations of moral judgments from other realms. As Kohlberg (1971) explained:

> The individual whose judgments are at stage 6 asks "Is it morally right?" and means by morally right something different from punishment (stage 1), prudence (stage 2), conformity to authority (stages 3 and 4) etc. Thus, the responses of lower-stage subjects are not moral for the same reasons that responses of higher-stage subjects to aesthetic or other morally neutral matters fail to be moral...This is what we had in mind earlier when we spoke of our stages as representing an increased differentiation of moral values and judgments from other types of values and judgments. (p. 216)

In this type of differentiation model, distinct moral judgments emerge through a lengthy process of distinguishing issues of welfare, justice, and rights from other judgments (punishment and prudence at first, and then authority, rules, and conventions). It is not until the highest stages (in terms of age, late adolescence at the earliest) that understandings of morality are distinguished from understandings based on commitments to following rules, adherence to authority dictates, and respect for society (i.e., in the shift from stage 4 to stages 5 and 6). Moreover, in these formulations, it is implicitly assumed that decisions are bounded within the moral domain, without consideration of how domains are coordinated. This is because embedded in the idea of progressive differentiations of domains is the idea that moral judgments displace other and developmentally lower types of judgments. The types of moral understandings that characterize the highest stages involve overarching principles that serve to organize priorities in decisions. At the highest stages, moral principles are given priority over other domains because the process of development is understood to involve the formation of judgments out of prior confusions. Because development here entails a disentanglement of morality from other social considerations, it is presumed that morality will then be given priority over the "less adequate" forms of judgment represented in the lower stages.

We have seen, however, that research examining children's judgments in the different domains—without assuming they are undifferentiated—yielded a different picture than that proposed by the differentiation theories. In the research on domains, components of social situations were disentangled in ways not done in the methods used by Kohlberg (1963a). Many social situations include moral and nonmoral components, often posing people with conflicts, with the need to coordinate the different domains of judgment, and the need to draw priorities among them (Turiel, 2008b). Many of the situations used by Kohlberg to elicit responses were multifaceted in these ways, but the various components were not separated. An example is the story in which a doctor is deciding whether to adhere to the request of a dying woman in pain that he give her drugs to make her die sooner. Although this situation raises moral issues regarding the value of life, the responsibilities of doctors to patients, and legal issues, it also raises issues about the quality of life and personal choices in that regard, and when it is legitimate for an individual to end her life in the context of a terminal illness and great pain. The responses of a 10-year-old boy in Kohlberg's study illustrate how these issues might be disentangled. The boy recognized that the decision has pragmatic consequences for the doctor in stating, "From the doctor's point of view, it

could be a murder charge" (Kohlberg, 1963a, p. 23). Recognizing that the situation confronted the dying woman with personal choices about the quality of her life and the great pain she was experiencing, he said, "From her point of view, it isn't paying her to live anymore if she's just going to be in pain," and "It should be up to her; it's her life, not the law's life" (Kohlberg, 1963a, p. 23).

These responses were coded solely in terms of judgments of a moral kind: That morality for the 10-year-old is instrumental, hedonistic (pleasure and pain), and based on a person's ownership rights (which fit into his second stage). A domain theory alternative interpretation is that the boy viewed the woman's wishes in terms of her legitimate realms of personal jurisdiction and the doctor's choices, which the boy assumed to be one of helping her or putting himself in legal jeopardy. As noted earlier, research shows that children of this age, as well as younger and older people, do form judgments in domains of personal choices, including pragmatics, that are different from moral considerations (Nucci, 1981, 1996). Therefore, it may well be that the 10-year-old was making judgments about what he saw as nonmoral features of the situation that he attempted to coordinate with moral considerations. We do not know whether this boy was making differentiations between the moral and personal domains, because his responses to those complex and domain-multifaceted situations were not analyzed for such a possibility. If he were making such differentiations, it would mean that he was not defining morally right action instrumentally or in terms of hedonistic calculations.

LIFE IS NOT EASY: DECISIONS ARE COMPLICATED AND TAKE INTO ACCOUNT MULTIPLE CONSIDERATIONS

If we look beyond the linguistic expression of the 10-year-old boy responding to questions about euthanasia, his concerns with the doctor's perspective on serious legal jeopardy and his appreciation for the plight of a person in great pain nearing the end of life are not very different from how many adults approach the question of euthanasia (which is not to say that adults would not see even greater complexities and raise additional issues). A better way to analyze the thinking of children and adults about multifaceted issues such as this one is to examine if they discriminate the varying components and how they coordinate them in coming to decisions.

It is usually recognized that an issue like euthanasia is complicated even for adults. However, many issues are often regarded as morally straightforward. An example is the issue of honesty. It might be thought that it is good to act honestly and wrong to act dishonestly. Indeed, this simplicity of what is morally correct is presumed in many positions, including those that portray morality as the acquisition and implementation of traits of character or virtue. Whereas it is thought that people do not always act honestly because of a lack of inner strength and inability to resist temptation, it is thought that acting honestly is morally right in a straightforward way.

But then again, perhaps honesty is not so straightforward. Consider the following example taken from philosophical discourse regarding Kant's contention that it is always wrong to lie. The scenario they have raised to show that it is not always wrong to lie is the following: Suppose someone goes past a bystander who is soon thereafter asked by a murderer where his intended victim has gone (Bok, 1979/1999). It has been maintained that in such a situation, the moral prescription to save a life should take precedence over the moral prescription to be honest. It could be argued that there is a moral obligation for the bystander to engage in deception. An obvious real-life example of giving precedence to saving lives over honesty is when people hid Jews from Nazis and lied about it during World War II. In those cases, people engaged in deception at great risk to themselves to save lives.

People generally do value honesty, but deception is also judged necessary in some contexts. Deception is judged acceptable to spare the feelings of others, to protect people from physical harm and avoid injustices, and to promote perceived legitimate personal ends in the face of relationships of unequal power (Abu-Lughod, 1993; Lewis, 1993; Perkins & Turiel, 2007; Turiel, 2002; Turiel & Perkins, 2004; Wikan, 1996). Studies with adolescents and adults in the context of adolescent–parent relationships and in the context of marital relationships have shown that judgments about deception vary systematically by the domain of issues involved and types of relationships. The findings demonstrate how several features of situational contexts are coordinated in coming to decisions. In one study (Perkins & Turiel, 2007), adolescents of two age groups, 12- to 13-year-olds and 16- to 17-year-olds, made judgments about deception of parents or peers with regard to moral, personal, and prudential activities. They were presented with hypothetical situations in which parents or peers insist in their objections to an adolescent's choice of an activity and the adolescent continues the activity but lies about

it. In one set, the adolescent is directed to engage in acts considered morally wrong (racial discrimination and fighting). For the personal (who to date, which club to join) and prudential (not riding a motorcycle, doing school work) domains, the parents or peers object to the adolescent's choices. The findings showed that adolescents weigh and try to balance issues of honesty and other considerations in different ways for each type of activity and for relationships with parents and peers. It was found that almost all participants in each age group judged deception of parents to be acceptable for the moral activities. In weighing honesty against unfairness and harm, honesty was given less priority. Similarly, the majority judged deception acceptable for the personal activities. In these cases, priority was given to perceived legitimate personal choices in the context of unequal relationships of power. However, the majority of adolescents judged deception of parents unacceptable for the prudential acts because they accepted the legitimacy of parental authority in directing such acts (but not in directing the moral and personal acts). It was also found that deception of peers in the moral and personal domains was judged to be less legitimate than deception of parents. In relationships of equality and mutuality, honesty was given greater priority than in relationships of inequality. The study also showed that the adolescents judged dishonesty to be wrong in the abstract and in situations where it was used to cover up misdeeds and for self-serving purposes.

Another study yielded analogous results with older people in the context of marital relationships (Turiel, Perkins, & Mensing, 2009). College undergraduates and older married adults (35–55 years of age) made judgments about deception in marital relationships involving inequalities. Participants were presented with hypothetical situations in which a spouse objects to the other spouse's activities, and the other spouse continues the activities and lies about it. Two conditions were used: one in which a husband works outside the home and the wife does not, and a second in which the wife works outside the home and the husband does not. Nonworking spouses were depicted as engaging in deception with regard to four activities: attending meetings of Alcoholics Anonymous for a drinking problem, which involves issues of physical and psychological welfare; maintaining a secret bank account, involving issues of financial welfare; shopping for goods; and seeing a friend (the last two involving personal choices). In this study as well, findings varied by the type of activity. Almost all in each age group judged deception to attend meetings of Alcoholics Anonymous acceptable, thus giving priority to welfare over honesty. The majority also accepted deception with regard to the secret bank account and seeing a friend, but they were more likely to accept deception on the part of a wife (whether working or not) than a husband. It appears, therefore, that honesty is coordinated not only with inequalities in the family, but also with power relations in the general structure of society.

Both studies revealed some age-related differences. In the study on judgments of the deception of parents, the older adolescents (16–17 years) were more likely to judge deception for the personal and prudential domains to be acceptable than the younger ones. However, these findings do not necessarily mean there is a developmental shift in ways of coordinating honesty with personal and prudential issues. In the study of judgments of deception in marital relationships, it was found that in some situations, the older and married adults were more likely to judge deception acceptable than the younger adults (i.e., the undergraduates). Therefore, there is not a linear increase with age in acceptance (or rejection) of deception when the activities and relationships differ. In some situations and relationships, the undergraduates gave greater weight to honesty than personal choices than the 16- to 17-year-olds in other situations and relationships.

The problem of how to coordinate honesty and the protection or promotion of welfare is faced by adolescents and adults (and even by children when they lie to spare the feelings of others). Variations in judgments about honesty and welfare by situational contexts were demonstrated in another study with adults (Freeman, Rathore, Weinfurt, Schulman, & Sulmasy, 1999). In that study, female and male physicians (mean age, 42 years) made judgments about hypothetical stories that depicted doctors who consider deceiving an insurance company as the only means to obtain approval for a treatment or diagnostic procedure for a patient. The stories depicted medical conditions of different degrees of severity. In the two most severe conditions (life-threatening ones), the majority thought that the doctor was justified in engaging in deception. In other conditions, the percentages accepting deception were considerably lower, with the fewest (only 3%) judging that deception was legitimate for purposes of cosmetic surgery. Whereas we can assume that, in the abstract, the physicians would judge honesty to be good and dishonesty wrong, many judged deception acceptable in some situations as a means of helping assure the physical well-being of their patients.

The issue of the coordination of different considerations, of course, is not restricted to honesty. The concept of rights provides another example. For many years there have been

debates over whether most American adults have adequate understandings of rights. One source for these debates is the findings of several large-scale public opinion surveys of adult Americans from 18 to 60 years of age showing that they endorse rights in some situations and do not in other situations (Hyman & Sheatsley, 1953; McClosky & Brill, 1983; Stouffer, 1955). To some philosophers, psychologists, and political scientists (e.g., Protho & Grigg, 1960; Sarat, 1975), the findings mean that most Americans do not adequately understand or apply the concept of rights. In their view, an adequate understanding of rights would result in consistently upholding rights across situations.

However, some philosophers have put forth the alternative view that rights constitute one type of moral norm that, even when well understood, is weighed and balanced against other competing moral and social norms in particular situations (Dworkin, 1977; Gewirth, 1982). Adequate understandings of rights can lead to sometimes subordinating rights to other goals. For example, a right to free speech may be judged in relation to the harm to persons' physical welfare that might result from its exercise (Helwig, 1995a). Along those lines, the findings from the public opinion surveys can be interpreted to mean that individuals, though endorsing rights in the abstract, will evaluate the application of rights and freedoms in comparison with other moral and social goals (Turiel, Killen, & Helwig, 1987). In coordinating different considerations, individuals sometimes uphold rights and at other times subordinate rights toward the goals of preventing harm or promoting community interests.

Developmental and cultural research has examined the judgments children, adolescents, and adults make about rights (Helwig, 1995b, 1997; Turiel & Wainryb, 1998). These studies have included children and adolescents (from 7–17 years), as well as adults ranging in age from 34 to 70 years. It was found that at all ages, rights pertaining to such matters as freedom of speech and religion were upheld in the abstract, regarded as an obligatory norm in that they were judged to generalize across groups or cultures, and seen as serving needs for self-expression and autonomy. As found in the surveys, in some contexts, rights were subordinated to preventing psychological harm (e.g., a public speech with racial slurs), physical harm (a speech advocating violence), and inequality (advocating exclusion). At all the ages studied, individuals took into account the different considerations posed in a given situation and drew priorities between conflicting norms or goals. The coordination of judgments between different domains or between different judgments in a domain (e.g., rights and preventing physical harm) involves making choices about competing claims.

One more example comes from a series of studies with children and adolescents on social exclusion, as related to prejudice and discrimination (Killen, Lee-Kim, McGothlin, & Stagnor, 2002). The methods and findings are analogous to those in the research on deception and rights. Children do judge exclusion based on sex, race, or ethnicity to be morally wrong in the abstract and in particular situations. For instance, children and young adolescents judged that it is wrong to exclude a child from a group activity solely on the basis of sex or race (Killen & Stagnor, 2001). In that study, children judged it wrong to exclude someone from group activities like a ballet group or a baseball club because they are male or female, and used reasons of fairness and equality to justify their judgments. Similarly, excluding a European American child from a basketball club or an African American child from a math club was judged wrong for reasons of fairness and equality. However, when asked about choosing between less and more qualified children on sex lines or by race for a competitive activity, they were more likely to accept exclusion on the basis of sex or race. Therefore, children do consider the goals of group activities, such as in team competitions, in judging acts of exclusion. Group goals, efficiency of group functioning, and individual prerogatives are coordinated with moral considerations in coming to conclusions about the validity of excluding people from activities (see also Killen, Sinno, & Margie, 2007).

Process of Coordinating Different Components May or May Not Result in Errors

A great deal more research is needed to better understand processes of coordination, including research to understand when and why a given concept (e.g., trust, rights, inclusion) is or is not given priority over another moral or social concept. The research I have discussed, however, provides ample evidence that at different ages (7–70 years), people do recognize different components in moral and social situations, and do weigh and try to balance different considerations. There are bodies of research on heuristics, intuitions, and emotions that, in my view, fail to recognize that there are coordinations going on in decision making, and thereby come to erroneous conclusions about shortcomings in human cognition.

Research on heuristics is an example of a form of reductionism. Here, thought, rational processes, and reflection are reduced to more simple strategies, in the form of

heuristics, biases, and the influences of framing—all of which actors are largely unaware. Often, the starting point for heuristic work emerges from long-held assumptions in economics and psychology that rational decisions involve maximizing interests through considerations of risks and benefits (Tversky & Kahneman, 1983). Decisions that do not appear to maximize benefits through such considerations are defined within this perspective as nonrational.

The validity of this line of reasoning rests on the definition of rationality in economic decisions—a definition that reduces rationality to self-interest and to one type of self interest at that. Implicitly, it is assumed that if individuals acted rationally, then maximizing gains in economically related situations will prevail over all other considerations. However, if we recognize that although maximizing self-interest may be a goal, people are capable of maintaining a variety of goals at any one time, then it becomes apparent that it is simply incorrect to evaluate as nonrational decisions that do not maximize material gains. For example, a person may hold moral beliefs about equality and respect for persons, and these may be connected to the person's conceptions of the importance of promoting justice, insuring the rights of individuals, and maintaining the welfare of self and others. These moral ideas and goals may well involve reasoning and understandings about how one wants social interactions to proceed (Rawls, 1971). In this case, decision making involves weighing and balancing moral and personal considerations (including self-interest), as well as other social and prudential considerations.

A second assumption made in research on heuristics is that rational decisions require the understandings of probabilities and predictions of outcomes, but people often act irrationally and use simple strategies in the form of misleading heuristics (Kahneman, Slovic, & Tversky, 1982). It is important here, however, to distinguish between errors and the employment of modes of thinking that entail careful scrutiny and deeper processes of thought. This distinction was central to Piaget's theorizing about cognitive development (Piaget & Inhelder, 1969). Starting with a critique of standardized tests of intelligence, which assess only whether answers were correct or incorrect, Piaget argued that the appropriate study of thought or intelligence required analyses of how the answers were derived. As an example, incorrect answers to conservation tasks were examined by Piaget for the types of thinking leading to those answers. Children's conclusions that amounts of quantity are not conserved after pouring a liquid into a different shaped container were analyzed to explain the cognitive operations (in the form of preoperational thought) involved, as were correct answers that the amount is conserved (in the form of concrete operations).

The research on heuristics begins with tasks or problems that have a correct answer based on probabilities and predictions of outcomes, and draws a contrast between, on the one hand, the application of adequate understandings of probabilities and, on the other hand, heuristics resulting in incorrect answers. In this research, respondents are often asked for predictions of a future outcome or estimations of the likelihood that persons described in particular ways fit a category (e.g., a political affiliation or occupation). I present two examples from the work of Tversky and Kahneman (1983) to illustrate the approach and how decisions evaluated as the irrational substituting of heuristics for rational thought may, in fact, be a matter of the participants actually using deeper cognitive processes. In one example, respondents were presented with a sketch of a woman (Linda) along with potential occupations and avocations. The sketch is as follows (from Tversky & Khaneman):

> Linda is 31 years old, single, outspoken and very bright. She majored in philosophy. As a student, she was deeply concerned with issues of discrimination and social justice, and also participated in anti-nuclear demonstrations. (p. 297)

The presented list of potential occupations/avocations included:

Linda is active in the feminist movement. (designated F for feminist)

Linda is a bank teller. (T for teller)

Linda is a bank teller and is active in the feminist movement. (T & F)

The participants' task was to rank Linda's most probable vocation/avocation. Results demonstrated that the large majority ranked as more probable that Linda is a bank teller and active in the feminist movement (the conjunction of T & F) than that she is a bank teller (T). From the viewpoint of rational probabilistic thinking, this is in error because it is a violation of what Tversky and Kahneman (1983) refer to as the conjunction rule (that the likelihood of both occurring is less than one of the elements). This finding was interpreted to mean that a heuristic had been used and, thus, intuition rather than rational logic was at work.

Certainly this research demonstrates that errors (such as violations of the conjunction rule) can occur in judgments that demand probability assessments. It is also quite possible that probabilistic thought may develop both through experience without formal training, and through formal training designed to acquire specialized knowledge in a domain. However, none of this means that heuristics were, in fact, used in the case of Linda or in similar cases. What is missing in tasks of this sort are analyses of how participants may be thinking about the problem at deeper levels and more extensively than that entailed by mere heuristics.

In the Linda occupation task, the introduction of a biographical (psychological) sketch opens the possibility that participants were reasoning, not merely about probabilities, but about the psychology of choices of occupations/avocations. It is not unreasonable to suspect that participants may have been drawing the psychological inference that a 31-year-old bright woman with an education in philosophy and interests in social justice would not feel satisfied or fulfilled as a bank teller, and might be highly motivated to engage in political activism of one kind or another. If it were, in fact, the case that the participants reasoned in this fashion, then—regardless of accuracy in terms of probabilities—the participants were engaging in complex reasoning about psychological functioning. By contrast, the researchers presumed that respondents were not approaching the situation with complex reasoning regarding psychological processes but by simpler intuitions or heuristics. Indeed, in conditions that identified Linda only as a "31-year-old woman," the large majority thought it was less likely that she would be a bank teller and active feminist than a bank teller.

A second study by Tversky and Kahneman (1983, p. 307) further illustrates how decisions involving probability judgments can include other inferential considerations. The study was conducted in 1982, with professional forecasters as participants. The participants were asked to evaluate the probability of the following two forecasts: (1) a complete suspension of diplomatic relations between the United States and the Soviet Union, sometime in 1983; and (2) a Russian invasion of Poland, and a complete suspension of diplomatic relations between the United States and the Soviet Union, sometime in 1983. The conjunction of invasion and suspension of relations in (2) is less likely than suspension of relations in (1), as the suspension in (1) might have happened for a variety of reasons. Consistent with the previous example, participants' estimates of probability were higher for the incorrect depiction that included both invasion of Poland and suspension of diplomatic relations. It is possible that the participants acted nonrationally by not choosing the most probable outcome. However, it is also likely that the participants were seeking a plausible cause to suspension of diplomatic relations to make sense of the situation. Therefore, suspension of diplomatic relations because of an invasion of Poland was seen as more plausible than suspension for no given reason. Again, the issue is not whether the reasoning results in error, but whether the error is the result of a misapplied heuristic or the result of a complex process of reasoning.

Heuristic concepts have also been applied to the moral realm. Sunstein (2004) has argued that people sometimes use moral heuristics, which involve generalizing moral intuitions and rules of thumb (which may often work well) from one context to a superficially similar context. An issue used by Sunstein to illustrate how everyday morality consists of "simple rules" is that of lying. In Sunstein's view, the rule it is wrong to lie is a "heuristic" that does not work to moral effectiveness when a lie would save a human life. We have already seen that the evidence does not support this view of honesty and deception. Most individuals say lying is acceptable under many circumstances, including situations in which perceived benefits are to prevent harm and promote fairness. The studies discussed earlier showed that adults and adolescents accept that a lie is not wrong when it is aimed at preventing harm, promoting the welfare of others, preventing injustices, and preserving their realms of personal choice (Freeman et al., 1999; Perkins & Turiel, 2007). The research demonstrates that "it is wrong to lie" is far from a heuristic or a rule of thumb for most people, because they make nuanced judgments about circumstances in which lying is acceptable and circumstances in which it is not. Parallel findings were obtained, as already discussed, regarding another issue treated as a heuristic by Sunstein: the endorsement of freedom of speech as absolute. As with honesty, rights such as freedom of speech are not treated as absolute but are subordinated to other social and moral considerations in a variety of situations.

Thought as Rationalization and Not as a Way of Understanding

The work on heuristics fails to account for the various aspects of thinking that are brought to bear on tasks that involve elements of probabilistic thinking and predictions of outcomes. Predicting outcomes is generally not taken lightly, and when predicting human actions and choices, people think about the various factors that may be involved, including human psychology. Explaining decisions through heuristics is essentially a simplification of

thought to a set of strategies or, in Sunstein's terms, rules of thumb. Another general approach to morality that also reduces decision making to simple reactions claims that moral decisions are based primarily on intuitions, emotions, and nonconscious brain processes. Work done by Haidt (2001) is an example of this line of thought. From Haidt's perspective, emotions are the primary sources of morality. The claim is that emotions are manifested through intuitions about right and wrong that people maintain without being able to explain why that is the case (it is just so in their minds). Further, reasoning, reflection, and mental scrutiny are claimed to be unusual types of epiphenomena of rationalization in that they have little to do with the moral decisions people come to, and a great deal to do with after-the-fact explanations to oneself and to persuade others of what one believes in the first place.

Illusions, cognitive blindness (Haidt refers to it as "moral dumbfounding"), and the use of reason to rationalize loom large in these claims. We know not what we do and we know not why we think what we think! These are all part and parcel of Haidt's (2001) argument that morality is based on intuitions that are intertwined with emotional reactions. Immediate and reflexive reactions such as revulsion, disgust, and sympathy are claimed to trigger the response that the act is wrong without reasoning playing any substantive role. For Haidt, a key defining feature of moral intuitions is that they occur rapidly, without effort, and automatically. They are also assumed to occur without intentionality and without the use of evidence. Haidt further argues that intuitions themselves are explained by evolutionary adaptations shaped by culture.

In this perspective, reasoning, in contrast with intuitions, is slow and requires effort. Whereas moral evaluations and decisions are intuitive, moral reasoning occurs after the fact to justify to self and others why an act is wrong: "...when faced with a social demand for a verbal justification one becomes a lawyer building a case rather than a judge searching for the truth" (Haidt, 2001, p. 814). Moral reasoning is also used to persuade and to rationalize. Through the use of reasoning and steps of hypothesis testing, "people can maintain an illusion of objectivity about the way they think" (Haidt, p. 823).

There are at least five ways in which Haidt's arguments are flawed by limited evidence and inadequate interpretation. First, most of the evidence cited comes from nonmoral realms. This limited evidence is drawn primarily from social psychology studies, which appear to support the idea that people are biased, emotive, intuitive, and unconcerned with evidence. The second flaw with respect to evidence is that no account is taken of large bodies of research from developmental and cognitive psychology, including research on morality, which demonstrates that people make judgments that are not necessarily immediate, rapid, and categorical, and that such judgments can be intentional, deliberative, and reflective. The same research also shows that such reasoning can be applied in an immediate and rapid fashion (Kohlberg, 1969; Nucci, 2001; Piaget & Inhelder, 1969; Turiel, 1998). As examples, conceptualizations of number and arithmetic may be acquired laboriously over time but, once acquired, are applied rapidly. As another example, a large body of research shows that a good deal of cognitive work occurs from ages 3 to 5 years in the formation of understandings of others' minds (see Carpendale & Lewis, Chapter 17 of this volume, and Chandler & Birch, Chapter 19 of this volume, for an extended discussion of the development of a child's "theory of mind"). Once those understandings are formed, however, children use them in an immediate, rapid fashion. That a concept is used rapidly does not mean that it does not involve complex processes of reasoning.

The third flaw in Haidt's work lies in its failure to account for research findings that support other perspectives. It fails to account for the body of work described earlier on domain distinctions, coordination, and evaluations of acts like deception that involve violations of moral precepts for moral ends. The configuration of judgments within the moral, social, and personal domains, and their manifestations in coordinations provide evidence that people's moral judgments are much more complex and go deeper than the entire idea of intuition.

Research within the domain perspective has demonstrated that judgments about acts such as inflicting harm, which may appear on the surface to fit the interpretation of being unreflective and immediate, in fact, involve complex judgments and discriminations. Although children rapidly judge many acts of physical harm as wrong, they are also readily able to articulate reasons, especially that it is not good to inflict pain, and that people do not like to feel the experience of pain. In addition, children distinguish between acts of physical harm that are wrong in some circumstances (e.g., unprovoked acts of hitting) and acts of harm that are justified in other circumstances (e.g., in retaliation for provocations; see Astor, 1994). Children and adults also take intentions into account and, thereby, distinguish between spanking of a child by a father and a father who hits a child for other reasons (Wainryb, 1991).

A fourth flaw in Haidt's work is that no evidence is presented that moral reasoning (such as in understandings of welfare, justice, and rights) is used instrumentally only after decisions are reached and as a means of either justifying the decision to oneself. The unsubstantiated and reductionistic assertion that reasoning is used after the fact entails not only a deprecation of human thinking but also a misconstrual of what lawyers do in attempting to convince a jury. Sometimes lawyers believe in the case of the accused and argue about evidence to achieve justice. Sometimes lawyers may not know or be uncertain about the innocence or guilt of a client but will argue the case on the understood and generally agreed-on principle that the justice system requires due process and legal representation. People, regardless of whether they are lawyers, have much more complex and nuanced moral and legal understandings than is attributed to them in the intertwined propositions of intuition and post hoc rationalization.

The fifth flaw in Haidt's argument concerns the use of a combination of illustrative examples of an anecdotal nature and research evidence from isolated examples of supposedly moral items. Both types—anecdotal and research based—are not representative of the myriad moral issues that have been and could be investigated (including many of the issues in studies discussed earlier). The salient moral issues that confront people are generally quite familiar. They include physical assault, rape, killing, psychological and emotional harm, theft, violations of human rights, racial prejudice, inequalities in relationships, inequalities in the distribution of resources, inequalities based on sex and social class in cultural practices, poverty, genocide, peace and war, and many more. With all these issues as potential targets of research, two main issues used by Haidt in his analyses are incest and eating dog meat (Haidt, Koller, & Dias, 1993). Incest is treated as a prototypical moral issue—an issue that could be viewed as shared among members of culture, yet applicable across cultures, and as having come about through evolution. Incest is presumably prototypical because it is a type of act that even when specified as consensual and even when there is no risk for pregnancy, people react immediately with a gut reaction that it is wrong but are unable to explain why. It is proposed that because these types of issues evoke (supposedly) rapid emotional and unexplainable reactions, all of morality functions this way. The generalized interpretations drawn from such a limited and inadequate set of examples flies in the face of our notions of scientific validity. Moreover, empirical tests of Haidt's propositions regarding people's reactions to issues like incest have not confirmed them (Royzman, Leeman, & Baron, 2009).

Thought as Nonthought: Brain Processes, Emotions, and Determinism

The intuitionist position provides a contemporary example of the psychologizing of morality, with an emphasis on virtues "held to be obligatory by a culture or subculture" (Haidt, 2001, p. 917). In spite of this reliance on culture for the source of an individual's moral evaluations, it has been argued that the intuitionist position is compatible with contemporary neuroscience research, which places much more emphasis on biology than culture. In keeping with the spirit of E. O. Wilson's call for biologizing morality, a number of neuroscience researchers have taken an empiricist reductionistic approach and dismissed philosophical conceptual analyses. For example, Greene (2007) argued:

> As an empiricist, I believe that we can study things like life without defining them....This strategy, I believe, works just as well for the aspect of life that we call 'morality.' For empiricists, rigorously defining morality is a distant goal, not a prerequisite. If anything, I believe that defining morality at this point is more of a hindrance than help, as it may artificially narrow the scope of inquiry....Rather than seeking out morality by the light of a philosopher's definition (Kantian or otherwise), I and like-minded scientists choose to study decisions that ordinary people regard as involving moral judgment.

This neuroscientist's argument that reasoning constitutes after-the-fact rationalization is quite clearly compatible with the intuitionist perspective. The neuroscientist's justification for this position lies in the proposition that decisions are determined by subconscious brain functions, and decisions or responses are made before conscious awareness (Wegner, 2002). In this regard, Koenigs et al. (2007) contrast their neuroscience position with "traditional rationalist approaches to moral cognition that emphasize the role of conscious reasoning from explicit principles" (p. 908).

In an empiricist fashion, some neuroscience investigators have focused mainly on tasks presented to participants, emphasizing problems entailing life and death. For example, in several studies, research participants are presented with what are labeled "trolley car bystander" and "trolley car footbridge" scenarios (Cushman et al., 2006; Greene, et al., 2001; Koenigs et al., 2007). These scenarios

involve utilitarian calculations about saving more or fewer lives. The trolley car bystander scenario depicts a runaway trolley that will kill five people unless a bystander throws a switch that will prevent killing the five but would kill one person instead. In the trolley car footbridge scenario, the actor has to decide whether to push a man in front of the train to save the five, but which would result in the death of the man pushed. Research participants are asked if it is all right or permissible to throw the switch and push the man. Both scenarios are characterized as involving utilitarian calculations as to whether it is best to save five lives by sacrificing one life.

Studies have shown that most participants judge it acceptable to throw the switch to save five people, whereas most state it is not permissible to push a man even though that act would save the same number of people (Cushman et al., 2006; Greene et al., 2001). This finding forms the basis for the claim that the critical difference between the scenarios is that the footbridge version evokes emotions more than the bystander version, and that it is this difference in emotions that accounts for the difference in responses. The finding also forms the basis for the argument that many moral decisions are nonrational, intuitive, and determined by unconscious processes. As evidence for this argument, the authors point to research demonstrating that differential areas of the brain associated with rationality and emotions are activated in the two scenarios.

There are several reasons to question the interpretations drawn from the findings of these studies (Killen & Smetana, 2007; Miller, 2008; Turiel, 2009). First, both scenarios are complicated with regard to the value of life because participants are essentially posed with the problem of whether it is permissible for them to act as *executioners* by choosing whom to save and whom to sacrifice (see Turiel, 2009, for an extended discussion). The trolley car scenarios pose particular types of emotionally laden problems with multiple considerations that are difficult to reconcile without violating serious moral precepts to achieve serious moral goals. These scenarios are complex and emotionally laden because a strongly held value—the value and perceived sacredness of life—must be violated to preserve that very value. These situations are highly unusual and pose dilemmas because people are forced to repudiate morality with morality.

Another problem lies in the idea that because the footbridge scenario evokes emotions greater than the bystander scenario, the differences in decisions are accounted for by emotions. The intensity of the emotions in the footbridge scenario is not the sole difference between the two.

Although the footbridge problem is likely to evoke more intense emotions, the two situations are not otherwise the same. If we do not split emotions from judgments, then it is likely that people also make judgments about the act of physically pushing someone to his death. The footbridge scenario constitutes a different context of evaluation from the bystander scenario because in addition to the dilemma of saving lives by repudiating the prohibition on taking lives embedded in the bystander scenario, the footbridge scenario entails judgments and emotions about actively and physically causing another's death. The footbridge scenario includes the component of what might be interpreted as inflicting physical assault on another person, and thereby directly causing his death. This is to say that rationality does not solely entail utilitarian calculations in these situations, that judgments are made about the fundamental conflict in values in the situations, that judgments are made about the means used to achieve ends, and that people do take into account the different features of social situations and attempt to coordinate different types of judgments relevant to those features.

To a greater extent than the bystander scenario, the footbridge scenario presents a compounded problem involving the saving of lives, taking a life, the natural course of events, the responsibility of individuals altering natural courses, and causing someone's death in a direct way. The emotions and coordination of judgments involved are more complex in one than the other. The diversity of features embedded in social situations can be even more complex, as is evident in another scenario in which it is stated that a doctor can save five patients who are dying from organ failure by cutting up and killing a sixth healthy patient to use his organs for the others. Few judge it permissible for the doctor to use a healthy patient's organs to save five others (Greene et al., 2001). Although this scenario also includes the five versus one calculation, it also raises issues about a doctor's duties and responsibilities, the power granted to individuals to make life-and-death decisions, the legal system, and societal roles and arrangements.

It is likely that the bystander scenario also evokes strong emotions, even if not as strong as the footbridge scenario. The emotions involved in responding to that scenario have not been discussed in reports of the research. The impression given is that the bystander scenario does not activate parts of the brain presumably associated with emotions. If so, such findings would serve to question the validity of the functional magnetic resonance imaging findings because emotions associated with the trolley car scenario are undetected. A good deal may be undetected by functional magnetic resonance images because, according to some neuroscientists, a particular brain region is associated with more than one cognitive process, or emotional state, or behavioral response (Miller, 2008).

The differences among the scenarios used in the described neuroscience studies seem to be designed to confound people by presenting significantly different features in the guise of similar features (i.e., the utilitarian calculation). However, these scenarios constitute what philosophers call extreme, hard cases (Walzer, 2007). Such cases entail exceptions to rules and principles; therefore, judgments in these situations cannot simply be generalized to most moral decisions. Consequently, the trolley car situations are inadequate starting points for psychological analyses of people's moral decision making. These types of situations might be useful for the study of moral decisions in complex and extreme situations with a solid background of data and theory on people's judgments and decisions regarding more straightforward situations. Although that background is available, the described neuroscience research has ignored it and made inappropriate generalizations to morality in general. What are taken to be seeming inconsistencies in responses to the presumably similar (i.e., involving utilitarian calculations) situations have been used to assert that morality is due to evolutionarily determined, emotionally based intuitions, and that reasoning is rationalization for subconscious decisions.

The described intuitionist and neuroscience approaches to morality, with their emphasis on emotions and brain processes, and marginalization of rationality, fail to present a holistic, integrative systems perspective on biology, thought, emotions, and actions. Instead, they provide mechanistic causal explanations. At least one prominent neuroscientist, who has written about morality, has been more attentive to the need to integrate biological processes, thought, emotions, feelings, and actions. Damasio (1994, 2003) has argued for the study of the embodied mind: "I suggested that feelings are a powerful influence on reason, that the brain systems required by the former are enmeshed in those needed by the latter, and that such specific systems are interwoven with those that regulate the body" (Damasio, 2003, p. 245). Damasio takes a relational systems approach in arguing against the split-off reductionistic perspective that reasoning is less important than feelings or that thought is driven by emotions, whereas arguing for the holistic perspective that reasoning and moral judgments cannot be separated, except for analytic purposes, from emotions and feelings that involve physical pain and other emotional upheavals.

An important task within the moral domain is to determine the nature of various relations between emotions and reasoning. This task requires clear-cut and adequate definitions of morality, and conceptions of reasoning and emotions that are relevant to morality. Damasio, himself, approaches reasoning in a broad fashion, without differentiating alternatives, and approaches morality in the same general way, without a clear or detailed conceptual analysis. As a consequence, Damasio's work can provide only broad hints as to what a fully integrative relational developmental systems approach to morality will look like. It will certainly be one that entails an integrative perspective on the biological, the personal, the social, the brain, the mind (including thought and emotions), and the environmental contexts.

ANOTHER WAY OF THINKING ABOUT EMOTIONS AND THINKING

In the domain perspective on moral and social development presented in this chapter, it is important that the emotions associated with moral judgments be clearly specified and clearly differentiated from those associated with other types of social judgments. Research addressing this issue has demonstrated that children attribute positive emotions to actors, recipients, and observers in connection with positive actions, such as helping and sharing (Arsenio, 1998; Arsenio & Fliess, 1996; Arsenio & Ford, 1985). With respect to moral transgressions, children attribute hurt feelings to recipients of the acts, and mixed positive and negative emotions to instigators of the acts (see Wainryb et al., 2005). By contrast, the emotions attributed to transgressors in the conventional domain are attributed neutral emotions or feelings of sadness.

Another important task is to identify emotions that may be central organizing features of moral orientations (Turiel & Killen, 2010). Philosophical analyses, as well as a limited amount of psychological research, suggest that two general sentiments—the sanctity of life and respect for persons—are, in fact, such organizing features. In the previous section, the point was made that the neuroscience trolley car problems are emotionally laden and conceptually difficult because the strongly held value of the sacredness of life must be violated to preserve the value of life. It is safe to say that people everywhere are concerned in one way or another with preserving lives, act to save lives when they can, make strong judgments about the loss of life, and experience intense emotions like grief at the loss

of a loved one. The dynamics of the issue of life are complicated because people do take lives in war and for reasons of self-defense, and it is one of the condoned ways, through capital punishment, of responding to murder. It is largely unheard of that nations do not have laws about killing.

Although the issue of the sacredness of life is largely unexamined in psychological research, it is a topic some philosophers have pondered. A particularly informative analysis was provided by Dworkin (1993), who maintained that the intrinsic value of life includes the strong emotional-conceptual sense of the sacredness or inviolability of life. Dworkin's treatise was aimed at demonstrating that the sacredness of life is central to debates about abortion and euthanasia, but it was also intended to provide a general formulation of "a fundamental idea that almost all share in some form: that the individual human life is sacred" (Dworkin, 1993, p. 13).

Although a sharp division exists among people concerning whether abortion and euthanasia are right or wrong, Dworkin (1993) argued that, to understand the differences between "liberal" (pro-choice; abortion is generally acceptable) and "conservative" (pro-life; abortion is generally unacceptable) positions, it is necessary to go beyond the public utterances and to account for their common views that life is sacred and inviolable (the term *sacred* has religious connotations and the term *inviolable* has secular connotations). The idea, associated with pro-life positions, that the fetus is a human being at conception is ambiguous, as reflected in the exceptions that many taking a pro-life position make (e.g., acceptability of abortion to save the mother's life or in cases of rape and incest). Fundamental in pro-life positions is that life has intrinsic value, is sacred in itself, and that the sacred nature of life begins when biological life begins. These views do not presuppose any particular rights or interests for the fetus. Abortion is seen as wrong because it disregards the intrinsic value of any stage or form of human life. Similarly, euthanasia and suicide are seen as wrong because taking the life of a person in a vegetative state or in great pain and nearing death violates the sanctity of life—even if it would be in the person's interests not to continue living.

Although for some there may be religious underpinnings to the sense of the sacredness of life, it is also a secular view (in the form that life is inviolable). The sense of sacredness or inviolability of life is also maintained by those who are accepting of abortion and euthanasia. In Dworkin's view, those who take a pro-choice stance on abortion nevertheless almost always regard it as a "grave decision" because it does mean the extinction of human life already begun. There are many reasons for abortion that those maintaining a pro-choice position would not consider legitimate, such as to take a long-awaited trip, or a preference for a more comfortable time to be pregnant, or choice of the sex of the child (Dworkin, 1993).

In the context of viewing life as having intrinsic moral significance, for some people, abortion is acceptable when other serious life issues are involved. Pro-choice people regard abortion to be morally justified when issues of lives are in conflict, such as to save the life of the mother or in cases of known serious fetal abnormalities. For most people holding a liberal view, abortion entails a conflict between the inviolability of life and when "the consequences of childbirth would be permanent and grave for her or her family's life" (Dworkin, 1993, p. 33). The quality of lives is implicated in these types of conflict, as it is for decisions about euthanasia.

Dworkin's purpose in illuminating the nature of debates about abortion and euthanasia, even in the context of differences about their permissibility, was to demonstrate the force of the sacredness and inviolability of life. It becomes clear that most people hold to the sanctity and inviolability of life when we consider their common positions on the taking of life immediately after birth (or late in pregnancy). There are no debates over whether it is acceptable to take an infant's life after birth with regard to any of the reasons or justifications (or any others) evident in the controversies over abortion (Turiel, Hildebrandt, & Wainryb, 1991). As discussed elsewhere (Turiel & Killen, 2010), research into moral judgments needs to better account for people's sense that lives have intrinsic value and how the sentiment develops. This should be viewed as a general sentiment because people feel highly emotional about maintaining their own lives, the lives of close others (family, friends, etc.), and in a general way, human life (including those one does not know).

A related general sentiment that was part of developmental analysis in Piaget's (1932) research on moral judgments is respect for persons. For Piaget, respect for persons in relationships of mutuality and reciprocity is essential for moral concepts of equality and justice. An autonomous morality of mutual respect includes concerns with justice and fairness in serving the needs of persons and adjudicating competing interests. It may well be that the sentiment of respect for persons is intertwined with the sentiment of the sacredness of life.

Both the sentiments of the sanctity of life and respect for persons are likely to be related to emotions and judg-

ments pertaining to harm that develop in early childhood (Turiel, 2006; Turiel & Killen, 2010). Many studies have shown that children judge hitting to be morally wrong. Children perceive the negative effects of pain in self and others, but the primary emotions associated with their moral judgments are positive ones of sympathy, empathy, and caring for others. Part of those judgments is the sense of respect for the dignity of persons and their emotional states. Emotions, therefore, are not simply distinct from judgments; they do not in themselves, most of the time, motivate or drive judgments or actions. Emotions involve evaluative appraisals such that they are guided by ways of judging social relationships, can be part of people's aims, purposes, and goals in life, as well as their understandings of other people and events (Nussbaum, 1999, 2001).

I can illustrate the nature and components of emotions as evaluative appraisals through an analysis provided by Nussbaum (2001) of her own experiences of grief. Clearly, grief is an emotion associated with the sentiment of the value of life. Nussbaum's analysis is that "emotions always involve thought of an object combined with the thought of the object's salience or importance" (Nussbaum, 2001, p. 23). As she relates it, Nussbaum was in Dublin to give a lecture while her mother was recovering well in a Philadelphia hospital after routine surgery. While in Dublin, Nussbaum learned that her mother had suddenly experienced life-threatening complications. She flew back as soon as possible with fear about her mother's fate and hope that she would be well. However, her mother died before she arrived at the hospital. The fear and hope experienced while flying to Philadelphia, which were based on an awareness of the danger faced by a person very important to her, then turned to intense grief. Like the fear and hope, the grief was a complex emotion based on the perceived importance of the mother in the daughter's life—a person who was now forever unavailable.

The complexity of the intense feelings of grief is connected to the importance invested in persons, in parents, and in the particular person lost. A certain amount of sadness is felt for the loss of a person, especially a person one knows, because of the intrinsic worth of human beings. In addition, the loss of any mother adds a dimension of sadness and loss because of the recognition that most people cherish (or should be able to) their mothers. These general features of feelings are intensified to strong grief because of the personal connection. As is often the case with mothers, she constituted an important aspect of Nussbaum's relationships, and life goals and plans. This is neither selfish nor egoistic, but an important aspect of her personal sphere of life, and her understandings of relationships, a valued person, and significant life activities and goals. Appraisals and understandings of the person who died, the role of the person in one's life, and perceptions of what the loss means and life changes it brings are all intricately connected to the intense emotion of grief she felt because of her mother's death. This example allows for specification of the features of emotions as evaluative appraisals in that it shows how emotions involve judgments, conceptions, and perceptions of value. As Nussbaum (2001) summarized, emotions have an object (i.e., they are about something in the world); the object is intentional, in that the person experiencing the emotion perceives and interprets the object (e.g., the qualities of the person and the loss of the person); and they are connected to complex beliefs about the person.

Much of the emotion associated with grief at the death of one's parent is particularistic and personal (though it can be shared with others). The emotions associated with moral judgments, which can be generalized and impartial, do not necessarily have these personal features. Nevertheless, emotions as evaluative appraisals are associated with moral judgments. Moral judgments pertaining to harm or welfare, fairness or justice, and equality or rights include emotional appraisals and are not mainly related to negative emotions such as fear, anxiety, disgust, and guilt. As noted earlier, emotions associated with harm do involve attention to pain and hurt, but importantly stem from sympathy, empathy, affection, and respect.

ALL IS NOT JUST ACCEPTED: OPPOSITION AND MORAL RESISTANCE

The propositions that people are reasoning beings who attempt to understand the world around them and whose emotions involve evaluative appraisals do not imply that all is well understood, that harmony is the norm, or that people do not experience ambiguities and uncertainties. Together with reasoning that includes understandings of the world come incomplete and inadequate understandings of much of social life. Explanations of morality based on brain processes, emotions, and direct learning of given standards leave little room for life's ambiguities and uncertainties because the proposed processes do not involve scrutiny of social relationships. However, as reasoning beings, people attempt to understand all this, evaluate their world positively and critically, struggle with each other, and experience conflicts and disagreements. People evaluate societal arrangements and cultural practices, and thereby oppose perceived injustices in the social system and engage in acts of moral resistance.

Earlier in this chapter, research was discussed suggesting that adolescents and adults accept the legitimacy of acts of resistance through deception in relationships of inequality. Adolescent relationships with parents are seen as involving inequalities in the power and control parents can exert (Perkins & Turiel, 2007). The findings of that study showed that adolescents believe it is appropriate to resist certain directives coming from parents through covert acts—that is, continuing the activity and keeping it from parents with the use of deception. Deception with regard to activities in the moral and personal domains was judged more acceptable in relationships of inequality (parents) than in relationships of equality and mutuality (peers). It is telling, with regard to the use of deception for purposes of opposition and resistance, that adolescents did not judge deception of parents to be acceptable across the board. They judged it acceptable only when parents were seen to overstep boundaries of their legitimate authority to guide adolescents' actions. Similarly, findings in the study of deception in marital relationships revealed that college undergraduates and adults in their 40s and 50s judged it acceptable to deceive a spouse regarding individual choices within relationships of imbalances in power and control, as well as to promote welfare.

I believe that these judgments about deception reflect individuals' orientations to social opposition and moral resistance for the reasons stated regarding the patterns of findings bearing on the role of inequalities and concerns with preventing harm and promoting welfare. Those studies, however, only indirectly relate to the types of social opposition and moral resistance that entail critiques of societal arrangements and cultural practices. Before discussing research directly bearing on opposition and resistance, the ubiquitous role of deception in resistance can be illustrated with some nonresearch examples.

One example stems from events in Iran during the 1990s. After the revolution of 1979, governmental and religious authorities imposed restrictions on many personal and leisure activities. These included prohibitions on watching videos, listening to music, drinking alcohol, dancing, playing cards, as well as many other activities. Many restrictions were placed on females especially on dress and the use of makeup. Several journalistic reports detailed the ways women and men secretly violated many of these restrictions in private by wearing prohibited dress, watching videos, listening to music, dancing, and drinking (see Turiel, 2002, for an extended discussion of events in Iran and other Middle East countries). An Iranian woman succinctly portrayed the role of deception in the acts of opposition in discussing covert activities (Kinzer, *The New York Times*, May 27, 1997):

> We live a double-life in this country. My children know that when their school teachers ask whether we drink at home, they have to say no. If they are asked whether we dance or play cards, they have to say no. But the fact is we do drink, dance, and play cards, and the kids know it. So they are growing up as liars and knowing that to survive in this country we have to be. That's a terrible thing, and I want to change it. (p. A4)

Another illustrative example of the use of deception comes from the recollections of Fatima Mernissi (1994) of the lives of girls and women confined to the walls of the compound of her family in the patriarchal culture of Morocco in the 1940s. One of the stories told by Mernissi involved women secretly listening to a radio they were prohibited from using while the men were not home. To make a long story short, one time the men learned from the children that the women had listened to the radio, which they could have done only by obtaining a key to the locked cabinet with the radio. Although the men were angry, every woman denied knowing how the key was obtained. In spite of the fact that each woman was asked about the key separately, they were able to hold steadfastly to their resistance to the practices maintained by the men. Moreover, the women took the children to task for revealing the secret. When the children protested that they had only told the truth, Mernissi's mother asserted, "...some things were true, indeed, but you still could not say them: you had to keep them secret. And then she added that what you say and what you keep secret has nothing to do with truth and lies" (Mernissi, 1994, p. 8).

Resistance on the part of the women, according to Mernissi (1994), was not by any means restricted to pleasurable activities like listening to the radio. The women desired freedoms and rights in many respects, and especially the freedom to venture beyond the walls of the compound. The women also desired a future for their daughters with greater freedoms and opportunities than had been available to them.

These examples reveal how deception has been used in different times (1940s and 1990s), in different places (Morocco and Iran), and in different contexts (of religious restrictions and in patriarchal cultures) as ways of combating injustices and defying rules, laws, and practices that are seen as unfairly restricting a group of people in the context of power differences and inequalities. Findings from anthropological research reveal analogous activities of opposition and resistance. In ethnographic research with Bedouin groups in villages on the northwest coast of Egypt, Abu-Lughod (1993) found a good deal of opposition and resistance in daily life among girls and young, middle, and late adult women. Acts of opposition and resistance occurred in the context of a patriarchal system in which many cultural practices are designed to allow males to control the activities of females and for males to have greater access to activities that fulfill their autonomy and achievement of personal choices and entitlements. On a day-to-day basis females must contend with restrictions—restrictions that do not apply to males on their leisure activities, education, and work. Cultural practices also involve inequalities with regard to the distribution of resources, arranged marriages, and polygamy. In contradiction with theoretical formulations in which it is assumed that a primary concern with community, interdependence, and harmony in non-Western cultures exists (Markus & Kitayama, 1991; Shweder, Much, Mahaptra, & Park, 1997), Abu-Lughod found that women do not simply accept the situation imposed by authority and embedded in cultural practices. Instead, they find ways of circumventing the commands of fathers and husbands, and the requirements of cultural practices. Often, the strategies used for these purposes involved deception. In addition, open conflicts and disagreements were frequent between males and females.

Wikan (1996) also conducted ethnographic studies in urban areas of Egypt. She studied people living in poor areas of Cairo, where men and women were in lower positions in the social hierarchy of social classes, and where women were in subordinate positions to men within the community. Wikan reports a predominance of social struggle, conflict, and disagreement in her observations of family and social life. These struggles and conflicts are multifaceted because they involve conflicts with society, as well as within the family. As in Abu-Lughod's research with the Bedouins, there are conflicts between females and males and opposition on the part of females to the restrictions imposed on them by males.

We can infer from these findings of acts of opposition and resistance that aspects of societal organization and cultural practices are judged to be unfair by those who are placed in subordinate positions of inequality. Other research has addressed this question directly in non-Western cultures. One study was conducted with Druze Arabs in northern Israel who maintain a patrilineal and patriarchal family structure in which males are in dominant positions over females, and in which many restrictions are placed on females' dress, leisure activities, educational opportunities, work, and decision making (Wainryb & Turiel, 1994). Among other issues, the study assessed judgments of adolescents and adults (ages 17–50 years) about the jurisdiction of males and females in making decisions within the family. It was found that the main decision-making power was deemed to rest with male family members. Both male and female adolescents and adults recognized that males are accorded a good deal of autonomy, freedom of choice, and personal entitlements. It is evident from this and other studies that members of the Druze community are aware of cultural expectations regarding male independence; they used terms like *freedom, self-reliance,* and *rights* to characterize the expectations regarding males. As put by an 18-year-old female (Turiel, 2002): "He is free. Even when a baby is born, people are glad if it's a boy, and less glad if it's a girl. We live in a conservative culture. Maybe in the future I might want to treat my daughter in the same way as I would treat my son, but the culture wouldn't let me do it" (p. 249).

Implicit in the 18-year-old's statement is a criticism of, or at least dissatisfaction with, the cultural orientation to the prerogatives and status of males and females. Assessments of the moral evaluations of the entitlements accorded to males in decision making in the family revealed that the large majority thought the system was unfair (Wainryb & Turiel, 1994). It should also be noted that many females recognized a need to sometimes go along with the practices because of the serious negative consequences that would befall them if they did not do so. Using a variety of methods and examining different aspects of family relationships, investigators obtained similar results in research conducted in India (Neff, 2001), Colombia (Mensing, 2002), and Benin (Conry-Murray, 2009).

The studies discussed here suggest that conflicts and disagreements are not uncommon in social relationships, and that social opposition and resistance are part of people's everyday lives. Wikan (1996) characterized the lives of people of poverty in Cairo as follows: "… these lives I depict can be read as exercises in resistance against the state, against the family, against one's marriage, against the forces of tradition or change, against neighborhoods and society—even against oneself" (pp. 6–7). Judgments about justice, rights, and concerns with the welfare of others and self produce opposition and resistance in the face of inequalities and injustices that are embedded in societal arrangements and cultural practices.

In this view, people commonly scrutinize social relationships and make positive and critical evaluations. Therefore, opposition and resistance are not solely part of social movements or organized political groups. Opposition and resistance also are not solely instigated or motivated by leaders with special attributes of character or who have attained "high levels" of moral acuity (Turiel, 2003b). Social conditions motivate people to act insofar as they evoke perceptions of injustices. This is not to say that social organizations and political movements do not influence people. For instance, organized groups of women have engaged in protests in places like India (e.g., the Self-Employed Women's Association; see Nussbaum & Glover, 1995) and Afghanistan (e.g., the Revolutionary Association of the Women of Afghanistan; see Turiel, 2003b). However, accounts of the workings of these organizations indicate that there is a reciprocal relation between individual judgments and goals, and the activities of organized groups. People do not simply join groups for the sake of joining, and people do not simply suspend their judgments because they are members of such groups. The purposes and goals of organized groups are understood and evaluated by people who make choices about their life goals, occupations, and families, and who strive to better their own lives and those of others on the basis of understandings of welfare, rights, and justice.

MORALITY IN ADULTHOOD

I have discussed a fair amount of research that included adults as participants. Some of that research is on conceptions of rights, and has illuminated especially how concepts of rights are applied. There had been a tendency to presume that understandings of rights meant that they would be applied across contexts and given priority over other moral and social considerations. Insofar as people subordinated rights to other considerations, it was thought that they did not have sufficiently developed understandings of rights (Protho & Grigg, 1960; Sarat, 1975). The survey research (e.g., McClosky & Brill, 1983) noted earlier indicated that adults who do understand rights would subordinate them to other considerations in some situations. Research with children and adolescents (Helwig, 1995a, 1995b) demonstrated that decision making about rights involves the weighing and balancing of different considerations in a process of coordination.

The importance of understanding the process of coordinating different types of considerations in social and moral decision making has been a major theme of this chapter (see also Turiel, 2008b). Another issue that needs to be analyzed from the perspective of coordination is honesty or truth telling. As we have seen, the value of honesty is often weighed against other moral goals (e.g., preventing harm) in coming to a decision whether to be honest or lie. As detailed in the previous section, deception is one of the means used for purposes of social opposition and moral resistance. The roots of social opposition and moral resistance are in childhood (Turiel, 2003b), and as we have seen, they occur in adolescence. Adolescents accept the legitimacy of deception as a form of resistance to the commands of parents who have greater power and control (Perkins & Turiel, 2007). There is also a body of research on the related topic of adolescents' use of strategies to disclose activities or keep them secrets from parents (Finkenauer, Engels, & Meeus, 2002; Kerr & Stattin, 2000; Smetana, Metzger, Gettman, & Campione-Barr, 2006).

However, work on social opposition and moral resistance has involved the activities of adults to a greater extent than children or adolescents. An example is the types of activities just discussed regarding social opposition and moral resistance. For the most part, it is adults who participate in organized social and political groups and movements. This has been the case, for instance, in the civil rights and feminist movements in the United States during the latter part of the 20th century. It is the case for the types of women's groups in non-Western cultures discussed in the previous section. It is also the case for the loosely organized acts of resistance in countries such as Iran and Afghanistan. The anthropological research (Abu-Lughod, 1993; Wikan, 1996) that focused on opposition and resistance on the part of people in subordinate positions in the social hierarchy has mainly involved adults.

It makes sense that research on rights and moral resistance would focus on adults. It is adults, much more so than children or even adolescents, who are in positions to organize and join social and political movements for the furtherance of rights. It is also adults who are better able to have the understandings needed for protests and efforts at changing cultural practices, societal organization, and close relationships.

In spite of these investigations of adults, the study of adults in the context of life-span development of morality is not extensive, and not as extensive as in childhood and adolescence. What I mean by this is that there have been few investigations of changes in moral judgments that might occur with age past adolescence. Research by Piaget (1932), Kohlberg (1969), and others has focused

mainly on children and adolescents. Kohlberg's stage formulations were examined in some research that included longitudinal analyses into adulthood (Kohlberg & Kramer, 1969). However, Kohlberg's basic proposition of a six-stage sequence was based on studies of children and adolescents. In our own work on age-related changes in moral judgments (Nucci & Turiel, 2009), we have concentrated thus far on childhood and adolescence. It is still necessary to undertake systematic studies of possible age-related changes in moral reasoning during adulthood.

PEOPLE REALLY DO THINK, PLAN, AND CHOOSE

The field of psychology has been divided as to whether human beings can do or often do what psychological researchers can do and usually do. Researchers in the field of psychology actively construct explanations of human functioning using rational processes, critical analyses, debate and argumentation, and the gathering of evidence. Some broad theorists, notably psychoanalytic and behaviorist, carefully and methodically constructed theories about how people did not or could not engage in the types of thinking, rational analyses, and consideration of evidence used by them in generating their explanations. Those broad, general theories have largely gone by the wayside because the evidence did not support their positions. In part, those general theories were discounted because of much evidence indicating that children and adults do not solely act to reduce drives, achieve physiological satisfaction, reduce tensions, or adapt socially (e.g., Berlyne, 1961; Chomsky, 1959; Hunt, 1961; Piaget & Inhelder, 1969; White, 1959).

Broad theories premised on the idea that people are fundamentally nonthinking or nonrational are not present in the contemporary scene. Instead, we see research on smaller scale phenomena, and particular judgments and behaviors purporting to show that people act without thought, are driven by emotions, and are fooled into believing that they make conscious decisions and choices. A propensity to engage in this kind of research is especially evident in the subdiscipline of social psychology (Festinger, 1957). The predominance in social psychology of such approaches was portrayed by Asch (1952) when he wrote, "No assumption has spread more widely in modern psychology than that men are ruled by their emotions and that these are irrational" (p. 21).

Asch was, of course, referring to the modern psychology of the early 1950s. In the modern psychology of the first part of the 21st century, we still see (with a little help from neuroscience), as I have discussed, the view that men and women are ruled by emotions and irrationality. For the most part, researchers choose specific topics for study in experimental settings to demonstrate inconsistencies in responding, a lack of awareness of reactions, and the strength of emotions over thought. I have already noted some of the specific topics subjected to these types of analyses: evaluations of matters like incest and eating dog meat, and the hard and morally paradoxical cases of the trolley car scenarios entailing the choice of sacrificing one life to save more lives. In the trolley car scenarios, situations are set up to look for seeming inconsistencies in responding by presenting seemingly similar situations (one life versus five lives) with presumably irrelevant differences (throwing a switch or pushing a person). Many experiments are designed to look for inconsistencies by applying supposedly small changes in scenarios or the ways aspects of a situation are presented and framed (Lakoff, 2008). These experiments and surveys have examined topics such as political decisions on party affiliation and voting, stances on issues such as the death penalty and taxes, food preferences, choices of products to buy, choices of romantic partners, choices of friends, preferences for brands and styles of products like automobiles, preferences for types of advertisements of products, preferences in team sports, and many other like topics. As put by Kihlstrom (2004, p. 3), there is a "People are Stupid" school of psychology. Kihlstrom argues that it is necessary to replace that school with the study of "mind in social interaction," with a focus on reciprocal interactions (see also Kihlstrom, 2008).

The study of isolated topics of these types is usually not connected to systems of thought about more general aspects of people's understandings of the world or their goals in life. Much of the evidence demonstrating that individuals attempt to understand events and relationships, and form ways of thinking that are not motivated by the need to reduce drives and adjust to and comply with social demands comes from research on children's development. Developmental psychology, led especially by Piaget (1947) and Werner (1957), and followed up by many in subsequent years, has conducted research on logic, mathematics, concepts of the physical world, language, emotions, social cognition, and morality in efforts to understand development through individual–environment interactions. A wealth of data exists countering the views that deprecate human thinking. One feature characteristic of such developmental research is that people's answers and conclusions are a starting point for analyses of explanations of how people arrive at their answers and conclusions. Moreover, developmental research has shown that individuals form more than one system of thought and, thereby, maintain a variety of goals that can be in conflict with each other. Many contexts require the coordination of different domains of thought.

I have attempted to provide a systematic analysis of important domains of social development, focusing on morality, as well as the domains of the conventional systems of societies and arenas of personal jurisdiction. By placing analyses of decisions within the framework of different substantive domains of social considerations, we are able to see that people navigate complex social issues in a multifaceted world with complex forms of thought. People's thinking is flexible in that they do attempt to weigh and balance different considerations in situational contexts. Thinking is also flexible in that people seek harmony but also do not avoid conflict when judged necessary from moral and personal viewpoints. People recognize difficulties, ambiguities, and many unknowns in trying to navigate the complicated social issues in their lives. In planning life goals, making purposeful decisions about necessities, obligations, and personal choices, they accept aspects of social realities and attempt to change other aspects through critiques of society and culture. Planning, purposes, and understanding of the social world and self are not illusions.

REFERENCES

Abu-Lughod, L. (1993). *Writing women's worlds: Bedouin stories.* Berkeley, CA: University of California Press.

Aronfreed, J. (1968). *Conduct and conscience: The socialization of internalized control over behavior.* New York: Academic Press.

Arsenio, W. (1988). Children's conceptions of the situational affective consequences of sociomoral events. *Child Development, 59,* 1611–1622.

Arsenio, W., & Fleiss, K. (1996). Typical and behaviourally disruptive children's understanding of the emotional consequences of sociomoral events. *British Journal of Developmental Psychology, 14,* 173–186.

Arsenio, W., & Ford, M. (1985). The role of affective information in social-cognitive development: Children's differentiation of moral and conventional events. *Merril- Palmer Quarterly, 31,* 1–18.

Asch, S. E. (1952). *Social psychology.* Englewood Cliffs, NJ: Prentice-Hall.

Astor, R. A. (1994). Children's moral reasoning about family and peer violence: The role of provocation and retribution. *Child Development, 65,* 1054–1067.

Baldwin, J. M. (1906). *Social and ethical interpretations in mental development*. New York: Macmillan.

Bandura, A., & Walters, R. (1963). *Social learning and personality development*. New York: Holt, Rinehart, & Winston.

Benedict, R. (1934). *Patterns of culture*. Boston: Houghton Mifflin.

Bennett, W. J. (1993). *The book of virtues*. New York: Simon & Schuster.

Bennett, W. J. (1995). *The children's book of virtues*. New York: Simon & Schuster.

Bennett, W. J., & Delattre, E. J. (1978). Moral education in the schools. *The Public Interest, 50*, 81–99.

Berlyne, D. (1961). *Conflict arousal and curiosity*. New York: McGraw-Hill.

Bok, S. (1999). *Lying: Moral choice in public and private life*. New York: Vintage Books. (Original work published 1979)

Chomsky, N. (1959). A review of B. F. Skinner's *Verbal Behavior*. *Language, 35*, 26–58.

Chomsky, N. (1979). *Language and responsibility*. New York: Pantheon Books.

Conry-Murray, C. (2009). Adolescent and adult reasoning about gender roles and fairness in Benin, West Africa. *Cognitive Development, 24*, 207–219.

Cushman, F., Young, L., & Hauser, M. (2006). The role of conscious reasoning and intuition in moral judgment: Testing three principles of harm. *Psychological Science, 17*, 1082–1089.

Damasio, A. R. (1994). *Descartes' error: Emotion, reason, and the human brain*. New York: Harper Collins.

Damasio, A. R. (2003). *Looking for Spinoza: Joy, sorrow, and the feeling brain*. New York: Harcourt, Inc.

Davidson, P., Turiel, E., & Black, A. (1983). The effect of stimulus familiarity on the use of criteria and justifications in children's social reasoning. *British Journal of Developmental Psychology, 1*, 49–65.

Durkheim, E. (1961). *Moral education*. Glencoe, IL: Free Press. (Original work published 1925)

Durkheim, E. (1965). *The elementary forms of religious life*. New York: Free Press. (Original work published 1912)

Dworkin, R. (1977). *Taking rights seriously*. Cambridge, MA: Harvard University Press.

Dworkin, R. (1993). *Life's dominion: An argument about abortion, euthanasia, and individual freedom*. New York: Alfred A. Knopf.

Eisenberg, N., & Fabes, R. A. (1991). Prosocial behavior and empathy: A multimethod, developmental perspective. In P. Clark (Ed.), *Review of personality and social psychology* (Vol. 12, pp. 34–61). Newbury Park, CA: Sage.

Festinger, L. (1957). *A theory of cognitive dissonance*. Stanford, CA: Stanford University Press.

Finkenauer, C., Engels, R. C. M. E., & Meeus, W. (2002). Keeping secrets from parents: Advantages and disadvantages of secrecy in adolescence. *Journal of Youth and Adolescence, 31*, 123–136.

Frankena, W. K. (1963). *Ethics*. Englewood Cliffs, NJ: Prentice-Hall.

Freeman, V. G., Rathore, S. S., Weinfurt, K. P., Schulman, K. A., & Sulmasy, D. P. (1999). Lying for patients: Physician deception of third-party payers. *Archives of Internal Medicine, 159*, 2263–2270.

Freud, S. (1960). *The ego and the id*. New York: Norton. (Original work published 1923)

Freud, S. (1961). *The future of an illusion*. New York: Norton. (Original work published 1927)

Freud, S. (1961). *Civilization and its discontents*. New York: Norton. (Original work published 1930)

Gewirth, A. (1982). *Human rights: Essays on justification and applications*. Chicago: University of Chicago Press.

Glassman, M., & Zan, B. (1995). Moral activity and domain theory: An alternative interpretation of research with young children. *Developmental Review, 15*, 434–457.

Greene, J. (2007, October 9). The biology of morality: Neuroscientists respond to Killen and Smetana (1) [Online exclusive]. *Human Development—Letters to the Editor content. karger.com/produkteDB/ produkte.asp?aktion=PDF Letter&serial=0018716X&datei=HDE-Letters-to-Editor-10-09-2007*.

Greene, J., & Haidt, J. (2002). How (and where) does moral judgment work? *Trends in Cognitive Science, 6*, 516–523.

Greene, J. D., Sommerville, R. B., Nystrom, L. E., Darley, J. M., & Cohen, J. D. (2001). An fMRI investigation of emotional engagement in moral judgment. *Science, 293*, 2105–2108.

Habermas, J. (1990). *Moral consciousness and communicative action*. Cambridge, MA: MIT Press.

Haidt, J. (2001). The emotional dog and its rational tail: A social intuitionist approach to moral judgment. *Psychological Review, 108*, 814–834.

Haidt, J., Koller, S. H., & Dias, M. G. (1993). Affect, culture, and morality, or is it wrong to eat your dog? *Journal of Personality and Social Psychology, 65*, 613–628.

Hauser, M. D. (2006). *Moral minds*. New York: Harper Collins.

Helwig, C. C. (1995a). Social context in social cognition: Psychological harm and civil liberties. In M. Killen & D. Hart (Eds.), *Morality in everyday life: Developmental perspectives* (pp. 166–200). Cambridge: Cambridge University Press.

Helwig, C. C. (1995b). Adolescents' and young adults' conceptions of civil liberties: Freedom of speech and religion. *Child Development, 66*, 152–166.

Helwig, C. C. (1997). The role of agent and social context in judgments of freedom of speech and religion. *Child Development, 68*, 484–495.

Hoffman, M. L. (1970). Moral development. In P. H. Mussen (Ed.), *Carmichael's manual of child psychology* (pp. 261–359). New York: John Wiley & Sons.

Hoffman, M. L. (2000). *Empathy and moral development: Implications for caring and justice*. Cambridge: Cambridge University Press.

Hunt, J. McV. (1961). *Intelligence and experience*. New York: Ronald Press.

Hyman, H. H., & Sheatsley, P. B. (1953). Trends in public opinion on civil liberties. *Journal of Social Issues, 9*, 6–16.

Kahneman, D., Slovic, P., & Teversky, A. (Eds.). (1982). *Judgment under uncertainty: Heuristics and biases*. Cambridge: Cambridge University Press.

Kant, I. (1964). *Groundwork of the metaphysic of morals*. New York: Harper & Row. (Original work published 1785)

Kerr, M., & Stattin, H. (2000). What parents know, how they know it, and several forms of adolescent adjustment: Further support for a reinterpretation of monitoring. *Developmental Psychology, 36*, 366–380.

Kihlstrom, J. H. (2004). Is there a "People are Stupid" school in social psychology? [Commentary on "Towards a balanced social psychology: Causes, consequences, and cures for the problem-seeking approach to social behavior and cognition" by J. I. Krueger and D. C. Funder.] *Behavioral & Brain Sciences, 27*, 348–349.

Kihlstrom, J. H. (2008). The automocity juggernaut—or, are we automatons after all? In J. Baer, J. C. Kaufman, & R. F. Baumeister (Eds.), *Are we free? Psychology and free will* (pp. 155–180). New York: Oxford University Press.

Killen, M., Lee-Kim, J., McGlothlin, H., & Stagnor, C. (2002). How children and adolescents value gender and racial exclusion. *Monographs of the Society for Research in Child Development, 67*(4, Serial No. 271).

Killen, M., Sinno, S., & Margie, N. G. (2007). Children's experiences and judgments about group exclusion and inclusion. In R. V. Kail (Ed.), *Advances in child development and behavior* (Vol. 35, pp. 173–218). New York: Academic Press.

Killen, M, & Smetana, J. (2007). The biology of morality: Human development and moral neuroscience. *Human Development, 50,* 241–243.

Killen, M., & Stangor, C. (2001). Children's social reasoning about inclusion and exclusion in gender and race peer group contexts. *Child Development, 72,* 174–186.

Kinzer, S. (1997, May 27). Beating the system with the bribes and big lie. *The New York Times.*

Kochanska, G. (1993). Toward a synthesis of parental socialization and child temperament in early development of conscience. *Child Development, 64,* 325–347.

Koenigs, M., Young, L., Adolphs, R., Tranel, D., Cushman, F., Hauser, M., et al. (2007). Damage to the prefrontal cortex increases utilitarian moral judgements. *Nature, 446,* 908–911.

Kohlberg, L. (1963a). The development of children's orientations toward a moral order: 1. Sequence in the development of moral thought. *Vita Humana, 6,* 1–33.

Kohlberg, L. (1963b). Moral development and identification. In H. Stevenson (Ed.), *Child psychology, The sixty-second yearbook of the National Society for the Study of Education* (pp. 277–332). Chicago: University of Chicago Press.

Kohlberg, L. (1964). Development of moral character and moral ideology. In M. L. Hoffman & L. W. Hoffman (Eds.), *Review of child development research* (Vol. 1, pp. 383–432). New York: Sage.

Kohlberg, L. (1969). Stage and sequence: The cognitive-developmental approach to socialization. In D. Goslin (Ed.), *Handbook of socialization theory and research* (pp. 347–480). Chicago: Rand McNally.

Kohlberg, L. (1971). From is to ought: How to commit the naturalistic fallacy and get away with it in the study of moral development. In T. Mischel (Ed.), *Psychology and genetic epistemology* (pp. 151–235). New York: Academic Press.

Kohlberg, L., & Kramer, R. (1969). Continuities and discontinuities in childhood and adult moral development. *Human Development, 12,* 93–120.

Krebs, D. L., & Denton, K. (2005). Toward a more pragmatic approach to morality. A critical evaluation of Kohlberg's model. *Psychological Review, 112,* 629–649.

Lakoff, G. (2008). *The political mind: Why you can't understand 21st-century American politics with an 18th-century brain.* New York: Penguin.

Laupa, M. (1991). Children's reasoning about three authority attributes: Adult status, knowledge, and social position. *Developmental Psychology, 27,* 321–329.

Laupa, M., & Turiel, E. (1986). Children's conceptions of adult and peer authority. *Child Development, 57,* 405–412.

Lerner, R. M. (2006). Developmental science, developmental systems, and contemporary theories of human development. In W. Damon & R. M. Lerner (Series Eds.) & R. M. Lerner (Vol. Ed.), *Handbook of child psychology: Vol. 1. Theoretical models of human development* (6th ed., pp. 1–17). Hoboken, NJ: John Wiley & Sons.

Lerner, R. M., & Overton, W. F. (2008). Exemplifying the integrations of the relational developmental system: Synthesizing theory, research, and application to promote positive development and social justice. *Journal of Adolescent Research, 23,* 245–255.

Lewis, M. (1993). The development of deception. In M. Lewis & C. Saarni (Eds.), *Lying and deception in everyday life* (pp. 90–105). New York: Guilford Press.

Markus, H. R., & Kitayama, S. (1991). Culture and the self: Implications for cognition, emotion, and motivation. *Psychological Review, 98,* 224–253.

McClosky, M., & Brill, A. (1983). *Dimensions of tolerance: What Americans believe about civil liberties.* New York: Sage.

McDougall, W. (1926). *An introduction to social psychology.* Boston: John W. Luce.

Mensing, J. F. (2002). Collectivism, individualism, and interpersonal responsibilities in families: Differences and similarities in social reasoning between individuals in poor, urban families in Colombia and the United States. Unpublished doctoral dissertation, University of California, Berkeley.

Mernissi, F. (1994). *Dreams of trespass: Tales of a harem girlhood.* Reading, MA: Addison-Wesley.

Mikhail, J. (2007). Universal moral grammar: Theory, evidence, and the future. *Cognitive Science, 11,* 143–152.

Mill, J. S. (2001). *Utilitarianism.* Indianapolis, IN: Hackett. (Original work published 1863)

Miller, G. (2008). Growing pains for fMRI. *Science, 320,* 1412–1414.

Mischel, W., & Mischel, H. (1976). A cognitive social-learning approach to morality and self-regulation. In T. Lickona (Ed.), *Moral development and behavior: Theory, research, and social issues* (pp. 84–107). New York: Holt, Rinehart, & Winston.

Neff, K. D. (2001). Judgments of personal autonomy and interpersonal responsibility in the context of Indian spousal relationships: An examination of young people's reasoning in Mysore, India. *British Journal of Developmental Psychology, 19,* 233–257.

Nucci, L. (1977). *Social development: Personal, conventional, and moral concepts.* Unpublished doctoral dissertation, University of California, Santa Cruz.

Nucci, L. (1981). Conceptions of personal issues: A domain distinct from moral or societal concepts. *Child Development, 52,* 114–121.

Nucci, L. (1996). Morality and the personal sphere of actions. In E. Reed, E. Turiel, & T. Brown (Eds.), *Values and knowledge* (pp. 41–60). Hillsdale, NJ; Erlbaum.

Nucci, L. (2001). *Education in the moral domain.* Cambridge: Cambridge University Press.

Nucci, L., & Nucci, M. S. (1982a). Children's responses to moral and social conventional transgressions in free-play settings. *Child Development, 53,* 1337–1342.

Nucci, L., & Nucci, M. S. (1982b). Children's social interactions in the context of moral and conventional transgressions. *Child Development, 53,* 403–412.

Nucci, L., & Turiel, E. (1978). Social interactions and the development of social concepts in preschool children. *Child Development, 49,* 400–407.

Nucci., L., & Turiel, E. (2009). Capturing the complexity of moral development and education. *Mind, Brain, and Education, 3,* 151–159.

Nucci, L., Turiel, E., & Encarcion-Gawrych, G. (1983). Children's social interactions and social concepts: Analyses of morality and convention in the Virgin Islands. *Journal of Cross-Cultural Psychology, 14,* 469–487.

Nucci, L., & Weber, E. (1995). Social interactions in the home and the development of young children's conceptions of the personal. *Child Development, 66,* 1438–1452.

Nussbaum, M. C. (1999). *Sex and social justice.* New York: Oxford University Press.

Nussbaum, M. C. (2001). *Upheavals of thought: The intelligence of emotions.* Cambridge: Cambridge University Press.

Nussbaum, M. C., & Glover, J. (Eds.). (1995). *Women, culture, and development: A study of human capabilities.* New York: Oxford University Press.

Okin, S. M. (1989). *Justice, gender, and the family.* New York: Basic Books.

Overton, W. F. (2006). Developmental psychology: Philosophy, concepts, methodology. In W. Damon & R. M. Lerner (Series Ed.) & R. M. Lerner (Vol. Ed.), *Handbook of child psychology: Vol. 1. Theoretical models of human development* (6th ed., pp. 18–88). Hoboken, NJ: John Wiley & Sons.

Overton, W. F. (2007). Embodiment from a Relational Perspective. In W. F. Overton, U. Mueller & J. L. Newman (Eds.), (pp. 1–18). *Developmental Perspective on Embodiment and Consciousness.* Hillsdale, NJ: Erbaum.

Perkins, S. A., & Turiel, E. (2007). To lie or not to lie: To whom and under what circumstances. *Child Development, 78,* 609–621.

Piaget, J. (1932). *The moral judgment of the child.* London: Routledge and Kegan Paul.

Piaget, J. (1947). *The psychology of intelligence.* London: Lowe and Brydore.

Piaget, J. (1970). *Psychology and epistemology.* New York: Viking Press.

Piaget, J. (1981). *Intelligence and affectivity: Their relationships during child development.* Palo Alto, CA: Annual Reviews, Inc.

Piaget, J., & Inhelder, B. (1969). *The psychology of the child.* New York: Basic Books.

Protho, J. W., & Grigg, C. M. (1960). Fundamental principles of democracy: Bases of agreement and disagreement. *Journal of Politics, 22,* 276–294.

Rawls, J. (1971). *A theory of justice.* Cambridge, MA: Harvard University Press.

Royzman, E. B., Leeman, R. F., & Baron, J. (2009). Unsentimental ethics: Toward a content-specific account of the moral-conventional distinction. *Cognition, 112,* 159–174.

Ryan, K. (1989). In defense of character education. In L. P. Nucci (Ed.), *Moral development and character education: A dialogue* (pp. 3–18). Berkeley, CA: McCutchan.

Sarat, A. (1975). Reasoning in politics: The social, political, and psychological bases of principled thought. *American Journal of Political Science, 19,* 247–261.

Shweder, R. A., Much, N. C., Mahaptra, M., & Park, L. (1997). The "Big Three" of morality (Autonomy, Community, and Divinity) and the "Big Three" explanations of suffering. In A. Brandt & P. Rozin (Eds.), *Morality and health* (pp. 119–169). New York: Routledge.

Skinner, B. F. (1971). *Beyond freedom and dignity.* New York: Knopf.

Skinner, B. F. (1990). Can psychology be a science of mind? *American Psychologist, 45,* 1206–1210.

Smetana, J. G. (2006). Social domain theory: Consistencies and variations in children's moral and social judgments. In M. Killen & J. G. Smetana (Eds.), *Handbook of moral development* (pp. 119–153). Mahwah, NJ: Erlbaum.

Smetana, J. G., Metzger, A., Gettman, D. C., & Campione-Barr, N. (2006). Disclosure and secrecy in parent-adolescent relationships. *Child Development, 77,* 201–217.

Sommers, C. H. (1984). Ethics without virtue: Moral education in America. *American Scholar, 53,* 381–389.

Stouffer, S. (1955). *Communism, conformity and civil liberties.* New York: Doubleday.

Sunstein, C. (2004). Moral heuristics and moral framing. *Minnesota Law Review, 88,* 1556–1597.

Tisak, M. S. (1986). Children's conceptions of parental authority. *Child Development, 57,* 166–176.

Tisak, M. S. (1995). Domains of social reasoning and beyond. In R. Vista (Ed.), *Annals of child development* (Vol. 11, pp. 95–130). London: Jessica Kingsley.

Turiel, E. (1983). *The development of social knowledge: Morality and convention.* Cambridge: Cambridge University Press.

Turiel, E. (1998). The development of morality. In W. Damon (Series Ed.) & N. Eisenberg (Vol. Ed.), *Handbook of child psychology: Vol. 3. Social, emotional, and personality development* (5th ed., pp. 863–932). New York: John Wiley & Sons.

Turiel, E. (2002). *The culture of morality: Social development, context, and conflict.* Cambridge: Cambridge University Press.

Turiel, E. (2003a). Morals, motives, and actions. In L. Smith, C. Rogers, & P. Tomlinson (Eds.), *Development and motivation: Joint perspectives* (Monograph Series II, Serial No. 2, pp. 29–40). Leicester, United Kingdom: *British Journal of Educational Psychology.*

Turiel, E. (2003b). Resistance and subversion in everyday life. *Journal of Moral Education, 32,* 115–130.

Turiel, E. (2006). Thought, emotions, and social interactional processes in moral development. In M. Killen & J. G. Smetana (Eds.), *Handbook of moral development* (pp. 7–35). Mahwah, NJ: Erlbaum.

Turiel, E. (2008a). Thought about actions in social domains: Morality, social conventions, and social interactions. *Cognitive Development, 23,* 126–154.

Turiel, E. (2008b). Social decisions, social interactions, and the coordination of diverse judgments. In U. Mueller, J. I. Carpendale, N. Budwig, & B. Sokol (Eds.), *Social life, social knowledge: Toward a process account of development* (pp. 255–276). Mahwah, NJ: Erlbaum.

Turiel, E. (2009). The relevance of moral epistemology and psychology for neuroscience. In P. Zelazo, M. Chandler, & E. Crone (Eds.), *Developmental social cognitive neuroscience* (pp. 313–331). New York: Taylor & Francis.

Turiel, E., Hildebrandt, C., & Wainryb, C. (1991). Judging social issues: Difficulties, inconsistencies, and consistencies. *Monographs of the Society for Research in Child Development, 56*(2, Serial No. 224).

Turiel, E., & Killen, M. (2010). Taking emotions seriously: The role of emotions in moral development. In W. Arsenio & E. Lemerise (Eds.), *Emotions, aggression, and morality in children: Bridging development and psychopathology* (pp. 33–52). Washington, DC: American Psychological Association.

Turiel, E., Killen, M., & Helwig, C. C. (1987). Morality: Its structure, functions and vagaries. In J. Kagan & S. Lamb (Eds.), *The emergence of moral concepts in young children.* Chicago: University of Chicago Press.

Turiel, E., & Perkins, S. A. (2004). Flexibilities of mind: Conflict and Culture. *Human Development, 47,* 158–178.

Turiel, E., Perkins, S. A., & Mensing, J. (2009). *Honesty in Marriage: When is deception justified?* Unpublished manuscript, University of California, Berkeley.

Turiel, E., & Wainryb, C. (1998). Concepts of freedoms and rights in a traditional hierarchically organized society. *British Journal of Developmental Psychology, 16*(3), 375–395.

Tversky, A., & Kahneman, D. (1983). Extensional versus intuitive reasoning: The conjunction fallacy in probability judgment. *Psychological Review, 90,* 293–315.

Twain, M. (1876/1936). *The adventures of Tom Sawyer.* New York: The Heritage Press.

Twain, M. (1885/1958). *The adventures of Huckleberry Finn.* Cambridge, MA: Harvard University Press.

Wainryb, C. (1991). Understanding differences in moral judgments: The role of informational assumptions. *Child Development, 62,* 840–851.

Wainryb, C., Brehl, B. A., & Matwin, S. (2005). Being hurt and hurting others: Children's narrative accounts and moral judgments of their own interpersonal conflicts. *Monographs of the Society for Research in Child Development, 70*(3, Serial No. 281).

Wainryb, C., & Turiel, E. (1994). Dominance, subordination, and concepts of personal entitlements in cultural contexts. *Child Development, 65,* 1701–1722.

Walzer, M. (2007). *Thinking politically: Essays in political theory.* New Haven: Yale University Press.

Watson, J.B. (1924). *Behaviorism.* New York: The People's Institute.

Wegner, D. M. (2002). *The illusion of conscious will.* Cambridge, MA: MIT Press.

Werner, H. (1957). *Comparative psychology of mental development.* New York: International Universities Press.

White, R. (1959). Motivation reconsidered: The concept of competence. *Psychological Review, 66,* 297–333.

Wikan, U. (1996). *Tomorrow, God willing: Self-made destinies in Cairo.* Chicago: University of Chicago Press.

Wilson, E. O. (1975). *Sociobiology: The new synthesis.* Cambridge, MA: Harvard University Press.

Wynne, E. A. (1985). The great tradition in education: Transmitting moral values. *Educational Leadership, 43,* 4–9.

CHAPTER 17

The Development of Social Understanding
A Relational Perspective

JEREMY I. M. CARPENDALE and CHARLIE LEWIS

Social cognition refers to our understanding of social features of the world, of ourselves and others in psychological terms, as persons with beliefs, intentions, wishes, emotions, and desires. Other people are perhaps the most complex aspect of our worlds, and they are also the most interesting. They respond in lively and appropriate ways to the infant's gestures, the child taking a toy, and the adult's or older adult's announcement of good or bad news. Social understanding is visible in everyday exchanges within interpersonal relationships. Examining such interpersonal activity in early development, we see the young child's increasing grasp of the social world in these relationships. For this reason, the question of how we come to understand the mind and how this understanding changes across the life span has been of central interest to an interdisciplinary group of scholars, including developmental scientists, primatologists, philosophers, and social and cognitive scientists.

This work was supported by the Social Sciences and Humanities Research Council of Canada and the Human Early Learning Partnership (to J.I.M.C.) and the Economic and Social Research Council (grant RES-576–25–0019, to C.L.).

Within developmental science, this interest has been pursued in a number of different research literatures including "person perception," "role taking," and "metacognition" (Chandler, 1978; Chandler & Boyes, 1982; Flavell, 1992; Shantz, 1983). These terms all refer to thinking about social matters, although each derives from a different theoretical tradition. Metacognition, for example, refers to thinking about thinking and reflects an assumption that more complex thinking involves a hierarchy of nested relations between thoughts, thought about thoughts, thoughts about thoughts about thoughts, and so on, linked recursively together (see Mascolo & Fischer, Chapter 6 of this volume). This idea has been a driving force behind the cognitive revolution since the 1950s, and most developmental scientists are paid-up members of this movement. The term *social cognition* is not restricted to life-span developmental psychology. Indeed, many of the ideas emerge from the social psychology of the 1950s (e.g., Heider, 1958), in which the main question concerned the nature of everyday thinking that makes social interaction possible.

This chapter focuses primarily on the research and theory since the late 1970s on what has come to be referred to as "theory of mind." This research accelerated in momentum from the early 1980s (for earlier reviews, see Chandler, 1978; Chandler, & Boyes, 1982; Flavell, 1992; Shatz, 1975; Shantz, 1983; see also more recent reviews by Carpendale & Lewis, 2006; Harris, 2006; Lewis & Carpendale, 2002, 2010; Moore, 2006; see also Chandler & Birch, Chapter 19 of this volume). The topic of social cognition has taken on many names in its various reincarnations, including "folk psychology," "commonsense psychology," "belief-desire psychology," "mentalizing," "theory of mind," and "mind reading." Everyday folk psychology is conceptualized as organized around understanding mental states, like beliefs and desires; that is, "we see each other as executing acts that we *think* will get us what we *want*" (Wellman & Miller, 2008, p. 107, emphasis in original; for a critical analysis of conceptualizations of "mental states," see Racine & Carpendale, 2008). The popular phrase "theory of mind" is derived from the theory that children form theories about their and others' minds— the "theory theory." The use of the phrase "theory of mind" can, in some cases, refer broadly to social cognition; in other cases, to the theoretical perspective called "theory-theory," and in yet other cases, merely to children's understanding that beliefs can be false. This is one reason why we place the term in scare quotes. Names often implicate specific theories, which is the reason that some have been cautious about using phrases such as "theory of mind," and

the more recent "mind reading," preferring the more neutral "social understanding" or "social cognition" instead. We will follow in the tradition that uses the latter labels.

Since the cognitive revolution, developmental psychology's explorations in the area of social cognition have tended to tilt heavily toward cognitive explanations of social phenomena (e.g., intersubjectivity explained by terms such as "theory of mind" and "theory-theory"). That is, developmental psychology has increasingly come to depict social cognition in terms of cognitive processes. This chapter examines an alternative stance: reviewing social understanding through a wide-angle lens, which takes into account both the breadth of individuals' social experiences and the range of theories that have been drawn on to explain social cognition. The approach we take attempts to reassert a balance between the social and the cognitive. Rather than limiting our examination to the role of cognitive processes, we follow a tradition that gives equal weight to the role of interpersonal processes in social understanding.

As background to structure our critical review of the literature on the development of social understanding, we consider the generally unexamined metatheoretical assumptions on which theories in the area are based (Jopling, 1993; Lerner, 2006; Overton, 2006). Theories of social cognition are generally based on one of two contrasting sets of metatheoretical assumptions: split, or individualistic, and relational. Many theories in this area take the individual mind as the starting point and assume a split between self and other. Thus, from this perspective, the problem faced by the developing person is how to learn about other minds. The difficulty faced by the child, according to this approach, is that other minds are assumed to be hidden and private, and thus inaccessible. This individualistic, split metatheoretical framework leads to asking only certain kinds of questions and accepting only certain kinds of answers. That is, it assumes the way the problem is set up and the solutions considered possible. It turns the spotlight on the individual cognitive dimension and marginalizes the way in which social understanding is embedded in interpersonal engagement. This chapter critically reviews the impact of individualistic, split frameworks, particularly in the areas of infant social development, disorders of social understanding, and primatology.

The second metatheoretical approach to social cognition, the relational approach, contrasts sharply with the split approach. This chapter is broadly contextualized by the relational framework. From this perspective, rather than assuming individual minds as a starting point, the social process is considered primary from which minds develop.

Here a primordial intersubjectivity is assumed, and individual minds arise from the differentiations of this intersubjectivity through interpersonal actions (see Jopling, 1993; Overton, 2006; see also Mascolo & Fischer, Chapter 6 of this volume). The relational framework begins with the perspective that life starts as a relatively undifferentiated and fused *developmental system* that might be termed the "infant-caregiver system." Initially, this system is a biosocial action matrix, and through actions in the world, it becomes differentiated and articulated into infant and caregivers. According to this perspective, from the start, social intercourse is a necessary prerequisite for social understanding. Rather than imposing an adult experience of mind on infants, as the split position does, the relational starting point is engagement, and the distinction between self and other gradually differentiates out of this activity matrix. The adult experience of mind is thus the outcome of a developing system and cannot be the explanation of social development. Stated slightly differently, from a relational perspective, it is not assumed that infants first understand others—in a Cartesian-inspired fashion—as physical bodies, like furniture, and only later as mental agents. Instead, right from the start, in the context of embodied sensorimotor actions, the infant experiences others as intentional agents. Action is not split from intention; activity is not split into physical movement and mental states. In place of the individualistic, split approach of representing beliefs, desires, and intentions as separate from and causing behavior, we argue that it is both less problematic and more productive to consider them as aspects of action that children come to learn about and articulate through everyday interactions, resulting in ways of talking about human activity in psychological terms. We examine these two frameworks—split and relational—as they structure research on the development of social understanding.

The individualistic approach has tended to be standard in psychology and some, but not all, versions of cognitive science. Descartes is the philosopher most closely associated with the assumptions of split metatheory, whereas important figures in the relational movement include Baldwin (e.g., 1906), Mead (1934), Piaget (e.g., 1936/1963), Werner (1957), Winnicott (1965, 1971/2005), and Wittgenstein (1968) (see Jopling, 1993; Overton, 2006). Although classifying particular theories may not always be clear-cut, being aware of these two sets of metatheoretical assumptions, on which theories are based, is useful in understanding debates in this area.

Psychology has a long history of claims that such philosophical/metatheoretical issues are irrelevant to science. These claims arose from the assumption that all knowledge must be based on error-free, direct observations, termed *data*. But this itself is a philosophical assumption, not an empirical finding (Overton, 2006). The standard individualistic formulation of "theory of mind" has historically been accepted with few questions and with little recognition of its metatheoretical foundations; and yet this formulation was certainly not induced from any set of empirically pure facts. This is why an analysis at the level of the metatheoretical assumptions, on which questions, problems, and theories are based, is necessary for an adequate critical review of how we explain the development of social understanding (Jopling, 1993; Overton, 2006).

This chapter is divided into six sections. The first describes how and why the "theory of mind" metaphor became such a driving force within the study of social cognition. This also helps to narrow this massive area of research to manageable proportions. Here, we sketch out the research over the life course that has pinpointed the individual's grasp of the mind as the basis of the study of social cognition. The second section focuses on the classical standard individualistic theoretical analyses and demonstrates the manner in which each promotes the cognitive at the expense of marginalizing the social. Here, we discuss foundations of these theories and expand on the criticism that they are too narrowly focused on the workings of a detached mind. We also argue that more recent work, which attempts to broaden the framework to include general cognitive processes and links between typical and atypical development, is too narrow to take into account the social nature of social cognition. The third section explores some of the key topics currently under investigation in the "theory of mind" literature. Rather than embracing the sort of relational stance that we propose, we argue that some of these theoretical accounts have split the mind from social processes as radically as the standard theories described in the second section. The remaining three sections of the chapter describe what a relational account of social understanding must entail—and what, therefore, is lacking in the majority of contemporary accounts. The fourth section returns to the relational perspective of the embedding of the person's understanding of the social world in a range of social processes that makes social life complex and intertwined. We explore the range of these social factors including culture, family interaction, and relationships, as well as implications for increasing sophistication in social understanding for individuals' social lives. As a result, the following two sections consider how social understanding may develop. The fifth section reviews the origins of social

skills in infancy and summarizes a growing literature suggesting that achievements in infancy form a basis of later social understanding. Given that the "theory of mind" literature is dominated by the child's acquisition of a grasp of mental state terms, such as "beliefs," "desires," "intentions," and various emotions, the sixth section considers the role of language and communication in the development of social cognition. Like others (e.g., Astington & Baird, 2005), we argue that the child's early grasp of the relation between language and social understanding is crucial for a theoretical account of more complex forms of social understanding.

SOCIAL COGNITION AS "THEORY OF MIND": EVIDENCE ACROSS THE LIFE COURSE

As mentioned previously, an earlier social cognition literature was referred to as "perspective taking" or "role taking." This literature derived part of its inspiration from the research on visual perspective taking identified and explored by Piaget and Inhelder (1948/1967) using assessment tools such as the three-mountain task. This task was designed to explore the child's developing ability to construct another's visual perspectives on the same object: a model of three mountains. When combined with Piaget's earlier studies of language and moral reasoning, this line of research was influential in the study of children's social perspective taking or role taking. In this approach, the development of social understanding was conceived of in terms of a decline of egocentrism. This led to an extensive research effort and numerous tests designed to assess children's perspective taking (e.g., Flavell et al., 1968). Debates concerned exactly when children develop this skill, and attempts were made to discover it earlier and earlier in the child's development. The field declined, perhaps because of the conceptual difficulties raised by the lack of correlations between many tests, all designed to measure perspective taking, based on the assumption that it is a single factor rather than a range of gradually developing skills of varying complexity.

At that time, a literature on the development of children's so-called theory of mind began to emerge and can be traced to a target article by Premack and Woodruff in 1978 on the question of "Do chimpanzees have a theory of mind?" Three philosophers commenting on the article each argued that what was required to provide evidence of an understanding of belief was to demonstrate an understanding

of *false* beliefs. Daniel Dennett (1978), in particular, discussed the need to assess an understanding that beliefs can be false as essential in demonstrating an understanding of beliefs. He used the example of Punch and Judy puppet shows, which tend to turn on Punch's mistaken beliefs for generating humor. This suggestion was taken up by Heinz Wimmer and Josef Perner (1983) in their highly cited article that reported the use of the now-famous false belief *unexpected transfer* task—the Maxi task (Perner, 1991). The story involves Maxi returning from shopping with his mother and helping to put away groceries. Maxi puts his chocolate away and goes out to play. While he is out, his mother moves it to another location. The key issue here concerns where a child watching this story unfold would say Maxi thinks his chocolate is, or where he would go to look for it, once he returns from outside. In the preschool period, there is a developmental shift from children incorrectly stating that Maxi will look for the chocolate where it actually is, to coming to answer that Maxi will search where he put it in the first place. This is the crucial demonstration that 4-year-old children develop an awareness of other people's perspectives on events that is not present in younger children. The key question, which is discussed next, is why this happens.

The Primacy of False Belief Understanding

Wimmer and Perner's (1983) research generated great interest, perhaps because it seemed so counterintuitive that 3-year-old children cannot attribute false beliefs to others or themselves. This task, once regarded as a "litmus test" of children's understanding of the nature of the mind, takes a variety of forms in addition to the unexpected transfer test. For example, in the *unexpected contents* task, or the Smarties task, the child is shown a popular chocolate box and asked what is inside (all say excitedly "Smarties!" or "Chocolates!"); they are then shown that the box contains something else (e.g., pencils) and are asked, "What did you think was in the box?" or "What will [name of friend who has not seen the box] think is in here?" As with unexpected transfer, in the unexpected contents task, 3-year-olds tend to provide an egocentric answer ("Pencils!"), whereas only 4-year-olds come to recognize that someone's belief can be out of date or false (Hogrefe, Wimmer, & Perner, 1986; Perner, Leekam, & Wimmer, 1987).

One reason why these simple tasks had a significant influence on social cognitive theory is that it is easy to use simple controls to show that the errors made by younger children are not caused by factors that are peripheral to the task. In 1987, Perner, Leekam, and Wimmer added two control questions to the procedure of the unexpected transfer task to ensure that the child's memory of the procedure ("Where did Maxi put his chocolate in the beginning?") and knowledge of the object's current location ("Where is the chocolate now?") did not explain young children's failure. These have become key additional questions in the standard procedure. Many other checks and balances on the standard procedure have been used. For example, in their original article, Wimmer and Perner (1983) found that telling children to "stop and think" before asking them the test question did not help, suggesting that 3-year-olds were not simply blurting out the true whereabouts of Maxi's chocolate.

A second reason for the task's resilience comes from its apparent reliability. Although an early test-retest study (Mayes, Klin, Tercyak, Cicchetti, & Cohen, 1996) failed to demonstrate correlations indicating an underlying cognitive skill, a later study demonstrated positive associations across tasks administered in sessions a few weeks apart (Hughes, Adlam, Happé, Taylor, & Caspi, 2000). This evidence of reliability was further strengthened with the aggregated data from many individual studies, leading to the common conclusion that there is a developmental shift between 3 and 4 years of age in success on the task. Wellman, Cross, and Watson (2001) reported a meta-analysis of 178 experiments and 591 different manipulations of the task conducted in a wide range of, mainly Western, cultures. Their analysis suggested that there is a rapid increase in numbers of children passing the test in the fourth year of life, confirming the findings of the original study.

Wellman et al. (2001) also analyzed whether type of manipulation influenced preschoolers' performances on the task. Five of these manipulations were found to lead to improved success: (1) when the child participated in the procedure as opposed to simply observing it; (2) if the desired object is either destroyed or not shown at all to the child (following Zaitchik, 1991); (3) when the child is told that Maxi cannot see the object being moved; (4) if a pictorial representation is used as an aide-mémoire for the protagonist's belief; or (5) when the protagonist's motive is articulated to the child. Wellman et al. also found that temporal marking in the test question, like "What did you think was in the box *before* I took the top off?" (following Lewis & Osborne, 1990), had a consistent influence on performance, but only for 4-year-olds who were likely to be on the verge of acquiring this skill, not for younger children. Although questions remain about whether the

meta-analysis masked some undetected effects (e.g., those that might be engendered by grouping studies inappropriately; Moses, 2001), evidence presented by Wellman and colleagues has supported the claim that there is a developmental shift at around the age of 4.

The developmental shift at age 4 does not mean a lack of development before this age. Hogrefe, Wimmer and Perner (1986) found that 3-year-olds were aware of the protagonist's ignorance (in response to the question "Does [name of another person] *know* what is really in the box or does she not know that?"), but still failed the question about *what* the other person thinks is in the box. Since this study, there has been a line of research that has explored prerequisites to understanding the standard false belief question. The question of prerequisites led Clements and Perner (1994) to a study in which a story involving an unexpected transfer test is enacted and just as the protagonist is coming to find the object, the experimenter states, "I wonder where he's [the protagonist] going to look." The experimenter does this to assess the child's direction of gaze. With this prompt, even children younger than 3 years looked at the correct location (i.e., where the protagonist should falsely believe it to be), but then went on to fail the standard false belief question. This discrepancy between looking and verbal responses led Clements and Perner to suggest that children first develop an "implicit" understanding, which children cannot articulate because they do not have a full understanding of mental states as representations. Further experiments have suggested that implicit looks are initially related to a strong commitment to the erroneous verbal judgment, followed by a transition to a successful verbal judgment that initially is less confident (e.g., Ruffman, Garnham, Import, & Connolly, 2001). The common theme here is that these accounts focus only on the child's mind-cognitive system and its capacity to understand representations as representations; a theme that is further examined later in this chapter.

After False Belief Understanding: Social Cognitive Development in Childhood and Beyond

The "theory of mind" literature has focused attention on preschoolers from 3 to 5 and their acquisition of false belief understanding. Thus, it is easy to get the impression that by 5, children are assumed to have mastered social understanding. Older literatures on social cognitive development and perspective taking, however, showed greater interest in development following the preschool years (e.g., Selman, 1980). From early on in the "theory of mind" literature, Chandler (1988) argued that the narrow focus on false belief understanding resulted in a "one miracle" view of social development, with little interest in what comes before and after false belief understanding. Together with the prerequisite issue, there is the question of whether children older than 5 still have more to learn about mind. It turns out, not surprisingly, they do, including an understanding of the relation of mind to other psychological processes. For example, there is the relation of false beliefs and emotions. Here, one would expect that if a preschooler understands that Little Red Riding Hood does not know that the Wolf is dressed up as her grandmother, her false belief understanding would be linked to her understanding of emotions; that is, Little Red Riding Hood should not be afraid. However, even if children pass a false belief test, some of them still fail this application of such understanding (Bradmetz & Schneider, 1999; de Rosnay, Pons, Harris, & Morrell, 2004; Harris, Johnson, Hutton, Andrews, & Cook, 1989). A further application of understanding how beliefs are acquired is to draw inferences about others' knowledge. For example, if it is known that a boy bought something at a store selling only blue marbles, it can be inferred that he bought a blue marble (e.g., Sodian & Wimmer, 1987; Varouxaki, Freeman, Peters, & Lewis, 1999).

Another ability that seems to develop after false belief understanding is recursive thinking, or thinking about thinking (Flavell et al., 1968; see also Mascolo & Fischer, Chapter 6 of this volume, and Müller & Racine, Chapter 11 of this volume, for extended discussions of the development of recursive thought). This form of thinking was explored with what Perner and Wimmer (1985) termed a *second-order* false belief task. In this task, on seeing an ice-cream van at the park, John and Mary go home to get money. As John is on his way home, he sees that the van has moved to the church, and he does not know that Mary has also, but independently, found out that the van has moved. In contrast with the false belief test, it was not until the age of 6 to 7 years that most children realized John would look for Mary at the park when told that she had gone to buy ice cream, rather than the church, suggesting a 2-year lag between false belief understanding and mastering this more complex situation involving beliefs about others' beliefs. However, Sullivan, Zaitchik and Tager-Flusberg (1994) suggested that children's difficulty in the "ice-cream van" task lay in the complexity of the situation rather than a new level of conceptual understanding. They modified the task to reduce the information-processing demands. With a simplified procedure and shorter stories, they found that

most 5½-year-olds and 40% of the 4-year-olds passed the new tasks.

The recursive application of belief understanding in second-order false belief is not the only increase in the complexity in children's social understanding. Another step in the process of knowledge acquisition that young children have yet to achieve is an understanding of interpretation. To illustrate, consider two people watching a movie together. If one person leaves to buy popcorn and so misses an important part of the film, he or she may end up with different beliefs about the movie compared with the person who watches the entire film. This is equivalent to the false belief task, because Maxi is out of the room when the key event—his chocolate being moved—occurs. Adults, however, know more; even if two people do watch an entire movie or play together or read the same novel, they may still hold different beliefs about it because they may interpret the same event differently. This is an insight about the nature of knowledge and the mind that 5-year-olds have yet to master (Carpendale & Chandler, 1996; Chandler & Carpendale, 1998; Chandler & Lalonde, 1996; Lalonde & Chandler, 2002).

The age at which children first begin to understand interpretation has been debated, with some researchers arguing that this ability is equivalent to false belief understanding because the false belief test shows that children can grasp the possibility of two "interpretations" of the same situation (e.g., Meltzoff & Gopnik, 1993; Perner, 1991; Sodian, 1990; Wellman, 1990). One way to view this debate sympathetically is that dictionaries often list two, somewhat different, meanings of interpretation. It is legitimate, for example, to talk about the interpretation of an aerial photograph, where what is meant is whether there is enough information present to make out what the structures in the photograph actually are. In contrast, a second meaning of interpretation turns on how an event is construed from different perspectives. For example, if we talk about interpretations of *Hamlet*, we are not concerned with whether there is enough information to get at exactly what Shakespeare actually meant, but rather the point is that multiple interpretations can be equally legitimately grounded in available evidence. This second, and more complex, meaning of interpretation is distinct from and a step beyond simple false belief understanding, and this ability typically begins to develop between 6 and 8 years of age (Carpendale & Chandler, 1996; Carpendale & Lewis, 2006; Lalonde & Chandler, 2002).

One line of research taking a step from false belief understanding toward interpretation is Pillow's (1991) research on children's understanding of biased interpretation. He presented children with an ambiguous action by a story character named Joan, such as holding a doll in front of a donation box full of toys for poor children. This same scene was observed by two other story characters differing in their preexisting biases or knowledge about Joan—Cathy likes Joan, whereas Sarah does not. Children with some understanding of the biased nature of interpretation realize that Cathy may think that Joan is donating the doll, whereas Sarah may think she is stealing it. Pillow found that, although the results depend somewhat on the complexity of the situation and the nature of the questions asked, this understanding develops between the ages of 5 and 8 (see also Pillow & Mash, 1999). However, in addition to grasping the particular interpretations that people arrive at, there is the understanding that more than one interpretation is, in fact, possible at all regardless of individuals' particular likes and dislikes, and that in ambiguous situations multiple interpretations may be legitimate.

Two general approaches have been used to assess children's understanding of interpretation. One is to use ambiguous stimuli that are without particular form, like Rorschach inkblots, to assess when children understand that it is unlikely that two individuals would arrive at exactly the same interpretation. This approach was taken by Lalonde and Chandler (2002; Chandler & Lalonde, 1996) in their use of ambiguous pictures known as droodles, in which only a keyhole, restricted view of a larger drawing is visible, making it ambiguous. For example, the restricted view of a droodle entitled, "a ship arriving too late to save a drowning witch," shows only two triangles, depicting the bow of the ship and the witch's hat in the larger picture. Without knowledge of the larger picture, the restricted view of the two triangles would be completely ambiguous. By the age of 7 to 8, children provide evidence of an understanding of interpretation by recognizing that two individuals would most likely interpret the ambiguous restricted views in different ways.

A second approach is based on a class of stimuli, which provide strong evidence for two distinct interpretations. Such stimuli can be drawn from pictures, sentences, or words, such as ambiguous figures (e.g., Jastrow, 1900), ambiguous referential communication (e.g., Robinson & Robinson, 1983), or homonyms. In taking this approach, it was found that even though 5-year-olds could see both views of the ambiguous figures, knew both meanings of the homonyms, and could understand both meanings of the ambiguous referential message, they still tended to think that one had to be right and that the other one must be wrong. In contrast, the majority of the 8-year-olds easily acknowledged the ambiguity and the fact that both interpretations were equally legitimate (Carpendale & Chandler, 1996).

This understanding that people may interpret events or words differently may be associated with other aspects of children's social development such as their understanding of communication and humor. At about the age of 6 to 7 years, children's sense of humor seems to change, and they can understand and appreciate jokes based on puns; that is, they understand humor that turns on multiple meanings of words (McGhee, 1979). Similarly, children younger than 5 or 6 years old tend to be unaware that ambiguous messages can be understood in different ways, and it is not until about the age of 7 or 8 that children come to understand that the same message can have two different meanings (e.g., Robinson & Robinson, 1983).

Another possible link to an understanding of multiple interpretations may be children's grasp of sarcasm and irony. Initial findings indicated that it is not until children are older than 6 to 7 years that they typically come to understand ironic utterances (Winner & Leekam, 1991). Such communicative purposes have been interpreted within a "theory of mind" framework as requiring a second-order mental understanding because they require a grasp of an agent's representation of another's perspective on the world (Happé, 1994; Winner & Leekam, 1991). However, younger children do have some grasp of the ironical component of language (Filippova & Astington, 2008; Pexman & Glenwright, 2007). By the age of 6, children show a grasp of the negative intention of a sarcastic remark when valance options (e.g., "nice" or "nasty") are given to them (Dews et al., 1996). Indeed, there is evidence to suggest that the acquisition of this complex aspect of language might have its origins earlier in development. For example, Recchia, Howe, Ross, and Alexander (in press) recorded pairs of 4- and 6-year-olds siblings' conversations with their parents. They found that parents used irony in their talk to these children, using proportionately more understatement and rhetorical questions when disagreements arose. They also replicate earlier research (e.g., Ely & McCabe, 1994) showing children's use of some spontaneous ironical utterances. Indeed, there is emerging evidence that, with careful questioning, even 3-year-olds have some understanding of sarcasm (Yasui & Lewis, 2005). One way to resolve these conflicting results is to think about the process by which children come to understand forms of communication like sarcasm and understatement. A key feature of social-cognitive development concerns the role of language, which is explored in depth in the final section of this chapter.

Clearly, the examples of interpretation used with children in the research reported earlier are very simple, and older children and adults encounter far more complex circumstances involving interpretation. This understanding continues to develop through childhood and adolescence (Chandler, 1988; Hallet, Chandler, & Krettenauer, 2002; King & Kitchener, 1994; Kuhn, Amsel, & O'Laughlin, 1988; Mansfield & Clinchy, 2002). More complex understanding of the process of knowledge acquisition has been studied in adolescence and young adulthood, from adolescents' relativistic thinking (Chandler, 1987) through further development in university students' understanding of the process of knowledge acquisition (Perry, 1970; Chandler & Birch, Chapter 19 of this volume). The general pattern in this understanding of the nature of knowledge moves from certainty to relativity, and finally to some commitment in relativism (Chandler, 1987).

Does Social Understanding Decline in Older Adults?

Social cognition is a vital resource for navigating the social world that is essential throughout the life span. Although research has focused mainly on infancy and childhood, a few pioneering studies have extended the "theory of mind" approach into adulthood and, particularly, late adulthood. Happé, Winner, and Brownell (1998) reported that the ability to make inferences about others' thoughts, beliefs, and desires did not decline in a group of older adults with a mean age of 73 compared with a group of young adults (mean age, 21 years); in fact, the older age group showed superior performance. Subsequent findings, however, contradict this result. In a small study, a group of older adult participants scored lower on social inference tasks compared with university-aged participants, but this was due to one of four tasks only; on the other tasks, both groups performed at ceiling (Saltzman, Strauss, Hunter, & Achibald, 2000). Also in contrast with Happé et al.'s study, Maylor, Moulson, Muncer, and Taylor (2002) found a decline in social understanding comparing groups with mean ages of 19 and 67, but not when memory load was removed. However, in an older group with a mean age of 81, there was a decline relative to the other groups even with no memory load. In a second study more closely replicating Happé et al. by using the same stories involving inference about double bluffs, persuasions, white lies, and mistakes, Maylor et al. compared groups with mean ages of 21 and

81, and again found significantly better performance in the younger group. Differences were not found, however, on control tasks requiring understanding short passages of text and drawing correct inferences. The older participants in these studies were active and living independently, and most were members of a whist society, a card game requiring keeping track of what cards have been played. Maylor et al. suggest that if social reasoning involves frontal processing, then their findings fit with known functional decline in late adulthood.

Sullivan and Ruffman (2004) also found a decline in social cognition in late adulthood. For some tasks, but not others, this was mostly explained by a decline in fluid intelligence. On other tasks requiring less working memory, however, elderly participants still tended to have somewhat impaired social understanding. However, Sullivan and Ruffman also note that on the various tasks used, between 13% and 33% of the older adult participants were not impaired in social understanding. There is also additional evidence that, on average, social understanding declines with age between 50 and 90 years on stories requiring inference about others' beliefs and intentions, but not on control stories (Charlton, Barrick, Markus, & Morris, 2009). This decline was partially or fully explained by decline in other cognitive abilities. Decline in performance on the social understanding tasks was associated with reduced integrity of white matter, but performance on the control stories was not correlated with brain imaging measures.

Beyond drawing inferences about others' beliefs and emotions, another important aspect of social understanding is emotion recognition. Lack of such competence may lead to problems in communication and impairment in social functioning. Ruffman, Henry, Livingstone, and Phillips (2008) conducted a meta-analytic review of studies of emotion recognition in adult and late adult development, comparing emotion recognition in young and older adults based on identifying emotions in four modalities: faces, voices, bodies and contexts, and matching faces to voices. Across the 28 datasets reviewed, older adults performed more poorly recognizing anger and sadness in all modalities, and more poorly on fear, surprise, and happiness in some modalities compared with the younger adults, who were mostly at ceiling. However, recognition of disgust seemed to be preserved in the older adult participants. Ruffman et al. (2008, p. 874) suggest the possibility that "structural changes in grey or white matter as well as changes in neurotransmitters might be related to older adults' recognition difficulties" rather than an overall general cognitive decline. They note the caveats that a cohort effect cannot be ruled out, or that older adults' performances on stimuli using young and middle-aged adults who have been instructed how to move their facial muscles to produce a conventional expression may not be an accurate reflection of their competence in more naturalistic situations.

It is known that performance tends to be lower on laboratory-based tests of social understanding compared with real-life performance; thus, Charlton et al. (2009) question whether reported decline in social understanding with age actually reflects any reduction in "real-world" ability in this area. Exploring this possibility would require more naturalistic measures of social understanding. The tasks used so far in research with older adult participants involve complex recursive thinking about what someone else is thinking, and recognition of emotions seems to require working memory. These are important aspects of social cognition, but throughout this chapter, we continue to argue for the need to broaden research on social cognition from that focused on in the current "theory of mind" tradition. Considering social understanding in older adults highlights this point. To get a better picture of social cognition and late adult development, an assessment of older adults' actual competence in social situations is needed. More typical, everyday uses of social understanding may not require complex recursive thinking, and instead may rely more on practiced social skills. It is possible that some aspects of social understanding may be based on more extensive experience, tact, social insight, judgment, and cultural knowledge. Crystallized abilities such as vocabulary and general knowledge are relatively intact in late adulthood compared with fluid abilities requiring more working memory. Therefore, it is possible that aspects of social understanding depending more on social and cultural knowledge such as self-presentation (Goffman, 1959) may be more preserved compared with aspects requiring inference.

THEORIES OF "THEORY OF MIND": THE QUEST FOR A MIND DETACHED FROM SOCIAL PROCESSES

The data from research with the false belief task have been used since the 1980s to differentiate several theoretical perspectives in children's social understanding. This section describes the four theoretical accounts based on individualistic, split metatheoretical assumptions that dominated discussion in the 1980s and 1990s. These share the assumption that theory should focus on the mental

architecture required for understanding the mind, and they marginalize the role of social processes in the construction of this architecture. The following section describes how these four approaches have changed since the late 1990s.

The perspective that served as an iconic metaphor for the field was termed "theory theory" because it proposed that the child is like a miniature theoretician, and it posited the child as an armchair philosopher who simply had to devise theoretical speculations about how the mind works. The metaphor of the child-as-scientist creating a sequence of domain-specific naïve theories was enlisted to explain the child's grasp of physical (e.g., Karmiloff-Smith & Inhelder, 1974) and biological concepts (Carey, 1985). This work was coupled with social psychological analyses of adults' naïve psychology (Heider, 1958) to inspire an explosion of research in the 1980s on the child's grasp of psychological processes. A landmark was Henry Wellman's (1990) book, claiming that the child's grasp of the mind can be defined as a "theory." This was based, first, on a series of philosophical claims: (1) that the child makes "ontological" distinctions between "mind versus matter" (p. 14) and further distinctions between different mental states, like beliefs and desires; (2) that the understanding of the mind is "coherent" (a grasp of beliefs desires intentions, etc. are connected); and (3) these understandings fit together into a causal-explanatory framework to mediate our interpretations of our experiences. Second, Wellman justified the use of the theory metaphor by claiming that the child goes through a series of mini-scientific revolutions—from having no grasp of mental states, to an understanding of desires at the age of 2, to a belief-desire psychology at around 4 years, to a belief-desire-emotion psychologist by 6 years. He claimed that these transitions occur as a result of a subtle balance between the child's grasp of mental state terms (Bartsch & Wellman, 1995) and her or his interpretation of the available data. So, the 3-year-old who does not have a sound understanding of beliefs will answer the false belief test question in terms of the protagonist's desires and, therefore, fail the task. Wellman and Liu (2004) devised a scale of integrated measures, which demonstrate that children seem to follow his predicted sequence of understanding different mental states.

James Russell (1992) once quipped that "theory theory" is so good that they named it twice. In fact, it is so "good" that there are two versions of it. The alternative account that also uses the "theory" metaphor, put forward by Josef Perner (1991), is that it is not the content of belief desire reasoning that changes, but the very nature of thinking itself, and this drives "theory" development. Perner claimed that the key shift at age 4 is the ability to compare mental representations—we might know that the chocolate is in the red cupboard, but Maxi might think that it is in the yellow cupboard, and we need to have the cognitive capacity to be able to hold both perspectives in mind and compare them. Perner described this skill as "metarepresentation": It allows us to hold competing, yet compatible, mental representations of the World. He used the metaphor of the child-as-scientist, but for him the paradigm shift at age 4 is a move to an understanding that the mind is not simply a reflection of reality. He described a second shift, at about age 6, involving the understanding that it is possible to have a false belief about others' beliefs—"second-order" false belief (Perner & Wimmer, 1985).

Wellman's and Perner's positions have not been tested as explanatory competitors. This may be because they are generally viewed as *the* "theory-theory" approach, and when joined as one, the perspective has been broadly attacked by proponents of two opposing perspectives: the Innate Module approach and the Simulation approach. We outline these two perspectives briefly here before discussing more recent developments. The first opposition to theory-theory came from a group arguing that understanding the mind is innately constrained: the *Innate Module* account. According to this perspective, nature does not take the risk of allowing us to construct an understanding of the mind. Instead, the "mind-brain" system is *innately* equipped with discrete skills termed *modules*, which initially have separate functions (e.g., an ability to attend to another's direction of gaze, or an awareness of shared attention [Baron-Cohen, 1995]). Leslie (1987) defends the idea of this innate "Theory of Mind Mechanism" because toddlers demonstrate a proclivity for pretence—an ability to represent an object "as if" it were another—which is claimed to be a nascent meta-representational skill. He suggests that 3-year-olds fail the false belief task because usually people's beliefs correspond to what is actually true, whereas 4-year-olds have a greater capacity for applying their "theory of mind" skills (Leslie, 1991). Development occurs not in the child's changing attitude but in a broader change in the child's general processing capacities (Fodor, 1992; Leslie, 1987, 2005).

The second opposition to theory-theory—arising from philosophers (e.g., Gordon, 1986; Hurley, 2008) and psychologists (Harris, 2000; Johnson, 1988)—attacks the notion of the child—or adult—being considered a "theoretician." These critics argue that an understanding of the mind occurs through the capacity to imagine, or "simulate," another's perspective, not through the acquisition of a "theory." Harris (1991) proposed four stages of development of this *Simulation approach*. According to Harris, the child begins with an innate ability to synchronize interactional gestures with others (following Trevarthen, 1979), moving to acquiring an ability to take turns by the first birthday, then to anticipating others' gestures at age 3, and finally to placing oneself in the shoes of another at age 4.

Critical Reflections on "Theory of Mind"

The debate of the 1980s and 1990s between the three perspectives just described (theory theory, the innate module account and simulation theory; the two versions of theory theory are considered one position) appeared to be stagnating as the new millennium approached. First, there were moves within the "theory" and "simulation" perspectives toward reconciliation, and an effort aimed at marginalizing the innate module account (Carruthers & Smith, 1996; Stone & Davies, 1996). Second, there were critiques of all three accounts from both within "theory of mind" discussions and from those who had been critical from the outset.

Perhaps the most significant criticisms to arise from within the "theory of mind" discussion came from James Russell (1992, 1996). Russell's main attack against the "theory-theory" approach involved the loose manner in which the term *theory* is applied. Similar criticisms of the use of the term *theory* came from others (Campbell & Bickhard, 1993; Gellatly, 1997; German & Leslie, 2000; Leudar & Costall, 2009; Sharrock & Coulter, 2004). If all that is meant is that individuals' psychological knowledge is interlinked and changes with development, then using the term *theory* is not required.

With respect to the simulation account, Russell attacked the assumption—actually common to all three perspectives—that successful understanding of another's mental state requires the means to identify one's own mental state and to compare that with the other. Russell's critique draws from the later philosophy of Wittgenstein (1968), who argued that internal mental states are not private events that can be introspected on and used to understand others through analogy. This is also a core feature of our own critique of these three theories, and we return to and explicate this argument as advanced by other critics in the Language and Social Understanding section later in this chapter. As a result of such criticisms, developmental psychology broadly rejected the simulation account of the 1990s. However, as discussed in the next major section, a new form of simulation theory has recently emerged.

Another form of criticism focused on the reliance of each explanatory account on one critical test: the false belief task (Chandler, 1988). For example, Bloom and German (2000) argued that the test should be "abandoned" because children require other cognitive abilities to pass the test; thus, the general processing demands of the task make it unlikely to be a pure test of mental state understanding. Bloom and German also argued that "there is more to theory of mind than passing the false belief task" (p. B28), because even at the age of 2, children demonstrate some understanding of others' knowledge. We return to these issues later in this chapter (see Development of Social Understanding in Infancy).

Another series of critiques of the three accounts of the understanding of other's mental states emerges from a fundamental concern about cognitive science's isolated and internalist view of the mind, which neglects the embeddedness of human psychosocial functioning within a social context—again, a core feature of our own critique. These critiques were spearheaded by Jerome Bruner (1986), one of the leaders of the "cognitive revolution" that began in the mid-1950s. Bruner attacked the metaphor of the mind-as-computer, particularly the idea that individuals calculate the rules of interpersonal interaction in an abstract, theoretical way. Instead, understanding is based on the subtle interweaving of individual skills and the cultural processes which give rise to narratives that comprise folk psychology, and are so neglected in the "theory of mind" movement. Bruner (1990) argued that we have a propensity for the interpersonal, but this requires stimulation by the flow of everyday social interaction and story-making.

Michael Chandler (1988; Chandler & Birch, Chapter 19 of this volume), an early critic of the "theory of mind" approach, argued that the movement ignored development and focused too narrowly on the 3- to 4-year shift. Chandler, Fritz, and Hala (1989) devised a task demonstrating that even 2-year-olds could deceive—erasing trails to a container where a desired object was located and laying false trails to other locations—and deception entails taking into account the other's mental state.

Bruner's and Chandler's analyses led to a broad concern about the focus on the "individual" mind in the "theory of mind" approach (Feldman, 1992; Jopling, 1993; Nelson, 2005; Raver & Leadbeater, 1993). The relational account of social understanding argued for in this chapter takes as its foundation the primacy of interpersonal relationships, not the exclusivity of cognitive operations of the individual mind (Mead, 1934; Vygotsky, 1978). Given the backdrop of these early critiques of "theory of mind," the final

two parts of this section turn to debates that have fueled the tension between the "theory of mind" tradition and its cognitive critics: links with executive functions and disorders of social understanding.

Is Social Understanding Best Understood as a General Cognitive Process?

As a result of the fact that the "theory of mind" debate has been narrowly focused on cognitive components, one of the central questions *within* this tradition has been whether social cognition derives from general cognitive skills or ones specific to social understanding. Since the 1990s, this has centered on the role of executive function processes in the emergence of "theory of mind" (e.g., Russell, 1997). For example, according to Leslie's (e.g., 1991) innate modular account, children become able to pass false belief tasks because of an increase in their general processing capacities, which allow them to realize this innate skill. However, other approaches assume that "theory of mind" and executive cognitive skills are both constructed developmentally by the child. We briefly explore this literature before suggesting that the association between executive processes and "theory of mind" poses interesting empirical questions from a contemporary cognitive perspective but does little to expand on social understanding from a social point of view.

Although several tasks have been designed to measure various dimensions of executive function, a great deal of the research in this area has used the Dimensional Change Card Sort test (DCCS). In this procedure, the child has to sort cards by shape (e.g., cars vs. flowers) into two trays in front of target cards the opposite color of the sorting cards; for example, blue flowers where the target card is a red flower and red cars where the target car is blue. Three-year-olds find this easy. After a few trials, the child is told, "We're going to play the color game now, put the blue ones in here and the red ones in here," using the color rather than the shape of the model as a guide. Three-year-olds usually continue to use shape as the guiding rule, whereas 4-year-olds can switch easily between color and shape (Zelazo, Müller, Frye, & Marcovitch, 2003).

Tasks that measure executive function (see Jacques & Marcovitch, Chapter 13 of this volume, for an extended discussion of the development of executive function across the life span) are believed to reflect at least three sets of cognitive skills (see Dick & Overton, 2010, for an extended list of executive function skills). The first of these is *attentional flexibility*, which entails the ability to switch from one rule to another. In the DCCS, described earlier, this is the central issue under investigation. A second is *inhibitory control* (Hughes, 1998), which refers to the ability to inhibit a prepotent response, like responding to the instruction in Simon Says. The third cognitive skill thought to be entailed by executive function is *working memory*, which concerns the ability to maintain and manipulate verbal and visual information (see Demetriou, Mouyi, & Spanoudis, Chapter 10 of this volume, for an extended discussion of the development of the architecture of mind, including working memory). Just how distinct these skills are is itself open to a great deal of negotiation. Although these sets of skills are distinguishable in adults (Miyake et al., 2000), this is not the case for studies of young children (Huizinga, Dolan, & van der Molen, 2006). Individual tasks may draw on a range of skills. Thus, for example, the ability to switch sorting rules on the DCCS may also involve the ability to inhibit the first rule when sorting by the second, and even the ability to hold information in mind and apply it in particular circumstances—working memory.

One issue concerning the relation between social understanding and executive function skills is the question of whether any association between the two is increased depending on whether a single or multiple executive function skills are assessed. Perner, Kain, and Barchfeld (2002) maintain that the self-insight caused by the development of a grasp of the mind as a representational device, as indicated by the false belief task, leads to the development of self-control. That is, false belief understanding facilitates the development of executive functions. However, longitudinal evidence for this claim has not been found. The contrasting hypothesis that executive skills predict later "theory of mind" has been supported in several studies (Carlson, Mandell, & Williams, 2004; Flynn, O'Malley, & Wood, 2004; Hughes, 1998), but for only a subset of measures in each study. For example, Carlson and Moses (2001) tested the relation between inhibitory control derived from a factor analysis of many measures and "theory of mind" in 3- to 4-year-olds. The "theory of mind" tasks were found to correlate strongly with measures of inhibitory control in 3- to 4-year-olds, even when language and age were taken into account. There are also grounds for assuming that it is the combination of inhibitory control and working memory that is important for "theory of mind." For example, Hala, Hug, and Henderson (2003) found that only if combined with working memory was the association of inhibitory control with false belief understanding significant.

A second, and fundamental, question addressed in the literature concerns possible causal relations between executive functions and social understanding. Establishing causal relations between constructs is, of course, enormously difficult. Training studies facilitate the process, but here the evidence is contradictory. In an effort to assess whether attentional flexibility influences "theory of mind" or the reverse, Kloo and Perner (2003) trained children either on the DCCS or on false belief tasks. They found an improvement on the task that children had not been trained on, suggesting that they may be two sides to the same coin. Research on inhibitory control has been more informative but not conclusive. The combination of working memory and conflict inhibition was found in several studies to be the best longitudinal predictor of false belief understanding (e.g., Carlson, Moses, & Breton, 2002; Hala et al., 2003). We know that these executive skills are associated with adjacent loci in the prefrontal cortex (Diamond, 1990), suggesting that these skills may be linked at the neuroanatomical level. Even though such links are only causal by implication, this perspective is still in the ascendancy and is supported in longitudinal findings (Carlson, Mandell, & Williams, 2004). However, it has not met with universal agreement. For example, Zelazo and Müller (2002) point out that the notion of "inhibitory control" does not explain the selection of what is to be inhibited or the process of inhibition. Partly as a result, Moses and colleagues (Moses & Carlson, 2004; Moses & Sabbagh, 2007) propose an "emergence" argument: that the skills of inhibitory control and working memory are necessary, but not sufficient, for a grasp of "theory of mind."

Another recent exploration of the relation between executive skills and social understanding has entailed a focus on cross-cultural data. Support for the emergence account comes from a comparison of these skills in Europe, Africa, and Latin America (Chasiotis, Kiessling, Winter, & Hofer, 2006), following initial studies solely in Britain and North America. Attention has recently focused on children in Northeast Asia because they show advanced working memory (Tardif, So, & Kaciroti, 2007) and other executive skills (Oh & Lewis, 2008; Sabbagh, Xu, Carlson, Moses, & Lee, 2006) compared with their Western counterparts. Sabbagh et al. found that these advanced executive skills in Chinese children still correlated with concurrent false belief understanding, which is consistent with the emergence approach. However, our own work does not support such a view. In both China (Lewis, Huang, & Rooksby, 2006) and Korea (Oh & Lewis, 2008), inhibitory control and working memory did not predict false belief once general skills such as language were factored in. These results cannot completely refute the emergence account, because children's levels of inhibition and memory are in place long before false belief understanding. However, Korean children's impressive mastery of inhibitory control was achieved more than a year in advance of their more modest understanding of false beliefs. The length of this lag questions whether there are any necessary links between the two skills and this, in turn, opens the question of whether it may be the case that social processes specific to a culture are central to the development of these skills (Lewis, Koyasu, Oh, Ogawa, & Short, 2009) and must, therefore, be built into theories of each type of skill.

Support for the contention that social processes play a central role with respect to both executive and false belief skills comes from a diversity of sources. First, on a cultural level, it has long been known that children in Japan lag up to 2 years behind those in other cultures in passing false belief tests (Naito & Koyama, 2006). When combined with advanced executive skills in this culture, this Japanese lag in false belief understanding suggests that cultural processes may be exerting a strong influence on the acquisition of false belief understanding. At a behavioral level, social processes have not been explored in depth. However, an interesting study hints at social process influences by examining how specific social understanding tasks relate, within one culture, to specific behavioral skills. Peskin and Ardino (2003) tested children on two false belief tasks described at the beginning of this chapter—the unexpected transfer and the unexpected contents tests. Performance on these tasks was explored in relation to two common social activities—keeping a secret and the skills involved in playing hide-and-seek. Once age had been taken into account, unexpected contents test performance was correlated only with the child's ability to keep a secret. The authors suggested that this may be because both involve beliefs about the nature and/or identity of an object. At the same time, the unexpected transfer test was predicted by children's ability to play hide-and-seek, perhaps because both tasks involve the location of an object. Thus, Peskin and Ardino's evidence suggests that specific false belief skills may be developed in the context of particular social experiences.

Other evidence also supports the idea that social processes may play an important role in the acquisition of executive skills. For example, a series of studies in the 1970s found that children's performances on delay inhibition tasks was influenced by a simple comment made by an adult about how well the child could control his or her behavior (Toner, Moore, & Emmons, 1980; Toner & Smith, 1977). Recent work has started to revisit Soviet ideas inspired by Luria (Subbotsky, 1976) to explore social influences on conflict inhibition. For example, Moriguchi, Lee, and Itakura (2007) examined the association between the child seeing an adult model making errors on the preswitch trials of the DCCS and performance on this task. Viewing the adult model was associated with making fewer errors when following the same rule on the postswitch trials themselves, especially when the actor said he had been unsure about what he had done. Using another conflict inhibition test, the Windows task, it has been found that 3-year-olds are also less likely to point to the baited box for the experimenter (pointing to the baited box means the child loses the sweet) if they use a pointer (a pointing hand) to alert the experimenter to the box that she should open (Hala & Russell, 2001). Hala and Russell suggest that this action serves as a means of marking the link between the experimenter and the box in a symbolic way. It is further suggested that this helps children perform the deceptive act required in the Windows task—pointing to the empty box knowing that this will lead to them receiving the reward.

The lesson, therefore, of some recent work on the relations between executive function and "theory of mind" is that both are connected to social processes, and that both may emerge from the child's everyday interactions. Together with critiques of other studies, it is empirical evidence of this sort that suggests that taking a relational approach to the development of social understanding may be more than simply speculative musings (Lewis, Carpendale, Towse, & Maridaki-Kassotaki, 2010; Sokol, Müller, Carpendale, Young, & Iarocci, 2010).

Disorders of Social Understanding

A key reason that the "theory of mind" approach to social cognition came to dominate the literature stems from the early optimism that typical development could be compared directly with atypical development, notably autism. That is, as the movement emerged in the 1980s, autism was viewed as a deficit in "theory of mind." We select this disorder because although problems in social understanding have been found in children with other clinical syndromes, these are less well specified. For example, individuals with Williams syndrome show problems with a range of verbal and nonverbal false belief tests, but the variation within this group's performance on social understanding tasks is wide (Porter, Coltheart, & Langdon, 2008).

Soon after Wimmer and Perner's first experiment, Baron-Cohen, Leslie, and Frith (1985) showed that children with autism with a mental age higher than 4 failed a version of the unexpected transfer task that was passed by typically developing children matched for mental age and those of a comparable chronological age but with Down syndrome. These findings were quickly replicated (e.g., Leslie & Frith, 1988) and extended to the unexpected contents task (Perner, Frith, Leslie, & Leekam, 1989), deception (Oswald & Ollendick, 1989), and for children with an elementary grasp of first-order false belief, second-order false belief tasks (Baron-Cohen, 1989). So compelling was the evidence of a specific problem in "mind reading" in autism that it led to the speculation that this ability is "innate, biological, [and] modular" (Baron-Cohen, 1995, p 12; for a similar view see Leslie, 1992). If children with autism, or another special population, have specific problems with understanding mental states, whereas appearing intact in other areas of cognitive functioning, this would appear to support the modular account.

In the 1990s, much debate concerned whether the evidence from autism supports one theory over another. Yet, from the outset, the data failed to support the idea that individuals with autism have clear deficits in social skills, as predicted by the innate module account. Research demonstrated that once children with autism develop sufficient language skills, they passed false belief tests (e.g., Eisenmajer & Prior, 1991). Similarly, individuals with Asperger syndrome pass second-order false belief tests (Bowler, 1992). Such inconsistencies in the link between false belief and autism have been further supported in a meta-analysis of some 40 studies (Yirmiya, Erel, Shaked, & Solomonica-Levi, 1998). As a result of the inconsistent links with false belief understanding, the 1990s witnessed the development of a series of laboratory tests of advanced mental state understanding involving a grasp of "strange stories" in which an actor's utterance is nonliteral (Happé, 1994), understanding emotions when presented only with photographs of a person's eyes (Baron-Cohen, Jolliffe, Mortimore, & Robertson, 1997), and understanding when someone commits a faux pas (Baron-Cohen, O'Riordan, Jones, Stone, & Plaisted, 1999). In series of studies involving each of these skills, individuals with autism performed less well on these tasks than those in comparison groups with similar levels of intellectual performance.

Two concerns have been raised about the relevance of these laboratory tasks. First, the ecological validity of these "high-level" assessments has been questioned. For example, in the Eyes Test (Baron-Cohen et al., 1997), adults are presented with a photograph of part of a face showing a person's eyes. They have to select which of four words characterizes the displayed emotion. Individuals with autism perform poorly on this task. However, if this restricted view of the face is made more ecologically valid, by having the participant view a video of a person's eyes, the difference between autistic individuals and control participants is no longer found (Back, Ropar, & Mitchell, 2007). Second, Rajendran and Mitchell (2007) point out that the Eyes Test, the Strange Stories, and Faux Pas Tests do not have the same underpinning in theory as the false belief tasks, which were designed specifically to contrast a protagonist's beliefs with reality. Rajendran and Mitchell suggest that "the development of advanced tests could be viewed as a post hoc response in finding data anomalous to the 'theory of mind' hypothesis that some individuals with autism pass tests of false belief" (p. 229).

The application of the "theory of mind" approach to autism has also long been criticized for other reasons. For example, Uta Frith (2003) pointed out that the "theory of mind" explanation of autism cannot take into account a range of problems and skills in autism that do not relate to social understanding. Individuals with autism are reported to show "islets of ability" in identifying smaller patterns within the Embedded Figures Test (Shah & Frith, 1983), but do not see visual illusions (Happé, 1996), because they focus on the component parts of the array and not its overall configuration. Frith interprets these differences in terms of a general cognitive deficit, "central coherence," in which individuals with autism process visual stimuli at local rather than general levels. The fact that "theory of mind" approaches do not explain these differences undermines this theory as an explanation for autism (Tager-Flusberg, 2003).

A second general area of research, also questioning the idea that autism consists solely of a deficit in "theory of mind," comes from a long tradition of research showing that children with autism have difficulties with executive functions. For example, in the Windows task, discussed earlier, Russell, Mauthner, Sharpe, and Tidswell (1991) found that older children with autism, like typically developing 3-year-olds, failed over repeated trials to select the empty box for the experimenter to open, and thus lost out repeatedly on a reward. They concluded that such failure is caused by a general executive problem in inhibiting salient responses. This evidence also generalized to the other executive tests. As with typically developing children, such performance correlated with scores on batteries of false belief tests (Colvert, Custance, & Swettenham, 2002). As a result, in the 1990s, there was confidence that autism is an "executive disorder" (Russell, 1997). However, individuals with autism do not show across-the-board problems with executive tests (Hill, 2004); as a consequence, there has been growing criticism of the idea that the problems in social understanding are caused by an executive dysfunction (Rajendran & Mitchell, 2007).

Although the "theory of mind" literature has influenced popular depictions of autism since the 1980s, more mainstream accounts of autism argue and provide empirical evidence that children with autism have fundamental problems engaging in shared affective exchanges with others (Mundy & Sigman, 1989; Mundy, Sullivan, & Mastergeorge, 2009; Sigman, Mundy, Sherman, & Ungerer, 1986), orienting to others (Leekam, López, & Moore, 2000; Osterling & Dawson, 1994), sharing attention with objects (see Bruinsma, Koegel, & Koegel, 2004, for a review), and switching attention (Courchesne et al., 1994).

Autism research illustrates the problems with the cognitive approach of the "theory of mind" movement. The evidence we have presented has led to a broad shift away from viewing autism as simply a deficit in the ability to theorize about mind. In its place, investigators have begun to take a more relational stance, not denying the significance of cognitive processes, but focusing on the role played by fundamental social-affective relationships. And the work in this area has supported the contention that early difficulty with interpersonal relations is a key antecedent to the diagnosis of autism. For example, eye tracking studies have demonstrated that individuals with autism show a lack interest in other people when watching social interactions in movies (Klin, Jones, Schultz, & Volkmar, 2003). Another suggestion is that such children may differ in their emotional reactivity, which could lead to a lack of interpersonal engagement required for social cognitive development (Shanker, 2004). These examples open the possibility that small differences in infants' social-emotional status may significantly influence the nature of their experience of interpersonal relationships and, thus, their social cognitive development.

Peter Hobson (1993, 2002/2004) argues that the self-other relationship must be the basic unit of analysis in the area of social and social cognitive development to understand the nature of autism, as well as to illuminate typical development. For Hobson, the major features of autism are social relational. Typical development begins from an interpersonal connectedness—as stated earlier, a core assumption of the relational stance—and requires identification with the psychological stance of other people. The

atypical development of those with autism, Hobson argues, demonstrates disruptions in these processes.

The theoretical and empirical movement away from an exclusive reliance on cognitive processes to explain both the typical and atypical development of social understanding, combined with the movement toward a more relational stance, suggests the need for a greater focus on the fundamental interpersonal building blocks of social understanding. This is the focus of the final three sections of this chapter.

CURRENT STATE OF PLAY: MOVES TO INCREASED INDIVIDUALIZATION

This section explores the contemporary cognitive approach to social understanding, as represented in four related, but distinct, research literatures. The aim here is to demonstrate that despite, or perhaps partly as a result of, the continuing criticism of the split individualistic approach of theories discussed earlier, work in the area of the "theory of mind" has become increasingly insular in its outlook. Indeed, the trend has been to locate social understanding within increasingly narrow areas of the mind-brain system, even at the level of the individual neuron. We contrast each of the four areas of research with alternatives offered by the relational approach.

Neuroscience and Social Understanding

Studies since the 1990s have used neuroimaging techniques to explore the possible localization of social skills in adult brain functioning. Two brain areas have been identified as being active when individuals are assumed to be "mentalizing," or thinking about others as intentional agents. First, when adults think they are competing with another person in a simple game while in a functional magnetic resonance imaging (fMRI) scanner, there is increased activity in and around the anterior cingulate cortex (ACC) (Gallagher, Jack, Roepstorff, & Frith, 2002). Second, the area around the temporoparietal junction (TPJ; including the adjacent posterior superior temporal sulcus region) is thought to be important. This region has been identified in a number of studies when participants are asked to attribute mental states in other individuals (Gallagher & Frith, 2003; Saxe, 2006), when they either look at cartoons with a "mental state" component (Gallagher et al., 2000) or are read stories describing a character's beliefs (Saxe & Wexler, 2005). Sommer et al. (2007) suggest that the two areas might serve different functions, with the ACC associated with monitoring action and the TPJ involved in the computation of mental representations that make the contrast between two different perspectives on beliefs possible.

Some authors are optimistic that imaging studies will allow us to choose between the main theories of "theory of mind." In one study, Mitchell, Banaji, and Macrae (2005; Mitchell, Macrae, & Banaji, 2006) analyzed individuals' judgments of the emotions displayed in photographs of faces, and comparisons between themselves and the person. They found that the dorsal medial prefrontal cortex appeared to be related to social judgments about others who were considered to be like the self. They infer that this provides support for simulation theory's emphasis on introspection as a basis of social understanding. However, Applerly (2008) argues that such data do not, and perhaps cannot, allow us to distinguish a simulation account from, for example, a theory-based one. Indeed, Apperly suggests that if we look at processing costs involved in making false belief and related inferences, as judged in adult reaction times when processing false belief judgments (Samson, Apperly, Kathirgamanathan, & Humphreys, 2005), then this favors an account based largely on executive functions as it emphasizes the role of general processing demands rather than specific "mind-reading" skills.

Although the recent neuroimaging studies of adults are interesting, they do not yet focus on frames of reference that are shared with the main "theory of mind" enterprise involving the development of particular skills. They examine the brain structures that appear to be active when individuals think about situations involving others' emotions and beliefs, but they tell us little about the processes by which individuals acquire and utilize such skills. Furthermore, it is quite unclear whether developmental and neuropsychological studies will sufficiently combine to address overlapping or identical questions. This is particularly the case as the research identified in this section is small in its quantity compared with the explosion of studies on preschool children. There is a need to relate this work to studies on children throughout the school years. There is also a danger of merely assessing adults and assuming that we understand the developmental story. Currently, there is a problematic move to dismiss the developmental story as being uninformative in the debate between the major theoretical positions (Carruthers, 2009).

There is also, however, critical discussion regarding the interpretation of neuroimaging studies. To begin with, fMRI data indicates blood flow, which does not necessarily indicate the firing of neurons (Logothetis, 2008); thus, "a brain region can activate according to the fMRI measure without producing any outputs" (Page, 2006, p. 432). In addition, it is known that the same brain regions can be active but for different functions (Kagan, 2006; Miller, 2008; Page, 2006). Furthermore, regarding controversies about which brain regions may be involved in social understanding, Gallese (2007) has argued that such thinking likely involves "the activation of large regions of our brain, certainly larger than a putative and domain-specific theory of mind module" (p. 667).

Although a complete explanation of social cognition must involve neurological processes, there are different neuroscience approaches to social cognition. The reductionistic position views cognitive neuroscience as "the study of the mind through the brain" that "holds the promise of explaining the operations of the mind in terms of the physical operations of the brain" (Greene & Cohen, 2004, p. 1775). This sort of approach, however, already buys into individualistic assumptions about the nature of thinking. An alternative relational perspective recognizes human activity as an interpersonal process based on reasons. Although neurological processes are involved, understanding human activity in terms of intentions and beliefs, and so forth, must be approached through interpersonal processes. This approach fits with relational developmental systems approaches (Lerner, 2006; Lerner & Overton, 2008; Overton, 2006) and examines the ways in which social experience shapes neurological processes (e.g., Griffiths & Stotz, 2000).

Mirror Neurons

Great interest has been generated by the recent discovery of a special type of neuron, which, some have argued, may form the neural basis for social cognition. These neurons, referred to as *mirror neurons*, were first found in the ventral premotor cortex (area F5) of macaque monkeys. They are activated both during a monkey's performance of a particular action, as well as when the monkey observes another performing the same act. For example, these neurons fire when a monkey grasps a nut, as well as when that monkey sees a human experimenter grasp a nut. Many of these neurons even fire in conditions where the action is partially hidden but the monkey can predict the outcome; that is, when the monkey has seen that there is an object behind the screen but cannot see the part of the action in which the hand grasps the object. Some neurons fire even when the action cannot be seen but only heard, for example, breaking nuts (Gallese, 2007; Gallese, Keysers, & Rizzolatti, 2004).

There is indirect evidence for a mirror neuron system in humans (Gallese et al., 2004), but this claim has also been challenged (Hickok, 2008; Lingnau, Gesierich, & Caramazza, 2009). It has been suggested "that, in our brain, there are neural mechanisms (mirror mechanisms) that allow us to directly understand the meaning of the actions and emotions of others by internally replicating ('simulating') them without explicit reflective mediation" (Gallese et al., p. 396). It is claimed that this system allows us to "directly understand the meaning of the actions and emotions of others" (Gallese et al., p. 396), and that this supports a simulation view of social cognition. That is, it is claimed that our brains "have developed a basic functional mechanism, embodied simulation, which can provide a direct access to the meanings of the actions and intentions of others" (Gallese, 2007, p. 662) and, thus, solve the problem of how we understand other minds (Colle, Becchio, & Bara, 2008; Iacoboni, 2009).

Iacoboni et al. (2005, pp. 529–530) recognize, however, that although this might explain how an individual understands a grasping action (e.g., grasping an apple), remaining questions are: "Why is she grasping it? Does she want to eat it, or give it to her brother, or maybe throw it away?" It appears that Iacoboni et al. recognize this problem, and as well as mirror neurons they are also investigating other "logically related" mirror neurons that fire in different contexts. Whether they recognize the far-reaching extent of this issue remains to be seen. A strength of Gallese's approach, however, is his attempt to root understanding in embodied interaction, and he suggests that "ascribing intentions would therefore consist in predicting a forthcoming new goal" (Gallese, 2007, p. 662). This way of linking intentions to observable human activity has a resonance with G. H. Mead's (1934) view of psychological notions as manifest in observable attitudes.

If mirror neurons were demonstrated to be associated with behaviors indexing social understanding, we would still have to examine exactly how this discovery could explain even "the simplest social action" (Colle et al., 2008, p. 337), pointing gestures. Infants at 12 months may, in some circumstances, understand or respond correctly to pointing, but these gestures may at times not be understood even by adults without the appropriate shared experience (Carpendale & Lewis, 2008; Moll & Tomasello, 2007). As Tomasello, Carpenter, and Liszkowski (2007) put it: "Pointing can convey an almost infinite variety of meanings" (p. 705). Thus, even if the same neurons fire

when an individual points or sees others point, this would not help in understanding the meaning of a particular gesture without shared experience. Yet, by 18 months, infants can understand that the same pointing gesture to the same object can convey different meaning if used by different people with whom they have shared different experiences (Liebal, Behne, Carpenter, & Tomasello, 2009). That is, they rely on shared experience to understand the gestures (Mead, 1934; Wittgenstein, 1968), and mirror neurons alone would not be sufficient.

Another difficulty with mirror neuron explanations is that it is often assumed that mirror neurons are "probably present from early on in development" (Colle et al., 2008), in which case they presumably must "acquire their function by genetic pre-wiring." But the "critical issue of *how* MNs could be pre-programmed to perform their task is rather unclear" (Del Giudice, Manera, & Keysers, 2009, p. 351, emphasis in original). Alternatively, the mirror neuron system may be the result of a Hebbian learning process through which neurons develop stronger connections with each other (Del Giudice et al., 2009; Keysers & Perrett, 2004). That is, the neurons may be the outcome of the infant's and child's shared social experience; that is, neurological processes are shaped by social experience (e.g., Griffiths & Stotz, 2000).

Although these neural systems may play a role in social cognition, the gap between the firing of neurons and the experience of understanding another person is large. In contemporary relational developmental systems approaches and in contemporary evolutionary developmental biology (see Greenberg & Partridge, Chapter 5 of this volume), it is accepted that novel systems are emergent and exhibit novel qualities that cannot be reduced to (explained by) lower order systems. Thus, although a causal, neurological side to the story of social cognition is necessary, an adequate account of social understanding cannot be restricted to the firing of neurons, and instead must recognize that meaning has to be rooted in shared social experience. This makes language possible, which vastly extends social understanding.

Social Cognition in Nonhuman Primates

One way to learn about the evolution of human social cognition is by studying other closely related species, especially chimpanzees, because they shared a common ancestor with humans 5 to 7 million years ago. Chimpanzees are good at a number of social skills such as following gaze (Call & Tomasello, 2008; see also Emery & Clayton,

2009). Also, in competitive circumstances, chimpanzees seem to understand what another has seen, and they base their action accordingly (Tomasello, Call, & Hare, 2003). Furthermore, chimpanzees can understand others' goals in many different contexts (Call & Tomasello, 2008). Although there seems to be consensus that in the wild, chimpanzees do not appear to point, many nonlanguage trained chimpanzees held in captivity do use pointing gestures to request food when an experimenter is present, perhaps because this is the sort of situation that human infants experience (Leavens, Racine, & Hopkins, 2009). Interestingly, observations of gestures used by wild chimpanzees suggest that they use "directed scratching" to request grooming, and perhaps also in a particular area of their body (Pika & Mitani, 2006).

These findings have led to a somewhat paradoxical debate. Povinelli and Vonk (2003) claimed that a chimpanzee's ability with such tasks is merely due to forming behavioral abstractions rather than an ability to conceive of the mental world. They question whether "chimpanzees construe behavior in terms of mental states" (p. 157). Instead, they suggest that chimpanzees: "(a) construct abstract categories of behavior, (b) make predictions about future behaviors that follow from past behaviors, and (c) adjust their own behavior accordingly" (Povinelli & Vonk, p. 157). If it is assumed that chimps grasp only the "surface behavior" without going "beneath" the surface, what is the secret ingredient that is added in the case of humans, and how do we account for the transitional phase of human infancy? The debate is set up as if the only two options are behaviorism or mentalism. This problematic way of conceptualizing the issue even extends to interpreting the activity of scrub-jays, ravens and jackdaws as based on behavior or understanding others' mental states (Emery & Clayton, 2009). But this splitting of intentions and beliefs from action is a philosophical assumption, not an empirical conclusion.

It is only behavior, or rather, activity, that chimpanzees, as well as humans, have access to. Understanding others in psychological terms may involve far more complex understanding than mere isolated physical movement, but there is no separate Cartesian-inspired space "beneath the surface." Behavior now has a bad name because behaviorism was also Cartesian inspired in splitting physical movement from intentions, and so on. For G. H. Mead (1934), in contrast, action is inextricably tied up with goals, beliefs, and desires; thus, understanding intentions involves anticipating the upcoming act. More recently, Gallese (2007) suggested that "ascribing intentions would therefore consist in

predicting a forthcoming new goal" (p. 662). From Mead and Wittgenstein's perspective, mental states are a dimension of action—a way of talking about or redescribing action. Mental states are not being denied, but the problematic conception of them in a Cartesian-inspired sense as separate from and causing action can be questioned (Racine & Carpendale, 2008; Ryle, 1949).

Can Infants Understand False Beliefs?

Given that much of the focus of attention within the "theory of mind" tradition has been on the shift in children's cognitive development around their fourth birthdays, the field experienced an earthquake in 2005 when Onishi and Baillargeon published findings suggesting that 15-month-old infants have some grasp of false beliefs, in that they look longer when an agent appears to act contrary to what would be expected from her previous actions. The experimental paradigm involved the agent having placed a toy in a green box, then reaching to that box if she has seen it move to the yellow box ("true belief") or reaching to the yellow box having been absent when it moved to that box ("false belief"). Increased looking is taken to be a sign of an understanding of these violations of expectations. These findings have been replicated in a related paradigm (Surian, Caldi, & Sperber, 2007), adding to the rekindling of the heated debate started by the original false belief test with preschoolers.

This research has been cited as evidence for an innate module dedicated to understanding mental state representations, which emerges in the second year of life. Onishi and Baillargeon (2005) propose a "representational theory of mind" that is "already in place" at 15 months, whereas Alan Leslie (2005, p. 459) describes "a specialized neurocognitive mechanism that matures during the second year of life. This allows infants "to attribute beliefs to agents" (Surian et al., 2007). There is no obvious empirical way to assess these claims in comparison with the simpler possibility that infants learn something in a practical, lived sense about their social world during their first year and a half. Onishi and Baillargeon's experiment has led to much current discussion about the influence of innate knowledge on social understanding. However, the old battle lines have been reoccupied. Protagonists of theory theory claim that a grasp of an agent's beliefs, particularly false ones, must come later because they hold that the child must have the capacity for theory construction. Theory theory's explanation of preferential looking times in infants toward surprising events (e.g., looking where a toy is without seeing it move to the current location) resorts to the associationism of learning theory to explain such patterns (Perner & Ruffman 2005; Ruffman & Perner, 2005). According to this explanation, the infant simply acts on the premise that an agent will look for an object where she last saw it as a result of the regularity of the familiarization trials, in the same way as can be identified in rat search patterns (Wan, Aggleton, & Brown, 1999). A problem with this interpretation is that if infants "solve" false belief in this simple way, so could 4-year-olds in solving the standard false belief test of Wimmer and Perner (1983). Another problem concerns the rather tenuous neurological evidence cited by Perner and Ruffman (Csibra & Southgate, 2005) with its own "top-down" reliance on theoretical inferences of the nature of associations (Sirois & Jackson, 2007).

The results of Onishi and Baillargeon's (2005) experiment are intriguing, but do they mean that we must reduce our interpretation either to the dramatic appearance of innate knowledge or to simple rules of association without any recourse to mental state understanding? Stack and Lewis (2008) outline arguments against each position. To begin, the experimental paradigm used is based on two methods, preferential looking and violation of expectations, which have been extensively criticized. For example, it has been argued by several authors that preferential looking is easily overinterpreted (Aslin, 2007; Bremner, 1994; Fischer & Biddell, 1991; Haith, 1998). It measures looking times, not necessarily the beliefs and representations suggested by Onishi and Baillargeon's interpretation.

Second, Stack and Lewis (2008) draw on a long tradition of critiques (e.g., Haith, 1998; Sirois & Jackson, 2007), which argue that nativist explanations for findings like Onishi and Baillargeon's (2005) turn us away from the crucial question of the developmental course of an understanding of beliefs. Perner and Ruffman's (2005) associationist account, described earlier, may on one level be more plausible than the nativist account, because it attempts closely to describe infants' developing skill. However, Stack and Lewis identified the emergence of an alternative explanation based on the gradual differentiation of infants' grasp of a person's levels of perceptual awareness within shared and nonshared experiences (e.g., O'Neill, 1996; Sodian & Thoermer, 2008; Tomasello & Haberl, 2003). This view argues that infants initially are not as firm in their "false belief" understanding as Onishi and Baillageon maintain. For example, Sodian and Thoermer (e.g., Experiment 2A) demonstrated that a 16-month-old's grasp of another's commitment to one box is disrupted if a screen briefly comes between her and the array after she has seen the toy move to the box.

In this debate, the grip of individualistic, mechanistic metatheoretical assumptions can be clearly seen as researchers grapple with the apparent contradiction that children seem to first understand false beliefs about the age of 4, yet much earlier at 15 months they seem to pass other tasks apparently requiring knowledge of false beliefs. Apperly and Butterfill's (2009) proposed solution is that humans have two "systems" for understanding false beliefs, one that accounts for the earlier competence and a second that explains the later developing ability. This proposal neglects Occam's advice to avoid multiplying entities, or in this case, "systems," beyond what is needed. It is only from a computational approach to mind that the evidence is mysterious. From a relational developmental systems and constructivist approach, an embodied, practical, or sensorimotor form of knowledge naturally occurs before reflective, self-conscious forms are possible (see Mascolo & Fischer, Chapter 6 of this volume, for an extended discussion), so the evidence of different forms of knowing is not surprising.

This section has explored four key contemporary issues, all indicating that accounting for the development of human social understanding must begin with an appreciation of the roots of development in interpersonal engagement. When considering neuroscience approaches to social development, we find some approaches that attempt to reduce social understanding to the localization of evolved neurological circuits. How it is possible to get from genes to forms of thinking is left as an untold story. We suggest that taking a relational developmental systems approach in which multiple levels of factors are considered will provide a better chance of filling in the details of this story. Relational approaches consider forms of understanding to be the result of multiple relational bidirectional interactions between biological and social processes. Research with nonhuman primates and nonlinguistic human infants raises key issues that bring out the difficulties with unexamined assumptions. This is because in both areas we encounter difficulties with imposing the experience of our adult commonsense view of the mind on nonlinguistic organisms. The split between mind and body or now between mind/brain and body emerged from a philosophical tradition and has become a part of our folk psychology, but it is important to recognize that this perspective emerged from linguistically competent adults. The Cartesian-inspired view of mental states that underlie and cause behavior (e.g., Meltzoff, Gopnik, &

Repacholi, 1999) results in many problems, including difficulties in thinking about whether other species have and understand mental states, and the age at which this emerges in human infants.

INTERPERSONAL INTERACTION AND SOCIAL UNDERSTANDING

Critics of the "theory of mind" tradition have argued that the dominant theories have treated social cognition as an entirely cognitive phenomenon, isolating it from the interpersonal processes in which it is embedded. The remaining sections of this chapter outline the range of social factors related to the development of social understanding. On the one hand, the social world can be understood as a set of external factors that impinge on the child's functioning—a kind of distal causal factor. On the other hand, the social process can be understood as what makes human development and social understanding possible. Unfortunately, Bruner (1986) was interpreted by proponents of the "theory of mind" position as if he were advocating the former understanding, arguing merely that adopting a "theory of mind" was simply a matter of enculturation, like learning a convention such as "forks go on the left" (Astington & Gopnik, 1991), and his ideas were marginalized as a result. The relations between social interaction and social understanding were taken up by Judy Dunn in two longitudinal studies of the development of sibling relationships within the context of interaction between mothers and their children (Dunn, Brown, Slomkowski, Tesla, & Youngblade, 1991; Dunn & Kendrick, 1982). Dunn's (1996) work was instrumental in leading the movement to address the relations between social interaction and social understanding. This section explores cultural and subcultural differences, and how they might emerge, before focusing on particular relationships and the issue of the role of social interaction in the development of social understanding.

Differences Across and Within Cultures

Evidence for differences in social understanding across different cultures is equivocal. Avis and Harris (1991) found that Baka children of Cameroon were similar to Western children in the age at which they passed a false belief task, but Wellman et al.'s (2001) meta-analysis of false belief studies found differences between children in the various countries studied: "If at 44 months of age children in the United States are 50% correct, then children in Australia are 69% correct and children in Japan are 40% correct" (pp. 667–668). Larger effects were found in cultures that differ more radically. Junín Quechuan children in Peru, for example, lagged behind Western children in performance on false belief tasks by at least 3 years (Vinden, 1996). In further research, Vinden (1999) compared Western children and three non-Western cultures: the Mofu of Cameron, and the Tolai and Tainae of Papua, New Guinea. She found delays in false belief understanding and the ability to predict an emotion based on a false belief in the non-Western cultures relative to Western children. Callaghan et al. (2005), however, argue that some of the differences between cultures may be explained by differences in the tests used in some cross-cultural studies. Although they present data demonstrating the same general advances across five cultures, their evidence cannot downplay the differences in Wellman's meta-analysis or Vinden's specific studies, which used batteries of tests based on those used across the industrialized world.

The cross-cultural evidence is consistent with comparisons of social groups within cultures. Cutting and Dunn (1999) found that children with mothers having more education were advanced in false belief understanding, and this was also related to both parents' occupational status. Similarly, Holmes, Black, and Miller (1996) and Pears and Moses (2003) found that children's performance on false belief tasks was delayed for children from families of lower socioeconomic circumstances. However, this link has not always been found (Hughes, Deater-Deckard, & Cutting, 1999; Ruffman, Perner, & Parkin, 1999). Recent studies have turned to examine those unfortunate circumstances in which children have experienced horrendous conditions of profound social deprivation. Children in institutions tend to be delayed in false belief understanding (Tarullo, Bruce, & Gunar, 2007; Yagmurlu, Berument, & Celimli, 2005). Studies of Romanian adoptees show that conditions of profound deprivation are found to be associated with quasi-autism, disinhibited attachment, and inattention/overactivity (Colvert et al., 2008; Kreppner et al., 2007; Rutter, Kreppner, O'Connor, & the English and Romanian Adoptees study team, 2001). This raises the question of *how* early social deprivation exerts its influence.

Siblings

One of the early empirical indications from the "theory of mind" literature of the importance of social interactions in social cognitive development was the so-called sibling effect. Perner, Ruffman, and Leekam (1994) reported that having siblings was positively correlated with false belief understanding. This result was replicated with larger studies in the United Kingdom, as well as Japan, and extended with the finding that the association is due to older rather than young siblings (Ruffman, Perner, Naito, Parkin, & Clements, 1998). In an Australian population, it was found that children with siblings between 1 and 12 years of age performed better on false belief tests compared with children with no siblings (Peterson, 2000). Going beyond sibling relationships, Lewis, Freeman, Kyriakidou, Maridaki-Kassotaki, and Berridge (1996) found positive association between having older kin living nearby and false belief understanding for children living in Greece.

Further research has suggested nuances in this interesting pattern. For example, the sibling effect has *not* been found for children with a twin but no other siblings (Cassidy, Fineberg, Brown, & Perkins, 2005). Other studies (Cole & Mitchell, 2000; Cutting & Dunn, 1999; Peterson & Slaughter, 2003) have reported no effect of siblings. In addition, in China, where most children have no siblings, not only was Lewis et al.'s (2005) finding concerning older kin not replicated, but preschoolers with older cousins actually showed lower performance on false belief than those without. Where the sibling effect is in evidence, it is not likely to be the mere number of people in a home, but rather something about the nature of the interaction that facilitates development in preschoolers' understanding. For example, Jenkins and Astington (1996) found that the advantage of having siblings held mostly for children with lower linguistic ability.

Parenting

In the exploration of various social factors related to social understanding, the examination of parenting style has yielded complex findings. Ruffman et al. (1999) examined parents' descriptions of how they respond to their children in various disciplinary situations. Their responses ranged from sending the child to his or her room to discussing the event. These researchers found that parents who reported talking to their children about the other person's feelings had children who were advanced in false belief understanding. Furthermore, Pears and Moses (2003) found that parents who reported using assertive styles, including yelling and spanking, had children with a poorer grasp of beliefs. Extending this methodology to an observation of parental warmth and discipline, Hughes, Deater-Deckard, and Cutting (1999) reported a sex-specific relation between adults' interaction styles. As might be expected

from Ruffman et al.'s (1999) finding, parental warmth to girls was positively linked to their advanced false belief understanding. However, severity of parental discipline, even including physical punishment was, unexpectedly, associated with boys' greater false belief understanding. At the same time, parental criticism of both boys and girls was associated with poorer performance on false belief, so we cannot make definitive conclusions from these interesting sex differences. In cross-cultural research, however, authoritarian parenting was associated with lower performance for European-American families but not Korean-American families (Vinden, 2001).

These parenting style findings are open to alternative explanations. Pears and Moses (2003), for example, admit that parental style might be a reaction to, rather than an influence on, the level of the child's social understanding. But they found no correlation between parenting style with child maturity, suggesting that parents do not adjust their parenting style to fit their child's maturity.

In another investigation, Sabbagh and Seamans (2008) found associations between parents' skills on a test of adult "mind reading" (Baron-Cohen, Wheelwright, Hill, Raste, & Plumb's [2001] Eyes Test) and their children's level of social understanding. As Sabbagh and Seamans pointed out, if this is evidence for intergenerational transmission of a sensitivity to mental states, it could reflect the effects of socialization or of inheritance. However, simply contrasting environment versus genes is based on the assumption that they are separate. From a relational developmental systems perspective, there are many levels of bidirectionally interacting factors (e.g., Gottlieb, 2007; Griffiths & Stotz, 2000).

Dynamics of Relationships: Attachment and "Mindmindedness"

In keeping with its predecessor, object relations theory (Winnicott, 1965, 1971/2005), attachment theory (Bowlby, 1969) provides an account of development in which the interpersonal is a central feature in the development of social understanding, and the child's self-understanding emerges from an initially undifferentiated relationship between infant and caregiver. The infant's construction of a model of the self in relation to others occurs within a process of differentiation and reintegration. This perspective contrasts with the individualistic view that assumes that self is split from the other as preexisting, discrete entities that require the glue of associations, through drive reduction or social reinforcement to form relationships. According to the attachment relational position, differentiation is achieved developmentally through a few central attachment relationships. Most of the research in this area has tended to focus on individual differences in security of attachment.

Several studies have identified associations between secure attachment status and false belief understanding. Fonagy, Redfern, and Charman (1997) found that 3- to 6-year-old children classified as securely attached on a projective measure of attachment, the Separation Anxiety Test, were advanced on a belief-dependent emotion task. In a longitudinal analysis, Symons and Clark (2000) rated attachment with a Q-sort measure when children were 2 years of age and found a positive correlation with performance when the children were 5 years of age on a false belief task involving the location of a mother character but not with a standard false belief task. Another longitudinal study was conducted by Meins, Fernyhough, Russell, and Clark-Carter (1998), in which they assessed attachment status within the Strange Situation (a procedure involving a series of separations and reunions between parent and infant designed to assess the infant's form of attachment) when the infants were 11 or 13 months of age. They reported a number of links between security of attachment and the children's social development, including the fact that securely attached children were more likely to pass a false belief task at 4 years of age. Attachment security at 2 years of age has also been found to be positively associated with young children's knowledge of emotions when they are 3 years of age (Raikes & Thompson, 2006). This facilitative effect seems to be due to the increase in talk about emotions in security attached dyads. Maternal depression in this low-income sample was negatively associated with the children's understanding of emotions at age 3.

However, the link between attachment and social understanding does not necessarily reveal how these relationships facilitate development. The correlations reported earlier may need to be explained by another aspect of parenting. In a follow-up study, Meins et al. (2002) compared the predictive power of attachment status at 12 months with that of the mother's propensity to treat the infant as a psychological being when assessed when the infants were 6 months old. Later false belief understanding was predicted by the latter notion, "mind-mindedness" (as assessed by mothers' tendencies to describe their children in psychological terms), but not attachments. Subsequent research has replicated this association on the basis of observed mother–infant (Ereky-Stevens, 2008) and mother–preschooler (Ruffman, Slade, Devitt, & Crowe, 2006) interaction, but the association that Meins et al. (2002) reported between

mothers' mental state language and their child's later social understanding was not replicated by Ereky-Stevens. De Rosnay et al. (2004) found that mothers' descriptions of their children in psychological terms were associated with their children's understanding of belief-based emotions. It has been suggested that "mind-mindedness" is mediated by the sensitivity of mothers to their infants (Laranjo, Bernier, & Meins, 2008; Ontai & Thompson, 2008), "joint engagement" with their toddlers (Nelson, Adamson, & Bakeman, 2008), or responsiveness (Ensor & Hughes, 2008) to their preschoolers' utterances. This research is consistent with a relational view of social understanding developing within interpersonal engagement.

As well as the facilitation of social development by the individual's social experience, increasing sophistication in social understanding may also have implications for the forms of interpersonal interaction in which individuals can engage. We turn to this in the next subsection.

Social Understanding and Social Lives

In concentrating on some aspects of social understanding, particularly beliefs, we have omitted many stalwarts of the social cognition literature, notably the affective components and other aspects such as morality and values. We believe that the debates we have summarized allow us to better reflect on these more traditional topics. We demonstrate here that the topics we have covered form the basis of developments over the rest of individuals' social lives. Supporting this intuition, a number of researchers have found correlations between social skills and first-order (Astington, 2003; Lalonde & Chandler, 1995) and second-order (Baird & Astington, 2004) belief understanding. These associations carry over into social conduct. Children who are relatively advanced in understanding beliefs and emotions tend to have fewer conflicts with their friends and engage in more cooperative play (Dunn & Cutting, 1999; see Dunn, 2004). Children's performance on false belief tasks is also correlated with more sophisticated arguments in conflicts with their siblings (Foote & Holmes-Lonergan, 2003), and at least for children older than 5 years, false belief understanding has been linked to peer popularity (Peterson & Siegal, 2002; Slaughter, Dennis, & Pritchard, 2002).

The link between children's social understanding and their social competence continues beyond preschool and into preadolescence. Children from 7 to 8 years of age show more sophisticated understanding of interpretation within the context of their sibling interaction (Ross,

Recchia, & Carpendale, 2005). At the ages of 11 to 12, understanding of possible interpretations and emotions regarding ambiguous social situations are associated with peer rating of the child's ability to deal with social situations, although not with teacher ratings of social skills (Bosacki & Astington, 1999).

The flip side to this positive story is that some children might use their advanced social understanding for Machiavellian ends. Repacholi, Slaughter, Pritchard, and Gibbs (2003) found no clear evidence of this, although they did find that 9- to 12-year-old children who self-reported as high in Machiavellianism did have more negative interpretations of story characters' intentions than other children. This thinking about the uses of social understanding for negative purposes can be extended to bullying. Sutton, Smith, and Swettenham (1999a, 1999b) have argued that bullies are socially skilled: "The bully may be a cold, manipulative expert in social situations, organizing gangs and using subtle, indirect methods" (p. 435). They found positive correlations between bullying and social cognitive abilities in 7- to 10-year-olds, and a negative correlation between social cognition and tendency to be a victim of bullying (see also Gini, 2006).

This research raises a further apparent paradox with the previous evidence of links between social understanding and social skills—that social skills may actually have a negative impact rather than promoting harmonious social interaction. However, we should add that the bullies in Sutton et al.'s (1999b) study did not, in fact, differ in level of social understanding from other children in their study who were not involved in bullying. Thus, level of social understanding "says nothing about how that knowledge will be utilized" (Arsenio & Lemerise, 2001, p. 62). Aggression can, however, be classified as proactive or "cold-blooded," or as reactive or "hot-headed" and impulsive. Social understanding and inhibition may be differentially related to these two types of aggression. Sutton et al.'s (1999b) argument may hold for proactive aggression, but reactive or impulsive aggression may not be associated with social understanding in the same way (Carpendale & Lewis, 2006). Advanced social understanding may be used in bullying, but whether a child becomes a bully must be explained by factors other than their social cognitive ability such as empathy and values (e.g., Arsenio & Lemerise, 2001; Sutton et al., 1999b). This debate is relevant for appropriate interventions designed for different types of bullies.

A further link concerns children's understanding of emotions. The "theory of mind" literature has been criticized for neglecting emotions (e.g., Banerjeee, 2004; Dunn, 1996). However, some studies do combine an examination of beliefs with an analysis of understanding emotions (e.g., Ruffman, Slade, & Crowe, 2002). And a number of investigators have concluded that understanding most social situations requires an understanding of beliefs, as well as emotions (Wellman & Banerjee, 1991). However, some researchers have suggested that belief and emotion are separate domains because they appear to be differentially related to different aspects of later development (Dunn, 1995). At the same time, there are reports of positive correlations between the two (Cutting & Dunn, 1999; Hughes & Dunn, 1998). These correlations, however, may be because of shared variance with other factors such as children's family background and language ability (Cutting & Dunn, 1999). The belief–emotion relation becomes more complex if we consider emotions in social situations of varying complexity and emotions of varying complexity such as happy and sad versus surprise, embarrassment or guilt (Bennett & Matthews, 2000; Hadwin & Perner, 1991; Ruffman & Keenan, 1996; Tangney & Fischer, 1995). Emotions and beliefs can be interrelated because understanding emotions in some contexts depends on understanding the person's beliefs (e.g., Bradmetz & Schneider, 1999; Chandler & Greenspan, 1972; Harris, Johnson, Hutton, Andrews, & Cooke, 1989). Further, development in understanding emotions involves mixed emotions (Dunn, 1995).

An essential aspect of social life that the "theory of mind" movement should relate to is, of course, morality. There has been continuing discussion of these links (e.g., Baird & Sokol, 2004; Chandler, Sokol, & Hallet, 2001; Chandler, Sokol, & Wainryb, 2000; Dunn, 1995; Dunn, Brown, & Maguire, 1995; Dunn, Cutting, & Demetriou, 2000). As with social understanding, much depends on one's theory of moral development. If morality is conceived of as merely conforming to local rules, then social understanding may not have a large role to play (see Turiel, Chapter 16 of this volume, for an extended discussion of thought and emotion in several domains of social understanding, including morality). But if morality is identified as the understanding and coordination of conflicting perspectives in social situations, then it would appear that social understanding should be closely linked to moral understanding (Carpendale, 2000). One example of such a link is that between false belief understanding and deception and lying. Lying has been a topic of research interest for some time (Piaget, 1932/1965). It seems that the whole point about lying is to instill a false belief in someone else; therefore, it would seem that false belief understanding would be a necessary condition, and that engaging in deception could be an indicator of an understanding of beliefs (Chandler et al., 1989; Hala, Chandler, & Fritz, 1991). However, there are different forms of deception, and lying itself may be a skill at which children can improve, coming to correct their flawed early attempts such as "I didn't break the lamp and I won't do it again" (Vasek, 1986). Another side to lying is learning when it is appropriate to tell a white lie, which emerges between 3 and 11 years of age (Talwar & Lee, 2002; Talwar, Murphy, & Lee, 2007).

Only when the links between social understanding and more traditional domains, such as emotions and morality, are developed will this area of research truly come of age. This sentiment is echoed in recent analyses of the field from within the "theory of mind" movement itself. For example, Wellman and Miller (2008) argue that the traditional framework of belief-desire folk psychology is incomplete, and they propose to include not just belief-desire reasoning but also "conceptions of social influences on action and thought, in particular, obligations and permissions" (p. 105). They propose that a broadened perspective on "theory of mind" would recognize that behavior is situated within social contexts, and thus may be influenced not just by the individual's wishes but also constrained by social rules, obligations, duties, and responsibilities. This chapter has attempted to identify the nature of these social contexts and some of the processes by which social cognition fuses cognitive and social processes.

Once again, the data from social interactions suggest a need to develop an understanding of the development of social understanding that accounts for the links with interpersonal interactions in which children are engaged. To do this, we turn to examining how social cognitive development in infancy is rooted in interpersonal engagement.

DEVELOPMENT OF SOCIAL UNDERSTANDING IN INFANCY

Social understanding does not, of course, just begin when children can pass a false belief test. Research on social understanding in infancy has burgeoned, and it converges with a previous research literature on infant social development (e.g., Bates, 1976, 1979; Trevarthen, 1979; Trevarthen & Hubley, 1978). There is evidence that some form of social understanding is available to the infant quite early in development (Bretherton, McNew, & Beeghly-Smith, 1981). A significant body of research has emerged since the 1970s

exploring infants' emerging ability to coordinate attention with others, referred to as *joint attention* (Bakeman & Adamson, 1984). One interpretation of this joint, or shared, attention characterizes it as triadic interaction involving the coordination of attention between self, other, and an object or event.

Social referencing is an example of this type of interaction, in which the infant apparently refers to her parent's expression to interpret ambiguous situations such as encountering toy spiders or being faced with crawling across a visual cliff (Walden & Ogan, 1988). However, the meaning of infants' looks toward their parents is controversial; that is, it is not clear whether the infants look to their parents to seek information or comfort (Baldwin & Moses, 1996; Striano, Vaish, & Benigno, 2006).

Paradigmatic joint attention behaviors consist of using pointing gestures and responding to others' pointing gestures. Two classic forms of pointing gestures have been described (Bates, 1979; Bates, Camaioni, & Volterra, 1975). A *protoimperative* is pointing to make a request, whereas a *protodeclaritive* is pointing to direct another person's attention. A third use of pointing gestures more recently described is to inform. For example, when an experimenter appears to have lost an object, many 12-month-old infants will point toward it (Liszkowski, Carpenter, Striano, & Tomasello, 2006). Infants typically begin pointing in the months around their first birthdays (e.g., Tomasello, 2008). Although the way to do it may vary across cultures (e.g., with the lips instead of the index finger), it seems that some way to direct others' attention with gestures would be important in any human culture (Kita, 2003). How this everyday ability develops, however, remains controversial (Carpendale & Lewis, 2006).

Joint attention has been considered of "cosmic importance" (Bates, 1979) because it forms the foundation for further communicative interaction and the acquisition of language (Baldwin, 1995), as well as making participation in culture possible, so it has been argued that the rest of social cognitive development is just "icing on the cake" compared with the importance of the development of this human adaptation for culture (Tomasello, 1999). The importance of joint attention is revealed in longitudinal studies showing that infants' skills in sharing attention with others are correlated with their later social competence (Charman, Baron-Cohen, Swettenham, Baird, Cox, & Drew, 2000; Vaughan Van Hecke et al., 2007) and with cognitive and language development (Baldwin, 1995; Brooks & Meltzoff, 2008; Carpenter et al., 1998; Mundy et al., 2007; Vaughan Van Hecke et al., 2007). In addition, difficulties in infants' joint attention interaction, in particular, a lack of pointing to direct attention at 18 months, have been linked to the later diagnosis of autism (Baron-Cohen, Allen, & Gillberg, 1992; Baron-Cohen, Baird, Swettenham, Nightingale, Morgan, Drew, & Charman, 1996).

Although research and theory have focused on the development of joint attention toward the end of the infant's first year of life, there is also the important problem of how triadic interaction develops from earlier dyadic interaction during the first year of life (Striano & Reid, 2006). For example, in the paradigm known as the "still face" procedure, mothers, after engaging in face-to-face dyadic interaction with their 4- to 5-month-old infants, are asked to stop normal interaction and simply present a "still face" to their infant for one minute and then begin interacting normally again. The fact that, for example, mothers who responded contingently had infants who made more social bids during the still face phase by looking at their mother and smiling and vocalizing, appearing to expect further response from their mothers (Mcquaid, Bibok, & Carpendale, 2009), suggests some early social competence is emerging in dyadic interaction as a step toward later triadic interaction.

Joint attention might appear to be straightforwardly defined as jointly attending to the same object or event. And, in fact, Butterworth (1998, p. 171) defined it as "looking where someone else is looking." However, this could also include cases of "simultaneous looking" or "onlooking" (Bakeman & Adamson, 1984; Tomasello, 1995) without mutual awareness that attention is shared. Joint attention also seems to involve some shared understanding of mutual engagement; it "is not just a geometric phenomenon concerning two lines of visual attention" (Tomasello, 1995, p. 105). It also requires that "two individuals know that they are attending to something in common" (Tomasello, 1995, p. 106). But this requires interpretation of infants' behaviors, and there are rich and lean views of such interpretation.

What does following others' direction of gaze indicate about infants' understanding? Meltzoff and Brooks (2007) suggest that gaze following "entails the ascription of a mental life to a viewer. We follow where another person looks because we want to see what they are seeing. When we see people direct their gaze somewhere, we wonder what object is catching their attention" (p. 232). Although this could be an appropriate claim for some levels of development, Moore and colleagues (2008; Moore & Corkum, 1994) argue that this is an overly rich interpretation of what young infants are doing when they first begin to follow

gaze. Some early indication of this ability is even evident at 3 months (D'Entremont, 2000), and has been observed in other primates and other mammals such as dogs and domestic goats (Call & Tomasello, 2008; Emery & Clayton, 2009). Scaife and Bruner (1975) first used what has become the standard research paradigm for studying gaze following in which an experimenter—sitting across from an infant—first engages with the infant and then turns to look to one side of the room. An infant's ability to follow the experimenter's gaze depends on a number of factors. At 3 months, infants may turn to the correct side when the objects the experimenter looks toward are close by and in the infant's visual field (D'Entremont, 2000). Infants can follow gaze to more distant objects by 6 months, but they have a tendency to stop at the first object they encounter, which is overcome by 12 months (Butterworth, 2001; Butterworth & Jarrett, 1991). And at this age, they will move around a barrier to see what an adult is looking at (Moll & Tomasello, 2004).

Thus, it appears that gaze following develops over a protracted period, and infants may first follow head turns and only later eye direction (Butterworth & Jarrett, 1991; Moore & Corkum, 1998). Moore and colleagues (2008; Corkum & Moore, 1998; Moore & Corkum, 1994) argue that rather than understanding others as seeing things, instrumental learning or attentional cueing could account for the early emergence of gaze following, and further learning occurs within such interaction. Although much of the research on joint attention has addressed visual attention, there is also potential for other dimensions such as touch and gaze in interpersonal engagement (Akhtar & Gernsbacher, 2008).

The same problem of interpreting the meaning of infants' actions arises in the case of pointing. Simply extending an index finger might not be a social act, but if the infant looks toward the adult, perhaps to check if he or she is paying attention, this seems to indicate some understanding of the social function of the gesture (Bates, 1979; Bates et al., 1975). In one study, it was found that between 12 and 16 months, the timing of visual checking moved from after the infant pointed, to during the act, to before pointing (Franco & Butterworth, 1996), suggesting increasing sophistication in infants' understanding of the social nature of gestures. However, from a more skeptical perspective, infants might look toward the adult for other reasons, such as expecting some response from them (Moore, 1998; Moore & Corkum, 1994), or they might not look toward the adult because they are confident that the adult is engaged with them (Bates, 1976).

Another way to assess infants' understanding of their pointing gestures is to examine how satisfied they are with adults' responses to their gestures. In setting gestures within a sequence of interaction, Liszkowski, Carpenter, Henning, Striano, and Tomasello (2004) found that when 12-month-old infants were pointing, they were satisfied only when the experimenter responded appropriately by sharing attention with them and the object. The infants were not satisfied if the experimenter looked only at the object or only at them, and they expressed this through continuing gesturing in an apparent attempt to communicate with the obtuse experimenter. Liszkowski et al. (2004) interpret this as evidence of a declarative motive at this age. As further evidence that 12-month-olds use gestures with communicative intent, Liszkowski, Albrecht, Carpenter, and Tomasello (2008) report that infants are more likely to point when an adult is looking toward them and to repeat their gesture if they are not successful in their communicative act.

Theories of Joint Attention

This area has been the focus of extensive research and theoretical debate (see Carpendale & Lewis, 2006; Flom, Lee, & Muir, 2007; Hobson, 2002/2004; Moore, 1996, 2006; Racine & Carpendale, 2007a, 2007b). One way to group theories concerns whether they assume that joint attention behaviors are possible for infants because of their understanding of others, or whether early cases of interaction involving coordinated attention with others result from other factors and infants develop their understanding through such experience. These approaches have been described as "rich" versus "lean" interpretations. An example of a rich position is Trevarthen's (1979; Trevarthen & Aitken, 2001, p. 40) assumption that infants are born with innate intersubjectivity.

Relatedly, Meltzoff, Gopnik, and Repacholi (1999) argue that infants' social cognitive development begins with an innate ability to understand others as like themselves. The infant then reasons by analogy—from self to other—to an understanding of the other. This approach has been criticized for, among other reasons, its reliance on the analogical argument, which already assumes infants' ability to distinguish self and other (Müller & Carpendale, 2004; Müller & Runions, 2003). Meltzoff's position that infants see others as like them is based on the empirical claim that newborn infants can imitate. This claim, however, is itself controversial (Moore & Corkum, 1994; Tissaw, 2007; Welsh, 2006). A part of the controversy concerns the

fact that infants lose the ability to imitate at around 2 to 3 months, and then begin to do so again at about 12 months, with imitation continuing to develop over the first 2 years (Jones, 2007). Another facet of the controversy is the argument that rather than the ability to imitate a range of facial expressions, there is only reliable evidence of early imitation of tongue protrusions (Anisfeld, 1996; Anisfeld, Turkewitz, & Rose, 2001). If this is the case, then simpler explanations for infants' matching of tongue protrusions would be more likely, such as "early attempts at oral exploration of interesting objects" (Jones, 1996, p. 1952).

In contrast with the view that joint attention behaviors are the result of infants' understanding of others, a lean alternative approach is that such behavior is the result of other factors, and understanding develops in this context (Carpendale & Lewis, 2004a, 2004b, 2006; Moore, 1998, 2006; Moore & Corkum, 1994). Consistent with this view, relational approaches (Overton, 2004, 2006) begin from infants' activities, and explain communication and mind as emerging from a field of relational bidirectional interactions (e.g., Carpendale & Lewis, 2006; Hobson, 2002/2004; Mead, 1934; Müller & Carpendale, 2004; Reddy, 2008; Soffer, 1999; Winnicott, 1965, 1971/2005).

Tomasello and his colleagues attempt to include aspects of both approaches because he accounts for the way in which chimpanzees learn gestures in terms of social shaping or "ontogenetic ritualization" (Tomasello, 1999), and he acknowledges that some human infants may learn pointing gestures in this way, especially infants younger than 12 months (Tomasello, 2003). This follows Vygotsky's (1978) classic view, inspired by Wundt (1973), that pointing develops through failed grasping attempts that are responded to by the infant's parent, and the infant gradually learns how to make a request by pointing. It appears that most infants learn the "arms up" gesture in this way by an average of 10½ months as a means for getting picked up (Bretherton et al., 1981). Tomasello (1995) and colleagues' primary emphasis, however, and especially more recently (Tomasello, Carpenter, & Liszkowski, 2007), is that the various joint attention skills are "all manifestations of infants' emerging understanding of other persons as intentional agents whose attention and behavior to outside objects and events may be shared, followed into, and directed in various ways" (Carpenter et al., 1998, p. 118). The predication from this perspective is that all of the various joint attention behaviors should be correlated in development because they are all based on the same insight.

Such correlations have been reported in Carpenter et al.'s (1998) longitudinal study, but other research has reported a lack of correlation between a range of joint attention behaviors (Slaughter & McConnell, 2003), for example, responding to and initiating joint attention (Mundy et al., 2007), or pointing gestures with gaze following (Brooks & Meltzoff, 2008). There also appears to be a lack of correlation between the joint attention skills of producing versus understanding pointing gestures, with some studies reporting that children understand others' pointing before producing their own gestures (e.g., Carpenter et al., 1998), whereas other studies report the opposite; that is, infants first produce their own pointing gestures before understanding others' gestures (Desrochers, Morissette, & Ricard, 1995; Murphy & Messer, 1977).

One way of making sense of this apparent lack of correlation among joint attention skills is to think of these various forms of interaction as a set of converging social skills rather than as derived from a single insight (Bibok, Carpendale, & Lewis, 2008). Soon after their first birthday, these skills converge to the point that observers could describe infants' social skills as an insight. These skills, however, initially develop in a piecemeal fashion depending on the infant's experience. For example, Brune and Woodward (2007) found that 10-month-old infants who used pointing gestures showed more understanding of such gestures in an experimental procedure, whereas, conversely, those infants who engaged more extensively in sharing of attention were better at understanding gaze following in an experimental procedure. Such evidence of piecemeal development of particular social skills does not fit with the typical way of thinking about understanding, which Chapman (1987) termed the "measurement model." That is, understanding is assumed to be based on an insight, and attempts are made to measure it with the best indicator. An alternative approach, however, is the "membership model" of understanding, according to which understanding is best thought of as set of skills that children gradually acquire (Chapman; see also Mascolo & Fischer, Chapter 6 of this volume).

Another way in which the contrast between rich and lean interpretations arises concerns interpreting the motives for infants' pointing gestures. From a lean perspective, these gestures only gradually become social (Bates, 1976; Moore & D'Entremont, 2001; Vygotsky, 1978) in the sense that the infant already understands their effect on adults, whereas from a rich perspective, they are social to begin with (Tomasello et al., 2007). Tomasello et al. (2007, pp. 705–706) defend a rich interpretation of infants' pointing and contrast the two perspectives as following: "The question is whether young infants are attempting in their prelinguistic communication to influence the intentional/mental states of others (cause them to "know" something) or whether, alternatively, they are simply aiming to achieve certain behavioral effects in others (cause them to "do" something)." This way of setting up the alternatives involves philosophical assumptions regarding how action and mental states are conceptualized. It appears to assume a split between action and mental states, and it is a matter of understanding either behavior or mental states. This is parallel to the debate regarding animal cognition reviewed in a previous section.

Movement toward a resolution of this debate would be to consider the forms of knowledge that Moll et al. (2007, p. 827) remind us of in terms of the contrast between the German terms *kennen* and *wissen*. *Kennen* refers to a developmentally earlier form of knowledge—practical, lived, sensorimotor knowledge, or knowledge in action (Piaget, 1936/1963). According to this distinction between forms of knowledge, present in classic relational theories of development, infants first know about other people at this practical or lived level before later developing more reflective forms of understanding (see Mascolo & Fischer, Chapter 6 of this volume). For theorists such as Mead (1934), people's attitudes are evident in their orientation to the world, and understanding others' intentions involves anticipating their upcoming act (cf. Gallese, 2007; Gómez, 2007). The key question concerns whether infants first understand others in a Cartesian-inspired fashion as physical bodies, like furniture, and only later as mental agents. As an alternative, we suggest a relational perspective according to which action is not split from intention, and on a practical level, infants experience others as intentional agents. Their understanding of others continues to develop to advanced levels through social experience and improving competence in social interactions.

The research that Tomasello et al. (2007) reviewed focuses on infants at 12 months and older. The important question of the developments that occur in the months leading up to infants' first birthdays and resulting in actions such as pointing gestures is still left open. Tomasello et al. (2007) note Wittgenstein's (1968) insight that understanding pointing always requires "some 'form of life' or shared context" (p. 706). Thus, we must consider the development of these routines or shared patterns of interaction or joint attentional frames within which actions become meaningful (Racine & Carpendale, 2007a, 2007b). Reddy (2008) details the patterns of very early interaction to suggest that at some level, even very young infants "know minds" in the sense that they develop some level of awareness of themselves in interaction with others, as we see, for example, in displays of "coyness" (Reddy, 2003).

Joint Attentional Frames

Pointing is ambiguous. It can be used to convey many different meanings, depending on shared experiences. An extended index finger alone cannot convey meaning; this hand configuration could be used to check if a cake is cooked or the paint is dry, but within the appropriate context of shared experience, it could also be used to perform any number of actions from ordering a gin and tonic to suggesting that a child do his homework. Infants as young as 9 to 15 weeks have been observed to extend their index finger in a pointing gesture (Fogel & Hannan, 1985), but these hand configurations do not perform a social act. Moll and Tomasello (2007) provide the example of an encounter in an aisle of a hardware store with someone apparently pointing to a bucket. This illustrates that the meaning of the gesture would be ambiguous without some shared framework of understanding. For a pointing gesture to be meaningful, it has to be set in a history of shared interaction (Carpendale & Lewis, 2008). Within such a framework, such as searching with a friend for a particular type of bucket, the gesture would be meaningful. The hand configuration is not by itself sufficient to convey meaning. What is required is some shared history of interpersonal relational engagement (Racine & Carpendale, 2007a, 2007b). This is shown in a study by Liebal, Behne, Carpenter, and Tomasello (2009). They presented 18-month-old infants with the same pointing gesture to the same object but made by different experimenters with which the infants had had different experiences. The infants could understand that different meaning was being conveyed because of the difference in the experience that they had shared with the two experimenters—making a puzzle versus cleaning up. Furthermore, infants at 14 months also had some success with a simpler procedure.

Another series of studies also shows the important role of shared engagement and common ground. For example, in one study, 14- and 18-month-old infants played with two new objects with an experimenter (Moll et al., 2007). Then while that experimenter was out of the room, the infant played with a third new object with a second experimenter. The first experimenter returned and expressed excitement in the general direction of the three objects arrayed in front of the infant and asked the infant to give "it" to her. These infants were able to make sense of the ambiguous request in light of their shared experience with the experimenter

and their experience that others are excited when they see something new (see also Moll, Richter, Carpenter, & Tomasello, 2008).

In this brief review, we have highlighted the importance of the routines and patterns of interaction infants share with others in the way infants come to understand other people (Racine & Carpendale, 2007b). The social skills and activity patterns infants develop in their engagement with others then form the foundation on which language is based, and this, in turn, makes more complex forms of social understanding possible.

LANGUAGE AND SOCIAL UNDERSTANDING

Although general agreement exists that language is central to social cognitive development, this relation has been conceptualized in various ways, and these ways are used to organize this section into subsections: (1) the speech that young children use may be an indication of their understanding of mind, (2) the psychological terms children are exposed to may facilitate social cognitive development, and (3) children's linguistic ability may be linked to their development of social understanding. Two further subsections review theories regarding the links between language and social understanding, and discuss critiques of the view of language and mind assumed in much of this research.

Language as a Window on Child Development

One of the first approaches to the links between language and social cognition focused on the psychological terms used by young children as a window to their understanding; that is, "children's talk about the mind reveals their thoughts about this intriguing subject" (Bartsch & Wellman, 1995, p. 3). Bretherton and Beeghly (1982) claimed that children's use of words referring to the mind reveals their *explicit, verbally expressible* theory of mind that begins to emerge at the end of the second year" (p. 356, emphasis in original). Bartsch and Wellman examined transcripts of young children's use of language to track their use of words such as want, wish, afraid, think, know, believe, expect, wonder, and dream. They found that children used desire terms at around 2½ years of age, and their use of belief terms increased and often exceeded desire terms by 4 years of age. A type of utterance that is especially convincing for indicating an understanding of the psychological world is referred to as a contrastive; for example, "It's a bus; I thought a taxi" (Adam, at 3 years, 3 months). Shatz, Wellman, and Silber (1983) cautioned that children's use of mental state terms does not necessarily indicate an adult understanding; it is important to go beyond just counting these words, and instead examine how they are used in conversation. Furthermore, Nelson (1996, 2005) argues that children begin using words without full adult meaning and gradually acquire more complete understanding.

A focus on the frequency of particular words should not overlook the fact that words are used in different ways, as illustrated in a study of children and their mothers' uses of the same mental term, "want," for different functions (Budwig, 2002). The 18- to 36-month-old children used the word in asserting what they wanted, whereas mothers used the word to clarify their child's desires. For children younger than 2, the word functioned mainly as a request, but for children older than 2, who were able to do things for themselves, the word functioned as a request for permission. In addition to the words children used, researchers are interested in the possibility that language may provide an essential context for social cognitive development.

Language as a Context for Development

A number of studies have addressed the relations between the language children are exposed to and their social understanding. For example, deaf children tend to be delayed in their development of false belief understanding, but only when their parents are not deaf. This is likely to be because deaf parents tend to be fluent in sign language, and thus expose their children to complex communication, whereas this may not be the case for those deaf children whose parents are not deaf (e.g., de Villiers & de Villiers, 2000; Schick, de Villiers, de Villiers, & Hoffmeister, 2007; Woolfe, Want, & Siegal, 2002).

In research on how parents' ways of talking to their children is related to their children's false belief understanding, Peterson and Slaughter (2003) extended Ruffman et al. (1999)'s research on disciplinary situations with a questionnaire assessing mothers' styles of talking about everyday psychological events. Like Ruffman et al. (1999), they found that mothers who reported discussing and elaborating on mental states when talking to their young children had children who were advanced in false belief understanding. However, because these studies are correlational, it is possible that children who are advanced somehow elicit more talk about psychological events from

their parents than other children, or alternatively, a third factor, such as verbal intelligence, could be involved.

One way to begin addressing these possibilities is with longitudinal studies. In one such analysis of naturalistic in-home observation of 50 families, Dunn et al. (1991) observed daily interactions in a first visit when the target child was 33 months old. When these children were assessed 7 months later at 40 months of age, it was found that more family talk about feelings and the reasons for social events at the first visit was linked with advanced understanding of beliefs at the second visit (see Chapter 7 of Carpendale & Lewis, 2006, for a review). In a closer examination of mothers' talk, Slaughter, Peterson, and Mackintosh (2007) found in two cross-sectional studies that it was not just the simple mention of cognitive terms, but rather mothers' explanatory, causal, and contrastive talk about cognition, that was correlated with children's performance on false belief tasks. For children on the autism spectrum, it was mothers' explanatory, causal, and contrastive talk about emotions that was associated with these children's social understanding.

Similar longitudinal studies have also found correlations between parents' talk about emotions and their child's later talk about, and understanding of, emotions (e.g., Garner, Jones, Gaddy, & Rennie, 1997). Although sex differences in understanding beliefs are quite minor in the "theory of mind" literature (Charman, Ruffman, & Clements, 2002), differences between boys and girls have been found in their understanding of emotions. Kuebli, Butler, and Fivush (1995) found that parents used more, and a greater variety of, emotion words when talking to their daughters compared with their sons. The boys and girls did not differ in their talk about emotions at the beginning of the study, but by the end, the daughters were talking more about emotions with a greater variety of terms than the sons.

Caution is required, however, in concluding that parental talk facilitates their children's social cognitive development, because longitudinal studies are still not conclusive. It is possible that the correlations between the mothers' earlier use of mental state terms and the child's later performance on false belief tests could be because of the mothers' understanding that their children were precocious in social understanding or because these children elicited more of this talk from their mothers. In a longitudinal study designed to address this problem, Ruffman, Slade, and Crowe (2002) assessed children's social understanding (false belief and emotion understanding), children's language ability, and mothers' tendencies to use mind-related talk at three time points over one year. They found that mothers' use of psychological words at earlier time points predicted children's social understanding at later time points, even when accounting for the child's linguistic ability and level of social understanding at the earlier time point, and independently of mothers' education. In contrast, children's earlier social understanding did not predict mothers' later mental talk. This suggests that it is parental talk involving psychological terms that is influential in the development of children's social understanding. A similar finding has been reported in another longitudinal study with children up to the age of 7, in which Adrián, Clemente, and Villanueva (2007) found a correlation between mothers' earlier use of cognitive verbs and their children's later social understanding after controlling for children's age, verbal ability, and earlier social understanding, but they did not find the converse relation between children's earlier social understanding and later linguistic ability.

In extending this general finding to younger children, Taumoepeau and Ruffman (2006) found that mothers' use of desire terms in talking with their 15-month-old child was a predictor of their child's later understanding of emotions and their child's use of mental state language when they were 24 months old. In extending this study, Taumoepeau and Ruffman (2008) found that mothers' talk about others' thoughts and knowledge predicted their children's later use of mental language when they were 33 months old. Moving from these empirical results toward an understanding of how such language facilitates social cognitive development, Taumoepeau and Ruffman (2008) interpret their results in terms of Vygotsky's notion of mothers scaffolding their children in the "zone of proximal development." The children's use of psychological terms did not correlate with their mothers' later use of such words, suggesting that it is not children's social understanding that is driving the relation between social understanding and language, but rather it is the exposure to parental talk that facilitates social cognitive development (see also Fernyhough, 2008, for a Vygotskian interpretation of the development of social understanding).

The next step is to compare language and social interaction in relation to children's social cognitive development. In a longitudinal study on this topic, Ruffman et al. (2006) reported that mothers' psychological talk predicted social understanding, whereas general parenting style did not. Intuitively, some role for the parent–child relationship in addition to the content of what they talk about might be expected. We would expect that boring lectures or enraged shouting, even if containing many psychological terms, would not be helpful in children coming to understand their social worlds. This view is supported by the finding that children whose mothers used talk about causes while trying to control them did not do as well later on tests of emotion understanding as children whose mothers used such talk but in the context of shared play, comforting, or joking (Brown & Dunn, 1996). Ruffman et al. (2006) acknowledge that most of the middle- to upper-class mothers in their study tended toward the optimal end of their measure of parental warmth. Thus, it may be that they had a good enough relationship with their child so that the main source of variance was in the content of their talk. This possibility was supported in a study showing that beyond mothers' use of psychological terms, parental engagement with their children was associated with children's false belief understanding (Susswein, 2007).

Another step in moving from *what* is talked about to *how* it is talked about is to consider what is referred to as the *connectedness* of conversation. This is the degree to which maternal–child conversation is related to what their partner has just said in the previous turn; that is, they are responding to each other. Children who are advanced in false belief tests tend to engage in frequent and extended conversations with their friends that are connected in this sense; that is, they are responding to what each other has just said (Dunn & Cutting, 1999). Ensor and Hughes (2008) assessed the connectedness of conversation between mothers and their children when they were 2, 3, and 4 years old, and found more reference to beliefs, desires, and intentions within connected conversation. They also found that connectedness of conversational turns between mothers and their 2-year-olds was a significant and independent predictor of children's social understanding later when they were age 4 after controlling for mothers' use of mental terms. Ensor and Hughes suggest that "engagement with, rather than exposure to, mental-state talk appears to be valuable in promoting children's social understanding" (p. 213).

Children's Linguistic Ability and Social Understanding

There are also consistent links between children's own language ability and their social cognitive development (e.g., Astington & Jenkins, 1999; Cutting & Dunn, 1999; Happé, 1995; Hughes & Dunn, 1998; Jenkins & Astington, 1996; Ruffman, Slade, Rowlandson, Rumsey, & Garnham, 2003). This relation has been supported in a meta-analysis of 104 studies with a total of close to 9,000 participants (Milligan, Astington, & Dack, 2007). The overall relation was found to be moderate to strong ($r = 0.43$) and remained moderate in those studies controlling for age ($r = 0.31$), so that children's linguistic ability accounts for 18% of the variance in their performance on false belief tasks and 10% when controlling for the child's age. As stated earlier, there is also evidence that the positive effect of having siblings is far weaker for those children who are linguistically advanced (Jenkins & Astington, 1996). The reason for this relation between linguistic ability and false belief understanding, however, is controversial. Three possibilities have been discussed: social understanding depends on language, language depends on social understanding, or a third factor accounts for both.

Some evidence suggests that it is children's early language ability that predicts later false belief understanding and not the other way around (Astington & Jenkins, 1999; Ruffman et al., 2003), suggesting that language makes false belief understanding possible. Slade and Ruffman (2005) also found that early language ability predicts later false belief understanding, but in addition, they found a weaker effect of earlier false belief understanding associated with later language ability. These bidirectional effects were replicated in Milligan et al.'s (2007) meta-analysis in which they found significant effects in both directions; that is, earlier language was related to later false belief, as well as earlier false belief being related to later language, but the effect for language to false belief was significantly stronger. Increases in linguistic skill may lead to an increase in the complexity of social interaction children experience, which, in turn, may result in increases in social skills. Milligan et al. also addressed whether it is a particular aspect of linguistic competence that is driving this relation, and they found that of the five different types of language measure—general language, semantics, receptive vocabulary, syntax, and memory for complements—all were significantly related to false belief understanding (see also Slade & Ruffman, 2005).

Language and social understanding are complex and closely related phenomena, which may be difficult to clearly differentiate. If social understanding is narrowly defined as false belief understanding and language competence is defined by vocabulary, then we could look for correlations; but if we approach both more broadly, the relation becomes more complex. Early forms of social understanding involved in coordinating attention with others are required for learning words. Then later aspects of language such as pragmatics, humor, and irony turn on understanding others' intentions, and thus are intertwined with social competence. Pragmatics is usually considered an aspect of language, but it involves social understanding. So perhaps social understanding and language should be conceptualized as two related aspects of social competence.

Why Does Language Matter for Children's Social Understanding?

Several theories have been proposed to account for the link between language and social understanding. Language is important, according to Harris (e.g., 2005), because conversation is a constant reminder that other people have different beliefs, desires, and intentions. An alternative theory has been proposed by Jill and Peter de Villiers (2000; de Villiers, 2005), who argue that the syntax of complementation is essential as a representational format for dealing with false beliefs because this aspect of English mental verbs makes it possible for an overall sentence, such as "Sarah thought *the earth was flat*" (de Villers & Pyers, 2002, p. 1038, emphasis original), to be true, although the embedded complement (in italics) can be false (de Villiers & de Villiers, 2000). Their theory has been supported by a correlational study showing a link between children's understanding of beliefs and their grasp of nonmental verbs, which also take complements (e.g., *say* and *tell*). Further support comes from a training study in which children who were trained with complementation were found to significantly increase their performance on false belief tasks (Hale & Tager-Flusberg, 2003).

It has also been argued that rather than a specific aspect of syntax, it is a general grasp of syntax that is important (Astington & Jenkins, 1999), or that syntax and semantics are intertwined and it is general language ability that is essential (Ruffman et al., 2003; Slade & Ruffman, 2005). It may not be possible to completely separate syntax from semantics, so that in the training to use complements, children may also be trained to talk about false beliefs (Hale & Tager-Flusberg, 2003). De Villers and Pyers (2002, p. 1040) acknowledge that there is a link between the syntax and semantics of complementation, and that their claim is that false belief understanding "rests on the children's mastery of the grammar (semantics and syntax) of complementation." Because other languages have different complement structures, predictions can be derived from the de Villierses' position, but these have not been supported in cross-language studies in Mandarin and Cantonese (Cheung, Hsuan-Chih, Creed, Ng, Wang, & Mo, 2004; Tardiff & Wellman, 2000) and German (Perner, Sprung, Zauner, & Haider, 2003). Cheung et al. found that general language ability appeared to be most important, although it was highly correlated with complementation.

A further way to address these issues is with training studies. Lohmann and Tomasello (2003) used four conditions in an intervention study exposing children to a series of deceptive objects that appeared to be one thing, such as a flower, but on closer examination turned out to be something else, like a writing pen. In a *no language* training condition, the experimenter indicated the deceptive nature of the objects primarily nonverbally by drawing children's attention to the different functions by saying "Look!" and then "But now look!" In *discourse only* training, the experimenter talked about the deceptive nature of the objects but without using sentential complement constructions. In the *sentential complement only* training condition, the deceptive nature was not pointed out; instead, the experimenter used short stories to talk to the children about the objects using mental or communication verbs and sentential complements. Finally, the *full training* condition combined the features of the discourse only and the sentential complement training conditions, and the experimenter talked to the children about the deceptive nature of the objects using either mental terms (think, know) or communication verbs (say, tell) within sentential complement constructions. Lohmann and Tomasello found significant improvement in false belief understanding for training in the syntax of complementation, as well as the discourse only condition; but for the full training condition, they found significantly greater improvement than for either of the two conditions separately, suggesting that both may play a role. It is also interesting to note that they found no differences between conditions in which "think" and "know" were used compared with "say" and "tell."

Debate and further clarification are continuing (de Villiers, 2005; Perner, Zauner, & Sprung, 2005). However, as Lohmann, Tomasello, and Meyer (2005) point out, there is no real conflict between the position that discourse is important in social cognitive development because it reveals different perspectives and the view that the grammar of complementation is important. They suggest that what is of "greatest importance is reflective discourse in which adult and child comment on the ideas contained in the discourse turn of the other (or the self)" (Lohmann et al., p. 262). This reflective function has become part of the grammar of complementation. At this point, a reasonable suggestion is that "language in its totality provides a way to think and talk about other minds" (Cheung et al., 2004, p. 1168).

The evidence discussed earlier that parents' use of psychological terms is associated with their children's false belief understanding suggests that this talk may facilitate the development of social understanding. This possibility was assessed in a training study in which Peskin and Astington (2004) had approximately 70 picture books read to kindergarten children by parents, teachers, and research assistants over a 4-week period. The experimental group had books with added cognitive terms such as know, think, guess, wonder, and figure out, whereas the control group received the same books but with no additional cognitive terms. The additional exposure to cognitive terms did result in the children in the experimental group using more cognitive terms, but their comprehension of such words was not improved compared with the control group, and in fact, the control group, unexpectedly, did better at explaining false beliefs. In understanding these unexpected results, it is important to note that the control group was exposed to the same events in the picture books and to words such as "hide" and "look." These words, however, can also be used to talk about human activity in psychological terms, and we have just seen in Lohmann and Tomasello's (2003) study that there was no difference between the training conditions when cognitive terms such as "think" and "know" were used or communication verbs such as "say" and "tell." Thus, it seems that what is of primary importance is for children to understand people's actions—using excessively complex terms might have hampered this in the experimental condition. Words that are not usually considered psychological terms such as "because," "hide," and "trick" are also related to understanding human activity in psychological terms, and they were used on the control condition (Russell, 1992; Turnbull & Carpendale, 1999).

In a further study, rather than just the use of psychological terms, it was mothers' talk about the important events regarding a false belief situation that accounted for additional significant variance in children's false belief understanding beyond mothers' use of mental terms (Turnbull, Carpendale, & Racine, 2008, 2009). This suggests that although mental terms may be a useful indicator of the extent of talk about the psychological world, in fact, what is important is that children understand the events in question, and thus talk that facilitates this is beneficial in the development of social understanding.

Psychological Talk and Social Understanding

The underlying issue in this section on language is how children learn the meaning of psychological terms. However, assumptions about this process also entail views of the nature of mind and language. The general assumption is that the meaning of psychological terms is arrived at through mapping between psychological words and private inner experience, and the problem children face is figuring out the referent of psychological terms. For example, from German and Leslie's (2004) perspective, it is the "theory of mind" mechanism that "allows the young brain to attend to...mental states despite the fact that such states cannot be seen, heard, felt of otherwise sensed" (p. 107). Other theories begin with the same problem, although their proposed solution to it varies. From the theory theory perspective, children must infer hidden mental states, whereas from the simulation perspective, children draw on their own inner experience and reason by analogy about others. What is common here is a particular picture of the nature of the mind, according to which "intentions underlie and cause bodily movements" (Meltzoff et al., 1999, p. 24). This view of the mind is usually attributed to Descartes, and it has been described as a "ghost in the machine" (Ryle, 1949): a "picture of a purely mental willing entity trapped, as it were, inside the body, able, if it pulls the right levers, to cause the body to move as it intends it to move" (Russell, 1996, p. 173). It is assumed that the child must learn about how the various mental entities such as beliefs, desires, and intentions underlie and cause outer behavior.

This way of setting up the problem children face and the underlying assumptions about the nature of mind and language have already been discussed in the sections of nonhuman primates and infants. These assumptions are conceptual, not empirical, and have been extensively criticized (e.g., Carpendale & Lewis, 2004a, 2004b, 2006; Chapman, 1987; Montgomery, 2002; Racine & Carpendale, 2007a, 2007b; Sharrock & Coulter, 2004). These critics do not deny beliefs, desires, and intentions, but, rather, they criticize the Cartesian-inspired view of them. Instead of thinking of beliefs, desires, and intentions as separate from and causing behavior, they suggest that it may be less problematic to consider them as ways of talking about human actions. It is not behaviorism that is being suggested because this also assumes a Cartesian-inspired split between mind and physical movement. Instead, it is argued that beliefs, desires, and intentions are internally related to action, and human action is not viewed as split into mere physical movement and causal mental states.

The proposed alternative relational approach is that children learn about psychological terms such as want, look, happy, sad, pain, and fear through their natural reactions (Canfield, 1993; Carpendale & Lewis, 2004a, 2004b, 2006; Carpendale, Lewis, Susswein, & Lunn, 2009). For example, an infant's desires are manifest in actions such as reaching, and within a social context, these actions may

gradually become requests (Bibok, Carpendale, & Lewis, 2008). Words derive their meaning from their regular use and the role they play in patterns of human interaction. These routines of interpersonal interaction in which both adult and child has developed expectations about what happens are the shared practices on which language can be based. From this perspective, language is part of and built onto human activity (Tomasello, 2003; Turnbull, 2003; Wittgenstein, 1968) as a means for directing others' attention within shared frames. Therefore, what is helpful from family interaction for social cognitive development is talk about situations that children understand. This is what is required for children to understand human activity and learn language for talking about it in such terms. It then becomes possible for children to think about others in psychological terms.

CONCLUSIONS

Agreement about the importance of social understanding across the life span for making life within our complex social worlds possible contrasts with the diversity in theories proposed to account for this understanding. To organize our critical review of this literature, we began this chapter by outlining two frameworks or sets of metatheoretical assumptions on which theories of the development of social understanding are based (Jopling, 1993; Overton, 2004, 2006). These frameworks define the questions asked and the nature of problems studied, as well as solutions that are considered possible. An awareness of the unexamined philosophical/conceptual assumptions that underlie theories not only helps to organize the field, but also assists in critical evaluation and reveals why some theories run into conceptual difficulties. From our review of the literature, it can be seen that the individualistic or split framework has dominated much of the research in this area, focusing attention on the structure of individuals' social cognitions rather than their relation to the social processes that enable the emergence of such capabilities. This general framework structures the problems and at the same time constrains the solutions that are considered possible. Thus, although theories such as the theory theory, simulation theory, and the innate module account may appear to be quite different, in fact, they share common and problematic assumptions about the nature of the mind. A further reason for an analysis of underlying assumptions is that these are not just single theories, but rather they are research programs in the sense of Lakatos (1970). Thus, they cannot be rejected simply through critical experiments because they can be, and are, modified in the light of new evidence. This process can be clearly seen in the history of the "theory of mind" tradition (e.g., Carpendale & Lewis, 2004a, 2004b, 2006). These research programs can, however, be evaluated in light of the coherence of the assumptions they are based on, as well as relevant research.

We suggest that a relational or relational developmental systems approach (Lerner, 2006; Lerner & Overton, 2008; Overton, 2006) is a more fruitful framework with which to address the development of social understanding. In contrast to the individualistic or split framework's starting point of the individual from which it is then necessary to explain how the infant and child come to know about others, from a relational perspective, the starting point is the infant in relation to his or her caregivers. Knowledge develops through the infant's action on the physical and social worlds; although to begin with, these are not differentiated for the infant. Thus, social understanding is rooted in early emotional engagement with others, and infants gradually develop distinctions between self and other, and self and the physical world. Within interpersonal engagement, infants learn routine patterns of social activities. Understanding of such human forms of life, typically based on natural reactions, provides the foundation for language to begin, and children then learn words for these patterns of interaction. It is an interdisciplinary task to account for the development of social understanding. There is, of course, a necessary evolutionary side of the story, but this does not mean the evolution of neural modules. Rather, from a developmental systems perspective, the task is to look for adaptations that facilitate the infant's entry into typical human forms of interaction in which the infant learns about these patterns of activity.

Humans develop within a social and cultural niche, and also create, and change, cultures. We have evolved within this social environment and have evolved the ability to create culture. Infants are adapted to bring forth a socially interactive environment and to develop within this environment. Within this social environment, humans develop a form of social understanding with which they can understand the meaning of their own acts for others in routine situations (Mead, 1934). This is a form of meaning in which the self is aware of the significance of his or her own acts for others. That is, the self can take the attitude of the other toward her own act and understand the meaning of that act for the other. This form of interaction is the foundation that makes language possible. Language, in turn, then makes other, more complex forms of social understanding possible. Thus, human forms of social understanding are inextricably linked with language and the nature of human thinking.

REFERENCES

Adrián, J. E., Clemente, R. A., & Villanueva, L. (2007). Mothers' use of cognitive state verbs in picture-book reading and the development of children's understanding of mind: A longitudinal study. *Child Development, 78,* 1052–1067.

Akhtar, N., & Gernsbacher, M. A. (2008). On privileging the role of gaze in infant social cognition. *Child Development Perspectives, 2,* 59–65.

Anisfeld, M. (1991). Neonatal imitation. *Developmental Review, 11,* 60–97.

Anisfeld, M. (1996). Only tongue protrusion modeling is matched by neonates. *Developmental Review, 16,* 149–161.

Anisfeld, M., Turkewitz, G., & Rose, S. (2001). No compelling evidence that newborns imitate oral gestures. *Infancy, 2,* 111–122.

Apperly, I. A. (2008). Beyond simulation–theory and theory–theory: Why social cognitive neuroscience should use its own concepts to study "theory of mind." *Cognition, 107,* 266–283.

Apperly, I. A., & Butterfill, S. A. (2009). Do humans have two systems to track beliefs and belief-like states? *Psychological Review, 116,* 953–970.

Arsenio, W. F., & Lemerise, E. A. (2001). Varieties of childhood bullying: Values, emotional processes and social competence. *Social Development, 10,* 59–73.

Aslin, R. (2007). What's in a look? *Developmental Science, 10,* 48–53.

Astington, J. W. (2003). Sometimes necessary, never sufficient: False belief understanding and social competence. In B. Repacholi & V. Slaughter (Eds.) *Individual differences in theory of mind: Implications for typical and atypical development* (pp. 13–38). New York: Psychology Press.

Astington, J. W., & Baird, J. A. (Eds.). (2005). *Why language matters for theory of mind.* New York: Oxford University Press.

Astington, J. W., & Gopnik, A. (1991). Theoretical explanations of children's understanding of mind. *British Journal of Developmental Psychology, 9,* 7–29.

Astington, J. W., & Jenkins, J. M. (1999). A longitudinal study of the relations between language and theory-of-mind development. *Developmental Psychology, 35,* 1311–1320.

Avis, J., & Harris, P. L. (1991). Belief-desire reasoning among Baka children: Evidence for a universal conception of mind. *Child Development, 62,* 460–467.

Back, E., Ropar, D., & Mitchell, P. (2007). Do the eyes have it? Inferring mental states from animated faces in autism. *Child Development, 78,* 397–411.

Baird, J. A., & Astington, J. W. (2004). The role of mental state understanding in the development of moral cognition and moral action. In J. A. Baird & B. W. Sokol (Eds.), Connections between theory of mind and sociomoral development. *New Directions for Child and Adolescent Development, 103,* 37–49.

Baird, J. A., & Sokol, B. W. (Eds.). (2004). *Connections between theory of mind and sociomoral development: New directions for child and adolescent development, No. 103.* Hoboken, NJ: Jossey-Bass.

Bakeman, R., & Adamson, L. B. (1984). Coordinating attention to people and objects in mother-infant and peer-infant interaction, *Child Development, 55,* 1278–1289.

Baldwin, D. A. (1995). Understanding the link between joint attention and language. In C. Moore & P. J. Dunham (Eds.), *Joint attention: Its origins and role in development* (pp. 131–158). Hillsdale, NJ: Erlbaum.

Baldwin, D. A., & Moses, L. J. (1996). The ontogeny of social information gathering. *Child Development, 67*, 1915–1933.

Baldwin, J. M. (1906). *Thoughts and things: Vol. 1. Functional logic.* New York: Macmillan.

Banerjee, R. (2004) The role of social experience in advanced social understanding. *Behavioral and Brain Sciences, 27*, 97–98.

Baron-Cohen, S. (1989). The autistic child's theory of mind—a case of specific developmental delay. *Journal of Child Psychology and Psychiatry, 30*, 285–297.

Baron-Cohen, S. (1995). *Mindblindness: An essay on autism and theory of mind.* Cambridge, MA: MIT Press.

Baron-Cohen, S., Allen, J., & Gillberg, C. (1992). Can autism be detected at 18 months? The needle, the haystack, and the CHAT. *British Journal of Psychiatry, 161*, 839–843.

Baron-Cohen, S., Cox, A., Baird, G., Swettenham, J., Nightingale, N., Morgan, K., et al. (1996). Psychological markers of autism at 18 months of age in a large population. *British Journal of Psychiatry, 168*, 158–163.

Baron-Cohen, S., Jolliffe, T., Mortimore, C., & Robertson, M. (1997). Another advanced test of theory of mind: Evidence from very high functioning adults with autism or Asperger syndrome. *Journal of Child Psychology and Psychiatry, 38*, 813–822.

Baron-Cohen, S., Leslie, A. M., & Frith, U. (1985). Does the autistic child have a "theory of mind"? *Cognition, 21*, 37–46.

Baron-Cohen, S., O'Riordan, M., Jones, R., Stone V., & Plaisted, K. (1999). A new test of social sensitivity: Detection of faux pas in normal children and children with Asperger syndrome. *Journal of Autism and Developmental Disorders, 29*, 407–418.

Baron-Cohen, S., Wheelwright, S., Hill, J., Raste Y., & Plumb, I. (2001). The "Reading the Mind in the eyes" test revised version: A study with normal adults, and adults with Asperger Syndrome or High-Functioning autism. *Journal of Child Psychology and Psychiatry, 42*, 241–252.

Bartsch, K., & Wellman, H. M. (1995). *Children talk about the mind.* Oxford: Oxford University Press.

Bates, E. (1976). *Language and context.* New York: Academic Press.

Bates, E. (1979). *The emergence of symbols: Cognition and communication in infancy.* New York: Academic Press.

Bates, E., Camaioni, L., & Volterra, V. (1975). The acquisition of performatives prior to speech. *Merrill-Palmer Quarterly, 21*, 205–226.

Bennett, M., & Matthews, L. (2000). The role of second-order belief-understanding and social context in children's self-attributions of social emotions. *Social Development, 9*, 126–130.

Bibok, M. B., Carpendale, J. I. M., & Lewis, C. (2008). Social knowledge as social skill: An action based view of social understanding. In U. Müller, J. I. M. Carpendale, N. Budwig, & B. Sokol (Eds.), *Social life and social knowledge: Toward a process account of development* (pp. 145–169). New York: Taylor Francis.

Bloom, P., & German, T. P. (2000). Two reasons to abandon the false belief task a test of theory of mind. *Cognition, 77*, B25–B31.

Bosacki, S., & Astington, J. W. (1999). Theory of mind in preadolescence: Relations between social understanding and social competence. *Social Development, 8*, 237–255.

Bowlby, J. (1969) *Attachment and loss: Vol. 1. Attachment.* Harmondsworth, United Kingdom: Pelican.

Bowler, D. M. (1992). Theory of mind in Asperger's syndrome. *Journal of Child Psychology and Psychiatry, 33*, 877–893.

Bradmetz, J., & Schneider, R. (1999). Is Little Red Riding Hood afraid of her grandmother? Cognitive vs. emotional response to a false belief. *British Journal of Developmental Psychology, 17*, 501–514.

Bremner, J. G. (1994). *Infancy* (2nd ed.). Oxford: Blackwell

Bretherton, I., & Beeghly, M. (1982). Talking about internal states: The acquisition of an explicit theory of mind. *Developmental Psychology, 18*, 906–921.

Bretherton, I., McNew, S., & Beeghly-Smith, M. (1981). Early person knowledge as expressed in gestural and verbal communication: When do infants acquire a "theory of mind"? In M. E. Lamb & L. R. Sherrod (Eds.), *Infant social cognition: Empirical and theoretical considerations* (pp. 333–373). Hillsdale, NJ: Erlbaum.

Brooks, R., & Meltzoff, A. N. (2008). Infant gaze following and pointing predict accelerated vocabulary growth through two years of age: A longitudinal, growth curve modeling study. *Journal of Child Language, 35*, 207–220.

Brown, J. R., & Dunn, J. (1996). Continuities in emotion understanding from three to six years. *Child Development, 67*, 789–802.

Bruinsma, Y., Koegel, R. L, & Koegel, L., K. (2004). Joint attention and children with autism: A review of the literature. *Mental Retardation & Developmental Disabilities Research Reviews, 10*, 169–175.

Brune, C. W., & Woodward, A. L. (2007). Social cognition and social responsiveness in 10-month-old infants. *Journal of Cognition and Development, 8*, 133–158.

Bruner, J. (1983). *Child's talk.* New York: Norton.

Bruner, J. (1986). *Actual minds, possible worlds.* Cambridge, MA: Harvard University Press.

Bruner, J. (1990). *Acts of meaning.* Cambridge, MA: Harvard University Press.

Budwig, N. (2002). A developmental-functionalist approach to mental state talk. In E. Amsel & J. P. Byrnes (Eds.), *Language, literacy, and cognitive development: The development and consequences of symbolic communication* (pp. 59–86). Mahwah, NJ: Erlbaum.

Butterworth, G. (2001). Joint visual attention in infancy. In G. Bremner & A. Fogel (Eds.), *Blackwell handbook of infant development* (pp. 213–240). Oxford: Blackwell.

Butterworth, G., & Jarrett, N. (1991). What minds have in common is space: Spatial mechanisms serving joint visual attention in infancy. *British Journal of Developmental Psychology, 9*, 55–72.

Butterworth, G. E. (1998). What is special about pointing in babies? In F. Simion & G. Butterworth (Eds.), *The development of sensory, motor and cognitive capacities in early infancy: From perception to cognition* (pp. 171–190). Hove, United Kingdom: Psychology Press.

Call, J., & Tomasello, M. (2008). Does the chimpanzee have a theory of mind? 30 years later. *Trends in Cognitive Science, 12*, 187–192.

Callaghan, T., Rochat, P., Lillard, A., Claux, M. L., Odden, H., Itakura, S. T., et al. (2005). Synchrony in the onset of mental-state reasoning. *Psychological Science, 16*, 378–384.

Campbell, R. L., & Bickhard, M. H. (1993). Knowing levels and the child's understanding of mind. *Behavioral and Brain Sciences, 16*, 33–34.

Canfield, J. V. (1993). The living language: Wittgenstein and the empirical study of communication. *Language Sciences, 15*, 165–193.

Carey, S. (1985). *Conceptual change in childhood.* Cambridge, MA: MIT Press.

Carlson, S. M., Mandell, D. J., & Williams, L. (2004). Executive function and theory of mind: Stability and prediction from ages 2 to 3. *Developmental Psychology, 40*, 1105–1122.

Carlson, S. M., & Moses, L. J. (2001). Individual differences in inhibitory control and children's theory of mind. *Child Development, 72*, 1032–1053.

Carlson, S. M., Moses, L. J., & Breton, C. (2002). How specific is the relation between executive function and theory of mind? Contribution of inhibitory control and working memory. *Infant and Child Development, 11,* 73–92.

Carpendale, J. I. M. (2000). Kohlberg and Piaget on stages and moral reasoning. *Developmental Review, 20,* 181–205.

Carpendale, J. I. M., & Chandler, M. J. (1996). On the distinction between false belief understanding and subscribing to an interpretive theory of mind. *Child Development, 67,* 1686–1706.

Carpendale, J. I. M., & Lewis, C. (2004a). Constructing an understanding of mind: The development of children's social understanding within social interaction. *Behavioral and Brain Sciences, 27,* 79–96.

Carpendale, J. I. M., & Lewis, C. (2004b). Constructing understanding, with feeling. *Behavioral and Brain Sciences, 27,* 130–151.

Carpendale, J. I. M., & Lewis, C. (2006). *How children develop social understanding.* Oxford: Blackwell.

Carpendale, J. I. M., & Lewis, C. (2008). Mirroring cannot account for understanding action. *Behavioral and Brain Sciences, 31,* 23–24.

Carpendale, J. I. M., Lewis, C., Susswein, N., & Lunn, J. (2009). Talking and thinking: The role of speech in social understanding. In A. Winsler, C. Fernyhough, & I. Montero (Eds.), *Private speech, executive function, and the development of verbal self-regulation* (83–94). Cambridge: Cambridge University Press.

Carpenter, M., Nagell, K., & Tomasello, M. (1998). Social cognition, joint attention, and communicative competence from 9 to 15 months of age. *Monographs of the Society for Research in Child Development, 63* (Serial No. 255).

Carruthers, P. (2009). How we know our own minds: The relationship between mindreading and metacognition. *Behavioral & Brain Sciences, 32,* 121–182.

Carruthers, P., & Smith, P. K. (Eds.). (1996). *Theories of theories of mind.* Cambridge: Cambridge University Press.

Cassidy, K. W., Fineberg, D. S., Brown, K., & Perkins, A. (2005). Theory of mind may be contagious, but you don't catch it from your twin. *Child Development, 76,* 97–106.

Chandler, M. J. (1978). Social cognition: A selected review of current research. In H. Furth, W. Overton, & J. Gallagher (Eds.), *Knowledge and development: Yearbook of development epistemology* (pp. 93–147). New York: Plenum Press.

Chandler, M. J. (1987). The Othello effect: The emergence of skeptical doubt. *Human Development, 30,* 137–159.

Chandler, M. J. (1988). Doubt and developing theories of mind. In J. W. Astington, P. L. Harris, & D. R. Olson (Eds.), *Developing theories of mind* (pp. 387–413). New York: Cambridge University Press.

Chandler, M. J., & Boyes, M. (1982). Social-cognitive development. In B. B. Wolman (Ed.), *Handbook of developmental psychology* (pp. 387–402). Englewood Cliffs, NJ: Prentice-Hall.

Chandler, M. J., & Carpendale, J. I. M. (1998). Inching toward a mature theory of mind. In M. Ferrari & R. J. Sternberg (Eds.), *Self-awareness: Its nature and development* (pp. 148–190). New York: Guilford Press.

Chandler, M. J., Fritz, A. S., & Hala, S. (1989). Small scale deceit: Deception as a marker of 2-, 3- and 4-year-olds' theories of mind. *Child Development, 60,* 1263–1277.

Chandler, M. J., & Greenspan, S. (1972). Ersatz egocentrism: A reply to Borke. *Developmental Psychology, 7,* 104–106.

Chandler, M. J., & Lalonde, C. (1996). Shifting to an interpretive theory of mind: 5- to 7-year-olds' changing conceptions of mental life. In A. Sameroff & M. Haith (Eds.), *Reason and responsibility: The passage through childhood* (pp. 111–139). Chicago: University of Chicago Press.

Chandler, M. J., Sokol, B. W., & Hallett, D. (2001). Moral responsibility and the interpretive turn: Children's changing conceptions of truth and rightness. In B. F. Malle, L. J. Moses, & D. A. Baldwin (Eds.), *Intentions and intentionality* (pp. 345–365). Cambridge, MA: MIT Press.

Chandler, M. J., Sokol, B. W., & Wainryb, C. (2000). Beliefs about truth and beliefs about rightness. *Child Development, 71,* 91–97.

Chapman, M. (1987). Inner processes and outward criteria: Wittgenstein's importance for psychology. In M. Chapman & R. A. Dixon (Eds.), *Meaning and the growth of understanding: Wittgenstein's significance for developmental psychology* (pp. 103–127). Berlin: Springer-Verlag.

Charlton, R. A., Barrick, T. R., Markus, H. S., & Morris, R. G. (2009). Theory of mind associations with other cognitive functions and brain imaging in normal aging. *Psychology and Aging, 24,* 338–348.

Charman, T., Baron-Cohen, S., Swettenham, J., Baird, G., Cox, A., & Drew, A. (2000). Testing joint attention, imitation, and play as infancy precursors to language and theory of mind. *Cognitive Development, 15,* 481–498.

Charman, T., Ruffman, T., & Clements, W. (2002). Is there a gender difference in false belief development? *Social Development, 11,* 1–10.

Chasiotis, A., Kiessling, F., Winter, V., & Hofer, J. (2006). Sensory motor inhibition as a prerequisite for theory of mind: A comparison of clinical and normal preschoolers differing in sensory motor abilities. *International Journal of Behavioral Development, 30,* 178–190.

Cheung, H., Hsuan-Chih, C., Creed, N., Ng, L., Wang, S. P., & Mo, L. (2004). Relative roles of general and complementation language in theory-of-mind development: Evidence from Cantonese and English. *Child Development, 75,* 1155–1170.

Clements, W. A., & Perner, J. (1994). Implicit understanding of belief. *Cognitive Development, 9,* 377–395.

Cole, K., & Mitchell, P. (2000). Siblings in the development of executive control and a theory of mind. *British Journal of Developmental Psychology, 18,* 279–295.

Colle, L., Becchio, C., & Bara, B. G. (2008). The non-problem of other minds: A neurodevelopmental perspective on shared intentionality. *Human Development, 51,* 336–348.

Colvert, E., Custance, D., & Swettenham, J. (2002). Rule-based *reasoning* and theory of mind in autism. *Infant and Child Development, 11,* 197–200.

Colvert, E., Rutter, M., Kreppner, J., Beckett, C., Castle, J., Groothues, C., et al. (2008). Do theory of mind and executive function deficits underlie the adverse outcomes associated with profound early deprivation? Findings from the English and Romanian adoptees study. *Journal of Abnormal Child Psychology, 36,* 1057–1068.

Corkum, V., & Moore, C. (1998). The origins of joint visual attention in infants. *Developmental Psychology, 34,* 28–38.

Courchesne, E., Townsend, J., Akshoomoff, N. A., Saitoh, O., Yeung-Courchesne, R., Lincoln, A. J., et al. (1994). Impairment in shifting attention in autistic and cerebellar patients. *Behavioral Neuroscience, 108,* 848–866.

Csibra, G., & Southgate, V. (2005). Evidence for infants' understanding of false beliefs should not be dismissed. *Trends in Cognitive Sciences, 10,* 4–5.

Cutting, A. L., & Dunn, J. (1999). Theory of mind, emotion understanding, language, and family background: Individual differences and interrelations. *Child Development, 70,* 853–865.

Del Giudice, M., Manera, V., & Keysers, C. (2009). Programmed to learn? The ontogeny of mirror neurons. *Developmental Science, 12,* 350–363.

Dennett, D. C. (1978). Beliefs about beliefs. *Behavioral and Brain Sciences, 4,* 568–570.

D'Entremont, B. (2000). A perceptual-attentional explanation of gaze-following in 3- and 6-month-olds. *Developmental Science, 3,* 302–311.

de Rosnay, M., Pons, F., Harris, P. L., & Morrell, J. M. B. (2004). A lag between understanding false belief and emotion attribution in young children: Relationships with linguistic ability and mothers' mental-state language. *British Journal of Developmental Psychology, 22,* 197–218.

Desrochers, S., Morissette, P., & Ricard, M. (1995). Two perspectives on pointing in infancy. In C. Moore & P. J. Dunham (Eds.), *Joint attention: Its origins and role in development* (pp. 85–101). Hillsdale, NJ: Erlbaum.

de Villiers, J. G. (2005). Can language acquisition give children a point of view? In J. W. Astington & J. A. Baird (Eds.), *Why language matters for theory of mind* (pp. 186–219). New York: Oxford University Press.

de Villiers, J. G., & de Villiers, P. A. (2000). Linguistic determinism and the understanding of false beliefs. In P. Mitchell & K. J. Riggs (Eds.), *Children's reasoning and the mind* (pp. 191–228). Hove, United Kingdom: Psychology Press.

de Villiers, J. G., & Pyers, J. E. (2002). Complements to cognition: A longitudinal study of the relationship between complex syntax and false-belief-understanding. *Cognitive Development, 17,* 1037–1060.

Dews, S., Winner, E., Kaplan, J., Rosenblatt, E., Hunt, M., Lim, K., et al. (1996). Children's understanding of the meaning and functions of verbal irony. *Child Development, 67,* 3071–3085.

Diamond, A. (1990). The development and neural bases of memory functions, as indexed by the A-not-B and delayed response tasks, in human infants and infant monkeys. *Annals of the New York Academy of Sciences, 608,* 267–317.

Dick, A. S., & Overton, W. F. (2010). Executive function: Description and explanation. In B. W. Sokol, U. Müller, J. I. M. Carpendale, A. R. Young, & G. Iarocci (Eds.), *Self- and social-regulation* (pp. 7–34). New York: Oxford University Press.

Dunn, J. (1995). Children as psychologists: The later correlates of individual differences in understanding of emotions and other minds. *Cognition and Emotion, 9,* 187–201.

Dunn, J. (1996). Children's relationships: Bridging the divide between cognitive and social development. *Child Psychology and Psychiatry, 37,* 507–518.

Dunn, J. (2004). *Children's friendships: The beginnings of intimacy.* Oxford: Blackwell.

Dunn, J., Brown, J., & Maguire, M. (1995). The development of children's moral sensibility: Individual differences and emotional understanding. *Developmental Psychology, 31,* 649–659.

Dunn, J., Brown, J., Slomkowski, C., Tesla, C., & Youngblade, L. (1991). Young children's understanding of other people's feelings and beliefs: Individual differences and their antecedents. *Child Development, 62,* 1352–1366.

Dunn, J., & Cutting, A. L. (1999). Understanding others, and individual differences in friendship interactions in young children. *Social Development, 8,* 201–219.

Dunn, J., Cutting, A. L., & Demetriou, H. (2000). Moral sensibility, understanding others, and children's friendship interactions in the preschool period. *British Journal of Developmental Psychology, 18,* 159–177.

Dunn, J., & Kendrick, C. (1982). *Siblings: Love, envy and understanding.* Oxford: Blackwell.

Eisenmajer, R., & Prior, M. (1991). Cognitive linguistic correlates of theory of mind ability in autistic-children. *British Journal of Developmental Psychology, 9,* 351–364.

Ely, R., & McCabe, A. (1994). The language play of kindergarten children. *First Language, 40,* 19–35.

Emery, N. J., & Clayton, N. S. (2009). Comparative social cognition. *Annual Review of Psychology, 60,* 87–113.

Ensor, R., & Hughes, C. (2008). Content or connectedness? Mother-child talk and early social understanding. *Child Development, 79,* 201–216.

Ereky-Stevens, K. (2008). Associations between mothers' sensitivity to their infants' internal states and children's later understanding of mind and emotion. *Infant and Child Development, 17,* 527–543.

Feldman, C. F. (1992). The new theory of theory of mind. *Human Development, 35,* 107–117.

Fernyhough, C. (2008). Getting Vygotskian about theory of mind: Mediation, dialogue, and the development of social understanding. *Developmental Review, 28,* 225–262.

Filippova, E., & Astington, J. W. (2008). Further development in social reasoning revealed in discourse irony understanding, *Child Development, 79,* 126–138.

Fischer, K. V., & Bidell, T. (1991). Constraining nativist inferences about cognitive capacities. In S. Carey & R. Gelman (Eds.), *The epigenesist of mind: essays on biology and cognition* (pp. 199–235). Hillsdale, NJ: Erlbaum.

Flavell, J. H. (1992). Perspectives on perspective taking. In H. Beilin & P. B. Pufall (Eds.), *Piaget's theory: Prospects and possibilities* (pp. 107–139). Hillsdale, NJ: Erlbaum.

Flavell, J. H., Botkin, P. T., Fry, C., Wright, J., & Jarvis, P. (1968). *The development of role-taking and communication skills in children.* New York: John Wiley & Sons.

Flom, R., Lee, K., & Muir, D. (Eds.). (2007). *Gaze-following: Its development and significance.* Mahwah, NJ: Erlbaum.

Flynn, E., O'Malley, C., & Wood, D. (2004). A longitudinal, microgenetic study of the emergence of false belief understanding and inhibition skills. *Developmental Science, 7,* 103–115.

Fodor, J. (1992). A theory of the child's theory of mind. *Cognition, 44,* 283–296.

Fogel, A., & Hannan, T. E. (1985). Manual actions of nine- to fifteen-week old human infants during face-to-face interaction with their mothers. *Child Development, 56,* 1271–1279.

Fonagy, P., Redfern, S., & Charman, T. (1997). The relationship between belief-desire reasoning and a projective measure of attachment security (SAT). *British Journal of Developmental Psychology, 15,* 51–61.

Foote, R. C., & Holmes-Lonergan, H. A. (2003). Sibling conflict and theory of mind. *British Journal of Developmental Psychology, 21,* 45–58.

Franco, F., & Butterworth, G. E. (1996). Pointing and social awareness: Declaring and requesting in the second year. *Journal of Child Language, 23,* 307–336.

Frith, U. (2003). *Autism: Explaining the enigma* (2nd ed.). Oxford: Blackwell.

Gallagher, H. L., & Frith, C. D. (2003). Functional imaging of "theory of mind." *Trends in Cognitive Science, 7,* 77–83.

Gallagher, H. L., Happé, F., Brunswick, N., Fletcher, P. C., Frith, U., & Frith, C. D. (2000). Reading the mind in cartoons and stories: An fMRI study of "theory of mind" in verbal and nonverbal tasks. *Neuropsychologia, 38,* 11–21.

Gallagher, H. L., Jack, A. I., Roepstorff, A., & Frith, C. D. (2002). Imaging the intentional stance in a competitive game. *Neuroimage, 16,* 814–821.

Gallese, V., (2007). Before and below "theory of mind": Embodied simulation and the neural correlates of social cognition. *Philosophical Transactions of the Royal Society, B, 362,* 659–669.

Gallese, V., Keysers, C., & Rizzolatti, G. (2004). A unifying view of the basis of social cognition. *Trends in Cognitive Science, 8,* 396–403.

Garner, P., Jones, D., Gaddy, D., & Rennie, K. (1997). Low income mothers' conversations about emotion and their children's emotional competence. *Social Development, 6,* 125–142.

Gellatly, A. (1997). Why the young child has neither a theory of mind nor a theory of anything else. *Human Development, 40,* 32–50.

German, T. P., & Leslie, A. M. (2000). Attending to and learning about mental states. In P. Mitchell & K. J. Riggs (Eds.), *Children's reasoning and the mind* (pp. 229–252). Hove, United Kingdom: Psychology Press.

German, T. P., & Leslie, A. M. (2004). No (social) construction without (meta) representation: Modular mechanisms as a *basis* for the capacity to acquire an understanding of mind. *Behavioral and Brain Sciences, 27,* 106–107.

Gini, G., (2006). Social cognition and moral cognition in bullying: What's wrong? *Aggressive Behavior, 32,* 528–539.

Goffman, E. (1959). *The presentation of the self in everyday life.* New York: Anchor.

Gómez, J-C. (2007). Pointing behavior in apes and human infants: A balanced interpretation. *Child Development, 78,* 729–734.

Gordon, R. M. (1986). Folk psychology as simulation. *Mind and Language, 1,* 156–171.

Gottlieb, G. (2007). Probabilistic epigenesis. *Developmental Science, 10,* 1–11.

Greene, J., & Cohen, J. (2004). For the law, neuroscience changes nothing and everything. *Philosophical Transaction of the Royal Society, 359,* 1775–1785.

Griffiths, P. E., & Stotz, K. (2000). How the mind grows: A developmental perspective on the biology of cognition. *Synthese, 122,* 29–51.

Hadwin, J., & Perner, J. (1991). Pleased and surprised: Children's cognitive theory of emotion. *British Journal of Developmental Psychology, 9,* 215–234.

Haith, M. M. (1998). Who put the cog in infant cognition? Is the rich interpretation too costly? *Infant Behavior and Development, 21,* 167–179.

Hala, S., Chandler, M. J., & Fritz, A. (1991). Fledgling theories of mind: Deception as a marker of 3-year-olds' understanding of false belief. *Child Development, 62,* 83–97.

Hala, S., Hug, S., & Henderson, A. (2003). Executive function and false belief understanding in preschool children: Two tasks are harder than one. *Journal of Cognition and Development, 4,* 275–298.

Hala, S., & Russell, J. (2001). Executive control within strategic deception: A window on early cognitive development? *Journal of Experimental Child Psychology, 80,* 112–141.

Hale, C. M., & Tager-Flusberg, H. (2003). The influence of language on theory of mind: A training study. *Developmental Science, 6,* 346–359.

Hallett, D., Chandler, M. J., & Krettenauer, T. (2002). Disentangling the course of epistemic development: Parsing knowledge by epistemic content. *New Ideas in Psychology, 20,* 285–307.

Happé, F. G. E. (1994). An advanced test of theory of mind: Understanding story characters' thoughts and feelings by able autistic, mentally handicapped, and normal children and adults. *Journal of Autism and Developmental Disorders, 24,* 129–154.

Happé, F. G. E. (1995). The role of age and verbal ability in the theory of mind task performance of subjects with autism. *Child Development, 66,* 843–855.

Happé, F. G. E. (1996). Studying weak central coherence at low levels: Children with autism do not succumb to visual illusions. A research note. *Journal of Child Psychology and Psychiatry, 37,* 873–877.

Happé, F. G. E., Winner, E., & Brownell, H. (1998). The getting of wisdom: Theory of mind in old age. *Developmental Psychology, 34,* 358–362.

Harris, P. L. (1991). The work of the imagination. In A. Whiten (Ed.), *Natural theories of mind* (pp. 283–304). Oxford: Blackwell.

Harris, P. L. (2000). *The work of the imagination.* Oxford: Blackwell.

Harris, P. L. (2005). Conversation, pretense, and theory of mind. In J. W. Astington & J. A. Baird (Eds.), *Why language matters for theory of mind* (pp. 70–83). New York: Oxford University Press.

Harris, P. L. (2006). Social cognition. In D. Kuhn & R. Sielgler (Eds.), *Handbook of child psychology: Vol. 2. Cognition, perception, and language* (6th ed., pp. 811–858). Editors in chief: W. Damon & R. M. Lerner. Hoboken, NJ: John Wiley & Sons.

Harris, P. L., Johnson, C. N., Hutton, D., Andrews, G., & Cooke, T. (1989). Young children's theory of mind and emotion. *Cognition and Emotion, 3,* 379–400.

Heider, F. (1958). *The psychology of interpersonal relations.* Chichester, United Kingdom: John Wiley & Sons.

Hickok, G. (2008). Eight problems for the mirror neuron theory of action understanding in monkeys and humans. *Journal of Cognitive Neuroscience, 21,* 1229–1243.

Hill, E. L. (2004). Evaluating the theory of executive dysfunction in autism. *Developmental Review, 24,* 189–233.

Hobson, R. P. (1993). *Autism and the development of mind.* Hove, United Kingdom: Erlbaum.

Hobson, R. P. (2004). *The cradle of thought.* London: Macmillan/ Oxford University Press. (Original work published 2002)

Hogrefe, G. J., Wimmer, H., & Perner, J. (1986). Ignorance versus false belief: A developmental lag in the acquisition of mental states. *Child Development, 57,* 567–582.

Holmes, H. A., Black, C., & Miller, S. A. (1996). A cross-task comparison of false-belief understanding in a Head Start population. *Journal of Experimental Child Psychology, 63,* 263–285.

Hughes, C. (1998). Executive function in preschoolers: Links with theory of mind and verbal ability. *British Journal of Developmental Psychology, 16,* 233–253.

Hughes, C., Adlam, A., Happé, F., Jackson, J., Taylor, A., & Caspi, A. (2000). Good test-retest reliability for standard and advanced false-belief tasks across a wide range of abilities. *Journal of Child Psychology & Psychiatry, 41,* 483–490.

Hughes, C., Deater-Deckard, K., & Cutting, A. L. (1999). "Speak roughly to your little boy"? Sex differences in the relations between parenting and preschoolers' understanding of mind. *Social Development, 8,* 143–160.

Hughes, C., & Dunn, J. (1998). Understanding mind and emotions: Longitudinal associations with mental-state talk between young friends. *Developmental Psychology, 34,* 1026–1037.

Huizinga, M., Dolan, C. V., & van der Molen, M. W. (2006) Age-related change in executive function: Developmental trends and a latent variable analysis, *Neuropsychologia, 44,* 2017–2036.

Hurley, S. (2008). The shared circuits model (SCM): How control, mirroring, and simulation can enable imitation, deliberation, and mindreading. *Behavioral and Brain Sciences, 31,* 1–58.

Iacoboni, M. (2009). Imitation, empathy, and mirror neurons. *Annual Review of Psychology, 60,* 653–670.

Iacoboni, M., Molnar-Szakacs, I., Gallese, V., Buccino, G., Mazziotta, J. C., & Rizzolatti, G. (2005). Grasping the intentions of others with one's own mirror neuron system. *PLoS Biology, 3,* 529–535.

Jastrow, J. (1900). *Fact and fable in psychology.* Boston: Houghton-Mifflin.

Jenkins, J. M., & Astington, J. W. (1996). Cognitive factors and family structure associated with theory of mind development in young children. *Developmental Psychology, 32,* 70–78.

Johnson, C. N. (1988). Theory of mind and the structure of conscious experience. In J. W. Astington, P. L. Harris, & D. R. Olson (Eds.), *Developing theories of mind* (pp. 47–63). New York: Cambridge University Press.

Jones, S. S. (1996). Imitation or exploration? Young infants' matching of adults' oral gestures. *Child Development, 67,* 1952–1969.

Jones, S. S. (2007). Imitation in infancy: The development of mimicry. *Psychological Science, 18,* 593–599.

Jopling, D. (1993). Cognitive science, other minds, and the philosophy of dialogue. In U. Neisser (Ed.), *The perceived self* (pp. 290–309). Cambridge, MA: MIT Press.

Kagan, J. (2006). Biology's useful contribution: A comment. *Human Development, 49,* 310–314.

Karmiloff-Smith, A., & Inhelder, B. (1974). If you want to get ahead get a theory. *Cognition, 3,* 195–212.

Keysers, C., & Perrett, D. I. (2004). Demystifying social cognition: A Hebbian perspective. *Trends in Cognitive Science, 8,* 501–507.

King, P. M., & Kitchener, K. S. (1994). *Developing reflective judgment.* San Francisco, CA: Jossey-Bass.

Kita, S. (Ed.) (2003). *Pointing: Where language, culture, and cognition meet.* Mahwah, NJ: Erlbaum.

Klin, A., Jones, W., Schultz, R., & Volkmar, F. (2003). The enactive mind, or from actions to cognition: lessons from autism. *Philosophical Transactions of the Royal Society of London Series B-Biological Sciences, 358,* 345–360.

Kloo, D., & Perner, J. (2003). Training transfer between card sorting and false belief understanding: Helping children apply conflicting descriptions. *Child Development, 74,* 1823–1839.

Kreppner, J. M., Rutter, M., Beckett, C., Castle, J., Colvert, E., Goothues, C., et al. (2007). Normality and impairment following profound early institutional deprivation: A longitudinal follow-up into early adolescence. *Developmental Psychology 43,* 931–946.

Kuebli, J., Butler, S., & Fivush, R. (1995). Mother-child talk about past emotions: Relations of maternal language and child gender over time. *Cognition and Emotion, 9,* 265–283.

Kuhn, D., Amsel, E., & O'Laughlin, M. (1988). *The development of scientific thinking skills.* Orlando, FL: Academic Press.

Lakatos, I. (1970). Falsification and the methodology of scientific research programmes. In I. Lakatos & A. Musgrave (Eds.), *Criticism and the growth of knowledge* (pp. 91–196). New York: Cambridge University Press.

Lalonde, C. E., & Chandler, M. J. (1995). False belief understanding goes to school: On the social-emotional consequences of coming early or late to a first theory of mind. *Cognition and Emotion, 9,* 167–185.

Lalonde, C. E., & Chandler, M. J. (2002). Children's understanding of interpretation. *New Ideas in Psychology, 20,* 163–198.

Laranjo, J., Bernier, A., & Meins, E. (2008). Associations between maternal mind-mindedness and infant attachment security: Investigating the mediating role of maternal sensitivity, *Infant Behavior and Development, 31,* 688–695.

Leavens, D. A., Racine, T. P., & Hopkins, W. D. (2009). The ontogeny and phylogeny of non-verbal deixis. In R. Botha & C. Knight (Eds.), *The cradle of language: Vol. 1. Multidisciplinary perspectives* (pp. ·142–165). Oxford: Oxford University Press.

Leekam, S. R., López, B., & Moore, C. (2000). Attention and joint attention in preschool children with autism. *Developmental Psychology, 36,* 261–274.

Lerner, R. M. (2006). Developmental science, developmental systems, and contemporary theories of human development. In R. M. Lerner (Ed.), *Handbook of child psychology: Vol. 1. Theoretical models of human development* (6th ed., pp. 1–17). Editors in chief: W. Damon & R. M. Lerner. Hoboken, NJ: John Wiley & Sons.

Lerner, R. M., & Overton. W. F. (2008). Exemplifying the integrations of the relational developmental system: Synthesizing theory, research, and application to promote positive development and social justice. *Journal of Adolescent Research, 23,* 245–255.

Leslie, A. M. (1987). Pretense and representation: The origins of "theory of mind." *Psychological Review, 94,* 412–426.

Leslie, A. M. (1991). The theory of mind impairment in autism: Evidence for a modular mechanism of development? In A. Whiten (Ed.), *Natural theories of mind* (pp. 63–78). Oxford: Blackwell.

Leslie, A. M. (1992). Pretense, autism, and the "theory-of-mind" module. *Current Directions in Psychological Science, 1,* 18–21.

Leslie, A. M. (2005). Developmental parallels in understanding minds and bodies. *Trends in Cognitive Sciences, 9,* 459–462.

Leslie, A. M., & Frith, U. (1988). Autistic children's understanding of seeing, knowing and believing. *British Journal of Developmental Psychology, 6,* 315–324.

Leudar, I., & Costall, A. (2009). Against "theory of mind". In I. Leudar & A. Costall (Eds.), *Against theory of mind.* London: Routledge.

Lewis, C., & Carpendale, J. I. M. (2002). Social cognition. In P. K. Smith & C. Hart (Eds.), *The Blackwell handbook of childhood social development* (375–393). Oxford: Blackwell.

Lewis, C., & Carpendale, J. I. M. (2010). Social cognition. In P. K. Smith & C. H. Hart (Eds.), *Blackwell handbook of childhood social development* (2nd ed.). Oxford: Blackwell.

Lewis, C., Carpendale, J. I. M., Towse, J., & Maridaki-Kassotaki, K. (2010). Epistemic flow and the social making of minds. In B. Sokol, U. Müller, J. I. M. Carpendale, A. Young, & G. Iarocci, (Eds.), *Self- and Social-Regulation: Social interaction and the development of social understanding and executive functions* (pp. 80–110). New York: Oxford University Press.

Lewis, C., Freeman, N. H., Kyriakidou, C., Maridaki-Kassotaki, K., & Berridge, D. M. (1996). Social influences on false belief access: Specific sibling influences or general apprenticeship? *Child Development, 67,* 2930–2947.

Lewis, C., Huang, Z., & Rooksby, M. (2006). Chinese preschoolers' false belief understanding: Is social knowledge underpinned by parental styles, social interactions or executive functions? *Psychologia, 49,* 252–266.

Lewis, C., Koyasu, M., Oh, S., Ogawa, A., & Short, B. (2009) Culture, executive function and social understanding. *New Directions in Child and Adolescent Development, 123,* 69–76.

Lewis, C., & Osborne, A. (1990) Three-year-olds' problems with false belief: Conceptual deficit or linguistic artifact? *Child Development, 61,* 1514–1519.

Liebal, K., Behne, T., Carpenter, M., & Tomasello, M. (2009). Infants use shared experience to interpret pointing gestures. *Developmental Science, 12,* 264–271.

Lingnau, A., Gesierich, B., & Caramazza, A. (2009). Asymmetric fMRI adaptation reveals no evidence for mirror neurons in humans. *Proc National Academy of Science U S A, 106,* 9925–9930.

Liszkowski, U., Albrecht, K., Carpenter, M., & Tomasello, M. (2008). Infants' visual and auditory communication when a partner is or is not visually attending. *Infant Behavior and Development, 31,* 157–167.

Liszkowski, U., Carpenter, M., Henning, A., Striano, T., & Tomasello, M. (2004). Twelve-month-olds point to share attention and interest. *Developmental Science, 7,* 297–307.

Liszkowski, U., Carpenter, M., Striano, T., & Tomasello, M. (2006). Twelve- and 18-month-olds point to provide information for others. *Journal of Cognition and Development, 7,* 173–187.

Logothetis, N. (2008). What we can and what we cannot do with fMRI. *Nature, 453,* 869–878.

Lohmann, H., & Tomasello, M. (2003). The role of language in the development of false belief understanding: A training study. *Child Development, 74,* 1130–144.

Lohmann, H., Tomasello, M., & Meyer, S. (2005). Linguistic communication and social understanding. In J. W. Astington & J. A. Baird (Eds.), *Why language matters for theory of mind* (pp. 245–265). New York: Oxford University Press.

Mansfield, A. F., & Clinchy, B. (2002). Toward the integration of objective and subjectivity: Epistemological development from 10 to 16. *New Ideas in Psychology, 20,* 225–262.

Mayes, L. C., Klin, A., Tercyak Jr, K. P., Cicchetti, D. V., & Cohen, D. J. (1996). Test-retest reliability for false belief tasks. *Journal of Child Psychology & Psychiatry, 37,* 313–319.

Maylor, E. A., Moulson, J. M., Muncer, A-M., & Taylor, L. A. (2002). Does performance on theory of mind tasks decline in old age? *British Journal of Psychology, 93,* 465–485.

McGhee, P. E. (1979). *Humor: Its origin and development.* San Francisco: W. H. Freeman.

Mcquaid, N., Bibok, M., & Carpendale, J. I. M. (2009). Relationship between maternal contingent responsiveness and infant social expectation. *Infancy, 14,* 390–401.

Mead, G. H. (1934). *Mind, self and society.* Chicago: University of Chicago Press.

Meins, E., Fernyhough, C., Russell, J., & Clark-Carter, D. (1998). Security of attachment as a predictor of symbolic and mentalising abilities: A longitudinal study. *Social Development, 7,* 1–24.

Meins, E., Fernyhough, C., Wainwright, R., Das Gupta, M., Fradley, E., & Tuckey, M. (2002). Maternal mind-mindedness and attachment security as predictors of theory of mind understanding. *Child Development, 73,* 1715–1726.

Meltzoff, A., & Gopnik, A. (1993). The role of imitation in understanding persons and developing a theory of mind. In S. Baron-Cohen, H. Tager-Flusberg, & D. J. Cohen (Eds.), *Understanding other minds: Perspectives from autism* (pp. 335–366). Oxford: Oxford University Press.

Meltzoff, A. N., & Brooks R. (2007). Eyes wide shut: The importance of eyes in infant gaze-following and understanding other minds. In R. Flom, K. Lee, & D. Muir (Eds.), *Gaze-following: Its development and significance* (pp. 217–241). Mahwah, NJ: Erlbaum.

Meltzoff, A. N., Gopnik, A., & Repacholi, B. M. (1999). Toddlers' understanding of intentions, desires, and emotions: Explorations of the dark ages. In P. D. Zelazo, J. W. Astington, & D. R. Olson (Eds.), *Developing theories of intention* (pp. 17–41). Mahwah, NJ: Erlbaum.

Miller, G. (2008). Growing pains for fMRI. *Science, 320,* 1412–1414.

Milligan, K., Astington, J. W., & Dack, L. A. (2007). Language and theory of mind: Meta-analysis of the relations between language ability and false-belief understanding. *Child Development, 78,* 622–646.

Mitchell, J. P., Banaji, M. R., & Macrae, C. N. (2005). The link between social cognition and self-referential thought in the medial prefrontal cortex. *Journal of Cognitive Neuroscience, 17,* 1306–1315.

Mitchell, J. P., Macrae, C. N., & Banaji, M. R. (2006). Dissociable medial prefrontal contributions to judgments of similar and dissimilar others. *Neuron, 50,* 655–663.

Miyake, A., Friedman, N. P., Emerson, M. J., Witzki, A. H., Howerter, A., & Wager, T. D. (2000). The unity and diversity of executive functions and their contributions to complex "frontal lobe" tasks: A latent variable analysis. *Cognitive Psychology, 41,* 49–100.

Moll, H., Carpenter, M., & Tomasello, M. (2007). Fourteen-month-olds know what others have experienced only in joint engagement with them. *Developmental Science, 10,* 826–835.

Moll, H., Richter, N., Carpenter, M., & Tomasello, M. (2008). Fourteen-month-olds know what "we" have shared in a special way. *Infancy, 13,* 90–101.

Moll, H., & Tomasello, M. (2004). 12- and 18-month-old infants follow gaze to spaces behind barriers. *Developmental Science, 7,* F1–F9.

Moll, H., & Tomasello, M. (2007). Cooperation and human cognition: The Vygotskian intelligence hypothesis. *Philosophical Transactions of the Royal Society, 362,* 639–648.

Montgomery, D. E. (2002). Mental verbs and semantic development. *Journal of Cognition and Development, 3,* 357–384.

Moore, C. (1996). Theories of mind in infancy. *British Journal of Developmental Psychology, 14,* 19–40.

Moore, C. (1998). Social cognition in infancy. In M. Carpenter, K. Nagell, & M. Tomasello, Social Cognition, joint attention and communicative competence from 9 to 15 months of age. *Monographs of the Society for Research in Child Development, 63,* 167–174.

Moore, C. (2006). *The development of commonsense psychology.* Mahwah, NJ: Erlbaum.

Moore, C. (2008). The development of gaze following. *Child Development Perspectives, 2,* 66–70.

Moore, C., & Corkum, V. (1994). Social understanding at the end of the first year of life. *Developmental Review, 14,* 349–372.

Moore, C., & Corkum, V. (1998). Infant gaze following based on eye direction. *British Journal of Developmental Psychology, 16,* 495–503.

Moore, C., & D'Entremont, B. (2001). Developmental changes in pointing as a function of parent's attentional focus. *Journal of Cognition and Development, 2,* 109–129.

Moriguchi, Y., Lee, K., & Itakura, S. (2007). Social transmission of disinhibition in young children. *Developmental Science, 10,* 481–491.

Moses, L. J. (2001). Executive accounts of theory-of-mind development. *Child Development, 72,* 688–690.

Moses, L. J., & Carlson, S. M. (2004). Self-regulation and children's theories of mind. In C. Lightfoot, C. Lalonde, & M. Chandler (Eds.), *Changing conceptions of psychological life* (pp. 127–146). Mahwah, NJ: Erlbaum.

Moses, L. J., & Sabbagh, M. A. (2007). Interactions between domain general and domain specific processes in the development of children's theories of mind. In M. J. Roberts (Ed.), *Integrating the mind: Domain general versus domain specific processes in higher cognition* (pp. 375–391). Hove, United Kingdom: Psychology Press.

Müller, U., & Carpendale, J. I. M. (2004). From joint activity to joint attention: A relational approach to social development in infancy. In J. I. M. Carpendale & U. Müller (Eds.), *Social interaction and the development of knowledge* (pp. 215–238). Mahwah, NJ: Erlbaum.

Müller, U., & Runions. K. (2003). The origins of understanding of self and other: James Mark Baldwin's theory. *Developmental Review, 23,* 29–54.

Mundy, P., Block, J., Delgado, C., Pomares, Y., van Hecke, A. V., & Parlade, M. V. (2007). Individual differences and the development of joint attention in infancy. *Child Development, 78,* 938–954.

Mundy, P., & Sigman, M. (1989). The theoretical implications of joint attention deficits in autism. *Development and Psychopathology, 1,* 173–183.

Mundy, P., Sullivan, L., & Mastergeorge, A. M. (2009). A parallel and distributed-processing model of joint attention, social cognition and autism. *Autism Research, 2,* 2–21.

Murphy, C. M., & Messer, D. J. (1977). Mothers, infants and pointing: A study of gesture. In H. R. Schaffer (Ed.), *Studies in mother-infant interaction* (pp. 325–354). London: Academic Press.

Naito, M., & Koyama, K. (2006). The development of false belief understanding in Japanese children: Delay and difference? *International Journal of Behavioral Development, 30,* 290–304.

Nelson, K. (1996). *Language in cognitive development: The emergence of the mediated mind.* New York: Cambridge University Press.

Nelson, K. (2005). Language pathways into the community of minds. In J. W. Astington & J. Baird (Eds.), *Why language matters for theory of mind* (pp. 26–49). Oxford: Oxford University Press.

Nelson, P. B., Adamson, L. B., & Bakeman, R. (2008). Toddlers' joint engagement experience facilitates preschoolers' acquisition of theory of mind. *Developmental Science, 11,* 840–845.

Oh, S, & Lewis, C. (2008). Korean preschoolers' advanced inhibitory control and its relation to other executive skills and mental state understanding. *Child Development, 79,* 80–99.

O'Neill, D. K. (1996). Two-year-old children's sensitivity to a parent's knowledge state when making requests. *Child Development, 67,* 659–677.

Onishi, K., & Baillargeon, R. (2005). Do 15-month-old infants understand false beliefs? *Science, 308,* 255–258.

Ontai, L. L., & Thompson, R. A. (2008). Attachment, parent-child discourse and theory-of-mind development. *Social Development, 17,* 47–60.

Osterling, J., & Dawson, G. (1994). Early recognition of children with autism: A study of first birthday home videotapes. *Journal of Autism & Developmental Disorders, 24,* 247–257.

Oswald, D. P., & Ollendick, T. H. (1989). Role-taking and social competence in autism and mental-retardation. *Journal of Autism and Developmental Disorders, 19,* 119–127.

Overton, W. F. (2004). A relational and embodied perspective on resolving psychology's antinomies. In J. I. M. Carpendale & U. Müller (Eds.), *Social interaction and the development of knowledge* (pp. 19–44). Mahwah, NJ: Erlbaum.

Overton, W. F. (2006). Developmental psychology: Philosophy, concepts, methodology. In R. M. Lerner (Vol. Ed.), *Handbook of child psychology: Vol. 1. Theoretical models of human development* (6th ed., pp. 18–88). Editors in chief: W. Damon & R. M. Lerner. Hoboken, NJ: John Wiley & Sons.

Page, M. P. A. (2006). What can't functional neuroimaging tell the cognitive psychologist? *Cortex, 42,* 428–443.

Pears, K. C., & Moses, L. J. (2003). Demographics, parenting, and theory of mind in preschool children. *Social Development, 12,* 1–20.

Perner, J. (1991). *Understanding the representational mind.* Cambridge, MA: MIT Press.

Perner, J., Frith, U., Leslie, A. M., & Leekam, S. R. (1989). Exploration of the autistic child's theory of mind: Knowledge, belief, and communication. *Child Development, 60,* 688–700.

Perner, J., Kain, W., & Barchfeld, P. (2002). Executive control and higher-order theory of mind in children at risk of ADHD. *Infant and Child Development, 11,* 141–158.

Perner, J., Leekam, S. R., & Wimmer, H. (1987). 3-year-olds difficulty with false belief—the case for a conceptual deficit. *British Journal of Developmental Psychology, 5,* 125–137.

Perner, J., & Ruffman, T. (2005). Infants' insight into the mind: how deep? *Science, 308,* 214–216.

Perner, J., Ruffman, T., & Leekam, S. R. (1994). Theory of mind is contagious: You catch it from your sibs. *Child Development, 65,* 1228–1238.

Perner, J., Sprung, M., Zauner, P., & Haider, H. (2003). Want that is understood well before say that, think that, and false belief: A test of de Villier's linguistic determinism on German-speaking children. *Child Development, 74,* 179–188.

Perner, J., & Wimmer, H. (1985). "John thinks that Mary thinks that…": Attribution of second-order beliefs by 5- to 10-year-old children. *Journal of Experimental Child Psychology, 39,* 437–471.

Perner, J., Zauner, P., & Sprung, M. (2005). What does "that" have to do with point of view? Conflicting desires and "want" in German. In J. W. Astington & J. A. Baird (Eds.), *Why language matters for theory of mind* (pp. 220–244). New York: Oxford University Press.

Perry, W. G. (1970). *Forms of intellectual and ethical development in the college years.* New York: Holt, Rinehart, & Winston.

Peskin, J., & Ardino, V. (2003). Representing the mental world in children's social behavior: Playing hide-and-seek and keeping a secret. *Social Development, 12,* 496–512.

Peskin, J., & Astington, J. W. (2004). The effects of adding metacognitive language to story texts. *Cognitive Development, 19,* 253–273.

Peterson, C., & Slaughter, V. (2003). Opening windows into the mind: Mothers' preferences for mental state explanations and children's theory of mind. *Cognitive Development, 18,* 399–429.

Peterson, C. C. (2000). Kindred spirits: Influences of siblings' perspectives on theory of mind. *Cognitive Development, 15,* 435–455.

Peterson, C. C., & Siegal, M. (2002). Mindreading and moral awareness in popular and rejected preschoolers. *British Journal of Developmental Psychology, 20,* 205–224.

Pexman, P. M., & Glenwright, M. (2007). How do typically developing children grasp the meaning of verbal irony? *Journal of Neurolinguistics, 20,* 178–196.

Piaget, J. (1963). *The origins of intelligence in children.* New York: Norton. (Original work published 1936)

Piaget, J. (1965). *The moral judgment of the child.* New York: The Free Press. (Original work published 1932)

Piaget, J., & Inhelder, B. (1967). *The child's conception of space.* New York: Norton. (Original work published 1948)

Pika, S., & Mitani, J. (2006). Referential gestural communication in wild chimpanzees (*Pan troglodytes*). *Current Biology, 16,* R191–R192.

Pillow, B. H. (1991). Children's understanding of biased social cognition. *Developmental Psychology, 27,* 539–551.

Pillow, B., & Mash, C. (1999). Young children's understanding of interpretation, expectation and direct perception as sources of false belief. *British Journal of Developmental Psychology, 17,* 263–276.

Porter, M., Coltheart, M., & Langdon, R. (2008). Theory of mind in Williams syndrome assessed using a nonverbal task. *Journal of Autism and Developmental Disorders, 38,* 806–814.

Povinelli, D. J., & Vonk, J. (2003). Chimpanzee minds: Suspiciously human? *Trends in Cognitive Sciences, 7,* 157–160.

Premack, D., & Woodruff, G. (1978). Does the chimpanzee have a theory of mind? *Behavioral and Brain Sciences, 4,* 515–526.

Racine, T. P., & Carpendale, J. I. M. (2007a). Shared practices, understanding, language and joint attention. *British Journal of Developmental Psychology, 25,* 45–54.

Racine, T. P., & Carpendale, J. I. M. (2007b). The role of shared practice in joint attention. *British Journal of Developmental Psychology, 25,* 3–25.

Racine, T. P., & Carpendale, J. I. M. (2008). The embodiment of mental states. In W. F. Overton, U. Müller, & J. Newman (Eds.), *Developmental perspectives on embodiment and consciousness* (pp. 159–190). Mahwah, NJ: Erlbaum.

Raikes, H. A., & Thompson, R. A. (2006). Family emotional climate, attachment security and young children's emotion knowledge in a high risk sample. *British Journal of Developmental Psychology, 24,* 89–104.

Rajendran, G., & Mitchell, P. (2007). Cognitive theories of autism. *Developmental Review, 27,* 224–260.

Raver, C. C., & Leadbeater, B. J. (1993). The problem of the other in research on theory of mind and social development. *Human Development, 36,* 350–362.

Recchia, H., Howe, N., Ross, H., & Alexander, S. (in press). Children's understanding and production of verbal irony in family conversations. *British Journal of Developmental Psychology*.

Reddy, V. (2003). On being the object of attention: Implications for self–other consciousness. *Trends in Cognitive Sciences, 7,* 397–401.

Reddy, V. (2008). *How infants know minds.* Cambridge, MA: Harvard University Press.

Repacholi, B. M., Slaughter, V., Pritchard, M., & Gibbs, V. (2003). Theory of mind, Machiavellianism, and social functioning in childhood. In B. Repocholi & V. Slaughter (Eds.), *Individual differences in theory of mind: Implications for typical and atypical development* (pp. 67–97). New York: Psychology Press.

Robinson, E. J., & Robinson, W. P. (1983). Children's uncertainty about the interpretation of ambiguous messages. *Journal of Experimental Child Psychology, 36,* 81–96.

Ross, H. S., Recchia, H. E., & Carpendale, J. I. M. (2005). Making sense of divergent interpretations of conflict and developing an interpretive understanding of mind. *Journal of Cognition and Development, 6,* 571–592.

Ruffman, T., Garnham, W., Import C., & Connolly, D. (2001). Does eye gaze indicate implicit knowledge of false belief? Charting transitions in knowledge. *Journal of Experimental Child Psychology, 80,* 201–224.

Ruffman, T., Henry, J. D., Livingstone, V., & Phillips, L. H. (2008). A meta-analytic review of emotion recognition and aging: Implications for neuropsychological models of aging. *Neuroscience and Biobehavioral Reviews, 32,* 863–881.

Ruffman, T., & Keenan, T. R. (1996). The belief-based emotion of surprise: The case for a lag in understanding relative to false belief. *Developmental Psychology, 32,* 40–49.

Ruffman, T., & Perner, R. (2005). Do infants really understand false belief? *Trends in Cognitive Sciences, 9,* 462–463.

Ruffman, T., Perner, J., Naito, M., Parkin, L., & Clements, W. A. (1998). Older (but not younger) siblings facilitate false belief understanding. *Developmental Psychology, 34,* 161–174.

Ruffman, T., Perner, J., & Parkin, L. (1999). How parenting style affects false belief understanding. *Social Development, 8,* 395–411.

Ruffman, T., Slade, L., & Crowe, E. (2002). The relation between children's and mothers' mental state language and theory-of-mind understanding. *Child Development, 73,* 734–751.

Ruffman, T., Slade, L., Devitt, K., & Crowe, E. (2006). What mothers say and what they do: The relation between parenting, theory of mind, language and conflict/cooperation. *British Journal of Developmental Psychology, 24,* 105–124.

Ruffman, T., Slade, L., Rowlandson, K., Rumsey, C., & Garnham, A. (2003). How language relates to belief, desire, and emotion understanding. *Cognitive Development, 18,* 139–158.

Russell, J. (1992). The theory theory: So good they named it twice? *Cognitive Development, 7,* 485–519.

Russell, J. (1996). *Agency: Its role in mental development.* Hove, United Kingdom: Erlbaum (UK) Taylor & Francis.

Russell J. (Ed.). (1997). *Autism as an executive disorder.* Oxford: Oxford University Press.

Russell, J., Mauthner, N., Sharpe, S., & Tidswell, T. (1991). The windows task as a measure of strategic deception in preschoolers and autistic subjects. *British Journal of Developmental Psychology, 9,* 331–349.

Rutter, M. L., Kreppner, J. M., O'Connor, T. B., & the English and Romanian Adoptees study team. (2001). Specificity and heterogeneity in children's responses to profound institutional privation. *British Journal of Psychiatry, 179,* 97–103.

Ryle, G. (1949). *The concept of mind.* Middlesex, United Kingdom: Penguin Books.

Sabbagh, M. A., & Seamans, E. L. (2008). Intergenerational transmission of theory-of-mind. *Developmental Science, 11,* 354–360.

Sabbagh, M., Xu, F., Carlson, S. M., Moses, L. J., & Lee, K. (2006). The development of executive functioning and theory of mind: A comparison of Chinese and U.S. preschoolers. *Psychological Science, 17,* 74–81.

Saltzman, J., Strauss, E., Hunter, M., & Achibald, S. (2000). Theory of mind and executive functions in normal human aging and Parkinson's disease. *Journal of the International Neuropsychological Society, 6,* 781–788.

Samson, D., Apperly, I. A., Kathirgamanathan, U., & Humphreys, G. W. (2005). Seeing it my way: A case of selective deficit in inhibiting self-perspective. *Brain, 128,* 1102–1111.

Saxe, R. (2006). Why and how to study Theory of Mind with fMRI. *Brain Research, 1079,* 57–65.

Saxe, R., & Wexler, A. (2005). Making sense of another mind: The role of the right temporo-parietal junction. *Neuropsychologia, 43,* 1391–1399.

Scaife, M., & Bruner, J. (1975) Capacity for joint visual attention in infant. *Nature, 253,* 256–266.

Schick, B., de Villiers, P., de Villiers, J., & Hoffmeister, R. (2007). Language and theory of mind: A study of deaf children. *Child Development, 78,* 376–396.

Selman, R. (1980). *The growth of interpersonal understanding.* New York: Academic Press.

Shah, A., & Frith, U. (1983). An islet of ability in autistic children: A research note. *Journal of Child Psychology and Psychiatry, 24,* 613–620.

Shanker, S. G. (2004). Autism and the dynamic developmental model of emotions. *Philosophy, Psychiatry & Psychology, 11,* 219–233.

Shantz, C. V. (1983). Social cognition. In J. H. Flavell & E. M. Markman (Eds.), *Handbook of child psychology: Cognitive development,* (pp. 495–555). New York: John Wiley & Sons.

Sharrock, W., & Coulter, J. (2004). ToM: A critical commentary. *Theory & Psychology, 14,* 579–600.

Shatz, M. (1975). The development of social cognition. In E. Hetherington (Ed.), *Review of child development research* (Vol. 5, pp. 257–323). Chicago: University of Chicago Press.

Shatz, M., Wellman, H. M., & Silber, S. (1983). The acquisition of mental verbs: A systematic investigation of the first reference to mental state. *Cognition, 14,* 301–321.

Sigman, M., Mundy, P., Sherman, T., & Ungerer, J. (1986). Social interactions of autistic, mentally retarded and normal children and their caregivers. *Journal of Child Psychology & Psychiatry, 27,* 647–655.

Sirois, S., & Jackson, I. (2007). Social cognition in infancy: A critical review of research on higher order abilities. *European Journal of Developmental Psychology, 4,* 46–64.

Slade, L., & Ruffman, T. (2005). How language does (and does not) relate to theory-of-mind: A longitudinal study of syntax, semantics, working memory and false belief. *British Journal of Developmental Psychology, 23,* 117–141.

Slaughter, V., Dennis, M. J., & Pritchard, M. (2002). Theory of mind and peer acceptance in preschool children. *British Journal of Developmental Psychology, 20,* 545–564.

Slaughter, V., & McConnell, D. (2003). Emergence of joint attention: Relationships between gaze following, social referencing, imitation, and naming in infancy. *Journal of Genetic Psychology, 164,* 54–71.

Slaughter, V., Peterson, C. C., & Mackintosh, E. (2007). Mind what mother says: Narrative input and theory of mind in typical children and those on the autism spectrum. *Child Development, 78,* 839–858.

Sodian, B. (1990). Understanding verbal communication: Children's ability to deliberately manipulate ambiguity in referential messages. *Cognitive Development, 5,* 209–222.

Sodian, B., & Thoermer, C. (2008). Precursors to a theory of mind in infancy: Perspectives for research on autism. *The Quarterly Journal of Experimental Psychology, 61(1),* 27–39.

Sodian, B., & Wimmer, H. (1987). Children's understanding of inference as a source of knowledge. *Child Development, 58,* 424–433.

Soffer, G. (1999). The other as alter ego: A genetic approach. *Husserl Studies, 15,* 151–166.

Sokol, B. W., Müller, U., Carpendale, J. I. M., Young, A. R., & Iarocci, G. (Eds.). (2010). *Self- and social-regulation: Social interaction and the development of social understanding and executive functions.* New York: Oxford University Press.

Sommer, M., Döhnel, K., Sodian, B., Meinhardt, J., Thoermer, C., & Hajak G. (2007). Neural correlates of true and false belief reasoning. *Neuroimage, 35,* 1378–1384.

Stack, J., & Lewis, C. (2008). Steering towards a developmental account of infant social understanding. *Human Development, 51,* 229–234.

Stone, T., & Davies, M, (1996). *Theories of theories of mind: The mental simulation debate.* Cambridge: Cambridge University Press.

Striano, T., & Reid, V. M. (2006). Social cognition in the first year. *Trends in Cognitive Science, 10,* 471–476.

Striano, T., Vaish, A., & Benigno, J. P. (2006). The meaning of infants' looks: Information seeking and comfort seeking? *British Journal of Developmental Psychology, 24,* 615–630.

Subbotsky, E. V. (1976). *Psychology of partnership relations in preschoolers* [in Russian]. Moscow: Moscow University Press.

Sullivan, K., Zaitchik, D., & Tager-Flusberg, H. (1994). Preschoolers can attribute second-order beliefs. *Developmental Psychology, 30,* 395–402.

Sullivan, S., & Ruffman, T. (2004). Social understanding: How does it fare with advancing years? *British Journal of Developmental Psychology, 95,* 1–18.

Surian, L., Caldi, S., & Sperber, D. (2007). Attribution of beliefs by 13-month-old infants. *Psychological Science, 18,* 580–586.

Susswein, N. (2007). Maternal engagement, mental state terms, and children's understanding of the mind. Master's thesis, Simon Fraser University, Burnaby, British Columbia, Canada.

Sutton, J., Smith, P. K., & Swettenham, J. (1999a). Bullying and "theory of mind": A critique of the "social skills deficit" view of anti-social behaviour. *Social Development, 8,* 117–127.

Sutton, J., Smith, P. K., & Swettenham, J. (1999b). Social cognition and bullying: Social inadequacy or skilled manipulation? *British Journal of Developmental Psychology, 17,* 435–450.

Symons, D. K., & Clark, S. E. (2000). A longitudinal study of mother-child relationships and theory of mind during the preschool period. *Social Development, 9,* 3–23.

Tager-Flusberg, H. (2003). Exploring the relationship between theory of mind and social communicative functioning in children with autism. In B. Repacholi & V. Slaughter (Eds.), *Individual differences in theory of mind* (pp. 197–212). Hove, United Kingdom: Psychology Press.

Talwar, V., & Lee, K. (2002). Emergence of white-lie telling in children between 3 and 7 years of age. *Merrill-Palmer Quarterly, 48,* 160–180.

Talwar, V., Murphy, S. M., & Lee, K. (2007). White lie-telling in children for politeness purposes. *International Journal of Behavioral Development, 31,* 1–11.

Tangney, J. P., & Fischer, K. W. (Eds.). (1995). *Self-conscious emotions.* New York: Guilford Press.

Tardif, T., So, C. W.-C., & Kaciroti, N. (2007). Language and false belief: Evidence for general, not specific, effects in Cantonese-speaking preschoolers. *Developmental Psychology, 43,* 318–340.

Tardiff, T., & Wellman, H. M. (2000). Acquisition of mental state language in Mandarin- and Cantonese-speaking children. *Developmental Psychology, 36,* 25–43.

Tarullo, A. R., Bruce, J., & Gunnar, M. R. (2007). False belief and emotion understanding in post-institutionalized children. *Social Development, 16,* 57–78.

Taumoepeau, M., & Ruffman, T. (2006). Mother and infant talk about mental states relates to desire language and emotion understanding. *Child Development, 77,* 465–481.

Taumoepeau, M., & Ruffman, T. (2008). Stepping stones to others' minds: Maternal talk relates to child mental state language and emotion understanding at 15, 24, and 33 months. *Child Development, 79,* 284–302.

Tissaw, M. A. (2007). Making sense of neonatal imitation. *Theory & Psychology, 17,* 217–242.

Tomasello, M. (1995). Joint attention as social cognition. In C. Moore & P. J. Dunham (Eds.), *Joint attention: Its origins and role in development* (pp. 103–130). Hillsdale, NJ: Erlbaum.

Tomasello, M. (1999). *The cultural origins of human cognition.* Cambridge, MA: Harvard University Press.

Tomasello, M. (2003). *Constructing a language: A usage-based theory of language acquisition.* Cambridge, MA: Harvard University Press.

Tomasello, M. (2008). *Origins of human communication.* Cambridge, MA: The MIT Press.

Tomasello, M., Call, J., & Hare, B. (2003). Chimpanzees understand psychological states: The question is which ones and to what extent. *Trends in Cognitive Science, 7,* 153–156.

Tomasello, M., Carpenter, M., & Liszkowski, U. (2007). A new look at infant pointing. *Child Development, 78,* 705–722.

Tomasello, M., & Haberl, K. (2003). Understanding attention: 12- and 18-month-olds know what is new for other persons. *Developmental Psychology, 39,* 906–912.

Toner, I. J., Moore, L. P., & Emmons, B. A. (1980). Effect of being labelled on subsequent self control in children. *Child Development, 51,* 618–621.

Toner, I. J., & Smith, R. A. (1977). Age and overt verbalisations in delay maintenance behaviour in children. *Journal of Experimental Child Psychology, 12,* 334–348.

Trevarthen, C., & Aitken, K. J. (2001). Infant intersubjectivity: Research, theory, and clinical applications. *Journal of Child Psychology and Psychiatry, 42,* 3–48.

Turnbull, W. (2003). *Language in action: Psychological models of conversation.* Hove, United Kingdom: Psychology Press.

Turnbull, W., & Carpendale, J. I. M. (1999). A social pragmatic model of talk: Implications for research on the development of children's social understanding. *Human Development, 42,* 328–355.

Turnbull, W., Carpendale, J. I. M., & Racine, R. P. (2008). Relations between mother-child talk and 3- to 5-year-old children's understanding of belief: Beyond mental state terms to talk about the mind. *Merrill-Palmer Quarterly, 54,* 367–385.

Turnbull, W., Carpendale, J. I. M., & Racine, T. (2009). Talk and children's understanding of the mind. *Journal of Consciousness Studies, 16,* 140–166.

Varouxaki, A., Freeman, N. H., Peters, D., & Lewis, C. (1999). Inference neglect and inference denial. *British Journal of Developmental Psychology, 17,* 483–499.

Vasek, M. E. (1986). Lying as a skill: The development of deception in children. In R. W. Mitchell & N. S. Thompson (Eds.), *Deception:*

Perspectives on human and nonhuman deceit (pp. 271–292). Albany, NY: State University of New York Press

Vaughan Van Hecke, A., Mundy, P. C., Acra, C. F., Block, J. J., Delagado, C. E. F., Parlade, M. V., et al. (2007). Infant joint attention, temperament, and social competence in preschool children. *Child Development, 78,* 53–69.

Vinden, P. G. (1996). Junin Quechua children's understanding of mind. *Child Development, 67,* 1701–1716.

Vinden, P. G. (1999). Children's understanding of mind and emotion: A multi-cultural study. *Cognition and Emotion, 13,* 19–48.

Vinden, P. G. (2001). Parenting attitudes and children's understanding of mind: A comparison of Korean American and Anglo-American families. *Cognitive Development, 16,* 793–809.

Vygotsky, L. S. (1978). *Mind in society: The development of higher psychological processes.* Cambridge, MA: Harvard University Press.

Walden, T., & Ogan, T. (1988). The development of social referencing. *Child Development, 59,* 1230–1240.

Wan, H., Aggleton, M. W., & Brown, J. (1999). Different contributions of the hippocampus and perirhinal cortex to recognition memory. *Neuroscience, 19,* 1142.

Wellman, H. M. (1990). *The child's theory of mind.* Cambridge, MA: MIT Press.

Wellman, H. M., & Banerjee, M. (1991). Mind and emotions: Children's understanding of the emotional consequences of beliefs and desires. *British Journal of Developmental Psychology, 9,* 191–214.

Wellman, H. M., Cross, D., & Watson, J. (2001) Meta-analysis of theory of mind development: The truth about false belief. *Child Development, 72,* 655–684.

Wellman, H. M., & Liu, D. (2004). Scaling of theory of mind tasks. *Child Development, 75,* 523–541.

Wellman, H. M., & Miller, J. G. (2008). Including deontic reasoning as fundamental to theory of mind. *Human Development, 51,* 105–135.

Welsh, T. (2006). Do neonates display innate self-awareness? Why neonatal imitation fails to provide sufficient grounds for innate self- and other-awareness. *Philosophical Psychology, 19,* 221–238.

Werner, H. (1957). The concept of development from a comparative and organismic point of view. In D. B. Harris (Ed.), *The concept*

of development: An issue in the study of human behavior (pp. 125–148). Minneapolis, MN: University of Minnesota Press.

Wimmer, H., & Perner, J. (1983). Beliefs about beliefs: Representation and constraining function of wrong beliefs in young children's understanding of deception. *Cognition, 13,* 103–128.

Winner, E., & Leekam, S. (1991). Distinguishing irony from deception: Understanding the speaker's second-order intention. *British Journal of Developmental Psychology, 9,* 257–270.

Winnicott, D. W. (1965). *The maturational processes and the facilitating environment.* New York: International Universities Press.

Winnicott, D. W. (2005). *Playing and reality.* New York: Routledge. (Original work published 1971)

Wittgenstein, L. (1968). *Philosophical investigations.* Oxford: Blackwell.

Woolfe, T., Want, S. C., & Siegal, M. (2002). Signposts to development: Theory of mind in deaf children. *Child Development, 73,* 768–778.

Wundt, W. (1973). *The language of gestures.* The Hague: Mouton.

Yagmurlu, B., Berument, S. K., & Celimli, S. (2005). The role of institution and home contexts in theory of mind development. *Applied Developmental Psychology, 26,* 521–537.

Yasui, M., & Lewis, C. (2005, April 7) "'Oh great!' can mean nasty": *A message from three-year-olds understanding of sarcasm.* Paper presented at the biennial meeting of the Society for Research in Child Development, Atlanta, GA.

Yirmiya, N., Erel, O., Shaked, M., & Solomonica-Levi, D. (1998). Meta-analyses comparing theory of mind abilities of individuals with autism, individuals with mental retardation, and normally developing individuals. *Psychological Bulletin, 124,* 283–307.

Zaitchik, D. (1991). Is only seeing really believing?: Sources of the true belief in the false belief task. *Cognitive Development, 6,* 91–103.

Zelazo, P. D., & Müller, U. (2002). Executive function in typical and atypical development. In U. Goswami (Ed.), *Handbook of childhood cognitive development* (pp. 445–469). Oxford: Blackwell.

Zelazo, P. D., Müller, U., Frye, D., & Marcovitch, S. (2003). The development of executive function in early childhood. *Monographs of the Society for Research in Child Development, 68*(Serial No. 274).

CHAPTER 18

The Emergence of Consciousness and Its Role in Human Development

MICHAEL LEWIS

INTRODUCTION

This chapter explores several issues, all of which have to do with consciousness. To begin, I discuss intentions and intentionality to argue that much of what is currently ascribed to the infant in regard to its ability rests on the problem of confusing competence with comprehension (Dennett, 2009). As Putnam (1963) has warned us, just because an ant might be able to trace a face in the sand does not necessarily imply that the ant knows anything about faces. Indeed, just because a 3-month-old infant can perceptually discriminate between two conditions does not necessarily mean that the infant knows about them if we mean that they know as adults know. I will come back to this distinction between the development of "I know" versus "I know I know."

Having discussed intentions and their development, I will turn next to the idea of the role of the knower in knowing, and again argue for the centrality of a self and consciousness in the act of knowing. Indeed, much of what we know about the social world involves our relationship to it. Once I have established the epistemological necessity of a knower, a self, I turn to the question of what is a self and explore how historically the idea of a self has been conceived. Here the role of the social world as a mirror for the infant is contrasted with the idea that the self emerges as a function of our maturing brains. Again taking up the idea of a self, I will explore the issue of knowing that I know. "I know I know" is distinctly different from "I know" and is the gateway to understanding the particular human ability found in the recursive statement, "I know, you know, I know." Although I have done considerable work on the measurement of a knower, a self-referencing organism, I spend only a little time on its measurement, saving the time for a lengthy discussion on the central role of consciousness in the development of the human child. Here I wish to argue that the child is the central organizing principle, and with the development of a self system and consciousness, the early organism competencies give way to comprehension in which the self expresses its social, emotional, and cognitive skills, converting early and possibly preadapted capacities into the rich fabric of the human condition.

INTENTION IS NOT INTENTIONALITY

Two Worldviews

Two views of human nature have predominated in our theories development. In the first, the human psyche is acted on by its surrounding environment—both its biological and its external physical and social environments. In the second view, the human organism acts on and in a bidirectional fashion interacts with the biological, physical, and social environments. The reactive view has generated a dichotomy of two major theoretical paradigms: biological determinism and social determinism. The active view, in contrast, has generated what has recently come to be known as the *relational developmental systems perspective* (Lerner, 2006; Lerner & Overton, 2008; Overton, 2006). The place of intention and the self within these two worldviews differs greatly. Let us consider the views in their extreme forms to show how their respective theories might treat the issue of intention.

In both the biological-motivational and social-determinism paradigms, the causes of behavior or action are forces that act on the organism, causing it to behave. These may be internal biological features of the species, including species-specific features. In all cases, within this worldview, the organism is acted on and the causes of its action (including its development) are external to it. Thus, for example, the major determinant of sex-role behavior is thought to be biological, that is, determined by sex, and in this case, by the effects of hormones (Money & Ehrhardt, 1972) or lateralization (Buffery & Gray, 1972). Alternatively, sex-role behavior can be determined externally by the shaping of effect of the social environment, either the differential rewards of conspecifics (Fagot, 1973) or the differential construction of the social world. Examples of the former are already well-known (e.g., parental praising or punishing of specific sex-role–appropriate actions, such as playing with particular toys; see Goldberg & Lewis, 1969; Rheingold & Cook, 1975). Examples of determinism by the social world include giving the child a male or female name. These do not imply reinforcement control but structural control. In such external control paradigms, we need not infer a self or consciousness and with it a will, intention, or plan.

In contrast with this passive or reactive view is the relational developmental systems perspective based on the worldview that the organism is inherently active, acting on and being acted on the biological, physical, and social environment in a bidirectional fashion (Lewis & Rosenblum, 1974). Within this perspective the organism has a self and consciousness and as such has desires and plans. These desires and goals are constructed, as are most of the actions enabling the organism to behave adaptively. This view does not necessitate discarding either biological imperatives or social control as potential determinants of behavior, because from this relational perspective, humans are both biological and social creatures, and both must impact on behavior. I prefer to think of these biological and social features as nothing more than the raw materials or resources for the construction of cognitive structures subsumed under a self and consciousness, which include goals and desires, plans, and action patterns (see Fodor, 1981, for a similar view). Taking the example of sex-role behavior, I have argued that hormones and social control become material for the construction of self-cognitive structures. These structures might take the form "I am male or female," "Males or females behave this way or that way," or "To receive the praise of others (a desired goal) I should act either this way or that." Cognitions of this sort, and their accompanying goals and desires, together with cognitions concerning information about the world, enable the child to *intend,* that is, to will to act in a particular fashion.

These two worldviews are present in all psychological inquiry. The reactive organism mechanistic model receives support in the case of the biological study of action (e.g., T cells tracing foreign proteins that have entered the body). Relational developmental systems views are supported by theories of the mind (Neisser, 1967). It should not go unnoticed that with the growth of cognitive science, the idea of constructing mental representations, in particular of the self (that do not correspond in any one-to-one fashion with the "real" world) and with it, plans and intentions, had become more acceptable to psychology proper by the 1980s (see Gardner's [1985] review).

The Problem of Intention

The problem of intention and its development is central to the problem of consciousness and self-development. In so stating the problem, I beg the question of whether there is such a thing as intention. Intuitively, most of us are comfortable in believing that intention exists. There is no difficulty for any of us in using terms such as "I intend to go to the market tomorrow," or in understanding that an intentional act of violence is a more serious transgression than an unintentional one. Nor do we have difficulty in explaining our actions as intentional: "I went to the refrigerator because I intended to get the butter."

Even so, accepting the notion of intentionality raises difficulties. Some forms of action are more difficult to explain as intentional, such as unaware action, "I did not realize I was angry and did not intend to push you away." Freud suggested that action we are unaware of is unconsciously intentional. Other actions appear so rote and mechanical, we hardly believe that they were planned or were intentional, for example, walking actions, or even talking or listening. However, if we recognize that intentions can be "intentions in action" (Searle, 1984, p. 65), these actions are intentional. I argue that adult human acts are intentional, or if not so, then at least we *believe* that the acts of ourselves and others are intentional (Dennett, 1987).

Make no mistake: The claim that adult human acts are intentional is made without observational evidence. I claim only that *we* have such an idea; there might be cultures and times that would deny such a concept. The same, however, might be said for any mental structure or operation. Here I am willing to consider Rorty's (1989) analysis of truth. If we follow his analysis correctly, we cannot make the claim that intentionality exists out there, only that our understanding of it exists and is "real." There is no Truth out there to which some language (read the *worldview* or *model*) is better than another.

> Truth cannot be out there—cannot exist independently of the human mind—because sentences cannot so exist, or be out there, but descriptions of the world are not, only descriptions of the world can be true or false. The world on its own unaided by the describing activities of human beings—cannot. (Rorty, 1989, p. 5)

Adopting this conceptualization permits us to choose between alternative descriptions of reality and allows us to test our choice for truthfulness vis-à-vis another description. In this context, our choice is between a model that does not require intention and consciousness, and one that

does. Because I wish to focus on the topic of ontogenetic change in intentional behavior and ultimately to discuss the development of a self and consciousness, I chose the model asserting that it exists. Our problem then becomes how to study the development of this concept. I chose to focus on the topic of development, for it seems to capture the problems inherent in any discussion of intention; for example, the question of intention in animals (Griffin, 1984), in machines (Newell, 1982), and in different cultures (D'Andrade, 1981). The ontogenesis of humans allows us to consider the issue of intention from a broad perspective in *the same organism at different points in its life.* Because we have some idea of the similarities and difference among infants, children, and adults, we may have more information to aid us in understanding intention. The problem of generalizing from animals or machines to humans or from one culture to another is avoided. For these reasons, the study of the development of intention is of some general interest.

One way to pursue this topic is to ask how children come to understand the concept of intention. We might, for example, ask at what age children come to understand the differences between accidental or intentional behavior (e.g., see Dunn, 1988). The difficulty here is that the terms *accidental* versus *intentional* tell us only about the child's knowledge of intention. Another difficulty is that studies of this type require that children be able to speak or at least understand the language. Because the language has terms such as *intention* and *accidental,* we may be inquiring into the child's socialization rather than into its logical structures. There is clear evidence that children show behaviors, before language, that would lead the observer to believe they have an understanding of intention and of causality, a closely related problem (e.g., see Leslie & Keeble, 1987; Michotte, 1963).

Development of Intentionality

It was Piaget (1936/1952) who offered us a developmental blueprint of the development of causality and intention in the opening years of life. In summary, in the earliest stages of development, children's actions are simply preadapted action patterns. After a time, these action patterns produce (still without intention) outcomes. It is these outcomes that, in turn, produce the action patterns. Thus, *A* accidentally causes *B* (an effect), and *B,* in turn, produces *A.* Piaget characterizes this chain of events as a *simple circular action* pattern. Notice that the control of the action is associated with the simplest of mental representations.

The representation is the association that *A* and *B* are mutually connected. Nevertheless, it is *B,* an environmental event (an effect in the world) that causes *A* (the action) to occur. I think it is safe to conclude that, for Piaget, the child starts the developmental process without intentions.

However, by the end of the first year of life, children "set out to obtain a certain result" (Piaget & Inhelder, 1969, p. 10). By now, the mean, formerly *A* (both action and representation), has become independent of outcome, *B.* The mental representation associating *A* and *B,* which appeared at the beginning of life, has now been separated. In a sense, Piaget describes the child as changing from reactive to active and from rote associative reproduction to the pursuit of a goal. Here, then, he starts to speak of intention. However, it is still a limited intentionality; it is only the separation of means and end in the utilization of an *available* means for a new end. It is not until the end of the fifth stage (somewhere around 15 months) that intentionality is assumed. Interestingly, this age will reappear when I talk about the onset of consciousness. For Piaget, intentionality makes possible the creation of goals and plans in the absence of external events and in the establishment of new schemata—multiple means associated with multiple ends.

Piaget's model denies the existence of intentionality at the beginning of life but allows for its development over the first 2 years. The difficulty with such a model of development is in the question of how intention is created. If we accept, for example, a nativist's biological determinism perspective, we can dismiss intention as an unnecessary mentalistic construct having little utility at any point in development. The problem remains of how to go from the absence of the mental state—intention—to its presence. A mechanistic, reactive organism stance might ask, "If in the beginning of development you do not claim intention, even though one might describe the behavior that way, then why do you claim later for similar behaviors?" In other words, if we do not need it in one case, what allows us to claim it for another? As I argue later, consciousness is an aspect of the emerging self that has intentions because it can reflect on itself.

Piaget's model—a relational developmental systems perspective—requires that we address this question: "Where does intention come from?" How can an infant discover intentions if he does not already possess them? Like other ideas, intention needs to be discovered. However, the problem of discovering something that one does know becomes an issue. This problem of how to know of something one does not know is too complex to deal with here. Fodor (1975), in his critique of Piaget's theory of concept acquisition, raises the same problem of how children can learn a new concept unless they already have the ability to hypothesize the concept. If they already have this ability, then they already possess the concept. This is a problem for Piaget, because the idea of the intention is part of the logicomathematical structure existing in the child's head. As such, it does no good to argue that the child does not create it, but rather borrows it from the language of the adults around him. The utilization of the development of a mental representation of the self may provide some help in addressing this problem.

RELATION OF COGNITION AND EMOTION

This idea led readily to our consideration of the connection between cognition, emotion, and action. Here we need to keep in mind that the role of emotions is in its action capacity. That is, emotions are action patterns, adaptive responses linked to cognitions and these linked to environmental pressures. It is not unlike J.J. Gibson's (1979) concept of affordance.

To explore the relation between thought and action, I turn to a discussion of the association between cognition (representations) and emotion (action and motives). The association is often discussed as one leading to the other, either cognition leading to emotion or emotion leading to cognition. Thus, in either case we have assumed a connection between them, a position not unlike that held by those who would see in representations an action potential, that is, a desire for or a desire to do something (e.g., Searle, 1984).

Cognition Before Emotion?

From the point of view of cognition leading to emotion, appraisal theories regard emotion as the product of information processing. Arnold's (1960, 1970) theory of emotion had as its central construct the cognitive act of appraisal, whereas I have held to the view that it is chiefly the self-conscious emotions that are dependent on appraisal. It is the appraisal itself that leads to the emotion (Lewis, 1992b). As a part of general appraisal theories, discrepancy theory argues for an even more direct connection between cognition and emotion (Hebb, 1946, 1949). Berlyne (1960), for example, suggested that unfamiliar events evoke fear, a view taken by others (Kagan, 1974;

Lewis & Goldberg, 1969). Siminov (1970) defined emotion in terms of information processing. In his model, emotion is the consequence of the organism's need for information with respect to reaching a goal, multiplied by the difference between "necessary" and "available" information. Notice that here emotion is defined at the cognitive-process level rather than at the goal level. If, on the other hand, we defined emotion as the goal or the desire to achieve the goal, we would consider emotion as a precursor to cognition. This point is important, because if emotion is to be defined at this point, then emotions are not only caused by cognitions, but, in turn, produce cognitions, the fundamental position taken by the relational developmental systems perspective.

Emotion Before Cognition?

We can approach this problem from another perspective. Emotions have been viewed as preceding cognitions from three perspectives: as motive, markers, and instigator.

Emotions as Motive

Since Darwin's (1872) findings, the notion of emotions as sources of action has been useful as a theory of motivation. Theories that consider emotions as motives can be divided into two classes: (1) those viewing emotion as a consequence of thought, and thereby reinforcing thought; and (2) those viewing emotion as causing thought based on evolutionary history of the species. The central issue of the hedonic tradition is the belief that people think in such ways as to reproduce pleasure and to avoid pain. The emotional consequence of a thought is regarded as the primary cause of that action.

This view of emotions as motivating action through the emotional consequences of that action appears reasonable. For example, students may study for examinations because it feels good to pass and it feels bad to fail; children engage in symbolic play to experience the pleasures in solving a problem. It should be noted that this view of emotion considers thought to be motivated by the *possibility* of its emotional consequence. Even though the emotional experience occurs after the thought, it is believed that the reinforcement value of this experience serves to produce the same set of behaviors to reexperience the particular emotion. So although emotion is initially a consequence of thought, the expectation or memory of the emotional state may precede and influence subsequent thought; again, this is a relational developmental systems perspective.

If one thinks of emotion in this way, then emotions, especially feeling good and feeling bad, act as rewards to particular patterns of thought. In many cases, these hedonic events seem to be unlearned. For example, it is unlikely that the good feeling produced by eating when hungry is learned. Rather, eating feels good because of an innate biological connection between food in the digestive tract and relief from hunger. On the other hand, some emotional reinforcers seem, at least at first glance, to be learned. There is no intrinsic reason that it should feel good to get an "A" on a French examination.

Emotion may not only be the rewarding outcome of thought, but, in a bidirectional fashion, also its antecedent. This view of emotion is usually associated with biological explanations of emotion. Darwin (1872/1969) argued that the process of evolution applies not only to anatomical structures but to intellectual and expressive behaviors as well. Emotions are by their nature action patterns that the organism needs for survival. For example, the sight of a predator will elicit fear in the organism, the action pattern of which is not only a fear face but the motor act of fleeing. Or a baby's cry will elicit nurturance in the mother with a concomitant behavioral repertoire of nursing, holding, or retrieving the infant. Viewed in this way, emotion is both a state of the organism and an action that is basic to life and survival. In all cases of positive and negative emotions, the emotional *elicitor* produces specific action patterns (including cognitions) as a part of the emotion.

Plutchik (1980) enumerated eight basic functional patterns of behavior that have adaptive significance for all organisms in their struggle for survival. The prototypic patterns include incorporation, rejection, destruction, protection, reproductions, reintegration, orientation, and exploration. These basic adaptive patterns are thought to be the functional bases for all emotions recognized in humans and animals. Eight emotions accompany the functional patterns: acceptance, disgust, anger, fear, joy, sadness, surprise, and expectancy. Although the specific behaviors that accompany these patterns may vary across different species, their survival function is common to all species.

Zajonc (1980) offered a view similar to the evolutionary position. For Zajonc, some of the behaviors associated with an emotional state may have "hardwired" cognitive representations; that is, they may be independent of cognitive systems and, in fact, may precede perceptual and cognitive operations. Zajonc discussed the primacy of emotion with regard to preferences and attitudes, but his argument was essentially that emotion "accompanies all cognitions, that it arises early in the process of registration and retrieval…and it derives from a parallel, separate, and partly independent system in the organism" (p. 154). In short, emotions may be associated with basic adaptive functions and have as their biological consequence a set of dispositions, including actions and thoughts.

Emotions as Markers

Attention has been focused on the roles of "hot" versus "cold" cognitions. The general assumption underlying this belief is that cognitive processes have different levels of efficiency or outcome depending on how these cognitive processes are tagged with specific emotional tones (see Zajonc, 1980; Zelazo, Gao, & Todd, 2007). One might argue that certain cognitive processes marked with emotion might be more efficient than those not marked. For example, the retrieval of past events, both in short-term and long-term memory, is facilitated by specific affective markers (Norman & Rumelhard, 1975). It is reasonable to assume that information may enter memory not only as a function of the content or sequence of the material, but also as a function of the type of emotional tag; clearly, the schema of a man in a white coat is more likely to be remembered if it is associated with high fear than if it is marked with low interest and fear. Markers also may be associated with the emotional content of events as they relate to the emotional state of the organism. The research on state-dependent learning indicates that emotions may have a powerful influence on cognitive processes, including free recall, imaginative fantasies, and social perception. For example, Bower (Marsh, Edelman, & Bower, 2002; Wright & Bower, 1992) found that people recall more events that are affectively congruent with their mood recall. Here, emotions as markers refer not only to the emotional tag attached to the cognitive event but also to the emotional state of the subject as the subject interacts with the cognitive event.

Emotions as Instigators

The third role of emotion in cognition addresses the following question: Do certain feelings necessarily lead people to think in particular ways? One way to approach this issue is to consider patterns as related to specific emotions. Emotions may not only lead in some biological fashion to action patterns, but emotions may produce specific thinking patterns. One aspect of this issue is related to the nature or the content of the thought. For instance, someone may tell you that your cousin was hit by a car, or someone may tell you that your cousin won the lottery. The emotions produced by the information affect subsequent thoughts.

Isen (2007), for example, demonstrated that happy moods produce more associations than unhappy moods.

This discussion suggests that, as argued by the relational developmental systems perspective, it is unreasonable to consider cognition and emotion as unrelated. Within the organism, these processes coexist and are interdependent. That we separate them reflects a Cartesian split perspective (Overton, 2006). In fact, it is difficult to think without action, because for the most part, either intentions have action patterns associated with them or are themselves the goals of thought. Such an analysis again leads us to the connection and interdependence between thought and desire; that is, intentions consist of actions and thoughts, although as we shall see, the level of thought may vary considerably.

Behaviors as Measures of Intention

It might be the case that Piaget's observations, and those of others before him (e.g., Baldwin, 1894/1903), could allow us to come to understand how one can claim intentionality from the observation of behavior. In some way, it may be useful to use Piaget's observations to construct a model of the development of intention from a single stance. Piaget, in thinking about the development of intention, introduces two central features of mental life: (1) means and end, and (2) scheme development. Let us consider each in turn to see whether these mental operations and the behaviors associated with them aid our understanding of the developmental process.

Means and End

The 3-day-old infant is attached to an apparatus that delivers sweet liquid if it sucks at a certain rate. Within a few minutes, the infant is able to alter its behavior to get the liquid. It is clear that, for Piaget, conditioning in a very young child does not represent intentionality. The child at very early ages may be taught to suck on a nipple "to produce" an effect (Lipsitt, 1976); however, the behavioral connection between the sucking response and the outcome are not intended. These he saw as habits, acquired through relational bidirectional interactions with the world. There is no mental separation between the means and end, and therefore no intentionality. Piaget acknowledged this when he spoke of multiple means to the same end (i.e., equifinality) or, alternatively, the same means to multiple ends. Although Piaget inferred the development of mental structures that logically must be associated with such actions, to infer intention requires only that multiple means and ends are available. When they are, we need to infer some mechanism within the organism enabling the choice. In doing so, we assume that there are no simple habits that can account for our observation.

However, we are not helped as much by this observation as we might at first assume. In the case of a repeated similar action, we cannot assume that the same means to an end does not reflect intention. First, no action is ever the same; thus, even a child's kick is different each time (Thelen, Kelso, & Fogel, 1987). Moreover, certain means may be preferred and are repeated not because they are controlled externally, but because they are valued. I may put my left shoe on first each day because I prefer it, not because the perception of shoes compels me to put the left one on first.

For the case of multiple means to an end, there also may be logical problems. For example, it seems possible to construct a system (or instruct a child) to produce any one of several reaction to produce a given result. The training of such a complex habit or rule (or its programming, using the computer metaphor) requires only that a particular response be selected and its effect vis-à-vis the end be evaluated. If a particular means succeeds, alternative means are not needed.

Scheme Development

On this topic, Piaget (1936/1952) suggested that the infant shows us that she is not passive to events around her, but takes an active stance in her development. The child in Stage 5 begins to coordinate different combinations into new and meaningful schemata. So, for example, the child knows how to pull on a rug to bring the rug toward itself. The child sees an object that she wants possess but is out of reach. By pulling the rug, the object comes into reach and is possessed. This is for the child the coordination of previously independent schemes.

> Now, in order that two scheme(s), until then detached, may be coordinated with one another in a single act, the subject must *aim* to attain an end which is not directly within reach and to put to work, with this intention, the schemata hitherto related to other situations. (Piaget, 1936/1952, p. 211)

The child moves from a trial-and-error behavior pattern, in which a solution is eventually found, to an insightful period. In this latter period, possible solutions are presumed to occur as mental representations, which are created and combined, and only later displayed as action.

Here, too, it is difficult to see how such behavior can help us assume intention. Piaget's language uses an intentional stance to show it is intentional. It is not clear—unless we believe that by sensorimotor Stage 4 the child has gained, at least, primitive intention—the actions and combinations themselves satisfy our need. Consider reaching for an object no longer in sight, at about 8 months. We know that before this age, the child's reaching is related to a complex scheme, which combines reaching with seeing. If seeing is blocked, reaching ceases. The development of active memory at this point may allow the child to continue to see the object, but now in memory, thus reaching continues. Alternatively, children might reach for something they see because they want it. They cease to reach when the wanted object is out of sight because they cannot remember it, but with the advent of a maturing memory system, they can remember, and so continue to reach for it. Piaget's argument for intention at a particular point in development, but not before, strikes me as assuming a selective ontogenetic intentional stance, something akin to a limited intentional stance (Dennett, 1987). Something more is needed for the development of intentions. This needs to come from another system than action, emotions, and scheme development. Here the idea of consciousness becomes important and will be considered in due time.

Our studies of infants as young as 2 months speak to this general issue as well. These infants can learn to pull a string and obtain an award, and do so within 3 to 5 minutes (Lewis, Allesandri, & Sullivan, 1990). When their pulling suddenly does not produce the previously obtained reward, infants significantly increase their arm pulling and show an angry face in an attempt to regain the picture. For some, this would seem that they intend to get the picture to turn on by pulling the string. We have suggested that following Darwin (1872/1969), organisms innately respond to a blocked goal by anger and increasing approach responses previously learned to reinstate the goal. This might be called a *first-order intention*, but it is not a mental act.

Attention, Desire, and Consciousness

It seems obvious that our very description of what happens in this experiment assumes an interpretive and, therefore, a particular stance (see Hirsch, 1967, for an analysis of this problem). Given that I assume a particular stance, let me restate it explicitly: All goal-directed systems are intentional; it is their level that develops. By sensorimotor Stage 5, with the emergence of self-reflecting systems, a new level of self-reflecting intentionality is reached.

How these levels of goal-directed systems differ depends on the process underlying the goals. For all goals, intention is determined by the affective states comprising part of the goal. However, some goals contain both affective and knowledge states (or knowledge systems; see Newell, 1982), and some consciousness (see Duval & Wicklund, 1972; Lewis & Michalson, 1983).

The idea of levels of intentionality, when developed, enables us to deal with such diverse questions as "Does a T cell have intention when it moves after a foreign protein?" "Does a leaf have intention when it moves toward the sun?" "Does an 8-week-old intend to learn, or intend to try to get the lost objects back?" "Do adults intend to go to work each day?" In each case, the answer to the question is "yes," and we need to see how it might be the case. Changes in cognitive capacities result in changes in levels of intentions.

This analysis is presented to support the argument that our reasoning regarding the meaning of very young infants' behaviors should not be based on an intentional stand that requires the type of mental act that includes consciousness. Perhaps what is needed is to make certain that we clearly distinguish between levels of intentions and intentionality, with the latter term reserved for self-reflective levels of intentions. Moreover, there is reason to consider the fact that the same actions may be in the service of different processes. Thus, although it might be said that the infant intends to get the reward to occur again, this intention is quite different from that formed by an adult who intends to write about intentions. Some intentions, those at levels of intentionality, imply a self-reflective intender, a self system including consciousness. This leads to a parallel question: What do we mean by a self system? Before discussing this issue, however, I should like to argue that, in any system of epistemology, we need to consider the role of the knower in what can be known.

ROLE OF THE KNOWER IN KNOWING

Contemporary scientific method is designed to generate theory and predict events. These goals are achieved, in part, though the separation of the scientist from the phenomena being investigated. Thus, the experimenter's word and belief are replaced by a method. This distancing of the individual from the phenomena of study through a commonly accepted method of empirical proof, reliability of measures, and logic, represents a major event in the development of the scientific method.

Indeed, on an individual level, intellectual abstraction serves to distance the individual from events or objects. One function of a symbol is to separate the thinker from that which the symbol has come to represent. This process of separation serves the same function for both the individual and the science. It is an attempt to know through the reification of the thing to be known and assumes, in a Platonic sense, that there exists a reality or ideal independent of the knower.

One founder of these ideas was Francis Bacon, who in the early 17th century offered the Western mind one of the first strongly empirical views of a philosophy of science. In *Advancement of Learning*, Bacon (see Durant, 1954) urged more systematic experimentation and documentation: "The [physicians] rely too much on mere haphazard, uncoordinated *individual experience*; let them experiment more widely…and about all, let them construct an easily accessible and intelligible record of experiments and result" (p. 121). In his first book of the *Novum Organum,* Bacon (see Durant, 1954) challenged existing metaphysical views: "Man, as the minister and interpreter of nature, does and understands as much as his observations on the order of nature…permit him, and neither knows nor is capable of more" (p. 129). He argued (see Durant, 1954) that science must rid itself of the structure established by Aristotle and must become as "little children, innocent of ism and abstractions, washed clear of prejudices and preconceptions" (p. 129). In a word, Bacon counseled scientists to separate themselves form that which they wished to study.

Toward this goal, Bacon outlined the famous set of errors. The first is the *idols of the tribe*, which are fallacies considered natural to all human beings. Bacon rejected Protagoras' assertion that "man is the measure of all things" and wished to substitute a logical method free from the distortions of the human mind. This need for the scientist to become objective also implied that passions or emotions (anything hinting of subjectivity) be removed (see Durant, 1954): "In general let every student of nature take this as a rule that whatever his mind seizes and dwells upon with peculiar satisfaction, is to be held in suspicion; and that so much the more care is to be taken, in dealing with such questions, to keep the understanding even and clear" (p. 131).

The second class of errors, *idols of the cave*, is caused by particular characteristics of the individual. They may be caused by prejudices, personality traits, history, or socialization. For Bacon (see Durant, 1954), such errors are a personal cave, "which refracts and discolors the light of nature" (p. 131).

The third type of errors, *idols of the marketplace,* arises between individuals as a result of differences in communication styles, in language usage, and imperfections caused by the commerce of ideas. Finally, there are *idols of theatre,* which are caused by the errors of others. These are the errors of dogma, the errors of "-isms."

From this list of errors, Bacon proceeded to explicate his scientific method of inquiry with its hypothesis generation, empirical methodology, results, and conclusions. Bacon's view of science flourished, first in the founding of the Royal Society in 1660 and then in the work of Newton, who articulated a particular view of the universe and the role of science in comprehending that universe.

This view of science and the role of the scientist was carried into modern time, infusing the entire scientific enterprise. However, Bacon's view, together with the universe as constructed by Newton, was to be radically altered in the 20th century by modern physics. Einstein's revolutionary insight into the nature of relativity, and Planck and Bohr's development of quantum mechanics profoundly altered our understanding of the relation of knower to known, not only in physics but in other scientific domains as well. Before we apply these thoughts in developmental psychology to our own problems, a brief description of Newton's ideas and the emergence of modern physics is necessary.

Around the time of the founding of the Royal Society, Newton was ready to deliver his views, which became the foundation of contemporary science. With gravity as its center and the use of mathematical laws to explain planets, stars, small particles, and the actions of people, Newton constructed a simple but bold synthesis of the physical world and universe. The cornerstone of his entire system was the belief in the absolute nature of time and space. For Newton (see Clark, 1972):

> Absolute time and mathematical time of itself and from its own nature, flows equally, without relations to anything external, and by another name is called duration…

> Space could be absolute space, in its own nature, without relation to anything external which remains always similar and immovable; or relative space which was some moveable dimension or measure of the absolute space. (p. 103)

To the degree that Newton went beyond the merely observable and constructed these theories, he had acted contrary to both Bacon's prescription and his own stated intention of investigating only tangible facts.

Newton's conception of the universe as an absolute and orderly system stood for more than 200 years. Indeed, his view held so strong a sway over the minds of the physicists (see Clark, 1972) that they could say: "In the beginning… God created Newton's laws of motion together with necessary masses and forces. This is all; everything beyond this follows the development of appropriate mathematical methods by means of deduction" (p. 59). In this view, a person could examine the workings of this orderly universe, and extract general principles and laws that could further explain the observed relations. Newton's theories represent the most powerful example of the separation between the role of the knower and the known. Scientific objectivity, for Newton, rested on the belief that there is an external world "out there" as opposed to an internal world, the "I" which is "in here." Nature is "out there," and the task of the scientist is to study those phenomena "out there."

The Newtonian universe, however, was imperfect, and toward the end of the 19th and early part of the 20th century, many scientists began to question its truths. The planet Mercury refused to conform to Newton's laws. Ernst Mach and Henri Poincare, among others, challenged Newton's notions of absolute space and time. However, a radically new vision of the universe was provided by Einstein and 20th century quantum mechanics, accompanied by a totally new view of the nature of the scientific enterprise. Moreover, the new view of the universe and science brought with it a new view of the friendship between the knower and the known.

Einstein produced in a single year three articles that were to change forever the cherished view of the universe. To trace Einstein's influences, or indeed to expound his theory, is beyond the scope of this chapter. Nevertheless, it is important to note that this contribution took the form of a statement of relativity. No longer was the notion of "absolute" to dominate our ideas of the universe. Instead, the terms "relativity" and "probability" entered our discussions. For Einstein, relativity meant that the existing laws of nature were valid only when all observers moved at rates uniformly relative to one another. Einstein described relativity in many forms (see Clark, 1972), such as one in which he speaks of simultaneity as the perceived relation between two things: "So we see that we cannot attach any absolute significance to the concept of simultaneity, but that two events which, viewed from a system of coordinates, are simultaneous, can no longer be looked upon as simultaneous events when envisaged from a system which is in motion relatively to that system" (p. 182).

Einstein's view of time, speed, and space changed the view of an absolute universe. The properties of objects, time, and space were not independent but dependent and changing according to the particular system from which they were viewed. Events became dependent on probabilities rather than absolute certainties. The impact of these ideas was profound on all of our notions of what was "absolute" and what was "real." For example, Arthur Eddington (see Clark, 1972), in talking about the changing notions regarding property of objects, included a statement that suggested the perspective of knower to the known was not only of interest but was a necessity for proper interpretations of the data:

> When a rod is started from reset into uniform motion, nothing whatever happens to the rod. We say that it contracts; but length is not a property of the rod; it is a relation between the rod and the observer. Until the observer is specified, the length of the rod is quite indeterminate. (p. 120)

Such statements capture a profound change in our view of nature. Although this new view may have had little impact on the everyday lives of most people and their perceptions of the world of objects and people, the effect on philosophers was profound. In Eddington's statement, "Until the observer is specified, the length of the rod is quite indeterminate," the knower and the known enter into a relationship unthought of in the Newtonian period.

Einstein's theory of relativity and the study of quantum mechanics changed the notion of what science is and the perceived relation of the scientist to science. No longer could one think of either scientists or knowers studying a phenomenon without considering their relation to that phenomenon. The phenomenon no longer was believed to possess absolute properties, as scientists once believed.

Modern physics soon went beyond even Einstein's conception. Born, Heisenberg, and Bohr, working within the discipline of quantum physics, conceptualized the universe in a way that leveled all remaining notions of absolute and certainty. No longer is anything certain; probabilities are all that govern. No longer could one say that at a certain time a particle will be found in a certain place with a certain amount of energy or momentum. Such statements of certainty had to be altered to statements of probabilities.

However, in the study of subatomic particles, quantum mechanics was to go beyond merely stating probabilities. Not only was the notion of certainty shown to be incorrect, but the belief in a reality unaffected by human action was undermined. To some degree, human observation and measurement actually create the phenomenon of study. Quantum physicists began to consider questions such as: "Did a particle with momentum exist before we measure its momentum?" Thus, the relation of the knower to known became one of the major questions of quantum mechanics. A statement by John Wheeler illustrates this well:

> May the universe in some strange sense be "brought into being" by the participation of those who participate?...The vital act is the act of participation. "Participator" is the incontrovertible new concept given by quantum mechanics. It strikes down the term "observer" of classical theory, the man who stands safely behind the thick glass wall and watches what goes on without taking part. It can't be done, quantum mechanics says. (see Zukav, 1979, p. 54)

The developments of quantum mechanics produced startling consequences. Not only was our view of the universe changed, but we found we could no longer describe the universe with physical models. The universe was no longer reflected in ordinary sensory perceptions. It no longer allowed for the description of things but only the relation between things, a relation that was probabilistic. Furthermore, the distinction between an "out there" and an "in here," or an objective reality independent of the observer, was not feasible because it was impossible to observe anything without distorting it. Finally, the new view of the universe destroyed our belief that we could measure absolute truth; rather, we learned we can only correlate experience.

Although it is beyond this chapter to detail more recent developments in quantum mechanics, it should be noted that theories, which go beyond the issue of participation and observation as causes of the phenomenon of study, continue to evolve. For example, it is no longer the case that we believe that only one of many possibilities occurs at a given time; possible events happen but in different worlds that coexist with ours.

The reduction of the absolute was complete. This new worldview went beyond Einstein's personal belief. Until the end of his life, Einstein resisted the notions of chance and probability and sought to find lawful absolute principles that could be used to predict events with certainty. His now famous statement, "God does not play dice," reflected his displeasure with the new conception. The nature of movement and the properties of matter, time, and space were relative. Epistemology, too, was changed. Referring to this change in view of science and knowing, Born writes that we had been:

taught there exists an objective physical world, which unfolds itself according to immutable laws independent of us. We are watching this process like the audience watches a play in a theater…Quantum mechanics, however, interprets the experience gained in atomic physics in a different way. We may compare the observer of a physical phenomenon not unlike the audience of a theatrical performance, but with that of a football game where the act of watching, accompanied by applauding or hissing, has a marked influence on the speed and concentration of the players, and thus on what is watched. In fact, a better simile is life itself, where audience and actors are the same persons. It is the action of the experimentalist who designs the apparatus which determines the essential features of the observations. Hence, there is no objectively existing situation, as was supposed to exist in classical physics. (see Clark, 1972, p.143)

In summary, under the influence of Bacon and Newton, the object of the scientist was to remain uninvolved with the phenomena being studied. Indeed, the entire scientific enterprise and its methods revolved around this goal. Accompanying these aims was the notion of a reality that was independent of the scientist. New developments in the study of relativity and quantum physics, however, denied us this belief. Bohr's notion on "complementarity" directly affects the knower: The common denominator of all experiences is "I." Zukav (1979) states that experience, then, does not mirror external reality but "our interaction with it" (p. 116). The effect of such a conclusion on our role in knowing is profound. Zukav, speaking of quantum physics, has the final word:

> Transferring the properties that we usually ascribe to light to our interaction with light deprives light of an independent existence. Without us, or by implication, anything else to interact with, light does not exist. This remarkable conclusion is only half the story. The other half is that, in a similar manner, without light, or, by implication, anything else to interact with, we do not exist! As Bohr himself put it…"an independent reality in the ordinary physical sense can be ascribed neither to the phenomena nor the agencies of observation." (p. 118)

Properties belong to the relational bidirectional interaction of the phenomena and observer. It is to the notion of this relation that our developmental inquiries need turn. It is of interest to see how broad this idea of known and knower is, and I take the example of religious inquiry to make this point.

In Christianity, several texts are not considered part of the core of the religion, such as the Greek Gospel of Thomas and the Apocryphon ("secret book") of John. In Pagels's (1979) The Gnostic Gospels, the issue of the relation between knower and known is to be found in the meaning of gnosis.

The Greek word gnosis is usually translated as knowledge. The Greek language, however, distinguishes between scientific and reflective knowledge (e.g., "she knows historical facts" vs. "she knows me" or knowing through observation or experience). It is the latter form of knowing that is gnosis. From the Gospel of Truth, one of the discovered texts, it is clear that one group of early Christians believed that to know God required that they also know themselves. This was the heresy of these believers. According to Pagels (1979), although the group now considered orthodox Christians "insisted that a chasm separates humanity from its creator. God is wholly other…the Gnostics contradicted this. They held that self-knowledge is knowledge of God; the self and the divine are identical" (p. 101).

In short, this gnostic view broke down the barrier between what was to be known and the knower. The orthodox view held that what was to be known, God, could be known only through some intermediary. The intermediaries were the true disciples, those to whom God had given authority. Thus, the Gnostics posed a threat to the structure of the church and to clerical authority. Consequently, this form of Gnostics was declared heretical.

In this example, the issue of the knower and the known is again central. For orthodox Christians, knowing is a process of distancing oneself from the known, found in the process of knowing oneself: Through the use of oneself, the barrier separating the knower from the known could be broken.

Another example of this relational bidirectional interaction between the knower and known is in the nature of the scientist and the science created. In thinking about the scientific enterprise or, for that matter, any intellectual enterprise, I cannot help being struck by something almost too obvious to mention. On virtually any topic, there are people who subscribe to very different views. Although it is not surprising to find disagreement between a learned and ignorant person, to find disagreement between two learned people is something of a surprise. These differences of opinion within a discipline cannot be accounted for by claiming that one side is more intelligent than the other (although this might be the case). Rather, such differences are more often explained by basic models or paradigmatic differences between the combatants (e.g., Overton, 2006). It is usually at this level that the consideration of difference is left.

This problem could be pursued further, however, by asking where and how these different paradigms arise. How is it that two highly intelligent scientists, each possessing similar information, can arrive at discrepant sets of conclusions? The answer again involves the relation between the knower and the known. In this example, one must move beyond the paradigmatic view and ask what it is about an individual that facilitates thinking about a problem in a particular way. It is important then to examine characteristics of the knower to understand what is known (or at least thought to be known). In particular, certain characteristics of scientists may affect the truth value they assign to an event, as well as the inclination of the scientific community to accept an event as fact. Thus, the announcement of an unusual and unexpected discovery is more readily accepted when made by a well-known and respected scientist than by an unknown student. Thus, the acceptance of what is known goes well beyond mere statistical probability levels and involves the personal attributes of the scientist.

The scientist is related to science in other ways as well. As every sociology major student is taught, one must be somewhat suspicious of an informant, especially when the informant is telling something that he or she wishes to be true. Are we more or less likely to believe a finding when it was predicted in advance by the investigator than when it was not? Predicted facts have a higher regard than nonpredicted ones, as is suggested by the difference between one- and two-tailed statistical tests. However, we would be much less likely to believe that smoking is injurious to health if the investigator is someone who does not smoke and believes smoking to be vile.

The scientific enterprise usually assumes that the characteristics of the scientist are orthogonal to the phenomenon investigated. A corollary to this is the belief that whenever a relation exists between the knower and the known, the facts discovered are likely to be suspect. For example, if we were to give a personality inventory to two groups of scientists who held different theories and found that the groups differed along some personality dimension, both theories might be challenged. Consequently, one of the primary goals of Western science is to separate the scientist from the science, or the knower from the known.

Unfortunately, relatively little research on the characteristics of scientists has been conducted. Exceptions to this are provided by Roe (1951, 1953), Eiduson (1962), and Hudson (1972), all of whom have found significant and interesting scientist differences between and within various scientific disciplines. Thus, although much of the

scientific enterprise since the time of Bacon has tried to separate, isolate, and distance the scientist from the phenomena being studied, this may be impossible.

This discussion has direct bearing on the relational bidirectional interaction between the knower and known, the nature of the knower, and the issue of the self. The following summary of the self-knowledge demonstrates, in part, that in the study of cognitive and social development, we need to consider the knower in relation to the known.

Many examples can be found to document the interrelatedness of what is known and the knower. For instance, Bower's demonstration that who you identify within a story will affect and change the interpretation of the story (Owens, Bower, & Black, 1979) suggests that the role of the self has an important influence in constructing information. Even more central to our concern is the demonstration that memory is facilitated if what is to be remembered is made relevant to the self (Hyde & Jenkins, 1969; Kuiper & Rogers, 1979; Rogers, Kuiper, & Kirker, 1977).

Language acquisition is another area in which the relation between self and knowing can be demonstrated. In researching the acquisition of prepositions, we have found a developmental sequence: The prepositions in and out, on or under, and in front of or behind are learned in that order. Almost all 2-year-olds know that meanings of in and out, but far fewer know on or under, and almost none know in front of or behind. Although 2-year-olds could demonstrate "on-under" knowledge by manipulating two objects, they had far less difficulty when asked to "get on the table" or "get under the table." That is, when they were one of the two objects that was to be related to another, the children had far less difficulty in demonstrating their knowledge than when they had to manipulate two objects in the same way. In a similar vein, Huttenlocher (1980) reports that intentional verbs are applied to the self before being applied to others.

The foregoing examples indicate that there is a difference in cognitive activity when the self is engaged. The influence of self on the outcome does not prove the nonexistence of a self-independent "factual" world, but it does point out that in some forms of knowing, the self plays an important role. This can also be seen in the effect of self on classification behavior.

Age is one particular social feature that young children appear to learn and that is relatively easy to study. Because age is usually considered in terms of number of years, the acquisition of age knowledge or classification has not been studied before children are able to use number concepts and seriation. However, covarying with numerical age are physical features of the face and body, which children and adults may use to determine age apart from number of years. Indeed, number concepts may be mapped on these initial features at a later time. In our earlier work, we found that young children rarely make age errors; that is, when asked to point to a picture of their father's face, when the father's picture is embedded in a set of pictures containing other people of varying ages and sex, children between 15 and 24 months almost never make an error on age. They may pick the wrong adult, but seldom do they point to a child. Sex errors are also quite rare (Brooks-Gunn & Lewis, 1979; Lewis & Weinraub, 1976).

Another study that can be used to exemplify the role of the knower in classification extends this research (Lewis, Edwards, Weistuch, & Cortelyou, 1981). Three- to 5-year-old children were asked to sort a set of pictures of faces. The faces of people aged 1 to 20 years in the first study and 1 to 70 years in the second study. All children were given the same task; they were asked to sort the pictures into three piles (in the first study) and four piles (in the second study). The labels given to the piles were little girls and boys, big girls and boys, mother and fathers, and in the second study, grandmothers and grandfathers. The children were allowed to move pictures back and forth from one pile to another.

Of importance for our discussion is the age of transition; approximately 60% of subjects placed 5-year-old faces in the little girl and boy pile, whereas approximately 70% placed the 7-year-old faces in the big girl and boy pile. We infer from this information that 6 years is the commonly preferred transition age between little and big children. Remember, no years were used in the study. Likewise, the transition age for children to parents appears to be 13 years and for parent to grandparent 40 years. Adults (20–60 years old) also have little difficulty with the same task. However, the ages of transition change. The age of transition between little and big children is now 13 years, between big children and parents is between 17 and 20 years, and between parents and grandparents 40 years. These results are not surprising. They show that the classification of age into groups, not by number of years old but by features, varies with the age of the respondent. For the 3-year-old child, the 7-year-old is big, whereas for the 20-year-old, the 7-year-old is little.

We gave a similar task to students in a graduate seminar by asking them to divide an imagined set of faces and ages into four groups. Inasmuch as the graduate students were not given any labels for the groups, they were free to select age ranges that fit their own classification system.

Five of the students were in their early 20s and two were in their late 30s. The younger students all considered the first group to contain ages 1 to 10 years, whereas the two older students created groups to 1 to 14 years and 1 to 20 years. Even more interesting was the final grouping. The younger students' both started at age 50 to 55 years and went to 70 years, whereas the older students both started at 65 years of age. Thus, using imaginary stimuli, the effect of one's own age on age classification is apparent. We have since given this task to 40 subjects varying in age from 31 to 65 years and have obtained similar results. Age classification appears to be dependent on the respondent's age. The classifications differ and none is incorrect; however, they use their own age to construct the classification system.

Both the historical account and that data on subject's age influence on age classification provide support for the proposition that the role of the knower cannot be overlooked in either the scientific enterprise or the study of knowing. The epistemological issue of the knower and the known has been recognized by Piaget (1960) and others (Polyani, 1958). For them, knowing involves the relational bidirectional interaction of the knower with objects, events, or people. The structures of knowledge (e.g., schemes) are assumed to originate from this interaction; they are the structures of mind. The mind of the knower, although formed through relational bidirectional interactions, is understood to operate independently of the known. Indeed, it is often argued that the degree to which the knower remains embedded in the known is a measure of the immaturity (egocentrism) of the knower. On the other hand, the development of consciousness provides a means of distancing the knower from the known, which, in turn, is a necessary condition for the use of a self concept in the formation of other cognitions or thoughts.

Although it may be possible to separate the knower from the structures of the knowledge for some forms of knowledge (i.e., abstract knowledge), there are structures of knowledge that, by necessity, depend on the knower. Rather than a dichotomy between two types of cognition, it is perhaps more useful to think of knowing as a continuum (see Mascolo & Fischer in Chapter 6 of this volume), for an extended discussion of levels of knowing). Thus, the following discussion rests on the view that cognition, in general, represents a continuum of involvement of the knower (or self) with what is known. Social cognition represents that part of the continuum where there is a markedly close relation between the knower and the known. In other words, without the use of the self, some things are impossible to know. The distinction between hot and cold cognitions contains some of the same difference as stated here. Hot cognition (emotions) appears to involve the self and, as such, may be different from those that do not.

Social cognition has been defined as social perception (Bruner & Tagiuri, 1954), as the learning of social rules and obligations (Kohlberg, 1969), sex-role knowledge (Mischel, 1970), and in terms of features such as age and sex (Edwards & Lewis, 1979). In each of these cases, the knowledge is considered social in that it applies to human beings, human attributes, and human products as rule and obligations. Social cognition has also been defined to include communicative competence (Krauss & Glucksberg, 1969), inferences about other (Flavell, 1974), role tasking (Selman, 1971a, 1971b), and emotional experiences such as empathy involving events that are inside the person (e.g., intentions, attitudes, perceptions, consciousness, self-determination) and events between persons (e.g., friendship, love; see Carpendale & Lewis, this volume, for an extended discussion of social cognition). These forms of knowledge are not independent of the knower, or self, because they pertain to knowledge that necessarily requires the use of the self. Role taking and empathy, for example, require that knowers put themselves in the place of another.

Cognitions about self and other are not separate processes but rather are part of a duality of knowledge. This view is shared by others. For example, Bannister and Agnew (1977) note: "The ways in which we elaborate our construing of self must be essentially those ways in which we elaborate our construing of others, for we have not a concept of self but a bipolar construct of self—not self or self-other" (p. 99). If this is the case, then social cognitions, as something different from cognitions in general, are not really content differences but differences based on the role of the self, or knower, in relation to what is known. The definition of social cognition involves the relation between knower and known (they are relational cognitions) rather than features that apply to people.

By making cognitions independent of the knower, it becomes possible to talk about general cognitions that refer to objects. That is, when cognitions about humans do not involve the knower or self, they are not social cognitions; conversely, when cognition about objects involves the knower or self, they become social. As can be readily seen, the degree of the knower-to-known relational bidirectional interaction becomes the definition of social cognition. The degree to which any cognition is so constructed is the degree to which social cognitions differ from nonsocial cognitions in their formal properties. One could say, then,

that cognitions that do not involve the knower can be considered absolute and are Newtonian. Cognitions that rely on the knower are relative and, as such, are Einsteinian. Inasmuch as the study of the known excludes the knower in genetic epistemology, it can be linked to a Newtonian study of absolute properties; when the self enters into the known, the study of the knower becomes relative.

An examination of cultural differences in these different types of knowing is beyond the scope of this chapter, but it should come as no surprise to find that cultural needs and values influence these differences. In fact, it may be a particular cultural requirement, a demand for abstraction and reification, that requires the knower be separated from the known. Thus, as Luria (1976) suggests, different developmental levels are not controlled by some genetic program but chiefly by cultural requirements. Similar arguments can found in Polyani (1958). Merleau-Ponty (1964) captures the spirit of social cognition in the following quote: "If I am a consciousness turned toward things, I can meet in things the actions of another and find in them a meaning because they are themes of possible activity for my own body" (p. 113). Social knowledge and social action are dependent on the role of the knower. Like Asch (1952), Heider (1958) reflects this as a central theme when he states: "Social perceptions in general can best be described as a process between the center of one person and the center of another person, from life space to life space...A, through psychological processes in himself, perceives psychological processes in B" (p. 33). The concept of self is a very compelling idea, especially for the modern Western societies. It seems difficult to imagine that such an idea did not always exist in people's minds but may have developed over long periods (see Jaynes, 1976, for one historical analysis of its genesis), or that it may take different forms between contemporary cultures (Geertz, 1984). It is even harder to imagine that a self does not exist from the beginnings of life (Lewis, 1992b; Neisser, 1988; Stern, 1985). That the concept of self now is so compelling suggests that it possesses important meaning for us all.

Finally, I am reminded of Nozick's (1981) analysis of identity. You may recall, for example, people are able to maintain the rowboat's identity (it remains the same boat) over many years even though each year another piece of the boat was removed and replaced. After many years, there was not a piece of the original boat left, yet people still think of it as the same boat. However, if the pieces of the boat are all replaced at once, the boat ceases to be the same boat and becomes a new one. This example of the boat impressed on me at least one good reason for a sense of self, because this concept of ourselves allows for elaborate change and transformation whereas preserving who we think we are. As a corollary, cultures that change more rapidly and cultures less bounded interpersonally (defined by others) are more likely to be cultures for which the concept of self, located especially in the individual, is to be found. This may explain, at least in part, why the topic of the self has become so focused for us in the last part of the century and now.

WHAT IS AND IS NOT A SELF

The following four questions are essential to understand our notion of consciousness: (1) What is a self? (2) How do we measure a self? (3) Are there cultural and historical differences in a self? and (4) What does a self do?

What Is a Self?

T cells are capable of intentions; they go after foreign protein and kill them. T cells also are capable of self-versus-nonself recognition. Do these cells have a self? Rat pups soon after birth engage in what some have called *nonverbal communication*, others have called *social reflexive behavior*, and still others, *intersubjectivity*. Do these pups have a self? Even more important, from the perspective of human ontogeny, do both the newborn infant who imitates its mother and the child who says "me drink bottle" while reaching for the bottle have selves? If they do—a claim made by many—then what develops? The problem is solved by considering that term *self* is inadequate to the task. A self is made up of many features or types (e.g., Lewis, 1979, 1992b; Neisser, 1988; Stern, 1985). For example, all living creatures have self-regulating and self-organizing capabilities, and all creatures that have social lives have the ability to interact with regard to other conspecifics. Whether we call these processes "self" does not alter the fact that human and nonhumans share these features. What we might not share with most other creatures—great apes being the exception—is our ability to reflect on and focus our attention on ourselves (consciousness). We are also not likely to share, again except with great apes, the ability to have a symbolic-linguistic understanding of recursive propositions such as, "I know that you know that I know how to chop wood." The role of language and conversation and the role of playing and play do bear on the features of self described in this unique way. It is clear that

the field remains plagued by definitional vagrancies for the different aspects of a self. One problem in particular is to be noted; namely, that even the most basic aspects of self are often discussed in ways that assume that they exhibit a self-reflection that is, in fact, found only in older children and adults.

How Do We Measure a Self?

Of course, measurement must follow from theory. If that aspect of self we wish to observe is related to self-other differentiation, self-regulation, self-other relational bidirectional interaction (called by some *intersubjectivity*), or self-reference, the way we choose to measure the particular feature of self will differ. It would be foolish to confuse measurement of one feature of self with another, and to make the claim that one measure reflects all aspects of self. Imitation, perceptual-motor organization, language, role taking, and self-directed behavior are all methods that should inform us about features of the self. Measurement issues, as always, must be tied to the particular construct of the self studied.

Are There Cultural and Historical Differences in a Self?

The issue of cultural differences in the concept of self, certainly those features requiring objective self-awareness, vary markedly (e.g., Lewis, 1992b, discusses the cultural and natural changes in some features of self). On the other hand, one might wish to argue for some universal features of self. For example, the self-other discrimination, self-regulating, and self-other interactions observed in the very young infant are likely to be found across cultures and historical time. Moreover, other features of the self may also be pan-cultural. If, as some believe, the left temporal lobe, is necessary for consciousness (objective self-awareness), then the development that occurs in this brain area in the middle of the second year of life may also exist across cultures. Its expression, however, may be quite different depending on cultural specifics. The "terrible twos," described in our culture as the emergence of the child's will independent of the parent's wishes, may not be as marked in cultures less interested in individual autonomy (see Geertz, 1984).

However, as William James suggested a century ago, it is probably wise to separate structural from content features. There is no reason to assume that the structural features of self (e.g., the emergence of consciousness) is much affected by cultural or caregiving techniques. Except for severely bad treatment, children are likely to develop this structural feature. What is affected, however, is how the child comes to view himself or herself. Poor or violent care is likely to result in different and negative (even pathological) views of the self. However, it should not affect the emergence of the self-reflective aspect of self.

Only our particular idea of self is culturally specific. The Western idea of a single self, standing alone and in opposition other such selves—the I-self—stands in opposition to the we-self found in Japanese and Indian cultures (Roland, 1988) is an example of cultural specificity. A structural feature of self such as consciousness is, on the other hand, likely to be universal.

What Does a Self Do?

The question of what a self does has to do with why we need the construct of self at all. For example, instead of the term *self-regulation*, we could simply use the term *system regulation*. Self-regulation implies something unique about the self. For each of the features of self that we articulate, we can have the same question: What would the child be like if he does not have that self feature? It is obvious that for the earliest features of self, their absence would result in such maladaptive behavior that the organism could not survive. Thus, failures of self-other differentiation or self-other interaction results in disorders that we term *autism* or *retardation*. What happens when the final structural feature of self-reference (termed *consciousness* or *objective self-awareness*) emerges? What are the differences between children who have self-referential and those who are developmentally less advanced? From a modeling point of view, if we found no differences between a child who does or does not have self-reference, then our model might need revision. If, in contrast, there was a difference, this difference may inform us as to the role and importance of this capability.

In case of a self-referential organism, we could expect the child to show a variety of capabilities, including role-playing empathy, embarrassment, shame, guilt, pride (Lewis, 1992b), and achievement motivation (Heckhausen, 1984). It is that feature of the self, the self that can place itself in the role of other, that creates mature forms of empathy, that shows pride in its achievement, and that shows shame or guilt in its failure. Before the emergence of the skills, these behaviors remain absent or, at best, controlled by reflexive-like behavior. From my point of view, humans and nonhumans share many features of self. Those features that we do not share, self-referential behaviors, identity, and self-concept, are what makes us different from other creatures.

THE SELF SYSTEM

My daughter Felicia, an infectious disease physician, knowing of my interest in self system, some time ago sent me an article by Von Boehmer and Kisielow (1990) entitled "Self-Nonself Discrimination by T Cells," and one by Harding, Gray, McClure, Anderson, and Clarke (1990) entitled "Self-Incompatibility: A Self Recognition System in Plants." We use the terms *self* and *nonself* in reference to plants and to cells, as well as to humans. If the term self used here is confusing, consider several examples from the human literature. We use the term self-regulation when we talk about newborn infants (Kopp, 1982) and intersubjectivity in 6-month-olds (Rochat, 2009; Stern, 1984). Things do not get much better when we consider adult humans; for example, the Western view of self as "I self" versus an Eastern view of self as "we self" (see Geertz, 1984). We even have identified multiple personality disorder, the idea of multiple selves rather than a single self (Ross, 1989).

Even in our everyday lives we are confronted with explaining selves. Much of my motor action, although initially planned, is carried out by core processes of my body that include, by definition, self regulation and self-other differentiation. The same, of course, is true of thinking. A self is necessary to formulate, at least sometimes, what it is that we wish to think about. But self does not appear to be involved in the processes that actually conduct the task of thinking. Consider this example: we give a person the problem of adding a 7 to the sum of 7s that precede it (e.g., $7 + 7 = 14 + 7 = 21 + 7 = 28$, etc.). It is clear that as she carries out this task, she cannot reflect on herself doing the arithmetic. One aspect of the self has set up the problem, another solves it. These diverse examples from plants, cells, human newborns, and adults all address the single topic of what it is that we mean when we use the term *self*. To anticipate what is to follow, I should like to make a few declarative statements; statements that, if we could figure out a way to test, might prove useful. Following Duval and Wicklund (1972), I have considered two major aspects of "self," which I have called subjective self-awareness (the core processes of our system) and objective self-awareness (the ability to reflect on and focus attention on our selves, thoughts, actions, and feelings):

1. All living systems self-regulate. By this we mean that within any living system, there needs to be communication between parts of that system. This can include a unit as small as a cell, a plant or animal, or even a more complex organism. As I sit here writing, my systems are self-regulating my temperature, producing shivering as the room cools, or regulating my blood sugar level and informing me that it is time to have a snack. Self-regulation is a property of living matter. Self-regulation makes no assumptions about a mental state or objective self-awareness (see also, McClelland, Ponitz, Messersmith & Tominey, this volume, for an extended discussion of self-regulation).

2. Some minimal differentiation between self and other is a necessary condition for action. Whether this differentiation is a product of experience or part of the process of action—including perceiving, feeling, and thinking—is unknown (see Butterworth, 1992). What appears to be so is that organisms cannot act without at some level being able to distinguish between self and other.

3. The ability to self-regulate or to distinguish self from other is part of the core processes of all living systems (Von Bertalanffy, 1967).

4. Even higher order functions such as perception, thinking, and complex actions, such as driving a car, can be performed by adult humans without a mental state or objective self-awareness, that is, without their being able to reflect on, look at, and observe the processes that allow these behaviors to be carried out. I cannot watch myself think. I can only look at the product of my thinking.

5. A unique aspect of some self systems is objective self-awareness. By objective self-awareness I mean the capacity of a self to know it knows or to remember it remembers. It is this "meta" ability that we refer to when we say self-awareness, the reflective capacity of objective self-awareness, may be uniquely human (perhaps we need to include the great apes who also are capable of this).

The notion of a self and its development can also be viewed in relation to emotion. Elsewhere (Lewis, 1992b; Lewis & Michalson, 1983) I have discussed emotion as including emotional states and experiences. People can have certain emotional states and yet be unaware that they have them; that is, they have states but no experience of them. Emotional states refer to the subjective self-awareness or the core processes of our system. These core processes can

have goals, can learn and profit from experience, can control functions, and can react to events including people. The experience of our emotional states refers to objective self-awareness or what Damasio (2003) refers to as "feelings."

As an illustration of the self distinction between states and experience or between subjective versus objective self-awareness, consider Pribram's description of a patient in whom the medial part of the temporal lobe, including the amygdala, had been removed bilaterally. Here we see a distinction between the subject's objective self-experience or mental state and her subjective state of hunger.

> I once had the opportunity to examine some patients in whom the medial part of the temporal lobe—including the amygdale—had been removed bilaterally. There patients, just as their monkey counterparts, typically ate considerably more than normal and gained up to a hundred pounds in weight. At least I could *ask* the subject how it felt to be so hungry. But much to my surprise, the expected answer was not forthcoming. One patient who gained more than 100 pounds in the several years since surgery was examined at lunchtime. "Was she hungry?" She answered, "No." "Would you like a piece of rare, juicy steak?" "No." "Would she like a piece of chocolate candy?" She answered, "um-hum," but when no candy was offered she did not pursue the matter. A few minutes later when the examination was completed, the doors to the common room were opened, and she saw the other patients already seated at a table eating lunch. She rushed to the table, pushed the others aside, and began to stuff food into her mouth with both hands. She was immediately recalled to the examining room, and questions about food were repeated. The same negative answers were obtained again, even after they were pointedly contrasted with her recent behavior at the table. Somehow the lesion had impaired the patient's feelings of hunger and satiety, and this impairment was accompanied by excessive eating! (Pribram, 1984, p. 25)

Given the definition of objective and subjective self-awareness, we are confronted with the following question: Is all information that is subjectively known capable of being objectively known? The answer is, not always and, in fact, most often not. Subjective self-processes may be available to an objective self-awareness but only at times. I may be able to learn to focus on my core processes, such as controlling my heart rate or pressure; however, when I focus on this, I am unable to focus on other aspects of the system's core processes. Some subjective awareness may never be available to objective awareness. The process of thinking is an example. This suggests the likelihood that objective self-awareness is limited.

The problem also can be stated from an epistemological point of view. For example, when I say "I know X," is it the case that I *must* know that I know X. If it is the case that I can know that I know X, when is it the case that I do know that I know X? These kinds of epistemological questions require different ways of knowing.

It seems to me that these epistemological questions are best addressed by our analysis of different aspects of self. As we have discussed, there are at least two aspects of self, an objective versus a subjective self. From an epistemological point of view, knowledge can be subjective or objective, but the knowledge of the knowledge is always objective. Knowledge of the knowledge is the capacity of the self to reflect on itself. This ability to reflect on itself is what makes the self so important to understand.

HISTORICAL VIEWS OF SELF-DEVELOPMENT: DUALITY OF THE SELF

The development of the self is a topic that has received much thought and has a long history. I cannot do justice to this history, but I will attempt to touch on some significant theories. A hundred years ago, William James, in *The Principles of Psychology*, considered the problem of self, and mentioned its duality:

> Whatever I may be thinking of, I am always, at the same time more or less aware of myself, of my personal existence. At the same time, it is I who am aware, so that the total self or me, being as it were duplex, partly known and partly knower, partly object and partly subject, must have two aspects discriminated in it, of which, for shortness, we may call one the "me" and the other the "I." (James, 1895, p. 43)

James went on to distinguish a hierarchy of selves, with a "bodily me" at the bottom and a "spiritual me" at the top, and various social selves in between. He envisioned a developmental trajectory, from the earliest physical experiences of the self as an entity to the later spiritual or nonmaterial experiences.

James's duality of self can be noted in the philosophical literature from Descartes to Wittgenstein. However, James's duality and Wittgenstein's were relational in nature, not split into a dichotomy as was Descartes (see Overton, 2006). Nevertheless, Descartes considered two classes of experience, with pain as an example of one, grief of the other. The first, pain, comes to us through our senses, or what we might refer to as James's "bodily me." Grief, in contrast, does not arise from immediate sense impressions.

James's thinking about the self and self-development branched in two directions, one cognitive and the other social. Within a cognitive framework, Baldwin described the development of the self in terms of its relationship to others, whereas Piaget viewed this development in terms of the evolving mathematical/logical constructions, as the child moved from egocentricism to decentering. Though Piaget's discussion focuses on ages beyond the period of most interest for study of the emergence of the objective self, his views are still intriguing. If we ignore the fact that he is talking about children between the ages of 2 and 6, his formalization fits with those of others who are talking about 2-year-olds. Piaget writes:

> That the child being ignorant of his own ego, take his own point of view as absolute, and fails to establish between himself and the external world of things, that reciprocity, which alone would ensure objectivity...Whenever relationship dependent upon the ego are concerned—they are at the crux of the matter—the child fails to grasp the logic of relations for lack of having established reciprocity, first between himself and other people, and between himself and things. (Piaget, 1960, p. 272)

According to Piaget, having reached a symbolic level of functioning—which permits early reflection—at around age 2, complete decentering is a slow process that may not be completed until around age 6. It is with this decentering that the child becomes capable of taking the perspective of another. This permits viewing himself as others might view him, thereby indicating movement from a subjective to an objective self point of view.

At about the same time as James, Charles Cooley, a sociologist, struggled with similar problems concerning the self and its origins. Cooley, writing about the social nature of human beings and social organization, posited a reflector or "looking glass" self. The self is reflected through other; thus, other people are the "looking glass" for oneself. In addition, Cooley stressed the relational idea that self and society form a common whole, with neither existing in the absence of the other. Cooley believed that infants are not conscious of the self, or the "I," nor are they aware of society or other people. Infants experience a simple stream of impressions, impressions that gradually become discriminated as the young child differentiates itself, or "I," from the society, or "we."

Following Cooley, George Herbert Mead also drew a distinction between the objective and subjective self, using James's "I" and "me." The "I" is the subjective self and the "me" is the objective self reflecting on the "I." Mead assumed that the movement from the subjective "I" to the objective "me" takes place within a social nexus and is made possible only thorough social learning. Mead saw taking the perspective of another as the way the child was able to develop an objective self, and like Cooley, argued the relational position that knowledge of the self and others developed simultaneously, with both forms of knowledge dependent on social interaction. Heavily influenced by Darwin, he felt that the human infant is active rather than passive, selectively responding to stimuli rather than indiscriminately responding to all events. Hence, Mead believed that the infant actively constructs the self (here he is referring to the objective self). He stated:

> Self has a character which is different from that of the physiological organism proper, the self is something which has a development; it is not initially there at birth, but arises in the process of social experience and activity. That is, it develops in the given individual as a result of his relations to that process as a while and to other individuals within that process. (Mead, 1934, p. 135)

The similarity between Mead's and Cooley's ideas is considerable: They share belief in the relational duality of self, subjective and objective, and the role of the child's social interaction in promoting his development from subjective to objective.

Although I cannot present psychoanalytical views of the self in detail, we need to keep in mind two of Freud's central ideas concerning the self's conscious and unconscious processes, and tripartite structure. The id and ego can be characterized as representing a subjective and an objective self, although Freud's ideas about this tripartite division of personality have recently been questioned.

In general, classical psychoanalytic theory has not paid much attention to the self, although self psychology has redressed the balance. I will restrict my discussion of self psychology, only briefly mentioning the work of Erikson, Mahler, and Stern. Each takes a developmental perspective like my own. Erikson does not deal directly with self-development except from the point of view of the self's struggle at each stage. Nevertheless, the challenge of the stages bears directly on issues of self-development. Mahler and her colleagues articulate a self system that clearly develops in a sequence. There is some similarity between Mahler's point of view and Erikson's in that she describes the development of the self as a struggle between separateness and relatedness, and calls this the separation/individuation process. This process and struggle continues across the life course. Of special interest for us is Mahler's description of the child in the last half of the second year. She posits an increased awareness of self, and a concomitant heightened concern with the mother. In addition, she feels that both empathy and understanding of what it means to be separate and autonomous emerge between ages 18 and 24 months. The child's "love affair" with the world is modified as he learns about frustrations and limitations. In the third year, individuality is consolidated, separations from the mother become easier to bear, and the ability to take another's role becomes more pronounced. The child has developed a self that is separate from, but also related to, others. Stern, a student of Mahler, speaks of four forms of self, which, although developing over time, are all available to both child and adult: the emergent self, the core self, the subjective self, and the verbal self (see Santostefano, this volume, for an extended discussion of these forms of self in relation to the development of psychopathology). This scheme is useful, although it bears much resemblance to others (Stern, 1985).

In most theories, the mechanism of self-development has to do with the child's actions in a social world. A second proposed mechanism is associated with developmental processes related to change in biological structures; and a third concerns bidirectional interactions between the social world and biological change.

Baldwin, Mead, and Cooley all focused on the child's action in a social world. Although it is unclear whether Mead saw any biological processes at work in the process of the development of objective self-awareness, he certainly argues for the child's involvement with its social world as the mechanism of its development. The child cannot develop a sense of the self, or objective self-awareness, alone. Mead uses the example of a boy running down a road. The boy has a rudimentary awareness of his body (subjective), but this awareness does not constitute a genuine self (objective). For Mead, the child's developmental task is to detach his awareness from within himself and assume an outside point of view. That is, individuals need to gain a vantage point external to themselves and then look back at themselves. This ability to look back at oneself implies taking the role of another, as if the boy enters the head of the other and observes himself through the other's way of characterizing him. For Mead, the way others characterize one's self leads to objective self-awareness. We need to keep the idea of an outside point of view because the metaphor is useful. The development of the self system allows us to take this outside point of view, providing the opportunity to change our behavior, to deceive ourselves and others, and to alter our view of the world and of the emotions we experience. Moreover, this process has a function that occurs throughout our lifetimes. The infant has to learn this outside perspective. This, I believe, is associated with brain-process–related activity, the coming online (through maturation or myelination of the left lobes and especially the left temporal lobe).

Caregivers, through their actions, have an impact on the child as the child moves through the various levels of self-development. Poor caregiving, then, should logically result in disruptions of objective self-awareness. This view is held by almost all social theorists. Although such a view is appealing, and on its face reasonable, closer examination reveals this view's flaws. Most importantly, except for special classes of psychotic or autistic children, there is no evidence that poor caregiving results in failure to develop objective self-awareness. Although poor parenting has been shown to be associated with how children think of themselves (i.e., whether they see themselves as good or bad people), to reduce their capacity for empathy, and to impair their ability to self-reflect, there is no support for the idea that poor parenting leads to the lack of objective self-awareness. Mahler's studies and theory grew out of her work with autistic children. Her explanations of individuation might be reasonable for this special category of children, but even here I have some doubt. Autism in children is now thought to be strongly biologically influenced. In some sense, then, the theory of social origin of self-awareness remains in doubt. There is no doubt, however, that the qualities that we consider ourselves to possess, those aspects of our objective self, are influenced by social factors.

The parent as mirror plays an important role in developing self-concept but not in developing objective self-awareness. It has been argued that through children's interactions with their parents, the meaning system attributed to the child by the parent is the mechanism of change (Kaye, 1982). The adult's meaning system, as expressed in behavior toward the child, produces that which that parent thought the child already possessed. In a sense, parents believe that their children possess self-awareness. This is a reasonable position from the standpoint of hermeneutics: Meaning is not found within the individual but results from collective agreement as to meaning. The achievement of objective self-awareness might not be different from

the achievement of other forms of meaning, because self-awareness is an idea we have about ourselves. The social cognitive theorists, and their position in terms of a looking glass, are extremely similar to the views of Kohut (1971) and Fairbairn (1952), who argued for the development of knowledge through the social milieu.

Duval and Wicklund (1972) have suggested that at least three conditions need to be met if the child is to develop objective self-awareness: (1) There must be an entity who has a different point of view than the child; (2) the two different points of view must concern the same object; and (3) the child must be aware of these two different opinions simultaneously. They base their position on their belief that the objective self becomes differentiated from the subjective self. To begin with, the infant acts, perceives, and thinks but does not turn his attention on himself. The turning of attention on the self requires a conflict between the child's action and the actions of others. This conflict enables the child to objectify his actions, thoughts, and feelings, and thus to develop objective self-awareness.

This conflict is most likely to occur in the social world. However, for this conflict to occur, the child has to be able to compare two events simultaneously. Simultaneity requires that the child look at event A in space/time, have a memory of event A, and then look at event B. If the child is not able to retain a memory of A when she looks at B, then B will be quite novel, and thus no comparison will be possible. I have suggested that this ability to make comparisons requires memory capacity, and that memory capacity becomes sufficient for comparison somewhere around age 8 months. What is important here is that certain cognitive capacities, specifically memory development, are essential to the acquisition of the ability to make comparisons, and these are prerequisites for consciousness. Another person with a differing point of view is necessary only to the extent that simultaneity of difference is an important feature in allowing the child to make a comparison, and the simultaneous and discrepant events in the child's world are other social objects, especially parents. Therefore, when the child starts to, let us say, reach for a toy, and the mother tells him not to, the desire and action pattern to reach for the toy is interrupted. This simultaneous comparison is what facilitates the objective self. As Duval and Wicklund wrote:

> The interaction must generate an opposition between the child's own perception, thinking or doing at one point in time, and those same processes at another point in time. Accordingly, out of all the contacts the child has with the world, we are left with just two possibilities. One, the child

could differ with a previous opinion. By notes a contrast with the earlier. Two, the second possibility is disagreement with the perceptions of another. It now remains to be seen if both of these alternatives satisfy the requisite condition for activating the perceptual differentiating mechanism. (Duval & Wicklund, 1972, p. 140)

By referring to Piaget's work on decentering, they reached the conclusion that, in fact, the parent–child relationship is likely to lead to this objectification. This occurs, in part, because interactions eliminate the time gap between the two perceptions, the child's own perception and the child's perception of the other as different from one's own.

It is the simultaneity of differing opinions and perceptions that is important. It is conflictual situations, ones in which there are punishments and negative prohibitions, that are likely to be the most effective in generating this perceptual difference. Interestingly, this analysis bears a similarity to the psychoanalytic view of the emergence of secondary thought processes. The inability of the id to achieve its purpose in the world creates ego mechanisms. Thus, wishing for something to eat causes lawful planning in the world only to the degree that the environment is in some conflict with the id's desires. However, there is not much empirical support for this social interaction as the mechanism of the emergence of a self-representation. In fact, there is no empirical evidence for it at all. We have found that the attachment relationship between mother and child is unrelated to the emergence of self-representation (Lewis, Brooks-Gunn, & Jaskir, 1985; see also Schneider-Rosen & Cicchetti, 1984; Tajima, 1982). Given that there appears to be a developmental onset, no infant shows self-representation before 15 months, given that a mental age of 15 to 18 months is necessary for its display (see Lewis & Brooks-Gunn, 1979a), and given that it is absent or delayed in children with autism (Carmody & Lewis, in press), it is likely that developing biological processes play an important role in the development of self-representation. Finally, given that monkeys cannot, but the great apes and humans can (possibly also dolphins), suggests a phylogenetic and an ontogenetic pattern. These findings provide strong support for the idea that brain development may strongly associated with the onset of an objective self or of a mental representation of the self. But to be clear, brain development itself is not a split-off feature of an encapsulated brain; the brain develops epigenetically through complex relational bidirectional interactions with other bodily processes and environmental contexts.

This idea of the significance of brain development is further supported by the findings that specific brain region activation is associated with self-representational behaviors. The left superior temporal gyrus and the left medial frontal gyrus are activated when subjects engage in a theory-of-mind task relative to reading sentences (Fletcher et al., 1995; Gallagher et al., 2000; Mitchell, Heatherton, & Macrae, 2002). Activation of the left superior temporal cortex (Brodmann area 22), the left inferior parietal cortex, and the left and right occipital cortexes (BA 18) occurs when subjects judge whether adjectives are relevant to themselves (Fossati et al., 2003; Macrae, Moran, Heatherton, Banfield, & Kelley, 2004). In a study of brain activation to hearing one's own name, Carmody and Lewis (2006) found activation in the middle and superior temporal cortex and the left middle frontal cortex. In general, there is agreement that self-representational behaviors activate regions near the temporoparietal junction, although there are data suggesting activation of the medial frontal cortex as well (Fletcher et al., 1995; Kampe, Frith, & Frith, 2003).

To measure brain activation developmentally as a function of the capacity to show self-representation, one would need to study the relation between the emergence of this representational ability and changes in brain function. Obtaining functional magnetic resonance imaging (fMRI) or positron emission tomography (PET) scans in very young children has been shown to be difficult (Souweidane et al., 1999), and there are few, if any, published fMRI studies of children between 15 and 30 months of age, which is the critical age range for the development of self-representational behaviors (Saxe, Carey, & Kanwisher, 2004). Paus (2005) has suggested that the mapping of brain development and its relation to social cognition should be undertaken.

One way to study brain development is to use magnetic resonance imaging (MRI) to measure the relative amounts of gray and white matter in different cortical brain regions (Toga, Thompson, & Sowell, 2006). MR images show a gray–white matter contrast in a sequence that reflects the time course of brain development (Barkovich, 2000, 2005; Paus et al., 2001), and changes in MRI features are informative in determining the developmental changes in white and gray matter for normal and clinical cases (Barkovich, 2002). Different MRI techniques are available to assess brain development and involve either qualitative judgments or quantitative measures. The qualitative judgments have been used to describe the general developmental changes during infancy and early childhood in regional brain development and in gray–white differentiation shown on T1 and T2 images (Barkovich, Kjos, Jackson, & Norman, 1988; Bird et al., 1989; Dietrich et al., 1988; Holland, Haas, Norman, Brant-Zawadzki, & Newton, 1986; Konishi et al., 1993; Martin et al., 1988; McArdle et al., 1987). Although the qualitative descriptions help characterize brain development, computational analysis of MR images allows the detection of individual changes in white matter that signal the biological underpinnings of development of motor, sensory, cognitive, and perhaps social changes. To that end, quantitative measures may prove more valuable than the qualitative judgments of change.

Quantitative measures include volumetric analyses of gray and white matter (Giedd et al., 1999; Thompson et al., 2007), development of white matter relative to gray matter (Carmody, Dunn, Boddie-Willis, DeMarco, & Lewis, 2004), and the more recent diffusion tensor imaging (DTI) techniques to assess white matter integrity (Anjari et al., 2007; Dubois, Hertz-Pannier, Dehaene-Lambertz, Cointepas, & Le Bihan, 2006; Hermoye et al., 2006; Mukherjee et al., 2001). DTI provides data on the anatomy and the density of white matter fibers and development (Dubois et al., 2006; Hermoye et al., 2006), as well as providing images of the cortical association tracts (Mori et al., 2002).

As indicated in a review of MRI studies of brain development, a majority of MRI studies provided qualitative descriptions of images with a focus on gray–white matter contrast and estimates of the degree of development (Paus et al., 2001). In many pediatric studies, MRI examinations are obtained for clinical reasons, and the subjects are screened for MR abnormalities, leaving normal subjects for analyses. We are interested in using the standard clinical MRI scans to assess brain development in both clinical and nonclinical groups. Quantitative scores based on the difference between white matter and gray matter were obtained using quantitative assessments of T2-weighted MR images for specific brain regions, which generate age changes in white matter development (Barkovich, 2002; Carmody et al., 2004; Dietrich et al., 1988; McArdle et al., 1987). Given this technique, it is possible to measure individual differences in development by region and relate these individual regional differences in development to individual differences in children's self-representation.

To study this problem, we studied 15 infants from 15 to 30 months of age and related their development of particular brain regions to their scores on a self-referential scale made up of mirror self-recognition, personal pronouns, and pretend play (Lewis & Carmody, 2008). Figure 18.1 shows the correlations between specific brain regions and scores on the self-representation scale.

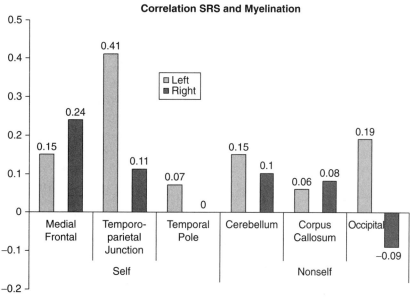

Figure 18.1   Relation between brain development and self-representational behavior. *Solid bars* represent left; *dotted bars* represent right hemispheres.

The findings from this study indicate that the degree of brain development in a specific region, independent of age, is related to the emergence of children's self-representation. This held for the self-representation score, as well as the three components that make up the score. It is the degree of development in the left temporoparietal junction that is most related to self-representational behavior. This is consistent with other findings that implicate the temporoparietal junction in its role in self-representational behavior (Samson, Apperly, Chiavarino, & Humphreys, 2004; Saxe et al., 2004; Saxe & Kanwisher, 2003). This brain region, as well as regions located nearby, have been found to be activated during several types of self-representational behaviors, such as when subjects engage in a theory-of-mind task relative to reading sentences (Fletcher et al., 1995; Gallagher et al., 2000; Mitchell, Heatherton, & Macrae, 2002), when subjects judge whether adjectives are relevant to themselves (Fossati et al., 2003; Macrae et al., 2004), and when subjects hear their own name (Carmody & Lewis, 2006).

Studies have found evidence for both left- and right-hemisphere involvement in self-representation; the left hemisphere showing greater activation on tasks involving self-representation, whereas the right hemisphere showing activation in tasks involving self in comparison with others. For example, Ruby and Decety (2001), using PET, reported left parietal activation when subjects mentally simulated an action with a first-person perspective and right parietal activation when subjects simulated an action with a third-person perspective (i.e., imagining the action of the other). In addition, Turk et al. (2002) found in a study of face recognition in a split-brain patient that the left hemisphere in comparison with the right hemisphere showed more activation to self than to a familiar face, whereas the right hemisphere showed more activation to familiar faces of others than to the self. Interestingly, similar findings of brain activation are found in adults when drawing a picture of themselves and another they know (Carmody & Lewis, 2006).

WHAT A SELF IS AND HOW I KNOW I KNOW

As I sit here in my study looking out at the garden, the late-afternoon sun blinds my sight. The taste of my coffee in my mouth lingers as I think about the paper I am writing. I have no trouble recognizing myself. I know where I am and why I am here. I feel my arm and hand move as I write. When I answer my wife's calls, my voice sounds like me. Sitting here, I can think about myself. I can wonder whether I will go to New York tonight. I wonder about my appearance. Do I need to wear a tie and jacket? Is my hair combed properly? As I get up to leave the room, I pass a mirror; there I see myself, the reflected surface of my being. "Yes, that is me," I say, fixing my hair.

I know a great deal about me. One of the things I know is how I look; for example, there is a scar in my left eyebrow. I look familiar to myself, even though I have changed considerably with age. Pictures taken of me 30 years ago look like me. Nevertheless, I know when I look at myself in the mirror I will not look as I did then; my hair and beard are now white, not the brown they were then. My face will be less smooth, and I will have to tuck in my belly to look like anything I wish to be. This self-deception I also know. It is complex knowledge. I know that if I stand a certain way I will look thinner, so I turn that way. I confirm that I am still thin but know I know that I am not. This ability to know and yet to be able to deceive myself clearly deserves a name—I call it objective self-awareness or consciousness.

I know many people might argue that the concept of self is merely an idea. I would agree, and argue that this idea of self is a particularly powerful one; it is an idea with which I cannot part. It is one around which a good portion of the network of many of my ideas center. This is not to say that what I know explicitly about myself is all I know. In fact, this idea of myself is only one part of myself; there are many other parts of which I do not know. These have been called implicit knowledge by some. They also go by the name of unconscious or bodily knowledge. There are the activities of my body—the joints and muscles moving, the blood surging, the action potentials of my muscle movements, as well as the calcium exchange along the axons. I have no knowledge of a large number of my motives—organized, coherent thoughts and ideas that have been called unconscious—that control large segments of my life. I have no explicit knowledge of how my thoughts occur. Nevertheless, I know that I do not know about how my thoughts occur. This part of me is explicit, it is my consciousness.

Although it might be true that I could explicitly know more of some parts of my implicit self if I chose to, it is nonetheless the case that what is known by my self-system is greater than what I can state I know. If such facts are true, then, it is fair to suggest a metaphor of myself. I imagine myself to be a biological system that is an evolutionarily fit complex of processes: doing, feeling, thinking, planning, and learning. One aspect of this system is explicit; it is the idea of me. This idea or mental state knows itself and knows it does not know all of itself! My self, then, is greater than the me, the explicit me being only a small portion of myself. The difference between myself and me also can be understood from an epistemological point of view. The idea that I know is not the same as the idea that I know I know. The explicit aspect of the self that I refer to is that which knows it knows.

In the adult, we can refer to the core processes of self as implicit consciousness, whereas the idea of me is explicit consciousness. From this perspective, we can say that, for the adult human, both spheres of consciousness are functional. The implicit sphere of the self is composed of the core processes of the body, or implicit consciousness; the other sphere is the idea of me, explicit consciousness, that represents an emergent transformation of these core processes. Implicit consciousness may develop, entail a form of memory, and operate even in sleep. Explicit consciousness, in contrast, is transient; that is, it can be functioning some of the time, or not functioning, much like Hilgard's (1977) idea of divided attention. From a developmental perspective, the core processes of self exist at birth, and the mental state of the idea of me emerges as a developmental transformation in the first 2 years of the child's life.

CONSCIOUSNESS: THE CORE PROCESSES OF SELF AND THE MENTAL STATE OF ME

To deal with the problem of how to understand the development of the mental state of the idea of me, we need to return to our discussion of intention and intentionality, in particular, to address the issue of the meaning of a behavior. It is a problem in development with a long history (Werner, 1948). The equivalence of a behavior across age is the problem. One can often observe that a very young infant can perform some action that, when performed at an older age, would be considered to represent some complex mental state. Take our studies of the 2-month-old pulling a string to turn on a picture. This pulling can imply some intention on the part of the infant and constitutes a challenge for our notion of development, of intentions, and the development of an intender. Another example is in newborn imitation. Imitation has been particularly of concern since Baldwin (1973) argued that true imitation heralds the child's understanding of himself.

However, the newborn infant can imitate certain body movements. For example, a tongue protrusion by an adult will produce a tongue protrusion in the infant (Meltzoff & Moore, 1977). Other forms of imitative behavior have been reported (Field, Woodson, Greenberg, & Cohen, 1982). Although there may be some question as to the reliability of this behavior (Anisfeld et al., 2001), such actions have been called imitation. Imitation has a particular meaning, usually implying some intention on the part of the imitator (Piaget, 1954). The finding that matching behavior exists in the newborn constitutes a challenge for developmental theory. We could claim that intentional behavior exists in the newborn, and therefore, that imitation takes place. However, this is a nativistic explanation, implying that there is no development in the process of intention or in imitation.

Alternatively, the same behavior can be said to have different meanings. We can say that the behavior at Time 1 is called X, whereas at Time 2 it is called Y. This solution has the effect of saying that Y, the more mature behavior, does not exist until Time 2. Thus, for example, imitation in the newborn can be called a *matching behavior*, whereas in the 18-month-old, it can be called *imitation* (Jacobson, 1979). It is much like stage theory, because X at Time 1 is not Y, nor is it Y-like.

Another way of handling this problem of the meaning of behavior is to consider that X and Y are functionally similar, but that they represent different developmental levels of the same meaning. In this case, X and Y could be called the same behavior, but it would be acknowledged that X represents a lower level of the behavior than Y. In the imitation example, we may call both behaviors "imitation," but we recognize that newborn "imitation" is an earlier level of imitation than is 18-month-old "imitation." This position requires us to consider that a particular ability may have multiple levels. These levels are ordered and emergent, and may be controlled by different processes. Moreover, the level of the ability may be found as both a phylogenetic and an ontogenetic function. From a phylogenetic perspective, a nonhuman animal (e.g., a rat) may imitate, but this imitation is controlled by different processes than that of a 1-year-old child. Likewise, from an ontogenetic perspective, a newborn human may imitate, but this imitation is controlled by implicit consciousness, whereas the imitation of a 2-year-old is explicit. Whether the levels found phylogenetically match those found ontogenetically is unknown, although there is every reason to assume that they might.

The problem of equivalence is especially relevant to the understanding of self and consciousness. In my theory of the development of explicit consciousness, we see that the same behavior at two ages may be a function of different processes, one having to do with the core processes of the self, which will become part of implicit consciousness, and the other the mental state of the idea of me, which will become explicit consciousness. For me, implicit consciousness of the core processes of self precedes the idea of me or explicit consciousness, with each dependent on different processes and different brain structures.

Two early features of the self that can be relegated to the core processes of the system are well-known and have been given considerable attention: These are self-other differentiation and the conservation of self across time and place (Rochat & Striano, 2002). By 3 months, and most likely from birth, the infant can differentiate itself from other. Self-other differentiation also has associated with it a type of recognition. This type of recognition—the self-other differentiation—is part of the core processes of any living complex system. This differentiation does not contain, nor is it analogous to, explicit consciousness. For example, T cells can recognize and differentiate themselves from foreign protein. The rat does not run into a wall but knows to run around it. The newborn infant recognizes intersensory information. These examples indicate that both simple and complex organisms possess the ability to differentiate self from other. We should not expect this aspect of self to be a differentiating feature when we compare widely different organisms because all organisms have this capacity. The single T cell must organize the information needed to distinguish self from other in a less complex manner than the multicell creature having a central nervous system. Nevertheless, in both cases, self-other differentiation exists for the organism to survive. This is built into the biological core processes and is not predicated on any mental state or explicit consciousness.

Another aspect of the core processes of the system has to do with the idea of conservation of the self across time and place. What formal aspects imply conservation? It could entail responding the same way to similar occurrences, or it could mean adapting to them, as in habituation. The ability to maintain conservation appears in all creatures. For example, the ability to reach for an object requires some implicit consciousness, as it requires one to act as if there is something other than the self in space–time. This relation to the other in space–time has consistency. Habituation, if used as a measure of conservation, also suggests its general appearance. Very simple organisms are able to habituate to redundant information. This suggests that in almost all organisms, from one-cell organisms on, biological core processes exist that are capable of maintaining information and utilizing that information in making a response. There is also self-conservation in the process we call identity: "This is me regardless of how I look." This type of conservation, unlike the former, requires explicit consciousness, or the mental state(s) that involves the idea of me.

These two features—self-other and self-conservation—appear relatively early in the child's life. They are based on the biological embodied core processes of the self and are a part of implicit consciousness; they are simple aspects of the functioning of a complex process. All complex creatures, by definition, contain many parts. These parts must be in communication with one another; that is a feature of the very definition of a system (Overton, 1975; Von Bertalanffy, 1967). Moreover, for the parts to work, they need to be interacting or coacting with each other and with the environment; this is again a feature of the very definition of a system. To be in interaction with the environment, they need to be able to differentiate self from other. The processes that allow this to occur are multidetermined but do not require explicit consciousness.

The ontogenetic and phylogenetic coherences found to date support the idea that to understand the concept of self, we need to disentangle the common term, *self*, into at least these two aspects: the core processes of the self that is a part of implicit consciousness; and explicit consciousness, or the mental state of the idea of me. They have been referred to by other terms, for example, as *objective self-awareness*, which reflects the idea of "me," and *subjective self-awareness*, which reflects the core processes of self (Lewis, 1990a, 1991, 1992a). The same objective-subjective distinctions have been considered by Duval and Wicklund (1972). In any consideration of the concept of self, especially in regard to adult humans, it is important to keep in mind that both aspects exist. There is, unbeknownst to us most of the time, an elaborate complex of core processes that controls much of our behavior, learns from experience, has states and affects, and effects our bodies, most likely including what and how we think. The implicit processes are, for the most part, unavailable to us. What is available is explicit consciousness.

Both the core processes of the self, as part of implicit consciousness, and explicit consciousness, or the mental state involving the idea of me, appear to be the consequences of different biological processes and perhaps different brain structures. LeDoux's work (1990) suggests that specific brain regions may be implicated in different kinds of self-processes. LeDoux's findings indicate that the production of a fear state can be mediated by subcortical regions, the thalamic-amygdala sensory pathways. Similar findings have been reported in humans, which suggests that implicit emotional states can exist without one part of the self explicitly experiencing them (Bechara et al., 1995). Weiskrantz (1986), among others, has reported on a phenomena called *blindsightedness*. Patients have been found who lack the visual cortex, at least in one hemisphere. When they were asked if they could see an object placed in their blind spot, they report that they cannot see it—that is, they do not have the experience of the visual event. They have no explicit consciousness. When they are asked to reach for it, they show that they can reach for it. Thus, they can see the event, implicit consciousness, but cannot experience their sight, explicit consciousness. These findings, as well as Gazzaniga's work (1988) on split-brain patients, suggest that separate brain regions are associated with the production and maintenance of both the implicit and the explicit consciousness.

A similar analysis involving memory has been suggested by Tulving (1985). Karmeloff-Smith (1986), from a developmental-cognitive perspective, has also taken up this type of distinction, arguing as we do that early in the developmental process, knowledge is part of the system and, therefore, implicit, whereas later knowledge became explicit (see also Dienes & Perner, 1999). The difference between implicit and explicit consciousness is easily seen as we observe our emotional lives. I have tried, in the past, to distinguish between emotional states and experiences, and have argued that adults can have emotional states and yet may have no experience of them (Lewis, 1990b; Lewis & Michalson, 1983). Thus, if I say "I am happy," it can be assumed that I mean by the statement that I am in a state of happiness and I can experience that state. Emotional states, therefore, refer to implicit consciousness. Implicit consciousness can have goals, can learn and profit from experience, can control functions, and can react to events, including people. The experiences of our emotional states refer to explicit consciousness.

MEASUREMENT OF EXPLICIT CONSCIOUSNESS

Measurement follows from the constructs we make; therefore, if we are interested in the development of explicit consciousness, then we need to measure explicit rather than implicit consciousness. Because early imitation,

intersensory integration, and coordination between infant and mother all are likely to reflect the core processes of self as part of implicit consciousness, they are not adequate measures of explicit consciousness.

The study of the idea of me or explicit consciousness requires, for the most part, symbolic language capacity. If the emergence of this mental state occurs before 2 years of age, using language as a measure of this mental state is difficult. In an adult or older child, we can ask, "Who are you?" "Tell me something about yourself," or "Tell me something that you know that others don't know." Alternatively, following R. D. Laing (1970), we can see whether the child understands statements such as "I know, you know that I know where you put your teddy bear." As is readily understood, all of these questions imply some idea about me or explicit consciousness since the recursive knowledge about what others know about what you know explicitly implies a self referent.

Without language, however, the child cannot through language explain this idea to us. One alternative is to require, without using language, that the child do certain tasks and see whether he or she can do them. If the child understands the task given, it is possible to demonstrate that the child has the idea, even though he does not have language. Thus, for example, in the work on deception (Lewis, Stanger, & Sullivan, 1989) and in the research on theories of mind, Wellman (1990) and others (Moses & Chandler, 1992) have been able to show that the child can intentionally deceive and also place herself in the role of another. In each of these types of studies, there is an implicit theory of mind that includes the mental state or explicit consciousness (see Carpendale & Lewis; Chandler, this volume for extended discussions of theory of mind).

Unfortunately, even these studies require that children understand complex language although they do not have to produce it. Thus, for example, in the deception studies, children have to understand the experimenters' instructions and, therefore, cannot be much younger than 3 years. By this age, it seems clear that children have explicit consciousness. The question, then, is whether explicit consciousness emerges earlier, and if so, how might it be measured. We could still focus on language and argue that explicit consciousness can be measured by whether children have acquired their names; after all, we are what we are called. The risk of accepting this as proof is that the child may have been taught to use its name by associating it with a visual array, a photograph of itself, without explicit consciousness being present (see Putnam, 1981, for a discussion of this type of problem).

Another language measure, a bit less suspect, is that of personal pronoun usage. Because parents do not use the label "me" or "mine" when referring to the child or teaching him to recognize pictures of himself, the use of these terms by the child is likely to be a reasonable measure of explicit consciousness. This appears even more the case when we observe children's use of the terms and how they behave when using them. One can observe a child saying "mine" as he or she pulls the object away from another child and toward himself or herself. Because moving the object toward oneself does not move the object as far away from the other as possible, the placement of the object next to the body, together with the use of the term "me" or "mine," appears to reference explicit consciousness. Children begin to use personal pronouns including "me" and "mine" by the latter part of the second year of life, which can provide a linguistic demonstration of the emerging mental state (Harter, 1983; Hobson, 1990).

Another procedure that can be used to measure explicit consciousness is self-recognition. We have studied self-recognition in infants and young children in detail (Lewis, 2003; Lewis & Brooks-Gunn, 1979c; Lewis & Ramsay, 2004). The procedure is simple. Unknown to the child, her nose is marked with rouge and then the child is placed in front of a mirror, where it is possible to observe whether the child, looking in the mirror, touches her marked nose or whether she touches the image in the mirror. The data from a variety of studies indicate that infants even as young as 2 months, when placed in front of mirrors, will show interest and respond to the mirror image. Children will smile, coo, and try to attract the attention of the child in the mirror, although they do not behave as if they recognize that it is they in the mirror. At older ages, when locomotion appears, on occasion, infants have been observed going behind the mirror to see whether they can find the child in the mirror. In addition, they often strike the mirror as if they are trying to touch the other. Somewhere around 15 to 18 months of age, they appear to know that the images are themselves, because they touch their noses or comment about their noses when looking in the mirror. The mental state of the idea of me or explicit consciousness is captured by the children's use of self-directed referential behaviors. The touching of their noses when they look in the mirror seems to reveal that they know that it is "me" there.

The ability to use the mirror to reference herself has been mistaken for the child's understanding of the reflective property of mirrors. There is ample evidence that although children are able to produce self-referential behavior through the use of the mirror-mark technique, they do not know many of the properties of reflected surfaces; for example, they cannot use the mirror to find an object reflected in its surface (Butterworth, 1990). What is important about the self-referential behaviors in the mirror is that they need not be a marker of general knowledge about reflected surfaces, but rather a marker for the child's knowledge about himself. They are the equivalent of the phrase "that's me." This recognition, if put into words, says, "That is me over there; this is me here."

Measuring other aspects of explicit consciousness is possible, pretend play in particular. From a variety of theoretical perspectives (Huttenlocher & Higgins, 1978; Leslie, 1987; McCune-Nicolich, 1981; Piaget, 1962), it is apparent that pretense is an early manifestation of the ability to understand mental states including one's own and others'. Pretense involves double knowledge or dual representation of the literal and pretend situation. The dissociable relation between the two allows the child to distinguish between appearance and reality. Research by Piaget (1962) and subsequent investigators (Fein, 1975; Lowe, 1975; McCune, 1995; Nicolich, 1977) indicates that pretense emerges in children by the middle to latter part of the second year of life. The capacity for pretense not only marks explicit consciousness but also the beginning of a theory of mind, the process that leads to the 3- to 4-year switch when children know that what they know is not necessarily what another knows (Flavell, 1988; Perner, 1991; Rosen, Schwebel, & Singer, 1997; Wellman, 1990; Wimmer & Perner, 1983). The mental state of me seen in pretense distinguishes children's early explicit consciousness from abilities likely to reflect implicit rather than explicit consciousness seen earlier in development such as joint attention, social referencing, and preverbal communication abilities (Bretherton, 1991; Carpenter, Nagel, & Tomasello, 1999).

There have been studies that have examined the relation between verbal measures of self-recognition (including the use of the personal pronoun "me" and one's name) and the mark-directed behavior (Bertenthal & Fischer, 1978; Lewis & Ramsay, 2004; Pipp, Fischer, & Jennings, 1987). These studies have generally found that verbal measures appear after the mark-directed behavior (Harter, 1983). It also is apparent that self-awareness and pretense emerge at approximately the same point in development (see Lewis & Ramsay, 2004) because it is necessary for pretend play. A mental state of the idea of me (or explicit consciousness) is taken for granted in Leslie's (1987) model on the relation between pretend play and theory of mind. That pretend play emerges as soon as the onset of self-recognition would support the belief that both reflect the emergence of explicit consciousness, as well as a source for a theory of mind.

Lewis and Ramsay (2004) have studied the relation among these three measures of explicit consciousness. There appears to be a relatively strong association among them, supporting our belief that they can be used to measure the onset of explicit consciousness. Moreover, there is a developmental sequence in the acquisition of these behaviors in the following order: self-recognition, personal pronoun use, and pretend play. Self-recognition by itself or together with personal pronoun use and/or pretend play was most likely to emerge first in development.

Self-recognition, personal pronoun use, and pretend play all indicate explicit consciousness. It is apparent that, with development, self-representation increasingly becomes a more complex and multifaceted phenomenon that progressively includes other cognitive and evaluative aspects of self-knowledge (Lewis & Brooks-Gunn, 1979b, 1979c). Nonetheless, the results suggest that in terms of emergent time, self-recognition is earliest in the formation of a complex self-representation. Of the three self abilities assessed, self-recognition was the one most likely to emerge first in development, suggesting that physical self-recognition may provide the core aspect of self-representation that continues to develop beyond the second year of life.

Consistent with the present findings is work that indicates children's emerging understanding of a theory of mind by the middle of the second year of life. Meltzoff (1995) reports that 18-month-old toddlers have the ability to understand the intentions of others. After observing adult models demonstrate the intention to act in a certain way by starting, but not completing, a given activity, the toddlers, when given the opportunity, performed the complete acts the adult intended. Similarly, Asendorph and colleagues (Asendorph & Baudonniere, 1993; Asendorph, Warkentin, & Baudonniere, 1996) found increases in imitative play linked to the presence of self-recognition in 20-month-old infants. Indeed, many studies link self-recognition to other abilities that mark more broadly the emergence of self-representation. For example, self-recognition is related to children's self-conscious emotions, in particular, embarrassment (Lewis, Sullivan, Stanger, & Weiss, 1989) and empathy (Bischof-Kohler, 1994), as well as altruism (Zahn-Waxler, Radke-Yarrow, Wagner, & Chapman, 1992). Self-recognition is related to autobiographical memories (Harley & Reese, 1999) and is associated with imitation (Asendorpf, 2002). Other measures of self-representation are possible. Pretense is an early manifestation of the ability to understand mental states, including one's own (Leslie, 2002; Piaget, 1951/1962), as well as understanding

a negation by the self that "this is what I pretend it to be" rather than what it actually is. A third measure of self representation is the use of personal pronouns, including "me" and "mine" (Stipek, Gralinski, & Kopp, 1990).

The degree of correspondence between self-recognition, pretend play, language self-referents, and object permanence suggests the emergence of explicit consciousness (measured in a multitude of ways) and with it the organizing role of self-knowledge in cognitive development (Lewis, 1992b; Lewis & Brooks-Gunn, 1979c; Lewis & Carmody, 2008; Lewis & Michalson, 1983; Lewis & Ramsay, 2004; Mounoud & Vinter, 1981).

ROLE OF EXPLICIT CONSCIOUSNESS IN DEVELOPMENT

The problem in studying development or, for that matter, adult behavior is that our studies usually divide the organism's cognitive, social, and emotional life into separate, discrete domains. Lost in this epistemological division is the relational idea of the organism itself. In terms of infants and young children, different studies provide information, but with little attempt at unifying these separate domains. Thus, although we shall separate out the role of explicit consciousness in cognitive, social, and emotional development, it should be understood that these domains are connected with each other through the child's developing mental state of herself (see McClelland, Ponitz, Messersmith, & Tominey; Santostefano; Turiel, this volume, for extended discussions of the relational perspective on the unity of cognitive, social, and emotional spheres of development). The organization of development follows from the assumption that social, emotional, and cognitive knowledge are features of the same unified relational development system that is fundamental to the individual's explicit consciousness. Individuals develop social, emotional, and cognitive knowledge in relational bidirectional interactions with each other. Moreover, development is understood as a gradual differentiation among the various domains (Werner, 1948). The change from a unified system of knowledge based on the emergence of consciousness to one that is differentiated, integrated, and specialized occurs as a function of development (see Mascolo & Fischer, this volume, for an extended discussion of development as a process of differentiation). I see this system like a tree, the trunk representing the unified and integrated system generated by consciousness, whereas the branches represent the separate areas of knowledge, some of which are

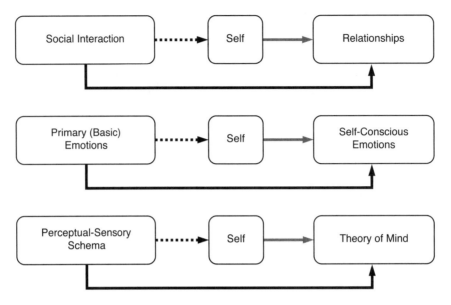

Figure 18.2   Role of the self in development.

interrelated, whereas others are independent. This model allows for both the integration of knowledge from a developmental perspective and the functional independence of the end product. Thus, as a central premise, the development of explicit consciousness provides the scaffolding for the development, integration, and separation of the various other behaviors of the child.

Figure 18.2 presents in schematic form the proposed relations. As can be seen, each of the early classes of behavior is transformed by the emergence of explicit consciousness. Thus, perceptual-sensory become a theory of mind, social interactions become social relationships, and the early or basic emotions become the self-conscious emotions. Each is considered in the following section.

Social Cognition, Theory of Mind, and Explicit Consciousness

The work on social cognition predates and provides the logical basis for the newer work called "theory of mind" (see Chandler & Birch, Chapter 19 of this volume). We address both from the need to include explicit consciousness as the basis of their development. When we use the term *social cognition,* we imply that there is a role of the self in knowing. To the degree that the self as knower is part of the process of knowing that is the degree to which the cognition is social (Lewis, 1993, 1997). So, for example, I may know about a sunset over the Chianti hills of Tuscany

by watching it, or I may know of it by reading a guidebook. In both cases, I have knowledge, but in one, that knowledge is gained through the self's experience of the phenomenon, whereas in the other, it is through the self's knowledge of words.

Another example has to do with knowledge that involves the self. This is best captured by the sentence, "I know that you know that I know your name." Such sentences and their meaning cannot be independent of explicit consciousness because the self knows something about what another self knows about itself. The meaningfulness of such a sentence is dependent on the knowledge of myself and knowledge of another self's knowledge of myself. This aspect of explicit consciousness has been studied under the heading of a theory of mind, a topic that is considered later in this chapter.

As I have tried to show, the epistemological issue of the relation between the knower and the known has been widely recognized for more than a half century (Merleau-Ponty, 1964; Overton, 2006; Piaget, 1960; Polyani, 1958). Explicit consciousness involves the relational bidirectional interaction of the knower with objects, events, or people. Social cognition depends on just such a connection. Following the work of Mead (1934) and Cooley (1902), explicit knowledge of the self and knowledge of others are dependent on one another: "I cannot know another unless I have knowledge of myself." Furthermore, a child's knowledge of self and others is developed through interactions with these others, social interaction and consciousness being the basic unit out of which social cognition derives. Many who subscribe to a relational interactionist position agree that knowledge of others and the world in general is derived through relational interaction: "To understand that a person is…involves understanding what sorts of relations can exist between mere things and between people and things" (Hamlyn, 1974).

Because what a child knows of the other through relational bidirectional interactions—usually nonsocial "other," characterized by physical properties such as weight, length, etc.—has been the major focus of researchers, the fact that knowledge of other, gained through interaction, must provide information about oneself has been ignored. If I find one object hard and the other soft by holding them, then not only do I know something about objects, in this case, hardness, but I know something about myself, how hard the object feels to me. As Merleau-Ponty (1964) states, "If I am a consciousness turned toward things, I can meet in things the actions of another and find in them a meaning, because they are themes of possible activity for my own body" (p. 113).

A "theory of mind," like social cognition, involves explicit knowledge of one's own and others' mental states (Gallup, 1991; Leslie, 1987; Povinelli & Eddy, 1996; Premack & Woodruff, 1978). The origins of a theory of mind can be found in the early work of psychologists such as Shantz (1975), Youniss (1975), and Chandler (1978; Chandler & Birch, Chapter 19 of this volume). From the broad social cognition perspective, children's perspective-taking or role-taking abilities, their abilities to "put themselves in the place of the other," or their "theory of mind" has been examined in various situations including those that assess children's capacity for the expression of empathy. It has long been recognized that taking the point of view of another presupposes explicit knowledge of one's own self (Leslie, 1987; McCune, 1995).

With this in mind, especially given our work on the development of explicit consciousness, let me suggest a brief outline in the development of a theory of mind. There are at least three or four aspects to its development: (1) I know; (2) I know I know; (3) I know you know; and (4) I know you know I know.

Level 1 is called *knowing* (or I know). This level prevails from birth until the middle of the second year of life and is likely to be driven by basic processes common to other animals. It is based on implicit consciousness and involves little or no language; it is not supported by the mental state of the idea of me or explicit consciousness. Many organisms can share in this kind of knowledge. For example, when an object in the visual field rapidly expands, infants, as well as adults and animals, show surprise and discomfort. This response is simply built into the core features of perceptual-motor knowledge. Likewise, a rat running toward a wall perceptually knows it is a wall and does not run into it. In the last 30 years there has been an expanded test of infant competencies that reflect such a knowledge level. Infants' competencies however, are not the same as understanding, and the distinction between competence and understanding is necessary in order not to confuse the level of knowledge.

Level 2 is *I know I know*. This level involves explicit consciousness and self-referential behavior. It is based on the mental state of me, and allows for the capacity to reflect on one's self and to reflect on what one knows. This mental state is a metarepresentation. It is similar to a memory of a memory. Whereas a child at the first level may have a memory, it is at the second level that metamemory is possible. Here the child remembers that he or she remembers. As we have seen, this capacity emerges somewhere in the middle of the second year of life (Lewis, 1990a, 1990b).

Level 3 is *I know you know*. This form of knowing takes into account the mental state that not only do I know something, but I believe others know it as well; it is the ability and basis of shared meaning. This representation, that you know what I know, does not need to be accurate. Adults know more than children know; thus, the child may not really know what the adult knows. The child is likely to make errors, something called egocentric errors. That is, she assumes that what she know is what the other knows. At this level, children know, they know they know, and they also know you know. What they cannot yet do is place themselves in opposition to what they know. This level, in combination with the earlier ones, accounts in part for the early ability to deceive. A 2½-year-old child who deceives knows that he knows and he knows that you know; thus, deception is possible. It is also the reason why children are likely to make the traditional false belief error.

Before going on to the fourth level, it is worth mentioning that the third level may not be distinct from the one before it in which children know they know. It is possible that the mental state of the idea of me and what I know may emerge at the same time as the mental state of what I know about what others know. In other words, it is not possible that what I know about me is not part of what I know about the other. If this, indeed, is the case, then a separate level might not be called for.

Level 4 is the adult-like level. It addresses the interactive and recursive nature of cognition. It is characterized as *I know you know I know* or recursive knowledge. At this level, not only are there two actors, as at level 3, but each actor has a perspective. These perspectives can be different. It is when there are two perspectives that one has the ability to recognize false belief. Only when one has reached the level of knowing that "they know I know" can one's knowledge about what they know be corrected, because you can check their knowledge of what they know about you against what you know. That is, once a child knows that she can be the subject and also the object of the knowledge of another, she is capable of recognizing the difference in perspectives between individuals. It is at this final level of perspective taking that mature meta-knowledge can emerge.

As these levels of knowing are reached and mastered, there is at the same time an increase in general cognitive competence, in particular, language usage. Language ability is laid down on the general cognitive scaffolding that allows the language to reflect increasingly the available cognitive ability. Our problem in studying children's early development is that language ability may not precede this general cognitive capacity but may follow it. Thus, children's observed social behavior and cognition may reflect a level higher than their verbal capacities.

Social Relationships and Explicit Consciousness

When I think about relationships, by definition, they involve me; and when I think about relationships, one of the things that I may think about is what the other thinks of me. Recursive knowledge can become quite complex, as, for example, when I think of what others think that I think of them. In his discussion of interpersonal relationships, Asch (1952) makes a similar point: "The paramount fact about human interactions is that they are happenings that are psychologically represented in each of the participants. In our relationship to an object, perceiving, thinking, and feeling take place on one side, whereas in relations between persons, these processes take place on both sides and are dependent upon one another" (p. 212).

Knowledge about self and other, whether they occur sequentially or at the same time, eventually become a part of the duality of knowledge. For example, Bannister and Agnew (1977) note, "The ways in which we elaborate our construing of self must be essentially those ways in which we elaborate our construing of others. For we have not a concept of self, but a bipolar construct of self-not self,

or self-other" (p. 101). The definition of social knowledge involves the relation between the knower and the known, rather than characteristics of people as objects. By utilizing the self in knowing, we can differentiate when we are treating people as objects from when we are treating them as people. If the self is not involved, then the people are being treated as objects; when the self is involved, people are being treated as people.

Relational Interactions and Relationships

The developmental issue in social relationships is quite complex, especially given the wide acceptance of attachment theory and the argument that children form relationships with their mothers, at least by one year of age. Some have argued that this occurs even earlier, perhaps by three months. If, however, we believe that social relationships require explicit consciousness, then children cannot form relationships that early, although adults do. We would do well to consider Hinde's (1976, 1979) discussion of the nature of relationships. He has argued for eight dimensions that can be used to characterize relationships. The first six describe what can be considered to be interactions while the last two characterize relationships. These six are (1) goal structures, (2) diversity of interactions, (3) degree of reciprocity, (4) meshing of interactions, (5) frequency, and (6) patterning and multidimensional qualities of interactions. These six features describe interaction that are likely supported by the core processes of the system or implicit consciousness, at least on the part of the infant. Interactions, however, are not relationships. This is often misunderstood and, again, has to do with the difference between competency and understanding, this time in the social realm. Infants can engage in interactions, as can their mothers, and it is the infants' core processes that allow for this. While mothers can form relationships with their infants because they possesses consciousness, infants can not. Thus, the nature of the infant–mother relationship is complex and one-sided, as it is the mother but not the child who possesses Hinde's last two features. Relationships require explicit consciousness of both parties. In this regard, Hinde's two additional features are relevant. These two features include: (7) cognitive factors, or those mental processes that allow members of an interaction to think of the other member as well as of themselves; and (8) something that Hinde (1979) calls penetration, which I would interpret as something having to do with ego boundaries, which also has to do with the explicit consciousness of the two participants.

If bidirectional interactions alone (features 1–6) are insufficient to describe a higher level human relationship, then a rather asymmetrical pattern exists between the infant and his mother. This pattern is likely to be supported by the core processes of the self in the case of the infant and by explicit consciousness in the case of the mother. Because of this, it needs to be distinguished from adult relationships because two sets of explicit consciousnesses are needed (Lewis, 1987). Such a view was suggested by Sullivan (1953) who argued that a relationship is by necessity the negotiation of at least two selves. Higher level abilities are vital for a relationship because without two selves (one has only an I-it, not an I-thou), there can be no relationship (Buber, 1958). Emde (1988) makes reference to the "we" feature of relationships, and in support of the timetable of consciousness (self-awareness) points to the second half of the second year of life for its appearance.

Our model of mature human relationships requires that we consider different levels in the development of a relationship over time, rather than seeing it exist in the adult form from the first. Uniquely mature human relationships may arise from interactions only after the development of explicit consciousness and the ability to represent self and other on the part of the child. From this point of view, the achievement of adult human relationships for the child has a developmental progression. This progression involves first, bidirectional interactions built into core processes which may be similar to those shown by all social creatures, and second, cognitive structures or mental states, in particular, explicit consciousness, and with it such skills as empathy and the ability to place the self in the role of other (Lewis, 1987). The relationships of one-year-olds do not contain these cognitive structures and, therefore, may not be that of adults. By two years, most children have explicit consciousness and the beginning of such skills as empathy (Borke, 1971; Zahn-Waxler & Radke-Yarrow, 1981). Their behavior toward others now approximate more closely those of the adult level. Mahler's concept of individuation is relevant here, for as she has pointed out, only when the child is able to individuate can it be said that the mature level of relationship exists (Mahler, Pine, & Bergman, 1975).

Such an analysis raises the question of the nature of the child's relationships before the emergence of explicit consciousness. For me, relationships not built on mental states are complex social species-patterned processes, which through adaptive processes, may be a fundamental feature of the social organisms. It is not unlike the action of one bird's flying off a fence, which sets off the other birds' flight. Some social interactions are related to complex core processes which influence other's core processes (Waldrop, 1992). In humans, the best example of this is when the yawning of one person sets off yawning in another.

The nature of higher level relationships is dependent on many factors. These include core processes, the nature of socialization practices, mental states related to the idea of me or explicit consciousness, and the cognitions about the interactions of self and other; that is, the meaning given to them by the selves involved (Bowlby, 1980).

Main and colleagues (Main, Kaplan, & Cassidy, 1985) and Bretherton (1987) consider a more cognitive view of attachment, as suggested by Bowlby (1980), that of a "working model." By a working model, these authors suggest a schema concerning the mother as a secure base. By focusing attention on the child's cognitive construction rather than on just the interactive patterns of the dyad, the theory of attachment and relationships moves toward a greater realization that an attachment relationship involves the self and the mental states involved in self and other. Leaving aside the question of at what ages this occurs, we find Bowlby (1973) stating, "The model of the attachment figure and the *model of the self* are likely to develop so as to be complementary and mutually nonconforming. Thus, an unwanted child is likely not only to feel unwanted by his parents, but to believe that he is essentially unwanted" (*emphasis added*, p. 208).

Such a view of relationships is much more similar to the one that we posit but assumes incorrectly a more adult-like form in early infancy. The level of representation of relationship, including the self, is far different from relationships formed by simple interactions. Notice that in Bowlby's quote, children believe that they—their selves—are unwanted. Such a representation must involve a child capable of the mental state of the idea of me or explicit consciousness.

As soon as we come to consider relationships in terms of mental states or representations, we need to return to the child's capacity for explicit consciousness. This, we believe, occurs after the first year of life, somewhere toward the middle of the second year. If this is so, then our observation of the attachment relationship at one year reflects: (1) the relational bidirectional interactions based on socialization patterns that the child will subsequently use to form a working model of the relationship; and (2) the adult caregiver's relationship, which includes the adult's explicit consciousness, as well as the working model of the parents attachment relationship with their parents.

Emotions and Explicit Consciousness

I have spent considerable time researching and writing about the relation between emotion and consciousness and my recent book, *Consciousness and the Development of Emotional Life* (in press) deals with this relationship in some detail. Here, briefly, I will summarize this association, leaving many of the details to be read elsewhere. I have proposed a model of emotional development where core processes, here referred to as primary emotions (early action patterns such as joy, sadness, fear, and anger), are altered by the development of explicit consciousness, giving rise to the self-conscious emotions such as embarrassment, pride, guilt, and shame. In particular, explicit consciousness creates two sets of self-conscious emotions, those I refer to as self-conscious exposed emotions and self-conscious evaluative emotions (Lewis, 1992a, 2002). All of these self-conscious emotions require explicit consciousness, although, as in the case of the evaluative self-conscious emotions, more is required.

Although the emotions that appear early—such as joy, sadness, fear, and anger—have received considerable attention, the set of later-appearing emotions that I wish to consider has received relatively little attention. There are likely to be many reasons for this; one reason is that these self-conscious emotions cannot be described solely by examining a particular set of facial movements, necessitating the observation of bodily action, as well as facial cues. A second reason for the neglect of study of these later emotions is the realization that there are no clear specific elicitors of these particular emotions. Although happiness can be elicited by seeing a significant other, and fear can be elicited by the approach of a stranger, few specific situations will elicit shame, pride, guilt, or embarrassment. These self-conscious emotions are likely to require classes of events that only can be identified by the individuals in relation to themselves.

The elicitation of self-conscious emotions involves elaborate cognitive processes that have, at their heart, mental states about the self or explicit consciousness. Although some theories, such as psychoanalysis (Erikson, 1950; Freud, 1963; Tomkins, 1963), have argued for some universal elicitors of self-conscious emotions, such as failure at toilet training or exposure of the backside, the idea of an automatic noncognitive elicitor of these emotions does not make much sense. Cognitive processes must be the elicitors of these complex emotions (Lewis, 1992b; see also Darwin, 1872/1969). It is the way we think or what we think about that becomes the elicitor of these emotions.

There may be a one-to-one correspondence between thinking certain thoughts and the occurrence of a particular emotion; however, in the case of this class of emotions, the elicitor is a cognitive event. This does not mean that the earlier emotions, those called primary or basic, are elicited by noncognitive events. Cognitive factors may play a role in the elicitation of any emotion; however, the nature of cognitive events are much less articulated and differentiated in the earlier ones (Plutchik, 1980).

The need for cognitive elicitors having to do with the self was known to Darwin (1872/1969). He suggested that these emotions were a consequence of our thoughts about other's thoughts of us, there being, therefore, no clear or universal elicitors. Darwin saw these latter emotions as involving the self, although he was not able to distinguish among the various types (see also Tomkins, 1963, and Izard, 1977, for similar problems). His observation in regard to blushing indicates his concern with the issue of appearance and the issue of explicit consciousness. He repeatedly makes the point that these emotions depend on sensitivity to the opinion of others, whether good or bad.

We have attempted to clarify those specific aspects of self that are involved in self-conscious emotions. First, let us consider self-conscious exposed emotions. The self-conscious exposed emotions have been differentiated from the self-conscious evaluative emotions because the latter require fairly elaborate socialized cognitions around standards, rules, and goals, and around attributions relevant to the self (Lewis, 1992a; Lewis & Michalson, 1983). The exposed emotions consist, at least, of embarrassment, empathy, and jealousy. Although some work has been done observing empathy (Bischof-Kohler, 1991), most of the work has been conducted on embarrassment (Lewis, 1995). I have tried to distinguish between two different types of embarrassment—one related to exposure and one related to evaluation, which has much in common with shame.

Exposure embarrassment emerges once self-recognition (explicit consciousness) can be shown, around 15 to 24 months of age, whereas evaluative embarrassment does not emerge until 2½ years. An example of exposure embarrassment is the embarrassment that occurs when one is complimented. Praise rather than a negative evaluation is the source of this type of embarrassment. Another example of this type of embarrassment can be seen in our reactions to public display. When people observe someone looking at them, they are apt to become self-conscious, look away, and touch or adjust their bodies. In few cases do the observed people look sad. If anything, they appear pleased by the attention.

This combination—gaze turned away briefly, no frown, and nervous touching—is exposure embarrassment.

Another example of embarrassment as exposure can be seen in the following example. When I wish to demonstrate that embarrassment can be elicited just by exposure, I announce that I am going to point randomly to a student. I repeatedly mention that my pointing is random and that it does not reflect a judgment about the person. I close my eyes and point. My pointing invariably elicits embarrassment in the student pointed to. When we experimentally point to a child and call his or her name, it invariably leads to exposure embarrassment. In a series of studies, we have demonstrated the effectiveness of complimenting, pointing to the child, and asking him or her to perform (e.g., dance to music) in front of us as three different elicitors of exposure embarrassment (Lewis et al., 1989; Lewis, Stanger, Sullivan, & Barone, 1991).

The relation between self-recognition measuring explicit consciousness and exposure embarrassment has been explored (Lewis et al., 1989), and the findings are quite clear. Exposure embarrassment is seen once the child shows self-recognition. However, the earlier emotions, such as wariness or fearfulness, are unaffected by the child's emerging explicit consciousness (Lewis et al., 1989). Thus, whereas the emotions such as joy, sadness, fearfulness, disgust, anger, and interest all emerge before self-recognition and explicit consciousness, the exposed self-conscious emotions require its emergence. Looking at another nonevaluative self-conscious emotion, empathy, finds a similar result (Bischof-Kohler, 1991). This should not be surprising given that adult empathic responses require that one be able to place oneself in the role of the other, an ability that obviously requires explicit consciousness.

Self-conscious evaluative emotions not only require explicit consciousness but also an elaborate set of other cognitive capacities. Because of this, these emotions do not emerge until 2½ to 3 years of age (Lewis, 1992a). They all require explicit consciousness, because they require knowledge about standards, rules, or goals. These standards are inventions of the culture that are transmitted to the child and involve the child's learning of and willingness to consider them as their own. This process of incorporating the standards has been discussed by Stipek, Recchia, and McClintic (1992). What is apparent from this work is that learning starts quite early in life. Standards, rules, and goals imply self-evaluation, and therefore explicit consciousness, for it would make little sense if we had standards but no evaluation of our action vis-à-vis them.

Having self-evaluative capacity allows for two distinct outcomes: we can evaluate our behavior and hold ourselves responsible for the action that is being evaluated, or we can hold ourselves not responsible. In the attribution literature, this distinction has been called either an internal or an external attribution (Weiner, 1986). If we conclude that we are not responsible, then evaluation of our behavior ceases. However, if we evaluate ourselves as responsible, then we can evaluate our behavior as successful or unsuccessful vis-à-vis the standard. Finally, global self-attributions refer to the whole self, whereas specific self-attributions refer to specific features or actions of the self (Dweck & Leggett, 1988; Weiner, 1986). These are sometimes referred to as *performance versus task orientation* (Dweck, 1996). In every one of these processes, the mental state of the idea of me needs to be considered.

The terms *global* and *specific* are used to specify the tendency of individuals to make specific evaluations about themselves (Beck, 1967, 1979; Seligman, 1975). Global evaluations about themselves refers to an individual's focus on the total self and on his or her performance. Thus, for any particular behavior violation, an individual can focus on the totality of the self and then use such self-evaluative phrases as, "Because I did this, I am bad [or good]." Janoff-Bulman's (1979) distinction is particularly relevant here. In global attributions, the focus is on the self and performance. The self becomes embroiled in the self. The focus is not on the self's behavior as in task focus, but on the self. There is little wonder that in using such global attribution one can think of nothing else, and one becomes confused and speechless (H. B. Lewis, 1971). We turn to focus on ourselves, not on our actions. Because of this, we are unable to act and are driven from the field of action into hiding or disappearing.

Specific, in contrast, refers to the individual's propensity to focus on specific actions of the self and on the task. It is not the total self that has done something wrong or good, it is specific behaviors in context that are judged. Individuals use such evaluative phrases as, "My behavior was wrong, I mustn't do it again." Notice that the individual's focus is on the task in a specific context, not on the totality of the self. These cognitions, which focus on the self, create the self-conscious evaluative emotions. Our research indicates that these emotions do not emerge until after the onset of explicit consciousness, in the middle of the second year of life, and not until the child is capable of the complex cognitions associated with standards. By 2½ to 3 years, these cognitive capacities are present and so is the emergence of these self-conscious evaluative emotions (Lewis, 1992a).

We can see, therefore, that the role of explicit consciousness in both classes of emotion is quite elaborate, involving the following factors: (1) explicit consciousness; (2) knowledge of standards, rules, and goals; (3) evaluation of one's behavior vis-à-vis the standards; (4) distribution of the blame to oneself or to others; and (5) attribution focus, either global or performance focus or specific and task focus. In each one of these processes, mental structures around the idea of me, therefore, rest on the emergence of explicit consciousness.

SOME WORDS ON THE IMPLICIT-EXPLICIT PREDICAMENT

This chapter has used a variety of terms, including the idea of me, mental structures, metarepresentations, and explicit consciousness, in talking about issues of epistemology and the development of emotions, cognitions, and social behavior. It is clear that although explicit consciousness is needed, it often seems that much of what we do, think, and feel seems automatic, that is, with the minimum of attention directed at ourselves. Indeed, this provides the basis in adults to posit implicit consciousness. It also seems that when too much attention is paid to the self, too much explicit consciousness, psychopathology is often the consequence (Wegner, 2009). Thus, explicit consciousness, although necessary, also is potentially disruptive. Moreover, explicit consciousness can become implicit consciousness. So, for example, we know that early learning of complex motor acts (like skiing) requires explicit consciousness, but that by becoming well-learned, the acts become implicit. Likewise, it is possible that implicit consciousness can become explicit. In this regard, it appears that Eastern traditions, such as Yoga, urge us to get in touch with processes usually not open to explicit consciousness. Thus, it may be possible to make explicit, implicit consciousness.

From a developmental perspective, we have argued that the core processes of the system are the first example of implicit consciousness and are part of the primitives that infants are born with. In the middle of the second year of life explicit consciousness emerges and provides the scaffolding for all other development. Thus, the human child, by the middle of the second year, has both implicit and explicit consciousness. After the development of explicit consciousness, the young child as the adult can move between implicit and explicit consciousness, although much of implicit consciousness in the core processes of the system is not open to explicit consciousness. For example, I

may never know directly what my amygdala knows. To address this problem in the adult, we need to consider that adults have the capacity to direct their attention inward toward themselves or outward toward the world. Even without directing their attention inward toward themselves (e.g., their actions and emotional states), they are capable of performing highly complex and demanding tasks. In fact, the example of solving complex mental problems without focusing on them explicitly is well-known. Solutions to mental problems often "come to us" as if someone inside our heads has been working on it while we go about attending to other problems.

The term *consciousness* is used in talking about attention directed inward toward the self, as well as outward to the world. To understand this, we may wish to consider Hilgard (1977) and, before him, Janet (1929), who talked about divided consciousness, whereas others have talked about subconsciousness or unconsciousness and consciousness (Freud, 1960). Modularity of brain function has demonstrated that areas of the brain are quite capable of conducting complex tasks or learning complex problems without other areas having explicit knowledge of them (Bechara et al., 1995; Gazzaniga, 1985; LeDoux, 1990). It has been demonstrated that both perceptual processes and complex learning can take place in the amygdala and hippocampus without cortical involvement or without explicit knowledge of that learning.

Such findings lend support to the idea of modularity of brain function—that is, for the involvement of some brain areas without the involvement of others—as well as the idea that complex operations can take place without the subject's own knowledge or self-attention (what we call *explicit consciousness*) of these operations, although they could. These new findings of brain function fit with our own well-known experiences of sudden insight or spontaneous solution to complex mental problems, as well as a set of common phenomena that require intrapsychic differentiation and even conflict. Some of these well-known phenomena are hypnotism, perceptual defenses, self-deception, active forgetting, loss of will or acrasia, and multiple personalities. These processes, although receiving some attention, have not been given the study they need. Hilgard (1977), for one, has called the underlying processes involved in each of them *disassociation*, a term once in favor but now not used. This is because Freud (1960) argued for an active process of repression rather than splitting off of consciousness, a concept more favored by Charcot (1889) and Janet (1929). Each of these phenomena appears to rest on a process involving the idea of divided consciousness, or as we now call it, *implicit and explicit consciousness*, which may be supported by the modularity of brain functions.

The ability to reflect and direct attention both toward ourselves (explicit) and toward the outer world is an adaptive strategy. The adaptive significance of divided consciousness is that it allows us to check on our own internal responses in addition to our behavior in the world and quite separately to act in the world. It is obvious from observations of animals, or even cells, that it is possible to behave in a highly complex fashion in the world as a function of internally generated plans and programs. This action-in-the-world does not require that we reflect on or pay attention by thinking about our actions. Thus, when I want to cross a busy street, it is probably adaptive not to be thinking about how well I am doing, but rather coordinating action in context. In contrast, if I have almost had an accident, then thinking about myself and my fear at being almost hit allows me to modify my plans for the future. Both directions of consciousness are important.

From a developmental perspective, this distinction may mean that initially attention focused outward is reflected by the core processes of the self, processes that are likely to be a fundamental feature of the nervous system. It is only after development of mental states, in particular, the mental state about the idea of me, that the human child becomes capable of looking inward, that is, to have explicit consciousness. Thus, for the adult human, divided attention is the consequence of the development of explicit consciousness in addition to the given primitives or core processes of the self. While considering these two types of consciousness is useful, it also leads to confusion. Perhaps it might be better to consider that implicit consciousness is not consciousness at all, rather it is the core processes as given to begin with and then made more complex as a consequence of learning. Explicit consciousness is the only consciousness we have. For example, Mihaly has discussed the idea of flow. In flow, the core processes do their work and there is no consciousness at all. When we are deeply involved in a task, we forget where we are, what time it is, etc. We have no awareness of ourselves. In such a state of flow there is no consciousness, just the core processes doing their job, a job our consciousness has set up but then does not participate in. In some metaphorical sense, then, there is only the humming of the machine, the core processes learned and unlearned carrying out the task. Consciousness, what we have been calling explicit consciousness or the mental state of or idea of me, is all that there is. The metaphor is of a biological

adaptive process carrying out much of life's work. My consciousness serves as a director of the tasks as well as the processor of failure, interruption, or completion of a task (Mandler, 1975).

LIFE SPAN OF CONSCIOUSNESS

This essay has been about the origins of consciousness. I have tried to locate the beginnings of the mental state of the idea of me, calling it variously objective self-awareness, the idea of me, and explicit consciousness. I have also tried to consider what I have called subjective self-awareness, core processes of the self, and implicit consciousness. The argument is that subjective, core processes, and implicit consciousness exist as a given within the human child, and that the later explicit consciousness develops but does not replace the former; thus, the 3-year-old, as the adult human, possesses both. Although some, notably Freud, saw them as competing entities and tried to understand their development as competing forces, others, for example, Hilgard (1977) thought of them as more like a divided attention and less as competing entities. The competition, as I see it, is that some of the self is not available to other aspects of the self; this is based on the nature of our brains and its modularity.

However, we might ultimately conceptualize this development. I for one see explicit consciousness as closely associated with development of specific regions of the brain; it does not exist at birth but requires the first three years of the child's life to develop. This consciousness can be considered similar to Piaget's idea of object permanence; that is, it is a quality of the person—its existence. The content of explicit consciousness is a function of the child's embedment into its family, friends, community, and culture. The features of the person, including sex identity and age, are some of the early emerging and presumably universal features (Lewis, 1980). Others include agency, the ability to achieve a goal, the nature of her relationships to her mother, father, siblings, and others. It also includes her relationship to herself, in particular, whether she is morally good.

These features develop, and they develop within a child who knows he exists and whose fundamental task is to maintain his identity. Because we have selves and minds that conceive of ourselves, it may be difficult to show that earlier events have an impact on subsequent events. The self and its construction of reality interrupt the chain of events between past and present.

We give meaning to our behavior, both in the past and in the present. The task of the self is to construct a narrative that allows us to explain events that are occurring now. This explanation may require that we reconstruct our past to make it fit with what it is we are now, a point made by Kierkegaard in his description of existential contingency. Developmental processes serve the pragmatic function of allowing us to adapt to the present, so we might say that the end point of development is the need for meaning now. Moreover, because we are constructing organisms, we are capable of having an enduring idea about ourselves, and we have a need to find meaning that will preserve that idea.

The preservation of our identities is necessary for our adaptation. How could we exist in the world if we did not know who we are? The stories we create about our lives, our narratives, allow us to reconstruct our histories to fit with what we are now or want to be in the future, and thus preserve our identity.

Our idea of a good story, whether it be of our own life or of some other person, is one which the pieces fit together, they touch, and one event flows into another. So we create our histories, even as historians do, by tying the actual discontinuities together to make them match our perception of human lives as continuous and directional. These life narratives also fit with our notion of causality, in that events that happen earlier affect events that happen later. Our personal life narratives must explain how we got from one point to another, so they are likely designed to eliminate discontinuities. Our narratives are, by their nature, attempts at continuity because it is our nature, at least in this age, to think of ourselves as a unity even though we may contain conflicting parts. No matter how difficult these parts may be to reconcile, in the picture we paint of ourselves, all the disparate parts somehow get together and form a single me, a personality we can understand. We need to maintain our identity, and our narratives serve that need by showing how we are the same or, if we are different, how that difference came about.

Of course, it does not have to be this way. We do not have to construct a narrative that has continuity as one of its chief features. We could live with the idea that what we are now bears only a slight resemblance to what we were. This shift in perspective about ourselves would have great impact on our notions of causality and on our notion of self. It would violate our belief that we have a history whose parts fit a linear progression.

In what way can we truly view ourselves as being the same people we were at age three anyway? We do not look, act, think, or feel like those people. It is our memory that helps us identify ourselves in those earlier individuals. How can we do this? Following Nozick, perhaps we can understand this problem if we use a rowboat rather than a person as an example. Imagine we have a rowboat built of wood and each year we replace one board of the rowboat with a new board. At the end of 50 years, none of the original boards of the rowboat remains, and yet at no point in this sequence of events have we said that this is not "the same rowboat," nor, for that matter, would we think that there was not a continuous change in this boat. But if we had replaced all of the boards of the rowboat at once, we would say that "this is not the same rowboat" and that the change was not continuous. When the parts of the rowboat were slowly replaced with new ones, what we call *gradualism*, we were willing to assume a continuous process of change, a change that did not alter the identity of the rowboat (Lewis, 1997). However, when we change the boards too quickly, we see that identity cannot be maintained, nor can continuity. In like fashion, people are willing to assume that the changes that occur over their seventy years are continuous and, therefore, do not alter their identity.

In this regard, it is interesting to note that if change occurs too quickly, that is, there are too many events in a unit of time, then we are likely to experience discontinuity. Here I am reminded of at least two periods in the life cycle when this is likely to occur, adolescence and middle age, when there are many changes in a relatively short time. In adolescence, the physical body changes rather quickly, and emotional, psychological, and brain events also appear to undergo rapid alterations. The same is true in middle age, when physical abilities begin to change, and our body shape again changes. At such a point, one of the most noticeable characteristics is the loss of identity. That is, when the changes occur very quickly, as in the rowboat, that ability to maintain identity becomes difficult. Both adolescence and middle age are characterized by rather large and sudden changes; therefore, they are associated with problems in personal identity.

Because of the pragmatics of current adaptation, people's histories are rewritten as often as necessary to maintain the idea of themselves in time. They are rewritten to give meaning to the things around them. Rather than accept the passive developmental models, which have forces acting on people through either the biology within them or the social control from without, we need a model of development that focuses on the meaning for the individual in interaction with its world, social and physical. Meaning for individuals not only speaks to how they reconstruct the past but also addresses how they are to understand how the past may or may not influence the future. Thinking, planning, active minds are capable of having desires, of creating goals, and of making plans to reach those goals. Those goals obviously undergo change. The degree to which they change is the degree to which people's behavior in the present will be altered to reach those goals. People are capable of altering the course and trajectory of their lives on the basis of the goals they seek to achieve, rather than on the events that occurred in the past. Indeed, people alter past events to provide a better opportunity for achieving their future goals.

The task of maintaining our identity is necessitated by having consciousness and the idea of me. The core processes that govern much of our lives do not have this problem. It is only our consciousness that makes this requirement. For me, consciousness and identity is one of the most important psychological functions in human lives; it affects what we remember about our pasts, and how we plan for the future (Lewis, 1997). It affects how we behave to others and, therefore, how they behave toward us, which in turn defines us (Lewis & Rosenblum, 1974). As has been said, our consciousness allows us to see in the others our own actions and allows us as well to understand that what we know of ourselves we know of others. Equally important are the social connections produced by our cognitions of I know, you know, I know. Thus, consciousness, once it emerges in the early years of life, continues to exert its influence across the life span, allowing us to be us, and allowing us to influence and be influenced by our world in ways that the core processes cannot do. It is what really distinguishes us from other living biological organisms. Parenthetically, it is also the idea of ourselves as "not being" (i.e., our death), that drives us toward maintaining our identity and the construction of complex ideas of religion and life after death where we continue to be us.

REFERENCES

Anisfield, M., Turkewitz, G., Rose, S. A., Rosenberg, F. R., Sheiber, F. J., Couturier-Fagan, D. A., et al. (2001). No compelling evidence that newborns imitate oral gestures. *Infancy, 2,* 111–122.

Anjari, M., Srinivasan, L., Allsop, J. M., Hajnal, J. V., Rutherford, M. A., Edwards, A. D., et al. (2007). Diffusion tensor imaging with tract-based spatial statistics reveals local white matter abnormalities in preterm infants. *Neuroimage, 35*(3), 1021–1027.

Arnold, M. B. (1960). *Emotion and personality* (Vols. 1 and 2). New York: Columbia University Press.

Arnold, M. B. (1970). Brain function in emotion: A phenomenological analysis. In P. Black (Ed.), *Physiological correlates of emotion* (pp. 261–286). New York: Academic.

Asch, S. E. (1952). *Social psychology.* Englewood Cliff, NJ.: Prentice-Hall.

Asendorpf, J. B. (2002). Self-awareness, and secondary representation. In A. N. Meltzoff & W. Prinz (Eds.), *The imitative mind: Development, evolution, and brain bases. Cambridge studies in cognitive perceptual development* (pp. 63–73). New York: Cambridge University Press.

Asendorph, J. B., & Baudonniere, P. M. (1993). Self-awareness and other-awareness: Mirror self-recognition and synchronic imitation among unfamiliar peers. *Developmental Psychology, 29*(1), 88–95.

Asendorph, J. B., Warkentin, V., & Baudonniere, P. M. (1996). Self-awareness and other-awareness II: Mirror self-recognition, social contingency awareness, and synchronic imitation. *Developmental Psychology, 32*(2), 313–321.

Baldwin, J. M. (1903). *Mental development in the child and the race* (2nd ed.). New York: Macmillan. (Original work published 1894)

Baldwin, J. M. (1973). *Social and ethical interpretations in mental development.* New York: Arno. (Original work published 1899)

Bannister, D., & Agnew, J. (1977). The child's construing of self. In J. Cole (Ed.), *Nebraska symposium on motivation* (Vol. 25). Lincoln, NE: University of Nebraska Press.

Barkovich, A. J. (2000). Concepts of myelin and myelination in neuroradiology. *American Journal of Neuroradiology, 21*(6), 1099–1109.

Barkovich, A. J. (2002). Magnetic resonance imaging: Role in the understanding of cerebral malformations. *Brain Development, 24*(1), 2–12.

Barkovich, A. J. (2005). Magnetic resonance techniques in the assessment of myelin and myelination. *Journal of Inherited Metabolic Disease, 28*(3), 311–343.

Barkovich, A. J., Kjos, B. O., Jackson, D. E., Jr., & Norman, D. (1988). Normal maturation of the neonatal and infant brain: MR imaging at 1.5 T. *Radiology, 166,* 173–180.

Bechara, A., Tranel, D., Damasio, H., Adolphs, R., Rockland, C., & Damasio, A. R. (1995). Double dissociation of condition and declarative knowledge relative to the amygdala and hippocampus in humans. *Science, 269,* 1115–1118.

Beck, A. T. (1967). *Depression: Clinical, experimental, and theoretical aspects.* New York: Harper & Row.

Beck, A. T. (1979). *Cognitive therapy and emotional disorders.* New York: Times Mirror.

Berlyne, D. E. (1960). *Conflict, arousal and curiosity.* New York: McGraw-Hill.

Bertenthal, B. L., & Fischer, K. W. (1978). Development of self-recognition in the infant. *Developmental Psychology, 14,* 44–50.

Bird, C. R., Hedberg, M., Drayer, B. P., Keller, P. J., Flom, R. A., & Hodak, J. A. (1989). MR assessment of myelination in infants and children: Usefulness of marker sites. *American Journal of Neuroradiology, 10*(4), 731–740.

Bischof-Kohler, A. (1991). The development of empathy in infants. In M. E. Lamb & H. Keller (Eds.), *Development: Perspectives from German-speaking countries* (pp. 245–273). Hillsdale, NJ: Erlbaum.

Bischof-Kohler, D. (1994). Self-objectification and other-oriented emotions: Self-recognition, empathy, and prosocial behavior in the second year. *Zeitschrift fur Psychologie, 202,* 349–377.

Borke, H. (1971). Interpersonal perception of young children: Egocentrism or empathy. *Developmental Psychology, 5,* 263–269.

Bowlby, J. (1973). *Attachment and loss: Vol. 2. Separation: Anxiety and anger.* London: Hogarth Press.

Bowlby, J. (1980). *Attachment and loss: Vol. 3. Loss, sadness, and depression.* New York: Basic Books.

Bretherton, I. (1987). New perspectives on attachment relations: Security, communication, and internal working models. In J. D. Osofsky (Ed.), *Handbook of infant development* (2nd ed., pp. 1061–1100). New York: John Wiley & Sons.

Bretherton, I. (1991). *Intentional communication and the development of an understanding of mind.* Hillsdale, NJ: Erlbaum.

Brooks-Gunn, J., & Lewis, M. (1979). "Why mama and papa?" The development of social labels. *Child Development, 50,* 1203–1206.

Bruner, J. S., & Tagiuri, R. (1954). The perception of people. In G. Lindzey (Ed.) *Handbook of social psychology* (Vol. 2). Cambridge, MA: Addison-Wesley.

Buber, M. (1958). *I & thou* (2nd ed.) (R. G. Smith, Trans.). New York: Scribner.

Buffery, A. W. H., & Gray, J. A. (1972). Sex differences in the development of spatial and linguistic skills. In C. Ounsted & D. C. Taylor (Eds.), *Gender differences: Their ontogeny and significance* (pp. 123–157). Baltimore, MD: Williams & Wilkins.

Butterworth, G. (1990). Origins of self-perception in infancy. In D. Cicchetti & M. Beeghly (Eds.) *The self in transition: Infancy to childhood* (pp. 119–137). Chicago: University of Chicago Press.

Butterworth, G. (1992). Origins of self-perception in infancy. *Psychological Inquiry, 3,* 103–111.

Carmody, D. P., Dunn, S. M., Boddie-Willis, A. S., DeMarco, J. K., & Lewis, M. (2004). A quantitative measure of myelination development in infants, using MR images. *Neuroradiology, 46,* 781–786.

Carmody, D. P., & Lewis, M. (2006). Brain activation when hearing one's own and others' names. *Brain Research, 1116,* 153–158.

Carmody, D. P., & Lewis, M. (in press). Self representation in Autism. *Journal of Autism and Developmental Disorders.*

Carmody, D. P., & Lewis, M. (in press). Regional white matter development in children with Austim spectrum disorders. *Developmental Psychobiology.*

Carpenter, M., Nagel, K., & Tomasello, M. (1999). Social cognition, joint attention, and communicate competence from 9 to 15 months of age. *Monographs of the Society for Research in Child Development, 63,* 1–212.

Chandler, M. J. (1978) Social cognition: A selected review of current research. In W. Overton & J. Gallagher (Eds.), *Knowledge and development: Yearbook of development epistemology.* New York: Plenum.

Charcot, J. M. (1889). *Clinical lectures on diseases on nervous system.* London: New Sydenham Society.

Clark, R. W. (1972). *Einstein: The life and times.* New York: Avon.

Cooley, C. H. (1902). *Human nature and social order.* New York: Scribner's.

Cooley, C. H. (1962). *Social organization: A study of the larger mind.* New York: Schocken. (Original work published in 1909)

Csikszentmihaly, M. (1991) *Flow: The Psychology of Optimal Experience.* New York: Harper Collins.

D'Andrade, R. (1981). The cultural part of cognition. *Cognitive Science, 5,* 179–195.

Damasio, A. (2003). *Looking for Spinoza: Joy, sorrow, and the feeling brain.* London: Heinemann.

Darwin, C. (1965/1969). *The expression of the emotions in man and animals.* Chicago: University of Illinois Press. (Original work published 1872)

Dennett, D. C. (1987). *The intentional stance.* Cambridge, MA: MIT Press/Bradford.

Dennett, D. C. (2009). Darwin and the evolution of "why" (Abstract). Darwin Festival, Cambridge.

Dienes, Z., & Perner, J. (1999). A theory of implicit and explicit knowledge. *Behavioral and Brain Sciences, 22,* 735–808.

Dietrich, R. B., Bradley, W. G., Zaragoza, E. J. T., Otto, R. J., Taira, R. K., Wilson, G. H., et al. (1988). MR evaluation of early myelination patterns in normal and developmentally delayed infants. *American Journal of Roentgenology, 150*(4), 889–896.

Dubois, J., Hertz-Pannier, L., Dehaene-Lambertz, G., Cointepas, Y., & Le Bihan, D. (2006). Assessment of the early organization and maturation of infants' cerebral white matter fiber bundles: A feasibility study using quantitative diffusion tensor imagining and tractography. *Neuroimage, 30*(4), 1121–1132.

Dunn, J. (1988). *The beginnings of social understanding.* Cambridge, MA: Harvard University Press.

Durant, W. (1954). *The story of philosophy.* New York: Pocket Books.

Duval, S., & Wicklund, R. A. (1972). *A theory of objective self-awareness.* San Diego, CA: Academic Press.

Dweck, C. S. (1996). Social motivation: Goals and social-cognitive processes. In J. Juvonen & K. R. Wentzel (Eds.), *Social motivation: Understanding children's school adjustment* (pp. 181–195). New York: Cambridge University Press.

Dweck, C. S., & Leggett, E. L. (1988). A social cognitive approach to motivation and personality. *Psychological Review, 95,* 256–273.

Edwards, C. P., & Lewis, M. (1979). Young children's concepts of social relations: Social functions and social objects. In M. Lewis & L. Rosenblum (Eds.), *The child and its family: The genesis of behavior* (Vol. 2). New York: Plenum.

Eiduson, B. T. (1962). *Scientists: Their psychological world.* New York: Basic Books.

Emde, R. N. (1988). Developmental terminable and interminable II: Recent psychoanalytical theory and therapeutic considerations. *International Journal of Psychoanalysis, 69,* 283–296.

Erikson, E. (1950). *Childhood and society.* New York: Norton.

Fagot, B. I. (1973). Sex-related stereotyping of toddlers' behaviors. *Developmental Psychology, 9,* 429.

Fairbairn, W. R. D. (1952). *Object-relations theory of the personality.* New York: Basic Books.

Fein, G. G. (1975). A transformational analysis of pretending. *Developmental Psychology, 11,* 291–296.

Field, T., Woodson, R., Greenberg, R., & Cohen, O. (1982). Discrimination and imitation of facial expression by neonates. *Science, 218,* 179–181.

Flavell, J. H. (1974). The genesis of our understanding of persons: Psychological studies. In T. Mischel (Ed.), *Understanding other persons.* Totowa, NJ: Rowman & Littlefield.

Flavell, J. H. (1988). The development of children's knowledge about the mind: From cognitive connections to mental representations. In J. W. Astington, P. L. Harris, & D. R. Olson (Eds.), *Developing theories of mind* (pp. 244–267). Cambridge: Cambridge University Press.

Fletcher, P. C., Happe, F., Frith, U., Baker, S. C., Dolan R. J., Frackowiak, R. S., et al. (1995). Other minds in the brain: A functional imaging study of "theory of mind" in story comprehension. *Cognition, 57*(2), 109–128.

Fodor, J. A. (1975). *The language of thought.* New York: Crowell.

Fodor, J. A. (1981). *Representations: Philosophical essays on the foundation of cognitive science.* Cambridge, MA: MIT Press.

Fossati, P., Hevenor, S. J., Graham, S. J., Grady, C., Keightley, M. L., Craik, F., et al. (2003). In search of the emotional self: An FMRI study using positive and negative emotional words. *Am J Psychiatry, 160*(11), 1938–1945.

Freud, S. (1960). *The psychopathology of everyday life.* (A. Tyson, Trans.) New York: Norton. (Original work published in 1901)

Freud, S. (1963). *The psychopathology of everyday life* (A. Tyson, Trans.). New York: Norton.

Gallagher, H. L., Happe, F., Brunswick, N., Fletcher, P. C., Frith, U., Frith, C. D. (2000). Reading the mind in cartoons and stories: An fMRI study of "theory of mind" in verbal and nonverbal tasks. *Neuropsycholgia, 38*(1), 11–21.

Gallup, G. G., Jr. (1991). Toward a comparative psychology of self-awareness: Species limitations and cognitive consequences. In G. R. Goethals & J. Strauss (Eds.), *The self: An interdisciplinary approach* (pp. 121–135). New York: Springer Verlag.

Gardner H. (1985). *The mind's new science.* New York: Basic.

Gazzaniga, M. S. (1985). *The social brain: Discovering the networks of the mind.* New York: Springer Verlag.

Gazzaniga, M. S. (1988). Brain modularity: Towards a philosophy of conscious experience. In A. J. Marcel & E. Bisiach (Eds.), *Consciousness in contemporary science.* New York: Oxford University Press.

Geertz, C. (1984). On the nature of anthropological understanding. In R. A. Shweder & R. A. Levine (Eds.), *Cultural theory: Essays on mind, self, and emotion.* Cambridge: Cambridge University Press.

Gibson, J. J. (1979). *The ecological approach to visual perception.* Boston: Houghton-Mifflin.

Giedd, J. N., Blumenthal, J., Jeffries, N. O., Castellanos, F. X., Liu, H., Zijdenbos, A., et al. (1999). Brain development during childhood and adolescence: A longitudinal MRI study. *Nature Neuroscience, 2*(10), 861–863.

Goldberg, S., & Lewis, M. (1969). Play behavior in the year-old infant: Early sex differences. *Child Development, 40,* 21–31.

Griffin, D. R. (1984). *Animal thinking.* Cambridge, MA: Harvard University Press.

Hamlyn, D.W. (1974). Person-perception and our understanding of others. In T. Mischel (Ed.), *Understanding other persons.* Totowa, NJ: Rowman & Littlefield.

Harding, V., Gray, J. E., McClure, B. A., Anderson, M. A., & Clarke, A. E. (1990). Self-incompatibility: A self recognition system in plants. *Science, 250,* 937–941.

Harley, K., & Reese, E. (1999). Origins of autobiographical memory. *Developmental Psychology, 35,* 1338–1348.

Harter, S. (1983). Developmental perspectives on the self-system. In E. M. Hetherington (Ed.), *Handbook of child psychology: Vol. 4. Socialization, personality and social development* (pp. 275–385). New York: John Wiley & Sons.

Hebb, D. O. (1946). On the nature of fear. *Psychological Review, 53,* 256–276.

Hebb, D. O. (1949). *The organization of behavior.* New York: John Wiley & Sons.

Heckhausen, H. (1984). Emergent achievement behavior: Some early developments. In J. Nicholls (Ed.), *The development of achievement motivation* (pp. 1–32). Greenwich, CT: JAI Press.

Heider, F. (1958). *The psychology of interpersonal relations.* New York: John Wiley & Sons.

Hermoye, L., Saint-Martin, C., Cosnard, G., Lee, S. K., Kim, J., Nassogne, M. C., et al. (2006). Pediatric diffusion tensor imaging: Normal database and observation of the white matter maturation in early childhood. *Neuroimage, 29*(2), 493–504.

Hilgard, E. R. (1977). *Divided consciousness: Multiple controls in human thought and action.* New York: John Wiley & Sons.

Hinde, R. N. (1976). Interactions, relationships and social structure. *Man, 11,* 1–17.

Hinde, R. N. (1979). *Towards understanding relationships.* London: Academic Press.

Hirsch, E. D. (1967). *Validity in interpretation.* New Haven, CT: Yale University Press.

Hobson, R. P. (1990). On the origins of self and the case of autism. *Development and Psychopathology, 2,* 163–181.

Holland, B. A., Haas, D. K., Norman, D., Brant-Zawadzki, M., & Newton, T. H. (1986). MRI of normal brain maturation. *American Journal of Neuroradiology, 7*(2), 201–208.

Hudson, L. (1972). *The cult of the fact.* London: Cape.

Huttenlocher, J. (1980). Personal Communication.

Huttenlocher, J., & Higgins, E. T. (1978). Issues in the study of symbolic development. In W. Collins (Ed.), *Minnesota symposia on child psychology* (Vol. 11, pp. 98–140). Hillsdale, NJ: Erlbaum.

Hyde T. S., & Jenkins, J. J. (1969). The differential effects of incidental tasks on the organization of recall a list of highly associated words. *Journal of Experimental Psychology, 82,* 472–481.

Isen, A. M. (2007). Some ways in which positive affect influences decision making and problem solving. In M. Lewis, J. M. Haviland-Jones, & L. F. Barrett (Eds.), *The Handbook of Emotions.* (3rd ed.) Guilford Press.

Izard, C. E. (1977). *Human emotions.* New York: Plenum Press.

Jacobson, S. W. (1979). Matching behavior in young infants. *Child Development, 50,* 425–430.

James, W. (1895) *The principles of psychology.* New York: Holt.

Janet, P. (1929). *Major symptoms of hysteria.* New York: Hafner.

Janoff-Bulman, R. (1979). Characterological versus behavioral self-blame: Inquiries into depression and rape. *Journal of Personality and Social Psychology, 37,* 1798–1809.

Jaynes, J. (1976). *The origins of consciousness in the breakdown of the bicameral mind.* Boston: Houghton Mifflin.

Kagan, J. (1974). Discrepancy, temperament, and infant distress. In M. Lewis & L. Rosenblum (Eds.), *The origins of fear* (pp. 229–248). New York: John Wiley & Sons.

Kampe, K. K., Frith, C. D., & Frith, U. (2003). "Hey John": Signals conveying communicative intention toward the self-activate brain regions associated with "metalizing," regardless of modality. *Journal of Neuroscience, 23*(12), 5258–5263.

Karmeloff-Smith, A. (1986). From meta-processes to conscious access: Evidence from children's metalinguistic and repair data. *Cognition, 23,* 95–147.

Kaye, K. (1982). *The mental and social life of babies.* Chicago: University of Chicago Press.

Kohlberg, L. (1969). Stage and sequence: The cognitive-developmental approach to socialization. In D. A. Goslin (Ed.), *Handbook of socialization theory and research.* Chicago: Rand McNally.

Kohut, H. (1971). *The analysis of the self.* New York: International Universities Press.

Konishi, Y., Hayakawa, K., Kuriyama, M., Fujii, Y., Sudo, M., Konishi, K., et al. (1993). Developmental features of the brain in preterm and fullterm infants on MR imaging. *Early Human Development, 34*(1–2), 155–162.

Kopp, C. B. (1982). Antecedent of self-regulation: A developmental perspective. *Developmental Psychology, 18,* 199–214.

Krauss, R. M., & Glucksberg, S. (1969). The development of communication: Competence as a function of age. *Child Development, 40,* 255–266.

Kuiper, N. A., & Rogers, T. B. (1979).Encoding of personal information: Self-other differences. *Journal of Personality and Social Psychology, 37*(4), 499–514.

Laing, R. D. (1970). *Knots.* New York: Pantheon.

LeDoux, J. (1990). Cognitive and emotional interactions in the brain. *Cognition and Emotions, 3*(4), 265–289.

Lerner, R. M. (2006). Developmental science, developmental systems, and contemporary theories of human development. In R. M. Lerner (Ed.), *Handbook of child psychology: Vol. 1. Theoretical models of human development* (6th ed., pp. 1–17). Editors in chief: W. Damon & R. M. Lerner. Hoboken, NJ: John Wiley & Sons.

Lerner, R. M., & Overton, W. F. (2008). Exemplifying the integrations of the relational developmental system: Synthesizing theory, research and application to promote positive development and social justice. *Journal of Adolescent Research, 23,* 245–255.

Leslie, A. M. (1987). Pretense and representation: The origin of "Theory of Mind." *Psychological Review, 94,* 412–426.

Leslie, A. M., & Keeble, S. (1987). Do six-month-old infants perceive causality? *Cognition, 24,* 265–274.

Leslie, M. (2002). Pretense and representation revisited. In N. L. Stein & P. J. Bauer (Eds.), *Representation, memory, and development: Essays in honor of Jean Mandler* (pp. 103–114). Mahwah, NJ: Erlbaum.

Lewis, H. B. (1971). *Shame and guilt in neurosis.* New York: International Universities Press.

Lewis, M. (1979). The self as a developmental concept. *Human Development, 22,* 416–419.

Lewis, M. (1980). Self-knowledge: A social-cognitive perspective on gender identity and sex role development. In M. E. Lamb & L. R. Sherrod (Eds.), *Infant social cognition: Empirical and theoretical considerations* (pp. 395–414). Hillsdale, NJ: Erlbaum.

Lewis, M. (1987). Social development in infancy and early childhood. In J. Osofsky (Ed.), *Handbook of infant development* (2nd ed., pp. 419–493). New York: John Wiley & Sons.

Lewis, M. (1990a). Social knowledge and social behavior. *Special Issue of Merrill-Palmer Quarterly, 36*(1), 93–116.

Lewis, M. (1990b). Thinking and feeling—the elephants tail. In C. A. Maher, M. Schwebel, & N. S. Fagley (Eds.), *Thinking and problem solving in the developmental process: International perspectives* (the WORK) (pp. 89–110). Hillsdale, NJ: Erlbaum.

Lewis, M. (1991). Ways of knowing: Objective self-awareness or consciousness. *Developmental Review, 11,* 231–243.

Lewis, M. (1992a). *Shame, The exposed self: Zero to three, 7*(4), 6–10.

Lewis, M. (1992b). *Shame, The exposed self.* New York: The Free Press.

Lewis, M. (1993). Commentary. (Raver, C. C., & Leadbeater, B. J., The problem of the other in research on theory of mind and social development. *Human Development, 36,* 350–362). *Human Development, 36,* 363–367.

Lewis, M. (1995). Embarrassment: The emotion of self exposure and evaluation. In J. P. Tangney & K. W. Fischer (Eds.), *Self-conscious emotions: The psychology of shame, guilt, embarrassment, and pride* (pp. 198–218). New York: Guilford Press.

Lewis, M. (1997). *Altering fate: Why the past does not predict the future.* New York: Guilford Press.

Lewis, M. (2000). The emergence of human emotions. In M. Lewis & J Haviland-Jones (Eds.), *Handbook of emotions* (2nd ed., pp. 265–280). New York: Guilford Press.

Lewis, M. (2001). The origins of self-conscious child. In R. Crozier & L. E. Alden (Eds.), *International handbook of social anxiety: Concepts, research, and interventions relating to the self and shyness* (pp. 101–118). Sussex, United Kingdom: John Wiley & Sons, Ltd.

Lewis, M. (2003). The development of self-consciousness. In J. Roessler & N. Eilan (Eds.), *Agency and self-awareness: Issues in philosophy and psychology* (pp. 275–295). New York: Oxford University Press.

Lewis, M., Allesandri, S., & Sullivan, M. W. (1990). Violation of expectancy, loss of control, and anger in young infants. *Developmental Psychology, 26*(5), 745–751.

Lewis, M., & Brooks-Gunn, J. (1979a). *Social cognition and the acquisition of self.* New York: Plenum.

Lewis, M., & Brooks-Gunn, J. (1979b). *The search for the origins of self: Implications for social behavior and intervention.* Paper presented at Symposium on the Ecology of Care and Education of Children under Three, Berlin, West Germany, February 23–26, 1977.

Lewis, M., & Brooks-Gunn, J. (1979c). Toward a theory of social cognition: The development of self. In I. Uzgiris (Ed.), *New directions in child development: Social interaction and communication during infancy* (pp. 1–20) San Francisco, CA: Jossey-Bass.

Lewis, M., Brooks-Gunn, J., & Jaskir, J. (1985). Individual differences in visual self recognition as a function of mother-infant attachment relationship. *Developmental Psychology, 21,* 1181–1187.

Lewis, M., & Carmody, D. (2008). Self-representation and brain development. *Developmental Psychology, 44*(5), 1329–1334.

Lewis, M., Edwards, C. P., Weistuch, L., & Cortelyou, S. (1981). *Age as a social cognition.* Unpublished manuscript.

Lewis, M., & Goldberg, S. (1969). Perceptual-cognitive development in infancy: A generalized expectancy model as a function of the mother-infant interaction. *Merrill-Palmer Quarterly, 15*(1), 81–100.

Lewis, M., & Michalson, L. (1983). *Children's emotions and moods: Developmental theory and measurement.* New York: Plenum.

Lewis, M., & Ramsay, D. (2004). Development of self-recognition, personal pronoun use, and pretend play during the 2nd year. *Child Development, 75*(6), 1821–1831.

Lewis, M., & Rosenblum, L. (Eds.). (1974). *The effect of the infant on its caregiver: The origins of behavior.* New York: John Wiley & Sons.

Lewis, M., Stanger, C., & Sullivan, M. W. (1989). Deception in three-year-olds. *Developmental Psychology, 25,* 439–443.

Lewis, M., Stanger, C., Sullivan, M. W., & Barone, P. (1991). Changes in embarrassment as a function of age, sex and situation. *British Journal of Developmental Psychology, 9,* 439–443.

Lewis, M., Sullivan, M. W., Stanger, C., & Weiss, M. (1989). Self-development and self-conscious emotions. *Child Development, 60,* 146–156.

Lewis, M., & Weinraub, M. (1976). The father's role in the infant's social network. In M. Lamb (Ed.), *The role of the father in child development* (Vol. 1). New York: John Wiley & Sons.

Lipsitt, L. (Ed.). (1976). *Developmental psychobiology: The significance of infancy.* Hillsdale, NJ: Earlbaum.

Lowe, M. (1975). Trends in the development of representational play in infants from one to three years—An observational study. *Journal of Child Psychology and Psychiatry, 16,* 33–47.

Luria, A. R. (1976). *Cognitive development: Its cultural and social foundations.* Cambridge, MA: Harvard University Press.

Macrae, C. N., Moran, J. M., Heatherton, T. F., Banfield, J. F., & Kelley, W. M. (2004). Medial prefrontal activity predicts memory for self. *Cerebral Cortex, 14*(6), 647–654.

Mahler, M. S. (1968). *On human symbiosis and the vicissitudes of individuation (Vol. 1). Infantile Psychosis.* New York: International Universities.

Mahler, M. S., Pine, F., & Bergman, A. (1975). *The psychological birth of the infant.* New York: Basic Books.

Main, M., Kaplan, N., & Cassidy, J. (1985). Security in infancy, childhood, and adulthood: A move to the level or representation. In I. Bretherton & W. Waters (Eds.), *Growing points of attachment theory and research. Monographs of the Society for Research in Child Development, 50,* (1–2, Serial No. 209), 66–104.

Mandler, G. (1975). *Mind and emotion.* New York: John Wiley & Sons.

Martin, E., Kikinis, R., Zuerrer, M., Boesch, C., Briner, J., Kewitz, G., et al. (1988). Developmental stages of human brain: An MR study. *Journal of Computer Assisted Tomography, 12*(6), 917–922.

McArdle, C. B., Richardson, C. J., Nicholas, D. A., Mirfakhraee, M., Hayden, C. K., & Amparo, E. G. (1987). Developmental features of the neonatal brain: MR imaging. Part I. Gray-white matter differentiation and myelination. *Radiology, 162,* 223–229.

McCune, L. (1995). A normative study of representation play at the transition to language. *Developmental Psychology, 31,* 198–206.

McCune-Nicolich, L. (1981). Toward symbolic functioning: Structure of early pretend games and potential parallels with language. *Child Development, 52*(3), 785–797.

Mead, G. H. (1934). *Mind, self, and society: From the standpoint of a social behaviorist.* Chicago: University of Chicago Press.

Meltzoff, A. N. (1995). Understanding the intentions of others: Re-enactment of intended acts by 18-month-old children. *Developmental Psychology, 31,* 838–850.

Meltzoff, A. N., & Moore, M. K. (1977). Imitation of facial and manual gestures by human neonates. *Science, 198,* 75–78.

Merleau-Ponty, M. (1964). *Primacy of perception* (J. Eddie, Ed.; W. Cobb, Trans.). Evanston, IL: Northwestern University Press.

Michotte, H. (1963). *The perception of causality.* London: Methuen.

Mischel, W. (1970). Sex-typing and socialization. In P. Mussen (Ed.), *Carmichael's manual of child psychology* (Vol. 2). New York: John Wiley & Sons.

Mitchell, J. P., Heatherton, T. F., & Macrae, C. N. (2002). Distinct neural systems subserve person and object knowledge. *Proceedings of the National Academy of Sciences of the USA, 99*(23), 15238–15243.

Money, J., & Ehrhardt, A. (1972). *Man and woman, boy and girl.* Baltimore, MD: Johns Hopkins University Press.

Mori, S., Kaufmann, W. E., Davatzikos, C., Stieltjes, B., Amodel, L., Fredericksen, K., et al. (2002). Imagining cortical association tracts in the human brain diffusion-tensor-based axonal tracking. *Magnetic Resonance in Medicine, 47*(2), 215–223.

Moses, J., & Chandler, M. J. (1992). Traveler's guide to children's theories of mind. *Psychological Inquiry, 3,* 285–301.

Mounoud, R., & Vinter, A. (1981). (Eds.). *La reconnaissance de son image chez l'enfant et l'animal.* Paris: L Delachanx et Niestle.

Mukherjee, P., Miller, J. H., Shimony, J. S., Conturo, T. E., Lee, B. C., Álmli, C. R., et al. (2001). Normal brain maturation during childhood: Developmental trends characterized with diffusion-tensor MR imaging. *Radiology, 221*(2), 349–358.

Neisser, U. (1967). *Cognitive psychology.* New York: Appleton-Century-Crofts.

Neisser, U. (1988). Five kinds of self-knowledge. *Philosophical Psychology, 1,* 35–59.

Newell, A. (1982). The knowledge level. *Artificial Intelligence, 18,* 81–132.

Nicolich, L. (1977). Beyond sensorimotor intelligence: Assessment of symbolic maturity through analysis of pretend play. *Merrill-Palmer Quarterly, 23,* 89–102.

Norman, D. A., & Rumelhard, D. F. (1975). *Explorations in cognition.* San Francisco: Freeman.

Nozick, R. (1981). *Philosophical explanations.* Cambridge, MA: Harvard University Press.

Overton, W. F. (1975). General systems, structure and development. In K. Riegel & G. Rosenwald (Eds.), *Structure and transformation: Developmental aspects* (pp. 61–81). New York: Wiley Interscience.

Overton, W. F. (2006). Developmental psychology: Philosophy, concepts, methodology. In R. M. Lerner (Ed.), *Handbook of child psychology: Vol. 1. Theoretical models of human development* (6th ed., pp. 18–88). Editors in chief: W. Damon & R. M. Lerner. Hoboken, NJ: John Wiley & Sons.

Owens, J., Bower, G. H., & Black, J. B. (1979). The soap opera effect in story recall. *Memory & Cognition, 1,* 185–191.

Pagels, E. (1979). *The gnostic gospels.* New York: Random House.

Paus, T. (2005). Mapping brain maturation and cognitive development during adolescence. *Trends in Cognitive Sciences, 9*(2), 60–68.

Paus, T., Collins, D. L., Evans, A. C., Leonoard, G., Pike, B., & Zijdenbos, A. (2001). Maturation of white matter in the human brain: A review of magnetic resonance studies. *Brain Research Bulletin, 54*(3), 255–266.

Perner, J. (1991). *Understanding the representational mind.* Cambridge, MA: MIT Press.

Piaget, J. (1952). *The origins of intelligence in children* (M. Cook, Trans.) New York: International Universities Press. (Original work published 1936)

Piaget, J. (1954). *Construction of reality in the child.* Paterson, NJ: Littlefield, Adams.

Piaget, J. (1960). *The psychology of intelligence.* New York: Littlefield, Adams.

Piaget, J. (1962). *Play, dreams, and imitation in childhood* (C. Gatlegno & F. M. Hodgson, Trans.). New York: Norton. (Original work published 1951 in French)

Piaget, J., & Inhelder, B. (1969). *The psychology of the child.* New York: Basic.

Pipp, S., Fischer, K. W., & Jennings, S. (1987). Acquisition of self- and mother knowledge in infancy. *Developmental Psychology, 23,* 86–96.

Plutchik, R. (1980). A general psychoevolutionary theory of emotion. In R. Plutchik & H. Kellerman (Eds.), *Emotion: Theory, research, and experience* (Vol. I, pp. 3–33). New York: Academic.

Polyani, M. (1958). *Personal language: Toward a post-critical philosophy.* London: Routledge & Kegan Paul.

Povinelli, D. J., & Eddy, T. J. (1996). What young chimpanzees know about seeing. *Monographs of the Society for Research in Child Development, 61*(3, Serial No. 247).

Premack, D., & Woodruff, G. (1978). Does the chimpanzee have a theory of mind? *The Brain and Behavioral Sciences, 4,* 515–526.

Pribram, K. H. (1984). Emotion: A neurobehavioral analysis. In K. R. Scherer & P. Ekman (Eds.), *Approaches to emotion* (pp. 13–38). Hillsdale, NJ: Erlbaum.

Putnam, H. (1963). Brains and behavior. In R. J. Butler (Ed.), *Analytical philosophy, second series* (pp. 211–235). Oxford: Basis Blackwell.

Putnam, H. (1981). *Reason, truth, and history.* Cambridge: Cambridge University Press.

Rheingold, H. L., & Cook, K. V. (1975). The content of boys' and girls' rooms as an index of parents' behavior. *Child Development, 46,* 459–563.

Rochat, P. (2009). *Others in mind: Social origins of self-consciousness.* New York: Cambridge University Press.

Rochat, P., & Striano, T. (2002). Who's in the mirror? Self-other discrimination in specular images by four- and nine-month-old infants. *Child Development, 73*(1), 35–46.

Roe, A. (1951). A psychological study of eminent physical scientists. *General Psychology Monographs, 43,* 121–135.

Roe, A. (1953). *The making of a scientist.* New York: Dodd/Mead.

Rogers, T. B., Kuiper, N. A., & Kirker, W. S. (1977). Self-reference and the encoding of personal information. *Journal of Personality and Social Psychology, 35,* 677–688.

Roland, A. (1988). *In search of self in India and Japan.* Princeton, NJ: Princeton University Press.

Rorty, R. (1989). *Contingency, irony and solidarity.* Cambridge, MA: Cambridge University Press.

Rosen, C. S., Schwebel, D. C., & Singer, J. L. (1997). Preschoolers' attributions of mental states in pretense. *Child Development, 68,* 1133–1142.

Ross, C. A. (1989). *Multiple personality disorder.* New York: John Wiley & Sons.

Ruby, P., & Decety, J. (2001). Effect of subjective perspective taking during simulation of action: A PET investigation of agency. *Nature Neuroscience, 4*(5), 546–550.

Samson, D., Apperly, I. A., Chiavarion, C., & Humphreys, G. W. (2004). Left temporoparietal junction is necessary for representing someone else's belief. *Nature Neuroscience, 7,* 499–500.

Saxe, R., Carey, S., & Kanwisher, N. (2004). Understanding other minds: Linking developmental psychology and functional neuroimaging. *Annual Review of Psychology, 55,* 87–124.

Saxe, R., & Kanwisher, N. (2003). People thinking about thinking people. The role of the temporo-parietal junction in "theory of mind." *Neuroimage, 19*(4), 1835–1842.

Schneider-Rosen, K., & Chicchetti, D. (1984). The relationship between affect and cognition in maltreated infants: Quality of attachment and the development of visual self-recognition. *Child Development. 55,* 648–658.

Searle, J. (1984). *Minds, brains and science.* Cambridge, MA: Harvard University Press.

Seligman, M. E. P. (1975). *Helplessness: On depression, development and death.* San Francisco: Freeman.

Selman, R. (1971a). The relation of role-taking ability to the development of moral judgment in children. *Child Development, 42,* 79–91.

Selman, R. (1971b). Taking another's perspective: Role taking development in early childhood. *Child Development, 42,* 1721–1734.

Shantz, C. U. (1975). *The development of social cognition.* Chicago: University of Chicago Press.

Siminov, P. V. (1970). The information theory of emotion. In M. B. Arnold (Ed.), *Feelings and emotions* (pp. 145–150). New York: Academic.

Souweidane, M. M., Kim, K. H., McDowall, R., Ruge, M. I., Lis, E., Krol, G., et al. (1999). Brain mapping in sedated infants and young children with passive-functional magnetic resonance imaging. *Pediatric Neurosurgery, 30*(2), 86–92.

Stern, D. (1984). *The interpersonal world of the child.* New York: Basic Books.

Stern, D. N. (1985). *The interpersonal world of the infant.* New York: Basic Books.

Stipek, D. J., Gralinski, J. H., & Kopp, C. B. (1990). Self-concept development in the toddler years. *Developmental Psychology, 26,* 972–977.

Stipek, D., Recchia, S., & McClintic, S. (1992). Self evaluation in young children. *Monographs of the Society for Research in Child Development, 57*(40), 385–398.

Sullivan, H. S. (1953). *The interpersonal theory of psychiatry.* New York: Norton.

Tajima, N. (1982). Self awareness and attachment at 12 months. Paper presented at Tune Conference, Hokkadio, Japan.

Thelen, E., Kelso, S. J., & Fogel, A. (1987). Self-organizing systems and infant motor development. *Developmental Review, 7*(1), 39–65.

Thompson, D. K., Warfield, S. K., Carlin, J. B., Pavlovic, M., Wang, H. X., Bear, M., et al. (2007). Perinatal risk factors altering regional brain structure in the preterm infant. *Brain, 130,* 667–677.

Toga, A. W., Thompson, P. M., & Sowell, E. R. (2006). Mapping brain maturation. *Trends in Neurosciences, 29*(3), 148–159.

Tomkins, S. S. (1963). *Affect, imagery, and consciousness: Vol. 2. The negative affects.* New York: Springer,

Tulving, E. (1985). How many memory systems are there? *American Psychologist, 40,* 385–398.

Turk, D. J., Heatherton, T. F., Kelley, W. M., Funnell, M. G., Gazzaniga, M. S., & Macrae, C. N. (2002). Mike or me? Self-recognition in a split-brain patient. *Nature Neuroscience, 5,* 148–159.

Von Bertalanffy, L. (1967). *Robots, men, and minds.* New York: Brazilles.

Von Boehmer, H., & Kisielow, P. (1990). Self-nonself discrimination by T cells. *Science, 248,* 1369–1372.

Waldrop, M. M. (1992). *Complexity: The emerging science at the edge of order and chaos.* New York: Simon & Schuster

Wegner, D. M. (2009). How to think, say, or do precisely the worst thing for any occasion. *Science, 325,* 48–51.

Weiner, B. (1986). *An attributional theory of motivation and emotion.* New York: Springer-Verlag.

Weiskrantz, L. (1986). *Blindsight: A case study and implications.* Oxford: Oxford University Press.

Wellman, H. M. (1990). *The child's theory of mind.* Cambridge, MA: MIT Press.

Werner, H. (1948). *Comparative psychology of mental development.* New York: International Universities Press. (Original work published 1940)

Wimmer, H., & Perner, J. (1983). Beliefs about beliefs: representation and constraining function of wrong beliefs in young children's understanding of deception. *Cognition, 13,* 103–128.

Wright, W. F., & Bower, G. H. (1992). Mood effects on subjective probability assessment. *Organizational Behavior and Human Decision Processes, 52,* 276–291.

Youniss, J. (1975). Another perspective on social cognition. In A. D. Pick (Ed.) *Minnesota symposium on child psychology* (Vol. 9). Minneapolis, MN: University of Minnesota Press.

Zajonc, R. B. (1980). Feeling and thinking: Preferences need no inferences. *American Psychologist, 35,* 151–175.

Zahn-Waxler, C., & Radke-Yarrow, M. (1981). The development of prosocial behavior: Alternative research strategies. In N. Eisenberg-Berg (Ed.). *The development of prosocial behavior behavior* (pp. 109–138). New York: Academic Press.

Zahn-Waxler, C., Radke-Yarrow, M., Wagner, E., & Chapman, M. (1992). Development of concern for others. *Developmental Psychology, 28,* 126–136.

Zelazo, D. P., Gao, H. H., & Todd R. (2007). The development of consciousness. In P. D. Zelazo, M. Moscovitch, & E. Thompson (Eds.), *The Cambridge handbook of consciousness.* Cambridge, UK: Cambridge University Press.

Zukav, G. (1979). *The dancing Wu Li masters.* New York: Morrow.

CHAPTER 19

The Development of Knowing

MICHAEL J. CHANDLER and SUSAN A. J. BIRCH

This chapter is meant to be about "knowing" (whatever, exactly, that is), and about how (one way or another) it supposedly develops across the life span. "Not nearly good enough," you could easily be thinking; or, less harshly, "probably not the most auspicious way of beginning." Who could blame you? Later on, perhaps, as page leads on to page, uncertainties of this caliber might well seem less jarring. Here, at the very outset, before things have hardly gotten under way, one ordinarily expects, and usually gets, more in the way of upfront clarity. As it is, however, and for reasons to which we will quickly come, little in the way of such front-end precision seems to be on offer when it comes to matters of "knowing." We all do, naturally enough, have a lot of impromptu things to say about knowing and knowledge, but as you will see, even among the experts from whom we might have hoped for more, there is surprisingly little in the way of real consensus concerning what knowing actually is, and even less consensus on how it develops. It remains a serious question whether knowing even qualifies as a bona fide psychological concept.

High on the list of problems with the concepts of knowledge and knowing is that they are so epistemically unforgiving. At least since Plato's *Meno* and *Theaetetus* (c. 400 B.C.), the so-called standard analysis of knowing demands that it be understood as something like "justified true belief" (Audi, 1999). All such easy "tripartite" talk aside, however, what remains is a preternaturally long and especially thorny list of perpetually unsettled philosophical questions. Included among these is whether being knowledgeable presupposes some defensible insight into "how things really are," some capacity to recognize the "truth" should we encounter it, and whether we are able to reliably sort justifiable (i.e., epistemically good or permissible) from deontologically unjustifiable (i.e., epistemically bad or unwarrantable) beliefs. All of these disputed matters leave open the still further question of whose business it is to speak to such normative issues, and what we are all meant to do in the interim while such open questions are hopefully being settled.

Given standard divisions of labor, tradition has it that it is philosophers (not psychologists or related "cognitive scientists") who are meant to have, as part of their usual job description, the task of working out the defining features, substantive conditions, and limits of "justified true belief." Psychologists and cognitive scientists of varying sorts—whether because they are judged to be somehow lacking in the right stuff or are, otherwise, simply constitutionally reluctant to traffic in such matters—have characteristically tended to shy away from explicit talk of knowledge and knowing, and have ordinarily opted instead to focus their collective attention on a range of potentially more answerable, if no less contested, matters having to do with the holding of "beliefs." The same is true of this chapter.

BELIEFS AND BELIEFS ABOUT BELIEFS

Whether having elected to forego certain normative considerations regarding issues of knowing, and having chosen instead to refocus attention on more psychologically saturated matters having to do with believing, will ultimately succeed in allowing contemporary developmentalists to avoid some of philosophy's more vicious circles (see Overton, 2006) remains an open question. To take only one example, the whole point of talk about beliefs, as Davidson (1984) reminds us, is that beliefs can be, and often are, mistaken—a backdoor opportunity through which questions about how things "really are" once again threaten to enter. As such, research into matters of so-called false belief understanding (arguably the hot-button topic that has taken up the lion's share of things written on the subject of children's so-called developing theories of mind) automatically threatens to plunge us all back into those same murky justification waters that traditionally swirl around classical philosophic inquiries into

knowledge and knowing. All such cautionary tales aside, however, and not withstanding the fact that there is also less than uniform agreement about what beliefs are and are not, it remains the case that talk of "belief," in contrast with talk of knowledge or knowing, is widely seen to hold the best promise of bringing the conversation about epistemic matters back to a domain of discourse in which behavioral scientists are meant to be articulate, and where their traditional research tools and methods hold some hope of gaining traction.

On similar prospects, attention throughout this chapter is also turned away from disputed matters of knowing and redirected to issues of belief about belief, and about how they supposedly develop across the life span. What makes this otherwise promising shift in attention more problematic than it might otherwise be is that beliefs, whatever else they might be, are clearly not things in the world of the same ontological caliber as are, for example, heads and shoulders, knees and toes. No one, for instance, has ever seen a belief. Rather, beliefs would appear to require being understood as working parts of some larger "folk" or "commonsense" conception of mental life—parts that are closer to what philosophers of science have dubbed "hypothetical constructs" or, better still, "intervening variables"—imagined (some would say "theoretical") things whose existence we posit as parts of an explanatory system meant to help advance our appreciation of our own and one another's behavior, or even lack of behavior. Presumably, in a world where there was some direct link between what happened to us and what we did next, there would be no need for talk of beliefs. Things are, however, rarely this simple, and so we (or at least we as adults) are standardly given to imagining that there are, hidden somewhere behind our own eyes and the eyes of others, various internal "psychological states" that mediate our behaviors. Such mental states, we commonly assume, come in various stripes, including those typically understood as moods or values or affective dispositions, and so forth. Key among these supposed mental states are said to be "beliefs" that have been classically viewed as "dispositional psychological states"—possibly "propositional attitudes"—in virtue of which putative belief holders are thought to be disposed to assent to, or behave in accordance with, some proposition under consideration (Audi, 1999). A mere string of words that reads "Person X believes" (full stop) does not, therefore, constitute a well-formed sentence. Rather, to qualify as properly exemplifying such an epistemic attitude, the word *belief* requires being followed by some version of the word *that*, and then finished off by the listing out of some supposed propositional content (e.g., "Person X believes: *that* the cat is on the mat; *that* the moon is made of green cheese; *that* killing is wrong"). It is also commonly, although not universally (e.g., see Bickhard, 2006), supposed that the holders of such beliefs have somehow managed to form certain mental "representations" of the world—representations that may or may not actually accord with "reality." Without some appreciation of the possibility that beliefs may be, in some sense, mistakenly held, or are otherwise "false" or counterfactual, an important and apparently constitutive part of what it could possibly mean for something to be a belief would necessarily go missing.

The rationale for there being a chapter such as this rests on the broad expectation that there is an interesting developmental story to be told about how and when "beliefs" that satisfy some or all of the foregoing conditions are actually formed, and how we come to act, not with reference to how the world actually is, but in terms of how we believe it to be. As such—and this is where the developmental story gains its primary foothold—it is widely imagined that, although those who are first credited with subscribing to such a notion of belief may be quite young (or at least "youngish"), others of a still younger age actually proceed differently by relying on something more prosaic—something perhaps as simple as appreciating that we are changed by the mere wear and tear of direct experience. Once in place, however, such notions of belief are thought to reference many different things, some of which have as their propositional content still other beliefs or other mental states, and thus are seen to legitimately bear on the topics of so-called mind reading, developing theories of mind, or the folk epistemologies that will prove so central to this chapter.

With regard to all of those emerging matters that actually do concern beliefs about mental life, and especially about peoples' changing beliefs about belief, it has been widely imagined that some or all of the following propositions hold:

1. There is some young age before which actually subscribing to various notions about beliefs is thought to be possible.

2. Those who are judged to be too young to actually represent their experience (or represent such things *as* being a particular way), although not held to be entirely uninformed about their environment, fail to behave in ways that warrant their being credited with employing any *bona fide* notions about beliefs.

3. There not only exists some developmental moment before which trafficking in beliefs is ontogenetically possible, but there is also some later and especially auspicious, watershed moment after which, in addition to acting in ways informed by experience, young persons can be fairly credited with holding to some beginning notion of beliefs about the material world, or (and there is a lot of confusion on this point) more complicated still, with having beliefs about their own and others' beliefs.

4. The newly acquired capacity to actually hold to ideas or beliefs about belief is either: (a) a singular, once-in-a-lifetime accomplishment such that, for ever afterward, all seemingly new insights about beliefs actually constitute minor procedural variations on what has already become a standard set of epistemic marching orders; or, alternatively, (b) an early step in a drawn-out developmental process within which several distinguishable steps divide later from earlier insights into what holding to a belief could possibly mean.

5. There is some usually less auspicious moment in the course of epistemic development after which it is "all over but the shouting"; a time subsequent to which every seemingly new thing having to do with beliefs that may appear on the ontogenetic scene is, on closer inspection, really and truly no more than the endless cranking out of still older ways of thinking about the knowing relation, plus (perhaps) a certain theoretically uninteresting measure of experiential water under the dam.

One could, more or less effortlessly, go on extending this presuppositional list to almost any length, but with these few planks already in place, the foundational platform supporting most of the weight of the available literature concerned with epistemic development has already assumed its signature form. What naturally follows from such a lining out of foundational assumptions—what most readers especially want to know—are straightforward answers to an equally short list of compelling questions. When, for example, would it be fair to say that young persons actually acquire their first fledgling insights into that belief-driven and representationally dominated world in which ordinary adults ordinarily live? Once "in the game," exactly how many interesting, qualitatively distinct levels, or steps or stages separate the first from the last of such insights? If there is some developmental trajectory to be seen in all of this, then what drives it or causes its wheels to come off? Is there some likely age

(4 or 8 or 16, or perhaps in late adulthood) after which any subsequent questions about epistemic development become fundamentally uninteresting? Again, it would be easily possible to also further elaborate this list, but it would hardly matter. Serious answers (i.e., answers about which there is real professional agreement—some "justified true belief") to even this small starter-set of questions simply do not exist, and convincing answers to just one of them would put us so far ahead of where things currently stand that to ask for more would seem greedy. That is the bad news.

Here is some other news that, as you will see, necessarily plays to mixed reviews. Despite having come from radically different theoretical orientations, and having used almost entirely nonoverlapping methodologies and study populations, the broad picture of the development of believing so far painted by almost every cognitive scientist who has set her or his hand to this task awkwardly turns out, against all odds, to be, if not identical, then at least eerily similar. That is, with surprisingly few exceptions, whole armies of researchers (some studying infants, others studying young adults, and everyone in-between) have ended up describing what seem suspiciously like the exact same set of developmental achievements.

Although this much in the way of apparent consensus has at least the outward trappings of a good thing, the fact that more or less interchangeable claims are all being made about radically different sorts of persons of radically different ages or developmental stations needs to be seen as deeply problematic. The watershed insight that others fervently hold to and act on beliefs that contradict our own has, for example, been argued to occur for the first time ever in persons as young as 13 or 15 months (Onishi & Baillargeon, 2005; Surian, Caldi, & Sperber, 2007; see also Buttelmann, Carpenter, & Tomasello, in press); no, that's not right, it's really 2 or perhaps 4; no, wait, it's 6, or maybe 8 years of age; take that back, its really only true of young adolescents; sorry, wrong again, it's college sophomores; no, now we get it, it all happens in those last days of their postgraduate years (for review, see Chandler, Hallett, & Sokol, 2002). In this theater of confusion, the exits are definitely not clearly marked. Although more will need to be said on this later, what should be already apparent is that the difficult job facing anyone assigned the task of summarizing the wildly scattered, and radically disunified literature on epistemic development is faced with an especially difficult job—one that has less to do with getting the details of the story straight than with working out who it is, exactly, that the story is supposedly about.

BALKANIZATION AND THE COLLAPSE OF THE ONTOGENETIC EMPIRE

Tackling this assignment would, of course, prove to be a great deal simpler than it actually is if more of the various contributors to this literature had looked back over their shoulders at the claims of others who have studied still younger individuals, or, alternatively, had looked forward across the full life-span trajectory at all of those competing claims being put out by those whose work focuses on still older age groups. As it is, however, developmentalists, many sporting nonoverlapping and highly *balkanized* states of mind, keep asking more or less the same set of questions, and often unbeknown to one another, incredibly coming up with more or less the same answers. This, it seems clear enough, is not good news either. "Balkanization"—originally a geopolitical term intended to describe conflicts that arose in the aftermath of the bloody dissolution of what was once the Ottoman Empire—has subsequently come to refer not only to the process of dismantling once larger nation states into smaller and often hostile political bits and pieces, but also references other and broader forms of fragmentation or disintegration. The creation of "gated communities," the introduction of separate enclaves within the once seamless Internet, and the "silo-ing" of various public health services are all contemporary instances of such balkanization.

Developmentalists hardly need look far afield to find homegrown instances of the effects of such processes of balkanization. For all intents and purposes, students of infant cognition, for example, live on entirely separate conceptual planets from similarly degreed specialists whose work centers on the epistemic understanding of young adults, or even the "beliefs about beliefs" held by preschool and early school-aged children. Babes in arms, ruddy-cheeked children in short pants, and aspiring young adults are all treated, for every practical purpose, as if they were not members of the same species. Nor, it would seem, are those who study them. Members of our breakaway and often warring scientific tribes regularly use entirely nonoverlapping methodologies, speak mutually uninterpretable languages, subscribe to different journals, and can and do easily spend whole professional lifetimes without ever experiencing a real encounter with bona fide members of other theoretically alien groups.

All of this could be all that anyone has a right to expect in a world so supersaturated with new information that "specializing" is generally understood not simply as a necessary evil, but as a positive mark of the maturity of one's field. That is, notwithstanding a certain fading but wistful nostalgia for earlier and simpler times, we, as residents of the early 21st century, regularly imagine ourselves as no longer having the luxury of being broadly concerned about matters lying beyond the immediate purview of whatever restricted domain or specific age group about which we have become local experts.

Whatever one's attitude about such pressures toward increasing specialization, our hope for collective salvation—the thing commonly imagined to pull us all back from the brink of having our best efforts dissolve into fractured and incommensurable knowledge claims—is regularly seen to lie in the prospect that the final aggregation of all such atomic facts will ultimately add up to a more complete and, therefore, truer big picture. That is, however much merit there may prove to be in the "divide-and-conquer" strategy that increasingly drives our specialized subdisciplines, their cumulative success necessarily presupposes that the localized facts unearthed in any separate patch of inquiry must, at the very least, avoid the spectacle of directly contradicting other "facts" unearthed elsewhere. Awkwardly, this does not seem to be how things are currently shaping up. Rather, and all too frequently, each and every chapter intended to contribute to the full story of knowledge development appears to make more or less the same claims about the same epistemic accomplishment, while incomprehensibly attributing them to radically different age groups. To gain some understanding of how this unsuitable state of affairs might have arisen, it will prove useful to first step briefly back in time in an effort to examine the historical circumstances that have led us to our current theater of confusion.

SHORT HISTORICAL SKETCH

Even casual observation would appear to confirm that adults regularly operate in a world that requires them to mark the differences between their own and others' psychological lives. Perhaps just as obviously, infants seem to do little or none of this, and instead, regularly find themselves confused about who believes what, collapse "true" and "taken for true," and otherwise badly bungle everything that naturally depends on even a fledgling reading of their own and others' mental states. Infants and toddlers, who do seemingly have some early insights about things such as referential pointing (e.g., Bretherton, 1991), and even the prospects for pretense (e.g., Leslie, 1988), still

regularly confuse seeing with knowing, and act as if they can hardly imagine that others could conceivably subscribe to beliefs that are false (e.g., Wellman, Cross, & Watson, 2001). Those who are a bit older (e.g., preschoolers) are often not that much better at solving such "mind-reading" problems, and thus, although having noticed the possibilities of deception and "false beliefs," nevertheless go on behaving in ways that leave us questioning the future of sociability. Shortly into their early school years, those of 6 or 8 may begin to intuit something of the "interpretive" nature of knowing (Chandler & Carpendale, 1994; Chandler & Lalonde, 1996), but all of this seems to do little to advance their appreciation of the situated character of all beliefs. Through middle school, and on into adolescence, young people are notoriously bad at knowing about (or, perhaps, it is caring about) the thoughts and feelings of others (Selman, 1980). As if this were not enough, even young adults (one's own postsecondary students, for example) are themselves often insensitive to the conceptual differences that divide us, and often reflexively imagine that those who hold to beliefs different from their own are necessarily and sadly mistaken. Because all of this is so nakedly the case, effectively every celebrated account of human development offered up in the course of the last century has had something poignant to say regarding these age-related epistemic matters.

In a more perfect world, all of these resulting story fragments, painstakingly described by generation after generation of developmental scholars, would have, by now, already begun to coalesce into some overarching "grand narrative." As already hinted at, this is not the conceptual world in which we currently find ourselves. Instead, scholars of this or that age, or one or another theoretical persuasion, have all separately contributed to an account that, in the aggregate, simply fails to add up. Perhaps it is true that, in our present era, all such "grand narratives" actually deserve, as Lyotard (1984) and other postmodern theorists have argued, to be dead.

As a way of refusing such know-nothing conclusions, an alternative strategy—the one being urged here—is to proceed on the hope that, even if it is not currently possible to touch bottom (Bernstein, 1983), we can all still hope to keep afloat the thin prospect that, by carefully examining the diverse claims about epistemic development already on offer, it may still be possible to pick out certain continuous threads running through the scattered research materials currently available—threads that, on closer inspection, might well amount to a real and seamless story to be told. One way to begin such a search—a way taken up in the sections that immediately follow—is to first try to gain enough altitude to accomplish some bird's-eye view of the recent history of research into the problems of belief entitlement, all in the continuing hope that adulthood is not simply childhood, plus accumulated experience. From such a heightened viewing distance, it is, we suggest, both possible and useful to identify what amounts to three such distinct and often contradictory story lines that may still add up to some overarching plot.

One of these prospects has to do with Piaget, and the mid-century sequelae of his and Inhelder's insights about childhood egocentrism (see Chandler, 2001 for a review). A second concerns the reputedly contradictory accounts put out by those self-proclaimed "theory theorists," whose work on false-belief understanding began by presuming that Piaget was largely mistaken on all counts (Gopnik, Meltzoff, & Kuhl, 1999). A third thread running through this loosely braided history turns on the seminal work of William Perry (1970), and what he had to say about the course of epistemic development in the lives of college students and other young adults. As a way of beginning, a brief analysis needs to be made about each of these competing historical strands.

Piaget and the Prospects of Childhood Egocentrism

What is perhaps the most well-known of these competing accounts of young people's changing conceptions of psychological life is owed to the seminal ideas of Piaget and Inhelder (1963/1948)—ideas that, during the 1960s and 1970s (the period that William Kessen [1996] dubbed "the decades of the rebirth of Piaget"), fueled a whole genre of research into the course of "social-cognitive" development. While triggering a broad array of different research programs, the attention of the hundreds of contributors to this literature was especially focused on so-called childhood egocentrism, and the range of slow to develop role- and perspective-taking competencies, the absence of which was thought to collectively act as a break on the wheel of preschoolers' and young school-aged children's social-emotional development. In those early days, well before subsequent, usually unwarranted, attacks, this broad program of research (including a whole *pharmikea* of studies of social, conceptual, affective, and visual perspective-taking competencies) was everywhere the talk of the town. An electronic search of the literature of the day yields well over a thousand "hits" that related childhood egocentrism to almost everything that children

ordinarily do, or do badly. For the better part of 20 years, books and journal articles given over to such topics were commonplace, and the programs of various developmental congresses became dedicated conduits for any and everything to do with the shifting fortunes of children's supposed role-taking abilities.

If the early contributors to this role-taking literature had it right (for reviews, see Chandler, 1978; Chandler & Boyes, 1982; Elkind, 1985; Selman, 1980), then the focal problem facing young school-aged persons, as they struggle to get a grip on their own and others' mental lives, all turn on an early developmental incapacity to set aside one's own thoughts and feelings while undertaking to properly infer the thoughts and feeling of others. Preschool children, it was commonly said—although, interestingly, not by Piaget and Inhelder—were, in virtue of their age, all thought to be more or less "egocentric," and, because of this cognitive limitation, were thought to have an especially tenuous grasp on the differences that divide various people's mental lives. To be sure, there were some investigators who, while working well inside the tent of the Piaget-inspired role- and perspective-taking research enterprise, introduced evidence meant to suggest that preschoolers were a lot more clever at "mind reading" than most were prepared to allow (for a review, see Chandler, 1978). It was, nevertheless, generally thought to be true that the weight of evidence indicated that, before entering the public school system, most young persons are strongly inclined to confuse the differences between what they and others thought they knew.

As a way of seeing what these investigators repeatedly saw, picture a pair of 4-, 5-, or even 6-year-olds thrown together in a psychologist's laboratory where they sit opposite one another at a common desk, and where they are asked to participate in a kind of board game. Call it a "referential communication" task, one in which each player has arrayed before them an identical checkerboard-like matrix of differently colored squares, as well as the same selection of differently shaped and colored bits and pieces. The job of the first, and later the other, of these children is to begin by filling up the matrix in front of her or him with some selection of the "shapes" at their disposal. At the same time, participants must communicate about what they are doing in such a way that their partner could follow their lead and create an identical matrix on their own side of the table. Although the children working on this measurement task can see and hear one another, a low screen running down the middle of their shared table makes it impossible for them to see the board and pieces of their partner. The obvious point of this more or less straightforward assessment task is to determine how well young research participants of various ages can anticipate and take into account the informational needs of their partner. As it turns out, preschoolers and kindergartners are hopelessly bad at such tasks (Carpendale & Chandler, 1996). Preschool and kindergarten children commonly begin and end by saying especially unhelpful things like "I have one and I am putting it here," whereas their partner standardly responds with comments like "good" or "me too," all without any apparent appreciation that everything that they should be saying or need to know has been inadvertently left out. In the end, when the occluding screen is removed, both children in such procedures are typically flabbergasted that their respective matrices fail to look anything alike (Carpendale & Chandler).

Given that, on good authority, this is precisely what young children regularly do, how is this possible? How could two such children, who otherwise manage their lives with some skill, regularly behave so stupidly? What could possibly be going on in their "unlettered" minds that could have led them to mistakenly imagine that they had both performed so well? Multiply research findings such as this hundreds of times and you will begin to approach the sense of warranted conviction that persuaded generations of developmentalists that they knew, on good evidential grounds, that children younger than 5 or 6 simply do not properly understand that others, differently situated than themselves, processed the world differently. Why else, everyone thought, did preschoolers so regularly imagine that their parents automatically knew of their worst misdeeds?

Now, in the perhaps more methodologically chastened era in which we currently live, many who were originally involved in amassing such evidence might well grudgingly agree that, once again, certain potentially confounding methodological matters may have crept in and prevented all of us from seeing everything as clearly as might have been done. Perhaps some such measures were unnecessarily linguistically encumbered. Perhaps a more sensitive set of assessment tasks would have inched back by some number of months the age at which perspective-taking and referential communication skills "really" do put in their first ontogenetic appearance? Still, and this is our point, it seems unlikely that all of those relatively "tough-minded" investigators of not so by-gone years—colleagues, some of whom are still among us and who originally and judiciously collected such data—were all deeply misled and so fundamentally mistaken. As it turns out, research participants younger than 5 or 6 (whoever's research participants they are) just do ordinarily appear to be "thick as posts" when it comes

to the complicated business of keeping their own and other people's thoughts and feelings separate, and just do seem generally bad at working out what it is that others know or have a right to know. As any divorce lawyer could tell you, such shortcomings are not all that uncommon, even among persons decades older than 4 or 5 (e.g., Bernstein, Atance, Loftus, & Meltzoff, 2004; Birch & Bloom, 2007; Epley, 2008; Epley, Morewedge, & Keysar, 2004; Keysar, Lin, & Barr, 2003). As such, any account of epistemic development that failed to take such compelling evidence properly into account is simply poorer for not having done so.

Notwithstanding all of the vaguely supportive things just said about what is an increasingly "ancient" role- and perspective-taking literature, it is also equally true that at the heyday of this research enterprise, it occurred to certain of its contributors (e.g., Coie, Costanzo, & Farnhill, 1973; Flavell, 1974, 1977; Kurdek & Rodgon, 1975; Masangkay, et al., 1974; Mossler, Marvin, & Greenberg, 1976) to ask the up-until-then unspoken question: Do all of the diverse procedural ways and means of measuring what are deemed to be expressions of the same childhood egocentrism actually demonstrate one and the same thing? In short, is childhood egocentrism—the cognitive stuff that reputedly prevents young persons from achieving a mature grasp of their social or interpersonal circumstances—really the "unitary construct" it has been held out to be? The short answer is "no." When all of these unifying hopes proved empirically unsupported (i.e., when multiple measures of childhood egocentrism turned out not to correlate; see, for example, Kurdek & Rodgon), the entire social-cognitive enterprise suddenly fell under suspicion, threatened bankruptcy, and, by the early 1980s, was fully into receivership (for a review, see Chandler & Boyles, 1982).

Study of Children's So-Called Developing "Theories of Mind"

Owed, perhaps, to nature's tendency to abhor a vacuum, all of the loose equity that had been previously tied up in the increasingly moribund role-taking enterprise was quickly bought up by a new generation of investigators, a predominately "commonwealth consortium" of British, Australian, and Canadian researchers preoccupied, this time, with what came to be called the study of children's "developing theories of mind." Rising phoenix-like out of the still smoking ashes of the childhood egocentrism literature, this new collective enterprise, emboldened by its thin but real conceptual ties to British analytic philosophy, worked to distance itself from all things Piagetian. The rallying cry of this self-anointed group of "theory theorists" was that, rather than conflating their own and others' points of view, young school-aged children—children who, for as much as half of their young lifetimes, had already well appreciated the prospect of representational diversity—had been mistakenly judged to have failed one or another routine test of childhood egocentrism, all for no better reason than that these earlier measures were judged to be unnecessarily verbally encumbered (Perner, 1991). That is, children as young as 4 now came to be said to already grasp the prospect of so-called false beliefs, and thus already properly understood that putative knowledge is always a direct function of the slice of reality to which one had been exposed. In short, it was broadly maintained, on the basis of new and generally compelling evidence, that children as young as 4 had already undergone some largely unspecified, but age-graded transformation that miraculously causes the scales to fall from their eyes, allowing them to see for the first time the possibility of "representational diversity" and the potential corrigibility of beliefs. The signature claim of such theory-theorists was, then, that during their preschool years, young persons had already come to the insight that the whole point of talk about "beliefs" is that one's ideas (i.e., representations, interpretations, constructions) of the world can be, and often are, mistaken. All of this was, at the time, new news. Not just ordinary, run-of-the-mill local news, but for many a blinding new insight. There had always existed, hidden beneath the obfuscating surface structure of generations' worth of wrong-headed methodologies, new and compelling evidence that there existed a heretofore unrecognized joint in the body of child development; an auspicious and so far previously undetected watershed moment before and after which everything was different. Who would have imagined that such a critical ontogenetic milestone was present at 4, and could have laid there for so long, trodden over, but unrecognized by countless generations of otherwise serious scholars—scholars who, perhaps because of their theory blindness, had failed to alert us all to what was now so painfully obvious?

One way of getting a grip on the proper importance attached to the new discoveries of this "theories-of-mind" cabal is, as Dennett (1978) suggested, to imagine this: Imagine yourself, years ago, on the boardwalk of England's Brighton Beach. Near the water's edge you see a crowd—mostly children—gathered around the striped tent of a traveling Punch and Judy show. Punch is standing by as Judy rummages through a large steamer trunk. Suddenly, Judy slips and falls into the trunk. Punch, quick to seize any opportunity to get rid of her at last, clamps the lid resoundingly shut. Muttering something about needing to find a bit of rope to lash the trunk shut, Punch then exits stage-left. While Punch is off-stage, Judy succeeds in freeing herself from the trunk and surreptitiously sneaks away (stage-right). Punch (none the wiser) returns, secures everything with his rope, and pointlessly attempts to push the now-empty trunk over the edge of the stage/cliff. Quick to get the point, the older children in the audience are beside themselves, laughing and ridiculing Punch for stupidly believing to be true what they themselves grandly know to be false. Other, mostly younger children—children presumably younger than 4—look on in bewilderment and are not amused. In all of this you have the germ of what Dennett (1978) described as a "minimally complex" measure—a "litmus test," if you will—for sorting out who should and should not be credited with at least a fledging "theory of mind." All of this is convincing and especially important, regardless of whether it tells us anything of significance about Piaget's and others' different claims about childhood egocentrism.

In the more than two decades since Heinz Wimmer and Josef Perner first published their now classic 1983 article, taking up Dennett's challenge to find a "minimally complex" measure of children's developing "theories of mind," some two dozen books, and several thousand journal articles and conference presentations have appeared, the great bulk of which make it plain that 4-year-olds are simply better at solving standard false belief puzzles than are their still younger counterparts. What is widely called into question, however, is whether their doing so ought to be counted as evidence for the existence of some new, heretofore undiscovered joint in the body of human development. Offering up some opinion about all of this, and about whether "false belief understanding" is or is not the singular watershed event that it is standardly held up as being (i.e., whether it does, in fact, arrive de novo and without precedent, and whether, once in place, it actually marks the real end of epistemic development) will be the subject of much that needs to be said here. In particular, it will prove important to open up the question whether other, so far unmentioned, transformations in epistemic thought also evolve during either infancy or the middle-school years.

William Perry and the College Counseling Movement: Epistemic Development Grows Up

While all of the above was happening, elsewhere, on an entirely different intellectual planet far, far away, an entirely separate breed of cognitive development researchers—individuals primarily concerned with the epistemic growth of college students and young adults—had already been hard at work for most of two score years attempting to verify or extend or rewrite the seminal work of the Harvard educator William Perry (1970). If all of our earlier comments about the fractious and distressingly balkanized nature of research into the life-span course of epistemic development are accurate, then many who are reading these lines (especially those whose insights into matters of belief entitlement are owed exclusively to Piaget and subsequent generations of "theory theorists") may well be hearing Perry's name for the first time. If true, that is especially unfortunate. As it turns out, Perry conducted one of the relatively few truly longitudinal studies of young people's (in his case, male Harvard undergraduate) developing notions of belief entitlement. What he did, over a period of decades, was to individually meet with successive waves of students during each of their four undergraduate years, and to interview them at length about their ideas concerning where knowledge comes from, how truth is established, and how one is meant to react in the face of competing knowledge claims. On his account, these students followed a predictable sequence of steps or stages, beginning with a strictly objectivistic view of the knowing process. As they aged, or as their education progressed, these same students were shown to pass through a series of intermediate levels according to which some or all putative knowledge claims were first dismissed as unassuageably person-relative matters of taste or opinion, before eventually progressing to a view that saw knowledge as the arbitrated outcome of various "evaluativistic" efforts to pit better against worse reasons to believe (Kuhn, 1991). In the decades following the 1970 publication of his book *Forms of Intellectual and Ethical Development in the College Years*, successive generations of educators and college counselors found in Perry's writing a new way of accounting for many of the intellectual struggles that commonly arise in the course of students being exposed to an ever-expanding diet of new ideas. As a result, a long list of investigators have undertaken studies and reported findings that, for the most part, qualify rather than broadly challenge the general outline of Perry's original claims. Some (e.g., Benack & Basseches, 1989; Commons et al., 1989; Sinnot, 1989) have suggested that Perry's description of the shift from realism to relativism may count as the next logical step in Piaget's developmental framework. Using modest variations on Perry's scheme, still others such as Kuhn (e.g., Kuhn, 1991; Kuhn, Amsel, & O'Laughlin, 1988) and Kitchener and King (e.g., King & Kitchener, 1994; Kitchener & King, 1981) have examined a broader range of age groups than did Perry, whereas others still (e.g., Belenky, Clinchy, Goldberger, & Tarule, 1986) have explored the interesting question of whether movement through such epistemic stages is somehow "gendered," and so different for young men and women. Not surprisingly, given all of these efforts, there is a William Perry Society that meets biannually and always attracts more than a thousand participants, and whole journals that are largely given over to publishing Perry-related research.

FINDING SOME FOLLOWABLE PATH THROUGH ALL OF THE INCOMMENSURABLE THINGS COMMONLY SAID ABOUT THE PROCESS OF BELIEF ENTITLEMENT

Given all of the competing claims that have so far been listed out concerning the possible ontogeny of beliefs about beliefs, it should already be clear enough that, if there is some developmental pathway connecting these various dots, it will not be easily found lying about. Rather, coming to some fuller account about the full course of epistemic development, if possible at all, will require sorting through the details of numerous competing and often contradictory claims about what exactly happens, and when. To do this will require some sort of road map with some assigned starting point and some ideas about where to head next. Although, given the level of disagreement that is afoot, the choice of any such jumping-off place will necessarily be a bit arbitrary, the spot that we have chosen is on that densely populated patch of literature concerned with the study of children's so-called theory of mind. High on any list of the reasons driving this choice are the following facts: (1) the developmental accomplishment said to mark the first appearance of legitimate, "theory-like" ideas about beliefs is widely held out to be a "watershed" moment such that still younger children fail to qualify; and (2) once such *true* beliefs about beliefs are in evidence, then all of the fundamental architecture responsible for governing subsequent epistemic development is said to be in place. A possible virtue of this fundamentally antidevelopmental claim is that it drives an explicit stake in the ground, marking out a clear before and after. We use this marker as an organizational tool for lining out a sequence of three major chapter headings. First, in Part I, we attempt to make clear what has been intended by talk of children's developing theories of mind, presenting along the way key research findings that have been judged to give legitimacy to such theorizing. In Part II, we explore various claims and lines of evidence concerning children still younger than the celebrated watershed age of 3½ or 4, all in an effort to examine what we take to be the suspect claim that infants and toddlers are actually bereft of anything that would qualify as a working (and perhaps theory-like) understanding of their own and others' mental lives. Here research on deception, lying, pretense, and various referential actions are selectively reviewed. Having at least partially covered the relevant research literatures dealing with the epistemic accomplishments of infant and preschool children, we turn, in Part III, to an examination of what is said to happen in the early school years and beyond. Because what needs to be said in the final section concerns events unfolding across the remaining nine tenths of the life span, this section is subdivided into two parts: Part IIIA concerns research involving middle-school children, with a special focus on what has been termed their "interpretive theories of mind"; and Part IIIB summarizes some of the research on epistemic development in adolescence and young adulthood. The final Conclusion section identifies whatever developmental threads appear to run through the whole of this scattered literature, and, if better fleshed out, could contribute to an eventual life-span account of the topic of belief entitlement.

PART I: CHILDREN'S DEVELOPING THEORIES OF MIND—A PRIMER

Piagetian Background

Given that the theories-of-mind literature "arose like a phoenix" from the presumably discredited ashes of Piaget's earlier account of childhood egocentrism, it easily could have happened that serious efforts might have been made to rehabilitate all of those things that seemingly went wrong with first-generation studies of social role taking. After all, studies of childhood egocentrism had been the "bread and butter" of child development for most of a generation. As things have turned out, however, there was seen to be less merit in any such backward glance than might have been expected. The key reason that (at least in this case) knowledge about past "mistakes" seems to do such a poor job of preventing us from repeating them is that much of the received knowledge about Piaget's views concerning childhood egocentrism is, if not seriously mistaken, at least a poor and badly anglicized version of what Piaget and Inhelder actually had to say on this subject in

their classic 1948 book *The Child's Conception of Space*. True enough, this volume did serve to prime the pumps of more than a hundred studies that all involved the use of some variation on Piaget and Inhelder's classic "Test of Three Mountains" (for a detailed review of this literature, see Chandler, 2001). Beyond serving as a procedural template, however, little of the original message that Piaget and Inhelder worked to convey appears to have actually survived its North Americanization.

Rather than constituting an across-the-board indictment of the egocentric ways of preschoolers and young school-aged children, as is commonly claimed, or a search for some singular witching hour when the clouds of egocentrism were meant to lift, *The Child's Conception of Space* actually offers up a wide-ranging account of young people's early success at and only gradual progress toward the eventual achievement of an adult-like understanding of the spatial relations that exist between the objects that make up one's visual field. That is, rather than having been written off as hopelessly egocentric, even the youngest of Piaget and Inhelder's research participants were actually described as already having achieved a surprisingly sophisticated grasp of the difference between their own and other people's perspectives, just as other older participants were characterized as continuing to struggle with the coordination of such multiple perspectives well into their early adolescent years. In short, in the account of childhood egocentrism that Piaget and Inhelder actually provided, no threshold moments are offered, no age is specified before which egocentrism is the rule, or after which it was assumed to have disappeared entirely from the epistemic landscape. Instead, the whole affair is refreshingly portrayed as a rather drawn-out developmental process spread out across most of the childhood years; a process with no salutary, watershed moments anywhere in sight; and with no lines drawn in the sand that, if wrongly stepped across, could easily provoke the sort of infighting that later generations of psychometrically more punctilious role-taking and theory theorists were evidently spoiling for.

All such turning of the tables notwithstanding, by the time the 1970s had run their course, and as it came to be increasingly clear that the sundry ways of measuring social and conceptual, and affective and spatial perspective taking actually had little to do with one another, what Piaget and Inhelder may or may not have originally said about childhood egocentrism no longer seemed particularly pertinent. What mattered instead was that whatever they did or did not say was automatically taken to be yesterday's badly mistaken news. Given this Whiggish form of presentist historiography, the stage for the emergence of the then "new" theories-of-mind enterprise seemed well and truly set.

False Belief Understanding and Other "Minimally Complex" Measures of Children's "Developing" Theories of Mind

The signature publication that is widely held out as both a capstone on Piaget and Inhelder's presumably discredited past, and a signpost for the theories-of-mind enterprise still to come, was Premack and Woodruff's 1978 article, "Does the Chimpanzee Have a Theory of Mind?" published in *Behavioral and Brain Sciences*. Clearly, the common expectation of the day was that, on the prospect that "lower" animals may also have some "theory-like" understanding of mental life, any inclination to deny some counterpart theory of mind to preschoolers would need to count as churlish and withholding at best. That is, with everyone rooting for the prospect that young children were at least as complex as their nearest neighbors on some lower branch of the evolutionary tree, expectations were naturally high that your typical preschooler would also be shown to legitimately harbor some workable theory of mind.

As a consequence of such expectations, Premack and Woodruff's now classic *Behavioral and Brain Sciences* "target article"—which concluded that chimpanzees do, in fact, have something akin to a "theory of mind" (but see Premack, 1988, for a later retraction)—seems to have done exactly what a proper target article is optimally meant to do—it drew a lot of fire, friendly and otherwise. That is, it drew an amazingly long list of some 27 commentaries, contributed by a wide-ranging international roster of well-positioned philosophers, psychologists, and sundry cognitive scientists, the large bulk of whom viewed the results presented by Premack and Woodruff as a harbinger of what was to come.

What has subsequently been marked as the most generative of these several commentaries was a submission by Daniel Dennett (1978), entitled "Beliefs about Beliefs." What was especially memorable about Dennett's short commentary is that it included what he described as the minimally complex experimental paradigm necessary to successfully impute a theory of mind. What, in particular, Dennett claimed was that anyone wishing to ascribe some theory of mind to an "organism" would need to demonstrate: (1) that Y believes that H believes that *p*; (2) that Y believes that H desires that *q;* and (3) that Y infers from his

or her belief in (1) and (2) that H will do some observable thing *x*. As a case in point, it might be: (1) that You (Y) believe that Homer (H) believes that *(p)* there is beer in the refrigerator; (2) that You believe that Homer desires/ wants *(q)* a beer; and (3) that, given (1) and (2), You believe that Homer will *(x)* go to the refrigerator, where he believes that the beer is kept, and get one. Dennett went on to caution that various things can complicate such an otherwise straightforward experimental arrangement. One of these arises when (as is often the case) *p* is true (e.g., when Homer is right in assuming that there actually is beer in the fridge). Under such fortuitous circumstances, Y might well anticipate that H would do *x* (i.e., go to the refrigerator) for any number of reasons (such as he is drawn to refrigerators like a magnet), none of which need have anything to do with imagined mental states such as beliefs. The way around such eventualities is to further arrange things experimentally such that H's doing *x* only makes sense if it is also imagined that H harbors a "false belief" about the likely consequences of doing *x* (by arranging, for example, that the refrigerator is stripped of beer, but doing so in a way that leaves H unaware of this "unexpected transfer"). Under such experimental circumstances, it might still be imagined (assuming that Y had the capacity to entertain the possibility of false beliefs) that Homer will be expected to go to the refrigerator anyway, given that he is likely laboring under the misapprehension that there is still beer there to be had. All of this amounts to a seemingly roundabout, but methodologically well-oiled, way of demonstrating that some Y (e.g., you, or some child subject) does or does not subscribe to the "theory" that, true or false, Homer and others all behave with reference to the way they have come to "believe" the world is, rather than how it might objectively be.

Taking Dennett Seriously

Persuaded by the stringency of the semantically dense, but otherwise straightforward arguments put forward by Dennett, the large bulk of subsequent theory-theorists have chosen to follow his methodological recommendations and have put into play various tests of "false belief understanding," purposely built to require only minimal responses on the part of target subjects. By the late 1980s and early 1990s, publications dealing with such measures of false belief understanding, and related aspects of children's so-called developing theories of mind, had reached something of a fever pitch. In the 4-year window between 1988 and 1991, for example, there appeared, in rapid succession, a total of at least 10 volumes devoted to this common theme. The year 1988, for instance, saw the publication of both Astington, Harris, and Olson's flagship volume *Developing Theories of Mind*, and Dunn's *The Beginnings of Social Understanding*. In 1989, Harris's *Children and Emotion: The Development of Psychological Understanding*, Forguson's *Common Sense*, and Frith's book *Autism: Explaining the Enigma* all appeared. The year 1990 saw the publication, not only of Bruner's more generic *Acts of Meaning*, but also Wellman's *The Child's Theory of Mind*; immediately followed in 1991 by Carey and Gelman's *Epigenesis of Mind: Essays in Biology and Knowledge*, Frye and Moore's *Children's Theories of Mind*, and Whiten's *Natural Theories of Mind*. More than half of this long list of books is edited volumes and contains more than 50 chapters by authors who became regular contributors to the mushrooming theory-of-mind literature. Many of these same authors appear again in a 1991 special theories-of-mind issue of the *British Journal of Developmental Psychology*, further swelling the ranks of what was already more than a hundred related journal articles, and perhaps double that number of presentations to learned societies.

All of this early upheaval was, of course, hardly the end of it. A rough machine count of articles given over, in whole or part, to matters pertaining to various folk psychologies of mental life, so-called mind reading, and children's developing theories of mind all published in the intervening 20 years now easily exceeds 4,000! In extreme cases such as this, words like *deluge* and *maelstrom*—words that we are sometimes guilty of bandying about much too casually—actually do seem to apply.

Although this onslaught of published articles has obviously been viewed as welcome news by many of theory of mind's most avid "boosters," it also serves to create an impossible task for anyone—anyone such as ourselves—faced with the task of trying to say something interestingly synoptic about all of these speckled efforts. What, in the absence of a better alternative, we are reduced to here is more simply compiling—not a bona fide review, but, rather, something more on the order of CliffsNotes—something that will, at best, provide a kind of "Traveler's Guide" (Moses & Chandler, 1992) to this runaway theories-of-mind literature.

Quick Reprise of "Standard" Tests of False Belief

Without imagining that any particular set of measures of false belief understanding is somehow coextensive with the full range of potential markers of children's growing appreciation of mental life (why not, for example, also include an account of children's developing understanding of mental-state terms, or referential communication skills, or deception, or pretense, or the telling of lies, to name only a few), it is, nevertheless, also true that an understanding of the possibility of false belief has served as a paradigm case for (and for many is all but definitional of) what having a theory of mind could possibly be taken to mean. For such reasons, special attention is focused here on Wimmer and Perner's (1983) so-called unexpected transfer task, and the claims that these and subsequent authors have made on its behalf.

Getting Wimmer and Perner Right

In their now classic measure of false belief understanding, Wimmer and Perner presented children with a set of illustrated stories in which a protagonist acquired a false belief about an object's location by virtue of not having seen (as the child participants clearly saw) that object being surreptitiously moved from one place to another.

Picture a puppet theater outfitted with two cabinets, A and B, two doll figures meant to represent "Maxi" and his mother, together with a chocolate bar they are bringing back from the store. Together, Maxi and his mother place the chocolate in cabinet A. Later, while he is outside playing, and consequently in no position to be any the wiser, Maxi's mother (operating with no intent to deceive) moves the chocolate to the second cabinet B. On Maxi's return, child participants, who had witnessed all of these events, were asked to predict where, on his return, Maxi would look for his chocolate, or otherwise think it might be.

Remarkably, children younger than, first 6, but later 5, and eventually 4, typically failed to take account of the difference between the true (i.e., updated) location of the chocolate and what Maxi otherwise has every reason to believe (on earlier, but now outdated evidence) concerning its whereabouts. That is, children younger than what eventually turned out to be 4 were reported to confuse their own more up-to-date knowledge concerning the current location of the chocolate with the now mistaken belief appropriate to Maxi. In short, such young children seemingly found themselves unable to entertain the possibility that they would think one thing and Maxi another. By contrast, children older than 4 routinely responded in ways indicative of their new-found appreciation that, out of ignorance about the "unexpected change" in the location of the chocolate, Maxi would proceed on his now false belief that the chocolate remained back in cabinet A where he had put it.

In the more than quarter of a century that has passed since Wimmer and Perner first published their results, the main outlines of their findings have been widely replicated, and young children's difficulties with such "unexpected transfer" tasks have been shown to persist in the face of at least some significant task simplifications (e.g., for a review, see Carpendale & Lewis, 2006). As a result, few have seriously doubted that 4-year-olds do standardly pass such false belief tests, just as young 3-year-olds regularly do not.

What *is* subject to especially serious doubts, however, are all of the far-reaching conclusions that Wimmer and Perner (and subsequent theory-theorists) have wished to draw from such data. Altogether, three such large-scale doubts will be focused on in the course of this chapter, but only the last of these are the focus here in the balance of Part I.

The first of these concerns centers on the view, staunchly defended by most theory-theorists, that children who fail such "unexpected transfer" and later "unexpected contents" tests (Gopnik & Astington, 1988; Perner, Leekam, & Wimmer, 1987) actually suffer from some across-the-board cognitive "deficit" that not only deeply undermines their ability to entertain the possibility of false belief, but also renders children of 3 years and still younger children fundamentally incapable of appreciating the representational nature of mental experience, of adopting an intentional stance, or of otherwise joining in with those of 4 years in understanding the representational nature of mental life. The task of reporting on the work and contrary claims of other investigators who often share with theory-theorists an abiding interest in the folk psychologies of young persons, but who reject the notion that young preschoolers suffer some cognitive deficit that categorically denies them access to anything like a bona fide belief about belief is the subject of Part II.

The second major bone of contention picked with Wimmer and Perner and subsequent theory-theorists (e.g., Gopnik, et al., 1999; Meltzoff & Gopnik, 1993; Perner, 1991; Ruffman, Olson, & Astington, 1991; Wellman, 1990) turns on their common claim that once an appreciation of the possibility of false belief is well in place, usually sometime around 4 years of age, such children can be fairly credited with a theory-like understanding of the mind that is adult-like in all of its essential characteristics. Although some quantitative improvements in fluency and proficiency are envisioned, and some progression from novice to expert status is tolerated in such "one miracle" views, all possibilities of further qualitative transformations in

the architectural structure of such mentalist theories are ruled out of court. In direct opposition to all such views, other contributors to the literature on epistemic development have rejected all such claims of singularity, and have undertaken to identify various other different and later-occurring mental models. Part III of this chapter is given over to a discussion of these subsequent turns of the epistemic wheel.

The third set of broad concerns that have been raised by critics of the theory-theory enterprise—concerns that are voiced in what still remains of this Part I—are neither about whether children younger than 4 already possess some or all of the competencies differently measured by various tests of false belief understanding, nor are they focused on whether there is continuing epistemic development beyond the fourth year. Rather, the concerns we now turn our attention to here are of a different and more root-and-branch sort—concerns that grow out of certain faults that are found with the whole theory-theory enterprise. As detailed here, these larger caliber concerns can be seen to turn on a small handful of foundational assumptions common to most theory-theorists. Included on this short list are what we call the "theory" question, the "developmental" question, and the "agency" question.

The "Theory" Question

High on the list of the things that have especially rankled those looking on from outside of the theory-of-mind tent has been the stubborn insistence among the theories-theorists that what they are studying actually warrants being called children's "theories" of mental life in the first place. Perhaps as a result of professional lifetimes often spent in the service of trying to educate undergraduates about what holding to a theory might conceivably mean, or more generally, because it has seemed to many to be much too much of a stretch to credit preschoolers, who still have difficulty in speaking in full sentences, with anything as toplofty as an already adult-like theory of mind, even onlookers who are otherwise broadly sympathetic often bridal, wishing that there were some less grand-eloquent way of framing the whole theories-of-mind enterprise.

Although there is, perhaps, an element of rightness in such disgruntlement, such critics would appear to be right, but not necessarily for the right reason. Although claims to the effect that children subscribe to such "theories" are commonplace, it is important to appreciate that such talk does not come out of nowhere. Rather, imagining that persons of every stripe necessarily rely on some more or less implicit "theory" about mental matters participates in a long and distinguished philosophical tradition.

In a continuing effort to slip the leash on the various "other minds problems" endemic to Cartesian dualism, and working to avoid a certain circularity inherent in the "verificationist accounts" of meaning promoted by philosophical behaviorists such as Ryle (1949), a long list of late 20th-century philosophers of mind (e.g., Armstrong, 1968; Lewis, 1972; Morton, 1980; Putnam, 1960; Stich, 1996) have effectively promoted the idea that the meanings of mental-state terms are not best given individually or exclusively by observable behaviors. Instead, proponents of such "functionalist" accounts have argued that mental-state terms get their meaning collectively through their association with clusters of related terms, all of which are embedded within a common empirical theory. As they bear on efforts to explicate notions of "belief" or "desire," for example, such functionalist accounts promote the view that we all construct various commonsense or folk psychologies that, in ways not unlike the operations of scientific theories, allow us to explain certain regularities between stimuli and responses.

Certain "eliminativist" versions of such broadly functional accounts have been used in the service of arguing that commonsense or folk psychologies are not only theories but massively mistaken and untenable theories that deserve to be eliminated outright (e.g., Churchland, 1981). More commonly, however, a growing consortium of philosophers of mind, psychologists, and other cognitive scientists (e.g., Stich & Nichols, 2003) have pushed forward the idea that, because the meaning of ordinary mental state terms is best determined by the role they play in commonsense psychological theories, anyone committed to the serious developmental study of beliefs must, necessarily, attempt to make plain what particular theory or theories of mind young people actually use.

Among the contemporary psychologists who defend this view, perhaps the most clearly spoken has been Wellman (2002), who, together with some of his close collaborators (e.g., Gopnik & Wellman, 1994; Wellman & Bartsch, 1988), has worked to make plain what he describes as "three theory-relevant features" (Wellman, 1988, p. 67)—features that are supposedly common to any and all theories. He argued that all who subscribe to a theory share "a basic conception of what phenomena are encompassed by the theory; a sense of how these phenomena and propositions about them are mutually interdependent; and, consequently, what counts as a relevant and informative explanation of changes and relationships [sic] among the various phenomena" (Wellman, 1988, p. 66). According to Morton (1980), "theory-theory" is the contention that, at least in the case of ordinary adults, our knowledge of the mental world—the realm of beliefs, desires, intentions, thoughts, and so on—is a theory, a naive or undisciplined theory, even, perhaps, as Forguson (1989) suggests a "theorette," but a theory nonetheless. It is Wellman's contention, and that of all of the theory-theorists discussed here (e.g., Gopnik et al., 1999), that after a certain not yet fully agreed on but still tender age, children do come to subscribe to such a mentalistic theory.

Right or wrong, this has proved to be a very productive idea. If, as we are told that they should, theories are to be judged, not by some correspondence to the illusive "truth," but by their capacity to promote serious research, then theory-theory is clearly on the short list of the very best theories psychology has dreamed up. Perhaps Russell (1992) was more right than he knew or intended when he quipped that theory-theory is "so good that they had to name it twice." Perhaps all of those who find any talk of "children's developing theories of mind" sticking in their craw should just get over it.

That is not the problem. The real problem lies in automatically proceeding as though any account of children's developing insights about mental life must necessarily be a "representational" theory. This is hardly the case. Piaget, for example, had it that young children make it through most of their so-called sensorimotor period without "representing" anything at all. Enthusiasts of such representational theories should, of course, be entitled to a certain leeway in how forcefully they intend to press their point, but even serious readers of the theory-of-mind literature could be forgiven for coming away with the idea that young children automatically "have" a representational theory of mind in just the same way that they have heads, shoulders, knees, and toes. What makes this not only unfortunate but misleading is, of course, that there is no shortage of equally interesting alternative explanations afoot (see Bickhard, 2006, for a review of this literature). Perhaps the most serious of these contenders has come to be known as "simulation theory."

The Challenge from Simulation Accounts

Rather than imagining that children in short pants are running about inventing and putting into practice elaborate mentalistic theories, it is considerably more plausible, many (e.g., Davies & Stone, 1995; Goldman, 1989; Gordon, 1986; Harris, 2006; Johnson, 1988; Markman, Klein, & Suhr, 2009) have argued, that children's success at predicting and explaining what others will think and do is not the result of a rich body of well-theorized information about the mind, but comes about instead by means of a process of projective simulation—by first imagining "stepping into the shoes" of the other and then figuring out what they themselves would perceive, think, or feel in that circumstance. As such, proponents of this view tend to place special emphasis on children's introspective access to their own mental states, arguing that phenomenological awareness of such states provides a rich source of information about the mind that does not rely on theoretical inferences.

Stich and Nichols (2003) try to convey how such a simulation approach might work by analogy to the problem of trying to work out how some new airplane design might work in certain wind conditions. One way to proceed, they suggest, would be to derive a prediction from aeronautical theory, together with various particulars about the plane in question. Another would be to build a model of the plane, put it in a wind tunnel that reproduces the wind conditions in question, and then simply observe how the model behaves—a strategy that does not require a rich body of theory. Simulation theorists maintain that we can act as our own wind tunnel. All that is required to predict what another person's mind will do, especially if it is supposed that that person's mind is similar to one's own, is to imagine that such an individual would do and think as we would under similar circumstances. All of this, plus some capacity to go "off-line," and to imagine or "pretend" to have beliefs and desires different from one's own, is enough, such simulation theorists argue, to get the same result as theory-theorists, but without all of the excess "theoretical baggage."

The point here is not to necessarily plump for simulation theory at the expense of theory-theory. Rather, we only mean to emphasize that available accounts of children's theories of mind are not objective descriptions of how the world actually is, but are, rather, "theories" about how the world is, in active competition with other and different theories. Consequently, if you don't fancy talk about young children's mentalistic "theories," then there are other alternatives from which to freely choose.

The "Developmental" Question

Although most of the several thousand publications broadly concerned with the possibility of false belief understanding that have appeared since the early 1980s are about children, and thus constitute a contribution to

"child psychology," few of these efforts qualify as truly "developmental" studies, all for the reason that they fail to satisfy even the minimal condition of entertaining the possibility that development actually unfolds in real time. Instead, most champion what amounts to a singular, "one miracle" view of change by paradigm revolution—that is, a "now-you-see-it, now-you-don't," one-off, salutary sort of accounting strategy that imagines the process of becoming representational as arriving without prefix and as having no sequel—a process, if you can still call it that, which effectively "begins and ends all in the same breath."

Clearly, as we have tried to show, the new proud-as-punch insight that effectively binds together all card-carrying members of the theories-of-mind group has been the renunciation of Piaget and all of his supposed "powers" (e.g., Gopnik et al., 1999). Most particularly, they have objected to Piaget and Inhelder's allegedly mistaken insistence that, well into their adolescence, young school-aged children continue to suffer a persistently egocentric frame of mind. Quite to the contrary, all seriously committed theory-theorists have insisted instead that preschoolers of 3½ or 4 already subscribe to an epistemic view that makes adult-like beliefs about beliefs (including false beliefs) fully available to them (e.g., Perner, 1991; Wellman et al., 2001).

As if it were not enough to have declined to see in the epistemic struggles of young school-aged children anything that might oblige a re-envisioning of the folk epistemologies attributable to those living beyond the familiar 5- to 7-year shift (Chandler & Lalonde, 1996), theory-theorists have also gone the second mile by attributing to toddlers, and other preschoolers still younger than 3½ or 4, a disqualifying "conceptual deficit" (e.g., Perner et al., 1987)—one that reputedly renders the world of mental representation essentially opaque. Having so completely truncated their search pattern both fore and aft, theory-theorists have come to be seen by many as guilty of having so thoroughly narrowed the focus of their research attention that all conceivable forms of epistemic growth and development end up collapsed onto a single and ultimately nondevelopmental vanishing point.

It is true, of course, that several key contributors to the theories-of-mind literature have speculated about and collected evidence pertaining to what are described as developmentally later occurring "beliefs about beliefs about belief" (see Harris, 2006, for a review). In one such series of studies, for example, it was shown that, although 4-year-olds were perfectly able to unpack nested situations concerning Mary's beliefs about John's beliefs about the location of an ice-cream truck, only children of 7 or 8 could get their minds successfully wrapped around multiple embedded problems involving Mary's beliefs about John's beliefs about Mary's beliefs concerning the location of the truck (Perner & Wimmer, 1985). These and related studies, to be discussed more fully later in this chapter, are commonly brought out whenever there is a felt need to defend against the accusation that theory-theory lacks a developmental dimension.

It is also the case that some potential developmental scope may have been added by theorists such as Wellman (1990; Wellman & Liu, 2004) and Perner (1991), both of whom have written importantly about some of what might go on before 4. For his part, Wellman has developed an elaborate theory about how, before acquiring any effective understanding about the possibility of false beliefs, even young 3-year-olds understand and mentally operate on notions of "desire." In short, Wellman defends the view that before first using anything like a standard "belief-desire psychology," they already have in place at least half of that story (e.g., Wellman & Liu, 2004).

Although certainly aware of the problem, what Wellman's postulated "Desire Psychology" does not effectively address is what Duhem (1906/1962) called the problem of *holism*. According to this widely accepted view, our various mentalistic concepts, including various intentional states such as beliefs and desires, cannot be treated in isolation. Rather, all of these concepts need to be seen as entrenched in a common network of related concepts. Thus, as Armstrong (1981) has argued, "The corresponding concepts must be introduced together or not at all" (p. 24). On this view, concepts of desire, denuded of necessarily associated beliefs, would be fundamentally nonsensical (Bennett, 1978). For example, it is not clear what it would mean to say that Homer wanted a beer unless one was also prepared to say that he knew what a beer was. By such more holistic lights, our concepts of belief and desire necessarily come as a "package deal" and must necessarily share a yoked developmental history. On this account, it would then not be possible for a genuine conception of desire to be in place before a corresponding conception of belief. The upshot of all of this would seem to be that theory-theory is back where it started, that is, with a well-marketed set of assumptions about a particular watershed achievement, but little or nothing to say about what might have come before or might come after (Chandler, 2001).

More generally, it is worth noting that, seen through the eyes of many theory-theorists (e.g., Gopnik, 1991; Gopnik & Wellman, 1992; Morton, 1980), any later-life changes that might conceivably occur in young people's conceptions of mental life would need to be understood as instances of some revolutionary "paradigm shift"—a shift of the sort often thought to mark the slow, episodic course of scientific theory change (Kuhn, 1970). Given that theory-theorists are generally committed to the view that there is no real qualitative light between the theory of mind subscribed to by 4-year-olds and that held by your average adult, it is hard to imagine where the requisite incommensurabilities required to spark such a paradigm revolution might come from, or how any of us would be able to recognize such revolutionary changes if they were to somehow occur. Interestingly, rather than taking scientific change as a source model for ontogenetic change, developmentalists such as Piaget (1972/1965) have tended to move in the opposite direction by taking children as source models for science. Although this is perhaps not the place to attempt to arbitrate between these contrasting views, it should at least be clear enough that, although nothing about theory-theory would lead us to expect epistemic growth beyond the preschool years, more constructivist accounts of the sort promoted by Piaget do provide some grounds for hope that the ontogenetic study of epistemic change across the life span may impact on our collective efforts to better understand scientific change (Chapman, 1988; Garcia, 1987; Murray, 1979).

The "Agency" Question

The thrust of this concern over precisely when, in the course of development, growing persons can be fairly credited with a "mature" theory of mind turns on the child-as-scientist metaphor that has dominated the theory-theory enterprise, and the "causal" language that commonly attends it. More specifically, it is argued (e.g., Blasi, 1995; Bickhard, 2006; Carpendale & Chandler, 1996; Greenwood, 1989; Russell, 1996) that, in its push to situate children's conceptions of others' beliefs and desires within a "scientistic" framework of folk psychological "laws" (e.g., Gopnik & Wellman, 1994), the theories-of-mind enterprise has promoted an impoverished conception of agency, that, to borrow from the Enlightenment philosopher Thomas Reid (1788/1863), works to wrongly locate the "active powers of man" [sic] outside of, or external to, the individual. Bandura (1986, p. 12) similarly characterizes such accounts as promoting only a notion of "mechanical agency" where all activity or movement originates from outside of persons. The upshot of such an externalist view, as Blasi

(1995, p. 235) points out, is that "the idea that knowledge belongs to, [and] is an intrinsic possession of the conscious person, who intentionally pursues it" is lost, and all talk of subjectivity, at least as it is commonly understood to operate in the personal construction of meaning, takes a back seat to more "object-centered" notions that work to reduce genuine interpretive diversity to mundane instances of simple ignorance and *mis*interpretation (see Carpendale & Chandler, 1996, p. 1693). Although some of the evidence required to show this more clearly better belongs to Part III of this account, where attention is focused on the distinction between passive "copy theories" and more active "interpretive" conceptions of mental life (Chandler & Boyes, 1982), it will hopefully be enough to point out here that all standard "unexpected transfer tasks" succeed in driving a wedge between one and another representation of the world by simply gerrymandering access to information so that some target person (Maxi, for example) is left in ignorance, whereas the subject himself or herself is better informed.

What remains more or less hidden in the background of this description is exactly where such a "copy theory of mind" leaves children in terms of their understanding of the source of the mind's activity and their consequent notions of epistemic agency. A copy theory, we would argue, naturally leads children to view epistemic agency as originating outside, or external to, the individual. This follows from the fact that, based on such a view, the mind is, as Rorty (1979) claims, no more than a "mirror of nature" that essentially reflects internally on the mind's eye what can be seen externally in the world outside our skins. Although some (e.g., Perner & Davies, 1991) have claimed that the mind, even in this evident state of passive accommodation, is nevertheless "doing" something, it is no more "active," we would counter, than is any other mirror or reflective surface when light strikes it. The mind's activity, in this case, is neither a process that is initiated nor controlled by an active subject, and is akin instead to what philosophers of action (e.g., Frankfurt, 1988; Taylor, 1966; Velleman, 2000) have characterized as behavioral *re*-actions, or mere internal events, that pale by comparison with more "full-blooded" (Velleman, 1993) and "meaningful" (Moya, 1990) real *actions* belonging to, and initiated by, autonomous, self-moving agents. For the young copy-theorist, mental life amounts to "psychological and physiological *events*" that, as Velleman (1993) notes, may be said to "take place inside a person," but then (and here's the catch) "the person serves merely as the arena for these events: he takes no active part" (p. 189). In other words, for those children who hold a copy theory of mind, it is best to say that they recognize the mere *activities* of epistemic "patients" rather than the meaning-making *actions* of knowing "agents" (Sokol & Chandler, 2003).

Questions about all of these disputed matters abound. Why, except for certain persnickety methodological considerations, are "true" beliefs not just as interesting, for example, as those that happen to be "false"? Are chimpanzees really a hard enough case? What about our cats, dogs, and goldfish, or, still closer to our hearts, our infant children? Given that your average adult lives late into their 70s, and that children of 4 are commonly credited with having a theory of mind that is already adult-like in all of its major particulars, what are we all meant to be doing epistemically in the remaining 70 plus years of our lives? Is that all there is? There is every reason to suppose that any complete list of such uncertain and disputed matters could, in principle, be extended almost indefinitely.

PART II: IS THERE METAREPRESENTATIONAL LIFE BEFORE AGE 4?

Given a quarter-century's worth of near and far replications of Wimmer and Perner's 1983 initial results, whether children younger than 4 years can or cannot pass "standard" tests of false belief understanding is neither particularly open nor, we suggest, especially interesting. What is of theoretical moment, however, is whether there is some early age before which beliefs about beliefs can otherwise be shown to be possible, and whether theory-theorists' own theoretically charged reasons, and not some other reading of the evidence, best fit the generally agreed-on fact that children older than "X" are typically successful and children younger than "Y" unsuccessful in navigating the intricacies of standardized "unexpected transfer" tasks.

Boosters and Scoffers

Among the groups of strange bedfellows that have assembled around these empirical and interpretive challenges, two, in particular, stand out as sufficiently oppositional in character to allow some real light to pass between them. The catechetical claim common to the historically first and most orthodox of these groups—call them the *Scoffers*—is that there really exists an early stretch of developmental time before which nothing about young people's behavior warrants their being credited with anything like a bona fide theory of mind—a supposedly "mind-blind" period (typically said to occupy the first 3 or 4 years of a child's life) that then gives way, at some decisive watershed moment, to what are essentially adult-like insights about the representational nature of mental life.

Although practitioners of this "one miracle" view tend to be unified in their common condemnation of more "gradualist" alternatives, there is among them room for important differences of opinion about what constitutes a truly "minimally complex" set of methods for indexing the exact age of onset of children's first and purportedly last theory of mind. Consequently, among the crowd currently taking issue with the claim that 4-year-olds, but not still younger children, already subscribe to a truly representational theory of mind, there is a subset of otherwise committed *Scoffers* who, although seemingly comfortable with the enterprise of specifying some exact age at which true representations of representations first become possible, is, nevertheless, still prepared to quibble over whether this happens to be at age 4 or some still earlier age (for a review, see Carpendale & Lewis, 2006). The shared hope of this reformist wing of the *Scoffer* group is that by holding to the same demanding standards of proof subscribed to by more orthodox theory-theorists, it will be possible to lower even further the age at which research participants are ordinarily seen to "pass" such procedures.

Standing out in sharp contrast with this *Scoffer* group of theory-theorists, there also exists a second, but more loosely organized, assemblage of *Boosters* that all participate in the common view that children much younger than 4 have already achieved and effectively practice some real, if fledgling, understanding of epistemic life. The reservations that representatives of this *Booster* group generally hold about classic theory-theory tend to be of a broad and transcendental sort that leads them to object, not just to the particular claim that children younger than 4 lack a genuine theory of mind, but to any line of evidence purporting to specify any other age before which some important modicum of representational complexity can be said to be at least tacitly present. In its most orthodox form—practiced by those whom Olson (1993) calls "intentional realists"— various neonativist *Boosters* (e.g., Fodor, 1987; Leslie, 1987; Macnamara, 1989) argue that nothing as "powerful" as a truly representational system could possibly arise out of an antecedent system of less complexity, and so some nascent, perhaps modularized, beliefs about belief are said to have existed from the outset. For example, Fodor (1987) writes:

Here is what I would have done if I had been faced with this problem in designing Homo sapiens. I would have made a knowledge of commonsense Homo sapiens psychology innate; that way nobody would have to spend time learning it…The empirical evidence that God did it the way I would have isn't, in fact unimpressive. (p. 132)

Still others (e.g., Dunn, 1991), spurred on by the discovery of so many previously unrecognized capabilities on the part of the very young, tend to also be deeply suspicious of all categorical claims about what children cannot even begin to do, especially when such claims are based on an inability to pass some artfully arranged laboratory procedure. As such, representatives of this *Booster* group tend to be somewhat dismissive of the whole false belief assessment enterprise that has spawned so much of the present theory-of-mind literature. Operating instead in full recognition of the lurking possibility that their own commitments to greater ecological validity come equipped with some heightened risk for errors made on the side of leniency, such investigators, nevertheless, typically see methodological trade-offs that err on the side of the in situ as generally preferable to the more pristine process of holding out until the last possible false-positive dog is dead.

Finally, among this loosely federated *Booster* group, there are those (and here we mean to especially count ourselves) whose first commitment is to the working principle that nothing, or next to nothing, in the ontogenetic course ever truly qualifies as a bona fide one-trick pony, capable of arriving on the scene without antecedent or departing without constantly changing structural consequences. By this way of reckoning, anything that is alleged to simply "pop up" at the age of 4, or any other age, and that is subsequently imagined to go on being relentlessly self-same through subsequent thick and thin, automatically falls under suspicion.

Unlike their *Scoffer* counterparts, whose collective efforts have been, at least historically, unified by a common methodological commitment to some variant of standard "unexpected change" and "unexpected transfer" measures of false belief understanding, *Boosters* have not tended to rally around any single assessment strategy. Rather, they have variously used sundry measures of deception, pretense, and referential communication as methodological vehicles for getting at young children's early insights into mental life. Representative examples drawn from this scattered body of research are lined out under the broad heading of *Deception, Lying, Pretense, Referential Behavior, and Other Markers of Early Insights into Mental Life.*

Before any of this, however, attention is first turned to the efforts of those who have tinkered with more standard measures of false belief understanding, all in the hope of better identifying whatever lower bound threshold there may be in children's earliest beliefs about beliefs.

Bending Over Backward to Lower the Bar on False Belief Understanding

As skilled Limbo dancers are well aware, success at lowering the bar depends on just how far one is prepared to bend over backward. In this case, various efforts to pick out the lower bound of false belief understanding have all involved inventing modified methods and procedures calculated to remove incidental impediments that might work to prevent young children from demonstrating their best understanding of other people's earliest beliefs about belief. By working to denude such measures of unnecessary mental-state terms (Moore, Pure, & Furrow, 1990), by allowing respondents to simply point (rather than explain in words) where Maxi would first search for his chocolate (Siegal & Beattie, 1991), by carefully rehearsing the plot lines of the various story problems used (Lewis, 1994), by otherwise providing children with various memory aids (Mitchell & Lacohee, 1991), or by otherwise modifying these tasks in ways meant to more fully engage the interests of young subjects (Hala & Chandler, 1993a, 1993b, 1996; Moses, 1993; Wellman & Banerjee, 1991), more or less everyone who has worked to strip standard false-belief measures of their unessential processing requirements has found the same thing—children as young as 3 years standardly demonstrate an understanding of the possibility of false beliefs.

For similar reasons, Wellman and colleagues (Wellman, et al., 2001) worked to draw attention to the fact that our collective theoretical interests are, or should be, in children's understanding of true belief, and that the common preoccupation in the literature with false belief understanding is primarily owed to methodological difficulties encountered in attempting to distinguish actions that are based on beliefs that are true from actions that implicate no representations of beliefs at all. As such, if it were methodologically possible to determine with some confidence that young children's understanding of their own and others' actions are, in fact, belief driven, even though these beliefs happened to be true, then it would be possible to eliminate many of the awkward procedural steps required to orchestrate standard false belief scenarios. Through a series of 10 interrelated studies, Wellman and his colleagues worked

to overcome various confounds associated with inquiring about true (as opposed to false) beliefs and, in the process, found that children as young as 3 performed at or near ceiling levels.

In brief, it would appear that the problems in false belief understanding encountered by children younger than 4 are not due to some conceptual deficit, or lack of understanding of false beliefs per se, but are better laid at the door of various other processing limitations, including executive function limitations, language problems, natural biases, or difficulties with counterfactual reasoning (for studies demonstrating these links, and for reviews of this extensive literature, see Jacques and Markovitch, Chapter 13 of this volume, and also see, for example, Bloom & German, 2002; Carlson, Moses, & Claxton, 2004; Carpendale & Lewis, 2006; German & Leslie, 2000; Harris, 1991; Milligan, Astington, & Dack, 2007; Moses, 1993; Muller, Zelazo, & Imrisek, 2005; Zelazo, 2000).

The broad conclusion that belief reasoning makes significant demands on various cognitive processes—demands that call into question whether so-called classic measures of false belief understanding are, as advertised, minimally complex—is further supported by correlations between belief reasoning and executive functioning in adults (e.g., German & Hehman, 2006), and by evidence that belief reasoning is impaired if executive functions are disrupted because of brain injury (e.g., Samson, Apperly, Kathirgamanathan, & Humphreys, 2005). Taken together, what these and other related findings show is that, by simplifying various task requirements, or eliminating various troublesome procedural complications associated with standard "unexpected change" and "unexpected transfer" false belief tasks, it is possible to systematically lower the age at which young children first give evidence of understanding the intentional nature of beliefs, both true and false.

The general thrust of these several rehabilitative efforts has, then, been to show that there is something psychometrically inhospitable about standard false belief measures that oblige young preschoolers to sit through verbally saturated, third party, "as-if" narratives concerning matters in which they have no personal stake, all as a prelude to answering a barrage of temporally ill-marked, hypothetical, and computationally complex questions that regularly pit children's known salience biases against their otherwise good intelligence. Alternatively, by simply taking steps to further clarify or to better temporally mark the questions being posed, by better equating the salience of both false and true beliefs (Mitchell & Lacohee, 1991;

Zaitchik, 1991), by working to reduce the memory load and other computational demands of the usual story narratives (Lewis, 1994), or by otherwise modifying these tasks in ways meant to more fully engage the interest of young subjects (Chandler, Fritz, & Hala, 1989; Hala & Chandler, 1993a, 1993b, 1996; Hala, Chandler, & Fritz, 1991; Moses, 1993; Wellman & Banerjee, 1991), it is clearly possible to show that if there is a special witching hour when young children first acquire an understanding of the possibility of false beliefs, it most likely occurs nearer 3 than 4 years of age.

It remains true, of course, that children who are 4 and older typically do a better job of understanding others' false beliefs, and of remembering their own false beliefs than do their still younger counterparts, often without the benefit of the various procedural modifications just described. For many orthodox theory-theorists, all that such boundary-altering findings are dismissively said to show is that, when given "special assistance," somewhat younger research participants can be "artificially" helped to succeed on tasks that they would normally fail (e.g., Wellman et al., 2001). What each reader will need to decide for himself or herself is whether it is the so-called standard measures of false belief understanding, or the various procedural variations just reported here, that should be judged as most indicative of children's natural abilities. In weighing these alternatives, it is, perhaps, useful to also factor into one's judgments the fact that adults also frequently experience difficulties of their own in sorting out what they and others believe (e.g., see Birch, 2005; Birch & Bernstein, 2007; Birch & Bloom, 2003, 2004; Bernstein, et al., 2004; Epley et al., 2004; Keysar et al., 2003; Royzman, Cassidy, & Baron, 2003).

Whatever you, as a reader, choose to conclude about the likely merits of any or all of the methodological and procedural modifications offered up as a way of "improving" on more traditional measures of false belief understanding, and whether you are convinced that false belief understanding occurs at age 4 or much earlier, what you will likely have still more difficulty with is the prospect to which we now turn attention: A working theory of mind may well be available even to infant children, and possibly even to various nonhuman animals, all of whom have especially limited resources for language and executive control. For instance, Onishi and Baillargeon (2005) report that 15-month-old infants look longer when an agent with a false belief acts as if she has a true belief (see also Surian et al., 2007). *Similarly*, chimpanzees (who got all of this started in the first place) are known to exploit what

a dominant competitor sees, or "believes," to obtain food without threat from the more dominant chimp (Hare, Call, & Tomasello, 2001; Tomasello, Call, & Hare, 2003). Not surprisingly, these findings are controversial. Some have argued, for instance, that such evidence shows that infants understand false beliefs, whereas similar evidence in nonhuman primates has been viewed as indicators of perception and knowledge understanding, but not beliefs (e.g., Call & Tomasello, 2008). Still leaner interpretations of these findings have also been provided (see Penn & Povinelli, 2007; Perner & Ruffman, 2005).

Leaving nonhuman primates aside, what are we to make of the possibility that infants and children much younger than 3 or 4 might be more competent at reasoning about mental life than the classic literature on false belief understanding would lead one to believe? Is there other evidence to suggest that before age 3 or 4 children should be credited with some understanding of mental activity? Are the differences between infants and older children simply ones of degree? Are there two separate mental-state reasoning systems, one that is dependent on language and executive abilities, and another that relies on more automatic processes? These are the kinds of questions we turn to in the following section.

Deception, Lying, Pretense, Referential Behavior, and Other Markers of Early Insights into Mental Life

Since the 1980s, charter members of what we have called the *Booster* group have collectively pointed to an impressively long list of early arising competencies, each of which, when taken piecemeal, pose some serious, if limited, challenge to the delayed onset view, and when combined, collectively constitute a rather impressive challenge to any would-be *Scoffer*. Any such list of possible challenges to the claim that only 4-year-olds appreciate the propositional nature of their own and others' representations would include the facts that, well in advance of any supposed 48-month-watershed, still younger children are uncommonly good at the following tasks: (1) taking active steps to disinform others by purposefully leading them into beliefs that are patently false (e.g., Chandler et al., 1989, Hala & Chandler, 1993a, 1993b, 1996); (2) engaging in elaborate acts of social pretense that arguably require a working understanding of the distinction between things and their possible counterfactual representations (e.g., Dunn & Dale, 1984; Leslie, 1987); (3) salting their usual talk with mental-state terms that attach to their own and others' belief states (e.g., Bretherton, 1991); (4) behaving cooperatively and competently with others in ways that seem difficult to interpret without crediting them with knowledge of true belief states (e.g., Dunn, 1991; Reddy, 1990); (5) grasping the referential intent of adults interested to teach them the meaning of various words (e.g., Baldwin et al., 1996; Bloom, 2000; Tomasello & Barton, 1994); and (6) declaratively pointing to interesting matters that lay outside another's perceptual field (e.g., Astington, 1993; Bretherton, 1991; Bretherton & Beeghly, 1982) Although none of these claims is free of controversy, or somehow immune to a host of possible reductive reinterpretations, the combined weight of these various demonstrations, some of which present evidence of an ability to appreciate representation as representation in infant children hardly able to walk or talk, would seem to be enough to cause anyone not already fully committed to a delayed onset view to seriously rethink their position. In difficult situations such as this, the open question is always, "Would a lie help?"

Lies and Deceit

We are not of one mind about lies and deceits. Notwithstanding the fact that bearing false witness easily made it into Judeo-Christianity's top 10 "thou shall nots" (Exodus 20: 2–17), few among us are entirely free of the sin of pride about having successfully lied our way out of some tightly painted corner, or having privately admired the elegance of some especially well-crafted deceit. Not to put too fine a point on it, pulling off a good lie or deceit is widely (although rarely publicly) counted as a point in one's intellectual favor. Taking someone in—pulling the wool over their eyes, so to speak—clearly requires skills, including the skillful reading of other people's mental states.

It seems intuitively compelling that certain well-placed lies or acts of deceit, especially those purposely built to lead others to take as true what is known to be false, offer something close to proof positive that the young deceivers who author them must have at least some working understanding of the possibility of false belief, and thus deserve to be credited with some bona fide theory of mind. Coupled with this evident link, if not an identity relation, between deceit and false belief understanding is the fact that there is a good deal of at least anecdotal evidence indicating that the ability to use mental-state terms, to perpetrate lies and deceits (Dunn, 1991; Dunn & Munn, 1985; Reddy 1990), and to recognize them in the actions of others (e.g., Lewis, Stanger, & Sullivan, 1989), first come to children at a surprisingly young age.

None of this has escaped the watchful eye of typical theory-theorists, most of whom have been quick to appreciate that if any important part of such naturalistic evidence about the alleged deceits of infants and young preschoolers is allowed to stand, then still further efforts to go on endlessly replicating standard measures of false belief understanding become pointless, and all claims about a mysterious watershed in false belief understanding said to emerge at age 4 will need to be abandoned. The battle lines are, therefore, clearly drawn. Either toddlers do sometimes behave deceitfully, and do so with a clear intent to cause others to believe to be true what they themselves know to be false (thus necessitating a dramatic rewriting of theory-theory as we have come to know it), or alternatively, perhaps such children are simply repeating things they have heard others say, regurgitating social scripts and routines, or mindlessly going through the motions of these games for the sheer pleasure of the responses they get from others. What follows is an attempt to line out available evidence on both sides of this controversy, beginning with the deflationary arguments standardly run by classic theory-theorists.

Before turning to these competing accounts, however, one quick clarification is in order. Hopefully it is already clear enough that what is at stake here has nothing to do with whether persons of any given age are or are not skillful liars. In fact, evidence that young children are terrible (often comical) liars and regularly fail in their attempts to deceive is abundant. They deny, for example, having eaten the cookies despite being smeared with chocolate and cookie crumbs, they "hide" under the couch without bothering to tuck in their protruding feet, and they regularly bumble the parts that would actually make for convincing lies. Such preschoolers are similarly notorious for their transparent and patently self-serving attempts to rewrite history in accordance with their own liking (e.g., LaFerniere, 1988; Vasek, 1988), and are otherwise quick to confuse ignorance-based mistakes with lies, or to wrongly imagine that deceit can be measured by its distance from the truth and the amount of punishment it draws. As Piaget reported (1965/1932), for example, even 5- and 6-year-olds believe that a lie about a 100-pound canary is twice as bad, and deserves twice as much punishment, as does a lie about a 50-pound canary. Bloom (2004) relays a related story about a 3-year-old who having been repeatedly told to keep the existence of a pie a secret from the guest of honor, walked up to him and shrieked, "There is no pie!" Clearly, if you wanted to draft someone to carry off a good lie on your behalf, it would not be wise to choose a young child.

What all of these examples help to show is that precisely where appropriate definitional lines ought to be drawn will ultimately depend on what sorts of research questions one aims to answer. For certain investigations, what is of most interest are the ages at which young persons begin to grasp the "tells" or "give-aways" that otherwise prevent them from being accomplished liars. A lifetime could obviously be spent in honing such Machiavellian skills. None of this, however, is to the present point, in so far as this point turns on the broad question of when in their development children are first capable of entertaining the very possibility of deceit, however badly equipped they may be to *successfully* pull off such a trick. All that having been said, what is it exactly that standard-issue theory-theorists find so wanting in what others have been quick (perhaps too quick) to see as early evidence of bona fide lying and deception?

Defending the Ramparts of Theory-Theory against Childish Lies and Deceits

Not surprisingly, an important part of the work of shoring up the ramparts of theory-theory against the possible incursion of childish lies and deceits has involved taking pages from the book meant to ward off similar threats of possible acts of deception in other species (see Mitchell & Thompson, 1986; Whiten, 1991). It is worth remembering, in this context, that Premack and Woodruff's seminal 1978 article, "Does the Chimpanzee Have a Theory of Mind? was all about the prospect that, by acting deceitfully, our nearest primate relatives might also possess an appreciation of the possibility of false belief. It is also relevant that, rather than simply arising out of nowhere, Premack and Woodruff's classic article actually bookends some four-score years during which comparative psychologists were left staring down the mussel of Lloyd Morgan's 19th-century "canon of parsimony"—a weapon [sic] leveled against interpretive excesses that entreated ethologists of the day to abandon their suspect anthropomorphic ways and to "in no case interpret an action as the outcome of the exercise of a higher physical faculty, if it can be interpreted as the outcome of one standing lower in the psychological scale" (Morgan, 1894, p. 54).

Consider, for example, Dennett's (1987) often repeated example of "Ashley's dog" that, with the definite aim of getting interlopers out of its favorite armchair, routinely applied the ruse of scratching at the door, "as if" it needed to be let out. Of course when it comes to dogs, which do not otherwise seem to especially bristle with further evidence of deceptive intent, those who most live in fear of being felled by Morgan's canon are perhaps within their

rights for worrying over the prospect that all this scratching is nothing more than the automatic result of some well-oiled contingent association between still earlier scratching and subsequently finding one's chair empty. That is, it is perhaps enough in such cases to simply assume that this or that seemingly deceptive behavior has been unwittingly associated with some favorable outcome, and thus simply executed without any recognition of what others may or may not be thinking about.

As you will have guessed, none of those who routinely keep track of such seemingly deceitful behavior on the part of animals or young children is required to read such events in exactly the same way. Some (e.g., standard theory-theorists) elect to opt for a reductive reading of such evidence—one that guarantees that they will never be duped into prematurely labeling something as truly deceptive when it is not. At the same time, the real world to which children are apprenticed needs to be seen as riddled with deceit (Anderson, 1986), and any analytical strategy that denies them the early prospect of participating in such charades runs the risk for confusing interpretive caution with an exaggerated fear of type 1 error. As William James (1910) aimed to show, there are worse things that can happen to a man [sic] in this world than to be duped.

All such to-ing and fro-ing notwithstanding, it obviously remains judicious to exercise appropriate methodological cautions in deciding what should and should not be seen to legitimately qualify as deception. At a minimum, such cautions would need to include, as Sweetser (1987) suggests, the promotion of the idea that all bona fide instances of deceit must, necessarily, involve assertions that: "a) are false quite apart from any telling; b) that are understood to be false by those putting them forward (by whatever means); and c) that are promoted with the full intent of leading credulous others into false beliefs about some true state of affairs" (p. 59). It is simply not enough to merely say or do on purpose something that coincidentally happens to be false to qualify as being authentically deceptive. Rather, if you want your actions to qualify as uncontested instances of deceit, you must also appreciate that you are purposefully misrepresenting some real truth of the matter, all with the aim of actively disinforming others by leading them into some false belief.

Having adopted some variation on such attempts at methodological rigor, a large number of investigators have reported that they failed to come up with convincing evidence that 2- and 3-year-olds are capable of deceit. LaFreniere (1988), Selman (1980), and Shultz and Cloghess (1981), to name only a few, reported that their young preschool subjects regularly failed to lie or otherwise act deceptively in various laboratory-based competitive game situations. As interesting as all of this is, it remains unclear, however, whether such reported failures were the result of some real, foundational inability to deceive, or were instead the by-products of failures on the part of these young research participants to appreciate how behaving deceptively might have been of service to them in what were generally novel and heavily rule-bound games. As with other equally rigorous laboratory-based practices, the methods applied in these studies also offered few response options to those who might have otherwise been inclined to deceive, provided little in the way of license for those uncertain about what was and was not permissible, and generally made it hard to weigh the likelihood of being caught. In this context, Lewis et al. (1989) report, for example, that the lion's share of their 3-year-old subjects were actually quick to attempt what appeared to be difficult to verify lies when asked whether they had touched a forbidden toy. All in all, then, few, if any, of the studies that have aimed to play methodological "hard ball" could be said to have effectively laid the groundwork for bringing prospective liars and deceivers out of the closet.

In response to such criticisms, first Russell (1989) and then Russell, Mauthner, Sharpe, and Tidswell (1991), and Peskin (1992) each took special pains to develop procedures that not only implicated respondents' own best interests, but also excused them from the necessity of explaining themselves in words. All of these tasks involved preschoolers in a seemingly simple game that only required them to point incorrectly as a way of disinforming an opponent. In most of these cases, 3- and 4-year-olds were required to first express their own preferences for one or the other of two items (e.g., decorative stickers). The twist in this "game" was that subjects had to compete with a puppet who got first pick and who always kept for himself whichever sticker the child indicated that he or she preferred. For an adult, the obvious way out of this situation would be to lie about one's true preferences, thereby promoting the false belief that the preferred sticker was the opposite of their own real choice. As things turned out, only a few 4-year-olds, and almost no 3-year-olds, were able to use such a strategy for disinforming others about their true preferences. Rather, trial after trial, these young children continued to act against their own best interests.

In response to these findings, all of which clearly support a standard theory-theory interpretation, Chandler and his colleagues (e.g., Chandler et al., 1989; Chandler & Hala, 1994; Hala & Chandler, 1993a, 1993b, 1996; Hala

et al., 1991) argued that such studies required respondents not only to behave deceptively, but to also respond in ways that ran counter to their own initial impulses, a capacity that subsequent studies of executive functioning suggest is slow to develop.

In response to this limitation, Chandler and his colleagues undertook a series of more than a dozen studies that also required children to act deceptively in their own best interests, but not in ways that obliged them to misrepresent their own interests. In the first half of these experiments, a hide-and-seek game was fashioned in which 2½- to 5-year-old children were encouraged to hide a treasure in one of a series of differently colored containers, with the "help" of a push-toy doll that left tell-tale footprints clearly marking out its movements across a white playing surface. Faced with this dilemma, subjects could undertake to deceive a returning opponent by lying, by wiping away incriminating evidence of the doll's progress across the playing surface, by laying additional sets of false and misleading trails to empty containers, or by using various combinations of all of these strategies. Although there was some evidence of building competence with increasing age, 70 percent of even the young 2½-year-olds in these studies took active steps to misinform their opponent by laying false trails to empty containers. They also wiped up offending tracks, behaved surreptitiously, occasionally lied, and in more than half the cases, gave credible explanations for their having done so. Clearly, if such evidence is left to stand, then false belief understanding has a considerably earlier age of onset than the 4 years that is more generally insisted on. Clearly, these were fighting words.

Two groups (Ruffman, Olson, Ash, & Keenan, 1993; Sodian, 1991) quickly responded with hide-and-seek studies of their own, and others still (e.g., Wellman, 1990) reacted only with words. Perhaps not surprisingly, the new evidence offered in rebuttal ended up exactly matching the unshakable faith these theory-theorists are known to maintain in the rightness of the proposition that only 4-year-olds, but not still younger children, have any real comprehension of the possibility of false belief. In one of these studies (Sodian), 3- to 5-year-olds were told an elaborate story about good and bad puppets that needed help or hindering, but were allowed only a single means of acting deceptively. In the other study (Ruffman et al., 1993), children were offered the opportunity to trick a Mr. Bubby, whose forbidden cookies could be approached only by crossing a field of spilled flour. The options available to the puppet figures of this study boiled down to whether they tracked through the flour while wearing their own or someone else's shoes. Deception, in this case, turned on keeping all of this straight while working it out that Mr. Bubby might be misled by a plan that involved stealing the cookies while wearing someone else's oversized shoes. Given enough tangled rope, children can, it would appear, be made to hang themselves using almost any sufficiently twisted procedure. Small wonder, then, that such purported replications of the work of Chandler and colleagues have seemingly failed to show any evidence of the early onset of deception.

As a way of strengthening the theory-theory case, Wellman (1990) suggested, for example, that the intention of the typical 2- and 3-year-olds in Chandler and company's studies (Hala et al., 1991; Chandler & Hala, 1994; Hala & Chandler, 1996) was not, as it would appear, to actively disinform an opponent by laying false trails to empty containers, but was, more simply, to rid himself or herself of a competitor: "His actions essentially say 'go away,' not 'believe this mistaken information so that you will go away'" (p. 265). Similarly, but somewhat less extravagantly, Sodian (1991) has suggested that Chandler et al.'s subjects were simply caught up in the fun of making and wiping up of tracks, and might well have behaved similarly if they were trying to help rather than hinder.

As a way of countering these reductive readings of their work, Hala, Chandler, and Fritz (1991) undertook a second series of studies that were intended, not only to replicate their earlier findings, but: (1) to make room for a direct test of the seemingly extravagant possibility that their successful subjects were simply undertaking to manipulate the behaviors and not the beliefs of their opponents; and (2) to ensure that these same respondents would actually behave differently if instructed to help rather than mislead an opponent. What, in particular, was done in these studies was to arrange things in such a way that it was up to these young subjects themselves (rather than a puppet figure) to move the equivalent of the standard chocolate bar in an otherwise standard Maxi task from its original container A into some new container B, all for reasons that were clearly meant to be deceptive in intent, that is, to "hide" the chocolate from Maxi. The common finding across all of these studies was that young 3-year-olds almost always succeeded in their deceptive hiding efforts, and did so for the express and openly stated purpose of leading others into false beliefs. That is, the new 3-year-old subjects in this second series of studies not only explicitly indicated that their efforts would lead others into definite false beliefs, but dutifully helped rather than hindered others when asked to do so. All of this, we suggest, goes some consid-

erable distance in showing that children as young as 2½ or 3 years of age can and do regularly take definite and deceptive steps to lead others into false beliefs. Clearly, then, young children cannot be counted among those who you can fool all of the time, nor are they quite as innocent as certain earlier talk about "pure as the undriven snow" or "unblemished as the newborn lamb" might lead you to expect. A young child can very well trick you, and will do so if your guard is not up. Perhaps, given all of this, the developmental window during which young persons begin their slow progress toward a mature theory of mind is actually a good deal wider than first-generation theory-theorists have insisted.

Pretend Play as a Marker of Mental-State Understanding

Like both false belief understanding and intentional efforts to deceive, the ability to meaningfully engage in pretend play is widely thought to similarly mark an important milestone in young children's growing understanding of their own and other's mental lives. Pretending, for example, that a banana is a telephone, or making some sort of playful sense out of seeing someone else do so, would be impossible, it has been argued (e.g., Leslie, 1987), unless or until some wedge had already been driven between how things are presumed to actually be, on the one hand, and how one might playfully imagine them to be, on the other. Among the unsettled questions to be taken up in this section are: What ought to count as bona fide instances of pretense? When, in the usual course of ontogenetic developments, do such acts of pretense first occur? And what sort of mental model or theory of mind would need to be in place before such acts of pretense could be reasonably understood?

An important driver in the debate over how such questions might best be answered turns on the age at which young children first appreciate and participate in such acts of pretense. Although any precise answer to this question naturally depends on what is assumed to count as pretense, there is a great deal of observational evidence to suggest that, between 18 and 24 months of age (e.g., Leslie, 1987; Piaget, 1962/1945), many children already actively participate in what looks very much like shared acts of pretense. Still others (e.g., Bosco, Friedman, & Leslie, 2006; Fenson & Ramsay, 1981; Onishi, Baillargeon, & Leslie, 2007; Walker-Andrews & Kahana-Kalman, 1999) have argued that such evidence is already to be had as early as the 15th or 16th month.

If any of these claims are right, then such evidence poses a serious problem for anyone committed to the view that children younger than 3 or 4 sport a "cognitive deficit" that robs them of the very possibility of a representational or mentalistic understanding of the mind. That is, (a) if children are otherwise said to be of preschool age before having a reliable grip on the earliest possibility of false belief, and (b) if, before they are half of that age, these same children already happily participate in acts of pretense, then, (c) unless such claims about the early onset of pretense are seriously mistaken, or otherwise mean something different than is commonly supposed, anyone committed to the view that false belief understanding provides the best and truest "litmus test" of an introductory-level theory of mind would have some tall explaining to do. Given all of these star-crossed possibilities, how, you might well ask, have standard-issue theory-theorists undertaken to dodge this bullet, and how successful have they been in doing so?

Efforts to beat back the implications of the apparent early onset of pretense have generally taken one or the other of two general forms. The first of these (call it the Behavioral Gambit) proceeds by arguing that those actions routinely held up as evidence for the early onset of pretense are, in fact, little more than a kind of mindless pantomime and, consequently, do not actually signal anything of special moment about young children's representational understanding of mental life. Clearly, the possible success of this sort of salvage operation turns on somehow winning the argument that what (to the untrained eye) look like full-blown acts of pretense—acts that come equipped with all of their commonly associated mentalist overtones—are, in fact, better understood as examples of some less representationally encumbered form of "protopretense" that may look like, but, nevertheless, falls short of constituting genuine acts of pretense.

The second of these defensive maneuvers (referred to here as the Decoupling Gambit) consists of first stipulating to the fact that children as young as 15 or 18 months can, after all, engage in bona fide acts of pretense (and that such acts of pretense do mark an important advance in young children's fledgling grasp of mental life), although still insisting that such behaviors, nevertheless, fall importantly short of the sort of representational competencies required to hold to a fully representational theory of mind. Each of these separate attempts to slip the leash on the theory-altering implications of pretense is taken up separately next.

Behavioral Gambit

What is generally held up as the best available evidence in support of the first of these strategies—the one given over

to discounting the possibility that what preschoolers actually intend by their fledgling acts of pretense is not the same thing as what we would mean if we were the ones doing the pretending—is the work of Lillard and her colleagues (e.g., Lillard, 1993, 1994, 2001; Lillard & Flavell, 1992). The thrust of Lillard's program of research has been to show that young children's pretend behaviors are importantly different from those of still older children and adults, all because such early instances of "protopretense" are actually devoid of any usual reference to, or reliance on, the mental goings-on of those whose behavioral acts they seek to imitate.

The usual form that this work has taken has been to show that, for children who could not otherwise pass a standard measure of false belief (and even for many 4- and 5-year-olds who could), it is typically enough, in order to brand a target's behavior as an act of "pretense," to recognize certain behavioral similarities between the pretender and the "pretendee." Such children, it is said, wrongly believed that someone hopping like a rabbit is actually pretending to be a rabbit, even when such target individuals are pointedly said not to be thinking about rabbits while hard at work doing their hopping (Lillard, 1993). The presumptive point of this inquiry was to determine whether mental representations or actions are more important in the framing of preschool children's judgments concerning whether a particular behavior is or is not a case of pretense. In response to such questions, Lillard reports that the majority of 4-year-olds, and a significant minority of 5-year-olds, claimed that the target child was pretending to be a rabbit, even though he or she knows nothing about rabbits. Lillard (1996) also demonstrated that many 4- and 5-year-old children classify pretense together with physical activities such as clapping one's hands, rather than mental activities such as thinking. It is not until age 7 to 8, she has argued, that most children responded like adult subjects to such tasks, by insisting that pretense actions involved mental activities. What Lillard took away from such demonstrations is that, whatever young preschoolers standardly understand pretense to be, it is all largely behavioral in character and does not include any of the mental modeling presupposed by a more adult-like appreciation of what pretense ordinarily entails. These findings, and others like them, have led Lillard to argue that, rather than understanding pretense as mental representation, children's earliest understandings of pretense actually amount to no more than "acting as if."

It is, of course, one thing to argue that (for preschoolers at least) labeling an action as an instance of pretense is not the same thing as embellishing such an act with mentalistic overtones, and quite another to specify what it is, then, that such young persons actually take such acts of pretense to be. According to Lillard (1994) and other advocates of such behavioral accounts of pretense (e.g., Nichols & Stich, 2000, 2003), children younger than 4 or 5 typically regard others as behaving "as if" a specific scenario were true, or as behaving in a way that would be appropriate if a specific scenario were true. On this account, to engage in and to recognize pretense in others, one need *not* draw on any representational understanding at all; these tasks require only an ability to appreciate that, in certain instances (e.g., pretending that a broom is a horse), people behave in a way that would be appropriate if the broom were a horse (e.g., by straddling it and exclaiming "Giddy-up!").

Such attempts to substitute "as-if" scenarios for other more mentally encumbered notions of pretense have not escaped criticism. One such critique centers on the question of how it is that young children determine which instances of behavior denote pretense and which do not. Simple appeals to the fact that some such behaviors (e.g., galloping a broom, talking into a banana) would stand out as odd or inappropriate were they not somehow marked as acts of pretense will hardly do. As Friedman and Leslie (2007) note, our lives are full of inappropriate actions caused by false beliefs, accidents, simple ignorance, and so forth, none of which is routinely mistaken for acts of pretense. We would all be surprised, for example, if a preschooler mistakenly imagined that a classmate who accidentally spilled his or her juice was pretending to be a fireman or was behaving "as if" the juice were a waterfall. On such grounds, Friedman and Leslie argue that "behaving as if" can include virtually any action at all, and that behavioral theories such as those of Lillard (1994) or Nichols and Stich (2000, 2003) are inadequate explanations of how children manage to avoid regularly confusing various nonpretend behaviors with genuine instances of pretense, mistakes for which, they claim, there is no evidence at all.

Such criticisms have not gone unanswered. In addition to sometimes being inappropriate, acts of pretense have also been shown to be marked by certain specific behavioral cues or mannerisms such as exaggerated motions, "knowing" looks, smirks, and intonation changes (Dias & Harris, 1990; Lillard & Witherington, 2004; Piaget, 1962/1945; Richert & Lillard, 2004). One potential way, then, of rescuing various behavioral accounts from the "Whoa, too-broad-it-can't-separate-pretense-from-other-actions" critique spelled out earlier has been to assert that the recognition of these cues help young children to differentiate the "real" world from the world of pretense (e.g., Lillard & Witherington, 2004).

Against such views, others have argued that the existence of such "giveaway" cues actually poses an even greater threat to behavioral accounts of pretense. Friedman and Leslie (2007) suggest that the presence of such cues has the effect of actually decreasing the extent to which pretense behaviors match the behavior being pantomimed. Take, for example, a mother who pretends that some object, such as a Lego block, is a cookie: She may pick up the block with a wink or a smile, make exaggerated mouth movements and exclamations (Mmm…Good!) when placing the block near (but not in) her mouth, and so on. According to Freidman and Leslie, all such exaggerated behaviors only serve to decrease the extent to which the mother behaves *as if* the block really was a cookie. As such, the extent to which such "mannerism markers" of pretense help or hinder behavioral accounts of pretense remains unclear.

Decoupling Gambit

In contrast with researchers who posit that early pretense is initially understood as a special sort of behavior rather than a special sort of mentalizing, Leslie (1987) argues that as soon as children begin to engage in or otherwise appreciate acts of pretense, it can be shown that they understand such acts as necessarily implicating mental states. Indeed, he argues that pretense is the first clear sign of an ability to understand another's mental states. Early pretense, on his account, requires the same cognitive machinery implicated in any understanding of beliefs as representations—"innate," "modularized" machinery that he terms the "theory of mind mechanism," or TOMM—machinery assumed to come online through a combination of biological maturation and exogenous influences. According to Leslie's version of metarepresentation, toddlers' understanding of what telephones are called or used for is not "contaminated" by observing their mothers talking into bananas because the TOMM allows them to decouple their primary representations of bananas from their secondary representations of bananas as telephones. Primary representations are veridical representations of the world (e.g., "It is raining" when, in fact, it is raining). Secondary representations, such as beliefs about beliefs, are different from primary representations because they are said to be "decoupled" from reality and do not carry the same truth value that primary representations do (e.g., Mom mistakenly thinks or believes or pretends it is raining). According to Leslie, the TOMM is the presumptive cognitive system required to allow for the embedding of primary representations into secondary representations (e.g., Mom is pretending the banana is a telephone), thereby isolating or decoupling them from reality.

People are, of course, often locked away for making up similarly elaborate stories about previously unheard of machinery whirring away inside their heads. What sets Leslie's imagined TOMM apart from such indictable offenses is that, in addition to laying out a hypothesized blueprint descriptive of the sorts of machinery that would theoretically need to be in place if pretense were to function as it is known to do, his account also anticipates other empirical relations that might not have otherwise been anticipated. One such example is that Leslie's model provides a promising (although often contested) account of what goes awry in development in children with autism. Children with autism do not spontaneously engage in pretend play (Baron-Cohen, 1987, 1995; Ungerer & Sigman, 1981) and typically fail false-belief tasks (e.g., Baron-Cohen, Leslie, & Frith, 1985). These findings have led Leslie and others (e.g., Baron-Cohen, 1995) to posit that autism is the result of a specific impairment or "characteristic breakdown" in the TOMM.

The point in rehearsing even this much of Leslie's generally well-known TOMM is not to necessarily advocate its use, but to illustrate the point that children's early appreciation of pretense need not automatically lead to attempts to entirely redescribe it in behavioral terms. Assuming that pretense under some description is here to stay, it seems important to take it seriously.

Taking Pretense Seriously

In addition to all of those whose ideological commitments to the proposition that children younger than 4 are, because of some presumed cognitive deficit, structurally excluded from the possibility of engaging in genuine acts of pretense, there also has been a long list of others who have, in one way or another, assigned special importance to the fact that, like false beliefs, pretense also seems to imply some capacity to envision and act on propositions that are known to be untrue (e.g., Flavell, 1988; Fodor, 1992; Forguson & Gopnik, 1988). In Paul Harris's (1991, 1995) simulation account, for instance, the child is said to learn about others' mental states through a capacity to simulate or pretend about nonexistent situations. As such, for Harris and other "simulation" theorists, pretense is not only another manifestation of counterfactual reasoning, it is also a description of the primary means by which full participation in adult-like versions of some folk psychology eventually come about.

Still others, less inclined to see pretense as a burr under the saddle of their theory building efforts, have accumulated data showing that children who engage in more

pretend play, or role enactment, or are otherwise "fantasy predisposed," show more advanced performance on theory-of-mind tasks than do their less fantasy-predisposed counterparts (Dunn, 1993; Jenkins & Astington, 1993; Taylor & Carlson, 1997). Moreover, individuals with autism, who show marked deficits in other theory-of-mind tasks, have also been shown to fail to engage in pretend play (Baron-Cohen et al., 1985). More extravagant still, recent neuroimaging work also supports some link between pretense and theory of mind by showing that brain regions typically associated with theory-of-mind reasoning are likewise activated when adults watch pretend scenarios (German, Niehaus, Roarty, Giesbrecht, & Miller, 2004).

Although suggestive, none of these bits of correlational evidence showing links between pretense and theory of mind successfully addresses the provocative question of whether early manifestations of pretense are precursors to, or previously unheralded expressions of, a bona fide theory of mind. As such, the reader is awkwardly left to wonder whether the existence of developmentally early outcroppings of pretense should cause us to worry over, or congratulate, our favorite candidate account of the emergence of mentalistic or representational theory of mind.

Referential Behaviors and Other Potential Markers of Early Insights into Beliefs about Belief

Infants seem to show some rather sophisticated abilities suggestive of the operation of some naïve or "folk" psychology from very early in development. For example, infants seem to construe humans, and human-like agents, as special, or uniquely different from inanimate objects. Six-month-old infants are not surprised (as evidenced by longer looking times) if people move without making contact with other objects in their environment, but they are surprised if inanimate objects do the same (Spelke, Phillips, & Woodward, 1995). Six-month-old infants expect a human arm to behave in a goal-directed manner (i.e., following the same goal over time), but do not expect a mechanical arm to be goal oriented (Woodward, 1998). At 9 months of age, infants seem surprised if agents act in an irrational manner to achieve their goal (Csibra et al., 1999) and interpret new goal-directed actions based on previously witnessed behavior (Kuhlmeier, Wynn, & Bloom, 2003). Furthermore, when an object moves out of sight, 12-month-old infants try to reach toward its place of disappearance. In contrast, when a person moves out of sight, infants vocalize (Legerstee, 1992). Also at 12 months, infants will orient in the same direction as a novel agent that either has a face or acts contingently with them, but not one that acts in a random manner. These findings suggest that infants perceive that the agents with a face and the agents that acted contingently with them had attentional, and perhaps intentional, states (Johnson, Slaughter, & Carey, 1998).

Also around 1 year of age, an infant can point where he or she wants a social partner (e.g., his or her mother) to look. Interestingly, by around 15 months of age, the infant will first check to see that his or her mother is looking at him or her before pointing (Astington, 1993). But what, if anything, does this tell us about the infant's understanding of knowledge? Do such children understand that people's behaviors are governed, not simply by what is in the visible physical world, but also by an invisible world of mental activity; one that may be incomplete or even in conflict with reality? Do such children know that their mother won't know they are pointing if she isn't looking; that not everyone knows what they know? Does he or she know that perception can lead to knowledge, or more specifically that, in this case, it is "looking" that will lead to knowing rather than, for example, smelling or tasting?

Whatever the answer to such questions is, at around 18 months of age, it becomes increasingly difficult to deny that infants have at least a rudimentary understanding of the minds of others. For instance, at this age, infants understand that someone else can have desires that are inconsistent with their own. In one study, for example, an experimenter demonstrated that she likes broccoli but does not like crackers. When she then stuck out her hand indicating that she wanted something, 18-month-olds, but not 14-month-olds, tended to give her broccoli, even though this was inconsistent with their own preference for crackers (Repacholi & Gopnik, 1997).

Similarly, children at least as young as 2 understand that one's emotional reaction is governed by whether the outcome of an event is consistent with his or her desire, rather than the outcome per se that leads to an emotion. For example, 2-year-olds were able to judge that a boy who was looking for his rabbit would be sad if he found his dog, whereas a boy who was looking for his dog would be happy. That is, such children do not assume that emotions are inherent to the object or situation—that everyone would be happy to find a dog (Wellman, 1990).

At 18 months, infants will also "imitate" the action a person intended to perform even though that person's actual action was unsuccessful (e.g., pulling the ends off a dumbbell). That is, they can infer what the person wanted to do and perform this action even though they have never seen that action performed. They do not, however, engage in such behavior when they see the same actions performed by a machine (Meltzoff, 1995). Thus, by 18 months, if not before, infants appreciate that human action, but not mechanical action, is governed by underlying mental states such as goals and intentions.

Children at this age, and perhaps earlier, also use their understanding of the mental states of others to facilitate word learning (see Bloom, 2000, for a review). For instance, 18-month-old children will use the direction of the speaker's gaze as a cue to the referent of a new word (Baldwin, 1991). This is the case even if the children are attending to a different object when the word is spoken. They do not assume that the word applies to the object that they themselves are attending to. Instead, they use the speaker's direction of gaze as a cue to what that person intended to refer.

Tomasello and Barton (1994) explored a different role of theory of mind in word learning. In their study, 24-month-olds were presented with an array of five buckets each containing a novel object. The children heard the experimenter say, "Let's find the 'toma.' Where's the 'toma'?" Then the experimenter withdrew an object from the first bucket and scowled, placing it back in the bucket. This was repeated for a second bucket. On retrieving an object from the bucket, the experimenter held it up and exclaimed excitedly, "Ah!", before continuing to pick up objects from the remaining buckets. The contents of all of the buckets were then emptied out and the children were then asked to find the "toma." Children regularly selected the object that the experimenter seemed pleased with, despite the fact that it was not the last object that they saw and not the first. To succeed at such a task, they could not simply rely on the speaker's direction of gaze. Instead, it required being sensitive to the speaker's goal and cues as to when it was achieved.

Thus far, we have provided an abbreviated review of the literature on children's early understanding of mental states such as goals, intentions, and desires. But what about their understanding of knowledge and belief states? At the very least, 2-year-olds have some basic understanding that familiarity or experience tends to correlate with knowing, whereas never seeing or being absent leads to ignorance. For example, if a speaker uses a proper name (e.g., "There's Jessie.") ambiguously in the presence of two individuals, one she has "played with before" and one she has "never seen before," children as young as 2 assume the proper name applies to the individual with whom the speaker is familiar. The same assumption is not made when a common noun is used (e.g., "There's the dog."). These results suggest that, by 2 years of age, children have a rudimentary appreciation of how knowledge is acquired—that someone cannot know about an individual's unobservable properties, such as their proper name, without prior experience with that individual (Birch & Bloom, 2002).

Similarly, if a 2-year-old's mother is absent when an attractive toy is placed onto a high shelf, the child will gesture toward the toy when she returns, more so than if the mother was present when the toy was hidden. Again, these results demonstrate that children as young as 2 have a rudimentary understanding of how knowledge is acquired; they appreciate that if the mother was absent when the toy was moved, she is unlikely (or at least less likely) to know about the toy's new location (O'Neill, 1996).

Also by 2 years of age, children are able to ensure that when showing an adult a picture it is facing toward them (Lempers, Flavell, & Flavell, 1977). By 18 months, Perner (1991) grants them some awareness of others' mental states that he denies to younger children. He and his colleagues gave 18-month-olds a task that they were unlikely to have encountered in a natural setting, such as showing an adult a picture fixed inside the bottom of a hollow cube. When children first showed these pictures to an adult, they tried to show them in such a way that they themselves could also see the picture. For example, some of them would hold the cube down low, and tilt it back and forth between themselves and the adult. Perner suggests that because they are just coming to an understanding that looking leads to seeing, they give themselves the same visual experience as the adult to assure themselves that the adult sees the picture. Other experimental work (e.g., Pillow, 1989) has shown that by the age of 3, children understand that looking leads to knowing and will attribute knowledge of a box's contents to someone who has looked inside the box and ignorance of the contents to someone who has not looked (see Robinson, 2000, for a review).

Of course, in some sense, even very young children know how information is acquired. If we pointed to two identical toys on the shelf and asked a toddler to bring us the wet one, not the dry one, it is doubtful she or he would just stare at the toys. More likely she or he would touch the toys to determine which one is wet. Does this mean she or he knows that knowledge about an object's moisture content is best garnered through tactile observation rather than visual observation? It depends on your meaning of knowing.

In summary, across all of the sundry efforts cited earlier to either repair the evident shortcomings of once standard tests of false belief understanding, or to look elsewhere within young children's rich repertoires of social communicative practices, the conclusion best afforded by the available evidence is that the claim that only 4-year-olds deserve to be credited with a capacity to represent their own and others' representation is simply misleading. Rather, there now seems to be sufficient evidence to suggest that the task of first coming to a working understanding of their own and others' mental lives—a theory of mind, if you will—involves a developmental process that reaches back all the way to some especially early moment in the developmental course. At the very least, the development of representational competence and beliefs about beliefs is not a process that can be fairly said to begin without precedent at something like 4 years of age. What this conclusion leaves still untouched, however, and what remains to be unpacked in Part III of this chapter is what further development has in store concerning the subsequent achievements of other even more grown-up representational views about belief formation and the management of competing knowledge claims.

PART IIIA: IS THERE EPISTEMIC DEVELOPMENT AFTER AGE 4?

It will not have escaped notice that, despite having already moved well past the midpoint of this chapter, there has been, at least so far, little or no mention of anyone older than 4 or 5—a shortcoming that we now mean to work to belatedly repair. Success here will not come easily. Spending so much of our page allotment in detailing research involving children still too young to read or write was not, however, an entirely free choice. As it is, something like 9 of 10 of the studies in the existing literature just are about such young children, and to describe things differently would have constituted another kind of arbitrary. If responsibility for this lopsided arrangement is to be taken on, it is, perhaps, best worn by all those wellspring specialists who attach special gravitas to anything and everything that happens to occur early rather than late in the developmental course. On this familiar account, the die of human affairs is said to be cast uncommonly early, and anyone holding out real hope of getting in on the scientific ground floor would do well to avoid getting caught up in the tangled business of whatever circumstance-driven matters happen next. Quick to buy into this "early-good, later-bad" mentality, those studying the early course of epistemic development have taken this message perhaps too much to heart, regularly imagining that what is of most interest is over and done with before children are out of short pants.

Notwithstanding what has, then, been a broad fascination with all things early occurring, there are, nevertheless, two notable exceptions to what has otherwise been an exception-less rule of thumb. The first of these, detailed below, concerns the efforts of those scattered few whose work follows closely on the heels of that of more classical theory-theorists. What sets this new rump group of investigators apart from other more mainstream theorists of mind is not that their study samples are all that much older, but the difference hinges instead on their shared conviction that the achievement of simple false belief understanding is not the last real turn of the epistemic wheel.

By contrast, members of the second and last of these two working groups to be discussed here tend to live in a developmental world seemingly light-years removed from the usual orbit of theory-theorists and their critics—a world occupied primarily by college undergraduates and the occasional young adult or precocious adolescent. These research efforts, described earlier as having as their collective center of gravity the inspirational work of William Perry (1970), are briefly summarized in Part IIIB, the final substantive section in this chapter.

Epistemic Development in the Middle-School Years

The handful of researchers who have elected to study young persons marginally older than 4 or 5 tend to fall into one or the other of three small groups, arrayed along a continuum running from near to far extensions of the now familiar theory-of-mind enterprise. The first and most proximate of these includes the work of stalwart theory-theorists such as Perner (1988) and Perner and Wimmer (1985), who, although still committed to the views that false belief understanding heralds, not only the first but also the last real revolution in the course of human epistemic growth, remain open to the thin prospect that these same unitary capacities can, nevertheless, become self-embedding, or otherwise recursively stacked one on the other in ways that allow for the possibility of higher order beliefs about beliefs about beliefs. Call such studies explorations into the possibility of *false beliefs squared.*

The second of these research forays extrudes just beyond what Chandler and Sokol (1999) have called "the usually impenetrable thicket of self-citations that otherwise ring in the theory-of-mind literature," by exploring the prospect that false belief understanding may vary, not simply as a function of information access, but as a result of other more personalized factors such as attitudes and values and prejudices. Call these studies, primarily owed to Pillow and

his colleagues (e.g., Pillow, 1991, 1999; Pillow & Weed, 1995), forays into the study of *misinterpretation.*

Finally, there is a small, but more radical, subset of studies, all predicated on the assumption that standard measures of false belief understanding are mistaken in their claims, all as a result of having restricted their focus to only those occasional instances of representational diversity in which different onlookers have access to *different* information. Proponents of this more differentiated account (e.g., Carpendale, 1995; Carpendale & Chandler, 1996; Chandler & Carpendale, 1998; Chandler & Lalonde, 1996; Lalonde & Chandler, 2002) have generally promoted the view that simple ignorance-driven false belief understanding, although perhaps marking a real qualitative juncture in young people's early beliefs about beliefs, is perhaps not the first, and certainly not the last, such major architectural shift in the course of epistemic development. Because this line of research is especially focused on how young persons attempt to make sense of instances of representational diversity that cannot be laid solely at the door of different experiences, but is owed instead to whatever endogenous factors ordinarily lead persons to "interpret" the *same* information differently, this work will be lined out under the heading *Children's Interpretive Theories of Mind.* In what immediately follows, each of these distinctive programs of research is taken up in turn.

False Beliefs Squared

Few are inclined to doubt that there are differences in the ways that preschoolers and adults think about the mind. What is open to dispute is the particular shape such differences are imagined to take. Traditional theory theorists such as Wimmer and Perner (1983), who are committed to the view that all of the major planks that make up the platform on which representational life necessarily rests are fundamentally in place by 4 years of age, have left themselves only limited maneuvering room for imagining the possible shapes that beliefs about beliefs might take. Beyond easy claims about growing expertise, one of the few remaining options left open is to imagine that, as they grow older, people newly acquire the capacity to not only hold to beliefs about beliefs, but to recursively embed such thoughts in ways that enable them to have beliefs about beliefs about beliefs, and so on. The fundamental move here is captured by Augustus de Morgan's (1872/1915) expansion of Jonathan Swift's *On Poetry: A Rhapsody:*

> Great fleas have little fleas upon their backs to bite 'em,
> and little fleas have lesser fleas, and so ad infinitum. And

the great fleas themselves, in turn, have greater fleas to go on, while these again have greater still, and greater still, and so on. (p. 377)

To the extent that some such process is actually afoot in the course of epistemic development, it would follow that older persons can still be said to differ from their younger counterparts, all without the necessity of introducing a whole new layer of cognitive machinery.

As a way of putting this hypothesis to the test, Perner and Wimmer (1985) told children a story about John and Mary and an ice-cream van. Both John and Mary see an ice-cream van at the park and go back to their respective homes to get spending money. On his way home, John discovers that the ice-cream van has moved to the church. What he doesn't know is that Mary has also been informed that the van is now at the church. When asked where John would think that Mary would think the ice-cream van now is, many of the 6- and 7-year-olds succeeded in reporting that John would "correctly" think that Mary thinks that the van is still at the park, whereas still younger children tended to fail by indicating that she somehow mysteriously knew the van has made its way to the church. On the basis of such results, Perner and Wimmer have laid claim to having discovered the future course of epistemic development—it is recursions all the way down.

In an earlier study, Flavell, Botkin, Fry, Wright, and Jarvis (1968) provided a related example of how some such recursive process might play out, by asking 7- to 17-year-olds to solve a competitive strategy puzzle that involved their trying to outthink an opponent in a kind of shell game. The game involved two inverted cups, one labeled with one nickel and the other with two nickels. In each case, the cups covered the same number of nickels indicated by the money glued to their top. The game consisted of encouraging participants to "remove the money from under one or the other cup," all as a way of limiting the winnings of their opponent, who was allowed to keep whatever money was found beneath the cup he or she picked up. Importantly, the participants were told that their opponents knew that they would be taking the money from one of the cups. Given these arrangements, the majority of 7- to 10-year-olds simply assumed that their opponents would choose the cup with the most nickels. However, from age 11 on, many began to use various strategies that involved recursively thinking about the other person's thoughts (e.g., "he's gonna know we're gonna take the most money out so I took the small one"—the one-nickel cup; Flavell et al., 1968, p. 47). What even the oldest of these participants failed to appreciate was the impossibility of knowing where the reiterative wheel turning in the other person's mind might stop spinning. Had they recognized that no amount of "mind reading" could solve this problem, they would, of course, have always chosen the two-nickel cup.

The limitations of such recursive thought processes are entertainingly captured by a contest of wits between the thief Vizzini and the swashbuckling Man in black in S. Morgenstern's classic tale of *The Princess Bride*. As a way of settling the fate of Princess Buttercup, The Man in Black persuades Vizzini to enter into an intellectual duel to the death requiring them to choose between two identical goblets of wine, one of which the Man in Black had presumably laced with the tasteless and odorless poison "Iocaine." Vizzini is meant to chose, then both will drink and one will die. Vizzini, who prides himself on his intellectual prowess, quickly agrees to this battle of wits. Excerpts [paraphrased] from Vizzini's tortuous line of reasoning read like this:

> But it's so simple. All I have to do is divine it from what I know of you. Are you the sort of man who would put the poison into his own goblet or his enemy's? Now, a clever man would put the poison into his own goblet because he would know that only a great fool would reach for what he was given. I am not a great fool so I can clearly not choose the wine in front of me…But you must have known I was not a great fool; you would have counted on it, so I can clearly not choose the wine in front of you. [He reasons further that] Iocaine comes from Australia. As everyone knows, Australia is entirely peopled with criminals. And criminals are used to having people not trust them, as you are not trusted by me. So, I can clearly not choose the wine in front of you. And you must have suspected I would have known the powder's origin, so I can clearly not choose the wine in front of me…

Finally, a half dozen more turns of contorted logic later, Vizzini makes up his mind and they both drink. Moments later, Vizzini lies dead because the Man in Black, having carefully cultivated an immunity to Iocaine, has poisoned both glasses. Whatever else may be true about this vignette, two things are clear enough. The first is that Vizzini is older than, and does not think like, a young 4- or 7-year-old. The second is that, had he lived, Vizzini, perhaps like us all, obviously still had room for intellectual growth—room to discover (among other things) that there is more to epistemic maturity than endlessly stacking one recursive thought on another.

Not only are there good reasons, therefore, to suppose that there is more to epistemic maturity than endlessly stacking one recursive thought on another, there is also evidence to suggest that even 4- and 5-year-olds can successfully navigate such nested problems when spared some of the burdens of keeping such details simultaneously in mind. Sullivan, Zaitchik, and Tager-Flusberg (1994) hypothesized, and found, that by shortening Perner and Wimmer's (1985) recursive story problems, and otherwise reducing the cognitive demands of their task (e.g., adding a memory aid and a deceptive component), 90% of 5½-year-olds and 40% of 4-year-olds passed these tasks. The implication drawn by these authors was that, not only do such multiple-recursion tasks not portend the real future of epistemic development, but they do not even generate evidence that children older than 4 actually use some qualitatively different, higher order form of reasoning not already on display among preschool children.

Despite the apparent failures of Perner and Wimmer's (1985) assessment procedure in picking out what might be the next real turn of the epistemic wheel, one should not automatically assume that all other candidate possibilities will necessarily suffer the same fate. Two such prospects are considered in the balance of this section. One of these is owed to the work of Pillow and his colleagues (e.g., Pillow, 1988, 1989, 1991, 1995), and concerns the role that children come to assign to person-attributes in accounting for acts of interpretation and misinterpretation. The second involves the emergence of what has come to be termed children's *interpretive* or *constructivist* theories of mind.

Notions of Interpretation and Misinterpretation

A frequent and widely accepted claim in theories-of-mind circles is that young children are first committed to a "causal," or passive (Pillow, 1988, 1995), conception of the knowing process. On this account, persons younger than 4 begin their epistemic journey by effectively treating their own and others' minds as "passive recorders" that simply "bear the scars of information which has been embossed upon them" (Chandler & Boyes, 1982, p. 391). That is, before understanding the interpretive or constructive or subjective nature of knowing, children seem to conceptualize knowledge as simply given, and consequently equally available to anyone and everyone with eyes to see things as they objectively are.

More mature conceptions of the mind, by contrast, are seen to go beyond understanding knowledge as a direct function of perceptual access, and involve instead an appreciation that knowledge is somehow interpretive, in that the mind itself influences how the world is experienced. That is, in addition to appreciating that two "minds" exposed to different things will suffer different representations or beliefs about the world, children must also come to realize that two minds exposed to one-and-the-same-thing can, and often do, arrive at different representations. This distinction is well captured by what Searle (1983) called the "mind-to-world" versus "world-to-mind" direction of fit between thinkers and the things they think about.

As Flavell (1988) has argued, a key marker of children's emerging theories of mind is that those who can be said to have such a theory necessarily exhibit a robust appreciation of the "one-to-many" relations that exist between objects in the world and their many possible representations of them. That is, most, if not all, theory-of-mind researchers contend that the crucial feature of a mature theory-of-mind—the thing that makes it a *representational* theory of mind in the first place—is the insight that minds may represent what is objectively identical in subjectively different ways. Thus, in order to empirically test whether or not children of a given age actually do subscribe to an adult-like representational theory-of-mind, it is critical to insure that research participants actually demonstrate an awareness that one and the same object, event, or state of affairs can legitimately give rise to different beliefs.

Given all of this, the open question is whether the experimental measures of false belief understanding commonly reported in the literature meet this simple test. It would seem that they do not. Rather, such measures all turn on the existence of carefully engineered discrepancies in perceptual access (i.e., Maxi is always absent when the critical transfer of his chocolate occurs). As a result, the contradictory beliefs held, for example, by Maxi and the child participant in standard false belief tasks are plainly *not* beliefs about the *same* event or state of affairs, and, consequently, there is no need for participants to represent the "same" situation in two different ways. Rather, in all of these cases, there are two different beliefs because there are two different objects of belief. Under these or similar assessment circumstances, all that is required to demonstrate an understanding of the possibility of false belief is for participants to realize that anyone not currently informed about all the relevant facts will, all things equal, be mistaken. As such, rather than providing foundational insight into the "one-many" relations between things in the world and their possible representation, ignorance-based false-belief tasks only reveal an understanding of how different events and states of affairs in the external world dictate how different beliefs are formed.

To make this especially clear, imagine (together with Chandler & Sokol, 1999) two couples, the Wimmers and the Perners, who all go to the same movie. At some ill-chosen moment in the plot line of the film, one of the Wimmers goes out for popcorn. Later, they end up arguing over the meaning of what they saw. By contrast, the Perners remain glued to their seats throughout the film but also exit in sharp disagreement about what they had both seen together from curtain to credits. Clearly, the Wimmers are in a situation not unlike that of Maxi and the usual respondents in standard false belief tasks who each have access to differing amounts of information, and the basis of any disagreements that they might have are easily laid at the door of the fact that going out to play, or out for popcorn, at the wrong moment can often lead to false beliefs. By contrast, the Perners are also in disagreement, but this time about the meaning of events they both saw clearly—a situation that more closely approximates an ideal test case of what Flavell had in mind by talk of a "one-to-many" relation between objects and their many possible representations.

If traditional false belief tasks only tap into "ignorance-based" or "perceptual access-driven" beliefs, then *what* is needed, one might well ask, to measure children's understanding of the more subjective and interpretive kinds of beliefs of the sort illustrated by the Perners in the foregoing movie scenario? And *when* do children begin to develop an early understanding of the interpretive nature of knowledge?

Study of Misinterpretation

One reason two minds might construe the same event differently is because of differences in the histories or preexisting biases belonging to one or both of the people in question. That adults ordinarily appreciate this fact is evidenced, for example, in the fact that those with personal connections to a defendant are not allowed to serve on that person's jury, just as peer reviewers are expected to recuse themselves when asked to judge manuscripts or grant submissions of former students, friends, and immediate colleagues (Mills & Keil, 2008).

One line of research meant to address children's understanding of the role of such preexisting biases was pursued by Pillow (1991; Pillow & Weed, 1995). In short, what Pillow demonstrated was that 5-, 6-, and 7-year-olds, but not still younger children, seem to appreciate that people's likes and dislikes will dictate how they end up viewing a range of morally and factually ambiguous events. Joan, for example, a story character in one of Pillow's studies, is shown holding a doll in front of a donation box containing toys for poor children. The open question is how other story characters, Cathy (who likes Joan) and Sarah (who thinks Joan is a troublemaker), will view this ambiguous event. Perhaps not surprisingly, 7- and 8-year-olds anticipated that Joan's behavior might be read differently by these two onlookers. By contrast, 5- and 6-year-olds were much less likely to anticipate that prior beliefs might influence interpretations of this event.

When it comes to understanding how two minds can construe the same event differently, there are obviously a number of dimensions of subjectivity that children must appreciate. For instance, Mills and Keil (2005) examined children's developing cynicism regarding others' self-interested beliefs, finding that by second grade, children first begin discounting others' self-interested statements regarding the outcomes of contests, because they recognize that such statements may be skewed by personal motivations. It is also around this age that children have been shown to recognize that a person's personality traits can influence their perspectives (Gnepp & Chilamkurti, 1988; Heyman & Gelman, 1999; Yuill & Pearson, 1998). Similarly, by fourth grade, children also apparently know to discount self-report as a source of information for learning about evaluative traits in others, suggesting that they realize that desires to be viewed in a positive manner can contaminate such reports (e.g., Heyman, Fu, & Lee, 2007; Heyman & Legare, 2005). Again, by fourth grade, and to a limited extent in second grade, children also appear to appreciate that the same state of affairs can be interpreted differently because of favoritism, or one's personal relationships or connections. For instance, they appreciate that the parent of one of the contestants in a dance contest might come to different conclusions as to who is the best dancer than would a judge who did not have any personal relationships with the dancers (Mills & Keil, 2008).

Children must also come to realize that the degree to which two minds can differ in their evaluations of the same state of affairs depends on contextual factors. That is, they must come to appreciate that certain situations allow for more variability in interpretation than others. For instance, Mills and Keil (2008) suggest that even kindergartners appreciate that judging who won a footrace or spelling bee leaves much less room for preexisting biases to worm their way in than does judging who should win an art or beauty contest, suggesting that even young school-aged children recognize that beauty is "in the eye of the beholder."

What this leaves untouched, however, are all of those matters of interpretation that revolve around issues of legitimacy. That is, it is one thing for young children to anticipate the possibility of misinterpretation, and something quite different to imagine that two individuals may hold to different but equally warrantable beliefs. It is this second dimension of interpretation that we turn to next.

Children's Interpretive Theory of Mind

What seems largely missing from the studies just cited is some better means of capturing the changing ways in which developing persons actually imagine where frank matters of personal bias leave off, and where some range of legitimate interpretations might reasonably begin.

One expression of such more fully fledged matters of interpretation can be seen in two programs of research that test young persons' awareness that different minds can legitimately interpret the same event differently. In one such research program, Carpendale (1995) and Carpendale and Chandler (1996) focused attention on a small class of stimuli that, whether by nature or design, tend to have the special feature of reliably prompting two especially compelling interpretations. Homophones are instances of this class for the obvious reason that they ordinarily promote just two distinct interpretations, as do certain line drawings such as Jastrow's (1900) famous duck-rabbit and Bugelski's (1960) rat-man drawings, which each share the common property of being easily taken to be one or the other of two distinctively different things.

In these study sequences, 5- to 8-year-olds (all of whom had been shown to easily succeed on a standard measure of false belief understanding) were given problems involving such ambiguous stimuli. Despite the fact that all of these subjects were able to "see" for themselves both of the alternative meanings offered, only the 7- and 8-year-olds, and not the 5- or 6-year-olds, were able to regularly *acknowledge* the legitimacy of the two different interpretations offered by two different puppet figures. This was true despite the fact that, young or old, these same subjects found no difficulty in crediting different characters with the right to exercise different likes and dislikes regarding matters of taste.

In a second such study sequence, Chandler and Lalonde (1996; Lalonde, 1996) took the different tack of choosing as test items stimuli drawn from that general class of fundamentally amorphous stimuli that include Rorschach ink blots, and clouds and puddles of spilled milk, all of which easily afford an almost infinite variety of defensibly different interpretive possibilities. More particularly, the specific stimuli chosen for inclusion were part of a set of cryptic puzzle pictures originally popularized by the cartoonist Roger Price (1953). Such drawings are perhaps better il-

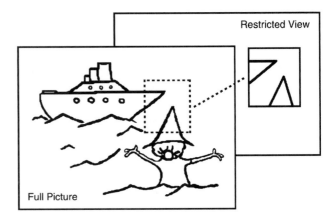

Figure 19.1 "A ship arriving too late to save a drowning witch."

Source: From Price, R. (1953). *Droodles.* New York: Simon & Schuster, by permission.

lustrated than explained. Figure 19.1, for example, depicts a variation on a so-called droodle originally published by Price over the caption "A ship arriving too late to save a drowning witch." The humor in this and related drawings by Price uniformly turns on the fact that, given the restricted view offered, it would be farfetched to imagine that anyone could ever intuit the larger scene of which the droodle itself is only a fractional part. Once alerted by the captions, however, these otherwise nondescript fragments fall into place, and it becomes possible to imagine—even difficult not to imagine—that they are other than fractional parts of what is now understood to be a partially obscured larger drawing.

Several things especially recommend the use of these materials in the study of the development of children's emerging understanding of the interpretive character of mental life. One of these is that, when stripped of their captions, these drawings are sufficiently ambiguous that, at least for adults, it is not just "conceivable" that two different persons might interpret them differently, but something more like a felt necessity.

In close agreement with the findings of the Carpendale (1995) and Carpendale and Chandler (1996) studies, a half-dozen experiments utilizing these droodle materials (e.g., Chandler & Lalonde, 1996) all make it clear that 7-year-olds, but not still younger subjects, appreciate the possibility that two different doll figures might somehow be within their rights to find different meanings in one and the same ill-defined stimulus event. Younger children of 5 or 6, by contrast, predictably showed themselves committed to the immature proposition that, no matter how vague the task, each and every ambiguous event still allows for one and only one legitimate "interpretation."

Taken together, these two study sets provide support for the conclusion that false belief understanding is demonstrably different from the conceptually distinct ability to eventually appreciate that one and the same stimulus event can be open to more than one legitimate interpretation. By focusing attention on stimuli that especially call out for two equally compelling interpretations, or that easily afford almost any interpretation at all, the series of studies just summarized likely provides a lower bound estimate of children's earliest insights into the interpretive nature of knowing. For this reason, it is unlikely that this is really the end of the story. Instead, there are good reasons to suppose that what 7- or 8-year-old children know about interpretation is only a first chapter in a continuing developmental story that, in all likelihood, extends at least through adolescence, and very likely into adulthood as well (e.g., Chandler, 1987). The research to which we now turn in Part IIIB is representative of the efforts of many whose work provides strong evidence of just such a continuing trajectory in epistemic development.

PART IIIB: EPISTEMIC DEVELOPMENT BEYOND THE CHILDHOOD YEARS

Given the summary findings reported in Part IIIA, many of which support the emergence of something like an "interpretive theory of mind" in the early school years—findings that call into deep question the suspect "one miracle view" that age 4 is somehow both the first and last watershed moment in the course of epistemic development—the obvious follow-up question is, given all of that, what, if anything, happens next? That is, assuming that some fledgling insights into the interpretive or constructive nature of knowing really do put in an appearance as early as the primary-school years, then, is that all there is? Could it really be the case that young school-aged children already have in hand all of the important intellectual tools necessary to work out a lifetime's worth of hard epistemic problems? Is it really the case that everything else is just a matter of getting up to speed? Why, otherwise, do we, as parents or teachers, work so hard to alert everyone to the multiply-perspectival nature of human experience ("How would you like it if your sister put *your* pigtails in the ink well?"), and why do we keep on insisting that people achieve some specified "age of majority" before

being entrusted to hold high office, or to otherwise manage their own and others' affairs? And more to the present point, why should there otherwise exist, as we now mean to show, a substantial research enterprise, stretching back over at least the last 40 years, all given over to detailing what happens next in the subsequent course of epistemic development?

Outside of the restricted theory-theory compound, most remain confident that children of 6 or 8 often make a poor job of many "mind-reading" tasks that require them to carefully sort out who believes what, and for what reason. It is also widely assumed that still older persons are not only generally more efficient at dealing with some of these same problem-solving tasks, but that they approach them in radically different ways. As a way of understanding such hypothesized age-graded differences, a minimum of two broad possibilities are seen to present themselves. The *first* of these boils down to the observation that there are a whole lot of experiences and opportunities for practice that school-aged children have not yet had, and so it is thought to be at least conceivably the case that whatever subsequent changes do still occur in their later arriving beliefs about beliefs may be because of the simple fact that practice sometimes makes perfect. With rare exception (e.g., see Schommer, 1990, 1993), few contributors to the available literature on epistemic development have, however, opted for this generally mundane prospect.

Rather, the lion's share of the concerned research community has chosen instead for a second class of possibilities, all of which share a commitment to the general prospect that there actually arises in the subsequent course of cognitive development some qualitatively different ways of thinking about thinking—something that your typical shiny-faced school child still does not get.

Oddly, working out *what* it is, exactly, that supposedly happens next seems not to have been generally seen to be the problem. Almost everyone involved in the so-called personal epistemologies literature (for a review, see Hofer & Pintrich, 1997) would appear to be in broad agreement that, once young persons have come to appreciate that all knowledge claims necessarily bear rifling marks laid down by the particular minds through which they pass, what most remains to be understood is *how* developing persons actually go about the business of identifying serviceable criteria for sorting better from worse ideas. Although a lot of the details about how all of this is accomplished remain open to dispute, the real bone of contention that contributors to this literature have been actively worrying over the last 40-plus years has been (somewhat disappointedly) the more pedestrian question of not *what* but *when* it is, exactly, that such newer insights first occur.

Although there is nothing especially unusual about finding developmentalists squabbling over the particular threshold moment at which some new achievement is thought to first appear, what is especially unseemly and uncommonly strange in this case is the extravagant array of candidate ages that have been seriously proposed for this same inaugural role. Modest differences of professional opinion, such as to whether a given developmental accomplishment first occurs at age 3 or 5, can, perhaps, be written off to measurement error or sample variability. This is not like that. Rather, as we mean to show, various contributors to the literature on personal epistemologies have presented evidence meant to demonstrate that, if not at age 2 or 4 or 6, then the next and last turn of the epistemic wheel actually occurs at age 8 or 16 or 32 (for a review, see Chandler et al., 2002).

Although there are, no doubt, occasions on which certain kinds of disagreements of this magnitude prove to be all to the good, this is not one of them. Rather, what you have here is a deeply problematic situation in which largely indistinguishable claims are being made about individuals of wildly different ages. Given this level of radical disagreement, a fair-minded reader could easily come away from an exhaustive review of this literature justifiably convinced that young people reach epistemic maturity at just about any age you might care to imagine. In the end, unless some reconciliatory explanation of these seeming disparities can be put forth, somebody—actually several somebody(s)—implicated in this ramshackle literature will obviously need to take back a lot of what they have mistakenly said about the ensuing course of epistemic development. Working out precisely who it is that, in the end, will need to do all of this radical retracting or revising is not a job that can be completed inside the confines of this chapter. What is obvious, however, is that any hope of assisting readers in moving toward some judgment of their own necessarily depends on gaining some oversight of exactly what sorts of claims are actually on offer.

As a way of advancing this agenda, we mean to do four quick things. First, it will be useful to begin by saying something synoptic about the touchstone work of William Perry (1970), who, it is widely acknowledged, almost single-handedly jump-started what has gone on to become a veritable cottage industry given over to the study of epistemic development in the lives of college students and young adults. Having laid this groundwork, we will proceed to detail some of the largely "in-house" efforts of

others, who, although generally in close accord with the broad outlines of Perry's scheme, nevertheless argue that people are actually slower to achieve epistemic maturity than Perry imagined (e.g., King & Kitchener, 1994, 2002; Kitchener & King, 1981). Finally, we will consider the work of others who have insisted that, well before their college years, adolescents, and even preadolescents have already arrived at some or all of these same epistemic insights considerably earlier than Perry seemed to think possible. Some of these (e.g., Clinchy, 2002; Kuhn & Weinstock, 2002) have understood their own efforts as downward extensions of Perry's earlier work, whereas others (e.g., Boyes & Chandler, 1992; Broughton, 1978; Chandler, 1987; Chandler, Boyes, & Ball, 1990; Mansfield & Clinchy, 1997; Reich, Oser, & Valentin, 1994) have largely positioned themselves well outside of Perry's usual tent. In the end, all of this will be followed by a Summary section, in which we venture a reading of all of these divergent claims and findings—one that is intended to describe a common developmental arc that begins in infancy and runs all the way to adulthood.

William Perry's *Forms of Intellectual and Ethical Development in the College Years: A Scheme*

Perhaps the earliest and still most authoritative voice in the mounting chorus of investigators who have contributed to the literature on epistemic development in late adolescence and early adulthood is William Perry (1970). In a way that was largely without precedence, Perry conducted a series of short longitudinal studies in which he repeatedly interviewed cohorts of Harvard undergraduates (then all male students) concerning their changing views about the process of belief entitlement. That is, he interviewed them at length during each of their 4 undergraduate years, pressing them for answers about where knowledge comes from, how it is best authenticated, and what we are to do when confronted with competing knowledge claims.

Drawing on these interview protocols, Perry concluded **that** these students followed what, at the limit, was a nine-level developmental process. The first of these levels was said to begin with a strictly "objectivistic" view of the knowing process—a view according to which the truth of any matter is thought to be at least potentially available to anyone with the eyes to see reality for what it actually is. Through the next two levels, this extreme objectivist position was qualified by the growing suspicion that some so-called experts may actually distort the truth because of their own potentially correctable biases. At level 4, Perry described a more qualitative shift within which at least some contested knowledge claims are unmasked as mere matters of arbitrary personal opinion about which everyone is imagined to be equally entitled to their own views. At level 5, a stage of unbridled skepticism, resolvable issues of truth and falsity come to be seen as rare exceptions to the no-rule rule, with everything else understood to be unassuageably personally relative. Levels 6 through 9 are described as sequential steps toward achieving reasoned "commitments" in an uncertain world. Although it was never Perry's view that everyone arrived at university necessarily sporting the first of these epistemic stances, or proceeded at the same pace through his various periods, his stagelike theory (especially levels 1–6) has, nevertheless, come to be broadly viewed as something of a template for progress through the course of a liberal arts education.

Much of the special appeal of what Perry had to say about his elite sample of college undergraduates arises out of the fact that most academics are quick to recognize their own students (if not themselves) in his accounts. Many "freshmen," it would seem, are, just as Perry described, naive realists—objectivists at heart—hopelessly committed to the idea that somewhere, waiting in the wings, there is a brute fact capable of resolving any competing knowledge claim. Similarly, who among us would fail, on reading Perry, to be reminded of all of those "multiplicitists" and uncommitted "relativists" who have riled their way through our second- and third-year classes, smugly insisting that everything is a matter of opinion. Since Perry's (1970) *Forms of Intellectual and Ethical Development in the College Years: A Scheme*, the large bulk of what a great number of others have gone on to add can, without serious prejudice, be characterized as an elaborate footnote to Perry's original and richly textured account. Together with many others, a following army of educators or college counselors has, for example, created not only a William Perry Society, but also something of a college counseling industry based on his work. Motivated primarily by the conviction that much of the business of postsecondary education naturally turns on the course of epistemic development, a long train of such investigators have explored various ways in which such epistemic matters need to be taken into account in the following ways: (1) guiding efforts in the areas of student counseling or curricular reform (for a review, see Hofer & Pintrich, 1997); (2) identifying pedagogic practices that especially promote or frustrate epistemic development (e.g., Schommer, 1990, 1993); (3) determining how epistemic level might influence the choice of one as opposed to another area of study (Paulsen & Wells, 1998); and (4) in deciding whether the course

of epistemic development unfolds differently in persons with and without the benefit of a college education (Kuhn, 1991). Over and above these and other content-bearing matters, still others have developed various paper-and-pencil tests meant to help avoid the necessity of conducting lengthy interviews of the sort that consumed so much of Perry's time (see Hofer & Pintrich, 1997, for a review of these various psychometric efforts).

Perhaps the closest thing to a palace revolt among those otherwise traveling well within the orbit of Perry's scheme has been the work of those who, out of concern that Perry's research participants (like those of Kohlberg) were exclusively Harvard undergraduate male students, have challenged the legitimacy of generalizing from his original elite male sample to college populations, in general, and to female students, in particular (e.g., Baxter Magolda, 1992; Baxter Magolda & Porterfield, 1985; Belenky, Clinchy, Goldberger, & Tarule, 1986; Clinchy, 2002; Moore, 1994). Although providing important caveats to Perry's model, the findings of these investigators have generally qualified, rather than broadly challenged, the general outline of his original scheme.

Driven by various practical concerns, and by the largely untested conviction that they were already working on the ground floor, the large majority of these close camp-followers have, as a consequence, had little or nothing to say about what might have transpired in the years before college admission, and have shown even less interest in detailing the sorts of cognitive limitations that are presumably responsible for preventing still younger persons from having already moved beyond the sorry absolutist and objectivist state thought to characterize standard-issue college freshmen.

Late-Game Changes in Epistemic Development

Perhaps because Perry's original account made room for a total of nine supposed stages in the course of epistemic development, and because few college undergraduates seem to manage to make it beyond stages 5 or 6, a considerable number of investigators whose work orbits at greater or lesser distance from the gravitational center of Perry's model have chosen to include still older respondents in their research (e.g., Hofer & Pintrich, 1997; King, 1977; King & Kitchener, 1994, 2002; Kuhn, 1991). Clearly, the most tenacious of this group has been Kitchener and King (e.g., see King & Kitchener, 2002), who have contributed to the epistemic development literature since the 1970s, and who, as early as 1994, report having tested in excess of 1,700 high-school, college-aged, and still older graduate students using their so-called Reflective Judgment Interview. Though conceding (as did Perry, 1970) that epistemic development begins before the college years, these authors generally agree that the most highly developed levels are reached by only a few people—more often than not by the occasional advanced doctoral student. Be this as it may, the evidence in hand does little to encourage the belief that this continuing program of research will tell us anything new about the early course of epistemic development.

Like Kitchener and King, Kuhn and her colleagues (Kuhn, 1991; Kuhn, Amsel, & O'Loughlin, 1988; Kuhn, Weinstock, & Flaton, 1994) have also explored dimensions of epistemic reasoning in respondents beyond the usual college years—research that is primarily about argumentative reasoning regarding various ill-formed, but everyday social problems, and thus only partially overlaps with the work of Perry scholars. Kuhn's 1991 book, which usefully focuses on subjects in their 40s and 60s, as well as more usual 20-year-olds, is relevant to this discussion primarily for the reason that no clear age differences were observed in the frequency with which these broad samples of subjects endorsed what Kuhn and her colleagues described as absolutist, multiplist, and evaluative epistemic views. There is, of course, a spotty literature concerned with the late-arriving matter of "wisdom" (e.g., Holliday & Chandler, 1986; Karelitz, Jarvin, & Sternberg, Chapter 23 of this volume; Sternberg, 1990), but the bulk of this work is intellectually isolated, and more of a carbuncle on, than a living part of, more traditional developmental theory. In keeping with the work emanating more directly from Perry's model, however, there is a body of evidence generated by Kuhn and others suggesting that the inherently subjective or interpretive nature of the knowing process is evident for the first time only among their 12th graders, and is only found to be well consolidated in their sample of graduate student subjects. Although Kuhn and her colleagues do make efforts to interpret progress through their proposed stage sequence as turning on the achievement of something like Piagetian Formal Operations (Inhelder & Piaget, 1958), these data, like those of Kitchener and King, contain little to suggest that epistemic development gets seriously off the ground before the college years.

Epistemic Development in the Adolescent and Preadolescent Years

Although, as just outlined, only a small fraction of the many studies concerned with possible changes in the natural epistemologies of young adults have also included samples of primary- or secondary-school students, fewer still were undertaken with any serious expectation that such young persons would score beyond the lowest entry levels in Perry's nine-level scheme. Not surprisingly, most of these studies proved themselves right. By contrast, there does exist a scattered and still smaller handful of studies, most of which have their intellectual roots in soil different from that which has nourished work in the Perry tradition and which were undertaken by investigators often full of hopes that such young persons might have already made real progress toward epistemic maturity. Advocates of this second, "early-onset" position, although often in agreement about little else, all appear broadly committed to these ideas: (1) that progress in epistemic understanding is a fundamental part of all social-cognitive development (Broughton, 1978); (2) that an awareness of representational diversity is a natural by-product of fading egocentrism and the growth of those role-taking abilities common to the middle-school years (Elkind, 1967; Selman, 1980); and (3) that the capacities for abstraction and the metarepresentational skills that help to define early Formal Operational thought likely make important contributions to a growing appreciation of the ineluctably subjective nature of knowledge (e.g., Boyes & Chandler, 1992; Chandler, 1975, 1987, 1988; Chandler et al., 1990).

As a result of these shared assumptions, advocates of such "early-onset" views have been quick to argue that there is nothing in principle to prevent young adolescents from coming to some, if not all, of the same insights about the subjective nature of belief entitlement that those working within the Perry tradition have reserved for only the most deserving of college graduates. Of course, there is likely no end to the list of possible mitigating factors that might intrude to prevent the typical adolescent from *always* showcasing his best epistemic insights, but this is not, these investigators have argued, the same thing as supposing that such young persons are bereft of any such intuitions until they make their way to the college of their choice.

What is obviously needed, if such "early-onset" views are to make any headway, is some line of evidence that shows that real flesh-and-blood adolescents actually do, as a matter of empirical fact, possess at least some of the epistemic abilities otherwise thought to be reserved for young and not so young adults. Some of this evidence on offer (e.g., Chandler et al., 1990) is owed to efforts meant to better ensure that the contested knowledge claims involved, not just bookish matters of fact under the control of "experts," but familiar and "live" issues of serious personal concern to young people (e.g., whether 16-year-olds are responsible enough to drive). Under these more favorable assessment conditions, Boyes and Chandler (1992) and Chandler et al. (1990) found that more than half of the 8th through 12th graders they tested already gave evidence of a clear appreciation of the relativized or subjective nature of beliefs, whereas fewer than a third responded in ways that still betrayed anything like a consistently "objectivist," or "absolutist," or "naively realistic" commitment to the idea that there is always some singular truth hiding behind every difference of opinion.

In a related series of studies, Oser and Reich (e.g., Oser & Reich, 1987; Reich, 1998), working with groups of 9- to 22-year-old Swiss youths, similarly report that recognition of the active contribution of the knower to the known begins to emerge in preadolescence, and that even the youngest of these recognized the contribution of internal and external features of the knowing process. Much earlier, Broughton (1978) found similar evidence of "nascent skepticism" among 12-year-olds, and reported that, by age 18, his respondents regularly voiced the view that knowing is a "constructive" enterprise guaranteed only by social convention. Clinchy and Mansfield (1985, 1986) and Mansfield and Clinchy (1997) similarly tracked the "natural epistemologies" of young persons—this time from their preschool years through adolescence—and report that children as young as 4 already realize that knowledge is not simply absorbed, but is rather constructed by people with individual personalities and unique pasts; that as many as half of their 7-year-olds, and nearly all of their 10-year-olds, believed that diversity of opinion was legitimate; and that between 9 and 13 participants in their studies regularly came to "portray the knower as an active constructer, rather than a passive receiver of knowledge" (Mansfield & Clinchy, 1997, p. 1). As they put it, "by 13, not a single objectivist was left" (Mansfield & Clinchy, p. 10) in their sample. Although using a sharply different set of methodologies, Schwanenflugel, Fabricius, and their colleagues (e.g., Schwanenflugel, Fabricius, & Noyes, 1996) also report that children of 8 or 10 years of age regularly "move toward a constructivist theory of mind" in which they recognize that the same event may legitimately be interpreted differently. Similarly, Kuhn and Weinstock (2002) have also demonstrated that, particularly in domains removed from the imagined certainty of "hard" or impersonal facts, even middle-school children are often quick to entertain the possibility that equally well-informed others are free to differ in their beliefs about what is right or true. Related

research by Smith, Maclin, Houghton, and Hennessey (2000) has gone further by suggesting that even grade 6 students can begin to appreciate the constructive nature of "scientific thinking" if they receive the right kind of prior instruction. Finally, Walton (2000), who examined the epistemological expressions present in the spontaneous utterances of kindergarten through fourth-grade children, reports that, in talking about knowing and believing, all of her especially young subjects commonly used epistemological expressions that concerned uncertainty, contrasting knowledge with belief.

Although it would be possible to go on piling up more examples, the general point made by all of the investigators cited in this context is that preadolescents and adolescents do not appear obliged to hang back until they have entered college before observing that people take note of, and struggle to comprehend, what they take to be legitimate interpretive diversity.

Summary

However encouraging or discouraging one might find having all of the foregoing evidence of early epistemic development paraded about, it is important not to lose sight of the numerous arguments previously rehearsed in Part II, all of which have repeatedly been taken as proof positive that, by age 5 or earlier, young children who can pass tests of false belief have already begun "to understand knowledge as representation with all its essential characteristics" (Perner, 1991, p. 275); already appreciate that beliefs are "active interpretations or construals of them from a given perspective" (Meltzoff & Gopnik, 1993, p. 335); already hold to "an interpretive or constructive understanding of representation" (Wellman, 1990, p. 244); and have already acquired the view that the contents of mental life are actively constructed "on the basis of inference and subject biases, misrepresentations, and active interpretations" (Wellman & Hickling, 1994, p. 1578).

Given these, together with all of the other competing sets of knowledge claims so far rehearsed about the ontogenetic course of everyone's emerging understanding of competing knowledge claims, one could hardly have hoped for more complete research coverage. That is, some *200-plus* citations later, it is by now obvious that small armies of dedicated researchers have painstakingly explored the epistemic insights of just about every conceivable age group between 6 months and 60 years. That is the good news. The bad news is that they all make more or less the same claim: group X (where X is defined as persons of whatever age group one happens to be studying) is the first age group to ever give evidence of an appreciation of the constructive nature of belief formation. In the following Conclusion section, an attempt is made to find a congruous explanation for this tendency of the epistemic research community to endlessly repeat itself, while describing every age group imaginable.

CONCLUSION

The strong conclusion to which the preceding pages lead is that epistemic development both begins and ends more or less whenever one likes to imagine. Clearly, this is not nearly good enough. How can whole armies of investigators soberly insist that the full warp and woof of epistemic development fully transpires within the confines of just exactly that particular idiosyncratic patch of the full life course on which their own professional careers have come to roost? Isn't this all just too self-serving, chaotic, and caviler?

What we mean to put on offer here, in response to all of this balkanized caprice, is a candidate way of potentially unsnarling at least some of these tangled bits and pieces—of somehow lining them all up end for end. This attempt to posit something of a developmental arc begins with two facts and ends with a third. Fact one is that, from a surprisingly early age, young children appear to have a remarkably precocious understanding of the fact that not everyone likes or values precisely the same thing. As various investigators whose work has already been reviewed help to make clear (e.g., Flavell, Flavell, Green, & Moses, 1990; Repacholi & Gopnik, 1997), somewhere between 18 and 36 months, children already seem to appreciate that cats like cat food and we don't, whereas at least some adults like broccoli better than the goldfish crackers children themselves tend to prefer. Do things, can things, in the personal preference department get a lot better than this? Regardless of whether they do, the domain of personal tastes seems not to be a place that encourages holding out any special hopes of finding evidence of steady epistemic growth.

More or less the same prospects seem to apply to young people's early thoughts about competing knowledge claims, especially as they apply to so-called matters of brute fact. Neither the fact that the cat is or is not on the mat, nor the exact location of Maxi's chocolate, appear to be the sort of thing about which equally well-informed persons are likely to disagree. As it is, a close reading of the evidence concerning young children's understanding of false beliefs would suggest that, despite all of the importance attached to matters of "representational diversity," there actually appears to be no such thing, or at least nothing that is not directly owed to carefully gerrymandered differences in informational access. Once again, then, it is hardly surprising that epistemic development (at least in so far as it is indexed by ignorance-driven false beliefs) occurs early and then never goes anywhere at all.

Given all of this, the only unexplored place to search for possible evidence for such age-graded change is, we suggest, in the shifting ways that persons of every age work to understand what John Searle (1983) and others (e.g., Elgin, 1989; Hanson, 1958; Kuhn, 1970; Rorty, 1979) have described as "social" or "institutional" facts. The trouble with suggesting this is, of course, that next to nothing has so far been said about the possibility that there exists some as yet unexamined class of epistemically relevant matters that are neither brute facts nor matters of personal taste—something like whatever it might mean to speak of "social" facts. What immediately follows, then, is some 11th-hour attempt to explicitly introduce this category of possibilities—the only remaining place, we mean to suggest, that epistemic development has any real hope of gaining much new ground.

The question of what, if anything, might be sandwiched between "objective" beliefs concerning brute facts, on the one hand, and issues of largely arbitrary personal taste, on the other, has been answered in a variety of only partially overlapping ways. By some accounts, this interstitial space is occupied by a confusing variety of other things variously labeled "opinions," "sentiments," "convictions," among others—mental objects that, according to Webster's dictionary, are said to constitute belief-like entities that are greater than a mere "impression" and less than an instance of "positive knowledge."

Alternatively, and without turning our backs on such matters of opinion, it is also possible to envision a still broader class of "social facts" that have been widely understood to shoulder their way between brute facts and residual mental attitudes such as matters of tastes. Putnam (1987), for example, among others (e.g., Elgin, 1989; Hanson, 1958; Kuhn, 1970; Latour, 1993; Overton, 2006; Rorty, 1979; Searle, 1983), has argued strenuously against any two-note fact-value dichotomy and in favor of an alternative view that seeks to arrange various forms of knowledge along a rough continuum, the bulk of which is taken up with so-called social facts of the middle range. That is, facts that, although still thought to be true or false, seem not to hinge on evident sense-based data, but are instead socially constructed. It is not, for example, a simple matter of opinion as to who won the most recent World Series. It is, instead, an already decided matter of fact on which careers and heavy money turn. At the same time, however, questions about what is to count as a "run," as opposed to an "out," or how many "innings" make up a game, are widely agreed-on facts, but not facts of the same caliber as are those about whether lead is heavier (or has a higher atomic number) than tin.

Armed with such an account of social and institutional facts, it becomes potentially more understandable why some of the things once written off as mere values or tastes or opinions may actually have enough of a factual nature to begin bracketing them with beliefs about brute fact. In much the same way, other things that once counted as "brute" facts come to be revealed as institutional or social facts. For reasons such as this, the class of social facts would appear to grow at the expense of brute facts and matters of mere opinion. The same set of distinctions also potentially offers a way of better understanding why the literature on epistemic development appears so fractured and contradictory.

"Social Facts" as the Dark Horse in the Epistemic Race

The ordinary notion of a "dark horse" refers to instances of persons or things that surprisingly emerge, often at the last minute, from the back of the pack, and that rise to prominence after having been previously little considered. So-called social facts, we mean to argue, are like that. As it is, one could easily review a thousand journal articles having to do with early epistemic development without ever once encountering a whiff of the prospect that, in addition to personalized issues about what tastes best, or locally disputed matters of so-called brute facts, there actually exists a whole class of fact-bearing epistemic matters that require being arbitrated. Given that a good case has been made for the prospect that early epistemic development, particularly as it bears on disputes regarding either aesthetics or issues of raw facticity, is evidently short-lived, the possibility that there exists a third category involving novel matters of social or institutional facts that may have longer legs seems especially deserving of our attention.

Wholesale versus Retail Doubt

It is entirely possible, at least in principle, that the class of social facts exists as just described, but the way they come to be understood across development is no different from

that followed for brute facts. That is, it could happen that young people's grasp of social facts also involves some single watershed moment at which the possibility of false social beliefs is initially intuited, followed only by a gradualist lifetime spent building a repertoire of experiences and opportunities for practice. Were this to be the case, then classical theory theorists would be right on all counts, all claims about structural changes in epistemic development beyond the preschool years would once again become fraudulent, and scores of research programs described earlier would need to be seen as a waste of time. Before everyone rushes to prematurely cash in their developmental chips, however, all of the differences that potentially divide social facts from other matters of epistemic import must first be carefully considered. The most important of these, we suggest, turns on the fact that, although disputes about brute facts tend to be decided by appeals to sense-based evidence, disputes about social fact more often engender still more doubts, which are only temporarily held in check by the fact that children typically lack the cognitive wherewithal to take the "wholesale" measure of all of this generic uncertainty (Chandler, 1975, 1987).

This difference is owed to the fact that, although competing claims about matters of brute facts do turn up on occasion, most of these are easily written off to simple ignorance. On still other, and even rarer occasions when, for example, even experts in possession of all the facts continue to disagree, faith in the certainty of some more enlightened future where new facts will intrude to settle such contested matters is widely thought to be warranted by all of the "progress" otherwise happening all around us. That is, we ordinarily think of ourselves as entitled to certain local doubts about the truth of this or that particular "retail" matter, but to doubt too many brute facts all at once, including the truth of one's own experiences, is rare.

Competing matters of taste tend to be handled differently but no less confidently. We automatically expect that different people may differ in their beliefs about matters of taste. That is why we talk about issues of "personal" taste in the first place, and why it is so often mistakenly said that such matters are entirely lacking in epistemic content. If too many people failed to differ in this expected, even constitutive, way, then we would likely reassign such outlier cases by deciding that they were brute facts after all.

Differences of "opinion" about social or institutional facts are, however, a different matter entirely. Rather than rooting out competing knowledge claims, as is regularly assumed to be the proper thing to do with disputes concerning brute fact, here, in the case of social facts, increased knowledge and experience tends not to rid us of such competing views but to multiply them exponentially. In this sense, social facts are like matters of taste in that they often seem to invite disagreement. It is in this sense that social facts earn their dark horse status, shooting up the middle, as they do, between impossible to agree-on matters of taste, on the one hand, and ultimately settleable matters of brute fact, on the other.

As tends to be true of dark horses more generally, social facts often aggravate the status quo, and thus, at least initially, tend to be driven back. That is, perhaps, why young (and sometimes not so young) people often work so hard to empty out their own growing category of social facts by reassigning them, whenever possible, to the more stable categories of brute facts and matters of personal taste. We even have names for people who excel at this. Those who see a brute fact hidden behind every candidate social fact are often regarded as "dogmatists" (e.g., an ordained marriage just *is* a union between a man and a woman), whereas those who wish to regard *everything* as a matter of personal taste tend to be labeled as rabid "relativists."

We, as developing persons, could, in principle, go on dealing individually with every aspiring social fact that appeared on our own epistemic horizon by attempting to banish them to the less troublesome categories of taste and brute facticity, but there is no economy of scale to such a one-off, "retail" enterprise. Rather, what seems to happen is that as the number of contending social facts continues to grow, some developmental tipping point is reached when everything "turns turtle," when retail goes wholesale, and for better or worse, we convince ourselves that, in some measure, everything is a social fact.

Such turning points are often crisis moments. Having drunk from the poisoned well of generic doubt, Descartes, for example, described, on finding himself "forced to deny that there are determinate and unambiguous criteria for knowledge," that he was overtaken by a "dread of madness and chaos where nothing is fixed and where we can neither touch bottom nor support ourselves on the surface" (Bernstein, 1983, p. 18). Similarly, Hume (1938) reported that he became so wrought by what he perceived to be irreconcilable differences in human understanding that he was "ready to reject all belief and reason, and look upon no opinion ever as more likely than another" (p. 267). More positively, Lovejoy (1936) assigned to such experiences responsibility for a new appreciation for a "certain complicatedness" in our worlds, one that also allows for a measure of connoisseurship with regard to matters of taste (Gadamer, 1960/1982), and a way of regarding what were

once held to be especially "brute" facts as drawing their meaning from the socially constructed paradigm in which they are situated.

The point in rehearsing these matters about social facts is not to proselytize for some particular metaphysical framework for helping others to recover from their "Cartesian anxiety" (Bernstein, 1983). Rather, our hope is to use these distinctions to sketch a possible descriptive framework within which all of the sundry investigators who have contributed to the literature on epistemic development might conceivably find a place. It is, we think, not helpful, and almost certainly wrong, to go down some cynical road casting doubts on the likelihood that the research participants in every study cited here did, in fact, do and say what has been claimed. The job, rather, is to envision a way in which all of these redundant and (because they are said about persons of wildly different ages) contradictory claims can find some place.

The CliffsNotes version of our claims goes something like this: (1) Even infant children evidently make certain baby steps toward eventual epistemic maturity by intuiting the legitimacy of at least personal tastes; (2) preschoolers, and quite possibly those much younger, because they come to grasp the possibility of false beliefs, begin prying open the door to acknowledging representational diversity, but only in the instance of what might be called "brute" facts, and only when the different knowledge claims they are prepared to acknowledge are seen as caused by differences in information access; (3) there is little evidence to suggest that there is much room for further development in the case of matters of either personal taste, or "brute" facts, at least until these are later "bracketed" and reunderstood in light of the constructive nature of all knowing; (4) the "executive functions" of early school-aged children allow them to engage in recursive patterns of thought, but these advances largely happen to the side of real epistemic growth; (5) during their middle-school years, young persons finally acquire some fledgling grasp of the real "interpretive" nature of the knowing process but are cognitively ill-prepared to grasp the wholesale implications of this retail discovery; (6) armed with whatever capacities for abstract thought that ordinarily accompany the move into adolescence, teenagers begin to drink from the poisoned well of generic doubt, and as a result are frequently catapulted into either regressive forms of dogmatic thinking, or enter some "moratorium" period especially marked by thoughts of radical relativism; (7) the "Cartesian anxiety" that often marks the adolescent years also helps to author new insights into the dark horse possibility that, in a sense, all facts are social facts, although some are less arguable or less worthy of being argued over than are others; and (8) with burgeoning adulthood, those who are about to or have already entered their college years slowly begin to reach back to and bracket some of their earlier absolutist thoughts about brute facts and know-nothing matters of taste, and slowly come to appreciate that, if there is an ineluctable subjective component to all knowledge claims, then it is necessary to begin hammering out criteria for sorting out better from worse ideas. Perhaps you will find all of this too accommodating, but it at least makes room for a very long list of competing knowledge claims about competing knowledge claims.

REFERENCES

Anderson, M. (1986). Cultural concatenation of deceit and secrecy. In R. W. Mitchell & N. S. Thompson (Eds.), *Deception: Perspectives on human and nonhuman deceit* (pp. 323–348). Albany, NY: State University of New York Press.

Armstrong, D. (1968). *A materialist theory of mind.* New York: Humanities Press.

Armstrong, D. M. (1981). The causal theory of the mind. In D. M. Armstrong (Ed.), *The nature of mind and other essays* (pp. 16–31). Ithaca, NY: Cornell University Press.

Astington, J. W. (1993). *The child's discovery of the mind.* Cambridge, MA: Harvard University Press.

Astington, J. W., Harris, P. L., & Olson, D. R. (1988). *Developing theories of mind.* New York: Cambridge University Press.

Audi, R. (1999). *The Cambridge dictionary of philosophy.* Cambridge: Cambridge University Press.

Baldwin, D. A. (1991). Infants' contribution to the achievement of joint reference. *Child Development, 62,* 875–890.

Baldwin, D. A., Markman, E. M., Bill, B., Desjardins, R. N., Irwin, R. N., & Tidball, G. (1996). Infants' reliance on a social criterion for establishing word-object relations. *Child Development, 67,* 3135–3153.

Bandura, A. (1986). *Social foundations of thought and action: A social cognitive theory.* Englewood Cliffs, NJ: Prentice-Hall.

Baron-Cohen, S. (1987). Autism and symbolic play. *British Journal of Developmental Psychology, 5,* 139–148.

Baron-Cohen, S. (1995). *Mindblindness: an essay on autism and theory of mind.* Cambridge, MA: MIT Press.

Baron-Cohen, S., Leslie, A., & Frith, U. (1985). Does the autistic child have a "theory of mind"? *Cognition, 21,* 37–46.

Baxter Magolda, M. B. (1992). *Knowing and reasoning in college: Gender-related patterns in students' intellectual development.* San Francisco: Jossey Bass.

Baxter Magolda, M. B., & Porterfield, W. D. (1985). *Assessing intellectual development: The link between theory and practice.* Alexandria, VA: American College Personnel Association.

Belenky, M. F., Clinchy, B. M., Goldberger, N. R., & Tarule, J. M. (1986). *Women's way's of knowing: The development of self, voice and mind.* New York: Basic Books.

Benack, S., & Basseches, M. A. (1989). Dialectical thinking and relativistic epistemology: Their relation in adult development. In M. L. Commons, J. D. Sinnott, F. A. Richards, & C. Armon (Eds.), *Adult development: Comparisons and applications of developmental models* (pp. 95–109). New York: Praeger.

Bennett, J. (1978). Some remarks about concepts. *Behavioral and Brain Sciences, 4,* 557–560.

Bernstein, D. M., Atance, C., Loftus, G. R., & Meltzoff, A. N. (2004). We saw it all along: Visual hindsight bias in children and adults. *Psychological Science, 15,* 264–267.

Bernstein, R. (1983). *Beyond objectivism and relativism.* Philadelphia: University of Pennsylvania Press.

Bickhard, M. H. (2006). Developmental normativity and normative development. In L. Smith & J. Voneche (Eds.), *Norms in human development* (pp. 57–76). Cambridge: Cambridge University Press.

Birch, S. A. J. (2005). When knowledge is a curse: Children's and adults' mental state reasoning. *Current Directions in Psychological Science, 14,* 25–29.

Birch, S. A. J., & Bernstein, D. (2007). What kids can tell us about hindsight bias: A fundamental constraint on perspective-taking? *Social Cognition, 25,* 98–113.

Birch, S. A. J., & Bloom, P. (2002). Preschoolers are sensitive to the speaker's knowledge when learning proper names. *Child Development, 73,* 434–444.

Birch, S. A. J., & Bloom, P. (2003). Children are cursed: An asymmetric bias in mental-state attribution. *Psychological Science, 14,* 283–286.

Birch, S. A. J., & Bloom, P. (2004). Understanding children's and adults' limitations in mental state reasoning. *Trends in Cognitive Science, 8,* 255–260.

Birch, S. A. J., & Bloom, P. (2007). The curse of knowledge in reasoning about false beliefs. *Psychological Science, 18,* 382–386.

Blasi, A. (1995). Moral understanding and the moral personality: The process of moral integration. In W. M. Kurtines & J. L. Gewirts (Eds.), *Moral development: An introduction* (pp. 229–253). Boston: Allyn & Bacon.

Bloom, P. (2000). *How children learn the meanings of words.* Cambridge, MA: MIT Press.

Bloom, P. (2004). *Descartes' baby: How the science of child development explains what makes us human.* New York: Basic Books.

Bloom, P., & German, T. (2000). Two reasons to abandon the false belief task as a test of theory of mind. *Cognition, 77,* B25–B31.

Bosco, F. M., Friedman, O., & Leslie, A. M. (2006). Recognition of pretend and real actions in play by 1- and 2-year-olds: Early success and why they fail. *Cognitive Development, 21,* 3–10.

Boyes, M., & Chandler, M. J. (1992). Cognitive development, epistemic doubt, and identity formation in adolescence. *Journal of Youth and Adolescence, 21*(3), 277–304.

Bretherton, I. (1991). Intentional communication and the development of an understanding of mind. In D. Frye & C. Moore (Eds.), *Children's theories of mind: Mental states and social understanding.* Hillsdale, NJ: Erlbaum.

Bretherton, I., & Beeghly, M. (1982). Talking about internal states: The acquisition of an explicit Theory of Mind. *Developmental Psychology, 18,* 906–921.

Broughton, J. (1978). Development of concepts of self, mind, reality, and knowledge. *New Directions for Child Development, 1,* 70–100.

Bruner, J. (1990). *Acts of meaning.* Cambridge, MA: Harvard University Press.

Bugelski, B. R. (1960). *An introduction to the principles of psychology.* New York: Holt, Rinehart, and Winston.

Buttelmann, D., Carpenter, M., & Tomasello, M. (2009). Eighteen-month-old infants show false belief understanding in an active helping paradigm. *Cognition, 112,* 337–342.

Call, J., & Tomasello, M. (2008). Does the chimpanzee have a theory of mind? 30 years later. *Trends in Cognitive Science, 12,* 187–192.

Carey, S., & Gelman, R. (Eds.). (1991). *Epigenesis of mind: Essays in biology and knowledge.* Hillsdale, NJ: Erlbaum.

Carlson, S. M., Moses, L. J., & Claxton, L. J. (2004). Individual difference in executive functioning and theory of mind: An investigation of inhibitory control and planning ability. *Journal of Experimental Child Psychology, 87,* 299–319.

Carpendale, J. I. M. (1995). *On the distinction between false belief understanding and the acquisition of an interpretive theory of mind.* Unpublished doctoral dissertation, University of British Columbia, Vancouver, Canada.

Carpendale, J. I. M., & Chandler, M. J. (1996). On the distinction between false belief understanding and subscribing to an interpretive theory of mind. *Child Development, 67*(4), 1686–1706.

Carpendale, J. I. M., & Lewis, C. (2006). *How children develop social understanding.* Oxford: Blackwell.

Chandler, M. J. (1975). Relativism and the problem of epistemological loneliness. *Human Development, 18,* 171–180.

Chandler, M. J. (1978). Social cognition: A selected review of current research. In W. Overton & J. Gallagher (Eds.), *Knowledge and development: Yearbook of development epistemology.* New York: Plenum.

Chandler, M. J. (1987). The Othello effect: An essay on the emergence and eclipse of skeptical doubt. *Human Development, 30,* 137–159.

Chandler, M. J. (1988). Doubt and developing theories of mind. In J. W. Astington, P. L. Harris, & D. R. Olson (Eds.), *Developing theories of mind* (pp. 387–413). New York: Cambridge University Press.

Chandler, M. J. (2001). Perspective taking in the aftermath of theory-theory and the collapse of the social role-taking enterprise. In A. Tryphon & J. Voneche (Eds.), *Working with Piaget: Essays in honour of Barbel Inhelder* (pp. 39–63). London: Psychology Press.

Chandler, M. J., & Boyes, M. (1982). Social-cognitive development. In B. B. Wolman (Ed.), *Handbook of developmental psychology* (pp. 387–402). Englewood Cliffs, NJ: Prentice-Hall.

Chandler, M. J., Boyes, M. C., & Ball, L. (1990). Relativism and stations of epistemic doubt. *Journal of Experimental Child Psychology, 50,* 370–395.

Chandler, M. J., & Carpendale, J. I. M. (1994). Concerning the rumored falling to earth of Time's Arrow. *Psychological Inquiry, 5,* 245–248.

Chandler, M. J., & Carpendale, J. I. M. (1998). Inching toward a mature theory of mind. In M. Ferrari & R. Sternberg (Eds.), *Self-awareness: Its nature and development* (pp. 148–190). New York: Guilford Press.

Chandler, M. J., Fritz, A. S., & Hala, S. M. (1989). Small scale deceit: Deception as a marker of 2-, 3- and 4-year-old's theories of mind. *Child Development, 60,* 1263–1277.

Chandler, M. J., & Hala, S. (1994). The role of personal involvement in the assessment of false belief skills. In C. Lewis & P. Mitchell (Eds.), *Origins of an understanding of mind.* Hove, United Kingdom: Erlbaum.

Chandler, M. J., Hallett, D., & Sokol, B. W. (2002). Competing claims about competing knowledge claims. In B. K. Hofer & P. R. Pintrich (Eds.), *Personal epistemology: The psychology of beliefs about knowledge and knowing* (pp. 145–168). Mahway, NJ: Erlbaum.

Chandler, M. J., & Lalonde, C. (1996). Shifting to an interpretive theory of mind: 5- to 7-year-olds' changing conceptions of mental life. In A. J. Sameroff & M. M. Haith (Eds.), *The five to seven year shift: The age of reason and responsibility* (pp. 111–139). Chicago: University of Chicago Press.

Chandler, M. J., & Sokol, B. W. (1999). Representation once removed: Children's developing conceptions of representational life. In I. E. Sigel (Ed.), *Development of mental representation: Theories and applications* (pp. 201–230). Mahwah, NJ: Erlbaum.

Chapman, M. (1988). *Constructive evolution: Origins and development of Piaget's thought.* Cambridge: Cambridge University Press.

Churchland, P. (1981). Eliminative materialism and propositional attitudes. *Journal of Philosophy, 78,* 67–90.

Clinchy, B. M. (2002). Revisiting women's ways of knowing. In B. K. Hofer & P. R. Pintrich (Eds.), *Personal epistemology: The psychology of beliefs about knowledge and knowing* (pp. 63–87). Mahwah, NJ: Erlbaum.

Clinchy, B. M., & Mansfield, A. F. (1985, March). Justifications offered by children to support positions on issues of "fact" and "opinion." Paper presented that the 56th annual meeting of the (U.S.) Eastern Psychological Association, Philadelphia.

Clinchy, B. M., & Mansfield, A. F. (1986, May). The child's discovery of the role of the knower in the known. Paper presented that the 16th Annual Symposium of the Jean Piaget Society, Boston.

Coie, J. D., Costanzo, P. R., & Farnhill, D. (1973). Specific transitions in the development of spacial perspective-taking ability. *Developmental Psychology, 9,* 167–177.

Commons, M. L., Armon, C., Richards, F. A., Schrader, D. E., Farrell, E. W., Tappan, M. B., et al. (1989). A multidomain study of adult development. In M. L. Commons, J. D. Sinnott, F. A. Richards, & C. Armon (Eds.), *Adult development: Comparisons and applications of developmental models* (pp. 33–56). New York: Praeger.

Csibra G., Gergely, G., Biró, S., & Koós, O., & Brockbank, M. (1999). Goal-attribution without agency cues: The perception of "pure reason" in infancy. *Cognition, 72,* 237–267.

Davidson, D. (1984). Thought and talk. In D. Davidson (Ed.), *Inquiries into truth and interpretation* (pp. 155–170). Oxford: Oxford University Press.

Davies, M., & Stone, T. (Eds.). (1995). *Folk Psychology.* Oxford: Blackwell.

De Morgan, A. (1872/1915). On poetry: A rhapsody. *A budget of paradoxes.* New York: Dover.

Dennett, D. C. (1978). Beliefs about beliefs. *Behavioral and Brain Sciences, 4,* 568–570.

Dennett, D. C. (1987). *The intentional stance.* Cambridge, MA: Bradford Books/MIT Press.

Dias, M. G., & Harris, P. L. (1990). The influence of the imagination on reasoning by young children. *British Journal of Developmental Psychology, 8,* 305–317.

Duhem, P. (1906/1962). *The aim and structure of physical theory.* New York: Atheneum.

Dunn, J. (1988). *The beginnings of social understanding.* Cambridge, MA: Harvard University Press.

Dunn, J. (1991). Understanding others: Evidence from naturalistic studies of children. In A. Whiten (Ed.), *Natural theories of mind. Evolution, development and simulation of everyday mindreading* (pp. 51–61). Oxford: Basil Blackwell.

Dunn, J. (1993). Children's understanding of "other minds": Antecedents and later correlates in interaction with family and friends. Paper presented at a Symposium at the Biennial Meeting of the Society for Research in Child Development, New Orleans, LA.

Dunn, J., & Dale, N. (1984). I a daddy: 2-year-olds' collaboration in joint pretend with sibling and with mother. In I. Bretherton (Ed.), *Symbolic play* (pp. 131–158). New York: Academic Press.

Dunn, J., & Munn, P. (1985). Becoming a family member: Family conflict and the development of social understanding in the second year. *Child Development, 56,* 764–774.

Elgin, C. (1989). The relativity of the fact and the objectivity of value. In M. Krausz (Ed.), *Relativism: Interpretation and confrontation* (pp. 86–98). Notre Dame, IN: University of Notre Dame Press.

Elkind, D. (1967). Egocentrism in adolescence. *Child Development, 38,* 1025–1034.

Elkind, D. (1985). Egocentrism redux. *Developmental Review, 5,* 218–226.

Epley, N. (2008). Solving the (real) other minds problem. *Social and Personality Psychology Compass, 2,* 1455–1474.

Epley, N., Morewedge, C. K., & Keysar, B. (2004). Perspective taking in children and adults: Equivalent egocentrism but differential correction. *Journal of Experimental Social Psychology, 40,* 760–768.

Fenson, L., & Ramsay, D. S. (1981). Effects of modeling action sequences on the play of twelve-, fifteen- and nineteen-month-old children. *Child Development, 52,* 1028–1036.

Flavell, J. (1974). The development of inferences about others. In T. Mischel (Ed.), *Understanding other persons.* Oxford: Blackwell, Basil, & Mott.

Flavell, J. (1977). *Cognitive development.* Englewood Cliffs, NJ: Prentice.

Flavell, J. H. (1988). The development of children's knowledge about the mind: From cognitive connections to mental representations. In J. W. Astington, P. L. Harris, & D. R. Olson (Eds.), *Developing theories of mind* (pp. 244–267). New York: Cambridge University Press.

Flavell, J. H., Botkin, P. T., Fry, C. L., Wright, J. W., & Jarvis, P. E. (1968). *The development of role-taking and communication skills in children.* New York: John Wiley & Sons, Inc.

Flavell, J. H., Flavell, E. R., Green, F. L., & Moses, L. J. (1990). Young children's understanding of fact beliefs versus value beliefs. *Child Development, 61,* 915–928.

Fodor, J. A. (1987). *Psychosemantics: The problem of meaning in the philosophy of mind.* Cambridge, MA: Bradford Books/MIT Press.

Fodor, J. (1992). A theory of the child's theory of mind. *Cognition, 44,* 283–296.

Forguson, L. (1989). *Common sense.* London: Routledge.

Forguson, L., & Gopnik, A. (1988). The ontogeny of common sense. In J. W. Astington, P. L. Harris, & D. R. Olson (Eds.), *Developing theories of mind* (pp. 226–243). New York: Cambridge University Press.

Frankfurt, H. G. (1988). *The importance of what we care about: Philosophical essays.* Cambridge: Cambridge University Press.

Friedman, O., & Leslie, A. M. (2007). The conceptual underpinnings of pretense: Pretending is not "behaving-as-if." *Cognition, 105*(1), 103–124.

Frith, U. (1989). *Autism: Explaining the enigma.* Oxford: Blackwell.

Frye, D., & Moore, C. (1991). *Children's theories of mind.* Hillsdale, NJ: Erlbaum.

Gadamer, H. G. (1960/1982). *Truth and method.* New York: Seabury Press.

Garcia, R. (1987). Sociology of science and sociogenesis of knowledge. In B. Inhelder, D. de Caprona, & A. Cornu-Wells (Eds.), *Piaget today* (pp. 127–140). Hove, United Kingdom: Erlbaum.

German, T. P., & Hehman, J. A. (2006). Representational and executive selection resources in "theory of mind": Evidence from compromised belief–desire reasoning in old age. *Cognition, 101,* 129–152.

German, T. P., & Leslie, A. M. (2000). Attending to and learning about mental states. In P. Mitchell & K. Riggs (Eds.), *Children's reasoning and the mind.* Hove, United Kingdom: Psychology Press.

German, T. P., Niehaus, J. L., Roarty, M. P., Giesbrecht, B., & Miller, M. B. (2004). Neural correlates of detecting pretense: Automatic engagement of intentional stance under covert conditions. *Journal of Cognitive Neuroscience, 16,* 1805–1817.

Gnepp, J., & Chilamkurti, C. (1988). Children's use of personality attributions to predict other people's emotional and behavioral reactions. *Child Development, 59,* 743–754.

Goldman, A. (1989). Interpretation psychologized. *Mind and Language, 4,* 161–185.

Gopnik, A. (1991, April). Is the child's theory of mind really a theory? Paper presented at the biennial meeting of the Society for Research in Child Development, Seattle, WA.

Gopnik, A., & Astington, J. W. (1988). Children's understanding of representational change and its relation to the understanding of false belief and the appearance-reality distinction. *Child Development, 59,* 26–37.

Gopnik, A., Meltzoff, A. N., & Kuhl, P. K. (1999). *The scientist in the crib: Minds, brains, and how children learn.* New York: William Morrow.

Gopnik, A., & Wellman, H. M. (1992). Why the child's theory of mind really is a theory. *Mind and Language, 7,* 145–171.

Gopnik, A., & Wellman, H. M. (1994). The theory theory. In L. A. Hirschfeld & S. A. Gelman (Eds.), *Mapping the mind: Domain specificity in cognition and culture* (pp. 257–293). New York: Cambridge University Press.

Gordon, R. M. (1986). Folk psychology as simulation. *Mind and Language, 1,* 158–171.

Greenwood, J. D. (1989). *Explanation and experiment in social psychological science: Realism and the social constitution of action.* New York: Springer-Verlag.

Hala, S., & Chandler, M. J. (1993a, March). Intentional action and early false belief understanding. Presented at the Biennial Meetings of The Society for Research in Child Development, New Orleans, LA.

Hala, S., & Chandler, M. J. (1993b). Plans of action and 3-year-olds' understanding of false belief. Presented at the Twenty-Third Annual Symposium of the Jean Piaget Society, Philadelphia.

Hala, S., & Chandler, M. J. (1996). The role of strategic planning in accessing false-belief understanding. *Child Development, 67,* 2948–2966.

Hala, S., Chandler, M. J., & Fritz, A. (1991). Fledgling theories of mind: Deception as a marker of 3-year-old's understanding of false belief. *Child Development, 62,* 83–97.

Hanson, N. R. (1958). *Patterns of discovery.* London: Cambridge University Press.

Hare, B., Call, J., & Tomasello, M. (2001). Do chimpanzees know what conspecifics know? *Animal Behaviour, 61,* 139–151.

Harris, P. (1991). The work of the imagination. In A. Whiten (Ed.), *Natural theories of mind.* Oxford: Blackwell.

Harris, P. (2006). Social cognition. In D. Kuhn & R. S. Siegler (Eds.), *Handbook of child psychology: Vol. 2. Cognition, perception, and language* (pp. 811–858). Hoboken, NJ: John Wiley & Sons.

Harris, P. L. (1989). *Children and emotion: The development of psychological understanding.* Oxford: Blackwell.

Harris, P. L. (1995). Imagining and pretending. In M. Davies & T. Stone (Eds.), *Mental simulation: Evaluations and applications* (pp. 170–184). Oxford: Blackwell.

Heyman, G. D., Fu, G., & Lee, K. (2007). Evaluating claims people make about themselves: The development of skepticism. *Child Development, 78,* 367–375.

Heyman, G. D., & Gelman, S. A. (1999). The use of trait labels in making psychological inferences. *Child Development, 70,* 604–619.

Heyman, G. D., & Legare, C. H. (2005). Children's evaluation of sources of information about traits. *Developmental Psychology, 41,* 636–647.

Hofer, B. K., & Pintrich, P. R. (1997). The development of epistemological theories: Beliefs about knowledge and knowing and their relation to learning. *Review of Educational Research, 67*(1), 88–140.

Holliday, S. G., & Chandler, M. J. (1986). Wisdom: Explorations in adult competence. *Contributions to Human Development, 17,* 1–100.

Hume, D. (1938). *An abstract of a treatise of human nature.* Cambridge: Cambridge University Press.

Inhelder, B., & Piaget, J. (1958). *The growth of logical thinking.* London: Routledge & Kegan Paul.

James, W. (1910) *Psychology: The briefer course.* New York: Holt and Co.

Jastrow, J. (1900). *Fact and fable in psychology.* Boston: Houghton-Mifflin.

Jenkins, J. M., & Astington, J. W. (1993). Cognitive, linguistic, and social factors associated with theory of mind development in young children. Paper presented at the Biennial Meeting of the Society for Research in Child Development, New Orleans, LA.

Johnson, C. N. (1988). Theory of mind and the structure of conscious experience. In J. W. Astington, P. L. Harris, & D. R. Olson, (Eds.), *Developing theories of mind.* New York: Cambridge University Press.

Johnson, S., Slaughter, V., & Carey, S. (1998). Whose gaze will infants follow? The elicitation of gaze-following in 12-month-olds. *Developmental Science, 1,* 233–238.

Kessen, W. (1996). American psychology just before Piaget. *Psychological Science, 7*(4), 196–199.

Keysar, B., Lin, S., & Barr, D. J. (2003). Limits on theory of mind use in adults. *Cognition, 89,* 25–41.

King, P. M. (1977). The development of reflective judgment and formal operational thinking in adolescents and young adults. *Dissertation Abstracts International, 38,* 7233A.

King, P. M., & Kitchener, K. S. (1994). *Developing reflective judgment: Understanding and promoting intellectual growth and critical thinking in adolescents and adults.* San Francisco: Jossey-Bass.

King, P. M., & Kitchener, K. S. (2002). The reflective judgment model: Twenty years of research on epistemic cognition. In B. K. Hofer & P. R. Pintrich (Eds.), *Personal epistemology: The psychology of beliefs about knowledge and knowing* (pp. 37–61). Mahwah, NJ: Erlbaum.

Kitchener, K. S., & King, P. M. (1981). Reflective judgment: Concepts of justification and their relationship to age and education. *Journal of Applied Developmental Psychology, 2,* 89–116.

Kuhlmeier, V., Wynn, K., & Bloom, P. (2003). Attribution of dispositional states by 12-month-olds. *Psychological Science, 14,* 402–408.

Kuhn, D. (1991). *The skills of argument.* Cambridge: Cambridge University Press.

Kuhn, D., Amsel, E., & O'Loughlin, M. (1988). *The development of scientific thinking skills.* San Diego: Academic Press.

Kuhn, D., & Weinstock, M. (2002). The development of epistemological understanding. In B. K. Hofer & P. R. Pintrich (Eds.), *Personal epistemology: The psychology of beliefs about knowledge and knowing* (pp. 121–144). Mahwah, NJ: Erlbaum.

Kuhn, D., Weinstock, M., & Flaton, R. (1994). Historical reasoning as theory-evidence coordination. In M. Carretero & J. F. Voss (Eds.), *Cognitive and instructional processes in history and the social sciences* (pp. 377–401). Hillsdale, NJ: Erlbaum.

Kuhn, T. S. (1970). *The structure of scientific revolutions* (2nd ed.) Chicago: University of Chicago Press.

Kuhn, T. S. (1991). The natural and human sciences. In D. R. Hiley, J. F. Bohman, & R. Shusterman (Eds.), *The interpretive turn: Philosophy, science, culture* (pp. 17–24). Ithaca, NY: Cornell University Press.

Kurdek, L., & Rodgon, M. (1975). Perceptual, cognitive, and affective perspective taking in kindergarten through six-grade children. *Developmental Psychology, 11,* 643–650.

LaFreniere, P. (1988). The ontogeny of tactical deception in humans. In R. W. Byrne & A. Whiten (Eds.), *Machiavellian intelligence: Social expertise and the evolution of intellect in monkeys, apes, and humans* (pp. 238–252). Oxford: Clarendon Press.

Lalonde, C. E. (1996). *Children's understanding of the interpretive character of the mind.* Unpublished doctoral dissertation. University of British Columbia, Vancouver, British Columbia, Canada.

Lalonde, C. E., & Chandler, M. J. (2002). Children's understanding of interpretation. *New Ideas in Psychology: Special Issue on Folk Epistemology, 20,* 163–198.

Latour, B. (1993). *We have never been modern.* Cambridge, MA: Harvard University Press.

Legerstee, M. (1992). A review of the animate-inanimate distinction in infancy: Implications for models of social and cognitive knowing. *Early Development and Parenting, 1,* 57–67.

Lempers, J. D., Flavell, E. R., & Flavell, J. H. (1977). The development in very young children of tacit knowledge concerning visual perception. *Genetic Psychology Monographs, 95,* 3–53.

Leslie, A. (1988). Some implications of pretense for the development of theories of mind. In J. W. Astington, P. L. Harris, & D. R. Olson (Eds.), *Developing theories of mind* (pp. 19–46). New York: Cambridge University Press.

Leslie, A. M. (1987). Pretense and representation: The origins of "theory of mind." *Psychological Review, 94,* 412–426.

Lewis, C. (1994). Episodes, events, and narratives in the child's understanding of mind. In C. Lewis & P. Mitchell (Eds.), *Children's early understanding of mind: Origins and development* (pp. 457–480). Hove, United Kingdom: Erlbaum.

Lewis, D. (1972). Psychophysical and theoretical identifications. *Australian Journal of Philosophy, 50,* 249–258.

Lewis, M., Stanger, C., & Sullivan, M. W. (1989). Deception in 3-year-olds. *Developmental Psychology, 25,* 439–443.

Lillard, A. S. (1993) Young children's conceptualization of pretense: Action or mental representational state? *Child Development, 49,* 642–648.

Lillard, A. S. (1994). Making sense of pretense. In C. Lewis & P. Mitchell (Eds.), *Children's early understanding of mind: Origins and development.* Hove, United Kingdom: Erlbaum.

Lillard, A. S. (1996). Body or mind: Children's categorizing of pretense. *Child Development, 67,* 1717–1734.

Lillard, A. S. (2001). Pretend play as twin earth: A socio-cognitive analysis. *Developmental Review, 21,* 495–531.

Lillard, A. S., & Flavell, J. H. (1992). Young children's understanding of different mental states. *Developmental Psychology, 28,* 626–634.

Lillard, A. S., & Witherington, D. S. (2004). Mothers' behavior modifications during pretense snacks and their possible signal value for toddlers. *Developmental Psychology, 40,* 95–113.

Lyotard, J. F. (1984). *The postmodern condition: A report on knowledge* (G. Bennington & B. Massiuri, Trans.). Minneapolis, MN: University of Minnesota Press.

Macnamara, J. (1989). Children as common sense psychologists. *Canadian Journal of Behavioural Science, 21,* 426–429.

Mansfield, A. F., & Clinchy, B. M. (1997, April 3). Toward the integration of objectivity and subjectivity: A longitudinal study of epistemological development between the ages of 9 and 13. Paper presented at the biennial meeting of the Society for Research in Child Development, Washington, DC.

Markman, K. D., Klein, W. M. P., & Suhr, J. A. (2009). *The handbook of imagination and mental simulation.* New York: Psychology Press.

Masangkay, Z. S., McCluskey, K. A., McIntyre, C. W., Sims-Knight, J., Vaughn, B. E., & Flavell, J. H. (1974). The early development of inferences about the visual percepts of others. *Child Development, 45,* 357–366.

Meltzoff, A. N. (1995). Understanding the intentions of others: Re-enactment of intended acts by 18-month-old children. *Developmental Psychology, 31,* 838–850.

Meltzoff, A. N., & Gopnik, A. (1993). The role of imitation in understanding persons and developing a theory of mind. In S. Baron-Cohen, H. Tager-Flusberg, & D. J. Cohen (Eds.), *Understanding other minds: Perspectives from autism* (pp. 335–366). Oxford: Oxford University Press.

Milligan, K., Astington, J. W., & Dack, L. A. (2007). Language and theory of mind: Meta-analysis of the relation between language ability and false-belief understanding. *Child Development, 77,* 622–646.

Mills, C. M., & Keil, F. C. (2005). The development of cynicism. *Psychological Science, 16,* 385–390.

Mills, C. M., & Keil, F. C. (2008). Children's developing notions of (im)partiality. *Cognition, 107,* 528–551.

Mitchell, P., & Lacohee, H. (1991) Children's understanding of false belief. *Cognition, 39,* 107–128.

Mitchell, R. W., & Thompson, N. S. (Eds.). (1986). *Deception: Perspectives on human and nonhuman deceit.* Albany, NY: State University of New York Press.

Moore, C., Pure, K., & Furrow, D. (1990). Children's under- standing of the modal expression of certainty and un-certainty and its relation to the development of a representational theory of mind. *Child Development, 61,* 722–730.

Moore, W. S. (1994). Student and faculty epistemology in the college classroom: The Perry schema of intellectual and ethical development. In K. W. Prichard & R. A Sawyer (Eds.), *Handbook of college teaching: Theory and applications* (pp. 45–67). Westport, CT: Greenwood Press.

Morgan, C. L. (1894). *An introduction to comparative psychology.* London: Walter Scott.

Morton, A. (1980). *Frames of mind.* Oxford: Clarendon Press.

Moses, L. (1993). Young children's understanding of belief constraints on intention. *Cognitive Development, 8,* 1–25.

Moses, L. J., & Chandler, M. J. (1992). Traveler's guide to children's theories of mind. *Psychological Inquiry, 3,* 286–301.

Mossler, D. G., Marvin, R. S., & Greenburg, M. T. (1976). Conceptual perspective taking in 2 to 6-year-old children. *Developmental Psychology, 12*(1), 85–86.

Moya, C. J. (1990). *The philosophy of action: An introduction.* Cambridge: Polity Press.

Muller, U., Zelazo, D. P., & Imrisek, S. (2005).Executive function and children's understanding of false belief: How specific is the relation? *Cognitive Development, 20,* 173–189.

Murray, F. B. (1979). Preface. In F. B. Murray (Ed.), *The impact of Piagetian theory: On education, philosophy, psychiatry, and psychology* (pp. ix–xiii). Baltimore, MD: University Park Press.

Nichols, S., & Stich, S. (2000). A cognitive theory of pretense. *Cognition, 74,* 115–147.

Nichols, S., & Stich, S. (2003). *Mindreading: An integrated account of pretense, self-awareness and understanding other minds.* Oxford: Oxford University Press.

Olson, D. R. (1993). The development of representations: The origins of mental life. *Canadian Psychology, 34*(3), 293–306.

O'Neill, D. K. (1996). Two-year-old children's sensitivity to a parent's knowledge state when making requests. *Child Development, 67,* 659–677.

Onishi, K. H., & Baillargeon, R. (2005). Do 15-month-old infants understand false belief? *Science, 308,* 255–258.

Onishi, K. H., Baillargeon, R., & Leslie, A. M. (2007). 15-month-old infants detect violations in pretend scenarios. *Acta Psychologica, 124,* 106–128.

Oser, F. K., & Reich, K. H. (1987). The challenge of competing explanations: The development of thinking in terms of complementarity of "theories." *Human Development, 30,* 178–186.

Overton, W. F. (2006). Developmental psychology: Philosophy, concepts, methodology. In W. Damon & R. M. Lerner (Series Eds.) & R. M. Lerner (Ed.), *Handbook of child psychology: Vol. 1. Theoretical models of human development* (6th ed., pp. 18–88). Hoboken, NJ: John Wiley & Sons.

Paulsen M. B., & Wells C. T. (1998). Domain differences in the epistemological beliefs of college students. *Research in Higher Education, 39,* 365–384.

Penn, D., & Povinelli, D. J. (2007). Causal cognition in human and nonhuman animals: A comparative, critical review. *Annual Reviews of Psychology, 58,* 97–118.

Perner, J. (1988). Higher-order beliefs and intentions in children's understanding of social interaction. In J. W. Astington, P. L. Harris, & D. R. Olson (Eds.), *Developing theories of mind* (pp. 271–294). New York: Cambridge University Press.

Perner, J. (1991). *Understanding the representational mind.* Cambridge, MA: MIT Press.

Perner, J., & Davies, G. (1991). Understanding the mind as an active information processor: Do young children have a "copy theory of mind"? *Cognition, 39*(1), 51–69.

Perner, J., Leekam, S. R., & Wimmer, H. (1987). Three-year-old's difficulty with false belief: The case for conceptual deficit. *British Journal of Developmental Psychology, 5,* 125–137.

Perner, J., & Ruffman, T. (2005). Infants' insight into the mind: How deep? *Science, 308,* 214–216.

Perner, J., & Wimmer, H. (1985). "John thinks that Mary thinks that…": Attribution of second-order beliefs by 5- to 10-year-old children. *Journal of Experimental Child Psychology, 39,* 437–471.

Perry, W. G. (1970). *Forms of intellectual and ethical development in the college years: A scheme.* New York: Holt, Rinehart, & Winston.

Peskin, J. (1992). Ruse and representation: On children's ability to conceal their intentions. *Developmental Psychology, 28,* 84–89.

Piaget, J. (1962/1945). *Play, dreams, and imitation in childhood.* New York: Norton.

Piaget, J. (1965/1932). *The moral judgment of the child.* New York: The Free Press.

Piaget, J. (1972/1965). *Insights and illusions of philosophy.* London: Routledge & Kegan Paul.

Piaget, J., & Inhelder, B. (1963/1948). *The child's conception of space* (F. J. Langdon & J. L. Lunzer, Trans.). London: Routledge & Kegan Paul.

Pillow, B. H. (1988). The development of children's beliefs about the mental world. *Merrill-Palmer Quarterly, 34,* 1–32.

Pillow, B. H. (1989). Early understanding of perception as a source of knowledge. *Journal of Experimental Child Psychology, 47,* 11–129.

Pillow, B. H. (1991). Children's understanding of biased social cognition. *Developmental Psychology, 27*(4), 539–551.

Pillow, B. H. (1995). Two trends in the development of conceptual perspective-taking: An elaboration of the passive-active hypothesis. *International Journal of Behavioural Development, 18*(4), 649–676.

Pillow, B. H. (1999). Epistemological development in adolescence and adulthood: A multidimensional framework. *Genetic, Social, and General Psychology Monographs, 125*(4), 413–432.

Pillow, B. H., & Weed, S. T. (1995). Children's understanding of biased interpretation: Generality and limitations. *British Journal of Developmental Psychology, 13,* 347–366.

Premack, D. (1988). 'Does the chimpanzee have a theory of mind?' Revisited. In W. Byrne & A. Whiten (Eds.), *Machiavellian intelligence. Social expertise and the evolution of intellect in monkeys, apes and humans* (pp. 160–179). Oxford: Clarendon Press.

Premack, D., & Woodruff, G. (1978). Does the chimpanzee have a theory of mind? *The Behavioral and Brain Sciences, 4,* 515–526.

Price, R. (1953). *Droodles.* New York: Simon & Schuster.

Putnam, H. (1960). Minds and Machines. In S. Hook (Ed.), *Dimensions of mind* (pp. 138–164). New York: New York University Press.

Putnam, H. (1987). *The many faces of realism.* LaSalle, IL: Open Court.

Reddy, V. (1990). Playing with others' expectations: teasing and mucking about in the first year. In A. Whiten (Ed.) *Natural theories of mind. Evolution, development and simulation of everyday mindreading* (pp. 143–158). Oxford: Basil Blackwell.

Reich, K. H. (1998, September 21–24). Relational and contextual reasoning and its relationships with other forms of thought. Poster presented at the 15th advanced course of the Archives Jean Piaget, Geneva, Switzerland.

Reich, K. H., Oser, F. K., & Valentin, P. (1994). Knowing why I now know better: Children's and youth's explanations of their worldview changes. *Journal of Research on Adolescence, 4*(1), 151–173.

Reid, T. (1863/1788). Essays on the active powers of man. In *The works of Thomas Reid, D.D.* (6th ed., Vol. 2, pp. 509–679). Edinburgh, United Kingdom: Maclachlan and Stewart.

Repacholi, B. M., & Gopnik, A. (1997). Early reasoning about desires: Evidence from 14- and 18-month-olds. *Developmental Psychology, 33*(1), 12–21.

Richert, R. A., & Lillard, A. S. (2004). Observers' proficiency at identifying pretense acts based on behavioral cues. *Cognitive Development, 19*(2), 223–240.

Robinson, E. J. (2000). Belief and disbelief: Children's assessments of the reliability of sources of knowledge about the world. In K. P. Roberts & M. Blades (Eds.), *Children's source monitoring* (pp. 59–83). Mahwah, NJ: Erlbaum.

Rorty, R. (1979). *Philosophy and the mirror of nature.* Princeton, NJ: Princeton University Press.

Royzman, E. B., Cassidy, K. W., & Baron, J. (2003). "I know, you know": Epistemic egocentrism in children and adults. *Review of General Psychology, 7,* 38–65.

Ruffman, T., Olson, D. R., Ash, T., & Keenan, T. (1993). The ABC's of deception: Do young children understand deception in the same way as adults? *Developmental Psychology, 29,* 74–87.

Ruffman, T., Olson, D. R., & Astington, J. W. (1991). Children's understanding of visual ambiguity. *British Journal of Developmental Psychology, 9,* 89–102.

Russell, J. (1989) Cognisance and cognitive science. Part two: Towards an empirical psychology of cognisance. *Philosophical Psychology, 2,* 187–223.

Russell, J. (1992). The Theory-Theory: So good they named it twice? *Cognitive Development, 7,* 485–519.

Russell, J. (1996). *Agency: Its role in mental development.* Hove, United Kingdom: Erlbaum.

Russell, J., Mauthner, N., Sharpe, S., & Tidswell, T. (1991). The "windows task" as a measure of strategic deception in preschoolers and autistic subjects. *British Journal of Developmental Psychology, 9,* 331–349.

Ryle, G. (1949). *The concept of mind.* London: Hutchinson.

Samson, D., Apperly, I. A., Kathirgamanathan, U., & Humphreys, G. W. (2005). Seeing it my way: A case of a selective deficit in inhibiting self-perspective, *Brain, 128,* 1102–1111.

Schommer, M. (1990). Effects of beliefs about the nature of knowledge on comprehension. *Journal of Educational Psychology, 82,* 498–504.

Schommer, M. (1993). Epistemological development and academic performance among secondary students. *Journal of Educational Psychology, 85*(3), 406–411.

Schwanenflugel, P. J., Fabricius, W. V., & Noyes, C. R. (1996). Developing organization of mental verbs: Evidence for the development of a constructivist theory of mind in middle childhood. *Cognitive Development, 11,* 265–294.

Searle, J. R. (1983). *Intentionality: An essay in the philosophy of mind.* Cambridge: Cambridge University Press.

Selman, R. L. (1980). An analysis of "pure" perspective taking: Games and the delights of deception. In R. L. Selman (Ed.), *The growth of interpersonal understanding: Developmental and clinical analyses* (pp. 49–68). New York: Academic Press.

Shultz, T. R., & Cloghess, K. (1981). Development of recursive awareness of intention. *Developmental Psychology, 17,* 456–471.

Siegal, M., & Beattie, K. (1991). Where to look first for children's knowledge of false beliefs. *Cognition, 38,* 1–12.

Sinnot, J. D. (1989). Life-span relativistic postformal thought: Methodology and data from everyday problem-solving studies. In M. L. Commons, J. D. Sinnott, F. A. Richards, & C. Armon (Eds.), *Adult development: Vol. 1. Comparisons and applications of developmental models* (pp. 239–278). New York: Praeger.

Smith, C. L., Maclin, D., Houghton, C., & Hennessey, M. G. (2000). Sixth-grade students' epistemologies of science: The impact of school science experiences on epistemological development. *Cognition and Instruction, 18*(3), 349–422.

Sodian, B. (1991). The development of deception in young children. *British Journal of Developmental Psychology, 9,* 173–188.

Sokol, B. W., & Chandler, M. J. (2003). Taking agency seriously in the theories-of-mind enterprise: Exploring children's understanding of interpretation and intention. *British Journal of Educational Psychology Monograph Series II, 2* (Development and Motivation), 125–136.

Spelke, E. S., Phillips, A., & Woodward, A. L. (1995). Infants' knowledge of object motion and human action. In D. Sperber, D. Premack, & A. J. Premack (Eds.), *Causal cognition: A multidisciplinary debate. Symposia of the Fyssen Foundation* (pp. 44–78). New York: Oxford University Press.

Sternberg, R. (1990). *Wisdom: Its nature, origins, and development.* New York: Cambridge University Press.

Stich, S., & Nichols, S. (2003). Folk epistemology. In S. Stich & T. A. Warfield (Eds.), *The Blackwell guide to philosophy of mind* (pp. 235–255). Oxford: Basil Blackwell.

Stich, S. P. (1996). *Deconstructing the mind.* Oxford: Oxford University Press.

Sullivan, K., Zaitchik, D., & Tager-Flusberg, H. (1994). Preschoolers can attribute second-order beliefs. *Developmental Psychology, 30,* 395–402.

Surian, L., Caldi, S., & Sperber, D. (2007). Attribution of beliefs by 13-month-old infants. *Psychological Science, 18,* 580–586.

Sweetser, E. E. (1987). The definition of a lie: An examination of the folk models underlying a semantic prototype. In D. Holland & N. Quin (Eds.), *Cultural models in language and thought.* New York: Cambridge University Press.

Taylor, M., & Carlson, S. M. (1997). The relation between individual differences in fantasy and theory of mind. *Child Development, 68,* 436–455.

Taylor, R. (1966). *Action and purpose.* Englewood Cliffs, NJ: Prentice-Hall.

Tomasello, M., & Barton, M. (1994). Learning words in nonostensive contexts. *Developmetal Psychology, 30,* 639–650.

Tomasello, M., Call, J., & Hare, B. (2003). Chimpanzees understand psychological states—The question is which ones and to what extent. *Trends in Cognitive Sciences, 7*(4), 153–156.

Ungerer, J. A., & Sigman, M. (1981). Symbolic play and language comprehension in autistic children. *American Academy of Child Psychiatry, 20,* 318–337.

Vasek, M. E. (1988). Lying as a skill: The development of deception in children. In R. W. Mitchell & N. S. Thompson (Eds.), *Deception: Perspectives on human and nonhuman deceit* (pp. 271–292). Albany, NY: State University of New York Press.

Velleman, J. D. (1993). What happens when someone acts? In J. M. Fischer & M. Ravizza (Eds.), *Perspectives on moral responsibility* (pp. 188–210). Ithaca, NY: Cornell University Press.

Velleman, J. D. (2000). *The possibility of practical reason.* Oxford: Clarendon Press.

Walker-Andrews, A. S., & Kahana-Kalman, R. (1999). The understanding of pretence across the second year of life. *British Journal of Developmental Psychology, 17*(4), 523–536.

Walton, M. D. (2000). Say it's a lie or I'll punch you: Naïve epistemology in classroom conflict episodes. *Discourse Processes, (29)*2, 113–136.

Wellman, H. M. (1988). First steps in the child's theorizing about the mind. In J. W. Astington, P. L. Harris, & D. R. Olson (Eds.), *Developing theories of mind* (pp. 64–92). New York: Cambridge University Press.

Wellman, H. M. (1990). *The child's theory of mind.* Cambridge, MA: MIT Press.

Wellman, H. M. (2002). Understanding the psychological world: Developing a theory of mind. In U. Goswami (Ed.), *Handbook of childhood cognitive development* (pp. 167–187). Oxford: Blackwell.

Wellman, H. M., & Banerjee, M. (1991). Mind and emotion: Children's understanding of the emotional consequences of beliefs and desires. *British Journal of Developmental Psychology, 9,* 191–214.

Wellman, H. M., & Bartsch, K. (1988). Young children's reasoning about beliefs. *Cognition, 30,* 239–277.

Wellman, H. M., Cross, D., & Watson, J. (2001). Meta-analysis of theory-of-mind development: The truth about false belief. *Child Development, 72,* 655–684.

Wellman, H. M., & Hickling, A. K. (1994). The mind's "I": Children's conceptions of the mind as an active agent. *Child Development, 65,* 1564–1580.

Wellman, H. M., & Liu, D. (2004). Scaling of theory of mind tasks. *Child Development, 75,* 523–541.

Whiten, A. (Ed.). (1991). *Natural theories of mind: Evolution, development, and simulation of everyday mindreading.* Cambridge, MA: Basil Blackwell.

Wimmer, H., & Perner, J. (1983). Beliefs about beliefs: Representation and constraining function of wrong beliefs in young children's understanding of deception. *Cognition, 13,* 103–128.

Woodward, A. L. (1998). Infants selectively encode the goal object of an actor's reach. *Cognition, 6,* 1–34.

Yuill, N., & Pearson, A. (1998). The development of bases for trait attribution: Children's understanding of traits as causal mechanisms based on desire. *Developmental Psychology, 34,* 574–586.

Zaitchik, D. (1991). Is only seeing really believing?: Sources of the true belief in the false belief task. *Cognitive Development, 6,* 91–103.

Zelazo, P. D. (2000). Self-reflection and the development of consciously controlled processing. In P. Mitchell & K. Rigs (Eds.), *Children's reasoning and the mind* (pp. 445–469). Oxford: Blackwell.

CHAPTER 20

Spatial Development

MARINA VASILYEVA and STELLA F. LOURENCO

Spatial thinking encompasses a diverse set of skills that are essential to everyday life and have been implicated in major scientific breakthroughs (Committee on Support for Thinking Spatially, 2006). The diversity of spatial cognition makes it difficult to provide a concise definition of this field of study. Whereas some spatial tasks may require mental rotation of small-scale objects, others may require distance estimation in a large-scale environment. The common thread among these tasks is that they involve reasoning about key properties of space captured by concepts such as distance and direction. Considering these spatial properties allows us to identify individual objects and their locations, and to establish relations among multiple objects and places. The study of spatial development is concerned with identifying the starting points and subsequent changes in people's reasoning about spatial properties of objects and environments, as well as understanding the mechanisms underlying developmental change.

The ability to reason about spatial properties is critically important for the functioning of all mobile organisms. Animals rely on spatial information to find food, return to shelter, and avoid danger. Likewise, humans are constantly confronted with a variety of problems that require perceiving and reasoning about space. Many spatial activities are so basic and mundane that most people do not view them as spatial problem solving. Yet, packing a lunch bag, grocery shopping, or even simple locomotion all involve processing information about space. Other spatial tasks that are embedded in our daily activities present more serious cognitive challenges, causing some people to complain about their impoverished spatial skills. Many people, for example, comment on the difficulty of assembling furniture or equipment, a task that requires transforming spatial relations among the component parts of objects. Another set of spatial challenges concerns navigating through and locating objects in unfamiliar environments, such as finding the best route through a neighborhood or locating a car in a large parking lot.

In addition to playing an integral role in everyday functioning, spatial reasoning provides a foundation for successful performance in a variety of scientific and technological fields (Ackerman & Cianciolo, 2002; Hegarty & Waller, 2005; Kozhevnikov, Motes, & Hegarty, 2007). Reasoning about spaces and their properties is at the core of such professional fields as geography, geology, astronomy, architecture, and engineering (Cheng, 2002; Golledge, 2002). The involvement of spatial reasoning in other fields of science and technology may be less obvious. Nevertheless, its significance is underscored by major scientific breakthroughs. Consider, for example, the scientific domains of biology and chemistry. Whereas much of the knowledge in the natural sciences can be gained through the application of verbal logic and analytical skills, current and future progress in these domains depend on the understanding of spatial configurations and properties of molecules.

A striking illustration of the power of spatial thinking is provided by the discovery of the DNA structure (Committee on Support for Thinking Spatially, 2006). Before the seminal work by Watson and Crick (1953), multiple researchers attempted and failed to specify the three-dimensional configuration that would be compatible with the existing experimental data. The accurate spatial visualization of DNA enabled researchers to explain its properties, suggesting the mechanism implicated in the reproduction of genetic material. Other powerful illustrations of spatial reasoning can be seen in the use of spatial representations as tools of scientific thinking. One of the well-known historical examples is the formulation of the periodic law that captured regularities in the world of chemical elements. Biographers of Dmitri Mendeleev relate the story of how he created a card for each known chemical element and tried to arrange these cards in several different configurations by grouping elements with similar properties together (Emsley, 2001; Gordin, 2004). The final arrangement in order of ascending atomic weight led Mendeleev to develop the periodic law that guided future work on the atomic structure of chemical elements.

These historical cases are complemented by the contemporary research that has highlighted the association between spatial skills and academic achievement. For example, studies of college students have shown that sex differences in mathematics test scores can be largely accounted for by differences in students' performance on spatial tasks (e.g., Casey, Nuttall, & Pezaris, 1997). A study of talented youth revealed that spatial ability assessed at 12 to 14 years of age predicted educational and vocational outcomes at 23 and 33 years (Shea, Lubinski, & Benbow, 2001). The measures of spatial skills predicted later outcomes above and beyond, and sometimes better than, measures of verbal and quantitative skills. The significance of spatial thinking, highlighted by current evidence and the history of science, perhaps explains the profound interest among psychologists in the issues related to the development of spatial skills.

The following section outlines the major themes in the study of spatial development. The subsequent sections discuss empirical findings characterizing the trajectory and nature of age-related changes in the spatial domain. Throughout the chapter, we trace the major themes of spatial development in the context of different age groups. The next two sections are organized in order of chronological age, starting with research on infants and continuing through work on late adulthood. The chapter ends with a discussion of individual differences and the related issue of malleability of spatial skills across the life span.

MAJOR THEMES IN THE STUDY OF LIFE-SPAN SPATIAL DEVELOPMENT

This section outlines some of the key issues guiding past and current research in the domain of spatial development. It begins with the role of biological and environmental factors, an issue that has generated much discussion across different areas of developmental psychology. Next, issues that are unique to the domain of spatial cognition are considered. These include questions about the types of information (e.g., landmarks vs. geometry) and frames of reference (allocentric vs. egocentric) that are used to identify and locate objects. Another major theme in the study of spatial development concerns the role of symbolic cultural tools. Successful spatial functioning in humans relies on the combination of basic and culturally acquired skills, and it is important to understand how these skills develop and interact. A final theme addressed in this section concerns the diversity of spatial skills. Considering the wide range of spatial tasks, researchers have examined the relation between different aspects of spatial thought, attempting to determine whether they represent a single or multiple constructs.

Role of Biological and Environmental Factors in Spatial Intelligence

One of the central issues addressed in developmental psychology concerns the relative contributions of biological and environmental factors to the developmental process. Whereas most contemporary psychologists agree that both biology and environment play a role in cognitive development, the two contrasting views, nativism and empiricism, differ in the emphasis they put on each of these components. Some researchers have made a case for innate core knowledge of space, based primarily on the findings of impressive spatial abilities in early childhood and even in infancy (e.g., Spelke & Newport, 1998). Others point to significant limitations of early spatial skills and a gradual course of development of competence following particular types of experience in the spatial domain (e.g., Liben, 2002). Given the current state of knowledge, Newcombe (2002) has argued for an interactionist approach that acknowledges strong starting points and seeks to identify specific mechanisms implicated in the transformation of early abilities into mature competence. The interactionist approach also acknowledges the relational bidirectional character of interactions of developmental systems (Lerner, 2006; Overton, 2006). This chapter considers evidence for both biological and experiential factors in spatial development, and points to interactions at different points across the course of development.

Whereas this discussion primarily follows common trends in the typical developmental process, it also highlights the existence of substantial individual differences in spatial skills. Because spatial reasoning is critical to the survival of all mobile organisms, one could expect a high degree of uniformity in its development, and yet spatial tasks are known to reveal considerable individual variability (Allen, 1999; Hegarty & Waller, 2005; Newcombe & Huttenlocher, 2006). This variability may reflect differences among individuals in their biological makeup, prior experiences, or a complex bidirectional pattern of interactions between biological predispositions and specific experiential activities. It should be noted that the involvement of biological factors in the development of spatial skills does not exclude developmental plasticity (Lerner, 2006), the possibility that these skills are malleable in relation to variations in contextual conditions. Understanding the nature of variability and the extent of plasticity of spatial skills is a matter of both theoretical and practical significance because of the vital role of spatial cognition in human functioning and achievement.

Use of Metric and Nonmetric Cues in Representing Location

A major direction in the research on spatial development involves the study of location coding (e.g., Bushnell, McKenzie, Lawrence, & Connell, 1995; Hermer & Spelke, 1996; Huttenlocher, Newcombe, & Sandberg, 1994; Piaget & Inhelder, 1967; Rieser & Rider, 1991). The ability to represent location is among the most fundamental of cognitive capacities. Without knowing where things are, we would be unable to get to school or work, find restaurants, meet with friends, and so on. We have all experienced personal frustration about time wasted while trying to find our way when we get lost. On a societal scale, errors associated with misrepresenting location information can have disastrous consequences, as was the case with the Mars Orbiter spacecraft, which crashed because of an error in the measurement of distance to the landing site. Throughout the chapter, we consider developmental changes in how children and adults approach the task of locating objects. This section defines key terms and concepts that are unique to this area of research. Further, it outlines the main lines of discussion that have dominated the field of spatial development in the last decades.

There are several kinds of information that one can use to represent location. In some situations, people use nonspatial properties, such as color, to locate an object. In other situations, they must rely on spatial properties of the environment. With respect to spatial properties, one could further distinguish the use of *categorical* and *metric information*. Examples of categorical information involve representing an object's location in a large region of space (e.g., as being in front of the house as opposed to behind the house) without precise metric information about the exact location within that region. In contrast, metric representations, also referred to as *fine-grained* or *coordinate*, specify location in terms of distance and direction from a point of reference (e.g., 2 feet to the left of the door in front of the house).

Historically, it was assumed that young children relied exclusively on categorical coding, and in the course of development they acquired the ability to code location using metric cues, such as distance (Piaget & Inhelder, 1967). However, more recent work has revealed much earlier sensitivity to metric information. Rather than relying only on categorical cues, children as young as toddler age appear to combine categorical and metric information in reproducing an object's location (Huttenlocher et al., 1994). Another key question in the area of spatial development concerns the possibility of combining spatial and nonspatial properties in representing location. It has been proposed that spatial performance may be guided by distinct modules that process only certain types of information. In particular, a geometric module posited by Hermer and Spelke (1994) can process information about length but not information about color. This chapter discusses the nature of early spatial competence and provides evidence that different types of information are combined by children and adults in the representation of location.

Egocentric versus Allocentric Framework

Researchers distinguish two fundamental ways in which spatial cues can be used to determine location. The first is known as *egocentric* (or *viewer-centered*) *coding*—that is, coding location with respect to oneself. The second is known as *allocentric* (or *environment-centered*) *coding*— that is, coding location with respect to external features of the environment. Because the egocentric strategy specifies a target location relative to the observer, it can be used either when the observer remains stationary or when he/she moves but is able to keep track of this movement, updating the changing relation between him- or herself and the target location. This updating is known as *dead reckoning* (or *path integration*). In some situations, the observer may become sufficiently disoriented so that it is impossible to reconstruct the changes that led to the new position. In this case, one must rely on an allocentric strategy to locate an object. As discussed in subsequent sections, research indicates that both egocentric and allocentric types of coding are available to young children and adults, and that these types of coding may be more tightly connected than generally discussed.

Role of Symbolic Tools in Spatial Reasoning

Spatial functioning relies on basic cognitive processes, such as the ability to encode distance and shape or mentally transform objects and arrays. Symbolic spatial representations (e.g., maps and models) significantly augment these basic spatial abilities by providing information that is not always available to direct experience. Throughout history, using maps has led to changes in people's thinking about the physical space and social world (Liben & Downs, 1993; Uttal, 2000). In the process of individual development, acquiring symbolic spatial tools influences the growth and flexibility of spatial cognition (Liben & Myers, 2007; Uttal, 2000). Yet, the task of learning how to use a map or model presents multiple challenges as it depends

on the development of general cognitive skills (e.g., appreciating the correspondence between a symbol and its referent) (see Müller & Racine, Chapter 11 of this volume for an extended discussion of symbol development), as well as specific spatial skills (e.g., scaling distance). This chapter reviews work on the trajectory of development in children's symbolic spatial skills and the reciprocal relation between reasoning about symbolic spaces and functioning in real spaces.

Diversity of Spatial Thinking

Mirroring the wide range of spatial problems arising in everyday life, the experimental paradigms used to examine spatial cognition range from paper-and-pencil tasks (e.g., mental rotation and paper folding) to tasks that require problem solving in large spaces (e.g., map reading and way-finding). It has turned out to be rather difficult to identify a small number of basic underlying spatial factors that could account for performance on such diverse tasks. Researchers have attempted to categorize spatial tasks from both psychometric and cognitive perspectives (Carpenter & Just, 1981; Carroll, 1993; Hegarty & Waller, 2005; Linn & Petersen, 1985). Recent studies, using a combination of these approaches, separated tasks that rely on spatial perception, such as estimating length or judging the orientation of line segments, from tasks that involve mental transformation, such as mental rotation (Johnson & Bouchard, 2005, 2007).

Other investigators emphasize differences in spatial processes as a function of space size. Traditionally, researchers distinguished between *small-scale spaces* that can be seen from a single viewpoint and *large-scale spaces* that require movement to be perceived in their entirety (e.g., Hegarty, Montello, Richardson, Ishikawa, & Lovelace, 2005; Zacks, Mires, Tversky, & Hazeltine, 2000). A more differentiated view identifies three psychological scales: object-sized spaces, room-sized spaces, and larger environmental spaces (Montello, 1993). Differences between tasks that involve the manipulation of objects versus movement in large-scale spaces have been reported in work with children and adults (Acredolo, 1981; Zacks et al., 2000). At the same time, there are indications that spatial skills associated with different scales of space are not completely unrelated (Kirasic, 2000). In this chapter, as we trace changes in spatial cognition across the life span, we consider a variety of tasks, pointing out dissociations, as well as links, between different aspects of spatial thought in children and adults.

SPATIAL DEVELOPMENT DURING CHILDHOOD

Early Investigations: The Work of Jean Piaget

The systematic study of spatial development began with the work of Jean Piaget and his colleagues (Piaget & Inhelder, 1967; Piaget, Inhelder, & Szeminska, 1960). They proposed that children initially have an impoverished understanding of space, and that they progress through several developmental stages gradually acquiring a more advanced understanding of spatial relations. The earliest spatial conceptual system, *topological*, is characterized by a limited ability to encode spatial relations. Although this system allows children to represent proximity (adjacent vs. nonadjacent), order (in front vs. behind), and enclosure (inside vs. outside), it does not allow them to encode distances and lengths as features of objects in the environment. Rather, distances are specified in terms of action, or what Piaget referred to as *sensorimotor* understanding, such as the amount of reach or movement. A major limitation of the topological system is the egocentric nature of spatial coding, which involves information about location preserved from the child's initial viewing position.

More advanced spatial conceptual systems, *projective* and *Euclidean*, emerge later on; sometimes their development has been described as sequential and sometimes as concurrent. The main development characterizing the transition from the topological to the projective system is the emergence of allocentric coding. Piaget demonstrated this development with a series of perspective-taking tasks. In the best known of these, the three mountains task, children had to indicate how a spatial array would look to a person who viewed it from a different position. The predominant response of 5- to 6-year-olds was to choose a picture that showed the array from their own point of view. Only at around 9 years of age were children able to select the correct picture, which corresponded to the view of the other person. Piaget concluded that at this age children start using actual spatial relations between objects rather than relying on egocentric information.

A major change associated with the Euclidean spatial conceptual system is from nonmetric to metric spatial coding. As discussed earlier, nonmetric coding refers to the use of categorical spatial relations, for example, coding an object's location as being adjacent to a particular landmark or left/right of the target without differentiating the distance from the target. In contrast, metric coding refers to the use of more fine-grained (coordinate) information

about distance and direction, for example, distinguishing objects that are located 3 versus 5 feet away from a landmark. Piaget argued that at around 9 to 10 years of age, children become accurate in coding locations of objects that are not immediately adjacent to landmarks, thus demonstrating the use of distance cues. Recent empirical investigations have raised questions about some of Piaget's views, especially with respect to the timing of emergence of more advanced aspects of spatial coding (cf. Newcombe & Huttenlocher, 2000). However, the major contribution of Piaget's work has been in outlining the set of critical issues in spatial development that have guided subsequent investigations in this area of research.

Spatial Development in Infancy

Extending empirical investigations of spatial reasoning to infancy has been made possible largely through the use of looking-time paradigms (Baillargeon, 1986, 1987; Baillargeon & Graber, 1987; Baillargeon, Spelke, & Wasserman, 1985; Quinn, 1994). In this methodology, infants are repeatedly shown the same display and, after being familiarized with the scene, presented with a novel display. An increase in looking time indicates that children have noticed and reacted to the difference between the two displays. Using this methodology, researchers have demonstrated infants' ability to distinguish between different spatial categories, such as above versus below (Quinn, 1994; Quinn, Cummins, Kase, Martin, & Weissman, 1996), as well as the early sensitivity to metric properties of space, such as lengths/distances and angles (Baillargeon, 1987, 1991; Lourenco & Huttenlocher, 2008; Newcombe, Huttenlocher, & Learmonth, 1999; Slater, Mattock, Brown, & Bremner, 1991).

Categorical Coding of Location

Even newborns are sensitive to the relative positions of distinct, unconnected objects. That is, they can discriminate pairs of objects when the only difference is the top-bottom position (e.g., a cross above a square vs. a square above a cross; Antell & Caron, 1985). Quinn and colleagues have also found that spatial-relational sensitivity applies to groups of objects. In particular, there is evidence that infants between 3 and 10 months of age can group stimuli into spatial categories, including above versus below, left versus right, and between (Quinn, 1994; Quinn, Adams, Kennedy, Shettler, & Wasnik, 2003; Quinn et al., 1996). Reasoning about these spatial relations undergoes developmental changes during infancy. Younger infants (age, 3–4 months) show sensitivity to categorical distinctions only in limited contexts, when both familiarization and test trials involve the same objects, whereas older infants (age, 6–7 months) appear to form more generalized spatial categories that are not tied to particular objects (Quinn, Norris, Pasko, Schmader, & Mash, 1999).

Sensitivity to Metric Information

Other studies utilizing the looking-time paradigm have reported that not only do infants represent categorical spatial information, but they also show sensitivity to metric cues, such as object size, shape, and angular relations. For example, the work of Baillargeon and colleagues has suggested that infants represent spatial features of objects, such as their height (Baillargeon, 1987; Baillargeon & Graber, 1987; Baillargeon et al., 1985). Baillargeon and Graber presented infants with short and tall objects, which moved behind a screen. The screen contained a window at a particular height so that the taller object, but not the shorter one, would be seen as it moved from one side of the screen to the other. It was found that 5.5-month-olds expected such a relation to hold true; that is, infants looked longer at the display if the shorter object appeared in the window or if the taller object did not. This looking behavior indicates that infants were sensitive to the height of each object.

Using a different task, Baillargeon (1987, 1991) examined the precision with which infants represent height information. Infants were shown a block, placed behind a screen that rotated along an arc. The rotation of the screen was either consistent or inconsistent with the height of the block behind it. In the consistent case, the screen stopped rotating when it reached the top of the block. In the inconsistent cases, the screen either rotated a full 180 degrees or partway through the top of the block. The older infants (age, 6.5 months) looked longer at both inconsistent events, whereas the younger infants (age, 4.5 months) looked longer only when the screen rotated the entire way, that is, through the space that was occupied by the box. These findings indicate that, although infants can represent height information by 4.5 months of age, the nature of the representation changes with development—younger infants represent object height less precisely than older infants.

Other studies have revealed infants' ability to code even more complex metric properties of objects, such as their contour length and area (Clearfield & Mix, 1999, 2001). Furthermore, in addition to coding metric dimensions of an object, infants have been shown to code object location based on distance cues. For example, 5-month-olds who have seen a toy being repeatedly hidden and then retrieved at a particular location within a sandbox looked longer if the toy hidden in that location emerged from a new location (Newcombe et al., 1999; Newcombe, Sluzenski, & Huttenlocher, 2005). In some experimental conditions, the distance between the original hiding location and the location where the object was retrieved was only 8 inches, and yet 5-month-old infants were able to discriminate these locations. In summary, a growing body of empirical work suggests that children code information about extent, including object size and distance between objects.

However, to specify the shape or location of an object, distance information is not always sufficient; it must be supplemented by information about angular size or direction. There is evidence that even newborns can represent angular size. When presented with line segments joined by either an acute or obtuse angle, from different orientations, infants distinguished these angles, looking longer at the angular relation they had not previously seen (Cohen & Younger, 1984; Slater et al., 1991). The stimuli in these studies were fairly simple; they included only two connected lines, which might have served to highlight the angular relations. Recently, Lourenco and Huttenlocher (2008) examined infants' sensitivity to angular and length cues in the context of a connected array. Using a looking-time procedure, 4.5- to 6.5-month-olds were tested on whether they could distinguish among the corners of a triangle. The stimulus, a triangle with a dot in the target corner, appeared in different orientations across familiarization trials, ensuring that only cues related to the triangle itself could be used to differentiate the corners. On test trials, infants looked longer when the dot appeared in a different corner, thus demonstrating the ability to distinguish between corners on the basis of length cues, angular size, or both.

The reviewed evidence suggests that starting in infancy, children display sensitivity to metric information, including distance/length and angles. However, it must be pointed out that the nature and extent of infants' spatial reasoning is not fully understood. Most of the information concerning this developmental period comes from studies utilizing looking-time paradigms, and a number of questions have been raised regarding the use of these techniques (see Goswami, 2008, for review). One critique centers on the fact that looking paradigms engage perceptual skills, and thus differences in looking times may not reveal conceptual representations in infants as much as they reveal underlying perceptual mechanisms (Bogarts, Shinskey, & Speaker, 1997; Haith, 1998). For example,

Haith suggested that traces of lingering sensory information acquired during familiarization trials could lead to changes in looking behavior on test trials. Although these types of explanations cannot account for all of the existing results, they certainly point to the need for a better understanding of the nature and extent of early competence. The work on older children has the potential to shed light on some of the phenomena observed in earlier developmental periods by providing researchers with more direct ways of evaluating spatial cognition, and its accompanying limitations, in children.

Spatial Representation in Toddlers

Coding Metric Information

Investigations that focused on the use of distance cues in toddlers have utilized search tasks as a major methodological tool (Bushnell et al., 1995; Huttenlocher et al., 1994; Newcombe, Huttenlocher, Drummey, & Wiley, 1998). In these tasks, children are shown an object being hidden in a target location and are then asked to find that object. By varying the characteristics of the target's location, researchers have been able to explore children's sensitivity to different types of cues. For example, if a target object is not immediately adjacent to a salient landmark, children would need to use metric information, such as the distance between the target and edge of the surrounding spatial layout. Existing findings indicate that 1- and 2-year-old children search for an object hidden in a continuous space with impressive metric accuracy (Bushnell et al., 1995; Huttenlocher et al., 1994). Thus, they can code and reproduce distance, at least in the small spaces where they have mostly been tested.

A closer look at the studies demonstrating the early coding of distance reveals a common feature that could be critical to children's successful performance. These studies typically present children with an object that is contained within a salient frame of reference, such as a sandbox. The frame may provide a perceptually available standard, allowing children to code extent (distance or length) in relation to that standard. This hypothesis was tested in a series of experiments in which children had to match a target dowel to one of the choice dowels on the basis of vertical extent, namely, height (Huttenlocher, Duffy, & Levine, 2002). The results showed that 2-year-olds performed well when the target and choices were presented along with a standard, for example, when each dowel was presented in a container of a fixed height. However, when the target and choice dowels were presented without containers,

2-year-olds performed at chance and only 4-year-olds were able to identify the dowel of the same height as the target. Thus, it appears that in younger children, success depends on the ability to encode the height of an object in relation to another (comparison) object.

The findings suggesting an early use of relative cues in the coding of spatial extent may seem counterintuitive given the complexities associated with reasoning about relations. Encoding relative size requires considering the size of the target object, the size of the comparison standard, and the relation between them. It is unlikely that the use of relational information in preschoolers is based on a mathematical computation of ratios for lengths and distances. It is more likely that early metric coding involves a form of perceptually based judgments, which automatically register the relation between the object and its surroundings (Bryant, 1974; Jeong, Levine, & Huttenlocher, 2007; Vasilyeva & Huttenlocher, 2004). Indeed, research in both spatial and quantitative domains shows that young children can solve a variety of tasks that require comparing relations between distances and sizes long before they acquire formal knowledge of proportions (Singer-Freeman & Goswami, 2001; Sophian, 2000; Spinillo & Bryant, 1991).

Another interesting feature of metric coding in toddlers is how it combines with categorical information in a hierarchical coding system. The model of hierarchical coding was originally proposed in work with adults to describe a process of adjusting metric estimates on the basis of categorical information, such as prototypical locations (Huttenlocher, Hedges, & Duncan, 1991). An example of hierarchical coding involves representing the location of a picture on a page as being a certain distance away from the edge (metric coding) and in the top part of the page (categorical coding). Because metric representations can be imprecise and tend to fade quickly, categorical information may prove useful in reconstructing location (Hund & Plumert, 2003). That is, if one had to guess where a target might be located, having some idea about the general region of its location would serve to rule out unlikely possibilities.

The work with toddlers has provided evidence of early categorical adjustments in their location estimates. Specifically, when looking for an object hidden in a narrow rectangular box, children's responses were systematically biased toward the center of the box (Huttenlocher et al., 1994). This bias has been interpreted as evidence that children treat the rectangular frame of the box as a single spatial category with a prototypical location at its center. As a result, children adjust their estimates toward the center of the space—the category's prototype. Note that in adjusting their location estimates, toddlers rely on categories formed by perceptually available boundaries. As discussed later, older children and adults also use mentally imposed categorical boundaries to code locations.

Using Egocentric and Allocentric Frameworks to Locate Objects

Research on the early use of spatial frameworks has utilized search tasks similar to those described in the previous section. However, a critical feature of the studies that examine children's ability to use allocentric versus egocentric frameworks is that they involve a change in the child's viewing perspective. That is, children observe an object hidden in a particular location and are then required to locate that object after they have been moved to a new position. These tasks can be solved by relying on either an allocentric (environment-centered) or an egocentric (viewer-centered) framework.

An example of allocentric coding would consist of representing an object in relation to environmental landmarks. In the simplest case, when a landmark is adjacent to the target object, it can be used as a direct cue to the object's location, and indeed both infants and toddlers can locate objects by relying on adjacent landmarks (Acredolo, 1981; Piaget & Inhelder, 1967). When there are no salient landmarks next to the target, one can use distal landmarks as fixed reference points and encode the target location in terms of distance and direction from those referents (Newcombe, 2002). Although the ability to locate objects in relation to distal landmarks has been shown to emerge around 2 years of age (Newcombe et al., 1998), this ability is quite limited and continues to develop throughout childhood (Overman, Pate, Moore, & Peuster, 1996).

It is also possible to identify a target location from a new position when this location has been coded egocentrically (with respect to the self). This can be accomplished by keeping track of changes in the relation between the self and the target location in a process known as *dead reckoning*. That is, as a person moves through the environment, the representation of the target location can be adjusted by taking into account the distance and direction of one's movements. Research on the development of dead reckoning indicates some basic capacity within the first year of life, as children develop the ability to code rotational movements (Rieser & Heiman, 1982; Tyler & McKenzie, 1990) and translational movement along a straight line (Landau & Spelke, 1988). Problems involving both translation and rotation, however, pose a greater challenge and can be solved at 12 months only when infants are not prevented from viewing the target location while they are moving (Acredolo, Adams, & Goodwyn, 1984).

Newcombe and colleagues (1998) examined dead reckoning abilities in children aged 16 to 36 months. Children were asked to search for objects hidden in a long rectangular box, after being turned around and moved to the opposite side of the box. In the absence of landmarks, locating the hidden object after movement required that children update both lateral and rotational components of this movement. Although children across the age range performed at levels above chance, they were reliably less accurate than when they remained stationary. The size of the decrement due to movement did not decrease with age, suggesting that, although the dead reckoning system undergoes considerable development between 12 and 16 months of age, there appears to be little improvement in lateral and rotational updating through 3 years.

Note that when tracking is difficult or becomes impossible, as when organisms become disoriented, location must be specified in terms of distance or direction, or both, from particular environmental features. Anyone who has traveled by underground subway and remembers feeling disoriented when returning aboveground can understand the importance of being able to reorient oneself relative to the environment. Investigators have studied the developmental origins of this critical ability, and there has been a proliferation of studies examining young children's performance in tasks that require locating objects after disorientation (Hupach & Nadel, 2005; Learmonth, Nadel, & Newcombe, 2002; Lee, Shusterman, & Spelke, 2006; Lourenco, Huttenlocher, & Vasilyeva, 2005). The use of environmental cues in the context of disorientation was originally studied in animal models (Cheng, 1986; Cheng & Gallistel, 1984). In one study, after being trained to find food in a particular corner of a rectangular chamber, rats were disoriented and then returned to the chamber (Cheng, 1986). They searched mostly at the two geometrically appropriate corners (e.g., the ones with the longer wall to the left of the shorter wall), ignoring landmark cues (e.g., a different-colored wall) that were available to disambiguate the target corner from its geometric equivalent.

Hermer and Spelke (1994, 1996) adapted the disorientation task used by Cheng (1986) with rats for use with human children (18–24 months of age). Toddlers were tested in a small rectangular room with four identical containers, one in each corner. They were shown which corner contained the hidden object (toy) and then they were disoriented; that is, the parent picked up the child, covered the child's eyes, and spun him/her around several times. After disorientation, children were allowed to search for the hidden toy. Similar to Cheng's findings with rats, children searched for the toy at the two geometrically appropriate corners. Even when the room contained landmark cues that could be used to distinguish the two corners, children seemed to rely only on the geometric information about the shape of the space.

Geometry versus Landmarks

Because young children appear to favor geometry after disorientation, Spelke and colleagues have argued that the process of reorientation is modular, based on geometry alone (e.g., Hermer & Spelke, 1994, 1996; Hermer-Vasquez, Spelke, & Katsnelson, 1999; Lee et al., 2006). In their view, other types of environmental cues are not used to represent location on disorientation tasks; only geometric information about the shape of an enclosed space is used for this purpose. The idea is that the processing of geometric information is task specific and encapsulated, preventing the use of nongeometric cues (landmarks) for the purpose of reorientation. Other research, however, has not supported the modular view of geometric processing. For example, in larger spaces, young children have been shown to rely on nongeometric cues (e.g., a different-colored wall) to locate a hidden object (Learmonth et al., 2002; Learmonth, Newcombe, & Huttenlocher, 2001).

Nevertheless, despite disagreements concerning the nature of geometric representation, there is reason to believe that geometric information is highly salient and may be especially prepotent to young children. Toddlers use geometric information to represent the location of a target object under a variety of conditions, including spaces of different shapes (i.e., *isosceles triangle:* Huttenlocher & Vasilyeva, 2003; Lourenco & Huttenlocher, 2006; *rhombus:* Hupach & Nadel, 2005) and sizes (i.e., *larger rooms:* Hupach & Nadel, 2005; Learmonth et al., 2001, 2002; *smaller rooms:* Lourenco & Huttenlocher, 2006; Lourenco et al., 2005; *models:* Huttenlocher & Vasilyeva, 2003).

What might account for the prepotency of geometric information in specifying location, especially under conditions of disorientation? Recent work points to the more general property of scalar dimensions, which feature ordered information. Anywhere along a scale, unequal values in a pair are ordered such that one member is always more or less than the other. Consider a rectangular-shaped space used in studies with young children (e.g., Hermer & Spelke, 1994; Learmonth et al., 2001; Lourenco et al., 2005). In that space, the location task requires the mapping

of metric information onto left and right directions. That is, combining relative length (shorter/longer) and sense information (left/right) allows for the differentiation of pairs of corners (i.e., corners with the shorter wall to the left of the longer wall vs. corners with the shorter wall to the right of the longer wall). The mapping of scalar information, such as wall length, onto directions in space may be facilitated by the inherent direction (order) along the scale. It is this directional analogy that may support the left/right mapping needed to locate a hidden object after disorientation (cf. Bryant & Squire, 2003).

To test this hypothesis, Huttenlocher and Lourenco (2007) examined location representation in a square-shaped space. The task was identical to that in previous studies (e.g., Hermer & Spelke, 1996). An object was hidden at one of the corners; the child was disoriented and then allowed to search for the hidden object. The only difference from previous studies was that the shape of the surrounding space could not be used to distinguish the corners. What could be used, however, were the cues on the walls. In one condition, the cues were scale-like in nature, that is, ordered in terms of more/less relations along the magnitude scale of size (i.e., smaller vs. larger dots). In two other conditions, the cues were nonscalar—they could be considered discrete and unordered (i.e., blue vs. red, pattern vs. no pattern). In the scalar condition, children searched at the appropriate corners (e.g., the corners with smaller dots to the left of larger dots). However, in the other two conditions, children searched randomly, failing to restrict their choices to the appropriate corners, suggesting that scalar properties may be critical for supporting location representation on tasks that involve disorientation.

Studies using disorientation techniques have produced a significant body of evidence relevant to the ongoing discussion about the nature of early spatial representation. It is remarkable that after being disoriented in a spatial environment, young children can reconstruct an object's location from a novel position using the features of that environment. Notably, however, although toddlers perform equally well from any position within an enclosed space, their performance varies as a function of their position relative to the entire space—that is, whether they are inside versus outside. This has been demonstrated when children were tested with a spatial enclosure that had short walls so that they could see the space while standing either inside or outside (Huttenlocher & Vasilyeva, 2003; Lourenco et al., 2005). Performance was at chance when children's position relative to the enclosure changed after disorientation, for example, when they were shown an object's location and disoriented outside the space and then moved inside to search for the object, suggesting that the viewer's perspective on the entire space is encoded in the representation of the object's location.

Findings from animal research suggest a possible way in which egocentric and allocentric representations of location can be combined. Cheng (1988, 1989) provided evidence that pigeons learn to find a hidden target by coding two kinds of information—the target's relation to nearby landmarks (i.e., landmark-to-target vectors) and their own relation to these landmarks (i.e., self-to-landmark vectors). By coding both kinds of relations, the animals may be able to compute the distance and direction they need to move to retrieve the target (i.e., self-to-target vectors). It is possible that toddlers similarly incorporate their own position when encoding the relation between the object and the spatial layout, which would explain their performance on disorientation tasks when their position relative to the space (inside vs. outside) is varied.

Further Spatial Developments in Older Children

Reasoning about Size and Location

While infants and toddlers show early sensitivity to metric cues, the accuracy of coding metric information continues to increase through the primary school years. Between the ages of 5 and 10, children's performance improves substantially on a variety of tasks that require estimating and reproducing object size and location (Sandberg, Huttenlocher, & Newcombe, 1996; Vasilyeva, Duffy, & Huttenlocher, 2007). It remains to be determined whether improvements in accuracy during school years represent a fundamental change in the mechanisms that underlie reasoning about the metric properties of space or a refinement of an existing less developed representational system. Newcombe and Huttenlocher (2000, 2006) proposed that age-related improvements in spatial performance may be, at least in part, caused by the development of a hierarchical coding system.

As discussed earlier, this coding system involves combining categorical and metric information. Although the combination of different information sources has been reported in toddlers, they appear to use this process in limited situations—they rely on spatial categories formed by perceptually available boundaries and adjust their estimates only along a single dimension. Older children (age, 6–10 years) impose mental subdivisions on spatial layouts, thus forming categories for which there are no physically defined boundaries. For example, when reproducing

location in a rectangular-shaped space, the pattern of responses reflects the division of the rectangle into two categories (left and right halves) and using the categorical prototype (center) of each half to adjust estimates of location (Huttenlocher et al., 1994).

In addition, around the age of 7, the ability to use hierarchical coding extends to situations involving categorical information defined along two dimensions (Sandberg et al., 1996). This marks an important development in children's spatial reasoning as most real-life location-finding tasks require considering at least two dimensions (as in Cartesian coordinates). The development of categorization involving two dimensions has been examined in a series of experiments in which children were presented with a dot inside a circle and later asked to reproduce, from memory, the dot's location (Sandberg et al.). The pattern of responses suggested that 10-year-olds, but not younger children, subdivided the circle into quadrants at the vertical and horizontal lines of symmetry, and then used the mentally imposed categorization in conjunction with their inexact memories of the specific locations. Their estimates of specific locations were systematically biased toward the prototypes (centers) of the four quadrants formed by dividing the circle along vertical and horizontal axes.

These and other findings clearly demonstrate that the process of using categorical information to adjust location estimates undergoes substantial development through elementary school age (Hund & Plumert, 2005; Hund & Spencer, 2003; Plumert & Hund, 2001). The advantage of a coding system involving a more differentiated division of space is that, despite the slight categorical bias in reproducing each individual location, it significantly constrains the variability of responses, leading, on average, to higher accuracy. It is not currently clear what mechanisms underlie the observed developmental changes in the hierarchical coding system. It has been proposed that early experiences with hierarchical coding in simple situations may lead older children to apply this system in less obvious situations (Huttenlocher et al., 1994; Newcombe & Huttenlocher, 2000).

In addition to the development of basic cognitive processes of distance coding, which may reflect everyday experiences with space, improvements in children's performance may be related to their educational experiences. For example, the acquisition of measurement skills may lead to increased accuracy in tasks that involve considering and manipulating metric properties of objects and spaces. Practice in measuring objects presented in different spatial contexts may help children gain the ability to focus on the size of the object independently of its context. Specifically, learning about measurement units provides children with additional tools for representing object size and distance (Clements & Bright, 2003; Miller, 1989). Internalizing cultural tools may augment children's ability to reason about and reproduce metric information.

Advances in the Use of the Allocentric Framework

The work with younger children shows that the ability to locate objects in relation to the features of the environment emerges initially in the form of "cue learning"—that is, using a salient landmark as a cue to locating objects that are adjacent to the landmark. This type of location coding, however, is not useful in situations where a target object is not adjacent to a landmark. Infants and toddlers also have been shown to use distance in locating objects, but this ability appears to be initially restricted to small-scale spaces with clear boundaries where location can be coded along a single dimension (e.g., Huttenlocher et al., 1994). The ability to code location in relation to a set of distal landmarks in large-scale spaces emerges gradually during later years (Lehnung, Leplow, Friege, Herzog, Mehdorn, & Ferstl, 1998; Leplow, Lehnung, Pohl, Herzog, Ferstl, & Mehdorn, 2003; Overman, et al., 1996; Rieser & Rider, 1991).

One study, which examined place learning in children up to 12 years of age, used a series of tasks that required finding an object in a radial arm maze, a large circular enclosure, or an open field (Overman et al., 1996). In all of these tasks, children showed significant improvement as a function of age when locating objects in the absence of adjacent cues. Consider, for example, a task of finding an object in a circular enclosure. In this task, a round cardboard "pool" filled with packing chips was placed inside a larger room, with a box hidden underneath the chips. Performance was measured by the distance traveled in the pool before locating the box. The results showed that children younger than 7 years performed significantly worse than older children in the conditions that required using spatial relations with distal landmarks; children between the ages of 7 and 12 performed equally well and better than younger children.

Other studies provided further support for the view that children's ability to locate objects in relation to distal landmarks emerges gradually during childhood. In Leplow et al.'s (2003) study, children had to navigate a circular platform placed in a larger room to locate a reward. The platform contained several toys and the larger room contained landmarks, which could be used as cues to object location. In one condition, the toys on the platform were moved (while the child was blindfolded) so that the platform cues were put in conflict with the room cues. In this condition, children younger than 7 years tended to rely only on the platform cues. At the age of 7, about half the children used distal landmarks, and starting at the age of 10, almost all children solved the task successfully by using a configuration of distal landmarks as their guide.

Thus, there appears to be a significant delay between the time when children can locate objects by coding distance along a single dimension in an enclosed space (Huttenlocher et al., 1994) and the time when they start integrating distance from multiple landmarks to infer location (Leplow et al., 2003; Overman et al., 1996). It has been proposed that this time lag in the development of relational place learning may be linked to the functional maturation of the hippocampal brain system (O'Keefe, 1991; Overman et al., 1996). In addition, children's accumulating experience walking around larger spaces and using landmarks to locate objects may play a role in this development. Newcombe and Huttenlocher (2000) suggested that children may begin by using single salient landmarks that are fairly close to the target location and, with age, gradually realize the value of using distant landmarks. It is also possible that learning about spatial models and maps, in which landmarks that are far from each other in the real space can be seen at once in the symbolic space, may help children take advantage of using distal landmarks when reasoning about locations.

Reasoning about Large- and Small-Scale Spaces

A number of investigations have demonstrated that children's use of metric information, as well as their reliance on viewer- versus environment-centered cues, vary as a function of space size (Acredolo, 1977, 1981; Bell, 2002; Herman & Siegel, 1978; Huttenlocher et al., 1994; Overman et al., 1996; Quaiser-Pohl, Lehmann, & Eid, 2004; Siegel & White, 1975). There are several key differences between small- and large-scale spaces that might relate to differences in children's performance.

A small-scale space, by definition, can be seen in its entirety from a single perspective, whereas large-scale spaces usually surround the viewer and require the coordination of different viewpoints (Acredolo, 1981; Hegarty et al., 2005; Siegel, 1981). Older children may be better able to coordinate multiple viewpoints, constructing the representation of a large-scale space that allows them to use environmental features to infer locations within that space. Younger children, having more difficulty integrating multiple viewpoints, may be more inclined to use an egocentric strategy when reasoning about large-scale spaces. This hypothesis was tested by Acredolo (1977) in a task that involved locating a hidden object either in a model or in a larger room. The child's position during the test trials was different from that during the demonstration trials. Children younger than 5 produced a large number of egocentric responses when inside the large space, even though they made virtually no egocentric errors with the small-scale model.

The need to integrate multiple perspectives is related to another important feature of large-scale spaces—their structure is often inferred over time, across several sequential observations (Siegel, 1981). Siegel and White (1975) proposed that there is a long developmental period, over which children acquire the ability to combine spatial information obtained at different time points in a single representation of space. Although preschoolers can notice individual landmarks, they do not form fully integrated spatial representations. The next stage after the use of individual landmarks involves combining landmark sequences into routes, and only after that do elementary school children start combining individual routes into survey-like representations of large-scale spaces (Hazen, Lockman, & Pick, 1978; Herman, 1980; Pick, 1993; Siegel & White, 1975). It has been suggested that the difficulty of integrating information acquired over time may be related to limitations of processing capacity in younger children (Siegel, 1981). In addition, investigators have pointed to the acquisition of effective spatial strategies as a possible explanation for improved performance in large-scale spaces. Between the ages of 6 and 12 years, there are substantial improvements in children's strategic behavior when exploring large environmental spaces; for example, when they reach a turn, they look around to view key locations from different perspectives (Cornell, Heth, & Alberts, 1994).

In examining tasks that involve small- and large-scale spaces, researchers also point to another potentially important difference between them. A small-scale model is usually presented inside a larger space that provides additional information (Acredolo, 1981). This information can be useful in reasoning about the model if it remains stationary with respect to the larger space. However, when the relation between the model and the larger space changes, it may create additional challenges in locating objects within the model. That is, when the model is moved relative to the larger space, viewers have to deal with the conflict between the frame of reference provided by the model itself and the frame of reference provided by the larger space.

Newcombe (1989) showed that the ability to deal with conflicting information provided by a small layout and a surrounding space emerges around 9 years of age.

Despite the differences observed on tasks involving small- and large-scale spaces, there are some commonalities in the cognitive processes underlying these tasks, as they require reasoning about spatial relations, including distance and direction. Work with adults points to a correlation between individuals' ability to solve spatial tasks with small-scale stimuli and their ability to navigate large environments (e.g., Kirasic, 2000). A recent study with 7- to 12-year-olds, however, reported a very low correlation between children's performance in large- and small-scale spatial tasks (Quaiser-Pohl et al., 2004). It is important to further explore this finding and determine whether there is a developmental change in the integration of abilities involved in reasoning about spaces of different scales. A related line of inquiry involves research on the development of children's ability to transfer information between small- and large- scale spaces, as in mapping tasks, which is reviewed in the next section.

Acquisition of Symbolic Spatial Tools

A critical aspect of development in spatial thinking involves the acquisition of symbolic spatial tools (Liben, 2002; Newcombe & Huttenlocher, 2000). The uniquely human ability to use symbolic representations, such as maps and models, augments spatial capabilities by allowing humans to acquire and communicate information about space beyond that available from direct experience (Liben & Downs, 1989; Uttal, 2000). Symbolic spatial representations come in a variety of forms, from two-dimensional "you are here" maps to three-dimensional models and interactive media, such as GPS. These representations allow us to function more efficiently because they often save us countless hours of random searching in unfamiliar environments.

As with any symbolic system, certain aspects of maps and models are arbitrary in nature. For example, a location of a village on a map may be marked with a red star or a black dot, or the map designer may decide not to show villages and indicate only the locations of big cities. However, unlike words whose linguistic form is completely unrelated to the concepts they represent, maps/models typically preserve characteristics of the spaces they represent. Because the properties of symbolic spatial representations are systematically linked to the properties of the referent spaces, some researchers call maps and models "motivated symbols" (Liben & Yekel, 1996).

A map or model must convey information about spatial relations among objects in the referent space. Depending on the purpose of the map, some of them accurately preserve metric relations among places, whereas others may preserve certain aspects of spatial relations while distorting others (Liben, 2001). For example, many geographic maps are designed to convey information about distances: If a village is located halfway between two large cities, the relative distances between these geographic units are generally preserved on the map of a region. In contrast, a subway map preserves the order of stations and the relative positions of major line intersections, but not the distance or angular relations among lines. In either case, however, at least some aspects of spatial relations (categorical or metric) are preserved.

Learning how to use symbolic spatial representations is a gradual process that depends on the level of cognitive development in general and spatial reasoning in particular. To be able to use a map, one has to establish the correspondence between individual symbols on the map and objects in the real world (*representational*, or *object correspondence*), and also between the spatial relations on the map and those in the real world (*geometric*, or *relational correspondence*). A large body of research has examined the development of children's ability to establish these two kinds of correspondence between representation and referent space (e.g., Blades & Cook, 1994; DeLoache, 1995; Marzolf, DeLoache, & Kolstad, 1999; Loewenstein & Gentner, 2001).

Solving Map Tasks on the Basis of Object Correspondence

The emergence of children's abilities to use simple representations of space has been explored in a series of studies by DeLoache (1989, 1995). In these studies, children had to make inferences about the object's location in a spatial layout based on information obtained from another layout. For example, after having observed the experimenter hide a toy under a piece of furniture in a model of a room, the child was asked to find the toy in the corresponding location in the room itself. The results showed that 2.5- to 3-year-old children performed successfully on this task, whereas younger children failed to find the toy. An important question concerning the interpretation of these findings is whether children who were successful on the task fully recognized the correspondence of spatial relations between the room and the model, not just the correspondence between individual items (Blades & Cook, 1994; Marzolf et al., 1999; Perner, 1991). Because the target location was marked by objects with unique features, the mapping task did not require children to establish the correspondence of spatial relations but could be carried out by matching object attributes (e.g., if a toy is hidden behind the chair in the model, the child can find it in the room by looking for a big chair with similar features).

Solving Map Tasks on the Basis of Relational Correspondence

To investigate whether children can use relational correspondence in mapping, researchers have presented them with map tasks in which information about particular object features is not sufficient to identify the target location. Spatial layouts used in these tasks either contained multiple identical objects (Blades & Spencer, 1994; Bluestein & Acredolo, 1979) or open spaces (Huttenlocher, Newcombe, & Vasilyeva, 1999; Liben & Yekel, 1996; Uttal, 1996; Vasilyeva & Huttenlocher, 2004). In these situations, children had to rely on spatial cues, such as distance or direction, which allow for distinguishing identical objects or determining a specific location within the open space. The findings have generally indicated that preschoolers have more difficulty with mapping tasks that require the use of spatial cues compared with tasks that can be solved by matching object features (Blades & Spencer; Liben & Yekel).

The earliest use of distance cues in mapping was demonstrated with a task in which children had to find an object location in a sandbox based on the picture of the sandbox with a dot marking the target's location (Huttenlocher et al., 1999). The results showed that 4-year-olds and some 3.5-year-olds were able to translate the distance presented in the picture to the distance in the sandbox. Even though these results indicate that the ability to use distance in mapping location emerges almost a year after the ability to use object correspondence, it may still appear somewhat surprising that preschoolers are able to carry out scaling operations, or to translate distances between spaces of different sizes. However, this early scaling ability may share particular features with the coding of relative extent seen in younger children (Bryant, 1974; Duffy, Huttenlocher, & Levine, 2005). Recall that Duffy et al. showed that toddlers coded the height of an object relative to the container in which it was presented. In the context of a map task, the frame of a map can be thought of as a container and the outline of the referent space as another container. If children coded distance on the map in a relative, rather than absolute, manner, they would be able to identify the same relative distance in the referent space (Vasilyeva et al., 2007; Vasilyeva & Huttenlocher, 2004).

Despite the early demonstrations of scaling ability, most researchers find that the use of relational correspondence in preschoolers is limited, and children fail many tasks that involve maps and models until the age of 5 or older (Blades & Spencer, 1994; Liben & Downs, 1989; Liben & Yekel, 1996; Uttal, 1996). Preschoolers often ignore differences in scale between the two spaces or disregard spatial cues and focus on object features as a basis for mapping, which leads them to incorrect responses. Several factors appear to increase the difficulty of the mapping task for younger children. One such factor is the presence of competing cues, which may be particularly challenging given preschoolers' difficulties with inhibiting irrelevant information (Newcombe, 1989). For example, the presence of salient unique landmarks that mark some of the target locations may lead children to focus on object features and disregard spatial information even when it is relevant (Liben & Yekel). Another factor that may affect children's performance on a map task is the size of the referent space. The accuracy of distance scaling is inversely related to the magnitude of the scaling transformation (Vasilyeva & Huttenlocher, 2004); thus, children's performance may become very inaccurate when the map represents a much larger space. Furthermore, children may have general difficulty conceptualizing large-scale environments, which may explain their poor performance with actual geographic maps even at the early elementary school age (Liben & Downs, 1989).

Using maps or models is especially challenging when they are not aligned with the referent space. Children often fail to correct for the lack of alignment, as demonstrated by Liben and Downs (1993). In this study, 5- to 12-year-old children were shown a map of the classroom; the map was either aligned with the room or rotated by 180 degrees. As the adult moved to different positions in the room, the child's task was to place arrow stickers on the map to indicate the adult's location and heading. Children's accuracy in the unaligned condition was significantly lower than in the aligned condition in all but the oldest age group. In another set of experiments, Blades and Spencer (1994) presented children with a mapping task in which the corresponding spatial layouts were either aligned or rotated 180 degrees relative to each other. The layouts contained both unique objects that could be identified by their surface features and identical objects that could be distinguished only using spatial cues (e.g., distance from other objects). The findings showed that the mapping of the unique objects was not affected by the rotation of the two layouts. However, the mapping of nonunique objects was directly affected: The level of performance was high when the layouts were

aligned, but at chance when the layouts were rotated 180 degrees.

In summary, the ability to solve mapping tasks on the basis of object correspondence appears during early preschool age (3 years old; DeLoache, 1995), but the ability to use spatial relations in mapping emerges later (around 4 years old; Huttenlocher et al., 1999) and initially manifests itself only in limited contexts. During the gradual development of map understanding, children extend the range of tasks in which they rely on relational correspondence to include tasks that involve competing cues, unaligned spaces, and configurations of multiple objects (5–6 years old; Blades & Spencer, 1994; Bluestein & Acredolo, 1979; Liben & Yekel, 1996; Uttal, 1996; Uttal, Gregg, Tan, Chamberlin, & Sines, 2001). In early elementary grades, mapping skills further extend to incorporate reasoning about large geographic spaces (Downs & Liben, 1991; Liben & Downs, 1989).

Reciprocal Relation between Map Skills and Spatial Reasoning

The relation between the acquisition of map-reading skills and the development of spatial cognition is reciprocal (Liben, 2000; Liben & Myers, 2007; Uttal, 2000). As children gain experience with symbolic representations of space, it facilitates their spatial reasoning, perhaps because they use insights from that experience to guide their thinking about actual spaces. Experience with maps may have particularly important implications for spatial reasoning, particularly in thinking about large-scale spaces that are typically represented on geographic maps. As argued by Uttal (2000), the influence of maps on spatial cognition is both specific and general. Using a map provides people with an opportunity to think about the multiple relations between different locations in a particular space, much as these relations are represented on maps. In addition, maps may also transform our understanding of space in a more general sense, by providing a structure that can be mentally imposed on a space in thinking about its overall shape, its constituent elements, and the relations among these elements. In a well-known example, when cases of cholera were plotted on a street map of London, the map revealed that the disease clustered around locations of water pumps, therefore suggesting that the disease was likely water borne (Gilbert, 1958). Thus, a spatial representation of cholera cases on a map helped uncover the pattern that could otherwise have gone unnoticed. This historical example illustrates the role of maps in reasoning about relations among individual entities in the physical world.

Summary

Research on spatial development reveals impressive abilities in young children. Toddlers and infants show sensitivity to metric information, such as distance/length and direction/angular size. Children's performance on tasks that require locating objects demonstrates their use of allocentric framework, as seen in their coding of distance to landmarks, and the egocentric framework, as seen in dead reckoning when they update their relation to the target location as they move. Disorientation tasks have demonstrated toddlers' ability to use the geometry of space in locating objects and suggested a possibility that egocentric information is integrated with allocentric representations of location. Taken together, these findings clearly indicate that the early points of spatial development are stronger than those posited by Piaget.

At the same time, the research shows limitations of early spatial behaviors, suggesting a long developmental progression between the starting points and a more mature spatial competence. Although the ability to code location relative to distal landmarks emerges earlier than proposed by Piaget, landmark use undergoes development through the elementary school age. During this period, children become progressively more accurate and flexible in the use of landmark information; they begin integrating their knowledge of individual landmarks to represent relations among multiple locations and to form routes that connect ordered sequences of landmarks. Substantial developments are also seen in the use of the hierarchical coding system; it becomes more differentiated with age, and its use extends to a wider range of spatial stimuli.

More generally, older children become more systematic in the use of spatial information. Although younger children demonstrate advanced spatial reasoning in certain contexts, they often revert to more primitive strategies (e.g., coding location only in terms of adjacent landmarks or relying solely on the egocentric frame of reference) in challenging situations, particularly when there is a conflict between different kinds of spatial cues. Older children, however, show a greater resistance to conflicting cues and an improved ability to transfer spatial information from one spatial context to another, as seen in their performance on map tasks.

Investigators have proposed that some of the observed developments during childhood may reflect the maturation of brain regions implicated in spatial reasoning. Other age-related changes may result from accumulating experience. Much of the experiences relevant to spatial development involve interactions with objects in the physical world, which are typical for most children in our and other societies. Other experiences are more culturally dependent, including learning conventional spatial tools, such as measurement, and acquiring information about symbolic spatial representations, such as maps and models. Still, more work is needed to better understand interactions between biological and environmental factors involved in the development of spatial reasoning.

SPATIAL REASONING IN ADULTS

Exploring the Nature of Mature Spatial Cognition

When researchers discuss a mature form of spatial cognition, mature form is often taken to mean the ability to accurately encode metric properties of objects and spaces, and to represent spatial relations independently of one's own viewpoint. Adults, indeed, are more precise in metric coding than children, and more flexible in the ability both to take different perspectives and to rely on allocentric cues. Nevertheless, a closer examination of strategies underlying performance of adults on spatial tasks reveals an influence of nonmetric information on their judgments of distance, as well as viewpoint specificity in reasoning about space.

Judging and Reproducing Size, Distance, and Location

When estimating spatial extent, such as the size of an object or the distance between objects, adults often demonstrate systematic errors or biases (Hirtle & Jonides, 1985; McNamara & Diwadkar, 1997; Sadalla, Burroughs, & Staplin, 1980; Stevens & Coupe, 1978; Tversky, 1981, 2005). It has been proposed that a complex pattern of distortion and bias observed in adult performance can be explained, at least in part, by the influence of categorical information on metric estimates (Newcombe & Huttenlocher, 2006; Tversky, 1981).

The distinct functions of categorical and metric (coordinate) information in adult cognition have been examined by Kosslyn and colleagues (Kosslyn, 1987; Kosslyn, Anderson, Hillger, & Hamilton, 1994). They posited that spatial relations are processed by two separate systems in the brain—metric information is processed primarily by the right hemisphere, whereas categorical relations are processed primarily by the left hemisphere. Further investigations of these two systems have led researchers to suggest that there is an interaction between them (Huttenlocher et al., 1991, 1994). This interaction introduces some degree of bias, but, critically, it may also serve to increase the average accuracy of performance by decreasing variability in the estimates of individual stimuli (Huttenlocher et al., 1991). Earlier in this chapter we presented evidence that categorical information plays a role in estimating location even in toddlers. The evidence from research with older children and adults points to a continuing transformation in the manner in which categorical information influences metric estimates. Adults impose a complex categorical structure on space and make extensive use of culturally created categories, such as geographic subdivisions.

Adults' reliance on geographic categories has been reported in studies where participants were asked to make judgments about the relative positions of various cities. For example, people often report that San Diego is located to the west of Reno (Stevens & Coupe, 1978). This error most likely reflects the knowledge that the state of California is largely west of Nevada, even though for some cities within these states the relation is reversed. Adults also demonstrate the influence of categorical information when judging distances. For example, people may report that the distance between two buildings located in the same town is smaller than between two buildings located in neighboring towns even when the second pair of buildings is actually closer (Hirtle & Jonides, 1985). Thus, natural and geographic boundaries (e.g., rivers, mountain ranges, cities, regions) provide the basis for the hierarchical organization of space, which is then used to reason about spatial relations.

In the absence of preexisting boundaries, adults tend to impose categorical distinctions on spatial layouts similar to those observed in 10- to 12-year-old children. That is, rather than simply using spatial categories defined by perceptually available boundaries, they mentally subdivide the space and use information about the boundaries of these imposed categories, as well as their prototypical locations, to adjust their estimates of location (Crawford, Huttenlocher, & Engebretson, 2000; Huttenlocher et al., 1991). In addition to object location tasks, adults demonstrate combined use of categorical and fine-grained information in reasoning about length, width, and other metric dimensions of objects. Thus, when estimating or reproducing individual stimuli, they show a tendency to bias their responses toward the central value of the category to which these stimuli belong.

Category effects on size estimates have been examined in a series of experiments in which participants were presented with objects that belonged to the same category but varied in size (Crawford et al., 2000). They were asked to reproduce the size of each object after some delay. Results showed that following several trials, participants' responses began to reflect the distribution of stimuli seen on previous trials, suggesting that people keep track of the range of stimulus values and form a corresponding representation of the presented objects as a specific category with a central value (i.e., average size of the objects) that serves as the prototype. When reproducing a stimulus value on a given trial, people combine information about the size of that particular stimulus with information about the prototypical size for that type of stimuli. Thus, the same stimulus may be overestimated when it is embedded in a set of items larger than it and underestimated when embedded in a set of smaller items.

Similar to the hierarchical coding model positing the combination of categorical and metric information, many current models of spatial representation in adults posit the use of multiple sources of information in judging and reproducing spatial properties (Ernst & Banks, 2002; Hartley, Trinkler, & Burgess, 2004; Hills, Ernst, Banks, & Landy, 2002; Knill & Saunders, 2003). A common feature of these models is that adults are viewed as assigning greater weights to information sources that are more reliable and less variable. For example, Hills et al. examined performance on tasks that required judging the size of an object, which was presented visually, haptically, or in both modalities. In general, people weighted visual information more heavily; however, when visual information was less reliable, greater weight was placed on haptic information. Hartley et al. proposed that location within an enclosed space is coded using both absolute and relative distance information, and that relative information is weighted more or less heavily depending on how accurately one can estimate the absolute distance. In both of these examples, people adjust their estimates of stimulus values in near-optimal fashion; they automatically take into consideration the reliability and variability of the available information.

These different approaches have been characterized as adaptive combination models because they serve to increase the accuracy of spatial performance (Newcombe & Huttenlocher, 2006). Given the adaptive importance of accuracy in estimating size and location, as well as evidence of the early use of hierarchical coding in children, it is possible that some of the basic processes of combining spatial information across levels and modalities may involve neurobiological constraints. At the same time, developmental changes in the differentiation of spatial information and the complexity of spatial categories suggest that experience plays a significant role in fine-tuning these basic cognitive processes (Huttenlocher & Lourenco, 2007).

Viewpoint Dependence versus Viewpoint Independence

Parallel to the issue of egocentric versus allocentric coding addressed in the research on children, much of the work on spatial reasoning in adults focuses on the issue of viewpoint dependence versus independence. Although adults are capable of coding spatial relations in terms of external features of the environment and, therefore, independent of their own perspectives, questions have been raised whether they tend to rely on this type of coding in solving spatial tasks. One line of research in which this issue has been addressed concerns object recognition (Biederman & Bar, 2000; Hayward & Tarr, 1997; Tarr & Bülthoff, 1998; Tarr, Williams, Hayward, & Gauthier, 1998). To examine factors that may affect object recognition, researchers have used matching tasks, in which participants are shown two objects, one after another, and then are asked whether the objects are the same or different. The critical manipulation is whether the pair of objects is presented from the same or a different perspective. Using this methodology, Tarr and colleagues (Tarr et al., 1998; Tarr & Bülthoff, 1998) have demonstrated an *alignment effect*—people find it easier to match objects if they are aligned (i.e., presented from the same viewpoint) than if they are rotated relative to each other.

In contrast with viewpoint-dependent mechanisms of object recognition, Biederman and colleagues (Biederman & Bar, 1999; Biederman & Gerhardstein, 1995) have argued that the perception of certain features of objects is virtually unaffected by rotation, and that the matching of objects with the same component features is equally easy regardless of whether the objects are aligned. Some examples of spatial features that can uniquely specify the structural description of an object include straight versus curved contours and parallel versus perpendicular lines. It has been proposed that this type of information allows people to represent objects as an arrangement of viewpoint invariant parts or *geons*, each with their own uniquely identifiable shape (Biederman & Gerhardstein). Such representations may be involved in everyday object recognition. Indeed, it seems that we recognize common objects, such as a mug or fork, regardless of the angle at which they are presented, as long as their defining features are apparent. However, even within an account of viewpoint independence, researchers allow for a degree of viewpoint-dependent mental processing. For example, solving a matching task (i.e., deciding whether two objects are identical or not) requires identifying and matching distinctive structural features. Searching for these features may take longer if the second object is presented from a different perspective than from the same perspective.

A second line of research exploring the issues of viewpoint independence involves studies examining scene recognition and location coding (Diwadkar & McNamara, 1997; Holmes & Sholl, 2005; McNamara, Rump, & Werner, 2003; Sholl & Bartels, 2002). A spatial scene or array usually consists of multiple objects, whose locations can be determined using distance and direction cues. Research on adults' representations of spatial arrays has commonly used a perspective-change paradigm. In this paradigm, people learn the positions of objects in a spatial array from a particular perspective and then are asked to imagine themselves facing the array from the same or a different perspective; in either case, the task is to point to various objects in the layout. Most studies report alignment effects—performance suffers, both in terms of pointing error and reaction time, when the viewing perspective at the time of testing is not the same as at the time of learning. Furthermore, the results show a roughly linear increase in reaction time as a function of angular difference between the two perspectives (Diwadkar & McNamara, 1997). These findings suggest that people may solve the task by transforming the view of the layout at testing into the view of the layout formed during learning, possibly by mental rotation. Larger transformations take longer and result in greater errors.

Notably, under certain conditions, particularly in tasks involving larger spatial layouts, adults show a lack of alignment effects (Presson, DeLange, & Hazelrigg, 1989; Sholl & Nolin, 1997). Presson and Hazelrigg (1984), for example, presented participants with a layout of a specific path within a large space. After learning the path from a single position, they were asked to point (while blindfolded) toward different targets along the path. The responses were equally accurate when produced from the original viewing position as from a novel position. In a follow-up study, Presson and colleagues (1989) found that small paths spanning the area of less than 1 m^2 produced alignment effects, whereas large paths (about 14 m^2) did not. The finding that spatial behavior varies as a function of space size thus appears to be common to children and adults. Sholl and colleagues' work indicates that the nature of one's representation of a spatial array depends not only on the size of the space but also on other contextual factors, such as the viewing angle during encoding (Sholl & Bartels, 2002; Sholl & Nolin).

The accumulating evidence suggests that multiple specific conditions have to be met to produce orientation-independent performance (McNamara & Valiquette, 2004; Sholl & Nolin, 1997). This has led researchers to suggest that information about a spatial layout is generally acquired in an orientation-specific manner, but when people acquire multiple representations of the layout from different perspectives (i.e., snapshots), they can infer locations from new perspectives, creating an impression of orientation-free representation (Diwadkar & McNamara, 1997). However, researchers disagree whether multiple perspectives are integrated in a unified viewpoint-independent representation, or whether they exist as a collection of viewpoint-specific snapshots that provides a basis for "computing" location from a novel perspective (e.g., Shelton & McNamara, 1997; Sholl & Nolin).

Near versus Far Space Representations

Perceiving the immediate space around us is crucial for successful action. Given that we cannot act at indefinite distance, it is of primary importance to represent the space closest to us. Accordingly, many researchers in diverse fields have differentiated the near space surrounding the body from the far space at greater distances (Brain, 1941; Cutting & Vishton, 1995; Hall, 1966). Brain, for example, described two patients with opposite localization deficits—one unable to localize objects within arm's reach, and the other unable to localize objects farther than a yard from his body. Following Brain, numerous studies have found that the near space immediately surrounding the body is represented differently than the space farther away (Berti & Frassinetti, 2000; Cowey, Small, & Ellis, 1994; Gamberini, Seraglia, & Priftis, 2008; Rizzolatti, Matelli, & Pavesi, 1983).

Recently, Longo and Lourenco (2006) examined the representation of near space in adults via lateral attentional biases on a line bisection task. Participants were asked to indicate the perceived midpoint of different-length lines using a laser pointer while standing at different distances. In near space, participants showed a slight leftward bias, a phenomenon known as *pseudoneglect* (for review, see Jewell & McCourt, 2000). When participants bisected lines at farther distances, the bias shifted rightward. Interestingly, people with longer arms showed a more gradual shift in bias than people with shorter arms, suggesting a systematic relation between the length of one's arms and the "size" of near space (Longo & Lourenco, 2007). People

with longer arms appear to have a correspondingly larger near space. These findings are consistent with earlier work by Warren (1984) in which it was found that perceptual judgments of spatial extent were represented in body-centered coordinates. These findings are also consistent with early work by Piaget and colleagues, who argued that young children learn about the external environment via their sensorimotor actions (e.g., Piaget & Inhelder, 1967). More recently, the idea that mental representations are not completely devoid of perceptual and bodily experiences has come to be known as embodied cognition (Overton, Mueller, & Newman, 2007).

The distinction between near and far space, however, is far from rigid. Not only does arm length not restrict one's interactions with the world, but there are also tools that can be used to alter these interactions. Longo and Lourenco (2006) showed tool effects and extension of near space in adults. Recall that when bisecting a line with a laser pointer, participants showed a slight leftward bias in near, but not in far, space. When participants used sticks, instead of a laser pointer, to bisect lines, they showed leftward bias at all distances from the body, suggesting that near space had expanded to incorporate the range within reach of the tool. These findings provide evidence for the flexibility of spatial representations in adults and the role of tools in altering the representation of space by extending the range of effective action.

Age-Related Changes in Spatial Cognition in Late Mature Adulthood

The studies of spatial cognition in adults discussed in the previous section have been conducted mostly with young and middle-aged participants. In fact, much of this work has been done with college students, primarily because of practical convenience and easy access to this population. At the same time, a growing body of research is focusing specifically on late mature adulthood (e.g., Aartsen, Smith, van Tilburg, Knopscheer, & Deeg, 2002; Kirasic, 2000; Kirasic, Allen, Dobson, & Binder, 1996; Salthouse, 2005, 2009; Schaie, 2005, 2009). These studies generally point to a decline in performance on reasoning and memory tasks at an older age (see, however, Bialystok & Craik, Blair, and Ricco, Chapters 7, 8, and 12 of this volume, respectively). However, although the existence of age-related decline in cognitive functioning is a widely recognized fact, a number of questions remain open and subject to debate concerning the nature of this phenomenon.

One set of questions has to do with the time course of cognitive changes in adult development. In particular, there is ongoing discussion about the age period when the decline begins (cf. Salthouse, 2009; Schaie, 2009). Another set of questions has to do with the proper characterization of cognitive tasks that reveal substantial age-related decreases in performance. The course of late adult development varies across different aspects of cognition. Some of the most dramatic declines have been noticed in spatial performance, but even within the spatial domain, certain aspects of functioning appear to be more preserved across the life span than others (Kirasic, 1991). Finally, there remain questions about the causes of the observed changes. Whereas age-related reductions in activity level (e.g., walking through a neighborhood) may lead to the decline in corresponding cognitive functions (e.g., orientation in a large-scale environment), many researchers point out that the relation between decreased levels of activity and functioning are most likely reciprocal (e.g., Aartsen et al., 2002; Walsh, Krauss, & Regnier, 1981). Addressing the questions concerning the timing and characterization of cognitive development in late mature adulthood is critical for the understanding of potential causes of age-related declines. For example, if the evidence points to a decline in spatial performance beginning as early as 30 years of age, it eliminates certain types of explanations involving biological and experiential factors associated with older ages.

Starting Points of Age-Related Decline in Spatial Functioning

Many researchers investigating cognitive development in late adulthood have come to the conclusion that relatively little decline occurs during early and middle adulthood, and only around the age of 60 or 70 do the changes in cognitive functioning become more apparent (Aartsen et al., 2002; Plassman et al., 1995; Schaie, 2009). In accord with this view, investigations of age-related changes in spatial functioning often focus on late mature adults (e.g., Janowsky, Oviat, & Orwoll, 1994; Walsh et al., 1981) or compare performance of young adults (age range, 20–30 years) with participants who are older than 60 (e.g., Kirasic, 1991, 2000). Yet, the evidence produced by some studies that include a range of ages between 20 and 90 suggests a nearly monotonic decrease in reasoning (but see Blair and Ricco, Chapters 8 and 12 of this volume, respectively, for a contrasting view) and spatial orientation (e.g., Salthouse, Atkinson, & Berish, 2003). These findings led Salthouse (2009) to argue that cognitive decline in several domains, including spatial functioning, begins shortly after reaching

maturity (but see Bialystok & Craik, Chapter 7 of this volume, for a contrasting view).

A potential source of discrepancy between the findings of different studies on late adult development has to do with study design. In particular, whereas cross-sectional studies reveal a gradual decline on certain spatial tasks starting in early adulthood, longitudinal studies tend to show stable, or even improving, levels of performance during early and middle adulthood. For example, when examining longitudinal changes over a 7-year period in different age cohorts, Schaie (2005) found improvements in performance on a spatial orientation task until about 40 years of age, no significant changes until the late 50s, and declines starting in the early 60s. A cross-sectional comparison of performance on a parallel spatial orientation task showed a decrease in performance starting around 30 years of age (Salthouse, 2009). It has been suggested that the differences in the trends revealed by cross-sectional and longitudinal studies may be caused by practice effects associated with longitudinal investigations. That is, individuals who have been tested on prior occasions have more familiarity and experience with the task, which may improve their subsequent performance. It is thus possible that negative age-related effects may be offset by the positive effects of test-retest practice.

It should be noted, however, that even though practice effects present a legitimate concern for the interpretation of longitudinal studies, they are usually relatively short-lived (Schaie, 2009). It is not clear whether they can completely account for the lack of decline observed in longitudinal studies during earlier adulthood. Furthermore, some negative trends observed in cross-sectional studies may by exaggerated by cohort effects, such as differences in educational and other relevant experiences across age groups. Finally, it is important to emphasize that despite the differences in findings reported across studies, there are also important commonalities in age trends. That is, even cross-sectional studies that reveal some differences in spatial functioning early on show that the magnitude of age-related decrease in performance accelerates with age. Specifically, the decline in perceptual speed and spatial memory for adults in the 60- to 90-year-old range is two to four times greater than for adults younger than 60 (Salthouse, 2009). Thus, even though questions concerning the starting age of spatial cognitive decline remain open, converging evidence across studies and methodologies indicates that significant changes do take place in the late 60s or early 70s, suggesting a precipitous decline in spatial performance in late mature adult populations.

Tasks Revealing Age-Related Differences in Performance

The relation between age and the level of performance during adulthood varies across cognitive domains. Much of the existing evidence indicates that spatial cognition is more vulnerable to age-related decline than verbal cognition (Jenkins, Myerson, Joerding, & Hale, 2000). Many verbal tasks, particularly those based on accumulated knowledge (i.e., vocabulary, general information, discourse processing), show increases in performance until at least age 60, with little or no decline in healthy late mature adults (Salthouse, 2009; Blair, Chapter 8 of this volume). In contrast, the signs of declining performance in the spatial domain are evident in late mature adult populations across a wide variety of tasks. In particular, age-related changes have been consistently reported on tasks involving visualization and the mental manipulation of objects, location memory, and way-finding in large-scale environments (Barash, 1994; Blair, Chapter 8 of this volume; Cherry & Park, 1993; Dobson, Kirasic, & Allen, 1995; Kirasic & Mathes, 1990; Moffat & Resnick, 2002; Wilkniss, Jones, Korol, Gold, & Manning, 1997).

The studies on age-related changes in spatial performance can be roughly divided into two groups. The first group involves the assessment of spatial performance via psychometric tests, often as part of more general intelligence testing (e.g., Dobson et al., 1995; Hertzog & Rypma, 1991; Plassman et al., 1995; Schaie, 2005). Psychometric testing has consistently produced evidence of age-related differences in mental rotation: Young adults outperform older adults in accuracy and response time (Dobson et al.; Hertzog & Rypma; Mayr & Kliegl, 1993). The second group of investigations focuses on age-related changes in way-finding and reasoning about realistic large-scale environments (e.g., Barash, 1994; Kirasic & Mathes, 1990; Salthouse & Siedlecki, 2006). The ability to reason about large-scale spaces is commonly tested with tasks that require learning routes, selecting landmarks, and judging distances.

Kirasic (2000) investigated the relations among age, general spatial abilities assessed by psychometric tests, and performance in a realistic spatial layout. Participants' performance on psychometric tests was assessed in a laboratory setting and included a variety of tasks on pattern recognition, mental rotation, and visualization. Performance in a realistic layout was tested in a large supermarket where, following a guided tour, the participants were asked to locate items and judge distances between different points. Consistent with prior studies, the results showed significant differences in performance between the younger participants (age range, 18–28 years) and the older participants (age range, 60–85 years), with lower levels of performance in older participants. The age differences in learning the environmental layout were mediated by general spatial abilities. These findings suggest that the widely recognized age-related decline in the ability to acquire environmental knowledge and navigate large-scale environments is, at least in part, due to a decrease in general spatial abilities captured by psychometric tests. At the same time, even when the influence of the general spatial ability is accounted for, there still is a significant relation between age and environmental learning, suggesting that some age-related spatial challenges are unique to reasoning about large-scale spaces.

The extent of age-related differences varies not only across different types of spatial tasks, but also as a function of task-specific variables, such as task complexity (Cerella, Poon, & William, 1980; Dobson et al., 1995; Mayr & Kliegl, 1993). Dobson et al., for example, examined interactions between age and task complexity in performance on a figure comparison task. Participants were presented with two figures formed by two to four line segments and their task was to judge whether the two figures were the same or different. Task complexity was varied by manipulating two stimulus characteristics: the number of lines comprising each figure and the relative orientation of the two figures (aligned or rotated). Findings showed that errors in older adults increased with the increase in the number of line segments, whereas younger adults performed equally accurately with different numbers of line segments. Response times increased as a function of additional line segments in all age groups, but the increase was most dramatic in the older participants. Similarly, misalignment affected both error rates and response times in all age groups, but the effects were most pronounced among the older adults.

Factors Related to Age-Related Decline in the Spatial Domain

In the search for potential sources of age-related differences in spatial performance, researchers have suggested explanations at different levels of analysis. At the psychological level, investigations focus on the cognitive mechanisms involved in tasks that show age-related decline compared with the tasks that show relative stability across age. Analyses of the component processes involved in these tasks have allowed researchers to identify key cognitive factors that appear to play a critical role in a variety of tasks showing age-related decline. One such factor is working memory, or the ability to maintain and operate on relevant information whereas simultaneously thinking about a problem (see Bialystok & Craik, Chapter 7 of this volume, Blair, Chapter 8 of this volume, and Demetriou, Mouyi, & Spanoudis, Chapter 10 of this volume, for extended discussions of development and working memory). Several studies have documented decreases in working memory capacity, which correlate with the decrease in performance on spatial tasks. Furthermore, when controlling for differences in working memory, researchers found a significant reduction in age-related variance on spatial tasks, such as geometric analogies and matrix reasoning (Salthouse, 1992, 1993). These findings suggest the possibility that working memory mediates the relation between age and level of spatial functioning during adulthood.

Another cognitive factor that has been implicated in late adult cognitive development is information-processing speed (see Demetriou, Mouyi, & Spanoudis, Chapter 10 of this volume). This factor accounts for additional age-related variance in spatial performance (Salthouse, 1993). Thus, both processing speed and working memory may modulate age-related differences in spatial functioning, sometimes referred to as a *resource reduction* model of cognitive late adult development (Kirasic et al., 1996). Some researchers have pointed out that age-related decrements in processing capacity are greater than storage decrements (Dobson et al., 1995; Salthouse, Babcock, & Shaw, 1991). That is, older participants may do as well as younger participants on tasks (or components of cognitive tasks) that require keeping and retrieving information in the form in which it was originally presented, but they show lower levels of performance when the information not only has to be maintained but also manipulated.

Although cognitive-level explanations increase our understanding of the extent and nature of late adult development in the spatial domain, they leave open questions concerning the mechanisms underlying age-related cognitive changes. These questions have been addressed in the studies exploring the biology of late adult development and the role of experiential factors. Among the biological factors, changes in hormonal levels have been frequently discussed with respect to age-related declines in spatial functioning (e.g., Berenbaum & Resnick, 2007; Gouchie & Kimura, 1991; Janowsky et al., 1994; Moffat & Hampson, 1996; see Liben et al., 2002, for review). The idea that hormones may be implicated in spatial reasoning is based on several well-documented findings. First, spatial tasks

represent a domain of cognition that has most consistently produced evidence of sex differences, and such differences could be linked to hormonal differences in males versus females. Second, the levels of certain hormones, such as testosterone, decrease with age, corresponding to a decline in spatial performance.

To address a possible link between testosterone and spatial performance, Janowsky and colleagues (1994) conducted an experimental study in which they manipulated the levels of testosterone in healthy older men. The participants were randomly assigned to either treatment or placebo group in a double-blinded design. The treatment group received a testosterone supplement for 3 months, which increased the level of this hormone approximately to the level of normal younger men. At the end of this 3-month period, testosterone levels of the treatment group were significantly greater than that in the placebo group. Both groups of participants were administered cognitive assessments at the start and end of the study, which included measures of vocabulary, cognitive flexibility, and spatial reasoning. There were no differences between the two groups before treatment. At the end of the study, however, men in the treatment group performed significantly better than the placebo group on the spatial task, but not on any of the other cognitive measures. The selective effect of testosterone on spatial skills has been replicated in a 10-year longitudinal study with older adult men, which showed a positive association between the amount of free testosterone and performance on a variety of spatial tasks, but no association with language measures (Moffat & Resnick, 2002).

Other studies, however, failed to find an association between the level of testosterone and spatial functioning (e.g., Alexander, Swerdloff, Wang, Davidson, McDonald, Steiner, & Hines, 1998; Wolf, Preut, Hellhammer, Kudielka, Schürmeyer, & Kirschbaum, 2000). For example, a short-term experimental study with healthy older men that involved a single testosterone injection showed that the spatial performance of this group did not differ from that of the control group who received a placebo injection (Wolf et al.). The difference between the findings of this study and those of Janowsky et al. (1994) may be caused, in part, by differences in the length and dosage of the hormone treatment. Work with younger men has shown that higher levels of testosterone are not necessarily related to higher levels of spatial abilities. In fact, several studies report a negative relation between these two variables in younger males (e.g., Gouchie & Kimura, 1991; Moffat & Hampson, 1996). It is possible, then, that the relation between levels of testosterone and spatial functioning is curvilinear, with both too high and too low levels associated with poorer performance (Janowsky et al.).

Whereas the investigation of hormonal links to late adult cognitive development in males has generally focused on testosterone, parallel investigations in women have tended to focus on estrogen, which declines dramatically after menopause. In work with late adult women, greater levels of estrogen appear to be associated with increased verbal memory and decreased spatial abilities, but there are some inconsistencies in the findings, perhaps because of differences in the methods used to assess hormonal levels and the instruments used to measure cognitive skills (e.g., Drake et al., 2000; Hampson, 1990). Nevertheless, a growing body of evidence suggests that specific hormones may be related to distinct cognitive processes, and age-related changes in hormonal levels may lead to changes in the levels of spatial and other cognitive functioning.

Experiential explanations generally attribute the decrease in cognitive functioning in older adults to reduced levels of sufficiently stimulating cognitive activities. In this view, maintaining an optimal level of cognitive functioning requires experiences that involve exercising and challenging the relevant skills (Hultsch, Hertzog, Small, & Dixon, 1999). Hultsch et al. proposed that their findings were consistent with two explanatory models. Under the first scenario, intellectual activities serve to buffer individuals against decline, and under the second scenario, high-ability individuals lead more intellectually stimulating lives until the time when decline in their cognitive skills constrains their participation in these activities.

Some researchers argue that the level of activity is more likely a consequence than a cause of age-related cognitive changes (Aartsen et al., 2002; Salthouse, 2005). Indeed, Aartsen et al. found no effect of activity level on cognitive functioning. However, that study examined only regular everyday activities, whereas the maintenance of cognitive functions may depend on the intensity of cognitively stimulating experience. Evidence from several recent studies supports this view (Newson & Kemps, 2006; Tranter & Koutstaal, 2008; Wilson, Barnes, & Bennett, 2003). Tranter and Koutstaal used an intervention design to test the role of cognitively challenging activities in spatial performance. After an intervention that involved mentally stimulating exercises for 10 to 12 weeks, experimental participants showed greater pretest to post-test gains on a spatial-perceptual task than did a control group. Thus, accumulating evidence demonstrates the effects of stimulating activities on spatial performance in late mature adults.

Summary

This section has examined research exploring the nature of mature spatial cognition, as well as work on age-related changes in spatial functioning in late adult development. The analysis of this body of work suggests that on many spatial tasks, the peak level of performance is demonstrated in young and middle adulthood. When compared with children, young and middle-aged adults show greater accuracy and flexibility in spatial thinking. Interestingly, a close analysis of adults' performance reveals certain features of their representations that had been viewed by Piaget as more characteristic of young children' spatial thinking. These include, for example, viewpoint dependence in scene recognition. Of course, in adults, such features have a more subtle effect on performance than in children. Whereas young children have difficulty identifying a spatial array presented from a different perspective, adults tend to show a decline in speed rather than accuracy of performance in a parallel situation.

Other features of adult spatial cognition, such as the influence of categorical information on metric representations, although leading to slightly biased responses, actually serve to increase the average accuracy of performance. Generally, adults tend to combine various sources of information in estimating object size or location in a way that automatically takes into account the reliability and variability of these sources. The process of integrating information and assigning greater weights to more reliable sources serves an adaptive purpose of optimizing spatial performance across different contexts.

Compared with younger adults, older adults show a decline both in the accuracy and speed of performance on several spatial tasks, including mental rotation and way finding. Existing studies provide evidence of the relation between experiential factors (e.g., activity level) and age-related changes in spatial functioning. Although some researchers argue that a decrease in everyday activity may be an outcome rather than a cause of the decrease in cognitive skills, others suggest that late adult cognitive development is moderated by mentally challenging activities. Based on the existing evidence, it appears likely that the relation between changes in activity level and cognitive performance is reciprocal. Evidence of the malleability of cognitive skills in late mature adulthood suggests that it may be possible to reduce cognitive decline, such as that associated with spatial reasoning, through targeted interventions.

INDIVIDUAL DIFFERENCES IN SPATIAL COGNITION

Exploring Individual-Level Differences

It is commonly known that people differ substantially in the level of their spatial functioning in everyday situations. This is true both for tasks involving navigating a large-scale space, and for tasks involving manipulating objects and small-scale spatial arrays. Some individuals appear to know their way around even after brief exposure to a new place, whereas others have great difficulty learning new environments even after relatively long exposure. People also vary in the ability to manipulate and transform objects; some enjoy household projects that require assembling equipment out of component parts, whereas others try to avoid putting together a piece of furniture. It is quite likely that these individual differences in everyday functioning reflect differences in basic spatial processes that can be explored in experimental settings. However, the study of individual variability presents a number of challenges in spatial and other cognitive domains, especially for developmental psychologists.

First, differences among individuals may reflect random fluctuations in performance, which may be due to factors such as motivation or level of stress and alertness during the test. Second, the pattern of differences between any two individuals may undergo substantial changes with development, possibly due to differential availability of experiences relevant to the development of spatial skills. Given these issues, it is perhaps not surprising that much of the current developmental research focuses on average performance, treating individual differences primarily as error variance. In work with children, it is common to see reports that at the time of emergence of a new spatial skill, about half of the children of a certain age display the skill and the other half does not. Yet, we know little about whether these differences in the age of acquisition of spatial skills are related to later variability in performance on more advanced spatial tasks. In adult research, more work focuses on individual variability in spatial skills. Much of this research examines how differences in performance on one type of task may be related to differences in performance on other types of tasks (Hegarty et al., 2005; Kozhevnikov & Hegarty, 2001; Pazzaglia & De Beni, 2001, 2006).

The earliest work on individual differences in adults was done in the context of psychometric analyses that aimed to determine whether spatial cognitive abilities across tasks can be captured by a single spatial factor or should be conceptualized as a collection of different factors (McGee, 1979; Thurstone, 1950). These analyses examined patterns of correlation across tasks. If the rank order based on the level of performance on one spatial task closely corresponded to the rank order for the same participants on another task, it was concluded that these different tasks reflected the same basic underlying cognitive process. Several investigators have pointed to the limitations of inferring underlying cognitive processes based on factor analytic techniques (Hegarty & Waller, 2005). Depending on the type of tasks that are included in the exploratory factor analysis, one can arrive at different patterns of individual differences and, as a result, different conceptualizations of the underlying structure of spatial cognition (Carroll, 1993; McGee, 1979).

Another approach to the investigation of individual differences in spatial cognition focuses on a theoretical analysis of the perceptual and cognitive variables involved in various spatial tasks. As we have seen in the research with late mature adults, processing speed and working memory have been identified as critical cognitive factors implicated in age-related changes in spatial reasoning. There is also evidence to suggest that these aspects of cognition may differentiate high- from low-performing individuals within a particular age group. In particular, differences among individuals in speed of mental rotation and in the initial encoding of unfamiliar stimuli can account for a large portion of variance in performance on a variety of spatial tests (Just & Carpener, 1985; Pellegrino & Kail, 1982). Some spatial tests can be solved by most people given unlimited time, but imposing a time limit often leads to noticeable individual differences (Pellegrino & Kail). In more complex problem-solving situations, where people need to manipulate and transform spatial representations in memory, slow processing speed may lead to a decay of information from the earliest stages of problem solving, leading to poor performance (Salthouse, 1992).

The importance of maintaining and manipulating spatial information highlights the role of working memory in spatial problem solving. Several studies have suggested that differences in working memory can explain some of the observed differences in spatial ability (Miyake, Rettinger, Friedman, Shah, & Hegarty, 2001; Shah & Miyake, 1996). Another potential source of individual differences has to do with the strategy chosen by the individual to solve a spatial problem. For example, Just and Carpenter (1985) uncovered systematic differences in strategy use on a mental rotation task between high- and low-performing individuals. In their study, the participants were shown two pictures of a cube, with each side marked by a different letter. The task was to decide whether the two pictures involved the same object seen from a different perspective or two different objects. Some participants imagined mentally moving the cube, others imagined moving themselves, and yet others tried to solve the task analytically by analyzing the relative positions of different letters on the sides of the cube. The most common strategy involved mentally moving the cube. However, low-performing individuals rotated the cube around canonical axes (i.e., orthogonal to the faces of the cube), whereas high-performing individuals rotated the cube around noncanonical axes, which often reduced the number of steps needed to align the two pictures and allowed for solving the task more quickly.

Differences in strategy choice and the level of performance have been observed not only in tasks involving manipulation of small objects and arrays, such as mental rotation, but also in large-scale spatial tasks, such as wayfinding in realistic spaces. For example, when learning novel environments, some individuals tend to use a route-learning strategy where they encode successive views of landmarks on a path through the environment, whereas others prefer to use a survey strategy, learning the space from an aerial perspective provided by a map. It remains to be determined why individuals differ in their preference for a particular strategy, and whether these differences in strategy choice reflect individual differences in underlying ability, such that people avoid strategies they are less able to implement.

A recent line of research has revealed a complex pattern of relations among basic spatial abilities, choice of strategy, and underlying neural mechanisms (Pazzaglia & De Beni, 2001, 2006; Shelton & Gabrieli, 2004). When examining cognitive factors associated with differences in strategies on tasks that require learning novel environments, it has been shown that a link exists between strategy preference and mental rotation ability. Individuals who prefer to use a survey strategy are significantly better on mental rotation than those who prefer landmark-based strategies (Pazzaglia & De Beni, 2001). Further, functional magnetic resonance imaging studies examining brain activity during the learning of novel environments have revealed different patterns of activation when using survey- versus route-learning strategies in people with high versus low mental rotation ability (Shelton & Gabrieli). Relatively little is currently known about distinct patterns of brain functioning among people with different levels of spatial abilities. Although this type of research is in only the initial stages, it may prove particularly informative for the understanding

of naturally occurring variability, as well as experience-related changes in spatial functioning.

Exploring Group-Level Differences

A large body of research on variability in spatial cognition has focused on group-level differences rather than differences at the level of the individual. Within this body of research, substantial progress has been made in exploring the nature of sex differences. Spatial tasks have produced the most consistent evidence of sex-related variability compared to other cognitive domains. On average, males outperform females on many spatial tasks; males also tend to show greater variance in cognitive functioning, with a larger number of men than women at both high and low ends of the score distribution (Hedges & Nowell, 1995). The combination of these factors may explain the large proportion of males at the highest levels of performance (Halpern, 2000; Halpern & Collaer, 2005). In interpreting the group-level variability, however, it is important to realize that there is substantial overlap between the two groups and large variation within each group. Thus, particular women may outperform particular men on tasks, but males, on average, have an advantage. Yet, the presence of even small, but statistically significant, differences between males and females raises questions concerning the role of biological and experiential factors in spatial cognition. The following section reviews evidence concerning sex differences in children and adults, and discusses possible sources of sex-related differences in spatial reasoning.

Early Sex Differences in Spatial Cognition

It has long been believed that sex-related differences in spatial cognition emerge around the age of puberty. However, more recent evidence indicates the existence of sex differences in younger children (Levine, Huttenlocher, Taylor, & Langrock, 1999; Levine, Vasilyeva, Lourenco, Newcombe, & Huttenlocher, 2005; Vasilyeva & Bowers, 2006). In particular, such differences have been demonstrated in tasks that involve mental rotation. In one study, for example, children were shown a target shape, and were required to rotate and fit together component pieces to form that shape (Levine, et al., 1999). Sex differences were observed on this task in preschool-aged children.

Using looking-time paradigms, recent investigations have shown that the male advantage on mental rotation is present even in infancy. Moore and Johnson (2008) familiarized 5-month-olds with a three-dimensional object revolving along a 240-degree arc. During the test phase, they were shown the same object or its mirror image, as these objects revolved along a previously unseen arc. In this experiment, only the male infants looked longer at the mirror image. In another study, Quinn and Liben (2008) familiarized 3- to 4-month-olds with a two-dimensional object shown in different orientations. The infants were then presented with a novel orientation of the familiar stimulus paired with its mirror image. Male infants tended to look longer at the mirror image than at the familiar stimulus, whereas most of the female infants divided their attention relatively equally between the two test stimuli. These studies suggest that boys were more likely than girls to recognize the difference in object orientation, which would only be possible if they engaged in mental rotation.

Sex Differences in Spatial Cognition in Adults

Mental rotation tasks, especially those that require maintaining and transforming three-dimensional images, have produced the most consistent evidence of a male advantage and are characterized by large effect sizes (Masters & Sanders, 1993). The observed differences on these tasks concern both the accuracy of responses and the time it takes to arrive at the correct response. It has been suggested that these differences in performance are partly due to the difference in strategies used to solve mental rotation tasks. In particular, on matching tasks, males may favor the strategy of mentally rotating the whole object and comparing the result of this rotation with the target, whereas females may approach the task by comparing the component parts of the target and choice figures. Both strategies can lead one to the right solution, but the latter may be less efficient and more prone to error.

It has been suggested that generating an image may be more difficult for females than males (Loring-Meier & Halpern, 1999). However, the pattern of performance on image generation tasks varies greatly depending on the complexity of the image. Some investigators have argued that image manipulation rather than generation per se may be the critical factor associated with a male advantage (Johnson & Bouchard, 2007). Differences in the average level of performance can also be seen in spatial tasks that involve large visuoperceptual components, but these differences are usually relatively small (Halpern & Collaer, 2005). In particular, a moderate male advantage has been shown on tasks that require ignoring irrelevant spatial perceptual cues. An example of such tasks is the water-level task, in which participants are asked either to draw a horizontal line showing the water level in a tilted glass or to identify a picture that shows the water level

correctly (Vasta & Liben, 1996). As the degree of tilt increases, females have greater difficulty than males drawing or choosing a perfectly horizontal line.

Consistent findings of sex differences have also been reported on tasks involving navigation and reasoning about large-scale spaces. The pattern of performance on these tasks depends on the type of information (i.e., landmarks vs. distance and cardinal direction) used in representing target location in the spatial environment. In route-planning or direction-giving tasks, one can represent a path as a series of right and left turns at particular landmarks. Alternatively, one can represent the same path in terms of distances and cardinal directions, starting from the point of departure. Of course, in many situations, people rely on a combination of these two approaches. It has been well documented that when asked to provide directions, males are more likely to indicate distance and cardinal information whereas females are more likely to use landmark information (Brown, Lahar, & Mosley, 1998; Galea & Kimura, 1993; Ward, Newcombe, & Overton, 1986).

It should be noted, however, that when participants are explicitly asked to use distance information or when cardinal direction is made more salient, the difference between females and males in strategy use virtually disappears (Ward et al., 1986). Nevertheless, differences in the preferred approach observed when participants are not directed toward a particular strategy correspond to differences in accuracy. For example, when learning a novel route, males are more accurate with distance information but females show better recall of individual landmarks along the route (Galea & Kimura, 1993). Montello and colleagues (Montello, Lovelace, Golledge, & Self, 1999) obtained similar findings in a task where participants walked through a novel route and then were asked to draw a map of this route. As expected, male subjects tended to make fewer errors for distance and direction, whereas female subjects tended to make fewer errors in reporting landmarks that lie along the route. Notably, however, when people were familiarized with the area not by walking through it but rather by studying a picture of it, sex differences disappeared. Thus, the differential sensitivity to landmark versus metric cues may apply more to information acquired in large-scale than small-scale spaces.

Biological and Experiential Factors Associated with Sex Differences

A number of factors have been proposed as possible explanations for the observed variation in spatial performance between males and females. Biological theories often emphasize the relation between hormone levels and spatial ability. As discussed earlier, sex hormones have been implicated in age-related changes in spatial functioning. In addition, differences in sex hormones between males and females may be related to sex differences in spatial performance. A potential role of sex hormones in spatial development is suggested by studies of individuals with atypical hormonal profiles (Bushbaum & Henkin, 1980; Resnick, Berenbaum, Gottesman, & Bouchard, 1986; Williams, Barnett, & Meck, 1990). It has been shown, for example, that males who have androgen deficiency early in life have low spatial ability compared to males with normal hormonal levels (Bushbaum & Henkin, 1980). However, males who acquire androgen deficiency after puberty do not exhibit spatial impairments, suggesting important differences between organizational and activational effects of hormones (Williams et al., 1990). The presence of certain hormones may be particularly consequential during earlier periods because these hormones are instrumental in organizing the process of neural development.

The evidence of biological effects does not exclude, however, a role of experiential factors. It has been proposed that early play experiences, such as playing with construction sets and other spatially relevant toys, may be an important factor in the development of spatial abilities (Voyer, Nolan, & Voyer, 2000). Indeed, there are numerous reports of an association between participation in spatially stimulating activities and performance on spatial tasks (e.g., Newcombe, Bandura, & Taylor, 1983; Serbin & Sprafkin, 1986). There are alternative interpretations for such an association, however. One possibility is that, in Western societies, boys are encouraged more than girls to engage in block play and mechanical tasks. Another possibility is that certain biological predispositions may lead boys to engage with spatial toys and elicit spatially related activities from caregivers. The previously discussed findings suggest that an increased level of androgen in girls is related to a greater interest in male-type toys and activities (Berenbaum & Resnick, 2007). It is thus an open question whether gender-stereotyped play mediates the relation between biological differences and spatial development.

Another way of examining the relation between specific experiences and spatial reasoning is to look for cultural variation across populations. Only a handful of studies have examined whether a male spatial advantage is present across different population groups. There are reports that this sex difference is present in African, Asian, and Western cultures (Mann, Sasanuma, Sakuma, & Masaki, 1990). However, Eastern Canadian Eskimos from the Baffin Islands do not show a sex difference on a variety of spatial tasks, possibly because both men and women in this culture hunt, which involves navigating across land and sea environments sparse in landmarks (Berry, 1966).

Traditional experiences for males versus females may vary not only cross-nationally but also across socioeconomic groups. A recent study reported that sex differences on spatial tasks in elementary school children varied as a function of socioeconomic status (SES) (Levine et al., 2005). In high and middle SES groups, boys performed better than girls on tasks involving mental rotation and aerial map reading. In contrast, these sex differences were not present in a lower SES group, raising the possibility that differential levels of engagement in the kinds of activities that promote the development of spatial skill may play a critical role in supporting a male advantage. In lower SES groups, these kinds of spatial activities (e.g., playing with Lego blocks and putting together puzzles) may be relatively unavailable to both boys and girls. Children from lower SES groups certainly engage in gender-typed play, but they may have less access than their higher SES counterparts to the toys and games that promote spatial reasoning.

The studies discussed so far were based on naturally occurring variability, either in the individuals' biological makeup or in the environmental context. Experimental research may provide the strongest evidence concerning the role of specific activities in the development of spatial skills. The next section reviews research in which the extent of malleability of spatial skills was evaluated through experimentally designed interventions.

Malleability of Spatial Skills

The benefits of training on spatial performance have been observed in children and adults on a variety of spatial tasks, thus demonstrating malleability in spatial reasoning across the life span (e.g., Baenninger & Newcombe, 1989, 1995). Several key questions guide contemporary research on training effects. One concerns the nature of effective input with respect to specific spatial skills. Despite the mounting evidence that training enhances spatial skill, it has been difficult to characterize the specific qualities of input that may lead to the greatest gains in performance. Another issue concerns the nature of improvement as a result of training. The question is whether training can produce generalizable effects or whether it simply improves performance with the type of stimuli used during practice. Further, it is important to understand the extent of differences in susceptibility to training and whether individuals with lower initial skills may benefit from training more than those with higher skills.

The types of input provided during spatial training vary from simple practice to explicit instructions about effective strategies (Ehrlich, Levine, & Goldin-Meadow, 2006; Kail, 1986; Leone, Taine, & Droulez, 1993; Lizarraga & Ganuza, 2003). A recent study compared the effects of different types of training on preschoolers' performance on a two-dimensional mental rotation task (Ehrlich et al.). The authors examined children's performance after either observing the physical movements of the stimuli or being told to imagine comparable movements. Although children showed significant improvement after different types of training, this improvement was not substantially different from practice alone. The effects of practice are often so substantial that they can alleviate preexisting differences among age groups. For example, extended practice on mental rotation led to better performance in children and adolescents than in unpracticed adults (Kail, 1986).

Other studies showing effects of training have focused on how specific types of information can facilitate spatial reasoning. Loewenstein and Gentner (2001, 2005), for example, suggest that providing children with spatial language capturing relevant spatial relations can help learners arrive at a spatial encoding that is optimal for a given task. In other experiments, Liben and Yekel (1996) have shown that even brief exposure to more iconic maps facilitated preschoolers' use of abstract maps. Finally, Plumert and Hund have examined how additional information about salient boundaries and nearby locations experienced in close temporal proximity affect the representation of spatial categories in children (e.g., Hund & Plumert, 2003; Plumert & Hund, 2001). In most cases, additional experience with critical category features promoted the use of spatial categories, not spontaneously used previously, to solve location problems.

Note that, in many training studies, test stimuli that are used to evaluate the effectiveness of training are similar in kind to the stimuli used during the training phase. This is true, for example, of several studies demonstrating that practice with mental rotation improves the speed and accuracy of mental rotation (Ehrlich et al., 2006; Kail, 1986; Kail & Park, 1990). Sims and Mayer (2002) have demonstrated that people who have extensive experience playing a computer game of Tetris, which involves the use of mental rotation skills, are better on mental rotation tasks that involve objects similar to those used in Tetris, but this improvement does not appear to transfer to other spatial

tasks. In contrast, some other studies provide evidence consistent with training-related generalization to novel stimuli (De Lisi & Wolford, 2002; Leone et al., 1993).

To understand the extent of generalizability of spatial training, researchers have recently examined whether training effects transfer not only to different types of stimulus but also to different types of tasks (Terlecki, Newcombe, & Little, 2008; Wright, Thompson, Ganis, Newcombe, & Kosslyn, 2008). For example, in a study by Wright et al. (2008), college students engaged in extensive practice with either a mental rotation or a mental paper folding task. The paper folding task required mental transformation but did not include a typical mental rotation component. The question was whether practice with mental rotation would improve performance on mental transformation and vice versa. The results provided a clear positive answer: There was symmetrical transfer of practice between spatial tasks. The investigators also gave participants a verbal task at pretest and post-test to examine the domain specificity of the training effect. They found that the effects of spatial practice on the novel spatial task were significantly larger than on the verbal task. Thus, spatial training can lead to generalized improvement in spatial reasoning.

In examining the effects of spatial training, researchers have been eager to determine whether benefits are particularly pronounced for the initially underperforming group, which would suggest that training may reduce or eliminate the existing gap in performance. An extensive review of prior work by Baenninger and Newcombe (1989, 1995) concluded that most studies find comparable improvement in male and female subjects. A closer examination of training effects indicated different dynamics in the two sex groups, with males showing faster initial growth and females showing more improvement later on (Terlecki et al., 2008). A few recent studies have demonstrated an interaction between sex and training effects; males outperformed females on mental rotation before training, but the differences disappeared after training. This has been shown in work with children (De Lisi & Wolford, 2002) and adults (Wright et al., 2008). Both of these studies included extended practice and examined generalized practice effects, either with novel stimuli (De Lisi & Wolford, 2002) or a novel task (Wright et al., 2008). Future research should explore the possibility that it is generalized rather than task-specific effects that show a decrease in the performance gap between males and females.

From a developmental perspective, it is also important to determine whether training effects vary with age. Relatively few studies have examined the effects of spatial interventions developmentally. A study by Kail (1986), which included children, adolescents, and adults, found comparable improvement in all age groups, suggesting that the mechanism underlying practice may be the same from childhood to adulthood. Intervention studies with older adults have demonstrated significant improvements with training (e.g., Tranter & Koutstaal, 2008), comparable in effect sizes to the improvements seen in younger adults. The combined evidence from research reviewed in this section points to substantial malleability in spatial skills in children and adults. These findings clearly have significant practical implications for a variety of applied fields concerned with improving educational outcomes, extending opportunities for underperforming groups, and improving the quality of life across the life span.

CONCLUSIONS

This chapter reviewed some of the key issues guiding research on spatial development. Throughout the history of psychology, there has been a profound interest in this area of development, evidenced by an extraordinary amount of research on spatial intelligence, only part of which could be presented here. This interest is based both on fascinating theoretical questions that arise in the analysis of spatial development and on the practical implications of spatial skills in everyday life, science, and technology. The existing body of literature covers the entire life span, starting with work on newborns and continuing into late adulthood. Common research themes can be traced across studies involving different age groups. Whether investigators are concerned with the spatial functioning of infants or adults, they explore what kinds of spatial information (e.g., metric or categorical) and frameworks (egocentric or allocentric) individuals use in reasoning about objects and their locations.

Despite the commonalities, however, there are significant differences in the research focus across age groups. Some of these differences have to do with developmental constraints. For example, the study of map skills cannot occur in infancy because maps and other symbolic spatial representations involve culturally acquired information that is not likely to be systematically directed at infants. Other differences, however, have to do more with established traditions. For example, there are quite disparate approaches to the study of individual variability in research with children versus adults. Over the years, work with children has focused on larger group differences, perhaps because of

the vast age-related changes that occur during childhood. Work with adults, in contrast, concerns mature forms of reasoning, and thus has been able to focus more directly on differences at the individual level. A relative lack of integration of research with respect to this and other issues may slow progress in the continued study of spatial development, particularly in identifying mechanisms underlying age-related changes.

Understanding the nature of variability in spatial performance perhaps presents one the most vital lines of current research in spatial development, with significant potential for practical applications. One aspect of this investigation concerns within-individual variability in performance across spatial tasks. The other aspect concerns the extent and nature of differences among individuals. Over the last few decades, some progress has been made in identifying specific biological and environmental factors related to individual differences. It may take substantial advances in neurobiological research to fully understand the involvement of biological factors in the development of spatial cognition. Meanwhile, as argued by Newcombe (2002), a concerted effort is required of psychologists and educators to understand what kinds of interventions work to maximize spatial competence.

REFERENCES

Aartsen, M. J., Smith, C. H. M., van Tiburg, T., Knopscheer, K. C. P. M., & Deeg, D. J. H. (2002). Activity in older adults: Cause or consequence of cognitive functioning? A longitudinal study on everyday activities and cognitive performance in older adults. *Journal of Gerontology: Psychological Science, 57,* 153–162.

Ackerman, P. L., & Cianciolo, A. (2002). Ability and task constraint determinants of complex task performance. *Journal of Experimental Psychology: Applied, 8,* 194–208.

Acredolo, L. P. (1977). Developmental changes in the ability to coordinate perspectives of a large-scale space. *Developmental Psychology, 13,* 1–8.

Acredolo, L. P. (1981). Small- and large-scale spatial concepts in infancy and childhood. In L. S. Liben, A. H. Patterson, & N. Newcombe (Eds.), *Spatial representation and behavior across the life span* (pp. 63–81). New York: Academic Press.

Acredolo, L. P., Adams, A., & Goodwyn, S. (1984). The role of self-produced movement and visual tracking in infant spatial orientation. *Journal of Experimental Child Psychology, 38,* 312–327.

Alexander, G. M., Swerdloff, R. S., Wang, C., Davidson, T., McDonald, V., Steiner, B., et al. (1998). Androgen-behavior correlations in hypogonadal men and eugonadal men: II. Cognitive abilities. *Hormones and Behavior, 33,* 85–94.

Allen, G. L. (1999). Spatial abilities, cognitive maps and wayfinding: Bases for individual differences in spatial cognition and behavior. In R. G. Golledge (Ed.), *Wayfinding behavior: Cognitive mapping and other spatial processes* (pp. 46–80). Baltimore: Johns Hopkins Press.

Antell, S. E. G., & Caron, A. J. (1985). Neonatal perception of spatial relationships. *Infant Behavior & Development, 8,* 15–23.

Baenninger, M., & Newcombe, N. (1989). The role of experience in spatial test performance: A meta-analysis. *Sex Roles, 20,* 327–344.

Baenninger, M., & Newcombe, N. (1995). Environmental input to the development of sex-related differences in spatial and mathematical ability. *Learning and Individual Differences, 7,* 363–379.

Baillargeon, R. (1986). Representing the existence and location of hidden objects: Object permanence in 6- and 8-month-old infants. *Cognition, 23,* 21–41.

Baillargeon, R. (1987). Young infants' reasoning about the physical and spatial properties of a hidden object. *Cognitive Development, 2,* 179–200.

Baillargeon, R. (1991). Reasoning about the height and location of a hidden object in 4.5- and 6.5-month-old infants. *Cognition, 38,* 13–42.

Baillargeon, R., & Graber, M. (1987). Where's the rabbit? 5.5-month-old infants' representation of the height of a hidden object. *Cognitive Development, 2,* 375–392.

Baillargeon, R., Spelke, E. S., & Wasserman, S. (1985). Object-permanence in 5-month-old infants. *Cognition, 20,* 191–208.

Barash, J. (1994). Age-related decline in route learning ability. *Developmental Neuropsychology, 10,* 189–201.

Bell, S. (2002). Spatial cognition and scale: A child's perspective. *Journal of Environmental Psychology, 22,* 9–27.

Berenbaum, S. A., & Resnick, S. M. (2007). The seeds of career choices: Prenatal sex hormone effects on psychological sex differences. In S. J. Ceci & W. M. Williams (Eds.), *Why aren't more women in science?* (pp. 147–157). Washington, DC: APA Books.

Berry, J. W. (1966). Emne and Eskimo perceptual skills. *International Journal of Psychology, 1,* 207–229.

Berti, A., & Frassinetti, F. (2000). When far becomes near: Remapping of space by tool use. *Journal of Cognitive Neuroscience, 12,* 415–420.

Biederman, I., & Bar, M. (1999). One-shot viewpoint invariance in matching novel objects. *Vision Research, 39,* 2885–2899.

Biederman, I., & Bar, M. (2000). Differing views on views: Response to Hayward and Tarr (2000). *Vision Research, 40,* 3901–3905.

Biederman, I., & Gerhardstein, P. C. (1995). Viewpoint dependent mechanisms in visual object recognition: Reply to Tarr and Bülthoff (1995). *Journal of Experimental Psychology: Human Perception and Performance, 21,* 1506–1514.

Blades, M., & Cook, Z. (1994). Young children's ability to understand a model as a spatial representation. *Journal of Genetic Psychology, 155,* 201–218.

Blades, M., & Spencer, C. (1994). The development of children's ability to use spatial representations. In H. W. Reese (Ed.), *Advances in child development and behavior* (pp. 157–199). New York: Academic Press.

Bluestein, M., & Acredolo, L. (1979). Developmental changes in map reading skills. *Child Development, 50,* 691–697.

Bogartz, R. S., Shinskey, J. L., & Speaker, C. (1997). Interpreting infant looking: The event set X event set design. *Developmental Psychology, 33,* 408–422.

Brain, W. R. (1941). Visual disorientation with special reference to lesions of the right cerebral hemisphere. *Brain, 64,* 244–272.

Brown, L. N., Lahar, C. J., & Mosley, J. L. (1998). Age and gender-related differences in strategy use for route information. *Environment and Behavior, 30,* 123–143.

Bryant, P. (1974). *Perception and understanding in young children: An experimental approach.* New York: Basic Books.

Bryant, P., & Squire, S. (2003). Children's mathematics: Lost and found in space. In M. Gattis (Ed.), *Spatial schemas and abstract thought* (pp. 175–201), Cambridge, MA: MIT Press.

Bushbaum, M. S., & Henkin, R. I. (1980). Perceptual abnormalities in patients with chromatin negative gonadal dysgenesis and hypogonadotropic hypogonadism. *International Journal of Neuroscience, 11,* 201–209.

Bushnell, E. W., McKenzie, B. E., Lawrence, D. A., & Connell, S. (1995). The spatial coding strategies of one-year-old infants in a locomotor search task. *Child Development, 66,* 937–958.

Caroll, J. (1993). *Human cognitive abilities: A survey of factor-analytical studies.* New York: Cambridge University Press.

Carpenter. P. A., & Just, M. A. (1981). *Spatial ability: An information-processing approach to psychometrics.* Unpublished manuscript, Carnegie-Mellon University, Pittsburgh, PA.

Casey, M. B., Nuttall, R., & Pezaris, E. (1997). Mediators of gender differences in mathematics college entrance test scores: A comparison of spatial skills with internalized beliefs and anxieties. *Developmental Psychology, 33,* 669–680.

Cerella, J., Poon, L. W., & William, D. (1980). Age and the complexity hypothesis. In L. W. Poon (Ed.), *Aging in the 1980s: Psychological issues* (pp. 332–340). Washington, DC: American Psychological Association.

Cheng, K. (1986). A purely geometric module in the rat's spatial representation. *Cognition, 23,* 149–178.

Cheng, K. (1988). Some psychophysics of the pigeon's use of landmarks. *Journal of Comparative Physiology, 162,* 815–826.

Cheng, K. (1989). The vector sum model of pigeon landmark use. *Journal of Experimental Psychology: Animal Behavior and Processes, 15,* 366–375.

Cheng, K., & Gallistel, C. R. (1984). Testing the geometric power of an animal's spatial representation. In H. L. Roitblat, T. G. Bever, & H. S. Terrace (Eds.), *Animal cognition: Proceedings of the Harry Frank Guggenheim Conference* (pp. 409–423). Hillsdale, NJ: Erlbaum.

Cheng, P. C. (2002). Electrifying diagrams for learning: Principles for complex representational systems. *Cognitive Science, 26,* 685–736.

Cherry, K. E., & Park, D. C. (1993). Individual differences and contextual variables influence spatial memory in younger and older adults. *Psychology and Aging, 8,* 517–526.

Clearfield, M. W., & Mix, K. S. (1999). Number versus contour length in infants' discrimination of small visual sets. *Psychological Science, 10,* 408–411.

Clearfield, M. W., & Mix, K. S. (2001). Amount versus number: Infants' use of area and contour length to discriminate small sets. *Journal of Cognition and Development, 2,* 243–260.

Clements, D. H., & Bright, G. (2003). *Learning and teaching measurement: 2003 yearbook.* Reston, VA: National Council of Teachers of Mathematics.

Cohen, L. B., & Younger, B. A. (1984). Infant perception of angular relations. *Infant Behavior & Development, 7,* 37–47.

Committee on Support for Thinking Spatially. (2006). *Learning to think spatially: GIS as a support system in the K-12 curriculum.* Washington, DC: National Academies Press.

Cornell, E. H., Heth, C. D., & Alberts, D. M. (1994). Place recognition and wayfinding by children and adults. *Memory and Cognition, 22,* 633–643.

Cowey, A., Small, M., & Ellis, S. (1994). Left visuo-spatial neglect can be worse in far than in near space. *Neuropsychologia, 32,* 1059–1066.

Crawford, L. E., Huttenlocher, J., & Engebretson, P. H. (2000). Category effects on estimates of stimuli: Perception or reconstruction? *Psychological Science, 11,* 280–395.

Cutting, J. E., & Vishton, P. M. (1995). Perceiving layout and knowing distances. The integration, relative potency, and contextual use of different information about depth. In W. Epstein & S. Rogers (Eds.), *Handbook of perception and cognition* (Vol. 5, pp. 69–117). San Diego, CA: Academic Press.

De Lisi, R., & Wolford, J. L. (2002). Improving children's mental rotation accuracy with computer game playing. *Journal of Genetic Psychology, 163,* 272–282.

DeLoache, J. S. (1989). Young children's understanding of the correspondence between a scale model and a larger space. *Cognitive Development, 4,* 121–139.

DeLoache, J. S. (1995). Early symbol understanding and use. In D. L. Medin (Ed.), *The psychology of learning and motivation: Advances on theory and research* (Vol. 33, pp. 65–114). New York: Academic Press.

Diwadkar, V. A., & McNamara, T. P. (1997). Viewpoint dependence in scene recognition. *Psychological Science, 8,* 302–307.

Dobson, S. H., Kirasic, K. C., & Allen, G. L. (1995). Age-related differences in adults' spatial task performance: Influences of task complexity and perceptual speed. *Aging and Cognition, 2,* 19–38.

Downs, R. M., & Liben, L. S. (1991). The development of expertise in geography: A cognitive-developmental approach to geographic education. *Annals of the Association of American Geographers, 8,* 304–327.

Drake, E. B., Henderson, V. W., Stanczyk, F., McClear, C., Brown, W. S., Smith, C. A., et al. (2000). Associations between circulating sex steroid hormones and cognition in normal elderly women. *Neurology, 54,* 599–602.

Duffy, S., Huttenlocher, J., & Levine, S. (2005). It's all relative: How young children encode extent. *Journal of Cognition and Development, 6,* 51–63.

Ehrlich, S. B., Levine, S., & Goldin-Meadow, S. (2006). The importance of gesture in children's spatial reasoning. *Developmental Psychology, 42,* 1259–1268.

Emsley, J. (2001). *Nature's building blocks.* New York: Oxford University Press.

Ernst, M. O., & Banks, M. S. (2002). Human integrate visual and haptic information in a statistically optimal fashion. *Nature, 415,* 429–433.

Galea, L. A. M., & Kimura, D. (1993). Sex differences in route learning. *Personality and Individual Differences, 14,* 53–65.

Gamberini, L., Seraglia, B., & Priftis, K. (2008). Processing of peripersonal and extrapersonal space using tools: Evidence from visual line bisection in real and virtual environments. *Neuropsychologia, 46,* 1298–1304.

Gilbert, E. W. (1958). Pioneer maps of health and disease in England. *Geographic Journal, 124,* 172–183.

Golledge, R. G. (2002). The nature of geographic knowledge. *Annals of the Associations of American Cartographers, 92,* 1–14.

Gordin, M. (2004). *A well-ordered thing: Dmitri Mendeleev and the shadow of the periodic table.* New York: Basic Books

Goswami, U. (2008). *Cognitive development: The learning brain.* New York: Psychology Press.

Gouchie, C., & Kimura, D. (1991). The relationship between testosterone levels and cognitive ability patterns. *Psychoneuroendocrinology, 16,* 323–334.

Haith, M. M. (1998). Who put the cog in infant cognition? Is rich interpretation too costly? *Infant Behavior & Development, 21,* 167–179.

Hall, E. T. (1966). *The hidden dimension.* Garden City, NY: Doubleday.

Halpern, D. F. (2000). *Sex differences in cognitive abilities.* Hillside, NJ: Erlbaum.

Halpern, D. F., & Collaer, M. L. (2005). Sex differences in visuospatial abilities: More than meets the eye. In P. Shah & A. Miyake (Eds.), *The Cambridge handbook of visuospatial thinking.* New York: Cambridge University Press.

Hampson, E. (1990). Estrogen-related variations in human spatial and articulatory motor skills. *Psychoneuroendocrinology, 15,* 97–11.

Hartley, T., Trinkler, I., & Burgess, N. (2004). Geometric determinants of human spatial memory. *Cognition, 94,* 39–75.

Hayward, W. G., & Tarr, M. J. (1997). Testing conditions for viewpoint invariance in object recognition. *Journal of Experimental Psychology: Human Perception and Performance, 23,* 1511–1521.

Hazen, N. L., Lockman, J. J., & Pick, H. L. (1978). The development of children's representations of large-scale environments. *Child Development, 49,* 623–636.

Hedges, L. V., & Nowell, A. (1995). Sex differences in mental test scores, variability and numbers of high-scoring individuals. *Science, 269,* 41–45.

Hegarty, M., Montello, D. R., Richardson, A. E., Ishikawa, T., & Lovelace, K. (2005). Spatial abilities at different scales: Individual differences in aptitude-test performance and spatial-layout learning. *Intelligence, 34,* 151–176.

Hegarty, M., & Waller, D. (2005). Individual differences in spatial abilities. In P. Shah & A. Miyake (Eds.), *The Cambridge handbook of visuospatial thinking* (pp. 121–169). New York: Cambridge University Press.

Herman, J. F. (1980). Children's cognitive maps of large-scale spaces: Effects of exploration, direction, and repeated experience. *Journal of Experimental Child Psychology, 29,* 126–143.

Herman, J., & Siegel, A. W. (1978). The development of cognitive mapping of the large-scale environment. *Journal of Experimental Child Psychology, 26,* 389–406.

Hermer, L., & Spelke, E. (1994). A geometric process for spatial reorientation in young children. *Nature, 370,* 57–59.

Hermer, L., & Spelke, E. (1996). Modularity and development: A case of spatial reorientation. *Cognition, 61,* 195–232.

Hermer-Vasquez, L., Spelke, E. S., & Katsnelson, A. S. (1999). Sources of flexibility in human cognition: Dual-task studies of space and language. *Cognitive Psychology, 39,* 3–36.

Hertzog, C., & Rypma, B. (1991). Age differences in components of mental-rotation task performance. *Bulletin of the Psychonomic Society, 29,* 209–212.

Hills, J. M., Ernst, M. O., Banks, M. S., & Landy, M. S. (2002). Combining sensory information: Mandatory fusion within, but no between, senses. *Science, 298,* 1627–1630.

Hirtle, S. C., & Jonides, J. (1985). Evidence of hierarchies in cognitive maps. *Memory and Cognition, 13,* 208–217.

Holmes, M. C., & Sholl, M. J. (2005). Allocentric coding of object-to-object relations in overlearned and novel environments. *Journal of Experimental Psychology: Learning, Memory, and Cognition, 31,* 1069–1087.

Hultsch, D. F., Hertzog, C., Small, B. J., & Dixon, R. (1999). Use it or loose it: Engaged lifestyle as a buffer of cognitive decline in aging? *Psychology and Aging, 14,* 245–263.

Hund, A. M., & Plumert, J. M. (2003). Does information about what things are influence children's memory for where things are? *Developmental Psychology, 39,* 939–948.

Hund, A. M., & Plumert, J. M. (2005). The stability and flexibility of spatial categories. *Cognitive Psychology, 50,* 1–44.

Hund, A. M., & Spencer, J. P. (2003). Developmental changes in the relative weighting of geometric and experience-dependent location cues. *Journal of Cognition and Development, 4,* 3–38.

Hupach, A., & Nadel, L. (2005). Reorientation in a rhombic environment: No evidence for an encapsulated geometric module. *Cognitive Development, 20,* 279–302.

Huttenlocher, J., Duffy, S., & Levine, S. (2002). Infants and toddlers discriminate amount: Are they measuring? *Psychological Science, 13,* 244–249.

Huttenlocher, J., Hedges, L. V., & Duncan, S. (1991). Categories and particulars: Prototype effects in estimating spatial location. *Psychological Review, 98,* 352–376.

Huttenlocher, J., & Lourenco, S. F. (2007). Coding location in enclosed spaces: Is geometry the principle? *Developmental Science, 10,* 741–746.

Huttenlocher, J., Newcombe, N., & Sandberg, E. H. (1994). The coding of spatial location in young children. *Cognitive Psychology, 27,* 115–148.

Huttenlocher, J., Newcombe, N., & Vasilyeva, M. (1999). Spatial scaling in young children. *Psychological Science, 10,* 393–398.

Huttenlocher, J., & Vasilyeva, M. (2003). How toddlers represent enclosed spaces. *Cognitive Science, 27,* 749–766.

Janowsky, J. S., Oviat, S. K., & Orwoll, E. S. (1994). Testosterone influences spatial cognition in older men. *Behavioral Neuroscience, 108,* 325–332.

Jenkins, L., Myeron, J., Joerding, J., & Hale, S. (2000). Converging evidence that visuospatial cognition is more age sensitive than verbal cognition. *Psychology and Aging, 15,* 157–175.

Jeong, Y., Levine, S. C., & Huttenlocher, J. (2007). The development of proportional reasoning: Effect of continuous versus discrete quantities. *Journal of Cognition and Development, 8,* 237–256.

Jewell, G., & McCourt, M. E. (2000). Pseudoneglect: A review and meta-analysis of performance factors in line bisection tasks. *Neuropsychologia, 38,* 93–110.

Johnson, W., & Bouchard, T. J. (2005). Constructive replication of the visual–perceptual-image rotation model in Thurstone's (1941) battery of 60 tests of mental ability. *Intelligence, 33,* 417–430.

Johnson, W., & Bouchard, T. J. (2007). Sex differences in mental abilities: g makes the dimensions on which they lie. *Intelligence, 35,* 23–39.

Just, M. A., & Carpenter, P. A. (1985). Cognitive coordinate systems: Accounts of mental rotation and individual differences in spatial ability. *Psychological Review, 92,* 137–171.

Kail, R. (1986). The impact of extended practice on rate of mental rotation. *Journal of Experimental Child Psychology, 42,* 378–391.

Kail, R., & Park, Y. (1990). Impact of practice on speed of mental rotation. *Journal of Experimental Child Psychology, 49,* 227–244.

Kirasic, K. C. (1991). Spatial cognition and behavior in young and elderly adults: Implications for learning new environments. *Psychology and Aging, 6,* 10–18.

Kirasic, K. C. (2000). Age differences in adults' spatial abilities, learning environmental layout, and wayfinding behavior. *Spatial Cognition and Computation, 2,* 117–134.

Kirasic, K. C., Allen, G. L., Dobson, S. H., & Binder, K. S. (1996). Aging, cognitive resources, and declarative learning. *Psychology and Aging, 11,* 658–670.

Kirasic, K. C., & Mathes, E. A. (1990). Effects of different means of conveying environmental information on elderly adults spatial cognition and behavior. *Environment and Behavior, 22,* 591–607.

Knill, D. C., & Saunders, J. A. (2003). Do humans optimally integrate stereo and texture information for judgments of surface slant? *Vision Research, 43,* 2539–2558.

Kosslyn, S. M. (1987). Seeing and imagining in the cerebral hemispheres: A computational approach. *Psychological Review, 94,* 148–175.

Kosslyn, S. M., Anderson, A. K., Hillger, L. A., & Hamilton, S. E. (1994). Hemispheric differences in sizes of receptive fields or attentional biases? *Neuropsychology, 8,* 139–147.

Kozhevnikov, M., & Hegarty, M. (2001). A dissociation between object-manipulation spatial ability and spatial orientation ability. *Memory and Cognition, 29,* 745–756.

Kozhevnikov, M., Motes, M. A., & Hegarty, M. (2007). Spatial visualization in physics problem solving. *Cognitive Science, 31,* 549–579.

Landau, B., & Spelke, E. (1988). Geometric complexity and object search in infancy. *Developmental Psychology, 24,* 512–521.

Learmonth, A. E., Nadel, L., & Newcombe, N. S. (2002). Children's use of landmarks: Implications for modularity theory. *Psychological Science, 13,* 337–341.

Learmonth, A. E., Newcombe, N., & Huttenlocher, J. (2001). Toddlers' use of metric information and landmarks to reorient. *Journal of Experimental Child Psychology, 80,* 225–244.

Lee, S. A., Shusterman, A., & Spelke, E. S. (2006). Reorientation and landmark-guided search by young children: Evidence for two systems. *Psychological Science, 17,* 577–582.

Lehnung, M., Leplow, B., Friege, L., Herzog, A., Ferstl, R., & Mehdorn, M. (1998). Development of spatial memory and spatial orientation in preschoolers and primary school children. *British Journal of Psychology, 89,* 463–480.

Leone, G., Taine, M. C., & Droulez, J. (1993). The influence of long-term practice on mental rotation of 3-D objects. *Cognitive Brain Research, 1,* 241–255.

Leplow, B., Lehnung, M., Pohl, J., Herzog, A., Ferstl, R., & Mehdorn, M. (2003). Navigational place learning in children and young adults as assessed with a standardized locomotor search task. *British Journal of Psychology, 94,* 299–317.

Lerner, R. M. (2006). Developmental science, developmental systems, and contemporary theories of human development. In R. M. Lerner (Ed.), *Handbook of child psychology: Vol. 1. Theoretical models of human development* (6th ed., pp. 1–17). Editors in chief: W. Damon & R. M. Lerner. Hoboken, NJ: John Wiley & Sons.

Lerner, R. M., & Overton. W. F. (2008). Exemplifying the integrations of the relational developmental system: Synthesizing theory, research, and application to promote positive development and social justice. *Journal of Adolescent Research, 23,* 245–255.

Levine, S. C., Huttenlocher, J., Taylor, A., & Langrock, A. (1999). Early sex differences in spatial skill. *Developmental Psychology, 35,* 940–949.

Levine, S. C., Vasilyeva, M., Lourenco, S. F., Newcombe, N. S., & Huttenlocher, J. (2005). Socioeconomic status modifies the sex differences in spatial skill. *Psychological Science, 16,* 841–845.

Liben, L. S. (2000). Map use and the development of spatial cognition: Seeing the bigger picture. *Developmental Science, 3,* 270–274.

Liben, L. S. (2001). Thinking through maps. In M. Gattis (Ed.), *Spatial schemas and abstract thought* (pp. 45–77). Cambridge, MA: MIT Press.

Liben, L. S. (2002). Spatial development in childhood: Where are we now? In U. Goswami (Ed.), *Blackwell handbook of childhood cognitive development* (pp. 326–348). Malden, MA: Blackwell Publishing.

Liben, L. S., & Downs, R. (1989). Understanding maps as symbols. In H. W. Reese (Ed.), *Advances in child development and behavior* (pp. 145–201). New York: Academic Press.

Liben, L. S., & Downs, R. M. (1993). Understanding person-space-map relations: Cartographic and developmental perspectives. *Developmental Psychology, 29,* 739–752.

Liben, L. S., & Myers, L. J. (2007). Developmental changes in children's understanding of maps: What, when and how? In J. M. Plumert & J. P. Spencer (Eds.), *The emerging spatial mind.* New York: Oxford University Press.

Liben, L. S., Susman, E. J., Finkelstein, J. W., Chinchilli, V. M., Kunselman, S., Schwab, J., et al. (2002). The effects of sex steroid on spatial performance: A review and an experimental clinical investigation. *Developmental Psychology, 38,* 236–253.

Liben, L. S., & Yekel, C. (1996). Preschoolers' understanding of plan and oblique maps: The role of geometric and representational correspondence. *Child Development, 67,* 2780– 2796.

Linn, M. C., & Petersen, A. C. (1985). Emergence and characterization of sex differences in spatial ability: A meta-analysis. *Child Development, 56,* 1479–1498.

Lizarraga, M. L, & Ganuza, J. M. (2003). Improvement of mental rotation in girls and boys. *Sex Roles, 49,* 277–286.

Longo, M. R., & Lourenco, S. F. (2006). On the nature of near space: Effects of tool use and the transition to far space. *Neuropsychologia, 44,* 977–981.

Longo, M. R., & Lourenco, S. F. (2007). Space perception and body morphology: Extent of near space scales with arm length. *Experimental Brain Research, 177,* 285–290.

Loewenstein, J., & Gentner, D. (2001). Spatial mapping in preschoolers: Close comparisons facilitate far mappings. *Journal of Cognition and Development, 2,* 189–219.

Loewenstein, J., & Gentner, D. (2005). Relational language and the development of relational mapping. *Cognitive Psychology, 50,* 315–353.

Loring-Meier, S., & Halpern, D. F. (1999). Sex differences in visuo-spatial working memory: Components of cognitive processing. *Psychonomic Bulletin & Review, 6,* 464–471.

Lourenco, S. F., & Huttenlocher, J. (2006). How do young children determine location? Evidence from disorientation tasks. *Cognition, 100,* 511–529.

Lourenco, S. F., & Huttenlocher, J. (2008). The representation of geometric cues in infancy. *Infancy, 13,* 103–127.

Lourenco, S. F., Huttenlocher, J., & Vasilyeva, M. (2005). Toddlers' representations of space: The role of viewer perspective. *Psychological Science, 16,* 255–259.

Mann, V. A., Sasanuma, S., Sakuma, N., & Masaki, S. (1990). Sex differences in cognitive abilities: A cross-cultural perspective. *Neuropsychologia, 28,* 1063–1077.

Marzolf, D. P., DeLoache, J. S., & Kolstad, V. (1999). The role of relational similarity in young children's use of a scale model. *Developmental Science, 2,* 296–305.

Masters, M. S., & Sanders, B. (1993). Is the gender difference in mental rotations disappearing? *Behavior Genetics, 23,* 337–341.

Mayr, U., & Kliegl, R. (1993). Sequential and coordinative complexity: Age-based processing limitations in figural transformations. *Journal of Experimental Psychology: Learning, Memory, and Cognition, 19,* 1297–1320.

McGee, M. G. (1979). Human spatial abilities: Psychometric studies and environmental, genetic, hormonal, and neurological influences. *Psychological Bulletin, 86,* 899–918.

McNamara, T. P., & Diwadkar, V. A. (1997). Symmetry and asymmetry in human spatial memory. *Cognitive Psychology, 34,* 160–190.

McNamara, T. P., Rump, B., & Werner, S. (2003). Egocentric and geocentric frames of reference in memory of large-scale space. *Psychonomic Bulletin & Review, 10,* 589–595.

McNamara, T. P., & Valiquette, C. M. (2004). Remembering where things are. In G. L. Allen (Ed.), *Human spatial memory* (pp. 3–24). Mahwah, NJ: Erlbaum.

Miller, K. (1989). Measurement as a tool for thought: The role of measuring procedures in children's understanding of quantitative invariance. *Developmental Psychology, 25,* 589–600.

Miyake, A., Rettinger, D. A., Friedman, N. P., Shah, P., & Hegarty, M. (2001). Visuospatial working memory, executive functioning and spatial abilities. How are they related? *Journal of Experimental Psychology: General, 130,* 621–640.

Moffat, S. D., & Hampson, E. (1996). A curvilinear relationship between testosterone and spatial cognition in humans: Possible influence of hand preference. *Psychoneuroendocrinology, 21,* 323–337.

Moffat, S. D., & Resnick, S. M. (2002). Effects of age on virtual environment place navigation and allocentric cognitive mapping. *Behavioral Neuroscience, 116,* 851–859.

Montello, D. R. (1993). Scale and multiple psychologies of space. In A. U. Frank & I. Campari (Eds.), *Spatial information theory: A theoretical basis for GIS. Proceedings of COSIT '93. Lecture notes in Computer Science* (Vol. 716, pp. 312–321). Berlin: Springer-Verlag.

Montello, D. R., Lovelace, K. L., Golledge, R. G., & Self, C. M. (1999). Sex-related differences and similarities in geographic and environmental spatial abilities. *Annals of the Association of America Geographers, 89,* 515–534.

Moore, D. S., & Johnson, S. P. (2008). Mental rotation in human infants: A sex difference. *Psychological Science, 19,* 1063–1066.

Newcombe, N. (1989). Development of spatial perspective taking. In H. W. Reese (Ed.), *Advances in child development and behavior* (pp. 203–247). New York: Academic Press.

Newcombe, N., Bandura, M., & Taylor, D. G. (1983). Sex differences in spatial ability and spatial activities. *Sex Roles, 9,* 377–386.

Newcombe, N., & Huttenlocher, J. (2006). Development of spatial cognition. In D. Kuhn, R. S. Siegler, W. Damon, & R. Lerner (Eds.), *Handbook of child psychology* (Vol. 2, pp. 734–776). Hoboken, NJ: John Wiley & Sons.

Newcombe, N., Huttenlocher, J., Drummey, A. B., & Wiley, J. G. (1998). The development of spatial location coding: Place learning and dead reckoning in the second and third years. *Cognitive Development, 13,* 185–200.

Newcombe, N. S. (2002). The nativist-empiricist controversy in the context of recent research on spatial and quantitative development. *Psychological Science, 13,* 395–401.

Newcombe, N. S., & Huttenlocher, J. (2000). Making space: The development of spatial representation and reasoning. *Learning, development, and conceptual change.* Cambridge, MA: MIT Press.

Newcombe, N. S., Huttenlocher, J., & Learmonth, A. (1999). Infants' coding of location in continuous space. *Infant Behavior & Development, 22,* 483–510.

Newcombe, N. S., Sluzenski, J., & Huttenlocher, J. (2005). Preexisting knowledge versus on-line learning: What do young infants really know about spatial location? *Psychological Science, 16,* 222–227.

Newson, R. S., & Kemps, E. B. (2006). The influence of physical and cognitive activities on simple and complex cognitive tasks in older adults. *Experimental Aging Research, 32,* 341–362.

O'Keefe, J. (1991). The hippocampal cognitive map and navigational strategies. In J. Paillard (Ed.), *Brain and space* (pp. 273–295). New York: Oxford University Press.

Overman, W. H., Pate, B. J., Moore, K., & Peuster, A. (1996). Ontogeny of place learning in children as measured in the Radial Arm Maze, Morris Search Task, and Open Field Task. *Behavioral Neuroscience, 110,* 1205–1228.

Overton, W. F. (2006). Developmental psychology: Philosophy, concepts, methodology. In R. M. Lerner (Ed.), *Handbook of child psychology: Vol. 1. Theoretical models of human development* (6th ed., pp. 18–88). Editors in chief: W. Damon & R. M. Lerner. Hoboken, NJ: John Wiley & Sons.

Overton, W. F., Mueller, U., & Newman, J. L. (Eds.). (2007). *Developmental perspective on embodiment and consciousness.* Hillsdale, NJ: Erlbaum.

Pazzaglia, F., & De Beni, R. (2001). Strategies of processing spatial information in survey and landmark-centred individuals. *European Journal of Cognitive Psychology, 13,* 493–508.

Pazzaglia, F., & De Beni, R. (2006). Are people with high and low mental rotation abilities differently susceptible to the alignment effect? *Perception, 35,* 369–383.

Pellegrino, J. W., & Kail, R. V. (1982). Process analysis of spatial aptitude. In R. J. Sternberg (Ed.), *Advances in the psychology of human intelligence* (pp. 311–365). Hillsdale, NJ: Erlbaum.

Perner, J. (1991). *Understanding the representational mind.* Cambridge, MA: Bradford Books/MIT Press.

Piaget, J., & Inhelder, B. (1967). *The child's conception of space.* New York: Norton. (Original work published 1948)

Piaget, J., Inhelder, B., & Szeminska, B. (1960). *The child's conception of geometry.* New York: Basic Books.

Pick, H. L. (1993). Organization of spatial knowledge in children. In N. Eilan, R. A. McCarthy, & B. Brewer (Eds.), *Spatial representations: Problems in philosophy and psychology* (pp. 31–42). Oxford: Blackwell.

Plassman, B. L., Welsh, K. A., Helms, M., Brandt, J., Page, W. F., & Breitner, J. C. S. (1995). Intelligence and education as predictor of cognitive state in late life: A 50-year follow-up. *Neurology, 45,* 1446–1450.

Plumert, J. M., & Hund, A. M. (2001). The development of memory for location: What role do spatial prototypes play? *Child Development, 72,* 370–384.

Presson, C. C., DeLange, N., & Hazelrigg, M. D. (1989). Orientation specificity in spatial memory: What makes a path different from a map of the path? *Journal of Experimental Psychology: Learning, Memory, and Cognition, 15,* 887–897.

Presson, C. C., & Hazelrigg, M. D. (1984) Building spatial representation through primary and secondary learning. *Journal of Experimental Psychology: Learning, Memory, and Cognition, 10,* 716–722.

Quaiser-Pohl, C., Lehmann, W., & Eid, M. (2004). The relationship between spatial abilities and representations of large-scale space in children—a structural equation modeling analysis. *Personality and Individual Differences, 36,* 95–107.

Quinn, P. C. (1994). The categorization of above and below spatial relations by young infants. *Child Development, 65,* 58–69.

Quinn, P. C., Adams, A., Kennedy, E., Shettler, L., & Wasnik, A. (2003). Development of an abstract category representation for the spatial relation *between* in 6- to 10-month-old infants. *Developmental Psychology, 39,* 151–163.

Quinn, P. C., Cummins, M., Kase, J., Martin, E., & Weissman, S. (1996). Development of categorical representations for above and below spatial relations in 3- to 7-month-old infants. *Developmental Psychology, 32,* 642–650.

Quinn, P. C., & Liben, L. S. (2008). A sex difference in mental rotation in young infants. *Psychological Science, 19,* 1067–1070.

Quinn, P. C., Norris, C. M., Pasko, R., Schmader, T. M., & Mash, C. (1999). Formation of categorical representation for the spatial relation between by 6- to 7-month-old infants. *Visual Cognition, 6,* 569–585.

Resnick, S. M., Berenbaum, S. A., Gottesman, I. I., Bouchard, T. J. (1986). Early hormonal influences on cognitive functioning in congenital adrenal hyperplasia. *Developmental Psychology, 22,* 191–198.

Rieser, J. J., & Heiman, M. L. (1982). Spatial self-reference systems and shortest-route behavior in toddlers. *Child Development, 53,* 524–533.

Rieser, J. J., & Rider, E. A. (1991). Young children's spatial orientation with respect to multiple targets when walking without vision. *Developmental Psychology, 27,* 97–107.

Rizzolatti, G., Matelli, M., & Pavesi, G. (1983). Deficits in attention and movement following the removal of postarcuate (area 6) and prearcuate (area 8) cortex in macaque monkeys. *Brain, 106,* 655–673.

Sadalla, E. K., Burroughs, W. J., & Staplin, L. J. (1980). Reference points in spatial cognition. *Journal of Experimental Psychology: Human Learning and Memory, 6,* 516–528.

Salthouse, T. A. (1992). Why do adult age differences increase with task complexity? *Developmental Psychology, 28,* 905–918.

Salthouse, T. A. (1993). Speed mediation of adult age differences in cognition. *Developmental Psychology, 29,* 722–738.

Salthouse, T. A. (2005). Effects of aging on reasoning. In K. J. Holyoak & R. G. Morrison (Eds.), *The Cambridge handbook of thinking and reasoning* (pp. 589–605). New York: Cambridge University Press.

Salthouse, T. A. (2009). When does age-related cognitive decline begin? *Neurobiology of Aging, 30,* 507–514.

Salthouse, T. A., Atkinson, T. M., & Berish, D. E. (2003). Executive functioning as a potential mediator of age-related cognitive decline in normal adults. *Journal of Experimental Psychology: General, 132,* 566–594.

Salthouse, T. A., Babcock, R. L., & Shaw, R. L. (1991). Effects of adult age pm structural and operational capacities in working memory. *Psychology and Aging, 6,* 118–127.

Salthouse, T. A., & Siedlecki, K. L. (2006). Efficiency of route selection as a function of adult age. *Brain and Cognition, 63,* 279–286.

Sandberg, E. H., Huttenlocher, J., & Newcombe, N. (1996). The development of hierarchical representation of two-dimensional space. *Child Development, 67,* 721–739.

Schaie, K. W. (2005). *Developmental influences on adult intelligence: The Seattle Longitudinal Study.* New York: Oxford University Press.

Schaie, K. W. (2009). When does age-related cognitive decline begin? Salthouse again reifies the "cross-sectional fallacy." *Neurobiology, 30,* 528–529.

Serbin, L. A., & Sprafkin, C. (1986). The salience of gender and the process of sex typing in middle childhood. *Child Development, 57,* 1188–1199.

Shah, P., & Miyake, A. (1996). The separability of working memory resources for spatial thinking and language processing: An individual differences approach. *Journal of Experimental Psychology: General, 125,* 4–27.

Shea, D. L., Lubinski, D., & Benbow, C. P. (2001). Importance of assessing spatial ability in intellectually talented adolescents: A 20-year longitudinal study. *Journal of Educational Psychology, 93,* 604–614.

Shelton, A. L., & Gabrieli, J. D. E. (2004). Neural correlates of individual differences in spatial learning strategies. *Neuropsychology, 18,* 442–449.

Shelton, A. L., & McNamara, T. P. (1997). Multiple views of spatial memory. *Phychonomic Bulletin & Review, 4,* 102–106.

Sholl, M. J., & Bartels, G. P. (2002). The role of self-to-object updating in orientation-free performance on spatial-memory tasks. *Journal of Experimental Psychology: Learning, Memory, and Cognition, 28,* 422–436.

Sholl, M. J., & Nolin, T. L. (1997). Orientation specificity in representations of place. *Journal of Experimental Psychology: Learning, Memory, and Cognition, 23,* 1494–1507.

Siegel, A. W. (1981). The externalization of cognitive maps by children and adults: In search of ways to ask better questions. In L. S. Liben, A. H. Petersen, & N. Newcombe (Eds.), *Spatial representation and behavior across the life span* (pp. 167–194). New York: Academic Press.

Siegel, A. W., & White, S. H. (1975). The development of spatial representations of large-scale spatial environments. In H. W. Reese (Ed.), *Advances in child development and behavior* (pp. 9–55). New York: Academic Press.

Sims, V. K., & Mayer, R. E. (2002). Domain specificity of spatial expertise: The case of video game players. *Applied Cognitive Psychology, 16,* 97–115.

Singer-Freeman, K. E., & Goswami, U. (2001). Does half a pizza equal half a box of chocolates? Proportional matching in an analogy task. *Cognitive Development, 16,* 811–829.

Slater, A., Mattock, A., Brown, E., & Bremner, J. G. (1991). Form perception at birth: Cohen and Younger (1984) revisited. *Journal of Experimental Child Psychology, 51,* 395–406.

Sophian, C. (2000). Perceptions of proportionality in young children: Matching spatial ratios. *Cognition, 75,* 145–170.

Spelke, E. S., & Newport, E. L. (1998). Nativism, empiricism, and the growth of knowledge. In R. M. Lerner (Ed.), *Handbook of child psychology* (pp. 275–340). New York: John Wiley & Sons.

Spinillo, A., & Bryant, P. (1991). Children's proportional judgments: The importance of "half." *Child Development, 62,* 427–440.

Stevens, A., & Coupe, P. (1978). Distortions in judged spatial relations. *Cognitive Psychology, 10,* 422–437.

Tarr, M. J., & Bülthoff, H. H. (1998). Image-based object recognition in man, monkey and machine. *Cognition, 67,* 1–20.

Tarr, M. J., Williams, P., Hayward, W. G., & Gauthier, I. (1998). Three-dimensional object recognition is viewpoint dependent. *Nature Neuroscience, 1,* 275–277.

Terlecki, M. S., Newcombe, N. S., & Little, M. (2008). Durable and generalized effects of spatial experience on mental rotation: Gender differences in growth patterns. *Applied Cognitive Psychology, 22,* 996–1013.

Thurstone, L. L. (1950). *Some primary abilities in visual thinking.* Chicago: University of Chicago, Psychometric Laboratory.

Tranter, L. J., & Koutstaal, W. (2008). Age and flexible thinking: An experimental demonstration of the beneficial effects of increased cognitively stimulating activity on fluid intelligence in healthy older adults. *Aging, Neuropsychology, and Cognition, 15,* 184–207.

Tversky, B. (1981). Distortions in memory for maps. *Cognitive Psychology, 13,* 407–433.

Tversky, B. (2005). Visuospatial reasoning. In K. J. Holyoak & R. G. Morrison (Eds.), *The Cambridge handbook of thinking and reasoning* (pp. 209–242). New York: Cambridge University Press.

Tyler, D., & McKenzie, B. E. (1990). Spatial updating and training effects in the first year of human infancy. *Journal of Experimental Child Psychology, 50,* 445–461.

Uttal, D. H. (1996). Angles and distances: Children's and adults' reconstruction and scaling of spatial configurations. *Child Development, 67,* 2763–2779.

Uttal, D. H. (2000). Seeing the big picture: Map use and the development of spatial cognition. *Developmental Science, 3,* 247–286.

Uttal, D. H., Gregg, V. H., Tan, L. S., Chamberlin, M. H., & Sines, A. (2001). Connecting the dots: Children's use of a systematic figure to facilitate mapping and search. *Developmental Psychology, 37,* 338–350.

Vasilyeva, M., & Bowers, E. (2006). Children's use of geometric information in mapping tasks. *Journal of Experimental Child Psychology, 95,* 255–277.

Vasilyeva, M., Duffy, S., & Huttenlocher, J. (2007). Developmental changes in the use of absolute and relative information: The case of spatial extent. *Journal of Cognition and Development, 8,* 455–471.

Vasilyeva, M., & Huttenlocher, J. (2004). Early development of scaling ability. *Developmental Psychology, 40,* 682–690.

Vasta, R., & Liben, L. S. (1996). The water-level task: An intriguing puzzle. *Current Directions in Psychological Science, 5,* 171–177.

Voyer, D., Nolan, C., & Voyer, S. (2000). The relation between experience and spatial performance in men and women. *Sex Roles, 43,* 891–915.

Walsh, D. A., Krauss, I. K., & Regnier, V. A. (1981). Spatial ability, environmental knowledge, and environmental use: The elderly. In L. S. Liben, A. Patterson, & N. Newcombe (Eds.), *Spatial representation and behavior across the life span* (pp. 321–357). New York: Academic Press.

Ward, S. L., Newcombe, N., & Overton, W. F. (1986). Turn left at the church or three miles north: A study of direction giving and sex differences. *Environment and Behavior, 18,* 192–213.

Warren, W. H. (1984). Perceiving affordances: Visual guidance of stair climbing. *Journal of Experimental Psychology: Human Perception Performance, 10,* 683–703.

Watson, J. D., & Crick, F. H. C. (1953). Molecular structure of nucleic acids. *Nature, 171,* 737–738.

Wilkniss, S. M., Jones, M. G., Korol, D. L., Gold, P. E., & Manning, C. A. (1997). Age-related differences in an ecologically based study of route learning. *Psychology and Aging, 12,* 372–375.

Williams, C. L., Barnett, A. M., & Meck, W. H. (1990). Organizational effects of early gonadal secretions on sexual differentiation in spatial memory. *Behavioral Neuroscience, 104,* 84–97.

Wilson, R. S., Barnes, L. L., & Bennett, D. A. (2003). Assessment of life participation in cognitively stimulating activities. *Journal of Child and Experimental Neuropsychology, 25,* 634–642.

Wolf, O. T., Preut, R., Hellhammer, D. H., Kudielka, B. M., Schürmeyer, T. H., & Kirschbaum, C. (2000). Testosterone and cognition in elderly men: A single testosterone injection blocks the practice effects in verbal fluency, but has no effect on spatial or verbal memory. *Biological Psychiatry, 47,* 650–654.

Wright, R., Thompson, W. L., Ganis, G., Newcombe, N. S., & Kosslyn, S. M. (2008). Training generalized spatial skills. *Psychonomic Bulletin & Review, 15,* 763–771.

Zacks, J. M., Mires, J., Tversky, B., & Hazeltine, E. (2000). Mental spatial transformations of objects and perspectives. *Spatial Cognition and Computation, 2,* 315–332.

CHAPTER 21

Gesturing across the Life Span

SUSAN GOLDIN-MEADOW and JANA M. IVERSON

SITUATING GESTURE IN RELATION TO NONVERBAL BEHAVIOR AND SIGN LANGUAGE

People move their hands when they talk—they gesture—and they do so at every stage of the life span. Some people gesture more than others, but everyone gestures. The question is why? Everyone's first guess is that gesture is nothing more than hand waving, something that we do when we are nervous or excited, but that has no purpose. But this guess turns out to be wrong. Gesturing plays an important role in how we communicate and also we think. This chapter explores both roles.

Gesture has been an object of attention for at least 2,000 years, across domains as diverse as philosophy, rhetoric, theater, divinity, and language. It came into modern-day focus, this time in the semiotic world, as one of five

nonverbal behaviors catalogued by Ekman and Friesen in 1969. The five behaviors are distinguished along a number of dimensions, the most important of which for our purposes is the behavior's connection to speech. Four of the nonverbal behaviors can be produced with speech, but need not be. The fifth—gesture—is tied to speech.

The first nonverbal behavior listed by Ekman and Friesen (1969) is the *affect display,* whose primary site is the face. Affect displays convey emotions whether or not the person is talking. The second nonverbal behavior is the *regulator,* which typically involves head movements or slight changes in body position. Regulators maintain the give-and-take between individuals when talking, but also when not talking. The third nonverbal behavior, the *adaptor,* is a fragment or reduction of a previously learned adaptive hand movement maintained by habit (e.g., pushing one's glasses up when the glasses are already perfectly positioned). Adaptors are performed with little awareness and no intent to communicate. They can be used at any time. The fourth behavior, the *emblem*, is what typically comes to mind when people say they are talking about gesture. Emblems have conventional forms and meanings, and therefore vary across cultures. For example, the *thumbs-up*, the *okay*, and the *shush* gestures are all immediately recognizable in American culture. We are always aware of having produced an emblem, and we use them to communicate, often to control someone else's behavior. But emblems need not be produced with speech. Indeed, one of their defining features is that they are interpretable on their own without speech.

The last category, called *illustrators*, in Ekman and Friesen's (1969) classification scheme, is, by definition, tied to speech and often illustrates the speech it accompanies. For example, a child says that one container is taller than another and illustrates the point by indicating with her hand first the height of one container and then the height of the other. This chapter focuses on illustrators, called *gesticulation* by Kendon (1980) and plain old *gesture* by McNeill (1992), the term we will use. Gestures can mark the tempo of speech (beat gestures), point out referents of speech (deictic gestures), or exploit imagery to elaborate the contents of speech (iconic or metaphoric gestures). In every case, gesture has some relation to the speech it accompanies (although, as we will see, the relation need not be a redundant one). Gesture is not only tied to speech semantically but also temporally. Gesture and speech are integrated into a single system serving the functions of communication (Goldin-Meadow, 2003; McNeill, 1992).

Although gestures share the burden of communication with the speech they accompany, they are different from speech. They convey meaning but do so only in conjunction with the words that frame them. They do not need to, and indeed cannot, stand on their own. As a result, there is no need for the form of a gesture to be standardized, and it is, unlike speech, created on the fly to capture the meaning of the moment.

Gesture is also very different from sign languages of the deaf, despite the fact that both are produced in the manual modality. Sign languages are autonomous systems that are not based on the spoken languages of the hearing cultures that surround them (Bellugi & Studdert-Kennedy, 1980; Klima & Bellugi, 1979; Lane & Grosjean, 1980). The structure of American Sign Language, for example, is distinct from the structure of English. Indeed, the structure of *American* Sign Language is distinct from the structure of *British* Sign Language, a comparison that dramatically

underscores the point that sign languages are not derivative from spoken languages. Nevertheless, sign languages are structurally similar to spoken languages and, as such, different from gesture.

For example, lexical items in a sign language, like all languages, have a right and a wrong form. The sign for "candy" in American Sign Language is made by rotating the tip of the index finger on the cheek. A signer cannot arbitrarily choose to, say, rotate the knuckle of her index finger on her cheek to mean "candy." In fact, if she does use her knuckle, she produces the sign for "apple." If she uses her middle finger instead of her index finger, she produces no sign at all. It is easy to produce a sign incorrectly, but it is not even clear what it means to talk about producing a gesture incorrectly. For example, three speakers described Sylvester the cat's ascent up a drainpipe and used different gestures along with their verbal descriptions. The first flicked a flat palm upward to denote the ascent. The second wiggled the two fingers of a V hand shape as he moved his hand upward. The third produced a basket-like hand shape and moved it upward (McNeill, 1992, pp. 125–126). Each of the three speakers used a different hand shape (palm, V, basket-like shape)—clearly, there is more than one way to represent a cat in gesture.

The fact that gesture plays a role in communication but is not itself codified is precisely why it is of interest to us. Gesture is free to take on forms and meanings that are not dictated by a shared linguistic code. It, therefore, has the potential to tell us about thoughts that do not fit neatly into categories established by our language (Goldin-Meadow & McNeill, 1999). This chapter begins by providing evidence that gesture takes advantage of this potential, often conveying information that is not found in a speaker's words.

We then explore the role of gesture in communication over the life span. If the information conveyed in gesture is accessible to listeners, even those not trained in gesture coding, then gesture adds a second track to every conversation. There is now compelling evidence that this second track has a substantial effect on what speakers and listeners get out of the conversation.

We also explore the role of gesture in cognition over the life span. Gesture conveys information that is not found in speech and, in this sense, reflects a speaker's unspoken thoughts. But evidence is mounting that gesture does more than reflect thought. It can play a role in changing thought and, thus, is a factor in learning.

Our next step is to explore the role of gesture in communication and cognition early in the life span when children are first learning language, and later in the life span when older adults may be losing some of their linguistic skills (e.g., the ability to hear or to deal with complex sentential structures). The question is whether gesture does the same kind of work with respect to communication and cognition throughout the life span.

Finally, we explore what gesture can tell us about developmental disorders and disorders of adulthood. Because gesture is a good index of what a speaker knows, it can also be used to index what a speaker does not know. It, therefore, has the potential to serve as a diagnostic tool in identifying children who are, and who are not, on the road to developmental delay or disability, and perhaps in identifying skills that are spared in adults who have become disabled. Moreover, because gesture can change what we know, it has the potential to serve as an effective tool for intervention for child and adult alike. We end by considering whether gesture plays the same role throughout the life span.

GESTURE IS A WINDOW TO THE MIND

The folk view of nonverbal behavior, including gesture, is that it expresses our emotions and attitudes, and perhaps our personality (see Argyle, 1975). For example, we instinctively believe that gesture marks a speaker as a liar, but it does not give away the content of his lies. The folk view is correct, but only in part. A speaker's hand gestures can, indeed, identify him as a liar (Ekman, Friesen, & Ellsworth, 1972, p. 367). But gesture can also give away the content of the speaker's lies and, of course, his truths. As an example of a truth, a speaker says "I ran all the way upstairs" while spiraling his hand upward. The speaker has conveyed through his gesture, and only through his gesture, that the staircase he mounted was a spiral. Perhaps if his spiral movement were produced slowly and with little enthusiasm, it would also convey the speaker's attitude toward his climb. But at the least, the gesture provides specific information that goes beyond feelings and attitudes.

Gesture Conveys Substantive Information

The gestures that speakers produce together with their talk are symbolic acts that convey meaning. It is easy to overlook the symbolic nature of gesture simply because its encoding is iconic. A gesture looks like what it represents—for example, a shoe-tying motion in the air resembles the action used to tie a shoe—but the gesture is no more the actual act of tying than is the word *tie*.

Because gesture can convey substantive information, it can provide insight into a speaker's mental representation (Kendon, 1980; McNeill, 1992). For example, a speaker in one of McNeill's (1992, p. 12) studies says "and he bends it way back" while his hand appears to grip something and pull it from a space high in front of him back and down to his shoulder. The speaker is describing a scene from a comic book in which a character bends a tree back to the ground. The gesture reveals the particular point of view that the speaker takes to the event—he is gripping the tree as though he were the tree-bender, making it clear by his actions that the tree was anchored on the ground. He could, alternatively, have represented the action from the point of view of the tree, producing the same motion without the grip and perhaps in a different space (one that was not tied to his shoulder), a movement that would have conveyed the tree's trajectory but not the actions done on it.

As an example from a more abstract domain, consider a speaker gesturing about a moral dilemma (Church, Schonert-Reichl, Goodman, Kelly, & Ayman-Nolley, 1995). An adult is asked to judge whether a father has a right to ask his son to give up the money he earned to go camping so that the father can go fishing (Kohlberg, 1969). The adult gives a relatively abstract explanation of his beliefs in speech: "I think about opportunities like this where you have two interests that compete with one another. This is the point where people develop the skills of negotiation." At the same time, he conveys an equally abstract set of ideas in gesture: The speaker holds both hands out in front 6 to 8 inches apart, with the thumb and index finger of each hand resembling an equal sign (illustrating two sets of interests). He then brings his hands in toward one another and holds them in the air (highlighting the fact that the two set of interests are not aligned). Finally, he pivots both wrists in an alternating manner so that while one is forward, the other is back (illustrating how the interests can be brought together in a process of negotiation). This gesture, like the speech that accompanies it, conveys the notion that there are two equal points of view coming into a dynamic interaction with one another.

School-aged children also use hand gestures as they speak (Jancovic, Devoe, & Wiener, 1975), gesturing when asked to narrate a story (e.g., McNeill, 1992) or when asked to explain their responses to a problem (e.g., Church & Goldin-Meadow, 1986). The gestures children produce in a problem-solving situation provide insight into the way they represent those problems. For example, Evans and Rubin (1979) taught children to play a simple board game and then asked them to explain the game to an adult. The children's verbal statements of the rules were routinely accompanied by gestures that conveyed information about their knowledge of the game. As a second example, Crowder and Newman (1993) found that gestures were a frequent mode of communication in a science lesson on the seasons. A child discussing the seasons used both hands to produce a symmetrical gesture, laying down temperature bands on either side of the equator, and thus revealing, through her hands, knowledge of the symmetry of the hemispheres.

Gesture and Speech Form an Integrated System

Gesture not only conveys meaning, it does so in a manner that is integrated with speech. Several types of evidence lend support to the view that gesture and speech form a single, unified system. First, gestures routinely occur with speech. Although emblems may be delivered in utter silence, the spontaneous gestures that speakers generate are almost always produced when the speaker is actually talking. McNeill (1992) found that 90% of gestures were produced during talk. Thus, acts of speaking and gesturing are bound to each other.

Second, gestures and speech are semantically and pragmatically coexpressive. Each type of gesture has a characteristic type of speech with which it occurs (McNeill, 1992). For example, iconic gestures accompany utterances that depict concrete objects and events, and fulfill a narrative function—they accompany the speech that "tells the story." The bend-back gesture described earlier is a concrete description of an event in the story and is a good example of an iconic gesture. In contrast, metaphoric gestures often accompany utterances that refer to the structure of the discourse rather than to a particular event in the narrative. For example, when announcing that what he had just seen and was about to recount was a cartoon, a speaker produced the following metaphoric gesture (McNeill, 1992, p. 14): The speaker raised his hands as though he were offering an object to the listener while saying, "It was a Sylvester and Tweety cartoon," an utterance that sets up and introduces the topic of discussion rather than forming part of the story line.

Finally, gesture and speech are temporally synchronous, and thus form a unified system in this sense. The gesture and the linguistic segment representing the same information as that gesture are cotemporal. Specifically, the gesture movement—the *stroke*—lines up in time with the equivalent linguistic segment. For example, in the bending-back gesture, the speaker produced the stroke of the gesture just as he said, "bends it way back" (see Kita, 1993, for more subtle examples of how speech and gesture adjust to each other in timing, and Nobe, 2000). Typically, gesture precedes the word with which it is coexpressive, and the amount of time between the onset of the gesture and the onset of the word is systematic—the timing gap between word and gesture is larger for unfamiliar words than for familiar words (Morrel-Samuels & Krauss, 1992). The systematicity of the relation suggests that gesture and speech are part of a single production process. Indeed, gesture and speech are systematically related in time even when the speech production process goes awry. For example, gesture production is halted during bouts of stuttering (Mayberry & Jaques, 2000). Synchrony of this sort underscores once again that gesture and speech form a single integrated system.

Gesture and Speech Represent Information Differently

As mentioned earlier, speech conforms to a codified, recognizable system. Gesture does not. We are forced to package our thoughts using the words and structures that our language offers us, whereas gesture gives us a measure of flexibility. For example, it is difficult to adequately describe the coastline of the eastern seaboard of the United States using words alone (Huttenlocher, 1973, 1976). A gesture, unencumbered by the standards of form that language imposes, and able to take advantage of visual imagery, can convey the shape of the coastline far better than even a large number of words.

For the most part, gesture conveys information through imagery. A fist moves in a winding motion, conveying the action performed on the wind-up crank of an old car (Beattie & Shovelton, 1999). A loose palm traces an arc in the air, conveying the trajectory of a cat's flight on a rope into a wall (Ozyurek & Kita, 1999). A pointing finger moves back and forth between two rows of checkers, pairing the checkers and thus conveying the one-to-one correspondence between the checkers in the two rows (Church & Goldin-Meadow, 1986). In each case, the hand in motion makes use of visual imagery to convey meaning.

One feature of visual imagery is that it can present simultaneously information that must be presented sequentially in speech. For example, when commenting on a spider that he sees on the kitchen counter, a speaker says, "There's a spider running across the counter," while moving his hand, all five fingers wiggling, over the counter. The gesture presents, in a single motion, information about the spider (it has many legs, as indicated by all five fingers moving), the manner of motion (running, as indicated by the wiggling fingers), the path (across, as indicated by the path of the hand), and location (the counter, as indicated by the place where the gesture is produced).

In contrast, the scene must be broken up into parts when it is conveyed in speech. The effect is to present what had been a single instantaneous picture in the form of a string of segments: the spider, the running, the direction, the location. These segments are organized into a hierarchically structured string of words. Speech then has the effect of segmenting and linearizing meaning. Segmentation and linearization are essential characteristics of all linguistic systems (including sign languages), but not of gesture (Goldin-Meadow, McNeill, & Singleton, 1996).

Thus, gesture conveys meaning globally, relying on visual and mimetic imagery. Speech conveys meaning discretely, relying on codified words and grammatical devices.

Gesture Can Convey Information Not Found in Speech

Because gesture and speech use such different forms of representation, it is difficult for the two modalities to contribute identical information to a message. Indeed, even deictic pointing gestures are not completely redundant with speech. For example, when a child says the word *shoe* while pointing at the shoe, the word labels and thus classifies (but does not locate) the object. The point, in contrast, indicates where the object is but not what it is. Word and gesture do not convey identical information, but they work together to more richly specify the same object.

But word and gesture can, at times, convey information that overlaps very little, if at all. A point, for example, can indicate an object that is not referred to in speech—the child says "Daddy" while pointing at the shoe. Word and gesture together convey a simple proposition —"the shoe is Daddy's"—that neither modality conveys on its own.

As another example, consider a child participating in a Piagetian conservation task and asked whether the amount of water changed when it was poured from a tall, skinny container into a short, wide container. The child says that the amount of water has changed "cause that's down lower than that one," while first pointing at the relatively low water level in the short, wide container and then the higher water level in the tall, skinny container. Again, word and gesture do not convey identical information—speech

tells us that the water level is low, gesture tells us how low—yet they work together to more richly convey the child's understanding.

In contrast, another child gives the same response in speech, "cause this one's lower than this one," but indicates the *widths* (not the heights) of the containers with her hands (two C-shaped hands held around the relatively wide diameter of the short, wide container, followed by a left C-hand held around the narrower diameter of the tall, skinny container). In this case, word and gesture together allow the child to convey a contrast of dimensions that neither modality conveys on its own (this one's lower but wide, and that one's higher but skinny).

We can posit a continuum based on the overlap of information conveyed in gesture and speech. At one end of the continuum, gesture elaborates on a topic that has already been introduced in speech. At the other end, gesture introduces new information that is not mentioned at all in speech. Although at times it is not clear where to draw a line to divide the continuum into two categories, the ends of the continuum are obvious and relatively easy to identify. In previous work (Church & Goldin-Meadow, 1986), we have called cases in which gesture and speech convey overlapping information *gesture–speech matches,* and cases in which gesture and speech convey nonoverlapping information *gesture–speech mismatches* (see also Goldin-Meadow, Alibali & Church, 1993).

The term *mismatch* adequately conveys the notion that gesture and speech convey different information. However, for many, mismatch also brings with it the notion of conflict, a notion that we do not intend. The pieces of information conveyed in gesture and in speech in a mismatch need not conflict and, in fact, they rarely do. There is almost always some framework within which the information conveyed in gesture can be fitted with the information conveyed in speech. For example, it may seem as though a conflict between the *height* information conveyed in the child's words ("lower") and the *width* information conveyed in her gestures. However, in the context of the water conservation problem, the two dimensions actually compensate for one another. Indeed, it is essential to understand this compensation—that the water may be lower than the original dish, but it is also wider—to master conservation of liquid quantity. Thus, the information conveyed in gesture in a mismatch is different from, but has the potential to be integrated with, the information conveyed in speech.

Gesture–speech mismatches are produced throughout the life span and in a wide variety of situations. Mismatches have been observed in toddlers going through a vocabulary spurt (Gershkoff-Stowe & Smith, 1997); preschoolers explaining a game (Evans & Rubin, 1979) or counting a set of objects (Alibali & DiRusso, 1999; Graham, 1999); elementary school children explaining Piagetian conservation problems (Church & Goldin-Meadow, 1986), mathematical equations (Perry, Church, & Goldin-Meadow, 1988), and seasonal change (Crowder & Newman, 1993); children and adults discussing moral dilemmas (Church et al., 1995); children and adults explaining how they solved Tower of Hanoi puzzles (Garber & Goldin-Meadow, 2002); adolescents explaining when rods of different materials and thicknesses will bend (Stone, Webb, & Mahootian, 1991); adults explaining how gears work (Perry & Elder, 1997; Schwartz & Black, 1996); adults describing pictures of landscapes, abstract art, buildings, people, machines, and so on (Morrel-Samuels & Krauss, 1992); adults describing problems involving constant change (Alibali, Bassok, Olseth, Syc, & Goldin-Meadow, 1999); and adults narrating cartoon stories (Beattie & Shovelton, 1999; McNeill, 1992; Rauscher, Krauss, & Chen, 1996).

Thus, we find gesture–speech mismatches in all sorts of speakers and situations. Sometimes the mismatching gesture is absolutely essential for the spoken sentence to make sense. For example, an adult narrating a cartoon story says, "so the hand is now trying to start the car," an odd formulation and one that is difficult to make sense of without the accompanying gesture—a hand moving in a winding motion, which lets the listener know that the car is an old one started with a crank (Beattie & Shovelton, 1999, p. 5). In other instances, speech *can* stand on its own, but it takes on a different sense when interpreted in the context of gesture. For example, Kendon (1985, p. 225) describes a husband sitting in the living room and talking with his wife about what the children had done that day. He says, "They made a cake, didn't they?"—a sentence that appears quite straightforward. However, while producing the word *cake,* the speaker gestured toward the garden, thereby indicating that the activity had taken place not in the kitchen but in the garden, and implying that the cake was of the mud variety. In both cases, gesture conveys information that cannot be found in, and is not even implied by, the accompanying speech.

The fact that gesture can, and often does, convey information that is distinct from the information conveyed in speech creates an opportunity for gesture to have its own unique impact on communication. This is the topic to which we turn in the next section.

ROLE OF GESTURE IN COMMUNICATION OVER THE LIFE SPAN

Do Speakers Intend Their Gestures to Communicate?

We first ask whether speakers intend to communicate information with their gestures. The easiest way to explore this question is to ask people to talk when they can and cannot see their listener. If we gesture in order to convey information to our listeners, we ought to gesture more when our listeners can see our hands than we they cannot see them.

A number of studies have manipulated the presence of a listener and observed the effect on gesture. In most studies, the speaker has a face-to-face conversation with a listener in one condition, and a conversation in which a barrier prevents the speaker and listener from seeing one another in the second condition. In some studies, the second condition is conducted over an intercom, and in some, the first condition is conducted over a videophone. In some studies, the camera is hidden so that the speakers have no sense that they are being watched. It does not really seem to matter—speakers gesture more when they can see their listener than when they cannot see them (Cohen & Harrison, 1973; Emmorey & Casey, 2001; Krauss, Dushay, Chen, & Rauscher, 1995; but see Rimé, 1982; Lickiss & Wellens, 1978). However, speakers do not increase their production of all gestures. For example, Bavelas, Chovil, Lawrie, and Wade (1992) found that speakers produced more interactive gestures (gestures that refer to the listener) when they could see their listener than when they could not, but not more topic gestures (gestures that refer to the topic of conversation). Similarly, Alibali, Heath, and Myers (2001) found that speakers produced more representational gestures (gestures that depict semantic context) when they could see their listener than when they could not, but not more beat gestures (simple, rhythmic gestures that do not convey semantic context).

Another way to explore whether speakers intentionally use their gestures to communicate is to vary some aspect of the listener, rather than merely varying the listener's presence or absence. Ozyurek (2000, 2002) asked speakers to retell a cartoon story to different numbers of listeners sitting in different locations. She found that speakers changed their gestures as a function of the positioning of their listeners, in particular, as a function of how the speaker's and listeners' gesture spaces intersected—their shared space. For example, when describing how Granny threw Sylvester the cat onto the street, speakers would change the direction of their gesture so that it moved out of the shared gesture space, wherever that space was. If the speaker shared the space with two listeners sitting at her right and left sides, that space was larger than it would be if the speaker shared the space with one listener sitting at one side—and the outward motion of the speaker's gesture varied accordingly. Perhaps not surprisingly, "out of" looked different depending on what was considered "in." What's important for our discussion here is that the speakers took their listeners into account when fashioning their gestures, suggesting that they were, at least in part, making those gestures for the listeners.

But do speakers really intend to produce gestures for their listeners? There is no doubt that speakers change their *talk* in response to listeners. Perhaps the changes in gesture come about as a by-product of these changes in speech. Speakers could alter the form and content of their talk, and those changes could "automatically" bring with them changes in gesture. To address this possibility, we need to examine not only changes that occur in gesture as a function of who the listener is, but also changes that occur in the accompanying speech. Alibali, Heath, and Myers (2001) examined the amount, fluency, and content of the speech in their face-to-face and screen conditions, and found no evidence to support this hypothesis—speakers used essentially the same number of words, made the same number of speech errors, and said the same things whether a listener was present or not. Thus, when speakers produced more gestures with visible than nonvisible listeners, it was not because they had changed their talk—it looks like they meant to change their gestures.

Up to this point, we have been stressing the fact that speakers gesture more when they address visible listeners than nonvisible listeners. There does appear to be a communicative aspect to gesturing. However, in each of these studies, speakers continued to gesture even when there was no listener there at all. Although statistically less likely, gesture was produced in *all* of the experimental conditions in which there was no possibility of a communicative motive. It looks like we gesture not only for others but also for ourselves (cf. Overton, 2006, who argues that all acts have an expressive-constitutive and an instrumental-communicative function).

Perhaps the most striking bit of evidence for this claim comes from congenitally blind individuals who have never seen speakers move their hands as they talk, and thus have no model for gesturing. Nonetheless, congenitally blind

speakers gesture when they talk. They even gesture when speaking to a blind listener. Iverson and Goldin-Meadow (1998, 2001) asked 12 children and adolescents blind from birth to participate in a series of conservation tasks, and compared their speech and gesture on these tasks to age- and sex-matched sighted individuals. They found that all 12 blind speakers gestured as they spoke, despite the fact that they had never seen gesture or their listeners. The blind group gestured at the same rate as the sighted group, and conveyed the same information using the same range of gesture forms. In addition, Iverson and Goldin-Meadow (1998) asked four more children each blind from birth to participate in conservation tasks conducted by a blind experimenter. Here again, the blind speakers gestured and gestured at the same rate as the sighted-with-sighted dyads and the blind-with-sighted dyads. Speakers apparently do not gesture solely to convey information to a listener.

The issue of communicative intention still remains: Do we really intend to convey information to others with our gestures? In the end, the debate seems difficult, perhaps impossible, to resolve. On the one hand, we adjust our gestures to our listeners, and thus seem to be taking their needs into account. On the other hand, we gesture when no one is around, even when addressing blind listeners who cannot possibly profit from the information conveyed in our gestures. Even if it turns out that speakers do not tailor their gestures to the needs of their listeners, gesture may still play an important role in communication. It may not matter whether we intend to use our hands to convey information to our listeners. All that may matter is that our listeners are able to grasp whatever information lies in our hands. We explore whether listeners have this skill in the next section.

Can Listeners Glean Information from the Gestures They See?

There is clearly information to be gotten out of gesture. If individuals are trained to code hand shape and motion forms, and to attribute meanings to those forms, they are able to reliably describe the information that gesture conveys. But just because trained individuals can get meaning from gesture does not mean that untrained listeners can.

How can we tell if untrained listeners can understand gesture? At first blush, it might seem that the best way to approach this question would be to present gesture to listeners without speech and ask them what they think it means. Listeners can, in fact, glean a small amount of information from gesture when it is viewed without speech

(Feyereisen, van de Wiele, & Dubois, 1988; Krauss, Morrel-Samuels, & Colasante, 1991). However, unless our goal is to examine emblems (which are meant to be interpreted without speech), we are taking gesture out of its normal habitat in this type of manipulation—the gestures that accompany speech are not meant to be interpreted away from the framework provided by speech. As a result, studies of this type cannot tell us whether listeners glean information from the gestures they routinely see speakers produce.

There are a number of ways to figure out how much information listeners glean from gestures produced along with speech, some more convincing than others. We review the approaches that have been taken, beginning with a look at how listeners respond to speech when it is presented with and without gesture, and ending with what we think is the most convincing way to address this question (we look at gesture that conveys information not found in the speech it accompanies; in other words, we look at the gestural component of a gesture–speech mismatch and whether listeners can glean information from it).

There are hints that we pay attention to gesture from observations of how listeners behave in naturalistic conversations (see, for example, Kendon, 1994). Although naturalistic examples are suggestive, they cannot be definitive simply because we have no idea what a listener is actually understanding when he nods his head. The listener may *think* he's gotten the point of the sentence, but he may be completely mistaken. He may even be pretending to understand. We need to know exactly what listeners are taking from gesture to be sure that they have truly grasped its meaning. To accomplish this goal, we turn to experimental approaches.

Graham and Argyle (1975) conducted one of the very first studies designed to explore the effect of gesture on the listener. A speaker described a series of abstract line figures to listeners who could not see the figures and were asked to make drawings of the shapes described to them. Each speaker described half of the pictures using gesture freely, and half with his or her arms folded. A separate panel of judges analyzed the listeners' drawings for similarity to the original drawing and assigned each drawing an "accuracy" score—an assessment of how much information the listener took from the speaker's message. This measure can be compared for drawings done following messages with gesture versus messages without gesture.

The effect was large. Listeners created significantly more accurate drawings when presented with messages that were accompanied by gesture than when presented with messages that were gesture free. The effect was particularly large for line drawings that were difficult to describe in words. Allowing gesture to accompany speech improves the accuracy with which shapes can be communicated. The problem, however, is that the speakers could be changing their speech when they are not permitted to gesture (see Graham & Heywood, 1975), and listeners could be responding to the difference in speech (rather than to the presence of gesture) in the two conditions.

To get around this problem, we need to control speech. Thompson and Massaro (1986) did just that in a study exploring how pointing gestures affect listeners' perception of speech sounds. Listeners saw two objects, a ball and a doll, and heard synthesized speech sounds that corresponded either to /ba/ or /da/, or to sounds intermediate between these two syllables. The listener's job was to indicate whether the ball or the doll had been referred to in speech. Listeners either heard the sounds on their own, or they heard them in conjunction with a gesture (a person was seated behind the objects and pointed to one of the two objects). Sometimes the object that was pointed to was the same as the object referred to in speech (point at ball + /ba/) and sometimes it wasn't (point at doll + /ba/). The listeners' decision about which object had been referred to was strongly influenced by the pointing gesture: They were more likely to choose the ball when they saw a point at the *ball* while hearing /ba/ than when they saw a point at the *doll* while hearing /ba/. Moreover, the pointing gesture influenced the listeners' judgments to a greater extent when the speech information was ambiguous (i.e., when points were used in conjunction with the intermediate sounds between /ba/ and /da/).

However, it is more difficult to tell whether gesture is playing a communicative role when the gesture is iconic simply because the information conveyed in an iconic gesture often overlaps with the information conveyed in the speech it accompanies. When gesture and speech convey overlapping information, we can never really be sure that the listener has gotten *specific information* from gesture (e.g., Riseborough, 1981). Even if a listener responds more accurately to speech accompanied by gesture than to speech alone, it could be because gesture is heightening the listener's attention to the speech—gesture could be serving as an energizer or focuser, rather than as a supplier of information.

One way we can convince ourselves that the listener is gleaning specific information from gesture is to look at instances where that information is not conveyed *anywhere* in speech. Under these circumstances, the information must be coming from gesture. McNeill, Cassell, and McCullough (1994) created stimuli in which gesture conveyed different information from the information conveyed in speech. Several types of mismatches were included in the narrative, some that never occur in natural communication and some that are quite common. As an example of a match, the narrator wiggles the fingers of a downward-pointing V hand shape as he moves his hand forward while saying, "And he's running along ahead of it"—gesture and speech both convey running across. In the mismatch, a relatively uncommon one in natural discourse, the narrator produces precisely the same gesture while saying, "And he's climbing up the inside of it"—gesture again conveys running across, but speech conveys climbing up. Do listeners notice discrepancies of this sort, and if so, how do they resolve them?

Listeners did, indeed, notice the discrepancies and often resolved them by incorporating information conveyed in the gestures they saw into their own speech (McNeill et al., 1994). For example, the narrator on the videotape says, "He comes out the bottom of the pipe," while bouncing his hand up and down—a verbal statement that contains no mention of how the act was done (i.e., no verbal mention of manner), accompanied by a gesture that does convey manner. The listener resolves the mismatch by inventing a staircase. In her retelling, the listener turns the sentence into "and then goes down stairs across—back across into," while producing a manner-less gesture, a dropping straight down motion. Notice that the listener has not only picked up the information conveyed uniquely in gesture (the bouncing manner), but has incorporated it into her speech. The listener must have stored the bouncing manner in some form general enough to serve as the basis for her *linguistic* invention ("stairs").

Listeners can even glean information from gesture–speech mismatches that are spontaneously produced. In these studies, listeners are shown videotapes of children explaining their responses to conservation (Goldin-Meadow, Wein, & Chang, 1992) or math (Alibali, Flevares, & Goldin-Meadow, 1997; see also Goldin-Meadow & Sandhofer, 1999) tasks. In half of the explanations, children are producing gestures that convey the same information as their speech; in the other half, children are producing gestures that convey different information from their speech. If adults are responding only to the fact that the children are moving their hands, they should react to mismatches in the same way that they react to matches. However, if adults are responding to the *content* of the children's gestures, they ought to react differently to mismatches than to matches. In particular, because a mismatch contains two

messages, one in speech and one in gesture, adults who are gleaning information from gesture might say more when they assess a child who produces a mismatch than when they assess a child who produces a match. And they did. In both studies, adults produced many more "additions"—that is, they mentioned information that could not be found anywhere in the speech of the child they were assessing—when evaluating children who produced mismatches than when evaluating children who produced matches. Moreover, more than half of the additions that the adults produced could be traced back to the gestures that the children produced in their mismatches.

One additional point deserves mention. Some of the adults in the study were very aware of the children's gestures and remarked on them in their assessments of the children's knowledge. Interestingly, however, these adults were no better at gleaning substantive information from the children's gestures than were the adults who failed to mention gesture. Thus, being explicitly aware of gesture (at least enough to talk about it) is not a prerequisite for decoding gesture.

The gesture-reading situation in the studies we have just reviewed seems a bit removed from the real world. It would be more convincing to examine adults interacting with real-live children producing whatever gestures they please. Goldin-Meadow and Singer (2003; see also Goldin-Meadow, Kim, & Singer, 1999) asked teachers to instruct a series of children individually in mathematical equivalence, and then looked at how the *teachers* responded to the children's gestures, as well as how the *children* responded to the teachers' gestures. They found that both teachers and children reiterated the problem-solving strategies that their partner produced in the gesture half of a gesture–speech mismatch. Moreover, both teachers and children often recast the strategy that had appeared uniquely in gesture into their own words. In other words, they were able to read their partner's gestures, even in a relatively naturalistic setting.

ROLE OF GESTURE IN COGNITION OVER THE LIFE SPAN

We have seen that gesture can play an influential role in communication. It is part of the give-and-take between speakers and listeners, often conveying information that is not found in speech, but that listeners are nonetheless able to interpret. But gesture does more than contribute to communication. It plays an equally important role in cognition.

Some of the most convincing evidence that gesture plays a role in cognition comes from the fact that speakers' gestures, in particular, their gesture–speech mismatches, are a reliable index that they are at a transitional point and on the verge of change.

Gesture Predicts Change

We begin by noting that a person who produces gesture–speech mismatches on one task will not necessarily produce them on another. For example, children who produce many mismatches when explaining how they solved a mathematical equivalence task may produce none at all when explaining how they solved an (easier) conservation task (Perry et al., 1988). Even within the same domain, a speaker may produce many mismatches on a hard task and few on an easy task. For example, 2-year-olds produce more mismatches when counting a relatively large set of objects (four or six objects) than when counting a small set (two objects). For 3-year-olds, who know more about counting, the pattern is the same but the line between easy and hard falls at a different point—they produce mismatches only when counting six object sets and not when counting two or four object sets (Graham, 1999).

Rather than reflecting who a person is, gesture–speech mismatch reflects how ready a person is to learn about a particular task. A speaker who produces gesture–speech mismatches on a task is likely to be in a state of transition with respect to that task, ready to profit from whatever input manages to come her way. The evidence for this claim comes from experimental training studies, as well as studies of more naturalistic learning situations.

Church and Goldin-Meadow (1986) gave 5- to 8-year-old children a pretest of six conservation problems to assess their understanding of conservation and to determine whether the children produced a relatively large number of gesture–speech mismatches (mismatchers) or a small number (matchers). They then gave all of the children instruction in the task: half were given explicit instruction in conservation, and half were given experience in manipulating the task objects but no training or feedback. After the instruction, children were given the six conservation problems again and their improvement from pretest to post-test was assessed. Church and Goldin-Meadow (1986) found, not surprisingly, that children given explicit instruction made more progress than children given only the opportunity to manipulate the objects. However, the important point is that, no matter what type of instruction the children received, mismatchers made significantly more progress than matchers. Importantly, the matchers and the mismatchers did *not* differ on the pretest. Before instruction, the *only* way to tell the groups apart was by the number of gesture–speech mismatches each produced.

Gesture–speech mismatch in a child's explanations of conservation is thus a sign that the child is ready to learn about conservation. But is gesture–speech mismatch a general index of readiness-to-learn, or is it specific to the conservation task or to 5- to 8-year-olds? To address this question, Perry, Church and Goldin-Meadow (1988) gave older children (9- to 10-year-olds) instruction in mathematical equivalence, instantiated in problems of the following type: $4 + 5 + 3 = \_\_ + 3$. When asked to explain how they arrived at the number they put in the blank, children typically gesture while talking and often produce gesture–speech matches. For example, for the problem $6 + 3 + 4 = \_\_ + 4$, a child puts 13 in the blank and says "6 plus 3 is 9, 9 plus 4 equals 13," while pointing at the 6, the 3, the 4 on the left side of the equation, and the 13 in the blank. The child has produced an add-to-equal-sign strategy in both speech and gesture, a gesture–speech match. However, children also produce gesture–speech mismatches. Another child says he added the 6, the 3, and the 4 (an add-to-equal-sign strategy), while at the same time pointing at all four numbers in the problem (an add-all numbers strategy). This child has conveyed one strategy in speech and another in gesture, a gesture–speech mismatch.

Perry et al. (1988) gave children in the fourth and fifth grades a pretest of six addition problems to assess their understanding of mathematical equivalence and to determine whether the children were mismatchers or matchers. They then gave the children instruction in the principle underlying the addition problems—the children were told that the goal of the problem was to make both sides of the equation equal. After the instruction session, the children were again given six addition problems, and a series of novel addition and multiplication problems that tested their ability to generalize what they had learned. Here again, significantly more mismatchers were successful after instruction than matchers, on both the post-test and a generalization test. Similar results have been found for other tasks and other ages (balance scale problems: Pine, Lufkin, & Messer, 2004; gears task: Perry & Elder, 1997).

One advantage of a training study (as opposed to waiting for learners to change on their own) is time; the changes we want to observe occur over a short rather than a long period (hours as opposed to weeks). Another advantage is that we can control the instruction that the learner gets, which means that if we find differential effects after instruction (as we do), those effects cannot be attributed to differences in input, but rather to differences in the learners themselves (their status as a matcher or mismatcher). However, there are also benefits to looking at learning as it occurs in more naturalistic circumstances, not the least of which is that it would be nice to know whether gesture–speech mismatch has anything to do with learning in the real world. A study of math teachers suggests that it does.

Goldin-Meadow and Singer (2003) asked math teachers to instruct 9- and 10-year-old children individually in mathematical equivalence. The teacher watched while an experimenter gave the child a pretest consisting of six mathematical equivalence problems. Children who solved even one problem correctly were eliminated from the study. The teacher then instructed the child using any techniques that he or she thought appropriate. After the tutorial, the child was given a post-test comparable with the pretest. The children could be divided into three groups on the basis of the explanations they produced during the pretest and training: those who never produced mismatches at any point during the testing or instruction, those who produced mismatches only during instruction, and those who produced mismatches during the pretest and typically during instruction as well.

The interesting result is that the children's post-test scores reflected these groupings: Children who produced mismatches on the pretest solved more problems correctly on the post-test than children who produced mismatches only during instruction, who, in turn, solved more problems correctly than children who never produced mismatches. Thus, the children who produced mismatches were far more likely to profit from the teacher's instruction than the children who did not. Of course, the teachers may have altered their instruction as a function of the children's gestures, treating matchers differently from mismatchers. If so, it may have been the child's gestures that let the teacher know the child was ready for a different kind of input, thus playing a pivotal role in the learning process. We return to this very real possibility in a later section.

Why does gesture predict learning? Expressing information in gesture and not in speech is a type of variability, and variability seems to be good for learning. Siegler (1994) describes three types of within-child variability common to children. First, a child may solve the same type of problem in different ways. For example, a child uses the "add-to-equal-sign" strategy to solve the problem $4 + 5 + 3 = \_\_ + 3$, but the "add-all-numbers" strategy to solve $7 + 5 + 4 = \_\_ + 4$. The second problem has the

same structure as the first and differs from it only in its particular numbers. The child thus has more than one way of solving problems of this type at her disposal. Second, a child may solve precisely the same problem in different ways. If the child were given the $4 + 5 + 3 = \_\_ + 3$ problem twice, such a child might solve it first using an "add-to-equal-sign" strategy and then an "add-all-numbers" strategy (cf. Siegler & McGilly, 1989; Siegler & Shrager, 1984; Wilkinson, 1982). Finally, a child may use two different strategies when solving a single problem. The prototypical example of this type of within-child variability is mismatch—the child solves the problem using an "add-to-equal-sign" strategy that she expresses in speech while at the same time expressing an "add-all-numbers" strategy in gesture. By definition, a mismatch is an utterance in which gesture conveys different information from speech. It is a response that, in a sense, contains two responses.

Why should we care about variability? There are both theoretical and empirical reasons to believe that variability is important to change (see Nesselroade & Molenaar, Chapter 2 of this volume for an extended discussion of the significance of variability to change). Theories that posit internal conflict as a mechanism of change (e.g., Piaget's equilibration theory, 1975/1985) assume that the impetus for transition comes from having more than one rule for solving a problem, and noting discrepancies among those rules. Detecting discrepancy leads to disequilibrium, which then acts as an impetus for change (see, for example, Langer, 1969; Overton & Ennis, 2006; Snyder & Feldman, 1977; Strauss, 1972; Strauss & Rimalt, 1974, within the Piagetian tradition; and Turiel, 1974, Chapter 16 of this volume, within the domain of moral development). Even traditions that are distinctly non-Piagetian have proposed that multiple solutions to a problem may be characteristic of a changing state. Take, for example, Keil (1984), who lists resolution of internal inconsistencies as a possible mechanism of change, and Fischer (1980), who argues that change comes about when two or more skills with an old structure are transformed into skills with a new structure. From an information-processing perspective, Klahr (1984) lists conflict-resolution rules—rules that apply when two productions are eligible to be activated on a single problem—as an important mechanism of change in self-modifying systems. From a Vygotskian perspective, Griffin and Cole (1985) argue that the zone of proximal development embodies multiple levels, both next steps and previous steps. Finally, a number of more contemporary descriptions of cognitive change argue that new understanding emerges when two different levels of knowledge are integrated (e.g., Bidell & Fischer, 1992; Smith, 2005; Smith & Breazeal, 2007; Thelen & Smith, 1994; Zelazo, Frye, & Rapus, 1996). The common thread running through all these theories is the notion that more than one approach is activated or considered in solving a problem, and that the simultaneous activation of a variety of approaches is good for learning.

Empirical work supports the link between variability and change. Across a range of tasks, individuals display variability just before making a cognitive change (Thelen & Smith, 1994; Turiel, 1969, 1974; Walker & Taylor, 1991). Take, for example, children in the process of discovering a new way to solve a simple addition problem. The children exhibit variable behavior on trials immediately before the discovery and when the discovery itself is made (Siegler & Jenkins, 1989). As another example, adults who profited from instruction in how gears work had a variety of approaches to the problem in their repertoires before instruction—many more than adults who did not profit from the instruction or who understood how gears work from the start (Perry & Elder, 1997). And, of course, there is our own finding that children who produce many mismatches on a task (two responses on a single problem) are more likely to profit from instruction on that task than children who produce few (Church & Goldin-Meadow, 1986; Goldin-Meadow & Singer, 2003; Perry et al., 1988). Variability is associated with learning.

Gesture–speech mismatch is clearly one type of variability that is associated with change. But is it special in any way? Mismatch does, in fact, have some unique features. First, the different approaches are activated on a single problem in a mismatch, which could encourage comparison across the approaches. Second, the different approaches are expressed in different modalities, one in speech and the other in gesture. Perhaps having a variety of representational formats is itself an important catalyst leading to change (see Church, 1999).

We have seen that gesture is associated with learning. It can index moments of cognitive instability and reflect thoughts not found in speech. Gesture is, therefore, an ideal tool for researchers interested in identifying who is on the verge of learning and figuring out what those learners know that they cannot say. But might gesture do more than just reflect learning? The following sections explore whether gesture is involved in the learning process itself.

Gesture Brings About Change by Affecting the Learning Environment

We have seen that an undercurrent of conversation takes place in gesture alongside the acknowledged conversation in speech. Children who are on the verge of change gesture differently from children who are not. When a student's gestures convey information that is different from the information found in speech, those gestures can inform the teacher of thoughts that the student has but cannot (or at least does not) express in speech. Gesture may be one of the best ways that teachers have of discovering thoughts that are on the edge of a student's competence—what Vygotsky (1978) called the child's "zone of proximal development" (the set of skills a child is actively engaged in developing).

In fact, teachers do notice, and rely on, the gestures children produce in a classroom situation. For example, students in a science lesson were asked by the teacher whether the shadows cast by a streetlight (actually a light bulb hung from a ladder) on a line of 20-cm sticks would get longer, shorter, or stay the same as the sticks got farther away from the ladder. In response, one child said, "I think that the longer one's gonna have a longer shadow and the shorter one's shadow gonna be…," while pointing to sticks *farthest* from the ladder. The teacher restated his ideas for the classroom as follows: "So the ones up here closer to the light bulb are gonna have shorter ones and the ones further away are gonna have longer ones" (Crowder, 1996, p. 196). The teacher focused on the objects that the student had referred to in gesture rather than speech (see also Roth & Welzel, 2001). It is not clear, in this instance, whether the teacher knew he was making inferences about his student's thoughts on the basis of the student's gestures. However, at times, teachers can be quite aware of their students' gestures and even ask the students directly to make their gestures more explicit (Crowder & Newman, 1993).

But teachers do not always notice the comments that their students make in gesture. When students produce gesture-rich but lexically limited expressions, teachers at times overlook those gestured contributions even if they are key to the discussion (Crowder & Newman, 1993). Not being ratified by the teacher, the comments that appear in gesture and not speech—which often are at the forefront of the student's knowledge—may then be lost to the group and to subsequent discussion.

Responding in a tailored way to a child's individual needs is difficult in a classroom situation. But teachers might be able to use children's gestures to tailor instruction to them in a one-on-one tutorial. As described earlier, Goldin-Meadow and Singer (2003) asked teachers to individually instruct children in mathematical equivalence. Before instructing each child, the teacher observed the child solving a series of math problems and explaining her solutions. Would teachers adjust their instruction as a function of the gestures that the children spontaneously produced during the lesson? As it turns out, they did. Teachers taught children who produced gesture–speech mismatches more and different kinds of strategies for solving the problems than they taught children who did not produce mismatches. In addition, the teachers produced more gesture–speech mismatches of their own when teaching children who produced gesture–speech mismatches than they produced when teaching children who did not produce mismatches. Thus, the teachers gave the mismatching children instruction that was more varied than the instruction they gave the matching children.

Did the instruction that the teachers spontaneously offered their pupils facilitate learning? To find out, Singer and Goldin-Meadow (2005) designed lessons based on the teachers' spontaneous instructional strategies and used those lessons to teach groups of fourth graders mathematical equivalence. The instruction varied along two dimensions: (1) Some lessons contained only one spoken strategy, and others contained two; (2) some lessons contained gestures conveying a different strategy from speech, some contained gestures conveying the same strategy as speech, and some contained no gestures at all. They found that giving children instruction containing two instructional strategies was effective, but only when the two strategies were conveyed in different modalities, one in speech and another in gesture, or in other words, when the two strategies were produced in a gesture–speech mismatch.

The following picture is emerging from these findings: Children produce gestures that reveal the edges of their knowledge. Teachers read these gestures and adjust their instruction accordingly. Children then profit from this instruction that has been tailored to their needs. Children are able to shape their own learning environments just by moving their hands.

Although adults are able to glean information from children's gestures, they do not do it all of the time. Can we get teachers to improve their rates of gesture reading, which, in turn, might then help them get as much as they can out of their students' hands and mouths? To address this question, Kelly, Singer, Hicks, and Goldin-Meadow (2002) gave adults instruction in how to read gesture. They did a number of studies teaching adults to read the gestures that

children produce on either conservation or mathematical equivalence tasks, and varying the instructions they gave the adults from giving a hint ("Pay close attention not only to what the children on the videotape say with their words, but also to what they express with their hands."), to giving general instruction in the parameters that experts use when describing gesture (hand shape, motion, placement), to giving specific instruction in the kinds of gestures children produce on that particular task. The adults were given a pretest, then the instructions, and finally a post-test to determine improvement.

The adults improved with instruction, even with just a hint; they picked up 30% more explanations that the child had expressed uniquely in gesture after getting a hint to attend to gesture than before, and 50% more after getting specific instruction in the gestures on the task than before. In fact, after the adults were given specific training, they were able to accurately decode the children's gestures 90% of the time on the conservation task and 60% on the math task (improvement was the same on the two tasks—before instruction, the adults were at a 40% level on conservation, but at a 10% level on math). Moreover, on both tasks, the adults were able to generalize the instruction they received to new gestures they had not seen during training. Importantly, improvement in reading gesture did not affect the adults' abilities to glean information from the children's speech on the conservation task—they identified the child's spoken explanations perfectly before and after instruction. There was, however, a slight decrement in the number of spoken explanations the adults reported after instruction on the math task (as in naturalistic situations, this decrement was offset by an increase in the number of gestured explanations the adults reported after instruction).

The challenge for us in future studies is to figure out ways to encourage teachers to glean information from their students' gestures, whereas at the same time not losing their students' words. The technique that seems fruitful is to instruct teachers to look for a framework that can unite the information the student conveys in both gesture and speech. Having such a framework in mind should make it easier for the teacher to process the information coming in from the two modalities. The added benefit is that the teacher can also make the framework explicit to the student—and the framework may be just what the student needs at this particular moment. The student already has the pieces but lacks the whole that could unify those pieces. If the student's gesture and speech are any indication, she may be particularly ready to accept such a framework.

Gesture Brings about Change by Affecting the Learner

This section considers whether gesture plays a role in the learning process more directly by influencing the learners themselves. Gesture externalizes ideas differently from speech and, therefore, may draw on different resources. Using both modalities to convey ideas may therefore allow different ideas to enter the system, or it may allow ideas to enter the system earlier and with less effort than if the ideas had been encoded in speech alone. If so, the act of gesturing may itself change thought.

Gesturing Lightens the Learner's Cognitive Load

If the act of gesturing is itself beneficial, we might expect that gesturing will increase as problems get harder. And it does. Gesturing increases when the speaker hears his own voice continuously echoing back to him (under conditions of delayed auditory feedback; McNeill, 1992); when the speaker has suffered a stroke, trauma, or tumor and has greatly impaired language abilities (Feyereisen, 1983); when the number of problems in a task increases (Graham, 1999; Saxe & Kaplan, 1981); when the speaker can choose among options (Melinger & Kita, 2007); when the speaker is describing a scene from memory (De Ruiter, 1998; Wesp, Hesse, Keutmann, & Wheaton, 2001); and when the speaker is reasoning rather than merely describing (Alibali, Kita, & Young, 2000). These observations provide evidence that gesturing is associated with thinking hard. But they do not yet convince us that gesturing contributes to making the task easier. To make that argument, we need to manipulate gesture—that is, take it away and see if doing so affects the amount of effort the speaker expends. If gesturing merely reflects effort expended and does not contribute in any way to making the task easier, we would expect no change in effort when speakers are prevented from gesturing (or, for that matter, when they are encouraged to gesture). If, however, gesturing actually makes the task easier, we would expect that speakers will increase the amount of effort they expend on a task when prevented from gesturing on the task (to make up for the lost benefits of gesture).

How can we measure the amount of effort an individual expends on a task? One technique often used by cognitive psychologists is to give individuals a second task to perform at the same time as they are performing the original task. If the first task is very costly (from a cognitive effort point of view), they will perform less well on the second task than they would have if the first task was less effortful (Baddeley, 1986). In other words, we can use performance on the second task to gauge how much effort an individual is expending on the simultaneously performed first task.

Goldin-Meadow, Nusbaum, Kelly, and Wagner (2001) explored how gesturing on one task (explaining a math problem) affected performance on a second task (remembering a list of words or letters) performed at the same time. If gesturing reduces cognitive load, gesturing while explaining the math problems should free up resources available for remembering. Memory should then be *better* when speakers gesture than when they do not gesture. If, however, gesturing increases cognitive load, gesturing while explaining the math problems should take away from the resources available for remembering. Memory should then be *worse* when speakers gesture than when they do not gesture. Finally, if gesturing merely reflects cognitive load but has no role in causing it, gesturing while explaining the math problems should have no effect on the resources available for remembering. Memory should then be *same* when speakers gesture and when they do not gesture. Goldin-Meadow and colleagues (2001) individually tested children on addition problems of the form, $4 + 5 + 3 = \_\_ + 3$, and adults on factoring problems of the form, $x^2 - 3x - 10 = (\ )(\ )$. Children and adults were asked to solve a math problem at the blackboard. After doing so, they were given a list of items to remember (words for children, letters for adults) and were then asked to explain how they arrived at their solutions to the math problem. After completing the explanation, children and adults were asked to recall the list. The crucial part of the design is that the children and adults had to keep the to-be-remembered list in mind while explaining how they solved the math problem—the two tasks were performed simultaneously. The memory task could then serve as a gauge of how much effort each child and adult expended on the explanation task (Logan, 1979; Shiffrin & Schneider, 1984).

Children and adults gave explanations under two conditions: (1) gesture permitted, in which their hands were unconstrained; and (2) gesture not permitted, in which they were instructed to keep their hands still on the tabletop. Both children and adults remembered a significantly larger proportion of items when gesturing than when not gesturing, particularly on the long lists that taxed their memories. Thus, gesturing does not merely reflect cognitive load but appears to have an impact on the load itself. Moreover, that impact is beneficial—gesturing reduces rather than increases cognitive load.

There is, however, an alternative explanation: being forced not to gesture could itself hurt memory. If so, the effect might be not because of the beneficial effects of gesture, but the deleterious effects of the constraining instructions. Asking speakers not to gesture is, in effect, asking them to do yet another task, which could add to their cognitive load. To deal with this concern, Goldin-Meadow and colleagues (2001) reanalyzed the data focusing on a subset of the children and adults who spontaneously (and presumably, unconsciously) gestured on only some of the problems where gesturing was permitted. In other words, there were problems on which these individuals could have gestured but chose not to, allowing the researchers to compare the effects on memory of removing gesture by experimental design versus by the individual's spontaneous inclination. They reanalyzed the data from these children and adults, separating memory when they did not gesture *by choice* from memory when they did not gesture *by instruction.* Both children and adults remembered more when gesturing than when not gesturing either by choice or by instruction, suggesting that the act of gesturing really does lighten the burden on the speaker's working memory.

What might gesture be doing to reduce cognitive effort? There are a number of possibilities, all of which might be correct. First, gesture could lighten cognitive load by raising the overall activation level of the system so that words reach a firing level more quickly (Butterworth & Hadar, 1989). Under this view, any movement would do to raise activation, and the beneficial effects of gesture would have nothing to do with its ability to convey meaning. We know that this extreme view is not correct—the type of gesture speakers produce (in particular, whether it matches or mismatches the speech it accompanies) affects how much the speakers can recall on the secondary memory task (Wagner, Nusbaum & Goldin-Meadow, 2004). Nevertheless, it is possible that part of the reason gesture is effective in lightening load is because it engages the motor system.

Second, gesture might help speakers retrieve just the right word in their explanations (which would, in turn, save them cognitive effort so that they could perform better on the memory task). Gesture, particularly iconic gestures, might assist word finding by exploiting another route to the phonological lexicon, a route mediated by visual coding (Butterworth & Hadar, 1989). To test the role of gesture in lexical access, Rauscher, Krauss, and Chen (1996) prevented speakers from gesturing, whereas at the same time making lexical access more difficult (they asked speakers to try to use as many obscure words as possible, or to avoid using words that contain a specific letter). They found that preventing speakers from gesturing had the same effects as increasing the difficulty of lexical access by the other means. However, several studies designed to test the role of gesture in lexical access have found negative results. Beattie and Coughlan (1998) asked speakers to tell the same story on six consecutive trials. One would imagine that, at some point in the retellings, all of the words that the speaker might have had difficulty accessing in the first telling would have been accessed. The need for gesture (assuming that its function is to access words) ought to then decline. But gesture did not decline over the six retellings. It stayed constant throughout (see also Alibali, Kita & Young, 2000). Rather than manipulate the need for lexical access and observe the effects on gesture, Beattie and Coughlan (1999) manipulated gesture and observed the effects on lexical access. They gave speakers definitions of rare words and asked them to come up with the word that matched the definition. All of the words were rated high in imageability, and thus ought to have been easy to gesture. Half of the speakers were free to gesture and the other half was instructed to fold their arms. Speakers who were free to gesture actually reached the target word *less* often than those who had their arms folded (see Pine, Bird, & Kirk, 2007, for similar findings in children). Thus, although gesturing may reflect the fact that a speaker is in the throes of searching for a word (or has completed such a search, cf. Christenfeld, Schachter, & Bilous, 1991), it does not necessarily help the speaker find that word. Moreover, even when there seems to be little need to access a lexical item, speakers continue to gesture. Gesture could, of course, increase a speaker's access to a temporarily inaccessible lexical item on some occasions (cf. Pine et al., 2007). However, this function does not appear to be sufficiently widespread to account for gesture's beneficial effects on cognitive load.

A third possibility is that gesturing makes it easier to link a speaker's words to the world (cf. Glenberg & Robertson, 1999). Alibali and DiRusso (1999) asked preschool children to count objects. Sometimes the children were allowed to gesture while they counted and sometimes they weren't. The children counted more accurately when they gestured than when they did not gesture, suggesting that hooking word to world is easier for speakers when they can use their hands. Indeed, the children rarely made "coordination" errors (errors in coordinating the set of number words with the action of tagging each item) when they were allowed to gesture but made errors of this sort when they were prevented from gesturing. Alibali and DiRusso also included a third condition—they asked children to count aloud while a puppet gestured for them. Here, too, the children counted more accurately than when there was no gesture at all. However, unlike the self-gesturing trials, the errors that the children made on the puppet-gesturing trials tended to be coordination errors. Gesture helps speakers link words to the world, but apparently only when the speakers themselves produce those gestures. Note that the gestures in this study are what we might call *grounded* gestures—they refer concretely to objects in the world. Indeed, that is why these gestures serve the indexing function so well. The gestures in the math cognitive load studies were, for the most part, also grounded gestures (points at numbers strung together in different ways to convey problem-solving strategies). However, Ping and Goldin-Meadow (2008) recently conducted a cognitive load study using a task that tends to elicit nongrounded gestures (the conservation task). In addition, they asked half of the speakers to give their explanations with no objects around at all. They found that here again speakers remembered more when they gestured than when they did not, regardless of whether the objects were present, suggesting that indexing cannot be the sole explanation for the ability of gesture to reduce cognitive load.

Finally, gesturing could help speakers organize information, particularly spatial information, for the act of speaking and in this way ease the speaker's cognitive burden. Kita (2000) has argued that gesture helps speakers "package" spatial information into units appropriate for verbalization. If this hypothesis is correct, speakers should find it easier to convey spatial information when they gesture than when they do not. Alibali, Kita, Bigelow, Wolfman, and Klein (2001) asked children to explain their answers to a series of conservation tasks under two conditions: when they could move their hands freely, and when their hands were placed in a muff and therefore restrained. As expected, under the view that gesture helps speakers organize spatial information, children produced more perceptual-based explanations when they were allowed to move their hands freely than when they were not. Of course, the children could have changed the content of their explanations for the listener, that is, they could have adjusted their response to make up for the fact that the listener was or was not seeing gesture (as opposed to making the adjustment to benefit themselves). However, in a second study, Alibali and colleagues (2001) had a different set of children participate in the same task, with the exception that a curtain blocked the listener's view of the child's gestures. The results were unchanged—children produced more perceptual-based explanations when they were allowed to gesture than when they were not (see also Rime, Schiaratura, Hupet, & Ghysselinckx, 1984, for comparable results with adults).

Although not conclusive, these studies suggest that gesture might play a role in helping speakers (as opposed to, or in addition to, listeners) organize spatial information into speech. This mechanism could well account for the beneficial effects that gesture has on a speaker's cognitive load in the math tasks, which do call on spatial skills. The open question is whether gesturing will also lighten cognitive load when the task is a nonspatial one (a moral reasoning task, for example).

More than one, or even all, of these hypotheses might explain how gesture lightens a speaker's cognitive load. Moreover, a theme underlies all of them: Gesture and speech form an integrated and, indeed, synergistic system in which effort expended in one modality can (at times, but probably not always) lighten the load on the system as a whole.

Gesturing Brings New Ideas into the Learner's Repertoire

We have seen that gesturing can aid thinking by reducing cognitive effort. Gesturing saves effort on a task. That effort can then be used on some other task, one that would have been performed less well had the speaker not gestured on the first task. Gesturing thus allows speakers to do more with what they have and, in this way, can lead to cognitive change. But gesturing may contribute to cognitive change in other ways as well. Gesture offers a route, and a unique one, through which new information can be brought into the system. Because the representational formats underlying gesture are mimetic and analog rather than discrete, gesture permits speakers to represent ideas that lend themselves to these formats (e.g., shapes, sizes, spatial relationships)—ideas that, for whatever reason, may not be easily encoded in speech. Indeed, gesture may serve as a medium in which learners are able to experiment with new ideas. For example, a child learning about conservation of number may recognize, at some level, that pairing the checkers in one row with the checkers in another row can tell him whether the two rows have the same number of checkers. The child may not yet be able to express the notion of one-to-one correspondence in words, but by tracing a zigzag path between the checkers in the two rows, she can express the notion in gesture. Once an idea is expressed in the manual modality, it may be able to serve as a catalyst for change. In other words, gesture sneaks ideas in through the back door, and once in, those ideas take up residence and flourish.

Experimental evidence for this hypothesis comes from a series of studies in which children were told to gesture while explaining their solutions to a math problem. These children produced more new—and correct—ideas in their gestures than children told not to gesture, and more than children given no instructions about their hands. Interestingly, at the same time that the children were producing these correct ideas in gesture, they continued to solve the problems incorrectly and articulated incorrect problem-solving strategies in their speech. However, when given instruction in how to solve the problems, children who were told to gesture were more likely to profit from the instruction than children who were told not to gesture (Broaders, Cook, Mitchell, & Goldin-Meadow, 2007). Gesturing thus brings out implicit ideas, which, in turn, lead to learning.

Even more striking, we can introduce new ideas into children's cognitive repertoires by telling them how to move their hands. For example, if we make children sweep their left hands under the left side of the mathematical equation $3 + 6 + 4 = \_\_ + 4$ and their right hands under the right side of the equation during instruction, they are more likely to learn how to correctly solve problems of this type than if they are told to say, "The way to solve the problem is to make one side of the problem equal to the other side" during instruction (Cook, Mitchell, & Goldin-Meadow, 2008). Telling children how to move their hands thus seems to introduce new ideas into their repertoires.

But just *how* does gesturing promote new ideas? Learners may extract meaning from the hand movements they produce. If this is the case, then learners should be sensitive to the particular movements they produce and learn accordingly. Alternatively, all that may matter is that learners move their hands. If so, they should learn regardless of the particular movements they produce. In fact, children who were told to produce movements instantiating a *correct* rendition of the grouping strategy during instruction (e.g., a V-hand placed under the 3 and 6 in the $3 + 6 + 4 = \_\_ + 4$ problem, followed by a point at the blank) solved more problems correctly after instruction than children told to produce movements instantiating a *partially correct* strategy (e.g., a V-hand placed under the 6 and 4, followed by a point at the blank; the gesture highlighted grouping two numbers but focused on the wrong two numbers), who, in turn, solved more problems correctly than children told not to gesture at all (Goldin-Meadow, Cook, & Mitchell, 2009). Importantly, this effect was mediated by whether children added the grouping strategy to their postinstruction spoken repertoires. Because the grouping strategy was never expressed in speech during instruction by either child or teacher, nor was it expressed in gesture by the teacher, the information that children incorporated

into their postinstruction speech must have come from their own gestures.

Although the findings suggest that the children extracted information relevant to solving the problem from their hand movements, an alternative possibility is that the children's hand movements merely helped them focus their attention on the particular numbers that needed to be manipulated. Note, however, that the gestures children produced in the *partially correct* condition focused their attention on the wrong numbers. Nevertheless, children in this condition improved on the post-test, and did so more than children who did not gesture, making it unlikely that the sole function of gesture was to regulate attention. Rather, the gestures that the children produced appeared to help them learn the grouping operation, as evidenced by the fact that they added grouping to their spoken repertoires after the lesson. We may be able to lay foundations for new knowledge simply by telling learners how to move their hands. If this view is correct, even inadvertent movements of the hand have the potential to influence thinking, as has been suggested for adults solving mental rotation problems (Chu & Kita, 2008).

Thus, gesture does not just reflect the incipient ideas that a learner has; it can play a role in helping the learner formulate and, therefore, develop these new ideas. In other words, the course of cognitive change is different by virtue of the fact that the learner has gestured.

GESTURING EARLY IN DEVELOPMENT

We have seen that gesture plays a role in both communication and cognition in proficient language users. We next ask whether gesture plays the same kind of role at the earliest stages of development, during the period before language is mastered.

Role of Gesture in Communication in the Early Stages of Development

School-aged children seem to look just like adults in terms of their abilities to get meaning from gesture. Kelly and Church (1997, 1998) asked 7- and 8-year-old children to watch the videotapes of other children participating in conservation tasks. In half of the examples, the children on the videotape produced gesture–speech mismatches; in the other half, they produced gesture–speech matches. The children in the study watched the videotape twice. On one pass through, they simply described to the experimenter how they thought the child in the videotape explained his or her answer. On the other pass through, they filled out a checklist after watching each child on the videotape. No matter which technique the children used, they were able to get substantive information from other children's gestures. They produced more information when responding to mismatches, and much of the additional information could be traced back to the gestures on the videotape. They checked off explanations on the checklist that had appeared only in the gestures on the videotape. Like adults, they are able to glean specific meaning from gestures that are produced together with speech yet convey different meaning from speech.

The ability to interpret the gestures that accompany speech is not limited to school-aged children and adults—very young children can do it too. In fact, very early on, gesture-plus-word combinations seem to offer an easier route to the speaker's message than word-plus-word combinations. Young children respond to others' pointing gestures by directing their attention to the object indicated by the point, and do so months before they produce their own pointing gestures to orient another's attention toward an object (Allen & Shatz, 1983; Lempers, Flavell, & Flavell, 1976; Leung & Rheingold, 1981; Macnamara, 1977; Murphy & Messer, 1977).

But do young children integrate the information they get from the pointing gesture with the message they are getting from speech? Morford and Goldin-Meadow (1992) gave children, all of whom were in the one-word stage, "sentences" composed of a word and a gesture. For example, the experimenter said "push" while pointing at a ball, or "clock" while producing a give gesture (flat hand, palm facing up, held at chest level). If the children can integrate information across gesture and speech, they ought to respond to the first sentence by pushing the ball and to the second by giving the clock. If not, they might throw the ball or push some other object in response to the first sentence, and shake the clock or give a different object in response to the second sentence. The children did just as we might expect. They responded by pushing the ball and giving the clock—that is, their responses indicated that they were indeed able to integrate information across gesture and speech. Moreover, they responded more accurately to the "push" + point at ball sentence than to the same information presented entirely in speech—"push ball." For these one-word speakers, gesture + word combinations were *easier* to interpret than word + word combinations conveying the same information.

One more point deserves mention. The gesture + word combinations were more than the sum of their parts; that is, the number of times the children pushed the ball when presented with the word *push* alone, when added to the number of times the children pushed the ball when presented with the point at ball gesture on its own, was significantly smaller than the number of times the children pushed the ball when presented with the "push" + point at ball combination. In other words, the children needed to experience *both* parts of the gesture + word combination to produce the correct response. Gesture and speech together evoked a different response from the child than either gesture alone or speech alone (see also Kelly, 2001, who found a similar effect in 3- to 5-year-olds).

Role of Gesture in Cognition in the Early Stages of Development

Even before children produce meaningful gestures, they move their hands and, interestingly, those hand movements seem to set the stage for the synchronization between gesture and speech that we see in adult speakers. Couplings between the manual and oral/vocal systems are in place from very early in development (Iverson & Thelen, 1999) A well-established characteristic of systems such as these (known as *coupled oscillators*) is that each tries to draw the other into its characteristic oscillation pattern. Entrainment is said to occur when the activation of one oscillator "pulls in" the activity of the other and yields an ordered patterning of coordinated activity. Iverson and Thelen suggest that entrainment is the driving developmental force behind speech–gesture synchrony.

The evidence comes from a cross-sectional study of 6- to 9-month-old infants in which Iverson and Fagan (2004) found an increase in the coordination of vocalizations with rhythmic *manual* movements (e.g., hand banging, arm swinging), together with a decrease in the coordination of vocalizations with rhythmic *nonmanual* movements (e.g., leg kicking, torso bouncing). In addition, infants were significantly more likely to coordinate vocalizations with single-arm (as opposed to both arms) rhythmic movements, and with right arm (as opposed to left arm) movements, a pattern that presages the predominance of single-handed gestures executed with the right hand in adults. Finally, in most of the infants' vocal-motor coordinations, the onset of the limb or body movement either slightly anticipated or was synchronous with the onset of the vocalization, the temporal pattern found when adults produce gesture along with speech. Although the findings are cross-sectional and need to be replicated with a longitudinal sample, they suggest that, by the time infants reach 9 to 12 months, when first gestures and first words typically appear, the link between manual activity and vocalization is strong, specific, and stable, and available to serve a platform for gesture–speech integration (cf., Butcher & Goldin-Meadow, 2000; Pizzuto, Capobianco, & Devescovi, 2005).

Gesture Precedes Speech

Despite the fact that hand and mouth are integrated early in development, meaningful gestures are produced several months before meaningful words. Beginning around 10 months, children produce gestures that indicate an interest in objects—holding an object up for an adult's inspection, pointing at an object to draw an adult's attention to it, reaching for an object to indicate to an adult that they want it (Bates, 1976; Bates, Benigni, Bretherton, Camaioni & Volterra, 1979). Children often refer to a particular object first using gesture and only after several weeks add the word for that object to their vocabularies. For example, a child might refer to a ball first by pointing at it and only later produce the word *ball*. Children refer to an object for the first time using both modalities relatively rarely, and refer to an object for the first time using speech only even less often (Iverson & Goldin-Meadow, 2005). Gesture may reflect the child's interest in learning the name for a particular object, and as discussed in subsequent sections, it may even pave the way for the child to learn that name.

In addition to pointing gestures, children also produce what McNeill (1992) calls *iconic gestures.* For example, a child might open and close her mouth to represent a fish, or flap her hands to represent a bird (Acredolo & Goodwyn, 1985; Iverson, Capirci, & Caselli, 1994). Unlike a pointing gesture, the form of an iconic gesture captures aspects of its intended referent—its meaning is consequently less dependent on context. These gestures, therefore, have the potential to function like words, and for some children they do (Goodwyn & Acredolo, 1998). Acredolo and Goodwyn (1988) compared the ages at which children first used words and iconic gestures symbolically. They found that the onset of words occurred at the same time as the onset of gestures for only 13 of their 22 children. The other nine children began producing gestural symbols at least 1 month before they began producing verbal symbols—some even began 3 months before. Importantly, none of the children produced verbal symbols before they produced gestural symbols. In other words, none of the children found words easier than gestures, but some did find gestures easier than words.

Not surprisingly, children drop their reliance on symbolic gestures over time. They use fewer gestural symbols once they begin to combine words with other words, whether the language they are learning is English (Acredolo & Goodwyn, 1985, 1988) or Italian (Iverson et al., 1994). There thus appears to be a shift over developmental time: The young child seems to be willing to accept either gestural or verbal symbols; as the child ages, she begins to rely uniquely on verbal symbols (see also Capirci, Contaldo, Caselli, & Volterra, 2005). Namy and Waxman (1998) have found experimental support for this developmental shift. They tried to teach 18- and 26-month-old children novel words and novel gestures. Children at both ages learned the words, but only the *younger* children learned the gestures. The older children had already figured out that words, not gestures, carry the communicative burden in their worlds.

Gesture Predicts Speech

Gesture not only precedes speech, it also predicts changes in speech. Children combine a gesture and a word several months before they combine two words. More to the point, children who are the first to produce gesture + speech combinations in which the gesture conveys one idea and the speech another idea (e.g., point at hat combined with the word *dada* to indicate that the hat belongs to the child's father) are the first to produce two-word sentences conveying the same type of idea ("dada hat"; Goldin-Meadow & Butcher, 2003; Iverson, Capirci, Volterra, & Goldin-Meadow, 2008; Iverson & Goldin-Meadow, 2005; Ozcaliskan & Goldin-Meadow, 2005). Importantly, the type of gesture + speech combination matters—the pattern does *not* hold if we look at the age at which children first produce combinations in which gesture and speech convey essentially the same information (point at hat combined with the word *hat*). Thus, it is the ability to use gesture and speech to convey different components of a proposition (a type of gesture–speech mismatch)—and not just the ability to use gesture and speech in a single utterance—that predicts the onset of two-word utterances (see also Capirci, Iverson, Pizzuto, & Volterra, 1996; Goodwyn & Acredolo, 1998; McEachern & Haynes, 2004).

Gesture thus forecasts the earliest stages of language learning. It might do so because gesture use is an early index of global communicative skill. If so, children who convey a large number of different meanings in their early gestures might be generally verbally facile and, therefore, not only have large vocabularies later in development but also produce relatively complex sentences. Alternatively, particular types of early gesture use could be specifically related to particular aspects of later language use. In fact, we find that gesture *selectively* predicts later language learning. The number of different meanings children convey in gesture at 18 months predicts their spoken vocabulary at 42 months, but the number of gesture–speech combinations they produce at 18 months does not. In contrast, the number of gesture–speech combinations, particularly those conveying sentence-like ideas, children produce at 18 months predicts sentence complexity at 42 months, but the number of meanings they convey in gesture at 18 months does not (Rowe & Goldin-Meadow, 2009a). We can thus predict particular language milestones by watching the particular ways in which children move their hands 2 years earlier.

Gesture Has the Potential to Bring About Change in Language Learning

Gesture has the potential to bring about change in language learning in the same two ways it can influence change at later stages. First, child gesture could elicit verbal responses from parents that are targeted to the child's level. For example, consider a child who does not yet know the word *dog* and refers to the animal by pointing at it. If the mother is attentive to her child's gestures, she is likely to respond, "Yes, that's a dog," thus supplying the child with just the word he is looking for. Or consider a child who points at her father's hat while saying the word "Dada." Her father may reply, "That's Dada's hat," thus translating the child's gesture–speech combination into a simple sentence. Because they are responses to the child's gestures and therefore finely tuned to the child's current state, parental responses of this sort could be particularly effective in teaching children how an idea is expressed in the language they are learning.

Mothers do respond to the gestures their children produce (Golinkoff, 1986; Masur, 1982). For example, mothers frequently translate the gestures that children produce without speech into words, thus providing a verbal label for the object that is on the child's mind at that moment (Goldin-Meadow, Goodrich, Sauer, & Iverson, 2007). In addition, mothers produce relatively long sentences when they respond to their children's combinations in which gesture conveys one idea and speech another (point at hat + "dada")—longer than the sentences they produce when responding to combinations in which gesture and speech convey the same idea (point at hat + "hat"; Goldin-Meadow et al., 2007).

If child gesture is, indeed, playing a communicative role in language learning, mothers' translations ought to be related to later word and sentence learning in their children. In fact, we find evidence for an effect of mother translations on both word and sentence learning (Goldin-Meadow et al., 2007). In terms of learning words, when mothers produce words in response to the gestures that their children produce without speech, children later add those words to their vocabularies. In terms of learning sentences, children whose mothers frequently translate their gestures into speech are first to produce two-word utterances, suggesting that mothers' targeted responses to their children's gestures might be playing a role in helping the children take their first step into multiword combinations. Thus, a child's readiness to learn a word or sentence, as evidenced by the child's gestures, elicits particular responses from parents, which, in turn, facilitate learning in the child.

The second way in which gesture can play an active role in language learning is by giving children repeated opportunities to practice expressing particular ideas before they can express those ideas in speech. Evidence for this hypothesis comes from the fact that early child gesture use is an excellent predictor of later vocabulary size, better than other predictors that have been examined. Rowe, Ozcaliskan, and Goldin-Meadow (2008) videotaped 53 English-speaking parent–child dyads in their homes during their daily activities for 90 minutes every 4 months between children ages 14 and 34 months. At 42 months, children were given the Peabody Picture Vocabulary Test (PPVT). Child gesture use at 14 months (the number of different meanings children expressed in gesture) was a significant predictor of child spoken vocabulary 2½ years later, accounting for a third of the variance. And the relation between early child gesture and later child receptive vocabulary in speech was robust—it held even after the child's speech (number of different words expressed) at 14 months was controlled. Adding parent speech at 14 months and family income to the analysis increased the variance accounted for, but in this model, neither parent speech nor child speech at 14 months was a significant predictor of later child spoken vocabulary. However, child gesture at 14 months continued to be a significant predictor and, indeed, was a more potent predictor than family income. Indeed, child gesture at 14 months has been found to partially explain the differences in vocabulary size that children from low versus high socioeconomic status families bring with them to school (Rowe & Goldin-Meadow, 2009b).

Thus, one of the best predictors of the size of a child's vocabulary at school entry is the number of different meanings the child expresses in gesture at 14 months. It is possible, of course, that the number of different meanings a child expresses in gesture is nothing more than a reflection of the child's interest in communicating. However, it is also possible that the act of expressing these meanings in the manual modality paves the way for future vocabulary development. Future research is needed to decide between these alternatives. We would need to randomly select children and manipulate their gestures early in development, encouraging some to gesture and discouraging others. If the act of gesturing itself contributes to progress in language development, the children who are encouraged to gesture should have larger vocabularies than the children who are discouraged from gesturing.

GESTURING AND LATE ADULT DEVELOPMENT

Spoken language changes in a number of ways in late adulthood. Cross-sectional research suggests that, relative to younger adults (typically between the ages of 18 and 28 years), older adults (between the ages of 70 and 80) typically speak more slowly, are less fluent, produce more clauses with fillers, and make use of shorter, less complex constructions than younger adults, giving the impression that older adults utilize a simplified speech register (see Kemper, 2006, for a review). Differences of this sort have been attributed to age-related declines in a variety of cognitive processes, including working memory and verbal processing.

The best evidence for age-related changes in spoken language comes from a longitudinal study of 30 healthy older adults (Kemper, Thompson, & Marquis, 2001) who were between the ages of 65 and 75 years at the beginning of the study and were seen annually over a period of 7 to 15 years. At each session, an oral language sample (produced in response to elicitation questions such as "describe an unexpected event that happened to you") of at least 50 utterances was collected. Two aspects of speech were tracked over time—grammatical complexity and propositional content (i.e., the informational content of an utterance relative to the number of words)—and declines were apparent in both. The most pronounced decline in grammatical complexity occurred between the ages of 74 and 78, with relatively little change before or after this period. A similar, though less pronounced decline was evident for propositional content, with the greatest change also apparent in the mid-70s. There was, however, considerable

individual variability in both initial levels of grammatical complexity and propositional content, and in their relative rates of decline.

Overall, these longitudinal findings suggest that, with age, speech declines in syntactic and informational complexity in at least some individuals. Because, as we have seen, gesture production varies in relation to the content and complexity of its co-occurring speech, we might expect age-related differences in speech to be reflected in older adults' gestures. Surprisingly, however, only a handful of studies to date have examined spontaneous gesture production in older adults and its relation to communication and cognition.

Role of Gesture in Communication During Late Adult Development

A substantial body of evidence suggests that working memory operations are slower in older adults than in younger adults (e.g., Salthouse, 1992). One implication of this age-related slowing is that older adults may experience a disadvantage in spoken language comprehension, particularly when it requires relatively fast processing. Do older adults use gesture to compensate for reduced processing speed?

Thompson (1995) examined whether older adults between the ages of 64 and 85 years use facial articulatory information (visible speech), gestures, or both, when understanding language and whether they rely on this type of information more than younger adults (age range, 17–31 years). Older and younger adults watched and listened to a female speaker videotaped in three conditions: spoken language with facial articulatory movements (visible speech), spoken language with both visible speech and iconic gestures (visible speech + gesture), and spoken language with no view of the speaker at all (speech only). On each trial, the speaker produced a single sentence, which participants were asked to repeat word-for-word immediately after its presentation. Each sentence consisted of 16 words (18–25 syllables); sentences in the visible speech + gesture condition also contained three to four iconic gestures that were, for the most part, redundant with speech. Responses were scored for the number of words correctly repeated, regardless of the order in which they were produced.

Thompson (1995) found that the older adults performed significantly better on sentences in the visible speech condition than in the speech only condition, but the younger adults did not, suggesting that the articulatory cues helped older adults more than younger adults (although the younger adults did well overall, leaving less room for them to improve). Interestingly, adding iconic gestures to visible speech in the visible speech + gesture condition had virtually no effect on older adults' performances but had a significant impact on younger adults' performances: Younger adults performed better on sentences in the visible speech + gesture condition than in either the speech only or visible speech conditions. Thus, although older adults were more influenced by the seeing mouth movements than younger adults, they did not use hand movements as much as younger adults did.

Although this research sheds some light on the extent to which gesture is used during the late adult years when processing spoken language, it is limited in two ways. First, the sentences all contained multiple clauses and were accompanied by three to four iconic gestures, each of which conveyed a distinct meaning. This configuration may have created competition between visible speech and gestures; the sheer amount of additional information conveyed in gestures, combined with more limited processing resources during the late adult years, may have influenced the extent to which older adults were able to attend to and process the gestures. Second, task demands created by the instructions to reproduce the sentences word-for-word may have encouraged the older adults to focus their attention on cues from the mouth and to ignore information from the hand. Although this pattern may not generalize to all communicative situations, it is very clear that whether an older (or younger, for that matter) listener relies on gesture to compensate for difficulties with language processing depends on the listener's task in the communicative context (e.g., to encode the message for verbatim recall vs. to recall the gist of the message).

Role of Gesture in Cognition During Late Adult Development

Two studies to date have attempted to make inferences about age-related cognitive changes by examining older adults' gesture production. In an initial study, Cohen and Borsoi (1996) compared the gestures produced spontaneously by older adults (age range, 62–80 years) versus younger adults (age range, 18–34 years) in a communication-description task to explore whether gesture use increases or decreases with age. On the one hand, given the tight link between speech and gesture, the relatively short descriptions that older adults produce might be accompanied by fewer gestures (assuming, of

course, that decline in older adults' verbal skills leads to shorter verbal descriptions relative to younger adults). On the other hand, older adults might use gesture to compensate for poorer verbal abilities, and thus might make greater use of gesture relative to younger adults. In two experiments, groups of older and younger adults (all women) were asked to describe a set of four unfamiliar objects to a video camera. Descriptions were rated by four independent judges for overall quality (on a nine-point scale) and quality of the verbal description (rated with video off). The total number of gestures produced was recorded, and gestures were classified according to whether they were descriptive (i.e., iconic gestures) or nondescriptive (i.e., beats).

Surprisingly, the descriptions produced by older adults were slightly (although not significantly) longer than those of younger adults. Thus, there was no reason to expect differences in the gestures the two groups produced. Nevertheless, in both experiments, older adults used fewer iconic gestures than younger adults; there was no age difference in beat gestures. This result is difficult to interpret without information on the content and complexity of the accompanying speech (which were not analyzed), but it does suggest that separate mechanisms underlie the production of iconic and beat gestures. Cohen and Borsoi (1996) argue that the production of beat gestures is driven by the speech system, whereas the production of iconic gestures is driven by the visual or visuomotor imagery system. They suggest that the apparent decline in iconic gestures in older adults may be driven by an age-related decline in the ability to generate mental images.

Cohen and Borsoi (1996) provide no data in support of a link between iconic gestures and mental imagery, but there is evidence that the two are related. Feyereisen and Havard (1999) assessed the production of representational (including iconic) gestures versus beat gestures in relation to the activation of mental imagery. If production of representational gestures depends on activation of mental images, and if activation of mental imagery declines with age, differences between older and younger adults should be most evident in descriptions of motor actions and/or visual scenes (assumed to elicit images), and less evident in descriptions of abstract, less imageable topics. In addition, the ratio of representational gestures to beat gestures should be positively related to the imagery content of speech.

In this study, older adults (age range, 61–80 years) and younger adults (age range, 18–25 years) were videotaped responding to questions designed to elicit a visual image (e.g., "Could you describe a favorite painting or sculpture?"), a motor image (e.g., "Could you explain how to change the tire on a car?"), or no image (e.g., "What do you think about a single currency in Europe?"). Responses were coded for duration, and speech transcripts were scored for imagery using a computer program that assigns an imagery value (on a seven-point scale) to each word. Participants' responses were then divided into 5-second intervals, and each interval was coded for gestures (occurrence and type). The two primary measures of gesture use were the proportion of intervals containing at least one gesture (a global gesture production score) and the proportions of intervals containing representational gestures versus beat gestures.

Older adults generally produced longer responses and spoke at a slower tempo than younger adults. But there were no age differences for either speech imagery scores or overall gesture production. Furthermore, both groups gestured most in the motor imagery condition, followed by the visual imagery and no image (abstract) conditions, in that order, and both groups produced the greatest number of beat gestures in the abstract condition. Despite these similarities, however, one important age difference was found, and this difference replicated Cohen and Borsoi's (1996) findings—representational gestures were observed less frequently in the older than in the younger adults.

Contrary to Cohen and Borsoi's (1996) hypothesis, however, the absence of age differences in the production of imagery words in Feyereisen and Havard's (1999) data suggests that the decline of representational gestures in older adults is *not* caused by age-related declines in mental imagery. Feyereisen and Havard suggest instead that the infrequent use of representational gestures in older adults is related to differences in the speech styles adopted by older versus younger adults. They note that beats are often associated with metanarrative speech (e.g., repairs, personal comments, provisional clauses), which they suggest is more frequent in older than younger adults. In addition, they suggest that there is a trade-off between beats and representational gestures over the life span such that beats gradually replace iconic gestures as older speakers come to rely more heavily on speech as a primary means of communication. Beats emerge relatively late in children and are initially infrequent. But as linguistic knowledge becomes more sophisticated and more elaborate forms of language are used in communication, beats become increasingly frequent. If there is less demand on gesture to carry the informational load when the verbal message is rich, the increase in beats could bring with it a concomitant decrease in representational gestures. This developmental story rests on two assumptions: that gesture is richest when spoken language is most impoverished, and that older adults have richer spoken language than younger adults. There is currently no evidence in support of either assumption (see Kemper et al., 2001, for evidence against the second assumption).

Although the two studies described in the preceding paragraphs hint at an intriguing developmental phenomenon (i.e., a decline in representational gestures during the late adult years), they raise several issues that will need to be addressed in future research. First, neither study analyzed the speech that co-occurred with gesture so the nature of the reported age differences is unclear. In light of the findings on age-related changes in expressive language described earlier, this is a particularly significant limitation. Second, despite the reported declines in speech complexity and informational content in late adulthood (cf. Kemper et al., 2001), vocabulary size appears to increase consistently into late adulthood (e.g., Schaie & Willis, 1993). Indeed, in both the Cohen and Borsoi (1996) and Feyereisen and Havard (1999) studies, older adult scored higher on vocabulary measures than younger adults.

Finally, although we know relatively little about the ways in which the gesture–speech relation changes in healthy individuals in late adulthood, we know even less about how gesture is affected by the changes in speech that occur in adult disorders such as dementia. The pattern of linguistic decline described in healthy late adult development appears to be accelerated in individuals with dementia, particularly in terms of propositional content (Kemper et al., 2001). There is some indication that, relative to healthy older adults, patients with Alzheimer disease, whose speech is fluent and grammatical but frequently contains circumlocutions and indefinite vague terms, produce more referentially ambiguous gestures (i.e., gestures that are unclear in form or content; Carlomagno, Pandolfi, Marini, Di Iasi, & Cristilli, 2005; Glosser, Wiley, & Barnoski, 1998). Indeed, ambiguous gestures have been found to increase with severity of dementia symptoms (Glosser et al., 1998). But because these studies used relatively small samples and reported extensive individual variability, the effects need to be replicated with larger samples. In particular, longitudinal research is needed to determine whether an increase in ambiguous gestures over time goes hand in hand with a decline in the informational complexity of speech.

WHAT GESTURE TELLS US ABOUT COMMUNICATION DISORDERS OVER THE LIFE SPAN

As previously discussed, the gestures that accompany speech can provide insight into a speaker's underlying thought processes. It is no surprise then that, in children and adults with a variety of language and communication disorders, gesture can provide unique information about the nature and extent of those underlying deficits (see also Capone & McGregor, 2004). This section reviews evidence from a range of disordered populations suggesting that gesture: (1) provides information about diagnostic status and prognostic outcome, (2) reveals subtle language-related deficits that may not be apparent through analyses of speech alone, and (3) provides a means for speakers to compensate for difficulties with spoken language.

Role of Gesture in Diagnosis and Prognosis

A common feature of empirical studies conducted with language-disordered populations is the wide individual variability observed in language and communication skills, even in samples selected on the basis of stringent inclusion criteria. Equally variable are the participants' language outcomes. Thus, for example, some children with autism never acquire any speech, whereas others develop language that is nearly indistinguishable from their typically developing (TD) peers (e.g., Tager-Flusberg, Paul, & Lord, 2005). Similarly, some toddlers with early language delays catch up to their peers by preschool entry, whereas others experience persistent language difficulties (e.g., Ellis & Thal, 2008). In light of this variation, one approach taken by researchers and clinicians has been to, first, identify subgroups of individuals who share a common behavioral profile within a given population, and then examine the extent to which the candidate behavior predicts future language outcomes. Studies of a range of disordered populations across the life span have identified subgroups on the basis of gesture use, and have then examined current and/or future language in relation to subgroup membership.

Children with Early Focal Brain Injury

Children with prenatal or perinatal brain injury exhibit remarkable plasticity in language development, unlike adults (even those with comparable brain injuries), who typically exhibit persistent language difficulties (e.g., Bates & Dick, 2002; Feldman, 2005; Levine, Kraus, Alexander, Suriyakham, & Huttenlocher, 2005; Reilly, Levine, Nass,

& Stiles, in press; Stiles, Reilly, Paul, & Moses, 2005; Woods & Teuber, 1978). However, there is great variability across children. Children typically go through an initial, often protracted, period of language delay. This delay resolves for some children but not for others (Bates et al., 1997; Feldman, Holland, Kemp, & Janosky, 1992; Thal et al., 1991; Vicari, Albertoni, Chilosi, Cipriani, Cioni, & Bates, 2002). The variability in outcome across individuals has led researchers to ask whether early gesture can index the likelihood of recovery from initial language delay.

Some indirect evidence on this issue comes from a series of case studies reported by Dall'Oglio and colleagues (Dall'Oglio, Bates, Volterra, Di Capua, & Pezzini, 1994). They described cognitive and language development in six children with early focal brain lesions. Parents completed the Infant form of the Italian version of the Macarthur-Bates Communicative Development Inventory, the *Primo Vocabolario del Bambino* (PVB; Caselli & Casadio, 1995). The PVB includes a list of gestures and actions commonly produced by young children, and parents are asked to indicate the gestures that their child produces. Although these data were not the primary focus of the research, the authors noted that the children who had larger repertoires of gestures and actions also had better language outcomes in their third year.

More recently, Sauer, Levine, and Goldin-Meadow (2010) examined the relation between gesture use at 18 months and vocabulary comprehension at 30 months in a group of 11 children with prenatal or perinatal unilateral brain injury. At 18 months, children were videotaped at home for 90 minutes as they played and interacted with a parent, and all speech and gestures were transcribed from the videos. The primary measures of interest were word types (number of different words, with repetitions excluded) and gesture types (number of unique gesture meanings; pointing gestures used to refer to distinct objects, events, or people were counted as unique meanings). At 30 months, the PPVT-3 was administered to children as a measure of vocabulary comprehension.

Sauer and colleagues (2010) found that the number of different words the children produced at 18 months was not significantly related to PPVT-3 standard scores at 30 months (presumably because the children produced relatively few word types at 18 months). The interesting result, however, is that there was a strong, positive relation between gesture types at 18 months and vocabulary comprehension at 30 months, even after controlling for word types at 18 months. Thus, children who used gesture to communicate a broad array of meanings at 18 months developed vocabularies that were in the normative range 1 year later. In contrast, children who conveyed more limited information in gesture exhibited persistent delays with respect to vocabulary comprehension. These findings suggest that early delays in gesture production can be used to identify those children with unilateral prenatal or perinatal lesions whose language learning is likely to be delayed in the future. If so, we may be able to offer these children interventions while their language-learning trajectory is likely to be most malleable.

Children with Autism

Autism is a neurodevelopmental disorder characterized by impairments in social interaction and communication, and by restricted and repetitive behaviors and interests (American Psychiatric Association, 2000). Atypicality in gesture use is one among several diagnostic indicators of impairment in social interaction and communication. Descriptions of deficits in gesture are present in the classic descriptions of autism (Asperger, 1944/1991; Wing, 1981), and assessment of gestures and their production with speech is an integral component of the gold standard for autism evaluation, the Autism Diagnostic Observation Schedule–Generic (ADOS-G; Lord et al., 2000).

A majority of children with autism exhibit significant language impairment (LI). Indeed, a "delay in, or total lack of, the development of spoken language" is one of the core symptoms in the communication domain (American Psychiatric Association, 2000). However, because many children exhibit delayed language development but are not given a diagnosis of autism (see later), and because gesture impairments are evident in older children and adults with autism, recent work has begun to ask whether the gestures of very young children who eventually receive an autism diagnosis differ from the gestures of TD children. In particular, studies have asked whether there are differences in the gesture forms that are used and the communicative functions those forms serve.

On the surface, this question seems like it should be relatively straightforward to address. But addressing the question empirically has proved to be a challenge. Because an autism diagnosis involves impairment in a variety of domains that typically develop only over the first 2 to 3 years (e.g., language, symbolic play, peer relationships), it is difficult to make a reliable diagnosis of autism before age 2 (e.g., see Rogers, 2001). Indeed, many children with autism do not receive a diagnosis until they enter a school setting (e.g., Mandell, Novak, & Zubritsky, 2005). As a result, it is difficult to collect data on the early development of gestures. In addition, because the prevalence rate of autism in the general population is approximately 1:150 (Wing & Potter, 2002), an impossibly large sample of children would be needed to provide longitudinal data on what would end up being a very small number of children ultimately diagnosed with autism.

In light of these difficulties, one strategy that researchers have used is the retrospective analysis of home videos of children with autism. In this approach, parents of children with an autism diagnosis are asked to provide videotapes made during the child's infancy (e.g., at a first birthday party). These videos are then transcribed and coded for the child's use of gestures. Studies taking this approach have consistently reported differences in the gestures produced by children who are later diagnosed with autism compared with the gestures observed in videos collected from parents of TD infants under comparable conditions.

One of the most widely cited investigations of this sort compared videos recorded at the first birthday parties of 11 children later diagnosed with autism with those of 11 TD children (Osterling & Dawson, 1994). The first birthday party was assumed to provide a context for assessing early social communication that would be fairly similar across children. Results of this comparison suggest that, relative to TD infants, infants subsequently diagnosed with autism produced fewer gestures overall and almost no instances of pointing. This latter finding has been confirmed by a number of other researchers (e.g., Bernabei, Camaioni, & Levi, 1998), leading some to suggest that failure to point by 12 months may be a red flag for autism (Filipek et al., 2000).

Retrospective home video studies have also reported that the relatively infrequent use of gestures observed at 12 months in children later diagnosed with autism is characteristic of the entire 12- to 24-month period (Adrien et al., 1992). Indeed, between 12 and 18 months, the gap in gesture production between TD children and children with autism appears to widen substantially, with gesture production continuing to increase in TD children but remaining relatively flat in children later diagnosed with autism, a pattern that may be specific to autism (Crais, Watson, Baranek, & Reznick, 2006).

In addition to differences in frequency of gesture use, children later diagnosed with autism demonstrate a more restricted repertoire of gestures, and use gestures for a more limited range of communicative functions, than do TD children. Thus, for example, in a study that compared home videos of 9- to 12-month-old children who eventually received an autism diagnosis with home videos of

children who were developing along a typical trajectory, Colgan and colleagues (2006) reported that 60% of the autism group (compared with only 29% of the TD group) failed to use any "social interaction" gestures (conventional/ representational gestures such as "shake head no," "wave," "so big"), and when they did use these gestures, the gestures were significantly less varied than those of the TD children. In addition, in a recent study, Clifford and Dissanayake (2008) compared home video observations of children later receiving an autism diagnosis with those of TD children across two age ranges: 12 to 18 months and 18 to 24 months. The initiation of joint attention (involving the deictic gestures point and show, among other behaviors) did not vary by group in the early period. However, by 18 to 24 months, TD toddlers used gesture to initiate joint attention four times more often than the group with autism. This finding is consistent with frequent reports in the literature that, although older children with autism use gesture to request objects or events and do so at rates that are roughly comparable with those of TD peers, they rarely use gesture to establish shared attention or to comment on a particular object of interest (e.g., Buitelaar, van Engeland, de Kogel, de Vries, & van Hooff, 1991; Wetherby, Yonclas, & Bryan, 1989).

The retrospective home video methodology has provided valuable insight into the nature and development of gesture in very young children later diagnosed with autism. However, the technique does have a number of serious limitations (e.g., inadvertent sampling bias introduced by parents in deciding when to video, substantial variation in amount of footage available for individual children, atypicality of contexts such as the first birthday party). Researchers have, as a result, turned to prospective longitudinal study of infant behavior in an attempt to observe indices of a later autism diagnosis as they occur. To circumvent the need for an unmanageably large general population sample to obtain even a small sample of children receiving an eventual autism diagnosis (given the low incidence of autism in the general population), investigators have recruited samples from a high-risk population, namely, the younger, infant siblings of older children already diagnosed with autism. The probability of receiving a diagnosis of autism is approximately 200 to 300 times higher in younger siblings of children diagnosed with autism (hereafter *infant siblings*) than in the TD population (e.g., Ritvo et al., 1989). This approach has two significant advantages: (1) It significantly increases the chances of studying children who will eventually receive an autism diagnosis (approximately 18–20% of infant siblings

eventually receive an autism diagnosis; Yirmiya, Gamliel, Shaked, & Sigman, 2007; Zwaigenbaum et al., 2005); and (2) it permits the design of prospective, longitudinal studies in which behaviors can be assessed in contexts and for periods that are consistent across participants.

Longitudinal work with infant siblings suggests that gesture may be a potentially useful indicator of risk for a future autism diagnosis. For example, in a parent report study using the MacArthur-Bates Communicative Development Inventory (Fenson et al., 1993), infant siblings later diagnosed with autism had significantly smaller gesture repertoires at 12 and 18 months than infant siblings who did not eventually receive such a diagnosis and than a comparison group of infants with no family history of autism. What is especially noteworthy about this finding is that, before the age of 18 months, gesture was more informative about future diagnostic status than word comprehension or production. Differences between infant siblings later diagnosed with autism and the two comparison groups did not emerge in speech until 18 months of age (Mitchell et al., 2006).

Recent research making use of direct behavioral observation during home visits has reported results consistent with these parent-report data. In a longitudinal study of 21 infant siblings, Iverson and colleagues (Iverson, Poulos-Hopkins, Winder, & Wozniak, 2008) reported that, at 13 and 18 months, three children subsequently diagnosed with autism were at the very bottom of the distribution on all measures of deictic gesture production. Specifically, they produced few gestures overall, and the few gestures they did produce were primarily giving and reaching (i.e., gestures that serve a requesting function), rather than pointing and showing (i.e., gestures that are more likely to involve the establishment of joint attention; see also Parladé, Koterba, & Iverson, 2009).

Additional work is, of course, needed to establish gesture use (or its lack) as a specific marker of autism (as opposed to a general marker of language and communication delay independent of cause). Nevertheless, current evidence indicates that the relative lack of gesture production and, in particular, the virtual absence of pointing and infrequent use of gestures to initiate joint attention is a highly sensitive index of autism. Indeed, failure to point may be a hallmark of autism in very young children. Importantly, because these differences may be evident as early as 12 months, well before the period when language delay becomes apparent, gesture impairment may be of particular value as a source of information about diagnostic risk for autism in very young children.

Late-Talking Toddlers

"Late talkers" are young children who exhibit delays in expressive language in the absence of hearing loss, mental retardation, behavioral disturbances, or other known forms of neurological impairment. Data from prevalence studies indicate that approximately 15% to 19% of 2-year-olds are delayed in expressive language, defined as having a vocabulary of fewer than 50 words or no productive two-word combinations, or both (e.g., Klee, Pearce, & Carson, 2000; Rescorla, 1989). For some children, this early delay is transient, with language abilities appearing to "catch up" by about age 3. For others, however, initial delays persist and may be an indicator of a more significant LI. This pattern suggests that early language delay may stem from a variety of different factors, ranging from difficulties with oral articulation to difficulties with symbolic communication (e.g., Rescorla & Merrin, 1998). Thus, the question of prognostic indicators has become a critical issue for diagnosticians and clinicians attempting to identify appropriate interventions for late talkers.

In a series of studies, Thal and colleagues have provided evidence that gesture may be one such indicator. They have demonstrated that gesture production can distinguish between children who are late bloomers (i.e., children who recover from initial delays and begin to produce age-appropriate language) and those who remain delayed. In an initial study (Thal & Bates, 1988), 18- to 32-month-old late talkers (all still in the one-word stage of language development) were presented with two tasks: (1) a single gesture imitation task in which children imitated object-related gestures produced by an experimenter (e.g., drinking from a cup, making a toy airplane fly); and (2) a gesture-sequencing task in which children were asked to reproduce a series of familiar, scripted actions modeled by an experimenter (e.g., feeding a teddy bear by putting him in a highchair, putting on his bib, feeding him an apple, and wiping his mouth). Each late talker was individually matched to two TD comparison children: one on the basis of expressive vocabulary size (language-matched control subject), and one on the basis of sex and age (age-matched control subject). Thal, Tobias, and Morrison (1991) examined these children 1 year later to determine whether any of the measures from the initial observation reliably predicted language outcome. At the follow-up visit, 6 of the 10 late talkers were classified as *late bloomers;* they had caught up and had language skills comparable with the skills of TD peers. The remaining four children continued to exhibit language delay and were classified as *truly delayed.* Two

measures from the initial visit distinguished between the late bloomers and the truly delayed children: Truly delayed children were delayed in comprehension (as measured by parent inventory and an experimenter-administered picture identification task) and also performed significantly worse than late bloomers on all gesture task measures. Taken together, these findings suggest that vocabulary comprehension measures, combined with the imitation of conventional object-related gestures embedded in familiar scripts, provide valuable prognostic information about recovery from early language delay.

Although gesture production on an experimental imitation task can distinguish among subgroups of late talkers, the measure provides little information about how late talkers use gesture to communicate and whether spontaneous gesture can be used for diagnosis. Thal and Tobias (1992) addressed this issue by analyzing communicative gestures in a new cohort of 18- to 28-month-old late talkers, all in the one-word stage, and a group of younger, language-matched comparison children participating in a series of structured play sessions. Relative to language-matched control subjects, late talkers used significantly more communicative gestures, particularly as answers to adult questions. Moreover, late talkers who were eventually identified as late bloomers produced significantly more communicative gestures at the initial visit than late talkers who were eventually identified as truly delayed. The truly delayed children used only as many gestures as their language-matched control subjects.

On the basis of these data, Thal and Tobias (1992) suggest that late bloomers are using gesture to compensate for their delay in oral language, whereas truly delayed children do not. They speculate that the relatively low frequency of communicative gesture in truly delayed children reflects more substantial difficulties with language (e.g., deficiencies in symbolic representation and in recognizing that symbols can have communicative value). That late bloomers made extensive use of gesture suggests that symbolic abilities and a desire to communicate are in place in these children. Their delayed language production may therefore be a product of difficulties in word retrieval and production, articulatory problems, or other temporary obstacles to language, rather than a symbolic or communicative deficit. The findings also underscore the role that gesture can play as an assessment tool in evaluating toddlers suspected of language delay. Gesture can provide information about the nature, severity, and prognosis of the delay not readily accessible in evaluations of language alone.

Adults with Aphasia

One frequently occurring and widely recognized adult syndrome, Broca's aphasia, is of particular interest in the study of gesture and speech because it provides the opportunity to examine the relation between these two systems after damage to areas of the brain known to be involved in language production. The speech of individuals with Broca's aphasia is often referred to as nonfluent, and is marked by incomplete and syntactically simplified sentences, reduced phrase length, awkward articulation, and disturbances in the rate, stress, pitch, and intonation of speech (e.g., Kearns, 2005). For example, an adult with Broca's aphasia might attempt to describe how to use a cup by saying "cocoa...a...a...uh soup...coffee." Models that posit a tightly linked, integrated system between gesture and speech would predict that, in the presence of a language breakdown of this sort, gesture ought to break down as well, displaying characteristics parallel to halting speech (e.g., McNeill, 1992, 2005).

Although only a handful of studies have examined gesture production in adults diagnosed with Broca's aphasia, this prediction has generally been confirmed. For example, relative to adults with Wernicke's aphasia (who typically produce fluent but semantically empty speech) and healthy adults, adults with Broca's aphasia produce fewer gestures overall (presumably reflecting their limited speech output). When they do gesture, adults with Broca's aphasia use more iconic and fewer beat gestures, and a greater proportion of gestures in the absence of speech compared with adults with Wernicke's aphasia and healthy adults (Cicone, Wapner, Foldi, Zurif, & Gardner, 1979; Glosser, Wiener, & Kaplan, 1986; Pedelty, 1987). The findings suggest that language and gesture break down in parallel. Just as the speech of adults with Broca's aphasia is characterized by short utterances filled with content words, and lacking function words and grammatical markers, so are their gestures more likely to convey substantive information (i.e., iconics) rather than mark the rhythm of fluent speech (i.e., beats).

One limitation of these findings, however, is that they are based on observations taken at a single point in time in adults who vary widely in the amount of time that has passed since the onset of their symptoms (from weeks to years). Although the adult brain exhibits less plasticity in the face of injury than the child brain, language abilities often exhibit measurable recovery over time in adults with aphasia (Cappa et al., 1997; Kertesz, Harlock, & Coates, 1979). This observation raises two questions: (1) How does gesture change as language recovers, and (2) can gesture predict the likelihood of language recovery?

Braddock (2007) addressed both questions by following a group of six men with Broca's aphasia over the first 6 months after the onset of their symptoms. The initial observation was completed approximately 4 to 8 weeks after symptoms appeared (usually caused by stroke), with five additional monthly follow-up visits. At each observation, adults completed an object description task. All speech and gestures produced in this task were transcribed and coded, and compared with speech and gesture in a group of men with no neurological impairment matched on age and education. In addition, at the initial and 6-month visits, the Western Aphasia Battery (Kertesz, 1982) was administered to assess change in language abilities.

As a group, the adults with aphasia demonstrated significant improvement in verbal communication over the 6-month recovery period (although their verbal skills remained significantly below those of the comparison adults throughout the period of study). With regard to whether these verbal improvements were accompanied by changes in gesture, the data provide a mixed picture. At the initial observation, adults with aphasia gestured at a significantly higher rate than the comparison group; indeed, the distributions of the two groups were almost completely nonoverlapping. Six months later, however, this difference had decreased substantially, primarily because of a decrease in the gestures the aphasia group produced with speech. There was no change in how often the aphasic group used gesture without speech (15% and 12% of their communications at the initial and 6-month follow-up visits, respectively, consisted of gestures without speech, compared with none for the comparison group), and no change in the types of gestures the aphasic group used (the majority of their gestures at the initial and 6-month follow-up visits were emblems, whereas the comparison group primarily used iconic gestures).

Although these group-level patterns are intriguing, there was also considerable variability among individual adults with aphasia on both measures. The sample size was too small to allow for statistical analysis of differences. Nevertheless, there was a natural split in the distribution of gesture rates within the aphasia group at Time 1: three adults fell above and three fell below the median (high vs. low gesturers, respectively). The high gesturers produced shorter utterances and fewer different words across the 6-month period than the low gesturers. Indeed, there was a remarkably high correlation between gesture rate at the initial observation and utterance rate at the 6-month follow-up examination ($r = -0.87$; $p = 0.015$) in the aphasic group. In short, although adults in both subgroups exhibited comparable levels of difficulty with spoken language immediately after the onset of their aphasic symptoms, the adults who made the most extensive use of gesture initially were also the adults most likely to have *poor* language outcomes after 6 months of recovery.

Overall, the findings suggest that, as language abilities recover, gesture changes, and that gesture assessed within the first months after aphasia onset may be a useful clinical indicator of the extent to which language abilities can be expected to recover. Adults who present initially with comparable profiles of language abilities and impairments may, in fact, vary widely in prognosis. Paradoxically, an initial pattern of compensation via gesture may not be a positive prognostic indicator for language recovery. Unlike children, for whom early gesture use is a sign of resilience and an indicator that they may *not* be delayed in the future, adults with aphasia who gesture may expect worse outcomes than adults who do not gesture. Although replication of these findings with a larger sample is clearly needed, the results suggest the importance of including systematic assessments of gesture in evaluations of adults with aphasia.

Gesture as a Window Onto the Nature of Language Deficits

Just as gesture can provide a window onto speakers' underlying thought processes, so, too, can it yield unique information about the nature of the language deficits exhibited by individuals with communication disorders. Findings from two set of studies, one focused on individuals with Down syndrome (DS) and one on individuals with Williams syndrome (WS), suggest that variation in patterns of gesture use can offer insight into the nature of language difficulties that are not readily apparent in analyses of speech alone.

In keeping with the nature of the cognitive impairments characteristic of DS, young children with DS exhibit significant delays in early language development (e.g., Chapman & Hesketh, 2000). Recent research, however, suggests that young children with DS exhibit an additional cognitive delay over and above the delay evident in their level of language use, a delay that is apparent only when their gesture-word combinations are taken into account. Iverson and her colleagues (Iverson, Longobardi, & Caselli, 2003) observed the spontaneous communication of five children with DS (age range, 37–53 months; mental age range, 18–27 months) as they played with their mothers,

and individually matched them to TD children on number of different words (i.e., vocabulary types) produced during a 30-minute play session.

When children were matched on vocabulary types, no significant differences between groups were found for total number of words, gestures, or gesture-word combinations produced (i.e., tokens). However, the two groups did differ in the types of gesture-word combinations they produced. The TD children produced a relatively large number of supplementary combinations in which gesture conveys different information from the information conveyed in speech (e.g., "dada" + point at hat). In addition, in line with previous findings reviewed earlier indicating that supplementary combinations herald the onset of two-word speech (e.g., Capirci et al., 1996; Goldin-Meadow & Butcher, 2003; Iverson & Goldin-Meadow, 2005; Pizzuto et al., 2005), three of the TD children were already producing a small number of two-word utterances. In contrast, the children with DS produced almost no supplementary combinations and no two-word combinations. Thus, in addition to the well-documented global delay in language, children with DS appear to exhibit an additional, specific delay in the ability to combine two ideas within a single communicative act (either two words or a word plus a gesture).

WS is a genetic disorder that has captured particular attention because individuals with WS exhibit an unusual pattern of strengths and weaknesses across domains (e.g., very poor visuospatial processing with relatively intact face recognition; Bellugi, Lichtenberger, Jones, Lai, & St. George, 2000). Although language has traditionally been thought to be relatively "spared" in WS (but see Karmiloff-Smith et al., 1997; Volterra, Capirci, Pezzini, Sabbadini, & Vicari, 1996), recent research suggests that here, too, individuals with WS exhibit a profile of varying strengths and weaknesses. Thus, for example, although individuals with WS are generally reported to have rich vocabularies and fluent speech in everyday conversational interactions, performance on laboratory-based tasks requiring rapid picture naming is relatively poor (Rossen, Klima, Bellugi, Bihrle, & Jones, 1997; Stevens & Karmiloff-Smith, 1997; Vicari, Carlesimo, Brizzolara, & Pezzini, 1996).

In an attempt to clarify the nature of the picture-naming impairment in WS, Bello, Capirci, and Volterra (2004) examined gestures produced during a picture-naming task (the Boston Naming Test) in school-aged children with WS and two groups of TD children: one matched to the WS children on chronological age and the other on mental age. Because speakers often use iconic gestures when they are having difficulty retrieving particular lexical items (Krauss, Chen, & Gottesman, 2000), the researchers reasoned that gesture production during naming might provide insight into the nature of the picture-naming impairment in WS. The children with WS were found to produce comparable numbers of correct and incorrect naming responses, and to make similar types of errors as the mental age-matched comparison TD children, suggesting that semantic representations may not be impaired in children with WS. However, the children with WS took more than twice as long to name the pictures as the children in both of the TD comparison groups. Furthermore, the children with WS were more likely to report that they could not remember the names of the pictures, to exhibit uncertainty about their responses, to produce irrelevant speech (e.g., "What's that?") before providing a naming response, and to accompany their spoken responses with iconic gesture. Indeed, children with WS not only produced iconic gestures together with their verbal circumlocutions (a pattern found in the TD children as well), they also produced gestures together with their correct responses and when they failed to respond at all (which the TD children did not do). Taken together, these differences suggest that, despite a relatively high level of accuracy in picture naming, children with WS do experience difficulty in the process of lexical retrieval.

In summary, differences in how gesture is used in relation to speech in young children with DS point to a specific delay in packaging two distinct ideas within a single communicative act, and in children with WS point to impairments in the processes underlying lexical retrieval. Both findings underscore the importance of including gesture together with speech in assessments of disordered language systems.

Gesture as a Compensatory Device

When speech is difficult, gesture can serve as an alternate communicative route, compensating for limited oral language and providing a more complete picture of the speaker's knowledge than the view seen in speech on its own. Studies of children with DS and children with specific language impairment (SLI) offer cases in point.

As described earlier, children with DS generally have expressive language abilities that are less advanced than their cognitive skills. They might, therefore, be able to use gesture to compensate for their linguistic difficulties. Research based on parent reports of child gesture use (e.g., the Macarthur-Bates Communicative Development Inventory; Fenson et al., 1993) has generally supported this prediction; relative to TD children, children with DS

were reported by their parents to have enhanced gestural repertoires (Caselli, Vicari, Longobardi, Lami, Pizzoli, & Stella, 1998; Singer Harris, Bellugi, Bates, Jones, & Rossen, 1997). However, studies of spontaneous communication have failed to find a "gesture advantage" in children with DS (Chan & Iacono, 2001; Iverson et al., 2003).

Laboratory research on somewhat older children has also reported compensatory use of gesture in individuals with DS. Stefanini, Caselli, and Volterra (2007) examined speech and gesture produced during picture naming in children with DS (ranging in age from 3 years 8 months to 8 years 3 months) and in two groups of TD children individually matched to the DS sample on the basis of developmental and chronological age, respectively. For each picture, the child's spoken response was classified as correct, incorrect, or a failure to respond. During picture presentation, all gestures, whether produced with or without speech, were transcribed and coded by type (deictic, iconic, and other, including beat and conventional). Each overall response was then classified as unimodal (speech alone or gesture alone) or bimodal (containing both speech and gesture). All bimodal responses containing iconic gestures were then further examined to determine whether the gesture expressed a meaning similar to or different from the expected target word.

Relative to both TD comparison groups, children with DS produced a significantly greater number of incorrect spoken answers and failures to respond. There were also reliable group differences in overall gesture production, with children with DS producing more iconic (but not deictic or other) gestures than children in either of the TD comparison groups. Indeed, children with DS produced nearly twice as many iconic gestures as children in the developmental age-matched group and three times as many as their same-aged peers. Consistent with their increased use of iconic gesture, children with DS were also significantly more likely than TD children to produce bimodal or unimodal gestural responses to the pictures and, importantly, to use those iconic gestures to convey "correct" information about the picture that was lacking in their speech. This difference was so substantial that when naming accuracy was recoded to include not only correct spoken responses but also iconic gestures that conveyed meanings similar to those of the target words, naming accuracy for children with DS increased dramatically (although it remained below accuracy for both comparison groups).

The fact that children with DS can convey correct information in their gestures that is not evident in their speech suggests that using speech alone to assess their knowledge may substantially underestimate that knowledge. It also underscores the fact that their ability to represent the meaning of a picture exceeds their capacity to link meaning with speech. Along these lines, Capone (2007) has suggested that if a child's meaning representation is intact but is poorly linked to phonological representation, the meaning representation may be readily expressed in gesture.

Unlike children with DS who have known cognitive deficits, children with SLI have no identifiable intellectual impairments yet fail to acquire age-appropriate language skills. Although the language of children with SLI has been extensively characterized (e.g., Leonard, 1998), relatively little attention has been devoted to their gestures. However, two studies to date, one with preschoolers and one with older children, suggest that children with SLI do use gesture, that they use it to compensate for poor oral language, and that their gestures often convey information that is not found in their speech.

Iverson and Braddock (2009) examined speech and gesture on two picture narration tasks in preschoolers with LI and in age- and sex-matched TD peers. As anticipated, the language of the children with LI was significantly less advanced across a variety of measures than the language of their TD peers. Strikingly, however, the children with LI produced significantly more gestures per utterance than the TD children. Moreover, for children with LI (but not for the TD children), gesture rate was negatively correlated with expressive language ability (indexed by a composite measure derived from spontaneous speech). In other words, in the LI group, the poorer the child's language, the higher that child's gesture rate.

In a study of older children with SLI, Evans, Alibali, and McNeil (2001; see also Mainela Arnold, Evans, & Alibali, 2006) gave children a series of Piagetian conservation tasks and compared their performance with a group of chronologically younger TD children matched to the children with SLI on number of correct conservation judgments. The children with SLI did not use gesture more often than the judgment-matched TD children. However, they were significantly more likely to express information in their explanations that could *only* be found in gesture. For example, when given a water conservation task, a child with SLI might express the essential components of a conserving explanation—the fact that the tall container is not only taller than the short container but is also thinner (i.e., the two dimensions compensate for one another)—by indicating the height of the container in speech and its width in gesture. When Evans and colleagues considered the spoken and gestured components of children's explanations

together, children with SLI were found to produce significantly more conserving explanations than the judgment-matched comparison children. It is not surprising that the children with SLI knew more about conservation than their task-matched peers—they were, after all, older than the comparison group. What is of interest is the fact that *all* of the additional knowledge that the children with SLIs displayed was expressed uniquely in gesture and not in speech.

In summary, just as gesture can "fill in" when speech is difficult in unimpaired speakers (e.g., McNeill, 1992), so, too, can it be used by speakers with language disorders to compensate for poor oral language. Notably, however, the gestures produced with atypical language do not form a substitute system that replaces speech. The gestures produced by individuals with disordered language appear no different from the gestures that any speaker produces with speech. Speakers with atypical language appear to utilize the gesture-speech system that all speakers use, but they may do so more frequently to compensate for language difficulties.

GESTURING ACROSS THE LIFE SPAN

We have seen that speakers of all ages gesture when they talk. Moreover, gesturing appears to play the same roles throughout development. The gestures that speakers produce play an important role in communication, often conveying information that the speaker does not convey in her words. And listeners pay attention to those gestures (albeit not necessarily consciously), often changing the way they respond to a speaker as a function of her gestures. Even young children are able to glean meaning from gesture, seamlessly integrating it into the meaning that they glean from speech. Gesture is part of the conversation, regardless of whether we acknowledge it.

Gesture is also part of our cognition. At the least, the gestures that a speaker produces reflect the speaker's thoughts—at times, thoughts that the speaker does not (and perhaps cannot) express in speech. But there is mounting evidence that the gesture does more than reflect a speaker's knowledge. It can play a role in changing that knowledge; in other words, it can play a role in the learning process itself. Does the role of gesture in cognition change over time? Proficient language users, like beginning language learners, convey information in gesture that is different from the information conveyed in speech and often do so when describing tasks that they are on the verge of mastering. However, the learning task facing the young child is language itself. When gesture is used in these early stages, it is used as an assist into the linguistic system, substituting for words that the child has not yet acquired. But once the basics of language have been mastered, children are free to use gesture for other purposes—in particular, to help them grapple with new ideas in other cognitive domains, ideas that are often not easily translated into a single lexical item. As a result, although gesture conveys ideas that do not fit neatly into speech throughout development, there may be a transition in the kinds of ideas that gesture conveys as children become proficient language users. Initially, children use gesture as a substitute for the words they cannot yet express. Later, once they master language and other learning tasks present themselves, they use gesture to express more global ideas that do not fit neatly into wordlike units. Future work is needed to determine when this transition takes place.

Because gesture reflects thought, it can be used by researchers, parents, teachers, and clinicians as a window onto the child's mind, a window that provides a perspective that is often different from the perspective that speech provides. Early delays in gesture production can be used to identify children whose language learning is likely to go awry in the future, allowing clinicians to identify children likely to have persistent language difficulties well before those difficulties appear in speech. One of the interesting differences that we see in gesturing over the life span is the role it plays in compensating for language disabilities. Young children who are suffering from language delays and who gesture to compensate for those impairments have an excellent prognosis, better than the prognosis for children who have language delays and do not gesture. In contrast, adults who are suffering from aphasia and who gesture to compensate for their language losses appear to have a worse prognosis than adults who have aphasia and do not gesture. Thus, although gesture appears to play the same kind of role in communication and cognition throughout development in healthy individuals, it may take on different roles over the life span in individuals suffering from LIs. The interesting question for future research is why?

Finally, because gesture has the potential to change thought, it can be used in the home, the classroom, and the clinic to alter the pace, and perhaps the course, of learning and development. We have good evidence that gesturing can change the course of learning in school-aged children. Future work is needed to determine whether gesturing can be used to influence learning in the early and late stages in the life span. If we find that gesture is causally involved in change throughout the life span, its effect is likely to be widespread. As we have seen throughout this chapter, gesture is pervasive and, as listeners, we pay attention to gesture even though we typically do not realize that we are doing so. The time seems ripe for researchers to notice gesture, too, looking beyond speakers' words to the thoughts held in their hands.

REFERENCES

Acredolo, L. P., & Goodwyn, S. W. (1985). Symbolic gesture in language development: A case study. *Human Development, 28,* 40–49.

Acredolo, L. P., & Goodwyn, S. W. (1988). Symbolic gesturing in normal infants. *Child Development, 59,* 450–466.

Adrien, J. L., Perrot, A., Sauvage, D., Leddet, I., Larmande, C., Hameury, L., et al. (1992). Early symptoms in autism from family home movies. *Acta Psychopaediatrica, 55,* 71–75.

Alibali, M. W., Bassok, M., Olseth, K. L., Syc, S. E., & Goldin-Meadow, S. (1999). Illuminating mental representations through speech and gesture. *Psychological Sciences, 10,* 327–333.

Alibali, M. W., & DiRusso, A. A. (1999). The function of gesture in learning to count: More than keeping track. *Cognitive Development, 14,* 37–56.

Alibali, M. W., Flevares, L., & Goldin-Meadow, S. (1997). Assessing knowledge conveyed in gesture: Do teachers have the upper hand? *Journal of Educational Psychology, 89,* 183–193.

Alibali, M. W., Heath, D. C., & Myers, H. J. (2001). Effects of visibility between speaker and listener on gesture production: Some gestures are meant to be seen. *Journal of Memory and Language, 44,* 1–20.

Alibali, M. W., Kita, S., Bigelow, L. J., Wolfman, C. M., & Klein, S. M. (2001). Gesture plays a role in thinking for speaking. In C. Cave, I. Guaitella, & S. Santi (Eds.), *Oralite et gestualite: Interactions et comportements multimodaux dans la communication* (pp. 407–410). Paris: L'Harmattan.

Alibali, M. W., Kita, S., & Young, A. J. (2000). Gesture and the process of speech production: We think, therefore we gesture. *Language and Cognitive Processes, 15,* 593–613.

Allen, R., & Shatz, M. (1983). "What says meow?" The role of context and linguistic experience in very young children's responses to *what*-questions. *Journal of Child Language, 10,* 14–23.

American Psychiatric Association. (2000). *Diagnostic and statistical manual of mental disorders* (4th ed., text revision). Washington, DC: American Psychiatric Association.

Argyle, M. (1975). *Bodily communication.* New York: International Universities Press.

Asperger, H. (1991). "Autistic psychopathy" in childhood. In U. Frith (Ed.), *Autism and Asperger syndrome* (pp. 37–92). Cambridge: Cambridge University Press. (Original work published 1944)

Baddeley, A. D. (1986). *Working memory.* Oxford: Oxford University Press.

Bates, E. (1976). *Language and context: The acquisition of pragmatics.* New York: Academic Press.

Bates, E., Benigni, L., Bretherton, I., Camaioni, L., & Volterra, V. (1979). *The emergence of symbols: Cognition and communication in infancy.* New York: Academic Press.

Bates, E., & Dick, F. (2002). Language, gesture, and the developing brain. *Developmental Psychobiology, 40,* 293–310.

Bates, E., Thal, D., Trauner, D., Fenson, J., Aram, D., Eisele, J., et al. (1997). From first words to grammar in children with focal brain injury. *Developmental Neuropsychology, 13*(3), 275–343.

Bavelas, J. B., Chovil, N., Lawrie, D. A., & Wade, A. (1992). Interactive gestures. *Discourse Processes, 15,* 469–489.

Beattie, G., & Coughlan, J. (1998). Do iconic gestures have a functional role in lexical access? An experimental study of the effects of repeating a verbal message on gesture production. *Semiotica, 119,* 221–249.

Beattie, G., & Coughlan, J. (1999). An experimental investigation of the role of iconic gestures in lexical access using the tip-of-the-tongue phenomenon. *British Journal of Psychology, 90,* 35–56.

Beattie, G., & Shovelton, H. (1999). Do iconic hand gestures really contribute anything to the semantic information conveyed by speech? An experimental investigation. *Semiotica, 123,* 1–30.

Bello, A., Capirci, O., & Volterra, V. (2004). Lexical production in children with Williams syndrome: Spontaneous use of gesture in a naming task. *Neuropsychologia, 42,* 201–213.

Bellugi, U., Lichtenberger, L., Jones, W., Lai, Z., & St. George, M. (2000). The neurocognitive profile of Williams syndrome: A complex pattern of strengths and weaknesses. *Journal of Cognitive Neuroscience, 12,* 7–30.

Bellugi, U., & Studdert-Kennedy, M. (Eds.). (1980). *Signed and spoken language: Biological constraints on linguistic form.* Deerfield Beach, FL: Verlag Chemie.

Bernabei, P., Camaigni, L., & Levi, G. (1998). An evaluation of early development in children with autism and pervasive developmental disorders from home movies: Preliminary findings. *Autism, 2,* 243–258.

Bidell, T. R., & Fischer, K. W. (1992). Beyond the stage debate: Action, structure, and variability in Piagetian theory and research. In R. Sternberg & C. Berg (Eds.), *Intellectual development* (pp. 100–140). New York: Cambridge University Press.

Braddock, B. A. (2007). *Links between language, gesture, and motor skill: A longitudinal study of communication recovery in Broca's aphasia.* Unpublished doctoral dissertation, University of Missouri-Columbia.

Broaders, S., Cook, S. W., Mitchell, Z., & Goldin-Meadow, S. (2007). Making children gesture brings out implicit knowledge and leads to learning. *Journal of Experimental Psychology: General, 136*(4), 539–550.

Buitelaar, J. K., van Engeland, H., de Kogel, K. H., de Vries, H., & van Hooff, J. A. R. A. M. (1991). Differences in the structure of social behavior of autistic children and non-autistic controls. *Journal of Child Psychology and Psychiatry, 32*(6), 995–1015.

Butcher, C., & Goldin-Meadow, S. (2000). Gesture and the transition from one- to two-word speech: When hand and mouth come together. In D. McNeill (Ed.), *Language and gesture* (pp. 235–257). New York: Cambridge University Press.

Butterworth, B., & Hadar, U. (1989). Gesture, speech, and computational stages: A reply to McNeill. *Psychological Review, 96,* 168–174.

Capirci, O., Contaldo, A., Caselli, M. C., & Volterra, V. (2005). From action to language through gesture: A longitudinal perspective. *Gesture, 5,* 55–77.

Capirci, O., Iverson, J. M., Pizzuto, E., & Volterra, V. (1996). Communicative gestures during the transition to two-word speech. *Journal of Child Language, 23,* 645–673.

Capone, N. (2007). Tapping toddlers' evolving semantic representation via gesture. *Journal of Speech, Language, and Hearing Research, 50,* 732–745.

Capone, N. C., & McGregor, K. K. (2004). Gesture development: A review for clinical and research practices. *Journal of Speech Language and Hearing Research, 47,* 173–186.

Cappa, S. F., Perani, D., Grassi, F., Bressi, S., Alberoni, M., Francheschi, M., et al. (1997). A PET follow-up study of recovery in stroke in acute aphasics. *Brain and Language, 56,* 55–67.

Carlomagno, S., Pandolfi, M., Marini, A., Di Iasi, G., & Cristilli, C. (2005). Coverbal gestures in Alzheimer's type dementia. *Cortex, 41,* 535–546

Caselli, M. C., & Casadio, P. (1995). *Il Primo Vocabolario del Bambino.* Milan: Franco Angeli.

Caselli, M. C., Vicari, S., Longobardi, E., Lami, L., Pizzoli, C., & Stella, G. (1998). Gestures and words in early development of children with Down syndrome. *Journal of Speech, Language, and Hearing Research, 41,* 1125–1135.

Chan, J., & Iacono, T. (2001). Gesture and word production in children with Down syndrome. *AAC: Alternative and Augmentative Communication, 17,* 73–87.

Chapman, R. S., & Hesketh, L. J. (2000). Behavioural phenotype of individuals with Down syndrome. *Mental Retardation and Developmental Disabilities Research Reviews, 6,* 84–95.

Christenfeld, N., Schachter, S., & Bilous, F. (1991). Filled pauses and gestures: It's not coincidence. *Journal of Psycholinguistic Research, 20,* 1–10.

Chu, M., & Kita, S. (2008). Spontaneous gestures during mental rotation tasks: Insights into the microdevelopment of the motor strategy. *Journal of Experimental Psychology: General, 137,* 706–723.

Church, R. B. (1999). Using gesture and speech to capture transitions in learning. *Cognitive Development, 14,* 313–342.

Church, R. B., & Goldin-Meadow, S. (1986). The mismatch between gesture and speech as an index of transitional knowledge. *Cognition, 23,* 43–71.

Church, R. B., Schonert-Reichl, K., Goodman, N., Kelly, S. D., & Ayman-Nolley, S. (1995). The role of gesture and speech communication as reflections of cognitive understanding. *Journal of Contemporary Legal Issues, 6,* 123–154.

Cicone, M., Wapner, W., Foldi, N., Zurif, E., & Gardner, H. (1979). The relation between gesture and language in aphasic communication. *Brain and Language, 3,* 324–349.

Clifford, S. M., & Dissanayake, C. (2008). The early development of joint attention in infants with autistic disorder using home video observations and parental interview. *Journal of Autism and Developmental Disorders, 38*(5), 791–805.

Cohen, A. A., & Harrison, R. P. (1973). Intentionality in the use of hand illustrators in face-to-face communication situations. *Journal of Personality and Social Psychology, 28,* 276–279.

Cohen, R. L., & Borsoi, D. (1996). The role of gestures in description-communication: A cross-sectional study of aging. *Journal of Nonverbal Behavior, 20,* 45–63.

Colgan, S. E., Lanter, E., McComish, C., Watson, L. R., Crais, E. R., & Baranek, G. T. (2006). Analysis of social interaction gestures in infants with autism. *Child Neuropsychology, 12,* 307–219.

Cook, S. W., Mitchell, Z., & Goldin-Meadow, S. (2008). Gesturing makes learning last. *Cognition, 106,* 1047–1058.

Crais, E. R., Watson, L. R., Baranek, G. T., & Reznick, J. S. (2006). Early identification of autism: How early can we go? *Seminars in Speech and Language, 27,* 143–160.

Crowder, E. M. (1996). Gestures at work in sense-making science talk. *Journal of the Learning Sciences, 5,* 173–208.

Crowder, E. M., & Newman, D. (1993). Telling what they know: The role of gesture and language in children's science explanations. *Pragmatics and Cognition, 1,* 341–376.

Dall'Oglio, A. M., Bates, E., Volterra, V., Di Capua, M., & Pezzini, G. (1994). Early cognition, communication and language in children with focal brain injury. *Developmental Medicine and Child Neurology, 36,* 1076–1098.

Ekman, P., & Friesen, W. (1969). The repertoire of nonverbal behavioral categories. *Semiotica, 1,* 49–98.

Ekman, P., Friesen, W. V., & Ellsworth, P. (1972). *Emotion in the human face.* New York: Pergamon Press.

Ellis, E., & Thal, D. J. (2008). Early language delay and risk for language impairment. *Perspectives on Language Learning and Education, 15,* 93–100.

Emmorey, K. E., & Casey, S. (2001). Gesture, thought, and spatial language. *Gesture, 1,* 35–50.

Evans, J. L., Alibali, M. W., & McNeil, N. M. (2001). Divergence of embodied knowledge and verbal expression: Evidence from gesture and speech in children with Specific Language Impairment. *Language and Cognitive Processes, 16,* 309–331.

Evans, M. A., & Rubin, K. H. (1979). Hand gestures as a communicative mode in school-aged children. *Journal of Genetic Psychology, 135,* 189–196.

Feldman, H. M. (2005). Language learning with an injured brain. *Language Learning and Development, 1*(3&4), 265–288.

Feldman, H. M., Holland, A. L., Kemp, S. S., & Janosky, J. E. (1992). Language development after unilateral brain injury. *Brain and Language, 42*(1), 89–102.

Fenson, L., Dale, P., Reznick, J. S., Thal, D., Bates, E., Hartung, J., et al. (1993). *The MacArthur Communicative Development Inventories: User's guide and technical manual.* San Diego, CA: Singular Publishing Group.

Feyereisen, P. (1983). Manual activity during speaking in aphasic subjects. *International Journal of Psychology, 18,* 545–556.

Feyereisen, P., & Havard, I. (1999). Mental imagery and production of hand gestures while speaking in younger and older adults. *Journal of Nonverbal Behavior, 23,* 153–171.

Feyereisen, P., van de Wiele, M., & Dubois, F. (1988). The meaning of gestures: What can be understood without speech. *Cahiers de Psychologie Cognitive/European Bulletin of Cognitive Psychology, 8,* 3–25.

Filipek, P., Accardo, P., Ashwal, S., Baranek, G., Cook, E., Dawson, G., Gordon, B., Gravel, J., Johnson, C., Kallen, R., Levy, S., Minshew, N., Ozonoff, S., Prizant, B., Rapin, I., Rogers, S., Stone, W., Teplin, S., Tuchman, R., & Volkmar, F. (2000). Practice parameter: Screening and diagnosis of autism. *Neurology, 55,* 468–479.

Fischer, K. W. (1980). A theory of cognitive development: The control and construction of hierarchies of skills. *Psychological Review, 87*(6), 477–531.

Garber, P., & Goldin-Meadow, S. (2002). Gesture offers insight into problem-solving in children and adults. *Cognitive Science, 26,* 817–831.

Gershkoff-Stowe, L., & Smith, L.B. (1997). A curvilinear trend in naming errors as a function of early vocabulary growth. *Cognitive Psychology, 34,* 37–71.

Glenberg, A. M., & Robertson, D. A. (1999). Indexical understanding of instructions. *Discourse Processes, 28,* 1–26.

Glosser, G., Wiener, M., & Kaplan, E. (1986). Communicative gesture in aphasia. *Brain and Language, 27,* 345–359.

Glosser, G, Wiley, M. J., & Barnoski, E. J. (1998). Gestural communication in Alzheimer's disease. *Journal of Clinical and Experimental Neuropsychology, 20,* 1–13.

Goldin-Meadow, S. (2003). *The resilience of language: What gesture creation in deaf children can tell us about how all children learning language.* New York: Psychology Press.

Goldin-Meadow, S., Alibali, M. W., & Church, R. B. (1993). Transitions in concept acquisition: Using the hand to read the mind. *Psychological Review, 100,* 279–297.

Goldin-Meadow, S., & Butcher, C. (2003). Pointing toward two-word speech in young children. In S. Kita (Ed.), *Pointing: Where language, culture, and cognition meet.* Mahwah, NJ: Erlbaum.

Goldin-Meadow, S., Cook, S. W., & Mitchell, Z. A. (2009). Gesturing gives children new ideas about math. *Psychological Science, 20,* 267–272.

Goldin-Meadow, S., Goodrich, W., Sauer, E., & Iverson, J. M. (2007). Young children use their hands to tell their mothers what to say. *Developmental Science, 10,* 778–785.

Goldin-Meadow, S., Kim, S., & Singer, M. (1999). What the teacher's hands tell the student's mind about math. *Journal of Educational Psychology, 91,* 720–730.

Goldin-Meadow, S., & McNeill, D. (1999). The role of gesture and mimetic representation in making language the province of speech. In Michael C. Corballis & Stephen Lea (Eds.), *The descent of mind* (pp. 155–172). Oxford: Oxford University Press.

Goldin-Meadow, S., McNeill, D., & Singleton, J. (1996). Silence is liberating: Removing the handcuffs on grammatical expression in the manual modality. *Psychological Review, 103,* 34–55.

Goldin-Meadow, S., Nusbaum, H., Kelly, S. D., & Wagner, S. (2001). Explaining math: Gesturing lightens the load. *Psychological Sciences, 12,* 516–522.

Goldin-Meadow, S., & Sandhofer, C. M. (1999). Gesture conveys substantive information about a child's thoughts to ordinary listeners. *Developmental Science, 2,* 67–74.

Goldin-Meadow, S., & Singer, M. A. (2003). From children's hands to adults' ears: Gesture's role in teaching and learning. *Developmental Psychology, 39*(3), 509–520.

Goldin-Meadow, S., Wein, D., & Chang, C. (1992). Assessing knowledge through gesture: Using children's hands to read their minds. *Cognition and Instruction, 9,* 201–219.

Golinkoff, R. (1986). I beg your pardon? The preverbal negotiation of failed messages. *Journal of Child Language, 13,* 455–476.

Goodwyn, S. W., & Acredolo, L. P. (1998). Encouraging symbolic gestures: A new perspective on the relationship between gesture and speech. In J. M. Iverson & S. Goldin-Meadow (Eds.), *The nature and functions of gesture in children's communication: New directions for child development* series (no. 79, pp. 61–73). San Francisco: Jossey-Bass.

Graham, J. A., & Argyle, M. (1975). A cross-cultural study of the communication of extra-verbal meaning by gestures. *International Journal of Psychology, 10,* 57–67.

Graham, J. A., & Heywood, S. (1975). The effects of elimination of hand gestures and of verbal codability on speech performance. *European Journal of Social Psychology, 2,* 189–195.

Graham, T. A. (1999). The role of gesture in children's learning to count. *Journal of Experimental Child Psychology, 74,* 333–355.

Griffin, P., & Cole, M. (1985). Current activity for the future: The zo-ped. In B. Rogoff & J. V. Wertsch (Eds.), *Children's learning in the "zone of proximal development": New Directions for Child Development* (no. 23, pp. 45–64). San Francisco: Jossey-Bass Inc.

Huttenlocher, J. (1973). Language and thought. In G. A. Miller (Ed.), *Communication, language and meaning: Psychological perspectives* (pp. 172–184). New York: Basic Books.

Huttenlocher, J. (1976). Language and intelligence. In L. B. Resnick (Ed.), *The nature of intelligence* (pp. 261–281). Hillsdale, NJ: Erlbaum.

Iverson, J. M., & Braddock, B. A. (2010). *Links between language, gesture, and motor skill in relation to children with language impairment.* Submitted for publication.

Iverson, J. M., Capirci, O., & Caselli, M. C. (1994). From communication to language in two modalities. *Cognitive Development, 9,* 23–43.

Iverson, J. M., Capirci, O., Volterra, V., & Goldin-Meadow, S. (2008). Learning to talk in a gesture-rich world: Early communication of Italian vs. American children. *First Language, 28,* 164–181.

Iverson, J. M., & Fagan, M. K. (2004). Infant vocal-motor coordination: Precursor to the gesture-speech system? *Child Development, 75,* 1053–1066.

Iverson, J. M., & Goldin-Meadow, S. (1998). Why people gesture as they speak. *Nature, 396,* 228.

Iverson, J. M., & Goldin-Meadow, S. (2001). The resilience of gesture in talk: Gesture in blind speakers and listeners. *Developmental Science, 4,* 416–422.

Iverson, J. M., & Goldin-Meadow, S. (2005). Gesture paves the way for language development. *Psychological Science, 16,* 367–371.

Iverson, J. M., Longobardi, E., & Caselli, M. C. (2003). Relationship between gestures and words in children with Down's syndrome and typically developing children in the early stages of communicative development. *International Journal of Language and Communication Disorders, 38,* 179–197.

Iverson, J. M., Poulos-Hopkins, S., Winder, B., & Wozniak, R. H. (2008, May). *Gestures and words in the early communication of infant siblings of children with autism.* Poster session presented at the International Meeting for Autism Research, London.

Iverson, J. M., & Thelen, E. (1999). Hand, mouth, and brain: The dynamic emergence of speech and gesture. *Journal of Consciousness Studies, 6,* 19–40.

Jancovic, M. A., Devoe, S., & Wiener, M. (1975). Age-related changes in hand and arm movements as nonverbal communication: Some conceptualizations and an empirical exploration. *Child Development, 46,* 922–928.

Karmiloff-Smith, A., Grant, J., Berthoud, I., Davies, M., Howlin, P., & Udwin, O. (1997). Language and Williams syndrome: How intact is "intact"? *Child Development, 68,* 274–290.

Kearns, K. P. (2005). Broca's aphasia. In L. L. LaPointe (Ed.), *Aphasia and related neurogenic language disorders* (3rd ed.). New York: Thieme.

Keil, F. C. (1984). Mechanisms of cognitive development and the structure of knowledge. In R. J. Sternberg (Ed.), *Mechanisms of cognitive development* (pp. 81–100). New York: W. H. Freeman.

Kelly, S. D. (2001). Broadening the units of analysis in communication: Speech and nonverbal behaviours in pragmatic comprehension. *Journal of Child Language, 28,* 325–349.

Kelly, S. D., & Church, R. B. (1997). Can children detect conceptual information conveyed through other children's nonverbal behaviors? *Cognition and Instruction, 15,* 107–134.

Kelly, S. D., & Church, R. B. (1998). A comparison between children's and adults' ability to detect conceptual information conveyed through representational gestures. *Child Development, 69,* 85–93.

Kelly, S. D., Singer, M. A., Hicks, J., & Goldin-Meadow, S. (2002). A helping hand in assessing children's knowledge: Instructing adults to attend to gesture. *Cognition and Instruction, 20,* 1–26.

Kemper, S. (2006). Language in adulthood. In E. Bialystok & F. I. M. Craik (Eds.), *Lifespan cognition: Mechanisms of change* (pp. 223–237). New York: Oxford University Press.

Kemper, S., Thompson, M., & Marquis, J. (2001). Longitudinal change in language production: Effects of aging and dementia on grammatical complexity and propositional content. *Psychology and Aging, 16,* 600–614.

Kendon, A. (1980). Gesticulation and speech: Two aspects of the process of utterance. In M. R. Key (Ed.), *Relationship of verbal and nonverbal communication* (pp. 207–228). The Hague: Mouton.

Kendon, A. (1985). Some uses of gesture. In D. Tannen & M. Saville-Troike (Eds.), *Perspectives on silence* (pp. 215–234). Norwood, NJ: Ablex.

Kendon, A. (1994). Do gestures communicate?: A review. *Research on Language and Social Interaction, 27,* 175–200.

Kertesz, A. (1982). *Western Aphasia Battery (WAB).* San Antonio, TX: Harcourt Assessment, Inc.

Kertesz, A., Harlock, W., & Coates, R. (1979). Computer tomographic localization, lesion size, and prognosis in aphasia and nonverbal impairment, *Brain and Language, 8,* 34–50.

Kita, S. (1993). *Language and thought interface: A study of spontaneous gestures and Japanese mimetics.* Unpublished doctoral dissertation, University of Chicago.

Kita, S. (2000). How representational gestures help speaking. In D. McNeill (Ed.), *Language and gesture* (pp. 162–185). New York: Cambridge University Press.

Klahr, D. (1984). Transition processes in quantitative development. In R. J. Sternberg (Ed.), *Mechanisms of cognitive development* (pp. 101–140). New York: W. H. Freeman.

Klee, T., Pearce, K., & Carson, D. K. (2000). Improving the positive predictive value of screening for developmental language disorder. *Journal of Speech, Language, and Hearing Research, 43,* 821–833.

Klima, E., & Bellugi, U. (1979). *The signs of language.* Cambridge, MA: Harvard University Press.

Kohlberg, L. (1969). Stage and sequence: The cognitive-developmental approach to socialization. In S. Goslin (Ed.), *Handbook of socialization theory and research* (pp. 347–480). Chicago: Rand McNally.

Krauss, R., Chen, Y., & Gottesman, R. (2000). Lexical gestures and lexical access: A process model. In D. McNeill (Ed.), *Language and gesture* (pp. 261–283). New York: Cambridge University Press.

Krauss, R. M., Dushay, R. A., Chen, Y., & Rauscher, F. (1995). The communicative value of conversational hand gestures. *Journal of Experimental Social Psychology, 31,* 533–553.

Krauss, R. M., Morrel-Samuels, P., & Colasante, C. (1991). Do conversational hand gestures communicate? *Journal of Personality and Social Psychology, 61,* 743–754.

Lane, H., & Grosjean, F. (1980). *Recent perspectives on American Sign Language.* Hillsdale, NJ: Erlbaum.

Langer, J. (1969). Disequilibrium as a source of development. In P. Mussen, J. Langer, & M. Covington (Eds.), *Trends and issues in developmental psychology* (pp. 22–37). New York: Holt, Rinehart & Winston.

Leonard, L. B. (1998). *Children with specific language impairment.* Cambridge, MA: MIT Press.

Leung, E., & Rheingold, H. (1981). Development of pointing as a social gesture. *Developmental Psychology, 17,* 215–20.

Levine, S. C., Kraus, R., Alexander, E., Suriyakham, L., & Huttenlocher, P. (2005). IQ decline following early unilateral brain injury: A longitudinal study. *Brain and Cognition, 59,* 114–123.

Lickiss, K. P., & Wellens, A. R. (1978). Effects of visual accessibility and hand restraint on fluency of gesticulator and effectiveness of message. *Perceptual and Motor Skills, 46,* 925–926.

Logan, G. D. (1979). On the use of a concurrent memory load to measure attention and automaticity. *Journal of Experimental Psychology: Human Perception and Performance, 5,* 189–207.

Lord, C., Risi, S., Lambrecht, L., Cook, Jr., E. H., Leventhal, B. L., DiLavore, P. C., Pickles, A., & Rutter, M. (2000). The Autism Diagnostic Observation Schedule-Generic: A standard measure of social and communication deficits associated with the spectrum of autism. *Journal of Autism and Developmental Disorders, 30,* 205–223.

Macnamara, J. (1977). From sign to language. In J. Macnamara (Ed.), *Language learning and thought.* New York: Academic Press.

Mainela Arnold, E., Evans, J. L., & Alibali, M. W. (2006). Understanding conservation delays in children with Specific Language Impairment: Task representations revealed in speech and gesture. *Journal of Speech, Language, and Hearing Research, 49,* 1267–1279.

Mandell, D., Novak, M. M., & Zubritsky, C. D. (2005). Factors associated with age of diagnosis among children with Autism Spectrum Disorders. *Pediatrics, 116,* 1480–1486.

Masur, E. F. (1982). Mothers' responses to infants' object-related gestures: Influences on lexical development. *Journal of Child Language, 9,* 23–30.

Mayberry, R. I., & Jaques, J. (2000). Gesture production during stuttered speech: Insights into the nature of gesture-speech integration. In D. McNeill (Ed.), *Language and gesture* (pp. 199–214). Cambridge: Cambridge University Press.

McEachern, D., & Haynes, W. O. (2004). Gesture–Speech combinations as a transition to multiword utterances. *American Journal of Speech-Language Pathology, 13,* 227–235.

McNeill, D. (1992). *Hand and mind: What gestures reveal about thought.* Chicago: University of Chicago Press.

McNeill, D. (2005). *Gesture and thought.* Chicago: University of Chicago Press.

McNeill, D., Cassell, J., & McCullough, K.-E. (1994). Communicative effects of speech-mismatched gestures. *Research on Language and Social Interaction, 27,* 223–237.

Melinger, A., & Kita, S. (2007). Conceptualisation load triggers gesture production. *Language and Cognitive Processes, 22,* 473–500.

Mitchell, S., Brian, J., Zwaigenbaum, L., Roberts, W., Szatmari, P., Smith, I., et al. (2006). Early language and communication development of infants later diagnosed with autism spectrum disorder. *Developmental and Behavioral Pediatrics, 27,* S69–S78.

Morford, M., & Goldin-Meadow, S. (1992). Comprehension and production of gesture in combination with speech in one-word speakers. *Journal of Child Language, 19,* 559–580.

Morrell-Samuels, P., & Krauss, R. M. (1992). Word familiarity predicts temporal asynchrony of hand gestures and speech. *Journal of Experimental Psychology: Learning, Memory, and Cognition, 18,* 615–622.

Murphy, C. M., & Messer, D. J. (1977). Mothers, infants and pointing: A study of gesture. In H. R. Schaffer (Ed.), *Studied in mother-infant interaction.* New York: Academic Press.

Namy, L. L., & Waxman, S. R. (1998). Words and gestures: Infants' interpretations of different forms of symbolic reference. *Child Development, 69,* 295–308.

Nobe, S. (2000). Where do *most* spontaneous representational gestures actually occur with respect to speech? In D. McNeill (Ed.), *Language and gesture* (pp. 186–198). New York: Cambridge University Press.

Osterling, J., & Dawson, G. (1994). Early recognition of children with autism: A study of first birthday home videotapes. *Journal of Autism and Developmental Disorders, 24,* 247–257.

Overton, W. F. (2006). Developmental psychology: Philosophy, concepts, methodology. In R. M. Lerner (Ed.), *Handbook of child psychology: Vol. 1. Theoretical models of human development* (pp. 18–88, 6th ed.). Editors in chief: W. Damon & R. M. Lerner. Hoboken, NJ: John Wiley & Sons.

Overton, W. F., & Ennis, M. (2006). Cognitive-developmental and behavior-analytic theories: evolving into complementarity. *Human Development, 43,* 143–172.

Ozcaliskan, S., & Goldin-Meadow, S. (2005). Gesture is at the cutting edge of language development. *Cognition, 96,* B101–B113.

Ozyurek, A. (2000). The influence of addressee location on spatial language and representational gestures of direction. In D. McNeill (Ed.), *Language and gesture* (pp. 64–82). New York: Cambridge University Press.

Ozyurek, A. (2002). Do speakers design their co-speech gestures for their addressees: The effects of addressee location on representational gestures. *Journal of Memory and Language, 46*(4), 688–704.

Ozyurek, A., & Kita, S. (1999). Expressing manner and path in English and Turkish: Differences in speech, gesture, and conceptualization. In M. Hahn & S. C. Stoness (Eds.), *Proceedings of the twenty-first annual conference of the Cognitive Science Society* (pp. 507–512). Mahwah, NJ: Erlbaum.

Parladé, M. V., Koterba, E. A., & Iverson, J. M. (2009). Early joint attention and relations to preschool socioemotional competence in infant siblings of children with autism spectrum disorders. Manuscript in preparation.

Pedelty, L. L. (1987). *Gesture in aphasia.* Unpublished doctoral dissertation, University of Chicago.

Perry, M., Church, R. B., & Goldin-Meadow, S. (1988). Transitional knowledge in the acquisition of concepts. *Cognitive Development, 3,* 359–400.

Perry, M., & Elder, A. D. (1997). Knowledge in transition: Adults' developing understanding of a principle of physical causality. *Cognitive Development, 12,* 131–157.

Piaget, J. (1975/1985). *The equilibration of cognitive structures.* Chicago: University of Chicago Press.

Pine, K. J., Bird, H., & Kirk, E. (2007). The effects of prohibiting gestures on children's lexical retrieval ability. *Developmental Science, 10,* 747–754.

Pine, K. J., Lufkin, N., & Messer, D. (2004). More gestures than answers: Children learning about balance. *Developmental Psychology, 40,* 1059–1106.

Ping, R., & Goldin-Meadow, S. (2008). Hands in the air: Using ungrounded iconic gestures to teach children conservation of quantity. *Developmental Psychology, 44,* 1277–1287.

Pizzuto, E., Capobianco, M., & Devescovi, A. (2005). Gestural-vocal deixis and representational skills in early language development. *Interaction Studies, 6,* 223–252.

Rauscher, F. H., Krauss, R. M., & Chen, Y. (1996). Gesture, speech, and lexical access: The role of lexical movements in speech production. *Psychological Science, 7,* 226–231.

Reilly, J., Levine, S. C., Nass, R., & Stiles, J. (in press). Brain plasticity: Evidence from children with prenatal brain injury. In J. Reed & J. Warner (Eds.), *Child neuropsychology.* Oxford: Blackwell.

Rescorla, L. A. (1989). The Language Development Survey: A screening tool for delayed language in toddlers. *Journal of Speech and Hearing Disorders, 54,* 587–599.

Rescorla, L., & Merrin, L. (1998). Communicative intent in late-talking toddlers. *Applied Psycholinguistics, 19,* 393–414.

Rimé, B. (1982). The elimination of visible behaviour from social interactions: Effects on verbal, nonverbal and interpersonal variables. *European Journal of Social Psychology, 12,* 113–129.

Rimé, B., Schiaratura, L., Hupet, M., & Ghysselinckx, A. (1984). Effects of relative immobilization on the speaker's nonverbal behavior and on the dialogue imagery level. *Motivation and Emotion, 8,* 311–325.

Riseborough, M. G. (1981). Physiographic gestures as decoding facilitators: Three experiments exploring a neglected facet of communication. *Journal of Nonverbal Behavior, 5,* 172–183.

Ritvo, E. R., Jorde, L. B., Mason-Brothers, A., Freeman, B. J., Pingree, C., Jones, M. B., et al. (1989). The UCLA-University of Utah epidemiologic survey of autism: Recurrence risk estimates and genetic counseling. *American Journal of Psychiatry, 146,* 1032–1036.

Rogers, S. J. (2001). Diagnosis of autism before the age of 3. In L. G. Masters (Ed.), *International review of research in mental retardation* (Vol. 23, pp. 1–31). New York: Academic Press.

Rossen, M., Klima, E., Bellugi, U., Bihrle, A., & Jones, W. (1997). Interaction between language and cognition: Evidence from Williams syndrome. In J. H. Beitchman, N. Cohen, M. Konstantareas, & R. Tannock (Eds.), *Language, learning and behaviour disorders: Developmental, biological and clinical prospectives* (pp. 367–392). New York: Cambridge University Press.

Roth, W.-M., & Welzel, M. (2001). From activity to gestures and scientific language. *Journal of Research in Science Teaching, 38,* 103–136.

Rowe, M. L., & Goldin-Meadow, S. (2009a). Early gesture selectively predicts later language learning. *Developmental Science, 12*(1), 182–187.

Rowe, M. L., & Goldin-Meadow, S. (2009b). Differences in early gesture explain SES disparities in child vocabulary size at school entry. *Science, 323,* 951–953.

Rowe, M. L., Ozcaliskan, S., & Goldin-Meadow, S. (2008). Learning words by hand: Gesture's role in predicting vocabulary development. *First Language, 28,* 185–203.

Salthouse, T. A. (1992). Influence of processing speed on adult age differences in working memory. *Acta Psychologica, 79,* 155–170.

Sauer, E., Levine, S. C., & Goldin-Meadow, S. (2010). Early gesture predicts language delay in children with pre- and perinatal brain lesions. *Child Development, 81,* 528–539.

Saxe, G. B., & Kaplan, R. (1981). Gesture in early counting: A developmental analysis. *Perceptual and Motor Skills, 53,* 851–854.

Schaie, K. W., & Willis, S.L. (1993). Age differences in patterns of psychometric intelligence in adulthood. *Psychology and Aging, 8,* 44–55.

Schwartz, D. L., & Black, J. B. (1996). Shuttling between depictive models and abstract rules: Induction and fallback. *Cognitive Science, 20,* 457–497.

Shiffrin, R. M., & Schneider, W. (1984). Automatic and controlled processing revisited. *Psychological Review, 84,* 127–190.

Siegler, R. S. (1994). Cognitive variability: A key to understanding cognitive development. *Current Directions in Psychological Science, 3,* 1–5.

Siegler, R. S., & Jenkins, E. (1989). *How children discover new strategies.* Hillsdale, NJ: Erlbaum.

Siegler, R. S., & McGilly, K. (1989). Strategy choices in children's time-telling. In I. Levin & D. Zakay (Eds.), *Time and human cognition: A life span perspective.* Amesterdam: Elsevier.

Siegler, R. S., & Shrager, J. (1984). Strategy choices in addition and subtraction: How do children know what to do? In C. Sophian (Ed.), *The origins of cognitive skills.* Hillsdale, NJ: Erlbaum.

Singer, M. A., & Goldin-Meadow, S. (2005). Children learn when their teachers' gestures and speech differ. *Psychological Science, 16,* 85–89.

Singer Harris, N., Bellugi, U., Bates, E., Jones, W., & Rossen, M. (1997). Contrasting profiles of language development in children with Williams and Down syndromes. *Developmental Neuropsychology, 13,* 345–370.

Smith, L. B. (2005) Cognition as a dynamic system: Principles from embodiment. *Developmental Review, 25,* 278–298.

Smith, L. B., & Breazeal, C. (2007) The dynamic lift of developmental process. *Developmental Science, 10,* 61–68.

Snyder, S. S., & Feldman, D. H. (1977). Internal and external influences on cognitive developmental change. *Child Development, 48,* 937–943.

Stefanini, S., Caselli, M. C., & Volterra, V. (2007). Spoken and gestural production in a naming task by young children with Down syndrome. *Brain and Language, 101,* 208–221.

Stevens, T., & Karmiloff-Smith, A. (1997). Word learning in a special population: Do individuals with Williams syndrome obey lexical constraints? *Journal of Child Language, 24,* 737–765.

Stiles, J., Reilly, J., Paul, B., & Moses, P. (2005). Cognitive development following early brain injury: Evidence for neural adaptation. *Trends in Cognitive Sciences, 9*(3), 136–143.

Stone, A., Webb, R., & Mahootian, S. (1991). The generality of gesture-speech mismatch as an index of transitional knowledge: Evidence from a control-of-variables task. *Cognitive Development, 6,* 301–313.

Strauss, S. (1972). Inducing cognitive development and learning: A review of short-term training experiments. I. The organismic developmental approach. *Cognition, 1*(4), 329–357.

Strauss, S., & Rimalt, I. (1974). Effects of organizational disequilibrium training on structural elaboration. *Developmental Psychology, 10*(4), 526–533.

Tager-Flusberg, H., Paul, R., & Lord, C. (2005). Language and communication in autism. In F. Volkmar, R. Paul, A. Klin, & D. Cohen, (Eds.), *Handbook of autism and pervasive developmental disorders: Diagnosis, development, neurobiology, and behavior* (pp. 335–364). Hoboken, NJ: John Wiley & Sons.

Thal, D., Marchman, V., Stiles, J., Aram, D., Trauner, D., Nass, R., et al. (1991). Early lexical development in children with focal injury. *Brain and Language, 40,* 491–527.

Thal, D., Tobias, S., & Morrison, D. (1991). Language and gesture in late talkers: A one year followup. *Journal of Speech and Hearing Research, 34,* 604–612.

Thal, D. J., & Bates, E. (1988). Language and gesture in late talkers. *Journal of Speech and Hearing Research, 31,* 115–123.

Thal, D. J., & Tobias, S. (1992). Communicative gestures in children with delayed onset of oral expressive vocabulary. *Journal of Speech and Hearing Research, 35,* 1281–1289.

Thelen, E., & Smith, L. B. (1994). *A dynamic systems approach to the development of cognition and action.* Cambridge, MA: MIT Press.

Thompson, L. A. (1995). Encoding and memory for visible speech and gestures: A comparison between young and older adults. *Psychology and Aging, 10,* 215–228

Thompson, L. A., & Massaro, D. (1986). Evaluation and integration of speech and pointing gestures during referential understanding. *Journal of Experimental Child Psychology, 57,* 327–354.

Turiel, E. (1969). Developmental processes in the child's moral thinking. In P. Mussen, J. Langer, and M. Covington (Eds.), *Trends and issues in developmental psychology* (pp. 92–133). New York: Holt, Rinehart & Winston.

Turiel, E. (1974). Conflict and transition in adolescent moral development. *Child Development, 45,* 14–29.

Vicari, S., Albertoni, A., Chilosi, A., Cipriani, P., Cioni, G., & Bates, E. (2002). Plasticity and reorganization during language development in children with early brain injury. *Cortex, 36*(1), 31–46.

Vicari, S., Carlesimo, G., Brizzolara, D., & Pezzini, G. (1996). Short-term memory in children with Williams syndrome: A reduced contribution of lexical—semantic knowledge to word span. *Neuropsychologia, 34,* 919–925.

Volterra, V., Capirci, O., Pezzini, G., Sabbadini, L., & Vicari, S. (1996). Linguistic abilities in Italian children with Williams syndrome. *Cortex, 32,* 663–677.

Vygotsky, L. S. (1978). *Mind in society: The development of higher psychological processes* (M. Cole, V. John-Steiner, S. Scriber, & E. Souberman, Eds.). Cambridge, MA: Harvard University Press.

Wagner, S., Nusbaum, H., & Goldin-Meadow, S. (2004). Probing the mental representation of gesture: Is handwaving spatial? *Journal of Memory and Language, 50,* 395–407.

Walker, L. J., & Taylor, J. H. (1991). Stage transitions in moral reasoning: A longitudinal study of developmental processes. *Developmental Psychology, 27,* 330–337.

Wesp, R., Hesse, J., Keutmann, D., & Wheaton, K. (2001). Gestures maintain spatial imagery. *American Journal of Psychology, 114,* 591–600.

Wetherby, A., Yonclas, D. G., & Bryan, A. A. (1989). Communicative profiles of preschool children with handicaps: Implications for early identification. *Journal of Speech and Hearing Disorders, 54,* 148–158.

Wilkinson, A. C. (1982). Partial knowledge and self-correction: Developmental studies of a quantitative concept. *Developmental Psychology, 18*(6), 876–893.

Wing, L. (1981). Language, social, and cognitive impairments in autism and severe mental retardation. *Journal of Autism and Developmental Disorders, 11,* 31–44.

Wing, L., & Potter, D. (2002). The epidemiology of autistic spectrum disorders: Is the prevalence rising? *Mental Retardation and Developmental Disabilities Research Reviews, 8,* 151–161.

Woods, B., & Teuber, H. (1978). Changing patterns of childhood aphasia. *Annals of Neurology, 3,* 273–280.

Yirmiya, N., Gamliel, I., Shaked, M., & Sigman, M. (2007). Cognitive and verbal abilities of 24- to 36-month-old siblings of children with autism. *Journal of Autism and Developmental Disorders, 37,* 218–229.

Zelazo, P. D., Frye, D., & Rapus, T. (1996). An age-related dissociation between knowing rules and using them. *Cognitive Development, 11,* 37–63.

Zwaigenbaum, L., Bryson, S., Rogers, T., Roberts, W., Brian, J., & Szatmari, P. (2005). Behavioral manifestations of autism in the first year of life. *International Journal of Developmental Neuroscience, 23,* 143–152.

CHAPTER 22

Developmental Psychopathology—Self, Embodiment, Meaning
A Holistic-Systems Perspective

SEBASTIANO SANTOSTEFANO

In 1975, in his introduction to a textbook on child psychiatry that had been dedicated to him, Piaget used the opportunity to say that he was looking forward "with great expectations to the emergence of developmental psychopathology as a new discipline" (p. ix). About the same time, Achenbach (1974) noted that the field of developmental psychopathology "hardly exists yet" (p. 3). Ten years later, a special issue of the journal *Child Development* announced the birth of "developmental psychopathology" (Cicchetti, 1984) whose ancestors were traced back for more than a century to clinical psychiatry and clinical psychology, as well as to disciplines such as clinical neurology and embryology. A decade after the birth of developmental psychopathology, observing that there had been many publications addressing this new discipline, Overton and Horowitz (1991) noted that the volume "suggests the impression that developmental psychopathology has passed its early formative years and has begun the kind of rapid spurt characteristic of adolescence" (p. 1). They also added the following important recommendation that has not yet been adequately addressed. "Like any adolescent, developmental psychopathology is entering a phase in which identity issues emerge that must be confronted and worked through to resolution if a productive maturity is to be assumed" (p. 1). This chapter follows this recommendation in presenting and exploring a conceptual matrix—and associated empirical studies—that represents critical identity features of developmental psychopathology that the discipline must confront for the sake of its own development. The concepts of this matrix emerge from the integrated perspective on the nature and roles of cognition, emotion, behavior, and environment in both normal and pathological development. As Overton (2006) suggests, however, "it is essential that psychology, or any empirical science, focus some significant portion of its energy on the clarification of concepts that are central to its theories and methods" (p. 19). This is accomplished in the present chapter.

Accordingly, at the start, several questions are raised. How should we define developmental psychopathology and the meaning of cognition, emotion, behavior, and environment? And if we set out to examine developmental psychopathology from each of these perspectives, is it necessary that we wear a different pair of glasses when each domain is examined? Is it possible that we can bring into focus, and examine, all four of these perspectives while wearing only one pair of glasses? Throughout this discussion, the position taken is that these perspectives, classically considered as alternatives, do not operate as independent domains. Rather, the position taken in this chapter is that these concepts form a single, holistic organization that is essentially a relational developmental system perspective (Lerner, 2006; Lerner & Overton, 2008; Overton, 2006). But the goal of this chapter is broader than encouraging theoreticians, clinicians, and researchers to consider the concepts and methods discussed and the questions they raise. The overarching goal is to encourage a search for other related theoretical questions and methods that will assist the discipline of developmental psychopathology to confront and work through identity issues as it steps into maturity. This chapter begins with a

description of the current dominant understanding of the nature of psychopathology and contrasts this with a relational developmental systems approach.

WHAT THE CONCEPT OF PSYCHOPATHOLOGY MEANS IN THE GENERAL FIELD OF PSYCHOLOGY

It is well-known that the model of nosology (i.e., diagnostic categories defining different pathologies) has a long, successful history in medical science, dating back to the ancient Egyptians (Temkin, 1965), and has dominated how psychopathology is defined in the fields of clinical psychology and psychiatry. This model proposes that, to understand psychopathology, it is necessary to locate diseases in separate, independent classifications that help clinicians and researchers organize the phenomena patients present, communicate with each other, and make decisions concerning treatment. When looking through the many lenses provided by diagnostic categories, the investigator and clinician typically select the one that brings into focus those aspects of a person's behavior that are causing the most concern as reported by the patient, parents, spouse, school, and work environments. But what strategy is typically used to construct this understanding? This question involves epistemology, the study of knowledge and how it is acquired. In the history of science, two approaches to this question have opposed each other, one usually referred to as "objectivism" and the other as "interpretationism" (Overton, 2006).

The position of objectivism accepts that knowledge is split off, existing independent of the observer's mental activity, and that the observer gathers what are accepted to be neutral observations of a person's behaviors. This dualistic view has dominated the meaning of psychopathology. Overton (2006) illustrates how "psychology has implicitly used the philosophical assumptions of a seventeenth-century ontological dualism" (p. 18) that handles a series of dichotomies such as conscious versus unconscious, internal versus external, and normal versus abnormal. This orthodox approach, Overton notes, elevates one concept of a pair to a privileged position, builds a research program around it, and attempts to illustrate why the alternative can be subordinated if not dismissed. That a dualistic position dominates Western psychological sciences converges with Wilbur's (1979) discussion, which elaborates that for centuries Western cultures have drawn a mental boundary casting any issue as one of a pair of opposites; for example, success versus failure, appearance versus reality. The tendency to draw a boundary, and elevate one of the polarized pairs over the other, began with Greek philosophers, was adopted by American psychology and psychiatry, and persists to this day.

The following is one example of how, in the early history of American psychology, the strategy of objectivism dominated long before the model of psychological diagnostic categories emerged, an example that relates to the concepts and methods discussed later. A brief look at this moment in history provides the opportunity to observe that most investigators of the time were taking a dualistic position and how one investigator, who disagreed with this position, responded. A century ago, Frederick Lyman Wells (1912) took issue with one dichotomy that was being constructed when he published his experiments with the "free association method." This procedure had already been introduced in Europe in 1883 by its originator, Sir Frances Galton, as a method to study a person's "emotional life," and was introduced into the United States in 1887 by James McKeen Cattell (Santostefano, 1976). The examiner spoke a word to which the subject was to reply with "the first thing it makes you think of." The participant's associations were then examined in search of clues about "mental and affective processes." Following Cattell's pioneering work, numerous reports of this technique appeared. When Wells reviewed this literature, he noticed a trend that disturbed him, namely, that most investigators were avoiding the "unpleasant task" of learning about a person's emotional life by "hiding themselves" in more pleasant studies that focused on grammatical connections between a person's associations and the stimulus words. Accordingly, Wells concluded, "Such experiments [of word associations] lay bare the mental and emotional life in a way that is startling…so startling…in fact, that workers…seem long to have been effectively blocked from any progress…" (p. 436).

The dualistic position continued to be followed by behavioral scientists into the 1940s but became prominent when, in 1952, the American Psychiatric Association published a *Diagnostic and Statistical Manual of Mental Disorders* (DSM), the first manual describing categories of psychopathology. In 1965, however, the National Institutes of Mental Health (NIMH) invited professionals to discuss whether and how the classifications of nosology benefit the mental health field (Katz, Cole, & Barton, 1965). The invited guests did more than discuss; they vigorously debated the advantages and disadvantages of diagnostic categories. For example: (a) Do the benefits of categorizing people outweigh the loss of information about their individuality? (b) Would the mental health field advance more effectively if behav-

ioral characteristics revealed by individuals are viewed as interacting in a complex manner, rather than as fixed, diagnostic entities? (c) Are diagnostic types that are based on self-description, interviews, and questionnaires limited in some way? Shakow (1965), for example, emphasized that classifying mental disorders could result in reifying a diagnostic category and accepting a simpler understanding of a complex phenomenon. He also questioned the methodology of forming diagnoses by clustering behavioral traits observed to occur together and assume the cluster has meaning. To emphasize this point, he cited a scientist who, in 1939, pointed out that pencils of yellow wood have a greater incidence than pencils of other colors (at least in 1939). The question remained, however, whether the color yellow is essential to the function of pencils. George Kelly (1965) pointed out that developing categories of emotional problems "proves itself to be almost completely sterile in suggesting something new to be looked for" (p. 158), and invented his own diagnosis of clinicians and researchers of his day who followed the model of nosology. These professionals, Kelly proposed, were suffering from "hardening of the categories" (p. 158). And in the summary remarks of this conference, Katz and Cole (1965) asked very telling questions: "Are the mental disorders really made up of these particular configurations of symptoms and characteristics? And why is it that when we think about diagnosis it is difficult not to think of types?" (p. 563).

Notably, the issues raised at this conference did not influence the second edition of the *Diagnostic and Statistical Manual of Mental Disorders* (DSM-II), which was published 3 years later in 1968 and now included diagnostic categories for children and adolescents. A few years later, Piaget (1975) pointed out that the discipline of child psychiatry was still placing too much emphasis on diagnostic categories, viewing individuals in terms of traits they share considered abnormal, and loosing sight of the observation that some individuals may behave adequately in one moment and pathologically at another. Piaget (1975) also recommended that developmental psychopathology go beyond comparing diagnostic groups and pursue the goal of constructing "a common language" that would help us understand a psychological disorder in terms of the "ensemble of elements involved" (p. vii). Neither Piaget's (1975) remarks, nor the deliberations of the NIMH conference, influenced the third edition of the *Diagnostic and Statistical Manual of Mental Disorders* (DSM-III), which was released in 1980 and then revised in 1987 (DSM-III-R). During this period, several volumes appeared indicating that most clinicians and researchers were still focusing their efforts on pathological groups defined in terms of diagnostic categories (e.g., Erlenmeyer-Kimling & Miller, 1986). The next edition, published in 1994 (DSM-IV), described criteria for more than 200 disorders, and showed some evidence that the deliberations of the NIMH conference and Piaget's comments had exerted some influence. In a brief section submerged in the introduction and titled "Limitations of the Categorical Approach" (American Psychiatric Association, 1994, p. xxii), two issues are discussed. The reader is cautioned not to assume that each diagnostic category is a completely discrete entity with boundaries dividing it from other disorders, and not to assume that all individuals "described as having the same mental disorder are alike in all important ways" (American Psychiatric Association, 1994, p. xxii). This brief section also notes that some workers have suggested that, instead of following a categorical model, a dimensional model should be considered that addresses deep and surface behaviors (in other words, Piaget's "ensemble of elements"). But DSM-IV rejects the dimensional model because it is "much less familiar and vivid then are the categorical names for mental disorders" (American Psychiatric Association, 1994, p. xxii).

In 2000, the American Psychiatric Association published a text revision of DSM-IV (DSM-IV-TR), not only to construct a bridge leading to DSM-V, but also "to ensure that all information is still up to date" and "to make improvements that will enhance the educational value of DSM-IV" (American Psychiatric Association, 2000, p. xxix). In spite of these goals, the brief section titled "Limitations of the Categorical Approach" is identical to that in DSM-IV (noted earlier), except for a brief paragraph. Here the reader is reminded that valid application of the manual requires the clinician and researcher to evaluate the criteria that must be met if a person is to qualify for membership in a diagnostic category (e.g., the length of time a symptom must persist). The reader is also informed that assessments relying on "psychological testing not covering the criteria content (e.g., projective testing) cannot be validly used as the primary source of diagnostic information" (American Psychiatric Association, 2000, p. xxxii). In simpler terms, methods assessing features of a person's inner self (e.g., cognitive functioning and meanings assigned to experiences) do not qualify. This position not only differs from Piaget's and others noted earlier, but also disagrees with investigators discussed later. That DSM-IV and DSM- IV-TR reject the dimensional model because diagnostic categories are "more vivid" relates, in my opinion, to the caution Shakow (1965) expressed at the NIMH conference decades earlier, namely, that diagnostic categories are "reified," and to Wells' (1912) question whether some professionals avoid the "unpleasant task" of learning about a person's emotional life. It is an open question whether professionals who focus solely on diagnostic categories do so partially to avoid the task of engaging the complex ensemble of elements involved in a person's psychological, emotional functioning. Notably, DSM-IV and DSM-IV-TR conclude their brief comments on the limitations of the categorical approach with a statement that is relevant to the conceptual matrix and empirical studies discussed in this chapter: "Nonetheless, it is possible that increasing research on, and familiarity with, dimensional systems may eventually result in their acceptance both as a method of conveying clinical information and as a research tool" (American Psychiatric Association, 2000, p. xxii).

Thus, from the studies of the free association method to the present time, the viewpoint of objectivism and the method of nosology have dominated the concept of psychopathology (e.g., Beutler & Malik, 2002; McHugh, 2005). This viewpoint, however, is being challenged. Levy-Warren and Levy-Warren (2005), for example, discuss the misuses of diagnostic categories, noting that a diagnostic label becomes who the person is. Horwitz and Wakefield (2007) argue that the DSM has transformed normal sorrow into a disorder of depression. Murrie, Boccaccini, McCoy, and Cornell (2007) discuss whether diagnostic labels influence judges in juvenile courts, and Patten (2006) wonders whether the high frequency of the diagnosis of bipolar disorder raises the question whether everyone qualifies for this category. The model of nosology has also received criticism from the lay public. For example, in a provocative article, Davis (1997) notes that "according to DSM-IV human life is a form of mental illness" (p. 62), and creatively examines diagnoses to illustrate that, from the viewpoint of nosology, there is no behavior observed in everyday life that does not fall into one. In spite of the challenge from professionals and the lay public, it is not surprising that, with the rapid and widespread use of diagnostic manuals over five decades, the most common way of thinking about psychological functioning has become either viewing it as pathological, and therefore qualifying for membership in a diagnostic category, or as normal, namely, failing to fit a diagnosis.

A HOLISTIC RELATIONAL APPROACH TO DEFINING THE CONCEPT OF PSYCHOPATHOLOGY

The concept of psychopathology to be offered in this chapter is emphatically not based on diagnostic categories. The conceptual matrix offered here, together with associated empirical methods, forms a developmental model that understands person and environment as a holistic system of dialectical relational parts. This view of psychopathology converges with the position that Overton and Horowitz (1991) presented, which holds that "developmental psychopathology is a system of concepts that explores individual differences in adaptational patterns as these patterns arise in the context of normative development and as they become dysfunctional" (p. 1). To set the stage for the proposed conceptual matrix, and how it introduces a quite divergent understanding of psychopathology from that offered by nosology, the reader is asked to consider John, a 16-year-old, 10th grader who, after visiting the high-school counselor, asked his parents to arrange a consultation with me because he felt "very confused about some things." Throughout our first meeting, he oscillated between very different moods and themes: He spontaneously shared with pride his accomplishments as a gymnast and that he made the honor role last year; he stared at the floor, anxiously clutched his hands, or passed his fingers over the leaves of a nearby Dieffenbachia plant, mumbling that he now has difficulty listening to what teachers are saying and to his parents complaining that, before leaving for school, he always carefully aligns pictures hanging on the wall and the chairs around the dining room table. Near the end of the meeting, without commenting, he leaned forward and pushed aside his wavy hair, revealing an area of about one square inch that was bald. During our second meeting, John shared that every day he carefully felt the bald area with his fingertips and, if he detected a hair stub, plucked it out, experiencing a surge of pleasure, which is why he has been doing this since he was "a kid." Also, recently, he has enjoyed nuzzling against his neck the furry head of a toy lion, which he has kept since early childhood. From this, he associated to an issue he declared was the reason for his requesting a consultation. With difficulty, he described the surge of excitement and anger he experiences when interacting with one of his teachers who maintains a beard and when in the locker room after gymnastics, if a particular classmate, who has developed considerable body hair, is there. In closing this sketch, one observation made several times needs to be underlined because it eventually carried significance, especially in terms of one of the concepts to be introduced. I noticed that when John talked about his hair pulling, the science teacher, the classmate with body hair, and his toy lion, he sometimes arched his shoulders back ever so slightly, pushing his abdomen out. Because this occurred with such regularity I became convinced that it expressed an embodied meaning that held importance in John's personality.

With John's permission, I met with his parents, who shared that although his hair pulling was a concern, they were more concerned about his poor academic performance. When we focused on John's hair pulling, they agreed on when and how it began. John's sister was born when he was 17 months old. During the next several months, he made clear he did not accept her because, in his mother's opinion, she was struggling with postpartum depression and her inability to control her anger. One day when she spotted John poking his sister, she screamed with anger and slapped him. John ran off, crawled under the parents' bed, and refused to come out. His father arrived shortly thereafter and coaxed him out. Both parents noticed a couple of strands of hair in his fist. In the following months, when they observed that an area of his scalp remained sparse, they and the pediatrician concluded he was still pulling out hair, and believed that the mother's angry scream and slap had caused this behavior. Between the ages of 5 and 13, John participated in a behavior modification program on three occasions. Each time the hair pulling was eliminated, but the habit returned. The parents emphasized that except for his recent academic difficulties, John has always done very well in school.

Influenced by hypotheses suggested by my meetings with John, I asked his father if he ever maintained a beard. Surprised by the question, he acknowledged he did, spontaneously sharing that he enjoyed snuggling his beard on John's belly and neck when he was a baby. John's mother added that she also enjoyed caressing John's belly with her shoulder-length hair. Both parents laughed, acknowledging they were "ticklers." The mother shared she "stopped being a tickler" when John was a year old because she focused on her pregnancy. The father recalled with amusement that when John began to walk, he would arch his back and push out his stomach, inviting his father to tickle him, and then run away as father playfully searched for him. The mother asked the father to recall what happened when he shaved his beard. The father thought John seemed "stressed," but in the mother's opinion, he was "terrified," avoiding his father for weeks. The father offered that, for some reason, after he shaved his beard, he stopped playing games with John like searching for him when he hid behind the couch. Both parents agreed that the father had shaved his beard before the incident when the mother slapped John.

This sketch, which we will return to later, is intended to illustrate the limitations of diagnostic categories and set the stage for the conceptual matrix that is introduced shortly. If we consider John in terms of diagnostic categories, we are left with several questions. Should we view him through the lens of trichotillomania (hair pulling), one of the impulse-control disorders, or through the lens of obsessive–compulsive disorder, because of his preoccupation with aligning whatever is hanging on walls and adjusting chairs, or through the lens of anxiety disorder, and focus on how he experiences waves of anxiety that include twisting his hands? Or should we focus on the times he appeared very sad when staring at the floor with his head hanging low and select the diagnosis of depressive disorder, or examine him through the lens of attention deficit disorder and focus on the extreme difficulty he is having concentrating on what teachers and parents are saying? Whichever diagnosis we select, we are still faced with confusion. For example, what about the fact that he performed

well academically and socially since kindergarten until the last semester? And what about his achievements in gymnastics? Whether a diagnostic category exists that helps us understand John's personality development and functioning leads to several other questions that introduce the concepts outlined in Figure 22.1. How and why was the hair pulling established? What was the original meaning of this behavior, and did this meaning undergo change? How did the hair pulling persist from the age of 2 years to adolescence in a boy who had, until recently, functioned quite adequately? And how do we understand that, as he approached his 16th birthday, he felt pressed to talk to someone about his main concern which, as it turned out, involved the surge of excitement and anger he experienced whenever he was in the presence of a particular teacher and friend?

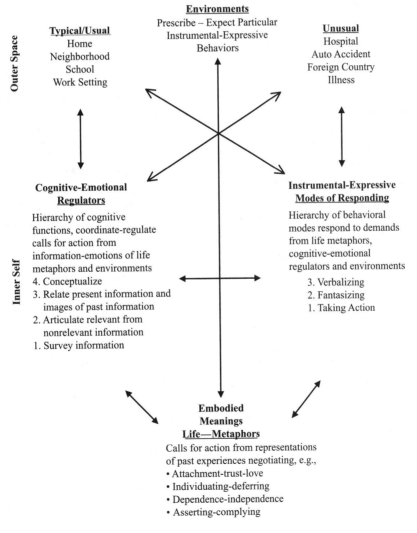

Figure 22.1 Matrix of concepts depicting dialectical relations within and between a person's inner self and environments.

A CONCEPTUAL MATRIX ADDRESSING DEVELOPMENTAL PSYCHOPATHOLOGY FROM THE PERSPECTIVE OF COGNITION-EMOTION-BEHAVIOR-ENVIRONMENT

It is necessary to summarize the metatheoretical and theoretical principles that shape them to adequately describe the concepts of this matrix that addresses developmental psychopathology from the perspective of cognition-emotion-behavior-environment. As Overton (2006) suggests, metatheory "defines the context in which theoretical concepts are constructed...[and]...functions not only to ground, constrain and sustain theoretical concepts but also functions to do the same thing with observational methods" (p. 20). Guided by this advice and that of others (Granic, 2005), the following is a list of each of the planks that form the metatheoretical scaffold that shapes the concepts and methods proposed, a scaffold following a relational developmental systems perspective:

A. A person is a unique self-organizing and self-regulating system, and an active agent, negotiating with her physical and social environments, registering information and giving meaning to these experiences. New forms of cognition, emotion, and behavior emerge through this process of self-organization.

B. The meanings a person gives to experiences form the foundation of the person's self-structure.

C. Change is not always linear, occurring in what a person perceives, the meanings and related emotions he gives to experiences, and actions he takes.

D. Development consists of two complementary processes of change: (1) transformational change, namely, change in the organization or structure of some behavior or cognitive activity that results in the emergence of novel, increasingly complex, differentiated, and integrated forms; and (2) variational change, namely, the degree to which a change varies from some standard or average (Overton, 2006).

E. Behavior contains both instrumental qualities that serve to achieve some outcome and expressive qualities that reflect meanings associated with the behavior (Overton, 2006). Of particular importance, these qualities are viewed as coequal, complementary processes that function within a dialectical-relational context when a person is interacting and negotiating with environments.

F. Cause and effect is a relational, bidirectional, circular process. Lower order features provide the foundation from which higher order features emerge. But these higher order features, in turn, exert a top-down influence.

G. Concepts guide the construction of methods to evaluate processes and change that take place in real time. The method that is most effective in revealing the various psychological processes available to a system is to perturbate the system (Granic, 2005).

Given these metatheoretical principles, we now consider the theoretical principles that further shape the matrix of concepts and associated methods of the three-story "developmental house" depicted in Figure 22.1. These principles derive from the developmental theories of Jean Piaget (e.g., 1967), Heinz Werner (e.g., 1964), and psychoanalytic relational theory (e.g., Aron, 1996) elaborated by Overton (e.g., 2006) and Granic (2005). Each principle builds on and elaborates the others. (A more detailed discussion of these theoretical principles is presented, together with related research findings, in Santostefano's [1978, 1998] work.)

1. *Principle of holism.* The principle of holism states that the meaning and psychological properties of any behavior (e.g., perception, action, fantasy, emotion, social interaction) are determined by the psychological context of which the behavior is a part.

2. *Principle of psychological givens and directiveness of behavior.* An individual does not passively experience and react to stimulation. Rather, from birth, the organism makes use of preadapted modes of functioning (e.g., motoric rhythm patterns, emotional and cognitive regulators), which enable the individual to approach, avoid, select and organize stimulation, and to take action, in the service of accomplishing some intention and/or changing his or her relationship with the environment.

3. *Principle of mobility of behavioral functions, stages of development, and multiple behavioral modes and goals.* At an early stage of development, the individual functions with a limited, less flexible, hierarchy of behavioral modes that require physical contact with environments. At a later stage, the individual functions with a broader, more flexible hierarchy of behavioral modes, sometimes operating at a level characteristic of earlier development (regression), and

at other times at a more advanced level (progression) in response to changes in stimulation. Progressing from one stage to the next results in the individual having available multiple means to achieve a goal and multiple goals that serve the same mode of functioning. In the absence of developmental interferences, these progressive and regressive shifts in functioning result in a positive fit between the individual's developmental goals and opportunities, limits, and expectations presented by environments, fostering development and adaptive success.

4. *Principle of developmental goals as motivating forces.* Long-range and short-range developmental goals stimulate the individual to make use of behavioral, cognitive, and emotional functions to reach a goal that requires particular qualities, types, tempos, and degrees of stimulation. Long-range developmental goals are meanings a child constructs from the first weeks of life through embodied actions and negotiations with human and nonhuman environments, meanings that are directed toward particular types of interactions; for example, trust-love-attachment with and unconditional availability of others; separating-individuating; and asserting/competing. Short-range developmental goals include, for example, curiosity and the need for change and complexity. Illustrated by Piaget's concept of alimentation and the psychodynamic concept of stimulus nutriment, an individual looks for ways to "nourish" his developmental goals by repeatedly assimilating environmental stimuli related to them.

5. *Principle of adaptation.* A relational dialectic exists between an individual and her environments, each defining and defined by the other. In this process, the individual makes use of an evolving hierarchy of average-expectable behavioral modes that more or less match opportunities presented by environments, and environments act on the individual with an evolving series of average-expectable types of stimulation and demands that more or less fit the behavioral modes available to the individual. Demands and stimulation from the individual and environments, however, are never perfectly matched. To cope with these mismatches, the individual moves from a more recently acquired organization to an earlier level or develops a more differentiated organization (the principle of mobility of functions noted earlier).

6. *Principle of developmental intrusions and interferences* (Nagera, 1981; Winnicott, 1965). At certain periods in development, psychological systems are ready to deal with and accommodate to particular types of stimulation. If this stimulation is not made available, the behavioral system in question assumes a deviant line of development. In addition, if a particular class of stimulation is presented to an individual who, however, has not yet constructed the behavioral system that deals with that type, the individual's developmental course is also derailed.

These developmental principles converge with those defined by others who have examined and evaluated requirements for a sound scientific theory of development (e.g., Harris, 1957; Overton, 2006). At this point, Figure 22.1 should be examined from the altitude of a helicopter, so to speak. The matrix consists of two broad organizations, one labeled Outer Space and the other Inner Self. If we lower our altitude, we notice that Outer Space, that is, the ecological perspective (Bronfenbrenner & Morris, 2008), consists of two suborganizations: Typical/Usual Environments and Unusual Environments. Inner Self consists of three suborganizations: Cognitive-Emotional Regulators, Instrumental-Expressive Behaviors, and Embodied Meanings—Life Metaphors. As discussed later, each subsystem is engaged in a relational dialectic with the others, each defining and defined by the others. In general terms, then, as a person acts in the context of a typical/usual or unusual human or nonhuman environment, negotiating his developmental goals, three interrelated, dialectical processes take place: (1) the person's embodied meanings construe the environment and prescribe some plan of action; (2) cognitive-emotional regulators gather information simultaneously from these embodied meanings and related environments, and regulate associated emotions; and (3) an instrumental-expressive behavior that meets the opportunities afforded by the structure of the environment is formed and effected. Usually, these dialectical interactions among the subsystems promote development but sometimes produce some form of maladaptation in response to developmental interferences. In what follows, each concept is addressed as a probe to emphasize it is not elevated to a privileged position and to stimulate other investigations. With each probe, the history and research that create the concept is summarized, and an evaluation is made of recent research to assess its metatheoretical coherence. In addition, specific research methods are proposed to illustrate how the concept may serve developmental psychopathology across the life span.

THE FIRST PROBE: THE FOUNDATION AND FIRST FLOOR OF THE INNER SELF: EMBODIED MEANINGS–LIFE METAPHORS

Wolfe (2003) points out that the concept of "Self" has become a very hot topic in the general field of psychology but still lacks clarity and requires elaboration. To address this need, I have proposed that embodied meanings (body image) form the foundation of a person's inner self (Overton, Müller, & Newman, 2008; Santostefano, 1998, 2004). Before elaborating this concept, the reader is reminded of the classic, dualistic mind-body split, initially crafted by Descartes, which historically has dominated the general field of psychology (e.g., Overton, 2006; Wilbur, 1979). Because of this split, as Müller and Newman (2008) noted, "Until recently the body has been almost completely ignored in theories and empirical research in psychology in general and in developmental psychology in particular" (p. 313). Before we consider the recent surge of studies of body image, however, a review of the history of this concept will serve our considering different definitions and related methods in current use.

Lessons from the Past

When neurology and psychoanalysis emerged at the dawn of the 20th century, the body was not split off from the mind and subordinated because the methods of these disciplines relied on patients closely scrutinizing and sharing accounts of their body experiences. In 1926, the neurologist Henry Head proposed "unconscious body schema" to conceptualize how body perceptions are integrated, forming a frame of reference and integrating body experiences (Fisher, 1990). Although giving little attention to how a person's body experiences are tied to his or her personality, early neurologists legitimized the study of body image phenomena. Paul Shilder is credited with being the first to construct a bridge connecting body experiences with personality. In his major work, Shilder (1935) conceptualized a person's body image as representing an integration of her goals, emotions, body experiences, and interactions. For example, Shilder noted:

[T]here is unity in the body…we may call it body image (p. 11)…the body contracts when we hate, it becomes firmer, and its outlines towards the world are more marked…We expand the body when we feel friendly and lovingly… When…the body is not sufficient for expression…we add clothes…jewelry which again expand, contract, disfigure, or emphasize the body image… (pp. 210–211)

Shilder (1935) conceptualized body image as expressions of meanings in everything from one's body movements to one's clothing. Although he followed Freud, who proposed that a "body ego" is constructed first forming the foundation of higher mental functions, he differed in placing emphasis on body image as an entity that continues to change and develop. Of particular relevance regarding my proposed concepts, Shilder concluded that the construction of a person's body image, and how it changes, depends on interactions and experiences the person has with human and nonhuman environments. For example, he suggested that, in Freud's clinical case of Dora, her hysterical coughing was not so much an expression of erotic sensations in the throat but expressions of her early attachment to, and identification with, attributes of her mother.

It is interesting to note that decades before the concept of body image was introduced, Francis Galton (1884) devised a method to assess what could be viewed as one aspect of a person's embodied meanings. Noticing that persons who "have an inclination to one another [seem to]…incline or slope together when sitting side by side" (Galton, p. 182), he attached pressure gauges to the legs of chairs, located in a room in which meetings were held, in an effort to study the meaning of this behavior. After each of several meetings, he recorded the measures to assess who leaned toward whom. Although he reported that he could not complete his experiment because of other commitments, Galton advocated that methods should be designed to increase the likelihood of observing behaviors that represent some combination of body activity, emotion, and meaning. Galton's proposal received some attention, such as Fernald assessing "persistence" by recording the length of time a person stands on tiptoes (Symonds, 1931), Allport and Vernon (1933) proposing that various actions a person performs (e.g., body postures, type of gait) are determined by and reveal his personality, and Werner Wolff (1943) observing how a child punched a balloon and manipulated a jar of cold cream to study whether the child was expressing embodied meanings such as aggression, insecurity, and caution.

During the following years, several psychoanalysts addressed the concept of body image (Santostefano, 1998): for example, Carl Jung noticed that some persons experience their bodies as a protective enclosure within which they can find safety and fend off attack, and Theodore Rich that some persons image their bodies after an object with hard surfaces when coping with mental conflicts. And Mahl (1987) proposed that when a person repeats some action during treatment sessions, the embodied meaning of the action is sometimes transformed into fantasies and conscious thoughts. He described an adult who, during psychoanalytic treatment sessions, repeatedly rubbed the back of her hand against a nearby roughly plastered wall. When stimulated by this body experience, this patient remembered how her father rubbed his beard against her face, leaving her tingling with excitement.[1] In spite of these studies of body image/embodied meanings, the concept received only isolated attention in mainstream psychology until it entered through the doorway of cognitive research in the 1950s and 1960s. For example, Wapner and Werner (1965) demonstrated that one's body posture in space reflected attitudes that influence perceptions of objects. After these programs peaked in the 1970s, interest in body image research declined (Tiemersma, 1989).

Current Approaches to Investigating Embodied Meanings/Body Image

Beginning in 1990 the tide began to change, reflected by an edited volume addressing body image (Cash & Pruzinsky, 1990). In these presentations, however, the methods used to assess body image are very different from Galton's, who assessed the meaning of the direction in which a person leans. For example, Thompson, Penner, and Altabe (1990) reviewed more than 40 methods that ask a person to respond to a questionnaire or rate satisfaction with each of a series of silhouettes. Research addressing body image as related to physical and interpersonal conditions also relies on questionnaires and rating scales, for example, chronic illness (Vamos, 1993), parental divorce (Spigelman & Spigelman, 1991), and social anxiety (Edelman & Skov, 1993). The reliance on questionnaires reflects the conceptual and methodological tendency, as noted earlier, to segregate body and mind. A decade later, another edited

volume appeared. In the introduction, addressing the need to understand the concept of body image, Pruzinsky and Cash (2002) cited a publication that lists 16 "definitions" of body image (e.g., weight satisfaction, appearance satisfaction, size perception accuracy) and noted "the concept of body image has remained rather elusive in the past because it has meant different things to different scientists and practitioners" (p. 7). The presentations in this volume, however, illustrate that, for most investigators, the concept of body image is still defined in terms of how a person construes her/his appearance, size, and weight. For example, Levine and Smolak (2002) report, "Longitudinal studies reveal that, for girls, satisfaction with body parts and overall appearance declines significantly over the years 12–15, before leveling off..." (p. 75). Similarly, studies of body image development in adulthood and late adulthood (Whitbourne & Skultety, 2002) focus on a person's reaction to changes in body appearance, which Tiggermann (2002) relates to the influence of the media. And Tantleff-Dunn and Gokee (2002) report studies comparing self-ratings of appearance with ratings by the persons' romantic partners, emphasizing that "many of the available instruments are easily administered questionnaires..." (p. 114).

Questionnaires have also been used to assess body image related to, for example, adolescent suicidal ideation (Brausch & Muehlenkamp, 2007), breast cancer (Bredart, Verdier, & Dolbeault, 2007), and out-of-body experiences (Murray & Fox, 2008). The questionnaire method also dominates studies addressing body image issues related to gender and race (e.g., Chen, Jackson, & Huang, 2006; Martins, Tiggermann, & Churchett, 2008; Penkal & Kurdek, 2007; Reddy & Crowther, 2007; Sabik, Cole, & Ward, 2007). Conceptualizing body image primarily in terms of appearance, and the method of self-report/questionnaire, has also stimulated interest in other countries, resulting in the translation of body image questionnaires (e.g., Albani et al., 2006; Gailego, Perpina, Botella, & Banos, 2006; Legenbauer, Vocks, & Schult-Stromel, 2007). In addition, other related methods are also used. For example, a life-size image of the person is projected on a screen, and she adjusts the width of the image, which is taken as a measure of the degree to which the person distorts her perception of the body, and the person selects which of eight figure changes represents her current size and the one that depicts the size the person would like to be (Thompson & Gardner, 2002). From this review of past and current methods used to asses body image, we now turn to consider methods used in life-span investigations of body image.

---

[1] I have described previously the meanings children expressed with their body activity during intensive treatment and demonstrated how these body meanings are related to experiences from the first years of life (Santostefano, 2004).

Approaches to Assessing Body Image across the Life Span

The focus on appearance, and the method of questionnaires and figure drawings to assess body image also dominate investigations of life-span changes in body image. The following are examples: questionnaires completed by women (age range, 20–65 years) show that the relationship between body dissatisfaction and self-esteem declines with age (Weber & Tiggermann, 2003); questionnaires completed by European American, Asian American, Hispanic American, and African American women (age range, 18–81) indicate no significant ethnic differences, (Gilmore, 2001); and negative comments made when 54-year-old females were children had a significant negative effect on their current body dissatisfaction as reported in questionnaires (McLaren, Kirk, Hardy, & Gauvin, 2004). One review of studies concludes that body dissatisfaction is stable across the adult life span for women into late adult years (Tiggermann, 2004), and another that the desire for physical beauty is at the highest point among adolescents (Bybee & Wells, 2006).

The Need to Clarify the Concept of Body Image and Select Related Methods

Research conducted during PE during recent years demonstrates that body image is conceptualized, for the most part, as a person's view of her physical appearance, expressed in a questionnaire, which differs considerably from the original conceptualization and methods used before the 1970s. This conceptualization is reflected by Thompson and Gardner (2002), who noted that when selecting a method "the assessor should have a clear sense of which 'aspect' of body image is relevant (size, weight, masculinity) and which 'dimension' is relevant (general dissatisfaction, affective...)" (p. 151). Cash and Pruzinsky (2002) emphasized, however, that we must go beyond conceptualizing and assessing body image as a trait-like phenomenon concerning physical appearance, "We must enhance our understanding of how body image affects and is affected by...social functioning...[and of]...the longitudinal development of body image..." (p. 511). Cash (2002) also argued that investigation of body image requires the assessment of "body image states in specific contexts or in response to environmental manipulation" (p. 164). And in their review of methods investigators use to assess body image, Thompson and van den Berg (2002) noted, "Behavioral measures have received limited analysis in body image literature" (p. 150).

Current Approaches to Conceptualizing and Assessing Body Image Related to the Original View of Body Image as Expressions of Meaning

A groundbreaking volume (Overton et al., 2008) recently appeared that addresses the challenges noted earlier and comprehensively explores the role of body experiences in the development of meaning, consciousness, and psychological functioning. As Overton (2008) noted, "The kind of body we have is a precondition for our having the kind of behaviors, experiences and meanings we have" (p. 1). In broad terms, this volume clarifies that body experiences result in multiple *meanings*, rather than in a singular "image" or trait. Some chapters of this volume reflect efforts to put the mind back into the body by focusing on the body as experienced and actively engaged with environments. Other chapters that focus on how the mind forms particular images or meanings of body experiences reflect efforts to put the body back in the mind.

In contrast with the bulk of research on body image noted earlier, a few studies used methods that perturbate a person's body to express meanings. For example, to assess the relation between the tendency to take risks and abuse alcohol, Skeel, Pilarski, Kimberley, and Neudecker (2008) projected a balloon on a computer screen and asked the participant to "pump it up," making the balloon as large as possible without causing it to explode. The participant received points for each pump and decided when to "cash out." Kring and Sloan (2007) rated meanings conveyed by facial expressions, and Tracy and Robins (2007) rated meanings such as pride, fear, and disgust represented, for example, by direction of eye gaze, posture, and arm position. Carrick and Quas (2006) used a method reported decades ago by Overton and Jackson (1973) that focused on meanings conveyed by gestures. And to study fear of heights, Teachman, Stefanucci, Clerkin, Cody, and Proffitt (2008) asked a participant to climb a 12-foot ladder and measured the time taken to ascend to the top. Along the same line, in my own research, I have examined the development of a person's body image by designing methods assessing embodied meanings as they are expressed in response to environmental manipulations (e.g., Santostefano, 1998, 2004, 2008). Before describing examples of these methods and preliminary results, to illustrate how they could serve assessing embodied meanings across the life span, it is important that we discuss how body-image–embodied meanings are constructed beginning in the first years of life, forming the foundation of a person's inner self.

How Embodied Meanings That Form the Foundation of the Inner Self Are Constructed During the First Years of Life

An integration of Jean Piaget's (e.g., 1951, 1967), Daniel Stern's (1985) and Louis Sander's (e.g., 1964, 1989) infancy research programs present a developmental systems perspective on the construction of a matrix of embodied meanings. In turn, this matrix system represents the point of origin of instrumental-expressive actions and cognitive-emotional regulators during the first years of life (see Santostefano, 1998, 2004, for an elaborated discussion). Piaget's pioneering research program demonstrated how infants construct knowledge and meanings while physically engaging and interacting with environments. Stern's research elaborates Piaget's by centering on the role of emotions the infant experiences during interactions and how these emotions contribute to the development of meanings and the infant's sense of self. To conceptualize how the meanings of repeated experiences and associated emotions with persons and things are conserved, Stern introduces the concept of "representations of interactions [that have] generalized" (RIGs). When the infant repeatedly experiences activity-emotions that differ in only minor ways, the infant gradually constructs a generalized meaning that prescribes what the infant expects and how the infant performs. When an infant has an experience that is not similar to previously repeated experiences, elements of the ongoing experience activate the RIG that has already been constructed, a memory Stern terms *evoked companion*; for example, if a mother now plays peekaboo in a different way because she is depressed, the infant uses the evoked companion to check whether the mother's emotional tone is a variation of the past or defines an entirely new type of self-other experience. Stern proposes that constructing RIGs contributes to the development of five "senses of self," each one building on the previous one and organizing interpersonal experiences in a new way. Sander's research elaborates Piaget's and Stern's by focusing on a series of interpersonal issues infant and caregiver "negotiate" that contribute to the embodied meanings an infant constructs. These meanings represent successes and failures of previous negotiations, and influence how the infant seeks, engages, and avoids subsequent interactions with others and objects. The success that infant and caregiver achieve in negotiating each issue influences the success with which the next issue in the hierarchy is negotiated. An integration of these infant research programs defines the following stages in the development of a person's inner self consisting of a matrix of embodied meanings representing experiences with persons and objects.

Emergent Self (0–3 months): Acquired Adaptation, the Evaluation of Primary Reactions, and Negotiating Initial Adaptation

From birth, experiences involving a variety of body sensations (e.g., sucking, tactile perceptions, body movements, sounds) are integrated when the infant contacts his own body, the bodies of others, and objects in the environment. Although these experiences are uncoordinated, they gradually shift from being reflexes to becoming "acquired adaptations." The infant elaborates these bodily sensations by engaging in activity that integrates and coordinates schemas representing them with different modalities (e.g., vision with touch, sound with touch) and repeats these activities many times. During this activity, initial adaptation is negotiated as the infant enacts cues about her physical and emotional state (e.g., various cries, fussing, being content). In response, the caregiver coordinates, for example, the way the baby is held, fed, and bathed. If this issue is successfully negotiated, the infant develops, for example, a predictable rhythm of sleeping and wakefulness, and the caregiver begins to develop a sense that he "knows" the child.

Core Self (3–7 months): Secondary Circular Reactions and Negotiating Reciprocal Exchange

At 3 to 7 months of age, the infant begins to be oriented beyond the self, repeating behaviors to sustain contact with aspects of human and nonhuman environments that, for various reasons, have appeal. For example, the infant deliberately imitates a sound or movement performed by another person so that she will repeat the sound or movement and participate in a cycle of interactions. Constellations of actions, sensations, and emotions that occur during these repeated interactions are summarized and conserved in RIGs, which equip the infant to anticipate what should be expected during future interactions and determine whether a given experience/emotion is the same or different from previous ones. In addition, the infant begins to sense that he and caregivers are separate physically and have different emotional experiences. Caregiver and infant also negotiate reciprocity by taking turns being active and passive while they are sharing a crescendo of emotions (e.g., mother smiles and pauses, allowing the infant to respond; the infant adds new giggles and movements). The rhythmicity and emotions with which caregiver and child respond to each other, and the emotions they share during, for example, feeding and bathing define the success with which this issue is negotiated.

Subjective Self (7–14 months): Coordinating Secondary Circular Reactions, Imitating the Actions of Others, and Negotiating Early Directed Activity and Focalization

The circular reactions of the previous stage, and the mental schemas and images that result from them, are integrated and coordinated forming a matrix of meanings that deals with new situations and enables the infant to imitate the actions of others with behaviors that are analogous. For example, when Piaget opened and closed his eyes, the infant first opened and closed her hand and then her mouth. In this way, the infant begins to define herself by sensing and understanding the motives, intentions, and emotions of other persons that are shared and guide or influence interactions. To this point, the interactions between caregiver and infant have been initiated, for the most part, by the caregiver. Now the infant begins to use smiles and gestures to initiate and direct interactions, and begins to show preferences for types of stimulation. Becoming physically more mobile and exploring larger spaces, the toddler sends more differentiated cues to the caregiver that concern the need to explore the unknown and to be protected from stressful stimulation, that is, negotiating the caregiver's unconditional availability. If the caregiver responds appropriately, while she is maintaining the reciprocity negotiated earlier, the toddler begins to explore increasingly larger geographies with confidence, individuates, and asserts himself with the caregiver and the larger environment.

Symbolic-Verbal Self (15–24 months): Tertiary Circular Reactions, Deferred Imitation, Negotiating Self-Assertion, and Testing Aggression

The infant uses repetitive behaviors to experiment actively with the environment, in the service of discovering new ways of accomplishing goals, and transforms these circular reactions into play rituals. For example, Piaget (1951) described his infant daughter who one day pressed her nose against her mother's check, which caused the infant to breathe loudly. "This phenomenon at once interested her... she drew her nose back...sniffed and breathe very hard (as if blowing her nose) then again thrust her nose against her mother's check, laughing heartily" (Piaget, 1951, p. 94). Piaget reported that the infant repeated these actions at least once a day for more than a month as a "play ritual." The infant also continues to invent new ways of accomplishing goals by combining schemas before taking action.

For example, if a carriage is set against the wall, instead of pushing the carriage in trial-and-error experiments, the toddler looks over the situation and pushes the carriage away from the wall. With the capacity to combine schemas without including experimental action, the infant develops another important capacity Piaget termed *deferred imitation*. This capacity is a clear sign that the budding toddler has moved from the ability to represent objects to symbolically representing objects, persons, and events. When an important person is absent, the toddler performs some action representing and conserving the meaning of that person. For example, a toddler was sitting in a highchair with a nanny nearby. He observed his mother place a hat on her head and leave the room; the toddler then placed a napkin on his head, expressing the meaning, "although you're gone, you're still with me." In addition, the budding toddler and caregiver now begin to share meanings with symbolic language and action signals that they coauthor. Negotiating self-assertion emerges gradually in this phase as the budding toddler begins to walk, cultivate the beginning sense of autonomy, and show the first signs of negativism and possessiveness. In response, the caregiver attempts to set limits and also gives permission with both physical and emotional reactions. To negotiate this issue successfully, the child should experience that some of his victories are being accepted, and become explicitly aggressive toward persons and things while he is negotiating self-assertion. For example, while hurling a toy, the child exclaims emotionally and with a body posture. During these negotiations, the caregiver should distinguish among various aggressive intentions the child displays, coordinate her responses accordingly, and provide the child with opportunities to repair the disruption.

Narrative Self (24–36 months): Modifying Aggressive Intentions, Inventing Symbolic Behavior During Interactions, and Consolidating a Body Image

The toddler begins to share with others the content of his private representational world with action and language symbols, and develops multiple ways to express assertiveness, internalize the standards of others, and render in more realistic ways his sense of power. If this issue is successfully negotiated, the child does not surrender her ambition and assertiveness. While the child and caregiver are negotiating the previous issues, they develop ways of communicating through symbolic behaviors (e.g., body postures, gestures, facial expressions, emotional tones, and verbal metaphors), and negotiate whether and how they coauthor symbols during interactions. If this negotiating is successful, the child internalizes the actions and verbal symbols that have been invented. During negotiations throughout the first 3 years of life, then, the child constructs a body image representing the many meanings that define her self (e.g., self-worth, assertiveness, loving, and being loved).

Beebe and Lachmann (2002) incorporate the concepts of Piaget, Stern, and Sander to emphasize particular developmental principles that operate during interactions between infant and caregiver; for example, the principle of disruption and repair focuses on the issue that some interactions fail to fulfill what an infant expects from a caregiver. Beebe and Lachmann review studies showing that as early as the age of 2 months, infants and their mothers match their behaviors (e.g., facial expressions, body movements) only 30% of the time whether interacting in real-life or experimentally designed situations. When involved in a disruption, however, they return to mutual regulation 70% of the time. Infants who have opportunities to successfully repair disruptions show more secure attachments with others, and a greater sense of competence at 1 year of age, than do infants who do not have opportunities to repair disruptions. Beebe and Lachmann also emphasize that the body is involved in everyday interactions between infant/toddler and caregiver, and that representations of these interactions influence how interactions are experienced throughout life, a position consistent with embodiment theory (Overton et al., 2008). Along the same line, Mark Johnson (2008) proposes that body image schemas constructed during the first years of life are "metaphorically projected," influencing meanings a person gives to experiences later in life, illustrated and elaborated by Overton (1994), Santostefano (1994), and the research of Brandtstädter and Heckhausen (Poulin, Haase, & Heckhausen, 2005).

These developmental models and related research, therefore, address how the body remains in the mind, forming the foundation of all meanings experienced and expressed later, and how this foundation creates organizations of cognitive-emotional regulators and instrumental-expressive behaviors that coordinate and regulate the goals of the self and environments. The next section discusses examples of methods used in studies conducted to explore embodied meanings, methods that differ significantly from questionnaires in popular use.

Meanings Generated by Body Experiences: When the Body Speaks, What Does It Say?

Relying on infant research and models we just reviewed, I define body image as an organized matrix of embodied life metaphors, or embodied meanings, representing experiences and related emotions involved in negotiating interactive-intrapersonal goals with environments from the first years of life throughout the life span—for example, attachment/trust/love, loss/detachment, separation-individuation, dependence-autonomy, safety-risk taking, initiating-reciprocating, deferring-dominating, asserting/competing, self-love-idealizing others. The first edition of an embodied life metaphor emerges at the age of 8 to 12 months, when a child organizes and repeats nonverbal, play rituals negotiating developmental goals. For a play ritual to create an embodied life metaphor, the infant should have achieved the following developmental landmarks (see earlier): (1) constructed the beginnings of a subjective self within which the infant comes to understand the motives of others and is able to share meanings; (2) reached the stage of cognitive development when circular reactions uncover new ways of accomplishing goals and become play rituals; (3) negotiated reciprocal exchange and directed activity, and become involved in negotiating self-assertiveness, conveying more differentiated directions to others; and (4) distinguished whether the disruption of a negotiation was repaired. This first edition of an embodied life metaphor undergoes revisions during interactions throughout the life span. With each revision, an individual constructs a series of interrelated meanings in each behavioral modality (action, fantasy, and language), each building on previous editions. Converging with Shilder's (1950) formulation of body image, Francis Galton's (1884) assessing how a person leans when sitting next to someone, research with infants and toddlers noted earlier, my observations of children and adults in treatment situations (Santostefano, 1998, 2004), and presentations devoted to embodiment theory (Overton et al., 2008), the following are examples of methods I devised to help a person's body speak.

Examples of Methods That Assess Embodied Meanings

The *Action Test of Body Image* (ATBI) asks the participant to assume various body postures or perform different movements and share what each body experience brings to mind (Santostefano, 1998). Some items involve the total body; for example: (1) stand on one leg, lift the other leg, and spread arms out to each side; (2) lean over and push an arm back and forth with fist closed. Other items involve body parts; for example: (1) repeatedly spread open and close the fingers of both hands; (2) open and close eyelids several times. Responses are evaluated with six-point scales; for example, body imbalance-balance (e.g., "makes me think of how it feels when you fall off a cliff"; "I feel like I'm a ballet dancer"), body constriction-assertion (e.g., "I feel like I'm handcuffed"; "I'm thinking of a salmon swimming up stream"). Responses are also evaluated in terms of whether a particular meaning is experienced; for example, aggression toward others (e.g., "I feel like I'm punching a wise guy I know"), body-self deformed-inadequate (e.g., "reminds me of this cripple guy I saw in a wheelchair"), affiliation (e.g., "hanging out with my friends"), and self-competence (e.g., "throwing the shot put really far").

The *Touch Association Test* (Santostefano, 1998) asks the participant to feel a series of clay objects placed one at a time under a cloth, not to look at them, and share what each experience brings to mind. The objects include, for example, a sphere, a cone, and a human-like figure. Responses are evaluated with several scales; for example: Body Orientation—concrete to abstract representations of events and inanimate objects (e.g., sphere: "it's just something round and smooth"; "reminds me of the Epcot Center"); Action Taken—the participant acts on the stimulus object (e.g., sphere: "a marble," the participant taps the object on the table); See—the participant pulls the cloth away to examine the object visually; Emotion—for example, aggression toward others (e.g., sphere: "makes me think of a rock to hit someone on the head with"); Nurture (e.g., rectangle: "a chocolate candy bar"); and Noxious texture/temperature (e.g., cube: "it feels cold; scratchy").

Embodied Meanings Individuals Experience and Express When Participating with These Methods

The ATBI was administered to 78 children and adolescents on admission to a psychiatric inpatient facility (age range, 5–17 years; 38 girls, 40 boys; Santostefano, 1998). No significant sex or age differences were observed, and the following are examples of results: Participants who experienced embodied meanings of imbalance also experienced meanings representing fatigue, aggression toward others, and the body as deformed; those who experienced embodied meanings representing balance also experienced assertion and did not experience aggression toward others or fatigue. And participants who experienced meanings of body constriction also experienced meanings representing fear. The ATBI was also administered to 63 eleventh-grade public school students (36 girls, 27 boys) who volunteered, and written permission was obtained from their parents. No sex differences were observed. In general, the results resemble the configurations produced by the psychiatric,

inpatient population. For example, adolescents who experienced body imbalance also tended to experience aggression toward others and the body as unsafe, those who experienced body constriction also expressed meanings of the body as incompetent, and those who experienced meanings of fatigue also experienced the body-self as deformed.

From the viewpoint of nosology, the inpatient population represented many different diagnostic categories. Yet, as a group, they produced relations among embodied meanings that resemble those produced by the public school population. This preliminary result suggests that pathological groups are not represented by categories of embodied meanings and raises questions related to the introduction to this chapter that require further study. For example, did individuals in the inpatient group not have sufficient opportunities to negotiate and repair developmental interferences that occurred during their first years of life? Are embodied meanings experienced by a person related to other elements of his inner self, resulting in differences in overt behavior? In terms of life-span studies, would individuals who participate in the ATBI at age 15 produce the same embodied meanings at ages 20 and 60? These questions relate to the position noted earlier that developmental psychopathology is a system of concepts that explores individual differences in adaptational patterns.

The Touch Association Test was administered to 207 youths admitted to an inpatient psychiatric facility (age range, 5–18 years; mean age, 13 years; 98 girls, 109 boys; Santostefano, 1998). Analyses resulted in several significant relations; for example, participants who experienced symbolic-abstract meanings when touching the objects also produced a higher number of responses representing emotions, especially nurture, whereas those who experienced concrete-descriptive meanings tended not to experience meanings representing emotions; participants who experienced meanings representing noxious textures/temperatures also experienced representations of aggression toward others and tended to perform some action with the stimulus object; and participants who pulled the cloth to one side to see the object produced fewer meanings representing something or someone as deformed, and fewer meanings representing fear.

A second analysis was conducted to explore relations between meanings experienced with touch perceptions and suicidal or violent behavior. Participants whose histories showed no evidence of suicide or violence were selected from the same population to serve as control subjects. Those who had committed violent acts tended to act on and look at the stimulus objects, produced more responses representing aggression toward others and objects, and experienced more representations of noxious textures. Suicidal youths tended not to act on or look at the objects and more often experienced meanings representing a symbolic-abstract body orientation. In addition, while feeling the human-like figure, violent youths experienced meanings representing a concrete-descriptive orientation, whereas suicidal youths experienced meanings representing a symbolic-abstract orientation.

These results illustrate that embodied meanings can also be assessed with the Touch Association Test method, and raise questions that could guide future studies with nonclinical and clinical populations of all ages. As one example, this population defined a construct suggesting that looking at the stimulus objects was a way of avoiding experiencing representations of fear and body deformation. Would a nonclinical population use the same instrumental-expressive behavior to cope? And does this finding suggest that persons who look at stimulus objects, when instructions ask that they engage them only by touch, have experienced interferences during the development of the Core Self (see earlier)? If so, the caregivers involved in these interferences did not give them sufficient opportunities, while they negotiated taking turns being active and passive, to repeat tactile-interactive experiences, construct representations of these interactions, and share a crescendo of emotions.

Exploring Relations between Embodied Meanings and Experiences a Person Defines as Stressful

The developmental principle of heightened affective moments emphasizes that intense emotional experiences that cannot be averaged with others could play a unique role in the construction of meanings representing these events (Beebe & Lachmann, 2002). But how do we decide which events that occur during a person's interactions cannot be averaged with other experiences. To address this question, investigators typically use questionnaires listing events that parents, teachers, and mental health professionals designate as stressors and ask the child to check those she experienced during the recent past. Such questionnaires have been used, for example, to study the effects on children of their parents being deployed in Operation Desert Storm (Jensen, Marten, & Watanabe, 1996), differences in stressors experienced by black, white, and Hispanic children (Kilmer, Cowen, Wyman, Work, & Magnus, 1998), and the relation between life events and mood disorders

(Johnson & McMurrich, 2006). Reviews of research reflect the extent to which investigators have relied on questionnaires (e.g., Pfefferbaum, 1997). The results of other studies, however, question the heuristic value of this positivistic position. For example, only moderate agreement was observed between mothers and their children regarding events each designated as stressful (Beasley & Kearney, 1996). And self-report checklists completed by adolescents captured only 32% of stressful events they discussed in interviews (Duggal et al., 2000).

In contrast with the positivistic approach, a few authors have argued that stressful events should be defined by meanings a child gives to experiences (e.g., Pynoos, Steinberg, & Goenjian, 1996). Following this point of view and assuming a relational, constructivist position, I designed an interview method (Life Stressor Interview [LSI]) to explore the types of events a child shares as having been especially upsetting to her, when examples of events are not suggested by the examiner (e.g., Santostefano, O'Connell, MacAuley, & Quiroga-Estevez, 2005). After the examiner and child establish sufficient rapport, the examiner asks the child to describe whether anything happened "that upset you a lot," joins the child in discussing the event, provides empathic support indicated, and is careful not to guide the child in some direction. If the child spontaneously describes one upsetting event, the examiner asks only once, "Is there anything else that upset you a lot?" Responses are scored in terms of types of stressors, for example, global events (war, terrorism, social crises), aggressive events, harm to loved ones, disruptions in family relations, and natural disasters. This method was used, for example, in studies exploring what children and adolescents who reside in inner-city or rural areas of the United States, or in residential treatment centers in Spain, construe as stressful (Santostefano et al., 2005). At this point, two studies are summarized that illustrate relations between heightened affective moments a person defines as upsetting and embodied meanings he experiences.

During two successive years, 93 kindergarten children attending an inner-city public school were administered, with parental consent, the ATBI and LSI (39 girls, 54 boys; 37 African American, 51 Latino, 4 white, and 1 Asian student; Santostefano, 1998). Although no significant gender or race differences were observed in the total number and types of stressful events reported, correlations were observed between stressful events and embodied meanings these children experienced; for example, children who reported shootings/fights as a stressor experienced fewer embodied meanings representing competence and more representing the self as deformed/inadequate, children who reported illness/hospitalization of a loved one as especially upsetting experienced embodied meanings of pain/danger and aggression toward others, and children who reported the death of a loved one as upsetting experienced embodied meanings of constriction.

The LSI was also administered to the 63 eleventh graders whose performance with the ATBI was discussed earlier (the second study). Thirty-eight of these participants reported experiencing one or more upsetting event (e.g., death of a family member or relative, divorce of parents), and 25 shared they had not. Several relations were observed between ATBI responses and whether the adolescent reported experiencing an upsetting event. For example, adolescents who discussed an upsetting event also experienced meanings representing the body as constricted, unsafe, deformed, and fatigued.

These preliminary results raise questions that should stimulate future research in developmental psychopathology across the life span. For example, would different races of an adult population also show no differences in the embodied meanings they have constructed? And would adults produce correlations such as experiencing the embodied meaning of danger, when participating in the ATBI, and reporting being upset by the illness or death of a loved one when responding to the LSI? Another issue concerns the time when the upsetting event occurred. Would adults show that particular events that occurred during childhood exert a lasting and significant influence within their inner selves in terms of embodied meanings they experience?

THE SECOND PROBE: COGNITIVE-EMOTIONAL REGULATORS AND INSTRUMENTAL-EXPRESSIVE BEHAVIORS

With this probe, we enter the second floor of the developmental house depicted in Figure 22.1. Before considering the concepts and related research at this level, however, the history and metatheory of each concept is reviewed first, as was the case with our discussion of body image, to evaluate definitions and methods in current use. This probe is concluded by illustrating why it is important to the understanding of normal and pathological functioning across the life span to consider embodied meanings, cognition, emotion, and various modes of behavior as forming a relational developmental system of part processes operating within the self as the person interacts with environments to negotiate goals.

Cognitive-Emotion Regulation

Similar to the divide that was maintained between body and mind (see the first probe), another dualistic boundary was established and maintained between cognition and emotion. The philosophical rationale for this boundary was that it preserved cognition or thought as right and rational, and protected it from emotions that were viewed as irrational (Bruner, 1986). In addition, during the early decades of the 20th century, whether thought is related to emotion was dismissed by the discipline of psychology when orthodox behaviorism renounced the mind and cognition, declaring that overt behavior is the only legitimate topic for psychological study (Bearison & Zimiles, 1986). John B. Watson, who is credited with launching behaviorism, made clear what this movement was splitting off and renouncing. For Watson, psychology should be "the [science of behavior]…never to use the terms consciousness, mental states, mind…imagery, and the like…" (cited in Messer & Winokar, 1984 p. 64). With the emergence of the research program and associated concepts of Jean Piaget, (e.g., 1951), Heinz Werner (e.g., 1964), and Jerome Bruner (1951), however, new ways were formed to reintroduce and understand the previously forbidden mind. Although psychologists embraced their viewpoints, cast aside the boundary between body and mind, and conducted research leading to a cognitive science (Gardner, 1985), many others maintained the boundary. One primary reason was that a group of the new cognitive scientists accepted the digital computer as a model of the mind. This mechanistic devise is by its very nature a simple aggregate of independently defined elements, not a holistic system. As a consequence, cognitive science moved toward a focus on "information-processing" approaches to knowledge and understanding that treated the emotional side of life as irrelevant to its goals. But some psychologists, who were not captured by the computational model of the mind, protested that emotions were being neglected and sparked a cognitive revolution that created what became known as the "New Look" in cognitive science (Blake & Ramsey, 1951).

Lessons from the Past: The New Look Approach to Relating Cognition with Emotions and Personality

The New Look approach to cognition was launched by three symposia. The first, held at the 1948 convention of the American Psychological Association, was titled "Interrelationship between Perception and Personality." In his introduction to the presentations, Heinz Werner (1949) emphasized that psychology had done little to integrate perception with personality and offered his "sensoritonic-field theory of perception," which located perception within the individual and individual within the environment. Klein and Schlesinger (1949) presented research conceptualizing "perceptual attitudes" that coordinate information from environments, and from meanings and emotions located within "the personal world of the perceiver." Because their conceptualization of cognition-emotion relations and methods forecast issues that are raised later, several features of their research are sketched here. In one study, they asked participants, who were World War II refugees, to estimate the size of each of a series of disks by adjusting a variable circle. On each disk were placed symbols, including the swastika, which the subject was asked to ignore, and which were presumed to arouse emotions-meanings. They observed that participants made greater errors in size estimation with particular disks and inferred that the meanings-emotions provoked by the symbols in question were not adequately regulated by the cognitive process involved (focusing attention on information defined as relevant). In their "thirst study," Klein and Schlesinger selected participants who showed either considerable or no difficulty regulating stress associated with the task of naming as rapidly as possible the ink color of words when the color disagrees with the word name (e.g., the word *red* is printed in blue ink; the person is to say "blue"). After half of each group was served a thirst-inducing meal, participants were asked to scan a picture of an ice-cream soda surrounded by numbers and place a dot on a sheet of gridded paper at the spot where he perceived each number. The thirsty subjects who performed best on the pretest (i.e., ignored words while naming colors) were the most accurate (i.e., regulated thirst-related emotions while articulating the field of information).

The issues raised in this symposium received further attention the following year in a conference organized at the University of Texas to address the view that "perceptual activity supplies the material from which the individual constructs his own personally meaningful environment" (Blake & Ramsey, 1951, p. iii). For example, Hilgard (1951) pointed out, "We are trying to discover how perception may be influenced by the realities outside and by the realities within ourselves" (p. 95), and proposed that individuals attempt to maintain "dynamic equilibrium" between these two realities. Frenkl-Brunswick (1951) emphasized that the best way to assess a person's dynamic equilibrium is in "his natural, cultural habitat." And Klein (1951) elaborated his concept of cognition as actively maintaining a dynamic balance between a person's emotions and

the demands of the environment as perceived. The topic of unconscious cognitive processes also received attention when Bronfenbrenner (1951) encouraged psychologists to consider that mental processes of which a person is not fully aware could occur. The third symposium, held at the University of Colorado in 1955 (Gruber, Hammond, & Jesser, 1957), emphasized the position of interpretationism (for a very useful discussion of interpretationism, see Overton [1994]) and articulated three motifs: (1) cognition is a process at the center of a person's adaptations to environments; (2) the environments to which a person adapts are cognitive representations rather than actual things; and (3) unconscious cognitive structures code or determine what pictures a person takes, so to speak, of the ingredients in the environment.

The New Look approach to cognition as processes regulating environmental and personal stimulation (e.g., emotions, meanings, goals) flourished in the 1960s and 1970s (see Santostefano, 1978, for a review) but was then eclipsed by a second revolution (H. Gardner, 1985). In sharp contrast with the interpretationist view, the second revolution assumed the objectivist position, shifted the focus to cognition as involving "processing information," and ignored emotion. When Bruner (1992) reviewed this second revolution, and recalled his participation in the first, he urged that cognitive science return to the original New Look emphasis. Curiously, Jean Piaget, who was credited with being one of the researchers who freed American psychology from the ethos of orthodox behaviorism, conducted only a few studies on the role of emotions in development, in contrast with his many studies of reasoning, problem solving, and logic. But unlike other investigators, Piaget recognized that cognition and emotion were conceptual conveniences serving research. When Decarie (1978) brought to his attention that he seldom referred to emotional processes, Piaget replied, in a personal communication to her, "Freud focused on emotion, I chose intelligence" (p. 183), and gave the reason for his choice: "I have always [preferred]…the study of normalcy and the workings of the intellect over that of the tricks of the unconscious" (p. 116). He also shared that he preferred the study of normalcy because his mother's poor mental health had a profound effect on him when he was a young child. Recognizing that the boundary between cognition and emotion is a conceptual convenience, Piaget was able to make significant contributions to the understanding of unconscious cognitive and emotional activity (Piaget, 1973), and how cognitive emotional processing are related during child development (Piaget, 1981). Moreover, his legacy was illustrated by the annual conference of the Piaget Society held in 1983 on the topic of developmental perspectives of thought and emotion (Bearison & Zimiles, 1986).

Current Approaches to Conceptualizing and Assessing Relations between Cognition and Emotion

The focus of the New Look on the relation between cognition and emotion continues to grow (see also Mascolo & Fisher, Chapter 6 of this volume, and McClelland, Ponitz, Messersmith, & Tominey, Chapter 15 of this volume, for an extended discussion of the cognitive-emotion relation). As Rottenberg and Gross (2007) noted, "the pace of research on…emotion regulation has become 'vigorous'…" (p. 323). In this surge of interest, however, it is important to note that many studies do not conceptualize cognition-emotion relations following the interpretationist view of the New Look, and do not use New Look methodology illustrated by Klein's "thirst study," which emphasized perturbating a person's inner self with test stimuli or evocative situations, or both. In this regard, Sokol and Müller (2007) noted, "The classic antinomy between thought and emotion continues to persist as one of the 'great divides' for self regulation research" (pp. 401–402) reflected by the question, "Do cognition and emotion share one head or does each have its own head?" (Stein, 1987). From the viewpoint of this metaphor, one domain of the literature reviewed by Solomon (2002) focuses on identifying "basic emotions," conceptualized as separate from cognition and, therefore, as having its own head, a concept with origins in Descartes' "six primitive passions" (wonder, love, hatred, desire, joy, sadness) reflected in recent research on "hard-wired" affect programs that define emotion as specific neurological processes. And Rottenberg and Gross (2007) propose that emotion regulation may be distinguished from "an individual's efforts to manage relations with an environment…coping includes non emotional actions taken to achieve non emotional goals…" (p. 325). From the position of the New Look, the reductionism reflected by the concept of basic emotions, and the emphasis on emotion regulation as neurologically based, neglects the role of conscious and unconscious meanings-emotions a person assigns to information and the role of unique cognitive processes involved in registering information and regulating emotions in the service of negotiating a goal.

A comprehensive research program guided by the concept of "cognitive emotion regulation strategies" (e.g., Garnefski & Kraaij, 2007) provides one example of a conceptualization depicting cognition and emotion as sharing one head. Although making a contribution, aspects of this conceptualization and methodology, however, differ significantly from that of the New Look revolution. Garnefski and Kraaij define cognitive emotion regulation as "the *conscious* cognitive way of handling the intake of emotionally arousing information…[and] cognitive emotion regulation theory is based upon the assumption that *thinking and acting refer to different processes and, therefore, considers cognitive strategies in a conceptually pure way, separate from behavioral strategies*" (p. 141, emphasis added). In addition, Garnefski, Rieffe, Jellesma, Terwogt, and Kraaij (2007) hold that cognitive emotion regulation is a process that "helps to manage emotions *after the experience of stressful events* (p. 1, emphasis added). To assess cognitive emotion regulation strategies, Garnefski devised a questionnaire organized into subscales, each assessing a conceptually distinct cognitive strategy; for example, blaming oneself for the event, blaming the environment or someone else, or focusing on thoughts about more pleasant experiences (Garnefski, Rieff, Jellesma, & Kraaij, 2007). This questionnaire has been administered to children, adolescents, and adults to study cognitive emotional strategies they use after experiencing different types of events and also to individuals who displayed various symptoms.

Although interest in cognitive emotional regulation is growing, so is the use of questionnaires as a method to assess the concept. Discussing measurement issues in emotion research, Zeman, Kilmes-Dougan, Cassano, and Adrian (2007) noted that the use of a structured questionnaire "provides an efficient, systematic approach to assessing the frequency or intensity of an emotional behavior…" (p. 385). Sloan and Kring (2007) also reviewed questionnaires devised to assess emotion regulation; for example, each of 10 items is rated on a 7-point scale from agree to disagree (e.g., I control my emotions by changing the way I think about the situation that I am in). With a related approach, Rye, Cahoon, Ali, and Daftary (2008) assess "counterfactual thinking" by asking participants to describe a negative event and then complete a questionnaire assessing the degree to which they experience "If only…" thoughts (e.g., If only I had listened to my friend, things would have turned out better."). Amone-P'Olak, Garnefski, and Kraai (2007), proposing that "cognitive emotional strategies should be studied in a conceptually pure way, separate from behavioral strategies" (p. 657), administered a questionnaire to assess cognitive emotional strategies of adolescents who had lived in captivity. And although Sloan and Kring (2007) noted that "emotions can be defined as action dispositions that prepare organisms to respond to their environment" (p. 308), the procedures they describe are questionnaires. Another review of studies (Kramer & Erickson, 2007) indicates that a divide is also maintained by many researchers between cognition and action dispositions. It should be clear that the popularity of questionnaires as a method to assess cognitive emotional regulation disagrees with the New Look, which advocates devising methods that assess different cognitive processes operating outside of awareness that regulate information and to related emotions, in the service of the individual taking some action to achieve a goal.

Approaches to Assessing Cognition and Emotion across the Life Span

The divide between cognition and emotion has also been maintained by life-span studies that examine relations between changes in the volume of gray matter (evaluated with neuroimaging) and cognitive functioning (e.g., speed of responding; e.g., Casey, Tottenham, Listen, & Durston, 2006; Kramer & Madden, 2008). Other life-span studies have also maintained the divide by focusing on age-related changes in the efficiency of a particular cognitive function with stimuli that do not evoke emotions, for example, immediate and delayed verbal memory, and numerical tasks (e.g., Gomez-Perez & Ostrosky-Solis, 2006). In a review of research on changes in cognitive functioning associated with normal, late adult development, Hassing and Johansson (2006) organized results in terms of two conceptualizations of cognitive functioning: "crystallized abilities" (e.g., knowledge, vocabulary) and "fluid abilities" (e.g., speed, working memory; see also Blair, Chapter 8 of this volume). And another review of studies of memory and late adult development (Hess, 2005) emphasized a characteristic that applies to the examples just noted: "The unidimensional research approach...often neglects the adaptive nature of cognition as well as contextual factors..." (p. 383). Similarly, studies of emotion across the life span also maintain a divide by ignoring cognition, reflected by one literature review (Izard & Ackerman, 1997) supporting the concept that particular "situational emotions" are a function of non-cognitive activities (e.g., exercise increases endorphins in the brain, leading to pleasant feelings).

Current Approaches to Cognition and Emotion That Relate to the New Look

Voices can be heard that call for a return to exploring relations among cognition, emotion, meaning, and adaptation; for example, Burum and Goldfried (2007) noted that "emotion is a basic component of human experience inexorably interwoven with thought and action" (p. 407); Greenberg (2007) emphasized that "affective and cognitive processes act as a dynamic system to mutually regulate each other" (p. 414); Campos, Frankl, and Camras (2004) argued that "emotion regulation [is a] process dealing with a person-environment problem" (p. 391); Mennin and Farach (2007) cited recent evidence supporting "the role of emotion as a regulator of cognitive processes such as directing attention and perception...and...guiding decision making" (p. 335); and Leahy (2007) reminded us that Plato represented the relation between reason (cognition) and emotion with the metaphor of a charioteer regulating a horse as it gallops about. This same metaphor was used by Freud (1923) to represent drives (emotions) as a galloping horse and the ego (cognition) as the rider trying to regulate its direction in the service of achieving some goal.

Also converging with the New Look Approach, a few studies used methods perturbating participants with stimuli that call for cognition to regulate the galloping horse of meanings and related emotions in the service of accomplishing a goal. For example, in one study concerning fear associated with heights, Teachman and colleagues (2008) asked each participant to stand on a two-story-high balcony ledge and estimate the size of a disk placed on the ground beneath the balcony. In another study, McGrath (2008) asked each participant to view a computer screen and, in one block of trials, hit the D key if a positive word or a picture of flowers appeared and the K key if a negative word or a picture of a snake appeared. Reaction time was recorded. With another block of trials, he was asked to hit the D key if a positive word or a picture of a snake appeared and the K key if a negative word or the picture of a flower appeared. Along the same line, Yeo and Neal (2004) assessed the personal world of the perceiver by asking the participant to view a computer screen on which was projected a series of four aircraft, and press one key if she decided the aircraft would pass within 5 km of each other (termed a *conflict*) and another if not (termed *non-conflict*). In one life-span study, Williams, and Strauss, David, Hultsch, and Hunter (2007) asked participants (age range, 5–76 years) to view a screen on which was projected a fish swimming either to the left or right, and press either the left or right button corresponding with the direction in which the fish was swimming. The trials were classified as "congruent" (e.g., the fish is swimming to the left and located on the left side of the screen), "incongruent" (e.g., the fish is swimming to the right and located on the left side of the screen), and "neutral" (e.g., the fish is located in the center of screen).

In what follows, a similarity to these studies and a sharp difference from studies investigating cognitive emotion regulation with a questionnaire method is presented. In broad terms, the approach presented here conceptualizes and assesses a hierarchy of cognitive processes, occurring outside of awareness, that gather information while at the same time regulate related meanings-emotions. Moreover, these cognitive processes interact with and contribute to the behavior a person uses to negotiate a goal.

Developmental Hierarchy of Cognitive-Emotional Regulators

Influenced by the New Look Revolution and, in particular, by Klein's formulation of "cognitive controls" based on research with adults, I devised cognitive tests to explore how many distinctively different processes account for the ways in which children and adolescents gather and use information, and regulate related emotions, to meet the demands of environments and personal meanings (Santostefano, 1978, 1988, 1998). This research supports the view that the process of each of the following cognitive-emotional regulators is defined by levels of organization from global, characterizing early stages of development, to differentiated, characterizing later stages of development:

1. *Body-tempo regulation* is the manner in which a person uses images/symbols to represent and regulate body motility and associated emotions.
2. *Focal attention* is the manner in which a person surveys a field of information and related emotions.
3. *Field articulation* is the manner in which a person regulates information and related emotions containing elements both relevant and irrelevant to the task at hand.
4. *Leveling-sharpening* is the manner in which a person constructs an image of information and related emotions, holds the image in memory over time, and compares it with perceptions of present stimulation.
5. *Equivalence range* is the manner in which a person categorizes information in terms of a concept or meaning.

The methods constructed to assess each of these cognitive-emotional regulators (illustrated later) consist of stimuli experienced either as neutral or as evoking conscious/unconscious meanings-emotions. These methods, for example, were administered annually in longitudinal studies, to public school children (age range, 5–15 years),

to children living in an orphanage and attending a nearby public school, to brain damaged children enrolled in a residential center, and to maltreated children (e.g., Santostefano, 1978, 1988, 1998). A modified version of the method designed to assess the focal attention cognitive emotional regulator was also used in a study comparing selective attention skills in late mature adult participants who showed evidence of Alzheimer disease or depression, or were free of major symptoms (Foldi, Jutagir, Davidoff, & Gould, 1992). Results from these studies support the reliability and validity of the proposed methods constructed to assess a developmental hierarchy of cognitive processes.

Emergence of Cognitive-Emotional Regulators and the Relations Among Them

Observations of infants suggest that these functions begin to be organized during the first 2 years of life and become structured by the third year of life (see Santostefano, 1978, for a review of studies). Although the organization of each cognitive-emotional regulator changes throughout development from global to differentiated, the process of each remains the same, when functioning adequately, and relies on and integrates the process of other mechanisms lower in the hierarchy. For example, imagine a person who, when entering a large room for the first time with the goal of turning on the lights, experiences a wave of tension associated with the meaning of being alone in the dark. The person quickly walks to the center of the room, slowly comes to a halt, remains still for a moment (body-tempo regulation), looks about, scanning the many objects in the room (focal attention), and continues to regulate tension and surrounding information (e.g., furniture, paintings, drapes). The person then focuses attention selectively on a row of items fixed on the wall alongside of a doorway (field articulation), steps forward, stares at these items, and compares the attributes of each with memory images of items the person encountered in the past (leveling-sharpening). Still regulating tension, the person decides one item on the wall is a dial for the heating system, another a dial for the air conditioner, another a switch for the fan hanging from the ceiling, and another a switch to turn on the lights (equivalence range).

Adaptation, Stability, and Mobility of Cognitive-Emotional Regulators: The Concept of Cognitive-Emotional Orientation

An individual's cognitive-emotional functioning is conceptualized as both a single level within each of these cognitive processes and as a range of levels. In long-term development, cognitive-emotional regulators become accommodated to the pace and complexity of information and related emotions unique to the person's usual environments. When the environment shifts to one that is unusual for the person (e.g., a mother becomes depressed; a tornado strikes the neighborhood), cognitive-emotional regulators reorganize regressively (shift to a more undifferentiated level) or progressively (shift to a more differentiated level). The degree and direction of the reorganization results in an adaptive fit between the person's inner self and the requirements of the external context as construed. The concept of regressions and progressions that occur in the functioning of cognitive-emotional regulators brings us to the matrix depicted in Figure 22.1. In brief, environments whether molar (e.g., classroom; dentist's office) or molecular (e.g., a light switch) are viewed as containing "a call for action," that is, a prescription for particular motoric, cognitive, and emotional responses. Similarly, a meaning with roots in embodied experiences of the past also contains a call for action when construing a current environment. Cognitive-emotional regulators coordinate attributes and calls for action from both the particular environmental ingredients and meanings a person assigns to them. This coordinating process is referred to as "cognitive-emotional orientation" or "cognitive-affective balance."

Two interrelated issues are central to evaluating the efficiency and success with which a particular cognitive-emotional orientation serves adaptation: the extent the environment limits the degree to which the individual can actively engage the information, and whether the demands and stimulation of the environment are usual (i.e., average and expectable), given the individual's history. If the context permits the person to participate and is usual, the person's cognitive-emotional orientation organizes to form a balance between the demands of external stimulation and of meanings-emotions that construe it, promoting adaptation, development, and learning. If the situation limits or interferes with the person's active participation, and is also unusual, cognitive-emotional regulation shifts either to an "inner orientation" (i.e., focusing on meanings-emotions) or to an "outer orientation" (i.e., focusing on the demands of the environment) to avoid personal meanings-emotions.

Course of Cognitive-Emotional Orientation in Normal Development

Research resulted in the view that there are three phases in the developmental course of cognitive-emotional orientation (Santostefano & Reider, 1984). Before the age of 4, cognitive-emotional regulators are oriented more toward information from embodied meanings so that information in the environment is typically experienced in highly personal terms. From the age of 5 to 9 years, cognitive-emotional regulators become more oriented toward information presented by environments, enabling the child to keep some distance from emotionally laden embedded meanings and fantasies. From age 9 years to early adolescence, cognitive-emotional regulation gradually shifts to an orientation that is both outer and inner, enabling the individual to respond more flexibly to the demands of embodied meanings and environments.

Maladaptive Cognitive-Emotional Orientations

Research also demonstrates that children representing a wide range of "behavioral difficulties" use the same cognitive-emotional regulators as do "normals" to respond to or avoid stimulation from personal meanings-emotions and environments, but differ in terms of the orientation that dominates. For example, brain-damaged children showed a cognitive-emotional orientation that combines narrow scanning (focal attention) with an organization of field articulation that focuses excessively on external stimuli and subordinates meanings-emotions-fantasies. For this population, then, an outer cognitive-emotional orientation serves to limit the disruptive influence of fantasies/emotions/meanings in order to cope with environmental demands. In another study (Reider & Cicchetti, 1989), maltreated children, when compared with control subjects, displayed an inner orientation, focusing on irrelevant information that evokes meanings-emotions related to interpersonal aggression (field articulation), and holding in memory more efficiently information related to interpersonal aggression (leveling-sharpening). These and other studies have shown that long-standing, traumatic, heightened-emotional experiences result in one of three types of maladaptive cognitive-emotional orientations: (1) outer orientation, which centers inflexibly on external stimuli, permitting little or no contribution from personal meanings-emotions; (2) inner orientation, which centers excessively on personal meanings, permitting little or no contribution from environments; and (3) excessive shifts in orientation—that is, when the call for action of a personal meaning-life metaphor is experienced, cognition rapidly shifts back and forth to an outer orientation, centering on a detail in the environment unrelated to the meaning being experienced as a way of avoiding its demands, and to an inner orientation, centering on an unrelated meaning-emotion as a way of avoiding the environment's expectations.

*Examples of Methods That Assess
Cognitive-Emotional Regulators*

In this section, two of the several methods constructed to assess cognitive-emotional regulators are described. These methods are, in turn, used in the studies discussed later. The construction of these methods followed one particular principle of Relational Developmental Systems Theory discussed earlier that emphasizes "the importance of studying real-time (moment to moment) processes…real time behaviors…" and stipulates "one can not know about various behavioral states available to a system without perturbating it" (Granic, 2005, p. 390; see also Nesselroade & Molenaar, Chapter 2 of this volume; Mascolo & Fisher, Chapter 6 of this volume). Age norms are available, as well as studies that support the reliability and construct validity of each procedure (e.g., Santostefano, 1978, 1988, 1998; Santostefano & Rieder, 1984).

Fruit Distraction Test (FDT) evaluates how a person attends selectively to information defined as relevant and at the same time regulates personal thoughts, fantasies, and emotions irrelevant to the task at hand (field articulation cognitive-emotional regulator). In five trials, the participant is asked to name as quickly as possible 50 colors randomly arranged in rows: Card I (Practice) has rows of colored bars (red, yellow, blue, green); Card II has rows of yellow bananas, red apples, bunches of blue grapes, heads of green lettuce; Card III is the same as Card II except that next to each fruit is located a picture of a nurture-related object (e.g., bottle of milk) that the participant is asked to ignore; Card IV presents the same fruit in the same locations, but each is colored incorrectly (e.g., a banana is colored red, blue, or green, but never yellow), and the person is asked to ignore the colors and name the colors that should be there; and Card V is the same as Card III except that a picture of a weapon (e.g., pistol) is placed next to each fruit that the participant is asked to ignore. Card II reading time and naming errors are compared with those of Cards III, IV, and V to obtain a measure of the extent to which each type of distraction affected a person's cognitive-emotional regulation.

Leveling Sharpening Shoot-Out Test (LSSOT) and the *Leveling Sharpening Friends Test* (LSFT) assess the manner in which a person holds images of information in memory and compares these images with perceptions of ongoing information (the leveling-sharpening cognitive emotional regulator). LSSOT and the LSFT are identical in makeup, procedure, and task requirement. With each, 63 pictures of a scene are displayed in succession, 5 seconds each display.

Gradually throughout the series, 20 details are omitted accumulatively from the scene. The person is asked to report any changes in the scene she notices. The LSSOT for male subjects consists of a scene of two cowboys in a shoot-out; for female subjects, two cowgirls in a shoot-out. The LSFT consists of two cowboys (cowgirls) greeting each other. Performance is evaluated with two scores: (1) the number of correct changes detected and how soon a change is perceived once it is introduced; and (2) the total number of changes reported that do not occur, reflecting "slips of cognition" triggered by conflicted meanings-emotions.

Here two other procedures are described that were used in studies reported later, which explored relations between embodied meanings and cognitive-emotional regulators. For the Binoculars Test, the examiner asks the participant to look at some object in the room through a pair of binoculars and experience how looking through one end magnifies the object and "moves it close to you," whereas looking through the other end "moves it far away," and then asks him to look at the examiner "Either from the end that moves me closer to you or the end that moves me further away." The Body Regulation Test II (BRT II) asks the participant to draw a continuous line on a spiral pathway with a pencil, from the beginning to the end, in each of three trials: (1) "Your regular speed"; (2) "As slowly as possible without stopping"; and (3) "As slowly as possible without stopping while the examiner speaks 6 words at 25-cm intervals, for example, 'bad,' 'mother,' 'blood,' which the participant is asked to ignore."

Exploring Relations Between Embodied Meanings and Cognitive-Emotional Regulators

Seventy-five youths (35 girls, 40 boys; age, 6–18 years) admitted to a psychiatric facility were administered the Binoculars Test, LSFT, and LSSOT. Significant relations were observed only with the LSFT. Youths who drew the examiner nearer when peering through the binoculars detected fewer correct changes and later (cognitive leveling), whereas children who moved the examiner farther away detected more correct changes and sooner (cognitive sharpening). If pushing the examiner away represents self-other differentiation, this developmentally more advanced stage in self-development was associated with a more mature organization of a cognitive-emotional regulator when dealing with stimuli-emotions representing interpersonal affiliation, whereas drawing the examiner closer was associated with a less mature organization. The number of incorrect changes produced by younger versus older children adds an interesting dimension. Young children who pushed the examiner away when peering through binoculars produced more errors with the LSFT (suggesting more cognitive-emotional conflict concerning affiliation) than did young children who drew the examiner nearer. Older youths who drew the examiner nearer produced more errors, suggesting cognitive conflict in these children who have not yet individuated. The heuristic value of this illustration is supported by the observation that no differences were observed with the LSSOT, which presented stimuli representing interpersonal aggression.

In another study, parental permission was obtained for 20 public school children (10 girls, 10 boys) in each of three age groups (6, 9, and 12 years) to be administered the BRT II and the FDT. In one analysis, the time a child took to move the pencil slowly during the silent condition, versus when the examiner spoke emotionally evocative words, showed no age or sex differences. Nearly half of each age group, however, displayed a quicker tempo when hearing evocative words. These children were designated the "Emotion-Body-Quick-Tempo Group," the others the "Emotion-Body-Slow-Tempo Group." The Emotion-Body-Quick-Tempo Group displayed a faster cognitive tempo with Card III (vs. Card II) when naming the colors of the fruit while regulating emotions/fantasies evoked by irrelevant pictures and made more naming errors. The Emotion-Body-Slow-Tempo Group displayed a slower cognitive tempo and made significantly fewer naming errors. These results provide one illustration of relations among embodied meanings, tempo regulation, and cognitive-emotional regulation. In need of further study, the findings suggest that children who quicken their body tempo in microspace when dealing with fantasies and related emotions evoked by the environment also experience cognitive imbalance, or slips in cognition-emotional regulation, when focusing attention in the face of distraction. In contrast, children who shift to a slower body tempo experience more efficient cognitive-emotion regulation and make fewer cognitive errors.

Instrumental-Expressive Behaviors

We noted earlier that any behavior is conceptualized as containing both instrumental and expressive qualities viewed as coequal. For example, a child frequently invites his parent to sit with him under a large bush and makes clear that the instrumental quality of this behavior contains the expressive quality of enjoying the sense of attachment. The same instrumental action could, however,

contain other expressive qualities. For example, another child who invites a parent to sit with him under a large bush conveys that the expressive quality of this behavior is fear of the outer world. We also noted that the same expressive quality could be contained in different instrumental behaviors (e.g., the child who experiences fear of the environment also requests that lights be left on at bedtime). A brief look at history indicates that conceptualizing behavior in terms of instrumental-expressive qualities was commonly accepted.

Lessons from the Past: Approaches to Assessing Instrumental-Expressive Behaviors

Similar to Galton examining the meanings expressed by the way a person leans when seated with others (described earlier), Hugh Hartshorne and Mark A. May (Symonds, 1931) assessed "honesty" by presenting a person with 10 circles of varying diameters printed randomly on a sheet of cardboard. The person was instructed to close his eyes and try to write in each circle the appropriate number from the smallest (#1) to the largest (#10). Successful subjects, of course, opened their eyes while performing this task. As another example, June Downey asked each subject to choose between two envelopes and later to state which envelope was chosen, whereupon the examiner contradicted the subject. The subject was scored high in persistence if he insisted that he was correct. Allport and Vernon (1933) evaluated behavior in terms of a person's quality of writing and manner of speaking, on the basis of which they coined the term *expressive movements*. And R. B. Cattell (1957) assessed the degree to which fright impairs performance by asking participants to complete a finger maze under normal conditions, and again while a rat and cockroaches in a cage surrounded the maze. From these experiments, investigators began to grapple with the observation that there seemed to be no consistent relations among what a person displayed in action, in fantasy, and verbally (e.g., Rader, 1957). Lindzey (1952) reminded psychologists that fantasy behavior, for example, does not always mirror overt behavior, and Brown (1958) noted, "We do not understand the relationship between modes of inner experiencing and overt behavior" (p. 66).

Current Approaches to Investigating and Assessing Instrumental-Expressive Behaviors

Since the latter 1980s, interest in understanding the relations between inner experiences and modes of overt behavior has declined, and the focus has been on developing methods that assess what is broadly termed *personality*. A comprehensive handbook (Hersen, 2003) delineates two broad categories of methods to assess behavior: "objective methods" (e.g., inventories, questionnaires) and "projective methods" (e.g., the Rorschach Inkblot Test, the Thematic Apperception Test). And researchers (e.g., Widiger & Samuel, 2005) note that questionnaires appear to have become the most widely used method to assess personality, paralleling the assessment of cognitive emotional regulation discussed earlier. For example, questionnaires were used by Herrington and colleagues (2008) to assess disharmony in relationships, Guy, Poythress, Douglas, Skeem, and Edens (2008) to assess antisocial behavior of offenders in court-mandated substance-abuse treatment programs, MacKillop, Murphy, Ray, Eisenberg, and Lisman (2008) to assess personality characteristics related to cigarette consumption, Sonnentag and Fritz (2007) to assess how individuals unwind during leisure time, Lauterbach and Hosser (2007) to assess empathy in male prisoners, Mufson and Mufson (1998) to assess possible performance of police officers, and Osborne, Kenny, and Holsomback (2005) to assess anxiety associated with music performance.

Similar to questionnaires, the Q-sort method is also popular, illustrated by the Shelder-Westen Assessment Procedure (SWAP) used with adolescents and adults (e.g., Shelder, Westen, & Bradley, 2006). Each of 200 statements derived from DSM-IIIR and DSM-IV that describe some aspect of behavior and psychological functioning is printed on a card. On the basis of what the researcher or clinician knows about a person, she sorts these cards into one of seven categories in terms of the degree to which the statement accurately describes the person under evaluation: from 0 (irrelevant) to 7 (highly descriptive). Along the same line, a growing literature, referred to as "trait psychology" proposes that various behaviors fall within one of five basic traits that underlie personality functioning and remain stable across the life span—that is, neuroticism, extraversion, openness, agreeableness, and conscientiousness (Costa & Widiger, 2001). Kagan (2005) criticizes this focus on traits and self-report, and Reinecke and Freeman (2007) propose that an alternative solution "may be to adopt a dimensional approach" (p. 690), a view we noted earlier that Piaget (1975) expressed more than three decades ago when he recommended that investigators and clinicians understand psychological functioning in terms of the "ensemble of elements involved" (p. vii). In contrast with self-report, Wakschlag and colleagues (2008) describe a method that makes use of real-life behaviors. Although the study relates to whether preschool children exhibit disruptive behavior, it could stimulate researchers to develop similar methods

for older individuals. The child participates in three different interpersonal contexts: (1) interacting with the parent; (2) interacting with the examiner, who enacts being busy and then leaves the room for a moment; and (3) interacting with the examiner, who enacts being actively engaged with the child.

A Developmental Hierarchy of Instrumental-Expressive Behaviors

A series of developmental studies was conducted in my laboratory designed to explore, from a developmental viewpoint, the relations among various instrumental-expressive qualities of a person's behavior (e.g., Santostefano, 1965, 1968a, 1968b, 1970, 1985, 1998). These studies were influenced by several sources; for example, methods researchers used in the past; Brown's (1958) challenge that we need to understand the relations between overt behavior and inner experiences; Piaget's (1975) recommendation that we explore the ensemble of elements involved as a person negotiates with environments to achieve some goal. In addition, the methods follow the point of view noted earlier that instrumental and expressive qualities of behaviors are coequal processes.

Results support the concept that taking action, fantasizing, and verbalizing are alternative modalities with which a person symbolizes meanings (expressive qualities) and achieves some goal (instrumental qualities). In addition, the results indicate that, although the three modalities are available throughout the life span, a developmental principle defines the relations among them, as well as the modality that dominates a person's functioning at different phases. Young children (2–7 years) express meanings and negotiate goals for the most part with actions and gestures. With development (8 to about 11 years), the action mode is subordinated by and assimilated into the fantasy mode so that images and fantasies are vehicles used more often to express meanings and rehearse actions before taking action physically. Still later (12 years and beyond), the action and fantasy modes are subordinated and assimilated into the language mode that dominates. Although subordinated, earlier modes are not replaced but remain potentially active so that a person may shift from one to another. The transition from action to fantasy to language, as alternative ways of expressing meanings and achieving goals, is determined by simultaneously occurring and complementary processes each defined by the developmental principle of directness and delay. When fantasizing the person distances himself from persons and objects, and delays taking action at least for the duration of the fantasy; when verbalizing, the instrumental qualities of the behavior are the least direct and most delayed in terms of physical contact with persons and objects. These studies also illustrate that each modality is organized in terms of developmental levels from expressions that are most direct and immediate to expressions that are indirect and delayed. The availability of action, fantasy, and language as behavioral modes, and the availability of a range of degrees of directness and delay within each mode, provide an individual with multiple, alternative behavioral means to express an embodied meaning, and to negotiate and achieve some goal with the environment. Notably, Stoops (1974) reviewed 55 studies by other investigators who compared two or more modes of expression (action, fantasy, language) and reported that, although different assessment techniques were used, 35 of the studies support the model outlined earlier. The following are examples of methods devised to assess each modality and the relations among them.

The Miniature Situations method assesses the action mode, each item consisting of two possible actions a person could perform, requiring only a few seconds to complete. (See Santostefano [1968b] for a review of the history of situational testing in personality assessment.) One study illustrates that the manifest qualities of different instrumental actions could share the same expressive quality. For example, high-school boys who elected to play a "hard" game without knowing the requirements of the task, also elected to have the examiner give them a mild electric shock on one hand (rather than shock the examiner's hand) and explored an unfamiliar object located behind a screen (rather than pop a balloon). Participants who elected to play the "easy" unknown game performed the alternative actions. These relations suggest that the instrumental behavior of giving the examiner an electric shock and popping a balloon contained the expressive quality of avoiding unknown situations rather than aggressing toward a person and object.

In terms of population differences, this method was administered, to public school, brain-damaged, and orphaned children (age range, 6–13 years). Brain-damaged children, for example, performed aggressive actions more often (e.g., tore a sheet of paper vs. repairing a torn sheet with tape); orphaned children expressed lower self-esteem (e.g., stood on a short box rather than a taller one) and a need for nurture (e.g., drank from a baby's bottle rather than from a cup). As another example, the method was also administered to two populations confined in the same institution. One group resided in an "Honor Dormitory,"

having demonstrated sufficient behavioral control, another in a maximum security unit ("Cell House"). The Honor group, for example, expressed the meaning of deferring to and honoring authority; for example, they helped the examiner put on a pair of gloves rather than tie a piece of rope around his wrists, and mounted an American flag before a picture of Abraham Lincoln rather than measure their strength with a hand dynamometer. The Cell House group performed the alternative actions.

The Miniature Situations method was also used to evaluate parent–child interactions (Santostefano, 1968a). With some situations, the child and mother act on each other and with others on objects for each other. One result illustrates that the same instrumental action could reflect different expressive qualities. The procedure was administered to a mother and her 14-year-old son, Tom, and during a separate session to the mother and her 15-year-old daughter, Mary. In one situation, Tom chose to place a bracelet on mother's wrist rather than tie an apron around her waist, commenting, "Maybe I'd like to see her need me." Mary also chose to place the bracelet on mother's wrist, noting that her mother enjoys jewelry and "likes to look pretty."

The Miniature Situations method is also used to assess developmental levels within each modality and relations between modalities. The participant is asked to perform three actions, from direct-immediate to indirect-delayed, in whatever order she chooses, for example, tear up a sheet of paper, crumple another, and carefully cut another with a pair of scissors along a penciled line. Following the same design, the Structured Fantasy method presents the participant with a series of pictures, the first depicting the beginning of a fantasy (e.g., a dog with an injured paw). The participant is asked to select which one of three response pictures displays what she imagines certainly happened (e.g., the dog stepped on a stone, a porcupine accidently stuck the dog's paw with a needle, another dog bit the paw), and then select one of the remaining pictures that displays what also could have happened. With the Continuous Word Association method, the examiner asks the participant to say aloud every word that comes to mind for 60 seconds, after hearing the stimulus word the examiner speaks. Each association is assigned a score ranging from 1, representing verbalizations symbolizing directness and no delay (e.g., stimulus word mouth: "swallowing"), to a score of 8, representing verbal expressions symbolizing indirectness and delay (e.g., "take your time"). With the Action Versus Fantasy method, each item is presented behind two screens and the participant is asked to perform some action (e.g., knock down a building of blocks with a toy bulldozer), or look at a picture of someone performing the action and imagine what is going on. With the Action Versus Fantasy Versus Language method, items are set behind three screens, and the participant is invited to perform in any order he chooses: taking action, examining a picture of someone performing that action, and speaking into a microphone describing the situation (e.g., water a plant, look at a picture of someone watering a plant, and say, "The plant is hungry, I will feed it.")

These methods, for example, were administered to boys in each of three age groups (6, 8, and 10 years) with no history of psychological problems. With the Miniature Situation method, 6-year-olds significantly more often performed the most direct and immediate action first (e.g., broke a light bulb, then hammered a nail, and then turned a screw into wood with a screwdriver), 10-year-olds more often performed the most delayed and indirect action first, and 8-year-olds fell between. Similar age trends were observed with the Structured Fantasy method. With the Continuous Word Association method, 6-year-olds, for example, verbalized fewer words to the stimulus word "knife" but spoke more words representing direct and immediate expressions (e.g., "stab," "smash"). In contrast, 10-year-olds verbalized the greatest number of words, most representing indirect and delayed meanings (e.g., "chip," "peel"). With the Action Versus Fantasy Versus Language method, 6-years-olds tended to take action first, 10-year-olds tended to verbalize first, and the performance of 8-year-olds fell between.

Exploring Relations Among Embodied Meanings, Cognitive-Emotional Regulators, and Instrumental-Expressive Behaviors

To explore relations between embodied meanings and fantasizing activity, 78 children and adolescents of an inpatient facility were administered, on admission, the ATBI and the Fantasy Activity Test (i.e., the Rorschach Inkblot Test), and asked to describe what each inkblot "reminds you of or what you imagine it could be" (Santostefano, 1998). In contrast with the popular Rorschach scoring systems that focus on structured determinants of images, responses are evaluated as expressions in the fantasy mode of different forms of activity performed by humans and nonhumans; for example, whether the activity is vigorous (e.g., "This is a rocket zooming through space.") or attenuated (e.g., "This is a maple leaf floating to the ground.") (The ATBI is discussed earlier—the first study.) As one example of results, children who experienced embodied meanings of

constriction tended not to express fantasies representing motion, and those who experienced embodied meanings representing aggression constructed fantasies representing slow, attenuated activity. These results suggest that with this inpatient population, a boundary segregates embodied meanings from meanings expressed in the fantasy mode. In other words, fantasizing does not seem to serve as an alternative "theater" or modality in which meanings-emotions can be expressed, negotiated, rehearsed, and revised, raising questions for future study. For example, why did the fantasy mode fail to experience and express motion, to compensate for the embodied meaning of the self as constricted?

To explore relations between cognitive-emotional regulators and instrumental-expressive behaviors, a group of 185 public school children participated in this study with parental permission (kindergarten to grade 8; 99 girls, 86 boys). Half of the group was administered the LSSOT, LSFT (described earlier), and the Two Person Drawing Test, which assesses representations/fantasies of persons interacting (Santostefano, 1998). With this method, the participant is asked to draw "two persons doing something." Drawings are scored in terms of representing one of three forms of interpersonal interacting; (1) aggression-competition ranging from more to less direct (e.g., "This kid is kicking this one." "These kids are racing."); (2) parallel activity either segregated or shared (e.g., "This kid is playing a game on his computer and this kid is reading." "These two girls are watching TV."); (3) affiliation from less to more direct (e.g., "This girl is jumping rope, and this kid is clapping." "These kids are shaking hands."). On the basis of his drawing, each youth was assigned to one of three groups: Aggressive Drawing Group, Parallel Drawing Group, and Affiliative Drawing Group.

The results of this study provide one illustration with a nonclinical population of how the process of the leveling-sharpening cognitive-emotional regulator interacts with the process of the fantasy mode of instrumental-expressive behaviors. Children who fantasized interpersonal relationships as aggressive used a developmentally higher cognitive organization of the leveling-sharpening process when regulating information-emotions associated with interpersonal violence (LSSOT), and shifted to a developmentally lower cognitive organization and experienced more imbalance (made errors) when regulating information-emotions associated with interpersonal affiliation (LSFT). Conversely, children who fantasized interpersonal interactions as affiliative used a developmentally lower cognitive organization, and experienced more imbalance (errors), when regulating information-emotions depicting interpersonal violence (LSSOT), and shifted to a developmentally higher cognitive organization when dealing with information-emotions depicting interpersonal affiliation (LSFT). The Parallel Drawing Group made use of the same organization of the leveling-sharpening cognitive-emotional regulator with each type of interpersonal information, illustrating that because they fantasize relationships as "side by side," the leveling-sharpening process remains relatively impervious to changes that occur in interpersonal contexts. Further studies of these issues are needed, with clinical and normal groups of all ages, and should include information about how the fantasized representations of interpersonal interactions are related to overt participation in relationships.

Ninety-three kindergarten children (48 boys, 45 girls) who did not present learning or adjustment problems were administered, with parental permission, the ATBI, FDT, LSSOT, LSFT, and the Fears Interview, which provides an assessment of the language mode, to explore relations among embodied meanings, cognitive-emotional regulators, and instrumental-expressive behaviors. With this procedure, once sufficient rapport is negotiated, the examiner comments, "Usually there's something that makes a person afraid or very nervous. Please tell me the three things you're afraid of most of all." Responses are rated in terms of several categories; for example: (1) General Conditions-Circumstances (e.g., "the dark"); (2) Animals/Insects (e.g., "rats," "spiders"); (3) Type I Aggression (e.g., "people shooting"); (4) Type II Aggression (e.g., "getting kidnapped"); and (5) Type III Aggression (e.g., "when the kids at school call me names"). Another analysis explored relations between embodied meanings (ATBI performance) and the cognitive-emotional regulator of focusing attention in the face of distracting information-emotions (FDT performance). For example, children who experienced embodied meanings representing nurture were not distracted by the irrelevant, food-related pictures surrounding the fruit and produced fewer errors than did children who did not experience embodied meanings of nurture. In terms of the leveling-sharpening cognitive-emotional regulator, children who experienced embodied meanings representing body balance detected more changes and sooner when dealing with both the LSFT and LSSOT than children who experienced embodied meanings representing body imbalance. Another analysis explored relations between embodied meanings and the instrumental-expressive language mode (i.e., fears the child discussed during the interview). We should first note that typically a child is

not aware of the symbolic meanings revealed by her associations to body postures. On the other hand, while discussing with the examiner what he is afraid of, the child is consciously aware of what is being verbalized. Children who experienced embodied meanings of assertion discussed fewer fears, whereas children who experienced embodied constriction discussed significantly more types of fears. And children who experienced the body-self as deformed-inadequate discussed being afraid of shootings/fights in their neighborhood.

These results also raise issues that deserve further study with older children and adults, as well as with clinical populations. For example, at first glance, the finding that experiencing embodied meanings representing nurture correlated with not being distracted by irrelevant pictures of food items appears discordant given, for example, that the performance of orphaned children with the FDT showed that they were distracted by this information (see earlier). Requiring further study, one possible hypothesis is that because the population consisted of 5-year-old children, the need for nurture is age appropriate, which, in turn, is related to a developmentally more mature organization of the Field-Articulation Cognitive-Emotional Regulator. Stated another way, children at this age who did not experience embodied meanings representing nurture may have experienced developmental interferences when negotiating need/nurture, which, in turn, is associated with a less mature developmental organization of the Field-Articulation Cognitive-Emotional Regulator. This speculation converges with one finding that concerns the number of errors a child made. Children who experienced embodied meanings representing nurture made fewer errors (experienced less disruption in cognitive-emotional regulation) while managing Card III than did children who did not experience embodied meanings of need/nurture. Along the same line, that children who experienced embodied meanings of constriction (instead of assertion) also discussed having more types of fears suggests they could have experienced interferences when negotiating self-assertion during the developmental stage of the Subjective Self (see earlier).

In another study, on admission to an inpatient psychiatric facility, 45 youths (20 girls, 25 boys; age range, 6–15 years) were administered the FDT, the Rorschach Test to assess fantasized activity (see earlier), and the BRT I, which assesses regulating representations of the body in large, medium, and small spaces. The child is asked to move her body and representations of the body (i.e., a doll and a pencil) in three tempos—regular, fast, and slow—and in three space dimensions—Floor Maze, Table Maze, and Paper Maze. The time participants took to regulate body tempos in three spaces did not correlate with time to name colors of the FDT cards but did correlate with FDT error scores. The slower the child moved his body on the floor, table, and paper mazes, both when requested to move slowly and quickly, the more color-naming errors he made and the more peripheral, irrelevant items the child recalled after Card III was removed (i.e., reflecting the amount of attention the child paid to information instructions designated as irrelevant). For this inpatient population, then, restraining physical activity did not facilitate the field articulation process of regulating information-emotions but was associated with cognitive-emotional imbalance, which is the opposite of what has been observed with nonclinical populations, who show that delaying body motion correlates with efficiency in cognitive-emotional regulation. In terms of the relation between body tempos and the activity they fantasized in response to inkblots, the slower the tempo the child performed (whether attempting to move in a regular, fast, or slow tempo in macrospace, medium space, or microspace), the more the child fantasized humans, animals, and objects in motion.

These relations produced by an inpatient population, representing many different diagnostic categories, suggests another element of "the ensemble" within the inner self that could be related to developmental interferences, and that should be studied further to contribute to our understanding of developmental psychopathology across the life span. For example, during interpersonal negotiations with caregivers in the first years of life were these individuals required to "sit still," "stop jumping around," interferences that contributed to a rigid outer orientation of the field articulation cognitive-emotional regulator focusing on irrelevant information in the service of avoiding paying attention to the caregiver, and to the development of an exaggerated use of fantasizing motion.

THE THIRD PROBE: EXPLORING RELATIONS AMONG ENVIRONMENTS, INSTRUMENTAL-EXPRESSIVE BEHAVIORS, COGNITIVE-EMOTIONAL REGULATORS, AND EMBODIED MEANINGS

With this probe we enter the third floor of the developmental house depicted in Figure 22.1, and address the relations between environments and a person's inner self.

This issue also requires an identification of the metatheoretical concepts that generate alternative understandings of the nature and impact of the environment. The literature demonstrates that the field has been dominated by two metatheories, each of which frames a different meaning of the environment as it relates to psychological development and functioning. In reviewing these alternatives, we arrive at a concept of environment that underlies the matrix of proposed concepts.

Lessons from the Past: Approaches to the Role of the Environment in Psychological Functioning

The first conceptualization of the environment emerged in the 1920s influenced by the research of John B. Watson and the model of behaviorism. In its broadest form, behaviorism constructed a dualistic metatheory that erected a boundary between a person and environment, thus defining the environment as the person-independent context that delivers some form of stimulation-information and to which the person responds. Watson did not pay attention to the person's inner self, except for taking the position that it should be ignored. As mentioned earlier, he rejected concepts of the mind (consciousness, thought, imagery) and advocated that psychological explanation could be encapsulated in terms of predictions from particular environmental stimuli to particular responses. Accordingly, Watson's metaphor of human functioning viewed a person as a machine; that is, inputs (stimuli from independent environments) activate the machine to produce outputs (responses). This metaphor was elaborated, to some degree, by B. F. Skinner (1974), who introduced his principle of "operant learning," characterized as the A:B:C of behavioral theory. "A" is the *antecedent* environmental condition that evokes a person to produce some form of *behavior* (B), which, in turn, produces some *consequence* (C) in the environment. The environment responds with a reward, so that the behavior is maintained, or responds with punishment, so that the behavior decreases in frequency or is eliminated. At the time, because attention to a person's inner self was steadily gaining momentum because of the influence of psychodynamic psychology, Allan Paivio (1975) reminded behaviorists that "Skinner warned us against...fascination with the inner life...mentalistic ideas are so seductive that one is in danger of being lead by them down the garden path of intraspectionism and mysticism forever" (p. 263).

Bandura (1977) attempted to look inside the person with his "social learning theory" by conceptualizing that, between antecedent stimuli and behaviors they evoke

(A and B), and between behaviors and consequences (B and C) are "internal" stimuli and responses connected to them, referred to as *symbols* and *cognitions*. The relation between these symbols and environments, however, is defined by the same principle of reinforcement. Accordingly, once an experience is acquired, it is cast as a "cognitive representation" evaluated in terms of how well it fits the "real event." Problem behaviors, therefore, are defined as "cognitive distortions" of what the environmental event really means. In addition, although Bandura also introduced the concept of "reciprocal determinism," holding that the environment and person act on each other, a boundary was still maintained between them. Either the person constructs the environment and acts accordingly, or the environment constructs the person and acts accordingly, defining a linear relation.

The dualistic models of behaviorism and social learning theory contributed to the foundations of two new disciplines: environmental psychology and ecopsychology. Emerging in the 1950s, environmental psychology set out to construct a scientific understanding of the relation between human behavior and environment, and chose to follow the view of behaviorism that environments determine behaviors (Bonauito & Bonnes, 2000). Elaborating this position, ecopsychology (Roszak, 1992) embraced the concept that environments contain stimulation that automatically influences a person in positive ways, a view articulated a century ago by Fredrick Law Olmsted, the renowned architect, when he noted in 1865, "Nature employs the mind without fatigue and exercises it, tranquilizes it and yet enlightens it...and gives...reinvigoration to the whole system" (cited in Ulrich & Parsons, 1992, p. 95).

Current Approaches to Investigating the Role of Environment in Psychological Functioning

Hollin (1990) applied behavioral theory to assess young offenders and noted, "[since] the consequences of an individual's behavior are delivered by the environment in which the behavior occurs, then the cause or determinants of behavior are to be found *outside* of the person" (p. 8, emphasis added). As another example, following the view of environmental psychology, Sako (1997) compared the behavior of children attending small schools with that of children attending large schools, and reported that small schools stimulate students to participate more responsibly. Other researchers studied differences in behaviors observed in urban versus rural environments (reviewed by Wapner, Demick, Yamomoto, & Takahashi, 1997). The

position of ecopsychology that nature automatically heals emotional pain and stress has also stimulated considerable research (see Santostefano [2004] for a detailed review and citations of these and related studies); for example: (a) After completing a demanding cognitive task, adults who walked through an area filled with trees and vegetation were more relaxed than subjects who walked in an urban area; (b) adults sitting in a waiting room of a dental clinic were less stressed when a large mural depicting mountains and trees was hung on the wall than were subjects who sat in the same waiting room when the wall was blank; and (c) university students who were experiencing mild stress because of a final examination recovered to a greater degree after viewing slides of rural settings than did students who viewed slides of urban settings. The momentum of ecopsychology has reached a high pitch evidenced by newspaper articles informing the general public that flowers have power and how gardening can improve a person's mental health (e.g., Waldholz, 2003).

Other models have been proposed that differ in significant ways from these viewpoints. The model of "transactionalism" (Wapner & Demick, 2000) selects the alternative conceptualization, namely, that a person and environment form a holistic organization. One contribution to the roots of this discipline came from Heinz Hartmann (1939/1958), who introduced "autoplasticity" and "alloplasticity" to conceptualize a dialectical-reciprocal relation between an individual and the environment in which the person both changes and is changed by environmental stimulation. He also emphasized the importance of conceptualizing environments in terms of whether the stimulation is usual or unusual given the person's history. At the foundation of transactionalism—a model quite compatible with a relational developmental systems perspective—is the concept that the unit of analysis consists of the person-in-the-environment, and the holistic notion that a change in any part of the system affects the whole system. This model also proposes that each level of body-self experience with the environment does not replace but integrates earlier levels, a view converging with embodiment theory (Overton, Müller, & Newman, 2008), and advocates that people interpret environments in terms of personal intentions and act accordingly. This viewpoint relies on the orthogenetic principle (Werner, 1964), which holds that whenever development occurs, the entire system shifts from a relatively global state to a more differentiated and integrated state, to define change. This model was used in one study (Wapner & Demick, 2000) to examine differences in behavior displayed by two diagnostic groups of hospitalized, psychiatric patients before and after the physical relocation of the entire hospital community.

The bioecological model of human development launched by Bronfenbrenner (1986) decades ago, and recently elaborated and supported by investigations (Bronfenbrenner & Morris, 2008) also differs significantly from the metatheoretical assumptions of environmental psychology and ecopsychology. This model advocates the importance of observing individuals in real-life settings and of the dynamic, relational, bidirectional interaction among four principle components: (1) proximal processes, that is, particular forms of interactions that take place between a person and the environment; (2) characteristics of the developing person, that is, unique cognitive, emotional, behavioral qualities; (3) contexts that involve interactions with objects and symbols in addition to persons; and (4) time, ranging from some ongoing episode, to an episode that occurs over a broad interval, and to changes in events and expectations that occur in the larger society. This model also emphasizes that the environment is not only considered in terms of its objective makeup, but also in terms of how the properties of the environment are subjectively experienced by the person dealing with those ingredients.

The ecological approach to social psychology and social cognition presented by Good (2007) also defines a metatheory converging with transactionalism and the bioecological model. To set the stage, Good reviews the "skirmishes" that have taken place regarding the relation between an individual and environment. Particular aspects of this history are especially relevant to the thesis of this chapter. Beginning in 1896, and for the next 30 years, Dewey urged psychologists and sociologists to conceptualize a person and environment as forming one interdependent, holistic system,[2] a viewpoint that contributed to the emergence of the transactional approach (see earlier) and that attempts to dissolve obstacles presented by dualisms (e.g., body/mind, organism/environment). Good also reviews Gibson's (1979) ecological approach to perception that emphasizes the mutuality of person and environment, and the reciprocity of perception and action (a view that contributed to and converged with the New Look revolution in cognitive science discussed earlier). In addition, Good outlines Gibson's concept of "affordances," which is particularly relevant to the studies to be described later,

conducted to illustrate ways of exploring a person's inner self and the environment as forming a relational interdependent system. In these studies, positive affordances are conceptualized as opportunities the environment provides for an individual to take some form of action that serves achieving a goal, and negative affordances as environments that inhibit/limit action to achieve a goal. These opportunities are both physical and psychical, dissolving the dichotomy of subjective versus objective. In addition to emphasizing the importance of the concept of affordance, Good stresses that "the growing interest in cognition as embodied and embedded is seen…as guaranteeing the continuing relevance of the ecological approach with its emphasis on the reciprocity of perception and action and its relational ontology" (p. 268). And that "mind, body and environment cannot be understood in isolation, but are constructions from the flow of purposive activity in the world" (p. 269).

Of the models reviewed that represent current approaches to the role of the environment in psychological functioning and development, Wapner's model of transactionalism, Bronfenbrenner's bioecology, and Good's ecological approach to social psychology set the stage for the studies summarized later. As one example, the reader should take note that the methods used to assess cognitive-emotional regulators and instrumental-expressive behaviors, as a person negotiates with environments, evaluate these processes in terms of the orthogenetic principle emphasized by transactionalism; that is, whenever change in the environment occurs, a person's cognitive and behavioral processes shift either to a more differentiated and integrated organization (progression) or to a more global organization (regression). In addition, transactionalism emphasizes that a person interprets the environment in terms of meanings representing body experiences that took place in the past and acts accordingly. This emphasis converges with one aspect of the bioecological model that articulates why it is important to specify the core characteristics of a person that interact with the environment and how a person's subjectivity experiences the environment. In terms of the proposed conceptual matrix, therefore, the characteristics detailed here concern a person's unique cognitive-emotional regulators, instrumental-expressive behaviors, and embodied meanings.

The studies described later also illustrate the bioecological emphasis on the importance of observing persons in real-life settings and the concept of affordances. The various environments in which participants are assessed either provide/permit or limit/prohibit opportunities for the

---

[2] I attempted with clinical observations to illustrate how a person and environment grow together and become one in healthy psychological development (Santostefano, 2008).

participant to take some action in the service of negotiating a goal. Last, these studies also follow a position that Frenkl-Brunswick (1951) articulated in his presentation at the second symposium that created the New Look Revolution's approach to the personal world of the perceiver (see earlier). He emphasized that the best method for assessing a person's attempts to maintain a dynamic equilibrium between environments and her personal world is to assess the person in "natural habitats." Accordingly, the studies to which we now turn are intended to illustrate the potential, heuristic value of the models of transactionalism, bioecology, and ecological social psychology—all framed within a relational developmental systems perspective—in studies of psychopathology across the life span, especially whether the environment with which a person negotiates provides opportunities for her to take some form of action to achieve a goal. The studies are also intended to stimulate interest in investigating interrelations among environments, cognitive-emotional regulators, instrumental-expressive behaviors, and embodied meanings.

Exploring Relations between the Inner Self and Environments

Three studies explored changes in the leveling-sharpening cognitive-emotional regulator associated with changes in environments that provide opportunities permitting the person to take some form of action to negotiate a goal. In one study (Santostefano, 1978), participants are 44 members of a parachute club involved in the first phase of training; that is, performing eight jumps with a static line attached to the doorway of the airplane so that the parachute automatically opens when the person jumps from the airplane. After a club member takes the eighth jump, he performs the first "free-fall" jump without the aid of this static line. All participants had made at least one jump with the static line, but fewer then eight. Half of the participants formed the experimental group because they were scheduled to perform a jump at the end of a 2-week period. Members of the control group had not scheduled a jump at the end of a 2-week period. In terms of methods, two tests of the leveling-sharpening cognitive-emotional regulator were constructed, paralleling those described earlier, each presenting a scene designed to perturbate embodied meanings-emotions unique to the environment of parachute jumping. Parachute Test Form A presents a scene of a parachutist falling through the air performing a free-fall jump; that is, the parachute is not yet deployed. Parachute Test Form B consists of a scene of a parachutist descending with parachute fully

deployed. With each test, 20 details are omitted accumulatively throughout the series of 60 cards. The Leveling-Sharpening House Test (Santostefano, 1988) was also used to serve as a stimulus that had no relation to parachute jumping: a two-dimensional line drawing of a house is presented and 20 details, ranging from less to more conspicuous, are omitted accumulatively (e.g., doorknob, tree next to the house). As with the Leveling-Sharpening Tests described earlier, each card is presented for 5 seconds, and the participant is asked to report any changes in the scene. Performance is evaluated in terms of the number of correct changes detected, how soon a change is perceived once it is introduced, and the number of changes reported that do not occur.

These procedures were administered individually to each participant in his home, and readministered 7 days later to members of the experimental group at the airport within an hour of his performing a jump, and to members of the control group again in his home environment. Half of each group was administered Parachute Test Form A in Session 1 and then Parachute Test Form B in Session 2. The other half received the reverse sequence. In both the first and second sessions, the House Test was administered after one of the Parachute Tests. The experimental group detected more changes and sooner with both Parachute Tests, and the House Test when at the airport versus in their home environments. The control subjects showed no difference in their performance from the first to the second evaluation. This result indicates that when the participant is in the environment of an airport, and permitted to take action to achieve the goal of ensuring his safety, the leveling-sharpening cognitive-emotional regulator reorganizes progressively. Unexpected findings were obtained when performances with the Parachute Tests were compared. The experimentals who dealt with Form A (parachute in free fall) when at the airport showed a significantly greater reorganization toward increased sharpening than experimentals administered Form B (parachute in slow descent). This result suggests that because none of the subjects had yet experienced a free-fall jump, a scene depicting a free fall was construed with embodied meanings that evoked more anxiety-alertness related to the goal of ensuring personal safety, which, in turn, resulted in an even higher progressive reorganization of the cognitive-emotional regulator. Another finding supports this hypothesis. Recall that the LS-House Test was administered in both Sessions 1 and 2 immediately after one of the forms of the Parachute Test. Participants who engaged the House Test immediately after they had experienced Form A (free fall) showed a significantly greater shift toward increased sharpening with the House Test than did subjects who dealt with the House Test after experiencing Form B (slow descent). These findings suggest that when a person can actively engage stimulation in the environment from usual (e.g., one's home) to less usual (e.g., airport in the service of achieving the goal of personal safety), a progressive reorganization of a cognitive-emotional regulator occurs, at least with a nonclinical population. These findings also suggest that for a novice parachutist, a picture itself of a jumper performing a free-fall perturbates to a greater degree the embodied meaning associated with the "unusual" environment with which the person is negotiating.

The second study explored changes in the organization of the leveling-sharpening cognitive emotional regulator responding to the goal of taking a college course final examination (Santostefano, 1978). Participants in the experimental group (11 females, 11 males) were administered the LSHT (described earlier) in their dormitory rooms and again 2 weeks later within hours before taking a final examination. The control subjects (11 females, 11 males) were administered the LSHT in their dormitory rooms on two occasions, separated by 2 weeks; no final examination was scheduled near the time of either administration. The performance of the two groups did not differ during the first evaluation. On the second evaluation, the group anticipating a final examination detected the first change sooner and detected more changes (a progressive reorganization).

The participants of a third study (Santostefano et al., 2006) were 106 abandoned youths (age range, 5–19 years) residing in villages maintained by the Spanish government. The procedures administered included the LSI (see earlier) and the FDT (described earlier). Forty-eight of these youths were invited several times by relatives to visit them and they accepted. These children, when compared with those who did not visit relatives, produced significant differences. For example, they discussed less often being upset by aggressive events and discussed more often being upset by the death of a loved one; they showed a more mature developmental organization of the field articulation cognitive-emotional regulator, focusing more efficiently when naming the colors of the fruit while regulating information and associated emotions represented by the surrounding irrelevant pictures of food-related objects.

These three studies illustrate changes in the organization of cognitive-emotion regulators occurring in response to unusual environments. One aspect of these studies is of special relevance. The participants elected to enter and

negotiate with the unusual environment (airport, final exam, home of relative) that permitted taking action to achieve a goal (e.g., engaging parachute equipment, classroom notes, relatives), while at the same time regulating information and related emotions.

Two other studies explored changes in cognitive-emotional regulators associated with changes in the environment that a person does not voluntarily select to engage and that restricts the actions a person can take to negotiate goals. In one study (Santostefano, 1998), three groups participated: Group A—15 hospitalized male patients scheduled for surgery within 24 hours (mean age, 32 years); Group B—20 male patients at the same hospital but not scheduled for a surgical procedure (mean age, 47 years); and Group C—11 male subjects attending a nearby university (mean age, 22 years). The Leveling-Sharpening Hospital Test was constructed to assess the leveling-sharpening cognitive-emotional regulator following the same guidelines used in constructing and administrating other tests described earlier. The scene consists of a doctor holding a syringe and standing in a hospital room. Members of Groups A and B volunteered and understood that participation was not related to his treatment and were individually administered the Leveling-Sharpening Hospital Test while seated at a table by their hospital bed. The members of Group C were administered the same test in their homes. Group A detected fewer changes and after more presentations (a developmentally less mature organization). The nonhospitalized control subjects detected the largest number of changes and sooner (a more mature organization), and Group B fell between.

The participants of the second study (Santostefano, 1978) were three groups of boys of the same age (age range, 7–11 years): one scheduled to be hospitalized for hernia repair, another scheduled for dental work for the first time to repair tooth decay, and the third attending a public school in the same city. All children participated with parental permission, and their histories did not suggest physical or emotional difficulties. The Leveling-Sharpening Hospital Test and the Leveling-Sharpening House Test (described earlier) were administered in addition to the following procedures assessing the instrumental expressive fantasy modality: (1) The examiner read a brief story describing a monkey who has "a big, pretty tail," and the monkey's keeper notices that the tail looks different. The child was asked, "What do you think happened?" The child's fantasy was ranked from representing direct, immediate injury (e.g., "The tail was chopped off") to indirect, delayed outcomes (e.g., "The hair was trimmed"); (2) the child was asked to look over a picture of two persons (the hands of one near the head and neck of the other) and make up a story about what is going on. Responses were ranked from fantasies depicting one figure engaged in some form of immediate, direct, aggressive behavior directed toward the other (e.g., "This lady is strangling that person.") to fantasies representing interpersonal affiliation-compassion (e.g., "This one has a toothache, and she's looking at it to help."); and (3) the child was asked to describe what each inkblot of the Rorschach Test brought to mind; responses were evaluated in terms of the degree the body-self is depicted as free of barriers and differentiated from environments (e.g., "This looks like a wall." "This looks like two kids dancing around a tree.").

These procedures were administered individually to each child of the surgical group in his home 1 week before hospitalization (Time I), readministered in his hospital room at bedside one day before the scheduled surgery (Time II), and 3 weeks after discharge from the hospital, again in his home (Time III). Similarly, each child in the dental group was evaluated at home 1 week before his dental appointment (Time I), at the dentist's office (Time II), and 3 weeks later at home (Time III). Each child in the control group was evaluated in his home, and again 1 and 3 weeks later. In addition, only mothers of the children in the surgical group were interviewed at home during Times I and III and asked to discuss several issues; for example, her child's behavior that reflected fear-anxiety, difficulty with sleeping, or moodiness with friends.

The three groups did not differ in their performance at Time I with the Leveling-Sharpening Hospital Test and Leveling-Sharpening House Test. At Time II, the Surgical Group shifted the most toward a developmentally earlier organization (increased leveling) with both tests and maintained this organization 3 weeks after leaving the hospital environment. The Dental Group showed the same trends but to a lesser degree. The performance of the Control Group did not vary over the three assessments. These results indicate that the leveling-sharpening cognitive-emotional process reorganized regressively, when the children shifted from their usual environments and coped with an unusual, stressful environment that limited/prevented taking action and negotiating. Another series of analyses explored whether and how the degree and direction of cognitive-emotional reorganization related to changes that took place with other elements of the inner self that were assessed. The Surgical Group produced the highest number of statistically significant correlations when assessments of Time I and Time II were compared. At Time II, they fantasized

more direct-literal forms of body injury (Fables Test; e.g., "The monkey's tail was chopped off.") and interpersonal interactions as aggressive (e.g., "This person is choking this one."), and produced few barriers between persons and environments. The Dental Group produced similar relations, but fewer reached statistical significance. The Control Group showed chance variations.

The interviews held with mothers of the children in the Surgical Group resulted in significant relations at Time I. Children who showed the most mature developmental organization of the Leveling-Sharpening Cognitive Emotional Regulator were rated, for example, as less irritable, not displaying fears, having little difficulty sleeping, and feeling free to venture outside the home. The correlations obtained 3 weeks after hospitalization resulted in a striking finding. Now the relations are in the *opposite* direction; that is, children who showed the less mature cognitive organization (i.e., perceived the first change later, and detected fewer changes) were rated by their mothers as not irritable, afraid, having difficulty sleeping, or moody. The finding that a regressive cognitive organization, taking place when negotiating a stressful environment that prohibits taking action, is associated with successful adaptation after hospitalization-surgery converges with the correlations observed at Time II. Recall that a shift toward leveling information-emotions when in the hospital environment (compared with the home environment at Time I) correlated with experiencing more fantasies representing body injury and aggressive interpersonal interactions, and fewer representing barriers from environments. These relations led to the speculation that when in a stressful, unusual environment that limits taking action, a regressive reorganization of the leveling-sharpening cognitive-emotional regulator is associated with changes in other elements of the inner self that contribute to successfully coping with the stress and meaning of facing surgery. We noted earlier that the fantasy mode is viewed as providing a person with alternative opportunities to negotiate developmental goals when the environment does not make available opportunities to take some action. On the basis of the results obtained, one could argue, for example, that when a child is coping with the environment of a hospital that limits the use of the action mode, if the child expresses and rehearses in fantasy various forms of body harm and interpersonal aggressive interactions, the child's inner self is taking the opportunity to negotiate with instrumental-expressive fantasy behavior the stress associated with anticipating and experiencing bodily harm.

These five studies illustrate methods and issues that could contribute to investigations of life-span development and psychopathology, and support the following hypothesis. When dealing with an unusual environment that provides positive affordances allowing the instrumental-expressive action mode to engage ingredients in the environment (e.g., parachute jumping), a progressive reorganization of the leveling-sharpening cognitive-emotional regulator serves the adaptive process because more information in the environment, and related emotions, can be engaged. In contrast, when dealing with an unusual environment that limits participation of the instrumental-expressive action mode (e.g., hospital-surgery), a regressive reorganization serves the adaptive process because information and related emotions in question are more effectively negotiated in the instrumental-expressive fantasy mode. Similarly, the results suggest that when individuals interact with usual environments that permit action (positive affordances), no noteworthy progressive or regressive shifts take place with cognitive-emotional regulators, as well as other elements of the inner self.

The next study explores whether and how an environment that invites expressions of physical aggression, versus an environment that invites fantasizing aggressive behavior, influences a person's preferred mode of instrumental-expressive behavior (Santostefano, 1998). The Action versus Fantasy Test (see earlier) was administered to a large number of first- and fifth-grade boys, inviting the child to perform an action or look at a picture of someone performing the action and "imagine what's going on." Ten boys from each grade who performed only actions were selected as the "action-oriented group," and 10 who examined only pictures were selected as the "fantasy-oriented group." A week after the preliminary evaluation, each child was administered two procedures: (1) the Miniature Situations Test II (described earlier) to assess the degree of directness and delay the child exhibits in the instrumental-expressive action mode; and (2) the Structured Fantasy Test (described earlier) to assess the degree of directness and delay the child exhibits in the instrumental-expressive fantasy mode. Immediately after these evaluations, each child participated individually in one of two experimental "environments." Half of the action-oriented group and half of the fantasy-oriented group were randomly assigned to participate in an "action-activity" environment (e.g., punch a BoBo clown for 1 minute; break 10 wooden sticks in half); half were assigned to participate in a "fantasy" environment (e.g., view aggressive moments of a film of a boxing match; examine magazine pictures depicting violence).

Immediately after the child participated in one of these environments, he was readministered the Miniature Situations Test II and the Structured Fantasy Test. Results show that action-oriented boys who experienced an action environment displayed a progressive reorganization of that mode (e.g., they turned a screw into wood first, then hammered a nail, and then smashed a light bulb) and a regressive reorganization of the nonpreferred mode (e.g., a dog's paw was bitten by another dog). On the other hand, fantasy-oriented boys who participated in the fantasy environment expressed more direct-immediate actions (e.g., they smashed the light bulb first) and more indirect-delayed fantasies (e.g., they imagined the dog stepped on a stone). The boys who experienced an environment opposite to their preferred mode of expression displayed confusion and conflict when responding to the assessment procedures. These results suggest that when an environment provides opportunities to engage ingredients converging with one's preferred instrumental-expressive mode, the dialectical relation between action and fantasy facilitates a transfer from the preferred mode as the instrument of expression to the other. And when the environment emphasizes engaging ingredients that oppose one's preferred instrumental-expressive mode, the inner self experiences cognitive-emotional-behavioral confusion that, if it continues, could result in the development of psychopathological functioning. These results also raise questions and should stimulate studies of the relations between environments and cognitive, behavioral, and emotional elements. For example, given the growing use by youths of computer games, how does this environment affect the processes of cognitive-emotional regulators and instrumental-expressive behaviors in school? As another example, how would adults of different ages who watch two or three movies a week differ from those who do not?

CONCLUSIONS

We noted at the start that the discipline of developmental psychopathology emerged in the early 1980s in a conceptual atmosphere dominated by the viewpoint of nosology, which had gained momentum when the American Psychiatric Association published the first manual of mental disorders in 1952. We also noted that this viewpoint continued to dominate, stimulated by the influence of four editions released in the following years, conceptualizing psychopathology in terms of more than 200 segregated diagnostic categories, each defined by a fixed set of symptoms. We considered how this conceptualization continues to influence research and stimulates the use of questionnaires and self-report as methods to assess cognitive and personality traits. We also discussed that nosology has been challenged over the years, beginning with an NIMH-sponsored conference held after the first manual was released. Of particular relevance to my presentation, recall that after the second edition of this manual was released, Piaget (1975) advocated that psychiatry places too much emphasis on the principle of syndromes, and that psychological difficulties should not be conceptualized as fixed, behavioral traits because a person may function adequately at one moment and not at another. Piaget's position forecast the criticism, which we summarized, that has been levied against the DSM approach, illustrated by Kutchins and Kirk (1997), who argue that nosology defines ordinary behavior as pathological, "making all of us crazy." Another investigator (Watson, 2005), anticipating the next edition (DSM-V) scheduled for publication in 2012, proposes that it may help if diagnostic categories are organized to form a hierarchy. Criticisms continue to be levied, however, at the manual under preparation; for example, the degree to which the pharmaceutical industry influences DSM revisions because specific medications are designated for particular diagnostic categories (Bradshaw, 2008), and the secrecy surrounding the preparation of DSM-V (Bradshaw, 2009).

To avoid the misconception of psychological functioning as fixed categories of behavioral traits, recall that Piaget (1975) also encouraged investigators to study the "ensemble of elements involved at different levels of functioning" (p. vii), a recommendation followed by some investigators and supported by results. For example, relying on research conducted by Sidney Blatt and colleagues, Luyten (2006) noted "psychopathological disorders should be seen as a result of various distortions of normal, dialectical interactions between the development of self-definition and relatedness...situated on a continuum" (p. 524). Luyten also points out that research shows individuals are not "passive recipients of intrapersonal (biological and psychological) factors and of their environments..." but "... in part generate their own internal and external stressors..." (p. 526). The perspective offered in this chapter also endorses Piaget's position proposing that the various alternative approaches to conceptualizing psychopathology across the life span should step beyond nosology and follow a developmental viewpoint investigating interrelated parts (i.e., psychological processes) of a person's self-system as goals are negotiated. This proposal emphasizes two particular

challenges: (1) the need to identify, assess, and explore the various parts/processes that constitute a person's self-system and how this system of parts becomes transformed beginning in early childhood; and (2) the need to expand our understanding of how particular features of human and nonhuman environments provide goals that promote the development of these parts/processes of the system, whereas other features require short-term regressive or progressive reorganizations, and why still other features may derail their development across the life span.

To illustrate this challenge, I proposed four system parts/processes, a matrix that, metaphorically speaking, forms a developmental house. The foundation and first floor of a person's Inner Self consists of a system of embodied meanings-life metaphors the individual constructs during the first years of life. These reflect the relational, bidirectional interactions/experiences between the embodied living system—the person—and her social and physical environment. These embodied meanings themselves become transformed throughout development as the person negotiates and renegotiates core developmental goals. The second floor consists of two parts/processes: (1) a hierarchy of cognitive-emotional regulators that gather information and regulate related emotions from the person's embodied meanings/life metaphors and from environmental affordances with which the person is negotiating; and (2) a hierarchy of instrumental-expressive behaviors with which a person responds both to the demands of embodied meanings and to the goals and requirements of environments as perceived by cognitive-emotional regulators. Although the top floor involves Outer Space, these environments are experienced in terms of personal, embodied meanings/life metaphors assigned to the goals environments make available and limits they present.

The parts/processes of this developmental house converge with a conceptualization William James (1890) proposed more than a century ago that has had an impact on discussions of the self (Harter, 1999). James distinguished between two dialectically related aspects of a person's sense of self that he termed *Me-Self* and *I-Self*. The Me-Self includes a person's tactile, kinesthetic, and emotional experiences with her body, the bodies of others, social interactions, and material things. The I-Self includes perceiving, knowing, and giving meaning to what is going on within and around oneself, the sense of being the author of one's thoughts and actions, the sense of understanding one's experiences, and remaining the same person over time. Based on observations of traumatized adults, Aron (1996) conceptualized a dialectical relation between the

I-Self and Me-Self, which he termed *self-reflexive functioning*. In the absence of protracted, intense, emotional experiences, the self that experiences and the self that gives meaning to experiences continuously and reflexively communicate with and define each other. But when a developmental interference is experienced, the link between the experiencing Me-Self and the observing I-Self is broken. Accordingly, these persons are left "out of touch with their feelings and emotions (p. 15)…unable to utilize their body sensations…traumatized patients are unable to reflect on their traumatic experiences, self-reflexive functioning fails" (p. 25). Steven Stern's (2002) emphasis on the process of constructing an identification also contributes to conceptualizing the elements I propose within the self. Relying on infant investigations by Jean Piaget, Daniel Stern, and Louis Sander, which we considered earlier, Steven Stern emphasizes that as an infant negotiates various goals (e.g., trust, reciprocity, asserting) by coordinating circular reactions, imitating the actions of others, and initiating and coauthoring play rituals, these experiences do not become psychologically real until the infant/toddler identifies with and internalizes within herself the responses and representations of others. Recall that Daniel Stern viewed these representations of interactions as "memories" and Piaget as "deferred imitation." For Steven Stern, identifying with the behaviors-emotions of others is so fundamental to psychological development that it is "something analogous to our need for oxygen…I view identification as fundamental to psychological life" (p. 725).

Interrelating Aron's (1996) and Steven Stern's (2002) views with the matrix of concepts that form the developmental house, I have argued (Santostefano, 2004), on the basis of longitudinal observations of traumatized children, that the behaviors of others that abused or interfered with a child's negotiating goals, and that the child internalized, form a significant part of the child's matrix of embodied life metaphors, which dominate the meanings the child gives to environments, the orientation of his cognitive-emotional regulators, and the instrumental-expressive behaviors the child uses when negotiating. In addition, given that the dialectical relation between the I-Self and Me-Self has been severed, the I-Self has difficulty using environments and interactions that make available developmentally appropriate goals that could revise the original pathological, interactive meaning. Accordingly, the individual continues to repeat some form of instrumental-expressive behavior that satisfies what the embodied meaning of the original developmental interference prescribes.

To illustrate these concepts and issues as a potentially heuristic approach to developmental psychopathology across the life span, I return to John, whose development and difficulties were summarized at the start of my discussion. I begin with two questions. How and why was the hair pulling established? What was the original meaning, and was this meaning revised? Two major embodied meanings John constructed within his Core and Subjective selves (age, 3–14 months), *before* father shaved his beard, condensed, represented, and conserved the following experiences with mother and father: (1) regarding mother—initially affectionate; extreme bodily excitement when she frequently engaged in the ritual of brushing her hair across John's belly; then withdrawn, detached, depressed, irritable; a few months later, elements were added of mother cooing and caressing the new sibling; and (b) regarding father—vigorous body sensations and explosive excitement when father repeatedly rubbed and nuzzled his beard against John's belly, neck, and cheeks; father's excitement; the sense of being one with father when John initiated the play ritual of arching his stomach, running off, and hiding, with father always gleefully responding as he searched for John; father as security and protection from mother's depression and angry moods.

When the father shaved his beard, only the embodied meanings within John's Subjective Self, representing the first edition of his identification with his father, were severely disrupted. Given the central position his father's beard held in most of John's interactions with him and, therefore, in the key meanings that formed his Subjective Self, John faced a major developmental task; that is, reconstructing a representation of his father without a beard and at the same time preserving other meanings such as well-being, excitement, security, and individuation. John could not accomplish this task, however, because his father withdrew, failing to initiate other play rituals to substitute for the "beard games." John probably tried to negotiate these developmental interferences. For example, when he tried to engage his father in games of hide-and-seek, he was calling up the still well-established representations of "father with beard" as an evoked companion, which disagreed, however, with the father who is now without a beard. To cope with this predicament, John, who was now capable of *deferred imitation* (a behavior noted earlier that is central to this phase of development and the emergence of symbolic behavior), pulled hair from his head (imitating his father, who had removed hair from his face), experiencing and preserving the meaning of well-being and security within his Subjective Self.

From this formulation of the original meaning of John's hair pulling, we consider how and why the hair pulling persisted uninterrupted from the age of nearly 2 years to adolescence while, until recently, he functioned very adequately. To address this issue requires that we focus on activities in a child's environment that interfere with goals required by each stage of development (Nagera, 1981); for example, the unique psychology of a parent, resulting in either overstimulation or failure to participate in interactions. To cope with these interferences, Nagera proposed the child uses adaptations that persist unchanged and that may not produce conscious stress until later stages of development when the child is negotiating typical developmental tasks and/or biological changes that introduce new demands on cognition, emotion, and behavior. This position is elaborated by Daniel Stern (1985) in ways that serve our discussion. On the basis of infant research we considered, he proposes that although the Verbal Self (age, 15–24 months) and Narrative Self (age, 24–36 months) typically build on embodied meanings constructed during physical-emotional interactions and play rituals that took place during the development of the Core Self and Subjective Self (age, 3–14 months; see earlier discussion), when developmental interferences occur, "some experiences … continue underground, non-verbalized, to lead an unnamed (and to that extent only, unknown) but nonetheless very real existence" (p. 173). Piaget's (1973) discussion of the cognitive unconscious elaborates this issue, proposing that "the functional utility" the translation serves determines why some nonverbal experiences become translated into shared symbols (fantasies, words), whereas others are not. He notes that a sensorimotor schema (i.e., representations of interactions) are not translated, and remain unconscious yet operational whenever the schema is incompatible with, or in conflict with, conscious thoughts and perceptions already constructed and accepted. Piaget noted, "The child has not constructed a conscious hypothesis and then set it aside…he had repressed it from the conscious territory before it penetrated there in any conceptualized form…" (1973, p. 255).

Viewing John with these concepts, the protracted, intensely stimulating "beard playing rituals" he experienced, followed by his father's abrupt withdrawal and his mother's withdrawal and angry rejection, constituted a developmental interference that resulted in an embodied life metaphor that dominated John's Core and Subjective Self, and prescribed excessive investment in bodily excitement and hair. To cope with this interference, John used the instrumental-expressive behavior of pulling hair from his head as a deferred imitation of his father without a beard. Because the embodied meanings representing interactions with father and mother remained unconscious (i.e., sensorimotor fixation points that were not translated into the fantasy and language modes), John's development proceeded unimpaired for the most part. But how do we understand that in recent months he experienced major difficulty concentrating on school work and felt pressed to talk to someone about a major concern, namely, the excitement and anger he experienced when in the presence of a particular teacher and male friend? When John entered puberty, heightened biological changes produced intense body excitation, imposing new burdens on his psychological resources. Under this sudden impact, the original father-beard life metaphor made demands that influenced John's cognitive-emotion regulators to which I now turn and illustrate.

Recall that cognitive-emotional regulators coordinate attributes and calls for action from ingredients (goals and limits) in the environment with the calls for action from embodied meanings and related emotions a person's inner self assigns to these ingredients. In the absence of major developmental interferences, this regulating-coordinating process operates flexibly so that one of the instrumental-expressive modalities (action, fantasy, language) adequately manages the goal being negotiated. We also noted that whenever developmental interferences occur, the process of cognitive-emotional regulation becomes inflexible, assuming a maladaptive orientation; for example, either centering on attributes in the environment unrelated to the embodied meaning to avoid its demands, or centering on an embodied meaning to avoid demands in the environment. John provides us with one opportunity to observe how elements of the inner self can result in adequate functioning during one stage of development and produce emotional turmoil in another, when the power of an embodied meaning is magnified by new psychological/biological demands. Although he had functioned quite adequately until recently, now each time he prepared to leave home and enter the school environment, John's cognitive-emotional regulators immediately assumed a rigid outer orientation by carefully aligning chairs around tables and adjusting pictures hanging on the walls, to avoid the embodied meanings/emotions evoked by his anticipating the teacher who maintained a beard and the classmate with body hair. On the other hand, when he was at home, his cognitive-emotional regulators assumed a rigid, inner orientation, centering on embodied meanings/emotions representing play rituals with father's beard, and avoiding goals in the environment (e.g., homework), in the service of experiencing the explosion of bodily excitement when he plucked a strand of hair from his scalp or nuzzled the head of his toy lion against his neck.

These rigid maladaptive cognitive orientations occurred during my initial meeting with John. For example, when we first met and I asked him to share why he had asked for a consultation, his cognitive-emotional regulators shifted to an outer orientation. He immediately pointed to a painting on the wall, commented he liked it, stood up, and carefully manipulated its alignment. At other times, his cognitive-emotional regulators shifted to a rigid inner orientation when he ignored me, clenched his hands, stared at the floor for several minutes, and then slowly passed his fingertips over the leaf of a Dieffenbachia plant as if he were touching hair. In general, the significant interference John experienced in the first years of life severed the link between his Me-Self and I-Self, limiting his capacity to reflect on these experiences and construct developmentally more advanced alternatives. Accordingly, the embodied meanings that derived from his play ritual with his father remained nonverbal, unnamed but still very active, because, as Piaget (1973) noted (see earlier), this schema was never revised and conflicted with conscious thoughts. For example, during our meetings, John frequently arched his shoulders back and pushed out his abdomen whenever he experienced thoughts/feelings related to body hair (e.g., when discussing the science teacher and his toy lion). In addition, the hair pulling persisted with alternative, related expressions taking place only with the action mode (e.g., touching the leaves of plants) instead of advancing to instrumental-expressive behaviors in the fantasy and language modes, a developmental progression, we noted, that is characteristic when an individual does not experience significant developmental interferences.

Consider now the studies described earlier that assessed changes that took place in the cognitive-emotional orientation of participants when they were evaluated in the context of usual environments, and again in unusual environments that presented different goals and limits. In contrast with John's rigid cognitive-emotion regulation, these studies demonstrate that flexibility in the orientation of cognitive-emotional regulators serves adaptation. Recall that the cognitive-emotional orientation of children and adults who were about to experience surgery flexibly reorganized to an inner orientation in the service of avoiding ingredients in the environment, by centering on embodied meanings/emotions and related fantasies. The question whether this reorganization served adaptation receives support from the study that showed that the more a child's cognitive orientation reorganized to an inner position when in the context

of a hospital, the more positive the mother's rating of the child's behavior and social functioning 30 days after surgery. In contrast, young novice adult parachutists who were at an airport about to execute a jump, and college students who were about to take an exam, showed that their cognitive-emotional regulators shifted to an outer orientation when negotiating with environments that permitted active negotiating and interacting. These studies create questions that serve developmental psychopathology. For example, if we focus on individual differences, would college students whose cognitive-emotional regulators shift most to an outer orientation before taking an exam achieve higher grades? Would novice parachutists whose cognitive-emotional regulators shift most to an outer orientation achieve higher performance ratings from their instructors? And would patients whose cognitive-emotional regulators shift most to an inner orientation show the most adaptive behavior after surgery?

To illustrate how studies exploring another part of the inner self, namely, instrumental-expressive behaviors, could serve studies of developmental psychopathology across the life span, consider a study of generativity conducted by McAdams and St. Aubin (1992). The concept of generativity was introduced into life-span theory by Erik Erikson (1950), who proposed that once an individual consolidates an identity and establishes bonds of intimacy (e.g., friendships, marriage), than she is psychologically ready to make a commitment to, and help improve, the next generation. To explore this model, McAdams and St. Aubin administered four questionnaires to females and males aged 19 to 68 years. With one scale, for example, designed to assess "social desirability," the participant rated items (e.g., "I have kind thoughts about everybody") on a 4-point scale, from 0 ("the statement never applies to you") to 4 ("the statement applies to you often"). In terms of the concept of a hierarchy of instrumental-expressive behaviors we considered, the results obtained in this study relate only to the language mode. This study's contribution could be increased through the inclusion of assessments of instrumental-expressive actions (e.g., participants would be asked to water a plant or nibble on a cookie, and to repair a torn sheet of paper or measure the strength of their handgrip). Participants might also be asked to draw a picture of two persons doing something (see earlier discussion) to assess generativity at the instrumental-expressive fantasy modality (e.g., one drawing depicts a person helping another person carry a box; another depicts two persons each seated before a computer doing their work). And in terms of our discussion of environments, what if, for example, cognitive-emotional regulators are assessed when the participant is in his home environment and again when he is visiting a special needs classroom of high-school ninth graders.

Last, in terms of the system parts at the foundation (i.e., embodied meanings), Murray and Farrington's (2008) study provides another illustration. Based on histories of participants who were followed from the ages of 8 to 48, these investigators describe differences in DSM diagnoses associated with the type of parental separation participants experienced (e.g., because of imprisonment, hospitalization, death, disharmony). If these participants were administered the ATBI (see earlier discussion), resulting data might have significantly contributed to an understanding of how these early experiences influenced the construction of different embodied meanings, which, in turn, contributed to the expression of different behaviors later in life.

In conclusion, the conceptual matrix that has been discussed in this chapter as an integrative cognitive-emotional-behavioral-environmental approach to developmental psychopathology across the life span converges with relational developmental systems (Lerner, 2006; Lerner & Overton, 2008; Overton, 2006) and dynamical systems theory (e.g., Camras & Witherington, 2005; Granic, 2005), both descendents of general systems theory (von Bertalanffy, 1968; Overton, 1975) and cousins of functionalist theory (Barrett & Campos, 1987). From the viewpoint of these converging perspectives, in both normal and pathological development, the person (i.e., the developing system) is constituted as a holistic interrelation of dynamic parts/processes who acts to negotiate developmental goals in the context of physical and interpersonal environments that are reciprocally constructed (principle of self-regulation). From this viewpoint of a person's parts/processes and environment forming a holistic, relational, developmental system, any concept of theoretical reductionism becomes irrelevant. It is the dialectical relation among the parts, not the aggregate of elements, that constitutes the ever-changing developmental system. And one cannot observe these parts/processes without perturbating the systems with stimulation.

REFERENCES

Achenbach, T. (1974). *Developmental psychopathology.* New York: Ronald Press.

Albani, C., Blaser, G., Geyer, M., Daig, L., Schmutzer, G., Bailer, H., et al. (2006). Testing and Standardization of the "Body Image Questionnaire." *Zeitschrift fur Medizinsche Psychologie, 15,* 99–109.

Allport, G. W., & Vernon, P. E. (1933). *Studies in expressive movement.* New York: Macmillan.

American Psychiatric Association. (1994). *Diagnostic and statistical manual of mental disorders* (4th ed., revised). Washington, DC: APA.

American Psychiatric Association. (2000). *Diagnostic and statistical manual of mental disorders* (4th ed., text revision). Arlington, VA: APA.

Amone-P'Olak, K., Garnefski, N., & Kraai, V. (2007). Adolescents caught between fires: Cognitive emotion regulation in response to war experiences in Northern Uganda. *Journal of Adolescence, 30,* 655–669.

Aron, L. (1996). *A meeting of minds: Mutuality in psychoanalysis.* Hillsdale, NJ: Analytic Press.

Bandura, A. (1997). *Social learning theory.* Englewood cliffs, NJ: Prentice Hall.

Barrett, K., & Campos, J. (1987). Perspectives on emotional development II. A functionalist approach to emotions. In J. Osofsky (Ed.), *Handbook of infant development* (2nd ed., pp. 555–578). New York: John Wiley & Sons.

Bearison, D. J., & Zimiles, H. (1986). Developmental perspectives of thought and emotion: An introduction. In D. J. Bearison & H. Zimiles (Eds.), *Thought and emotion: Developmental perspectives* (pp. 1–10). Hillsdale, NJ: Erlbaum.

Beasley, J. F., & Kerney, C. A. (1996). Source agreement in assessing youth stress and negative affectivity. New evidence for an old problem. *Journal of Anxiety Disorder, 10,* 465–475.

Beebe, B. & Lachmann, F. M. (2002). Infant research and adult treatment: Co-constructing interaction. Hillsdale, NJ: Analytic Press.

Beutler, L. E., & Malik, M. L. (Eds.). (2002). *Rethinking the DSM. A psychological perspective.* Washington, DC: American Psychological Association.

Blake, R. R., & Ramsey, G. V. (Eds.). (1951). *Perception: An approach to personality.* New York: Ronald Press.

Bonaiuto, M., & Bonnes, M. (2000). Social-psychological approaches in environment behavior studies. In S. Wapner, J. Demick, & T. Yamomoto (Eds.), *Theoretical perspectives in environment-behavior research: Underlying assumptions, research problems, and methodologies* (pp. 67–78). New York: Kluwer Academic/Plenum Press.

Bradshaw, J. (2008). Drug controversy envelopes DSM-IV. *The National Psychologist, 17,* 12.

Bradshaw, J. (2009). Concerns voiced over secrecy surrounding DSM-V. *The National Psychologist, 18,* 5.

Brausch, A. M., & Muehlenkamp, J. J. (2007). Body image and suicidal ideation in adolescents. *Body Image, 4,* 207–212.

Bredart, A., Verdier, A. S., & Dolbeault, S. (2007). French translation and adaptation of Body Image Scale (BIS) assessing body image perception in women following breast cancer. *Psycho-Oncologie, 1,* 24–30.

Bronfenbrenner, U. (1951). Toward an integrated theory of personality. In R. R Blake & G. V. Ramsey (Eds.), *Perception: An approach to personality* (pp. 206–257). New York: Ronald Press.

Bronfenbrenner, U. (1986). Recent advances in research on the ecology of human development. In R. K. Silbereisen, K. Eyferth, & G. Rudinger (Eds.), *Development as action in context. Problem behavior and normal youth development* (pp. 286–309). New York: Springer Verlag.

Bronfenbrenner, U., & Morris, P. A. (2008). The bioecological model of human development. In W. Damon & R. M. Lerner (Eds.), *Handbook of child psychology: Vol. 1. Theoretical models of human development* (pp. 793–828). Hoboken, NJ: Wiley Interscience.

Brown, F. (1958). The psychodiagnostic test battery. In D. Brower & L. E. Abt (Eds.), *Progress in clinical psychology* (pp. 60–71). New York: Grune & Stratton.

Bruner, J. S. (1951). Personality dynamics and the process of perceiving. In R. R. Blake & G. V. Ramsey (Eds.), *Perception: An approach to personality* (pp. 121–147). New York: Ronald Press.

Bruner, J. S. (1986). Thought and emotion: Can Humpty Dumpty be put back together again? In D. J. Bearison & H. Zimiles (Eds.), *Thought and emotion: Developmental perspectives* (pp. 11–20). Hillsdale, NJ: Erlbaum.

Bruner, J. S. (1992). Another look at the New Look I. *American Psychologist, 47,* 780–785.

Burum, B. A., & Goldfried, M. R. (2007). The centrality of emotion to psychological change. *Clinical Psychology: Science and Practice, 14,* 407–413.

Bybee, J. A., & Wells, Y. V. (2006). Body themes in descriptions of possible selves: Diverse perspectives across the lifespan. *Journal of Adult Development, 13,* 95–101.

Campos, J. J., Frankl, C. B., & Camras, L. (2004). On the nature of emotion regulation. *Child Development, 75,* 377–394.

Camras, L. A., & Witherington, D. C. (2005). Dynamic systems approaches to emotional development. *Developmental Review, 25,* 328–350.

Carrick, N., & Quas, J. A. (2006). Effects of discrete emotions on young children's ability to discern fantasy and reality. *Developmental Psychology, 42,* 1278–1288.

Casey, B. J., Tottenham, N., Listen, C., & Durston, S. (2006). Imaging the developing brain: What have we learned about cognitive development? *Trends in Cognitive Sciences, 9,* 104–110.

Cash, T. F. (2002). Beyond traits. Assessing body image states. In T. F. Cash & T. Pruzinsky (Eds.), *Body image. A handbook of theory, research and clinical practice* (pp. 163–170). New York: Guilford Press.

Cash, T. F., & Pruzinsky, T. (Eds.). (1990). *Body images: Development, deviance and change.* New York: Guilford Press.

Cash, T. F., & Pruzinsky, T. (2002). Future challenges for body image theory and clinical practice. In T. F. Cash & T. Pruzinsky (Eds.), *Theory, research and clinical practice* (pp. 509–516). New York: Guilford Press.

Cattell, R. B. (1957). *Personality and motivation structure and measurement.* New York: World Book.

Chen, H., Jackson, T., & Huang, X. (2006). The Negative Physical Self Scale: Initial development and validation in samples of Chinese adolescents and young adults. *Body Image, 3,* 401–412.

Cicchetti, D. (1984). The emergence of developmental psychopathology. *Child Development, 55,* 1–7.

Costa, P. T., & Widiger, T. A. (Eds.). (2001). *Personality disorders and the five factor model of personality* (2nd ed.). Washington, DC: American Psychological Association.

Davis, L. T. (1997, February). The encyclopedia of insanity: A psychiatric handbook lists a madness for everyone. *Harpers Magazine.*

Decarie, T. G. (1978). Affect development and cognition in a Piagetian context. In M. Lewis & L. A. Rosenblum (Eds.), *The development of affect* (pp. 183–230). New York: Plenum Press.

Duggal, S., Malkoff-Schwartz, S., Brimaher, B., Anderson, B. P., Matty, M. K., & Houck, P. R. (2000). Assessment of life stress in adolescents: Self-report versus interview methods. *Journal of the American Academy of Child and Adolescent Psychiatry, 39,* 445–452.

Edlemann, R. J., & Skov, V. (1993). Blushing propensity, social anxiety and awareness of bodily sensations. *Personality and Individual Differences, 14,* 495–498.

Erikson, E. H. (1950). *Childhood and society.* New York: Norton.

Erlenmeyer-Kimling, L., & Miller, N. E. (Eds.). (1986). *Life-span research on the prediction of psychopathology.* Hillsdale, NJ: Erlbaum.

Fisher, S. (1990). The evolution of psychological concepts about the body. In T. F. Cash & T. Pruzinsky (Eds.), *Body images: Development, deviance, and change* (pp. 3–20). New York: Guilford.

Foldi, N. S., Jutagir, R., Davidoff, D., & Gould, T. (1992). Selective attention skills in Alzbeimer's disease: Performance on graded cancellation tests varying in intensity and complexity. *Journal of Gerontology, 47,* 146–153.

Frenkl-Brunswik, E. (1951). Personality theory and perception. In R. R. Blake & G. V. Ramsey (Eds.), *Perception: An approach to personality* (pp. 356–420). New York: Ronald Press.

Freud, S. (1923). The ego and the id. *Standard Edition, 19,* 12–66.

Gailego, M. J., Perpina, C., Botella, C., & Banos, R. M. (2006). Psychometric properties of the Situational Inventory of Body Image Dysphoria (SIBID) in a Spanish population. *Psicologia Conductual Revista Internacional de Psicologia Clinica de las Salud, 14,* 19–40.

Galton, F. (1884). Measurement of character. *The Fortnightly Review, 36,* 179–185.

Gardner, H. (1985). *The mind's new science: A history of the cognitive revolution.* New York: Basic Books.

Garnefski, N., & Kraaij, V. (2007). The Cognitive Emotion Regulation Questionnaire: Psychometric features and prospective relationships with depression and anxiety in adults. *European Journal of Psychological Assessment, 23,* 141–149.

Garnefski, N., Rieffe, C., Jellesma, F., Terwogt, M. M., & Kraaij, V. (2007). Cognitive emotion regulation strategies and emotional problems in 9–11-year-old children. *European Child Adolescent Psychiatry, 16,* 1–9.

Gibson, J. J. (1979). *The ecological approach to visual perception.* Boston, MA: Houghton Mifflin.

Gilmore, T. E. (2001). Influence of shame, female identity and ethnic identity on body image across women's life-span. *Dissertation Abstracts International: Section B: The Sciences and Engineering, 61*(9-B), 4982.

Gomex-Perez, E., & Ostrosky-Solis, F. (2006). Attention and memory evaluation across the life span. Heterogeneous effects of age and education. *Journal of Clinical and Experimental Neuropsychology, 28,* 477–494.

Good, J. M. (2007). The affordances for social psychology of the ecological approach to social knowing. *Theory and Psychology, 17,* 265–295.

Granic, I. (2005). Development as self-organization: New approaches to the psychology and neurobiology of development. *Developmental Review, 25,* 386–407.

Greenberg, L. S. (2007). Emotion coming of age. *Clinical Psychology Science and Practice, 14,* 414–428.

Gruber, H. E., Hammond, K. R., & Jesser, R. (Eds.). (1957). *Contemporary approaches to cognition.* Cambridge, MA: Harvard University Press.

Guy, L. S., Poythress, N. G., Douglas, K. S., Skeem, J. L., & Edens, J. F. (2008). Correspondence between self report and interview-based assessments of antisocial personality disorder. *Psychological Assessment, 20,* 47–54.

Harris, D. B. (1957). Problems in formulating a scientific concept of development. In D. B. Harris (Ed.), *The concept of development: An issue in the study of human behavior* (pp. 3–14). Minneapolis, MN: University of Minnesota Press.

Harter, S. (1999). *The construction of the self: A developmental perspective.* New York: Guilford Press.

Hartmann, H. (1939, published in German). *Ego psychology and the problem of adaptation* (1st English ed.). New York: International Universities Press, 1958 published in English.

Hassing, L. B., & Johansson, B. (2006). Aging and cognition. *Nordisk Psykologi, 57,* 4–20.

Herrington, R. L., Mitchell, H. E., Castellani, A. M., Joseph, J. I., Snyder, D. K., & Gleares, D. H. (2008). Assessing disharmony and disaffection in intimate relationships: Revision of the Martial Satisfaction Inventory Factor Scales. *Psychological Assessment, 20,* 341–350.

Hersen, M. (Ed.). (2003) *Comprehensive handbook of psychological assessment.* Hoboken, NJ: John Wiley & Sons.

Hess, T. M. (2005). Memory and aging in context. *Psychological Bulletin, 131,* 383–406.

Hilgard, E. R. (1951). The role of learning in perception. In R. R. Blake & G. V. Ramsey (Eds.), *Perception: An approach to personality* (pp. 95–120). New York: Ronald Press.

Hollin, C. R. (1990). *Cognitive-behavioral interventions with young offenders.* New York: Pergammon Press.

Horwitz, A. V., & Wakefield, J. C. (2007). *The loss of sadness: How psychiatry transformed normal sorrow into depressive disorder.* New York: Oxford University Press.

Izard, C. E., & Ackerman, B. P. (1997). Emotion and self-concept across the life span. *Annual Review of Gerontology and Geriatrics, 17,* 1–26.

James, W. (1890). *Principles of psychology.* Chicago: Encyclopedia Britannica.

Jensen, P. S., Marten, D., & Watanabe, H. (1996). Children's response to parental separation during Operation Desert Storm. *Journal of American Academy of Child and Adolescent Psychiatry, 35,* 433–441.

Johnson, M. (2008). The meaning of the body. In W. F. Overton, U. Müller, & J. L. Newman (Eds.), *Developmental perspectives on embodiment and consciousness* (pp. 19–44). New York: Erlbaum.

Johnson, S. L., & McMurrich, S. (2006). Life events and juvenile bipolar disorder: Conceptual issues and early findings. *Development and Psychopathology, 18,* 1169–1179.

Kagan, J. (2005). Temperament and personality. In M. Rosenbluth, S. H. Kennedy, & M. F. Bagby (Eds.), *Depression and personality: Conceptual and clinical challenges* (pp. 3–18). Washington, DC: American Psychiatric Press.

Katz, M. M., & Cole, J. O. (1965). Reflections on the major conference issue. In M. M. Katz, J. O. Cole, & W. E. Barton (Eds.), *The role of classification in psychiatry and psychopathology* (pp. 563–568). Chevy Chase, MD: U.S. Department of Health, Education and Welfare.

Katz, M. M., Cole, J. O., & Barton, W. E. (Eds.). (1965). *The role of classification in psychiatry and psychopathology.* Chevy Chase, MD: U.S. Department of Health, Education and Welfare.

Kelly, G. A. (1965). The role of classification in personality theory. In M. Katz, J. O. Cole, & W. E. Barton (Eds.), *The role and methodology of classification in psychiatry and psychopathology* (pp. 155–162). Chevy Chase, MD: U.S. Department of Health, Education and Welfare.

Kilmer, R. P., Cowen, E. L., Wyman, P. A., Work, W. C., & Magnus, K. B. (1998). Differences in stressors experienced by urban African American, White and Hispanic Children. *Journal of Community Psychology, 26,* 415–428.

Klein, G. S. (1951). The personal world through perception. In R. R. Blake & G. V. Ramsey (Eds.), *Perception: An approach to personality* (pp. 328–355). New York: Ronald Press.

Klein, G. S., & Schlesinger, H. J. (1949). Where is the perceiver in perceptual therapy? *Journal of Personality, 18,* 32–47.

Kramer, A. F., & Erickson, K. J. (2007). Capitalizing on cortical plasticity: Influence of physical activity on cognition and brain function. *Trends in Cognitive Sciences, 11,* 342–348.

Kramer, A. F., & Madden, D. J. (2008). Attention. In T. I. Craik & T. A. Salthouse (Eds.), *The handbook of aging and cognition* (pp. 189–249). New York: Psychology Press.

Kring, A. M., & Sloan, D. M. (2007). The facial coding system (FACES): Development, validation, and utility. *Psychological Assessment, 19,* 210–224.

Kutchins, H., & Kirk, S. A. (1997). *Making us crazy. DSM: The psychiatric bible and the creation of mental disorders.* New York: Free Press.

Lauterbach, O., & Hosser, D. (2007). Assessing empathy in prisoners—a shortened version of the Interpersonal Reactivity Index. *Swiss Journal of Psychology, 66,* 91–101.

Leahy, R. L. (2007). Emotion and psychotherapy. *Clinical Psychology: Science and Practice, 14,* 353–358.

Legenbauer, T., Vocks, S., & Schult-Stromel, S. (2007). Validation of a German version of the Body Image Avoidance Questionnaire (BAQ). *Diagnostica, 53,* 218–225.

Lerner, R. M. (2006). Developmental science, developmental systems, and contemporary theories of human development. In R. M. Lerner (Ed.), *Handbook of child psychology: Vol. 1. Theoretical models of human development* (6th ed., pp. 1–17). Editors in chief: W. Damon & R. M. Lerner. Hoboken, NJ: John Wiley & Sons.

Lerner, R. M., & Overton, W. F. (2008). Exemplifying the integrations of the relational developmental system: Synthesizing theory, research and application to promote positive development and social justice. *Journal of Adolescent Research, 23,* 245–255.

Levine, M. P., & Smolak, L. (2002). Body image development in adolescence. In T. F. Cash & T. Pruzinsky (Eds.), *Body image: A handbook of theory, research and clinical practice* (pp. 74–82). New York: Guilford Press.

Levy-Warren, M. H., & Levy-Warren, A. L. (2005). I am/might be/ am not my diagnosis: A look at the use and misuse of diagnoses in adolescence. *Journal of Infant, Child, and Adolescent Psychotherapy, 4,* 282–295.

Lindzey, G. (1952). TAT: Interpretive assumptions and related empirical evidence. *Psychological Bulletin, 49,* 1–25.

Luyten, P. (2006). Psychopathology: A twist of fate or a meaningful distortion of normal development? Toward an etiologically based alternative for the DSM approach. *Psychoanalytic Inquiry, 26,* 519–533.

MacKillop, J., Murphy, J. G., Ray, L. A., Eisenberg, D. T., & Lisman, S. A. (2008). Further validation of a cigarette purchase task for assessing the relative reinforcing efficacy of nicotine in college smokers. *Experimental and Clinical Psychopharmacology, 20,* 81–85.

Mahl, G. F. (1987). *Explorations in nonverbal and vocal behavior.* Hillsdale, NJ: Erlbaum.

Martins, Y., Tiggermann, M., & Churchett, L. (2008). The shape of things to come. Gay men's satisfaction with specific body parts. *Psychology of Men and Masculinity, 9,* 248–256.

McAdams, D. P., & St. Aubin, E. (1992). A theory of generativity and its assessment through self-report, behavioral acts, and narrative themes in autobiography. *Journal of Personality and Social Psychology, 62,* 1003–1015.

McGrath, R. E. (2008). The Rorschach in the context of performance based personality assessment. *Journal of Personality Assessment, 90,* 465–476.

McHugh, P. R. (2005). Striving for coherence: Psychiatry's efforts over classifications. *Journal of the American Medical Association, 293,* 2526–2528.

McLaren, L., Kirk, D., Hardy, R., & Gauvin, L. (2004). Positive and negative body related comments and their relationship with body dissatisfaction in middle-aged women. *Psychology and Health, 19,* 261–272.

Mennin, D., & Farach, F. (2007). Emotion and evolving treatments for adult psychopathology. *Clinical Psychology: Science and Practice, 14,* 329–352.

Messer, S. B., & Winoker, M. (1984). Ways of knowing and visions of reality in psychoanalytic therapy and behavior therapy.

In H. Arkowitz & S. B. Messer (Eds.), *Psychoanalytic therapy and behavioral therapy: Is integration possible?* (pp. 63–100). New York: Plenum.

Mufson, D. W., & Mufson, M. A. (1998). Predicting police officer performance using Inwald Personality Inventory: An illustration form Appalachia. *Professional Psychology: Research and Practice, 29,* 59–62.

Müller, U., & Newman, J. L. (2008). The body in action: Perspectives on embodiment and development. In W. F. Overton, U. Müller, & J. L. Newman (Eds.), *Developmental perspectives on embodiment and consciousness* (pp. 313–342). New York: Erlbaum.

Murray, C. D., & Fox, J. (2008). Differences in body image between people reporting near-death and spontaneous our-of-body experiences. *Journal of the Society for Psychical Research, 70,* 98–109.

Murray, J., & Farrington, D. P. (2008). Parental imprisonment: Long-lasting effects on boys internalizing through the life course. *Development and Psychopathology, 20,* 273–290.

Murrie, D. C., Boccaccini, M. T., McCoy, W., & Cornell, D. G. (2007). Diagnostic labeling in Juvenile Court. How do descriptions of psychopathology and conduct disorders influence judges? *Journal of Clinical Child and Adolescent Psychology, 36,* 228–241.

Nagera, H. (1981). *The developmental approach to child psychopathology.* New York: Jason Aronson.

Osborne, M. S., Kenny, D. I., & Holsomback, R. (2005). Assessment of music performance anxiety in later childhood. A validation of the Music Performance Anxiety Inventory for Adolescence. *International Journal of Stress Management, 12,* 312–330.

Overton, W. F. (1975). General systems, structure and development. In K. Riegel & G. Rosenwald (Eds.), *Structure and transformation: Developmental aspects* (pp. 61–81). New York: Wiley Interscience.

Overton, W. F. (1994). The arrow of time and the cycle of time: Concepts of change, cognition, and embodiment. *Psychological Inquiry, 5,* 215–237.

Overton, W. F. (2006). Developmental psychology: Philosophy, concepts, methodology. In R. M. Lerner (Ed.), *Handbook of child psychology: Vol. 1. Theoretical models of human development* (6th ed., pp. 18–88), Editors in chief: W. Damon & R. M. Lerner. Hoboken, NJ: John Wiley & Sons.

Overton, W. F. (2008). Embodiment from a relational perspective. In W. F. Overton, U. Müller, & J. Newman (Eds.), *Developmental perspectives on embodiment and consciousness* (pp. 1–18). New York: Erlbaum.

Overton, W. F., & Horowitz, H. A. (1991). Developmental psychopathology: Integrations and differentiations. In D. Cicchetti & S. L. Toth (Eds.), *Rochester Symposium on Developmental Psychopathology: Vol. 3. Models and integration* (pp. 1–42). Rochester, NY: University of Rochester Press.

Overton, W. F., & Jackson, J. P. (1973). The representation of imagined objects in action sequences: A developmental study. *Child Development, 44,* 309–314.

Overton, W. F., Müller, U., & Newman, J. (Eds.). (2008). *Developmental perspectives on embodiment and consciousness.* New York: Erlbaum.

Paivio, A. (1975). Neomentalism. *Canadian Journal of Psychology, 29,* 263–291.

Patten, S. B. (2006). Does almost everybody suffer from bipolar disorder? *The Canadian Journal of Psychiatry, 51,* 6–8.

Penkel, J. L., & Kurdek, L. A. (2007). Gender and race differences in young adults' body dissatisfaction. *Personality and Individual Differences, 43,* 2270–2281.

Pfefferbaum, B. (1997). Post-traumatic stress disorder in children: A review of the past 10 years. *Journal of American Academy of Child and Adolescent Psychiatry, 36,* 1503–1511.

Piaget, J. (1951). *Play, dreams and imitation in childhood.* New York: Norton.

Piaget, J. (1967). *Six psychological studies.* New York: Random House.

Piaget, J. (1973). The affective unconscious and the cognitive unconscious. *Journal of the American Psychoanalytic Association, 21,* 249–266.

Piaget, J. (1975). Foreword. In E. J. Anthony (Ed.), *Explorations in child psychiatry* (pp. vii–ix). New York: Plenum.

Piaget, J. (1981). *Intelligence and affectivity: Their relationship during child development.* Palo Alto, CA: Annual Reviews.

Poulin, M., Haase, C. M., & Heckhausen, J. (2005). Engagement and disengagement across the life span: An analysis of two-process models of developmental regulation. In W. Greve, K. Rothermund, & O. Wentura (Eds.), *The adaptive self: Personal continuity and intentional self-development* (pp. 117–136). Ashland, OH: Hogrefe & Haber Publishers.

Pruzinsky, T., & Cash, T. F. (2002). Understanding body images: Historical and contemporary perspectives. In T. F. Cash & T. Pruzinsky (Eds.), *Body image: A handbook of theory, research and clinical practice* (pp. 3–12). New York: Guilford Press.

Pynoos, R. S., Steinberg, A. M., & Goenjian, A. (1996). Traumatic stress in childhood and adolescence: Recent developments and current controversies. In B. A. Van der Kole, A. C. McFarlane, & L. Weisaeth (Eds.), *Traumatic stress: The effects of overwhelming experience on mind, body and society* (pp. 331–358). New York: Guilford Press.

Rader, G. E. (1957). The prediction of overt aggressive verbal behavior from Rorschach content. *Journal of Professional Technology, 21,* 294–306.

Reddy, S. D., & Crowther, J. H. (2007). Teasing, acculturation, and culture conflict: Psychosocial correlates of body image and eating attitudes among South Asian women. *Cultural Diversity and Ethnic Minority Psychology, 13,* 45–53.

Reider, C., & Cicchetti, D. (1989). Organizational perspective in cognitive control functioning and cognitive affective balance in maltreated children. *Developmental Psychology, 25,* 382–393.

Reinecke, M. A., & Freeman, A. (2007). Development and treatment of personality disorder: Summary. In A. Freeman & M. A. Rinecke (Eds.), *Personality disorders in childhood and adolescence* (pp. 681–697). Hoboken, NJ: John Wiley & Sons.

Roszak, T. (1992). *The voice of the earth.* New York: Simon & Schuster.

Rottenberg, J., & Gross, J. J. (2007). Emotion and emotion regulation: A map for psychotherapy researchers. *Clinical Psychology: Science and Practice, 14,* 323–328.

Rye, M. S., Cahoon, M. B., Ali, R. S., & Daftary, T. (2008). Development and validation of the counterfactual thinking for negative events scale. *Journal of Personality Assessment, 90,* 261–269.

Sabik, N., Cole, E. R., & Ward, M. L. (2007, August 18). *Assessing body satisfaction among Black, Asian American and White women.* American Psychological Association Annual Convention, San Francisco, CA.

Sako, T. (1997). Big school, small school revisited: A case study of large-scale comprehensive high school based on the campus plan. In S. Wapner, J. Demick, & Y. Takiji (Eds.), *Handbook of Japan-United States environment-behavior research: Toward a transitional approach* (pp. 273–282). New York: Plenum Press.

Sander, L. W. (1964). Adaptive relationships in early mother-child interaction. *Journal of the American Academy of Child Psychiatry, 3,* 231–264.

Sander, L. W. (1989). Investigations of the infant and its care giving environments as a biological system. In S. I. Greenspan & G. H. Pollack (Eds.), *The course of life* (2nd ed., pp. 359–391). Madison, WI: International Universities Press.

Santostefano, S. (1965). Construct validity of the Miniature Situations Test. I: The performance of public school, orphaned and brain-damaged children. *Journal of Clinical Psychology, 21,* 418–421.

Santostefano, S. (1968a). Miniature situations and methodological problems in parent-child interaction research. *Merrill-Palmer Quarterly of Behavior and Development, 14,* 285–312.

Santostefano, S. (1968b). Situational testing in personality assessment. In D. L. Sills (Ed.), *International encyclopedia of the social sciences* (pp. 48–55). New York: Macmillan Company and Free Press.

Santostefano, S. (1970). Assessment of motives in children. *Psychological Reports, 26,* 639–649.

Santostefano, S. (1976). On the relation between research and practice in psychiatry and psychology: The laboratory of the McLean Hospital, 1889. *McLean Hospital Journal, 1,* 120–129.

Santostefano, S. (1978). *A biodevelopmental approach to clinical child psychology cognitive controls and cognitive control therapy.* New York: John Wiley & Sons.

Santostefano, S. (1985). Metaphor: Integrating action, fantasy and language in development. *Imagination, Cognition and Personality, 4,* 127–146.

Santostefano, S. (1988). *The Cognitive Control Battery.* Los Angeles: Western Psychological Services.

Santostefano, S. (1994). The arrow of time and developmental psychopathology. *Psychological Inquiry, 5,* 248–253.

Santostefano, S. (1998). *A handbook of integrative psychotherapies for children and adolescents.* Northvale, NJ: Jason Aronson.

Santostefano, S. (2004). *Child therapy in the great outdoors: A relational view.* Hillsdale, NJ: Analytic Press.

Santostefano, S. (2008). The sense of self inside and environments outside: How the two grow together and become one in healthy psychological development. *Psychoanalytic Dialogues, 18,* 513–535.

Santostefano, S., MacAuley, L., O'Connell, B., Quiroga-Estevez, M., Santostefano, S. R., & Burke, P. (2006). What abandoned children construe as stressful experiences: Implications for psychoanalytic relational theory and child psychotherapy. *Journal of Infant Child and Adolescent Psychotherapy, 5,* 1–23.

Santostefano, S., O'Connell, B., MacAuley, L., & Quiroga-Estevez, M. (2005). Stressful events viewed through the eyes of children. *Journal of Infant Child and Adolescent Psychotherapy, 4,* 58–76.

Santostefano, S., & Rieder, C. (1984). Cognitive controls and aggression in children: The concept of cognitive-affective balance. *Journal of Consulting and Clinical Psychology, 52,* 46–56.

Shakow, D. (1965). The role of classification in the development of science of psychopathology. In M. M. Katz, J. O. Cole, & W. E. Barton (Eds.), *The role and methodology of classifications in psychiatry and psychotherapy* (pp. 116–142). Chevy Chase, MD: U.S. Department of Health, Education and Welfare.

Shelder, J., Westen, D., & Bradley, R. (2006). A prototype approach to personality disorder diagnosis. *American Journal of Psychiatry, 103,* 846–856.

Shilder, P. (1935). *The image and appearance of the human body.* New York: International Universities Press.

Skeel, R. L., Pilarski, C., Kimberley, P., & Neudecker, J. (2008). Personality and performance-based measures in the prediction of alcohol use. *Psychology of Addictive Behaviors, 22,* 402–409.

Skinner, B. F. (1974). *About behaviorism.* New York: Knopf.

Sloan, D. M., & Kring, A. M. (2007). Measuring changes in emotion during psychotherapy: Conceptual and methodological issues. *Clinical Psychology: Science and Practice, 14,* 307–322.

Sokol, B. W., & Müller, U. (2007). The development of self-regulation: Toward the integration of cognition and emotion. *Cognitive Development, 22,* 401–405.

Solomon, R. C. (2002). Back to basics: On the very idea of "basic emotions." *Journal for the Theory of Social Behavior, 32,* 115–144.

Sonnentag, S., & Fritz, C. (2007). The Recovery Experience Questionnaire: Development and validation of a measure for assessing recuperation and unwinding from work. *Journal of Occupational Health Psychology, 12,* 204–221.

Spigelman, A., & Spigelman, G. (1991). The relationship between parental divorce and the child's body boundary definiteness. *Journal of Personality Assessment, 56,* 96–105.

Stein, N. L. (1987). Do thought and emotion have one head or two? *Contemporary Psychology, 32,* 346.

Stern, D. N. (1985). *The interpersonal world of the infant: A view from psychoanalysis and developmental psychology.* New York: Basic Books.

Stern, S. (2002). Identification, repetition and psychological growth: An expansion of relational theory. *Psychoanalytic Psychology, 19,* 722–738.

Stoops, J. W. (1974). *The assessment of aggression in children: Arguments for a multimodal approach.* Unpublished doctoral dissertation, Kent State University, Kent, OH.

Symonds, P. M. (1931). *Diagnosing personality and conduct.* New York: Appleton-Century-Crofts.

Tantleff-Dunn, S., & Gokee, J. L. (2002). Interpersonal influences on body image development. In T. F. Cash & T. Pruzinsky (Eds.), *Body image: A handbook of theory, research and clinical practice* (pp. 108–116). New York: Guilford Press.

Teachman, B. A., Stefanucci, J. K., Clerkin, E. M., Cody, M. W., & Proffitt, D. R. (2008). A new mode of fear expression: Perceptual bias in height fear. *Emotion, 8,* 296–301.

Temkin, O. (1965). The history of classification in the medical sciences. In M. Katz, J. O. Cole, & W. E. Marton (Eds.), *The role and methodology of classification in psychiatry and psychopathology* (pp. 11–19). Chevy Chase, MD: U.S. Department of Health, Education and Welfare.

Thompson, J. K., & Gardner, R. M. (2002). Measuring perceptual body image among adolescents and adults. In T. F. Cash & T. Pruzinsky (Eds.), *Body image: A handbook of theory, research and clinical practice* (pp. 135–141). New York: Guilford Press.

Thompson, J. K., Penner, L. A., & Altabe, M. N. (1990). Procedures, problems and progress in the assessment of body images. In T. F. Cash & T. Pruzinsky (Eds.), *Body images: Development, deviance and change* (pp. 21–50). New York: Guilford Press.

Thompson, J. K., & van den Berg, P. (2002). Measuring body image attitudes among adolescents and adults. In T. F. Cash & T. Pruzinsky (Eds.), *Body image: A handbook of theory, research and clinical practice* (pp. 142–154). New York: Guilford Press.

Tiemersma, D. (1989). *Body schema and body image.* Amsterdam/Lisse: Swets and Zeitlinger.

Tiggermann, M. (2002). Media influences on body image development. In T. F. Cash & T. Pruzinsky (Eds.), *Body image: A handbook of theory, research and clinical practice* (pp. 91–98). New York: Guilford Press.

Tiggermann, M. (2004). Body image across the life span: Stability and change. *Body Image, 1,* 29–41.

Tracy, J. L., & Robins, R. W. (2007). The prototypical pride expression: Development of a nonverbal behavior coding system. *Emotion, 7,* 789–801.

Ulrich, R. S., & Parsons, R. (1992). Influences of passive experience with plants in individual well-being and health. In D. Relf (Ed.), *The role of horticulture in human well-being and social development* (pp. 93–105). Portland, OR: Timber Press.

Vamos, M. (1993). Body image in chronic illness: A reconceptualization. *International Journal of Psychiatry in Medicine, 23,* 163–178.

von Bertalanffy, L. (1968). *General systems theory: Foundations, development, applications.* New York: George Braziller.

Wakschlag, L. S., Hill, C., Carter, A. S., Danis, B., Egger, H., Keenan, K., et al. (2008). Observational assessment of preschool disruptive behavior, Part 1: Reliability of the disruptive behavior disorder diagnostic observation schedule (DB-DOS). *Journal of American Academy of Child and Adolescent Psychiatry, 46,* 622–631.

Waldholz, M. (2003, August 26). Flower power: How gardens improve your mental health. *The Wall Street Journal.*

Wapner, S., & Demick, J. (2000). Assumptions, methods, and research problems of the holistic, developmental, systems-oriented perspective. In S. Wapner, J. Demick, T. Yamomoto, & H. Minami (Eds.), *Theoretical perspectives in environment-behavior research: Underlying assumptions, research problems and methodologies* (pp. 7–19). New York: Kluwer Academic/Plenum Press

Wapner, S., Demick, J., Yamomoto, T., & Takahashi, T. (Eds.). (1997). *Handbook of Japan-United States environment-behavior research: Toward a transitional approach.* New York: Plenum Press.

Wapner, S., & Werner, H. (Eds.). (1965). *The body perfect.* New York: Random House.

Watson, D. (2005). Rethinking the mood and anxiety disorders. A quantitative hierarchical model for DSM-V. *Journal of Abnormal Psychology, 114,* 522–536.

Weber, J., & Tiggermann, M. (2003). The relationship between women's body satisfaction and self-image across the life span: The role of cognitive control. *Journal of Genetic Psychology, 164,* 241–252.

Wells, F. L. (1912). The association experiment. *Psychological Bulletin, 9,* 435–438.

Werner, H. (1949). Introductory remarks. *Journal of Personality, 18,* 2–5.

Werner, H. (1964). *Comparative psychology of mental development* (Rev. ed.). New York: International Universities Press.

Whitbourne, S. K., & Skultety, K. M. (2002). Body image development: Adulthood and aging. In T. F. Cash & T. Pruzinsky (Eds.), *Body image: A handbook of theory, research and clinical practice* (pp. 83–90). New York: Guilford Press.

Widiger, T. A., & Samuel, D. B. (2005). Diagnostic categories or dimensions? A question for the Diagnostic and Statistical Manual of Mental Disorders (5th ed.). *Journal of Abnormal Psychology, 114*(4), 494–504.

Wilber, K. (1979). *No boundary: Eastern and Western approaches to personal growth.* Boston: Shambhala Publishing.

Williams, B. R., Strauss, E. H., David, F. H., Hultsch, D. F., & Hunter, M. A. (2007). Reaction time inconsistency in a spatial Stroop task: Age related differences through childhood and adulthood. *Aging, Neuropsychology and Cognition, 14,* 417–439.

Winnicott, D. W. (1965). *The maturational processes and the facilitating environment.* New York: International Universities Press.

Wolfe, B. E. (2003). Knowing the self: Building a bridge from basic research to clinical practice. *Journal of Psychotherapy Integration, 13,* 83–95.

Wolff, W. (1943). *The expressions of personality experimental depth psychology.* New York: Harper and Brothers.

Yeo, G. B., & Neal, A. (2004). A multilevel analysis of effort, practice and performance: Effects of ability, conscientiousness, and goal orientation. *Journal of Applied Psychology, 89,* 231–247.

Zeman, J., Kilmes-Dougan, B., Cassano, M., & Adrian, M. (2007). Measurement issues in emotion research with children and adolescents. *Clinical Psychology Science and Practice, 14,* 377–401.

CHAPTER 23

The Meaning of Wisdom and Its Development Throughout Life

TZUR M. KARELITZ, LINDA JARVIN, and ROBERT J. STERNBERG

We are made wise not by the recollection of our past, but by the responsibility for our future.
—*George Bernard Shaw*

As this chapter was first being written, the United States of America was facing the worst economic crisis in years. A decline in standards of and supervision over lending practices led to an increase in borrowers committing to mortgages that they could not afford. Consequently, the housing and lending bubbles burst in the summer of 2008, leading the U.S. Congress to debate an unprecedented economic rescue plan, at a time when the U.S. debt was at an all-time high. Meanwhile, the United States was fighting two wars overseas, the energy and environmental crises were (and still are) taking their toll all over the world, and all eyes were directed toward the change that would happen after the inauguration of a new president, Barack Obama. The hope of many was that a new administration would take the necessary actions to make things better. It was not just the United States but the whole world that needed things to be better.

The "better" that people around the world have hoped for remains far off. Terrorist attacks have continued around the world, killing indiscriminately people of various nationalities and ethnicities. For those interested in "wisdom," where do such attacks leave them? At the beginning of the 21st century, the world is still plagued with injustice, poverty, sickness, war, and crime. Essentially, we expect our leaders to be wise and to make wise decisions.

What do we actually know about wisdom or about being wise? How do we know if someone, or some action, is wise or foolish? How does one become wise? How can we develop or enhance our wisdom? What does wisdom mean throughout our life span? This chapter aims to answer or, at the least, to address these questions.

Wisdom is a valuable virtue that has long been praised and appreciated; practically every culture has had an ideal of wisdom (Rudolph, 2005). The breadth of knowledge about wisdom spans centuries—from the writings of ancient cultural, philosophical, and religious perspectives, through the truths captured in maxims and proverbs, to research on theories of wisdom as a psychological construct.

The concept of wisdom has acquired many definitions (see Birren & Svensson, 2005), no one of which is entirely accepted by either laypersons or scholars. It has been described as the ability to make proper judgments based on good sense and moral values, the possession of insight or wealth of knowledge, the reflective ability to discern inner qualities and relations, and the emotional-spiritual strength needed to deal with life's uncertainties or to show compassion to others. One conclusion that connects all these perspectives is that being wise is beneficial for both the individual and the society. The various definitions are discussed throughout the chapter.

Throughout time, great thinkers have contemplated the nature of wisdom, how it develops, and how it can be enhanced. This chapter summarizes the knowledge that has been gained from centuries of human thinking about wisdom. It is by no means a complete account of the topic. It would be unwise to assume otherwise. Specifically, we focus on two main questions:

What is wisdom?

How does wisdom develop from birth through late adulthood?

The first two sections of the chapter provide some of the main perspectives about the nature of wisdom. Although they deal primarily with the first question, they also suggest a substantive framework needed to answer the second question. The first section, Historical Conceptions of Wisdom, describes how the concept of wisdom evolved from ancient civilizations to modern times. Religious, cultural, and societal aspects of wisdom are also discussed. The second section, Psychological Research about the Meaning of Wisdom, summarizes how wisdom is currently studied and measured in psychological research.

The last section, Development of Wisdom, discusses the development of wisdom throughout the life span. Different theories and studies on how wisdom changes from birth to late adulthood are presented. We also discuss wisdom specifically with respect to four stages of life: childhood, adolescence, adulthood, and late adulthood. Finally, the chapter concludes with a summary of the main issues that concern the development of wisdom.

Concepts regarding the meaning of wisdom have shifted and evolved as the notion of wisdom has been reinvented throughout the history of humankind. A main theme of this chapter is that wisdom is an elusive, complex, sometimes changing, and multifaceted concept. Not only does it involve multiple human and social characteristics, but it is also highly context dependent. What we consider wise today might be deemed foolish tomorrow; what is considered wise in one culture or situation may be inappropriate in another. However, several themes connect all knowledge about wisdom, from the very early text to modern-day science. These few "truths" are shared by laypeople and experts throughout the world. The conventional wisdom about wisdom is that it is essential for the development of humans—individually, culturally, and globally.

Although the concept of wisdom is multidimensional in how we perceive it with respect to our lives, its essence is perhaps quite simple: *Do the right thing for yourself, for others, and for the world, and it will usually pay off in the end.* The reason this simple truth is so elusive is that what is right or good for you now may not be what is right or good for others, or even for yourself, at a later time. The ability to comprehend this inherent uncertainty in life, and the ability to act in accordance with this knowledge of truth and doubt, is typical of those who exhibit wisdom.

> It is unwise to be too sure of one's own wisdom.
> It is healthy to be reminded that the
> strongest might weaken and the wisest might err.
> —*Mahatma Gandhi*

HISTORICAL CONCEPTIONS OF WISDOM

How was wisdom perceived in ancient societies? On the one hand, wisdom was commonly considered to be practical and pragmatic, dealing with the proper and prosperous conduct of life. Throughout time, all civilizations have recognized the importance of wisdom and have passed it on to future generations through spoken, sung, and written stories. For common people, wisdom in the form of proverbs and simple rules of conduct was important and useful. It helped the layperson in an uneducated society to capitalize on past generations' experiences and knowledge. On the other hand, wisdom was also considered a moral and theological system, exclusive to the religious and social elites (Perdue, 2002). Overall, the way wisdom was perceived in the past is not much different from how it is perceived today.

The meaning of wisdom, whether referring to a quality possessed by a person or to a collection of knowledge, is bounded by our interpretation of the words used to describe it. Some of the meaning may be lost as text is translated and as the meanings of words within a language change as well. Many languages have several words describing different aspects of wisdom that are all broadly translated as "wisdom" in modern translations. This simplification of terminology limits our ability to fully understand the meaning of wisdom in ancient times.

This section discusses several historical perspectives: proverbial wisdom, wisdom and the ruling class, and religious and philosophical conceptions from Eastern and Western cultures. The reader interested in more details should consult other historical overviews (e.g., Assmann, 1994; Baltes, 2004; Birren & Svensson, 2005; Brugman, 2006; Clayton & Birren, 1980; Robinson, 1990; Rudolph, 2005; Takahashi & Overton, 2005; Trowbridge, 2005).

Proverbial Wisdom

> The wise man has long ears and a short tongue.
> —*German Proverb*

In every culture of the world, the accumulated knowledge about pragmatic life issues, as well as overarching truths, has been preserved in the form of proverbs, maxims, and adages. These short, pithy sayings are designed to be easily remembered and are used extensively in daily speech and writings. The way proverbial wisdom has been disseminated across centuries and societies can be investigated through the etymology of specific proverbs (Kunstmann, 1994). The study of proverbial wisdom has been reviewed in detail by Mieder (1993, 1997, 2002), Mieder and Dundes (1994), and Perry (1993).

Given the extensive history of proverbs and their cardinality in our cultural discourse, one is tempted to ask: Do proverbs hold the ultimate truth about life? The answer is probably, "It depends." It depends on which proverbs one uses and under what circumstances; also, choosing

the "right" proverbs, itself, would require tremendous wisdom. Proverbs can be problematic because, as a collection, they contain inner contradictions and complexities. Many proverbs can be interpreted in multiple and even opposite ways (Milner, 1971). In certain situations, one proverb is relevant, whereas in another situation, the opposite may be relevant (e.g., "Many hands make light work." vs. "Too many cooks spoil the broth."). Essentially, proverbs and maxims are usually best understood within a given context (Nichols, 1996; Rogers, 1990). Maxims from a specific culture can be confusing if one does not understand the society in which the statement developed. The essence of a very "good" proverb or maxim is that it has contextual flexibility, which allows it to translate well across cultures and languages.

With this in mind, how can a maxim purport to provide a clear solution to life issues? The answer appears to lie in knowing when and where to apply certain maxims. Thus, maxims themselves cannot be classified as wisdom. They may point toward what may eventually turn out to be wisdom, but only if the user can appropriately match the maxims' historical meaning and situational usage. Many maxims are more concerned with describing *what* should be done, rather than *why* it should be done that way. In this sense, they may hide the wisdom-based reasoning behind the actions they seem to support. (Samuel Palmer [1710] argued, "Wise men make proverbs but fools repeat them.") Maxims, in themselves, rely on tension and contradiction as a way of showing that pragmatic life issues are rarely, if ever, black and white. The seeker of wisdom must understand that, in complex situations, there is no one simple answer. Proverbs do not provide solutions to complex problems. Instead, they provide multiple insights into a given situation, within a given context, and then show how wisdom could be used to reason and make judgments based on all the information available.

Wisdom and the Ruling Class

> By me [Wisdom] kings reign, and rulers decree justice. By me princes rule, and nobles, All who judge rightly.
> —*Proverbs, 8:15–16*

For generations, wisdom was preserved within circles of the societal elite by means of written knowledge and wisdom-based education that was exclusively available to children of the aristocrats. This perpetual conservation of wisdom created a reality in which faith, wealth, power, and wisdom were inherently intertwined. Contributing to this was the common belief that good fortune was the reward of the wise, who acted according to the will of God, whereas poverty and misfortune were God's punishment to the foolish and the wicked. This was a direct consequence of God's creation of the world based on principles of justice and causality. Thus, the leaders of the past were considered wise because their education was wisdom based, but mainly because by inherited authority they possessed power and wealth that were seen as God's reward to the wise. With time and political turmoil, the teaching of wisdom to the ruling class diminished, and those who were taught in wisdom-oriented schools became counselors to the leaders, rather than the leaders themselves (Perdue, 2002). Recent studies on common conceptions of wisdom suggest that people still associate wisdom with the educational, religious, and social elite (Hershey & Farrell, 1997). The development of hierarchical societies leads to a situation where influential military, religious, and economic groups had complete control over the collection and distribution of information and wisdom. Consequently, Csikszentmihalyi (1990) warns us that wisdom may represent the interests of particular groups and not the common good.

Conceptions of Wisdom in Eastern Cultures

> Knowledge is not necessarily wisdom.
>
> —*Proverb from an ancient Egyptian temple*

The writings left on clay tablets by the Sumerian culture (around 4000–2000 B.C.) show that wisdom was expressed in the form of practical advice for daily life, such as "Don't build your house so that it extends into a public place." Other tablets unfold wisdom-related epic tales such as *Gilgamesh,* where the search after ancestral wisdom leads to understandings about the mortality of men (Sandars, 1972). The maxims found on these clay-made time capsules provide practical advice on how to conform to the norms of society, and for the most part, do not contain a strong religious dimension. Because writing was limited to the educated scribes, it is thought that these tablets were produced by the governing institutions and used as educational material to promote and maintain civil order (Rudolph, 2005).

The early Egyptians (around 3000 B.C. to A.D. 300) have also left written traces of their wisdom (e.g., the Wisdom of Amenemope, the Instructions of Ptah-Hotep). Many of their precepts for behavior survived and can be found in Hebrew and early Christian cultures as discussed in the Old Testament (Boadt, 1985). The writings of the early Egyptians focus mostly on practical advice for good behavior. However, the Egyptians went beyond the direct utilitarian advice of proverbs and introduced a spiritual dimension with the notion of the goddess *Maat,* who symbolizes both cosmic order and social justice (Fontaine, 1981). This supreme order became a pivotal aspect of wisdom. The concept of Maat served as the moral basis for the ruling authority of Egyptian kings, thus establishing the heavenly order here on Earth.

> Who is wise? The one who sees what will be.
>
> —*Hebrew Talmud, Tamid, 32*

Similar to other Mesopotamian wisdom cultures, ancient Hebrews often viewed wisdom in a secular, practical sense. The wise person was seen as a productive, efficient, and successful member of the community. Thus, wisdom was associated with the shrewdness, skillfulness, and artistry of professionals (Assmann, 1994; Fritsch, 1955). However, wisdom in Biblical times was mainly theocentric; all wisdom was believed to have originated from God. Most significantly, the wisdom of God was revealed to humankind through the ethical code embedded in the Ten Commandments. This set of moral rules embodies the essence of humans' "contract" with God.

Seven Biblical books are regarded as encompassing much of ancient Hebrew wisdom: Psalms, Proverbs, Job, Song of Songs, Ecclesiastes, Wisdom of Solomon, and Ecclesiasticus (Ben Sira). They provide slightly different perspectives on wisdom—optimistic in the case of Proverbs and pessimistic in the case of Job and Ecclesiastes (Baltes, 2004). The books represent a collective outlook on wisdom contained within statements about the nature of the world, instructions about daily life, contemplations about the meaning of life, and descriptions of the divine nature of wisdom. A pivotal theme in the Hebrew wisdom literature is that the fear of God constitutes the first step toward attaining wisdom. The Old Testament also provides multiple perspectives on the meaning of wisdom, including the benefits to its beholders and to society as a whole. The texts offer deep contemplation of wisdom's elusive and multifaceted nature in light of life's uncertainties. Within the Hebrew Scriptures, the moral, ethical, and religious aspects of wisdom are also discussed at length. Specifically, reciprocity ("Love your fellow as yourself," Leviticus 19:18) is commonly seen as the essence of the Bible and the Hebrew moral code.

Contrary to Western philosophies, which are discussed later, Eastern traditions downplay the role of rational thought in the path to enlightenment (Clayton & Birren,

1980). Emphasis on intelligence seems detrimental to the attainment of wisdom. Consequently, the meaning of wisdom in many Eastern philosophies is often ambiguous, flexible, and broad. Specifically, more emphasis is given to noncognitive aspects of wisdom such as spiritual, transformational, and integrative aspects of human consciousness (Takahashi & Overton, 2005).

The Chinese thinker Confucius (551–479 B.C.) believed that wisdom is a learned and highly refined state of mind or character (Yutang, 1994). Confucius led his students through intellectual and spiritual inquiry into the purpose of life, or "How to be human?" The Confucian teachings are based on the belief that humans are inherently good and anyone has the ability to be wise. The principles of Confucianism are thought to be universal, and the ways people often strayed from this path are mostly through a lack of desire or will.

The Golden Rule: "What you do not wish for yourself, do not do to others."

—*Confucius*

The wisdom of Confucius comes from the pursuit of perfection within oneself, a life-long journey that includes good mentorship, education, and self-reflection. Good mentorship is based on experience in following a good path. Love, compassion, and reciprocity (the Golden Rule) are pivotal themes in the Confucian way to achieving one's human potential (Wattles, 1996). Through this journey, the learner can find moral harmony within himself or herself and within the greater social system; Earthly peace can be achieved by intrapersonal peace (Yutang, 1994).

Wisdom, as captured in the vast Buddhist literature, is an understanding of the nature and meaning of life, and living accordingly (Harvey, 2000). Buddhism was initiated by Prince Siddhārtha Gautama (approximately 560–480 B.C.), whose title, the enlightened one (Buddha), represents his achievement of Nirvana. In this ideal state of mind, one understands the causes of all human suffering, and consequently one is liberated from all those sufferings. The enlightened one has overcome his own passions, hatred, and ignorance (Buddharakkhita, 1985; Nanamoli, 2001). Enlightenment is difficult to express in words— one needs to experience it. By following the "right" path, practically anyone can attain this ultimate wisdom and see reality in its true form (although that may not happen in a single life circle). Buddha's Noble Eightfold Path provides practical steps toward enlightenment, based on taking the "middle way" between extremes. The eight components represent interconnected concepts of good thought and behavior. The essence of Buddhist wisdom is represented by the right knowledge (view) and direction (intention), which are necessary for succeeding at following Buddha's path (Bodhi, 1994). A person who holds the right view and intention can become liberated from destructive and negative impulses, thoughts, or deeds. Consequently, his or her actions, words, and thoughts will lead to happiness.

Both Confucianism and Buddhism emphasize the interconnectedness of individuals and their environments to foster a shared sense of responsibility. Both philosophies relate wisdom to a way of life that is oriented toward self-actualization and leading to an ideal state of being. Moreover, in both traditions, moral, ethical, balanced, and peaceful conducts of life are all directly related to wisdom. A wise person would denounce greed and selfishness, and embrace compassion, calmness, and a genuine desire to improve oneself and one's surroundings. In this sense, the Eastern philosophies perceive wisdom as a utopian state of mind, but one that can be achieved by education, dedication, and experience.

Ancient thought contains profound understandings about human nature and the meaning of good conduct. The perception of wisdom includes both pragmatic and moral issues about how one should live. Wisdom is associated with some ultimate truth, a divine entity, or an ideal state of being. A wise person is one who both possesses that truth and acts accordingly. Such a person will live a happy and successful life. In other words, reality is based on the rules of cause-and-effect; thus, being, thinking, and doing good will lead to good fortune (Trowbridge, 2005).

Conceptions of Wisdom in Western Societies

Wisdom is the supreme part of happiness.

—*Sophocles*

Greek Philosophers

The study of wisdom in philosophy is marked by a huge discrepancy between how it was studied in the past and how it is studied today. The exploration of wisdom by philosophers has a long and rich history, dating back to the Greeks in the 5th century B.C., who gave the first intensive Western analysis of the concept of wisdom. The Greeks emphasized intellectual, systematic inquiry into wisdom, applying both dialectical discourse and pedagogy. A pivotal element in all forms of wisdom is the ability to perceive the reality behind appearances. The study of philosophy and wisdom began as part of the quest for knowledge about human nature and a life of good conduct. To the early Greeks, prudence or practical wisdom was one of the four Cardinal Virtues of human excellence (together with justice, temperance, and fortitude). Here we describe three main Greek philosophers' approaches to wisdom: Socrates, Plato, and Aristotle. For in-depth reviews on Greek wisdom, see also Annas (1992), Labouvie-Vief (1990), Osbeck and Robinson (2005), and Robinson (1989).

> I am wiser than that man. Neither of us knows anything that is great and good; but he thinks that he does, while I know that I do not. So I am that much wiser than he is.
>
> —Socrates

Socrates (470–399 B.C.) devoted his life to describing the connection between mind and virtue. Wisdom was a prime concept in the Socratic dialogues, which were inquiries focused on how to conduct a good and just life. Socrates believed that a wise person is one who seeks the undistorted truths. Being wise meant "possession of knowledge…which provides a basis for infallibly good judgment in decisions pertinent to how one should live" (Smith, 1998, p. 753). However, Socrates differentiated between being skilled or smart, and being wise. Wisdom is driven by the ability to suppress passions and desires to the authority of rationality in thoughts and actions, which has nothing to do with a person's intellect, but rather, with the person's spirit, morality, and self-control (Robinson, 1990).

Socrates' way of pursuing wisdom was through persistent questioning. The Socratic dialogues are a systematic and pedagogical study of one's thoughts and actions. Through this study, Socrates revealed the difference between knowledge (knowing the truth) and opinion (thinking you know). The possessors of the former are wise, and the possessors of the latter need to learn by discovering their ignorance (Benson, 1996). Socrates is known to have said that he does not know, nor does he think he knows. To him, admitting your ignorance is a sign of wisdom; believing otherwise is an illusion. His perspectives on mind and soul, his systematic inquiries and his teaching methods, profoundly shaped the Western culture (see further discussions in Ahbel-Rappe & Kamtekar, 2005; Guthrie, 1969; Kekes, 1995; Ryan, 1997).

> Is there anything more closely connected with wisdom than truth?
>
> —Plato

Socrates never wrote, and his views were mostly given to us by his loyal student, Plato (428–347 B.C.). Through the Socratic dialogues, Plato offers an opportunity to gain wisdom by challenging the reader to actively engage in philosophical inquiry with Socrates himself. According to Plato, wisdom is knowledge of the ultimate truth—an absolute good, an ideal. As such, wisdom resides in the metaphysical world; therefore, it is divine. Humans could not reach it, but merely be "lovers" or "seekers" of wisdom (philos-sophia) who attempt to understand wisdom through reason (Rice, 1958). Essentially, the lover of wisdom is searching for the governing principles of the soul (psyche, which can also be translated as mind). Plato contemplated the structure and function of the soul as consisting of three parts: appetite (desires), reason, and spirit. The possibility of seeing the truth can only be realized if the spirit is released from its earthly pleasures. Thus, in a just man, the appetite is strictly controlled by reason and spirit (Santas, 2006). Being wise requires the innate intention (soul) and ability (virtues) to use this knowledge in the right ways, thus leading to a good and happy life (Eudemonia). However, Plato believed it is extremely difficult to attain wisdom. The extent to which we actually achieve this ultimate state of being is contingent on how well we exhibit each of the virtues: justice, wisdom, courage, and temperance.

According to Robinson (1990), the Platonic dialogues have three different senses of wisdom: (1) theoretical, sophia, the optimal goal of the rational soul, which is found in those who seek a contemplative life in search of truth; (2) practical, phronesis, which is the application of good judgment to human conduct, as shown by those who take the prudent course of action, not affected by passions or the inaccuracy of the senses; and (3) episteme, an intellectual sense like knowledge, which is found in those who understand the nature of things and the principles that govern their behavior from a scientific or technical point of view.

> Knowing yourself is the beginning of all wisdom.
>
> —Aristotle

Aristotle (384–322 B.C.) elaborated on Socrates' views and presented a complex and sophisticated account of wisdom. To Aristotle, wisdom is knowledge of the truth—the reality behind the perception of circumstances. Such knowledge is needed for one to behave in accordance with nature and can be acquired through logical means. A wise person is one who is ruled by right reason—rational and moral principles—and whose knowledge and desires are disposed to promote growth of one's human attributes. Such a person consequently enjoys a perfect state of well-being—a successful and complete life (eudaimonia).

Aristotle believed that this state cannot be achieved by humankind in isolation, but rather through the flourishing of a community (Jeannot, 1989; Young, 2005). Thus, the key to societal stability and human happiness is a well-oriented application of both intellectual and moral virtues. Being wise encompasses deep knowledge about oneself, the ability to grow in accordance with one's true self, and a sustained effort to achieve moral perfection in all of life's matters (Natali, 2001).

Aristotle discussed two kinds of wisdom: theoretical wisdom, which involves contemplation about knowledge of invariant truths; and practical wisdom, which involves context-dependent choices. Aristotle suggested the contemplative life was superior to the practical one (Robinson, 1990). Theoretical wisdom is both scientific knowledge *(episteme)* and philosophical wisdom *(sophia)*. To Aristotle, scientific knowledge is the pursuit of observable, invariant knowledge. Such knowledge is based on logic and gained by deduction (e.g., through the use of syllogisms). Thus, this knowledge consists of the principles that are not specific to any particular science, but that reflect a common body of knowledge. This body of "first principles" is the nexus of the term and study of *metaphysics*.

Aristotle differentiated between four types of causes (or explanations) of things and events: material, formal, efficient, and final. For example, a textbook is made out of paper (material cause), it is a bounded collection of written pages (formal cause), it is produced by an author and a printing machine (efficient cause), and it is meant to transfer information to the readers (final cause). To Aristotle, a wise individual knows more than the mere causes but also knows the final cause. The final cause is of greater importance in the sense that it is the main reason something exists in the first place (Osbeck & Robinson, 2005). The knowledge of the first principles of being—the causal structure of the world and the extent of what is known—is *sophia*. To discern the best course of action in a particular situation is *phronesis*.

Practical wisdom concerns rational behavior, situational insight, and moral character (Noel, 1999). To Aristotle, this wisdom stems from experience and is based on action oriented toward achieving a good life. The two principles underlying practical wisdom are invariant: goodness and health. At the same time, practical wisdom varies depending on who or what is under consideration; thus, "what is good or healthy is different for men and fishes" (Ethics, VI, 7, in Osbeck & Robinson, 2005). However, not everything in practical wisdom is variable. Human nature is not variable, and so practical wisdom involves the appropriately balanced judgment of circumstance and morally based reasoning to produce desirable outcomes.

Following Socrates, Plato, and Aristotle, many Greek philosophers continued to deliberate the meaning and function of wisdom. For example, Pyrrho (360– 272 B.C.) argued that it is impossible to know things in their own nature, and that every statement can be contradicted with equal justification. The Skeptic view is one of extreme questioning, leading to the understanding that if nothing can be known, then the best approach is the absence of action. Wisdom, therefore, stems from suspending any judgment and being free from desire to know, thus avoiding any stress and emotion, and reaching a peace of mind (Bailey, 2002; Sinnott-Armstrong, 2004). Advocating hedonism, Epicurus (341–270 B.C.) believed that a prudent life will help avoid possible physical pain and sustain mental serenity (Annas, 1992). Wisdom, in his eyes, would be to live as long as possible with as little pain and grief as possible. Another philosophic movement, the Stoical one, sought serenity through self-discipline. Stoics viewed philosophy as an art of living and developing expertise in matters beneficial to life. The Stoics reasserted reason-based knowledge as the foundation for wisdom and suppressed the role of emotions. To them, wisdom was seen through the rational and divine order that underlies nature and is the root of all cardinal virtues (Osbeck & Robinson, 2005).

The Greek philosophers had a tremendous effect on the Western world. They connected wisdom and knowledge of truth as it applies to the conduct of the good life (i.e., moral, ethical, rational). They helped us understand that, although wisdom itself may be of divine nature, we can and should contemplate it, and by doing so, we will also cultivate it in ourselves and our society. Their discussion of theoretical and practical wisdom has helped establish wisdom as a valid and important topic for scientific inquiry. Their observation that true wisdom, at the very best, can only be approximated by humans, echoes every day in the media, scientific journals, and web pages. As we know more about ourselves and the world around us, we discover there is much more to be learned and uncovered.

Christian Views on Wisdom

Christian conceptions of wisdom arose from a complex combination of Hebraic and Hellenic thought. Hebraic thought prepared Christians for "revealed" truth. Christians accepted that God's love is the only remedy for what is otherwise humankind's "irremediable ignorance" (Robinson, 1990). The Hellenic view, rich in analysis, observation, and naturalism, influenced Christian thought in its quest for perfection through harmony. The emergent Christian view emphasized faith and revelation but also showed some inclination toward finding supportive reasoning behind it. In this sense, Christian thinkers elaborated on the question of the source of wisdom, whether it stemmed from God, and thus is driven by faith, or whether it stemmed from humankind, and thus is driven by reason (Baltes, 2004).

> Patience is the companion of wisdom.
> —*De Patientia, 4, St. Augustine*

Augustine (354–430) believed that truth and happiness could be found only through God's grace and the authority of his revelation (Rice, 1958). True wisdom is based solely on divine knowledge, whereas science is based on knowledge of human things. Augustine argued that true wisdom could not be achieved by rationality alone; reason has to be founded on faith and knowledge of God's expectations for humanity. Without humility and the guidance of faith, humans cannot grasp truth or attain wisdom (Harrison, 2006).

For centuries, the commonly accepted view among Christian scholars was that wisdom is the absolute truth captured in the word of God. The writings of Thomas Aquinas (1225–1274) mark the beginning of a shift toward a more secular treatment of wisdom. Aquinas argued that the autonomy of human reason was conditioned on faith and the reality of the world as created by God. Thus, the laws of rationality and logic could operate within the framework of religious belief (Chenu, 1984; Stump, 2003). Moreover, he believed that although human reasoning may err, the idea that truth could be discovered by natural law is, nevertheless, valid.

Aquinas argued that it is possible to acquire wisdom through reason, although that wisdom would be lacking. He believed theological (divine) wisdom is superior to metaphysical (human) wisdom, although the two are not opposed (Rice, 1958). Aquinas also holds a Christian conviction that simplicity is at the foundation of all wisdom, and profound wisdom can be found in a "simple faith" in God as the cause of all things. This discovery of a simple cause for the complexity of things exemplifies the belief that wisdom is a form of "seeing through things," which was a Christian view held until the dawn of the modern scientific age (Robinson, 1990).

Early Christian philosophers emphasized seven virtues needed for human growth toward excellence: Prudence, Temperance, Fortitude, Justice, Faith, Hope, and Love (or Charity). The first four are the cardinal virtues that originated in the ancient and Greek worlds. The last three are the theological or Christian virtues. More than anything else, the theological virtues capture the essence of the divine. Not only do they originate from the grace of God, but they are also free of vice. The cardinal virtues can be harmful when taken to the extreme, but the theological virtues cannot; thus, they essentially help the wise person to refrain from wrongdoing.

The early Christian view emphasized the importance of a life lived in pursuit of divine and absolute truth. Indeed, most religions aim for wisdom through an understanding of the relation between the material and spiritual worlds. Although the search for truth may be very beneficial for one's own development of wisdom, it is not clear that such ultimate truth exists in every respect (Sternberg, 2005a).

Wisdom in the Renaissance and Enlightenment Periods

During most of the Middle Ages, the philosophical study of wisdom was practically nonexistent. The stronghold of religion in Europe in those days limited open philosophical discourse about wisdom. Neo-Platonic ideas resurfaced in the early 15th century, as the notion of wisdom became secularized, and thus removed from its ties to religion. For example, Carolus Bovillus (Charles de Bovelles, 1479–1553) defined wisdom as an "encyclopedic knowledge of all things, created and uncreated, divine and human: the world, the human body and soul, angels, God, the end of all things" (Rice, 1958, p. 113). For Bovillus, humans are capable of attaining wisdom because the soul is "the natural mirror of the universe" and is influenced by everything around it. We have the potential to know all the substantial things in the world. Wisdom lies in the balance of self-contemplation and worldly contemplation. It is a perpetual becoming, "a life-long passage from potency to act" (Rice, p. 120).

With the rise of Renaissance and Humanism, wisdom became more humanly rather than divinely based, representing a moral virtue related to liberal learning and self-development, leading to human perfection. For example, Charron (1541–1603) speculated that human wisdom as a moral virtue can be naturally acquired. God's gift to humankind is a virtuous willpower leading us toward love, respect, and a moral attitude. Humans are predisposed to be good, and thus could use their reasoning to distinguish between right and wrong. Intellect alone cannot lead to the absolute truth; but through knowledge, contemplation, and action, humans can reach wisdom as a desirable moral virtue, independent of any practice of religion (Rice, 1958). Similar ideas were echoed by the great French philosopher René Descartes (1596–1650). In the preface to the *Principles of Philosophy*, he wrote, "God is in truth the only being who is absolutely wise, that is, who possesses a perfect knowledge of all things; but we may say that men are more or less wise as their knowledge of the most important truths is greater or less" (1644/2004, p. 3). To him, all sciences are exercises of common sense and wisdom, may it be human, universal, or natural wisdom. Such practice of wisdom operates without support from any divine revelation.

The 17th and 18th centuries brought further separation of wisdom from religion and challenged the classical conceptions of wisdom, as well as its desirability as a form of knowledge. British Empiricism, exemplified by the works of Francis Bacon (1561–1626), John Locke (1632–1704), and David Hume (1711–1776), emphasized evidence-based human experience and natural science as the only valid sources of knowledge and truth (Levi, 1994). From the belief of the mind as a *tabula rasa,* free at birth from inherent knowledge, thinkers from the Empiricist era held that ultimate knowable reality was, in fact, *observable* reality, a state of knowledge in which everyone theoretically has the same access to verifiable facts. Because wisdom is a claim about understanding reality, it is dependent on a metaphysical assumption of what is real, while also necessitating an epistemological position on how one can know anything at all (Robinson, 1990). This effectively reduced the basis of wisdom to scientific laws. Furthermore, previous notions of wisdom were forced to be verified by the public experience that was the accepted source of epistemic authority, reducing wisdom to mere technical knowledge. Thus, the Empiricists viewed wisdom as what could be induced through scientific methodology about the structure, conduct, and meaning of life. Lacking the proper scope of knowledge and evidence needed to make such a contribution, the Empiricists left the scientific study of wisdom to future generations (Baltes, 2004). No single Empiricist offered a complete theory of wisdom per se, but their views leveled the interdisciplinary playing field, and effectively took wisdom out of the hands of philosophy and into the hands of general science.

> Science is organized knowledge.
> Wisdom is organized life.
> —*Immanuel Kant*

During the age of Enlightenment, the German philosopher Immanuel Kant (1724–1804) strongly believed wisdom was a human, rather than a divine, product. To him, wisdom deals with the metaphysical world, at the limits of human reasoning or intellect. He argued that science, in the form of evidence-based reasoning, is the basis for the development of wisdom, but also that wisdom encompasses principles beyond mere science such as morality and the common good (Baltes, 2004). Wisdom based on scientific knowledge is more rational and less prone to having "speculative" and "irrational" features. Pure reasoning can help illuminate what is considered good and moral, but to act wisely and morally, practical wisdom needs to be utilized through the regulation of passions and desires. Kant suggested that wise people should exhibit self-control over their passions and act out of good will (Wood, 1999). Wisdom cannot be judged simply by the outcomes of human actions, but rather through the intent behind them. The outcomes may be affected by many factors that are not under the control of the person taking the action. Thus, a person who intends to act wisely, but fails to do so as a result of the foolishness of others, should be considered wiser than a person who did not intend to act wisely but, as a result of circumstances, ended up producing a desirable outcome.

Post-Enlightenment and Contemporary Philosophers

The beginning of the modern era marked a further separation of the concept of wisdom from its faith-based interpretation. The new concept included moral reasoning and civic good at its core. The new thinkers of the Enlightenment era emphasized that humanity should be concerned with the quest for wisdom through contemplation, observation, and scientific inquiry. In that era, science and wisdom began to converge, and the concept of human morality and good deeds became more salient. Although many still believed that true wisdom could not be achieved by humans, they also believed that wisdom could be developed and nurtured, and they supported this endeavor in their writings.

Commentaries on wisdom from the post-Enlightenment period tend to be accidental reflections rather than a sincere embracing of wisdom as a concept. For the many years following, there was practically no significant work on wisdom. Technology-based modern society perhaps overemphasizes the ability of science, rather than wisdom, to find solutions to complex problems. Contributing to this is the narrow and distorted view of common wisdom as representing archaic metaphysic influence, related to religion, art, and folklore (Freeman, 2003). Science offers highly specialized clarity in distinct knowledge domains, but it rarely looks at the bigger picture, whereas wisdom as a means of knowing is holistic and interdisciplinary (Csikszentmihalyi & Rathunde, 1990). Important nontechnical attributes of wisdom (e.g., intuition, reflection, virtue) have lost their practical appeal as a result of historical factors such as the scientific tradition, economic rationalism, and the normalization of bureaucracy and formal measurement. In discussing the genealogical decline of wisdom's social status, Rooney and McKenna (2007) claimed that "the rationalist principles of the modern scientific tradition valorized the rational processes of the mind and distrusted the role of the body's instincts and feelings, which we identify as crucial to wise practice" (p. 119).

In recent years, interest in wisdom-related research and practice has been revived, possibly because of the emphasis given to it in psychological research (discussed in the next section). Many contemporary philosophical views of wisdom have veered back toward a practical perspective. The following three definitions of wisdom demonstrate this return:

> Robert Nozick's (1989) definition: "Wisdom is what you need to understand in order to live well and cope with the central problems and avoid the dangers in the predicaments human beings find themselves in" (p. 267).
>
> Richard Garrett's (1996) definition: "Wisdom is that understanding which is essential to living the best life" (p. 221).
>
> Sharon Ryan's (1997) definition:[1] Wisdom is knowing, in general, how to live well at a certain time, and having a general appreciation for the true value of living well.

Although technically different, these contemporary philosophical thoughts on wisdom show strong similarities; they all consider wisdom as essentially linked to living well or living the best life possible. Contemporary definitions have seemingly come full circle, returning again to Aristotle's *Phronesis*—knowledge required for flourishing and representing a culmination of skeptical views toward wisdom. In these definitions, wisdom is no longer considered a higher truth, but rather practical truths that relate to pragmatic ends.

Wisdom has always represented an ideal. Each age and thinker has had his own thoughts on wisdom because the ideals of each generation and culture are different. Contemporary theories follow these conditions, drawing on our own age's collective ideals: that human flourishing and the elimination of suffering is the greatest end we can hope to achieve. Kekes (1995) identifies moral wisdom as a necessity for living a good life. To him, wisdom is a reflective virtue that can be gained by improved judgment and increased control over one's life. Kekes builds on the Greek philosophers by acknowledging the theoretical and practical aspects of moral wisdom, which involve knowledge of what is right and wrong, and sound sense in life matters, respectively. The knowledge of moral truth involves those invariant values that are beneficial for individuals and societies as a whole, as well as the various ways in which these values are manifested in real life. When faced with life's adversities, moral wisdom emerges through our deliberations about finding the best course of action. Kekes discusses three modes for attaining this wisdom: moral imagination (the ability to perceive the contextualized moral basis of others' actions), self-knowledge (the ability to know one's own strengths and weaknesses, and thus be more effective in executing moral thought), and moral depth (the inner motivation to live a good moral life).

Summary of Historical Perspectives of Wisdom

The conceptual evolution of wisdom exemplifies its multifaceted nature. Wisdom was always seen as the practical know-how essential for a successful and constructive life. As such, wisdom encompasses many good personal qualities related to one's mind, soul, spirit, and behavior. Even in the most ancient wisdom texts, we find a sense of order, where one's actions are reason driven, and aim to benefit oneself and the society in which one lives. Then the meaning of wisdom expanded and evolved. People associated wisdom with the divine, and so respect and faith in God could help one attain wisdom. Behaving wisely was seen as a commitment to live a moral and just life, following a divine ethical code.

Later, people began to think of wisdom in ways that are more practical and human based. Throughout history, unique individuals reflected on their own path to wisdom. Western thinkers emphasized rationally driven cognition and behavior. In particular, the possession of knowledge of the right rationale was considered wisdom. Eastern thinkers generally left the definition of wisdom somewhat vague. As in Western thought, Eastern wisdom is seen as an advanced stage of the mind. However, Eastern thinkers also emphasized noncognitive features, such as holistic experiences involving the integration of mind, affect, intuition, and behavior (Takahashi & Overton, 2005). These historic wisdom texts strongly influenced other thinkers;

---

[1] This definition was rephrased to fit with the format of the other definitions. For a person S at time t, the definition is: "S is wise at t if and only if at t (i) S knows, in general, how to live well, and (ii) S has a general appreciation of the true value of living well." (Ryan, 1997, p. 135)

around the world, people began to ponder how one attains, or develops, wisdom.

Although the meaning and usefulness of wisdom, as captured in proverbs and maxims, has remained relatively constant throughout history (yet somewhat fuzzy), societal events and movements continued to shape the philosophic and academic discourse of wisdom. At different times, wisdom was "studied" through different lenses: religious, scientific, practical, moral, experiential, and societal; each body of text emphasizes different aspects of the same phenomena. In some centuries, wisdom (or at least writing about it) seems simply to have disappeared from the face of the earth. Yet, there is one line of thought that permeates almost all these historical perspectives. Wisdom requires both the intent and the knowledge to act according to higher principles (may these be based on supreme reason, divine knowledge, impeccable morals, or a utopian state of being). Wisdom involves the application of sound sense to all matters of life with the purpose of becoming and remaining a good person. In some views, the essence of wisdom seems to be captured in a positive interpretation of the natural law of cause and effect: "Good begets good." Being good toward yourself and being good toward others will eventually lead to flourishing. This basic truth summarizes the goal of wisdom: to protect us and to help us grow. The next section discusses how our understanding of wisdom continued to evolve as the modern psychological inquiry "picked up" on this historical line of thought.

The wise in all ages have always said the same thing, and fools, who at all times form the immense majority, have in their way, too, acted alike, and done just the opposite; and so it will continue.

—*The Wisdom of Life,*
Arthur Schopenhauer

PSYCHOLOGICAL RESEARCH ABOUT THE MEANING OF WISDOM

With the emergence of psychology as a field of study separate from philosophy, the concept of wisdom has been studied as a psychological construct. Various theoretical frameworks have been developed to explain and measure it. Psychological inquiries diverge from the path of previous treatments of wisdom. The emphasis here is on an attempt to decipher the meaning of wisdom as a concept inherent within the individual. The psychological field considers wisdom both componentially and holistically, both broadly and deeply.

The psychological study of wisdom began to flourish in the late 20th century. For example, Erik Erikson discussed wisdom as an optimal stage of human development, Abraham Maslow related wisdom to mental health and authenticity, Lawrence Kohlberg presented advanced stages of moral reasoning that are highly related to wisdom, and Viktor Frankel associated wisdom with finding a meaning in life. Recent research has inspected wisdom more directly, through theory-based measurement methodologies. These studies have produced a significant number of findings about the antecedents, correlates, and consequences of wisdom.

One reason for the renewed interest in wisdom, as noted by Baltes (2004), is the desire to "identify the facets of the…[older adult's] mind associated with opportunities for gains. It also may help us to…[develop] more successfully, to integrate mind and body at a new level of insight and efficacy" (p. 32). Researchers began to inquire about the types of cognitive and emotional components needed in late adulthood, and suggested new and integrated forms of advanced cognitive and emotional development that can be found in adulthood. For example, theorists began to diverge from the path set by the Greeks and seriously to study the implications of the idea that there is no objective truth that holds in every context.

Current psychological studies of wisdom can be categorized as research on either implicit or explicit theories. In the former, researchers focus on people's everyday conceptions of wisdom, whereas in the latter, researchers offer a theory of their own and design studies to test it. Usually, explicit theories of wisdom stem from findings on people's implicit conceptualizations. Hershey and Farrell (1997) noted that both implicit and explicit approaches aim to provide a complete definition of wisdom, using different methods. Indeed, a clear definition of wisdom is essential for any serious inquiry of the concept. However, researchers do not share a single definition of wisdom (Ardelt, 2004; Staudinger, Lopez, & Baltes, 1997). Consider, for example, the *Oxford English Dictionary*'s (2nd ed., 1989) definition of wisdom: "Capacity of judging rightly in matters relating to life and conduct; soundness of judgment in the choice of means and ends; sometimes, less strictly, sound sense, esp. in practical affairs: opp. to *folly*." If we are interested in studying wisdom as a psychological construct based on such a definition, we need to understand what "judging rightly" and "soundness of judgment" mean. Otherwise, how can we operationalize these concepts in scientific studies? How can we know whether someone is wise?

Most psychological research on wisdom aims at specifying the components of wisdom (Staudinger, 2001). Some researchers design methodologies to measure wisdom based on a specific theoretical framework. Studies on implicit and explicit theories illuminate not only what wisdom means today, but also how it applies to the complexities of modern life, how it develops throughout the life span, and how it can be enhanced. Current research emphasizes the relation of wisdom and positive aspects of life, and the relation of wisdom to elevated human performances (e.g., of experts) with regard to attributes such as intelligence, creativity, and practical thinking. This section describes main findings from implicit-theoretical and explicit-theoretical research on wisdom as a psychological construct (for further review, see Baltes, 2004; Kramer, 2000; Sternberg, 1990; Sternberg & Jordan, 2005; Taranto, 1989; Trowbridge, 2005).

Implicit-Theoretical Approaches

Implicit-theoretical approaches to wisdom aim to describe people's folk conceptions of wisdom. They provide an account that is true with respect to people's beliefs about wisdom, whether these beliefs are right or wrong. Social-science researchers have used the wisdom captured by proverbs and maxims as a source for developing hypotheses and designing studies of human nature and behavior. For instance, Zajonc's (1968) work on the "mere exposure effect" challenges the proverb "Familiarity breeds contempt" (see Rogers, 1990). Such studies are motivated by the implicit theories conveyed in a proverb and aim to test their validity in real life. The results can be illuminating for the meaning of the proverb in different current contexts. More recently, implicit theories have been studied more directly in relation to wisdom. (A comprehensive review can be found in Bluck & Glück, 2005.)

Many studies have focused on the dimensions underlying the concept of wisdom, as perceived by different individuals. In her classic article, Clayton (1976) asked participants from different age groups to describe a wise person. Responses included terms such as *experienced, intuitive, introspective, pragmatic, understanding, gentle, empathic, intelligent, peaceful, knowledgeable, sense of humor,* and *observant*. Her participants then rated similarities between these characteristics, including three more descriptors: wise, aged, myself. A multidimensional scaling analysis was used to recover three components of wisdom: *reflective* (e.g., introspection, intuition), *affective* (e.g., compassion, empathy), and *cognitive* (e.g., experience,

intelligence). Later studies identified similar dimensions (Hershey & Farrell, 1997; Jason et al., 2001). Clayton and Birren (1980) also found that implicit theories of wisdom consist of an integration of these dimensions and that, for older participants, the meaning of wisdom was more varied and less related to age, when compared with younger participants.

Holliday and Chandler (1986a, 1986b) studied implicit theories to determine whether wisdom is a "prototype-organized concept." In one study, participants listed attributes of wise, shrewd, perceptive, intelligent, spiritual, and foolish people. In a second study, another group rated these attributes on how well they describe a wise person. The researchers uncovered five factors that are most prototypical of wisdom: *exceptional understanding, sound judgment and communication skills, general competence* (e.g., *curiosity, intelligence,* and *thoughtfulness*), *proper interpersonal skills,* and *social adeptness.*

Sternberg (1985, 1990) has reported a series of studies investigating implicit theories of wisdom. In one study, professors from different fields were asked to rate the distinctness of a list of behaviors with respect to their conception of an ideally wise, intelligent, or creative individual in their occupation (laypersons were also asked to provide ratings without regard to occupation). In each academic field except philosophy, the highest correlation between the ratings was between wisdom and intelligence; in philosophy, the highest correlation was between intelligence and creativity. For all the fields, the lowest correlation was between wisdom and creativity (and this correlation was negative for the group of business professors). Other participants were asked to rate descriptions of hypothetical individuals for intelligence, creativity, and wisdom. The results suggested again that wisdom and intelligence are highly correlated in people's implicit theories.

In a second study, college students were asked to sort sets of the top-rated wisdom, intelligence, and creativity behaviors from previous studies into as many or as few piles as they wished. Using multidimensional scaling, the researchers uncovered three dimensions with dual interpretations: *strong reasoning ability* (e.g., can solve problems, logical) versus *sagacity* (e.g., fair, considering others advice), *learning from ideas and environment* (e.g., attaches importance to ideas, perceptive) versus *judgment* (e.g., aware of own limitations, sensible), and *expeditious use of information* (e.g., experienced, detail oriented) versus *perspicacity* (e.g., has intuition, good advice).

Hershey and Farrell (1997) asked participants to rate personal characteristics and occupations on a scale from very unwise to very wise. Their findings suggest that wise individuals can make perceptive judgments and have a quiet and reflective nature. They also found that people tended to associate wisdom with professions that require significant levels of education or provide high social status. Overall, wisdom was weakly linked with all other professions in the study, suggesting that people can be wise in any occupation.

Bluck and Glück (2005) argued that the studies described earlier produced many subcomponents of wisdom but only a few distinct conceptual categories. The authors organized the competencies and motivations related to wisdom into five categories: *cognitive ability, insight, reflective attitude, concern for others,* and *real-world skills.* Wisdom involves a personal disposition to successfully integrate these components and the ability to appropriately use that disposition in response to real-life problems.

Other researchers, using various methods, found similar components of wisdom, as well as additional ones. For example, among Hungarian and Swiss teachers and students, Oser, Schenker, and Spychiger (1999) found three components of perceived wisdom with respect to specific actions: *solidarity, situated intelligence,* and *calculated risk taking.* Montgomery, Barber, and McKee (2002) conducted phenomenological interviews with six people whose background was considered "wisdom facilitative" (i.e., aged and experienced; see Baltes & Staudinger, 1993). The themes that emerged from this study included *guidance, experience, moral principles, time,* and *compassionate relationships.* Glück, Bluck, Baron, and McAdams (2005) used an autobiographical approach to study people's conception of wisdom as it applies to their own lives. Three dual forms of wisdom emerged with respect to important life events: *empathy* and *support, self-determination* and *assertion,* and *knowledge* and *flexibility.*

A consistent finding among studies of implicit theories is that conceptions of wisdom differ with respondents' characteristics, such as age (Clayton & Birren, 1980; Heckhausen, Dixon, & Baltes, 1989), spiritual beliefs (Hershey & Farrell, 1997; Jason et al., 2001), professions (Sternberg, 1985), culture (Takahasi & Overton, 2005), and gender (Denney, Dew, & Kroupa, 1995; Hira & Faulkender, 1997; Orwoll & Perlmutter, 1990). For example, Denney et al. found that although both genders share similar understanding of the meaning of wisdom, males were nominated as being wise with respect to specific skills, whereas females were nominated as being interpersonally wise. Cultural studies indicate that a common meaning of wisdom is shared by people from the same culture, but that meaning differs across cultures.

Cultural Perspective on Implicit Theories

For the most part, the research described thus far was conducted in Western societies. Several studies focusing on implicit theories in Eastern cultures have also been conducted. For example, Yang (2001) studied wisdom among Taiwanese Chinese. She found four pairs of components for wisdom: *competencies* and *knowledge, benevolence* and *compassion, openness* and *profundity,* and *modesty* and *unobtrusiveness.* Takayama (2002) identified similar components among behaviors rated by Japanese men and women of various ages. Generally, the Japanese participants associated wisdom more with practically based experience than with intellectual reasoning. The four factors that emerged were *knowledge* and *education, understanding* and *judgment, sociability* and *interpersonal relationships,* and an *introspective attitude.*

Takahashi and Bordia (2000) compared implicit theories of wisdom in Western and Eastern participants. For the Western participants, the adjective *wise* was semantically most similar to *experienced* and *knowledgeable.* It was least similar to *discreet.* The Eastern participants, conversely, viewed *wise* as closest to *discreet,* followed by *aged* and *experienced.* All cultural groups thought that being wise was very desirable (most similar to descriptors of an ideal self), but that being aged was very undesirable (see also Takahashi & Overton, 2005).

Other researchers used in-depth interviews with people who are considered wise in their culture to learn about their conception of wisdom. For example, Levitt (1999) found that, for Tibetan Buddhist monks, wisdom is distinct from education, intelligence, and religion. A wise person exhibits *good judgment, self-examination, efficient conduct, compassion, honesty, humility, respect,* and *genuine acts to meet the needs of others.* The monks' belief encompasses a deep understanding of Buddhist concepts such as the illusion of the worldly self and the interconnectedness of all things through multiple lifetimes. Yang (2008) also studied the characteristics of Taiwanese Chinese people nominated as wise. Their wisdom-related experiences were those in which integration, embodiment, and positive affect were made explicit. Yang (2008) concluded that wisdom is "a special kind of real-life process that is achieved after a person cognitively makes an unusual integration, embodies his or her ideas through action, and hence brings forth positive effects to both self and others" (p. 64). In another study, Valdez (1994) found spiritual and interpersonal, rather than cognitive aspects, to be related to perceived wisdom in Hispanic Americans nominated as wise in their community.

Limas and Hansson (2004) studied the relation between wisdom and work-related factors such as well-being and work environment. In one study, they surveyed employees' beliefs about the match between wise leaders and organizational culture. Overall, wise leadership appeared most important in cultures valuing *supportiveness* (trust and collaboration) and *team orientation* (a shared fate and mutual support). It was least important in cultures valuing *attention to detail, aggressiveness*, and *decisiveness.*

Baltes and Kunzmann (2004) noted that some theorists, consistent with Western cultural views, see wisdom as an "analytic theory of expert knowledge, judgment and advice about difficult and uncertain matters of life," whereas others, consistent with Eastern cultures, associate it with wise people and their products. Takahashi and Overton (2005) concluded that Eastern cultures, compared with Western cultures, associate wisdom less with cognitive abilities such as the accumulation of knowledge; instead, Eastern conceptions involve qualities that focus on the prudence and the good judgment needed to effectively use existing knowledge in real-life situations. They argued that researchers of wisdom should "avoid cultural egocentrism and acknowledge the broadest and most inclusive meanings entailed by the concept" (Takahashi and Overton, 2005, p. 42). The authors offer an explicit model based on an extensive review of the implicit-theories literature. Their model is an integration of analytic and synthetic modes of wisdom. The analytic mode, exemplary of the West, simplifies human experience into manageable pieces of information and examines their relations. The synthetic mode, exemplary of the East, focuses on a more holistic view of experience, emphasizing the dialectical, reflective, integrative, and transformational aspects of the mind.

Rational Decision Making

Another related line of studies can be found in research on cognitive heuristics that deviate from normative rational rules for decision making (Kahneman, Slovic, & Tversky, 1982; Kahneman & Tversky, 2000). These studies investigated how people form implicit beliefs about the likelihoods of uncertain events. Such situations call for the rational decision-making process typical of wisdom. For example, people's tendency to agree to give a life-saving treatment to a group of 100 terminal patients should not change depending on whether the treatment is said to have a 90% chance of success as opposed to a 10% chance of failure. Multiple studies have shown that people rely on heuristic principles to decrease the cognitive complexity of decision making under uncertainty, thus simplifying the process of daily-life judgments (Gilovich, Griffin, & Kahneman, 2002). For the most part, these heuristics are pragmatic, efficient, and successful (Gigerenzer, Todd, & ABC Research Group, 1999), but under certain circumstances, they may lead to irrational behavior.

Some authors pointed out that the rules of rationality are based on unreasonable expectations of the human mind in real-world situations. Wise, rational thought requires superior levels of knowledge, analysis, and objectivity. However, in real life, humans have very limited mental resources, and they tend to judge things based on the context and not on their absolute value (Ariely, 2008). Essentially, studies on decision-making examine aspects of wisdom related to how people interpret the uncertainty in their lives. In uncertain situations, people vary in the extent to which their thoughts and actions are motivated by an absolute rational truth (theoretical wisdom) or by heuristics and circumstances (practical wisdom).

Summary of Implicit Theories of Wisdom

Implicit theories play an important role in the development of scientific research on wisdom. These studies explicate the multidimensional meaning of wisdom, emphasizing competencies and motivations, particularly those related to helping others (Bluck & Glück, 2005). Wisdom is conceived as the integration of characteristics related to one's mind, spirit, and conduct. Being wise requires the ability appropriately to apply one's skills and capabilities in the face of life's complexities, uncertainties, and challenges. In addition, the ability to lead, guide, or teach is commonly associated with wise people.

In almost all of the studies described here, wisdom is viewed as having a cognitive component related to possessing and using knowledge and experience, an affective component related to moral principles, and a reflective component related to intrapersonal and interpersonal perceptions. However, respondents from different cultures, age groups, and professions seem to emphasize different components. In other words, people's views of wisdom are highly contextualized and contingent on respondents' characteristics. Explicit-theoretical approaches attempt to describe wisdom in a more nearly universal sense. These approaches try to synthesize existing knowledge about wisdom with known psychological theories, and provide methodological frameworks for identifying and describing wise behavior.

Explicit-Theoretical Approaches

Explicit theories are models of wisdom based on the implicit theories of experts rather than of laypeople. The models suggested by researchers are inclusive, integrated, and aimed at explaining what wisdom is and how it is manifested in our lives. Most researchers base their theories on models of human-developmental psychological constructs. Wisdom is commonly seen as an advanced development of cognitive and affective aspects of one's personality. Some theories suggest that wisdom can also be understood as developing from an evolutionary perspective. Some theories characterize wisdom as the development of expertise in life matters, whereas others emphasize various kinds of balance needed to be wise. Birren and Svensson (2005) note that psychological studies of wisdom are top-down in the sense that they build from the simple to the complex, from purpose and intention to behavior. We now review some of the main explicit theories about wisdom and its relation to cognition, personality, experience, and their integration (for more about this topic, see Baltes & Staudinger, 2000; Brugman, 2006; Kramer, 2000; Staudinger, 2008; Sternberg, 1990, 2005b; Sternberg & Jordan, 2005; Trowbridge, 2005).

Wisdom and Cognition

As we have seen in the historical review, wisdom always has been associated with knowledge and the cognitive ability to obtain it. Echoing Socrates' famous quote, some researchers emphasize the importance of knowing the limits of one's own extant knowledge and attempting to go beyond it. For example, based on a thorough review of the literature, Taranto (1989) defined wisdom as the individual's recognition of, and response to, human limitations. This distinction does not represent the discrepancy between what the individual knows and does not know, but rather the awareness that the unknowns are greater than what one can possibly know. Meacham (1983, 1990) suggested that all knowledge-based wisdom is essentially uncertain. In his view, the awareness of one's own fallibility and the knowledge of what one does and does not know is an important aspect of wisdom; one has to strive for a balance between knowledge and doubt. A wise person will know when to give advice, but also when not to do so.

Another view defines wisdom as seeing through illusion (McKee & Barber, 1999). Wisdom is seen through keen judgment and the ability to evade life's temptations and universal errors. Brugman (2000, 2006) defined an *epistemic model of wisdom* as expertise in uncertainty, which involves metacognitive, affective, and behavioral components leading to the good life. The epistemic model builds on stoic and empiricist views of wisdom, emphasizing attitude toward knowledge rather than knowledge itself. Brugman's belief is that wisdom is mainly associated with increasing doubt regarding the comprehensibility of reality. This acknowledgment of the uncertainty in life leads to emotional stability, which translates into the ability to act effectively in the face of such situations. Brugman (2000) reports partial empirical support for the epistemic model. An epistemic wisdom scale is significantly correlated with well-being and openness to experience, but not with emotional stability.

Wisdom is also commonly associated with the development of metacognitive skills (Flavell, 1979), such as those related to reflective or dialectical/relativistic thought. Dialectical thought involves the recognition of multiple points of view and the limitations of knowledge. Such processes are exemplified by the acceptance of contradictions (e.g., incompatible knowledge) and their resolution through synthesis of opposing systems or frames of reference (see also Basseches, 1984a, 1984b; Blanchard-Fields & Hess, 1996; Kramer, 1983, 1990; Riegel, 1973; Sinnott, 1993). The dialectical process can be seen as the contemplation or evolution of opinions (Hegel, 1931). Sternberg (1998, 2001, 2005a) noted that wisdom encompasses the understanding that truth is not always absolute, but rather, it evolves in a historical context of theses, antitheses, and syntheses. That is, truth, the concept sought by wisdom, lies in the transition from what we think we know to be true at this point in time, which is then challenged by new and conflicting information, understandings, or circumstances, to finally culminating in an integration of perspectives.

Reflective thought is an inwardly oriented process associated with good judgment in one's life. This process requires self-awareness, self-examination, and insight. It is seen as the ability to contemplate problems while being aware of one's own limitation of knowledge, as well as integrating information from various sources. For example, Kitchener and Brenner (1990) suggested that wisdom requires a synthesis of knowledge from opposing points of view to deal with difficult, ill-defined problems. This reflective judgment is manifested as people shift from understanding of what can be known with certainty to awareness of the uncertainties that underlie any knowledge (see also Kitchener, 1986; Kitchener & King, 1981, 1990).

Some theorists built on Piaget's cognitive stages (1972) by considering wisdom in terms of postformal-operational thinking (e.g., Alexander & Langer, 1990; Labouvie-Vief,

1990; Pascual-Leone, 1990, 2000). Labouvie-Vief (1990) emphasized the importance of a smooth and balanced dialogue between logical (objective) forms of processing knowledge and more socioemotional (subjective) forms of processing (see also Carstensen, 1995; Staudinger, 1999). Her view of wisdom is that of an "integrated thought," where abstract and mechanical forms of knowledge (*logos*) are seamlessly combined with holistic, nonrational, and contextual knowledge (*mythos*). Labouvie-Vief (1990) emphasized the role of reflective thought in balancing the "paradoxical tension of thought between being both immanent and transcendent" (p. 77).

Arlin (1984, 1990) linked wisdom to identifying problems and contemplating their solution. Problem finding involves reflection on the nature of the problem and its solution, while balancing multiple perspectives and sources of information. She also noted that "one can be a problem finder without being particularly wise, but it is difficult to conceive of a wise person who does not ask questions whose forms reflect the highest level of problem finding" (Arlin, 1990, p. 231). Arlin views problem finding as a possible stage of postformal-operational thinking, evolving from the process of problem resolution, which is common in adolescence. Such a view is not necessarily inconsistent with the view of dialectical thinking. Both dialectical thinking and problem finding could represent distinct postformal-operational stages, or two manifestations of the same postformal-operational stage.

Wisdom and Personality Development

In addition to cognition as the foundation for wisdom, many researchers emphasize the development of emotional, motivational, and moral aspects of personality. For example, Erikson (1959, 1968) viewed wisdom as a key element of late-life psychosocial development. During the middle adult years, the most common psychosocial crisis is in the tension between *generativity* versus *stagnation*: Individuals deal with their concern to establish and guide future generations, as opposed to a tendency to slow down and stop progressing. In later adulthood, the psychosocial crisis concerns *integrity* versus *despair*, as individuals experience a sense of mortality: Integrity is conceived as acceptance of the human life cycle, including death. Despair, in contrast, is experienced when individuals fail to find meaning in their life and ultimately fear death. Erikson viewed this final stage of moral development as leading to wisdom.

Other researchers continued this line of thought. Orwoll and Perlmutter (1990) argued that wisdom is an integration

of cognition and personality. Based on a review of theories by Erikson, Jung, and Kohut, they identified two key indicators of personality-based wisdom: exemplary *self-development* and *self-transcendence* (moving beyond individualistic concerns toward universal concerns). They suggested that these levels of affective clarity, in combination with advanced cognitive attributes, foster self-insight and form the basis of wisdom. Achenbaum and Orwoll (1991) used the biblical story of Job, the righteous man who suffers great misfortunes but remains strong willed, to demonstrate the "complex, dynamic yet integrative nature of growing wise." In their synthetic view, becoming wise involves certain personality characteristics, cognition, and conation (motivation) that transform one's intrapersonal, interpersonal, and transpersonal experiences.

Staudinger, Dörner, and Mickler (2005) examined the connections between wisdom and personality (see also Staudinger, 2008). The authors pointed out that much of the psychological research on wisdom focused on two types of wisdom: personal wisdom (a person's insight into his or her own life) and general wisdom (insight into life in general). Research on personal wisdom views it as unique personality characteristics related to maturity and adaptation, both from social (life satisfaction, positive relationships) and personal perspectives (openness to experience and personal growth). Research on general wisdom considers both nonpersonal manifestations of wisdom (e.g., wisdom literature) and personality characteristics that are associated with wisdom (i.e., traits that either facilitate the development of wisdom or increase as a result of it). The authors argued that one's wisdom evolves through life experiences, where the dynamic relation between general and personal knowledge affect one's decisions and actions.

Pascual-Leone (1990) has argued for the importance of developing dialectical integration of all aspects of a person's affect, cognition, motivation, and life experience. This integration is the outcome of the struggle to resolve the ego's inner conflicts induced by our life. Wisdom is associated with the will-driven development of advanced emotional and behavioral stages that lead to a stronger sense of the "true self" and weaker ego-centered concerns (similar to Kohlberg's moral development and Erikson's psychosocial development). These qualities oriented at human growth strengthen intuition, empathy, and intrapersonal/interpersonal understandings. Pascual-Leone (1990) also has considered three forms of wisdom: (1) wisdom-as-will within vital reason (typical of philosophical, religious and psychological literature), (2) wisdom as valid existential counseling (e.g., a good advice), and (3) wisdom as the ability for empathic experiencing of the other or of nature.

Birren and Fisher (1990) compared the views of wisdom given by the theories presented in Sternberg's (1990) edited book on wisdom. Their conclusion was that wisdom is "integration of the affective, conative and cognitive aspects of human abilities in response to life's tasks and problems. Wisdom is a balance between the opposing valences of intense emotion and detachment, action and inaction, and knowledge and doubts" (Birren & Fisher, p. 326). They noted that such balance is likely to be achieved through experience; hence wisdom is correlated with, but not exclusive to, age. This definition reflects not only psychological approaches to wisdom, but historical approaches as well (Birren & Svensson, 2005).

The importance of the integration of cognitive and affective development as a basis for wisdom is also echoed in Kramer's organicist model (1990). The organismic approach is dynamic; change occurs in a systematic way through the resolution of conflicts, leading to greater integration and coherence (Overton & Reese, 1973). The pivotal idea in the model is that the development of wisdom is facilitated by integration of cognitive and affective processes, which result from using relativistic and dialectical modes of thinking to respond to life's challenges. Kramer (2000) argued that wisdom is "an integration of cognitive, affective, and behavioral dimensions to produce a rare but adaptive form of judgment that is conducive to exceptional insight and judgment about important life issues and situations" (Kramer, p. 95). The integration of all aspects of oneself allows greater acceptance of others. Kramer (1990) also distinguishes five interrelated functions of wisdom: *solution of problems confronting self, advising others, management of social institutions, life review,* and *spiritual introspection.*

According to Kramer, wise people seem to better utilize their emotional experiences to foster personal growth and well-being. Blanchard-Fields and Norris (1995) also suggested that effective regulation of emotion in the face of life complexities is a pivotal ability related to wisdom (see also Ardelt, 1997). Emotions can either help or hinder the ability to make rational decisions in matters important to life. Similarly, Csikszentmihalyi and Nakamura (2005) noted that research on wisdom and affect focuses on adaptive and effective emotion regulation (Gross, 1999). This view is also supported by the connection between emotional intelligence and many characteristics associated with wisdom (Feldman-Barrett & Salovey, 2002; Sternberg, 2001).

Based on Clayton and Birren (1980), Ardelt (1997, 2003, 2004) has proposed that wisdom involves the integration of three personality characteristics: (1) *cognitive*, a desire to know the truth and the ability to understand the deeper meaning of life, its uncertainties, and the limits of knowledge; (b) *reflective,* an awareness to multiple perspectives of life, and the use of self-examination and insight to transcend one's subjectivity and projections; and (c) *affective*, the ability to express genuine empathy and compassion for others. She argued that these components are both necessary and sufficient for the development of wisdom. Ardelt (2000a, 2003, 2008) sees the reflective component as a prerequisite for proper cognitive development. Through reflective and insightful self-examination based on the willingness to learn from experience, one can achieve a deeper understanding of life. This process reduces the personality characteristics that distort the perception of reality (self-absorption, subjectivity, and projections) and increases one's ability to see the true nature of objects, people, and relationships. As a result, affective characteristics are improved, specifically those related to self-transcendence as a compassionate concern for others. Similar views of wisdom as integration are shared by other researchers (e.g., Clayton & Birren; Csikszentmihalyi & Rathunde, 1990; Kramer, 1990; Labouvie-Vief, 1990; Pascual-Leone, 1990).

Ardelt emphasized that, for a person to be wise, all three components (reflective, cognitive, and affective) need to be present simultaneously. Therefore, people who only partially integrate these components would probably not be considered wise. For example, those who have some cognitive and reflective attributes, but who lack empathy and compassion, may not be considered wise (see also Sternberg, 1998). Similarly, those who have cognitive and affective attributes sometimes lack the reflective attributes needed to help themselves (the "helpless helper" syndrome, Schmidbauer, 1977). And finally, those who have affective and reflective attributes may not be considered wise if they lack the desire for knowing the truth.

Ardelt (2004) further noted that the object of wisdom pursuit is knowledge of the truth—universal answers to fundamental questions of life. Wisdom emerges when this "theoretical, abstract, and detached" knowledge becomes "applied, concrete, and involved." She argued that wisdom cannot exist independently of individuals; "even the most profound 'wisdom literature' remains intellectual or theoretical knowledge until its inherent wisdom is realized by a person" (Ardelt, 2004, p. 260; see also Assmann, 1994; Labouvie-Vief, 1990). This view of wisdom seems to unify both Western and Eastern perspectives.

The following sections describe three explicit theories that consider wisdom within broader conceptual frameworks. Csikszentmihalyi and his colleagues have placed wisdom within a societal evolutionary perspective; Baltes and his colleagues have described wisdom as a form of expertise development; and Sternberg has presented wisdom as a balance of decisions and actions oriented toward the common good.

Evolutionary Perspectives on Wisdom

Csikszentmihalyi and Rathunde (1990) presented a phylogenetic or evolutionary approach to the study of wisdom. They argued that, at least in a cultural sense, constructs such as wisdom must have been selected over time. Within each society, wise ideas should survive better over time than do unwise ideas. Given the problems found in the world today—hunger, poverty, war, terrorism, to name a few—it is not clear that such selection has occurred, at least in any obvious way. The authors reviewed the continuity of the meaning of wisdom across more than 25 centuries. Consequently, they defined wisdom as having three basic dimensions of meaning: (1) that of a cognitive process, an attempt to understand reality by seeking the ultimate causes and consequences of events while preserving integration of knowledge; (2) that of a virtue, or a socially valued pattern of behavior; and (3) that of a personal good, or an intrinsically desirable state/condition.

Csikszentmihalyi and Nakamura (2005) further expanded on this view of wisdom and suggested that the concept of wisdom defines a type of cognitive process motivated by values and emotions. This process is perceptive and considers multiple perspectives and related frameworks. The authors described wise people as having a "disinterested interest"; that is, they view reality objectively, and yet they are concerned with every aspect of it. Wisdom also encompasses a deep understanding of human nature and of one's own strengths and weaknesses. The authors emphasized that wisdom depends on identifying relevant past experiences and applying them to current problems: "Wisdom is definitely not 'in the head' but rather in the relationship between an inquiring mind and the results of inquiries of bygone minds" (Csikszentmihalyi & Nakamura, p. 224). Wise individuals seek out, maintain, and apply useful knowledge in life's matters, and also transmit it to others. From the dawn of society, different cultures used myths, maxims, songs, and rituals to pass on important information about their lives, first verbally, and later by writing (Csikszentmihalyi, 2000). Texts about past knowledge became a source of important and useful

ideas. True wisdom, therefore, lies in identifying the right information to communicate to future generations.

Wisdom as Expertise: The Berlin Paradigm

The most extensive program of research has been that conducted by the late Paul Baltes and his colleagues at the Max Planck Institute in Berlin (e.g., Baltes, 2004; Baltes & Smith, 1990, 2008; Baltes & Staudinger, 1996, 2000; Baltes & Kunzmann, 2003; Staudinger & Baltes, 1996). Their goal was to develop tools objectively to measure performance related to wisdom. The Berlin group's approach is grounded in the wisdom literature, neo-Piagetian research, life-span development, and research on expertise (Staudinger & Baltes, 2001). Baltes and Staudinger (2000) described wisdom as a "metaheuristic to orchestrate mind and virtue toward excellence" (p. 122). It aims at the development of one's well-being, as well as others', and involves an effective integration of cognitive, motivational-emotional, interpersonal, social, and spiritual characteristics (see also Baltes, 2004; Baltes & Kunzmann, 2004; Baltes & Smith, 2008). The Berlin paradigm is based on a notion of wisdom as expert knowledge about fundamental issues. Specifically, wisdom is seen as good judgment, commentary, and advice in difficult but uncertain matters of life (Baltes & Staudinger, 1993; Smith & Baltes, 1990). Three types of factors are seen as antecedents and correlates to the development and application of wisdom: *general person factors* (e.g., mental health, cognitive style, creativity, openness to experience), *expertise-specific factors* (e.g., experience or mentorship in dealing with life matters, heuristics, motivational dispositions), and *facilitative experiential contexts* (age, education, profession, culture). The development of wisdom requires a synthesis (an "orchestrated coalition") of these factors (Baltes & Staudinger, 2000). Thus, wisdom is not simply expert knowledge, but rather knowledge applied to the practical aspects of life, which are essential to one's own development, as well as that of others.

In the studies that Baltes and his colleagues conducted, participants responded to questions about life planning, life management, and life review. These are seen as examples of processes that regulate the development of wisdom by transferring life's experiences into insights (Staudinger, 2001). Five components of wisdom can be drawn on in response to these situations: (1) *rich factual (declarative) knowledge* (e.g., general and specific knowledge about the conditions of life and its variations); (2) *rich procedural knowledge* (e.g., general and specific knowledge about strategies of judgment and advice concerning matters of life); (3) *life-span contextualism* (e.g., knowledge about the contexts of life and how they change over time); (4) *relativism* (e.g., knowledge about differences in values, goals, and priorities); and (5) *uncertainty* (e.g., knowledge about the relative indeterminacy and unpredictability of life, and ways to manage it). The first two components represent the basic development of expertise as a shift from declarative to procedural knowledge about the fundamental pragmatics of life. Stemming from these basic criteria are the three knowledge components that are essential for the development of wisdom. These metacriteria represent concepts commonly addressed in research on life-span development of cognition, personality, and their integration.

Over time, Baltes and his colleagues have collected an impressive amount of data showing the utility of the proposed theoretical and measurement approaches to wisdom. Their research shows a wide range of cognitive, emotional, motivational, social, and contextual factors related to the development of wisdom (e.g., Baltes & Staudinger, 2000; Kunzmann & Baltes, 2005; Pasupathi, Staudinger, & Baltes, 2001). Specific studies are described further under the Measurement of Wisdom subsection and Development of Wisdom section.

Wisdom as Balance

Sternberg's balance theory of wisdom (Sternberg, 1998, 2000, 2001, 2003, 2004, 2005c; Sternberg & Lubart, 2001) views wisdom as inherent in the interaction between a person and the context. The theory specifies the processes needed (balancing of interests and of responses to environmental contexts) in relation to the *goal* of wisdom (achievement of a common good). According to the balance theory, wisdom is the application of intelligence,

creativity, and knowledge, as mediated by positive ethical values, toward the achievement of a common good through a balance among (a) intrapersonal, (b) interpersonal, and (c) extrapersonal interests, over the (a) short- and (b) long-term, to achieve a balance among (a) adaptation to existing environments, (b) shaping of existing environments, and (c) selection of new environments. Figure 23.1 is a visual presentation of this conception of wisdom.

According to this model, wise individuals rely on their values and knowledge to help them find a balanced solution to problems and situations they encounter in life. Wise decisions do not merely require intelligence, creativity, and explicit knowledge; rather, they typically draw on tacit or implicit knowledge gained through experience. The term *tacit knowledge* (Polanyi, 1966) describes knowledge that is (1) implicit, or acquired without instructional support or even conscious awareness; (2) procedural, or "knowing how" rather than "knowing what"; and (3) practical or instrumental to obtaining a particular goal (Sternberg et al., 2000). Tacit knowledge allows people to appreciate the nuances of a given situation that are not obtainable from any formalized, or even verbalized, set of rules. It is the ability to be attuned to the unique complexities of one's rich environment and to use this understanding to reach one's desired objectives. Although important for making wise decisions, tacit knowledge is not a substitute for other types of knowledge, such as declarative or explicit procedural knowledge.

Sternberg (2000, 2001) also differentiates among the analytical, creative, and practical aspects associated with wisdom (see Sternberg, 1990). Although all involve utilization of metacomponents for the acquisition of knowledge and its processing, they differ in the kinds of

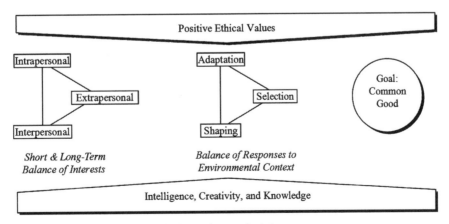

Figure 23.1   Illustration of the balance theory of wisdom.

contexts in which they are applied. Analytical thinking is used for relatively familiar, well-defined, and abstract problems, commonly found in academic settings. Creativity is used in relatively novel, unfamiliar tasks and situations (e.g., Simonton, 1990). Practical thinking, however, is called for in highly contextualized situations, commonly encountered in one's life. Sternberg (2001) describes one view of the dialectical relation among the three constructs. Intelligence can be seen as the thesis—the reasoning used to advance current societal agendas. Creativity can be seen as the antithesis, questioning and opposing current agendas, as well as proposing new ones. Wisdom can be seen as the synthesis of the two perspectives, balancing the old (intelligence) with the new (creativity), to achieve both stability and change.

Sternberg's definition of wisdom draws heavily on the idea of *balance*: the balances among multiple interests, immediate and long-term consequences, and differentiated environmental responses. The psychological theories of wisdom summarized earlier propose different kinds of balances. However, each theory usually emphasizes only one aspect of balance. For example, Labouvie-Vief (1990) discussed balance among objective and subjective forms of thinking; Kramer (1990) emphasized balance between different self-systems, such as cognitive, conative, and affective; Kitchener and Brenner (1990) considered wisdom as a balance among various points of view; and Takahashi and Overton (2005) viewed wisdom as the balance of analytic-synthetic moments of experience. In contrast, Sternberg's theory applies the idea of balance to the affective processes within one's self, to the interactions between people, and to the ways people operate within their environment. Thus, emotional, intrapersonal, and interpersonal skills are closely related to wisdom (Sternberg, 2001). Specifically, *intrapersonal interests* affect only the individual. They have to do with one's own sense of identity and may include such things as the desire for self-actualization, popularity, prestige, power, prosperity, or pleasure (e.g., "I want a promotion because I want to be viewed as successful by myself and others."). *Interpersonal interests* involve other people. They relate not only to one's sense of self but also to desirable relationships with others (e.g., "I want a promotion because my spouse expects me to get paid well."). *Extrapersonal interests* are those that affect a wider organization, community, or environment (e.g., "I want a promotion because my organization needs someone with my skills in a high-level position."). Naturally, wise solutions would weigh more heavily on the interpersonal and extrapersonal interests, and less on the individual's

(intrapersonal) perspective. However, wise people tend to hold values that foster growth in others. Thus, in acting to promote the interests of others, wise people also act in accordance with their own interests.

In addition to multiple interests, the consequences of each decision are assessed to balance short- and long-term objectives. For example, Norway is the world's third-largest oil exporter, yet has one of the highest gas prices in the world at the pump (and one of the lowest carbon emission levels in the Western world). Recently, the Norwegian government decided to advocate conservation despite the country's vast resources. Most of the revenues from its oil profits are directed into a national savings account, dedicated to future generations. The government's reasoning was that it would be irresponsible to spend revenues from a natural resource in the span of a generation or two. This decision shows a balance of short- and long-term needs.

Notably, the balance in Sternberg's theory of wisdom does not mean that each interest, action, or consequence is weighed equally. For example, when working out a solution, self-interests can, and typically should, be weighed less than the interests of others, although both are considered in the final decision. The relative "weightings" are determined by the extent to which a particular alternative contributes to the achievement of wisdom's end result—a common good. A wise person will take into account all of these considerations and try to balance multiple interests and consequences in a way that maximizes the outcome for everyone. For example, a driver who bumped into a parked car might decide to leave a note identifying himself or herself. In this way, the driver suppresses his or her own interests (not getting into trouble), compared with those of others (the owner of the car who would like to keep it intact) and the interest of society as a whole (where people are expected to be responsible for their actions and honest toward others).

Similar to other theories of wisdom, Sternberg's theory is oriented toward action. Applying relevant values and knowledge, together with considering multiple interests and consequences, must lead to choosing a particular behavior.[3] Here, action in response to a situation is seen as a balance among *adaptation*, *shaping*, and *selection* of environments. *Adaptation* involves changing oneself to fit the environment. For instance, for a new student to fit in with an existing study group, he or she may need to change aspects of his or her own behavior (e.g., not be late, inhibit chatty tendencies). *Shaping,* on the contrary, involves modifying parts of the environment to fit one's own interests and values. For example, the student may choose not to change him or herself, but instead, convince members of a study group to change their conception of what is allowed in the group (e.g., "It's okay if people are late, as long as they bring food with them."). Finally, if people cannot adapt to an existing environment or change the environment to meet their needs, they can *select* a new environment. For instance, the student may choose to look for a different study group—one that better fits his or her personality. A particular solution may also combine the environmental responses, such as adaptation and shaping, when one concurrently changes oneself and one's environment.

What is evident from Sternberg's theory is that choosing the right balance depends on one's system of values. Values can help tip the triangular balances less toward oneself and more toward global needs. Sternberg's is not the only theory that places *values* at the core of wise decision making. According to Csikszentmihalyi and Rathunde (1990), "Wisdom becomes the best guide for what is the *summum bonum*, or 'supreme good'" (p. 32). Pascual-Leone (1990) also considered "moral feelings and ethical evaluations (right–wrong or bad–good judgments) of motives and possible acts (e.g., morality)" (p. 267) as an important component of wisdom. In the balance theory of wisdom, ethical values not only establish what constitutes the common good, they also influence the relative weightings of conflicting interests, environments, and consequences. This view is consistent with Dewey's (1938) conception of the common good as the outcome of the process of valuation—a continuous interplay between personal and cultural values. Thus, Sternberg (2004) concluded, "Wisdom is especially important in current times. Humans have made enormous strides in technology, including destructive technology, without corresponding advances in the wisdom required to use this technology for the common good. The result is a world at risk" (p. 119).

The central place of positive ethical values in Sternberg's theory brings up the question of who determines what the "right" ethical values are. Although there are certain universal values, such as *respect for human life, honesty, reciprocity, integrity, responsibility, compassion, sincerity, fairness,* and *enabling people to fulfill their potential,* still, there are many cultural, religious, and political differences in value systems throughout the world. Moreover, within a given culture, values differ at various points in history. Our own democratic values dictate that we respect others' differences in deciding what is right or wrong. When we speak of "our" values, we need to remember that not so long ago in the United States, women

had few rights, and African Americans, essentially none at all. So our ethical "values" have changed, or at least, those to whom we apply them. The danger here is of succumbing to moral relativism and proclaiming that any value framework is equally justifiable, and that there is no principle to distinguish right from wrong. In a way, this view is similar to the idea that knowledge of reality can never be objectively understood. There are two ways to avoid such relativism. First, although there could be more than one acceptable ethical-value system and there is no—and will never be—well-defined and exhaustive list of ethical values that is culturally and temporally invariant, some values can be considered ultimately unacceptable and unwise (e.g., disrespect for human life). Such values are contrary to all major religious and ethical systems. Second, one can subscribe to Charles Taylor's (2005) position, according to which core values are those that cannot be denied without being incoherent. For example, one cannot say, "Life has no value," and keep on living; if one really believed one's life had no value, one would presumably commit suicide.

It may seem that the balancing act among values, interests, consequences, and responses to environment has by now become overwhelmingly complex and will not help us understand the psychological processes and outcomes involved in wise decision making. Some authors (Paris, 2001) have criticized the model for making the concept of wisdom more opaque and harder to understand, rather than the reverse (see Reznitskaya & Sternberg, 2004, for a discussion). The presence of balance, values, knowledge, and action in a conceptualization of wise thinking is not unique to Sternberg's theory. What is unique is the inclusion of so many relevant factors involved in making wise judgments, as well as the explication of the relations among these factors. The theoretical model is complex because real behavior in real environments is complex, and in particular, wisdom is complex.

Wisdom and Leadership

Recently, Sternberg (1985, 1997) combined the balance theory of wisdom with his theory of successful intelligence into a unified model of leadership. The Wisdom, Intelligence, Creativity, Synthesized (WICS) model (Sternberg, 2002, 2003, 2004, 2005c, 2005d, 2007, 2008; Sternberg & Vroom, 2002) stipulates that "effective leadership is, in large part, a function of creativity in generating ideas, analytical intelligence in evaluating the quality of these ideas, practical intelligence in implementing the ideas and convincing others to value and follow the ideas, and wisdom to ensure that the decisions and their implementation are for the common good of all stakeholders" (Sternberg, 2005c, p. 29). Wisdom here is the essential nexus of decision making. Intelligence and creativity are necessary for effective leadership, but wisdom is the apparatus through which leadership becomes truly successful in a globally desirable sense.

According to Sternberg, wisdom is the skill set leaders are most likely to lack, and also the skill set that most distinctly defines leaders as good or bad. It is the quality that would distinguish between Stalin and Gandhi, for example. Both used skills of intelligence and creativity to accomplish their goals as leaders, but only Gandhi would be considered a good leader in the sense that his wise actions were oriented toward achieving the common good of his people (as well as of all living creatures). The WICS model suggests that successful leadership requires a synthesis of all of these desirable qualities—creativity, intelligence, and wisdom. As such, the WICS model encompasses the major qualities that differentiate among good, bad, successful, and unsuccessful leaders.

Recent literature has been studying wisdom with respect to functions and characteristics of our modern global-technological society. These studies discussed the importance of wisdom in management (Bigelow, 1992; Boal & Hooijberg, 2000; Kriger & Malan, 1993; Malan & Kriger, 1998; Rooney, 2005; Rooney & McKenna, 2007), in leadership (Korac-Kakabadse, Korac-Kakabadse, & Kouzmin, 2001; Ludema, Wilmot, & Srivastva, 1997; Srivastva & Cooperrider, 1998, Whittington, Pitts, Kageler, & Goodwin, 2005), in information management (Ackoff, 1999; Rowley, 2007), and in organizational settings overall (Bierly, Kessler, & Christensen, 2000; Kessler, 2006; Kessler & Bailey, 2007; Limas & Hansson, 2004). Furthermore, collaborative efforts, such as the University of Chicago project *Defining Wisdom* (see www.wisdomresearch.org), advocate research on the nature of wisdom and its benefits in multiple areas of life. Nevertheless, the current state of research about wise leadership is sparse and fragmented. We view wisdom as a desirable line of research because understanding what makes some people wise leaders has the potential to positively advance our society and other societies. After all, individuals in powerful positions make decisions that affect millions, shaping our planet and our lives. Humanity has had its share of foolish, irresponsible, and evil leaders; we can learn from their mistakes. If we ever want to better our global state, we need to know how to choose wise people to be our leaders in the 21st century. Given some of the selections, it is hard to be wholly optimistic.

Italy has a president, Silvio Berlusconi, at this time whose main goal seems, at least to us, to be the use of his position to advance his own financial interests and to squelch corruption charges against him. Worse, he was reelected after doing the same in his earlier term. This is a man who was not imposed on the country—he was chosen. George W. Bush, too, was reelected, proving that people were willing to reelect a man who would become the most unpopular president (and, in the view of some, most incompetent and unwise president) since records of popularity started to be kept. It is characteristic of people who are foolish that they fail to recognize this trait in themselves, and Berlusconi and Bush seem to us to exemplify this tendency. It is not only in politics that we find unwise leaders. The former chairman of the NASDAQ stock market, Bernard Madoff, admitted to committing what seems to be the greatest financial fraud of all time. True, his creativity and intelligence helped him make his clients, as well as himself, very wealthy, but in the larger scheme of things, he was acting against the common good, digging a financial "black hole" for millions around the world. Selfish and careless leaders have plagued society from the dawn of time. Leaders who show good-oriented decisions and actions are rare and precious. It becomes pivotal to our global progress that we learn to distinguish wise and unwise decisions, support actions that are based on the former, and avoid those based on the latter.

Measurement of Wisdom

The earlier review of thinking about wisdom, dating back to ancient times, through philosophical and religious perspectives, to current-day psychological inquiry, has shown that wisdom is an elusive, complex, and multifaceted construct. As such, wisdom poses unequivocal challenges for those interested in its measurement. First and foremost, a theory describing wisdom and its observable manifestations is a necessary step toward any explicit measurement, as the measures need to be based on some theory as to what it is that is to be measured. Second, researchers need to develop appropriate tasks to elicit behaviors indicative of wisdom. Third, a set of criteria for evaluating performance on the tasks is needed to obtain a valid and reliable assessment of wise people.

Researchers have made serious attempts to overcome these hurdles and design various measures of wisdom. Such measures can be valuable tools in operationalizing the meaning of wisdom, of how it develops, and of how it can be enhanced. Moreover, such measures of wisdom can be used to study constructs that reflect its ontogenesis, and the consequences of wisdom and individual differences associated with being wise.

Several assessments of wisdom have been proposed in the literature: the Berlin Paradigm (e.g., Baltes & Smith, 1990, 2008; Baltes & Staudinger, 2000; Kunzmann & Baltes, 2005; Staudinger & Leipold, 2002), the Three-Dimensional Wisdom Scale (Ardelt, 2003), the Self-Assessed Wisdom Scale (Webster, 2003, 2007), the Practical Wisdom Scale and the Transcendent Wisdom Ratings (Wink & Helson, 1997), the Foundational Value Scale (Jason et al., 2001), and the Wisdom Development Scale (Brown & Greene, 2006). The assessments differ in their underlying conceptualization of wisdom, the ways in which these definitions were operationalized, the ways in which responses are obtained, the methods used for determining scores, and the psychometric rigor of the assessments that have been done of the measures. We review the measures, the assessments of the measures, and the main findings of studies using the measures. Other studies involving measurement of implicit theories of wisdom were discussed earlier in this chapter.

Similar to other theorists, Wink and Helson (1997) differentiated between practical and theoretical or transcendent wisdom (based on the work of Achenbaum & Orwoll, 1991). Practical wisdom involves practical knowledge and good judgment about life's issues, whereas transcendent wisdom involves more contemplative, spiritual, and emancipatory knowledge. Although both types of wisdom are related to personality and cognitive development, the authors hypothesized that practical wisdom would be more strongly associated with interpersonal aspects of development, whereas transcendent wisdom would be more strongly associated with transpersonal aspects, such as recognition of one's limits and self-transcendence. Different instruments were used to measure each type of wisdom. Practical wisdom was measured by a scale consisting of adjectives, taken from the Adjective Check List (Gough & Heilbrun, 1983), describing a wise person. Transcendent wisdom was measured by analyzing participant-provided examples of personally meaningful wisdom. These measures of practical and transcendent wisdom were administered to participants in a longitudinal study, together with demographic surveys and multiple personality and cognitive assessments. The research goal was to study the connection between the two types of wisdom and an array of personality correlates and life-satisfaction measures. People who scored high on both wisdom scales were "cognitively complex, perceptive, insightful, and healthily

self-directed." As expected, practical wisdom and transcendent wisdom were exclusively associated with interpersonal and transcendental constructs, respectively.

Jason et al. (2001) developed their scale based on a study of implicit theories of wisdom. They asked participants to name the wisest person they know, describe this person's qualities, provide demographic information about that wise person, and give an example of that person's wisdom and how it relates to the participant. The themes that emerged (motivation, insight, love, intellect, and practical skills), together with ideas from the spirituality literature, were used to construct the Foundational Value Scale. This instrument measures people's conceptions of wisdom, based on 38 wisdom-related qualities. Participants used a Likert-type scale to rate how well each quality describes a wise person. In addition, participants completed assessments of depression, stress, life orientation, social support, and social desirability. For the most part, the Foundational Value Scale did not correlate with those additional measures, thus supporting its divergent validity. A factor analysis of participants' responses uncovered five dimensions of wisdom: *harmony, warmth, intelligence, connection to nature*, and *spirituality*. Perry et al. (2002) adapted the Foundational Value Scale to examine its associations with adolescent substance abuse and other problematic behaviors. The revised instrument, named the Adolescent Wisdom Scale, significantly correlated with desirable behaviors, though not after controlling for other known risk factors (e.g., peer influence, low self-efficacy, and access to alcohol).

Webster (2003, 2007) developed the Self-Assessed Wisdom Scale, which measures five interrelated dimensions that he views as necessary, but not sufficient, for wisdom: *critical life experience, emotional regulation, reminiscence* and *reflectiveness, openness*, and *humor*. These dimensions, apart from humor, were discussed earlier in the chapter. Humor is considered a mature defense mechanism, associated with wisdom, which is also used to enhance experiences and interpersonal relations (Frecknall, 1994; Vaillant, 1977). Webster's assessment consists of self-report items with a Likert-type scale. Webster (2007) has given some evidence for the scale's reliability and construct validity. The scale correlates positively with measures of generativity and ego integrity, and negatively with attachment avoidance.

Brown and Greene (2006) created the Wisdom Development Scale based on Brown's (2004) model of wisdom as a construct subsuming integrated learning outcomes. Brown studied the development of wisdom in college students by looking at different aspects of their "learning-from-life" process and the conditions that facilitate it. Brown's model, based on both implicit and explicit theories of wisdom, consists of six dimensions: *self-knowledge, interpersonal understanding, judgment, life knowledge, life skills,* and *willingness to learn.* The Wisdom Development Scale consists of 141 self-report, Likert-type items. Brown and Greene (2006) discussed exploratory and confirmatory factor analyses of the scale. The results supported the first five dimensions in the model, and indicated that interpersonal understanding involves both altruism and inspirational engagement; life skills also involve emotional management. The authors suggested that the scale could be potentially useful for higher education purposes.

Ardelt's (2003, 2004) research deals with the role of wisdom in late adulthood, including its antecedents and consequences. Her 3-Dimensional Wisdom Scale is based on Clayton and Birren's (1980) and Ardelt's (1997) view of wisdom as an "integration of cognitive, reflective, and affective dimensions." The questionnaire contains 39 self-report, Likert-type items that target these dimensions (Ardelt's scale can be accessed online at: http://www.nytimes.com/ref/magazine/20070430_WISDOM.html). Cognitive items tap the disposition and ability to understand life thoroughly, knowledge of positive and negative aspects of human nature, awareness of life's ambiguities, and the ability to make decisions under uncertainty. Reflective items tap the disposition and ability to consider situations from multiple perspectives, and the absence of subjective tendencies and projections. Affective items tap the existence of positive emotions and behaviors toward others, and the lack of negative or indifferent emotions and behaviors toward others. Ardelt (2003) has shown that the scale has significant positive correlations with various measures of well-being, and significant negative correlations with measures of depression, stress, and avoidance. Moreover, those who score high on the scale are more likely to be rated as wise by their peers. Based on these findings, she concluded that cognitive, reflective, and affective qualities are both necessary and sufficient for a person to be considered wise.

The most comprehensive effort to objectively measure wisdom has been made by the Berlin group. As mentioned earlier, their research focused on positive aspects of late adult development, specifically, the exceptional ability to apply one's knowledge to the fundamental pragmatics of life. Their view is that wisdom, as an integration of multiple aspects of human development, can be seen as expert-like performance in response to specific situations

(e.g., those involving planning, reviewing, or management of life). Baltes and his colleagues' main interest was to develop a standardized task that would allow a comparison of responses obtained by different individuals or by the same individual at different times.

Unlike the measurement approaches described earlier, participants in the Berlin paradigm are not asked to report on how they typically behave in certain situations. Instead, the paradigm is based on a maximal-performance approach, similar to that of ability tests, where participants are required to "do their best" by attempting to solve challenging problems. Generally, Baltes and his colleagues studied wisdom using short hypothetical vignettes about complicated life matters, to which participants were asked to answer while thinking aloud (e.g., Maercker, 1992; Smith, 1998; Staudinger, Smith, & Baltes, 1992). For example, participants were asked to respond to the following prompt: "A fourteen-year-old girl is pregnant. What should she consider and do?" or "A fifteen-year-old girl wants to marry soon. What should one consider and do?"

The quality of participants' answers was usually judged by two groups of raters using different wisdom scales (although both used a seven-point scoring system). One group gave an overall wisdom score by answering, "How wise is this response?" whereas the other group rated responses separately on each of the five criteria suggested by the Berlin group (i.e., rich factual knowledge, rich procedural knowledge, life-span contextualism, relativism, and uncertainty). The ratings from both groups were compared to support the validity of this measurement. Overall, an expert answer should reflect more components of wisdom, by exhibiting practical expert knowledge about important matters of life (i.e., high ratings on all five scoring criteria). Since the 1980s, the Berlin paradigm, and its different variations, have been repeatedly shown to be reliable, valid, and useful (see Baltes & Kunzmann, 2004; Baltes & Smith, 2008; Baltes & Staudinger, 2000; Smith & Baltes, 1990; Smith, Staudinger, & Baltes, 1994, for reviews). The Berlin paradigm has been used to study wisdom with respect to many of its components, antecedents, correlates, and consequences. We describe some of their main results here, and discuss findings on wisdom and late adult development in the Development of Wisdom section.

Staudinger et al. (1997) found that measures of intelligence and personality, as well as their interface, overlap with, but are not identical to, measures of wisdom in terms of constructs measured. They concluded that wisdom may be a construct in its own right, measuring an important quality, different from what has been measured thus far by psychologists. Wisdom scores were correlated with scores on measures of fluid and crystallized intelligence, and with personality measures of psychological-mindedness (sagacity) and openness to experience. The personality-intelligence interface measures were most strongly associated with wisdom. Specifically, wisdom-related performance was highly correlated with measures of creativity and cognitive styles (e.g., judicial style, progressive style; see Sternberg, 1996). Other studies have shown the validity of wisdom as a psychological construct (for reviews, see Baltes & Smith, 2008; Baltes & Staudinger, 2000). For example, higher levels of wisdom-related knowledge were found more frequently in people nominated as wise compared with an old control group. In addition, people nominated as wise were more likely than control subjects to be within the highest scoring group for wisdom-related knowledge (Baltes, Staudinger, Maercker, & Smith, 1995). In addition, those who score high on the Berlin paradigm are more adaptive and display more healthy behaviors related to conflict resolution (Kunzmann & Baltes, 2003).

Although wisdom nominees tend to be middle-aged adults, contrary to common belief, age during adulthood was not found to be associated with wise performance on the Berlin paradigm (we discuss this further in the next section). Simply being old does not guarantee that one possesses wisdom-related knowledge or the capability to make wise decisions (Smith & Baltes, 1990; Staudinger, 1999). In fact, Pasupathi et al. (2001) have found evidence that wisdom-related knowledge and judgment capability is acquired relatively early in life, with few changes during most of adulthood (see also Richardson & Pasupathi, 2005). Nevertheless, the "age-match effect" does seem to play a role in the Berlin paradigm. When the task matches the age of the respondent, people tend to perform better in life-planning and life-review situations (see Smith & Baltes, 1990; Smith et al., 1994; Staudinger, 1989, 1999; Staudinger et al., 1992).

Baltes and Staudinger (2000) summarized findings from multiple studies, showing that predictive correlates for performance on their wisdom paradigm consist of personality traits, intelligence, the intelligence-personality interface, and life experiences. Generally speaking, personality factors are more strongly correlated with wisdom than intelligence factors. The best predictors of wisdom, however, are factors that involve the intelligence-personality interface (e.g., social-cognitive characteristics such as social intelligence, openness to experience, creativity) and life experience (e.g., presence of wise role models, professional experience). The two strongest predictors explain

about 30% of the variation in wisdom-related performance (see also Staudinger, Maciel, Smith, & Baltes, 1998). Age is generally not a significant predictor of wisdom. Baltes and Staudinger (2000) concluded that wisdom is "not simply another variant of intelligence or personality. Rather, wisdom implies a coordinating configuration of multiple attributes, including knowledge associated with specific life experiences. The outcome is the orchestration of mind and virtue toward excellence" (Baltes & Staudinger, 2000, p. 129).

Kunzmann and Baltes (2005) argued that wisdom develops through "a complex coalition of expertise-enhancing factors" (p. 122). Most importantly, the development of wisdom is seen through the infusion of social factors, such as social dispositions (e.g., openness to experience) and wisdom-facilitative experiences (e.g., the presence of wise role models; see Maercker, Böhmig-Krumhaar, & Staudinger, 1998; Smith & Baltes, 1993; Staudinger et al., 1998). Some studies have shown that people in certain professions (e.g., psychologists, human-services professionals) generally score about the same on wisdom assessments, regardless of age. However, they tend to score higher than people who are not in those professions. Thus, the professional training and practice seem to offer some advantage to those individuals in attaining wisdom (Smith & Baltes, 1990; Smith et al., 1994; Staudinger et al., 1992). Baltes and his colleagues examined whether the clinical psychologists who scored higher than nonpsychologists also share other characteristics related to their "constellation of mind and virtue." They discovered that profession was the most important factor in the model, followed by personality traits and, to a much lesser extent, intelligence (Staudinger et al., 1998). Thus, some life choices (education, career), coupled with certain personal characteristics (e.g., high openness to experience), seem to be facilitative for wisdom development.

Baltes and Staudinger (1996) found interesting evidence for the reflective nature of wisdom (see also Staudinger, 1996). Responses given by participants who completed the task alone were evaluated as less wise than those given by participants who either discussed the task with someone else or were instructed to consult their "inner voice" before completing the task. Intervention studies also showed that participants can exhibit higher levels of wisdom by following knowledge-search strategies or by being exposed to a broader context (Böhmig-Krumhaar, Staudinger, & Baltes, 2002; Staudinger & Baltes, 1996; but see also Glück & Baltes, 2006). These findings suggest not only that people probably have a greater potential than their regular performance suggests, but also that wisdom can be developed and enhanced through cognitive and emotional regulation.

Recent work by the Berlin group has emphasized social and emotional-motivational aspects of wisdom (Baltes, Glück, & Kunzmann, 2002; Kunzmann & Baltes, 2005; Stange, 2005; Staudinger, 2008). Their views of wisdom suggest that its holistic nature will help people take a broader, more relativistic perspective on life's challenges, thus exhibiting a less emotionally labile attitude. At the same time, wise people have a deep understanding of the meaning of life's events, and so they are expected to display strong empathy toward those in dire situations. Kunzmann and Baltes (2003) found that wise people's values were enhancing of both others and self; they oriented toward insightful and positive growth for themselves, others, and the environment. Wiser people exhibited more cooperative attitudes toward the resolution of social conflicts, and reported less self-centered, pleasant emotions. Generally, possessing wisdom-related knowledge was negatively correlated with hedonistic values. Finally, the authors showed that, after controlling for age, the association between wisdom and affective experience became nonsignificant. Similarly, the relation between wisdom and other-enhancing values (well-being of friends, societal engagement, and ecological protection) is related to age. With age, people hold more other-enhancing values, which constitute an important feature of wisdom development.

Building on the wisdom and late adult development literature, Mickler and Staudinger (2007; cited in Staudinger, 2008) expanded the Berlin paradigm to include social, emotional, and motivational aspects of wisdom (see also Staudinger et al., 2005; Staudinger, Kessler & Dörner, 2006). Their model consists of five criteria to measure personal wisdom: (1) *rich self-knowledge,* a deep insight into one's life, competencies, emotions, and goals; (2) *available heuristics for growth and self-regulation,* effective strategies to regulate emotions and social situations (e.g., through humor); (3) *interrelating the self,* a reflective understanding and insightful awareness of human nature; (4) *self-relativism,* the ability to evaluate oneself and others objectively, critically, and sympathetically; and (5) *tolerance of ambiguity,* the ability to identify and respond to life's uncertainties (e.g., openness to experience, trust). This new measure of personal wisdom showed good convergent and discriminant validity; out of the Big Five personality measures, only openness to experience had a strong association with personal wisdom. Similarly, Stange (2005) found that, within the context of advice giving,

nonverbal and social behaviors (e.g., attentiveness, empathy, and tempered concern) were associated with people's wisdom.

In conclusion, the main distinction between approaches taken to measure wisdom is the type of task to which people respond. Baltes and his colleagues used hypothetical scenarios requiring one to judge wisely in giving advice to others in difficult matters of life. Thus, they measured wisdom-related performance in solving problems removed from one's own life. The other approach, for example, Ardelt (2003), is based on people's self-report of how they typically think, feel, and act in situations from their own life. Both methods have disadvantages, as performance on such assessments is always affected by the quality of the instrument, the objectivity of the scoring system, and the presence of intervening variables, biases, and contexts. Nevertheless, these studies produced a wealth of knowledge about the nature of wisdom and how to identify, describe, and quantify it. Studies using measurement methodologies enable us to discuss wisdom in concrete terms, and empirically to examine its relation to other individual and environmental factors.

Summary of Psychological Research on the Meaning of Wisdom

Although there are many different psychological approaches to the study of wisdom, they seem to converge on six attributes of wisdom. First, wisdom is a relatively rare and unique human ability, related to, yet distinct from, other psychological constructs. Second, wisdom is associated with positive aspects of one's life and development. Third, wisdom is seen as an integration of advanced cognitive, affective, motivational, and social aspects of life. Wisdom can be seen as an integration or a balance of different mental and emotional qualities, human relations, and interests, types of knowledge, and time frames. Fourth, wisdom develops throughout life. By attempting to improve ourselves, we can strengthen certain qualities that would enhance our level of wisdom. Fifth, wisdom is seen as occurring in thought and deed, not solely in thought. Wisdom is at least as much about what one does as it is about what one thinks or feels. Sixth, wisdom is represented by the effective application of skills and knowledge toward a common good.

In his dissertation, Trowbridge (2005) discussed many qualities of wisdom that emerge from psychological research and that we have covered in this section as well: *good judgment, reflectivity, insight, intuition, relativistic/dialectical and critical thinking, ability to deal with complex problems, intelligence, deep general knowledge, creativity, experience, virtuous character, self-control, autonomy, self-knowledge, decentering, knowledge of limits, humility, openness, comfort with uncertainty, social skills, benevolence, empathy, compassion, generativity, humor,* and *serenity.* Some of these different facets of wisdom have been recognized almost since the dawn of civilizations, whereas others represent more modern conceptualizations of wisdom. Nevertheless, the research shows that wisdom permeates multiple desirable aspects of our lives.

Psychologists have developed models to represent the meaning of wisdom and to describe it concretely. However, we ended up with so many terms, connections, and perspectives, that for some, the concept may now seem even vaguer than before. Thus, attempts to summarize wisdom in simple axiomatic truths are bound to fail to capture its multifaceted nature, whereas attempts to delineate what wisdom encompasses fail to capture its singular nature.

As people move through the stages of life, their personal development, infused with experiences, knowledge, and social interactions, helps them form a meaning of wisdom unique to their own lives. The next section presents psychological research aimed at studying how wisdom develops throughout the life span.

DEVELOPMENT OF WISDOM

Life's tragedy is that we get old too soon and wise too late.

—*Benjamin Franklin*

Wisdom and Late Adult Development

Relation between Wisdom and Age

The common belief about the inevitable connection between wisdom and late adulthood began with ancient societies, continued with thinkers of the world's wisdom literature, and lasts to this very day. Traditional societies gave respect to their elders, whose wisdom assured a successful continuity of past experiences to future generations (Assmann, 1994; Kekes, 1983). Most researchers also believe that wisdom, as a proxy for good life, can be a positive outcome of late adulthood (e.g., Baltes et al., 2002; Birren & Fisher, 1990; Jordan, 2005; Kramer, 2000; Kunzmann & Baltes, 2003; Taranto, 1989). However, many studies have shown that wisdom is not correlated with age, at least during adulthood and late adulthood

(e.g., Baltes & Staudinger, 2000; Brugman, 2006; Jordan, 2005; Staudinger, 1999). For example, Smith and Baltes (1990) have found that both older and younger adults are equally likely to be among the top scorers on wisdom-related knowledge. Generally, the younger adults scored higher than middle-aged and older adults, although this pattern was not statistically significant and completely disappeared when the problem included a non-normative situation encountered by an older person.

Brugman (2000), after reviewing empirical studies regarding the development of wisdom, concluded that wisdom does not, on average, increase in later life. Ironically, he noted that "one needs to be old and wise to see that wisdom does not come with age" (p. 115). Baltes and Staudinger (2000) concluded that wisdom is best predicted by factors related to the intelligence-personality interface and life experience, rather than by age. In most studies conducted thus far, age was not found to be a significant predictor of wisdom. Similarly, others have claimed that whereas adolescents and young adults show increases in wisdom (Anderson, 1998; Pasupathi et al., 2001; Richardson & Pasupathi, 2005), adults after the age of 25 rarely do. Although these findings seem to contradict the "older and wiser" belief, one must consider the context in which this belief was first created. As a result of the increase in life expectancy, the chronological age that was considered old in previous centuries is equivalent to what may be considered today as midlife. Thus, the prototypical age for wisdom may not have changed at all, only how we define that age in terms of life's stages. This might be one reason why age is not positively correlated with wisdom during adult life, at least according to these studies.

Yet, other studies suggest a more complex relation between age and wisdom. For example, Takahashi and Overton (2002, 2005) found that older adults scored higher than younger adults on their assessment of wisdom. In a longitudinal study, Wink and Helson (1997) found that practical wisdom tended to increase during adult life. Similarly, other researchers report age-related increases in different components of wisdom, such as openness to experience (Labouvie-Vief, DeVoe, & Bulka, 1989), reflective judgment (Kitchener & Brenner, 1990; Kitchener, Lynch, Fischer, & Wood, 1993), dialectical thinking (Basseches, 1984a), and social reasoning (e.g., Happé, Winner, & Brownell, 1998). Ardelt (2008) found evidence that wisdom might increase with age for people who are motivated and able to pursue it. She concluded that "the relation between wisdom and age is *potentially* positive as long as the individual remains willing (and able) to learn from experiences and to engage in self-reflection and self-examination" (Ardelt, 2008, p. 96). However, because studies use different measures of wisdom, it is possible that age-related findings depend on how wisdom is defined and operationalized.

Sternberg (2005b) concluded that age, in and of itself, is not a valid variable for indexing the development of wisdom; it is an "empty" variable that may distract us from understanding the mechanisms involved in the development and decline of wisdom. It is better to view age as a proxy for other characteristics related to wisdom, such as personal growth, accumulated knowledge, openness to experience, and ability to learn from experience. As people age, they accrue valuable knowledge pertaining to cognitive, affective, and social aspects of the human experience. This knowledge can be used to foster development but can also be used ineffectively or destructively, or it can be completely ignored. Thus, the accumulation of experience through one's increasing age does not automatically lead to the attainment of wisdom. Rather, one's ability to reflectively utilize experiences toward personal and social growth is what determines whether and how wisdom develops. Nevertheless, most researchers agree that age-related aspects of wisdom are both important and relevant for current life. The next section explains why it is important to study wisdom with respect to late adult development, discusses the challenges involved in such studies, describes developmental aspects of wisdom, and presents the main findings about wisdom at specific stages of life.

Promises and Challenges

During the last century, the average life expectancy throughout much of the world rose dramatically, thanks to advances in health care, nutrition, and medicine (Riley, 2001). Jordan (2005) noted that, by 2020, about 23% of the North American population will be older than 65 years of age. These days, more individuals than ever before experience late adulthood, and this period of late adulthood lasts longer too. However, Baltes and Smith (2008) noted, "Neither societies nor individuals have the necessary theoretical and practical knowledge that would assist them to anticipate and master the uncertainties of this life period" (p. 63). In other words, the increase in average life expectancy was not paralleled by a rise in people's possession and use of wisdom.

One reason why wisdom research is promising is because it illuminates the potential benefits of late adulthood, and offers hope and vitality to people in a challenging period of physical and mental decline. It is crucial to investigate ways to help this segment of our population

age well, and the study of wisdom seems to be one useful way to do so (Ardelt, 2000a, 2000b; Baltes & Smith, 2008; Jordan, 2005). The revived research on wisdom is largely motivated by a pressing interest in gerontology—the multidisciplinary study of social, psychological, and biological aspects of late adult development (Ardelt, 2003; Baltes, 2000). Wisdom research can provide practical insights to this field concerning factors and strategies that can lead to optimal levels of human development, a desired goal for the older adult. Moreover, given that wisdom can be so beneficial, it now becomes important to study the facilitative circumstances of wisdom in early life. This study will help reveal factors that may enable us to foster wisdom sooner and maintain it longer throughout life. Indeed, current perspectives emphasize the development of wisdom in adolescence (e.g., Pasupathi et al., 2001) and the importance of teaching wisdom in schools (e.g., Sternberg, 2001; Sternberg, Reznitskaya, & Jarvin, 2007).

Still, studying the connection between wisdom and late adult development comes with major challenges. For example, different researchers have different conceptualizations of what wisdom is and how it should be measured, leading to great difficulties in synthesizing findings across multiple studies. Another major challenge stems from the common knowledge, shared by researchers and laypeople alike, that wisdom is a rare attribute (Clayton & Birren, 1980; Jordan, 2005; Smith & Baltes, 1990). Thus, not only do researchers attempt to study a hard-to-define, multifaceted, and complex phenomenon; it is also quite difficult to find people who possess wisdom in significant measure! Contributing to this situation is the fact that many psychological and philosophical perspectives describe wisdom in utopian, almost superhuman terms, making it practically impossible for people to achieve high levels on wisdom-related assessments.

Another major challenge is that wisdom is not all or nothing: People cannot simply be categorized as wise or foolish; rather, they exhibit varying levels of wisdom over time. Wisdom can develop throughout life, and is highly dependent on life's contexts and experiences. Therefore, the study of wisdom must consider its trajectory over the life span. However, there is a dearth of longitudinal studies about wisdom. Brugman (2006) and others have noted that most research on wisdom is cross sectional (comparing different age cohorts at the same point in time) rather than sequential (comparing the same cohort during different points in time). Unfortunately, cross-sectional differences probably do not reflect different stages in the developmental trajectory of wisdom (Baltes & Smith, 2008). Rather, findings are likely to be biased by period and cohort effects. For example, it is possible that differences with respect to wisdom-related knowledge are due to differences between cohorts in their level of familiarity with, access to, and use of information in the modern technological age (Brugman, 2006). Similarly, Sternberg (2004) points to the existence of cohort effects in intelligence tests (e.g., Flynn, 1987) and suggests that we could expect similar trends in wisdom measures. Another shortcoming of cross-sectional studies is that if some people gain wisdom with age, whereas others lose wisdom, the net result would seem to suggest that wisdom is not related to age, *on average* (Ardelt, 2008; Sternberg, 2005b). Given that people may vary in their trajectories of wisdom, this caveat of cross-sectional studies seems to be quite problematic. Differences in cohorts in wisdom may reflect cohort rather than developmental effects. For example, the Flynn effect (Flynn, 1987) refers to increases in intelligence, and especially fluid intelligence, over secular time. Alleged decreases in wisdom over time may reflect the higher fluid intelligence later generations bring to the table. In other words, the findings may be artifactual, reflecting a Flynn effect for wisdom whereby the higher scores of younger generations are similar to their higher scores on measures of fluid intelligence, reflecting unknown factors in the environment that promote wisdom more in the present than they did in the past.

Furthermore, some wisdom-related knowledge is primarily age specific. For example, adolescents are more likely to be familiar with multiple perspectives and deeper contextual meanings of problems that relate to their lives at present, as opposed to adult life in general, and vice versa, thus causing age differences in wisdom-related performance. Generally speaking, when using a scenario-based wisdom assessment like those assessments of the Berlin paradigm, participants perform better when their ages roughly match the ages of the main character in the wisdom assessment (the "age-match effect," see Smith et al., 1994).

The few longitudinal studies that do exist show evidence for increased levels of practical wisdom with age (Wink & Helson, 1997) and positive effects on life-satisfaction beyond environmental contexts (e.g., Ardelt, 1997, 2000a). Other studies show connections between the development of wisdom and creativity throughout life, and that particular career choices (spiritual or psychotherapeutic) are strong predictors of wisdom later in life (Helson & Srivastava, 2002). However, current longitudinal studies suffer from some methodological shortcomings. For example, because wisdom research is a relatively new

field in psychology, and because the development of a valid and reliable theory-based measurement framework takes quite a bit of time, some of these studies use existing data collected under different research goals and with nonrepresentative samples. More tightly controlled longitudinal studies are needed to answer the basic questions about how wisdom develops within individuals over time.

Finally, because the development of wisdom is highly dependent on life's contexts and experiences, great individual differences exist in terms of the age, and the rate, at which wisdom develops. For example, some young people may become wise beyond their years as they face difficult circumstances early in their life (e.g., death of a friend, parents' separation) and attempt to cope in a healthy and successful way (Bluck & Glück, 2004; Glück et al., 2005; Kinnier, Tribbensee, Rose, & Vaughan, 2001). Similarly, wisdom-facilitative life experiences such as certain types of professional training are associated with higher levels of wisdom performance (e.g., Staudinger et al., 1998). Consequently, age-related findings about wisdom can be strongly influenced by the particular life experiences of individuals in the sample.

Trajectories of Wisdom

Technically speaking, there is no one trajectory of wisdom with age; rather, individuals differ in their paths to wisdom (see also Baltes, 2004; Jordan, 2005; Sternberg, 2005b). We discuss several generalized views of the relation of wisdom and age that help position findings within larger frameworks. However, we caution the reader that most findings on the topic are based on cross-sectional studies that are ultimately unable to answer the question in full.

"Received" View of Wisdom

The first view is the positive outlook implicitly held by most people, namely, that wisdom increases monotonically with age; it is never lost, only gained with time (e.g., Denny et al., 1995; Hendrick, Knox, Gekoski, & Dyne, 1988; see also the section on implicit theories in this chapter). People are generally expected to use more common sense and make wiser decisions as they grow. Thus, although late adulthood may bring with it physical decline, it also brings with it a sort of spiritual awakening that enables one to become wise. There is mixed evidence to support this view. For example, Birren and Fisher (1990) concluded that "wisdom tends to increase with experience and therefore age but is not exclusively found in…[older adults]" (p. 326). As mentioned earlier, some studies showed that specific aspects of wisdom may increase with age, such as practical wisdom, emotional empathy, reflective judgment, and openness to experience (e.g., see Blanchard-Fields, 1986; Carstensen, 1995; Kitchener et al., 1993; Labouvie-Vief et al., 1989; Takahashi & Overton, 2002, 2005; Wink & Helson, 1997).

In an extensive narrative analysis, Pennebaker and Stone (2003) found that, with increasing age, people use more language typical of different aspects of wisdom, for example, increased cognitive complexity and positive affect, and reduced egocentrism. Other narrative studies have found that older people associate wisdom with increased knowledge, experience, compassion, guidance, moral motivation, reflective apprehension of actions, and effective and creative problem-solving strategies (Montgomery et al., 2002; Sowarka, 1989). These findings suggest that people do exhibit components of wisdom in their thoughts and self-descriptions, and that these tendencies increase and develop over time. Ardelt (2008) has argued that such studies show that wisdom has the potential to increase with age. She distinguished wisdom from intellectual knowledge; the latter tends to increase with age as people learn and experience more, but is likely to decline in late adulthood because of physical/mental decline or becoming outdated (see also Baltes et al., 1995; Clayton, 1982; Moody, 1986). Intellectual knowledge is useful and important in life but not sufficient to become personally and globally wise (Baltes & Staudinger, 2000; Kramer, 2000; Kunzmann & Baltes, 2005; Kupperman, 2005; Sternberg, 1998). Wisdom, in contrast, "requires motivation, determination, self-examination, self-reflection, and an openness to all kinds of experiences to do the necessary inner work that the development of wisdom demands" (Ardelt, 2008, p. 98).

This argument seems to suggest, again, that the development of wisdom is contingent on having high levels of specific cognitive, affective, and conative characteristics; without them, wisdom will not be achieved. Not only are some of these qualities rare (e.g., dialectical thinking; Kramer, 1990), the full coalition of mind and virtue is indeed exceptional. Although many aspects of wisdom are positively correlated with age, a specific individual may have only some of those characteristics, but likely not enough actually to become wise when he or she is older. Consequently, being older does not necessarily mean one will perform better on a wisdom assessment. Thus, on this view, we can conclude that currently, for most people, wisdom does not seem to increase automatically with age, although it well may.

"Declining" View of Wisdom

The second view pessimistically suggests that, starting in early life, wisdom generally decreases with age (Meacham, 1983, 1990). Meacham believes that individuals can be characterized by the ratio between what they know and their knowledge of what they do not know. A child may know little compared with an adult, but if the child is aware of how much else there is to know, he or she is relatively wise compared with adults who think they know almost everything. Thus, wisdom lies in the right balance between certainty and doubt; being close to either extreme goes against the fundamentals of wisdom. Meacham suggested that, with life experience, people gain great amounts of knowledge, which causes them to be too confident that they know everything, which, in turn, drives them further from wisdom. Alternatively, tragic events and increased uncertainty in life may cause some to become much less confident in themselves, again, leading them further from wisdom. Thus, Meacham argues provocatively that wisdom decreases with age (at least with respect to the ratio between knowledge and doubt). Children are wise because of their sensitivity to their own lack of knowledge, and as this sensitivity decreases, either extreme certainty or uncertainty emerges in adulthood, thus diminishing one's wisdom. Those few people who exhibit wisdom in late adulthood were simply able to maintain their level of wisdom from childhood. Meacham's (1990) model of wisdom is a two-dimensional model. The first dimension, which we have described, is the attitude toward wisdom (knowledge vs. doubt) that generally decreases with time. However, people can attain the right attitude toward knowledge at any age; therefore, this dimension is relatively age independent. The second dimension, which reflects the quality of wisdom (simple vs. profound), is age dependent because it depends on accumulation of information, experiences, and insights.

Although no direct empirical evidence supports the declining view, per se, several findings add to its viability. First, as discussed earlier, many of the research findings support the view of an age-independent dimension of wisdom. Second, some studies support the view that the "seeds of wisdom" can be found in earlier ages (e.g., Pasupathi et al., 2001). Third, there is empirical evidence that wisdom decreases in very late adulthood, probably because of declines in physical health, and thus brain functioning (e.g., for many people older than 75 years; see Baltes & Staudinger, 2000).

Another issue related to this view is that the rapid technological and social changes in the world have made some of the knowledge and value systems of older generations, on the one hand, rather outdated or even possibly irrelevant (Birren & Svensson, 2005). On the other hand, the wisdom-facilitative conditions of children who are born today include experiences that are increasingly high-tech and multimedium based. Currently, a wealth of information, good or bad, is literally at one's fingertips; wisdom-related knowledge can be found on the Web in the form of strategies to deal with the uncertainties of life, and reciprocal thoughts and deeds, such as humanistic, interdisciplinary, or globally-oriented actions. Thus, the knowledge and experience these children gain in their lifetime is significantly more relevant for today and tomorrow than the knowledge possessed, for instance, by their grandparents. In other words, wisdom declines because the value of the knowledge one possesses can change over time.

The rate of change perhaps was slower in previous centuries and may still be slower in some places than in the Western world (see also Brugman, 2006; Sternberg, 2005b). When the world in which one grows to become an older adult is pretty much the same as the world in which one first became an older adult, the wisdom one accumulated might be beneficial. But in current times of rapid change, one's wisdom may become irrelevant, applying to a world that no longer exists. For example, in a study comparing wisdom performance among adolescents and young adults, Pasupathi et al. (2001) found that adolescents performed similarly regardless of the problem's age context (i.e., involving either adolescence or adult issues). On the contrary, young adults performed worse on the adolescence-related problems. The authors suggest that early in adulthood, people begin to lose some of their expert knowledge about issues relevant to adolescence. It may be the case that, in rapidly changing societies, the experience of the older adult actually is worth less, and hence they are valued less (Csikszentmihalyi & Nakamura, 2005; Willis & Dubin, 1990). Thus, as the children of today become older adults, their knowledge, too, may become outdated, unless they know how to sustain or even increase it throughout their life span.

Another way to understand the "declining" view is to think of wisdom as a time-based potential we all possess at birth. When born, we are given a certain amount of time on this planet, time we can use to gain experiences and apply the knowledge we acquire from them into wise choices in the face of new experiences. Every minute that passes without our utilizing our experiences to gain and apply such wisdom is a minute lost to becoming wiser. Every time we miss an opportunity to transform experiences into wisdom, our potential for wisdom decreases. Thus, as we grow older, we have fewer opportunities to become wise. Pessimistic as this view may seem, it may motivate people to seek out wisdom more actively. At the very least, people might find comfort in the fact that there currently is no direct evidence to support this view.

"Fluid" and "Crystallized" Views of Wisdom

The remaining views are based on the late adult developmental patterns related to two types of intelligence commonly discussed in the literature (Horn, 1994; Horn & Cattell, 1966; Schaie, 1996, and see Blair, Chapter 8 of this volume). Crystallized intelligence deals with the storage, access, and use of declarative knowledge such as vocabulary, arithmetic, and general information. This type of intelligence tends to increase with age, as we accumulate more knowledge and get better at retrieving it when needed. Fluid intelligence, in contrast, deals with the ability to think flexibly in novel ways to solve problems, such as through inference and analysis of relations (e.g., figural analogies). This type of intelligence tends to increase gradually during early life and stays relatively constant across adulthood, before it typically begins to decline in late life. The development of wisdom throughout life can be conceived as contingent on the trajectory of either fluid or crystallized intelligence, or some combination of both.

For instance, the "crystallized" view of wisdom proposes that wisdom begins to increase relatively early in life and then continues to increase into late adulthood, perhaps until 10 or so years before one's death, when disease processes or social conditions might impair its continued growth (see Baltes et al., 1995; Sternberg, 1998, 2005b). In a way, this view is very similar to the "received" view, only it puts the emphasis on one's intelligence rather than age. That is, on this view, those who do not actively develop their crystallized intelligence through the continuous acquisition of knowledge are not necessarily becoming any wiser, no matter how old they are.

Baltes and his colleagues have regarded wisdom-related knowledge as prototypical of crystallized intelligence rather than of fluid intelligence (Baltes, 1993; Baltes & Smith, 1990; Dittmann-Kohli & Baltes, 1990; Smith et al., 1989). This aspect of wisdom is considered as related to the cognitive pragmatics of the mind; the kind of information encompassed in human- and social-related knowledge that is passed along within and across cultures (Baltes & Staudinger, 1993). Within this framework, wisdom is believed to be relatively stable late into late adulthood. Indeed, Baltes and his group have found participants beyond

75 years of age to be among some of the top scorers in wisdom-related performance (e.g. Baltes et al., 1995; Smith & Baltes, 1990). There is also some empirical evidence from longitudinal work to support the "crystallized" point of view (Hartman, 2000; Wink & Helson, 1997).

The "fluid" perspective on wisdom, on the other hand, considers most relevant cognitive mechanics based on the mind's biological "hardware," which are expected to decline in late adulthood (Baltes, 1993; Baltes & Staudinger, 1993; Salthouse, 1991). According to this view, wisdom increases until early adulthood and then levels off for a period of time before it begins to decline in late middle age or early in late adulthood (see Jordan, 2005; McAdams & de St. Aubin, 1998; Sternberg, 2005b). The connection between fluid intelligence and wisdom can be related to the view that wisdom is connected to problem solving and requires rational inference based on relations between things. Thus, a wise person may rely on his or her fluid abilities when confronting novel and complex situations that call for a wise solution.

Current studies suggest that the development of wisdom is, in part, similar to that of fluid intelligence. Staudinger et al. (1998) have found that although fluid intelligence measures were negatively correlated with age (as expected), they were positively correlated with wisdom performance. Crystallized intelligence, however, was not significantly correlated with wisdom. The overall effect of intelligence in a model predicting wisdom was negligible. Some studies show that, up to about age 65, the improvement in crystallized intelligence is about the same in magnitude as the decline in fluid intelligence (e.g., see Papalia, Camp, & Feldman, 1996). In the Berlin model, the development of wisdom plateaus toward the end of the college years—in the early 20s. Most findings show that levels of wisdom are relatively stable across adulthood and begin to decline much later in life. Thus, the overall shape of wisdom's trajectory seems to be similar to that of fluid intelligence, but perhaps more long-lasting.

An integrated view of wisdom's trajectory considers both fluid and crystallized aspects (Baltes & Smith, 2008). Wisdom relies on fluid abilities but involves extensive access to and use of different kinds of knowledge. In the larger scheme of things, a wise culture is one that optimizes the transfer of knowledge to its people, and a wise person is one who makes the best use of that knowledge by making more productive decisions. The culture instills the declarative knowledge needed for wisdom relevant to life, and individuals are responsible for learning it and using it to better their lives and the lives of others. Thus, wisdom

as a human trait includes both knowledge and process, or both crystallized and fluid aspects (Birren & Svensson, 2005).

The integrated view makes wisdom's pattern of development more complex than that of either kind of intelligence individually. According to this view, intelligence will increase until somewhere in the middle or later part of the adult life span, but then, as fluid abilities start to decline, the increase in crystallized abilities may not be enough to offset the decline in fluid abilities (Sternberg, 2005b). So there will be decline somewhat earlier than the crystallized view alone would predict, but perhaps not as early or rapidly as the fluid view alone would predict. More specifically, as people age, some wisdom-related abilities decline, whereas others develop further. Individual characteristics (e.g., cognitive style, personality, behavior, life contexts) can help foster one's ability in areas beneficial for wisdom development (e.g., developing expertise). Thus, on average, all these factors would correlate well with wisdom across individuals. However, it is likely that for specific individuals, only a subset of these factors is actually "responsible" for their own development of wisdom. Figure 23.2 illustrates what the fluid and crystallized trajectories might look like. The integrated view would suggest a trajectory of wisdom that is somewhere between these two intelligence-based developmental paths, and possibly varies greatly from individual to individual. Thus, any cross-sectional findings are simply averages of many individual paths, and not necessarily the typical, or "true" trajectory of wisdom. Longitudinal studies might help shed more light on this question.

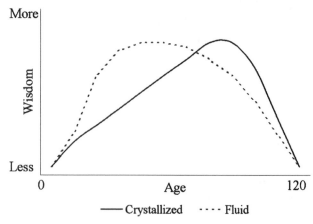

Figure 23.2   Illustration of fluid *(dashed line)* and crystallized *(solid line)* views of wisdom trajectory.

Trajectories Connected to Individual Differences in Wisdom

Trajectories of wisdom can be inspected with respect to the characteristics that make certain individuals score higher or lower on wisdom assessments. Current research on wisdom and late adult development emphasizes the individual differences related to the correlates, antecedents, and consequences of wisdom (Brugman, 2006; Sternberg & Jordan, 2005). Many studies measure wisdom in people from different age groups who share certain characteristics (e.g., knowledge, personal traits, education/profession). Essentially, such studies examine the relations between factors that help classify different "types" of paths to wisdom. For example, Ardelt (2008) reported findings that wisdom scores on her three-dimensional scale not significantly higher for older adults (around 70 years) compared with college students. However, older adults who had a college degree did score significantly higher than the students and were overrepresented in the group of top wisdom scores. Thus, increased wisdom with age might occur when people have the motivation and opportunity to pursue it, for example, through education or professional training.

Other studies examined other inner qualities that may explain wisdom-related differences. For example, Glück et al. (2005) analyzed wisdom narratives from people in different age groups. They identified three forms of wisdom present in their language. Across all participants, self-determination and assertion jointly were the most prevalent form, followed by empathy and support, and knowledge and flexibility (which were mentioned to about the same degree). However, each form of wisdom was more strongly associated with a specific age group: Adolescents most often mentioned empathy and support, and adults (of all ages) most often mentioned determination and assertion. Older adults also mentioned knowledge and flexibility. In a second study, however, empathy and support was found in more than 80% of the narratives across all age groups. These findings suggest that people may perceive some aspects of wisdom differently at various points along their life span, whereas other aspects stay constant (see also Pennebaker & Stone, 2003). The way people view wisdom depends on the historic and personal events they have encountered in their lifetime.

Other studies connect age differences in wisdom performance to different aspects of personality development. For example, Pasupathi and Staudinger (2001) found that wisdom and moral reasoning are positively correlated, just as wisdom correlates with other personal characteristics found before, such as creativity, cognitive styles, personality, and intellectual ability (Baltes & Staudinger, 2000; Staudinger et al., 1998). Among the top scorers for wisdom were many of the top moral reasoners, and almost none of the low moral reasoners. Thus, the authors concluded that, although association between wisdom and moral reasoning was mediated by personal characteristics, high levels of wisdom seem to require high levels of moral reasoning. The authors also found that wisdom generally did not correlate with age. However, for adults who performed at above-median levels on a task of moral reasoning, wisdom did increase with age. Thus, moral reasoning seems to be a moderator of the relation between wisdom and age. In addition, the adolescents' performance was also found to be more variable than the adults'. Staudinger and Pasupathi (2003) have found that the best predictors of wisdom-related performance for adolescents were constructs of intelligence (e.g., crystallized intelligence) and personality (e.g., openness to experience), whereas for adults, the best predictors were related to their interface (e.g., creativity). Thus, it seems that the basic psychological components are important in adolescence, but their synthesis seems more important in adulthood. The authors suggested that the kind of integration that would eventually lead to wisdom in adulthood "may require the basic structure provided by personality and intelligence" (p. 258).

Kunzmann and Baltes (2003) found an association between wisdom-related knowledge and values that promote insightful growth in self and others. Wisdom was also found to be related to a reduction in emotional experience (less negative *and* less positive emotions). The relation between wisdom and affective experience or other-enhancing values was found to be related to age. In other words, these values seem to emerge as people get older and gain more wisdom-related knowledge and experiences. Ardelt (2005) argued that by showing more compassion toward and understanding of others, people are more likely to feel satisfaction with life. Indeed, in samples from different age groups, wisdom was found to be associated with life satisfaction and subjective well-being (Ardelt, 2003; Brugman, 2000; Takahashi & Overton, 2002), regardless of contextual circumstances (Ardelt, 1997).

Wisdom at Different Stages of Life

We now describe studies of wisdom at specific stages of life. We discuss childhood and adolescence followed by adult life and late adulthood. These studies draw a more detailed picture of wisdom, with respect to specific characteristics of each life stage. Findings suggest that each stage is associated with different wisdom-related knowledge. Many studies compare multiple age groups, so each subsequent section contains findings that relate to all stages of life.

Childhood and Adolescence

In the tale "Little Girls Wiser than Men," Tolstoy (1885/2009) described how a minor quarrel between two young girls escalated and incited the whole village. As the adults in the village proceeded to fight each other, the young girls soon made up and were out playing again. The moral of the story is that adults can learn from the forgiveness, understanding, and friendship shown by children. Wisdom is so strongly associated with age in our collective conception that it seems counterintuitive to think about what form it takes in childhood. Wisdom represents a supreme functioning of the human mind and spirit, based on experience and knowledge; none of these is characteristic of young children, in particular. Yet, children possess some qualities that grownups may never have again. For example, children's simplified views of reality can be seen in their ability to say exactly what is on their mind. As children experience and learn from life, their personal characteristics evolve. This process is described in developmental theories that have been linked to the emergence of wisdom; for example, theorists built on Erikson's stages of psychosocial development (e.g., Orwoll & Perlmutter, 1990; Pascual-Leone, 1990; Ryff, 1995; Staudinger et al., 1997; Takahashi & Overton, 2002), Kohlberg's stages of moral development (e.g., Pasupathi & Staudinger, 2001; Sternberg, 2001), Loevinger's stages of ego development (e.g., Helson & Wink, 1987; Staudinger et al., 2005), and Piaget's theory of cognitive development (e.g., Labouvie-Vief, 1990; Pascual-Leone, 2000).

We know little about how wisdom is perceived or experienced in childhood. Most of the research suggests that antecedents and correlates of wisdom emerge in early years, but it does not directly assess children's wisdom. There is, however, some evidence that wisdom-related knowledge increases between adolescence and early adulthood (i.e., between ages 14 and 25; see Anderson, 1998; Pasupathi et al., 2001). Pasupathi and her colleagues compared adolescents and adults on the Berlin wisdom paradigm. Adolescents scored lower than did the young adults on all wisdom-related criteria but also showed major improvements with age. Pasupathi et al. concluded, "Adolescents are, like adults, not wise. Unlike adults, however, they are becoming wiser with advancing years, and understanding this process may teach us much about the origins of

wisdom" (p. 360). Indeed, youth seems to be the prime time for studying the development of wisdom, as it begins to stabilize in adulthood. Still, research on this life stage is quite sparse (Brugman, 2006; Lerner & Galambos, 1998; Takanishi & Hamburg, 1997).

Richardson and Pasupathi (2005) reviewed research related to the development of wisdom in youth. They concluded that there is not much direct evidence that this is a period of normative growth for wisdom, compared with the amount of indirect evidence about developing capacities that relate to wisdom in later life. The authors described a wide range of studies that show early-life development related to intelligence, personality, and their interface. For example, in adolescence, constructs involving cognitive and intellectual development undergo important changes. During these years, there are increases in the ability to think abstractly and reflectively, to process information from multiple points of view, to allocate attention, and to use different and more diverse strategies to understand and solve problems. In addition, adolescents exhibit increased breadth of knowledge and autobiographical experience, improved decision-making skills, and more awareness of uncertainty. All these characteristics can be seen as prerequisites for the development of wisdom (see also Brugman, 2006; Sternberg, 2005a).

Personality development during adolescence marks the emergence of personal characteristics found later in adulthood. As children develop their self-identity (e.g., Erikson & Erikson, 1997), they begin to commit to certain ideologies. Adolescents, with their increased capacities to think more broadly and abstractly, are capable of developing the moral principles and conduct typical of wisdom (see Damon, 2000; Kohlberg, 1973; Richardson & Pasupathi, 2005). Other wisdom-related qualities are known to develop in this stage of life. For example, adolescents experience increasing open-mindedness with age, until it stabilizes in early adulthood (e.g., Roberts & Caspi, 2003). Research on adolescence also supports age-related development of the ego, moving away from self-centered patterns toward more other-oriented patterns (e.g., Cohn, 1998). At the same time, all this positive growth can be offset by negative aspects of development associated with adolescence (e.g., anxiety, low self-esteem, peer pressure, risky behavior). Through this interplay of forces, adolescents may face the type of uncertain and fundamental situations that are seen as facilitative of wisdom. Thus, their experiences help shape their personalities and, ultimately, their wisdom.

Other lines of research have investigated how adolescents develop on constructs related to the intelligence-personality interface, such as integrated or transcendent thought related to social and moral reasoning, improved interpersonal skills, and increased comprehension of the "common good" (see Blanchard-Fields, 1986; Richardson & Pasupathi, 2005). Although the development of these wisdom-related constructs begins in adolescence, studies suggest that the emphasis in those years is on basic cognitive and personality factors, as opposed to their integration (Anderson, 1998; Pasupathi & Staudinger, 2001; Staudinger & Pasupathi, 2003).

Overall, we do not know much about when children begin to acquire knowledge about wisdom, or what form it takes at that point. Baltes (2004, p. 24) noted that "living long and growing older also result in a deeper experience with and understanding of the dynamic between gains and losses in life." Although much of childhood and adolescence deals with growth and gains, adulthood is increasingly concerned with stability and avoiding losses (Baltes, 1997). It is very likely that, with greater wisdom-oriented growth in adolescence, one would experience continued growth and positive outcomes in late adulthood.

Adulthood and Later Adulthood

Following the widespread belief that wisdom increases with age, people tend to associate wisdom with adult life (e.g., Holliday & Chandler, 1986b; Orwoll & Perlmutter, 1990). For example, people nominated as wise are usually also in their middle to late stages of adulthood (e.g., Ardelt, 2008; Baltes et al., 1995; Maercker et al., 1998). People implicitly assume that, throughout adulthood, there will be an increase in practical wisdom, such as in the ability to make effective everyday decisions (Berg & Sternberg, 1992). At the same time, people perceive development between early and late adulthood to be capable of both increase and decrease. Whereas memory is expected to decline during adulthood, older adults are perceived as more likely to build on their experiences to better their lives and understand others. Heckhausen et al. (1989) found that people believe that, overall, the gains in adulthood would outweigh the losses. The participants in their study thought that wisdom would increase from around 55 to about 85 years of age, when it would begin to decrease. Clayton and Birren (1980), however, found that older adults were less likely to associate wisdom with age than were young and middle-aged adults. Moreover, older people were found to have a more differentiated view of wisdom compared with younger adults.

As seen from our review of the literature, wisdom is a multidimensional construct. Different aspects of wisdom increase during adulthood: Some aspects stay relatively stable, whereas others decrease. Because the onset and rate of increase and decrease are largely dependent on idiosyncratic qualities and experiences, the development of wisdom in adulthood may differ greatly across individuals, leading to null findings, on average. Indeed, as discussed earlier, researchers have found few age-group differences on wisdom performance across adulthood (e.g., Baltes & Smith, 2008; Brugman, 2006; Jordan, 2005; Staudinger, 1999). Younger adults generally perform at about the same level as older adults (up to about 80 years), and are equally likely to be among the top scorers on wisdom-related tasks. At the same time, studies suggest that the relation between wisdom and age during adulthood is more complex; specifically, when one considers how different constructs related to wisdom develop simultaneously throughout the life span (e.g., see Baltes, Staudinger, & Lindenberger, 1999).

For example, crystallized intelligence tends to increase with age, fluid intelligence is relatively stable across the first part of adult life and tends to decrease afterward, and other cognitive abilities such as problem finding and high levels of dialectic or reflective thought seem to emerge only in midlife (e.g., Arlin, 1984; Kitchener et al., 1989; Kramer, 1990). Similar patterns can be seen in personality characteristics. For instance, between adolescence and adulthood, people become more agreeable, conscientious, and emotionally stable, but at the same time, less extroverted and less open to experiences (e.g., Helson, Kwan, John, & Jones, 2002; Loehlin & Martin, 2001; McCrae & Costa, 1997). Personal growth, in contrast, tends to increase into midlife and then begins to decline (Ryff & Keyes, 1995). Baltes and Smith (2008) concluded, based on multiple studies, that during adulthood, the best predictors of wisdom are not intelligence or personality factors alone, but rather "a combination of psychosocial characteristics and life history factors, including openness to experience, generativity, cognitive style, contact with excellent mentors, and some exposure to structured and critical life experiences" (p. 60).

Certain personal characteristics of the intelligence-personality interface seem to contribute to the development of wisdom with age (e.g., moral reasoning). More broadly, Kunzmann and Baltes (2003) found that wisdom is correlated with a higher affective involvement combined with reduced emotionality, the existence of values oriented toward growth of oneself, as well as others, and cooperative tendency to resolve conflicts. For the most part, controlling for gender or the Big Five (neuroticism, extraversion, openness to experience, conscientiousness, and agreeableness) did not alter the relation between the study variables. However, once age was introduced as a covariate in the model, the relation with reduced emotionality and other-enhancing values (e.g., well-being of friends, societal engagement, and ecological protection) became negligible. Thus, it seems that reduced emotionality and increased social perspective are related to both wisdom and age, but it is mainly their age-related growth that drives the association with wisdom.

Studies on wisdom in adult samples indicate the importance of certain facilitative conditions that seem to happen later, rather than earlier, in life. Ardelt (2000a) reported findings from longitudinal data suggesting that a supportive social environment in early adulthood is positively associated with wisdom later in life, whereas the quality of childhood and personality characteristics was generally unrelated to wisdom in later adulthood. In general, challenging life experiences, both personal (e.g., divorce, poverty) and social-historical (e.g., the great depression), are seen as pivotal for the development of wisdom, although they do not automatically lead to wisdom (e.g., Assmann, 1994; Bianchi, 1994; Pascual-Leone, 2000). Difficult, uncertain, and complex situations can shift the balance between gains and losses in life, leading people to reflect more critically and holistically about their values and purpose in life (Baltes, 2005; Dittmann-Kohli & Baltes, 1990; see also Hartman, 2000). Some see the ability to reminisce on, analyze, and possibly reconstruct one's life story as a necessary step in the development of wisdom (e.g., Brugman & ter Laak, 2004; Randall & Kenyon, 2001, 2002). To achieve higher levels of insight, a person must reflect on these difficult experiences, integrate them with existing knowledge, and use that knowledge when needed (Staudinger, 1999). Ardelt (1998, 2004, 2005) argued that being able to cope successfully with crises and obstacles in life seems to be one pathway to wisdom. Her findings suggest that a difficult personal history can lead to wisdom if people are able and willing to learn from their life's experiences and "be transformed in the process."

The gaining of wisdom is perceived as one of the positive aspects of later life (Baltes, 1993; Baltes & Smith, 2003; Heckhausen et al., 1989; Jordan, 2005). However, few studies empirically test the relation between wisdom and late adult development well. Moreover, in many cross-sectional studies, very late adult people constitute a minor part of the sample. Overall, studies suggest that a decline in cognitive abilities related to wisdom is expected very late in life as a result of the biological deterioration of the older adult brain (Baltes et al., 1995; Salthouse, 1991; Schaie, 1989; Smith & Baltes, 1993; Staudinger & Baltes, 1996). In addition, societal structure and norms are leading older adults to have more isolated lives, which can be less conducive to the development of wisdom (Jordan, 2005). Nevertheless, those who attain wisdom earlier may be able to accept biological and social decline in a more healthy way (Ardelt, 2008; Clayton, 1982). For example, in a longitudinal study, Ardelt (1997, 2000a) found that wise older adult women had greater satisfaction with life, better interpersonal relationships, and overall a healthier life than women with lower levels of wisdom. Thus, developing wisdom is an important goal as it can help one deal with life's adversities in a more effective and healthy way. The next section elaborates on the perception that wisdom-oriented education, both at an early stage, but also throughout the full span of one's life, can be beneficial for attaining and maintaining wisdom.

Wisdom and Education

By three methods we may learn wisdom: First, by reflection which is noblest; second, by imitation, which is the easiest; and third, by experience, which is the bitterest.

—*Confucius*

The emphasis on education exists throughout the ancient, religious, and philosophical literature on wisdom. In many cultures over time, the educated elites were perceived as wise and, in many cases, were also the generators of wisdom texts. The exact type of education related to developing and enhancing wisdom took different forms, such as apprenticeship or mentorship in a particular field and the study of the meaning of life and nature through religion or science. In the dawn of the 21st century, new ideas have emerged about what might be important for future generations. The modern technological world offers a wealth of information and opportunities for growth, and at the same time great risks and challenges and different types of "misinformation." What tools do people need today to make the most out of their lives ahead?

Educational systems, for both youths and adults, are pivotal in preparing individuals for life. Such institutes play a major role in fostering the kind of wisdom needed to create a better, more harmonious world. Schools, for example, are a natural setting to cultivate wisdom in our society, as wise students will later be those most likely to become wise parents, citizens, and leaders. Wisdom is relevant here not only because schools help students gain knowledge and skills, but also because schools intersect multiple groups with different needs and interests, including issues of high stakes and uncertain nature. These intersections lead to a multitude of complex problems that require wise decision making. Therefore, schools should offer many opportunities to infuse wise thoughts and actions into student's experiences.

Sternberg (2001, 2008) proposed to integrate wisdom into the practices of teachers and principals. In his eyes, the goal of schooling should be not only to impart knowledge but also to help students develop the skills necessary for using that knowledge wisely. That is, the goal of schooling should be to teach students how best to use their knowledge and abilities for good rather than bad causes (see also Reznitskaya & Sternberg, 2004; Sternberg, 2002, 2004). Currently, schools mainly nurture memory and analytical abilities. These skills are important, but they are not enough. Schools should also provide students with a framework in which to develop positive and productive values. Such conditions are seen as essential for the development of wisdom, according to the balance theory (Sternberg, 1998).

Wisdom in the balance theory is defined as the application of knowledge and abilities mediated by positive ethical values toward the achievement of a common good through a balance among competing interests and responses to environmental contexts. Thus, knowledge is important for wisdom because people need it to draw on in rendering judgments—knowledge of human nature, of life circumstances, or of strategies that succeed and those that fail. Similarly, analytical, creative, and practical abilities are important, as they provide the tools through which ideas turn into effective actions. Schools do promote knowledge and abilities in their students, albeit to varying degrees of success. However, Sternberg (2001, 2008) argued that schools should more explicitly integrate wisdom-related skills into their curricula. Specifically, the content of instructional activities should emphasize reflective and dialectical modes of thinking by considering multiple perspectives and the balance among them. This sort of wisdom depends on teaching the right things, but also on teaching things right. The idea here is that wisdom, as a form of tacit knowledge, cannot be directly taught, but rather needs to be acquired through experience, specifically experience that requires using cognitive skills and moral attitudes to make wise decisions and to act accordingly. Sternberg (2001, 2004) offered principles, procedures, and guidance for developing

a curriculum for teaching to wisdom (see also Sternberg et al., 2007). For instance, under this framework, students will learn about the usefulness of interdependence ("a rising tide raises all ships; a falling tide can sink them"), and learn to recognize and balance their own interests, those of other people, and those of institutions.

Sternberg's ideas initiated a critical discussion about the role of wisdom in education (Halpern, 2001; Kuhn & Udell, 2001; Paris, 2001; Perkins, 2001; Stanovich, 2001; Sternberg, 2001). Recently, similar ideas have been advocated by different authors, researchers, and organizations. For example, Craft, Gardner, and Claxton (2008) emphasized the need to educate students for "wise creativity"— the ability to consider multiple perspectives and to utilize personal qualities responsibly within one's community and in the real world. The authors advocated the role of educators as "trustees," or respected and impartial role models of wise creativity in the classroom (see also Ferrari, 2004). Brown (2004) argued for the need to promote wisdom in higher education. For example, colleges and universities should provide learning environments that foster reflection, integration, and application, enabling students to learn better from their experiences. Others have called for teaching spiritual practices in educational institutes (Rockefeller, 2006; Wall, 2005) as a way to increase mindfulness, awareness, and reflective thought, and decrease self-centeredness. Such practices are likely to lead to better understanding of oneself, to greater consideration of others, and ultimately, to wisdom (Ardelt, 2008; Pascual-Leone, 2000).

Ideas about infusing wisdom into our lives have also manifested themselves in new organizations and large-scale initiatives. For example, the Partnership for 21st Century Learning (http:// www.21stcenturyskills.org) is a multiperspective collaboration whose goal is to improve education in the 21st century and to prepare a better workforce for the future. Based on an extensive dialogue among educators, academics, leaders, and businesses, the partnership identified the essential knowledge and skills needed to be learned today, to ensure successful communities and workplaces in the future. For example, the core subjects include languages, arts, mathematics, economics, science, geography, history, and civics. The skills identified include learning and innovation skills (e.g., creativity, critical thinking, problem solving, communication, and collaboration), information, media and technology literacy, and life and career skills (e.g., adaptability, self-direction, social skills, productivity, leadership, and responsibility). Many of the themes advocated by the partnership are aligned with different aspects of wisdom: creativity, integrative thoughts, effective use of knowledge and strategies, and will-driven actions to benefit oneself and others.

If we want wisdom to have a lasting effect further into our future, we must sustain wisdom-based knowledge and skills throughout life. Thus, the call to bring wisdom into education also resonates in lifelong learning, professional training, and practice. Current initiatives are set to study how such sustainability can be achieved and what that requires from us. This practical wisdom can then be disseminated to current and future generations. For example, the investigation led by Csikszentmihalyi, Damon, Gardner, and the collaborators of the GoodWork project (e.g., Gardner, 2007; see http://www.goodworkproject.org) analyzed exemplars of work that is deemed to be of high quality and socially responsible. The researchers showed how motivation, cultural factors, and professional norms are integrated into our working environment and habits. These aspects of work should be driven by responsibility to good personal and social goals and purposes that should be embedded in every profession. Under these conditions, our working experience can be more personally, socially, and economically beneficial.

The GoodWork initiative has generated many parallel lines of inquiry. For example, current projects investigate implications for schooling and child development, the role of spirituality and meditation in promoting GoodWork, different platforms to bring these ideas to a wider audience, and ways to sustain it across generations. The GoodWork project exemplifies the study of work-related wisdom, which encompasses practical, personal, and social forms of wisdom. Essentially, initiatives such as GoodWork and the 21st Century Partnership produce new forms of "wisdom texts" for the modern age. These new forms are more interactive, interconnected, holistic, applied, and accessible than most of the psychological, philosophical, or religious texts.

To conclude, our task as individuals, communities, nations, and as a global world is to achieve a state of peace and progress. Wisdom is seen by many as an important feature of this process. Apart from the scientific inquiry of wisdom, which mostly remains within the academic realm, different ideas advocated by current movements and organizations emphasize various aspects of wisdom. For instance, ideas like globalization, environmentalism, and human rights highlight the importance of rational, moral, and practical knowledge needed to ensure our survival and healthy growth. At the same time, they emphasize sustainability, responsibility, reciprocity, moderation,

good judgment, and purposeful action. These ideas shape the reality in which we live by infusing it with wise decisions and actions designed to help individuals and societies flourish (see Halpern, 2008).

Summary of Research About Wisdom and Late Adult Development

In conclusion, findings on wisdom and late adult development, although largely cross sectional, draw a detailed and interconnected picture of wisdom's trajectory. Overall, findings suggest that individuals are able to develop and maintain wisdom until later stages of life in which health problems impair thinking. But whether wisdom actually will develop depends not on age per se, but rather on cognitive variables, personality variables, and life experiences. Recent studies explore the relations between different personal characteristics related to wisdom. Some researchers compare people from different groups (e.g., types of profession, level of education, personality traits) by inspecting their observed differences in wisdom within and across age cohorts. Most findings are in line with the theories on which the measurement instruments used were developed. Because many of the theories of wisdom share some basic features (e.g., integration of cognitive, affective, and behavioral qualities oriented toward growth within one's life context), findings tend to show similar trends.

Overall, the studies describe empirical associations between wisdom and various constructs that are hypothesized to be related or unrelated. Consequently, we know more about what wisdom is and what it is not, specifically in terms of components that can be clearly identified (and possibly modified) in one's life. This knowledge about multiple aspects of wisdom gives us a holistic view of its structure and meaning.

The course of the development of wisdom across chronological age is different than might be expected. This may be because our expectations are too simple compared with the complexities of real trajectories. Possibly, there is much variation in how experiences accumulated across age interact with different personal constructs associated with wisdom. Thus, the development of high levels of wisdom may be contingent on a unique combination of circumstances. On the one hand, it is unique in the sense that, although there are many qualities that relate to wisdom, only a few people actually attain it. On the other hand, this combination is unique in the sense that every person has a different set of characteristics and experiences that may foster or hinder their individual wisdom. Wisdom depends on the level of integration of such personal qualities within oneself, and with one's life experiences, which consequently produces a complex trajectory across the life span.

Most importantly, individuals need to utilize life experience in a way that is consistent with the development of wisdom. People must want to acquire and maintain wisdom-related knowledge and skills, and then must adopt the attitudes toward life—reciprocity, openness to experience, reflectivity on experience, and willingness to profit from experience—that will enable wisdom to develop. Educational and social systems can facilitate this process by providing conditions facilitative for wisdom; however, the real change toward wisdom must originate from within each individual.

We must become the change we want to see in the world.

—*Mahatma Gandhi*

REFERENCES

Achenbaum, W. A., & Orwoll, L. (1991). Becoming wise: A psycho-gerontological interpretation of the Book of Job. *International Journal of Aging and Human Development, 32,* 21–39.

Ackoff, R. L. (1999). On learning and the systems that facilitate it. *Reflections, 1*(1), 14–25.

Ahbel-Rappe, S., & Kamtekar, R. (Eds.). (2005). *A companion to Socrates.* Hoboken, NJ: Wiley-Blackwell.

Alexander, C. N., & Langer, E. J. (Eds.). (1990). *Higher stages of human development.* New York: Oxford University Press.

Anderson, B. J. (1998). *Development of wisdom-related knowledge in adolescence and young adulthood.* Unpublished doctoral dissertation, University of Toronto, Toronto, Ontario, Canada.

Annas, J. (1992). *Hellenistic philosophy of mind.* Berkeley, CA: University of California Press.

Ardelt, M. (1997). Wisdom and life satisfaction in old age. *Journal of Gerontology, 52B,* 15–27.

Ardelt, M. (1998). Social crisis and individual growth: The long-term effects of the Great Depression. *Journal of Aging Studies, 12*(3), 291–314.

Ardelt, M. (2000a). Antecedents and effects of wisdom in old age. *Research on Aging, 22*(4), 360–394.

Ardelt, M. (2000b). Intellectual versus wisdom-related knowledge: The case for a different kind of learning in the later years of life. *Educational Gerontology, 26,* 771–789.

Ardelt, M. (2003). Empirical assessment of a three-dimensional wisdom scale. *Research on Aging, 25*(3), 275–324.

Ardelt, M. (2004). Wisdom as expert knowledge system: A critical review of a contemporary operationalization of an ancient concept. *Human Development, 47,* 257–285.

Ardelt, M. (2005). How wise people cope with crises and obstacles in life. *ReVision: A Journal of Consciousness and Transformation, 28*(1), 7–19.

Ardelt, M. (2008). Being wise at any age. In S. J. Lopez (Ed.), *Positive psychology: Exploring the best in people: Vol. 1. Discovering human strengths* (pp. 81–108). Westport, CT: Praeger.

Ariely, D. (2008). *Predictably irrational: The hidden forces that shape our decisions.* New York: Harper Collins.

Arlin, P. K. (1984). Adolescent and adult thought: A structural interpretation. In M. L. Commons, F. A. Richards, & C. Armon (Eds.). *Beyond formal operations: Late adolescent and adult cognitive development* (pp. 258–271). New York: Praeger.

Arlin, P. K. (1990). Wisdom: The art of problem finding. In R. J. Sternberg (Ed.), *Wisdom: Its nature, origins, and development* (pp. 230–243). New York: Cambridge University Press.

Assmann, A. (1994). Wholesome knowledge: Concepts of wisdom in a historical and cross-cultural perspective. In D. L. Featherman, R. M. Lerner, & M. Perlmutter (Eds.), *Life-span development and behavior* (Vol. 12, pp. 187–224). Hillsdale, NJ: Erlbaum.

Bailey, A. (2002). *Sextus empiricus and pyrrhonean scepticism.* Oxford, U.K.: Oxford University Press.

Baltes, P. B. (1993). The aging mind: Potential limits. *Gerontologist, 33*(5), 580–594

Baltes, P. B. (1997). On the incomplete architecture of human ontogeny: Selection, optimization, and compensation as foundation of developmental theory. *American Psychologist, 52,* 366–380.

Baltes, P. B. (2000). Autobiographical reflections: From developmental methodology and lifespan psychology to gerontology. In J. E. Birren & J. J. F. Schroots (Eds.), *A history of geropsychology in autobiography* (pp. 7–26). Washington, DC: American Psychological Association.

Baltes, P. B. (2004). *Wisdom as orchestration of mind and virtue.* Unpublished manuscript. Retrieved June 25, 2009, from http://www.library.mpib-berlin.mpg.de/ft/pb/PB_Wisdom_2004.pdf.

Baltes, P. B. (2005). Introduction: The future of aging. Potentials and challenges. In G. Stock, M. Lessl, & P. B. Baltes (Eds.), *The future of aging: Individual and societal implications* (pp. 11–18). Berlin, Germany: Ernst Schering Research Foundation.

Baltes, P. B., Glück, J., & Kunzmann, U. (2002). Wisdom: Its structure and function in regulating successful lifespan development. In C. R. Snyder & S. J. Lopez (Eds.), *Handbook of positive psychology* (pp. 327–347). London: Oxford University Press.

Baltes, P. B., & Kunzmann, U. (2003). Wisdom. *The Psychologist, 16,* 131–132.

Baltes, P. B., & Kunzmann, U. (2004). The two faces of wisdom: Wisdom as a general theory of knowledge and judgment about excellence in mind and virtue vs. wisdom as everyday realization in people and products. *Human Development, 47,* 290–299.

Baltes, P. B., & Smith, J. (1990). Toward a psychology of wisdom and its ontogenesis. In R. Sternberg (Ed.), *Wisdom: its nature, origins and development* (pp. 87–120). Cambridge: Cambridge University Press.

Baltes, P. B., & Smith, J. (2003). New frontiers in the future of aging: From successful aging of the young old to the dilemmas of the fourth age. *Gerontology, 49,* 123–135.

Baltes, P. B., & Smith, J. (2008). The fascination of wisdom: Its nature, ontogeny, and function. *Perspectives on Psychological Science, 3*(1), 56–64.

Baltes, P. B., & Staudinger, U. M. (1993). The search for a psychology of wisdom. *Current Directions in Psychological Science, 2,* 75–80.

Baltes, P. B., & Staudinger, U. M. (1996). Interactive minds in a life-span perspective: Prologue. In P. B. Baltes & U. M. Staudinger (Eds.), *Interactive minds: Life-span perspectives on the social foundation of cognition* (pp. 1–32). New York: Cambridge University Press.

Baltes, P. B., & Staudinger, U. M. (2000). Wisdom: A metaheuristic (pragmatic) to orchestrate mind and virtue toward excellence. *American Psychologist, 55,* 122–136.

Baltes, P. B., Staudinger, U. M., & Lindenberger, U. (1999). Lifespan psychology: Theory and application to intellectual functioning. *Annual Review of Psychology, 50,* 471–507.

Baltes, P. B., Staudinger, U. M., Maercker, A., & Smith, J. (1995). People nominated as wise: A comparison study of wisdom-related knowledge. *Psychology and Aging, 10,* 155–166.

Basseches, M. A. (1984a). *Dialectical thinking and adult development.* Norwood, NJ: Ablex.

Basseches, M. A. (1984b). Dialectic thinking as a metasystematic form of cognitive orientation. In M. L. Commons, F. A. Richards, & C. Armon (Eds.), *Beyond formal operations* (pp. 216–328). New York: Praeger.

Benson, H. H. (1996). The aims of the Socratic Elenchos. In K. Lehrer, B. J. Lum, B. A. Slichta, & N. D. Smith (Eds.), *Knowledge, teaching and wisdom* (pp. 21–33). Dordrecht, the Netherlands: Kluwer.

Berg, C. A., & Sternberg, R. J. (1992). Adults' conceptions of intelligence across the adult life span. *Psychology and Aging, 7*(2), 221–231.

Bianchi, E. C. (1994). *Elder wisdom. Crafting your own elderhood.* New York: Crossroad

Bierly III, P. E., Kessler, E., & Christensen, E. (2000). Organizational learning, knowledge and wisdom. *Journal of Organizational Change Management, 13*(6), 595–618.

Bigelow, J. (1992). Developing managerial wisdom. *Journal of Management Inquiry, 1*(2), 143–153.

Birren, J. E., & Fisher, L. M. (1990). Conceptualizing wisdom: the primacy of affect-cognition relations. In R. J. Sternberg (Ed.), *Wisdom: Its nature, origins, and development* (pp. 317–332). New York: Cambridge University Press.

Birren, J. E., & Svensson, C. M. (2005). Wisdom in history. In R. J. Sternberg & J. Jordan (Eds.), *A handbook of wisdom: Psychological perspectives* (pp. 3–31). New York: Cambridge University Press.

Blair, C. See Chapter 8 in this volume.

Blanchard-Fields, F. (1986). Reasoning on social dilemmas varying in emotional saliency: An adult developmental perspective. *Psychology and Aging, 1,* 325–333.

Blanchard-Fields, F., & Hess, T. M. (1996). *Perspectives on cognitive change in adulthood and aging.* New York: McGraw-Hill.

Blanchard-Fields, F., & Norris, L. (1995). The development of wisdom. In M. A. Kimble, S. H. McFadden, J. Wellor, & J. F. Seeber (Eds.), *Aging, spirituality, and religion: A handbook* (pp. 102–118). Minneapolis, MN: Fortress Press.

Bluck, S., & Glück, J. (2004). Making things better and learning a lesson: Experiencing wisdom across the lifespan. *Journal of Personality, 72*(3), 543–572.

Bluck, S., & Glück, J. (2005). From the inside out: People's implicit theories of wisdom. In R. J. Sternberg & J. Jordan (Eds.), *A handbook of wisdom: Psychological perspectives* (pp. 84–109). New York: Cambridge University Press.

Boadt, L. (1985). *St. Thomas Aquinas and the biblical wisdom tradition.* Retrieved May 22, 2005, from http://www.thomist.org/journal/1985/October/1985%20Oct%20A%Boadt%20web.htm.

Boal, K. B., & Hooijberg, R. (2000). Strategic leadership research: Moving on. *Leadership Quarterly, 11*(4), 515–549.

Bodhi, B. (1994). *A Buddhist response to contemporary dilemmas of human existence.* Retrieved June 25, 2009, from http://www.accesstoinsight.org/lib/authors/bodhi/response.html.

Böhmig-Krumhaar, S. A., Staudinger, U. M., & Baltes, P. B. (2002). Mehr Toleranz tut Not: Läßt sich wert-relativierendes Wissen und Urteilen mit Hilfe einer wissensaktivierenden Gedächtnisstrategie verbessern? *Zeitschrift für Entwicklungspsychologie und Pädagogische Psychologie, 34,* 30–43.

Brown, S. C. (2004). Learning across campus: How college facilitates the development of wisdom. *Journal of College Student Development, 45,* 134–148.

Brown, S. C., & Greene, J. A. (2006). The Wisdom Development Scale: Translating the conceptual to the concrete. *Journal of College Student Development, 47*(1), 1–19.

Brugman, G. (2000). *Wisdom: Source of narrative coherence and eudaimonia.* Unpublished doctoral dissertation, University of Utrecht, Delft, the Netherlands.

Brugman, G. M. (2006). Wisdom and aging. In J. E. Birren & K. W. Schaie (Eds.), *Handbook of the psychology of aging* (6th ed., pp. 445–476). Amsterdam, The Netherlands: Academic Press.

Brugman, G. M., & ter Laak, J. (2004). Narrative change: An analysis of the narratives of three confirmed Russian communists after the collapse of the Soviet Union. *Tidschrift voor Ontwikkelingspsychologie, 25*(1), 43–58.

Buddharakkhita, A. (1985). *Dhammapada translations.* Retrieved June 25, 2009, from http://www.accesstoinsight.org/tipitaka/kn/dhp/index.html.

Carstensen, L. L. (1995). Evidence for a life-span theory of socioemotional selectivity. *Current Directions in Psychological Science, 4,* 151–156.

Chenu, M.-D. (1984). Thomas Aquinas, Saint. In R. P. Gwinn, C. E. Swanson, & P. W. Goetz (Eds.), *The new encyclopaedia Britannica* (15th ed., Vol. 18, pp. 363–368). Chicago, IL: Encyclopaedia Britannica.

Clayton, V. (1976). *A multidimensional scaling analysis of the concept of wisdom.* Unpublished dissertation, University of Southern California, Los Angeles.

Clayton, V. (1982). Wisdom and intelligence: The nature and function of knowledge in the later years. *International Journal of Aging and Development, 15,* 315–321.

Clayton, V. P., & Birren, J. E. (1980). The development of wisdom across the life span: A reexamination of an ancient topic. In P. B. Baltes & J. O. G. Brim (Eds.), *Life-span development and behavior* (Vol. 3, pp. 103–135). New York: Academic Press.

Cohn, L. D. (1998). Age trends in personality development: A quantitative review. In P. M. Westenberg, A., Blasi, & L. D. Cohn (Eds.), *Personality development: Theoretical, empirical, and clinical investigations of Loevinger's conception of ego development.* Mahwah, NJ: Erlbaum.

Craft, A., Gardner, H., & Claxton, G. (Eds.). (2008). *Creativity, wisdom, and trusteeship: Exploring the role of education.* Thousand Oaks, CA: Corwin Press.

Csikszentmihalyi, M. (1990). The domain of creativity. In M. A. Runco & R. S. Albert (Eds.). *Theories of creativity* (pp. 190–212). Thousand Oaks, CA: Sage.

Csikszentmihalyi, M. (2000). Happiness, flow, and economic equality. *American Psychologist, 55*(10), 1163–1164.

Csikszentmihalyi, M., & Nakamura, J. (2005). The role of emotions in the development of wisdom. In R. J. Sternberg & J. Jordan (Eds.), *A handbook of wisdom: Psychological perspectives* (pp. 220–242). New York: Cambridge University Press.

Csikszentmihalyi, M., & Rathunde, K. (1990). The psychology of wisdom: An evolutionary interpretation. In R. J. Sternberg (Ed.), *Wisdom: Its nature, origins, and development* (pp. 25–51). New York: Cambridge University Press.

Damon, W. (2000). Setting the stage for the development of wisdom: Self-understanding and moral identity during adolescence. In W. S. Brown (Ed.), *Understanding wisdom: Sources, science, and society* (pp. 339–360). West Conshohocken, PA: Templeton Foundation Press.

Denney, N. W., Dew, J. R., & Kroupa, S. L. (1995). Perceptions of wisdom: What is it and who has it? *Journal of Adult Development, 2*(1), 37–47.

Descartes, R. (2004). *Principia Philosophiae* [The principles of philosophy]. Whitefish, MT: Kessinger. (Original work published 1644)

Dewey, J. (1938). *Logic: The theory of inquiry*. New York: Holt.

Dittmann-Kohli, F., & Baltes, P. B. (1990). Toward a neofunctionalist conception of adult intellectual development: Wisdom as a prototypical case of intellectual growth. In C. Alexander & E. Langer (Eds.), *Higher stages of human development: Perspectives on adult growth* (pp. 54–78). New York: Oxford University Press.

Erikson, E. H. (1959). Identity and the life cycle: Selected papers. *Psychological Issues, 1*, 1–171.

Erikson, E. H. (1968). *Identity, youth and crisis*. New York: Norton.

Erikson, E. H., & Erikson, J. M. (1997). *The life cycle completed*. New York: W. W. Norton.

Feldman-Barrett, L. F., & Salovey, P. (Eds.). (2002). *The wisdom in feeling: Psychological processes in emotional intelligence*. New York: Guilford Press.

Ferrari, M. (2004). Educating selves to be creative and wise. In L. V. Shavinina & M. Ferrari (Eds.), *Beyond knowledge: Extracognitive aspects of developing high ability* (pp. 211–238). Mahwah, NJ: Erlbaum.

Flavell, J. H. (1979). Metacognition and cognitive monitoring: A new area of cognitive developmental inquiry. *American Psychologist, 34*, 906–911.

Flynn, J. R. (1987). Massive IQ gains in 14 nations: What IQ tests really measure. *Psychological Bulletin, 95*, 29–51.

Fontaine, C. R. (1981). A modern look at ancient wisdom: The instruction of Ptahhotep revisited. *Biblical Archaeology, 44*, 155–160.

Frecknall, P. (1994). Good humor—A qualitative study of the uses of humor in everyday life. *Psychology: A Quarterly Journal of Human Behavior, 31*(1), 12–21.

Freeman, C. (2003). *The closing of the Western mind*. London: Pimlico.

Fritsch, C. F. (1955). The book of proverbs. Introduction and exegesis. In *The Interpreters Bible* (pp. 765–967). New York: Abingdon Press.

Gardner, H. (Ed.). (2007). *Responsibility at work: How leading professionals act (or don't act) responsibly*. San Francisco, CA: Jossey-Bass.

Garrett, R. (1996). Three definitions of wisdom. In K. Lehrer, B. J. Lum, B. A. Slichta, & N. D. Smith (Eds.), *Knowledge, teaching and wisdom* (pp. 221–232). Dordrecht, the Netherlands: Kluwer.

Gigerenzer, G., Todd, P. M., & ABC Research Group. (1999). *Simple heuristics that make us smart*. New York: Oxford University Press.

Gilovich, T., Griffin, D., & Kahneman, D. (2002). *Heuristics and biases: The psychology of intuitive judgment*. Cambridge: Cambridge University Press.

Glück, J., & Baltes, P. B. (2006). Using the concept of wisdom to enhance the expression of wisdom knowledge: Not the philosopher's dream but differential effects of developmental preparedness. *Psychology and Aging, 21*, 679–690.

Glück, J., Bluck, S., Baron, J., & McAdams, D. P. (2005). The wisdom of experience: Autobiographical narratives across adulthood. *International Journal of Behavioral Development, 29*(3), 197–208.

Gough, H. G., & Heilbrun, A. B. (1983). *Adjective Check List Manual*. Palo Alto, CA: Consulting Psychologists Press.

Gross, J. J. (1999). Emotion regulation: Past, present, future. *Cognition and Emotion, 13*, 551–573.

Guthrie, W. K. C. (1969). *History of Greek philosophy*. Cambridge: Cambridge University Press

Halpern, C. (2008). *Making waves and riding the currents. Activism and the practice of wisdom*. San Francisco, CA: Berrett-Koehler.

Halpern, D. F. (2001). Why wisdom? *Educational Psychologist, 36*(4), 253–256.

Happé, F. G. E., Winner, E., & Brownell, H. (1998). The getting of wisdom: Theory of mind in old age. *Developmental Psychology, 34*(2), 358–362.

Harrison, C. (2006). *Rethinking Augustine's early theology: an argument for continuity*. Oxford: Oxford University Press.

Hartman, P. S. (2000). *Women developing wisdom: Antecedents and correlates in a longitudinal sample*. Unpublished doctoral dissertation, University of Michigan, Ann Arbor, MI.

Harvey, P. (2000). *An introduction to Buddhist ethics*. Cambridge: Cambridge University Press.

Heckhausen, J., Dixon, R. A., & Baltes, P. B. (1989). Gains and losses in development throughout adulthood as perceived by different age groups. *Developmental Psychology, 255*, 109–121.

Hegel, G. W. F. (1931). *The phenomenology of mind* (J. B. Baillie, Trans.). London: G. Allen and Unwin. (Original work published 1807)

Helson, R., Kwan, V. S. Y., John, O. P., & Jones, C. (2002). The growing evidence for personality change in adulthood: Findings from research with personality inventories. *Journal of Research in Personality, 36*, 287–306.

Helson, R., & Srivastava, S. (2002). Creativity and wisdom: Similarities differences, and how they develop. *Personality and Social Psychology Bulletin, 28*, 1430–1440.

Helson, R., & Wink, P. (1987). Two conceptions of maturity examined in the findings of a longitudinal study. *Journal of Personality and Social Psychology, 53*(3), 531–541.

Hendrick, J. J., Knox, V. J., Gekoski, W. L., & Dyne, K. J. (1988). Perceived cognitive ability of young and old targets. *Canadian Journal on Aging, 7*(3), 192–203.

Hershey, D. A., & Farrell, A. H. (1997). Perceptions of wisdom associated with selected occupations. *Current Psychology, 16*(2), 115–130.

Hira, F. J., & Faulkender, P. J. (1997). Perceiving wisdom: Do age and gender play a part? *International Journal of Aging and Human Development, 44*, 85–101.

Holliday, S. G., & Chandler, M. J. (1986a). *Wisdom: Explorations in adult competence*. Basel, Switzerland: Karger.

Holliday, S. G., & Chandler, M. J. (1986b). Wisdom: Explorations in adult competence. In J. A. Meacham (Ed.), *Contributions to human development* (Vol. 17, pp. 1–96). Basel, Switzerland: Karger.

Horn, J. L. (1994). The theory of fluid and crystallized intelligence. In R. J. Sternberg (Ed.), *The encyclopedia of human intelligence* (Vol. 1., pp. 443–451). New York: Macmillan.

Horn, J. L., & Cattell, R. B. (1966). Refinement and test of the theory of fluid and crystallized intelligence. *Journal of Educational Psychology, 57*, 253–270.

Jason, L. A., Reichler, A., King, C., Madsen, D., Camacho, J., & Marchese, W. (2001). The measurement of wisdom: A preliminary effort. *Journal of Community Psychology, 29*(5), 585–598.

Jeannot, T. M. (1989). Moral leadership and practical wisdom. *International Journal of Social Economics, 16*(6), 14–38.

Jordan, J. (2005). The quest for wisdom in adulthood: A psychological perspective. In R. J. Sternberg & J. Jordan (Eds.), *A handbook of wisdom: Psychological perspectives*. New York: Cambridge University Press.

Kahneman, D., Slovic, P., & Tversky, A. (1982). *Judgment under uncertainty: Heuristics and biases*. New York: Cambridge University Press.

Kahneman, D., & Tversky, A. (Eds.). (2000). *Choices, values, and frames*. New York: Cambridge University Press and the Russell Sage Foundation.

Kekes, J. (1983). Wisdom. *American Philosophical Quarterly, 20*, 277–286.

Kekes, J. (1995). *Moral wisdom and good lives.* Ithaca, NY: Cornell University Press.

Kessler, E. (2006). Organizational wisdom: Human, managerial, and strategic implication. *Group and Organization Management, 31*(3), 296–299.

Kessler, E., & Bailey, J. R. (Eds.). (2007). *Handbook of organizational and managerial wisdom.* Thousand Oaks, CA: Sage.

Kinnier, R. T., Tribbensee, N. E., Rose, C. A., & Vaughan, S. M. (2001). In the final analysis; more wisdom from people who have faced death. *Journal of Counseling & Development, 79*(2), 171–177.

Kitchener, K. S. (1986). Formal reasoning in adults: a review and critique. In R. A. Mines & K. S. Kitchener (Eds.), *Adult cognitive development.* New York: Praeger.

Kitchener, K. S., & Brenner, H. G. (1990). Wisdom and reflective judgment: Knowing in the face of uncertainty. In R. J. Sternberg (Ed.), *Wisdom: Its nature, origins, and development* (pp. 212–229). New York: Cambridge University Press.

Kitchener, K. S., & King, P. M. (1981). Reflective judgment: Concepts of justification and their relationship to age and education. *Journal of Applied Developmental Psychology, 2,* 89–116.

Kitchener, K. S., & King, P. M. (1990). The Reflective Judgment model: Ten years of research. In M. L. Commons, C. Armon, L. Kohlberg, F. A. Richards, T. A. Grotzer, & J. D. Sinnott (Eds.), *Adult development: Vol. 2. Models and methods in the study of adolescent and adult thought* (pp. 63–78). New York: Praeger.

Kitchener, K. S., King, P. M., Wood, P. K., & Davison, M. L. (1989). Sequentiality and consistency in the development of reflective judgment: A six-year longitudinal study. *Journal of Applied Developmental Psychology, 10,* 73–95.

Kitchener, K. S., Lynch, C. L., Fischer, K., & Wood, P. K. (1993). Developmental range of Reflective Judgment: The effect of contextual support and practice on developmental stage. *Developmental Psychology, 29,* 893–906.

Kohlberg, L. (1973). The claim to moral adequacy of a highest stage of moral judgment. *Journal of Philosophy, 70,* 630–646.

Korac-Kakabadse, N., Korac-Kakabadse, A., & Kouzmin, A. (2001). Leadership renewal: Towards the philosophy of wisdom. *International Review of Administrative Sciences, 67*(2), 207–227.

Kramer, D. A. (1983). Post-formal operations? A need for further conceptualization. *Human Development, 26,* 91–105.

Kramer, D. A. (1990). Conceptualizing wisdom: The primacy of affect–cognition relations. In R. J. Sternberg (Ed.), *Wisdom: Its nature, origins, and development* (pp. 279–313). New York: Cambridge University Press.

Kramer, D. A. (2000). Wisdom as a classical source of human strength: Conceptualization and empirical inquiry. *Journal of Social and Clinical Inquiry, 19,* 83–101.

Kriger, M. P., & Malan, L. C. (1993). Shifting paradigms: The valuing of personal knowledge, wisdom, and other invisible processes in organizations. *Journal of Management Inquiry, 2*(4), 391–398.

Kuhn, D., & Udell, W. (2001). The path to wisdom. *Educational Psychologist, 36*(4), 261–265.

Kunstmann, J. G. (1994). The bird that fouls its nest. In W. Mieder & A. Dundes (Eds.), *The wisdom of many* Madison, WI: University of Wisconsin Press.

Kunzmann, U., & Baltes, P. B. (2003). Beyond the traditional scope of intelligence: Wisdom in action. In R. J. Sternberg, J. Lautrey, & T. Lubart (Eds.), *Models of intelligence: International perspectives* (pp. 329–343). Washington, DC: American Psychological Association.

Kunzmann, U., & Baltes, P. B. (2005). The psychology of wisdom: Theoretical and empirical challenges. In R. J. Sternberg, & J. Jordan (Eds.), *A handbook of wisdom: Psychological perspectives* (pp. 110–135). New York: Cambridge University Press.

Kupperman, J. J. (2005). Morality, ethics, and wisdom. In R. J. Sternberg & J. Jordan (Eds.), *A handbook of wisdom: Psychological perspectives* (pp. 245–271). New York: Cambridge University Press.

Labouvie-Vief, G. (1990). Wisdom as integrated thought: Historical and developmental perspectives. In R. J. Sternberg (Ed.), *Wisdom: Its nature, origins, and development* (pp. 52–83). New York: Cambridge University Press.

Labouvie-Vief, G., DeVoe, M., & Bulka, D. (1989). Speaking about feelings: Conceptions of emotion across the life span. *Psychology and Aging, 4,* 425–437.

Lerner, R. M., & Galambos, N. L. (1998). Adolescent development: Challenges and opportunities for research, programs, and policies. *Annual Review of Psychology, 49,* 413–446.

Levi, A. W. (1994). Classical British empiricism. In R. McHenry (Ed.), *The new Encyclopaedia Britannica* (Vol. 25, pp. 751–752). Chicago, IL: Encyclopaedia Britannica.

Levitt, H. M. (1999). The development of wisdom: An analysis of Tibetan Buddhist experience. *Journal of Humanistic Psychology, 39,* 86–105.

Limas, M. J., & Hansson, R. O. (2004). Organizational wisdom. *International Journal of Aging and Human Development, 59,* 85–103.

Loehlin, J. C., & Martin, N. G. (2001). Age changes in personality traits and their heritabilities during the adult years: Evidence from the Australian twin registry samples. *Personality and Individual Differences, 30,* 1147–1160.

Ludema, J., Wilmot, T., & Srivastva, S. (1997). Organizational hope: Reaffirming the constructive task of social and organizational inquiry. *Human Relations, 50*(8), 1015–1052.

Maercker, A. (1992). Weisheit im Alter. *Münchner Medizinische Wochenschrift, 134,* 518–522.

Maercker, A., Böhmig-Krumhaar, S., & Staudinger, U. M. (1998). Existentielle Konfrontation als Zugang zu weisheitsbezogenem Wissen und Urteilen: Eine Untersuchung von Weisheitsnominierten. *Zeischrift für Entwichlungs- und Pädagogische Psychologie, 1.*

Malan, L. C., & Kriger, M. P. (1998). Making sense of managerial wisdom. *Journal of Management Inquiry, 7*(3), 242–251.

McAdams, D. P., & de St. Aubin, E. (Eds.). (1998). *Generativity and adult development: How and why we care for the next generation.* Washington, DC: American Psychological Association.

McCrae, R. R., & Costa, P. T. (1997). Personality structure as a human universal. *American Psychologist, 52*(5), 509–516.

McKee, P., & Barber, C. (1999). On defining wisdom. *International Journal of Aging and Human Development, 49,* 149–164.

Meacham, J. A. (1983). Wisdom and the context of knowledge: Knowing that one doesn't know. In D. Kuhn & A. Meacham (Eds.), *On the development of developmental psychology* (pp. 111–134). Basel, Switzerland: Karger.

Meacham, J. A. (1990). The loss of wisdom. In R. J. Sternberg (Ed.), *Wisdom: Its nature, origins, and development* (pp. 181–211). New York: Cambridge University Press.

Mieder, W. (1993). *Proverbs are never out of season: Popular wisdom in the Modern Age.* New York: Oxford University Press.

Mieder, W. (1997). *The politics of proverbs.* Madison, WI: University of Wisconsin Press.

Mieder, W. (2002). Proverbium. In *Yearbook of international proverb scholarship* (Vol. 19). Burlington, VT: University of Vermont.

Mieder, W., & Dundes, A. (1994). *The wisdom of many.* Madison, WI: University of Wisconsin Press.

Milner, G. B. (1971). The quartered shield: Outline of a semantic taxonomy (of proverbs). In E. Ardener (Ed.), *Social anthropology and language* (pp. 243–269). London: Tavistock.

Montgomery, A., Barber, C., & McKee, P. (2002). A phenomenological study of wisdom in later life. *International Journal of Aging and Human Development, 52,* 139–157.

Moody, H. R. (1986). The meaning of life and the meaning of old age. In T. Cole & S. Gadow (Eds.), *What does it mean to grow old? Views from the humanities.* Durham, NC: Duke University Press.

Nanamoli, B. (2001). *The life of the Buddha. According to the Pali Canon.* Seattle, WA: BPS Pariyatti Editions.

Natali, C. (2001). *The wisdom of Aristotle.* Albany, NY: State University of New York Press.

Nichols, R. (1996). Maxims, "practical wisdom," and the language of action. *Political Theory, 24,* 687–705.

Noel, J. (1999). On the varieties of *Phronesis. Educational Philosophy and Theory, 31*(3), 273–289.

Nozick, R. (1989). What is wisdom and why do philosophers love it so? In R. Nozick (Ed.), *The examined life: Philosophical meditation* (pp. 267–278). New York: Simon & Schuster.

Orwoll, L., & Perlmutter, M. (1990). The study of wise persons: Integrating a personality perspective. In R. J. Sternberg (Ed.), *Wisdom: Its nature origins, and development* (pp. 160–180). New York: Cambridge University Press.

Osbeck, L. M., & Robinson, D. N. (2005). Philosophical theories of wisdom. In R. J. Sternberg & J. Jordan (Eds.), *A handbook of wisdom: Psychological perspectives.* New York: Cambridge University Press.

Oser, F. K., Schenker, D., & Spychiger, M. (1999). Wisdom: An action-oriented approach. In K. H. Reich, F. K. Oser, & W. G. Scarlett (Eds.), *Psychological studies on spiritual and religious development: Being human: The case of religion* (Vol. 2, pp. 155–172). Lengerich, Germany: Pabst Science Publishers.

Overton, W. F., & Reese, H. W. (1973). Models of development: Methodological implications. In J. R. Nesselroade & H. W. Reese (Eds.), *Life-span developmental psychology; methodological issues* (pp. 65–86). New York: Academic Press.

Oxford English Dictionary (2nd ed.). (1989). Oxford: Oxford University Press.

Palmer, S. (1710). *Moral essays on some of the most curious and significant English, Scotch and Foreign proverbs.* London: Hodgkin.

Papalia, D. E., Camp, C. J., & Feldman, R. D. (1996). *Adult development and aging.* New York: McGraw-Hill.

Paris, S. G. (2001). Wisdom, snake oil, and the educational marketplace. *Educational Psychologist, 36,* 257–260.

Pascual-Leone, J. (1990). An essay on wisdom: toward organismic processes that make it possible. In R. J. Sternberg (Ed.), *Wisdom: Its nature, origins, and development* (pp. 244–278). New York: Cambridge University Press.

Pascual-Leone, J. (2000). Mental attention, consciousness, and the progressive emergence of wisdom. *Journal of Adult Development, 7*(4), 241–254.

Pasupathi, M., & Staudinger, U. M. (2001). Do advanced moral reasoners also show wisdom? Linking moral reasoning and wisdom-related knowledge and judgment. *International Journal of Behavioral Development, 25,* 401–415.

Pasupathi, M., Staudinger, U. M., & Baltes, P. B. (2001). Seeds of wisdom: Adolescents' knowledge and judgment about difficult life problems. *Developmental Psychology, 37*(3), 351–361.

Pennebaker, J. W., & Stone, L. D. (2003). Words of wisdom: Language use over the lifespan. *Personality Processes and Individual Differences, 85*(2), 291–301.

Perdue, L. G. (2002). The rhetoric of wisdom and postcolonial hermeneutics. *Scriptura, 81,* 437–452.

Perkins, D. N. (2001). Wisdom in the wild. *Educational Psychologist, 36*(4), 265–268.

Perry, C. L., Komro, K. A., Jones, R. M., Munson, K., Williams, C. L., & Jason, L. (2002). The measurement of wisdom and its relationship to adolescent substance use and problem behaviors. *Journal of Child and Adolescent Substance Abuse, 12*(1), 45–63.

Perry, T. A. (1993). *Wisdom literature and the structure of proverbs.* University Park, PA: Pennsylvania State University Press.

Piaget, J. (1972). *The psychology of intelligence.* Totowa, NJ: Littlefield-Adams.

Polanyi, M. (1966). *The tacit dimensions.* Garden City, NY: Doubleday.

Randall, W., & Kenyon, G. (2001). *Ordinary wisdom: Biographical aging and the journey of life.* Westport, CT: Praeger.

Randall, W., & Kenyon, G. (2002). Reminiscence as reading our lives: Toward a wisdom environment. In J. Webster & B. Haight (Eds.), *Critical advances in reminiscence: Theoretical, empirical, and clinical perspectives* (pp. 233–53). New York: Springer.

Reznitskaya, A., & Sternberg, R. J. (2004). Teaching students to make wise judgments: The "teaching for wisdom" program. In P. A. Linley & S. Joseph (Eds.), *Positive psychology in practice* (pp. 181–196). Hoboken, NJ: John Wiley & Sons.

Rice, E. F. (1958). *The renaissance idea of wisdom.* Cambridge, MA: Harvard University.

Richardson, M. J., & Pasupathi, M. (2005). Young and growing wiser: Wisdom during adolescence and young adulthood. In R. J. Sternberg & J. Jordan (Eds.), *A handbook of wisdom: Psychological perspectives.* New York: Cambridge University Press.

Riegel, K. F. (1973). Dialectic operation: The final period of cognitive development. *Human Development, 16,* 346–370.

Riley, J. C. (2001). *Rising life expectancy: A global history.* Cambridge: Cambridge University Press.

Roberts, B. W., & Caspi, A. (2003). The cumulative continuity model of personality development: Striking a balance between continuity and change in personality traits across the life course. In U. M. Staudinger & U. Lindenberger (Eds.), *Understanding human development: Lifespan psychology in exchange with other disciplines* (pp. 183–214). Dordrecht, the Netherlands: Kluwer.

Robinson, D. N. (1989). *Aristotle's psychology.* New York: Columbia University Press.

Robinson, D. N. (1990). Wisdom through the ages. In R. J. Sternberg (Ed.), *Wisdom: Its nature, origins, and development* (pp. 13–24). New York: Cambridge University Press.

Rockefeller, S. C. (2006). Meditation, social change, and undergraduate education. *Teachers College Record, 108*(9), 1775–1786.

Rogers, T. B. (1990). Proverbs as psychological theories. Or is it the other way around? *Canadian Psychology, 31,* 195–207.

Rooney, D. (2005). Knowledge, economy, technology and society: The politics of discourse. *Telematics and Informatics, 22*(3), 405–422.

Rooney, D., & McKenna, B. (2007). Wisdom in organizations: Whence and whither. *Social Epistemology, 21*(2), 113–138.

Rowley, J. (2007). The wisdom hierarchy: Representations of the DIKW hierarchy. *Journal of Information Science, 33*(2), 163–180.

Rudolph, K. (2005). Wisdom. In L. Jones (Ed.), *Encyclopedia of religion* (2nd ed., Vol. 14, pp. 9746–9754). Detroit: Thomson Gale—Macmillan.

Ryan, S. (1997). What is wisdom? *Philosophical Studies, 93,* 119–139.

Ryff, C. D. (1995). Psychological well-being in adult life. *Current Directions in Psychological Science, 4,* 99–104.

Ryff, C. D., & Keyes, C. L. M. (1995). The structure of psychological well-being revisited. *Journal of Personality and Social Psychology, 69,* 719–727.

Salthouse, T. A. (1991). *Theoretical perspectives on cognitive aging.* Hillsdale, NJ: Erlbaum.

Sandars, N. K. (1972). *The epic of Gilgamesh.* New York: Penguin Classics.

Santas, G. X. (2006). *The Blackwell guide to Plato's Republic.* New York: Blackwell.

Schaie, K. W. (1989). Perceptual speed in adulthood: Cross-sectional and longitudinal studies. *Psychology and Aging, 4,* 443–453.

Schaie, K. W. (1996). *Intellectual development in adulthood: The Seattle Longitudinal Study.* New York: Cambridge University Press.

Schmidbauer, W. (1977). *Die Hilflosen Helfer (The helpless helpers).* Reinbek, Germany: Rowohlt.

Simonton, D. K. (1990). Creativity and wisdom in aging. In J. E. Birren & K. W. Schaie (Eds.), *Handbook of the psychology of aging* (3rd ed., pp. 320–329). New York: Academic Press.

Sinnott, J. D. (1993). Use of complex thought and resolving intragroup conflicts: A means to conscious adult development in the workplace. In J. Dernick & P. M. Miller (Eds.), *Development in the workplace.* Mahwah, NJ: Erlbaum.

Sinnott-Armstrong, W. (Ed.). (2004). *Pyrrhonian skepticism.* New York: Oxford University Press.

Smith, J., & Baltes, P. B. (1990). Wisdom-related knowledge: Age/cohort differences in response to life-planning problems. *Developmental Psychology, 26,* 494–505.

Smith, J., & Baltes, P. B. (1993). Differential psychological ageing: Profiles of the old and very old. *Ageing and Society, 13,* 551–587.

Smith, J., Dixon, R. A., & Baltes, P. B. (1989). Expertise in life-planning: A new research approach to investigating aspects of wisdom. In M. L. Commons, J. D. Sinnott, F. A. Richards, & C. Armon (Eds.), *Beyond formal operations II* (Vol. 1, pp. 307–331). New York: Praeger.

Smith, J., Staudinger, U. M., & Baltes, P. B. (1994). Occupational settings facilitating wisdom-related knowledge: The sample case of clinical psychologists. *Journal of Consulting and Clinical Psychology, 62,* 989–999.

Smith, S. D. (1998). *The constitution and the pride of reason.* New York: Oxford University Press.

Sowarka, D. (1989). Weisheit und weise Personen: Common-Sense-Konzepte älterer Menschen. *Zeitschrift für Entwicklungspsychologie und Paedagogische Psychologie, 21,* 87–109.

Srivastva, S., & Cooperrider, D. L. (Eds.). (1998). *Organizational wisdom and executive courage.* San Francisco, CA: New Lexington Press.

Stange, A. (2005). *The social dimension of wisdom: Conditions for perceiving advice-giving persons as wise.* Unpublished doctoral dissertation, Free University of Berlin, Germany.

Stanovich, K. E. (2001). The rationality of educating for wisdom. *Educational Psychologist, 36,* 247–251.

Staudinger, U. M. (1989). *The study of life review: An approach to the investigation of intellectual development across the life span* (Dissertation). Berlin, Germany: Edition Sigma. Doctoral dissertation, Max Planck Institute of Human Development and Education, Berlin, and Verlag Klett-Cotta, Stuttgart, Germany.

Staudinger, U. M. (1996). Wisdom and the social-interactive foundation of the mind. In P. B. Baltes & U. M. Staudinger (Eds.), *Interactive minds: Life-span perspectives on the social foundation of cognition* (pp. 276–318). New York: Cambridge University Press.

Staudinger, U. M. (1999). Older and wiser? Integrating results on the relationship between age and wisdom-related performance. *International Journal of Behavioral Development, 23*(3), 641–664.

Staudinger, U. M. (2001). Wisdom. In G. L. Maddox (Ed.). *The encyclopedia of aging* (3rd ed., Vol. 2, pp. 1059–1062). New York: Springer.

Staudinger, U. M. (2008). A psychology of wisdom: History and recent developments. *Research in Human Development, 5,* 107–120.

Staudinger, U. M., & Baltes, P. B. (1996). Interactive minds: A facilitative setting for wisdom-related performance? *Journal of Personality and Social Psychology, 71,* 746–762.

Staudinger, U. M., & Baltes, P. B. (2001). Entwicklungspsychologie der Lebensspanne. In H. Helmchen, F. A. Henn, H. Lauter, & N. Sartorius (Eds.), *Psychiatrie der Gegenwart: Vol. 1. Wissenschaftliche Grundlagen der Psychiatrie* (4th ed., pp. 3–17). Berlin: Springer.

Staudinger, U. M., Dörner, J., & Mickler, C. (2005). Wisdom and personality. In R. J. Sternberg & J. Jordan (Eds.), *A handbook of wisdom: Psychological perspectives.* New York: Cambridge University Press.

Staudinger, U. M., Kessler, E. M., & Dörner, J. (2006). Wisdom in social context. In K. W. Schaie & L. Carstensen (Eds.), *Social structures, aging, and self-regulation in the elderly* (pp. 33–54). New York: Springer.

Staudinger, U. M., & Leipold, B. (2002). The assessment of wisdom-related performance. In S. J. Lopez & C. R. Snyder (Eds.), *The handbook of positive psychology assessment* (pp. 171–184). Washington, DC: American Psychological Association.

Staudinger, U. M., Lopez, D. F., & Baltes, P. B. (1997). The psychometric location of wisdom-related performance: Intelligence, personality, and more? *Personality and Social Psychology Bulletin, 23,* 1200–1214.

Staudinger, U. M., Maciel, A. G., Smith, J., & Baltes, P. B. (1998). What predicts wisdom-related performance? A first look at personality, intelligence, and facilitative experiential contexts. *European Journal of Personality, 12,* 1–17.

Staudinger, U. M., & Pasupathi, M. (2003). Correlates of wisdom-related performance in adolescence and adulthood: Age-graded differences in "paths" toward desirable development. *Journal of Research on Adolescence, 13*(3), 239–268.

Staudinger, U. M., Smith, J., & Baltes, P. B. (1992). Wisdom-related knowledge in a life review task: Age differences and the role of professional specialization. *Psychology and Aging, 7*(2), 271–281.

Sternberg, R. J. (1985). Implicit theories of intelligence, creativity, and wisdom. *Journal of Personality and Social Psychology, 49,* 607–627.

Sternberg, R. J. (1990). Wisdom and its relations to intelligence and creativity. In R. J. Sternberg (Ed.), *Wisdom: Its nature, origins, and development* (pp. 142–159). New York: Cambridge University Press.

Sternberg, R. J. (1996). Styles of thinking. In P. B. Baltes & U. M. Staudinger (Eds.), *Interactive minds: Life- span perspectives on the social foundation of cognition* (pp. 347–365). New York: Cambridge University Press.

Sternberg, R. J. (1997). *Successful intelligence.* New York: Plume Books.

Sternberg, R. J. (1998). A balance theory of wisdom. *Review of General Psychology, 2,* 347–365.

Sternberg, R. J. (2000). Intelligence and wisdom. In R. J. Sternberg (Ed.), *Handbook of intelligence* (pp. 629–647). New York: Cambridge University Press.

Sternberg, R. J. (2001). Why schools should teach for wisdom: The balance theory of wisdom in educational settings. *Educational Psychologist, 36*(4), 227–245.

Sternberg, R. J. (Ed.). (2002). *Why smart people can be so stupid.* New Haven, CT: Yale University Press.

Sternberg, R. J. (2003). *Wisdom, intelligence, and creativity synthesized.* New York: Cambridge University Press.

Sternberg, R. J. (2004). Teaching for wisdom: What matters is not what students know, but how they use it. In D. R. Walling (Ed.), *Public education, Democracy, and the common good* (pp. 121–132). Bloomington, IN: Phi Delta Kappan.

Sternberg, R. J. (2005a). What is wisdom and how can we develop it? In D. L. Evans, E. Foa, R. Gur, H. Hendin, C. O'Brien, M. E. P. Seligman, & B. T. Walsh (Eds.), *Treatments that work for adolescents* (pp. 664–674). New York: Oxford University Press.

Sternberg, R. J. (2005b). Older but not wiser? The relationship between age and wisdom. *Ageing International, 30*(1), 5–26.

Sternberg, R. J. (2005c). WICS: A model of leadership. *Psychologist-Manager Journal, 8*(1), 29–43.

Sternberg, R. J. (2005d). WICS: A model of positive educational leadership comprising wisdom, intelligence, and creativity synthesized. *Educational Psychology Review, 17*(3), 191–262.

Sternberg, R. J. (2007). A systems model of leadership: WICS. *American Psychologist, 62*(1), 34–42.

Sternberg, R. J. (2008). The WICS approach to leadership: Stories of leadership and the structures and processes that support them. *Leadership Quarterly, 19*(3), 360–371.

Sternberg, R. J., Forsythe, G. B., Hedlund, J., Horvath, J. A., Wagner, R. K., Williams, W. M., et al. (2000). *Practical intelligence in everyday life.* New York: Cambridge University Press.

Sternberg, R. J., & Jordan, J. (Eds.). (2005). *A handbook of wisdom: Psychological perspectives.* New York: Cambridge University Press.

Sternberg, R. J., & Lubart, T. I. (2001). Wisdom and creativity. In J. E. Birren & K. W. Schaie (Eds.), *Handbook of the psychology of aging* (5th ed., pp. 500–522). San Diego, CA: Academic Press.

Sternberg, R. J., Reznitskaya, A., & Jarvin, L. (2007). Teaching for wisdom: What matters is not what students know, but how they use it. *London Review of Education, 5*(2), 143–158.

Sternberg, R. J., & Vroom, V. H. (2002). The person versus the situation in leadership. *Leadership Quarterly, 13,* 301–323.

Stump, E. (2003). *Aquinas.* New York: Routledge.

Takahashi, M., & Bordia, P. (2000). The concept of wisdom: A cross cultural comparison. *International Journal of Psychology, 35*(1), 1–9.

Takahashi, M., & Overton, W. F. (2002). Wisdom: A culturally inclusive developmental perspective. *International Journal of Behavioral Development, 26*(3), 269–277.

Takahashi, M., & Overton, W. F. (2005). Cultural foundations of wisdom: An integrated developmental approach. In R. J. Sternberg & J. Jordan (Eds.), *A handbook of wisdom: Psychological perspectives.* New York: Cambridge University Press.

Takanishi, R., & Hamburg, D. A. (Eds.). (1997). *Preparing adolescents for the twenty-first century: Challenges facing Europe and the United States.* Cambridge: Cambridge University Press.

Takayama, M. (2002). *The concept of wisdom and wise people in Japan.* Unpublished doctoral dissertation, Tokyo University, Japan.

Taranto, M. A. (1989). Facets of wisdom: A theoretical synthesis. *International Journal of Aging and Human Development, 29,* 1–21.

Taylor, C. (2005). *The ethics of authenticity.* Cambridge, MA: Harvard University Press.

Tolstoy, L. (2009). Little girls are wiser than men. In L. Wiener (Ed.), *Walk in the light and twenty-three tales* (pp. 126–127). Lawrence, KS: Digireads.com Publishing. (Original work published 1885)

Trowbridge, R. H. (2005). *The scientific approach to wisdom.* Unpublished doctoral dissertation, Union Institute & University, Cincinnati, OH. Retrieved from www.cop.com/ TheScientificApproachtoWisdom.doc. Accessed November 21, 2008.

Vaillant, G. E. (1977). *Adaptation to life.* Boston, MA: Little, Brown.

Valdez, J. M. (1994). Wisdom: A Hispanic perspective (Doctoral dissertation, Colorado State University, 1993). *Dissertation International Abstract, 54,* 6482-B.

Wall, R. B. (2005). Tai chi and mindfulness-based stress reduction in a Boston public middle school. *Journal of Pediatric Health Care, 19*(4), 230–237.

Wattles, J. (1996). *The golden rule.* New York: Oxford University Press.

Webster, J. D. (2003). An exploratory analysis of a self-assessed wisdom scale. *Journal of Adult Development, 10*(1), 13–22.

Webster, J. D. (2007). Measuring the character strength of wisdom. *International Journal of Aging & Human Development, 65*(2), 163–183.

Whittington, J. L., Pitts, T. M., Kageler, W., & Goodwin, V. L. (2005). Legacy leadership: The leadership wisdom of the apostle Paul. *Leadership Quarterly, 16*(5), 749–770.

Willis, S. L., & Dubin, S. S (Eds.). (1990). *Maintaining professional competence: Approaches to career enhancement vitality, and success throughout a work life.* San Francisco, CA: Jossey-Bass.

Wink, P., & Helson, R. (1997). Practical and transcendent wisdom: Their nature and some longitudinal findings. *Journal of Adult Development, 4,* 1–15.

Wood, A. W. (1999). *Kant's ethical thought.* Cambridge: Cambridge University Press.

Yang, S. (2001). Conceptions of wisdom among Taiwanese Chinese. *Journal of Cross-Cultural Psychology, 32*(6), 662–680.

Yang, S. (2008). A process view of wisdom. *Journal of Adult Development, 15*(2), 62–75.

Young, M. A. (2005). *Negotiating the good life: Aristotle and the civil society.* Burlington, VT: Ashgate.

Yutang, L. (Ed.). (1994). *The wisdom of Confucius.* New York: Random House.

Zajonc, R. B. (1968). Attitudinal effects of mere exposure. *Journal of Personality and Social Psychology, 9*(2), 1–27.

CHAPTER 24

Thriving across the Life Span

MATTHEW J. BUNDICK, DAVID S. YEAGER, PAMELA EBSTYNE KING, and WILLIAM DAMON

By common definition, the word *thrive* implies a desirable life condition. Virtually any rational person who is not bent on self-destruction wishes to thrive, and virtually anybody who cares about the well-being of others wants to see them thrive. Certainly the question is not whether it is a good thing to thrive throughout life, but rather what exactly it means for a person to thrive. This question is difficult enough when asked about a single individual at a single point in time. Adding greatly to the complexity of the question is that individuals and their needs change over time. Moreover, what it takes to thrive in one social, cultural, and historical setting may not work well at all in a different time and place. Because of these daunting complexities, together with a lack of conceptual consensus

and limited empirical study of the construct, no one has yet fully reviewed and put forth a detailed set of criteria that could define *thriving* in a manner that could be studied across all of life's stages and contexts.

As a developmental goal or *telos, thriving* retains considerable appeal to those who wish to explore optimal conditions of human development. Most parents, teachers, youth workers—indeed, anyone who has a stake in the positive development of young people—would likely agree to the benefits of promoting more than mere competence. Thus, a term is required that identifies a telos *and* draws attention to the more elevated aspects of human thought and behavior. The study of thriving is consistent with recent shifts in the psychological sciences toward interest in

---

We thank the Thrive Foundation for Youth for their generous support of this work, and their many colleagues on the Thriving Indicators Project for their conceptual contributions.

the positive dimensions of our life goals and experiences (see Seligman & Csikszentmihalyi, 2000). Not surprisingly, then, the term appears frequently in current writings about individual growth over the life span. But often the term is left undefined or ambiguous, and there have been few attempts to build a scientific knowledge base of what thriving means, how it comes about over the life course of individual lives, and how it can be studied empirically.

This chapter advances a set of definitional criteria synthesizing previous work that we intend to function as the basis for the systematic study of thriving across diverse social and cultural contexts, and at all phases of the life span. We then outline a number of essential assumptions that follow from this definition, and consider the condition of thriving from developmental and more broadly defined psychological perspectives, reviewing the existing scientific literature that has examined thriving and its closely related constructs. Finally, we derive several conclusions regarding the nature and facilitators of thriving throughout the course of human development. The general goals of this chapter are to establish the concept of thriving as a scientifically useful means of analyzing progress toward positive developmental ends and to offer a conceptualization of thriving that represents a first step toward a unifying theory of positive development across the life span.

CONCEPT OF THRIVING IN DEVELOPMENTAL STUDY

The term *thriving* has been used in various ways during its century-long history in developmental study. Holt's (1897) *The Diseases of Infancy and Childhood* may be the first research publication to introduce the term, describing inadequate growth and development in infancy as a *failure to thrive* (FTT). The phrase failure to thrive soon became a measurable (if not quite general) syndrome in pediatric medicine, and retained that status for most of the 20th century until falling out of favor after it was replaced by a number of more specific behavioral deficits.

More recently, thriving has been conceptualized by both medical and social scientists in a variety of ways (and with a variety of labels) across the entire life span, from optimal development in adolescence to growth as a response to adversity in adulthood through the reemergence of the notion of FTT in late adulthood. A major advantage of developing and using this concept lies in its potential to capture the unique features of optimal development, rather than to note a deficit by its inverse or absence. In

this chapter, therefore, we shall introduce a concept of thriving and its associated principles derived primarily from the frameworks of positive psychology (Seligman & Csikszentmihalyi, 2000) and positive youth development (PYD) (Benson, 2008; Damon, 2004; Lerner, 2007). In the context of these perspectives, we review the ways in which the term has been used by scholars from a number of research traditions, as well as a number of closely related concepts dealing with positive development and optimal human functioning across the life span.

Fundamental to our viewpoint is the notion that human development must be understood from not only a deficit-centered perspective, but also a strengths-based one. Indeed, recent decades have seen a mushrooming of strengths-based research, such as studies of positive psychology (Seligman & Csikszentmihalyi, 2000), happiness (Diener, 1984), psychological well-being (Ryff, 1989), flourishing (Keyes, 2002), optimal experience or "flow" (Csikszentmihalyi, 1990), character strengths (Peterson & Seligman, 2004), developmental assets (Benson, 1997), purpose (Damon, 2008), "sparks" (Benson, 2008), and healthy adolescence (Lerner, 2007). In the field of developmental psychology, the positive perspective has its roots in seminal writings on cognitive development by Jean Piaget (1952) and Heinz Werner (1948), as well as those on resilience by Norman Garmezy (1983) and Emmy Werner (1985; Werner & Smith, 1982), which accentuated rather than discounted the capacities of youth. In the years since the groundbreaking work of these scholars, researchers and practitioners of youth development (who were once focused solely on the prevention and remediation of problem behaviors such as alcohol and drug use, delinquency, and violence) have heard and responded to Karen Pittman's (1991) call to arms: "Problem-free is not fully prepared." The PYD movement has thus "introduced a more affirmative and welcome vision of young people [which] envisions young people as resources rather than as problems for society [and] emphasizes the manifest potentialities rather than the supposed incapacities of young people" (Damon, 2004, p. 15).

Research on late adult development and gerontological health has followed suit, redirecting some of its focus from primarily cataloging declining mental and physical health in later adulthood to emphasizing their potential to effectively deal with losses and capacity for "successful" development at this stage of life (Baltes & Baltes, 1990; Baltes & Smith, 2003; Heckhausen, 1999; Rowe & Kahn, 1998; Schulz & Heckhausen, 1996). Though conceptualizations of successful late adult development vary somewhat, Rowe and Kahn (1998) offer a concise and straightforward three-component definition, which includes the capacity for high cognitive and physical functioning, active engagement in life, and a low probability and existence of disease and disease-related disability. In particular, Baltes and his colleagues have advanced their notions of wisdom and selective optimization with compensation as integral to successful development in late adulthood (Baltes, 1997; these concepts are covered in more detail later in this chapter; see also Karelitz, Jarvin, & Sternberg, Chapter 23 of this volume, for an extended discussion of the development of wisdom). This notion of successful late adult development, in particular the Selection, Optimization, Compensation (SOC) model, provides a framework for understanding the continuation of positive development through later life, and may be brought to bear on how we understand optimal development across the life span (Baltes, Staudinger, & Lindenberger, 1999; Lerner, Freund, De Stefanis, & Habermas, 2001).

The findings of this ever-growing body of research on positive development at all stages of the life span have not only presented a more encouraging view of human development where the headlines had too often focused on deficiencies and personal problems (or "crises"; Erikson, 1968), but they also have demonstrated the value of drawing attention to personal strengths as a way to prevent such problems and to provide protection when life crises do occur. For example, Hawkins, Catalano, and Miller (1992) have proposed a social-development model through which children's and adolescents' increased opportunities for involvement, social skills, and reinforcement from important others (such as parents) can lead to social bonding, which acts as a buffer against drug and alcohol use. Other scholars of youth development such as Peter Benson, Peter Scales, and their colleagues at the Search Institute have demonstrated that the presence of certain developmental strengths, or "developmental assets," during adolescence is associated with a decrease in problem behaviors such as depression, suicidal thoughts, violence, and drug and alcohol abuse (Leffert, Benson, Scales, Sharma, Drake, & Blyth, 1998; Scales, Benson, Leffert, & Blyth, 2000; for a review, see Benson, 2007). In older adult populations, the presence of certain developmental strengths, such as a sense of purpose in life, is predictive of better mental and physical health (Pinquart, 2002); similarly, greater wisdom has been shown to be related to an increased ability to exercise self-restraint when tempted to engage in one's vices (Baltes, Staudinger, & Lindenberger, 1999).

Together, the combination of a developmental perspective (see Overton, 2006) with a strengths-based approach (see Damon, 2004) brings us closer to an understanding of what it means to "thrive." Such knowledge may have vital implications for, among other things, the education system, youth development programs, parenting practices, elder care, human longevity, personal fulfillment across the life span, and even the stability of civil society (Lerner, 2004). We now turn to the current definition of thriving and an explication of a set of principles we have distilled from the literature that are core to the construct. First, we offer a brief history of the theorizing around and conceptualizations of thriving leading up to the current definition and set of principles.

DEFINITION AND PRINCIPLES OF THRIVING

Brief History of the Conceptualization of Thriving

Generally speaking, researchers in the PYD tradition agree that thriving refers to, broadly speaking, the optimal development of adolescents; however, disagreement and conceptual confusion about what constitutes "optimal" development has pervaded the literature. Indeed, it has proved difficult to keep pace with this moving conceptual target, let alone the specific contextual-temporal factors that make thriving appear different for different people across time and place. Although it is promising that the notion of *thriving* has received serious attention by scholars, and recent work has advanced both the theory and measurement of the construct (e.g., Benson & Scales, 2009; Gestsdottir & Lerner, 2007), it is time for consensus—the current review of this literature together with the definition and principles advanced herein are intended to serve that end. This section identifies and explores some of the more prominent conceptualizations of thriving in the PYD literature, which have formed the foundation for the current definition.

Since Benson (1990) first used the term "thriving" to refer to a set of positive "vital signs" in adolescence (e.g., academic success, caring for others and their communities, the affirmation of cultural and ethnic diversity, commitment to healthy lifestyles; see Benson & Scales, 2009), scholars of PYD have referred to thriving in a variety of ways, including as the process of positive development, successful regulation of one's development, a variety of outcomes of positive development, a variety of behaviors thought to be reflective of this process, an individual orientation toward positive development, and/or some combination of the above (Benson & Scales, 2009; Dowling, Steinunn, Anderson, von Eye, & Lerner, 2003; Gestsdottir & Lerner, 2007; Jelicic, Bobek, Phelps, Lerner, & Lerner, 2007; King, Dowling, et al., 2005; Lerner, Fisher, & Weinberg, 2000; Scales et al., 2000; Theokas et al., 2005). Further, thriving has at different times been operationalized by many different indicators, ranging from one's social competencies (such as compassion and connection) to one's engagement in discrete behaviors (such as attending church and volunteering). There has been a decided lack of consistency in the sets of indicators different researchers use; for example, sometimes religion or spirituality, or both, are considered indicators of thriving (e.g., Dowling et al., 2004; King & Benson, 2005); sometimes they are not (e.g., Lerner, Phelps, Alberts, Forman, & Christiansen, 2007). If this brief overview is any indication, the confusion in the literature over what thriving is, not to mention what it includes and how to measure it, is apparent (see Benson & Scales, 2009, for a similar perspective).

Although the first mention of thriving in the empirical PYD literature can be found in Benson, Leffert, Scales, and Blyth (1998), the first study in the PYD tradition to operationalize thriving was performed by Scales et al. (2000). These authors constructed a composite "thriving index" from items of an existing self-assessment tool known as the Search Institute Profiles of Student Life: Attitudes and Behaviors (PSL-AB) survey. To create this index, they summed the scores of single items that measured engagement in the following behaviors and individual characteristics: (1) school success, (2) leadership, (3) helping others, (4) maintenance of physical health, (5) delay of gratification, (6) valuing diversity, and (7) overcoming adversity. The authors chose these indicators to represent thriving because, in their review of the literature on adolescent development, they found these categories to be "generally related to other positive outcomes" and, as a group, "collectively reflect some of the developmental tasks of adolescence" (Scales et al., 2000, p. 28). Scales et al. (2000) used primarily cross-sectional, correlational analyses to explore the relations between these seven thriving outcomes and the Search Institute's well-established model of 40 Developmental Assets, which present a set of individual and environmental building blocks of positive development (Benson, 1997; additional review of the 40 Developmental Assets model can be found later in this chapter). The authors found that the presence of four of the eight theoretical groupings of developmental assets (planning and decision making, time in youth programs,

cultural competence, and self-esteem) predicted higher scores on their measure of thriving; the results for the other groupings of assets were mixed as a function of race and in their magnitude.

Although Scales et al.'s (2000) efforts to operationalize thriving represent an important early step in the scientific study of the construct, their work reflects the growing pains of an emerging field of inquiry. For example, it is unclear whether developmental assets were considered by these authors to be necessary inputs for optimal development, whether they are themselves indicators of the thriving process, or perhaps instead whether thriving is actually defined by the presence of these assets. It is also unclear whether thriving is a cause or a consequence of the assets, or both, in the short and long term. Moreover, although comprehensive in its multidimensionality, their thriving index suffered from a number of psychometric shortcomings, including issues of validity (such as the use of one-item measures) and low reliability. As such, this study might be viewed more symbolically as a success in the direction of putting an early theory of thriving to the empirical test and in laying the groundwork for future empirical work in the field.

Though suffering from the same limitations regarding their operationalization of thriving, Theokas et al. (2005) extended Scales et al.'s (2000) investigation through an exploration of the factor structure of the 40 Developmental Assets and these factors' relations with thriving behaviors. Following an exploratory factor analysis of the assets, the authors used multivariate analyses to uncover relations among two second-order factors of "individual assets" (such as personal values and social consciousness) and "ecological assets" (such as family support and adult mentorship), and thriving behaviors. These factors, both by themselves and in combination, accounted for unique variance in the prediction of thriving behaviors. Specifically, they found that, on average, the more overall assets an individual has, the more thriving behaviors they report engaging in, and that those high in either individual or ecological assets are more likely to report greater thriving, regardless of the number of assets in the other factor. These findings support the notion that a combination of positive individual and contextual attributes is conducive to positive development, a notion to which we return later in the chapter in a discussion of relational developmental systems theory (Lerner, 2006; Lerner & Overton, 2008; Overton, 2006).

Benson and Saito's (2001) report on the scientific foundations for youth development further fleshed out Benson and his colleagues' thinking on thriving. These authors defined thriving outcomes as positive developmental outcomes that are opposite of high-risk unhealthy behaviors, including both short-term outcomes (through adolescence) and long-term outcomes (into adulthood). Their indicators of youth thriving included school success, affirmation of diversity, and positive nutrition, whereas adult thriving outcomes included work effectiveness, parenting effectiveness, and civic engagement. More recently, Benson and Scales (2009; Benson, 2008) have sharpened their conceptualization of thriving as having three "key interconnected parts," which suggest that thriving has the following characteristics:

1. Represents a dynamic and bi-directional relational interplay over time of a young person intrinsically animated and energized by discovering his/her specialness, and the developmental contexts (people, places) that know, affirm, celebrate, encourage and guide its expression [see Figure 24.1];

2. Involves "stability" or "balance" of movement toward something; that is, thriving is a process of experiencing a balance between continuity and discontinuity of development over time that is optimal for a given individual's fused relations with her or his contexts; and

3. Reflects both where a young person is currently in their journey to idealized personhood, and whether they are on the kind of path to get there that could rightly be called one of exemplary adaptive development regulations. (Benson & Scales, 2009, p. 90)

Benson and Scales (2009) importantly note that they "prefer to describe a young person at any point in time as more or less thriving *oriented*, rather than as thriving or not" (p. 12). This reflects (and has helped inform) the current view that there exists a distinction between the thriving process and thriving as a descriptor of an individual person at a given point in time, a point to which we return shortly.

Beyond offering their conceptualization of thriving, Benson and Scales (2009) further present a new measurement tool for assessing thriving (see Table 24.1). Revealing its theoretical underpinnings, the authors have constructed this tool to measure a profile of thriving youth composed of four groupings of thriving indicators: (1) the young person, (2) the young person's developmental contexts, (3) the young person's active role in shaping contexts, and (4) developmental contexts' active role in shaping the young person. These must be considered in unison to obtain a complete picture of the thriving process and one's thriving

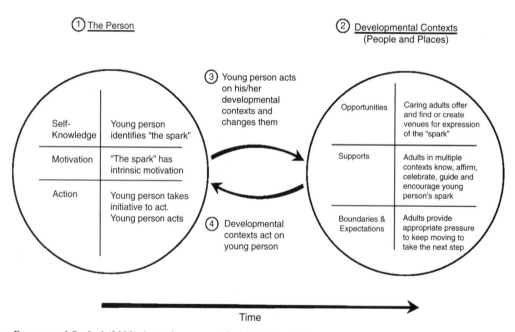

Figure 24.1 Benson and Scales' (2009) dynamic process of thriving in adolescence.
Source: Reprinted from Benson, P. L., & Scales, P. C. (2009). The definition and preliminary measurement of thriving in adolescence. *Journal of Positive Psychology, 4*(1), 85–104, with permission from Taylor & Francis Ltd. This article can be accessed at http://www.informaworld.com.

TABLE 24.1 Benson and Scales's (2009) Theoretical Measurement Markers of Thriving in Adolescence

Elements of Thriving	Measurement Markers of Thriving
1. Young Person	**1. Spark identification.** Young person can name, describe talents and interests that give them energy and purpose.
	2. Positive emotionality. Young person is positive and optimistic.
	3. Stability/growth of spark. Young person reports growth in developing and pursuing sparks over the last 12 months.
	4. Motivation. Young person has intrinsic desire to pursue their sparks and enjoys challenges.
	5. Purpose. Young person has a sense of purpose and a goal to make a positive difference in the world.
	6. Hopeful future. Young person sees self as on the way to a happy and successful future.
	7. Prosocial orientation. Young person sees helping others as a personal responsibility and intends to volunteer in the next year.
	8. Spiritual development. Young person affirms importance of a sacred or transcendent force and the role of their faith or spirituality in shaping everyday thoughts and actions.
2. The Young Person's Developmental Contexts	**Opportunities.** Young person experiences chances to grow and develop their sparks from multiple individuals and life contexts.
	9. Family
	10. Friends
	11. School
	12. Neighborhood
	13. Youth organizations
	14. Religious congregations
	Supports. Young person experiences encouragement and support in pursuing their sparks from multiple life contexts.
	15. Family
	16. Friends
	17. School
	18. Neighborhood
	19. Youth organizations
	20. Religious congregations
	Positive pressure. Young person is pushed to develop their sparks by people in multiple life contexts.
	21. Family
	22. Friends
	23. School
	24. Neighborhood
	25. Youth organizations
	26. Religious congregations
3. Young Person's Active Role in Shaping Contexts	**27. Action to develop and pursue sparks.** Young person seeks and acts on adult guidance, studies or practices, and takes other actions to develop their sparks.
4. Developmental Contexts Act on the Young Person	**28. Frequency of specific adult actions.** How often adults do concrete things to motivate, enable, and push young people to develop their sparks and connect them to others who can help.
	29. Adult role models of sparks. Young person has several adult role models who have sparks like theirs and who inspire young people to develop their sparks.

Additional Constructs Measured in Thriving Youth Survey

Positive Developmental Outcomes	**Life satisfaction.** Young person feels good about their life.
	Positive health perceptions. Young person feels strong and healthy.
	Contribution to social good. Young person volunteers or does things to make their world a better place.
	School success. Young person earns a B or higher average in school.
	Values diversity. Young person considers it important to know people of different races.
	Leadership. Young person has been a leader in a group or organization in the last 12 months.

Continued

TABLE 24.1 (*Continued*)

Other Correlates of Thriving	**Personal power/confidence.** Young person feels confident about reaching goals.
	Competence:
	Social. Young person is good at making friends and cares about others' feelings.
	Behavioral (Self-control). Young person can control emotions and delay gratification.
	Academic. Young person is confident about ability to do school work.
	Moral compass/character. Young person says others would describe them as respectful, responsible, helpful, and hard working, among other virtues, and says they live their values.
	Fulfillment of potential. Young person takes the initiative and takes advantage of opportunities.
	Personal growth. Young person sets goals and seeks the help needed to reach them.
	Resourcefulness. Young person adjusts and meets challenges well.

Reprinted from Benson, P. L., & Scales, P. C. (2009). The definition and preliminary measurement of thriving in adolescence. *Journal of Positive Psychology, 4*(1), 85–104, with permission from Taylor & Francis Ltd. This article can be accessed at http://www.informaworld.com.

orientation. Among them, the authors propose an indicator of thriving missing from previous conceptualizations: the development of a "spark." They refer to the thriving process as "animated by a passion for, and the exercise of action to nurture, a self-identified interest, skill, or capacity…the pursuit and exercise [of which] is done for its own sake…the motivation is intrinsic, not extrinsic" (Benson & Scales, p. 13). Adding to this, Benson (2008) suggests thriving may be thought of as "the dynamic interplay of a young person animated and energized by discovering his or her specialness, and the developmental contexts (people, places) that know, affirm, celebrate, encourage, and guide its expression" (p. 174).

As Benson and Scales (2009) noted, this new measure still requires further validation and confirmation of its factor structure; furthermore, their inclusion of the "spark" among their indicators invites both broad discussion and empirical testing to better understand the degree to which it is a component, predictor, and/or outcome of thriving. Nonetheless, Benson and Scales's new conceptualization and measurement tool represent an important advance in thriving research and will no doubt move the field forward.

The term "thriving" as an optimal developmental construct has received attention from other scholars of youth development as well. Together with a number of other terms related to PYD, thriving was one of the main foci in King, Shultz, et al.'s (2005) evaluation of the adolescent development literature. Their comprehensive scan of the titles and abstracts of nearly 1,200 articles from prominent developmental journals published between 1991 and 2003

revealed that the term "thriving" only showed up once. The authors concluded that "there exists a wide disparity between what theory and practice suggest is the importance of the PYD perspective and what researchers…indicate through their actions" (King, Shultz, et al., p. 223). Pam King and her colleagues (King, Dowling, et al., 2005) further sought to determine whether their scholarly definition of thriving as an optimal developmental construct was similar to everyday conceptions of thriving. The authors spoke with research investigators in the field and practitioners of youth development, as well as parents and youths, about their understanding of the meaning of the term "thriving." Results suggest that although thriving was conceived of by community members and practitioners of PYD in much the same way as it is by scientists in this field, there nonetheless exists little consistency in the specific terminology used to describe thriving, and there remains a general lack of agreement on a set of indicators. Taken together, this work further highlights the need for a common understanding (and usage) of the term "thriving."

Rich Lerner and his colleagues have also contributed significantly to the study of thriving and optimal development, drawing (as did Benson and his colleagues, and King and her colleagues) on relational developmental systems theory and the concept of adaptive developmental regulation (Ford & Lerner, 1992; Lerner, 2006; Lerner & Overton, 2008). From this perspective, to understand the concept of thriving, one must first understand the tenets of relational developmental systems theory. Damon and Lerner (2008) describe the defining features of this theory, summarized as follows:

1. Relational developmental systems theory espouses a synthetic and integrated approach to understanding development, which involve the integration of all levels of organization from biological and physiological through the cultural and historical.

2. Developmental regulation involves mutually influential individual ←→ context relations (i.e., bidirectional relations among people and their environments) among all levels of the developmental system.

3. The integration of actions of the individual on the context and of the multiple levels of the context on the individual (individual ←→ context) constitutes the fundamental unit of analysis in the study of the basic process of human development.

4. The relational developmental system is characterized by the potential for systematic change, or plasticity, which at the individual level may vary in its trajectory across time and place, and its magnitude across the life span and history.

5. The integrated levels of organization within the relational developmental system will result in individual and contextual differences in plasticity, which makes the study of diversity essential to understanding human development. (Relative plasticity thus implies that there is no "ideal" developmental pathway that applies to all people [Ford & Lerner, 1992].)

Following from these assumptions, the development of an individual cannot be fully understood in isolation; people must take into account their relation to the many levels of systems or ecologies in which their development is embedded. Integral to development, and foundational to the idea of relative plasticity, is the idea advanced by Lerner and his colleagues of temporal embeddedness (Lerner, 2002; Lerner, Dowling, & Anderson, 2003), which acknowledges that the individual's potential for change in person–context relations exists across situations and throughout the life span.

These notions are closely associated with Bronfenbrenner's (1979) ecological systems theory, which suggests development may be viewed as a function of the reciprocal interactions between individuals and the many environments and systems in which they interact. Bronfenbrenner emphasized the significance of bidirectional relational interaction, arguing that to understand an individual's development, one must examine how the individual influences his or her many ecological systems, and how each of these systems impact the individual. This dynamic

process between the person and context is further characteristic of Elder's (1998) life-span theory, Cicchetti and Lynch's (1995) ecological-transactional model of development, Overton's (2006) relational embodied action theory, and Magnusson's (1988; Magnusson & Mahoney, 2003; Magnusson & Stattin, 1998) holistic-interactionistic framework. Indeed, Magnusson and Mahoney suggest that any "definition of positive development cannot be made with reference to an isolated individual; it must be formulated with reference to the characteristics features, resources, and restrictions of the individual considered and the social, cultural, psychical, and historical contexts in which he or she is embedded" (p. 230).

The relational developmental systems theory notion of relative plasticity further stresses that across the life span, development involves the integration of changing relations among the multiple levels of organization that comprise the ecology of human life (Ford & Lerner, 1992; Lerner, 2002; Overton, 2006), and thus that all humans have the potential for systematic change in structure and function at any age (Baltes, 1997; Lerner, 1984, 2002; Thelen & Smith, 1998). Relational developmental systems theory also integrates action theory (Brandstädter, 1984, 2006), which holds that humans are active producers of their own development through these individual ←→ context relations. Lerner, Dowling, and Anderson (2003) offer a succinct summary statement of relational developmental systems theory, suggesting that "changes across the life span are seen as propelled by the dynamic relations between individuals and the multiple levels of the ecology of human development, all changing interdependently across time" (p. 675).

Taking together these notions of relationism and integration, bidirectionality, active production of one's own development, relative plasticity, and relational developmental systems theory suggest that human development can be strengthened through what has been termed *adaptive developmental regulation* (Lerner, 2004). Reflecting the fundamentals of relational developmental systems theory, adaptive developmental regulation refers to engagement in mutually beneficial interrelations between an individual and the multiple ecologies in which he or she is embedded, maintaining and perpetuating healthy, positive functioning for all facets of these relations.

In their discussion of thriving, Lerner et al. (2003) focus much of their attention on their notion of adaptive developmental regulation, which emphasizes the ability for a young person to effectively gather resources and shape the environment to meet personal goals. These authors imply that developmental regulation is, in essence, the sum total of thriving behavior, arguing that "adaptive regulation of person-context relations constitutes the basic process of ontogenetic change" and have "conceptualized the idealized version of this ontogenetic change process as thriving" (Lerner et al., 2003, p. 175).

Reflecting his principle of temporal embeddedness, Lerner (2004) argues that what behaviors constitute thriving at one time and in one context may look quite different under other circumstances. As a result, he suggests that a theory of thriving should first clarify what effective developmental regulation entails in a given time and place; however, he believes there exists a set of thriving indicators that are temporally and contextually standard. All six of his theoretical categories start with the letter C: confidence, competence, character, compassion, connection, and contribution. Thus, according to this perspective,

thriving is the idealized ontogenetic process of developmental regulation and occurs when persons have the first five Cs. The developmental end point of thriving in adolescence is an adulthood status marked by the sixth C: contribution (Figure 24.2). Thus, a person could be said to be thriving when "he or she is involved across time in such healthy, positive relations with his or her community and on the path to what Csikszentmihalyi and Rathhunde (1998) called 'idealized personhood,' and adult status marked by making culturally valued contributions to self, others, and institutions" (Lerner et al., 2003, p. 172).

Taking these assertions together, Lerner and his colleagues (e.g., Lerner, 2004; Lerner et al., 2003) conceptualize thriving as a marker of successful developmental regulation in adolescence, which leads to healthy and contributing adulthood. Furthermore, Lerner (2004, Lerner et al., 2000) has linked this conceptualization of thriving to the notions of

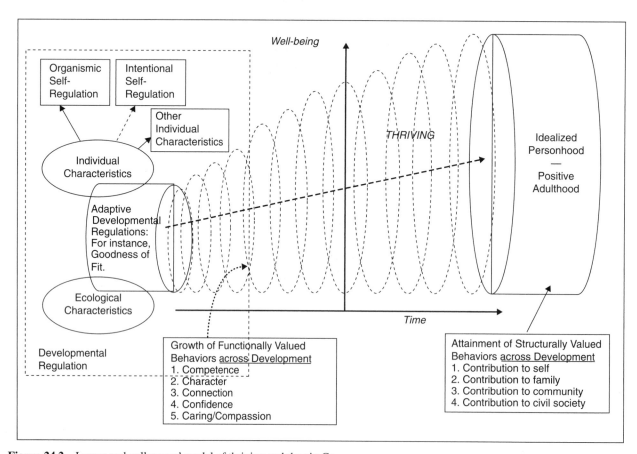

Figure 24.2 Lerner and colleagues' model of thriving and the six Cs.

Source: Reprinted from Gestsdottir, S., & Lerner, R. M. (2007). Intentional self-regulation and positive youth development in early adolescence: Findings from the 4-H Study of Positive Youth Development. *Developmental Psychology, 43*(2), 508–521, with permission of the American Psychological Association.

liberty and the advancement of the common good, suggesting that thriving "is a developmental concept that denotes a healthy change process linking a youth with an adulthood status enabling society to be populated by healthy individuals oriented to integratively serve self and civil society" (Lerner, Brentano, Dowling, & Anderson, 2002, p. 22).

Current Definition of Thriving

Although there are many points of overlap between these conceptualizations of thriving, for the field to move forward, it is essential to have a common understanding and usage of the term. Based on our review of the literature, we propose the following as an integrative (yet succinct) definition of thriving:

> Thriving refers to a dynamic and purposeful process of individual ←→ context interactions over time, through which the person and his/her environment are mutually enhanced.

Most of the aspects of this definition follow directly from relational developmental systems theory and incorporate the notion of adaptive developmental regulation. *Dynamic* draws directly on these theories, particularly invoking the idea of relative plasticity (that human beings are constantly developing over time, and both across and within multiple ecologies), and thus must adaptively self-regulate as they grow and encounter new situations, and select, pursue, and adjust their life goals (Baltes, 1997; Lerner, 1984; Lerner, Dowling, & Anderson, 2003; Thelen & Smith, 2006). By purposeful, we are suggesting there is intentionality to the thriving process, which reflects Brandstädter's (1984) notion that humans are active producers of their own development. In particular, thriving entails goal-setting and goal-striving in accordance with one's individual talents and unique skills (with the individual's understanding and consideration of how these talents and skills might uniquely equip him or her to contribute to the common good), and from the pursuit of which one derives some degree of meaning. Of course, not every interaction will constitute an explicit step in the pursuit of one's life goals, but over time, the thriving process ought to include many interactions that do. The relational *individual ←→ context interactions* component follows directly from Lerner's and Overton's (and their colleagues') relational developmental systems theory (Ford & Lerner, 1992; Lerner, 2006; Lerner & Overton, 2008), suggesting that people and their environments interact with and influence each other throughout

development. The final component of the definition that highlights *mutual enhancement* implies that these interactions are beneficial for both the context (i.e., the individual contributes to his or her surroundings) and the individual (i.e., the environment in which one is embedded has a positive influence on one's development). Brandstädter's (1984) action theory also applies to this component, in that individuals may actively choose environments that are more conducive to their positive development.

Five Core Principles of Thriving

The fundamental components of thriving may best be understood through a set of core principles. As with the definition of thriving, these principles are largely derived from and reflect the defining features of relational developmental systems theory, and are meant to represent an amalgamation of the essential components of the existing theories of thriving. Furthermore, they are meant to be applicable to the entire life span, encompassing the processes and individual capacities that are necessary to thrive at any age—in this way, these principles were designed to go beyond the focus on adolescent development as has been the case in the thriving literature to date. Indeed, positive development certainly does not occur only in youth; in one form or another, it happens (and thus needs to be understood) at every life stage. The five core principles of thriving are as follows:

1. Thriving is an essentially *developmental* construct, which entails a general orientation toward and, over time, the realization of relatively stable movement along an upward (though perhaps nonlinear) life trajectory.

2. Thriving focuses on aspects of development beyond merely the absence of the negative, and beyond mere competence or simple achievement of developmental tasks—in this way, we might think of thriving as a *theory of optimal development* (not just *adequate* development).

3. Thriving refers to the functioning of the *integrated, whole person across all life domains*; thus, the term implies personal balance, such that one is not considered to be thriving if he or she is functioning and developing positively in one aspect or area of his or her life but having serious developmental problems in others.

4. Thriving recognizes the multidirectional nature of relations between person and context, through which both

the individual and his or her contexts are mutually enhanced. This notion of mutual enhancement implies a moral component of thriving—when thriving individuals act on (and thus help create) their environments, they seek to in some way contribute to others and/or the multiple ecologies in which they are embedded.

5. Thriving entails the *engagement of one's unique talents, interests, and/or aspirations.* In this lies the assumption of one's self-awareness of his or her uniquenesses, and the opportunities to purposefully manifest them. Through such engagement, one might be thought of as actively working toward fulfilling his or her full potential.

These principles of thriving are intended to function as general rules of thumb. Under their umbrella, at the person level, one can expect to find more specific psychosocial and behavioral *indicators* of thriving, such as future orientation; optimism; openness to experience; the ability to adapt to new situations and regulate one's emotions, thoughts, and actions; resilience in the face of adversity; and a sense of meaning and purpose in one's actions and decisions. The quest for a comprehensive list of individual indicators and capacities of thriving is ongoing (we review some of these efforts later in the chapter). Also notable is that these principles of thriving may apply not only to individuals, but to families, communities, and societies as well. An ecological setting can develop positively just as can an individual; a community may engage in mutually enhancing relationships with both individuals and other communities, and in turn facilitate their thriving (see Lerner & Benson, 2003).

Thriving: Process versus Orientation

An analysis of the literature suggests that the term thriving has commonly taken on both the forms of intransitive verb (e.g., "The young boy is clearly thriving as he moves forward on a path to a hopeful future.") and attributive adjective (e.g., "The thriving young girl is involved in a variety of volunteering activities."). Unfortunately, this distinction has not been clearly elucidated, which may lead to some conceptual confusion. In its verb form, thriving refers to a process, namely, that of actual ongoing positive development; the current definition of thriving stems from this understanding. Following from this process-oriented notion of thriving, the adjectival use of the term thriving refers to an *orientation toward life* that reflects the tenets of the thriving process (see also Benson & Scales, 2009). This

"thriving orientation" is marked by individual characteristics such as (but not limited to) the maintenance of personal balance (i.e., one devotes attention to all facets of their well-being and domains of their lives), a sense of purpose and meaning (which is often derived from the purposeful pursuit of one's life goals and positive values), and an openness and adaptiveness to experience (which is integral to adaptive developmental regulation). Further essential to the notion of a thriving orientation is that one knows, acts on, and finds resources that foster one's talents, interests, and aspirations (i.e., "sparks"; Benson, 2008), and through which one contributes to the common good.

To be clear, thriving is understood herein as a developmental process, which may be *characterized* by the orientation toward life as described earlier. Put another way, thriving is an active process (verb) that implies actual, observable growth, marked by successful and mutually beneficial engagement with others and one's multiple levels of ecologies, along with forward motion on an upward developmental trajectory aimed toward a hopeful and purposeful future. A thriving orientation, which provides a descriptive status (adjective), suggests a point-in-time assessment of the developmental direction in which one appears to be pointed (i.e., toward a hopeful, positive future), as well as capacities of the person that might suggest positive growth (see also Benson & Scales, 2009). This emphasis on the developmental nature of thriving suggests that the appearance of well-being (or its lack) at a given point in time may not provide the necessary information on which to judge whether a person is optimally developing. Thus, a thriving orientation does not merely constitute point-in-time mental health or happiness but must also consider one's developmental trajectory. In this sense, there may be some indicators of both current well-being and a thriving orientation. For example, although one's level of positive affect at a given point in time is a clear indicator of subjective well-being (Watson, Clark, & Tellegen, 1988), it may not reflect whether that individual will be experiencing positive affect at any given time in the future, or develop in a positive manner. In contrast, having a sense of purpose in life has also been considered a hallmark of well-being (e.g., Ryff, 1989); but at the same time, the goal-directed and future-oriented aspects of having a purpose reflect an increased prospect of positive development (see Damon, 2008).

As further evidence, Mahoney and Bergman (2002) point out that developmental studies of children in high-risk environments (such as low socioeconomic status, high crime neighborhoods) have revealed the unexpected prevalence of a combination of behaviors that may at the same time appear to indicate both negative *and* positive development, such as poor academic achievement coupled with high peer acceptance (popularity) and avowed happiness (e.g., Luthar, 1999). According to these authors, given the disadvantaged background of these children, this combination may actually be viewed positively by others under similar circumstances, but the long-term educational and job prospects for these low-achieving, high-popularity kids may be less than promising. In this case, apparent high current well-being may mask suboptimal future prospects. Conversely, apparent low well-being in times of stress may reflect a temporary dip in one's sense of well-being, though that person may emerge even better equipped to deal with stress once the difficult situation is resolved (a.k.a., the "steeling effect"; Garmezy, 1986; Rutter, 1985). Thus, any person may at a given time be thriving in the developmental sense even though they may appear to be struggling from a well-being perspective.

REVIEW OF THE LITERATURE RELATED TO THRIVING THROUGHOUT THE LIFE SPAN

With the definition and these principles of thriving laid out, we turn to a review of the research literature that has addressed the construct of thriving and other closely related concepts at each stage of life, from infancy to the late mature years. This review incorporates both the developmental and social psychological literatures on thriving as a theory of optimal development and functioning, as well as the broader social and medical science literature that has addressed other conceptualizations that have incorporated the term thriving in some way. To underline the breadth of related research, we include understandings of thriving from perspectives that differ from our own; in these cases, we highlight important distinctions. To date, no conceptualization of thriving or positive development has taken a full life-span perspective from infancy to late adulthood; however, the principles of thriving we have outlined underlie many related constructs used throughout the life span. As a consequence, this section is organized by life stage, starting in infancy and ending in late adulthood.

Usage of the Term Thriving in Infancy

As previously noted, historically the first scientific use of the term thriving occurred in the pediatric medical field. Because the term thrive in this conceptualization is referred to only in terms of its absence or failure (i.e., FTT), this usage runs counter to the positive perspective espoused in this chapter. Nevertheless, findings from this research tradition are informative for a life-span account of thriving.

Since the time of Holt's (1897) influential article in *The Diseases of Infancy and Childhood*, FTT syndrome had been used broadly in the pediatric medical literature to describe inadequate infant growth and development. The *Gale Encyclopedia of Childhood and Adolescence* indicates that "failure to thrive occurs when an infant, toddler, or child fails to grow at a normal rate, either due to organic or environmental causes" (Kagan & Gall, 1998). The APGAR score method (Apgar, 1953) and Bayley Scales of Infant Development (Bayley, 1969) are among the two more commonly used tools for assessing FTT in infants.

Despite over a century of medical observation, there remains little consensus on a specific definition of FTT, and a general lack of uniformity of indices and criteria for abnormality (Wilcox, Nieburg, & Miller, 1989). Although Olsen (2006) has asserted that "agreement exists as to defining failure to thrive solely by anthropometrical indicators" (p. 5), with weight gain as the preferred choice of indicator (and weight-to-length ratio as an additional option), much of the literature suggests that the definition should also include criteria that address psychological capacities (Schwartz, 2000). Indeed, several studies have explored infant FTT in terms of impairments in intellectual functioning, some showing links between infant FTT and cognitive performance early in life. For example, Singer and Fagan (1984) found that deficits in performance at 20 months on the Bayley Mental Scale of Infant Development predict deficits in performance at 3 years on the Stanford-Binet Intelligence Scale.

FTT in infancy has been shown to have implications for physical functioning later in life, though the long-term consequences of infant FTT on cognitive performance are less clear. In their review of the infant FTT literature, Boddy, Skuse, and Andrews (2000) found that "there is consistent evidence that infant growth failure [FTT] has a long-term impact on physical development" (p. 1004). For example, Drewett, Corbett, and Wright (1999) found that children who failed to thrive in the first 18 months had lower weights, body mass indexes, and head circumferences at ages 7 to 9 when compared with a matched sample. Practitioners generally suggest that early diagnosis of and interventions regarding FTT are important for preventing malnutrition and negative developmental consequences (Krugman & Dubowitz, 2003). In contrast with the physical outcomes, Drewett, Corbett, and Wright

(1999) found no statistical difference in cognitive functioning between 7- to 9-year-olds who had FTT as infants and matched samples. Similarly, the results of Boddy, Skuse, and Andrews's (2000) follow-up study of 6-year-old children who were diagnosed as FTT in the first year of life "provided limited evidence that infant growth faltering had a long-term negative impact on cognitive development" (p. 1012).

FTT has traditionally been divided into organic (biological) FTT and nonorganic (environmental) FTT. However, the causes of FTT can be traced to both biological and environmental factors (Kagan & Gall, 1998; Rosenn, Loeb, & Bates, 1980). Among others, Wright, Parkinson, and Drewett (2006) found that parental and other environmental factors (especially maternal handling of the feeding dynamic) together with intrinsic characteristics of the child are important determinants of FTT. Indeed, many now believe that the organic/nonorganic distinction is not practical because of the prevalence of mixed causative factors (Krugman & Dubowitz, 2003). These findings suggest one commonality of understandings of thriving from both the FTT and positive development perspectives, namely, the impact of both the individual and the environment.

Though most developmental research in infancy has focused on preventing and remediating deficits, some have attended to the positive aspects of infant development. For example, Bowlby (1969), Ainsworth (1969; Ainsworth, Blehar, Waters, & Wall, 1978), and Sroufe (1979; Sroufe & Waters, 1977), among others, conducted seminal research on secure attachment between infant and mother (as well as infant and father), which has been suggested to set the stage for the development of certain "character strengths" later in life (see Park, 2004) and are likely to undergird the relational aspects of thriving. Erikson (1968) explored the role of the positive virtue of trust at the very early stages of psychosocial development. Tronick (1989) investigated positive exchanges between infant and adult, and the positive emotions these exchanges elicited, leading him to hypothesize that "positive development may be associated with the experience of coordinated interactions characterized by frequent reparations of interactive errors and the transformation of negative affect into positive affect" (p. 112).

Despite the lack of a broad theory of positive development in infancy, this literature may form the foundation for an understanding of developmental building blocks of thriving in these formative years of life. The capacity for healthy attachment and trust, empathy, and positive interactions with one's environment is likely integral toward developing a thriving orientation in childhood and adolescence. It is also likely that the physiological focus of the FTT perspective is equally vital toward understanding the early development of the cognitive capacities that underlie the psychological, social, and emotional components related to thriving. It will be important for future research to bridge this gap in our understanding of how such positive development in infancy might lead to positive development in childhood and beyond.

Concepts Related to Thriving and Positive Development in Childhood

The term thriving has not been widely used in developmental research focusing on the childhood years, though there has been some scholarly work at this life stage that has embraced the strengths-based perspective. For the most part, the progression through stages of cognitive and psychosocial development, the achievement of age-appropriate developmental tasks, and the development of competence have dominated the child development literature on various aspects of optimal development in this life period. Because such accounts have helped form the developmental foundation for theorizing on thriving and positive development through the life span, we now briefly review some of the most prominent of these theories.

Many of the classic theories of development focused extensively on infancy, childhood, and adolescence, including Werner's (1948) broad organismic developmental theory, Piaget's (1952) cognitive developmental theory, Havighurst's (1948/1972) theory of developmental tasks, Bowlby's (1958, 1969) attachment theory, and (though not focused solely on these early years) Erikson's (1968) theory of psychosocial stages. In Piaget's (1952) theory of cognitive development, young people develop a system of cognitive capacities through four sequential stages (sensorimotor, preoperational, concrete operational, and formal operational). These cognitive processes are the means through which developing persons understand and reason about their world. According to this theory, at each point in the child's development there is a tension between current understanding and novel information that challenges this understanding. Any action in the world entails both "assimilation"—interpreting new information through the lens of current thought patterns or "schemes"—and "accommodation"—changes in the scheme based on the novelty of the information. It is this imbalance, or lack of "equilibrium," between assimilation and accommodation that drives cognitive development. With the achievement of equilibrium at any given developmental stage, the system advances to a new higher or more "adapted" level of thought and reasoning. Thus, the telos of cognitive development is represented by a movement toward increasingly higher levels of "adaptation," where adaptation itself is defined as any behavior that increases the probability of the survival of the child, and "higher levels of adaptation" are defined by increased flexibility, mobility, and generalizability of thought and reasoning. This perspective is very much in the spirit of relational developmental systems and (as evinced by the preponderance of the notion of adaptation throughout this chapter) provides a building block for any theory of thriving.

Werner (1948; Werner & Kaplan, 1963) focused on cognitive and emotional features of development, and the processes of differentiation and reintegration that underlie this development. Werner's "orthogenetic principle" formulates these processes into an explanatory principle stating that "whenever development occurs, it proceeds from a state of relative globality and lack of differentiation to a state of increasing differentiation, articulation, and hierarchic integration" (p. 126). From this principle follows the idea that as humans develop, they become less bound to the stimuli of their concrete immediate environments and more open to goal-setting, planning, motivation, and self-regulation, all of which have direct bearing on the thriving process (see Mascolo & Fischer, Chapter 6 of this volume, and Müller & Racine, Chapter 11 of this volume, for extended discussions of similar ideas).

Havighurst's (1948/1972) theory of developmental tasks understands human development as involving a series of problems and challenges that naturally emerge at different points in the life course. These developmental tasks have their sources in physical and biological development, one's personal value system, and social expectations. Childhood, in particular, presents a set of such tasks, such as learning to play and share with other children, developing self-knowledge and a moral conscience, and understanding social roles, which are likely to lay the foundation for many of the capacities of thriving. Indeed, according to Havighurst (1973), these tasks "give direction, force, and substance" to one's life and one's development over the life course (p. 11).

Erikson's (1968) developmental theory of psychosocial stages primarily concerns the development of "ego identity" across the life span, which he conceptualized as the sense of self that individuals develop and come to understand primarily through social interaction. Erikson's eight stages each involve the confrontation and resolution of a "crisis," which is conceptually similar to the notion of a developmental task. Successful progression through these stages is thought to develop in a young person the capacities of trust, autonomy, social skills, confidence, competence, pride, and self-esteem. Such development at this stage may lay the foundation for many of the psychosocial capacities implicit in the principles of thriving.

Bowlby's (1958, 1969) attachment theory, like Erikson's theory of psychosocial development, was constructed within a relational metatheoretical context (see Overton, 2006), and was influenced by the work of Piaget and Werner. Bowlby believed primary relationships (e.g., the attachment bond formed between mother and child) were the principal source of cognitive, social, and emotional development. He, together with his colleague Mary Ainsworth (e.g., Ainsworth, 1969), emphasized the role of attachment figures (especially parents) in laying the early groundwork for positive social relations throughout life, which is, in turn, likely foundational to adaptive developmental regulation (see also Sroufe, 1979; Sroufe & Waters, 1977).

Although Piaget, Werner, Havighurst's Erikson, and Bowlby would all accept the notions of holism, relational bidirectionality, epigenesis, and dynamically progressive change that are at the conceptual core of thriving, each fails to consider development beyond mere competence. Moreover, none of them directly addresses young people's orientation toward and optimism about the future, their self-exploration and engagement of their unique talents and aspirations, or their capacity and desire to positively affect others and benefit their surrounding environments.

Contemporary work on the development of competence has its roots in these early theories of development, to which Havighurst's (1948/1972) notion of developmental tasks is particularly relevant. Masten, Coatsworth, Neeman, Gest, Tellegen, and Garmezy (1995) define competence as "a pattern of effective performance in the environment, evaluated from the perspective of salient developmental tasks in the context of [a given point in history]" (p. 1636). Building off the work of Havighurst (1948/1972) and clearly integrating some of the tenets of relational developmental systems theory, Roisman, Masten, Coatsworth, and Tellegen (2004) suggest these "salient developmental tasks" represent "the benchmarks of adaptation that are specific to a developmental period and are contextualized by prevailing sociocultural and historically embedded expectations" (p. 123).

Masten and Obradovic (2006) have more recently suggested a refinement of developmental tasks theory, enumerating a set of new perspectives that have evolved since

Havighurst, including (among others) that "adaptation is multidimensional and developmental in nature," "success in salient tasks of particular developmental periods forecast success in future age-salient tasks, even in new domains," "success or failure in multiple developmental task domains can have cascading consequences that lead to problems in other domains of adaptation, both internal and external," and "interventions to promote success in these tasks have preventive effects on behavioral and emotional problems" (p. 15). The first of these propositions is very Piagetian in that it explicitly acknowledges the multidimensionality of adaptation; this is due, in large part, to the complexity of the multiple ecologies in which one is embedded. The second suggests competence is likely to be relatively stable across time and situations. The third proposition reflects the interconnectedness of individual ←→ context relations. And the fourth provides further support for an earlier claim in this chapter, that the presence of the positive (or at least the adequate) often provides protection against the negative.

The net of these perspectives reveals four basic tenets of competence: (1) It entails the organization and coordination of multiple mental and physical processes; (2) there are generally multiple routes to the achievement of adaptive developmental outcomes (a view shared by Piaget); (3) competence involves the complex interplay of individual and ecological processes; and (4) competent "outcomes" are part of ongoing processes and, therefore, are inherently dynamic rather than static (Masten et al., 1995, p. 1636). Though the authors do not make explicit reference to relational developmental systems theory, their integrative, transactional approach appears to be cut from the same cloth.

Competence has often been studied alongside the related construct of resilience with regards to one's response to adversity. From this perspective, competence is designated as good adaptation in the relative absence of adversity (at present or in one's life history), whereas resilience refers to good adaptation in the presence of such adversity (Masten et al., 1999). Though there is still a lack of full consensus in the field, resilience can be more formally defined as "a class of phenomena characterized by good outcomes in spite of serious threats to adaptation or development" (Masten, 2001, p. 228). Notably, resilience is not the same thing as recovery—the latter refers to a trajectory in which normal functioning temporary suffers (e.g., via depressive symptoms or signs of post-traumatic stress disorder) for some period before returning to normal, whereas the former reflects the ability to at least maintain a stable

equilibrium, if not demonstrate even improved functioning, in the wake of adversity (Bonanno, 2004). Of course, like competence, the phenomenon of resilience is not limited to the young; however, research on the development of resilience has focused primarily on children (and to a certain degree, adolescents), as these life stages represent a formative period for such development.

As noted earlier, a focus on the strengths of young people rather than their deficits took hold in the perspective espoused by a group of researchers investigating resilience in the 1980s and early 1990s. In one of the most well-known of these studies, Garmezy (1983) introduced and explored the notion of the "invulnerable child." Garmezy found in his longitudinal investigation of children growing up in poverty and other difficult life situations that, despite the adversity, the majority of these kids were able to successfully adapt to their life circumstances, deal with life's most severe stressors, and overcome very difficult odds. Most of these young people developed into perfectly normal functioning (and some quite high-achieving) adults. Similarly, in their cross-cultural study of children in Hawaii and the mainland United States, Werner and Smith (1982) found that most children have the capacity for what they termed *resiliency,* or the personality characteristic that enables many young people to positively develop in the face of adversity. Building off the work of Garmezy and Werner, Benard (1991) suggested that, contrary to the once-popular belief, *every* child possesses the potential to develop resiliency, and claimed that this capacity could be learned by all young people (albeit perhaps to differing degrees; see also Masten, 2001). This more hopeful perspective on youth development provided the underpinnings for the PYD approach.

Increasingly, researchers in this field have emphasized the process-like nature of resilience, making a clear distinction from the terms *resiliency* and *resilient child,* which are descriptive of a personality attribute. The resilience process consists of two primary components: the challenge (also referred to as the threat, adversity, or risk), and the achievement of adaptive developmental outcomes in the face of that challenge. The challenge may constitute one specific negative life experience, such as one's parents suffering a divorce, or a constellation of negative life events or conditions across a span of time, such as growing up in a disadvantaged neighborhood.

Just as there is a lack of consistency in defining the challenge, there is variation in how "good" developmental outcomes are defined and operationalized, ranging from growth specific to the area affected by the challenge (e.g., strengthened interpersonal relationships with friends amidst a parental divorce) to adjustment across life domains. Some have suggested that the criteria for assessing these outcomes might consider the quality of adjustment to one's external environment, as well as improvement in one's internal psychological states (Luthar, Cicchetti, & Becker, 2000). In this way, contemporary models of resilience have begun to incorporate the transactional-ecological model of human development (Bronfenbrenner & Morris, 2006; Masten, 2001).

The resilience process is enhanced in the presence of what are known as "protective factors." Werner (1995) referred to protective factors as "the mechanisms that moderate (ameliorate) a person's reaction to a stressful situation or chronic adversity," and argued for their indispensability to positive adaptation (p. 81). Jessor, van den Bos, Vanderryn, Costa, and Turbin (1995) demonstrated that protective factors may act as moderators between risk factors and negative behavior (such as delinquency). Masten (2001) asserts that the absence of protective factors in youth, such as good parenting and intellectual functioning, may increase the likelihood of a traumatic event having long-term negative effects. Garmezy (1983) outlined three categories of protective factors characteristic of resilience: (1) positive personality dispositions, (2) a supportive family milieu, and (3) an external supportive system outside the family of one's origin.

Spencer's (1995) Phenomenological Variant of Ecological Systems Theory (PVEST) has brought into this conversation the notion of vulnerability, defined as "the net experience of risk and protective factors that an individual encounters" (Spencer, 2006, p. 628). According to Spencer (2006), resilience involves "successful negotiation of exacerbated challenges" and "is not possible without significant challenge [first] being encountered" (p. 628). PVEST addresses resilience and vulnerability in terms of the existence and degree of risk and protective factors present in an individual and his/her environment. Spencer's "Dual-Axis" model attempts to account for these interactions by considering how these factors come together to increase or decrease the likelihood one will behave adaptively when confronted with adversity.

Though again we see similarities between these conceptualizations of competence and resilience, and the current conceptualization of thriving, the differences are also evident. The principles of thriving explicitly note that the construct implies development beyond mere competence (see also Benson & Scales, 2009); and although the notion of resilience by definition refers to functioning beyond what is expected given one's level of risk or challenge and is clearly a strengths-based approach, it is predicated on the existence of the negative in the form of that risk. Although the notion of thriving certainly allows for risk and challenge in one's life—indeed, in the face of adversity the resilience process likely quite closely resembles the thriving process—the current conceptualization of thriving is not yoked to the risk in the same way. According to Ryff and Singer (2003a), it is not necessary for one to experience great adversity at any point in his or her development to live a good life and function optimally in adulthood. From this perspective, resilience is one integral aspect of the larger, more balanced picture of human strengths and adaptive development. One may thrive both in the presence and absence of such risk; within the traditional resilience framework, the optimal developmental trajectory appears to be no greater than simple competence. Beyond these distinctions, neither competence nor resilience integrates the moral component of contribution to the common good inherent in a thriving framework, and one's uniqueness and purposeful pursuits are not particularly salient in these concepts.

Another strand of research in the child development literature, that which addresses moral development, has also helped lay the conceptual groundwork for our understanding of thriving, specifically with regard to the dimension that incorporates mutual enhancement and contribution to the common good. Scholarly investigations of empathy, for example, have demonstrated that children have the capacity to recognize and understand another's feelings from early in life, and that the development of empathy leads to growth in both the moral and social domains (Collins, Maccoby, Steinberg, Hetherington, & Bornstein, 2000; Eisenberg & Fabes, 1998; Kagan, 1984). Indeed, the presence of a strong moral sense in childhood has been shown to contribute to greater engagement in prosocial behaviors, especially in disadvantaged youth (Hart, Yates, Fegley, & Wilson, 1995). Madsen (1971), Feshbach (1983), and others have further demonstrated that the capacity for such moral awareness and prosocial behavior is universal across cultures, though these dispositions may develop and manifest themselves differently once children have the exposure and the cognitive capacity to understand the belief systems and values particular to their cultures (Damon, 2004; see Turiel, Chapter 16 of this volume, for an extended discussion of moral development domains theory, constructed within a relational developmental systems approach).

Also of great importance to the positive development of children is the development of a moral identity, in which one uses moral ideas to define the self (Damon, 1999). With the development in late childhood of the cognitive capacity to analyze and understand the self and others, moral identity may take shape. One's moral identity becomes evident when he or she moves from simply understanding a general moral precept (such as "people should be kind") to adopting it as a central part of his or her personal identity ("I want to be a kind person"). Not surprisingly, there are individual differences in the degree to which children adopt a sense of moral identity (e.g., Walker, Pitts, Hennig, & Matsuba, 1995); however, the development of a moral identity can be facilitated by encouragement from loved ones and respected others, as well as educational and social interventions such as character education and community service programs (Youniss & Yates, 1997). According to Damon (2004), "Acquiring a moral identity is an essential part of [young people's] positive development as future citizens" (p. 23); it is also essential to better understanding the thriving process.

Thriving and Positive Development in Adolescence

It is at the life stage of adolescence that we find the bulk of the efforts directed toward an understanding of thriving as conceptualized in this chapter, and more broadly as part of the PYD movement. As noted earlier, the strengths-based perspective espoused in the resilience literature helped spur the wave of both research- and practice-focused work that has emerged on risk prevention, asset promotion, and youth development. Yet, in itself, the research on resilience was limited as a developmental approach to thriving. The notion of "resilience" focuses on the strengths and growth that come about in reaction to adversity, rather than as a natural part of the human condition. In the words of Damon (2004):

> While the positive youth development approach recognizes the existence of adversities and developmental challenges that may affect children in various ways, it resists conceiving of the developmental process mainly as an effort to overcome deficits and risk....Although the resiliency research put a number of important positive youth attributes squarely on the psychological map, it did not provide a sufficient basis for a universal model of youth development. (p. 15)

In the decades since the seminal resilience research emerged, significant efforts have been made to better understand the capacities of young people beyond those geared toward responding to adversity.

Some of the most well-established work on PYD related to (indeed, that foreshadowed) thriving began in the early 1990s at the Search Institute in Minneapolis, Minnesota, under the leadership and direction of Peter Benson. The flagship of the Search Institute's foundational work in this area surrounded their 40 Developmental Assets framework. Developmental assets refer to "key relationships, opportunities, values, skills, and self-perceptions that help young people limit their engagement in high-risk behaviors, enjoy resilience in the face of adversity, and thrive" (Benson & Scales, 2009). They were originally identified by way of a review of the strengths-based literature that existed at the time of their formation in the 1990s, which primarily constituted the constructs of resilience, competence, and developmental tasks (Scales & Leffert, 2004). These 40 distinct developmental assets are grouped into 8 asset categories. Support, empowerment, boundaries and expectations, and constructive use of time are the four categories that make up the external assets, provided to youth by parents, school, peers, and community. Commitment to learning, positive values, social competencies, and positive identity are internal assets that youths develop; they are thought to be the self-processes that eventually become the guideposts of effective self-regulation (Benson, 2003).

As noted earlier in this chapter, research has consistently shown that these developmental assets are reliable negative predictors of problem behaviors such as risky sex, substance abuse, and gambling, among others (Leffert et al., 1998; Scales et al., 2000), and are positive predictors of academic achievement (Scales, Benson, Roehlkepartain, & van Dulmen, 2006). Benson, Scales, Hamilton, and Sesma (2006) refer to the ideas of "vertical pile up" and "horizontal pile up" of assets, which suggest that the more total assets one demonstrates over time, and the more assets one experiences across settings, the better. Benson et al. (2006) also proposed that these assets are universally relevant (though they may be experienced or express themselves differently in different contexts and cultures), and that they will be enhanced under certain conditions, and in certain contexts and ecologies. The authors referred to these assets as "dynamically interconnected 'building blocks' that, in combination, prevent high risk health behaviors and enhance many forms of developmental success (i.e., thriving)" (Benson et al., 2006, p. 906). The connections between developmental assets and thriving are further disccussed later in this chapter.

In addition to the pioneering work performed by Benson, Scales, and their colleagues at the Search Institute, the field of PYD has flourished in large part because of the work of researchers exploring the efficacy of youth development programs themselves, and the ways in which such programs, together with schools, communities, government, and so forth, can actively help our children and adolescents optimally develop. One of the most comprehensive reviews of youth development programs in the United States was conducted by Catalano, Berglund, Ryan, Lonczak, and Hawkins (2002). In this review, the authors echoed the drum beat of many researchers and practitioners before them who believed youth development programs have benefited greatly from the shift in focus from deficit-centered to risk prevention- and strengths-based models (Blum, 1998, 2003; Connell, Gambone, & Smith, 2000; Henderson, Barnard, & Sharp-Light, 1999; Pittman, 1991; Pittman, Irby, & Ferber, 2000; Roth, Brooks-Gunn, Murray, & Foster, 1998). In the spirit of the PYD movement and influenced by the relational developmental systems model, Catalano and his colleagues took a holistic approach to understanding youth in the context of these youth development programs, noting the importance of considering each level of individual, family, school, and community factors. They rigorously evaluated 25 youth development programs, measuring both positive and negative outcomes across diverse youth, and found that intrapersonal and interpersonal competencies can both prevent the occurrence of problems and create a positive developmental pathway. Catalano, Berglund, et al. (2002) suggest a set of common themes of successful youth development programs, including that their standards are clear, consistent, and integrated with the messages promoted by the families and in the community; that they strengthen interpersonal bonds with peers, family, and other adults, whereas also building intrapersonal competencies (social, emotional, and behavioral); and that they expand opportunities for youth across the span of the program and beyond.

Whereas Catalano, Berglund, et al. (2002) focused primarily on the risk-reduction approach as a means toward PYD (see also Catalano, Hawkins, Berglund, Pollard, & Arthur, 2002), others have centered on and promote a more explicitly strengths-based focus (e.g., Blum, 1998, 2003; Bumbarger & Greenberg, 2002; Durlak & Weissberg, 2005; Durlak et al., 2007; Greenberg et al., 2003; Pittman et al., 2000; Roth et al., 1998; Roth & Brooks-Gunn, 2003a, 2003b). One prominent model of the strengths-based approach is known as the "social and emotional learning" process (SEL; Bumbarger & Greenberg, 2002; Durlak & Weissberg, 2005; Durlak et al., 2007; Greenberg et al., 2003; Weissberg & O'Brien, 2004). The SEL approach was designed as a comprehensive framework for integrating social and emotional instruction across academic, physical health, prevention, and PYD activities. Proponents of this approach logically contend that youths benefit from strong and supportive relationships with teachers, parents, and the community. It espouses five "teachable competencies": (1) self-awareness, (2) social awareness, (3) self-management, (4) relationship skills, and (5) responsible decision making. Studies have shown the benefits of SEL for students' academic performance, social competence, emotional regulation, and a reduction in risk behaviors (Durlak & Weissberg; Durlak et al.; Greenberg et al.; Weissberg & O'Brien).

In other investigations of the benefits of youth development programs, some researchers have adopted approaches from the PYD research-based literature (Blum, 1998, 2003; Edwards, Mumford, & Serra-Roldan, 2007; Henderson, Barnard, & Sharp-Light, 1999; Pittman et al., 2000; Roth & Brooks-Gunn, 2003a, 2003b). For example, in their expansive review of the literature on youth development programs, Roth and Brooks-Gunn (2003a) draw on Lerner's "6 Cs" model of positive development suggesting that "youth development programs [should] seek to enhance not only adolescents' skills, but also their confidence in themselves and their future, their character, and their connections to other people and institutions by creating environments" more amenable to PYD (p. 180). Pittman et al. (2000) call for more integrative efforts between research and practice (as they have accomplished in their own work with Child Trends, an independent research group). Edwards et al. (2007) reviewed the PYD and resilience literatures as they apply specifically to at-risk children, and addressed the ways in which youth development programs and asset-building initiatives, based on the Developmental Assets model (Benson, 1997), are beneficial to at-risk students, and suggested ways in which asset building can be directly integrated into schools.

In what may be the most comprehensive review of the PYD literature to date, the National Research Council and Institute of Medicine's national report on youth development (Eccles & Gootman, 2002) covers ground from across a variety of PYD perspectives in what effectively amounts to a guidebook for building, evaluating, and sustaining youth development programs. This report summarized and evaluated the current state of the field of adolescent health and development, with a focus on community programs for youth. Although this report is not centered only on understanding PYD, it offers some insights of particular relevance to the current exploration in their chapter entitled "Personal and Social Assets That Promote Well-Being."

In their approach, the contributors wisely integrate theory, practical wisdom, and findings from empirical research to arrive at their own definition of optimal positive development, which bears certain resemblance to the current definition of thriving, as "development that is headed along a positive trajectory toward finding a meaningful and productive place in one's cultural milieu" (Eccles & Gootman, p. 66). The contributors to this report were clearly of much the same mind regarding positive development as the authors of this chapter.

Furthermore, the contributors to the Eccles and Gootman (2002) report endeavored to compile a list of indicators of positive development and well-being from across developmental theories in psychology, anthropology, and sociology, integrating empirical findings that incorporated three types of evidence:

> (1) [E]vidence that particular characteristics are either positively related concurrently to other indicators of well-being or negatively related concurrently to indicators of problematic development; (2) evidence that particular characteristics predict positive indicators of adult well-being and of a "successful" transition to normative adult statuses; and (3) evidence that the experimental manipulation or training of particular characteristics produces changes on other indicators of either current well-being and adequate functioning or a successful transition into adulthood. (p. 68)

In addition, the committee included insights from practitioners whose experience informed a better understanding of indicators that might be revealed only in practice. Integrating all of these sources and perspectives, the authors presented a comprehensive (though somewhat less-than-parsimonious) list of personal and social assets that facilitate their conceptualization of optimal positive development. They grouped these assets into four categories: social development, psychological and emotional development, intellectual development, and physical development. Examples of social developmental assets included "perceived good relationships and trust with parents, peers, and some other adults" and "commitment to civic engagement"; among the psychological and emotional developmental assets were emotional self-regulation, confidence, prosocial values and purpose in life; intellectual developmental assets included school success and critical thinking skills; and good health habits and "health risk management skills" comprised the assets of physical development (Eccles & Gootman, pp. 74–75).

Although each of the approaches outlined in this section advance scholarly research and guide practice, there is a notable lack of uniformity in the research approaches, theoretical models, desired outcomes, and program recommendations. As Small and Memmo (2004) pointed out, the "lack of an integrative conceptual scheme and consistent terminology" (p. 3) hinders our overall understanding of what exactly constitutes PYD (cf. Roth & Brooks-Gunn, 2003b). Moore and Lippman (2005; see also Moore, Lippman, & Brown, 2004) likewise lament the lack of a universally accepted set of indicators of PYD and offer a set of criteria for positive outcome indicators, including that they have the following functions: (1) predict desirable adult outcomes, (2) are intrinsically important, (3) provide age-appropriate measures, (4) are psychometrically rigorous, (5) consider possible moderating and mediating effects, and (6) meaningfully inform practice.

These PYD approaches to adolescent development certainly share much conceptual space with the current theory of thriving. They celebrate the positive approach (while also addressing the reduction of risk behaviors), and focus squarely on development (though all-too-often use point-in-time assessments). However, they generally do not adopt all of the principles of thriving; relational bidirectionality is often not considered, future orientation and purpose are rarely included as key indicators of positive development, and contribution to the common good is sometimes, but not always, hailed as a necessary component of PYD programming. There are also methodological shortcomings; longitudinal research is relatively sparse, and unit of analysis is typically a variable of interest (such as increased confidence or reduced drug use) rather than the whole person. This line of research has helped the field of PYD make tremendous strides in its understanding of many aspects of youth development, especially in ways that inform practice, which is particularly laudable. At the same time, even greater strides are in store in this area when the principles of relational developmental systems theory and thriving are integrated more directly into the research agenda.

As noted earlier, the current conceptualization of thriving is borne out of research on this construct from the PYD tradition and is very much in alignment with this work. Although much of this research has already been reviewed earlier in this chapter regarding the early theorizing, underpinnings, and evolving definition of the construct, further work in this tradition has deepened our understanding of thriving. For example, Pam King and her colleagues have extended beyond their earlier conceptual contributions to the literature regarding the use and understanding of the term *thriving* (e.g., King, Dowling, et al., 2005; King, Shultz, et al., 2005) and have formulated and empirically tested a set of thriving indicators that mark advances from the relatively simple (and in some ways, problematic) measures used in early empirical studies of thriving. For example, Shultz, Wagener, and King (2006) explored the relation between an established group of developmental resources (including parent involvement, positive school orientation, adult support, neighborhood resources, and social ties with peers) and a set of thriving indicators that included future orientation, positive values, resourcefulness, fulfillment of potential, religion, happiness, and contribution to the common good. This investigation uncovered a factor structure of thriving including five factors, which they labeled future orientation, positive values, resourcefulness, fulfillment of potential, and religion. Religion was later dropped from their model when it was shown to weaken the link between the thriving indicators and developmental resources; however, the authors noted, this may have been because of their use of a measure of religiosity, rather than using a more general consideration of spirituality. Indeed, it is worth noting that the contribution of spirituality to positive development in adolescence has garnered significant attention in recent years (e.g., Dowling et al., 2004; King & Benson, 2005; King & Furrow, 2004) and remains a possible indicator of thriving. Shultz et al.'s (2006) final set of four factors of indicators was found to strongly predict the developmental resources and provides one of the few examples of the empirical validation of a set of thriving indicators in the literature.

In addition, Bill Damon's work on moral development (e.g., 1978, 1990), self-understanding (e.g., Damon & Hart, 1982, 1988), moral exemplarity (Colby & Damon, 1992), character building through school and community programs (e.g., Damon, 1995, 1997), work-related adult ethical and prosocial behavior (e.g., Damon, 2004; Gardner, Csikszentmihalyi, & Damon, 2001), PYD (e.g., Damon, 2004; Damon & Gregory, 2002), and most recently, the development of purpose (e.g., Damon, 2008; Damon, Menon, & Bronk, 2003) has significantly advanced both the thinking and research agenda related to optimal youth development and thriving. Damon and his colleagues' contemporary work on the development of purpose reflects the future-oriented, prosocial, and motivational aspects inherent in any positive developmental definition of thriving, as denoted in the current definition by inclusion of the term *purposeful*. The stability of movement in the direction of one's purpose reflects the stability of upward movement of the thriving process. According to Damon (2008):

More revealing than any particular behavioral signposts, such as tests passed, prizes won, or popularity gained, is the *direction* and *meaning* of a young person's efforts.... When two crucial conditions apply: (1) forward movement toward a fulfilling purpose, and (2) a structure of social support consistent with that effort, there is every likelihood that the child will thrive. (pp. 37–38)

The focus here is on the idea that an individual is on track, that he or she has forward momentum in life, not necessarily that he or she is always feeling extremely happy or is popular or "succeeding" at some given task at any given point in time. In accordance with relational developmental systems theory, Damon (2008) explicitly noted that one "must be observed over time in order to make this determination" that he or she is thriving (p. 38; see Nesselroade & Molenaar, Chapter 2 of this volume, and McArdle, Chapter 3 of this volume, for extended discussions of multiple observations). Like Benson and his colleagues, Damon and his colleagues are currently engaged in a multiyear longitudinal research project that addresses and is beginning to sort out the ways in which purpose and thriving are interrelated (e.g., Bundick, Yeager, & Damon, 2008).

Although Lerner and his colleagues have significantly advanced the theory of thriving (e.g., Lerner, 2006), they have further been engaged in empirical work seeking to confirm the structure of the 6 Cs (confidence, competence, character, compassion, connection, and contribution) model, and its relevance to PYD and thriving (Dowling et al., 2004; Gestsdottir & Lerner, 2007; Lerner et al., 2005, 2006, 2007; Theokas et al., 2005). For example, studies by Dowling et al. (2003, 2004) used factor analysis to test the structure and relevance of spirituality and religiosity to the seven thriving outcomes used by Scales et al. (2000). As summarized earlier in the chapter, the authors found that the best fit for the data was one where both spirituality and religiosity are indirectly related to thriving outcomes through a mediating factor, though it is not clear whether either or both of them should be considered indicators of thriving.

As with many of the other major scholars in the field of thriving research, Lerner and his colleagues are engaged in a multiyear longitudinal study investigating youths involved with 4-H Youth Development programs and the presence of indicators of PYD (i.e., the 6 Cs), which he suggests represent the thriving process. Lerner et al. (2005) used the first wave of these 4-H study data to confirm five first-order latent factors representing the first five of the 6 Cs of PYD (not including "contribution"). The second wave of the 4-H study data confirmed that factor structure (Jelicic et al., 2007), and further found that the presence of these 5 Cs (i.e., thriving) in fifth grade predicts lower levels of risk behaviors (i.e., substance use and delinquent behaviors) and depression, as well as (moderately) increased levels of contribution to the common good (the "6th C" of PYD) in sixth grade.

Furthermore, Lerner et al. (2007) found that urban girls exhibit signs of thriving, and provided further confirmation of the developmental hypothesis that presence of the first 5 Cs not only predicts thriving behaviors but also contribution to the common good. Notably, in this study, the authors distinguished "thriving" from "well-being" by claiming that well-being is embedded in a time and place (namely, at the time of measurement), whereas thriving occurs "across time" and signifies being on the path to an idealized personhood. Although Lerner et al. (2007) did not explicitly explore the relations between thriving and well-being, they did speculate that when a young person exhibits thriving behavior, when coupled with adult support, negative outcomes and risky behaviors will be diminished.

Here, Lerner et al. (2007) appear to depart from previous thriving research, which has typically explored predictors of thriving (i.e., thriving as the outcome variable; e.g., Scales et al., 2000), in that thriving (operationalized as the presence of the first 5 Cs) is used to predict contribution to the common good as the outcome variable of interest (see also Lerner et al., 2005). Empirically, as in all of the research stemming from the 4-H longitudinal study, the first 5 Cs were measured using a collection of items from four instruments: the Search Institute's PSL-AB survey, the Self-Perception Profile for Children (Harter, 1982), the Peer Support Scale (Armsden & Greenberger, 1987) from the Teen Assessment Project Question Bank (Small & Rodgers, 1995), and the Eisenberg Sympathy Scale (Eisenberg, Fabes, Murphy, Karbon, Smith, & Maszk, 1996). Depression and risk behaviors (which they also incorporated into their outcome variables) were measured by the Center for Epidemiological Studies Depression scale (Radloff, 1977) and the PSL-AB, respectively. Also notable is that because they used open-ended questions in their assessment, Lerner et al. (2007) were able to uncover that some subgroups (such as urban girls) use many other terms for and indicators of their thriving beyond the 6 Cs, leading them to suggest that further research may be necessary to provide a more robust understanding of thriving and a more inclusive set of thriving indicators.

Tying this contemporary approach to the study of thriving to the life-span development literature, Gestsdottir

and Lerner (2007) explored the relation between thriving (again operationalized as the first 5 Cs) and self-regulation, as conceptualized by Baltes's (1997) SOC model. This approach marks another advance in Lerner and his colleagues' work related to thriving: the hypothesized relation between two well-established models of positive human development from different stages of the life span. Gestsdottir and Lerner (2007) concluded that young adolescents (in 5th and 6th grade) are still learning to self-regulate, but that the SOC approach to development in these years is, in fact, adaptive, as evident in the significant and positive relations between their measures of self-regulation and all of the first 5 Cs. Furthermore, the authors found evidence that these 5 Cs are orthogonal, and that a young person may develop positively in some of the Cs, but not in others. This may inform thriving research by suggesting that a young person need not have all the indicators of thriving to be on a path to a hopeful future.

Though the current PYD-inspired conceptualization of thriving has not been broadly investigated beyond adolescence, much research has been conducted related to positive development emerging in the adulthood years. Although conceptually distinct from thriving, the concepts of flourishing and character strengths in the domain of positive psychology speak directly to the kind of understanding researchers of thriving in adolescence seek, yet from a broad social/personality rather than developmental psychology perspective. These constructs, together with another related (but also distinct) usage of the term thriving, are reviewed in the following section. We again note that, as with resilience and competence, these phenomena are not restricted to one phase of life (i.e., the adult years); however, it is the life stage at which the bulk of the research on the topic has been conducted, and thus the life stage at which they are best understood.

Thriving and Positive Development in Adulthood

The term thriving shows up in a strand of psychological research that appears to have evolved separately from the pediatric medical research on FTT, as well as the PYD literature on thriving, but has a genealogy that can be traced back to the resilience literature reviewed earlier. In their work studying female adults who have overcome significant adversity (such as divorce, disability, or severe illness), O'Leary and Ickovics (1995) encountered many who not only fully recovered but appeared to have actually improved psychologically (and perhaps even physically) from where they were before experiencing the trauma. The authors termed this phenomenon thriving in the face of adversity.

Within this perspective, Ickovics and Park (1998) define thriving as "the effective mobilization of individual and social resources in response to risk or threat, leading to positive mental or physical outcomes and/or positive social outcomes…[it is] an adaptive response to challenge [which] represents something more than a return to equilibrium" (p. 122). This conceptualization of thriving is essentially synonymous with the notions of "stress-related growth" and "post-traumatic growth" seen in this same research tradition (e.g., Park, Cohen, & Murch, 1996; Tedeschi, Park, & Calhoun, 1996).

Carver (1998) makes the distinction between resilience and this definition of thriving explicit, noting that the former should be "reserved to denote homeostatic return to a prior condition" (before an adverse event) whereas thriving refers to "the better-off-afterward experience" (p. 247). Following from the resilience model, he restricts the word thriving to refer to a response to adversity; the term cannot apply to a person who has never faced a significant trauma, threat, or risk (even if he or she is developing quite positively). Further, thriving is a particular type of response ("better-off-afterward") to a particular type of stimulus (trauma). Carver (1998) categorizes the responses an individual could have to significant life trauma into four groups: succumbing (which entails a long-term loss of normal functioning), survival with impairment (in which one could maintain a functional life, only at a lower level than before the trauma), resilience (return to normal functioning), and thriving (see Figure 24.3). It follows from this conceptualization that thriving and resilience are mutually exclusive; a person may be said to be thriving or resilient, but not both (at least not in the same domain).

Some of the empirical research on thriving from this perspective has demonstrated the breadth of the phenomenon and its relation with other similar psychological characteristics such as mental health. Research using Tedeschi, Park, and Calhoun's (1996) Post-Traumatic Growth Inventory, a measure of growth after a significant adverse life event, has cataloged a variety of circumstances in which such growth can occur, such as after war, heart problems, arthritis, and cancer (see Tedeschi, Park, & Calhoun, 2006, for a review). Park (1998) found a consistent relation between this model of thriving and psychological well-being, and others have found associations with other personal strengths such as existential wisdom, empathy, and strong interpersonal relationships (Tedeschi & Calhoun, 1995; Calhoun & Tedeschi, 1989–1990).

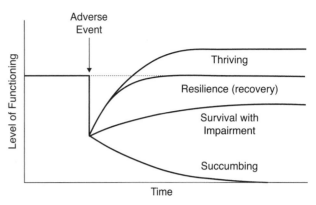

Figure 24.3 Carver's (1998) possible responses to adversity, including thriving.
Source: Reprinted from Carver, C. S. (1998). Resilience and thriving: Issues, models, and linkages. *Journal of Social Issues, 54,* 245–266, with permission from Wiley-Blackwell.

Interestingly, according to this conceptualization, thriving and poor mental health can coexist. Calhoun and Tedeschi (1998) cite a case study of a woman who they considered to be both thriving and depressed at the same time. In this particular example, several months after her husband was murdered in a robbery, this woman was depressed and still experiencing significant grief, yet she also reported growth in "her sense of strength, her ability to live independently, and her general sense of being closer to something transcendent" (Calhoun & Tedeschi, 1998, p. 363). As this example demonstrates, a thriving individual in this framework may experience growth in some domains of his or her life whereas at the same time suffering in others; this suggests, in this model, thriving need not be domain general, which is contrary to how this chapter defines thriving. We return to the issue of the domain generality versus domain specificity of thriving later in the chapter.

The "better-off-after-trauma" model of thriving clearly differs from the definition put forth in this chapter, but it does share the perspective that thriving should refer to something that goes beyond what is expected (homeostasis and competence, respectively). It focuses on the strengths that emerge from difficulties, rather than the absence of loss or other negative outcomes after trauma. However, as noted earlier, and again similar to the concept of resilience, this model of thriving is, by definition, tied to the experience of adversity; in fact, it requires a specific traumatic event, which is even more limiting in scope than some of the perspectives on resilience that consider adversity to include general backgrounds of vulnerability/risk (such as socioeconomic status or race; see Spencer, 2006). This is because, according to O'Leary (1998), thriving is (in her model) representative of a "transformational" process (from initial state before the trauma, to significantly worse directly following the trauma, to better than the initial state following recovery from the trauma), and such a process requires an event that "shakes the foundations of one's life…because these are the ones that provide the opportunity for a heroic response" (p. 430).

Also unlike this chapter's conceptualization of thriving, the "better-off-after-trauma" model does not represent a full model of positive development. Furthermore, it fails to embrace the relational developmental systems theory approach: Although it acknowledges the interaction of person and environment, and implies plasticity, it does not integrate the notion of relational bidirectionality (the focus is about a direct *effect of* the traumatic context *on* the individual). In addition, at no place in this model is there any consideration of the relational enhancement of person and context, or following from that the opportunity for one to positively impact one's environment as part of the reaction to the adversity (e.g., one might devote oneself to making sure others do not suffer the same trauma). Moreover, thriving from this perspective has no particular relevance to one's unique talents and skills; perhaps, if coupled with the idea that a thriving response to adversity might include a commitment to improving the conditions related to the trauma or some other related contribution to society, we might see one using one's talents and skills to that end, and thus a closer conceptual link between the two definitions.

At the beginning of this chapter, we noted the role of the positive psychology movement (Seligman & Csikszentmihalyi, 2000) in advancing the strengths-based approach to psychological research. Though most of the positive psychological research is focused on individual well-being, and very little directly addresses development (cf., Park, 2004), it has produced a number of relevant (and some very similar) perspectives on human functioning that inform the current perspective on thriving (see also Benson & Scales, 2009). Indeed, some of the more prominent frameworks in the positive psychological literature, such as flourishing (Keyes, 2002) and character strengths (Peterson & Seligman, 2004), posit models of optimal human functioning that, on many levels, overlap and can coexist with—indeed, mutually inform—thriving research.

Before delving into a review of the positive psychology literature, it is important to recognize that the positive, strengths-based approach to psychology in general, and life-span human development in particular, shares roots with the work of earlier developmentalists, including Piaget, Werner, and Lev Vygotsky; humanistic psychologists such as Abraham Maslow and Carl Rogers; and one of the founding fathers of personality and social-cognitive psychology, Gordon Allport.

As presented earlier, Piaget's adaptation and equilibration processes, and Werner's orthogenetic principle speak directly to the presence of human strengths (namely, cognitive capacities) in development, and do not focus on the mere absence of weaknesses. Piaget further revealed an orientation toward the positive in his book *Six Psychological Studies* (1967), in which he not only elaborates on his cognitive developmental theories but also discusses human capacities such as cooperation and personal autonomy. Another of the classic developmental theorists, Vygotsky was also interested in the development of a child's capacities. His theory of the "zone of proximal development" (Vygotsky, 1978) addresses the potentialities of the child; he described it as "the distance between the actual developmental level as determined by independent problem solving and the level of potential development as determined through problem solving under adult guidance or in collaboration with more capable peers" (p. 85).

Though humanistic theories have been criticized for their dubious methodologies, sparse databases, and social and political repercussions (e.g., Prilleltensky, 1992), they, too, succeeded in orienting psychological research and practice away from human inadequacies and toward human potential. In his exploration of human motivation, Maslow (1968) placed atop his hierarchy of human needs the notion of "self-actualization." He defined striving toward self-actualization as one's "desire to become more and more what one idiosyncratically is, to become everything that one is capable of becoming" (Maslow, 1970, p. 22). His notion focuses less on an end point to be attained and more on the process of ongoing striving toward the maximization of one's individual full potential. He suggested many attributes he thought to be characteristic of the self-actualized person, including acceptance of self and others, spontaneity, autonomy, appreciation of life, having peak experiences, feeling of kinship or connectedness with others, strong interpersonal relations, a sense of morality, creativity, and the ability to transcend one's culture and biases (Maslow, 1970). Rogers (1961) likewise sought to understand the pursuit of human potential and optimal functioning in his notion of the "fully-functioning person." He theorized the existence of an underlying "actualizing tendency" in all humans, which serves to motivate them to develop all capacities in the pursuit of autonomy, positive regard from others, and positive self-regard. Rogers's fully functioning person represents the optimal human condition, described by the characteristics of openness to experience, the capacity to live existentially, trust, self-expression, independence, and creativity. This fully functioning person seeks to live "the good life," which Rogers insightfully (and consistent with the position taken in this chapter) considers to be "a *process* not a state of being… it is a direction, not a destination" (p. 186, emphasis in original).

This dialectic between being and becoming was also addressed by Gordon Allport. Allport is well-known for his work as a personality and social-cognitive psychologist; however, it is often overlooked that beyond his investigations of basic human traits, motives, and biases, he sought to understand personality from a decidedly positive perspective. This was perhaps most on display in his book *Becoming* (Allport, 1955/1983), in which he suggested "the process of becoming is governed…by a disposition to realize [one's] possibilities, i.e., to become characteristically human at all stages of development" (p. 27). These notions of possibilities and potential, capacities and becoming are at the core of the thriving process.

The concept of "flourishing" in many ways represents a contemporary version of the humanists' orientation toward the maximization of human potential. Broadly speaking, flourishing is a universal model of optimal human functioning. Keyes (2003) has defined flourishing as "a state in which an individual feels positive emotion toward life and is functioning well psychologically and socially" (p. 294). It lies at the positive end of a continuum of functioning that has "languishing" as its opposite. Flourishing describes individuals who are not only doing well in many areas of life but are largely free of negative indicators of health such as mental illness. In other words, flourishing considers well-being to include both the presence of the positive and the absence of the negative.

The concept of flourishing emerged out of, and is largely based in, Ryff's (1989) conceptualization of psychological well-being together with Keyes's (1998) notion of social well-being. Ryff helped to usher in the era of positive psychology through her efforts to reconceptualize well-being and devise an instrument to measure her theoretically derived constructs of psychological well-being. Picking up where Jahoda (1958) left off decades earlier, Ryff was interested in exploring the positive side of mental health, and in her approach addressed the theoretical literature on mental health/illness, humanistic psychology, identity, maturity, and life-span development. She found a set of core themes in this literature and reformulated

them into her six dimensions of psychological well-being (Ryff; see also Ryff & Keyes, 1995). These dimensions include positive evaluations of oneself and one's life (self-acceptance), a sense of personal growth and development (personal growth), the ability to effectively manage one's life and world around them (environmental mastery), a sense of self-determination (autonomy), the sense that one's life has purpose and meaning (purpose in life), and engagement in positive relationships with other people (positive relations with others).

This sixth dimension of Ryff's psychological well-being model segues conceptually into Keyes's (1998) overall conception of social well-being. Social well-being also comprises multiple dimensions, including social coherence, social integration, social acceptance, social contribution, and social actualization. Seeking a more comprehensive model of positive human functioning, Keyes (2002) combined the notions of psychological and social well-being, and integrated a third component he called *emotional well-being* to formulate a theory of human flourishing (see Table 24.2). According to Keyes (2007), whereas psychological well-being and social well-being represent the Aristotelian notion of *eudaimonia*, emotional well-being aligns with Aristotle's *hedonia*. Emotional well-being thus includes one's experiences of positive and negative affect (Watson et al., 1988) and what Keyes (2007) referred to as one's "avowed quality of life," which is akin to subjective well-being (Diener, 1984).

It should be noted that subjective well-being, although considered here primarily under the umbrella of flourishing, has enjoyed a long and deep history of research in its own right (Diener, 1984, 2000). Seligman and Csikszentmihalyi (2000) recognized the importance of the study of positive subjective experience by advancing it as the first area of investigation within positive psychology. Happiness, high positive affect and low negative affect, and life satisfaction are generally considered the major components of subjective well-being, which has itself been shown to have many desirable correlates (e.g., strong relationships, physical health; see Diener, 1984, 2000; Myers, 2000) and has been advanced by some as an indicator of positive development (e.g., Park, 2004; Shultz et al., 2006).

However, Ryff (1989), Keyes (1998), and others have argued that subjective well-being, although an essential piece of the larger well-being puzzle, is limited in its ability to capture the full breadth of "the good life"—this is where Aristotle's distinction between *eudaimonia* and *hedonia* is particularly important. Keyes, Shmotkin, and Ryff (2002) suggest that, whereas *hedonia* refers to a certain kind of

TABLE 24.2 Keyes's (2007) Components of Flourishing

Dimension	Definition
	Positive emotions (i.e., emotional well-being)
Positive affect	Regularly cheerful, interested in life, in good spirits, happy, calm and peaceful, full of life
Avowed quality of life	Mostly or highly satisfied with life overall or in domains of life
	Positive psychological functioning (i.e., psychological well-being)
Self-acceptance	Holds positive attitudes toward self, acknowledges, likes most parts of self, personality
Personal growth	Seeks challenge, has insight into own potential, feels a sense of continued development
Purpose in life	Finds own life has a direction and meaning
Environmental mastery	Exercises ability to select, manage, and mold personal environs to suit needs
Autonomy	Is guided by own, socially accepted, internal standards and values
Positive relations with others	Has, or can form, warm, trusting personal relationships
	Positive social functioning (i.e., social well-being)
Social acceptance	Holds positive attitudes toward, acknowledges, and is accepting of human differences
Social actualization	Believes people, groups, and society have potential and can evolve or grow positively
Social contribution	Sees own daily activities as useful to and valued by society and others
Social coherence	Interested in society and social life and finds them meaningful and somewhat intelligible
Social integration	A sense of belonging to, and comfort and support from, a community

Adapted from Keyes, C. L. M. (2007). Promoting and protecting mental health as flourishing: A complementary strategy for improving national mental health. *American Psychologist, 62,* 95–108, with permission of the American Psychological Association.

happiness characterized by pleasure-seeking pursuits, *eudaimonia,* though often also translated to mean *happiness,* "is more accurately characterized as the striving toward realization of one's true potential" (p. 1018; cf. Ryan & Deci, 2000). It is from the well of this humanistic pursuit of self-actualization that these authors (as well as the current authors) believe the good life more fruitfully springs. Importantly, Keyes et al. (2002) acknowledge that the demands of such striving "may compromise contentment or more hedonic aspects of well-being" (p. 1009); this is highly consistent with the thriving conception presented in this chapter that at any given point in time one may not be especially happy or joyous, but this temporarily reduced well-being is in the service of a greater developmental benefit.

Research on flourishing has substantiated the component structure of the construct and demonstrated a variety of desirable associations (e.g., Keyes, 2002, 2005). Empirical studies of flourishing and languishing have explored their relations with, among other things, sociodemographic variables such as gender and age, depression, work productivity, and physical health. The results of this work showed significant relations between flourishing and increased psychosocial functioning, as well as between languishing and psychological impairment, greater chronic physical health

problems, emotional distress, and more lost work days (see Keyes, 2007, for a summary).

Notably, the measurement of flourishing does not follow the traditional additive scale score approach. Keyes (2002, 2005) believes that mental health can be diagnosed in a manner analogous to how mental illness has been traditionally diagnosed using rubrics such as the *Diagnostic and Statistical Manual of Mental Disorders* (4th ed., text rev.; American Psychiatric Association, 2000), because mental health and mental illness both consist of sets of symptoms. For example, in the case of depression, the symptoms include unhappiness, emotional distress, and maladaptive behaviors; on the flip side of this coin, symptoms of flourishing include happiness, emotional vitality, and engagement in positive relationships. Specifically, according to Keyes (2005), "to be diagnosed as flourishing in life, individuals must exhibit high levels on one of the two scales of hedonic well-being and high levels on 6 of the 11 scales of positive functioning" (p. 540).

Though flourishing stands alone as a model of complete mental health incorporating both positive and negative indicators, a number of researchers in the positive psychology tradition have explored and discussed various constructs that may be individual components of flourishing, some of which are particularly relevant to the understanding of the current definition of thriving. In Keyes and Haidt's (2003) recent compendium on flourishing entitled *Flourishing: Positive Psychology and the Life Well-Lived*, many of the foremost scholars in the positive psychology movement weighed in on some of these theorized components. Baltes and Freund (2003b) explained the relation of flourishing to wisdom (especially in later adulthood, to which we return later in this chapter), which they define as "an expert knowledge system concerning the fundamental pragmatics…and conduct and meaning of life" (p. 252). Nakamura and Csikszentmihalyi (2003b) addressed the role of creativity in flourishing, using creativity exemplars to better understand how meaning arises in people's daily lives through what they call *vital engagement*, defined as "participation in an enduring relationship that is at once enjoyed and meaningful" (p. 86). They are careful to point out that flourishing is not simply a string of flow-like experiences, and go on to put forth a theory of emergent meaning that is derived from their research on flow (see Csikszentmihalyi, 1990).

Another concept considered to be a component of flourishing (as well as thriving) is optimism. Importantly, the old notion that optimism and pessimism are simply ends of the same continuum is challenged by Peterson and Chang (2003); these authors suggested that much of the existing research provides an incomplete understanding of the construct because the measures used typically do not assess both negative and positive outcomes. However, these authors did not distinguish between realistic and unrealistic optimism, a point that might have bearing on the prospect of positive outcomes (Schneider, 2001). Schneider defined realistic optimism as "the tendency to maintain a positive outlook within the constraints of the available 'measurable phenomena situated in the physical and social world' (DeGrandpre, 2000, p. 733)…[that] involves enhancing and focusing on the favorable aspects of our experiences…and hoping, aspiring, and searching for positive experiences while acknowledging what we do not know and accepting what we cannot know" (2001, p. 253). Along these lines, taking a developmental perspective, Damon (2008) pointed out the benefits of a combination of optimism, ambition, and "realistic humility" toward the fruitful pursuit of one's purpose. On the other hand, unrealistic optimism includes processes such as self-deception, wherein one seeks out only information that confirms one's desired beliefs, and may undermine positive development (see Baumeister, 1993).

Meaning and purpose in life are also components of flourishing, as explained by Emmons (2003). Establishing and pursuing personal goals, or what he called *personal*

strivings, plays a central role in mental health. Emmons proposed four categories of life meaning, derived from across three different perspectives in meaning research: (1) achievements/work, (2) relationships/intimacy, (3) religion/spirituality, and (4) self-transcendence/generativity, which have much conceptual overlap with the current definition of thriving. One source of meaning and an opportunity for self-transcendence come from what Piliavin (2003) referred to as *doing good*, which may take the form of community involvement and volunteerism. Another moral component related to flourishing is what Haidt (2003) called *elevation*, which in moral-emotional terms refers to the opposite of disgust.

Further empirical work by Fredrickson and Losada (2005) addressed flourishing by incorporating the idea of a "positivity ratio." One's positivity ratio is simply one's level of positive affect in relation to one's level of negative affect. Fredrickson and Losada proposed that to flourish, individuals (or groups) must achieve a certain minimum positivity ratio (approximately 3:1 positive affect to negative affect). Interestingly, their results also suggested that there is an upper limit to the beneficial effect of the positivity ratio on flourishing (signs of disintegration of flourishing emerge at a positivity ratio of 11.6:1), and that a certain level of "appropriate negativity" may, in fact, be important toward flourishing. These authors concluded by suggesting that they believe flourishing is primarily characterized by four key components, including goodness (indexed by happiness, satisfaction, and superior functioning), generativity (indexed by broadened thought–action repertoires and behavioral flexibility), growth (indexed by gains in enduring personal and social resources), and resilience (indexed by survival and growth in the aftermath of adversity).

Similar to flourishing, character strengths comprise a set of personality attributes that are together thought to provide a virtuous path to overall well-being (Peterson & Seligman, 2004). In this research tradition, the concept of character is considered a "multidimensional construct comprised of a family of positive traits manifest in an individual's thoughts, emotions and behaviors" (Park & Peterson, 2006b). After an extensive review of Western and Eastern philosophical and theological traditions, Peterson and Seligman proposed 24 character strengths and grouped them into six categories: wisdom and knowledge, courage, humanity, justice, temperance, and transcendence (see Table 24.3). These character strengths may be assessed via a self-report questionnaire known as the Values in Action Inventory (Peterson & Seligman, 2004), and have been investigated through a number of both theoretical

TABLE 24.3   Values in Action Classification of Character Strengths

1. **Wisdom and knowledge**—cognitive strengths that entail the acquisition and use of knowledge.

- *Creativity:* Thinking of novel and productive ways to do things
- *Curiosity:* Taking an interest in all of ongoing experience
- *Love of learning:* Mastering new skills, topics, and bodies of knowledge
- *Open-mindedness:* Thinking things through and examining them from all sides
- *Perspective:* Being able to provide wise counsel to others

2. **Courage**—emotional strengths that involve the exercise of will to accomplish goals in the face of opposition, external or internal

- *Authenticity:* Speaking the truth and presenting oneself in a genuine way
- *Bravery:* Not shrinking from threat, challenge, difficulty, or pain
- *Persistence:* Finishing what one starts
- *Zest:* Approaching life with excitement and energy

3. **Humanity**—interpersonal strengths that involve "tending and befriending" others

- *Kindness:* Doing favors and good deeds for others
- *Love:* Valuing close relations with others
- *Social intelligence:* Being aware of the motives and feelings of self and others

4. **Justice**—civic strengths that underlie healthy community life

- *Fairness:* Treating all people the same according to notions of fairness and justice
- *Leadership:* Organizing group activities and seeing that they happen
- *Teamwork:* Working well as member of a group or team

5. **Temperance**—strengths that protect against excess

- *Forgiveness:* Forgiving those who have done wrong
- *Modesty:* Letting one's accomplishments speak for themselves
- *Prudence:* Being careful about one's choices; *not* saying or doing things that might later be regretted
- *Self-regulation:* Regulating what one feels and does

6. **Transcendence**—strengths that forge connections to the larger universe and provide meaning

- *Appreciation of beauty and excellence:* Noticing and appreciating beauty, excellence, and/or skilled performance in all domains of life
- *Gratitude:* Being aware of and thankful for the good things that happen
- *Hope:* Expecting the best and working to achieve it
- *Humor:* Liking to laugh and tease; bringing smiles to other people
- *Religiousness:* Having coherent beliefs about the higher purpose and meaning of life

Adapted from Park, N., & Peterson, C. (2006b). Moral competence and character strengths among adolescents: The development and validation of the Values in Action Inventory of Strengths for Youth. *Journal of Adolescence, 29,* 891–905, with permission from Elsevier.

works and empirical studies (e.g., Biswas-Diener, 2006; Park, Peterson, & Seligman, 2004; Peterson, 2006; Park & Peterson, 2006a, 2006b; Peterson, Park, Pole, D'Andrea, & Seligman, 2008; Peterson, Park, & Seligman, 2006; Seligman, Steen, Park, & Peterson, 2005; Steen, Kachorek, & Peterson, 2003).

The category of wisdom and knowledge represents the cognitive strengths that involve the acquisition of information and use of this understanding of the self and the world; examples include open-mindedness, curiosity, and the love of learning. Courage is the domain of emotional strengths such as persistence and bravery, which help to enable one to accomplish goals in the face of challenges. Humanity involves kindness, love, and social intelligence, which are interpersonal strengths and reflect aspects of Keyes's notion of social well-being. Justice involves moral reasoning and civic duty—examples include fairness and leadership. Temperance refers to the capacity to resist excess and regulate the self, and involves strengths such as forgiveness, humility, and prudence. And transcendence can be seen as "strengths that forge connections to the larger universe and provide meaning" (Peterson, Park, & Seligman, 2006, p. 18), such as spirituality, hope, and gratitude. Character strengths have been linked to a number of different positive outcomes, including recovery and growth after illness (Peterson et al., 2006), which fits with the research on the conceptualization of thriving as growth after trauma (Carver, 1998).

As in the emerging research tradition of flourishing, the bourgeoning work on character strengths has also been celebrated in a recent book compilation entitled *A Psychology of Human Strengths: Fundamental Questions and Future Directions for a Positive Psychology* (Aspinwall & Staudinger, 2003). As in *Flourishing,* this edited volume provided an opportunity for leading psychologists to contribute to the conversation regarding human strengths, expanding on the strengths enumerated in Peterson and Seligman's (2004) seminal work in this new tradition.

Many of the topics in this volume overlap directly with notions covered in *Flourishing,* including wisdom, resilience, and meaning/purpose (see Karelitz, Jarvin, & Sternberg, Chapter 23 of this volume, for an extended discussion of the life-span development of wisdom). Wisdom and the SOC model are again addressed by Baltes and Freund (2003a), who suggest they combine to represent an "important facet of human strengths that can be viewed as an ideal outcome of development" (p. 27). Carver and Scheier (2003) explored one specific task of wisdom as it relates to goal selection and perseverance. Somewhat counterintuitively (yet persuasively), the authors asserted that despite almost universal accord about the positive value of continued perseverance toward one's goals, "giving up" is often the most adaptive decision and reflective of the SOC process. Ryff and Singer (2003b) alluded to the role of resilience as a character strength that is necessary toward the appreciation of all aspects of human experience, both positive and negative. According to these authors, the "challenges of 'engaged living' are the essence of what it means to be well" (p. 282). Larsen, Hemenover, Norris, and Cacioppo's (2003) conceptualization of resilience mirrored O'Leary and Ickovics's (1995), Carver's (1998), and others' takes on thriving, as growth after adversity. They addressed both the affective and cognitive components of resilience, showing that the activation of both positive and negative emotions predicts positive adjustment, and the ability to imagine positive coping with a stressful event predicts increased actual engagement coping (Carver, Scheier, & Weintraub, 1989). Larsen et al. concluded that "beneficial health outcomes are associated more strongly with coactivation [of positive and negative emotions] than with neutrality" (p. 218). And as in *Flourishing*, Nakamura and Csikszentmihalyi (2003a) again took on the construct of meaning and its motivational power. These authors

suggested that having a sense of purpose or vocation in one's career might organize and provide meaning to daily work, and as a result, one becomes motivated to continue that meaningful pursuit.

However, this volume highlights a number of additional psychological constructs beyond those that overlap flourishing and character strengths. The importance of self-regulation as a human strength is evident in *A Psychology of Human Strengths*, as 4 of its 23 chapters are allotted to covering it (see McClelland, Ponitz, Messersmith, & Tominey, Chapter 15 of this volume, for an extended discussion of the life-span development of self-regulation). Caprara and Cervone (2003) suggested the self-regulatory system serves several functions: It evaluates one's actions, plans and sets goals, assesses one's efficacy for challenges, and motivates after self-evaluation. As such, this approach accords closely with the SOC model. They further argued that an individual's perceived self-efficacy is related to their self-regulatory system, insofar as self-efficacy beliefs influence motivation, goal choice, performance, strategy choice, and attributions, and therefore development. Eisenberg and Wang (2003) also advanced their thinking about self-regulation as a human strength. They considered it in terms of optimal levels of self-control, which is similar to Block and Block's (1980) personality attribute of ego resiliency. Individuals who exhibit appropriate levels of self-control are more likely to be resilient and cope effectively (Asendorpf & van Aken, 1999; Eisenberg, Fabes, Guthrie, & Reiser, 2000). Further, the authors noted, people who regulate themselves tend to experience more positive and fewer negative emotions (Derryberry & Rothbart, 1988). Mischel and Mendoza-Denton (2003) described self-regulation as involving willful and strategic mental representations to achieve homeostatic affective conditions. In this model, self-regulation is a cognitive process using strategies such as reimagining stimuli to control the less cognitive systems in one's mind. Cantor (2003) also suggested that the ability to strategically imagine situations, which she called *constructive cognition*, is a strength that can lead to more efficient goal pursuit. This human strength is useful in goal selection, such as in social situations where an individual might imagine the probable actions of others, or toward a personal life goal pursuit, when an individual imagines creative probable outcomes from his or her behavior.

The notions of intelligence and judgment also come into play in the conceptualization of character strengths. Sternberg (2003) called for a reconceptualization of the traditional notion of intelligence to be more in line with his principles of positive psychology, which state: (1) people's definitions of success does not always correspond to societal ones; (2) people adapt to, select, and shape their environments; and (3) people do so most effectively when they capitalize on other human strengths. These principles led him to advance the notion of "successful intelligence" (Sternberg, 1996) as more befitting of a character strength than the traditional definition. Sternberg (2003) defined successful intelligence as "the set of skills needed to achieve success in life, as defined by the individual within his or her sociocultural context, in order to adapt to, shape, and select environments by identifying and capitalizing on strengths and identifying and compensating for or correcting weaknesses through a balance of analytical, creative, and practice skills" (p. 321). This definition seems to nicely encapsulate the individual qualities that underlie one's ability to adaptively regulate one's development through individual $\longleftrightarrow$ context relations, and thus may be considered a competency of thriving.

The literature reviewed in this section makes clear the conceptual overlap between the notions of optimal human *functioning* put forth in the models of character strengths and flourishing, and the model of optimal human *development* advanced in the current theory of thriving. However, as pointed out at the beginning of this section, there are many ways in which these social/personality- and cognitive-oriented research traditions of character strengths and flourishing differ from the developmental notion of thriving. Most obviously, as noted earlier, character strengths and flourishing are models of well-being, which primarily view human functioning as one's current status on some continuum or a desired end state; although they might be explored developmentally, such explorations are rare and do not claim to focus on the process of, or attempt to explain, development. In addition, the focus of both character strengths and flourishing is generally on the individual, one's personality characteristics or traits; rarely do they fully consider person-environment interactions and contextual variation. Although character strengths at their core do address human virtues and morality, flourishing does not incorporate moral well-being into its psychological, social, and emotional framework. However, a few recent studies have endeavored to fill some of these conceptual gaps.

Park (2004) reviewed some of the literature that demonstrates linkages between character strengths and PYD. She pointed out that many youth development programs (in and out of school) promote character strengths such as kindness, altruism, and personal responsibility, and touted the research-validated benefits of such programs

(see Larson, 2000; Piliavin, 2003). She referred to the work of Catalano and his colleagues (Hawkins et al., 1992; see also Catalano, Hawkins, et al., 2002) to highlight the salubrious effects of promoting the character strengths of self-control and social intelligence. She concluded her review by declaring there is "consistent evidence that character strengths play important roles in positive youth development as enabling conditions that *facilitate thriving*," but is careful to point out that "just how character strengths…work as buffers against problems and contribute to thriving is not clear" (p. 50, emphasis added).

In addition, Park and Peterson (2006b) uncovered some possible developmental differences in their cross-sectional study comparing adolescents' and adults' scores on the Values in Action survey measure of character strengths. They showed that the character strengths of hope, teamwork, and zest are relatively more common in adolescence, and appreciation of beauty, authenticity, leadership, and open-mindedness are relatively more common in adulthood. They noted that these latter strengths may require more advanced maturation. The authors also explored some differences in the relation between character strengths and life satisfaction in the adolescent versus the adult years. Results showed that whereas life satisfaction is highly correlated with the strengths of zest, hope, love, wisdom, social intelligence, self-regulation, and perseverance across all ages, teamwork and prudence are more powerful predictors of life satisfaction in young people than in adults, and curiosity and spirituality are better predictors of life satisfaction for adults than for young people. Following from these findings, Park (2004) suggested that PYD programs should strategically target those strengths that have demonstrated associations with life satisfaction.

The emergence of these developmental studies of character strengths and the prospect of similar studies integrating flourishing signal the potential for the advancement of the field's understanding of the nature of thriving in adulthood. Although there are clear differences between the approaches taken by those studying thriving as a value-added response to adversity, those taking the more personality-oriented perspective on optimal human functioning, and the conceptualization of thriving presented in this chapter, it is important to note that these perspectives seem to have more in common than they do in distinction. For example, it is likely that the capacities that enable one to achieve better-than-baseline outcomes after trauma likewise contribute to adaptive developmental regulation; the characteristics of a thriving orientation integrate many of the character strengths, and the core components of flourishing.

(Indeed, it would seem those in the positive development movement would benefit from a greater integration of these concepts into its understanding and research agenda on the thriving orientation.) In these ways, thriving in adulthood may look quite similar to thriving in adolescence. Though the time horizon of a hopeful future may appear different in adulthood compared with the teenage years, it is nonetheless quite adaptive to continue looking forward, planning for whatever is next, to continue to explore one's identity and life purpose, and the ways in which one might contribute to the world beyond the self. Alternatively, these psychosocial markers of thriving in adulthood might be thought to function as developmental goals or benchmarks toward which optimal adolescent development points. Regardless, insofar as it is the case that people are developing at every stage of life, it follows that a set of principles of thriving applies at every life stage—including later life.

Thriving and Positive Development in Later Life

Until recently, the developmental literature on late adult development has focused on the identification and, namely, in the medical and nursing literature, remediation of losses, especially in the physical and cognitive domains (Rowe & Kahn, 1987). However, there was a shift in the final two decades of the 20th century toward a greater understanding of positive development in later life (e.g., Baltes, 1987). Although this is encouraging, for the purposes of this review, it is perhaps ironic that, as in infancy, the primary usage of the word *thrive* in the research literature on later life development is deficit-centered, again in the form of a medical diagnosis of FTT. Symptoms of FTT in late adult populations, such as nutritional problems and severe weight loss, surfaced in the medical/geriatrics literature in the late 1980s (Robbins, 1989; Verdery, 1990), and FTT has been further explored in the gerontological nursing literature in recent years. In its 1991 report on late adult development in the United States, the Institute of Medicine described FTT in late adult patients (a.k.a. "inanition") as "a syndrome of weight loss, decreased appetite and poor nutrition, and inactivity, often accompanied by dehydration, depressive symptoms, impaired immune function, and low cholesterol levels" (Lonergan, 1991, p. 60). Late adulthood FTT is now recognized in the *International Classification of Diseases, Ninth Revision, Clinical Modification* under the code "783.7—Adult failure to thrive."

Newbern and Krowchuk (1994) provided an oft-cited summary of FTT literature that addresses both infant and older adult FTT, and offered a conceptual analysis of the proper application of FTT to late adult populations. Building on the notion that FTT includes both anthropomorphic and psychosocial indicators, these authors propound seven "critical attributes" of FTT in older populations. These attributes are broken into two categories: (1) "problems in social relatedness," which include disconnectedness, inability to give of oneself, inability to find meaning in life, and inability to attach to others; and (2) "physical/cognitive dysfunction," including consistent and unplanned weight loss, decline in cognitive function, and signs of depression. They additionally provide a list of five antecedents to FTT in late adult populations, including loss, dependency, feelings of exclusion, shame, helplessness, and worthlessness, loneliness, and inadequate nutritional intake.

In contrast with the infant FTT literature, research on FTT in late adult populations, especially that in the nursing literature, emphasizes psychosocial factors on an equal plane with biological ones (Bergland & Kirkevold, 2001; Kimball & Williams-Burgess, 1995; Newbern & Krowchuk, 1994; Walker & Grobe, 1999). Bergland and Kirkevold asserted that, with regard to physically frail nursing-home residents, "to be useful, the concept of thriving must integrate physical and psychosocial aspects" (p. 431). Whereas others asserted that FTT should be viewed as the negative end of single thriving continuum (where the positive end is defined by high level of psychosocial and nutritional well-being; see Walker & Grobe), these authors proposed that FTT and thriving should be addressed separately. Thriving, in their conceptualization, is a theoretical concept that integrates "the perspective of growth and development and the psychological perspective" (p. 431), whereas FTT should be viewed as more akin to how infant FTT is generally considered, with a greater emphasis on physical factors.

At the same time, some believe the lack of definitional consistency and coherence in the late adult FTT literature is grounds for abandoning it as a medical diagnosis altogether. Sarkisian and Lachs (1996) asserted "the label 'failure to thrive' promotes an intellectual laziness that needs to be balanced by a considered and thoughtful deconstructionist approach, wherein the areas of impairment would be carefully identified, quantified, and, most importantly, scrutinized for potential interactions" (p. 1074). They believed it is impractical to attempt to diagnose late adult patients under a single pathophysiologic process such as FTT and called for a more measurement-oriented approach to declining health in older populations that takes into consideration what they called the *four major contributor domains:* impaired physical functioning, malnutrition, depression and decreasing socialization, and dementia (i.e., cognitive impairment; see also Robertson & Montagnini, 2004). Though Sarkisian and Lachs claimed FTT is "a stigmatizing label [that] distracts the clinician from a systematic evaluation" using these four domains, and thus not a useful diagnosis in geriatric populations (p. 1075), their domains nonetheless largely reflect the indicators to which much of the late adult FTT literature adheres, and the preponderance of the literature supports FTT as a clinically meaningful diagnosis in late adult populations.

However, whereas the term *thrive* appears only in the late adult development literature in this context, many aspects of the current notion of thriving are nonetheless well-represented in the literature on what has been dubbed "successful aging" (referred to here as *successful late adult development*; see p. 616 in Baltes, 1987; see also Baltes & Baltes, 1980; Heckhausen & Schulz, 1995; Rowe & Kahn, 1987). Paul Baltes and his colleagues (Baltes, 1987, 1997; Baltes & Baltes, 1980) are often credited with laying the groundwork for much of the theory and research on positive development in the late mature years. Previously, the psychosocial and medical literature on late adult and life-span development had largely grouped the late mature years into two groups: "normal," which represented the typical late adult development where losses are expected; and "diseased," an unfortunate but functional categorization of those who suffered from subnormal development. Baltes (1987), Rowe and Kahn (1987), and others observed the significant variability of functioning among those in the "normal" category, and challenged the idea that the two categories captured all of the meaningful differences in development during the late adult years. From this, normal late adult development was bifurcated into "usual" and "successful" late adult development. "Usual" might be thought of as akin to the notion of "adequate" development or "competence" in the youth development literature; it represents what is expected, no worse and no better. However, "successful" late development described those who developed along trajectories "above the curve"—they were more vibrant, in better physical health, demonstrated above-average cognitive skills, and felt in more control of their lives. "Successful" late adult developers were also found to have stronger systems of social support. According to Rowe and Kahn (1998), there are three main characteristics of successful late adult developers: (1) low risk for disease and disability, (2) high cognitive and physical functioning, and (3) active engagement with life (p. 53).

Baltes, Baltes, and their colleagues' (e.g., Baltes, 1987; Baltes & Baltes, 1980) work on successful late adult development stemmed from their exploration of cognitive development during this life period. They posited their theory of "selective optimization with compensation" to help explain the relation of gains and losses that naturally accompany the developmental process; in this early iteration of what is now known as the SOC model, Baltes (1987) acknowledged the potential for continual development (i.e., plasticity) throughout the late mature years (albeit decreasing with age), together with the role of one's selective and compensatory efforts to deal with age-related loss.

Baltes, Baltes, and their colleagues (Baltes & Baltes, 1990; Baltes & Freund, 2003; Baltes, Lindenberger, & Staudinger, 2006) have since updated and refined this model for a broader application to phases across the life span. In this model, "selection" involves choosing and committing to goals that give direction and focus to the developmental journey, "optimization" refers to the acquiring and refining of expertise needed to accomplish the goals one has selected, and "compensation" involves finding alternative means toward maintaining a given level of functioning when existing means are lost. By way of this model, Baltes and his colleagues remind us that adulthood and late adulthood, like the developmental stages before them, continue to be about not just "being" but "becoming" (Allport, 1955/1983), as development across the life span is perpetually marked by transitions and the ongoing process of selection, optimization, and compensation. According to Baltes and Freund (2003a), "it is arguable that the modern world accentuates a condition where the central point is not the definition of a particular end state, but the delineation of a behavioral system that promotes as a 'whole' the continued adaptation to and mastery of new life circumstances" (p. 25). Connecting this literature on later life with the PYD literature, Gestsdottir and Lerner (2007) refer to the SOC model as it applies to adolescence as one of "intentional self-regulation" (p. 508). Such self-regulatory capacities have been shown to predict higher levels of functioning (Freund & Baltes, 2002) and moderate one's actions (Baltes et al., 2006; see McClelland, Ponitz, Messersmith, & Tominey, Chapter 15 of this volume, for an extended discussion of self-regulation theories, including Baltes and Heckhausen's).

Heckhausen and her colleagues (1999; Heckhausen & Schulz, 1995; Schulz & Heckhausen, 1996) built from Baltes' and colleagues (Baltes, 1987; Baltes & Baltes, 1980, 1990) SOC model, particularly the selectivity and compensation dimensions, and advanced their own conceptualization of successful late adult development. They posited two keys mechanisms of developmental regulation:

primary and secondary control. Primary control is directed toward influencing and shaping the external world, to bring it in closer accordance with one's desires; in this way, it is thought to be instrumental, or *primary*. If the primary control strategies fail to change the environment, secondary control kicks in; this control mechanism is instead focused internally, and involved changing one's goals or individual standards, or perhaps drawing on self-protective strategies. According to Heckhausen and Schulz (1995), adaptive functioning and development occurs when primary control is operational; simply put, people are better off being able to change their environments to suit them than having to change themselves (e.g., their goals, priorities, attributions) to suit their environments. However, in late adulthood, for most people, primary control becomes more difficult as a function of normal age-related decline in functioning, so secondary control strategies become more salient and more important.

Heckhausen and her colleagues (Heckhausen & Schulz, 1995; Wrosch & Heckhausen, 1999) further break down these types of control by the selection and compensation components of the SOC model, resulting in four forms of control: selective primary control, which is aimed at goal achievement; selective secondary control, which denotes an allocation of internal resources toward the goal(s) selected; compensatory primary control, which entails the gathering of external resources to achieve one's goal(s); and compensatory secondary control, which enables internal buffering strategies against the potential negative effects of failure to achieve one's goal(s). According to Heckhausen and Schulz, successful late adult development does not privilege any one of these forms over the others; instead, one must be capable of using any combination of them in varying degrees contingent on the constraints of the goal(s) one has selected and the environment.

Before moving on from this discussion of concepts related to thriving and positive development, it is important to highlight one additional conceptualization of optimal development and functioning that has helped inform our and others' (e.g., Lerner, 2004) thinking about the nature of thriving. Csikszentmihalyi and Rathunde (1998) quite elegantly presented a set of guidelines for optimal development by way of six "conditions for complex adulthood" (p. 640). They viewed these conditions as the ontological end points toward which optimal development might point, and thus reflecting many of the hallmarks of successful late adult development, and to a degree, thriving. These conditions include: (1) health and physical fitness (though they are careful to stipulate that physical well-being is not a precondition of successful late adult development); (2) the preservation of an alert and vital mind; (3) continuity of a vocation (by which the authors simply mean continued involvement in a meaningful activity, not necessarily a career); (4) keeping up with family and friends (i.e., having a strong social network and support system); (5) continued involvement in the community (which entails not just the personal benefits of social support but also opportunities to remain engaged in purposeful pursuits and contribute to society); and (6) wisdom (following, in part, from Sternberg, 1990; see also Karelitz, Jarvin, & Sternberg, Chapter 23 of this volume). They suggested this final condition includes the following attributes: the ability to get at the essence of problems, holistic thinking rather than specialized knowledge, virtue or behavior toward the common good, and joyful engagement in everyday life (Csikszentmihalyi & Rathunde, p. 642). Taken together, these characteristics represent the kind of "idealized personhood" toward which the thriving process aims. Life's quest to achieve such idealized personhood is never ending; as human beings, we can—and should—constantly strive to improve ourselves, and the conditions in the lives of others and the world around us. There are no age limits to such noble and vital pursuits.

TOWARD A SCIENTIFIC INVESTIGATION OF THRIVING

We have suggested that adolescence marks a formative period in the development of the psychosocial, cognitive, and emotional capacities necessary for thriving. Though the current approach to thriving has only explicitly been tackled in the research literature covering the adolescent years, it may apply as a model of optimal development from this life stage (if not childhood) through late adulthood. Only recently has one of the literatures reviewed herein, in PYD, begun to articulate a solid research agenda that will advance our scientific understanding of thriving. Although it is beyond the scope of this chapter to review the methodologies best suited to thriving research (see Nesselroade & Molenaar, Chapter 2 of this volume, and McArdle, Chapter 3 of this volume, for extended methodological discussions), some methodological principles central to conducting empirical research on thriving are worth noting.

As suggested earlier, adaptive developmental regulation is considered a hallmark of PYD and the basis for optimal growth (Lerner, 2004). However, what constitutes the "optimal environmental conditions" for such development is likely to vary, perhaps substantially, among individuals and across time (Magnusson & Stattin, 1998). Thriving may thus be reflected in the process of an individual simply making the best of his or her environment. For example, we know that youth in disadvantaged settings generally have fewer opportunities for developmentally rich activities, such as volunteer service, compared with those living in less impoverished communities (Atkins & Hart, 2003). Still, individuals may thrive in this setting by making the most of the opportunities they do have. This observation leads to many questions: Might what is considered thriving in some settings, such as high-risk neighborhoods, not be considered thriving in others, such as communities with ample resources? In what ways might thriving appear different in these different contexts? Which external developmental assets (e.g., family, friends, community resources) best support the thriving process, and under what conditions might these relations differ? These kinds of questions reflect but a few of the unresolved issues in the study of thriving.

Conceptual and methodological issues stemming from distinctions between thriving *within* one's context and thriving *despite* one's context are among these unresolved issues. As noted earlier in this chapter, it is also important to consider whether thriving ought to be construed as domain general or domain specific. Can one be thriving in school or at work, but not in one's family life? We would suggest that the answer to this question is "no." Thriving represents the integration of all relational individual ←→ context interactions over time across all environments. Supporting this view, Benson and Scales (2009) offered that "implicit in a conception of thriving as a more global construct is the acknowledgement of countless paths of adolescent thriving whose integrity derives from the ongoing negotiation of each individual's unique bidirectional relations with her or his contexts" (p. 9).

Along these lines, there has been some discussion in the literature regarding the role of culture in thriving (see Benson & Scales, 2009). Lerner, Dowling, and Anderson's (2003) understanding of thriving is based on the notion that a young person over time makes *culturally appropriate* contributions to their society; it is implied that although the specific ways in which one may contribute may differ across cultures, the *idea* of contribution is universal to thriving. However, Eisenberg and Wang (2003) cautioned that what is conceptualized as a strength positive may differ across cultures. For example, individualism and uniqueness

are prized in many Western contexts (and implicitly celebrated in the notion of the "spark"; Benson, 2008) but may not be perceived as positive in collectivist societies. Empirical cross-cultural explorations of thriving, such as one ongoing study conducted by researchers at the Fuller Theological Seminary in Pasadena, California, are necessary to address this critical issue.

It also remains unresolved whether the application of the label *thriving* should entail a certain developmental baseline across all domains of life. Benson and Scales (2009) suggested that "*adequacy* in the social, conduct, and academic dimensions is a necessary foundation for thriving" (p. 14, emphasis added). If thriving, in fact, takes into consideration all relational individual ←→ context interactions over time and across all environments, and it is unreasonable (as we believe it is) to expect all of those interactions across every context to always be mutually enhancing, do we allow for decline in some of those areas? Or do we set "baselines" of functioning and development that must be minimally achieved to consider one thriving? Keyes (2005) has taken an approach akin to setting baselines in his diagnosis method for applying the labels *flourishing* and *languishing* to people; however, the diagnosis approach may not be appropriate for a developmental process such as thriving. And what are we to make of the person who is already functioning very highly in all areas and on an upward developmental trajectory? Is there a ceiling effect where growth cannot be expected (or necessary) to warrant the label *thriving*? These are among the many issues in this field that require more research and greater theoretical consideration.

Perhaps the most elusive (yet arguably most important) goal of researchers of thriving has been that of establishing a well-defined and consensual set of behavioral and psychosocial indicators. As alluded to earlier, this is due, in part, to the fact that the developmental principles of temporal embeddedness and diversity would suggest an expectation of somewhat different indicators of thriving by life stage and by context (including culture), even by historical time (e.g., what might have indicated thriving in the early 20th century might not in the present day). However, we should also expect there to be some indicators of thriving that transcend these categories; indeed, efforts have been made to establish a functional set of these indicators (e.g., the Thriving Indicators Project and the 4-H Study of Positive Youth Development; see the section entitled Conclusions, which follows). Currently, the two most prominent sets of indicators of thriving are those put forth in the 6 Cs model of PYD from Lerner and his colleagues (e.g., Lerner, 2004; Lerner et al., 2003; Theokas et al., 2005), and the recent "Measurement Markers of Thriving" advanced by Benson and Scales (2009), both reviewed earlier. Although the efficacy and theoretical fit of these models are still in the process of being fully tested, each is instrumental toward advancing our understanding of thriving as both a process and an orientation. Research should be encouraged to use both frameworks and assessment tools together, for purposes of comparison and because of the complementary strengths of the models (such as the focus on process in the Lerner model—wherein the first 5 Cs of PYD predict the 6th C of contribution—and the focus on orientation toward thriving and the "spark" in the Benson and Scales model).

Though we do not undertake endorsing or advancing a new a list of thriving indicators here, three issues on this point warrant particular attention. First, the role of subjective well-being in the process of optimal development has been debated among thriving scholars. Although it is clear that being happy or more generally satisfied with one's life is not necessary at all times to ensure optimal development—indeed, according to Ryff and Singer (2003b), "'interpersonal flourishing' is profoundly about the mix of positive and negative emotions" (p. 279)—it is much less clear to what extent happiness and life satisfaction must exist over time to allow for the thriving process. At any given point, happiness may or may not be an indicator of thriving; however, over time, one might expect it to be, on average, present. If a person is perpetually unsatisfied with her or his life but appears to be on an upward developmental trajectory marked by mutually beneficial relationships with others, can we consider this person to be thriving? One approach might follow from Fredrickson and Losada's (2005) notion of a positivity ratio, wherein an optimal range or moderate oscillation of subjective well-being over time might function as an indicator of thriving.

Second, there is much interindividual diversity in the degree to which people know and understand both themselves and their environments. The literature on self-understanding, self-knowledge, and self-concept is vast, and we do not review it here; however, the role of self-knowledge is key to self-regulation (see Higgins, 1996; Markus & Wulf, 1987), and thus integral to the thriving process as well. All normally developing people eventually have the capacity to appraise their goals (including purposes and sparks) and abilities via self-appraisal; the extent to which people actually engage in accurate

self-appraisal may have important ramifications toward their ability to thrive (see Bandura, 1989). Analogously, context appraisal addresses the degree to which one can accurately assess his or her environmental assets and risks; this, too, is likely to facilitate thriving. Though the field has largely overlooked these capacities, the thriving process may be predicated on their development.

Finally, scholars of thriving have commonly addressed the roles of psychological, social, and emotional development, but there remains little consensus on the roles of spiritual and physical development. Increasingly across the human sciences, scholars are recognizing spirituality as an intrinsic component of the human condition. As noted earlier, some theoretical models of thriving and positive development advance spiritual development as essential (e.g., King & Benson, 2005; King & Furrow, 2004), whereas others do not (e.g., Lerner et al., 2007); to date, empirical explorations have been inconclusive (e.g., Shultz et al., 2006). Similarly, some PYD scholars suggest aspects of physical development—such as "maintenance of physical health" (Scales et al., 2000), "positive health perceptions" (Benson & Scales, 2009), and "good health habits" and "good health risk management skills" (Eccles & Gootman, 2002)—are important indicators of thriving, whereas others pay little attention to the role of physical development (e.g., Gestsdottir & Lerner, 2007; Lerner, 2004; Lerner et al., 2003, Theokas et al., 2005). Some take a middle stance; Jelicic et al. (2007) noted the importance for young people to "maintain their health and fitness," not as an explicit indicator of thriving but instead as necessary to avoid "being a physical burden to others [thus] enabling effective interactions with their social world" (p. 271). As suggested earlier in the chapter, it may be the case that physical development takes a more prominent position in thriving at different life stages: The FTT perspective in infancy is based on proper physical development, and the maintenance of physical health from adulthood into late adulthood is viewed as an essential indicator of successful late adult development (Baltes & Smith, 2003; Schulz & Heckhausen, 1996). Furthermore, the interaction of psychological and physical capacities may come into play; for example, successful late adult development entails the ability to appropriately psychologically cope with and compensate for physical losses (Stern & Carstensen, 2000). Although we strongly believe that the presence of physical ailments (such as a physical disability, chronic medical disease, etc.) in no way precludes thriving, it is important that the role of physical health—be it actual health or engagement in healthy habits (such as proper hygiene maintenance, wholesome eating habits, etc.)—is explored more deeply in these conceptualizations and assessments of thriving.

CONCLUSIONS

The driving philosophy behind the PYD movement—and many of its cousins in the positive psychology, cognitive development, and successful late adult development perspectives—hold that individuals, cultures, and nations ought to believe, and act on the belief, that all humans, young and old, are (to paraphrase Benson, 1997, and Resnick, 2000) resources to be nourished and developed, not problems to be solved and managed. Damon and Lerner (2008) asserted that "the potential for and instantiations of plasticity legitimate an optimistic and proactive search for characteristics of individuals and of their ecologies that, together, can be arrayed to promote positive human development *across life*" (p. 8, emphasis added). Taking these statements together, we submit that a more positive, strengths-based view of development—as embraced in the concept of thriving presented in this chapter—is not only warranted but essential for fully understanding ontogeny across the human life span. Furthermore, the perspective espoused by "applied developmental science" (Lerner, 2002), and shared by scholars of thriving, emphasizes the applied nature of relational developmental systems theory in which the current concept of thriving is rooted. As such, additional scholarly work is needed not only toward the construction and validation of research assessments for a better scientific understanding of thriving, but the development of practical tools for parents and communities to put into these principles of thriving into action. It is one of the tasks of developmental inquiry to seek an understanding of optimal human development, and to communicate this understanding to both the research community and the broader public. Investigators in this area also need to partner with organizations and practitioners who are in the position to deliver on the promises of thriving and positive development.

There are already numerous examples of such collaborations currently in progress, many focusing on the formative developmental stages of childhood and adolescence. For example, a research initiative known as the Thriving Indicators Project has partnered researchers of thriving in the PYD tradition (including Peter Benson, Peter Scales, and their colleagues at Search Institute; Pamela King and

her colleagues at the Fuller Theological Seminary; and William Damon and his colleagues at Stanford University) with members of the Thrive Foundation for Youth and practitioners of thriving such as Friends of the Children (a national nonprofit organization that provides mentoring for at-risk teens) to help better understand PYD in practice. Similarly, the 4-H Study of Positive Youth Development is a joint initiative between Richard Lerner and his colleagues in the Institute of Applied Research in Youth Development at Tufts University and the National 4-H Council, which aims "to conduct good science that enhances the abilities of practitioners, parents, policy makers, and young people themselves to promote positive human development" (Lerner, Lerner, Phelps, & Colleagues, 2008, p. 3). Furthermore, the Search Institute has over the years partnered with thousands of communities across the country, as well as America's Promise Alliance, to advance the PYD agenda. Damon and his colleagues are working hand in hand with nonprofit organizations to explore avenues for fostering purpose and thriving in schools both in the United States and abroad. Child Trends, an independent, nonpartisan research center in Washington, DC, has conducted significant research on PYD and is dedicated to putting their findings directly into practice to improve the lives of children and their families. These are but a few of the many examples of such positive collaborations.

At the outset of this chapter, we noted that despite the growing knowledge base and the excellent work by many scholars in the field of PYD and fields adjacent, the construct of thriving remains by and large ill-defined and ill-understood. We have sought to remedy these conceptual ills by proposing a synthetic definition rooted squarely in relational developmental systems theory, and have laid the groundwork for advances in the existing knowledge base to be built around a set of core principles we have distilled from the literature. These principles are designed to highlight the fundamentally developmental nature of thriving, focus on optimal (not merely adequate) development, acknowledge the whole person across all life domains, consider the relational multidirectional (and inherently moral) nature of mutually enhancing interactions among people and their environments, and integrate the humanistic notion of maximizing one's full potential. Although each of these principles may act as stand-alone guidelines for thriving-related research and practice, they must be considered en bloc for thriving to be truly understood in all its complexity. Indeed, the greater this understanding we can achieve, the greater the likelihood that we can help people at all stages of life to thrive.

REFERENCES

Ainsworth, M. D. (1969). Object relations, dependency, and attachment: A theoretical review of the infant-mother relationship. *Child Development, 11*(4), 969–1025.

Ainsworth, M. D., Blehar, M., Waters, E., & Wall, S. (1978). *Patterns of attachment: A psychological study of the strange situation.* Hillsdale NJ: Erlbaum.

Allport, G. (1983). *Becoming: Basic considerations for a psychology of personality.* New Haven, CT: Yale University. (Original work published 1955)

American Psychiatric Association. (2000). *Diagnostic and statistical manual of mental disorders* (4th ed., text rev.). Washington, DC: American Psychiatric Press.

Apgar, V. (1953). A proposal for a new method of evaluation of the newborn infant. *Current Research in Anesthesia & Analgesia, 32*(4), 260–267.

Armsden, G., & Greenberger, M. (1987). The inventory of parent and peer attachment: Individual differences and their relationship to psychological well-being in adolescence. *Journal of Youth and Adolescence, 16*, 427–452

Asendorpf, J. B., & van Aken, M. A. G. (1999). Resilient, overcontrolled, and undercontrolled personality prototypes in childhood: Replicability, predictive power, and the trait-type issue. *Journal of Personality and Social Psychology, 77*, 815–832.

Aspinwall, L. G., & Staudinger, U. M. (Eds.). (2003). *A psychology of human strengths: Fundamental questions and future directions for a positive psychology.* Washington, DC: APA Books.

Atkins, R., & Hart, D. (2003). Neighborhoods, adults, and the development of civic identity in urban youth. *Applied Developmental Science, 7*(3), 156–164.

Baltes, P. B. (1987). Theoretical propositions of life-span developmental psychology: On the dynamics between growth and decline. *Developmental Psychology, 23*, 611–626.

Baltes, P. B. (1997). On the incomplete architecture of human ontogeny: Selection, optimization, and compensation as foundation of developmental theory. *American Psychologist, 52*, 366–380.

Baltes, P. B., & Baltes, M. M. (1980). Plasticity and variability in psychological aging: Methodological and theoretical issues. In G. E. Gurski (Ed.), *Determining the effects of aging on the central nervous system* (pp. 41–66). Berlin: Schering.

Baltes, P. B., & Baltes, M. M. (1990). Psychological perspectives on successful aging: The model of selective optimization with compensation. In P. B. Baltes & M. M. Baltes (Eds.), *Successful aging: Perspectives from the behavioral sciences* (pp. 1–34). New York: Cambridge University Press.

Baltes, P. B., & Freund, A. M. (2003a). Human strengths as the orchestration of wisdom and selective optimization with compensation (SOC). In L. G. Aspinwall & U. M. Staudinger (Eds.), *A psychology of human strengths: Fundamental questions and future directions for a positive psychology* (pp. 23–35). Washington, DC: APA Books.

Baltes, P. B., & Freund, A. M. (2003b). The intermarriage of wisdom and selective optimization with compensation: Two meta-heuristics guiding the conduct of life. In C. L. M. Keyes & J. Haidt (Eds.), *Flourishing: Positive psychology and the life well-lived* (pp. 249–274). Washington, DC: American Psychological Association.

Baltes, P. B., Lindenberger, U., & Staudinger, U. M. (2006). Lifespan theory in developmental psychology. In R. M. Lerner (Ed.), *Handbook of child psychology: Vol. 1. Theoretical models of human development* (6th ed., pp. 569–664). Editors in chief: W. Damon & R. M. Lerner. Hoboken, NJ: John Wiley & Sons.

Baltes, P. B., & Smith, J. (2003). New frontiers in the future of aging: From successful aging of the young old to the dilemmas of the fourth age. *Gerontology, 49*, 123–135.

Baltes, P. B., Staudinger, U. M., & Lindenberger, U. (1999). Lifespan psychology: Theory and application to intellectual functioning. *Annual Review of Psychology, 50*, 471–507.

Bandura, A. (1989). Human agency in social cognitive theory. *American Psychologist, 44*, 1175–1184.

Baumeister, R. F. (1993). *Self-esteem: The puzzle of low self-regard.* New York: Plenum Press.

Bayley, N. (1969). *The Bayley scales of infant development.* New York: Psychological Corporation.

Benard, B. (1991). *Fostering resiliency in kids: Protective factors in the family, school and community.* San Francisco: Western Regional Center for Drug Free Schools and Communities, Far West Laboratory.

Benson, P. L. (1990). *The troubled journey.* Minneapolis, MN: Search Institute.

Benson, P. L. (1997). *All kids are our kids: What communities must do to raise caring and responsible children and adolescents.* San Francisco: Jossey-Bass.

Benson, P. L. (2003). Developmental assets and asset-building community: Conceptual and empirical foundations. In R. M. Lerner & P. L. Benson (Eds.), *Developmental assets and asset building communities: Implications for research, policy, and practice* (pp. 19–43). Norwell, MA: Kluwer.

Benson, P. L. (2007). Developmental assets: An overview of theory, research, and practice. In R. K. Silbereisen & R. M. Lerner (Eds.), *Approaches to positive youth development* (pp. 33–58). Thousand Oaks, CA: Sage.

Benson, P. L. (2008). *Sparks: How parents can help ignite the hidden strengths of teenagers.* San Francisco: Jossey-Bass.

Benson, P. L., Leffert, N., Scales, P. C., & Blyth, D. A. (1998). Beyond the "village" rhetoric: Creating healthy communities for children and adolescents. *Applied Developmental Science, 2*, 138–159.

Benson, P. L., & Saito, R. (2001). The scientific foundation of youth development. In *Youth development: Issues, challenges, and directions.* Philadelphia: Public/Private Ventures.

Benson, P. L., & Scales, P. C. (2009). The definition and preliminary measurement of thriving in adolescence. *Journal of Positive Psychology, 4*(1), 85–104.

Benson, P. L., Scales, P. C., Hamilton, S. F., & Sesma, A., Jr. (2006). Positive youth development: Theory, research and applications. In R. M. Lerner (Ed.), *Handbook of child psychology: Vol. 1. Theoretical models of human development* (6th ed., pp. 894–941). Editors in chief: W. Damon & R. M. Lerner. Hoboken, NJ: John Wiley & Sons.

Bergland, A., & Kirkevold, M. (2001). Thriving—A useful theoretical perspective to capture the experience of well-being among frail elderly in nursing homes? *Journal of Advanced Nursing, 36*, 426–432.

Biswas-Diener, R. (2006). From the equator to the North Pole: A study of character strengths. *Journal of Happiness Studies, 7*, 293–310.

Block, J. H., & Block, J. (1980). The role of ego-control and ego-resiliency in the organization of behavior. In W. A. Collins (Ed.), *The Minnesota Symposia on Child Psychology* (Vol. 13, pp. 39–101). Hillsdale, NJ: Erlbaum.

Blum, R. W. (1998). Healthy youth development as a model for youth health promotion. *Journal of Adolescent Health, 22*, 368–375.

Blum, R. W. (2003). Positive youth development: A strategy for improving adolescent health. In R. M. Lerner, F. Jacobs, & D. Wertlieb (Eds.), *Handbook of applied developmental science: Promoting positive child, adolescent, and family development through research, policies, and programs: Vol. 2. Enhancing the life chances of youth and families: Public service systems and public policy perspectives* (pp. 237–252). Thousand Oaks, CA: Sage.

Boddy, J., Skuse, D., & Andrews, B. (2000). The developmental sequelae of nonorganic failure to thrive. *Journal of Child Psychology and Psychiatry and Allied Disciplines, 41,* 1003–1014.

Bonanno, G. A. (2004). Loss, trauma, and human resilience: Have we underestimated the human capacity to thrive after extremely aversive events? *American Psychologist, 59,* 20–28.

Bowlby, J. (1958). The nature of the child's tie to his mother. *International Journal of Psychoanalysis, 39*(5), 350–73.

Bowlby, J. (1969). *Attachment and loss: Vol. 1. Attachment.* New York: Basic Books.

Brandstädter, J. (1984): Personal and social control over development. In P. B. Baltes & O. G. Brim, Jr. (Eds.), *Life-span development and behaviour* (Vol. 6, pp. 1–32). New York: Academic Press.

Brandtstädter, J. (2006). Action perspectives on human development. In R. M. Lerner (Ed.), *Handbook of child psychology: Vol. 1. Theoretical models of human development* (6th ed., pp. 516–568). Editors in chief: W. Damon & R. M. Lerner. Hoboken, NJ: John Wiley & Sons.

Bronfenbrenner, U. (1979). *The ecology of human development.* Cambridge, MA: Harvard University Press.

Bronfenbrenner, U., & Morris, P. A. (2006). The bioecological model of human development. In R. M. Lerner (Ed.), *Handbook of Child Psychology: Vol. 1. Theoretical models of human development* (6th ed.). Editors in chief: W. Damon & R. M. Lerner. Hoboken, NJ: John Wiley & Sons.

Bumbarger, B., & Greenberg, M. T. (2002). Next steps in advancing research on positive youth development. *Prevention & Treatment, 5,* 1–7.

Bundick, M. J., Yeager, D. S., & Damon, W. (2008, August 14). Correlates and developmental trends of thriving in adolescence. Presented at the Annual Meeting of the American Psychological Association, Boston.

Calhoun, L. G., & Tedeschi, R. G. (1989–1990). Positive aspects of critical life problems: Recollections of grief. *Omega, 20,* 265–272.

Calhoun, L. G., & Tedeschi, R. G. (1998). Beyond recovery from trauma: Implications for clinical practice and research. *Journal of Social Issues, 54*(2), 357–371.

Cantor, N. (2003). Constructive cognition, personal goals, and the social embedding of personality. In L. G. Aspinwall & U. M. Staudinger (Eds.), *A psychology of human strengths: Fundamental questions and future directions for a positive psychology* (pp. 49–60). San Francisco: Berrett-Koehler.

Caprara, G. V., & Cervone, D. (2003). A conception of personality for a psychology of human strengths: Personality as an agentic, self-regulating system. In L. G. Aspinwall & U. M. Staudinger (Eds.), *A psychology of human strengths: Fundamental questions and future directions for a positive psychology* (pp. 61–74). Washington, DC: APA Books.

Carver, C. S. (1998). Resilience and thriving: Issues, models, and linkages. *Journal of Social Issues, 54,* 245–266.

Carver, C. S., & Scheier, M. F. (2003). Three human strengths. In L. G. Aspinwall & U. M. Staudinger (Eds.), *A psychology of human strengths: Fundamental questions and future directions for a positive psychology* (pp. 87–102). Washington, DC: APA Books.

Carver, C. S., Scheier, M. F., & Weintraub, J. K. (1989). Assessing coping strategies: A theoretically based approach. *Journal of Personality and Social Psychology, 56,* 267–283.

Catalano, R. F., Berglund, M. L., Ryan, J. A., Lonczak, H. S., & Hawkins, J. D. (2002). Positive youth development in the United States: Research findings on evaluations of Positive Youth Development Programs. *Prevention & Treatment, 5,* Article 15.

Catalano, R. F., Hawkins, J. D., Berglund, M. L., Pollard, J. A., & Arthur, M. W. (2002). Prevention science and positive youth development: Competitive or cooperative frameworks. *Journal of Adolescent Health, 31,* 230–239.

Cicchetti, D., & Lynch, M. (1995). Failures in the expectable environment and their impact on individual development: The case of child maltreatment. In D. Cicchetti & D. J. Cohen (Eds.), *Developmental psychopathology: Risk, disorder, and adaptation* (Vol. 2, pp. 32–71). New York: John Wiley & Sons.

Colby, A., & Damon, W. (1992). *Some do care: Contemporary lives of moral commitment.* New York: Free Press.

Collins, W. A., Maccoby, E. E., Steinberg, L., Hetherington, E. M., & Bornstein, M. H. (2000). Contemporary research on parenting: The case for nature and nurture. *American Psychologist, 55,* 218–232.

Connell, J. P., Gambone, M. A., & Smith, T. J. (2000). *Youth development in community settings: Challenges to our field and our approach.* Philadelphia: The Community Action for Youth Project.

Csikszentmihalyi, M. (1990). *Flow: The psychology of optimal experience.* New York: Harper & Row.

Csikszentmihalyi, M., & Rathunde, K. (1998). The development of the person: An experiential perspective on the ontogenesis of psychological complexity. In R. M. Lerner (Ed.), *Handbook of child psychology: Vol. 1. Theoretical models of human development* (5th ed., pp. 635–684). Editors in chief: W. Damon & R. M. Lerner. New York: John Wiley & Sons.

Damon, W. (Ed.) (1978). *Moral development.* San Francisco: Jossey-Bass.

Damon, W. (1990). *The moral child.* New York: Free Press.

Damon, W. (1995). *Greater expectations: Overcoming the culture of indulgence in our homes and schools.* New York: Free Press.

Damon, W. (1997) *The youth charter: How communities can work together to raise standards for all our children.* New York: Free Press.

Damon, W. (1999). The moral development of children. *Scientific American, 281,* 72–88.

Damon, W. (2004). What is positive youth development? *Annals of the American Academy of Political and Social Science, 591*(1), 13–24.

Damon, W. (2008). *The path to purpose: Helping our children find their calling in life.* New York: Simon & Schuster.

Damon, W., & Gregory, A. (2002). Bringing in a new era in the field of youth development. In R. L. Lerner, F. Jacobs, & D. Wertlieb (Eds.), *Handbook of applied developmental science* (Vol. 1, pp. 407–420). Hoboken, NJ: John Wiley & Sons.

Damon, W., & Hart, D. (1982). The development of self-understanding from infancy through adolescence. *Child Development, 53,* 841–864.

Damon, W., & Hart, D. (1988). *Self-understanding in childhood and adolescence.* New York: Cambridge University Press.

Damon, W., & Lerner, R. L. (2008). The scientific study of child and adolescent development: Important issues in the field today. In W. Damon & R. L. Lerner (Eds.), *Child and adolescent development: An advanced course* (pp. 696–735). Hoboken, NJ: John Wiley & Sons.

Damon, W., Menon, J., & Bronk, K. C. (2003). The development of purpose during adolescence. *Applied Developmental Science, 7*(3), 119–128.

DeGrandpre, R. J. (2000). A science of meaning: Can behaviorism bring meaning to psychological science? *American Psychologist, 55,* 721–739.

Derryberry, D., & Rothbart, M. K. (1988). Arousal, affect, and attention as components of temperament. *Journal of Personality and Social Psychology, 55*(6), 958–966.

Diener, E. (1984). Subjective well-being. *Psychological Bulletin, 95,* 542–575.

Diener, E. (2000). Subjective well-being: The science of happiness, and a proposal for a national index. *American Psychologist, 55,* 34–43.

Dowling, E., Gestsdottir, S., Anderson, P., von Eye, A., Almerigi, J., & Lerner, R. M. (2004). Structural relations among spirituality, religiosity, and thriving in adolescence. *Applied Developmental Science, 8,* 7–16.

Dowling, E. M., Steinunn, G., Anderson, P. M., von Eye, A., & Lerner, R. (2003) Spirituality, religiosity and thriving among adolescents: Identification and confirmation of factor structures. *Applied Developmental Science, 7*(4), 253–260.

Drewett, R., Corbett, S., & Wright, C. (1999). Cognitive and educational attainment at school age of children who failed to thrive in infancy: A population-based study. *Journal of Child Psychology and Psychiatry, 40,* 551–561.

Durlak, J. A., Taylor, J. D., Kawashima, K., Pachan, M. K., DuPre, E. P., Celio, C., et al. (2007). Effects of positive youth development programs on school, family, and community systems. *American Journal of Community Psychology, 39*(3), 269–286.

Durlak, J. A., & Weissberg, R. P. (2005, August). A major meta-analysis of Positive Youth Development Programs. Presentation at the Annual Meeting of the American Psychological Association, Washington, DC.

Eccles, J., & Gootman, J. A. (Eds.). (2002). *Community programs to promote youth development.* Board on Children, Youth, and Families, Division of Behavioral and Social Sciences and Education, National Research Council & Institute of Medicine. Washington, DC: National Academies Press.

Edwards, O. W., Mumford, V. E., & Serra-Roldan, R. (2007). A positive youth development model for students considered at-risk. *School Psychology International, 28*(1), 29–45.

Eisenberg, N., & Fabes, R. A. (1998). Prosocial development. In W. Damon (Ed.), *Handbook of child psychology* (Vol. 3, pp. 701–78). New York: John Wiley & Sons.

Eisenberg, N, Fabes, R. A., Guthrie, I. K., & Reiser, M. (2000). Dispositional emotionality and regulation: Their role in predicting quality of social functioning: Their role in predicting quality of social functioning. *Journal of Personality and Social Psychology, 78,* 136–157.

Eisenberg, N., Fabes, R. A., Murphy, B. C., Karbon, M., Smith, M., & Maszk, P. (1996). The relations of children's dispositional empathy-related responding to their emotionality, regulation, and social functioning. *Developmental Psychology, 32,* 195–209.

Eisenberg, N., & Wang, V. O. (2003). Toward a positive psychology: Social developmental and cultural contributions. In L. G. Aspinwall & U. M. Staudinger (Eds.), *A psychology of human strengths: Fundamental questions and future directions for a positive psychology* (pp. 117–130). Washington, DC: APA Books.

Elder, G. H., Jr. (1998). The life course and human development. In R. M. Lerner (Ed.), *Theoretical models of human development* (Vol. 1, 5th ed., pp. 939–991). New York: John Wiley & Sons.

Emmons, R. A. (2003). Personal goals, life meaning, and virtue: Wellsprings of a positive life. In C. L. M. Keyes & J. Haidt (Eds.), *Flourishing: Positive psychology and the life well-lived* (pp. 105–128). Washington, DC: American Psychological Association.

Erikson, E. H. (1968). *Identity, youth and crisis.* New York: Norton.

Feshbach, N. (1983). Sex differences in empathy and social behavior in children. In N. Eisenberg (Ed.), *The development of prosocial behavior* (pp. 11–47). New York: Academic Press.

Ford, D. L., & Lerner, R. M. (1992). *Developmental systems theory: An integrative approach.* Newbury Park, CA: Sage.

Fredrickson, B. L., & Losada, M. F. (2005). Positive affect and the complex dynamics of human flourishing. *American Psychologist, 60,* 678–686.

Freund, A. M., & Baltes, P. B. (2002). Life-management strategies of selection, optimization, and compensation: Measurement by self-report and construct validity. *Journal of Personality and Social Psychology, 82,* 642–662.

Gardner, H., Csikszentmihalyi, M., & Damon, W. (2001). *Good work: When excellence and ethics meet.* New York: Basic Books.

Garmezy, N. (1983). Stressors of childhood. In N. Garmezy (Ed.), *Stress, coping, and development in children* (pp. 43–84). Baltimore, MD: Johns Hopkins University Press.

Garmezy, N. (1986). On measures, methods, and models. *Journal of the American Academy of Child and Adolescent Psychiatry, 25,* 727–729.

Gestsdottir, S., & Lerner, R. M. (2007). Intentional self-regulation and positive youth development in early adolescence: Findings from the 4-H Study of Positive Youth Development. *Developmental Psychology, 43*(2), 508–521.

Greenberg, M. T., Weissberg, R. P., O'Brien, M. U., Zins, J. E., Fredericks, L., Resnik, H., et al. (2003). School-based prevention: Promoting positive social development through social and emotional learning. *American Psychologist, 58*(6/7), 466–474.

Haidt, J. (2003). Elevation and the positive psychology of morality. In C. L. M. Keyes & J. Haidt (Eds.), *Flourishing: Positive psychology and the life well-lived* (pp. 275–290). Washington, DC: American Psychological Association.

Hart, D., Yates, M., Fegley, S., & Wilson, G. (1995). Moral commitment in inner-city adolescents. In M. Killen & D. Hart (Eds.), *Morality in everyday life: Developmental perspectives* (pp. 317–342). Cambridge: Cambridge University Press.

Harter, S. (1982). The Perceived Competence scale for children. *Child Development, 53,* 87–98.

Havighurst, R. J. (1972). *Developmental tasks and education* (3rd ed.). New York: McKay. (Original work published 1948)

Havighurst, R. J. (1973). History of developmental psychology: Socialization and personality development through the life span. In P. B. Baltes & K. W. Schaie (Eds.), *Life-span developmental psychology: Personality and socialization* (pp. 3–24). New York: Academic Press.

Hawkins, J. D., Catalano, R. F., & Miller, J. Y. (1992). Risk and protective factors for alcohol and other drug problems in adolescence and early adulthood: Implications for substance abuse prevention. *Psychological Bulletin, 112,* 64–105.

Heckhausen, J. (1999). *Developmental regulation in adulthood: Age-normative and sociocultural constraints as adaptive challenges.* New York: Cambridge University Press.

Heckhausen, J., & Schulz, R. (1995). A life-span theory of control. *Psychological Review, 102,* 284–304.

Henderson, N., Barnard, B., & Sharp-Light, N. (Eds.). (1999). *Resiliency in Action: Practical ideas for overcoming risks and building strengths in youth, families and communities.* Gorham, ME: Resiliency in Action.

Higgins, E. T. (1996). Knowledge activation: Accessibility, applicability, and salience. In E. T. Higgins & A. W. Kruglanski (Eds.), *Social psychology: Handbook of basic principles* (pp. 133–168). New York: Guilford.

Holt, L. E. (1897). *The diseases of infancy and childhood.* New York: D. Appleton and Co.

Ickovics, J. R., & Park, C. L. (1998). Paradigm shift: Why a focus on health is important. *Journal of Social Issues, 54*(2), 237–244.

Jahoda, M. (1958). *Current concepts of positive mental health.* New York: Basic Books.

Jelicic, H., Bobek, D., Phelps, E. D., Lerner, J. V., & Lerner, R. M. (2007). Using positive youth development to predict contribution and risk behaviors in early adolescence: Findings from the first two waves of the 4-H Study of Positive Youth Development. *International Journal of Behavioral Development, 31*(3), 263–273.

Jessor, R. J., van den Bos, J., Vanderryn, J., Costa, F. M., & Turbin, M. S. (1995). Protective factors in adolescent problem behavior: Moderator effects and developmental change. *Developmental Psychology, 31,* 923–933.

Kagan, J. (1984). *The nature of the child.* New York: Basic Books.

Kagan, J., & Gall, S. (Eds.). (1998). *The Gale encyclopedia of childhood and adolescence.* Detroit, MI: Gale Group. Retrieved November 13, 2008, from http://www.healthline.com/galecontent/failure-to-thrive-ftt.

Keyes, C. L. M. (1998). Social well being. *Social Psychology Quarterly, 61,* 121–140.

Keyes, C. L. M. (2002). The mental health continuum: From languishing to flourishing in life. *Journal of Health and Social Behavior, 43,* 207–222.

Keyes, C. L. M. (2003). Complete mental health: An agenda for the 21st century. In C. L. M. Keyes & J. Haidt (Eds.), *Flourishing: Positive psychology and the life well-lived* (pp. 293–312). Washington, DC: American Psychological Association.

Keyes, C. L. M. (2005). Mental health *and/or* mental illness? Investigating axioms of the complete state model of health. *Journal of Consulting and Clinical Psychology, 73,* 539–548.

Keyes, C. L. M. (2007). Promoting and protecting mental health as flourishing: A complementary strategy for improving national mental health. *American Psychologist, 62,* 95–108.

Keyes, C. L. M., & Haidt, J. (Eds.). (2003). *Flourishing: Positive psychology and the life well lived.* Washington DC: American Psychological Association.

Keyes, C. L. M., Shmotkin, D., & Ryff, C. D. (2002). Optimizing well-being: The empirical encounter of two traditions. *Journal of Personality and Social Psychology, 82,* 1007–1022.

Kimball, M. J., & Williams-Burgess, C. (1995). Failure to thrive: the silent epidemic of the elderly. *Archives of Psychiatric Nursing, IX,* 99–105.

King, P. E., & Benson, P. L. (2005). Adolescent spiritual development and well-being and thriving. In E. C. Roehlkepartain, P. E. King, L. M. Wagener, & P. L. Benson (Eds.), *The handbook of spiritual development in childhood and adolescence.* Thousand Oaks, CA: Sage.

King, P. E., Dowling, E. M., Mueller, R. A., White, K., Schultz, W., Osborn, P., et al., (2005). Thriving in adolescence: The voices of youth-serving practitioners, parents, and early and late adolescents. *Journal of Early Adolescence, 25*(1), 94–112.

King, P. E., & Furrow, J. L. (2004). Religion as a resource for positive youth development: Religion, social capital, and moral outcomes. *Developmental Psychology, 40,* 703–713.

King, P. E., Shultz, W., Mueller, R. A., Dowling, E. M., Osborn, P., Dickerson, E., et al. (2005). Positive youth development (PYD): Is there a nomological network of concepts used in the developmental literature? *Applied Developmental Science, 9*(4), 216–228.

Krugman, S. D., & Dubowitz, H. (2003). Failure to thrive. *American Family Physician, 68*(5), 879–884.

Larsen, J. T., Hemenover, S. H., Norris, C. J., & Cacioppo, J. T. (2003). Turning adversity to advantage: On the virtues of the coactivation of positive and negative emotions. In L. Aspinwall & U. Staudinger (Eds.), *A psychology of human strengths: Perspectives on an emerging field* (pp. 211–225). Washington, DC: American Psychological Association.

Larson, R. (2000). Toward a psychology of positive youth development. *American Psychologist, 55*(1), 170–183.

Leffert, N., Benson, P., Scales, P., Sharma, A., Drake, D., & Blyth, D. (1998). Developmental assets: Measurement and prediction of risk behaviors among adolescents. *Applied Developmental Science, 2*(4), 209–230.

Lerner, R. M. (1984). *On the nature of human plasticity.* New York: Cambridge University Press.

Lerner, R. M. (2002). *Concepts and theories of human development* (3rd ed.). Mahwah, NJ: Erlbaum.

Lerner, R. M. (2004). *Liberty: Thriving and civic engagement among American youth.* Thousand Oaks, CA: Sage.

Lerner, R. M. (2006). Developmental science, developmental systems, and contemporary theories of human development. In R. M. Lerner (Ed.), *Handbook of child psychology: Vol. 1. Theoretical models of human development* (6th ed., pp. 1–17). Editors in chief: W. Damon & R. M. Lerner. Hoboken, NJ: John Wiley & Sons.

Lerner, R. M. (2007). *The good teen: Rescuing adolescents from the myths of the storm and stress years.* New York: Crown.

Lerner, R. M., & Benson, P. L. (2003). *Developmental assets and asset-building communities: Implications for research, policy, and practice.* New York: Kluwer Academic/Plenum.

Lerner, R. M., Brentano, C., Dowling, E. M., & Anderson, P. M. (2002). Positive youth development: Thriving as the basis of personhood and civil society. *New directions for youth development, 95,* 11–33.

Lerner, R. M., Dowling, E. M., & Anderson, P. M. (2003). Positive youth development: Thriving as the basis of personhood and civil society. *Applied Developmental Science, 7*(3), 172–180.

Lerner, R. M., Fisher, C. B., & Weinberg, R. A. (2000). Toward a science for and of the people: Promoting civil society through the application of developmental science. *Child Development, 71,* 11–20.

Lerner, R. M., Freund, A. M., De Stefanis, I., & Habermas, T. (2001). Understanding developmental regulation in adolescence: The use of the selection, optimization, and compensation model. *Human Development, 44,* 29–50.

Lerner, R. M., Lerner, J. V., Almerigi, J., Theokas, C., Phelps, E., Gestsdottir, S., et al. (2005). Positive youth development, participation in community youth development programs, and community contributions of fifth grade adolescents: Findings from the first wave of the 4-H study of positive youth development. *Journal of Early Adolescence, 25*(1), 17–71.

Lerner, R. M., Lerner, J. V., Almerigi, J., Theokas, C., Phelps, E., Naudeau, S., et al., (2006). Towards a new vision and vocabulary about adolescence: Theoretical, empirical, and applied bases of a "Positive Youth Development" perspective. In L. Balter & C. S. Tamis-LeMonda (Eds.), *Child psychology: A handbook of contemporary issues* (pp. 445–469). New York: Psychology Press/Taylor & Francis.

Lerner, R. M., Lerner, J. V., Phelps, E., & Colleagues (2008). *The 4-H study of positive youth development: Report of the findings from the first four waves of data collection: 2002–2003, 2003–2004, 2004–2005, and 2005–2006.* Institute for Applied Research in Youth Development, Tufts University. Retrieved October 18, 2008, from http://www.ase.tufts.edu/iaryd/documents/4HStudyFindings2008.pdf.

Lerner, R. M., & Overton, W. F. (2008). Exemplifying the integrations of the relational developmental system: Synthesizing theory, research, and application to promote positive development and social justice. *Journal of Adolescent Research, 23,* 245–255.

Lerner, R. M., Phelps, E., Alberts, A., Forman, Y., & Christiansen, E. D. (2007). The many faces of urban girls: Features of positive development in early adolescence. In B. Leadbeater & N. Way (Eds.), *Urban girls revisited: Building strengths* (Vol. 2, pp. 19–53). New York: New York University Press.

Lonergan E. T. (Ed.). (1991). *Extending life, enhancing life: A national research agenda on aging.* Washington, DC: National Academy Press.

Luthar, S. S. (1999). *Poverty and children's adjustment.* Thousand Oaks, CA: Sage.

Luthar, S. S., Cicchetti, D., & Becker, B. (2000). The construct of resilience: A critical evaluation and guidelines for future work. *Child Development, 71*(3), 543–562.

Madsen, M. C. (1971). Developmental and cross-cultural differences in the cooperative and competitive behavior of young children. *Journal of Cross-Cultural Psychology, 2,* 365–371.

Magnusson, D. (1988). Individual development from an interactional perspective. In D. Magnusson (Ed.), *Paths through life* (Vol. 1, pp. 3–31). Hillsdale, NJ: Erlbaum.

Magnusson, D., & Mahoney, J. L. (2003). A holistic person approach for research on positive development. In L. G. Aspinwall & U. M. Staudinger (Eds.), *A psychology of human strengths: Fundamental questions and future directions for a positive psychology* (pp. 227–244). Washington, DC: APA Books.

Magnusson, D., & Stattin, H. (1998). Person-context interaction theories. In R. M. Lerner (Ed.), *Handbook of child psychology: Vol. 1. Theoretical models of human development* (5th ed., pp. 685–760). Editor in chief: W. Damon. New York: John Wiley & Sons.

Mahoney, J. L., & Bergman, L. R. (2002). Conceptual and methodological considerations in a developmental approach to the study of positive adaptation. *Applied Developmental Psychology, 23,* 195–217.

Markus, H. R., & Wulf, E. (1987). The dynamic self-concept: A social psychological perspective. *Annual Review of Psychology, 38,* 299–337.

Maslow, A. H. (1968). *Toward a psychology of being* (2nd ed.). New York: Van Nostrand.

Maslow, A. H. (1970). *Motivation and personality* (2nd ed.). New York: Harper & Row.

Masten, A. S. (2001). Ordinary magic: Resilience processes in development. *American Psychologist, 56,* 227–238.

Masten, A. S., Coatsworth, J. D., Neeman, J., Gest, S. D., Tellegen, A., & Garmezy, N. (1995). The structure and coherence of competence through adolescence. *Child Development, 66,* 1635–1659.

Masten, A. S., Hubbard, J. J., Gest, S. D., Tellegen, A., Garmezy, N., & Ramirez, M. (1999). Competence in the context of adversity: Pathways to resilience and maladaptation from childhood to late adolescence. *Development & Psychopathology, 11*(1), 143–169.

Masten, A. S., & Obradovic, J. (2006). Competence and resilience in development. *Annals of the New York Academy of Sciences, 1094,* 13–27.

Mischel, W., & Mendoza-Denton, R. (2003). Harnessing willpower and socioemotional intelligence to enhance human agency and potential. In L. G. Aspinwall & U. M. Staudinger (Eds.), *A psychology of human strengths: Fundamental questions and future directions for a positive psychology* (pp. 245–256). Washington, DC: APA Books.

Moore, K. A., & Lippman, L. (2005). *What do children need to flourish? Conceptualizing and measuring indicators of positive development.* New York: Kluwer Academic/Plenum.

Moore, K. A., Lippman, L., & Brown, B. (2004). Indicators of child well-being: The promise for positive youth development. *Annals of the American Academy of Political and Social Science, 591,* 125–45.

Myers, D. G. (2000). The funds, friends, and faith of happy people. *American Psychologist, 55*(1), 56–67.

Nakamura, J., & Csikszentmihalyi, M. (2003a). The construction of meaning through vital engagement. In C. L. M. Keyes & J. Haidt (Eds.), *Flourishing: Positive psychology and the life well-lived* (pp. 83–104). Washington, DC: American Psychological Association.

Nakamura, J., & Csikszentmihalyi, M. (2003b). The motivational sources of creativity as viewed from the paradigm of positive psychology. In L. G. Aspinwall & U. M. Staudinger (Eds.), *A psychology of human strengths: Fundamental questions and future directions for a positive psychology* (pp. 257–270). Washington, DC: APA Books.

Newbern, V. B., & Krowchuk, H. V. (1994). Failure to thrive in elderly people: A conceptual analysis. *Journal of Advanced Nursing, 19*(5), 840–849.

O'Leary, V. E. (1998). Strength in the face of adversity: Individual and social thriving. *Journal of Social Issues, 54,* 425–446.

O'Leary, V. E., & Ickovics, J. R. (1995). Resilience and thriving in response to challenge: An opportunity for a paradigm shift in women's health. *Women's Health: Research on Gender, Behavior, and Policy, I,* 121–142.

Olsen E. M. (2006). Failure to thrive: Still a problem of definition. *Clinical Pediatrics, 45,* 1–6.

Overton, W. F. (2006). Developmental psychology: Philosophy, concepts, methodology. In R. M. Lerner (Ed.), *Handbook of child psychology: Vol. 1. Theoretical models of human development* (6th ed., pp. 18–88). Editors in chief: W. Damon & R. M. Lerner. Hoboken, NJ: John Wiley & Sons.

Park, C. L. (1998). Stress-related growth and thriving through coping: The roles of personality and cognitive processes. *Journal of Social Issues, 54,* 267–277.

Park, C. L., Cohen, L. H., & Murch, R. L. (1996). Assessment and prediction of stress-related growth. *Journal of Personality, 64,* 71–105.

Park, N. (2004). Character strengths and positive youth development. *The Annals of the American Academy of Political and Social Science, 591,* 40–54.

Park, N., & Peterson, C. (2006a). Character strengths and happiness among young children: Content analysis of parental descriptions. *Journal of Happiness Studies, 7,* 323–341.

Park, N., & Peterson, C. (2006b). Moral competence and character strengths among adolescents: The development and validation of the Values in Action Inventory of Strengths for Youth. *Journal of Adolescence, 29,* 891–905.

Park, N., Peterson, C., & Seligman, M. (2004). Strengths of character and well-being. *Journal of Social and Clinical Psychology, 23,* 603–619.

Peterson, C. (2006). Strengths of character and happiness: Introduction to special issue. *Journal of Happiness Studies, 7,* 289–291.

Peterson, C., & Chang, E. C. (2003). Optimism and flourishing. In C. L. M. Keyes & J. Haidt (Eds.), *Flourishing: Positive psychology and the life well-lived* (pp. 55–80). Washington, DC: American Psychological Association.

Peterson, C., Park, N., Pole, N., D'Andrea, W., & Seligman, M. E. P. (2008). Strengths of character and posttraumatic growth. *Journal of Traumatic Stress, 21,* 214–217.

Peterson, C., Park, N., & Seligman, M. E. P. (2006). Greater strengths of character and recovery from illness. *Journal of Positive Psychology, 1*(1), 17–26.

Peterson, C., & Seligman, M. E. P. (2004). *Character strengths and virtues: A handbook and classification.* New York: Oxford University Press & American Psychological Association.

Piaget, J. (1952). *The origins of intelligence in children.* New York: Norton.

Piaget, J. (1967). *Six psychological studies.* New York: Random House.

Piliavin, J. A. (2003). Doing well by doing good: Benefits for the benefactor. In C. L. M. Keyes & J. Haidt (Eds.), *Flourishing: Positive psychology and the life well-lived* (pp. 227–248). Washington, DC: American Psychological Association.

Pinquart, M. (2002). Creating and maintaining purpose in life in old age: A meta-analysis. *Ageing International, 27*(2), 90–114.

Pittman, K. J. (1991). *Promoting youth development: Strengthening the role of youth-serving and community organizations.* Washington, DC: U.S. Department of Agriculture Extension Services.

Pittman, K. J., Irby, M., & Ferber, T. (2000). Unfinished business: Further reflections on a decade of promoting youth development. In Youth development: Issues and challenges. Philadelphia: Public/Private Ventures. Retrieved July 31, 2007, from http://www.ppv.org/ppv/publications/assets/74_sup/ydv_1.pdf.

Prilleltensky, I. (1992). Humanistic Psychology, Human Welfare and the Social Order. *The Journal of Mind and Behaviour, 13*(4), 315–327.

Radloff, L. S. (1977). The CES-D scale: A self-report depression scale for research in the general population. *Applied Psychological Measurement, 1,* 385–401.

Resnick, M. D. (2000). Protective factors, resiliency, and healthy youth development. *Adolescent Medicine: State of the Art Reviews, 11,* 157–164.

Robbins, L. (1989). Evaluation of weight loss in the elderly. *Geriatrics, 44*(4), 31–37.

Robertson, R. G., & Montagnini, M. (2004). Geriatric failure to thrive. *American Family Physician, 70*(2), 343–50.

Rogers, C. (1961). *On becoming a person: A therapist's view of psychotherapy.* London: Constable.

Roisman, G. I., Masten, A. S., Coatsworth, J. D., & Tellegen, A. (2004). Salient and emerging developmental tasks in the transition to adulthood. *Child Development, 75*(1), 123–133.

Rosenn, D. W., Loeb, L. S., & Bates, M. (1980). Differentiation of organic from non-organic failure to thrive syndrome in infancy. *Pediatrics, 66,* 698–704.

Roth, J. L., & Brooks-Gunn, J. (2003a). Youth development programs: Risk, prevention, and policy. *Journal of Adolescent Health, 32,* 170–182.

Roth, J. L., & Brooks-Gunn, J. (2003b). What exactly is a youth development program? Answers from research and practice. *Applied Developmental Science, 7,* 94–111.

Roth, J. L., Brooks-Gunn, J., Murray, L., & Foster, W. (1998). Promoting health adolescents: Synthesis of youth development program evaluations. *Journal of Research on Adolescence, 8,* 423–459.

Rowe, J. W., & Kahn, R. L. (1987). Human aging: Usual and successful. *Science, 237,* 143–149.

Rowe, J. W., & Kahn, R. L. (1998). *Positive aging.* New York: Pantheon.

Rutter, M. (1985). Resilience in the face of adversity. *British Journal of Psychiatry, 147,* 598–611.

Ryan, R. M., & Deci, E. L. (2000). Self-determination theory and the facilitation of intrinsic motivation, social development, and well-being. *American Psychologist, 55,* 68–78.

Ryff, C. D. (1989). Happiness is everything, or is it? Explorations on the meaning of psychological well-being. *Journal of Personality and Social Psychology, 57,* 1069–1081.

Ryff, C. D., & Keyes, C. L. M. (1995). The structure of psychological well-being revisited. *Journal of Personality and Social Psychology, 69,* 719–727.

Ryff, C. D., & Singer, B. (2003a). Flourishing under fire: Resilience as a prototype of challenged thriving. In C. L. M. Keyes & J. Haidt (Eds.), *Flourishing: Positive psychology and the life well-lived* (pp. 15–36). Washington, DC: American Psychological Association.

Ryff, C. D., & Singer, B. (2003b). Ironies of the human condition: Well-being and health on the way to mortality. In L. G. Aspinwall & U. M. Staudinger (Eds.), *A psychology of human strengths: Fundamental questions and future directions for a positive psychology* (pp. 271–288). Washington, DC: APA Books.

Sarkisian, C. A., & Lachs, M. S. (1996). Failure to thrive in older adults. *Annals of Internal Medicine, 124*(12), 1072–1078.

Scales, P., Benson, P., Leffert, N., & Blyth, D. A. (2000). The contribution of developmental assets to the prediction of thriving among adolescents. *Applied Developmental Science, 4,* 27–46.

Scales, P. C., Benson, P. L., Roehlkepartain, A. S., & van Dulmen, M. (2006). The role of developmental assets in predicting academic achievement: A longitudinal study. *Journal of Adolescence, 29,* 691–708.

Scales, P. C., & Leffert, N. (2004). *Developmental assets: A synthesis of the scientific research on adolescent development* (2nd ed.). Minneapolis, MN: Search Institute.

Schneider, S. L. (2001). In search of realistic optimism: Knowledge, meaning, and warm fuzziness. *American Psychologist, 56,* 250–263.

Schulz, R., & Heckhausen J. (1996). A life span model of successful aging. *American Psychologist, 51,* 702–714.

Schwartz, I. D. (2000). Failure to thrive: An old nemesis in the new millennium. *Pediatric Review, 21*(8), 257–264.

Seligman, M. E. P., & Csikszentmihalyi, M. (2000). Positive psychology: An introduction. *American Psychologist, 55,* 5–14.

Seligman, M. E. P., Steen, T. A., Park, N., & Peterson, C. (2005). Positive psychology progress: Empirical validation of interventions. *American Psychologist, 60,* 410–421.

Shultz, W., Wagener, L., & King, P. E. (2006, March 24). Predictors of thriving in adolescence. Presented at the Society for Research on Adolescence Biennial Conference, San Francisco, CA.

Singer, L. T., & Fagan, J. F. (1984). Cognitive development in the failure-to-thrive infant: A three-year longitudinal study. *Journal of Pediatric Psychology, 9,* 363–383.

Small, S., & Memmo, M. (2004). Contemporary models of youth development and problem prevention: Toward an integration of terms, concepts, and models. *Family Relations,* 3–11.

Small, S. A., & Rodgers, K. B. (1995). *Teen Assessment Project Survey Question Bank.* Madison, WI: University of Wisconsin–Madison.

Spencer, M. B. (1995). Old issues and new theorizing about African American youth: A phenomenological variant of ecological systems theory. In R. L. Taylor (Ed.), *Black youth: Perspectives on their status in the United States.* Westport, CT: Praeger.

Spencer, M. B. (2006). Phenomenology and ecological systems theory: Development of diverse groups. In R. M. Lerner (Ed.), *Handbook of child psychology: Vol. 1. Theoretical models of human development* (6th ed., pp. 829–893). Editors in chief: W. Damon & R. M. Lerner. Hoboken, NJ: John Wiley & Sons.

Sroufe, L. (1979). The coherence of individual development: Early care, attachment, and subsequent developmental issues. *American Psychologist, 34,* 834–841.

Sroufe, L. A., & Waters, E. (1977). Attachment as an organizational construct. *Child Development, 48,* 1184–1199.

Steen, T. A., Kachorek, L. V., & Peterson, C. (2003). Character strengths among youth. *Journal of Youth and Adolescence, 32,* 5–16.

Stern, P. C., & Carstensen, L. L. (2000). *The aging mind: Opportunities in cognitive research.* Washington, DC: National Academy Press.

Sternberg, R. J. (Ed.). (1990). *Wisdom: Its nature, origins, and development.* Cambridge: Cambridge University Press.

Sternberg, R. J. (1996). *Successful intelligence.* New York: Simon & Schuster.

Sternberg, R. J. (2003). Driven to despair: Why we need to redefine the concept and measurement of intelligence. In L. G. Aspinwall & U. M. Staudinger (Eds.), *A psychology of human strengths: Fundamental questions and future directions for a positive psychology* (pp. 319–330). Washington, DC: APA Books.

Tedeschi, R. G., & Calhoun, L. G. (1995). *Trauma and transformation: Growing in the aftermath of suffering.* Thousand Oaks, CA: Sage.

Tedeschi, R. G., Park, C. L., & Calhoun, L. G. (1996). The posttraumatic growth inventory: Measuring the positive legacy of trauma. *Journal of Traumatic Stress, 9,* 455–471.

Thelen, E., & Smith, L. B. (2006). Dynamic systems theories. In R. M. Lerner (Ed.), *Handbook of child psychology: Vol. 1. Theoretical models of human development* (6th ed., pp. 258–312). Editors in chief: W. Damon & R. M. Lerner. Hoboken, NJ: John Wiley & Sons.

Theokas, C., Almerigi, J. B., Lerner, R. M., Dowling, E. M., Benson, P. L., Scales, P. C., et al. (2005). Conceptualizing and modeling individual and ecological asset components of thriving in early adolescence. *Journal of Early Adolescence, 25*(1), 113–143.

Tronick, E. (1989). Emotions and emotional communication in infant. *American Psychologist, 44,* 112–119.

Verdery, R. B. (1990). Fatigue, failure to thrive, weight loss and cachexia. In W. R. Hazzard, R. Andres, E. L. Bierman, & J. P. Blass (Eds.), *Principles of geriatric medicine and gerontology* (2nd ed., pp. 1102–1108). New York: McGraw Hill.

Vygotsky, L. S. (1978). *Mind and society: The development of higher psychological processes.* Cambridge, MA: Harvard University Press.

Walker, L. J., Pitts, R. C., Hennig, K. H., & Matsuba, M. K. (1995). Reasoning about morality and real-life moral problems. In M. Killen & D. Hart (Eds.), *Morality in everyday life: Developmental perspectives* (pp. 371–407). New York: Cambridge University Press.

Walker, L. O., & Grobe, S. (1999). The construct of thriving in pregnancy and postpartum. *Nursing Science Quarterly, 12,* 151–157.

Watson, D., Clark, L. A., & Tellegen, A. (1988). Development and validation of brief measures of positive and negative affect: The PANAS scales. *Journal of Personality and Social Psychology, 54,* 1063–1070.

Weissberg, R., & O'Brien, M. U. (2004). What works in school-based social and emotional learning programs for positive youth development. *Annals of the American Academy of Political and Social Science, 591*(1), 86–97.

Werner, E. E. (1985). Stress and protective factors in children's lives. In A. R. Nicol (Ed.), *Longitudinal studies in child psychology and psychiatry* (pp. 335–355). New York: John Wiley & Sons.

Werner, E. E. (1995) Resilience in development. *Current Directions in Psychological Science, 3,* 81–85.

Werner, E. E., & Smith, R. S. (1982). *Vulnerable but invincible: A study of resilient children.* New York: McGraw-Hill.

Werner, H. (1948). *Comparative psychology of mental development.* New York: International Universities Press.

Werner, H., & Kaplan, B. (1963). *Symbol formation: An organismic-developmental approach to language and the expression of thought.* New York: John Wiley & Sons.

Wilcox, W. D., Nieburg, P., & Miller, D. S. (1989). Failure to thrive: A continuing problem of definition. *Clinical Pediatrics, 28,* 391–394.

Wright, C. M., Parkinson, K. M., & Drewett, R. F. (2006). How does maternal and child feeding behavior relate to weight gain and failure to thrive? Data from a prospective birth cohort. *Pediatrics, 117*(4), 1262–1269.

Wrosch, C., & Heckhausen, J. (1999). Control processes before and after passing a developmental deadline: Activation and deactivation of intimate relationship goals. *Journal of Personality and Social Psychology, 77,* 415–427.

Youniss, J., & Yates, M. (1997). *Community service and social responsibility in youth.* Chicago: University of Chicago Press.

THE HANDBOOK OF LIFE-SPAN DEVELOPMENT:

COGNITION, BIOLOGY, AND METHODS

VOLUME 1

Author Index

Subject Index